HoX

The Shorter New Cambridge Bibliography of English Literature

The Shorter New Cambridge Bibliography of English Literature

Edited by
GEORGE WATSON

CAMBRIDGE UNIVERSITY PRESS

CAMBRIDGE
LONDON   NEW YORK   NEW ROCHELLE
MELBOURNE   SYDNEY

Published by the Press Syndicate of the University of Cambridge
The Pitt Building, Trumpington Street, Cambridge CB2 1RP
32 East 57th Street, New York, NY 10022, USA
296 Beaconsfield Parade, Middle Park, Melbourne 3206, Australia

First published 1981

Printed in Great Britain at
the Alden Press, Oxford

British Library Cataloguing in Publication Data
The shorter new Cambridge bibliography of
English literature.
1. English literature – Bibliography
I. Watson, George, *b. 1927*
016.82 Z2011 80-49948
ISBN 0 521 22600 7

TO THE MEMORY OF
ALAN SPILMAN
1929–1980

CONTENTS

CONTENTS

Part II 1600–1800

CONTENTS

Part III 1800–1900

CONTENTS

Part IV 1900–1950

EDITOR'S PREFACE

This book is largely, though not wholly, the epitome of another. The *New Cambridge Bibliography of English Literature 600–1950* appeared in five volumes between 1969 and 1977, edited by I. R. Willison (who was responsible for the fourth volume) and myself, the fifth volume or Index being by J. D. Pickles. *New CBEL*, in its turn, had been based on the *CBEL* of 1940 edited by F. W. Bateson, and its *Supplement* of 1957, which I edited. And it was new in more ways than one. Its conventions were new, and much of its data; and so on the whole were its contributors, who totalled nearly two hundred. Since its appearance a few years ago, it has established itself as the chief bibliographical aid to the literature of the British Isles since its beginnings in the seventh century.

The scale and cost of *New CBEL*, however, have not always helped it to reach the shelves of those who might wish to own it. These include school as well as university libraries, and private scholars and collectors as well as booksellers and publishers. For the private person, above all, a one-volume condensation is now clearly needed, as well as for libraries anxious to reserve the five-volume edition for special use. Many will find the shorter version more convenient for student and general reader.

With all these purposes in view, the Bibliography of 1969–77 has been distilled into its present compass, or a fifth and less of its original extent. Its conventions, which are by now familiar to thousands of readers, have been entirely kept. So has its general design of six historical periods from the Anglo-Saxon to the first half of the present century. So has its arrangement within those periods, notably into sections called Poetry, Novel and Drama; though certain marginal sections such as Book Production and Distribution, and Literary Relations with the Continent, have been abandoned altogether.

All the major authors in *New CBEL*, and many minor ones, have been included here, with the familiar distinction between primary and secondary works. In each case the primary section, or the canon of an author's works, has been wholly or largely kept; the secondary section, however, which consists of books and articles concerning that author, has usually been reduced substantially with the interests of general reader and student in mind. An index of primary authors, together with certain useful headings, is appended. I have also made additions, usually of newly published items, most notably in the twentieth century, and have entered a number of corrections as well.

ACKNOWLEDGEMENTS

My chief debt, as ever, is to the contributors of *New CBEL*, who laboured on that work from the early 1960s till the mid 1970s; to F. W. Bateson, editor of the 1940 *CBEL*, who left no more fitting monument when he died in October 1978; and to I. R. Willison of the British Library for his advice on volume 4. Once again, P. G. Burbidge of the Cambridge University Press has guided and inspired the undertaking, and Alan Spilman gave valuable editorial aid.

More than that, the present work has profited in its corrections from the alertness of countless correspondents in many lands, some of them total strangers, who have generously responded to my earlier prefatorial entreaties for advice and help. I entreat that help again. It is only by the particular knowledge of many individuals, scattered and yet impelled by a common devotion to English studies, that a work of this scale can over the years be perfected and refined.

GEORGE WATSON

St John's College, Cambridge

ABBREVIATIONS

Acad	Academy	illustr	illustrated by
addn	addition	Inst	Institute
Amer	American	introd	introduction
anon	anonymous	JEGP	Journal of English and Germanic
Archiv	Archiv für das Studium der		Philology
	neueren Sprachen	JHI	Journal of the History of Ideas
AS	Anglo-Saxon	Jnl	Journal
Assoc	Association	Lang	Language
b.	born	Lib	Library
Bibl	Bibliographical	Lit	Literature
bk	book	MÆ	Medium Ævum
BM	British Museum	Mag	Magazine
Br	British	ME	Middle English
Bull	Bulletin	ML	Muses' Library
BNYPL	Bulletin of New York Public	MLN	Modern Language Notes
	Library	MLQ	Modern Language Quarterly
c.	circa	MLR	Modern Language Review
ch	chapter	MP	Modern Philology
CHEL	Cambridge History of English	ms	manuscript
	Literature	Nat	National
col	column	nd	no date
CQ	Critical Quarterly	no	number
d.	died	N & Q	Notes and Queries
DNB	Dictionary of National	OE	Old English
	Biography	OHEL	Oxford History of English
ed	edited by		Literature
edn	edition	OSA	Oxford Standard Authors
E & S	Essays and Studies	p.	page
et al	and others	pbd	published
EC	Essays in Criticism	pbn	publication
EETS	Early English Text Society	PBSA	Publications of the Biblio-
EHR	English Historical Review		graphical Society of America
EL	Everyman's Library	PMLA	Publications of the Modern
ELH	Journal of English Literary		Language Association of
	History		America
EML	English Men of Letters	PQ	Philological Quarterly
Eng	English	priv	privately
E Studien	Englische Studien	Proc	Proceedings
E Studies	English Studies	prop	proprietor
facs	facsimile	pt	part
fl.	floruit	ptd	printed
GM	Gentleman's Magazine	Quart	Quarterly
HLQ	Huntington Library Quarterly	REL	Review of English Literature

ABBREVIATIONS

rev	revised by	STS	Scottish Text Society
Rev	Review	Stud	Studies
RES	Review of English Studies	suppl	supplement
rptd	reprinted	TLS	Times Literary Supplement
SB	Studies in Bibliography (University of Virginia)	tr	translated by
		trn	translation
SE	Studies in English (University of Texas)	Univ	University
		unpbd	unpublished
ser	series	UTQ	University of Toronto Quarterly
Sh Jb	Shakespeare Jahrbuch	vol	volume
Soc	Society	WC	World's Classics
SP	Studies in Philology		

GENERAL INTRODUCTION

For bibliographies, literary histories, journals etc wholly or mainly related to a single period see under the period concerned.

I. BIBLIOGRAPHIES

(1) LISTS OF BIBLIOGRAPHICAL SOURCES

Courtney, W. P. A register of national bibliography. 3 vols 1905–12.

Cross, T. P. A list of books and articles designed to serve as an introduction to the bibliography and methods of English literary history. Chicago 1919, 1951 (10th edn rev), 1962 (rev and enlarged D. F. Bond as A reference guide to English studies).

Northup, C. S. A register of bibliographies of the English language and literature. New Haven 1925.

Esdaile, A. The sources of English literature. Cambridge 1928.

Spargo, J. W. A bibliographical manual for students of the language and literature of England and the United States. Chicago 1939, 1941, New York 1956 (rev).

Kennedy, A. G. A concise bibliography for students of English. Stanford 1940, 1945, 1954, 1960 (rev and enlarged D. B. Sands).

Watson, G. The concise Cambridge bibliography of English literature 600–1950. Cambridge 1958, 1965 (rev).

— and I. R. Willison. The new Cambridge bibliography of English literature [600–1950]. 5 vols Cambridge 1969–77.

Altick, R. D. and A. Wright. Selective bibliography for the study of English and American literature. New York 1960, 1963 (rev).

Bateson, F. W. A guide to English literature. 1965, 1968 (rev).

McNamee, L. F. Dissertations in English and American literature: theses accepted by American, British and German universities 1865–1964. New York 1968; Supplement one for 1964–8, New York 1969.

Howard-Hill, T. H. Bibliography of British literary bibliographies. Oxford 1969.

(2) CURRENT LISTS OF NEW BOOKS

The English catalogue of books from 1835– (with retrospective vol for 1801–36 by R. A. Peddie and Q. Waddington, 1914). 1864– (now annual with a 5-year cumulation).

The publishers' trade list annual (Uniform trade list annual, 1873–7). New York 1873–; Books in print: an index to the publishers' trade list annual, New York 1948–.

British books in print (superseding Reference catalogue of current literature, 1874–1940, 1951, 1961, 1965). 1967– (annual).

The British Museum list of accessions. 1881– (now monthly, formerly fortnightly).

The United States catalog: books in print. New York 1899–1928; Cumulative book index: a world list of books in English supplementing the United States catalog, ed M. Burnham et al, New York 1933–.

The times literary supplement. 1902–.

The British national bibliography: a subject list of new British books. Ed A. J. Wells 1950– (annual).

The library of Congress author catalog 1948–52. 24 vols Ann Arbor 1953; continued as National union catalog: a cumulative author list, 1953–7, 26 vols Ann Arbor 1958; for 1952–5 imprints, 30 vols Ann Arbor 1961; for 1958–62, 50 vols New York 1963; for 1963–7, 59 vols Ann Arbor 1969; for 1968, 12 vols Washington 1969; 1969– (9 issues annually with quarterly and annual cumulations and 5-year cumulations projected).

American book publishing record. New York 1960– (monthly, then annual cumulations from Publishers' weekly).

National union catalog, pre-1956 imprints. Chicago 1968–.

(3) CURRENT LISTS OF ENGLISH STUDIES

The year's work in English studies. 1919–.

Annual bibliography of English language and literature. Cambridge 1921– (Modern Humanities Research Assoc).

The review of English studies. Oxford 1925– (quarterly lists of articles and periodicals).

Research in progress in the modern languages and literatures. PMLA 63–75 1948–60.

MLA international bibliography of books and articles on the modern languages and literatures. New York 1963– (replacing Annual bibliography 1956–63, and American bibliography 1922–55).

MLA abstracts of articles. New York 1970–.

(4) REFERENCE WORKS

General

Watt, R. Bibliotheca britannica: or a general index to British and foreign literature. 4 vols Edinburgh 1824.

Chambers, R. Cyclopaedia of English literature. 2 vols Edinburgh 1843–4, 4 vols 1857–60 (rev R. Carruthers); ed D. Patrick 3 vols 1901–3; rev J. L. Geddie 3 vols Philadelphia 1938.

Allibone, S. A. A critical dictionary of English literature and British and American authors (suppl by J. F. Kirk).

5 vols Philadelphia 1858–91.

Brewer, E. C. Dictionary of phrase and fable. 1870, 1970 (rev).

Halkett, S., J. Laing et al. A dictionary of the anonymous and pseudonymous literature of Great Britain. 4 vols 1882–8; rev J. Kennedy, W. A. Smith and A. F. Johnson 7 vols Edinburgh 1926–34; vols 8 (for 1900–50) and 9 (addns for vols 1–8) ed D. E. Rhodes and A. E. C. Simoni, Edinburgh 1956–62.

Stephen, L., S. Lee et al. The dictionary of national biography from the earliest times to 1900 [with 6 decennial suppls]. 69 vols 1885–1901, 22 vols 1908–9; Compact edition, 2 vols Oxford 1975. *See* Corrections and additions, cumulated from the Bulletin of the Institute of Historical Research, University of London 1923–63, Boston 1966.

Murray, J., H. Bradley, W. A. Craigie and C. T. Onions. A new English dictionary on historical principles. 20 vols (10 pts) Oxford 1888–1928; The Oxford English dictionary, 13 vols Oxford 1933 (with suppl); Compact edition, 2 vols Oxford 1971; Supplement, ed R. W. Burchfield, Oxford 1972–.

Cousin, J. W. A short biographical dictionary of English literature. 1910, 1938 (EL) (rev); rev D. C. Browning 1958 (EL).

Harvey, P. The Oxford companion to English literature. Oxford 1932, 1946 (rev), 1967 (rev D. Eagle).

The author's and writer's who's who. 1934 etc.

Ghosh, J. C. and E. G. Withycombe. Annals of English literature 1475–1925. Oxford 1935, 1961 (rev).

Oxford dictionary of quotations. Oxford 1941, 1953 (rev).

Union list of microfilms. 4 vols Philadelphia 1942, Ann Arbor 1951 (rev); suppl 1949–59, Philadelphia 1961.

Shipley, J. T. Dictionary of world literature. New York 1943, 1953 (rev).

—— Encyclopaedia of literature. 2 vols New York 1946.

Smith, H. Columbia dictionary of modern literature. New York 1947.

Baldensperger, F., and W. P. Friederich. Bibliography of comparative literature. Chapel Hill 1950.

Matthews, W. British diaries: an annotated bibliography of British diaries written between 1442 and 1942. Berkeley 1950.

—— British autobiographies: an annotated bibliography of British autobiographies published or written before 1951. Berkeley 1955.

Steinberg, S. H. Cassell's encyclopaedia of literature. 2 vols 1953, 3 vols 1973 (enlarged).

Bibliography and Bookmanship

Lowndes, W. T. The bibliographer's manual of English literature. 4 vols 1834; rev H. G. Bohn 11 pts 1857–64, 6 vols 1890.

Book-prices current. 1888– (annual, with indexes for 1887–1916 3 vols 1901–20).

American book-prices current. New York 1895– (annual, with indexes every 4 to 9 years).

Book auction records. 1903–

British Museum. List of catalogues of English book sales 1676–1900. 1915.

de Ricci, S The book collector's guide. Philadelphia 1921, New York 1967.

—— English collectors of books and mss 1530–1930 and their marks of ownership. Cambridge 1930, New York 1969.

McKerrow, R. B. Introduction to bibliography for literary students. Oxford 1927, 1928 (corrected).

Sawyer, C. J., and F. J. H. Darton. English books 1475–1900. 2 vols 1927.

Carter, J. New paths in book-collecting. 1934.

—— Taste and technique in book-collecting. 1934.

—— ABC for book-collectors. New York 1951, London 1953, 1961 (both rev), 1967 (corrected).

—— Books and book-collectors. 1956.

Hayward, J. English poetry: a catalogue of first and early editions from Chaucer to the present day, exhibited at the National Book League. 1947, 1950 (rev).

Bowers, F. T. Principles of bibliographical description. Princeton 1949.

Glaister, G. A. An encyclopaedia of the book. Cleveland 1960.

Munby, A. N. L. et al. Sale catalogues of libraries of eminent persons. 12 vols 1971–5.

II. GENERAL HISTORIES

Bale, J. Illustrium majoris Britanniae scriptorum, hoc est Angliae, Cambriae ac Scotiae summarium. Ipswich 1548, Basle 1557–9 (enlarged).

—— Index Britanniae scriptorum. Ed R. L. Poole and M. Bateson, Oxford 1902.

Leland, J. Commentarii de scriptoribus britannicis. Ed A. Hall 2 vols Oxford 1709.

Taine, H. Histoire de la littérature anglaise. 4 vols Paris 1863–4; tr 2 vols Edinburgh 1871; tr H. Van Laun 4 vols New York 1965.

Handbooks of English literature. Ed J. Hales 10 pts 1895–1903.

Periods of European literature. Ed G. Saintsbury 12 vols Edinburgh 1897–1908.

Saintsbury, G. A short history of English literature. 1898.

The Cambridge history of English literature. Ed A. W. Ward and A. R. Waller 14 vols Cambridge 1907–16 (vol 15, Index, 1927), 1932 (without bibliographies).

Legouis, E. and L. Cazamian. Histoire de la littérature anglaise. Paris 1924; tr 2 vols 1926–7, 1964 (16th edn rev R. Las Vergnas).

Legouis, E. A short history of English literature. Tr Oxford 1934. Abridged from Legouis and Cazamian, above.

Sampson, G. The concise Cambridge history of English literature. Cambridge 1941, 1961, 1970 (rev).

Wilson, F. P. and B. Dobrée (ed). The Oxford history of English literature. Oxford 1945–.

Baugh, A. C. (ed). A literary history of England. New York 1948.

Craig, H. (ed). A history of English literature. New York 1950.

Ford, B. (ed). A guide to English literature. 7 vols 1954–63 (Pelican), 1961 (rev).

Bolton, W. F., C. Ricks et al. Sphere history of literature in the English language. 12 vols 1970–.

Part I
600–1660

THE ANGLO-SAXON PERIOD
(TO 1100)

A. GENERAL WORKS

(1) BIBLIOGRAPHIES

Wülcker, R.-P. Grundriss zur Geschichte der angelsächsischen Litteratur. Leipzig 1885.

Kennedy, A. G. A bibliography of writings on the English language. Cambridge Mass 1927, 1961.

Loomis, R. S. Introduction to medieval literature chiefly in England: a reading list and bibliography. New York 1939, 1948 (rev).

Ker, N. R. Catalogue of manuscripts containing Anglo-Saxon. Oxford 1957.

Bonser, W. An Anglo-Saxon and Celtic bibliography 450–1087. 2 vols Oxford 1957.

Anderson, G. K. Beowulf, Chaucer and their backgrounds. In Contemporary literary scholarship: a critical review, ed L. Leary, New York 1958.

— Old English literature. In The medieval literature of Western Europe, ed J. H. Fisher, New York 1966.

Greenfield, S. B. An Old English bibliographical guide. In D. M. Zesmer, Guide to English literature from Beowulf through Chaucer and medieval drama, New York 1961.

Robinson, F. C. Old English research in progress. Neuphilologische Mitteilungen 66– 1965–.

— Old English literature: a select bibliography. Toronto 1970.

Matthews, W. Old and Middle English literature. New York 1968.

(2) HISTORIES

Hickes, G. Linguarum veterum septentrionalium thesaurus grammatico-criticus et archaeologicus. 3 vols Oxford 1703–5.

Earle, J. Anglo-Saxon literature. 1884.

Brooke, S. A. History of early English literature to the accession of King Alfred. 2 vols 1892.

— English literature from the beginning to the Norman Conquest. 1898.

Ker, W. P. Epic and romance. 1897, 1931.

— The Dark Ages. Edinburgh 1904.

— Medieval English literature. Oxford 1912 (Home Univ Lib).

Wardale, E. E. Chapters on Old English literature 1935.

Malone, K. The Old English period to 1100. In A literary history of England, ed A. C. Baugh, New York 1948, 1967 (rev).

Anderson, G. K. The literature of the Anglo-Saxons. Princeton 1949, 1966 (rev).

— Old and Middle English literature from the beginnings to 1485. New York 1950.

Whitelock, D. The beginnings of English society. 1952 (Pelican), 1965 (rev).

Hunter Blair, P. An introduction to Anglo-Saxon England. Cambridge 1956.

Greenfield, S. B. A critical history of Old English literature. New York 1965.

— The interpretation of Old English poems. Boston 1972.

Stanley, E. G. (ed). Continuations and beginnings: studies in Old English literature. 1966.

Wrenn, C. L. A study of Old English literature. 1967.

Cross, J. E. Old English literature. In The Middle Ages, ed W. F. Bolton 1970.

Shippey, T. A. Old English verse. 1972.

Pearsall, D. Old and Middle English poetry. 1977.

(3) ANTHOLOGIES

In Old English

Thorpe, B. Analecta anglo-saxonica. 1834, 1846.

Zupitza, J. Altenglisches Übungsbuch. Vienna 1874, 1882 (as Alt- und mittelenglisches Übungsbuch); rev J. Schipper 1897; rev A. Eichler 1922; rev 1932.

Sweet, H. An Anglo-Saxon reader. Oxford 1876; rev C. T. Onions, Oxford 1922–59; rev D. Whitelock, Oxford 1967 (15th edn).

— An Anglo-Saxon primer. Oxford 1882; rev N. Davis 1953 (9th edn).

— The oldest English texts. 1885 (EETS).

— A second Anglo-Saxon reader: archaic and dialectal. Oxford 1887.

— First steps in Anglo-Saxon. Oxford 1897.

Bright, J. W. An Anglo-Saxon reader. New York 1891; rev J. R. Hulbert 1935; rev Hulbert and B. C. Monroe 1965.

Wyatt, A. J. An elementary Old English reader (early West Saxon). Cambridge 1901.

— An Anglo-Saxon reader. Cambridge 1919.

Krapp, G. P. and A. G. Kennedy. An Anglo-Saxon reader. New York 1929.

Mossé, F. Manuel de l'anglais du Moyen Age des origines au xive siècle: 1, vieil-anglais: 1, grammaire et textes; 2, notes et glossaire. Paris 1945, 1950 (rev).

Brook, G. L. An introduction to Old English. Manchester 1955.

Bolton, W. F. An Old English anthology. 1963, Evanston 1966 (rev).

Fowler, R. Old English prose and verse. 1966.

In Translation

Magoun, F. P. and J. A. Walker. An Old-English anthology: translation of Old-English prose and verse. Dubuque 1950.

Whitelock, D. English historical documents: 1, c. 500–1042. 1955.

B. POETRY

(1) DICTIONARIES

Grein, C. W. M. Sprachschatz der angelsächsischen Dichter. Cassel and Göttingen 1861–4, Heidelberg 1912 (rev J. J. Köhler).

Bessinger, J. B. A short dictionary of Anglo-Saxon poetry. Toronto 1960, 1961 (rev).

(2) COLLECTIONS AND ANTHOLOGIES

In Old English

Conybeare, J. J. Illustrations of Anglo-Saxon poetry. 1826.

Wülcker, R. P. Bibliothek der angelsächsischen Poesie. 3 vols Cassel 1881–98, Hamburg 1922.

— Kleinere angelsächsische Dichtungen. 2 vols Halle 1874–82.

Schücking, L. L. Kleines angelsächsisches Dichterbuch. Cöthen 1919.

Sedgefield, W. J. An Anglo-Saxon verse book. Manchester 1922.

Krapp, G. P. and E. V. K. Dobbie. The Anglo-Saxon poetic records. 6 vols New York 1931–53.

Magoun, F. P. The Anglo-Saxon poems in Bright's Anglo-Saxon reader, done in a normalized orthography. Cambridge Mass 1965.

Pope, J. C. Seven Old English poems. Indianapolis 1966.

Hamer, R. F. S. A choice of Anglo-Saxon verse. 1970. With trns.

In Translation

Grein, C. W. M. Dichtungen der Angelsachsen stabreimend übersetzt. 2 vols Göttingen 1857–9, Heidelberg 1930.

Cook, A. S. and C. B. Tinker. Select translations from Old English poetry. Boston 1902, Cambridge Mass 1926 (rev).

Gordon, R. K. Anglo-Saxon poetry. 1926, 1954 (rev), 1964. Contains most of the poetry in prose trn.

Malone, K. Ten Old English poems put into modern English alliterative verse. Baltimore 1941.

Bone, G. Anglo-Saxon poetry: an essay with specimen translations in verse. Oxford 1943.

Kennedy, C. W. Early English Christian poetry translated into alliterative verse. 1952, Gloucester Mass 1965.

— An anthology of Old English poetry. Oxford 1960.

Crossley-Holland, K. The battle of Maldon and other Old English poems. Ed B. Mitchell 1965.

Alexander, M. The earliest English poems. 1966 (Penguin).

(3) INDIVIDUAL POEMS AND AUTHORS

ALDHELM

Ms : Corpus Christi College Cambridge 326, pp. 5–6.
Krapp-Dobbie 6 1942.

ALMS-GIVING

Ms : Exeter book 121b–2b.
Krapp-Dobbie 3 1936.

ANDREAS

Ms : Vercelli book 29b–52b.
Grimm, J. Andreas und Elene. Cassel 1840.
Krapp, G. P. Andreas and the Fates of the apostles. Boston 1906.
Krapp-Dobbie 2 1932.
Brooks, K. R. Andreas and the Fates of the apostles. Oxford 1961.

Translations

Root, R. K. Andreas: the legend of St Andrew. New York 1899.
Kennedy, C. W. The poems of Cynewulf. 1910.
Hall, J. L. Judith, Phoenix and other Anglo-Saxon poems. New York 1912.

AZARIAS

Ms : Exeter book 53a–5b.
Schmidt, W. Die altenglischen Dichtungen Daniel und Azarias. Bonner Beiträge zur Anglistik 23 1907.
Krapp-Dobbie 3 1936.

BATTLE OF BRUNANBURH

Mss : in 4 mss of the Anglo-Saxon Chronicle : Corpus Christi College Cambridge 173, Cotton Tiberius A vi, Cotton Tiberius B i, Cotton Tiberius B iv.
Crow, C. L. Maldon and Brunanburh: two Old English songs of battle. Boston 1897.

Sedgefield, W. J. The battle of Maldon and short poems from the Saxon chronicle. Boston 1904.
Kershaw, N. Anglo-Saxon and Norse poems. Cambridge 1912.
Campbell, A. The battle of Brunanburh. 1938.
Krapp-Dobbie 6 1942.
See also edns of the Chronicle, below.

Translations

Tennyson, A. Battle of Brunanburh. In Ballads and other poems, 1880. In verse.
Hall, J. L. Judith, Phoenix and other Anglo-Saxon poems. New York 1912.
Garmonsway, G. N. In his Anglo-Saxon chronicle, 1953 (EL).
Whitelock, D. In her English historical documents c. 500–1042 vol 1, 1955; rptd in her Anglo-Saxon chronicle: a revised translation, 1962.

BATTLE OF FINNSBURH

Ms not known. Transcript by G. Hickes in his Linguarum veterum septentrionalium thesaurus vol 1, Oxford 1705.

Bibliographies

Fry, D. K. Beowulf and the Fight at Finnsburh: a bibliography. Charlottesville 1969.

§ 1

Dickins, B. Runic and heroic poems of the old Teutonic peoples. Cambridge 1915. With trn. Ed D. K. Fry 1974.
Krapp-Dobbie 6 1942.

Translations

Scott-Moncrieff, C. K. Widsith, Beowulf, Finnsburgh, Waldere, Deor. 1921.

Lattimore, R. Finnsburg. Hudson Rev 16 1963.
See also edns and trns of Beowulf, *below.*

BATTLE OF MALDON

Ms: Cotton Otho A. xii 57a–62b, burnt in library fire 1731. Transcript by J. Elphinston in Bodley Rawlinson B 203, from which T. Hearne ptd the earliest extant record in his Johannis Glastoniensis chronica, *2 vols Oxford 1726.*

Crow, C. L. Maldon and Brunanburh: two Old English songs of battle. Boston 1897.
Sedgefield, W. J. The battle of Maldon and short poems from the Saxon chronicle. Boston 1904.
Ashdown, M. English and Norse documents relating to the reign of Ethelred the Unready. Cambridge 1930. With trn.
Laborde, E. D. Byrhtnoth and Maldon. 1936.
Gordon, E. V. The battle of Maldon. 1937, 1957 (corrected).
Krapp-Dobbie 6 1942.

Translations

Hall, J. L. Judith, Phoenix and other Anglo-Saxon poems. New York 1912.

BEDE'S DEATH SONG

Mss: 29 known to exist, of which 11 give the song in the Northumbrian dialect, 17 in West Saxon, and one (Hague ms 70.H.7) in a mixed Northumbrian-West Saxon. See Krapp-Dobbie 6 pp. ci–civ.

Smith, A. H. Three Northumbrian poems. 1933.
Dobbie, E. V. K. The manuscripts of Cædmon's hymn and Bede's death song. New York 1937.
Brotanek, R. Nachlese zu den Hss. der Epistola Cuthberti und des Sterbespruches Bedas. Anglia 64 1940.
Ker, N. R. MÆ 8 1939; Krapp-Dobbie 6 1942.

BEOWULF

Ms: BM Cotton Vitellius A. xv 132a–201b (new foliation).

Concordances

Bessinger, J. B. with P. H. Smith. A concordance to Beowulf. Ithaca 1969.

Bibliographies

Fry, D. K. Beowulf and the Fight at Finnsburh: a bibliography. Charlottesville 1969.
See also Klaeber's edn, 1922, 1950, and in R. W. Chambers, Beowulf: an introduction, *1921, 1959.*

§1

Thorkelin, G. J. De Danorum rebus gestis seculis III et IV poema danicum dialecto anglosaxonica. Copenhagen 1815. With Latin trn.
Kemble, J. M. The Anglo-Saxon poems of Beowulf, the Traveller's song and the Battle of Finnesburh 1. 1833, 1835.
Thorpe, B. The Anglo-Saxon poems of Beowulf, the Scop or gleeman's tale, and the Fight at Finnsburg. Oxford 1855, 1875 (with trn); ed V. F. Hopper, Great Neck NY 1963.
Arnold, T. Beowulf. 1876. With trn.
Harrison, J. A. and R. Sharp. Beowulf; The fight at Finnsburh. Boston 1883, 1894 (4th edn).
Wyatt, A. J. Beowulf. Cambridge 1894, 1898.
Sedgefield, W. J. Beowulf. Manchester 1910, 1935 (3rd edn).
Chambers, R. W. Beowulf with the Finnsburg Fragment. Cambridge 1914, 1920. Nominally a revision of Wyatt, above, but really a new edn.
Klaeber, F. Beowulf and the Fight at Finnsburg. Boston

1922, 1936 (3rd edn), 1941, 1950 (both with suppls).
Krapp-Dobbie 4 1953.
Wrenn, C. L. Beowulf with the Finnsburg fragment. 1953, 1958, 1973 (rev W. F. Bolton).
Magoun, F. P. The poems of British Museum ms Cotton Vitellius A.xv. Cambridge Mass 1955, 1959 (expanded as Beowulf and Judith, done in a normalized orthography), 1966 (rev J. B. Bessinger).

Translations

Earle, J. The deeds of Beowulf. Oxford 1892.
Hall, J. L. Beowulf: an Anglo-Saxon epic poem. Boston 1892.
Morris, W. and A. J. Wyatt. The tale of Beowulf. Hammersmith 1895, London 1898.
Hall, J. R. Clark. Beowulf and the Fight at Finnsburg. 1901, 1950 (rev C. L. Wrenn, with prefatory remarks by J. R. R. Tolkien).
— Beowulf: a metrical translation. Cambridge 1914.
Tinker, C. B. Beowulf. New York 1902.
Child, C. G. Beowulf and the Finnesburh fragment. Boston 1904.
Scott-Moncrieff, C. K. Beowulf translated. 1921; rptd in his Widsith, Beowulf, Finnsburgh, Waldere, Deor, 1921.
Gordon, R. K. The song of Beowulf. 1923.
Leonard, W. E. Beowulf: a new verse translation. 1923.
Strong, A. Beowulf translated into modern English rhyming verse. 1925.
Crawford, D. H. Beowulf translated into English verse. 1926.
Kennedy, C. W. Beowulf: the oldest English epic. New York 1940.
Bone, G. Beowulf in modern verse. Oxford 1945.
Waterhouse, M. E. Beowulf in modern English. Cambridge 1949.
Morgan, E. Beowulf: a verse translation into modern English. Aldington Kent 1952, Berkeley and Los Angeles 1962.
Wright, D. Beowulf: a prose translation. 1957 (Penguin Classics).
Pearson, L. D. Beowulf. Bloomington 1965.
Donaldson, E. T. Beowulf. New York 1966.
Hieatt, C. B. Beowulf and other Old English poems. New York 1967. Introd by A. K. Hieatt.
Crossley-Holland, K. Beowulf. 1968. Introd by B. Mitchell.
Garmonsway, G. N. and J. Simpson. Beowulf and its analogues. 1968.

§2

Leo, H. Beowulf: das älteste deutsche, in angelsächsischer Mundart erhaltene Heldengedicht. Halle 1839.
Ker, W. P. In his Epic and romance, 1897.
Schücking, L. L. Die Grundzüge der Satzverknüpfung im Beowulf part 1. Halle 1904.
— Beowulfs Rückkehr. Halle 1905.
Lawrence, W. W. Some disputed questions in Beowulf-criticism. PMLA 24 1909.
— The haunted mere in Beowulf. PMLA 27 1912.
— The Breca episode in Beowulf. In Anniversary papers [for] G. L. Kittredge, Boston 1913.
— Beowulf and the tragedy of Finnsburg. PMLA 30 1915.
— The dragon and his lair in Beowulf. PMLA 33 1918.
— Beowulf and epic tradition. Cambridge Mass 1928.
— Grendel's lair. JEGP 38 1939.
Chambers, R. W. Beowulf: an introduction to the study of the poem with a discussion of the stories of Offa and Finn. Cambridge 1921, 1959 (3rd edn, with suppl by C. L. Wrenn).
— Beowulf and the heroic age. Foreword to Strong's trn, 1925; rptd in his Man's unconquerable mind, 1939.

Malone, K. The burning of Heorot. RES 13 1937.
—— Young Beowulf. JEGP 36 1937.
—— Swerting. Germanic Rev 14 1939; rptd as part of Tale of Ingeld in his Studies in heroic legend, Copenhagen 1959.
—— Time and place in the Ingeld episode of Beowulf. JEGP 39 1940; rptd as part of Tale of Ingeld, ibid.
—— Symbolism in Beowulf: some suggestions. In English studies today: 2nd series, ed G. A. Bonnard, Berne 1961.
—— Widsith, Beowulf and Bravellir. In Festgabe für L. L. Hammerich, Copenhagen 1962.
Williams, R. A. The Finn episode in Beowulf. Cambridge 1924.
Magoun, F. P. Danes, North, South, East and West, in Beowulf. In Philologica: the [Kemp] Malone anniversary studies, Baltimore 1949.
—— Oral-formulaic character of Anglo-Saxon narrative poetry. Speculum 28 1953; rptd in Essential articles for the study of OE poetry, ed J. B. Bessinger and S. J. Kahrl, Hamden Conn 1968, and in Nicholson and Fry, below.
—— Béowulf B: a folk-poem on Beowulf's death. In Early English and Norse studies presented to Hugh Smith, 1963.
Girvan, R. Beowulf and the seventh century. 1935, 1971 (with new ch by R. Bruce-Mitford).
—— Finnsburuh. Proc Br Acad 26 1940.
Tolkien, J. R. R. Beowulf: the monsters and the critics. Proc Br Acad 22 1936; 1937 (separately); rptd in Nicholson and Fry, below.
Whitelock, D. Beowulf 2444–71. MÆ 8 1939.
—— The audience of Beowulf. Oxford 1951.
Andrew, S. O. Syntax and style in Old English. Cambridge 1940.
—— Postscript on Beowulf. Cambridge 1948.
Bonjour, A. The use of anticipation in Beowulf. RES 16 1940; rptd in his Twelve Beowulf papers, 1962.
—— Twelve Beowulf papers 1940–60, with additional comments. Neuchâtel 1962.
Pope, J. C. The rhythm of Beowulf: an interpretation of the normal and hypermetric verse-forms in Old English poetry. New Haven 1942, 1966 (rev).
Brodeur, A. G. The art of Beowulf. Berkeley 1959.
Sisam, K. Anglo-Saxon royal genealogies. Proc Br Acad 39 1953.
—— Liber monstrorum and English heroic legend. In his Studies in the history of OE literature, Oxford 1953.
—— Beowulf's fight with the dragon. RES new ser 9 1958.
—— The structure of Beowulf. Oxford 1965.
Bliss, A. J. The metre of Beowulf. Oxford 1958.
Chadwick, N. K. The monsters and Beowulf. In The Anglo-Saxons: studies presented to B. Dickins, 1959.
Creed, R. P. The making of an Anglo-Saxon poem. ELH 26 1959; rptd in Essential articles for the study of OE poetry, ed J. B. Bessinger and S. J. Kahrl, Hamden Conn 1968; in Fry, below, with addns.
—— A new approach to the rhythm of Beowulf. PMLA 81 1966.
Greenfield, S. B. Beowulf and epic tragedy. Comparative Lit 14 1962; rptd in Studies in OE literature in honor of A. G. Brodeur, Eugene 1963.
—— The canons of Old English criticism. ELH 34 1967.
—— Grammar and meaning in poetry. PMLA 82 1967.
—— Grendel's approach to Heorot: syntax and poetry. In Old English poetry: fifteen essays, ed R. P. Creed, Providence RI 1967.
Stanley, E. G. 'Hæthenra hyht' in Beowulf. In Studies in OE literature in honor of A. G. Brodeur, Eugene 1963.
—— The search for Anglo-Saxon paganism. N & Q Sept 1964.
—— Beowulf. In Continuations and beginnings, ed E. G. Stanley 1966.

Fry, D. K. (ed). The Beowulf poet. Englewood Cliffs NJ 1968.
Irving, E. B. A reading of Beowulf. New Haven 1968.
Bloomfield, M. W. Episodic motivations and marvels in epic and romance. In his Essays and explorations, Cambridge Mass 1970.
Goldsmith, M. E. The mode and meaning of Beowulf. 1970.

CÆDMON

The poems of the Junius ms, as well as the Hymn, were once thought to be by Cædmon; a certain body of literature developed around this misconception.

§1

Junius, F. Cædmonis monachi paraphrasis poetica Genesios. Amsterdam 1655.
Thorpe, B. Cædmon's metrical paraphrase of parts of the Holy Scriptures in Anglo-Saxon. 1832 (Soc of Antiquaries). With trn.
Krapp-Dobbie 1 1931.
Kennedy, C. W. The Cædmon poems. 1916, Gloucester Mass 1965.

§2

Crawford, S. J. The Cædmon poems. Anglia 49 1926.
Klaeber, F. Analogues of the story of Cædmon. MLN 42 1927.
—— Bede's story of Cædmon again. MLN 53 1938.
Wrenn, C. L. The poetry of Cædmon. Proc Br Acad 32 1946; rptd in Essential articles for the study of OE poetry, ed J. B. Bessinger and S. J. Kahrl, Hamden Conn 1968.
Shepherd, G. The prophetic Cædmon. RES new ser 5 1954.
—— Scriptural poetry. In Continuations and beginnings, ed E. G. Stanley 1966.
Malone, K. Cædmon and English poetry. MLN 76 1961.
See also under Junius ms above, under Cædmon's Hymn, Christ and Satan, Daniel, Exodus and Genesis.

CÆDMON'S HYMN

Mss: 17 known to exist, ranging in date from the eighth to the fifteenth centuries; 4 in the Northumbrian dialect, 13 in West Saxon; of the latter, 8 in Latin mss of Bede's Ecclesiastical history, and 5 in OE trns of Bede. See Krapp-Dobbie 6 pp. xcv–xcvii for an account.

§1

Smith, A. H. Three Northumbrian poems. 1933.
Dobbie, E. V. K. The manuscripts of Cædmon's hymn and Bede's death song. New York 1937.
Krapp-Dobbie 6 1942.
Arngart [Anderson], O. S. The Leningrad Bede. Copenhagen 1952 (facs).
Kroll, J. Translations from Old English. Cambridge Quart 4 1969.
The text is included in most OE readers as part of the story of Cædmon.

§2

Pound, L. Cædmon's dream song. In Studies in English philology in honor of F. Klaeber, Minneapolis 1929.
Anderson, O. S. Old English material in the Leningrad ms of Bede's Ecclesiastical history. Lund 1941.
Ross, A. S. C. Miscellaneous notes on Cædmon's hymn and Bede's death song. Eng & Germanic Stud 3 1950.
Magoun, F. P. Bede's story of Cædman: the case history of an Anglo-Saxon oral singer. Speculum 30 1955.

Huppé, B. F. Doctrine and poetry: Augustine's influence on Old English poetry. New York 1959.

Bloomfield, M. W. Patristics and Old English literature. Comparative Lit 14 1962; rptd in Studies in OE literature in honor of A. G. Brodeur, Eugene 1963; and in Essential articles for the study of OE poetry, ed J. B. Bessinger and S. J. Kahrl, Hamden Conn 1968.

Henry, P. L. The early English and Celtic lyric. 1966.

CHRIST

The 3 pts of this poem are no longer considered to be a unity, but are treated together here for convenience.

Ms: Exeter Book 8a–32b.

§ 1

Gollancz, I. Cynewulf's Christ. 1892. With trn.

Cook, A. S. The Christ of Cynewulf: a poem in three parts, the Advent, the Ascension and the Last Judgment. Boston 1900.

Krapp-Dobbie 3 1936.

Campbell, J. J. The Advent lyrics of the Exeter book. Princeton 1959. With trn.

Whitman, C. H. The Christ of Cynewulf. Boston 1900. Trn.

§ 2

Shepherd, G. Scriptural poetry. In Continuations and beginnings, ed E. G. Stanley 1966.

Burlin, R. B. The Old English Advent: a typological commentary. New Haven 1968.

Clemoes, P. Cynewulf's image of the Ascension. In England before the Conquest: studies presented to Dorothy Whitelock, Cambridge 1971.

See also under Cynewulf, below.

CHRIST AND SATAN

Ms: Bodley, Junius xi, numbered pp. 213–29.

Clubb, M. D. Christ and Satan. New Haven 1925.

Krapp-Dobbie 1 1931.

See also under Manuscripts, above, and under Cædmon, above.

CREED

Ms: Bodley, Junius 121, 46a–7a.

Feiler, E. Das Benedikter-Offizium. Heidelberg 1901.

Krapp-Dobbie 6 1942.

Ure, J. M. The Benedictine office: an old English text. Edinburgh 1957.

CYNEWULF

§ 1

Kennedy, C. W. The poems of Cynewulf, translated into English prose. 1910, 1949.

§ 2

Sisam, K. Cynewulf and his poetry. Proc Br Acad 18 1932; rptd in his Studies in the history of OE literature, Oxford 1953.

Schaar, C. Critical studies in the Cynewulf group. Lund 1949.

Derolez, R. Runica manuscripta: the English tradition. Bruges 1954.

DANIEL

Ms: Bodley, Junius xi, numbered pp. 173–212.

Hunt, T. W. Cædmon's Exodus and Daniel. Boston 1883.

Blackburn, F. A. Exodus and Daniel. Boston 1907.

Schmidt, W. Die altenglische Dichtung Daniel. Halle 1907.

Krapp-Dobbie 1 1931.

DEOR

Ms: Exeter book 100.

Dickins, B. Runic and heroic poems of the Old Teutonic peoples. Cambridge 1915. With trn.

Malone, K. Deor. 1933, 1966 (rev).

Krapp-Dobbie 3 1936.

Translations

Scott-Moncrieff, C. K. Widsith, Beowulf, Finnsburgh, Waldere, Deor. 1921.

Kroll, J. Translations from Old English. Cambridge Quart 4 1969.

Also in many readers and collections, including those of the Elegies, as well as in edns of the Exeter book.

DESCENT INTO HELL

Ms: Exeter book 119b–21b.

Cramer, J. Quelle, Verfasser und Text des altenglischen Gedichtes Christi Höllenfahrt. Anglia 19 1897.

Krapp-Dobbie 3 1936.

DREAM OF THE ROOD

Ms: Vercelli book 104b–6a.

§ 1

Cook, A. S. The dream of the rood. Oxford 1905.

Dickins, B. and A. S. C. Ross. The dream of the rood. 1934, 1963 (rev).

Krapp-Dobbie 2 1932.

Swanton, M. The dream of the rood. Manchester 1970.

Brooks, H. F. The dream of the rood. Dublin 1942. Trn.

Tr H. Gardner, Essays and poems presented to Lord David Cecil, 1970.

§ 2

Schlauch, M. The dream of the rood as prosopopoeia. In Essays and studies in honor of C. Brown, New York 1940; rptd in Essential articles for the study of OE poetry, ed J. B. Bessinger and S. J. Kahrl, Hamden Conn 1968.

Woolf, R. Doctrinal influences on the Dream of the rood. MÆ 27 1958.

Burrow, J. A. An approach to the Dream of the rood. Neophilologus 43 1959.

Huppé, B. F. The web of words. Albany NY 1970. With text and trn.

Raw, B. C. The dream of the rood and its connections with early Christian art. MÆ 39 1970.

DURHAM

Mss: Cambridge Univ Lib Ff.i.27, p. 202 (col 101b); formerly also in Cotton Vitellius D.xx, destroyed in fire of 1731, but ptd by G. Hickes in his Thesaurus 1703–5.

Krapp-Dobbie 6 1942.

DURHAM PROVERBS

Ms: Durham Cathedral B.III.32.

Arngart, O. S. The Durham proverbs. Lund 1956. Not in Krapp-Dobbie.

ELEGIES

§1

Kershaw, N. Anglo-Saxon and Norse poems. Cambridge 1922. With trn.

Translations

Kennedy, C. W. Old English elegies, translated into alliterative verse. Princeton 1936.

See also under individual elegies: Deor, *above;* Husband's message, Resignation, Ruin, Seafarer, Wanderer, Wife's lament, Wulf and Eadwacer, *below.*

§2

Jackson, K. Studies in early Celtic nature poetry. Cambridge 1935.

Greenfield, S. B. The formulaic expression of the theme of exile in Anglo-Saxon poetry. Speculum 30 1955; rptd in Essential articles for the study of OE poetry, ed J. B. Bessinger and S. J. Kahrl, Hamden Conn 1968.
— The Old English elegies. In Continuations and beginnings, ed E. G. Stanley 1966.

Elliott, R. W. V. Form and image in the Old English lyrics. EC 11 1961.

Henry, P. L. The early English and Celtic lyric. 1966.

ELENE

Ms: Vercelli book 121a–33b.
Grimm, J. Andreas und Elene. Cassel 1840.
Zupitza, J. Cynewulf's Elene. Berlin 1877, 1899 (rev).
Holthausen, F. Cynewulf's Elene. Heidelberg 1905, 1936 (rev).
Cook, A. S. The Old English Elene, Phoenix and Physiologus. New Haven 1919.
Krapp-Dobbie 2 1932.
Gradon, P. Cynewulf's Elene. 1958.

EXODUS

Ms: Bodley, Junius xi, numbered pp. 143–71.
Hunt, T. W. Cædmon's Exodus and Daniel. Boston 1883, 1888 (rev).
Krapp-Dobbie 1 1931.
Irving, E. B. The Old English Exodus. New Haven 1953.

FATES OF THE APOSTLES

Ms: Vercelli book 52b–4a.
Thorpe, B. Appendix B to Cooper's report on Rymer's Foedera. 1869 (ptd 1836).
Krapp, G. P. Andreas and the Fates of the apostles. Boston 1906.
Krapp-Dobbie 2 1932.
Brooks, K. R. Andreas and the Fates of the apostles. Oxford 1961.

Translations

Olivero, F. The Fates of the apostles: translation and critical commentary. Milan 1927. *See also under* Andreas, *above.*

GENESIS

Ms: Bodley, Junius xi, numbered pp. 1–142. Genesis A (The older Genesis) consists of ll. 1–234, 852–2936; Genesis B (The later Genesis) of ll. 235–851.
Sievers, E. Der Heliand und die angelsächsische Genesis. Halle 1875.
Behagel, O. Heliand und Genesis. Halle 1903, 1922 (rev).

Klaeber, F. The later Genesis and other Old English and Old Saxon texts relating to the fall of man. Heidelberg 1913.
Holthausen, F. Die ältere Genesis. Heidelberg 1914.
Krapp-Dobbie 1 1931.
Timmer, B. J. The later Genesis. Oxford 1948, 1954 (rev).

GUTHLAC

Ms: Exeter book 33a–52b. Guthlac I (or A) consists of ll. 1–818; Guthlac II (or B), of ll. 819–1379.
Krapp-Dobbie 3 1936.
For other edns and trns see under Cynewulf, *above.*

HUSBAND'S MESSAGE

Ms: Exeter book 123a–b.
Krapp-Dobbie 3 1936.
Leslie, R. F. Three Old English elegies: The Wife's lament, The husband's message, The ruin. Manchester 1961.

JUDITH

Ms: BM Cotton Vitellius A. xv, 199a–206.
Cook, A. S. Judith: an Old English epic fragment. Boston 1888.
Timmer, B. J. Judith. 1952, 1961 (rev).
Krapp-Dobbie 4 1953.

Translations

Elton, O. Judith [ll. 1–121]. In An English miscellany presented to Dr [F. J.] Furnivall, Oxford 1901.
Hall, J. L. Judith, Phoenix and other Anglo-Saxon poems. New York 1912.

JULIANA

Ms: Exeter book 65b–76a.
Strunk, W. Juliana. Boston 1904.
Krapp-Dobbie 3 1936.
Woolf, R. E. Juliana. 1955, New York 1966 (corrected with addns).

Translations

Kennedy, C. W. The legend of St Juliana, translated from the Latin of the Acta sanctorum and the Anglo-Saxon of Cynewulf. Princeton 1906.
See also under Cynewulf, *above.*

METRES OF BOETHIUS

Ms: BM Cotton Otho A. vi, 1a–129b (alternating with prose); paper transcript, Junius 12 (17th century).
Fox, S. King Alfred's Anglo-Saxon version of the Metres of Boethius. 1835. With trn.
— King Alfred's Anglo-Saxon version of Boethius De consolatione philosophiæ. 1864. With verse trns of Metres by M. F. Tupper.
Sedgefield, W. J. King Alfred's version of Boethius De consolatione philosophiae. Oxford 1899.
Krapp-Dobbie 5 1932.

Translations

Sedgefield, W. J. King Alfred's version of the Consolations of Boethius, done into modern English. Oxford 1900.

METRICAL CHARMS

Mss: BM Cotton Caligula A. vii (for unfruitful land), 176a–8a.
BM Harley 585 (nine herbs), 160a–3b; (against a dwarf), 167a–7b; (for a sudden stitch), 175a–6a; (for loss of cattle), 180b–1a; (for delayed birth), 185a–b.

BM Royal ms 12D. xvii (for the water-elf disease), 125a–b.
Corpus Christi College Cambridge 41 (for a swarm of bees), numbered p. 182; (for theft of cattle), numbered p. 206; (for loss of cattle), ibid; (a journey charm), numbered pp. 350–3.
BM Royal ms 4A. xiv (against a wen), 106b.
Cockayne, O. Leechdoms, wortcunning and starcraft of early England. 3 vols 1864–6. With trn.
Grendon, F. The Anglo-Saxon charms. Jnl of Amer Folklore 22 1909; New York 1909 (separately). With trn.
Krapp-Dobbie 6 1942.
Storms, G. Anglo-Saxon magic. Hague 1948. With trn.
Grattan, J. H. G. and C. Singer. Anglo-Saxon magic and medicine. New York 1952. Pt 2 is an edn of Lacnunga (in Harley 585), containing 5 metrical charms.

METRICAL PREFACE TO THE PASTORAL CARE

Mss: Bodley, Hatton 20, 2b; Bodley, Junius 53, numbered p. 4; Corpus Christi College Cambridge 12; Trinity College Cambridge R.5.22, 72a.
Sweet, H. King Alfred's West-Saxon version of Gregory's Pastoral care. 1871 (EETS).
Holthausen, F. Die Gedichte in Alfreds Übersetzung der Cura pastoralis. Archiv 106 1901.
Krapp-Dobbie 6 1942.

PHOENIX

Ms: Exeter book 55b–65b.
Grundtvig, N. F. S. Phenix-Fuglen. Copenhagen 1840. With Danish trn.
Cook, A. S. The Old English Elene, Phoenix and Physiologus. New Haven 1919.
Krapp-Dobbie 3 1936.
Blake, N. F. The Phoenix. Manchester 1964.

Translations

Stephens, G. The King of birds: or the lay of the phoenix. Archaeologia 30 1844. Also pbd separately.
Hall, J. L. Judith, Phoenix and other Anglo-Saxon poems. New York 1912.

PHYSIOLOGUS

Ms: Exeter book 95b–6b (Panther); 96b–7b (Whale); 97b–8b (Partridge).
Cook, A. S. The Old English Elene, Phoenix and Physiologus. New Haven 1919. Text of Physiologus alone rptd 1922, with verse trn by J. H. Pitman.
Krapp-Dobbie 3 1936 (as 3 poems).

POEMS OF THE ANGLO-SAXON CHRONICLE

Here are considered the Capture of the Five Boroughs, Coronation of Edgar, Death of Edgar, Death of Alfred and Death of Edward. See also Battle of Brunanburh, above.
Mss: in 4 mss of the Chronicle: Corpus Christi College Cambridge 173, Cotton Tiberius A. vi, Cotton Tiberius B. i, Cotton Tiberius B. iv. The 2 poems on Edgar are not found in Cambridge ms; those on Alfred and Edward appear only in last 2. See under respective dates: 942, 973, 975, 1036, 1065.
Sedgefield, W. J. The battle of Maldon and short poems from the Saxon Chronicle. Boston 1904.

Craigie, W. A. Specimens of Anglo-Saxon poetry III. Edinburgh 1931.
Krapp-Dobbie 6 1942.
See also under Prose: Anglo-Saxon Chronicle, below, for edns and trns. Individual poems appear in many readers.

A PRAYER

Mss: BM Cotton Julius A. ii, 136a–7a; Lambeth Palace Lib 427, 183b.
Junius, F. Cædmonis monachi paraphrasis poetica Genesios. Amsterdam 1655.
Thomson, E. Select monuments of the doctrine and worship of the Catholic Church in England before the Norman Conquest. 1849. With trn.

RIDDLES

Ms: Exeter book 101a–15a, 122b–3a, 124a–130b.
Tupper, F. The riddles of the Exeter book. Boston 1910.
Wyatt, A. J. Old English riddles. Boston 1912.
Krapp-Dobbie 3 1936.

Translations

Baum, P. F. The Anglo-Saxon riddles of the Exeter book. Durham NC 1963 (complete).
Abbott, H. H. The riddles of the Exeter book. Cambridge 1968.
Crossley-Holland, K. Storm and other Old English riddles, 1970.
See also under Exeter book, above. Selected riddles and trns appear in many readers and literary histories; some recent trns by B. Raffel, in his Poems from the Old English, Lincoln Nebraska 1960, 1964 (rev and enlarged), and by K. Crossley-Holland, in his Battle of Maldon and other Old English poems, 1965.

RUIN

Ms: Exeter book 123b–4b.
Krapp-Dobbie 3 1936.
Leslie, R. F. Three Old English elegies: the Wife's lament, the Husband's message, the Ruin. Manchester 1961.

Translations

Abbott, C. C. Three Old English elegies. Durham Univ Jnl 36 1944.
Massingham, H. The ruin (after the Anglo-Saxon). TLS 18 Aug 1966.
See also under Elegies, above.

RUTHWELL CROSS

Runic inscriptions on east and west faces of lower shaft.
Viëtor, W. Die northumbrischen Runensteine. Marburg 1895.
Cook, A. S. The dream of the rood. Oxford 1905.
Dickins, B. and A. S. C. Ross. The dream of the rood. 1934.
Krapp-Dobbie 6 1942.

SEAFARER

Ms: Exeter book 81b–3a.
Krapp-Dobbie 3 1936.
Gordon, I. L. The seafarer. 1960.

Translations

Pound, E. The seafarer from the Anglo-Saxon. In his Personae, New York 1926.

Bone, G. The seafarer. MÆ 3 1934; rptd in his Anglo-Saxon poetry, Oxford 1943.
Abbott, C. C. The seafarer. Durham Univ Jnl 35 1943.
Whitelock, D. In her English historical documents vol 1, c. 500–1042, 1955.

WALDERE

Ms: 2 leaves in the Royal Library at Copenhagen, Ny kgl. saml. 167b.
Stephens, G. Two leaves of King Waldere's lay. Copenhagen 1860. With trn.
Holthausen, F. Die altenglischen Waldere-Bruchstücke. Gothenburg 1899. With facs.
Norman, F. Waldere. 1933, 1949 (rev).
Dickins, B. Runic and heroic poems of the old Teutonic peoples. Cambridge 1915. With trn.
Krapp-Dobbie 6 1942.
Also in many edns of Beowulf and in many collections.

Translations

Gummere, F. B. The oldest English epic. New York 1909.
Scott-Moncrieff, C. K. Widsith, Beowulf, Finnsburgh, Waldere, Deor. 1921.
Magoun, F. P. and H. M. Smyser. Walter of Aquitaine: materials for the study of his legend. New London 1950.

WANDERER

Ms: Exeter book 76b–8a.
Krapp-Dobbie 3 1936.
Leslie, R. F. The wanderer. Manchester 1966.
Dunning, T. P. and A. J. Bliss. The wanderer. 1969.

Translations

Abbott, C. C. Three Old English elegies. Durham Univ Jnl 36 1944.
Whitelock, D. In her English historical documents vol 1, c. 500–1042, 1955.
See also under Elegies, above, and in most collections, both in Old English and in trn.

WIDSITH

Ms: Exeter book 84b–7a.
Chambers, R. W. Widsith: a study in Old English heroic legend. Cambridge 1912. With trn.
Krapp-Dobbie 3 1936.
Malone, K. Widsith. 1936, Copenhagen 1962 (rev).
Also in many edns of Beowulf and in readers and collections.

Translations

Gummere, F. B. The oldest English epic. New York 1909.
Scott-Moncrieff, C. K. Widsith, Beowulf, Finnsburgh, Waldere, Deor. 1921.

WIFE'S LAMENT

Ms: Exeter book 115a–b.
Krapp-Dobbie 3 1936.
Leslie, R. F. Three Old English elegies: the Wife's lament, the Husband's message, the Ruin. Manchester 1961.

Translations

Abbott, C. C. Three Old English elegies. Durham Univ Jnl 36 1944.
See also under Elegies, above.

C. PROSE

For a description of all the mss and their contents and for a list of the main edns and the mss on which they draw, see N. R. Ker, Catalogue of manuscripts containing Anglo-Saxon, Oxford 1957.

(1) COLLECTIONS AND ANTHOLOGIES

Bibliothek der angelsächsischen Prosa. Ed C. W. M. Grein, R. Wülcker and H. Hecht 13 vols Cassel, Leipzig and Hamburg 1872–1933.
Sweet, H. Anglo-Saxon primer. Oxford 1882, 1953 (9th edn, rev N. Davis).
Craigie, W. A. Specimens of Anglo-Saxon prose. 2 pts Edinburgh 1923–5.
Sedgefield, W. J. An Anglo-Saxon prose book. Manchester 1928.

Translations

Cook, A. S. and C. B. Tinker. Select translations from Old English prose. Boston 1908.
For trns of numerous OE prose texts see D. Whitelock, English historical documents c. 500–1042, 1955.

(2) GENERAL CRITICISM

Chambers, R. W. On the continuity of English prose from Alfred to More and his school. In Nicholas Harpsfield, Life of Sir Thomas Moore, ed E. V. Hitchcock and R. W. Chambers 1932 (EETS); rptd separately 1966.
Wright, C. E. The cultivation of saga in Anglo-Saxon England. Edinburgh 1939.
Campbell, A. Verse influences in Old English prose. In Philological essays in honour of H. D. Meritt, Hague 1970.

(3) MAJOR TRANSLATORS OF KING ALFRED'S REIGN (871–99)

KING ALFRED
849–99

§ 1

Pastoral Care

King Alfred's West Saxon version of Gregory's Pastoral care. Ed H. Sweet 2 vols 1871–2 (EETS). With trn.
The metrical preface and epilogue to the Pastoral care. In The Anglo-Saxon minor poems, ed E. V. K. Dobbie, New York 1942. *See also under Poetry, col 17, above.*

The pastoral care. Ed N. R. Ker, Early English mss in facsimile vol 6, Copenhagen 1956. Facs of mss Hatton 20, Cotton Tiberius B. xi and Kassel.

Boethius

King Alfred's Old English version of Boethius De consolatione philosophiae. Ed W. J. Sedgefield, Oxford 1899.
The meters of Boethius. In The Paris Psalter and the meters of Boethius, ed G. P. Krapp, New York 1932.
Tr W. J. Sedgefield, Oxford 1900.

Soliloquies

King Alfred's version of St Augustine's Soliloquies. Ed T. A. Carnicelli, Cambridge Mass 1969.
Tr H. L. Hargrove, New York 1904.
For trns of Orosius and Bede, formerly thought to be by Alfred, see below.

§2

Brooke, S. A. King Alfred as educator of his people and man of letters. 1901.
Asser's Life of King Alfred. Ed W. H. Stevenson, Oxford 1904, 1959 (with addn by D. Whitelock).
Sisam, K. The publication of Alfred's Pastoral care. In his Studies in the history of Old English literature, Oxford 1953.
—— The authorship of the verse translation of Boethius's Metra. Ibid.
Whitelock, D. The prose of Alfred's reign. In Continuations and beginnings, ed E. G. Stanley 1966.
—— William of Malmesbury on the works of King Alfred. In Medieval literature and civilization: studies in memory of G. N. Garmonsway, 1969.
Payne, F. A. King Alfred and Boethius: an analysis of the Old English version of the Consolation of philosophy. 1968.

WÆRFERTH
d. by 915

Gregory's Dialogues

§1

The metrical preface to Wærferth's translation of Gregory's Dialogues. In The Anglo-Saxon minor poems, ed E. V. K. Dobbie, New York 1942.

§2

Timmer, B. J. Studies in Bishop Wærferth's translation of the Dialogues of Gregory the Great. Wageningen 1934.

Sisam, K. The verses prefixed to Gregory's Dialogues. In his Studies in the history of Old English literature, Oxford 1953.
Whitelock, D. *See under Alfred, above.*

ANONYMOUS TRANSLATORS
Orosius

King Alfred's Anglo-Saxon version of Orosius. Ed J. Bosworth 1859. With trn.
King Alfred's Orosius. Ed H. Sweet 1883 (EETS).
The Tollemache Orosius: BM additional ms 47967. Ed A. Campbell, Early English mss in facsimile vol 3, Copenhagen 1953.
Tr B. Thorpe in R. Pauli, The life of Alfred the Great, 1853.

The Old English Bede

§1

Historia ecclesiastica. Strasbourg [c. 1475]; ed A. Wheloc(k) 2 vols Cambridge 1643–4 (with OE version).
The Old English version of Bede's Ecclesiastical history. Ed T. Miller 4 pts 1890–8 (EETS). With trn.
The metrical epilogue to ms 41, Corpus Christi College, Cambridge. In The Anglo-Saxon minor poems, ed E. V. K. Dobbie, New York 1942.

§2

Chambers, R. W. In his Man's unconquerable mind, 1939.
Whitelock, D. The Old English Bede. Proc Br Acad 48 1963.
Hunter Blair, P. The world of Bede. 1970.

For Anglo-Saxon Chronicle, first compiled in Alfred's reign, see below.

(4) MAJOR WRITERS OF THE LATER PERIOD

ÆLFRIC
c. 955–c. 1010(?)

For the Ælfric canon see P. Clemoes, The chronology of Ælfric works, in The Anglo-Saxons: studies presented to Bruce Dickins, 1959.

Catholic Homilies

The homilies of the Anglo-Saxon church: the first part, containing the Sermones catholici or Homilies of Ælfric. Ed B. Thorpe 2 vols 1844–6 (Ælfric Soc). With trn.
Ælfric: selected homilies. Ed H. Sweet, Oxford 1885.
Ælfric's first series of Catholic homilies: BM Royal 7 C. xii. Ed N. Eliason and P. Clemoes, Early English mss in facsimile vol 13, Copenhagen 1966.
Early English homilies from the 12th century ms Vespasian D. xiv. Ed R. D.-N. Warner 1917 (EETS). Contains mainly items from the Catholic homilies but also other works by Ælfric and some anon pieces.

Other Homilies

De duodecim abusivis. Ed R. Morris, Old English homilies: first series, 1867–8 (EETS), p. 299 line 1– p. 304.
Wulfstan: Sammlung der ihm zugeschriebenen Homilien. Ed A. S. Napier, Berlin 1883. Nos viii, xxxi and the Latin part of no vii are by Ælfric.

Angelsächsische Homilien und Heiligenleben. Ed B. Assmann, Bibliothek der angelsächsischen Prosa vol 3, 1889; rptd with supplementary introd by P. Clemoes, Darmstadt 1964. Nos i–ix are by Ælfric.
Twelfth-century homilies in ms Bodley 343. Ed A. O. Belfour 1909 (EETS). With trn. Items i–iv, vii–ix, xiii and xiv are by Ælfric, but i–ii have been re-ed Pope, below, and xiii–xiv are extracts from Catholic homilies II xxx and Pope no vi respectively.
Zwei Homilien des Ælfric. Ed R. Brotanek, Texte und Untersuchungen, Halle 1913. Only the first by Ælfric.
Exameron anglice. Ed S. J. Crawford, Bibliothek der angelsächsischen Prosa vol 10, 1921. With trn.
Homilies of Ælfric: a supplementary collection. Ed J. C. Pope 2 vols 1967–8 (EETS).

Lives of Saints

Lives of saints. Ed W. W. Skeat 4 pts 1881–1900 (EETS). With trn. Nos xxiii, xxiiib, xxx and xxxiii are not by Ælfric.
Gloucester fragments. Ed J. Earle 1861. With facs and trn. Includes fragments of Skeat no xxi, St Swithun, and xxiiib, St Mary of Egypt (latter not by Ælfric).
Lives of three English saints. Ed G. I. Needham 1966. SS Oswald, Edmund, Swithun; Skeat nos xxvi, xxxii, xxi.

Letters

Die Hirtenbriefe Ælfrics. Ed B. Fehr, Bibliothek der angelsächsischen Prosa vol 9, 1914; rptd with suppl by P. Clemoes to introd, Darmstadt 1966.

Letter to the monks of Eynsham (Latin). Ed M. Bateson as Excerpta ex institutionibus monasticis, in Compotus rolls of the obedientiaries of St Swithun's priory, ed G. W. Kitchin 1892.

Items i–ii in Assmann's collection, above, and Ælfric's treatise on the Old and New testaments, below, are also letters.

Other Works

Admonitio ad filium spiritualem. Ed H. W. Norman 1849 (with Hexameron) (with trn).

Ælfric's version of Alcuini Interrogationes Sigewulfi in Genesin. Ed G. E. MacLean, Halle 1883.

The Old English Heptateuch, Ælfric's treatise on the Old and New testament, and his preface to Genesis. Ed S. J. Crawford 1922 (EETS); rptd with text of two additional mss 1969. The Heptateuch is only partly by Ælfric.

Colloquy. Ed G. N. Garmonsway 1939, 1947 (rev). Only the Latin is by Ælfric.

Grammatik und Glossar: Text und Varianten. Ed J. Zupitza, Berlin 1880; rptd with preface by H. Gneuss, Berlin 1966.

De temporibus anni. Ed H. Henel 1942 (EETS).

Vita, S. Æthelwoldi. Ed J. Stevenson, Chronicon monasterii de Abingdon, 1858 (Rolls ser); tr S. H. Gem 1912, below, and D. Whitelock, English historical documents vol 1, 1955.

Ely charter. Ed J. Pope, England before the Conquest: studies presented to Dorothy Whitelock, Cambridge 1971.

WULFSTAN
d. 1023

§1

Wulfstan: Sammlung der ihm zugeschriebenen Homilien. Ed A. S. Napier, Berlin 1883; rptd with bibliographical suppl by K. Ostheeren, 1967. Not all by Wulfstan; *see* K. Jost, Wulfstanstudien, below.

Sermo Lupi ad Anglos. Ed D. Whitelock 1939, 1963 (rev); tr D. Whitelock in her English historical documents vol 1, 1955.

Homilies. Ed D. Bethurum, Oxford 1957.

Die Institutes of polity, civil and ecclesiastical. Ed K. Jost, Berne 1959.

A Wulfstan ms containing institutes, laws and homilies: BM Cotton Nero A.i. Ed H. R. Loyn, Early English mss in facsimile vol 17, Copenhagen 1971.

Canons of Edgar. Ed. R. G. Fowler 1972 (EETS).

§2

Napier, A. S. Über die Werke des altenglischen Erzbischofs Wulfstan. Weimar 1882.

Kinard, J. P. A study of Wulfstan's homilies, their style and sources. Baltimore 1897.

Dodd, L. H. A glossary of Wulfstan's homilies. New York 1908.

Becher, C. F. Wulfstans Homilien. Leipzig 1910.

Whitelock, D. A note on the career of Wulfstan the homilist. EHR 52 1937.

—— Wulfstan and the so-called Laws of Edward and Guthrum. EHR 56 1941.

—— Archbishop Wulfstan, homilist and statesman. Trans Royal Historical Soc 4th ser 24 1942.

Bethurum, D. Archbishop Wulfstan's commonplace book. PMLA 57 1942.

—— Six anonymous Old English codes. JEGP 49 1950.

—— Episcopal magnificence in the eleventh century. In Studies in OE literature in honor of A. G. Brodeur, Eugene 1963.

—— In Continuations and beginnings, ed E. G. Stanley 1966.

—— (D. Bethurum Loomis). Regnum and sacerdotium in the early eleventh century. In England before the Conquest: studies presented to Dorothy Whitelock, Cambridge 1971.

Ker, N. R. Hemming's cartulary. In Studies in medieval history presented to F. M. Powicke, Oxford 1948.

—— The handwriting of Archbishop Wulfstan. In England before the Conquest: studies presented to Dorothy Whitelock, Cambridge 1971.

McIntosh, A. Wulfstan's prose. Proc Br Acad 35 1949.

Jost, K. Wulfstanstudien. Berne 1950.

(5) OTHER RELIGIOUS PROSE

TRANSLATIONS OF THE BIBLE
General

Cook, A. S. Biblical quotations in Old English prose writers. Sers 1–2, 1898–1903.

Hargreaves, H. From Bede to Wiclif: medieval English Bible translations. Bull John Rylands Lib 48 1965.

Shepherd, G. English versions of the scriptures before Wyclif. In The Cambridge history of the Bible vol 2, ed G. W. H. Lampe, Cambridge 1969.

West Saxon Gospels

Ða halgan godspel on englisc. Ed B. Thorpe 1842.

The Gothic and Anglo-Saxon gospels, with the versions of Wyclif and Tyndale. Ed J. Bosworth 1865.

The gospels in Anglo-Saxon, Northumbrian and Old Mercian versions. Ed W. W. Skeat 4 vols Cambridge 1871–87.

The gospel of St Luke in Anglo-Saxon. Ed J. W. Bright, Oxford 1893.

The gospels in West Saxon. Ed J. W. Bright 4 vols Boston 1904–6.

The West-Saxon gospels: a study of the gospel of St Matthew with text of the four gospels. Ed M. Grünberg, Amsterdam 1967.

Paris Psalter

Liber psalmorum: the West Saxon psalms being the prose portion of the Paris Psalter. Ed J. W. Bright and R. L. Ramsay, Boston 1907.

The Paris Psalter: Bibliothèque Nationale Paris Lat. 8824. Ed J. Bromwich et al, Early English mss in facsimile vol 8, Copenhagen 1958.

HOMILIES
Blickling

The Blickling homilies. Ed R. Morris 3 pts 1874–80 (EETS). With trn.

The Blickling homilies. Ed R. Willard, Early English mss in facsimile vol 10, Copenhagen 1960.

Vercelli

Förster, M. Der Vercelli-Codex cxvii nebst Abdruck einiger altenglischer Homilien der Handschrift (nos ix, xv, xxii). Studien zur Englischen Philologie 50 1913.

Die Vercelli-Homilien i–viii. Ed M. Förster, Bibliothek der angelsächsischen Prosa vol 12, 1932.

Il codice vercellese riprodotto in fototipia. Ed M. Förster, Rome 1913.

Others

An Old English homily on the observance of Sunday. Ed A. S. Napier, An English miscellany presented to Dr [F. J.] Furnivall, Oxford 1901. From ms CCCC 162.

A new version of the Apocalypse of Thomas in Old English. Ed M. Förster, Anglia 73 1955.

Three Old English texts in a Salisbury pontifical, Cotton Tiberius C. i. Ed N. R. Ker, The Anglo-Saxons: studies presented to Bruce Dickins, 1959.

SAINTS' LIVES

St Chad

Ein altenglisches Leben des heiligen Chad. Ed A. S. Napier, Anglia 10 1888.

The life of St Chad: an Old English homily. Ed R. Vleeskruyer, Amsterdam 1953.

St Christopher

Brüchstuck einer ae. Legende. Ed G. Herzfeld, E Studien 13 1889.

Three Old English prose texts. Ed S. Rypins 1924 (EETS).

The Nowell Codex: BM Cotton Vitellius A. xv, second ms. Ed K. Malone, Early English mss in facsimile vol 12, Copenhagen 1963.

Sisam, K. The compilation of the Beowulf ms. In his Studies in the history of OE literature, Oxford 1953.

St Guthlac

Das angelsächsische Prosa-Leben des heiligen Guthlac. Ed P. Gonser, Anglistische Forschungen 27 1909.

St Margaret

Ed O. Cockayne, Narratiunculae, 1861. Version from ms Cotton Tiberius A. iii. Another version, from ms CCCC 303, is no xv in Assmann's collection, col 22, above.

St Mildred

Ed O. Cockayne, Leechdoms, wort-cunning and star-craft, 3 vols 1864–6 (Rolls ser).

MARTYROLOGY

An Old English martyrology. Ed G. Herzfeld 1900 (EETS).

APOCRYPHA AND LEGENDS

Gospel of Nicodemus

The Old English version of the gospel of Nicodemus. Ed W. H. Hulme, PMLA 13 1898.

Crawford, S. J. The gospel of Nicodemus. Edinburgh 1927.

Jamnes and Mambres

A fragment of the Penitence of Jamnes and Jambres [sic]. Ed M. R. James, Jnl Theological Stud 2 1901. Ms Cotton Tiberius B. v.

Marvels of the East. Ed M. R. James, Oxford 1929. Facs.

Legends of the Cross

Legends of the holy rood. Ed R. Morris 1871 (EETS). Includes OE text from ms Bodley Auct. F.4.32.

History of the holy rood-tree. Ed A. S. Napier 1894 (EETS). Ms Bodley 343.

Ker, N. R. An eleventh-century Old English legend of the cross before Christ. MÆ 9 1940. Fragment from ms CCCC 557 of text ed Napier, above.

Colgrave, B. and A. Hyde. Two recently discovered leaves from Old English mss. Speculum 37 1962. Another fragment of text ed Napier, above.

Leofric

An Old English vision of Leofric, Earl of Mercia. Ed A. S. Napier, Trans of Philological Soc 1909.

Phoenix (prose version)

Kluge, F. Zum Phoenix. E Studien 8 1885. With text from mss CCCC 198 and Cotton Vespasian D. xiv.

(6) THE CHRONICLE

Versions

A   Corpus Christi College Cambridge 173 (Parker; to 1070)
B   BM Cotton Tiberius A. vi (to 977)
C   BM Cotton Tiberius B. i (to 1066)
D   BM Cotton Tiberius B. iv (to 1079)
E   Bodley, Laud Miscellaneous 636 (Peterborough; to 1154)
F   BM Cotton Domitian A. viii (bilingual; to 1058)
G   BM Cotton Otho B. xi (fragments of a copy of A to 1001)
H   BM Cotton Domitian A. ix (fragment; 1113–14).

Venerabilis Bedae Historia ecclesiastica. Ed A. Whelock, Cambridge 1640. Includes text of G copied from the ms before it was burnt.

The Anglo-Saxon chronicle. Ed B. Thorpe 2 vols 1861 (Rolls ser). With trn.

Two of the Saxon chronicles parallel (A and E). Ed C. Plummer on the basis of an edn by J. Earle 2 vols Oxford 1892–9, 1952 (with addns by D. Whitelock).

An Anglo-Saxon chronicle from BM Cotton ms Tiberius B. iv. Ed E. Classen and F. E. Harmer, Manchester 1926.

The Anglo-Saxon chronicle (C), annals 978–1017. Ed M. Ashdown, English and Norse documents relating to the reign of Ethelred the Unready, Cambridge 1930. With trn.

The Parker chronicle 832–900. Ed A. H. Smith 1935.

The C-text of the Old English chronicles. Ed H. A. Rositzke, Bochum 1940.

The Parker chronicle and laws: a facsimile. Ed R. Flower and H. Smith 1941 (EETS).

Annales Domitiani Latini. Ed F. P. Magoun, Mediaeval Stud 9 1947.

The genealogical preface to the Anglo-Saxon chronicle: four texts edited to supplement Earle-Plummer. Ed B. Dickins, Cambridge 1952.

The Peterborough chronicle. Ed D. Whitelock, Early English mss in facsimile vol 4, Copenhagen 1955. With appendix by C. Clark.

The Peterborough chronicle 1070–1154. Ed C. Clark, Oxford 1958, 1970 (rev).

Translations

Rositzke, H. A. The Peterborough chronicle translated with an introduction. New York 1951.

Garmonsway, G. N. The Anglo-Saxon chronicle. 1953 (EL).

Tucker, S. I. The Anglo-Saxon chronicle 1042–1154. In English historical documents vol 2, ed D. C. Douglas and G. W. Greenaway 1953.

Whitelock, D. The Anglo-Saxon chronicle 60 BC–AD 1042.
In her English historical documents vol 1, 1955.
—— The Anglo-Saxon chronicle: a revised translation.
1961. With D. C. Douglas and S. I. Tucker. Based on
2 preceding items, with full bibliography.

(7) LAWS, CHARTERS etc

Laws

Ancient laws and institutes of England. Ed B. Thorpe
2 vols 1840. With trn.
Gerefa. Ed F. Liebermann, Anglia 9 1886.
The legal code of Ælfred the Great. Ed M. H. Turk,
Halle 1893.
Gesetze der Angelsachsen. Ed F. Liebermann 3 vols
Halle 1903–16.
The laws of the earliest English kings. Ed F. L. Atten-
borough, Cambridge 1922. With trn.
The laws of the kings of England from Edmund to
Henry I. Ed A. J. Robertson, Cambridge 1925. With
trn.
Textus Roffensis part I: Rochester Cathedral library
A.3.5 ff. 1–118. Ed P. Sawyer, Early English mss in
facsimile vol 7, Copenhagen 1957.
The Parker Chronicle and laws: a facsimile. Ed R.
Flower and H. Smith 1941 (EETS).
A Wulfstan ms. Ed H. R. Loyn 1971. *See under Wulf-
stan, above.*
For trns of several codes see D. Whitelock, English historical
documents vol 1, c. 500–1042, *1955.*

Charters

Sawyer, P. H. Anglo-Saxon charters: an annotated list
and bibliography. 1968 (Royal Historical Soc).
Codex diplomaticus aevi saxonici. Ed J. M. Kemble 6 vols
1839–48 (Eng Historical Soc).
Diplomatarium anglicum. Ed B. Thorpe 1865. With trn.
Cartularium saxonicum. Ed W. de G. Birch 3 vols
1885–93.

Birch, W. de G. Index saxonicus: an index to all the
names of persons in the Cartularium saxonicum. 1899.
A handbook to the land charters and other Saxonic documents. Ed J. Earle, Oxford 1888.
The Crawford collection of early charters and documents. Ed A. S. Napier and W. H. Stevenson, Oxford
1895.
Select English historical documents of the ninth and tenth
centuries. Ed F. E. Harmer, Cambridge 1914. With
trn.
Anglo-Saxon charters. Ed A. J. Robertson, Cambridge
1939. With trn.
Textus Roffensis part II: Rochester Cathedral library
A.3.5 ff. 119–235. Ed P. Sawyer, Early English mss in
facsimile vol 11, Copenhagen 1962.

Other Documents

Anglo-Saxon wills. Ed D. Whitelock, Cambridge 1930.
With trn.
The will of Æthelgifu. Ed Lord Rennell, Oxford 1968
(Roxburghe Club). With discussion and trn by D.
Whitelock, notes by N. Ker and facs.
Anglo-Saxon writs. Ed F. E. Harmer, Manchester 1952.
With trn.
Facsimiles of royal writs to AD 1100 presented to V. H.
Galbraith. Ed T. A. M. Bishop and P. Chaplais,
Oxford 1957.
For trns of many charters, wills etc see D. Whitelock,
English historical documents vol 1, c. 500–1042, *1955.*

(8) SCIENCE, MEDICINE AND MAGIC, AND FOLKLORE

Byrhtferth's Manual

Byrhtferth's manual. Ed S. J. Crawford 1929 (EETS).
Byrhtferth's preface. Ed G. F. Forsey, Speculum 3 1928.
With trn.

Medicine and Magic

Leechdoms, wort-cunning and starcraft. Ed O. Cockayne
3 vols 1864–6 (Rolls ser).
Peri Didaxeon: eine Sammlung von Rezepten. Ed M.
Löweneck, Erlangen 1896.
Herbarium Apuleii. Ed H. Berberich, Heidelberg 1902.
Das Læceboc; die Lacnunga. Ed G. Leonhardi, Kleinere

angelsächsische Denkmäler, Bibliothek der angel-
sächsischen Prosa vol 6, 1905.
The Anglo-Saxon charms. Ed F. Grendon, Jnl Amer
Folklore 22 1909.
Medicina de quadrupedibus. Ed J. Delacourt, Heidelberg
1914. With trn.
Cotton ms Vitellius C. iii of the Herbarium Apuleii.
Ed A. J. G. Hilbelink, Amsterdam 1930.
Storms, G. Anglo-Saxon magic. Hague 1948.
Bald's leechbook: BM Royal 12 D. xvii. Ed C. E.
Wright, Early English mss in facsimile vol 5, Copen-
hagen 1955.
Brackman, W. Some minor Old English texts II: various
herb recipes (from Nowell transcript of ms Cotton
Otho B. xi). Archiv 202 1966.

THE MIDDLE ENGLISH PERIOD
(1100–1500)

1. INTRODUCTION

(1) BIBLIOGRAPHIES ETC

Geddie, W. Bibliography of Middle Scots poets. Edinburgh 1912 (Scottish Text Soc).

Wells, J. E. Manual of the writings in Middle English 1050–1400. New Haven 1916; 9 suppls to 1951; Manual 1050–1500, ed J. B. Severs, New Haven 1967– (rev and enlarged).

Tucker, L. L. and A. R. Benham. Bibliography of fifteenth-century literature. Seattle 1928.

Lawrence, W. W. Selected bibliography of medieval literature in England. New York 1930.

Brown, C. and R. H. Robbins. Index of Middle English verse. New York 1943; suppl ed Robbins and J. L. Cutler, Lexington Kentucky 1965.

Farrar, C. P. and A. P. Evans. Bibliography of English translations from medieval sources. New York 1946.

Williams, H. F. Index of mediaeval studies published in Festschriften 1865–1946. Berkeley 1951.

Zesmer, D. M. and S. B. Greenfield. Guide to English literature from Beowulf through Chaucer and medieval drama. New York 1961.

Matthews, W. Old and Middle English literature. New York 1968.

Sawyer, P. H. et al. International medieval bibliography. Leeds 1968–.

Ker, N. R. Medieval manuscripts in British libraries. 3 vols Oxford 1969–.

Preston, M. J. A concordance to the Middle English shorter poem. 2 pts Leeds 1975.

(2) LITERARY HISTORY AND CRITICISM

Warton, Thomas (the younger). History of English poetry. 3 vols 1774–81; ed W. C. Hazlitt 4 vols 1871.

Ritson, Joseph. Bibliographia poetica. 1802.

Morley, H. English writers [to Dunbar]. 2 vols 1864–7.

— English writers. 11 vols 1887–95. Vols 3–7.

Brink, B. ten. Geschichte der englischen Literatur. 2 vols Berlin 1877–93 (vol 1 rev A. Brandl, Strasbourg 1899); tr 3 vols 1883–96.

Ker, W. P. Epic and romance. 1897.

— Essays on medieval literature. 1905.

— English literature, medieval. 1912 (Home Univ Lib).

Saintsbury, G. The flourishing of romance and the rise of allegory. Edinburgh 1897.

Snell, F. J. The fourteenth century. 1899.

— Age of Chaucer. 1901.

— Age of transition. 2 vols 1905.

Smith, G. G. The transition period. 1900.

Cambridge history of English literature vols 1–2. Cambridge 1907–8.

Lawrence, W. W. Medieval story. New York 1911.

Baldwin, C. S. Introduction to English medieval literature. 1914.

— Medieval rhetoric and poetic (to 1400). 1928.

— Three mediæval centuries of literature in England 1100–1400. Boston 1932.

Krapp, G. P. The rise of English literary prose. New York 1915.

Chaytor, H. J. The troubadours and England. Cambridge 1923.

— From script to print. Cambridge 1945.

Thomas, P. G. English literature before Chaucer. 1924.

Chambers, R. W. On the continuity of English prose. Oxford 1932 (EETS).

— Man's unconquerable mind. 1939.

Lewis, C. S. The allegory of love. Oxford 1936.

— The discarded image. Cambridge 1964.

— Studies in medieval and Renaissance literature. Ed W. Hooper, Cambridge 1966.

— Selected literary essays. Ed W. Hooper, Cambridge 1969.

Bennett, H. S. The author and his public in the fourteenth and fifteenth centuries. E & S 23 1937.

— Science and information in English writings in the fifteenth century. RES 39 1944.

— Medieval literature and the modern reader. E & S 31 1945.

— Chaucer and the fifteenth century. Oxford 1947 (OHEL), 1973 (rev N. Davis).

Thompson, J. W. The literacy of the laity in the Middle Ages. New York 1939.

Wilson, R. M. Early Middle English literature. 1939, 1968 (rev).

— The lost literature of medieval England. 1952, 1970 (rev).

Wyld, H. C. Aspects of style and idiom in fifteenth-century English. E & S 26 1940.

Weiss, R. Humanism in England during the fifteenth century. Oxford 1941.

Atkins, J. W. H. English literary criticism: the medieval phase. Cambridge 1943.

Utley, F. L. The crooked rib. Columbus 1944.

Chambers, E. K. English literature at the close of the Middle Ages. Oxford 1945 (OHEL).

Baugh, A. C. and K. Malone. The Middle Ages. In Literary history of England, ed Baugh, New York 1950.

Girvan, R. The medieval poet and his public. In English studies to-day, ed C. L. Wrenn and G. Bullough, Oxford 1951.

Kane, G. Middle English literature. 1951.

Ford, B. (ed). The age of Chaucer. 1954 (Pelican Guide to Eng Lit).

Everett, D. Essays on Middle English literature. Oxford 1955.

Schlauch, M. English medieval literature and its social foundations. Warsaw 1956.

Clark, J. W. Early English. 1957, 1967 (rev).

Speirs, J. Medieval English poetry: the non-Chaucerian tradition. 1957.

Bethurum, D. (ed). Critical approaches to medieval literature. Eng Inst Essays 1959.

Spearing, A. C. Criticism and mediaeval poetry. 1964, 1972 (rev and enlarged).

— Medieval dream-poetry. Cambridge 1976.

Matthews, W. (ed). Medieval secular literature: four essays. Berkeley 1965.

Brewer, D. S. et al. Chaucer and Chaucerians. Edinburgh 1966.

Fisher, J. H. (ed). The medieval literature of Western Europe: a review of research, mainly 1930–60. New York 1966.

Lawlor, J. (ed). Patterns of love and courtesy: essays in memory of C. S. Lewis. 1966.

Tuve, R. Allegorical imagery: some mediaeval books and their posterity. Princeton 1966.

Salter, E. Medieval poetry and the figural view of reality. Proc Br Acad 54 1968.

—— Medieval poetry and the visual arts. E & S new ser 22 1969.

Bloomfield, M. W. Essays and explorations. Cambridge Mass 1970.

Gradon, P. O. E. Form and style in early English literature. 1971.

Burrow, J. A. Ricardian poetry. 1971.

Pearsall, D. Old and Middle English poetry. 1977.

(3) COLLECTIONS

Original Texts

Morris, R. Specimens of early English 1250–1400. Oxford 1867.

Skeat, W. W. Specimens of English literature 1394–1579. Oxford 1871.

Morris, R. and W. W. Skeat. Specimens of early English. 2 pts Oxford 1872–82.

Sweet, H. First Middle English primer. Oxford 1884, 1938.

—— Second Middle English primer. Oxford 1886.

Emerson, O. F. Middle English reader. New York 1905.

Cook, A. S. Literary Middle English reader. Boston 1915.

Hall, J. Selections from early Middle English 1130–1250. 2 pts Oxford 1920.

Sisam, K. Fourteenth-century verse and prose. Oxford 1921, 1922 (with vocabulary by J. R. R. Tolkien).

Hammond, E. P. English verse between Chaucer and Surrey. Durham NC 1927.

Chambers, R. W. and M. Daunt. A book of London English 1384–1425. Oxford 1931. Mainly local records.

Mossé, F. Manuel de l'anglais du Moyen Age. Paris 1949; tr 1952.

Dickins, B. and R. M. Wilson. Early Middle English reader. Cambridge 1951.

Bennett, J. A. W. and G. V. Smithers. Early Middle English verse and prose. Oxford 1966, 1968 (rev).

Sisam, C. The Oxford book of medieval English verse. Oxford 1970.

Gray, D. A selection of religious lyrics. Oxford 1975.

Modernized Texts

Pollard, A. W. Fifteenth-century verse and prose. 1903.

Rickert, E. (ed and tr). Early English romances in verse. 2 vols 1908.

Weston, J. L. (ed and tr). Romance, vision and satire. 1912.

—— Chief Middle English poets. [1914].

Benham, A. R. (ed and tr). English literature from Widsith to the death of Chaucer. New Haven 1916.

Neilson, W. A. and K. G. T. Webster. Chief British poets of the 14th and 15th centuries. [1916].

Reinhard, J. R. (ed and tr). Medieval pageant. 1939.

Matthews, W. Later medieval English prose. 1962.

Stone, B. (ed and tr). Medieval English verse. 1965 (Penguin).

2. MIDDLE ENGLISH LITERATURE

References

Index   The index of Middle English verse, ed C. Brown and R. H. Robbins, New York 1943; Supplement, ed R. H. Robbins and J. L. Cutler, Lexington Kentucky 1965.

Severs   A manual of the writings in Middle English 1050–1500, ed J. B. Severs, fascicule 1: Romances, by M. J. Donovan et al, New Haven 1967.

(1) GENERAL

Bibliographies etc

Ward, H. L. D. and J. A. Herbert. Catalogue of romances in the department of manuscripts of the British Museum. 3 vols 1883–1910.

Wells, J. E. Manual of the writings in Middle English. New Haven 1916; Supplements 1–9, 1919–51.

Hibbard, L. A. Medieval romance in England: a study of the sources and analyses of the non-cyclic metrical romances. New York 1924.

Thompson, S. Motif-index of folk literature: a classification of narrative elements in folk-tales, ballads, myths, fables, mediaeval romances etc. Bloomington 1932.

Brown, C. and R. H. Robbins. The index of Middle English verse. New York 1943; Supplement by R. H. Robbins and J. L. Cutler, Lexington Kentucky 1965.

Farrar, C. P. and A. P. Evans. Bibliography of English translations from medieval sources. New York 1946.

Bordman, G. Motif-index of the English metrical romances. Helsinki 1963.

Severs, J. B. A manual of the writings in Middle English 1050–1500. Fascicule 1: Romances, by M. J. Donovan, C. W. Dunn, L. Hornstein, R. M. Lumiansky, H. Newstead, H. M. Smyser. New Haven 1967.

Collections

Ritson, J. Ancient English metrical romances. 3 vols 1802.

Laing, D. Select remains of the ancient popular poetry of Scotland. 1822, 1885 (rev).

—— Early metrical tales. 1826, 1889 (rev).

—— Early popular poetry of Scotland and the Northern border. Rev W. C. Hazlitt 1895.

Thoms, W. J. Collection of early prose romances. 3 vols 1828, 1907 (rev).

Halliwell(-Phillipps), J. O. Thornton romances. 1844 (Camden Soc).

Hazlitt, W. C. Remains of the early popular poetry of England. 4 vols 1864–6.

Hales, J. W. and F. J. Furnivall. Percy folio manuscript. 4 vols 1867–9.

Sisam, K. Fourteenth-century verse and prose. Oxford 1921, 1937 (rev).

Dickins, B. and R. M. Wilson. Early Middle English texts. 1951.

Mossé, F. A handbook of Middle English. Tr J. A. Walker, Baltimore 1952.

Bennett, J. A. W. and G. V. Smithers. Early Middle

English verse and prose. Oxford 1966, 1968 (rev).

Gibbs, A. C. Middle English romances. 1966 (York Medieval Texts).

Sands, D. B. Middle English verse romances. New York 1966.

Modern Versions

Ellis, G. Specimens of early English metrical romances. 3 vols 1805, 1848 (rev).

Rickert, E. Early English romances in verse. 2 vols 1908.

Weston, J. L. Romance, vision and satire. Boston 1912.

—— Chief Middle English poets. Boston 1914.

Loomis, R. S. and L. H. Medieval romances. New York 1957.

Brengle, R. L. Arthur King of Britain: history, romance, chronicle and criticism, with texts in modern English from Gildas to Malory. New York 1964.

General Studies

Saintsbury, G. The flourishing of romance. Edinburgh 1897.

Ker, W. P. Epic and romance. 1897, 1908 (rev).

Lawrence, W. W. Medieval story. New York 1911, 1931 (rev).

Weston, J. L. Legendary cycles of the Middle Ages. Cambridge 1929 (Cambridge medieval history vol 6).

Oakden, J. P. Alliterative poetry in Middle English. 2 vols Manchester 1930–5.

Bezzola, R. R. Le sens de l'aventure et de l'amour. Paris 1947.

Kane, G. Middle English literature. 1951.

Ford, B. (ed). The age of Chaucer. 1954 (Pelican).

Schlauch, M. English medieval literature. Warsaw 1956.

—— Antecedents of the English novel 1400–1600. Warsaw and London 1963.

Speirs, J. Medieval English poetry: the non-Chaucerian tradition. 1957.

Mehl, D. Die mittelenglischen Romanzen des 13 und 14 Jahrhunderts. Heidelberg 1967; tr 1969.

Loomis, R. S. Studies in medieval literature. 1970.

Stevens, J. Medieval romance. 1973.

(2) ARTHURIAN ROMANCES: THE MATTER OF BRITAIN

Bibliographies

Parry, J. J. A bibliography of critical Arthurian literature 1922–9. 2 vols New York 1931–6. Annually in MLQ 1940–.

Harding, J. The Arthurian legend: a check list of books in the Newberry Library. Chicago 1933; suppl 1938.

Northup, C. S. and J. J. Parry. The Arthurian legends, modern retellings of the old stories: an annotated bibliography. JEGP 43 1944, 49 1950.

Ackerman, R. W. et al. Arthurian bibliography for 1948. Bulletin Bibliographique de la Société Internationale Arthurienne 1– 1949– (annually).

See also Malory, col 74, below.

General Studies

Paris, P. Romans de la Table Ronde. 5 vols Paris 1868–77.

Rhys, J. Arthurian legend. Oxford 1891.

Weston, J. L. King Arthur and his knights. 1899, 1905 (rev).

Fletcher, R. H. Arthurian material in the chronicles. Harvard Stud 10 1906; New York 1966 (rev).

Sommer, H. O. Vulgate version of the Arthurian romances. 8 vols Washington 1908–16.

—— Structure of the Livre d'Artus and its function in the evolution of the Arthurian prose romances. Paris and London 1914.

Jones, W. L. King Arthur in history and legend. Cambridge 1911.

Bruce, J. D. Evolution of Arthurian romance to 1300. 2 vols Göttingen 1923–4, 1928 (rev).

—— Mordred's incestuous birth. In Medieval studies in memory of G. S. Loomis, Paris and New York 1927.

Loomis, R. S. Celtic myth and Arthurian romance. New York 1927.

—— Some names in Arthurian romance. PMLA 45 1930.

—— Arthurian tradition and Chrétien de Troyes. New York 1949.

—— Wales and the Arthurian legend. Cardiff 1956.

—— (ed). Arthurian literature in the Middle Ages. Oxford 1959.

Chambers, E. K. Arthur of Britain. 1927.

Faral, E. La légende arthurienne: études et documents. 3 vols Paris 1929.

—— The development of Arthurian romance. 1963.

Reid, M. J. C. Arthurian legend: comparison of treatment in medieval and modern literature. Edinburgh 1938.

Ackerman, R. W. An index of the Arthurian names in Middle English. Stanford 1952.

—— The English rimed and prose romances. In Arthurian literature in the Middle Ages, ed R. S. Loomis, Oxford 1959.

Barber, R. W. Arthur of Albion: an introduction to the Arthurian literature and legends of England. 1961.

Owen, D. D. R. (ed). Arthurian romance: seven essays. 1970.

The Historical Arthur: Gildas, Nennius, Geoffrey of Monmouth, Wace

Giles, J. A. (tr). Six Old English chronicles. 1848, 1901 (rev).

Mommsen, T. (ed). Nennius, Historia Britonum. In Monumenta Germaniae historica vol 13, Berlin 1898.

Fletcher, R. H. Arthurian materials in the chronicles. Harvard Stud 10 1906; New York 1966 (rev).

Mason, E. (tr). Arthurian chronicles represented by Wace and Layamon. 1912.

Chambers, E. K. Arthur of Britain. 1927.

Griscom, A. (ed). Historia regum Britanniae. New York 1929.

Hammer, J. (ed). Geoffrey of Monmouth: a variant version. Cambridge Mass 1951.

Tatlock, J. S. P. The legendary history of Britain; Geoffrey of Monmouth's History and its early vernacular versions. Berkeley 1950.

Jackson, K. The Arthur of history. In Arthurian literature in the Middle Ages, ed R. S. Loomis, Oxford 1959.

Wade-Evans, L. History of the Britons. 1938.

Hutson, A. E. British personal names in the History of Geoffrey. Berkeley 1940.

Houck, M. Sources of the Roman de Brut of Wace. Berkeley 1941.

Kendrick, T. D. British antiquity. 1950.

Dunn, C. W. (tr). Geoffrey of Monmouth's History of the kings of Britain. New York 1958.

Parry, J. J. and R. A. Caldwell. Geoffrey of Monmouth. In Arthurian literature in the Middle Ages, ed R. S. Loomis, Oxford 1959.

Foulon, C. Wace. Ibid.

Thorpe, L. (tr). Geoffrey of Monmouth's History of the Kings of Britain. 1966.

Hanning, R. W. The vision of history in early Britain from Gildas to Geoffrey of Monmouth. New York 1966.

Lindsay, J. Arthur and his times: Britain in the Dark Ages. New York 1966.

Ashe, G. The quest for Arthur's Britain. 1968.

—— Camelot and the vision of Albion. 1971.

Morte Arthure

Index 2322. 4346 alliterative long lines.
Ms: Lincoln Cathedral 91 (Thornton).
Ed J. O. Halliwell (-Phillipps), The alliterative romance of the death of King Arthur, 1847; ed G. G. Perry 1865 (EETS), rev E. Brock 1871; ed M. M. Banks 1900; ed E. Björkman, Heidelberg 1915; ed J. Finlayson 1967 (York Medieval Texts) (extracts; about half the text); ed L. D. Benson, Indianapolis 1974.
Selections in Mossé; modern version by A. Boyle 1912 (EL).

Le Morte Arthur

Index 1994. 3834 lines in 8-line stanza.
Ms: BM Harley 2252.
Ed G. A. Panton 1819 (Roxburghe Club); ed F. J. Furnivall 1864; ed J. D. Bruce 1903 (EETS); ed S. B. Hemingway, New York 1912; ed L. D. Benson, Indianapolis 1974.
Modern version by L. A. Paton 1912 (EL).

Gawain

Weston, J. L. The legend of Sir Gawain. 1897.
—— (tr). Sir Gawain at the Grail castle. 1903.

Sir Gawain and the Green Knight

Index 3144. 2530 lines in unrhymed alliterative stanza with bob and wheel.
Ms: BM Cotton Nero A.x; ed I. Gollancz 1923 (EETS) (facs).
Kottler, B. and A. M. Markman. Concordance to five Middle English poems. Pittsburgh 1966.

§1

Ed R. Morris 1864, 1869, 1897 (both rev); ed J. R. R. Tolkien and E. V. Gordon, Oxford 1925, rev N. Davis 1967; ed I. Gollancz, M. Day and M. S. Serjeantson 1938 (EETS); ed A. C. Cawley 1962 (EL) (with Pearl); ed R. A. Waldron 1970 (York Medieval Texts); ed W. R. J. Barron, Manchester 1974 (text and trn).
Modern versions by E. J. B. Kirtlan 1912; K. Hare 1918, 1948 (rev); G. H. Gerould, New York 1929; M. R. Ridley, Leicester 1944; B. Stone 1959; J. Gardner, Chicago 1965; M. Borroff 1968.

§2

Kittredge, G. L. Gawain and the Green Knight. Cambridge Mass 1916.

Everett, D. The alliterative revival. In her Essays on Middle English literature, Oxford 1955.
Burrow, J. A reading of Sir Gawain and the Green Knight. 1965.
—— In his Ricardian poetry, 1971.
Spearing, A. C. The Gawain-poet: a critical study. Cambridge 1971.
Blanch, R. J. (ed). Sir Gawain and Pearl: critical essays. 1966.
Howard, D. R. and C. K. Zacher (ed). Critical studies of Sir Gawain. 1968.

Perceval

Weston, J. L. The legend of Sir Perceval. 2 vols 1906–9.
Nitze, W. A. Perceval and the Holy Grail. Berkeley 1949.
Thompson, A. W., O. Springer, P. le Gentil and W. A. Nitze. In Arthurian literature in the Middle Ages, ed R. S. Loomis, Oxford 1959. Chs 17–20.

The Holy Grail

Nutt, A. Studies on the legend of the Holy Grail. 1888.
—— Legends of the Holy Grail. 1902.
Kempe, D. The legend of the Holy Grail. 1905 (EETS).
Weston, J. L. The quest of the Holy Grail. 1913.
—— From ritual to romance. Cambridge 1920.
Nitze, W. A. On the chronology of the Grail romances. MP 17 1919; rptd in J. M. Manly anniversary studies, Chicago 1923.
Loomis, R. S. The Grail: from Celtic myth to Christian symbol. Cardiff and New York 1963.
Owen, D. D. R. The evolution of the Grail legend. Edinburgh 1968.
Bogdanow, F. The Romance of the Grail: a study of the structure and genesis of a 13th-century Arthurian prose romance. Manchester 1966.

Tristram

Bédier, J. (ed). Le roman de Tristan par Thomas. 2 vols Paris 1902–5.
Bossert, A. La légende chevaleresque de Tristan et Iseult. Paris 1902.
Loomis, R. S. (tr). The romance of Tristram by Thomas. New York 1931, 1951 (rev).
Adams, R. D. A. A Tristan bibliography. Los Angeles 1943.
Sharpe, R. C. Tristram of Lyonesse. New York 1949.
Eisner, S. The Tristan legend: a study in sources. Evanston 1969.

(3) CHARLEMAGNE ROMANCES: THE MATTER OF FRANCE

Lee, S. The Charlemagne romances in France and England. 1882 (EETS).
Weston, J. L. The romance cycle of Charlemagne. 1901.
Ker, W. P. Epic and romance. 1908.

Riquer, M. de. Les chansons de geste françaises. Paris 1957.
Menéndez Pidal, R. La Chanson de Roland et la tradition épique des Francs. Paris 1960.

(4) THE MATTER OF ANTIQUITY

Alexander

Meyer, P. Alexandre le Grand dans la littérature du Moyen Age. 2 vols Paris 1886.
Budge, E. A. W. History of Alexander the Great. Cambridge 1889.
—— The life and exploits of Alexander the Great. 1896.
Kroll, W. (ed). Historia Alexandri Magni (Pseudo-Callisthenes). Berlin 1926; tr H. E. Haight as The life of Alexander of Macedon, New York 1955.

Magoun, F. P. (ed). Gests of King Alexander of Macedon. Cambridge Mass 1929.
Armstrong, E. C. et al (ed). The medieval French Roman d'Alexandre. 5 vols Princeton 1937–55.
Cary, G. The medieval Alexander. Cambridge 1956.

Troy

See also Chaucer, Troilus and Criseyde, col 55, below.
Constans, L. (ed). Le roman de Troie par Benoît de Sainte-Maure. 6 vols 1904–12.

Griffin, N. E. Dares and Dictys: introduction to the study of the medieval versions. Baltimore 1907.
—— (ed). Guido de columnis, Historia destructionis Troiae. Cambridge Mass 1936.
Atwood, E. B. and V. K. Whitaker (ed). The Excidium Troiae. Cambridge Mass 1944.
Tatlock J. S. P. The legendary history of Britain. Berkeley 1950.

Scherer, M. R. Legends of Troy in art and literature. New York 1963.
Frazer, R. M. (tr). The Trojan war: the chronicles of Dictys of Crete and Dares the Phrygian. Bloomington 1966.
Marcello, G. (ed). Dares Phrygius, De excidio Troiae. Rome 1967.

(5) THE 'MATTER OF ENGLAND'

Wilson, R. M. Early Middle English literature. 1939.
—— Lost literature of medieval England. 1952.
Legge, M. D. Anglo-Norman literature and its background. Oxford 1963.

King Horn
Index 166. 1569 lines in irregular short couplet.
Mss: Bodley 1486 (Laud miscellany 108); Cambridge Univ Lib Gg.4.27 (11); BM Harley 2253.
Ed F. Michel, Horn et Rimenhild, Paris 1845 (Bannatyne Club); ed J. R. Lumby 1866 (EETS), rev G. H. McKnight 1901; ed E. Mätzner, Altenglische Sprachproben vol 1, Berlin 1867; ed C. Horstmann, King Horn nach Laud 108, Archiv 50 1872; ed T. Wissman,

Quellen und Forschungen 16 1876, 45 1881; ed J. Hall, Oxford 1901; ed W. H. French, Essays on King Horn, Ithaca 1940 (reconstructed text).

Havelok
Index 114. 3001 lines in short couplet.
Mss: Bodley 1486 (Laud misc 108); Cambridge Univ Lib additional 4407 (19) (4 fragments).
Ed F. Madden 1828 (Roxburghe Club) (with French); ed W. W. Skeat 1868 (EETS), Oxford 1902, rev K. Sisam, Oxford 1915; ed Skeat, A new Havelok ms, MLR 6 1911 (Cambridge fragments); ed F. Holthausen, Heidelberg 1901, 1910, 1928 (both rev).

(6) 'BRETON LAYS'

Mason, E. (tr). French mediaeval romances from the lays of Marie de France and other French legends. 1911 (EL).
Ewert, A. (ed). Marie de France, Lais. Oxford 1944.
Lods, J. (ed). Les lais de Marie de France. Paris 1959.
Rumble, T. C. (ed). The Breton lays in Middle English. Detroit 1965.
Rychner, J. (ed). Les lais de Marie de France. Paris 1966.
Donovan, M. J. The Breton lay: a guide to varieties. Notre Dame 1969.

Sir Orfeo
Index 3868. 604 lines in short couplet.
Mss: Nat Lib of Scotland 19.2.1 (Auchinleck); Bodley 6922 (Ashmole 61); BM Harley 3810.
Ed D. Laing, Selected remains of the ancient popular poetry of Scotland, 1822, rev W. C. Hazlitt 1895; ed J. O. Halliwell(-Phillipps), Illustrations of the fairy mythology of A midsummer night's dream, 1845, ed W. C. Hazlitt 1875; ed A. J. Bliss, Oxford 1954, 1966 (rev).

(7) CHRONICLES

General Studies
Poole, R. L. Chronicles and annals: a brief outline of their origins and growth. Oxford 1926.
Douglas, D. C. The Norman Conquest and British historians. Glasgow 1946.
Wilson, R. M. The lost literature of medieval England. 1952. Ch 2.
Bagley, J. J. Historical interpretation. 1965 (Pelican).
Taylor, J. The use of medieval chronicles. 1965.

Laȝamon's Brut
Mss: 1, BM Cotton Caligula A 9; 2, BM Cotton Otho c 13.
Laȝamon's Brut or Chronicle of England. Ed F. Madden 3 vols 1847 (ms 1–2).
Laȝamon's Brut. Ed G. L. Brook and R. F. Leslie vol 1 1963 (EETS). Lines 1–8020.

Brut or the Chronicles of England
Mss: 1, Bodley Rawlinson B 171; 2, Bodley Douce 323; 3, Trinity College Dublin 490.
Brie, F. The Brut or the Chronicles of England. 2 vols 1906–8 (EETS) (ms 1 with collation of 2–3).

Robert Mannyng of Brunne's Story
Mss: 1, Inner Temple Lib Petyt no 511, no 7; 2, Lambeth 131; 3, Lincoln Cathedral ms; 4, Bodley Rawlinson Miscellany 1370.
Hearne, T. Peter Langtoft's Chronicles as illustrated and improved by Robert of Brunne. 2 vols Oxford 1725.

Zetsche, A. Chronik des Robert von Brunne. Anglia 9 1886 (ms 2).
Furnivall, F. J. The story of England by Robert Mannyng. 2 vols 1887 (Rolls ser).
Kölbing, E. Ein Fragment von Robert Mannings Chronik. E Studien 17 1892 (ms 4).

Barbour's Bruce
Mss: 1, St John's College, Cambridge G 23; 2, Nat Lib of Scotland 19.2.2.
Pinkerton, J. The Bruce of the history of Robert I. 1790.
Jamieson, J. The Bruce and Wallace. Edinburgh 1820.
Innes, C. The Brus. Aberdeen 1856 (Spalding Club).
Skeat, W. W. Barbour's Bruce. 4 vols 1870–89 (EETS); rptd 2 vols 1894 (STS), 1968 (EETS).
MacKenzie, W. M. The Bruce. 1909.

Translations
Todd, G. E. The Bruce. Glasgow 1907.
MacMillan, M. The Bruce of Bannockburn. Stirling 1914.
Weston, J. E. Chief ME poets. Boston 1914.

JOHN TREVISA
c. 1330–1402
Mss: 1, St John's College, Cambridge H.1; 2, BM additional 24,194; 3, BM Harley 1900; 4, Cotton Tiberius D.7.
Polychronicon. 1482 (Caxton); ed C. Babington and J. R. Lumby 9 vols 1865–86 (Rolls ser) (with Latin

original). A trn, completed 1387, of Ranulf Higden's history.

A dialogue betwene a knyght and a clerke. [c.1540] (with Latin original); ed A. J. Perry 1925 (EETS) (from Harley ms). A trn from William of Occam (d. 1349?).

De proprietatibus rerum. 1494 (de Worde); ed M. C. Seymour 2 vols Oxford 1974–. A trn, completed 1398, of the encyclopaedia of natural science by Bartholomew Anglicus.

(8) TRAVEL

General Works

Freeling, G. H. (ed). Informacõn for pylgrymes unto the Holy Londe. 1824 (Roxburghe Club); facs of De Worde's 1498 edn ed E. G. Duff 1893.

Wright, T. (ed). Early travels in Palestine. 1848. Includes modernized version of Mandeville's travels.

Ellis, H. (ed). The pylgrymage of Sir Richard Guylforde to the Holy Land. 1851 (Camden Soc).

Williams, G. (ed). The itineraries of William Wey, Fellow of Eton College, to Jerusalem AD 1458 and AD 1462; and to Saint James of Compostella AD 1456. 1857 (Roxburghe Club). Also facs of companion map 1867 (Roxburghe Club).

Library of Palestine Pilgrims' Text Society. 13 vols and index 1887–97. Especially vol 6 pt 3, Guide-book to Palestine (c. 1350 AD), tr J. H. Bernard; vol 6 pt 4, John Poloner's description of the Holy Land (c. 1421 AD), tr A. Stewart; vol 11 pt 2, The history of Jerusalem, AD 1180, by Jacques de Vitry, tr A. Stewart.

Rockhill, W. W. (ed and tr). The journey of William of Rubruck, with two accounts of the earlier journey of John of Pian de Carpine. 1900 (Hakluyt Soc).

Newton, A. P. (ed). Travel and travellers of the Middle Ages. 1926.

James, M. R. (ed). Marvels of the East. 1929 (Roxburghe Club) (facs).

Woodruff, C. E. (ed and tr). A xvth-century guide-book to the principal churches of Rome. 1933.

Crone, G. R. The Hereford world map. 1948 (Royal Geographical Soc).

Penrose, B. Travel and discovery in the Renaissance 1420–1620. Cambridge Mass 1952.

Carus-Wilson, E. M. English merchant venturers. 1954.

Parks, G. B. The English traveler to Italy: vol 1, The Middle Ages (to 1525). Rome 1954.

Parry, J. H. The age of reconnaissance. 1963.

Mitchell, R. J. The spring voyage: the Jerusalem pilgrimage in 1458. 1964.

Skelton, R. A. et al. The Vinland map and the Tartar relation. 1965. Plates; with bibliography.

Stations of Rome

Ms 1, Vernon ms (ms Bodley 3938); ms 2, BM additional ms 22,283; with prologue; ed F. J. Furnivall 1867 (EETS), and prologue only, 1901 (EETS).

Ms 3, BM ms Cotton Caligula A ii; ms 4, Lambeth ms 306; ed F. J. Furnivall 1866 (EETS).

Ms 5, BM additional ms 37,787 (incomplete). Ed N. S. Baugh, A Worcestershire miscellany, Philadelphia 1956.

Ms 6, Public Record Office ms SC 6/956/5 (roll). See Scattergood, below.

Ms 7, BM ms Cotton Vespasian D ix (incomplete).

Ms 8, Newberry Library ms Gen add 12 (roll; formerly Condover Hall ms).

Ms 9, National Library of Wales Porkington ms 10 (prose); ed F. J. Furnivall 1867 (EETS).

Stations of Jerusalem

Ms 1, Bodley ms Ashmole 61; ed C. Horstmann, Altenglische Legenden, Heilbronn 1881.

Ms 2, Bodley 565; pbd in The itineraries of William Wey, above.

Ms 3, Huntington Library ms HM 144 (formerly Huth ms); not pbd; see Ricci Census p. 58, and Manly and Rickert, Text of the Canterbury tales vol 1, pp. 289 f.

Travels of Sir John Mandeville

There are some 250 mss in most West European languages; see J. W. Bennett, Rediscovery, 1954. For the 40 English mss, see Seymour, Edinburgh Bibl Soc Trans 4 1966.

Ms 1, BM ms Cotton Titus C xvi; ed P. Hamelius 2 vols Oxford 1919–23 (EETS); ed M. C. Seymour, Oxford 1967 (with bibliography). Modernized edns: A. W. Pollard 1901, 1923; M. C. Seymour, Oxford 1968 (WC). Selections in R. Morris and W. W. Skeat, Specimens of early English pt 2, Oxford 1894; K. Sisam, 14th-century verse and prose, Oxford 1921; W. Matthews, Later medieval English prose, 1962 (modernized).

Ms 2, BM ms Egerton 1982; ed G. F. Warner 1889 (Roxburghe Club) (with French text, plates). Modernized version ed M. Letts 2 vols 1953 (Hakluyt Soc) (with French text, bibliography etc; see also below). Selections in A. S. Cook, Reader, Boston 1915.

Ms 3, Bodley ms Rawlinson D 99; ed M. Letts above.

Ms 4, Bodley ms e Musæo 116; ed M. C. Seymour, Oxford 1963 (EETS) (with Latin text).

Also the defective version, represented by 32 mss and a collection of extracts; pbd in pre-18th-century edns and in modernized form ed J. Bramont 1928 (EL).

Ms 5, The epitome, in BM additional ms 37049;

Ms 6, The metrical version, in a Coventry Record Office ms; unpbd.

Ms 7, The stanzaic fragment, in Bodley ms e Musæo 160.

(9) VERSIONS OF THE BIBLE

Deanesly, M. The Lollard Bible and other medieval biblical versions. Cambridge 1920, 1966 (with note).

Craigie, W. A. The English versions (to Wyclif). In The Bible in its ancient and English versions, ed H. W. Robinson, Oxford 1940.

Butterworth, C. C. The literary lineage of the King James Bible. Philadelphia 1941.

Grierson, H. J. C. The English Bible. 1943.

Smalley, B. The study of the Bible in the Middle Ages. 1941, 1952 (rev).

Shepherd, G. English versions of the scriptures before Wyclif. In The Cambridge history of the Bible vol 2, Cambridge 1969.

(10) SERMONS

General Studies

Owst, G. R. Preaching in medieval England. Cambridge 1926.

—— Literature and pulpit in medieval England. Cambridge 1933, Oxford 1961 (rev).

Pfander, H. G. The popular sermons of the medieval friar in England. New York 1937.

Hinnebusch, W. A. The early English friars preachers. Rome 1951. Ch 16.

Robson, C. A. Maurice of Sully and the medieval vernacular homily. Oxford 1952.

Pantin, W. A. The English church in the 14th century. Cambridge 1955.

Blench, J. W. Preaching in England. Oxford 1964.

Auerbach, E. 'Sermo humilis'. In his Literary language and its public in late Latin antiquity and in the Middle Ages, 1965.

Ormulum

Ms: Junius I (Bodley).

Ed R. M. White, Oxford 1852; rev R. Holt, Oxford 1878.

(11) JOHN WYCLIF AND WYCLIFFITE WRITINGS

c. 1325–84

Bibliographies

Shirley, W. W. A catalogue of the original works by Wyclif. Oxford 1865, London 1924 (as Catalogue of the extant works) (rev J. Loserth).

§1

This section is concerned only with English works by Wyclif and his supporters, not distinguished.

Wycklyffes wycket. 1546; ed T. P. Pantin, Oxford 1828.

The last age of the Church. Ed J. H. Todd, Dublin 1840.

Treatise of miraclis pleyinge. Ed T. Wright and J. O. Halliwell (-Phillipps), Reliquiae antiquae vol 1, 1841.

An apology for Lollard doctrines. Ed J. H. Todd 1842 (Camden Soc).

Three treatises by Wyclif. Ed J. H. Todd, Dublin 1851.

Thirty-seven conclusions of the Lollards. Ed J. Forshall, Remonstrance against Romish corruptions, 1851.

— Ed H. F. B. Compston, EHR 26 1911.

Select English works of Wyclif. Ed T. Arnold 3 vols Oxford 1869–71.

English works of Wyclif hitherto unprinted. Ed F. D. Matthew 1880 (EETS).

Twelve conclusions of the Lollards. Ed H. S. Cronin, EHR 22 1907.

The holi prophete Dauid seith. Ed M. Deanesly, Lollard Bible, Cambridge 1920.

A3ens hem that seyn that hooli wri3t schulde not or may not be drawun into Englische. Ed M. Deanesly, ibid.

— Ed C. F. Bühler, MÆ 7 1938.

Select English writings. Ed H. E. Winn, Oxford 1929.

Jack Upland, Friar Daw's reply and Upland's rejoinder. Ed P. L. Heyworth, Oxford 1968.

§2

Lewis, J. The history of the life and sufferings of Wicliffe. 1720, Oxford 1820.

Vaughan, R. Life and opinions of John de Wycliffe DD. 1828.

Shirley, W. W. Fasciculi zizaniorum magistri Johannis Wyclif cum tritico. 1858 (Rolls ser).

Trevelyan, G. M. England in the age of Wycliffe. 1899, 1909 (rev).

Gairdner, J. Lollardry and the reformation in England. 1908.

Workman, H. B. Wyclif: a study of the English medieval Church. Oxford 1926.

Hargreaves, H. Wyclif's prose. E & S new ser 19 1966.

Wycliffite Translations of the Bible

The New testament translated out of the Latin Vulgat by Wiclif about 1378. Ed J. Lewis 1731.

The New testament translated from the Latin in the year 1380 by Wiclif. Ed H. H. Baber 1810.

The English Hexapla, exhibiting the six important English translations of the New testament scriptures. [1841].

The New testament in English, translated by Wycliffe circa mccclxxx. Ed Lea Wilson 1848.

The Holy Bible translated by Wycliffe and his followers. Ed J. Forshall and F. Madden 4 vols Oxford 1850.

The New testament in English. Ed W. W. Skeat, Oxford 1879.

The books of Job, Psalms, Ecclesiastes, Song of songs. Ed W. W. Skeat, Oxford 1881.

The New testament in Scots. Ed T. G. Law and J. Hall 3 vols 1901–4 (STS).

Ms Bodley 959: Genesis–Baruch 3.20 in the earlier version of the Wycliffite Bible. Ed C. Lindberg 5 vols Stockholm 1959–69.

(12) OTHER RELIGIOUS WRITINGS

Ancrene Riwle and Wisse [AR] [AW]

Mss: English 1, Corpus Christi College Cambridge 402; 2, BM Cotton Titus D XVIII; 3, Cotton Nero A XIV; 4, Cotton Cleopatra C VI; 5, Caius College Cambridge 234; 6, Vernon (Bodley 3938); 7, Magdalene College Cambridge Pepys 2498; 8, Lord Robartes – one leaf, Bodmin Cornwall; 9, Royal 8 C I; French, 1, Cotton Vitellius F VII; 2, Trinity College Cambridge R 14 7; 3, Bibliothèque Nationale F.Fr. 6276; 4, Bodley 90; Latin, 1, Magdalen College Oxford 67; 2, Cotton Vitellius E VII (fragments).

Ed J. R. R. Tolkien, The English text of the AR, AW, 1962 (EETS); G. Shepherd, AW, pts 6–7, 1959; 2, F. M. Mack, The English text of the AR, together with the Lanhydrock fragment (ms Bodley Eng. th. c. 70) ed A. Zettersten 1963 (EETS); 3, with some variants of 2 and 4, J. Morton 1853 (Camden Soc); M. Day and J. A. Herbert 1952 (EETS); 5, R. M. Wilson, The English text of AR, 1954 (EETS); 7, Pahlsson, The recluse, Lund 2 pts 1911–18; 8, JEGP 2 1898; 9, A. C.

Baugh 1956 (EETS); Modern English, The AR (from ms 1) tr M. B. Salu, introd by Dom G. Sitwell, preface by J. R. R. Tolkien 1956; The Cleopatra ms, ed E. J. Dobson 1972 (EETS); ed A. Zettersten 1976 (EETS) (ms Pepys 2498); French, 1, J. A. Herbert 1944 (EETS); 2, W. H. Trethewey 1958 (EETS); Latin, C. d'Evelyn 1944 (EETS).

See E. J. Dobson, Moralities on the Gospels, *Oxford 1975;* The origins of AW, *Oxford 1976.*

Ayenbite of Inwyt (Dan Michel)

Ms: Arundel 57.

Ed J. Stevenson 1885 (Roxburghe Club); R. Morris 1866 (EETS), 1965 (rev P. Gradon).

Pricke of Conscience

Ed R. Morris, Berlin 1863 (Philological Soc); G. Horstmann, Yorkshire writers vol 1, 1895 pp. 129, 372; vol 2, 1896 pp. 36, 67, 70.

Robert Mannyng

For Mannyng's Chronicle see Chronicles, above.

Handlyng Synne

Mss: 1, BM Harley 1701; 2, Bodley 415; 3, Univ Lib Cambridge Ii IV 9; 4, Dulwich College XXIV.

Ed F. J. Furnivall 1862 (Roxburghe Club); 1901 (EETS), 1903 (EETS).

Testament of Love (Thomas Usk)

Ed W. Thynne, Workes of Chaucer, 1532; W. W. Skeat, Complete works of Chaucer vol 7, Oxford 1897.

Proverbs of Alfred

Mss: 1, Jesus College Oxford 29 (Bodley); 2, Trinity College Cambridge B 14 39; 3, BM Cotton Galba A XIX (fragments); 4, Bodley James 6 (complete copy of 3); 5, Maidstone Museum A 13.

Ed J. Hall, Selections from early ME, Oxford 1920 (ms 1); T. Wright and J. O. Halliwell (-Phillipps), Reliquiae antiquae vol 1, 1841 (mss 1–2); R. Morris, 1872 (EETS); W. W. Skeat, Oxford 1907; J. M. Kemble, Dialogue of Salomon and Saturnus, 1848 (ms 2); E. Borgström, Lund 1908, 1911 (ms 3); A. Brandl and O. Zippel, Mittelenglische Sprach- und Literaturproben, Berlin 1917; C. Brown, MLR 21 1926 (mss 4–5); O. S. Anderson Arngart, Lund 1955 (mss 4–5); tr J. L. Weston, Chief ME poets, Boston 1914; M. G. Segar, A medieval anthology, 1916 (selected).

Proverbs of Hendyng

Mss: 1, Digby 86 (Bodley); 2, BM Harley 2253; 3, Univ Lib Cambridge Gg I 1; 4 (parts), Univ Lib Cambridge 4407 (19); 5, St John's College Cambridge F 8 (145); 6, Worcester Cathedral Lib F 19; 7, Bodley 410; 8, Rawlinson C 670 (Bodley); 9, Eton College 34; 10–11, Laud 111 and 213 (Bodley).

Ed J. M. Kemble, Salomon and Saturnus, 1848 (appendix) (ms 2); K. Böddeker, Altenglische Dichtungen des ms Harley 2253, Berlin 1878 (ms 2); E. Mätzner, Altenglische Sprachproben pt 1, Berlin 1867 (ms 2); R. Morris and W. W. Skeat, Specimens of early English vol 2, Oxford 1894 (ms 2); T. Wright and J. O. Halliwell (-Phillipps), Reliquiae antiquae vol 1, 1841 (ms 2); H. Varnhagen, Anglia 4 1881 (1 and 3, with comparison of 2); W. W. Skeat, MLR 7 1912 (ms 4); C. Brown, Register vol 1, Oxford 1916, pp. 450–1 (ms 6); G. Schleich, Anglia 51 1927; tr J. L. Weston, Chief ME poets, Boston 1914.

The Owl and the Nightingale

Mss: 1, BM Cotton Caligula A IX; 2, Jesus College Oxford 29 (Bodley).

Ed J. Stevenson 1838 (Roxburghe Club); T. Wright 1843 (Percy Soc); F. H. Stratmann, Krefeld 1867, and see E Studien 1 1877; J. E. Wells, Boston and London 1907 (parallel texts); W. Gadow, Das mittelenglische Streitgedicht Eule und Nachtigall, Palaestra 65 1909; J. H. G. Grattan and G. F. H. Sykes 1935 (EETS); J. W. H. Atkins, Cambridge 1922 (with trn); G. Eggers 1955 (trn); E. G. Stanley 1960; N. R. Ker 1963 (EETS) (ms facs with introd).

The Body and the Soul

Mss: Version 1, Exeter Book (Cathedral Lib Exeter); Version 2, Worcester Cathedral Lib (fragments); Version 3, Bodley 343 (25vv); Version 4a, Laud 108 (Bodley); b, Auchinleck (Nat Lib of Scotland 19.2.1); c, Royal 18 A X; e, Vernon (Bodley 3938); e, BM additional 22,283; f, Digby 102 (Bodley); g, BM additional 37,787; Version 5a, Digby 86 (Bodley); b, Trinity College Cambridge B.14.39; c, Harley 2253; Version 6, Trinity College Cambridge B.14.39 (f27r.22vv).

Ed C. W. M. Grein, Bibliothek der angelsächsischen Poesie vol 1, Göttingen 1857 (version 1); R. Wülcker, Leipzig 1894 (version 1); T. Phillipps, Fragment of Aelfric's grammar, 1838 (version 2); S. W. Singer, Departing soul's address to the body, 1845 (version 2); E. Haufe, Greifswald 1880 (version 2); R. Buchholz, Erlanger Beiträge 6 1890 (version 2); J. Hall, Selections from early ME, Oxford 1920 (version 3); Archaeologia 17 1814 (version 3); T. Thorpe, Analecta anglosaxonica, 1846 (version 3); F. L. M. Rieger, Alt- und angelsächsisches Lesebuch, Giessen 1861 (version 3); A. Schröer, Anglia 5 1882 (version 3); R. Buchholz, Erlanger Beiträge 6 1890 (version 3); (with Latin and French), T. Wright, Latin poems attributed to W. Mapes 1841 (Camden Soc) (version 4a, d); 1–2, W. Linow, Erlanger Beiträge 1 1889 (version 4a, b, d, f with variants of e); E. Mätzner, Altenglische Sprachproben pt 1, Berlin 1867 (version 4a); O. F. Emerson, Reader, New York 1915 (4a); D. Laing, Owain Miles, Edinburgh 1837 (version 4b); H. Varnhagen, Anglia 2 1879 (version 4c); E. M. Stengel, Codicem manu scriptum, Digby 86, Halle 1871 (version 5a); T. Wright, Latin poems attributed to W. Mapes, 1841 (Camden Soc) (5c); K. Böddeke, Altenglische Dichtungen der Handschrift Harley 2253, Berlin 1878 (version 5c); T. Wright, Latin poems attributed to W. Mapes, 1841 (Camden Soc) (version 6); H. Varnhagen, Anglia 3 1880 (version 6); tr C. G. Child, Boston 1908; J. L. Weston, Chief ME poets, Boston 1914.

Bestiary

Ms: Arundel 292.

Ed T. Wright, Altdeutsche Blätter vol 2, 1837; T. Wright and J. O. Halliwell (-Phillipps), Reliquiae antiquae vol 1, 1841; R. Morris, 1872 (EETS), and Archiv 88 1891; E. Mätzner, Altenglische Sprachproben pt 1, Berlin 1867; J. Hall, Selections from early ME, Oxford 1920; J. A. W. Bennett and G. V. Smithers, Early ME verse and prose, Oxford 1968; tr M. H. Shackford, Legends and satires, Boston 1913; J. L. Weston, Chief ME poets, Boston 1914.

RICHARD ROLLE

c. 1300–49

Bibliographies

Allen, H. E. Writings ascribed to Rolle and materials for his biography. New York 1927.

Collections

Latin Works

De emendatione peccatoris. Antwerp 1533.
De emendatione peccatoris opusculum cum aliis aliquot appendicibus. Cologne 1535.
In psalterium davidicum atque alia quaedam sacrae scripturae monumenta. Cologne 1536.
M. de la Bigne, Magna bibliotheca vol 15. Cologne 1622.
M. de la Bigne, Maxima bibliotheca vol 26. Lyons 1677.

English Works

English prose treatises. Ed G. G. Perry 1866 (EETS), 1921 (rev).
Yorkshire writers: Rolle and his followers. Ed C. Horstman 2 vols 1895–6.
Some minor works. Ed G. E. Hodgson 1923 (modernized).
Selected works. Ed G. C. Heseltine 1930 (modernized).
English writings. Ed H. E. Allen, Oxford 1931.

§ I

English Works

Commentary on the psalter. Ed H. R. Bramley, Oxford 1884; commentary on canticles ed G. C. Heseltine, Selected works 1930; ed H. E. Allen, English writings of Rolle, Oxford 1931 (excerpts).

Ego dormio. Ed C. Horstman, Yorkshire writers vol 1, p. 5; ed R. H. Benson 1904 (modernized); ed G. C. Hodgson, Some minor works, 1923; ed G. C. Heseltine, Selected works, 1930; ed H. E. Allen, English writings, Oxford 1931; ed E. Colledge, The mediaeval mystics of England, 1962 (modernized).

The commandment. Ed C. Horstman, Yorkshire writers vol 1, p. 61; ed G. E. Hodgson, Some minor works, 1923; ed G. C. Heseltine, Selected works, 1930; ed H. E. Allen, English writings, Oxford 1931.

The form of living. Ed C. Horstman, Yorkshire writers vol 1, p. 3; ed G. E. Hodgson 1910 (modernized); ed G. C. Heseltine, Selected works, 1930; ed H. E. Allen, English writings, Oxford 1931.

Short prose pieces. Ed C. Horstman, Yorkshire writers vol 1, p. 193, p. 81; ed G. C. Heseltine, Selected works, 1930; ed H. E. Allen, English writings, Oxford 1931.

Meditations on the passion. [Shorter version], ed J. Ullman, E Studien 7 1884; [longer version], ed C. Horstman vol 1, p. 92; ed H. Lindqvist, Upsala 1917; ed C. Horstman, Yorkshire writers vol 1, p. 83; ed E. Burton 1906 (modernized); ed G. C. Heseltine, Selected works, 1930; ed H. E. Allen, English writings, Oxford 1931.

Lyrics. Ed C. Horstman, Yorkshire writers vol 1 pp. 72–81, 363, 367, 370; vol 2 p. 247; ed F. M. M. Comper, Life and lyrics of Rolle, 1928 (modernized); ed H. E. Allen, English writings, Oxford 1931.

Our daily work [authorship uncertain]. Ed G. E. Hodgson 1910 (with The form of perfect living); Rolle and Our daily work, 1929 (modernized).

§2

The English martyrologe, by a Catholicke priest. 1608.
The English martyrologe. [St Omer] 1672.
Officium de sancto Ricardo de Hampole. Ed G. G. Perry, English prose treatises of Rolle, 1866 (EETS); ed F. Proctor, Breviarium ad usum ecclesie eboracensis, ed S. W. Lawley, Durham 1883 (Surtees Soc); ms fragment ed H. Lindqvist in his edn of Meditatio de passione domini, Upsala 1917; ed R. M. Woolley 1919; tr F. M. M. Comper 1914 (with Fire of love).

Allen, H. E. The authorship of the Prick of conscience. Boston 1910.
Knowles, D. In his English mystics, 1927.
—— In his English mystical tradition, 1961.
Comper, F. M. M. The life of Rolle. 1928.
Wilson, R. M. Three middle English mystics. E & S new ser 10 1956.

WILLIAM OF NASSYNGTON
d.c. 1359

Tractatus Willelmi Nassyngtone quondam advocati curiae Eboraci. Ed G. G. Perry, Religious pieces in prose and verse, 1867 (EETS).
The mirror of life. Lines 1–370 ed J. Ullman, E Studien 7 1884; fragment ed C. Wordsworth, Horae eboracenses, Durham 1920 (Surtees Soc).
Metrical version of Richard Rolle's Form of living. Ed C. Horstman, Yorkshire writers vol 2 p. 283, 1896. Authorship uncertain.

AUTHOR OF THE CLOUD OF UNKNOWING
late 14th century

Collections

Deonise hid divinite and other treatises. Ed P. Hodgson 1955 (EETS).

§1

The cloud of unknowing. Ed H. Collins 1871 (modernized); ed E. Underhill 1912 (modernized); ed J. McCann 1924 (modernized), 1952 (rev); ed P. Hodgson 1944 (EETS), 1958 (rev); ed L. Progroff 1959 (modernized); ed C. Wolters 1961.
Epistle of privy counselling. Ed J. McCann 1924 (with Cloud, above); ed P. Hodgson 1944 (with Cloud); ed E. Colledge, The mediaeval mystics of England, 1962 (modernized); ed J. Walsh, Verona 1963 (modernized).
Deonise hid divinite. Ed J. McCann 1924 (with Cloud, above); ed P. Hodgson 1955 (EETS).
A veray devoute treatyse named Benyamyn, A pistle of preier, A pistle of discrecioun of stirings, A tretis of discrescyon of spirites. 1521 (H. Pepwell); ed J. E. G. Gardner, The cell of self-knowledge, 1910 (modernized); ed P. Hodgson 1955 (with Deonise hid diuinite); A tretyse that men clepen Beniamyn, ed C. Horstman, Richard Rolle vol 1 p. 162, 1895.

WALTER HILTON
d. 1396

Collections

Minor works. Ed D. Jones 1929 (modernized).

§1

The scale of perfection. 1494 (de Worde), 1507 (Notary), 1519 (de Worde), 1525, 1533, 1659 (de Worde edn rev); ed E. Guy 1869; ed J. B. Dalgairns 1870 (modernized); ed E. Underhill 1923 (BM ms Harley 6579) (modernized); tr G. Sitwell 1953; ed L. Sherley-Price 1957 (Penguin) (modernized); ed E. Colledge, The mediaeval mystics of England, 1962 (excerpts).
Epistle to a devout man in temporal estate. 1494 (de Worde) (shorter text with Scale of perfection, above), 1507 (Notary) (longer text with Scale of perfection), 1519 (de Worde), 1525, 1533; 1516 (Pynson) (with Kalendre of the newe legende of England), [1531] (Wyer), 1659 (with Scale of perfection), 1869, 1870; ed G. G. Perry, English prose treatises of Richard Rolle, 1866 (EETS); ed C. Horstman, Yorkshire writers vol 1 p. 264, 1895; ed D. Jones, Minor works, 1929.
The song of angels. In A veray deuoute treatyse named Benyamyn, 1521 (H. Pepwell); ed G. G. Perry, English prose treatises of Richard Rolle, 1866 (EETS); ed C. Horstman, Yorkshire writers vol 1 p. 175, 1895; ed E. G. Gardner, The cell of self-knowledge, 1910 (modernized).
Eight chapters on perfection. Ed D. Jones, Minor works, 1929; ed F. Kuriyagawa, Tokyo 1967.
Qui habitat and Bonum est. Ed D. Jones, Minor works, 1929; ed B. Wallner, Lund 1954.
Benedictus. Ed D. Jones, Minor works, 1929; ed B. Wallner, Lund 1957.
The goad of love. Ed C. Kirchberger 1952 (modernized). Trn of Stimulus amoris.
Epistola ad solitarium [in Latin]. Tr Way July 1966.

§2

Knowles, D. In his English mystics, 1927.
—— In his English mystical tradition, 1961.
Gardner, H. L. Hilton and the authorship of the Cloud of unknowing. RES 9 1933.
—— The text of the Scale of perfection. MÆ 5 1936.
—— Hilton and the mystical tradition in England. E & S 22 1936.
White, V. Hilton: an English spiritual guide. 1944.

Hughes, A. C. Hilton's direction to contemplatives. Rome 1962.

Milosh, J. E. The scale of perfection and the English mystical tradition. Madison 1966.

Wilson, R. M. Three Middle English mystics. E & S new ser 10 1956.

Molinari, P. Julian of Norwich: the teaching of a fourteenth-century mystic. 1958.

JULIAN OF NORWICH

c. 1343–c. 1413

§ 1

Sixteen revelations of divine love. Ed R. F. S. Cressy 1670 (longer version, Paris ms); ed G. H. Parker 1843; ed G. Tyrrell 1902; ed J. Walsh 1961 (modernized); ed H. Collins 1877 (longer version, Sloan ms) (modernized); ed G. Warrack 1901 (modernized), 1949 (rev); ed R. Hudleston 1927 (modernized); ed G. Wolters 1966 (modernized); ed D. Harford 1911 (shorter version, Amherst ms); ed A. M. Reynolds 1958. 15th-century excerpts ed J. Walsh and E. Colledge, The knowledge of our self and God, 1961 (modernized); ed P. F. Chambers 1955 (excerpts); ed Colledge, The medieval mystics of England 1962 (modernized excerpts).

§ 2

Chambers, P. F. Juliana of Norwich. 1955.

MARGERY KEMPE

c. 1373–c. 1439

§ 1

A short treatyse of contemplacyon taken out of the boke of Margerie Kempe of Lyn. [1501] (de Worde), 1521 (with A veray devoute treatyse named Benyamyn)(H. Pepwell); ed J. E. G. Gardner, The cell of self knowledge, 1910 (modernized).

The book of Margery Kempe. Ed W. Butler-Bowden 1936 (modernized); ed S. B. Meech and H. E. Allen 1940 (EETS); ed E. Colledge, The medieval mystics of England, 1962 (modernized excerpts).

§ 2

Cholmeley, K. Margery Kempe. 1947.
Thornton, M. Margery Kempe. 1960.
Collis, L. The apprentice saint. 1964.

(13) SAINTS' LEGENDS

Alliterative Katherine Group

General Studies

Gerould, G. H. Saints' legends. Boston 1916.
Tolkien, J. R. R. Ancrene wisse and Hali meiðhad. E & S 14 1928.

Hali Meidenhad

Mss: 1, Bodley 34; 2, BM Cotton Titus D. XVIII.
1 and 2. Ed O. Cockayne 1866 (EETS); re-ed F. Furnivall 1922 (EETS); ed A. F. Colborn, Copenhagen 1940; ed N. R. Ker, Facsimile of ms Bodley 34, 1960 (EETS).

Sawles Warde

Mss: 1, Bodley 34; 2, BM Cotton Titus D. XVIII; Royal 17 A. XXVII.
1, Ed R. Morris 1868 (EETS); ed J. Hall, Selections from early ME, Oxford 1920 (part of 3); ed N. R. Ker 1960 (EETS); ed J. A. W. Bennett and G. V. Smithers, Early ME verse and prose, Oxford 1966; 3, ed W. Wagner, Bonn 1908; 1–3, ed R. M. Wilson, Leeds 1936. *See also* R. Morris, Ayenbite of inwit, 1886 (EETS) p. 263 (Kentish: ms Arundel LVII, College of Arms).

Katherine

Mss: 1, Bodley 34; 2, BM Cotton Titus D. XVIII; 3, Royal 17 A. XXVII.
1, Ed N. R. Ker 1960 (EETS) (facs); 2, ed J. Morton 1841 (Abbotsford Club); ed C. Hardwick 1849 (Cambridge Antiquarian Soc); ed J. Hall, Selections from early ME, Oxford 1920; 3, ed E. Einenkel 1884 (EETS).

Juliana

Mss: 1, Bodley 34; 2, BM Royal 17 A. XXVII.
1, Ed N. R. Ker 1960 (EETS) (facs); 1–2, ed O. Cockayne and E. Brock 1872 (EETS); ed J. Hall, Selections from early ME, Oxford 1920; ed S. T. R. O. d'Ardenne 1961 (EETS).

Seinte Marherete

Mss: 1, Bodley 34; 2, BM Royal 17 A. XXVII.
1, Ed N. R. Ker 1960 (EETS) (facs); 2, ed O. Cockayne 1886 (EETS); 1–2, ed F. M. Mack 1934 (EETS).

General Studies

Morris, R. Legends of the Holy Rood. 1871 (EETS).
Napier, A. S. History of the Holy Rood Tree. 1894 (EETS).
Lovewell, B. E. Life of St Cecilia. New Haven 1898.
Foster, F. A. Northern Passion. 1912–13 (EETS); suppl 1930 (EETS).
Day, M. The Wheatley ms. 1921 (EETS). Legend of Adam and Eve.
Peebles, R. J. The dry tree. New Haven 1923. Cross legend.
Brown, B. Southern Passion. 1927 (EETS).
Brown, P. A. The development of the legend of Thomas Becket. Philadelphia 1930.
Rosenthal, C. L. The Vitae patrum in Old and Middle English literature. Philadelphia 1936.
Attwater, D. A dictionary of saints. 1939.
Moore, G. E. The ME verse life of Edward the Confessor. Philadelphia 1942.
Klenke, Sr M. A. Three saints' lives by Nicholas Bozon. New York 1947 (Franciscan Stud).
Loomis, C. G. White Magic: an introduction to the folklore of Christian legend. Cambridge Mass 1948.
Garth, H. M. St Mary Magdalene in medieval literature. Baltimore 1950.
Patch, H. R. The other world according to descriptions in medieval literature. Cambridge 1950.
Lawrence, C. H. St Edmund of Abingdon: a study in hagiography and history. Oxford 1960.

Particular Collections

Northern Homily Cycle

Mss: See Register, and Index, appendix 4; G. H. Gerould, Northern homily collection, Lancaster Pa 1902, and Saints' legends, Boston 1916.
Ed J. Small, English metrical homilies, Edinburgh 1862 (ms Edinburgh Royal College of Physicians); ed E. Mätzner, Altenglische Sprachproben pt i, Berlin 1877, p. 278 (2 items); ed R. Morris and W. W. Skeat, Specimens of early English vol 2, Oxford 1894, p. 83

(2 items); Signs of doom, ed O. F. Emerson, Reader, New York 1915; Northern Passion 1912–13 (EETS), suppl 1930 (EETS); ed R. Morris 1871 (EETS) (Cross story only).

Southern Legend Collection

Mss: See C. Horstmann, Altenglische Legenden, Paderborn 1875, p. i; Heilbronn 1881, p. xliv; 1887 (EETS), p. vii; C. d'Evelyn and A. J. Mill 1959 (EETS).

Ed F. J. Furnivall, Early English poems and lives of saints, Berlin 1862 (various items from BM ms Harley 2277).
Ed C. Horstmann, 1887 (EETS) (Laud 108); Archiv 82 1889, pp. 307, 369 (Bodley 779, later addns).
Ed C. d'Evelyn and A. J. Mill 1956–9 (EETS) (Corpus Christi College, Cambridge 154, Harley 2277, with variants from Bodley Ashmole 43 and BM Cotton Julius D. IX).

(14) WILLIAM LANGLAND

c. 1332–1400

Piers Plowman

Mss:
A-text: 17 mss. Listed and described in G. Kane, Piers Plowman: the A version, 1960.
B-text: 17 mss. Listed and classified in E. Blackman, Notes on the B-text mss of Piers Plowman, JEGP 17 1918.
C-text: 19 mss. Listed and classified in E. T. Donaldson, Piers Plowman: the C-text and its poet, New Haven 1949.
See also C. Brown, Register of Middle English verse vol 2, Oxford 1920, items 880–1; R. H. Robbins, Index of Middle English verse, New York 1943, items 745, 1458, 1459.

§ 1

A-text: ed W. W. Skeat, 1867 (EETS); ed T. A. Knott and D. C. Fowler, Baltimore 1952; ed G. Kane 1960.
B-text: ed R. Crowley 1550; ed O. Rogers 1561; ed T. Wright 1842, 1856 (rev), 1895; ed W. W. Skeat 1869 (EETS); ed G. Kane and E. T. Donaldson 1975; ed. A. V. C. Schmidt 1978 (EL).
C-text: ed T. D. Whitaker 1813; ed W. W. Skeat 1873 (EETS); ed R. B. Haselden and H. C. Schulz, The Huntington Library ms (HM 143), San Marino 1936 (facs) (introd by R. W. Chambers).
Notes to A-, B- and C-texts by W. W. Skeat, 1885 (EETS); ed Skeat, Oxford 1886 (parallel texts), 1954 (with bibliography); ed Skeat 1886 (EETS) (parallel extracts).
Selections: Ed W. W. Skeat, Oxford 1869, 1923 (B Prologue, i–vii); ed E. Salter and D. Pearsall 1967 (selections from C i–xxiii); ed J. A. W. Bennett, Oxford 1972 (B Prologue, i–vii).

§ 2

Chambers, R. W. The authorship of Piers Plowman. MLR 5 1910; rptd 1910 (EETS).
— The original form of the A-text of Piers Plowman. MLR 6 1911.
— The three texts of Piers Plowman and their grammatical forms. MLR 14 1919.
— Long Will, Dante and the righteous heathen. E & S 9 1923.
— Piers Plowman: a comparative study. In his Man's unconquerable mind, 1939.
— Poets and their critics: Milton and Langland. Proc Br Acad 27 1941.
Dunning, T. P. Piers Plowman: an interpretation of the A-text. Dublin 1937; partly rptd in Vasta, below.
— Langland and the salvation of the heathen. MÆ 12 1943.
— The structure of the B-text of Piers Plowman. RES new ser 7 1956; rptd in Blanch, below.
— Action and contemplation in Piers Plowman. In Piers Plowman: critical approaches, ed S. S. Hussey 1969.
Bloomfield, M. W. Piers Plowman as a fourteenth-

century apocalypse. New Brunswick NJ 1962.
Bennett, J. A. W. The date of the A-text of Piers Plowman. PMLA 58 1943.
— The date of the B-text of Piers Plowman. MÆ 12 1943.
— Chaucer's contemporary. In Piers Plowman: critical approaches, ed S. S. Hussey 1969.
Coghill, N. The pardon of Piers Plowman. Proc Br Acad 30 1944; partly rptd in Blanch, below.
— Langland: Piers Plowman. 1964 (Br Council pamphlet).
Kane, G. Piers Plowman: problems and methods of editing the B-text. MLR 43 1948.
— Piers Plowman. In his Middle English literature, 1951; partly rptd in Vasta, below.
— Piers Plowman: the evidence for authorship. 1965.
— The autobiographical fallacy in Chaucer and Langland studies. 1965.
Frank, R. W. Piers Plowman and the scheme of salvation. New Haven 1957; partly rptd in Vasta, below.
Lawlor, J. Piers Plowman: an essay in criticism. 1962.
Robertson, D. W. and B. F. Huppé. Piers Plowman and scriptural tradition. Princeton 1951.
Smith, A. H. Piers Plowman and the pursuit of poetry. 1951; rptd in Blanch, below.
Donaldson, E. T. The texts of Piers Plowman: scribes and poets. MP 50 1953.
— Piers Plowman: the C-text and its poet. New Haven 1949.
Hussey, S. S. Langland, Hilton and the three lives. RES new ser 7 1956; rptd in Vasta, below.
— (ed). Piers Plowman: critical approaches. 1969.
Zeeman, E. Piers Plowman and the pilgrimage to Truth. E & S new ser 11 1958; rptd in Blanch, below.
— (E. Salter). Piers Plowman: an introduction. Oxford 1962.
Woolf, R. Some non-mediaeval qualities of Piers Plowman. EC 12 1962.
— The tearing of the pardon. In Piers Plowman: critical approaches, ed S. S. Hussey 1969.
Vasta, E. The spiritual basis of Piers Plowman. Hague 1965.
— (ed). Interpretations of Piers Plowman. Notre Dame 1968.
Blanch, R. J. (ed). Style and symbolism in Piers Plowman. Knoxville 1969.

The following poems have in the past been associated with Langland:

Pierce the Ploughman's Crede

Mss: BM Royal 18 B.xvii; Trinity College Cambridge R.3.15.

Ed R. Wolfe 1553, 1814; ed T. Wright in Piers Plowman, 1842, 1856 (rev), 1895; ed W. W. Skeat 1867 (EETS); ed Skeat, Specimens of English literature 1394-1579, Oxford 1879 (2nd edn rev); ed A. S. Cook, Literary Middle English reader, Boston 1915.

Richard the Redeless, or Mum and the Sothsegger

Mss: Cambridge Univ Lib Ll.4.14; BM additional 41,666. Both fragmentary.

Ed T. Wright 1838 (Camden Soc); ed T. Wright, Political poems and songs vol 1, 1859 (Rolls ser); ed W. W. Skeat 1873 (EETS); ed Skeat, Piers Plowman vol 1, Oxford 1886; ed M. Day and R. Steele 1936 (EETS).

Tr A. R. Benham, English literature from Widsith to the death of Chaucer, New Haven 1916 (in part).

Complaint of the Ploughman or Plowman's Tale

For mss see Wells p. 1613; S. de Ricci and W. J. Wilson, Census of mediaeval and Renaissance mss, Washington 1937, vol 2, p. 2157 (Univ of Texas 8).

Ed W. Thynne, Workes of Chaucer, 1542 (2nd edn); ed T. Wright, Political poems and songs vol 1, 1859 (Rolls ser); ed W. W. Skeat, Complete works of Chaucer vol 7, Oxford 1897.

Jack Upland

No ms extant.

Ed J. Gough [c. 1540 or c. 1536]; ed T. Wright, Political poems and songs vol 2, 1861 (Rolls ser); ed W. W. Skeat, Complete works of Chaucer vol 7, Oxford 1897; ed P. L. Heyworth, Oxford 1968.

Other Alliterative Poems
Parlement of the Thre Ages

Ms: BM additional 31,042; imperfect copy in 33,994.

Ed I. Gollancz 1897 (Roxburghe Club), 1915; ed F. Berry, The age of Chaucer, ed B. Ford 1954 (Pelican), 1959 (rev); ed M. Y. Offord 1959 (EETS).

Tr H. S. Bennett, England from Chaucer to Caxton, 1928 (in part) and Life on the English manor, 1937 (in part).

Wynnere and Wastoure

Ms: BM additional 31,042.

Ed I. Gollancz 1897 (Roxburghe Club), 1920, 1930 (for 1931) (with trn); ed F. Berry, The age of Chaucer, ed B. Ford 1954 (Pelican), 1959 (rev); ed R. Kaiser, Mediaeval English, Berlin 1958 (3rd edn of Alt- und mittelenglische Anthologie, rev and enlarged) (in part).

(15) THE PEARL POET

Ms: BM Cotton Nero A.x+4 (once A.x); ed I. Gollancz 1923 (EETS)(facs). See W. W. Greg, MLR 19 1925.

Indexes and Concordances

Chapman, C. O. An index of names in Pearl, Purity, Patience and Gawain. Ithaca 1951.

Kottler, B. and A. M. Markman. A concordance to five Middle English poems: Cleanness, St Erkenwald, Sir Gawain and the Green Knight, Patience, Pearl. Pittsburgh 1966.

Collections

Ed R. Morris 1864 (EETS), 1869 (rev); The Pearl poet: his complete works, ed M. Williams, New York 1967.

Tr J. Gardner, Complete works of the Gawain poet in a modern English version, Chicago 1965; tr J. R. R. Tolkien 1975 (Pearl, Sir Gawain, Sir Orfeo).

General Studies

Everett, D. Patience, Purity and Sir Gawain and the Green Knight. In her Essays on Middle English literature, Oxford 1955.

Savage, H. L. The Gawain poet: studies in his personality and background. Chapel Hill 1956.

Brewer, D. S. Courtesy and the Gawain poet. In Patterns of love and courtesy: essays in memory of C. S. Lewis, 1966.

—— The Gawain poet: a general appreciation of the four poems. EC 17 1967.

Spearing, A. C. Patience and the Gawain poet. The Gawain-poet: a critical study. Cambridge 1970.

Pearl

§1

Ed R. Morris 1864 (EETS), 1869 (rev); ed I. Gollancz 1891 (with trn), 1897 (rev), 1907, 1921 (rev with trn of Olympia); ed C. G. Osgood, Boston 1906; ed F. Olivero, Turin 1926, Bologna 1936 (both with Italian trn); ed S. P. Chase et al, Boston 1932; ed E. V. Gordon, Oxford 1953; ed M. V. Hillman, New York 1961 (with trn); ed A. C. Cawley 1962 (EL); ed S. de Ford, New York 1967 (with trn).

Selections: Ed A. Brandl and O. Zippel, Mittelenglische

Sprach- und Literaturproben, Berlin 1917, 1927, tr 1947, 1949; ed K. Sisam, Fourteenth-century verse and prose, Oxford 1921, 1937 (corrected).

Translations: G. G. Coulton 1906 (in original metre); C. G. Osgood, Princeton 1907 (prose); S. O. Jewett, New York 1908 (in original metre), rptd in R. S. Loomis, Medieval English verse and prose, New York 1948; S. W. Mitchell, New York 1908 (selection in verse); J. L. Weston, Romance, vision and satire, Boston 1912 (in original metre); W. A. Neilson and K. G. T. Webster, Chief British poets of the 14th and 15th centuries, Boston 1916 (prose); I. Gollancz 1918 (and in his edns above); E. Kirtlan 1918 (verse); S. P. Chase, Oxford 1932 (verse); B. Stone, Medieval English verse, 1964 (Penguin).

§2

Blanch, R. J. (ed). Sir Gawain and Pearl: critical essays. Bloomington 1966.

Kean, P. M. The Pearl: an interpretation. 1967.

Patience

Ed R. Morris 1864 (EETS), 1869 (rev); ed H. Bateson, Manchester 1912, 1918 (rev); ed I. Gollancz 1913, 1924 (rev); ed J. J. Anderson, Manchester 1969.

Selections: Ed J. Zupitza, Altenglisches Übungsbuch, Vienna 1874; ed R. Wülcker, Altenglisches Lesebuch pt 2, Halle 1879; ed G. E. MacLean, Old and ME reader, New York 1893; ed F. Kluge, Mittelenglisches Lesebuch, Halle 1904, 1912; ed G. Sampson, Cambridge book of prose and verse, Cambridge 1924.

Translations: J. L. Weston, Romance, vision and satire, Boston 1912 (selection); B. Stone, Mediaeval English verse, 1964 (Penguin).

Purity or Cleanness

Ed R. Morris 1864 (EETS), 1869 (rev); ed R. J. Menner, Yale Stud 61 1920; ed I. Gollancz 1921.

Selections: Ed R. Morris and W. W. Skeat, Specimens of early English vol 2, Oxford 1894.

Translations: J. L. Weston, Romance, vision and satire, Boston 1912 (selections); B. Stone 1971 (Penguin).

Sir Gawayne and the Grene Knight

See under Arthurian Romances, col 35, above.

Erkenwald

Ms: BM Harley 2250.

Ed C. Horstmann, Altenglische Legenden, Heilbronn 1881; ed I. Gollancz 1922 (with trn); ed H. L. Savage, New Haven 1926; tr B. Stone 1971 (Penguin).

(16) JOHN GOWER

1330?–1408?

Collections

Complete works. Ed G. C. Macaulay 4 vols Oxford 1899–1902.
Selections. Ed J. A. W. Bennett, Oxford 1968.

§1

Confessio amantis. 1483 (Caxton); ed R. Pauli 3 vols 1857; The English works in Complete works, ed G. C. Macaulay 2 vols 1901; ed R. A. Peck, New York 1968; Selections, ed H. Morley 1889; ed M. W. Easton, Halle 1896 (as Readings in Gower); ed Macaulay, Oxford 1903; ed T. Tiller 1968 (modernized). In English. At least 60 mss; *see* Macaulay, Complete works, above vol 2 p. cxxxviii; H. Spies, E Studien 28 1900, JEGP 4 1902, E Studien 32 1903, 34 1904; Archiv 110 1903; J. H. Fisher, Gower, New York 1964, appendix A (omits Christ Church Oxford ms, unknown to Macaulay).
Vox clamantis. Ed H. O. Coxe 1850 (Roxburghe Club); tr E. W. Stockton, Seattle 1962 (in Major Latin works of Gower). In Latin.
Mirour de l'omme. In Complete works, ed Macaulay, above. In French.

The minor French and Latin poems were ed H. O. Coxe with Vox clamantis, above; see also Political poems and songs, ed T. Wright 1859 (Rolls ser).
In praise of peace. In Wright, above.
For Balade moral of gode counsayle see M. Forster, Archiv 102 1899.
Un traité: Quixley's translation. Ed H. N. MacCracken, Yorkshire Archaeological Jnl 20 1909.

§2

On Gower's tomb in Southwark Cathedral, see Berthelette's edn of Confessio, 1532–4; also J. Stow, Survey of London, 1633 p. 450; R. Gough, Sepulchral monuments vol 2, 1786 p. 24.
Thynne, F. In his Animadversions, 1599.
Leland, J. In his Commentarii de scriptoribus britannicis, Oxford 1709.
Todd, H. J. Illustrations of Gower and Chaucer. 1810.
Ker, W. P. In his Essays on medieval literature, 1905.
Lewis, C. S. In his Allegory of love, Oxford 1936.
Bennett, J. A. W. Caxton and Gower. MLR 45 1950.
—— Gower's 'honeste love'. In Patterns of love and courtesy: essays in memory of C. S. Lewis, 1966.
Fisher, J. H. Gower: moral philosopher and friend of Chaucer. New York 1964.

GEOFFREY CHAUCER

c. 1343–1400

Bibliographies etc

Hammond, E. P. Chaucer: a bibliographical manual. New York 1908.
Spurgeon, C. F. E. Five hundred years of Chaucer criticism and allusion. 7 pts 1914–24 (Chaucer Soc), 3 vols Cambridge 1925, New York 1960.
French, R. D. A Chaucer handbook. New York 1927, 1947 (rev).
Tatlock, J. S. P. and A. G. Kennedy. A concordance to the complete works of Chaucer and to the Romaunt of the rose. Washington 1927, Gloucester Mass 1963.

Collections

Complete Works

Ed R. Pynson 3 vols 1526; ed W. Thynne 1532, 1542, [1545?], 1561, ed W. W. Skeat 1905 (facs), D. S. Brewer, Menston 1970 (facs); ed J. Stow 1561; ed T. Speght 1598, 1602, 1687; ed J. Urry 1721; 1810; 5 vols Chiswick 1822; 1843; 6 vols 1845, rev R. Morris 1866; New York [1880]; ed A. Gilman 3 vols Boston 1880; ed W. W. Skeat 7 vols Oxford 1894–7, 1 vol Oxford 1895, 3 vols Oxford 1909; ed F. S. Ellis 1896 (Kelmscott), ed J. T. Winterich, Cleveland 1958 (facs); ed A. W. Pollard et al 1898; 2 vols New York 1901; 1903; 1906; ed A. W. Pollard 8 vols Oxford 1928–9; 2 vols Oxford 1929–30; Boston 1930; ed F. N. Robinson, Boston 1933, 1957 (rev); ed K. Malone, Baltimore 1953.

Selections

Ed F. N. Paton 1888; ed J. L. Robertson, Edinburgh 1902; ed E. A. Greenlaw, Chicago 1907; ed W. W. Skeat, Oxford 1907; ed C. G. Child, Boston 1912; ed O. F. Emerson, New York 1911; ed H. N. MacCracken, New Haven 1913; ed M. Kaluza, Leipzig 1915, 1927 (rev); ed L. J. Lloyd 1952; ed C. W. Dunn, New York 1952; ed R. A. Jeliffe, New York 1952; ed E. T. Donaldson, New York 1958; ed A. C. Baugh, New York 1963; ed R. A. Pratt, Boston 1966; ed K. Kee 1967; ed L. O. Coxe, New York 1969.

§1

Romaunt of the Rose

Ed F. J. Furnivall 1911 (Chaucer Soc; Thynne's text); ed R. Sutherland, Oxford 1967; ed S. G. Nichols 1967.

Book of the Duchess

Ed F. J. Furnivall 1871 (Chaucer Soc), Lexington Kentucky 1954.

Hous of Fame

Ed W. Caxton [1484]; ed H. Willert, Berlin 1888; ed W. W. Skeat 1893, 1896; ed C. M. Drennan 1921; tr Skeat 1908.

Parlement of Foules

Ed W. Caxton [1477]; ed W. de Worde [1530]; ed [J. Rastell 1525]: ed T. R. Lounsbury, Boston 1877; ed J. Koch, Berlin 1904; ed C. M. Drennan 1911; ed D. S. Brewer 1960; tr W. W. Skeat 1908.

Troilus and Criseyde

Ed W. Caxton [1484]; ed W. de Worde 1517; ed R. Pynson [1526?]; ed W. S. McCormick and R. K. Root 1914 (Chaucer Soc) (incomplete); ed R. K. Root, Princeton 1926; ed R. C. Goffin 1935 (selections); ed G. Bonnard, Berne 1943 (selections); ed J. Warrington 1953 (EL) (modernized); ed D. Cook, Garden City NY 1966 (selections); ed D. S. and L. E. Brewer 1969 (selections); tr F. Kynaston, Oxford 1635 (Latin); G. P. Krapp, New York 1932; R. M. Lumiansky, Columbia SC 1952; M. Stanley-Wrench 1965.
Everett, D. In her Essays on Middle English literature, Oxford 1955.
Bayley, J. Love and the code: Troilus and Criseyde. In his Characters of love, 1960.
Dunning, T. P. God and man in Troilus and Criseyde. In English and medieval studies presented to J. R. R. Tolkien, 1962.
Donaldson, E. T. The ending of Chaucer's Troilus. In Early English and Norse studies presented to H. Smith, 1963; rptd in his Speaking of Chaucer, 1970.
Gordon, I. L. The narrative function of irony in Chaucer's Troilus and Criseyde. In Medieval miscellany presented to E. Vinaver, Manchester 1965.
Salter, E. Troilus and Criseyde: a reconsideration. In Patterns of love and courtesy: essays in memory of C. S. Lewis, 1966.
Shepherd, G. T. In Chaucer and Chaucerians, ed D. S. Brewer, Edinburgh 1966.

Legend of Good Women

Ed H. Corson, Philadelphia 1864; ed F. J. Furnivall 3 vols 1871–90 (Chaucer Soc); ed W. W. Skeat, Oxford 1889; tr Skeat 1907.

Canterbury Tales

Ed W. Caxton [1478], [1484]; ed R. Pynson 1492; ed W. de Worde 1498; ed T. Morell 1737; ed T. Tyrwhitt 5 vols 1775–8, 2 vols Oxford 1798; ed T. Wright 3 vols 1847–51 (Percy Soc); ed F. J. Furnivall 36 pts 1868–79 (Chaucer Soc, 6-text edn), 1901–2 (Chaucer Soc, Cambridge ms); ed A. W. Pollard 2 vols 1886–7, 1894; ed J. S. P. Tatlock 1907 (Chaucer Soc); ed A. Burrell 1908, 1912 (EL); ed W. W. Skeat 1908 (Chaucer Soc, 8-text edn); 2 vols Manchester 1911 (Ellesmere ms facs); ed J. Koch, Heidelberg 1915; ed J. M. Manly, New York 1928; Boston 1930; ed W. van Wyck 2 vols 1930; ed J. M. Manly and E. Rickert 8 vols Chicago 1940; ed I. A. Kashkin and O. B. Runner, Moscow 1943; ed A. C. Cawley 1958 (EL); Major tales, ed M. Hoy and M. Stevens 1970; ed N. Coghill 1972.

Selections

Ed R. Morris, Oxford 1867 (General prologue, Knight's tale, Nun's priest's tale), 1889 (rev W. W. Skeat); ed S. H. Carpenter, Boston 1873 (General prologue, Knight's tale); ed Skeat, Oxford 1874 (Clerk's tale, Squire's, Prioress's, Summoner's, Monk's); ed Skeat, Oxford 1877 (Man of law's tale, Pardoner's, second nun's, Canon's yeoman's); ed A. W. Pollard 1886 (General prologue, Knight's tale, Man of law's, Clerk's, Prioress's); ed A. J. Wyatt, Cambridge 1895 (General prologue, Knight's tale); ed H. Corson, New York 1896; ed F. J. Mather, Boston 1898 (General prologue, Knight's tale, Nun's priest's); ed M. H. Liddell, New York 1901 (General prologue, Knight's tale, Nun's priest's); ed A. Ingraham 1902 (General prologue, Knight's tale, Nun's priest's); ed A. J. Wyatt

1903 (General prologue, Squire's tale); ed M. B. Smith, Cambridge 1908 (General prologue, Knight's tale); ed L. Winstanley, Cambridge 1908 (Clerk's tale, Squire's); ed A. M. van Dyke 1909 (General prologue, Knight's tale); ed L. Winstanley, Cambridge 1922 (Prioress's tale, Summoner's); ed G. Boas 1926 (General prologue Knight's tale, Clerk's, Monk's, Nun's priest's); ed A. J. Wyatt 1930; ed C. M. Drennan and Wyatt 1933 (Prioress's tale, Summoner's, Monk's); ed G. H. Cowling 1934 (General prologue, Prioress's tale, Nun's priest's, Pardoner's); ed G. H. Gerould 1935; ed anon, Edinburgh 1938 (General prologue, Squire's tale, Nun's priest's); ed E. J. Howard and G. D. Wilson, Oxford Ohio 1942; ed J. Delacourt, Paris 1946; ed R. D. French 1948; ed C. W. Dunn, New York 1952; ed N. H. Wallis 1957; ed M. J. Barber 1961; ed D. Cook, Garden City NY 1961; ed D. R. Howard and J. Dean, New York 1969; ed F. King and B. Steele, Melbourne 1969.

Modernizations and Translations

Tr F. E. Hill 1935; J. U. Nicholson, New York 1935; H. L. Hitchins 1946; V. F. Hopper, Brooklyn 1948; R. M. Lumiansky, New York 1948; N. Coghill 1952 (Penguin); D. Wright 1964.

Studies

Skeat, W. W. The evolution of the Canterbury tales. 1907 (Chaucer Soc).
Lawrence, W. W. Chaucer and the Canterbury tales. New York and Toronto 1950.
Donaldson, E. T. Chaucer the pilgrim. PMLA 69 1954; rptd in his Speaking of Chaucer, 1971 and in Chaucer criticism vol 1, ed R. Schoeck and J. Taylor, Notre Dame 1960.
—— The ordering of the Canterbury tales. In Medieval literature and folklore studies: essays in honor of F. L. Utley, New Brunswick NJ 1970.
Craik, T. W. The comic tales of Chaucer. 1963.

General Prologue

Ed W. McLeod 1871; ed B. ten Brink, Marburg 1871; ed J. Zupitza, Marburg 1871, Berlin 1882, 1920; ed A. Monfries, Edinburgh 1875; ed E. F. Willoughby 1881, Chicago 1907, London 1940; ed J. M. D. Meiklejohn 1882; ed W. W. Skeat, Oxford 1891; ed A. J. Wyatt 1900, 1927; ed A. W. Pollard 1903, 1920; ed C. T. Onions 1904; ed H. van Dyke, New York 1909; ed M. B. Smith 1929; ed A. Burrell, Portland Oregon 1937; ed R. F. Patterson 1940; ed F. W. Robinson 1940, 1954 (rev); ed R. T. Davies 1953; ed J. Winny, Cambridge 1965; ed P. Hodgson 1969; tr Skeat 1907.

Prose

Astrolabe

Ed A. E. Brae 1870; ed W. W. Skeat 1872 (Chaucer Soc), 1928 (EETS); ed R. T. Gunther, Oxford 1930.

Boethius

Ed W. Caxton 1478; ed R. Morris, Oxford 1868; ed F. J. Furnivall 1886 (Chaucer Soc).

Minor Poems

Ed W. Caxton [1477] (Anelida, Empty purse, Envoy to the King), rptd F. Jenkinson, Cambridge 1905 (facs); ed Caxton 1477 (Envoy to Scogan, Good counceyl, Gentilesse); ed J. Notary [1500?] (Mars and Venus); ed F. J. Furnivall 5 vols 1868–91 (Chaucer Soc; minor poems); ed J. Koch, Berlin 1883, Heidelberg 1925 (minor poems), E Studien 53 1919 (Against women); ed W. W. Skeat, Oxford 1883 (minor poems); Berkeley 1936 (Merciles beaute); tr Skeat 1909.

§2

Root, R. K. The poetry of Chaucer. Boston 1906, 1922 (rev), Gloucester Mass 1957.

Kittredge, G. L. Chaucer and his poetry. Cambridge Mass 1915.

Manly, J. M. Some new light on Chaucer: lectures delivered at the Lowell Institute. New York 1926.

Chesterton, G. K. Chaucer. 1932.

Clemen, W. Der junge Chaucer: Grundlagen und Entwicklung seiner Dichtung. Bochum-Langendreer 1938, Göttingen 1963 (enlarged as Chaucers frühe Dichtung); tr 1963.

Bennett, H. S. In his Chaucer and the fifteenth century, Oxford 1947 (OHEL).

Everett, D. Some reflections on Chaucer's art poetical. Proc Br Acad 36 1950; rptd in her Essays on ME literature, Oxford 1955; and in Chaucer's mind and art, ed A. C. Cawley 1969.

Tatlock, J. S. P. The mind and art of Chaucer. Syracuse NY 1950.

Malone, K. Chapters on Chaucer. Baltimore 1951.

Speirs, J. Chaucer the maker. 1951, 1960 (rev).

Bloomfield, M. W. Chaucer's sense of history. JEGP 51 1952; rptd in his Essays and explorations, Cambridge Mass 1970.

—— Authenticating realism and the realism of Chaucer. Thought 39 1964; rptd ibid.

Gerould, G. H. Chaucerian essays. Princeton 1952.

Ford, B. (ed). The age of Chaucer. 1954 (Pelican).

Coghill, N. Geoffrey Chaucer. 1956 (Br Council pamphlet).

—— The poet Chaucer. Oxford 1949 (Home Univ Lib), 1960 (corrected), 1967 (with addns).

Muscatine, C. Chaucer and the French tradition: a study in style and meaning. Berkeley 1957.

Wagenknecht, E. (ed). Chaucer: modern essays in criticism. New York 1959.

Schoeck, R. J. and J. Taylor (ed). Chaucer criticism. 2 vols Notre Dame 1960–1.

Robertson, D. W., jr. A preface to Chaucer: studies in medieval perspectives. Princeton 1962.

Hussey, M., A. C. Spearing and J. Winny. An introduction to Chaucer. Cambridge 1965.

Brewer, D. S. (ed). Chaucer and Chaucerians: critical studies in Middle English literature. Edinburgh 1966.

—— Chaucer and his world. 1978.

Burrow, J. A. Chaucer. 1969 (Penguin). An anthology of Chaucer criticism.

—— In his Ricardian poetry, 1971.

Donaldson, E. T. Speaking of Chaucer. 1970.

—— Chaucer and the elusion of clarity. E & S new ser 25 1972.

Hussey, S. S. Chaucer: an introduction. 1971.

Kean, P. M. Chaucer and the making of English poetry. 2 vols 1972.

Sources, Analogues and Literary Relations

Furnivall, F. J. et al. Originals and analogues of Chaucer's Canterbury tales. 1872–88 (Chaucer Soc).

—— and R. E. G. Kirk. Analogues of Chaucer's Canterbury pilgrimage. 1903 (Chaucer Soc).

Young, K. Chaucer's use of Boccaccio's Filocolo. MP 4 1907.

—— The origin and development of the story of Troilus and Criseyde. 1908 (Chaucer Soc), 1968.

Gordon, R. K. (ed and tr). The story of Troilus as told by Benoît de Sainte-Maure, Giovanni Boccaccio, Chaucer and Robert Henryson. 1934.

Bryan, W. F. and G. Dempster (ed). Sources and analogues of the Canterbury tales. Chicago 1941.

Language, Style and Metre

Marshall, I. and L. Porter. Rhyme index to the manu-

script texts of Chaucer's minor poems. 1887 (Chaucer Soc).

Kittredge, G. L. Observations on the language of Chaucer's Troilus. 1891–4 (Chaucer Soc).

Skeat, W. W. A rhyme-index to Chaucer's Troilus and Criseyde. 1892 (Chaucer Soc).

Tolkien, J. R. R. Chaucer as a philologist: the Reeve's tale. Trans Philological Soc 1934.

Whiting, B. J. Chaucer's use of proverbs. Cambridge Mass 1934.

Everett, D. Chaucer's good ear. RES 23 1947; rptd in her Essays in ME literature, Oxford 1955.

Moore, A. K. The eyen greye of Chaucer's prioress. PQ 26 1947.

Kökeritz, H. A guide to Chaucer's pronunciation. Stockholm and New Haven 1954.

Southworth, J. G. Verses of cadence: an introduction to the prosody of Chaucer and his followers. Oxford 1954.

—— The prosody of Chaucer and his followers: supplementary chapters to Verses of cadence. Oxford 1962.

Baum, P. F. Chaucer's verse. Durham NC 1961.

Kean, P. M. Chaucer and the making of English poetry. 2 vols 1972.

Elliott, R. W. V. Chaucer's English. 1974.

Manuscripts, Chronology and Text

Furnivall, F. J. Autotype specimens of the chief Chaucer manuscripts. 1877–86 (Chaucer Soc).

Koch, J. The chronology of Chaucer's writings. 1890 (Chaucer Soc).

—— A detailed comparison of the eight manuscripts of the Canterbury tales as printed by the Chaucer Society, second series 43. 1913, Amsterdam 1967.

Skeat, W. W. The Chaucer canon. Oxford 1900.

—— The eight-text edition of the Canterbury tales; with remarks upon the classification of the manuscripts and upon the Harleian manuscript 7334. 1909.

Tatlock, J. S. P. The development and chronology of Chaucer's works. 1907 (Chaucer Soc), Gloucester Mass 1964.

—— The Harleian ms 7334 and the revision of the Canterbury tales. 1909 (Chaucer Soc).

Kittredge, G. L. The date of Chaucer's Troilus and other matters. 1909 (Chaucer Soc), New York 1969.

Root, R. K. The manuscripts of Chaucer's Troilus, with collotype facsimiles of the various handwritings. 1914 (Chaucer Soc).

—— The textual tradition of Chaucer's Troilus. 1916 (Chaucer Soc).

Brusendorff, A. The Chaucer tradition. London and Copenhagen 1925; 1967.

Manly, J. M. and E. Rickert. The text of the Canterbury tales. 8 vols Chicago 1940.

Donaldson, E. T. Chaucer's Miller's tale A. 3483–6. MLN 69 1954; rptd in his Speaking of Chaucer, 1970.

—— Chaucer, Canterbury tales D. 117: a critical edition. Speculum 40 1965; rptd ibid.

Life and Background

Furnivall, F. J., W. D. Selby, E. A. Bond and R. E. G. Kirk. Life-records of Chaucer. 4 pts 1871–1900 (Chaucer Soc).

Crow, M. M. Materials for a new edition of the Chaucer life-records. SE 31 1952.

—— and C. C. Olson (ed). Chaucer life-records. Oxford and Austin 1966.

Brewer, D. S. Chaucer. 1953, 1960 (rev).

—— Chaucer in his time. 1963.

Howard, D. R. Chaucer the man. PMLA 80 1965; rptd in Chaucer's mind and art, ed A. C. Cawley 1969.

Kane, G. The autobiographical fallacy in Chaucer and Langland studies. 1965.

Bennett, J. A. W. Chaucer at Oxford and at Cambridge. Oxford 1974.

Manly, J. M. A knight there was. Trans Amer Philosophical Soc 38 1907; rptd in Chaucer: modern essays in criticism, ed E. Wagenknecht, New York 1959.
—— Chaucer and the rhetoricians. Proc Br Acad 12 1926; rptd in Chaucer criticism vol 1, ed R. Schoeck and J. Taylor, Notre Dame 1960.

Coulton, G. G. Chaucer and his England. 1908, 1963 (with bibliography by T. W. Craik).
Rickert, E., M. M. Crow and C. C. Olson (ed). Chaucer's world. 1948.
Loomis, R. S. A mirror of Chaucer's world. Princeton 1965.

3. THE FIFTEENTH CENTURY

I. THE ENGLISH CHAUCERIANS: LYDGATE, HOCCLEVE, HAWES AND OTHERS

References

Index   Brown, C. and R. H. Robbins, The index of ME verse, 1943;
Index Supplement   Robbins, R. H. and J. L. Cutler, Supplement to the index of ME verse, 1966.

JOHN LYDGATE
1370?–1449

A full discussion of the mss will be found in the Lydgate canon appended to (1) H. N. MacCracken's edn of Minor poems, 1911; (2) W. F. Schirmer, John Lydgate, 1961. Complete lists are in Index and Index Supplement. Much incidental information on mss containing Lydgate items is included in E. Seaton, Sir Richard Roos, 1961.

Selections

Minor poems. Ed J. O. Halliwell (-Phillipps) 1840 (Percy Soc). Includes London lackpenny; Moral of horse, goose and sheep; Bycorne and Chichevache; Churl and the bird; Testament etc.
Minor poems. Ed H. N. MacCracken 2 pts 1911–34 (EETS). Includes St Margaret; St Giles; Testament etc.
Poems. Ed J. Norton-Smith, Oxford 1966. Includes Letter to Gloucester; As a mydsomer rose; A complaynt of a loveres lyfe; Temple of glas etc.
Other poems are in T. Wright, Political poems and songs *vol 2, 1861; W. W. Skeat*, Complete works of Chaucer *vol 7, Oxford 1897; E. P. Hammond*, English verse between Chaucer and Surrey, *Durham NC 1927; R. H. Robbins*, Historical poems of the xivth and xvth centuries, *New York 1959; C. and K. Sisam*, The Oxford book of medieval verse, *Oxford 1970*.

§ I

Aesop. Ed P. Sauerstein, Anglia 9 1885 (from BM Harley ms 225); ed J. Zupitza, Archiv 85 1890 (from other mss); ed H. N. MacCracken, Minor poems, 1934.
[Assembly of the gods]. The interpretacion of the names of goddis and goddises. [1498] (de Worde), nd (de Worde), [1500?] (de Worde), nd (Pynson), [after 1529] (Redman), 1540; ed O. L. Triggs, Chicago 1895, 1896 (EETS) (from Trinity College Cambridge ms); ed F. Jenkinson, Cambridge 1906 (facs of 2nd edn). But *see* C. F. Bühler, The assembly of gods and Christine de Pisan, Eng Lang Notes 4 1967, who dates it after 1475.
A calendar. Ed C. Horstmann, Archiv 80 1888; ed H. N. MacCracken, Minor poems, 1911; ed A. Clark, The English register of Godstow nunnery, 1911 (EETS).
Chichevache and Bycorne. In Old plays vol 12, R. Dodsley 1780; ed J. O. Halliwell (-Phillipps), Minor poems, 1840; ed E. P. Hammond, English verse between Chaucer and Surrey, Durham NC 1927; ed H. N. MacCracken, Minor poems, 1934.

The chorle and the birde. [1477?] (Caxton), [nd] (Caxton), [1493] (Pynson), nd (de Worde), [1520] (de Worde), [1550?] (Mychel), [after 1561] (Copland), 1652 (in Ashmole's Theatrum chemicum britannicum); ed M. M. Sykes 1822 (Roxburghe Club); ed F. Jenkinson, Cambridge 1906 (facs of first edn), 1929; ed E. P. Hammond, English verse between Chaucer and Surrey, Durham NC 1927; ed H. N. MacCracken, Minor poems, 1934.
[The complaint of the black knight]. The complainte of a lovers lyfe. nd (de Worde), 1508 (as The maying or disport of Chaucer in The knightly tale of Golagrus and Gawane), 1532 (in Thynne's Works of Chaucer and subsequent edns until discovered to be Lydgate's by Shirley's testimony); ed K. Krausser, Anglia 19 1896; ed W. W. Skeat, Complete works of Chaucer vol 7, Oxford 1897; ed G. Stevenson 1918 (STS) (from 1508 edn); ed H. N. MacCracken, Minor poems, 1934; ed J. Norton-Smith, Poems, Oxford 1966.
[Danse macabre]. The daunce machabree. 1554 (in Fall of princes); rptd in W. Dugdale, History of St Paul's Cathedral, 1658, and in Hans Holbein's Alphabet of death, 1856; ed E. P. Hammond, English verse between Chaucer and Surrey, Durham NC 1927; ed F. Warren and B. White 1931 (EETS).
The departing of Thomas Chaucer. Ed E. P. Hammond, MP 1 1903; ed H. N. MacCracken, Minor poems, 1934; ed J. Norton-Smith, Oxford 1966.
Fabula duorum mercatorum. Ed J. Zupitza and G. Schleich, Quellen und Forschungen 83 1897; ed H. N. MacCracken, Minor poems, 1934.
The falle of princis. 1494 (Pynson), 1527 (Pynson), 1554 (Tottell), [1555?] (Wayland); ed H. Bergen, Washington 1923–4, 1924–7 (EETS). E. P. Hammond, English verse between Chaucer and Surrey, Durham NC 1927 contains extracts. *See also* Proverbs of Lydgate, below, which contains extracts.
Flour of curtesye. 1532 (in Thynne's Chaucer and later edns to Chalmers); ed W. W. Skeat, Complete works of Chaucer vol 7, 1897; ed H. N. MacCracken, Minor poems, 1934.
Of Gloucester's wedding, and Complaint for my lady of Gloucester. Ed E. P. Hammond, Anglia 27 1904; ed H. N. MacCracken, Minor poems, 1934; ed E. P. Hammond, English verse between Chaucer and Surrey, Durham NC 1927.
The governance of kings and princes. *See* Secrets of old philosophers, below.
The grateful dead. Ed A. Beatty, A new ploughman's tale, 1902 (Chaucer Soc).
Guy of Warwick. Ed J. Zupitza, Sitzungsberichte der Königlichen Akademie der Wissenschaften (philo-

logische-historische Klasse) 74 1873; ed F. N. Robinson, Harvard Stud 5 1896; ed H. N. MacCracken, Minor poems, 1934.

The hystorye, sege and dystruccyon of Troye. 1513 (Pynson), 1555 (Marshe), 1614 (modernized by T. Heywood as The life and death of Hector); ed H. Bergen 4 pts 1906–35 (EETS). See also under Romances of Troy, col 36, above.

The horse the ghoos and the sheep. 1477 (Caxton), [1477–8] (Caxton), [1500] (de Worde), [1500?] (de Worde), 1500 (de Worde); ed M. M. Sykes 1822 (Roxburghe Club); ed M. Degenhart 1900; ed F. J. Furnivall 1903 (in Political, religious and love poems) (EETS); ed F. Jenkinson, Cambridge 1906 (facs of 1500 edn); ed H. N. MacCracken, Minor poems, 1934; ed C. F. Bühler, MLN 55 1940 (additional stanzas in Huntington ms HM 144).

King Henry's triumphal entry in London. Ed H. N. MacCracken, Archiv 126 1911; ed H. N. MacCracken, Minor poems, 1934.

On the kings of England. Ed J. Gairdner, The historical collections of a citizen of London in the fifteenth century, 1876 (Camden Soc); ed R. H. Robbins, Historical poems, New York 1959.

The lyf of our lady. [1484] (2 issues) (Caxton), 1531 (Redman); ed C. E. Tame, Early English religious literature 1871–9; ed J. A. Lauritis, R. A. Klinefelter and V. F. Gallagher, Duquesne Stud: Philological ser 2 1961.

The lyfe of Seint Albon and the lyfe of Saint Amphabel. St Albans 1534; ed C. Horstmann, Festschrift der Realschule zu Berlin, Berlin 1882.

Merita missae. Ed T. F. Simmons, Lay folks mass book, 1879 (EETS). Also contains Venus mass and extracts from Virtutes missarum, not to be confused with Virtue of the mass.

Mummings. Ed E. P. Hammond, Mumming at Hertford, Anglia 22 1900; ed R. Brotanek, Die englischen Maskenspiele, Vienna 1902; ed H. N. MacCracken, Minor poems, 1934; ed J. Norton-Smith, Mumming at Bishopswood, Poems, Oxford 1966.

New year's valentine. Ed E. P. Hammond, Anglia 32 1909; ed H. N. MacCracken, Minor poems, 1934.

Two nightingale poems. Ed O. Glauning 1900 (EETS).

The pilgrimage of the life of man. Ed F. J. Furnivall 1899–1904 (EETS); ed F. J. Furnivall and K. B. Locock 1905 (Roxburghe Club). On Deguileville, see edn by J. J. Sturzinger 1893 (Roxburghe Club).

The puerbes [proverbs] of Lydgate. [1515?] (de Worde), [1520?] (de Worde), 1526 (Pynson). Extracts from Fall of princes; Loke in thy merour; Consulo quisquis eris; and Chaucer's Fortune and Truth.

Queen Margaret's entry into London. Ed C. Brown, MLR 7 1912; ed R. Withington, MP 13 1915 (additional stanzas in BM ms Harley 542).

Reason and sensuality. Ed E. Sieper 1901–3 (EETS).

St Edmund and Fremund. Ed C. Horstmann, Altenglische Legenden, Heilbronn 1881; ed F. Harvey, Corolla sancti Eadmundi, 1907.

St Giles. Ed C. Horstmann, Altenglische Legenden, Heilbronn 1881; ed H. N. MacCracken, Minor poems, 1911.

[Secrets of old philosophers]. The governaunce of kynges and prynces. 1511 (Pynson); ed R. Steele 1894 (EETS) (from Sloane ms). T. Prosiegel, The book of the governaunce of kynges and prynces, 1903, corrects this edn and collates with other mss.

The serpent of division. nd (fragment) (Treverys), 1559 (Rogers), 1590 (with Gorboduc); ed H. N. MacCracken, New Haven 1911.

[Siege of Thebes]. The storye of Thebes. [1495?] (de Worde), [1500?] (de Worde), 1561 (in Stow's Chaucer and later edns to Chalmers); pt 1 ed A. Erdmann 1911 (Chaucer Soc and EETS); pt 2 ed Erdmann and E.

Ekwall 1930 (EETS); Prologue, ed E. P. Hammond, Anglia 36 1912.

Stans puer ad mensam. nd (Caxton), [1545?] (appended to Hugh Rhodes, Book of nurture); ed W. C. Hazlitt, Remains of the early popular poetry of England vol 3, 1866; ed F. J. Furnivall, The Babees book, 1868 (EETS); ed H. N. MacCracken, Minor poems, 1934.

Two tapestry poems: (a) The life of St George; (b) The falls of seven princes. Ed E. P. Hammond, E Studien 43 1910.

The temple of glass. [1477–8] (Caxton), nd (de Worde), [1500] (de Worde), nd (de Worde), [1505?] (Pynson), [1530?] (Berthelet); ed J. Schick 1891 (EETS); ed F. Jenkinson, Cambridge 1905 (facs of first edn); ed J. Norton-Smith, Poems, Oxford 1966.

The testament of J. Lydgate. [1515?] (Pynson); rptd in Halliwell's and MacCracken's edns of Minor poems.

Troy book. See History of Troy, above.

The vertue of the masse. nd (de Worde); rptd in Fugitive tracts vol 3, 1875; ed H. N. MacCracken, Minor poems, 1911.

Works attributed to Lydgate

Cartae versificatae. In Memorials of St Edmund's abbey vol 3, ed T. Arnold 1896. Attributed on internal evidence by Arnold, MacCracken and Index.

The child of Bristow. Ed C. Hopper, Camden Miscellany vol 4, 1859; ed T. Burke, The charm of the West Country, 1913. Attributed by Ritson.

The complaint of Mary Magdalen. 1526 (Pynson), 1561 (in Stow's Chaucer); ed C. E. Tame [1871] (as The lamentation of St Mary Magdalene). Attributed in Harleian catalogue.

[The Court of Sapience]. De curia sapiencie. [1490] (Caxton), 1510 (de Worde); ed R. Spindler, Leipzig 1927; [selections] ed E. P. Hammond, English verse between Chaucer and Surrey, Durham NC 1927.

The lamentation of our lady. [before 1519] (de Worde); ed C. E. Tame [1871]. Attributed by Ritson and Tanner.

London lickpenny. Ed E. P. Hammond, Anglia 20 1898; ed F. Holthausen, Anglia 43 1919. Attributed by Stow, Tanner and Ritson.

The medicine of the stomach. In The governayle of helthe, [c. 1491] (Caxton), nd (de Worde), [c. 1491] (Caxton); ed W. Blades 1858. Attributed in BM Harley ms 116, which contains nothing but Lydgate's work.

[The pilgrimage of the soul]. The boke of the pylgremage of the sowle. 1483 (Caxton); [selections] ed K. I. Cust 1859. For facs of several pages of 1483 edn see Apollo 14 1931.

The seven virtues. [1500?].

A treatise of a gallant. [1516?] (de Worde). In W. C. Hazlitt, Remains of the early popular poetry of England vol 3, 1866 and F. H. Furnivall, Academy 29 Aug 1896. Attributed by Bishop John Alcock.

A treatise of the smith. nd (Copland). In W. C. Hazlitt, Remains of the early popular poetry of England vol 3, 1866. Attributed by Bale, Ritson.

§2

Schirmer, W. F. Lydgate: ein Kulturbild aus dem 15 Jahrhundert. Tübingen 1952; tr and rev as Lydgate: a study in the culture of the 15th century, 1961.

Pearsall, D. A. The English Chaucerians. In Chaucer and Chaucerians, ed D. S. Brewer, Edinburgh 1966.

THOMAS HOCCLEVE
1368?–1426?

For complete lists see Index *and* Index Supplement; *for addns etc, M. C. Seymour, RES new ser 20 1969. Since Index the Corpus Christi ms 237 has been refoliated.*

Collections

Poems. Ed G. Mason 1796.
Works. Vol 1: The minor poems, ed F. J. Furnivall 1892; vol 2: The minor poems in the Ashburnham ms [now Huntington HM 144], ed I. Gollancz 1925; vol 3: The regiment of princes and 14 minor poems, ed F. J. Furnivall 1897 (EETS).

§1

Address to Sir John Oldcastle. Ed L. T. Smith, Anglia 5 1882; ed F. J. Furnivall, Minor poems vol 1, 1892 (EETS).
Balade au tres honourable compaignie du garter. 1542 (in Thynne's Chaucer); ed W. W. Skeat, Complete works of Chaucer vol 7, Oxford 1897.
Balade au tres noble Henry le quint. 1542 (in Thynne's Chaucer); ed W. W. Skeat, Complete works of Chaucer vol 7, Oxford 1897.
Balade to my Lord Chancellor. Ed R. H. Robbins, Secular lyrics of the 14th and 15th centuries, Oxford 1952.
The letter of Cupid. 1532, [1545?] (in Thynne's Chaucer), 1561 (in Stow's Chaucer); ed E. Arber, An English garner vol 4, 1882; ed W. W. Skeat, Complete works of Chaucer vol 7, Oxford 1897. For Christian de Pisan herself see Roy, Oeuvres poétiques vol 2, Paris 1888–96.
The mother of God. In edns of Chaucer from 1532; ed J. Leyden, The complaynt of Scotland, Edinburgh 1801; re-ed 1872 (EETS); ed F. J. Furnivall, Minor poems vol 1, 1892 (EETS).
De regimine principium. Ed T. Wright 1869 (Roxburghe Club).
Tale of Jonathas. In W. Browne, The shepherds pipe, 1614. Modernized and abridged.
Of the virgin and her sleeveless garment. Ed A. Beatty, A new ploughman's tale, 1902 (Chaucer Soc); ed I. Gollancz, Minor poems vol 2, 1925 (EETS); ed B. Boyd, ME miracles of the Virgin, San Marino 1964.

§2

Pearsall, D. A. The English Chaucerians. In Chaucer and Chaucerians, ed D. S. Brewer, Edinburgh 1966.
Mitchell, J. Hoccleve: a study in early 15th-century English poetic. Urbana 1968.

STEPHEN HAWES
fl. 1503–11

Comfort of lovers. [1512?] (de Worde), [1515?].
The convercyon of swerers. 1509 (de Worde), [1510? de Worde?], [c. 1530] (Butler), 1551 (Copland); ed D. Laing 1865 (Abbotsford Club).

The example of vertu. [1504?] (de Worde), [1510?] (de Worde), [1520?] (de Worde), 1530.
A joyfull medytacyon to all Englande of the coronacyon of Kynge Henry the Eyght. [1509] (de Worde); ed D. Laing 1865 (Abbotsford Club); ed E. Flügel, Neuenglisches Lesebuch, Halle 1895 (Prologue only).
The pastyme of pleasure (otherwise titled the Historie of graunde amoure and la bel pucel). [1509] (de Worde), 1517 (de Worde), 1554 (adds 3 verses) (Wayland), 1555 (Tottell), 1555 (Waley); ed T. Wright 1845 (Percy Soc) (from Tottell's 1555 edn); ed W. E. Mead 1928 (EETS).
Minor poems. Ed F. W. Gluck and A. B. Morgan, Oxford 1974 (EETS).

PSEUDO-CHAUCERIAN PIECES

The following are the most important 15th-century poems, other than works by Lydgate and Hoccleve, that were included in the early edns of Chaucer. They have been rptd in Skeat's Complete works of Chaucer vol 7, Oxford 1897, and summaries of criticism are in E. P. Hammond, Chaucer: a bibliographical manual, New York 1908—referred to as Skeat and Hammond respectively. More recent criticism is contained in E. P. Hammond, English verse between Chaucer and Surrey, Durham NC 1927; C. S. Lewis, The allegory of love, Oxford 1936; E. Seaton, Sir Richard Roos, 1961; D. A. Pearsall, The English Chaucerians, in Chaucer and Chaucerians, ed D. S. Brewer, Edinburgh 1966.

The assembly of ladies. 1532 (in Thynne's Chaucer); Skeat pp. 380–404; ed D. A. Pearsall, Edinburgh 1962. Hammond pp. 408–9.
[Roos, Sir Richard]. La belle dame sans mercy. [1526?] (in Pynson's Boke of fame, Chaucer); extracts ed R. Southey in Select works of the British poets from Chaucer to Jonson, 1831; Skeat pp. 299–326. Hammond pp. 432–3. For biography, criticism and anagrammatical evidence for new canon, see E. Seaton, Sir Richard Roos, 1961.
The Court of Love. 1561 (in Stow's Chaucer); Skeat pp. 409–47. Hammond pp. 418–19.
The floure and the leaf. 1598 (in Speght's Chaucer); ed J. Dryden, Fables ancient and modern, 1700 etc (modernized); Skeat; ed D. A. Pearsall, Edinburgh 1962. Hammond pp. 423–4.
[Scogan, Henry]. A moral ballade. [1477?] (in Caxton, Temple of glas), [1478?] (in Caxton, Temple of glas), 1532 (in Thynne's Chaucer); Skeat pp. 237–44. Hammond p. 455.
The tale of Beryn. 1561 (in Stow's Chaucer), 1721 (in Urry's Chaucer); ed F. J. Furnivall and W. G. Stone 1876 (Chaucer Soc) (EETS). Hammond p. 412.

II. MIDDLE SCOTS POETS

JAMES I, HENRYSON, DUNBAR, GAVIN DOUGLAS AND OTHERS

(1) ANTHOLOGIES

Manuscript Collections

Arundel ms 285 and Harleian ms 6919 [BM]. Ed J. A. W. Bennett, Devotional pieces in verse and prose from ms Arundel 285 and ms Harleian 6919, 1955 (STS).
Asloan ms [written c. 1515 by John Asloan, formerly in possession of the Boswell family at Auchinlech; now in Nat Lib of Scotland]. Ed W. A. Craigie 2 vols 1923–5 (STS).

Bannatyne ms [said to be compiled 1568, now in Nat Lib of Scotland]. Ed J. B. Murdoch 6 vols 1873–1901 (Hunterian Club); ed W. T. Ritchie 4 vols 1928–34 (STS).
Gray ms [written c. 1500 by James Gray: the Scots pieces are interpolated; now in Nat Lib of Scotland]. Ed G. Stevenson, Pieces from the Makculloch and the Gray mss together with the Chepman and Myllar prints, 1918 (STS).

Maitland folio ms [compiled c. 1580 by Sir Richard Maitland of Lethington, now in Pepys Lib, Magdalene College Cambridge]. Ed W. A. Craigie 2 vols 1919–27 (STS).

Maitland quarto ms [written by Sir Richard's daughter in 1586; also in Pepys Lib]. Ed W. A. Craigie 1920 (STS).

Makculloch ms [a collection of lecture notes in Latin, the Scots pieces being written on blank pages; written after 1477; now in Edinburgh Univ Lib]. Ed G. Stevenson 1918 (STS).

Bibliographies

Geddie, W. A bibliography of Middle Scots poets. 1912 (STS).

Printed Collections

Chepman and Myllar prints. Edinburgh 1508 (unique copy in Nat Lib of Scotland); ed D. Laing, Edinburgh 1827 (facs); ed G. Stevenson 1918 (STS); ed W. Beattie 1950 (facs) (Edinburgh Bibl Soc).

Ramsay, Allan. The ever green: being a collection of Scots poems wrote by the ingenious before 1600. 2 vols Edinburgh 1724, 1761. Mainly from Bannatyne ms.

Dalrymple, D., Lord Hailes. Ancient Scottish poems, published from the ms of George Bannatyne. Edinburgh 1770, [1815].

Pinkerton, J. Ancient Scotish poems never before in print but now published from the ms collections of Sir Richard Maitland. 2 vols 1786.

—— Scotish poems reprinted from scarce editions. 3 vols 1792.

Dalyell, J. G. Scottish poems of the sixteenth century. Edinburgh 1801.

Sibbald, J. Chronicle of Scottish poetry. 4 vols Edinburgh 1802.

Laing, D. Select remains of the ancient popular and romance poetry of Scotland. Edinburgh 1822; ed J. Small, Edinburgh 1885.

—— Early Scottish metrical tales. Edinburgh 1826, 1889.

—— Early popular poetry of Scotland and the northern border, re-arranged and revised by W. C. Hazlitt. 2 vols 1895.

Amours, F. J. Scottish alliterative poems in riming stanzas. 1892–7 (STS).

Mackie, R. L. A book of Scottish verse. 1934; rev M. Lindsay 1967.

Gray, M. M. Scottish poetry from Barbour to James VI. 1935.

Girvan, R. Ratis raving and other early Scots poems on morals. 1939 (STS).

MacQueen, J. and T. Scott. The Oxford book of Scottish verse. Oxford 1966.

MacQueen, J. Ballatis of lufe. Edinburgh 1970.

Scott, T. Late medieval Scots poetry. 1967.

—— The Penguin book of Scottish verse. 1970.

Kinghorn, A. M. The Middle Scots poets. 1970.

(2) GENERAL STUDIES

Gregory Smith, G. The transition period. Edinburgh 1900.

—— Specimens of Middle Scots. Edinburgh 1902.

—— Scottish literature: character and influence. 1919.

Millar, J. H. A literary history of Scotland. 1903.

Lewis, C. S. In his Allegory of love, Oxford 1936.

—— In his English literature in the sixteenth century, Oxford 1954 (OHEL).

Speirs, J. The Scots literary tradition. 1940, 1962 (rev).

Craigie, W. A. The Scottish alliterative poems. Proc Br Acad 28 1942.

Kinsley, J. (ed). Scottish poetry: a critical survey. 1955.

Wittig, K. The Scottish tradition in literature. Edinburgh 1958.

Fox, D. The Scottish Chaucerians. In Chaucer and Chaucerians, ed D. S. Brewer, Edinburgh 1966.

Aitken, A. J., A. McIntosh and H. Palsson (ed). Edinburgh studies in English and Scots. 1971.

JAMES I, King of Scotland
1394–1437

Collections

Poetical remains of James the First, King of Scotland. [Ed W. Tytler], Edinburgh 1783.

The works of James I, King of Scotland. Perth 1786 (ptd R. Morison).

Poetical remains of King James I of Scotland. Ed C. Rogers, Edinburgh 1873.

§ I

Kingis quair

There is one late fifteenth-century ms, Bodley Arch. Selden B 24.

Chronicle of Scottish poetry vol 1. Ed J. Sibbald, Edinburgh 1802.

The King's quair. Ed E. Thomson, Ayr 1815, 1824, Glasgow 1877.

The Kingis quair, together with a ballad of good counsel. Ed W. W. Skeat 1884 (STS), 1911 (rev).

The Kingis quair. Ed J. Norton-Smith, Oxford 1971.

Other Poems Attributed to James I

1. *For W. W. Skeat's ascription to James I of fragment B of the* Romaunt of the rose *(ll. 1706–5810), see his introd to*

Oxford Chaucer, pp. 3–6; The Chaucer canon, Oxford 1900, pp. 75–89

2. Ballad of good counsel (Sen throw vertew incressis dignitie). Attributed to James I in Ane compendious buik of godly and spirituall songis, 1578, 1600, 1621; ed D. Laing, Edinburgh 1868; ed A. F. Mitchell 1897 (STS). 2 other versions are extant in the Bannatyne ms and ms Cambridge Univ Lib Kk.1.5, ed R. Girvan, Ratis raving and other early Scots poems on morals 1939 (STS).

3. Peblis to the play, Christis kirk on the green. Early texts of these poems are in Maitland folio. Another text of Christis kirk occurs in the Bannatyne ms, where it is attributed to James I. Peblis to the play was first ptd in Select Scotish ballads, ed J. Pinkerton 1783.

A merrie ballad, called Christ's kirk on the green. 1643. Single folio sheet.

A ballad of a country wedding. 1660. Single folio sheet.

Polemo-middinia [by William Drummond of Hawthornden?]; accedit cantilena rustica vulgo inscripta Christs kirk on the green. Ed E.G[ibson], Oxford 1691.

Christ's kirk on the green, in three cantos [cantos 2–3 by A. Ramsay]. Edinburgh 1718.

Christ's kirk on the green: poems in the Scottish dialect. 1748, [1750], Glasgow 1768.

Two ancient Scottish poems: the gaberlunzie man and Christ's kirk on the green, with notes by J. Callander. Edinburgh 1782, Glasgow 1794, Stirling [1820?], Falkirk [1821].

Chryste-kirk on the green, supposed to be written by King James I: attempted in Latin heroic verse [with text; by John Skinner]. In Carminum rariorum macaronicorum delectus, Edinburgh 1801, 1813.

§2

Memoirs relating to the restoration of King James I. 1716; Scotia redivivia vol 1, [1826]; Tracts illustrative of the antiquities of Scotland vol 1, 1836.
Life and death of King James the First of Scotland. [Ed J. Stevenson] 1837 (Maitland Club).
Brown, J. T. T. The authorship of the Kingis quair. Glasgow 1896.
Rait, R. S. The Kingis quair and the new criticism. Aberdeen 1898.
Balfour-Melville, E. W. M. James I, King of Scots.1936.
Craigie, W. A. The language of the Kingis quair. E & S 25 1939.
MacQueen, J. Tradition and the interpretation of the Kingis quair. RES new ser 12 1961.

ROBERT HENRYSON
1425?–1506?

Henryson's poems survive in a number of mss and prints, most later than his lifetime. The minor poems attributed to him survive almost entirely in the ms collections (Bannatyne, Maitland folio, Makculloch and Gray). 2 short poems and an incomplete version of his Orpheus and Eurydice are found in the Chepman and Myllar prints. The most important ms collection of the fables is that in the Bannatyne ms; other mss containing one or more of the fables are Harley ms 3865 (BM), the Makculloch ms and the Asloan ms. No authoritative complete ms of the Testament of Cresseid survives; it is listed in the Asloan ms table of contents, but the leaves on which it was written have been lost. 2 late English mss (Kinaston in Bodley, and that in St John's College Cambridge) are thought to derive from the version of the poem ptd in Speght's edn of Chaucer.

Collections

Poems and fables. Ed D. Laing, Edinburgh 1865.
Poems. Ed G. Gregory Smith 3 vols 1906–14 (STS).
Poems and fables. Ed H. Harvey Wood, Edinburgh 1933, 1958 (rev).
Selections from the poems. Ed D. Murison, Edinburgh 1952.
Poems. Ed C. Elliott, Oxford 1963.

§1

Moral Fables

The morall fabillis of Esope the Phrygian compylit in eloquent and ornate Scottis meter. Edinburgh 1570 (unique copy in BM), Amsterdam 1970 (facs).
The morall fabillis of Esope. Edinburgh 1571. Unique copy in Nat Lib of Scotland.
The fabulous tales of Esope now lately englished. 1577. Unique copy in Nat Lib of Scotland.
The morall fables of Esope the Phrygian. Edinburgh 1621 (unique copy in Nat Lib of Scotland); rptd for Maitland Club, 1832, with unsigned preface by D. Irving.
Henrisones Fabeln. Ed A. R. Diebler, Anglia 9 1886. Edn of Harley ms.

Testament of Cresseid

In Workes of Geoffrey Chaucer, ed W. Thynne 1532.
The testament of Cresseid. Edinburgh 1593 (unique copy in BM); rptd with Robene and Makyne, ed G. Chalmers 1824 (Bannatyne Club); Amsterdam 1969 (facs).

The testament of Cresseid printed in the year 1663. Unique copy in Trinity College Cambridge. Rptd in D. Fox, The 1663 Anderson edition of Henryson's Testament of Cresseid, Stud in Scottish Lit 8 1971.
In Chaucerian and other pieces. Ed W. W. Skeat, Oxford 1897.
The testament of Cresseid. Ed B. Dickins 1925, 1931, 1943 (rev).
The testament of Cresseid. Ed A. Attwater, Cambridge 1926.
The story of Troilus. Ed R. K. Gordon 1934.
A modernization of Henryson's testament of Cresseid, by M. W. Stearns. Bloomington 1945.
The testament of Cresseid. Tr F. Cogswell, Toronto 1957.
The testament of Cresseid. Ed D. Fox, Edinburgh 1968.

§2

Tillyard, E. M. W. In his Five poems 1470–1870, 1948, 1955 (as Poetry and its background).
Muir, E. In his Essays on literature and society, 1949, 1965 (rev).
Stearns, M. W. Robert Henryson. New York 1949.
Cruttwell, P. Two Scots poets: Dunbar and Henryson. In The age of Chaucer, ed B. Ford 1954 (Pelican).
Spearing, A. C. Conciseness and the Testament of Cresseid. In his Criticism and medieval poetry, 1964.
Wood, H. H. Two Scots Chaucerians [Henryson and Dunbar]. 1967.
MacQueen, J. Henryson: a study of the major narrative poems. Oxford 1967.

WILLIAM DUNBAR
1460?–1513?

Apart from the 6 poems in the Chepman and Myllar prints, 1508, there are no early ptd texts of Dunbar's poems. The two most important sources are the Bannatyne ms (with 60 poems attributed to Dunbar) and the Maitland folio (with 61 poems attributed to Dunbar). Other mss which contain poems by or attributed to Dunbar are the Asloan ms, the Makculloch ms, Arundel ms 285 and the Aberdeen Register of Sasines. During the eighteenth century selections from his poems were ptd in the collections of Ramsay, Dalrymple, Pinkerton and Sibbald.

Collections

Select poems of Will Dunbar: part I. Perth 1788 (ptd R. Morison).
Poems. Ed D. Laing 2 vols Edinburgh 1834; Supplementary vol, 1865.
The life and poems of Dunbar. Ed J. Paterson, Edinburgh 1860.
Poems. Ed J. Small 3 vols 1884–93 (STS).
Poems. Ed W. M. Mackenzie, Edinburgh 1932, 1960 (rev).
Selections from the poems. Ed 'Hugh MacDiarmid' (C. M. Grieve), Edinburgh 1952.
Selected poems. Ed 'Hugh MacDiarmid' (C. M. Grieve), Glasgow 1955.
Poems. Ed J. Kinsley, Oxford 1958.

§1

Chepman and Myllar prints. Edinburgh 1508.
The thistle and the rose: a poem in honour of Margaret, Queen to James IV King of Scots, with a poem addrest to James V by J. Bellentyne. Glasgow 1750.
Two married women and the widow, translated into English verse. Edinburgh 1840.

§2

Mackay, A. J. G. William Dunbar 1460–1520. Edinburgh 1889.

Smeaton, W. H. O. William Dunbar. Edinburgh 1898.

Taylor, R. A. Dunbar: the poet and his period. 1932.

Baxter, J. W. Dunbar: a biographical study. Edinburgh 1952.

Cruttwell, P. Two Scots poets: Dunbar and Henryson. In The age of Chaucer, ed B. Ford 1954 (Pelican).

Scott, T. Dunbar: a critical exposition of the poems. Edinburgh 1966.

Wood, H. H. Two Scots Chaucerians [Henryson and Dunbar]. 1967.

Hope, A. D. A midsummer eve's dream: variations on a theme by Dunbar. Canberra 1970. On The tua mariit wemen and the wedo.

GAVIN DOUGLAS
1474?–1522

No ms survives of Douglas's Palice of honour (c. 1501). *For the fragments of an early edn (c. 1530–40) see D. Laing, Adversaria 1867 (Bannatyne Club), p. 19; W. Beattie, Fragments of the Palyce of honour, Edinburgh Bibl Soc Trans 3 1951 (pt 1). Douglas's trn of the Aeneid, 1513, is extant in 5 mss, of which the earliest and most authoritative is that in Trinity College Cambridge; 2 other mss are in Edinburgh Univ Library, one in Lambeth Palace Library, and another the property of the Marquess of Bath. 2 poems* King Hart *and* Conscience *have been attributed to Douglas; they are extant only in the Maitland folio ms. King Hart was first ptd by Pinkerton, Ancient Scotish poems vol 1, 1786.*

Collections

Select works of Gawin Douglas: containing memoirs of the author, the Palace of honour, prologues to the Aeneid and a glossary. Perth 1787 (ptd by R. Morison).

Poetical works of Gavin Douglas, Bishop of Dunkeld. Ed J. Small 4 vols Edinburgh 1874.

A selection from his poetry. Ed S. Goodsir Smith, Edinburgh 1959.

Selections. Ed D. F. C. Coldwell, Oxford 1964.

Shorter poems. Ed P. J. Bawcutt 1967 (STS).

Palice of Honour

The palis of honoure compyled by Gawyne Dowglas. [1553?], Amsterdam 1969 (facs).

Ane treatise callit the palice of honour. Edinburgh 1579 (2 copies extant, one in Edinburgh Univ Lib, the other in the Nat Lib of Scotland); ed J. G. Kinnear 1827 (facs) (Bannatyne Club).

Aeneid

The xiii bukes of Eneados of the famose poete Virgill translatet into Scottish metir. 1553.

Virgil's Aeneis translated into Scottish verse. Edinburgh 1710.

The Aeneid of Virgil translated into Scottish verse. [Ed G. Dundas] 2 vols 1839 (Bannatyne Club).

Virgil's Aeneid translated into Scottish verse by Gavin Douglas. Ed D. F. C. Coldwell 4 vols 1957–64 (STS).

The prologues have often been anthologized.

III. ENGLISH PROSE OF THE FIFTEENTH CENTURY

CAPGRAVE, PECOCK, FORTESCUE, CAXTON, MALORY, BERNERS

JOHN CAPGRAVE OSA
1393–1464

Nova legenda Angliae. 1516 (de Worde); tr 1516 (abridged, Pynson); ed C. Horstmann 2 vols Oxford 1901. Capgrave is at best an editor of this collection of saints' lives, originally compiled by John of Tynemouth.

The chronicle of England. Ed F. C. Hingeston 1858 (Rolls ser).

Liber de illustribus Henricis. Tr F. C. Hingeston 1858 (Rolls ser).

The life of St Katharine of Alexandria. Ed C. Horstmann (forewords by F. J. Furnivall) 1893 (EETS).

The life of St Augustine; The life of St Gilbert of Sempringham; A treatise of the orders under the rule of St Augustine. Ed J. J. Munro 1910 (EETS).

Ye solace of pilgrimes. Ed C. A. Mills (introductory note by H. M. Bannister) 1911 (Br & Amer Soc of Rome).

REGINALD PECOCK
1390/5–c. 1460

§1

[The book of faith]. Ed H. Wharton 1688 (incomplete); ed J. L. Morison, Glasgow 1909.

The repressor of over much blaming of the clergy. Ed C. Babington 2 vols 1860 (Rolls ser).

The reule of Crysten religioun. Ed W. C. Greet 1927 (EETS).

The donet. Ed E. V. Hitchcock 1921 (EETS).

The folower to the donet. Ed E. V. Hitchcock 1924 (EETS).

§2

Green, V. H. H. Bishop Reginald Pecock. Cambridge 1945.

Jacob, E. F. Pecock Bishop of Chichester. Proc Br Acad 37 1951; rptd in his Essays in late medieval history, Manchester 1968.

SIR JOHN FORTESCUE
c. 1394–c. 1476

Collections

The works of Sir John F[ortescue]. Ed Thomas [Fortescue] Lord Clermont 2 vols 1869 (priv ptd). Contains all Latin and English works attributed to Fortescue, though the attribution of some is now questioned.

§1

[De laudibus legum Angliæ]. Prenobilis militis cognomento Forescu de politica administratione et legibus civilibus florentissimi regni Angliæ commentarius. [1546]; 1567 (Latin, and tr R. Mulcaster as A learned commendation of the politique lawes of Englande); 1573, 1599; ed and tr J. Selden 1616; ed and tr F. Gregor 1737, 1741, 1775, Cincinnati 1874, London 1917 (trn only); ed and tr S. B. Chrimes, Cambridge 1942, 1949. Chrimes's edn has a full introd.

Sir John Fortescue on the governance of England: the difference between an absolute and limited monarchy. Ed J. Fortescue-Aland 1714; ed C. Plummer, Oxford 1885, 1926; rptd in Complaint and reform in England 1436–1714, ed W. H. Dunham and S. Pargellis, New York 1938. Plummer's edn contains a biography, historical study and fragments of works attributed to Fortescue.

§2

Waterhous, E. Fortescutus illustratus: or a commentary on that nervous treatise De laudibus legum Angliæ. 1663.
Jacob, E. F. Fortescue and the law of nature. Bull John Rylands Lib 18 1934; rptd in his Essays in the conciliar epoch, Manchester 1953.
—— In his Fifteenth century 1399–1485, Oxford 1961.
Chrimes, S. B. English constitutional ideas in the fifteenth century. Cambridge 1936.
Hinton, R. W. K. English constitutional theories from Fortescue to Sir John Eliot. EHR 75 1960.

WILLIAM CAXTON
1415/24–1490/1

Bibliographies

de Ricci, S. A census of Caxtons. 1909 (Bibl Soc).
Wilson, R. H. In A manual of the writings in Middle English 1050–1500 vol 3, ed A. E. Hartung, New Haven 1972.

Collections

Prologues and epilogues. Ed W. J. B. Crotch 1928 (EETS).
Selections from Caxton. Ed N. F. Blake, Oxford 1973.

§1

Texts are arranged chronologically under the author or translator, where known. For works by English authors other than Caxton, only Caxton's edns or direct reprints are listed; further details of these works will be found elsewhere in the bibliography. Many texts not tr Caxton have addns by him.

Caxton, W. The recuyell of the historyes of Troye. [Bruges 1473/4], 1502 (de Worde), [1503] (de Worde), 1553 (Copland), 1596 (Creede), 1607, 1617, 1636, 1663, 1670, [1676], 1680, 1684, 1702, 1708, 1738, 1802, [1810], 2 vols 1892 (priv ptd); ed H. O. Sommer 2 vols 1894.
Caxton, W. The game and play of the chess. [Bruges 1475/6], [1483]; ed V. Figgins 1855 (facs of 1483 edn), 1860; [1857] (phonetic spelling); 1860; ed W. E. A. Axon 1883.
d'Ailly, P. Septenuaire de pseaulmes de penitence. [Bruges 1475/6].
Lefèvre, R. Le recueil de histoires de Troyes. [Bruges 1475/6].
Lefèvre, R. Les fais et proesses du Jason. [Bruges 1475/6].
Mielot, J. Les quatre choses derrenieres. [Bruges 1475/6].
Russell, J. Propositio clarissimi oratoris magistri Johannis Russell. [Bruges or Westminster 1476]; ed H. Guppy, Manchester 1909 (facs).
Caxton, W. The advertisement. [1477].
Burgh, B. Parvus Cato; Magnus Cato. [1477], [1477], 1481; ed F. Jenkinson, Cambridge 1906 (facs).
Chaucer, G. Anelida and the false Arcite; The complaint of Chaucer to his purse: Th'envoy of Chaucer. [1477];

ed F. J. Furnivall 1868–80 (Chaucer Soc); ed F. Jenkinson, Cambridge 1905 (facs).
Chaucer, G. The parliament of fowls (ptd as Temple of brass); A treatise which John Scogan sent; The good counsel of Chaucer; Balade of a village; Th'envoy of Chaucer. [1477]; ed F. J. Furnivall 1868–80 (Chaucer Soc).
Horae. [1477], [1480], [1489], [1490].
Infantia salvatoris. [1477]; ed F. Holthausen, Halle 1891.
Caxton, W. Jason. [1479], Antwerp 1492 (Leeu); ed J. Munro, Oxford 1912 (EETS).
Lydgate, J. The churl and the bird. [1477], [1477]; ed F. Jenkinson, Cambridge 1906 (facs).
Lydgate, J. The horse, sheep and goose. [1477], [1477].
Lydgate, J. Stans puer ad mensam; An holy salve regina in English. [1477]. The latter not by Lydgate.
Ordinale secundum usum Sarum. [1477]; ed C. Wordsworth 1894 (Bradshaw Soc).
Woodville, A. The dicts or sayings of the philosophers. 1477, 1479, [1489]; ed W. Blades 1877 (facs).
The book of courtesy. [1477/8]; ed F. J. Furnivall, Oxford 1868 (EETS); ed F. Jenkinson, Cambridge 1907 (facs).
Chaucer, G. Boethius de consolatione philosophiae. [1478].
Chaucer, G. The Canterbury tales. [1478], [1484].
Woodville, A. The moral proverbs of Christine. 1478; ed W. Blades 1859 (facs).
Woodville, A. The cordial. 1479; ed J. A. Mulders, Nijmegen [1962].
Traversagni, L. G. Nova rhetorica. [1479]; ed R. H. Martin and J. E. Mortimer, Proc Leeds Philosophical & Literary Soc 14 1971.
Caxton, W. The metamorphoses of Ovid. Ed G. Hibbert 1819 (Roxburghe Club); ed S. Gaselee and H. F. B. Brett-Smith, Oxford 1924; 2 vols New York and Cambridge 1968 (facs). Survives only in ms (Pepys 2124 and the Phillipps ms, both in Magdalene College Cambridge).
Chronicles of England. 1480, 1482.
De curia sapienciae. [1480]; ed R. Spindler, Leipzig 1927.
Festum visitationis beatae virginis Mariae. [1480].
Psalter. [1480].
Traversagni, L. G. Epitoma sive isagogicum margarite castigate eloquentie. [1480].
Trevisa, J. Description of Britain. 1480. An extract from Trevisa's trn of Higden's Polychronicon.
[Vocabulary in French and English]. [1480]; ed H. Bradley, Oxford 1900 (EETS); ed J. C. T. Oates and L. C. Harmer, Cambridge 1964 (facs).
Caxton, W. Godfrey of Boloyne. 1481; ed W. Morris 1892; ed M. N. Colvin, Oxford 1893 (EETS).
Caxton, W. The mirror of the world. [1481], [1490], 1527 (Andrewe); ed O. H. Prior, Oxford 1913 (EETS).
Caxton, W. Reynard the Fox. [1481], [1489], [1500] (Pynson), [1515] (de Worde), 1550 (Gaultier), 1620, 1629, 1640, 1640, 1656, 1667, 1681, 1694, 1701; ed W. J. Thoms 1844 (Percy Soc); ed E. Arber 1878, 1895; ed E. Goldsmid 1884; ed H. Morley 1889; ed H. H. Sparling, Edinburgh 1892; ed F. S. Ellis 1897; ed W. S. Stallybrass 1924; ed D. B. Sands, Cambridge Mass 1960; ed N. F. Blake, Oxford 1970 (EETS). All modern edns except Blake's are modernized.
Tiptoft, J. Of old age; Of friendship; The declamation of noblesse. 1481, 1530 (Rastell, Of friendship only); ed E. G. Duff 1912 (Of old age and Of friendship); ed H. Susebach, Halle 1933 (Of old age); ed R. Mitchell 1938 (The declamation). The first text is not a Tiptoft trn.
[Deathbed prayers]. [1482].
Trevisa, J. Polychronicon. [1482]. With a continuation added by Caxton.
Carmeliano, P. Sex epistolae. [1483]; ed G. Bullen and J. Hieatt 1892 (facs).
Caxton, W. Caton. [1483].

Caxton, W. The golden legend. [1483], [1487], 1493 (de Worde) (abridged), 1498 (de Worde), 1503 (Notary), [1510] (de Worde), 1512 (de Worde), 1527 (de Worde); ed A. Aspland 1878; ed F. S. Ellis 3 vols 1892; ed G. V. O'Neill 1914 (selection).

Chaucer, G. The book of fame. [1483]; ed F. J. Furnivall 1868–80 (Chaucer Soc).

Chaucer, G. Troilus and Criseyde. [1483]; ed W. S. McCormick and R. K. Root 1914 (Chaucer Soc).

Gower, J. Confessio amantis. 1483.

Lydgate, J. The pilgrimage of the soul. 1483; ed K. I. Cust 1859.

Mirk, J. The festial. [1483], [1491], 1883 (Roxburghe Club).

Caxton, W. Fables of Aesop. 1484, [1497] (Pynson), [1500] (Pynson), 1550 (Myddelton), 1551 (Powell), [1560] (Walley), [1570] (Wykes), 1585 (Bollifant), 1596 (Adams), 1625, 1634, 1647, 1658; ed J. Jacobs 2 vols 1889; San Francisco 1930; Newtown 1931; ed P. M. Zall, Lincoln Nebraska 1963 (selection); ed R. T. Lenaghan, Cambridge Mass 1967.

Caxton, W. The curial. [1484]; ed P. Mayer and F. J. Furnivall, Oxford 1888 (EETS).

Caxton, W. The knight of the tower. 1484; ed G. B. Rawlings 1902 (selection); ed M. Y. Offord, Oxford 1971 (EETS).

Caxton, W. The order of chivalry. [1484]; ed F. S. Ellis 1892; ed A. T. P. Byles, Oxford 1926 (EETS).

Caxton, W. The royal book. 1484?

Lydgate, J. The life of Our Lady. [1484].

Caxton, W. The life of Charles the Great. 1485; ed S. J. H. Herrtage, Oxford 1880–1 (EETS).

Caxton, W. Paris and Vienne. 1484, Antwerp 1492 (Leeu), [1510] (de Worde), 1621, [1628], [1632], 1650; ed W. C. Hazlitt 1868 (Roxburghe Club); ed M. Leach, Oxford 1957 (EETS).

Caxton, W. The life of St Winifred. [1485]; ed C. Horstmann, Anglia 3 1890.

Malory, Sir T. Le morte d'Arthur. 1485; ed H. O. Sommer 2 vols 1889–1900.

The mirror of the life of Christ. [1486], [1490], 1494 (de Worde); ed L. F. Powell 1908 (Roxburghe Club) (from ms).

Caxton, W. The book of good manners. 1487.

Commemoratio lamentationis sive compassionis beatae Mariae. [1487]; ed E. G. Duff, Oxford 1901 (facs) (Bibl Soc of Lancs).

[Image of pity]. [1487], [1490]; ed W. Cooke and C. Wordsworth 2 vols 1900–1 (Bradshaw Soc).

Mancinello, A. Donatus. [1487].

Maydeston, C. Directorium sacerdotum. [1487], [1489]; ed W. Cooke and C. Wordsworth 2 vols 1900–1 (Bradshaw Soc).

Caxton, W. Blanchardin and Eglantine. [1489]; ed L. Kellner, Oxford 1890 (EETS).

Caxton, W. Doctrinal of sapience. [1489].

Caxton, W. Feats of arms. 1489–90; ed A. T. P. Byles, Oxford 1932 (EETS).

Caxton, W. [Four sons of Aymon]. [1489], 1504 (de Worde), 1554 (Copland); ed O. Richardson, Oxford 1884–5 (EETS).

Governal of health; Medicina stomachi. [1489]; ed W. Blades 1858 (facs).

Statutes of Henry VII. [1489]; ed J. Rae 1869 (facs).

Caxton, W. The art and craft to know well to die. [1490], 1875 (facs).

Caxton, W. Eneydos. [1490]; ed M. T. Culley and F. J. Furnivall, Oxford 1890 (EETS).

[The book of divers ghostly matters]. Horologium sapientiae; The twelve profits of tribulation; The rule of St Benedict. [1491]; ed C. Horstmann, Anglia 10 1888 (Horologium); ed C. Horstmann, 1895–6 (Twelve profits); ed E. A. Kock, Oxford 1902 (EETS) (The rule).

Caxton, W. (?) The craft for to die for the health of a

man's soul. [1491]; ed E. W. B. Nicholson 1891 (facs); ed F. M. M. Comper 1917.

Festum transfigurationis Jesu Christi. [1491].

Fifteen oes. [1491]; ed S. Ayling 1869 (facs).

Caxton, W. Vitas patrum. 1495 (de Worde). Tr in 1491 from French.

§2

Lewis, J. The life of mayster Wyllyam Caxton of the Weald of Kent. 1737.

Ames, J., W. Herbert and T. F. Dibdin. In their Typographical antiquities vol 1, 1810.

Knight, C. Caxton: the first English printer. 1844, 1877.

Blades, W. The life and typography of Caxton. 2 vols London and Strasbourg 1861–3, 1 vol 1882 (as The biography and typography of Caxton); ed J. Moran 1971. First edn contains prologues and epilogues and Liber ultimus of Polychronicon.

—— How to tell a Caxton. 1870.

Bradshaw, H. In his Collected papers, Cambridge 1889.

Duff, E. G. Caxton. Chicago 1905 (Caxton Club).

—— Fifteenth-century English books. 1909 (Bibl Soc).

Plomer, H. R. William Caxton 1424–91. London and Boston 1925.

Aurner, N. S. Caxton, mirrour of fifteenth-century letters: a study of the literature of the first English press. 1926, New York 1965. Includes Caxton's prologues and epilogues.

Winship, G. P. Caxton and the first English press: a bio-bibliographical essay. New York 1938.

Bennett, H. S. Caxton and his public. RES 19 1943.

—— In his Chaucer and the fifteenth century, Oxford 1947 (OHEL vol 2 pt i). With bibliography of Caxtoniana.

—— In his English books and readers 1475 to 1557, Cambridge 1952, 1969 (rev).

Blake, N. F. Caxton and his world. 1969.

—— Caxton: England's first publisher. 1976.

Painter, G. D. William Caxton. 1976.

SIR THOMAS MALORY
fl. c. 1470

Kato, T. A concordance to the works of Malory. Tokyo 1974.

§1

Le morte Darthur reduced in to Englysshe. 1485 (Caxton), 1498 (de Worde), 1529 (de Worde), 1557 (Copland), 1585? (East), 1634; [ed J. Haslewood] 1816; ed R. Southey 1817; ed T. Wright 3 vols 1865–6; ed E. Strachey 1884; ed H. O. Sommer 3 vols 1889–91 (diplomatic edn); ed F. J. Simmons 3 vols 1893–4; ed J. Rhys 1893–4; ed I. Gollancz 1897; ed A. W. Pollard 2 vols 1900; [1913] (priv ptd); [1923] (abridged); ed C. R. Sanders and C. E. Ward, New York 1931 (abridged); ed E. Vinaver 3 vols Oxford 1947, 1 vol Oxford 1954 (OSA), 3 vols Oxford 1967 (rev), 1 vol Oxford 1969 (OSA); ed E. Vinaver, Oxford 1955 (8th bk), New York 1956 (selection); ed R. T. Davies 1967 (selection); ed D. S. Brewer 1968 (bks 7–8); ed J. Cowen 2 vols 1969 (Penguin) (Caxton's text modernized). All texts before Vinaver's 1947 edn were based on Caxton's; Vinaver's and subsequent texts have been based on the Winchester ms, discovered in 1934, which showed the work to be 8 narratives. Vinaver's 1967 edn is now standard.

§2

Kittredge, G. L. Who was Malory? Boston 1897.

Chambers, E. K. Malory. 1922 (Eng Assoc); rptd and rev in his Sir Thomas Wyatt and some collected studies, 1933.

Vinaver, E. Le roman de Tristan et Iseult dans l'oeuvre de Malory. Paris 1925.
—— Malory. Oxford 1929.
—— Epic and tragic patterns in Malory. In Friendship's garland: essays presented to Mario Praz on his seventieth birthday, Rome 1966.
Oakeshott, W. F. The text of Malory. TLS 27 Sept 1934. First detailed account of Winchester ms, by its discoverer.
Loomis, R. S. In his Arthurian literature in the Middle Ages, Oxford 1959.
—— In his Development of Arthurian romance, 1963.
Williams, C. Arthurian torso. Ed C. S. Lewis 1948.
Bradbrook, M. C. Malory. 1958 (Br Council pamphlet).
Bennett, J. A. W. (ed). Essays on Malory. Oxford 1963.
Matthews, W. The ill-framed knight: a skeptical inquiry into the identity of Malory. Berkeley 1966.
Lewis, C. S. The Morte Darthur. In his Studies in medieval and Renaissance literature, ed W. Hooper, Cambridge 1966.

JOHN BOURCHIER, BARON BERNERS
1467–1533
Collections
Berners: a selection from his works. Ed V. de Sola Pinto 1937.

§ 1

The first volum [the third and fourthe boke] of Sir Johan Froyssart: of the cronycles of Englande, Fraunce, Spayne, Portyngale, Scotlande, Bretayne, Flaunders; and other places adioynynge. 2 vols 1523–5 (Pynson), [1545]; ed G. C. Macaulay 1895 (modernized and abridged); ed W. P. Ker 6 vols 1901–3, 8 vols Oxford 1927–8.
The boke of Duke Huon of Burdeux. [1534?] (de Worde?), [possible 2nd edn by Copland 1570 not extant], 1601 (Purfoot; rev); ed S. Lee 4 pts 1882–7 (EETS); ed R. Steele 1895 (modernized). Trn of French edn by Michel Lenoir 1513.
The golden boke of Marcus Aurelius. 1535 (Berthelet), 1537 (colophon, 1536 title-page), 1539, 1542, 1546, 1553, 1557, 1559, 1566, 1573, 1586; ed J. M. Galvez, Berlin 1916. Trn from French version of Guevara's Spanish.
The castell of love. [1549] (Turke), [1550] (Wyer), [1560]; ed W. G. Crane, Gainesville 1950 (facs). Trn of Diego de San Pedro's Spanish, probably via French.

The hystory of Arthur of lytell Brytayne. [1555] (Copland), [1582]; ed E. V. Utterson 1814. Trn from French.
Ordinances for watch and ward at Calais. Ed J. G. Nichols 1846 (in Chronicle of Calais) (Camden Soc) from ms Cotton Faustina E vii. Often attributed to Berners, doubtfully.

PASTON LETTERS

Paston letters. Ed J. Fenn 5 vols 1787–1823; rev J. Gairdner 3 vols 1872–5, 4 vols 1901, 6 vols 1904, 1965; ed J. Warrington 2 vols 1956; ed N. Davis 1958 (selection, 1963 (selection), modernized), 3 vols Oxford 1971– (standard edn).
Bennett, H. S. The Pastons and their England. Cambridge 1922.
Davis, N. The language of the Pastons. Proc Br Acad 40 1954.
Marshall, K. N. The Pastons 1378–1732. Norwich 1956.

JULIANA BERNERS etc
d. 1388?

The book of hawking, hunting and blasing of arms. St Albans 1486, London 1496 (de Worde; includes The treatyse of fysshynge wyth an angle), 1540 (Tab), [1561] (Copland), [1563] (Vele), 1586, 1595 etc.
The book of hawking, hunting, coat-armour, fishing and blasing of arms, as printed at Westminster by Wynkyn de Worde. Ed J. Haslewood 1810 (facs).
The treatyse of fysshynge. Ed M. G. Watkins 1880 (facs).
The boke of St Albans by Dame Juliana Berners 1486. Ed W. Blades 1881 (facs).
An older form of the treatyse of fysshynge wyth an angle. Ed T. Satchell 1883.
The treatyse of fysshynge. Ed 'Piscator', Edinburgh 1885 (facs).
The book of hawking, hunting and blasing of arms. Ed W. Blades [1905] (facs).
The booke of hawkyng after Prince Edwarde Kyng of Englande and its relation to the Book of St Albans. Ed A. E. H. Swaen, Studia Neophilologica 16 1944. BM ms Harley 2340.
The book of St Albans and the origins of its treatise on hawking. Ed N. J. S. Leggatt, Studia Neophilologica 22 1950. BM ms Sloane 3488 xviii F.
Julians Barnes: boke of huntyng. Ed G. Tilander, Karlshamn 1964 (Cynegetica 11). Bodley ms Rawlinson poetry 143.

IV. MEDIEVAL DRAMA

(1) BIBLIOGRAPHIES

Chambers, E. K. The mediaeval stage. 2 vols Oxford 1903.
Wells, J. E. A manual of the writings in Middle English 1050–1400. New Haven 1916; 9 suppls 1919–51.
Harbage, A. Annals of English drama 975–1700. Philadelphia 1940, London 1964 (rev S. Schoenbaum); 2 suppls 1966–70.
Brown, C. and R. H. Robbins. The index of Middle English verse. New York 1943.
Farrar, C. P. and A. P. Evans. Bibliography of English

translations from medieval sources. New York 1946.
Stratman, C. J. Bibliography of medieval drama. Berkeley and Los Angeles 1954, 2 vols New York 1972 (rev).
Robbins, R. H. and J. L. Cutler. Supplement to the Index of Middle English verse. Lexington Kentucky 1965.
Fisher, J. H. (ed). The medieval literature of Western Europe. New York 1966.
Current projects: medieval. Research Opportunities in Renaissance Drama 10– 1967–. In progress.

(2) HISTORIES

Chambers, E. K. The mediaeval stage. 2 vols Oxford 1903.
—— English literature at the close of the Middle Ages.

Oxford 1945 (OHEL), 1947 (corrected).
Nicoll, A. The development of the theatre. 1927.

—— Masks, mimes and miracles. 1931.

Rossiter, A. P. English drama from early times to the Elizabethans. 1950.

Wickham, G. Early English stages 1300 to 1660 vol 1. 1959.

Kinghorn, A. M. Mediaeval drama. 1968.

Sticca, S. (ed). The medieval drama. Albany NY 1972.

Taylor, J. and A. H. Nelson (ed). Medieval English drama: essays critical and contextual. Chicago 1972.

(3) COLLECTIONS

The anthologies are later referred to by the names of the editors.

Hawkins, T. The origin of the English drama. 3 vols 1773.

Collier, J. P. Five miracle plays. 1836.

Marriott, W. A collection of English miracle-plays or mysteries. Basle 1838.

Pollard, A. W. English miracle plays moralities and interludes. Oxford 1890, 1927 (rev).

Manly, J. M. Specimens of the pre-Shaksperean drama. 2 vols Boston 1897.

Hemingway, S. B. English nativity plays. New York 1909.

Adams, J. Q. Chief pre-Shakespearean dramas. Cambridge Mass 1924.

Loomis, R. S. and H. W. Wells. Representative medieval and Tudor plays. New York 1942 (tr and modernized).

Cawley, A. C. Everyman and medieval miracle plays. 1956 (EL), 1957 (rev).

Browne, E. M. Religious drama 2: mystery and morality plays. New York 1958 (modernized).

Franklin, A. Seven miracle plays. Oxford 1963 (adapted).

Gassner, J. Medieval and Tudor drama. New York 1963 (modernized).

Thomas, R. G. Ten miracle plays. 1966.

Robertson, D. W. The literature of medieval England. 1970.

(4) ENGLISH MYSTERY AND MIRACLE PLAYS

Surveys and Special Studies

Whiting, B. J. Proverbs in the earlier English drama. Cambridge Mass 1938.

Wilson, R. M. The lost literature of medieval England. 1952. Ch 11.

Pantin, W. A. The English Church in the fourteenth century. Cambridge 1955. Pt 3.

Salter, F. M. Mediaeval drama in Chester. Toronto 1955.

Southern, R. The medieval theatre in the round: a study of the staging of the Castle of Perseverance and related matters. 1957.

Prosser, E. Drama and religion in the English mystery plays: a re-evaluation. Stanford 1961.

Anderson, M. D. Drama and imagery in English medieval churches. Cambridge 1963.

Kolve, V. A. The play called Corpus Christi. Stanford 1966.

Wickham, G. In his Shakespeare's dramatic heritage, 1969. Ch 1.

—— The staging of saint plays in England. In The medieval drama, ed S. Sticca, Albany 1972.

Texts and Criticism
The Cycles

The Chester Plays

§1

Ed T. Wright 2 vols 1843–7 (Shakespeare Soc); ed H. Deimling and Dr Matthews 2 pts 1892–1916 (EETS); ed I. and O. Bolton King 1930 (abridged and modernized); ed M. Hussey 1957 (16 plays modernized).

One or more plays: Ed J. H. Markland 1818 (Noah, Innocents) (Roxburghe Club); Collier; Marriott; Pollard; Manly; Hemingway; Adams; ed P. E. Dustoor, Allahabad 1930 (Fall of Lucifer); ed W. W. Greg, Oxford 1935 (Antichrist); ed F. M. Salter, Oxford 1935 (Trial and flagellation) (Malone Soc); ed W. W. Greg in Trial and flagellation, Oxford 1935 (Malone Soc) (fragment of the Resurrection and banns); Cawley; Browne; Franklin; Gassner; Thomas.

§2

[Salter, F. M. and W. W. Greg]. The trial and flagellation with other studies in the Chester cycle. Oxford 1935 (Malone Soc).

Salter, F. M. The banns of the Chester plays. RES 15–16 1939–40.

—— Mediaeval drama in Chester. Toronto 1955.

The Coventry Plays (or True-Coventry Plays)

Shearmen and tailors' play. [Ed T. Sharp], Coventry 1817; ed T. Sharp, A dissertation on the Coventry mysteries, Coventry 1825; Marriott; Manly; ed A. W. Pollard, Fifteenth-century prose and verse, 1903 (modernized); Browne; Gassner.

Weavers' play. [Ed J. B. Gracie? and T. Sharp], Edinburgh 1836 (Abbotsford Club).

[Both plays]. Ed H. Craig 1902, 1957 (rev) (EETS).

Ludus Coventriae (or Hegge Plays or N-Town Cycle)

Ed J. O. Halliwell 1841 (Shakespeare Soc); ed K. S. Block 1922 (EETS); ed R. T. Davies 1972 (abridged and modernized).

One or more plays: Collier; Marriott; Pollard; Manly; Hemingway; ed W. W. Greg, Oxford 1915 (Assumption of the Virgin); Adams; Loomis; Cawley; Browne; Thomas.

The Towneley Plays (or Wakefield Plays)

[Ed J. Gordon and J. Hunter] 1836 (Surtees Soc); ed G. England and A. W. Pollard 1897 (EETS); ed M. Rose 1961 (modernized).

One or more plays: [Ed F. Douce] 1822 (Judicium, Roxburghe Club); Marriott; Manly; Hemingway; Adams; Loomis; Gassner; Thomas.

The 'Wakefield Master's' Plays
(plays 2–3, 12–13, 16 and 21 in the Towneley cycle)

Ed A. C. Cawley, Manchester 1958.

One or more plays: Collier; Marriott; Pollard; Manly; Hemingway; Adams; Loomis; Cawley; Browne; Franklin; Gassner; Thomas; Robertson.

The York Plays

Ed L. T. Smith, Oxford 1885; ed J. S. Purvis 1957 (modernized).

One or more plays: Pollard; Manly; Hemingway; Adams; ed A. C. Cawley, Leeds 1952 (Sykes ms of the Scriveners' play); Cawley; Browne; Franklin; Gassner; Thomas.

THE RENAISSANCE TO THE RESTORATION (1500-1660)

1. INTRODUCTION

I. GENERAL WORKS

(1) BIBLIOGRAPHIES

Leland, J. (1506?–52). Commentarii de scriptoribus britannicis. Ed A. Hall 2 vols Oxford 1709; ed T. Hearne, Collectanea, Oxford 1715, 1770 (enlarged), 1774. Used by Bale for his Summarium and Catalogus, below.

Bale, J. Illustrium majoris Britanniae scriptorum summarium. Ipswich (Wesel?) 1548. Rev and enlarged as Scriptorum illustrium majoris Brytanniae catalogus, 2 pts Basle 1557–9. His notebook, c. 1549–57, used as material for the Catalogus, pbd as Index Britanniae scriptorum, ed R. L. Poole and M. Bateson, Oxford 1902.

Wood, A. Athenae oxonienses: a history of writers educated at Oxford 1500–1695. 2 vols 1691–2; rev and enlarged T. Tanner 1721; ed P. Bliss 4 vols 1813–20 (with addns), New York 1967.

Ames, J. Typographical antiquities: an historical account of printing in England to 1600. 1749; augmented W. Herbert 3 vols 1785–90; rev T. F. Dibdin 4 vols 1810–19, Detroit 1969. Index to Dibdin's edn, 1899.

Watt, R. Bibliotheca britannica: or a general index to British and foreign literature. 4 vols Edinburgh 1824 (with subject-index).

Lowndes, W. T. The bibliographer's manual of English literature. 4 vols 1834, 1864 (rev and enlarged H. G. Bohn), 8 vols Detroit 1967.

Hazlitt, W. C. Handbook to the popular, poetical and dramatic literature of Great Britain from the invention of printing to the Restoration. 1867; Supplements, 1876, 1882, 1887–92, 1903; Index (1867–89) by G. J. Gray, 1893; 8 vols New York 1961 (complete).

Arber, E. A transcript of the registers of the Company of Stationers 1554–1640. 4 vols 1875–7; with Index, Birmingham 1894, 5 vols New York 1950. Supplement: Registers 1640–1708, ed G. E. B. Eyre 3 vols 1913–14, New York 1950; The Court records of the Company 1576–1602, ed W. W. Greg and E. Boswell 1930; 1602–40, ed W. A. Jackson 1957. See also A companion to Arber: a calendar of documents in Arber's transcript, with text and calendar of supplementary documents, ed W. W. Greg with C. E. Blagden and I. G. Philip, Oxford 1967.

Huth library: catalogue of books. Ed F. S. Ellis 5 vols 1880.

British Museum. Catalogue of English books to 1640. Ed G. Bullen 3 vols 1884.

—— Catalogue of the pamphlets, books, newspapers and manuscripts relating to the Civil War, the Commonwealth and Restoration (1640–61). Collected G. Thomason and ed G. K. Fortescue 2 vols 1908.

Madan, F. Oxford books: a bibliography of works printed by the Press '1468'–1680. 3 vols Oxford 1895–1931.

Cambridge University Library. Early English printed books 1475–1640. Ed C. E. Sayle 4 vols with appendix, Cambridge 1900–7.

Aldis, H. G. A list of books printed in Scotland before 1700. Edinburgh 1904.

Marsh's Library, Dublin. A short catalogue of its books before 1641. Ed N. J. D. White, Oxford 1905.

Pierpont Morgan Library. Catalogue of manuscripts and early printed books. Ed A. W. Pollard et al 4 vols 1906–7.

Pollard, A. W. and G. R. Redgrave. A short-title catalogue of books printed in England, Scotland and Ireland, and of English books printed abroad 1475–1640. 2 vols 1926 (Bibl Soc), 1946, 1976– (rev K. Pantzer); P. G. Morrison, Index of printers, publishers and booksellers in the STC, Charlottesville 1950, 1961; D. Ramage et al, A finding list of English books to 1640 in libraries in the British Isles (excluding Cambridge, Oxford and the national libraries), Durham 1958; F. B. Williams jr, Photofacsimiles of STC books: a cautionary check list, SB 21 1968. The microfilming of STC books by University Microfilms, Ann Arbor 1938–; A. F. Allison and V. F. Goldsmith, Titles of English books vol 1: 1475–1640, 1976. For a continuation of the STC, see Wing below.

Davies, G. Bibliography of British history: Stuart period 1603–1714. Oxford 1928, 1970 (rev M. F. Keeler); C. Read, Tudor period 1485–1603, Oxford 1933, 1959 (rev).

The Britwell handlist: or short-title catalogue of the principal volumes to 1800, formerly in the library of Britwell Court. 2 vols 1933.

Case, A. E. A bibliography of English poetical miscellanies 1521–1750. Oxford 1935 (Bibl Soc).

de Ricci, S. and W. J. Wilson. Census of medieval and Renaissance manuscripts in the United States and Canada. 3 vols New York 1935–40, 1961; Supplement, ed W. H. Bond, New York 1962.

Noyes, G. E. Bibliography of courtesy and conduct-books in 17th-century England. New Haven 1937.

Tannenbaum, S. A. and D. R. Elizabethan bibliographies. Nos 1–40, New York 1937–49; Supplements, London 1967–.

Pforzheimer, Carl H., Library. English literature 1475–1700. Compiled E. V. Unger and W. A. Jackson 3 vols New York 1940.

Taylor, A. Renaissance reference books: a checklist of some bibliographies printed before 1700. Berkeley 1941.

—— Renaissance guides to books: an inventory and some conclusions. Berkeley 1945.

Folger, H. The Folger Shakespeare Memorial Library: a report on progress 1931–41, by J. Q. Adams, Amherst Mass 1942. See also G. E. Dawson, The resources and policies of the Folger Library, Lib Quart 19 1949. For its STC holdings *see* W. W. Bishop under Pollard and Redgrave, above. Catalogues of manuscripts, 3 vols, and printed books, 28 vols Boston 1971–.

Seventeenth-century News. 1942–. Since 1950 ed J. M. Patrick. Reviews of current pbns.

Wing, D. G. A short-title catalogue of books printed in England, Scotland, Ireland, Wales and British America, and of English books printed in other countries 1641–1700. 3 vols New York 1945–51; Suppls by M. I. Fry and G. Davies, HLQ 16 1953; J. E. Tucker, Wing's STC and translations from the French 1641–1700, PBSA 49 1955; W. G. Hiscock, The Christ Church supplement to Wing, Oxford 1956; J. Alden, Bibliographica hibernica: additions and corrections to Wing, Charlottesville 1955; also his Wing addenda and corrigenda, Charlottesville 1958; E. Wolf, A check-list of the books in the Library Company of Philadelphia in and supplementary to Wing, Philadelphia 1959; and Wing, A gallery of ghosts: books published between 1641–1700 not found in the STC, New York 1967. *See also* P. G. Morrison, Index of printers, publishers and booksellers, Charlottesville 1955. The microfilming of STC books by University Microfilms, Ann Arbor 1961–.

Matthews, W. British diaries: an annotated bibliography to 1942. Berkeley 1950.
—— British autobiographies: an annotated bibliography to 1951. Berkeley 1955.

Mish, C. C. English prose fiction 1600–1700: a chronological checklist. Charlottesville 1952, 1967 (rev).

O'Dell, S. A chronological list of prose fiction in English 1475–1640. Cambridge Mass 1954.

Allison, A. F. and D. M. Rogers. A catalogue of Catholic books in English printed abroad or secretly in England 1558–1640. Bognor Regis 1956; Supplement, Recusant History 6 1961.

Jayne, S. Library catalogues of the English Renaissance. Berkeley 1956.

Williams, F. B., jr. Index of dedications and commendatory verses in English books before 1641. 1962 (Bibl Soc).

Adams, H. M. Catalogue of books printed on the Continent of Europe 1501–1600 in Cambridge libraries. 2 vols Cambridge 1967.

Watson, G. The English Petrarchans: a critical bibliography of the Canzoniere. 1967 (Warburg Inst).

Crum, M. First-line index of English poetry 1500–1800 in manuscripts of the Bodleian Library, Oxford. 2 vols Oxford 1969.

(2) COLLECTIONS

The Harleian miscellany: a collection of pamphlets and tracts. 8 vols 1744–6; ed W. Oldys 1746 (with catalogue); ed T. Park 10 vols 1808–13; ed J. Malham 12 vols 1808–11 (chronologically arranged).

Somers tracts: a collection of scarce and valuable tracts. 16 vols 1748–52; ed W. Scott 13 vols 1809–15 (rev and enlarged).

Harington, J. Nugae antiquae: a miscellaneous collection of prose and verse written from the reign of Henry VIII to the reign of King James. 2 vols 1769–75, 3 vols 1779 (enlarged); ed T. Park 2 vols 1804, New York 1966.

Nichols, J. The progresses and public processions of Queen Elizabeth. 3 vols 1823, New York 1964.
—— The progresses, processions and magnificent festivities of King James I. 4 vols 1828, New York 1964.

Percy Society publications. Early English poetry, ballads and popular literature of the Middle Ages. 30 vols 1840–52, New York 1965.

Parker Society publications. 55 vols Cambridge 1841–55; Index by H. Gough, Cambridge 1855. Includes works of the early writers of the Reformed English church.

Library of Anglo-Catholic theology. 88 vols 1841–63.

Wright, T. and J. O. Halliwell(-Phillipps). Reliquiae antiquae: scraps from ancient manuscripts illustrating chiefly early English literature. 2 vols 1841–3, 1845, New York 1966.

Collier, J. P. Shakespeare's library: a collection of the romances, novels, poems and histories used as the foundation of his dramas. 2 vols 1843; rev W. C. Hazlitt 6 vols 1875, New York 1965.
—— Illustrations of early English popular literature. 2 vols 1863, 1864, New York 1966.
—— Illustrations of old English literature. 3 vols 1866, New York 1966.

Hakluyt Society publications. 1st series, 100 vols 1847–99, New York 1963; 2nd series, 1899–; Extra series, Cambridge 1903–.

Halliwell(-Phillipps), J. O. Contributions to early English literature 15th–17th century. 6 pts 1849.
—— Literature of the 16th and 17th centuries illustrated by reprints of tracts. 1851.

Hazlitt, W. C. Shakespeare jest-books. 3 vols 1864, New York 1964.
—— Inedited tracts illustrating the manners, opinions and occupations of Englishmen during the 16th and 17th centuries. 1868, New York 1964.

Spenser Society publications. 55 vols Manchester 1867–95, New York 1966.

Arber, E. English reprints. 30 pts 1868–95.
—— An English garner. 8 vols 1877–97; ed T. Seccombe 12 vols 1903–4 (enlarged); Analytical catalogue, ed H. Guppy, Manchester 1909 (John Rylands Lib).
—— The English scholars library of old and modern works. 5 vols 1878–84, New York 1967.

Ashbee, E. W. Occasional facsimile reprints (of the 16th and 17th centuries). 30 pts 1868–72.

Grosart, A. B. Fuller Worthies' library. 39 vols Edinburgh 1868–76.
—— Miscellanies of the Fuller Worthies' library. 4 vols Blackburn 1871–6, New York 1966.
—— Early English poets. 9 vols 1876–7.
—— The Huth Library of Elizabethan-Jacobean books. 29 vols 1881–6.

Tudor translations. Ed W. E. Henley 44 vols 1892–1909; 2nd series ed C. Whibley 12 vols 1924–7. Both rptd, New York 1970.

Pollard, A. F. Tudor tracts 1532–88. 1903, New York 1964. Suppl by C. H. Firth, Stuart tracts 1603–93, 1903, New York 1964.

Smith, G. G. Elizabethan critical essays. 2 vols Oxford 1904.

Spingarn, J. E. Critical essays of the 17th century. 3 vols Oxford 1908–9, Bloomington 1957.

Wilson, J. D. Life in Shakespeare's England: a book of Elizabethan prose. Cambridge 1911.

Smith, D. N. Characters from the histories and memoirs of the 17th century. Oxford 1918.

Bodley Head quartos. Ed G. B. Harrison 15 vols 1923–6, Edinburgh 1966.

Hebel, J. W. and H. H. Hudson. Poetry of the English Renaissance 1509–1660. New York 1929; Prose, New York 1952; collected as Tudor poetry and prose, New York 1953.

Luttrell Society reprints. Oxford 1946–61.

English reprints series. 22 nos Liverpool 1948–67.

Pelican book of English prose. Vol 1, Elizabethan and Jacobean prose 1550–1620, ed K. Muir 1956; vol 2, Seventeenth-century prose 1620–1700, ed P. Ure 1956.

Bullough, G. Narrative and dramatic sources of Shakespeare. 8 vols 1957–75.

Clarendon medieval and Tudor series. Ed J. A. W. Bennett et al, Oxford 1958–.

Donno, E. S. Elizabethan minor epics. 1963; suppl by P. S. Miller, Seven minor epics 1596–1624, Gainesville 1967.

English recusant prose. Menston 1970–. Facs of 300 vols listed in Allison and Rogers, Catalogue of Catholic books 1558–1640.

(3) LITERARY HISTORY AND CRITICISM

Fuller, T. The history of the Worthies of England. 1662.

Walton, I. The lives of Donne, Wotton, Hooker, Herbert. 1670.

Phillips, E. Theatrum poetarum: or a complete collection of the poets of all ages, particularly those of our own nation. 1675; ed S. E. Brydges, Canterbury 1800, Hildesheim 1970.

Winstanley, W. The lives of the most famous English poets. 1687; ed W. R. Parker, Gainesville 1963 (facs).

Warton, T. The history of English poetry from the close of the 11th to the commencement of the 18th century. 3 vols 1774–81; rev W. C. Hazlitt 4 vols 1871, New York 1968. Completed to c. 1600.

Aubrey, J. Lives. 1813.

Hazlitt, W. Lectures on the English poets. 1818.

—— Lectures on the literature of the age of Elizabeth. 1820.

Coleridge, S. T. Literary remains. Ed H. N. Coleridge 4 vols 1836–9.

—— Coleridge on the seventeenth century. Ed R. F. Brinkley, Durham NC 1955.

Hallam, H. Introduction to the literature of Europe 15th–17th centuries. 4 vols 1837–9.

Gosse, E. W. Seventeenth-century studies: a contribution to the history of English poetry. 1883.

—— From Shakespeare to Pope. Cambridge 1885, New York 1968.

—— The Jacobean poets. 1894.

Spingarn, J. E. A history of literary criticism in the Renaissance. New York 1899; tr Italian, 1905 (rev and enlarged), tr 1908; ed B. Weinberg, New York 1963.

Greg, W. W. Pastoral poetry and pastoral drama. 1906, New York 1959.

Grierson, H. J. C. The first half of the 17th century. Edinburgh 1906.

Swinburne, A. C. The age of Shakespeare. 1908.

Mackail, J. W. The springs of Helicon: the progress of English poetry from Chaucer to Milton. New York 1909, Lincoln Nebraska 1962.

Williamson, G. The Donne tradition: a study in English poetry from Donne to the death of Cowley. Cambridge Mass 1930.

—— Seventeenth-century contexts. 1960, 1969 (rev).

—— The proper wit of poetry. 1961.

—— Milton and others. 1965.

Chambers, R. W. On the continuity of English prose from

Alfred to More and his school. In N. Harpsfield, The life and death of Sir Thomas More, ed E. V. Hitchcock 1932 (EETS), 1950 (separately).

Garvin, K. (ed). The great Tudors. 1935.

Bush, D. English literature in the earlier seventeenth century 1600–60. Oxford 1945 (OHEL), 1962 (rev).

Wilson, F. P. Elizabethan and Jacobean. Oxford 1945.

—— Seventeenth-century prose. Cambridge 1960.

Knights, L. C. Explorations: essays in criticism mainly on the literature of the 17th century. 1946.

—— Further explorations. 1965.

Atkins, J. W. H. English literary criticism: the Renascence. 1947.

—— English literary criticism: 17th and 18th centuries. 1951.

Craig, H. The literature of the English Renaissance. Pt 2 of A history of English literature, ed Craig, New York 1950, 1962 (rev).

Mahood, M. M. Poetry and humanism. 1950.

Wedgwood, C. V. Seventeenth-century English literature. Oxford 1950 (Home Univ Lib), 1970 (rev).

Danby, J. F. Poets on fortune's hill. 1952, 1964 (as Elizabethan and Jacobean poets).

Smith, H. Elizabethan poetry: a study in conventions, meaning and expression. Cambridge Mass 1952, Ann Arbor 1968.

Lewis, C. S. English literature in the sixteenth century, excluding drama. Oxford 1954 (OHEL).

Ford, B. (ed). A guide to English literature vol 2: The age of Shakespeare; vol 3: From Donne to Marvell. 1955 (Pelican), 1962 (rev).

Walton, G. Metaphysical to Augustan: studies in tone and sensibility in the 17th century. 1955.

Tillyard, E. M. W. The Metaphysicals and Milton. 1956.

Ellrodt, R. Les poètes métaphysiques anglais. 3 vols Paris 1960.

Alvarez, A. The school of Donne. 1961.

Keast, W. R. (ed). Seventeenth-century English poetry: modern essays in criticism. New York 1962, 1971 (rev).

Buxton, J. Elizabethan taste. 1963.

—— A tradition of poetry. 1967.

Ricks, C. (ed). English poetry and prose 1540–1674. 1970.

Gordon, D. J. The Renaissance imagination. Ed S. Orgel, Berkeley 1975.

2. POETRY

I. INTRODUCTION

(1) BIBLIOGRAPHIES ETC

Rollins, H. E. An analytical index to the ballad-entries in the Stationers' Registers. Chapel Hill 1924.
Case, A. E. A bibliography of English poetical miscellanies 1521–1750. 1935 (Bibl Soc).
White, E. A. and M. Dean-Smith. An index of English songs. 1951 (English Folk-Dance & Song Soc).

Crum, M. First-line index of English poetry 1500–1800 in manuscripts of the Bodleian Library, Oxford. 2 vols Oxford 1969.
Preston, M. J. A complete concordance to the songs of the early Tudor court. Leeds 1972.

(2) MISCELLANIES AND REPRESENTATIVE BALLAD-COLLECTIONS

For miscellanies in languages other than English, largely university productions, see Case, above.

The Court of Venus. [1538] (fragment in Bodley), [1548] (as A boke of balettes) (fragment in Univ of Texas), [1562] (as The Courte of Venus) (fragment in Folger Lib); ed R. A. Fraser, Durham NC 1955.
Songes and sonettes. 5 June 1557, 31 July 1557 (rev with addns), 31 July 1557, 1559, 1559, 1565, 1567, 1574, 1585, 1587; ed G. Sewell 1717; ed T. Percy [1767] (not pbd); ed G. F. Nott [1814] (not pbd); ed J. P. Collier, Seven English poetical miscellanies, 1867; ed E. Arber 1870 (as Tottel's miscellany); ed H. E. Rollins 2 vols Cambridge Mass 1928–9 (as Tottel's miscellany), 1965 (with addns).
The paradyse of daynty devises. 1576, 1578 (rev), 1580 (rev), 1585 (rev), [1590], 1596, [1596], 1600, 1606; ed S. E. Brydges 1810; ed J. P. Collier, Seven English poetical miscellanies, 1867; ed H. E. Rollins, Cambridge Mass 1927.
A gorgious gallery of gallant inventions. 1578; ed T. Park, Heliconia vol 1, 1815; ed H. Ellis, Three collections of English poetry, 1845 (Roxburghe Club); ed J. P. Collier, Seven English poetical miscellanies, 1867; ed H. E. Rollins, Cambridge Mass 1926.
Syr P. S. his Astrophel and Stella. 1591, [1591].
The phoenix nest. 1593; ed T. Park, Heliconia vol 2, 1815; ed J. P. Collier, Seven English poetical miscellanies, 1867; ed H. Macdonald 1926; ed H. E. Rollins, Cambridge Mass 1931.
Politeuphia: wits commonwealth, by John Bodenham. 1597, 1598, [1608], [1610], [1620], [1626], [1630], [1640], [1641], 1647, 1650, 1653, 1655 (17th edn), 1661, 1663, 1667, 1669, 1671, 1674, 1678, 1684, 1687, 1688, 1698, 1699, 1706.
The passionate pilgrime, by W. Shakespeare. 1599, 1612 (3rd edn).
Bel-vedere: or the garden of the Muses. 1600, 1610 (as The garden of the Muses), 1875 (Spenser Soc).
Englands Helicon. 1600, 1614 (with addns); ed S. E. Brydges, Br Bibliographer 3 1812; ed J. O. Halliwell(-Phillipps) 1865 (selection); ed J. P. Collier, Seven English poetical miscellanies, 1867; ed A. H. Bullen 1887; ed H. Macdonald 1925, 1950 (ML); ed H. E. Rollins 2 vols Cambridge Mass 1935.
Englands Parnassus. 1600; ed T. Park, Heliconia vol 3, 1815; ed J. P. Collier, Seven English poetical miscellanies, 1867; ed C. Crawford, Oxford 1913
Strange histories of kings, princes, dukes etc by Thomas Deloney et al. 1600, 1602, 1607, 1612 (rev), 1631 (rev), 1674 (rev as The royal garland of love and delight); ed J. P. Collier 1841 (Percy Soc); ed F. O. Mann in his edn of Deloney, Oxford 1912.

Loves martyr: or Rosalins complaint by Robert Chester. 1601, 1611 (as The annals of Great Brittaine).
A poetical rhapsody. 1602, 1608 (rev), 1611 (rev), 1621 (rev); ed S. E. Brydges 3 vols 1814–17; ed N. H. Nicolas 2 vols 1826; ed J. P. Collier, Seven English poetical miscellanies, 1867; ed A. H. Bullen 2 vols 1890–1; ed H. E. Rollins 2 vols Cambridge Mass 1931–2.
Jonsonus virbius: or the memorie of Ben Johnson revived by the friends of the Muses. 1638.
Justa Edouardo King naufrago. Cambridge 1638.
Three poems upon the death of his late Highnesse Oliver Lord Protector. 1659, 1682 (as Three poems upon the death of the late usurper Oliver Cromwell), 1709 (as A panegyrick on Oliver Cromwell).
Park, T. Heliconia. 3 vols 1815.
Collier, J. P. Old ballads from early printed copies. 1840 (Percy Soc).
—— Eight ballads, from the original black-letter copies. 1846 (priv ptd).
—— A book of Roxburghe ballads. 1847.
—— Broadside black-letter ballads. 1868 (priv ptd).
—— Twenty-five old ballads and songs from mss. 1869 (priv ptd).
Wright, T. Political ballads published in England during the Commonwealth. 1841 (Percy Soc).
—— Songs and ballads chiefly of the reign of Philip and Mary. 1860 (Roxburghe Club).
Child, F. J. English and Scottish ballads. 8 vols Boston 1857–8, 5 vols 1882–98 (rev as The English and Scottish popular ballads).
Rollins, H. E. Old English ballads 1553–1625. Cambridge 1920.
—— A Pepysian garland 1595–1639. Cambridge 1922.
—— Cavalier and Puritan: ballads of the Great Rebellion. New York 1923.
—— The pack of Autolycus. Cambridge Mass 1927.
—— The Pepys ballads. 8 vols Cambridge Mass 1929–32.
Ault, N. Elizabethan lyrics. 1925, 1949 (rev).
—— Seventeenth-century lyrics. 1928, 1950 (rev).
—— A treasury of unfamiliar lyrics. 1938.
Hammond, E. P. English verse between Chaucer and Surrey. Durham NC 1927.
Hebel, J. W. and H. H. Hudson. Poetry of the English Renaissance 1509–1660. New York 1929.
Howarth, R. G. Minor poets of seventeenth century. 1931 (EL), 1953 (rev).
Chambers, E. K. The Oxford book of sixteenth-century verse. Oxford 1932.
Grierson, H. J. C. and G. Bullough. The Oxford book of

seventeenth-century verse. Oxford 1934.
Green, R. L. The early English carols. Oxford 1935.
Hughey, R. The Arundel Harington manuscript of Tudor

poetry. 2 vols Columbus 1960.
Lucie-Smith, E. The penguin book of Elizabethan verse. 1965 (Penguin).

(3) GENERAL STUDIES

Berdan, J. M. Early Tudor poetry. New York 1920.
Bush, D. Mythology and the Renaissance tradition in English poetry. Minneapolis 1933.
Miles, J. Major adjectives in English poetry from Wyatt to Auden. Berkeley 1946.
— The primary language of poetry in the 1640's. Berkeley 1948.
— The continuity of poetic language. Berkeley 1951.
Tuve, R. Elizabethan and metaphysical imagery. Chicago 1947.
Pattison, B. Music and poetry of the English Renaissance. 1948.
Mahood, M. M. Poetry and humanism. 1950.
Nicolson, M. H. The breaking of the circle: studies in the effect of the 'New Science' upon seventeenth-century poetry. Evanston 1950.

Wallerstein, R. Studies in seventeenth-century poetic. Madison 1950.
Ing, C. M. Elizabethan lyrics: a study of the development of English metres. 1951.
Smith, H. Elizabethan poetry: a study in conventions, meaning and expression. Cambridge Mass 1952, 1968 (rev).
Danby, J. F. Poets on Fortune's Hill: studies in Sidney, Shakespeare, Beaumont and Fletcher. 1952, 1964 (rev as Elizabethan and Jacobean poets).
Lever, J. W. The Elizabethan love sonnet. 1956.
Davis, H. and H. Gardner (ed). Elizabethan and Jacobean studies presented to F. P. Wilson. Oxford 1959.
Stevens, J. E. Music and poetry in the early Tudor court 1480–1530. 1961.

II. TUDOR POETRY

JOHN SKELTON
1460?–1529

Bibliographies
Kinsman, R. S. and T. Yonge. Skelton: canon and census. [Darien Conn 1968].

Collections
Certayne bokes. [1545], [1554], [1560].
Pithy pleasaunt and profitable workes. Ed J. Stow 1568, 1736.
Poetical works. Ed A. Dyce 2 vols 1843, 3 vols Boston 1856 (with addns [by F. J. Child]).
Skelton (laureate). Ed R. Graves 1927.
Complete poems. Ed P. Henderson 1931, 1948 (rev), 1959 (rev), 1964 (rev).
Poems. Ed R. S. Kinsman, Oxford 1969.

§1
The bowge of Courte. [1499], [1510]. Anon.
A ballade of the Scottysshe Kynge. [1513] (anon); ed J. Ashton 1882.
The tunnyng of Elynour Rummyng. [1521] (fragment), 1624, 1718; ed H. Stearns 1928; ed anon 1930; Worcester Mass 1953.
A goodly garlande or chapelet of laurell. 1523; ed E. P. Hammond, English verse between Chaucer and Surrey, Durham NC 1927.
Dyvers balettys and dyties solacyous. [1527].
Agaynste a comely coystrowne. [1527].
A replycacion agaynst certayne yong scolers. [1528].
Magnyfycence. [1533], 1821 (Roxburghe Club); ed R. L. Ramsay 1905, 1908 (EETS); ed J. Farmer 1910.
Collyn Clout. [1530], [1545], [1554], [1560].
Phyllyp Sparowe. [1545], [1554], [1560].
Why come ye nat to Courte. [1545], [1554], [1560]; ed J. Zupitza, Archiv 85 1890 (ms fragment).
Speculum principis. Ed F. M. Salter, Speculum 9 1934.
The bibliotheca historica of Diodorus Siculus. Ed F. M. Salter and H. L. R. Edwards 2 vols 1956–7 (EETS).

§2
Auden, W. H. In The great Tudors, ed K. Garvin 1935.
Nelson, W. Skelton laureate. New York 1939.
Gordon, I. A. Skelton: poet laureate. Melbourne 1943.
Edwards, H. L. R. Skelton: the life and times of an early Tudor poet. 1949.
Forster, E. M. In his Two cheers for democracy, 1951.
Fish, S. E. Skelton's poetry. New Haven 1965.

ALEXANDER BARCLAY
1475?–1552
Collections
The ship of fools. 1570.
Certayne egloges. Manchester 1885 (Spenser Soc).
Eclogues. Ed B. White 1928 (EETS).

§1
The castell of laboure. Paris [1503], London [1505], 1506, 1506; ed A. W. Pollard 1905 (Roxburghe Club).
The shyp of folys. 1509; ed T. H. Jamieson 2 vols Edinburgh 1874.
[Eglog 1]. [1510] (fragment), [Cambridge 1523] (fragment).
The lyf of saynt George. 1515; ed W. Nelson 1955 (EETS).
The famous cronycle of the warre agaynst Jugurth. [1520], [1525], 1557 (rev T. Paynell).
The lyfe of the blessed martyr Saynte Thomas. [1520]. Anon.
The fyfth eglog. [1518].
The fourth eglog. [1521].
The myrrour of good maners. [1523], Manchester 1885 (Spenser Soc).
A lytell cronycle. 1525. Anon.
The eglogs. [1530], [1548], [1560]. Eclogues 1–3.

SIR THOMAS WYATT
1503?–42

Ms: BM Egerton 2711 has 12 autograph poems and 6 others with autograph corrections.

Hangen, E. C. A concordance to the complete poetical works of Wyatt. Chicago 1941.

Collections

Works. Ed G. F. Nott 1816.
Poetry. Ed E. M. W. Tillyard 1929. A selection.
Collected poems. Ed K. Muir 1949 (ML).
Collected poems. Ed K. Muir and P. Thomson, Liverpool 1969. First complete edn.
Collected poems. Ed J. Daalder, Oxford 1975.

§ 1

Plutarckes boke of the quyete of mynde. [1528]; ed C. R. Baskervill, Cambridge Mass 1931 (facs).
Certayne psalmes chosen out of the psalter of David. 1549.
Songes and sonnettes. 5 June 1557. Tottel includes 97 poems by Wyatt. *For edns see col 85, above.*
Unpublished poems. Ed K. Muir, Liverpool 1961.

§ 2

[Howard, H.] An excellent epitaffe of Wyat. [1542].
Leland, J. Naeniae in mortem Viati. 1542.
Foxwell, A. K. A study of Wyatt's poems. 1911.
Chambers, E. K. In his Wyatt and some collected studies, 1933.
Muir, K. Life and letters of Wyatt. Liverpool 1963.
Southall, R. The courtly maker. 1964.
Thomson, P. Wyatt and his background. 1964.
—— (ed). Wyatt: the critical heritage. 1974.

HENRY HOWARD, EARL OF SURREY
1517?–47

Collections

Poems. Ed F. M. Padelford, Seattle 1920, 1928 (rev).
Poems. Ed E. Jones, Oxford 1964.

§ 1

An excellent epitaffe of Syr Thomas Wyat. [1542].
The fourth boke of Virgill. [1554]; ed H. Hartman, Purchase NY 1935 (with facs).
Certain bokes of Virgiles Aenaeis. 1557, 1814 (Roxburghe Club); ed F. H. Ridley, Berkeley 1963.
Songes and sonnettes. 1557. *For edns see col 85, above.* Tottel includes 40 poems by Surrey.

A MIRROR FOR MAGISTRATES

Thomas Sackville's Induction was first ptd in 1563 edn. The ms of his Buckingham is at St John's College, Cambridge.

Collections

The mirrour for magistrates. Ed J. Higgins 1587. First and last pts.
A mirrour for magistrates. Ed R. Niccols 1610, 1619 (as The falles of unfortunate princes), 1620. 3 pts.
Mirror for magistrates. Ed J. Haslewood 3 vols 1815. 3 pts.
Parts added to the mirror for magistrates. Ed L. B. Campbell, Cambridge 1946. First and 2nd pts.

§ 1

A memorial of suche princes as have been unfortunate in the realme of England. [1555]. Fragments of a suppressed edn.

A myrroure for magistrates. Ed W. Baldwin 1559, 1563 (with addns), 1571, 1574 (as The last part), 1575, 1578 (with addns); ed L. B. Campbell, Cambridge 1938.
The first parte of the mirror for magistrates. Ed J. Higgins 1574, 1575 (with addns); ed J. Haslewood, Br Bibliographer 4 1814.
The seconde part of the mirroure for magistrates, by T. Blenerhasset. 1578.
The complaint of Henry Duke of Buckingham. Ed M. Hearsey, New Haven 1936.

GEORGE GASCOIGNE
1542?–77

Collections

The pleasauntest workes. 1587. Another issue as The whole woorkes.
Complete poems. Ed W. C. Hazlitt 2 vols 1869–70.
Complete works. Ed J. W. Cunliffe 2 vols Cambridge 1907–10.

§ 1

A hundreth sundrie flowres. [1573]; ed B. M. Ward 1926; ed C. T. Prouty, Columbia Missouri 1942.
The glasse of gouernement. 1575; ed J. S. Farmer, Amersham 1914 (facs).
The posies. 1575.
The whole arte of venerie or hunting. [1575], 1611, 1908.
A delicate diet, for daintiemouthde droonkardes. 1576; ed F. G. Waldron 1789.
The droomme of doomes day. 1576, 1586.
The princelye pleasures at the Courte at Kenelwoorth. 1576 (no known copy), 1821.
The spoyle of Antwerpe. 1576.
The steele glas. 1576; ed E. Arber 1868.
The tale of Hemetes the heremite. In Synesius, A paradoxe, 1579; in The Queenes Majesties entertainment at Woodstocke, 1585.

§ 2

Whetstone, G. A remembrance of the wel imployed life and godly end of Gascoigne. 1577.
Schelling, F. E. The life and writings of Gascoigne. Boston 1893.
Prouty, C. T. Gascoigne: Elizabethan courtier, soldier and poet. New York 1942.

NICHOLAS BRETON
1545?–1626?

Collections

The works in verse and prose. Ed A. B. Grosart 2 vols 1879 (priv ptd).
A mad world my masters and other prose works. Ed U. Kentish-Wright 2 vols 1929.
Poems not hitherto reprinted. Ed J. Robertson, Liverpool 1952.

§ 1

A smale handfull of fragrant flowers. 1575; ed T. Park, Heliconia vol 1, 1815.
A floorish upon fancie. 1577, 1582 (with addns), [1585] (fragment); ed T. Park, Heliconia vol 1, 1815.
The workes of a young wyt. 1577.
A discourse in commendation of maister Frauncis Drake. 1581.
The historie of the life and fortune of don Federigo di Terra Nuova. 1590.
Brittons bowre of delights. 1591, 1597 (with omissions); ed H. E. Rollins, Cambridge Mass 1933.
Marie Magdalens love; A solemne passion. 1595, 1598 (A solemne passion, alone), 1622, 1623, [1625].

Auspicante Jehova. 1597.
The wil of wit, wits wil or wils wit. 1597, 1599, 1606 (5th edn); ed J. O. Halliwell-Phillipps 1860.
Wits trenchmour. 1597.
The passions of the spirit. 1599; ed J. O. Halliwell-Phillipps, A brief description of manuscripts in the Public Library at Plymouth, 1853 (as The Countesse of Penbrooke's passion); ed N.B.G. 1862 (as A poem on our Saviour's passion by Mary Sidney Countess of Pembroke).
Pasquils mad-cap and mad-cappes message. 1600, 1626.
The second part of Pasquil's mad-cap, intituled the fooles-cap. 1600, 1600 (as Pasquils fooles-cap).
Pasquils mistresse. 1600.
Pasquils passe, and passeth not. 1600.
Melancholike humours. 1600; ed S. E. Brydges 1815; ed G. B. Harrison 1929.
No whipping nor tripping. 1601; ed C. Edmonds 1895.
The strange fortunes of two excellent princes. 1600.
A divine poeme. 1601; ed S. E. Brydges, Excerpta tudoriana vol 2, 1817.
An excellent poeme. 1601; ed S. E. Brydges 1814.
The soules heavenly exercise. 1601.
The mothers blessing. 1602, 1621 (with addns).
Olde mad-cappes new gally-mawfrey. 1602.
The passion of a discontented minde. 1602.
A poste with a madde packet of letters. 1602, 1603 (with addns), 1605, 1605 (2nd pt), 1606, 1607 (with addns), 1609, 1613, 1620, 1623, 1630, 1633, 1634, 1637, 1650, 1660, 1669, 1678, 1685.
The soules harmony. 1602, 1622 (6th edn), 1630, 1635 (9th edn), 1676 (11th edn).
Wonders worth the hearing. 1602.
A true description of unthankfulnesse. 1602.
A dialogue full of pithe and pleasure. 1603.
A merrie dialogue betwixt the taker and the mistaker. 1603, 1635 (as A mad world my masters).
Grimellos fortunes. 1604; ed E. G. Morice, Two pamphlets, Bristol 1936.
The passionate shepheard. 1604; ed F. Ouvry 1877 (priv ptd).
A piece of Friar Bacons brazen-heads prophesie. 1604.
An olde mans lesson 1605; ed E. G. Morice, Two pamphlets, Bristol 1936.
Honest counsaile. 1605.
The honour of valour. 1605.
I pray you be not angrie. 1605, 1624, 1632.
The soules immortall crowne. 1605.
Choice, chance and change. 1606; ed A. B. Grosart, Manchester 1881.
A murmurer. 1607.
Wits private wealth. 1607, 1611, 1612, 1613, 1615, 1625, 1629, 1639, 1643, 1664, 1670 (7th edn).
Divine considerations of the soule. 1608.
The uncasing of Machivils instructions to his sonne. 1613, 1613, 1615, 1635 (abridged), 1681 (as Machiavil's advice).
I would and would not. 1614.
Characters upon essaies. 1615; ed S. E. Brydges, Archaica vol 1, 1815.
The good and the badde. 1616, 1643 (as Englands selected characters).
Crossing of proverbs. 1616, 1631.
Crossing of proverbs: the second part. [1616], 1632, 1668, [1670] (as The last part).
The hate of treason. 1616.
Machiavells dogge. 1617.
The Court and country. 1618; ed W. C. Hazlitt, Inedited tracts, 1868; ed S. Pargellis and W. H. Dunham jr, Complaint and reform in England 1436–1714, New York 1938.
Conceyted letters newly layde open. 1618, 1632, 1638.
Strange newes out of divers countries. 1622.
Soothing of proverbs. 1626.
Fantasticks. 1626; ed J. O. Halliwell-Phillipps, Books of

character, 1857 (extracts); ed B. Rhys, The twelve moneths, Waltham St Lawrence 1927 (extracts).
The figure of foure. 1631, 1636.
The figure of four: the second part. 1626, 1636, 1653 (as The last part), 1654.
Character of Queen Elizabeth. Ed J. Nichols, The progresses and public procession of Queen Elizabeth vol 2, 1788.

EDMUND SPENSER
1552?–99

Bibliographies etc

Osgood, C. G. A concordance to the poems of Spenser. Washington 1915, Gloucester Mass 1963.
Whitman, C. H. A subject-index to the poems of Spenser. New Haven 1918, New York 1966.
Carpenter, F. I. A reference guide to Spenser. Chicago 1923, New York 1950; A bibliographical supplement by D. F. Atkinson, Baltimore 1937, New York 1967; Annotated bibliography 1937–60 by W. F. McNeir and F. Provost, Pittsburgh 1962 (Duquesne Stud).
Johnson, F. R. A critical bibliography of the works of Spenser printed before 1700. Baltimore 1933, London 1966.

Collections

The Faerie Queen; The shepheards calendar; together with the other works of England's arch-poet Edm. Spenser, collected into one volume. 1611[–12, –13] (first folio), 1617.
The works of that famous English poet, Mr Edmond Spenser. 1679.
Works. Ed H. J. Todd 8 vols 1805 (with selection of notes from various commentators), 1 vol 1845, 1850 etc.
Poetical works. Ed J. C. Smith and E. de Selincourt 3 vols Oxford 1909–10 (with bibliographical and textual notes), 1 vol Oxford 1912 (OSA) (with Spenser-Harvey correspondence, abridged textual notes and essay by de Selincourt).
Works. Ed W. L. Renwick 4 vols 1928–34. With notes; omits Faerie Queene but includes all the other poems and A view).
Works. Ed W. L. Renwick 8 vols Oxford 1930–2.
Works: a variorum edition. Ed E. Greenlaw, C. G. Osgood, F. M. Padelford and R. Heffner 10 vols Baltimore 1932–49, 1958.

§1

A theatre [for] voluptuous worldlings, devised by S. John van-der-Noodt. 1569, New York 1936 (facs). Contains Epigrams and Sonets tr Spenser, rev in Complaints, 1591, below.
The shepheardes calender: conteyning twelve æglogues proportionable to the twelve moneths. 1579 (anon), 1581, 1586, 1591, 1597, 1653 (with Bathurst's Latin trn); ed H. O. Sommer 1890 (facs), New York 1967; ed C. H. Herford 1895 (with introd and notes); San Marino 1926 (facs of 1597); San Marino 1927 (facs of 1579); Menston 1968 (facs).
The Faerie Queene, disposed into twelve books, fashioning xii morall vertues. 1590 (bks 1–3). *For later edns see below.*
Complaints: containing sundrie small poemes of the worlds vanitie. 1591. Contains The ruines of time; The teares of the Muses; Virgils gnat; Prosopopoia: or Mother Hubberds tale; Ruines of Rome, by Bellay; Muiopotmos: or the fate of the butterflie (dated 1590); Visions of the worlds vanitie; The visions of Bellay; The visions of Petrarch.
Daphnaida: an elegie upon the death of the noble and vertuous Douglas Howard. 1591, 1596 (with Fowre hymnes), San Marino 1927 (facs).

Sonnet to M. Gabriell Harvey. Appended to Harvey's Foure letters, 1592; dated 1586.

Axiochus: a most excellent dialogue, written in Greeke by Plato, translated by Edw. Spenser. 1592; ed F. M. Padelford, Baltimore 1934.

Amoretti and Epithalamion. 1595; ed S. Lee, Elizabethan sonnets, 1904, New York 1964; ed C. Van Winkle, New York 1926 (Epithalamion only), London and New York 1927 (facs); Menston 1968 (facs); Epithalamion, ed E. Welsford, New York 1969 (with Fowre hymnes); New York 1969 (facs).

Colin Clouts come home againe 1595. Includes Astrophel: a pastorall elegie upon the death of Sidney, together with other poems on Sidney's death by other hands (The dolefull lay of Clorinda has been attributed to Spenser);

Commendatory sonnet prefixed to Nennio: or a treatise of nobility, written by Sir John Baptiste Nenna of Bari; done into English by William Jones 1595.

The Faerie Queene, disposed into twelve bookes, fashioning xii morall vertues. 2 vols 1596. Bks 1–3, first pbd 1590, with The second part containing books 4–6; *for later edns see below.*

Fowre hymnes. 1596 (with 2nd edn of Daphnaida); ed L. Winstanley, Cambridge 1907 (Hymnes only); San Marino 1927 (facs of 1596); ed E. Welsford, New York 1969 (with Epithalamion, essay and notes).

Prothalamion: or a spousall verse in honour of the double marriage of Ladie Elizabeth and Ladie Katherine Somerset. 1596, San Marino 1927 (facs).

Commendatory sonnet prefixed to the Historie of George Castriot surnamed Scanderbeg, newly translated out of French by Z.I. 1596.

Commendatory sonnet prefixed to the Commonwealth and government of Venice, written by the Cardinall Gasper Contareno and translated by Lewis Lewkenor. 1599.

The Faerie Queene. 1609 (containing first edn of fragment of bk vii or the Mutabilitie cantos); ed T. Birch 3 vols 1751 (with life); ed R. Church 4 vols 1758–9 (with notes); ed J. Upton 2 vols 1758 (with detailed notes); ed T. J. Wise 6 vols 1895–7; ed A. C. Hamilton 1977; ed T. P. Roche 1978 (Penguin).
Mutability cantos. Ed S. P. Zitner 1968.

A view of the present state of Ireland. In The historie of Ireland, ed J. Ware, Dublin 1633, 1763 etc, New York 1970; in Works, 1679, above; ed H. Morley 1890; ed W. L. Renwick, Works, 1928–34, above (modernized with notes); Oxford 1970 (with notes). Written 1596.

Letters

Three proper, and wittie, familiar letters. 1580; Two other, very commendable letters, 1580 (by Spenser and Gabriel Harvey); portions ed G. G. Smith, Elizabethan critical essays vol 1, Oxford 1904; Poetical works, Oxford 1912 (OSA), above.

§2

Jortin, J. Remarks on Spenser's poems. 1734, 1790 (expanded in his Tracts).

Spence, J. In his Polymetis, 1747.

Warton, T. Observations on the Faerie Queene. 1752, 1762 (enlarged), New York 1969.

Upton, J. Preface to the Faerie Queene. 1758.

Hurd, R. In his Letters on chivalry and romance, 1762.

Jones, H. S. V. A Spenser handbook. New York 1930.

Renwick, W. L. Edmund Spenser. 1952.

Greenlaw, E. Studies in Spenser's historical allegory. Baltimore 1932.

Spens, J. Spenser's Faerie Queene: an interpretation. 1934, New York 1967.

Lewis, C. S. In his Allegory of love, Oxford 1936.

—— Studies in medieval and Renaissance literature. Ed W. Hooper, Cambridge 1966. Includes Edmund Spenser (1954); On reading the Faerie Queene (1941);

Neoplatonism in the poetry of Spenser (1961); Spenser's cruel Cupid (previously unpbd); Genius and genius (1936).

—— Spenser's images of life. Ed A. Fowler, Cambridge 1967.

Williams, K. Spenser's Faerie Queene: the world of glass. 1966.

Hamilton, A. C. The structure of allegory in the Faerie Queene. Oxford 1961.

Hough, G. A preface to the Faerie Queene. 1962.

Fowler, A. D. S. Spenser and the numbers of time. 1964.

Kermode, J. F. In his Shakespeare, Spenser, Donne, 1971.

Tuve, R. Allegorical imagery: some mediaeval books and their posterity. Princeton 1966.

—— Essays: Spenser, Herbert, Milton. Ed T. P. Roche jr, Princeton 1970.

Alpers, P. J. The poetry of the Faerie Queene. Princeton 1967.

—— (ed). Spenser: a critical anthology. 1969 (Penguin).

Hamilton, A. C. (ed). Essential articles on Spenser. Hamden Conn 1972.

SIR PHILIP SIDNEY
1554–86
Collections

The Countesse of Pembrokes Arcadia: the third time published with new additions. 1598 (with Certaine sonets, Defence of poesie, Astrophel and Stella, Her most excellent Majestie [or Lady of May]), Edinburgh 1599, London 1605, 1613 (as 4th edn, with A dialogue betweene two shepherds), Dublin 1621 (with suppl by Sir W. A[lexander]—*see* Mitchell 1969 below; reissued London 1622, 1623), London 1627 (with Sixth booke by R. B[ellings] dated 1628, separately ptd Dublin 1624), reissued as 7th edn London 1629, 1633, 1638 (with 2nd suppl by Ja. Johnstoun), 1655 (with portrait, life, spurious Remedie for love), 1662 (11th edn), 1674 (as 13th edn), 3 vols 1724–5 (as Works, 14th edn, [ed J. Henley], with new life), Dublin 1739.

Englands Helicon. 1600, 1614. 14 poems.

Complete works. Ed A. Feuillerat 4 vols Cambridge 1912–26.

Poems. Ed W. A. Ringler jr, Oxford 1962.

Miscellaneous prose. Ed K. Duncan-Jones and J. van Dorsten, Oxford 1973.

§1

The Countesse of Pembrokes Arcadia. 1590 (3 bks, New Arcadia); ed H. O. Sommer 1891 (facs with bibliographical introd, rptd C. Dennis, Kent Ohio 1970); ed A. Feuillerat, Cambridge 1912 (with variants from 1593–1674 edns). The Arcadia augmented and ended 1593 (5 bks, last 3 from ms of Old Arcadia); ed A. Feuillerat 1922 (last 3 bks, with variants from 1598–1674 edns); 13 edns 1598–1739; Old Arcadia, ed. J. Robertson, Oxford 1973 (critical text with commentary); ed M. Evans 1977 (Penguin) (from 1593).

Syr P. S. his Astrophel and Stella; sundry other rare sonnets [by Daniel, Campion, Greville and anon]. 1591 (Newman; corrupt text); ed E. Flügel 1889; A. Feuillerat 1922 (with variants from Newman's 2nd quarto, BM ms additional 15,232, Arcadia 1598–1674), Menston 1970 (facs); [1597–1600] (Lownes; omits Newman's dedication and Nashe's preface); Sir P.S. his Astrophel and Stella, 1591 (Newman; partly corrected through sonnet 95, without prose preliminaries and Other sonnets). In Arcadia 1598 (from an authoritative ms); 12 edns 1599–1739; ed E. Arber, An English garner vol 1, 1877, rptd S. Lee, Elizabethan sonnets vol 1, 1904; ed A. W. Pollard 1888; ed M. Wilson 1931.

The defence of poesie. 1595 (Ponsonby); rptd in 13 edns of Arcadia 1598–1739; Glasgow 1752; [ed J. Warton] 1787 (with Jonson's Discoveries); ed A. Feuillerat 1923 (with variants from Olney, De L'Isle and Dudley ms, 1598–1674 Arcadia); 1928 (facs); Menston 1968 (facs); An apologie for poetrie, 1595 (Olney); ed E. Arber 1868; ed G. Gregory Smith, Elizabethan critical essays vol 1, Oxford 1904 (with valuable notes). Mss: Viscount De L'Isle and Dudley 1226; Norwich Public Lib, ptd M. R. Mahl, Northridge Cal 1969; substantive quotations in W. Temple's ms Analysis. More than 10 19th-century and 20 20th-century edns, many often rptd, of which the most useful are: ed A. S. Cook, Boston 1890; ed E. S. Shuckburgh, Cambridge 1891; ed G. Shepherd 1965 (with elaborate notes); ed J. A. van Dorsten, Oxford 1966 (modernized critical text without apparatus).

Certaine sonets. In 13 edns of Arcadia 1598–1739; Cleveland 1890, Boston 1904, London 1906 (with Defence of poesie), 1909 (with Defence of poesie).

[The lady of May]. In 13 edns of Arcadia 1598–1739; rptd J. Nichols, Progresses of Queen Elizabeth vol 1, 1788, 1823; ed E. W. Parks and R. C. Beatty, The English drama, New York 1935. Arthur A. Houghton jr (Helmingham Hall) ms, ed R. Kimbrough and P. Murphy, Renaissance Drama new ser 1 1968.

Defence of the Earl of Leicester. Pierpont Morgan Lib ms MA 1475 (holograph), ptd A. Collins, Letters and memorials of state vol 1, 1746.

Psalms (1–43 by Sidney, rest by the Countess of Pembroke). For 14 mss see Poems, ed Ringler, 1962, and Huntington Lib ms Ellesmere 11,636. The Psalmes of David, [ed S. W. Singer] 1823; J. Ruskin, Rock honeycomb, 1877 (selections with comment); ed J. C. A. Rathmell, Garden City NY 1963.

§ 2

Churchyard, T. The epitaph of Sidney. [1587]; rptd S. Butler, Sidneiana, 1837.

Academiae cantabrigiensis lachrymae. Ed A. Neville 1587.

Philip, J. The life and death of Sidney. 1587; rptd S. Butler, Sidneiana, 1837.

Whetstone, G. Sidney. [1587]; rptd A. Boswell, Frondes caducae, 1816.

Peplus. Ed J. Lloyd, Oxford 1587.

Exequiae. Ed W. Gager, Oxford 1587.

Epitaphia in mortem Sidneii. Ed G. Benedictus, Leyden 1587.

Lant, T. Sequitur celebritas et pompa funeris. 1588. 30 engravings of funeral.

Fraunce, A. The Arcadian rhetorike: made plaine by examples out of Homer, Virgil, Sydnei, Tasso, Salust, Boscan and Garcilasso. [1588]; ed E. Seaton, Oxford 1950 (Luttrell Soc).

Moffet, T. Nobilis [1589]; Lessus lugubris 1593. Ms ed and tr V. B. Heltzel and H. H. Hudson, San Marino 1940.

Breton, N. Amoris lachrimae. In Brittons bowre of delights, 1591; ed H. E. Rollins, Cambridge Mass 1933.

Stow, J. In his Annales of England, 1592. On Netherlands campaign.

Spenser, E. Colin Clouts come home again; Astrophel: a pastorall elegie upon the death of Sidney (with other elegies by L. B[ryskett, M. Roydon, Sir W. Ralegh] and anon [last 3 rptd from Phoenix nest 1593]). 1595.

Hoskyns, J. Directions for speech and style exemplified out of Arcadia [written 1599]; ed H. H. Hudson, Princeton 1935 (from ms).

Greville, F. The life of Sidney. 1652; ed N. Smith, Oxford 1907. Written 1610–12.

Aubrey, J. In his Lives, 1813. Written c. 1687.

Winstanley, W. In his Lives of the most famous English poets, 1687.

Wood, A. In his Athenae oxonienses vol 1, 1691; with addns by P. Bliss 1813.

Zouch, T. Memoirs of the life and writings of Sidney. York 1808, 1809.

Lamb, C. Defence of Sidney's sonnets. London Mag Sept 1823; rptd in his Last essays of Elia, 1833.

Bourne, H. R. Fox. A memoir of Sidney. 1862.

Wallace, M. W. The life of Sidney. Cambridge 1915.

Zandvoort, R. W. Sidney's Arcadia: a comparison between the two versions. Amsterdam 1929.

Wilson, M. Sidney. 1931.

Kalstone, D. Sidney's poetry: contexts and interpretations. Cambridge Mass 1965.

Osborn, J. M. Young Philip Sidney 1572–7. New Haven 1972. A biography with trns of letters from Languet et al.

Hamilton, A. C. Sidney: a study of his life and works. Cambridge 1977.

FULKE GREVILLE, 1st BARON BROOKE

1554–1628

Collections

Certaine learned and elegant workes written in his youth and familiar exercise with Sir Philip Sidney. 1633. Humane learning, Fame and honour, Warres, Alaham, Mustapha, Caelica, 2 prose letters to a lady and G. Varney.

The remains: poems of monarchy and religion. 1670; ed G. A. Wilkes, Oxford 1965 (from ms).

The works in verse and prose complete. Ed A. B. Grosart 4 vols Blackburn 1870 (Fuller Worthies' Lib).

Poems and dramas. Ed G. Bullough 2 vols Edinburgh [1939], New York 1945. Contents of 1633 Workes, above, except prose, from mss.

Selected poems. Ed T. Gunn, Chicago 1968. Caelica and 5 choruses.

Selected writings. Ed J. Rees 1973.

§ 1

The tragedy of Mustapha. 1609; rptd R. Dodsley, A collection of old plays vol 2, 1744.

Caelica. In Workes, 1633; ed M. F. Crow, Elizabethan sonnet cycles vol 4, 1898; ed U. M. Ellis-Fermor, Newtown 1936. No 29 attributed to E.O. in Other sonnets appended to Syr P.S. his Astrophel and Stella, 1591, [1597–1600]; no 52 in J. Dowland, The first booke of songes or ayres, 1597; no 1 in M. Cavendish, Ayres in tabletorie, 1598; no 52 anon in Englands Helicon, 1600, 1614 (with 2 other poems, nos 77 and 79 in H. E. Rollins edn 1935, attributed to M.F.G. but cancelled as Ignoto); no 29 in J. Dowland, The second booke of songs or ayres, 1600; 13 Caelica poems and another on death of Greville in M. Peerson, Mottects, 1630.

The life of the renowned Sir Philip Sidney. 1652; ed S. E. Brydges 2 vols Lee Priory 1816; ed N. Smith, Oxford 1907.

§ 2

Croll, M. The works of Greville. Philadelphia 1903.

Rebholz, R. A. The life of Greville. Oxford 1971.

Rees, J. Greville: a critical biography. 1971.

ROBERT SOUTHWELL SJ

c. 1561–95

Collections

S. Peters complaint; Saint Mary Magdalens funerall teares [prose]; sundry other poems, by R. S. [St Omer] 1616, 1620.

St Peters complaint; Mary Magdal[ens] teares [prose];

with other workes by R.S. 1620 (set up from 1615 Saint Peters complaint and 1595 Moeniae, adds prose Mary Magdalens teares, Triumphs over death, and Short rules of good life), 1630, 1636 (for 1634); ed W. B. Turnbull 1856 (as Poetical works, from 1636 poems and ms, with memoir).

Complete poems. Ed A. B. Grosart 1872 (with memoir).
Complete works. 1876. Omits Epistle of comfort.
Poems. Ed J. H. McDonald and N. P. Brown, Oxford 1967. Standard edn.

§ I

Marie Magdalens funerall teares. 1591, 1592, 1594, 1602, 1609; ed W. Tooke 1772; rptd 1823 (from 1636, above), 1827. Prose.
Saint Peters complaint; other poemes. 1595, 1595 (rev with 8 new poems), 1595, 1597, 1599, Edinburgh [1599], 1634, London 1602 ('newlie augmented' with 7 new poems), [1607–9], 1615 (all anon); ed W. J. Walter 1817 (from 1595 and ms, with memoir).
Moeniae: or certaine excellent poemes omitted in the last impression of Peters complaint, all composed by R.S. 1595 (3 edns).
The triumphs over death. 1595, 1596, 1596; rptd S. E. Brydges in Archaica vol 1, 1815; ed J. W. Trotman 1914 (from ms). Prose.
A short rule of good life; Advice of a sonne. [1596–7?], [1598?], St Omer 1622. Advice of a sonne rptd 1632 (4 edns), 1633, 1636. Anon; prose. See col 299, below.
An epistle of comfort. Paris [1604?], [no place], 1605, [St Omer] 1616; ed M. Waugh 1965. Anon; prose.
An humble supplication to her Majestie. [English secret press] 1595 (for 1601?) (anon); ed R. C. Bald, Cambridge 1953. Prose, written 1591.
A hundred meditations on the love of God. Ed J. Morris 1873 (from ms). Prose trn of Diego de Estella.
[A foure-fold meditation, by R.S. 1606; ed C. Edmonds 1895, who attributes it to Southwell, is probably by Philip Howard, Earl of Arundel.]

§ 2

Devlin, C. The life of Southwell, poet and martyr. 1956.

SAMUEL DANIEL
1563–1619

Collections

Delia; An ode; the Complaint of Rosamond. 1592, 1592, Menston 1969 (facs); ed J. P. Collier 1870.
Delia and Rosamond augmented; Cleopatra. 1594, 1595, 1598.
Poeticall essayes. 1599. Sheets of 1595 Civile wars (5 bks), Musophilus, Letter from Octavia, Cleopatra, Rosamond.
Works. 1601, 1602. Contents of 1599, above, and 6th bk of Civil wars, Delia (57 sonnets), An ode, A pastorall.
A panegyrike congratulatorie to the Kings Majestie; certaine epistles (to Sir Tho. Egerton, Lord Henry Howard, Margaret Countesse of Cumberland, Lucie Countesse of Bedford, Lady Anne Clifford, Henry Earle of Southampton); A defence of ryme. [1603], 1603, Menston 1969 (facs).
Certaine small poems; the Tragedie of Philotas. 1605. Letter from Octavia, Cleopatra, Rosamond, An ode, A pastorall, Ulisses and the Syren, Philotas.
Certaine small workes. 1607 (contents of 1605, above, except Philotas, with Musophilus, Queenes Arcadia, Funerall poeme upon the Earle of Devonshire), 1611 (with Delia, Philotas).
The tragedie of Philotas. 1607. Philotas, A panegyrike congratulatorie, Certaine epistles, The passion of a distressed man, A defence of ryme.

The whole workes in poetrie. 1623 (sheets of 1609 Civile wares; contents of 1607 Philotas, except Defence of ryme, and 1611 Workes; with A description of beauty, To the angell spirit of Sr Phillip Sidney [by Mary Herbert Countess of Pembroke], Letter to a worthy Countesse, To James Montague Bishop of Winchester, Hymens triumph, Vision of the twelve goddesses—edited by Daniel's brother John), 1635 (sheets Aa–Tt8 reissued as Drammaticke poems).
The poetical works of Mr S. Daniel. 2 vols 1718 (from 1623, above); rptd in [R. Anderson], Poets of Great Britain vol 4, Edinburgh 1793; A. Chalmers, English poets vol 3, 1810.
Complete works in verse and prose. Ed A. B. Grosart 5 vols 1885–96, New York 1963.
Poems and A defence of ryme. Ed A. C. Sprague, Cambridge Mass 1930.

§ I

The worthy tract of Paulus Jovius contayning a discourse of imprese. 1585. Prose trn of Dialogo dell' imprese militari et amorose, 1555.
Syr P. S. his Astrophel and Stella; other sonnets of divers gentlemen. 1591, [1597–1600], Menston 1970 (facs). Other sonnets, which include 28 by Daniel, rptd E. Arber, An English garner vol 1, 1877; S. Lee, Elizabethan sonnets vol 1, 1904.
Delia. In collections, above, 1592 (50 sonnets), 1592 (54 sonnets), 1594 (55 sonnets), 1595, 1598, 1601 (57 sonnets), 1611, 1623; ed E. Arber, An English garner vol 3, 1880; ed M. F. Crow, Elizabethan sonnet cycles vol 2, 1896; ed S. Lee, Elizabethan sonnets vol 2, 1904; ed A. Esdaile 1908 (with Drayton's Idea).
Rosamond. In collections, above, 1592, 1592, 1594, 1595, 1601, 1611, 1623; ed N. Alexander, Elizabethan narrative verse, 1967.
The tragedie of Cleopatra. In collections, above, 1594, 1595, 1599, 1601, 1605, 1607, 1611, 1623; rptd Glasgow 1751; ed M. Lederer, Louvain 1911 (from 1611); ed G. Bullough, Narrative and dramatic sources of Shakespeare vol 5, 1964 (from 1599).
The first fowre bookes of the civile warrs; the fift booke. 1595; rptd in Poeticall essayes, 1599; Works, 1601 (with 6th bk); The civile wares corrected and continued, 1609 (8 bks); ed L. Michel, New Haven 1958.
Musophilus. In collections, above, 1599, 1601, 1607, 1611, 1623; ed R. Himelick, West Lafayette Ind [1965].
Letter from Octavia. In collections, above, 1599, 1601, 1605, 1607, 1611, 1623.
A panegyrike congratulatorie. [1603]; in collections, above, [1603], 1603, 1607, 1623; rptd J. Nichols, Progresses of James I vol 1, 1828.
A defence of ryme. In collections, above, [1603], 1603, 1607, 1623; ed J. Haslewood, Ancient critical essays vol 2, 1815; ed E. Rhys, Literary pamphlets vol 1, 1897; ed G. G. Smith, Elizabethan critical essays vol 2, Oxford 1904; ed E. D. Jones, English critical essays, Oxford 1922; ed G. B. Harrison 1925 (with Campion's Observations), Edinburgh 1966.
The true description of a royal masque. 1604 (surreptitious edn); The vision of the 12 goddesses, 1604; rptd in Workes, 1623; ed J. Nichols, Progresses of James I vol 1, 1828; ed E. Law 1880; ed H. A. Evans, English masques, 1897; ed J. Rees, A book of masques in honour of A. Nicoll, Cambridge 1967.
The tragedie of Philotas. In collections, above, 1605, 1607, 1611, 1623; ed L. Michel, New Haven 1949.
The Queenes Arcadia: a pastorall trage-comedie. 1606; rptd in Workes, 1607, 1611, 1623.
A funerall poeme upon the Earle of Devonshyre. [1606]; rptd in Workes, 1607, 1611, 1623.
Danyel, J. Songs for the lute, viol and voice. 1606. Music for 2 poems.
Tethys festival [a masque]. In The order of the creation of Prince Henrie, Prince of Wales, 1610; rptd Somers

tracts vol 1, 1750, vol 2, 1809; J. Nichols, Progresses of James I vol 2, 1828.

The first part of the historie of England. 1612 (to Stephen), 1613; The collection of the historie of England, [1618] (to Edward III), 1621, 1621, 1626, 1626, 1634, 1650 (with J. Trussell's continuation), 1685; in A complete history of England vol 1, 1706, 1719. Prose.

Hymens triumph: a pastorall tragicomaedie. 1615; rptd in Workes, 1623; partly rptd J. Nichols, Progresses of James I vol 2, 1828.

An introduction to a breviary of the history of England. 1693. Prose; attributed to Sir W. Ralegh.

The prayse of private life. Ed N. E. McClure, Letters and epigrams of Sir John Harington, Philadelphia 1930. Prose paraphrase of Petrarch, De vita solitaria. Attributed to Daniel.

§2

Oldmixon, J. Reply to the Bp of Rochester's vindication: an account of the alterations in Daniel's History. 1732.

Rees, J. Daniel: a critical and biographical study. Liverpool 1964.

MICHAEL DRAYTON
1563–1631

Bibliographies etc

Juel-Jensen, B. Bibliography of the early editions of Drayton. In Works of Drayton vol 5, ed Hebel, Tillotson and Newdigate, Oxford 1961.

Tannenbaum, S. A. Drayton: a concise bibliography. New York 1941; G. R. Guffey, Supplement 1941–65, 1967.

Donow, H. S. A concordance to the sonnet sequences of Daniel, Drayton, Shakespeare, Sidney and Spenser. Carbondale 1969.

Collections

The tragicall legend of Robert Duke of Normandy; The legend of Matilda; The legend of Peirs Gaveston, the latter two newly corrected and augmented. 1596.

Englands heroicall epistles newly corrected; Idea. 1600, 1602.

The barrons wars [revised text of Mortimeriados]; Englands heroicall epistles [reissue of 1602, above]. 1603.

Poems. 1605 (Barrons warres; Englands heroicall epistles; Idea (63 sonnets); legends of Robert, Matilda and Gaveston, 1888 (Spenser Soc), 1608 (newly corrected), 1610, 1613, [c. 1616], 1619 (2 issues; with Cromwell and rev contents of 1606? Poemes lyrick and pastorall), 1630, 1637, Menston 1969 (facs of 1619).

Poemes lyrick and pastorall: Odes; Eglogs; The man in the moone. [1606?], 1891 (Spenser Soc).

The battaile of Agincourt [different from the Ballad]; The miseries of Queene Margarite; Nimphidia; The quest of Cinthia; The shepheards Sirena; The moone-calfe; Elegies upon sundry occasions. 1627, 1631, Menston 1970 (facs of 1627).

The Muses Elizium: ten nymphalls; Noahs floud; Moses his birth and miracles [revision of 1604 Moyses]; David and Golia. 1630, 1892 (Spenser Soc).

Works. [Ed C. Coffey] 1748 (Agincourt from 1627 or 1631, Polyolbion, Poems from 1630 or 1637); Appendix, [c. 1752] (Owl, Man in the moon, Odes and Eclogues from 1619, Muses elysium from 1630), 4 vols 1753 (reprint of 1748 and Appendix).

Complete works. Ed J. W. Hebel 4 vols Oxford 1931–3; vol 5, 1941 (variant readings by J. W. Hebel, introds and notes by K. Tillotson and B. H. Newdigate, bibliography by G. Tillotson), 5 vols 1961 (with new bibliography by B. Juel-Jensen). The standard edn.

Poems. Ed J. Buxton 2 vols 1953 (ML).

§1

The harmonie of the Church: spirituall songes and holy hymnes. 1591, 1610 (as A heavenly harmonie); ed A. Dyce 1843 (Percy Soc).

Idea: the shepheards garland in nine eglogs. 1593; ed J. P. C[ollier] [1870] (facs).

Peirs Gaveston. [1593–4], [1595?]; rptd in collections, above, 1596, 1605, 1608, 1610, 1613, [c. 1616], 1619, 1630, 1637.

Ideas mirrour: amours in quaterzains. 1594 (51 sonnets); rptd in collections, above (as Idea, rev and expanded), 1599, 1600, 1602, 1605, 1608, 1610, 1613, [c. 1616], 1619, 1630, 1637; ed E. Arber, An English garner vol 6, 1883; ed M. F. Crow, Elizabethan sonnet cycles vol 3, 1897; ed S. Lee, Elizabethan sonnets vol 2, 1904; ed A. Esdaile 1908 (with Daniel's Delia). A total of 103 sonnets with 4 other poems.

Matilda, the daughter of Lord Fitzwater. 1594, 1594; rptd in collections above, 1596, 1605, 1608, 1610, 1613, [c. 1616], 1619, 1630, 1637.

Endimion and Phoebe: Ideas Latmus. 1595; ed J. P. C[ollier] [1870] (facs); ed J. W. Hebel, Oxford 1925; ed E. S. Donno, Elizabethan minor epics, New York 1963.

Mortimeriados: the civell warres of Edward the Second and the barrons. 1596, [1596?]; rev as The barrons wars in collections, above, 1603, 1605, 1608, 1610, 1613, [c. 1616], 1619, 1630, 1637.

Englands heroicall epistles. 1597, 1598 (enlarged), 1599; rptd in collections, above, 1605, 1608, 1610, 1613, [c. 1616], 1619, 1630, 1637; separately rptd nd, 1697 (same setting of type), 1737, 1788; epistles of Rosamond and Henry tr Latin by N. Hookes in Amanda, 1653.

The first part of the historie of Sir John Oldcastle. 1600, 1600 (for 1619); in W. Shakespear's Comedies, histories and tragedies, 1664 (2nd issue of 3rd folio), 1685 (4th folio); ed C. F. T. Brooke, The Shakespeare apocrypha, Oxford 1908; ed P. Simpson, Oxford 1908 (Malone Soc). A play written with A. Munday, R. Hathway and R. Wilson.

Englands Helicon. 1600, 1614; ed H. E. Rollins, Cambridge Mass 1935. 5 poems: nos 7, 14, 56, 74, 126.

To the Majestie of King James: a gratulatorie poem. 1603, 1603, Amsterdam 1969 (facs).

Moyses in a map of his miracles. 1604; rptd in The Muses elizium, 1630 (as Moses his birth and miracles).

The owle. 1604 (4 edns); rptd in collections, above, 1619, 1630, 1637.

A paean triumphall for the societie of goldsmiths congratulating his Highnes entring the citie. 1604; rptd J. Nichols, Progresses of King James vol 1, 1828.

The legend of great Cromwell. 1607, 1609 (as The historie of the life and death of the Lord Cromwell); rptd in A mirour for magistrates, 1610; in collections, above, 1619, 1630, 1637.

Poly-Olbion [pt 1]. [1612], 1613, 1622 (18 songs with notes by J. Selden); pt 2, 1622 (songs 19–30); [c. 1630] (both pts reissued as The faerie land), 1889–90 (Spenser Soc).

Ward, J. The first set of English madrigals. 1613. 3 songs, with music by Ward.

Certain elegies done by sundrie excellent wits; satyres and epigrams [by H. Fitzgeffrey]. 1618, 1620 (on Lady P. Clifton and sons of Lord Sheffield); rptd in collections, above, 1627, 1631.

The ballad of Agincourt. In 1606? collection, above; rptd B.H.N[ewdigate], Oxford 1926 (with Ode to the Virginian voyage); [ed B. Juel-Jensen] Oxford 1951 (from 1619 with new holograph stanza from R. Butcher's copy).

The battaile of Agincourt. In 1627 collection, above; ed R. Garnett 1893.

Epistle to H. Reynolds. In 1627 collection, above; ed J. E. Spingarn, Seventeenth-century critical essays,

Oxford 1908; tr Greek by H. Stubbe in Deliciae poetarum anglicanorum in graecum verse, Oxford 1658.
Nymphidia. In 1627 collection, above; rptd as The history of Queen Mab: the story upon which the entertainment now exhibiting at Drury-lane is founded, 1751, 1751; ed S. E. Brydges, Lee Priory 1814; ed J. Gray 1896 (with the Muses elizium); ed H. F. B. Brett-Smith, Oxford 1921; ed J. C. Squire, Oxford 1924.
The quest of Cynthia. In 1627 collection, above; rptd [1923] (Medici Soc).

§2

Elton, O. An introduction to Drayton. 1895 (Spenser Soc).
—— Drayton: a critical study. 1905, New York 1966.
Newdigate, B. H. Drayton and his circle. Oxford 1941.

THOMAS CAMPION
1567–1620
Collections

Works. Ed P. S. Vivian, Oxford 1909. Complete, with biography.
Works: complete songs, masques and treatises, selection of Latin verse. Ed W. R. Davis, Garden City NY 1967. With trns of Latin verse.

§1

Syr P.S. his Astrophel and Stella; other sonnets of divers gentlemen. 1591, [1597–1600], Menston 1970 (facs). Includes 5 songs signed Content, identified as Campion's by G. C. Moore Smith in his edn of A. Fraunce, Victoria, 1906.
Poemata: Ad Thamesin; Fragmentum umbrae; Liber elegiarum; Liber epigrammatum. 1595.
A booke of ayres to be song to the lute, orpherian and base violl by P. Rosseter. 1601; music ed E. H. Fellowes, English school of lutenist song writers, 1st ser 4, 13, 1922; words ed E. H. Fellowes, English madrigal verse, Oxford 1920, rev F. W. Sternfeld and D. Greer, Oxford 1967. Words and music of pt 1 by Campion.
Observations in the art of English poesie. 1602; ed G. Gregory Smith, Elizabethan critical essays vol 2, Oxford 1904; ed G. B. Harrison 1925, Edinburgh 1966 (with Daniel's Defence of ryme); Menston 1968 (facs of 1602).
The discription of a maske at White-Hall in honour of the Lord Hayes and his bride; other small poemes. 1607; rptd J. Nichols, Progresses of James I vol 2, 1828; ed K. Talbot 1924 (for a production at Hatfield); Amsterdam 1969 (facs of 1607).
The first booke of ayres. [1613?].
Two bookes of ayres. [c. 1613]; music ed E. H. Fellowes, English school of lutenist song writers, 2nd ser 1–2, 1925; words ed E. H. Fellowes, English madrigal verse, Oxford 1920, rev F. W. Sternfeld and D. Greer, Oxford 1967.
A relation of the entertainment given by Lord Knowles; the lords maske on the marriage night of the Count Palatine and the Ladie Elizabeth. 1613; rptd J. Nichols, Progresses of James I vol 2, 1828; Lords maske ed H. A. Evans, English masques, 1897; ed I. A. Shapiro, A book of masques in honour of A. Nicoll, Cambridge 1967.
Songs of mourning bewailing the death of Prince Henry. 1613.
A new way of making fowre parts in counterpoint. [c. 1614]; rptd J. Playford, Brief introduction to the skill of musick, 1660, 1661, 1667, 1671.
The description of a maske at the mariage of the Earle of Somerset; ayres by severall authors sung in the maske. 1614; rptd J. Nichols, Progresses of James I vol 2, 1828.
The third and fourth booke of ayres. [1617?]; music ed

E. H. Fellowes, English school of lutenist song writers, 2nd ser 10–1, 1926; words ed E. H. Fellowes, in his English madrigal verse, Oxford 1920, rev F. W. Sternfeld and D. Greer, Oxford 1967.
Ayres that were sung and played at Brougham Castle. 1618; words rptd E. H. Fellowes, English madrigal verse, Oxford 1920, rev F. W. Sternfeld and D. Greer, Oxford 1967. 10 songs with music by G. Mason and J. Earsden, words possibly by Campion.
Epigrammatum libri II; Umbra; Elegiarum liber unus. 1619, [1628–9].
A friends advice in [a] ditty concerning the variable changes in this world. [c. 1625?], [after 1640].
The man of life upright, illustrated by R. Graham. Leicester 1962. From R. Alison, An howres recreation in musicke, 1606.

§2

Daniel, S. A defence of ryme. [1603]. Reply to Observations.
Lowbury, E., T. Salter and A. Young. Campion: poet, composer, physician. 1970.

SIR JOHN DAVIES
1569–1626
Collections

Nosce teipsum; Hymnes of Astraea. 1619.
Nosce teipsum; Hymnes of Astraea; Orchestra. 1622.
On the immortality of the soul [Nosce teipsum, from Tate's edn] with an essay by Dr T. Sheridan; A discovery of the causes why Ireland was never entirely subdued [prose]. Dublin 1733.
Works in prose and verse. Ed A. B. Grosart 3 vols Blackburn 1869–76.
Complete poems. Ed A. B. Grosart 2 vols 1876.
Poems. Ed C. Howard, New York 1941. Facs of Orchestra, Nosce teipsum, Astraea, Epigrames, and reprint of Gulling sonnets.
Poems. Ed R. Krueger and R. Nemser, Oxford 1974 (from mss).

§1

Orchestra: a poeme of dauncing. 1596; ed R. S. Lambert, Wembley Hill 1922; ed E. M. W. Tillyard 1945.
Epigrammes and elegies by J. D[avies] and C.M[arlowe]. Middleburg [Edinburgh? 1598?], [1599?], Menston 1970 (facs of first edn); Ovids elegies: three bookes by C.M.; Epigrames by J.D., 'Middleburg' [i.e. London c. 1600] (2 edns), [c. 1630], [c. 1640]; ed C. F. T. Brooke, Works of Marlowe, Oxford 1910; 1925 (Haslewood Books).
Hymns of Astraea in acrosticke verse. 1599.
Nosce teipsum in two elegies: of humane knowledge, of the soule of man. 1599 (2 edns), 1602, 1608; ed T. Jenner 1653 (pt 2 only, as A work for none but angels and men), 1682; ed W. R[avenhill] 1688; ed N. Tate 1697, 1714, 1715, Glasgow 1749; ed E. Capell, Prolusions, 1760.
A poetical rapsody. Ed F. Davison 1602 (contains A hymne in prayse of musicke, ten sonnets to Philomel), 1608 (with Yet other 12 wonders of the world, A lotterie 1601, A contention betwixt a wife a widdowe and a maide), 1611, 1621. The xii wonders of the world rptd with music by J. Maynard 1611; ed E. V. Utterson, Ryde 1842 (without music). A lotterie rptd with music by R. Jones, Ultimum vale, 1608; Conway ms version, Shakespeare Soc Papers 2 1845.
Gullinge sonnets. Chetham ms 8012; ed A. B. Grosart, Dr Farmer Chetham ms vol 1, Manchester 1873.
Epithalamion: 10 sonnets on marriage of Elizabeth Vere to William Stanley Earl of Derby 1595. Ed R. Krueger, RES new ser 13 1962 (from ms).

§2

Tillyard, E. M. W. Orchestra. In his Five poems, 1948.

Simpson, P. Unprinted epigrams of Davies. RES new ser 3 1952.

Eliot, T. S. In his On poetry and poets, 1957.

Sanderson, J. L. Unpublished epigrams of Davies. RES new ser 12 1961.

Krueger, R. Orchestra complete, epigrams, unpublished poems. RES new ser 13 1962.

Wilkes, G. A. The poetry of Davies. HLQ 25 1962.

Spencer, T. Two classic Elizabethans: Daniel and Davies. In his Selected essays, New Brunswick NJ 1966.

III. THE ELIZABETHAN SONNET

The Earliest English Sonnets to 1590

This list attempts to be complete. J. Bale (Index, ed Poole p. 66) said that Edmund first Baron Sheffield (d. 1549) wrote 'Sonettos Italico more', but no trace of these remains. Thomas Warton, History of English poetry vol 3, 1781, p. 58, said on the authority of Oldys that 'Henry Lord Berners translated some of Petrarch's sonnets'; there was no Henry Lord Berners, and John Bourchier Lord Berners (d. 1533) is not known to have written verse. Warton's mention (p. 58) of a ms owned by Lord Eglinton containing sonnets by Henry VIII refers to BM ms additional 31,922 which contains no quatorzains. The anon sonnet ptd from a ms of G. Bowes by Wright and Halliwell, Reliquiae antiquae vol 2, 1843, is by Gascoigne.

Wyatt, Sir Thomas (d. 1542): 29 (24 in BM ms Egerton 2711, 5 more in R. Tottel, Songes and sonettes, 1557, in Rollins' edn nos 75, 84, 101 (double), 102, plus 3 rondeaux rewritten as sonnets, nos 69–70, 103); all ptd G. F. Nott, Works of Surrey and Wyatt vol 2, 1816.

BM ms additional 17,492 (Devonshire ms): 4 (3 anon, folios 75, 77, 81, ptd as Wyatt's by Nott pp. 143–5; one by E.K. [Sir Edmund Knyvet d. 1546], ptd K. Muir, Proc Leeds Philosophical Soc 6 1947).

Surrey, Earl of, Henry Howard (d. 1547): 15 (14 in Tottel; Tottel no 9 is not Surrey's; one in W. Camden, Remaines, 1605); rptd G. F. Nott, Works of Surrey and Wyatt vol 1, 1815.

Lambeth ms 265, folio 106: one in Surreyan form by 'TER' in early 16th-century hand?; ptd C. F. Bühler, MLN 72 1957.

Baldwin, William (d. 1563): one in C. Langton, Treatise of phisick, 1547; rptd T. W. Camp, MLN 52 1937.

Morley, Lord, Henry Parker (d. 1556): one in BM ms Royal A xv, probably before 1547, ptd E. Flügel, Anglia 13 1891; cf his Epitaph on Lord Delaware (d. 1554) in G. Legh, Accedens of armory, 1562 (15 lines), rptd J. Loveday, 1887 (Roxburghe Club).

Hall, John (d. 1566?): one in his The proverbes of Salomon, [1549] A5; rptd as anon in Tottel, no 285; see H. E. Rollins, TLS 14 Jan 1932.

Cambridge University Library ms Mm.3.12 p. 287: one anon on Bp W. Rugg, c. 1549.

BM ms additional 36,529, folios 44ᵛ–8 and 66ᵛ: 14 anon mid 16th-century; 12 ptd K. Muir, Proc Leeds Philosophical Soc 6 1950.

Bieston, Roger: one in his The bayte and snare of fortune, [1550?] B4ᵛ.

Trinity College Dublin ms D.2.7 (Blage ms): 3 anon before 1551; ptd K. Muir, Unpublished poems from the Blage ms, Liverpool 1960, pp. 6, 9, 17.

Whythorne, Thomas (d. 1596): one in Bodley ms English Miscellaneous c. 33, written c. 1555; ptd J. M. Osborn, The autobiography of Whythorne, Oxford 1961, p. 70.

Vaux?, Baron, Thomas (d. 1556): one in Tottel, no 9 (attributed to 'L Vawse' in BM ms additional 28,635 folio 139ᵛ).

Grimald, Nicholas (d. 1562): 3 in Tottel, nos 137, 146, 156.

Tottel, R. Songes and sonnettes 1557: 9 anon (nos 173, 179, 186, 218–19, 232–3, 241, 300).

Harington? John, the elder (d. 1582): 2 written after 1558 ptd in Nugae antiquae, ed H. Harington 1769 pp. 87, 198.

Anon: 26 in A meditation of a penitent sinner in maner of a paraphrase upon the 51 psalme, appended to A.L., Sermon of Calvin upon Ezechias, 1560.

Dorset, Earl of, Thomas Sackville (d. 1608): one in T. Hoby's trn of Castiglione's Courtyer, 1561; rptd E. Flügel, Anglia 13 1891.

Blundeville, Thomas: one written 1561 in his Three morall treatises 1580 B5ᵛ.

Broke, Arthur (d. 1563): 5 (3 in his Tragicall historye of Romeus and Juliet, 1562; rptd P. A. Daniel 1875 (New Shakespeare Soc); 2 in L. Humphrey, The nobles, 1563; ed V. B. Heltzel, Shakespeare Quart 22 1971).

Googe, Barnabe (d. 1594): 3 in his Eglogs, epytaphes and sonettes, 1563 (2 by Googe and one tailed by L. Blundeston); ed E. Arber 1871 pp. 95, 98, 105; cf 91. See H. H. Hudson, Poetry of the English Renaissance, New York 1929 p. 952, and P. N. U. Hartung, E Studies 11 1929.

Garter, Bernard (fl. 1563–78): 3 in his Tragicall historie between two English lovers 1563, 1565.

Gascoigne, George (d. 1577): 37 (one in his Jocasta 1566, ptd 1575, 31 in his A hundreth sundrie flowres 1573, one even in his Posies 1575, one in his Hemetes the heremyte [BM ms Royal 18A.xlviii 1576], one in 2nd edn of [T. Bedingfield's] trn of Cardanus comforte 1576, one in Sir Humphrey Gilbert, A discourse of a new passage to Cataia 1576, one in C. Holyband, Frenche Littleton [1576]); all rptd in Works of Gascoigne, ed J. W. Cunliffe 2 vols Cambridge 1907–10.

Fulwood, W.: one in his Enimie of idlenesse, 1568 A5.

Fyldinge, Ferdinand: one in T. Jeney, Discours of the present troobles in France, 1568 D4ᵛ; ed J. A. van Dorsten, The radical arts, Leyden 1970.

Spenser, Edmund (d. 1599): 87 (2 in J. van der Noodt, A theatre [of] worldlings 1569 (with 14 unrhymed quatorzains), one written c. 1580 in ms (Cambridge Univ Dd.5.75 folio 37ᵛ, Bodley Rawlinson Poetry 85 folio 7ᵛ, BM Harley 1392 (2) folio 28, later ptd as Amoretti no 8; see L. Cummings, Stud in Eng Lit 1500–1900 4 1964), one dated 1586 in G. Harvey, Foure letters 1592, 17 in his Faerie Queene 1590, 66 in his Complaints 1591 (entered 1590, with 2 ptd 1569]). Written later: 87 more in his Amoretti 1595, 3 commendatory 1595, 1596, 1599; all rptd in Poetical works, ed Smith and de Selincourt 3 vols Oxford 1909–10.

Arundel Harington ms: 4 anon written in 1560's?; ed R. Hughey, Columbus 1960, nos 146, 150, 256, 258.

Goodyer, Sir Henry (d. 1595) and Thomas Norton (d. 1584): 6 written 1572 (3 each in Bodley ms Gough Norfolk 43 folio 53ᵛ (ed J. P. Collier, Camden Miscellany 3 1855), Arundel Harington ms ed Hughey nos 147–8, and Goodyer's 3 only in Marsh's Library Dublin ms Z.3.5.21 folios 2–3).

Tusser, Thomas (d. 1580): 2 in his Five hundreth points of good husbandry 1573; ed W. Payne and S. J. Herrtage 1878 (English Dialect Soc) pp. 150–1.

M.C. and R.S.: 2 (one each in Gascoigne's Posies 1575); rptd Cunliffe vol 1, 1907.

Bowyer, Nicholas: one in Gascoigne's Steele glas 1576; rptd Cunliffe vol 2, 1910.

E.S.: one in Paradyse of daynty devises 1576; ed H. E. Rollins, Cambridge Mass 1927, no 38.

Sidney, Sir Philip (d. 1586): 139+3? (18 in his Old Arcadia 1577–80, 13 in his Certain sonnets 1577–81, 108 in his Astrophel and Stella c. 1582, 2 possibly his in H. Goldwel, A briefe declaration [1581]; see E. G. Fogel, MLN 75 1960; one possibly his in Bodley ms Rawlinson Poetry 85); all rptd in Poems, ed Ringler, Oxford 1962.

Whetstone, George (d. 1587?): 2 (one in his A remembraunce of G. Gaskoigne [1577?], rptd A. Chalmers, English poets vol 2, 1810; one in his A mirror of Frauncis Earle of Bedford 1575, rptd T. Park, Heliconia vol 2, 1815).

P[roctor], T[homas], A gorgious gallery of gallant inventions 1578: 5 anon F4ᵛ, H1ᵛ, I3, O2ᵛ, O4; ed H. E. Rollins, Cambridge Mass 1926.

W.A., A speciall remedie against the furious force of lawlesse love 1578: 2 e4ᵛ; rptd H. Ellis 1844 (Roxburghe Club).

J.C., A poor knight his pallace of private pleasures 1579: 3 I1ᵛ–2; rptd H. Ellis 1844 (Roxburghe Club).

Churchyard, Thomas (d. 1604): 2 (one in his Chance 1580 [entered 1578] K2, one in his Charge 1580 D2ᵛ).

Dyer, Sir Edward (d. 1607): one written c. 1581 ptd with Sidney's Certain sonnets 1598; rptd R. M. Sargent, Life and lyrics of Dyer, Oxford 1935.

Howell, Thomas H. his devises 1581: 14 (12 by Howell, one by E.L., one by J[ohn] K[eeper]); ed W. Raleigh, Oxford 1906 (facs).

Watson, Thomas (d. 1593): 3 (one in his Hecatompathia [1582], ed E. Arber 1870; 2 in his Italian madrigalls englished 1590, rptd F. I. Carpenter JEGP 2 1899). One later probably his in Phoenix nest 1593 O1ᵛ, ed H. E. Rollins, Cambridge Mass 1931.

Bucke, G[eorge] (d. 1623): one in Watson's Hecatompathia [1582], ed E. Arber 1870.

Yates, James: 2 in his The castell of courtesie 1582 Q1ᵛ.

Brooke, Baron, Fulke Greville (d. 1628): 41 in his Caelica, written after 1582; ptd in Workes written in his youth with Sir P. Sidney 1633; ed G. Bullough, Poems and dramas of Greville vol 1, 1939.

BM ms additional 15,232 fols 9ᵛ–11ᵛ: 5 anon after 1582.

Harvard ms f MS English 1015 folio 17: 2 anon before 1583.

Young, Bartholomew: 29 tr 1583 in his Diana of George of Montemayor 1598; pts 1 and 3 ed J. M. Kennedy, Oxford 1968.

Soowthern, John, Pandora 1584: 25; ed G. B. Parks, New York 1938 (facs).

BM ms additional 41,499A folio 6: one anon 1584; ptd E. K. Chambers, Review quarterly 1936, p. 271.

Gorges, Sir Arthur (d. 1625): 27 in BM ms Egerton 3165 written 1584–9 (with 4 written after 1599); ed H. E. Sandison, Poems of Gorges, Oxford 1953.

Dymoke, [Sir] Edward (d. 1625): 3 in Univ of Edinburgh ms De.5.96 folios 2–3, on Sir Philip Sidney after 1586.

Byrd, W. Psalmes sonets and songs 1588: 2 anon (nos 18, 20); rptd E. H. Fellowes, English madrigal verse, Oxford 1920.

Yonge, N. Musica transalpina 1588: 6 anon; rptd A. H. Bullen, Some shorter Elizabethan poems [1903].

Bodley ms Rawlinson Poetry 85: 6 anon after 1588, folios 9, 16ᵛ, 18ᵛ(2), 25ᵛ, 108ᵛ.

Byrd, W. Songs of sundrie natures 1589: 6 anon (nos 10, 12, 15, 17, 26, 36); rptd Fellowes 1920.

Lodge, Thomas (d. 1625): 4 (2 in his Scillaes metamorphosis 1589, 2 in his Rosalynde 1590). Later 40 in his Phillis 1593, one in Phoenix nest 1593, one in his Margarite of America 1596; all ed E. Gosse, Works of Lodge, 4 vols Glasgow 1883.

Breton, Nicholas (d. 1626?): 3 in his Historie of Don Frederigo 1590; rptd J. Robertson, Poems by Breton, Liverpool 1952 pp. xlix–l. Others later.

Constable, Henry (d. 1613): 66 (63 in South Kensington Museum ms Dyce 44, 2 more in Marsh's Library Dublin ms Z.3.5.21, one more in his Diana 1592 A3; all written by 1590). Probably his, written later: 17 'Spirituall sonnettes by H:C:' in BM ms Harley 7553 folios 32–40, one in Edmund Bolton, Elements of armories 1160 A1ᵛ; all ed J. Grundy, Poems of Constable, Liverpool 1960.

Greene, Robert (d. 1592): one in his Never too late 1590; one later in his Groatsworth of wit 1592; ed J. C. Collins, Plays and poems of Greene vol 2, Oxford 1905 pp. 295, 315.

Ralegh, Sir Walter (d. 1618): one in Spenser, Faerie Queene 1590; 2 written later; ed A. M. C. Latham, Poems of Ralegh 1951, nos 13 and 11, 12, 23.

Sylvester, Joshua (d. 1618): one in his trn of du Bartas, A canticle of the victorie obtained by Henrie the Fourth at Ivry, 1590. Others later.

Collections of Sonnets Printed after 1590

For Scottish sonneteers (William Fowler, King James VI and I, Alexander Montgomerie), see cols 361 f., below.

Sidney, Sir Philip. Astrophel and Stella; other sonnets of divers gentlemen. 1591, [1597–1600] (107 by Sidney, 28 by Daniel), 1591 (corrected text, without Other sonnets), 1598 (in Arcadia) (108, best text); rptd in 12 folio edns 1599–1674.

Spenser, Edmund. Complaints. 1591 (entered 1590) (Ruines of Rome 33, Visions of the worlds vanitie 12, Visions of Bellay 15, Visions of Petrarch 7).

—— Amoretti. 1595 (88).

Constable, Henry. Diana by H.C. 1592 (23); Diana of H.C. augmented, [1594–7] (2 edns) (77: 27 by Constable, 8 by Sidney, one by R. Smyth, 41 anon).

Daniel, Samuel. Delia. 1592 (50), 1592 (54), 1595 (55), 1598, 1601 (in Works) (57), 1602 (another issue), 1611, 1623.

Harvey, Gabriel. Foure letters and certaine sonnets. 1592, 1592 (19, with 4 in blank verse).

Barnes, Barnabe. Parthenophil and Parthenophe. 1593 (112).

—— A divine centurie of spiritual sonnets. 1595 (100).

Fletcher, Giles, the elder. Licia. 1593 (54).

Lodge, Thomas. Phillis. 1593 (40).

T.W. The tears of fancie. 1593 (53, with 8 lost).

Lok, Henry. Sundry Christian passions. 1593 (200).

—— Ecclesiasticus; sundrie sonets of Christian passions augmented; other sonets of a feeling conscience. 1597 (88 new).

Drayton, Michael. Ideas mirrour. 1594 (51); rev and enlarged in collections as Idea, 1599, 1600, 1602, 1605, 1608, 1610, 1613, [c. 1616], 1619, 1630, 1637 (total 107, of which 4 not sonnets).

Percy, William. Sonnets to the fairest Coelia. 1594 (20).

Zepheria. 1594 (35). Anon.

Barnfield, Richard. Cynthia; certaine sonnets [20]; Cassandra. 1595.

E.C. Emaricdulfe. 1595 (40).

Chapman, George. Ovids banquet of sence; a coronet for his mistresse philosophie [10]; amorous zodiacke. 1595.

Griffin, Bartholomew. Fidessa. 1596 (62).

R.L. Diella: certain sonnets [38]; Don Diego and Gynevra. 1596.

Smith, William. Chloris. 1596 (50).

Salusbury, Sir John. The patrone his pathetical posies, appended to Robert Parry, Sinetes passions, 1597 (32).

Rogers, Thomas. Celestiall elegies. 1598 (41).

Davies, Sir John. Hymnes of Astraea in acrosticke verse. 1599 (26).

—— Gulling sonnets (9), written 1596–1604; ptd from ms 1873.

—— Epithalamion on the marriage of Elizabeth Vere and

the Earl of Derby (10), written 1595; ptd from ms 1962.

Newton, Thomas. Atropoion Delion: the death of Delia [Queen Elizabeth]. 1603 (26).

Stirling, Earl of, Sir William Alexander. Aurora: the first fancies of the authors youth. 1604 (106), probably written before 1592.

Shakespeare, William. Sonnets. 1609 (154), written in 1590's?

C[onstable], H[enry]. Spiritual sonnettes (17), written in 1590's; ptd from ms 1815.

Alabaster, William. Divine meditations (77), written 1597-8; ptd from ms 1959.

IV. MINOR TUDOR POETRY

Lee, S. Elizabethan sonnets. 2 vols 1904. Texts and first-line index of 15 collections.

English madrigal verse 1588–1632. Ed E. H. Fellowes, Oxford 1920; rev F. W. Sternfeld and D. Greer, Oxford 1967. Texts, with first-line and author-indexes, of contents of all the song books.

Rollins, H. E. Edns of ptd Tudor anthologies 1920-37. See col 85 f., above.

— Index to ballad entries in the Stationers' Registers. SP 21 1924.

Crum, M. First-line index of English poetry 1500–1800 in mss of the Bodleian Library. 2 vols Oxford 1968. Contains author-index, and identifies many anon items.

WILLIAM ALABASTER
1568–1640

Manuscripts

Elisaeis: apotheosis poetica principis Elizabethae, liber primus. Mss Bodley Rawlinson D 293, Emmanuel College Cambridge 68, Newberry Library 210,756.

The conversion of Alabaster. Ms English College Rome. Prose autobiography written 1598.

Epigrammata. Bodley mss Rawlinson D 283, 293.

§ I

Roxana tragædia. 1632 (anon), 1632 (a plagiarii unguibus vindicata, aucta et agnita).

Sonnets. Ed G. M. Story and H. Gardner, Oxford 1959. 77 sonnets written 1597-8, from mss.

SIR WILLIAM ALEXANDER, EARL OF STIRLING
1567?–1640

Collections

· The monarchick tragedies. 1604 (Croesus and Darius only; probably part of Woorkes with 1604 Aurora and 1604 Paraenesis), 1607 (reissue of Croesus and Darius with cancel title, adding Alexandræan tragedy and Julius Caesar), 1616.

Recreations with the Muses. 1637. Foure monarchicke tragedies, Doomes-day, A paraenesis to Prince Henry, Jonathan an heroicke poeme.

Poetical works. Ed R. Alison 3 vols Glasgow 1870–2.

Poetical works. Ed L. E. Kastner and H. B. Charlton 2 vols 1921–9 (STS).

§ I

A short discourse of the late attemptat against his Majesties person. [Edinburgh] 1600, [London] 1600 (piracy). Anon prose, on Gowrie conspiracy.

The tragedie of Darius. Edinburgh 1603, London 1604 (probably part of Monarchick tragedies).

Aurora: containing the first fancies of the authors youth. 1604. 106 sonnets and 20 other poems, probably written before 1592.

A paraenesis to the Prince [Henry]. 1604.

An elegie on the death of Prince Henrie. Edinburgh 1612, 1613 (variant issue).

Doomes-day. [Edinburgh] 1614, London 1720.

Supplement by Sir W. A[lexander], to bk 3 of Sir Philip Sidney's Arcadia. 1616–18 (2 settings), bound in 1613, Dublin 1621, London 1622–3 (Arcadia); rptd in 8 edns of Arcadia 1627–1739, and in edn by E. A. Baker 1907, 1921. Prose.

An encouragement to colonies. 1624, 1625 (variant issue), 1630 (another issue as The mapp of New-England); rptd 1867 (Bannatyne Club); ed E. F. Slafter, Alexander and American colonization, Boston 1873 (Prince Soc). Prose.

The psalmes of King David translated by King James. Oxford 1631 etc; Edinburgh 1712 (as part of The book of common prayer for the use of the Church of Scotland). Partly the work of Alexander.

Anacrisis: or a censure of some poets ancient and modern. In Works of William Drummond of Hawthornden, Edinburgh 1711; ed J. E. Spingarn, Critical essays of the 17th century vol 1, Oxford 1908. Prose; written c. 1634.

WILLIAM BALDWIN
c. 1515–63

Collections

The mirror for magistrates. Ed L. B. Campbell, Cambridge 1938. Item no below refer to this edn.

Beware the cat; Funerals of Edward VI. Ed W. P. Holden, New London Conn 1963.

§ I

Sonnet before C. Langton, Treatise of phisick, 1547; ed T. W. Camp, MLN 52 1936; Holden p. 86.

A treatise of morall phylosophie. 1547 (for 1548) (4 bks, prose and 62 verse tags), 1550 (for 1551), [1551?], [1552?], [c. 1555], [c. 1555] (enlarged T. Paulfreyman; 7 bks, 104 verse tags), 1557 (for 1558?), 1564 ('again enlarged by the first authour'; 10 bks, 151 verse tags), 1567 (3rd time enlarged T. Paulfreyman), 1571, 1575, 1579 (4th time enlarged), 1584, 1587, 1591, 1596, 1600, 1605, 1610, [c. 1620] ('sixt time enlarged'), [c. 1620], [c. 1620], [c. 1637], [c. 1640], 1651; ed E. Arber 1908 (from 4-bk c. 1555); ed R. H. Bowers, Gainesville 1967 (facs of c. 1620).

The canticles or balades of Salomon in Englysh metres. 1549.

A memorial of suche princes as have been unfortunate in England. [1554?]. Fragment of suppressed edn of Mirror; probably contained 21 tragedies: the 19 ptd 1559, with Ferrer's Duke Humfrey and Elianor Cobham ptd 1578.

A myrroure for magistrates. [1559]. Contains 19 tragedies: dedication, to the reader, prose links and nos 4, 8, 13, 18 by Baldwin; 2, 7, 9–12, 14–17 probably by Baldwin.

The funeralles of King Edward the Sixt. 1560 (for 1561?), 1610 (wrongly attributed to Sir J. Cheke), 1817 (Roxburghe Club, from 1560); ed W. Trollope, History of

Christ's Hospital, 1834 (from 1610). 2 poems written 1553.

A myrrour for magistrates. 1563. Adds Induction and 8 tragedies: prose links and probably nos 20 and 23 by Baldwin.

Beware the cat. 1570 (J. Alde, preserved only in transcript in BM additional ms 24,628, ptd J. O. Halliwell[-Phillipps] 1864), 1570 (W. Gryffith, fragment), 1584; preliminaries ed W. C. Hazlitt, Prefaces dedications epistles, 1874; ed Holden 1963 (from 1584). Satirical prose fiction, one poem, written c. 1553.

RICHARD BARNFIELD
1574–1627

Ms of Shepherdes confession *etc, Folger Lib 300.2.*

Collections

Complete poems. Ed A. B. Grosart 1876 (Roxburghe Club). Wrongly attributes My flocks feed not and Isham ms items.

Poems. Ed E. Arber, Birmingham 1882.

Poems. Ed M. Summers [1936]. Text from Arber, above.

§1

The affectionate shepheard. 1594; ed J. O. Halliwell(-Phillipps) 1847 (Percy Soc). Anon, but claimed in Cynthia, below.

[Greenes funeralls, by R.B. gent. 1594; ed R. B. McKerrow 1911, Stratford 1922. Attributed to Barnfield on slender evidence by McKerrow].

Cynthia; certaine sonnets; the legend of Cassandra. 1595, 1595; ed E. V. Utterson, Ryde 1841.

The encomion of Lady Pecunia; the complaint of poetrie for the death of liberalitie; the combat betweene conscience and covetousnesse; poems in divers humors. 1598 (separate title-pages, but continuous signatures for last 3 items), 1605 (Pecunia expanded, only 2 Poems in divers humors); ed A. Boswell 1816 (Roxburghe Club); ed J. P. Collier, Illustrations of Old English literature vol 1, 1866.

The passionate pilgrim by W. Shakespeare. 1599. Contains 2 of Barnfield's poems.

A lovers newest curranto. [c. 1620]. Anon broadside.

THOMAS BLENERHASSET
1550?–1624(5?)

The seconde part of the mirrour for magistrates from the conquest of Caesar to Williame the Conquerour. 1578 (12 tragedies), 1610 (in A mirrour for magistrates, newly enlarged, ed R. Niccols, 10 tragedies), 1619, 1620, 1621; ed J. Haslewood, Mirror for magistrates in five parts pt 2, 1815 (from 1578); ed L. B. Campbell, Parts added to the Mirror for magistrates, Cambridge 1946 (from 1578, with biography).

A revelation of the true Minerva [Queen Elizabeth]. 1582; ed J. W. Bennett, New York 1941 (facs).

A direction for the plantation in Ulster. 1610. Prose.

RICHARD CAREW of Anthony
1555–1620

Godfrey of Bulloigne: the recoverie of Hierusalem, by T. Tasso, the first part containing five cantos imprinted in both languages. [1594]; ed A. B. Grosart, Manchester 1881.

A herrings tayle: a poeticall fiction of divers matters. 1598; abridged in The survey of Cornwall, ed F. E. Halliday 1953.

GEORGE CHAPMAN
1559?–1634

The shadow of night [etc]. 1594; Ovids banquet of sence [etc], 1595; continuation of Marlowe's Hero and Leander, 1598 etc; Seaven bookes of the Iliades of Homere, 1598 (bks 1–2, 7–11); Achilles shield, 1598 (from Iliad bk 18). *See col 223, below.*

THOMAS CHURCHYARD
c. 1530–1604

Unique ms poems in BM Cotton Caligula B.v (variant of Siege of Lieth *in* Chippes *1575; Egerton 2877 (The welcome home of the Earle of Essex from Cales 1596); Egerton 3165 (ed H. E. Sandison, Poems of Sir Arthur Gorges, Oxford 1953); Royal 17.B.vii (A rebuke to rebellion, ptd Nichols vols 2–3, 1788–1823); Bodley Rawlinson Poetry 172 (ptd Goldwyn 1967); Harvard Typographical 19 (ptd Goldwyn 1967).*

Collections

The contention bettwyxte Churchyeard and Camell upon David Dycers dreame. 1560.

The first parte of Churchyardes chippes. 1575, 1578; rptd G. Chalmers 1817 (with memoir and bibliography); ed J. P. Collier, Illustrations of early English poetry, [1870]. 13 poems and prose.

A generall rehearsall of warres [prose]; some tragedies and epitaphes. [1579] (2 issues).

A pleasaunte laborinth called Churchyardes chance. 1580. 70 poems.

A light bondell of livly discourses called Churchyardes charge. 1580; ed J. P. Collier, Illustrations of early English poetry, [1870]. 10 poems.

A revyving of the deade. 1591. 5 epitaphs.

A feast full of sad cheere. 1592. 8 poems.

Churchyards challenge. 1593. 18 poems, 5 prose discourses.

Nichols, J. In his Progresses of Queen Elizabeth, 3 vols 1788–1805, 1823. Pageants and verses to the Queen.

Collman, H. L. Ballads and broadsides. 1912 (Roxburghe Club). 9 broadsides.

§1

[Churchyard-Camel flyting c. 1552: see R. Lemon, Catalogue of printed broadsides in Soc of Antiquaries London, 1866]. Davy Dycars dreame, rptd in Westerne Wyll upon the debate betwyxte Churchyard and Camell, c. 1552, in Chance, 1580; ed H. E. Rollins and H. Baker, The Renaissance in England, Boston 1954; A replication to Camels objection; The surrejoinde unto Camels rejoinder; A playn and fynall confutacion of cammells corlyke oblatracion; all 4 rptd in Contention, 1560, and Collman nos 19, 21 ,23, 25.

A myrour for man. [1552], 1594 (rev in The mirror of man).

Shores wife. In A myrrour for magistrates, 1563 etc, 1593 (rev in Challenge); ed E. Cooper, Muses' library, 1737; ed S. E. Brydges, Censura literaria vol 2, 1806; ed Rollins and Baker, The Renaissance in England, Boston 1954.

A farewell cauld Churcheyeards rounde. [1566]; ed J. P. Collier, Old ballads, 1840 (Percy Soc); Collman no 26.

A greatter thanks for Churchyardes welcome home. [1566]; Collman no 28.

Churchyardes lamentacion of freyndshyp. [1566]; ed J. P. Collier, Roxburghe ballads, 1847; Collman no 29.

Churchyardes farewell. [1566]; Collman no 30; Arundel Harington ms, and R. Hughey 1960, no 321.

Commendatory poem in Pithy workes of maister Skelton, collected by J. S[tow]. 1568.

The epitaphe of the Earle of Penbroke. 1570; Collman no 31.

Come bring in Maye with me: a discourse of rebellion. 1570.

The thre first bookes of Ovids De tristibus translated. [1572], 1578, 1580, 1816 (Roxburghe Club).

Commendatory verse to Huloets dictionarie. Ed J. Higgins 1572; ed L. B. Campbell, Parts added to the Mirror for magistrates, Cambridge 1946.

Commendatory verse to L. Lloyd, Pilgrimage of princes, [1573].

He perswadeth his freend. In Paradise of dainty devices, 1576 etc (no 23).

A prayse of maister M. Forboishers voyage to Meta Incognita. 1578. Prose, with one poem.

A discourse of the Queenes Majesties entertainment in Suffolk and Norffolk [prose and verse]; a welcome home to M. Frobusher; a commendation of Sir H. Gilberts ventrous journey. [1578]; ed Nichols vol 2, 1788, 1823; 1851.

A lamentable description of the wofull warres in Flaunders. 1578. Prose, with 2 poems.

The miserie of Flaunders, calamitie of Fraunce, misfortune of Portugall. [1579], 1876.

The moste true reporte of James Fitz Morrice death. [1579?]. Prose.

A warning for the wise of the late earthquake. 1580. Prose, with one poem.

A plaine report of the takyng of Macklin. [1580]. Prose.

A scourge for rebels. 1584. Prose.

The epitaph of Sir Phillip Sidney. [1587]; ed S. Butler, Sidneiana, 1837 (Roxburghe Club).

Thomas Wolsey. In Mirour for magistrates, 1587 etc; ed H. Morley, Cavendish's Wolsey, 1885.

The worthines of Wales. 1587; ed T. Evans 1776; ed C. E. Simms 1876 (Spenser Soc). Verse and prose.

A sparke of friendship [prose]; a description of a paper-mill built by M. Spilman. 1588; rptd in Harleian miscellany vol 3, 1774, vol 2, 1809; Nichols vol 2, 1788, 1823.

A handeful of gladsome verses given to the Queenes Majesty at Woodstocke. 1592.

A pleasant conceite presented to the Queenes Majestie. [1593]; Nichols vol 2, 1788, vol 3, 1823.

Giacomo di Grassi his true arte of defence englished by I.G. 1594. Ed Churchyard, who wrote prose dedication and To the reader.

The mirror of man [rev from 1552, above]; and manners of men. 1594; ed A. Boswell, Frondes caducae, 1816.

A musicall consort called Churchyards charitie; a praise of poetrie out of Sir Phillip Sidney. 1595; ed A. Boswell, with above.

The honor of the lawe. 1596.

A sad funerall of Sir F. Knowles. 1596; ed A. Boswell, with above.

A pleasant discourse of Court and wars called his cherrishing: a commendation of those that serve prince and countrie. 1596; ed A. Boswell, with above.

The welcome home of the Earle of Essex. 1598 (fragment). On 1596 Cadiz expedition; full text in BM Egerton ms 2877.

A wished reformation of wicked rebellion. 1598.

The fortunate farewel to the Earle of Essex. 1599; ed Nichols vols 2–3, 1788–1823.

The wonders of the ayre, the trembling of the earth. 1602.

A true discourse of the Governours in the Netherlands and the civill warres there. 1602. Prose, tr with R. Robinson from E. van Meteren; autobiographical passages added.

Sorrowful verses on [the] death of Queene Elizabeth. [1604]; Collman no 32; Rollins and Baker, The Renaissance in England, Boston 1954.

Churchyards good will: an epitaph for the Abp of Canterbury. 1604; T. Park, Heliconia vol 3, 1815; H. Huth, Fugitive tracts vol 2, 1875.

[The history of Fortunatus, abstracted in English by T.C., 1676 etc, has been attributed to Churchyard]. Prose.

HENRY CONSTABLE
1562–1613

Collections

Poems. Ed J. Grundy, Liverpool 1960.

§I

Commendatory sonnet to James VI, Poeticall exercises, 1591.

Examen pacifique de la doctrine des Huguenots. 'Paris' (for London) 1589, 'Caen' (for London) 1590; tr W.W. as The Catholike moderator, 1623 (4 edns), 1624. Anon; prose.

Diana. 1592. 23 sonnets.

Diana: augmented with divers quatorzains of honorable and lerned personages. [1594], [1595]; ed J. Littledale 1818 (Roxburghe Club); [ed S. W. Singer] 1818; ed E. Arber, English garner vol 2, 1879; ed M. F. Crow, Elizabethan sonnet cycles vol 2, 1896; ed S. Lee, Elizabethan sonnets vol 2, 1904. Reprints 27 of Constable's sonnets, adds 41 by unknown authors, 8 by Sidney, one by R. Smith.

Four commendatory sonnets to Sir P. Sidney, Apologie for poetry, 1595.

A poetical rapsody. 1602. Includes 2 poems by Constable.

Harleian miscellany vol 9, ed T. Park 1812. Sonnets from the Todd ms, now Victoria & Albert Museum ms Dyce 44.

Spirituall sonnettes [from BM Harley ms 7553]. In Heliconia vol 2, ed T. Park 1815.

JOHN DAVIES of Hereford
1565–1618

Collections

Complete works. Ed A. B. Grosart 2 vols Edinburgh 1878.

§I

Mirum in modum: a glimpse of Gods glorie and the soules shape. 1602.

Microcosmos: the discovery of the little world. Oxford 1603, 1605, 1611.

Wittes pilgrimage through a world of amorous sonnets and other passages. [1605?].

Bien venu: Greate Britaines welcome to the Danes. 1606; ed P. Birkelund, Copenhagen 1957 (with German trn of H. Roberts, Relatio wie Christianus Quartus zu Dennemarck im Königreich Engellandt angelanget).

Summa totalis: an addition to mirum in modum. 1607.

The holy roode: Christ crucified described in speaking-picture. 1609.

Humours heav'n on earth; the civile warres of death; the triumph of death: the picture of the plague in 1603. 1609.

The scourge of folly: satyricall epigrammes; a descant upon English proverbes; to worthy persons; papers complaint. [1611?]. Papers complaint rptd as A scourge for paper-persecutors, preceded by A continu'd inquisition by A. H[olland], 1624.

[Verses below engraved portrait of Princess Elizabeth. c. 1611.]

The Muses sacrifice: divine meditations; rights of the living and dead. 1612.

The Muses-teares for the losse of Henry Prince of Wales. 1613.

An eclogue between Willy and Wernocke. In W. Browne, The sheapherdes pipe, 1614; rptd in George Withers, Workes, 1620.

A select second husband for Sir Thomas Overburies wife. 1616.

Wits bedlam. 1617. Epigrams and epitaphs.

[Verses for portrait of Queen Elizabeth. Before 1625.]

The writing schoolemaster. [c. 1625] (fragment), 1631 (6th edn), 1636 (16th edn). Handwriting manual with engraved plates.

A divine psalme; an elogie upon the patron [i.e. pattern] of Scripture; divine epigrams. 1652.

THOMAS DRANT
d. 1578

Impii cuiusdam epigrammatis quod edidit R. Shaklockus in mortem C. Scoti. 1565. Latin and English verse.

A medicinable morall: two bookes of Horace his satyres englyshed; waylyngs of Hieremiah; epigrammes [Latin and English]. 1566.

Horace his arte of poetrie, pistles and satyrs englished. 1567.

Epigrams and sentences spirituall in vers of Gregori Nazanzen englished. 1568.

In Selomonis Ecclesiasten paraphrasis poetica. 1572. Latin verse.

Praesul; sylva. [1576]. Latin verse.

Commendatory verses. In J. Sadler, Four books of Vegetius, 1572; L. Lloyd, A pilgrimage of princes, 1573; A. Neville, Kettus, 1582.

SIR EDWARD DYER
d. 1607

Collections

Writings in verse and prose. Ed A. B. Grosart 1872. 12 poems.

Sargent, R. M. At the Court of Queen Elizabeth: the life and lyrics of Dyer. Oxford 1935. Adds 3 poems.

§ 1

A sweet sonet: my minde to me a kingdome is. [1624?]. Anon, ascribed to Edward de Vere Earl of Oxford by Harvard fMS 1015 folio 14ᵛ.

QUEEN ELIZABETH I
1533–1603

Queen Elizabeth's englishings of Boethius, Plutarch and Horace. Ed E. C. Pemberton 1889 (EETS).

Flügel, E. Poems by Queen Elizabeth. Anglia 14 1892.

Phillips, J. E. Elizabeth I as a Latin poet. Renaissance News 16 1963.

Poems. Ed L. Bradner, Providence 1964.

Black, L. G. A lost poem by Queen Elizabeth. TLS 23 May 1968.

EDWARD FAIRFAX
d. 1635

Godfrey of Bulloigne done into English heroicall verse. 1600, 1624, 1687, Dublin 1726, London 1749, 1817, 1817, 1844, 1853; ed H. Morley 1890, 1901; ed R. Weiss, Carbondale 1962. Trn of Tasso, Gerusalemme liberata.

Eclogue the fourth: Egon and Alexis. Ed E. Cooper, Muses' library, 1737; ed W. Grainge, Harrogate 1882 (with A discourse of witchcraft).

Eclogue: Hermes and Lycaon. Ed W. Grainge, Harrogate 1882 (from ms).

GILES FLETCHER the elder
1546–1611

Bibliographies

Berry, L. E. Fletcher the elder: a bibliography. Trans Cambridge Bibl Soc 3 1961.

Collections

English works. Ed L. E. Berry, Madison 1964. Licia, Russe commonwealth, Tartars, letters.

§ 1

Of the Russe commonwealth. 1591, 1643, 1657; epitomized in R. Hakluyt, Voyages vol 1, 1598; S. Purchas, Pilgrimes vol 3, 1625; J. Harris, Compleat collection of voyages vol 1, 1705; ed E. A. Bond 1856 (Hakluyt Soc); ed R. Pipes and J. V. A. Fine jr, Cambridge Mass 1966; A. J. Schmidt, Ithaca 1968. Prose.

Licia: poems of love; the rising to the crowne of Richard the Third. [1593?] (anon); ed A. B. Grosart, Manchester 1871; ed E. Arber, English garner vol 8, 1896; Licia, ed M. F. Crow, Elizabethan sonnet cycles vol 1, 1896; ed S. Lee, Elizabethan sonnets vol 2, 1904. 54 sonnets adapted from Angerianus et al with 7 other poems.

De literis antiquae Britanniae. 1633. Latin verse.

The Tartars or Ten Tribes. In S. Lee, Israel Redux, 1677; in Memoirs of the life and writings of W. Whiston, 1749, 1753. Prose.

ABRAHAM FRAUNCE
fl. 1582–1633

The lamentations of Amyntas for the death of Phillis. 1587, 1588, 1589, 1591 (in Yvychurch), 1596; ed F. Dickey, Chicago 1967. Trn in English hexameters of T. Watson's Latin Amyntas.

The Arcadian rhetorike. [1588]; ed E. Seaton, Oxford 1950 (Luttrell Soc); Menston 1969 (facs of 1588). Prose with verse quotations.

Insignium, armorum, emblematum, hieroglyphicorum et symbolorum explicatio. 1588. Latin prose.

The lawiers logike. 1588, Menston 1969 (facs). Prose.

The Countesse of Pembrokes Yvychurch. 1591. Trns in English hexameters: Amyntas pastorall [Tasso's Amintas], Phillis funerall [Watson's Amyntas], Lamentation of Corydon for Alexis [Virgil's Eclogue 2], The beginning of Heliodorus his Æthiopical history.

The Countesse of Pembrokes Emanuel: the nativity, passion, buriall and resurrection of Christ, with certaine psalmes of David, all in English hexameters. 1591; ed A. B. Grosart, Manchester 1872.

The third part of the Countesse of Pembrokes Yvychurch: Amintas dale, wherein are conceited tales of the pagan gods in English hexameters. 1592. Verse with prose comment explaining allegory.

Victoria. Ed G. C. M. Smith, Louvain 1906 (Bang's Materialien 14) (from ms). Latin verse play tr from L. Pasqualigo, Il Fidele; biographical introd.

The shepheardes logike. Menston 1969 (facs of BM additional ms 34,361).

ARTHUR GOLDING
1536?–1606

The fyrst fower bookes of P. Ovidius Nasos Metamorphosis translated into Englishe meter. 1565.

The xv bookes of P. Ovidius Naso entytuled Metamorphosis translated into English meeter. 1567, 1575, 1584, 1587, 1593, 1603, 1612, 1675; ed W. H. D. Rouse 1904 (as Shakespeare's Ovid); ed J. M. Cohen, Carbondale 1961 (from Rouse).

A briefe discourse on the late murther of George Saunders. 1573, 1577; ed R. Simpson, School of Shakespeare vol 2, 1878; ed L. T. Golding 1937. Prose.

A tragedie of Abrahams sacrifice, written in French by T. Beza and translated into Inglish. 1577; ed M. W. Wallace, Toronto 1906.

A discourse upon the earthquake. 1580; ed L. T. Golding above. Prose.

Commendatory poem to Barrets Alvearie, 1580; ed L. T. Golding above.

BARNABE GOOGE
1540–94

The first thre bokes of the zodyake of lyfe. 1560; The firste syxe bokes, 1561; The zodiake of life by Marcellus Palingenius, 1565 (12 bks), 1576, 1588; ed R. Tuve, New York 1947 (facs of 1576 edn).

Eglogs, epytaphes and sonettes. 1563; ed E. Arber 1871; Selected poems, ed A. Stephens, Denver 1961.

A newe booke called the shippe of safegarde. 1569.

The popish kingdome or reigne of Antichrist, written in Latin verse by T. Naogeorgus [Kirchmeyer] and englyshed. 1570; ed R. C. Hofe 1880.

Foure bookes of husbandry collected by C. Heresbachius. 1577, 1578, 1586, 1596, 1601, 1614 (enlarged), 1631 (enlarged G. Markham). Prose trn.

The overthrow of the gout written in Latin verse by C. Balista. 1577. Verse trn.

The proverbes of Sir J. Lopez de Mendoza with the paraphrase of P. Diaz of Toledo, translated out of Spanishe. 1579. Verse proverbs with prose commentary.

The vertues of a new terra sigillata lately found out in Germany, by A. Bertholdus. 1587. Prose trn from Latin.

A prophecie lately transcribed from an old manuscript of Doctor Barnaby Googe predicting the rising and falling of the United Provinces. 1672.

SIR ARTHUR GORGES
1557?–1625

Collections
Poems. Ed H. E. Sandison, Oxford 1953.

§I
Lucans Pharsalia. 1614.

The wisedome of the Ancients. 1619, 1622. Prose trn of F. Bacon, De sapientia veterum liber, 1609.

Essays moraux. 1619. French prose trn of F. Bacon, Essayes.

Observations concerning the Royall Navy. 1650. Attributed to Gorges by Sandison; also attributed to Sir W. Ralegh.

The Olympian catastrophe. Ed R. Davies 1925 (from ms).

NICHOLAS GRIMALD
1519?–62?

Collections
Life and poems. Ed L. R. Merrill, New Haven 1925.

§I
Christus redivivus: comoedia tragica. Cologne 1543; ed J. M. Hart, PMLA 14 1899. Latin verse.

Archipropheta: tragoedia. Cologne 1548. Latin verse.

Latin and English commendatory verse. In W. Turner, A preservative agaynst the poyson of Pelagius, 1551.

M.T. Ciceroes thre bokes of duties. 1556, 1558, 1568, 1574, 1583, 1596, [1600?]. Prose trn.

Songes and sonettes by the Earle of Surrey and other. 1557 (40 poems by Grimald); 8 edns 1557–87 (10 poems). *See col 85, above.*

Oratio ad pontifices in aede Paulina 1553. 1583. Latin prose.

In P. V. Maronis quatuor libros Georgicorum in oratione soluta paraphrasis. 1591. Virgil's text with Latin prose paraphrase, written 1549.

JOSEPH HALL
Bishop of Norwich
1574–1656

Collections
Complete poems. Ed A. B. Grosart, Manchester 1879.
Collected poems. Ed A. Davenport, Liverpool 1949.

§I
Virgidemiarum: first three bookes of tooth-lesse satyrs. 1597, 1598, 1602.

Virgidemiarum: the three last bookes of byting satyres. 1598, 1599. All 6 bks rptd W. Thompson, Oxford 1753, and 13 other edns (*see* Davenport, above); ed S. W. Singer, Chiswick 1824 (with notes by T. Warton); Works of J. Hall, vol 12, ed P. Hall, Oxford 1839; ed K. Schulze, Berlin 1910 (with commentary).

The Kings prophecie. 1603; ed W. E. Buckley 1882 (Roxburghe Club).

Some fewe of Davids psalms metaphrased. In Holy observations, 1607; rptd with other works 8 times to 1639.

For prose see col 308, below.

SIR JOHN HARINGTON
1560–1612

Collections
Letters and epigrams. Ed N. E. McClure, Philadelphia 1930.

§I
Orlando furioso in English heroical verse. 1591, 1607, 1634; ed G. Hough 1962; ed R. Gottfried, Bloomington 1963 (selection); ed R. McNutty, Oxford 1972. Verse trn of Ariosto.

A new discourse of a stale subject called the Metamorphosis of Ajax; an anatomie [by T. Combe]; an apologie. 1596 (4 edns); ed S. W. Singer, Chiswick 1814; ed P. Warlock and J. Lindsay 1927; ed E. S. Donno 1962. Prose.

The Englishmans docter: or the school of Salerne. 1607, 1608, 1609, Edinburgh 1613, London 1617, 1624; ed F. R. Packard and F. H. Garrison, New York 1920; Salerno 1953 (with Latin). Verse trn of J. de Mediolano.

Epigrammes by Sir J.H. and others. In J.C., Alcilia, 1613, 1628 (20 epigrams); Epigrams both pleasant and serious, 1615, 1615 (116 epigrams); The most elegant and witty epigrams digested into foure bookes, 1618 (ed N. E. McClure, Philadelphia 1926, with 80 additional), 1625, 1633 (appended to 1634 Orlando furioso, above). 346 epigrams.

A briefe view of the state of the Church of England. Ed J. Chetwind 1653; ed T. Park, Nugae antiquae vol 2, 1804 (with corrections from autograph ms BM Royal 17 B xxii). Prose.

Nugae antiquae. Ed H. Harington 2 vols 1769–75, 3 vols 1779, 1792; ed T. Park 2 vols 1804 (with addns). Poems and prose from family papers.

A tract on the succession to the crown. Ed C. R. Markham 1880 (from York ms) (Roxburghe Club). Prose.

The Arundel Harington ms of Tudor poetry. Ed R. Hughey 2 vols Columbus 1960. Ms anthology of 324 poems compiled by John the elder and his son, including some of their own composition.

The prayse of private life. BM ms additional 30,161; in McClure, above. Prose; also attributed to Samuel Daniel.

§2

Rich, T. Harington and Ariosto. New Haven 1940.
Lea, K. M. Harington's folly. In Elizabethan and Jacobean studies presented to F. P. Wilson, Oxford 1959.

MARY HERBERT(née SIDNEY), COUNTESS OF PEMBROKE
1561–1621

§1

Discourse of life and death written in French by Ph. Mornay [prose]; Antonius: a tragedie written also in French by Ro. Garnier. 1592, 1600, 1606, 1607; 1595 (Antonie alone); ed A. Luce, Weimar 1897; ed G. Bullough, Narrative and dramatic sources of Shakespeare vol 5, 1964. *See col 196, below.*
Sir P. Sidney, The Countesse of Pembrokes Arcadia augmented and ended. 1593, 1598 (with new addns) etc. Ed Lady Mary with H. S[tanford]; *see col 94, above.*
A dialogue betweene two shepheards, Thenot and Piers, in praise of Astraea. In A poetical rapsody, ed F. Davison 1602 etc; rptd J. Nichols, Progresses of Queen Elizabeth vol 3, 1823.
To the angell spirit of Sir P. Sidney. In S. Daniel, Whole workes in poetrie, 1623. Shorter version, wrongly attributed to Daniel. Longer version ed W. A. Ringler jr, Poems of Sidney, Oxford 1962 (from B. Juel-Jensen ms of Psalms, which also contains an unpbd dedicatory poem by Lady Mary to Queen Elizabeth).
The psalmes of David translated into divers and sundry kindes of verse. [Ed S. W. Singer], Chiswick 1823; ed J. C. A. Rathmell, Garden City NY 1963 (both from De L'Isle and Dudley ms). Lady Mary translated psalms 43–150.
The triumphe of death translated out of Italian [of Petrarch]. Inner Temple Petyt ms 538.43.1; ed F. B. Young, PMLA 27 1912; rptd in her Mary Sidney, 1912.

§2

Donne, John. Upon the translation of the psalmes by Sir P. Sydney and his sister. In his Poems, 1635.
Walpole, H. In his Catalogue of royal and noble authors vol 2, 1758.
Young, F. B. Mary Sidney Countess of Pembroke. 1912.

JOHN HEYWOOD
1497?–1580?

A dialogue of proverbes concernyng two maner of mariages. 1546 (10 edns to 1598); An hundred epigrammes, 1550 (9 edns to 1598 expanded to 600 epigrams); A balade specifienge the mariage betwene our soveraigne lord and lady, [1554]; The spider and the flie, 1556; A balet touching the takynge of Scarborow Castell, [1557]; A ballad against sklander and detraccion, [1562]; Of a number of rattes, [c. 1562]. *See col 178, below.*

THOMAS LODGE
1558–1625

Complaint of truth. In An alarum against usurers, 1584; Scillaes metamorphosis, 1589. 16 poems in Phoenix nest, 1593. Phillis; Elstred, 1593; A fig for Momus, 1595. Scattered poems in prose works. *See col 185, below.*

GERVASE MARKHAM
1568?–1637

The tragedie of Sir Richard Grinvile. 1595; The poem of poems: the song of King Salomon devided into eight eclogues, [1596]; Devoreux: teares for the losse of King Henry Third of Fraunce and the death of Walter Devoreaux, written in French by Madam G. Petau Maulette and paraphrastically translated, 1597; The teares of the beloved: the lamentation of St John concerning the death and passion of Christ, 1600; The newe metamorphosis, BM ms additional 14,824–6 (narrative poem in 24 bks written 1600–14); Marie Magdalens lamentations for the losse of her master Jesus, 1601, 1604; Rodomonths infernall: Ariostos conclusions of the marriage of Rogero with Bradamanth, written in French by P. de Portes and paraphrastically translated, 1607; The famous whore: the complaint of Paulina mistres unto Cardinall Hypolito of Est, 1609. *See col 319, below.*

CHRISTOPHER MARLOWE
1564–93

Hero and Leander. [Lost edn 1593?], 1598; finished by G. Chapman, 1598 etc; Certaine of Ovids elegies, Middleburgh (for Edinburgh? 1598?), [1599?] (10 only with Davies' Epigrammes); All Ovids elegies: 3 bookes, Middleburg (for London c. 1600) (with Davies' Epigrames) etc; Lucans first booke, 1600 etc; The passionate sheepheard to his love, in Passionate pilgrime, 1599 (4 stanzas attributed to Shakespeare); in Englands Helicon, 1600 (6 stanzas attributed to Marlowe). *See col 188, below.*

JOHN MARSTON
1576–1634

The metamorphosis of Pigmalions image and certaine satyres. 1598; The scourge of villanie: three bookes of satyres, 1598, 1599, 1599. *See col 240, below.*

ANTHONY MUNDAY
1560–1633

The mirrour of mutabilitie. 1579; The paine of pleasure, 1580; [Ballad in praise of the navy, c. 1584] (fragment); A banquet of daintie conceits, 1588 (entered 1584); Englands Helicon, 1600 (contains 7 poems signed Shepherd Tony, some probably from the lost Sweet sobs and amorous complaints of shepherds and nymphs, entered 1583). Scattered verses in prose works; *see col 193, below.*

THOMAS NASHE
1567–1601?

The choice of valentines (written before 1593, 3 mss); Dido Queene of Carthage, by C. Marlowe and T. Nash, 1594 (play); Summers last will and testament, 1600 (play). Scattered verses in prose works; *see col 190 below.*

HENRY PARKER, 8th Baron Morley
1476–1556

The exposition of the psalme [94] Deus ultionem. 1539. Prose, tr 1534.

The tryumphes of F. Petrarcke. [1555?]; ed J. E. T. Loveday 1887 (Roxburghe Club); in E. P. Hammond, English verse between Chaucer and Surrey, Durham NC 1927 (extracts); ed D. D. Carnicelli, Cambridge Mass 1971. Tr before 1547.

Epitaph on Sir T. West Lord Delaware. In G. Legh, The accedens of armory, 1562; ed T. Park in his edn of H. Walpole, A catalogue of the royal and noble authors of England vol 1, 1806; ed S. E. Brydges in his edn of A. Collins, The peerage of England vol 5, 1812; ed Loveday above; ed L. I. Guiney, Recusant poets, 1939. Written 1554.

Forty-six lives translated from Boccaccio's De claris mulieribus. In F. G. Waldron, Literary museum, 1792 (extracts); ed H. G. Wright 1943 (EETS). Prose, tr 1534–7.

Masuccio novella 49. BM ms Royal 18 A.lxii; ed F. Brie, Archiv 124 1920. Prose, tr 1543–7.

An Italion ryme called soneto. BM ms Royal A. xv; ed E. Flügel, Verschollene Sonette, Anglia 13 1891; in his Neuenglisches Lesebuch, Halle 1895; Hammond as above. Tr before 1547.

2 poems in Bodley ms Ashmole 48; 2nd ed P. Bliss in his edn of A. Wood, Athenae oxonienses vol 1, 1810; both ed T. Park in S. E. Brydges, The British bibliographer vol 4, 1814; ed Flügel, Lesebuch above; E. Arber, in his Surrey and Wyatt anthology, 1900; ed Guiney above (first poem only with notes).

THOMAS SACKVILLE, 1st EARL OF DORSET
1536–1608

Collections

Works. Ed R. W. Sackville-West 1859. Gorboduc, Induction and Buckingham, letters, biography.

§1

Sonnet before T. Hoby's translation of Castiglione's Courtyer. 1561, 1577, 1588; ed W. Raleigh 1900; ed W. B. D. Henderson, nd (EL).

The tragedie of Gorboduc: three actes wrytten by Thomas Norton and the two last by T. Sackville, shewed before the Quenes Majestie [at] Whitehall, 18 Jan 1561 (for 1562). 1565, [1570], 1590 (with Lydgate's Serpent of devision). See col 256, below.

Induction and Complaynt of Henrye Duke of Buckingham. In A myrrour for magistrates, 1563 etc; ed L. B. Campbell, Cambridge 1938 (Induction and no 22). St John's College Cambridge ms 364, ed M. Hearsey, New Haven 1936.

§2

Davie, D. A. Sixteenth-century poetry and the common reader: the case of Sackville. EC 4 1954.

Bacquet, P. Un contemporain d'Elisabeth I: Sackville. Geneva 1966.

See Mirror for magistrates, col 89, above.

WILLIAM SHAKESPEARE
1564–1616

Venus and Adonis. 1593; Lucrece, 1594; The passionate pilgrim, 1599 (wrongly attributed); The Phoenix and turtle, in R. Chester, Loves martyr, 1601; Sonnets; A lovers complaint, 1609. *See col 217, below.*

SIR THOMAS SMITH
1513–77

§1

Certaigne psalmes translated in the Tower with other prayers and songues. BM ms Royal 17 A xvii, dated 1549; ed B. Danielsson, Stockholm Stud in Eng 12 1963. *See col 334, below.*

§2

Strype, J. The life of Smith. 1698 (anon), Oxford 1820 (rev).

Dewar, M. Smith: a Tudor intellectual in office. 1964.

RICHARD STANYHURST
1547–1618

Thee first foure bookes of Virgil his Aeneis; oother poetical devises. Leyden 1582, London 1583; ed J. Maidment, Edinburgh 1836; ed E. Arber, English scholars' library 1880, 1895; ed D. van der Haar, Amsterdam 1933; ed G. Gregory Smith, Elizabethan critical essays vol 1, Oxford 1904 (extracts from prose dedication and preface); 2 Oother devises rptd in R.B.'s Greenes funeralls, 1594.

JOSHUA SYLVESTER
1563–1618

A canticle of the victorie obteined by Henrie the Fourth at Ivry, written in French by William Salustius lord of Bartas. 1590; reissued with following item.

The triumph of faith; the sacrifice of Isaac; the ship-wreck of Jonas; a song of the victorie obteined by the French King at Yvry, written in French by W. Salustius lord of Bartas. 1592.

The profit of imprisonment: a paradox, written in French by Odet de la Noue lord of Teligni. 1594.

Monodia: an elegie in commemoration of Dame Hellen Branch widowe. [1594] (with Triumph of faith, above, appended).

The second weeke or childhood of the world. 1598. Trn of du Bartas.

Bartas his devine weekes and workes. 1605 (includes Τετράστιχα: the quadrains of G. de Faur [French and English, another edn 1614]), 1605, 1608 (with T. Hudson's trn of The historie of Judith), 1611, 1613, 1621 (with a collection of all the other workes translated and written by J. Sylvester), 1633, 1641; ed F. C. Haber, Gainesville 1965 (facs).

Posthumous Bartas: the third day of his second week. 1606.

Posthumus Bartas: the fore-noone of the fourth day of his second week. 1607.

Automachia: the self-conflict of a Christian. 1607. Trn from Latin of George Goodwin.

The heroyk life of Henry the Fourth, translated by E. Grimeston; a panegyre of Henry the Fourth, translated J. Sylvester. 1612. Tr from Pierre Matthieu.

Lachrimae lachrimarum. 1612, [1612], 1613 (with Other elegies).

The parliament of vertues royal. 1614. 5 pts, tr from Jean Bertaut et al.

The second session of the parliament of vertues reall. 2 pts 1615.

Tobacco battered and the pipes shattered. [1617–20]. Also issued as part of Second session, above.

The sacred workes of that famous poet Silvester. 1620.

The maidens blush: or Joseph. 1620. Trn of Girolamo Fracastoro.

The wood-mans bear: a poeme. 1620.

Panthea: or divine wishes and meditations. 1630.
Nebuchadnezzars fierie furnace, nach dem Ms Harley
7576. Ed M. Rösler, Louvain 1936 (Bang's Materialien
12). Anon play, attributed to Sylvester by Rösler.

ROBERT TOFTE
1562–1620

Laura: the toyes of a traveller, by R.T. gent. 1597; ed E.
Arber, English garner vol 8, 1896; ed S. Lee, Elizabethan
sonnets vol 2, 1904. 124 short poems, 30 said not to be
by R.T.
Two tales translated out of Ariosto, the one in dispraise
of men the other in disgrace of women, by R.T. gent.
1597. K–N4, probably continuation of Orlando inamorato below.
Alba: the months minde of a melancholy lover; certaine
divine poems by R.T. gent. 1598; ed A. B. Grosart,
Manchester 1880.
Orlando inamorato: the three first bookes of Boiardo done
into English heroicall verse, by R.T. 1598. Entered
1592.
A controversy between the two Tassi [Ercole and Tor-
quato] of marriage and wiving, done into English by
R.T. gent. 1599. Prose.
The batchelars banquet. 1603, 1604, 1630, 1631 (all anon);
ed F. P. Wilson, Oxford 1929, who attributes to Tofte;
also attributed to T. Dekker. Based on Les quinze joyes
de mariage attributed to Antoine de la Sale. Prose.
Ariostos satyres by Garvis Markham. 1608, 1609, 1611
(as Ariostos seven planets, with a new addition of three
Elegies, anon). Claimed by Tofte in Blazon of jealousie,
below.
Honours academie: the famous pastorall of the faire
shepherdesse Julietta; divers histories, englished by
R.T. 1610. Entered 1607; tr from French of N. de
Montreaux.
The blazon of jealousie, translated by R.T. 1615. From
Italian of B. Varchi.

CYRIL TOURNEUR
1575?–1626

The transformed metamorphosis. 1600; A funerall poeme
upon Sir Francis Vere, 1609; A griefe on the death of
Prince Henrie, 1613. *See col 241, below.*

GEORGE TURBERVILE
c. 1544–c. 1597

The eclogs of B. Mantuan [Spagnuoli] turned into English.
1567, 1572, 1594; ed D. Bush, New York 1937 (facs).
Entered 1566–7.
The heroycall epistles of Ovidius, with Aulus [Angelus]
Sabinus aunsweres. 1567 (3 edns), 1569, [1570?],
[c. 1584], 1600; ed F. S. Boas 1928. Entered 1566–7.
Epitaphes, epigrams, songs and sonets, with a discourse of
the affections of Tymetes to Pyndara. 1567 (newly
corrected with addns), 1570; ed A. Chalmers, English
poets vol 2, 1810; ed J. P. Collier [1867]. Entered
1566–7.
Commendatory verses to G. Fenton, Certaine tragicall
discourses, 1567; D. Roulands's trn of Lazarillo de
Tormes, 1586 (entered 1568–9).
A plaine path to perfect vertue devised by [D.] Mancinus.
1568. Entered 1567–8.
The booke of faulconrie or hauking collected out of the
best aucthors. 1575, 1611 (corrected, 2 issues). Prose.
The noble arte of venerie or hunting, translated out of the
best authors. [1575] (anon), 1611; rptd in Tudor and
Stuart library, 1908. Prose, 15 poems; by George
Gascoigne;

The author being in Muscovia [1568–9] wrytes to certaine
his frendes in England of the state of the place. In his
Tragical tales, 1587; in R. Hakluyt, The principall
navigations of the English nation, 1589.
Tragical tales translated out of sundrie Italians. 1587,
Edinburgh 1837.

WILLIAM WARNER
1558–?1609

Pan his syrinx or pipe. [1584], 1597 (as Syrinx or a seaven-
fold historie newly perused); ed W. A. Bacon, Evanston
1950 (with biography). Prose fiction.
Albions England. 1586 (4 bks from Noah to Norman
Conquest), 1589 (rev and continued, 6 bks to Henry VII),
1592 (3rd time corrected and augmented, 9 bks to
Elizabeth), 1596 (rev and newly enlarged, 12 bks with
prose epitome), 1597 (another issue), 1602 (13 bks),
1612; ed A. Chalmers, English poets vol 4, 1810 (from
1596, without epitome).
Menaecmi out of Plautus by W.W. 1595; ed J. Nichols,
Six old plays vol 1, 1779; ed W. C. Hazlitt, Shakespeare's
library vol 1, 1875; 1905 (with Comedy of Errors); ed
W. H. D. Rouse 1912 (with Latin text); ed G. Bullough,
Narrative and dramatic sources of Shakespeare vol 1,
1957. Prose trn.
A continuance of Albions England. 1606 (bks 14–16 to
James I).

THOMAS WATSON
1557?–92

Collections

Poems. Ed E. Arber 1870, Westminster 1895, 1910.
Hekatompathia, Meliboeus, An eglogue, T.W.'s Tears
of fancie (not by Watson), commendatory poems and
dedications.

§1

Sophoclis Antigone interprete T. Watsono; huic adduntur
pompae quaedam. 1581. Latin verse.
The Ἑκατομπαθία: or passionate centurie of love.
[1582], 1869 (Spenser Soc); ed S. K. Henninger jr,
Gainesville 1964 (facs).
Amyntas. 1585 (Latin verse); tr Abraham Fraunce, The
lamentations of Amyntas translated into English
hexameters, 1587, 1588, 1589, 1591 (in The Countesse
of Pembrokes Yvychurch), 1596; both ed W. F. Staton
jr and F. M. Dickey, Chicago 1967.
Compendium memoriae localis. [1585?]. Latin prose.
Coluthi Thebani Helenae raptus Latinus paraphraste.
1586. Latin verse.
A gratification unto John Case for his booke in praise of
musicke. [1586?] (anon, music by W. Byrd); ed M. C.
Boyd, Elizabethan music and musical criticism, Philadelphia 1940 (facs); attributed to Watson in Bodley
ms Rawlinson poetry 148, ed J. Haslewood, British
bibliographer vol 2, 1812.
Meliboeus: sive ecloga in obitum D. Francisci Walsing-
hami. 1590. Latin verse.
An eglogue upon the death of Sir Francis Walsingham.
1590. Watson's own trn of his Meliboeus.
The first sett of Italian madrigalls englished. 1590 (music
by W. Byrd); ed F. I. Carpenter, JEGP 2 1899 (with
sources); ed W. Bolle, Palaestra 29 1903; English
madrigal verse, ed E. H. Fellowes, Oxford 1967 (3rd
edn rev F. W. Sternfeld and D. Greer).
A dialogue of Bernard Palessy concerning waters and
fountains translated out of French. Harvard ms English
707. Prose, written c. 1590.
Amintae gaudia. 1592 (Latin verse); tr I.T. as An ould
facioned love, 1594.
The Phoenix nest. 1593. 3 poems.

GEORGE WHETSTONE
c. 1551–87

§ 1

Commendatory poems to G. Gascoigne, Posies, 1575; T. Kendall, Floweres of epigrammes, 1577.

The rocke of regard. 1576; ed J. P. Collier [1870]. Verse and prose fiction.

A remembraunce of George Gaskoigne. [1577]; ed A. Chalmers, Works of the English poets vol 2, 1810; Bristol 1815, London 1821 (with Gascoigne, Princely pleasures); ed E. Arber 1868 (with Gascoigne, Notes of instruction etc); Edinburgh 1885.

The right excellent historye of Promos and Cassandra devided into two commicall discourses. 1578; [ed J. Nichols], Six old plays vol 1, 1779; ed W. C. Hazlitt, Shakespeare's library vol 6, 1875; ed I. Gollancz, Oxford 1909; ed J. S. Farmer, Tudor facsimile texts, 1910; ed G. Bullough, Narrative and dramatic sources of Shakespeare vol 2, 1958; ed G. G. Smith, Elizabethan critical essays vol 1, Oxford 1904 (epistle only). 2-pt verse play, unacted.

Verses of 20 good precepts. In The paradyse of daynty devises, 1578 etc.

A remembrance of Sir Nicholas Bacon. [1579]; ed A. Boswell, Auchinleck 1816.

An heptameron of civill discourses. 1582, 1593 (as Aurelia the paragon of pleasure). Prose fiction, some verse.

A remembraunce of Sir James Dier. [1582–3?]; ed A. Boswell, Auchinleck 1816.

A remembraunce of Thomas [Radcliffe], late Earle of Sussex. 1583; ed A. Boswell, Auchinleck 1816.

A mirour for magestrates of cyties; a touchstone for the time. 1584, 1586 (as The enemie to unthryftinesse). Prose.

A mirror of the life of Frauncis [Russell] Earle of Bedford. 1585; ed T. Park, Heliconia vol 2, 1815.

The honorable reputation of a souldier. 1585, Leyden 1586 (with Dutch trn). Prose.

The English myrror. 1586. Prose.

The censure of a loyall subject. 1587 (2 issues); ed J. P. Collier, Illustrations of early English popular literature vol 1, 1863. Prose dialogue on Babington conspiracy.

Sir Philip Sidney his honorable life. [1587]; ed A. Boswell, Auchinleck 1816.

§ 2

Izard, T. C. Whetstone: mid-Elizabethan gentleman of letters. New York 1942.

THOMAS WHYTHORNE
1528–96

Songes for three, fower, and five voyces. 1571; ed R. Immelmann, Sh Jb 39 1903 (words of 76 songs, music of 3rd pt only).

Duos or songs for two voices. 1590; ed W. Bergmann, Fifteen duos in canon for divers recorders, 1955 (last pt only). Words and music of 51 songs.

A book of songs and sonetts, with discoorses of the chylds, yoong mans and entring old mans lyfe. Bodley ms English Miscellaneous c.33, written c. 1576; ed J. M. Osborn, Autobiography of Thomas Whythorne, Oxford 1961 (old spelling), 1962 (modernized). Prose with 197 poems.

See also col 163, below.

V. JACOBEAN AND CAROLINE POETRY

(1) COLLECTIONS AND ANTHOLOGIES

Saintsbury, G. Minor poets of the Caroline period. 3 vols Oxford 1905–21.

Fellowes, E. H. English madrigal verse 1588–1632. Oxford 1920, 1929 (rev), 1967 (rev and enlarged by F. W. Sternfeld and D. Greer).

Grierson, H. J. C. Metaphysical lyrics and poems. Oxford 1921.

—— and G. Bullough. The Oxford book of seventeenth-century verse. Oxford 1934.

Ault, N. Seventeenth-century lyrics from the original texts. 1928, 1950 (rev).

Howarth, R. G. Minor poets of the seventeenth century. 1931 (EL), 1953 (rev).

Brinkley, R. F. English poetry of the seventeenth century. New York 1936.

Cutts, J. P. Seventeenth-century songs and lyrics, from the original music manuscripts. Columbia Missouri 1959.

Gardner, H. The metaphysical poets. 1957 (Penguin), Oxford 1961 (rev), London 1967 (Penguin), 1972 (rev).

Martz, L. L. The meditative poem: an anthology of seventeenth-century verse. New York 1963.

(2) GENERAL STUDIES

Gosse, E. From Shakespeare to Pope. 1885.

—— The Jacobean poets. 1894.

Quiller-Couch, A. T. In his Studies in literature: first series, Cambridge 1918.

Eliot, T. S. The metaphysical poets. TLS 20 Oct 1921; rptd in his Homage to John Dryden, 1924 and Selected essays, 1932. A review of Grierson's anthology, above. The unpbd ms of his 1926 Clark lectures on the Metaphysicals is in the library of King's College Cambridge.

Grierson, H. J. C. In his Cross-currents in seventeenth-century literature, 1929.

Williamson, G. The Donne tradition: English poetry from Donne to Cowley. Cambridge Mass 1930.

—— Seventeenth-century contexts. 1960.

—— The proper wit of poetry. 1961.

—— Six metaphysical poets: a reader's guide. New York

1967, London 1968 (as A reader's guide to the metaphysical poets).

Leishman, J. B. The metaphysical poets: Donne, Herbert, Vaughan, Traherne. Oxford 1934.

Praz, M. Studi sul concettismo. Milan 1934; tr with addns and new bibliography as Studies in seventeenth-century imagery, 2 vols 1939–47 (Warburg Inst), 1 vol Rome 1964 (rev).

—— The flaming heart: essays on Crashaw, Machiavelli and other studies of the relations between Italian and English literature from Chaucer to T. S. Eliot. Garden City NY 1958.

Tuve, R. Elizabethan and metaphysical imagery: Renaissance poetic and twentieth-century critics. Chicago 1947.

Mahood, M. M. In her Poetry and humanism, 1950.

Nicolson, M. H. The breaking of the circle. Evanston 1950.

Jones, R. F. et al. The seventeenth century. Stanford 1951.

Martz, L. L. The poetry of meditation: a study in English religious literature of the seventeenth century. New Haven 1954, 1962 (with addns).

—— The paradise within: studies in Vaughan, Traherne and Milton. New Haven 1964.

—— The wit of love: Donne, Carew, Crashaw, Marvell. Notre Dame Ind 1969.

Røstvig, M.-S. The happy man: studies in the metamorphosis of a classical idea 1600–1700. 2 vols Oslo and Oxford 1954–8, 1962 (rev).

Walton, G. Metaphysical to Augustan: studies in tone and sensibility in the seventeenth century. Cambridge 1955.

Ford, B. (ed). From Donne to Marvell. 1956 (Pelican), 1968 (rev).

Hibbard, G. R. The country house poem of the seventeenth century. Jnl Warburg & Courtauld Inst 19 1956.

Ellrodt, R. Les poètes métaphysiques anglais. 3 vols Paris 1960.

Wedgwood, C. V. Poetry and politics under the Stuarts. Cambridge 1960.

Keast, W. R. (ed). Seventeenth-century poetry: modern essays in criticism. New York 1962, 1971 (with addns).

Donne, Sandys, Phineas Fletcher, Drummond, Giles Fletcher, Wither, Browne, Herrick, King, Quarles, Herbert, Carew, Habington, Davenant, Waller, Suckling, Crashaw, Denham, Cowley, Lovelace, Marvell, Vaughan, Traherne

JOHN DONNE
1572–1631

Bibliographies etc

Keynes, G. L. A bibliography of Donne. Cambridge 1914, 1932, 1958, Oxford 1973 (rev and enlarged).

Combs, H. C. and Z. R. Sullens. Concordance to the English poems of Donne. Chicago 1940.

Collections and Selections

Poems. 1633, 1635, 1639, 1649, 1650, 1654, 1669, 1719, Edinburgh 1779 (Bell's poets); ed E. K. Chambers, introd by G. Saintsbury 1896 (ML); ed H. J. C. Grierson 2 vols Oxford 1912, 1 vol Oxford 1929 (OSA) (without notes); ed J. Hayward, Complete poetry and selected prose, 1929 (Nonesuch Lib), 1930; ed R. S. Hillyer, New York [1941] (with Blake's poems); ed R. E. Bennett, Chicago [1942]; ed F. Kermode, [New York] 1968.

LXXX sermons. 1640. With Walton's life.

Fifty sermons. 1649.

XXVI sermons. 1660, 1661 (2 issues).

Works. Ed H. Alford 6 vols 1839.

Selected passages from the sermons. Ed L. P. Smith, Oxford 1919.

Ten sermons. Ed G. L. Keynes 1923 (Nonesuch Press).

Complete poetry and selected prose. Ed J. Hayward 1929 (Nonesuch Lib), 1936 (rev).

Poetry and prose, with Walton's life. Ed H. W. Garrod, Oxford 1946.

Poems. Ed J. Hayward 1950 (Penguin). A selection.

Divine poems. Ed H. Gardner, Oxford 1952, 1978 (rev); Elegies, and Songs and sonnets, ed Gardner, Oxford 1965; Satires, epigrams and verse letters, ed W. Milgate, Oxford 1967; Anniversaries, epithalamions and epicedes, ed Milgate, Oxford 1978.

Complete sermons. Ed G. R. Potter and E. M. Simpson 10 vols Berkeley and Los Angeles 1953–62.

Songs and sonets. Ed T. Redpath 1956.

Sermons on the Psalms and Gospels, with a selection of prayers and meditations. Ed E. M. Simpson, Berkeley 1963.

Complete English poems. Ed A. J. Smith 1971 (Penguin).

Donne's prebend sermons. Ed J. M. Mueller, Cambridge Mass 1971.

§1

Pseudo-martyr. 1610. A Protestant prose text for English Catholics.

Conclave Ignati. [1611], [1611]; Ignatius his conclave, 1611 (3 edns), 1626, 1634, 1635, 1653, 1680; ed C. M. Coffin, New York 1941 (facs of first English edn); ed T. S. Healy, Oxford 1969 (both versions, Latin and English).

An anatomy of the world. 1611, ed G. L. Keynes, Cambridge 1951 (Roxburghe Club) (facs); The second anniversary: of the progress of the soule, 1612 (with First anniversary), 1621, 1625; ed J. Sparrow, New York 1927 (facs); Shaftesbury 1929; The anniversaries, ed F. Manley, Baltimore 1963. In Second anniversary, only Of the progress of the soul is by Donne.

[Sermon of valediction at his going into Germany preached at Lincoln's Inn April 18 1619. Ed E. M. Simpson 1932; ed G. R. Potter, Stanford 1946.]

Sermon on Acts i, 8. 1622, 1624.

Sermon on Judges xx. 15 [i.e. v. 20]. 1622 (3 issues).

Encaenia: the feast of Dedication celebrated at Lincoln's Inn in a sermon on Ascension day. 1623.

Three sermons. 1623, 1624.

Devotions upon emergent occasions. 1624, 1624, 1624, 1626, 1627, 1634, 1638, Oxford 1841; ed J. Sparrow, Cambridge 1923 (with bibliographical note by G. L. Keynes); ed W. H. Draper [1925].

First sermon preached to King Charles. 1625.

Four sermons. 1625.

Sermon preached at Whitehall. 1626.

Five sermons. 1626, Menston 1970 (facs).

Sermon of Commemoration. 1627.

Death's duell. 1632, 1633, 1633.

Juvenilia: or certaine paradoxes and problems. 1633, 1633, 1652 (with addns as Paradoxes, problems, essayes, characters; usually bound with Essayes in divinity, below), 1652 (slightly rev); ed R. E. Bennett, New York 1936 (facs).

Sermon on John viii. 15. 1634. Part of Six sermons, below.

Six sermons. 1634.

Two sermons. 1634.

Sermon upon Ecclesiastes xii. 1. In Sapientia clamitaus, 1638, 1639.

Biathanatos. 1646, 1648, 1700; ed J. W. Hebel, New York [1930] (facs).

Essayes in divinity. 1651 (usually bound with Juvenilia 1652, above); ed A. Jessopp 1855; ed E. M. Simpson, Oxford 1952.

To Mr E[verard] G[uilpin]. In E. Gosse, Life and letters of Donne, 1899.

Sermon on Psalm xxxviii. 9. 1921 (facs of Dowden ms).

Cataiogus librorum. Ed E. M. Simpson 1930 (with trn). Rptd from Poems 1650, 1654, 1669, 1719.

An elegy. Ed E. K. Chambers, RES 7 1931. From Holgate ms, Pierpont Morgan Lib, New York.

Letters, Diaries etc

Poems. 1633, 1635, 1639, 1649, 1650, 1654, 1669, 1719. Each contains same 11 letters. 1635–1719 add 4.
LXXX sermons. 1640. Letter in Walton's Life.
Letters to several persons of honour. 1651, 1654; ed E. E. Merrill jr, New York 1910.
Cabala. 1654, 1663, 1691. 2 letters.
Walton, I. Life of Donne. 1658. 5 letters.
—— Life of Herbert. 1670. 4 letters.
—— Lives of Donne, Wootton, Hooker, Herbert. 1670. 9 letters.
Collection of letters made by Sir Tobie Matthew. 1660, 1692. 38 letters to and from Donne.
The Loseley manuscripts. Ed A. J. Kempe 1835. 10 letters.
Works of Donne vol 6. Ed H. Alford 1839.
Gosse, E. Life and letters of Donne. 2 vols 1899. Includes 19 unpbd letters.
Simpson, E. M. A study of the prose works of Donne. Oxford 1924. 32 unpbd letters.
Letter to Sir Nicholas Carey (Carew, 21 June 1625). Ed T. Spencer, Cambridge Mass 1929.

§2

For early criticism see Donne: the critical heritage, *ed A. J. Smith 1975.*

Walton, I. The life of Donne. 1640 (in Lxxx sermons), 1658 (enlarged).
Gosse, E. The life and letters of Donne. 2 vols 1899.
Simpson, E. M. A study of the prose works of Donne. Oxford 1924, 1948 (rev).
Wilson, F. P. The early life of Donne. RES 3 1927.
Legouis, P. Donne the craftsman. Paris 1928.
Williamson, G. The Donne tradition. Cambridge Mass 1930.
—— In his Proper wit of poetry, 1961.
Spencer, T., T. S. Eliot et al. A garland for Donne 1631–1931. Cambridge Mass 1931.
Lewis, C. S. Donne and love poetry. In Seventeenth-century studies presented to Sir Herbert Grierson, Oxford 1938. Reply by J. Bennett, ibid. Both rptd in Seventeenth-century English poetry, ed W. R. Keast, New York 1962.
Bald, R. C. Donne and the Drurys. Cambridge 1959.
—— Donne: a life. Ed W. Milgate, Oxford 1970.
Garrod, H. W. The date of Donne's birth. TLS 30 Dec 1944.
—— Donne and Mrs Herbert. RES 21 1945.
—— The Latin poem addressed by Donne to Dr Andrews. RES 21 1945.
Moloney, M. F. Donne: his flight from medievalism. Urbana 1944.
—— Donne's metrical practice. PMLA 65 1950.
Wiggins, E. L. Logic in the poetry of Donne. SP 42 1945.
Lederer, J. Donne and emblematic practice. RES 22 1946.
Brooks, C. In his Well wrought urn, New York 1947.
Martz, L. L. Donne in meditation: the Anniversaries. ELH 14 1947.
—— Donne and meditative tradition. Thought 34 1959.
—— Donne: the meditative voice. Massachusetts Rev 1 1960.
—— In his Wit of love, Notre Dame Ind 1969.
Grierson, H. J. C. Donne and the via media. MLR 43 1948.
—— The metaphysics of Donne and Milton. In his Criticism and creation, 1949.

Empson, W. Donne and the rhetorical tradition. Kenyon Rev 11 1949; rptd in Seventeenth-century poetry: modern essays in criticism, ed W. R. Keast, New York 1962.
—— Donne the space man. Kenyon Rev 19 1957.
—— Donne in the new edition. CQ 8 1966.
Pafford, J. H. P. Donne's library. TLS 2 Sept 1949 f.
Leishman, J. B. Donne: the monarch of wit. 1951, 1962 (rev).
Gardner, H. (ed). Donne: a collection of critical essays. Englewood Cliffs NJ 1962.
Gardner, H. On editing Donne. TLS 24 Aug 1967.
Donne: essays in celebration. Ed A. J. Smith 1972.

GEORGE SANDYS
1578–1644

Bibliographies

Bowers, F. T. and R. B. Davis. Sandys: a bibliographical catalogue of printed editions in England to 1700. BNYPL April–June 1950.

Collections

Selections from the paraphrases, with memoir [by H. J. Todd]. 1839.
Poetical works. Ed R. Hooper 2 vols 1872.

§1

A relation of a journey. 1615, 1621, 1627, 1632, 1637, 1652 (as Sandys travailes), 1658, 1670, 1673, 1864.
The first five books of Ovid's Metamorphosis. 1621 (3 issues).
Ovid's Metamorphosis englished by G.S. 1626, 1628 (unauthorized), Oxford 1632 (rev and with An essay to the translation of Virgil's Aeneis), 1638, 1640, 1656, 1664, 1669, 1678, 1690.
A paraphrase upon the Psalmes, by G.S. 1636.
A paraphrase upon the divine poems. 1638, 1648, 1676. An enlarged edn of preceding.
Christ's passion: a tragedie. 1640, 1640, 1687, 1693. Tr from Hugo Grotius.
A paraphrase upon the song of Solomon, by G.S. 1641, 1642.

§2

Davis, R. B. Sandys: poet-adventurer. New York 1955.

PHINEAS FLETCHER
1582–1650

Collections

Poems. Ed A. B. Grosart 4 vols 1869 (Fuller Worthies' Lib).
Poetical works of Giles and Phineas Fletcher. Ed F. S. Boas 2 vols Cambridge 1908–9.

§1

Locustae: vel pietas Jesuitica. 2 pts [Cambridge] 1627. The locusts or apollyonists.
Brittain's Ida written by that renowned poët Edmond Spencer. 1628. Really by Fletcher.
Sicelides a piscatory. 1631. Anon. Variant texts in BM additional ms 4453 and Bodley Rawlinson poetry ms 214.
Joy in tribulation: or consolations for afflicted spirits. 1632.

The way to blessedness: or a treatise on the first psalme. 1632.

Sylva poetica. Cambridge 1633. Part of Giles Fletcher, De literis antiquae Britanniae.

The purple island. Cambridge 1633, 1633. Includes Piscatorie eclogs, Poetical miscellanies, and Elisa or an elegie upon the unripe decease of Antonie Irby. The Piscatorie eclogs and Elisa have separate title-pages, each with imprint Cambridge 1633. Purple island rptd 1783, ed H. Headley 1816. Piscatorie eclogs and Poetical miscellanies rptd Edinburgh 1771, Amsterdam 1971 (facs of 1633).

A father's testament. 1670.

Venus and Anchises—Britain's Ida—and other poems. Ed E. Seaton 1926 (Royal Soc of Lit) (from ms).

WILLIAM DRUMMOND OF HAWTHORNDEN
1585-1649
Collections

The history of Scotland 1423-1542. 1655, 1680, 1681, 1682. Virtually a collected edn of Drummond's prose; includes Cypresse grove, various political tracts and selected letters. Preface by 'Mr Hall of Grayes Inn'.

Poems. 1656, 1659. Preface by Edward Phillips. Contains most pbd poems and 35 new poems, 2 probably not Drummond's.

Works. [Ed J. Sage and T. Ruddiman], Edinburgh 1711. Adds about 40 poetical pieces and hymns, many of doubtful authenticity, various tracts and papers, a selection of Drummond's correspondence, and a memoir by Bishop Sage.

Poems. Ed W. C. Ward 2 vols 1894 (ML), [1905].

Poetical works, with A cypresse grove. Ed L. E. Kastner, Manchester 1913, Edinburgh 1913 (STS).

Poetry and prose. Ed R. H. MacDonald, Edinburgh 1976. A selection.

§1

Tears on the death of Meliades. Edinburgh 1613, 1614 (3rd edn), 1614.

Mausoleum: or the choisest flowres of the epitaphs. Edinburgh 1613; rptd D. Laing, Fugitive Scottish poetry of the seventeenth century ser 1, Edinburgh 1853. 3 poems by Drummond.

Poems. [Edinburgh? 1614?] (priv ptd for distribution to Drummond's friends?), Edinburgh 1616 (expanded and rev as Poems: amorous, funerall, divine, pastorall, in sonnets, songs, sextains, madrigals); rptd [by T. Maitland], Edinburgh 1832. Edn of 1616 includes, with separate undated title-page, Madrigals and epigrams by W.D., Menston 1969 (facs of 1614?), Amsterdam 1969 (facs of 1616).

In memory of Euphemia Kyninghame. [Edinburgh 1616].

Forth feasting: a panegyricke to the King's most excellent Majestie. Edinburgh 1617, 1618 (in The Muses welcome [to King James]); ed J. Adamson with a new sonnet by Drummond prefixed 1656.

A midnight's trance. 1619, 1630 (as A cypresse grove, with Flowers of Sion), 1905, 1907 (with note by A. H. Bullen); ed S. Clegg 1919; ed R. Ellrodt, Oxford 1951 (from 1619).

Flowres of Sion; to which is adjoyned his Cypresse grove. [Edinburgh] 1623 (3 issues), Edinburgh 1630 (adds 4 poems).

Auctarium bibliothecae Edinburgenae. 1627.

The entertainment of the high and mighty monarch Charles King of Great Britaine. Edinburgh 1633.

To the exequies of the honourable Sr Antonye Alexander, knight: a pastorall elegie. Edinburgh 1638.

Polemo-Medinia inter Vitarvam et Nebernam. [Edinburgh? 1645?], [Aberdeen? 1670?], Oxford 1691 (as

Accedit Jacobi id nominis quinti regis Scotorum cantilena rustica etc), Edinburgh 1742, Glasgow 1748, 1768, 1813 (in Carminum variorum macaronicorum of the Conventus gymnasticus of Edinburgh). Macaronic verse.

The drunkards character. 1646.

The drunkard forewarn'd. 1680.

Muckomachy: or the midden-fecht. Edinburgh 1846. Poem in 3 cantos, with addns by later hands.

The diary. Miscellany of Scottish Soc 5 1942.

§2

Conversations of Ben Jonson with Drummond. Ed D. Laing 1842 (Shakespeare Soc); ed R. F. Patterson 1923; ed C. H. Herford and P. Simpson, Ben Jonson vol 1, Oxford 1925.

Laing, D. A brief account of the Hawthornden manuscripts in the possession of the Society of Antiquaries of Scotland; with extracts, containing unpublished letters and poems of Drummond. Trans Soc Antiquaries of Scotland 4 1831.

Masson, D. Drummond. 1873.

Joly, A. Drummond. Lille 1935.

Fogle, F. R. A critical study of Drummond. Oxford 1952.

MacDonald, R. H. The library of Drummond of Hawthornden. Edinburgh 1971.

GILES FLETCHER the younger
1588?-1623
Collections

Poems. Ed A. B. Grosart 1868 (Fuller's Worthies' Lib).

Complete poems. Ed A. B. Grosart 1876.

Poetical works of Giles and Phineas Fletcher. Ed F. S. Boas 2 vols Cambridge 1908-9.

Complete poems. Ed D. C. Sheldon, Madison 1938.

§1

Sorrowes joy: or a lamentation for our late deceased soveraigne Elizabeth, with a triumph for the prosperous succession of our gratious King James. Cambridge 1603. Attributed to Fletcher.

Christs victorie and triumph in heaven and earth, over and after death. Cambridge 1610, 1610, 1632, 1640, London 1640; 1783 (with The purple island), 1824 (with life and extracts from George Herbert); ed R. Cattermole and H. Stebbing 1834; ed W. T. Brooke [1888]; ed N. Alexander, Elizabethan narrative verse, 1967.

The reward of the faithfull. 1623, 1923. Prose.

GEORGE WITHER
1588-1667
Collections

Workes: containing satyrs, epigrams, eclogues, sonnets and poems. 1620. Pirated.

Juvenilia. 1622, 1626, 1633, 3 pts 1871 (Spenser Soc). Abuses stript and whipt, The scourge, Epigrams, Prince Henries obsequies, A satyre, Epithalamia, Shepheards hunting; Menston 1970 (facs of 1622). 1633 and some copies of 1622 add Wither's Motto, Faire-virtue and some minor verse.

Ecchoes from the sixth trumpet. [1666], 1668 (as Nil ultra: or the last works of Captain George Wither), 1669 (as Fragmenta prophetica: or the remains of George Wither). Excerpts from Wither's prophetic poems connected by short prose paragraphs, and some new verse.

Miscellaneous works. 6 vols 1872-3 (Spenser Soc). These, together with the other Spenser Soc reprints, form an almost complete edn of Wither.

Poems. Ed H. Morley 1891.

Poetry. Ed F. Sidgwick 2 vols 1902. With important biographical introd.

§I

Prince Henries obsequies or mournefull elegies upon his death. 1612, 1622, 1633.

Epithalamia: or nuptiall poems. 1612, 1633.

Abuses stript and whipt; also the Scourge, Epigrams. 1613 (at least 4 edns), 1614, 1615, 1617, 1622.

[W. Browne], Shepheard's pipe. 1614. Contains Wither's Thirsis and Alexis and Another eclogue, rptd as Eclogues 5–6 of Shepheard's hunting, below, as well as To his Melissa, which may be Wither's.

A satyre: dedicated to his most excellent Majestie. 1614, 1615 (at least 2 edns), 1616.

Fidelia. 1615, 1617, 1619, 1622; ed S. E. Brydges 1815 (text of 1619 collated with 1633); ed E. Arber, English garner vol 6, 1883 (from 1615).

The shepheards hunting. 1615 (3 edns); ed S. E. Brydges 1814 (text of 1633 collated with 1615 and 1622); ed R. Southey, Select works of the British poets, 1831.

A preparation to the Psalter. 1619, 1884 (Spenser Soc).

Exercises upon the first psalme. 1620, 1892 (Spenser Soc).

The songs of the Old testament, translated into English measures. 1621.

Wither's motto: Nec habeo, nec careo, nec curo. [London] 1621, nd (with engraved title-page), 1621 (engraved title-page), 1623 (with postscript, at least 2 edns); ed S. E. Brydges, Restituta vol 1, 1814.

Faire-virtue, the mistresse of Phil'arete. 1622, 1622, 1622 (both with new title-pages, once perhaps as part of Juvenilia), 1626, 1633; ed S. E. Brydges 1818 (text of 1622); ed E. Arber, English garner vol 4, 1882.

The hymnes and songs of the Church, translated and composed by G.W. 1623, 1623, [1624?]; ed S. E. Brydges 1815; ed H. E. Havergall 1846; ed E. Farr 1856; 1881 (Spenser Soc).

The schollers purgatory, discovered in the stationers commonwealth, and described in a discorse apologeticall. [1625?].

Britain's remembrancer. 1628, 2 pts 1880 (Spenser Soc). Extracts rptd 1642, 1643, both as Mr Wither his prophesie and as Wither's remembrancer; 1691 (in A collection of many wonderful prophecies), 1734 (in A warning to the inhabitants of Europe).

The psalmes of David translated into lyrick verse. Netherlands 1632, 2 pts 1881 (Spenser Soc).

A collection of emblemes, ancient and moderne. 4 bks 1635 (bks 2–4 dated 1634, various issues same year); ed J. Horden, Menston 1968 (facs); Zug [1969] (facs).

The nature of man written in Greek by Nemesius, englished. 1636, 1657.

A new song of a young mans opinion of the difference between good and bad women. Broadside, before 1640.

Heleluiah: or Britans second remembrancer. 1641; ed E. Farr 1856, 3 pts 1879 (Spenser Soc). Extracts as Wither's remembrancer, 1643.

A prophesie written long since. 1641.

Read and wonder: a warre between two entire friends, the Pope and the Divell. 1641.

Campo-Musae: or the field-musings of Captain George Wither. 1643, 1643, 1644, 1661.

Se defendendo: a shield, and shaft, against detraction. [1643].

Mercurius rusticus: or a countrey messenger. [1643]. Anon.

Letters of advice: touching the choice of knights and burgesses for the Parliament. [1644], 1645.

The speech without doore. [1644].

[?] The two incomparable Generalissimo's of the world briefly described. [1644?]. Signed G.W.

Wither's prophesie of the downfal of Antichrist. 1644.

The Great Assises holden in Parnassus by Apollo. 1645.

Vox pacifica: a voice tending to the pacification of God's wrath. 1645.

To the most honourable the Lords and Commons: petition. [1646].

Justitiarius justificatus: justice justified. [1646].

Opobalsamum anglicanum: an English balme, lately pressed out of a shrub and spread upon these papers. 1646.

What peace to the wicked? 1646. Anon. Attributed by Thomason.

Amygdala britannica, almonds for parrets. 1647. Anon. Attributed by Thomason.

Carmen expostulatorium. 1647.

Major Wither's disclaimer. 1647.

Articles presented against this Parliament, by Terrae-Filius. 1648.

A si quis, or queries. 1648. Excerpts in Ecchoes, 1666, 1840 (priv ptd).

Carmen-ternarium semi-cynicum. [1648?].

Prosopopoeia britannica: Britans genius, or good-angel, personated. 1648.

The tired petitioner. [1648]. Excerpts in Ecchoes, 1666.

A thankful retribution. 1649. Excerpts in Ecchoes, 1666.

An allarum from Heaven: or a memento to the great councell, by G.W. 1649.

Vaticinium votivum: or Palaemon's prophetick prayer. [1649] (2 edns, one with cancel). Anon.

Carmen eucharisticon: a private thank-oblation. 1649.

Respublica anglicana: or the historie of Parliament in their late proceedings. 1650, 1883 (Spenser Soc).

The true state of the case of. 1650.

Three grains of spirituall frankincense. 1651.

British appeals, with Gods mercifull replies. 1651, 1651.

A timely caution. 1652.

The dark lantern: containing a dim discoverie. 1653 (with A perpetuall Parliament).

Westrow revived. 1653.

The modern states-man. 1654.

To the Parliament of the Common-wealth: the humble petition of GW. [1654].

The protector. 1655.

Vaticinium causuale. 1655.

Boni ominis votum: a good omen to the next Parliament. [1656].

A cause allegorically stated. 1657. Excerpts in Ecchoes, 1666.

A suddain flash timely discovering some reason wherefore the stile of Protector should not be deserted by these nations. 1657.

The petition and narrative of Geo. Wither esq. [1659].

Epistolium-vagum-prosa-metricum: or an epistle at random. 1659.

A cordial confection, to strengthen their hearts whose courage begins to fail. 1659.

Salt upon salt: made out of certain ingenious verses upon the late storm and the death of his Highness ensuing. 1659.

Speculum speculativum, or a considering-glass: being an inspection into the present and late sad condition of these nations. 1660 (3 edns).

Furor-poeticus propheticus. 1660.

Fides-anglicana: or a plea for the publick-faith of these nations. 1660. Concludes with a list by Wither of his works—including many never ptd and some lost in ms.

Predictions of the overthrow of Popery. 1660, 1688.

The prisoners plea. 1661.

An improvement of imprisonment, disgrace, poverty, into real freedom; honest reputation; perdurable riches. 1661.

Joco-serio, Strange news, of a discourse between two dead giants. 1661. A retort to A dialogue between Colbrant and Brandamore.

A triple paradox: affixed to a counter-mure raised against the world, the flesh and the Devil. 1661.

Paralellogrammaton, An epistle to the three nations of

England, Scotland and Ireland. 1662, 1882 (Spenser Soc).

A proclamation in the name of the King of Kings, to all the inhabitants of the Isles of Great Brittain. 1662. Re-issued same year with Sig. A re-set.

Verses intended to the King's Majesty. 1662, 1662.

Tuba-pacifica, Seasonable precautions, whereby is sounded forth a retreat from the war intended between England and the United-Provinces. 1664.

A memorandum to London, occasioned by the pestilence. 1665. Includes Warning-piece to London, and Single sacrifice offered to almighty God.

Meditations upon the Lords Prayer. 1665.

Three private meditations. 1665, 1666.

Sigh for the Pitchers [upon the engagement expected 31 May 1666 with the Dutch]. 1666, 1666 (title corrected to Sighs).

Majesty in misery. 1681.

Mr Geo Withers revived. 1683. An extract from Britains remembrancer.

Divine poems (by way of paraphrase) on the Ten Commandments. 1688, 1728.

The grateful acknowledgement of a late trimming regulator. 1688.

The strange and wonderful prophecy. 1689. 1646 edn apparently not extant.

Withers redevivus. 1689.

A paraphrase of the Ten Commandments. 1697.

Vox vulgi: a poem in censure of the Parliament of 1661. Ed W. D. Macray 1880 (from ms).

The history of the pestilence 1625. Ed J. M. French, Cambridge Mass 1932 (from Magdalene College Cambridge ms, perhaps autograph).

[To the King when he was Prince of Wales]. Ed A. Pritchard, An unpublished poem by Wither, MP 61 1963.

WILLIAM BROWNE OF TAVISTOCK
1590?-1645?

Collections

Works. Ed W. Thompson [and T. Davies] 3 vols 1772.

Whole works. Ed W. C. Hazlitt 2 vols 1868-9 (Roxburghe Lib).

Poetical works. Ed G. Goodwin, with introd by A. H. Bullen 2 vols 1894 (ML).

§1

An elegie on the never inough bewailed death [of Henry Prince of Wales]. 1613. With another by Fulke Greville.

Britannia's pastorals. Bk 1, 1613; bks 1 (rev)-2, 1616, 1623; ed W. Thompson 1845; bk 3 (incomplete), ed T. C. Croker 1852 (Percy Soc) (from ms); Menston 1969 (facs of bks 1-2).

[An elegy, signed WB]. In Thomas Overbury (elder), Sir Thomas Overbury his wife, 1616.

The Inner Temple masque. (Acted 13 Jan 1614). In Works, 1772; ed G. Jones 1954 (with essay on Browne and the English masque; ed R. F. Hill, A book of masques in honour of Allardyce Nicoll, Cambridge 1967.

The shepherd's pipe. 1614, 1620 (as part of Wither's works).

[Commendatory poem, signed WB]. In Massinger, The Duke of Millaine, 1623.

[Commendatory poem, signed WB]. In Massinger, The bondman, 1624.

The history of Polexander [by Marin Le Roy] done into English by William Browne. 1647 (with 2nd title-page dated 1648).

Original poems never before published. Ed S. E. Brydges, Ickham 1815 (for 1816). From BM ms Lansdowne 777.

An uncollected poem by Browne. G. Tillotson, N & Q 20 Jan 1940.

ROBERT HERRICK
1591-1674

Bibliographies etc

Kerr, M. M. A bibliography of Herrick. Oxford 1936.

MacLeod, M. L. A concordance to the poems of Herrick. Oxford 1936.

Collections

Witts recreations. 1650 (4th edn). Many of Herrick's poems are included.

Select poems from the Hesperides. Ed J. N[ott], Bristol [1810].

Works. [Ed T. Maitland] 2 vols Edinburgh 1823 (with life), 2 vols 1825 (as Poetical works).

Complete poems. Ed A. B. Grosart 3 vols 1876.

Hesperides and Noble numbers. Ed A. W. Pollard, with preface by A. C. Swinburne 2 vols 1891 (ML).

Poetical works. Ed G. Saintsbury 2 vols 1893.

Poetical works. Ed F. W. Moorman, Oxford 1915, 1921 (text only), 2 vols 1935.

Poems. Oxford 1935 (WC).

Poetical works. Ed L. C. Martin, Oxford 1956, 1965.

Selected poems. Ed J. Hayward 1961.

Complete poetry. Ed J. M. Patrick, New York 1963, 1968 (with introd and new foreword).

§1

Hesperides: or, the works both humane and divine. 1648. Includes, with a separate title and pagination, His noble numbers, 1647, Menston 1969 (facs).

Poor Robin's visions. 1677. Sometimes attributed to Herrick.

A song for two voices. 1700 [?].

§2

Moorman, F. W. Herrick: a biographical and critical study. 1910, [1924].

Rollin, R. B. Herrick. New York 1966.

HENRY KING
Bishop of Chichester
1592-1669

Collections

Minor Caroline poets vol 3. Ed G. Saintsbury, Oxford 1921. King's English poems and critical introd.

Poems. Ed J. Sparrow 1925. With bibliography by G. L. Keynes.

Poems. Ed M. Crum, Oxford 1965.

§1

Elegy upon Charles I. 1648. Anon.

A groane at the funerall of Charles the first. 1649, 1649 (as A deepe groane).

Psalmes of David turned into meeter. 1651, 1654, 1671.

Poems, elegies, paradoxes and sonnets. 1657 (unauthorized), 1664 (with addns), 1700 (as Ben Johnson's poems, elegies, paradoxes and sonnets).

For prose see col 310, below.

§2

Berman, R. King and the seventeenth century. 1964.

FRANCIS QUARLES
1592–1644

Bibliographies

Horden, J. Quarles: a bibliography of his works to the year 1800. Oxford 1953 (Oxford Bibl Soc).

Collections

Divine poems [A feast for wormes, Hadassa, Job militant, Sions elegies, Sions sonets, Alphabet of elegies (on Dr Ailmer)]. 1630, 1633, 1634 (with The historie of Samson, Elegy on Dr Wilson, and Mildreiados (on Lady Luckyn)), 1638, 1642.
The loyall convert, with the New distemper. 1645.
The profest royalist [Loyall convert, New distemper, Whipper whipt]. 1645.
Solomons recantation with Enchiridion. 1649.
Complete works in prose and verse. Ed A. B. Grosart 3 vols Edinburgh 1880–1.
Hosanna and Threnodes. Ed J. Horden, Liverpool 1960.

§1

A feast for wormes: a poeme of the history of Jonah. 1620, 1626.
Hadassa: or the history of Queene Ester. 1621.
Job militant. 1624.
Sions elegies, wept by Jeremie the prophet. 1624, 1625.
Sions sonets, sung by Solomon. 1625, 1905.
Argalus and Parthenia. 1629, 1630, 1632, 1632, [c. 1632] (3 edns), 1647 etc.
Historie of Samson. 1631.
Divine fancies. 1632, 1633, 1636, 1638, 1641.
Quarlëis [Lusus poeticus poetis]. 1634.
Emblemes. 1635, 1635 (some copies with Quarlëis, above), 1639, 1643. From 1639 usually pbd with Hieroglyphikes; many edns and reissues before 1900.
An elegie upon Sir Julius Caesar. 1636, 1875.
An elegie upon Mr John Wheeler. 1637.
Hieroglyphikes of the life of man. 1638 (from 1639 usually pbd with Emblemes, above); ed J. Horden, Leeds 1969 (facs).
Memorials upon the death of Sir Robert Quarles. 1639.
Enchiridion. 1640 (enlarged), 1641, 1644 etc, 1695 (as Institutions, essays and maxims, political, moral and divine), 1698, 1698 (as Wisdom's better than money).
Sighes at the contemporary deaths of the Countess of Cleaveland and Mistrisse Cicily Killegrue with An elegie upon the death of Sir John Wolstenholme. 1640.
Threnodes on Lady Masham and William Cheyne. 1641.
Observations concerning princes and states upon peace and warre. 1642.
The loyall convert. 1644 (5 edns, one counterfeit dated 1643), 1645.
The whipper whipt. 1644.
Barnabas and Boanerges. 1644 (2nd pt of completed work), 1646 (as Judgement and Mercie); Judgement and Mercy, 1646 (first pt of completed work); Boanerges and Barnabas: or judgement and mercie, 1646 (complete work) etc.
The shepheards oracle. 1644 (one Eclogue); The Shepheards oracles, 1646 (10 Eclogues); 1646 (with The shepheards oracle added as Eclogue XI), 1646.
The new distemper. 1645.
Solomons recantation, entituled Ecclesiastes, paraphrased. 1645, 1648, 1649, 1680 (with Enchiridion).
Hosanna: or divine poems on the passion of Christ. 1647.
The virgin widow. 1649.

GEORGE HERBERT
1593–1633

Bibliographies etc

Palmer, G. H. A Herbert bibliography. Cambridge Mass 1911.
Mann, C. A concordance to the English poems of Herbert. Boston 1927.

Collections

Herbert's remains. 1652. Ed Barnabas Oley 3 pts, with separate title-page. Includes: A priest to the temple; Jacula prudentum; Apothegmes); 1836 (as The remains of that sweet singer of the Temple, George Herbert), 1841 (with lives by Izaak Walton and Oley), 1848; Menston 1970 (facs of 1652).
Works. Preface by W. Pickering, annotations of S. T. Coleridge 2 vols 1835–6, 1846, 1859.
Complete works. Ed A. B. Grosart 3 vols 1874 (Fuller Worthies' Lib).
English works newly arranged and annotated by G. H. Palmer. 3 vols 1905.
Works. Ed F. E. Hutchinson, Oxford 1941, 1945 (corrected).
Poems. Ed H. Gardner, Oxford 1961 (WC).
English poems. Ed C. A. Patrides 1974 (EL).

§1

Epicedium cantabrigiense. Cambridge 1612. 2 Latin poems by Herbert.
Lacrymae cantabrigienses. Cambridge 1619. One Latin poem by Herbert.
Ecclesiastes Solomonis, by J[ames] D[uport]. 1622. Contains Musae responsoriae, ad Andreae Melvini anti-tami-cami-categoriam.
Oratio habita coram dominus legatis. 1623.
Oratio quâ Principis Caroli reditum ex Hispaniis celebravit Georgius Herbert. Cambridge 1623.
Memoriae Francisci, Baronis de Verulamio, sacrum. 1626. One Latin poem by Herbert.
A sermon of commemoration of the Lady Danvers by John Donne. 1627. Contains Herbert's Parentalia.
The temple: sacred poems and private ejaculations. Cambridge 1633, 1633, 1634, 1635, 1638, 1641, 1660, 1667, 1674 (with Walton's life, and portrait by R. White), 1678 (some copies dated 1679), 1695, Bristol 1799, Lowell Mass 1834 (first American edn); ed F. Meynell 1927 (from Bodley ms); Menston 1968 (facs of 1633).
Hygiasticon by L. Lessius. 1634, 1634, 1636, 1678 (as The temperate man), Oxford 1935 (as How to live for 100 yrs). A treatise of temperance and sobrietie, by Luigi Cornaro (1475–1566), tr Herbert from Lessius' Latin version 1613.
Prefatory epistle [and 'briefe notes'] in The hundred and ten considerations of Signior John Valdesso. Oxford 1638, 1646 (a garbled edn); ed F. Chapman 1905.
Outlandish proverbs selected by Mr G.H. In Witts recreation, 1640, 1651 (separately as Jacula prudentum); ed T. Park, Facetiae, 2 vols 1817.
A priest to the temple: or the countrey parson his character, and rule of holy life. 1652, 1671 (with a new preface by B[arnabas] O[ley], 1675, 1701 etc; ed H. C. Beeching 1898, 1916; ed G. M. Forbes 1949 (selected passages).

Letters

Epistolary curiosities. Ed R[ebecca] W[est] 2 pts 1818. Includes unpbd letters; all collected in Works, ed Hutchinson 1941.

§2

Walton, Izaak. The life of Herbert. 1670, 1674 (with Temple), 1675 etc.

Addison, J. False wit. Spectator 7 May 1711.
Herbert, Edward (Baron Herbert of Cherbury). [Autobiography]. Strawberry Hill 1765; ed S. Lee 1886, [1906] (rev). By George's elder brother; *see col 156, below.*
—— Poems English and Latin. Ed G. C. Moore Smith, Oxford 1923.
Coleridge, S. T. Biographia literaria vol 2. 1817. Chs 19–20.
Ferrar, N. Two lives. Ed J. E. B. Mayor, Cambridge 1855.
Leishman, J. B. In his Metaphysical poets, Oxford 1934.
Knights, L. C. Herbert. Scrutiny 12 1944; rptd in his Explorations, 1946.
Tuve, R. A reading of Herbert. Chicago 1952.
Summers, J. H. Herbert: his religion and art. Cambridge Mass 1954.
Martz, L. L. In his Poetry of meditation, New Haven 1954, 1962 (with addns).

THOMAS CAREW
1595?–1640
Collections

Poems, songs and sonnets; together with a masque. [Ed T. Davies?] 1772.
Poems. Ed A. Vincent 1898 (ML).
Ed R. G. Howarth, Minor poets of the seventeenth century, 1931 (EL), 1953 (rev).
Poems, with his masque Coelum britannicum. Ed R. Dunlap, Oxford 1949.

§ I

The heire [by Thomas May]. 1622, 1633. Includes To Thomas May.
The just Italian [by William Davenport]. 1630. Includes To M. D'avenant.
Madrigals and ayres [by Walter Porter]. 1632. 2 songs by Carew.
Poems [by John Donne]. 1633. Includes An elegie upon Donne.
Coelum britannicum: a masque at Whitehall. 1634 (anon), 1640.
The witts [by William Davenant]. 1636. Includes a commendatory poem.
A paraphrase upon the divine poems [by George Sandys]. 1636. Includes a commendatory poem.
Romulus and Tarquin [by M. V. Malvezzi, tr H. Cary of Lepington]. 1637. Includes a commendatory poem.
Madagascar [by Davenant]. 1638. Includes a commendatory poem.
Poems. [Ed Aurelian Townshend?] 1640 (includes, with separate title but continuous pagination, Coelum britannicum), 1642 ('revised and enlarged', adds 8 poems, one by Waller), 1651 (as Poems, with a maske; adds 3 poems), 1670 (as Poems, songs and sonnets, together with a masque), 1671; Menston 1969 (facs, including Wyburd ms).

WILLIAM HABINGTON
1605–54
Collections

Castara: a collation of the editions of 1634, 1635 and 1640. Ed H. C. Combs, Evanston 1939.
Poems. Ed K. Allott, Liverpool 1948.

§ I

Castara. 2 pts 1634 (anon), 1 vol 1635 (corrected and augmented; adds 3 prose characters and 26 poems), 1636 (a variant of 1635), 1640 (adds 3rd pt: character A holy man and 22 poems); ed C. A. Elton, Bristol [1812]; ed R. Southey, Select works of the British poets, 1831; ed E. Arber 1870, 1895 (with collation of 3 original edns).
The Queen of Arragon. 1640 (anon); rptd Dodsley's Old plays vol 10, 1744; ed R. Thyer 1759; ed W. C. Hazlitt vol 13, 1875. *See* Samuel Butler's Remains vol 1, ed Thyer. A tragi-comedy.
The historie of Edward the Fourth. 1640; rptd and attributed to Habington, W. Kennett, Complete history of England vol 1, 1706.
Observations upon historie. 1641.
Several books contain commendatory verses by Habington, e.g. the 1647 folio of Beaumont and Fletcher, Jonsonus virbius 1638 (name given as W. Abington).

SIR WILLIAM DAVENANT
1606–68
Collections

Madagascar, with other poems. 1638, 1648.
Works. 1673.
Dramatic works. Ed J. Maidment and W. H. Logan 5 vols Edinburgh 1872–4, 1964.
Selected poems. Ed D. Bush, Cambridge Mass 1943.
Shorter poems and songs from the plays and masques. Ed A. M. Gibbs, Oxford 1972. Adds 6 poems to the canon.

§ I

The tragedy of Albovine. 1629.
The cruel brother. 1630. A tragedy.
The just Italian. 1630.
The temple of love. 1634 (for 1635). A masque.
The platonick lovers. 1636, 1665 (with The witts). A tragi-comedy.
The witts. 1636, 1665 (with The platonick lovers, as Two excellent plays); ed I. Reed, Dodsley's Old plays vol 8, 1780; ed W. Scott, Ancient British drama vol 1, 1810; ed J. P. Collier, Dodsley's Old plays vol 8, 1825–7. A comedy.
The triumphs of the Prince d'Amour. 1635. A masque.
Britannia triumphans. 1637 (for 1638). A masque.
Luminalia or the festivall of light. 1637 (anon); ed A. B. Grosart [1876]. A masque, attributed to Davenant.
Salmacida spolia. 1639; ed W. R. Chetwood, Select collection of old plays, Dublin 1750; ed H. A. Evans, English masques, 1879. A masque.
To the honourable knights, citizens etc. 1641 (at least 2 edns, one undated).
The unfortunate lovers. 1643, 1649. A tragedy.
London, King Charles his Augusta. 1648. Although ascribed to Davenant in the printer's epistle, T. H. Banks states it is not his.
Love and honour. 1649; ed J. W. Tupper, Boston 1909.
A discourse upon Gondibert. Paris 1650. Also issued as The preface to Gondibert. Ed J. E. Spingarn, Seventeenth-century critical essays vol 2, Oxford 1908.
Gondibert: an heroick poem. 1651 (8° and 4°), Menston 1970 (facs); ed D. F. Gladish, Oxford 1971.
The siege of Rhodes. 1656, 1659, 1663 (rev and expanded as The siege of Rhodes: the first and second part), 1670.
The first days entertainment at Rutland House. 1657.
The cruelty of the Spaniards in Peru. 1658.
The history of Sr Francis Drake. Pt 1 (all ptd), 1659.
Panegyrick to his Excellency the Lord Generall Monck. 1659. Folio sheet.
Prologue to his Majesty at the first play presented. 1660. Single folio.
Poem upon his sacred Majesties return. 1660.
Poem to the King's most sacred Majesty. 1663.
The rivals. 1668, 1669. A comedy.
The man's the master. 1669, 1775. A comedy.
The tempest. 1670, 1695 (with Works of John Dryden); ed M. Summers, Shakespearian adaptations, 1922. With John Dryden. A comedy, adapted from Shakespeare.
The law against lovers. 1673, 1970.

Macbeth, with all the alterations, amendments, additions
and new songs. 1674, 1674, 1687, 1695, 1697, 1710; ed
C. Spencer, New Haven 1961 (from Yale ms). Adapted
from Shakespeare.
The seventh and last canto of the third book of Gondibert.
1685; ed J. G. McManaway, MLQ 1 1940 (from 2 known
copies).
[Shakespeare's] Julius Caesar [with alterations by Davenant and John Dryden]. In A collection of plays by
eminent hands, 1719.

§2

Firth, C. H. Davenant and the revival of drama during the
Protectorate. EHR 18 1903.
Dowlin, C. M. Davenant's Gondibert, its preface and
Hobbes' answer: a study in English neo-classicism.
Philadelphia 1934.
Harbage, A. Davenant. Philadelphia 1935.
Nethercot, A. H. Davenant: poet laureate and playwright-
manager. Chicago 1938, New York 1967 (with additional
notes).

EDMUND WALLER
1606–87

Bibliographies
Osborne, M. T. Advice-to-a-painter poems 1633–1856.
Austin 1949. An annotated list.

Collections
Poems. 1645 (3 edns), 1664, 1668, 1682, 1686 (2 issues),
1693, etc, Menston 1971 (facs).
Divine poems. 1685.
The second part of Mr Waller's poems. 1690, 1690, 1705,
1711, 1712, 1722. The anon preface is generally attri-
buted to Francis Atterbury.
Works in verse and prose. Ed E. Fenton 1729, 1730, 1742,
1752, 1758 etc, 1772 (with a life by P. Stockdale) etc.
Poems. Ed S. Johnson, Works of English poets vol 8,
1779 etc.
Poems. Ed G. Thorn-Drury 1893, 2 vols [1905] (ML).

§1

Rex redux. Cambridge 1633. Contains Waller's To the
King on his return.
[Commendatory poem to George Sandys]. In Sandys, A
paraphrase upon the divine poems, 1638.
[Commendatory poem upon Ben Jonson]. In Jonsonus
virbius, 1638.
An honourable and learned speech against prelates' innova-
tions. 1641.
Mr Waller's speech in the Painted Chamber 6 July 1641.
1641.
A worthy speech. 1641. That parliaments are only way
for advancing the King's affairs; and that the restoring
of goods and freedom is a chief means to maintain
religion and obedience.
To the Kings most excellent Majesty. 1642.
Speech 4 July 1643. 1643. In defence of himself before
the House of Commons.
The works of Waller in this Parliament. 1645. Some copies
dated 1644.
The life and death of William Laud. 1645.
Witts recreations. 1645 (3rd edn).
A discourse upon Gondibert. Paris 1650. Contains
Waller's To Davenant. Rptd with Gondibert 1651.
[Commendatory poem To Davenant]. In A discourse
upon Gondibert, Paris 1650; rptd with Gondibert, 1651
etc.
Ayres and dialogues. 1653.
Poems by Francis Beaumont gent. 1653.
A panegyrick to my Lord Protector. 1655 (folio), 1655 (4°).
Upon the late storme, and the death of his Highnesse.
[1658], 1659 (in Three poems upon the death of his
late Highnesse).

The passion of Dido. 1658, 1679. By Waller and Sidney
Godolphin.
To the King, upon his Majesties happy return. [1660].
To my Lady Morton. 1661. Signed E.W.
A poem on St James's Park. 1661.
To the Queen, upon her Majesty's birthday. [1663].
Pompey the great: a tragedy, translated out of the French
by certain persons of honour. 1664. Act 1 by Waller.
[Pandoras not being approved]. In Three plays by Sir
William Killigrew, 1665. Commendatory poem to
Killigrew.
Instructions to a painter for the drawing of the posture and
progress of his Majesties forces at sea. 1666.
[To a friend of the author]. In Historical applications by
George, first Earl of Berkeley. 1666.
Of the Lady Mary. 1677.
A poem on the present assembling. [1679].
[Upon the Earl of Roscommon's translation]. In Horace's
Art of poetry made English, by the Earl of Roscommon,
1680.
The new masque for [F. Beaumont's and J. Fletcher's] The
maids' tragedy. [1683?].
A poem upon the present assembly of Parliament. 1685.
The maid's tragedy, altered. 1690.
[Poem upon the death of Oliver Cromwell]. In The life
of Oliver Cromwell [by Isaac Kimber], 1724, 1725, 1731
etc.

§2

Stockdale, P. Life of Waller. 1772.
Johnson, S. In his Lives of the poets, 1779–81.
Chernaik, W. L. The poetry of limitation: a study of
Waller. New Haven 1968.

SIR JOHN SUCKLING
1609–42

Bibliographies
Yeo, C. M. Suckling: a bibliography. 1948.

Collections
Works. 1676, 1696 (contains the 4 plays, each dated 1694),
1709, 1719, Dublin 1766, 2 vols 1770.
Poems, plays and other remains. Ed W. C. Hazlitt 2 vols
1874, 1892 (rev).
Works. Ed A. H. Thompson 1910, New York 1964.
Works. Ed T. Clayton and L. A. Beaurline 2 vols Oxford
1971. Vol 1, Non-dramatic works; vol 2, Plays.

§1

[To Lord Lepington]. In Romulus and Tarquin, 1638.
H. Cary's trn from Malvezzi's Italian.
[To William Davenant]. In Davenant's Madagascar, 1638.
Aglaura. 1638 (anon), 1646, Menston 1970 (facs).
The copy of a letter written to the Lower Houses of
Parliament. 1641.
A letter by ... from France. 1641.
Copy of a letter found in the privy lodgeings. 1641.
The discontented colonel. [1642] (unauthorized); rptd in
Fragmenta aurea, below, as Brennoralt.
Fragmenta aurea. 1646. Contains, each with separate
title and pagination: Poems, Aglaura, Goblins, Bren-
noralt, An account of religion by reason, and Letters to
divers eminent personages, all dated 1646; 1648 (in
4 pts, each dated 1648), 1658 (in Last remains of
Suckling, 1659 (includes, each with separate title-page
dated 1659 and separate pagination: Letters to several
persons of honor, and The sad one).
A letter from Sir J.S. to Mr H. German. [1660?].
Written 1640.

RICHARD CRASHAW
1612 or 1613–49

Collections

Epigrammata sacra selecta, cum anglica versione: sacred epigrams englished. 1682. Crashaw is not named, but all the Latin epigrams are his. The anon trns are by Clement Barksdale.
Complete works. Ed A. B. Grosart 2 vols 1872–3; suppl 1887–8.
Poems. Ed A. R. Waller, Cambridge 1904.
Poems. Ed J. R. Tutin, with introd by H. C. Beeching [1905] (ML).
Poems English, Latin and Greek. Ed L. C. Martin, Oxford 1927, 1957.
Complete poetry. Ed G. W. Williams, Garden City NY 1970.

§1

Epigrammatum sacrorum liber. Cambridge 1634. Dedication signed R.C.
Steps to the temple: sacred poems, with other delights of the Muses. 1646, 1648 ('second edition wherein are added divers pieces not before extant'), 1670 (2nd edn, with Carmen deo nostro); Menston 1970 (facs of 1646). Grosart vol 2 p. viii records an undated reissue of this with 'the third edn' on the title-page, but it has not been traced.
Carmen deo nostro, te decet hymnus, sacred poems. Paris 1652 (ed Thomas Car, alias Miles Pinkney, the poet's friend; 3 engravings probably by Crashaw); ed J. R. Tutin [1897].
A letter from Crashaw to the Countess of Denbigh, against irresolution and delay in matters of religion. [1653]. No printer's name or date. A contemporary hand has 1653, and G. Thomason has added 'Sept 23' above the year. It differs widely from the version in Carmen, 1652, above; see Martin, pp. 236, 348, 446.
Poemata et epigrammata: editio secunda, auctior et emendatior. Cambridge 1670, 1674 (with new title-leaf).
Musicks duell [from Steps to the temple 1646]. 1935.
Caritas nimia. Worcester [1964].

§2

Praz, M. In his Secentismo e Marinismo in Inghilterra, Florence 1925.
—— Richard Crashaw. Brescia 1946.
—— The flaming heart: Crashaw and the baroque. Garden City NY 1958.
Eliot, T. S. In his For Lancelot Andrewes, 1928.
Warren, A. Crashaw: a study in baroque sensibility. Ann Arbor 1939.

SIR JOHN DENHAM
1615–69

Bibliographies
Osborne, M. T. Advice-to-a-painter poems. 1633–1856. Austin 1949. An annotated list.

Collections
Poems and translations. 1668, 1671, 1684, 1703, 1709 (for 1710), 1719; ed S. Johnson 1779, 1790 etc.
Poetical works. Ed T. H. Banks, New Haven 1928 (with a bibliography).

§1

A letter sent to William Laud. 1641. Attributed to Denham.
The Sophy. 1642, 1667 (separate title-page but ptd with Poems and translations 1668), 1671, 1684.

Coopers Hill. 1642, 1643, 1650, 1655, 1709 (in A collection of the best English poetry vol 1) etc; ed B. O Hehir, Expans'd hieroglyphics, Berkeley 1969; Latine redditum, 1675 (a Latin trn by Moses Pengry).
Mr Hampdens speech. [1643, 2 edns]. Anon; rptd in Rump: or an exact collection etc, 1662, [1874].
[On Mr John Fletcher's works]. In Comedies and tragedies by Beaumont and Fletcher, 1647 etc.
[Commendatory poem to Richard Fanshaw]. In Fanshawe's trn of Guarini, Il pastor fido, 1648 etc, rptd with Coopers hill 1650 etc.
[Elegie upon Lord Hastings]. In R.B., Lachrymae musarum, 1649, 1650.
The anatomy of play. 1651. Anon.
Certain verses to be reprinted with Gondibert. 1653. Contains poems by Denham.
The destruction of Troy. 1656. Anon.
Panegyrick on Monck. 1659. Anon.
A relation of a Quaker. [1659] (anon); ptd as News from Colchester in The Rump 1660 etc.
Prologue to his Majesty at the first play at the Cock-pit. 1660. Anon.
The true Presbyterian without disguise. 1661, 1680. Authorship uncertain.
[To five principal members of the honourable House of Commons]. In The Rump, 1662.
Second advice to the painter. 1667, 1667 (enlarged as The second and third advice to a painter), 1667, 1667 (as Directions to a painter). Sometimes attributed to Marvell.
[On Mr Abraham Cowley]. In Several copies of verses on the death of Cowley, 1667. Also issued separately.
The famous battel of the catts. 1668. Authorship uncertain.
Cato Major, of old age. 1669, 1717 (in A collection of the best English poetry vol 2).
[Commendatory poem to Edward Howard]. In Howard, The Brittish princes, 1669.
Horace, by Corneille. 1678. 5th act tr Denham.
To his mistress. In C. Gildon, Chorus poetarum, [1694].
A version of the psalms. 1714.

§2

Johnson, S. In his Lives of the poets, 1779–81.
O Hehir, B. Harmony from discords: a life of Denham. Berkeley 1968.

ABRAHAM COWLEY
1618–67

Collections

Works. 1668 (also re-issued with corrections), 1669, 1672, 1674, 1678, 1680, 1680 etc.
The second part of the works. 1681, 1681, 1682, 1684.
The second and third part of the works. 1689, 1700, 1708, 1711, 1721.
Poems of Cowley and others composed into song by William King. Oxford 1668. 16 poems by Cowley, 15 from Mistress.
Songs set by Pietro Reggio. [1680]. Contains 33 songs from Anacreontiques and Mistress.
Complete works in verse and prose. Ed A. B. Grosart 2 vols Edinburgh 1881.
English writings. Ed A. R. Waller 2 vols Cambridge 1905–6.
Prose works. Ed J. R. Lumby, Cambridge 1887, 1923 (rev A. Tilley).
Essays and other prose writings. Ed A. B. Gough, Oxford 1915.
The mistress, with other select poems. Ed J. Sparrow 1926 (Nonesuch Press).
Poetry and prose, with Thomas Sprat's life and observations by Dryden, Addison, Johnson and others. Ed L. C. Martin, Oxford 1949.

§ 1

Poeticall blossomes. 1633 ('by A.C.'), 1636 ('enlarged', adds Sylva: or divers copies of verses), 1637.

Loves riddle: a pastorall comaedie. 1638.

Naufragium joculare: comedia. 1638. Tr C. Johnson as Fortune in her wits, 1705.

Prologue and epilogue [from Guardian]. 1642, 1650.

A satyre against separatists. 1642 ('by A.C.', 2 edns), 1660, 1675. Not by Cowley?

A satyre: the puritan and the papist. 1643 (anon); rptd as Cowley's in Wit and loyalty reviv'd, 1682; rptd Somers tracts vol 5, 1811.

The mistress: or several copies of love-verses. 1647.

The foure ages of England. 1648, 1675, 1705. Ascribed to Cowley on title-page, but disowned by him in preface to Poems 1656.

The guardian: a comedie. 1650. Performed 12 March 1641.

Poems. 1656, Menston 1971 (facs). Contains Preface, Miscellanies, Mistress, Pindarique odes, Davideis.

Ode, upon the blessed restoration and returne of his sacred Majestie Charles the Second. 1660.

A proposition for the advancement of experimental philosophy. 1661, Menston 1969 (facs).

Visions and prophecies. 1661 (for 1660), 1688 (as Definition of a tyrant), 1745 (as A vision concerning Cromwell; in Harleian miscellany vol 5), 1808, 1810.

A. Couleii plantarum libri duo. 1662, 1668 (enlarged to 6 bks as Abrahami Couleii Angli poemata latina), 1678; partly tr as A translation of the sixth book of Mr Cowley's Plantarum, 1680, 1683 (as An heroick poem); tr Nahum Tate as Cowley's History of plants, 1795.

Verses lately written upon several occasions. 1663. Publisher's note refers to unauthorized edn, Dublin 1663, of which no copy is known.

Cutter of Coleman street: a comedy. 1663; ed C. M. Gayley, Representative English comedies vol 4, 1903.

The garden, by A.C. In Poems upon divers occasions, with a character of a London scrivener, by J. Wells, 1667, 1679 (in John Evelyn, Sylvae); rptd in Evelyn, Kalendarium hortense, 1691 etc; ed A. A. Hyatt 1911.

[To the Royal Society]. In Thomas Sprat, History of the Royal Society, 1667 etc.

A poem on the late civil war. 1679; in John Dryden (ed), The third part of Miscellany poems, 1716, 1727; ed A. Pritchard, Toronto 1973 (3 bks, from ms). An extensive fragment.

Verses to Mr Hobbes. In Thomae Hobbes vita, 1681.

Drinking song [by Cowley], scolding wife and the jolly sailor. Boston and Middelburg [1840?].

§ 2

Johnson, S. In his Lives of the poets, 1779–81.

Hinman, R. B. Cowley's world of order. Oxford 1960.

RICHARD LOVELACE
1618–57?

Bibliographies

Ker, C. S. A bibliography of Lovelace. 1949.

Collections

Lucasta. Ed S. W. S[inger], 1817–18. Originally issued as vols 1 and 4 of Select Early English poets.

Poems. Ed C. H. Wilkinson 2 vols Oxford 1925, 1 vol Oxford 1930.

§ 1

Lucasta: epodes, odes, sonnets, songs etc; to which is added Amarantha: a pastorall. 1649 (3 issues).

Lucasta; posthume poems. Ed D. P. Lovelace 2 pts 1659–60. Includes Elegies sacred to the memory of the author, 1660.

ANDREW MARVELL
1621–78

Collections

For anthologies, in which Marvell's poems have had an important place, see Legouis pp. 473–5. For Poems on affairs of state, in which Marvell's satires were included, see Margoliouth pp. 209–12; Poems on affairs of state, New Haven 1963–.

Miscellaneous poems by Andrew Marvell esq. 1681, Menston 1969 (facs). In all but 2 known copies the 3 Cromwell poems have been cancelled.

Complete works in verse and prose. Ed A. B. Grosart 4 vols 1872–5.

Poems and letters. Ed H. M. Margoliouth 2 vols Oxford 1927 (complete except for prose), 1952 (corrected with addns), 1971 (rev P. Legouis and E. E. Duncan-Jones).

Poems printed from the unique copy in the British Museum with some other poems. Ed H. Macdonald 1952 (ML).

Complete poetry. Ed G. de F. Lord, New York 1968; ed E. S. Donno 1972 (Pelican).

§ 1

An elegy upon the death of my Lord Francis Villiers. [1648]. Only known copy at Worcester College Oxford; anon; attribution not conclusively proved.

The first anniversary of the government under his Highness the Lord Protector. 1655.

The character of Holland. 1665, 1672.

Advice to a painter. [1679?]; rptd in State poems, 1689, 1697 etc. See also John Denham, above.

The rehearsal transpros'd. 1672, 1672, 1672 (pirated), 1672 (censored edn with addns and amendments), 1673.

The rehearsal transpros'd: the second part. 1673, 1674; ed D. I. B. Smith, Oxford 1971 (both pts).

Mr Smirke. 1676, 1681.

An account of the growth of Popery. Amsterdam 1677, [1678]; rptd in State tracts 1689, 1693.

Remarks upon a late disingenuous discourse by T.D. 1678; ed J. Brown, Theological tracts vol 3, Edinburgh 1853–4.

A short historical essay. 1680, 1687, 1703.

§ 2

Aubrey, J. In his Brief lives, 1813.

Birrell, A. Marvell. 1905 (EML).

Legouis, P. Marvell: poète, puritain, patriote. Paris 1928; tr Oxford 1965 (abridged), 1968 (rev).

Eliot, T. S. Andrew Marvell. TLS 31 March 1921; rptd in his Homage to John Dryden, 1924 and in his Selected essays, 1932.

Empson, W. Marvell's Garden. In his Some versions of pastoral, 1935.

Bradbrook, M. C. and M. G. Lloyd Thomas. Andrew Marvell. Cambridge 1940.

Leishman, J. B. Some themes and variations in the poetry of Marvell. Proc Br Acad 47 1961.

—— The art of Marvell's poetry. Ed J. Butt 1966, 1968 (rev).

Carey, J. (ed). Marvell: a critical anthology. 1969 (Pelican).

HENRY VAUGHAN
'Silurist'
1622–95

Collections

Complete works. Ed A. B. Grosart 4 vols 1870–1. With poems of Thomas Vaughan.

Poems. Ed E. K. Chambers, introd by H. C. Beeching 2 vols 1896 (ML).

Works. Ed L. C. Martin 2 vols Oxford 1914, 1 vol Oxford 1957 (rev). With bibliography.

Selected prose and verse. Ed L. C. Martin, Oxford 1963 (OSA).

Complete poetry. Ed F. Fogle, New York 1965.

Complete poems. Ed A. Rudrum 1976 (Penguin).

§ 1

Poems, with the tenth satyre of Juvenal englished. 1646.

Silex scintillans: or sacred poems and private ejaculations. 1650, 1655 ('second edition in two books', i.e. an augmented reissue), 1847 (with memoir by H. F. Lyte), Boston 1856, 1858, 1883; ed W. Clare 1885 (facs); ed I. Gollancz 1900; ed W. A. Lewis Bettany [1905]; Leeds 1968 (facs).

Olor iscanus: a collection of some select poems, and translations, published by a friend. 1651, 1679. Prose trn from Plutarch, Maximus Tyrius and Guevara.

The Mount of Olives: or solitary devotions. 1652; ed L. I. Guiney 1902; ed B. H. Wall 1904.

Flores solitudinis: certaine rare and elegant pieces, viz two excellent discourses of 1, temperance and patience; 2, life and death, by I[ohannes] E[usebius] Nierembergius; The world contemned, by Eucherius, Bp of Lyons, and the life of Paulinus, Bp of Nola, collected in his sickness and retirement by Vaughan. 1654. Each of the 3 sections has separate title-page; all are trns from Jesuit works.

Hermetical physick, by Henry Nollius, englished. 1655.

The chymists key to open and to shut: or the true doctrine of corruption and generation, written by Hen. Nollius, published by Eugenius Philalethes. 1657 (for 1655?). Trn of Nollius, De generatione, 1615. Attributed by L. C. Martin, below.

Thalia rediviva: the pass-times and diversions of a country-muse, in choice poems on several occasions; with some learned remains of the eminent Eugenius Philalethes [Thomas Vaughan]. 1678.

§ 2

Blunden, E. On the poems of Vaughan, with his principal Latin poems translated into English verse. 1927.

Holmes, E. Vaughan and the Hermetic philosophy. Oxford 1932.

Martin, L. C. Vaughan and the theme of infancy. In Seventeenth-century studies presented to Sir Herbert Grierson, Oxford 1938.

— Vaughan and Hermes Trismegistus. RES 18 1942.

— Vaughan and the Chymists key. TLS 11 Dec 1953.

Hutchinson, F. E. Vaughan: a life and interpretation. Oxford 1947.

Martz, L. L. In his Poetry of meditation, New Haven 1954, 1962 (with addns).

— Vaughan: the man within. PMLA 78 1963.

— In his Paradise within, New Haven 1964.

Pettet, E. C. Of paradise and light: a study of Vaughan's Silex Scintillans. Cambridge 1960.

Durr, R. A. On the mystical poetry of Vaughan. Cambridge Mass 1962.

THOMAS TRAHERNE
1637–74

Collections

Poetical works, now first published from the original manuscripts. Ed B. Dobell 1903.

Poetical works. Ed G. I. Wade 1932. The poems ptd in 1903, above, but in ms spelling, with poems from the Burney ms.

Centuries, poems and thanksgivings. Ed H. M. Margoliouth 2 vols Oxford 1958.

Poems, centuries and three thanksgivings. Ed A. Ridler, Oxford 1966 (OSA).

§ 1

Roman forgeries. 1673.

Christian ethicks: or divine morality opening the way to blessedness. 1675 (8 poems); ed M. Bottrall 1962 (modernized); ed G. R. Guffey and C. L. Marks, Ithaca 1968.

A serious and patheticall contemplation of the mercies of God. 1699 (anon, but identified by Dobell); ed R. Daniells, Toronto 1941.

Hexameron: or meditations on the six days of creation. 1717 (pt i of A collection of meditations and devotions by S. Hupton); ed G. R. Guffey, Los Angeles 1966 (Augustan Reprint Soc).

Centuries of meditations, now first printed from the author's manuscripts. Ed B. Dobell 1908, 1960 (as Centuries, with note by H. M. Margoliouth); ed J. Farrar, New York 1960.

Traherne's poems of felicity. Ed H. I. Bell 1910 (from ms). The ms (BM Burney 392) was prepared for the press, probably by the poet's brother Philip; it contains 39 poems not in Dobell's edn. There are considerable variations in the 23 poems which appear in both ms collections.

Felicities. Ed A. T. Quiller-Couch 1935.

Of magnanimity and charity. Ed J. R. Slater, New York 1942.

§ 2

Wade, G. I. Traherne, with a selected bibliography by R. A. Parker. Princeton 1944, 1946 (rev).

Martz, L. L. In his Paradise within, New Haven 1964.

Clements, A. L. The mystical poetry of Traherne. Cambridge Mass 1969.

VI. JOHN MILTON
1608–74

For mss and their locations see W. R. Parker, Milton, 1968; H. Darbishire, The ms of Paradise lost bk i, 1931; M. Treip, Milton's punctuation, 1970.

(1) BIBLIOGRAPHIES ETC

Bradshaw, J. A concordance to the poetical works of Milton. 1894.

Cooper, L. A concordance of the Latin, Greek and Italian poems of Milton. Halle 1923.

Patterson, F. A. and F. R. Fogle. An index to the Columbia edition of the works of Milton. 2 vols New York 1940.

Hanford, J. H. In his A Milton handbook, New York 1946, 1970 (rev).

Ingram, W. and K. Swaim. A concordance to Milton's English poetry. 1972.

(2) COLLECTIONS

Verse and Prose

The student's Milton. Ed F. A. Patterson, New York 1930, 1933 (rev).

Works. Ed F. A. Patterson et al 18 vols New York 1931–8. The Columbia edn.

Complete poems and major prose. Ed M. Y. Hughes, New York 1957.

Poems and selected prose. Ed M. H. Nicolson, New York 1962.

Verse

Poems of Mr John Milton, both English and Latin, compos'd at several times. 1645.

Poems etc upon several occasions. 1673.

Facsimile of the ms of Milton's minor poems preserved in the library of Trinity College. Ed W. A. Wright, Cambridge 1899.

Poetical works. Ed H. C. Beeching, Oxford 1900, 1940 (WC) (adapted).

Complete poems. Ed F. A. Patterson, New York 1930.

The Cambridge ms of Milton: Lycidas and some of the other poems. Ed F. A. Patterson, New York 1933 (facs).

Complete poetical works reproduced in photographic facsimile. Ed H. F. Fletcher 4 vols Urbana 1943–8.

The portable Milton. Ed D. Bush, New York 1949, 1969 (as The essential Milton).

Poems of Mr John Milton: the 1645 edition. Ed C. Brooks and J. E. Hardy, New York 1951.

Comus and the shorter poems. Ed E. M. W. and P. B. Tillyard 1952.

Poetical works. Ed H. Darbishire 2 vols Oxford 1952–5.

Poems. Ed J. Carey and A. Fowler 1969, 2 vols 1971 (corrected).

Variorum commentary. Ed M. Y. Hughes et al 1970–.

The Cambridge Milton. Ed J. B. Broadbent et al, Cambridge 1972–.

The Macmillan Milton. Ed C. A. Patrides et al 1972–.

Prose

A complete collection of the historical, political and miscellaneous works. Ed J. Toland 3 vols 1694–8.

A complete collection of the historical, political and miscellaneous works of Milton, containing several original papers of his never before published. Ed T. Birch 2 vols 1738, 1753 (enlarged).

Private correspondence and academic exercises. Ed and tr P. B. and E. M. W. Tillyard, Cambridge 1932.

Complete prose works. Ed D. M. Wolfe et al 8 vols New Haven 1953–. The Yale edn.

Prose. Ed J. M. Patrick, New York 1967.

§1

An epitaph on the admirable dramaticke poet W. Shakespeare. In Shakespeare's second folio, 1632; also in folios of 1664, 1685, and in Shakespeare, Poems, 1640.

['Comus']. A maske presented at Ludlow Castle 1634 on Michaelmas night, before the Right Honorable John Earle of Bridgewater. 1637; ed F. T. Prince 1968 etc.

Lycidas. In Justa Edovardo King naufrago, ab amicis mœrentibus, amoris et μνείας χάριν, Cambridge 1638; ed C. A. Patrides, New York 1961 etc.

Epitaphium Damonis. [1640?]; tr W. W. Skeat 1933; H. Waddell 1943, UTQ 16 1947 and in Milton's Lycidas, ed C. A. Patrides, New York 1961.

[Sonnet to Henry Lawes. In Choice psalmes, put into musick by Henry and William Lawes. 1648].

Of reformation touching Church discipline in England, and the causes that hitherto have hindered it. 1641 (May); ed W. T. Hale, New Haven 1916.

Of prelatical episcopacy, and whether it may be deduc'd from the Apostolical times. 1641 (June?), 1654.

Animadversions upon the remonstrant's defence, against Smectymnuus. 1641 (Aug), 1954.

The reason of Church-government urg'd against prelaty. 1641 (Dec?), 1654.

An apology against a pamphlet call'd A modest confutation of the animadversions upon the remonstrant against Smectymnuus. 1642, 1654; ed M. C. Jochums, Urbana 1950.

The doctrine and discipline of divorce, restor'd to the good of both sexes from the bondage of canon law and other mistakes to Christian freedom, guided by the rule of charity. 1643 (Aug), 1644 (Feb) (rev).

Of education, to Master Samuel Hartlib. 1644 (June), 1673; ed O. Browning, Cambridge 1883 (facs).

The judgement of Martin Bucer concerning divorce now englisht. 1644 (Aug).

Areopagitica: a speech of Mr John Milton for the liberty of unlicenc'd printing, to the Parliament of England. 1644 (Nov); ed J. W. Hales, Oxford 1866; ed E. Arber 1868.

Colasterion: a reply to a nameless answer - against the Doctrine and discipline of divorce. 1645 (March).

Tetrachordon: expositions upon the foure chiefe places in Scripture which treat of mariage, or nullities in mariage. 1645 (March).

Poems of Mr John Milton, both English and Latin, compos'd at several times. 1645, 1673; 1926 (facs of 1645); ed C. Brooks and J. E. Hardy, New York 1951. The Trinity ms. Ed W. A. Wright, Cambridge 1899; 1933; Menston 1970. 3 facs of autograph ms in Trinity College, Cambridge, written c. 1633–48, including Arcades, Comus, Lycidas, 17 sonnets etc.

The tenure of kings and magistrates. 1649 (Feb), 1650 (Feb); ed W. T. Allison, New York 1911.

Observations upon the articles of peace with the Irish rebels, on the letter of Ormond to Col Jones. 1649.

ΕΙΚΟΝΟΚΛΑΣΤΗΣ, in answer to a book intitl'd ΕΙΚΩΝ ΒΑΣΙΛΙΚΗ, the portrature of his sacred Majesty in his solitudes and sufferings. 1649 (Oct), 1650 (rev), 1690.

Pro populo anglicano defensio, contra Claudii anonymi, alias Salmasii, defensionem regiam. 1651 (Feb), 1651, 1658; tr J. Washington 1692.

Pro populo anglicano defensio secunda, contra infamen libellum anonymum cui titulus, Regii sanguinis clamor ad cœlum adversus parricidas anglicanos. 1654 (May); ed G. Crantzius, Hague 1654; tr R. Fellowes 1806; F. Wrangham 1816.

Pro se defensio contra Alexandrum Morum ecclesiasten libelli famosi, cui titulus, Regii sanguinis clamor ad cœlum adversus parricidas anglicanos. 1655 (Aug); tr G. Burnett 1809.

The Cabinet-Council. 1658. Attributed to Sir Walter Ralegh.

A treatise of civil power in ecclesiastical causes, shewing that it is not lawfull for any power on earth to compell in matters of religion. 1659 (Feb).

Considerations touching the likeliest means to remove hirelings out of the church. 1659 (Aug), 1839.

The readie and easie way to establish a free commonwealth, and the excellence thereof compar'd with the inconveniences and dangers of readmitting kingship in this nation. 1660 (March), 1660 (April); ed E. M. Clark, New Haven 1915.

Brief notes upon a late sermon titl'd the Fear of God and the King; preach'd and sinc publish'd by Matthew Griffith DD and chaplain to the late King. 1660 (April).

Paradise lost: a poem written in ten books. 1667, 1674 (rev as A poem in twelve books), 1678, 1688, 1691–2, 1693; ed P. Hume 1695, 1705, 1720 (with Addison's essays); ed R. Bentley 1732, 1738; Menston 1968 (facs) etc.

The manuscript of Milton's Paradise lost book 1. Ed H. Darbishire, Oxford 1931.

Accedence commenc't grammar, supply'd with sufficient rules for the use of such as, younger or elder, are desirous, without more trouble than needs, to attain the Latin tongue. 1669.

The history of Britain, that part especially now call'd England. 1670; ed F. Maseres 1818.

Paradise regain'd: a poem, in iv books; to which is added Samson Agonistes. 1671,|1680, 1688; ed L. C. Martin, Oxford 1925.

Samson Agonistes. 1681, 1688; ed F. T. Prince, Oxford 1957.

Artis logicae plenior institutio, ad Petri Rami methodum concinnata; adjecta est praxis analytica et Petri Rami vita. 1672.

Of true religion, hæresy, schism, toleration, and what best means may be urg'd against the growth of Popery. 1673.

A declaration: or letters patents of the election of this present King of Poland, John the Third, now faithfully translated from the Latin copy. 1674.

Epistolarum familiarum liber unus: quibus acceserunt, ejusdem, jam olim in collegio adolescentis, prolusiones quaedam oratoriae. 1674; tr J. Hall, Philadelphia 1829; Private correspondence and academic exercises, tr P. B. Tillyard, Cambridge 1932.

Literae pseudo-senatus anglicani, Cromwelli reliquorumque perduellium nomine ac jussu conscriptae a Joanne Miltono. 1676, 1690.

Character of the Long Parliament and Assembly of Divines, in MDCXLI. 1681; rptd Harleian miscellany vol 5, 1810.

A brief history of Moscovia and of other less known countries lying eastward of Russia as far as Cathay. 1682; ed D. S. Mirsky 1929; ed R. R. Cawley, Princeton 1941.

Milton's republican letters: or a collection of such as were written by command of the late Commonwealth of England. 1682.

Letters of State from the year 1649 till the year 1659. 1694; ed H. Fernow, Hamburg 1903.

Examen poeticum duplex. 1698. Contains 4 of the early Latin poems.

Original letters and papers of State addressed to Oliver Cromwell concerning the affairs of Great Britain from the year 1649 to 1658. Ed J. Nickolls 1743.

De doctrina christiana libri duo posthumi, quos ex schedis manuscriptis deprompsit et typis mandari primus curavit C. R. Sumner. 1825; tr C. R. Sumner 1825.

Original papers, illustrative of the life and writings of John Milton, including 16 letters of State written by him, now first published. Ed W. D. Hamilton 1859.

A common-place book. Ed A. J. Horwood 1876, 1877 (rev).

§2

For 17th-century comments on Milton, see W. R. Parker, Milton's contemporary reputation, Columbus 1940; for early biographies, The early lives of Milton, ed H. Darbishire 1932;

Toland, John. The life of Milton. 1699, 1761.

Addison, Joseph. [Notes upon the twelve books of Paradise lost]. Spectator 5 Jan–3 May 1712; 1719.

Bentley, R. Dr Bentley's emendations on the twelve books of Paradise lost. 1734.

Johnson, S. In his Lives of the poets, 1779–81.

Macaulay, T. B. Milton. Edinburgh Rev 83 1825.

Arnold, M. In his Mixed essays, 1879.

— In his Essays in criticism series 2, 1888.

Pattison, M. Milton. 1879 (EML).

Garnett, R. Life of Milton. 1890.

Bridges, R. Milton's prosody. Oxford 1893, 1901 (rev), 1921 (with A chapter on accentual verse and notes).

Raleigh, W. Milton. 1900.

Hanford, J. H. A Milton handbook. New York 1926, 1946 (rev); rev J. G. Taaffe, New York 1970.

— John Milton, Englishman. New York 1949.

— Milton: poet and humanist. Cleveland 1966. Reprints 8 essays.

Tillyard, E. M. W. Milton. 1930, 1966 (rev).

— The Miltonic setting. Cambridge 1938.

— Studies in Milton. 1951.

Lewis, C. S. A note on Comus. E & S 8 1932; rptd in his Studies in medieval and Renaissance literature, Cambridge 1966.

— A preface to Paradise lost. Oxford 1942.

Williams, C. In his English poetic mind, Oxford 1932.

— Introduction to English poems of Milton, Oxford 1940 (WC); rptd in his Image of the city, ed A. Ridler 1958.

Leavis, F. R. Milton's verse. Scrutiny 2 1933; rptd in his Revaluation, 1936.

— Mr Eliot and Milton; In defence of Milton. Both in his Common pursuit, 1952.

Eliot, T. S. A note on the verse of Milton. E & S 21 1935.

— Milton. Proc Br Acad 33 1947; rptd in his On poetry and poets, 1957 (shortened).

Empson, W. Milton and Bentley: the pastoral and the innocence of man and nature. In his Some versions of pastoral, 1935.

— 'All' in Paradise lost. In his Structure of complex words, 1951.

— Milton's God. 1961, 1965 (rev with addns).

Cawley, R. R. Milton's literary craftsmanship: a study of A brief history of Muscovia, with an edition of the text. Princeton 1941.

— Milton and the literature of travel. Princeton 1951.

Chambers, R. W. Poets and their critics: Langland and Milton. Proc Br Acad 27 1941.

Bush, D. Paradise lost in our time. Ithaca 1945.

— John Milton. New York 1964.

Waldock, A. J. A. Paradise lost and its critics. Cambridge 1947.

French, J. M. (ed). The life records of Milton. 5 vols New Brunswick NJ 1949–58.

Prince, F. T. The Italian element in Milton's verse. Oxford 1954.

Adams, R. M. Ikon: Milton and the modern critics. Ithaca 1955, 1966 (as Milton and the modern critics).

Sayers, D. L. Dante and Milton. In her Further papers on Dante, 1957.

Blisset, W. Caesar and Satan. JHI 18 1957.

Damon, S. F. Blake and Milton. In The divine vision, ed V. de S. Pinto 1957.

Duncan, J. E. Milton's four-in-one Hell. HLQ 20 1957.

Ethel, G. Hell's marching music. MLQ 18 1957.

Holloway, J. Milton and Arnold. EC 7 1957.

— Paradise lost and the quest for reality. Forum (St Andrews) 3 1967.

Kerslake, J. F. The Richardsons and the cult of Milton. Burlington Mag Jan 1957.

Maclean, H. N. Milton's fair infant. ELH 24 1957.

Mayoux, J.-J. Un classique de la liberté. Critique 118 1957. On Areopagitica.

— Aspects de l'imagination de Milton. Etudes Anglaises 20 1967.

Moloney, M. F. The prosody of Milton's Epitaph, L'Allegro and Il Penseroso. MLN 72 1957.

— Plato and Plotinus in Milton's cosmogony. PQ 40 1961.

Broadbent, J. B. Some graver subject: an essay on Paradise lost. 1960.

— Milton: Comus and Samson Agonistes. 1961.

Kermode, F. (ed). The living Milton. 1960. 10 essays.

Martz, L. L. Paradise regained: the meditative combat. ELH 27 1960; rptd as Paradise regained: the interior teacher, in his Paradise within, New Haven 1964.

—— Paradise lost: the journey of the mind. ibid.
—— (ed). Milton: a collection of critical essays. Englewood Cliffs NJ 1966. 12 essays.
Nicolson, M. H. Milton: a reader's guide to his poetry. New York 1963.
Ricks, C. Milton's grand style. Oxford 1963.
—— Milton, Poems 1645; Paradise regained and Samson Agonistes. In English poetry and prose 1540–1674, ed Ricks 1970.
Fixler, M. Milton and the kingdoms of God. Evanston 1964.
Frye, N. The return of Eden. Toronto 1965, London 1966 (as Five essays on Milton's epics).
Gardner, H. A reading of Paradise lost. Oxford 1965.

Lewalski, B. K. Milton's brief epic: the genre, meaning and art of Paradise regained. Providence 1966.
Patrides, C. A. Milton and the Christian tradition. Oxford 1966.
—— (ed). Milton's epic poetry: essays on Paradise lost and Paradise regained. 1967 (Peregrine). With 16 essays and bibliography.
—— (ed). Approaches to Paradise lost: the York tercentenary lectures. 1968. With 13 papers.
Fish, S. E. Surprised by sin: the reader in Paradise lost. 1967.
Parker, W. R. Milton: a biography. 2 vols Oxford 1968.
Carey, J. Milton. 1969.

VII. MINOR JACOBEAN AND CAROLINE POETRY (1603–60)

Saintsbury   Minor poets of the Caroline period, ed G. Saintsbury 3 vols Oxford 1905–21.

WILLIAM ALABASTER
1568–1640

Sonnets. Ed G. M. Story and H. Gardner, Oxford 1959. *See col 107, above.*

SIR ROBERT AYTON (or AYTOUN)
1570–1638
Collections

[Latin poems]. In Arthur Johnston, Delitiae poetarum scotorum pt 1, 1637.
Poems. Ed C. Rogers 1844, 1871 (with memoir and Latin poems).
A choice of poems and songs. Ed H. M. Shire, Cambridge 1961.
The English and Latin poems. Ed C. B. Gullans, Edinburgh 1963.

§ 1

De foelici et semper augusto Jacobi. Paris 1603. Latin panegyric on James I.
Basia: sive strena Cal. Jan. ad Jacobum Hayum. 1605.
In obitum Thomae Rhaedi, epicidium. 1624. Signed R.A.
Lesus in funere R. Thorii. 1626. Latin elegy.
Poems. 1827 (Bannatyne Miscellany vol 1).
New poems by Ayton. Ed C. B. Gullans, MLR 55 1960.

SIR JOHN BEAUMONT
1583–1627
Collections

Poems. Ed A. B. Grosart 1869.

§ 1

The metamorphosis of tobacco. 1602; ed J. P. Collier, Illustrations of early English popular literature vol 1, 1863. A mock-heroic poem.
Bosworth Field, with a taste of the variety of other poems. 1629, 1710.
The theatre of Apollo: an entertainment written by Sir John Beaumont in 1625. Ed W. W. Greg 1926.

JOSEPH BEAUMONT
1616–99
Collections

Original poems in English and Latin. Ed J.G. [John Gee?], Cambridge 1749.
Poetical works. Ed A. Grosart 2 vols 1877–80.
Minor poems. Ed E. Robinson 1914. From autograph ms.

§ 1

Psyche: or love's mysterie, displaying the intercourse betwixt Christ and the soule. 1648, 1651; ed C. Beaumont, Cambridge 1702 (with corrections and 4 new cantos).

EDWARD BENLOWES
1603?–76

Sphinx theologica: sive musica templi. Cambridge [1636]. Includes Latin poems.
Papa perstriclus, (Echo) ictus. 1645. Verse attacks on Pope Innocent X.
A poetic descant upon a private musick-making. [1649]. Signed E. Benevolus.
Theophila, or loves sacrifice: a divine poem by E.B. 1652; Saintsbury.
The summary of wisedome. 1657; Saintsbury.
A glance at the glories of sacred friendship. 1657.
Oxonii encomium. Oxford 1672. One English poem, the rest in Latin.
Magia coelestis. Oxford 1673. Latin couplets; broadsheet.
Oxonia elogia. [Oxford 1673]. Latin poems.

ANNE BRADSTREET
1612–72
Collections

Works. Ed J. H. Ellis, Charlestown 1867, New York 1932.
Works. Ed J. Hensley, Cambridge Mass 1967.
Poems. Ed R. Hutchinson, New York 1969.

§ 1

The tenth muse lately sprung up in America. 1650, Boston 1678 (as Several poems), 1758; ed J. K. Piercy, Gainesville 1965 (facs). Contains letters and occasional pieces.

§2

Berryman, J. Homage to Mistress Bradstreet. New York 1956. Poems.
Piercy, J. K. Anne Bradstreet. New York 1965.
White, E. W. Anne Bradstreet: the tenth muse. New York 1972.

ALEXANDER BROME
1620–66

A Canterbury tale translated out of Chaucers Old English. 1641. Attributed to Brome.
Cromwell's panegyrick. 1647. Verse satire; signed Charolophilos.
A copie of verses, said to be composed by his Majestie. [1648]. Attributed to Brome.
The cunning lovers: a comedy as it was acted at the private house in Drury Lane. 1654.
A record in rithme. [1659?]. Verse satire.
Arsy versy: or the second martyrdom of the Rump. [1660]. A ballad.
Bumm-foder: or waste-paper proper to wipe the nations rump with. [1660?]. A ballad.
A congratulatory poem [on] the return of King Charls [sic]. 1660.
Poems upon several occasions. 1660.
Songs and other poems. 1661, 1664, 1668; rptd A. Chalmers, English poets vol 6, 1810.
Rump: or an exact collection of the choycest poems and songs. 1662; rptd as A collection of loyal songs written against the Rump Parliament, 1731.

WILLIAM CARTWRIGHT
1611–43

Comedies, tragi-comedies, with other poems 1651.
Plays and poems. Ed G. B. Evans, Madison 1951.

PATRICK CARY (or CAREY)
1624–56

Poems, from a ms written in the time of Oliver Cromwell. 1771. Ms dated 1651.
Trivial poems and triolets. Ed Sir Walter Scott 1819, 1820; Saintsbury. The whole, of which 1771 above gave only a part.
Poems. Ed V. Delany, Oxford 1978 (from ms).

MARGARET CAVENDISH, DUCHESS OF NEWCASTLE
1623–73

§1

Philosophicall fancies. 1653. Prose and verse.
Poems and fancies. 1653, 1664, 1668 (as Poems: or several fancies in verse).
The worlds olio. 1655, 1671. Contains 2 poems: But I would have this monarchy I make and Of all my works this work which I have writ.
Natures pictures. 1656, 1671. Stories in prose and verse, part-author with William Cavendish, below.
Philosophical letters. 1664. Contains one poem: Eternal God, infinite deity.
For her plays see col 252, below.

§2

Woolf, V. In her Common reader, 1925.
Grant, D. Margaret the First. 1957.

WILLIAM CAVENDISH, 1st DUKE OF NEWCASTLE
1592–1676

Natures pictures. 1656, 1671. Joint author with his wife Margaret.
Margaret Cavendish, Philosophical letters. 1664. One dedicatory poem.
The charms of liberty: a poem. 1709, 1709. With poems by various hands.
Phanseys. Ed D. Grant 1965. Written c. 1645.
For his plays see col 253, below.

SIR ROBERT CHESTER
1566?–1640?

Collections
Poems by John Salusbury and Chester. Ed C. Brown, Bryn Mawr 1913, London 1914 (EETS).

§1

Love's martyr. 1601, 1611 (as The anuals [sic] of Great Brittaine); ed A. B. Grosart, Occasional Issues 7 1878 (and New Shakespeare Soc).

JOHN CLEVELAND
1613–58

Bibliographies
Morris, B. R. Cleveland: a bibliography of his poems. 1967 (Bibl Soc).

Collections
Works. [Ed J. Lake and S. Drake] 1687, 1699.
Poems. Ed J. M. Berdan, New York 1903, New Haven Saintsbury. 1911.
Poems. Ed B. R. Morris and E. Withington, Oxford 1967.

§1

The character of a London-diurnal; with several select poems by the same author. 1644. Not all by Cleveland.
The character of a moderate intelligencer, with some select poems. [1647].
The Kings disguise. [1647].
The hue and cry after Sir John Presbyter. 1649. Verse satire.
Poems by J.C. with additions. 1651, 1653, 1654, 1656, 1657, 1658, 1659, 1661 etc.
The idol of the clownes, or the Insurrection of Wat the Tyler. 1654, 1654, 1658 (as The rustick rampant), [1658] (as The rebellion of the rude multitude).
J. Cleaveland revived. 1659, 1660, 1662, 1668.
Clievelandi vindiciae: or Clieveland's genuine poems, orations, epistles etc. 1677.

RICHARD CORBETT
1582–1635

Collections
Poems. Ed J. A. W. Bennett and H. R. Trevor-Roper, Oxford 1955. With account of mss, early edns and dubia.

§1

Certain elegant poems. 1647 etc. Amplified in later edns.
Poetica stromata, by R.C. [Holland or France?] 1648.
The time's whistle: or a new daunce of seven satires, and other poems. Ed J. M. Cowper 1871 (from ms). Signed R.C.

OWEN FELLTHAM
1602?–68

Poems annent the keeping of Yule. [1650?]. Taken from Resolves.
Lusoria: or occasional pieces. Appended to Resolves, 1661 (8th edn) and later edns.

JOSEPH FLETCHER
1582?–1637

Collections

Poems. Ed A. B. Grosart 1869.

§ I

Christes bloodie sweat. 1613, 1616. Signed I.F.
The historie of the perfect-cursed-blessed man. 1628, 1629. Contains emblems by Thomas Cecil.

SIDNEY GODOLPHIN
1610–43

Collections

Saintsbury.
Poems. Ed W. Dighton, Oxford 1931.

§ I

The passion of Dido for Aeneas. 1658, 1679. Completed by Waller. Verse trn of Virgil, Aeneid bk iv.

JOHN HALL
1627–56

Collections

Poems. Ed S. E. Brydges 1816; Saintsbury.

§ I

Poems. Cambridge 1646. Includes: The second booke of divine poems by J.H. (with separate title-leaf dated 1647).
Hierocles upon the golden verses of Pythagoras englished. 1657. Includes An account of the author, by John Davies, of Kidwelly.

CHRISTOPHER HARVEY
1597–1663

Collections

Complete poems. Ed A. B. Grosart 1874.

§ I

The synagogue. 1640, 1647, 1651, 1657, 1661, 1667, 1673, 1679, 1703, 1709, 1799, 1836. Often rptd with Herbert's Temple from 1641, though with separate title-page and pagination.
The school of the heart. 1647, 1664, 1675, 1723, 1777 (with Quarles), 1778, 1808 (with Quarles), 1812, 1816, 1823, 1838, 1844, 1845, 1853, 1857, 1859, 1863, 1866 (with Quarles). Trn of Benedict van Haeften's Scholar cordis; often rptd with Quarles's Emblemes and Hieroglyphikes.

EDWARD HERBERT, 1st BARON HERBERT OF CHERBURY
1583–1648

Collections

Poems. Ed J. C. Collins 1881.
Poems. Ed G. C. Moore Smith, Oxford 1923.
Minor poets of the seventeenth century. Ed R. G. Howarth 1931 (EL), 1953 (rev).

§ I

Occasional verses. 1665, Menston 1969 (facs); Poems, ed G. C. Moore Smith, Oxford 1923.
The life of Lord Herbert written by himself. Ed Horace Walpole, Strawberry Hill 1765 (from ms); ed S. Lee 1886, 1906 (rev); ed J. M. Shuttleworth, Oxford 1976 (with addns).
The Herbert correspondence. Ed W. J. Smith, Cardiff 1963.

SIR FRANCIS KYNASTON
1587–1642

Musae querulae de regis in Scotiam profectione. 1633. Latin poems by A. Johnstone with Kynaston's verse trns.
Amorum Troili et Creseidae: libri duo priores anglico-latini. Oxford 1635. Chaucer in rimed Latin.
Corona Minervae: or a masque. 1635. Anon. In verse.
Leoline and Sydonis: Cynthiades. 1642; Saintsbury. A romance.

HENRY PEACHAM the younger
1578?–1642?

The more the merrier. 1608. Epigrams.
Thomas Coryate, Odcombian banquet. 1611. 4 burlesque poems.
Arthur Standish, Commons complaint. 1611, 1611, 1612. With poems by Peacham.
The period of mourning disposed into six visions [on death of Henry, Prince of Wales], together with nuptiall hymns [on marriage of Frederick and Princess Elizabeth]. 1613, 1613 (with variant), 1789, 1792.
Prince Henry revived. 1615.
Thalias banquet. 1620. Epigrams, signed H.P.
An Aprill shower shed in abundance of teares. 1624. Elegy on Richard Sackville, Earl of Dorset.
Thestylis atrata. 1634. Elegy on Frances, Countess of Warwick.

THOMAS STANLEY the elder
1625–78

Bibliographies

Flower, M. Stanley: a bibliography of his writings in prose and verse. Trans Cambridge Bibl Soc 1 1950.

Collections

Poems and translations. Ed G. M. Crump, Oxford 1962.

§ I

Poems and translations. 1647 (priv ptd), 1651 (as Poems), 1652, 1657 (in John Gamble, Ayres and dialogues); ed S. E. Brydges 1814 (from 1651); ed L. I. Guiney, Hull 1907, 1923 (only trns from Joannes Secundus); Saintsbury.
The history of philosophy. 3 vols 1655–62, 1687, 1701. *Also trns from Anacreon, Bion, Moschus, Secundus, Ausonius etc.*

JOSHUA SYLVESTER
1563–1618

Collections

Collected works and trns pbd as pt of G. de Saluste du Bartas,
Bartas his devine weekes and workes, 1621. *See col 120,*
above.
Sacred workes gathered in one volume. 2 pts 1620, 1620
  (variant edn as All the small workes).
Works. Ed A. B. Grosart 2 vols 1880.

§ 1

Monodia. [1594]. Elegy on Dame Helen Branch.
[Dedicatory verses, signed J.S.]. In George Goodwin,
  Automachia, 1607, [1615?], 1621 (in Bartas his
  devine weekes).
Lachrimae lachrimarum. 1612, [1612], 1613, 1613,
  Amsterdam 1969 (facs).
The parliament of vertues royal. 2 vols 1614–15. Contains
  poems and trns by Sylvester.
Tobacco battered and the pipes shattered. [1617–20].
  Verse satire.
The wood-man's bear: a poeme. 1620.
[The mysterie of mysteries]. In Bartas his devine weekes,
  1621.
Panthea: or divine wishes and meditations. 1630. With
  poems by various hands.

EDWARD TAYLOR
1645?–1729

Collections

Poetical works. Ed T. H. Johnson, New York 1939,
  Princeton 1939.
Poems. Ed D. E. Stanford, New Haven 1960, 1963
  (abridged).

§ 1

Taylor requested that none of his poems be pbd and the mss
were deposited in Yale Univ Lib by his grandson.

A meditation upon the glory of God. Ed M. A. Neufield,
  Yale Univ Lit Gazette 25 1951. Written 13 Feb 1687.
A transcript of Taylor's Metrical history of Christianity.
  Ed D. E. Stanford, Cleveland 1962.
Kaiser, L. M. and D. E. Stanford. The Latin poems of
  Taylor. Yale Univ Lib Gazette 40 1965.
Mignon, C. W. Another Taylor manuscript at Yale. Yale
  Univ Lib Gazette 41 1966.

AURELIAN TOWNSHEND (or
TOWNSEND)
1583?–1643?

Collections

Poems and masks. Ed E. K. Chambers, Oxford 1912.

§ 1

Townshend's poems are scattered through ms miscellanies.

For poems in mss of Bodley see M. Crum, First-line index,
2 vols Oxford 1969.

[Commendatory verses]. In Henry Lawes, Choice psalmes
  set to music, 1648.
[Commendatory verses]. In Henry Lawes, Ayres and
  dialogues, 1655.
[2 poems set to music]. In Lawes, Second book of ayres,
  1655.
[Upon his constant mistress]. In Choice drollery, 1656
  (anon); ed J. W. Ebsworth 1876.
[Upon kind and true love]. In Wit's interpreter, 1655
  (anon); in Choice drollery, 1656 etc.
[Youth and beauty, Thou shepheard whose intentive eye].
  In W. Beloe, Anecdotes of literature vol 6, 1812.
[To the lady May, Upon kind and true love]. In A. H.
  Bullen, Speculum amantis, 1889.
[His mistress found]. In Richard Carew, Poems and a
  masque, ed J. W. Ebsworth 1893.
For plays and masques, see col 256, below.

SIR HENRY WOTTON (or
WOOTTON)
1568–1639

Collections

Reliquiae Wottonianae: or a collection of lives, letters,
  poems, with characters of sundry personages and other
  pieces. Ed Izaak Walton 1651 (with life), 1654 (with
  addns), 1672, 1685 (with letters to Lord Zouch). Prose
  with 14 poems.
Poems. Ed A. Dyce 1843 (Percy Soc).
Poems by Wooton and others. Ed J. Hannah 1845, 1870
  (as The courtly poets from Raleigh to Montrose), 1875
  (as Poems of Raleigh, Wotton and other courtly poets),
  1892.

§ 1

[You meaner beauties of the night]. In Michael East, Sixt
  set of bookes, 1624.
The elements of architecture. 1624; ed S. T. Prideaux
  1903; ed F. Hard 1968. Prose.
Ad regem e Scotia reducem HW plausus et vota. 1633.
  Latin prose.
A parallel betweene Robert late Earle of Essex and George
  late Duke of Buckingham. 1641; ed S. E. Brydges 1814.
  Prose.
A short view of the life and death of George Villiers Duke
  of Buckingham. 1642; rptd in Harleian miscellany vol
  8, 1744. Prose.
A panegyrick of King Charles. 1649. Prose.
The state of Christendom: or a discovery of many hidden
  mysteries of the times. 1657. Prose.

Letters

Letters to Sir Edmund Bacon. 1661.
Letters and dispatches from Wotton 1617–20. Ed G.
  Tomline 1850 (Roxburghe Club).
Smith, L. P. The life and letters of Wotton. 2 vols Oxford
  1907. With list of mss etc.
Crinò, A. M. Fatti e figure del Seicento anglo-toscano.
  Florence 1957. With unpbd letters.

VIII. EPIGRAMS AND FORMAL SATIRE

Crowley, Robert (1518?–88). One and thyrtye epigrammes.
  1550; ed J. M. Cowper 1872 (EETS).
Heywood, John (1497?–1580?). Two hundred epigrammes.
  1555.
—— An hundred epigrammes. 1556.

—— A fourth hundred of epygrams. 1560.
—— John Heywoodes woorkes, with one hundred of
  epigrammes; and three hundred of epigrammes; and a
  fifth hundred of epigrams; whereunto are now newly
  added a syxt hundred of epigrams. 1562.

Songes and sonettes. 1557. Tottel; includes Wyatt's satires.

Drant, Thomas (d. 1578). A medicinable morall: that is, the two bookes of Horace his satyres englyshed; also epigrammes. 1566.

Turbervile, George (c. 1544–97). Epitaphes, epigrams, songs and sonets. 1567.

Gascoigne, George (1542?–77). The steleglas: satyre. 1576.

Kendall, Timothy. Flowres of epigrammes out of sundrie the moste singular authors. 1577; rptd 1874 (Spenser Soc).

Epigrammes and elegies by J.D[avies] and C.M[arlowe]. 2 pts Middleburg [1598?].

Donne, John (1572–1631). Satires. In his Poems, 1633.

Lodge, Thomas (c. 1557–1625). A fig for Momus: containing satyres, eclogues and epistles. 1595; ed A. Boswell, Frondes caducae vol 3, Auchinleck 1817.

Hall, Joseph (1574–1656). Virgidemiarum: sixe bookes; first three bookes of tooth-lesse satyrs. 1597, 1598, 1602.

—— Virgidemiarum: sixe bookes; three last bookes of byting satyres. 1598, 1599.

Guilpin, Everard. Skialetheia: or shadow of truth in certain epigrams and satyres. 1598; rptd by A. B. Grosart 1878; ed G. B. Harrison 1931 (Shakespeare Assoc Facs).

—— The whipper of the satyre his pennance. 1601; ed A. Davenport, Liverpool 1951. With Breton.

Marston, John (1576–1634). The metamorphosis of Pigmalions image, and certaine satyres. 1598 (by W.K.).

—— The scourge of villanie: three bookes of satyres. 1598 (by W. Kinsayder).

Rankins, William (fl. 1587–1601). Seaven satyres applyed to the weeke. 1598; ed A. Davenport, Liverpool 1948.

Tyro, T. Tyros Roring Megge. 1598.

Bastard, Thomas (1566–1618). Chrestoleros: seven bookes of epigrames. 1598.

Barnfield, Richard (1574–1627). Encomion of Lady Pecunia. 1598.

Weever, John (1576–1632). Epigrammes in the oldest cut and newest fashion. 1599; ed R. B. McKerrow 1911.

—— Faunus and Melliflora. 1600; ed A. Davenport, Liverpool 1948.

—— The whipping of the satyre. 1601 (by 'W.I.'); ed A. Davenport, Liverpool 1951.

M., T. Micro-cynicon: six snarling satyres. 1599. Attributed Thomas Middleton and rptd in edns of his Works, ed Dyce 1840 and Bullen 1885–6.

Goddard, William. A mastif whelp, with other ruff-island-like currs. [Dort? 1599].

—— A neaste of waspes latelie found out in the Law Countreys. 1615; ed C. H. Wilkinson, Oxford 1921.

—— A satyricall dialogue betweene Alexander the Great and Diogynes. [Dort? 1616?].

Rowlands, Samuel (1570?–1630?). The letting of humors blood in the head-vaine. 1600.

—— Humors looking-glasse. 1608 (anon); ed J. P. Collier 1870. Sometimes attributed to Rowlands.

Tourneur, Cyril (1575?–1626). The transformed metamorphosis. 1600.

Thynne, Francis (1545?–1608). Emblemes and epigrames. Ed F. J. Furnivall 1876 (EETS). Written 1600.

Breton, Nicholas (1545?–1626?). Pasquils mad-cap and mad-cappes message. 1600.

—— The second part of Pasquils mad-cap, intituled the fooles-cap. 1600.

—— Pasquils mistresse. 1600.

—— Pasquils passe and passeth not. 1600.

—— No whipping nor tripping: but a kinde friendly snippinge. 1601; ed A. Davenport, Liverpool 1951.

Cooke, John. Epigrames, served out in 52 severall dishes. [c. 1604] (by 'I.C. Gent').

Woodhouse, Peter. Democritus his dream. 1605; ed A. B. Grosart 1877.

P[arrot], H[enry]. The mous-trap. 1606.

—— Epigrams. 1608.

—— Laquei ridiculosi: or springes for woodcocks. 1613.

—— The mastive, or young-whelpe of the old-dogge: epigrams and satyrs. 1615.

—— Cures for the itch: characters, epigrams, epitaphs. 1626.

West, Richard. The court of conscience: or Dick Whippers sessions. 1607.

—— Wits ABC: or a centurie of epigrams. [1608].

Middleton, Richard, of York. Epigrams and satyres. [1608]; rptd [Edinburgh 1840].

Peacham, Henry (1576?–1643?). The more the merrier. 1608.

—— Thalia's banquet furnished with newly devised epigrammes. 1620.

[Tofte, Robert (1562–1620)]. Ariostos satyres. 1608, 1609, 1611. Erroneously ascribed on title-page to G. Markham;

Heath, John. Two centuries of epigrammes. 1610.

—— The house of correction: or certayn satiricall epigrams. [1619].

Sharpe, Roger. More fooles yet. 1610. Epigrams.

Scot, Thomas. Philomythie or philomythologie, wherein outlandish birds, beasts and fishes are taught to speake true English verse. 2 pts 1616, 1616 (enlarged), 1622.

—— The second part of Philomythie. 1625.

Davies, John, of Hereford (1565–1618). The scourge of folly. [1611?].

—— Wits Bedlam. 1617.

Taylor, John (1580–1653). The sculler: or gallimawfry of sonnets, satyres and epigrams. 1612.

—— Epigrammes: being ninety in number; besides two new made satyres. 1651.

Gamage, William. Linsi woolsie: or two centuries of epigrammes. Oxford 1613.

Wither, George (1588–1667). Abuses stript and whipt. 1613.

Freeman, Thomas. Rubbe and a great cast: epigrams. 2 pts 1614.

N[iccols], R[ichard] (1584–1616). The furies, with vertues encomium, in two bookes of epigrammes. 1614.

C., R. The times whistle: or a new daunce of seven satires and other poems. [1614?]; ed J. M. Cowper 1871 (EETS).

Brathwait, Richard (1588?–1673). A strappado for the Divell: epigrams and satyres. 1615; ed J. W. Ebsworth, Boston 1878.

—— Natures embassie: or the wilde-mans measures, danced naked by twelve satyres. 1621.

Anton, Robert. The philosophers satyrs. 1616, 1617 (as Vices anotimie).

Fitzgeffrey, Henry. Satyres and satiricall epigrams. 1617.

—— Certain elegies done by sundrie excellent wits, with satyres and epigrammes. 1618.

Harington, Sir John (1560–1612). Epigrams both pleasant and serious. 1615.

—— The most elegant and witty epigrams. 1618; ed N. E. McClure, Philadelphia 1930.

Jonson, Ben (1572–1637). Epigrams. In his Workes, 1616.

Hutton, Henry. Follie's anatomie: or satyres and satiricall epigrams. 1619; rptd E. F. Rimbault 1842 (Percy Soc).

Owen, John (1560–1622). Epigrams of that most wittie and worthy epigrammatist Mr John Owen. Tr John Vicars 1619.

—— Certaine epigrams out of his first foure bookes. Tr Robert Hayman, Quodlibets, 1628, below.

[Wroth, Sir Thomas (1584–1672)]. The abortive of an idle hour: or a century of epigrams. 1620.

Ashmore, John. Certain selected odes of Horace englished, with epigrammes. 1621.

Martyn, Joseph. Newe epigrams, having in their company a mad satyre. 1621.

Hayman, Robert. Quodlibets lately come over from New Britaniola. 3 pts 1628.

Epigrammes. [Rouen before 1634]. Anti-Protestant; ms in Bodley.

Randolph, Thomas (1605–36). Aristippus: or the joviall philosopher. 1630.

Epigrammes, mirrour of new reformation. 1634.

Chamberlain, Robert (1607?–60). Nocturnall lucubrations; whereunto are added epigrams and epitaphs. 1638.

—— Conceits, clinches, flashes and whimsies. 1639, 1640 (rev as Jocabella); ed J. O. Halliwell (-Phillipps) 1860; ed W. C. Hazlitt 1864 (in Old English jest-books no 3).

Bancroft, Thomas. Two bookes of epigrammes and epitaphs. 1639.

Carew, Thomas (1595?–1640). In his Poems, 1640.

Urquhart, Sir Thomas (1611–60). Epigrams: divine and moral. 1641.

Herrick, Robert (1591–1674). In his Hesperides, 1648 (with epigrams).

Heath, Robert. Clarastella; together with poems occasional, elegies, epigrams, satyrs. 1650.

Sheppard, Samuel. Epigrams, theological, philosophical and romantick. 1651.

Eliot, John. Poems: consisting of epistles and epigrams, satyrs, epitaphs and elegies, songs and sonnets. 1658, 1661.

Pecke, Thomas. Parnassi puerperium: epigrams. 1659.

Studies

Hudson, H. H. The epigram in the English Renaissance. Princeton 1947.

Brooks, H. F. The imitation in English poetry, especially in formal satire, before the age of Pope. RES 25 1949.

Peter, J. Complaint and satire in early English literature. Oxford 1956.

Gransden, K. W. Tudor verse satire. 1970.

IX. SONG BOOKS

BIBLIOGRAPHIES ETC

Day, C. L. and E. B. Murrie. English song-books 1651–1702 and their publishers. Library 4th ser 16 1936.

—— English song-books 1651–1702: a bibliography with a first-line index of songs. 1940 (Bibl Soc).

Schnapper, E. B. The British union-catalogue of early music printed before the year 1801. 2 vols 1957.

STUDIES OF SONG, PART-SONG AND MADRIGAL

Fellowes, E. H. The English madrigal composers. 1921, 1948 (rev).

'Warlock, Peter' (P. Heseltine). The English ayre. 1926.

Greene, R. L. The early English carol. 1935.

Bontoux, G. La chanson en Angleterre au temps d'Elisabeth. Oxford 1936.

Pattison, B. Music and poetry of the English Renaissance. 1948.

Ing, C. M. Elizabethan lyrics: a study in the development of English metres. 1951.

Hollander, J. The untuning of the sky: ideas of music in English poetry 1500–1700. Princeton 1961.

Kerman, J. The Elizabethan madrigal: a comparative study. New York 1962.

Sternfeld, F. W. Music in Shakespearean tragedy. 1963, 1967 (rev).

Music in English Renaissance drama. Ed J. H. Long, Lexington Kentucky 1968.

Shire, H. M. Song, dance and poetry of the Court of Scotland under King James 6. Cambridge 1969.

COLLECTIONS (FROM 1800)

Chappell, W. Popular music of the olden time. 2 vols 1859; rev H. E. Wooldridge as Old English popular music 1893, New York 1961; ed F. W. Sternfeld, New York 1965 (from 1859).

Arkwright, G. E. P. The old English edition. 25 vols 1889–1902.

Cox, F. A. English madrigals in the time of Shakespeare. 1899. A selection of song book poetry with first-line index to ptd songbooks 1588–1638.

Fellowes, E. H. The English madrigal school. 36 vols 1913–24; rev R. T. Dart et al as The English madrigalists, 1956–.

—— The English school of lutenist song writers. Ser 1, 16 vols 1920–32; ser 2, 16 vols 1925–7; rev R. T. Dart et al as The English lute-songs, 1959–. Under this new title the following additional vols have been pbd: ser 1, 17 1959; ser 2, 17–21 1961–9.

—— Elizabethan and Jacobean part songs. 45 pts 1920–40. A selection of part-songs by Dowland, Bartlet, Campion, Cavendish, Ford, Pilkington, Jones.

—— English madrigal verse. Oxford 1920, 1929 (rev); rev and enlarged F. W. Sternfeld and D. Greer, Oxford 1967.

'Warlock, Peter' (P. Heseltine) and P. Wilson. English ayres. 4 vols 1922–5, 6 vols 1927–31 (enlarged), [1964].

'Warlock, Peter'. The first [second, third] book of Elizabethan songs. 3 vols 1926. Consort songs for voice and viols from mss.

Warlock also edited single sheet-music edns of part-songs by the lutenists in the Curwen edn and as English madrigals and part songs.

Scott, C. K. Euterpe: a collection of madrigals and other music of the 16th and 17th centuries. 70 pts 1928–36. Includes selected part-songs by lutenists.

Greenberg, N., W. H. Auden and C. Kallman. An Elizabethan song book. Garden City NY 1955.

Cutts, J. P. Seventeenth-century songs and lyrics. Columbia Missouri 1959. Poems selected from music mss.

Sabol, A. J. Songs and dances for the Stuart masque. Providence 1959. Mainly from mss.

Dart, R. T. Invitation to madrigals. Vols 1–, 1961–.

Souris, A. and J. Jacquot. Poèmes de Donne, Herbert et Crashaw mis en musique par leur contemporains. Paris 1961.

Stevens, J. Music and poetry in the early Tudor Court. 1961.

Elliott, K. Musa jocosa mihi. 1966. 12 songs by Lawes, Wilson et al to poems by Sir Robert Ayton.

Simpson, C. The British broadside ballad and its music. New Brunswick NJ 1966.

English lute songs 1597–1632: a collection of facsimile reprints. Ed D. Greer, I. Harwood, D. Poulton and F. Traficante 36 pts Menston 1967–71 (facs).

Doughtie, E. Lyrics from English airs 1596–1622. Cambridge Mass 1970. Contains all the lute-song lyrics except those by Campion.

Spink, I. English songs 1625–60. Musica britannica 33 1971.

English madrigals 1588–1630: a collection of facsimile reprints. Ed F. W. Sternfeld and D. Greer, Menston 1972–.

SEPARATE SONG BOOKS ETC 1500–1660

References to collections above are generally abbreviated to the surname of the editor and the opening words of the title, e.g. Spink, English songs. *The following special references are used:*

EM E. H. Fellowes, The English madrigalists (formerly The English madrigal school)
ELS E. H. Fellowes et al, The English lute-songs (formerly The English school of lutenist song writers)
els English lute songs: a collection of facsimile reprints

XX SONGES

xx songes, IX of IIII partes and XI of thre partes. 1530. Poems rptd in Flügel, Liedersammlungen. Songs by T. Ashwell, W. Cornysh, R. Cowper (Cooper), R. Fayrfax, R. Jones, R. Pygott, J. Qwynneth, T. Stretton, J. Taverner. Only the bassus pt-book survives complete (BM).

JOHN HALL
1529?–66?

[The Court of Vertue. 1565]. Title-page lacking: title from Stationers' register. Ed R. A. Fraser 1961.

THOMAS WHYTHORNE
1528–96

§ 1

Songes for three, fower and five voyces. 1571. Tenor pt rptd R. Imelmann, Sh Jb 39 1903; 11 songs ed 'Peter Warlock' (P. Heseltine), Oxford choral songs nos 354–64, 1927; 3 songs ed M. Bukofzer, New York 1947.
Duos: or songs for two voices. 1590.
Autobiography. Ed J. M. Osborn, Oxford 1961 (original phonetic spelling), 1962 (modernized).

§ 2

'Warlock, Peter' (P. Heseltine). Whythorne: an unknown Elizabethan composer. 1927.

WILLIAM BYRD
1543–1623

Collections

Ed Fellowes, EM 14–16 1920, 1962–5 (rev).
Collected vocal works. Ed E. H. Fellowes, vols 12–16, 1948–9, 1962– (rev). Includes ms works not listed below.

§ 1

A gratification unto Master John Case. [c. 1586–8]. A 6-pt motet; only Cantus II survives (Cambridge Univ Lib).
Psalmes, sonets and songs of sadnes and pietie. 1588, [c. 1599].
Songs of sundrie natures, some of gravitie and others of myrth. 1589, 1610; ed Arkwright, Old English edition 6–9, 1892–3.
Psalmes, songs and sonnets: some solemne, others joyfull, framed to the life of the words. 1611.
See also Yonge, Musica transalpina, *1588,* Watson, Italian madrigalls englished, *1590, and* Leighton, Teares or lamentacions, *1614.*

§ 2

Fellowes, E. H. Byrd: a short account of his life and work. Oxford 1923, 1928 (rev).
—— William Byrd. Oxford 1936, 1948 (rev).
Howes, F. William Byrd. 1928.

NICHOLAS YONGE
d. 1619

Selections

Ferrabosco: madrigals from Musica transalpina. Ed Arkwright, Old English edition 11–12, 1894.
Marenzio: 10 madrigals from Musica transalpina. Ed R. A. Harman 1955.

§ 1

Musica transalpina: madrigales translated of foure, five and six parts, chosen out of divers excellent authors, with the first and second part of La verginella made by Maister Byrd. 1588; poems rptd in Fellowes, English madrigal verse (3rd edn); ed D. Stevens 1972 (facs). An anthology of Italian madrigals compiled by Yonge.
Musica transalpina: the second booke of madrigalles to 5 and 6 voyces, translated out of sundrie Italian authors. 1597; ed D. Stevens 1972 (facs). Compiled by Yonge.

THOMAS WATSON
1557?–92

The first sett of Italian madrigalls englished. 1590. Poems rptd in Fellowes, English madrigal verse (3rd edn). Italian madrigals, mostly by Marenzio, tr Watson; also 2 by Byrd.

THOMAS MORLEY
1557–1602?

Collections

Ed Fellowes, EM 1–4, 1913, 1956– (rev), 32, 1923, 1962 (rev).

§ 1

Canzonets: or little short songs to three voyces. 1593, 1602 (enlarged), 1606, 1631; tr German, 1612 (lost), 1624; text of 1624 rptd Bolle, Die gedruckten englischen Liederbücher; ed J. E. Uhler, Baton Rouge 1957 (facs of 1624).
Madrigalls to foure voyces. 1594, 1600 (enlarged).
The first booke of canzonets to two voyces. 1595, 1619; ed D. H. Boalch, Oxford 1950; tr Italian, c. 1595 (lost); ed J. E. Uhler, Baton Rouge 1954 (facs of 1595).
The first book of balletts to five voyces. 1595, 1600; tr Italian, 1595; German, 1609; ed E. F. Rimbault, Musical Antiquarian Soc [5 1842]; rptd Bolle, Die gedruckten englischen Liederbücher (text of 1609); rptd Obertello, Madrigali italiani (English and Italian texts).
Canzonets or little short songs to foure voyces: celected out of the best and approv'd Italian authors. 1597. Compiled by Morley, with English texts; 2 pieces by Morley himself. Italian and English texts rptd Obertello, Madrigali italiani; ed C. A. Murphy in ¡Morley's editions of Italian canzonets and madrigals, Tallahassee 1964.
Canzonets or little short aers to five and six voices. 1597.

A plaine and easie introduction to practicall musicke. 1597, 1608, 1771; ed E. H. Fellowes 1937 (facs), 1970 (facs); ed R. A. Harman 1952.

Madrigals to five voyces celected out of the best approved Italian authors. 1598. Compiled by Morley, with English texts. Italian and English texts rptd Obertello, Madrigali italiani; ed C. A. Murphy in Morley's editions of Italian canzonets and madrigals, Tallahassee 1964.

The first booke of ayres. 1600; ed Fellowes ELS 1st ser 16 1932, 1958, 1966 (both rev); ed Greer, els no 33 1970 (facs). Unique copy (incomplete) in Folger Shakespeare Lib, Washington.

The triumphes of Oriana, to 5 and 6 voices: composed by divers severall authors. 1601, 1601; ed W. Hawes [1814]; ed Benson, Oriana collection [1905]. Compiled by Morley, and containing madrigals by M. East, D. Norcome, J. Mundy, E. Gibbons, J. Bennet, J. Hilton the elder, G. Marson, R. Carlton, J. Holmes, R. Nicholson, T. Tomkins, M. Cavendish, W. Cobbold, J. Farmer, J. Wilbye, T. Hunt, T. Weelkes, J. Milton the elder, G. Kirbye, R. Jones, J. Lisley, E. Johnson and Morley himself.

JOHN DOWLAND
1563–1623
Collections

Ed Fellowes, ELS 1st ser 1–2 1920–1, 1965 (rev), 5–6 1922, 1969 (rev), 10–11 1923, 1961 (rev), 12 1924, 1969 (rev), 14 1925, 1969 (rev).

Fifty songs. Ed E. H. Fellowes 2 vols 1925, 1971 (rev).

Ayres for four voices, transcribed E. H. Fellowes. Ed R. T. Dart and N. Fortune, Musica britannica 6 1953, 1963 (rev).

Ed Poulton, els nos 14–18 1968–70.

§ I

The first booke of songes or ayres of fowre partes with tableture for the lute. 1597, 1600, 1603, 1606, 1613; ed W. Chappell, Musical Antiquarian Soc [12 1844].

The second booke of songs or ayres. 1600.

The third and last booke of songs or aires. 1603.

A pilgrimes solace. 1612.

See also Robert Dowland A musicall banquet, 1610, and Leighton, Teares or lamentacions, 1614.

THOMAS WEELKES
1575?–1632
Collections

Ed Fellowes, EM 9–12 1916, 1967–8 (rev), 13 1916, 1965 (rev).

§ I

Madrigals to 3, 4, 5 and 6 voyces. 1597; ed E. J. Hopkins, Musical Antiquarian Soc [8 1843].

Balletts and madrigals to five voyces. 1598, 1608; ed Arkwright, Old English edition 13–15 1895.

Madrigals of 5 and 6 parts. 1600.

Ayres or phantasticke spirites for three voices. 1608; ed Arkwright, Old English edition 16–17 1895–6.

The cries of London. Ed Brett, Consort songs (ms).

See also Morley, Triumphes of Oriana, 1601, and Leighton, Teares or lamentacions, 1614.

PHILIP ROSSETER
1568–1623

A booke of ayres. 1601; poems ed A. H. Bullen, The works of Dr Thomas Campion, 1889; poems ed P. Vivian,

Campion's works, Oxford 1909, 1966; words and music ed Fellowes, ELS 1st ser 4 and 13 1922–4, 1960, 1969 (both rev) (Campion's songs), 8–9 1923, 1966 (rev) (Rosseter's songs); poems ed W. R. Davis, Works of Campion, Garden City NY 1967, London 1969; ed Greer, els no 36 1970 (facs). This book contains 21 songs by Campion and 21 by Rosseter.

THOMAS CAMPION

See col 101, above.

ALFONSO FERRABOSCO
the younger
c. 1575–1628

Ayres. 1609; ed Fellowes, ELS 2nd ser 16 1927; ed Greer, els no 20 1970 (facs).

See also Leighton, Teares or lamentacions, 1614. There are also some ms songs by Ferrabosco, ed I. Spink, ELS 2nd ser 19 1966.

THOMAS RAVENSCROFT
c. 1592–c. 1633
Collections

Fellowes, English madrigal verse (3rd edn). Reprints words only.

'Warlock, Peter' (P. Heseltine). Pammelia and other rounds and catches. 1928. Contains all Ravenscroft's rounds and catches.

§ I

Pammelia: musicks miscellanie, or mixed varietie of pleasant roundelayes and delightful catches. 1609, 1618; ed M. Leach, Pbns Amer Folklore Soc, bibl & special ser 12 Philadelphia 1961 (facs). Collected by Ravenscroft.

Deuteromelia: or the second part of musicks melodie. 1609. Collected by Ravenscroft.

Melismata: musicall phansies. 1611. Collected by Ravenscroft.

A briefe discourse. 1614. Compositions by Ravenscroft, John Bennet and Edward Peirs (Pearce).

ROBERT DOWLAND
c. 1586–1641

A musicall banquet. 1610; ed P. Stroud, ELS 2nd ser 20 1968; ed D. Poulton, els no 19 1969 (facs). Compiled by Robert Dowland and containing songs by J. Dowland, D. Batchelar, R. Martin, R. Hales, [G.] Tessier, P. Guédron, D. Megli, G. Caccini and anon.

ORLANDO GIBBONS
1583–1625

The first set of madrigals and mottets of 5 parts. 1612; ed G. Smart, Musical Antiquarian Soc [3 1841]; ed Fellowes, EM 5 1914, 1964 (rev).

See also Leighton, Teares or lamentacions, 1614; The Cries of London ed Brett, Consort songs (ms).

SIR WILLIAM LEIGHTON
d. 1616

The teares or lamentacions of a sorrowfull soule. 1613 (words only), 1614 (with musical settings by Leighton, J. Dowland, J. Milton the elder, R. Johnson, T. Ford, E. Hooper, R. Kindersley, N. Giles, J. Coprario

(Cooper), J. Bull, W. Byrd, F. Pilkington, T. Lupo, R. Jones, M. Peerson, O. Gibbons, T. Weelkes, J. Ward, J. Wilbye, A. Ferrabosco the younger, T. Thopull); selections ed J. F. Bridge, Sacred motets or anthems for four and five voices by W. Byrde and his contemporaries, [1922]; ed C. Hill 1970 (complete).

HENRY LAWES
1595–1662

Ayres and dialogues: the first booke. [Pbd by J. Playford] 1653; Select ayres and dialogues (bk 2 of Treasury of musick), 1669 (selection); The treasury, Ridgewood NJ 1966 (facs).

The second book of ayres, and dialogues. [Pbd by J. Playford] 1655; Select ayres and dialogues (bk 2 of Treasury of musick), 1669 (selection); The treasury, Ridgewood NJ 1966 (facs).

Ayres and dialogues: the third book. [Pbd by J. Playford] 1658, 1669 (as bk 3 of Treasury of musick); The treasury, Ridgewood NJ 1966 (facs).

See also Hilton, Catch that catch can, *1652*; Select musicall ayres, *1652*; Select musical ayres, *1653*; A brief introduction to the skill of music, *1660*; The musical companion, *1673*; New ayres and dialogues, *1678*; Synopsis of vocal musick, *1680*.

3. DRAMA

I. INTRODUCTION

(1) BIBLIOGRAPHIES AND DICTIONARIES

Lowe, R. W. A bibliographical account of English theatrical literature. 1888.

Arnott, J. F. and J. W. Robinson. English theatrical literature 1559–1900: a bibliography incorporating R. W. Lowe's A bibliographical account of English theatrical literature 1888. 1970.

Greg, W. W. A list of English plays written before 1643 and printed before 1700. 1892.

—— A list of masques, pageants etc, supplementary to A list of English plays. 1902.

—— A bibliography of the English printed drama to the Restoration. 4 vols 1939–59 (Bibl Soc).

Chambers, E. K. The medieval stage. 2 vols Oxford 1903.

—— The Elizabethan stage. 4 vols (and index vol) Oxford 1923.

Harbage, A. Annals of English drama 975–1700. Philadelphia 1940; rev S. Schoenbaum 1964.

Wells, H. W. A chronological list of extant plays produced in or about London 1581–1642. New York 1940, Oxford 1940.

Bentley, G. E. The Jacobean and Caroline stage. 7 vols Oxford 1941–68. Vols 3–5 on plays and playwrights.

Woodward, G. L. and J. G. McManaway. A check-list of English plays 1641–1700. Chicago 1945; F. T. Bowers, Supplement, Charlottesville 1949.

Stratman, C. J. Bibliography of English printed tragedy 1565–1900. Carbondale 1966.

(2) COLLECTIONS OF PLAYS

Dodsley, R. A select collection of old plays. 12 vols 1744; enlarged by I. Reed 12 vols 1780; ed O. Gilchrist and J. P. Collier 12 vols 1825–7; ed W. C. Hazlitt 15 vols 1874–6 (83 plays).

Lamb, C. Specimens of the English dramatic poets. 1808; ed I. Gollancz 2 vols 1893.

Bullen, A. H. A collection of old English plays. 4 vols 1882–5.

—— Old English plays. New ser 3 vols 1887–90.

The Mermaid series. 1887–1909. Selected plays separately edited.

Pollard, A. W. English miracle plays, moralities and interludes. Oxford 1890, 1927 (rev). Selected scenes.

Manly, J. M. Specimens of the pre-Shaksperean drama. 2 vols Boston 1897–8.

Bang, W. Materialien zur Kunde des älteren englischen Dramas. Louvain 1902–14. Continued by H. de Vocht as Materials for the study of old English drama, Louvain 1927–58. 69 vols in all.

Gayley, C. M. et al. Representative English comedies. 3 vols New York 1904–14.

Farmer, J. S. Early English dramatists. 12 vols 1905–8.

—— Tudor facsimile texts. 143 vols 1907–14. TFT.

Greg, W. W., F. P. Wilson and A. Brown. The Malone Society reprints. Oxford 1907–. Facs with introds usually on textual matters.

The Malone Society collections. Oxford 1907–.

Brooke, C. F. T. The Shakespeare apocrypha. Oxford 1908.

—— and N. B. Paradise. English drama 1580–1642. Boston 1933.

Bond, R. W. Early plays from the Italian. Oxford 1911.

Cunliffe, J. W. Early English classical tragedies. Oxford 1912.

Adams, J. Q. Chief pre-Shakespearean dramas. Boston 1924.

McIlwraith, A. K. Five Elizabethan comedies. Oxford 1934 (WC).

—— Five Elizabethan tragedies. Oxford 1938 (WC).

—— Five Stuart tragedies. Oxford 1953 (WC).

Regents Renaissance drama series. Lincoln Nebraska 1963–. Modernized texts of individual plays, separately edited. RRDS.

New Mermaids series. 1964–. Modernized texts of individual plays, separately edited.

Armstrong, W. A. Elizabethan history plays. Oxford 1965 (WC).

Fountainwell drama texts. Edinburgh 1968–. Old-spelling texts of individual plays, separately edited.

Masques

Nichols, J. The progresses and public processions of Queen Elizabeth. 4 vols 1788–1821, 3 vols 1823.

—— The progresses, processions and magnificent festivities of King James I. 4 vols 1828.

Spencer, T. J. B. and S. W. Wells (ed). A book of masques in honour of Allardyce Nicoll. Cambridge 1967.

(3) HISTORY AND CRITICISM

Dryden, J. Essays [1663–1700]. Ed W. P. Ker 2 vols Oxford 1900; Of dramatic poesy and other essays, ed G. Watson 2 vols 1962 (EL).

Rymer, T. The tragedies of the last age considered and examined. 1678.

—— A short view of tragedy. 1693.

Langbaine, G. An account of the English dramatick poets. Oxford 1691.

Hazlitt, W. Lectures on the dramatic literature of the age of Elizabeth. 1818.

Boas, F. S. Shakspere and his predecessors. 1896.

—— An introduction to Tudor drama. Oxford 1933.

—— An introduction to Stuart drama. Oxford 1946.
Swinburne, A. C. The age of Shakespeare. 1908.
—— Contemporaries of Shakespeare. 1919.
Schelling, F. E. Elizabethan drama 1558–1642. 2 vols Boston 1908.
—— Elizabethan playwrights: a short history of the English drama to 1642. 1925.
Eliot, T. S. The sacred wood. 1920.
—— Elizabethan essays. 1934.
Archer, W. The old drama and the new. 1923.
Reed, A. W. Early Tudor drama. 1926.
Sisson, C. J. The Elizabethan dramatists, except Shakespeare. 1928.

—— Lost plays of Shakespeare's age. Cambridge 1936.
Ellis-Fermor, U. M. The Jacobean drama: an interpretation. 1936, 1958 (rev).
—— The frontiers of drama. 1945.
Knights, L. C. Drama and society in the age of Jonson. 1937.
Wilson, F. P. Elizabethan and Jacobean. Oxford 1945.
—— The English drama 1485–1585. Oxford 1969 (OHEL).
Brown, J. R. and B. Harris (ed). Jacobean theatre. 1960.
—— (ed). Elizabethan theatre. 1966.
Ure, P. Elizabethan and Jacobean drama: critical essays. Liverpool 1974.

II. THEATRES AND ACTORS

(1) DOCUMENTARY SOURCES: *Public records, playhouse and private records*
(2) BIBLIOGRAPHIES AND GENERAL HISTORIES OF THE STAGE
(3) CENSORSHIP AND GOVERNMENT REGULATION OF THE STAGE

The material of this section is covered comprehensively in the following: E. K. Chambers, The Elizabethan stage, 4 vols Oxford 1923 (with index by B. White 1934); G. E. Bentley, The Jacobean and Caroline stage, 7 vols Oxford 1941–68; J. T. Murray, English dramatic companies 1558–1642, 2 vols 1910; L. Hotson, The Commonwealth and Restoration stage, Cambridge Mass 1928; G. Wickham, Early English stages 1300–1660, vol 1 1300–1576, vol 2 pt 1 1576– 1597–8, 1959, 1963– (in progress).

(1) DOCUMENTARY SOURCES

Public Records

Transcripts of the registers of the Company of Stationers 1554–1640. Ed E. Arber 5 vols 1875–94.
Malone Society collections. Vol 1, Dramatic records of the City of London: the Remembrancia, Records from the Lansdowne mss, Dramatic records from the patent rolls: company licences, Dramatic records from the Privy Council register 1603–42. Ed E. K. Chambers and W. W. Greg, Oxford 1907, 1908, 1909, 1911; vol 2, Dramatic records of the City of London: the repertories, journals and letter books, ed E. J. Mill and E. K. Chambers; Dramatic records of the Lord Chamberlain's office, ed E. Boswell and E. K. Chambers, Oxford 1931; vol 3, A calendar of dramatic records in the books of the livery companies of London 1485–1640, ed J. Robertson and D. J. Gordon, Oxford 1954; vol 4, More records from the Remembrancia, ed F. P. Wilson, Oxford 1956; vol 5, A calendar of dramatic records in the books of the London cloth-workers' company (addenda to Collections 3), ed J. Robertson. Companies of players entertained by the Earl of Cumberland and Lord Clifford 1607–39, ed L. Stone; The academic drama in Oxford: extracts from the records of four colleges, ed R. E. Alton, Oxford 1959; vol 6, Dramatic records in the declared accounts of the treasury of the chamber 1558–1642, ed D. Cook, Oxford 1961; vol 7, Records of plays and players in Kent 1450–1642, ed G. E. Dawson, Oxford 1965.
Documents relating to the office of the revels in the time of Queen Elizabeth. Ed A. Feuillerat. In Materialen vol 21, ed W. Bang, Louvain 1908.
Documents relating to the revels at Court in the time of King Edward 6 and Queen Mary. Ed A. Feuillerat, Materialien vol 44, ed W. Bang, Louvain 1914.
Dramatic records from the Privy Council register, James 1 and Charles 1. Ed C. C. Stopes, Sh Jb 48 1912.

Playhouse and Private Records
(listed in groups)

Stow, J. A survey of London. 1598, 1603 (rev); rev J. Strype 2 vols 1720; ed C. H. Kingsford 3 vols Oxford 1908–27.
Moryson, F. An itinerary. 1617; 4 vols Glasgow 1907–8.
Machyn, H. The diary of Henry Machyn, citizen and merchant taylor of London 1550–63. Ed J. G. Nichols 1848 (Camden Soc).
Forman, S. The autobiography and personal diary of Dr Simon Forman 1552–1602. Ed J. O. Halliwell(-Phillipps) 1849.
Alleyn, E. A collection of original documents illustrative of the life and times of Edward Alleyn. Ed J. P. Collier 1843 (Shakespeare Soc).
Warner, G. F. A catalogue of the manuscripts and muniments of Alleyn's college of God's gifts at Dulwich. 1881.
Henslowe, P. The diary of Philip Henslowe from 1591–1609. Ed J. P. Collier 1845 (Shakespeare Soc).
Greg, W. W. (ed). Henslowe's diary. 2 pts 1904– 8.
—— (ed). Henslowe's papers: being documents supplementary to Henslowe's diary. 1907.
—— A fragment from Henslowe's diary. Library 4th ser 19 1939. Addn by J. Q. Adams 20 1940.
—— Dramatic documents from the Elizabethan playhouse: stage plots, actor's part, prompt books. 2 vols Oxford 1931.
—— Collected papers. Ed J. C. Maxwell, Oxford 1966.
Foakes, R. A. and R. T. Rickert (ed). Henslowe's diary. Cambridge 1961.
Manningham, J. The diary of John Manningham of the Middle Temple 1602–3. Ed J. Bruce 1868 (Camden Soc).

(2) BIBLIOGRAPHIES AND GENERAL HISTORIES OF THE STAGE

Arnott, J. F. and J. W. Robinson. English theatrical literature 1559–1900: a bibliography incorporating

R. W. Lowe's A bibliographical account of English theatrical literature 1888. 1970.

Nungezer, E. A dictionary of actors and of other persons associated with the public representation of plays in England before 1642. New Haven 1929.

Flecknoe, R. A short discourse of the English stage. Appended to Love's kingdom, 1664; rptd W. C. Hazlitt, English drama and stage, 1869; ed J. E. Spingarn, Critical essays of the seventeenth century vol 2, Oxford 1928.

Wright, J. Historia histrionica: an historical account of the English stage. In A dialogue of plays and players, 1699; rptd in R. Dodsley, A select collection of old plays, ed W. C. Hazlitt 1874-6; ed W. Ashbee 1872 (facs); ed A. Lang 1903.

Malone, E. An historical account of the rise and progress of the English stage, and of the economy and usages of our ancient theatres. In his Plays and poems of William Shakespeare vol 1 pt 2, 1790; and in Boswell's Malone vol 3, 1821.

Adams, J. Q. Shakespearean playhouses. Boston 1917.

Southern, R. The seven ages of the theatre. 1962.

Jacquot, J. (ed). Les fêtes de la Renaissance. Paris 1956.

— (ed). Dramaturgie et société: xvie et xviie siècles. 2 vols Paris 1968.

Bentley, G. E. (ed). The seventeenth-century stage: a collection of critical essays. Chicago 1968.

(3) CENSORSHIP AND GOVERNMENT REGULATION OF THE STAGE

See particularly E. K. Chambers, The Elizabethan stage vol 1: the Revels office; the control of the stage; *and G. Wickham,* Early English stages *vol 2 pt 1.*

Chambers, E. K. Notes on the history of the revels office under the Tudors. 1906.

— The Elizabethan Lords Chamberlain. In Malone Society collections vol 1, Oxford 1907.

— and W. W. Greg (ed). Dramatic records from the Privy Council Register, James I and Charles I. In Malone Society collections vol 1, Oxford 1911.

Feuillerat, A. Le bureau des menusplaisirs et la mise en scène à la cour d'Elizabeth. Louvain 1910.

— (ed). Documents relating to the office of the revels in the time of Queen Elizabeth. In Materialien vol 21, ed W. Bang, Louvain 1908.

— (ed). Documents relating to the revels at Court in the time of King Edward 6 and Queen Mary. In Materialien vol 44, ed W. Bang, Louvain 1914.

Stopes, C. C. (ed). Dramatic records from the Privy

Council register, James I and Charles I. Sh Jb 48 1912.

— The seventeenth-century accounts of the Master of the Revels. 1922 (Shakespeare Assoc).

Adams, J. Q. The dramatic records of Sir Henry Herbert, Master of the Revels 1623-73. New Haven 1917.

Adair, E. R. The sources for the history of the [Privy] Council in the sixteenth and seventeenth centuries. 1924.

Marcham, F. The King's Office of the Revels. RES 2 1926.

— and J. P. Gilson (ed). The King's Office of the Revels 1610-22: fragments of mss. 1925.

Dawson, G. E. Copyright of plays in the early seventeenth century. Eng Inst Essays 1947.

Greg, W. W. Copyright in unauthorized texts. In Elizabethan and Jacobean studies presented to F. P. Wilson, Oxford 1959.

III. MORALITIES

Abbreviations (Adams, Malone Soc, TFT etc) refer to collections of plays, col 169, above.

(1) GENERAL STUDIES

Craig, H. Morality plays and Elizabethan drama. Shakespeare Quart 1 1950.

— Miracles and moralities. In his English religious drama of the Middle Ages, Oxford 1955.

Rossiter, A. P. English drama from early times to the Elizabethans. 1950.

Craik, T. W. The Tudor interlude. Leicester 1958.

— The Tudor interlude and later Elizabethan drama. In Elizabethan theatre, ed J. R. Brown and B. Harris 1966.

Bevington, D. M. From Mankind to Marlowe. Cambridge Mass 1962.

Wickham, G. Dramatic qualities of the English morality play and moral interlude. In his Shakespeare's dramatic heritage, 1969.

Wilson, F. P. The early Tudor morality and interlude; the late Tudor morality play. In his English drama 1485-1585, Oxford 1969 (OHEL).

(2) PRE-TUDOR MORALITIES

Wisdom, who is Christ. Ed W. B. D. Turnbull 1837 (Abbotsford Club) (as Mind, will and understanding); ed F. J. Furnivall, Digby plays, 1882 (New Shakspere Soc).

The Castell of Perseverance. Ed A. W. Pollard, English miracle plays, 1890 (in part).

The pride of life. Ed J. Mills, Proc Royal Soc Antiquaries of Ireland 1891; A fragment.

Mankind. Ed A. W. Pollard, English miracle plays, 1890 (in part); Manly vol 1; Brandl; ed J. S. Farmer, 'Lost' Tudor plays, 1907; Adams.

The four cardinall virtues. Ed W. W. Greg, Malone Society collections vol 4, 1957. A fragment.

The Macro plays (Mankind; Wisdom, who is Christ; the Castell of Perseverance). Ed F. J. Furnivall and A. W. Pollard 1904 (EETS); TFT 1907.

(3) EARLY TUDOR MORALITIES

JOHN BALE
1495–1563

Bibliographies
Davies, W. T. A bibliography of Bale. Proc Oxford Bibl Soc 4 1939, new ser 1 1947.

Collections
Dramatic writings. Ed J. S. Farmer 1907.

§1

King Johan. 1538 (first version), 1558–62 (2nd) (Huntington Lib ms); ed J. P. Collier 1838 (Camden Soc); Manly vol 1; Bang vol 25; ed J. H. P. Pafford 1931 (Malone Soc); ed W. A. Armstrong, English history plays, 1965; extracts in A. W. Pollard, English miracle plays, 1927.

[God's promises]. A tragedye or enterlude manyfestyng the chefe promyses of God unto man, compyled 1538. [1547?], 1577, 1578; rptd Dodsley vol 1; Hazlitt's Dodsley vol 1; TFT 1908; ed W. Marriott, Collection of English miracle plays, Basle 1838; ed E. Jones, Erlangen 1909; ed E. Rhys, Everyman with other interludes, 1909 (EL).

[John Baptist]. A briefe comedy or enterlude of Johan Baptystes, compyled 1538; rptd Harleian miscellany vol 1, 1744, 1808.

[Temptation]. A brefe comedy or enterlude concernynge the temptacyon of our Lorde, compyled 1538. [1548?]; rptd A. B. Grosart, Miscellanies of Fuller worthies' library vol 1, 1870; TFT 1909; ed P. Schwemmer, Nuremburg 1919.

[Three laws]. A comedy concernynge thre lawes, of nature, Moses and Christ, compyled 1538. [1548?], 1562; ed A. Schroeer, Anglia 5 1882; TFT 1908.

§2

Harris, J. W. Bale: a study in the minor literature of the Reformation. Urbana 1940.

McCusker, H. Bale: dramatist and antiquary. Bryn Mawr 1942.

Blatt, T. B. The plays of Bale. Copenhagen 1969.

SIR DAVID LINDSAY
1490?–1555

Ane satire of the thrie estaitis. Edinburgh 1602. *See col 363, below.*

HENRY MEDWALL
b. c. 1462

Nature [1516–20?]. Ptd W. Rastell [1530?]; Bang vol 12 1905; TFT 1908; ed J. S. Farmer, 'Lost' Tudor plays, 1907 (facs of fragment).

JOHN RASTELL
1475?–1536

[Four elements]. A new interlude of the nature of the four elements. [1517–27?]; rptd J. O. Halliwell(-Phillipps) 1848 (Percy Soc); Hazlitt's Dodsley vol 1; ed J. Fischer, Marburger Studien 1903; ed J. S. Farmer, Six anonymous plays, 1905; TFT 1908; ed A. W. Pollard, English miracle plays, 1927.

JOHN REDFORD
c. 1486–1547

Wyt and scyence. [1530?]; ed J. O. Halliwell(-Phillipps) 1848 (Shakespeare Soc); Manley vol 1; ed J. S. Farmer, 'Lost' Tudor plays, 1907; TFT 1908; Adams; ed A. Brown 1952 (Malone Soc). Ms BM additional 15,233, probably autograph.

JOHN SKELTON
1460?–1529

Magnyfycence. [1533]. *See col 87, above.*

RICHARD WEVER
fl. c. 1549–53

[Lusty juventus]. An enterlude called lusty Juventus. [1550?; entered Stationers' Register 1560], [1565?]; ed T. Hawkins, Origins of the English drama vol 1, 1773; Hazlitt's Dodsley vol 2; ed J. S. Farmer 1905 (Early Eng Drama Soc); TFT 1907.

ANONYMOUS PLAYS

[Albyon Knight]. [1537–65? entered Stationers' Register 1565], [1566?]; ed J. P. Collier, Shakespeare Soc Papers vol 1, 1844 (fragment); ed J. S. Farmer, Anonymous plays, 1906; ed W. W. Greg, Malone Society collections vol 1, 1909.

[The summoning of Everyman]. [1509–19]. Ptd Pynson, nd (2 edns), J. Skot, nd (2 edns); ed T. Hawkins, Origins of English drama vol 1, 1773; ed K. Goedeke, Hanover 1865; Hazlitt's Dodsley vol 1; H. Logemann, Ghent 1892 (with Dutch text); ed K. H. de Raaf, Groningen 1897; ed F. Sidgwick 1902; ed A. W. Pollard, Fifteenth-century prose and verse, 1903; ed M. J. Moses, New York 1903; ed J. S. Farmer 1905 (Early English Drama Soc); Bang vol 4, 1904 (Skot's edn), vol 24 1909 (Skot's other edn), vol 28 1910 (2 Pynson fragments); TFT 1912; ed J. S. Tatlock and R. G. Martin, Representative English plays, 1915; Adams; ed J. Allen, Three medieval plays, 1953; ed A. C. Cawley, Everyman and medieval miracle plays, 1959 (EL); ed Cawley, Everyman, Manchester 1961; Wellington 1968 (modernized text based on Skot).

[Godly Queene Hester] [1527] (entered Stationers' Register 1561); ed J. P. Collier, Early English popular literature vol 1, 1863; ed A. B. Grosart, Miscellanies of Fuller worthies' library, 1879; Bang vol 5, 1904; ed J. S. Farmer, Anonymous plays, 1906.

[Good Order]. 1533 (fragment).

Hyckescorner. [1512?] [1516?] (de Worde), [1526?] (J. Waley) (fragment), [1560?]; ed T. Hawkins, Origins of the English drama vol 1, 1773; Hazlitt's Dodsley vol 1; Manly vol 1; ed J. S. Farmer, Anonymous plays, 1906; TFT 1908.

[Impacyente poverte] [1560; entered Stationers' Register 1560]. 1560; ed J. S. Farmer, 'Lost' Tudor plays, 1907; Bang vol 33, 1911.

[Johan the Evangelyst] [1520?]. [1550?]; 1907 (Malone Soc); TFT 1907.

[Nice wanton] [1560? entered Stationers' Register 1560]. 1560, [1565?]; ed Hazlitt's Dodsley vol 2; Manly vol 1; ed J. S. Farmer, Anonymous plays, 1905; TFT 1908 (from undated edn), 1909 (from 1560 edn).

[Welth and Helth] [1554? entered Stationers' Register 1557]. [1557?]; TFT 1907; ed J. S. Farmer, 'Lost' Tudor plays, 1907; ed W. W. Greg and P. Simpson 1907 (Malone Soc) (corrected Malone Soc collections vol 1, 1908); ed F. Holthausen, Kiel 1908, 1922 (rev).

[The worlde and the chylde]. 1522, 1817 (Roxburghe Club); ed J. P. Collier, Dodsley's old plays vol 12, 1827; Hazlitt's Dodsley vol 1; Manly vol 1; ed J. S. Farmer,

Anonymous plays, 1905; TFT 1909; ed J. Hampden 1935.

[Youth] [1520?; entered Stationers' Register 1557]. [1530?] (fragment), [1557?], [1562?] (J. Waley, nd (Copland); ed J. O. Halliwell (-Phillipps) 1849; Hazlitt's Dodsley vol 2; Bang vol 12, 1905; TFT 1908, 1909 (first 2 edns).

(4) ELIZABETHAN MORALITIES

ULPIAN FULWELL
d. 1586

Like will to like. 1568 (entered Stationers' Register 1568), [1570?], 1587; ed Hazlitt's Dodsley vol 3; ed J. S. Farmer 1906 (Early Eng Drama Soc); TFT 1909 (edn of 1587).

ROBERT WILSON
fl. 1572–1600

The three ladies of London. 1584, 1592 (variant text); ed J. P. Collier, Five old plays, 1851; Hazlitt's Dodsley; TFT 1911.

The three lords and three ladies of London. 1590; ed J. P. Collier, Five old plays, 1851; Hazlitt's Dodsley vol 6; TFT 1912.

The cobler's prophesie. 1594; ed W. Dibelius, Sh Jb 33 1897; TFT 1911; ed A. C. Wood 1914 (Malone Soc).

NATHANIEL WOODES
fl. 1550–94

The conflict of conscience. 1581 (2 states: one has name of Francis Spera on title-page and a tragic ending; the other calls the author Philogus and has a happy ending);

ed J. P. Collier, Five old plays, 1851; Hazlitt's Dodsley; TFT 1911; 1952 (Malone Soc).

ANONYMOUS PLAYS

Liberalitie and prodigalitie. 1602; rptd Hazlitt's Dodsley; TFT 1912; 1913 (Malone Soc).

The story of King Daryus. 1577 (entered Stationers' Register 1565); ed J. O. Halliwell (-Phillipps) 1860; Brandl; ed J. S. Farmer, Anonymous plays, 1906; TFT 1907 (from 1577 edn); 1909 (from 1565 edn).

The mariage of witte and science. [1569?] (entered Stationers' Register 1569); rptd Hazlitt's Dodsley vol 2; TFT 1909; 1961 (Malone Soc).

The marriage of wit and wisdom [1570 or 1579 in ms]. Ed J. O. Halliwell (-Phillipps) 1846; ed J. S. Farmer, Anonymous plays, 1908; TFT 1909.

New custome. 1573; Dodsley vol 1; Hazlitt's Dodsley vol 3; ed J. S. Farmer, Anonymous plays, 1906; TFT 1908.

The pedler's prophecie. 1595 (entered Stationers' Register 1594); rptd TFT 1911; 1914 (Malone Soc). Sometimes attributed to Robert Wilson, above on analogy with the Cobler's prophecie.

The triall of treasure. 1567; ed J. O. Halliwell (-Phillipps) 1842 (Percy Soc); Hazlitt's Dodsley; ed J. S. Farmer, Anonymous plays, 1906; TFT 1908.

IV. THE EARLY COMEDIES

Medwall, Rastell, Heywood, Udall and their contemporaries

Abbreviations used in this section (Adams, Bang, Gayley, TFT etc) refer to collections of plays, col 169, above.

HENRY MEDWALL
b. c. 1462

Fulgens and Lucres. [c. 1515]; Bang 1905 (fragment); Malone Society collections 1909; ed S. de Ricci, New York 1920 (facs); ed F. S. Boas and A. W. Reed, Oxford 1926; ed F. S. Boas, Five pre-Shakespearean comedies, Oxford 1934.

For Medwall's morality Nature see col 175, above.

JOHN RASTELL
1475?–1536

[Calisto and Melebea]. [c. 1527]; rptd Hazlitt's Dodsley; ed J. S. Farmer, Anonymous plays, 1905; 1908 (Malone Soc); H. W. Allen 1908; TFT 1909.

Gentylnes and Nobylyte. [1527?], [1535?]; ed S. E. Brydges and J. Haslewood, British bibliographer vol 4, 1814; ed J. H. Burn 1829; ed J. S. Farmer 1908; TFT 1908; K. W. Cameron, Raleigh NC 1941; 1950 (Malone Soc).

Both plays attributed to Rastell, but also to Heywood. For Rastell's Four elements see col 175, above.

JOHN HEYWOOD
1497?–1580?
Collections

Woorkes. 1562, 1566, 1576, 1587, 1598; rptd 1867 (Spenser Soc); ed J. Sharman 1874; ed J. S. Farmer 1906 (with 3 ballads and 1534 birthday poem to Princess Mary).

Dramatic writings. Ed J. S. Farmer 1905 (Early Eng Drama).

Works and miscellaneous short poems. Ed B. A. Milligan, Urbana 1956.

§ I

Johan Johan. 1522, [1819] (Chiswick Press); Brandl; ed Gayley; ed J. S. Farmer, Two Tudor shrew plays, 1908; TFT 1909; Adams.

The pardoner and the frere. 1533; ed F. J. Child, Four old plays, 1848; Hazlitt's Dodsley; ed J. S. Farmer 1906; ed A. W. Pollard, English miracle plays, 1927 (in part).

A play of love. 1533; ptd Waley?; rptd Brandl; TFT 1909 (Waley); ed K. W. Cameron, Raleigh NC 1944.

The play of the wether. 1533; ptd Rastell?; Awdeley?; Kytson?; rptd Brandl; ed Gayley; TFT 1908–9 (1533 and Awdeley); Adams; ed K. W. Cameron, Raleigh NC 1941.

The foure PP. [1543–7?]; Myddylton; Copland?; 1569; rptd R. Dodsley, Collection of old plays vol 1; Ancient British Drama; Hazlitt's Dodsley; Manly; TFT 1908 (Myddylton); Adams; ed F. S. Boas, Five pre-Shakespearean comedies, Oxford 1934.

Wytty and wytless. Ed F. W. Fairholt 1846 (Percy Soc) (abridged); TFT 1909; K. W. Cameron, Raleigh NC 1941. Ms: BM Harley 367.

Non-dramatic Writings

[A dialogue conteining the number in effect of all the proverbes in the English tongue. [1549?] (signed J.H.; unique copy in BM lacks all before signature c), 1561 ('newly overseen and somewhat augmented').

An hundred epigrammes. 1550.

Two hundred epigrammes, upon the hundred proverbes, with a thyrde hundred newly added. 1555.

A fourth hundred of epygrams, newly invented. 1560.

The spider and the flie. 1556; rptd 1894 (Spenser Soc).

Maxwell, I. R. French farce and Heywood. Melbourne 1946.

Craik, T. W. Experiment and variety in Heywood's plays. Renaissance Drama 7 1964.

NICHOLAS UDALL
c. 1505–56

Ralph Roister Doister [written 1545–53. Entered Stationers' Register 1566]. [1566?]; ed T. Briggs 1818; ed F. Marshall 1821; ed T. White, Old English drama vol 1, 1830; ed W. D. Cooper 1847 (Shakespeare Soc); ed E. Arber 1869; Hazlitt's Dodsley vol 3; Manly vol 2; Gayley vol 1; Adams; ed J. S. Farmer 1906 (Early Eng Drama Soc), and Museum dramatists, 1907; ed C. G. Child 1913; ed F. S. Boas, Five pre-Shakespearian comedies, 1934; W. W. Greg 1935 (Malone Soc); Bang vol 14, 1939.

Respublica [written 1553]. Ed J. P. Collier, Illustrations of English literature vol 1, 1866; Brandl; ed J. S. Farmer, 'Lost' Tudor plays, 1907; TFT 1908; ed W. W. Greg 1952 (EETS) (superseding L. A. Magnus edn, 1905).

Ezechias. Lost play performed before Queen Elizabeth at King's College Cambridge, 3 Aug 1654. See A. R. Moon, TLS 19 April 1928.

Jacke Jugeler, Jacob and Esau, and Thersites have also been attributed to Udall.

Other Writings

Floures for Latine spekynge. 1533 (preface dated 1535), 1538, 1544, 1560; rev John Higgins 1575, 1581.

Apophthegmes compiled in Latin by Erasmus. 1542, 1564.

The first tome of the paraphrase of Erasmus upon the Newe testament. 1548, 1551.

A discourse concerning the Lordes Supper. [1550?]. From P. M. Vermigh.

Compendiosa totius anatomie delineatio. [1553], 1557, 1559 (enlarged). An English version from Thomas Geminus.

Verses made at the Coronation of Queen Anne. Ed J. Nichols, Progresses of Elizabeth vol 1, 1788; ed F. J. Furnivall, Ballads from manuscript, 1870 (Ballad Soc); ed E. Arber, English garner vol 2, 1879 (English only).

An answer to the articles of the comoners of Devonsheir and Cornwall. Ed N. Pocock, Troubles connected with the Prayer Book of 1549, 1844 (Camden Soc).

V. THE EARLY TRAGEDIES

Abbreviations (Manly, TFT etc) refer to collections of plays, col 169, above.

(1) GENERAL STUDIES

Cunliffe, J. W. The influence of Seneca on Elizabethan tragedy. 1893.
—— Early English classical tragedies. Oxford 1912. Introd.

Lucas, F. L. Seneca and Elizabethan tragedy. Cambridge 1922.

Eliot, T. S. Shakespeare and the stoicism of Seneca. In Selected essays, 1932.

Spencer, T. Death and Elizabethan tragedy. 1936.

Clemen, W. Tragödie vor Shakespeare. Heidelberg 1955; tr 1961.

Hunter, G. K. Seneca and the Elizabethans: a case-study in influence. Shakespeare Survey 20 1967.

(2) TRANSLATIONS FROM SENECA

Seneca his tenne tragedies. 1581; ed J. Leigh 1887 (Spenser Soc); ed T. S. Eliot 1927.

JASPER HEYWOOD
1535–98

The sixt tragedie of Seneca entituled Troas. 1559, 1559, [1560?]; ed H. de Vocht, Bang 41 1913. Comment by W. W. Greg, Library 3rd ser 11 1931.

The seconde tragedie of Seneca, entituled Thyestes. 1560; ed H. de Vocht, Bang 41 1913; ed A. K. McIlwraith, Five Elizabethan tragedies, Oxford 1938 (WC).

The first tragedie of Seneca, entituled Hercules Furens. 1561; ed H. de Vocht, Bang 41 1913.

ALEXANDER NEVYLE
1544–1614

The lamentable tragedie of Oedipus. 1563; rev in Tenne tragedies, 1581.

T[HOMAS] N[UCE]
d. 1617

The ninth tragedie of Seneca, called Octavia. [1566]; rptd in Seneca his tenne tragedies, 1581.

JOHN STUDLEY
b. c. 1547

The seventh tragedie of Seneca, entituled Medea. 1566; ed E. M. Spearing, Bang 38 1913.

The eyght tragedie of Seneca, entituled Agamemnon. 1566; ed E. M. Spearing, Bang 38 1913.

(3) OTHER TRAGEDIES

THOMAS NORTON
1532–84

and

THOMAS SACKVILLE
1536–1608

Gorboduc. 1565, [1570] (as The tragidie of Ferrex and Porrex), 1590; Dodsley; Manly; TFT 1908.

GEORGE GASCOIGNE
1542?–77

and

FRANCIS KINWELMERSHE
d. 1580?

Jocasta. Ed F. J. Child, Four old plays, Cambridge Mass 1848; ed J. W. Cunliffe, Boston 1906.

R.B.

Apius and Virginia. 1575; ed C. W. Dilke, Old English plays vol 5, 1815; ed J. P. Collier, Dodsley's old plays vol 8, 1826; Hazlitt's Dodsley 4; ed J. S. Farmer 1908 (Early Eng Drama Soc); TFT 1908; ed R. B. McKerrow 1911 (Malone Soc).

VI. LATER ELIZABETHAN DRAMA

Lyly, Kyd, Peele, Lodge, Greene, Marlowe, Nashe

See C. J. Stratman, Bibliography of English printed tragedy 1565–1900, Carbondale 1966.
For collections listed below as abbreviations (Bang, Gayley, TFT etc) see col 169, above. RP = Revels Plays

JOHN LYLY
1554–1606

Collections

Six Court comedies. Ed E. Blount 1632. Includes Endimion; Alexander and Campaspe; Sapho and Phao; Gallathea; Midas; Mother Bombie.
Complete works. Ed R. W. Bond 3 vols Oxford 1902, 1967.

§ 1

Euphues: the anatomy of wit. [1578], [1579], 1579 ('corrected and augmented'), 1580, 1581, 1585, 1587, 1595, 1597, 1601, 1605, 1606, 1607, 1613; ed J. Winny, The descent of Euphues, Cambridge 1957.
Euphues and his England. 1580 (3 edns), 1581, 1582, 1584, 1586, 1588, 1592, 1597, 1601, 1605, 1606, 1609, 1613.
　Euphues [both pts]. 1617, 1623, 1630, 1631, 1636; ed E. Arber 1868, 1895; ed M. W. Croll and H. Clemons 1916.
A moste excellent comedie of Alexander, Campaspe and Diogenes, played before the Queenes Majestie on New Yeares Day at night by her Majesties children and the children of Poules. 1584 (3 edns, all anon, 2nd–3rd as Campaspe; headlines in all edns, A tragicall comedie of Alexander and Campaspe), 1591; rptd in Dodsley's old plays vol 2, 1744; in Ancient British drama vol 1, 1810; ed J. M. Manly, Specimens vol 2, 1897; ed G. P. Baker, Gayley vol 1, 1903; ed W. W. Greg 1933 (Malone Soc); ed A. K. McIlwraith, Five Elizabethan comedies, Oxford 1935 (WC).
Sapho and Phao, played before the Queenes Majestie on Shrove-tewsday by her Majesties children and the boyes of Paules. 1584, 1591.
Pappe with an hatchett, alias a figge for my godsonne, or crack me this nut, or a countrie cuffe, that is, a sound boxe of the eare, for the idiot Martin. [1589] (anon); rptd J. Petheram 1844; ed G. Saintsbury, Elizabethan and Jacobean pamphlets, 1892. Probably by Lyly.
A whip for an ape: or Martin displaied. [1589], [1589] (as Rhythmes against Martin Marre-Prelate) (anon); rptd I. D'Israeli, Quarrels of authors vol 3, 1814. Possibly by Lyly.
Endimion, the man in the moone, playd before the Queenes Majestie at Greenewich on Candlemas day at night by the chyldren of Paules. 1591 (anon); rptd [C. W. Dilke], Old English plays vol 2, 1814; ed G. P. Baker 1894; Brooke and Paradise; Baskervill et al.
Gallathea, as it was playde before the Queenes Majestie at Greenewich on Newyeeres day at night by the chyldren of Paules. 1592 (anon); ed A. B. Lancashire 1969 (RRDS) (with Midas).
Midas, plaied before the Queenes Majestie upon Twelfe day at night by the children of Paules. 1592 (anon); rptd [C. W. Dilke], Old English plays vol 1, 1814; ed J. Winny, Three Elizabethan plays, 1959; ed A. B. Lancashire 1969 (RRDS) (with Gallathea).
Mother Bombie, as it was sundrie times plaied by the children of Powles. 1594 (anon), 1598; rptd [C. W. Dilke], Old English plays vol 1, 1814; ed K. M. Lea and D. N. Smith 1948 (Malone Soc).
The woman in the moone, as it was presented before her Highnesse. 1597.
Loves metamorphosis: a wittie and courtly pastorall, first playd by the children of Paules, and now by the children of the Chappell. 1601.
Queen Elizabeth's entertainment at Mitcham: poet, painter and musician. Ed L. Hotson 1953. Attribution to Lyly uncertain.
The maydes metamorphosis, *1600, col 198 below, and several anon entertainments and fragments of entertainments have also been assigned to Lyly, but without much plausibility.*

§ 2

Wilson, J. D. Lyly. Cambridge 1905, New York 1970.

Feuillerat, A. Lyly: contribution à l'histoire de la Renaissance en Angleterre. Cambridge 1910.

Croll, M. W. The sources of the Euphuistic rhetoric. In Euphues, ed Croll and Clemons, 1916; rptd in his Style, rhetoric and rhythm, Princeton 1966.

Tilley, M. P. Elizabethan proverb lore in Lyly's Euphues, and in Pettie's Petite pallace. New York 1926.

Hunter, G. K. Lyly: the humanist as courtier. 1962.

THOMAS KYD
1558–94

Bibliographies etc

Crawford, C. A concordance to the works of Kyd. 3 pts Louvain 1906–10 (Bang).

Collections

Works. Ed F. S. Boas, Oxford 1901, 1955 (with suppl).

§ I

The householders philosophie [by Torquato Tasso] now translated by T.K. 1588.

The Spanish tragedie, newly corrected and amended of such grosse faults as passed in the first impression. [1592] (anon), 1594, 1599, 1602 ('newly corrected, amended and enlarged with new additions of the Painters part, and others, as it hath of late been divers times acted'), 1603, 1610, 1615, 1618, 1623, 1633; rptd R. Dodsley, Collection of old plays vol 2, 1744; ed T. Hawkins, Origin of the English drama vol 2, 1773; ed I. Reed, Dodsley's Old plays vol 3, 1780; Ancient British drama 1; ed J. P. Collier, Dodsley's Old plays vol 3, 1825; Hazlitt's Dodsley 5; Manly 2; ed J. Schick 1898; ed J. Schick, Berlin 1901; ed W. W. Greg 1925 (1602 edn) (Malone Soc); Brooke and Paradise; Baskervill et al; ed A. K. McIlwraith, Five Elizabethan tragedies, Oxford 1938 (WC); ed W. W. Greg and D. N. Smith 1949 (1592 edn) (Malone Soc); ed C. T. Prouty, New York 1951; ed P. Edwards 1959 (RP); ed B. L. Joseph 1964 (New Mermaids); Leeds 1966 (facs of 1592); ed A. S. Cairncross 1967 (RRDS) (with the First part of Hieronimo); ed T. W. Ross 1968; ed J. R. Mulryne 1970.

The trueth of the most wicked and secret murthering of John Brewen. 1592; ed J. P. Collier, Illustrations of early English popular literature vol 1, 1863, New York 1966; ed A. F. Hopkinson, Play sources, 1913.

Cornelia. 1594, 1595 (as Pompey the Great his faire Corneliaes tragedie, effected by her father and husbandes downe-cast, death and fortune, written in French by that excellent poet Ro. Garnier, and translated into English by Thomas Kid); rptd R. Dodsley, Collection of old plays vol 11, 1744; Hazlitt's Dodsley 5; ed H. Gassner, Munich 1894.

Fragments. In England's Parnassus, 1600.

The following anon plays (see cols 215 f., below) have also been assigned to Kyd: Arden of Feversham, The contention of York and Lancaster, Edward III, The first part of Jeronimo, King Leir, The rare triumphs of love and fortune, Soliman and Perseda, The taming of a shrew, The true tragedy of Richard III, *as well as a lost* Hamlet *and Shakespeare's* Titus Andronicus. *See col 198, below.*

§ 2

Barish, J. A. The Spanish tragedy: or the pleasures and perils of rhetoric. In Elizabethan theatre, ed J. R. Brown and B. Harris 1966.

Edwards, P. Kyd and early Elizabethan tragedy. 1966.

Murray, P. B. Thomas Kyd. New York 1969.

GEORGE PEELE
1556–96

Collections

Works. Ed A. Dyce 2 vols 1828, 3 vols 1829–39.

Works. Ed A. H. Bullen 2 vols 1888, 1969 (with introd by H. W. Wells).

Life and works. Ed C. T. Prouty et al 3 vols New Haven 1952–70.

§ I

The araygnement of Paris: a pastorall presented before the Queenes Majestie by the children of her Chappell. 1584 (anon); ed O. Smeaton 1905; ed H. H. Child 1910 (Malone Soc); Brooke and Paradise; Baskervill et al.

The device of the pageant borne before Woolstone Dixi Lord Maior of the Citie of London. 1585; rptd Harleian miscellany vol 10, 1813; ed J. Nichols, Progresses of Elizabeth vol 2, 1823; ed F. W. Fairholt, Lord Mayors' pageants, 1843 (Percy Soc). Unique copy in Bodley.

A farewell entituled to the famous and fortunate generalls of our English forces, Sir John Norris and Syr Fraucis Drake knights, and all theyr brave and resolute followers; whereunto is annexed A tale of Troy. 1589. The Tale of Troy was rptd 1604 (rev); no copy is now extant, but the text is given in Dyce and Bullen, above.

An eglogue gratulatorie entituled to the Right Honorable and renowned shepheard of Albions Arcadia, Robert Earle of Essex and Ewe, for his welcome into England from Portugall. 1589. Unique copy in Bodley.

Polyhymnia: describing the honourable triumph at tylt before her Majestie on the 17 of November last past, being the three and thirtith yeare of her Highnesse raigne. 1590.

Descensus Astraeae: the device of a pageant borne before M. William Webb, Lord Maior of the Citie of London. [1591]; rptd Harleian miscellany vol 10, 1813; ed F. W. Fairholt, Lord Mayors' pageants, 1843 (Percy Soc). Unique copy in London Guildhall.

The honour of the Garter, displaied in a poem gratulatorie, entituled to the worthie and renowned Earle of Northumberland. [1593]; Englands Parnassus, 1600 (excerpts).

The famous chronicle of King Edward the First, sirnamed Edward Longshankes, with his returne from the Holy Land; also the life of Lleuellen rebell in Wales; lastly, the sinking of Queene Elinor, who sunck at Charingcrosse and rose again at Pottershith, now named Queenehithe. 1593, 1599; ed J. P. Collier, Dodsley's Old plays vol 11, 1827; ed W. W. Greg 1911 (Malone Soc).

The battell of Alcazar, fought in Barbarie betweene Sebastian King of Portugall and Abdelmelec King of Marocco, with the death of Captaine Stukeley, as it was sundrie times plaid by the Lord High Admirall his servants. 1594 (anon); ed W. W. Greg 1907 (Malone Soc).

The old wives tale: a pleasant conceited comedie played by the Queenes Majesties players. 1595 ('by G.P.'); ed F. B. Gummere, Gayley 1; ed W. W. Greg 1908 (Malone Soc); Brooke and Paradise; Baskervill et al; ed A. K. McIlwraith, Five Elizabethan comedies, Oxford 1934 (WC); Menston 1969 (facs).

The love of King David and fair Bethsabe, with the tragedie of Absalon, as it hath ben divers times plaied on the stage. 1599; ed T. Hawkins, Origin of English drama vol 2, 1773; Manly 2; ed W. W. Greg 1912 (Malone Soc).

Anglorum feriae: Englandes hollydayes, beginninge happyly the 38 yeare of the raigne of our soveraigne Ladie. Ed R. (or W. S.) Fitch, Ipswich [c. 1830] (from autograph ms BM additional 21,432).

The hunting of Cupid. Ed W. W. Greg, Malone Society collections vol 1, 1911 (from fragmentary excerpts in the commonplace book of William Drummond of Hawthornden). The original edn (Stationers' Register 26 July 1591) is lost.

Two Elizabethan stage abridgements: the Battle of Alcazar and Orlando Furioso. Ed W. W. Greg 1922 (Malone Soc).

[Merrie conceited jests of George Peele. 1607, [1620?], 1627, 1657, 1671; ed W. C. Hazlitt, Shakespeare's jest-books vol 2, 1864; ed C. Hindley, Old book collector's miscellany vol 1, 1871. No longer accepted as Peele].

The following plays have also been partially or wholly assigned to Peele: Alphonsus Emperor of Germany, Captain Thomas Stukeley, Clyomon and Clamydes, Contention of York and Lancaster, George a Greene, Histriomastix, Jack Straw, Troublesome reign of King John, Knack to know a knave, Leir, Locrine, Mucedorus, Soliman and Perseda, Taming of a shrew, True tragedy of Richard III, Wily beguiled, Wisdom of Dr Dodipoll, *and Shakespeare's* Henry VI *and* Titus Andronicus.

THOMAS LODGE
1558–1625

Collections
Complete works. Ed E. Gosse 4 vols Glasgow 1883 (Hunterian Club), New York 1963. Omits trns.

§1
[A defence of poetry, music and stage plays. Original title may have been Honest excuses; *see* J. D. Wilson, MLR 3 1908]. [1579?]; ed D. Laing 1853 (Shakespeare Soc); extracts rptd in Elizabethan critical essays vol 1, ed G. G. Smith, Oxford 1904. A reply to S. Gosson, The schoole of abuse, 1579.

An alarum against usurers, [with] the delectable historie of Forbonius and Prisceria [and] the lamentable complaint of Truth over England. 1584; ed D. Laing 1853 (Shakespeare Soc).

Scillaes metamorphosis, enterlaced with the unfortunate love of Glaucus, with sundrie other poems and sonnets. 1589, 1610 (as A most pleasant historie of Glaucus and Scilla); rptd S. W. S[inger], Chiswick 1819; ed E. S. Donno, Elizabethan minor epics, 1963; ed N. Alexander, Elizabethan narrative verse, 1967.

Rosalynde: Euphues golden legacie. 1590, 1592, 1596, 1598, 1604, 1609, 1612 (as Euphues golden legacie), 1614, 1623, 1634, 1642; ed W. W. Greg 1907, 1931; ed G. Bullough, Narrative and dramatic sources of Shakespeare vol 2, 1958.

Catharos: Diogenes in his singularitie. 1591 ('by T.L. gent').

The famous, true and historicall life of Robert second Duke of Normandy. 1591 ('by T.L.G.').

Euphues shadow, the battaile of the sences [with] the Deafe mans dialogue. 1592 ('by T.L. gent').

The life and death of William Long beard, with manye other histories. 1593 ('by T.L. gent'); ed J. P. Collier, Illustrations of old English literature vol 2, 1866, New York 1966.

Phillis: honoured with pastorall sonnets, elegies and amorous delights, [with] the Tragicall complaynt of Elstred. 1593; ed M. F. Crow, Elizabethan sonnet-cycles vol 1, Chicago 1896; ed S. Lee, Elizabethan sonnets vol 2, 1904 (selections).

The wounds of civill war, lively set forth in the true tragedies of Marius and Scilla, as it hath beene publiquely plaide in London by the Lord high Admirall his servants. 1594; ed J. P. Collier, Dodsley's Old plays vol 8, 1825; Hazlitt's Dodsley 7; ed J. D. Wilson 1910 (Malone Soc); ed J. W. Houppert 1969 (RRDS).

A looking glasse for London and England, made by Thomas Lodge, gentleman, and Robert Greene, in artibus magister. 1594, 1598, 1602, [1605?], 1617; rptd 1914 (TFT); ed W. W. Greg 1932 (Malone Soc); ed T.

Hayashi, Metuchen NJ and Folkestone 1970. *See also under Greene, below.*

A fig for Momus: containing satyres, eclogues and epistles. 1595 ('by T.L. gent'); ed A. Boswell, Frondes caducae no 3, Auchinleck 1817.

The Divel conjured. 1596 (signed T.L.).

A margarite of America. 1596; ed J. O. Halliwell (-Phillipps) 1859; ed G. B. Harrison 1927 (with R. Greene's Menaphon).

Wits miserie and the worlds madnesse. 1596 (signed T.L.), Amsterdam and New York 1969 (facs).

Prosopopeia: containing the teares of the mother of God. 1596 (dedication signed T.L.). Attribution doubtful.

The flowers of Lodowicke of Granado. 1601 ('by T.L.'). Trn of Michael ab Isselt, Flores Lodovici Granatensis.

The famous and memorable workes of Josephus. 1602, 1609, 1620, 1632, 1640, 1655, 1670, 1683, 1693.

A treatise of the plague. 1603. Trn of F. Valleriole, Traicté de la peste, Lyons 1566.

The workes of Lucius Annaeus Seneca. 1614, 1620, 1632. Selections: ed W. Clode 1888; ed W. H. D. Rouse 1899 (Temple Classics).

A learned summary upon the famous poem of William of Saluste Lord of Bartas, translated out of French. 1621 ('by T.L.'), 1637, 1638.

The poore mans talentt. Ed E. Gosse, Complete works vol 4, 1883 (from Norfolk-Collier ms). Another ms BM additional 34,212.

§2
Sisson, C. J. Lodge and his family. In his Lodge and other Elizabethans, Cambridge Mass 1933, 1966.

Tenney, E. A. Thomas Lodge. Ithaca 1935, New York 1969.

Rae, W. D. Thomas Lodge. New York 1967.

ROBERT GREENE
1558–92

Collections
Dramatic works, to which are added his poems. Ed A. Dyce 2 vols 1831.

Life and complete works in prose and verse. Ed A. B. Grosart 15 vols 1881–6 (Huth Lib), New York 1964.

Plays and poems. Ed J. C. Collins 2 vols Oxford 1905, New York 1970.

Complete plays. Ed T. H. Dickinson 1909 (Mermaid ser).

§1
Mamillia: a mirror or looking-glasse for the ladies of England. 1583, 1593.

Arbasto: the anatomie of fortune. 1584, 1589, 1594, 1617 (as The historie of Arbasto), 1626.

Gwydonius: the carde of fancie. 1584, 1587, 1593, 1608 (as Greenes carde of fancie); ed G. Saintsbury, Shorter novels vol 1, 1929 (EL); ed F. Ferrara, Due romanzi, Naples 1950 (with Greenes mourning garment).

The debate between Follie and Love, translated out of French by Robert Greene. 1584, 1587, 1593. From Louise Labé, Débat de Folie et d'Amour, Lyons 1555.

Morando: the tritameron of love. Pt 1, 1584; pts 1–2, 1587.

The myrrour of modestie. 1584; ed J. P. Collier, Illustrations of old English literature vol 3, 1866, New York 1966.

An oration or funerall sermon uttered at Roome, at the buriall of Gregorie the 13. 1585. Tr by Greene from the French. Not in Grosart, above.

Planetomachia. 1585.

Euphues his censure to Philautus. 1587, 1634.

Penelopes web. 1587, 1601.

Alcida: Greenes metamorphosis. 1588, 1617.

Pandosto: the triumph of time. 1588 (running title, The historie of Dorastus and Fawnia), 1592, 1595, 1607, 1609,

1614, 1619, 1621, 1629, 1632 etc; ed J. Winny, The descent of Euphues, Cambridge 1957.

Perimedes the blacke-smith. 1588.

Ciceronis amor: Tullies love. 1589, 1592, 1597, 1601, 1605, 1609, 1611, 1616, 1628, 1639; ed E. H. Miller, Gainesville 1954 (with A quip for an upstart courtier) (facs of 1589).

Menaphon: Camillas alarum to slumbering Euphues (with an epistle by Thomas Nashe). 1589, 1599, 1605, 1610 (as Greenes Arcadia, or Menaphon), 1616, 1632; rptd S. E. Brydges, Archaica vol 2, 1815; ed E. Arber 1880; ed G. B. Harrison 1927 (with Lodge's Margarite of America).

The Spanish masquerado. 1589, 1589.

Greenes never too late [in two pts; the second entitled Francescos fortunes]. 1590, 1600, 1607, 1611, 1616, [1620?], 1621, [1630?], 1631.

Greenes mourning garment. 1590, 1597, 1616; ed F. Ferrara, Due romanzi, Naples 1960 (with Gwydonius).

The Royal Exchange, fyrst written in Italian, and dedicated to the Signorie of Venice, now translated into Englishe and offered to the Cittie of London. 1590. An adaptation of Orazio Rinaldi, Dottrina della virtù et fuga de' vitii.

Greenes farewell to folly. 1591, 1617.

A maydens dream; upon the death of Sir Christopher Hatton. 1591.

A notable discovery of coosnage. 1591 (running title, The art of conny-catching), 1592; ed J. O. Halliwell (-Phillipps) 1859; ed G. B. Harrison 1923; ed A. V. Judges, Elizabethan underworld, 1930.

The second part of conny-catching. 1591, 1592; ed G. B. Harrison 1923 (with A notable discovery); ed A. V. Judges, Elizabethan underworld, 1930.

The thirde and last part of conny-catching. 1592; ed G. B. Harrison 1923; ed A. V. Judges, Elizabethan underworld, 1930; ed G. R. Hibbard, Three Elizabethan pamphlets, 1951.

A disputation betweene a hee conny-catcher and a shee conny-catcher. 1592, 1615 (as Theeves falling out, true men come by their goods), 1617, 1621, 1637; ed G. B. Harrison 1923 (with The thirde part of conny-catching); ed A. V. Judges, Elizabethan underworld, 1930.

The blacke bookes messenger. 1592; ed G. B. Harrison 1924 (with The defence of conny catching); ed A. V. Judges, Elizabethan underworld, 1930.

Philomela: the Lady Fitzwaters nightingale. 1592, 1615, 1631; rptd S. E. Brydges, Archaica vol 1, 1815.

The defence of conny catching by Cuthbert Cunny-catcher. 1592; ed J. E. Adlard 1859; ed G. B. Harrison 1924 (with Blacke bookes messenger). Possibly by Greene.

Greenes vision, written at the instant of his death. [1592]. Possibly by Greene, though disavowed by him.

A quip for an upstart courtier. 1592 (3 edns), 1606, 1620, 1622, 1635; rptd in Harleian miscellany vol 5, 1745; ed J. P. Collier, Miscellaneous tracts, 1870; ed C. Hindley, Old book collectors' miscellany vol 3, 1873; ed E. H. Miller, Gainesville 1955 (with Ciceronis amor) (facs of the unique copy of first edn, now in the Huntington Lib, containing the attack on the Harvey brothers cancelled in later issues).

Greenes groats-worth of witte, bought with a million of repentance. 1592, 1596, 1600, 1616, 1617, 1621, 1629, 1637 etc; ed S. E. Brydges, Lee Priory 1813; ed G. B. Harrison 1923 (with The repentance of Robert Greene); ed A. C. Ward, A miscellany of tracts and pamphlets, Oxford 1927 (WC); Menston 1969 (facs of 1592).

The repentance of Robert Greene Maister of Artes. 1592; ed G. B. Harrison 1923 (with Greenes groats-worth).

Mamillia: the second part of the triumph of Paris. 1593.

The first part of the tragicall raigne of Selimus, as it was playd by the Queenes Majesties players. 1594 (anon),

Doubtfully attributed to Greene; 6 passages assigned to him in R. Allot, Englands Parnassus, 1600.

The historie of Orlando Furioso, one of the twelve pieres of France, as it was plaid before the Queenes Majestie. 1594, 1599; ed W. W. Greg and R. B. McKerrow 1907 (Malone Soc).

The honorable historie of Frier Bacon and Frier Bongay, as it was plaid by her Majesties servants. 1594, 1630, 1655; ed J. P. Collier, Dodsley's Old plays vol 8, 1826; ed A. W. Ward, Old English drama, 1878; Gayley 1; rptd 1914 (TFT); ed W. W. Greg 1926 (Malone Soc); Brooke and Paradise; Baskervill et al; ed B. Cellini, Florence 1953 (with John of Bordeaux); ed D. Seltzer 1963 (RRDS); ed J. A. Lavin 1969 (New Mermaids ser).

The Scottish historie of James the Fourth, slaine at Flodden, entermixed with a pleasant comedie presented by Oboram King of Fayeries, as it hath bene sundrie times publikely plaide. 1598; Manly 2; ed A. E. H. Swaen and W. W. Greg 1921 (Malone Soc); ed J. A. Lavin 1967 (New Mermaids ser); ed N. Sanders 1970 (RP).

The comicall historie of Alphonsus King of Aragon, as it hath bene sundrie times acted, made by R.G. 1599; ed W. W. Greg 1926 (Malone Soc).

Greenes Orpharion, wherein is discovered a musicall concorde of pleasant histories. 1599.

A paire of turtle doves: or the tragicall history of Bellora and Fidelio. 1606. Trn of Juan de Flores, La historia de Grisel y Mirabella, 1529.

A looking glasse for London and England, made by Thomas Lodge, gentleman, and Robert Greene, in artibus magister. 1594, 1598, 1602, [1605?], 1617; rptd 1914 (TFT); ed W. W. Greg 1932 (Malone Soc); ed T. Hayashi, Metuchen NJ and Folkestone 1970.

Two Elizabethan stage abridgments: the Battle of Alcazar and Orlando Furioso. Ed W. W. Greg 1922 (Malone Soc).

A pleasant conceyted comedie of George a Greene, the pinner of Wakefield, as it was sundry times acted by the servants of the Right Honourable the Earle of Sussex. 1599; rptd Dodsley's Old plays vol 1, 1744; vol 3, 1780, vol 3, 1825; Ancient British drama vol 1, 1810; ed F. W. Clark 1911 (Malone Soc); rptd 1913 (TFT); Baskervill et al; ed E. A. Horsman, Liverpool 1956. Probably by Greene.

John of Bordeaux, or the second part of Friar Bacon. Ed W. L. Renwick 1936 (from ms in Duke of Northumberland's Lib at Alnwick) (Malone Soc); ed B. Cellini, Florence 1953 (with Friar Bacon). Possibly by Greene rev Chettle.

The following anon plays (see cols 215 f., below) have also been wholly or partially assigned to Greene: The contention of York and Lancaster, Edward III, Fair Em, The troublesome reign of King John, A knack to know a knave, The Thracian wonder, Leir, Locrine, Mucedorus, The taming of a shrew, Thomas Lord Cromwell, *as well as Shakespeare's* Titus Andronicus *and* Henry VI.

CHRISTOPHER MARLOWE
1564–93
Collections

Works. Ed C. F. T. Brooke, Oxford 1910.

Works and life. Ed R. H. Case et al 6 vols 1930–3, New York 1966.

Plays. Ed L. Kirschbaum, New York 1962; ed I. Ribner, New York 1963; ed J. B. Steane 1969 (Penguin).

Poems. Ed M. MacLure 1968 (RP); ed S. Orgel 1971 (Penguin); ed R. Gill 1971.

Complete works. Ed F. T. Bowers 2 vols Cambridge 1973.

Complete plays and poems. Ed E. D. Pendry and J. C. Maxwell 1976 (EL).

§1

Tamburlaine the Great, divided into two tragicall discourses, as they were sundrie times shewed upon stages in the Citie of London by the Lord Admyrall his servantes. 1590, 1593, 1597, 1605–6; ed J. D. Jump 1967 (RRDS); ed J. W. Harper 1971 (New Mermaids ser).

The troublesome raigne and lamentable death of Edward the Second, King of England, as it was sundrie times publiquely acted in the Citie of London, by the Earle of Pembrooke his servants. 1594, 1598, 1612, 1622; rptd Dodsley's Old plays vol 2, 1744; ed R. Gill 1967; ed W. M. Merchant 1967 (New Mermaids ser); ed I. Ribner, New York 1970.

The tragedie of Dido Queene of Carthage, played by the Children of her Majesties Chappell, written by Christopher Marlowe and Thomas Nash gent. 1594; ed R. B. McKerrow, Works of Nashe vol 2, 1904, 1958; rptd 1914 (TFT); ed H. J. Oliver 1968 (RP) (with the Massacre at Paris).

The massacre at Paris, with the death of the Duke of Guise, as it was plaide by the Lord High Admirall his servants. [1594?]; ed W. W. Greg 1928 (Malone Soc); ed H. J. Oliver 1968 (RP) (with Dido); Amsterdam and New York 1971 (facs). Ms fragment in Folger Lib.

Epigrammes and Elegies [of Ovid], by J[ohn] D[avies] and C[hristopher] M[arlowe]. Middleburg [1595?] (2 edns).

All Ovids Elegies: 3 bookes, by C[hristopher] M[arlowe]; epigrams by J[ohn] D[avies]. Middleburg [1595–1600?] (2 edns), [c. 1640] (2 edns); ed C. Edmonds 1870, 1925.

Hero and Leander. 1598 (unique copy in Folger Lib), 1598 (with Chapman's continuation), 1600, 1606, 1609, 1613, 1617, 1622, 1629, 1637; ed P. B. Bartlett, Poems of George Chapman, New York 1941, 1962; ed E. S. Donno, Elizabethan minor epics, 1963; Menston 1968 (facs of 1598, Marlowe and Chapman); ed L. L. Martz, Washington 1972 (facs of 1598 Marlowe) (Folger Lib).

Lucans first booke translated line for line. 1600.

The passionate shepherd to his love. In Englands Helicon, 1600.

The tragicall history of D. Faustus, as it hath been acted by the Earle of Nottingham his servants, written by Ch. Marl. 1604, 1609, 1611, 1616 (with addns), 1619, 1620, 1624, 1628, 1631, 1663; Parallel texts (1604 and 1616), ed W. W. Greg, Oxford 1950; A conjectural reconstruction by Greg, Oxford 1950; ed P. H. Kocher, New York 1950; ed J. D. Jump 1962 (RP); ed R. Gill 1965 (New Mermaids ser); ed I. Ribner, New York 1966; Menston 1970 (facs of 1604, 1616).

The famous tragedy of the rich Jew of Malta, as it was played before the King and Queene, in his Majesties Theatre at White-Hall, by her Majesties servants. 1633; ed R. Van Fossen 1964 (RRDS); ed T. W. Craik 1966 (New Mermaids ser); Menston 1970 (facs of 1633); ed I. Ribner, New York 1970; Amsterdam and New York 1971 (facs).

The following anon plays have also been wholly or partially ascribed to Marlowe: Alarum for London, Arden of Feversham, The contention of York and Lancaster, Edward III, Locrine, Lust's dominion, Selimus, The taming of a shrew, The troublesome reign of King John, *and Shakespeare's* Titus Andronicus, Henry VI *and* Richard III.

§2

Vaughan, W. The golden grove. 1600.

Symonds, J. A. In his Shakspere's predecessors, 1884.

Eliot, T. S. Notes on the blank verse of Marlowe. In his Sacred wood, 1920; rptd as Marlowe in his Selected essays, 1932, 1951, and in his Elizabethan essays, 1934.

Boas, F. S. Marlowe: a biographical and critical study. Oxford 1940, 1953 (rev).

Mahood, M. M. Marlowe's heroes. In her Poetry and humanism, 1950; rptd in Elizabethan drama: modern essays in criticism, ed R. J. Kaufmann, New York 1961.

Poirier, M. Christopher Marlowe. 1951.

Levin, H. The overreacher: a study of Marlowe. Cambridge Mass 1952.

Lewis, C. S. Hero and Leander. Proc Br Acad 38 1952; rptd in his Selected literary essays, Cambridge 1969; and in Elizabethan poetry: modern essays in criticism, ed P. J. Alpers, New York 1967.

Wilson, F. P. Marlowe and the early Shakespeare. Oxford 1953.

Weil, J. Marlowe: Merlin's prophet. Cambridge 1977.

THOMAS NASHE
1567–1601?

Collections

Works. Ed R. B. McKerrow 5 vols 1904–10, Oxford 1958 (with corrections and supplementary notes by F. P. Wilson).

Selected works. Ed S. W. Wells 1964. Includes Pierce Penniless; Summer's last will and testament; Terrors of the night; Unfortunate traveller etc.

§1

The anatomie of absurditie. 1589; ed J. P. Collier, Illustrations of old English literature vol 3, 1866, New York 1966.

Pierce Penilesse his supplication to the Divell. 1592 (3 edns), 1593, 1595; ed J. P. Collier 1842 (Shakespeare Soc), Miscellaneous tracts, 1870; ed G. R. Hibbard, Three Elizabethan pamphlets, 1951; Menston 1969 (facs of 1592).

Strange newes, of the intercepting certaine letters. 1592, 1593, 1593 (as The apologie of Pierce Pennilesse); ed J. P. Collier, Miscellaneous tracts, 1870; Menston 1969 (facs of 1592).

Christs teares over Jerusalem. 1593, 1594 (with new preliminary matter), 1613; ed S. E. Brydges, Archaica vol 1, 1815; Menston 1970 (facs of 1593 with appendix of 1594 revisions).

The terrors of the night. 1594.

The unfortunate traveller: or the life of Jacke Wilton. 1594, 1594 ('newly corrected and augmented'); ed E. Gosse 1892; ed S. C. Chew, New York 1926; ed H. F. B. Brett-Smith, Oxford 1927; illustr M. Ayrton 1948; ed J. Berryman, New York 1960; Menston 1971 (facs of 1594, 'newly corrected and augmented').

Have with you to Saffron-Walden. 1596; ed J. P. Collier, Miscellaneous tracts, 1870.

Nashes lenten stuffe: the praise of red herring. 1599; rptd Harleian miscellany vol 6, 1745, vol 2, 1809, vol 6, 1810; rptd C. Hindley, Old book collector's miscellany vol 1, 1871.

A pleasant comedie called Summers last will and testament. 1600; ed J. P. Collier, Dodsley's Old plays vol 9, 1826; Hazlitt's Dodsley 8.

The choise of valentines. Ed J. S. Farmer 1899. In subscribers' copies only of McKerrow 1904–10; in McKerrow 1958. Folger Lib has ms copy, giving name of the dedicatee, Lord Strainge, in full.

To the gentlemen students of both universities. Preface to R. Greene, Menaphon, 1589, col 187 above; ed G. G. Smith, Elizabethan critical essays vol 1, Oxford 1904.

An almond for a parrat. 1590; ed J. Petheram, Puritan discipline tracts, 1846. Included among the doubtful works by McKerrow, this pamphlet is now widely accepted as Nashe's. *See* D. J. McGinn, PMLA 59 1944.

Somewhat to reade for them that list. Preface to Sir P.
Sidney, Astrophel and Stella, 1591.
*For the Marprelate tracts conjecturally ascribed to Nashe see
col 301, below. For* The tragedie of Dido Queene of
Carthage, written by Christopher Marlowe and Thomas
Nash gent, *1594, see under Marlowe, above. It has
also been suggested that Nashe had a hand in the
anon* A knack to know a knave, *1594, in Marlowe's* Dr
Faustus, *and in Shakespeare's* 1 Henry VI. *Doubtfully
attributed to Nashe is* A wonderfull strange and miraculous astrologicall prognostication, *1591, rptd in* Elizabethan and Jacobean pamphlets, *ed G. Saintsbury 1892.*

§2

Barber, C. L. In his Shakespeare's festive comedy,
Princeton 1959. Ch 4. On Summer's last will and
testament.
Hibbard, G. R. Nashe: a critical introduction. 1962.

VII. MINOR ELIZABETHAN DRAMA (1560–1603)

The abbreviations (Hazlitt's Dodsley, TFT etc) refer to collections of plays listed col 169, above.

HENRY CHETTLE
1560?–1607?

Kind harts dreame. [1593]; ed E. F. Rimbault 1842
(Percy Soc); ed C. M. Ingleby, Shakspere allusion-
books pt 1, 1874 (New Shakspere Soc); ed G. B. Harri-
son 1923.
Piers Plainnes seaven yeres prentiship. 1595; ed H.
Varnhagen, Erlangen 1900; ed J. Winny, Descent of
Euphues, Cambridge 1957.
The downfall of Robert, Earle of Huntington, acted by the
Earle of Notingham, Lord High Admirall of England
his servants. 1601; ed J. P. Collier, Five old plays, 1828,
1833; Hazlitt's Dodsley 8; rptd 1913 (TFT); ed J. C.
Meagher 1965 (Malone Soc). With Anthony Munday.
The death of Robert, Earle of Huntington, acted by the
Earle of Notingham, Lord High Admirall of England
his servants. 1601; ed J. P. Collier, Five old plays, 1828,
1833; Hazlitt's Dodsley 8; rptd 1913 (TFT); ed J. C.
Meagher 1967 (Malone Soc). With Munday.
The pleasant comodie of Patient Grissil, as it hath beene
sundrie times lately plaid by the Earle of Nottingham
(Lord High Admirall) his servants. 1603; ed J. P.
Collier 1841 (Shakespeare Soc); ed A. B. Grosart,
Works of Dekker vol 5, 1886; ed G. Hübsch, Erlangen
1893; rptd 1911 (TFT); ed F. T. Bowers, Dramatic works
of Dekker vol 1, 1953. With William Haughton and
Thomas Dekker.
Englandes mourning garment. [1603]; rptd in Harleian
miscellany vol 3, 1809; ed C. M. Ingleby, Shakspere
allusion-books pt 1, 1874 (New Shakspere Soc).
The tragedy of Hoffman or a revenge for a father, as it
hath bin divers times acted with great applause at the
Phenix in Druery-lane. 1631; ed H. B. L[eonard] 1852;
ed R. Ackermann 1894; rptd 1913 (TFT); ed H. Jenkins
and C. J. Sisson 1951 (Malone Soc).
The blind-beggar of Bednal-Green. 1659. *See under* Day,
below.
*Most of Chettle's plays and collaborations, as recorded in
Henslowe's diary, have been lost. The Trial of chivalry,
The weakest goeth to the wall, Hand A in Sir Thomas
More and Yarrington's Two lamentable tragedies have
been ascribed to him.*

SAMUEL DANIEL
1563–1619

*For Daniel's tragedies (Cleopatra, Philotas), pastorals (The
Queenes Arcadia, Hymens triumph) and masks (The vision
of the 12 goddesses, Tethys festival), see col 97 f., above.*
The Maydes metamorphosis, *1600 (anon), has also been
ascribed to him without much plausibility.*

JOHN DAY
c. 1574–c. 1640

Collections

Works. Ed A. H. Bullen 2 vols 1881, West Orange NJ
1963 (with additional introd by R. Jeffs).

§1

The Ile of Guls, as it hath been often playd in the blacke
Fryars, by the Children of the Revels. 1606, 1606, 1633;
ed G. B. Harrison 1936 (Malone Soc).
The travailes of the three English brothers, Sir Thomas,
Sir Anthony, Mr Robert Shirley, as it is now play'd by
her Majesties servants. 1607 (Dedication signed John
Day, William Rowley and George Wilkins).
Humour out of breath: a comedie divers times latelie
acted, by the Children of the Kings Revells. 1608; ed
J. O. Halliwell (-Phillipps) 1860; ed A. Symons, Nero
and other plays, 1888 (Mermaid ser).
Law-trickes or, who would have thought it, as it hath bene
divers times acted by the Children of the Revels. 1608;
ed J. Crow and W. W. Greg 1950 (Malone Soc).
The Parliament of Bees, with their proper characters.
1641; ed A. Symons, Nero and other plays, 1888 (Mermaid ser). BM Lansdowne ms 725 is a variant text.
The blind-beggar of Bednal-Green, with the merry humor
of Tom Strowd the Norfolk yeoman, as it was divers
times publickly acted by the Princes servants. 1659;
ed W. Bang, Bang 1, 1902; rptd 1914 (TFT). With
Chettle.
Peregrinatio scholastica. In Bullen, where the text is
based on BM ms Sloane 3150. There is another ms in
Huntington Lib with a different dedication.
The following anon plays have also been ascribed to Day:
Edward IV, The fair maid of Bristol, The maid's
metamorphosis, The noble soldier, Three Parnassus
plays, Lust's dominion *and Yarington's* Two lamentable
tragedies.

MICHAEL DRAYTON
1563–1631

The first part of the true and honorable historie of the life
of Sir John Oldcastle, the good Lord Cobham, as it hath
been lately acted by the Earle of Notingham, Lord High
Admirall of England his servants. 1600. With Anthony
Munday, Richard Hathway and Robert Wilson.
*For general bibliography of Drayton's works, see col 99,
above.* Edward IV, The London prodigal, The merry
devil of Edmonton, Sir Thomas More, *and* Thomas Lord
Cromwell *have also been partially or wholly ascribed to
him.*

WILLIAM HAUGHTON
c. 1575–1605

English-men for my money: or a pleasant comedy called A woman will have her will. 1616, 1626, 1631; rptd C. Baldwyn, Old English drama vol 1, 1825; Hazlitt's Dodsley 10; rptd 1911 (TFT); ed W. W. Greg 1912 (Malone Soc); ed A. C. Baugh 1917.

The pleasant comodie of Patient Grissill. 1603. *See under Chettle, above.*

Grim the collier of Croyden: or the Devil and his dame, with the Devil and Saint Dunston. 1662 (in Gratiae theatrales, where it is ascribed to 'I.T.', who probably revised it for the press); rptd in Ancient British drama vol 3, 1810; Hazlitt's Dodsley 7; rptd 1912 (TFT).

Haughton may also have collaborated in Lust's dominion *and Yarington's* Two lamentable tragedies.

ANTHONY MUNDAY
1560–1633

The mirrour of mutabilitie: or principall part of the Mirrour for magistrates, selected out of the sacred scriptures by A.M. 1579.

The paine of pleasure. 1580.

A view of sundry examples, reporting many straunge murthers. [1580?].

Zelauto: the fountaine of fame. 1580; ed J. Stillinger, Carbondale 1963.

An advertisement and defence for trueth against her backbiters. 1581. Anon.

The true reporte of the prosperous successe which God gave unto our English soldiours in Ireland, gathered out of letters of most credit and circumstance and more at large than in the former printed copie. [1581] (signed A.M.).

A breefe discourse of the taking of Edmund Campion. 1581.

A courtly controversie betweene Loove and Learning betweene a ladie and a gentleman of Scienna. 1581.

A discoverie of Edmund Campion and his confederates, published by A.M. 1582.

A breefe aunswer made unto two seditious pamphlets. 1582.

A breefe and true reporte of the execution of certaine traytours at Tiborne, gathered by A.M. 1582.

The English Romayne life. 1582, 1590; rptd in Harleian miscellany vol 7, 1744, 1808; ed G. B. Harrison 1925.

A watch-woord to Englande, to beware of traytours. 1584 (2 edns, signed A.M.).

Fedele and Fortunio: the deceites in love, excellently discoursed in a very pleasaunt and fine conceited comoedie of two Italian gentlemen; translated out of Italian, and set downe according as it hath beene presented before the Queenes most excellent Majestie. 1585 (anon); ed P. Simpson 1909 (Malone Soc); ed F. Flügge, Archiv 123 1909. An adaptation of L. Pasqualigo, Il Fedele. Chapman and Gosson have also been suggested as translator.

A banquet of daintie conceits, written by A.M. 1588; rptd in Harleian miscellany vol 9, 1746, 1812.

Palmerin D'Oliva, written in the Spanish, Italian and French, and from them turned into English by A.M. 1588, 1597, 1597 (The second part of Palmerin D'Oliva), 1615 (pt 1), 1616 (2 pts), 1637 (2 pts).

The famous, pleasant and variable historie of Palladine of England, translated out of French by A.M. 1588.

The declaration of the Lord de la Noue, upon his taking armes, truely translated according to the French copie by A.M. 1589.

The honorable, pleasant and rare conceited historie of Palmendos, translated out of French by A.M. 1589, 1633, 1653.

[The first book of Amadis of Gaule]. [1590] (title-page and dedication missing in only extant copy), 1595 (The second booke of Amadis de Gaule, translated by L. Pyott [A. Munday?]), 1618 (The ancient and honourable history of Amadis de Gaule, pts 3 and 4, translated by A.M.), 1619 (pts 1–2 as The ancient, famous and honourable history of Amadis de Gaule, written in French by the Lord of Essars, Nicholas de Herberay).

The coppie of the Anti-Spaniard, translated out of French. 1590.

The masque of the League and the Spanyard discovered, faythfully translated out of the French coppie. 1592 (signed A.M.), 1605 (as Falshood in friendship). Trn of A., L.T., Le masque de la Ligue et de l'Hespagnol découvert.

Archaioplutos: or the riches of elder ages, written in French by Guil. Thelin, Lord of Gutmont and Morillonuilliers. 1592.

Gerileon of England: the second part of his historie, written in French by Estienne de Maisonneufve and translated into English by A.M. 1592.

The defence of contraries: paradoxes against common opinion, translated out of French by A.M. 1593, 1602 (anon as Paradoxes against common opinion). From Charles Estienne.

The first booke of Primaleon of Greece. 1595 (first 4 sheets only by Munday), 1596 (The second booke of Primaleon of Greece, translated out of French by A.M.), 1619 (The famous historie of Primaleon of Greece [bks 1–3] translated out of French and Italian into English by A.M.).

[The first part of Palmerin of England]. [1596] (title-page missing in only extant copy), 1596 (The second part of the no less rare then excellent and stately historie of Palmerin of England, translated out of French by A.M.), 1602 (The third and last part of Palmerin of England, translated into English by A.M.), 1609 (pt 1), 1616 (pt 2), 1639 (2 pts).

A breefe treatise of the vertue of the crosse, translated out of French. 1599.

The first part of the true and honorable historie of the life of Sir John Oldcastle. 1600; ed C. F. T. Brooke, Shakespeare apocrypha, Oxford 1908; ed P. Simpson 1908 (Malone Soc); rptd 1911 (TFT). With Drayton, Hathway and Wilson.

The downfall of Robert, Earle of Huntington, acted by the Earle of Notingham, Lord High Admirall of England his servants. 1601; ed J. P. Collier, Five old plays, 1828, 1833; Hazlitt's Dodsley 8; rptd 1913 (TFT); ed J. C. Meagher 1965 (Malone Soc). With Chettle.

The death of Robert, Earle of Huntington, acted by the Earle of Notingham, Lord High Admirall of England his servants. 1601; ed J. P. Collier, Five old plays, 1828, 1833; Hazlitt's Dodsley 8; rptd 1913 (TFT); ed J. C. Meagher 1967 (Malone Soc). With Chettle.

The strangest adventure that ever happened: containing a discourse concerning the King of Portugall Don Sebastian, all first done in Spanish [by J. Teixera], then in French. 1601 (signed A.M.); rptd in Harleian miscellany vol 4, 1809.

The true knowledge of a mans owne selfe, written in French by Monsieur du Plessis, Lord of Plessie Marly [Philippe de Mornay], translated by A.M. 1602.

A true and admirable historie of a mayden of Consolens in Poictiers. 1603 (signed A.M.), 1604.

The dumbe divine speaker, written in Italian by Fra. Giacomo Affinati d'Acuto Romano and truelie translated by A.M. 1605.

The triumphes of re-united Britannia, performed in honor of Sir Leonard Holliday Lord Mayor. 1605; rptd J. Nichols, Progresses of James I vol 2, 1828.

The admirable deliverance of 266 Christians by J. Reynard

[J. Fox], Englishman, from the Turkes. 1608. Anon.
The conversion of a most noble lady of Fraunce, truely
translated out of French. 1608.

Camp-bell: or the Ironmongers faire feild. [1609].
Pageant at the installation of Sir T. Campbell as Lord
Mayor.

Londons love to the royal Prince Henrie, meeting him
on the river of Thames. 1610 (anon); rptd J. Nichols,
Progresses of James I vol 2, 1828.

A briefe chronicle of the successe of times from the creation
of the world to this instant. 1611.

Chruso-Thriambos: the triumphes of gold, at the inaugu-
ration of Sir James Pemberton in the dignity of Lord
Maior, devised and written by A.M. 1611; ed J. H. P.
Pafford 1962 (priv ptd).

Himatia-Poleos: the triumphes of olde draperie, at the
entertainment of Sr. Thomas Hayes Lord Maior,
devised and written by A.M. 1614.

Metropolis Coronata, the triumphes of ancient drapery in
a second yeeres performance, in honour of Sir John
Jolles Lord Maior, devised and written by A.M. 1615;
rptd J. Nichols, Progresses of James I vol 3, 1828.

Chrysanaleia: the golden fishing, applauding the advancement of Mr John Leman to the dignitie of Lord Maior.
1616; rptd J. Nichols, Progresses of James I vol 3, 1828;
ed J. G. Nichols 1884 (as The Fishmongers' pageant,
1616).

Sidero-Thriambos: or steele and iron triumphing,
applauding the advancement of Sir Sebastian Harvey to
the dignitie of Lord Maior, devised and written by A.M.
1618.

The triumphs of the golden fleece, performed at the
enstaulment of Mr Martin Lumley in the Maioraltie.
1623.

Sir Thomas More: a play now first printed. Ed A. Dyce
1844 (Shakespeare Soc); ed A. F. Hopkinson 1902
(priv ptd); ed C. F. T. Brooke, Shakespeare apocrypha,
Oxford 1908; 1910 (TFT); ed W. W. Greg 1911 (Malone
Soc), 1961 (with minor corrections and suppl by H.
Jenkins). BM Harley ms 7368. See also under Shakespeare, col 215, below.

John a Kent and John a Cumber: a comedy printed from
the original manuscript. Ed J. P. Collier 1851 (Shakespeare Soc); rptd 1912 (TFT); ed M. St C. Byrne 1923
(Malone Soc). Autograph ms in Huntington Lib
(HM 500).

HENRY PORTER
d. 1599

The pleasant historie of the two angrie women of Abington, as it was lately playde by the Right Honorable the
Earle of Nottingham, Lord High Admirall, his servants.
1599, 1599; Hazlitt's Dodsley 7; ed H. Ellis, Nero and
other plays, 1888 (Mermaid ser); Gayley 1; rptd 1911
(TFT); ed W. W. Greg 1912 (Malone Soc).

SAMUEL ROWLEY
d. 1624

When you see me you know me, or the famous chronicle
historie of King Henry the Eight, with the birth and
vertuous life of Edward Prince of Wales, as it was playd
by the high and mightie Prince of Wales his servants.
1605, 1613, 1621, 1632; ed K. Elze, Dessau 1874; rptd
1912 (TFT); ed F. P. Wilson 1952 (Malone Soc).

*H. D. Sykes, Sidelights on Elizabethan drama, 1924,
ascribes to Rowley the Famous victories of Henry V, the
prose scenes in the Taming of a shrew, the clowning
passages in Greene's Orlando, and the prose scenes of
Wily beguiled. Rowley was also responsible, with William
Bird, for the addns to Marlowe's Faustus.*

MARY HERBERT (née SIDNEY), COUNTESS OF PEMBROKE
1561–1621

Discourse of life and death, written in French by Ph.
Mornay; Antonius: a tragoedie, written also in French
by Ro. Garnier; both done in English by the Countess
of Pembroke. 1592.

The tragedie of Anthonie. 1595; ed A. Luce, Weimar
1897; ed G. Bullough, Narrative and dramatic sources
of Shakespeare vol 5, 1964.

A dialogue betweene two shepheards, Thenot and Piers,
in praise of Astraea, by the excellent lady the Lady
Mary Countesse of Pembrook. In Davison's Poetical
rapsody, 1602. See col 117, above.

ROBERT YARINGTON
fl. 1594–1601

Two lamentable tragedies: the one of the murther of
Maister Beech, a chaundler in Thames-streete, and his
boye, done by Thomas Merry; the other of a young
childe murthered in a wood by two ruffins, with the
consent of his unckle, by Rob Yarington. 1601; ed
A. H. Bullen, Old English plays vol 4, 1885; rptd 1913
(TFT).

ANONYMOUS PLAYS 1580–1603

The troublesome raigne of King John of England, as it
was sundry times publikely acted by the Queenes
Majesties players in the honourable Citie of London.
1591.

The second part of the troublesome raigne of King John.
1591.

The first and second part of the troublesome raigne of
John, King of England, written by W. Sh. 1611, 1622;
rptd J. Nichols, Six old plays vol 2, 1779; ed W. C.
Hazlitt, Shakespeare's library vol 5, 1875; ed F. J.
Furnivall 1888 (facs); ed C. Praetorius 1888 (facs); rptd
1911 (TFT); ed F. J. Furnivall and J. Munro 1913; ed
H. H. Furness, New variorum edn of Shakespeare's
King John, 1919; ed G. Bullough, Narrative and
dramatic sources of Shakespeare vol 4, 1962.

The tragedye of Solyman and Perseda. [1592?], 1599,
[1815] (facs, with date 1599 and, in some copies, 'J.
Smeeton, printer, St Martin's Lane' on verso of title-
page); rptd T. Hawkins, Origin of the English drama
vol 2, 1773; Hazlitt's Dodsley 5; ed F. S. Boas, Works
of Kyd, Oxford 1901, 1955; rptd 1912 (TFT) (from
1815 reprint). See under Kyd, col 183, above.

The lamentable and true tragedie of M. Arden of Feversham in Kent. 1592, 1599, 1633. See under Shakespeare,
col 216, below.

The life and death of Jacke Straw, a notable rebell in
England, who was kild in Smithfield by the Lord Maior
of London. 1593 (colophon 1594), 1604; Hazlitt's
Dodsley 5; ed H. Schütt, Heidelberg 1901; rptd 1911
(TFT); ed K. Muir and F. P. Wilson 1957 (Malone
Soc).

A pleasant commodie of Faire Em, the Millers daughter
of Manchester, as it was sundrie times publiquely acted
by the Lord Strange his servants. [1593?], 1631. See
under Shakespeare, col 216, below.

The first part of the contention betwixt the two famous
houses of Yorke and Lancaster. 1594. See under
Shakespeare, col 203, below.

A most pleasant and merie new comedie, intituled A
knacke to knowe a knave, newlie set forth as it hath
sundrie tymes bene played by Ed. Allen and his com-
panie; with Kemps applauded merrimentes of the men
of Goteham in receiving the King into Goteham. 1594;

ed J. P. Collier, Five old plays, 1851; Hazlitt's Dodsley 6; rptd 1911 (TFT); ed G. R. Proudfoot 1964 (Malone Soc).

The first part of the tragicall raigne of Selimus, as it was playd by the Queenes Majesties players. 1594, 1638. *See under Greene, col 188, above.*

A pleasant conceited historie called the taming of a shrew, as it was sundry times acted by the Right Honorable the Earle of Pembrook his servants. 1594, 1596, 1607. *See under Shakespeare, col 205, below.*

The true tragedie of Richard the Third, as it was played by the Queenes Majesties players. 1594; ed B. Field 1844 (Shakespeare Soc); ed W. C. Hazlitt, Shakespeare's library vol 6, 1875; ed H. H. Furness, New variorum edn of Shakespeare's Richard III, 1909; ed W. W. Greg 1929 (Malone Soc); ed G. Bullough, Narrative and dramatic sources of Shakespeare vol 3, 1960 (selection).

The warres of Cyrus, King of Persia, played by the children of her Majesties Chappell. 1594; ed W. Keller, Sh Jb 37 1901; rptd 1911 (TFT); ed J. P. Brawner, Urbana 1942. Based on a play by Richard Farrant (fl. 1564–80)?

The lamentable tragedie of Locrine, newly set foorth, overseene and corrected, by W.S. 1595. *See under Shakespeare, col 217, below.*

The true tragedie of Richard Duke of Yorke and the death of good King Henrie the Sixt, with the whole contention betweene the two houses Lancaster and Yorke, as it was sundrie times acted by the Earle of Pembroke his servants. 1595. *See under Shakespeare, col 203, below.*

The raigne of King Edward the Third, as it hath bin sundrie times plaied about the Citie of London. 1596, 1599. *See under Shakespeare, col 215, below.*

A pleasant conceited comedie, called A knacke to know an honest man, as it hath beene sundrie times plaied about the Citie of London. 1596; ed H. de Vocht 1910 (Malone Soc); rptd 1912 (TFT).

The famous victories of Henry the Fifth: containing the honourable Battell of Agincourt, as it was plaide by the Queenes Majesties players. 1598, 1617; rptd J. Nichols, Six old plays vol 2, 1779; ed W. C. Hazlitt, Shakespeare's library vol 5, 1875; ed P. A. Daniel 1887 (facs); rptd 1912 (TFT); ed G. Bullough, Narrative and dramatic sources of Shakespeare vol 4, 1962 (selection).

A most pleasant comedie of Mucedorus, newly set foorth, as it hath bin sundrie times plaide in the honorable Cittie of London. 1598, 1606 etc. *See under Shakespeare, col 217, below.*

A pleasant conceyted comedie of George a Greene, the pinder of Wakefield, as it was sundry times acted by the servants of the Right Honorable the Earle of Sussex. 1599. *See under Greene, col 188, above.*

The first and second parts of King Edward the Fourth, as it hath divers times beene publikely played by the Earle of Derby his servants. 1599, 1600, 1605, 1613, 1619, 1626; ed B. Field 1842 (Shakespeare Soc); ed R. H. Shepherd, Dramatic works of Thomas Heywood. *See under Heywood, col 236, below.*

A warning for faire women: containing the most tragicall and lamentable murther of Master George Sanders of London, merchant, as it hath beene lately diverse times acted by the Lord Chamberlaine his servants. 1599; rptd R. Simpson, School of Shakespeare vol 2, 1878; rptd 1912 (TFT).

Adams, J. Q. The authorship of a Warning for fair women. PMLA 28 1913.

A pleasant commodie called Look about you, as it was lately played by the Lord High Admirall his servantes. 1600; Hazlitt's Dodsley 7; rptd 1912 (TFT); ed W. W. Greg 1913 (Malone Soc). May be the same play as Dekker's lost Bear a brain.

The maydes metamorphosis, as it hath beene sundrie times acted by the children of Powles. 1600; ed A. H. Bullen, Old English plays vol 1, 1882; ed R. W. Bond, Works of Lyly vol 3, Oxford 1902; rptd 1912 (TFT). *See also under Lyly, col 182, above.*

The weakest goeth to the wall, as it hath bene sundry times plaide by the Earle of Oxenforde, Lord Great Chamberlaine of England his servants. 1600, 1618; rptd 1911 (TFT); ed W. W. Greg 1912 (Malone Soc).

The wisdome of Doctor Dodypoll, as it hath bene sundrie times acted by the children of Powles. 1600; ed A. H. Bullen, Old English plays vol 3, 1884; rptd 1912 (TFT); ed M. N. Matson 1964 (Malone Soc).

A larum for London: or the siedge of Antwerpe, as it hath been playde by the Lord Chamberlaine his servants. 1602; ed R. Simpson 1872; rptd 1912 (TFT); ed W. W. Greg 1913 (Malone Soc).

A pleasant conceited comedie wherein is shewed how a man may chuse a good wife from a bad. 1602. *See under Thomas Heywood, col 236, below.*

Il pastor fido: or the faithfull shepheard, translated out of Italian into English. 1602, 1633. By John Dymocke?

The true chronicle historie of the whole life and death of Thomas Lord Cromwell, written by W.S. 1602. *See under Shakespeare, col 218, below.*

The first part of Jeronimo, with the warres of Portugall and the life and death of Don Andraea. 1605; Dodsley's Old plays vol 3, 1780, 1825; Ancient British drama vol 1; Hazlitt's Dodsley 4; ed F. S. Boas, Works of Kyd, Oxford 1901, 1955; ed A. S. Cairncross 1967 (with the Spanish tragedy) (RRDS).

The famous historye of the life and death of Captaine Thomas Stukeley, as it hath beene acted. 1605; rptd R. Simpson, School of Shakespeare vol 1, 1878; rptd 1911 (TFT).

The true chronicle history of King Leir and his three daughters, Gonorill, Ragan and Cordella, as it hath beene divers and sundry times lately acted. 1605; rptd J. Nichols, Six old plays vol 2, 1779; ed W. C. Hazlitt, Shakespeare's library vol 6, 1875; ed W. W. Greg 1907 (Malone Soc); ed S. Lee 1909; ed R. Fischer, Quellen zu König Lear, Bonn 1914. *See also under Shakespeare, 213, below.*

Sir Thomas More (BM ms Harley 7368). *See under Shakespeare, 215, below.*

Edmund Ironside, the English King: a trew chronicle history called War hath made all friends (BM ms Egerton 1994, fols 97–118). Ed E. Boswell 1927 (Malone Soc).

The tragedy of Thomas of Woodstock (BM ms Egerton 1994, fols 161–185b). Ed J. O. Halliwell (-Phillipps) 1870 (as A tragedy of King Richard the Second); ed W. Keller, Sh Jb 35 1899 (as Richard II part 1); ed W. P. Frijlinck 1929 (Malone Soc) (as The first part of the reign of King Richard the Second, or Thomas of Woodstock); ed A. P. Rossiter 1946 (as Woodstock); ed W. A. Armstrong, Elizabethan history plays, Oxford 1965 (WC) (as Woodstock).

John of Bordeaux: or the second part of Friar Bacon. *See under Greene, col 188, above.*

VIII. WILLIAM SHAKESPEARE
1564–1616

(1) BIBLIOGRAPHIES;

(2) CONCORDANCES, GLOSSARIES, DICTIONARIES ETC;

(3) SHAKESPEARE SOCIETIES AND PERIODICALS;

(4) COLLECTIONS;

(5) PLAYS;

(6) POEMS;

(7) LIFE AND PERSONALITY OF SHAKESPEARE;

(8) CRITICISM: *Technical criticism; Aesthetic criticism.*

For more detailed lists see Bibliographies, below, notably the annual bibliography in Sh Quart.
Sh   *Shakespeare*

(1) BIBLIOGRAPHIES

Current literature is listed in Sh Quart (jnl of Sh Assoc of America), Annual Bibliography of Eng Lang & Lit (Modern Humanities Research Assoc), Year's Work in Eng Stud (Eng Assoc), Sh Survey, Sh Jb. See (3), below.

Lee, S. A catalogue of Shakespeariana. 1899.
—— A Shakespeare reference library. 1910 (Eng Assoc); rev E. K. Chambers 1925, S. W. Wells 1969.
Greg, W. W. In his A list of English plays written before 1643 and printed before 1700, 1900 (Bibl Soc).
—— In his Catalogue of the books presented by Edward Capell to the library of Trinity College in Cambridge, Cambridge 1903.

—— A descriptive catalogue of the early editions of the works of Shakespeare preserved in the library of Eton College. Oxford [1909].
Pollard, A. W. Shakespeare folios and quartos 1594–1685. 1909.
Jaggard, W. Shakespeare bibliography: a dictionary of every known issue of the writings of our national poet and of recorded opinion thereon in the English language. Stratford 1911, New York 1959.
Ebisch, W. and L. L. Schücking. A Shakespeare bibliography. Oxford 1931; Supplement 1930–5, Oxford 1937.

(2) CONCORDANCES, GLOSSARIES, DICTIONARIES ETC

Onions, C. T. A Shakespeare glossary. Oxford 1911, 1953 (rev).
Halliday, F. E. A Shakespeare companion 1550–1950. 1952, 1964 (rev as A Shakespeare companion 1564–1964), 1969 (Pelican).
Kökeritz, H. Shakespeare's names: a pronouncing dictionary. New Haven 1959.

Campbell, O. J. and E. G. Quinn. The reader's encyclopedia of Shakespeare. New York 1966.
Spevack, M. A complete and systematic concordance to the works of Shakespeare. 6 vols Hildesheim 1968–70.
Howard-Hill, T. H. Oxford Shakespeare concordances. Oxford 1969–.

(3) SHAKESPEARE SOCIETIES AND PERIODICALS

Shakespeare Society. 1841–52. 48 pbns 1841–53.
Deutsche Shakespeare-Gesellschaft 1864–. Sh Jb, Berlin (later Weimar) 1865–. From 1964 also Deutsche Shakespeare-Gesellschaft West, Sh Jb (Heidelberg) 1965–.
New Shakspere Society. 1874–86. 27 pbns.
Shakespeare Association of America Inc. 1926–. Sh Assoc Bull 1926–49.

Shakespeare survey. Cambridge 1948–. Includes annual survey of scholarship.
Shakespeare quarterly. New York 1950–. Replaces Sh Assoc Bull as jnl of Sh Assoc of America, above. Includes annual bibliography.

(4) COLLECTIONS

(1) The Four Folios

(a) The First Folio

Mr William Shakespeares comedies, histories and tragedies, published according to the true originall copies [with Droeshout portrait]; London, printed by Isaac Jaggard and Ed. Blount. 1623. Colophon: Printed at the charges of W. Jaggard, Ed. Blount, J. Smethweeke and W. Aspley, 1623. The arrangement of the preliminary leaves varies in different copies. There are also textual variations, due to corrections in the press. Ed John Heming and Henry Condell, and contains: Tempest; Two gentlemen of Verona; Merry wives of Windsor; Measure for measure; Comedy of errours; Much adoo about nothing; Loves labour lost; Midsommer nights dreame; Merchant of Venice; As you like it; Taming of the shrew; Alls well that ends well; Twelfe-night; Winters tale; King John; Richard the Second; First part of Henry the Fourth; Second part of Henry the Fourth; Henry the Fift; First part of Henry the Sixt; Second part of Henry the Sixt; Third part of Henry the Sixt; Richard the Third; King Henry the Eight; [Troylus and Cressida]; Coriolanus; Titus Andronicus; Romeo and Juliet; Timon of Athens; Julius Caesar; Macbeth; Hamlet; King Lear; Othello, the Moore of Venice; Anthony and Cleopater; Cymbeline.

Reprints

H. Kökeritz and C. T. Prouty, New Haven 1954 (reduced facs); C. Hinman, New York 1968 (facs).

Studies

Pollard, A. W. The foundations of Shakespeare's text. Proc Br Acad 10 1923.

Studies in the First Folio. Ed I. Gollancz 1924. Includes J. D. Wilson, The task of Heminge and Condell; S. Lee, A survey of First Folios; W. W. Greg, The First Folio and its publishers.

Greg, W. W. The Shakespeare First Folio: its bibliographical and textual history. Oxford 1955.

Hinman, C. The printing and proof-reading of the First Folio of Shakespeare. 2 vols Oxford 1963.

(b) The Second, Third and Fourth Folios

Mr William Shakespeares comedies, histories and tragedies, published according to the true originall coppies: the second impression [with Droeshout portrait], London, printed by Tho. Cotes, for Robert Allot, and are to be sold at his shop at the signe of the Blacke Beare in Pauls Church-yard. 1632.

Mr William Shakespeares comedies, histories and tragedies, published according to the true original copies: the third impression; [with Droeshout portrait], London, printed for Philip Chetwinde. 1663. First issue of Third Folio.

Mr William Shakespear's comedies, histories and tragedies, published according to the true original copies: the third impression; and unto this impression is added seven plays, never before printed in folio, viz Pericles Prince of Tyre; The London prodigall; The history of Thomas Ld Cromwell; Sir John Oldcastle Lord Cobham; The Puritan widow; A Yorkshire tragedy; The tragedy of Locrine; London, printed for P.C. 1664. Second issue of Third Folio with the 7 additional plays.

Mr William Shakespear's comedies, histories and tragedies, published according to the true original copies; unto which is added seven plays, never before printed in folio, viz Pericles Prince of Tyre; The London prodigal; The history of Thomas Lord Cromwel; Sir John Oldcastle Lord Cobham; The Puritan widow; A Yorkshire tragedy; The tragedy of Locrine: the fourth edition. London, printed for H. Herringman, E. Brewster and R. Bentley, at the Anchor in the New Exchange, the Crane in St Paul's Church-Yard and in Russel-Street Covent-Garden. 1685. Also found with 2 other imprints.

(2) Principal Later Collections

Rowe, N. The works of Shakespeare, revis'd and corrected, with an account of the life and writings of the author. 6 vols 1709. A 7th vol, including the poems and critical essays by Charles Gildon, followed in 1710, probably without authority.

Pope, A. The works of Shakespeare, collated and corrected. 6 vols 1723–5 (separate title-leaves to vols dated 1723). A supplementary 7th vol of the poems, ed George Sewell, followed in 1725. Rptd 8 vols Dublin 1725–6, 10 vols 1728, 10 vols 1728 (corrected and adding Pericles and the spurious plays), 9 vols 1731 (plays only), 8 vols 1734–6 (plays only), 9 vols 1635 (for 1735; plays only), 16 vols Glasgow 1752–7, 8 vols Glasgow 1766, 9 vols Birmingham 1768.

Theobald, L. The works of Shakespeare, collated with the oldest copies, and corrected; with notes, explanatory and critical. 7 vols 1733, Dublin 1739, 8 vols 1740, 1752, 1757, 1762, 1767, 12 vols 1772, 8 vols 1773, 12 vols [1777?]. Plays only.

Hanmer, T. The works of Shakespeare, carefully revised and corrected. 6 vols Oxford 1743–4, 1744–6, 1745,

9 vols 1747, 1748, 1750–1, 1760, 6 vols Oxford 1770–1, 1771. Adds Theobald's and Capell's variant readings, Pope's preface, Rowe's life, new notes by Percy, Warton and John Hawkins, and Collins's verses epistle. Plays only.

Warburton, W. The works of Shakespeare: the genuine text, collated with all the former editions and then corrected and emended, is here settled; being restored from the blunders of the first editors, and the interpolations of the two last; with a comment and notes, critical and explanatory, by Mr Pope and Mr Warburton. 8 vols 1747, Dublin 1747. Plays only.

Johnson, S. The plays of Shakespeare, with the corrections and illustrations of various commentators, to which are added notes. 8 vols 1765, 10 vols Dublin 1766, 8 vols 1768.

Steevens, G. Twenty of the plays of Shakespeare: being the whole number printed in quarto during his life-time, or before the Restoration; collated where there were different copies and publish'd from the originals. 4 vols 1766.

[Capell, E.] Shakespeare: his comedies, histories and tragedies, set out by himself in quarto or by the players his fellows in folio and now faithfully republish'd with an introduction; whereunto will be added, in some other volumes, notes critical and explanatory and a body of various readings. 10 vols 1767–8. The promised notes and various readings did not appear until 1779–83 (3 vols), though a first pt was pbd [1774].

Johnson, S. and G. Steevens. The plays of Shakespeare, with the corrections and illustrations of various commentators; to which are added notes by Samuel Johnson and George Steevens, with an appendix [by Richard Farmer]. 10 vols 1773. Based on Johnson's edn, above.

[Steevens, G.] The plays of Shakespeare, with the corrections and illustrations of various commentators; to which are added notes by Samuel Johnson and George Steevens: the second edition, revised and augmented. 10 vols 1778. Includes Malone's Attempt to ascertain the order in which the plays attributed to Shakespeare were written. Malone also added a supplement, 2 vols 1780, with notes, the first draft of his History of the stage, and the poems and doubtful plays. He added a further appendix in 1783.

[Reed, I.] The plays of Shakespeare, with the corrections and illustrations of various commentators; to which are added notes by Samuel Johnson and George Steevens: third edition revised and augmented by the editor of Dodsley's Collection of old plays. 10 vols, 1785. Includes notes by Malone.

Malone, E. The plays and poems of Shakespeare, collated verbatim with the most authentick copies; with the corrections and illustrations of various commentators, to which are added, an essay on the chronological order of his plays; an essay relative to Shakespeare and Jonson; a dissertation on the three parts of King Henry VI; an historical account of the English stage; and notes by E. Malone. 10 vols 1790.

[Steevens, G.] The plays of Shakespeare, with the corrections and illustrations of various commentators; to which are added notes by Samuel Johnson and George Steevens: the fourth edition, revised and augmented with a glossarial index. 15 vols 1793.

Reed, I. The plays of Shakespeare, with the corrections and illustrations of various commentators; to which are added notes by Samuel Johnson and George Steevens: fifth edition, revised and augmented by Isaac Reed, with a glossarial index. 21 vols 1803. First variorum edn. Embodies Steevens's last corrections.

[Bowdler, T.] The family Shakespeare. 4 vols Bath 1807. 20 plays.

Reed, I. The plays of Shakespeare, with the corrections and illustrations of various commentators; to which are added notes by Samuel Johnson and George Steevens, revised and augmented by Isaac Reed: sixth edition.

21 vols 1813. 2nd variorum edn.

[Boswell, J.] The plays and poems of Shakespeare, with the corrections and illustrations of various commentators, comprehending a life of the poet, and an enlarged history of the stage. 21 vols 1821. 3rd variorum edn. Based on Malone's edn, above, and on his ms collections.

Furness, H. H. and H. H. Furness jr. A new variorum edition of the works of Shakespeare. Philadelphia 1871–.

Craig, W. J. The Oxford Shakespeare. [1891] etc. Also in 3 vols, with general introd by A. C. Swinburne and separate introds to plays and poems by E. Dowden.

Craig, W. J., R. H. Case et al. The Arden Shakespeare. 37 vols 1899–1924.

Cross, W. L., C. F. T. Brooke et al. The Yale Shakespeare. 40 vols New Haven 1918–28.

Quiller-Couch, A. T., J. D. Wilson et al. Works. Cambridge 1921–66. New Cambridge.

Farjeon, H. The works of Shakespeare. 7 vols 1929–34 (Nonesuch Press), 4 vols 1953 (with new introd by I. Brown). Nonesuch.

Kittredge, G. L. Works. Boston 1936, Chicago 1958.

Harrison, G. B. The Penguin Shakespeare. 1937–64.

Alexander, P. Complete works. 1951.

Craig, H. Complete works. Chicago 1951.

Ellis-Fermor, U., H. F. Brooks and H. Jenkins. The Arden Shakespeare. 1951–.

Sisson, C. J. Complete works. [1954].

Munro, J. The London Shakespeare. 6 vols 1957.

Harbage, A. The complete Pelican Shakespeare. Baltimore 1969.

Evans, G. B. et al. The Riverside Shakespeare. Boston 1974.

§1

(5) PLAYS

Arranged in the chronological order of composition adopted in Chambers.

A. Quartos

Shakspere quarto facsimiles: issued under the superintendence of F. J. Furnivall. 43 vols 1880–9.

Shakespeare's quartos in collotype facs. Oxford 1939–.

B. Plays in 1623 Folio

1, 2, 3 Henry VI; Richard III; Comedy of errors; Titus Andronicus; Taming of the shrew; Two gentlemen of Verona; Love's labour's lost; Romeo and Juliet; Richard II; A midsummer night's dream; King John; Merchant of Venice; 1, 2 Henry IV; Much ado about nothing; Henry V; Julius Caesar; As you like it; Twelfth night; Hamlet; Merry wives of Windsor; Troilus and Cressida; All's well that ends well; Measure for measure; Othello; King Lear; Macbeth; Antony and Cleopatra; Coriolanus; Timon of Athens; Cymbeline; Winter's tale; Tempest; Henry VIII.

1, 2, 3 Henry VI

The first part of the contention betwixt the two famous houses of Yorke and Lancaster, with the death of the good Duke Humphrey, and the banishment and death of the Duke of Suffolke, and the tragicall end of the proud Cardinall of Winchester, with the notable rebellion of Jacke Cade; and the Duke of Yorkes first claime unto the Crowne; London, printed by Thomas Creed, for Thomas Millington, and are to be sold at his shop under Saint Peters Church in Cornwall. 1594; ed F. J. Furnivall 1891 (facs).

The first part of the contention betwixt the two famous houses of Yorke and Lancaster. 1600.

The true tragedie of Richard Duke of Yorke and the death of good King Henrie the Sixt, with the whole contention betweene the two houses of Lancaster and Yorke, as it was sundrie times acted by the Right Honourable the Earle of Pembroke his servants; printed at London by P[eter] S[hort] for Thomas Millington, and are to be sold at his shoppe under Saint Peters Church in Cornwall. 1595; ed T. Tyler 1891 (facs); ed W. W. Greg, Oxford 1958 (facs).

The true tragedie of Richarde Duke of Yorke, and the death of good King Henrie the Sixt. 1600.

The whole contention betweene the two famous houses, Lancaster and Yorke, with the tragicall ends of the good Duke Humfrey, Richard Duke of Yorke and King Henrie the Sixt, divided into two parts and newly corrected and enlarged; written by William Shakespeare gent; printed at London for T[homas] P[avier]. [1619]; ed F. J. Furnivall 2 pts 1886 (facs).

Modern Editions

C. F. T. Brooke, 3 pts New Haven 1918–23 (Yale); J. D. Wilson, 3 pts Cambridge 1952 (New Cambridge); A. S. Cairncross, 3 pts 1957–64 (New Arden); W. W. Greg, Oxford 1958 (facs of True tragedy); F. Fergusson and C. J. Sisson, 3 pts New York 1963 (Laurel); L. B. Wright and V. A. LaMar, 3 pts New York 1967 (Folger); M. Crane, pt 3, New York 1968 (Signet); G. L. Kittredge, rev I. Ribner, 3 pts Waltham Mass 1969.

Studies

Shakspere's Holinshed. Ed W. G. Boswell-Stone 1896.

Malone, E. A dissertation on the three parts of King Henry VI, tending to show that these plays were not originally written by Shakespeare. 1787, 1792 (expanded); rptd in Third variorum Shakespeare vol 18, ed J. Boswell 1821.

Brockbank, J. P. The frame of disorder: Henry VI. In Early Shakespeare, ed J. R. Brown and B. Harris 1961.

Riggs, D. Shakespeare's heroical histories: Henry VI and its literary tradition. Cambridge Mass 1971.

Weiss, T. In his Breath of clowns and kings: Shakespeare's early comedies and histories, 1971.

Richard III

The tragedy of King Richard the Third: containing his treacherous plots against his brother Clarence, the pittiefull murther of his iunocent [sic] nephewes, his tyrannicall usurpation; with the whole course of his detested life, and most deserved death, as it hath beene lately acted by the Right Honourable the Lord Chamberlaine his servants; at London printed by Valentine Sims, for Andrew Wise, dwelling in Paules Chuch-yard [sic], at the signe of the Angell. 1597 (anon); ed J. O. Halliwell (-Phillipps) 1863 (facs); ed P. A. Daniel 1886 (facs); ed W. W. Greg, Oxford 1959 (facs).

The tragedie of King Richard the Third, by William Shake-speare. 1598, ed J. O. Halliwell (-Phillipps) 1867 (facs); 1602 ('newly augmented' but in fact identical with earlier edns), ed J. O. Halliwell (-Phillipps) 1865 (facs); ed P. A. Daniel 1888; 1605, ed Halliwell 1863 (facs); 1612, ed Halliwell 1871 (facs); 1622, ed P. A. Daniel 1889 (facs); 1629, 1634.

Modern Editions

J. R. Crawford, New Haven 1927 (Yale); J. D. Wilson, Cambridge 1954 (New Cambridge); F. Fergusson and

C. J. Sisson, New York 1958 (Laurel); G. B. Evans, Baltimore 1959 (Pelican); A. S. Downer 1959 (Oxberry's 1822 edn with Hackett's notes on Kean's performance); W. W. Greg, Oxford 1959 (facs of 4° 1); L. B. Wright and V. A. LaMar, New York 1960 (Folger); M. Eccles, New York 1964 (Signet); E. A. J. Honigmann 1968 (New Penguin).

Comedy of Errors
Modern Editions
H. Cuningham 1906 (Arden); A. T. Quiller-Couch and J. D. Wilson, Cambridge 1922 (New Cambridge); R. D. French, New Haven 1926 (Yale); R. A. Foakes 1962 (New Arden); P. A. Jorgensen, Baltimore 1964 (Pelican); H. Levin, New York 1965 (Signet); G. L. Kittredge, rev I. Ribner, Waltham Mass 1966.
For a concordance see T. H. Howard-Hill, Oxford 1969.

Studies
Rouse, W. H. D. The Menaechmi: the original of Shakespeare's Comedy of errors. 1912. Latin text and Elizabethan trn.
Baldwin, T. W. On the compositional genetics of the Comedy of errors. Urbana 1965.
Brooks, H. Themes and structure in the Comedy of errors. In Early Shakespeare, ed J. R. Brown and B. Harris 1961.

Titus Andronicus
The most lamentable Romaine tragedie of Titus Andronicus, as it was plaide by the Right Honourable the Earle of Darbie, Earle of Pembrooke and Earle of Sussex their servants; London, printed by John Danter, and are to be sold by Edward White and Thomas Millington, at the little north doore of Paules at the signe of the Gunne. 1594. Anon. The only copy known, now in Folger Lib, was discovered in Sweden in 1905.
The most lamentable Romaine tragedie of Titus Andronicus. 1600, ed J. O. Halliwell (-Phillipps) 1867; ed A. Symons 1885 (facs); 1611 (as The most lamentable tragedie).

Modern Editions
H. B. Baildon 1904 (Arden); A. M. Witherspoon, New Haven 1926 (Yale); J. Q. Adams, New York 1937 (facs of unique copy of 4° (1594) in Folger Lib); J. D. Wilson, Cambridge 1948 (New Cambridge); J. C. Maxwell 1953 (New Arden); S. Barnet, New York 1964 (Signet); L. B. Wright and V. A. LaMar, New York 1965 (Folger); G. L. Kittredge, rev I. Ribner, Waltham Mass 1969.

Taming of the Shrew
A pleasant conceited historie called the taming of a shrew, as it was sundry times acted by the Right Honorable the Earle of Pembrook his servants; printed at London by Peter Short and are to be sold by Cuthbert Burbie, at his shop at the Royall Exchange. 1594, ed J. O. Halliwell (-Phillipps) 1876 (facs); ed F. J. Furnivall 1886; TFT 1912; rptd T. Amyot 1844; ed F. S. Boas 1908; 1596, 1607. Alternatively held to be the source or a 'bad quarto' of the Folio 1 play.
A wittie and pleasant comedie called the taming of the shrew, as it was acted by his Majesties servants at the Blacke Friers and the Globe; written by Will. Shakespeare, printed by W.S. for John Smethwicke, and are to be sold at his shop in Saint Dunstones Churchyard under the Diall. 1631. Rptd from Folio 1.

Modern Editions
R. W. Bond 1904 (Arden), 1929; H. T. E. Perry, New Haven 1921 (Yale); A. T. Quiller-Couch and J. D. Wilson, Cambridge 1928 (New Cambridge); F. Fergusson and C. J. Sisson, New York 1958 (Laurel);

L. B. Wright and V. A. LaMar, New York 1963 (Folger); R. Hosley, Baltimore 1964 (Pelican); R. B. Heilman, New York 1966 (Signet); G. L. Kittredge, rev I. Ribner, Waltham Mass 1967; G. R. Hibbard 1968 (New Penguin).

Two Gentlemen of Verona
Modern Editions
R. W. Bond 1906 (Arden); A. T. Quiller-Couch and J. D. Wilson, Cambridge 1921 (New Cambridge); K. Young, New Haven 1924 (Yale); B. Evans, New York 1964 (Signet); F. Fergusson and C. J. Sisson, New York 1964 (Laurel); B. A. W. Jackson, Baltimore 1964 (Pelican); L. B. Wright and V. A. LaMar, New York 1964 (Folger); N. Sanders 1968 (New Penguin); G. L. Kittredge, rev I. Ribner, Waltham Mass 1969; C. Leech, 1969 (New Arden).
For a concordance see T. H. Howard-Hill, Oxford 1970.

Love's Labour's Lost
A pleasant conceited comedie called Loves labors lost, as it was presented before her Highnes this last Christmas, newly corrected and augmented by W. Shakespere; imprinted at London by W[illiam] W[hite] for Cutbert Burby. 1598; ed J. O. Halliwell (-Phillipps) 1869 (facs); ed F. J. Furnivall 1880 (facs); ed W. W. Greg, Oxford 1957 (facs).
Loves labours lost: a wittie and pleasant comedie, as it was acted by his Majesties servants at the Blacke-Friers and the Globe, written by William Shakespeare. 1631.

Modern Editions
H. C. Hart 1906 (Arden); H. B. Charlton 1917 (Heath); A. T. Quiller-Couch and J. D. Wilson, Cambridge 1923 (New Cambridge); W. L. Cross and C. F. T. Brooke, New Haven 1925 (Yale); R. W. David 1951 (New Arden); L. B. Wright and V. A. LaMar, New York 1962 (Folger); A. Harbage, Baltimore 1963 (Pelican); J. L. Calderwood, Dubuque Iowa 1970 (Blackfriars).

Romeo and Juliet
An excellent conceited tragedie of Romeo and Juliet, as it hath been often (with great applause) plaid publiquely, by the right Honourable the L. of Hunsdon his servants; London, printed by John Danter. 1597; ed H. A. Evans 1886 (facs); rptd P. A. Daniel 1874 (New Shakespeare Soc); W. A. Wright, Cambridge Shakespeare vol 9, 1893; ed F. G. Hubbard, Madison 1924. The 'bad' 4°.
The most excellent and lamentable tragedie of Romeo and Juliet, newly corrected, augmented and amended, as it hath bene sundry times publiquely acted, by the Right Honourable the Lord Chamberlaine his servants; London, printed by Thomas Creede for Cuthbert Burby, and are to be sold at his shop neare the Exchange. 1599; ed H. A. Evans 1886 (facs); rptd P. A. Daniel 1874 (New Shakespeare Soc); ed P. A. Daniel 1875 (New Shakespeare Soc). The 'good' 4°.
The most excellent and lamentable tragedie of Romeo and Juliet. 1609, nd (2 issues, 2nd adding 'written by W. Shakespeare', ed H. A. Evans 1887 (facs)), 1637.

Modern Editions
E. Dowden 1900 (Arden); W. H. Durham, New Haven 1917 (Yale); G. Sampson, Cambridge 1936; W. W. Greg, Oxford 1949 (William Drummond's copy of 4°2 1599); R. Hosley, New Haven 1954 (Yale); G. I. Duthie and J. D. Wilson, Cambridge 1955 (New Cambridge); F. Fergusson and C. J. Sisson, New York 1958 (Laurel); L. B. Wright and V. L. Freund, New York 1959 (Folger); J. E. Hankins, Baltimore 1960 (Pelican); G. W. Williams, Durham NC 1964; G. L. Kittredge, rev I. Ribner, Waltham Mass 1967; T. J. B. Spencer 1967 (New Penguin); M. Spevack, Dubuque Iowa 1970 (Blackfriars).

Richard II

The tragedie of King Richard the Second, as it hath beene publikely acted by the Right Honourable the Lorde Chamberlaine his servants; London, printed by Valentine Simmes for Androw Wise, and are to be sold at his shop in Paules Church yard at the signe of the Angel. 1597 (anon); ed J. O. Halliwell (-Phillipps) 1862 (facs); ed W. A. Harrison 1888 (facs); ed W. W. Greg, rev C. Hinman, Oxford 1966 (facs).

The tragedie of King Richard the Second, by William Shakespeare. 1598, ed J. O. Halliwell (-Phillipps) 1869 (facs); 1598, ed A. W. Pollard 1916 (facs); 1608, 1608 (as 'with new additions of the Parliament Sceane, and the deposing of King Richard', though the earlier issue also contains the new scene); ed J. O. Halliwell (-Phillipps) 1858 (facs); ed W. A. Harrison 1888; 1615, ed J. O. Halliwell (-Phillipps) 1870 (facs); 1634, ed P. A. Daniel 1887 (facs).

Modern Editions

I. B. John 1912 (Arden); L. M. Buell, New Haven 1921 (Yale); J. D. Wilson, Cambridge 1939 (New Cambridge); T. Spencer, New York 1949 (Crofts); M. W. Black, Philadelphia 1955 (New Variorum); P. Ure 1956 (New Arden); R. P. Petersson, New Haven 1957 (Yale); M. W. Black, Baltimore 1957 (Pelican); F. Fergusson and C. J. Sisson, New York 1961 (Laurel); L. B. Wright and V. A. LaMar, New York 1962 (Folger); K. Muir, New York 1963 (Signet); W .W. Greg, rev C. Hinman, Oxford 1966 (1597 4°); G. L. Kittredge, rev I. Ribner, Waltham Mass 1966; S. Wells 1969 (New Penguin).

A Midsummer Night's Dream

A midsommer nights dreame, as it hath beene sundry times publickely acted by the Right Honourable the Lord Chamberlaine his servants; written by William Shakespeare; imprinted at London, for Thomas Fisher, and are to be soulde at his shoppe, at the signe of the White Hart in Fleete-streete. 1600; ed J. O. Halliwell (-Phillipps) 1864 (facs); ed J. W. Ebsworth 1880 (facs).

A midsommer nights dreame, as it hath beene sundry times publikely acted by the Right Honourable the Lord Chamberlaine his servants; written by William Shakespeare; printed by James Roberts. 1600 (for 1619); ed J. O. Halliwell (-Phillipps) 1865 (facs); ed J. W. Ebsworth 1880 (facs).

Modern Editions

H.Cuningham 1905 (Arden); W. H. Durham, New Haven 1918 (Yale); A. T. Quiller-Couch and J. D. Wilson, Cambridge 1924 (New Cambridge); G. L. Kittredge, Boston 1939; F. W. Robinson, Melbourne 1940; L. B. Wright and V. A. LaMar, New York 1958 (Folger); M. Doran, Baltimore 1959 (Pelican); F. Fergusson and C. J. Sisson, New York 1960 (Laurel); W. Clemen, New York 1963 (Signet); G. L. Kittredge, rev I. Ribner, Waltham Mass 1967; S. Wells 1967 (New Penguin).

King John

Modern Editions

I. B. John 1907 (Arden); H. H. Furness jr, Philadelphia 1919 (New Variorum); S. T. Williams, New Haven 1927 (Yale); J. D. Wilson, Cambridge 1936 (New Cambridge); E. A. J. Honigmann 1954 (New Arden); F. Fergusson and C. J. Sisson, New York 1963 (Laurel); W. H. Matchett, New York 1963 (Signet); G. L. Kittredge, rev I. Ribner, Waltham Mass 1967.

The Merchant of Venice

The most excellent historie of the merchant of Venice, with the extreme crueltie of Shylocke the Jewe towards the sayd merchant, in cutting a just pound of his flesh, and the obtayning of Portia by the choyse of three chests; as it hath beene divers times acted by the Lord Chamberlaine his servants; written by William Shakespeare; at London, printed by J[ames] R[oberts] for Thomas Heyes, and are to be sold in Paules Churchyard, at the signe of the Greene Dragon. 1600; ed J. O. Halliwell (-Phillipps) 1870 (facs); ed F. J. Furnivall 1887 (facs); ed W. W. Greg, Oxford 1939 (facs).

The excellent history of the merchant of Venice, with the extreme cruelty of Shylocke the Jew towards the saide merchant in cutting a just pound of his flesh, and the obtaining of Portia, by the choyse of three caskets; written by W. Shakespeare; printed by J. Roberts. 1600 (for 1619), ed J. O. Halliwell (-Phillipps) 1865 (facs); ed F. J. Furnivall 1880 (facs); 1637, 1652.

Modern Editions

C. K. Pooler 1905 (Arden); W. L. Phelps, New Haven 1923 (Yale); A. T. Quiller-Couch and J. D. Wilson, Cambridge 1926 (New Cambridge); G. C. Taylor and R. Smith, Boston 1936 (interlinear); W. W. Greg, Oxford 1939 (Hayes 4°1); J. R. Brown 1955 (New Arden); L. B. Wright and V. L. Freund, New York 1957 (Folger); F. Fergusson and C. J. Sisson, New York 1958 (Laurel); B. Stirling, Baltimore 1959 (Pelican); A. D. Richardson, New Haven 1960 (Yale); K. Myrick, York 1965 (Signet); G. L. Kittredge, rev I. Ribner, Waltham Mass 1966; W. M. Merchant 1967 (New Penguin).

For a concordance see T. H. Howard-Hill, Oxford 1970.

1, 2 Henry IV

Part 1

The history of Henrie the Fourth; with the battell at Shrewsburie betweene the King and Lord Henry Percy, surnamed Henrie Hotspur of the North; with the humorous conceits of Sir John Falstalffe; at London, printed by P. S[hort] for Andrew Wise, dwelling in Paules churchyard, at the signe of the Angell. 1598; ed J. O. Halliwell (-Phillipps) 1866 (facs); ed H. A. Evans 1881 (facs); ed W. W. Greg, rev C. Hinman, Oxford 1966 (facs).

The history of Henrie the Fourth, with the battell at Shrewsburie betweene the King and Lord Henry Percy, surnamed Henry Hotspur of the North; with the humorous conceits of Sir John Falstalffe; newly corrected by W. Shake-speare. 1599, ed J. O. Halliwell (-Phillipps) 1861 (facs); 1604, ed Halliwell 1871 (facs); 1608, ed Halliwell 1867 (facs); 1613, ed Halliwell 1867 (facs); 1622, 1632, 1639, 1700.

Modern Editions

R. P. Cowl and A. E. Morgan 1914 (Arden); S. B. Hemingway, New Haven 1917 (Yale), Philadelphia 1936 (New Variorum); G. L. Kittredge, Boston 1940; R. C. Bald, New York 1946 (Crofts); J. D. Wilson, Cambridge 1946 (New Cambridge); M. A. Shaaber, Baltimore 1957 (Pelican); F. Fergusson and C. J. Sisson, New York 1959 (Laurel); A. R. Humphreys 1960 (New Arden); L. B. Wright and V. A. LaMar, New York 1961 (Folger); M. Mack, New York 1965 (Signet); W. W. Greg, rev C. Hinman, Oxford 1966 (facs of 4° 1); G. L. Kittredge, rev I. Ribner, Waltham Mass 1966; P. H. Davison 1968 (New Penguin).

Part 2

The second part of Henrie the Fourth, continuing to his death, and coronation of Henrie the Fift, with the humours of Sir John Falstaffe and swaggering Pistoll; as it hath been sundrie times publikely acted by the Right Honourable the Lord Chamberlaine his servants written by William Shakespeare; London, printed by V[alentine] S[immes] for Andrew Wise and William Aspley. 1600 (III. i, originally omitted, is found in some copies in cancel sheet of 6 leaves); ed J. O. Halliwell (-Phillipps) 1866 (facs); ed H. A. Evans 1882 (facs).

Modern Editions

S. B. Hemingway, New Haven 1921 (Yale); R. P. Cowl 1923 (Arden); M. A. Shaaber, Philadelphia 1940 (New Variorum); J. D. Wilson, Cambridge 1946 (New Cambridge); A. Chester, Baltimore 1957 (Pelican); L. B. Wright and V. A. LaMar, New York 1962 (Laurel); A. R. Humphreys 1966 (New Arden); G. L. Kittredge, rev I. Ribner, Waltham Mass 1966.

Much Ado about Nothing

Much adoe about nothing, as it hath been sundrie times publikely acted by the Right Honourable the Lord Chamberlaine his servants; written by William Shakespeare; London, printed by V. S[immes] for Andrew Wise and William Aspley. 1600; ed J. O. Halliwell (-Phillipps) 1865 (facs); ed P. A. Daniel 1886 (facs).

Modern Editions

C. F. T. Brooke, New Haven 1917 (Yale); A. T. Quiller-Couch and J. D. Wilson, Cambridge 1923 (New Cambridge); G. R. Trenery 1924 (Arden); A. G. Newcomer 1929; C. T. Prouty, New York 1948 (Crofts); J. W. Bennett, Baltimore 1958 (Pelican); F. Fergusson and C. J. Sisson, New York 1960 (Laurel); L. B. Wright and V. A. LaMar, New York 1964 (Folger); G. L. Kittredge, rev I. Ribner, Waltham Mass 1967; R. A. Foakes 1968 (New Penguin).

Henry V

The cronicle history of Henry the Fift, with his battell fought at Agin Court in France, togither with Auntient Pistoll, as it hath bene sundry times playd by the Right Honorable the Lord Chamberlaine his servants; London, printed by Thomas Creede for Tho. Millington and John Busby, and are to be sold at his house in Carter Lane, next the Powle head. 1600; ed J. O. Halliwell (-Phillipps) 1867 (facs); ed A. Symons 1886 (facs); ed W. W. Greg, Oxford 1956 (facs); rptd B. Nicholson 1875 (New Sh Soc), W. A. Wright 1893 (Cambridge Shakespeare vol 9).
The chronicle history of Henry the Fift, with his battell fought at Agin Court in France; together with Auntient Pistoll, as it hath been sundry times playd by the Right Honorable the Lord Chamberlaine his servants. 1602, ed J. O. Halliwell (-Phillipps) 1867 (facs); 1608 (for 1619), ed Halliwell 1870 (facs), ed A. Symons 1886.

Modern Editions

H. A. Evans 1903 (Arden); E. Roman, Marburg 1908 (parallel texts of 4° 1, 4° 3 and Folio 1); R. D. French, New Haven 1918 (Yale); K. Schrey, Frankfurt 1938; G. L. Kittredge, New York 1945; J. D. Wilson, Cambridge 1947 (New Cambridge); J. H. Walter 1954 (New Arden); W. W. Greg, Oxford 1956 (facs of 4° 1); R. J. Dorius, New Haven 1956 (Yale); L. B. Wright and V. Freund, Baltimore 1957 (Pelican); L. B. Wright and V. A. LaMar, New York 1960 (Folger); F. Fergusson and C. J. Sisson, New York 1962 (Laurel); J. R. Brown, New York 1965 (Signet); G. L. Kittredge, rev I. Ribner, Waltham Mass 1967; A. R. Humphreys 1968 (New Penguin).

Julius Caesar

Julius Caesar: a tragedy. 1684, nd, nd, nd, nd, 1691.

Modern Editions

M. Macmillan 1902 (Arden); F. H. Sykes 1909; H. H. Furness jr, Philadelphia 1913 (New Variorum); L. Mason, New Haven 1919 (Yale); G. C. Taylor and R. Smith, Boston 1936 (interlinear); P. Schultz, Münster

1936; K. Schrey, Frankfurt 1938; G. Skillan 1938; G. L. Kittredge, Boston 1939; J. D. Wilson, Cambridge 1949 (New Cambridge); H. T. Price, New York 1949 (Crofts); T. S. Dorsch 1955 (New Arden); F. Fergusson and C. J. Sisson, New York 1958 (Laurel); A. Kernan, New Haven 1959 (Yale), L. B. Wright and V. L. Freund, New York 1959 (Folger), S. F. Johnson, Baltimore 1960 (Pelican); W. and B. Rosen, New York 1963 (Signet); G. L. Kittredge, rev I. Ribner, Waltham Mass 1966; N. Sanders 1967 (New Penguin).

As You Like It

Modern Editions

J. W. Holme 1914 (Arden); J. R. Crawford, New Haven 1919 (Yale); A. T. Quiller-Couch and J. D. Wilson, Cambridge 1926 (New Cambridge); G. L. Kittredge, Boston 1939; S. C. Burchell, New Haven 1954 (Yale); F. Fergusson and C. J. Sisson, New York 1959 (Laurel); R. M. Sargent, Baltimore 1959 (Pelican); L. B. Wright and V. L. Freund, New York 1959 (Folger); A. Gilman, New York 1963 (Signet); G. L. Kittredge, rev I. Ribner, Waltham Mass 1967; H. J. Oliver 1968 (New Penguin).
For a concordance see T. H. Howard-Hill, Oxford 1970.

Twelfth Night

Modern Editions

M. Luce 1906 (Arden); G. H. Nettleton, New Haven 1922 (Yale); A. T. Quiller-Couch and J. D. Wilson, Cambridge 1930 (New Cambridge); M. Eccles, New York 1948 (Crofts); W. P. Holden, New Haven 1954 (Yale); C. T. Prouty, Baltimore 1958 (Pelican); F. Fergusson and C. J. Sisson, New York 1959 (Laurel); L. B. Wright and V. A. LaMar, New York 1960 (Folger); H. Baker, New York 1965 (Signet); G. L. Kittredge, rev I. Ribner, Waltham Mass 1966; M. M. Mahood 1968 (New Penguin).
For a concordance see T. H. Howard-Hill, Oxford 1970.

Hamlet

The tragical historie of Hamlet Prince of Denmarke by William Shake-speare, as it hath beene diverse times acted by his Highnesse servants in the Cittie of London; as also in the two universities of Cambridge and Oxford, and elsewhere; at London printed for N[icholas] L[ing] and John Trundell. 1603; ed J. O. Halliwell (-Phillipps) 1866 (facs); ed F. J. Furnivall 1880 (facs); A. B. Weiner, Great Neck NY 1962 (facs); ed L. Berger, Frankfurt 1967 (facs); rptd W. A. Wright 1893 (Cambridge Shakespeare, vol 9); ed F. G. Hubbard, Madison 1920; ed G. B. Harrison 1924; Cambridge Mass 1931; ed W. W. Greg, Oxford 1951.
The tragicall historie of Hamlet, Prince of Denmarke, by William Shakespeare, newly printed and enlarged to almost as much againe as it was, according to the true and perfect coppie; at London, printed by J[ames] R[oberts] for N[icholas] L[ing] and are to be sold at his shoppe under Saint Dunstons Church in Fleet-street. 1604 (in some copies 1605); ed J. O. Halliwell (-Phillipps) 1867 (facs); ed F. J. Furnivall 1880 (facs); ed W. W. Greg, Oxford 1940 (facs).
The tragedy of Hamlet Prince of Denmarke, by William Shakespeare. 1611, [1630?], 1637, 1676, 1676, 1683, 1695, 1695, 1703, 1703.

Modern Editions

E. Dowden 1899 (Arden); J. D. Wilson, Cambridge 1934 (New Cambridge); G. C. Taylor and R. Smith, Boston 1936 (interlinear); Second quarto, 1604: facsimile of Huntington Library copy, ed O. J. Campbell, San Marino 1938; A critical edition of the second quarto 1604, ed T. M. Parrott and H. Craig, Princeton 1938; G. L. Kittredge, Boston 1939; Second quarto 1604–5, 1940 (Shakespeare Quarto Facs); R. C. Bald, New York 1946 (Crofts); G. Rylands, Oxford 1947 (New Clarendon); E. Jones 1947 (with a psychoanalytical study); H. Oldendorf and H. Arguile, Cape Town 1948; First quarto 1603, 1951 (Shakespeare Quarto Facs); F. Fergusson and C. J. Sisson, New York 1958 (Laurel); L. B. Wright and V. L. Freund, New York 1959 (Folger); A. B. Weiner, Great Neck NY 1962 (facs 4° 1); E. Hubler, New York 1963 (Signet); L. Berger, Frankfurt 1967 (facs 4° 1); G. L. Kittredge, rev I. Ribner, Waltham Mass 1967.

Studies

Stoll, E. E. Shakespeare, Marston and the malcontent type. MP 3 1906.
— Hamlet: an historical and comparative study. Minneapolis 1919.
— Hamlet the man. 1935 (Eng Assoc lecture).
Murray, G. Hamlet and Orestes. Oxford 1914.
Wilson, J. D. What happens in Hamlet. Cambridge 1935.
Waldock, A. J. A. Hamlet: a study in critical method. Cambridge 1931.
Alexander, P. Hamlet: father and son. Oxford 1955.
Lewis, C. S. Hamlet: the Prince or the poem? Proc Br Acad 28 1942; rptd in his Selected literary essays, Cambridge 1969.
Empson, W. Hamlet when new. Sewanee Rev 61 1953.
Brown, J. R. and B. Harris (ed). Hamlet. 1963. Essays by various hands.

Merry Wives of Windsor

A most pleasant and excellent conceited comedie of Syr John Falstaffe and the merrie wives of Windsor, entermixed with sundrie variable and pleasing humors of Syr Hugh the Welch Knight, Justice Shallow and his wise cousin M. Slender, with the swaggering vaine of Auncient Pistoll and Corporall Nym; by William Shakespeare, as it hath bene divers times acted by the Right Honorable my Lord Chamberlaines servants, both before her Majestie and elsewhere; London, printed by T. C[reede] for Arthur Johnson, and are to be sold at his shop in Powles churchyard, at the signe of the Flower de Leuse and the Crowne. 1602; ed J. O. Halliwell (-Phillipps) 1866 (facs); ed P. A. Daniel 1881 (facs); ed W. W. Greg, Oxford 1910 (facs); rptd Halliwell 1842 (Shakespeare Soc); W. A. Wright 1893 (Cambridge Shakespeare vol 9).
A most pleasant and excellent conceited comedy of Sir John Falstaffe and the merry wives of Windsor; with the swaggering vaine of Ancient Pistoll and Corporal Nym; written by W. Shakespeare. 1619, ed J. O. Halliwell (-Phillipps) 1866 (facs); 1630, 1664.

Modern Editions

H. C. Hart 1904 (Arden); W. W. Greg, Oxford 1910 (facs of 4° 1); A. T. Quiller-Couch and J. D. Wilson, Cambridge 1921 (New Cambridge); G. van Santvoord, New Haven 1922 (Yale); F. T. Bowers, Baltimore 1963 (Pelican); L. B. Wright and V. A. LaMar, New York 1964 (Folger); W. Green, New York 1965 (Signet); H. J. Oliver 1971 (New Arden).
For a concordance see T. H. Howard-Hill, Oxford 1969.

Troilus and Cressida

The historie of Troylus and Cresseida, as it was acted by the Kings Majesties servants at the Globe; written by William Shakespeare; London, by G. Eld for R. Bonian and H. Walley, and are to be sold at the Spred Eagle in Paules churchyeard, over against the great north doore. 1609; ed J. O. Halliwell (-Phillipps) 1871 (facs); ed W. W. Greg, Oxford 1952 (facs).
The famous historie of Troylus and Cresseid, excellently expressing the beginning of their loves, with the conceited wooing of Pandarus Prince of Licia; written by

William Shakespeare; London, imprinted by G. Eld for R. Bonian and H. Walley, and are to be sold at the Spred Eagle in Paules church-yeard, over against the great north doore. 1609 (2nd issue with new title and epistle inserted); ed J. O. Halliwell (-Phillipps) 1863 (facs); ed H. P. Stokes 1886 (facs).

Modern Editions

K. Deighton 1906 (Arden); J. S. P. Tatlock, New York 1912 (Tudor); N. B. Paradise, New Haven 1927 (Yale); B. Dobrée 1938 (Warwick); W. W. Greg, Oxford 1952 (facs of 4° 1); H. N. Hillebrand and T. W. Baldwin, Philadelphia 1953 (New Variorum); A. J. Campbell, New Haven 1956 (Yale); J. D. Wilson and A. Walker, Cambridge 1958 (New Cambridge); V. K. Whitaker, Baltimore 1958 (Pelican); D. Seltzer, New York 1963 (Signet); L. B. Wright and V. A. LaMar, New York 1966 (Folger); G. L. Kittredge, rev I. Ribner, Waltham Mass 1967.

All's Well That Ends Well

Modern Editions

W. O. Brigstocke 1904 (Arden); A. E. Case, New Haven 1926 (Yale); A. T. Quiller-Couch and J. D. Wilson, Cambridge 1929 (New Cambridge); G. K. Hunter 1959 (New Arden); F. Fergusson and C. J. Sisson, New York 1961 (Laurel); J. A. Barish, Baltimore 1964 (Pelican); S. Barnet, New York 1965 (Signet); L. B. Wright and V. A. LaMar, New York 1965 (Folger); B. Everett 1970 (New Penguin).
For a concordance see T. H. Howard-Hill, Oxford 1970.

Measure for Measure

Modern Editions

H. C. Hart 1905 (Arden); A. T. Quiller-Couch and J. D. Wilson, Cambridge 1922 (New Cambridge); W. H. Durham, New Haven 1926 (Yale); D. Harding, New Haven 1954 (Yale); R. C. Bald, Baltimore 1956 (Pelican); F. Fergusson and C. J. Sisson, New York 1962 (Laurel); E. Leisi, Heidelberg 1964 (old spelling); S. Nagarajan, New York 1964 (Signet); J. W. Lever 1965 (New Arden); G. L. Kittredge, rev I. Ribner, Waltham Mass 1967; J. M. Nosworthy 1969 (New Penguin).
For a concordance see T. H. Howard-Hill, Oxford 1969.

Othello

The tragoedy of Othello, the Moore of Venice, as it hath beene diverse times acted at the Globe, and at the Black-Friers, by his Majesties servants; written by William Shakespeare; London, printed by N[icholas] O[kes] for Thomas Walkley, and are to be sold at his shop, at the Eagle and Child, in Brittans Bursse. 1622; ed J. O. Halliwell (-Phillipps) 1864 (facs); ed H. A. Evans 1855 (facs).
The tragoedy of Othello, the Moore of Venice. 1630, ed H. A. Evans 1885 (facs); 1655, 1681, 1687, 1695, 1705.

Modern Editions

H. C. Hart 1903 (Arden); L. Mason, New Haven 1918 (Yale); C. H. Herford 1920 (Warwick); M. Eccles, New York 1946 (Crofts); M. M. A. Schroer, Heidelberg 1949 (parallel texts of 4° 1 and Folio 1, with 4° 2 variants); J. D. Wilson and A. Walker, Cambridge 1955 (New Cambridge); L. B. Wright and V. L. Freund, New York 1957 (Folger); M. R. Ridley, 1958 (New Arden); G. E. Bentley, Baltimore 1958 (Pelican); F. Fergusson and C. J. Sisson, New York 1959 (Laurel).

Studies

Leavis, F. R. Diabolic intellect and the noble hero. Scrutiny 6 1938; rptd in his Common pursuit, 1952.
Granville-Barker, H. Othello. In his Prefaces to Shakespeare: series 4, 1946.
Flatter, R. The Moor of Venice. 1950.
Burke, K. Othello: an essay to illustrate a method. Hudson Rev 4 1951.
Gardner, H. The noble Moor. Proc Br Acad 41 1955.
—— Othello: a retrospect. Sh Survey 21 1968.
Bayley, J. In his Characters of love, 1961.

King Lear

M. William Shak-speare his true chronicle historie of the life and death of King Lear and his three daughters, with the unfortunate life of Edgar, sonne and heire to the Earle of Gloster, and his sullen and assumed humor of Tom of Bedlam, as it was played before the Kings Majestie at Whitehall upon S. Stephans night in Christmas hollidayes, by his Majesties servants playing usually at the Globe on the Bancke-side; London, printed for Nathaniel Butter, and are to be sold at his shop in Pauls Church-yard at the signe of the Pide Bull neere St Austins Gate. 1608; ed J. O. Halliwell (-Phillipps) 1868 (facs); ed P. A. Daniel 1885 (facs); ed W. W. Greg, Oxford 1939 (facs).
Mr William Shake-speare his true chronicle history of the life and death of King Lear and his three daughters, with the unfortunate life of Edgar, sonne and heire to the Earle of Glocester, and his sullen and assumed humour of Tom of Bedlam. 1608 (for 1619), ed J. O. Halliwell (-Phillipps) 1867 (facs), ed P. A. Daniel 1885 (facs); 1655.

Modern Editions

W. J. Craig 1901 (Arden); D. N. Smith 1902 (Warwick); W. L. Phelps, New Haven 1917 (Yale); W. W. Greg, Oxford 1939 (facs of 4° 1); G. I. Duthie, Oxford 1949; K. Muir 1952 (New Arden); L. B. Wright and V. L. Freund, New York 1957 (Folger); A. Harbage, Baltimore 1958 (Pelican); G. I. Duthie and J. D. Wilson, Cambridge 1960 (New Cambridge); F. Fergusson and C. J. Sisson, New York 1962 (Signet); G. L. Kittredge, rev I. Ribner, Waltham Mass 1967.
New York 1962 (Signet); G. L. Kittredge, rev I. Ribner, Waltham Mass 1967.

Studies

The true chronicle history of King Leir and his three daughters, Gonorill, Ragan and Cordella. 1605; rptd 1907 (Malone Soc facs); ed S. Lee 1909 (Sh Classics). See col 198, above.
Granville-Barker, H. In his Prefaces to Shakespeare: series 1, 1927.
Danby, J. F. Shakespeare's doctrine of nature: a study of King Lear. 1949.
Brooke, N. Shakespeare: King Lear. 1963.
Mack, M. King Lear in our time. Berkeley 1965.
Elton, W. R. King Lear and the gods. San Marino 1966.
Gardner, H. L. King Lear. 1967.

Macbeth

Modern Editions

H. Cuningham 1912 (Arden); C. M. Lewis, New Haven 1918 (Yale); G. C. Taylor and R. Smith, Boston 1939; J. D. Wilson, Cambridge 1947 (New Cambridge); K. Muir 1951 (New Arden); E. M. Waith, New Haven 1954 (Yale); A. Harbage, Baltimore 1956 (Pelican); F. Fergusson and C. J. Sisson, New York 1959 (Laurel); L. B. Wright and V. A. LaMar, New York 1960 (Folger); S. Barnet, New York 1963 (Signet); G. L. Kittredge, rev I. Ribner, Waltham Mass 1966; G. K. Hunter 1967 (New Penguin).

Antony and Cleopatra

Modern Editions

R. H. Case, 1906 (Arden); H. H. Furness jr, Philadelphia 1907 (New Variorum); H. S. Canby, New Haven 1921 (Yale); T. Spencer, New York 1948 (Crofts); J. D. Wilson, Cambridge 1950 (New Cambridge); M. R. Ridley 1954 (New Arden); P. G. Phialas, New Haven 1956 (Yale); M. Mack, Baltimore 1960 (Pelican); F. Fergusson and C. J. Sisson, New York 1961 (Laurel); L. B. Wright and V. A. LaMar, New York 1961 (Folger); B. Everett, New York 1964 (Signet); G. L. Kittredge, rev I. Ribner, Waltham Mass 1967.

Studies

Shakespeare's Plutarch vol 2. Ed C. F. T. Brooke 1909 (Sh Classics).
Granville-Barker, H. In his Prefaces to Shakespeare: series 2, 1930.
Cecil, D. Antony and Cleopatra. Glasgow 1944; rptd in his Poets and storytellers, 1949.

Coriolanus

Modern Editions

W. J. Craig and R. H. Case 1922 (Arden); C. F. T. Brooke, New Haven 1924 (Yale); H. H. Furness jr, Philadelphia 1928 (New Variorum); H. Levin, Baltimore 1956 (Pelican); J. D. Wilson, Cambridge 1960 (New Cambridge); F. Fergusson and C. J. Sisson, New York 1962 (Laurel); L. B. Wright and V. A. LaMar, New York 1962 (Folger); G. L. Kittredge, rev I. Ribner, Waltham Mass 1967; G. R. Hibbard, 1967 (New Penguin).

Studies

Shakespeare's Plutarch vol 2. Ed C. F. T. Brooke 1909 (Sh Classics).
Bradley, A. C. Coriolanus. Proc Br Acad 3 1912; rptd in his A miscellany, 1929.
Granville-Barker, H. Coriolanus. In his Prefaces to Shakespeare: series 5, 1947.

Timon of Athens

Modern Editions

K. Deighton 1905 (Arden); J. C. Maxwell, Cambridge 1957 (New Cambridge); H. J. Oliver 1959 (New Arden); F. Fergusson and C. J. Sisson, New York 1963 (Laurel); C. Hinman, Baltimore 1964 (Pelican); M. Charney, New York 1965 (Signet); G. L. Kittredge, rev I. Ribner, Waltham Mass 1967; L. B. Wright and V. A. LaMar, New York 1968 (Folger); G. R. Hibbard 1970 (New Penguin).

Cymbeline

Modern Editions

E. Dowden 1903 (Arden); H. H. Furness jr, Philadelphia 1913 (New Variorum); S. B. Hemingway, New Haven 1924 (Yale); J. M. Nosworthy 1955 (New Arden); J. C. Maxwell, Cambridge 1960 (New Cambridge); F. Fergusson and C. J. Sisson, New York 1964 (Laurel); R. B. Heilman, Baltimore 1964 (Pelican); L. B. Wright and V. A. LaMar, New York 1965 (Folger); R. Hosley, New York 1968 (Signet); G. L. Kittredge, rev I. Ribner, Waltham Mass 1969.
For a concordance see T. H. Howard-Hill, Oxford 1970.

Winter's Tale

Modern Editions

F. W. Moorman 1912 (Arden); F. E. Pierce, New Haven

1918 (Yale); A. T. Quiller-Couch and J. D. Wilson, Cambridge 1931 (New Cambridge); J. H. P. Pafford 1956 (New Arden); B. Maxwell, Baltimore 1956 (Pelican); F. Fergusson and C. J. Sisson, New York 1959 (Laurel); F. Kermode, New York 1963 (Signet); L. B. Wright and V. A. LaMar, New York 1966 (Folger); G. L. Kittredge, rev I. Ribner, Waltham Mass 1967; E. Schanzer 1969 (New Penguin).

Tempest

Modern Editions

M. Luce 1902 (Arden); W. Vickery 1911 (Rowfant Club); C. B. Tinker, New Haven 1918 (Yale); A. T. Quiller-Couch and J. D. Wilson, Cambridge 1921 (New Cambridge); G. L. Kittredge, Boston 1939; A. Harbage, New York 1946 (Crofts); F. Kermode 1954 (New Arden); D. Horne, New Haven 1955 (Yale); N. Frye, Baltimore 1959 (Pelican); F. Fergusson and C. J. Sisson, New York 1961 (Laurel); L. B. Wright and V. A. LaMar, New York 1961 (Folger); R. Langbaum, New York 1965 (Signet); G. L. Kittredge, rev I. Ribner, Waltham Mass 1967; A. Righter 1968 (New Penguin).
For a concordance see T. H. Howard-Hill, Oxford 1969.

Henry VIII

Modern Editions

C. K. Pooler 1915 (Arden); J. M. Berdan and C. F. T. Brooke, New Haven 1925 (Yale); R. A. Foakes 1957 (New Arden); J. C. Maxwell, Cambridge 1962 (New Cambridge); F. D. Hoeniger, Baltimore 1966 (Pelican); G. L. Kittredge, rev I. Ribner, Waltham Mass 1968; S. Schoenbaum, New York 1968 (Signet); L. B. Wright and V. A. LaMar, New York 1968 (Folger).

C. Plays Excluded from the Folio

Sir Thomas More, Edward III, Pericles, Two noble kinsmen, other ascribed plays.

Collections

The Shakespeare apocrypha. Ed C. F. T. Brooke, Oxford 1908. 14 plays in old spelling; detailed introd.
Six early plays related to the Shakespeare canon. Ed E. B. Everitt and R. L. Armstrong, Copenhagen 1965. Leir, Weakest goeth to the wall, Edmund Ironside, Troublesome reign, Edward III, Woodstock.

Sir Thomas More

The book of Sir Thomas Moore. Ed A. Dyce 1844 (Sh Soc); ed A. F. Hopkinson 1902; ed J. S. Farmer 1908 (facs); ed C. F. T. Brooke, Shakespeare apocrypha, Oxford 1908; ed W. W. Greg 1911 (Malone Soc), 1961 (with suppl); ed J. Shirley, Canterbury 1938; ed H. Jenkins, Complete works of Shakespeare, ed C. J. Sisson 1954. BM ms Harley 7368.

Edward III

The raigne of King Edward the Third, as it hath bin sundrie times plaied about the Citie of London. 1596; ed J. S. Farmer, TFT 1910 (facs).
The raigne of King Edward the Third. 1599.

Modern Editions

E. Capell, Prolusions, 1760; G. C. Moore Smith 1897 (Temple Dramatists); C. F. T. Brooke, Shakespeare apocrypha, Oxford 1908; E. B. Everitt and R. L. Armstrong, Six early plays related to the Shakespeare canon, Copenhagen 1965.

Pericles

The late and much admired play called Pericles, Prince of Tyre, with the true relation of the whole historie, adventures and fortunes of the said Prince; as also the no lesse strange and worthy accidents in the birth and life of his daughter Mariana, as it hath been divers and sundry times acted by his Majesties servants at the Globe on the Banck-side; by William Shakespeare; imprinted at London for Henry Gosson, and are to be sold at the signe of the Sunne in Pater-noster row etc. 1609; ed J. O. Halliwell (-Phillipps) 1862 (facs); ed P. Z. Round 1886 (facs); ed S. Lee, Oxford 1905 (facs).
The late and much admired play called Pericles, Prince of Tyre. 1609 (title identical with 4⁰ 1, above, differentiated by 'Eneer Gower' for 'Enter Gower' on signature A 2), ed J. O. Halliwell (-Phillipps) 1871 (facs); 1619, 1630, 1630, 1635.

Modern Editions

K. Deighton 1907 (Arden); A. R. Bellinger, New Haven 1925 (Yale); W. W. Greg, Oxford 1940 (facs of 4⁰ 1); J. C. Maxwell, Cambridge 1956 (New Cambridge); F. D. Hoeniger 1963 (New Arden); E. Schanzer, New York 1965 (Signet); J. G. McManaway, Baltimore 1967 (Pelican); L. B. Wright and V. A. LaMar, New York 1968 (Folger).

Two Noble Kinsmen

The two noble kinsmen: presented at the Blackfriers by the Kings Majesties servants, with great applause; written by the memorable worthies of their time, Mr John Fletcher and Mr William Shakspeare gent; printed at London by Tho. Cotes for John Waterson, and are to be sold at the signe of the Crowne in Pauls churchyard. 1634; ed J. S. Farmer, TFT 1920 (facs); rptd H. Littledale 1876 (New Shakspere Soc).
Fifty comedies and tragedies written by Francis Beaumont and John Fletcher gentlemen. 1679.

Modern Editions

W. W. Skeat 1875; H. Littledale 1885 (New Sh Soc); W. J. Rolfe, New York 1891; C. H. Herford 1897 (Temple); C. F. T. Brooke, Shakespeare apocrypha, Oxford 1908; F. O. Walker, Chicago 1957 (old spelling); C. Leech, New York 1966 (Signet); G. R. Proudfoot 1970 (Regents Renaissance Drama).

Other Plays Ascribed to Shakespeare

See B. Maxwell, Studies in the Shakespeare apocrypha, *New York 1956.*
The lamentable and true tragedie of M. Arden of Feversham in Kent. 1592, 1599, 1633; ed E. Jacob, Faversham 1770 (ascribed to Shakespeare); ed A. H. Bullen 1887; ed R. Bayne 1897 (Temple); ed C. F. T. Brooke, Shakespeare apocrypha, Oxford 1908; ed H. Macdonald 1947 (Malone Soc); ed M. L. Wine 1973 (Revels).
The birth of Merlin: or the childe hath found his father; written by William Shakespear and William Rowley. 1662; ed N. Delius, Pseudo-Shakspere'sche Dramen pt 3, Elberfeld 1856; ed K. Warnke and L. Proescholdt, Pseudo-Shakespearian plays pt 4, Halle 1887; ed A. F. Hopkinson, Shakespeare's doubtful plays vol 2, 1892; ed C. F. T. Brooke, Shakespeare apocrypha, Oxford 1908.
A pleasant commodie of faire Em, the millers daughter of Manchester, with the love of William the Conqueror. [1593?], 1631; ed N. Delius, Pseudo-Shakspere'sche Dramen pt 5, Elberfeld 1874; ed K. Warnke and L. Proescholdt, Pseudo-Shakespearian plays pt 1, Halle 1883; ed A. F. Hopkinson, Shakespeare's doubtful

plays vol 3, 1895; ed C. F. T. Brooke, Shakespeare apocrypha, Oxford 1908; ed W. W. Greg 1927 (Malone Soc).

The lamentable tragedie of Locrine, the eldest sonne of King Brutus, newly set foorth, overseene and corrected, by W.S. 1595; ed A. F. Hopkinson, Shakespeare's doubtful plays vol 2, 1892; ed C. F. T. Brooke, Shakespeare apocrypha, Oxford 1908; ed R. B. McKerrow, 1908 (Malone Soc).

The London prodigall, by William Shakespeare. 1605; Ancient British drama vol 1, 1810; ed A. F. Hopkinson, Shakespeare's doubtful plays vol 2, 1893; C. F. T. Brooke, Shakespeare apocrypha, Oxford 1908.

A most pleasant comedie of Mucedorus, the Kings sonne of Valentia. 1598, 1610, 1611, 1613, 1615 ('amplified with new additions'), 1618, 1619, 1621, [1626?], 1629, 1631, 1634, 1639; ed J. P. Collier 1824; ed N. Delius, Pseudo-Shakspere'sche Dramen pt 4, Elberfeld 1874; Hazlitt's Dodsley vol 7; ed K. Warnke and L. Proescholdt, Halle 1887; ed A. F. Hopkinson, Shakespeare's doubtful plays vol 2, 1893; ed C. F. T. Brooke, Shakespeare apocrypha, Oxford 1908.

The Puritaine: or the widdow of Watling-streete, written by W.S. 1607; Ancient British drama vol 1, 1810; ed A. F. Hopkinson, Shakespeare's doubtful plays vol 3, 1895; ed C. F. T. Brooke, Shakespeare apocrypha, Oxford 1908; ed S. Heaven [1955].

The first part of the true and honorable historie of the life of Sir John Old-castle, the good Lord Cobham. 1600, 1600 (for 1619, 'written by William Shakespeare'); Ancient British drama vol 1, 1810; ed A. F. Hopkinson, Shakespeare's doubtful plays vol 3, 1894; ed C. F. T. Brooke, Shakespeare apocrypha, Oxford 1908; ed P. Simpson 1908 (Malone Soc).

The true chronicle historie of the whole life and death of Thomas Lord Cromwell, written by W.S. 1602; Ancient British drama vol 1, 1810; ed A. F. Hopkinson, Shakespeare's doubtful plays vol 1, 1891; ed C. F. T. Brooke, Shakespeare apocrypha, Oxford 1908.

A Yorkshire tragedy, written by W. Shakespeare. 1608, 1619; Ancient British drama vol 1, 1810; ed A. F. Hopkinson, Shakespeare's doubtful plays vol 1, 1891; ed C. F. T. Brooke, Shakespeare apocrypha, Oxford 1908.

(6) POEMS

Modern Editions

Poems. Ed G. Wyndham 1898; Poems and sonnets, ed E. Dowden 1903; Poems and Pericles, ed S. Lee 5 vols Oxford 1905 (facs of earliest edns); Poems, ed C. K. Pooler 1911 (Arden); Poems, ed H. E. Rollins, Philadelphia 1938 (New Variorum); Sonnets, with A lover's complaint and the Phoenix and the turtle, ed W. Thomson, Oxford 1938; Sonnets, songs and poems, ed H. W. Simon, New York 1951, 1960; Narrative poems, ed G. B. Harrison 1959 (Penguin); Songs and poems, ed E. L. Hubler, New York 1959; Poems, ed F. T. Prince 1960 (New Arden); Poems: facsimile of earliest editions, ed J. M. Osborn, L. L. Martz and E. M. Waith, New Haven 1964; Sonnets, songs and poems, ed O. J. Campbell, New York 1967; Poems, ed W. Burto, New York 1968 (Signet); Poems, ed J. C. Maxwell, Cambridge 1969 (New Cambridge); Minor poems, ed G. L. Kittredge, rev I. Ribner, Waltham Mass 1970.

Studies

Baldwin, T. W. On the literary genetics of Shakespeare's poems and sonnets. Urbana 1950.
Ewbank, I.-S. Shakespeare's poetry. In A new companion to Shakespeare studies, ed K. Muir and S. Schoenbaum, Cambridge 1971.
Lever, J. W. Shakespeare's narrative poems. Ibid.

Venus and Adonis

Venus and Adonis; vilia miretur vulgus: mihi flavus Apollo Pocula Castalia plena ministret aqua; London, imprinted by Richard Field, and are to be sold at the signe of the white greyhound in Paules church-yard. 1593; ed J. O. Halliwell (-Phillipps) 1867 (facs) ed A. Symons 1886 (facs); ed S. Lee, Oxford 1905 (facs, with bibliography); Menston 1969 (facs).
Venus and Adonis. 1594 (rev), [1594–6?] (only extant copy in Folger Lib lacks title), 1596, 1599 (facs 1870), 1599, 1602, 1617, 1620, Edinburgh 1627, London 1630 [1630–6?] (only extant copy in Bodley lacks title), 1636.

Lucrece

Lucrece; London, printed by Richard Field, for John Harrison, and are to be sold at the signe of the white greyhound in Paules churhyard [sic]. 1594 (running-

title as The rape of Lucrece); ed J. O. Halliwell (-Phillipps) 1867 (facs); ed F. J. Furnivall 1886 (facs); ed S. Lee, Oxford 1905 (facs with bibliography).
Lucrece. 1598, 1600, 1607, 1616 (as The rape of Lucrece), 1624, 1632, 1655 (adds J. Quarles, The banishment of Tarquin).

Passionate Pilgrim

The passionate pilgrime, by W. Shakespeare; at London printed for W. Jaggard, and are to be sold by W. Leake at the Greyhound in Paules churchyard. 1599 (2nd title on C3, Sonnets to sundry notes of musicke); ed C. Edmonds 1870 (facs); E. Dowden 1883 (facs); ed S. Lee, Oxford 1905 (facs).
The passionate pilgrime: or certaine amorous sonnets, betweene Venus and Adonis, newly corrected and augmented, by W. Shakespeare; the third edition, whereunto is newly added two love-epistles, the first from Paris to Hellen, and Hellens answere backe againe to Paris. 1612. 2nd edn not known. The Epistles are by Thomas Heywood. Some copies are found without Shakespeare's name, possibly owing to Heywood's protest against piracy in his Apology for actors 1612.
Also ed J. Q. Adams, New York 1939 (facs of 1599 from Folger Lib); ed H. E. Rollins, New York 1940 (facs of 1612 from Folger Lib).

Phoenix and Turtle

Loves martyr: or Rosalins complaint, allegorically shadowing the truth of love, in the constant fate of the phoenix and turtle; a poeme translated out of the Italian by Robert Chester; to these are added some new compositions of severall moderne writers whose names are subscribed to their severall workes, upon the first subject: viz the phoenix and turtle; London, imprinted for E[dward] B[lount]. 1601, 1611 (as The anuals of Great Brittaine); ed A. B. Grosart 1878 (New Sh Soc).
Also ed B. H. Newdigate, Oxford 1937; G. Bullett 1938; W. H. Matchett, New York 1965 (with Chester's Love's martyr).

Sonnets

Shake-speares sonnets, never before imprinted; at London by G. Eld for T. T[horpe] and are to be solde by John

Wright, dwelling at Christ Church gate. 1609 (some copies have William Aspley instead of John Wright; appended is A lovers complaint, by William Shakespeare); ed T. Tyler 188 6(facs); ed S. Lee, Oxford 1905 (facs); 1925 (J. Cape); 1926 (N. Douglas).

Poems, written by Wil. Shake-speare gent. 1640. Includes sonnets and A lover's complaint, and interspersed among them the full contents of Passionate pilgrim 1612, together with some other poems, most not attributed to Shakespeare. Rptd 1885 (A. R. Smith).

Modern Editions

C. K. Pooler 1918 (Arden); E. B. Reed, New Haven 1923 (Yale); T. G. Tucker, Cambridge 1924; C. F. T. Brooke, New York 1936; T. Brooke, Oxford 1936; New York 1936 (facs); H. E. Rollins 2 vols Philadelphia 1944 (New Variorum); Thorpe's edition of Shakespeare's sonnets 1609, ed C. L. de Chambrun, Aldington 1950; F. Fergusson and C. J. Sisson, New York 1960 (Laurel); D. Bush and A. Harbage, Baltimore 1961 (Pelican); M. Seymour-Smith 1963; W. Burto, New York 1964; W. G. Ingram and T. Redpath 1964; A. L. Rowse 1964; J. D. Wilson, Cambridge 1966 (New Cambridge); L. B. Wright and V. A. LaMar, New York 1967 (Folger); Menston 1968 (facs of 1609); J. Fuzier, Paris 1970 (text, some trns, sources and bibliography).

For a concordance see H. S. Donow, A concordance to the sonnet sequences of Daniel, Drayton, Shakespeare, Sidney and Spenser, *Carbondale 1970.*

Studies

Knights, L. C. Shakespeare's sonnets. Scrutiny 3 1934; rptd in his Explorations, 1946.

Empson, W. They that have power. In his Some versions of pastoral, 1935.

Leishman, J. B. Variations on a theme in Shakespeare's sonnets. In Elizabethan and Jacobean studies presented to F. P. Wilson, Oxford 1959. The immortality conferred by poetry.

—— Themes and variations in Shakespeare's sonnets. 1961.

Hubler, E. et al. The riddle of Shakespeare's sonnets. New York 1962.

Wilson, J. D. An introduction to the sonnets of Shakespeare for the use of historians and others. Cambridge 1963.

Winny, J. M. The master-mistress: a study of Shakespeare's sonnets. 1968.

Booth, S. An essay on Shakespeare's sonnets. New Haven 1969.

A Lover's Complaint

Editions: *see Sonnets, above.*

(7) LIFE AND PERSONALITY OF SHAKESPEARE

(1) Documents

See E. K. Chambers, Shakespeare: a study of the facts and problems, *vol 2, appendix A, Oxford 1930; S. Schoenbaum, below.*

(2) Principal Biographies

Rowe, N. Some account of the life etc of Shakespeare. In his edn of Works, 1709.

Lee, S. A life of Shakespeare. 1898, 1925 (rev).

Raleigh, W. Shakespeare. 1907 (EML).

Adams, J. Q. A life of Shakespeare. Boston 1923.

Chambers, E. K. Shakespeare: a study of facts and problems. 2 vols Oxford 1930; abridged C. Williams 1933. Index by B. White, 1934 (Sh Assoc).

Wilson, J. D. The essential Shakespeare. Cambridge 1932.

Alexander, P. Shakespeare's life and art. 1939.

Schoenbaum, S. Shakespeare's lives. Oxford 1970.

—— The life of Shakespeare. In A new companion to Shakespeare studies, ed K. Muir and Schoenbaum, Cambridge 1971.

—— Shakespeare: a documentary life. Oxford 1975, 1977 (compact edn).

(8) CRITICISM

A. TECHNICAL CRITICISM

A companion to Shakespeare studies. Ed H. Granville-Barker and G. B. Harrison, Cambridge 1934.

A new companion to Shakespeare studies. Ed K. Muir and S. Schoenbaum, Cambridge 1971.

(1) Sources and Influences
Collections of Sources

[Nichols, J.] Six old plays on which Shakespeare founded his Measure for measure, Comedy of errors, the Taming of the shrew, King John, King Henry IV and King Henry V, King Lear. 2 vols 1779.

Collier, J. P. Shakespeare's library: a collection of the romances, novels, poems and histories, used by Shakespeare as the foundation of his dramas. 2 vols [1843] 1850; rev W. C. Hazlitt 6 vols 1875 (adding the plays).

Hazlitt, W. C. Shakespeare's jest-books. 3 vols 1864.

—— Fairy tales, legends and romances illustrating Shakespeare and other early English writers. 1875.

Bullough, G. Narrative and dramatic sources of Shakespeare. 8 vols 1957-75. The most complete collection.

Rouse, W. H. D. Shakespeare's Ovid: being Golding's translation of the Metamorphoses. 1961.

Spencer, T. J. B. Shakespeare's Plutarch. 1964 (Peregrine).

—— Elizabethan love stories. 1968 (Pelican).

Hosley, R. Shakespeare's Holinshed. New York 1968.

Modern Studies
General Studies

Farmer, R. Essay on the learning of Shakespeare. Cambridge 1767, 1767 (expanded); rptd in Eighteenth-century essays on Shakespeare, ed D. N. Smith, Glasgow 1903.

Muir, K. Shakespeare's sources 1: comedies and tragedies. 1957.

Jones, E. The origins of Shakespeare. Oxford 1977.

Classical Influences

Thomson, J. A. K. Shakespeare and the classics. 1952.

Simpson, P. Shakespeare's use of Latin authors. In his Studies in Elizabethan drama, Oxford 1955.

Spencer, T. J. B. Shakespeare and the Elizabethan Romans. Sh Survey 10 1959.

Wilson, J. D. Shakespeare's 'small Latin'—how much? Ibid.

Brower, R. A. Hero and saint: Shakespeare and the Graeco-Roman heroic tradition. Oxford 1971.

Continental Influences

Robertson, J. M. Montaigne and Shakespeare. 1897.

Thomas, H. Shakespeare and Spain. 1922.

Hunter, G. K. Shakespeare's reading. In A new companion to Shakespeare studies, ed K. Muir and S. Schoenbaum, Cambridge 1971.

English Influences

Pettet, E. C. Shakespeare and the romance tradition. 1950.

Watkins, W. B. C. Shakespeare and Spenser. Princeton 1950.

Bradbrook, M. C. Shakespeare and Elizabethan poetry. 1951.

— Shakespeare the craftsman. Cambridge 1968. On medieval background.

Wilson, F. P. Marlowe and the early Shakespeare. Oxford 1953.

— The proverbial wisdom of Shakespeare. Cambridge 1961; rptd in his Shakespearian and other studies, Oxford 1969.

Potts, A. F. Shakespeare and the Faerie Queene. Ithaca 1958.

Coghill, N. Shakespeare's reading in Chaucer. In Elizabethan and Jacobean studies presented to F. P. Wilson, Oxford 1959.

Muir, K. Shakespeare among the commonplaces. RES new ser 10 1959. On minor source material.

Rees, J. Shakespeare's use of Daniel. MLR 55 1960.

Sanders, N. The comedy of Greene and Shakespeare. In Early Shakespeare, ed J. R. Brown and B. Harris 1961.

(2) Textual Criticism

Theobald, L. Shakespeare restored: or a specimen of the many errors as well committed as unemended by Mr Pope in his late edition of this poet; designed to restore the true reading of Shakespeare in all the editions ever yet printed. 1726, 1740.

Capell, E. Notes and various readings to Shakespeare. [1774] (pt 1), 3 vols 1779–83 (extended, with addns by J. Collins).

Malone, E. A letter to Richard Farmer relative to the edition of Shakespeare published in 1790, and some late criticisms of that work. 1792, 1792. Replies to Ritson's Cursory criticism, 1792.

Greg, W. W. Principles of emendation in Shakespeare. Proc Br Acad 14 1928.

— The editorial problem in Shakespeare: a survey of the foundations of the text. Oxford 1942, 1951, 1954 (both rev).

— The Shakespeare First Folio: its bibliographical and textual history. Oxford 1955.

McKerrow, R. B. The treatment of Shakespeare's text by his earlier editors. Proc Br Acad 19 1933.

— Prolegomena for the Oxford Shakespeare: a study in editorial method. Oxford 1939.

Walker, A. Textual problems of the First Folio: Richard III, King Lear, Troilus and Cressida, 2 Henry IV, Othello. Cambridge 1953.

— Principles of annotation: some suggestions for editors of Shakespeare. SB 9 1957.

Sisson, C. J. New readings in Shakespeare. Cambridge 1956.

Brown, J. R. The rationale of old-spelling editions of the plays of Shakespeare and his contemporaries. SB 13 1960. Reply by A. Brown, ibid.

Honigmann, E. A. J. The stability of Shakespeare's text. 1965.

Wilson, F. P. Shakespeare and the new bibliography. Ed H. L. Gardner, Oxford 1970.

Evans, G. B. Shakespeare's text: approaches and problems. In A new companion to Shakespeare studies, ed K. Muir and S. Schoenbaum, Cambridge 1971.

(3) Language

Abbott, E. A. A Shakespearian grammar. 1869 etc.

Jespersen, O. Shakespeare and the language of poetry. In his Growth and structure of the English language, Leipzig 1905, 1938 (rev); rptd in Literary English since Shakespeare, ed G. Watson, New York 1970.

Bradley, H. Shakespeare's English. In Shakespeare's England vol 2, Oxford 1916.

Clemen, W. H. Shakespeares Bilder: ihre Entwicklung und ihre Funktionen im dramatischen Werk. Bonn 1935; tr and enlarged as The development of Shakespeare's imagery, 1951.

Wilson, F. P. Shakespeare and the diction of common life. Proc Br Acad 27 1941; rptd in his Shakespearian and other studies, Oxford 1969.

Empson, W. In his Structure of complex words, 1951. Fool in Lear, Timon's dog, Honest in Othello, Sense in Measure for measure.

Evans, B. I. The language of Shakespeare's plays. 1952.

Hulme, H. M. Shakespeare's language. In Works, ed C. J. Sisson 1954.

— Explorations in Shakespeare's language. 1962.

Mahood, M. M. Shakespeare's word play. 1956.

Vickers, B. Shakespeare's use of rhetoric. In A new companion to Shakespeare studies, ed K. Muir and S. Schoenbaum, Cambridge 1971.

B. AESTHETIC CRITICISM

(1) Anthologies of Criticism

Furnivall, F. J. Allusions to Shakespeare AD 1592–1693: supplement to Shakespeare's centurie of prayse. 1880 (New Sh Soc).

— Some three hundred fresh allusions to Shakespeare from 1594 to 1694. 1886 (New Sh Soc).

Smith, D. N. Eighteenth-century essays on Shakespeare. Glasgow 1903, Oxford 1963. With detailed introd.

— Shakespeare criticism. Oxford 1916 (WC).

Munro, J. The Shakespeare allusion-book: a collection of allusions from 1591 to 1700, originally compiled by C. M. Ingleby, L. Toulmin Smith and F. J. Furnivall, and now re-edited. 2 vols 1909, Oxford 1932 (rev E. K. Chambers).

Halliday, F. E. Shakespeare and his critics. 1949.

Ridler, A. (ed). Shakespeare criticism 1935–60. Oxford 1963 (WC).

Lerner, L. (ed). Shakespeare's tragedies. 1963 (Pelican).

Leech, C. (ed). Shakespeare, the tragedies: a collection of critical essays. Chicago 1965.

— Shakespeare's comedies. 1967 (Pelican).

Palmer, D. J. (ed). Shakespeare's later comedies: an anthology of modern criticism. 1971 (Pelican).

(2) The History of Criticism

Smith, D. N. Shakespeare in the eighteenth century. Oxford 1928.

Ralli, A. A history of Shakespearian criticism. 2 vols Oxford 1932.

Shaaber, M. A. Shakespeare criticism: Dryden to Bradley. In A new companion to Shakespeare studies, ed K. Muir and S. Schoenbaum, Cambridge 1971.

Wells, S. Shakespeare criticism since Bradley. Ibid.

(3) General Criticism

Coleridge, S. T. Notes and lectures upon Shakespeare and some of the old poets and dramatists. Ed Sara Coleridge 2 vols 1849; Shakespearean criticism, ed T. M. Raysor 2 vols Cambridge Mass 1930, London 1960 (EL); Coleridge on Shakespeare: the text of the lectures of 1811–12, ed R. A. Foakes 1971.

Dowden, E. Shakspere: a critical study of his mind and art. 1875 etc; ed W. D. Howe, New York 1918.

Swinburne, A. C. A study of Shakespeare. 1880.

Boas, F. S. Shakespeare and his predecessors. 1896.

Bradley, A. C. Shakespearean tragedy: lectures on Hamlet, Othello, King Lear, Macbeth. 1904.

Raleigh, W. Shakespeare. 1907 (EML).

Quiller-Couch, A. T. Shakespeare's workmanship. 1918.

Chambers, E. K. Shakespeare: a survey. 1925.

Granville-Barker, H. From Henry V to Hamlet. Proc Br Acad 11 1925.

—— Prefaces to Shakespeare. 5 sers 1927–47, 4 vols 1963.

Stoll, E. E. Shakespere studies. New York 1927.

—— Poets and playwrights. Minneapolis 1930.

—— Art and artifice in Shakespeare. New York 1933.

Knight, G. W. The wheel of fire: essays in interpretation of Shakespeare's sombre tragedies. Oxford 1930, 1949 (with addns).

—— The imperial theme: further interpretations of Shakespeare's tragedies. Oxford 1932, 1951 (rev).

—— The crown of life: Shakespeare's final plays. Oxford 1947.

Wilson, J. D. The essential Shakespeare. Cambridge 1932.

Alexander, P. Shakespeare's life and art. 1939.

—— A Shakespeare primer. 1951.

—— Shakespeare. Oxford 1964.

Knights, L. C. In his Explorations, 1946. Includes essays on Macbeth, Hamlet, sonnets etc.

—— Some Shakespearean themes. 1959.

—— In his Further explorations, 1965. Includes essays on Julius Caesar, Lear, Shakespeare's politics etc.

Sewell, A. Character and society in Shakespeare. Oxford 1951.

Rossiter, A. P. Angel with horns and other Shakespeare lectures. Ed G. Storey 1961.

Jones, E. Scenic form in Shakespeare. Oxford 1971.

IX. JACOBEAN AND CAROLINE DRAMA

Chapman, Middleton, Jonson, Dekker, Heywood, Marston, Tourneur, Webster, Massinger, Beaumont and Fletcher, Rowley, Ford, Shirley

For collections listed below as abbreviations (Bang, Gayley, TFT etc) see col 169, above.

GEORGE CHAPMAN
1559?–1634

Collections

Works. Ed R. H. Shepherd 3 vols 1874–5.

Plays. Ed T. M. Parrott 2 vols 1910–14.

Poems. Ed P. B. Bartlett, New York 1941.

Chapman's Homer: the Iliad, the Odyssey and the lesser Homerica. Ed A. Nicoll 2 vols New York 1956.

Plays: the comedies. Ed A. Holaday et al, Urbana 1970.

§ I

Σκία νυκτός: the shadow of night, containing two poeticall hymnes, devised by G.C. gent. 1594; rptd A. Acheson, Shakespeare and the rival poet, 1903.

Ovids banquet of sence, A coronet for his mistresse Philosophie, and his amorous zodiacke, with a translation of a Latin coppie written by a fryer. 1595, 1639; rptd A. Acheson, Shakespeare and the rival poet, 1903; ed E. S. Donno, Elizabethan minor epics, 1963; ed N. Alexander, Elizabethan narrative verse, 1968; Menston 1970 (facs). The trn The amorous contention of Phillis and Flora was rptd 1598 as by R.S. (Richard Stapleton?) who may be the author.

Achilles shield, translated as the other seven bookes of Homer out of his eighteenth booke of Iliades. 1598, Oxford 1931.

The blinde begger of Alexandria, most pleasantly discoursing his variable humours in disguised shapes full of conceite and pleasure, as it hath beene sundry times publickly acted in London by the Right Honorable the Earle of Nottingham, Lord High Admirall his servantes. 1598; ed W. W. Greg 1928 (Malone Soc).

Seaven bookes of the Iliades of Homere, prince of poets, translated according to the Greeke in judgement of his best commentaries. 1598. Bks 1–2, 7–11.

A pleasant comedy entituled An humerous dayes myrth, as it hath beene sundrie times publikely acted by the Right Honourable the Earle of Nottingham, Lord High Admirall his servants, by G.C. 1599; ed D. N. Smith 1938 (Malone Soc).

Peristeros: or the male turtle. In R. Chester, Love's martyr, 1601; ed A. B. Grosart 1878 (New Shakspere Soc); ed B. H. Newdigate, The phoenix and the turtle, Oxford 1937.

Al fooles, a comedy, presented at the Black fryers, and lately before his Majestie. 1605; ed I. Reed, Dodsley vol 4, 1780; Ancient British drama vol 2, 1810; ed J. P. Collier, Dodsley vol 4, 1825; ed T. M. Parrott 1907; ed F. Manley 1968 (Regents ser).

Eastward hoe, as it was playd in the Black-friers by the children of her Majesties revels, made by Geo. Chapman, Ben Jonson, Joh. Marston. 1605 (first edn reissued and 2 further edns ptd in this year); ed R. Dodsley, A select collection of old plays vol 4, 1744; ed W. R. Chetwood, Memoirs of Jonson, 1756; ed I. Reed, Dodsley vol 4, 1780; Ancient British drama vol 2, 1810; ed J. P. Collier, Dodsley vol 4, 1825; ed F. E. Schelling 1904; ed J. W. Cunliffe, Gayley vol 2, 1913; TFT 1914; ed J. H. Harris, New Haven 1926; ed C. F. T. Brooke and N. B. Paradise, English drama, 1933; ed H. Spencer, Elizabethan plays, 1933. Also included in collections of Marston, below, and in Herford–Simpson edn of Jonson, below.

The gentleman usher. 1606; ed T. M. Parrott 1907; ed J. H. Smith 1970 (Regents ser).

Monsieur D'Olive: a comedie, as it was sundrie times acted by her Majesties children at the Blacke-friers. 1606; ed C. W. Dilke, Old English plays vol 3, 1814.

Sir Gyles Goosecappe knight: a comedie presented by the chil. of the chappell. 1606, 1636 (both edns anon, but Chapman's authorship accepted); ed A. H. Bullen, Old English plays vol 3, 1884; ed W. Bang and R. Brotanek, Bang vol 26, 1909; TFT 1912.

Bussy D'Ambois: a tragedie, as it hath been often presented at Paules. 1607 (some copies dated 1608) (anon), 1641 ('being much corrected and amended by the author before his death'; re-issued 1641, 1646, 1657); ed C. W. Dilke, Old English plays vol 3, 1814; ed F. S. Boas 1905; ed W. A. Neilson, Chief Elizabethan dramatists, 1911; ed C. F. T. Brooke and N. B. Paradise, English drama 1933; ed H. Spenser, Elizabethan plays, 1933; ed C. R. Baskervill, Elizabethan and Stuart plays, 1934; ed A. K. McIlwraith, Five Stuart tragedies, Oxford 1953 (WC); ed J. Jacquot, Paris 1960; ed N. Brooke 1964 (Revels ser); ed R. Lordi 1964 (Regents ser); ed M. Evans 1965 (New Mermaid ser).

The conspiracie and tragedie of Charles Duke of Byron, Marshall of France, acted lately in two playes at the Black-friers. 1608, 1625.

Euthymiæ raptus: or the teares of peace, with interlocutions. 1609; rptd A. Acheson, Shakespeare and the rival poet, 1903.

Homer, prince of poets, translated according to the Greeke in twelve bookes of his Iliads. [1609?], 1611. Reprints the 7 bks of 1598 and adds 3–6 and 12.

The Iliads of Homer, prince of poets, never before in any language truely translated, with a comment uppon some of his chiefe places. [1611]; ed R. Hooper 2 vols 1857; ed H. Morley 1883. Adds bks 13–24 and substitutes new versions of 1–2.

May-day: a witty comedie, divers times acted at the Blacke fryers. 1611; ed C. W. Dilke, Old English plays vol 4, 1814.

An epicede or funerall song on the death of Henry Prince of Wales. 1612; ed S. E. Brydges 1818.

Petrarchs seven penitentiall psalmes, paraphrastically translated with other philosophicall poems and a Hymne to Christ upon the crosse. 1612.

The widdowes teares: a comedie, as it was often presented in the Black and White friers. 1612; ed R. Dodsley, A select collection of old plays vol 4, 1744; ed I. Reed, Dodsley vol 6, 1780; ed J. P. Collier, Dodsley vol 6, 1825; ed E. Smeak 1966 (Regents ser).

The memorable maske of the two honorable houses or Inns of Courte, the Middle Temple and Lyncolns Inne, as it was performed before the King at White-hall on Shrove Munday at night, being the 15 of February 1613, at the princely celebration of the most royall nuptialls of the Palsgrave and his thrice gratious Princesse Elizabeth, with a description of their whole show, invented and fashioned by our kingdomes most artfull and ingenious architect Innigo Jones, and written by Geo. Chapman. [1613?] (2 edns); ed J. Nichols, Progresses of James I vol 2, 1828.

The revenge of Bussy D'Ambois: a tragedie, as it hath beene often presented at the private play-house in the White-fryers. 1613; ed F. S. Boas 1905; Menston 1968 (facs).

Andromeda liberata: or the nuptials of Perseus and Andromeda. 1614.

Eugenia: or true nobilities trance for the most memorable death of William Lord Russell. 1614.

A free and offenceless justification of Andromeda liberata. 1614.

Homers Odysses. [1614?]. Bks 1–12.

Twenty-four bookes of Homers Odisses. [1615?]; ed R. Hooper 2 vols 1857; 2 vols 1897 (Temple Classics). Adds bks 13–24 to reissue of previous item.

The divine poem of Musaeus: first of all bookes, translated according to the originall. 1616; ed E. S. Donno, Elizabethan minor epics, 1963.

The whole works of Homer, prince of poetts, in his Iliads and Odysses. [1616] (re-issues edns of [1611], [1615?] with new general title-page), 1904, 4 vols Oxford 1930–1.

The Georgicks of Hesiod, translated elaborately out of the Greek. 1618.

Pro Vere autumni lachrymæ, inscribed to the immortal memorie of Sir Horatio Vere. 1622.

The crowne of all Homers workes, Batrachomyomachia or the battaile of frogs and mise, his hymn's and epigrams. [1624?], 1818; ed R. Hooper 1858; Oxford 1931.

A justification of a strange action of Nero in burying with a solemne funerall one of the cast hayres of his mistresse Poppæa; also a just reproofe of a Romane smell-feast: being the fifth satyre of Juvenall translated. 1629.

Caesar and Pompey: a Roman tragedy, declaring their warres, out of whose events is evicted this proposition, only a just man is a freeman. 1631 (some copies as The warres of Pompey and Caesar), 1652, 1653.

The tragedie of Chabot Admirall of France, as it was presented by her Majesties servants at the private house in Drury Lane, written by George Chapman and James Shirly. 1639; ed E. Lehman, Philadelphia 1906. A revision by Shirley of a play written by Chapman c. 1613.

For Hero and Leander, begun by Marlowe and completed by Chapman, see col 189, above.

§2

Swinburne, A. C. Chapman: a critical essay. 1875.

Jacquot, J. Chapman: sa vie, sa poésie, son théâtre, sa pensée. Paris 1951.

Lewis, C. S. Hero and Leander. Proc Br Acad 38 1952; rptd in his Selected literary essays, Cambridge 1969.

Kermode, F. The banquet of sense. Bull John Rylands Lib 44 1961; rptd in his Shakespeare, Spenser, Donne, 1971.

MacLure, M. Chapman: a critical study. Toronto 1966.

THOMAS MIDDLETON
1580–1627

Collections

Works. Ed A. Dyce 5 vols 1840; ed A. H. Bullen 8 vols 1885–6.

Thomas Middleton. Vol 1, ed A. C. Swinburne 1887 (A trick to catch the old one, The changeling, A chaste maid in Cheapside, Women beware women, The Spanish gipsy); vol 2, ed H. Ellis 1890 (The roaring girl, The witch, A fair quarrel, The mayor of Queenborough, The widow) (Mermaid ser).

Selected plays. Ed D. L. Frost, Cambridge 1978. 4 plays.

§1

The wisdome of Solomon paraphrased. 1597.

Micro-cynicon: sixe snarling satyres, by T.M. 1599, 1842.

The ghost of Lucrece, by T.M. 1600; ed J. Q. Adams 1937 (facs).

Blurt master-constable: or the Spaniards night-walke, as it hath bin sundry times privately acted by the children of Paules. 1602 (anon); rptd W. R. Chetwood, A select collection of old plays, Dublin 1750. Or by Dekker?

The ant and the nightingale: or Father Hubburds tales, by T.M. 1604, 1604 (as Father Hubburds tales). Anon.

The blacke booke, by T.M. 1604.

The honest whore, pt 1. 1604. With Dekker; *see col 234, below.*

Michaelmas terme, as it hath been sundry times acted by the children of Paules. 1607, 1630 (both edns anon); ed R. Levin 1966 (Regents ser).

The phoenix, as it hath beene sundry times acted by the children of Paules, and presented before his Majestie. 1607, 1630 (both edns anon).

The familie of love, acted by the children of his Majesties revells. 1608. Anon.

A mad world, my masters, as it hath bin lately in action by the children of Paules, composed by T.M. 1608, 1640; ed R. Dodsley, A select collection of old plays vol 5, 1744; ed I. Reed, Dodsley vol 5, 1780; Ancient British drama vol 2, 1810; ed J. P. Collier, Dodsley vol 5, 1825; ed S. Henning 1965 (Regents ser).

A tricke to catch the old-one, as it hath beene lately acted by the children of Paules. 1608 (anon), 1608–9 ('as it hath beene often in action both at Paules and the Black-fryers, presented before his Majestie on New-Yeares Night last, composde by T.M.'), 1616; ed C. W. Dilke, Old English plays vol 5, 1814; rptd Old English drama vol 3, 1830; ed W. A. Neilson, Chief Elizabethan dramatists, 1911; ed H. Spencer, Elizabethan plays, 1933; ed C. R. Baskervill, Elizabethan and Stuart plays, 1934; ed C. Barber 1968; ed G. J. Watson 1968 (New Mermaid ser).

Your five gallants, as it hath beene often in action at the Blackfriers. [1608?].

Sir Robert Sherley, sent ambassadour in the name of the King of Persia to Sigismond the third, King of Poland, his royal entertainment. 1609.

The roaring girle: or Moll Cut-purse, as it hath lately beene acted on the Fortune-stage by the Prince his players, written by T. Middleton and T. Dekkar. 1611; ed I. Reed, Dodsley vol 6, 1780; Ancient British drama vol 2, 1810; ed J. P. Collier, Dodsley vol 6, 1825; ed R. H. Shepherd, Dramatic works of Dekker, 1873; TFT 1914; ed F. T. Bowers, Dramatic works of Dekker, Cambridge 1958.

The manner of his Lordships entertainment on Michaelmas day last at that most famous and admired worke of the running streame from Amwell Head into the cesterne neere Islington, by T.M. 1613, 1613 (appended to reissue of Triumphs of truth, below); ed J. Nichols, Progresses of James I vol 2, 1828.

The triumphs of truth: a solemnity at the establishment of Sir Thomas Middleton, Knight, in the honorable office of Lord Mayor of London. 1613, 1613 (with Running-stream entertainment); ed J. Nichols, Progresses of James I vol 2, 1828.

Civitatis amor, the cities love: an entertainment by water at Chelsey and Whitehall. 1616; ed J. Nichols, Progresses of James I vol 3, 1828.

A faire quarrell, as it was acted before the King and divers times publikely by the Prince his Highnes servants, written by Thomas Midleton and William Rowley gentl. 1617, 1617 ('with new additions of Mr Chaughs and Trimtrams roaring and the bawds song'), 1622.

The tryumphs of honour and industry: a solemnity at establishment of G. Bowles, Lord Mayor. 1617.

The peace-maker: or Great Brittaines blessing. 1618.

The Inner-Temple masque: or masque of heroes, presented as an entertainement for many worthy ladies by gentlemen of the same ancient and noble house. 1619; ed R. C. Bald, A book of masques in honour of Allardyce Nicoll, Cambridge 1967.

The triumphs of love and antiquity: an honourable solemnitie at the establishment of Sir W. Cockayn, Lord Mayor. 1619; ed J. Nichols, Progresses of James I vol 3, 1828.

The mariage of the Old and New Testament. 1620 (dedication signed by Tho. Middleton, chronologer for the honourable citie of London), 1627 (as Gods parliament house: or the marriage of the Old and New testament).

A courtly masque: the device called the World tost at tennis, as it hath beene divers times presented to the contentment of many noble and worthy spectators by the Prince his servants, invented and set downe by Tho. Middleton and William Rowley gent. 1620.

Honorable entertainments, compos'de for the service of this noble cittie. 1621; ed R. C. Bald and F. P. Wilson 1953 (Malone Soc).

The sun in Aries: a noble solemnity at the establishment of Ed. Barkham, Lord Mayor. 1621.

An invention performed for the service of the Right Honorable Edward Barkham, Lord Mayor of the cittie of London. 1622. Ms in Conway Papers in Public Record Office (State Papers Domestic, James I, CXXIX, article 53).

The triumphs of honor and virtue: a noble solemnitie at the establishment of P. Proby, Lord Mayor. 1622; ed J. L. Pearson, Shakespeare Society's Papers 2, Publications 29 1845.

The triumphs of integrity: a noble solemnity at the establishment of M. Lumley, Lord Mayor. 1623.

A game at chaess as it was acted nine days to gether at the Globe on the Banks side. [1625] (3 undated edns, the 2nd reissued with date 1625) (anon); ed R. C. Bald, Cambridge 1929; ed C. F. T. Brooke and N. B. Paradise, English drama, 1933; ed J. W. Harper 1966 (New Mermaid ser).

The triumphs of health and prosperity: a noble solemnity at the inauguration of Cuthbert Hacket, Lord Mayor. 1626.

A chast mayd in Cheape-side: a pleasant conceited comedy never before printed, as it hath beene often acted at the Swan on the Banke-side by the Lady Elizabeth her servants. 1630; ed A. Brissenden 1968 (New Mermaid ser); ed R. B. Parker 1969 (Revels ser); Menston 1969 (facs); ed C. Barber 1969.

The widdow: a comedie, as it was acted at the private house in Black-fryers by his late Majesties servants, written by Ben Johnson, John Fletcher, Tho. Middleton gent. 1652; Ancient British drama vol 3, 1810; ed J. P. Collier, Dodsley vol 12, 1827. Principally if not entirely by Middleton.

The changeling, as it was acted at the privat house in Drury-Lane, and Salisbury Court, written by Thomas Midelton and William Rowley gent. 1653, 1668; ed C. W. Dilke, Old English plays vol 4, 1815; ed W. A. Neilson, Chief Elizabethan dramatists, 1911; ed C. F. T. Brooke and N. B. Paradise, English drama, 1933; ed H. Spencer, Elizabethan plays 1933; ed C. R. Baskervill, Elizabethan and Stuart plays, 1934; ed N. W. Bawcutt 1958 (Revels ser); ed P. Thompson 1964 (New Mermaid ser); ed M. W. Black 1966; ed G. W. Williams 1966 (Regents ser).

The Spanish gipsie, as it was acted at the privat house in Drury-Lane, and Salisbury Court, written by Thomas Midleton and William Rowley, gent. 1653, 1661; ed C. W. Dilke, Old English plays vol 4, 1815; ed E. C. Morris, Boston 1908; ed H. B. Clarke, Gayley vol 3, 1914.

The excellent comedy called the Old law: or a new way to please you, by Phil. Massinger, Tho. Middleton, William Rowley, acted before the King and Queene at Salisbury House and at severall other places. 1656. *Also included in collections of Massinger, col 243, below.*

No wit (help) like a womans: a comedy. 1657. Rev Shirley.

Two new plays: viz More dissemblers besides women, a comedy: Women beware women, a tragedy. 1657. More dissemblers ed C. W. Dilke, Old English plays vol 4, 1815; Women beware women ed C. W. Dilke, Old English plays vol 5, 1815; Old English drama vol 3, 1830; ed R. Gill 1968 (Mermaid ser).

The Mayor of Quinborough: a comedy, as it hath been often acted at Black-fryars by his Majesties servants. 1661, 1661; ed I. Reed, Dodsley vol 11, 1780; Ancient British drama vol 3, 1810; ed J. P. Collier, Dodsley vol 11, 1826; ed R. C. Bald 1938 (as Hengist, King of Kent: or the Mayor of Queenborough).

Any thing for a quiet life: a comedy, formerly acted at Black-fryers by his late Majesties servants. 1662; ed F. L. Lucas, Works of Webster vol 4, 1927.

A tragi-coomodie called the Witch, long since acted by his Majesties servants at the Black-friers. 1778 (first ptd from ms discovered by I. Reed, now Bodley ms Malone 12); Ancient British drama vol 3, 1810; ed L. Drees and H. de Vocht, Louvain 1945; ed W. W. Greg and F. P. Wilson 1950 (Malone Soc).

§2

Eliot, T. S. In his For Lancelot Andrewes, 1928; rptd in his Selected essays, 1932, and Elizabethan essays, 1934.

Empson, W. In his Some versions of pastoral, 1935. On Changeling.

Barker, R. H. Middleton. New York 1958.

Ricks, C. The moral and poetic structure of the Changeling. EC 10 1960.

—— Word-play in Women beware women. RES new ser 12 1961.

Frost, D. L. In his School of Shakespeare, Cambridge 1968.

Gibbons, B. In his Jacobean city comedy: a study of satiric plays by Jonson, Marston and Middleton, 1968.

Holmes, D. M. The art of Middleton. Oxford 1970.

BEN JONSON
1572?-1637

Collections

The workes of Benjamin Jonson. 1616. Contains Every man in his humour, Every man out of his humour, Cynthia's revels, Poetaster, Sejanus, Volpone, Epicoene, Alchemist, Catiline, Epigrammes, Forrest, and certain entertainments and masques.

The workes of Benjamin Jonson. 1640. The first vol reprints 1616, above. The 2nd (individual title-pages of which are variously dated 1631, 1640, 1641) contains Bartholomew fayre, Divell is an asse, Staple of newes, Magnetick lady, A tale of a tub, Sad shepherd, Underwood, Mortimer his fall, Horace his art of poetrie, English grammar, Timber, Execration against Vulcan, and entertainments and masques.

The workes of Ben Jonson. 1692 (adds New inne, Leges convivales), 1716-17.

Ben Jonson. Ed B. Nicholson, introd by C. H. Herford 3 vols 1893-4 (Mermaid ser).

Works. Ed C. H. Herford, P. and E. M. Simpson 11 vols Oxford 1925-52.

Poems. Ed H. H. Hudson, New York 1936 (fac); ed B. H. Newdigate, Oxford 1936.

Selected works. Ed H. Levin, New York 1938.

Five plays. Oxford 1953 (WC).

Complete masques. Ed S. Orgel, New Haven 1969.

§I

(in probable order of composition)

A tale of a tub. 1640 (licensed 7 May 1633, original version written c. 1596-7); ed H. Scherer, Bang vol 39, 1913; ed F. M. Snell, New York 1915.

The case is alterd, as it hath beene sundry times acted by the children of the Blacke-friers. 1609, 1609 (original version written c. 1597-8); ed W. E. Selin, New Haven 1917.

Every man in his humour, as it hath beene sundry times publickly acted by the Right Honorable the Lord Chamberlaine his servants. 1601 (acted 1598), 1616 (rev); 4° text of 1601 ed C. Grabau, Sh Jb 38 1902; ed W. W. Greg, Bang vol 10, 1905; folio text of 1616 ed W. Scott, Modern British drama vol 3, 1811; ed H. B. Wheatley 1877; ed W. M. Dixon 1901; ed H. Maas, Rostock 1901; ed W. A. Neilson, Chief Elizabethan dramatists, 1911; ed C. H. Herford, Gayley vol 2, 1913; ed P. Simpson, Oxford 1919; ed R. S. Knox 1923; ed G. B. Harrison 1926; ed C. F. T. Brooke and N. B. Paradise, English drama 1933; ed H. Spencer, Elizabethan plays 1933; ed C. R. Baskervill, Elizabethan and Stuart plays, 1934; ed A. Sale 1941, 1949 (rev); ed M. Seymour-Smith 1967 (New Mermaid ser); ed G. B.

Jackson, New Haven 1969. Parallel texts of 4° and folio versions ed H. H. Carter, New Haven 1921; ed J. W. Lever 1971 (Regents ser).

The comicall satyre of Every man out of his humor, as it was first composed by the author B.J. 1600 (3 4° edns) (acted 1599), 1616 (rev); first 4° text ed W. W. Greg and F. P. Wilson 1921 (Malone Soc); 2nd-3rd 4° texts ed W. Bang and Greg, Bang vols 16-17 1907.

The fountaine of selfe-love: or Cynthias revels, as it hath beene sundry times privately acted in the Black-friers by the children of her Majesties chappell. 1601 (acted 1600), 1616 (rev); 4° text of 1601 ed W. Bang and L. Krebs, Bang vol 22, 1908; folio text of 1616 ed A. C. Judson, New York 1912.

Poems. In R. Chester, Love's martyr, 1601; ed A. B. Grosart 1878 (New Shakspere Soc); ed B. H. Newdigate, The phoenix and the turtle, Oxford 1937.

Poetaster: or the arraignment, as it hath beene sundry times privately acted in the Blacke friers by the children of her Majesties chappell. 1602 (acted 1601), 1616 (rev); 4° text of 1602 ed H. de Vocht, Louvain 1934; folio text of 1616 ed H. S. Mallory, New York 1905; ed J. H. Penniman, Boston 1913.

Sejanus his fall. 1605 (acted 1603), 1616 (rev); 4° text of 1605 ed H. de Vocht, Louvain 1935; folio text of 1616 ed W. D. Briggs, Boston 1911; ed W. A. Neilson, Chief Elizabethan dramatists, 1911; ed C. R. Baskervill, Elizabethan and Stuart plays, 1934; ed J. A. Barish, New Haven 1965; ed W. Bolton 1966 (New Mermaid ser).

Part of King James his royall and magnificent entertainment [on his state-entry into London 15 March 1604]; also a briefe panegyre of his Majesties first and well auspicated entrance to his High Court of Parliament [19 March 1604], with other additions [Entertainment of the Queen and Prince at Althrope 25 June 1603]. 1604, 1616.

A private entertainment of the King and Queen at Highgate. 1616 (presented 1 May 1604). The Penates.

Eastward hoe. 1605. With Chapman and Marston; *see under Chapman, col 224, above.*

Volpone: or the foxe. 1607 (acted 1605), 1616, 1709; 4° text of 1607 ed V. O'Sullivan 1898; ed H. de Vocht, Louvain 1937; Menston 1968 (facs); folio text of 1616 ed W. Scott, Modern British drama vol 3, 1811; Old English drama vol 1, 1830; ed H. B. Wilkins, Paris 1906; ed W. A. Neilson, Chief Elizabethan dramatists, 1911; ed J. D. Rea, New Haven 1919; ed F. E. Schelling, Typical Elizabethan plays, New York 1926; ed C. F. T. Brooke and N. B. Paradise, English drama, 1933; ed H. Spencer, Elizabethan plays, 1933; ed C. R. Baskervill, Elizabethan and Stuart plays, 1934; ed A. Sale 1951; ed J. A. Barish, New York 1958; ed A. B. Kernan, New Haven 1962; ed J. B. Bamborough 1964; ed D. Cook 1967; ed P. Brockbank 1968 (New Mermaid ser); ed J. L. Halio 1968.

The characters of two royall masques, the one of blacknesse, the other of beautie. 1608 (performed respectively 6 Jan 1605, 10 Jan 1608), 1616. A ms of The masque of blackness is in BM ms Royal 17B.XXXI; rptd by J. P. Collier, Five Court masques, 1848 (Shakespeare Soc), and in Herford and Simpson edn of Jonson vol 7, pp. 195-201.

Hymenaei. 1606 (performed 5 Jan 1606), 1616.

The entertainment of the two Kings of Great Britaine and Denmarke at Theobalds. 1616 (presented 24 July 1606).

An entertainment of King James and Queene Anne at Theobalds. 1616 (presented 22 May 1607).

The description of the masque celebrating the marriage of John, Lord Ramsey, Viscount Haddington. 1608 (performed 9 Feb 1608), 1616; ed F. E. Schelling, Typical Elizabethan plays, New York 1926; ed C. R. Baskervill, Elizabethan and Stuart plays, 1934. Entitled

The masque of Queenes. 1609 (performed 2 Feb 1609), 1616. BM ms Royal 18A.XLV; ed J. P. Collier, Five

Court masques, 1848 (Shakespeare Soc); ed G. Chapman 1930 (facs, with Inigo Jones's designs).

Epicoene: or the silent woman. 1616 (acted 1609), 1620, 1709; Old English drama vol 3, 1830; ed A. Henry, New York 1906; ed C. M. Gayley vol 2, 1913; ed C. F. T. Brooke and N. B. Paradise, English drama, 1933; ed L. A. Beaurline 1966 (Regents ser).

The speeches at Prince Henries barriers. 1616 (performed 6 Jan 1610).

The alchemist. 1612 (acted 1610), 1616, 1709; 4° text of 1612, 1927 (facs); folio text of 1616 ed W. Scott, Modern British drama vol 3, 1811; ed C. M. Hathaway, New York 1903; ed F. E. Schelling, Boston 1903; ed W. A. Neilson, Chief Elizabethan dramatists, 1911; ed G. A. Smithson, Gayley vol 2, 1913; ed C. F. T. Brooke and N. B. Paradise, 1933; ed H. Spencer, Elizabethan plays, 1933; ed C. R. Baskervill, Elizabethan and Stuart plays, 1934; ed G. E. Bentley, New York 1947; ed R. J. L. Kingsford, Cambridge 1948; ed H. de Vocht, Louvain 1950; ed D. Brown 1966 (New Mermaid ser); ed J. Bamborough 1967; ed F. H. Mares 1967 (Revels ser); ed J. B. Steane, Cambridge 1967; ed S. Musgrove 1968.

Oberon: the Faery Prince. 1616 (performed 1 Jan 1611); ed R. Hosley, A book of masques in honour of Allardyce Nicoll, Cambridge 1967.

Love freed from ignorance and folly. 1616 (performed 3 Feb 1611); ed N. Sanders, A book of masques in honour of Allardyce Nicoll, Cambridge 1967.

Catiline his conspiracy. 1611 (acted 1611), 1616, 1635, 1635, 1669, 1674, 1739; ed L. H. Harris, New Haven 1916; ed W. Bolton and J. F. Gardner 1972 (Regents ser).

Love restored. 1616 (performed 6 Jan 1612).

Epigrammes. 1616 (S.R. 15 May 1612).

The Irish masque. 1616 (performed 29 Dec 1613, 3 Jan 1614).

A challenge at tilt. 1616 (performed 1 Jan 1614).

Bartholomew fayre. 1631, 1640 (acted 31 Oct 1614), 1739; ed C. S. Alden, New York 1904; ed H. Spencer, Elizabethan plays 1933; ed E. A. Horsman 1960 (Revels ser); ed E. M. Waith, New Haven 1963; ed M. Hussey 1964 (New Mermaid ser); ed E. B. Partridge 1964 (Regents ser).

The golden age restored. 1616 (performed presumably on 6, 8 Jan 1615).

Mercurie vindicated from the alchemists. 1616 (performed presumably on 1, 6 Jan 1616).

The forrest. 1616.

The Divell is an asse. 1631, 1640 (acted 1616), 1641, 1669; ed W. S. Johnson, New York 1905; ed M. Hussey 1967.

Christmas his masque. 1641 (performed 1616). Mss: (1) Folger Lib ms J.a.1; (2) Bodley ms Rawlinson poetry 160, ff. 173–4 (song of Christmas only); (3) BM ms Harley 4955, ff. 46–7 (song of Christmas only).

The vision of delight. 1641 (performed 6, 19 Jan 1617).

Lovers made men: a masque presented in the house of the Honorable the Lord Haye. 1617 (performed 22 Feb 1617), 1641; ed S. Wells, A book of masques in honour of Allardyce Nicoll, Cambridge 1967.

Pleasure reconciled to virtue. 1641 (performed 6 Jan 1618); ed R. A. Foakes, A book of masques in honour of Allardyce Nicoll, Cambridge 1967.

For the honour of Wales. 1641 (performed 18 Feb 1618).

Newes from the new world discover'd in the moone. 1641 (performed 17 Jan, 29 Feb 1620).

An entertainment at the Blackfriars (performed at christening of Charles Cavendish, May 1620). BM ms Harley 4955, ff.48–52; rptd Monthly Mag Feb 1816.

Pans anniversarie: or the shepherds holy-day. 1641 (performed 19 June 1620).

The gypsies metamorphos'd. 1640, 1640 (with extensive addns), 1641 (performed 3, 5 Aug, Sept 1621); ed G. W. Cole, New York 1931; ed C. F. T. Brooke and

N. B. Paradise, English drama, 1933; ed W. W. Greg 1952.

The masque of augures. [1622] (performed 6 Jan, 5 or 6 May 1622), 1641 (rev).

Time vindicated to himselfe and to his honors. [1623] (performed 19 Jan 1623), 1641.

Neptunes triumph for the returne of Albion. [1624] (planned for performance 6 Jan 1624), 1641.

The masque of owles. 1641 (performed 19 Aug 1624).

The fortunate isles and their union. [1625] (performed 9 Jan 1625), 1641. A revision of Neptunes triumph.

The staple of newes. 1631, 1640 (acted 1625); ed De Winter, New York 1905.

The new inne: or the light heart. 1631 (acted 1629), 1692; ed G. B. Tennant, New York 1908.

Loves triumph through Callipolis. 1630 (for 1631) (performed 9 Jan 1631), 1641.

Chloridia. [1631] (performed 22 Feb 1631), 1641.

The magnetick lady: or humors reconcild. 1640 (acted 1632); ed H. W. Peck, New York 1914.

The Kings entertainment at Welbeck. 1641 (presented 31 May 1633).

Loves wel-come at Bolsover. 1641 (performed 30 July 1634).

The sad shepherd: or a tale of Robin Hood. 1641 (3 acts only); ed F. G. Waldron 1783 (with continuation); ed W. W. Greg, Bang vol 11, 1905 (with Waldron's continuation); ed F. E. Schelling, Typical Elizabethan plays, New York 1926; ed L. J. Potts, Cambridge 1929; ed C. R. Baskervill, Elizabethan and Stuart plays, 1934; ed and completed A. Porter, New York 1944.

The under-wood. 1640, Cambridge 1905.

Mortimer his fall. 1640 (one scene only).

Horace his art of poetrie. 1640. Variant versions ptd in 12° and in folio collection; the 12° text rptd E. H. Blakeney 1928.

The English grammar. 1640; ed A. V. Waite 1909; ed S. Gibson 1928.

Timber: or discoveries made upon men and matter. 1641; ed H. Morley 1892; ed F. E. Schelling 1892; ed I. Gollancz 1898; ed M. Castelain, Paris [1906]; ed G. B. Harrison 1923; ed R. S. Walker, Syracuse NY 1953.

Execration against Vulcan, with divers epigrams. 1640 (edns in 4°, 12° and in folio collection).

Leges convivales. 1692.

Jonson has been connected with 2 plays in the Beaumont and Fletcher canon: Rollo Duke of Normandy: or the bloody brother, *col 246, below, and* Love's pilgrimage. *The title-page ascription to him (with Middleton and Fletcher) of* The widow *is generally rejected.*

Letters and Memoirs

Letters. Works vol 1, ed C. H. Herford and P. Simpson, Oxford 1925.

Heads of a conversation betwixt Ben Johnson and William Drummond. In Drummond's Works, Edinburgh 1711; ed D. Laing, Archaeologica scotica vol 4, 1833; 1842 (Shakespeare Soc); rptd in Gifford's Jonson vol 3, ed F. Cunningham 1871; ed P. Sidney 1906; ed G. B. Harrison 1923; ed R. F. Patterson 1923; ed C. H. Herford and P. Simpson, Works vol 1, Oxford 1925.

§2

Jonsonus virbius: or the memory of Ben Jonson revived by the friends of the Muses. Ed B. Duppa 1638.

Dryden, John. Examen of the Silent woman. In his Of dramatick poesie: an essay, 1668.

Aubrey, John. Lives. 1813.

Swinburne, A. C. A study of Ben Jonson. 1889.

Smith, G. G. Jonson. 1919 (EML).

Eliot, T. S. In his Sacred wood, 1920; rptd in his Selected essays, 1932, and Elizabethan essays, 1934.

Bradley, J. F. and J. Q. Adams. The Jonson allusion-book 1597–1700. New Haven 1922.

Knights, L. C. Tradition and Jonson. Scrutiny 4 1935.
—— Drama and society in the age of Jonson. 1937.
—— Ben Jonson, dramatist. In The age of Shakespeare, ed B. Ford 1955 (Pelican).
Bentley, G. E. 17th-century allusions to Jonson. HLQ 5 1942.
—— Shakespeare and Jonson: their reputations in the 17th century compared. 2 vols Chicago 1945.
Barish, J. A. Ben Jonson and the language of prose comedy. Cambridge Mass 1960.
Trimpi, W. Jonson's poems: a study of the plain style. Stanford 1962.
Orgel, S. The Jonsonian masque. Cambridge Mass 1965.
Bamborough, J. B. Ben Jonson. 1970.
McPherson, D. Jonson's library and marginalia. SP 71 1974.

THOMAS DEKKER
1572?–1632

Collections

Dramatic works. Ed R. H. Shepherd 4 vols 1873.
Non-dramatic works. Ed A. B. Grosart 5 vols 1884–6 (Huth Lib).
Thomas Dekker. Ed E. Rhys 1887 (Mermaid ser).
Dramatic works. Ed F. T. Bowers 4 vols Cambridge 1953–61, 1964–6 (vols 2–3 rptd with corrections) (standard edn); C. Hoy, Commentary, 2 vols Cambridge 1974.
Thomas Dekker. Ed E. D. Pendry 1968.

§1

The pleasant comedie of old Fortunatus, as it was plaied before the Queenes Majestie this Christmas by the Right Honourable the Earle of Nottingham, Lord High Admirall of England his servants. 1600 (anon); ed C. W. Dilke, Old English plays vol 3, 1814; ed H. Scherer, Erlangen 1901; ed O. Smeaton 1904; ed F. E. Schelling, Typical Elizabethan plays, 1926.
The shomakers holiday: or the gentle craft, with the humorous life of Simon Eyre, shoomaker and Lord Mayor of London, as it was acted before the Queenes most excellent Majestie on New-Yeares Day at night last by the Right Honourable the Earle of Notingham, Lord High Admirall of England his servants. 1600 (anon), 1610, 1618, 1624, 1631, 1657; ed J. R. Sutherland, Oxford 1928; ed C. F. T. Brooke and N. B. Paradise, English drama, 1933; ed H. Spencer, Elizabethan plays, 1933; ed C. R. Baskervill, Elizabethan and Stuart plays, 1934; ed A. K. McIlwraith, Five Elizabethan comedies, Oxford 1934 (WC); ed J. B. Steane, Cambridge 1965; ed P. C. Davies 1968.
Satiro-mastix: or the untrussing of the humorous poet, as it hath bin presented publikely by the Right Honorable the Lord Chamberlaine his servants, and privately by the children of Paules. 1602; ed T. Hawkins, Origin of the English drama vol 3, 1773; ed H. Scherer, Bang vol 20, 1907; ed J. H. Penniman, Boston 1913.
Patient Grissil. 1603. With Chettle and Houghton; see under Chettle, col 191, above.
The wonderfull yeare: wherein is shewed the picture of London lying sicke of the plague. 1603 (anon); 2 further edns before 1607; ed J. Morgan, Phoenix britannicus, 1731; ed G. B. Harrison 1924; ed F. P. Wilson, The plague pamphlets of Dekker, Oxford 1925; ed G. R. Hibbard, Three Elizabethan pamphlets, 1952.
Newes from Graves-end, sent to Nobody. 1604 (anon); ed F. P. Wilson, The plague pamphlets of Dekker, Oxford 1925.
The meeting of gallants at an ordinarie: or the walkes in Powles. 1604 (anon); ed J. O. Halliwell (-Phillipps) 1841 (Percy Soc); ed F. P. Wilson, The plague pamphlets of Dekker, Oxford 1925.

The honest whore, with the humours of the patient man and the longing wife. 1604, 1604 (as The converted curtezan), 1605, 1615 (some copies dated 1616), 1635; ed R. Dodsley, A select collection of old plays vol 3, 1744; ed I. Reed, Dodsley vol 3, 1780; ed H. Spencer, Elizabethan plays 1933; ed C. R. Baskervill, Elizabethan and Stuart plays, 1934. With Middleton.
The magnificent entertainment given to King James, Queene Anne his wife, and Henry Frederick the Prince upon the day of his Majesties tryumphant passage from the Tower through his honourable citie and chamber of London, being the 15 of March 1603, as well by the English as by the strangers, with the speeches and songes delivered in the severall pageants. 1604, 1604, Edinburgh 1604; ed R. Edwards, A collection of tracts from the Somers-collections, 1795; rptd in Somers tracts vol 3, 1810; ed J. Nichols, Progresses of James I vol 1, 1828.
The double pp: a Papist in armes, bearing ten severall sheilds, encountred by the Protestant at ten severall weapons, a Jesuite marching before them. 1606. Anon.
Newes from Hell, brought by the Divells carrier. 1606, 1607 (rev as A knights conjuring: done in earnest, discovered in jest); ed E. F. Rimbault 1842 (Percy Soc) (1607 text).
The seven deadly sinnes of London, drawne in seven severall coaches through the seven severall gates of the citie, bringing the plague with them. 1606; ed J. P. Collier, Illustrations of old English literature vol 2, 1866; ed E. Arber 1879; Cambridge 1905; ed H. F. B. Brett-Smith, Oxford 1922.
Jests to make you merie, with the conjuring up of Cock Watt, the walking spirit of Newgate, to tell tales, unto which is added the miserie of a prison and a prisoner, and a paradox in praise of serjeants; written by T.D. and George Wilkins. 1607.
North-ward hoe, sundry times acted by the children of Paules, by Thomas Decker and John Webster. 1607; ed A. Dyce, Webster's Works, 1830, 1859 (rev); ed W. Hazlitt, Webster's Dramatic works, 1857; TFT 1914.
The famous history of Sir Thomas Wyat, with the coronation of Queen Mary, and the coming in of King Philip, as it was plaied by the Queens Majesties servants, written by Thomas Dickers and John Webster. 1607, 1612; ed A. Dyce, Webster's Works, 1830, 1859 (rev); ed W. Hazlitt, Webster's Dramatic works, 1857; ed W. J. Blew, Two old plays by Dekker and Heywood, 1876; TFT 1914.
West-ward hoe, as it hath beene divers times acted by the children of Paules, written by Tho. Decker and John Webster. 1607; ed A. Dyce, Webster's Works, 1830, 1859 (rev); ed W. Hazlitt, Webster's Dramatic works, 1857; TFT 1914.
The whore of Babylon, as it was acted by the Princes servants. 1607.
The dead tearme, or Westminsters complaint for long vacations and short termes, written in manner of a dialogue betweene the two cityes London and Westminster. 1608.
The belman of London, bringing to light the most notorious villanies that are now practised in the kingdome. 1608 (4 edns with slight changes) (anon), 1616, 1640; ed O. Smeaton 1904. Mainly a cento compiled from pamphlets on beggars and coney-catchers by Awdely, Harman, Greene and Rowlands.
Lanthorne and candle-light: or the bellmans second nights walke, in which hee brings to light a broode of more strange villanies then ever were till this yeare discovered. 1608, 1609 ('the second edition, newly corrected and amended'); 1612 (with many addns and some omissions as O per se o, or a new cryer of lanthorne and candle-light, being an addition or lengthening of the bell-mans second night-walke), 1616 (with new chs on prisons as Villanies discovered by lanthorne and candle-light, and the helpe of a new cryer called O per se o), 1620 (with

slight addns), 1632 (with addns and omissions as English villanies six severall times prest to death by the printers), 1638 (as English Villanies seven severall times prest to death by the printers), 1648 (as English villanies eight severall times prest to death by the printers); ed O. Smeaton 1904.

Foure birds of Noahs arke: viz 1, the dove; 2, the eagle; 3, the pellican; 4, the phoenix. 1609; ed F. P. Wilson, Stratford 1924.

The guls horne-book. 1609; ed J. Nott, Bristol 1812; ed J. O. Halliwell(-Phillipps) 1862; ed C. Hindley 1872; ed G. Saintsbury 1892; ed R. B. McKerrow 1904; ed O. Smeaton 1904; Menston 1969 (facs). A satire on the Jacobean gallant. The early chs are indebted to Frederick Dedekind, Grobianus, 1549, tr R.F. as The schoole of slovenrie: or Cato turnd wrong side outward, 1605.

The ravens almanacke foretelling of a plague, famine and civill warre that shall happen this present yeare. 1609.

Worke for armorours, or the peace is broken: open warres likely to happin this yeare. 1609.

The roaring girl. 1611. With Middleton; see col 227, above.

If this be not a good play the Divel is in it: a new play as it hath bin lately acted by the Queenes Majesties servants at the Red Bull. 1612 (as If it be not good the Divel is in it).

Troia-nova triumphans, London triumphing: or the solemne, magnificent and memorable receiving of that worthy gentleman, Sir John Swinerton knight, into the citty of London after his returne from taking the oath of mayoralty at Westminster on the morrow next after Simon and Judes day. 1612; ed F. W. Fairhold, Lord Mayors' pageants vol 2, 1844; rptd R. T. D. Sayle, Lord Mayors' pageants of the Merchant Taylors, 1931.

A strange horse-race, at the end of which comes in the catch-poles masque, and after that the bankrouts banquet, which done, the Divell, falling sicke, makes his last will and testament this present yeare. 1613.

The artillery garden: a poem dedicated to the honour of all those gentlemen who there practize military discipline. 1616; ed F. P. Wilson, Oxford 1952.

Dekker his dreame, in which, beeing rapt with a poeticall enthusiasme, the great volumes of Heaven and Hell to him were opened, in which he read many wonderfull things. 1620; ed J. O. Halliwell (-Phillipps) 1860.

The virgin martir. 1622. With Massinger; see col 243, below.

A rod for run-awayes, Gods tokens of his fearefull judgements, sundry wayes pronounced upon this city and on severall persons, both flying from it and staying in it. 1625, 1625 (with addns and omissions); ed F. P. Wilson, The plague pamphlets of Dekker, Oxford 1925.

Brittania's honor, brightly shining in severall magnificent shewes or pageants to celebrate the solemnity of the Right Honorable Richard Deane at his inauguration into the mayoralty of the honourable citty of London. 1628.

Warres, warres, warres. 1628. A verse pamphlet in praise of war and of the officers of the Artillery Garden.

Londons tempe: or the feild of happines, in which feild are planted severall trees of magnificence, state and bewty to celebrate the solemnity of the Right Honorable James Campbell at his inauguration into the honorable office of praetorship or mayoralty of London. [1629]; ed F. W. Fairholt, Lord Mayors' pageants vol 10, 1843.

London looke backe at that yeare of yeares 1625, and looke forward upon this yeare 1630; written not to terrifie, but to comfort. 1630 (anon); ed F. P. Wilson, The plague pamphlets of Dekker, Oxford 1925.

The blacke rod and the white rod, justice and mercie, striking and sparing London. 1630; ed F. P. Wilson, ibid.

The second part of the honest whore, with the humors of the patient man, the impatient wife, the honest whore perswaded by strong arguments to turne curtizan againe,

her brave refuting those arguments, and lastly the comicall passages of an Italian Bridewell, where the scaene ends. 1630; ed R. Dodsley, A select collection of old plays vol 3, 1744; ed I. Reed, Dodsley vol 3, 1780; ed H. Spencer, Elizabethan plays, 1933.

A tragi-comedy called Match mee in London, as it hath beene often presented, first at the Bull in St Johns-street, and lately at the private-house in Drury-Lane called the Phoenix. 1631.

Penny-wise pound-foolish: or a Bristow diamond set in two rings and both crack'd. 1631 (anon); ed W. Bang, Bang vol 23, 1908. A version with English and Italian settings of the old story A pennyworth of wit.

The noble Spanish souldier, or a contract broken, justly reveng'd: a tragedy. 1634 (as The noble souldier, attributed to S. Rowley); ed A. H. Bullen, A collection of old English plays vol 1, 1882; TFT 1913.

The wonder of a kingdome. 1636; ed C. W. Dilke, Old English plays vol 3, 1814.

The sun's darling, a moral masque, as it hath been often presented at Whitehall by their Majesties servants, and after at the Cock-pit in Drury Lane, with great applause, written by John Ford and Tho. Decker gent. 1656.

Lust's dominion: or the lascivious Queen. 1657; ed C. W. Dilke, Old English plays vol 1, 1914; ed W. Oxberry, Old English drama, 1818, rptd in Dramatic works of Marlowe, 1827; ed G. Robinson, Works of Marlow vol 3, 1826; ed W. C. Hazlitt, Dodsley vol 14, 1875; ed J. Le G. Brereton, Louvain 1931.

The witch of Edmonton: a known true story composed into a tragi-comedy by divers well-esteemed poets: William Rowley, Thomas Dekker, John Ford etc, acted by the Princes servants often at the Cock-Pit in Drury-lane, once at Court. 1658; ed C. R. Baskervill, Elizabethan and Stuart plays, 1934.

The Welsh embassador. Ms Cardiff Public Lib; ed H. Littledale and W. W. Greg 1920 (Malone Soc).

19 verse passages attributed to Dekker are ptd in England's Parnassus, *1600. Dekker also wrote dedicatory verses to* Anthony Munday *in* The third and last part of Palmerin of England, *1602, and in* A true and admirable historie of a mayden of consolens, *1603; to* Stephen Harrison *in* The archs of triumph erected in honor of the high and mighty Prince James, *1604; to* John Taylor the Water Poet *in* Taylors Urania: or his heavenly Muse, *1615; to* Richard Brome *in* The northerne lasse: a comoedie, *1632. The songs in the 1632 edn of Lyly's plays have been assigned to Dekker.*

THOMAS HEYWOOD
1574?–1641

Bibliographies

Clark, A. M. A bibliography of Thomas Heywood. Proc Oxford Bibl Soc 1 1925.

Collections

Dramatic works. Ed J. P. Collier and B. Field 2 vols 1841–51 (Shakespeare Soc).

Dramatic works. Ed R. H. Shepherd 6 vols 1874.

Thomas Heywood. Ed A. W. Verity 1888 (Mermaid ser).

§ 1

Oenone and Paris. 1594; ed J. Q. Adams, Washington 1943; ed E. S. Donno, Elizabethan minor epics, New York 1963.

The first and second partes of King Edward the Fourth: containing his mery pastime with the Tanner of Tamwoorth, as also his love to fayre Mistresse Shoare, as it hath divers times been publiquely played by the Right Honorable the Earle of Derby his servants. 1599 (anon), 1600, 1605, 1613, 1619, 1626; ed S. de Ricci 1922 (facs).

A pleasant conceited comedie wherein is shewed how a man may chuse a good wife from a bad, as it hath bene sundry times acted by the Earle of Worcesters servants. 1602 (anon), 1605, 1608, 1614, 1621, 1630, 1634; ed C. Baldwin, Old English drama vol 1, 1825; ed W. C. Hazlitt, Dodsley vol 9, 1875; ed A. E. H. Swaen, Bang vol 35, 1912; TFT 1912.

If you know not me, you know no bodie: or the troubles of Queen Elizabeth. 1605 (anon), 1606, 1608, 1610, 1613, 1623, 1632, 1639; ed W. J. Blew, Two old plays by Dekker and Heywood, 1876; ed M. Doran 1935 (Malone Soc).

The second part of If you know not me, you know no bodie, with the building of the Royall Exchange, and the famous victorie of Queene Elizabeth in the yeare 1588. 1606 (anon), 1609 (as The second part of Queene Elizabeths troubles, Doctor Paries treasons, with the humors of Hobson and Tawney-cote), 1623, 1633; ed M. Doran 1935 (Malone Soc).

A woman kilde with kindnesse. 1607, 1617 ('The third edition, as it hath beene often times acted by the Queenes Majest. servants') (no 2nd edn known); ed R. Dodsley, A select collection of old plays vol 4, 1744; ed I. Reed, Dodsley vol 7, 1780; ed R. Van Fossen 1961 (Revelsser).

The rape of Lucrece: a true Roman tragedie, with the severall songes in their apt places by Valerius, the merrie lord amongst the Roman peeres, acted by her Majesties servants at the Red Bull neere Clarkenwell. 1608, 1609, 1614, 1630, 1638 ('revised, and sundry songs before omitted, now inserted in their right places'); ed C. Baldwin, Old English drama vol 1, 1825; ed A. Holaday, Urbana 1950.

The two most worthy and notable histories which remaine unmained to posterity, viz, the conspiracie of Cateline undertaken against the government of the senate of Rome, and the warre which Jugurth for many yeares maintained against the same state, both written by C. C. Salustius. 1608 (anon); ed C. Whibley 1924 (Tudor trns).

Troia britanica, or Great Britaines Troy. 1609. Extracts in The passionate pilgrim, 1612, and Poems written by Wil. Shakespeare gent, 1640.

The golden age, or the lives of Jupiter and Saturne, with the defining of the heathen gods, as it hath beene sundry times acted at the Red Bull by the Queenes Majesties servants. 1611 (certain copies read 'deifying' for 'defining' in the title).

An apology for actors, containing three briefe treatises: 1, their antiquity; 2, their ancient dignity; 3, the true use of their quality. 1612, [1658] (as The actors vindication); rptd Somers tracts vol 1, 1750; ed W. Scott, Somers tracts vol 3, 1810; ed J. P. Collier, Shakespeare Soc 1841; ed E. K. Chambers (condensed in Elizabethan stage vol 4, 1923).

The brazen age, the first act containing the death of the centaure Nessus, the second the tragedy of Meleager, the third the tragedy of Jason and Medea, the fourth Vulcans net, the fifth the labours and death of Hercules. 1613.

A funerall elegie upon the death of Henry Prince of Wales. 1613 (ptd in Three elegies on the most lamented death of Prince Henrie).

A marriage triumphe in memorie of the happie nuptials betwixt the high and mightie Prince Count Palatine and the most excellent Princesse the Lady Elizabeth. 1613; ed J. P. Collier, Percy Soc 1842; ed E. M. Goldsmid, Aungervyle Soc 1884.

The silver age, including the love of Jupiter to Alcmena, the birth of Hercules, and the rape of Proserpine, concluding with the arraignement of the moone. 1613. BM ms Egerton 1994, ff. 74a–95a includes Calisto or The escapes of Jupiter, made up of scenes from The golden and silver ages.

The foure prentises of London, with the conquest of Jerusalem, as it hath bene diverse times acted at the

Red Bull by the Queenes Majesties servants. 1615, 1632; ed I. Reed, Dodsley vol 6, 1780; Ancient British drama vol 3, 1810; ed J. P. Collier, Dodsley vol 6, 1825.

Γυναικεῖον: or nine bookes of various history concerning women, inscribed by the names of the nine Muses. 1624, 1657 (as The generall historie of women).

Publii Ovidii Nasonis de arte amandi: or the art of love. nd. Other edns under various titles nd (2 edns), 1650, 1662?, 1667, 1672, 1677, 1682, 1705.

A funeral elegie upon King James. 1625.

Englands Elizabeth: her life and troubles during her minoritie from the cradle to the crowne. 1631, Cambridge 1632, 1641; rptd Harleian miscellany vol 10, 1808.

The fair maid of the west: or a girle worth gold, the first part as it was lately acted before the King and Queen by the Queens Majesties comedians, written by T. H. 1631; ed K. L. Bates, Boston 1917; ed R. K. Turner 1967 (Regents ser).

The fair maid of the west: the second part. 1631; ed R. K. Turner 1967 (Regents ser).

Londons jus honorarium, exprest in sundry triumphs, pagiants and shews at the initiation or entrance of the Right Honourable George Whitmore into the mayoralty. 1631.

The iron age: contayning the rape of Hellen, the siege of Troy, the combate betwixt Hector and Ajax, Hector and Troilus slayne by Achilles, Achilles slaine by Paris, Ajax and Ulisses contend for the armour of Achilles, the death of Ajax etc. 1632.

The second part of the iron age: which contayneth the death of Penthesilea, Paris, Priam and Hecuba; the burning of Troy; the deaths of Agamemnon, Menelaus, Clitemnestra, Hellena, Orestes, Egistus, Pillades, King Diomen, Pyrhus, Cethus, Synon, Thersites etc. 1632.

Londini artium & scicentiarum scaturigo: or Londons fountaine of arts and sciences, exprest at the initiation of the Right Honorable Nicholas Raynton into the mayorty. 1632; ed A. M. Clark, Theatre miscellany, Oxford 1953 (Luttrell Soc).

The English traveller, as it hath beene publikely acted at the Cock-pit in Drury-lane by her Majesties servants. 1633; ed C. W. Dilke, Old English plays vol 6, 1815.

Londini emporia: or Londons mercatura at the inauguration of the Right Honorable Ralph Freeman into the mayorty. 1633; ed A. M. Clark, Theatre miscellany, Oxford 1953 (Luttrell Soc).

The late Lancashire witches: a well received comedy lately acted at the Globe on the Banke-side by the Kings Majesties actors, written by Thom. Heywood and Richard Brome. 1634; rptd L. Tieck, Shakespeares Vorschule vol 1, 1823; ed J. O. Halliwell (-Phillipps) 1853.

A pleasant comedy called A mayden-head well lost, as it hath beene publickly acted at the Cocke-pit in Drury-Lane by her Majesties servants. 1634; rptd C. Baldwin, Old English drama vol 2, 1824.

The hierarchie of the blessed angells. 1635.

Londini sinus salutis: or Londons harbour of health and happinesse at the initiation of the Right Honourable Christopher Clethrowe into the mayoralty. 1635.

Philocothonista: or the drunkard opened, dissected and anatomized. 1635.

The wonder of this age: or the picture of a man living who is one hundred and fifty two yeeres old and upward, this 12th day of November. 1635. Anon.

A challenge for beautie, as it hath beene sundry times acted by the Kings Majesties servants at the Blackefriers, and at the Globe on the Banke-side. 1636; ed C. W. Dilke, Old English plays vol 6, 1815.

Loves maistresse: or the Queens masque, as it was three times presented before their two excellent Majesties within the space of eight dayes in the presence of sundry forraigne ambassadors; publikely acted by the Queens comoedians at the Phoenix in Drury-lane. 1636, 1640, 1640 (for 1661?); ed H. M. Blake 1910.

The new-yeeres gift presented at Court from the Lady Parvula to the Lord Minimus (commonly called Little

Jefferie) her Majesties servant, with a letter written by Microphilus. 1636 (signed T.H.), 1638.

The three wonders of this age. 1636.

A true discourse of the two infamous upstart prophets, Richard Farnham Weaver of White-Chappell, and John Bull Weaver of Saint Butolphs Algate, now prisoners, as also of Margaret Tennis now prisoner, written by T.H. 1636.

A curtaine lecture as it is read by a countrey farmers wife to her good man, by a countrey gentlewoman or lady to her esquire or knight, by a souldiers wife to her captain or lieutenant, by a citizens or tradesmans wife to her husband, by a Court lady to her Lord, concluding with an imitable lecture read by a queene to her soveraigne Lord and King. 1637. Signed T.H.

Londini speculum: or Londons mirror at the initiation of the Right Honorable Richand Fenn into the mayrolty. 1637.

The phoenix of these late times: or the life of Mr Henry Welby esq. 1637, 1637.

Pleasant dialogues and dramma's, selected out of Lucian, Erasmus, Textor, Ovid etc. 1637; ed W. Bang, Bang vol 3, 1903. R. H. Shepherd includes most of Pleasant dialogues and dramas in Dramatic works vol 6, 1874.

The royall King and the loyall subject, as it hath beene acted by the Queenes Majesties servants. 1637; ed C. W. Dilke, Old English plays vol 6, 1815; ed K. W. Tibbals, Philadelphia 1906.

A true description of his Majesties royall ship built this yeare 1637 at Wooll-witch in Kent. 1637, 1638 (with addns). An extract rptd in The common-wealths great ship commonly called the Soveraigne of the Seas, 1653.

Porta pietatis: or the port or harbour of piety at the initiation of the Right Honourable Sir Maurice Abbot knight into the mayoralty. 1638; ed F. W. Fairholt, Lord mayors' pageants, 1843–4 (Percy Soc).

The wise-woman of Hogsdon: a comedie. 1638.

The life and death of Queene Elizabeth, written in heroicall verse. 1639. Anon.

Londini status pacatus: or Londons peacable estate at the innitiation of the Right Honourable Henry Garway into the mayoralty. 1639.

A true relation of the lives and deaths of the two most famous English pyrats, Purser and Clinton, who lived in the reigne of Queene Elizabeth. 1639. Anon.

The exemplary lives and memorable acts of nine the most worthy women of the world: three Jewes, three Gentiles, three Christians; written by the author of the history of women. 1640.

The black box of Roome opened, from whence are revealed the damnable bloody plots, practises and behaviour of Jesuites, priests, papists and other recusants in generall. 1641. Anon.

Brightmans predictions and prophecies. 1641. Anon.

A dialogue or accidental discourse betwixt Mr Alderman Abell and Richard Kilvert, the two maine projectors for wine, and also Alderman Abels wife etc. 1641. Anon.

The life of Merlin, sirnamed Ambrosius, his prophesies and predictions interpreted; being a chronographicall history of all the kings from Brute to the reigne of our royall soveraigne King Charles. 1641, 1651 (as Merlins prophesie and predictions interpreted). An extract rptd in Seven severall strange prophesies, 1642; Nine notable prophesies, 1644; and Twelve strange prophesies, nd.

Machiavels ghost, as he lately appeared to his deare sons, the moderne projectors. 1641 (anon), 1641 (as Machiavel, as he lately appeared). An extract rptd in Hogs caracter of a projector, 1642 etc.

A new plot discovered, practised by an assembly of Papists for the deliverance of William Waller, alias Walker, alias Ward, alias Slater, a Jesuite which was hang'd, drawn and quartered, revealed by John Hodgskins a porter, by a letter. 1641. Anon.

The rat-trap: or the Jesuites taken in their owne net etc. 1641. Anon.

Reader, here you'l plainly see judgement perverted by these three: a priest, a judge, a patentee. 1641.

A revelation of Mr Brightmans revelation, in a dialogue betweene a minister of the gospell, and a citizen of London, whereby it is manifest that Mr Brightman was a true prophet. 1641. Anon.

Fortune by land and sea: a tragi-comedy, as it was acted by the Queens servants, written by Tho. Haywood and William Rowly. 1655; ed J. E. Walker, Boston 1899.

The famo[us] and remarkable hist[ory of] Sir Richard Whittingto[n, three] times Lord Mayor of Lon[don], written by T.H. 1656, 1678, [1680?].

The captives: or the lost recovered. BM ms Egerton 1994, ff. 52ª–73ª; ed A. H. Bullen, Old English plays vol 4, 1885; ed A. C. Judson, New Haven 1921; ed A. Brown 1953 (Malone Soc).

JOHN MARSTON
1576–1634

Collections

The workes of Mr John Marston: being tragedies and comedies collected into one volume. Ed W. Sheares 1633, 1633 (as Tragedies and comedies).

Plays. Ed H. H. Wood 3 vols Edinburgh 1934–9.

Poems. Ed A. Davenport, Liverpool 1961.

§1

The metamorphosis of Pigmalions image and certaine satyres. 1598 (as by William Kinsayder); rptd J.C., Alcilia 1613, 1619, 1628; ed J. Bowle, Miscellaneous pieces of poesie, 1764; Waltham St Lawrence 1926; ed E. S. Donno, Elizabethan minor epics, New York 1963.

The scourge of villanie: three bookes of satyres. 1598 (as by William Kinsayder), 1599 (2 edns, with Satyra nova); ed J. Bowle, Miscellaneous pieces of poesie, 1764; ed G. B. Harrison 1925.

Jacke Drums entertainment: or the comedie of Pasquill and Katherine, as it hath bene sundry times plaide by the children of Powles. 1601, 1616, 1618; ed R. Simpson, The school of Shakespeare vol 2, 1878; TFT 1912.

Poems. In R. Chester, Love's martyr, 1601; ed A. B. Grosart 1878 (New Shakspere Soc); ed B. H. Newdigate, The phoenix and the turtle, Oxford 1937.

The history of Antonio and Mellida: the first part, as it hath beene sundry times acted by the children of Paules, written by J.M. 1602; ed W. W. Greg 1921 (Malone Soc); ed G. K. Hunter 1965 (Regents ser).

Antonios revenge: the second part, as it hath beene sundry times acted by the children of Paules, written by J.M. 1602; ed W. W. Greg 1921 (Malone Soc); ed G. K. Hunter 1965 (Regents ser).

The malcontent. 1604 (3 edns, the last 'with the additions played by the Kings Majesties servants, written by Jhon Webster'); ed R. Dodsley, A select collection of old plays vol 4, 1744; ed I. Reed, Dodsley vol 4, 1780; (Regents ser); ed B. Harris 1967 (New Mermaid ser); ed G. K. Hunter 1975 (Revels).

The Dutch courtezan, as it was playd in the Blacke-friars by the children of her Majesties revels. 1605; ed H. R. Walley and J. H. Wilson, Early 17th-century plays, 1930; ed M. L. Wine 1965 (Regents ser); ed P. Davison 1968.

Eastward hoe. 1605. With Chapman and Jonson; see under Chapman, col 224, above.

Parasitaster: or the fawne, as it hath bene divers times presented at the Black friars by the children of the Queenes Majesties revels. 1606 (2 edns, the 2nd 'corrected of many faults which by reason of the author's absence were let slip in the first edition'); ed C. W. Dilke, Old English plays vol 2, 1814; ed G. A. Smith 1965 (Regents ser).

The wonder of women: or the tragedie of Sophonisba, as it hath beene sundry times acted at the Blacke friars. 1606, 1606.

The argument of the spectacle presented to the sacred Majestys of Great Brittan and Denmark as they passed through London [31 July 1606]. BM Royal ms 18 A xxxi; ed A. Davenport, Poems of Marston, Liverpool 1961.

What you will. 1607; ed C. W. Dilke, Old English plays vol 2, 1814.

The honorable Lorde and Lady of Huntingdons entertainement of theire right noble mother Alice, Countesse Dowager of Darby the first night of her Honors arrivall att the house of Ashby [Aug 1607]; ed A. Davenport, Poems of Marston, Liverpool 1961.

Histrio-mastix: or the player whipt. 1610; ed R. Simpson, The school of Shakespeare vol 2, 1878; TFT 1912.

The insatiate Countesse: a tragedie, acted at Whitefryers. 1613, 1616, 1631 (2 issues, one as 'written by William Barksteed'). Probably a fragment by Marston written up by Barksted.

§2

Eliot, T. S. John Marston. TLS 26 July 1934 (anon); rptd in his Elizabethan essays, 1934.

Spencer, T. John Marston. Criterion 13 1934.

—— In his Death and Elizabethan tragedy, Cambridge Mass 1936.

Gibbons, B. Jacobean city comedy: a study of satiric plays by Jonson, Marston and Middleton. 1968.

CYRIL TOURNEUR
1575?–1626

Collections

Plays and poems. Ed J. C. Collins 2 vols 1878.

Webster and Tourneur. Ed J. A. Symonds 1888 (Mermaid ser).

Complete works. Ed A. Nicoll 1930.

Plays. Ed G. Parfitt, Cambridge 1978. 2 plays.

§1

The transformed metamorphosis. 1600.

The revengers tragaedie, as it hath beene sundry times acted by the Kings Majesties servants. 1607 (some copies dated 1608) (anon); ed R. Dodsley, A select collection of old plays vol 4, 1744; ed I. Reed, Dodsley vol 4, 1780; ed R. A. Foakes 1966 (Revels ser); ed L. J. Ross 1966 (Regents ser); ed B. Gibbons 1967 (New Mermaid ser).

A funerall poeme upon the death of Sir Francis Vere, knight. 1609. Anon.

The atheist's tragedie: or the honest man's revenge, as in divers places it hath often beene acted. 1611 (some copies dated 1612); ed I. Ribner 1964 (Revels ser).

A griefe on the death of Prince Henrie. In Three elegies on the most lamented death of Prince Henrie, 1613.

§2

Eliot, T. S. Cyril Tourneur. TLS 13 Nov 1930 (anon); rptd in his Selected essays, 1932, and in his Elizabethan essays, 1934.

Murray, P. B. The authorship of the Revenger's tragedy. PBSA 56 1962.

—— A study of Tourneur. Philadelphia 1964.

JOHN WEBSTER
c.1578?–c. 1634

Collections

Works. Ed A. Dyce 4 vols 1830, 1 vol 1857 (rev).

Webster and Tourneur. Ed J. A. Symonds 1888 (Mermaid ser).

Works. Ed F. L. Lucas 4 vols 1927.

Three plays. Ed D. C. Gunby 1972 (Penguin).

§1

North-ward hoe. 1607. With Dekker; see col 234, above.

The famous history of Sir Thomas Wyat. 1607. With Dekker; see col 234, above.

West-ward hoe. 1607. With Dekker; see col 234, above.

The White Divel: or the tragedy of Paulo Giordano Ursini, Duke of Brachiano, with the life and death of Vittoria Corombona the famous Venetian curtizan, acted by the Queenes Majesties servants. 1612, 1631, 1665, 1672; ed R. Dodsley, A select collection of old plays vol 3, 1744; ed I. Reed, Dodsley vol 6, 1780; ed J. R. Brown 1960 (Revels ser); ed E. Brennan 1966 (New Mermaid ser); ed J. R. Mulryne 1969 (Regents ser); ed C. Hart 1970.

A monumental columne erected to the living memory of the ever-glorious Henry, late Prince of Wales. In Three elegies on the most lamented death of Prince Henrie, 1613.

New characters (drawne to the life) of severall persons in several qualities. 1615. Anon. At end of 6th impression of Overbury's Characters.

The Devils law case: or when women goe to law the Devill is full of business, a new tragecomoedy, the true and perfect copie from the originall as it was approovedly well acted by her Majesties servants. 1623; ed F. Shirley 1972 (Regents ser); ed E. B. Brennan 1975 (New Mermaid).

The tragedy of the Dutchesse of Malfy, as it was presented privatly at the Blackfriers and publiquely at the Globe by the Kings Majesties servants: the perfect and exact coppy with diverse things printed that the length of the play would not beare in the presentment. 1623, 1640, [c. 1664] ('as it was acted by his late Majesties s[er]vants at Black fryers with great applause, thirty years since, and now acted by his Highnesse the Duke of York's servants'), 1678, 1708; ed J. R. Brown 1964 (Revels ser); Menston 1968 (facs).

Monuments of honor, celebrated in the honorable city of London at the sole munificent charge and expences of the right worthy and worshipfull fraternity of the eminent Merchant-Taylors at the confirmation of John Gore in the high office of his Majesties lieutenant over this his royall chamber. 1624; ed R. T. D. Sayle, Lord Mayors' pageants of the Merchant Taylors' Company in the 15th, 16th and 17th centuries, 1931.

Appius and Virginia: a tragedy. 1654, 1654, 1655, 1659, 1679; ed I. Reed, Dodsley vol 6, 1780; ed C. W. Dilke, Old English plays vol 5, 1815; ed A. H. Thorndike, New York 1912. With Heywood?

A cure for a cuckold: a pleasant comedy, as it hath been several times acted with great applause, written by John Webster and William Rowley. 1661, 1661, adapted S. Spring-Rice, Oxford 1885 (the main plot alone, as Love's graduate). With Heywood?

§2

Leech, C. Webster: a critical study. 1951.

Webster: a critical anthology. Ed G. K. and S. K. Hunter 1969 (Penguin).

Murray, P. B. A study of Webster. Hague 1970.

John Webster. Ed B. Morris 1970. 10 essays.
Berry, R. The art of Webster. Oxford 1972.

PHILIP MASSINGER
1583–1640
Collections

Plays. Ed W. Gifford 4 vols 1805 (adds Parliament of love), 1813 (rev; the standard edn).
Philip Massinger. Ed A. Symons 2 vols 1887–9 (Mermaid ser).
Plays and poems. Ed P. Edwards and C. Gibson 5 vols Oxford 1975.
Selected plays. Ed C. Gibson, Cambridge 1978. 4 plays.

§1

Sir John van Olden Barnavelt. 1619. With Fletcher; see col 247, below.
The virgin martir: a tragedie, as it hath bin divers times publickely acted by the servants of his Majesties revels, written by Phillip Messenger and Thomas Decker. 1622, 1622, 1631, 1651, 1661; ed J. S. Keltie, Works of the British dramatists, 1827; ed F. T. Bowers, Dekker's Dramatic works vol 3, Cambridge 1958.
The Duke of Millaine: a tragædie, as it hath beene often acted by his Majesties servants at the Blacke Friers. 1623, 1638; ed T. Dibdin, London theatre, 1816; ed T. W. Baldwin, Lancaster Pa 1918.
The bond-man: an antient storie, as it hath been often acted at the Cock-pit in Drury-lane by the most excellent Princesse the Lady Elizabeth her servants. 1624, 1638; Modern British drama vol 1, 1804; ed B. T. Spencer, Princeton 1932.
The Roman actor: a tragaedie, as it hath divers times beene acted at the private play-house in the Black-friers by the Kings Majesties servants. 1629; ed W. L. Sandidge, Princeton 1929; ed A. K. McIlwraith, Five Stuart tragedies, Oxford 1953 (WC).
The picture: a tragæcomedie, as it was often presented at the Globe and Blacke-friers play-houses by the Kings Majesties servants. 1630; ed R. Dodsley, A select collection of old plays vol 8, 1744.
The renegado: a tragæcomedie, as it hath beene often acted by the Queenes Majesties servants at the private play-house in Drurye-Lane. 1630.
The Emperour of the East: a tragæ-comœdie, the scæne Constantinople, as it hath bene divers times acted at the Black-friers and Globe play-houses by the Kings Majesties servants. 1632.
The fatall dowry: a tragedy, as it hath beene often acted at the private house in Blackefryers by his Majesties servants, written by P.M. and N.F. 1632; Modern British drama vol 1, 1804; ed C. L. Lockert, Lancaster Pa 1918; ed T. A. Dunn 1969. With Nathan Field.
The maid of honour, as it hath beene often presented at the Phoenix in Drurie-Lane by the Queenes Majesties servants. 1632; Cumberland's British theatre, 1829; ed E. A. W. Bryne 1927; ed C. R. Baskervill, Elizabethan and Stuart plays, 1934.
A new way to pay old debts: a comœdie, as it hath beene often acted at the Phoenix in Drury-Lane by the Queenes Majesties servants. 1633; ed R. Dodsley, A select collection of old plays vol 8, 1744; ed A. H. Cruickshank, Oxford 1926; ed C. F. T. Brooke and N. B. Paradise, English drama, 1933; ed H. Spencer, Elizabethan plays, 1933; ed C. R. Baskervill, Elizabethan and Stuart plays, 1934; ed M. St C. Byrne 1949; ed T. W. Craik 1964 (New Mermaid ser).
Sero, sed serio: to the Right Honourable my most singular good lord and patron Philip Earle of Pembrooke and Montgomerye, upon the deplorable and untimely death of his sonne Charles [1635]. Ms: BM P. 28,875,

Royal 18 A. xx, ff. 1ʳ–4ʳ; ed T. Coxeter, Massinger's Dramatic works, 1759 etc.
The great Duke of Florence: a comicall historie, as it hath beene often presented by her Majesties servants at the Phoenix in Drurie Lane. 1636; ed J. M. Stochholm, Baltimore 1933.
The unnaturall combat: a tragedie, the scaene Marsellis, as it was presented by the Kings Majesties servants at the Globe. 1639; ed R. Dodsley, A select collection of old plays vol 8, 1744; ed R. S. Telfer, Princeton 1932.
Three new plays, viz:
   The bashful lover: a tragi-comedy, as it hath been often acted at the private-house in Black-friers by his late Majesties servants. 1655.
   The guardian: a comical-history, as it hath been often acted at the private-house in Black-friars by his late Majesties servants. 1655; ed R. Dodsley, A select collection of old plays vol 8, 1744.
A very woman, or the Prince of Tarent: a tragi-comedy, as it hath been often acted at the private-house in Black-friars by his late Majesties servants. 1655. With Fletcher. Never printed before.
The old law. 1656. With Middleton and Rowley; see under Middleton, col 228, above.
The city-madam: a comedie, as it was acted at the private house in Black Friers. 1658 (some copies dated 1659); ed R. Dodsley, A select collection of old plays vol 8, 1744; ed R. Kirk, Princeton 1934; ed T. W. Craik 1964 (New Mermaid ser); ed C. Hoy 1964 (Regents ser).
To his sonne, upon his Minerva. Date uncertain; prefixed to James Smith, The innovation of Penelope and Ylysses in Wit restor'd in severall select poems, 1658. Rptd T. Coxeter, Massinger's Dramatic works, 1759 etc.
Believe as you list. BM ms Egerton 2828; ed T. C. Croker 1849 (Percy Soc); TFT 1907; ed C. J. Sisson 1927 (Malone Soc).
The parliament of love. Victoria and Albert Museum ms Dyce 39 (imperfect); ed K. M. Lea 1928 (Malone Soc).

Massinger has a share in the following plays in the Beaumont and Fletcher canon, col 245 f., below: Beggars' bush, Custom of the country, Double marriage, Elder brother, Fair maid of the inn, False one, Honest man's fortune, Knight of Malta, Little French lawyer, Lovers' progress, Love's cure, Prophetess, Queen of Corinth, Rollo Duke of Normandy or the bloody brother, Sea voyage, Spanish curate, Thierry and Theodoret.
Massinger contributed commendatory verses to J. Shirley, The gratefull servant, 1630; rptd in collections of Massinger and Shirley.

§2

Swinburne, A. C. Philip Massinger. Fortnightly Rev July 1889; rptd in his Contemporaries of Shakespeare, 1919.
Cruickshank, A. H. Philip Massinger. Oxford 1920.
—— Massinger and the Two noble kinsmen. Oxford 1922.
Eliot, T. S. In his Sacred wood, 1920; rptd in his Selected essays, 1932, and in his Elizabethan essays, 1934.
Garrod, H. W. In his Profession of poetry, Oxford 1929.

FRANCIS BEAUMONT
1585?–1616
and
JOHN FLETCHER
1579–1625
Collections

Comedies and tragedies written by Francis Beaumont and John Fletcher, gentlemen, never printed before, and now published by the authors originall copies. 1647. *34 plays all previously unptd.* Masque of the Inner

Temple and Gray's Inn *had been ptd c. 1613. Wild-goose chase was omitted because the copy had gone astray. When recovered, it was ptd separately in folio 1652.*

Fifty comedies and tragedies written by Francis Beaumont and John Fletcher, gent, published by the authors original copies, the songs to each play being added. 1679.

Beaumont and Fletcher. Ed A. Glover and A. R. Waller 10 vols Cambridge 1905–12.

The dramatic works in the Beaumont and Fletcher canon. Ed F. T. Bowers et al, Cambridge 1966–.

§ 1

Salmasis and 'Hermaphroditus. 1602 (anon); 1847 (Shakespeare Soc); ed E. S. Donno, Elizabethan minor epics, 1963; ed N. Alexander, Elizabethan narrative verse, 1968. By Beaumont.

The woman hater, as it hath beene lately acted by the children of Paules. 1607 (anon); 1648 ('as it hath beene acted by his Majesties servants, written by John Fletcher gent'), 1649 (as The woman hater, or the hungry courtier: a comedy written by Francis Beaumont and John Fletcher, gent).

The faithfull shepheardesse, by John Fletcher. [1609?]. 1629, 1634, 1656, 1665; ed F. W. Moorman 1896; ed W. A. Neilson, Chief Elizabethan dramatists, 1911; ed C. R. Baskervill, Elizabethan and Stuart plays, 1934.

The knight of the burning pestle. 1613 (anon), 1635 ('as it is now acted by her Majesties servants at the private house in Drury Lane, written by Francis Beaumont and John Fletcher'), 1635, [presumably ptd in the early 1650's]; ed J. Doebler 1967 (Regents ser); ed A. Gurr 1968.

The masque of the Inner Temple and Grayes Inne presented before his Majestie, the Queenes Majestie, the Prince, Count Palatine and the Lady Elizabeth their Highnesses in the Banqueting House at White-hall on Saturday the twentieth day of Februarie 1612 [i.e. 1613]. [1613]; in Beaumont's Poems, 1653; ed J. Nichols, Progresses of James I vol 2, 1828.

Cupids revenge, as it hath beene divers times acted by the children of her Majesties revels, by John Fletcher. 1615, 1630 ('written by Fran. Beaumont and Jo. Fletcher'), 1635.

The scornful ladie: a comedie, as it was acted by the children of her Majesties revels in the Blacke Fryers, written by Fra. Beaumont and Jo. Fletcher, gent. 1616, 1625, 1630, 1635, 1639, 1651, 1677, 1691, [1711?], 1717.

Certain elegies done by sundrie excellent wits (Fr. Beau., M. Dr., N.H.) with satyres and epigrames. 1618, 1843.

A King and no King, acted at the Globe by his Majesties servants, written by Francis Beaumont and John Fletcher. 1619, 1625, 1631, 1639, 1655, 1661, 1676, 1693; ed R. M. Alden, Boston 1910; ed H. R. Walley and J. H. Wilson, Early 17th-century plays, 1930; ed R. K. Turner 1963 (Regents ser).

The maides tragedy, as it hath beene divers times acted at the Blacke-friers by the Kings Majesties servants. 1619 (anon), 1622, 1630 ('written by Francis Beaumont and John Fletcher'), 1638, 1641, 1650 (for 1660?), 1661, 1686, 1704, 1717; ed A. H. Thorndike, Boston 1906; ed H. Norland 1968 (Regents ser); ed A. Gurr 1969.

Phylaster: or love lyes a bleeding, acted at the Globe by his Majesties servants, written by Francis Baymont and John Fletcher, gent. 1620, 1622, 1628, 1634, 1639, 1652, [c. 1661] (falsely dated 1652), [after 1661], 1687, 1717; ed F. S. Boas 1898; ed A. H. Thorndike, Boston 1906; ed A. Gurr 1969 (Revels ser).

The tragedy of Thierry King of France and his brother Theodoret, as it was diverse times acted at the Blacke-friers by the Kings Majesties servants. 1621 (anon), 1648 ('written by John Fletcher'), 1649 ('written by Francis Beamont and John Fletcher').

Henry VIII. In Shakespeare folio of 1623; for later edns *see under Shakespeare, col 215, above.*

The two noble kinsmen, presented at the Blackfriers by the Kings Majesties servants, written by the memorable worthies of their time, Mr John Fletcher and Mr William Shakespeare, gent. 1634; ed G. R. Proudfoot 1970 (Regents ser). Also included in collections of the Shakespeare Apocrypha, *col 216, above.*

The elder brother: a comedie, acted at the Blacke Friers by his Majesties servants, written by John Fletcher gent. 1637, 1637 (presumably ptd 1661), 1651 ('written by Francis Beaumont and John Fletcher'; some copies dated 1650), 1661, 1678; ed W. H. Draper 1916 ('with slight alterations and abridgement').

The bloody brother: a tragedy, by B.J.F. 1639, Oxford 1640 (as The tragoedy of Rollo Duke of Normandy, acted by his Majesties servants, written by John Fletcher, gent), 1686 (as Rollo, Duke of Normandy: or the bloody brother, by John Fletcher, gent), 1718 ('by Mr Francis Beaumont and Mr John Fletcher'); ed J. D. Jump, Liverpool 1948.

Monsieur Thomas: a comedy, acted at the private house in Blacke Fryers, the author John Fletcher, gent. 1639, [c. 1661] (as Fathers own son).

Wit with-out money: a comedie, as it hath beene presented at the private house in Drurie Lane by her Majesties servants, written by Francis Beaumont and John Fletcher, gent. 1639, 1661, [c. 1708] ('with alterations and amendments by some persons of quality'), 1718 (the unaltered play).

Poems, by Francis Beaumont. 1640 (containing Salmacis and Hermaphroditus, Remedie of love, Elegy to Lady Markham and other poems, some certainly not by Beaumont), 1653 (with addns), 1660 (as Poems: the golden remains of Frances Beaumont and John Fletcher).

The night-walker, or the little theife: a comedy, as it was presented by her Majesties servants at the private house in Drury Lane, written by John Fletcher, gent. 1640, 1661. Rev James Shirley.

Rule a wife and have a wife: a comoedy, acted by his Majesties servants, written by John Fletcher, gent. Oxford 1640, London 1697, 1717 etc; ed G. Saintsbury, Gayley vol 3, 1914.

The wild-goose chase: a comedie, as it hath been acted with singular applause at the Black-friers, being the noble, last, and onely remaines of those incomparable dramatists, Francis Beaumont and John Fletcher, gent. 1652; ed G. E. Bentley, The development of English drama, 1950.

The beggars bush, written by Francis Beaumont and John Fletcher, gentlemen. 1661, 1661, [1706?] (as The royal merchant, altered by H.N. [Henry Norris?]), 1717 (the unaltered play).

The island Princess, or the generous Portugal: a comedy, as it is acted at the Theatre Royal by his Majesties servants, with the alterations and new additional scenes. 1669 (altered anon), 1687 (altered by N. Tate), 1699 ('Made into an opera, as it is performed at the Theatre Royal, all the musical entertainments and the greatest part of the play new and written by Mr Motteux'), 1717 (the unaltered play); ed C. F. T. Brooke and N. B. Paradise, English drama 1933 (Fletcher's original play).

The chances: a comedy, as it was acted at the Theater Royal, corrected and altered by a person of honour [George Villiers, 2nd Duke of Buckingham]. 1682, 1692 (another edn of Buckingham's alteration), 1705 (altered by Buckingham), 1718 (the unaltered play), 1773 (altered by Garrick).

Valentinian: a tragedy, as 'tis alter'd by the late Earl of Rochester, and acted at the Theatre-Royal. 1685, 1717 (the unaltered play).

The prophetess: or the history of Diocleasian, written by Francis Beaumont and John Fletcher, with alterations and additions after the manner of an opera. 1690, 1690, 1719.

The humorous lieutenant, or generous enemies: a comedy, as it is now acted by his Majesties servants at the Theatre-Royal in Drury-Lane. 1697, 1717; ed M. Cook and F. P. Wilson 1951 (Malone Soc).

A wife for a month. 1697 (rev T. Scott as The unhappy kindness, or a fruitless revenge: a tragedy), 1717 (the unaltered play).

The pilgrim: a comedy, as it is acted at the Theatre-Royal in Drury-Lane, written originally by Mr Fletcher, and now very much alter'd, with several additions, likewise a prologue, epilogue, dialogue and masque written by the late great poet Mr Dryden just before his death. 1700 (2 issues; alterations by Vanbrugh), 1718 (the unaltered play).

The loyal subject: or the faithful general. 1706 (2 issues, one undated), 1706 (altered as The faithful general, written by a young lady [M.N.], 1717 (the unaltered play).

The custom of the country. 1717.

Bonduca. 1718; ed W. W. Greg 1951 (Malone Soc).

Love's cure: or the martial maid. 1718.

The maid in the mill. 1718.

The Spanish curate. 1718.

Wit at several weapons. 1718.

The tragedy of Sir John van Olden Barnavelt; ed A. H. Bullen, Old English plays vol 2, 1883; ed W. P. Frijlinck, Amsterdam 1922. By Fletcher and Massinger.

Verses by Frances Beaumont. TLS 15 Sept 1921.

The faire maide of the inne. Ed F. L. Lucas, Webster's Works vol 4, 1927.

Songs and lyrics from the plays of Beaumont and Fletcher with contemporary musical settings. Ed E. H. Fellowes 1928.

The honest mans fortune. Victoria and Albert Museum ms Dyce 9 (1625); ed J. Gerritsen, Groningen 1952.

The woman's prize: or the tamer tamed. Ed G. B. Ferguson, Hague 1966.

§ 2

Macaulay, G. C. Beaumont: a critical study. 1883.

Sprague, A. C. Beaumont and Fletcher on the Restoration stage. Cambridge Mass 1926.

Appleton, W. W. Beaumont and Fletcher: a critical study. 1956.

Beecham, T. John Fletcher. Oxford 1956 (Romanes lecture).

Edwards, P. The danger not the death: the art of Fletcher. In Jacobean theatre, ed J. R. Brown and B. Harris 1960.

Leech, C. The Fletcher plays. 1962.

WILLIAM ROWLEY
1585?–1626

The travailes of the three English brothers. 1607. With Day and Wilkins; see under Day, col 192, above.

A search for money: or the lamentable complaint for the losse of the wandring knight Mounsieur l'Argent, or come along with me, I know thou lovest money. 1609, 1840 (Percy Soc).

A faire quarrell. 1617. With Middleton; see col 227, above.

The world tost at tennis. 1620. With Middleton; see col 227, above.

A new wonder, a woman never vext: a pleasant conceited comedy, sundry times acted, never before printed. 1632; ed C. W. Dilke, Old English plays vol 5, 1815; ed W. C. Hazlitt, Dodsley vol 12, 1875.

A match at mid-night: a pleasant comœdie, as it hath been acted by the children of the revells, written by W.R. 1633; ed R. Dodsley, A select collection of old plays vol 6, 1744; ed I. Reed, Dodsley vol 7, 1780; Ancient British

drama vol 2, 1810; ed J. P. Collier, Dodsley vol 7, 1825; ed W. C. Hazlitt, Dodsley vol 13, 1875.

A tragedy called All's lost by lust, divers times acted by the Lady Elizabeths servants and now lately by her Majesties servants at the Phoenix in Drury Lane. 1633.

A merrie and pleasant comedy never before printed called A shoo-maker a gentleman, as it hath beene sundry times acted at the Red Bull and other theatres, by W.R. gentleman. 1637.

The maid in the mill. With Fletcher; see col 247, above.

The changeling. 1653. With Middleton: see col 228, above.

The Spanish gipsie. 1653. With Middleton; see col 228, above.

Fortune by land and sea. 1655. With Heywood; see col 240, above.

The old law. 1656. With Middleton and Massinger; see col 228, above.

The witch of Edmonton. 1658. With Dekker and Ford; see col 236, above.

A cure for a cuckold. 1653. With Webster; see col. 242, above.

The birth of Merlin: or the childe hath found his father. written by William Shakespeare and William Rowley, 1662; ed T. E. Jacob 1889; TFT 1910. Also included in collections of the Shakespeare Apocrypha; col 216, above.

Rowley has been suggested as partial author with Middleton of Wit at several weapons *in the Beaumont and Fletcher canon. Rowley wrote a series of verses on the death of Prince Henry included in John Taylor's* Great Britain all in black, *1612, and W. Drummond's* Mausoleum. or the choicest flowres of the epitaphs written on the death of Prince Henrie, *Edinburgh 1613. He wrote commendatory verses for John Taylor's* Nipping or snipping of abuses, *1614, and for Webster's* Duchess of Malfi, *1623.*

JOHN FORD
1586?–1639?

Collections

Dramatic works [with Fame's memorial]. Ed W. Gifford 2 vols 1827; rev A. Dyce 3 vols 1869, 1895.

John Ford. Ed H. Ellis 1888 (Mermaid ser).

Dramatic works. Ed W. Bang and H. de Vocht, Bang vol 23, 1908, new ser vol 1, 1927.

§ 1

Fames memoriall: or the Earle of Devonshire deceased, with his honourable life, peacefull end and solemne funerall. 1606; [ed S. E. Brydges], Lee Priory 1810.

Honor triumphant: or the peeres challenge by armes defensible at tilt, turney and barriers in honor of all faire ladies, and in defence of these four positions following: 1, Knights in ladies service have no freewill; 2, Beauty is the maintainer of valour; 3, Faire lady was never false; 4, Perfect lovers are onely wise, maintained by arguments; also the monarches meeting: or the King of Denmarkes welcome into England. 1606, 1843 (Shakespeare Soc).

A line of life, pointing at the immortalitie of a vertuous name. 1620, 1843 (Shakespeare Soc).

The lovers melancholy, acted at the private house in the Blacke Friers, and publikely at the Globe by the Kings Majesties servants. 1629.

The broken heart: a tragedy, acted by the Kings Majesties servants at the private house in the Black-friers, Fide Honor. 1633; ed B. Morris 1965 (New Mermaid ser); ed D. Anderson 1968 (Regents ser). Fide Honor is an anagram for John Forde.

Loves sacrifice: a tragedie acted by the Queenes Majesties servants at the Phoenix in Drury-lane. 1633.

Tis pitty shee's a whore, acted by the Queenes Majesties servants at the Phoenix in Drury-Lane. 1633; ed R. Dodsley, A select collection of old plays vol 5, 1744; ed I. Reed, Dodsley vol 8, 1780; ed N. W. Bawcutt 1966 (Regents ser); ed B. Morris 1969 (New Mermaid ser).

The chronicle historie of Perkin Warbeck: a strange truth, acted (some-times) by the Queenes Majesties servants at the Phoenix in Drurie lane, Fide Honor. 1634, 1714; ed D. Anderson 1965 (Regents ser); ed P. Ure 1968 (Revels ser).

The fancies chast and noble, presented by the Queenes Majesties servants at the Phoenix in Drury-lane, Fide Honor. 1638.

The ladies triall, acted by both their Majesties servants at the private house in Drury Lane, Fide Honor. 1639.

The Queen, or the excellency of her sex: an excellent old play found out by a person of honour, and given to the publisher Alexander Goughe. 1653 (anon); ed W. Bang, Bang vol 13 1906.

The sun's darling. 1656. With Dekker; see col 236, above.

The witch of Edmonton. 1658. With Dekker and W. Rowley; see col 236, above.

Ford wrote commendatory verses for Barnaby Barnes's Four books of elegies, 1606; Overbury's The wife, 1616; Henry Cockeram's English dictionary, 1623; Webster's Duchess of Malfi, 1623; Shirley's The wedding, 1629; Massinger's The Roman actor, 1629; Brome's The northern lass, 1632; Massinger's The great Duke of Florence, 1636; and Jonsonus virbius, 1638.

§2

Eliot, T. S. John Ford. TLS 5 May 1932 (anon); rptd in his Selected essays, 1932, and Elizabethan essays, 1934.

Oliver, H. J. The problem of Ford. 1955.

Leech, C. Ford and the drama of his time. 1957.

JAMES SHIRLEY
1596–1666

Collections

Dramatic works and poems. Ed W. Gifford and A. Dyce 6 vols 1833.

James Shirley. Ed E. Gosse 1888 (Mermaid ser).

§1

The wedding, as it was lately acted by her Majesties servants at the Phenix in Drury-Lane. 1629, 1633, 1660; ed A. S. Knowland, Six Caroline plays, Oxford 1962 (WC).

The gratefull servant: a comedie, as it was lately presented at the private house in Drury-Lane by her Majesties servants. 1630, 1637, [1662?].

The schoole of complement, as it was acted by her Majesties servants at the private house in Drury Lane, by J.S. 1631, 1637, 1667 (as Love tricks: or the school of complements, as it is now acted by his Royal Highnesse the Duke of York's servants at the theatre in Little Lincolns-Inne Fields).

Changes, or love in a maze: a comedie, as it was presented at the private house in Salisbury Court by the company of his Majesties revels. 1632.

A contention for honour and riches, by J.S. 1633.

The wittie faire one: a comedie, as it was presented at the private house in Drury Lane by her Majesties servants. 1633.

The bird in a cage: a comedie, as it hath beene presented at the Phoenix in Drury-Lane. 1633; ed R. Dodsley, A select collection of old plays vol 9, 1744; ed I. Reed, Dodsley vol 8, 1780; Ancient British drama vol 1, 1810.

The triumph of peace: a masque presented by the foure honourable houses or Innes of Court before the King and Queenes Majesties in the Banqueting-house at White Hall, February the third 1633 [i.e. 1634]. 1633 (3 edns, the 3rd re-issued with a new speech by Genius); ed H. A. Evans, English masques, 1897; ed C. Leech, A book of masques in honour of Allardyce Nicoll, Cambridge 1967.

The traytor: a tragedie, acted by her Majesties servants. 1635, 1692 ('with alterations, amendments and additions, as it is now acted at the Theatre Royal by their Majesties servants, written by Mr Rivers'); ed E. H. C. Oliphant, English dramatists other than Shakespeare, New York 1931; ed J. S. Carter 1965 (Regents ser).

Hide Parke: a comedie, as it was presented by her Majesties servants at the private house in Drury Lane. 1637.

The gamester, as it was presented by her Majesties servants at the private house in Drury-Lane. 1637; ed R. Dodsley, A select collection of old plays vol 9, 1744; ed I. Reed, Dodsley vol 9, 1780; Ancient British drama vol 2, 1810.

The young admirall, as it was presented by her Majesties servants at the private house in Drury Lane. 1637.

The example, as it was presented by her Majesties' servants at the private house in Drury-Lane. 1637.

The lady of pleasure: a comedie, as it was acted by her Majesties servants at the private house in Drury Lane. 1637; ed W. A. Neilson, Chief Elizabethan dramatists, 1911; ed H. Spencer, Elizabethan plays, 1933; ed A. S. Knowland, Six Caroline plays, Oxford 1962 (WC).

The Dukes mistris, as it was presented by her Majesties servants at the private house in Drury-Lane. 1638.

The royall master, as it was acted in the new theater in Dublin, and before the Right Honorable the Lord Deputie of Ireland in the Castle. 1638; ed A. W. Ward, Gayley vol 3, 1914.

The ball: a comedy, as it was presented by her Majesties servants at the private house in Drury Lane, written by George Chapman and James Shirly. 1639; rptd in collections of Chapman, above.

The maides revenge: a tragedy, as it hath beene acted at the private house in Drury Lane by her Majesties servants. 1639.

Loves crueltie: a tragedie, as it was presented by her Majesties servants at the private house in Drury Lane. 1640.

The opportunitie: a comedy, as it was presented by her Majesties servants at the private house in Drury Lane. 1640.

The coronation: a comedy, as it was presented by her Majesties servants at the private house in Drury Lane, written by John Fletcher, gent. 1640, 1679 (in 2nd Beaumont and Fletcher folio).

The constant maid: a comedy. 1640, 1661 (as Love will finde out the way: an excellent comedy, by T.B.), 1667 (as The constant maid: or love will finde out the way, a comedy by J. S.).

St Patrick for Ireland: the first part. 1640; ed W. R. Chetwood, A select collection of old plays, 1750. No 2nd pt is known.

The humorous courtier: a comedy, as it hath been presented at the private house in Drury-Lane. 1640.

A pastorall called the Arcadia, acted by her Majesties servants at the Phoenix in Drury Lane. 1640.

Poems. 1646 (1, Verses on various subjects; 2, Narcissus: or the self lover; 3, Several prologues and epilogues; 4, The triumph of beautie); ed R. L. Armstrong, New York 1941; Narcissus ed E. S. Donno, Elizabethan minor epics, 1963.

The triumph of beautie, as it was personated by some young gentlemen for whom it was intended at a private recreation. 1646. Appended to Poems.

Via ad latinam linguam complanata: the way made plain to the Latin tongue, the rules composed in English and Latine verse for the greater delight and benefit of learners. 1649, 1651 (as Grammatica anglo-latina).

Six new plays, viz:

The brothers: a comedie, as it was acted at the private house in Black Fryers. 1652.

The doubtful heir: a tragi-comedie, as it was acted at the private house in Black-friers. 1652.

The imposture: a tragi-comedie, as it was acted at the private house in Black Fryers. 1652.

The Cardinal: a tragedie, as it was acted at the private house in Black Fryers. 1652; ed C. R. Forker, Bloomington 1964.

The sisters: a comedie, as it was acted at the private house in Black Fryers. 1652.

The Court secret: a tragi-comedy, never acted but prepared for the scene at Black-friers. 1653.

All written by James Shirley. 1653.

Cupid and Death: a masque, as it was presented before his Excellencie the Embassadour of Portugal upon the 26 of March 1653, written by J.S. 1653, 1659 (as Cupid and Death, a private entertainment, represented with scenes and musick, vocall and instrumentall, written by J.S.) (2 issues); ed E. J. Dent, Musica britannica vol 2, 1951; ed B. A. Harris, A book of masques in honour of Allardyce Nicoll, Cambridge 1967.

The polititian: a tragedy, presented at Salisbury Court by her Majesties servants. 1655 (2 issues, one 8°, the other 4°).

The gentleman of Venice: a tragi-comedie, presented at the private house in Salisbury Court by her Majesties servants. 1655 (2 issues, one 8°, the other 4°).

The rudiments of grammar: the rules composed in English verse for the greater benefit and delight of young beginners. 1656, 1660 (enlarged as Manductio: or a leading of children by the hand through the principles of grammar).

Honoria and Mammon. [1658] (with the Contention of Ajax and Ulisses), nd, 1659. Honoria and Mammon is an altered and enlarged version of A contention for honour and riches.

The contention of Ajax and Ulysses for the armor of Achilles, as it was nobly represented by young gentlemen of quality at a private entertainment of some persons of honour. [1658] (with Honoria and Mammon), nd, 1659.

The true impartial history and wars of the kingdom of Ireland. 1693. Epistle to reader signed J.S.

X. MINOR JACOBEAN AND CAROLINE DRAMA
(1603–60)

ROBERT ARMIN
1565?–1610

Foole upon foole. 1599, 1605. Anon; enlarged below.

Quips upon questions. 1600, 1601, 1602; ed F. Ouvry 1875.

A nest of ninnies. 1608 (enlarged version of Foole upon foole, above), 1842 (Shakespeare Soc).

Phantasma the Italian tailor and his boy. 1609.

The history of the two maids of More-clacke, with the life and simple maner of John in the hospitall, played by the children of the Kings Majesties revels. 1609; ed A. B. Grosart, Works of Robert Armin, actor, Blackburn 1880; TFT 1913.

BARNABE BARNES
1570?–1609

Parthenophil and Parthenophe. 1593; ed A. B. Grosart, Occasional issues, 1875.

The Divils charter: a tragædie conteining the life and death of Pope Alexander the Sixt, as it was laide before the Kings Majestie upon Candlemasse night last by his Majesties servants. 1607, 1607; ed R. B. McKerrow, Bang vol 6, 1904; TFT 1913.

RICHARD BROME
1590?–1652 or 1653

Collections
Dramatic works. Ed R. H. Shepherd 3 vols 1873.

§ I

The northern lasse: a comoedie, as it hath beene often acted at the Globe and Black-fryers by his Majesties servants. 1632, 1663, 1684, 1706, 1717.

The late Lancashire witches. 1634. With Heywood; *see col 238, above.*

The sparagus garden: a comedie, acted in the yeare 1635 by the then company of revels at Salisbury Court. 1640.

The antipodes: a comedie, acted in the yeare 1638 by the Queenes Majesties servants at Salisbury Court in Fleetstreet. 1640; ed A. Haaker 1966 (Regents ser).

A joviall crew: or the merry beggars, presented in a comedie at the Cock-pit in Drury Lane in the yeer 1641. 1652, 1661, 1684; ed A. Haaker 1968 (Regents ser).

Five new plays, viz:

A mad couple well match'd. 1653; ed A. S. Knowland, Six Caroline plays, Oxford 1962 (WC).

The novella: a comedie, acted at the Black-friers by his Majesties servants, anno 1632. 1653.

The Court begger: a comedie, acted at the Cock-pit by his Majesties servants, anno 1632. 1653.

The city wit, or the woman wears the breeches: a comedy. 1653.

The damoiselle, or the new ordinary: a comedy. 1653.

By Richard Brome. 1653.

The Queenes exchange: a comedy, acted at the Black-friers by his Majesties servants. 1657, 1661 (as The royall exchange).

Five new plays, viz:

The English moor: or the mock-marriage, a comedy as it was often acted by her Majesties servants. 1658 (some copies dated 1659). Ms: Lichfield Cathedral Lib.

The love-sick Court, or the ambitious politique: a comedy. 1658.

The weeding of the Covent-Garden, or the Middlesex-Justice of Peace: a facetious comedy. 1658.

The new academy: or the new exchange. 1658.

The Queen and concubine: a comedie. 1659.

By Richard Brome. 1659.

MARGARET CAVENDISH, DUCHESS OF NEWCASTLE
1623–73

§ I

Playes written by the thrice noble, illustrious and excellent

Princess the Lady Marchioness of Newcastle. 1622. Contains the following plays, all unacted: Loves adventures (2 pts); Several wits: the wise wit, the wild wit, the cholerick wit, the humble wit; Youths glory and deaths banquet (2 pts); The lady contemplation (2 pts); Wits cabal (2 pts); The unnatural tragedie; The publick wooing; The matrimonial trouble (2 pts); Natures three daughters, beauty, love and wit (2 pts); The religious; The comical hash; Bell in campo (2 pts); The apocriphal ladies; The female academy.

Plays never before printed. 1668. Contains the following plays, all unacted: The social be companions, or the female wits; The presence; The bridals; The convent of pleasure; and fragments.

§ 2

Perry, H. T. E. The first Duchess of Newcastle and her husband as figures in literary history. Cambridge Mass 1921.

Grant, D. Margaret the First: a biography of Margaret Cavendish Duchess of Newcastle. 1957.

For the Duchess's non-dramatic works, see col 153, above.

WILLIAM CAVENDISH,
1st DUKE OF NEWCASTLE
1592-1676

The country captaine: a comoedye, lately presented by his Majesties servants at the Blackfryers. In The country captaine, and the Varietie: two comedies written by a person of honor, Hague 1649; ed A. H. Bullen and attributed to James Shirley as Captain Underwit, Old English plays vol 2, 1883.

The varietie: a comoedy, lately presented by his Majesties servants at the Black-friers. In Country captaine, and the Varietie, above.

Sir Martin Mar-all: or the feign'd innocence. 1668. With Dryden.

The humorous lovers: a comedy, acted by his Royal Highnes's servants. 1677.

A pleasant and merry humour of a rogue; ed F. Needham, Welbeck miscellany no 1, 1933.

The triumphant widow: or the medley of humours. 1677. An elaboration of A pleasant and merry humour of a rogue, above. With Shadwell.

For the Duke's non-dramatic works, see col 154, above.

SIR ASTON COKAYNE
1608-84

Collections

Small poems of divers sorts. 1658 (contains The obstinate lady, Trappolin and A masque), 1658 (as A chain of golden poems) (some copies dated 1659), 1662 (as Poems with the Tragedy of Ovid added), 1662, 1669 (as Choice poems of several sorts).

Dramatic works. Ed J. Maidment and W. H. Logan, Edinburgh 1874.

§ 1

The obstinate lady: a new comedy never formerly published; the scene London. 1657, 1658 (in Small poems), 1658 (in A chain of golden poems), 1662 (in Poems), 1662, 1669 (in Choice poems).

A masque presented at Bretbie in Darbyshire on twelfth-night 1639. 1658 (in Small poems), 1658 (in A chain of golden poems), 1662 (in Poems), 1662, 1669 (in Choice poems).

Trappolin creduto principe: or Trappolin suppos'd a Prince, an Italian trage-comedy, the scene part of Italy. 1658 (in Small poems), 1658 (in A chain of golden

poems), 1662 (in Poems), 1662, 1669 (in Choice poems).

The tragedy of Ovid. 1662 (in Poems), 1662, 1669 (in Choice poems).

SIR RICHARD FANSHAWE
1608-66

Il pastor fido, the faithful shepherd: a pastorall written in Italian by Baptista Guarini, and now newly translated. 1647 (anon), 1648 ('with an addition of divers other poems'), 1664, 1676, 1692, 1736; ed W. F. Staton and W. E. Simeone, Oxford 1964.

Selected parts of Horace, prince of lyricks, concluding with a piece out of Ausonius and another out of Virgil, now newly put into English. 1652.

The Lusiad: or Portugals historicall poem. 1655; ed J. D. M. Ford, Cambridge Mass 1940; ed G. Bullough 1963. Tr from Camoens.

La fida pastora [i.e. Fletcher's Faithful shepherdess]: comoedia pastoralis, autore F.F. Anglo-Britanno; adduntur nonnulla varii argumenti carmina ab eodem. 1658.

Querer por solo querer, To love only for love sake: a dramatick romance by Antonio de Mendoza, paraphrased in English anno 1654. 1670, 1671. BM additional ms 32,133.

Original letters of his Excellency Sir Richard Fanshawe during his embassies in Spain and Portugal. 2 vols 1702-24.

Memoirs of Lady Fanshawe, to which are added extracts from the correspondence of Fanshawe. Ed H. Nicholas 1829; ed B. Marshall 1905; ed E. J. Fanshawe 1907.

Historical Mss Commission. The mss of J. M. Heathcote of Conington Castle. Ed S. C. Lomas, Norwich 1899. Includes Fanshawe's correspondence.

The fourth book of Vergil's Aeneid. Ed A. L. Irvine, Oxford 1929.

Shorter poems and translations. Ed N. W. Bawcutt, Liverpool 1964.

NATHAN FIELD
1587-1619 or 1620

Collections

Plays. Ed W. Peery, Austin 1950.

§ 1

A woman is a weather-cocke: a new comedy, as it was acted before the King in White-hall, and divers times privately at the White-friers, by the children of her Majesties revels. 1612; ed A. W. Verity, Nero and other plays, 1888 (Mermaid ser).

Amends for ladies: a comedie, as it was acted at the Blacke-fryers, both by the Princes servants, and the Lady Elizabeths. 1618, 1618 (as Amends for ladies, with the humour of roring: a comedie), 1639 (Amends for ladies, with the merry prankes of Moll Cut-Purse, or the humour of roaring: a comedy full of honest mirth and wit); ed A. W. Verity, Nero and other plays, 1888 (Mermaid ser).

The fatall dowry: a tragedy, written by P.M. and N.F. 1632. With Massinger, *col 243, above.*

Four plays or moral representations in one. 1647. With Fletcher.

The honest man's fortune. 1647. With Fletcher and Massinger.

The knight of Malta. 1647. With Fletcher and Massinger.

The Queen of Corinth. 1647. With Fletcher and Massinger.

GEORGE GASCOIGNE
1542?-77

§ 1

Supposes. In A hundreth sundrie flowres, [1573] (performed at Gray's Inn 1566); 1575; Pleasantest works, 1587; Supposes and Jocasta, ed J. W. Cunliffe 1906, and Works, 2 vols Cambridge 1907-10; ed R. W. Bond, Early plays from the Italian, Oxford 1911; ed F. S. Boas, Five pre-Shakespearean comedies, Oxford 1934 (WC).

Jocasta. In A hundredth sundrie flowres, [1573] (performed at Gray's Inn 1566); 1575 (?), 1587; ed F. J. Child, Four old plays, Cambridge Mass 1848; ed J. W. Cunliffe, Supposes and Jocasta, 1906, and Early English classical tragedies, Oxford 1912. With Francis Kinwelmershe.

§ 2

Schelling, F. E. Life and writings of Gascoigne. Boston 1893.

Prouty, C. T. George Gascoigne. New York 1942.

THOMAS KILLIGREW
1612-83

The prisoners: a tragae-comedy, as it was presented at the Phoenix in Drury-Lane by her Majesties servants. 1640 (separate title-page in 12° edn of Prisoners and Claracilla; the joint title-page is dated 1641).

Claracilla: a tragae-comedy, as it was presented at the Phoenix in Drury-Lane by her Majesties servants. 1641 (separate title-page in 12° of 1641). Ms: Castle Howard lib.

Comedies and tragedies. 1644.

JAMES MABBE
1572-1642?

The Spanish bawd, represented in Celestina: or the tragicke-comedy of Calisto and Melibea. 1631, 1634 (with 3rd edn of Mabbe's trn of M. Aleman, The rogue: or the life of Guzman de Alfarache); ed J. Fitzmaurice-Kelly 1894; ed H. W. Allen 1908; 1923 (tr from de Rojas).

SHAKERLEY MARMION
1602-39

Collections

Dramatic works. Ed J. Maidment and W. H. Logan 1875.

§ 1

Hollands leaguer: an excellent comedy, as it hath bin lately and often acted by the high and mighty Prince Charles his servants at the private house in Salisbury Court. 1632.

A fine companion, acted before the King and Queene at White-Hall, and sundrie times at the private house in Salisbury Court by the Prince his servants. 1633.

A morall poem intituled the legend of Cupid and Psyche 1637, 1638, 1666; ed S. W. Singer 1820; ed A. J. Nearing, Philadelphia 1944.

The antiquary: a comedy, acted by her Majesties servants at the Cock-Pit. 1641; ed R. Dodsley, A select collection of old plays vol 7, 1744; ed I. Reed, Dodsley vol 10, 1780; Ancient British drama vol 3, 1810; ed J. P. Collier, Dodsley vol 10, 1826; ed W. C. Hazlitt, Dodsley vol 13, 1875.

THOMAS MAY
c. 1595-1650

The heire: an excellent comedie, as it was lately acted by the company of the revels. 1622, 1633; ed R. Dodsley, A select collection of old plays vol 7, 1744; ed I. Reed, Dodsley vol 8, 1780; ed W. C. Hazlitt, Dodsley vol 11, 1875.

The tragedy of Antigone, the Theban Princesse. 1631.

The tragedie of Cleopatra Queen of Ægypt. 1639, 1654 (singly and bound with Julia Agrippina as Two tragedies). Acted 1626.

The tragedie of Julia Agrippina, Empresse of Rome. 1639, 1654 (singly and bound with Cleopatra as Two tragedies); ed F. E. Schmid, Bang vol 43, 1914.

The old couple: a comedy. 1658; ed R. Dodsley, A select collection of old plays vol 7, 1744; ed I Reed, Dodsley vol 10, 1780; ed W. C. Hazlitt, Dodsley vol 12, 1875.

THOMAS NORTON
1532-84
and
THOMAS SACKVILLE
1536-1608

The tragedie of Gorboduc. 1565 (performed at Inner Temple 1561), [1570] (as Ferrex and Porrex), 1590; ed J. W. Cunliffe, Early English classical tragedies, Oxford 1912; ed J. Q. Adams, Chief pre-Shakespearean Dramas, [1924]; ed C. R. Baskervill, V. B. Heltzel and A. H. Nethercot, Elizabethan and Stuart plays, New York [1934]; A. K. McIlwraith, Five Shakespearean tragedies, Oxford 1938 (WC).

AURELIAN TOWNS(H)END
1583?-1643?

Albions triumph. 1631; Tempe restored, 1631. 2 masques with Inigo Jones, both ed E. K. Chambers, Oxford 1912. See col 157, above.

THOMAS RANDOLPH
1605-36

Collections

Poems with the Muses looking-glasse and Amyntas. 1638, 1640, 1664 (5th edn); rptd Dodsley; Ancient British drama vol 2.

Poetical and dramatic works. Ed W. C. Hazlitt 2 vols 1875.

§ 1

Aristippus: or the joviall philosopher. 1630 (3 edns), 1631, 1635? Added to 4th edn of Poems, above. Ms: BM Sloane 2531 (variants from ptd text).

The jealous lovers: a comedie. Cambridge 1632, 1634, 1640 (also in 1640 edn of Poems).

Hey for honesty, down with knavery, augmented and published by F.J. 1651. Adaptation of Aristophanes' Plutus.

The drinking academy. Ed H. E. Rollins, PMLA 39 1924; ed Rollins and S. A. Tannenbaum, Cambridge Mass 1930.

Cornelianum dolium: comoedia. 1638. Drafted by Randolph and completed by Richard Braithwait?

GEORGE WILKINS
fl. 1604–08

Three miseries of Barbary: plague, famine, civill warre. [1606?].

Jests to make you merie. 1607. With Dekker, *col 234, above*.

The miseries of inforst mariage, as it is now playd by his Majesties servants. 1607, 1611, 1629, 1637; ed I. Reed, Dodsley vol 5, 1780; Ancient British drama vol 2, 1810; ed J. P. Collier, Dodsley vol 5, 1825; ed W. C. Hazlitt, Dodsley vol 9, 1874; TFT 1913; ed G. H. Blayney 1964 (Malone Soc).

The travailes of the three English brothers. 1607. With Day and Rowley; *see Day, col 192, above*.

The painfull adventures of Pericles Prince of Tyre. 1608; ed T. Mommsen, Oldenburg 1857; ed K. Muir, Liverpool 1953.

ARTHUR WILSON
1595–1652

The inconstant lady: or better late than never [c. 1630]. Ed P. Bliss, Oxford 1814.

The Swisser [1631]. Ed A. Feuillerat, Paris 1904.

4. RELIGION

I. HUMANISTS AND REFORMERS

Linacre, Colet, More, Tindale, Gardiner, Latimer, Cheke, Coverdale, Cranmer,
Lupset, Fish, Elyot, Ridley, Parker, Caius, Ponet, Ascham, Wilson, Fulke

GENERAL STUDIES

Allen, P. S. The age of Erasmus. Oxford 1914.
Bush, D. Tudor humanism and Henry VIII. UTQ 7 1938.
— The Renaissance and English humanism. Toronto 1939.
Wright, L. B. The significance of religious writings in the English Renaissance. JHI 1 1940.
Southern, A. C. Elizabethan recusant prose 1559–82. 1950.

Porter, H. C. Reformation and reaction in Tudor Cambridge. Cambridge 1958.
Blench, J. W. Preaching in England in the late fifteenth and sixteenth centuries 1450–c. 1600. Oxford 1964.
McConica, J. K. English humanists and Reformation politics. Oxford 1965.

THOMAS LINACRE
1460?–1524

§ 1

Linacri progymnasmata. [1510?]. A Latin grammar written for Colet's school but not adopted. First surviving edn 1519?
De emendata structura latini sermonis libri sex. 1524, Paris 1527, Basle 1530, Paris 1532 (2nd edn), 1540; ed P. Melanchthon 1543; Lyons 1539, 1544, 1548, Paris 1550, Venice 1557, Lyons 1559, Menston 1968 (facs of 1524).
Rudimenta grammatices diligenter castigata denuo. [1523?], [1525], Menston 1971 (facs of 1525); tr G. Buchanan, Paris 1533, Lyons 1539, Paris 1540, 1545, Lyons 1548, Paris 1550, Lyons 1552, Paris 1556.

§ 2

Johnson, J. N. The life of Linacre. Ed R. Graves 2 vols 1835.
Osler, W. Thomas Linacre. Cambridge 1908.
O'Malley, C. D. English medical humanists: Linacre and Caius. Lawrence Kansas 1965.

JOHN COLET
1467?–1519

§ 1

Oratio habita ad clerum in convocatione anno 1511. [1511–12]; tr Thomas Lupset? [1530?], [1531?]; ed J. H. Lupton, Life of Colet, 1887.
Libellus de constructione. 1513, [Cambridge? 1521?], London 1531, 1533, 1539, 1539, 1540 (enlarged and rev). Also attributed to W. Lily and Erasmus.
Joannis Coleti aeditio una cum quibusdam G. Lilij Grammatices rudimentis [in English]. Antwerp 1527, 1533, 1534, 153[5], 1536, 1537, 1539, Menston 1971 (facs of 1527). Colet's initial catechism and the source for Erasmus' Christiani hominis institutum. Also London [1527?], 1529 (ptd by Wolsey for Ipswich grammar school), 1534, [1534?]. Extract ptd by R. Redman c. 1540 as De nominibus heteroclitis.
The vij petycions of the pater noster by Jhon Collet Deane of Powels. [Antwerp? c. 1530?].
A ryght frutefull monycion concerning the ordre of a good Chrysten mannes lyfe. 1534, 1534, 1563, 1577, 1582.
Opus de sacramentis ecclesiae. Ed J. H. Lupton 1867.

Two treatises on Hierarchies of Dionysius. Ed and tr J. H. Lupton 1869.
An exposition of St Paul's epistle to the Romans. Ed and tr J. H. Lupton 1873.
An exposition of St Paul's first epistle to the Corinthians. Ed and tr J. H. Lupton 1874.
Letters to Radulphus on the Mosaic account of the creation. Ed and tr J. H. Lupton 1876. Also includes shorter works by or attributed to Colet.

§ 2

Erasmus, D. The lives of Jehan Vitrier and Colet. Ed and tr J. H. Lupton 1883.
Knight, S. The life of Dr Colet. 1724, Oxford 1823.
Seebohm, F. The Oxford reformers of 1498: Colet, More, Erasmus. 1867, 1869 (enlarged).
Lupton, J. H. Life of Colet. 1887.
Jayne, S. Colet and Marsilio Ficino. Oxford 1963.

SIR THOMAS MORE
1478–1535

Bibliographies

Gibson, R. W. and J. M. Patrick. More: a preliminary bibliography of his works and of Moreana to 1750. New Haven 1961.
Reynolds, E. E. More: a bibliographical study. 1965.
Sullivan, F. and M. P. Moreana: materials for the study of More. 4 vols Los Angeles 1964–8; Index, 1971.

§ 1

The Utopia

Latin Text

Libellus vere aureus de optimo reip. statu, deque nova insula Utopiae cura P. Aegidii nunc primum editus. [Louvain 1516], Paris [1517?], Basle 1518, 1518, Leeds 1966 (facs of 1516). The Latin text accompanies Lupton's and Sampson's edns of Robinson's trn, below.
Utopia. Ed M. Delcourt, Paris 1936.
Utopia. Ed E. Surtz and J. H. Hexter. In Yale edn of Works of More vol 4, New Haven 1965.

Ralph Robinson's Translation

A fruteful and pleasaunt work of the newe yle called Utopia, translated into Englyshe by Raphe Robynson. 1551, 1556, 1597, 1624, 1639; ed T. F. Dibdin 1808; ed E. Arber 1869; ed J. R. Lumby 1897; ed J. H. Lupton,

Oxford 1895 (with Latin text and additional trns); ed
G. Sampson and A. Guthkelch 1910 (with Latin text
and bibliography); ed P. E. Hallett 1937. Facs:
Amsterdam 1969 (1551), Menston 1970 (1556).

Other Translations
[Burnet, G.] Utopia: written in Latin by Sir Thomas
More. 1684; ed H. Morley 1885; ed S. Lee 1906 (with
the poems).
[Cayley, Sir A.] Memoirs of Sir Thomas More; with a
new translation of his Utopia, History of King Richard
III and Latin poems. 2 vols 1808.
Surtz, E. In Selected works, New Haven 1964.
Marshall, P. K. Utopia: a new translation. New York
1965.
Turner, P. Utopia. 1965 (Pelican).
Surtz, E. and J. H. Hexter (ed). Utopia. Vol 4 of Complete
works, New Haven 1965. See A. B. Ferguson, The
Yale edition of More's Utopia, JHI 29 1968.

English Works
Collections
The workes of Sir Thomas More wrytten by him in the
Englysh tonge. Ed William Rastell 1557; ed W. E.
Campbell, with introd by R. W. Chambers and notes
and introds by A. W. Reed 2 vols 1931 (facs with
modernized texts).
Selections from his English works and from the lives by Eras-
mus and Roper. Ed P. S. and H. M. Allen, Oxford 1924.
English prayers and treatise on the Holy Eucharist. Ed
P. E. Hallett 1938.
Prayers made by More while he was prisoner in the Tower
of London. Ed E. F. Rogers, Madison 1952.
Complete works. Ed R. S. Sylvester et al 14 vols New
Haven 1963-.
Selected works. Ed E. Surtz, New Haven 1964.
The essential More. Ed J. J. Greene and J. P. Dolan 1967.

Separate Works
The lyfe of Johan Picus Erle of Myrandula (Here begin
xii rulys). [1510?] (J. Rastell), c. 1525 (de Worde);
ed J. M. Rigg 1890 (from de Worde).
A mery jest how the sergeant would lerne to play the frere.
[1516?] (Julian Notary).
The supplycacyon of soulys, agaynst the supplycacyon of
beggars. [1529], [1529] (W. Rastell). An answer to
Simon Fish. A transcript from Black Letter by E.
Morris 1970 (with text of S. Fish, The supplication of
beggars 1528), Amsterdam 1971 (facs).
A dyaloge of Syr Thomas More of ymages, praying to
sayntys, othere thynges touchyng the pestylent sect of
Luther and Tyndale. 1529 (J. Rastell), 1530 (W. Rastell,
'newly oversene'). See W. Tindale, An answere unto
Mores dialoge, [1530], 1850 (Parker Soc).
The confutacyon of Tyndales answere. 1532 (W. Rastell)
(bks i–iii); Complete works, ed F. Sullivan, Los Angeles
1957–8 (facs in part).
The second parte of the confutacion of Tyndales answere.
1533 (W. Rastell).
The debellacyon of Salem and Bizance. 1533 (W. Rastell).
The apologye of Syr T. More knyght. 1533 (W. Rastell);
ed A. I. Taft 1930 (EETS); Amsterdam 1970 (facs of
1533).
A letter of Syr Tho. More knyght impugnynge the
erronyous wrytyng of J. Fryth. 1533 (W. Rastell).
Syr Thomas Mores answere to the fyrst parte of the
poysoned booke which [Tindale] hath named the Souper
of the Lorde. 1534 (W. Rastell).
The boke of the fayre gentylwoman Lady Fortune. [c.
1540] (R. Wyer). 'Tho. Mo.'
A dialoge of comfort against tribulacion. 1553 (Tottell);
Antwerp 1573; ed P. E. Hallett 1937; ed M. Stevens
1951; ed L. Miles, Bloomington 1966; Menston 1970
(facs of 1573).
Versions of More's History of King Richard III originally

appeared in the chronicles of Hardyng and Hall. There
are modern edns by S. W. Singer 1821; J. R. Lumby 1883
(with omissions); R. S. Sylvester, New Haven 1964 (vol 2
of Yale edn of Works).

The More Circle
Rastell, John (1470?-1536). Of gentylnes and nobylyte
a dyaloge. [1529?]. Anon.
—— The pastyme of people: the cronycles of dyvers
realmys. [1530?]; ed T. F. Didbin 1811. A history of
England with remarkable woodcuts.
—— A newe boke of purgatory. 1530, 1530.
Frith, John. A disputacion of purgatory whiche answereth
unto Sir Thomas More. [Antwerp 1531?], [London
1537?].
—— A boke made by J.F. prisoner in the tower of London.
Münster 1533.
Smythe, Walter, Twelve merry jests of the widow Edith.
1525 (J. Rastell); ed W. C. Hazlitt, Shakespeare jest-
books vol 3, 1864. References to More household.
Tindale, William. The souper of the Lorde, wheryn
incidently M. Moris letter agenst J. Frythe is confuted.
Antwerp 1533. Anon.
Roy, William. Rede me and be nott wrothe. [1528],
[1546]; ed E. Arber 1871.
Literae virorum eruditorum ad F. Craneveldium 1522–8.
Ed H. de Vocht, Louvain 1928.

Letters, Diaries etc
Correspondence. Ed E. F. Rogers, Princeton 1947.
Selected letters. Ed E. F. Rogers, New Haven 1961.
Prayer book. Ed L. L. Martz and R. S. Sylvester, New
Haven 1969.

§2
Lives
For the Tudor lives see R. W. Chambers, Proc Br Acad 12
1926.
Harpsfield, N. The life and death of Sir Thomas Moore.
Ed E. V. Hitchcock 1932 (EETS) (from mss).
Stapleton, T. Tres Thomae. Douai 1588; tr P. E. Hallett
1928 (St Thomas, Thomas à Becket, More); Vita
Thomae Mori, Frankfurt 1689, Frankfurt 1964 (facs);
The life and illustrious martyrdom of More, tr P.
Hallett, ed E. E. Reynolds, New York 1966.
Roper, W. The mirrour of vertue in wordly greatnes: or
the life of More. Paris 1626; ed E. V. Hitchcock 1935
(EETS); ed J. M. Cline, New York 1950; ed R. S.
Sylvester and D. P. Harding, New Haven 1962 (with
Cavendish's Life of Wolsey); ed E. E. Reynolds 1963
(with Harpsfield's life) (EL); Menston 1970 (facs of
1626).
Ba., Ro. Ed C. Wordsworth, Ecclesiastical biography vol
2, 1810 (from ms); ed E. V. Hitchcock, P. E. Hallett
and A. W. Reed 1950 (EETS).
More, Cresacre. The life and death of More, written by
M.T.M. [Paris 1631?]; ed J. Hunter 1828, Menston
1971 (facs).
Chambers, R. W. Thomas More. 1935.
de Vocht, H. Acta Thomae Mori: history of the reports
of his trial and death with an unedited contemporary
narrative. Louvain 1947.
Bolt, R. Man for all seasons: a play in two acts. 1961.
Marc'hadour, G. L'univers de More: chronologie critique
de More, Erasme et leur époque 1477–1536. Paris 1963.
—— More: ou la sage folie. Paris 1971.

Studies
Chambers, R. W. The place of More in English literature
and history. 1937, New York 1964 (rev).
Visser, F. T. A syntax of the English language of More.
3 vols Louvain 1946–56.
Marc'hadour, G. The Bible in the works of More. 2 vols
Nieuwkoop 1969–72.

—— More et la Bible: la place des livres saints dans son apologétique et sa spiritualité. Paris 1969.
—— More vu par Erasme. Angers 1969.
Hanham, A. Richard III and his early historians 1483–1535. Oxford 1975.

WILLIAM TINDALE
1494?–1536
Collections

The whole works of W. Tyndall, J. Frith and Doct. Barnes. 2 vols 1572. Preface by Foxe.
Work. Ed G. E. Duffield, Appleford 1964.

§ 1

A compendious introduccion unto the pistle to the Romayns. [Worms 1520] (anon), London 1564.
The obedience of a Christen man. [Antwerp] 1528, 1535 ('diligently corrected'), 1537 ('diligently corrected'), [London 1537?], [1548], [1548?], [1548?], 1561, Menston 1970 (facs of 1528).
The parable of the wicked mannon. [Antwerp] 1528, 1528, Southwark 1536, [London] '1528' (for 1537?) ('lately corrected'), 1547, [1548] ('lately corrected'), 1549, [1561?].
An answere unto Sir T. Mores dialoge. [Antwerp 1530?].
The examinacion of Master William Thorpe; The examinacion of Syr J. Oldcastell. [Antwerp 1530]. Ed Tindale.
The practyse of prelates, whether the Kynges grace may be separated from hys Quene. [Antwerp] 1530, 1548, [1549?].
The exposition of the fyrste epistle of Seynt Jhon by W.T. [Antwerp] 1531, ed T. H. L. Parker, Library of Christian classics, 1966; Of the fyrste, seconde and thyrde epistles [second and third are trns of Bullinger], Southwark [1537?], 1538.
The praier and complaynte of the ploweman unto Christe. [Antwerp 1531?], [London c. 1532]. Ed Tindale.
An exposicion upon the v, vi, vii chapters of Mathew. [Antwerp? 1533?] (by W.T.), [London 1536?], [1536?], [1537?], [1548] ('newly set furth'), [1549?] ('and corrected').
A fruitefull and godly treatise expressinge the right institution of the sacraments. [1533?]. First surviving copy as A briefe declaration, [1548?].
The souper of the Lorde. [Antwerp?] '1533' (for 1546?) (anon), [London] '1533' [1547?], '1533' [1547?], '1533' (for 1547?).
The testament of W. Tracie esquier, expounded. Antwerp 1535. By Tindale and J. Frith.
A pathway into the holy scripture. [1536?] (anon), [1536?], 1564.
Tyndale's expositions and Practice of prelates. Ed H. Walter 1849 (Parker Soc).
An answer to More's Dialogue: the Supper of the Lord, and Wm Tracy's testament expounded. Ed H. Walter 1850 (Parker Soc).
Doctrinal treatises and introductions to different portions of the holy scriptures. Ed H. Walter 1858 (Parker Soc). Contains Parable of the wicked mammon, Obedience of a Christian man.
For Tindale's biblical trns see col 271, below.

§ 2

Demaus, R. Tyndale: a biography. 1871, 1886 (rev R. Lovett).
Reed, A. W. In K. Garvin (ed), The great Tudors, 1935.
Chambers, R. W. Tyndale and our Bible: the English prose tradition. TLS 3 Oct 1936; rptd in his Man's unconquerable mind, 1939.
Mozley, J. F. William Tyndale. 1937.
Campbell, W. E. Erasmus, Tyndale and More. 1949.

Davis, N. Tyndale's English of controversy. 1971.

STEPHEN GARDINER
1483?–1555

Stephani Winton. episcopi de vera obedientia oratio. 1535, [Wesel?] 1553; tr 1553, 1553; ed B. A. Heywood 1870; Leeds 1966 (facs of 1553).
Stephani Winton. Ad Bucerum de impudenti eiusdem pseudologia conquestio. Louvain 1544, Cologne 1545.
The rescuyunge of the Romishe fox: otherwyse called the examination of the hunted devised by Steven Gardiner. [Bonn 1545]. Pseudonym W. Wraghton; prints and answers Gardiner's Examination of the hunter, which apparently circulated only in ms.
Stephani Winton. ad Martinum Bucerum epistola. Louvain 1546, Ingolstadt 1546.
A declaration of such true articles as George Joye hath gone about to confute. 1546, 1546.
A detection of the Devils sophistrie, wherwith he robbeth the unlearned people, of the true byleef, in the sacrament of the aulter. 1546, 1546.
Theyr dedes in effect my lyfe wolde haue. [London 1548?]. 2 poems, the first signed Stephen Wynton, the 2nd in reply signed H.S.
An explication and assertion of the true catholique fayth, touchyng the moost blessed sacrament of the aulter. [Rouen] 1551; rptd in Cranmer's reply, An answer.
Confutatio cavillationum quibus sacrosanctum eucharistiae sacramentum ab impiis capernaitis impeti solet, authore Marco Antonio Constantio theologo lovaniensi. Paris 1552 (anon), Louvain 1554 (under Gardiner's name). Reply to Cranmer.
An admonishion to the Bishoppes of Winchester, London and others. [London] 1553.
The communication betwene my Lord Chauncelor and judge Hales. [London 1553]. Anon.
Exetasis testimoniorum quae M. Bucerus ex sanctis patribus non sancte edidit. Louvain 1554.
A traictise declaryng that the pretensed marriage of priests is no marriage. 1554. Attributed to Gardiner.
Concio habita dominica prima adventus. Rome 1555. Latin trn by Nicholas Harpsfield.
De pronunciatione linguae graecae et latinae. Basle 1555. Ptd with Cheke's treatise by C. S. Curio.
Responsio venerabilium sacerdotum Henrici Ioliffi & Roberti Ionson ad articulos Ioannis Hoperi una cum confutationibus Hoperi et replicationibus Stephani Gardineri. Antwerp 1564. Mostly by Gardiner.
Obedience in Church and State: three political tracts by Gardiner. Ed P. Janelle, Cambridge 1930. Prints from ms a tract on Fisher's execution 1535 and an answer to Bucer 1541; and reprints De vera obedientia, 1535 and English trn of 1553.
Letters. Ed J. A. Muller, Cambridge 1933.

HUGH LATIMER
1492?–1555
Collections

The sermons of Master Latimer. 2 vols 1758. With life.
Sermons of Latimer arranged, with life. Ed J. Watkins 2 vols 1824.
Sermons. Ed G. E. Corrie 1844 (Parker Soc).
Sermons and remains. Ed G. E. Corrie 1845 (Parker Soc).
Sermons. Ed H. C. Beeching [1906].
Selected sermons. Ed A. G. Chester, Charlottesville 1968.

§ 1

Concio quam habuit pater H. Latimer in conventu spiritualium. Southwark [1537], 1592 (as Oratio apud totum ecclesiasticorum conventum); tr 1537, 1537.

A notable sermon [on the plough] of Maister Latemer, preached in the shroudes at Paules Churche. 1548, [1548], [1548]; ed E. Arber 1868.

The fyrste sermon of mayster Latimer, preached before the Kinges Majestie at Westminster. [1549] (4 edns); ed E. Arber 1869.

The seconde [third, fourth, fifth, sixth, seventh] sermon preached before the Kynges Majestie. [1549] (3 edns), 1562 (as The seven sermons).

A most faithfull sermon preached before the Kynges Majestye. [1550], [1553?].

A sermon preached at Stamford. [1550?].

Sermons made before Katherine, Duches of Suffolke. Ed A. Bernher 1552, 1562.

Twenty-seven sermons preached by Latimer. 1562. Preface by T. Solme.

Frutefull sermons newly imprinted. 3 pts 1571–2, 1575, 1578, 1584, 1596, 1607, 1635. 38 sermons.

Seven sermons made upon the Lordes Prayer. 1572.

§2

Demaus, R. Latimer: a biography. 1869, 1881 (rev).
Carlyle, R. W. and A. J. Hugh Latimer. 1900.
Gray, C. M. Latimer and the sixteenth century. Cambridge Mass 1950.
Darby, H. S. Hugh Latimer. 1953.

SIR JOHN CHEKE
1514–57

§1

D. Ioannis Chrysostomi homiliae duae. 1543 (Latin and Greek), 1543. English trn of the second and of discourse on Job and Abraham, 'made out of Greke into Latin by master Cheke' by T. Chaloner, 1544, 1553.

D. Ioannia Chrysostomi de providentia Dei ac de fato orationes sex. 1545 (Latin trn).

The hurt of sedicion. 1549, 1549, 1549, 1569 ('newly perused and printed', running title, The true subiect to the rebell), 1576. Anon. Ptd in Holinshed's Chronicles, 1587, and by G. Langbaine with life of Cheke, Oxford 1641; Menston 1971 (facs of 1549).

De obitu doctissimi Buceri epistolae duae; item epigrammata varia. 1551, Basle 1587. First letter by Cheke to P. M. Vermigli, 2nd by N. Carr to Cheke. 2 letters also in C. Hubertus, Historia vera de vita Buceri, Strasbourg 1562.

Defensio verae et catholicae doctrinae de sacramento corporis et sanguinis Christi. 1553, Emden 1557, 1557. Latin trn from Cranmer's English.

Leonis imperatoris De bellico apparatu liber e graeco in latinum conversus I. Checo interp. Basle 1554, 1595.

De pronuntiatione graecae potissimum linguae disputationes cum Stephano Wintoniensi. Basle 1555, Menston 1968 (facs).

Reformatio legum ecclesiasticarum. 1571, 1640, 1641. Anon trn by Cheke with W. Haddon.

A treatise of superstition. In Strype, Life 1705. Trn by W. Elstob from Latin ms.

For Cheke's biblical trn see col 278, below; prose ed H. Craik, English prose selections, 1893.

§2

Strype, J. Life of Cheke. 1705, Oxford 1821.
Davies, H. S. Cheke and the translation of the Bible. E & S new ser 5 1952.

MILES COVERDALE
1488–1568

§1

Goostly psalmes. [1536?].

A confutacion of that treatise which one J. Standish made agaynst D. Barnes. [Zürich 1541?].

The order that the Churche in Denmarke doth use. [1549?].

Certain most godly letters of such true saintes as gaue their lyves. 1564; ed E. Bickersteth 1837. Preface only by Coverdale.

Memorials. Ed J. J. Lowndes 1838.

Writings. Ed G. Pearson 1844 (Parker Soc).

Remains. Ed G. Pearson 1846 (Parker Soc).

For Coverdale's trn of the Bible see col 273, below.

§2

Mozley, J. F. Coverdale and his Bibles. 1953.

THOMAS CRANMER
1489–1556

Collections

Remains. Ed H. Jenkyns 4 vols Oxford 1833.

Writings and Disputations relative to the sacrament of the Lord's supper. Ed J. E. Cox 1844–6 (Parker Soc).

Miscellaneous writings and letters. Ed J. E. Cox 1846 (Parker Soc).

Selected writings. Ed C. S. Meyer 1961. With bibliography.

§1

Cathecismus: that is to say, a shorte instruction into Christian religion. 1548 (3 edns). Tr from J. Jonas.

A defence of the true and catholike doctrine of the sacrament. 1550 (3 edns); tr French, 1552; tr Latin by Sir John Cheke 1553; [Emden] 1557 (rev); ed C. H. H. Wright 1907.

An answer unto a crafty and sophistical cavillation devised by Stephen Gardiner. 1551, 1580 ('revised and corrected by the Archbyshop').

An answere against the false calumniacion of Richarde Smyth. [1551?].

All the submyssyons and recantations of Cranmer. 1556 (first 4 in English, last 2 in Latin).

The copy of certain lettres sent to the Quene. [Emden 1556?].

The recantation of Cranmer translated out of Latin. [1556]. Original Latin is 5th recantation, above.

A confucation of vnwritten verities. Tr E.P. [Wesel? 1557?], 1582.

Reformatio legum ecclesiasticarum [anon]. Ed J. Foxe etc, tr W. Haddon and Sir John Cheke 1571, 1640.

Recantacyons. Ed Lord Houghton and J. Gairdner 1885 (Philobiblon Soc).

Cranmer's first litany. Ed J. E. Hunt, New York 1939.

§2

Pollard, A. F. Cranmer and the English Reformation. 1904.

Deane, A. C. Life of Cranmer. 1927.

Hutchinson, F. E. Cranmer and the English Reformation. 1951.

Sykes, N. Thomas Cranmer. 1956.

Ridley, J. G. Thomas Cranmer. Oxford 1962.

THOMAS LUPSET
1495–1530

The sermon of Doctor Colete made to the convocacion at Paulis. [1531?]. The anon trn is probably by Lupset.
A treatise of charite. 1533 (anon), 1535, 1539.
A compendious and a very fruteful treatyse, teachynge the waye of dyenge well. 1534, 1541.
Here be gathered counsailes of Saynct Isodorie. 1534, 1539, 1544.
An exhortation to yonge men, perswadinge them to walke in the pathe way that leadeth to honeste and goodnes. 1535, 1538, 1544.
A sermon of saint Chrysostome, translated into Englishe. 1542.
Workes. 1546, 1560.
The life and works of Lupset, with a critical text of the original treatises [2nd–4th items above] and the letters. Ed J. A. Gee, New Haven 1928.
Starkey, T. A dialogue between Reginald Pole and Lupset. Ed J. M. Cowper 1871 (as England in the reign of King Henry the Eighth) (EETS); ed K. M. Burton 1948 (preface by E. M. W. Tillyard).

SIMON FISH
d. 1531

A supplicacyon for the beggars. [ptd abroad 1528–9?] (anon); ed F. J. Furnivall 1871 (EETS); ed E. Arber, Birmingham 1878.
The summe of the holye Scripture and ordynance of Christen teachyng. [Antwerp] 1529, London [1535?], [1536?], [1540], [1547], 1548, [1550?]. Tr from Dutch.
A supplication of the poore commons, whereunto is added the Supplication of beggars. 2 pts [1546].

SIR THOMAS ELYOT
1499?–1546
Collections

Four political treatises: The doctrinal of princes; Pasquil the playne; The banquette of sapience; The image of governance. Gainesville 1967.

§ 1

Papyrii gemini eleatis hermathena: seu de eloquentia victoria. Cambridge 1522. By Elyot?
The education or bringinge up of children. [Before 1530], [1532?], [1550?]; ed R. D. Pepper, Gainesville 1966 (in Four Tudor books on education), Amsterdam 1969 (facs).
The boke named the governour. 1531, 1537, 1544, 1546, 1553, 1557, 1565, 1580; ed H. S. Croft 2 vols 1880 (with introd on life and works); ed F. Watson 1907; ed S. E. Lehmberg 1962; Menston 1970 (facs of 1531).
How one may take profyte of his enmyes. [1531?] (anon). Tr from Plutarch.
A dialoge betwene Lucian and Diogenes of life. [1532?].
Pasquil the playne: a dialogue on talkativeness and silence. 1532, 1533, 1540. Anon.
Of the knowledge which maketh a wise man. 1533, [after 1548?]; ed E. J. Howard, Oxford Ohio 1946.
The doctrinal of princes. [1533?], [c. 1550]. Tr from Isocrates.
A swete and devoute sermon of holy Saynte Ciprian of the mortalitie of man; [with] The rules of a Christian lyfe made by Picus Earle of Mirandula. 1534, 1539. Trns: Sermon, [1556], Rules, Rouen 1585, [English secret press] 1615.
The dictionary of Syr Thomas Elyot [Latin and English]. 1538, 1542 (as Bibliotheca Elyotae), 1545; rev and 'inriched' by T. Cooper 1548, 1552, 1559; Menston 1970 (facs of 1538).

The Castel of Helth. [1536–9], 1539 ('and augmented'), 1541, 1541, 1541 ('corrected') (for 1544?), 1547, [1550?], [1559?], [1560?], 1561, 1572, 1576, 1580, 1587, 1595, 1610; New York 1937 (facs of 1541 with title-page and preface to 1536–9).
The bankette of sapience. 1539 ('newly augmented'), 1542, 1545, 1545, 1557, 1564.
The defence of good women. [1540], 1545; ed E. J. Howard, Oxford Ohio 1940.
The image of governance compiled of the actes of Alexander Severus. 1541, 1544, 1544, 1549, 1549, 1556.
A preservative agaynste deth. 1545.

NICHOLAS RIDLEY
1500?–55
Collections

Works. Ed H. Christmas 1841 (Parker Soc).

§ 1

A brief declaracion of the Lordes supper. [Emden] 1555, [no place] 1559, London 1586; ed H. C. G. Moule 1895.
Certein godly, learned and comfortable conferences betwene Ridley and H. Latimer. [Emden] 1556, 1556, [Strasbourg 1556] (with A treatise agaynst transsubstantiation), London 1574 (newly againe imprinted).
A frendly farewel which master Ridley did write unto all his true louers and frendes in God, a little before that he suffred. [Ed J. Foxe] 1559 ('newly set forth').
A pituous lamentation of the miserable estate of the Churche of Christ in Englande, in the time of the late revolt from the gospel. 1566, 1566.
Praefatio et protestatio habita Aprilis 20 1555. [c. 1580]; tr and ed G. Ironside, Oxford 1688; 1792 (Latin).
The way to peace amongst all Protestants: being a letter of reconciliation sent by Bp Ridley to Bp Hooper with some observations upon it by Sam Johnson. 1688, 1703, 1846.

§ 2

Merrill, L. R. The life and poems of Nicholas Grimald. New Haven 1925. Introd.
Ridley, J. G. Ridley: a biography. 1957.

MATTHEW PARKER
1504–75

§ 1

How we ought to take the death of the godly: a sermon made in Cambrydge at the buriall of M. Bucer. [1551?]; tr T. Newton [1587] (tr from an abridged Latin version ptd abroad).
An admonition to all suche as shall intende to enter the state of matrimonye. 1560, [c. 1560], [c. 1560], 1563, 1571, 1594, [c. 1600] [c. 1600], [1605?], 1620, Oxford [c. 1630], London 1639.
Concio in funere Buceri habita. Latin trn in C. Hubertus, Historia de vita Buceri, Strasbourg 1562.
A briefe examination of a certaine declaration. [1566?]. Attributed to Parker.
The whole psalter translated into English metre. [1567?] (with four-part settings by T. Tallis).
De antiquitate britannicae ecclesiae cantuariensis, cum archiepiscopis ejusdem 70. 1572–4 (anon), 1605; ed S. Drake 1729; tr [Zürich] 1574.
The life off the 70 Archbishopp off Canterbury englished. [Zürich] 1574.
Registrum Matthei Parker 1559–75. Ed W. H. Frere 1907–35 (Canterbury & York Soc).
Parker also translated the canons and decrees of the Council of Trent, wrote preface to the anon Defence of priestes

mariages, [1567?] and notes to the next edn [1567?], edited a sermon of Aelfric's, the Anglo-Saxon version of the Gospels, and the following chroniclers: Asser, Matthew of Westminster, Matthew Paris, Thomas Walsingham.

Letters

Correspondence. Ed J. Bruce and T. T. Perowne 1853 (Parker Soc).

§ 2

Strype, J. The life and acts of Parker. 1711, 3 vols Oxford 1821.
Freeman, E. A. In his Historical essays, 1892.
Kennedy, W. P. M. Life of Archbishop Parker. 1908.
Brook, V.J.K. A life of Archbishop Parker. Oxford 1962

JOHN CAIUS
1510–73
Collections

Ioannis Caii opera aliquot et versiones. Louvain 1556.
Works. Ed E. S. Roberts, Cambridge 1912. With memoir by John Venn.

§ 1

De medendi methodo. Basle 1544.
A boke or counseill against the disease called the sweate. 1552 (Latin and English); rptd in J. C. F. Hecker, The epidemics of the Middle Ages, 1844; ed A. Malloch, New York 1937 (facs of 1552).
De antiquitate cantabrigiensis academiae libri duo. 1568, 1574.
De canibus britannicis liber unus; De rariorum animalium et stirpium historia; De libris propriis. 3 pts 1570. Pt 1 tr A. Fleming as Of English dogges, 1576, Amsterdam 1969 (facs).
De pronunciatione Graecae & Latine linguae cum scriptione noua libellus. 1574; tr J. B. Gabel, Leeds 1968 (with facs of 1574).
Historia cantabrigiensis academiae liber. 1574.
Caius also edited and translated Galen's works into Latin.

§ 2

Venn, J. Annals of Gonville and Caius College. Cambridge 1904.
O'Malley, English medical humanists: Thomas Linacre and Caius. Lawrence Kansas 1965.

JOHN PONET or POYNET
1514?–56

§ 1

A defence for mariage of priestes. 1549, [1567?].
A tragoedie or dialoge of the unjuste primacie of the Bishop of Rome. 1549; ed C. E. Plumptre 1899. Tr from Bernardino Ochino.
A notable sermon concerninge the ryght use of the Lordes supper. 1550.
Catechismus brevis. 1553; tr in Library of Christian classics, 1966. Probably compiled by Ponet.
The humble and unfained confession of certain poore banished men. [Wesel] 1554. Attributed to Ponet.
An apologie fully aunsweringe a blasphemose book by D. Steph. Gardiner. Strasbourg 1555, 1556.
A shorte treatise of politike power. [Strasbourg] 1556, [Paris?] 1639, Menston 1970 (facs).
Diallacticon. [Strasbourg] 1557.
Registra Stephani Gardiner et Johannis Poynet. Ed H. Chitty 1930 (Canterbury & York Soc).

§ 2

Hudson, W. S. Ponet: advocate of limited monarchy.

Chicago 1942. Biography, with facs of A shorte treatise.

ROGER ASCHAM
1515–68
Collections

English works. Ed J. Bennet 1761; rev J. G. Cochrane 1815.
Whole works. Ed J. A. Giles 4 vols in 3 1864–5.
English works: Toxophilus; Report of the affaires of Germany; The scholemaster. Ed W. A. Wright, Cambridge 1904.

§ 1

Toxophilus: the schole of shootinge conteyned in two bookes. 1545, 1571 ('newlye perused'), 1589; ed J. Walters, Wrexham 1788; ed E. Arber, Birmingham 1868; Wakefield 1968 (facs of 1788), Amsterdam 1969 (facs of 1545), Menston 1971 (facs of 1545).
A report and discourse of the affaires and state of Germany. [1570?].
The scholemaster: or plaine and perfite way of teachyng children the Latin tong. 1570, 1571, 1571, 1579, 1589; ed J. Upton 1711, 1743 (rev); ed J. E. B. Mayor 1863; ed E. Arber, Birmingham 1869; ed J. Holzamer, Vienna 1881; ed D. C. Whimster 1934; ed L. V. Ryan, Ithaca 1967; Menston 1967 (facs of 1570), Amsterdam 1968 (facs of 1570).
Apologia pro caena dominica; themata; expositiones in epistolas theologicas; cui accesserunt Pauli ad Titum & Philemonem. Ed E. Grant 1577.

Letters

Familiarium epistolarum libri tres. [1576], 1578 (rev), 1581, 1590, Hanover 1602; ed E. G[rant], Hanover 1610; ed W. Elstob, Oxford 1703.

§ 2

Ryan, L. V. Roger Ascham. Stanford 1963.

THOMAS WILSON
1524?–81

The rule of reason: conteining the arte of logique set forthe in Englishe. 1551, 1552, 1553, 1563, 1567, 1580, Amsterdam 1970 (facs of 1551).
Vita et obitus duorum fratrum Hen. et Car. Brandoni. 1551, nd. With Walter Haddon.
The arte of rhetorique for the use of all suche as are studious of eloquence sette forth in Englische. 1553, 1560 ('newlie sette forthe again'), 1562, 1563, 1567, 1580, 1584, 1585; ed G. H. Mair, Oxford 1909 (from 1560); Gainesville 1962 (facs of 1553), Amsterdam 1969 (facs of 1553).
Oratio habita Pataviae in mortem Domini Edowardi Courtenai 1556. In Strype, Ecclesiastical memorials vol 3, 1721.
The three orations of Demosthenes in favour of the Olynthians with fower orations against King Philip of Macedonie, englished by T. Wylson. 1570, Amsterdam 1968 (facs).
A discourse upon usurye. 1572, 1584; ed R. H. Tawney 1925.
A treatise of England's perils. 1578; ed A. J. Schmidt, Archiv für Reformationsgeschichte 46 1955.

WILLIAM FULKE
1537–89

Antiprognosticon contra inutiles astrologorum praedictiones. 1560; tr W. Painter, 1560 (whereunto is added a shorte treatise for the better subversion of that fained arte).

A goodly gallerye with a most pleasant prospect, into the garden of naturall contemplation. 1563, 1602, 1634 (2nd edn), 1639 (3rd edn).

The most noble auncient and learned playe, called the Philosophers game, 1563 (with Ralph Lever).

A sermon preached at Hampton Court 12 Nov 1570. 1570, 1571, 1572, 1574, 1579, 1580.

A confutation of a popishe libelle. 1571, 1573, 1574.

Οὐρανομαχία: hoc est astrologorum ludus. 1571, 1572.

In sacram diui Ioannis Apocalypsim praelectiones. 1573; tr 1573.

A comfortable sermon of faith, preached 1573. 1574, [1574?], 1578, 1586, 1611 ('newly corrected').

A sermon preached on 17 March at S. Alpheges. 1577; tr Latin by John Foxe, De Christo gratis justificante, 1583.

Two treatises written against the Papistes. 1577; 2nd treatise also issued separately with rev preface as An answer of a true Christian, 1577.

A commentarie upon Josue. 1578. Tr from Calvin, sometimes attributed to Fulke.

Gulielmi Fulconis Angli, ad epistolam Stanislai Hosii responsio. 1578.

Μετρομαχία: sive ludus geometricus. 1578.

Ad Thomae Stapletoni controversiarum cavillationes responsio. 1579.

D. Hoskins, D. Sanders, a. M. Rastel overthrowne. 1579.

A godly sermon preached 26 Februarie 1580. [1580?], [1580?]. Anon.

A retentive to stay good Christians. 1580. Includes 2nd work, A discovery of the daungerous rocke, ed R. Gibbings 1848 (Parker Soc).

T. Stapleton and Martiall confuted. 1580; ed R. Gibbings 1848 (Parker Soc).

A briefe confutation of a popish discourse by J. Howlet. 1581.

A rejoynder to Bristows replie. 1581.

A sermon preached upon Sunday the twelfth of March. 1581.

A defense of the sincere and true translations of the holie scriptures into the English tong; whereunto is added a briefe confutation. 1583, 1617, 1633; ed C. H. Hartshorne 1843 (Parker Soc).

Epistle to the reader. In Jean de Serres, A godlie commentarie upon Ecclesiastes 1585 (tr John Stockwood).

De successione ecclesiastica contra T. Stapletoni. 1584.

A treatise against the Defense of the censure. 1586. Includes 2 treatises by Fulke.

The text of the New testament translated by the Papists at Rhemes, with a confutation. 1589, 1601 ('perused and enlarged'), 1617, 1633.

Nowell, A. and W. Day. A true report of the Disputation had in the Tower. 1583. Includes account of Fulke's conferences with Campion, 1588, reported by John Field.

II. THE ENGLISH BIBLE

DMH   A. S. Herbert, Historical catalogue of printed editions of the English Bible 1525–1961, 1968 (rev and expanded from T. H. Darlow and H. F. Moule, 1903)

(1) BIBLIOGRAPHIES

[Ames, J.] A list of various editions of the Bible and parts thereof, in English, from the year 1526 to 1776, much enlarged and improved [by M. C. Tutet, A. C. Ducarel et al]. 1776, 1778 (rev).

Darlow, T. H. and H. F. Moule. Historical catalogue of the printed editions of holy scripture in the library of the British and Foreign Bible Society. 2 vols in 4 1903–11, New York 1963, London 1968 (rev A. S. Herbert) (vol 1).

(2) COLLECTIONS

The English hexapla, exhibiting the six important English translations of the New testament scriptures [ed S. Bagster]; preceded by an historical account of the English translations [by S. P. Tregelles]. 1841.

The New testament octapla: eight English versions of the New testament in the King James tradition. Ed L. A. Weigle, New York [1962].

The Genesis octapla. Ed L. A. Weigle, New York 1965.

(3) THE BIBLES

WILLIAM TINDALE
1494?–1536

Bibliographies

Fry, F. A bibliographical description of the editions of the New testament, Tyndale's version. 1878.

§ I

(a) New testament (with help from W. Roy): [Cologne 1525] (DMH 1: fragment only, to Matthew xxii.12; ed E. Arber 1871 (facs), ed A. W. Pollard 1926 (facs): DMH 1988, 2224; see H. F. Moule, Library 4th ser 7 1927), [Worms] 1526 (DMH 2: 2 incomplete copies, at Bristol Baptist College and St Paul's Cathedral; ed G. Offor 1831, ed J. P. Dabney, Andover Mass 1837,

ed F. Fry, Bristol 1862 (facs), ed J. Bosworth and G. Waring, The Gothic and Anglo-Saxon gospels in parallel columns with the versions of Wycliffe and Tyndale, 1865, 1874; DMH 1816, 1821, 1936); Antwerp 1526, [1530?] (Cambridge history of the Bible vol 3 p. 143), 1534 (rev) (DMH 13; in The English hexapla 1841 etc and separately ed N. H. Wallis, Cambridge 1938), 1535 (4 edns, the 'G.H.' [Godfrid van der Haghen] edn rev: DMH 15–16 and Kronenberg 1492; in Matthew's Bible, 1537–51, below, and The New testament octapla 1962), [Antwerp] 1536 (3 4° edns, the 'Mole', the 'Blank Stone' and the 'Engraver's Mark' edns, and 4 8°, one 16°: DMH 19–26), [London] 1536 (folio, the first New testament ptd in England: DMH 27), 1538, 1548 (DMH 36, 37; each with Latin of Erasmus), 1548 (3 edns: DMH 68–70), [1548–] 1549 (DMH 77);

London [Antwerp?] 1549 (3 edns, 2 with Latin of Erasmus: DMH 78, 79, 83), 1550 (DMH 88, with Latin of Erasmus), [Zürich] 1550 ('tr Miles Coverdal': DMH 90), [1550?] (DMH 91), 1551 (2 edns: DMH 96–7; also with Taverner's Old testament: DMH 93).

(b) Tyndale's New testament rev George Joye without Tyndale's authority: Antwerp 1534, 1535 (DMH 12, 17).

(c) Tyndale's New testament rev Richard Jugge: [1552?] (2 edns: DMH 99–100), 1553 (2 edns: DMH 104–5), [1561?] (5 edns: 111–15), [1566?] (DMH 121).

(d) Pentateuch, with help from Coverdale: 'Malborrow' [Antwerp] 1530 (5 pts: DMH 4), [Antwerp] 1534 (Genesis rev, the rest a reissue: DMH 8), 1537–51 in Matthew's Bible, below; the 1530 edn ed J. I. Mombert 1884, re-ed F. F. Bruce 1967; Genesis in The Genesis octapla, 1965.

(e) Jonah: [Antwerp 1531] (DMH 6); ed F. Fry, Bristol 1863 (facs); ed D. Daiches 1937 (with Authorized version).

(f) The liturgical 'Epistles' from the Old testament: first ptd as appendix to Tyndale's 1534 New testament (DMH 13); ed N. H. Wallis, Cambridge 1938.

(g) Joshua–II Chronicles: in Matthew's Bible, 1537–51, below.

See col 263, above.

MILES COVERDALE
1488–1568
Collections

Writings and translations. Ed G. Pearson 2 vols Cambridge 1844–6 (Parker Soc).

§1

(a) Psalms (paraphrase) 1534.

(b) Ecclesiastes: with Psalms 1535.

(c) Bible: The first 'Bug' Bible (Psalms xci.5), this rendering followed by Taverner and Matthew versions; also the first 'Treacle' Bible (Jeremiah viii. 22), followed in the Bishops' Bible. [Cologne or Marburg, not Zürich] 1535 (DMH 18; rptd S. Bagster 1838, 1847), Southwark 1537 (2 edns, the earliest English Bibles ptd in England: DMH 32–3), [ptd Zürich, pbd London] 1550 (DMH 84); [ptd Zürich, pbd London] 1553 (DMH 101).

(d) New testament: [Southwark? 1537?] (4 edns: DMH 40–3), Southwark 1538 (2 edns, both with Latin of Erasmus: DMH 37–8), ptd Paris, pbd London 1538 (with Latin of Erasmus: DMH 39), Antwerp 1539 (DMH 48), London 1549 (rev after Tindale: DMH 80).

(e) Proverbs, Ecclesiastes, Wisdom, Ecclesiasticus, The Story of Bel (The Books of Solomon): Southwark 1537 (St Paul's Cathedral Lib only: Mozley, Coverdale p. 327).

(f) Joshua; with annotations probably by Lancelot Ridley: [London? 1538?] (DMH 35: New York Public Lib only).

(g) Psalms (metrical) 1539.

(h) Psalms (prose) 1540.

(j) The 'Great Bible', rev Coverdale from 'Matthew' version, below.

See col 266, above.

JOHN ROGERS
1500?–55

The so-called 'Matthew' Bible ed Rogers under the (probable) pseudonym Thomas Matthew, adopting Tindale's Penta-teuch (1530), Joshua–II Chronicles (here first ptd), New testament (1535, 'G.H.' edn), Coverdale's Ezra-Malachi and Apocrypha, Rogers translating the Prayer of Manasses after the French of P. R. Olivetan (1535).

(a) Bible: [ptd Antwerp, pbd London] 1537 (DMH 34),

London 1549 (2 edns, one rev and ed E. Becke, called the 'Wife-beater's Bible' from a note to 1 Peter iii. 2: DMH 74–5), 1551 (6 versions: DMH 92 A–F). Selections in Roger's Collation 1847, above.

(b) New testament: [London] 1538 (DMH 44).

RICHARD TAVERNER
1505?–75

(a) Bible: 1539 (DMH 45). Rev from 'Matthew', above.

(b) New testament: 1539 (2 edns: DMH 49, 50).

(c) Liturgical Epistles and Gospels: 1540–[1545?] (6 edns).

(d) Old testament: 1549–51 (5 'parts': DMH 94, 81, 86–7, 82, the last containing the earliest English version of III Maccabees, but *see* (e) below), 1551 (with Tindale's New testament to constitute a Bible, ed E. Becke: DMH 93).

(e) III Maccabees: in W. Lynne (ed and tr), A briefe and compendiouse table in a maner of a concordaunce, 1550, 1563. Claims to be pbd before DMH 82, 1549, as (d) above.

GREAT BIBLE

Rev Coverdale from 'Matthew' Bible above; 1539 sometimes called after Thomas Cromwell under whose patronage Coverdale worked, 1540 after Thomas Cranmer, who con-tributed a prologue to the rev edns of 1540 etc.

§1

(a) Bible: [Paris and] London 1539 (DMH 46); rev T. Cranmer 1540 (3 edns: DMH 52–4), 1541 (4 edns: DMH 60–3), 1549 (DMH 76), 1550 (DMH 85), 1552 (DMH 98), 1553 (2 edns: DMH 102–3), 1561 (DMH 110), 1562 (2 edns, one Rouen: DMH 117, 119), [1566?] (DMH 120), 1568 (DMH 122), 1569 (3 edns: DMH 127–9). Genesis in The Genesis octapla, 1965.

(b) New testament: 1539 (DMH 51), 1540 (2 edns: DMH 58–9), 1546 (DMH 64), 1547 (DMH 65), 1548 (DMH 71), Worcester 1548 (2 edns: DMH 95 note), London 1548–9 (with Erasmus' paraphrase, 2 vols, 2 edns: DMH 72–3), 1550 (DMH 89), Worcester 1550–1 (2 or 3 edns: DMH 95), 1551–2 (as 1548–9: DMH 73 note); in The English hexapla, 1841 etc; The New testament octapla, 1962.

(c) Proverbs, Ecclesiastes, Song of Solomon, Wisdom, Ecclesiasticus: 1540 (DMH 57), [1544?], [1546?], [1547?], 1550, 1551, 1551.

(d) Psalter.

(e) Liturgical Epistles and Gospels: 1540, 1550, 1551, 1553 (7 edns in all).

§2

Fry, F. A description of the Great Bible 1539 and the six editions of Cranmer's Bible 1540 and 1541 etc. 1865.

Willoughby, H. R. The first authorized English Bible and the Cranmer preface. Chicago 1942.

GENEVA BIBLE

Tr W. Whittingham (1524?–79), with Coverdale, Chris-topher Goodman (1520–1603), William Cole (d. 1600), Anthony Gilby (d. 1585), Thomas Sampson (1517?–89) et al; the Old testament substantially rev from Great Bible. The earliest English New testament and Bible ptd in Roman type and with verse divisions. Called the 'Breeches' Bible from the trn of Genesis iii. 7, taken from Wyclif.

§1

(a) New testament, mostly tr Whittingham:
   (i) Geneva 1557 (DMH 106); [1842] (facs); in The English hexapla, 1841 etc.
   (ii) a different trn: Geneva 1560, London 1575, 1575-6, 1583, 1618-19 (DMH 109, 141, 147, 178, 371); in The New testament octapla, 1962.
   (iii) rev Laurence Tomson; more Calvinist than before: 1576, 1577, 1577, 1578, 1580 (3 edns), 1582, 1583 (rev) (DMH 146, 152-3, 156, 166-8, 175, 180); edns ptd at London most years till 1603 (DMH 189, 192-3, 196, 203-4, 213, 216-7, 231, 239-40, 242, 246, 260, 279), with edns ptd at Cambridge [1590?] (DMH 207) and Dort [pbd Edinburgh] 1601, 1603 (DMH 267, 278), London 1609, 1609, 1611, 1613, [1613?], 1615 (DMH 299, 299A, 311, 327, 329, 346).
   (iv) Tomson's revision with the commentary on Revelation tr from du Jon, below: 1602, 1610, 1616 (DMH 172, 305, 351).
(b) Psalms 1557.
(c) Bible:
   (i) with the 1560 New testament (above): Geneva 1560 (DMH 107; ed L. E. Berry, Madison 1969 (facs)), 1561-2 (DMH 116): the 'Whig' Bible, from Matthew v.9), 1568-70 (DMH 130), London 1576, ptd there almost every year till 1615, c. 64 edns (DMH 143-4, 148-9, 154, 159-161, 164-5, 170-1, 173-4, 179, 182-4, 187, 190-1, 195, 197, 199-201, 206, 211-12, 215, 219-23, 229, 234, 236, 243, 247, 256-7, 263, 269-70, 273, 276-7, 280-1, 286-7, 290, 293-4, 296, 303-4, 308, 330, 340-1) with edns pbd at Edinburgh 1576-9 (the 'Bassandyne' Bible, the earliest ptd in Scotland: DMH 158), Cambridge 1591 (the earliest ptd there: DMH 208), and Dort [pbd Edinburgh] 1601 (DMH 264); London 1610-11 called the 'Judas' Bible from John vi.67 (DMH 307); in Roger's Collation 1847, above; Genesis in The Genesis octapla, 1965.
   (ii) with Tomson's New testament: 1587, 1590, 1591-2, 1594, 1595, 1597, 1598, 1600, 1602, 1610 (DMH 194, 205, 210, 218, 225-6, 235, 244, 262, 268, 301).
   (iii) with Tomson's New testament and the du Jon-Barbar Apocalypse, 1592 (col 1886, below); without the Apocrypha: 'London' (Amsterdam, Dort '1599' [1616-33] (at least 8 edns: DMH 248-55), London 1603, 1603, 1606, 1607, 1608, 1609 (DMH 274-5, 285, 289, 295, 298), Edinburgh 1610 (DMH 302), London 1610-11, 1611-12, 1615, 1616 (DMH 306, 312, 342, 348), Amsterdam 1633, 1640, 1644 (DMH 473, 545, 579).
(d) Job, Psalms, Proverbs, Ecclesiastes, Song of Solomon ('The third part of the Bible'); in 1616 replaced by Authorized version: 1580, 1583, 1614 (DMH 169, 181, 336).

§2

Morison, S. The Geneva Bible. 1955.
Hall, B. The Genevan version of the English Bible. 1957.
Lupton, L. A history of the Geneva Bible. 7 vols 1966-.

BISHOPS' BIBLE

Rev from Great Bible by Matthew Parker et al.

§1

(a) Bible: 1568, 1569 (DMH 125-6), 1572 (rev, mainly in New testament, by Giles Lawrence; Psalms in both Coverdale's Great Bible and Prayer Book and Bishops' versions; the 'Leda' Bible, from initial at beginning of Hebrews: DMH 132), [1573?] (Psalms in Coverdale's Great Bible and Prayer Book version only, and in all subsequent edns except 1585: DMH 135), 1574-8

(14 edns, 9 in 1575: DMH 137, 139-40, 145, 150-1, 155), 1584 (2 edns: DMH 185-6), 1585 (Psalms in Bishops' version, the only edn thus since 1572: DMH 188), 1588, 1591, 1595, 1602 (DMH 198, 209, 227, 271), [not 1606: DMH 271 note]; in Roger's Collation 1847, above; Genesis in The Genesis octapla, 1965.
(b) New testament:
   (i) 1568 (2 edns: DMH 123-4), [1573-7?] (rev as in 1572 Bible; 3 edns: DMH 133-4, 136), 1575, [1578?], 1579, 1581, 1582 (DMH 142, 157, 163, 172, 176), 1595, 1596, 1597, 1598, 1600 (DMH 228, 232, 241, 245, 259), 1605 (3 edns), 1606, 1608 (DMH 282-4, 288, 297), 1613, 1613-14, 1615, 1617, 1617-19, 1618, nd (2 edns) (DMH 328, 337-8, 344, 356-8); in The New testament octapla, 1962.
   (ii) Bishops' and Rheims versions parallel, ed W. Fulke, below: 1589, 1601, 1601, 1617, 1617, 1633 (DMH 202, 265-6, 359-60, 480).
(c) Gospels, with the Anglo-Saxon, ed John Foxe for M. Parker: 1571 (DMH 131).

§2

Martin, G. A discoverie of the manifold corruptions of the holy scriptures by the heretikes of our daies, specially the English sectaries. Rheims 1582; rptd in Fulke.
Fulke, W. A defense of the sincere and true translations of the holie scriptures into the English tong, against Gregorie Martin. 1583, 1617, 1617, 1633; ed C. H. Hartshorne, Cambridge 1843 (Parker Soc).
Whitaker, W. Disputatic de sacra scriptura. Cambridge 1588, Herborn 1590, 1600; in Opera theologica, ed A. Assheton 2 vols Geneva 1610; tr W. Fitzgerald, Cambridge 1849 (Parker Soc).
Broughton, H. An epistle to the learned nobilitie of England touching translating the Bible. Middleburg 1597.

RHEIMS-DOUAI BIBLE

Roman Catholic; tr Gregory Martin (d. 1582), rev William Allen (1532-94) and Richard Bristow (1538-81).

(a) New testament:
   (i) Rheims 1582 (DMH 177), Antwerp 1600, 1621, (DMH 158, 382), 1630 (Pope p. 271), [Rouen?] 1633 (DMH 479), [Douai or London] 1738 (5th edn) (perhaps ed R. Challoner and F. Blyth: DMH 1041), Liverpool 1788 (6th edn), 1789, New York 1834 (Cotton p. 169); in Roger's Collation 1847, above; The English hexapla, 1841 etc, Firth's Holy Gospel, 1911-12, and New testament octapla, 1962.
   (ii) Rheims and Bishops' versions parallel, ed W. Fulke: 1589-1633, above.
   (iii) rev Robert Witham (d. 1738): [Douai] 2 vols 1730 (with notes: DMH 1009, Cambridge history of Bible p. 367); the notes rptd in the Manchester Bible, 1813 (DMH 1579).
   (iv) rev Richard Challoner (1691-1781): [Dublin?] 1749 (DMH 1086; rptd London 1815, 1818, 1823, 1825, Dublin 1826, 1834, 1835, 1837, 1840, 1850: Cotton p. 169), [Dublin?] 1750 (2nd edn) (DMH 1090; also as vol 5 of 1750 Bible; rptd 1818, Dublin 1820, 1825 etc: Cotton p. 169), [Dublin?] 2 vols 1752, 1 vol 1764 (also as vol 5 of 1763 Bible) (3rd-5th edns), London 1772 (DMH 1099, 1156, 1224), Edinburgh 1797 (from 1764 edn: DMH 1422; also as vol 5 of 1796-7 Bible); many subsequent revisions and reprints from that of B. MacMahon, Dublin 1783 (often called after J. T. Troy, who sanctioned the work: DMH 1292, 1538), Philadelphia 1805 (Hills no 126, DMH 1343 note) etc.
(b) Old testament:
   (i) 2 vols Douai 1609-10, [Rouen] 1635 (both as The

holy Bible, to be accompanied by the New testaments of 1582–1600 and 1633: DMH 300, 499); Genesis in The Genesis octapla, 1965.

(ii) rev R. Challoner: 4 vols [Dublin?] 1750, 1763, Edinburgh 1796 (all as The holy Bible, to be accompanied by the New testaments of 1750, 1764, 1797: DMH 1089, 1156, 1408).

(c) Bible:

(i) 3 vols Rheims or Antwerp-Douai 1582 or 1600–1609–10, [Rouen] 1633–5. Ed D. Rogers 3 vols 1975 (facs).

(ii) rev R. Challoner 5 vols [Dublin?] 1750, 1763–4 (a and b above), 2 vols Philadelphia 1790 (DMH 1343), 5 vols Edinburgh 1796–7 (Old testament 4 vols 1796, New testament 1 vol 1797: DMH 1408, 1422), 1805, Dublin 1811, Liverpool 1816–17.

(iii) many subsequent revisions and reprints from those of B. MacMahon, Dublin 1791 (often called after J. T. Troy, who sanctioned the work: DMH 1538 note), Philadelphia 1805 (Hills no 120, DMH 1343 note), Manchester 1811–13 (ed G. L. Haydock: DMH 1579) etc.

AUTHORIZED VERSION

§1

(a) Bible: 1611 (the Great 'He' Bible, from Ruth iii. 15: DMH 309; rptd Oxford 1833, together with Revised version, as The parallel Bible, 1885, ed W. A. Wright 5 vols Cambridge 1909, ed A. W. Pollard, Oxford 1911 (2 edns, one a facs: DMH 1792, 2040, 2166)); 1611–13 (the Great 'She' Bible, from Ruth iii. 15, or 'Judas' Bible, from Matthew xxvi. 36: DMH 319); 1612–60 London edns every year, often several in different formats (DMH 313–671), including the 'Revenge' Bible from Romans xii. 17, 1613, the 'Wicked' Bible, from Exodus xx. 14, 1631, the 'Forgotten Sins' Bible, from Luke vii. 47, 1638, the 'More Sea' Bible, from Revelation xxi. 1, 1641, and the 'Unrighteous' Bible, from I Corinthians vi. 9, 1653 (DMH 322, 444, 529–32, 553–5, 635–7), and edns ptd at Amsterdam 1625, 1638 [1656?], 1644, 1645 (DMH 399, 529–32, 582, 584, 586, 588, 599?; also Canne's edns listed below), Cambridge 1629, 1630, 1631, 1633, 1635, 1637, 1637–8, 1638, 1639, 1639–40, 1645, 1645–6, 1647?, 1648, 1657, 1659, 1660 (DMH 424, 432–3, 438, 474, 497, 513–14, 520–1, 540, 544, 585, 587, 589, 599?, 612–16, 656–7, 666, 668), Edinburgh 1633, 1636–7, 1637, 1638, 1648–9 (DMH 476, 510–12, 522, 618); edns of Cambridge 1629 and especially 1638 rev, the latter by S. Ward et al, remaining the standard text till rev F. S. Paris and H. Therold, Cambridge 1762, and rev B. Blayney, Oxford 1769 (DMH 424, 520, 1142, 1194); many other edns since 1661.

Scrivener, F. H. A. (ed). The Cambridge paragraph Bible of the Authorized English version, with the text revised by a collation of its early and other principal editions and a critical introduction prefixed. Cambridge 1873. Selections in Roger's Collation 1847, above.

Authorized version text with Geneva notes ed J. Canne, Amsterdam 1642, 1642–3, 1644?, 1647, 1662, 1664, 1672, 1679, 1682, 1683, London 1698, [ptd Amsterdam] pbd London 1700, [Amsterdam?] 1707–8, 1715, 1720?, Edinburgh 1727, 1747, 1754, 2 vols 1764–6 (as The pulpit and family Bible); tr Welsh,

Trefecca 1790, Caermarthen 1812.

The translators' preface separately rptd 1870, Oxford [1870], London [1880], [1911]; ed E. J. Goodspeed, Chicago 1935 (title varies).

(b) New testament: 1611 (DMH 310; rptd in The New testament hexapla 1841 etc; Firth's Holy gospel [etc] 1911–12, and The New testament octapla, 1962, and, together with the Revised version, as The parallel New testament, Oxford and Cambridge 1882 etc: DMH 1840, 2025), 1612–60 (London edns most years, often several in different formats: DMH 318–652), Edinburgh 1619, 1628, 1631, 1633, 1635, 1636, 1640, 1642, 1643, 1647 (DMH 373, 420, 457, 481, 496, 506, 508, 549, 568–9, 575, 603), Aberdeen 1631 (DMH 456), Cambridge 1628 (DMH 421–2); ed C. Hoole, parallel with Beza's Latin, 1659 (DMH 667) etc.

(c) Job, Psalms, Proverbs, Ecclesiastes, Song of Solomon ('The third part of the Bible'); replacing a similar Geneva collection: 1616, 1626, 1632, 1638 (DMH 350, 404, 470, 523), Edinburgh 1642 (DMH 570).

§2

Barlow, W. The summe and substance of the conference at Hampton Court. 1604, 1605, 1625, 1638; ed J. Dunton, Phenix, 2 vols 1707–8: reissued as A collection of choice, scarce and valuable tracts, 2 vols 1721.

Broughton, H. A censure of the late translation for our churches. [Middleburg 1612?].

Gell, R. An essay towards the amendment of the last English translation of the Bible. 1659.

MINOR VERSIONS

For the Golden legend, Westminster 1483 etc, W. Caxton's extended trn of a French version of the Legenda aurea of Jacobus de Voragine, into which Caxton inserts the Bible histories, including much of the Pentateuch and the Gospels, see col 73, above. For English versions of the Lord's Prayer, the Ten Commandments, and the Beatitudes 1500–26, see DMH p. xxxi.

Sir Thomas More
1478–1535

Miscellaneous passages tr incidentally in his writings, 1522–34.

(a) De quatuor novissimis: or the four last things 1522. In Workes, 1557; ed D. O'Connor 1903, 1935; in English works vol 1, ed W. E. Campbell 1931.

(b) A dialoge of comfort against tribulacion. 1553 (written 1534); in Workes, 1557; separately Antwerp 1573, London 1847; 1910 (EL) (with Utopia), 1951 (rev); ed P. E. Hallett 1937; ed M. Stevens 1951; extracts ed H. S. Bowden 1915 (Crumbs of comfort).

(c) A treatice to receave the blessed body of our Lorde 1534. In Workes, 1557.

(d) A treatice upon the passion of Chryste 1534. In Workes, 1557.

Sir John Cheke
1514–57

Matthew and Mark i, tr c. 1550 (ms at Corpus Christi College, Cambridge). Ed J. Goodwin 1843 (DMH 1847).

(4) STUDIES

Westcott, B. F. A general view of the history of the English Bible. 1868, 1872, 1905 (rev W. A. Wright).

Kenyon, F. G. Our Bible and the ancient manuscripts: being a history of the text and its translations. 1895, [1911] (rev), 1939 (rev), 1958 (rev A. W. Adams). Includes ch on English ptd Bible.

Pollard, A. W. Records of the English Bible: the documents relating to the translation and publication of the Bible in English 1525–1611. Oxford 1911.

Butterworth, C. C. The literary lineage of the King James Bible 1340–1611. Philadelphia 1941.

Daiches, D. The King James version of the English Bible, with special reference to the Hebrew tradition. Chicago 1941.

Grierson, H. J. C. The English Bible. 1943; rptd in W. J. Turner (ed), Impressions of English literature, 1944, New York 1945 (as Romance of English literature).

Greenslade, S. L. (ed). The Cambridge history of the Bible [vol 3]: the West from the Reformation to the present day. Cambridge 1963. Includes Greenslade, English versions of the Bible 1525–1611; L. A. Weigle, English versions since 1611; M. H. Black, The printed Bible.

III. THE PRAYER BOOK

Edward VI's First Prayer Book

The booke of common praier and administration of the sacramentes. 1549 (9 edns), Worcester 1549, 1549, London 1550 (with music by J. Marbeck), Dublin 1551, London 1551; 1910 (EL).

Calvinist Prayer Books

The forme of common praiers used in the churches of Geneva. 1550; The forme of prayers and ministration of the sacraments, used in the English congregation at Geneva and approved by John Calvyn, Geneva 1556; 1557 (bound with prose psalter) (Cambridge Univ Lib), 1558, 1561 (3 edns); Edinburgh 1562 (transitional between Genevan and Scottish orders; for subsequent Scottish revisions see below); A forme of prayers to be used in private houses, 1570 (in 3rd edn of Geneva Bible); A booke of the forme of common prayers, administration of the sacraments, agreable to the use of the reformed churches, [1584] (separately), Middelburg 1586, 1587, 1602, London 1643; tr Latin, Ratio et forma publice orandi Deum, Geneva 1556.

Edward VI's Second Prayer Book

The booke of common prayer. 1552 (9 edns), Worcester 1552, London 1553 (4 edns); 1910 (EL).

Queen Elizabeth's Prayer Book

The booke of common prayer and administration of the sacramentes. 1559 (5 edns), 1560, 1560, 1562, 1564, 1566, [Rouen?] 1566, London 1567, 1570, 1570, 1571, 1572, 1573, 1574, [1575], [1575], [1576], 1580 (3 edns), 1585, [1585], 1587, 1588, 1589, 1590, [1590], 1592, 1592, [1595], [1595], 1596, 1596, 1597, 1599, 1600, 1603.

Scottish Book of Common Order

The forme of prayers and ministration of the sacraments used in the English churche at Geneva. Edinburgh 1562; approved and received by the Churche of Scotland, 1564–5, 1565, [Geneva?] 1566, Edinburgh 1571, 1575, [Geneva?] 1584, London 1587, 1587, Middelburg 1594, Edinburgh 1595–6, [Middelburg 1599], Edinburgh 1599–1602, Dort 1601, Middelburg 1602, Edinburgh 1611, 1611, 1615, 1617, 1622, Aberdeen 1629, 1633, Edinburgh 1634, 1635, 1640 (3 edns, all incomplete); tr Gaelic, Edinburgh 1567.

Jacobean Prayer Book

1603[–4], 1604 (3 edns), 1605, 1605, 1606, 1606, 1607, 1608, 1609, [1610?], 1611, 1611, [1612?], 1613, 1613–14, 1613–14, 1614, 1614, 1615 (4 edns), 1616 (4 edns), 1617, 1618, 1619, 1619, 1619–20, 1620 (3 edns), 1621, 1621, 1622, 1622, 1623, 1623, 1624, 1625, 1625, 1626, 1626, 1627 (4 edns), 1628 (5 edns), 1629 (3 edns), Cambridge 1629, 1630, London 1630 (4 edns), 1631, 1631, 1632 (5 edns), 1632–3, 1632–3, 1633 (3 edns), Edinburgh 1633, London 1633–4, 1633–4, 1634, Edinburgh 1634, 1634, Cambridge 1635, London 1635, 1636, 1636, 1637, 1637, Cambridge 1637, Dublin 1637, London 1638 (4 edns), Cambridge 1638, 1638, London 1638–9, 1639 (7 edns), London 1640, 1640, Cambridge 1640, London 1641, 1642, 1645, 1660 (4 edns), Cambridge 1660, London 1661, 1661.

The 1604 Prayer book is a slight revision of Queen Elizabeth's, above; also called the Hampton Court book.

Scottish Prayer Book

§ 1

The booke of common prayer for the use of the Church of Scotland. Edinburgh 1636–7 ('Laud's Book', 3 edns); The new booke of common prayer, according to the forme of the Kirke of Scotland, 1644, Edinburgh 1712.

§ 2

Donaldson, G. The making of the Scottish Prayer-book of 1637. Edinburgh 1954.

Directory for Public Worship

1644 (2 edns) etc. Compulsory 1645–60.

Baxter's Proposed Savoy Liturgy

The reformation of the liturgy, as it was presented to the bishops by the divines appointed by his Majesties Commission [the Savoy Conference], to treat of the alteration to it [by R. Baxter]. In Baxter, A petition for peace, 1661; in E. Calamy, The history of nonconformity, 1704; in P. Hall, Reliquiæ liturgicæ vol 4, 1847.

Charles II's Prayer Book

The book of common prayer and administration of the sacraments. 1662 ('Sealed Book', 2 edns), Cambridge 1662, 1662, 1663, London 1663, 1663, 1665, Cambridge 1666, London 1667, Dublin 1668, London 1669, Cambridge 1670, London 1671, Cambridge 1673, Oxford 1675, Cambridge 1675, 1676, London 1676, 1678, Oxford 1679, Cambridge 1679, London 1680, 1680, Dublin 1680, Oxford 1680, 1681, 1682, 1683, London 1683, Cambridge 1683, Oxford 1684, 1685, 1686, 1687, London 1687, 1687, 1688, Oxford 1688, 1691, London 1692, 1693, Oxford 1693, Cambridge 1694, London 1695, Cambridge 1696, Oxford 1696, 1697, 1698, 1699, 1700, Dublin 1700 etc; with an exposition and preface by J. Fludger (Fludyer), 1735, 1739; illustrated and explained by L. Howard, 1761; with preface and notes by J. Reeves, 1801, 1802, 1804, 1807; with introd and notes by R. Warner, Bath 1806; with notes by Sir J. Bayley, 1813, 1816, 1824; with notes explanatory, practical, and historical, by R. Mant, Oxford 1820, 1822, 1825, 1836, London 1840, 1850;

illustrated so as to show its various modifications, by W. K. Clay, 1841; annotated, by J. H. Blunt, 1866; ed A. P. Stanley 1870.

William and Mary's Proposed Prayer Book

The revised liturgy. 1689; Being the Book of common prayer [1683–6] interleaved with the alterations proposed by the Royal Commissioners, ed J. Taylor 1855; A copy of the alterations in the Book of common prayer, prepared by the Royal Commissioners for the revision of the liturgy in 1689, printed by order [1854] of the House of Commons, 1856.

Polyglot

The book of common prayer in eight languages: namely English, French, Italian, German, Spanish, Greek ancient and modern, Latin. 1821, 1825, [1866].

IV. VERSIONS OF THE PSALMS

Complete and partial versions, metrical and prose, trns and paraphrases, liturgical and non-liturgical, pbd separately or in larger works other than Bibles and Prayer books, above.

References

Aston   [W. H. Aston, Baron (ed)], Select psalms in verse, with critical remarks by [R.] Lowth and others, 1811.
Cotton   H. Cotton, Editions of the Bible and parts thereof in English, Oxford 1852 (2nd edn).
Holland   J. Holland, The psalmists of Britain: records, biographical and literary, with specimens, 2 vols 1843.
Farr   E. Farr (ed), Select poetry, chiefly devotional, of the reign of Queen Elizabeth, 2 pts Cambridge 1845 (Parker Soc).
Farr 3   E. Farr (ed), Select poetry, chiefly sacred, of the reign of James I, Cambridge 1847.
Latham   [H. Latham (ed)], Anthologia Davidica, 1846 (with list of metrical versions, and specimens).
Glass   H. A. Glass, The story of the psalters: a history of the metrical versions of Great Britain and America, from 1549 to 1885, 1888.
Julian   J. Julian, A dictionary of hymnology, 1892, 2 vols 1907 (rev), 1925.
Steele   R. Steele, The earliest English music printing: a description and bibliography of English printed music to the close of the sixteenth century, 1903 (Bibl Soc).
Brooke   W. T. Brooke, Old English psalmody, from the accession of Edward VI to the restoration of Charles II 1547–1660, 1916 (with specimens).
BUCOEM   British union-catalogue of early music, ed E. B. Schnapper 2 vols 1957.
Aldis   H. G. Aldis, A list of books printed in Scotland before 1700, Edinburgh 1904 (Edinburgh Bibl Soc), 1970 (rev).

George Joye (1495?–1553). The psalter of David in Englishe purely and faithfully translated after the texte of ffeline. 'Argentine' (for Antwerp) 1530, London [1532–4] (DMH 3, 7). Prose; under the pseudonym Johan Aleph; from the Latin of 'Aretius Felinus' i.e. Martin Bucer, Strasbourg 1529; psalm 19 rptd in Cotton.
— Davids psalter diligently translated by G. Joye. [Antwerp] 1534, London [1541–2?] (DMH 9). Prose; a different trn from above; from the Latin of Felix Pratensis, Venice 1515, Hagenau 1522, Lyons 1530, Strasbourg 1545; psalm 19 rptd in Cotton.
Miles Coverdale (1488–1568). A paraphrasis upon al the psalmes of David, made by Johannes Campensis and translated out off Latyne into Englishe. [Antwerp] 1534 (Cambridge history of the Bible p. 148), [Antwerp] 1535, London 1539 (DMH 14). Prose paraphrase, from Latin of J. van Kampen (Campensis), Enchiridion psalmorum, Paris 1532, Paris and London 1534 etc.
— The psalter or booke of the psalmes; ther unto are added other devoute praiers. [1540?], 1540 (with Latin) 1548, [1550?] (DMH 55–6). Prose; extracted from Coverdale's Bible, 1535.
— A very excellent and swete exposition upon the two and twentye [i.e. 23] psalme, translated out of hye Almayne [of M. Luther] in to Englyshe. Southwark 1537, 1538; rptd in Cotton. Prose; from Luther's Warhafftig Widerlegung, der grossen Verferlogung der judischen Lehrer, des 22 Psalm, Nuremberg 1536, Wittenberg [1536] etc.
— The psalter or psalmes of David corrected and poyncted. 1549, [1549], Worcester 1549, Canterbury 1549, 1550, London [1553?], 1566, 1570, 1571, 1572, 1574, 1575, 1576, 1577, [1579]?, [1583], 1594, 1598, 1600, 1604, 1606, 1615, 1617, 1618, 1620, 1624, 1634, 1635 (DMH 162 etc); ed F. Wormald 1930. Great Bible version, 1539; used in the Book of common prayer, 1549, 1558, 1662.

— Goostly psalmes. [1536?] (DMH 47; Steele 13). Metrical trn, with music from various German metrical versions, of 13 psalms, 2 (50 and 127) in 2 trns: psalms 2, 11 [12], 13 [14], 24 [25], 45 [46], 50 [51], 66 [67] 123 [124], 127 [128], 129 [130], 132 [133], 136 [137], 146 [147]: psalm 137 rptd in Cotton, psalm 50 in Holland. 3rd and 5th rptd in G. Pearson (ed), Coverdale's Remains, Cambridge 1846 (Parker Soc); 2nd and 4th in The hexaplar psalter, 1911; 2nd, 4th and most of 5th in, E. Clapton (ed), Coverdale's Bible: our Prayer book psalter, 1934.
Willoughby, H. R. (ed). The Coverdale psalter and the quatro-centenary of the printed English Bible. Chicago 1935. Facs of 2nd psalter, with census of copies of all edns of Coverdale's Bible.
Thomas Becon (1512–67). The hundred and fiftene psalme, Credidi propter, with a fruitefull exposition and godly declaration. In Davids harpe ful of most delectable armony, newely stringed and set in tune, 1542; in his Worckes vol 1, 1564; in his Early works, ed J. Ayre, Cambridge 1843 (Parker Soc). Psalm 116.10–19 in prose, under pseudonym T. Basille.
— Confortable epistle. Strasbourg 1554; in his Worckes vol 3, 1563; in Prayers and other pieces, ed J. Ayre, Cambridge 1844 (Parker Soc). Contains psalms 103 and 112 in verse; from the German.
— Metrical trn of psalms 117 and 134, in the appendix to Sternhold and Hopkins 1560 etc, below; psalm 134 in Brooke.
Sir Thomas Smith (1513–77). Certaigne psalmes or songues of David, translated into Englishe meter. In BM Royal ms 17 A. xvii. Psalms 30, 40, 54, 70, 85, 102, 119, 142, 144–5, 152; ed B. Danielsson, Stockholm Stud in Eng 12 1963; psalm 54 in Holland.
Sir Thomas Wyatt (1503?–42). Certayne psalmes commonly called thee vii penytentiall psalmes, drawen into englyshe meter. [Ed J. Harington] 1549, [1550?]; in

edns of Wyatt's works, 1717 etc, R. Hughey, The Arundel Harington manuscript of Tudor poetry vol 1, Columbus 1960, and Collected poems, ed K. A. Muir and P. Thomson, Liverpool 1969; psalm 51 in Cotton, 102 in Holland, 130 in Brooke. The penitential psalms (6, 32, 38, 51, 102, 130, 143) and psalm 37; principally from parallel Latin trns of J. van Kampen (Campensis) and U. Zwingli in Enchiridion psalmorum, Lyons 1533, using also P. Aretino's Italian paraphrase, Venice 1536, Joye's English prose psalter of 1530, the Latin vulgate and Coverdale's Great Bible, 1539; trn generally regarded as made in 1542.

John Wedderburn (1500?–56). Psalmes of David with uther new pleasand ballatis translatit out of Enchiridion psalmorum. Pt 4 of Ane compendious buik of godlie psalmes and spirituall sangis, Edinburgh [1567–8], 1578, 1600, [1621] (Aldis 55, 148, 327, 570); ed D. Laing, Edinburgh 1868 (from edn of 1578); ed A. F. Mitchell, Edinburgh 1897 (STS) (from edn of 1567–8). Metrical version of 22 psalms (2, 12–13, 15, 23, 31, 33, 37, 51, 64, 67, 73, 79, 83, 91, 114–15, 124, 128, 130, 137, 145), ed and probably tr J. Wedderburn, vicar of Dundee, perhaps assisted by his brother Robert (1510?–57?), from the German; tr 1539–43 (Julian) or 1549 (Mitchell). Known as Dundee psalms.
Mitchell, A. F. The Wedderburns and their work. Edinburgh 1867.

Queen Elizabeth I (1533–1603). Metrical trn of psalm '13' [14], in her trn of A godly medytacyon of the Christen sowle, by Margaret d'Angoulême, Queen of Navarre, ed J. Bale 1548; only verse one in edn of [1568–70?]; ed P. Ames 1897; in T. Park (ed), A catalogue of the royal and noble authors of England by H. Walpole vol 1, 1806; in Holland, Farr, and Cotton. Tr 1544.

John Bale (1495–1563). Metrical trn of psalm 54 in The first examinacyon of Anne Askewe, Marburg 1546, London [1585?]; in his Select works, ed H. Christmas, Cambridge 1849 (Parker Soc).

—— Metrical trn of psalms 23 and 130 in An expostulation or complaynte agaynste the blasphemyes of a franticke papyst of Hamshyre, [1552?].

Sir John Croke (d. 1554). Thirteen psalms, and the first chapter of Ecclesiastes, translated into English verse. Ed A. Croke and P. Bliss 1844 (Percy Soc). Psalms 6, 13, 19, 31.1–6, 32, 38, 43, 51, 91, 102, 130, 139, 143. Tr by 1547.

Henry Howard, Earl of Surrey (1517–47). Metrical trn of psalms 31, 51, 88 in T. Sternhold, or rather J. Hall, Certayne chapters of the proverbes, [1549?] (later edns under Hall's name contain different psalms). Psalms 55, 73, 88 in J. Harington, Nugae antiquae vol 2, ed T. Park 1804.

Robert Crowley (Crole) (1518?–88). The psalter of David newely translated into Englysh metre. Holborn 1549 (BUCOEM 817; Steele 16). First complete English metrical version, from the Latin of Leo Juda et al, Biblia sacrosancta, Zürich 1543, 1543–4, 1544, Paris 1545, Salamanca 1584–5 etc; with music in 4 pts; psalm 19 rptd in Cotton, psalm 112 in Holland.

Sternhold and Hopkins, the 'Old Version'. See Holland 1 91–144, with psalm 9 (Sternhold), 37 (Whittingham), 84 (Hopkins), 125 (Kethe, Wisdom), 132 ('Mardley' or rather Marckant), 136 ('Churchyard' or rather Craig), 146 (Norton), 149 (Pullain); Farr xlvi–li, 480–99, with psalms 18, 103 (Sternhold), 84 (Hopkins), 147 (Norton), 51 (Whittingham), 125 (Kethe, Wisdom), 149 (Pullain), 145 ('Mardley' or rather Marckant); psalms 23, 35, 100, 104 (rev) in Latham; psalm 19 (1549, 1551, 1556, 1564) in Cotton; see Glass 65–6; Julian 857–66, 1538–41.
Long the standard Anglican metrical psalter; by Thomas Sternhold (d. 1549), John Hopkins (d. 1570), William Whittingham (1524?–79), John Pullain (1517–65), Thomas Norton (1532–84), William Kethe (d. 1608?), John Marckant (not Mardley), Robert Wisdom (d. 1568), John

Craig (1512–1600) and T. Becon (1512–67); after 1696 known as the 'Old Version' in distinction from Tate and Brady's 'New Version'.

Church of England

Certayne psalmes chosen out of the psalter of David, and drawen into English metre. [1547–8?] (19 psalms, all by Sternhold: 1–5, 20, 25, 28 (misprinted '27'), 29 ('19'), 32, 34 ('33'), 41, 49, 73, 78, 103, 120, 123 ('122'), 128 ('138'): DMH 66); Al such psalmes of David as T. Sternholde did draw into English metre, 1549, (37 psalms by Sternhold, 19 as before, with 6–17, 19, 21, 43–4, 63, 68, and 7 by Hopkins: 30, 33, 42, 52, 79, 82, 146); total 44); [1550?], 1551 (3 edns), 1553, 1553.

Church of Geneva

One and fiftie psalmes of David in English metre [pt 2 of The forme of prayers, and ministration of the sacraments, used at Geneva]. Geneva 1556 (44 as before, rev Whittingham, with 7 by Whittingham [23, 51, 114–15, 130, 133, 137], total 51; the first edn with music, adapted from that ed and composed by Bourgeois for the French psalter of C. Marot and T. de Bèze, 1552–54; BUCOEM 817); Psalmes [pt 2 of The forme of prayers], 1558 (51 as before, with 9 by Whittingham [37, 50, 67, 71, 119, 121, 124, 127, 129], and 2 by Pullain [148–9], total 62).

Church of England

Psalmes of David. 1560 (62 as before, with 2 by Wisdom [67, 125], one anon [95], 2 by Becon in an appendix [117, 134], total 67; 42 tunes: BUCOEM 817; Steele 36), 1561 (67 as before, the anon 95 being moved to the appendix, omitting Wisdom's 67 and Whittingham's 67 and 71, and adding 3 by Whittingham [18, 22–3], 14 by Hopkins [24, 26–7, 31, 62, 64–7, 69–72, 74], one by Norton [75], and one by Kethe [100], total 83; 40 tunes: Steele 38).

Church of Geneva

Foure score and seven psalmes [separately and in The forme of prayers]. [London or Geneva] 1561 (62 as before, with 25 by Kethe [27, 36, 47, 54, 58, 62, 70, 85, 88, 90–1, 94, 100–1, 104, 107, 111–13, 122, 125–6, 134, 138, 142], total 87; 62 tunes: Steele 37).

Complete edns:

The whole book of psalmes. Ed Hopkins 1562 (40 psalms by Sternhold: 19 first in 1547–8, 18 in 1549, 3 in 1561; 60 by Hopkins: 7 in 1549, 14 in 1561, 39 in 1562 [35–6, 38–40, 45–8, 50, 54–61, 76–7, 80–1, 83–99]; 10 by Whittingham: 5 of 7 from 1556 [51, 114, 130, 133, 137], and 5 of 9 from 1558 [37, 119, 121, 124, 127]; 26 by Norton: one in 1561, 25 in 1562 [51, 53, 101–2, 105–6, 108–10, 115–17, 129, 136, 138–45, 147, 149–50]; 4 by Marckant: 118, 131–2, 135, first in 1562; 9 by Kethe, from his 25 in 1561: 104, 107, 111–13, 122, 125–6, 134; one by Pullain: 148 from 1558, omitting 149, an anon psalm 100, and the anon 95 and 2 by Becon [1560] in appendix; total 150 psalms in 154 versions; with 65 tunes: DMH 118; BUCOEM 817; Steele 40); 291 edns 1563–1640 [London, except for 11 Cambridge edns 1628–38 and 7 undated Amsterdam edns c. 1630–3] (1563–4 restoring Whittingham's psalm 50, Kethe's 100 and Wisdom's 125; 1565 restoring Whittingham's 23; 1581 adding Craig's 136 from the Scottish psalter: 287 edns in BUCOEM 817–827; 80 edns 1563–1600 in Steele among 41–196), over 200 edns 1641–1700, at least 275 edns 1701–1852 (BM).
1601 (with Geneva version, parallel or in the margin), 1603, 1605, 1613, 1615, 1617, 1623, 1628, 1628, 1631. 1635 (with the Prayer book prose version, Coverdale 1539).

John Hall (1529?–66?). The proverbs of Salomon, three chapters of Ecclesiastes and certayn psalmes of David, drawen into metre. [1549?]. Contains 5 psalms (34,

54, 112, 114–15); the only copy is incomplete at the end.

—— Certayne chapters taken out of the proverbes of Salomon etc. [1548–9]. Contains 9 psalms: '21' [i.e. 24], 33, 53, 64, 111–13, 114 (unnumbered), 144.

—— The Courte of Vertu: contaynynge many holy songes, sonettes, psalmes and ballettes. 1565 (BUCOEM 817; Steele 49; contains 12 psalms: 25, 34, 54, 65, 112–15, 130, 137, 140, 145). Psalm 115 in Holland and Farr.

William Hunnis (d. 1597). Certayne psalmes chosen out of the psalter of David and drawen furth into Englysh meter. 1550. Psalms 51, 56–7, 113, 117, 147; supplementary to Sternhold and Hopkins 1549; 51 rptd in Cotton and Farr.

—— Seven sobs of a sorrowfull soule for sinne: comprehending these seven psalmes called pœnitentiall, reduced into meeter. 1583, 1587, 1589, 1597, 1600, 1604, 1609, 1615, 1618, 1629. (BUCOEM 516; Steele 86, 108, 122, 162). Psalms 6, 32, 38, 51 (different from above), 102, 130, 143; with 7 tunes; psalm 6 rptd in Holland and Farr.

John Knox (1505–72). A percel of the VI psalme expoundet. [Wesel 1554] (running title), [abroad 1556?] (as An exposition vpon the syxt psalme); ed A. Fleming 1580 (as A fort for the afflicted); in his Works vol 3, ed D. Laing, Edinburgh 1854.

Matthew Parker (1504–75). The whole psalter translated into English metre. [1567?] (BUCOEM 817; Steele 53). With 8 4-pt tunes by T. Tallis; completed in 1555; anon; authorship established by acrostic at psalm 119.

George Buchanan (1506–82). [Latin metrical versions of 18 psalms]. In Davidis psalmi aliquot latino carmine expressi a quatuor poetis, ed H. Estienne, [Paris] 1556.

The Geneva psalms. [Prose, probably by Anthony Gilby, based on Calvin's commentaries, 1557, and Sternhold and Hopkins]. [Geneva] 1557. Copies in Bodley and Cambridge Univ Lib.

—— [A different prose trn; the same as in 1560 Geneva Bible, above]. Geneva 1559, London 1576; ptd parallel with 10 edns of Sternhold and Hopkins, 1601–31, above; in The hexaplar psalter, 1911.

William Kethe (Keith) (d. 1608?). Psalme of David XCIII (XCIIII) turned in to metre. In J. Knox, The appellation from the cruell sentence, Geneva 1558; in Knox, Works vol 4, ed D. Laing, Edinburgh 1855.

—— [Metrical versions of psalms, 27, 36, 47, 54, 58, 62, 70, 85, 88, 90–1, 94, 100–1, 104, 107, 111–13, 122, 125–6, 134, 138, 142]. In Geneva psalter, 1561 etc and Scottish psalter 1564–5 etc. 9 psalms (between 104 and 134) are adopted in the English Sternhold and Hopkins 1562 and constantly thereafter.

John Craig (1512–1600). Verse trns of 15 psalms (24, 56, 75, 102, 105, 108, 110, 117–18, 132, 140–1, 143, 145) in Scottish psalter of 1564–5 below.

Robert Pont (Kylpont, Kynpont) (1524–1606). Verse trns of 6 psalms (57, 59, 76, 80–1, 83) in the Scottish psalter of 1564–5, below.

First Scottish Psalter. Ed John Knox and, specially after 1575, rev Robert Pont, above; the standard Presbyterian psalter till 1650; mainly derived from Sternhold and Hopkins.

William Byrd (Bird) (1543?–1623). [Metrical trn of psalms 12–13, 15, 112, 119 (2 sections only), 123, 130, with 6 and 55 in Sternhold and Hopkins version]. In Psalmes, sonets and songs of sadnes and pietie, made into musicke of five parts, 5 pts 1588, [1599?] (BUCOEM 147; Steele 113).

Abraham Fraunce (d. c. 1633). [Metrical trn of Certeine psalmes: 1, 6, 8, 29, 38, 50, 73, 104]. In The Countesse of Pembrokes Emanuell, 1591; in A. B. Grosart (ed), Miscellanies of the Fuller worthies' library vol 3, 1872.

Henry Lok (Lock) (1553?–1608?). Sundry psalms of David, translated into verse. 1594; in Ecclesiastes, otherwise called the preacher, 1597. Psalms 27, 71, 119,

121, 130; 121 rptd in Cotton and Farr, 27 in Holland and Farr.

Sir Philip Sidney (1554–86) and his sister Mary Herbert Countess of Pembroke (1555–1621). Metrical; psalms 1–43 by Sidney (probably tr c. 1585), 44–150 by the Countess (c. 1590–9); mainly from Les CL pseaumes mis en rime françoise par C. Marot et T. de Bèze, 1562, using also the Prayer book prose version from Coverdale's Great Bible 1539, Geneva Bible 1560, Bishops' Bible 1568 and Bèze's Latin metrical paraphrase 1580.

The psalmes of David, translated into divers and sundry kinds of verse, begun by Sir P. Sidney and finished by the Countess of Pembroke. [Ed S. W. Singer] 1823; Complete works vol 3, ed A. Feuillerat, Cambridge 1923 (1–43); Poems, ed W. A. Ringler, Oxford 1962 (1–43); ed J. C. A. Rathmell, Garden City NY 1963 (1–150).

Sir John Harington (1560–1612). 'The psalmes put into verse' in Bodley ms Douce 361. Psalms 24, 112, 137 ptd in Nugae antiquae vol 2, ed T. Park 1804; 112 and 137 in Farr; 112 in Brooke. All 150 psalms.

Charles Lumisden (c. 1561–1630). An exposition upon some select psalms of David, written by Robert Rollock, and translated out of Latine. Edinburgh 1600. Prose trn of 15 psalms (3, 6, 16, 23, 32, 39, 42, 49, 51, 62, 65, 84, 116, 130, 137); tr from In selectos aliquot psalmos Davidis commentarius, Edinburgh 1599, 1610.

Christopher Davison. Metrical trn c. 1602 of psalms 15 and 125 in BM ms Harley 6930, transcribed in Harley 3357 and Bodley ms Rawlinson poetry 61; psalms 15 and 125 in F. Davison, Poetical rhapsody vol 3, ed S. E. Brydges, Lee Priory 1817; vol 2 ed N. H. Nicolas 1826 (psalms from this edn also separately); vol 2 ed A. H. Bullen 1891 (psalm 15 only, also in Holland); 15 and 125, the latter misattributed to F. Davison, in Farr; 15 and 125 in G. Fletcher, Christ's victory and triumph, ed W. T. Brooke 1888.

Francis Davison (c. 1575–c. 1621). Metrical trn c. 1602 of 16 psalms in 18 versions (1. 2–4, 6, 13, 23 (3 versions), 30, 43, 73. 1–5, 79, 86, 123, 130–1, 133, 137, 142) in BM ms Harley 6930 (probably autograph; psalms 43, 123, 128 anon), transcribed in Harley 3357 (all attributed to F. Davison) and Bodley ms Rawlinson poetry 61; all except 43, 123 and 128 in Poetical rhapsody vol 3, ed Brydges (above) and Nicolas's edn vol 2 1826; 6, 13 and 23 (one version) in Bullen's edn vol 2 1891; all 18 versions in G. Fletcher, Christ's victory and triumph, ed W. T. Brooke 1888.

Henry Dod (1550?–1630?). Certaine psalmes of David reduced into English meter. 1603. Psalms 104, 111, 120, 122, 124–6, 130; with prose in the margin.

—— Al the psalmes of David with certeine songes and canticles, nowe faithfully reduced into easie meeter. 1620. With prose in the margin.

Elizabeth Grymeston (Grimstoun) née Barney (c. 1565–1603). Odes in imitation of the seven pœnitentiall psalmes, in seven severall kinde of verse. In Miscelanea, meditations, memoratives, 1604, [1606?], [1608?], [1610?]; psalm 51 in Farr.

Alexander Montgomerie (1556?–1610?). The mindes melodie: contayning certayne psalmes applyed to a new and pleasant tune. Edinburgh 1605 (Aldis 389). 15 psalms: 1, 4, 6, 8, 15, 19, 23, 43, 57, 91, 101, 117, 121, 125, 128; in Poems, ed D. Laing and D. Irving, Edinburgh 1821; ed J. Cranstoun and G. Stevenson vol 1 1887 (STS) (also trns of psalms 1 [rev], 2, 36 as Devotional poems); 19 in Cotton; 1 and 23 in A. Ramsay, The ever green vol 2, Edinburgh 1724 etc, and in Montgomerie's Poetical works, Glasgow 1754.

Joseph Hall (1574–1656). Some fewe of Davids psalms metaphrased, for a taste of the rest. Pt 2 of Holy observations, 1607, 1609; in edns of Works vol 1, 1614–48; Complete poems, ed A. B. Grosart, Manchester

1879. Psalms 1–10; in metre; 7 rptd in Holland and Latham; 8 in Cotton; 4 in Brooke.

Henry Ainsworth (1571–1623?). The book of psalmes englished, both in prose and metre, with annotations. Amsterdam 1612 (with music: DMH 317, BUCOEM 821), 1617–18 (as Annotations upon the book of psalmes) (BUCOEM 822); in Annotations upon the five books of Moses and the booke of psalmes, 1622, 1622, 1626–7, 1639 (DMH 385); The booke of psalmnes, Amsterdam 1644 (BUCOEM 827), Glasgow 1843; The booke of psalmes in English metre, [Amsterdam?] 1632 (with music; metrical version only: BUCOEM 825), Rotterdam 1638.

George Chapman (1559–1634). Petrarchs seven penitentiall psalms, paraphrastically translated. 1612; in his Works vol 2, ed A. C. Swinburne and R. H. Shepherd 1875; Poems, ed P. B. Bartlett, New York 1944.

John Davies of Hereford (1565?–1618). The dolefull dove: or Davids 7 penitentiall psalms, paraphrastically turned into verse. In The Muses sacrifice: or divine meditations, 1612; in his Works vol 2, ed A. B. Grosart 1878.

Sir William Leighton (fl. 1603–14). Seaven psalmes of Davids repentance. In The teares of lamentations of a sorrowfull sowle, 1613, 1614 (with music: BUCOEM 608). The 7 penitential psalms in verse.

Sir David Murray (1567–1629). A paraphrase of the civ psalme. Edinburgh 1615 (Aldis 478); in his Poems 1823; Blackwood's Mag April–May 1818.

Sir Edwin Sandys (1561–1629). Sacred hymns: consisting of fifti select psalms of David and others, paraphrastically turned into English verse. 1615 (BUCOEM 993).

George Wither (Wyther, Withers) (1588–1667). A preparation to the psalter. 1619, 1884 (Spenser Soc).

—— Exercises upon the first psalme, both in prose and verse. 1620, 1882 (Spenser Soc).

—— The psalmes of David, translated into lyrick-verse. [Netherlands] 1632, 2 vols 1881 (Spenser Soc).

Thomas Carew (Carey) (1595?–1640). 9 psalms in Poems, ed W. C. Hazlitt 1870, ed J. W. Ebsworth 1893, ed R. Dunlap, Oxford 1949; in R. G. Howarth (ed), Minor poets of the seventeenth century 1931 (EL); psalm 91 in G. Fletcher, Christ's victory and triumph, ed W. T. Brooke 1888.

John Milton (1608–74). Metrical paraphrases of psalms 114 and 136, made at age 15, influenced by G. Buchanan's Latin paraphrases; ptd in his Poems in English and Latin, 1645.

Sir John Davies (1570–1626). [Metrical 'metaphrase' c. 1624 of psalms 1–50, 67, 91, 95, 100, 103, 150]. In his Works vol 1, ed A. B. Grosart 1869.

Francis Bacon, Lord Verulam (1561–1626). Translation of certaine psalmes into English verse. 1625.

Alexander Top (fl. 1597–1629). The book of prayses, called the psalmes: the keyes and holly things of David, translated out of the Hebrew, according to the letter, and the mystery of them; opened in proper arguments upon every psalme. Amsterdam 1629. Prose trn.

William Slatyer (Slater) (1587–1647). Psalmes or songes of Sion, turned into the language and set to the tunes of a strange land, intended for Christmas carols. [1630–4], 1642.

—— The psalmes of David, in four languages and in four parts, set to the tunes of our Church. 1643, 1652 (BUCOEM 909–10). With music; psalms 1–22; Hebrew, Greek, Latin, English.

Sir William Alexander, Earl of Stirling (1567?–1640). The psalmes of King David, translated by King James. Oxford 1631 (DMH 452), [London?] 1631, London 1636 (rev), [1637?], 1637 (BUCOEM 826); in The book of common-prayer for the use of the Church of Scotland, Edinburgh 1712. Revision and completion of King James's ms version of 30 psalms, above; in 1627 Alexander was given the right of exclusive pbn for 31 years and in 1634 all other psalters were prohibited in Scotland, but opposition brought about a revision in 1636,

reissued with Laud's service book, above, then a General Assembly at Glasgow in 1638 which rescinded the privilege and prohibition; psalm 19 in Cotton.

John Vicars (1580/2?–1652). Divers of Davids psalmes, according to the French forme and metre. In Englands hallelu-jah: or Great Brittaines gratefull retribution for Gods gratious benediction, with divers of Davids psalmes, according to the French metre and measures, 1631.

John Donne (1572–1631). [Metrical trn of psalm 137]. In his Poems, 1633 etc.

Phineas Fletcher (1582–1650). Certain of the royal prophets psalmes metaphrased. In his Purple island, Cambridge 1633; in Poetical works, Edinburgh 1793, Poems 1810; ed A. B. Grosart 4 vols 1869. Psalms 1, 42, 63, 127, 130, 137.

George Herbert (1593–1633). [Metrical trn of psalm 23]. In his Temple: sacred poems and private ejaculations, Cambridge 1633 etc.

George Sandys (1578–1644). A paraphrase upon the psalmes of David, and upon the hymnes dispersed throughout the Old and New testaments. 1636, 1637 (in A paraphrase upon the divine poems, set to new tunes [by H. Lawes]), 1637–8, 1648, 1676, York 1789.

[Richard Brathwayte (Brathwait) (1588?–1673)]. The psalmes of David the King and prophet and of other holy prophets, paraphras'd in English: conferred with the Hebrew veritie, set forth by B. Arias Montanus, together with the Latin, Greek Septuagint, and Chaldee paraphrase. 1638; psalms 107, 133, 137 in Brathwayte's Barnabæ itinerarium vol 1, ed J. Haslewood 1820 (9th edn); psalms 18 (part), 23, 137 in T. Corser, Collectanea anglo-poetica vol 2, 1861 (Chetham Soc). In verse; by R.B., sometimes identified as Robert Burnaby, Robert Baillie (1599–1662), or Sir Richard Baker (1568–1645).

Francis Rous (Rouse) (1579–1659). The booke of psalmes in English meeter. Rotterdam 1638 (anon), London 1641, 1643 (rev as The psalmes of David in English meeter), 1646 (rev, with Authorized version in the margin). In 1643–5, with the authority of the Commons, this trn was approved by the Westminster Assembly, which in 1646 ordered its exclusive use; it was one of the principal sources for the Scottish psalter of 1650 and the New England psalter of 1651: psalm 19 (1641 and 1646 versions) in Cotton.

Sir William Mure (More, Muir) (1594–1657). Some psalmes translated and presented. Psalms 1–51 and 100–50 in his Works, vol 2, ed W. Tough 1898 (STS). In verse; composed 1622–39; psalms 52–99 lost; one of the versions ordered to be used for the Scottish psalter of 1650; psalms 15, 23, 122 also in Mure's The historie and descent of the house of Rowallane, ed W. Muir, Glasgow 1825.

Sir Henry Wotton (1568–1639). [Metrical trn of psalm 104]. In Reliquiæ Wottonianæ, 1651, 1654, 1672, 1685; in J. Hannah, The courtly poets from Raleigh to Montrose, 1870; Brooke.

'Bay Psalm Book'. The whole booke of psalmes faithfully translated into English metre. [Cambridge Mass] 1640; ed John Cotton and Thomas Shepard 1647; Cambridge Mass 1651 (3rd edn rev Henry Dunster, Richard Lyon(s) et al, using Rous, as The psalms, hymns, and spiritual songs; 'The New England Psalm Book'), [c. 1664], [1665] (5th edn as The whole book of psalms), London 1671, 1680, 1694; Boston 1695, 1697, London 1697; Boston 1698 (first edn with music) etc; c. 27 edns alleged for 1640–50.

William Barton (1598/1603–78). The book of psalms in metre, with musicall notes. 1644, 1645, 1646(?), 1654, 1655(?), 1672(?), 1682, 1691, 1692, 1696.

—— The choice and flower of the old psalmes, collected by John Hopkins and others and now revised and emended by W. Barton. 1645. With music.

—— Psalms and hymns composed for the public thanksgiving, October 24 1651. 1651. Psalms 46, 48, 76, 135,

mostly adapted from 1644, above.
—— Four centuries of select hymns, 1668 (unauthorized; the 3rd–4th centuries are based on the psalms); Two centuries of select hymns collected out of the psalms, 1672; Six centuries of select hymns and spiritual songs (The three last centuries of select hymns collected out of the psalms of David [rev and expanded from the edn of 1668]), ed E. Barton 1688.

Zachary Boyd (1585–1653). The psalmes of David in meeter, with the prose interlined. 1644 (?), Glasgow 1646, 1646, 1648 (rev). (Aldis 1215.5, 1216, 1311). In 1647 named by the General Assembly of Kirk of Scotland as one of versions to be used as a basis for new Scottish psalter 1650. Psalm 138 in Holland.

Francis Roberts (1609–75). The book of hymnes of praises: viz the (fourth) book of psalms [90–106], translated immediately out of the Hebrew, and analytically expounded. 1644 (Corpus Christi College, Oxford), [1648?] (Cambridge Univ Lib); The whole book of psalms, in Clavis bibliorum, the key to the Bible, 1665 (3rd edn), 1674. Not in first and 2nd edns, 1648, 1649, 1664; metrical. Psalm 22 in Holland.

Richard Crashaw (1613?–49). [Metrical trns of psalms 23 and 137]. In his Steps to the temple: sacred poems, 1646 etc.

John White of Dorchester (1574–1648). Davids psalms in metre, agreeable to the Hebrew, to be sung in usuall tunes. 1655. From the Latin of J. I. Tremellius, using the Authorized version. Psalm 52 in Holland.

Second Scottish psalter. The psalms of David in meeter, newly translated and diligently compared with the original text and former translations; more plain, smooth and agreeable to the text than any heretofore; allowed by the authority of the General Assembly of the Kirk of Scotland. Edinburgh 1650, 1651, 1653, 1655, 1656, 1658, 1659 (Aldis 1418–23.5, 1449.5–50, 1464.5–7, 1483, 1524–6, 1554–5, 1582, 1613.5); 18 further edns ptd at Edinburgh 1661–99.

Henry Vaughan (1622–95). [Metrical trn of psalm 121]. In his Silex scintillans: or sacred poems pt 1, 1650; psalms 65 and 104 in pt 2, 1655; Works ed L. C. Martin 2 vols Oxford 1914; psalm 121 in Brooke.

Thomas 3rd Baron Fairfax (1612–71). [Metrical trn of the psalms 1651]. In his Imployment of my solitude. 2 autograph mss in Bodley, Fairfax 38 and 40 (rev); psalm 137 in Cotton; 18 in C. R. Markham, A life of the great Lord Fairfax, 1870.

Henry King (1592–1669). The psalms of David, from the new translation of the Bible, turned into meeter. 1651, 1654, 1671; 15 psalms in J. Playford, Psalms and hymns in solemn musick, 1671; psalms 4, 24, 27 (part), 30, 46, 50 (part), 51, 80 (part), 102, 127, 130–1, 139 (part) in his Poems and psalms, ed J. Hannah 1843; 30, 46 in Aston; 26 in Holland; 30, 102 in Latham; 19 in Cotton; 46 in Brooke; 130 in his Poems, ed M. Crum, Oxford 1965.

Abraham Cowley (1618–67). [Metrical trn of psalm 114]. In his Davideis: a sacred poem of the troubles of David [book 1, section 42]. In his Poems, 1656 etc; English writings, ed A. R. Waller 2 vols Cambridge 1905–6.

Richard Baxter (1615–91). A paraphrase on the psalms of David. Ed M. Sylvester 1692. Probably written late in 1650's and rev 1691. Psalm 53 in Holland.

V. SERMONS AND DEVOTIONAL WRITINGS

LANCELOT ANDREWES

Bishop of Winchester
1555–1626

Collections

Scala coeli: nineteene sermons concerning prayer. 1611.
Sermons. Pt 1, 1618; pts 2–3, 1618; pt 4, 1620.
XCVI sermons. Ed W. Laud and J. Buckeridge 1629, 1631, 1632 (another issue with altered date), 1632, 1635 (with alphabetical table), 1641, 1661; ed J. P. Wilson 5 vols 1841–3.
Opuscula quaedam posthuma. 1629. Includes Latin sermons.
The moral law expounded whereunto is annexed nineteene sermons upon prayer; also seven sermons upon our Saviours tentations. 1642.
Seventeen sermons. Ed C. Daubeny 1821.
Sixteen sermons chiefly concerning fasts and festivals. Ed M. A. Davis 1831.
Works. Ed J. P. Wilson and J. Bliss 11 vols Oxford 1841–54 (Lib of Anglo-Catholic Theology).
Selections from the sermons. 1865; ed J. S. Utterton 1867.
Seventeen sermons on the Nativity. 1887, 1898.
Sermons, selected. Ed G. M. Story, Oxford 1967.

§ 1

Sermons

The wonderfull combate betweene Christ and Satan, opened in seven sermons. 1592 (anon), 1627.

The copie of the sermon preached on Good Friday [6 April 1604]. 1604, 1610, 1640.
A sermon before the King concerning the right and power of calling assemblies [28 Sept 1606]. 1606, 1610.
Concio coram Jacobo rege. [abroad?] 1608.
Concio Latine habita coram regia majestate, quinto Augusti 1606. 1610.
A sermon preached before his Majestie the fifth of August last. 1610.
A sermon preached Monday 25 December 1609. 1610.
A sermon preached Tuesday 25 December 1610. 1610, [1611?].
Two sermons preached before the King's Majestie, Christmas Day 1609. 1610, 1610.
A sermon on Easter day. 1611, 1611.
A sermon on Easter day. 1614.
A sermon on Easter day. 1618.
A sermon preached the fifth of November 1617. 1618.
A sermon on Easter day. 1620.
Sermon of the pestilence, preached 1603. 1636.
Sacrilege a snare: a sermon ad clerum, translated from Latin. 1646.
Of justification in Christ's name: a sermon preached 23 November 1600. 1740, 1765, 1846.
On the pillars of government. 1823.
Of convocation. In J. Brodgen, Catholic safeguards vol 3, 1851.
The duty of a nation and its members in time of war, preached before Elizabeth at Richmond. 1854.
Of being doers of the word. 1858 (Bishops Tracts no 2).
Two sermons concerning the Resurrection. Cambridge 1932.

Devotions

See F. E. Brightman, The preces privatae, 1903, pp: xiii–xxv, for detailed description of the mss and ptd texts.

I. Isaacson's version

Institutiones piae: or directions to pray. Ed H. Isaacson 1630, 1633, 1640, 1684 (7th edn); ed W. H. Hale 1839.
Holy devotions. 1655.
The true Church of England-man's companion in the closet collected from the writings of Archbishop Laud, Bishop Andrewes and others. 1749. Source of Andrewes's work is Institutiones piae.

II. Original versions

Verus christianus. Ed D. Stokes, Oxford 1668. First appearance of Preces, selections only.
Preces privatae, graece et latine. Ed J. Lamphire 1675 (first comprehensive edn); rev Patris Lanc. Andrewes, Preces privatae graece et latine, Oxford 1675, 1680; Editio tertia et emendatior [P. Hall], 1828, ed J. Barrow 1853 (Lib of Anglo-Catholic Theology), ed F. Meyrick 3 pts 1865–73; ed P. Hall 1828 (Preces privatae quotidianae); ed P. G. Medd 1892 (as The Greek devotions); ed H. Veale 1895, 1899.

III. Translations

(a) Moseley–Drake

The private devotions. Tr from the Greek, ed H. Moseley 1647.
A manual of the private devotions, translated out of a fair Greek ms by R. D[rake]. 1648, 1670, 1674, 1682, 1692. This differs considerably from preceding. Drake set out to correct the erroneous impression he considered Moseley to have made. The same text pbd as A manual of directions for the sick, tr from Greek ms by R. D[rake] 1648, 1670, 1682, 1692, 1853 (with corrections in Churchman's Lib); ed J. Bliss 1854 (Lib of Anglo-Catholic Theology); 1855 (selections in A manual of private devotions, Churchman's Lib) etc.

(b) Stanhope

Private prayers for every day in the week. Tr G. Stanhope 1730, 1778, 1808, 1818, 1826, 1832 (includes A manual of directions for the sick) etc. 2nd edn etc as The devotions of Bishop Andrewes.
Private devotions. Tr P. Hall 1830, 1839. A new version of Stanhope, above.
Prayers and offices of private devotion. Ed B. Bouchier 1834. Abridged from Stanhope, above.

(c) Newman–Neale

The Greek devotions of Bishop Andrewes. Tr J. H. Newman 1840 (78th Tract for the Times), Oxford 1842 (nearly all of Preces pt 1). Completed J. M. Neale, Private devotions of Bishop Andrewes translated from the Latin, 1844. 2 sections later combined.
Private devotions. Ed (from J. H. Newman and J. M. Neale) E. Venables 1883, 1885 (rev from Scriptural texts).
Private devotions of Bishop Andrewes, selected and arranged with variations adapted to general use. Ed J. E. Kempe 1897 (from Newman and Neale), New York 1950 (facs).
Private prayers. Ed H. Martin 1957.

(d) Brightman

The preces privatae. Tr F. E. Brightman 1903, New York 1961 (with T. S. Eliot, For Lancelot Andrewes 1928).

The preces privatae: selections from the translation of F. E. Brightman. Ed A. Burn 1908, 1949.

(e) Other translations

A manual of devotions. Ed A. Bettesworth 1700 (2nd edn).
Private prayers. Tr E. Bickersteth 1839. A new trn of pts 1–2.
The private devotions newly done into English by P. G. Medd. 1899.

IV. Miscellany

The moral law expounded. 1642. *See* Collections, above.
Εὐχαι ἰδιαι καθημεριναι ἐκδιδοντος φριδερικου Μερρικου. [1867].
Manual. Ed H. P. Liddon 1869–70, 1874, 1883; ed F. E. Brightman 1909.
Whyte, A. Lancelot Andrewes and his private devotions: a biography, a transcript and an interpretation. Edinburgh 1896.
An horology. Ed A. Gurney 1897.
Brief passages from his sermons and devotions. 1907.
Devotions. Ed T. S. Kepler, Cleveland 1957.

Other Works

Quaestiones, nunquid per ius divinum, magistratui liceat, a reo iusiurandum exigere? 1593.
Tortura torti. 1609; ed F. Meyrick 1872 (excerpts as De primatu sedis Romanae argumenta); tr 1877, 1884.
Responsio ad apologiam Cardinalis Bellarmini contra praefationem monitoriam Jacobi R. 1610.
Fides catholica antiqua revindicata in ecclesia anglicana. Ed F. Meyrick 1872. Excerpts from Responsio.
Stricturae: or a brief answer to Cardinal Perrons reply to King James. 1629 (pt of pt 2 of Opuscula quaedam posthuma).
A patterne of catechisticall doctrine. 1630, 1641, 1641, 1650, 1675.
A summarie view. Oxford 1641, 1641 (as Certain briefe treatises), 1661 (as The form of church government in N. Bernard, Clavi Trabales, pt 4).
Of episcopacy. 1647.
Of the right of tithes (Theologica determinatio de decimus). 1647, 1842 (as A dissertation upon tithes, ed C. E. Harles).
Reverendissimi Lanceloti Wintoniensis de synodo ablatis a D. Whitakero Articulis judicium. Pt 4 of Articuli Lambethani, 1651.
A defence of the thirty-nine articles of the Church of England with the judgment of Bishop Andrews. 1700, 1710. Trn of Reverendissimi, above.
A learned discourse of ceremonies. 1653.
Αποσπασματια sacra: posthumous and orphan lectures. 1657. By Andrewes?
The form of a consecration of a church. 1659, 1672, 1688, 1703 (rev). Form of a consecration of a churchyard 1898 (after the 1659 service which is of 1620).

§2

Isaacson, H. An exact narration of the life and death of Lancelot Andrewes. 1650, 1650; in Abel redevivus, 1651, 1817, 1829.
Russell, A. T. Memoirs of the life and works of Bishop Andrewes. Cambridge 1860, 1863.
Eliot, T. S. In his For Lancelot Andrewes, 1928.
Welsby, P. A. Lancelot Andrewes. 1958. With bibliography.
Wilson, F. P. In his Seventeenth-century prose, Cambridge 1960.
Bishop, J. G. Andrewes, Bishop of Chichester 1605–9. Chichester 1963.

RICHARD BANCROFT

Archbishop of Canterbury
1544–1610

A sermon preached at Paules Crosse [9 Feb 1588]. 1588, 1588, 1588 (with addns), 1636, 1637, 1709.

Daungerous positions and proceedings. 1593 (anon), 1640, 1641, 1712; ed R. G. Usher 1905 (Camden Soc).

A survay of the pretended holy discipline. 1593 (anon), 1663, 1663.

Tracts ascribed to Bancroft. Ed A. Peel (from a ms in Lib of St John's College, Cambridge), Cambridge 1953.

THOMAS BECON
1512–67

Collections

The worckes of Becon whiche he hath hytherto made and published. 3 vols 1560–4; ed J. Ayre 3 vols Cambridge 1843–4 (Parker Soc).

§I

Davids harpe ful of [h]armony, by T. Basille [pseudonym]. 1542. 114th Psalm.

The true defence of peace. 1542.

The floure of godly prayers. 1551.

The pomander of prayer. 1558 (anon) etc; 5 edns by 1578. Another book with this title ptd W. de Worde 1530.

The relikes of Rome. [1560?], 1563.

The syck mans salue. 1561 etc, 15 edns by 1632.

A new postil conteinyng sermons upon all the Sonday gospelles. 2 vols 1566, 1567.

JOHN FISHER

Bishop of Rochester
1469–1535

Mss, especially of correspondence, are in BM, Cambridge Univ Lib, St John's College Cambridge and Public Records Office.

Collections

Opera quae hactenus inveniri potuerunt omnia. Würzburg 1597, Farnborough 1967 (facs); tr R. Bayne and ed J. E. B. Mayor 1876 (EETS).

§I

This treatise concernynge the fruytfull saynges of Davyd in the seven penytencyal psalmes. 1508, 1509, 1509, 1509, 1510, [1516?], [1518?], 1525, 1529, 1555, 1714; ed J. E. B. Mayor 1876 (EETS); ed K. Vaughan 1888 (as Sermons on the seven penitential psalms); ed J. S. Phillimore 2 vols 1914 (as Commentary on the seven penitential psalms), 1915 (Catholic Lib vols 14, 16).

Here after foloweth a mornynge remembraunce had at the moneth mynde of Margarete Countesse of Rychemonde. [1509]; ed T. Baker 1708; ed J. Hymers, Cambridge 1840; ed J. E. B. Mayor 1876 (EETS); ed C. R. Ashbee 1906.

This sermon folowynge was compyled and sayd in the cathedrall chyrche of Saynt Poule, the body beynge present of the moost famouse prynce Kynge Henry the vii, the x daye of Maye mcccccix. 1509. Another edn 'enprinted the fyrst yere of the reygne of Henry the viij', [1509].

Eversio munitionis quam Jodocus Clichtobeus erigere moliebatur adversus unicam Magdalenam per Joannem Roffensis ecclesiae episcopum. Louvain [1519].

Reverendi patris J.F. confutatio secundae disceptationis per J. Fabrum Stapulensem habitae. Paris 1519, 1519. These 2 works were Fisher's answer to Faber and van Clichtove on the identity of Mary Magdalen.

The sermon of Johan the Bysshop of Rochester [on John 15.26] made agayn the pernicyous doctryn of M. Luuther [12 May 1521]. [1521?, 1521?]. Another edn as The sermon of John the Bysshop of Rochester made again the pernicious doctryn of M. Luther, [1528?], 1554, 1556; tr Latin by R. Pace, Cambridge 1521, Ditchling 1935 (rptd from first edn).

Convulsio calumniarum U. Veleni. Antwerp 1522, 1698.

Apologia S. Hessi adversus Roffensen Episcopum. [1523].

Von dem hochgelehrten und geistlichen Bischoff Johannes von Roffa. Strasbourg 1523, 1524.

Defensio Regie assertionis [of Henry VIII] contra Babylonice captivitate [of M. Luther] per D. D. Johannem Roffensem Episcopu. Cologne 1525, 1525, 1562.

Sacri sacerdotij defensio contra Lutherum jamprimum evulgata. Cologne 1525, 1525, Münster 1925 (Corpus Catholicorum no 9); tr P. E. Hallett 1935.

Was die christelilichen Alten von der Beycht haben gehalten. Dresden 1525.

De veritate corporis et sanguinis Christi in Eucharistia adversus J. Oecolanpadium. Cologne 1527, 1527.

A sermon had at Paulis upon quinquagesom Sonday [11 Feb 1525] concernynge certayne hereticks. [1526?]. This sermon is sometimes confused with The sermon agayn the pernicyous doctryn of Martin Luuther [1521]. It is not included in any modern edn. The BM copy (c.536.15) has several corrections, made in a contemporary hand, not Fisher's, but perhaps at his instance. *See* G. J. Gray, Fisher's sermon against Luther, 1912.

De causa matrimonii serenissimi Regis Angliae liber [Henry VIII with Catherine of Arragon]. [Alcalá 1530], [Compluti] 1530.

Here after ensueth two fruytfull sermons. 1532. Both on Matthew 5.20.

A spiritual consolation written by J. Fisher to hys sister Elizabeth. [1535]; ed D. O'Connor 1903, 1935.

Psalmi seu precationes ex variis Scripturae lacis collectae. Cologne [1525?], 1544, 1544, 1555, 1568, London 1554, 1572. Attributed to Fisher.

Reverendi patris D.J.F. opusculum de fiducia et misericordia Dei. Cologne 1556.

Tractatus de orando deum. Douai 1576; tr as A godlie treatisse declaryng the benefits of prayer, 1560, 1576, 1577.

A treatise of prayer. Tr R.A.B[att?], Paris 1640; ed a monk of Fort-Augustus 1887; 1969 (facs).

A position and testimony against all swearing. [1692?].

Oratio habita coram illustrissimo Rege Henrico Septimo Cantabrigiae AD 1506. 1770; rptd in J. Lewis, Life of Dr John Fisher vol 2, 1855.

Letters

Erasmus, D. The epistles of Erasmus. Ed F. M. Nichols 3 vols 1901–18.

—— Opus epistolarum Des. Erasmi Roterodami. Ed P. S. Allen 12 vols Oxford 1906–58.

Gray, G. J. Letters of Bishop Fisher 1521–3. Library 3rd ser 4 1913.

Thomson, D. F. S. and H. C. Porter. Erasmus and Cambridge: the Cambridge letters of Erasmus. Toronto 1963, 1970 (rev).

Rouschausse, J. (ed). Erasmus and Fisher: their correspondence 1511–24. Paris 1968. Latin text with English trn.

§2

Bayly, T. [R. Hall]. Life and death of that renowned John Fisher, Bishop of Rochester. 1655, Dublin 1835 (7th edn).

Lewis, J. Life of Dr John Fisher. Ed T. H. Turner 2 vols 1855.

Mayor, J. E. B. (ed). Early statutes of the College of St John the Evangelist. Cambridge 1859.

Bayne, R. The life of Fisher, transcribed from ms Harleian 6382. 1921 (EETS).

Macklem, M. God have mercy: the life of John Fisher of Rochester. Ottawa 1967.

JOHN HOOPER
Bishop of Worcester
d. 1555
Collections

Early writings. Ed S. Carr, Cambridge 1843 (Parker Soc).

Later writings. Ed C. Nevison, Cambridge 1852 (Parker Soc).

§ I

A declaration of Christe. Zürich 1547.

A declaration of the ten holy commaundementes. Zürich 1548.

A funerall oratyon made the xiiij day Januarij. 1549.

A lesson of the incarnation of Christe. 1549, 1549, 1550.

An oversight and deliberation upon the prophete Jonas. 1550.

Godly and most necessary annotations in the xiii chapyter to the Romaynes. 1551.

A godly confession and protestacion of the Christian fayth. [1551?].

An homelye to be read in the tyme of pestylence. 1553.

The wordes of Maister Hooper at his death. 1559.

An exposition upon the 23 psalmes. 1562.

Certeine comfortable expositions upon the xxiii, lxii, lxxiii and lxxvii psalmes. 1580.

A briefe and cleare confession of the Christian faith. Issued as part of J. Baker, Lectures, 1581 etc.

JOHN JEWEL
Bishop of Salisbury
1522–71
Collections

Seven godly sermons never before imprinted. 1607.

[Featley, D.] Works, and a briefe discourse of his life. 4 pts 1609, 1611.

Works. Ed J. Ayre 4 vols Cambridge 1845–50 (Parker Soc).

Works. Ed R. W. Jelf 8 vols Oxford 1848.

§ I

The copie of a sermon pronounced at Paules Crosse the second Sondaye before Easter 1560. [1560]. Jewel's challenge was first given in a sermon at Paul's Cross 26 Nov 1559; it was repeated in substance in a Court sermon 17 March 1560, and at Paul's Cross again 31 March. It was ptd 'as nere as the authour could call it to remembraunce' on 10 May, as above. The ensuing controversy led to Jewel's Apologia ecclesiae anglicanae, 1562.

An apologie or aunswer in defence of the Church of England. [Tr Ann, Lady Bacon] 1562; ed J. E. Booty, Ithaca 1963 (Folger Lib); Menston 1969 (facs).

[Cooper, T.] An apologie of private masse spredde abroade in writyng against the offer made in certain sermons by the Byshop of Salesburie, with an answere. 1562.

A replie unto M. Hardinges answeare to the sermon on I Cor. xi. 23. 1565.

A defence of the Apologie of the Churche of Englande: an answeare to a certain booke by M. Hardinge. 1567.

A viewe of a seditious bul sent into Englande 1569. 1582.

Certaine sermons preached before the Queenes Maiestie and at Paules crosse. 1583.

An exposition upon the two epistles to the Thessalonians. 1583, 1584, 1594.

A sermon made in Latine in Oxenforde. [1586?].

§2

Southgate, W. M. Jewel and the problem of doctrinal authority. Cambridge Mass 1962.

Booty, J. E. Jewel as apologist of the Church of England. 1965.

JOHN KNOX
1505–72
Collections

Works. Ed D. Laing 6 vols 1846–64.

§ I

An admonition that the faithful Christians in London, Newcastel, Barwycke and others, may avoide Gods vengeaunce. [Bremen?] 1554.

A confession and declaration of praiers. 1554; Upon the death of King Edward VI. Rome (for London) 1554.

A faythfull admonition unto the professours of Gods truthe in England. [Zürich] 1554.

A godly letter sent too the fayethfull in London, Newcastell etc; A confession and declaration of praiers etc. 2 pts Rome (for London) 1554; pt 2, 1581.

The copie of a letter sent to the ladye Mary dowagire, Regent of Scotland. [Geneva? 1556], Geneva 1558 (nowe augmented by the authour).

The appellation of J. Knoxe from the cruell sentence pronounced against him by the false bishoppes and clergey of Scotland. Geneva 1558. An admonition by A. Gilby.

The first blast of the trumpet against the monstruous regiment of women. [Geneva] 1558, [Edinburgh? 1687?]; ed E. Arber 1878.

The copie of an epistle sent unto the inhabitants of Newcastle and Barwike; in the ende whereof is added A brief exhortation to England. 2 pts Geneva 1559, 1560.

An answer to a great nomber of blasphemous cavillations. [Geneva] 1560, London 1591.

Heir followeth the coppie of the ressoning betuix the Abbote of Crossraguell and J. Knox. Edinburgh 1563, 1812.

A sermon [on Isaiah 26.13] preached in the publique audience of the church of Edenbrough, 19 August 1565. [Edinburgh] 1566.

To his loving brethren. [Edinburgh] 1571.

An answer to a letter of a Jesuit named Tyrie, be Johne Knox. St Andrews 1572.

A fort for the afflicted. 1580.

Exposition upon the fourth of Mathew. [1583].

The first book of the history of the reformation of religion within the realm of Scotland. 1587 (with bks 2–3); The historie of the reformation of the Church of Scotland, ed D. B[uchanan] 1644, Edinburgh 1644, London 1681, Edinburgh 1732, 1790, 2 vols 1816, 1 vol Glasgow 1831; ed R. S. Walker 1940 (selection); ed W. C. Dickinson 2 vols 1949.

The first booke of discipline, drawn up by J. Knox. Vol 2, 1719 (Church of Scotland Collections of Official Documents).

Knox's judgment on the true nature of Christian worship. 1842.

The source and bounds of kingly power. In H. C. Fish, History of the Repository of pulpit eloquence vol 2, 1857.

§ 2

Muir, E. Knox: portrait of a Calvinist. 1929.
Donaldson, G. In his Scottish Reformation, Cambridge 1960.
Ridley, J. John Knox. Oxford 1968.
See also col 366, below.

ROBERT PARSONS SJ
1546–1610

§ 1

The firste parte of the booke of the Christian exercise appertayning to resolution. Rouen 1582, [Rouen?] 1585 (with addns as A Christian directorie, guiding men to their salvation, commonly called the resolution, with reproofe of the falsified edition published by E. Buny). Edmund Bunny in 1584 edited a Protestant version of which there were many edns; *see* H. Thurston, Catholic writers and Elizabethan readers, Month Dec 1894, and 'N. Doleman', A conference about the next succession to the crowne of Ingland, 2 pts [Antwerp?] 1594.

WILLIAM PERKINS
1558–1602
Collections

A golden chaine: or the description of theologie [with 12 other treatises]. 13 pts Cambridge 1600 ('newly corrected according to his own copies'), 18 pts Cambridge 1603 (with 5 additional treatises), 1 vol Cambridge 1605 (enlarged), 3 vols Cambridge 1608, 1609 (vol 3), 1612–13 etc.
Works. Ed I. Breward, Abingdon 1971.

§ 1

A treatise tending unto a declaration whether a man be in the estate of damnation. [1588?].
The foundation of Christian religion. 1590, 1638 (13th edn), Hamburg 1688 (with J. Wallis, Grammatica linguae anglicanae).
Armilla aurea. Cambridge 1590, [1591?], 1592.
A golden chaine: or the description of theologie, containing the order of the causes of saluation and damnation according to Gods word. 1591, 1612 (5th edn).
An exposition of the Lords prayer. 1592.
A direction for the government of the tongue. Cambridge 1593.
Two treatises: 1, Of repentance; 2, Of the combat of the flesh and spirit. Cambridge 1593.
An exposition of the symbole or creed of the apostles. Cambridge 1595.
A salve for a sicke man. Cambridge 1595, 1632 (5th edn).
A declaration of the true manner of knowing Christ crucified. Cambridge 1596.
A discourse of conscience. [Cambridge] 1596.
A reformed Catholike. Cambridge 1598.
How to live and that well. Cambridge 1601, 1611, 1615.
A commentarie on the five first chapters of the Epistle to the Galatians. Cambridge 1604.
The first part of the cases of conscience. Cambridge 1604.
Lectures upon the three first chapters of the Revelation. 1604.
Of the calling of the ministerie. 2 pts 1605.
A Christian and plaine treatise of pre-destination. 1606.
A faithfull and plaine exposition upon the first two verses of the second chapter of Zephaniah. 1606.
A godly and learned exposition upon the whole epistle of Jude. 1606.
The whole treatise of the cases of conscience. Cambridge 1606, 1636 (7th edn).

A cloud of faithfull witnesses: a commentary on Hebrews 11. 1608.
A discourse of the damned art of witchcraft. Cambridge 1608.
A godly and learned exposition of Christ's sermon in the mount. Cambridge 1608.
Christian oeconomie: or a short survey of the right manner of ordering a familie according to the Scriptures. 1609.
A graine of musterd-seede. [Cambridge] 1611.
Deaths knell: or the sicke mans passing-bell. 1628.

JOHN RAINOLDS (or REYNOLDS)
1549–1607
Collections

The prophecie of Obadiah opened and applyed in sundry sermons preached by J. Rainolds. Ed W. Hinde, Oxford 1613.
V. Cl. D. J. Rainoldi Orationes duodecim, cum aliis quibusdam opusculis; edjecta est oratio funebris in obitu ejusdem habita a M. I. Wake. Oxford 1614, 1619, 1628.

§ 1

A sermon upon part of the prophesie of Obadiah. 1584.
The summe of the conference betwene J. Rainoldes and J. Hart touching the head and faith of the Church. 1584, 1588, 1598, 1609.
A sermon upon part of the eighteenth psalm preached in the Universitie of Oxford. Oxford 1586, 1613.
An answere to a sermon preached the 17 of April 1608 by G. Downame. 2 pts 1609. Anon.
A defence of the judgment of the reformed churches (touching adultery and remarriage). 1609, 1610.
The discovery of the man of sinne: sermons by J. R[ainolds]; published by W. H[inde]. Oxford 1614.
The prophesie of Haggai interpreted in sundry sermons, never before printed. 1649.

HENRY SMITH
1550–91
Collections

The sermons gathered into one volume. 1592; ed T. Fuller 1657 (with memoir), 1675, 2 vols 1866–7.
Works. Ed T. Smith, Edinburgh 2 vols 1866–7.
A selection of the sermons. Ed J. Brown, Cambridge 1908.

§ 1

The examination of usurie in two sermons, taken by characterie, and after examined. 1591. With a short preface, signed Thine H.S. These and other sermons of Smith were ptd in the author's lifetime, or immediately after his death; and for over 30 years after his death there were many edns of his sermons, singly, in small sets and in collections. On the use of shorthand for taking down sermons (the case with most of Smith's) *see* F. Watson, The English grammar schools, 1908.

ROBERT SOUTHWELL SJ
c. 1561–95
Collections

Prose works. Ed W. J. Walter 1828.
Complete poems. Ed A. B. Grosart 1872; ed J. H. Mc-Donald and N. P. Brown, Oxford 1967.
Spiritual exercises and devotions. Ed J. M. de Buck, tr P. E. Hallett 1931.

§ 1

An epistle of comfort to the reverend priestes. Secretly ptd in England 1587–8, Paris [1604?] (anon), 1605 [place?] (anon), [St Omer] 1616; ed M. Waugh 1965.

An epistle of a religious priest unto his father. [London? 1596–7]. Ptd anon at pt 2 of A short rule of good life, below; ed J. W. Trotman, The triumphs over death, 1914 below.

Marie Magdalens funerall teares. 1591, 1592, 1594, 1602, 1609; ed W. Tooke 1772; rptd 1823, 1827.

The triumphs over death: or a consolatorie epistle. 1595, 1596, 1596; ed S. E. Brydges, Archaica vol 1, 1815, ed J. W. Trotman 1914 (includes several letters) (from mss).

An humble supplication to her Majestie. 1595; ed R. C. Bald, Cambridge 1953.

A short rule of good life, newly set forth according to the author's direction before his death. [London? 1596–7], [1598?], St Omer 1622 (all anon); ed N. P. Brown, Charlottesville 1972 (as Two letters and short rules of a good life).

A foure-fold meditation: of the foure last things. 1606. Anon. Probably by Philip Howard, Earl of Arundel.

§ 2

Devlin, C. The life of Southwell, poet and martyr. 1956.

JOHN WHITGIFT
Archbishop of Canterbury
1530?–1604

Collections

Works. Ed J. Ayre 3 vols Cambridge 1851–3 (Parker Soc).

§ 1

An answere to a certen libel intituled An admonition to the Parliament [by J. Field and T. Wilcox]. 1572, 1572, 1573 (rev).

The defense of the aunswere to the Admonition. 1574.

A godlie sermon preached before the Queenes Maiestie. 1574, 1714.

A most godly and learned sermon, preached at Pauls Crosse. 1589.

§ 2

Paule, G. Life of Whitgift. 1612, 1699.

Strype, J. The life and acts of Whitgift. 1718, 3 vols Oxford 1822.

Brook, V. J. K. Whitgift and the English church. 1957.

VI. RICHARD HOOKER
1554–1600

Manuscripts

The fullest account of extant mss and of changes in the text of succeeding edns, and the best discussion of the last 3 bks of the Polity, *are in Keble's edn of Hooker's* Works, *1888 (rev). The only autograph of Hooker, A sermon of pride, is in Trinity College, Dublin.*

Bibliographies

Hill, W. S. Hooker: a descriptive bibliography of the early editions 1593–1724. Cleveland 1970.

Collections

Works. Ed J. Gauden 1662. With life.

Works, with life by I. Walton. 1666 (2nd edn), 1676, 1682, 1705, Dublin 1721, London 1723, 1724 (re-issue of Dublin edn with signature A reset), Oxford 1793, 1807, London 1822.

Works. Ed J. Keble 3 vols Oxford 1836, 1841, 1845, 1850, 1863, 1874, 1875, 1890; rev R. W. Church and F. Paget, Oxford 1888 (with much unpbd supplementary matter), New York 1967.

Of the laws of ecclesiastical polity. 2 vols 1907 (EL), 1954 (rev C. Morris). Based on Keble, above.

§ 1

Polity

Of the lawes of ecclesiastical politie: eyght bookes. [1593]. Entered at Stationers' Hall, 8 bks, 29 Jan 1593. Gives headings of 8 bks, but contains only preface and bks 1–4.

The fift booke. 1596. The last book of the Polity to appear in Hooker's lifetime. Bodley ms additional C.165, with corrections in Hooker's hand, was used by printers for bk 5.

Books i–v. 1604. Though styled 2nd edn, strictly a 2nd edn of preface and 1–4 only; bk 5 unchanged from 1597, and vol not continuously paged.

Books i–v. 1611. 3rd edn of preface and 1–4, 2nd of 5.

Books i–v. 1617 (first state, 4th edn of preface and 1–4,

3rd edn of 5), 1618 (2nd state, preface and 1–5 as before, pt 1; Certayne tractates, pt 2).

Books i–v. 1622 (5th edn of preface, bks 1–4, 4th edn of bk 5, 2nd collected edn of Tractates).

Books i–v. 1631–2 (first state, 2nd edn of preface, bks 1–4, issued with 5th edn bk 5, 3rd collected edn of Tractates), 1631–2 (2nd state, 6th edn of preface, bks 1–4, 5th edn of bk 5, 3rd collected edn of Tractates).

Books i–v. In Certain divine tractates 1638–9 (7th edn of preface and bks 1–4, 6th edn of bk 5, 5th collected edn of Tractates, 4th of 1635–6).

Books i–v. Menston 1969 (facs of 1593).

A discovery of the causes of these contentions concerning Church-government, out of the fragments of Richard Hooker. In Certain briefe treatises concerning the government of the Church, Oxford 1641. This composite volume was probably prepared by, or under direction of, Archbishop Ussher. Keble, who prints A discovery as appendix 2 to bk 8 of Polity, is doubtful if it is Hooker's.

The dangers of new discipline discovered [chs 8 and 9 of the preface, part of ch 79 of bk 5]. 1642.

The sixth and eighth books according to the most authentique copies. 1648 (first issue first state, 'London, printed by Richard Bishop, and are to be sold by John Crook, 1648'), 1648 (2nd state with cancel title, 'London, printed in the year 1648'), 1648 (3rd state, with cancel title, 'London, printed by Richard Bishop, 1648'), 1651 (2nd issue, with cancel title, 'London, printed by R.B. to be sold by George Badger, 1651').

Mr Hookers judgment of the Kings power in matters of religion. In Nicholas Bernard, Clavi trabales, 1661.

Works. Ed J. Gauden 1661–2. First complete edn of all 8 books of the Polity; includes bk 7 for the first time and adds 8 unpbd folio pages to the end of bk 8.

Works. Ed J. Keble 1836. Bk 8 ptd from a fuller and better arranged ms (120, Trinity College, Dublin).

Book i, with introduction and glossary by R. W. Church. 1868, 1868, 1873, 1896.

Book v, with Prolegomena and appendices by R. Bayne. 1902. Bayne reprints the Christian letter as well as

Hooker's ms replies, first ptd by Keble, above.
Book viii. Ed R. A. Houk, New York 1931 (from Trinity College Dublin ms 120).

Sermons and Tractates

A learned and comfortable sermon of the certaintie of faith. Oxford 1612. On Habakkuk 1, 4, first pt.

A learned discourse of justification. Oxford 1612, 1613. On Habakkuk 1, 4, 2nd pt.

The answere to a supplication preferred by Mr Walter Travers to the Privie Counsell. Oxford 1612. On the connection of Travers's appeal to the Privy Council with Hooker's 2 preceding sermons; *see* Walton's Life.

A learned sermon of the nature of pride. Oxford 1612. On Habakkuk 2, 4. Keble ptd for first time a large addn to this sermon from Trinity College, Dublin ms 121.

A remedie against sorrow and feare, delivered in a funerall sermon. Oxford 1612.

Two sermons upon part of S. Judes epistle. Oxford 1614.

A sermon of Richard Hooker found in the study of Bishop Andrews. Appendix to Walton, Life of Dr Sanderson, 1678.

§2

See also bibliography on Marprelate Controversy, below.

Walton, I. The life of Mr Rich Hooker. 1665. Prefixed to most edns of Hooker from 1666, and included in Walton's Lives from 1670.

Keble, J. Editor's preface. In his edn of Works, 1836. Walton's Life is included, with many corrections and addns.

Coleridge, S. T. In his Notes on English divines, ed D. Coleridge 2 vols 1853.

Paget, F. An introduction to the fifth book. Oxford 1899, 1907. The results of Paget's recension of Keble in 1888.

Craig, H. In his Enchanted glass, New York 1936.
—— Of the Laws of ecclesiastical polity: first form. JHI 5 1944.

Sisson, C. J. The judicious marriage of Mr Hooker and the birth of the Laws of ecclesiastical polity. Cambridge 1940.

Davies, E. T. The political ideas of Hooker. 1946.
—— In his Episcopacy and the royal supremacy, Oxford 1950.

Hill, W. S. (ed). Hooker: essays preliminary to an edition of his works. Cleveland 1972.

VII. THE MARPRELATE CONTROVERSY

Bibliographies

The best bibliographies are in W. Pierce, Historical introduction to the Marprelate Tracts, 1908 and The Marprelate tracts, 1911. On related literature, see E. Arber, Introductory sketch to the Martin Marprelate controversy, 1879. For the history of the Presbyterian movement whose left wing is represented by Marprelate, for information regarding original documents and for an account of the Puritan press etc see A. F. Scott Pearson, Thomas Cartwright and Elizabethan Puritanism, 1925. D. J. McGinn, John Penry and the Marprelate controversy, 1966 includes an extensive bibliography.

§1

The Marprelate Tracts

The Epistle

Oh read over D. John Bridges, for it is a worthy worke: or an epitome of the fyrste booke of that right worshipfull volume, written against the Puritanes, in the defence of the noble cleargie, by as worshipfull a prieste, John Bridges, Presbyter, priest or elder, doctor of divillitie, and Deane of Sarum; wherein the arguments of the Puritans are wisely prevented, that when they come to answere M. Doctor, they must needes say something that hath bene spoken; by the reverend and worthie Martin Marprelate gentleman, and dedicated to the Confocationhouse; the Epitome is not yet published: in the meanetime, let them be content with this learned Epistle; printed oversea, in Europe, within two furlongs of a bousing priest, at the cost and charges of M. Marprelate, gentleman. [1588] (secretly ptd by Waldegrave, East Molesey, October); ed J. Petheram 1842; ed E. Arber 1880; ed W. Pierce 1911.

The Epitome

Oh read over [as in Epistle, above]: by the reverend and worthie Martin Marprelat gentleman, and dedicated by a second epistle to the terrible priests; printed on the other hand of some of the priests. [1588] (secretly ptd by Waldegrave, Fawsley); ed J. Petheram 1843; ed W. Pierce 1911.

The Minerals

Certaine minerall and metaphisicall schoolpoints, to be defended by the reverende bishop and the rest of my cleargie masters of the Convocation house, against bothe the universities, and al the reformed Churches in Christendome. [1589] (broadside secretly ptd by Waldegrave at Coventry before 20 Feb 1589); ed W. Pierce 1911.

Hay any worke for Cooper

Hay any worke for Cooper: or a briefe pistle directed by way of an hublication to the reverende byshopps, counselling them, if they will needs be barrelled up, for feare of smelling in the nostrels of her Majestie and the State, that they would use the advise of reverend Martin, for the providing of their Cooper; penned and compiled by Martin the Metropolitane; printed in Europe, not farre from some of the Bounsing Priestes. [1589] (secretly ptd by Waldegrave at White Friars Coventry, March) 1641 (as Reformation no enemie), 1642 (under proper title); ed J. Petheram 1845; ed W. Pierce 1911.

Martin Junior or Theses Martinianae

Theses Martinianae: that is, certaine demonstrative conclusions, sette downe and collected (as it should seeme) by that famous and renowned Clarke, the reverend Martin Marprelate the great; published and set foorth as an after-birth of the noble gentleman himselfe, by a prety stripling of his, Martin Junior, and dedicated by him to his good neame and nuncka, Maister John Kankerbury; printed by the assignes of Martin Junior. [1589] (secretly ptd by John Hodgkins at the Priory, Wolston July); ed W. Pierce 1911.

Martin Senior or the just censure

The just censure and reproofe of Martin Junior: wherein the rash and undiscreete headines of the foolish youth, is sharply mette with, and the boy hath his lesson taught, him, I warrant you, by his reverend and elder brother, Martin Senior, sonne and heir unto the renowned Martin Marprelate the Great. [1589] (secretly ptd by John Hodgkins at the Priory, Wolston July); ed W. Pierce 1911.

Protestatyon

The protestatyon of Martin Marprelat: wherein not with standing the surprizing of the printer, he maketh it known unto the world that he feareth, neither proud priest, Anti-christian Pope, tiranous prellate not godlesse catercap; but defiethe all the race of them by these presents and offereth conditionally, as is farthere expressed hearin by open disputation to apear in the defence of his caus aginst them and theirs; published by the worthie gentleman D. Martin marprelat D. in all the faculties primat and metropolitan. [1589] (after seizure of main Puritan press and arrest of Hodgkins and his assistants at Manchester this tract was secretly and very imperfectly ptd probably in Sept 1589 at Wolston?); ed W. Pierce 1911.

§2

Burnet, G. History of the Reformation of the Church of England. 2 pts 1679–81; ed N. Pocock 7 vols Oxford 1865; Menston 1969–70 (facs).
Strype, J. Annals of the Reformation. 2 pts 1709–8, 4 vols 1725–31 (complete), 4 vols in 7 Oxford 1824, 1965.
—— Life of John Whitgift. 2 pts 1718, Oxford 1822.
Arber, E. An introductory sketch to the Martin Marprelate controversy. 1878. Reprints Diotrephes, Demonstration of discipline, Epistle, Admonition to the people of England.
Dickens, A. G. In his English Reformation, 1964.
—— The Marprelate tracts 1588–9. Leeds 1967 (facs).

VIII. THE CAROLINE DIVINES (1620–60)

GENERAL STUDIES

Fuller, T. Abel redivivus: the lives and deaths of the moderne divines. 1651, 1652.
—— The church-history of Britain. 1655.
Calamy, E. An abridgement of Mr Baxter's history of his life and times; with an account of many others of those worthy ministers who were ejected at the Restoration. 1702, 2 vols 1713; A continuation of the account, 2 vols 1727; rev S. Palmer 2 vols 1775, 3 vols 1802 (as The Nonconformist's memorial); A. G. Matthews, Calamy revised, Oxford 1934.
Coleridge, S. T. Notes on English divines. Ed D. Coleridge 2 vols 1853.
Campagnac, E. T. The Cambridge Platonists. Oxford 1901.
Powicke, F. J. The Cambridge Platonists. 1926.
Jones, R. F. The attack on pulpit eloquence in the Restoration. JEGP 30 1931; rptd in his The seventeenth century, Stanford 1951.
Mitchell, W. F. English pulpit oratory from Andrewes to Tillotson. 1932.
Tracts on liberty in the Puritan Revolution 1638–47. Ed W. Haller 3 vols New York 1934.
More, P. E. and F. L. Cross (ed). Anglicanism: the thought and practice of the Church of England illustrated from the religious literature of the seventeenth century. 1935.
Knox, R. A. Enthusiasm. Oxford 1950.
Haller, W. Liberty and reformation in the Puritan Revolution. New York 1955.
May, G. L. (ed). Wings of an eagle: an anthology of Caroline preachers. 1955.
Wilson, F. P. In his Seventeenth-century prose, Cambridge 1960.
Green, V. H. H. Religion at Oxford and Cambridge. 1964.
Trevor-Roper, H. R. Religion, the Reformation and social change. 1967. Includes Fast sermons before Long Parliament.
Cragg, G. R. (ed). The Cambridge Platonists. New York 1968. An anthology of selections from various writers, Whichcote, More et al.
Patrides, C. A. (ed). The Cambridge Platonists. 1969. Sermons and other selections of Whichcote, Cudworth, Smith and More, with introd and notes.
Thomas, K. Religion and the decline of magic. 1971.

GEORGE ABBOT

Archbishop of Canterbury
1562–1633

Bibliographies

Christophers, R. A. A bibliography of George Abbot, Archbishop of Canterbury. Charlottesville 1966.

§1

Questiones sex totidem praelectionibus in schola theologica oxoniae, pro forma habitis, discussae et discuptate anno 1597, in quibus e sacra scriptura et patribus, quid statuendum sit definitur. 1598.
A brief description of the whole world. 1599.
An exposition on the prophet Jonah, in certain sermons preached at St Mary's church in Oxford. 1600.
A sermon preached at Westminster, May 26 1608, at the funeral solemnities of the Right Hon Thomas Earl of Dorset. 1608.
Account, written by Dr George Abbot, Archbishop of Canterbury, with the speech he intended to have made, and King James's letter to him [Essex divorce]. 1613; rptd in W. Cobbett, Complete collection of state trials vol 2, 1809.
A treatise of the perpetual visibility and the succession of the true Church in all ages. 1624.
Archbishop Abbot in his narrative [concerning his sequestration]. 1627; rptd in J. Rushworth, Historical collections vol 1, 1721 and in W. Cobbett, Complete collection of state trials vol 2, 1809.

§2

A short apology for Archbishop Abbot, touching the death of Peter Hawkins, by an unknown hand. 1621; rptd in English works of Sir Henry Spelman, ed E. Gibson 1727.
Spelman, H. An answer to the foregoing apology [touching the death of Peter Hawkins]. 1621; rptd ibid.
Onslow, A. The character of Archbishop Abbot upon reading Lord Clarendon's account of him. 1723.
Welsby, P. A. Abbot: the unwanted Archbishop. 1962.

THOMAS ADAMS
c. 1583–c. 1660

Collections

The divells banket. 1614. 6 sermons.
A divine herball. 1616. 5 sermons.
Workes: being the summe of his sermons. 1629; ed J. Angus 3 vols Edinburgh 1861–2; ed J. Brown, Cambridge 1909 (selection).

§1

The gallants burden. 1612, 1614, 1616.
Heaven and earth reconcil'd. 1613.
The white devil: or the hypocrite uncased. 1613, 1613, 1615.

The blacke devill or the apostate, with the Wolf worrying the lambes and the Spirituall navigator. 3 pts 1615.
England's sickness. 1615. 2 sermons.
Mysticall bedlam. 1615. 2 sermons.
Diseases of the soule: a discourse. 1616.
The sacrifice of thankefulnesse. 1616.
The souldiers honour. 1617.
The happiness of the church. 1618.
The barren tree: a sermon. 1623.
The temple. 1624.
A commentary upon the second epistle by St Peter. 1633.
God's anger and man's comfort. 1652[3]. 2 sermons.

RICHARD BAXTER
1615–91

For a complete catalogue of Baxter's books, see his Compassionate counsel to all young men, *1691 (2nd edn).*

Collections

The practical works of the late reverend and pious Mr Richard Baxter, with a preface giving some account of the author. 4 vols 1707; ed W. Orme 23 vols 1830, 1833; 4 vols 1838, 1845–7, 1854.

§ 1

Aphorismes of justification, with their explication annexed; published especially for the use of the Church of Kidderminster in Worcestershire. 1640 (for 1649), 1655; ptd by J. Wesley, Newcastle 1745 (extract); 1831 (17th edn).
The saints everlasting rest: or a treatise of the blessed state of the saints in their enjoyment of God in glory. 4 pts 1650, 1659 (8th edn rev author), 1677 (11th edn rev author), 2 pts 1814 (13th edn, to which is added The dying thoughts of the Rev R. Baxter); ed W. Young 1907; ed J. T. Wilkinson [1962] (abridged); tr Dutch, 1677.
Apology against the modest exceptions of Mr T. Blake. 1654, 1654.
A sermon of judgement. 1655.
Gildas Salvianus: the first part, i.e. The reformed pastor; shewing the nature of the pastoral work, especially in private instruction and catechizing. 1656; abridged S. Palmer 1808; 1841 (from 1656 edn with appendix); ed J. Wilkinson 1939.
A call to the unconverted to turn and live. 1658, 1669 (13th edn); many later edns, many trns.
The crucifying of the world, by the cross of Christ; with a preface to the nobles, gentlemen and all the rich, directing them how they may be richer. 1658; ed J. Baillie 1861.
The life of faith, as it is the evidence of things unseen: a sermon preached—contractedly—before the King at Whitehall upon July the 22nd 1660. 1660, 1670.
A sermon of repentance, preached before the honourable House of Commons at their late solemn fast for the settling of these nations, April 30 1660. 1660.
A treatise of death, the last enemy to be destroyed: part of it was preached at the funerals of Elizabeth the late wife of Mr Joseph Baker. 1660.
Now or never: the holy, serious, diligent believer justified, encouraged, excited and directed, and the opposers and neglecters convinced by the light of Scripture and reason. 1662, 1689.
The divine life, in three treatises: the first, Of the knowledge of God; the second, Of walking with God; the third, Of co[n]versing with God in solitude. 1664, 1824.
The cure of church-divisions: or directions for weak Christians, to keep them from being dividers or troublers of the Church; with some directions to the pastors how to deal with such Christians. 1670.
A Christian directory: or a summ of practical theologie and cases of conscience. 4 pts 1673, 1678; ed J. Tawney 1925.

The poor man's family book: 1, teaching him how to become a true Christian; 2, how to live as a Christian; 3, how to die as a Christian; in plain familiar conferences between a teacher and a learner. 2 pts 1674.
Richard Baxter's Catholick theologie: plain, pure, peaceable, for pacification of the dogmatical word-warriors, in three books. 4 pts 1675. 3rd bk never pbd.
A sermon preached at the funeral of Mr Henry Stubbs. *See* T. Vincent, The death of ministers improved, 1678.
Church-history of the government of Bishops and their Councils abbreviated. 1680.
A sermon preached at the funeral of Mr John Corbet, with his true and exemplary character. [1680].
A breviate of the life of Margaret, the daughter of Francis Charlton and wife of Richard Baxter. 1681; ed J. Wilkinson 1928.
Compassionate counsel to all young men: especially I, London-apprentices; II, students of divinity, physick and law: III, the sons of magistrates and rich men. 1681, 1691 (2nd edn with complete catalogue of his books).
Poetical fragments: heart-imployment with God and it self; the concordant discord of a broken-healed heart. 1681, 1689, 1699, 1700 (with Additions to the poetical-fragments), 1821.
The poor husbandman's advocate to rich racking landlords. 1691; ed F. J. Powicke, Bull John Rylands Lib 10 1926. Baxter's last treatise.
Reliquiae Baxterianae: or Mr Richard Baxter's narrative of the most memorable passages in his life and times. Ed M. Sylvester 1696; abridged J. M. L. Thomas 1925 (EL).

§ 2

Calamy, E. An abridgement of Mr Baxter's history of his life and times. 1702, 2 vols 1713; rev S. Palmer 3 vols 1802–3; ed A. G. Matthews, Calamy revised, Oxford 1834, 1937.
Powicke, F. J. A Puritan idyll: or the Rev Baxter's love story. 1917.
—— Story and significance of the Rev Baxter's Saints' everlasting rest. 1920.
—— A life of the Reverend Baxter. 2 vols 1924.
—— The Reverend Baxter under the Cross 1622–91. 1927.
Nuttall, G. F. Baxter and Philip Doddridge. 1951.
—— The manuscript of Reliquiae Baxterianae. 1954.
—— Richard Baxter. 1966. Includes list of Baxter's works.

WILLIAM CHILLINGWORTH
1602–43

Collections

Works. 1704, 1719 (7th edn), 1727, 1742 (with life by T. Birch), 2 vols Dublin 1752, 3 vols 1820, Oxford 1838.

§ 1

The religion of Protestants a safe way to salvation. Oxford 1637, 1638, 1664, 1674, 1684, 1687, 3 vols 1820, 1838, 2 vols 1839.

JOHN COSIN
Bishop of Durham
1595–1672

Collections

Works. Ed J. Sansom 5 vols Oxford 1843–55 (Lib of Anglo-Catholic Theology). The autograph ms of Cosin's English sermons, ptd in Works vol 1, 1843, is in Durham Cathedral Chapter Library, A.IV.31.

§1

A collection of private devotions. 1627 (3 edns), 1635, 1638, 1655, 1664, 1672 (all anon), 1676 (signed); ed P. G. Stanwood, Oxford 1967 (text of first edn, with introd and commentary).
A forme of prayer, used in the King's chappel [in Paris] on Tuesdayes. 1649. BM copy with ms addns.
A scholastical history of the canon of the Holy Scriptures. 1657, 1672, 1683.
Argument proving that adultery works a dissolution of the marriage. [1665].
Historia transubstantiationis papalis [written 1655]. 1675; tr 1676, 1679, 1834; ed J. S. Brewer 1840; ed J. Brogden, Catholic Safeguards vol 2, 1846; Liverpool 1864 (as The history of Popish transubstantiation); both works rptd in Works vol 4, 1851.
The Right Reverend Doctor John Cosin his opinion for communicating rather with Geneva than Rome. 1684. Written as a letter to R. Watson, 19 June 1646.
Regni Angliae religio catholica [written c. 1652]. In T. Smith, 1707 below; ed W. Wekett 1729 (as Regni Angliae sub imperio serenissime); tr F. Meyrick 1853; tr 1870.

Letters

Correspondence. Ed G. Ornsby 2 vols Durham 1868–72 (Surtees Soc nos 52, 55); ed J. C. Hodgson, Northumbrian documents pt 2, Durham 1918 (Surtees Soc no 131). Most of the original letters are in Cosin's Lib, Durham Univ.
Stanwood, P. G. and A. I. Doyle. Cosin's correspondence. Trans Cambridge Bibl Soc 5 1969.

NICHOLAS FERRAR
1593–1637

Manuscripts

BM additional mss 34,657–9, 3 folio vols of the Story books or religious exercises of Little Gidding, Huntingdonshire.
Collection for the history of the memory of Little Gidding by Francis Peck, ms vol in Clare College Cambridge.
Ms letters in Magdalene College Cambridge.

§1

Hygiasticon by Leonard Lessius [Louvain 1613]. Cambridge 1634. Tr Ferrar.
Acta apostolorum. [1635?].
Actions and doctrine and other passages touching our Lord Jesus Christ. [1635].
Harmonies. [1636?].
The hundred and ten considerations of Signior John Valdesso [Basle 1550]. Oxford 1638, [London 1906]. Trn and introd by Ferrar, notes by George Herbert.
The story books of Little Gidding: being the religious dialogues recited in the great room 1631–2. Ed E. C. Sharland 1899.
The Ferrar papers. Ed B. Blackstone, Cambridge 1938.
Chronicles of Little Gidding. Ed A. L. Maycock 1954.
Conversations at Little Gidding: on the retirement of Charles V; on the austere life. Ed A. M. Williams, Cambridge 1970.

§2

Mayor, J. E. B. (ed). Ferrar: two lives by his brother John and by Doctor Jebb. Cambridge 1855.
Maycock, A. L. Ferrar of Little Gidding. 1938.
Eliot, T. S. Little Gidding. 1942; rptd in Four quartets, New York 1943.

JOHN GAUDEN
Bishop of Exeter
1605–62

The love of truth and peace. 1641, 1641. Sermon before House of Commons.
Three sermons preached upon severall publike occasions. 1642.
Certaine scruples and doubts of conscience. [1645].
Εἰκὼν Βασιλική: the pourtraicture of his sacred Majestie. 1648 etc (all anon); ed P. A. Knachel, Ithaca 1966. Once attributed to Charles I; probably written with Gauden.
The religious and loyal protestation. 1648 (for 1649).
Funerals made cordials. 1658. Funeral sermon for Robert Rich.
Ἱερὰ δάκρυα: ecclesiae anglicanae suspiria; the tears. 1659.
A sermon preached in the Temple-Chappel, at the funeral of Dr Brownrig. 1660.
Μεγαλεῖα θεοῦ: Gods great demonstrations. 1660. Sermon before House of Commons.
Anti-Baal-Berith: or the binding of the Covenant and all Covenanters to their good behaviors. 1661.
Considerations touching the liturgy. 1661.
Edited works of Richard Hooker with life, 1662. See Hooker, above.

JOSEPH HALL
Bishop of Norwich
1574–1656

Collections

A recollection of such treatises as have been heretofore severally published. 1615(–14), 1617, 1621.
Works. 1 vol 1625, 2 vols 1628(–7), 1633, 1634, 3 vols 1662 (vol 1 1634, 1647, 1648: vol 2 1634, 1648), 1 vol in 2 pts 1714 (pt 2 with separate title-page 1708); ed J. Pratt 10 vols Oxford 1808; ed P. Hall 12 vols Oxford 1837–9; ed P. Wynter 10 vols Oxford 1863.
The shaking of the olive-tree: remaining works. 1659, 1660 (with 14 of the sermons not before pbd, the first 10 tr French 1664).
Collected poems. Ed A. Davenport, Liverpool 1949.

§1
Sermons

See above: A recollection, Works, Shaking of the olive-tree.
Pharisaisme and Christianity [1 May 1608]. 1608, 1608, 1609, 1614, 1627, 1642.
The Passion sermon [14 April 1609]. 1609, 1614, 1627, 1642.
An holy panegyricke [24 March 1613]. 1613, 1627, 1642.
The righteous mammon: an hospitall sermon. 1618.
A sermon preached before his Majestie at Thebalds [15 Sept 1622]. 1622.
The great imposter [2 Feb 1623]. 1623, 1628, 1643.
The best bargaine [Theobalds 21 Sept 1623]. 1623.
A sermon preached at the reconcilement of the chappell of Exceter [St Stephen's day 1623]. 1624, 1627.
The true peace-maker [19 Sept 1624]. 1624, 1627.
Columba Noae olivum adferens jactatissimae Christi arcae. 1624; ed F. Meyrick 1874; tr Joseph Hall, Works, 1625 etc.
A sermon of publique thanksgiving for the wonderfull mitigation of the late mortalitie [Whitehall 29 Jan 1625]. 1626.
Westminster on the public fast [5 April 1628] and To H.M. before the fast [30 March 1628], Whitehall. 1628. 2 sermons pbd together as One of the sermons preacht at Westminster, on the day of the publike fast.

One of the sermons preacht to the Lords on Ash Wednesday, Feb 18. 1629.

The hypocrite [28 Feb 1629]. 1630.

Exeter—at the consecration of a new burial place, on St Bart's day 24 Aug 1637. 1637 (with The remedy of prophaneness).

The character of man [1 March 1634]. 1635.

A sermon preach't to his Majesty, Aug 8. 1641.

Other Works

Virgidemiarum: sixe books. 1598; pt 1, 1598, 1602; pt 2, 1599; Oxford 1753, [1808]; ed S. W. Singer, Chiswick 1824; Certaine worthy ms poems, 1597 (sometimes regarded as pt 3 of Virgidemiarum).

The anathomie of sin. 1603, 1608 (as Two guides to a good life). Attributed to Hall.

The Kings prophecie: or weeping joy. 1603; ed W. E. Buckley 1882 (Roxburghe Club).

Meditations and vowes divine and morall. 1605, 1606, 1607, 1609 (with Characters of vertues and vices), 1616, 1621, 1851; ed C. Sayle 1901.

Mundus alter et idem [signed Mercurius Brittanicus]. Frankfurt [1605?], Hanover 1607; ed W. Knight, Frankfurt [1640?], Utrecht 1643, Munich 1664; ed H. J. Anderson 1908; tr J. Healey [1609?]; tr Healey and ed H. Brown, Cambridge Mass 1937; ed H. Morley, Ideal commonwealths, 1885 (fragment).

Occasionall meditations. 1630, 1631, 1633, 1851; Meditations for Sundays and holydays, 1856.

Heaven upon earth. 1606, 1606, 1607, 1621 (with Meditations and vowes).

The arte of divine meditation. 1606, 1607, 1609, 1621 (with Meditations and vowes).

Holy observations. 1607, 1609, 1621 (with Meditations and vowes). All edns include Some fewe of David's psalmes metaphrased, which was not pbd separately.

Characters of vertues and vices. 1608, 1608, 1609, 1621 (with Meditations and vowes), 1691; ed R. Kirk, New Brunswick NJ 1948.

Epistles. Vols 1–2, 1608; vol 3, 1611; vol 3 pt 2, 1610; ed W. H. Hale 1846.

Salomon's divine arts (with paraphrase of the Song of songs). 1609.

The peace of Rome [with No peace with Rome]. 1609, 1844 (with A serious dissuasive from Poperie), 1852.

A common apologie of the Church of England. 1610.

Contemplations upon the principall passages of the holy storie. Vol 1, 1612, 1617; vol 2, 1614, 1617, 1661; vol 3, 1615, 1617; vol 4, 1618; vol 5, 1620; vol 6, 1622; vol 7, 1623; Contemplations upon the historicall part of the Old testament: eighth and last volume, 1626. Pbd as Contemplations on the historical passages of the Old and New testaments, 3 vols 1824 (Select British divines 12–14); ed C. Wordsworth 1871.

Polemices sacrae pars prior: Roma irreconciliabilis. 1611, 1612.

A recollection of such treatises as have bene heretofore severally published and are now revised. 1614, 1615, 1617, 1621 (augmented).

Quo vadis? a just censure of travell as it is commonly undertaken by the gentlemen of our nation. 1617, 1617.

The honor of the married clergie mayntayned. 1620.

The olde religion. 1627, 1628, 1630, 1636, 1686.

An answer to Pope Urban his inurbanitie. 1629.

The reconciler. 1629.

Occasionall meditations. 1630, 1631, 1633, 1851; Meditations for Sundays and holydays, 1856.

A plaine and familiar explication of the Old and New testament. 1632.

An explication by way of paraphrase of all the hard texts in the Old and New testament. 1633.

Propositiones catholicae. 1633 (anon); tr as Certaine Catholicke propositions, 1633.

The residue of the contemplation upon the New testament, with sermons. 1634.

Joseph Halli αὐτοσχεδιάσματα. 1635.

The remedy of prophanenesse. 1637, 1638.

Certaine irrefragable propositions. 1639.

An humble remonstrance to the High Court of Parliament. 1640, 1640; A defence of the humble remonstrance, 1641.

Christian moderation. 1640.

Episcopacie by divine right. 1640, 1640.

A letter sent to an honourable gentleman, in way of satisfaction. 1641.

Answer to the tedious vindication. 1641.

A short answer to the tedious vindication of Smectymnuus. 1641.

A survay of that foolish, seditious, scandalous, prophane libell. 1641.

Osculum pacis. 1641.

A letter lately sent by a reverend Bishop [Hall] from the Tower. 1642, 1642.

A modest confutation. 1642.

The lawfulness and unlawfulness of an oath. [Oxford?] 1643.

A modest offer of some meet considerations. [Oxford] 1644, 1660.

The devout soul. 1644, 1650, 1658.

The peace-maker. 1645, 1647.

The remedy of discontentment. 1645, 1652, 1684.

The balme of Gilead. 1646, 1650, 1652, 1655, 1660.

Three tractates. 1646.

Christ mysticall. 1647.

Satans fiery darts quenched. 1647.

The breathings of the devout soul. 1648.

Pax terris. 1648.

Select thoughts: one century. 1648, 1654, 1682.

Of resolutions and decisions of divers practicall cases. 1649, 1650, 1654, 1654, 1659.

Χειροθεσία: or the apostolique institution. 1649 (for 1659).

The revelation unrevealed. 1650.

Susurrium cum Deo. 1651, 1651, 1659, 1659.

Holy raptures. 1652, 1653.

The great mysterie of godliness. 1652, 1659, 1847.

The holy order. 1654; tr German, 1683.

An apologeticall letter to a person of quality. 1655.

A letter concerning Christmasse. 1659.

The invisible world. 1659.

Divers treatises: third tome. 1662.

Psicittacorum regis. 1669.

Contemplations upon the remarkable passages in the life of holy Jesus. 1679.

Episcopal admonition. 1681.

Bishop Hall's hard measure. 1647, 1710.

§2

Kinloch, T. F. The life and works of Hall. 1951.

HENRY KING

Bishop of Chichester
1592–1669

§1

A sermon preached at Paul's Crosse, the 25 of November 1621: upon occasion of that false and scandalous Report (lately printed) touching the supposed apostasie of the right Reverend Father in God, John King, late Lord Bishop of London. 1621.

David's Enlargement. In Two sermons upon the Act Sunday, being the 10th of July 1625, Oxford 1625.

A sermon of deliverance: preached at the Spittle on Easter Monday 1626. 1626.

Two sermons preached at White-Hall in Lent, March 3 1625 and February 20 1626. 1627.

An exposition upon the Lords Prayer delivered in certaine sermons in the Cathedrall Church of St Paul. 1628, 1634.

A sermon preached at St Pauls March 27 1640: being the anniversary of his Majesties happy inauguration to his crowne. 1640.

A sermon preached before the King's most excellent Majesty at Oxford. Oxford 1643.

A sermon preached at White-Hall on the 29th of May 1661: being the happy day of his Majesties inauguration and birth. 1661, 1713.

A sermon preached at the funeral of the Rt Reverend Father in God Bryan, Lord Bp of Winchester, April 24 1662. 1662.

A sermon preached at Lewis in the diocese of Chichester, by the Lord Bp of Chichester, at his visitation held there, October 8 1662. 1663.

A sermon preached the 30th of January at White-Hall 1664: being the anniversary commemoration of K. Charles the I, martyred on that day. 1665.

For King's poems, see cols 134, 290, above.

§2

Berman, R. King and the seventeenth century. 1964.

WILLIAM LAUD
Archbishop of Canterbury
1574–1645
Collections

Seven sermons preached upon severall occasions. 1651.
The second volume of the remains of William Laud. Ed H. and E. Wharton 1700.
Works. Ed W. Scott and J. Bliss 7 vols in 9 Oxford 1847–60 (Lib of Anglo-Catholic Theology).

§1

A sermon preached before his Majestie at Wansted. 1621.
A sermon preached at Whitehall on the 24 of March 1621. 1622.
A sermon preached before his Majestie [on Psalm 75, 2–3]. 1625.
A sermon preached on Munday, the sixt of February, at the opening of the Parliament at Westminster [on Psalm 122, 3–5]. 1625.
A sermon preached before his Majestie on the fifth of July at the solemn fast. 1626.
A sermon preached on Munday, the 17th of March, at Westminster. 1628.
A speech delivered in the starr-chamber, at the censure of J. Bastwick. 1637 (3 edns).
A relation of the conference betweene W. Laud and Mr Fisher, the Jesuite. 1639, 1639, 1673, 1686; ed C. H. Simpkinson 1901.
The Archbishop of Canterbury's speech: or his funeral sermon preacht by himself on the scaffold on Tower-Hill, on Friday the 10 of January 1644; all faithfully written by John Hinde. 1644, 1660; rptd Harleian miscellany vol 8, 1744, 1808. Another version, first ptd Oxford 1644, is rptd in Somers tracts vol 4, 1809.
A summarie of devotions. 1667.
The history of the troubles and tryal of William Laud, wrote by himself. [Ed H. Wharton] 1695, 1700 (with some of Laud's other writings).

§2

Trevor-Roper, H. R. Archbishop Laud. 1940.
Costin, W. C. William Laud. 1945.
Bourne, E. C. E. The Anglicanism of Laud. 1947.

WILLIAM SANCROFT
Archbishop of Canterbury
1617–93
Collections

Occasional sermons; with some remarks of his life and conversation, in a letter to a friend. 1694, 1703.

§1

Modern policies. 1652, 1653, 1657 (7th edn), 1690.
A sermon preached in S. Peter's Westminster, on the first Sunday in Advent. 1660. At Cosin's consecration.
A sermon preach'd November 13th 1678. 1678.

Letters

Familiar letters to Sir Henry North, to which is prefixed some account of his life and character. 1757.

ROBERT SANDERSON
Bishop of Lincoln
1587–1663
Collections

Works. Ed W. Jacobson 6 vols Oxford 1854.

§1

Two sermons preached at Boston. 1622.
Ten sermons. 1627, 1632 (enlarged as Twelve sermons), 1637 (enlarged as Twelve sermons; whereunto are added two sermons more), 1656 (enlarged as Twenty sermons), 1657 (rptd from 1637 edn as Fourteen sermons), 1671 (enlarged as 34 sermons), 1674, 1681 (enlarged as 35 sermons, with Walton's life), 1686, 1689; ed R. Montgomery 2 vols 1841.
Two sermons preached at Paules-Crosse. 1628.
Two sermons. 1635.
De juramenti. 1647, 1661, 1670 etc; tr as De juramento: seven lectures, 1655.
A resolution of conscience. 1649.
A sermon preached at Newport, October 1648. 1653.
Several cases of conscience. 1660.
Episcopacy. 1661, 1673, 1678, 1683.
Five causes of conscience. 1666, 1667 (enlarged as Eight cases of conscience), 1674 (enlarged as Nine cases of conscience), 1685; tr Latin as Casus conscientiae, Cambridge 1688.
De obligatione conscientiae. 1660, 1661, 1670 etc; tr as Ten lectures on the obligation of humane conscience, 1660; ed W. Whewell, Cambridge 1851; ed and tr C. Wordsworth, Lincoln 1877. Lectures given 1647.
Ad clerum: a sermon [1641]. Oxford 1670.
Bishop Sanderson's judgement concerning submission. 1678.
Judicium universitatis oxoniensis. 1682; tr as Reasons of the present judgement of the University of Oxford, 1647, 1647.
A discourse concerning the Church. 1688.
A preservative against schism and rebellion. 3 vols 1722. Includes trns of De juramenti and De obligatione conscientiae, above; Reasons of the present judgement of the University of Oxford, above.

§2

Walton, I. The life of Dr Sanderson. 1678.

JEREMY TAYLOR
Bishop of Down and Connor
1613–67

Bibliographies

Gathorne-Hardy, R. and W. P. Williams. A bibliography of the writings of Taylor to 1700. Dekalb Ill 1971.

Collections

Twenty-eight sermons preached at Golden Grove together with a discourse of the office ministeriall. 1651, 1654, 1668.

Twenty-five sermons preached at Golden Grove. 1653, 1655, 1668, 1673.

Ἐνιαυτός: a course of sermons for all the Sundays of the year. 1653, 1655, 1668, 1673, 1678 (all enlarged).

The righteous evangelicall described: the Christian's conquest over the body of sin; Fides formata: or faith working by love, in three sermons. 1663, Dublin 1663.

Ἑβδομάς ἐμβολιμαῖος: a supplement to the Ἐνιαυτός, or course of sermons for the whole year, being seven sermons preached since the Restoration. 1663.

Δεκάς ἐμβολιμαῖος: a supplement to the Ἐνιαυτός, being ten sermons preached since the Restoration. 1667, 1673, 1678.

Whole works. Ed R. Heber 15 vols 1822 (with life); rev C. P. Eden 10 vols 1847–54.

Poems and verse-translations. Ed A. B. Grosart 1870.

The golden grove: selected passages from the sermons and writings. Ed L. P. Smith, Oxford 1930.

§1

A sermon preached in Saint Maries church in Oxford, upon the anniversary of the gunpowder-treason. Oxford 1638.

Of the sacred order and offices of episcopacy, by divine institution, apostolicall tradition and Catholike practice. Oxford 1642, London 1647.

A discourse concerning prayer ex tempore or by pretence of the Spirit. 1646 (anon), 1647, 1649 (enlarged as An apology for authorised and set forms of liturgie).

A new and easie institution of grammar. 1647. With William Wyatt.

Θεολογία ἐκλεκτική: a discourse of the liberty of prophesying. 1647.

Treatises of 1, The liberty of prophesying; 2, Prayer ex tempore; 3, Episcopacie; together with a sermon preached at Oxon. 1648, 1650.

An apology for authorized and set forms of liturgie. 1649.

The great exemplar of sanctity and holy life according to Christian institution. 1649, 1653, 1657, 1667 etc.

A funerall sermon, preached at the obsequies of the right honorable and most vertuous lady the Lady Frances, Countesse of Carbery. 1650.

The rule and exercises of holy living. 1650, 1651, 1651, 1654, 1656, 1660, 1663, 1668 etc; ed A. R. Waller 2 vols 1900; ed T. S. Kepler 1956.

Clerus domini. 1651, 1655, 1668, 1672.

The rule and exercises of holy dying. 1651, 1652, 1655, 1658, 1663, 1666, 1668 etc; ed A. R. Waller 1900. Holy living and Holy dying are commonly bound together from 1658 on, and treated explicitly as one vol from 1676.

A short catechism for the institution of young persons in the Christian religion; to which is added An explication of the apostolicall Creed. 1652.

A discourse of baptisme: its institution and efficacy upon all believers. 1652, 1653.

Two discourses: 1, Of baptisme; 2, Of prayer ex tempore. 1652, 1653.

Rules and advices to the clergy of the diocese of Down and Connor. 1653, Dublin 1661, London 1661, 1663.

The real presence and spirituall of Christ in the Blessed Sacrament. 1654.

The golden grove: or a manuall of daily prayers and letanies, fitted to the dayes of the weeke. 1655, 1659 (4th edn), 1680 (12th edn), 1703 (21st edn) etc.

Unum necessarium: or the doctrine and practice of repentance. 1655.

An answere to a letter written by the R.R. 1656.

Deus justificatus: two discourses of original sin. 1656.

A further explication of the doctrine of original sin. 1656.

A discourse of the nature, offices and measures of friendship. 1657, 1657 (as The measures and offices of friendship), 1662, 1671, 1675, 1684, 1920.

Σύμβολον ᾽Ηθικο-πολεμικόν: or a collection of polemical and moral discourses. 1657, 1674 (3rd edn enlarged).

A collection of offices or forms of prayers in cases ordinary and extraordinary. 1658, 1690.

A sermon preached at the funerall of Sr George Dalston. 1658.

B. Taylor's opuscula: the measures of friendship, with additional tracts. 1658, 1675, 1678, 1684.

The worthy communicant or a discourse of the nature, effects and blessings consequent to the worthy receiving of the Lords Supper. 1660, 1661, 1667, 1671, 1674, 1683, 1686, 1689, 1695.

Ductor dubitantium: or the rule of conscience in all her general measures. 2 vols 1660, 1671, 1676, 1696; abridged R. Bancroft 2 vols 1725.

A sermon preached, May 8 1661. 1661.

A sermon preached at the consecraticn of two archbishops and ten bishops in the cathedral in Dublin. Dublin 1661, 1663.

A sermon preached at the opening of the Parliament in Ireland. 1661.

Via intelligentiae: a sermon preached to the university of Dublin. 1662.

A sermon preached in Christ-Church, Dublin: at the funeral of the Archbishop of Armagh; with a narrative of his whole life. Dublin 1663, 1663, 1663 ('enlarged').

Χρῖσις τελειωτικη: a discourse of Confirmation. Dublin 1663, 1664.

A choice manual. 1664.

A dissuasive from Popery to the people of Ireland. Dublin 1664, 1664, London 1664, 1668 (enlarged), 1686.

The second part of the dissuasive from Popery, in vindication of the first part. 1667.

Antiquitates christianae. 1675, 1678, 1684 (7th edn).

Christ's yoke an easy yoke, and yet the gate to heaven a strait gate, in two excellent sermons. 1675.

Toleration tolerated. 1687, 1688?

On the reverence due to the altar. Ed J. Barrow, Oxford 1848.

§2

Gosse, E. Jeremy Taylor. 1904 (EML).

Beaty, N. L. The craft of dying: a study in the literary tradition of the ars moriendi in England. New Haven 1970.

JAMES USSHER
Archbishop of Armagh
1581–1656

The largest collection of Ussher's mss is in Trinity College, Dublin.

Collections

Eighteen sermons preached in Oxford 1640. 1659, 1660, 1660.

Twenty sermons. 1678.

Whole works. Ed C. R. Elrington and J. H. Todd 17 vols Dublin 1847–64.

§ 1

The soveraignes power and the subjects duty: a sermon at Christ Church. Oxford 1644.

The rights of primogeniture, or the excellency of royall authority: a sermon before his Majesty upon the anniversary of his birthday. 1648.

§ 2

Parr, R. The life of Ussher, late Lord Archbishop of Armagh. 1686. Contains 323 letters to or from Ussher.

Carr, J. A. The life and times of Ussher, Archbishop of Armagh. 1895.

Knox, R. B. James Ussher Archbishop of Armagh. Cardiff 1967.

MATTHEW WREN

Bishop of Ely
1585–1667

Manuscripts

For Wren's mss see Common-place book, 2 vols in Pembroke College Library, Cambridge, and an extensive scriptural commentary in Peterhouse Library, Cambridge.

Bibliographies

Walker, T. A. In his A Peterhouse bibliography, Cambridge 1924.

§ 1

A sermon preached before the Kings Majestie. 1627.

Bishops Wren's petition to the Parliament. 1642.

Considerations on Mr Harrington's Commonwealth. 1657. *See col 359, below.*

Increpatio Bar Jesu: sive polemicae. 1660.

Monarchy asserted. Oxford 1659, 1660.

An abandoning of the Scottish covenant. 1662.

5. POPULAR AND MISCELLANEOUS PROSE

I. PAMPHLETEERS AND MISCELLANEOUS WRITERS

BARNABY RICH
1542–1617

A right exelent and pleasaunt dialogue, betwene Mercury and an English souldier. [1574].

Allarme to England, foreshewing what perilles are procured where the people live without regarde of martiall lawe. 1578, 1578, 1625 (as Vox militis, adapted by G. Marcelline).

Riche his farewell to militarie profession. 1581, 1583, 1594 (rev), 1606 (rev); ed J. P. Collier, Eight novels employed by English dramatic poets, 1846 (Shakespeare Soc); ed T. M. Cranfill, Austin 1959. Apolonius and Silla ed J. Boswell, Plays and poems of Shakespeare vol 11, 1821; ed J. P. Collier, Shakespeare's library vol 2, [1843]; ed H. Morley 1889 (with Twelfth night); ed H. H. Furness, New variorum vol 13, 1901 (with Twelfe night); ed M. Luce 1912; ed E. J. O'Brien, Elizabethan tales, 1937; ed G. Bullough, Narrative and dramatic sources of Shakespeare vol 2, 1958; ed M. Lawlis, Elizabethan prose fiction, New York 1968; ed T. J. B. Spencer, Elizabethan love stories, 1968 (Pelican). Phylotus and Emelia ed J. W. Mackenzie, Edinburgh 1835 (with Philotus). Two brethren and their wives ed G. Bullough, Narrative and dramatic sources vol 2, 1958.

The straunge and wonderfull adventures of Don Simonides. 1581.

The true report of a late practise enterprised by a Papist with a yong maiden in Wales. 1582.

The second tome of the travailes and adventures of Don Simonides. 1584.

A path-way to military practise. 1587.

The adventures of Brusanus, Prince of Hungaria. 1592.

A martial conference, pleasantly discoursed betweene two souldiers, the one Captaine Skil, the other Captaine Pill. 1598 (title-page only).

A souldiers wishe to Britons welfare. 1604. Also issued as The fruites of long experience.

Faultes, faults and nothing else but faultes. 1606; ed M. H. Wolf, Gainesville 1965 (facs).

A short survey of Ireland truely discovering who hath armed that people with disobedience. 1609 (for 1609).

Roome for a gentleman: or the second part of Faultes, collected for the true meridian of Dublin. 1609.

A new description of Ireland, wherein is described the disposition of the Irish. 1610, 1624 (as A new Irish prognostication, anon).

A true and a kinde excuse written in defence of that booke intituled A newe description of Irelande. 1612.

A Catholicke conference betweene Syr Tady MacMareall a popish priest and Patricke Plaine. 1612.

The excellency of good women. 1613.

Opinion diefied, discovering the ingins, traps and traynes that are set to catch opinion. 1613.

The honestie of this age. 1614, 1615, 1615, 1616, Edinburgh [1616?]; ed P. Cunningham 1844 (Percy Soc).

My ladies looking glasse, wherein may be discerned a wise man from a foole. 1616.

The Irish hubbub: or the English hue and crie. 1617, 1617 (rev), 1618, 1622.

Remembrances of the state of Ireland 1612. Ed C. L. Falkiner, Proc Royal Irish Acad 26 1906.

Rych's Anothomy of Ireland [1615], with an account of the author. Ed E. M. Hinton, PMLA 55 1940.

GABRIEL HARVEY
1550–1631

Collections
Works. Ed A. B. Grosart 3 vols 1884–5 (Huth Lib).

§1
Ode natalitia: vel opus eius feriae in memoriam P. Rami. 1575. Signed A.P.S., i.e. Aulae Pembr. socius?

Gabrielis Harveii Ciceronianus: vel oratio. 1577; ed H. S. Wilson, tr C. A. Forbes, Lincoln Nebraska 1945.

Gabrielis Harveii rhetor: vel duorum dierum oratio. 1577.

Gabrielis Harveii Valdinatis; Smithus; vel musarum lachrymae pro obitu Thomae Smithi. 1578.

Gabrielis Harveii gratulationum Valdinensium libri quatuor. 1578.

Three proper and wittie familiar letters. 1580; ed J. Haslewood, Ancient critical essays vol 2, 1815; ed E. de Selincourt, Poetical works of Edmund Spenser, Oxford 1912.

Crispinus Joannes. Lexicon graecolatinum. 1581. Orations by 'G.H.'.

Three letters and certaine sonnets, especially touching Robert Greene. 1592, 1592 (with 4th letter as Foure letters), 1592; ed S. E. Brydges, Archaica vol 2, 1815; ed J. P. Collier [1870]; ed G. B. Harrison, Edinburgh 1923; Menston 1969 (facs of 3rd edn).

Pierces supererogation: or a new prayse of the old asse. 1593; ed S. E. Brydges, Archaica vol 2, 1815; ed J. P. Collier [1870]; Menston 1970 (facs of 1593).

A new letter of notable contents. 1593 (with Pierces supererogation?); ed S. E. Brydges, Archaica vol 2, 1815; ed J. P. Collier [1870]; Menston 1970 (facs of 1593).

The trimming of Thomas Nashe gentleman, by the high-tituled patron Don Richardo de Medico campo. 1597; ed J. P. Collier [1870]; ed C. Hindley, The old book collector's miscellany vol 1, 1871. By Harvey?

Letter-book. Ed E. J. L. Scott 1884 (Camden Soc).

Marginalia. Ed G. C. Moore Smith, Stratford 1913.

§2
Moore Smith, G. C. In Bang's Materialien vol 8, Louvain 1905.

McKerrow, R. B. In Works of Thomas Nashe, 1910.

RICHARD HAKLUYT
1552?–1615

§1
Divers voyages touching the discoverie of America. 1582; ed J. W. Jones 1850.

The principall navigations, voiages and discoveries of the English nation. 1589, ed D. B. Quinn and R. A. Skelton

2 vols Cambridge 1965 (facs); 3 vols 1598–1600 (enlarged); ed W. Raleigh 12 vols Glasgow 1903–5; ed J. Masefield 10 vols 1927–8.
Western discoveries. 1877. Written 1584.
Original writings and correspondence of the two Richard Hakluyts. Ed E. G. R. Taylor 2 vols 1935.

§2

Froude, J. A. In his Short studies, 1867–83.
Raleigh, W. The English voyages of the sixteenth century. Glasgow 1906. Introd to his edn, above, rev.
Parks, G. B. Hakluyt and the English voyages. New York 1928.
Quinn, D. B. The Hakluyt handbook. 2 vols Cambridge 1973 (Hakluyt Soc).

SIR JOHN HARINGTON
1560–1612

Orlando furioso in English heroical verse. 1591, 1607, 1634 (rev, with The most elegant epigrams, 1633). See col 116, above.
A new discourse of a stale subject, called the Metamorphosis of Ajax, written by Misacmos to his friend Philostilpnos. 1596, 1596, 1596, 1596.
Ulysses upon Ajax, written by Misadiaboles to his friend Philaretes. 1596 (anon; probably not by Harington), 1596; ed S. W. Singer, Chiswick 1814 (with A new discourse, An anatomie, An apologie, above).
The Englishmans docter: or the schoole of Salerne. Tr 1607 (anon), 1608, 1609, Edinburgh 1613 (as Conservandae bonae valetudinis praecepta), London 1617 (under first title, with addn by H. Ronsovius), 1624; ed A. Croke, Oxford 1830; ed F. R. Packard and F. H. Garrison, New York 1920, London 1922; Salerno 1953.
C., I. Alcilia, Philoparthens loving folly. 1613 (2nd edn). With epigrammes by Sir J. H[arington].
Epigrams both pleasant and serious. 1615, 1615. Partly rptd in following.
The most elegant and witty epigrams of Sir J. Harrington. 4 bks 1618 (with some Epigrams, 1615, above), 1625, 1633 (also with Orlando, 1634, above); ed N. E. McClure, Philadelphia 1926; Menston 1970 (facs of 1618).
A briefe view of the state of the Church of England. 1653, 1779 (in Nugae, below). Harington's title was A supplie or addicion to the Catalogue of bishops to the year 1608.
Nugae antiquae: a miscellaneous collection of original papers. Ed Henry Harington 2 vols 1769–75, 3 vols 1779, 1792; ed T. Park 2 vols 1804.
A short view of the state of Ireland written in 1605. Ed W. D. Macray, Oxford 1879.
A tract on the succession to the Crown (AD 1602) by Sir John Harington. Ed C. R. Markham 1880 (Roxburghe Club).
The letters and epigrams of Sir John Harington together with the Prayse of private life [and bibliography]. Ed N. E. McClure, Philadelphia 1930. See also M. H. M. MacKinnon, PQ 37 1958.
The Arundel Harington manuscript of Tudor poetry. Ed R. Hughey 2 vols Columbus 1960.

GERVASE MARKHAM
1568?–1637

Bibliographies

Poynter, F. N. L. A bibliography of Markham. Oxford 1962 (Oxford Bibl Soc).

§1

A discource of horsmanshippe. 1593, 1595 (enlarged as How to chuse, ride, traine and diet horses), 1596, 1597, 1599, 1606 (enlarged), 1615 (abridged in Countrey contentments), 1616 (abridged in Cheape and good husbandry), 1639 (abridged in The complete farriar); ed T. Harris, Markham's masterpiece, [1883?] (as The complete jockey); ed H. J. Schonfield 1933.
The gentlemans academie: or the booke of S. Albans by Juliana Barnes. 1595.
The most honorable tragedie of Sir Richard Grinvile, knight. 1595; ed E. Arber, The last fight of the Revenge at sea, 1871; ed E. Goldsmid, The last fight of the Revenge, Edinburgh 1886.
The poem of poems, or Sions Muse: contayning the divine song of King Salomon. [1596].
Devoreux: vertues teares for the losse of King Henry III of Fraunce. 1597. From the French.
A health to the gentlemanly profession of servingmen. 1598; ed W. C. Hazlitt, Inedited tracts, 1868; ed A. V. Judges, Oxford 1931 (facs). Attributed to Markham.
The teares of the beloved: or the lamentation of Saint John. 1600 (by J.M.); ed A. B. Grosart, Miscellanies vol 2, 1871.
Marie Magdalens lamentations. 1601, 1604; ed A. B. Grosart, ibid. Attributed to Markham.
A most exact discourse, how to trayne and teach horses to amble. 1605.
Cavelarice: or the English horseman. 8 bks 1607, 1617.
The shape and porportion of a perfit horse. 1607 (probably issued with Cavelarice, above).
The English Arcadia, alluding his beginning from Sir Philip Sydnes ending. 2 pts 1607–13 (by G.M.).
Rodomonths infernall: or the divell conquered; Ariastos conclusions of the marriage of Rogero with Bradamanth. 1607. From the French.
The dumbe knight: a historicall comedy acted sundry times by the Children of his Majesties Revelles. 1608, 1633; ed R. Dodsley, Collection of old plays vol 6, 1744; rev I. Reed vol 4, 1780; rev J. P. Collier vol 4, 1825; rev W. C. Hazlitt vol 10, 1875; ed Sir Walter Scott, Ancient British drama vol 2, 1810. With Lewis Machin.
The famous whore: or noble curtizan Paulina, mistress unto Cardinall Hypolito of Est. 1609; ed F. Ouvry 1868.
A cure for all diseases in horses. 2 bks 1610, 1616 (as Markhams method).
Markhams maister-peece: or what doth a horse-man lacke. 1610, 1615, 1623, 1631 (for 1630), 1636, 1643, 1651, 1656, 1662, 1668, 1675, 1681, 1683, 1688, 1694; ed T. Harris [1883?]; tr French, 1666. See Markhams faithfull farrier, below.
The most famous and renowned historie of Mervine, sonne to Oger the Dane. 2 pts 1612. Tr from French by J. M[arkham]?
Hobsons horse-load of letters: or a president for epistles. Bk 1, 1613 (by G.M.); 2 bks 1617.
The English husbandman. Bk 1, 1613; bk 2, 1614 (with appendix, The pleasures of princes); 2 bks 1635. Pleasures of princes rptd 1631 with Country contentments in A way to get wealth; ed H. G. Hutchinson, The art of angling, 1927; ed J. M. French, Three books on fishing 1599–1659, Gainesville 1962 (in part).
Cheape and good husbandry for the well-ordering of all beasts and fowles. 1614, [1616?] (abridged in Markhams method), 1616 (including abridgement of A discource of horsmanshippe, 1606), 1623 (in A way to get wealth, below).
Countrey contentments. 1615. Bk 1, The whole art of riding great horses, including abridgement of A discource of horsmanshippe, rptd, with The pleasures of princes from English husbandman, above, as Country contentments: or the husbandman's recreations, in A way to get wealth, 1631 etc below. Bk 2, The English

huswife rptd as Country contentments: or the English huswife, in A way to get wealth, 1623 etc below, and as The English house-wife; ed Constance, Countess De la Warr 1907 (in part).

A schoole for young souldiers. [1615] (anon), 1616.

Maison rustique: or the countrey farme, by Charles Stevens and John Liebault, translated by Richard Surflet; reviewed, corrected and augmented by Gervase Markham. 1616.

Markhams method or epitome. [1616?] (abridgement of Cheape and good husbandry, 1614, above), 1616, 1623, 1628, 1630, 1633, 1641, 1650, 1671, 1684.

The horsemans honour. 1620. By Markham?

Markhams farwell to husbandry. 1620, 1623 etc (in A way to get wealth).

Hungers prevention: or the whole arte of fowling. 1621, 1655.

Verus pater: or a bundell of truths. 1622. Probably not by Markham.

A second part to the mothers blessing: or a cure against misfortunes. 1622. Nicholas Breton and Dorothy Leigh both wrote a Mothers blessing.

The true tragedy of Herod and Antipater, with the death of faire Marriam, as it hath beene acted at the Red Bull, by Gervase Markham and William Sampson. 1622.

Certaine excellent and new invented knots and mazes, for plots for gardens. 1623. Sometimes attributed to Markham.

Honour in his perfection: Henry Earle of Oxenford, Henry Earle of Southampton, Robert Earle of Essex, Robert Bartue, Lord Willoughby of Eresby. 1624 (by G.M.).

The inrichment of the Weald of Kent. 1625 (anon), 1631 etc (in A way to get wealth).

The souldiers accidence. 1625 (by G.M.), 1635, 1639 (in The souldiers exercise, below).

The souldiers grammar. Pt 1, 1626; pt 2, 1627; 2 pts 1639 (in The souldiers exercise, below).

The description of that ever to be famed knight, Sir John Burgh. 1628.

Markhams faithfull farrier. 1629 (from Markhams maister-peece, 1610, above), 1630, 1631, 1635, 1636, 1638, 1640, 1647, 1656, 1661, 1687.

A way to get wealth. 1623 (with Markhams farwell to husbandry, 1620, above; Cheape and good husbandry, 1623; Country contentments: or the English huswife, 1623; William Lawson, A new orchard and garden, 1623 augmented), 1625 (with Markhams farwell to husbandry, 1625), 1631 (Cheape and good husbandry, 1631; Country contentments: or the husbandmans recreations, 1631; The English house-wife, 1631; The inrichment of the Weald of Kent, 1631; Markhams farwell to husbandry, 1631; William Lawson, A new orchard and garden, 1631), 1638 (with later edns of same items), 1648 (for 1649), 1653, 1657, 1660, 1660, 1668, 1676, 1683, 1695.

Heresbatch, Conrade. The whole art of husbandrie. Tr Barnaby Googe 1631 (enlarged by Markham).

The art of archerie. 1634.

The complete farriar. 1639. Abridged from A discource of horsmanshippe, 1606.

The souldiers exercise. 1639 (with The souldiers accidence and The souldiers grammar), 1643 (3rd edn).

The perfect horseman: or the experienc'd secrets of Mr Markham's fifty years practice. 1655 (abridged from Cavelarice, above), 1656, 1660, 1668, 1671, 1680, 1684.

SAMUEL ROWLANDS
1570?–1630?

Collections

Complete works. Ed E. Gosse and S. J. H. Herrtage 3 vols Glasgow 1880 (Hunterian Club).

The four knaves. Ed E. F. Rimbault 1842 (Percy Soc).

Uncollected poems 1604?–17. Ed F. O. Waage, Gainesville 1970.

§ 1

The betraying of Christ: Judas in despaire. 1598.

The letting of humors blood in the head-vaine. 1600, 1600, 1600, [1605?] (as Humors ordinarie), 1607 (with addns), 1610, 1611 (as The letting of humours blood), 1613; ed Sir Walter Scott, Edinburgh 1814; ed F. O. Waage, Uncollected poems, Gainesville 1970 (facs of Humors ordinarie).

Tis merrie when gossips meete. 1602, 1609 (pt of A whole crew of kind gossips), [1613?] ('enlarged'), 1619 (as Well met gossip), 1627, 1673, Chiswick 1818.

Ave Caesar: God save the King. 1603; ed W. C. Hazlitt, Fugitive poetical tracts ser 2, 1875.

Looke to it, for Ile stabbe ye. 1604, 1604; ed E. V. Utterson, [Ryde] 1841.

Humors antique faces. 1605 (by E.M.); ed F. O. Waage, Uncollected poems, Gainesville 1970 (facs).

Hell's broke loose. 1605. By Rowlands?

A theater of delightfull recreation. 1605; ed F. O. Waage, Uncollected poems, Gainesville 1970 (facs).

A terrible battell betweene time and death. [1606?].

Diogines lanthorne. 1607, 1608, [1608?], 1628 (for 1608?), 1628, 1631, 1634, 1659.

Democritus: or Doctor Merry-Man his medicines against melancholy humors. [1607], 1609 (as Doctor Merrie-Man: or nothing but mirth), 1614 (title-page only), 1616, 1618, 1619, 1623, 1627, 1642, 1657, 1671, 1681.

Humors looking-glasse. 1608 (mainly from Humors antique faces and Humors ordinarie, 1607); ed J. P. Collier 1870.

The famous historie of Guy Earle of Warwick. 1609, [c. 1620], [c. 1625], 1632, 1635, 1649, 1654, 1667, [1680?], [1680?], [1699?].

A whole crew of kind gossips all met to be merry. 1609 (with Tis merrie when gossips meete), 1613 ('inlarged' as A crew of kind gossips), 1663 (in A crew of kind London gossips), 1684.

The knave of clubbes. 1609 (non-extant first edn A merry meeting: or 'tis merry when knaves meet, 1600), 1611, 161[2?], 1612, 1612, 1613; ed E. V. Utterson, [Ryde] 1841; ed E. F. Rimbault, The four knaves, 1843 (Percy Soc).

The knave of harts: haile fellow well met. 1612 (anon), 1613; ed E. V. Utterson, [Ryde] 1840; ed E. F. Rimbault, The four knaves, 1843 (Percy Soc).

More knaves yet? the knaves of spades and diamonds. [1613], [1613?] (with addns); ed E. V. Utterson, [Ryde] 1841; ed E. F. Rimbault, The four knaves, 1843 (Percy Soc).

Sir Thomas Overbury: or the poysoned knights complaint. [1614?].

A fooles bolt is soone shott. 1614.

The melancholie knight. 1615, 1615 (title-page only); ed E. V. Utterson, [Ryde] 1841.

The bride. 1617; ed A. C. Potter, Boston 1905; ed F. O. Waage, Uncollected poems, Gainesville 1970 (facs).

A sacred memorie of the miracles wrought by Jesus Christ. 1618.

The nigt-raven. 1620, 1634; ed E. V. Utterson, [Ryde] 1841.

A paire of spy-knaves. [1620?].

Good newes and bad newes. 1622; ed E. V. Utterson, [Ryde] 1841.

Heavens glory, seeke it; hearts vanitie, flye it; Hells horror, fere it. 1628 (with M. Sparke?), 1639 (as A most excellent treatise containing the way to seek Heavens glory), 1657 (as Time well improved).

II. CHARACTER-BOOKS AND ESSAYS

(1) CHARACTER-BOOKS

Bibliographies

Murphy, G. A bibliography of English character-books 1608–1700. Oxford 1925.

Greenough, C. N. A bibliography of the Theophrastan character in English. Cambridge Mass 1947.

§ 1

Hall, Joseph. Characters of vertues and vices. 1608 (24 characters), 1608, 1608, 1621 (as Meditations and vowes, and Characters of vertues and vices); rptd in his Works 1625, 1628, 1634, 1647, 1648, 1808, 1837, 1863; tr French, 1610, 1619, 1634; versified by Nahum Tate as Characters of virtue and vice, 1691.

H[eywood], T[homas]. Troia britannica. 1609 (one character).

— A true discourse of the two prophets. 1636 (one character).

— Machiavel as he lately appeared to his deare sons the moderne projectors. 1641 (also pt issued as Machiavels ghost; one character and 10 short sketches of particular projectors), 1642 (extract, as Hogs caracter of a projector).

Overbury, Thomas. A wife now the widdow of Sir Thomas Overburye; whereunto are added many witty characters. 1614 (2nd edn of A wife, 1614, adding 21 characters), 1614 (30 characters), 1614 (31 characters), 1614, 1615 (as New and choise characters; 73 characters, 32 of them by John Webster), 1616 (as Sir Thomas Overburie his wife, with new elegies upon his (now knowne) untimely death; whereunto are annexed new newes and characters; 72 characters), 1616 (72 characters), 1616 (81 characters), 1618, 1622 (82 characters including John Donne's A dunce, rptd with A Scot, in Paradoxes, problems, essayes, characters, 1652), [Dublin] 1626, 1627, 1628, 1630, 1632, 1638, 1655, 1664; 1756 (in Miscellaneous works in verse and prose); ed E. F. Rimbault, Miscellaneous works in prose and verse, 1856 (from 1616); ed W. J. Paylor, Oxford 1936; ed J. E. Savage, Gainesville 1968 (facs of 1616, as The conceited newes).

Brathwait, Richard. A strappado for the Divell. 1615 (3 characters).

— Essaies upon the five senses. 1620 (2 characters).

— The English gentleman. 1630 (one character).

— The English gentlewoman. 1631 (6 characters).

— Whimzies: or a new cast of characters. 1631 (28 characters); ed J. O. Halliwell (-Phillipps) 1859.

— A strange metamorphosis of man, transformed into a wildernesse, deciphered in characters. 1634 (anon; 40 characters); ed D. C. Allen, Baltimore 1949. Sometimes attributed to Brathwait.

Breton, Nicholas. Characters upon essaies morall and divine. 1615 (16 characters); ed S. E. Brydges, Archaica vol 1, 1815.

— The good and the badde: or descriptions of the worthies and unworthies of this age. 1616 (50 characters), 1643 (as England's selected characters; 28 characters, 5 new); ed S. E. Brydges, Archaica vol 1, 1815.

— Fantasticks: serving for a perpetuall prognostication. 1626 (38 characters); M. Stevenson, The twelve moneths, 1661 (12 characters from Fantasticks, 1626, adapted); ed B. Rhys 1927.

Earle, John. Micro-cosmographie: or a peece of the world discovered in essayes and characters, newly composed for the northerne parts of this kingdome. 1628 (anon:

54 characters), 1628, 1628, 1628, 1629 (77 characters), 1630, 1633 (78 characters), 1638, 1650 (54 characters), 1650 (71 characters), 1650, 1660, 1664 (78 characters), 1669; ed P. Bliss 1811; ed E. Arber 1868; ed H. Morley 1889; ed G. Murphy 1928; ed H. Osborne 1933. Selections: A true description of the pot-companion poet; also a character of the swibole cook, 1642; The character of a tavern, 1675; A gallery of portraits, Dublin 1813 (32 portraits adapted from Earle); A book of characters, selected from the writings of Overbury, Earle and Butler, Edinburgh 1865 (67 characters from Earle), 1869 (as The mirror of character); Menston 1966 (ms facs).

Saltonstall, Wye. Picturae loquentes: or pictures drawne forth in characters. 1631 (26 characters), 1635 (38 characters); ed C. H. Wilkinson, Oxford 1946 (Luttrell Soc).

Fuller, Thomas. The holy state; the profane state. Cambridge 1642 (51 characters), 1648, 1652, 1663, 1840, 1844 (9 characters and Lives omitted); The marvellous wisdom and quaint conceits of Fuller, abridged by A. L. J. Gosset 1893.

Cleveland, John. The character of a London diurnall. Oxford 1644 (for 1645), 1644 (for 1645), 1644 (for 1645), 1647 (17 poems), 1647 (18 poems), 1647 (20 poems), 1647, 1647 (21 poems), 1647 (22 poems), 1647 (23 poems), 1651 etc (in Poems), 1677 (in Clievelandi vindiciae: or Clieveland's genuine poems etc), 1657 (in Works), 1699.

— The character of a moderate intelligencer; with some select poems by J.C. [1647] (2 characters).

— The character of a country committee-man. 1649, 1651 etc (in Poems), 1677 (in Clievelandi vindiciae), 1687 (in Works), 1699.

— A character of a diurnal-maker, by J.C. 1654 (for 1653), 1654, 1654 etc (in Poems), 1677 (in Clievelandi vindiciae), 1687 (in Works), 1699.

— The Puritan. 1659 (in J. Cleaveland revived), 1660, 1662, 1668, 1687 (in Works), 1699.

See John Cleveland, col 154, above.

Flecknoe, Richard. Miscellania: or poems of all sorts, with divers other pieces. 1653 (4 characters).

— Enigmaticall characters, all taken to the life from severall persons, humours and dispositions. 1658 (69 characters), 1665 (as Fifty-five enigmatical characters), 1665 (as Sixty-nine enigmatical characters; with 69 characters as in 1658), 1665 (as Richard Flecknoe's Ænigmatical characters, 22 new).

— Heroick portraits with other miscellary pieces. 1660 (4 portraits, 15 characters); rptd in Richard Flecknoe, Ænigmatical characters, 1665, and in A collection, 1673.

— A farrago of several pieces. 1666 (7 characters).

— A collection of the choicest epigrams and characters of Richard Flecknoe. 1673 (63 characters, 19 new), 1677 (as Seventy-eight characters of so many vertuous and vitious persons; 63 characters, 2 new).

§ 2

Gordon, G. S. Theophrastus and his imitators. In his English literature and the classics, Oxford 1912.

Smith, D. N. The character. In his Characters from the histories and memoirs of the seventeenth century, Oxford 1918.

Boyce, B. The Theophrastan character in England to 1642. Cambridge Mass 1947.

(2) ESSAYS

Churchyard, Thomas. A sparke of frendship and warme goodwill. 1588; rptd Harleian miscellany vol 2, 1809.

Bacon, Francis. Essayes. 1597 etc.

—— Apophthegmes new and old. 1625, 1626 1674 (as A collection). *See col 353, below.*

Greenham, Richard. Works. Ed H. H[olland] 1599, 1599, 1600 (2nd pt), 1601 (both pts), 1605, 1612.

King James I. Βασιλικὸν Δῶρον, devided into three bookes. Edinburgh 1599. Anon.

Cornwallis, Sir William. Essayes. Pt 1, 1600; pt 2, 1601; 1610 (both pts 'newly enlarged', with Discourses upon Seneca), 1632 (for 1631) ('newly corrected' by H[enry] O[lney]); Essayes 1600–10, ed D. C. Allen, Baltimore 1946.

—— Discourses upon Seneca the tragedian. 1601.

—— Essayes: or rather encomions, prayses of sadnesse. 1616, 1616 (in following).

—— Essayes of certaine paradoxes. 1616 (anon), 1617 (with Essayes: or rather encomions).

Hall, Joseph. Meditations and vowes, divine and morall. 1605, 1606 (2 pts), 1606, 1607 (enlarged), 1609, 1616, 1621 (with Caracters of vertues and vices).

—— Contemplations upon the principall passages of the holie storie. 1612 (first vol in 4 bks), 1614 (2nd vol in 4 bks), 1615 (3rd vol in 3 bks), 1617 (in A recollection of treatises), 1618 (4th vol), 1620 (5th vol), 1622 (6th vol), 1623 (7th vol in 2 bks: Contemplations upon the historie of the Old testament), 1626 (8th vol), 1634 (in Complete works).

—— Occasionall meditations. 1630.

Rich, Barnaby. Faultes, faults and nothing else but faultes. 1606.

Breton, Nicholas. Divine considerations of the soule. 1608.

—— Characters upon essaies morall and divine. 1615.

Brathwait, Richard. Essaies upon the five senses. 1620.

Felltham, Owen. Resolves, divine, morall, politicall. [1623?], 1628 (with addns), 1628 (for 1629), 1631, 1634, 1636, 1647, 1661 (with addns), 1661, 1670, 1677, 1696; ed J. Cumming 1806; ed O. Smeaton 1904.

Donne, John. Devotions upon emergent occasions. 1624, 1624, 1626 (for 1627), 1634, 1638.

—— Essayes in divinity, interwoven with meditations and prayers. 1651.

—— Paradoxes, problemes, essayes, characters, with Ignatius his conclave. 1652, 1652. *See col 125, above.*

Ralegh, Walter. Instructions to his sonne and to posterity. 1632, 1632, 1633, 1633, 1634, 1636.

—— The Prince: or maxims of state. 1642.

Peacham, Henry. The truth of our times, revealed out of one mans experience by way of essay. 1638; ed R. R. Cawley, New York 1942 (facs).

—— The valley of varietie: or discourse fitting for the times. 1638.

Quarles, Francis. Enchyridion. 1640, 1641, 1644, 1646, 1654, 1658, 1664, 1667, 1670; Observations concerning princes, 1642 (collected from Enchyridion).

—— Boanerges and Barnabas: or judgement and mercy for afflicted soules. Pt 1, 1646, 1646; pt 2, 1644, 1646, 1646; 2 pts 1657, 1667, 1671, 1674, 1679.

Jonson, Ben. Timber: or discoveries. 1641 (in Works vol 2). *See col 229, above.*

Fuller, Thomas. The holy state, the profane state. Cambridge 1642.

—— Good thoughts in bad times. Exeter 1645.

—— Good thoughts in worse times. 1647.

—— Mixt contemplations in better times. 1660. *See col 343, below.*

Palmer, Herbert. Memorials of godlinesse and Christianitie. 1644, 1645, 1655 (5th edn), 1657 (7th edn), 1670 (10th edn), 1681; rptd in Bacon's Remaines, 1648 (in part); ed A. B. Grosart, Edinburgh 1865 (complete).

Howell, James. Epistolae Ho-Elianae: familiar letters domestic and forren. 4 vols 1645, 1650, 1655, 1673, 1678, 1688.

Hall, John (1627–56). Horae vacivae: or essays. 1646.

—— Paradoxes by J. de la Salle. 1650, 1653, 1656 (as Paradoxes by John Hall).

Wotton, Sir Henry. Aphorisms of education. 1654 (in Reliquiae Wottonianae, 2nd edn). *See col 158, above.*

Osborne, Francis. Advice to a son. Oxford 1656, 1656, 1656, 1656, 1656, 1658; pt 2, 1658.

—— A miscellany of sundry essayes. 1659, 1659.

III. PROSE FICTION

(1) BIBLIOGRAPHIES

Esdaile, A. A list of English tales and prose romances printed before 1740. 1912 (Bibl Soc).

Mish, C. C. English prose fiction 1600–1700. Charlottesville 1952, 1967 (rev).

(2) COLLECTIONS

Early prose romances. Ed W. J. Thoms 3 vols 1827–8, 1858 (rev), [1907] (rev).

Shakespeare's library: a collection of the romances, novels, poems and histories, used by Shakespeare as the foundation of his dramas. Ed J. P. Collier 2 vols [1843], 1850; rev W. C. Hazlitt 6 vols 1875.

The descent of Euphues: three Elizabethan romance stories. Ed J. Winny, Cambridge 1957.

Short fiction of the seventeenth century. Ed C. C. Mish, New York 1963.

Elizabethan love stories. Ed T. J. B. Spencer 1968 (Pelican).

(3) FICTION

Painter, William. The palace of pleasure: pleasaunt histories and excellent novelles. 1566, 1569, 1575 (corrected and augmented); Second tome, 1567, [1580?] (agayn corrected and encreased); [ed J. Haslewood] 1813; ed J. Jacobs 3 vols 1890; ed H. Miles 4 vols 1929.

Baldwin, William. A marvelous hystory intitulede beware the cat. 1570, 1584, 1652 (fragment); ed W. P. Holden, New London Conn 1963.

[Gascoigne, George]. A pleasant discourse of the adventures of master F.I. [1573] (in A hundreth sundrie flowres), 1575 (augmented, rev and transferred to an Italian setting), 1587 (as Whole woorkes); ed C. T.

Prouty, Columbia Missouri 1942; ed R. Ashley and
E. M. Moseley, Elizabethan fiction, New York 1953;
ed M. Lawlis, Elizabethan prose fiction, New York 1968.
—— The pleasant tale of Hemetes the hermite. 1579 (as
by Abraham Fleming in A paradoxe proving baldnesse
better than bushie haire), 1585 (in The Queen Majesty's
entertainment), 1587 (in Whole works), 1587.
Rich, Barnaby. A right exelent and pleasaunt dialogue,
betwene Mercury and an English souldier. [1574].
—— Riche his farewell to militarie profession. 1581, 1583,
1594 (rev), 1606 (rev).
—— The straunge and wonderfull adventures of Don
Simonides. 1581.
—— The second tome of the travailes and adventures of
Don Simonides. 1584.
—— The adventures of Brusanus, Prince of Hungaria.
1592.
Pettie, George. A petite pallace of Pettie his pleasure:
many pretie histories. [1576], [1578?], [c. 1585], [c.
1590], 1608, 1613; ed I. Gollancz 2 vols 1908; ed H.
Miles 4 vols 1930; ed H. Hartman, Oxford 1938.
Whetstone, George. The rocke of regard. 1576.
—— An heptameron of civill discourses: the Christmasse
exercise of sundrie gentlemen and gentlewomen. 1582,
1593 (as Aurelia).
Grange, John. The golden Aphroditis. 1577; ed H. E.
Rollins, New York 1939 (facs).
Lyly, John. Euphues: the anatomy of wyt. [1578].
—— Euphues and his England. 1580.
Gosson, Stephen. The ephemerides of Phialo. 1579, 1586.
Gifford, Humphrey. A posie of gilloflowers. 1580; ed
F. J. H. Darton 1933.
Munday, Anthony. Zelauto: the fountaine of fame. 1580.
Greene, Robert. Mamillia: a mirrour or looking-glasse
for the ladies of Englande. 1583, 1593 (The second part
of the triumph of Pallas).
—— Arbasto: the anatomie of fortune. 1584.
—— Gwydonius: the carde of fancie. 1584.
—— Morando the tritameron of love. Pt 1, 1584; 2 pts
1587.
—— The myrrour of modestie, by R.G. 1584.
—— Planetomachia. 1585.
—— Euphues his censure to Philautus. 1587.
—— Penelopes web. [1587].
—— Pandosto: the triumph of time. 1588.
—— Perimedes the blacke-smith. 1588.
—— Ciceronis amor: Tullies love. 1589.
—— The Spanish masquerado. 1589.
—— Menaphon Camilla's alarum to slumbering Euphues.
1589, 1599, [1605?], 1610 (as Greenes arcadia), 1616.
—— Greenes farewell to folly. 1591.
—— The blacke bookes messenger: the life and death of
Ned Browne, by R.G. 1592.
—— Greenes never too late. 1590.
—— Greenes mourning garment. 1590.
—— Philomela: the Lady Fitzwaters nightingale. 1592.
—— Greenes groats-worth of witte. 1592.
—— Greenes Orpharion: a musicall concorde of pleasant
histories. 1599.
—— Alcida Greenes metamorphosis. 1617.
Melbancke, Brian. Philotimus: the warre betwixt nature
and fortune. 1582 (for 1583).
Lodge, Thomas. An alarum against usurers: the delectable
historie of Forbonius and Prisceria. 1584.
—— Rosalynde: Euphues golden legacie. 1590.
—— The famous, true and historicall life of Robert second
Duke of Normandy, by T.L.G. 1591.
—— Euphues shadow: the battaile of the sences. 1592.
—— The life and death of William Longbeard. 1593.
—— A Margarite of America. 1596.
Warner, William. Pan his syrinx or pipe: seven tragical
and comicall arguments. [1584], 1597 (newly perused
and amended).
Sidney, Sir Philip. The Countesse of Pembrokes Arcadia.
1590. See col 94, above.

Fraunce, Abraham. The third part of the Countesse of
Pembrokes Yvychurch, entituled Amintas dale: the
most conceited tales of the pagan gods. 1592.
Johnson, Richard. The nine worthies of London. 1592;
rptd Harleian miscellany vol 8, 1811.
—— The most famous history of the seaven champions of
Christendome. Pt 1, 1596; pt 2, 1597; 1608 (both
pts), [1616], [1626], [1639?], [after 1640?], [1660],
1670, 1675, 1676, 1680, [1680], 1686, 1687, 1696; pt 3,
1686, 1689, 1694; abridged 1661, 1675, 1679; rptd R.
Kennedy, Portland Oregon 1967 (facs of 18th-century
edn).
—— The most pleasant history of Tom a Lincolne. 1631
(6th impression), 1635, 1655, 1668, 1682, 1682; abridged
[1695]; ed W. J. Thoms, Early prose romances vol 2,
1828 etc.
—— The pleasant conceites of old Hobson the merry
Londoner. 1607, 1610 (enlarged), 1634, 1640; ed J. O.
Halliwell(-Phillipps) 1843 (Percy Soc); ed W. C. Hazlitt,
Shakespeare jest-books vol 3, 1864.
—— The history of Tom Thumbe, by R[ichard?] J[ohn-
son?]. 1621; ed C. F. Bühler, Evanston 1965.
C[hettle], H[enry]. Kind-harts dreame. [1593].
—— Piers Plainnes seven yeres prentiship. 1595.
Nashe, Thomas. The unfortunate traveller: or the life of
Jacke Wilton. 1594.
Forde, Emanuel. The most pleasant historie of Ornatus
and Artesia. [1595?], 1607, 1619, 1634, 1650, 1662,
1669, 1683; abridged [1688?], [1694?] [c. 1700]; ed
P. Henderson, Shorter novels, Jacobean and Restoration, 1930.
—— Parismus, the renoumed Prince of Bohemia. 1598,
1599 (pt 2: Parismenos), 1604 (both pts), 1608, 1615,
1630, 1636, 1649, 1657, 1661, 1663, 1664 (pt 1 only),
1665 (pt 2 only), 1671–2 (pt 1), 1672 (pt 2), 1677
(complete), 1681, 1684, 1689, 1696; abridged [c. 1660],
1677, 1683, 1699, [1700?]; ed R. B. Johnson, The birth
of romance, 1928 (extracts).
—— The famous historie of Montelyon, knight of the
oracle. 1633, 1640, 1661, 1663, 1668, 1673, 1677, 1680,
1687, 1695, 1697.
Breton, Nicholas. The miseries of Mavillia. 1597 (in The
wil of wit), 1599, 1606 (corrected).
—— The strange fortunes of two excellent princes. 1600.
—— Grimellos fortunes. 1604.
See col 90, above.
Middleton, Christopher. The famous historie of Chinon of
England; with the worthy atchivement of Sir Lancelot
du Lake and Sir Tristram du Lions. 1597; ed W. E.
Mead 1925 (EETS).
Deloney, Thomas. The gentle craft. Pt 2, [c. 1598]
(fragment), 1639 (newly corrected and augmented),
1660; Pt 1, 1627, 1637, 164[0], 1648 (with pictures),
1652, 1660, [1670], 1672, 1674, [1675?], 1676, 1678,
[1680?], [1685], [1690?], 1696; ed A. F. Lange, Berlin
1903; ed W. H. D. Rouse 1926; pt 1 ed W. J. Halliday,
Oxford 1928. Sequel by L.P., The most pleasant
history of Bovinian, 1656.
—— The pleasant history of John Winchcomb, Jack of
Newberie. 1619 (8th edn), 1626 (10th edn), 1630, 1633,
1637, 1672, [1690?], [1700?]; abridged 1684; ed J. O.
Halliwell (-Phillipps) 1859; ed R. Sievers, Deloney,
Weimar 1903; ed W. H. D. Rouse 1920; ed G. Saintsbury, Shorter novels vol 1, 1929; ed R. Ashley and
E. M. Moseley, Elizabethan fiction, New York 1953.
—— Thomas of Reading: or the sixe worthy yeomen of the
west. 1612 (4th edn), 1623, 1632, 1636, 1672, 1690,
1690 (abridged); rptd Edinburgh 1812 (from 1632);
ed W. J. Thoms, Early prose romances vol 1, 1827; ed
C. Aldrich and L. S. Kirtland, New York 1903; ed
D. Senior, Some old English worthies, 1912; ed W. H. D.
Rouse 1920; ed G. Saintsbury, Shorter novels vol 1,
1929; ed M. Lawlis, Elizabethan prose fiction, New
York 1968; Menston 1969 (facs of 1612).

—— Works. Ed F. O. Mann, Oxford 1912; Novels, ed M. E. Lawlis, Bloomington 1961.

Armin, Robert. Foole upon foole: or six sortes of sottes, [by] Clonnico de Curtanio Snuffe. 1600, 1605, 1608 (with addns as A nest of ninnies); ed J. P. Collier, Fools and jesters, 1842 (Shakespeare Soc) (from 1608); ed A. B. Grosart, Manchester 1880 (from 1605); ed P. M. Zall 1963 (from 1608).

Dekker, Thomas. The wonderfull yeare. 1603.

—— Newes from hell. 1606, 1607 (as A knights conjuring).

—— and George Wilkins. Jests to make you merie. 1607. *See col 233, above.*

Pasquils jests, mixed with Mother Bunches merriments. 1604, 1609 (corrected with new addns), 1629, [1632?], 1635, [1650?]; ed W. C. Hazlitt, Shakespeare jest-books vol 3, 1864.

Dobsons drie bobbes: sonne and heire to Skoggin. 1607; ed E. Schulz, Die englischen Schwankbücher bis herab zu Dobsons Drie Bobs (1607), Berlin 1912; ed E. A. Horsman, Oxford 1955.

Peele, George. The merrie conceited jests of George Peale. 1607, [1620?], 1627, 1627, 1657, 1671; ed W. C. Hazlitt, Shakespeare jest-books vol 2, 1864; ed C. Hindley 1869.

Markham, Gervase. The English Arcadia, alluding his beginning from Sir Philip Sydnes ending. 1607.

—— The second and last part of the first booke of the English Arcadia. 1613.

Wilkins, George. The painfull adventures of Pericles Prince of Tyre: being the true history of the play of Pericles, as it was lately presented. 1608; ed T. Mommsen, Oldenburg 1857; ed K. Muir, Liverpool 1953.

The famous and renowned history of Morindos a King of Spain who maryed with Miracola a Spanish witch. 1609; ed C. C. Mish, Short fiction of the seventeenth century, New York 1963.

Tarlton, Richard. Tarltons jests, drawn into three parts. 1611, 1613, 1638; ed J. O. Halliwell (-Phillipps) 1844 (Shakespeare Soc); ed W. C. Hazlitt, Shakespeare jest-books vol 2, 1864; ed E. W. Ashbee [1876?] (facs).

The life and pranks of Long Meg of Westminster. 1620, 1635, 1636; ed R. Triphook, Miscellanea antiqua anglicana, 1816 (from 1635); ed C. C. Mish, Short fiction of the seventeenth century, New York 1963 (from 1620).

Reynolds, John. The triumphs of Gods revenege against murther, in thirty severall tragicall histories. Bk 1, 1621, 1629; bk 2, 1622; bk 3, 1623; bks 1–6, 1635 (for 1634), 1639, 1657, 1662, 1663, 1670, 1679 (enlarged), 1682, 1685 (abridged as The glory of God's revenge), 1686, 1687, 1688 (as God's revenge).

—— The flower of fidelitie: the various adventures of three foraign princes. 1650, 1654, 1655, 1660.

B[ernard], R[ichard]. The Isle of Man: or the legall proceeding in Man-shire against sinne. 1626, 1627, 1627 (4th edn 'much enlarged'), 1628, 1630 (7th edn), 1632, 1634, 1635 (10th edn), 1640, 1648, 1658, 1659, 1668, 1674, 1676, 1677, 1683; ed R. Edwards, Bristol 1803; rptd London 1834; ed D. F. Jarman 1851 (as Sin apprehended).

The famous historie of Fryer Bacon. 1627, 1629, [1640], 1661, 1666, 1679, 1683; ed W. G. Thoms, Early prose romances vol 1, 1828; ed H. Morley, Early prose romances, 1889; ed D. Senior, Some old English worthies, 1912.

Robin Good-Fellow his mad prankes. 2 pts 1628, 1639.

A pleasant history of the life and death of Will Summers. 1637, 1676; ed J. Caulfield 1794.

Godwin, Francis. The man in the moone: or a discourse of a voyage thither by D. Gonsales. 1638 (anon), 1657 (with Nuncius inanimatus, 1629); ed G. McColley, Northampton Mass 1937.

Brathwait, Richard. Ar't asleepe husband? 1640.

—— The two Lancashire lovers. 1640.

—— The penitent pilgrim. 1641.

H[owell], J[ames]. Δενδρολογία: Dodona's grove, or the vocall forrest. 1640, 1644, Cambridge 1645, [1649]; pt 2, 1650.

The pleasant history of Cawwood the rooke: or the assembly of birds. 1640, 1656, 1683; ed C. C. Mish, Short fiction of the seventeenth century, New York 1963.

Neville, Henry. The parliament of ladies: or divers remarkable passages of ladies in Spring-Garden in parliament assembled. 1647, 1647, 1647 (as The ladies' parliament), 1752 (Somers tracts), 1768, 1811 (Somers tracts; another version).

—— The ladies a second time assembled in parliament. 1647.

—— Newes from the New Exchange: or the commonwealth of ladies. 1650.

Boyle, Roger, Earl of Orrery. Parthenissa. 2 pts Waterford 1651; pt 1 (bks 1–6), 1654; pt 3 (bks 1–4), 1656; pt 3 (bks 5–8), 1669, 1676 (complete).

Cavendish, Margaret, Duchess of Newcastle. Natures pictures. 1656, 1671.

6. HISTORY, PHILOSOPHY, SCIENCE AND OTHER FORMS OF LEARNING

I. HISTORIANS, BIOGRAPHERS AND ANTIQUARIES

A. GENERAL WORKS

Stauffer, D. English biography before 1700. Cambridge Mass 1930.

Butt, J. The facilities for antiquarian research in the seventeenth century. E & S 24 1938.

Campbell, L. B. The use of historical patterns in the reign of Elizabeth. HLQ 1 1938.

Fox, L. (ed). English historical scholarship in the sixteenth and seventeenth centuries. Oxford 1956 (Dugdale Soc).

Pocock, J. G.·A. The ancient constitution and the feudal law: English historical thought in the 17th century. Cambridge 1957.

Baker, H. The race of time: three lectures on Renaissance historiography. Toronto 1967.

Levy, F. J. Tudor historical thought. San Marino 1967.

Delany, P. British autobiography in the seventeenth century. 1969.

For useful brief annotations on the 16th-century chronicles see C. Read, Bibliography of British history: Tudor period, *Oxford 1959 (rev)*.

B. 1500–58

POLYDORE VERGIL
1470?–1555?

§1

De inventoribus rerum. Venice 1499, Paris 1500, Strasbourg 1509, Basle 1521 etc. Many 16th-century edns and trns.

Polydori Vergilii urbinatis anglicae historiae libri xxvi. Basle 1534, 1546, 1555 (continued to 1538), 1556, 2 vols Ghent 1556–7, 1 vol Basle 1570, Leyden 1651; ed and tr H. Ellis 1844 (Camden Soc) (as Three bookes of Polydore Vergil's English history: comprising the reigns of Henry VI, Edward IV and Richard III); Polydore Vergil's English history: containing the first eight books, comprising the period prior to the Norman Conquest, ed H. Ellis 1846 (Camden Soc); ed and tr D. Hay 1950 (Camden Soc, Royal Historical Soc).

An abridgement of the notable woorke of Polydore Vergil. Tr T. Langley 1546, 1546, 1551, [c. 1560]; ed W. A. Hammond, New York 1868.

§2

Ferguson, J. Vergil: Renaissance historian and man of letters. Oxford 1952. With a list of letters.

EDWARD HALL
d. 1547

The union of the two noble and illustrate [illustre] femelies of Lancastre and York. 1548, 1550, [1560?], with some sheets ptd in 1547; [ed H. Ellis] 1809, New York 1965; Henry VIII, ed C. Whibley 2 vols 1904.

JOHN LELAND
1506–52

§1

Assertio inclytissimi Arturii regis Britanniae. 1544; tr R. Robinson 1582 (as A learned and true assertion of the life of prince Arthure); ed W. E. Mead 1925 (EETS) (appended to C. Middleton, The famous historie of Chinon of England, with Robinson's trn).

The laboryouse journey and serche of Johan Leylande, geven of hym as a newe yeares gyfte to Kynge Henry the VIII. 1549, 1596 (in R. Brooke, A discoverie of certaine errours), 1631 (in J. Weever, Funerall monuments), 1710 (in Itinerary ed T. Hearne vol 1), Oxford 1722, 1772 (in W. Huddesford, Lives of Leland etc); ed W. A. Copinger, Manchester 1895.

The itinerary of John Leland the antiquary. Ed T. Hearne 9 vols Oxford 1710–12, 1744–5, 1770; ed L. Toulmin Smith 11 pts in 5 vols 1906–10; 5 vols Carbondale [1964] (foreword by T. Kendrick).

§2

Huddesford, W. The lives of those eminent antiquaries John Leland, Thomas Hearne and Anthony à Wood. Ed W. Huddesford 2 vols Oxford 1772. Life of Leland by Huddesford.

Dorsch, T. S. Two English antiquaries: Leland and Stow. E & S new ser 12 1959.

NICHOLAS HARPSFIELD
1519?–75

A treatise on the pretended divorce between Henry VIII and Catherine of Aragon. Ed N. Pocock 1878 (Camden Soc).

Life of Sir Thomas More. Ed Lord Acton 1877 (in part, with historical portion of A treatise); ed R. W. Chambers and E. V. Hitchcock 1932 (EETS) (as The Tudor lives of Sir Thomas More).

WILLIAM ROPER
1496–1578[

The mirrour of vertue in worldly greatnes: or the life of Syr T. More. Paris [St Omer] 1626; ed T. Hearne, [Oxford] 1716, Cambridge 1879; ed J. Lewis 1720 (from better ms), 1731, Dublin 1765, 1835; ed S. W. Singer 1817, 1822; ed E. Rhys [1890]; ed I. Gollancz 1902, 1903, 1910 (Bohn's Lib); ed E. V. Hitchcock 1935 (EETS); ed J. M. Cline, New York 1950.

GEORGE CAVENDISH
1500–61

Life of Cardinal Wolsey. 1641 (as The negotiations of Thomas Woolsey), 1667, 1706, 1742 (in J. Grove, History of Cardinal Wolsey), 1745 (Harleian miscellany vol 5); ed J. Grove 1761 (more accurate version); ed R. S. Sylvester 1959 (EETS); ed R. Lockyer 1962.
Two early Tudor lives. Ed R. S. Sylvester and D. P. Harding, New Haven 1962. With Roper's Life of More.

C. 1558–1603

JOHN FOXE
1516–87
§1

Commentarii rerum in ecclesia gestarum: liber primus. Strasbourg 1554, 1564 (as Chronicon ecclesiae continens historiam rerum).
Rerum in ecclesia gestarum commentarii. 2 pts Basle 1559–63.
Actes and monuments. 1563, 2 vols 1570, 1576, 1583, 1596, 1610, 3 vols 1631–2, 1641, 1684; ed S. R. Cattley 8 vols 1837–41 (dissertation by G. Townsend); rev M. H. Seymour 1838; rev G. Townsend 8 vols 1843–9; rev J. Pratt 8 vols [1877] (with introd by J. Stoughton). An abridgement of the Acts and monumentes by T. Bright. 1589.
Foxe's Book of martyrs. Ed F. A. Williamson 1965 (abridged).
Μαρτυρολογία ἀλφαβετική: or an alphabetical martyrology. 1677.
Proposals for printing the Book of martyrs. [1683].
For trns and minor works see Mozley, below.

§2

Life. Prefixed to vol 2 of 1641 edn of Actes and monuments and attributed to Foxe's son Samuel.
Mozley, J. F. Foxe and his book. 1940, New York 1970. With a list of Foxe's minor works.
Haller, W. Foxe and the Puritan revolution. In Seventeenth-century studies by R. F. Jones et al, Stanford 1951.
—— Foxe's Book of martyrs and the elect nation. 1963, New York 1963 (as The elect nation: the meaning and relevance of Foxe's Book of martyrs).

MATTHEW PARKER
1504–75
§1

De antiquitate britannicae ecclesiae et privilegiis ecclesiae cantuariensis. [Lambeth] 1572[-4] (anon), Hanover 1605 (imperfect); ed S. Drake 1729.
Parker also edited:
Elegans, illustris et facilis rerum praesertim britannicarum narratio, quam Matthaeus westmonasteriensis Flores historiarum scripsit. 2 pts [London] 1567, 1570 (as Flores historiarum per Matthaeum westmonasteriensem collecti).
Matthaei Paris historia major. 1571.
Aelfredi regis res gestae ab Asserio conscriptae. 1574.
Historia brevis Thomae Walsingham et ypodigma Neustriae. 1574.
See also col 268, above.

§2

Strype, J. The life and acts of Parker. 1711, 3 vols Oxford 1821.
Brook, V. J. K. A life of Archbishop Parker. 1962.

RAPHAEL HOLINSHED
d. 1580?

The firste [laste] volume of the chronicles of Englande, Scotlande and Irelande. 4 pts 1577, 3 vols 1587, 6 vols 1807–8. The Privy Council ordered the excision of 8 ll. in vol 2 and 26 ll. in vol 3; some of these were replaced by new leaves. BM has all the original ll. among its copies. For 18th-century reprints of castrations *see* Masten, 1958, below.
Boswell-Stone, W. G. Shakespeare's Holinshed: the chronicle and the historical plays compared. 1896, 1907, New York 1966 (Shakespeare Lib).
Holinshed's chronicle as used in Shakespeare's plays. Ed A. and J. Nicoll 1927 (EL).

JOHN STOW
1525–1605

The workes of Geoffrey Chaucer, with divers addicions which were never in print before. 1561. The notes on Chaucer and list of Lydgate's works were also ptd in T. Speght's edn of Chaucer, 1598 and 1602.
A summarie of English chronicles. 1565, 1566, [1570], [1573], [1574], [1575], 1590.
The summarie of Englyshe chronicles abridged. 1566, [1567], [1573], [1579], 1584, [1587], 1598, 1598, 1604; continued by E.H[owes] [1607], 1611, 1618.
The chronicles of England from Brute unto this present year 1580. [1580], [1592] (as The Annales of England until 1592), [1600], [1601], [1605] (with addns probably by G. Eld); continued by E. Howes 1615 (with an appendix on the universities of Oxford, Cambridge and London by Sir G. Buck), 1631.
The Summary grows from 8° to 4° to folio, ending as the Annals; the Abridgement grows from 16° to 8°.
A survay of London. 1598, 1599 (with variants), 1603; rev A.M[unday] 1618; rev A.M[unday], D.D[yson] et al 1633 (one reissue after 1640); ed J. Strype 2 vols 1720, 1754–5; ed C. L. Kingsford 2 vols Oxford 1908; ed H. B. Wheatley [1912] (EL), [1960] (rev).
Three fifteenth-century chronicles (from Stow). Ed J. Gairdner 1880 (Camden Soc).
Two London chronicles from the collections of Stow. Ed H. L. Kingsford, Camden Miscellany 12 1910.

SIR THOMAS SMITH
1513–77

Many mss, both of works and letters, are in BM, Public Record Office and elsewhere. See col 120, above.

Collections

Literary and linguistic works. 1542, 1549, 1568. Pt 1 ed B. Danielsson, Stockholm [1963].

§1

De republica Anglorum: the maner of government of England. 1583, 1584, 1589 (as The commonwealth of England), 1594, 1601, 1609, 1612, 1621, 1633, 1635, 1640, 1691; ed L. Alston and F. W. Maitland, Cambridge 1906; Menston 1970 (facs of 1583).
An old mould to cast new lawes. [Oxford] 1643.
A discourse of the commonweal of the realm of England. Ed E. Lamond 1892, 1929; ed M. Dewar, Charlottesville 1969 (Folger Lib). Attributed to Smith.

§2

Strype, J. The life of the learned Sir Thomas Smith. 1698 (anon), Oxford 1820 (rev).
Dewar, M. Smith: a Tudor intellectual in office. 1964.

RICHARD CAREW of Anthony
1555–1620

Godfrey of Bulloigne or the recouverie of Hierusalem, translated into English by R.C. esquire, and now the first part containing five cantos imprinted in both languages. 1594; ed A. B. Grosart, Manchester 1881.
Examen de ingenios: the examination of mens wits by John Huarte, translated out of the Spanish tongue by M. Camillo Camilli, englished by R.C. esquire. 1594 (variant issues), 1596, 1604, 1616; ed C. Rogers, Gainesville 1959.
A herrings tayle: contayning a poeticall fiction of divers matters worthy the reading. 1598. Anon, attributed to Carew chiefly on the evidence of West Country words, many of which appear elsewhere only in the Survey.
The survey of Cornwall. 1602; ed H.C. (P. des Maizeaux) 1723, 1769 (with The excellencie of the English tongue); ed T. Tonkin and Francis Bacon de Dunstanville 1811; ed F. E. Halliday 1953 (with sketch of life).
The excellencie of the English tongue by R.C. of Anthony esquire, to W.C. In 2nd and later edns of William Camden, Remaines, 1614, 1623 etc, 1870; ed Des Maizeaux 1723 (with Survey), 1869; ed G. G. Smith, Elizabethan critical essays vol 2, Oxford 1904 (from ms).
The trn of Henri Estienne, A world of wonders, 1607, is also attributed to Carew.

D. 1603–60

WILLIAM CAMDEN
1551–1623

Britannia sive florentissimorum regnorum Angliae, Scotiae, Hiberniae chorographica descriptio. 1586, 1587, Frankfurt 1590, London 1590, 1594, 1600, 1607 (with addns in successive edns), 1616 etc; tr P. Holland 1610, 1637; ed E. Gibson 1695, 2 vols 1722, 1753; ed G. Scott 1772 (with corrections); ed R. Gough 3 vols 1789, 4 vols 1806, 1 vol Menston 1970 (facs of 1695).
Remaines of a greater worke concerning Britaine. 2 pts 1605, 1614, 1623, 1629 (all initialled M.N.); ed J. Philipot 1636, 1637 (variant with altered date) etc, 1870.
Annales rerum anglicarum et hibernicarum regnante Elizabetha. Pt 1 (to 1589), 1615, 1616; pts 1–2 (to 1603), Leyden 1625, pt 2, 1627, Leyden 1639, Amsterdam 1677; ed T. Hearne 3 vols [Oxford] 1717; tr French 1624 (pt 1), 1627 (pts 1–2); tr A. Darcie 1625 (pt 1 from French); T. Browne 1629 (pt 2); R. N[orton] 1630 pts 1–2), 1635. Later English edns 1675, 1688 and in White Kennett, Complete history vol 2, 1706; ed W. T. Macaffrey 1970 (selection).
Regni regis Jacobi I annalium apparatus; Memorabilia de seipso. Both in T. Smith, V. Cl. Gulielmi Camdeni epistolae, 1691; tr of the first with omissions in White Kennett, above.
Anglica, normannica, hibernica, cambrica a veteribus scripta. Ed W. Camden, Frankfurt 1602, 1603.
The abridgement of Camden's Britannia, with the maps. 1626.
Discourse concerning the prerogative of the crown, printed from ms by F. S. Fussner. Proc Amer Philological Soc 101 1957.

SIR WALTER RALEGH
1554–1618

Bibliographies

Brushfield, T. N. A bibliography of Raleigh. Plymouth 1886, 1908 (enlarged).

Collections

Judicious and select essayes and observations upon the first invention of shipping; the misery of invasive warre; the navy royall and sea-service; with his Apologie for his voyage to Guiana. 1650, 1667.
Maxims of state. 1650, 1651 (both with Instructions to his son; his son's advice to his father), 1656 (with all items of Remains, below, except 10).
Sir Walter Raleigh's sceptick. 1651.
Remains of Sir Walter Raleigh. 1657, 1661, 1664, 1669, 1675, 1681, 1702 (with new letters).
Three discourses: 1, Of a war with Spain; 2, Of the original cause of war; 3, Of ecclesiastical power, published by Philip Ralegh esq his only grandson. 1702. The ch On unnatural war pbd here for the first time.
Works, political, commercial and philosophical; together with his letters and poems. Ed T. Birch 2 vols 1751 (with a life).
Works. 8 vols Oxford 1829, New York 1965. With lives by W. Oldys and T. Birch.
Selections from the History of the world, letters etc. Ed G. E. Hadow, Oxford 1917.
Selected prose and poetry. Ed A. M. C. Latham 1965.

§1

Historical

The history of the world. 1614 (anon), 1617, 1621 (dated 1617; variant with date corrected), 1621, 1628, 1634, 1652, 1652, 1666, 1671, 1676, 1677, 1687, 1736, Edinburgh 1820 (with other pieces). Until 1652 engraved title-pages keep the date 1614.
An abridgement of Sir Walter Raleigh's History of the world; to which is added his Premonition to princes. [Ed L. Echard] 1698 (with variants).
An abridgement [etc], second edition with some genuine remains: 1, Of the first invention of shipping; 2, A relation of the action at Cadiz; 3, A dialogue between a Jesuite and a recusant; 4, An apology for his voyage to Guiana; publish'd by Philip Raleigh. 1700, 1702.

Naval and Military

A report of the fight about the iles of the Açores. 1591 (anon), Leeds 1967 (facs); rptd in Hakluyt, Voyages vol 2, 1599; in Somers tracts vol 1, 1751, 1809; ed E. Arber 1871 (with other tracts); ed E. Goldsmid, Edinburgh 1886 (with other documents).
The discoverie of the large, rich and bewtiful empyre of Guiana. 1596 (3 edns), Cleveland 1966 (facs), Leeds

1967 (facs), New York 1968 (facs); rptd in Hakluyt's Voyages vol 3, 1600; ed R. H. Schomburgk 1848 (Hakluyt Soc); ed V. T. Harlow 1928 (with Spanish documents).

Orders to the fleet. 1617.

Sir Walter Rawleigh his apologie for his voyage to Guiana. 1650.

A discourse of the originall and fundamentall cause of natural warre with the mysery of invasive warre. 1650.

A military discourse. 1734.

Arguments to manifest the advantages of a good fleet, added to Sir Clement Edmons's Observations on landing forces for invasion. 1759. An extract from History of the world, above.

Political and Philosophical

The prerogative of parlaments [sic; variant with reset title-page]. Hamburg (for London) 1628, Middelburg (from London) 1628 (3 edns), [London] 1640; rptd in Somers tracts vol 4, 1850, vol 3, 1809; Harleian miscellany vol 5, 1744, 1808.

Sir Walter Raleigh's instructions to his sonne and to posterity. 1632, 1632, 1633, 1633, Edinburgh 1634, London 1636, 1728; ed C. Whibley 1927; Manteo NC 1939; ed L. B. Wright, Ithaca 1962 (with Burghley's Precepts and Osborne's Advice) (Folger Documents).

The prince: or maxims of state. 1642; rptd in Somers tracts vol 3, 1809.

The interest of England with regard to foreign alliances explained in two discourses: 1, Concerning a match between the Lady Elizabeth and the Prince of Piemont; 2, Touching a marriage between Prince Henry of England and a daughter of Savoy. 1750.

A treatise of the soule. In Works, 1829.

Poems

Poems. Ed A. M. C. Latham 1929, 1951 (ML).

Letters

Edwards, E. The life of Raleigh, together with his letters. 2 vols 1868.

§2

Shirley, J. The life of the valiant and learned Sir Walter Raleigh. 1677.

Aubrey, J. In his Brief lives, 1813.

Stebbing, W. Ralegh: a biography. Oxford 1891, 1899.

Firth, C. H. Raleigh's History of the world. Proc Br Acad 8 1918; rptd in Essays literary and historical, Oxford 1938.

Edwards, P. Sir Walter Ralegh. 1953.

Quinn, D. B. The Roanoke voyages 1584–90. 2 vols 1955 (Hakluyt Soc).

Wallace, W. M. Sir Walter Raleigh. Princeton 1959.

Oakeshott, W. The Queen and the poet. 1960.

Davie, D. A reading of the Ocean's love to Cynthia. In Elizabethan poetry, ed J. R. Brown and B. Harris 1960.

Lefranc, P. Ralegh, écrivain: l'oeuvre et les idées. Paris 1968.

ROBERT BURTON
1577–1640

Bibliographies

Jordan-Smith, P. Bibliographia Burtoniana: a study of Burton's Anatomy of melancholy with a bibliography of Burton's writings. Stanford 1931.

—— and M. Mulhauser. Burton's Anatomy of melancholy and Burtoniana: a checklist. Claremont Cal 1959.

§1

The anatomy of melancholy, what it is; with all the kindes, causes, symptoms, prognostickes and several cures of it:

in three maine partitions with their several sections, members and subsections, philosophically, medicinally, historically opened and cut up, by Democritus Junior. Oxford 1621, 1624, 1628 (with engraved title-page, Latin elegiacs, Democritus Junior ad librum suum and the Author's abstract of melancholy), 1632 (with argument of frontispiece), Oxford, Edinburgh and London 1638, Oxford and London 1651 or 1652 (all edns after 1621 with substantial alterations and addns), London 1660, 1676; 2 vols 1925 (Nonesuch Press); ed Floyd Dell and P. Jordan-Smith 2 vols New York 1927, 1 vol 1930 (without marginal notes, with trns of all Latin); ed H. Jackson 3 vols 1932 (EL).

Philosophaster, comoedia; poemata adhuc sparsim edita, nunc in unum collecta. Ed W. E. Buckley, Hertford 1862 (Roxburghe Club). The poems had already appeared in Academiae oxoniensis pietas, Oxford 1603; Musa hospitalis ecclesiae Christi, Oxford 1605; Justa oxoniensum [in memory of Prince Henry], 1612; Death repealed: verses on Lord Bayning, Oxford 1638.

Philosophaster; with an English translation [and] Burton's minor writings in prose and verse. Ed P. Jordan-Smith, Stanford 1931.

§2

Madan, F. et al. Oxford Bibl Soc 1 1922–6. Contributions on Burton by F. Madan, W. Osler, E. G. Duff, E. Bensly, S. Gibson, F. D. R. Nedham; with list of Burton's books in Bodley and Christ Church.

Prawer, S. Burton's Anatomy of melancholy. Cambridge Jnl Aug 1948.

Babb, L. In his Elizabethan malady: a study of melancholy in English literature from 1580 to 1642, East Lansing 1951.

—— Sanity in Bedlam: a study of Burton's Anatomy of melancholy. East Lansing 1959.

Mueller, W. R. The anatomy of Burton's England. Berkeley 1952.

Simon, J. R. Burton et l'Anatomie de la mélancolie. Paris 1964.

IZAAK WALTON
1593–1683

Bibliographies etc

Butt, J. E. A bibliography of Walton's Lives. Proc Oxford Bibl Soc 2 1930.

Collections

The complete angler and lives. Ed A. W. Pollard 1901.

Waltoniana. Ed R. H. Shepherd 1878.

The compleat Walton. Ed G. L. Keynes 1929 (Nonesuch Press).

§1

The life and death of Dr Donne. 1640 (in LXXX sermons by John Donne), 1658 (much enlarged as The life of John Donne); [ed T. E. Tomlins] 1852, 1865.

The life of Sir Henry Wotton. 1651 (in Reliquiae Wottonianae), 1654 (ibid with addns and alterations), 1672 (ibid, with further addns and alterations), 1685.

The compleat angler: or the contemplative man's recreation. 1653 (rptd 1810, 1876 etc), 1655 (much enlarged), 1661 (with alterations), 1664, 1668, 1676 (as The universal angler, made so by three books of fishing; alterations in Walton's part, 2nd bk by Charles Cotton, 3rd by R. Venables); ed Moses Browne 1750; ed John Hawkins 1760.

The life of Mr Rich. Hooker. 1665, 1666 (with addns and alterations, in Works of Mr Richard Hooker), 1676, 1682, 1705, 1723; ed J. Keble, Oxford 1836 (in Works of Hooker vol 1).

The life of Mr George Herbert. 1670, 1674 (with alterations, in Temple, with which it has often been rptd; ed V. de Sola Pinto 1951 (in his English biography in the seventeenth century).

The life of Dr Sanderson (with some short tracts or cases of conscience by Sanderson, and a sermon of Hooker). 1678, 1681 (with addns and alterations in XXXV sermons by Sanderson), 1686, 1689; ed W. Jacobson, Oxford 1854 (in Works of Sanderson vol 6).

The lives of Dr John Donne, Sir Henry Wotton, Mr Richard Hooker, Mr George Herbert. 1670, Menston 1969 (facs) (with addns and alterations in first 3 lives, 2nd pbn of life of Herbert), 1675 (with addns or alterations in lives of Donne, Herbert, Hooker); ed T. Zouch, York 1796 etc (with life of Sanderson); ed A. H. Bullen 1884 (Bohn's Lib); ed H. Morley 1888 (without Sanderson); ed A. Dobson 2 vols 1898 (Temple Classics); ed G. Saintsbury, Oxford 1927 (WC) etc.

§2

Butt, J. E. Walton's methods in biography. E & S 19 1934.
— Biography in the hands of Walton, Johnson and Boswell. Los Angeles 1966.
Sisson, C. J. In his Judicious marriage of Mr Hooker and the birth of the Laws of ecclesiastical polity, Cambridge 1940. Against Walton's interpretation.
Bottrall, M. Izaak Walton. 1955.
Novarr, D. The making of Walton's Lives. Ithaca 1958.
Cooper, J. R. The art of the Compleat angler. Durham NC 1968.

WILLIAM PRYNNE
1600–69

Bibliographies etc

Sparke, M. A catalogue of printed books written by Prynne. 1643. 31 items.
— An exact catalogue. 1660. 160 items.
Gardiner, S. R. Documents relating to the proceedings against Prynne (with an unfinished biographical preface and a list of Prynne's works by J. Bruce). 1877 (Camden Soc).
Fry, M. A. and G. Davies. Prynne in the Huntington Library. HLQ 20 1957. Over 200 entries, with annotation on issues, reissues under different titles etc.

Collections

The works of William Prynne of Swainswick esquire since his last imprisonment. 1655. 6 works.

§1

The Church of Englands old antithesis to new Arminianisme. 1629, 1630 (with large addns as Anti-Arminianisme).
Histrio-mastix: the players scourge or actors tragædie. 1633.
Newes from Ipswich: discovering certaine late detestable practises of some domineering lordly prelates. Ipswich (for London, Edinburgh) 1636 (4 edns), London 1641. By 'Matthew White'.
The unbishoping of Timothy and Titus. [Amsterdam] 1636, London 1660, 1661, 1661. Initialled A.B.C.
A breviate of the prelates intollerable usurpations. 2 pts [Amsterdam] 1637 (called 3rd edn much enlarged). Sparke, above, refers to 2 edns of 1635. By 'W. Huntley'.
A catalogue of such testimonies as evidence bishops and presbyters to be both one. 1637, 1641, 1645, 1647. Anon.
The antipathie of the lordly English prelacie both to regall monarchy and civill unity. 2 pts 1641.
An humble remonstrance against the tax of ship-money. 1641 (anon), 1643.

A soveraigne antidote to prevent, appease and determine our unnaturall and destructive civil wars. 1642 (3 edns). Anon.
The soveraigne power of parliaments and kingdomes. 4 pts 1643. Anon. 2 edns of pt 1, enlarged from The treachery and disloyalty of papists to their soveraignes, 1642.
The popish royall favourite: or a full discovery of his Majesties extraordinary favour to notorious Papists. 1643 (with variants).
The opening of the great seale of England. 1643; rptd in Somers tracts vol 4, ed Sir Walter Scott 1810.
A breviate of the life of William Laud. 1644.
Hidden workes of darkenes brought to publike light: or a necessary introduction to the history of the Archbishop of Canterburies triall. 1645.
Canterburies doome: or the first part of a compleat history of the tryall, condemnation, execution of William Laud. 1646.
The levellers levelled to the very ground. 1647.
Irenarches redivivus: or a brief collection of sundry statutes concerning the dis-commissioning of Justices of Peace. 1648.
A breife memento to the present unparliamentary junto touching their present intentions to depose and execute Charles Steward. 1648 (3 edns), 1649.
Mr Pryn's last and finall declaration to the Commons it is high treason, to compasse or imagine the deposition or death of our sovereign lord King Charles. 1648.
A plea for the Lords: or a vindication of the judiciary and legislative powere of the Lords. 1648, 1649, 1658, 1659, 1675 (much enlarged).
The first part of a historical collection of the ancient parliaments of England from 673 till 1216. 1649.
A legall vindication of the liberties of England, against illegall taxes. 1649, 1649, 1660.
A seasonable, legal and historicall vindication of the good, old, fundamental liberties of all English freemen. 3 pts 1654–7, 1679; pts 1–2, 1655; pt 3 (as Historiarchos), 1659.
A new discovery of free-state tyranny: containing four letters to Mr John Bradshaw and his associates at White-Hall. 1655.
The Quakers unmasked and clearly detected to be but the spawn of Romish frogs. 1655, 1655 (enlarged), 1664.
A short demurrer to the Jewes long discontinued remitter into England. 2 pts 1656, 1656 (pt 1 enlarged).
A new discovery of some Romish emissaries, Quakers. 1656, 1658 (with new title-page).
A summary collection of the principal fundamental rights liberties and proprieties of all English freemen. 1656, 1656, 1658 (enlarged as Demophilos: or the assertor of the peoples liberty).
An exact abridgement of the records in the Tower of London, collected by Sir Robert Cotton, revised by William Prynne. 1657, 1679, 1689.
The first [second, fourth] part of a brief register, kalendar and survey of parliamentary writs. 4 pts 1659–64 (pt 3 as Brevia parliamentaria rediviva).
Mr Pryns letter and proposal to our gracious lord and soveraign King. 1660.
The signal loyalty and devotion of Gods true saints towards their Kings. 2 pts 1660; ed C. Wordsworth 1892 (in part) (Bradshaw Soc).
An exact chronological vindication of our [British, Roman etc] Kings supreme ecclesiastical jurisdiction. 3 vols 1665–8; vol 3 rptd 1670 as The history of King John, King Henry III and King Edward I; rptd as Antiquae constitutiones regni Angliae, 1672 (index 1675). Unique copy of 4th vol, without title-page but captioned An exact chronological history of the Popes intollerable usurpations, is in Library of Lincoln's Inn, London. Usually called Prynne's Records.
Aurum reginae: or a compendious tractate of records in the Tower concerning Queen-gold. 1668. Usually bound with an additional appendix, also 1668.
Brief animadversions on the fourth part of the Institutes

of the lawes of England, compiled by Sir Edward Cooke. 1669.

§2

Kirby, E. W. Prynne: a study in Puritanism. Cambridge Mass 1931.
Lamont, W. M. Marginal Prynne. 1963.

BULSTRODE WHITELOCKE
1605-75
§1

Speech. 1642.
Three speeches made. 1659. One by Whitelocke.
Monarchy asserted. 1660, 1679. Anon.
Memorials of the English affairs: from the beginning of the reign of King Charles the first to King Charles the Second his happy restauration. 1682 (initialled B.W.), 1732 (with addns), 4 vols Oxford 1853.
Essays ecclesiastical and civil; to which is subjoined a treatise of the work of the sessions of the peace. 1706.
Memorials of English affairs, from the suppos'd expedition of Brute to the end of the reign of James the First; with some account of his [Whitelocke's] life and writings by W. Penn, and a preface by J. Welwood. 1709.
Notes upon the Kings writt for choosing members of Parlement XIII Car. II. Ed C. Morton 2 vols 1766.
A journal of the Swedish embassy, in the years 1653 and 1654. Ed C. Morton 2 vols 1772; ed H. Reeve 2 vols 1855.
Annals of his life. 1860. Extracts in R. H. Whitelocke, Life, below.

§2

Oldmixon, J. Clarendon and Whitlock compar'd. 1727.
Whitelocke, R. H. Memoirs, biographical and historical, of Whitelock. 1860.

SIR THOMAS BROWNE
1605-82

None of the 17th-century mss of Religio medici are autograph, nor are there known autograph versions of Browne's principal works. But BM has mss of some of the minor works and much note-book material, some unpbd. There are also mss in Bodley, Norwich etc.

Bibliographies

Keynes, G. L. A bibliography of Browne. Cambridge 1924, Oxford 1968 (rev and enlarged).

Collections

The works of the learned Sr Thomas Browne: containing 1, Enquiries into vulgar and common errors; 2, Religio medici, with annotations and observations upon it; 3, Hydriotaphia: or urn-burial, together with the Garden of Cyrus; 4, Certain miscellany tracts. 1686.
Works. Ed G. L. Keynes 6 vols 1928-31, 4 vols 1964.

Selections

Religio medici and other works (Religio medici, Hydriotaphia, The garden of Cyrus, A letter to a friend with ms version, Christian morals). Ed L. C. Martin, Oxford 1964.
The prose of Browne (Religio medici, Hydriotaphia, The garden of Cyrus, A letter to a friend, Christian morals, with selections from Pseudodoxia epidemica, Miscellany tracts and ms notebooks and letters). Ed N. J. Endicott, New York 1967.
Selected writings (Religio medici, A letter to a friend, Hydriotaphia, The garden of Cyrus, and selections from

Christian morals, Pseudodoxia epidemica, Miscellany tracts and mss). Ed G. L. Keynes 1968.

§1

Religio medici. 1642 (2 anon unauthorized edns), 1643 (with addns and corrections), 1645, 1645, 1656 (with annotations by Thomas Keck included in later 17th-century edns), 1659, 1659 (with other works and Digby's Observations, included also in later 17th-century edns), 1669, 1672 (with Pseudodoxia), 1678, 1682, 1686 (in Works), 1736, 1736, 1738, 1754; ed T. Chapman, Oxford 1831; ed W. A. Greenhill 1881 (with Christian morals); ed Greenhill 1883 (facs of 1642); Oxford 1909 (facs of 1643); ed W. Murison, Cambridge 1922; ed J.-J. Denonain, Cambridge 1953, 1955 (without apparatus criticus; ed Denonain from Pembroke College Oxford ms, Algiers 1958; ed V. Sanna 2 vols Cagliari 1958 (the most complete apparatus criticus, with Italian trn); Menston 1968 (facs of 1643); ed R. H. Robbins, Oxford 1972 (with Hydriotaphia, Garden of Cyrus).
Pseudodoxia epidemica: or enquiries into very many received tenents and commonly presumed truths. 1646, 1650, 1658, 1658 (with Hydriotaphia and Garden of Cyrus, below), 1659 (reissue of 1658 folio with Religio, above, Hydriotaphia, Garden of Cyrus), 1669 (with Hydriotaphia and Garden of Cyrus), 1672 (with Religio), 1686 (in Works).
Hydriotaphia, urne-buriall: or a discourse of the sepulchrall urnes lately found in Norfolk; together with the Garden of Cyrus: or the quincunciall lozenge, or network plantations of the ancients, artificially, naturally, mystically considered. 1658, 1658, 1659 and 1669 (with other works), 1686 (in Works); 1736 (with Brampton urns, Of artificial hills, and 3 chs of Garden of Cyrus); ed J. Evans 1893; ed W. A. Greenhill 1896; ed W. Murison, Cambridge 1922; 1927 (facs); ed J. Carter, illustr J. Nash 1932, 1958 (without marginal notes and illustrations).
Certain miscellany tracts. 1683 (first issue), 1684, 1686 (in Works).
A letter to a friend upon occasion of the death of his intimate friend. 1690, 1712 (in Posthumous works); ed H. Macdonald 1924.
Posthumous works of the learned Sir Thomas Browne, printed from his original manuscripts: viz 1, Repertorium: or the antiquities of the cathedral church of Norwich; 2, An account of some urnes &c found at Brampton in Norfolk anno 1667; 3, Letters between Sir William Dugdale and Sir Tho. Browne; 4, Miscellanies, to which is prefix'd his life. 1712 (with variants), 1722, 1723.
Christian morals. Ed J. Jeffery, Cambridge 1716, Halle 1723, London 1756 (with life by Samuel Johnson), 1761; 1863; Cambridge 1904; ed S. C. Roberts, Cambridge 1927.
Notes and letters on the natural history of Norfolk, more especially on the birds and fishes, from the mss of Sir Thomas Browne. Ed T. Southwell 1902.

§2

Digby, Sir Kenelm. Observations upon Religio medici. 1643 (2 issues), 1644 (2 issues), 1659. From 1669 ptd with Religio.
Johnson, Samuel. Life. Prefixed to Christian morals, 1756.
Coleridge, S. T. In his Literary remains, 2 vols 1836.
Stephen, L. In his Hours in a library: ser 2, 1876.
Pater, W. In his Appreciations, 1889.
Gosse, E. Sir Thomas Browne. 1905 (EML).
Strachey, L. In his Books and characters, 1922.
Dunn, W. P. Browne: a study in religious philosophy. Menasha 1926, Minneapolis 1950 (rev).
Huntley, F. L. Browne: a biographical and critical study. Ann Arbor 1962.

THOMAS FULLER
1608–61

Bibliographies etc

Gibson, S. A bibliography of the works of Fuller. Proc Oxford Bibl Soc 4 1935. Addns and corrections, new ser 1 1927.

Collections

Poems and translations in verse. Ed A. B. Grosart, Edinburgh 1868.
Fuller's thoughts. Ed A. R. Waller 1902.
Selections, with [excerpts from] essays by Charles Lamb, J. Crossley, L. Stephen et al. Ed E. K. Broadus, Oxford 1928.

§ I

David's hainous sin, heartie repentance, heavy punishment. 1631, Edinburgh 1868 (in Poems and translations), 1869.
The historie of the holy warre. Cambridge 1639, 1640, 1647, 1647, 1651, London 1840.
Joseph's partly-coloured coat. 1640 (2 issues), 1867.
The holy state; the profane state. Cambridge 1642, 1648 (enlarged), London 1652, 1663; [ed A. Young], Cambridge Mass 1831; 1840; ed J. Nichols 1841; ed M. G. Walten 2 vols New York 1938 (with Andronicus 1648) (facs).
A fast sermon preached on Innocents day. 1642, 1654 (with A sermon preached at the collegiat church of St Peter).
A sermon on the day of his Majesty's inauguration. 1643, 1643, 1654.
A sermon of reformation. 1643, 1643 (with Truth maintained); ed J. E. Bailey 1875.
Truth maintained. Oxford 1643, 1643.
Jacob's vow: a sermon preached before his Majesty. Oxford 1644.
Good thoughts in bad times. Exeter 1645, London 1645, 1646.
Feare of losing the old light. 1646.
Andronicus: or the unfortunate politician. 1646 (3 issues), 1648 etc (in Profane state, above), 1649.
The cause and cure of a wounded conscience. 1647, 1649, 1810, 1812, 1815.
Good thoughts in worse times. 1647.
Good thoughts in bad times, together with good thoughts in worse times. 1649, 1649, 1652, 1657, 1659, 1665, 1669, 1680, Oxford 1810, 1830, 1831, 1841 (with Mixt -contemplations), 1863.
A sermon of assurance. 1647, 1648.
A sermon of contentment. 1648. Initialled T.F.
The just man's funeral. 1649, 1652, 1660, (in The house of mourning), 1672.
A pisgah-sight of Palestine. 1650, 1658, 1662, 1869.
Abel redivus: or the dead yet speaking. 1651 (several variants), 1652; ed J. W. Nichols 2 vols 1867. Preface and some lives by Fuller.
A comment on the eleven first verses of the fourth chapter of S. Matthew's gospel in 12 sermons. 1652.
Perfection and peace: delivered in a sermon. 1653 (2 issues).
The infants advocate: or circumcision on Jewish children and baptisme [on] Christian. 1653.
Two sermons. 1654.
A comment on Ruth, together with Two sermons. 1654, 1865.
A triple reconciler. 1654 (2 issues).
Ephemeris parliamentaria. 1654, 1658, 1660. Preface.
Life out of death: a sermon. 1655.
The church-history of Britain; with the history of the university of Cambridge and the history of Waltham Abbey in Essex. 1655 (one issue 1656); ed J. Nichols 3 vols 1837 etc; ed J. S. Brewer 6 vols 1845.

A collection of sermons, together with Notes upon Jonah. 1656, 1657.
The best name on earth, together with several other sermons lately preached. 1657, 1659 (2 issues).
A sermon preached at St Clemens Danes at the funeral of Mr George Heycock. 1657, 1660 (as The righteous man's service to his generation, in The house of mourning), 1672.
The sovereigns prerogative. 1657, 1658 (both anon), 1660.
The appeal of injured innocence. 1659.
Sermons of Mr Henry Smith. 1657, 1675. A brief life of Smith.
An alarum to the counties of England and Wales. 1660.
A happy handful. 1660. Anon. Title and dedication probably by Fuller.
A panegyrick to his Majesty on his happy return. 1660.
Mixt contemplations in better times. 1660, 1830 etc (with Good thoughts in bad times and Good thoughts in worse times).
The history of the worthies of England. 1662 (2 issues), 1684 (abridged by George Sandys as Anglorum speculum, several issues); ed J. Nichols 2 vols 1811; ed P. A. Nuttall 3 vols 1840, New York 1965; ed J. Freeman 1952 (abridged). An index pbd in 1744 is sometimes bound up with 1662.

§ 2

Lamb, Charles. Specimens from the writings of Fuller. Reflector 4 1811; rptd in Works, 2 vols 1818.
Coleridge, S. T. In Literary remains, ed H. N. Coleridge 4 vols 1836–9, and Notes on English divines ed D. Coleridge 2 vols 1853.
Fuller, M. J. The life, times and writings of Fuller. 2 vols 1884.
Houghton, W. E. The formation of Fuller's Holy and profane states. Cambridge Mass 1938.

SIR THOMAS URQUHART
1611–60

Collections

Tracts of the learned and celebrated antiquarian Urquhart. [Ed D. Herd], Edinburgh 1774, 1782.
The works of Urquhart. [Ed G. Maitland], Edinburgh 1834 (Maitland Club).
The admirable Urquhart: selected writings. Ed R. Boston 1975.

§ I

Epigrams: divine and moral. 1641, 1646.
The trissotetras: or a most exquisite table for resolving all manner of triangles. 1645, 1650 (as The most easy and exact manner of resolving all sorts of triangles).
Εκσκυβαλαμρον: or the discovery of a most exquisite jewel, found in the kennel of Worcester-streets, anno 1651. 1652. By 'Christianus Presbyteriomastix'.
Παντοχρονοχανον: or a peculiar promptuary of time, wherein is displayed a most exact directory for all particular chronologies, in what family soever: and that by deducing the true pedigree of the Urquharts, in the house of Cromartie, since the creation of the world until 1650. 1652.
Logopandecteison: or an introduction to the universal language. 1653.
The first book of the works of Mr Francis Rabelais, doctor in physick, now faithfully translated into English. 1653, 1654 (both anon); The second book, 1653 (by S.T.U.C.), 1664; The third book, 1693.
The works of F. Rabelais MD, done out of French by Sir Tho Urchard Kt and others. 5 vols 1694. P. A. Motteux edited the 3rd bk of Urquhart's trn, revised

the first 2, and himself translated bks 4–5. The 5 bks (including the 1693 vol) constituted the Works.

The whole works of F. Rabelais MD, done out of French by Sr Thomas Urchard Kt, Mr Motteux and others. 2 vols 1708; ed J. Ozell 5 vols 1737; ed T. Martin, Edinburgh 1838; ed A. Wallis 5 vols 1897; ed C. Whibley 3 vols 1900 (Tudor Translations); ed A. J. Knock and C. R. Wilson 2 vols New York 1931.

The history of the admirable Crichton (from 'Εκσκυβαλαυρον 1652]. Retrospective Rev 6 1822; ed H. Miles 1927 (as The life and death of the admirable Crichtoun).

A challenge from Urquhart. Ed C. H. Wilkinson, Oxford 1948 (Luttrell Soc).

SAMUEL DANIEL
1563–1619
Bibliographies

Sellers, H. A bibliography of the works of Daniel. Proc Oxford Bibl Soc 2 1927–30.

§ I

The first fowre books of the civile warres betweene the two houses of Lancaster and Yorke [also the fifth book]. 1595 (2 edns of 5th book), 1599 (in Poeticall essayes, one issue as The civill wars of England); bks 1–6, 1601 (in Works); complete text with bks 7–8 as The civile warres betweene the howses of Lancaster and Yorke corrected and continued, 1609; ed L. Michel, New Haven 1958.

The first part of the historie of England [to end of Stephen]. 1612, 1613; The collection of the historie of England [to end of Edward III], [1618], 1621, 1626, 1634; 2 pts (with continuation from Edward III by John Trussell), 1650, 1685, 1706 (in White Kennett, Complete history vol 1).

JOHN SPEED
1552?–1629

The theatre of the empire of Great Britaine: presenting an exact geography of England, Scotland, Ireland [etc]. 1611 (for 1612), 1615, 1623, 1627, 1627, 1646, 1650, 1676; tr Latin by P. Holland, 1616.

The history of Great Britaine. 1611, 1614, 1623, 1623, 1627, 1631 (variant 1632), 1650. A continuation of Theatre, above.

Speed's England: a coloured facsimile of the maps and text [of Theatre]. Ed J. Arlott 4 pts 1953–4.

An atlas of Tudor England and Wales: forty plates from Speed's pocket atlas of 1627. Ed E. G. R. Taylor 1951 (Penguin).

FYNES MORYSON
1566–1630

An itinerary containing his ten yeares trave lthrough the twelve dominions of Germany, Bohmerland, Sweitzerland, Netherland, Denmarke, Poland, Italy, Turky, France, England, Scotland and Ireland, divided in 3 parts. 1617, 4 vols Glasgow 1907–8; part of a 4th pt ed C. Hughes 1903 (as Shakespeare's Europe), New York 1967; 2nd pt and part of 3rd pt Dublin 1735 (as An history of Ireland from 1599–1603); Irish pt in Ireland under Elizabeth and James the First, ed H. Morley 1890.

EDWARD HERBERT, 1st BARON HERBERT OF CHERBURY
1583–1648

The life and raigne of King Henry the Eighth. 1649, 1672, 1682, 1706 (in White Kennett, Complete history vol 2).

Expeditio in Ream insulam. 1656. Latin version by T. Baldwin of The expedition to the Isle of Rhé, ed Earl of Powis 1860 (Philobiblon Soc) (from ms).

The life of Edward Lord Herbert of Cherbury, written by himself. Strawberry Hill 1764, London 1770, 1771, 1778, 1792, 1809, 1824 etc; in Lives of Lord Herbert of Cherbury and Thomas Elwood, with introductory essays by W. D. Howells, Boston 1877; ed S. Lee 1886, [1906] (rev); ed H. Dircks 1888; ed C. H. Herford, Newtown 1928.

SIR KENELM DIGBY
1603–65

Articles of agreement made between the French King and those of Rochell; also a relation of the brave sea-fight made by Sr Kenelam Digby. 1628 (with variants).

A coppy of 1, the letter sent by the Queene's Majestie concerning the collection of recusant mony for the Scottish warre; 2, the letter sent by Sir Kenelme Digby and Mr Montague concerning the contribution. 1641.

Sr Kenelme Digbyes honour maintained. 1641. Attributed.

Private memoirs of Sir Kenelm Digby, written by himself. Ed H. Nicolas 1827. Suppl (castrations) 1828, 1932 (in Bligh, below); ed V. Gabrieli, Rome 1968 (as Loose fantasies).

Journal of a voyage into the Mediterranean [1628]. Ed J. Bruce 1968 (Camden Soc).

II. LITERARY CRITICISM

(1) BIBLIOGRAPHIES

Wallace, K. R. Books on rhetorical theory 1500–1700. In his Francis Bacon on communication and rhetoric, Chapel Hill 1943.

Williams, F. B. Index of dedications and commendatory verses in English books before 1641. 1961 (Bibl Soc).

(2) COLLECTIONS

Gregory Smith, G. Elizabethan critical essays. 2 vols Oxford 1904. A full and representative collection with detailed introd and commentary; still standard. *Gregory Smith.*

Spingarn, J. E. Critical essays of the seventeenth century. 3 vols Oxford 1908–9. A sequel to Gregory Smith, above, with similarly full introd etc. *Spingarn.*

Bradley, J. F. and J. Q. Adams. The Jonson allusion-book 1597–1700. New Haven 1923.

Chambers, E. K. The Elizabethan stage. 4 vols Oxford 1923. Appendix C, vol 4, prints extracts from documents of literary criticism. *Chambers*.

Spurgeon, C. F. E. Five hundred years of Chaucer criticism and allusion. 3 vols Cambridge 1925.

Gebert, C. An anthology of Elizabethan dedications and prefaces. Philadelphia 1933.

(3) INDIVIDUAL CRITICS

ROGER ASCHAM
1515–68

Collections
English works. Ed W. A. Wright, Cambridge 1904.

§ I
Toxophilus. 1545, 1571 ('newlye perused') etc; ed E. Arber, Birmingham 1868.

A report and discourse of the affaires and state of Germany. [1570?]. Written 1553. Preface.

The scholemaster. 1570 etc; ed L. V. Ryan, Ithaca 1967.

RICHARD WILLES
fl. 1558–73

Ricardi Willeii poematum liber. In suorum poemat. librum scholia, 1573; ed and tr A. D. S. Fowler, Oxford 1958 (Luttrell Soc). With 3 theses: De re poetica; De poeticae natura atque ortu; Poeticam esse praestantiorem caeteris artibus.

GEORGE GASCOIGNE
1542?–77

Certayne notes of instruction concerning the making of verse or ryme in English. In his Posies, 1575; rptd in Gregory Smith.

HENRY PEACHAM the elder
fl. 1577

The garden of eloquence. 1577, 1593 ('corrected and augmented'), Gainesville 1954 (facs of 1593).

GABRIEL HARVEY
1550–1631

Collections
Letter-book. Ed E. J. L. Scott 1884 (Camden Soc).
Marginalia. Ed G. C. Moore Smith, Stratford 1913.

§ I
Rhetor: vel duorum dierum oratio, de natura, arte et exercitatione rhetorica. 1577.

Ciceronianus. 1577; ed H. S. Wilson, tr C. A. Foster, Lincoln Nebraska 1945.

Two other, very commendable letters of the same mens writing [Harvey and Spenser]. 1580 etc (written before Three letters); ed R. Gottfried in Works of Spenser: the prose works, Baltimore 1949.

Three proper, and wittie, familiar letters. 1580 etc; ed R. Gottfried, above.

Foure letters and certaine sonnets, especially touching Robert Greene. 1592; ed G. B. Harrison 1922; Menston 1969 (facs of 1592).

Pierces supererogation. 1593. Selections in Gregory Smith.

A new letter of notable contents. 1593. Selections in Gregory Smith.

GEORGE WHETSTONE
1544?–87?

The right excellent and famous historye of Promos and Cassandra. 1578. Epistle to William Fleetwood, rptd in Gregory Smith.

A touchstone for the time. 1584 (as an Addition to A mirour for magistrates of cyties).

STEPHEN GOSSON
1555–1624

The schoole of abuse. 1579, 1586; ed E. Arber, Birmingham 1868.

THOMAS LODGE
1558?–1625

[A defence of poetry, music, and stage plays]. [1579]; ed D. Laing 1853 (Shakespeare Soc); rptd in part in Gregory Smith.

'E.K.'

Spenser, Edmund. The shepheardes calender. 1579. Epistle dedicatory and notes by 'E.K.'

EDMUND SPENSER
1552?–99

Spenser-Harvey correspondence. 1580. *See* under Harvey, above.

A letter of the authors [to Ralegh]. 1596 etc; ed F. M. Padelford, Works of Spenser: Faerie Queene bk 1, Baltimore 1932.

SIR PHILIP SIDNEY
1554–86

An apologie for poetrie [written 1581–3?]. 1595, 1595 (as A defence of poesie), 1598 (appended to Arcadia) etc; ed G. Shepherd 1965.

ABRAHAM FRAUNCE
fl. 1582–1633

The lawiers logike. 1588.

The Arcadian rhetorike. 1588; ed E. Seaton, Oxford 1950 (Luttrell Soc); Menston 1970 (facs of 1588).

THOMAS NASHE
1567–1601?

Collections
Works. Ed R. B. McKerrow 5 vols 1904–10, Oxford 1958.

§ I
To the gentlemen students of both universities. Epistle prefixed to Greene, Menaphon, 1589 etc.

The anatomie of absurditie. 1589 etc. Selections in Gregory Smith.
Sidney, Sir Philip. Astrophel and Stella. 1591 etc. Preface.
Strange news. 1592 etc. Selections in Gregory Smith.

[GEORGE PUTTENHAM]
d. 1590

The arte of English poesie. 1589; ed E. Arber, Birmingham 1869; ed G. D. Willcock and A. Walker, Cambridge 1936; Menston 1968 (facs). Probably by Puttenham.

SIR JOHN HARINGTON
1560–1612

A preface: or rather a briefe apologie of poetrie, and of the author and translator [prefixed to his trn of Orlando furioso]. 1591 etc; ed R. McNulty in his edn of Harington's trn, Oxford 1972; rptd in Gregory Smith.
Commentary on Orlando furioso. 1591 (with above).

RICHARD CAREW of Anthony
1555–1620

The excellencie of the English tongue [written c. 1595]. 1614 (in 2nd edn of Camden's Remains); ed Gregory Smith (from BM ms Cotton F. xi, f. 265).

GEORGE CHAPMAN
1559?–1634

To Ma. Mathew Royden. Prefixed to Ovids banquet of sence, 1595.
To the reader. Prefixed to Seaven bookes of the Iliads, 1598; rptd in Gregory Smith.
To the Earle Marshall; To the understander. Prefixed to Achilles shield, 1598; rptd in Gregory Smith.
To the high borne prince of men, Henrie; To the reader. Epistle dedicatory and verses prefixed to the Iliads, [1609] etc.
The preface to the reader. In Iliads, [1611] etc.
To Robert, Earle of Somerset. Epistle dedicatory to the Odysseys, [1614] etc.
Andromeda liberata. 1614. Epistle to Earl and Countess of Somerset.
Justification of Andromeda Liberata. 1614.
Poems to the Iliads and Odysseys. Ed P. B. Bartlett, Poems of George Chapman, New York 1941.

FRANCIS BACON
1561–1626

Essayes. 1597, 1612 (enlarged), 1625 (enlarged) etc.
The twoo bookes: of the proficience and advancement of learning. 1605 etc; ed T. Case 1906.
De sapientia veterum. 1609; ed Spedding 1861 (in Works vol 6). *See col 353, below.*

THE BODENHAM SERIES
Aids to composition planned by John Bodenham (fl. 1600)

Politeuphia: wits commonwealth. Ed Nicholas Ling 1597 etc. A collection of 'sentences'.
Palladis Tamia: wits treasury. Ed Francis Meres 1598 etc; ed D. C. Allen, New York 1938 (facs). Similitudes or comparisons.
Wits theater of the little world. Ed Robert Allott 1599. Examples.

Belvedere: or the garden of the Muses. [Ed Anthony Mundy?] 1600, 1875 (Spenser Soc). Sentences, similitudes and examples in verse.
Englands Helicon. Ed Nicholas Ling 1600, 1614 (enlarged) etc; ed H. Macdonald 1925. Poems offered as models or sources.

SAMUEL DANIEL
1563–1619

Musophilus. 1599 (in The poeticall essayes) etc; ed R. Himelick, West Lafayette 1965.
A defence of ryme. [1603] etc; ed G. B. Harrison 1925 (with Campion, Observations); ed A. C. Sprague 1930 (with other pieces); rptd in Gregory Smith. *See Campion, below.*
Prefatory verses to Florio's Montaigne. 1603 etc.

JOHN HOSKYNS
1566–1638

§1

Directions for speech and style [written c. 1599]. Ed H. H. Hudson, Princeton 1936; ed L. B. Osborn 1937, below.

§2

Osborn, L. B. The life, letters, and writings of Hoskyns. New Haven 1937 (includes an edn of Directions).

FULKE GREVILLE
1554–1628

Caelica [written 1577–1600]. In Certaine learned and elegant workes of the Right Honorable Fulke, Lorde Brooke, 1633; ed G. Bullough, Poems and dramas of Fulke Greville, 2 vols 1939. Sonnets 66, 80.
Of humane learning [written 1603–6]. 1633, above; ed G. Bullough, above. Stanzas 107–15.
Life of Sir Philip Sidney [written c. 1611]. Ed 'P.B.' 1652; ed N. C. Smith, Oxford 1907.

THOMAS CAMPION
1567–1620

Observations in the art of English poesie. 1602; ed P. Vivian, Works, Oxford 1909; ed G. B. Harrison 1925 (with Daniel, Defence of ryme); ed W. R. Davis, Works, New York 1967. *Reply by Daniel, above.*

BEN JONSON
1572?–1637

Collections

Works. Ed C. H. Herford, P. and E. M. Simpson 11 vols Oxford 1925–52.
Literary criticism. Ed J. R. Redwine, Lincoln Nebraska 1970.

§1

Sejanus his fall. 1605 etc. Preface.
Volpone. 1607 etc. Epistle dedicatory.
To the memory of my beloved, the author Mr William Shakespeare. Verses prefixed to First Folio, 1623 etc.
Timber: or discoveries made upon men and matter [compiled c. 1623–35]. In Works vol 2, 1640 etc; ed Herford and Simpson, vol 8 1947 (text), vol 11 1952 (commentary); ed R. S. Walker, Syracuse NY 1953 (rearranged).

Conversations with Drummond. Edinburgh 1711 (in Drummond's Works); ed D. Laing 1842 (Shakespeare Soc) (from ms); ed R. F. Patterson 1923.

THOMAS HEYWOOD
1574?-1641

An apology for actors. 1612, 1658 (as Actors vindication); rptd 1841 (Shakespeare Soc); rptd A. H. Gilbert, Literary criticism Plato to Dryden, New York 1940.

HENRY PEACHAM the younger
1576?-1643?

The compleat gentleman. 1622, 1634, 1661; ed G. S. Gordon, Oxford 1906; ed V. B. Heltzel, Ithaca 1962 (with other pieces by Peacham).

SIR KENELM DIGBY
1603-65

Observations on the 22 stanza in the 9th canto of the 2d book of Spencers Faery Queen. 1643. Written 1628.
Concerning Spencer. Ed E. W. Bligh (in Digby and his Venetia, 1932). Written c. 1630; BM additional ms 41,846.

HENRY REYNOLDS
1563?-1635?

Mythomystes, wherein a short survay is taken of the nature and value of true poesy and depth of the Ancients above our moderne poets. [1632]; rptd Spingarn.

SIR WILLIAM ALEXANDER
1567?-1640

Anacrisis: or a censure of some poets ancient and modern [written c. 1634]. Edinburgh 1711 (in Works of William Drummond of Hawthornden); rptd Spingarn.

SIR JOHN SUCKLING
1609-42

A session of the poets [written 1637]. 1646 (in Fragmenta aurea); rptd Spingarn; ed L. A. Beaurline (in An editorial experiment, SB 16 1963) (from ms).

FRANCISCUS JUNIUS or DU JON
1589-1677

The painting of the Ancients. 1638. *See* especially bk 1 ch 4, bk 3 ch 1.

JOHN MILTON
1608-74

The reason of church-government. 1641 etc. Critical sections rptd Spingarn.
An apology [for] Smectymnuus. 1642 etc. Critical sections rptd Spingarn.
Areopagitica. 1644 etc; ed J. W. Hales, Oxford 1939; ed M. Davies 1963 (with Of education).
Of education. [1644] etc; ed O. M. Ainsworth, New Haven 1928; ed M. Davies 1963, above. Critical sections rptd Spingarn.
The verse. Prefixed in 1668 to copies then remaining of the first edn of Paradise lost, 1667.
Of that sort of dramatic poem which is call'd tragedy. Prefixed to Samson Agonistes, 1671 etc.

SIR WILLIAM DAVENANT
1606-68

A discourse upon Gondibert, an heroick poem written by Sir W. D'Avenant, with an answer to it by Mr Hobbs. Paris 1650, London 1651 (in Gondibert); rptd Spingarn.

THOMAS HOBBES
1588-1679

§ 1

Answer of Mr Hobbes to Sr Will. D'Avenant's preface before Gondibert. Paris 1650 (with Davenant's preface), London 1651 (with Gondibert); rptd Spingarn.
To the Honourable Edward Howard esq on his intended impression of his poem of the British princes. Prefixed to Howard's British princes, 1669.
To the reader concerning the vertues of an heroique poem. Prefixed to his trn of the Odyssey, 1675; rptd Spingarn.

§ 2

Dowlin, C. M. Davenant's Gondibert: its preface and Hobbes' answer. Philadelphia 1934.
Thorpe, C. D. The aesthetic theory of Hobbes. Ann Arbor 1940.

(4) GENERAL STUDIES

Spingarn, J. E. A history of literary criticism in the Renaissance. New York 1899, 1963 (with introd by B. Weinberg).
Saintsbury, G. History of criticism and literary taste in Europe. 3 vols Edinburgh 1900-4.
Croll, M. W. Attic prose in the seventeenth century. SP 18 1921; rptd in his Style, rhetoric and rhythm, ed J. M. Patrick et al, Princeton 1966.
—— Attic prose: Lipsius, Montaigne, Bacon. In F. E. Schelling anniversary papers, New York 1923, and with above.
Crane, W. G. Wit and rhetoric in the Renaissance: the formal basis of Elizabethan prose style. New York 1937.

Atkins, J. W. H. English literary criticism: the Renascence. 1947; Seventeenth and eighteenth centuries, 1951.
Jones, R. F. The triumph of the English language: a survey of opinions concerning the vernacular from the introduction of printing to the Restoration. Stanford 1953.
Howell, W. S. Logic and rhetoric in England 1500-1700. Princeton 1956.
Hardison, O. B. The enduring monument: a study of the idea of praise in Renaissance theory and practice. Chapel Hill 1963.
Vickers, B. Classical rhetoric in English poetry. 1970.

VII. PHILOSOPHY

General Studies – Francis Bacon – Thomas Hobbes – Other philosophical writers

GENERAL STUDIES

Powicke, F. J. The Cambridge Platonists. 1926.
Willey, B. The seventeenth-century background. 1934.
Jones, R. F. Ancients and Moderns: a study of the rise of the background of the Battle of the Books. St Louis 1936, 1961 (rev).
— et al. The seventeenth century. Stanford 1951.

FRANCIS BACON
Baron Verulam, Viscount St Albans
1561–1626

Bibliographies

Gibson, R. W. Bacon: a bibliography of his works and of Baconiana to the year 1750. Oxford 1950.

Collections

Opuscula varia posthuma: philosophica, civilia et theologica. Ed William Rawley 1658, Amsterdam 1663.
Philosophical works. Ed Peter Shaw 3 vols 1733, 1737.
Works. Ed J. Spedding, R. L. Ellis and D. D. Heath 14 vols 1857–74.
The life and letters of Bacon, including all his occasional works. Ed J. Spedding 7 vols 1861–74.
The New Organon and related writings. Ed F. H. Anderson, New York 1960.

§ 1

Essayes. 1597, 1598, 1606. 10 essays. *See* below for enlargements.
The twoo bookes of Francis Bacon: of the proficience and advancement of learning, divine and humane. 1605, 1629, Oxford 1633; ed A. Johnston, Oxford 1974 (with New Atlantis, below).
De sapientia veterum. 1609; tr 1619, 1622 etc (as The wisdom of the Ancients).
The essays of Sir Francis Bacon. 1612, 1613, Edinburgh 1614, 1624. 38 essays.
Novum organum: summi Angliae cancellarii instauratio magna. 1620, Leyden 1645, 1650, Amsterdam 1660; ed T. Fowler, Oxford 1889.
Historia naturalis et experimentalis. 1622.
Historia vitae et mortis. 1623, Amsterdam 1663; tr W. Rawley 1638.
De augmentis scientiarum: tomus primus, de dignitate et augmentis scientiarum, libros IX. 1623, Paris 1624; tr Oxford 1640 (Of the advancement of learning), London 1674; ed W. A. Wright 1900.
The essays, civil and moral. 1625, 1629, 1632; ed G. Grigson, Oxford 1937. 58 essays.
Sylva sylvarum: or a natural history in ten centuries. 1626, 1627, 1628; tr Latin, Amsterdam 1648. Also contains an early version of New Atlantis.
Nova Atlantis. Utrecht 1643; tr 1659.
A number of other individual works were pbd for the first time in collections, above.

§ 2

Rawley, E. (ed). Memoriae Francisci Baconis de Verulamio Sacrum. 1626; ed and tr E. K. Rand, Boston 1904.
Broad, C. D. The philosophy of Bacon. Cambridge 1926.
Wallace, K. R. Bacon on communication and rhetoric. Chapel Hill 1943.
Anderson, F. H. The philosophy of Bacon. Chicago 1948.
— Bacon: his career and his thought. Los Angeles 1962.
Righter, A. In The English mind: studies in the English moralists presented to Basil Willey, Cambridge 1964.

Vickers, B. Bacon and Renaissance prose. Cambridge 1968.
Jardine, L. Bacon: discovery and the art of discourse. Cambridge 1974.

THOMAS HOBBES
1588–1679

Bibliographies

Macdonald, H. and M. Hargreaves. Hobbes: a bibliography. 1952 (Cambridge Bibl Soc).

Collections

Opera philosophica. Amsterdam 1668.
A supplement to Mr Hobbes his works. 1675.
Tracts. 1681; 1682 (a 2nd collection).
Hobbes Tripos. In Three discourses of human nature, 1684 (3rd edn).
The English works. Ed W. Molesworth 11 vols 1839–45.

§ 1

Eight books of the Peloponnesian war written by Thucydides. 1629, 1634, 1676, 1822, 1960.
De mirabilibus pecci carmen. [1636 or 1666?], 1675, 1678, 1683.
Objectiones ad Cartesii meditationes de prima philosophia. In R. Descartes, Meditationes, Amsterdam 1641.
Preface to Ballistica and Tractatus opticus. In M. Mersenne, Cogitata physico-mathematica, Paris 1644.
Elementorum philosophiae sectio tertia: de cive. Paris 1642, Amsterdam 1647, 1669; ed S. P. Lamprecht, New York 1949. Tr as Philosophical rudiments, below. 3rd section of philosophical treatise, followed by first and 2nd sections, De corpore and De homine, below.
An answer to A discourse upon Gondibert: an heroic poem written by Sir William Davenant. Paris 1650 (in Gondibert).
Human nature: or the fundamental elements of policie. 1650, 1651.
De corpore politico: or the elements of law, moral and politick. 1650, 1652.
Epistolica dissertatio de principiis justis et decori. Amsterdam 1651.
Philosophical rudiments concerning government and society. 1651, 1659. Trn of De cive, above.
Leviathan: or the matter, forme and power of a commonwealth. 1651; ed A. R. Waller, Cambridge 1904; ed W. G. Pogson Smith 1909, 1958; ed M. Oakeshott, Oxford 1947, New York 1960 (with introd by R. S. Peters).
A brief of the art of rhetoric. In A compendium of the art of logick and rhetoric, 1651.
Of libertie and necessitie. 1654, Manchester 1839; ed C. von Brockdorff, Kiel 1938.
The questions concerning liberty, necessity and chance. 1656.
Elementorum philosophiae: sectio prima, de corpore. 1655; tr 1656; ed C. von Brockdorff 1934.
Elementorum philosophiae: sectio secunda, de homine. 1658.

Στιγμαί Ἀγεωμετρίας, Ἀγροικίας Ἀντιπολιτείας, Ἀμαθείας: or marks of the absurd geometry of John Wallis. 1657.

Examinatio et emendatio mathematicae hodiernae qualis explicatur in libris Johannis Wallisii. 1660.

Dialogus physicus: sive de natura aeris. 1661. Reply by Boyle in An examen of Mr Thomas Hobbes his Dialogus, 1662.

Problemata physica. 1662; tr 1682.

Mr Hobbes considered in his loyalty, religion, reputation and manners. 1662, 1680.

De principiis et ratiocinatione geometrarum. 1666.

Quadratura circuli. 1669.

Rosetum geometricum cum censura brevi doctrinae Wallisianae de motu. 1671; tr 1682.

Three papers presented to the Royal Society against Dr Wallis. 1671.

Lux mathematica excussa collisionibus Johannis Wallisii et Thomae Hobbesii. 1672.

The travels of Ulysses. 1673.

Principia et problemata aliquot geometrica. 1674; tr 1682, 1727.

The Iliads and Odyssey of Homer. 1673, 1674, 1675, 1676. Tr Hobbes.

A letter about liberty and necessity. 1676.

Behemoth: or an epitome of the civil wars of England. 1679, 1680 (corrected); 1682; F. Tönnies 1889 (from ms).

An historical narration concerning heresie and the punishment thereof. 1680.

A dialogue between a philosopher and a student of the common laws of England. 1681.

Historia ecclesiastica carmine elegiaco concinnata. 1688; tr 1722.

The elements of law, natural and politic. Ed F. Tönnies 1889, Cambridge 1928. Written and circulated in 1640.

Critique du De mundo de Thomas White. Ed J. Jacquot and H. W. Jones, Paris 1973 (from ms); tr Jones 1976. Written 1642–3?

§2

See Clarendon, col 670, below.

Strauss, L. Political philosophy of Hobbes. Tr Oxford 1936, Chicago 1952.

James, D. G. The life of reason: Hobbes, Locke, Bolingbroke. 1949.

Peters, R. Hobbes. 1956 (Pelican).

Warrender, H. The political philosophy of Hobbes: his theory of obligation. Oxford 1957.

Mintz, S. I. The hunting of Leviathan: seventeenth-century reactions to the materialism and moral philosophy of Hobbes. Cambridge 1962. With extensive bibliography of 17th-century attacks on Hobbes.

Oakeshott, M. The moral life in the writings of Hobbes. In his Rationalism in politics and other essays, 1962.

Skinner, Q. D. Hobbes' Leviathan. Historical Jnl 7 1964.

—— The ideological context of Hobbes' political thought. Historical Jnl 9 1966.

—— Hobbes and the nature of the early Royal Society. Historical Jnl 12 1969.

Watkins, J. W. N. Hobbes' system of ideas: a study of the political significance of philosophical theories. 1965.

JOHN SELDEN
1584–1654

The duello or single combat. 1610.

De dis syris syntagmata II. 1617.

The historie of tithes. 1618.

De successionibus ad leges Ebraeorum. 1631, 1636.

Mare clausum seu de dominio maris. 1635, 1636, Hague 1636, Leyden 1636, Amsterdam 1636.

De jure naturali & gentium juxta disciplinam Ebraeorum. 1640, Leipzig 1665, Strasbourg 1665.

A brief discourse of the powers of the Peeres and Comons. 1640.

Table-talk. Ed R. Milward 1689; ed S. H. Reynolds, Oxford 1892; ed F. Pollock 1927 (Selden Soc) (from ms).

Opera omnia. Ed D. Wilkins 3 vols 1726.

EDWARD HERBERT, 1st BARON HERBERT OF CHERBURY
1583–1648

De veritate. Paris 1624, 1633, 1636, London 1645; tr M. H. Carré, Bristol 1937.

De causis errorum. 1645, 1656.

De religione gentilium. Amsterdam 1663, 1700; tr 1705.

Religio laici. Ed H. G. Wright, MLR 28 1933; ed H. R. Hutcheson, New Haven 1944.

SAMUEL HARTLIB
c. 1600–62

§1

A description of the famous kingdome of Macaria. 1641.

Englands thankfulnesse: or an humble remembrance presented to Parliament. 1642.

The Parliaments reformation. 1646.

§2

Turnbull, G. H. Hartlib: a sketch of his life and his relations to J. A. Comenius. Oxford 1920.

—— Hartlib, Dury and Comenius. 1947.

Trevor-Roper, H. R. The three foreigners: the philosophers of the Puritan Revolution. In his Religion, the Reformation and social change, 1967.

Webster, C. (ed). Hartlib and the advancement of learning. Cambridge 1970.

HENRY MORE
1614–87
Collections

Philosophical poems. Cambridge 1647; ed A. B. Grosart 1876, 1878; ed G. Bullough, Manchester 1931 (selection).

A collection of several philosophical writings. 1662, 1712.

Henrici Mori cantabrigiensis opera. 3 vols 1675–9.

Theological works. 1708.

Philosophical writings. Ed F. I. Mackinnon, New York 1925.

§1

Ψυχωδία platonica: or a Platonicall song of the soul, consisting of foure severall poems, by H. M. Cambridge 1642.

Democritus platonissans: or an essay upon the infinity of worlds out of Platonick principles. Cambridge 1646; ed P. G. Stanwood, Los Angeles 1968. In verse.

Observations upon [Thomas Vaughan's] Anthroposophia theomagica and Anima magica abscondita, by Alazonomastix Philalethes. 1650.

The second lash of Alazonomastix. Cambridge 1651. Rptd with the preceding in Enthusiasmus triumphatus, 1656, below.

An antidote against atheism: or an appeal to the natural faculties of the mind of man, whether there be not a God. 1652, 1653, 1655 ('corrected and enlarged; with an appendix').

Conjectura cabbalistica: or a conjectural essay of interpreting the mind of Moses. 1653.

Enthusiasmus triumphatus: or a discourse of the nature, causes, kinds and cure of Enthusiasme. 1656; ed M. V. de Porte, Los Angeles 1965.

The immortality of the soule, so farre forth as it is demonstrable from the knowledge of nature and the light of reason. 1659.

An explanation of the grand mystery of godliness: or a true and faithful representation of the everlasting gospel. 1660. 4 chs rptd 1681 as Tetractys anti-astrologica.

Free-Parliament proposed to tender consciences, and published for the use of the Members now elected, by Alazonomastix Philalethes. 1660.

A modest enquiry into the mystery of iniquity. 1664. Appended is The apology of Dr Henry More.

Enchiridion ethicum, praecipua moralis philosophiae rudimenta complectens, illustrata ut plurimum veterum monumentis, et ad probitatem vitae perpetuo accommodata. 1667, 1668, 1669, Amsterdam 1679, 1695, 1695, 1696, 1711. Partial English version by More himself in Joseph Glanvill, Sadducismus triumphatus, 1681; rptd separately 1690, New York 1930 (facs).

Divine dialogues, containing sundry disquisitions and instructions concerning the attributes of God and his providence in the world, collected and compiled by Franciscus Palaeopolitanus. 1668, 1713, 3 vols Glasgow 1743. Appended is a brief discourse of the true grounds of the certainty of faith.

Philosophiae teutonicae censura. 1670. A criticism of Boehme.

Enchiridion metaphysicum: sive de rebus incorporeis succincta & luculenta dissertatio. 1671 (signed H.M.). An attack on Descartes.

A brief reply to a late Answer to Dr Henry More his Antidote against idolatry. 1672. Includes reprint of An antidote against atheism, above.

Remarks upon two late ingenious discourses [by Sir Matthew Hale]. 1676.

Apocalypsis Apocalypseos: or the Revelation of St John the Divine unveiled, containing a brief exposition of the whole Book of the Apocalypse. 1680.

A plain and continued exposition of the several prophecies or divine visions of the Prophet Daniel. 1681.

An answer to several Remarks upon Dr Henry More his expositions of the Apocalypse and Daniel by S.E. 1684.

A briefe discourse of the real presence of the body and blood of Christ in the celebration of the Holy Eucharist. 1686.

Discourses on several texts of Scripture. Ed J. Worthington 1692.

Letters on several subjects. Ed E. Elys 1694.

A collection of aphorisms, in two parts. 1704.

Divine hymns. 1706.

More also contributed to Kabbala denudata vol i, ed C. K. de Rosenroth 1677, tr 1677, and Joseph Glanvill, Sadducismus triumphatus, 1681, as well as providing elaborate notes to Glanvill and George Rust, Two choice and useful treatises, 1682. His letters to John Norris are in Norris, The theory and regulation of love, Oxford 1688, and The diary and correspondence of Dr John Worthington, ed J. Crossley 1847–86 (Chetham Soc), includes his letters to Worthington. Other letters will be found in Richard Ward, Life, and Conway letters, ed M. H. Nicolson, New Haven 1930.

§2

Lichtenstein, A. More: the rational theory of a Cambridge Platonist. Cambridge Mass 1962.

RALPH CUDWORTH
1617–88

Collections

Works. Ed T. Birch 4 vols Oxford 1829.
Works. Ed J. Harrison 1849.

§1

A discourse concerning the true notion of the Lords Supper, by R.C. 1642, 1670, 1676.

The union of Christ and the Church, in a shadow, by R.C. 1642.

A sermon preached before the honourable House of Commons, March 31 1647. Cambridge 1647, New York 1930 (facs).

Dantur rationes boni et mali aeternae et indispensabiles. Cambridge 1651. In verse.

A sermon preached to the honourable Society of Lincolnes-Inne. 1664.

The true intellectuall system of the universe: the first part, wherein all the reason and philosophy of atheism is confuted. 1678; ed T. Birch 2 vols 1743, 4 vols 1829; ed J. Harrison 3 vols 1845; tr Latin by J. L. von Mosheim 2 vols Jena 1733 (with elaborate biographical and critical notes, tr in Harrison's edn), abridged by Thomas Wise 2 vols 1706.

A treatise concerning eternal and immutable morality. Ed E. Chandler 1731.

A treatise on freewill. Ed J. Allen 1838.

§2

Passmore, J. A. Cudworth: an interpretation. Cambridge 1951.

JOHN BRAMHALL
1594–1663

Works. 4 vols Dublin 1674–7, 5 vols Oxford 1842.

§1

The serpent salve: or a remedy for the biting of an aspe. 1644. A defence of monarchy and criticism of the view that all power is derived from the people.

A defence of the true liberty of human actions from antecedent and extrinsicall necessity. 1655.

Castigations of Mr Hobbes his last animadversions in the case concerning liberty and universal necessity; with an appendix concerning the catching of Leviathan or the great whale. 1658.

SIR KENELM DIGBY
1603–65

§1

Two treatises, in the one of which the nature of bodies; in the other the nature of mans soule is looked into. Paris 1644, London 1645, 1658, 1665.

Of bodies, and of man's soul, to discover the immortality of reasonable souls; with two discourses of the powder of sympathy and of the vegetation of plants. 1669.

§2

Petersson, R. T. Sir Kenelm Digby. 1956.

ALEXANDER ROSS
1591–1654

The philosophicall touch-stone: or observations upon Sir K. Digbie's Discourses. 1645.

Arcana microcosmi. 1651, 1652.

Πανσέβεια: or a view of all religions in the world. 1653.

Leviathan drawn out with a hook: or animadversions on Mr Hobbes his Leviathan. 1653.

SIR ROBERT FILMER
1588?–1669

The necessity of the absolute power of all kings. 1648, 1680.
The free-holders grand inquest. 1648, 1679, 1680.
The anarchy of a limited or mixed monarchy. 1648, 1679, 1680.
Observations upon Aristotles politiques touching forms of government. 1652.
Directions for obedience to governors. 1652.
Observations concerning the original of government. 1652.
An advertisement to the jury-men of England touching witches. 1653.
Patriarcha: or the natural power of kings. 1680, 1685.
Patriarcha and other political works. Ed P. Laslett, Oxford 1949.

JAMES HARRINGTON
1611–77

Collections
The Oceana and other works collected by John Toland. 1700, 1737 (with addns).
Political works. Ed J. G. A. Pocock, Cambridge 1977.

§ I
The common-wealth of Oceana. 1656, 1658; ed H. Morley 1887; ed S. B. Liljegren, Lund 1924.
The prerogative of popular government. 2 pts 1657–8.
A discourse shewing that the spirit of Parliaments, with a Council in the interval, is not to be trusted for a settlement. 1659.
A discourse upon this saying 'the spirit of the nation is not yet to be trusted with liberty'. [1659].

The art of law-giving in III books. 1659.
Aphorisms political. [1659].
Political discourses: tending to the introduction of a free commonwealth in England. 1660.
See col 316, above.

JOHN SMITH
1618–52

Select discourses, as also a sermon preached by Simon Patrick at the author's funeral; with a brief account of his life and death. Ed J. Worthington 1660, Cambridge 1673; ed D. Dalrymple, Edinburgh 1756; ed H. G. Williams, Cambridge 1859.

ROBERT BOYLE
1627–91

Bibliographies
Fulton, J. F. A bibliography of Boyle. Oxford 1941, 1961 (rev).

Collections
Works. Ed T. Birch 5 vols 1744, 6 vols 1772.

§ I
The sceptical chymist. 1661.
An examen of Mr T. Hobbes his Dialogus physicus. 1662.
Some considerations touching the usefulnesse of experimentall naturall philosophy. Oxford 1663.
The origine of forms and qualities. Oxford 1666, 1667.
The excellency of theology compared with philosophy. 1674.

7. SCOTTISH LITERATURE

I. INTRODUCTION

(1) BIBLIOGRAPHIES

Aldis, H. G. A list of books printed in Scotland before 1700. 1904 (Edinburgh Bibl Soc).

Geddie, W. A bibliography of Middle-Scots poets. 1912 (STS).

(2) GENERAL STUDIES

Smith, G. G. Scottish literature. 1919.
Mackenzie, A. M. An historical survey of Scottish literature to 1714. 1933.
—— (ed). Scottish pageant 1513–1625. Edinburgh 1948. An annotated anthology.

Speirs, J. The Scots literary tradition. 1940, 1962 (rev).
Kinsley, J. (ed). Scottish poetry: a critical survey. 1955.

II. POETRY AND DRAMA

(1) COLLECTIONS AND ANTHOLOGIES

Ancient Scotish poems. Ed J. Pinkerton 2 vols Edinburgh 1786. *Pinkerton.*
Satirical poems of the time of the Reformation. Ed J. Cranstoun 3 vols 1884–93 (STS).
A book of Scottish verse, selected by R. L. Mackie. Oxford 1934 (WC), 1967 (rev).

Scottish poetry from Barbour to James VI. Ed M. M. Gray 1936.
The Oxford book of Scottish verse. Ed J. MacQueen and T. Scott, Oxford 1966.

(2) THE LATER SCOTTISH 'MAKARIS'

WILLIAM FOWLER
1560–1612

An answer to the calumnious letter and erroneous propositions of an apostat named M. Jo. Hammiltoun. Edinburgh 1581. Prose.
A funeral sonet, written vpon the death of the honorable and maist vertuous gentlewoman, Elizabeth Douuglas, spouse to M. Samuell Cobuurne, Laird of Temple-Hall. nd.
Sonet. Prefixed to James VI, Essayes of a prentise in the divine art of poesie, Edinburgh 1584.
Sonet. Prefixed to T. Hudson's Historie of Judith, Edinburgh 1584
Sonet, to the onely royal poet. Prefixed to James VI, Poeticall exercises at vacant houres, Edinburgh 1591.
Epitaphe upon the death of Sir John Seton of Barns, knight, ane of the lordes of our soveranes Privie Counsell and session. Edinburgh 1594.
A true reportarie of the most triumphant, and royal accomplishment of the baptisme of the most excellent, right high and mightie Prince, Frederik Henry; by the grace of God, Prince of Scotland, solemnized the 30 day of August 1594. Edinburgh [1594]. Prose.
A true accompt of the most triumphant, and royall accomplishment of the baptism of the most excellent, right high and mighty Prince Frederick Henry, by the grace of God, Prince of Scotland and now Prince of Wales, as it was solemnized to 30 day of August 1594. 1603; rptd in Somers' tracts vol 1, 1750, vol 2, 1809 (2nd edn); J. Nichols, Progresses of Queen Elizabeth

vol 3, 1805; rptd Edinburgh 1687, rptd in R. Buchanan, Scotia rediviva vol 1, 1826, and Tracts illustrative of the traditionary and historical antiquities of Scotland, Edinburgh 1836, 1703, 1745, Leith 1764. Prose.
The works of William Fowler. Ed H. W. Meikle, J. Purves and J. Craigie 3 vols 1914–40 (STS). Vol 1, Verse, including unpbd version of Petrarch's Trionfi and unpbd sonnet-sequence The tarantula of love; vol 2, Prose, including unpbd trn of portion of Machiavelli's Il Principe. Extracts from Triumphs of Petrarch ptd in J. Leyden, Scottish descriptive poems, Edinburgh 1803.
See J. Purves, Fowler and Scoto-Italian cultural relations in the sixteenth century, *in* Works of William Fowler, ed Meikle; Purves and Craigie vol 3, above; R. D. S. Jack, Fowler and Italian literature, MLR 65 1970.

JAMES VI of Scotland
1566–1625

The essayes of a prentise in the divine art of poesie. Edinburgh 1584, 1585; ed R. P. Gillies, Edinburgh 1814; ed E. Arber 1869, 1895.
His Majesties poeticall exercises at vacant houres. Edinburgh 1591; ed R. P. Gillies, Edinburgh 1818.
His Majesties Lepanto: or heroical song. 1603.
Rait, Sir Robert S. Lusus regius. 1901.
New poems by James I of England, from a hitherto unpublished manuscript [BM add ms 24,195]. Ed A. F. Westcott, New York 1911.
Poems. Ed J. Craigie 2 vols 1955–8 (STS). With bibliography.

SIR DAVID LINDSAY
1490?-1555

Collections

Works. Ed F. Hall, J. Small and J. A. H. Murray 5 pts
1865-71 (EETS), 1883 (pt i rev).
Poetical works. Ed D. Hamer 4 vols 1931-6 (STS).
Poems. Ed M. Lindsay, Edinburgh 1948 (Saltire Soc).
A selection.

§ 1

The complaynte and testament of a popinjay which lyeth
sore wounded and maye not dye, tyll every man hathe
herd what he sayth. 1583. English trn.
The tragedy of the late moste reverende father David, by
the mercie of God Cardinall and Archbishoppe of sainct
Andrewes, and of the whole realme of Scotland primate,
Legate and Chaunceler and Administrator of the
bishoprich of Merapois in Fraunce and Commendator
perpetuall of the Abbay of Aberbrothok. In The
tragicall death of David Beaton, [1548?] (by Robert
Burrant?]. English trn.
Ane dialog betuix Experience and ane Courteour off the
miserabill estait of the warld, compylit be Schir Dauid
Lyndesay of the mont knycht, and is devidit in foure
partis, as efter followis. [St Andrews? 1554?] (John
Scot), Rouen 1558, 1558.
A dialogue betweene Experience and a Courtier of the
miserable estate of the worlde, first compiled in the
Schottishe tongue, nowe newly corrected and made perfit
Englishe. 1566 (with anglicized versions of the Tragedie
of the late Cardinall Beaton, the Testament and complaynt of the papyngo and the Deploratioun of the deith
of Queene Magdalene), 1575 (with 20 lines of the
Complaynt and confession of Bagsche), 1581.
The warkis of the famous and vorthie knicht Schir David
Lyndesay of the Mont, alias Lyoun King of Armes,
newly correctit, and vindicate from the former errouris
quhairwith thay war befoir corruptit; and augmentit with
sindrie warkis quhilk was not befoir imprentit. Edinburgh 1568 (re-issued 1569, 1571), 1574, 1579? (reissued 1582), 1592, 1597.

The historie of ane nobil and wailzeand squyer William
Meldrum, umquhyle Laird of Cleische and Bynnis.
Edinburgh 1594 (rptd from lost edn c. 1579), 1610, 1634,
1683, Glasgow 1669, 1683, 1696, Aberdeen 1711; rptd
Pinkerton 1; ed J. Kinsley 1959.
Ane satyre of the thrie estaitis, in commendation of vertew
and vituperation of vyce. Edinburgh 1602; ed J.
Sibbald, Edinburgh 1802.
The satire of the three estates: acting text by R. Kemp.
Edinburgh 1948, London 1951.
Ane satire of the thrie estaitis. Ed J. Kinsley with essays
A satire of the three estates. Ed M. P. McDiarmid 1967.

§ 2

Murison, W. Sir David Lindsay. Cambridge 1938.
MacQueen, J. Ane satyre of the thrie estaitis. Stud in
Scottish Lit 3 1966.

ALEXANDER MONTGOMERIE
1556?-1610?

The cherrie and the slaye, composed into Scottis meeter.
Edinburgh 1597 ('prented according to a copie corrected
be the author himselfe'), 1615 (known only from reprint
in Ramsay's Evergreen), 1636, 1675, 1680, 1682, 1691,
Aberdeen 1645, Glasgow 1668, 1698, 1726, 1746, 1751,
1754, Belfast 1700, Kilmarnock 1782, Kirkcudbright
1842, Edinburgh 1885 (facs); ed H. H. Wood 1937.
The cherry and the sloe, corrected and modernised, by
J. D. Edinburgh 1779, Aberdeen 1792, Kilmarnock
1817.
The mindes melodie: contayning certayne Psalmes of the
kinglie prophete David, applyed to a new pleasant tune.
Edinburgh 1605.
The flytting betwixt Montgomerie and Sir Patrick Hume
of Polwart, newlie corrected and ammended. Edinburgh
1621, 1629, 1632, 1688, Glasgow 1665.
Poems. Ed J. Cranstoun 1887 (STS). Supplementary
volume, ed G. Stevenson 1910 (STS).
A selection from his songs and poems. Ed H. M. Shire,
1960 (Saltire Soc).

III. PROSE

See W. L. Matheson, Politics and religion: a study of Scottish history from the Reformation to the Revolution, *Glasgow
1902*; P. Hume Brown, History of Scotland vols 1-2, *Cambridge 1902-5*; W. C. Dickinson and G. Pryde, A new history
of Scotland, *2 vols Edinburgh 1961-2*; G. Donaldson, Scotland: James V-James VII, *Edinburgh 1965*.

JOHN BELLENDEN
c. 1500-c. 1548

Croniklis of Scotland with the cosmography and dyscrip-
tion thairof, compilit by the noble clerk maister Hector
Boece, chanoune of Aberdene, translatit laitly in our
vulgar and common language be maister John Bellenden.
Edinburgh [1540?]; ed T. Maitland, Edinburgh 1822.
The Dyscription was ptd in an anglicized form in the first
(1577) edn of Holinshed's Chronicles.
The first five books of the Roman history. Ed T. Maitland,
Edinburgh 1822; ed W. A. Craigie 2 vols 1901 (STS).
The chronicles of Scotland of Hector Boece. Tr John
Bellenden. Ed R. W. Chambers, E. C. Batho and H. W.
Husbands 2 vols 1938-41 (STS). Vol 2 contains a life
of Bellenden by E. A. Sheppard.

HECTOR BOECE or BOETHIUS
1465?-1536

Episcoporum Murthlacensium et Aberdonensium vitae.
Paris 1522; rptd 1825 (Bannatyne Club); ed and tr J.
Moir 1894 (New Spalding Club).
Scotorum historiae. Paris 1526, [1547?]. For Bellenden's
trn, *see* above.
The book of the croniclis of Scotland: a metrical version
of the History of Hector Boece by William Stewart.
Ed W. B. Turnbull 3 vols 1858 (Rolls ser). Apparently
undertaken by command of James V and completed
c. 1535.
Mar Lodge Boece. Ed G. Watson 1946 (STS). Vol 1 only.

BOOK OF COMMON ORDER
Bibliographies
Cowan, W. Bibliography of the Book of common order and Psalm book of the Church of Scotland. Edinburgh Bibl Soc 10 1913.

§I
The form of prayers and ministrations of the Sacraments. Geneva 1556, 1561, [place?] 1561, 1584, Edinburgh 1562, 1564–5, 1568, 1575, [1578]; tr Latin, 1556; tr Gaelic, Edinburgh 1567.
The cl psalmes of David in meeter. 1587, Edinburgh 1594, 1595–6, 1599, 1603, 1611, 1614, 1615, 1617, [1620?], 1621–2, 1625, 1630, 1632, 1633, 1634, 1635, 1640, 1640–1, 1643, 1644, Middelburgh 1594, 1596, 1602, Dort 1601, Aberdeen 1625, 1626, 1629, 1632, 1633, 1634, 1638.

GEORGE BUCHANAN
1506–82
Bibliographies
Murray, D. Catalogue of printed books, manuscripts, charters and other documents. In George Buchanan: Glasgow quatercentenary studies 1906, ed G. Neilson, Glasgow 1907.

Collections
Works of Buchanan in the Scottish language. Ed D. Webster, Edinburgh 1823.
Vernacular writings. Ed P. Hume Brown 1892 (STS).

§I
Rudimenta grammatices Thomae Linacri ex anglico sermone in latinum versa, interprete Georgio Buchanano. Paris 1533, 1536, 1537, 1540, 1545, 1546, 1550, 1556, Lyons 1539, 1541, 1544, 1548, 1552.
Medea Euripidis poetae tragici Georgio Buchanano Scoto interprete. Paris 1544.
Jephthes, sive votum: tragoedia; auctore Georgio Buchanano Scoto. Paris 1554, 1557, 1575, Orleans 1567, Glasgow 1775; tr W. Tait, Edinburgh 1750; C. C., Truro 1853; A. G. Mitchell, Paisley 1903.
Euripidis poetae tragici Alcestis Georgio Buchanano Scoto interprete. Paris 1556, 1557, Wittenberg 1581, Gotha 1776, Cambridge 1816, 1818, 1826, 1830, 1837, 1844.
De Caleto nuper ab Henrico II. Francorum rege invictiss, recepto Georgii Buchanani carmen. Paris 1558.
Psalmorum Davidis paraphrasis poetica, nunc primum edita, authore Georgio Buchanano, Scoto, poetarum nostri saeculi facilè principe. Paris [1564–5], 1566 etc, Strasbourg 1568.
Georgii Buchanani Scoti, franciscanus: varia eiusdem authoris poemata. [Paris?] 1566.
Tragoediae selectae Aeschyli, Sophoclis, Euripidis cum duplici interpretatione. Paris 1567.
Opinion anent the Reformation of the Universities of St Androis. In D. Irving, Memoirs of the life and writings of Buchanan, Edinburgh 1817 (2nd edn); in Bannatyne miscellany vol 2, 1836; P. Hume Brown, Vernacular writings of Buchanan, 1892 (STS). Written c. 1567.
The chamaeleon: or the crafty statesman, describ'd in the character of Mr Maitland of Lethington, Secretary of Scotland. 1701, 1741, Glasgow 1818.
Ane admonitioun direct to the trew Lordis, maintenaris of justice and obedience to the Kingis grace, M. G. B. Stirling 1571; D. Irving, Memoirs of the life and writings of George Buchanan, Edinburgh 1817 (2nd edn); in D. Calderwood, Historie of the Kirk of Scotland vol 2, 1843 (Wodrow Soc).
Ane detectioun of the duinges of Marie Quene of Scottes, touchand the murder of hir husband, and hir conspiracie,

adulterie and pretensed mariage with the Erle Bothwell: and ane defence of the trew Lordis, mainteineris of the Kingis graces actioun and authoritie, translated out of the Latin. [London? 1571?]. Probably ptd by John Day at London in Nov 1571; it contains more than the original Latin and is now doubtfully regarded as having been made by Buchanan himself, 1571, St Andrews 1572, Edinburgh 1577, 1578, in Anderson's Collections relating to the History of Mary Queen of Scotland vol 1, Edinburgh 1727.
De jure regni apud Scotos: dialogus, authore Georgio Buchanano Scoto. Edinburgh 1579, 1580, 1581, Glasgow 1750; tr Philalethes 1680, 1689; in The Presbyterian's armoury vol 3, Edinburgh 1846.
Rerum scoticarum historia, auctore Georgio Buchanano Scoto. Edinburgh 1582, 1700, 1727, [Oberwesel] 1583, Frankfurt 1584, 1594, 1624, Amsterdam 1643, 1697, Utrecht 1668, Aberdeen 1762; tr 1690, 1722, 1733; by J. Watkins 1827, 1840; Edinburgh 1751, 1762, 1766, 1821, 1827–9, Glasgow 1799, 1827.
Ad viros sui saeculi clarissimos eorumque ad eundem epistolae. 1711.
Medea et Alcestis, cum interpretatione latina Georgii Buchanani Scoti. In usum academicarum scoticarum, ed T. Ruddiman, Edinburgh 1722.

§2
Irving, D. Memoirs of the life and writings of Buchanan. Edinburgh 1807, 1817 (rev).
Brown, P. H. Buchanan: humanist and reformer. Edinburgh 1890.
Macmillan, D. Buchanan: a biography. Edinburgh 1906.
Buchanan: Glasgow quatercentenary studies 1906. Ed G. Neilson, Glasgow 1907.

WALTER CHEPMAN and ANDREW MYLLAR
The Chepman and Myllar prints. Edinburgh 1508; ed D. Laing, Edinburgh 1827 (facs); ed G. Stevenson 1918 (STS); ed W. Beattie, Edinburgh 1950 (Edinburgh Bibl Soc) (facs).

JOHN KNOX
1505–72
Collections
Works, collected and edited by D. Laing. 6 vols 1846–64; 1846 (Bannatyne Club) etc; 1846 (Wodrow Soc) etc.

§I
A confession and declaration of praiers added thrunto by Jhon Knox, minister of Christes most sacred Evangely, upon the death of that moste verteous and most famous King Edward the VI Kynge of Englande. Rome (for London) 1554.
A faythfull admonition made by John Knox, unto the professours of Gods truthe in England. Zürich 1554.
An admonition or warning that the faithful Christians in London, Newcastel, Barwycke and others, may avoide Gods vengeaunce, both in thys life and in the life to come. Wittonburge (for Bremen?) 1554, 1558.
A godly letter sent too the fayethfull in London, Newcastell, Barwyke; and to all other within the realme of Englande, that love the cominge of oure Lorde Iesus. Rome (for London) 1554; pt 2, 1581.
The copie of a letter sent to the ladye Mary dowagire, Regent of Scotland, by John Knox in the year 1556; there is also a notable sermon, made by the sayde John Knox, wherin is evidentlye proved that the masse is and

alwayes hath bene abhominable before God and idolatrye; scrutamini scripturas. [Geneva? 1556], Geneva 1558 (augmented).

The copie of an epistle sent unto the inhabitants of Newcastle and Barwike; in the ende whereof is added A brief exhortation to England for the spedie imbrasing of Christes gospel hertofore suppressed and banished. 2 pts Geneva 1559, 1560.

The first blast of the trumpet against the monstruous regiment of women. [Geneva] 1558, [Edinburgh? 1687?]; ed E. Arber 1878.

The appellation of John Knoxe from the cruell and most injust sentence pronounced against him by the false bishoppes and clergey of Scotland. Geneva 1558.

An answer to a great nomber of blasphemous cavillations written by an Anabaptist, and adversarie to Gods eternal predestination and confuted by John Knox, minister of Gods Word in Scotland. [Geneva] 1560, London 1591.

Heir followeth the coppie of the ressoning betuix the Abbote of Crosraguell [Quintin Kennedy] and J. Knox. Edinburgh 1563.

A sermon preached by Iohn Knox minister of Christ Iesus in the publique audience of the Church of Edenbrough, upon Sonday, the 19 of August 1565; for the which the said John Knox was inhibite from preaching for a season. [Edinburgh] 1566.

A sermon against the masse. [?].

To his loving brethren whome God ones gloriously gathered in the church of Edinburgh, and now ar dispersed for tryall of our faith. Stirling 1571.

An answer to a letter of a Jesuit named Tyrie. St Andrews 1572.

A brief discours off the troubles begonne at Franckford in Germany anno domini 1554 abowte the Booke of common praier and ceremonies. 1575.

A fort for the afflicted, in an exposition uppon the syxt psalme of David, wherein is declared hys crosse, complayntes and prayers. [London?] 1580.

Exposition upon the fourth of Matthew concerning the tentations of Christ. 1583.

A comfortable epistell sente to the afflicted church of Christ, exhorting them to beare his crosse with patience; wrytten by the man of God J. K. [?].

A most wholsome talke and communication betwixt the prentyse and the pryest touching the matter of auricular confession. [?].

A confutation of all such arguments as the Popes Catholykes doe bring for to prove the mutilate receavyng of the sacrament under one kynde. [?].

The history of the reformation of religion within the realm of Scotland. 1587 (imperfect); ed D. Buchanan 1644; Edinburgh 1644; ed M. Crawford, Edinburgh 1732, 1740, 1816; rev and ed C. Lennox 1905; ed R. S. Walker 1940 (Saltire Soc) (selection); ed W. C. Dickinson 2 vols 1949.

The liturgy of the Church of Scotland: or John Knox's Book of common order. Ed G. Cumming 1840; ed G. W. Sprott and T. Leishman, Edinburgh 1868.

Liturgy of the Church of Scotland since the Reformation. Ed S. A. Hurlburt, pt 2, Washington 1945.

§2

Brown, P. H. Knox: a biography. 2 vols 1895.

Muir, E. John Knox. 1929.

Ridley, J. John Knox. Oxford 1968.

See also col 296, above.

Part II
1660–1800

1. INTRODUCTION

I. GENERAL WORKS

A. BIBLIOGRAPHIES

Nichols, J. Literary anecdotes of the eighteenth century. 9 vols 1812–16.
— Illustrations of the literary history of the eighteenth century. 8 vols 1817–58.
Arber, E. The term catalogues 1668–1709, with a number for Easter term 1711. 3 vols 1903–6.
Tobin, J. E. Eighteenth-century English literature and its cultural background. New York 1939.
Hazen, A. T. A bibliography of the Strawberry Hill Press. New Haven 1942.
Wing, D. G. Short-title catalogue of books printed in England, Scotland, Ireland, Wales and British America, and of English books printed in other countries 1641–1700. 3 vols New York 1945–51 (Index Soc), 1972–; P. G. Morrison, Index of printers, publishers and booksellers, Charlottesville 1955.
The Rothschild library: a catalogue of the collection of eighteenth-century printed books and manuscripts formed by Lord Rothschild. 2 vols Cambridge 1954 (priv ptd).
Wiles, R. M. Serial publication in England before 1750. Cambridge 1957.
Gaskell, P. John Baskerville: a bibliography. Cambridge 1959.
— A bibliography of the Foulis Press. 1964.

Foxon, D. F. Libertine literature in England 1660–1745. Book Collector 12 1963; New Hyde Park NY 1965 (rev).
— (ed). English bibliographical sources: ser 1. 1964–6 (facs of 18th-century lists of books and pamphlets).
— English verse 1701–50: a catalogue of separately printed poems. 2 vols Cambridge 1975.
McKenzie, D. F. The Cambridge university press 1696–1712: a bibliographical study. 2 vols Cambridge 1966.

Current Bibliographies and Surveys

Crane, R. S. et al. English literature of the Restoration and eighteenth century: a current bibliography. PQ 5 1926–. Continued annually. The first 25 lists 1926–50 rptd 2 vols Princeton 1950–2; the next 10 lists 1951–60 rptd 2 vols Princeton 1962.
Graham, W. et al. The romantic movement: a current selective and critical bibliography. ELH 4–16 1937–49; PQ 29–43 1950–64; Eng Lang Notes 1 1965–. Continued annually.
Greene, D. J. et al. Recent studies in the Restoration and eighteenth century. Stud in Eng Lit 1500–1900 1 1961–. Continued annually.

B. LITERARY HISTORIES

Elton, O. The Augustan ages. Edinburgh 1899.
— A survey of English literature 1780–1830. 2 vols 1912.
— A survey of English literature 1730–80. 2 vols 1928.
Stephen, L. English literature and society in the eighteenth century. 1904, 1940.
Saintsbury, G. The peace of the Augustans. 1916, Oxford 1946 (WC).
Sherburn, G. The Restoration and eighteenth century 1660–1789. Bk 3 of A literary history of England, ed A. C. Baugh, New York 1948; rev D. F. Bond, New York 1967.
Butt, J. The Augustan age. 1950.

— The mid-eighteenth century. Oxford 1979 (OHEL vol 8).
Humphreys, A. R. The Augustan world. 1954, 1964.
Ford, B. (ed). Pelican guide to English literature vols 4–5: From Dryden to Johnson; From Blake to Byron. 1957.
Dobrée, B. English literature in the early eighteenth century 1700–40. Oxford 1959 (OHEL vol 7).
Renwick, W. L. English literature 1789–1815. Oxford 1963 (OHEL vol 9).
Sutherland, J. English literature of the late seventeenth century. Oxford 1969 (OHEL vol 6).
Rogers, P. The Augustan vision. 1974.

2. POETRY

I. HISTORIES AND SURVEYS

(1) LITERARY HISTORIES

Johnson, S. Prefaces biographical and critical to the works of the English poets. 10 vols 1779–81; ed G. B. Hill as Lives of the English poets, 3 vols Oxford 1905.

Hazlitt, W. Lectures on the English poets. 1818.

Gosse, E. From Shakespeare to Pope: an inquiry into the causes and phenomena of the rise of classical poetry in England. Cambridge 1885.

Sutherland, J. R. A preface to eighteenth-century poetry. Oxford 1948, 1962 (with additional notes).

Walton, G. Metaphysical to Augustan: studies in tone and sensibility in the seventeenth century. 1955.

Price, M. To the palace of wisdom: studies in order and energy from Dryden to Blake. New York 1964.

Trickett, R. The honest Muse: a study in Augustan verse [1660–1760]. Oxford 1967.

(2) CRITICAL SURVEYS

Smith, D. N. Some observations on eighteenth-century poetry. Oxford 1937.

Renwick, W. L. Notes on some lesser poets of the eighteenth century. In Essays in the eighteenth century presented to D. N. Smith, Oxford 1945.

Wilson, J. H. The Court wits of the Restoration: an introduction. Princeton 1948.

The age of Johnson: essays presented to C. B. Tinker, New Haven 1949.

Wimsatt, W. K. The Augustan mode in English poetry. ELH 20 1953; rptd in his Hateful contraries, Lexington Kentucky 1965.

(3) ANTHOLOGIES

Smith, D. N. The Oxford book of eighteenth-century verse. Oxford 1926 etc.

Rollins, H. E. The pack of Autolycus 1624–93. Cambridge Mass 1927.

—— The Pepys ballads vols 3–7. Cambridge Mass 1930–1. Ballads of 1666–1702.

Crane, R. S. A collection of English poems 1660–1800. New York 1932.

Gordon, I. A. Shenstone's Miscellany 1759–63. Oxford 1952. From ms.

Davie, D. The late Augustans: longer poems of the later eighteenth century. 1958 etc.

Cutts, J. P. Seventeenth-century songs and lyrics. Columbia Missouri 1959. From music mss.

Lord, G. de F. et al. Poems on affairs of state: Augustan satirical verse 1660–1714. 7 vols New Haven 1963–75, 1 vol New Haven 1975 (selection).

Sutherland, J. Early eighteenth-century poetry. 1965.

Holloway, J. and J. Black. Later English broadside ballads. 4 vols 1975.

II. RESTORATION POETRY

SAMUEL BUTLER
1613–80

Collections

Poetical works. Ed R. B. Johnson 2 vols 1893.

Complete works. 3 vols Cambridge 1905–28. Vol 1, Hudibras, ed A. R. Waller; vol 2, Characters and passages from notebooks, ed Waller; vol 3, Satires and miscellaneous poetry and prose, ed R. Lamar.

Hudibras I–II and selected other writings. Ed J. Wilders and H. de Quehen, Oxford 1973.

§ I

Mola asinaria by William Prynne. 1659; rptd in Posthumous works, below.

The Lord Roos his answer to the Marquesse of Dorchester's letter. [1660].

Hudibras: the first part. 1663 (9 edns).

Hudibras: the second part. 1664, 1664.

To the memory of the most renowned Du-Vall. 1671; rptd in Posthumous works and Genuine remains, below.

Two letters, one from John Audland to William Prynne; the other, William Prynnes answer. 1672; rptd in Posthumous works and Genuine remains, below.

Hudibras: the first and second parts, corrected and amended with several additions and annotations. 167 1678.

Hudibras: the third and last part. 1678 (3 edns), 1679, 1680.

Cydippe her answer to Acontius. In Ovid's epistles, 1680; rptd in Poetical works, ed R. B. Johnson, above.

Mercurius Menippeus: the loyal satirist. 1682; rptd in Posthumous works, below, and Somers tracts vol 7, 1810.

Hudibras in three parts. 1684, 1704 (includes biography), 1710 (illustr), 1726 (illustr Hogarth); ed Z. Grey 2 vols Cambridge 1744; ed T. R. Nash 3 vols 1793; ed J. Wilders, Oxford 1967.

The plagiary exposed. 1691; rptd in The secret history of the Calves Head Club, 1705 (5th edn), Posthumous works, Genuine remains, below, and Somers tracts vol 4, 1748. Variously entitled A vindication of the royal martyr, The case of King Charles I truly stated and The character of King Charles I.

Posthumous works in prose and verse. 3 vols 1715–17, 1732, 1754. Spurious apart from works listed above, admitted to the canon by Lamar.

Genuine remains. Ed R. Thyer 2 vols 1759; vol 1 (enlarged), 1822, 1827.

Prose observations. Ed H. de Quehen, Oxford 1978 (from ms).

§ 2

Aubrey, J. In his Brief lives, 1813.
Johnson, S. In his Lives of the poets, 1779–81.
Hazlitt, W. In his English comic writers, 1819.
Richards, E. A. Hudibras in the burlesque tradition. New York 1937.
Jack, I. In his Augustan satire, Oxford 1952.

CHARLES COTTON
1630–87
Collections

The genuine works: containing Scarronides, Lucian burlesqued, The wonders of the Peake, The planters manual. 1715, 1725 (as The genuine poetical works; omits Planters manual), 1734, 1741, 1765, Dublin 1770, London 1771.
Poems. Ed J. Beresford 1923.
Poems. Ed J. Buxton 1958 (ML).

§ 1

A panegyrick to the King's most excellent Majesty. 1660.
The morall philosophy of the Stoicks, written originally in French by Monsieur du Vair. 1664, 1667, 1671.
Scarronides, or Virgile travestie: being the first book of Virgil's Æneis in English burlesque. 1664, 1664.
Scarronides: or Virgile travestie, in imitation of the fourth book of Virgil's Æneis in English burlesque. 1665.
Scarronides, or Virgile travestie: a mock-poem on the first and fourth books of Virgil's Æneis. 1667, 1670, 1672, 1678, 1682, 1691, 1692, 1692, 1700, 1709 etc.
The nicker nicked: or the cheats of gaming discovered. 1669. An abbreviated version of the chapter Of gaming in general in Compleat gamester, below.
The history of the life of the Duke of Espernon, englished. 1670.
Horace: a French tragedy of Monsieur Corneille, englished. 1671, 1677.
The fair one of Tunis, out of French. 1674.
The commentaries of Messire Blaize de Montluc. 1674, 1688.
The compleat gamester. 1674, 1676, 1680, 1687 (as How to play at billiards, trucks, bowls and chess), 1696, 1709 (adds The game at basset), 1710, 1721, 1725, 1726; ed C. H. Hartmann 1930 (in Games and gamesters of the Restoration).
Burlesque upon burlesque, or the scoffer scoft: being some of Lucians dialogues newly put into English fustian. 1675, [1686].
The planters manual. 1675.
The compleat angler: part 2. 1676; ed M. Browne 1750; ed J. Hawkins 1760; ed N. H. Nicolas 2 vols 1836; ed R. B. Marston 2 vols 1888.
The wonders of the Peake. 1681, 1683, 1694, 1699, Nottingham 1725; rptd in Poems, ed Buxton, above.
Essays of Michael Seigneur de Montaigne and an account of the author's life, newly rendered into English. 3 vols 1685 (vol 2 1686), 1693, 1700, 1711, 1738, 1743 etc; ed W. C. Hazlitt 3 vols 1877, 1892, 4 vols 1902, 1923.
Poems on several occasions. 1689.
Memoirs of the Sieur de Pontis, faithfully englished. 1694.

The valiant knight: or the legend of St Peregrine. 1888. Perhaps spurious.

JOHN DRYDEN
1631–1700
Bibliographies etc

Macdonald, H. Dryden: a bibliography of early editions and of Drydeniana. Oxford 1939, 1967.
Monk, S. H. Dryden: a list of critical studies 1895–1950. Minneapolis 1950.
Montgomery, G. et al. Concordance to the poetical works of Dryden. Berkeley 1957.
Jensen, H. J. A glossary of Dryden's critical terms. Minneapolis 1969.

Collections
Works

The works of Mr John Dryden. 1695. 4°s bound together.
The works of the late famous Mr John Dryden. 4 vols 1701. This folio edn was made up from existing edns of the poems, plays and trns.
The works of John Dryden now first collected, illustrated with notes historical, critical and explanatory and a life of the author by Walter Scott. 18 vols 1808, Edinburgh 1821, 1882–92 (rev G. Saintsbury).
Poetry and prose. Ed D. Nichol Smith, Oxford 1925.
The best of Dryden. Ed L. I. Bredvold, New York 1933.
Poetry, prose and plays. Ed D. Grant 1952 (Reynard Lib).
Works. Ed E. N. Hooker, H. T. Swedenberg et al, Los Angeles 1956–.

Poems

Poetical works. Ed G. R. Noyes, Boston 1908, 1909 etc, 1950 (rev).
Poems. Ed J. Sargeaunt, Oxford 1910, 1935.
Prologues and epilogues. Ed W. B. Gardner, New York 1951.
Poems. Ed J. Kinsley 4 vols Oxford 1958, 1 vol 1962 (OSA).

Dramatic Works

Dramatick works. Ed William Congreve 6 vols 1717, 1725, 1735, 1762.
Selected plays. Ed G. Saintsbury 2 vols 1904 (Mermaid).
Selected dramas. Ed G. R. Noyes, Chicago 1910.
Dramatic works. Ed M. Summers 6 vols 1931–2.
Four comedies; Four tragedies. Ed F. T. Bowers and L. Beaurline 2 vols Chicago 1967.

Prose

The critical and miscellaneous prose works of John Dryden, now first collected, with notes and illustrations. Ed Edmond Malone 3 vols in 4 1800. Malone's annotated copy for a 2nd edn in Bodley.
Essays. Ed W. P. Ker 2 vols Oxford 1900, 1926.
Dryden and Howard 1664–8. Ed D. D. Arundell, Cambridge 1929.
Of dramatic poesy and other critical essays. Ed G. Watson 2 vols 1962 (EL).
The critical opinions of Dryden. Ed J. Aden, Nashville 1963.

§ 1

Dryden's dramatic works, including prologues and epilogues, are arranged by date of production. The following abbreviations are used: C = comedy; T = tragedy; TC = tragi-comedy; DO = dramatic opera; O = opera.

Upon the death of the Lord Hastings. Signed Johannes Dryden Scholae Westm. alumnus. In Lachrymae musarum: the tears of the Muses upon the death of Henry Lord Hastings, collected and set forth by R[ichard] B[rome?]. 1649, 1650; rptd in Miscellany poems 1st pt, 1702 (3rd edn).

To his friend the author on his divine epigrams. Signed J. Dryden of Trin C. In John Hoddesdon, Sion and Parnassus: or epigrams on severall texts of the Old and New Testament, 1650.

Three poems upon the death of his late Highnesse Oliver, Lord Protector of England, Scotland and Ireland, written by Mr Edm Waller, Mr Jo Dryden, Mr Sprat of Oxford. 1659, 1682 (as Three poems upon the death of the late usurper Oliver Cromwel), 1682.

To my honored friend Sr Robert Howard on his excellent poems. In Howard, Poems, 1660.

Astraea redux: a poem on the happy restoration and return of his sacred Majesty Charles the Second. 1660, 1660, 1688.

To his sacred Majesty: a panegyrick on his coronation. 1661, 1661, 1688; rptd in Complementum fortunatarum insularum, written originally in French by P. D. C[ardonnel], 1662, 1662.

To my Lord Chancellor, presented on New-years-day. 1662, 1688.

To my honour'd friend Dr Charleton, on his learned and useful works; and more particularly this of Stone-Heng, by him restored to the true founders. In W. Charleton, Chorea gigantum, 1663 (Dryden's poem in several states); rptd in Poetical miscellanies 5th pt, 1704.

The wild gallant. C (theatre in Vere St, 5 Feb 1663). 1669, 1669, 1684, 1694. 2 prologues and 2 epilogues; preface.

The Indian-queen. T (Theatre Royal, 25 Jan 1664). 1665 (in Four new plays), 1692 (in Five new plays), 1700 (ibid), 1722 (in Dramatick works of Sir Robert Howard). With Howard. Prologue and epilogue by Dryden?

The rival ladies. TC (Theatre Royal, June 1664). 1664, 1669, 1675, 1693. Prologue. Epilogue (not certainly Dryden's) ed R. G. Ham, RES 13 1937. Dedication.

The Indian Emperour: being the sequel of the Indian queen. T (Theatre Royal, April 1665). 1667, 1668, 1670, 1681, 1686, 1692, 1694, 1696, 1696, 1703, 1709. Prologue and epilogue. Dedication: Connexion of Indian emperour to the Indian Queen.

Annus mirabilis, the year of wonders 1666: an historical poem. 1667 (4 issues), 1668 (pirated edn preserving original stanzas 67 and 105), 1688; ed W. D. Christie, Oxford 1893; Oxford 1927 (facs of 1667). Dedication: An account of the ensuing poem.

Secret-love: or the maiden Queen. TC (Theatre Royal, late Feb 1667). 1668, 1669, 1669, 1679, 1691, 1698. 2 prologues. Preface. Prologue and epilogue spoken by the women only (ptd in Covent Garden drolery, 1672).

Sr Martin Mar-all. C (Lincoln's Inn Fields, 15 Aug 1667). 1668, 1668 (some copies of 2nd edn dated 1669), 1678, 1691, 1697. Prologue and epilogue.

The tempest: or the enchanted island. C (Lincoln's Inn Fields, 7 Nov 1667). 1670 (2 issues?), 1701 (in Comedies, tragedies and operas written by John Dryden esq); ed M. Summers 1922 (in Shakespearean adaptations). By Davenant and Dryden. Prologue and epilogue.

Of dramatick poesie: an essay. 1668, 1684 (rev), 1693; ed T. Arnold, Oxford 1889, rev W. T. Arnold 1903; ed D. Nichol Smith 1900; rptd 1928 (with A dialogue on poetic drama by T. S. Eliot).

Prologue to Albumazar, by Thomas Tomkis. (22 Feb 1668). In Covent Garden drolery, 1672, and Miscellany poems, 1684.

An evening's love: or the mock-astrologer. C (Theatre Royal, 12 June 1668). 1671, 1671, 1675, 1691. Prologue and epilogue. Dedication. Preface.

A defence of An essay of dramatique poesie: being an answer to the Preface of the Great favorite: or the Duke of Lerma. 1668; ed A. Mawer 1901. In early

copies of Indian Emperour, 2nd edn. Not rptd by Dryden, but in Congreve's edn, 1717.

Tyrannick love: or the royal martyr. T (Theatre Royal, 24 June 1669). 1670, 1672, 1677, 1686, 1695, 1702. Prologue and epilogue. Dedication (with extra paragraph added in 1672 edn). Preface.

The conquest of Granada by the Spaniards, in two parts. T (Theatre Royal, pt 1 c. Dec 1670; pt 2 Jan 1671). 1672, 1673, 1678, 1687, 1695, 1704. Pt 1: Prologue and epilogue. Dedication; Of heroique plays: an essay; Pt 2: Prologue and epilogue. Defence of the epilogue: or an essay on the dramatique poetry of the last age (some passages omitted in 1678 edn, and whole Defence not rptd in later 4° edns).

Prologue to Julius Caesar by William Shakespeare. (1672?). Ptd in Covent-garden drolery, 1672; accepted as Dryden's by J. Kinsley, Poems, Oxford 1958.

Prologue [to Beaumont and Fletcher, Wit without money], spoken the first day of the King's house acting after the fire. (Lincoln's Inn Fields, 26 Feb 1672). In Westminster-drollery, pt 2, 1672, Covent Garden drolery, 1672, Miscellany poems, 1684.

Marriage-a-la-mode. C (Lincoln's Inn Fields, April 1672). 1673, 1684, 1691, 1698; ed J. R. Sutherland 1934. Prologue and epilogue (also ptd in Covent Garden drolery, 1672). Dedication.

Prologue for the women when they acted at the old theatre in Lincoln's Inn Fields. (c. June 1672). In Miscellany poems, 1684.

The assignation: or love in a nunnery. C (Lincoln's Inn Fields, Nov 1672). 1673, 1678, 1692. Prologue and epilogue. Dedication.

Prologue to Arviragus and Philicia, by Lodowick Carlell. (At revival, 1673). In Miscellany poems, 1684.

Amboyna. T (Lincoln's Inn Fields, May 1673). 1673, 1691. Prologue and epilogue. Dedication.

Prologue and epilogue to the University of Oxford, spoken by Mr Hart at the acting of the Silent woman. (July 1673). In Miscellany poems, 1684.

The mistaken husband. C (Lincoln's Inn Fields, March 1674). 1675. Anon. Dryden possibly wrote one scene and the prologue and epilogue.

Prologue and epilogue spoken at the opening of the new house, March 26 1674. (Drury Lane). In Miscellany poems, 1684.

The tempest: or the enchanted island [rev Thomas Shadwell]. DO (Dorset Garden, 30 April 1674). 1674, 1676, 1690, 1676 (for c. 1692), 1695, 1701. The 1674 edn has the same title-page as the 1670 edn of Dryden's comedy, but the text differs.

To the Lady Castlemain. In A new collection of poems and songs, ed J. Bulteel 1674.

Notes and observations on the Empress of Morocco [by Elkanah Settle]: or some few erratas to be printed instead of the sculptures with the second edition of that play. 1674. Preface and Postscript probably by Dryden, and possibly further parts. Dryden was helped by Crowne and Shadwell.

Prologue and epilogue to the University of Oxford. (July 1674). In Miscellany poems, 1684.

Epilogue to Calisto or the chaste nymph, by John Crowne ['intended to have been spoken by the Lady Henrietta Maria Wentworth, who took the character of Jupiter when Calisto was acted at Court']. (15 Feb 1675). Not certainly Dryden's: in Miscellany poems, 1684.

Aureng-zebe. T (Drury Lane, 17 Nov 1675). 1676, 1685, 1690, 1692, 1694, 1699, 1704. Prologue and epilogue. Dedication.

Epilogue to the Man of mode: or Sir Fopling Flutter, by Sir George Etherege. (11 March 1676). 1676.

Prologue to the University of Oxford ['Tho' actors cannot much of learning boast']. (1676?). In Miscellany poems, 1684.

The state of innocence and fall of man. O (unacted). 1677, 1678, 1684, 1684, '1684' (pirated edn c. 1695?), 1690,

. 1692, 1695, 1695, 1703. Written c. 1674. Dedication: The author's apology for heroique poetry and poetique licence.

Prologue to Circe, by Charles Davenant. (12 May 1677). 1677. Shorter version entitled An epilogue in Miscellany poems, 1684.

To Mr Lee, on his Alexander. In The rival Queens: or the death of Alexander the Great, 1677.

All for love: or the world well lost. T (Drury Lane, 12 Dec 1677). 1678, 1692, 1696, 1703, 1709, San Francisco 1929 (facs of 1678); ed J. Encks, New York 1966. Prologue and epilogue. Dedication. Preface.

Epilogue to Mithridates, King of Pontus, by Nathaniel Lee. (c. Feb 1678). 1678. For Dryden's prologue and epilogue, written for a revival mid-Oct 1681, see below.

The kind keeper: or Mr Limberham. C (Dorset Garden, 11 March 1678). 1680, 1690, 1701. Prologue and epilogue. Dedication.

Prologue to A true widow, by Thomas Shadwell. (21 March 1678). Rptd with Aphra Behn, The widdow Ranter, 1690.

Oedipus. T (Dorset Garden, c. Sept 1678). 1679, 1682, 1687, 1692, [1696?], 1701, 1711. With N. Lee. Prologue and epilogue. Preface.

Troilus and Cressida: or truth found too late. T (Dorset Garden, c. April 1679). 1679, '1679' (for c. 1692), 1695. Prologue and epilogue. Dedication. A preface containing The grounds of criticism in tragedy.

Prologue to Caesar Borgia, by Nathaniel Lee. (May 1679). 1680.

Prologue to the University of Oxford, for Settle (1679?), altered for Sophonisba by Nathaniel Lee. (1680?). 1681 (2nd edn of Lee); rptd in Miscellany poems, 1684.

Prologue to the Loyal general, by Nahum Tate. (Dec 1679). 1680.

Ovid's epistles, translated by several hands. 1680, 1681. Canace to Macareus, Helen to Paris (with J. Sheffield, Earl of Mulgrave), Dido to Aneas, and Preface, are by Dryden.

Prologue to the University of Oxford ['Discord and plots which have undone our age']. (Nov 1680–March 1682). In Miscellany poems, 1684.

The Spanish fryar: or the double discovery. C (Dorset Garden, 1 Nov 1680). 1681, 1681, 1686, 1690, 1695, 1704 ('second edition'), 1717. Prologue. Dedication.

Prologue and epilogue to the Princess of Cleves, by Nathaniel Lee. (Late 1680–early 1682). In Miscellany poems, 1684.

Prologue to the University of Oxford. [1681]. In Examen poeticum, 1693.

Prologue to the University of Oxford ['The fam'd Italian Muse, whose rhymes advance']. (1681). In Examen poeticum, 1693.

Epilogue to Tamerlane the great, by Charles Saunders. (Mid–March 1681). 1681.

Epilogue [to above] spoke before his Majesty at Oxford, March 19 1680 [i.e. 1681] ['As from a darkened room some optick glass']. Single sheet, 1681, 1681; Oxford 1932 (facs).

Prologue to the King and Queen, at their coming to the house: epilogue for the Unhappy favourite: or the Earl of Essex, by John Banks. (May 1681). 1681.

His Majesties declaration defended. 1681; ed G. Davies, Los Angeles 1950 (Augustan Reprint Soc).

A prologue [and epilogue] spoken at Mithridates King of Pontus [by Nathaniel Lee], the first play acted at the Theatre Royal this year 1681. (Mid-Oct 1681). [1682]. Single sheet: Scott first ascribed the epilogue to Dryden, and R. G. Ham, TLS 27 Dec 1928, the prologue.

Absalom and Achitophel: a poem. 1681 (4 issues, 4°), [Dublin 1681?], London 1681 (2nd edn, but not so-called on title-page, folio), 1681 ('the second edition', 4°, containing addn of ll. 180–91, 957–60; 2 issues), [Dublin 1681?], 1682 (3rd–5th edns) etc; ed J. and H. Kinsley, Oxford 1961. For Second part, see below.

Prologue and epilogue to the Loyal brother: or the Persian prince, by Thomas Southerne. (4 Feb 1682). 1682. The prologue also ptd on a single sheet [1682].

The medall: a satyre against sedition, by the author of Absalom and Achitophel. 1682, 1682, Edinburgh 1682, Dublin 1682, London 1692. Prefaced by Epistle to the Whigs.

Prologue to his Royal Highness upon his first appearance at the Duke's Theatre since his return from Scotland, written by Mr Dryden, spoken by Mr Smith. (21 April 1682). Single sheet [1682], [1682]; rptd in Sylvae, 1702 (3rd edn).

Prologue to the Dutchess on her return from Scotland. (31 May 1682). 1682. Single sheet; rptd in Examen poeticum, 1693.

Mac Flecknoe: or a satyr upon the true-blew-Protestant poet T.S., by the author of Absalom and Achitophel. 1682, 1692 (with Absalom and Achitophel and Medall), 1924 (facs). Written 1678?

The second part of Absalom and Achitophel: a poem. 1682 (2 issues), 1682, Dublin 1682, London 1709, 1716 (with Key in 4th edn of first pt of Miscellany poems). By Nahum Tate, with addns by Dryden.

Prologue to the King and Queen, at the opening of their theatre, spoken by Mr Batterton, written by Mr Dryden, with epilogue; spoken by Mr Smith, written by the same author. (16 Nov 1682). 1683. 2 leaves.

The Duke of Guise. T (Drury Lane, 28 Nov 1682). 1683, 1687, 1699, 1699. With N. Lee. Prologue and epilogues (also ptd as Prologue, epilogue and second epilogue. 2 leaves). Dedication.

Religio laici, or a layman's faith: a poem. 1682 (3 issues), 1682 (perhaps pirated), 1683. Preface.

The vindication: or the parallel of the French Holy-League, and the English League and Covenant, turn'd into a seditious libell by Thomas Hunt. 1683. Running-title: The vindication of the Duke of Guise.

Plutarch's Lives, translated from the Greek by several hands. 5 vols 1683–6, 1693, 1700, 1703. Life of Plutarch as well as a Dedication and Advertisement of the publisher attributed by Malone.

Epilogue to Constantine the great, by Nathaniel Lee. (12 Nov 1683). 1684. Single sheet, 2 edns, one pirated; rptd in Miscellany poems, 1702 (3rd edn).

Soames, Sir William. The art of poetry, written in French by Boileau. 1683. Dryden revised and contributed some lines; rptd in The annual miscellany, 1708 (2nd edn); rptd separately, 1710, 1715, Glasgow 1755.

Miscellany poems. 1684. Contains trns: Ovid, Amours II xix; Theocritus, Idyll 3; Virgil, Eclogues 4, 9.

Prologue to Disappointment: or the mother in fashion, by Thomas Southerne. (April 1684). 1684. Single sheet; rptd in Miscellany poems, 1702 (3rd edn).

The history of the League written in French by M. Maimbourg. 1684. Dedication and Postscript.

To the Earl of Roscommon on his excellent Essay on translated verse. In An essay on translated verse, by the Earl of Roscommon, 1684, 1685.

To the memory of Mr Oldham. In Remains of Mr John Oldham in verse and prose, 1684.

Sylvae: or the second part of poetical miscellanies. 1685. Contains trns: Horace Odes, I iii, I ix, III xxix, 2nd Epode; Lucretius, portions of bks 1–5; Theocritus, Idylls 18, 23, 27 (rptd Poems, 1701); passages from Virgil etc.

Threnodia Augustalis: a funeral-pindarique poem sacred to the happy memory of King Charles II. 1685 (3 edns: 'the second edition' in fact a re-issue of first edn), Dublin 1685.

Albion and Albanius. DO (Dorset Garden, 3 June 1685). 1685, 1685, 1687, 1691. Prologue and epilogue (also ptd as single sheet). Preface.

To my friend Mr J. Northleigh. In The triumph of our monarchy over the plots and principles of our rebels and republicans, 1685.

To the pious memory of the accomplisht young lady Mrs Anne Killigrew, excellent in the two sister-arts of poesie and painting. In Poems by Mrs Anne Killigrew, 1686 (for 1685?); rptd with alterations in Examen poeticum, 1693.

A defence of the papers written by the late King of blessed memory, and Duchess of York, against the answer made to them [by Stillingfleet], by command. 1686. C. E. Ward, Life, 1960, p. 219, attributed all 3 defences to Dryden; earlier writers the 3rd only.

To my ingenious friend, Mr Henry Higden esq, on his translation of the tenth satyr of Juvenal. In Henry Higden, A modern essay on the tenth satyr of Juvenal, 1687.

The hind and the panther: a poem in three parts. 1687 (7 states of last leaf), 1687 (2nd–3rd edns), Edinburgh 1687, Dublin 1687; ed W. H. Williams 1900. To the reader.

A song for St Cecilia's Day 1687, written by John Dryden esq, and compos'd by Mr John Baptist Draghi. 1687 (single sheet), 1693 (in Examen poeticum).

Britannia rediviva: a poem on the birth of the Prince. 1688, Edinburgh 1688, London 1688 (for c. 1691).

Dedication to the life of St Francis Xavier, trnd from D. Bouhours. 1688.

An epitaph on Sir Palmes Fairborne's tomb. In Poetical recreations: part 1 by Mrs Jane Barker, part 2 by several gentlemen, 1688; rptd in Examen poeticum, 1693.

Prologue ['Gallants, a bashful poet bids me say']. 1689? In Examen poeticum, 1693.

Prologue and epilogue to the Widdow ranter: or the history of Bacon in Virginia, by Aphra Behn. (c. Nov 1689). 1689 (separately ptd).

Don Sebastian, King of Portugal. T (Drury Lane, 4 Dec 1689). 1690, 1692. Prologue and epilogue. Dedication. Preface.

Prologue to the Prophetess: or the history of Dioclesian [by Fletcher turned into an opera by Betterton]. (June 1690). 1690. In Poems of affairs of state pt 3, 1698, Muses Mercury Jan 1707, Annual Miscellany 1708 (2nd edn).

Amphitryon: or the two Socia's. C (Drury Lane, early Oct? 1690). 1690, 1691, 1694, 1706. Prologue and epilogue. Dedication.

Prologue to the Mistakes: or the false report, by Joseph Harris. (Mid-Dec 1690). 1691.

King Arthur: or the British worthy. DO (Dorset Garden, c. May 1691). 1691 (re-issued twice in same year with prologue and epilogue added). 1695; rptd (with alterations adopted by H. Purcell) Cambridge 1928.

Dedication to the vocal and instrumental musick of the Prophetess: or the history of Dioclesian, by Henry Purcell. 1691.

Preface to A dialogue concerning women: being a defence of the sex, by William Walsh. 1691. Walsh was assisted by Dryden's comments on the Dialogue.

A letter to Sir George Etheridge. In The history of Adolphus Prince of Russia, to which is added two letters in verse from Sir G.E. to the E. of M. with Mr D's answer to them, 1691; rptd in Familiar letters vol 2, 1697, and Sylvae, 1702 (3rd edn). Written c. 1686.

To Mr Southern on his comedy, called the Wives excuse. In The wives excuse, or cuckolds make themselves: a comedy, by Tho Southern[e], 1692.

Eleonora: a panegyrical poem dedicated to the memory of the late Countess of Abingdon. 1692. Dedication.

Cleomenes, the Spartan heroe. T (Drury Lane, mid-April 1692). 1692. Prologue and epilogue. Dedication. Preface.

Miscellaneous essays by Monsieur St Evremont, translated out of French, with a character by a person of honour here in England [Knightly Chetwood]; continued by Mr Dryden. 1692. A 2nd vol trn by Tom Brown was pbd in 1694.

Epilogue to Henry II, King of England [by John Bancroft]. (8 Nov 1692). 1693.

The character of Polybius and his writings. In The history of Polybius the megalopolitan, translated by Sir H[enry] S[heeres], 2 vols 1693 etc.

Homer, The last parting of Hector and Andromache. In Examen poeticum, 1693.

Ovid, Metamorphoses bk 1 and episodes from bks 9 and 13. Ibid.

Veni, creator spiritus, translated in paraphrase. Ibid.

The satires of Juvenalis, translated into English verse by Mr Dryden and several other eminent hands; together with the Satires of Persius, made English by Mr Dryden. 1693, 1697, 1697. Juvenal, Satires 1, 3, 6, 10, 16 and all Persius by Dryden; also A discourse concerning the original and progress of satire.

To my dear friend Mr Congreve on his comedy called the Double-dealer. In Congreve, The double-dealer: a comedy, 1694.

Love triumphant: or nature will prevail. TC (Drury Lane, mid-Jan 1694). 1694. Prologue and epilogue.

A parallel betwixt painting and poetry. In De arte graphica: the art of painting, by C. A. Du Fresnoy, 1695, 1716, 1750. Dryden's Parallel, ed E. Malone in Works of Sir Joshua Reynolds, 1797, 1801 (3rd edn).

Preface and epilogue to the Husband his own cuckold, by John Dryden jr. (Feb 1696). 1696.

An ode on the death of Mr Henry Purcell, late servant to his Majesty and organist of the Chapel Royal, and of St Peter's Westminster: the words by Mr Dryden, and sett to musick by Dr Blow. 1696; rptd in Orpheus britannicus, 1698.

The works of Virgil: containing his Pastorals, Georgics and Æneis: translated into English verse. 1697, 1698, 1709, 1716, 1721, 1730; ed J. Kinsley, Oxford 1961. The 4th and 9th Eclogues first pbd in Miscellany poems, 1684. 3 episodes from the Æneid in Sylvae, 1685, and bk 3 of the Georgics in Annual Miscellany 1694. Dryden wrote the Dedications for Pastorals, Georgics, Æneis; Discourse on epick poetry; Postscript.

Alexander's feast: or the power of musique; an ode in honour of St Cecilia's Day. 1697, 1700 (in Fables); Oxford 1925 (facs).

To Mr Granville on his excellent tragedy call'd Heroick love. In Heroick love: a tragedy, by George Granville afterwards Baron Lansdowne, 1698.

To my friend the author [Peter Anthony Motteux]. In Motteux, Beauty in distress: a tragedy, 1698.

Fables ancient and modern. 1700, 1713. Dedication and preface To her Grace the Dutchess of Ormond, 7 trns from Chaucer, 8 trns from Ovid's Metamorphoses, 3 trns from Boccaccio, trn of Homer's Iliad bk 1, To my honoured kinsman John Driden, lines on The monument of a fair maiden lady: ed A. Mawer 1901; Oxford 1910; ed W. H. W. Williams, Cambridge 1912; ed M. G. L. Thomas, Oxford 1928.

The secular masque etc. In The pilgrim as it is acted at the Theatre Royal, written originally by Mr Fletcher, and now very much alter'd with several additions [by Sir John Vanbrugh]; likewise a prologue, epilogue, dialogue and masque, written by the late great poet Mr Dryden, just before his death, being the last of his works, 1700.

Ovid, Amours I [iv]. In Poetical miscellanies, 5th pt, 1704.

Ovid's art of love, in three books. 1709. Bk 1 'translated some years since by Mr Dryden'.

Life of Lucian. In The works of Lucian, translated by several eminent hands, 4 vols 1711 etc.

[Heads of an answer to Rymer's remarks on the tragedies of the last age]. In Works of Mr Francis Beaumont and Mr John Fletcher vol 1, 1711, pp. xii–xxvi; another text in Johnson's Life, 1781.

Epitaph on the Marquis of Winchester. In Miscellaneous poems and translations by Mr Pope, 1712.

Ovid, Metamorphoses bk 11 (56 lines). In Ovid's Metamorphoses in fifteen books, 1717.

Lines to Honor Dryden. GM May 1785; rptd in Critical and miscellaneous prose works of Dryden, ed E. Malone 1800 I. i. 341–2. Probably written in 1653; *see* Works vol 1, ed E. N. Hooker and H. T. Swedenberg, Berkeley 1955.

Lines to Mrs Creed. In Critical and miscellaneous prose works of John Dryden, ed E. Malone 1800 I. i. 341–2.

Ode on the marriage of Mrs A. Stafford. In Tixall poetry, ed A. Clifford, Edinburgh 1813. Written c. 1687.

Epitaph on the poet's nephew, Erasmus Lawton. In J. Prior, Life of Malone, 1860.

Miscellanies

The successive edns of each vol vary greatly in content. See A. E. Case, Bibliography of English poetical miscellanies 1521–1750, 1935 (Bibl Soc); *and* Macdonald pp. 67–83.

Miscellany poems: containing a new translation of Virgills Eclogues, Ovid's Love elegies, Odes of Horace and other authors, with several original poems; by the most eminent hands. 1684, 1688, 1692, 1692, 1702, 1716, 1727.

Sylvae: or the second part of poetical miscellanies. 1685, 1685, 1692, 1693, 1702, 1716, 1727. Preface.

Examen poeticum, being the third part of miscellany poems: containing variety of new translations of the ancient poets; together with many original copies by the most eminent hands. 1693, 1693, 1706, 1716, 1727. Dedication.

The annual miscellany for the year 1694, being the fourth part of miscellany poems: containing great variety of new translations and original copies by the most eminent hands. 1694, 1708, 1716, 1727.

Poetical miscellanies: the fifth part. 1704, 1716, 1727. This and the 6th pt, below, were ed J. Tonson assisted by N. Rowe.

Poetical miscellanies: the sixth part. 1709, 1716, 1727.

Prose translations

The history of the League, written in French by Monsieur [L.] Maimbourg. 1684.

The life of St Francis Xavier by Dominick Bo[u]hours. 1688.

De arte graphica: the art of painting by C. A. De Fresnoy; with remarks; translated into English together with an original preface containing a Parallel betwixt painting and poetry; by Mr Dryden. 1695, 1716 (rev and abridged Charles Jervas assisted by Pope?), 1750.

Letters upon several occasions; with a new translation of select letters of Monsieur Voiture. Ed J. Dennis 1696. Dryden translated Voiture's letter 'To my Lord Cardinal de la Valette', p. 136.

The annals and history of Cornelius Tacitus, made English by several hands. 3 vols 1698. Bk 1 by Dryden.

Letters

Letters. Ed C. E. Ward, Durham NC 1942.

First attempts to collect were in the edns of Malone, Scott and Scott-Saintsbury.

§ 2

For early criticism see Dryden: the critical heritage, *ed J. and H. Kinsley 1971.*

Johnson, Samuel. In his Lives of the poets, 1779–81.

Saintsbury, G. Dryden. 1881 (EML).

Verrall, A. W. Lectures on Dryden. Cambridge 1914.

Van Doren, M. The poetry of Dryden. New York 1920, 1931 (rev), 1946 (as Dryden: a study of his poetry).

Eliot, T. S. Homage to John Dryden. 1924.

—— Dryden: the poet, the dramatist, the critic. New York 1932.

—— In his Use of poetry and the use of criticism, 1933.

Bredvold, L. I. The intellectual milieu of Dryden. Ann Arbor 1934.

Lewis, C. S. Shelley, Dryden and Mr Eliot. In his Rehabilitations, Oxford 1939.

Osborn, J. M. Dryden: some biographical facts and problems. New York 1940, Gainesville 1965 (rev).

Nichol Smith, D. Dryden. Cambridge 1950.

Purpus, E. R. A deistical essay attributed to Dryden. PQ 29 1950.

Sherwood, J. C. Dryden and the rules: the Preface to Troilus and Cressida. Comparative Lit 2 1950.

—— Dryden and the rules: the Preface to the Fables. JEGP 52 1953.

Davie, D. Dramatic poetry: Dryden's conversation piece. Cambridge Jnl June 1952.

Frost, W. Dryden and the art of translation. New Haven 1955.

Strang, B. M. H. Dryden's innovations in critical vocabulary. Durham Univ Jnl 51 1959.

Proudfoot, L. Dryden's Aeneid and its seventeenth-century predecessors. Manchester 1960.

Schilling, B. N. Dryden and the conservative myth: a reading of Absalom and Achitophel. New Haven 1961.

—— (ed). Dryden: a collection of critical essays. Englewood Cliffs NJ 1963.

Ward, C. E. The life of Dryden. Chapel Hill 1961.

Waith, E. M. The Herculean hero in Marlowe, Chapman, Shakespeare and Dryden. New York 1962.

Kirsch, A. C. Dryden's heroic drama. Princeton 1965.

Swedenberg, H. T. (ed). Essential articles for the study of Dryden. Hamden Conn 1966.

Miner, E. R. Dryden's poetry. Bloomington 1967.

Harth P. Contexts of Dryden's thought. Chicago 1968.

Myers, W. Dryden. 1973.

Pechter, E. Dryden's classical theory of literature. Cambridge 1975.

SIR CHARLES SEDLEY
1639?–1701

§ 1

Pompey the Great: a tragedy translated out of French [of Corneille] by certain persons of honour [Waller, Sedley, Godolphin, Filmer, Dorset]. 1664.

The mulberry garden: a comedy. (Theatre Royal 1668). 1668, 1675, 1688.

Antony and Cleopatra: a tragedy. (Drury Lane 1677). 1677, 1696.

Bellamira, or the mistress: a comedy. (Drury Lane 1687). 1687.

The oration of Cicero for M. Marcellus. 1689. Anon, attributed to Sedley in Works, 1722.

Reflections upon our late and present proceedings in England. 1689 (anon), Edinburgh 1689; rptd in Somers tracts, ed W. Scott vol 10, 1813.

The speech of Sir Charles Sidley in the House of Commons. 1691; rptd in Somers tracts, ed W. Scott vol 10, 1813.

The happy pair: or a poem on matrimony. 1702, 1705 (corrected).

The grumbler. In Works, 1722 with own title-page 1719. Tr from de Brueys and de Palaprat, adapted by Garrick 1754 (Larpent ms 112) and Goldsmith 1773 (ed A. I. P. Wood, Cambridge Mass 1931).

Poetical and dramatic works. Ed V. de S. Pinto 2 vols 1928.

§ 2

Pinto, V. de S. Sir Charles Sedley. 1927.

—— In his Restoration carnival, 1954. Selections with introd and notes.
—— In his Restoration Court poets, 1966.
Wilson, J. H. In his Court wits of the Restoration, Princeton 1948.

JOHN WILMOT,
2nd EARL OF ROCHESTER
1647–80

Bibliographies

Vieth, D. M. In his Attribution in Restoration poetry, New Haven 1963.

Collections

The early edns are classified as in Vieth, above.
Series A. Poems on several occasions by the Right Honourable the E. of R—. 1680 (at least 10 edns, with Antwerp or Antwerpen on title-page), 1685, 1690 (no known copy), 1701, 171[3], 1731; ed J. Thorpe, Princeton 1950 (facs).
Series B. Poems etc on several occasions; with Valentinian: a tragedy. 1691 (preface by T. Rymer), 1696, 1705, 1710, 1714, 1718, 1732 (4th edn).
Series C. Miscellaneous works of the Right Honourable the late Earls of Rochester and Roscommon. 1707, 1707, 1709 (2 3rd edns), 1711, 2 vols 1714 (with works of Dorset etc), 1718, 1721, 1721, 1731, 1 vol 1735, 2 vols 1739 (3 edns), 1752, 1756, 1756, 1757, 1758, 1767, 1771, 1774, 1777.
Series D. Remains from a manuscript found in a gentleman's lodging. 1718, 1761 (as Poetical works). This ser contains only one or two genuine poems.
Collected works. Ed J. Hayward 1926.
Poems by John Wilmot, Earl of Rochester. Ed V. de S. Pinto, 1953, 1964 (ML).
The Gyldenstolpe manuscript miscellany of poems by John Wilmot, Earl of Rochester and other Restoration authors. Ed B. Danielsson and D. M. Vieth, Stockholm 1967.
Complete poems. Ed D. M. Vieth, New Haven 1968.

§ 1

Corydon and Cloris: or the wanton shepherdess. [1676?]. Anon.
A satyr against mankind, by a person of honour. [1679].

A letter from Artemiza in the town to Chloe in the country, by a person of honour. [1679] (2 edns with varying titles).
Upon nothing: a poem. [1679], [1679], 1711.
A very heroical epistle from My Lord All-Pride to Dol-Common. 1679. Anon.
Sodom: or the quintessence of debauchery. 1684 (lost, perhaps never existent); ed L. S. A. M. von Römer, Paris 1904; Paris 1957, North Hollywood Cal 1966. In dramatic form, almost certainly not by Rochester.
Valentinian: a tragedy, as 'tis altered by the late Earl of Rochester. 1685.
The famous pathologist: or the noble mountebank, by Thomas Alcock and John Earl of Rochester. Ed V. de S. Pinto, Nottingham 1961. Rochester's mountebank bill, first rptd in Poems 1691, above, ed from transcript by Alcock.

Letters

A letter to Dr Burnet from the Earl of Rochester. 1680.
Familiar letters written by John late Earl of Rochester and several other persons of honour and quality. 2 vols 1697, 1697, 1699, 1705, 1705. Vol 1 ed T. Brown, vol 2 ed C. Gildon.
The Rochester-Savile letters 1671–80. Ed J. H. Wilson, Columbus Ohio 1941.

§ 2

For early criticism see Rochester: the critical heritage, *ed* D. Farley-Hills 1972.
Burnet, G. Some passages of the life and death of John Earl of Rochester. 1680.
Johnson, S. In his Lives of the poets, 1779–81.
Pinto, V. de S. Rochester: portrait of a Restoration poet. 1935, 1962 (as Enthusiast in wit).
—— In his Restoration Court poets, 1966.
Vieth, D. M. The text of Rochester and the editions of 1680. PBSA 50 1956.
—— Order of contents as evidence of authorship: Rochester's Poems of 1680. PBSA 53 1959.
—— Attribution in Restoration poetry: a study of Rochester's Poems of 1680. New Haven 1963.
Erskine-Hill, H. H. Rochester: Augustan or explorer? In Renaissance and modern essays presented to V. de S. Pinto, 1966.
Righter, A. John Wilmot, Earl of Rochester. Proc Br Acad 53 1968.
Griffin, D. H. Satires against man: the poems of Rochester. Berkeley 1973.
Greene, G. Lord Rochester's monkey. 1974. Written 1934.

III. MINOR POETRY 1660–1700

References
POAS Poems on affairs of state, ed G. deF. Lord 7 vols New Haven 1963–75.

PHILIP AYRES
1638–1712

Emblemata amatoria, emblems of love, emblemi d'amore, emblemes d'amour. 1683, [1687?–1700?] (3 edns entitled Emblems of love), 1714 (with first title), [1725?], [1750?]. Text engraved, same in all edns. English poems ed G. Saintsbury in Minor poets of the Caroline period vol 2, Oxford 1906.
Lyric poems made in imitation of the Italians, of which many are translations from other languages. 1687; ed G. Saintsbury, above.

Ayres also expanded Edward Chamberlayne, Angliae notitia, 1682, *edited* Voyages of B. Sharp and others, *and translated from French, Spanish and Italian.*

SIR RICHARD BLACKMORE
1654–1729

§ 1

Prince Arthur: an heroick poem. 1695, 1695 (corrected), 1696, 1697, 1714.
King Arthur: an heroick poem. 1697.

A short history of the last Parliament. 1699. Anon, rptd Somers tracts vol 11, ed W. Scott 1813 as by — Drake MD. Prose.

A satyr against wit. 1700 (3 edns), Dublin 1700; ed F. H. Ellis, POAS 6.

A paraphrase on the book of Job, as likewise on the songs of Moses, Deborah, David, on four select psalms, some chapters of Isaiah, and the third chapter of Habakkuk. 1700, 1716.

A hymn to the light of the world, with a short description of the cartoons of Raphael Urbin. 1703.

Eliza: an epick poem. 1705.

Advice to the poets: a poem occasion'd by the wonderful success of her Majesty's arms in Flanders. 1706, 1706 (corrected). Anon.

The Kit-cats: a poem. 1708 (3 edns), 1709, 1718. Anon.

Instructions to Vander Bank, a sequel to the Advice to the poets: a poem occasion'd by the glorious success of her Majesty's arms. 1709 (3 edns). Anon.

The nature of man: a poem in three books. 1711, 1720. Anon.

Creation: a philosophical poem in seven books. 1712, 1712, 1715, 1718, Dublin 1727.

The lay-monastery: consisting of essays, discourses etc, publish'd singly under the title of the Lay-monk. 1714. The lay-monk, a tri-weekly periodical by Blackmore and John Hughes, ran from 16 Nov 1713 to 15 Feb 1714.

Essays upon several subjects. 1716, 2 vols 1717; vol 1 Dublin 1716. An essay upon wit, ed R. C. Boys, Los Angeles 1946 (Augustan Reprint Soc).

A collection of poems on various subjects. 1718.

Just prejudices against the Arian hypothesis. 1721. Prose.

Modern Arians unmask'd. 1721. Prose.

A new version of the psalms of David. 1721.

Redemption: a divine poem. 1722.

A true and impartial history of the conspiracy against the person and government of King William in 1695. 1723. Prose.

Alfred: an epick poem. 1723.

Natural theology: or moral duties consider'd apart from positive. 1728. Prose.

The accomplished preacher: or an essay on divine eloquence. Ed J. White 1731. Prose.

Blackmore also published medical works.

§ 2

Dennis, J. Remarks on a book entitul'd Prince Arthur. 1696; ed E. N. Hooker in Critical works of Dennis vol 1, Baltimore 1939.

Johnson, S. In his Lives of the poets, 1779–81.

Boys, R. C. Blackmore and the Wits. Ann Arbor 1949.

Rosenberg, A. Sir Richard Blackmore. Lincoln Nebraska 1953.

CHARLES SACKVILLE, BARON BUCKHURST, 6th EARL OF DORSET AND 1st EARL OF MIDDLESEX
1638–1706

Bibliographies

Bagley, H. A. A checklist of the poems of Dorset. MLN 47 1932. Addns by R. G. Howarth 50 1935.

Collections

The works of the Earls of Rochester, Roscommon, Dorset etc. 2 vols 1714, 1718, 1721, 1731, 1735. At least 12 further edns before 1800.

§ 1

Pompey the great: a tragedy translated out of French [of Corneille] by certain persons of honour [Waller, Sedley,

Godolphin, Filmer, Dorset]. (Acted at Court, Duke's Company, Jan 1664). 1664.
Dorset's name appears on the title page of 15 miscellanies between 1697 and 1718.

§ 2

Johnson, S. In his Lives of the poets, 1779–81.

Harris, B. Charles Sackville, patron and poet. Urbana 1940.

Wilson, J. H. In his Court wits of the Restoration, Princeton 1948.

Pinto, V. de S. In his Restoration Court poets, 1966.

THOMAS ELLWOOD
1639–1713

§ 1

Rogero-mastix: a rod for William Rogers in return for his riming scourge. 1685.

A collection of poems on various subjects. [c. 1710–30, 2 edns].

Davideis: the life of David King of Israel, a sacred poem in five books. 1712, Dublin 1722 (2nd edn with addns), London 1727 (2nd edn), 1749 (3rd edn), Philadelphia 1751 (4th edn corrected), 1753 (4th edn), 1754 (5th edn), 1762, London 1763 (4th edn) etc; ed W. Fischer, Heidelberg 1936.

The history of the life of Thomas Ellwood written by his own hand. Ed J[oseph] W[yeth] 1714, 1714, 1765, 1791 etc; ed W. D. Howells, Boston 1877; ed C. G. Crump 1900; ed S. Graveson 1906. Includes hymns and religious verse.

§ 2

Snell, B. S. Ellwood: friend of Milton. 1934, 1949.

Patrick, J. M. Influence of Ellwood upon Milton's epics. In Essays in history and literature presented to Stanley Pargellis, Chicago 1965.

SIR SAMUEL GARTH
c. 1660–1719

§ 1

The dispensary: a poem. 1699 (anon), 1699 (corrected), 1699, 1700 (with addns), 1703, 1706 (6th edn with several descriptions and episodes never before ptd), 1709 (2 unauthorized edns), 1714 (7th edn), 1718, Dublin 1725 (9th edn), London 1726 (9th edn), Dublin 1730 (10th and 12th edns), London 1741 (10th edn), 1768 (11th edn); ed W. J. Leicht, Heidelberg 1905; F. H. Ellis, POAS 6.

A prologue to Tamerlane. London [i.e. Dublin] 1704.

Prologue spoken at the first opening of the Queen's new theatre in the Hay-market. [1705]. Anon.

A poem to the Earl of Godolphin, by Dr G—h. 1710.

A prologue for the 4th of November 1711. 1711.

Claremont. 1715, [1715?] (with corrections and annotations variorum). Anon.

Ovid's metamorphoses, translated by the most eminent hands. 1717. Garth signed dedication and translated bk 14.

§ 2

A compleat key to the Dispensary. 1706, 1709, 1714, 1718, 1726 (adds A continuation of the key), 1734 (3rd edn), 1746 (4th edn), 1768 (5th edn).

Johnson, S. In his Lives of the poets, 1779–81.

Boyce, B. The dispensary, Sir Richard Blackmore and the captain of the Wits. RES 14 1938.

CHARLES MONTAGU, 1st EARL OF HALIFAX
1661–1715

§ I

Ode on the marriage of the Princess Anne and Prince George. 1683. Anon.
On the death of his most sacred Majesty King Charles II. 1685. Anon.
The hind and the panther transvers'd to the story of the country-mouse and the city-mouse. 1687, Dublin 1687 (anon); ed G. M. Crump, POAS 4. Prose and verse, with M. Prior.
The man of honour, occasion'd by the postscript of Pen's letter. [1689?]; ed G. M. Crump, with above.
An epistle to the Earl of Dorset occasion'd by his Majesty's victory in Ireland. 1690, 1690, 1702, 1716.

§ 2

Johnson, S. In his Lives of the poets, 1779–81.
Hooker, H. M. Montagu's reply to the Hind and the panther. ELH 8 1941.
POAS 4.

JOHN SHEFFIELD, 3rd EARL OF MULGRAVE, MARQUIS OF NORMANBY, DUKE OF BUCKINGHAM AND NORMANBY
1648–1721

Collections

The works of John Sheffield, Earl of Mulgrave, Marquis of Normanby, Duke of Buckingham. Ed A. Pope 2 vols 1723, [Hague] 1726, London 1729 (2nd edn corrected), 1740 (3rd edn), 1752, 1753 (4th edn) etc.

§ I

A collection of poems written on several occasions by several hands. 1672, 1673, 1693, 1695 (as The temple of death by the Marquess of Normanby), 1701 (A collection of poems: viz The temple of death), 1702, 1716. Tr from French of P. Habert.
The character of a Tory. 1681. Anon. Prose.
An essay upon poetry. 1682 (anon), Dublin 1683 (anon), London 1691 (with Latin version by J. N[orris]), 1697 (with poems by others), 1709, Dublin 1731; ed J. E. Spingarn in Critical Essays of the seventeenth century vol 2, Oxford 1908.
A letter from the Earl of Mulgrave to Dr Tillotson. 1689, 1689 (as A true copy of the letter), 1689 (as To Dr Tillotson). Prose.
The character of Charles II. 1696 (anon), 1725 (7th edn), 1729. Prose.
The Earl of Mulgrave's speech. [1693?], 1712.
The Duke of Buck—g—m's speech relating to the sentence against Dr Henry Sacheverell. 1710.
The Duke of Buckingham's speech spoken in the House of Lords, Feb the 15th. 1715.
An unpbd account of the Revolution of 1688, Humanum est errare: or false steps on both sides, *is in BM ms Add 27382.*

§ 2

Gildon, C. The laws of poetry, as laid down by the Duke of Buckinghamshire in his Essay on poetry. 1721.
Johnson, S. In his Lives of the poets, 1779–81.
POAS 1.

JOHN OLDHAM
1653–83
Bibliographies

Brooks, H. F. Bibliography of Oldham. Oxford Bibl Soc Proc 5 1940.

Collections

The works of Mr John Oldham, together with his remains. 1684, 1684, 1686 (3 issues), 1692, 1694, 1695, 1698, 1703, 1704, 1710 (7th edn), 2 vols 1722 (with memoirs and notes).
Poetical works. Ed R. Bell 1854, [1870]; ed B. Dobrée 1960 (facs of 1854). A selection.

§ I

Upon the marriage of the Prince of Orange. 1677. Anon.
Garnet's ghost. [1679]. Anon, pirated. Included in Satyrs upon the Jesuits.
A satyr against vertue. 1679. Anon.
The clarret drinker's song. 1680, [1680?] (anon); rptd in Poems and translations, below, as The careless good fellow; ed E. F. Mengel jr, POAS 2.
Satyrs upon the Jesuits, together with the satyr against vertue and some other pieces. 1681, 1682 (anon); rptd in Works, above. Satyrs upon the Jesuits ed E. F. Mengel jr, POAS 2.
Some new pieces never before publisht. 1681, 1684. By the author of Satyrs upon the Jesuits.
Poems and translations. 1683, 1684.
Remains of Mr Oldham in verse and prose. 1684.
A second musical entertainment perform'd on St Cecilia's day. 1685.

§ 2

Williams, W. M. The genesis of Oldham's Satyrs upon the Jesuits. PMLA 58 1943.
—— The influence of Ben Jonson's Catiline upon Oldham's Satyrs upon the Jesuits. ELH 11 1944.
Vieth, D. M. Oldham, the Wits and A satyr against vertue. PQ 32 1953.
Mackin, C. R. The satiric technique of Oldham's Satyrs upon the Jesuits. SP 62 1965.

KATHERINE PHILIPS
1632–64

§ I

Pompey: a tragedy. (Smock Alley 1663). Dublin 1663, London 1663.
Poems by the incomparable, Mrs K.P. 1664. Pirated, suppressed.
Poems by Mrs Katherine Philips, the matchless Orinda; to which is added Corneille's Pompey and Horace. 1667, 1669, 1678, 1710; rptd except for plays in G. Saintsbury, Minor poets of the Caroline period vol 1, Oxford 1905.
Familiar letters written by the late Earl of Rochester, with letters written by Mr Thomas Otway and Mrs K. Philips. Ed T. Brown 1697.
Letters from Orinda to Poliarchus. 1705, 1729 (with new letter).

§ 2

Souers, P. W. The matchless Orinda. Cambridge Mass 1931.
Elmen, P. Some manuscript poems by the matchless Orinda. PQ 30 1951.

JOHN PHILLIPS
1631–1706

For a bibliography see W. R. Parker, Milton: a biography, 2 vols Oxford 1968.

Johannis Philippi Angli responsio ad apologiam anonymi cujusdam tenebrionis pro rege & populo anglicano infantissimam. 1652 (4 edns). Rptd in most edns of Milton's works, tr in Works of Milton vol 4, New Haven 1966. Probably with Milton's assistance.

A satyr against hypocrites. 1655 (3 edns), 1661, 1661 (as The religion of hypocritical presbyterians), 1671 (with first title), 1674, 1677, 1680, 1689, 1710 (as Mr John Milton's satyre); ed L. Howard, Los Angeles 1953 (Augustan Reprint Soc).

Montelion 1660: or the prophetical almanack. [1659]. Anon. Prose. Montelion 1661 is probably also by Phillips, though it and other works by 'Montelion' have been ascribed to T. Flatman.

An introduction to astrology. 1661. Anon. Prose.

Don Juan Lamberto: or comical history of the late times. Part 1, 1661, 1661; Part 2, 1661; 1664 (both pts). By Montelion knight of the oracle.

Typhon, or the gyants war with the gods: a mock poem. 1665. From Scarron.

Montelions predictions. 1672. Anon. Prose.

Maronides, or Virgil travestie: being a new paraphrase upon the fifth book of Virgil's Aeneids. 1672, 1672; Sixth book, 1673, 1678 (with 5th book). From Scarron.

Mercurius verax: or the prisoners prognostication for the year 1675, by the author of the first Mentelion and Satyr against hypocrites. 1675. Prose.

Duellum musicum. 1673 (added to M. Locke, The present practice of musick vindicated). Prose.

A brief account of the most memorable transactions in England, Scotland and Ireland, and foreign parts, from the year 1662 to the year 1675. 1676 (added to J. Heath, a chronicle of the late intestine war, 2nd edn). Prose.

Jockey's downfall: a poem on the defeat given to the Scotish covenanters. 1679. Anon.

Dr Oates's narrative of the Popish plot vindicated, by J. P. Gent. 1680. Prose.

Speculum crape-gownorum: or a looking-glass for the young academicks, with reflections on some of the late high-flown sermons, by a guide to the inferiour clergie. 1682, 1682 (enlarged); pt 2, 1682, 1732 (both pts). Prose.

The character of a Popish successor: part the second. 1681, 1681. Anon. Prose. Pt 1 by Elkanah Settle.

Horse-flesh for the Observator, by T.D. B.D. chaplain to the inferiour clergies guide. 1682. Prose.

An anniversary poem on the sixth of May. 1683. Anon.

An humble offering to the sacred memory of Charles II. 1685.

A poem on the coronation of King James II and his royal consort Queen Mary. [1685].

Modern history: or a monethly account of all considerable occurrences, civil, ecclesiastical and military. 1687–9. Prose.

Sam Ld Bp of Oxon his celebrated reasons for abrogating the test. [1688] (3 edns). Anon. Prose.

Advice to a painter. 1688. Anon.

In memory of our late most gracious Lady Mary, Queen of Great-Britain, France and Ireland. 1695.

A reflection on our modern poesy: an essay. 1695. Anon.

Augustus britannicus: a poem upon the conclusion of the peace. 1697.

The vision of Mons Chamillard concerning the battle of Ramillies, by a nephew of the late Mr John Milton. 1706.

Phillips edited Sportive wit 1656, *signed* J.P. *and* Wit and drollery, 1656, *signed* J.P. *He translated extensively from French, Spanish and Latin, including a trn of* Le Mercure histoire et politique 1690–1706. *Other attacks*

on L'Estrange's Observator *may be his. A life of Milton ascribed to Phillips, ed H. Darbishire in her* Early lives of Milton, 1932 *is probably by Cyriack Skinner.*

WENTWORTH DILLON, 4th EARL OF ROSCOMMON
1637–85

Collections

The miscellaneous works of the late Earls of Rochester and Roscommon. 1707, 1709, 1709, 1711, 2 vols 1714 etc.

Poems by the Earl of Roscom[m]on, to which is added An essay on poetry by the Earl of Mulgrave, together with poems by Mr Richard Duke. 1717.

§ 1

Horace's art of poetry made English. 1680, 1684, 1695, 1709 etc.

An essay on translated verse. 1684, 1685 (enlarged); ed J. E. Spingarn in Critical essays of the seventeenth century vol 2, Oxford 1908.

§ 2

Gildon, C. The laws of poetry, as laid down by the Duke of Buckinghamshire, by the Earl of Roscommon in his Essay on translated verse, and by the Lord Lansdowne. 1721.

Johnson, S. In his Lives of the poets, 1779–81.

POAS 2.

THOMAS SPRAT
1635–1713

§ 1

Three poems upon the death of his late Highness Oliver Lord Protector, written by Mr Edm Waller, Mr Jo Dryden, Mr Sprat. 1659, 1682, 1709.

The plague of Athens, first describ'd in Greek by Thucydides, then in Latin by Lucretius, now attempted in English after incomparable Dr Cowley's Pindarick way. 1659, 1665, 1667, 1676, 1683, 1688, 1703, 1709.

Observations on Monsieur de Sorbier's voyage into England. 1665, 1668, 1709. Prose.

The history of the Royal-Society of London. 1667, 1702, 1722, 1734; tr French, 1669; ed J. I. Cope and H. W. Jones, St Louis 1958. Prose.

Sprat also pbd sermons, pastoral letters and controversial pamphlets. He wrote the Life *prefixed to Cowley's* Works, 1668, *and probably assisted Buckingham in the* Rehearsal.

§ 2

Johnson, S. In his Lives of the poets, 1779–81.

SAMUEL WESLEY the elder
1662–1735

Maggots: or poems on several occasions, never before handled, by a schollar. 1685, 1685.

The life of our blessed lord and saviour Jesus Christ: an heroic poem; also a prefatory discourse concerning heroic poetry. 1693, 1694, 1697, 1809 (abridged); Essay on heroic poetry, ed E. N. Hooker, Los Angeles 1947 (Augustan Reprint Soc) (facs of 1697).

Elegies on the Queen and Archbishop. 1695, 1695.
An epistle to a friend concerning poetry. 1700; ed E. N. Hooker, Los Angeles 1947 (Augustan Reprint Soc).
History of the new testament attempted in verse. 1701, 1715, 1717.
History of the Old Testament in verse. 2 vols 1704, 1715.

With preceding item as History of the Old and New Testaments, 3 vols 1716.
Marlborough, or the fate of Europe: a poem. 1705.
A hymn on peace. 1713.
Wesley was also connected with Athenian Gazette, 1691–7, *and pbd religious works.*

IV. EARLY EIGHTEENTH-CENTURY POETRY

MATTHEW PRIOR
1664–1721

Collections

Poems on several occasions. 1709, 1709, 1711, 1713, 1717. For variants in the first edn *see* R. W. Chapman, RES 3 1927.
Poems on several occasions. 1718, Dublin 1719, London 1720, 1721, 1725, 1733, 1734, 1741, Glasgow 1751, London 1754, Aberdeen 1754, Glasgow 1759, London 1766, Berwick 1766, Glasgow 1771, Edinburgh 1773.
Writings. Ed A. R. Waller 2 vols Cambridge 1905–7.
Literary works. Ed H. B. Wright and M. K. Spears 2 vols Oxford 1959, 1971.

§ 1

On the coronation. 1685. Anon.
The hind and the panther transvers'd to the story of the country mouse and the city mouse. 1687 (anon), Dublin 1687, London 1709. With Charles Montagu, later Earl of Halifax.
The orange. 1688. Anon. A broadside.
An ode in imitation of the second ode of the third book of Horace. 1692.
For the New Year: to the sun. [1694].
To the King: an ode on his Majesty's arrival in Holland. 1695.
An English ballad in answer to Mr Despreaux's Pindarique ode on the taking of Namure. 1695.
Verses humbly presented to the King at his arrival in Holland. 1696.
A new answer to an argument against a standing army. 1697.
Carmen saeculare for the year 1700. 1700, 1701 (with Latin trn by T. Dibben).
To a young gentleman in love. 1702.
Prologue spoken at Court before the Queen on her Majesty's birth-day 1703/4. 1704.
A letter to Monsieur Boileau Depreaux occasion'd by the victory at Blenheim. 1704. Anon.
An English padlock. 1705.
Pallas and Venus: an epigram. 1706.
An ode humbly inscrib'd to the Queen. 1706.
Phaedra and Hippolitus, by Mr Edmund Smith. [1707]. Epilogue by Prior.
Horace lib I epist ix imitated. [1711].
To the Right Honorable Mr Harley, wounded by Guiscard. 1711.
Archibaldi Pitcarnii Scoti carmen imitated. [1712].
Walter Danniston ad amicos imitated. [1712?].
Earl Robert's mice. 1712 (H. Baldwin, unauthorized), 1712 (J. Morphew, authorized).
Two imitations of Chaucer. 1712. Susannah and the two elders, Erle Robert's mice.
A fable of the widow and her cat. 1712, 1712. Anon.
A memorial against the fortifying of the ports of Dunkirk and Mardike. 1715.
The dove. 1717.
Lucius, by Mrs Manley. 1717. Epilogue by Prior.
Upon Lady Katharine H-de's first appearing at the play-

house. 1718. Later called The female Phaeton. Probably by Simon Harcourt.
Chit-chat, by Mr Killigrew. [1719]. Prologue by Prior.
Verses spoke to the Lady Henrietta Cavendish Holles Harley in the library of St John's College Cambridge November the 9th 1719. Cambridge [1719], 1720.
Prologue to the Orphan. 1720.
The conversation. 1720.
Colin's mistakes. 1721.
The turtle and the sparrow. 1723 (3 edns).
Down-hall. 1723, 1727.
On Fleet Shepheards takeing. Oxford Bibl Soc Proc 1 1927.

Letters

Original letters from Prior [et al]. Ed R. Warner 1817.
Historical Mss Commission: calendar of the mss of the Marquis of Bath. Vol 2 (Prior papers), 1908.

§ 2

Johnson, S. In his Lives of the English poets, 1779–81.
Ketton-Cremer, R. W. Matthew Prior. Cambridge 1957.

EDWARD YOUNG
1683–1765
Collections

The works of the author of the Night-thoughts. 4 vols 1757, 1762, Dublin 1764, 5 vols 1767, 4 vols Edinburgh 1770, 5 vols 1773, 1774, 6 vols 1778–9, 3 vols 1792.

§ 1

An epistle [in verse] to Lord Lansdown. 1713.
A poem on the last day. Oxford 1713, 1713, London 1714, 1715, 1725, Dublin 1725, 1730, London 1741.
An epistle [in verse] to the Lord Viscount Bolingbroke, sent with A poem on the last day. 1714; rptd by C. K. Firman, An unrecorded poem by Edward Young, N & Q June 1963.
The force of religion, or vanquish'd love: a poem. 1714, 1715, Dublin 1725, 1735, London 1762.
On the late Queen's death, and His Majesty's accession to the throne. 1714, 1716 (in The loyal mourner for the best of princes: being a collection of poems, sacred to the immortal memory of Queen Anne).
Orationes duae Codringtone sacrae. Oxford 1716. One oration by Young.
Busiris, King of Egypt: a tragedy. 1719, 1719, [Hague?] 1719, London 1722, Dublin 1730, London 1733, 1735, Dublin 1761, London 1781.
A paraphrase on part of the Book of Job. 1719, 1719, Dublin 1719, London 1726.
A letter to Mr Tickell occasioned by the death of Joseph Addison. 1719, 1719.
The revenge: a tragedy. 1721, Dublin 1722, 1726, 1733, London 1735, Dublin 1749, London 1752, Glasgow 1755, Cork [1760], London 1764, 1769, 1775.
The universal passion: satire i. 1725; satire ii, 1725; satire iii, 1725; satire iv, 1725; satire the last, 1726,

Dublin 1726; satire v, 1727, Dublin 1727; satire vi, 1728. Collected as Love of fame, below.

Cynthio. 1727, [1872] (in Poetical works of Milton and Young), Paris 1901 (in W. Thomas, Le poète Young).

A vindication of providence, or a true estimate of human life, in which the passions are consider'd in a new light: a sermon preach'd soon after the late King's death; discourse I. 1728, Dublin 1728, London 1729, Dublin 1729, London 1737, 1747, 1765, 1802.

Love of fame, the universal passion, in seven characteristical satires: the second edition [the 7 pts of Universal passion, above, 'satire the last' becoming 'satire VII', the whole 'corrected and alter'd']. 1728, Dublin 1728, London 1730 ('third edition'), 1731, Dublin 1731, London 1741 ('fourth edition'), 1741 (in Collected works of Young, ed E. Curll, with 'key' to the satires), 1752 ('fifth edition'), 1762 (in Parnassium), 1763 ('sixth edition').

Ocean: an ode occasion'd by his Majesty's late royal encouragement of the sea-service; to which is prefix'd An ode to the King and A discourse on ode. 1728, Dublin 1728.

An apology for princes, or the reverence due to government: a sermon before the House of Commons, January 30 1728 [i.e. 1729]. 1729.

Imperium pelagi: a naval lyrick written in imitation of Pindar's spirit, occasion'd by his Majesty's return September 1729 and the succeeding peace. 1730, Dublin 1730 (as The merchant), London 1771 (as The merchant).

Two epistles [in verse] to Mr Pope concerning the authors of the age. 1730, Dublin 1730, London 1732 (in R. Savage, A collection of pieces in verse).

The foreign address [in verse]: or the best argument for peace; occasioned by the British fleet, and the posture of affairs, when the Parliament met 1734. 1735.

The complaint, or night-thoughts on life, death and immortality: night the first. 1742 (4 edns), 1743 (3 edns), 1744.

The complaint [etc]: night the second. 1742, 1742, 1743, 1744. Nights 1–2 rptd, illustr W. Blake, ed A. M. Butterworth 1911.

The complaint [etc]: night the third. 1742 (3 edns), 1743, 1744.

The complaint [etc]: night the fourth. 1743, 1743, 1744.

The complaint [etc] [nights 1–4]. 1743, 1743, Dublin 1744; ed R. Edwards, illustr W. Blake 1797.

The complaint [etc]: night the fifth. 1743.

The complaint [etc]: night the sixth. 1744.

The complaint [etc] [nights 1–6]. 1743 (for 1744), 1747, 1749.

The complaint [etc]: night the seventh. 1744. Nights 1, 2, 4–7 pirated by J. Wesley, Bristol 1744.

The complaint [etc]: night the eighth. 1745.

The consolation [night the ninth and last] and Some thoughts occasioned by the present juncture. 1745 (for 1746).

The complaint [etc]: volume II [nights 7–9]. 1748, 1749.

The complaint [etc] [nights 1–9]. 1750, 1750, 1751, 1751, 1755, 1756, 1758, 1760, 1767, 1769, 1769, Bristol 1770 (ed J. Wesley, without Night 3); ed J. R. Boyd, New York 1851 (with life); ed C. C. Clarke, Edinburgh 1853 (with life by G. Gilfillan); ed J. Nicholas 1853 (with life by J. Doran).

The brothers: a tragedy. 1753, Dublin 1753, London 1763, Dublin 1764, London 1776 (in New English theatre vol 12), 1776 (in Bell's British theatre vol 14), 1777, 1778.

The centaur not fabulous, in five [6 in 3rd and later edns] letters to a friend on the life in vogue. 1755 (3 edns), 1765.

A sea piece containing the British sailor's exultation and his prayer before engagement, occasioned by the rumour of war. 1755.

An argument drawn from the circumstances of Christ's death for the truth of his religion: a sermon preached before his Majesty at Kensington June 1758. 1758.

Conjectures on original composition in a letter to the author [S. Richardson] of Sir Charles Grandison. 1759, 1759.

Resignation [in 5 pts with A funeral epithalamium]. 1761 (priv ptd), 1762 (in 2 pts and a Postscript to Mrs B[oscawen]), 1762, 1764, 1767.

The beauties of Dr Young's Night thoughts. 1769.

Letters

The correspondence of Samuel Richardson. Ed A. L. Barbauld 6 vols 1804.

Correspondence. Ed H. Pettit, Oxford 1970.

§ 2

Johnson, S. In his Lives of the poets, 1779–81. Life by H. Croft, rev Johnson.

'Eliot, George' (M. A. Evans). Worldliness and otherworldliness: the poet Young. Westminster Rev 67 1857.

Keynes, G. L. Illustrations [30] to Young's Night thoughts by William Blake. Cambridge Mass 1927.

—— Blake's illustrations to Young's Night thoughts. In his Blake studies, 1949.

JOHN GAY
1685–1732

Collections

Poems on several occasions. 2 vols 1720, Dublin 1730, London 1731, 1737, 1745, Glasgow 1751, 1757, London 1767, Glasgow 1770, Edinburgh 1773, London 1775.

Plays; to which is added an account of the life and writings of the author. 1760, 1772.

Poetical dramatic and miscellaneous works, [with] Dr Johnson's biographical and critical preface. 6 vols 1795.

Poetical works: including Polly, The beggar's opera and selections from the other dramatic work. Ed G. C. Faber, Oxford 1926 (OSA).

Poetry and prose. Ed V. A. Dearing 2 vols Oxford 1974.

§ 1

Wine. 1708, 1708 (both anon), 1708 (with Old England's new triumph, not by Gay), 1709; 1926 (facs).

The present state of wit. 1711 (anon); ed J. C. Collins 1903 (in Critical essays: Arber's English garner); ed D. F. Bond, Ann Arbor 1947 (Augustan Reprint Soc).

The mohocks. 1712. Dedication signed W.B. Unacted.

An argument proving that the present mohocks and hawkubites are the Gog and Magog mention'd in the Revelations. 1712. Anon.

The wife of Bath. 1713, 1730 (rev), Vienna 1788. Drury Lane 12 May 1713.

Rural sports. 1713, 1713; ed O. Culbertson, New York 1930.

The fan. 1714, 1714.

The shepherd's week. 1714 (3 edns), 1721, 1728, Dublin 1729, London 1742; ed H. F. B. Brett-Smith, Oxford 1924.

A letter to a lady. 1714, 1714, Dublin 1714.

The what d'ye call it. 1715, 1715, Dublin 1715, London 1716, 1725, 1736, Dublin 1752; ed H. Patu, Paris 1756 (in Choix de petites pièces du théâtre anglais); London 1763, [1778?]. Drury Lane 23 Feb 1715.

Two epistles, one to the Earl of Burlington, the other to a lady. [1715?].

Trivia. [1716], Dublin [1716?], London [1720?], Dublin 1727, London 1730, 1740, 1807; ed J. P. Briscoe 1899; ed W. H. Williams 1922.

Three hours after marriage. 1717, 1757 (in A supplement to the works of Pope), Dublin 1758, 1761 (with key); ed

R. Morton and W. M. Peterson, Painesville Ohio 1961; ed J. H. Smith, Los Angeles 1961 (Augustan Reprint Soc). With Pope and Arbuthnot.

Horace epod iv, imitated by Sir James Baker Kt. [1717?]. Anon.

The poor shepherd. [1720?], [1730?].

Dione. In Poems, 1720, Glasgow 1752, London 1763. Unacted.

A panegyrical epistle to Mr Thomas Snow. 1721, 1721. Anon.

An epistle to her Grace Henrietta Dutchess of Marlborough. 1722.

A poem address'd to the Quidnunc's. 1724. Anon.

The captives. 1724, 1724. Drury Lane 15 Jan 1724.

Blueskin's ballad. 1725 (anon), [1725?].

To a lady on her passion for old china. 1725 (anon), 1925 (facs).

Daphnis and Cloe. [1725?].

Molly Mogg. [1726], [1727?], [1730].

Fables. 1727, 1728, 1729, Dublin 1730, London 1733, Amsterdam 1734, London 1737, 1746, 1753.

The beggar's opera. 1728, 1728, 1729, Dublin 1732, London 1733, 1735, 1737, 1742, 1749, 1754; ed O. Doughty 1922; ed F. W. Bateson 1934; ed H. Höhne, Halle 1959 (with Polly etc); Larchmont NY 1961 (facs of 1729); ed P. Lewis 1973. Lincoln's Inn Fields 29 Jan 1728.

Polly. 1729, [1729], 1729, Dublin 1729, London 1755; ed G. Sarrazin, Weimar 1898; ed O. Doughty 1922. Unacted.

Acis and Galatea. [1732] (anon), 1732, 1740, 1742, 1747, Oxford [1760?]. Lincoln's Inn Fields 26 March 1731.

Achilles. 1733. Lincoln's Inn Fields 10 Feb 1733.

Fables: volume the second. 1738, 1742, nd, 1747.

The distress'd wife. 1743, Dublin 1743, 1750. Covent Garden 5 March 1734.

Fables. 2 vols 1750 (numerous edns before 1800); ed A. Dobson 1884; ed W. H. K. Wright 1889 (with bibliography); ed V. A. Dearing, Los Angeles 1967 (Augustan Reprint Soc).

The rehearsal at Goatham. 1754. Unacted.

Gay's chair, poems never before printed. 1820. Probably spurious.

Some unpublished translations from Ariosto. Ed J. D. Bruce, Brunswick 1910.

Letters

Letters. Ed C. F. Burgess, Oxford 1966.

§ 2

Johnson, S. In his Lives of the English poets, 1779–81.

Melville, L. Life and letters of Gay. 1921.

Empson, W. In his Some versions of pastoral, 1935. On Beggar's opera.

Irving, W. H. Gay: favorite of the wits. Durham NC 1940.

Sutherland, J. R. Polly among the pirates. MLR 37 1942.

—— In Pope and his contemporaries: essays presented to George Sherburn, Oxford 1949.

ALEXANDER POPE
1688–1744

Bibliographies etc

Pope, A. A list of books, papers and verses in which our author was abused; a list of our author's genuine works. In The Dunciad, 1729 etc, Appendixes 2, 7.

Abbott, E. A concordance to the works of Pope. 1875.

Griffith, R. H. Pope: a bibliography. Vol 1, 2 pts Austin 1922–7, London 1962 (no more pbd).

Wise, T. J. A Pope library: a catalogue of plays, poems and prose writings by Pope. 1931. Both with facs of many title-pages.

Tobin, J. E. Pope: a list of critical studies 1895–1944. New York 1945.

Butt, J. [List of autograph manuscripts]. Proc Br Acad 40 1954. See also his Twickenham edn of Poems, below.

Guerinot, J. V. Pamphlet attacks on Pope 1711–44: a descriptive bibliography. 1969.

Bedford, E. G. and R. J. Dilligan. A concordance to the poems of Pope. 2 vols Detroit 1974.

Collections

The works of Mr Alexander Pope. 1717 (3 edns), 1737, 7 vols 1736–41.

Dunciad, 1743, Essay on man, 1743, Essay on criticism, [1743], and Four ethic epistles, 1748 (ptd 1744) were parts of a projected edn by Pope and Warburton.

Warburton, William. The works, with his last corrections, additions and improvements, together with commentaries. 9 vols 1751.

A supplement to the works: containing such poems, letters etc as are omitted in the edition by Dr Warburton; to which is added a key to the letters. 1757.

Sherburn, G. The best of Pope. New York 1929, 1940 (rev).

Ault, N. Prose works. Vol 1, [1711–20], Oxford 1936.

The Twickenham edition of the poems. Ed J. Butt et al 11 vols 1939–69. Vol 1, Pastoral poetry and An essay on criticism, ed E. Audra and A. Williams 1961; vol 2, The rape of the lock and other poems, ed G. Tillotson 1940, 1954 (rev), 1962 (3rd edn, reset); vol 3. i, An essay on man, ed M. Mack 1950; vol 3. ii, Epistles to several persons (Moral essays), ed F. W. Bateson 1951; vol 4, Imitations of Horace etc, ed Butt 1939, 1953 (rev); vol 5, The Dunciad, ed J. R. Sutherland 1943, 1953 (rev); vol 6, Minor poems, ed N. Ault and J. Butt 1954; vols 7–10, Translations of Homer, ed M. Mack et al 1967; Index, 1969. The standard edn of the poems. One vol edn, ed Butt 1963, 1968.

Selected poetry and prose. Ed W. K. Wimsatt, New York 1951, 1958.

Horatian satires and epistles. Ed H. H. Erskine-Hill, Oxford 1964.

Poetical works. Ed H. Davis, Oxford 1966 (OSA), 1978 (with introd by P. Rogers).

§ 1

January and May; The episode of Sarpedon; Pastorals. In Tonson's Poetical Miscellanies: sixth part, 1709 etc. Pastorals also in Miscellany pastorals, Dublin [1714]. Sarpedon rptd in the Iliad, 1717, 1718.

An essay on criticism. 1711, 1711, 1713 (3 edns), Dublin [1713], 1713 (in A select collection of modern poems), London 1714 (in Lintott's Miscellany, below), 1716 (T. Johnson piracy), 1716, 1719, 1722, 1744 (in An essay on man, below, with Warburton's notes); ed A. S. West, Cambridge 1896; ed J. C. Collins 1896; ed F. Ryland 1900; ed R. M. Schmitz, St Louis 1962 (with facs of ms).

The critical specimen. 1711.

Sapho to Phaon. In Tonson's Ovid's epistles, 1712 (8th edn) etc.

Messiah. Spectator no 378; in A collection of divine hymns and poems, 1719 (3rd edn); Lintott's Miscellany, 1720 (3rd edn); Windsor Forest, 1720 (4th edn).

Miscellaneous poems and translations by several hands. 1712, 1714, 2 vols 1720, 1722; Miscellany poems, 1727 (vol 1 sometimes 1726), 1732. Lintott's Miscellany, ed Pope. Edns vary in contents; first printings in each are separately noted.

The first book of Statius his Thebais; Vertumnus and Pomona; To a young lady with the works of Voiture; On silence; To the author of a poem entitled Successio;

Verses design'd to be prefix'd to Mr Lintott's Miscellany; The rape of the locke [in two-canto form]. In Lintott's Miscellany, 1712 (1st edn). The Rape rptd in Windsor Forest, Dublin 1713.

[Contributions to] Spectator nos 406, 452, 457, 532, 16 June–10 Nov 1712. Other attributions in Prose works, above.

[On a fan]. Spectator no 527, 4 Nov 1712.

Windsor-Forest, to the Right Honourable George Lord Lansdown. 1713, 1713, Dublin 1713, London 1714 (in Lintott's Miscellany, 2nd edn), 1716 (in pirated Essay on criticism), 1720; ed R. M. Schmitz, St Louis 1952 (with facs of holograph).

[Contributions to] Guardian nos 4, 11, 40, 61, 78, 91, 92, 132, 173, 16 March–29 Sept 1713. Other attributions in Prose works, above.

Prologue to Cato. Guardian no 33, 18 April 1713; in Cato, 1713 etc.

Ode for Musick [on St Cecilia's Day]. 1713, 1719 (3rd edn), 1722; tr Latin by C. Smart, 1743, 1746.

Proposals for a translation of Homer's Ilias. [1713 or 1714]. No original or reprint known to be extant.

The narrative of Dr Robert Norris, concerning the strange and deplorable frenzy of Mr John Denn—. 1713.

Upon a Tory lady who happen'd to open her floodgates at the tragedy of Cato. Poetical Entertainer no 5 1713.

The Wife of Bath her prologue; Prologue, designed for Mr D—'s last play; The arrival of Ulysses in Ithaca. In Steele's Poetical Miscellanies, 1714, 1714 etc. Wife of Bath her prologue rptd in Ogle, Canterbury tales of Chaucer moderniz'd, 1741. Arrival of Ulysses rptd in Odyssey, 1725.

The rape of the lock, in five canto's. 1714 (3 edns), Dublin 1714 (in Windsor Forest, 1713), 1715, 1716 (T. Johnson piracy), 1718, 1720 (in Lintott's Miscellany, 3rd edn), 1723, Dublin 1732 (in Swift-Pope Miscellanies), 1896 (9 drawings by A. Beardsley); ed A. S. West, Cambridge 1896; ed G. Tillotson 1941; ed J. S. Cunningham 1966; The rape observ'd, ed C. Tracy, Toronto 1974 (illustr).

Epigram upon two or three; Upon a girl of seven years old. In some copies of Lintott's Miscellany, 1714 (2nd edn).

The temple of fame: a vision. 1715, 1715, 1716 (in pirated Essay on criticism), 1727 (in Lintott's Miscellany, 5th edn).

A key to the lock: or a treatise proving beyond all contradiction the dangerous tendency of a late poem entitled the Rape of the lock to government and religion, by Esdras Barnivelt, apoth. 1715, 1715 (with commendatory verses added), 1718, 1723.

The dignity, use and abuse of glass-bottles. 1715, 1752 (as An ingenious and learned discourse, 5th edn).

The Iliad of Homer. Folio and 4°: Vol 1, 1715; vol 2, 1716; vol 3, 1717; vol 4, 1718; vols 5–6, 1720. 12° reprints: 1718–21 (T. Johnson piracy), 1720, 1720–1 (2nd edn), 1732 (3rd edn), 1736 (4th edn), 1743; ed G. Wakefield 5 vols 1806; ed R. A. Brower and W. H. Bond, New York 1965.

To Mr Jervas. In The art of painting, by C. A. Du Fresnoy, 1716 (2nd edn).

A full and true account of a horrid and barbarous revenge by poison on the body of Mr Edmund Curll, bookseller. [1716].

To the ingenious Mr Moore, author of the celebrated worm-powder. 1716 (3 edns).

A further account of the most deplorable condition of Mr Edmund Curll, bookseller, since his being poison'd on the 28th of March. 1716.

A Roman Catholick version of the first Psalm. 1716.

God's revenge against punning. 1716.

Prologue. In Three hours after marriage, 1717 etc. Pope and Arbuthnot collaborated with Gay in the play.

The Court ballad. [1717], [1717].

Epigrams, occasioned by an invitation to Court. In The parson's daughter, 1717.

The preface; A discourse on pastoral poetry; The fable of

Dryope; Two chorus's to the tragedy of Brutus; Verses to the memory of an unfortunate lady; To the same [a young lady] on her leaving the town after the Coronation; Epitaph [on Trumbull]; Epilogue to Jane Shore; Occasion'd by some verses of his Grace the Duke of Buckingham; Eloisa to Abelard. In Works [vol 1], 1717 etc. Eloisa to Abelard rptd (with Verses to the memory of an unfortunate lady and 6 poems by others), 1720 (2nd edn), in Lintott's Miscellany, 1720 (3rd edn); Eloisa, ed J. E. Wellington, Gainesville 1965.

Ode on solitude; Of a lady singing to her lute; Verses in imitation of Waller (5); Weeping; Verses in imitation of Cowley (2); On the statue of Cleopatra; Psalm xci; Stanzas from the French of Malherbe; From Boetius De cons philos; To Belinda on the Rape of the lock; Imitation of Martial; Written over a study. In Poems on several occasions, 1717, 1735 (Pope's Own Miscellany, ed N. Ault). Ed Pope.

The plot discover'd: or a clue to the comedy of the Non-juror. 1718 (3 edns).

Epitaph on John Hewett and Sarah Drew. White-hall Evening Post no 3, 20–3 Sept 1718.

What is prudery. Weekly Packet 11–18 Oct 1718.

The prayer of Brutus. In A. Thompson, The British history, 1718.

Mr Alexander Pope. In Giles Jacob, Historical account, 1720 etc.

Duke upon Duke. 1720, [1720] (as An excellent old ballad, called Pride will have a fall), [1720], 1723.

Epitaph design'd for Mr Rowe. In Lintott's Miscellany, 1720 (3rd edn).

Verses occasioned by Mr Addison's treatise of medals. In Works [vol 1], 1720.

Verses sent to Mrs T.B. with his Works; In behalf of Mr Southerne. In The grove, 1721.

To the Right Honourable Robert Earl of Oxford. In T. Parnell, Poems, 1722. Ed Pope.

If mean scorn Gil—n draws' [the Atticus satire upon Addison]. St James's Jnl no 34, 15 Dec 1722.

The works of John Sheffield, Duke of Buckingham. 2 vols 1723, 1724, 1726, 1729, 1740 etc. Ed Pope.

[On Simon Harcourt]. London Jnl 17 Oct 1724.

[To Mrs M. B. on her birthday]. Br Jnl 14 Nov 1724.

[Proposals for the Odyssey; Proposals for the Shakespear. No known copies].

The works of Shakespear in six volumes collated and corrected by Mr Pope. 1725 (separate title-leaves to vols are dated 1723), 1728, 1747 (re-edited by Warburton).

The Odyssey of Homer. [Folio, 4°, 12°]. Vols 1–3, 1725; vols 4–5, 1726; G. Wakefield 4 vols 1806.

Rondeau. Mist's Weekly Jnl 26 Feb 1726.

Letters to Henry Cromwell; Argus; Verses occasioned by Mr Durfy's adding an etc at the end of his name; An epistle to Henry Cromwell; The translator [epigram occasioned by Ozell's translation of Boileau's Lutrin]; Three gentle shepherds; Epigram in a maid of honor's prayerbook. In Curll's Miscellanea, 2 vols 1727.

Epitaph designed for Mr Dryden's monument. In Lintott's Miscellany, 1727 (5th edn).

The discovery. 1727, 1727, 1727 (as The 'Squire turn'd ferret).

A receipt to make a soop. [1727].

Epitaph on James Craggs. In Some memoirs of the life of Lewis Maximilian Mahomet, 1727.

'Tis thus that vanity'. 6 lines in J. M. Smyth, Rival modes, 1727, next ptd in the version of To Mrs M. B. on her birthday in the Swift-Pope miscellanies, 1727 ('last' vol).

Miscellanies in prose and verse. Vols 1–2, 1727; vol 'the last', 1727; vol 3, 1732. The Swift-Pope miscellanies, pbd by Motte. Apparently Pope edited only 4 vols, but the ser was often rptd and was ultimately extended to 11 vols. See under Swift, col 572, below. First pbns in the various vols are separately noted.

Preface; Memoirs of P.P. clerk of this parish; Stradling

versus Stiles; Thoughts on various subjects. In the Swift-Pope miscellanies vols 1–2, 1727.

To Quinbus Flestrin; The lamentation of Glumdalclitch; To Mr Lemuel Gulliver; Mary Gulliver to Captain Gulliver; The words of the King of Brobdingnag. In Swift, Travels by Lemuel Gulliver vol 1, 1727 (2nd edn).

To Kneller on his painting statues of Apollo. In Steele's miscellanies, 1727 (2nd edn).

Peri bathous: or the art of sinking in poetry; fragments of Alcander; The happy life of a country parson; A tale of Chaucer; The alley; Sandys's ghost; Umbra; Macer; Sylvia; Artimesia; Phryne; The capon's tale; The balance of Europe. In the Swift-Pope miscellanies, 1727 ('last' vol); Peri bathous, ed E. L. Steeves, New York 1952 (as The art of sinking in poetry) (facs).

Rapin of Gardens in four books, translated by James Gardiner. 1728 (3rd edn). Bks 1–2 corrected by Pope for this edn.

The Dunciad: an heroic poem in three books. 'Dublin' (actually London), 1728, 1728, 1728 ('Gold chains' edn, pirated), 1728 (2nd edn), 1728 (2nd edn), 1728 (3rd edn), 1728 (3rd edn), Dublin 1728, Oxford 1928 (type facs of larger London 8º). A key, pbd by Curll, ran through 3 edns in 1728; another 4 pp. 12º Key, with a dropped heading but no title-page, may have been prepared by Pope himself.

The Dunciad variorum. 1729 (3 edns), 1729 (8º as A Dob; a Curll piracy), 1729 (2nd edn), Dublin 1729, 1729, London [1735], (sheets of the large paper folio Works, vol 2, issued separately with a half-title leaf but without a title-page leaf), [1735], 1736; Princeton, 1929 (facs of 1729 4º). The document for the sale of the copyright from the noble lords to Gilliver, dated 16 Oct 1729, is preserved in BM as Egerton ms 1951, fol 6.

The new Dunciad. 1742 (3 edns; the 8º may be a piracy), 1742, 1742 (Hubbard piracies); Dublin 1742, 1742, London 1742 (The Dunciad, book the fourth, 2nd edn).

The Dunciad in four books. 1743, Dublin 1743, London 1749.

The bookseller to the reader; Table of contents; Letters to Wycherley; additions to Wycherley's poems. In Posthumous works of William Wycherley esq in prose and verse vol 2, 1729. Ed Pope. Suppressed?; unsold sheets used in Letters, 1735.

Prologue. In James Thomson, The tragedy of Sophonisba, 1730 etc. In part attributed to Pope by Johnson.

Kneller, by heaven. St James's Evening Post 21 April 1730. An epitaph.

When other ladies [epigram]; Adriani morientis ad animam translated [and] imitated; Epitaph on Mrs Corbet; Epitaph on Digby. In D. Lewis, Miscellaneous poems, 1730.

[Epigrams] On Mr M—re's going to law; A gold watch [on J.M.S. gent]; Here lyes what had [epitaph on James Moore Smyth]; On the candidates for the laurel; An epigram [on the same]; Epigram [on Dennis]; Occasion'd by seeing some sheets of Dr B—tl—y's edition of Milton's Paradise lost. Grub-street Jnl nos 25–6, 29, 45–6, 78, 100, 25 June 1730–2 Dec 1731.

Epitaph intended for Sir Isaac Newton. Present State of the Republick of Letters June 1730.

Epitaph on Mr Elijah Fenton. Daily Post-boy 22 Oct 1730.

Canticle. Grub-street Jnl no 46, 19 Nov 1730. Pope may be the author of the whole article.

Epitaph on General Henry Withers. Grub-street Jnl no 50, 17 Dec 1730.

To prove himself [on J.M.S. gent.] Evening Post 26–8 Aug 1731.

An epistle to the Right Honourable Richard Earl of Burlington. 1731, 1731, 1732 (as Of taste), 1731 (2nd edn), 1732 (in A miscellany on taste), 1732 (as Of false taste, 3rd edn) (3 edns), Dublin 1732, 1732, 1733 (in Stowe, The gardens of Viscount Cobham).

To J. Gay esq. Daily Post-boy 22 Dec 1731. A letter; see Correspondence 3, p. 254.

Horace, Satyr 4, lib 1, paraphrased. London Evening Post 22–5 Jan 1732.

To the Earl of Middlesex [dedication]; Postscript. In Richard Savage, A collection of pieces on occasion of the Dunciad, 1732.

A strange but true relation how Edmund Curll; An essay of the origine of sciences; Here Francis Ch—s lies; You beat your pate; Well then, poor, G—; On the toasts of the Kit-Cat Club; To a lady with the Temple of Fame; On the Countess of B—; On a certain lady at Court; Epitaph [Of by-words]; Epigram from the French; Epigram [Peter complains]; Verses to be placed under the picture of England's arch-poet. In the Swift-Pope Miscellanies vol 3, 1732.

Of the use of riches, An epistle to Bathurst. 1732, 1733, 1733 (2nd edn), 1733 (2nd edn), Dublin 1733, 1733; ed E. R. Wasserman, Baltimore 1960.

The first satire of the second book of Horace, imitated. 1733, 1733, Dublin 1733, London 1734 (with Second satire) (3 or 4 edns).

An essay on man: part i. [1733] (5, 6 or 7 edns; Griffith's books 294–5 may be the same; also 303 and 305), [1733] (Epistle I, corrected by the author), [1733], Dublin [1733], 1734, London 1735.

An essay on man: epistle ii. [1733] (4 edns), Dublin [1733], [1733].

An essay on man: epistle iii. [1733] (4 edns), Dublin [1733] (3 edns).

An essay on man: epistle iv. [1734], [1734], Dublin 1734, 1734.

An essay on man: being the first book of ethic epistles [4 epistles as one book]. 1734, 1734, Dublin 1734, [1735], London 1736 (for Witford; 2 7th edns, piracies), 1744 (with Warburton's notes); ed M. Pattison 1869; Oxford [1871], 1932; ed M. Mack 1962 (with facs of ms).

Epitaph on Mr Gay. GM June 1733.

The impertinent [Donne, Satire 4]. 1733, 1737, 1737, Dublin 1737.

An epistle to the Right Honourable Richard Lord Visct Cobham [Of the knowledge and characters of men]. 1733, 1734, Dublin 1734.

The second satire. In The first satire of the second book of Horace, imitated, to which is added the second satire of the same book, 1734 (5 edns), 1735.

Sober advice from Horace. [1734], 1735, 1735, Dublin 1737, London [1738] (reissue of 1735 folio sheets as A sermon against adultery).

An epistle to Dr Arbuthnot. 1734, 1734, Dublin 1735, Oxford 1926 (facs); ed J. Butt 1954. Title later changed to Prologue to the satires.

An essay on reason, by Walter Harte. 1735. Pope contributed lines to this poem.

Of the characters of women. 1735, 1735, Dublin 1735, Oxford 1924 (facs). Title changed in Works to Epistle ii: to a lady.

The author to the reader; Advertisement; The second satire of Dr John Donne; On the Earl of Dorset; On Mr Fenton; By the author a declaration. In Works vol 2, 1735. The original version of Second satire of Dr John Donne was first ptd from the ms in vol 4 of the Twickenham edn of the Poems, 1939. The Epitaph for Atterbury was cancelled before pbn and first ptd by Warburton in 1751.

Wrote by Mr P. in a volume of Evelyn on Coins. GM May 1735.

Letters of Mr Pope and several eminent persons. 1735 (21 or more edns, issues or varieties, often in 2-vol sets; rptd as Mr Pope's literary correspondence, annotated and continued by E. Curll; vols 1–3, 1735; vol 4, 1736; vol 5, 1737 (5 includes New letters of Mr Pope, also issued separately and rptd Dublin 1737 as Letters from Alexander Pope, and additional letters from Pope's authorized edn 1737); see Works in prose vol i.

A narrative of the method by which the private letters of Mr Pope have been procured and published by Edmund Curll. [1735], 1735 (in all 12° edns of Letters).

Epistle ii: to James Craggs. In 8° edn of Works vol 2, 1735.

Advertisement; The garden. In 8° edn of Works vol 3, 1736.

O fairest pattern [epitaph on John Knight]. Daily Gazetteer 17 July 1736.

To the Earl of Burlington. Grub-Street Jnl no 352, Sept 1736.

Bounce to Fop. 1736, Dublin 1736.

[Conclusion to A fit of the spleen]. White-hall Evening Post 19–22 March 1737. Later used as last 8 lines of To Mr Gay, first pbd in Dallaway's edn of Lady Mary Wortley Montagu's Works, 1803.

Horace his Ode to Venus lib iv, Ode i, Imitated, 1737, 1737.

The second epistle of the second book of Horace imitated. 1737 (3 edns), Dublin 1737, 1737.

The first epistle of the second book of Horace imitated. 1737 (3 edns), Dublin 1737.

The second book of the epistles of Horace, imitated. 1737. Reissues of the first edn of First epistle and 2nd edn of Second epistle.

The sixth epistle of the first book of Horace imitated. 1738, 1738, Dublin 1738.

An imitation of the sixth satire of the second book of Horace. 1738. By Swift and Pope; Swift's part rptd from Swift-Pope Miscellanies, 1727 ('last' vol).

The first epistle of the first book of Horace imitated. 1738, 1738, Dublin 1738.

One thousand seven hundred and thirty eight [Epilogue to the Satires, Dialogue i]. [1738], 1738, 1738, Dublin 1738.

The universal prayer. 1738, 1738.

One thousand seven hundred and thirty eight. Dialogue ii [Epilogue to the Satires]. 1738, 1738, Dublin 1738.

The seventh epistle of the first book imitated; On Edmund Duke of Buckingham; For one who would not be buried in Westminster ['Heroes and Kings']; Epigram on one who made long epitaphs; Engraved on the collar of a dog; Cloe; a character. In Works vol 2 pt 2, 1738.

Fair Mirror of foul times. In John Milton, Works vol 1, 1738.

May these put money in your purse. In J. Bancks, Miscellaneous works vol 2, 1738.

On lying in the Earl of Rochester's bed. London Mag Aug 1739.

On the benefactions in the late frost. GM March 1740.

Selecta poemata Italorum qui latine scripserunt. 2 vols 1740.

Epigram by Mr Pope, who had cut down three walnut trees. Publick Register no 1, 3 Jan 1741.

Under this marble [epitaph]; Verbatim from Boileau. Publick Register no 2, 10 Jan 1741.

A prologue by Mr Pope to a play for Mr Dennis's benefit. Publick Register no 3, 17 Jan 1741.

On the grotto at Twick'nham. GM Jan 1741. Latin and Greek trns by R. Dodsley and W.H., 1743.

The booksellers to the reader; Letters; Memoirs of Scriblerus. In Works in prose vol 2 1741; Dublin 1741 (Memoirs of Scriblerus alone). Memoirs of Scriblerus also in Aitken's edn of Arbuthnot's Works, 1892; in Eddy's edn of Swift's Satires and personal writings, Oxford 1932; and alone, ed C. Kerby-Miller, New Haven 1950.

To Lady Winchilsea. In A general dictionary vol 10, p. 180, 1741. Pope also revised the article on Gay in the Dictionary.

[Epigram on Shakespeare's monument]. In frontispiece to Shakespeare, Poems on several occasions, sold by Murden, Newton et al [1741?].

The idea of a patriot King. [1741?]. Pope edited and had Bolingbroke's pamphlet ptd, but never pbd it. The edn was burned after Pope's death. One copy is in BM, another in the Univ of Texas Lib.

Tom Southerne's birth-day dinner. GM Feb 1742.

Epigram [on Bishop Hough]. In the Swift-Pope miscellanies vol 4, 1742 (4th edn).

Epigram: on Cibber's declaration that he will have the last word with Mr Pope. In The summer miscellany, 1742.

A blast upon bays; or a new lick at the Laureate. 1742.

Epitaph on Mr Rowe. Common Sense 25 June 1743.

Posthumously pbd letters, some of which contain scraps of verse, are not noted.

The last will and testament. 1744.

Verses upon the late D—ss of M—. 1746, 1746. First pbn of lines added to Of the character of women in Four ethic epistles, 1738 (ptd 1744).

The character of Katharine, late Duchess of Buckinghamshire and Normanby, 1746.

Polyphemus and Acis. London Mag Dec 1749.

On seeing the ladies at Crux-Euston; Inscription on a grotto. In The student, Oxford 1750.

On receiving a Standish and two pens; Part of the ninth ode of the fourth book; On Dr Francis Atterbury; A letter to a noble lord. In Warburton's edn of Works, 1751, vol 4, p. 339; vol 6, pp. 37, 99; vol 8, p. 253.

[Plan of an epic poem]. In Ruffhead's Life, 1769, pp. 316 f.

To Mr C. Edinburgh Mag July 1774.

A farewell to London. St James's Chron 14–16 Sept 1775.

Lines suppressed at the end of the Epistle [to a young lady] on leaving the town. St James's Chron 10–12 Aug 1775.

A dialogue [Since my old friend]; Lord Coningsby's epitaph. St James's Chron 21–23 Sept 1775.

Couplets on wit. In Additions to the works, 1776.

A prayer of St Francis Xavier. GM Oct 1791.

On Queen Caroline's death-bed; On a picture of Queen Caroline; 1740: a poem. In Warton's edn of Works, 1797.

Lady M. W. Montagu's portrait. In Dallaway's edn of Lady Mary's Works, 1803.

Lines on Swift's ancestors. In Scott's edn of Swift's Works vol 1, 1814.

To the Right Honourable the Earl of Oxford upon a piece of news. GM July 1809.

Let Clarke make half his life. In Singer's edn of Spence's Anecdotes, 1820.

Inscription on a punch-bowl. In Supplemental volume, 1825.

A hymn written in Windsor Forest. In A. Dyce's Aldine edn of Poetical works, 1831.

Epitaph on Lady Kneller. In T. Hanmer's Correspondence, 1838.

Lines to Lord Bathurst. In J. Mitford's edn of Gray's Correspondence with Rev Norton Nicholls, 1843.

A paraphrase on Thomas à Kempis; Epitaph on John Lord Caryll. Athenaeum 15 July 1854.

Mss notes on Tickell's Homer. Fraser's Mag Aug 1860.

[Epigram on Shakespeare's monument]. In The autobiography of Mary Granville, Mrs Delaney vol 2, 1861.

A memorial list of departed relations and friends; [A character of Marlborough]; O all-accomplished Caesar. In Elwin and Courthope's edn of Works vol 1, 1871, 3, 1881 (facs), 8 p. 320, n. 2, 1872.

Epigrams occasioned by Cibber's verses in praise of Nash. In F. D. Senior, Life and times of Colley Cibber, 1928.

In the character of a legislator [fragment of Brutus]. In F. Brie, Pope's Brutus, Anglia 63 1939. Better transcript in H.-J. Zimmerman, Bemerkungen zum Manuscript und Text von Popes Brutus, Archiv 199 1963.

Presentation verses to Nathaniel Pigott. In G. Sherburn, An accident in 1726, Harvard Lib Bull 2 1948.

A master key to Popery. Ed J. Butt in Pope and his contemporaries: essays presented to George Sherburn, Oxford 1949.

Inscription, Martha Blount—A: P:; The six maidens. In N. Ault, New light on Pope, 1949.

[Lines on the monument to John Oliver and his wife]. In G. C. F. Mead, A Pope inscription, TLS 7 Oct 1949.

To Ld Hervey and Lady Mary Wortley. In Earl of Ilchester, Lord Hervey and his friends, 1950.

To Eustace Budgell esq; Lines on Ministers. In the Twickenham edn of Poems vol 6, 1954, which includes also a list of rejected attributions.

Letters

Correspondence. Ed G. Sherburn 5 vols Oxford 1956.

Sherburn, G. Letters of Pope, chiefly to Sir William Trumbull. RES new ser 9 1958.

Rawson, C. J. Some unpublished letters of Pope and Gay. RES new ser 10 1959.

Letters. Ed J. Butt, Oxford 1960 (WC).

§ 2

For early criticism see Pope: the critical heritage, *ed J. Barnard 1973.*

Addison, Joseph. Spectator no 253, 20 Dec 1711 (on the Essay on criticism); no 523, 30 Oct 1712.

Theobald, Lewis. The Odyssey of Homer. Bk I, 1716.

—— Shakespeare restored. 1726.

Spence, Joseph. An essay on Pope's Odyssey. 2 pts Oxford 1726–7, 1 vol 1737, 1747.

—— Anecdotes, observations and characters of books and men collected from the conversations of Mr Pope and other eminent persons of his time. Ed S. W. Singer 1820; ed E. Malone 1820; ed J. M. Osborn 2 vols Oxford 1966.

Voltaire, F. A. de. In his Letters concerning the English nation, 1733, 1741. Letter no 22 on Pope.

Warburton, William. Letters. In The works of the learned vol 4, Dec 1738 pp. 425 f.; vol 5, Jan–April 1739, pp. 56, 89, 159, 330; rptd in A vindication of Mr Pope's Essay on man from the misrepresentations of Mr de Crousaz in six letters, 1740, 1740; also in A critical and philosophical commentary on Mr Pope's Essay on man, 1742.

—— A seventh letter, which finishes the Vindication. 1740.

Johnson, Samuel. An essay on epitaphs. GM Dec 1740; rptd in Universal Visiter & Memorialist 1756, [1757]; Idler, 1767 (3rd edn); Life of Pope, 1781.

Cibber, Colley. An apology for the life of Mr Colley Cibber, comedian. 1740, 1740, 2 vols 1750, 1756; ed R. W. Lowe 2 vols 1888.

—— A letter from Mr Cibber to Mr Pope. 1742, 1742, 1742 (a pirated edn), Dublin 1742, Glasgow [1743?], London 1768, 1777.

—— A second letter from Mr Cibber to Mr Pope. 1743.

Warton, Joseph. An essay on the writings and genius of Mr Pope. 1756.

Ruffhead, Owen. The life of Alexander Pope from original manuscripts, with a critical essay. 1769. Ruffhead had the help of Warburton.

Wordsworth, William. Preface. In Lyrical ballads, 1800 (2nd edn) etc.

Hazlitt, William. In his Lectures on the English poets, 1818.

—— Pope, Lord Byron and Mr Bowles. London Mag June 1821.

De Quincey, Thomas. Pope. In Encyclopaedia britannica (7th edn); The poetry of Pope; Lord Carlisle on Pope. All in Collected works vols 4, 11, ed D. Masson 1888–90.

Stephen, L. Pope as a moralist. Cornhill Mag Nov 1873; rptd in his Hours in a library vol 1, 1874.

—— Alexander Pope. 1880 (EML).

Sherburn, G. Notes on the canon of Pope's works 1714–20. In J. M. Manly anniversary studies, Chicago 1923.

—— The early career of Pope 1688–1727. Oxford 1934.

—— Pope's letters and the Harleian Library. ELH 7 1940.

—— The Dunciad bk IV. (1944); rptd in Essential articles for the study of Pope, ed M. Mack, Hamden Conn 1964, 1968 (enlarged).

—— Pope at work. In Essays on the eighteenth century presented to David Nichol Smith, Oxford 1945.

—— Pope and 'the great shew of nature'. In The seventeenth century: studies by R. F. Jones et al, Stanford 1951.

Strachey, L. Pope. Cambridge 1925 (Stephen lecture); rptd; in his Characters and commentaries, 1933.

—— Pope, Addison, Steele and Swift. In his Characters and commentaries, 1933.

Sitwell, E. Alexander Pope. 1930.

Leavis, F. R. Pope. Scrutiny 2 1934; rptd in his Revaluation, 1935; in Essential articles for the study of Pope, ed M. Mack, Hamden Conn 1964, 1968 (enlarged).

—— The Dunciad. In his Common pursuit, 1952.

Williams, C. Reasoning but to err: the Essay on man. In his Reason and beauty in the poetic mind, Oxford 1933.

Fletcher, E. G. Belinda's game of ombre. SE 1935.

Sutherland, J. R. Pope or Arbuthnot? TLS 22 Nov 1935. On authorship of Annus mirabilis.

—— The Dunciad of 1729. MLR 31 1936.

—— Wordsworth and Pope. Proc Br Acad 30 1944.

—— The dull duty of an editor. RES 21 1945; rptd in Essential articles for the study of Pope, ed M. Mack, Hamden Conn 1964, 1968 (enlarged).

Butt, J. Pope's taste in Shakespeare. 1936 (Shakespeare Assoc Lecture).

—— The inspiration of Pope's poetry. In Essays on the eighteenth century presented to David Nichol Smith, Oxford 1945.

—— Pope's poetical manuscripts. Proc Br Acad 40 1954; rptd in Essential articles for the study of Pope, ed M. Mack, Hamden Conn 1964, 1968 (enlarged).

—— Pope: the man and the poet. In Of books and human-kind: essays and poems presented to Bonamy Dobrée, 1964.

Tillotson, G. Lady Mary Wortley Montagu and Pope's Elegy to the memory of an unfortunate lady. RES 12 1936.

—— On the poetry of Pope. Oxford 1938, 1950 (rev).

—— In his Essays in criticism and research, Cambridge 1942.

—— The moral poetry of Pope. Newcastle 1946.

—— Pope's epistle to Harley. In Pope and his contemporaries: essays presented to George Sherburn, Oxford 1949; rptd in his Augustan studies, 1961.

—— Pope and human nature. Oxford 1958.

Auden, W. H. In Anne to Victoria, ed B. Dobrée 1937; rptd in Essential articles for the study of Pope, ed M. Mack, Hamden Conn 1964, 1968 (enlarged).

Root, R. K. The poetical career of Pope. Princeton 1938.

Wilson Knight, G. The vital flame: an essay on Pope. In his Burning oracle, 1939.

—— Laureate of peace. 1955, 1965 (as The poetry of Pope).

Mack, M. The first printing of the letters of Pope and Swift. Library 4th ser 19 1939.

—— Pope's Horatian poems: problems of bibliography and text. MP 41 1943.

—— Letters of Pope to Atterbury. RES 21 1945.

—— Wit and poetry and Pope: his imagery. In Pope and his contemporaries: essays presented to George Sherburn, Oxford 1949.

—— The Muse of satire. Yale Rev 41 1951; rptd in Studies in literature of the Augustan age: essays collected in honor of A. E. Case, Ann Arbor 1952.

—— 'The shadowy cave': some speculations on a Twickenham grotto. In Restoration and eighteenth-century literature: essays in honor of A. D. McKillop, Chicago 1963.

—— (ed). Essential articles for the study of Pope. Hamden Conn 1964, 1968 (enlarged).

—— A poet in his landscape: Pope at Twickenham. In From sensibility to romanticism: essays presented to F. A. Pottle, New York 1965.

—— Secretum iter: some uses of retirement literature in the poetry of Pope. In Aspects of the eighteenth century, ed E. R. Wasserman, Baltimore 1965.

—— The garden and the city. Toronto 1969.

Quennell, P. C. Pope: the education of a genius. 1968.

Hooker, E. N. Pope and Dennis. ELH 7 1940.

—— Pope on wit: the Essay on criticism. Hudson Rev 2 1950; rptd in The seventeenth century: studies by R. F. Jones et al, Stanford 1951.

Brooks, C. The case of Miss Arabella Fermor. Sewanee Rev 51 1943; rptd in his Well wrought urn, New York [1947], and in Essential articles for the study of Pope, ed M. Mack, Hamden Conn 1964, 1968 (enlarged).

Bond, D. F. Pope's contributions to the Spectator. MLQ 5 1944.

—— The importance of Pope's letters. MP 56 1958; rptd in Essential articles for the study of Pope, ed M. Mack, Hamden Conn 1964, 1968 (enlarged).

Monk, S. H. A grace beyond the reach of art. JHI 5 1944; rptd in Essential articles for the study of Pope, ed M. Mack, Hamden Conn 1964, 1968 (enlarged).

Wimsatt, W. K. One relation of rhyme to reason. MLQ 5 1944; rptd in Studies in the literature of the Augustan age: essays collected in honor of A. E. Case, Ann Arbor 1952, and in Essential articles for the study of Pope, ed M. Mack, Hamden Conn 1964, 1968 (enlarged).

—— Rhetoric and poems: the example of Pope. Eng Inst Essays 1949.

—— The game of ombre in the Rape of the lock. RES new ser 2 1950.

—— 'Amicitiae causa': a birthday present from Curll to Pope. In Restoration and 18th-century literature: essays in honor of A. D. McKillop, Chicago 1963.

—— An image of Pope. In From sensibility to romanticism: essays presented to F. A. Pottle, New York 1965.

—— The portraits of Pope. New Haven 1965.

Ault, N. New light on Pope. 1949. Pope and Addison rptd in Essential articles for the study of Pope, ed M. Mack, Hamden Conn 1964, 1968 (enlarged).

Empson, W. Wit in the Essay on criticism. Hudson Rev 2 1950; rptd in his Structure of complex words, 1951, and in Essential articles for the study of Pope, ed M. Mack, Hamden Conn 1964, 1968 (enlarged).

Jack, I. Pope and the weighty bullion of Dr Donne's satires. PMLA 66 1951; rptd in Essential articles for the study of Pope, ed M. Mack, Hamden Conn 1964, 1968 (enlarged).

—— A complex mock-heroic: the Rape of the lock; Studies on the moral essays; Imitations of Horace; The Dunciad. In his Augustan satire: intention and idiom, Oxford 1952.

—— Pope. 1954 (Br Council pamphlet), 1962 (rev).

Brower, R. A. An allusion to Europe: Dryden and poetic tradition. ELH 19 1952; rptd in Essential articles for the study of Pope, ed M. Mack, Hamden Conn 1964, 1968 (enlarged).

—— Pope: the poetry of allusion. Oxford 1959.

—— Dryden and the 'invention' of Pope. In Restoration and 18th-century literature: essays in honor of A. D. McKillop, Chicago 1963.

Williams, A. L. Pope's Dunciad: a study of its meaning. Baton Rouge 1955.

—— Submerged metaphor in Pope. EC 9 1959.

—— The 'fall' of China and the Rape of the lock. PQ 41 1962; rptd in Essential articles for the study of Pope, ed M. Mack, Hamden Conn 1964, 1968 (enlarged).

—— Pope and Horace: the second epistle of the second book. In Restoration and 18th-century literature: essays in honor of A. D. McKillop, Chicago 1963.

—— Pope's 'knack' at versifying. In All these to teach: essays in honor of C. A. Robertson, Gainesville 1967.

Wasserman, E. R. Pope: Windsor Forest. In his Subtler language, Baltimore 1959.

—— Pope's Epistle to Bathurst: a critical reading with an edition of the mss. Baltimore 1960.

—— Pope's Ode for musick. ELH 28 1961; rptd in Essential articles for the study of Pope, ed M. Mack, Hamden Conn 1964, 1968 (enlarged).

Cunningham, J. S. Pope: the Rape of the lock. 1961.

Erskine-Hill, H. H. The 'new world' of Pope's Dunciad. Renaissance & Modern Stud 6 1962; rptd in Essential articles for the study of Pope, ed M. Mack, Hamden Conn 1964, 1968 (enlarged).

—— The medal against time: Pope's Epistle to Addison. Jnl of Warburg & Courtauld Inst 28 1965.

—— Pope: the Dunciad. 1972.

—— The social milieu of Pope. New Haven 1975.

Dixon, P. The world of Pope's satires: an introduction to the Epistles and Imitations of Horace. 1968.

—— (ed). Alexander Pope. 1972.

Rogers, P. An introduction to Pope. 1975.

Leranbaum, M. Pope's Magnum opus 1729-44. Oxford 1977.

JAMES THOMSON
1700-48
Collections

Works. 1736 (2nd vol of Seasons, 1730, 4°), 2 vols 1738, 1744 (rev), 3 vols 1749.

Works. [Ed Lyttelton] 4 vols 1750, 1752, 1756, 1757, 2 vols 1762 (with Murdoch's life and Collins's ode).

Complete poetical works. Ed J. L. Robertson, Oxford 1908, 1951.

The seasons and the Castle of Indolence. Ed J. Sambrook, Oxford 1972.

§ 1

The Edinburgh miscellany. Edinburgh 1720. Contains 3 poems by Thomson.

Winter. 1726 (March, 405 lines), 1726 (June, rev, adding 58 lines), 1726, 1726, Dublin 1726, London 1728, 1730 (787 lines), Dublin 1730, London 1734; ed W. Willis 1900; Oxford 1929 (type facs of 1st edn). In Seasons 1746, below, Winter is 1069 lines.

Summer. 1727 (1146 lines), Dublin 1727, London 1728, 1730 (1206 lines), Dublin 1730, London 1735, Dublin 1740. In Seasons 1746, below, Summer is 1805 lines.

A poem sacred to the memory of Sir Isaac Newton. 1727 (3 edns), Dublin 1727, London 1730; tr Italian, 1760.

Spring. 1728 (1082 lines), Dublin 1728, London 1729, 1731 ('second edn', 1087 lines), 1734, Dublin 1740. In Seasons 1746, below, Spring is 1176 lines.

Britannia. 1729, 1730 ('corrected'), 1730, 1925 (facs). Also rptd with the 1738 trn (by Thomson?) of Milton, Scriptum domini protectoris contra Hispanos, 1655.

A poem to the memory of Mr Congreve. 1729 (2 issues, anon); ed P. Cunningham 1843 (Percy Soc). Ascribed to Thomson by H. F. Cary.

Miscellaneous poems by several hands. Ed J. Ralph 1729. Contains 4 poems by Thomson.

The tragedy of Sophonisba. 1730 (3 issues), Dublin 1730. Performed Drury Lane 28 Feb 1730.

The seasons. 1730 (4°, 4464 lines), 1730 (8°, adding 6 lines to Winter), 1744 (5531 lines, Summer and Winter especially rev), 1744, 1746 (rev, adding 10 lines), 1752, 1758, Dublin 1758, London 1761, Edinburgh 1761, London 1761, 1764, 1766, 1767, 1768, Glasgow 1769; ed G. Wright [1770]; 1773, Dublin 1773, London 1774 (with Murdoch's life from Works 1762), Edinburgh 1774, London 1776, 1779 (with J. Aikin's Essay), Paris 1780; ed J. J. C. Timaeus, Hamburg 1791; ed R. Heron, Perth 1793; ed P. Stockdale 1793 (with glossary); ed J. Evans 1802; ed A. Cunningham 1841 (with

Castle of indolence); ed J. L. Robertson, Oxford 1891 (with Castle of indolence); ed O. Zippel, Berlin 1908 (variorum edn); ed J. Beresford 1927.

Winter, A hymn on the seasons, A poem to the memory of Sir Isaac Newton and Britannia. 1730, 1734.

Autumn. 1730 (2nd edn, 1269 lines). 1st edn in Seasons 1730, below.

The seasons, A hymn, A poem to the memory of Sir Isaac Newton and Britannia. 4 pts 1730, 1735. Some 1730 edns in 5 pts.

The four seasons and other poems. 4 pts 1735.

Antient and modern Italy compared: being the first part of Liberty. 1735.

Greece: being the second part of Liberty. 1735.

Rome: being the third part of Liberty. 1735.

Britain: being the fourth part of Liberty. 1736.

The prospect: being the fifth part of Liberty. 1736.

A poem to the memory of the right honourable the Lord Talbot, late Chancellor of Great Britain. 1737.

Liberty. 1738, Glasgow 1776 (Foulis).

Areopagitica. 1738. By Milton. Preface by Thomson.

Agamemnon. 1738, Dublin 1738. Performed Drury Lane 6 April 1738.

Edward and Eleonora. 1739, Dublin 1739, 1751, London 1758; tr German, 1764.

Alfred. 1740, 1745, 1751, 1753 (rev as Alfred the Great), 1754, 1773, 1781. Performed Cliefdon 1 Aug 1740. Written with David Mallet.

Tancred and Sigismunda. 1745, Dublin 1745, 1748, London 1752, 1755, Edinburgh 1755, London 1758, Glasgow 1759, London 1761, Edinburgh 1764, London 1766, Dublin 1767, 1768, Edinburgh 1768, London 1775, 1776, 1777, 1784 etc. Performed Drury Lane 18 March 1745.

The castle of indolence. 1748, 1748, 1779, [c. 1780], 1787; ed A. Cunningham 1841 (with Seasons); ed J. L. Robertson, Oxford 1891 (with Seasons); ed A. D. McKillop, Lawrence Kansas 1961.

Coriolanus. 1749, Dublin 1749, 1767. Performed Covent Garden 13 Jan 1749.

Poems on several occasions. 1750.

Poems: Britannia, The castle of indolence and lesser poems, with Alfred. Glasgow 1776 (Foulis).

Letters

A collection of letters written to Aaron Hill esq. 1751. Includes 14 from Thomson.

Unpublished letters from Thomson to Mallet. Ed F. Cunningham, Philobiblon Soc Miscellany 4 1854.

Letters and documents. Ed A. D. McKillop, Lawrence Kansas 1958.

§ 2

Aikin, J. An essay on the plan and character of Thomson's Seasons. 1778.

Johnson, S. In his Lives of the poets, 1779–81.

Macaulay, G. C. James Thomson. 1908 (EML).

McKillop, A. D. The background of Thomson's Seasons. Minneapolis 1942.

—— Thomson's visit to Shenstone. PQ 23 1944.

—— Ethics and political history in Thomson's Liberty. In Pope and his contemporaries: essays presented to George Sherburn, Oxford 1949.

Grant, D. Thomson: poet of the Seasons. 1951.

Cohen, R. The art of discrimination: Thomson's The seasons and the language of criticism. Los Angeles 1964.

WILLIAM SHENSTONE
1714–63

Collections

Poems upon various occasions. Oxford 1737 (anon), 1737. Includes The school-mistress in 12 stanzas.

Works in verse and prose. Ed Robert Dodsley 2 vols 1764, 3 vols 1765, 2 vols 1768, Edinburgh 1768.

§ 1

The judgment of Hercules. 1741.

The school-mistress. 1742 (anon), Oxford 1924 (facs). 28 stanzas; 35-stanza version in Dodsley's Collection vol 1, 1748 (2nd edn).

Cleone. 1758. By Dodsley; prologue by Shenstone.

Miscellaneous poems, revised and corrected by the late Mr William Shenstone. 1771. By Joseph Giles.

Shenstone's miscellany 1759–63. Ed I. A. Gordon, Oxford 1952. Verses by the Leasowes circle, ballads etc collected by Shenstone.

Shenstone also contributed a large number of poems to Dodsley's Collection vols 1, 3–5, 1748–58.

Letters

The works in verse and prose, vol 3: containing letters to particular friends. 1769.

Select letters between the late Duchess of Somerset, Lady Luxborough, Mr Whistler, Miss Dolman, Mr R. Dodsley, William Shenstone esq and others. Ed T. Hull 2 vols 1778.

Letters. Ed M. Williams, Oxford 1939. 300 letters.

Letters. Ed D. Mallam, Minneapolis 1939. 270 letters, including some new.

§ 2

Johnson, S. In his Lives of the poets, 1779–81.

Humphreys, A. R. William Shenstone. Cambridge 1937.

Tillotson, G. In his Essays in criticism and research, Cambridge 1942.

V. MINOR POETRY 1700–1750

This section is restricted to writers born between 1661 and 1715.

References

Johnson   The works of the English poets, ed S. Johnson 68 vols 1779–81, 75 vols 1790.
Anderson   The works of the British poets, ed R. Anderson 13 vols Edinburgh 1792–5; vol 14, 1807.
Chalmers   The works of the English poets, ed A. Chalmers 21 vols 1810.

JOHN ARMSTRONG
1709–79

Collections

Miscellanies. 2 vols 1770; ed R. Cohen, Los Angeles 1951 (Augustan Reprint Soc).
Medical essays. 1773.

§ 1

Dissertatio medica inauguralis de tabe purulenta. Edinburgh 1732.
An essay for abridging the study of physick; to which is added A dialogue relating to the practice of physick, as also An epistle from Usbek the Persian to J[oshua] W[ar]d. 1735.
The oeconomy of love: a poetical essay. 1736, 1737, 1745, 1747, 1749, 1753, 1763, 1768 (expurgated by Armstrong), 1777, 1781.
A synopsis of the history and cure of venereal diseases. 1737.
The art of preserving health: a poem. 1744, Dublin 1744, London 1745, 1748, 1754, 1757, Dublin 1765, London 1765, 1768, 1768, 1795 (with critical essay by J. Aikin).
The muncher's and guzzler's diary: in a word, the universal pocket almanack, by Noureddin Alrasxhin. 1749.
Of benevolence: an epistle to Eumenes. 1751.
Taste: an epistle to a young critic. 1753.
Sketches: or essays on various subjects, by Launcelot Temple. 1758.
A short ramble through some parts of France and Italy, by Launcelot Temple. 1771.
A day: an epistle to John Wilkes. 1661 (for 1761). With numerous omissions by Wilkes without Armstrong's permission.
Armstrong also contributed 4 stanzas to J. Thomson, The castle of indolence, 1748.
Anglo-Jewish letters 1158–1917. Ed C. Roth 1938.

§ 2

Knapp, L. M.   Armstrong: littérateur and associate of Smollett, Thomson, Wilkes and other celebrities. PMLA 59 1944.
—— Armstrong's Of benevolence. N & Q June 1959.
Maloney, W.   George and John Armstrong of Castleton. Edinburgh 1954.

WILLIAM BROOME
1689–1745

Collections

Johnson 43; Anderson 7; Chalmers 12.

§ 1

The Iliad of Homer done from the French by Mr Ozell. 1712. With Broome and Oldisworth.
The Iliad of Homer, translated from the Greek into blank verse, by Mr Ozell, Mr Broome and Mr Oldisworth. 1714, 1734.

The Iliad of Homer, translated by Mr Pope. 6 vols 1715–20. With notes partly by Broome.
The duty of publick intercession and thanksgiving for princes: a sermon preach'd on the 20th of October 1722, being the anniversary of the coronation of his Majesty. 1723.
The Odyssey of Homer. 5 vols 1725–6. Tr into verse by Pope, Broome (bks 2, 6, 8, 11–12, 16, 18, 23) and Fenton.
Poems on several occasions. 1727, 1739 (enlarged), 1750.
The oak and the dunghill. 1727. Attributed to Broome.
A sermon preach'd at the assizes of Norwich, August 8th 1737. 1737.
Odes d'Anacréon, traduites de français en vers anglais par Fawkes, Broome, Greene. Paris 1835. Broome's trns first pbd in GM over the pseudonym 'Chester'.

§ 2

Johnson, S. In his Lives of the poets, 1779–81.
Barlow, T. W.   Memoir of Broome with selections from his works. 1855.

WILLIAM DIAPER
1686?–1717

Collections

Complete works. Ed D. Broughton 1951 (ML).

§ 1

Nereides: or sea-eclogues. 1712.
Dryaides, or the nymphs prophecy: a poem. 1713 (for 1712).
An imitation of the seventeenth epistle of the first book of Horace, address'd to Dr S[wi]ft. 1714.
Oppian's Haliuticks of the nature of fishes and fishing of the ancients. Oxford 1722. Pt i tr Diaper.
Diaper also contributed to Rowe's version of Quillet's Callipaedia, 1712.

STEPHEN DUCK
1705–56

Collections

Poems on several subjects. 1730 (10 edns), 1731, 1733, 1736.
Poems on several occasions [with life by J. Spence]. 1736, 1737, 1738, 1753 (as The beautiful works of Duck), 1753, 1764.
Curious poems on several occasions, viz I: On poverty; II: The thresher's labour; III: The Shunamite; all newly corrected and much amended by the author. 1738.

§ 1

Royal benevolence: a poem; to which is annexed A poem on Providence. 1730.
To the Duke of Cumberland, on his birthday April the 15th 1732. 1732. Verse.
A poem on the marriage of the Prince of Orange: to which are added Verses to the author, by a divine, with the

author's answer and his poem on truth and falsehood. 1734.

Truth and falsehood: a fable. 1734. Verse.

The vision: a poem on the death of Queen Caroline. 1737, 1737.

The year of wonders. 1737.

Alrick and Isabel, or the unhappy marriage: a poem. 1740.

Hints to a school-master, address'd to Dr Turnbull. 1741.

Every man in his own way: an epistle to a friend. 1741.

An ode on the battle of Dettingen. 1743.

Caesar's camp, or St George's Hill: a poem. 1755.

The Shunamite: a poem. Canterbury 1830.

The thresher's labour. 1930.

§ 2

Spence, J. A full and authentick account of Duck. 1731.

Southey, R. Lives of uneducated poets. 1836; ed J. S. Childers, Oxford 1925.

Davis, R. M. Duck: the thresher-poet. Orono Maine 1926.

JOHN DYER
1699–1757
Collections

Miscellaneous poems and translations. Ed R. Savage 1726.

A collection of poems by several hands. Ed R. Dodsley vol 1 1748.

Poems: viz Grongar Hill, The ruins of Rome, The fleece. 1761, 1765 (as Poetical works of Dyer), 1770 (as Poems).

Poems. Ed E. Thomas 1903.

Johnson 53; Anderson 9; Chalmers 13.

§ 1

A new miscellany: being a collection of pieces of poetry from Bath, Tunbridge, Oxford, Epsom and other places in 1725. 1726 (with Grongar Hill, 1st version, 174 lines in octosyllabics).

Miscellaneous poems by several hands. Ed D. Lewis 1726. With final version of Grongar Hill, 157 lines in octosyllabics.

The ruins of Rome: a poem. 1740.

The fleece: a poem in four books. 1757.

Grongar Hill. Ed R. C. Boys, Baltimore 1941.

Letters to several eminent persons, including the correspondence of John Hughes. Ed W. Duncombe vol 3 1771 (2nd edn).

§ 2

Johnson, S. In his Lives of the poets, 1779–81.

Gilpin, W. In his Observations on the river Wye, 1782.

Williams, R. M. Thomson and Dyer: poet and painter. In The age of Johnson: essays presented to C. B. Tinker, New Haven 1949.

—— Poet, painter and parson: the life of Dyer. New York 1956.

LAURENCE EUSDEN
1688–1730
Collections

Original poems and translations by Mr Hill, Mr Eusden etc. 1714.

§ 1

Hero and Leander translated [from Musaeus]. In Tonson's Poetical miscellanies: the sixth part, 1709 etc; Glasgow 1750 (separately).

A letter to Mr Addison on the King's accession to the throne. 1714, 1714 (as The royal family: a letter).

Translations from Claudian and Statius: poem to Lord Halifax on reading the critique in the Spectator on Milton etc. In R. Steele, Poetical miscellanies, 1714.

Verses at the last publick commencement at Cambridge. 1714, 1714.

A poem on the marriage of his Grace the Duke of Newcastle. 1717.

Poems by the Earl of Roscommon [with Eusden's Latin version of his Essay on translated verse]. 1717.

Ovid's Metamorphoses in fifteen books, translated [into English verse] by the most eminent hands [J. Dryden, J. Addison, L. Eusden, A. Mainwaring, S. Croxall, N. Tate, J. Gay, W. Congreve, and the editor Sir S. Garth]. 1717.

A poem to the Royal Highness on the birth of the Prince. 1718.

An ode for the New Year. 1720.

An ode for the birthday. 1720.

An ode for the New Year. 1721.

An ode for the birthday. 1721.

Three poems, I: To the Lord High Chancellor; II: To Lord Parker, on his return from his travels; III: To Lord Parker, on his marriage. 1722.

An ode for the birthday, in English and Latin. Cambridge 1723.

The origin of the Knights of the Bath: a poem. 1725.

Three poems: the first, Sacred to the immortal memory of the last king; the second, On the happy succession and coronation of his present Majesty; and a third humbly inscrib'd to the Queen. 1727, 1727.

A poem humbly inscribed to his Royal Highness Prince Frederic. 1729.

ELIJAH FENTON
1683–1730
Collections

Miscellaneous poems and translations by several hands [including Fenton's]. 1712, 1714, 1720, 1722.

Poems on several occasions. 1717.

Poetical works, with the life of the author. 1802.

Johnson 29; Anderson 7; Chalmers 10.

§ 1

An ode to the sun, for the New-Year. 1707.

Oxford and Cambridge miscellany poems. 1708. Ed Fenton.

To the Queen, on her Majesty's birthday. [1710?].

An ode addressed to the Savoir Vivre Club. [1710?].

An epistle to Mr Southerne, from Mr El. Fenton, from Kent, Jan 28 1710/11. 1711.

Florelio: a pastoral lamenting the death of the Marquis of Blandford. In A. Pope, Eloisa to Abelard, 1720 (2nd edn).

Mariamne: a tragedy. 1723, Dublin 1723, London [1723], 1726, 1735, 1745, Dublin 1759, London 1760. Produced at Lincoln's Inn Fields 22 Feb 1723.

Life of John Milton. Prefixed to Paradise lost, 1725 etc.

The Odyssey of Homer, translated into English verse by Pope, Broome and Fenton. 1725–6 etc. Bks 1, 4, 19–20.

The works of Edmund Waller. 1729, 1730, 1744, 1752, 1772, 1796. Ed Fenton.

Observations on the works of Edmund Waller. 1730. Originally prefixed to his edn of Waller, above.

Fenton also contributed to D. Lewis, Miscellanies, 1726, 1730; and to G. Ogle's trn of Secundus, 1731.

§ 2

Johnson, S. In his Lives of the poets, 1779–81.

Harlan, E. Fenton. Philadelphia 1937

MATTHEW GREEN
1696–1737
Collections

The spleen and other poems, with a prefatory essay by J. Aikin. 1796.
The spleen and other poems. Ed R. K. Wood 1925.
Johnson 69; Anderson 10; Chalmers 15.

§ 1

The grotto: a poem written by Peter Drake, fisherman of Brentford. 1733, 1758 (in Dodsley's collection vol 5, with some omissions).
The spleen: an epistle inscrib'd to his particular friend Mr C. J[ackson]. Ed R. Glover 1737 (3 edns), Dublin 1737, London 1738 (with Some other pieces by the same hand), 1748, 1758; ed W. H. Williams 1936.

JOHN HUGHES
1677–1720
Collections

Poems on several occasions, with some select essays in prose. Ed W. Duncombe 2 vols 1735.
Johnson 22; Anderson 7; Chalmers 10.

§ 1

The triumph of peace. 1698.
The court of Neptune. 1699.
The house of Nassau: a Pindarick ode. 1702.
An ode in praise of music. 1703.
A review of the case of Ephraim and Judah. 1705.
Advices from Parnassus, all translated from the Italian by several hands, revis'd and corrected by Mr Hughes. 1706.
Fontenelle's Dialogues of the dead, translated from the French; and two original dialogues. 1708, 1730, Glasgow 1754.
Calypso and Telemachus: an opera. 1712, 1717, 1735 etc. Produced at Haymarket 17 May 1712.
The history of the revolution in Portugal by the Abbot de Vertot. 1712. Tr Hughes from French.
An ode to the creator of the world, occasion'd by the fragments of Orpheus. 1713, 1713.
The lay-monastery: consisting of essays, discourses etc publish'd singly under the title of the Lay-monk. 1714.
Apollo and Daphne: a masque set to musick. 1716 etc. Produced at Drury Lane 12 Jan 1716.
An ode for the birthday of her Royal Highness the Princess of Wales. 1716.
Orestes: a tragedy. 1717. Unacted.
A layman's thoughts on the late treatment of the Bishop of Bangor. 1717.
Charon, or the ferry-boat: a vision. 1719. Prose.
The ecstacy: an ode. 1720.
The siege of Damascus: a tragedy. 1720, 1721, 1744 etc.
The complicated guilt of the late Rebellion. 1745. Written 1716.
Letters by several eminent persons deceased. Ed J. Duncombe 1772, 1773, 2 vols 1773. Includes Hughes' correspondence, some new pieces and the original plan of Siege of Damascus.

§ 2

Johnson, S. In his Lives of the poets, 1779–81.

SOAME JENYNS
1704–87
Collections

Poems. 1752.
Miscellaneous pieces in verse and prose. 2 vols 1761.
Miscellanies. 1770.
Works. Ed C. N. Cole 4 vols 1790, 1793. With memoir.
Johnson 73; Anderson 11; Chalmers 17.

§ 1

The art of dancing: a poem in three cantos. 1729.
Versus inopes rerum, nugaeque canorae: commonly call'd poems on several occasions. [1730].
An epistle [in verse] to Lord Lovelace. 1735.
The modern fine gentleman. 1746.
An ode to the Hon Philip Y—ke, imitated from Horace, lib ii, ode xvi; to which is added the same ode imitated and inscribed to the Earl of B—on on his creation. 1747.
The 'squire and the parson: an eclogue. [1749].
The modern fine lady. 1751 (3 edns).
A free enquiry into the nature and origin of evil. 1757; tr French, 1791.
The objections to the taxation of our American colonies considered. 1765.
Thoughts on the causes and consequences of the present high price of provisions. 1767.
A scheme for the coalition of parties. 1772.
A view of the internal evidence of the Christian religion. 1776 (5 edns), Dublin 1776, London 1790, Edinburgh 1798, London 1799; tr Polish, 1782; French, 1797; Greek, 1804.
An ode. 1780.
Disquisitions on several subjects. 1782, Dublin 1782.
Thoughts on parliamentary reform. 1784.

GEORGE LYTTELTON,
1st BARON LYTTELTON
1709–73
Collections

Poems. Glasgow 1773, 1777.
The works of George Lord Lyttelton, now first collected together; with some other pieces never before printed. Ed G. E. Ayscough 1774, 2 vols Dublin 1774, London 1785, Dublin 1785, 3 vols 1776.
Poetical works. 1785, Glasgow 1787 etc.
Johnson 56; Anderson 10; Chalmers 14.

§ 1

Blenheim. 1728. Verse.
An epistle [in verse] to Mr Pope, from a young gentleman at Rome. 1730.
The progress of love, in four eclogues. 1732, 1732.
Advice to a lady. 1733. Verse.
Letters from a Persian in England to his friend at Ispahan. 1735 (4 edns, vol 2 not by Lyttelton).
Considerations upon the present state of our affairs at home and abroad. 1739, 1739.
Farther considerations on the present state of affairs, containing a true state of the South Sea Company's affairs in 1718. 1739, 1739.
Observations on the life of Cicero. 1741.
The Court secret: a melancholy truth. 1742, 1746 (as The new Court secret).
To the memory of a lady [Lyttelton's first wife] lately deceased: a monody. 1747, Dublin 1747, London 1748, 1748.
Observations on the conversion and apostleship of St Paul in a letter to Gilbert West. 1747, Dublin 1747, London

1748, 1749, 1754, 1799 etc; tr French, 1754, 1758.
A modesty apology for my own conduct. 1748.
The fourth ode of the fourth book of Horace. 1749. Tr Lyttleton.
Dialogues of the dead [nos 26–8 by E. Montagu]. 1760 (3 edns), 1765, 1768, Worcester Mass 1797; tr French, 1767.
An additional dialogue of the dead between Pericles and Aristides: being a sequel to the dialogue between Pericles and Cosmo. 1760.
Four new dialogues of the dead. 1765.
The history of the life of King Henry the second and of the age in which he lived. 4 vols 1767–71, 1767–71, 6 vols 1769–73, 1790.
A gentleman's tour through Monmouthshire. 1781.

§ 2

Johnson, S. In his Lives of the poets, 1779–81.
Roberts, S. C. An eighteenth-century gentleman. Cambridge 1930.
Davis, R. M. The correspondents. PMLA 51 1936.
—— The good Lord Lyttelton. Bethlehem Pa 1939.

DAVID MALLET, originally MALLOCH
1705?–65
Collections

Works. 4 pts 1743, 3 vols 1759.
Johnson 53; Anderson 9; Chalmers 14.

§ 1

William and Margaret: an old ballad. [1723].
A poem in imitation of Donaides. [1725].
The excursion: a poem in two books. 1728.
Eurydice: a tragedy. 1731, 1731, 1735, 1759, 1780. Produced at Drury Lane 22 Feb 1731.
Of verbal criticism: an epistle to Mr Pope, occasioned by Theobald's Shakespear and Bentley's Milton. 1733.
Verses presented to the Prince of Orange on his visiting Oxford. 1734. With W. Harte.
Mustapha: a tragedy. 1739, 1760. Produced at Drury Lane 13 Feb 1739.
Alfred: a masque. 1740, 1745. With J. Thomson. Produced at Cliefden, 1 Aug 1740. See Alfred, below.
The life of Francis Bacon. 1740, 1740, 1753, 1760, 1768.
Poems on several occasions. 1743.
Amyntor and Theodora, or the hermit: a poem in three cantos. 1747, 1747, Dublin 1747, 1748, 1748 (corrected).
A congratulatory letter to Selim on the three letters to the Whigs. 1748.
Letters on the spirit of patriotism: on the idea of a patriot king. 1749. By Bolingbroke, ed Mallet.
Alfred: a masque. 1751, 1753, 1754. Rev Mallet. Produced at Drury Lane 23 Feb 1751.
Works of Lord Bolingbroke. 5 vols 1754. Ed Mallet.
Britannia: a masque. 1755. Produced at Drury Lane 9 May 1755.
Observations on the twelfth article of war. 1757. On the case of Admiral Byng.
Edwin and Emma. Birmingham 1760, London 1777; ed F. T. Dinsdale 1849.
Verses on the death of Lady Anson. 1760.
Poems on several occasions. 1762. Different from 1743 edn, above.
Elvira: a tragedy. 1763, Edinburgh 1763, Dublin 1763, London 1778. Produced at Drury Lane 19 Jan 1763.
Ballads and songs. Ed F. T. Dinsdale 1857.

§ 2

Boswell, J., A. Erskine and G. Dempster. Critical strictures on the new tragedy of Elvira written by Mr David

Malloch. 1763; ed F. A. Pottle, Los Angeles 1952 (Augustan Reprint Soc).
Johnson, S. In his Lives of the poets, 1779–81.
D'Israeli, I. Bolingbroke and Mallet's posthumous quarrel with Pope. In his Quarrels of authors, 1814.

THOMAS PARNELL
1679–1718
Collections

Works in verse and prose, enlarged with variations and [7] poems not before publish'd. Glasgow 1755.
Johnson 44; Anderson 7; Chalmers 9.

§ 1

An essay [in verse] on the different stiles of poetry. 1713.
An essay on the life, writings and learning of Homer. Prefixed to Pope's Iliad vol 1, 1715.
Homer's battle of the frogs and mice, with the remarks of Zoilus, to which is prefix'd the life of the said Zoilus. 1717. Later appended to Pope's Iliad and Odyssey.
Poems on several occasions, published by Mr Pope. 1722, 1726, Dublin 1735, London 1737, Dublin 1744, Glasgow 1752, 1770 (with Goldsmith's Life), Dublin 1771.
Posthumous works. 1758, Dublin 1758.

§ 2

Goldsmith, O. The life of Parnell. 1770.
Johnson, S. In his Lives of the poets, 1779–81.
Cruickshank, A. H. Parnell: or what was wrong with the eighteenth century. E & S 11 1925.

AMBROSE PHILIPS
1674–1749
Collections

Three tragedies. 1725.
Pastorals, epistles, odes and other original poems, with translations from Pindar, Anacreon and Sappho. 1748, 1765.
A variorum text of four pastorals. Ed R. H. Griffith, Texas Univ Stud 12 1932.
Poems. Ed M. G. Segar, Oxford 1937 (with biography).
Ten new poems 1674–1749. Ed W. J. Cameron, N & Q Nov 1957.
Johnson 44; Anderson 9; Chalmers 13.

§ 1

Life of John Williams. 1700. Abridgement of J. Hacket, Scrinia reserata.
Persian tales. 1709. Tr from French of Pétis de la Croix.
Pastorals. 1710. First 4 pieces originally ptd in Fenton's Oxford and Cambridge miscellany [1706]; rptd with 2 more in Tonson's Poetical miscellanies: the sixth part, 1709.
The distrest mother: a tragedy. 1712, 1712, 1718, Hague [1723], 1726, London 1731, 1734, 1735, 1748, 1749, 1751, Dublin 1754, 1756 etc. Produced at Drury Lane 17 March 1712. Tr from Racine, Andromaque.
An epistle to the Right Honourable Charles Lord Halifax. 1714.
An epistle to the Honourable James Craggs esq. 1717.
The freethinker. 24 March 1718–28 July 1721, 3 vols 1722, 1733, 1739.
The Briton: a tragedy. 1722, 1725. Produced at Drury Lane 19 Feb 1722.

Humfrey, Duke of Gloucester: a tragedy. 1723, 1723, Dublin 1723, London 1725. Produced at Drury Lane 15 Feb 1723.
A collection of old ballads. 3 vols 1723–5, 1723–38, [1872]. Ed Philips?
An ode in the manner of Pindar on the death of the Right Honourable William, Earl Cowper. 1723.
To the Honourable Miss Carteret. 1725, Dublin 1725.
To Miss Georgiana, youngest daughter of Lord Carteret. Dublin 1725.
Supplication for Miss Carteret in the smallpox. Dublin 1726.
To Miss Margaret Pulteney, daughter of Daniel Pulteney esq. Dublin 1727.
Philips was a principal contributor to Grumbler, 1715.

§ 2

Pope, A. Guardian no 40 1713.
Johnson, S. In his Lives of the poets, 1779–81.

JOHN PHILIPS
1676–1709
Collections

Poems, to which is prefixed his life [by G. Sewell]. 1712, 1715, 1720, 1728, Dublin 1730, London 1744, 1762, Glasgow 1763, London 1776. Variously titled.
Poems. Ed M. G. L. Thomas, Oxford 1927.
Johnson 21; Anderson 6; Chalmers 8.

§ 1

The sylvan dream: or the mourning Muse. 1701.
The splendid shilling: an imitation of Milton. 1705. First ptd as In imitation of Milton in A collection of poems, viz The temple of death [etc], 1701, and in A new miscellany of original poems, ed C. Gildon 1701; pirated edn by B. Bragg, 1705.
Blenheim: a poem. 1705 (3 edns), 1709.
Cerealia: an imitation of Milton. 1706, 1706 (enlarged).
Honoratissimo viro Henrico Saint John, armigero: ode. 1707.
Ode gratulatoria Willielmo Cowper. 1707.
Cyder: a poem in two books. 1708, 1708, 1709, 1727; tr Italian, 1749, 1752.

§ 2

Johnson, S. In his Lives of the poets, 1779–81.

CHRISTOPHER PITT
1699–1748

§ 1

A poem on the death of the late Earl Stanhope. 1721.
Vida's Art of poetry, translated into English verse. 1725, 1726, 1742; rptd Chalmers 19.
Poems and translations. 1727.
An essay on Virgil's Æneid: being a translation of the first book. 1728.
The Æneid of Virgil, translated. 2 vols 1740, 1743; rptd Anderson 12, Chalmers 19.
Poems by the celebrated translator of Virgil's Aeneid. 1756.
Johnson 43; Anderson 8; Chalmers 12.

§ 2

Johnson, S. In his Lives of the poets, 1779–81.

JOHN POMFRET
1667–1702
Collections

Poems. 1699, 1702, 1707, 1710, 1710, 1716, 1724, 1727, 1735, 1736, 1740, 1751, 1773, 1790 (with remains).
Johnson 21; Anderson 6; Chalmers 8.

§ 1

An epistle to Charles, Earl of Dorset. 1690.
The sceptical Muse. 1699.
A prospect of death. [1700], 1709 (with Lady Winchilsea, Spleen).
Reason: a poem. 1700.
The choice or wish. 1700, 1700, 1701.
Two love poems. 1701.
Quae rara, chara: a poem on Panthea's confinement. 1707.

§ 2

Johnson, S. In his Lives of the poets, 1779–81.

RICHARD SAVAGE
1697?–1743
Collections

Various poems: The wanderer, The triumph of mirth and health and The bastard. 1761.
Works, with an account of the life and writings by Samuel Johnson. 2 vols 1775, 1777, Dublin 1777.
Poetical works. Ed C. Tracy, Cambridge 1962.
Johnson 45; Anderson 8; Chalmers 11.

§ 1

The convocation, or a battle of pamphlets: a poem. 1717.
Love in a veil: a comedy. 1719. Produced at Drury Lane 17 June 1718. Tr from Calderón.
The tragedy of Sir Thomas Overbury. 1724, 1777 (altered by W. Woodfall). Produced at Drury Lane 12 June 1723.
Miscellaneous poems and translations by several hands, publish'd by Savage. 1726 (with Savage's account of his early life).
A poem sacred to the glorious memory of our late King George. 1727, Dublin 1727.
Nature in perfections: or the mother unveil'd. 1728.
An author to be lett, by Iscariot Hackney. 1729; ed J. Sutherland, Los Angeles 1960 (Augustan Reprint Soc). With Pope.
The wanderer: a poem in five cantos. 1729.
Verses occasion'd by the Viscountess Tyrconnel's recovery at Bath. 1730.
A poem to the memory of Mrs Oldfield. 1730. Perhaps by Savage.
An epistle to the Right Honourable Sir Robert Walpole. 1732.
A collection of pieces in verse and prose, on the occasion of the Dunciad. 1732.
The volunteer laureat: a poem to her Majesty on her birthday. 1732. Similar verses yearly to 1738.
On the departure of the Prince and Princess of Orange: a poem. 1734.
The progress of a divine: a satire. 1735. Verse.
A poem on the birth-day of the Prince of Wales. 1735.
Of public spirit in regard to public works: an epistle. 1737, 1739. Verse.
A poem sacred to the memory of her Majesty. 1738.
London and Bristol compar'd: a satire. 1744.

§ 2

The life of Mr Richard Savage. 1727, 1728, 1728.

Johnson, S. An account of the life of Mr Richard Savage. 1744 etc; rev in his Lives of the poets vol 3, 1781.

Tracy, C. The artificial bastard: a biography of Savage. Cambridge Mass 1953.

THOMAS SHERIDAN
1687–1738
Collections

Poems by the celebrated translator of Virgil's Aeneid. 1756.

Johnson 43; Anderson 8; Chalmers 12.

§ 1

An easy introduction of grammar in English for the understanding of the Latin tongue. Dublin 1714.

Ars pun-ica, sive flos linguarum: the art of punning, or the flower of languages. Dublin 1719, London 1720 (3 edns). Ascribed to Swift, but mainly attributed to Sheridan.

Prologue spoke at the Theatre-Royal in behalf of the poor weavers of Dublin. Dublin 1721.

Mr Sheridan's prologue to the Greek play of Phaedra and Hypolitus. Dublin 1721.

The wonderful wonder of wonders. Dublin 1721.

The blunderful blunder of blunders: being an answer to the Wonderful wonder of wonders. Dublin 1721. Both pieces attributed to Sheridan.

To the Honourable Mr D[ick] T[igh,] great pattern of piety. Dublin 1725. Attributed to Sheridan.

Philoctetes. Dublin 1725. Tr from Sophocles.

A true and faithful inventory of the goods belonging to Dr Sw—t, Vicar of Lara Cor, upon lending his house to the Bishop of M[eath] till his own was built. Dublin 1726.

Tom Punsibi's letter to Dean Swift. Dublin 1727.

To the Right Honourable the Lord Viscount Mont-Cassell this fable is humbly dedicated by a person who had some share in his education. 1727.

The satyrs of Persius, translated into English. Dublin 1728, London 1728, 1739.

The intelligencer. Dublin 1728, London 1729. A periodical written with Swift.

An answer to the Christmas box, in defence of Doctor D[ela]n—y, by R[uper]t B[arbe]r. Dublin 1729. Attributed to Sheridan.

A new simile for the ladies with useful annotations. Dublin 1732.

The satires of Juvenal translated [into prose]. 1739, 1745, Dublin 1769, Cambridge 1777.

Correspondence of Jonathan Swift. Ed H. Williams vols 4–5, Oxford 1965.

THOMAS TICKELL
1685–1740

Oxford: a poem. 1707.

A poem to his Excellency the Lord Privy-Seal on the prospect of peace. 1713 (5 edns), 1714.

The prologue to the University of Oxford. 1713, 1714 (in R. Steele, Poetical miscellanies).

An imitation of the prophecy of Nereus, from Horace, book I, ode XV. 1715, 1715, 1716.

The first book of Homer's Iliad. 1715.

An epistle from a lady in England to a gentleman at Avignon. 1717 (5 edns), 1721 (in A miscellaneous collection of poems).

An ode occasioned by his Excellency the Earl Stanhope's voyage to France. 1718.

An ode inscribed to the Right Honourable the Earl of Sunderland at Windsor. 1720.

The works of the Right Honourable Joseph Addison esq. 4 vols 1721 etc. Ed with preface by Tickell.

Kensington Garden. 1722.

To Sir Godfrey Kneller, at his country seat. 1722.

Lucy and Colin: a song written in imitation of William and Margaret. Dublin 1725, 1729 (in The musical miscellany vol 1), 1730 (in The merry musician).

A poem in praise of the horn-book. 1726 (in D. Lewis, Miscellaneous poems), Dublin 1728, London 1732.

On her Majesty's re-building the lodgings of the Black Prince and Henry V at Queen's-College, Oxford. 1733.

Johnson 26; Anderson 8; Chalmers 11.

THOMAS WARTON the elder
1688?–1745

Poems on several occasions. 1748, New York 1930 (facs).

The three Wartons: a choice of their verse. Ed E. Partridge 1927.

ISAAC WATTS
1674–1748
Collections

Works. Ed D. Jennings and P. Doddridge 6 vols 1753; rev G. Burder 6 vols 1810–11, 9 vols Leeds 1812–13.

Johnson 46; Anderson 9; Chalmers 13.

§ 1

Horae lyricae, poems chiefly of the lyric kind. 1706, 1709 (enlarged), 1715, 1722, 1727, 1731, 1737, 1743, Boston 1748 etc; ed R. Southey 1834, 1837.

Hymns and spiritual songs. 1707, 1709 (enlarged), 1716, 1720, 1723, 1725, 1728, 1734, 1740, 1744, 1748 etc; ed S. L. Bishop 1962.

Divine songs attempted in easy language for the use of children. 1715, 1716, 1719, Boston 1719, London 1720, 1727, 1728, 1729 etc; ed J. H. P. Pafford, Oxford 1971 (facs).

The psalms of David imitated. 1719 etc.

Sermons on various subjects. 3 vols 1721–7. Includes hymns.

Logic. 1725.

The knowledge of the heavens and earth. 1726.

Reliquiae juveniles: miscellaneous thoughts in prose and verse. 1734, 1737, 1742, 1766 etc.

The improvement of the mind. 1741.

Watts also pbd many sermons and theological works; see col 666, below.

§ 2

Johnson, S. In his Lives of the English poets, 1779–81.

Escott, H. Watts, hymnographer: a study of the beginnings, development and philosophy of the English hymns. 1962.

LEONARD WELSTED
1688–1747
Collections

Works in verse and prose. Ed J. Nichols 1787.

§ 1

A poem occasioned by the late famous victory of Audenard. 1709.

The Duke of Marlborough's arrival: a poem. 1709.

A poem to the memory of the incomparable Mr [John] Philips. 1710.

Dionysius Longinus on the sublime; with some remarks on the English poets. 1712.

An epistle to Mr Steele on the King's accession. 1714.
An ode on the birth-day of the Prince of Wales [etc]. 1716.
Palaemon to Caelia, at Bath: or the triumvirate. 1717. Verse.
An epistle to his Grace the Duke of Chandos. 1720.
A prologue to the town, as it was spoken at the theatre in little Lincoln's-Inn fields. 1721. Verse.
An epistle to the late Dr Garth. 1722. Verse.
Epistles, odes etc written on several subjects. 1724, 1725. Preliminary essay rptd in Critical essays of the eighteenth century, ed W. H. Durham, New Haven 1915.
Oikographia: a poem. 1725.
An ode to Major General Wade. 1726.
A hymn to the creator, by a gentleman on the death of his only daughter. 1726.
The dissembled wanton, or my son get money: a comedy. 1727, 1728, 1787. Produced at Lincoln's Inn Fields 14 Dec 1726.
A discourse to Sir Robert Walpole; to which is annex'd Proposals for translating the whole works of Horace, with a specimen. 1727.
One epistle to Mr A. Pope [with James Moore Smythe]. 1730; ed J. V. Guerinot in Two poems against Pope, Los Angeles 1965 (Augustan Reprint Soc).
Of false-fame: an epistle to the Earl of Pembroke. 1732.
Of dulness and scandal, occasion'd by the character of Lord Timon, in Mr Pope's Epistle to the Earl of Burlington. 1732, 1732. Verse.
The scheme and conduct of providence from the creation to the coming of the Messiah. 1736.
The summum bonum: or wisest philosophy. 1741.

§ 2

Fineman, D. A. Welsted: gentleman poet of the Augustan age. Philadelphia 1950.

GILBERT WEST
1703–56

§ 1

Stowe, the gardens of the Right Honourable Richard Lord Viscount Cobham. 1732, 1732.
A canto of the Faery Queen [imitated]. 1739.
The institution of the Order of the Garter: a dramatick poem. 1742; altered by D. Garrick 1771.
Observations on the resurrection of Jesus Christ. 1747, Dublin 1747, London 1749, 1754, 1767 etc; tr German, 1748.
The odes of Pindar, with several other pieces translated. 1749, 1751; rptd Anderson vol 12.
Education: a poem in two cantos, written in imitation of the style and manner of Spenser's Faery Queen, canto the first. 1751. All pbd.

Two orations [by Thucydides] in praise of Athenians slain in battle. 1759, 1768. Plato's tr West.
Johnson 56; Anderson 9; Chalmers 13.

§ 2

Johnson, S. In his Lives of the poets, 1779–81.

ANNE FINCH,
COUNTESS OF WINCHILSEA
1661–1720

Collections

Miscellany poems on several occasions written by a lady. 1713, 1714 (as Poems on several occasions).
Poems and extracts, chosen by William Wordsworth [in 1819] for an album. 1905.
Poems. Ed J. M. Murry 1928. A selection.

§ 1

The spleen: a Pindarique ode by a lady; together with A prospect of death: a Pindarique essay [by J. Pomfret]. 1709. Spleen first ptd in C. Gildon, New miscellany, 1701.
Free-thinkers: a poem in dialogue. 1711.
Lady Winchilsea also contributed to Steele's Miscellany, *1714.*

§ 2

Brower, R. A. Lady Winchilsea and the poetic tradition of the seventeenth century. SP 42 1945.
Buxton, J. The poems of the Countess of Winchilsea. Life & Letters 65 1950.
— In his A tradition of poetry, 1967.

THOMAS YALDEN
1670–1736

§ 1

On the conquest of Namur: a Pindarique ode. 1695.
Temple of fame. 1700.
Aesop at court: or state fables. 1702. Verse.
An essay on the character of Sir Willoughby Aston. 1704.
The education of poor children: a sermon. 1728.
Johnson 45; Anderson 7; Chalmers 11.

§ 2

Johnson, S. In his Lives of the poets, 1779–81.

VI. LATER EIGHTEENTH-CENTURY POETRY

THOMAS GRAY
1716–71

Bibliographies etc

Cook, A. S. A concordance to the English poems of Gray. Boston 1908.
Northup, C. S. A bibliography of Gray. New Haven 1917.
Starr, H. W. A bibliography of Gray 1917–51. Philadelphia 1953. A continuation of Northup, above.

Collections

The poems of Mr Gray, with memoirs prefixed. Ed W. Mason, York 1775, 1775, 2 vols Dublin 1775, 4 vols 1778, 2 vols 1807 etc. Contains posthumous poems and fragments; Mason's memoirs are largely composed from Gray's letters, many in a garbled form.
Works, with memoirs by William Mason, to which are subjoined extracts philosophical, political and critical. Ed T. J. Mathias 2 vols 1814. Vol 1 adds letters from Gray to Walpole to Mason's edn and life; vol 2 contains extracts from Gray's commonplace book and postscript by Mathias on Gray.

Works. Ed J. Mitford 4 vols 1835–7, 1857–8. Vol 1, poems; vols 2–4, letters, many pbd for first time. Aldine edn. Gray's Correspondence with Nichols, 1843 (Letters, below) was also issued as vol 5 of this edn.
Works in prose and verse. Ed E. Gosse 4 vols 1884.
Gray's English poems. Ed D. C. Tovey, Cambridge 1898, 1922.
The poetical works of Gray and Collins. Ed A. L. Poole, Oxford 1917, 1937 (rev L. Whibley).
Poems. Ed L. Whibley, Oxford 1939 (WC).
Complete poems, English, Latin and Greek. Ed H. W. Starr and J. R. Hendrickson, Oxford 1966.
Poems. Ed R. H. Lonsdale 1969. With Collins and Goldsmith.
Johnson 56; Anderson 10; Chalmers 14.

§ I

Ode on a distant prospect of Eton College. 1747 (anon), Oxford 1924 (facs).
Ode [on the spring]; Ode on the death of a favourite cat. In Dodsley's Collection of poems, vol 2 1748 etc. Anon, with Eton ode, above.
An elegy wrote in a country church yard. 1751 (anon). 5 edns in 1751 and 8 more pbd by Dodsley 1752–71. 3rd and 8th edns rev Gray. 3rd and later edns entitled An elegy written in a country churchyard. Rptd Oxford 1927 (facs); facs of 1st edn and Eton ms in edn by G. Sherburn, Los Angeles 1951 (Augustan Reprint Soc); ed D. Flower and A. N. L. Munby 1938 (in their English poetical autographs, with facs of Wharton ms); ed R. P. T. Coffin, New York 1940.
Designs by Mr R. Bentley for six poems by Mr T. Gray. 1753. Adds to the above A long story and Hymn to adversity. Rptd with Odes, 1757, 1765, 1766, 1775, 1789. Poems by Mr T. Gray. Dublin 1756. Reprints 6 poems in Bentley edn.
Odes, by Mr Gray. Strawberry Hill 1757. The Progress of poesy and The bard. See A. T. Hazen, A bibliography of the Strawberry Hill press, New Haven 1942.
Epitaph on Mrs Clerke. GM Oct 1759.
The union. Dublin 1761. Contains poems in the Bentley edn and adds the Odes, 1757.
Poems by Mr Gray. 1768, 1768, Glasgow 1768, Dublin 1768, Cork 1768, 1770, Dublin 1771, Edinburgh 1773 (British poets, vol 42), 1774 (with life), Dublin 1775, 1776, Glasgow 1777, 1778, Dublin 1779, 1779, 1786, 1790, Parma 1793. Adds The fatal sisters, The descent of Odin, and The triumphs of Owen, but omits A long story.
Ode performed in the Senate-House at Cambridge July 1 1769, at the installation of his Grace Augustus Henry Fitzroy, Duke of Grafton, Chancellor of the University. Cambridge 1769, 1769. Anon.
On Lord Holland's seat near Margate, Kent. Anon and unauthorized, as Inscription for a villa of a decayed statesman on the sea coast, in The new foundling hospital for wit pt 3, 1769.
The candidate. Apparently first pbd, without title, in London Evening Post Feb 1777. The flysheet was printed after Gray's death, perhaps as late as 1787.
Ode on the pleasure arising from vicissitude. Ed L. Whibley 2 vols San Francisco 1933. Facs of Mason's trial printing of the text (with his own ending) ptd in his Memoirs of Gray in 1775.

Letters

See Collections, above.
The works of Lord Orford. Vol 5, 1798. Gray's letters to Walpole.
Letters. Ed D. C. Tovey 3 vols 1900–12.
The correspondence of Gray, Walpole, West and Ashton 1734–71. Ed P. Toynbee 2 vols Oxford 1915.
Correspondence. Ed P. Toynbee and L. Whibley 3 vols

Oxford 1935, 1971 (rev H. W. Starr).
Walpole's correspondence with Gray, West and Ashton. Ed W. S. Lewis, G. L. Lam and C. H. Bennett, New Haven 1948. Vols 13–14 of Yale edn of Walpole's correspondence.
Selected letters. Ed J. W. Krutch, New York 1952.

§ 2

Johnson, S. In his Lives of the poets, 1779–81.
Hazlitt, W. In his Lectures on the English poets, 1818.
[Bowles, W. L.] A letter to the Rt Hon Lord Byron, protesting against the immolation of Gray, Cowper and Campbell at the shrine of Pope. 1821. See Byron's Letter in reply, 1821.
Stephen, L. Gray and his school. Cornhill Mag July 1879.
Gosse, E. Gray. 1882 (EML).
Arnold, M. In T. H. Ward's English poets vol 3, 1884; rptd in his Essays in criticism ser 2, 1888.
Tovey, D. C. Gray and his friends. Cambridge 1890.
Correspondence of Hurd and Mason and letters of Hurd to Gray. Ed E. H. Pearce and L. Whibley, Cambridge 1932.
Ketton-Cremer, R. W. Thomas Gray. 1935.
—— In his Horace Walpole, 1940, 1946 (rev).
—— Gray: a biography. Cambridge 1955.
—— The poet who spoke out: the letters of Gray. In Familiar letter in the eighteenth century, ed H. Anderson, P. B. Daghlian and I. Ehrenpreis, Lawrence Kansas 1966.
Empson, W. In his Some versions of pastoral, 1935.
Tillotson, G. On Gray's letters; Gray the scholar poet. In his Essays in criticism and research, Cambridge 1942.
—— Gray's Ode on the spring; Gray's Ode on a favourite cat. In his Augustan studies, 1961.
Cecil, D. The poetry of Gray. Proc Br Acad 31 1945; rptd in Yale Rev 36 1947; and in his Poets and story-tellers, 1949.
—— School-days of Gray. Life & Letters Dec 1947; rptd in his Two quiet lives, 1948.
—— Gray at Cambridge. Life & Letters Jan 1948; rptd in his Two quiet lives, 1948.
Garrod, H. W. Notes on the composition of Gray's Elegy. In Essays on the eighteenth century presented to David Nichol Smith, Oxford 1945.
Brooks, C. Gray's storied urn. In his Well wrought urn, New York 1947.
Bateson, F. W. Gray's Elegy reconsidered. In his English poetry, 1950.

WILLIAM COLLINS
1721–59

Booth, B. A. and C. E. Jones. A concordance of the poetical works of Collins. Berkeley 1939.

Collections

Poetical works, with memoirs of the author; and observations on his genius and writings by J. Langhorne, 1765, 1765 (pirated?), 1771 (introd rev), 1776, 1781.
Poetical works. Ed C. Stone and A. L. Poole, Oxford 1917 (OSA); rev F. Page 1937; rev R. H. Lonsdale 1977. With Gray.
Poems. Ed R. H. Lonsdale 1969. With Gray and Goldsmith.
Anderson 9; Chalmers 13.

§ I

Persian eclogues, written originally for the entertainment of the ladies of Tauris and now first translated. 1742 (anon), 1757 (as Oriental eclogues), 1760; Oxford 1925 (facs of 1742 edn).

Verses humbly address'd to Sir Thomas Hanmer on his edition of Shakespeare's works, by a gentleman of Oxford. 1743 (anon), 1744 (rev as An epistle addrest to Sir Thomas Hanmer on his edition of Shakespear's works: the second edition, to which is added a song from the Cymbeline of the same author), 1755 (in Dodsley's Collection, vol 4).

Ode to a lady on the death of Colonel Ross in the action of Fontenoy. In Museum, ed M. Akenside no 6, 7 June 1746.

Odes on several descriptive and allegorical subjects. 1747 (pbd 20 Dec 1746), 1926 (facs), New York 1934.

Ode occasion'd by the death of Mr Thomson. 1749; in Union, ed T. Warton, 'Edinburgh' (for Oxford) 1753 (with Ode to evening); Oxford 1927 (facs).

The passions: an ode. Oxford [1750], Winchester [1750], Gloucester 1760.

An ode on the popular superstitions of the Highlands of Scotland, considered as the subject of poetry. Trans Royal Soc of Edinburgh 1 1788 (missing stanzas supplied by Henry Mackenzie), 1788 (Bell's spurious edn), 1789.

Drafts and fragments of verse, edited from the manuscripts. Ed J. S. Cunningham, Oxford 1956.

§ 2

Johnson, S. In his Lives of the poets, 1779–81.

Hazlitt, W. In his Lectures on the English poets, 1818.

[Murry, J. M.] William Collins. TLS 29 Dec 1921; rptd in his Countries of the mind, 1922.

Garrod, H. W. The poetry of Collins. Proc Br Acad 14 1928.

—— Collins. Oxford 1928.

Ainsworth, E. G. Poor Collins: his life, his art and his influence. Ithaca 1937.

Tillotson, G. Notes on Collins. In his Essays in criticism and research, Cambridge 1942.

Doughty, O. William Collins. 1964.

CHRISTOPHER SMART
1722–71

Collections

Poems: consisting of his prize poems, odes, sonnets and fables, Latin and English translations. 2 vols Reading 1791. Omits A song to David and much else.

Collected poems. Ed N. Callan 2 vols 1949 (ML). Excludes trns, libretti and Latin poems.

Poems. Ed R. E. Brittain, Princeton 1950. Selection, including some trns.

Anderson 11 (adds one poem); Chalmers 16 (omits one poem).

§ 1

The Horatian canons of friendship: being the third satire of the first book of Horace imitated. 1750.

On the eternity of the Supreme Being. Cambridge 1750, 1752, 1756. Seatonian Prize poem for 1750.

The student: or Oxford and Cambridge monthly miscellany 1750–1. 50 or more contributions; ed Smart.

An occasional prologue and epilogue to Othello. [1751], [1751].

A solemn dirge, sacred to the memory of Frederic, Prince of Wales. 1751.

The nut-cracker. 1751.

On the immensity of the Supreme Being. Cambridge 1751, 1753, 1757, 1761. Seatonian Prize poem for 1751.

An index to mankind: or maxims selected from the wits of all nations. 1751, 1754.

Poems on several occasions. 1752.

On the omniscience of the Supreme Being. Cambridge 1752, 1756, 1761. Seatonian Prize poem for 1752.

The Hilliad: an epic poem bk 1. 1753, 1753. All pbd.

On the power of the Supreme Being. Cambridge 1754, 1758, 1761. Seatonian Prize poem for 1753.

On the goodness of the Supreme Being. Cambridge 1756, 1756, 1761. Seatonian Prize poem for 1755.

Hymn to the Supreme Being on recovery from a dangerous fit of illness. 1756.

The apprentice, by Mr Murphy. 1756. Epilogue by Smart.

The works of Horace, translated literally into English prose. 2 vols 1756, 1762, 1770, Dublin 1772, 1780, 1790 etc; rptd 1911.

A song to David. 1763, 1819, 1827; ed E. Blunden 1924; rptd Oxford 1926 (facs); ed A. Hillyer, Los Angeles 1934; ed R. Todd 1947; ed J. B. Broadbent, Cambridge 1960.

Poems, viz Reason and imagination: a fable [and 3 other pieces]. [1763].

Poems on several occasions, viz Munificence and modesty [and 8 other pieces]. [1763].

Hannah: an oratorio, as perform'd at the King's Theatre in the Hay-market. [1764].

Ode to the Right Honourable the Earl of Northumberland on his being appointed Lord Lieutenant of Ireland, with some other pieces. 1764.

A poetical translation of the fables of Phaedrus. 1765, 1831, 1853 (Bohn's Lib).

A translation of the Psalms of David [including A song to David]. 1765. Selections in miscellaneous poems by Mrs Le Noir, 1825, and in a Song to David, ed E. Blunden 1924.

The works of Horace translated into verse. 4 vols 1767.

Abimelech: an oratorio as it is performed at the Theatre-Royal in Covent-Garden. [1768].

The parables of Our Lord and Saviour Jesus Christ, done into familiar verse, for the use of younger minds. 1768.

Hymns for the amusement of children. [?], Dublin 1772, London 1775 (3rd edn), Oxford 1947 (Luttrell Soc) (facs of 3rd edn).

Providence: an oratorio. 1777. Recitatives selected from Seatonian Prize poems.

Rejoice in the Lamb. Ed W. F. Stead 1939; ed W. H. Bond, Cambridge Mass 1954.

§ 2

Murry, J. M. In his Discoveries, 1924.

Havens, R. D. The structure of Smart's Song to David. RES 14 1938.

Stead, W. F. A Smart manuscript. TLS 5 March 1938.

—— Smart's metrical psalms. TLS 22 Oct 1938.

Bond, W. H. Smart's Jubilate agno. Harvard Lib Bull 4 1950.

—— Smart's last years. TLS 10 April 1953.

Devlin, C. Poor Kit Smart. 1961.

Grigson, G. Christopher Smart. 1961 (Br Council pamphlet).

Lonsdale, R. Smart's first publication in English. RES new ser 12 1961.

Sherbo, A. Smart: scholar of the University. East Lansing 1967.

Dearnley, M. The poetry of Smart. 1968.

CHARLES CHURCHILL
1731–64

Collections

Poems. 1763, 1765.

Poems. Vol II, 1765.

Poems. Ed J. Laver 2 vols 1933.

Poetical works. Ed D. Grant, Oxford 1956.
Johnson 66, 67; Anderson 10; Chalmers 14.

§ 1

The Rosciad. 1761 (5 edns), 1762, 1763 (61 lines not in
previous edns); ed R. W. Lowe 1891 (with Apology).
The apology. 1761 (5 edns), 1763; ed R. W. Lowe 1891
(with Rosciad).
Night: an epistle to Robert Lloyd. 1761, 1760 (for 1762)
(2nd-3rd edns), 1763.
The ghost, books I and II. 1762, 1762, 1763.
The ghost, book III. 1762, 1763.
The ghost, book IV. 1763.
The North Briton. 1762-3, 3 vols 1763. Churchill is said
to have written 'quite half', including a verse-satire,
The poetry professor, in nos 22 and 26.
The conference. 1763, 1764.
The author. 1763, 1764.
An epistle to William Hogarth. 1763 (3 edns), Dublin
1763.
The prophecy of famine: a Scots pastoral. 1763 (5
edns).
The duellist. 1764, 1764.
The candidate. 1764.
Gotham, bk I. 1764.
Gotham, bk II. 1764.
Gotham, bk III. 1764.
Independence. 1764.
The times. 1764.
The farewell. 1764.
The journey: a fragment. 1765.
Sermons. 1765, Dublin 1765, London 1774, Dublin 1774.
Contains satirical dedicatory verses to Warburton. The
sermons may be by the poet's father.
Letters of John Wilkes. Vol I, 1769.
The correspondence of John Wilkes, vol 3. Ed J. Almon
1805.
Correspondence of Wilkes and Churchill. Ed E. H.
Weatherley, New York 1954.

§ 2

Blunden, E. Charles Churchill. TLS 5 Feb 1931; rptd in
his Votive tablets, 1931.
Brown, W. C. Churchill: poet, rake and rebel. Lawrence
Kansas 1953.
Winters, Y. The poetry of Churchill. Poetry 98 1961;
rptd in his Forms of discovery, Denver 1967.

WILLIAM COWPER
1731-1800

Bibliographies etc

Neve, J. Concordance to the poetical works of Cowper.
1887.
Russell, N. H. Bibliography of Cowper to 1837. Oxford
1963.
Povey, K. Handlist of mss in the Cowper and Newton
Museum, Olney. Trans Cambridge Bibl Soc 4 1965.

Collections

Works. Ed John Johnson 10 vols (poems 3 vols, letters 3
vols, Iliad and Odyssey 4 vols) 1817.
Works: life and letters by W. Hayley, completed by
Cowper's private correspondence. Ed T. S. Grimshawe
8 vols 1835, 1836, 1 vol 1847.
Works: comprising his poems, correspondence and translations. Ed with life by R. Southey 15 vols 1835-7, 8
vols 1853-5 (Bohn's Lib).

§ 1

Olney hymns [66 by Cowper, 9 already pbd (see
Russell, above), the rest by J. Newton]. 1779, 1781,
1783, 1787, 1788, 1792, 1797, 1797, 1806, 1807, 1810.
Anti-Thelyphthora: a tale in verse. 1781. Anon.
Poems. 1 vol 1782 (a few copies have preface by J.
Newton); The task, 1785 (vol 2); 2 vols 1786 (2 issues of
Task), 1787, 1788, 1793 (with preface by Newton),
1794-5 (adding 9 poems), St Andrews 1797, London
1798 (adding 2 poems; 4 edns, one being the St
Andrews edn with cancel titles and the new poems),
1799, 1800 (3 edns, with appendixes of new poems),
1801, 1802 (incorporating appendixes), 1803, 1805, 1806
(3 edns), 1806 (1 vol 4° incorporating trns from Mme
Guyon and Olney hymns), 1808 (adding 3 poems, 3
edns), 1810, 1810 (Chalmers vol 18), 1811, 1812.
The history of John Gilpin. Public Advertiser 14 Nov
1782. Anon. Separately pbd J. Fielding [1785], [c.
1785] (3rd edn); with Life of John Gilpin, London and
Dublin 1785; with 6 illustrations by G. Cruikshank
1828; illustr R. Searle 1953; ed N. H. Russell 1968.
Stanzas subjoined to the bills of mortality for the parish of
All-Saints Northampton, for the years 1787, 1788, 1789,
1790, 1792, 1793. Northampton 1787-93. Anon.
A good song ('Here's a health to honest John Bull'). [c.
1792-3]. Anon; probably by Cowper. Also found with
variant titles 'John Bull: a song' etc.
Poems, I: On the receipt of my mother's picture; II: The
dog and the water-lily. 1798, Oxford 1926 (facs).
Adelphi. Ed J. Newton 1802, 1816. Extracts pbd during
Cowper's lifetime by the Rev David Simpson; abridged
in Religious Tract Soc no 161 [c. 1819]; ed H. P.
Stokes, Olney 1904 (in Cowper memorials).
Many new poems were first pbd in W. Hayley, Life of
Cowper, 1803-6; see §2, below.
Posthumous poetry [=Poems vol 3]. Ed John Johnson
1815. Contains nearly all the poems and trns pbd by
Hayley, with a few unpbd ones.
Memoir of the early life of William Cowper esq written by
himself. 1816, 1816, 1817, 1818, Birmingham 1817 (as
Narrative of the life) (all pbd Edwards), 1816 (pbd Cox,
as Memoirs of the most remarkable and interesting
parts of the life), 1822 (with Olney hymns by Cowper),
1835 (as Autobiography of Cowper); ed M. J. Quinlan,
Proc Amer Philosophical Soc 97 1953.
Poems, the early productions of Cowper, now first
published; with anecdotes of the poet. Ed J. Croft
1825.
Poetical works. Ed H. S. Milford, Oxford 1905 (OSA),
1913 (with addns), 1926 (enlarged), 1934 (with appendix
of new poems); rev N. H. Russell, Oxford 1967.
Selections from Cowper: poetry and prose; with essays
by Hazlitt and Bagehot. Ed H. S. Milford, Oxford
1921.
New poems. Ed F. Madan 1931.
Poetry and prose. Ed B. Spiller 1968 (Reynard Lib).
Selections.

Translations

Horace, Works in English verse by several hands, collected
by Mr Duncombe. 2 vols 1757-9, 4 vols 1767. Cowper's
trns of bk 1, satires 5 and 9 are in vol 2 of first edn and
vol 3 of 1767 edn.
Voltaire, The Henriade, translated by T. Smollett, T.
Francklin and others. 1762, 1772, 1781, Paris etc 1901,
New York 1927. Cantos 5-8 tr Cowper, anon.
Homer, The Iliad and Odyssey, translated into blank
verse by Cowper. 2 vols 1791, Dublin 1792, 4 vols
1802, 1809, 1810 (with 50 plates), 1817 (vols 7-10 of
Works), 2 vols 1820; in Poems, ed H. F. Cary 1839;
Odyssey, 1910 (EL).
Guyon, J. M. B. de la Motte. Poems translated from
the French by the late William Cowper. Ed W. Bull

1801 (adding a few uncollected poems), 1802, 1803, 1811.

Latin and Italian poems of Milton translated into English verse, and a fragment of a commentary on Paradise lost by the late William Cowper. Ed W. Hayley 1808. Extracts from Cowper's trns first pbd in Hayley's Life of Milton, 1796.

Cowper's Milton. Ed W. Hayley 4 vols 1810, 1811, 1835.

Letters

The letters in Hayley's Life of Cowper (*see* §2, *below*), *were rptd as vols 4–6 of* Works, *1817, and in 1 vol* 1820, 1827.

Private correspondence. Ed J. Johnson 2 vols 1824 (3 edns).

Correspondence. Ed T. Wright 4 vols 1904.

Selection. Ed E. V. Lucas, Oxford 1908 (WC); rptd with notes by M. L. Milford, Oxford 1911.

Letters. Ed J. G. Frazer 2 vols 1912.

Unpublished and uncollected letters. Ed T. Wright 1925.

§2

Hayley, W. Life and posthumous writings of Cowper. Vols 1–2, 1803, 1803; vol 3, 1804; Supplementary pages, 1806; 4 vols 1806, 1809 (as Life and letters), 1812, 3 vols 1824, 1 vol 1835. Contains letters and many unpbd poems.

Hazlitt, W. In his Lectures on the English poets, 1818.

Bagehot, W. Cowper. Nat Rev 1 1855; rptd in his Estimations in criticism, 1908.

Sainte-Beuve, C. A. Cowper: ou de la poésie domestique. In his Causeries du lundi vol 11, Paris 1856.

Stephen, L. Cowper and Rousseau. In his Hours in a library ser 3, 1879.

Smith, G. Cowper. 1880 (EML).

Wright, T. The life of Cowper. 1892, 1921 (rev).

Povey, K. Cowper's spiritual diary. London Mercury March 1927.

— The text of Cowper's letters. MLR 22 1927.

— Some notes on Cowper's letters and poems. RES 5 1929; Notes for a bibliography of Cowper's letters, RES 7–8 1931–2, 10 1934, 12 1936.

— Cowper and Lady Austen. RES 10 1934.

Cecil, D. The stricken deer: or the life of Cowper. 1929.

Thomas, G. Cowper and the eighteenth century. 1935, 1948 (rev).

Forster, E. M. Cowper, an Englishman. Spectator 16 Jan 1932.

Woolf, V. Cowper and Lady Austen. In her Common reader ser 2, 1932.

Strachey, G. L. Gray and Cowper. In his Characters and commentaries, 1933.

Hartley, L. C. Cowper, humanitarian. Chapel Hill 1938.

Nicholson, N. Cowper. 1951.

— Cowper. 1960 (Br Council pamphlet).

Davie, D. A. The critical principles of Cowper. Cambridge Jnl Dec 1953.

Sherbo, A. Cowper's Connoisseur essays. MLN 70 1955.

Bentley, G. E., jr. William Blake and 'Johnny of Norfolk'. SP 53 1956.

— Blake, Hayley and Lady Hesketh. RES new ser 7 1956.

Brooks, E. L. Cowper's periodical contributions. TLS 17 Aug 1956.

Letters of Dean Spencer Cowper. Ed E. Hughes, Surtees Soc 165 1956.

Huang, R. Cowper: nature poet. Oxford 1957.

Ryskamp, C. William Cowper of the Inner Temple esq. Cambridge 1959.

— The cast-away: text of original ms and first printing of Cowper's Latin translation. Princeton 1963.

— Johnson and Cowper. Princeton 1965.

— Richardson and Cowper. Library 5th ser 19 1968.

Keynes, G. L. The library of Cowper. Trans Cambridge Bibl Soc 3 pt 1 1959. Addns by Keynes, pt 2 1960; by N. H. Russell, pt 3 1961.

Golden, M. In search of stability: the poetry of Cowper. New Haven 1964.

JAMES MACPHERSON
1736–96

Collections

Fragments of ancient poetry collected in the highlands of Scotland. Edinburgh 1760, 1760 (rev with one addn), 1881; ed L. Jiriczek, Heidelberg 1915; Edinburgh 1917; ed J. J. Dunn, Los Angeles 1966 (Augustan Reprint Soc).

Fingal: an ancient epic poem, with several other poems translated from the Galic language. 1762, 1762.

Temora: an ancient epic poem, with several other poems translated from the Galic language. 1763.

The works of Ossian, translated by James Macpherson. 2 vols 1765 (with Hugh Blair, Critical dissertation), Dublin 1765, London 1773, Darmstadt 1773–5, 4 vols Frankfurt 1773–7, Frankfurt and Leipzig 1783, Paris 1783, 2 vols 1784–5, 1790, Dublin 1790, Philadelphia 1790, Edinburgh 1792, 1792, Berwick 1795, Perth 1795, London 1796, London and Glasgow [1796–7].

Ossian: Faksimile-Neudruck der Erstausgabe von 1762–3 mit Begleitband: die Varianten. Ed O. L. Jiriczek 3 vols Heidelberg 1940.

§1

The Highlander: an heroic poem in six cantos. 1758.

An introduction to the history of Great Britain and Ireland. 1771.

The Iliad translated into prose. 2 vols 1773.

The history of Great Britain from the Restoration to the accession of the House of Hanover. 2 vols 1775.

Original papers: containing the secret history of Great Britain from the Restoration to the accession of the House of Hanover. 2 vols 1775.

The rights of Great Britain asserted against the claims of America. 1776.

A short history of the opposition during the last session of Parliament. 1779.

§2

Blair, H. A critical dissertation on the poems of Ossian. 1763.

Saunders, T. B. The life and letters of Macpherson. 1894.

Thomson, D. S. The Gaelic sources of Ossian. Edinburgh 1952.

THOMAS CHATTERTON
1752–70

The major ms collections are in BM and Central Library, Bristol.

Collections

Poems, supposed to have been written at Bristol, by Thomas Rowley, and others, in the fifteenth century. [Ed T. Tyrwhitt] 1777, 1777, 1778 (with Tyrwhitt's An appendix tending to prove that they were written by Chatterton); ed J. Milles 1782 (with addns); ed L. Sharpe, Cambridge 1794; ed M. E. Hare, Oxford 1911 (from 1778).

Miscellanies in prose and verse. [Ed J. Broughton] 1778.

A supplement to the miscellanies. 1784.

Works. Ed R. Southey [and J. Cottle] 3 vols 1803. With G. Gregory's life.

Poems. Ed S. Lee 2 vols [1905], 1906-9.

Complete poetical works. Ed H. D. Roberts 2 vols 1906.

Complete works. Ed D. S. Taylor and B. B. Hoover 2 vols Oxford 1970.

§ 1

The execution of Sir Charles Bawdin. 1772.

Song to Ælle. Westminster Mag 1775.

A short account of William Cannings. Town & Country Mag 7 1775.

European Mag 20-1 1791-2. 6 pieces.

The revenge: a burletta, with additional songs. 1795.

During Chatterton's lifetime he pbd anon or pseudonymously in Felix Farley's Bristol Jnl 1768-9 (*2 pieces*), Bristol Jnl 1769 (*one piece*), Town & Country Mag 1769-70 (*29 pieces*), Universal Mag 1769 (*one piece*), Middlesex Jnl 1770 (*13 pieces*), Freeholder's Mag 1770 (*2 pieces*), Boddeley's Bath Jnl 1770 (*one piece*), Court & City Mag 1770 (*3 pieces*), London Mag 1770 (*2 pieces*). *After his death, pieces he had submitted were pbd in* Town & Country Mag 1770 (*one piece*), 1771 (*2 pieces*), 1783 (*one piece*). *For these periodicals, see index to E. H. W. Meyerstein, A life of Chatterton, 1930, below.*

Letters

[Croft, H.] Love and madness: a story too true in a series of letters. 1780 etc. Letter 49, a sketch of Chatterton, first prints 3 of his poems and 8 of his letters.

Walpole, H. Works. 1798. Vol 4 first prints 3 Chatterton letters.

Britton, J. An historical essay relating to Redcliffe church. 1813. First prints 2 letters to Dodsley.

Walpole's correspondence with Chatterton. Ed W. S. Lewis et al, New Haven 1951 (vol 16 of Yale Walpole).

§ 2

Interest in Chatterton and the Rowley controversy can be traced in GM, where articles appear annually 1777-92, thereafter frequently till 1840.

Warton, T. In his History of English poetry, 3 vols 1774-81 (vol 2 and addenda).

— An enquiry into the authenticity of the poems attributed to Rowley. 1782, 1782.

Walpole, H. A letter to the editor of the Miscellanies of Chatterton. Strawberry Hill 1779; rptd GM 1782.

[Malone, E.] Cursory observations on the poems attributed to Rowley. 1782; ed J. M. Kuist, Los Angeles 1966 (Augustan Reprint Soc).

Tyrwhitt, T. A vindication of the appendix to the poems called Rowley's. 1782.

Mathias, T. J. An essay on the evidence relating to the poems attributed to Rowley. 1783.

Gregory, G. The life of Chatterton. 1789; rptd in Biographia britannica, 1789; Works, 1803.

Browning, R. Foreign Quart Rev 29 1842; ed D. A. Smalley, Cambridge Mass 1948 (as Browning's essay on Chatterton). A review of R. H. Wilde, Tasso.

Masson, D. Chatterton: a biography. 1899.

Meyerstein, E. H. W. A life of Chatterton. 1930.

Ellinger, E. P. Chatterton: the marvelous boy. Philadelphia 1930.

Bronson, B. H. In The age of Johnson, New Haven 1949.

Taylor, D. S. Chatterton's suicide. PQ 31 1952.

— The authenticity of Chatterton's Miscellanies. PBSA 55 1961.

— Chatterton: the problem of Rowley chronology. PQ 46 1967.

Cottle, B. Thomas Chatterton. Bristol 1963 (Bristol Historical Assoc pamphlet).

GEORGE CRABBE
1754-1832

Collections

Poetical works (Poems, Borough, Tales). 4 vols 1816, 1816, 3 vols 1816?; Poems, Borough, Tales, Tales of the hall, 7 vols 1820, 5 vols 1820?; 5 vols 1823, 8 vols 1823; with letters and journals, and life by his son, 8 vols 1834 etc (includes Posthumous tales).

Poetical works. Ed A. J. and R. M. Carlyle, Oxford 1908 (OSA), 1914.

Crabbe: an anthology. Ed F. L. Lucas, Cambridge 1933.

Tales and miscellaneous poems. Ed H. Mills, Cambridge 1967.

A selection. Ed J. Lucas 1967.

§ 1

Poems

Inebriety: a poem in three parts. Ipswich 1775. Anon.

The candidate: a poetical epistle to the authors of the Monthly Review. 1780. Anon.

The library. 1781 (anon), 1783 (signed); rptd in Poems, 1807; A miscellany, ed H. Morley 1888.

The village: a poem in two books. 1783. Trial issue ptd by J. Nichols c. 1781? New York 1790, Boston 1791.

The news-paper. 1785; rptd in Poems, 1807.

Poems. 1807 (first pbn of The parish register), Philadelphia [1807], London 1808, 1808, New York 1808, Philadelphia 1808, 2 vols 1809, 1810, 1812, 1 vol 1812, 1813, 1816, 1817, 1820, 1835, 1837, 1840, [1850?], 1863 etc; ed H. Morley 1886.

A poem for the anniversary of the Literary Fund, April 20 1809. GM April 1809. Lines 188-336 of Borough iii, with variants.

The borough: a poem in twenty-four letters. 1810 (3 edns, one in 2 vols), Philadelphia 1810, 2 vols 1812, 1 vol 1813, 1816, 1820; ed H. Williams 1903.

Tales. 1812, 2 vols 1812, 1 vol 1813, 2 vols 1813, New York 1813, 1 vol 1814, 2 vols 1814, 1 vol 1816, 2 vols 1820, 1 vol 1854; ed H. Morley 1891 (selected).

Verses by the Rev G. Crabbe, written on the night of the 15th of April 17** [1782?]. Literary Gazette 16 Aug 1817.

Tales of the hall. 2 vols 1819, 1819, Boston 1819, 3 vols 1820.

Lines by the Rev George Crabbe LlB. [Edinburgh 1822]; rptd in Occasional verses on the King's visit to Scotland [Edinburgh 1822]; GM Sept 1822; in Royal Scottish minstrelsy, Leith 1824.

Posthumous tales. First pbd in Poetical works vol 8, 1834.

Literary anecdotes of the nineteenth century. Ed W. R. Nicoll and T. J. Wise 1896. Vol 2 includes Two poetical epistles.

New poems by Crabbe. Ed A. Pollard, Liverpool 1960. Hester, Joseph and Jesse, Poins, David Morris and 10 other unpbd poems.

Sermons and Prose Writings

A discourse on 2 Corinthians 1.9 read in the chapel at Belvoir Castle after the funeral of the Duke of Rutland. 1788.

The natural history of the Vale of Belvoir. In J. Nichols, The history and antiquities of the county of Leicester vol 1 pt 1, 1795.

A catalogue of plants growing in and near Framlingham. In R. Hawes, History of Framlingham ed R. Loder, Woodbridge 1798.

Memoirs of eminent persons: biographical account of the Rev G. Crabbe [written by himself]. New Monthly Mag Jan 1816; rptd in Annual biography and obituary for 1833; Catalogue of the bicentenary exhibition, Aldeburgh 1954.

The variation of public opinion and feelings considered as it respects religion: a sermon preached before the Lord Bishop of Sarum, 15 August 1817. 1817.

Posthumous sermons. Ed J. D. Hastings 1850.

§ 2

Hazlitt, W. Mr Crabbe. London Mag May 1821; rptd in part in his Spirit of the age, 1825 (in Mr Campbell and Mr Crabbe).

Crabbe, George, jr. The life of the Rev George Crabbe by his son. In Poetical works vol 1, 1834; rptd in edns of the Works; Cambridge Mass 1834; ed E. M. Forster, Oxford 1932 (WC); ed E. Blunden 1947.

Stephen, L. Hours in a library no 9: Crabbe's poetry. Cornhill Mag Oct 1874; rptd in his Hours in a library ser 2, 1876.

Saintsbury, G. Crabbe. Macmillan's Mag June 1889; rptd in his Essays in English literature 1780–1860, 1890.

Huchon, R. Un poète réaliste anglais: Crabbe. Paris 1906; tr 1907.

Pound, E. The Rev G. Crabbe Llb. In The Future, 1917; rptd in his Literary essays, 1954.

Forster, E. M. Crabbe. Spectator 20 Feb 1932.
—— Crabbe: the poet and the man. Listener 29 May 1941; rptd with alterations in Peter Grimes: an opera, 1945.
—— Crabbe and Peter Grimes. In his Two cheers for democracy, [1951].

Woolf, V. In her Captain's death bed, 1950.

Haddakin, L. The poetry of Crabbe. 1955.

Hodgart, P. and T. Redpath. Romantic perspectives: the work of Crabbe, Blake, Wordsworth and Coleridge as seen by their contemporaries and by themselves. 1964.

Chamberlain, R. L. Crabbe. New York 1965.

Sigworth, O. F. Nature's sternest painter: five essays on the poetry of Crabbe. Tucson 1965.

New, P. J. Crabbe's poetry. 1976.

WILLIAM BLAKE
1757–1827

Bibliographies etc

Keynes, G. L. A bibliography of Blake. New York 1921.
—— and E. Wolf. Blake's illuminated books: a census. New York 1953.

Keynes, G. L. Engravings by Blake: the separate plates, a catalogue raisonné. Dublin 1956.
—— Blake's illustrations to the Bible. 1957.

Bentley, G. E., jr and M. K. Nurmi. A Blake bibliography: annotated lists of works, studies and Blakeana. Minneapolis 1964, Oxford 1976 (as Blake books)

Erdman, D. V. et al. A concordance to the writings of Blake. 2 vols Ithaca 1967.

§ 1

Works in Illuminated Printing
The works are etched in relief unless otherwise stated.

There is no natural religion, series a and b. [c. 1788]. 19 plates. 13 very imperfect copies known.

All religions are one. [c. 1788]. 10 plates. The one known copy is in Huntington Library.

The book of Thel. 1789. 8 plates. 16 copies.

Songs of innocence. 1789. 31 plates. 22 copies.

The marriage of Heaven and Hell [including A song of liberty]. [c. 1793]. 27 plates. 10 copies.

Prospectus: to the public. 1793. One plate. Untraced.

For children: the gates of Paradise. 1793. 18 plates. 5 copies. Reissued, with additional text as For the sexes: the gates of Paradise, [c. 1818].

Visions of the daughters of Albion. 1793. 11 plates. 16 copies.

America: a prophecy. 1793. 18 plates. 17 copies.

Songs of innocence and of experience, shewing the two contrary states of the human soul. 1794. 54 plates. 27 contemporary copies, 5 incomplete.

Europe: a prophecy. 1794. 18 plates. 12 copies.

The first book of Urizen. 1794. 28 plates. 7 copies.

The book of Ahania. 1795. 6 plates in ordinary etching. The one known copy is in Library of Congress.

The book of Los. 1795. 5 plates in ordinary etching. The one known copy is in BM.

The song of Los. 1795. 8 plates. 5 copies.

Milton: a poem in 2 books. 1804 (completed c. 1808). 50 plates. 4 copies.

Jerusalem: the emanation of the giant Albion. 1804 (completed c. 1820). 100 plates. 8 copies traced, 3 posthumous.

For the sexes: the gates of Paradise. [c. 1818]. 21 engraved plates. 7 copies. A rev issue of For children: the gates of Paradise, 1793, with additional text.

[The Laocoon]. [c. 1818]. 2 copies. A line engraving of the Laocoon group with detached sentences inscribed in all directions around it.

On Homer's poetry [and] On Virgil. [c. 1820]. One plate. 6 copies.

The ghost of Abel: a revelation in the visions of Jehovah seen by William Blake. 1822. 2 plates. 4 copies.

Works Printed in Ordinary Type

Poetical sketches. 1783. 20 copies.

The French Revolution, a poem, in seven books: book the first. 1791. The one known copy is in Huntington Library.

Exhibitions of paintings in fresco, poetical and historical inventions. [May 1809]. A broadside leaflet. 2 copies.

Blake's Chaucer: the Canterbury pilgrims. [May 1809]. A broadside leaflet. The one known copy is in BM.

A descriptive catalogue of pictures, poetical and historical inventions. 1809. 18 copies.

Blake's Chaucer: an original engraving. [c. 1810]. A broadside leaflet. 2 copies.

Notebook. Ed G. L. Keynes 1935; ed D. V. Erdman, Oxford 1973 (facs of Rossetti ms).

Jerusalem [E]. 1951 (Blake Trust).

Jerusalem [C]. 1952, 1955 (Blake Trust).

Songs of innocence [b]. 1954 (Blake Trust).

Songs of innocence and of experience [Z]. 1955 (Blake Trust).

The book of Urizen [G]. 1958 (Blake Trust).

Visions of the daughters of Albion. 1959 (Blake Trust).

The marriage of Heaven and Hell [D]. 1960 (Blake Trust).

Vala, or the Four Zoas: facsimile, transcript and study by G. E. Bentley jr. Oxford 1963.

America [M]. 1963 (Blake Trust).

Milton [D]. 1967 (Blake Trust).

The gates of Paradise: for children [D]; for the sexes [F]. Introductory vol by G. L. Keynes 1968 (Blake Trust).

Europe [B, G]. 1969 (Blake Trust).

Tiriel: facsimile and transcript of the manuscript, and reproduction of the drawings, and a commentary on the poem by G. E. Bentley jr. Oxford 1967.

Typographical Reprints

Works. Ed E. J. Ellis and W. B. Yeats, with a memoir and interpretation 3 vols 1893.

Poems. Ed W. B. Yeats 1893 (ML).

Poetical works. Ed J. Sampson, Oxford 1905, 1947. The

Poetical works. Ed J. Sampson, Oxford 1913 etc. The text

of 1905, above, with the first pbn of French Revolution and with the shorter symbolic works, and a selection from the longer ones.

Writings. Ed G. L. Keynes 3 vols 1925, 1 vol 1957 (as Complete writings), 1966. The first comprehensive edn.

Prophetic writings. Ed D. J. Sloss and J. P. R. Wallis 2 vols Oxford 1926, 1957, 1964. A fresh text with an index of symbols.

Poetry and prose. Ed G. L. Keynes 1927, 1932, 1939, 1943 (reset), 1948, 1956. A popular revision of the text of 1925, above, omitting most variants, notes etc.

Vala: Blake's numbered text. Ed H. M. Margoliouth, Oxford 1956.

Selected poems. Ed F. W. Bateson 1957.

Poetry and prose. Ed D. V. Erdman, commentary by H. Bloom, Garden City NY 1965. A fresh text with Blake's punctuation.

Poems. Ed W. H. Stevenson and D. V. Erdman 1971.

The illuminated Blake. Ed D. V. Erdman, Oxford 1975.

Writings. Ed G. E. Bentley 2 vols Oxford 1977.

Reproductions of Drawings and Paintings

Illustrations to the Divine comedy of Dante. 1922; ed G. L. Keynes 1927; Blake's illustrations for Dante selections from the originals in the National Gallery of Victoria, Melbourne, Australia and the Fogg Art Museum, Cambridge Massachusetts, Cambridge Mass 1953; The Melbourne Dante illustrations, ed V. Hoff, Melbourne 1961.

Milton, John. Poems in English. Ed G. L. Keynes 2 vols 1926.

Illustrations to Young's Night thoughts. Ed G. L. Keynes 1927.

Pencil drawings by Blake. Ed G. L. Keynes 2 sers 1927, 1956.

Illustrations of the Book of Job by Blake: being all the water-colour designs, pencil drawings and engravings. Ed L. Binyon and G. L. Keynes, New York 1935; Illustrations of the Book of Job, reproduced in facsimile from the original New Zealand set, ed P. Hofer 1937.

Bunyan, John. The pilgrim's progress. Ed G. L. Keynes, New York 1941 (Limited Edns Club); New York 1942.

Letters

Letters to Thomas Butts 1800-3. Ed G. L. Keynes, Oxford 1926 (facs).

Letters. Ed G. L. Keynes 1956, 1968 (rev).

§ 2

See Blake records [1737-1831] ed G. E. Bentley, Oxford 1967; Blake: the critical heritage, ed Bentley 1975.

Gilchrist, Alexander. Life of Blake. 2 vols 1863, 1880 (rev); ed W. Graham Robertson 1906 etc; ed R. Todd 1942 (EL), 1945.

Swinburne, A. C. Blake: a critical essay. 1868.

Eliot, T. S. In his Sacred wood, 1920; rptd in his Selected essays, 1932, and in his Points of view, 1941.

Plowman, M. An introduction to the study of Blake. 1927, 1952; ed R. H. Ward 1967.

Wilson, M. The life of Blake. 1927, 1932 (without notes), 1948 (rev); ed G. L. Keynes, Oxford 1971.

Frye, N. Fearful symmetry: a study of Blake. Princeton 1947.

— (ed). Blake: a collection of critical essays. Englewood Cliffs NJ 1965.

Grigson, G. Palmer and Blake. In his Samuel Palmer: the visionary years, 1947.

Blackstone, B. English Blake. Cambridge 1949, Hamden Conn 1966.

— The traveller unknown. In his Lost travellers, 1962.

Keynes, G. L. Blake studies. 1949, Oxford 1971 (rev with addns).

Raine, K. William Blake. 1951 (Br Council pamphlet), 1965 (rev).

— Blake and tradition. 2 vols Princeton [1969].

Erdman, D. V. Blake: prophet against empire. Princeton 1954, 1970 (with addns).

Pinto, V. de S. (ed). The divine vision: studies in the poetry and art of Blake. 1957.

Gleckner, R. F. The piper and the bard: a study of Blake. Detroit 1959.

Hirsch, E. D., jr. Innocence and experience: an introduction to Blake. New Haven 1964.

Beer, J. Blake's humanism. Manchester 1968.

Holloway, J. Blake: the lyric poetry. 1968.

Raine, K. Blake and tradition. 2 vols 1969.

Blake: essays in honour of Sir Geoffrey Keynes. Oxford 1973.

Nurmi, M. K. William Blake. 1975.

VII. MINOR POETRY 1750–1800

MARK AKENSIDE

1720–71

Collections

Poems. [Ed J. Dyson] 1772, 1772, Edinburgh 1773.

Anderson 9; Chalmers 14; Johnson 55.

§ 1

A British philippic. GM Aug 1738; 1738, 1738 (as The voice of liberty: a British philippic).

The pleasures of imagination.1744, Dublin 1748, London 1754 (5th edn), Edinburgh 1758 (with Odes on several subjects), London 1763, 1765, Edinburgh 1768, London 1769, Glasgow 1771, 1775, 1777, 1780, London 1786, 1788, 1794 (with essay by Mrs Barbauld), 1795, New

York 1795, Portland Maine 1807 etc. Final revision and fragment of bk iv first ptd in 1772 collected edn.

An epistle to Warburton. 1744. Often attributed to J. Dyson.

An epistle to Curio. 1744.

Dissertatio medica inauguralis, de ortu et encremento foetus humani. Leyden 1744.

Odes on several subjects. 1745, 1745, 1760 (rev).

Friendship and love: a dialog; to which is added A song. 1745.

An ode to the Earl of Huntingdon. 1748, 1748.

An ode to the country gentlemen of England. 1758, 1758.

Notes on the postscript to a pamphlet by Alexander Monro. 1758.

Oratio anniversaria in theatro Collegii Regalis. 1760.

De dysenteria commentarius. 1764.

An ode to the late Thomas Edwards. 1766.

The works of William Harvey. 1766. Ed Akenside.

Williams, R. M. Two unpublished poems by Akenside. MLN 57 1942.

Akenside contributed to Dodsley's Collection vol 6, 1758 (*5 poems*) *and to* The new foundling hospital for wit vol 6, 1773. *He edited* The museum: or the literary and historical register 29 March 1746–12 Sept 1747. *He contributed medical papers to* Philosophical Trans of Royal Soc 1757, 1763 *and to* Medical Trans 1772.

§ 2

Johnson, S. In his Lives of the poets, 1779–81.

Houpt, C. T. Akenside: a biographical and critical study. Philadelphia 1944.

Renwick, W. L. Notes on some lesser poets of the eighteenth century. In Essays on the eighteenth century presented to David Nichol Smith, Oxford 1945.

CHRISTOPHER ANSTEY
1724–1805
Collections

The poetical works, with some account of the life and writings by his son John Anstey. 1808.

§ 1

Elegia scripta in coemeterio rustico latine reditta. Cambridge 1762, 1778. With W. H. Roberts.

On the death of the Marquis of Tavistock. 1767 (4 edns).

The new Bath guide: or memoirs of the B[lunde]R[hea]D family in a series of poetical epistles. 1766 (3 edns), Dublin 1766, London 1767, 1768 (6th edn), Dublin 1768, London 1772 (8th edn), 1773, 1776, 1784 (12th edn), 1788, 1797, 1804, 1830, 1832 etc; ed P. Sainsbury 1927.

The patriot: a pindaric address to Lord Buckhorse. Cambridge 1767, 1768 (with appendix), 1779.

Appendix to the Patriot. 1768.

Ode on an evening view of the Crescent at Bath. 1773.

The priest dissected: a poem addressed to the Rev Mr —— ——, author of Regulus, Toby, Caesar and other satirical pieces, canto 1. Bath 1774, 1774, nd.

An election ball in poetical letters in the Zomersetshire dialect from Mr Inkle of Bath to his wife at Glocester; with a poetical address to John Miller. 1776 (several edns), Dublin 1776, 1776, Bath 1776 ('the second edition with considerable additions'), 1779, 1787.

Fabulae selectae auctore Johanne Gay latine redditae. [1777], 1798.

Ad C. W. Bampfylde, arm: epistola poetica familiaris. Bath, London, Cambridge, Oxford 1776, 1776, Bath 1777. Tr anon as A familiar epistle from C. Anstey to C. W. Bampfylde, 1777, Dublin 1777.

Envy: a poem, addressed to Mrs Miller. [1778].

Winter amusements: an ode. [1778].

A paraphrase of the thirteenth chapter of first Corinthians. 1779.

Speculation, or a defence of mankind: a poem. 1780.

Liberality, or the decayed macaroni: a sentimental piece. 1788, [1790?].

The farmer's daughter: a poetical tale. Bath 1795, 1795.

The monopolist: a poetical tale. 1795.

Britain's genius: a song occasioned by the late mutiny at the Nore. Bath 1797.

Contentment: a poetical epistle. 1800.

Ad Edvardum Jenner: carmen alcaicum. Bath 1803. Tr J. Ring as A translation of Anstey's Ode to Jenner, 1804 (2nd edn).

§ 2

Powell, W. C. Anstey: Bath laureate. Philadelphia 1944. With bibliography.

ANNA LAETITIA AIKIN,
later BARBAULD
1743–1825
Collections

Miscellaneous pieces in prose. 1773, 1775, 1792. With J. Aikin.

Poems. 1773 (3 edns), 1774, 1777, 1792 (with Epistle to Wilberforce).

Works. 2 vols 1825, New York 1826. With memoir by L. Aikin.

Mrs Barbauld edited Collins, 1794, 1797; Akenside's Pleasures of imagination, 1794; Selections from the Spectator, Tatler etc, 3 vols 1804; Correspondence of Samuel Richardson, 6 vols 1804; The British novelists, 50 vols 1810; The female speaker, 1811.

§ 1

Corsica: an ode. 1768.

Lessons for children. 1778, 1779, 1787, 1788, 1808, 1812, 1821.

Hymns in prose for children. 1781, 1814 (16th edn), 1836 (28th edn), 1845 (30th edn).

Address to the opposers of the repeal of the corporation and test acts. 1790 (4 edns).

Epistle to Wilberforce. 1791, 1791.

Civic sermons to the people. 1792.

Remarks on Wakefield's Enquiry. 1792 (3 edns).

Sins of the government, sins of the nation, by a volunteer. 1793.

Eighteen hundred and eleven. 1812, Philadelphia 1812.

A discourse on being born again. Boston 1830 (2nd edn). A tract.

§ 2

Ellis, G. A. A memoir, letters and a selection from the writings of Anna Barbauld. 2 vols Boston 1874.

Le Breton, A. L. A memoir of Mrs Barbauld, including letters. 1874.

Rodgers, B. Georgian chronicle: Mrs Barbauld and her family. 1958.

JAMES BEATTIE
1735–1803
Collections

Original poems and translations. 1760, Aberdeen 1761.

Poems on several subjects. 1766.

Essays. Edinburgh 1776, 1776, 2 vols Dublin 1778, Edinburgh 1778, 1779.

Poems on several occasions Edinburgh 1776, 1780 (4th edn).

Dissertations moral and critical. 1783, 2 vols Dublin 1783, London 1786.

Chalmers 18.

§ 1

The judgment of Paris: a poem. 1765.

Verses occasioned by the death of Churchill. 1765.

An essay on the nature and immutability of truth. 1770, Edinburgh 1771, London 1772, 1773, 1774, Edinburgh 1774, 1777, London 1778, 1807, 1810 etc.

The minstrel, or the progress of genius: a poem, book the first. 1771, 1771, 1772, 1774, 1775; Book the second, 1774 (3 edns); In two books, with some other poems, 1775, Dublin 1775, London 1777, 1779, 1784, 1795, 1797, 2 vols 1799 (with life and miscellaneous poems), Edinburgh 1803, 1805, 1806, Alnwick 1807, 1807, Edinburgh 1807, London 1807, 1821, 1858.

A letter to the Rev H. Blair on the improvement of psalmody. 1778, Edinburgh 1829.

Scoticisms, arranged in alphabetical order. 1779, 1787, Edinburgh 1811.

Evidences of the Christian religion briefly stated. 2 vols Edinburgh 1786, Philadelphia 1787, London 1795, 1814 etc.

The theory of language. 1788.

Elements of moral science. 2 vols Edinburgh 1790–3, 1807, 1817.

Essays and fragments in prose and verse, by James Hay Beattie. 1794, 1799. Ed elder Beattie, with biographical sketch.

Letters and Diaries

Letters of Beattie. In British prose writers vol 5, 1819–21.

Mackie, A. Beattie, the Minstrel: some unpublished letters. Aberdeen 1908.

Beattie's London diary 1773. Ed R. S. Walker, Aberdeen 1946.

Day-book 1773–98. Ed R. S. Walker, Aberdeen 1948.

§ 2

Bower, A. An account of the life of Beattie. 1804.

Forbes, W. An account of the life and writings of Beattie, including many letters. 2 vols Edinburgh 1806, 3 vols 1807, 2 vols 1824.

Tave, S. M. Some essays by Beattie in the London Magazine 1771. N & Q 6 Dec 1952.

WILLIAM LISLE BOWLES
1762–1850
Collections

Fourteen sonnets, elegiac and descriptive, written during a tour. Bath and London 1789, 1789 (rev, 21 sonnets, as Sonnets written chiefly on picturesque spots), London 1794 (27 sonnets, 13 other poems, as Sonnets, with other poems), Bath 1796 (as Sonnets, and other poems), 1796, London and Bath 1798, Bath 1800 (with Poems, 1801, issued as suppl), 2 vols Bath and London 1801–2, London 1803, 2 vols 1805, Zürich 1950 (16 sonnets with trns).

§ 1

Verses to John Howard FRS. Bath, London and Oxford 1789.

The grave of Howard: a poem. Salisbury and London 1790.

Verses on the benevolent institution of the philanthropic society. Bath and London 1790.

A poetical address to Edmund Burke. 1791.

Elegy written at the Hot-wells, Bristol. Bath and London 1791.

Monody, written at Matlock. Salisbury, London and Bath 1791.

Elegiac stanzas, written during sickness at Bath. Bath and London 1796.

Hope: an allegorical sketch. London and Bath 1796.

St Michael's Mount: a poem. Salisbury, Shaftesbury and London 1798.

Coombe Ellen: a poem. Bath and London 1798.

Song of the battle of the Nile. 1799.

The sorrows of Switzerland: a poem. London and Bath 1801.

The picture: verses suggested by a landscape of Rubens. 1803.

The spirit of discovery, or the conquest of ocean: a poem in five books. Bath and London 1804, 1809. Issued as suppl to Poems, 1801 (see Fourteen sonnets, above).

Bowden Hill: the banks of the Wye. Southampton [1806].

The works of Pope. 10 vols 1806. Ed Bowles.

Poems, written chiefly at Bremhill. London and Bath 1809. Issued as vol 4, suppl to Spirit of discovery, above.

The missionary: a poem. 1813, 1815 (enlarged), 1816, 1835 (5th edn as The ancient missionary of Chili).

The invariable principles of poetry. Bath and London 1819.

A reply to the reviewer. Bath and London 1820.

A vindication of the editor of Pope's Works. 1821. Ptd as 2nd edn, first pbd in Pamphleteer.

Two letters to Lord Byron. 1821.

The grave of the last Saxon: a poem. London and Edinburgh 1822.

Ellen Gray: a poem. Edinburgh and London 1823.

Charity: a poem. Bath and London 1823.

The ark: a dramatic oratorio. Bath [1824?].

A final appeal relative to Pope. 1825.

Lessons in criticism. 1826.

Days departed: or Banwell Hill. London and Bath 1828, 1829 (with revision of Ellen Gray, above).

The parochial history of Bremhill. 1828.

The life of Thomas Ken. 2 vols 1830.

St John in Patmos: a poem. London and Bath 1832 (anon), 1835.

The grave of Anna. [Bath 1833]. From Spirit of discovery, above.

Annals and antiquities of Lacock Abbey. 1835.

Scenes and shadows of days departed. London and Bath 1835, 1837. Incomplete memoir.

Letters

Greever, G. A Wiltshire parson and his friends: the correspondence of Bowles. 1926.

§ 2

Byron. Letter to **** ****** on Bowles' strictures on Pope. 1821.

— Observations upon Observations: a second letter to Murray. [1832].

Hazlitt, W., jr. Pope, Byron and Bowles. Appendix to W. Hazlitt, Lectures on the English poets, 1841.

Waldock, A. J. A. Bowles: a lecture. Sydney 1928.

RICHARD OWEN CAMBRIDGE
1717–1802
Collections

Works. Ed G. O. Cambridge 1803. With biography. Chalmers 18.

§ 1

Verses. In Gratulatio in nuptias principium. Oxford 1736; rptd GM 1738.

The scribleriad: an heroic poem in six books. 1751, 1751, 1752. Books first pbd separately, Jan–March 1751.

A dialogue between a Member of Parliament and his servant, in imitation of Horace. 1752.

The intruder: in imitation of Horace book 1 satire 9. 1754.

The fable of Jotham: to the borough-hunters. 1754; Lady's Poetical Mag 1 1781.

An elegy written in an empty assembly room. 1756 (3 edns). Parody of Eloisa to Abelard.

The fakeer: a tale. 1756.

The genius of Britain: an iambic ode addressed to William Pitt. 1756.

An account of the war in India on the coast of Coromandel. 1761, 1761, 1762; tr French, 1766.

Altick, R. D. Cambridge serenades the Berry sisters. N & Q 12 Sept 1942. Prints several poems.

Cambridge contributed to Dodsley's collection vol 6, 1758, *to* World 1753–6 (*21 essays*), *to* Monthly Review 1783–6 *and to* Times 1789.

§2

Altick, R. D. Cambridge: belated Augustan. Philadelphia 1941. With bibliography.

GEORGE CANNING
1770–1827
Collections

Poetical works. [1823] (with biography), Glasgow 1825, 1827, Paris 1828.
Speeches; with a memoir by R. Therry. 6 vols 1828.

§1

Ulm and Trafalgar. 1806, 1806.
A letter to Earl Camden connected with the late duel. 1809, 1809.
Two letters to Earl Camden. 1809.
The doctor: a parody. In The man in the moon, 1820 (24 edns).
New morality. In The British satirist, Glasgow 1826.
The pilgrimage to Mecca. Warwick 1829; rptd in Translations of the Oxford prize poems, 1831.
An anglo-sapphic ode to Robert Beverley. 1833.
The knave of hearts. In Parodies of ballad criticism, ed W. K. Wimsatt, Los Angeles 1957 (Augustan Reprint Soc).

§2

Marriott, J. A. R. Canning and his times. 1903.
Temperley, H. W. V. Life of Canning. 1905.
Bagot, J. Canning and his friends. 2 vols 1909.
Petrie, C. A. George Canning. 1930, 1946.
Marshall, D. The rise of Canning. 1938.
Rolo, P. J. V. Canning: three biographical studies. 1965.

WILLIAM COMBE
1742–1823
§1

Nearly all of the following were issued anonymously or pseudonymously.
Clifton: a poem in imitation of Spenser. Bristol 1775, Bristol and London 1776, 1803.
The philosopher in Bristol. Bristol 1775; Part the second, Bristol 1775; 2 vols Bristol and London 1776.
The diaboliad: a poem, dedicated to the worst man in his Majesty's dominions. 1677, 1677 (both for 1777), Dublin 1777; Additions to the Diaboliad, 1677 (for 1777); The diaboliad: a new edition, 1677 (for 1777), 1778; The diaboliad, a poem: part the second, 1778 (3 edns).
A dialogue in the shades, between an unfortunate divine and a Welch member of Parliament. [1777].
The first of April, or the triumphs of folly: a poem. 1777 (3 edns).
An heroice pistle to the noble author of the Duchess of Devonshire's cow. 1777.
The justification: a poem. 1777, 1778.
A letter to the Duchess of Devonshire. 1777.
A poetical epistle to Sir Joshua Reynolds. 1777.
A second letter to the Duchess of Devonshire. 1777.
The auction: a town eclogue. 1778 (3 edns), 1780.
An interesting letter to the Duchess of Devonshire. 1778, 1779.
The r[oya]l register. 9 vols 1778–84.
An heroic epistle to Sir James Wright. 1779.
Letters supposed to have been written by Yorick and Eliza. 2 vols 1779, 1780; ed M. R. B. Shaw 1929 (as Sterne's Second journal to Eliza).

The world as it goes: a poem. 1779, 1779, 1781.
The fast-day: a Lambeth eclogue. 1780.
Letters of the late Lord Lyttelton. 1780 (3 edns), 2 vols 1782, 1806, Troy NY 1807.
Letters between two lovers. 1781.
Letters of an Italian nun and an English gentleman. 1781.
The traitor: a poetical rhapsody. 1781.
Original love letters, between a lady of quality and a person of inferior rank. 2 vols 1784, Dublin 1784, 1 vol Dublin 1811.
The royal dream, or the P[rince] in a panic: an eclogue. 1785, 1791.
Original letters of Sterne. 1788.
An history of the late important period. 1789.
A letter from a country gentleman to a Member of Parliament. 1789 (7 edns).
The royal interview. 1789 (3 edns).
Considerations on the approaching dissolution of Parliament. 1790.
The devil upon two sticks in England. 4 vols 1790, 6 vols 1791, 1811. *See* H. W. Hamilton, Doctor Syntax, Kent Ohio 1969.
Observations on the Royal Academy. 1790.
A word in season to the traders and manufacturers of Great Britain. 1792 (6 edns), 1793, 1793.
An history of the principal rivers of Great Britain. 2 vols 1794, 1796.
Two words of counsel and one of comfort. 1795.
Letter to a retired officer. 1796.
Plain thoughts of a plain man. 1797.
Brief observations on a letter to Pitt by W. Boyd. 1801.
The letters of Valerius. 1804. First pbd separately in Times.
The tour of Dr Syntax in search of the picturesque. [1812], 1813 (3 edns), 1815 (6th), 1819 (9th), 1823. Originally pbd in monthly pts in Poetical Mag 1809 as The schoolmaster's tour.
    The second tour of Doctor Syntax in search of consolation: a poem. 1820, 1820, 1855, 1903. First issued in monthly pts.
    The third tour of Doctor Syntax, in search of a wife: a poem. [1821], 1823, 1855. First pbd in pts.
    The three tours of Dr Syntax. 3 vols 1826; ed J. C. Hotten [1869] (with biography), [1871], 3 vols 1903. Variously titled.
The Thames. 2 vols 1811.
The history of the abbey church of St Peter's Westminster. 2 vols 1812. First pbd in 16 monthly pts.
Antiquities of York. 1813.
Six poems illustrative of engravings by the Princess Elizabeth. 1813.
A history of the university of Oxford. 2 vols 1814.
The English dance of death. 2 vols 1815–16, 1903. First pbd 24 monthly pts 1815–16.
The history of the colleges [etc]. 1816. First pbd in 12 monthly pts.
The dance of life. 1817, 1903. First pbd in 8 monthly pts.
Observations on Ackermann's patent moveable axles. 1819.
Swiss scenery. 1820.
A history of Madeira. 1821.
The history of Johnny Quae Genus. 1822, 1903. First pbd in 8 monthly pts 1821–2.
Views on the Thames. 2 vols 1822.
Letters to Marianne. 1823.
Letters between Amelia in London and her mother in the country. 1824.

§2

Hamilton, H. W. Doctor Syntax: a silhouette of Combe. Kent Ohio and London 1969. With bibliography.

ERASMUS DARWIN
1731-1802

Collections

Poetical works, with philosophical notes. 3 vols 1806.
Essential writings. Ed D. King-Hele 1968.

§ 1

Linnaeus, C., The families of plants. Lichfield 1787. Tr Darwin.
The loves of the plants. Lichfield 1789, 1790 (as The botanic garden: part II, 2nd edn).
The botanic garden, a poem in two parts: part I, containing The economy of vegetables, 1791; part II, The loves of the plants. Lichfield and London 1789, 1791 (pt II dated 1790, 2nd edn), 1791 (2nd edn pt I, 3rd edn pt II), 2 vols 1794-5, Dublin 1793-6, New York 1798, London 1799 (4th edn).
The golden age: a poetical epistle to T. Beddoes. 1794.
Zoonomia: or the laws of organic life. 2 vols 1794-6, 1796, Dublin 1800, 4 vols 1801, 1802, 1818.
A plan for the conduct of female education in boarding schools. 1797, Derby 1797.
Phytologia: or the philosophy of agriculture and gardening. 1800.
The temple of nature, or the origin of society: a poem. 1803, New York 1804; tr Russian, 1954.
Remembrance. In Poetical selections, 1812.

§ 2

Brown, T. Observations on the Zoonomia. Edinburgh 1798.
Seward, A. Memoirs of the life of Dr Darwin. 1804.
Butler, S. In his Evolution old and new, 1879.
—— In his Unconscious memory, 1880.
Darwin, C. Life of Erasmus Darwin. 1887.
King-Hele, D. Erasmus Darwin. 1963.

WILLIAM FALCONER
1732-69

A poem on the death of Frederick Prince of Wales. 1751.
The shipwreck, a poem in three cantos: by a sailor. 1762, 1764 (enlarged), 1769, 1772, Philadelphia 1774 (with Viaud's voyages); ed J. S. Clarke 1804; ed R. Dodd 1811; ed R. Carruthers 1858; ed W. H. D. A[dams] 1887 etc.
The fond lover. St James Mag 1 1762.
Ode on the Duke of York's departure. 1763.
The demagogue. 1766.
An universal dictionary of the marine. 1769, 1771, 1780, 1784, 1789 etc; ed W. Burney 1815, 1830; ed C. S. Gill 1930 (abridged as The old wooden walls).
An address to his mistress. Edinburgh Mag & Rev 1 1773.
Anderson 10; Chalmers 14; Johnson 67.

JOHN HOOKHAM FRERE
1769-1846

Collections

Aristophanes: a metrical version of the Acharnians, the Knights and the Birds. 1840, Malta 1839 (priv ptd); ed H. Morley 1886.
Works in verse and prose. 2 vols 1872, 3 vols 1874. Memoir by B. Frere.

§ 1

The microcosm. Eton 1786-7. Ed Canning: Frere contributed 5 papers.
Ode on Æthelstan's victory. In Ellis's Specimens of the early English poets, 1801.
Translations from the Cid. In R. Southey, Chronicle of the Cid, 1808.
Prospectus and specimen of an intended national work by William and Robert Whistlecraft relating to King Arthur. Cantos 1-2, 1817, 1818, 1818; Cantos 3-4, 1818; The monks and the giants: prospectus and specimen, 1818, 1821 (4th edn), Bath 1842; ed R. D. Waller 1926.
Fables for five-year-olds. Malta 1830.
Aristophanes, The frogs. 1839 etc.
Psalms etc. [1839?]. A metrical paraphrase.
Theognis restitutus, the personal history of the poet deduced from an analysis of his existing fragments: a hundred fragments in English metre. Malta 1842, 1856 (Bohn's Lib) (as The works of Theognis).

§ 2

Festing, G. Frere and his friends. 1899.

WILLIAM GIFFORD
1756-1826

§ 1

The baviad: a paraphrastic imitation of the first satire of Persius. 1791, 1793.
The maeviad, by the author of the baviad. 1795.
The baviad and maeviad. 1797, 1800 (6th edn), 1811 (8th edn), 1813, 1827 (with Epistle to Peter Pindar).
Epistle to Peter Pindar. 1800, 1800 (with Postscript), 1800 ('with considerable additions'); rptd with 1827 edn of Baviad and Maeviad, above.
The satires of Juvenal translated. 1802, Philadelphia and New York 1803, London 1806, 1906; ed J. Warrington 1954.
An examination of the strictures of the Critical reviewers on the translation of Juvenal. 1803; Supplement, 1804.
The satires of Persius translated. 1821.
The illiberal! verse and prose from the north!! [1822]. Suppressed before pbn.
Autobiography. 1827. Originally prefixed to the 1802 trn of Juvenal, above, as Memoir of Gifford written by himself.
Gifford edited Quart Rev 1809-24; *he also edited the works of* Massinger (1805, 4 vols 1813), Jonson (9 vols 1816), Ford (2 vols 1827) *and, with* A. Dyce, Shirley (6 vols 1833).

§ 2

Hazlitt, W. A letter to Gifford. 1819.
—— In his Spirit of the age, 1825.
Hunt, L. Ultra-crepidarius: a satire on Gifford. 1823.
Clark, R. B. William Gifford. New York 1930.
Shine, H. and H. C. Shine. The Quarterly Review under Gifford. Chapel Hill 1949.

WILLIAM HAYLEY
1745-1820

A poetical epistle to an eminent painter. 1778, 1779, 1781 (as An essay on painting, in two epistles to Romney), Dublin 1781 (An essay).
An elegy on the ancient Greek model. Cambridge and London 1779, Dublin 1783.
Epistle to Admiral Keppel. 1779.

Epistle to a friend on the death of John Thornton. 1780, 1780, 1782.

An essay on history in three epistles to Gibbon. 1780, 1781, Dublin 1781, 1782.

Ode inscribed to John Howard. 1780, 1781, 1782.

The triumphs of temper: a poem in six cantos. 1781, 1781, Dublin 1781, London 1782, Dublin 1782, London 1784, Philadelphia 1787, London 1788 (6th edn), Boston [1790?], Winchester 1792, London 1793, 1795, 1796, 1799, Newburyport [1800?], London 1801, Chichester 1803 (12th edn), Kennebunk 1804, New York 1806, Chichester 1807, London 1809, Chichester 1812.

An essay on epic poetry in five epistles to Mason. 1782, Dublin 1782; ed M. C. Williamson, Gainesville 1968 (facs).

Ode to Mr Wright of Derby. Chichester 1783.

The happy prescription, or the lady relieved from her lovers: a comedy in rhyme. Calcutta 1785.

A philosophical, historical and moral essay on old maids. 3 vols 1785, 1786, Dublin 1786, London 1793.

The two connoisseurs: a comedy in rhyme. Calcutta 1785.

Two dialogues: containing a comparative view of the Earl of Chesterfield and Dr Johnson. 1787, 1800 (as Anecdotes of Chesterfield and Johnson).

Occasional stanzas written at the request of the Revolution Society. 1788.

The young widow: or a history of Cornelia Sedley. 4 vols 1789, 2 vols Dublin 1789.

The eulogies of Howard. 1791.

An elegy on the death of Sir William Jones. 1795.

The national advocate. 1795.

The life of Milton; to which are added conjectures on the origin of Paradise lost. 1796, Dublin 1797, Basle 1799.

An essay on sculpture in a series of epistles to Flaxman. 1800.

Little Tom the sailor. [London?] 1800, Lambeth [1917]. Illustr Blake.

The life and posthumous writings of Cowper. 3 vols Chichester and London 1803–4, 2 vols Boston 1803, New York 1803, 3 vols Philadelphia 1805, 4 vols Chichester 1806; Supplementary pages, Chichester and London 1806; 4 vols Chichester 1809, London 1812.

The life of Cowper abridged. 1803.

The triumph of music. Chichester 1804.

Ballads founded on anecdotes relating to animals. Chichester and London 1805. Illustr Blake.

Latin and Italian poems of Milton, translated by Cowper. Chichester and London 1808. Ed Hayley.

Stanzas to the patriots in Spain. 1808.

The life of George Romney. Chichester and London 1809.

Cowper's Milton. 4 vols Chichester and London 1810. Ed Hayley.

Memoirs. 2 vols 1823.

SIR WILLIAM JONES
1746–94
Collections

Poems consisting chiefly of translations from the Asiatic languages, to which are added two essays: 1, On the poetry of the eastern nations; 11, On the arts commonly called imitative. Oxford 1772, London 1777.

Works. 8 vols 1799–1801, 13 vols 1807.

Poems. Ed J. Benthall, Cambridge 1961. Selection.

Chalmers 18.

§ 1

A grammar of the Persian language. 1771, 1785.

Lettre à Monsieur A[nquetil] du P[erron]. 1771.

The history of Nader Shah. 1770 (in French, with Traité sur la poésie orientale and trns from Hafiz), 1773 (abridged).

An oration intended to have been spoken at Oxford. 1773.

Poeseos asiaticae commentariorum libri sex. 1774, Leipzig 1777.

The speeches of Isaeus concerning property. 1779. Tr Jones.

An inquiry into the legal mode of suppressing riots. 1780 (with Oration, above and speech, 1780 below).

Julii Melesigoni ad libertatem. [1780].

A speech on the nomination of candidates to represent Middlesex. 1780.

An essay on the law of bailments. 1781, Dublin 1790.

The Muse recalled: an ode. Strawberry Hill 1781, Paris 1782; rptd in An asylum for fugitive pieces vol 1, 1785.

The Moullakát: or seven Arabian poems. 1782, 1891. Tr Jones.

Muhammad, I. A., The Mahomedan law of succession. 1782. Tr Jones.

An ode on imitation of Alcaeus. [1782].

The principles of government, in a dialogue. 1782, 1783, Norwich and London 1797, [London] [1800?], 1818.

A letter to a patriot senator. 1783.

Sacontala, or the fatal ring: an Indian drama, by Calidas. Calcutta 1789, London 1789, 1790, 1792, 1796, 1855, 1870. Tr Jones.

Muhammad, I. M., Al Sirájiyyah: or the Mohammedan law of inheritance. Calcutta 1792, 1869. Tr Jones.

An ode: what constitutes a state? [1796].

Institutes of Hindu law: or the ordinances of Menu. 1796, 1825, 1863, 1869, 1880, 1911. Tr Jones.

Jones was a major contributor to The Asiatick miscellany, 2 vols Calcutta 1785–6 (*rptd* Calcutta and London 1787) *and to* Asiatick researches (Calcutta) 1788–94.

Letters. Ed G. H. Cannon 2 vols Oxford 1970.

§ 2

Shore, J. Memoirs of Jones. 1804.

Arberry, A. J. Asiatic Jones. 1946.

Cannon, G. H. Oriental Jones: a biography. New York 1964.

Mukherjee, S. N. Jones: a study in eighteenth-century British attitudes to India. Cambridge 1968.

JOHN LANGHORNE
1735–79
§ 1

The death of Adonis, from Bion. 1759.

Job: a poem. 1760.

The tears of music: a poem to Handel, with an ode to the river Eden. 1760.

A hymn to hope. 1761.

Solyman and Almena: an Oriental tale. 1762, 1780, 1781.

Letters on religious retirement, melancholy and enthusiasm. 1762, 1772.

The Viceroy: a poem. 1762.

The visions of fancy, in four elegies. 1762.

The effusions of friendship and fancy, in several letters. 2 vols 1763, 1766 (enlarged), Dublin 1770.

The enlargement of the mind: epistle 1. 1763; Epistle 11, 1765.

The letters between Theodosius and Constantia. 1763, 1764, 1766 (4th); Correspondence, 1764, 1765, 1766; 2 vols 1770 (combined), 1778, 1782, 1 vol 1799, 1807.

Genius and valour: a Scotch pastoral. 1764, 1764.

Letters on the eloquence of the pulpit. 1765.

The fatal prophecy. 1766.

Precepts of conjugal happiness. 1767, 1769. Verse.

Sermons preached before the society of Lincoln's-Inn. 2 vols 1767 (2nd edn), 1773.

Verses in memory of a lady written at Sandgate castle. 1768.

Frederic and Pharamond: or the consolations of human life. 1769.

Letters supposed to have passed between St Evremont and Waller. 2 vols 1769.

A dialogue of the dead betwixt Lord Eglinton and Mungo Campbell. 1770.

Plutarch's lives. 6 vols 1770, 1774, 1778, 1780, 1792, 1795. With W. Langhorne.

The fables of Flora. 1771 (3 edns), Dublin 1772, London 1773 (5th edn), 1794, 1804 (with life by F. Blagdon).

The origin of the veil: a poem. 1773.

The country justice. 3 pts 1774, 1775, 1777; rptd in The late Augustans, ed D. Davie 1958.

Milton's Italian poems, translated. 1776.

Owen of Carron: a poem. 1778.

Anderson 11; Chalmers 16; Johnson (1790) 71.

WILLIAM MASON
1725–97

Bibliographies

Gaskell, P. First editions of Mason. Cambridge 1951 (Cambridge Bibl Soc).

Collections

Odes. Cambridge and London 1756, 1756.

Elegies. 1763, 1763.

Poems. 1764, Dublin 1764 (with 2 more poems), York 1771, 1773, 1774, 2 vols Glasgow 1774, 1 vol 1777, 2 vols Glasgow 1777, 1 vol London and York 1779, 3 vols York and London 1796–7 (with unpbd poems).

Satiric poems published anonymously by Mason, with notes by Walpole. Ed P. Toynbee, Oxford 1926.

Chalmers 18.

§ I

Musaeus: a monody to the memory of Pope, in imitation of Lycidas. 1747, 1747, 1748, Dublin 1748.

Isis: an elegy. 1749, 1749, 1766. Also in The Union, Edinburgh 1753.

Ode performed in the senate house at Cambridge. Cambridge 1749. Also pbd with music by Boyce, 1749.

Elfrida: a dramatic poem. 1752 (3 edns), Dublin 1752, London 1753, Edinburgh 1755, London 1757, 1759, 1773, 1773, 1779 ('altered for theatrical representation').

Caractacus: a dramatic poem. 1759, 1759, 1760, Dublin 1759, London 1762, Dublin 1764, York and London 1777 ('altered for theatrical representation').

A supplement to Watts' psalms and hymns. Cambridge 1769, 1807.

The English garden, a poem: book the first. 1772? (priv ptd), 1772, 1772, Dublin 1772, London 1778, 1781; Second, 1776 (priv ptd), 1777, 1777; Third, London and York 1779; Fourth, London and York 1781; A poem in four books, York and London 1771–81, Dublin 1782; York and London 1783, London 1803, 1813, 1825.

An heroic epistle to Sir William Chambers. 1773 (7 edns), 1774 (5 edns), 1776, 1777.

An heroic postscript to the public. 1774 (8 edns), 1777.

The poems of Gray, [with] memoirs. York and London 1775, 1775, 2 vols Dublin 1775, 4 vols York 1778, London 1807, 1814, 1820. Ed Mason.

Ode to Mr Pinchbeck upon his newly invented patent candle-snuffers, by Malcolm McGreggor. 1776 (5 edns), 1777.

An epistle to Dr Shebbeare, [with] an ode to Sir Fletcher Norton in imitation of Horace ode VIII book IV, by Malcolm MacGregor. 1777 (4 edns).

Ode to the naval officers of Great Britain. 1779.

Ode to Eliza Ryves. 1780. By Mason?

An archaeological epistle to Jeremiah Milles. 1782, 1782 ('corrected'), Dublin 1782.

A copious collection of portions of the Psalms, [with] a critical and historical essay on cathedral music. York 1782, London 1834.

The dean and the 'squire: a political eclogue dedicated to Jenyns. 1782 (4 edns).

King Stephen's watch: a tale founded on fact. 1782.

Ode to William Pitt. 1782.

Animadversions on the present government of the York lunatic asylum. York [1788].

An occasional discourse on the slave trade. York and London 1788.

Secular ode in commemoration of the Glorious Revolution. 1788.

Anecdotes of Reynolds. 1859.

Sappho: a lyrical drama with Italian translation by T. J. Mathias. London and Naples 1809, London 1810, 1816.

Religio clerici: a poem. 1810.

Letters

The correspondence of Walpole and Mason. Ed J. Mitford 2 vols 1851.

The correspondence of Gray and Mason. Ed J. Mitford 1853, 1855; rptd in edns of Gray's letters.

The correspondence of Hurd and Mason. Ed E. H. Pearce and L. Whibley, Cambridge 1932.

Walpole's correspondence with Mason. Ed W. S. Lewis et al 2 vols Hew Haven 1955.

ANNA SEWARD
1742–1809

Elegy on Captain Cook, to which is added an ode to the sun. 1780, 1780, 1781, Lichfield 1784 ('with additions').

Monody on Major Andre, Lichfield 1781, 1781.

Poem to the memory of Lady Miller. 1782.

Louisa: a poetical novel in four epistles. Lichfield 1784 (4 edns), 1792 (5th edn).

Ode on General Elliott's return from Gibraltar. 1787.

Variety: a collection of essays. 1788.

Llangollen vale, with other poems. 1796 (3 edns).

Original sonnets on various subjects, and odes paraphrased from Horace. 1799, 1799.

Memoirs of the life of Dr Darwin. 1804.

Memoirs of Abelard and Eloisa. 1805.

Blindness. Sheffield 1806.

Letters of Anna Seward written between 1784 to 1807. 6 vols Edinburgh 1811.

CHARLOTTE SMITH
1749–1806

§ I

Manon Lescaut. 2 vols 1785. From Prévost.

The romance of real life. 3 vols 1787, Philadelphia 1799, Aberdeen 1847. Based on the French of Pitaval.

Emmeline, or the orphan of the castle: a novel. 4 vols 1788, 1788, Belfast nd, Philadelphia 1802.

Ethelinde: or the recluse of the lake. 5 vols 1789, 1790.

Celestina: a novel. 4 vols 1791, 3 vols Dublin 1791, 4 vols 1791, 1792, 1794.

Desmond, a novel. 3 vols 1792, 1792, 2 vols Dublin 1792.

The emigrants: a poem. 1793, Dublin 1793.

The old manor house: a novel. 4 vols 1793, 3 vols Dublin 1793, London 1810; ed A. H. Ehrenpreis, Oxford 1968.

D'Arcy: a novel. Dublin 1793, Philadelphia 1796.

The wanderings of Warwick. 1794. Suppl to Old manor house, above.

The banished man: a novel. 4 vols 1794, 3 vols 1795.

Rural walks, in dialogues for young persons. 2 vols 1795, 1796.

Montalbert: a novel. 3 vols 1795, 2 vols Dublin 1795.

Rambles farther. 2 vols 1796, 1 vol 1796, Dublin 1796, 2 vols 1800.

A narrative of the loss near Weymouth. 1796.

Marchmont: a novel. 4 vols 1796, 2 vols Dublin 1797.

Minor morals. 2 vols 1798, 1 vol 1799, 2 vols Dublin 1800.

The young philosopher: a novel. 1798, 2 vols 1798.

What is she?: a comedy. 1799, Dublin 1799, London 1799, 1800.

Letters of a solitary wanderer. 2 vols 1799, 5 vols 1800–2, 1801.

Conversations introducing poetry, for the use of children. 2 vols 1804, 1819, 1 vol Edinburgh and London 1863.

History of England, in a series of letters to a young lady. 3 vols 1806. Vols 1–2 by Charlotte Smith.

The natural history of birds. 2 vols 1807, 1819.

§ 2

Hilbish, F. M. A. Charlotte Smith, poet and novelist. Philadelphia 1941. With bibliography.

McKillop, A. D. Charlotte Smith's letters. HLQ 15 1952.

JOSEPH WARTON
1722–1800
Collections

Odes on various subjects. 1746, 1747.

The three Wartons: a choice of their verse. Ed E. Partridge 1927.

Chalmers 18.

§ 1

The enthusiast: or the lover of nature. 1744.

Ranelagh house: a satire in prose. 1747.

T. Warton, Poems on several occasions. 1748. By the elder T. Warton, ed J. Warton.

An ode occasioned by reading West's translation of Pindar. 1749.

An ode to evening. 1749. English and Latin.

The works of Virgil in Latin and English. 4 vols 1753, 1763, 1778, 1 vol 1788. Eclogues, Georgics and notes throughout by Warton.

An essay on the writings and genius of Pope. 1, 1756, 1762, Dublin 1764, London 1772, 1782, 1782, 1786; 11, 1782, 1782; 2 vols 1806.

The works of Pope, with notes and illustrations by J. Warton and others. 9 vols 1797, Basle 1803.

The adventurer nos 127 and 133. 1754; ed E. N. Hooker, Los Angeles 1946 (with other essays on wit) (Augustan Reprint Soc).

Warton contributed 2 odes to his father's Poems on several occasions, 1748, *and miscellaneous verse to Dodsley's museum vol 6, 1746, Dodsley's collection 3–4 1748, 1755, Pearch's collection vol 2, 1768, Adventurer 1752–4 (24 essays), World 1753 (one essay).*

THOMAS WARTON the younger
1728–90
Collections

Poems: a new edition. 1777, 1777, 1779, [1789], 1791 (as Poems on various subjects).

Poetical works. Ed R. Mant 2 vols Oxford 1802. With memoir.

The three Wartons: a choice of their verse. Ed E. Partridge 1927.

Anderson 11; Chalmers 18.

§ 1

Five pastoral eclogues. 1745. Attributed to Warton.

The pleasures of melancholy. 1747.

The triumphs of Isis. [1749], 1750, 1750; rptd Dodsley's collection vol 1, 1768.

A description of Winchester. [1750], 1760.

Newmarket: a satire. 1751 (for 1750).

Ode for music as performed at Oxford 1751. Oxford [1751].

The Union: or select Scots and English poems. Edinburgh 1753, London 1759, Dublin 1761, Oxford 1796. Ed Warton.

Observations on the Fairy Queen. 1754, 2 vols 1762, 1807.

Inscriptionum romanarum metricarum delectus. [1758]. Ed Warton.

A companion to the guide and a guide to the companion: a supplement to all accounts of Oxford. [1760?], [1762?], [1770?], Oxford 1806.

The life and literary remains of Ralph Bathurst. 2 vols 1761.

The Oxford sausage: or select poetical pieces. 1764, Dublin 1766, Oxford 1772. Ed Warton.

The life of Sir Tho Pope. 1772, 1780, 1784.

The history of English poetry. 3 vols 1774–81 (2nd edn of vol 1, 1775); ed R. Price 4 vols 1824, 3 vols 1840, 1 vol 1870 (rptd from 1st); ed W. C. Hazlitt 4 vols 1871.

Specimen of the history of Oxfordshire. 1781, 1783 (as A history of Kidlington), 1815.

An enquiry into the authenticity of the poems attributed to Rowley. 1782, 1782.

Verses on Reynolds's painted window at Oxford. [1782], 1783, Oxford 1930, London 1932.

Milton, Poems upon several occasions. 1785, 1791. Ed Warton.

Verses left under a stone. [1790?].

Milton, Comus. 1799. With essay by Warton.

Essays on gothic architecture, by T. Warton [et al]. 1800, 1802, 1808.

Satires of Joseph Hall, with the illustrations of Thomas Warton. Chiswick 1824.

The hamlet: an ode. 1859, 1876.

A history of English poetry: an unpublished continuation. Ed R. M. Baine, Los Angeles 1953 (Augustan Reprint Soc).

Correspondence of Percy and Warton. Ed M. G. Robinson and L. Dennis, Baton Rouge 1951. Vol 3 of Percy letters, ed D. N. Smith and C. Brooks.

§ 2

[Ritson, J.] Observations on the History of English poetry. 1782.

Ker, W. P. Thomas Warton. Proc Br Acad 4 1912; rptd in his Collected essays vol 1, 1925.

Rinaker, C. Thomas Warton: a biographical and critical study. Urbana 1916. With bibliography.

Smith, D. N. Warton's History of English poetry. Proc Br Acad 15 1932.

—— Warton's miscellany: the Union. RES 19 1943.

HELEN MARIA WILLIAMS
1762–1827
Collections

Poems. 2 vols 1786, 1791.

Poems on various subjects, with introductory remarks on France. 1823.

§ 1

Edwin and Eltruda: a legendary tale. 1782.

An ode on the peace. 1783.

Peru: a poem. 1784.

Ode to peace. [1786?].

A poem on the bill lately passed for regulating the slave trade. 1788.

Julia: a novel, interspersed with poetical pieces. 2 vols 1790.

Letters written in France in the summer of 1790. 1790.

Letters on the French Revolution. 1790, Boston 1791, 2 vols 1792, 1796 (5th edn), Dublin 1802.

A farewell for two years to England. 1791.
Letters containing a sketch of the politics of France from May 1793 till July 1794. 2 vols Dublin 1794, London 1795, 3 vols Dublin 1796, 4 vols 1796.
J. H. B. de St Pierre, Paul and Virginia. Paris 1795. Tr H. M. Williams.
Sonnets. In Poems moral, elegant and pathetic, 1796, 1803.
A tour in Switzerland. 2 vols 1798, Dublin 1798.
Sketches of the state of manners and opinions in the French republic in a series of letters. 3 vols 1801.
The political and confidential correspondence of Lewis the sixteenth. 3 vols 1803.
Verses addressed to her two nephews. Paris 1809.
F. H. A. von Humboldt. Personal narrative of travels to the equinoctial regions of the new continent. 7 vols 1814–29. Tr H. M. Williams.
Researches concerning the institutions and monuments of the ancient inhabitants of America. 2 vols 1814. Tr H. M. Williams.
A narrative of the events in France from March 1815. 1815, 1816.
On the late persecution of the Protestants in the south of France. 1816.
J. de Maistre, The leper of the city of Aoste. 1817. Tr H. M. Williams.
The charter: lines addressed to her nephew. Paris 1819.
Letters on the events in France since the restoration in 1815. 1819.
Four new letters of Mary Wollstonecraft and Helen M. Williams. Ed B. P. Kurtz and C. C. Autry, Berkeley 1937.

JOHN WOLCOT, 'PETER PINDAR'
1738–1819
Collections

Works. Dublin 1788, 1791, 2 vols 1792, Dublin 1792, 3 vols Dublin 1792, 4 vols 1794–6, 1809, 5 vols 1812, 4 vols 1816, 1 vol 1824, [1856].
The beauties of Pindar. 1807, [1834?] (2 different selections).
Wolcot's various poems were bound together with general title-pages in one or 2 vols variously between 1790 and 1800. Besides the genuine issues there were many pirated edns. His pseudonym was usurped by several other satirists.

§ I

Persian love elegies. Kingston Jamaica 1773.
A poetical, supplicating, modest and affecting epistle to the reviewers. 1778, 1787, 1789.
Poems on various subjects. 1778.
Lyric odes to the Royal Academicians. 1782, 1784, 1786, 1787 (5th edn), 1787, 1788, 1790.
More lyric odes to the Royal Academicians. 1783, 1786 (3rd edn), 1789 (5th edn).
Lyric odes for the year 1785. 1785, 1786, 1787 (7th edn), 1791.
The lousiad: an heroi-comic poem. Canto I, 1785, 1786, 1786 (6th edn), 1787, 1788 (9th edn); Canto II, 1787, 1787, 1788, 1788 (6th edn); Canto III, 1791, Dublin 1791; Canto IV, 1792; Canto V and last, 1795, 1795; Cantos I–V, Paris [c. 1820].
Farewell odes for the year 1786. 1786 (4 edns), 1788 (5th edn).
Bozzy and Piozzi, or the British biographers: a town eclogue. 1786 (6 edns), Dublin 1786, London 1788 (9th–10th edn).
A poetical and congratulatory epistle to James Boswell. 1786 (5 edns), Dublin 1786, London 1787, 1788 (8th edn), 1789 (10th edn).
A congratulatory epistle to Peter Pindar. 1787.

Ode upon ode: or a peep at St James's. 1787 (7 edns), 1789 (9th edn).
An apologetic postscript to Ode upon ode. 1787, 1788.
Instructions to a celebrated laureat. 1787 (4 edns), 1788 (7th edn), 1790.
Brother Peter to brother Tom [Warton]: an expostulatory epistle. 1788 (3 edns), 1789 (5th edn).
Peter's pension: a solemn epistle to a sublime personage. 1788 (4 edns), 1792.
Peter's prophecy: or the president and poet. 1788.
Sir Joseph Banks and the Emperor of Morocco. 1788 (4 edns).
Tales and fables. 1788.
Expostulatory odes to a great Duke and a little lord. 1789, 1789.
Lyric odes to the academicians and subjects for painters. 1789, 1789, 1793.
A poetical epistle to a falling minister. 1789, 1789.
A benevolent epistle to Sylvanus Urban, alias John Nichols. 1790, 1790.
A complimentary epistle to James Bruce. 1790 (3 edns).
Advice to the future laureat: an ode. 1790, 1790, Dublin 1790.
Epistle to John Nichols. 1790, 1790.
A letter to the most insolent man alive. 1790.
The remonstrance; to which is added an ode to my ass. 1791, 1791.
Odes to Mr Paine author of Rights of man. 1791, 1791.
The rights of Kings: or loyal odes to disloyal Academicians. 1791, 1791.
A commiserating epistle to James Lowther. 1791, 1791.
A pair of lyric epistles to Lord Macartney and his ship. 1792, 1792.
Odes of importance. 1792, 1792.
More money: or odes of instruction to Mr Pitt. 1792, 1792, Dublin 1792.
The tears of St Margaret. 1792, 1792, Dublin 1792. With other poems.
Odes to Kien Long. 1792, 1792. With other poems.
The captive King. [1793?]. Song on Louis XVI.
A poetical, serious and possibly impertinent epistle to the Pope. 1792. With odes.
Pindariana. 1794.
Celebration, or the academic procession to St James's: an ode. 1794.
Pathetic odes. 1794.
Hair powder: a plaintive epistle to Pitt. 1795, 1795. With another poem.
The convention bill: an ode. 1795.
Liberty's last squeak. 1795, Dublin 1796. With several poems.
The royal tour and Weymouth amusements. 1795, 1795, Dublin 1796. With other poems.
The royal visit to Exeter. 1795.
The cap: a satiric poem. [1795?].
An admirable satire on Burke's defense of his pension. 1796.
One thousand seven hundred and ninety-six. 1797.
An ode to the livery of London. 1797.
Picturesque views with poetical allusions. 1797.
Tales of the Hoy: part the first. [1798?], 1798 (4th edn).
Nil admirari: or a smile at a bishop. 1799, 1799.
Pilkington's dictionary of painters. 1799. Ed Wolcot.
Lord Auckland's triumph: or the death of crim con. 1800.
Odes to ins and outs. 1801, 1801.
Out at last. 1801 ('new edition'), 1801 (6th edn).
A poetical epistle to Count Rumford. 1801, 1801.
Tears and smiles. 1801, Baltimore 1802, Philadelphia 1802. Collection.
Epistle to James Lowther. 1802, 1802.
'P. Hamlin', The horrors of bribery. 1802, 1802. By Wolcot.
Pitt and his statue. 1802.
The island of innocence. 1802, 1802.
The Middlesex election. 1802, 1802.

Great cry and little wool: I, 1804, 1804; II, 1804.
An instructive epistle to the Lord Mayor. 1804.
The beauties of English poetry, selected by Dr Wolcot.
  2 vols 1804. With new poems by Wolcot.
Tristia: or the sorrows of Peter. 1806.
One more peep at the Royal Academy. 1808.
The fall of Portugal, or the royal exiles: a tragedy. 1808.
  By Wolcot?
A solemn epistle to Mrs Clarke. 1809.
Epistle the second to Mrs Clarke. 1809.
Picture of Margate. 1809. With ode by Wolcot.
Carlton House fete: or the disappointed bard, in a series of
  elegies. 1811.
An address to be spoken at the opening of Drury Lane
  theatre by Peter Puncheon. 1813.
The Regent and the King. 1814.
Royalty fogbound. 1814.
Tom Halliard: a ballad. Penrith [1815?].
A most solemn epistle to the Emperor of China. 1817.

THE ANTI-JACOBIN

*See also under George Canning, John Hookham Frere and
William Gifford, above, and under Rolliad, below.*
The Anti-Jacobin. Nos 1–36, 20 Nov 1797–9 July 1798; 2
  vols 1799 (4th edn). Ed W. Gifford.

The beauties of the Anti-Jacobin; together with explana-
  tory notes etc. 1799.
Poetry of the Anti-Jacobin. 1799, 1800, 1801 (4th edn).
The poetry of the Anti-Jacobin. Ed C. Edmonds 1852,
  1854 (with etchings by Gillray), 1890. Assigns pieces
  to their authors.
Parodies and other burlesque pieces, by George Canning,
  George Ellis and John Hookham Frere, with the whole
  of the poetry of the Anti-Jacobin. Ed H. Morley 1890.
The poetry of the Anti-Jacobin. Ed L. Rice-Oxley,
  Oxford 1924.

THE ROLLIAD

Criticisms on the Rolliad. 1784, 1785, 1785, 1787, 1788
  (8th edn), 1791; Part the second, 1785, 1790 (4 edns).
The new rolliad: number 1. 1785.
Probationary odes for the laureatship, with a preliminary
  discourse by Sir John Hawkins. 1785.
Poetical miscellanies. 1790.
The rolliad in two parts: probationary odes and political
  eclogues. 1795, 1799 (21st edn), 1812 (22nd).
The Rolliad series of poems originally appeared in Morning
  Herald & Daily Advertiser *for 1784 and after.*

3. DRAMA

I. GENERAL WORKS

(1) COLLECTIONS OF PLAYS

Bell's British theatre: consisting of the most esteemed English plays. 21 vols 1776–81, 36 vols 1791–1802.

Supplement to Bell's British theatre: consisting of the most esteemed farces and entertainments. 4 vols 1784.

The British theatre: or a collection of plays with biographical and critical remarks, by Mrs Inchbald. 25 vols 1808, 20 vols 1824.

A collection of farces and other afterpieces selected by Mrs Inchbald. 7 vols 1809, 1815.

The modern theatre. Ed E. Inchbald 10 vols 1809.

The London theatre. Ed T. J. Dibdin 26 vols 1815–18.

Five Restoration tragedies. Ed B. Dobrée, Oxford 1928 (WC).

British dramatists from Dryden to Sheridan. Ed G. H. Nettleton and A. E. Case, Boston 1939.

Five heroic plays. Ed B. Dobrée, Oxford 1960 (WC).

Eighteenth-century tragedy. Ed M. R. Booth, Oxford 1965 (WC).

(2) HISTORIES ETC

Dictionaries and Bibliographies

Langbaine, Gerard. Momus triumphans: or the plagiaries of the English stage expos'd. 1688, 1688 (as A new catalogue of English plays).

— An account of the English dramatick poets. Oxford 1691. See A. W. Jones, E & S 21 1936.

Gildon, Charles. The lives and characters of the English dramatick poets. [1698], 1699, 1751. A revision of Langbaine, above.

[Reed, Isaac]. Biographia dramatica: or a companion to the playhouse. 2 vols 1782.

Lowe, R. W. A bibliographical account of English theatrical literature. 1888. Lowe lists many of the squibs and pamphlets in 18th-century theatrical history.

Summers, M. A bibliography of the Restoration drama. 1935.

Woodward, G. L. and J. G. McManaway. A check list of English plays 1641–1700. Chicago 1945. Supplement by F. T. Bowers, Charlottesville 1949.

Greg, W. W. A bibliography of the English printed drama to the Restoration. Vol 2, Plays 1617–89, Oxford 1951.

Hogan, C. B. Shakespeare in the theatre 1701–1800: a record of performances in London. 2 vols Oxford 1952–7.

Stratman, C. J. Bibliography of English printed tragedy 1565–1900. Carbondale 1966.

— Dramatic play lists 1591–1963. BNYPL Feb–March 1966.

Histories

Hazlitt, William. A view of the English stage. 1818.

Lamb, Charles. On the artificial comedy. In his Essays of Elia, 1821.

Hunt, Leigh. The dramatic works of Wycherley, Congreve, Vanbrugh and Farquhar. 1840. Introd.

Macaulay, T. B. The dramatic works of Wycherley, Congreve, Vanbrugh and Farquhar. Edinburgh Rev 62 1841. A review of Hunt, above.

Dobrée, B. Restoration comedy. Oxford 1924; Restoration tragedy, Oxford 1929.

Nicoll, A. A history of Restoration drama 1660–1700. Cambridge 1923, 1928, 1940, 1952 (rev).

— A history of early eighteenth-century drama 1700–50. Cambridge 1923, 1929, 1952 (rev).

— A history of late eighteenth-century drama 1750–1800. Cambridge 1927, 1937, 1952 (rev).

— Alphabetical catalogue of plays 1660–1900. Cambridge 1959.

Boas, F. S. Introduction to eighteenth-century drama. Oxford 1953.

Loftis, J. The London theatres in early eighteenth-century politics. HLQ 18 1955.

— Comedy and society from Congreve to Fielding. Stanford 1959.

— The politics of drama in Augustan England. Oxford 1963.

The London stage 1660–1800. Part 1 1660–1700, ed W. Van Lennep, E. L. Avery and A. H. Scouten, Carbondale 1965; Part 2 1700–29, ed E. L. Avery 2 vols Carbondale 1960; Part 3 1729–47, ed A. H. Scouten 2 vols Carbondale 1961; Part 4 1747–76, ed G. W. Stone 3 vols Carbondale 1962; Part 5 1776–1800, ed C. B. Hogan 3 vols Carbondale 1968.

(3) THE COLLIER CONTROVERSY

JEREMY COLLIER
1650–1726

§ I

A short view of the immorality and profaneness of the English stage; together with the sense of antiquity upon this argument. 1698 (3 edns), 1699.

A defence of the short view of the profaneness and immorality of the English stage etc: being a reply to Mr Congreve's amendments etc and to the vindication of the author of the Relapse. 1699.

A second defence of the short view of the profaneness and immorality of the English stage etc: being a reply to a

book entitled the Ancient and modern stages surveyed etc 1700.

Mr Collier's dissuasive from the play-house, in a letter to a person of quality occasion'd by the late calamity of the tempest. 1703, 1704 (with A letter written by another hand in answer to some questions sent by a person of quality).

A farther vindication of the Short view of the profaneness and immorality of the English stage, in which the objections of a late book entitled A defence of plays are consider'd. 1708.

A short view of the profaneness and immorality of the English stage etc, with the several defenses of the same. 1730, 1738. Includes all the above items except Mr Collier's dissuasive.

§ 2

Wright, James. Country conversations: being an account of some discourses that happen'd in a visit to the country last summer on divers subjects, chiefly of the modern comedies. 1694.
—— Historia histrionica: an historical account of the English-stage, shewing the ancient use, improvement and perfection, of dramatic representations in this nation. 1699; ed E. W. Ashbee 1872 (facs); ed W. C. Hazlitt in Dodsley's old plays vol 15 1876; ed R. W. Lowe in Colley Cibber's Apology vol 2 1889.
Blackmore, Sir Richard. Prince Arthur: an heroick poem. 1695. Preface.
—— King Arthur: an heroick poem. 1697. Preface.
—— A satyr against wit. 1700 (3 edns).
—— Essays upon several subjects. 1716.
D'Urfey, Thomas. The campaigners: or the pleasant adventures at Brussels, with a familiar preface upon a late reformer of the stage, ending with a satyrical fable of the dog and the ottor. 1698.
[Vanbrugh, Sir John]. A short vindication of the Relapse and the Provok'd wife, from immorality and profaneness. 1698.

Congreve, William. Amendments of Mr Collier's false and imperfect citations. 1698.
A vindication of the stage, with the usefulness and advantages of dramatic representations, in answer to Mr Collier's late book. 1698. By Charles Gildon?
Dennis, John. The usefulness of the stage, to the happiness of mankind, to government and to religion, occasioned by a late book, written by Jeremy Collier. 1698.
—— The person of quality's answer to Mr Collier's letters. In his Original letters, 1721.
—— The stage defended from Scripture, reason, experience and the common sense of mankind, occasion'd by Mr Law's late pamphlet against stage entertainments. 1726.
—— Critical works. Ed E. N. Hooker 2 vols Baltimore 1939–43.
[Gildon, Charles]. Phaeton: a tragedy, with some reflections on a book called A short view. 1698.
Oldmixon, John. Reflections on the stage and Mr Collier's Defence of the short view, in four dialogues. 1699.
Cibber, Colley. An apology for the life of Mr Colley Cibber, comedian, written by himself. 1740; ed R. W. Lowe 2 vols 1889; ed B. R. S. Fone, Ann Arbor 1968.

II. RESTORATION DRAMA

The abbreviations used in this section and the following:
Ba burletta, Bal ballet, BO ballad opera, Bsq burlesque, C comedy, CO comic opera, D drama, DO dramatic opera, Ext extravaganza, F farce, Int interlude, M masque, MD melodrama, MF musical farce, O opera, Oa operetta, P pantomime, T tragedy, TC tragi-comedy. *For theatres:* CG Covent Garden, DG Dorset Garden, DL Drury Lane, GF Goodman's Fields, Hay Haymarket (King's and Queen's Haymarket), New Hay Little Haymarket, LIF Lincoln's Inn Fields, TR Theatre Royal, Vere Street or Brydges Street. Larpent ms in Huntington Lib, California.

SIR GEORGE ETHEREGE
1635?–91
Collections

Works, containing his plays and poems. 1704, 1715, 1723, 1735.
Works: plays and poems. Ed A. W. Verity 1888.
Works. Ed H. F. B. Brett-Smith 2 vols Oxford 1927. Plays, introd and bibliography. Vol 3 unpbd.
Poems. Ed J. Thorpe, Princeton 1963.

§ 1

The comical revenge: or love in a tub. C LIF March 1664. 1664, 1664, 1667, 1669, 1689, 1690, 1697.
She wou'd if she cou'd. C LIF 6 Feb 1668. 1668, 1671, 1693, 1710, [c. 1711]; ed C. M. Taylor 1973.
The man of mode: or Sr Fopling Flutter. C DG March 1676. 1676, 1684, 1693, 1711, [c. 1711], 1733, Dublin [c. 1753], Edinburgh 1768; ed J. H. Wilson, Boston 1959; ed W. B. Carnochan, Lincoln Nebraska 1966; ed J. Conaghan, Edinburgh 1973.
Letterbook. Ed S. Rosenfeld, Oxford 1928.
Rosenfeld, S. The second letterbook of Etherege. RES new ser 3 1952.
Letters. Ed F. Bracher, Berkeley 1974.

§ 2

Dennis, John. A defense of Sir Fopling Flutter. 1722.
Fujimura, T. H. In his Restoration comedy of wit, Princeton 1952.
Underwood, D. Etherege and the seventeenth-century comedy of manners. New Haven 1957.
Holland, N. N. In his First modern comedies, Cambridge Mass 1959.

Powell, J. Etherege and the form of a comedy. In Restoration theatre, ed J. R. Brown and B. Harris 1965.

WILLIAM WYCHERLEY
1641–1716
Collections

Works. 1713, 2 vols 1720, 1 vol 1731, Dublin 1733, 2 vols 1735.
The posthumous works in prose and verse. 2 vols 1728–9. Vol 1 ed L. Theobald, with memoir by R. Pack; vol 2 ed Pope.
The dramatic works of Wycherley, Congreve, Vanbrugh and Farquhar. Ed Leigh Hunt 1840.
William Wycherley. Ed W. C. Ward 1888 (Mermaid ser).
Complete works. Ed M. Summers 4 vols 1924.
Complete plays. Ed G. Weales, New York 1966.
Plays. Ed A. Friedman, Oxford 1978.

§ 1

Hero and Leander, in burlesque. 1669. Anon.
Love in a wood: or St James's Park. C TR c. March 1671. 1672, 1693, 1694, 1711, etc.
The gentleman dancing-master. C DG c. Feb 1672. 1673, 1693, 1702.
The country-wife. C DL Jan 1675. 1675, 1683, 1688, 1688, 1695 etc; ed J. H. Wilson, Boston 1959; ed G. G. Falls, New York 1964; ed T. H. Fujimura, Lincoln Nebraska 1965; ed D. Cook and J. Swannell 1975 (Revels).
The plain dealer. C DL Dec 1676. 1677 (3 edns), 1678, 1681, 1686, 1691, 1694, 1700, 1709, 1710, 1711 etc; ed L. Hughes, Lincoln Nebraska 1967.
Epistles to the King and Duke. 1683.
Miscellany poems. 1704.

The idleness of business: a satyr. 1705 (2nd edn).
On his Grace the Duke of Marlborough. 1707.

§ 2

[Gildon, Charles]. Memoirs of the life of Wycherley. 1718.
Hazlitt, W. In his Lectures on the English comic writers, 1819.
Macaulay, T. B. The dramatic works of Wycherley, Congreve, Vanbrugh and Farquhar. Edinburgh Rev 72 1841.
Holland, N. N. In his First modern comedies, Cambridge Mass 1959.
Righter, A. In Restoration theatre, ed J. R. Brown and B. Harris 1965.

THOMAS SHADWELL
1642?–92
Collections

The Lancashire witches; The amorous bigot. 1691. Copies of separate edns of 2 plays issued with general title.
Works. 1693.
Thomas Shadwell. Ed G. Sainstsbury [1903] (Mermaid ser).
Complete works. Ed M. Summers 5 vols 1927 (Nonesuch Press).

§ I

The sullen lovers: or the impertinents. C LIF 2 May 1668. 1668, 1670, 1693.
The royal shepherdess. TC LIF 25 Feb 1669. 1669, 1691.
The humorists. C LIF Dec 1670. 1671, 1691.
The miser. C TR Jan 1672. 1672, 1691.
Epsom-wells. C DG Dec 1672. 1673, 1676, 1693, 1704; ed D. Walmsley, Boston [1930].
The tempest: or the enchanted island. DO DG April 1674. 1674, 1676, 1676, 1690, 1695, 1701.
Notes and observations on the Empress of Morocco. 1674. Anon. With Crowne and Dryden.
Psyche. DO DG 27 Feb 1675. 1675, 1690.
The libertine: a tragedy. C DG June 1675. 1676, 1692, 1697, 1704, 1705.
The virtuoso. C DG 25 May 1676. 1676, 1691, 1704; ed M. H. Nicolson and D. S. Rodes, Lincoln Nebraska 1966.
The history of Timon of Athens, the man-hater. T DG c. Jan 1678. 1678, 1688, 1696, 1703, [1705?].
A true widow. C DG 21 March 1678. 1679, 1689.
The woman-captain. C DG c. Sept 1679. 1680.
The Lancashire witches, and Tegue o Divelly the Irish priest. C DG c. Sept 1681. 1682, 1682, 1691, 1736.
The medal of John Bayes: a satyr against folly and knavery. 1682. Anon.
Satyr to his Muse, by the author of Absalom and Achitophel. 1682. Anon. Also ascribed to John, Baron Somers.
The Tory-poets: a satyr. 1682. Anon. Sometimes attributed to Shadwell.
A lenten prologue. 1683. Anon.
Some reflections upon the pretended parallel in the play called the Duke of Guise. 1683. Anon. Generally attributed to Shadwell.
The tenth satyr of Juvenal. 1687.
The squire of Alsatia. C DL May 1688. 1688, 1688, 1692, 1693, 1699, 1736 etc.
Bury-fair. C DL c. April 1689. 1689.
A congratulatory poem on his Highness the Prince of Orange his coming into England. 1689.
The amorous bigotte; with the second part of Tegue o Divelly. C DL c. March 1689. 1690, [1691?].

The address of John Dryden, laureat to his Highness the Prince of Orange. 1689. Anon.
A congratulatory poem to the most illustrious Queen Mary upon her arrival in England. 1689.
Ode on the anniversary of the King's birth. 1690.
Ode to the King, on his return from Ireland. [1690?].
The scowrers. C DL c. Dec 1690. 1691.
Votum perenne: a poem to the King on New-years-day. 1692.
Ode on the King's birth-day. 1692.
The volunteers: or the stock-jobbers. C DL Nov 1692. 1693; ed D. Walmsley, Boston [1930].

NATHANIEL LEE
1649?–92
Collections

Works. 1694, 2 vols 1713, 3 vols 1722, 1734, 1736 (as Dramatick works).
Works. Ed T. B. Stroup and A. L. Cooke 2 vols New Brunswick 1954–5.

§ I

The tragedy of Nero, Emperour of Rome. DL May 1674. 1675, 1696; ed R. Horstmann, Heidelberg 1914.
Sophonisba: or Hannibal's overthrow. T DL April 1675. 1675, 1676, 1681, 1685, 1691, 1693, 1697, 1704, 1709, 1712 etc; ed B. Dobrée, Oxford 1960 (WC) (in Five heroic plays).
Gloriana: or the Court of Augustus Caesar. T DL Jan 1676. 1676, 1699 etc.
The rival Queens: or the death of Alexander the Great. T DL 17 March 1677. 1677, 1684, 1690, 1691, 1694, 1699, 1702, 1704 etc; ed P. F. Vernon 1970.
To the Prince and Princess of Orange upon their marriage. 1677.
Mithridates King of Pontus. T DL c. March 1678. 1678, 1685, 1693, 1697, 1702, 1711 etc.
Oedipus. T DG c. Sept 1678. 1679, 1682, 1687, 1692, [1694?], 1701, 1711. With Dryden.
Caesar Borgia, son of Pope Alexander the Sixth. T DG c. May 1679. 1679, 1680, 1696, 1711.
Theodosius: or the force of love. T DG c. Sept 1680. 1680, 1684, 1692, 1697, 1708 etc.
Lucius Junius Brutus, father of his country. T DG Dec 1680. 1681, 1708; ed J. Loftis, Lincoln Nebraska 1967.
Prologue spoken at Mithridates. 1681.
To the Duke on his return. 1682.
The Duke of Guise. T DL 28 Nov 1682. 1683, 1687, 1699. With Dryden.
Constantine the Great. T DL Nov 1683. 1684; ed W. Häfele, Heidelberg 1933.
The Princess of Cleve. TC DG 1680 or 1681. 1689, 1697.
The massacre of Paris. T DL Nov 1689. 1689, 1690.
On the death of Mrs Behn. 1689. Verse.
On their Majesties coronation. 1689. Verse.

THOMAS OTWAY
1652–85
Collections

Works. 1692.
The works of Mr Thomas Otway: consisting of his plays, poems and love-letters. 2 vols 1712, 1717–18, 1722, 1728, 3 vols 1757, 1768.
Complete works. Ed M. Summers 3 vols 1926 (Nonesuch Press).
Works. Ed J. C. Ghosh 2 vols Oxford 1932. Plays, poems letters.

§ 1

Alcibiades. T DG Sept 1675. 1675, 1687.
Don Carlos, Prince of Spain. T DG June 1676. 1676, 1679, 1686, 1695, 1704 etc.
Titus and Berenice. T DG c. Dec 1676. 1677, 1701 etc.
The cheats of Scapin. F. Produced and ptd with Titus and Berenice.
Friendship in fashion. C DG April 1678. 1678 etc.
The history and fall of Caius Marius. F DG Sept or Oct 1679. 1680, 1692, 1696, 1703 etc.
The orphan: or the unhappy marriage. T DG Feb or March 1680. 1680, 1685, 1691, 1696, 1703, 1705 etc, Hague 1711.
The souldiers fortune. C DG c. June 1680. 1681, 1683, 1687, 1695 etc.
The poet's complaint of his muse: or a satyr against libells. 1680.
Phaedra to Hippolytus. In Ovid's epistles translated by several hands, 1680.
Venice preserv'd: or a plot discover'd. T DG 9 Feb 1682. 1682, 1696, 1704 etc; ed J. H. Wilson, Boston 1959; ed M. Kelsall 1969.
Epilogue to Venice preserv'd spoken upon the Duke of York's coming to the theatre. 1682.
Prologue to the City-heiress. 1682.
Epilogue to her Highness on her return from Scotland. 1682.
The atheist: or the second part of the souldiers fortune. C DG c. July 1683. 1684.
Prologue to Constantine the Great. 1683.
Windsor Castle in a monument to our late sovereign K. Charles II. 1685. Verse.
The history of the triumvirates, written originally in French, and made English by Tho Otway, lately deceased. 1686.
Love-letters written by the late most ingenious Mr Thomas Otway. In Familiar letters written by the Earl of Rochester, 1697.
Heroick friendship: a tragedy by the late Mr Otway. 1719. Perhaps by Otway.

§ 2

Johnson, Samuel. In his Lives of the poets, 1779–81.

SIR JOHN VANBRUGH
1664–1726
Collections

Plays. 2 vols 1719, 1730, 1734, 1735, 1759, Dublin 1765, London 1776.
The dramatic works of Wycherley, Congreve, Vanbrugh and Farquhar. Ed Leigh Hunt 1840.
Complete works. Ed B. Dobrée and G. Webb 4 vols 1927.

§ 1

The relapse: or virtue in danger. C DL 21 Nov 1696. 1697, 1698, 1708, [1709?], [1711?], 1727, 1734, 1735 etc; ed C. A. Zimansky 1970.
Aesop. C Pt 1 DL c. Dec 1696. 1697; pt 2 DL c. March 1697. 1697, 1697 (pts 1–2), 1702, 1711, Dublin 1725, London 1730, 1735 etc.
The provok'd wife. C LIF May 1697. 1697, 1698, 1709, 1710, 1727, 1734, 1735, Dublin 1743 (with new scenes in Act iv) etc; ed C. A. Zimansky 1970.
A short vindication of the Relapse and the Provok'd wife, from immorality and prophaneness, by the author. 1698.
The pilgrim. C DL April 1700. 1700 (anon), 1735.
The false friend. C DL c. Feb 1702. 1702. Anon.
The confederacy. C Hay 30 Oct 1705. 1705, 1734, 1751 etc.
The country house. F DL 18 Jan 1698. 1715, 1719, 1740 (as La maison rustique).

The mistake. C Hay 27 Dec 1705. 1706, Dublin 1726, London 1735.
Sir John Vanbrugh's justification, of what he depos'd in the Duchess of Marlborough's late tryal. [1718].
A journey to London. C 1728, 1730, 1735. Acted with Cibber's addns DL 10 Jan 1728 as The provok'd husband.

§ 2

Hazlitt, William. In A view of the English stage, 1818.
—— In Lectures on the English comic writers, 1819.
Harris, B. The dialect of those fanatic times. In Restoration theatre, ed J. R. Brown and Harris 1965.
—— Vanbrugh. 1967.

WILLIAM CONGREVE
1670–1729

See D. Mann, A concordance to the plays of Congreve, Ithaca 1973.

Collections

Works. 3 vols 1710, 1717, 1719–20 (adds 2 poems), Dublin 1731–29, London 1730, 1735, 1753, 1761, Birmingham 1761, Dublin 1773, 2 vols 1773, 1774 (rev text of all the plays).
The dramatic works of Wycherley, Congreve, Vanbrugh and Farquhar. Ed Leigh Hunt 1840.
Complete works. Ed M. Summers 4 vols 1923.
Works. Ed F. W. Bateson 1930. With textual variorum.
Complete plays. Ed H. Davis, Chicago 1967.

§ 1

Incognita, or love and duty reconcil'd: a novel. 1692, 1700, 1713, 1713; ed H. F. B. Brett-Smith, Oxford 1922; ed A. N. Jeffares 1966 (with Way of the world, below).
The old batchelour. C DL 9 March 1693. 1693 (4 'editions', re-issues with some pages re-set), 1694, 1697 ('corrected'), 1707, 1710, 1711, [1711?] etc.
The double dealer. C DL Oct 1693. 1694, 1706 (rev), 1711, [1711?], 1735, Dublin 1735, London 1739 etc.
The mourning Muse of Alexas: a pastoral, lamenting the death of Queen Mary. 1695 (3 edns), Dublin 1695.
A Pindarique ode, humbly offer'd to the King on his taking Namure. 1695.
Love for love. C LIF April 1695. 1695, 1695, 1697 (rev), 1704, 1711, [1711?], c. 1715 (2 reprints), 1733; ed E. L. Avery, Lincoln Nebraska 1966; ed A. N. Jeffares 1967.
The mourning bride. T LIF Feb 1697. 1697, 1697, 1703, 1711, [1711?], 1733 etc.
The birth of the Muse: a poem. 1698.
Amendments of Mr Collier's false and imperfect citations. 1698.
The way of the world. C LIF March 1700. 1700, 1706 ('revised'), 1711, [1711?], 1735 etc; ed J. H. Wilson, Boston 1959; ed K. Lynch, Lincoln Nebraska 1965; ed A. N. Jeffares 1966 (with Incognita, above); ed B. Gibbons 1971 (New Mermaid); ed J. Barnard, Edinburgh 1972.
The judgement of Paris. M DG March 1701. 1701.
A hymn to harmony. 1703.
The tears of Amaryllis for Amyntas: a pastoral. 1703.
A Pindarique ode on the victorious progress of her Majesties arms. 1706. With a prefatory discourse of the Pindarique ode.
Semele. In Works, 1710. An unacted opera.
The dramatic works of John Dryden. 6 vols 1717. Ed Congreve.
An impossible thing: a tale. 1720.
A letter from Mr Congreve to the Viscount Cobham. 1729.
Mr Congreve's last will and testament. 1729, 1730.

Letters

Letters upon several occasions. Ed John Dennis 1696. Several letters from Congreve.
Congreve: letters and documents. Ed J. C. Hodges, New York 1964.

§ 2

'Wilson, Charles' (John Oldmixon?). Memoirs of Congreve. 1730.
Voltaire, F. M. A. de. In his Letters concerning the English nation, 1733.
Johnson, Samuel. In his Lives of the English poets, 1779–81.
Walpole, Horace. Thoughts on comedy. In his Works vol 2, 1798.
Hazlitt, William. In his Lectures on the English comic writers, 1819.
Lamb, Charles. On the artificial comedy. In his Essays of Elia, 1821.
Macaulay, T. B. The dramatic works of Wycherley, Congreve, Vanbrugh and Farquhar. Edinburgh Rev 72 1841.
Gosse, E. Life of Congreve. 1888 (EML), 1924 (rev).
Hodges, J. C. Congreve the man: a biography from new sources. New York 1941.
— The library of Congreve. New York 1955.
Fujimura, T. H. In his Restoration comedy of wit, Princeton 1952.
Loftis, J. Comedy and society from Congreve to Fielding. Stanford 1959.
Holland, N. N. In his First modern comedies, Cambridge Mass 1959.

GEORGE FARQUHAR
1678–1707
Collections

Comedies. [1707], 1710, 1711, 1714, 1721, 1728, 2 vols 1736 (as Dramatick works).

The dramatic works of Wycherley, Congreve, Vanbrugh and Farquhar. Ed Leigh Hunt 1840.
George Farquhar. Ed W. Archer [1906] (Mermaid ser).
Complete works. Ed C. Stonehill 2 vols 1930.

§ I

Love and a bottle. C DL Dec 1698. 1699, [1705?], 1735, Dublin 1761.
The adventures of Covent Garden. 1699. Anon.
The constant couple: or a trip to the Jubilee. C DL Nov 1699. 1700, 1700, 1701 (with alterations), 1704, 1710, 1711, 1732, 1735 etc.
Sir Harry Wildair: being the sequel of the trip to the jubilee. C DL c. April 1701. 1701, 1735.
The stage-coach. F LIF c. April 1701. Dublin 1704 (anon), 1705, 1709, Dublin 1719. With P. A. Motteux.
The inconstant: or the way to win him. C DL c. Feb 1702. 1702, 1718, 1736 etc.
Love and business in a collection of occasionary verse and epistolary prose: a discourse likewise upon comedy in reference to the English stage. 1702.
The recruiting officer. C DL 8 April 1706. [1706] (3 edns, the 2nd 'corrected'), [1707?], 1711, 1714, 1736 etc; ed M. Shugrue, Lincoln Nebraska 1965; ed K. Tynan 1965.
The beaux' stratagem. C Hay 8 March 1707. [1707], 1707 (8 edns), 1711, 1715, 1730, 1736, 1748, 1752 etc; ed B. Dobrée, Bristol 1929; ed J. H. Wilson, Boston 1959; ed V. C. Hopper and G. B. Lahey, New York 1963.
Barcellona, a poem: or the Spanish expedition. 1710.

§ 2

Hazlitt, William. In his Lectures on the English comic writers, 1819.
Farmer, A. J. Farquhar. 1966.
Rothstein, E. Farquhar. New York 1967.

III. MINOR RESTORATION DRAMA 1660–1700

APHRA BEHN
1640–89
Collections

Plays. 2 vols 1702, 1716, 4 vols 1724.
Works. Ed M. Summers 6 vols 1915. Omits the Pindarics.

§ I

For the novels, see col 550, below.

The forc'd marriage: or the jealous bridegroom. TC LIF Sept 1670. 1671, 1690.
The amorous prince: or the curious husband. C LIF c. Feb 1671. 1671.
The Dutch lover. C DG Feb 1673. 1673.
Abdelazar: or the moor's revenge. T DG July 1676. 1677, 1693.
The town-fopp: or Sir Timothy Tawdrey. C DG c. Sept 1676. 1677, 1699.
The debauchee: or the credulous cuckold. C DG c. Feb 1677. 1677.
The rover: or the banish't cavaliers. C DG March 1677. 1677, [1697?], 1709; ed F. Link, Lincoln Nebraska 1966.
Sir Patient Fancy. C DG Jan 1678. 1678, [1681?].
The feign'd curtizans: or a night's intrigue. C DG c. March 1679. 1679.

The second part of the rover. C DG c. Jan 1681. 1681.
The revenge: or a match in Newgate. C DG c. June 1680. 1680. Anon.
The round-heads: or the good old cause. C DG c. Dec 1681. 1682, 1698.
The city-heiress: or Sir Timothy Treat-all. C DG c. March 1682. 1682, 1698.
The false count: or a new way to play an old game. C DG c. Dec 1681. 1682, 1697.
The young King: or the mistake. TC DG c. 1679. 1683, 1698.
Poems upon several occasions, with a voyage to the island of love. 1684, 1697 (with Lycidus, below).
Miscellany: being a collection of poems by several hands. 1685. Ed with preface by Aphra Behn, with her trn of La Rochefoucauld, Seneca unmasqued.
A Pindarick on the death of our late sovereign. 1685, 1685, 1686, Dublin nd.
A poem humbly dedicated to Catherine Queen Dowager. 1685.
A Pindarick poem on the happy coronation of his Sacred Majesty James II and his illustrious consort Queen Mary. 1685.
The luckey chance: or an alderman's bargain. C DL c. April 1686. 1687.
The emperor of the moon. F DG c. March 1687. 1687, 1688.

To Christopher Duke of Albemarle, on his voyage to Jamaica: a Pindarick. 1687.
To the memory of George Duke of Buckingham. 1687. Anon.
Lycidus: or the lover in fashion, from the French [of the Abbé Tallemant]; together with a miscellany of new poems by several hands. 1688, 1697 (with Poems upon several occasions).
A discovery of new worlds, from the French [of Fontenelle]. 1688, 1700 (as The theory etc). With a prefatory essay on translated prose.
A poem to Sir Roger L'Estrange. 1688.
A congratulatory poem to her Majesty. 1688, 1688.
A congratulatory poem to the King's Most Sacred Majesty. 1688, 1688.
Two congratulatory poems to their Majesties. 1688.
The history of oracles, and the cheats of the pagan priests. 1688, 1699. Tr from Fontenelle.
A congratulatory poem to her Sacred Majesty Queen Mary. 1689.
A Pindaric poem to the Rev Dr Burnet. 1689.
The widow ranter: or the history of Bacon in Virginia. TC DL Nov 1689. 1690.
The younger brother: or the amorous jilt. C DL c. Feb 1696. 1696. With a biographical preface by Charles Gildon.

§ 2

Sackville-West, V. Aphra Behn. 1927.
Cameron, W. J. New light on Aphra Behn. Auckland 1961.
Link, F. M. Aphra Behn. New York 1968.

THOMAS BETTERTON
1635?–1710

§ 1

Appius and Virginia. T LIF May 1669. 1679. Anon.
The amorous widow: or the wanton wife. C LIF c. Nov 1670. 1706 (anon), 1710, 1714, 1725, 1729.
The counterfeit bridegroom: or the defeated widow. C DG c. Sept 1677. 1677. Anon.
The prophetess: or the history of Dioclesian. O DG June 1690. 1690 (anon), 1719.
K. Henry IV, with the humours of Sir John Falstaff. TC LIF 9 Jan 1700. 1700. Anon.
The bondman: or love and liberty. TC DL 1719. Anon.
The sequel of Henry the Fourth; with the humours of Sir John Falstaffe. TC DL [1720].
A history of the English stage. 1741. A compilation by Oldys et al, partly based on Betterton's papers.

§ 2

Downes, John. Roscius anglicanus. 1708; ed T. Davies 1789; ed J. Knight 1886; ed M. Summers [1928]; ed J. Loftis, Los Angeles 1969 (Augustan Reprint Soc).
Gildon, Charles. The life of Mr Thomas Betterton. 1710.
Lowe, R. W. Thomas Betterton. 1891.

GEORGE VILLIERS,
2nd DUKE OF BUCKINGHAM
1628–87

Collections

Works. Ed T. Brown 1704, 2 vols 1704–5, 1715, 1721, 1754, 1775.

§ 1

The rehearsal. Bsq TR 7 Dec 1671. 1672 (anon), 1673, 1675 (with 'amendments and large additions'), 1683,

1687, 1692, 1701, 1709 ('with a key'), 1711 etc; ed E. Arber 1869; ed M. Summers, Stratford-on-Avon 1914; ed G. G. Falle, New York 1964. Samuel Butler, Thomas Sprat and Martin Clifford are supposed to have assisted Buckingham.
A letter to Sir Thomas Osborn upon the reading of a book called the Present interest of England. 1672.
Poetical reflections on a late poem entituled Absalom and Achitophel, by a person of honour. 1681, 1682. Ascribed (wrongly?) to Buckingham by Anthony Wood.
The chances. C DL Dec 1682. 1682, 1692, 1705 etc.
A short discourse upon the reasonableness of men's having a religion. 1685.

§ 2

Wilson, J. H. A rake and his times: Villiers. New York 1954.

THOMAS D'URFEY
1653–1723

Archerie reviv'd, or the bow-man's excellence: an heroick poem. 1676. With Robert Shotterel.
The siege of Memphis: or the ambitious Queen. T DL c. Sept 1676. 1676.
Madam Fickle: or the witty false one. C DG Nov 1676. 1677, 1682, 1691.
A fond husband: or, the plotting sisters. C DG May 1677. 1677, 1678, 1685, 1711, 1725.
The fool turn'd critick. C DL Nov 1676. 1678.
Trick for trick: or the debauch'd hypocrite. C DL c. March 1678. 1678.
Squire Oldsapp: or the night-adventurers. C DG c. June 1678. 1679.
The virtuous wife: or good luck at last. C DG c. Sept 1679. 1680.
Sir Barnaby Whigg: or no wit like a womans. C DL c. Sept 1681. 1681.
The progress of honesty, or a view of a Court and city: a Pindarique poem. 1681, 1681, 1739.
Butler's ghost, or Hudibras: the fourth part. 1682.
The royalist. C DG Jan 1682. 1682.
The injured princess: or the fatal wager. TC DL c. March 1682. 1682.
Scandalum magnatum, or Potapski's case: a satyr against Polish oppression. 1682. Anon.
A new collection of songs and poems. 1683.
Choice new songs never before printed. 1684.
Several new songs. 1684.
The malecontent, a satyr: being the sequel of the Progress of honesty. 1684.
A third collection of new songs, never printed before. 1685.
An elegy upon the late blessed monarch King Charles II; and two panegyricks upon their present Sacred Majesties King James and Queen Mary. 1685.
A common-wealth of women. C DL c. Aug 1685. 1686, 1688.
The banditti: or a ladies distress. C DL c. Feb 1686. 1686.
A compleat collection of Mr D'Urfey's songs and odes, whereof the first part never before published. 1687. The 2nd pt as A new collection of songs and poems pt II.
A poem congratulatory on the birth of the young Prince. 1688.
A fool's preferment: or the three Dukes of Dunstable; together with all the songs and notes to 'em, excellently compos'd by Mr Henry Purcell. C DG c. April 1688. 1688, 1917.
New poems: consisting of satyrs, elegies and odes. 1690.
Collin's walk through London and Westminster: a poem in burlesque. 1690, 1690.
Momus ridens: or comical remarks on the publick reports. 29 Oct 1690–11 March 1691. Anon; weekly.

Love for money: or the boarding school. C DL c. Jan 1691. 1691, 1691, 1696, 1724, 1726.

Bussy D'Ambois: or the husbands revenge. T DL c. March 1691. 1691.

A Pindarick ode on New-Year's-Day, perform'd by vocal and instrumental musick before their Sacred Majesties K. William and Q. Mary. 1691.

A Pindarick poem on the Royal Navy. 1691.

The moralist: or a satyr upon the sects. 1691. Anon.

The triennial mayor, or the new raparees: a poem. 1691. Anon.

The weesils: a satyrical fable. 1691. Anon.

The weesil trap'd: a poem. 1691. Anon.

The marriage-hater match'd. C DL Jan 1692. 1692, 1692, 1693.

A Pindarick ode upon the fleet. 1692.

The Richmond heiress: or a woman once in the right. C DL c. April 1693. 1693, 1693, 1718.

The canonical states-man's grand argument discuss'd. 1693. Anon.

The comical history of Don Quixote: part I. C DG c. May 1694. 1694, 1694, 1727, 1729, [1889].

The comical history of Don Quixote: part the second. C DG c. June 1694. 1694, 1702, 1729, [1889].

The songs to the new play of Don Quixote: part the first. 1694, 1694.

The songs to the new play of Don Quixote: part the second. 1694.

The comical history of Don Quixote: the third part. C DL c. Nov 1695. 1696, 1729, [1889].

Gloriana: a funeral Pindarique poem sacred to the blessed memory of that ever-admir'd and most excellent Princess, our late gracious soveraign Lady Queen Mary. 1695.

New songs in the third part of the comical history of Don Quixote. 1696.

A new opera call'd Cinthia and Endimion: or the loves of the deities. O DL c. Dec 1696. 1697.

The intrigues at Versailles: or a jilt in all humours. C LIF c. May 1697. 1697, 1697.

Albion's blessing: a poem panegyrical on his Sacred Majesty King William the III. 1698.

The campaigners: or the pleasant adventures at Brussels, with a familiar preface upon a late reformer of the stage, ending with a satyrical fable of the dog and the ottor. C DL c. June 1698. 1698.

A choice collection of new songs and ballads. 1699.

The famous history of the rise and fall of Massaniello, in two parts. T DL c. May 1699. 1700. The 2nd pt dated 1699 as The famous history and fall of Massaniello: or a fisherman a prince.

An ode for the anniversary feast made in honour of St Cecilia. 1700.

The Bath: or the western lass. C DL May 1701. 1701.

The old mode and the new: or country miss with her furbeloe. C DL March 1703. [1703].

Tales tragical and comical, viz Abradatus and Panthea: or love and honour in perfection; Hell beyond hell: or the devil and mademoiselle; Female revenge: or the Queen of Lombardy; The night-adventures: or the country intrigue; Fatal piety: or the royal converts; The broken commands: or the heirs adopted. 1704.

Wonders in the sun: or the Kingdom of the birds. CO Hay April 1706. 1706, 1706, Los Angeles 1964 (Augustan Reprint Soc).

Stories moral and comical: viz, The banquet of the gods; Titus and Gisippus: or the power of friendship; The prudent husband: or cuckoldom wittily prevented: Loyalty's glory: or the true souldier of honour. [1707].

The trophies: or Augusta's glory a triumphant ode. 1707.

Honor and opes, or the British merchant's glory: a poem. 1708.

The modern prophets: or new wit for a husband. C DL May 1709. [1709].

Musa et musica: or honour and musick. [1710].

Songs compleat, pleasant and divertive. 5 vols 1719. Ed D'Urfey. Vols 1–2 contain his songs.

Wit and mirth: or pills to purge melancholy. 6 vols 1719–20. Vols 1–5 are a re-issue of Songs compleat, pleasant and divertive, above, with new title-pages and head-lines. Vol 6 is dated 1720. Ed C. L. Day 3 vols New York 1959.

New opera's, with comical stories and poems, on several occasions. 1721. The two Queens of Brentford: or Bayes no poetaster, Bsq O; The Grecian heroine: or the fate of tyranny, T; Ariadne: or the triumph of Bacchus, O. All unacted.

Songs. Ed C. L. Day, Cambridge Mass 1933.

RICHARD FLECKNOE
c. 1620–78

The affections of a pious soule. 1640.

Miscellanea: or poems of all sorts with divers other pieces. 1653. Includes a Discourse of languages.

A relation of ten years travells. [1654?], 1665 (as A true narrative).

Love's dominion. TC Unacted. 1654.

The diarium: or journall, in burlesque rhime. 1656.

Enigmaticall characters. 1658, 1665 (rev).

The idea of Oliver, late Lord Protector. 1659.

The marriage of Oceanus and Britannia. 1659. No known copy.

Heroick portraits, with other pieces. 1660.

Erminia: or the fair and vertuous lady. TC Unacted. 1661, 1665.

Love's kingdom. TC LIF c. 1664. 1664, 1674. An alteration of Love's dominion. The Short treatise of the English stage appended is rptd in J. E. Spingarn, Critical essays of the seventeenth century vol 2, Oxford 1908.

Of one that Zany's the good companion; Of a bold abusive wit. 1665 (2nd edn) etc; ed E. N. Hooker, Ann Arbor 1946.

A farrago of several pieces. 1666.

The life of Tomaso the wanderer. 1667; ed G. Thorn-Drury 1925.

Sir William Davenant's voyage to the other world. 1668.

The damoiselles a la mode. C TR Sept 1668. 1667.

Epigrams of all sorts. 1669, 1670 (expanded), 1671 (further expanded), 1673 (as A collection of the choicest epigrams and characters; adds Characters made at several times).

SIR ROBERT HOWARD
1626–98

Collections

Four new plays. 1665. The surprisal, C TR April 1662; Committee, C TR before Nov 1662, ed C. N. Thurber, Urbana 1921; The Indian Queen, T TR Jan 1664; Vestal-virgin, T TR 1664.

Five new plays. 1692, 1700 ('corrected'), 1722 (as Dramatic works). Adds Duke of Lerma.

§ I

Poems. 1660, 1696. Includes The blind lady, C, unacted.

The duell of the stags: a poem. 1668, 1709.

The great favourite: or the Duke of Lerma. T TR 20 Feb 1668. 1668. Preface ed J. E. Spingarn, Oxford 1908 (in Critical essays of the seventeenth century vol 2) (with preface to Four new plays, above); ed D. D. Arundell, Cambridge 1929 (in Dryden and Howard).

An account of the state of his Majesties revenue. 1681.

The life and reign of King Richard the Second. 1681. Anon. Not by Howard?

Historical observations upon the reigns of Edward I, II, III and Richard II. 1689 (anon), 1690 (as The history of the reigns of Edward and Richard II, written in the year 1685 by Sᵣ Robert Howard).

A letter to Mr S. Johnson. 1692.

The history of religion. 1694 (anon), 1709 (as An account of the growth of deism).

§ 2

Dryden, John. Of dramatick poesie: an essay. 1668; A defence, 1668 (prefixed to The Indian Emperor).

Oliver, H. J. Howard: a critical biography. Durham NC 1963.

SIR WILLIAM KILLIGREW
1606–95
Collections

Three playes. 1664–5, 1674. Selindra TC TR March 1662; Pandora: or the converts; Ormasdes: or love and friendship, TC Unacted?

Four new playes. Oxford 1666. Adds The siege of Urbin, TC Unacted?; ed I. E. Taylor, Philadelphia 1946.

§ 1

Pandora. C TR c. 1662. 1664. Anon.

The imperial tragedy. T Unacted. 1669. Anon. Attributed to Killigrew.

Mid-night thoughts, by a person of quality. 1681 (prose), 1684 (with addns, mainly in verse, as The artless midnight thoughts of a gentleman at Court).

Mid-night and daily thoughts, in prose and verse. 1694.

PETER ANTHONY MOTTEUX
1663–1718
Bibliographies

Cunningham, R. N. A bibliography of the writings of Motteux. Proc Oxford Bibl Soc 3 1933.

§ 1

The gentleman's journal: or the monthly miscellany. Jan 1692–Nov 1694 (2 edns of Jan–April 1692). Ed Motteux.

The works of F. Rabelais, done out of French by Sir Tho Urchard and others. 5 bks 1694–3, 2 vols 1708, 5 vols 1737 (rev J. Ozell). Rev and concluded by Motteux.

The present state of the Empire of Morocco. 1695. From the French of Pidou de Saint Olon.

Maria: a poem occasioned by the death of her Majesty. 1695.

Christian conferences: demonstrating the truth of the Christian religion and morality. 1695. From the French of Malebranche.

Of pastorals. 1695, 2 vols 1719. From Fontenelle.

Words for a musical entertainment on the taking of Namur. Int LIF 1695. [1695].

Love's a jest. C LIF c. June 1696. 1696.

The loves of Mars and Venus. Int LIF c. Nov 1696. 1697, 1722, 1735.

The novelty: every act a play. C and T LIF c. June 1697. 1697.

Europe's revels for the peace. Int LIF Nov 1697. 1697.

Beauty in distress. T LIF c. April 1698. 1698.

The island Princess: or the generous Portuguese. O DL c. Nov 1698. 1699, 1701, 1701, 1724, 1726.

The four seasons: or love in every age. Int DL c. Feb 1699. 1699; rptd with Island Princess, 1699 etc, above.

The history of the renown'd Don Quixote. 4 vols 1700–3, 1712; rev J. Ozell 4 vols 1719 etc.

The masque of Acis and Galatea, with the musical entertainments in the mad lover. DL c. March 1701. 1701, 1723.

A banquet for gentlemen and ladies. 1701, 1703, 1712, 1718, nd. A collection of novels.

The stage-coach. F LIF c. April 1701. Dublin 1704, London 1705, 1709, Dublin 1719. With Farquhar.

Britain's happiness. Int DL and LIF c. Feb 1704. 1704. From Tomaso Stanzani.

Arsinoe, Queen of Cyprus. O DL 16 Jan 1705. 1705, 1705, 1707.

The amorous miser: or the younger the wiser. C Unacted? 1705. Anon.

The temple of love. O Hay 7 March 1706. 1706.

Camilla. O DL 30 March 1706. 1706, 1707, 1708, 1709, 1717, 1726. Dedication signed Owen Swiny, but perhaps really by Motteux. From Silvio Stampiglia.

Farewell folly: or the younger the wiser, with the Mountebank. C DL 18 Jan 1705. 1707. A recast of the Amorous miser?

Thomyris, Queen of Scythia. O DL 1 April 1707. 1707, 1708 (as The royal Amazon), 1709, 1719.

Love's triumph. O Hay 26 Feb 1708. 1708, 1713 (as The triumph of love). From Ottoboni, La pastorella.

A poem upon tea. 1712, 1712 (both folio), 1712 (8°); rptd Bee Oct 1715.

§ 2

Cunningham, R. N. Motteux: a bibliographical and critical study. Oxford 1933.

ROGER BOYLE,
1st EARL OF ORRERY
1621–79
Collections

Dramatic works. 2 vols 1739.

Dramatic works. Ed W. S. Clark 2 vols Cambridge Mass 1937. Includes Tragedy of Zoroastres (from ms).

§ 1

Parthenissa that most fam'd romance. 6 vols 1654–69, 1676.

The history of Henry the Fifth. T LIF Aug 1664. 1668, 1669, 1677, 1690.

The General. T LIF Sept 1664. Ed J. O. Halliwell [-Phillipps] 1853. One ms in Plymouth Lib; another at Worcester College, Oxford. Acted at Smock Alley, Dublin, 26 Feb 1663.

The tragedy of Mustapha, son of Solyman the magnificent. T LIF April 1665. Ptd with Henry the Fifth, above, ed B. Dobrée, Oxford 1960 (in Five heroic plays) (WC).

The Black Prince. T TR 19 Oct 1667. Ptd with Tryphon as Two new tragedies, 1669, 1672.

Tryphon. T LIF 8 Dec 1668.

Mr Anthony. C DG c. 1671. 1690.

Guzman. C LIF April 1669. 1693.

English adventures. 1676. Incomplete.

A treatise of the art of war. 1677.

Poems on most of the festivals of the Church. 1681.

Herod the great. T Unacted. 1694, 1694 (with the earlier plays, except Mr Anthony, as Six plays).

The tragedy of King Saul. T Unacted. 1703 (anon), 1739.

A collection of the state letters of Roger Boyle, the first Earl of Orrery. 1742, 2 vols Dublin 1743.

§ 2

Lynch, K. Roger Boyle. Knoxville 1965.

EDWARD RAVENSCROFT
c. 1650–c. 1700

The citizen turn'd gentleman. C DG July 1672. 1672, 1675 (as Mamamouchi).
The careless lovers. C DG March 1673. 1673.
The wrangling lovers: or the invisible mistress. C DG July 1676. 1677.
Scaramouch, a philosopher, Harlequin, a school-boy, bravo, merchant and magician. C DL May 1677. 1677.
King Edgar and Alfreda. TC DL c. Oct 1677. 1677.
The English lawyer. C DL c. Dec 1677. 1678.
The London cuckolds. C DG Nov 1681. 1682, 1683, 1688, 1697; ed M. Summers 1921 (in Restoration comedies).
Dame Dobson: or the cunning woman. C DG c. May 1683. 1684.
Titus Andronicus: or the rape of Lavinia. T DL c. Dec 1686. 1687.
The Canterbury guests: or a bargain broken. C DL Sept 1694. 1695.
The anatomist: or the sham doctor. C LIF c. 14 Nov 1696. 1697, 1722.
The Italian husband. T LIF c. Nov 1697. 1698.

ELKANAH SETTLE
1648–1724
§ 1

Mare clausum: or a ransack for the Dutch. 1666.
Cambyses King of Persia. T LIF c. Feb 1667. 1671, 1672, 1675 ('revised'), 1692.
The Empress of Morocco. T DG July 1673, probably produced at Court 1671. 1673, 1673, 1687, 1698; ed B. Dobrée, Oxford 1960 (in Five heroic plays) (WC).
Love and revenge. T DG Nov 1675. 1675.
Notes and observations on the Empress of Morocco revised. 1674.
The conquest of China, by the Tartars. T DG May 1675. 1676.
Ibrahim the illustrious Bassa. T DG c. March 1676. 1677, 1694; preface ed H. Macdonald, Oxford 1947 (Luttrell Soc).
Pastor Fido: or the faithful shepherd. M DG c. Dec 1676. 1677, 1689, 1694.
The female prelate: being the history of the life and death of Pope Joan. T DL 31 May 1680. 1680, 1689.
Fatal love: or the forc'd inconstancy. T DL c. Sept 1680. 1680.
The heir of Morocco, with the death of Gayland. T DL 11 March 1682. 1682, 1694.
Absalom Senior, or Achitophel transpros'd: a poem. 1682 (anon), 1682 ('revis'd, with additions'); ed H. W. Jones, Gainesville 1961.
Distress'd innocence: or the Princess of Persia. T DL c. Oct 1690. 1691.
The Fairy-Queen. O DG 2 May 1692. 1692 (anon), 1693 (rev).
The notorious impostor. 1692; Diego Redivivus, 1692; both ed S. Peterson, Los Angeles 1958 (Augustan Reprint Soc).
The new Athenian comedy. C Unacted. 1693.
The ambitious slave: or a generous revenge. T DL 21 March 1694. 1694.
Philaster: or love lies a-bleeding. TC DL c. Dec 1695. 1695.
The world in the moon. O DG May 1697. 1697, 1697.
A defence of dramatick poetry. 1698.
The virgin prophetesse: or the fate of Troy. O DL 15 May 1701. 1701, 1702 (anon as Cassandra).
The siege of Troy; Droll Bartholomew and Southwark Fairs. 1707, 1715, [1716].

The city-ramble: or a play-house wedding. O DL 17 Aug 1711. [1711]. Anon.
The lady's triumph. O LIF 22 March 1718. 1718. This version is at least partly by Lewis Theobald.

§ 2

Brown, F. C. Settle: his life and works. Chicago 1910.

THOMAS SOUTHERNE
1659–1746
Collections

Works. 2 vols 1713 (all the plays except Spartan dame and Money the mistress), 2 vols 1721 (adds Spartan dame).

§ 1

The loyal brother: or the Persian Prince. T DL Feb 1682. 1682; ed P. Hamelius, Liège 1911.
The disappointment: or the mother in fashion. T DL c. April 1684. 1684.
Sir Anthony Love: or the rambling lady. C DL c. Dec 1690. 1691, 1698.
The wives excuse: or cuckolds make themselves. C DL Dec 1691. 1692, 1726, 1735.
The maid's last prayer: or any, rather than fail. C DL Jan 1693. 1693.
The fatal marriage: or the innocent adultery. T DL Feb 1694. 1694, 1732, 1735.
Oroonoko. T DL c. Nov 1695. 1696, 1699, 1699, 1711, 1712, 1721, Dublin 1722, 1731, London 1735, 1736, 1740, 1744 etc.
The fate of Capua. T LIF c. April 1700. 1700.
The Spartan dame. T DL 11 Dec 1719. 1719 (3 edns), 1721 (5th edn).
Money the mistress. C LIF 19 Feb 1726. 1726.

§ 2

Dodds, J. W. Thomas Southerne, dramatist. New Haven 1933.

NAHUM TATE
1652–1715

Poems. 1677, 1684 ('enlarged').
Brutus of Alba: or the enchanted lovers. T DG c. July 1678. 1678.
The loyal General. T DG c. Dec 1679. 1680.
The history of King Richard the Second. T DL c. Jan 1681. 1681, 1691 (as The Sicilian usurper).
The history of King Lear. T DG c. March 1681. 1681, 1689, 1699, [1702?], 1703, 1712, 1733 etc; ed C. Spencer, Urbana 1965 (in Five Restoration adaptations of Shakespeare).
The ingratitude of a common-wealth: or the fall of Caius Martius Coriolanus. T DL c. Dec 1681. 1682.
The second part of Absalom and Achitophel. 1682. With Dryden.
A Duke and no Duke. F DL c. Aug 1684. 1685, 1693 (with a preface concerning farce).
Cuckolds-haven: or an alderman no conjurer. F DG c. July 1685. 1685.
Poems by several hands, collected by N. Tate. 1685.
On the sacred memory of our late Sovereign. 1685, 1685.
Syphilis: a poetical history of the French disease. 1686. Tr from Fracastoro.
The Island-Princess. TC DL April 1687. 1687.
A pastoral in memory of the Duke of Ormond. 1688.
Dido and Aeneas. O At Mr Josias Priest's boarding-school at Chelsey c. Dec 1689. Ed G. A. Macfarren 1841, 1926; 1961 (facs).

A poem occasioned by his Majesty's voyage to Holland. 1691.

A poem occasioned by the late discontents. 1691.

Characters of vertue and vice, attempted in verse from a treatise of the Reverend Joseph Hall. 1691.

An ode upon her Majesty's birth-day. 1693.

A present for the ladies. 1693.

A poem on the late promotion of several eminent persons. 1694.

In memory of Joseph Washington esq: an elegy. 1694.

The four epistles of A. G. Busbequius, done into English. 1694.

An ode upon the University of Dublin's foundation. Dublin 1694.

Mausolaeum: a funeral poem on our late Queen. 1695.

An elegy on the late Archbishop of Canterbury. 1695.

Miscellanea sacra: or poems on divine and moral subjects, collected by N. Tate. 1696, 1696, 1698 (with addns).

A new version of the psalms of David, by N. Tate and N. Brady. 1696, 1698 etc.

The innocent epicure. 1697. By J.S., ed Tate.

The anniversary ode for his Majesty's birthday. 1698.

A consolatory poem to Lord Cutts. 1698.

Elegies. 1699.

An essay of a character of Sir G. Treby. 1700.

Funeral poems. 1700.

Panacea: a poem upon tea. 1700, 1702 (as A poem upon tea).

An elegy in memory of Ralph Marshall. 1700.

A congratulatory poem on the new Parliament. 1701.

The Kentish worthies: a poem. 1701.

A monumental poem in memory of Sir George Treby. 1702.

Portrait-royal: a poem upon her Majesty's picture. 1703.

The song for new-year's-day. 1703.

The triumph: a poem on the glorious successes of the last year. 1705, 1705.

Britannia's prayer for the Queen. 1706.

Majestas imperii britannici, in Latin poems by Mr Maidwell, paraphras'd by N.T. 1706.

The triumph of union. 1707.

Injur'd love, or the cruel husband: a tragedy design'd to be acted at the Theatre Royal. 1707.

A congratulatory poem to Prince George of Denmark. 1708.

The celebrated speeches of Ajax and Ulysses, essay'd in English verse by Mr Tate and Aaron Hill gent. 1708. From Ovid.

An essay for promoting of psalmody. 1710.

The Muse's memorial of the Earl of Oxford. 1712.

The Muses bower. 1713.

The triumph of peace. 1713.

A poem sacred to the memory of Queen Anne. [1714].

Tate also collaborated in Dryden's version of Ovid, Juvenal and Lucian, and in the trn of Cowley's Latin history of plants.

SIR SAMUEL TUKE

c. 1620–74

The adventures of five hours. TC LIF 8 Jan 1663. 1663, 1664, 1671 (rev), 1704; ed R. Dodsley in Select collection of old plays vol 12, 1744; rev W. C. Hazlitt vol 15, 1876; ed A. E. H. Swaen, Amsterdam 1927 (from 1663 and 1671 edns); ed B. Van Thal and M. Summers [1927]. Swaen's edn contains a trn of the Spanish source, Coello's Los empeños de seis horas.

IV. EARLY EIGHTEENTH-CENTURY DRAMA

COLLEY CIBBER

1671–1757

Collections

Plays. 2 vols 1721. 10 plays, partially rev.

Dramatic works. 4 vols 1760. With anon life. Adds 6 plays.

Dramatic works. 5 vols 1777.

§ I

A poem on the death of our late sovereign lady Queen Mary. 1695.

Love's last shift: or the fool in fashion. C DL Jan 1696. 1696, 1702, 1711, Dublin 1725, London 1730, [1735], 1740, 1747, Dublin 1750.

Womans wit: or the lady in fashion. C DL c. Dec 1696. 1697, 1736.

Xerxes. T LIF c. Feb 1699. 1699, 1736.

The tragical history of King Richard III. T DL c. Feb 1700. [1700], 1718, Dublin [c. 1730], London 1734, 1736, 1754 etc; ed C. Spencer, Urbana 1965 (in Five Restoration adaptations of Shakespeare).

Love makes a man: or the fop's fortune. C DL 13 Dec 1700. 1701, [c. 1702], 1716, Dublin 1722, London 1726, 1735, 1745, 1751 etc.

She wou'd and she wou'd not: or the kind impostor. C DL 26 Nov 1702. 1703, 1717, 1719, 1725, 1736, 1748 etc.

The careless husband. C DL 7 Dec 1704. 1705, 1705, 1711, 1723, Dublin 1723, London 1725, 1731, 1733, 1734, 1735, 1735, Dublin 1752; rptd 1928; Amsterdam 1928; ed W. W. Appleton, Lincoln Nebraska 1966.

Perolla and Izadora. T DL 3 Dec 1705. 1706, 1736.

The school-boy: or the comical rival. F DL 1702. 1707 (anon), [1730], 1736. The subplot of Woman's wit, above.

The comical lovers. C Hay 4 Feb 1707. [1707] (anon), Dublin [1720?], London 1736, 1754.

The double gallant: or the sick lady's cure. C Hay 1 Nov 1707. [1707], 1707, 1719, 1723, Dublin 1725, London [1729], 1736, 1740 etc.

The lady's last stake: or the wife's resentment. C Hay 13 Dec 1707. [1708], 1732, 1747, Dublin 1750.

The rival fools. C DL 11 Jan 1709. [1709], 1753.

Cinna's conspiracy. T DL 1713. 1713. Anon. Not by Cibber?

The secret history of Arlus and Odolphus. 1714 (4 edns). Anon.

Myrtillo. M DL 5 Nov 1715. 1715, 1716, [1720] (with Venus and Adonis), 1736, 1736.

Venus and Adonis. M DL 12 March 1715. 1715, 1716, [1720] (with Myrtillo), 1736, 1736.

The non-juror. C DL 6 Dec 1717. 1718 (5 edns), 1736, 1746, Dublin 1759, London 1760.

Ximena: or the heroick daughter. T DL 28 Nov 1712. 1719, 1781.

The refusal: or the ladies philosophy. C DL 14 Feb 1721. 1721, 1722, 1735, 1736, 1737, Dublin 1749, London 1753, 1764.

Caesar in Aegypt. T DL 9 Dec 1724. 1725, 1736.

The provok'd husband: or a journey to London. C DL 10 Jan 1728. 1728, Dublin 1728 (8°), 1728 (12°), London 1729, 1730, 1734, 1735, 1741, 1743, 1748, Dublin 1748 London 1753, 1753 etc. An expansion of Vanbrugh's fragment A journey to London.

The rival queans, with the humours of Alexander the Great. Bsq Hay 29 June 1710. Dublin 1729; ed W. M. Peterson, Painesville Ohio 1965.

Love in a riddle. BO DL 7 Jan 1729. 1729 (2 issues).

Damon and Phillida. BO New Hay 16 Aug 1729. [1729], 1730 (different text), Edinburgh 1732, Dublin 1733, London 1734, 1737, 1765. Altered from Love in a riddle, above.

An ode to his Majesty for the new year. 1731.

An ode for his Majesty's birth-day. 1731.

The blind boy. [c. 1735]. A broadside.

An apology for the life of Mr Colley Cibber, comedian. 1740, 1740, Dublin 1740, 2 vols 1750 (with An account of English stage and dialogue on old plays), 1756 (with list of dramatic authors); ed E. Bellchambers 1822; ed R. W. Lowe 2 vols 1889; ed B. R. S. Fone, Ann Arbor 1968.

A letter from Mr Cibber to Mr Pope. 1742, 1742, Dublin 1742, Glasgow [1743?], London 1777.

A second letter from Mr Cibber to Mr Pope. 1743.

The egotist: or Colley upon Cibber. 1743, Dublin 1743.

Another occasional letter from Mr Cibber to Mr Pope. 1744, Dublin 1744, Glasgow [1744], London 1777.

Papal tyranny in the reign of King John. T CG 15 Feb 1745. 1745, Dublin 1745.

The character and conduct of Cicero considered. 1747.

The lady's lecture: a theatrical dialogue between Sir Charles Easy and his marriageable daughter. 1748.

A rhapsody upon the marvellous arising from the first odes of Horace and Pindar. 1751. Verse.

Verses to the memory of Mr Pelham. [1754].

§ 2

Leech, C. Shakespeare, Cibber and the Tudor myth. In his Shakespearean essays, Knoxville 1964.

Ashley, L. R. N. Cibber. New York 1965.

NICHOLAS ROWE
1674–1718
Collections

Tragedies. 2 vols 1714.

Poetical works. 1715, 1720, 1733 (as Miscellaneous works).

Dramatick works. 2 vols 1720.

Three plays: Tamerlane, The fair penitent, Jane Shore. Ed J. R. Sutherland 1929.

§ I

The ambitious step-mother. T LIF c. Dec 1700, 1701, 1702 (with new scene), 1714, Hague 1720, Dublin 1726, London 1727, 1733, 1735 etc.

Tamerlane. T LIF c. Dec 1701. 1702, 1703, 1714, 1717, Hague 1720, London 1730, 1733, 1736, Dublin 1750 etc; ed J. R. Sutherland 1929; ed L. C. Burnes 1966.

The fair penitent. T LIF c. May 1703. 1703, 1714, 1718, Hague [1723?], Dublin 1723, London 1730, Dublin 1732, London 1733, 1735, 1742, 1747, 1750 etc; ed S. C. Hart, Boston 1907; ed J. R. Sutherland 1929; ed J. H. Wilson, Boston 1963.

The biter. F LIF 4 Dec 1704. 1705, 1720, 1726, 1736.

Ulysses. T Hay 23 Nov 1705. 1706, 1714 ('revis'd'), 1726, Dublin 1726, London 1735.

The royal convert. T Hay 25 Nov 1707. 1708, 1714 (rev), 1720, 1726, 1735, 1738 etc.

A poem upon the late glorious successes of her Majesty's arms. 1707, 1719, 1726.

The life of Pythagoras [by Dacier], with his symbols and golden verses: the golden verses translated from the Greek by N. Rowe. 1707, 1719, 1726.

Boileau's Lutrin, render'd into English verse [by J. Ozell et al]; to which is prefix'd some account of Boileau's writings, by N. Rowe. 1708, 1711, 1714, 1730.

Callipaedia: a poem written in Latin by Claudius Quillet, made English. 1712, 1720. By Rowe et al.

The works of Mr William Shakespear, revis'd and corrected. 6 vols 1709, 9 vols 1714.

The tragedy of Jane Shore. T DL 2 Feb 1714. [1714], 1714, 1720, Dublin [1720?], [Hague? 1723?], London 1728, 1733, 1735, 1736, Glasgow 1748; ed S. C. Hart, Boston 1907; ed J. R. Sutherland 1929.

Poems on several occasions. 1714 (3 issues), 1720.

The tragedy of the Lady Jane Grey. T DL 20 April 1715. 1715, [Hague?] 1718, London 1720, 1727, 1730, 1736 etc.

Ode for the new year 1716. 1716.

Lucan's Pharsalia, translated into English verse. 1718 (with life of Rowe by James Welwood), Dublin 1719, 2 vols [Hague?] 1720, London 1722.

Rowe edited the Dryden Poetical miscellanies pts 5–6 1704–9, and had a hand in the composite Metamorphoses, 1717.

§ 2

Gildon, Charles. A new rehearsal: or Bays the younger. 1714, 1715 (with addns).

Johnson, Samuel. In his Lives of the English poets, 1779–81.

SUSANNA CENTLIVRE or CARROLL
c. 1670–1723
Collections

Works. 3 vols 1760–1, 1872 (as Dramatic works).

§ I

The perjur'd husband: or the adventures of Venice. TC DL c. Oct 1700. 1700, 1737.

The beau's duel: or a soldier for the ladies. C LIF c. June 1702. 1702, 1715 ('corrected'), 1719, Dublin 1727, London 1735, 1736 etc.

The stolen heiress: or the Salamanca doctor outplotted. C LIF 31 Dec 1702. [1703]. Anon.

Love's contrivance: or le medecin malgre lui. C DL 4 June 1703. 1703. Signed R.M.

The gamester. C LIF c. Jan 1705. 1705 (anon), 1708, 1714, Dublin 1725, London 1734, 1736, 1736, 1756, 1760 (re-issue of 1736 edn), Dublin 1765, London 1767.

Love at a venture. C Bath. 1706. Anon.

The basset-table. C DL 20 Nov 1705. 1706 (anon), [1706], 1735, 1736.

The platonick lady. C Hay 25 Nov 1706. 1707. Anon.

The busie body. C DL 12 May 1709. [1709], [1709], [c. 1715?], 1727, 1732, 1741, 1746, Norwich 1746, Dublin 1747, London 1749, 1753, 1759, 1765 etc; ed J. Byrd, Los Angeles 1949 (Augustan Reprint Soc).

The man's bewitch'd: or the devil to do about her. C Hay 12 Dec 1709. [1709], 1737, 1738.

A Bickerstaff's burying: or work for the upholders. F DL 27 March 1710. [1710], Dublin 1724.

Mar-plot: or the second part of the busie-body. C DL 30 Dec 1710. 1711, 1737.

The perplex'd lovers. C DL 19 Jan 1712. 1712, 1719, Dublin 1725, London 1734, 1736.

A trip to the masquerade: or a journey to Somerset-House. 1713. Anon. English and French, in verse.

The wonder: a woman keeps a secret. C DL 27 April 1714. 1714, 1714, Dublin 1725, London 1734, 1740, 1759 etc.

The Gotham election. F Unacted. 1715, 1737 (as The humours of elections).

A wife well manag'd. F DL 1715? 1715. Anon but frontispiece of Mrs Centlivre.

A poem humbly presented to his most sacred Majesty upon his accession to the throne. 1715 (for 1714).

An epistle to Mrs Wallup, now in the train of the Princess of Wales. 1715 (for 1714).

The cruel gift. T DL 17 Dec 1716. 1717 (with running title The cruel gift: or the royal resentment), 1734, 1736.

A bold stroke for a wife. C LIF 3 Feb 1718. 1718 (in A collection of plays by eminent hands, vol 3), 1719, 1724, Dublin 1727, London 1728, 1729, 1733, 1735, 1749 etc; ed T. Stathas, Lincoln Nebraska 1968.

A woman's case, in an epistle to Charles Joye esq. 1720. Verse.

The artifice. C DL 2 Oct 1722. 1723 (for 1722), 1735, 1736.

§ 2

Hazlitt, William. In his A view of the English stage, 1818.
—— In his Lectures on the English comic writers, 1819.
Sutherland, J. R. The progress of error: Mrs Centlivre and the biographers. RES 18 1942.

HENRY CAREY
1687?–1743

Collections

Dramatick works. 1743.
Poems. Ed F. T. Wood 1930.

§ 1

The records of love. 12 nos 1710. Anon.
Poems on several occasions. 1713, 1720 (enlarged), 1729 (enlarged).

The contrivances: or more ways than one. F DL 9 Aug 1715. 1715 (anon), 1719. Recast as BO DL 20 June 1729. 1729, Dublin 1731, London 1732, 1743, 1765 (7th edn) etc.

Hanging and marriage: or the dead-man's wedding. F LIF 15 March 1722. [1722]. Recast as BO, Betty: or the country bumpkin, DL 1 Dec 1732. Songs only ptd 1739.

Amelia: a new English opera after the Italian manner. New Hay 13 March 1732. 1732. Anon.

Teraminta. O LIF 20 Nov 1732. 1732.

The disappointment. BO New Hay 1732? 1732, 1732. Ptd as by John Randall, but probably Carey's.

The tragedy of Chrononhotonthologos. Bsq New Hay 22 Feb 1734. [1734], Edinburgh 1734, London 1743, 1744, 1753, 1760, 1765, 1770 (7th edn), 1777 etc.

The honest Yorkshireman. BO LIF 11 July 1735. 1736 (for 1735, pirated as A wonder: or an honest Yorkshireman), 1736, 1736, Belfast 1763, Glasgow 1770, London 1777. Songs, with score, c. 1743.

Of stage tyrants: an epistle. 1735.

The dragon of Wantley. Bsq CG 26 Oct 1737. [1737] (anon), 1737 (c. 6 edns), 1738 (14th edn), 1743, [1749?], 1755, 1762, 1763, 1770, 1777, 1777. Songs and duettos, with the score, 1738.

The musical century, in one hundred English ballads. 1737, 1740, 1743. With Carey's own settings.

Margery: or a worse plague than the dragon. Bsq CG 9 Dec 1738. 1738 (3 edns), 1743.

Nancy: or the parting lovers. Int CG 1 Dec 1739. 1739, 1755 (as The press gang), 1779, 1787 (as True blue).

An ode to mankind, address'd to the Prince of Wales. 1741.

Cupid and Hymen. 1748. Appendixes, probably all by Carey, also ptd singly.

V. MINOR DRAMA 1700–50

HENRY BROOKE
1703?–83

Collections

A collection of plays and poems. 4 vols 1778.

§ 1

Universal beauty: a poem. 6 pts 1735.

Tasso's Jerusalem: an epic poem translated. 1738. Bks 1–2 only.

Gustavus Vasa, the deliverer of his country, as it was to have been acted at the Theatre-Royal in Drury-Lane. T. 1739, 1739, Dublin 1739. DL performance prohibited but acted at Dublin in 1744 as The patriot.

The Canterbury tales of Chaucer, modernis'd by several hands. 3 vols 1741, 2 vols Dublin 1742. Ed George Ogle. Brooke contributed Constantia: or the Man of Lawes tale.

Prospectus of a work to be entitled Ogygian tales: or a curious collection of Irish fables. 1743.

Fables for the female sex. 1744, 1746, 1755 (4th edn), 1766 etc. 3 fables by Brooke, the rest by Edward Moore.

A history of Ireland from the earliest times proposed. 1744.

The farmer's six letters to the Protestants of Ireland. Dublin 1745, London 1746, Dublin 1746, Manchester [1750] (as Essays against Popery).

The secret history and memoirs of the barracks of Ireland. 1745.

The last speech of John the good, vulgarly called Jack the giant queller. 1748.

New fables. 1749.

The songs in Jack the gyant queller: an antique history. Dublin 1749, 1749, London 1749, 1749, 1757. Complete text in collected works as Little John and the giants.

A new collection of fairy tales. 1750.

The Earl of Essex. T Smock Alley Dublin May 1750. 1761, Dublin 1761, Edinburgh 1761.

A new system of fairery: or a collection of fairy tales, translated from the French of Comte de Caylus. 2 vols 1750.

A description of the College-Green Club: a satire, by the farmer. Dublin 1753.

The spirit of party. 2 pts 1753–4.

The interests of Ireland considered. Dublin 1759.

The case of the Roman Catholics of Ireland. Dublin 1760.

Tryal of the cause of the Roman Catholics. Dublin 1761, 1762, London 1762, 1764.

A proposal for the restoration of public wealth and credit. Dublin [1762?].

The fool of quality: or the history of Henry Earl of Moreland. 5 vols 1764–70 (vols 1–2 rptd 1767), 4 vols 1776, 5 vols 1777, 1781 (condensed by John Wesley) etc; ed C. Kingsley 2 vols 1859; ed E. A. Baker 1906.

Redemption: a poem. 1772.

Juliet Grenville: or the history of the human heart. 3 vols 1774.

§ 2

Wilson, C. H. Brookiana: anecdotes of Henry Brooke. 2 vols 1804.

D'Olier, Isaac. Memoirs of the life of the late excellent and pious Mr Henry Brooke. Dublin 1816.

THEOPHILUS CIBBER
1703–58

An historical tragedy of the civil wars in the reign of King Henry VI: being a sequel to the tragedy of Humphrey Duke of Gloucester; and an introduction to the tragical history of King Richard III, alter'd from Shakespeare, in the year 1720. T DL 3 July 1723. [1723?], 1724 (as King Henry VI).

Patie and Peggie: or the fair foundling. BO DL 25 Nov 1730. 1730.

The lover. C DL 20 Jan 1731. 1730, Dublin 1731, 1731.

The harlot's progress, or the ridotto al' fresco: a grotesque pantomime entertainment. Pant DL 31 March 1733.

A letter from Theophilus Cibber, comedian, to John Highmore esq. [1733].

Romeo and Juliet, revis'd and altered from Shakespeare. T New Hay 11 Sept 1744. [1744].

A lick at a liar, or calumny detected: being an occasional letter to a friend. [1752].

The lives and characters of the most eminent actors and actresses. Pt 1 (all pbd), 1753, Dublin 1753.

The lives of the poets of Great Britain and Ireland, to the time of Dean Swift. 5 vols 1753. Mainly compiled by Robert Shiels.

An epistle from Mr Theophilus Cibber to David Garrick esq. 1755, [1756?], 1759 (adds Dissertations).

Cibber's two dissertations on theatrical subjects. 3 pts [1756] (with Epistle to Garrick appended), 1759 (with Epistle).

The auction. F Unacted? 1757. Scenes from Fielding's Historical register.

ROBERT DODSLEY
1703–64
Collections

Trifles. 2 vols 1745–77.

§ 1

Servitude. [1729] (anon), [1731] (as The footman's friendly advice). Introd by Defoe? Verse.

An epistle from a footman to Stephen Duck. 1731. Anon. Verse.

A sketch of the miseries of poverty. 1731. Anon. Verse.

The muse in livery: or the footman's miscellany. 1732, 1732. Verse.

An entertainment for her Majesty's birthday. 1732. Anon. Verse.

An entertainment for the wedding of Governour Lowther. 1732. Anon. Verse.

The modern reasoners: an epistle to a friend. 1734. Anon. Verse.

An epistle to Mr Pope, occasion'd by his Essay on man. 1734. Verse.

Beauty: or the art of charming. 1735. Anon. Verse.

The toy-shop: a dramatick satire. CG 3 Feb 1735. 1735 (6 edns), 1737 (adds Epistles and poems on several occasions), [1739?], 1745, 1754, 1763, 1767.

The King and the miller of Mansfield: a dramatick tale. DL 29 Jan 1737. 1737, Dublin 1737, London 1745, [1751], Belfast 1764.

Sir John Cockle at Court, being the sequel of the King and the miller of Mansfield: a dramatick tale. DL 23 Feb 1738. 1738, Dublin 1738, London 1745, [1750?], Belfast 1767.

The art of preaching in imitation of Horace's Art of poetry. 1738 (anon), [1740], [1746], [1746], Glasgow 1790. Verse.

The chronicle of the Kings of England, written in the manner of the ancient Jewish historians, by Nathan Ben Saddi. 2 bks 1740–1, 1742, Dublin 1742, London 1745. Often ascribed to Chesterfield.

The blind beggar of Bethnal Green. BO DL 3 April 1741. 1741, 1745, Glasgow 1758, London 1761.

Colin's kisses: being twelve new songs. 1742. With and without music, anon. Verse.

Pain and patience: a poem. 1742.

A select collection of old plays. 12 vols 1744. Ed Dodsley.

Rex and Pontifex. Pant Unacted. 1745.

A collection of poems, by several hands. 3 vols 1748, 1748 (rev and enlarged, addns also separately as vol 4 1749), 1751, 2 vols Dublin 1751, 4 vols 1755 (vol 4 with new matter), 6 vols 1758 (vols 5–6 with new matter), 1763, 1765, 1766, 1770, 1775; ed I. Reed 6 vols 1782.

The triumph of peace M DL 21 Feb 1749. 1749.

The oeconomy of human life, translated from an Indian manuscript. 1751 (7 edns, anon), Dublin 1751, London 1758, 1761. Often ascribed to Chesterfield.

Public virtue: a poem in three books. 1753, Dublin 1754. Bk 1, Agriculture only. Verse.

Melpomene: or the regions of terror and pity. 1757. Anon. Verse.

Cleone. T CG 2 Dec 1758. 1758, 1758, 1759, Belfast 1759, London 1765, 1771, 1781, 1786.

Select fables in three books. 1761, Birmingham 1761, London, 1762, 1762, Birmingham 1764; An essay on fable, ed J. K. Welcher and R. Dircks, Los Angeles 1965 (Augustan Reprint Soc).

Fugitive pieces on various subjects. 2 vols 1761, 1762, 1765.

§ 2

Courtney, W. P. Dodsley's Collection of poetry: its contents and contributors. 1910.

Straus, R. Dodsley: poet, publisher and playwright. 1910.

GEORGE GRANVILLE, BARON LANSDOWNE
1667–1735
Collections

Three plays, viz The she-gallants, Heroick love and the Jew of Venice. 1713.

Four plays, viz Heroick love, the Jew of Venice, the She-gallants, the British enchanters. 1732.

The genuine works in verse and prose. 2 vols 1732, 3 vols 1736.

§ 1

The she-gallants. C LIF c. Dec 1695. 1696, 1700, [1720?], 1724, 1732.

Heroick love. T LIF c. Dec 1697. 1698.

The Jew of Venice. C LIF c. May 1701. 1701 (anon), 1713; ed C. Spencer, Five Restoration adaptations of Shakespeare, Urbana 1965.

The British enchanters: or no magick like love. O Hay 21 Feb 1706. 1706 (anon), 1710, Dublin 1732 ('revis'd and enlarg'd', in Poems upon several occasions), 1732.

Poems upon several occasions. 1712, 1716, 1721, 1726, Dublin 1732.

The genuine speech against repealing the occasional and schism bills. 1719.

A letter from a nobleman abroad to his friend in England. 1722.

A letter to the author of Reflexions historical and political. 1732.

§ 2

Johnson, Samuel. In his Lives of the English poets, 1779–81.

Handasyde, E. Granville the polite. Oxford 1933.

ELIZA HAYWOOD
1693?–1756
Collections

Works. 4 vols 1724.

§ 1

The fair captive. T LIF 4 March 1721. 1721. A revision of an unptd piece by Captain Hurst.
A wife to be lett. C DL 12 Aug 1723. 1724, 1724, 1729, 1735.
The tea table. 35 nos 21 Feb–22 June 1724. 1724.
Poems on several occasions. 1724.
The parrot. 4 nos 25 Sept–16 Oct 1728; Second ser 9 nos 2 Aug–4 Oct 1746, 1746 (with A compendium of the times).
Frederick, Duke of Brunswick-Lunenburgh. T LIF 4 March 1729. 1729, 1729, Dublin 1729.
The opera of operas: or Tom Thumb the great. Bsq New Hay 31 May 1733. 1733, 1733. Anon. Attributed to Mrs Haywood and William Hatchett.
The female spectator. 24 nos April 1744–March 1746. 4 vols Dublin 1747, London 1748, 1750, 1755, 1766; ed M. Priestley 1929 (selection).
For the novels, see col 553f., below.

§ 2

Whicher, G. F. The life and romances of Mrs Eliza Haywood. New York 1915.

AARON HILL
1685–1750
Collections

Works. 4 vols 1753.
Dramatic works. 2 vols 1760.

§ 1

Camillus. 1707. Verse.
The invasion: a poem to the Queen. 1708.
The celebrated speeches of Ajax and Ulysses. 1708. Tr Hill and Tate from Ovid. Verse.
A full account of the present state of the Ottoman Empire. 1709.
Elfrid: or the fair inconstant. T DL 3 Jan 1710. [1710].
The walking statue: or the devil in the wine-cellar. F DL Jan 1710. [1710] (with Elfrid, above).
Rinaldo. O Hay 24 Feb 1711. 1711. Italian and English. Tr from G. Rossi.
The dedication of the beech-tree. 1714. Verse.
The fatal vision: or the fall of Siam. T LIF 7 Feb 1716. [1716].
The northern star. 1718, 1724, 1725, 1739 (5th edn, 'revised and corrected by the author'). Verse.
Four essays. 1718. The first essay is by Hill.
The creation: a Pindaric, with a preface concerning the sublimity of the ancient Hebrew poetry and a material and obvious defect in the English. 1720. Preface ed G. G. Pahl, Los Angeles 1949 (Augustan Reprint Soc). Verse.
The fatal extravagance. T LIF 21 April 1721. 1720, Dublin 1721, London 1726, 1726 (enlarged to 5 acts), 1730 (one act). Given by Hill to Joseph Mitchell and ptd under Mitchell's name.
The judgment-day. 1721 (no copies extant?), [1721?]. Verse.
King Henry the Fifth: or the conquest of France by the English. T DL 5 Dec 1723. 1723, 1765 (3rd edn).
The plain-dealer. 23 March 1724–7 May 1725. A bi-weekly periodical by Hill and William Bond.

The progress of wit: a caveat, for the use of an eminent writer, by a Fellow of All-Souls. 1730. Verse.
Advice to the poets. 1731. Verse.
Athelwold. T DL 10 Dec 1731. 1731, 1732, Dublin 1732, London 1760. A recast of Elfrid, above.
The prompter. 12 Nov 1734–2 July 1736; ed W. A. Appleton and K. A. Burnim, New York 1966 (selection). A bi-weekly theatrical periodical.
The tragedy of Zara. DL 12 Jan 1736. 1736, 1736, Dublin 1737, London 1752. From Voltaire.
Alzira. T LIF 18 June 1736. 1736, Dublin 1736, London 1737, 1744, 1760, 1777, 1779, 1791. From Voltaire.
The tears of the Muses. 1737. Verse.
An enquiry into the merit of assassination. 1738.
The fanciad: an heroic poem. 1743. Anon.
The impartial: an address without flattery. 1744. Verse.
The art of acting. Pt 1 (all pbd), 1746. Verse.
Free thoughts on faith: or the religion of reason. 1746. Verse.
Merope. T DL 15 April 1749. 1749, Dublin 1749, London 1750 (corrected, with additional scene). From Voltaire.
Gideon, or the patriot: an epic poem. 1749.
A collection of letters between Mr Aaron Hill, Mr Pope and others. 1751.
The Roman revenge. T Bath c. 1753. 1753, 1754, 1759, 1760. From Voltaire.
The insolvent: or filial piety. T New Hay 6 March 1758. 1758, Dublin 1760.

GEORGE LILLO
1693–1739
Collections

Works. 1740.
Works. 2 vols 1775, 1810.
The London merchant and Fatal curiosity. Ed A. W. Ward 1906.

§ 1

Sylvia: or the country burial. O LIF 10 Nov 1730. Dublin 1730 (anon, unauthorized), London 1731 (authorized), 1731.
The London merchant: or the history of George Barnwell. T DL 22 June 1731. 1731 (3 edns), 1732, 1735 (6th edn), 1740, 1743, [1753?], 1763, Edinburgh 1768 etc: ed J. H. Wilson, Boston 1963; ed W. H. McBurney, Lincoln Nebraska 1965; ed M. R. Booth, Oxford 1965 (WC).
The Christian hero. T DL 13 Jan 1735. 1735, 1735.
Fatal curiosity. T New Hay 27 May 1736. 1737, 1762, 1768, 1780 etc; ed W. H. McBurney, Lincoln Nebraska 1966.
Marina. TC CG 1 Aug 1738. 1738.
Elmerick: or justice triumphant. T DL 23 Feb 1740. 1740.
Britannia and Batavia. M Unacted. 1740.
Arden of Feversham. T DL 12 July 1759. 1762, Dublin 1763 etc. Completed by John Hoadly.

LEWIS THEOBALD
1688–1744

The Persian Princess: or the royal villain. T DL 31 May 1708. 1715 (anon), 1717.
The perfidious brother. T LIF 21 Feb 1716. 1715, 1715.
Pan and Syrinx. O LIF 14 Jan 1718. 1718.
Decius and Paulina. M LIF March 1718. 1718 (in The entertainments for the Lady's triumph), 1718 (appended to Lady's triumph, by Settle), 1719 (expanded).
The tragedy of King Richard the II. LIF 10 Dec 1719. 1720.

Harlequin a sorcerer; with the loves of Pluto and Proserpine. Pant LIF 21 Jan 1725. 1725. Anon.

Vocal parts of an entertainment called Apollo and Daphne: or the burgomaster trick'd. Pant LIF 15 Jan 1726. 1726 (anon), 1729, 1731, 1734.

The rape of Proserpine. Pant LIF 13 Feb 1727. 1727 (anon, 4 edns), 1731.

Double falshood; or the distrest lovers, written originally by W. Shakespeare, and now revised. T DL 13 Dec 1727. 1728, 1728, 1767; ed W. Graham, Cleveland 1920.

Perseus and Andromeda. Pant LIF 2 Jan 1730. 1730 (anon), 1730 (rev, 3 edns), 1731.

Orestes. O LIF 3 April 1731. 1731.

The vocal parts of an entertainment call'd Merlin: or the devil of Stone-Henge. Pant DL 12 Dec 1734. 1734.

The fatal secret. T CG 4 April 1733. 1735.

Orpheus and Eurydice. Pant CG 12 Feb 1740. 1739. Anon.

The happy captive, with an interlude, in two comick scenes. New Hay 16 April 1741. 1741. Interlude, tr from Italian? rptd separately 1745 (with addns) as The temple of dullness.

VI. LATER EIGHTEENTH-CENTURY DRAMA

DAVID GARRICK
1717–79
Bibliographies

Knapp, M. E. A checklist of verse by Garrick. Charlottesville 1955.

Collections

Dramatic works. 3 vols 1768, 2 vols 1774. 16 plays, 9 original and 7 adapted.

Dramatic works, to which is prefixed a life of the author. 3 vols 1798.

§ I

The lying valet. F GF 30 Nov 1741. Dublin 1741, London 1742, 1743.

Mr Garrick's answer to Mr Macklin's case. 1743.

An essay on acting, in which will be considered the mimical behaviour of a certain fashionable faulty actor. 1744.

Lethe: or Aesop in the shades. F DL 15 April 1745. 1745 (pirated), 1749 (as Lethe a dramatic satire), Dublin 1749, London 1755, 1757 ('with additional character of Lord Chalkstone'), 1767, Glasgow 1767.

Miss in her teens; or the medley of lovers. F CG 17 Jan 1747. 1747 (anon), Dublin 1747, 1747, London 1748, 1749, 1759, 1771, Belfast 1775, London 1777.

Romeo and Juliet, by Shakespear, with alterations and an additional scene. T DL 29 Nov 1748. 1750, 1778, [1780].

The diary of Garrick: being a record of his trip to Paris in 1751. Ed R. C. Alexander, New York 1928.

Every man in his humour, by Ben Jonson, with alterations and additions. C DL 29 Nov 1751. 1752, 1754, 1755, 1759, Dublin 1759, Edinburgh 1768 (in Theatre vol 2), London 1769, Edinburgh 1774, London 1777.

An ode on the death of Mr Pelham. 1754, Dublin 1754.

The chances, by Beaumont and Fletcher, with alterations. C DL 7 Nov 1754. 1773, 1774, 1777 (in New English Theatre 11).

The fairies, taken from A midsummer night's dream, written by Shakespeare; the songs from Shakespear, Milton, Dryden, Waller, Lansdown, Hammond. O DL 3 Feb 1755. 1755, 1755.

Catherine and Petruchio, alter'd from Shakespear's Taming of the shrew. C DL 21 Jan 1756. 1756, 1786.

King Lear, alter'd from Shakespeare. T DL 28 Oct 1756. 1786 (Bell's Shakespeare).

Florizel and Perdita: a dramatic pastoral, alter'd from the Winter's tale of Shakespeare. DL 21 Jan 1756. 1758, 1762; Larpent ms.

The tempest, taken from Shakespear; the songs from Shakespear, Dryden etc. O DL 11 Feb 1756. 1756; Larpent ms.

Lilliput: a dramatic entertainment. Int DL 3 Dec 1756. 1757.

The male coquette: or seventeen fifty seven. F DL 24 March 1757 as The modern fine gentleman. 1757, Dublin 1758; Larpent ms.

Isabella, or the fatal marriage: a play alter'd from Southern. T DL 2 Dec 1757. 1757, 1758, Dublin 1769, Edinburgh 1773, London 1776 (in New English theatre vol 12).

The gamesters, alter'd from Shirley. C DL 22 Dec 1757. 1758; Larpent ms.

Antony and Cleopatra: an historical play, written by Shakespear, fitted for the stage by abridging only. DL 3 Jan 1759. 1758. Abridged by Garrick and Edward Capell.

The guardian. C DL 3 Feb 1759. 1759, 1759, 1771, 1773, 1779; Larpent ms.

High life below stairs. F DL 31 Oct 1759. 1759 (4 edns), 1775, 1787, 1795; Larpent ms.

Harlequin's invasion: a Christmas gambol, after the manner of the Italian comedy. Int DL 31 Dec 1759. Larpent ms.

Reasons why David Garrick esq should not appear on the stage, in a letter to John Rich esq. 1759. Generally ascribed to Garrick himself.

The enchanter; or love and magic: a musical drama. Int DL 13 Dec 1760. 1760; Larpent ms.

The fribbleriad. 1761. Verse.

Cymbeline, by Shakespear, with alterations. T DL 28 Nov 1761. 1762, 1767, 1770, 1784, 1795.

The farmer's return from London. Int DL 30 March 1762. 1762 (3 edns); Larpent ms.

A midsummer night's dream, written by Shakespear, with alterations and additions. C DL 23 Nov 1763. 1763; Larpent ms.

The clandestine marriage. *See under Colman, col 491, below.*

The sick monkey: a fable. 1765.

Neck or nothing. F DL 18 Nov 1766. 1766, 1767, 1774.

The country girl, alter'd from Wycherley. C DL 25 Oct 1766. 1766, 1790, 1791; Larpent ms.

Cymon: a dramatic romance. DL 2 Jan 1767. 1767, 1767, 1768, 1770, Dublin 1771, London 1778; 1792 ('with additional airs' for revival 31 Dec 1791), 1815, 1816 (songs only), Larpent ms.

Linco's travels. Int DL 6 March 1767. Larpent ms.

A peep behind the curtain: or the new rehearsal. Bsq DL 23 Oct 1767. 1767 (3 edns), 1770, 1772, 1778, 1786, Larpent ms (as The new rehearsal).

The elopement. Pant DL 26 Dec 1767. Not ptd.

An ode upon dedicating a building and erecting a statue to Shakespeare at Stratford upon Avon. 1769.

Shakespeare's garland being a collection of the new songs, ballads, roundelays, catches, glees, comic-serenatas etc performed at the Jubilee at Stratford-upon-Avon. 1769. 7 songs by Garrick.

The Jubilee. Int DL 14 Oct 1769. 1769, 1770, 1776, 1778 (songs only), Waterford 1773 (pirated, as The jubilee in honour of Shakespeare as performed at Waterford with additions).

King Arthur: or the British worthy, by Mr Dryden. M DL 13 Dec 1770. 1770, 1770, 1781, 1784 (abridged as Arthur and Emmeline), 1786.

The institution of the Garter: or Arthur's round table restored. M DL 28 Oct 1771. 1771 (songs and 'serious dialogue' only), Larpent ms (as The Order of the Garter). Based on Gilbert West, The institution of the Garter: a dramatic poem, 1742.

The Irish widow. F DL 23 Oct 1772. 1772, 1772, 1773, 1774, 1781, 1787.

Hamlet, as altered from Shakespear. T DL 18 Dec 1772. Not ptd. Garrick's copy now in Folger Lib, Washington. See G. W. Stone, PMLA 49 1934. An earlier acting version by Garrick was ptd 1763, 1755 (for 1765), 1767, 1768, 1770.

Albumazar, as it is now revived with alterations. C DL 19 Oct 1773. 1773, 1773, Dublin 1773, Larpent ms.

A Christmas tale: a dramatic entertainment. DL 27 Dec 1773. [1773] (songs only), 1774 (in 5 pts, 3 edns), Dublin 1774, London 1776 (in 3 acts), Larpent ms.

Bon ton: or high life above stairs. F DL 18 March 1775. 1775, 1776, 1781, 1784, Dublin 1785; Larpent ms.

The theatrical candidates: a musical prelude. DL Sept 1775. 1775 (appended on May day).

May Day, or the little gipsy: a musical farce. DL 28 Oct 1775. 1775, 1775 (songs only), 1776 (songs only), 1777 (songs only); Larpent ms.

The alchymist as altered from Ben Jonson. C DL 1766? 1777.

Journal describing his visit to France and Italy in 1763. Ed G. W. Stone, New York 1939.

Letters

Private correspondence. [Ed J. Boaden] 2 vols 1831–2, 1835. 242 letters by Garrick.

Letters of Garrick and Georgiana, Countess Spencer 1759–79. Ed Earl Spencer and C. Dobson, Cambridge 1960.

Letters. Ed D. M. Little and G. R. Kahrl 3 vols Cambridge Mass 1963.

§2

Davies, Thomas. Memoirs of the life of David Garrick esq. 2 vols 1780, 1780, 1781, 1784; rev S. Jones 2 vols 1808.

Murphy, Arthur. Life of David Garrick esq. 2 vols 1801, Dublin 1801.

Reynolds, Sir Joshua. Johnson and Garrick. 1816; ed R. B. Johnson 1927.

Stone, G. W. The god of his idolatry: Garrick's theory of acting and dramatic composition with especial reference to Shakespeare. In J. Q. Adams memorial studies, Washington 1948.

—— Garrick's significance in the history of Shakespearean criticism. PMLA 65 1950.

—— Bloody, cold and complex Richard: Garrick's interpretation. In Eight essays in English literature, Pullman 1968.

Oman, C. Garrick. 1958.

Stochholm, J. M. Garrick's folly: the Shakespeare Jubilee of 1769 at Stratford and Drury Lane. 1964.

SAMUEL FOOTE

1720–77

Collections

Dramatic works. Ed M. M. Belden, New Haven 1929.

§1

Genuine memoirs of Sir John Dinely Goodere, Bart who was murdered by his own brother near Bristol Jan 19 1740, by S. Foote of Worcester College, Oxford, nephew of the late Sir John D. Goodere. 1740, Worcester 1782. Foote's authorship has been doubted.

A treatise on the passions, so far as they regard the stage, with a critical enquiry into the theatrical merit of Mr G—k, Mr Q—n, and Mr B—y. [1747]. Anon.

The Roman and English comedy consider'd and compar'd, with remarks on The suspicious husband, and an examen into the merit of the present comic actors. 1747.

Taste. C DL 11 Jan 1752. 1752, 1753, Dublin 1762, London 1765, [1772], 1778, 1781; Larpent ms (dated 1761).

The Englishman in Paris. C CG 24 March 1753. 1753, Dublin 1753, London 1763, 1765, 1778, 1783.

The knights. C DL 9 Feb 1754. 1754, Dublin 1754, Glasgow 1758, London [1778], 1787; Larpent ms. Based on Two knights from the Land's End, acted New Hay 1749 but not ptd.

The Englishman returned from Paris: being the sequel to the Englishman in Paris. F CG 3 Feb 1756. 1756, Dublin 1756, London [1780], 1780, 1788.

The author. C DL 5 Feb 1757. 1757, Dublin 1757, London 1760, [c. 1760], 1778, 1782, 1794; Larpent ms.

The diversions of the morning: an entertainment. DL 17 Oct 1758. Act 2 ptd by Tate Wilkinson, The wandering patentee vol 4, 1795; W. Cooke, Memoirs of Foote vol 3, 1805; and Works of Foote, ed J. Badcock vol 1, 1830. Act 1 altered from Taste, above.

The minor. C Crow Street, Dublin 28 Jan 1760, and with alterations New Hay 28 June 1760. 1760 (4 edns), Dublin 1760, Belfast 1760, London 1761, 1762, 1764, 1767, 1778, 1781, 1792; Larpent ms.

A letter from Mr Foote to the reverend author [Martin Madan] of the Remarks critical and Christian on the Minor. 1760.

The orators. C New Hay 30 Aug 1762. 1762, Dublin 1762, London 1767, 1777, 1780, 1788.

The comic theatre: being a free translation of all the best French comedies, by Samuel Foote esq and others. 5 vols 1762. 'The first only, The young hypocrite, is to be attributed to him', Life of Foote, in Works, [1797].

The mayor of Garratt. C New Hay 20 June 1763. 1763 (no copy extant?), 1764, Dublin 1764, London 1769, Dublin 1774, London 1776, 1780, 1783, 1797; Larpent ms.

The tryall of Samuel Foote esq for a libel on Peter Paragraph. F New Hay 18 May 1763. Pbd in Tate Wilkinson, The wandering patentee vol 4, 1795; and W. Cooke, Memoirs of Foote vol 6, 1805.

The lyar. C CG 12 Jan 1762. 1764, 1764, Dublin 1764, London 1769, 1776, 1780, 1786, Dublin 1793; Larpent ms.

The patron. C New Hay 26 June 1764. 1764, 1764, Dublin 1764, London 1774, 1780, 1781.

The commissary. C New Hay 10 June 1765. 1765, 1765, Dublin 1765, London 1773, 1779, 1782.

An occasional prologue in prose. New Hay 29 May 1767. Monthly Mirror 1804; in W. Cooke, Memoirs of Foote vol 3, 1805. Extracts in London Mag July 1767.

The taylors: a tragedy for warm weather. Bsq New Hay 2 July 1767. 1778 (anon); ed R. Ryan 1836. Foote disclaimed authorship, not necessarily with truth. Rev Colman, who was responsible for pbn.

The Devil upon two sticks. C New Hay 30 May 1768. 1778, 1778, Dublin 1788, London 1794; Larpent ms.

Wilkes: an oratorio, as performed at the great room in Bishopsgate-Street, written by Mr Foote; the music by Signor Carlos Francesco Baritini. [1769]. Political burlesque of doubtful authorship.

The lame lover. C New Hay 22 June 1770. 1770, Dublin 1770, London 1794; Larpent ms.

An apology for the Minor in a letter to Mr Baine. Edinburgh 1771, 1771.

The maid of Bath. C New Hay 26 June 1771. 1771 (unauthorized, copy noted by E. Green, Bibliotheca

Somersetensis vol 1, Taunton 1902), 1778 (authorized), 1778, Dublin 1778, London [c. 1780]; Larpent ms.

The nabob. C New Hay 26 June 1772. 1778, 1795; Larpent ms.

Piety in pattens. C New Hay 15 Feb 1773. Larpent ms (as The handsome housemaid); synopsis in S. Jones, Biographia dramatica vol 3, 1812.

The bankrupt. C New Hay 21 July 1773. 1776, 1776, 1782; Larpent ms.

The cozeners. C New Hay 15 July 1774. 1778, 1778, Dublin 1778, London 1795; Larpent ms.

A trip to Calais. C Unacted. 1778, 1788, 1795. Prohibited by the Lord Chamberlain on a protest from the Duchess of Kingston.

The capuchin. C New Hay 19 Aug 1776. Larpent ms. Altered from A trip to Calais, above, with which it is pbd.

§ 2

Memoirs of the life and writings of Samuel Foote esq, the English Aristophanes; to which are added the bon mots, repartees and good things said by that great wit and excentrical genius. [1777].

Cooke, William. Memoirs of Samuel Foote. 3 vols 1805, 2 vols 1806.

Belden, M. M. The dramatic work of Foote. New Haven 1929.

GEORGE COLMAN the elder
1732–94
Collections

Dramatic works. 4 vols 1777.

§ 1

The connoisseur. 140 nos 31 Jan 1754–30 Sept 1756. 4 vols 1757, 1793. Conducted and largely written by Colman and Bonnell Thornton.

Poems by eminent ladies. 2 vols 1755, Dublin 1757, London 1773, 1780. Ed Colman and Thornton.

A letter of abuse to D—d G—k esq. 1757. Anon.

Two odes: 1, To obscurity; 2, To oblivion. 1760. With Robert Lloyd.

Polly Honeycombe: a dramatick novel. F DL 5 Dec 1760. 1760, 1761, Dublin 1761, London 1762 ('with alterations'), 1778; Larpent ms.

The jealous wife. C DL 12 Feb 1761. 1761, 1761, Dublin 1761, Oxford 1763, [1764], London 1775, Dublin 1775, London 1789, 1789.

The genius. 15 essays contributed to St James's Chron 11 June 1761–9 Jan 1762.

Critical reflections on the old English dramatick writers. 1761.

The musical lady. F DL 6 March 1762. 1762, Dublin 1762, London 1778; Larpent ms.

Terrae filius. 4 nos Oxford 5–8 July 1763.

Philaster, written by Beaumont and Fletcher with alterations. T DL 8 Oct 1763. 1763, Dublin 1763, London 1764, 1764, 1780.

The deuce is in him. F DL 4 Nov 1763. 1763, 1764, Dublin 1764, London 1769, 1776; Larpent ms.

A fairy tale, taken from Shakespeare. Int DL 26 Nov 1763. 1763, 1777 (altered); Larpent ms. From A midsummer night's dream via Garrick, The fairies, 1755.

The comedies of Terence translated into familiar blank verse. 1765, 1766 ('revised and corrected', with an appendix), 1802, 1810.

The clandestine marriage. C DL 20 Feb 1766. 1766 (3 edns), Dublin 1766, Edinburgh 1766, London 1770, 1778, Dublin 1788, London 1789 . With Garrick. See the younger Colman, Posthumous papers relating to the proportionate shares of authorship to be attributed to the elder Colman and Garrick, 1820.

The English merchant. C DL 21 Feb 1767. 1767, 1767.

The Oronian in town. C CG 7 Nov 1767. 1770 (for 1769), Dublin 1679; Larpent ms.

The history of King Lear. T CG 20 Feb 1768. 1768.

A true state of the differences [between the proprietors of Covent Garden Theatre]. 1768, 1768.

An epistle to Dr Kenrick. 1768.

T. Harris dissected. 1768.

Man and wife: or the Shakespeare Jubilee. C CG 9 Oct 1769. 1770 (3 edns), Dublin 1770; Larpent ms.

The portrait: a burletta. CG 22 Nov 1770. 1770, 1770, 1772; Larpent ms as The portrait: or a painter's easel.

The fairy prince from Ben Jonson. M CG 12 Feb 1771. 1771; Larpent ms. From Jonson, Masque of Oberon, with songs by Shakespeare, Dryden and Gilbert West.

Comus, altered from Milton. M CG 16 Oct 1773. 1772, 1774, 1780.

Achilles in petticoats, written by Mr Gay with alterations. BO CG 16 Dec 1773. 1774.

The man of business. C CG 29 Jan 1774. 1774 (4 edns), Dublin 1774, London 1775; Larpent ms.

The gentleman. 6 essays in London Packet 10 July–4 Dec 1775.

An occasional prelude. CG 21 Sept 1772. 1776; Larpent ms.

The spleen: or Islington Spa. F DL 24 Feb 1776. 1776; Larpent ms.

Epicoene: or the silent woman, written by Ben Jonson with alterations. C DL 13 Jan 1776. 1776.

New brooms! an occasional prelude. DL 21 Sept 1776. 1776; Larpent ms. With Garrick.

Polly: being a sequel to the Beggar's opera written by Mr Gay with alterations. BO New Hay 19 June 1777. 1777.

The sheep shearing: a dramatic pastoral taken from Shakespeare's A winter's tale. New Hay 18 July 1777. 1777.

The Spanish barber: or the fruitless precaution. C New Hay 30 Aug 1777. Larpent ms. From Beaumarchais.

The works of Beaumont and Fletcher. 10 vols 1778. Preface by Colman.

The suicide. C New Hay 11 July 1778. Larpent ms.

Bonduca, written by Beaumont and Fletcher, with alterations. T New Hay 30 July 1778. 1778 (3 edns), 1801, 1808.

The separate maintenance. C New Hay 31 Aug 1779. Larpent ms.

The manager in distress: a prelude. New Hay 30 May 1780. [1780?], 1820; Larpent ms.

The genius of nonsense: an extravaganza. New Hay 2 Sept 1780. 1781 (songs only); Larpent ms.

Preludio to the Beggar's opera. New Hay 8 Aug 1781. Larpent ms.

Harlequin Teague: or the giant's causeway. Pant New Hay 17 Aug 1782. 1782 (songs only); Larpent ms. With John O'Keeffe.

Fatal curiosity: a true tragedy, written by George Lillo, with alterations. New Hay 29 Aug 1782. 1783.

Q. Horatii Flacci epistola de arte poetica. 1783. English version and commentary, together with Latin text.

The election of the managers: a prelude. New Hay 2 June 1784. Larpent ms.

Tit for tat: or the mutual deception. C New Hay 29 Aug 1786. 1788, 1788; Larpent ms. From Joseph Atkinson, The mutual deception, 1785, an adaptation of Marivaux, Le jeu de l'amour et du hasard.

Poems on several occasions, accompanied by some pieces in verse. 3 vols 1787.

Ut pictura poesis! or the enraged musicians: a musical entertainment founded on Hogarth. New Hay 18 May 1789. 1789.

Some particulars of the life of George Colman, written by himself. 1795. Chiefly concerning affairs of 1767.

§ 2

Peake, R. B. Memoirs of the Colman family, including their correspondence with the most distinguished personages of their time. 2 vols 1841.

Page, E. R. George Colman the elder. New York 1935.

RICHARD CUMBERLAND
1732–1811

§ 1

The banishment of Cicero. T Unacted. 1761, Dublin 1741 (for 1761).

The summer's tale. CO CG 6 Dec 1765. 1765, Dublin 1766, London 1771; Larpent ms.

A letter to the Bishop of O—d, containing some animadversions upon a character of the late Dr Bentley. 1767, 1767.

Amelia. CO CG 12 April 1768. 1768, 1771 ('with alterations'). An abbreviation of Summer's tale, above.

The brothers. C CG 2 Dec 1769. 1770, Dublin 1770, London 1775, 1777, 1778, Perth 1792; Larpent ms.

The West Indian. C DL 19 Jan 1771. 1771 (several edns), Dublin 1771, London 1773, 1774, Dublin 1774, London 1775, Dublin 1775, Perth 1790, London 1792, Boston 1794; Larpent ms.

Timon of Athens: a tragedy altered from Shakespear. DL 4 Dec 1771. 1771, Dublin 1773; Larpent ms.

The fashionable lover. C DL 20 Jan 1772. 1772 (3 edns), Dublin 1772, London 1774, 1781, Perth 1790; Larpent ms.

The note of hand; or trip to Newmarket. F DL 9 Feb 1774. 1774, Dublin 1774; Larpent ms.

The choleric man. C DL 19 Dec 1774. 1775 (3 edns), Dublin 1775; Larpent ms.

Odes. 1776, Dublin 1776.

Miscellaneous poems: consisting of elegies, odes, pastorals; together with Calypso: a masque. 1778.

The battle of Hastings. T. DL 24 Jan 1778. 1778, Dublin 1778.

Calypso. M CG 20 March 1779. 1779, 1784, 1785; Larpent ms. Adapted from versions in Miscellaneous poems, 1778.

The widow of Delphi: or the descent of the deities. CO CG 1 Feb 1780. 1780 (songs only); Larpent ms.

The Walloons. C CG 20 April 1782. In Posthumous works vol 1, 1813; Larpent ms.

Anecdotes of eminent painters in Spain during the sixteenth and seventeenth centuries. 2 vols 1782.

A letter to Richard, Lord Bishop of Llandaff. 1783.

The mysterious husband. T CG 28 Jan 1783. 1783, Dublin 1783, London 1785; Larpent ms.

The Carmelite. T DL 2 Dec 1784. 1784, 1785, 1785, Dublin 1785; Larpent ms.

The natural son. C DL 22 Dec 1784. 1785, 1785, Dublin 1785; Larpent ms.

The Arab. T CG 8 March 1785. In Posthumous works vol 2, 1813 as Alcanor; Larpent ms.

The observer. 40 nos 1785, 5 vols 1788, 6 vols 1798 (with trn of Clouds), 1802–3; ed A. Chalmers, British essayists vols 38–40, 1817, 1823, 1856.

The character of the late Viscount Sackville. 1785.

An accurate catalogue of the paintings in the King of Spain's palace at Madrid. 1787.

Arundel: a novel. 1789, 1795.

The impostors. C DL 26 Jan 1789. 1789 (3 edns), Dublin 1789, 1790; Larpent ms.

The school for widows. C CG 8 May 1789; Larpent ms. Not pbd. Previously acted as The country attorney, New Hay 7 July 1787.

Curtius rescued from the gulph: or the retort courteous to the Rev Dr Parr. 1792.

Calvary or the death of Christ: a poem. 1792, 2 vols 1800, 1803, 1808, 1811.

The clouds of Aristophanes. [1793], 1798 (with Observer, above).

The armourer. CO CG 4 April 1793. 1793 (songs only); Larpent ms.

The box-lobby challenge. C New Hay 22 Feb 1794. [1794] (7 edns), Dublin 1794; Larpent ms.

The Jew. C DL 8 May 1794. 1794, 1794 (pirated), Dublin 1794, London 1795 (3 edns), Dublin 1796, London 1797, 1797, 1801; Larpent ms .

The wheel of fortune. C DL 28 Feb 1795. 1795 (4 edns), Dublin 1795, London 1796, Dublin 1801, London 1805; Larpent ms.

First love. C DL 12 May 1795. 1795, 1795, Dublin 1795, London 1796, 1799; Larpent ms.

The defendant. C DL 20 Oct 1795. Not pbd; Larpent ms.

Henry: a novel. 1795, 1798, 1821 (with preface by Sir Walter Scott).

The days of yore: a drama. CG 13 Jan 1796. 1796; Larpent ms.

Don Pedro: a play. New Hay 23 July 1796. In Posthumous works vol 2, 1813; Larpent ms.

The last of the family. C DL 8 May 1797. In Posthumous works vol 2, 1813; Larpent ms.

The village fete. Int CG 18 May 1797. Larpent ms. Not pbd and not certainly by Cumberland.

False impressions. C CG 23 Nov 1797. 1797, Dublin 1798.

The eccentric lover. C CG 30 April 1798. In Posthumous works vol 2, 1813; Larpent ms.

A word for nature. C DL 5 Dec 1798. In Posthumous works vol 1, 1813 as The passive husband; Larpent ms.

Joanna of Montfaucon: a dramatic romance. CG 16 Jan 1800. 1800, 1800, [1800] (songs only). Adapted from Maria Geisweiler's trn of Kotzebue.

A few plain reasons why we should believe in Christ. 1801, 1826 (as The Anti Carlile).

A poetical version of certain psalms of David. 1801.

Lover's resolutions. C DL 2 March 1802. In Posthumous works vol 1, 1813; Larpent ms.

The sailor's daughter. C DL 7 April 1804. 1804 (3 edns); Larpent ms.

The victory and death of Lord Viscount Nelson: a spectacle. DL 11 Nov 1805. 1805; Larpent ms. Cumberland wrote a similar piece for CG, which was interdicted.

A hint to husbands. C CG 8 March 1806. 1806 (4 edns); Larpent ms. In verse.

Memoirs of Richard Cumberland written by himself. 2 pts 1806–7, 1 vol New York 1806, 2 vols 1807; ed H. Flanders, Philadelphia 1856.

The exodiad: a poem, by the authors of Calvary and Richard the First [i.e. Sir James Bland Burgess]. 1807, 1808.

The Jew of Mogodore. CO DL 3 May 1808. 1808; Larpent ms.

The London review. 2 vols 1809. Conducted by Cumberland.

John de Lancaster: a novel. 3 vols 1809.

The widow's only son. C CG 7 June 1810. Not pbd; Larpent ms.

Retrospection: a poem in familiar verse. 1811.

The sybil, or the elder Brutus: a drama. DL 3 Dec 1818. In Posthumous works vol 1, 1813.

Posthumous dramatick works. 2 vols 1813.

§ 2

Mudford, William. The life of Richard Cumberland, embracing a critical examination of his various writings. 1812.

Williams, S. T. Cumberland: his life and dramatic works. New Haven 1917. With bibliography.

RICHARD BRINSLEY SHERIDAN
1751–1816
Collections

Speeches of the late Right Honourable Richard Brinsley Sheridan, several corrected by himself. Ed a constitutional friend 5 vols 1816, 3 vols 1842.

The works of the late Right Honourable Richard Brinsley Sheridan. 2 vols 1821, 1 vol Leipzig 1833; ed R. G. White 2 vols New York 1883. The first authorized collection, with preface by Thomas Moore.

Plays and poems. Ed R. C. Rhodes 3 vols Oxford 1928.

Dramatic works. Ed C. Price 2 vols Oxford 1973; Plays, ed Price, Oxford 1975 (OSA).

§ I

The ridotto of Bath: a panegyric written by a gentleman, resident in that city, published originally in the Bath Chronicle October 10th 1771. Bath 1771; rptd in Rival beauties, Bath 1773; and in Clio's protest, 1819.

The rival beauties: a poetical contest. London and Bath 1772. Contains The Bath picture [by Miles Peter Andrews?] and Clio's protest: or the picture varnished addressed to the Lady M[a]rg[a]r[e]t F[o]rd[y]ce [by Sheridan].

The rival beauties: a poetical contest; to which is added the Ridotto of Bath. Bath 1773.

Clio's protest: or the picture varnished, with other poems, [including Ridotto of Bath]. 1819.

The love epistle of Aristaenetus, translated from the Greek into English metre. 1771, 1773 ('corrected'); rptd in Erotica, 1854 (Bohn's Classics), 1883. With Nathaniel Brassey Halhed.

A familiar epistle to the author of the Heroic epistle to Sir William Chambers, and of the heroic postscript to the public. 1774, 1774; rptd in Plays and poems, ed R. C. Rhodes vol 3, Oxford 1928.

The rivals. C CG 17 Jan 1775. 1775, 1775, Dublin 1775, 1775, London 1776 ('corrected'), [1785], Dublin 1788, London 1791, Dublin 1793 (from 1st edn), 1793 (corrected), London 1798, Dublin 1802; Larpent ms. The Larpent version, ed R. L. Purdy, Oxford 1935, is that used for the first performance; the ptd texts all derive from the rev version, first produced CG 28 Jan 1775; ed A. S. Downer, New York 1953; ed A. N. Jeffares 1967.

St Patrick's day: or the scheming Lieutenant. F CG 2 May 1775. Dublin 1788, 1789; Larpent ms.

The duenna. CO CG 21 Nov 1775. The songs, duets, trios etc in The duenna: or the double elopement, 1775 (at least 6 edns), 1776 (at least 6 edns), Tamworth [1776?], London 1777 (at least one edn), Dublin 1777, London 1778 (25th edn), 1780 (27th edn), 1783 (29th edn), 1801.

The governess. Dublin 1777 (anon), London 1783 (as The duenna), [Dublin?] 1784, London 1785, Dublin 1785, 1786, 1786, 1788 (as The governess). This spurious text may have been the 'imitation' concocted by Tate Wilkinson (Wandering patentee vol 1; Memoirs vol 2) and acted at York as The duenna 9 April 1776.

The duenna: a comic opera, in three acts. 1794, Dublin 1794, [1795], New York 1808 ('second edition, from the original prompt book').

A trip to Scarborough, altered from Vanbrugh's Relapse: or virtue in danger. C DL 24 Feb 1777. 1781, Dublin 1781; Larpent ms.

The school for scandal. C DL 8 May 1777. Dublin 1780, 1781 (3 edns), 1782, 1782, Philadelphia 1782 (as The real and genuine school for scandal; see G. H. Nettleton, TLS 28 March 1935), London 1783 (as The real and genuine school for scandal), Dublin 1783, 1785, 1786, 1786, New York 1786, Dublin 1787, 1788, [Dublin?] 1788, Guernsey 1788, Paris 1789, Philadelphia 1789,

Guernsey 1789, Dublin 1792, Boston 1792, Dublin 1793, London 1798, [1799?] ('for J. Ewing'), Dublin 1799 ('taken from a correct copy'), 1800, Paris 1804, New York 1807, Dublin 1818; ed R. C. Rhodes, Oxford 1930; ed J. H. Wilson, Boston 1963; ed J. Loftis, New York 1966; ed A. N. Jeffares 1967; ed C. Price, Oxford 1971.

The camp: a musical entertainment. DL 15 Oct 1778; 1795; Larpent ms. Sheridan's authorship was denied by Moore, who ascribed it to Richard Tickell.

Verses to the memory of Garrick spoken as a monody. 1779, 1779, Dublin 1780 (as The tears of genius: a monody on the death of Mr Garrick).

The critic: or a tragedy rehearsed. Bsq 30 Oct 1779, 1781, Dublin 1781, 1785, 1790, 1806, New York, 1807, London 1808, 1811; Larpent ms.

Robinson Crusoe: or Harlequin Friday. Pant DL 29 Jan 1781. A short account of the situations and incidents, 1781; overture, comic-tunes and song, [1781].

The legislative independence of Ireland vindicated in a speech of Mr Sheridan's on the Irish propositions in the British House of Commons. Dublin 1785.

The genuine speech of Mr Sheridan delivered in the House of Commons on a charge etc against Warren Hastings esquire, late Governour-General of Bengal. [1787].

The speech of R. B. Sheridan in bringing forward the fourth charge [in the House of Commons] relative to the Begums of Oude. 1787, 1787 ('second edition enlarged').

The celebrated speech of Richard Brinsley Sheridan in Westminster Hall on his summing of the evidence on the Begum charge against Warren Hastings. 1788.

Speech before the High Court of Parliament in summing up the evidence on the Begum charge against Warren Hastings. 1788.

A short memoir of the life of the Right Honourable Richard Brinsley Sheridan; to which is added a report of his celebrated speech delivered in Westminster Hall. 1816.

Speeches in the trial of Warren Hastings. Ed A. E. Bond 4 vols 1859–61. From Gurney's original shorthand notes.

A comparative statement of the two bills for the better government of India brought into Parliament by Mr Fox and Mr Pitt, with explanatory observations. 1788 (4 edns).

Cape St Vincent: or British valour triumphant, altered from a dramatical performance performed in 1794 [i.e. The glorious First of June]. DL March 1797. Songs, duets, chorusses etc, 1797.

Speech in the House of Commons on the 21st of April 1798 on the motion to address his Majesty on the present alarming state of affairs. [London?] 1798.

Speech of R. B. Sheridan in the House of Commons, in reply to Mr Pitt's speech on the union with Ireland. Dublin 1799.

Pizarro: a tragedy taken from the German drama of Kotzebue adapted to the English stage. DL 24 May 1799. 1799 (at least 20 edns), Dublin 1799, 1799, Cork 1799, Philadelphia 1799, London 1800 (at least 4 edns), 1804 (27th edn), Paris 1804, London 1807, 1811, 1814.

Speech in the House of Commons in reply (December 8 1802) on the motion for the army establishment for the ensuing year. 1802, 1803.

The speech in the House of Commons, December 8th 1802, on the army estimates. Birmingham [1802].

The forty thieves: a grand romantic drama, in two acts, by R. B. Sheridan and Colman the younger. DL 8 April 1806. New York 1808, Philadelphia 1808, Boston 1810 (fuller text), Dublin 1814 (as Ali Baba: or the forty thieves). Sheridan wrote the scenario; the dialogue was by Charles Ward, rev younger Colman.

Death of Mr Fox: an elogium delivered by Mr Sheridan

at the Crown and Anchor Tavern on Thursday, September 13th 1806. Nottingham 1806.
Letters. Ed C. Price 3 vols Oxford 1966.

§ 2

Moore, Thomas. Memoirs of the life of the Right Honourable Richard Brinsley Sheridan. 2 vols 1825 (also large paper, 1 vol), 1827 (5th edn, with new preface).

Sichel, W. Sheridan, from new and original material. 2 vols 1909.
Sadleir, T. H. The political career of Sheridan. Oxford 1912.
Rhodes, R. C. Harlequin Sheridan: the man and the legends. Oxford 1933.
Loftis, J. Sheridan and the drama of Georgian England. Oxford 1976.

VII. MINOR DRAMA 1750–1800

ISAAC BICKERSTAFFE
d. 1812?

Leucothoe: a dramatic poem. 1756.
Thomas and Sally, or the sailor's return: a musical entertainment. CG 28 Nov 1760. 1761, 1765 (3rd edn), Dublin 1767, Belfast 1767, London 1780 ('with alterations').
Love in a village. CO CG 8 Dec 1762. 1763 (7 edns), Dublin 1763, London 1764 (10th edn), 1765, 1767, 1776, [1780], 1787, Dublin 1791.
The maid of the mill. CO CG 31 Jan 1765. 1765 (6 edns), Dublin 1765, London 1783, Dublin 1791.
Daphne and Amintor. CO DL 8 Oct 1765. 1765 (5 edns), 1766, 1788. Altered from The oracle of St Foix and Mrs Cibber.
The plain dealer, with alterations from Wycherley. C DL 7 Dec 1765. 1766, 1767; Larpent ms.
Love in the city. CO CG 21 Feb 1767. 1767, 1767, Dublin 1767.
Lionel and Clarissa. CO CG 25 Feb 1768. 1748 (for 1768), 1768 (3rd edn), Dublin 1769, London 1770, Dublin 1770, 1774; Larpent ms.
The absent man. F DL 21 March 1768. 1768, Dublin 1768; Larpent ms.
The padlock. CO DL 3 Oct 1768. 1768 (3 edns), 1769, Dublin 1770 ('with alterations'); Larpent ms.
The royal garland: a new occasional interlude in honour of his Danish Majesty. CG 10 Oct 1768. 1768, Larpent ms (as An occasional interlude: or the King of Denmark when in England).
The hypocrite taken from Molière and Cibber. C DL 17 Nov 1768. 1769, 1769, Dublin 1769. Based on Colley Cibber, The nonjuror.
Dr Last in his chariot. C New Hay 21 June 1769. 1769, Dublin 1769.
The captive. CO New Hay 21 June 1769. 1769.
The Ephesian matron, or the widow's tears: a comic serenata after the manner of the Italian. New Hay 31 Aug 1769. 1769, 1786.
The school for fathers. CO DL 8 Feb 1770. 1770, 1773. Altered from Lionel and Clarissa, above.
Tis well it's no worse. C DL 24 Nov 1770. 1770; Larpent ms.
The recruiting serjeant: a musical entertainment. DL 1770. 1770, 1787.
He wou'd if he cou'd, or an old fool worse than any: a burletta. DL 12 April 1771. 1771.
The sultan: or a peep into the seraglio. F DL 12 Dec 1775. 1787, 1787; Larpent ms.

JOHN BROWN
1715–66

Honour: a poem. 1743.

An essay on satire occasion'd by the death of Mr Pope. 1745, 1749.
On liberty: a poem. 1749.
Essays on the Characteristics [of Shaftesbury]. 1751, 1751, 1752, Dublin 1752, 1752, London 1755 (4th edn), 1764.
Barbarossa. T DL 17 Dec 1754. 1755, 1755, Dublin 1755, 1757, London [1760?] (4th edn), 1770, 1770, 1777; Larpent ms.
Athelstan. T DL 27 Feb 1756. 1756, 1756; Larpent ms.
An estimate of the manners and principles of the times. 1757 (6 edns), 1758 (7th edn), Boston 1758; vol 2, 1758.
An explanatory defence of the Estimate. 1758.
An additional dialogue of the dead between Pericles and Aristides: being a sequel to [Lyttelton's] Dialogue between Pericles and Cosmo. 1760, 1760.
The cure of Saul: a sacred ode. 1763, 1767.
A dissertation on the rise, union and power, the progressions, separations and corruptions, of poetry and music; to which is prefixed the Cure of Saul. 1763, Dublin 1763.
The history of the rise and progress of poetry, through its several species. Newcastle 1764. A recast of the Dissertation 'for the sake of such classical readers as are not particularly conversant with music'.
Sermons on various subjects. 1764.
Thoughts on civil liberty, on licentiousness and faction. Newcastle 1765, London 1765.
A letter to the rev Dr Lowth, occasioned by his late letter to the author [Warburton] of the Divine legation of Moses. Newcastle 1766 (4 edns).
Brown also pbd a number of sermons.

GEORGE COLMAN the younger
1762–1836

Collections

Dramatic works, with an original life of the author by J. W. Lake. 4 vols Paris 1827.

§ 1

Two to one. CO New Hay 19 June 1784. Dublin 1785; Larpent ms (dated 1783).
A Turk and no Turk. CO New Hay 9 July 1785. 1785 (songs only); Larpent ms.
Inkle and Yarico. CO New Hay 4 Aug 1787. [1787], 1788, Dublin 1788, London 1789, Dublin 1789, London 1792, 1806, New York 1806, Dublin 1807; Larpent ms.
Ways and means: or a trip to Dover. C New Hay 16 July 1788. 1788, 1788, Dublin 1788, London 1805, 1806.
The battle of Hexham. C New Hay 11 Aug 1789. 1790 (pirated text), Dublin 1790, London 1808 (authorized text); Larpent ms.
The surrender of Calais: a play. New Hay 30 July 1791.

Dublin 1792 (pirated), London 1808 (authorized); Larpent ms.

Poor old Haymarket, or two sides of the gutter: a prelude. New Hay 15 June 1792. 1792; Larpent ms.

The mountaineers: a play. New Hay 3 Aug 1793. 1794 (pirated), Dublin 1794, London 1795 (authorized, 3 edns), 1802, 1805, Dublin 1806, 1808; Larpent ms.

New Hay at the old market: an occasional drama. New Hay 9 June 1795. 1795, 1808 (altered, as Sulvester Daggerwood); Larpent ms.

The iron chest: a play. DL 12 March 1796. 1796 ('with a preface', attacking J. P. Kemble), 1796 ('with a preface and a postscript'), 1796 (without preface or postscript), Dublin 1796, London 1798, 1808; Larpent ms; ed M. A. Booth, Oxford 1965 (WC) (in Eighteenth-century tragedy). *See col 616, below.*

My night-gown and slippers or talks in verse. 1797; Larpent ms. Recited DL 28 April 1797.

The heir at law. C New Hay 15 July 1797. Dublin 1800 (pirated), 1806, London 1808 (authorized); Larpent ms.

Blue Beard: or female curiosity! a dramatick romance. DL 16 Jan 1798. 1798 (4 edns), Dublin 1798, London 1799, [1800], New York 1803, 1806, London 1808, 1811; Larpent ms.

Blue devils. F CG 24 April 1798. 1808, 1811; Larpent ms.

Feudal times, or the banquet-gallery: a drama. DL 19 Jan 1799. [1799], Dublin [1799], London 1808; Larpent ms.

The review: or the wags of Windsor. CO New Hay 2 Sept 1800. Dublin 1801 ('by Arthur Griffinhoof'), New York 1804, London 1808; Larpent ms.

The poor gentleman. C CG 11 Feb 1801, 1802, 1804, 1806, Dublin 1806; Larpent ms.

Broad grins: comprising with additional tales those published under the title of My nightgown and slippers. 1802, 1804, 1807, 1811 (5th edn), 1819 (7th edn), 1839.

Broad grins, my night-gown and slippers and other humorous works, with life and anecdotes of the author. Ed G. B. Buckstone [1872].

John Bull: or the Englishman's fireside. C CG 5 March 1803. Dublin 1803 (pirated), London 1805 (authorized); Larpent ms.

Love laughs at locksmiths: an operatic farce. New Hay 25 July 1803. 1803 ('by Arthur Griffinhoofe'; pirated), Dublin 1803, London 1808 (authorized); Larpent ms.

The gay deceivers, or more laugh than love: an operatic farce. New Hay 22 Aug 1804. 1808 ('by Arthur Griffinhoof'); Larpent ms.

Who wants a guinea? C CG 18 April 1805. 1805, 1805; Larpent ms.

We fly by night or long stories: an opera farce. CG 25 Jan 1806. 1806 ('by Arthur Griffinhoofe'); Larpent ms.

The forty thieves. *See under Sheridan, col 496, above.*

The Africans, or love, war and duty: a musical drama. New Hay 29 July 1808. 1808; Larpent ms.

XYZ. F CG 11 Dec 1810. 1810; Larpent ms.

The quadrupeds of Quedlinburgh: or the rovers of Weimar. Bsq New Hay 26 July 1811. Larpent ms.

Poetical vagaries. 1812, 1814 (with Vagaries vindicated), 1818.

Vagaries vindicated: or hypocritick hypercriticks. 1813, 1814 (with Poetical vagaries).

Doctor Hocus Pocus, or Harlequin wash'd white: a prelude. New Hay 12 Aug 1814. Larpent ms.

Eccentricities for Edinburgh. Edinburgh [1816].

The actor of all work: or first and second floor. F New Hay 13 Aug 1817. Larpent ms.

Posthumous papers relative to the proportionate shares of authorship [of the Clandestine marriage] to be attributed to the elder Colman and Garrick. 1820.

Posthumous letters addressed to Francis Colman and George Colman the elder, with annotations by George Colman the younger. 1820.

The law of Java: a musical drama. CG 11 May 1822. 1822; Larpent ms.

Stella and Leatherlungs: or a star and a stroller. Int DL 1 Oct 1873. Larpent ms.

Random records. 2 vols 1830. An autobiography to c. 1790.

§ 2

Peake, R. B. Memoirs of the Colman family. 2 vols 1841.

Bagster-Collins, J. F. Colman the younger. New York 1946.

JOSEPH CRADOCK
1742–1826
Collections

Literary and miscellaneous memoirs. Ed J. B. Nichols 4 vols 1828.

§ I

Letters from Snowdon, descriptive of a tour through the northern counties of Wales. 1770 (anon), Dublin 1770, London 1777 (enlarged).

Zobeide. T CG 11 Dec 1771. 1771, 1772, Dublin 1772.

The life of John Wilkes esq in the manner of Plutarch. 1773. Anon.

Village memoirs, in a series of letters between a clergyman and his family in the country. 1774 (anon), Dublin 1775.

An account of some of the most romantic parts of North Wales. 1777.

Four dissertations: moral and religious. 1815.

Fidelia. 1821.

The Czar: an historical tragedy. Unacted. 1824.

Literary and miscellaneous memoirs. 2 vols 1826.

CHARLES DIBDIN
1745–1814
§ I

For a complete list of plays etc, see E. R. Dibdin, A Dibdin bibliography, Liverpool 1937 (priv ptd).

The shepherd's artifice: a dramatic pastoral. CG 21 May 1764. 1765; Larpent ms.

The deserter: a new musical drama. DL 2 Nov 1773. 1773, 1773, Dublin 1775, London 1776, Dublin 1789; Larpent ms.

The waterman: or the First of August. BO New Hay 8 Aug 1774. 1774 (anon), 1776, 1777, 1783, Dublin 1785; Larpent ms.

The cobler: or a wife of ten thousand. BO DL 9 Dec 1774. 1774, Dublin 1775, 1776.

The Quaker. CO DL 7 Oct 1777. 1777 (anon), 1778, 1780, Belfast 1782, London 1784 (5th edn), 1787.

Poor Vulcan. Bsq CG 4 Feb 1778. 1778, 1778, Belfast 1784, [Dublin 1789] (as by O'Keefe); Larpent ms.

The Chelsea pensioner. CO CG 6 May 1779. 1779 (anon), 1779 (anon), Dublin 1779; Larpent ms.

The harvest-home. CO New Hay 16 May 1787. 1787, Dublin 1788; Larpent ms.

The musical tour. Sheffield 1788.

The bystander: or universal weekly expositor. 22 nos 15 Aug 1789–6 Feb 1790.

Hannah Hewit: or the female Crusoe. 3 vols (1792]. Anon.

The younger brother: a novel. 3 vols 1793.

How do you do? 8 nos 30 July–5 Nov 1796. With F. G. Waldron.

A complete history of the English stage. 5 vols [1800].

Observations on a tour through Scotland and England. 2 vols [1801–2].

The professional life of Mr Dibdin, written by himself; together with the words of six hundred songs. 4 vols 1803, 6 vols 1809 (800 songs).

§ 2

Kitchener, W. A brief memoir of Dibdin, with some letters and documents supplied by his grand-daughter. [1884].

THOMAS HOLCROFT
1745–1809

§ 1

Elegies: 1, On the death of Samuel Foote; 2, On age. 1777.
A plain and succinct narrative of the late riots and disturbances with an account of the commitment of Lord George Gordon to the Tower and anecdotes of the life by William Vincent [i.e. Holcroft]. 1780. The anecdotes by John Perry.
Alwyn: or the gentleman comedian. 2 vols 1780. With assistance from William Nicholson.
Duplicity. C CG 13 Oct 1781. 1781, 1781, 1782, Dublin 1782; Larpent ms.
The trial of the Hon George Gordon at the Court of King's Bench, taken in shorthand by William Vincent. 1781.
Human happiness, or the sceptic: a poem. 1783.
The family picture: or domestic dialogues on amiable subjects. 2 vols 1783.
The noble peasant. CO New Hay 2 Aug 1784. 1784, Dublin 1784; Larpent ms.
The follies of a day: or the marriage of Figaro, from the French of M. de Beaumarchais. C CG 14 Dec 1784. 1785, 1785; Larpent ms (as The marriage of Figaro).
The choleric fathers. CO CG 10 Nov 1785. 1785, Dublin 1786; Larpent ms.
Letter on Egypt by Mr Savary. 2 vols 1786, Dublin 1787.
An amorous tale of the chaste loves of Peter the Long and his most honoured friend Dame Blanche Bazu, imitated from the original French. 1786.
Seduction. C DL 12 March 1787. 1787 (3 edns), Dublin 1787; Larpent ms.
The secret history of the Court of Berlin. 2 vols 1789. Anon.
Posthumous works of Frederick King of Prussia. 13 vols 1789.
The school for arrogance. C CG 4 Feb 1791. 1791. 1791, Dublin 1791 New York 1807; Larpent ms.
The road to ruin. C CG 18 Feb 1792. 1792 (11 edns), Dublin 1792, New York 1792, 1806; Larpent ms.
Anna St Ives: a novel. 7 vols 1792.
The adventures of Hugh Trevor: a novel. 6 vols 1794, 4 vols 1801 (3rd edn). Largely autobiographical.
Love's frailties. C CG 5 Feb 1794. 1794, New York 1794; Larpent ms (as Love's frailties: or precept against practice).
The rival queens', or Drury Lane and Covent Garden: a prelude. CG 15 Sept 1794. Larpent ms.
The deserted daughter. C CG 2 May 1795. 1795 (4 edns), 1806, New York 1806; Larpent ms.
A narrative of facts relating to a prosecution for high treason, including the defence the author had prepared. 2 pts 1795.
A letter to the Right Honourable William Windham on the intemperance and danger of his public conduct. 1795.
The man of ten thousand. C DL 23 Jan 1796. 1796 (3 edns); Larpent ms.
The force of ridicule. C DL 6 Dec 1796. Larpent ms.
Travels through Germany, Switzerland and Italy, translated from the German of Frederick Leopold Count Stolberg. 2 vols 1796–7, 1797.
Knave or not? C DL 25 Jan 1798. 1798, Dublin 1798; Larpent ms.
He's much to blame. C CG 13 Feb 1798. 1798 (4 edns).
The inquisitor: a play. New Hay 23 June 1798. 1798 (4 edns); Larpent ms.

The old clothesman. Int CG 3 April 1799. Larpent ms.
Deaf and dumb, or the orphan protected: an historical drama, taken from the French of M Bouilly. DL 24 Feb 1801. 1801 (5 edns), 1802; Larpent ms.
A tale of mystery: a melodrama. CG 13 Nov 1802. 1802, 1802, New York 1803, 1808, London 1813 (4 edns); Larpent ms.
Hear both sides. C DL 12 Feb 1803. 1803 (4 edns), Philadelphia 1803; Larpent ms.
Travels from Hamburg through Westphalia, Holland and the Netherlands. 2 vols 1804, 1 vol Glasgow 1804 (abridged).
Memoirs of Bryan Perdue: a novel. 3 vols 1805.
The lady of the rock: a melo-drama. DL 12 Feb 1805. 1805, 1805, New York 1807; Larpent ms.
The theatrical recorder, edited by Thomas Holcroft. 2 vols 1805–6. Originally issued in 12 pts 1805; suppl 1806.
The vindictive man. C DL 20 Nov 1806. 1806, 1807; Larpent ms.
Memoirs of the late Thomas Holcroft, written by himself and continued [by William Hazlitt] to the time of his death from his diary, notes and other papers. 3 vols 1816, 1 vol 1852, 2 vols 1857; ed A. R. Waller and A. Glover, Hazlitt's Works vol 2, 1902; ed E. Colby 2 vols 1925, 1 vol Oxford 1926 (WC); ed P. P. Howe, Hazlitt's Works vol 3, 1932.

§ 2

Baine, R. M. Holcroft and the revolutionary novel. Athens Georgia 1965.

JOHN HOME
1722–1808

Collections

Dramatick works. 1760.
Dramatic works. 2 vols Edinburgh 1798. Complete.
Works now first collected, to which is prefixed an account of his life by Henry Mackenzie. 3 vols Edinburgh 1822.

§ 1

Douglas. T Edinburgh Dec 1756, CG 14 March 1757. 1757, Edinburgh 1757 (fuller text), Belfast 1758, Dublin 1761, London 1764; ed H. J. Tunney, Lawrence Kansas 1924.
Agis, by the author of Douglas. T DL 21 Feb 1758. 1758, Dublin 1758; Larpent ms.
The siege of Aquileia. T DL 21 Feb 1760. 1760. Edinburgh 1760, Dublin 1760; Larpent ms.
The fatal discovery. T DL 23 Feb 1769. 1769, Dublin 1769, London 1772.
Alonzo. T DL 27 Feb 1773. 1773, 1773, Dublin 1773; Larpent ms.
Alfred. T CG 21 Jan 1778. 1778, 1778; Larpent ms.
The history of the Rebellion in 1745. 1802.

ELIZABETH INCHBALD,
née SIMPSON
1753–1821

Bibliographies

Joughin, G. L. An Inchbald bibliography. SE 14 1934.

§ 1

A mogul tale: or the descent of the balloon. F New Hay 6 July 1784. Dublin 1788, London 1796; Larpent ms.
I'll tell you what. C New Hay 4 Aug 1785. 1786, 1786, 1787, Dublin 1787; Larpent ms.

Appearance is against them. F CG 22 Oct 1785. 1785, Dublin 1786; Larpent ms.

The widow's vow. F New Hay 20 June 1786. 1786, Dublin 1786, New York 1787.

Such things are: a play. CG 10 Feb 1787. 1788, 1788, Dublin 1788, 1790, London 1800 (12th edn), 1805; Larpent ms.

The midnight hour: or war of wits, translated from the French. F CG 22 May 1787. 1787, Dublin 1787, London 1788, Dublin 1788, Boston 1795; Larpent ms.

All on a summer's day. C CG 15 Dec 1787. Larpent ms.

Animal magnetism. F CG 29 April 1788. Dublin [1788?], 1789, 1792, New York 1808.

The child of nature: a dramatic piece from the French of the Marchioness of Sillery, formerly Countess of Genlis. CG 28 Nov 1788. 1788, 1789, Dublin 1789, Philadelphia 1790, London 1794, 1800 (6th edn).

The married man, from Le philosophe marié of Mr Nericault Destouches. C New Hay 15 July 1789. 1789, Dublin 1789; Larpent ms.

The hue and cry. F DL 11 May 1791. Larpent ms.

Next door neighbours, from the French dramas L'indigent [by L. S. Mercier] and Le dissipateur [by Destouches]. 1791, Dublin 1791; Larpent ms.

A simple story. 4 vols 1791, 2 vols Dublin 1791, 4 vols 1793 (3rd edn), 1799, 1 vol 1801, 2 vols Dublin 1804, 1 vol 1823, 1831 etc; ed W. B. Scott 1880; ed G. L. Strachey 1908; ed J. M. S. Tompkins, Oxford 1967.

Every one has his fault. C CG 29 Jan 1793. 1793 (5 edns), Dublin 1793, London 1794, 1794, Philadelphia 1794, Dublin 1795, London 1805; Larpent ms.

The wedding day. C DL 1 Nov 1794. 1794, Dublin 1795, London 1806; Larpent ms.

Nature and art. 2 vols 1796, Philadelphia 1796, London 1797, 1 vol 1810, 1821, 1823, 1824; ed W. B. Scott 1886. A novel.

Wives as they were and maids as they are. C CG 4 March 1797. 1797 (6 edns), Dublin 1799, Cork 1797, London 1806; Larpent ms (as The primitive wife and modern maid).

Lovers' vows: a play, from the German of Kotzebue. CG 11 Oct 1798. 1798 (11 edns), Dublin 1798, London 1799, 1799, Boston 1799, Cork 1799, London 1804, 1805, Dublin 1806; Larpent ms.

The wise men of the East: a play, from the German of Kotzebue. CG 30 Nov 1799. 1799 (4 edns), Dublin 1800; Larpent ms.

To marry or not to marry. C CG 16 Feb 1805. 1805, 1805, Baltimore 1805; Larpent ms.

The British theatre: or a collection of plays with biographical and critical remarks. 25 vols 1808, 20 vols 1824.

A collection of farces and other afterpieces. 7 vols 1809, 1815.

The modern theatre. 10 vols 1809.

§ 2

Boaden, James. Memoirs of Mrs Inchbald, including her familiar correspondence; to which are added the Massacre and A case of conscience now first published. 2 vols 1833.

Littlewood, S. R. Elizabeth Inchbald and her circle. 1921.

McKee, W. Elizabeth Inchbald, novelist. Baltimore 1935.

JOHN PHILIP KEMBLE
1757–1823

§ 1

Belisarius or injured innocence. T Liverpool and Hull 1778. Larpent ms.

The female officer. F Manchester 1778. Larpent ms (rev as The projects, DL 18 Feb 1786, also in Larpent ms).

Oh! it's impossible. C York 1780. Larpent ms.

Fugitive pieces. York 1780, nd (facs). Verse.

The maid of honour. C DL 27 Jan 1785. Larpent ms. Adapted from Massinger.

The pilgrim, with additions. C DL 26 Oct 1787. 1788. Vanbrugh's adaptation of Fletcher.

Shakespear's King Lear, as altered by N. Tate, newly revised. T DL 21 Jan 1788. 1788, 1800, 1808, 1815.

The pannel: an entertainment, altered from the comedy of 'Tis well it's no worse. F DL 28 Nov 1788. 1789, [1789]. From Bickerstaffe.

The farm house. F DL 1 May 1789. 1789, 1789, Dublin 1789. From Charles Johnson, The country lasses.

King Henry V: or the conquest of France. T DL 1 Oct 1789. 1789, 1801, 1806, 1815.

The tempest: or the enchanted island with additions from Dryden. C DL 13 Oct 1789. 1789, 1806 (with further alterations).

Love in many masks, as altered from Mrs Behn's Rover. C DL 8 March 1790. [1790]; Larpent ms.

Lodoiska. O DL 9 June 1794. [1794], [1794], 1801.

A select British theatre: being a collection of the most popular stock-pieces. 8 vols 1816.

Macbeth and Richard the Third: an essay, in answer to Remarks on some of the characters of Shakespeare [by T. Whateley]. 1817. The Macbeth essay was pbd separately 1786.

§ 2

Boaden, J. Memoirs of the life of John Philip Kemble esq. 2 vols 1825.

Fitzgerald, P. The Kembles. 2 vols [1871].

WILLIAM KENRICK
1725?–79

The town: a satire. 1748.

The kapélion: or poetical ordinary, consisting of great variety of dishes, in prose and verse; by Archimagirus Metaphoricus. 6 nos Aug 1750–Jan 1751. Ed Kenrick.

The grand question debated: or an essay to prove that the soul of man is not, neither can it be, immortal; by Ontologos. Dublin 1751. Answered by Kenrick himself in A reply to the grand question debated, 1751.

A monody to the memory of his Royal Highness Frederick Prince of Wales. 1751, 1751.

The so much talk'd of and expected Old woman's Dunciad, by Mary Midnight. 1751 (3 edns).

Fun: a parodi-tragi-comical satire. Unacted. 1752. Anon.

The pasquinade, with notes variorum: book the first [all pbd]. 1753. Anon.

The whole duty of woman, by a lady. 1753 (3 edns).

Epistles to Lorenzo. 1756 (anon), 1759 (rev as Epistles philosophical and moral), 1773 (4th edn, as Epistles to Lorenzo). Defended by Kenrick in A scrutiny: or the criticks criticis'd, 1759.

A review of Doctor Johnson's new edition of Shakespeare, in which the ignorance, or inattention, of that editor is exposed. 1765. Defended (by Kenrick himself?) against James Barclay, Examination in a defence of Mr Kenrick's review, by a friend, 1766 (signed R.R.).

Falstaff's wedding: being a sequel to the second part of the play of King Henry the Fourth, written in imitation of Shakespeare. C DL 12 April 1766. 1760 (for 1766), 1766, 1766, Dublin 1766, London 1773, 1781; Larpent ms.

The widow'd wife. C DL 5 Dec 1767. 1767, 1768, Dublin 1768; Larpent ms.

An epistle to G. Colman. 1768, 1768.

An epistle to James Boswell esq occasioned by his having transmitted the moral writings of Dr Samuel Johnson to Pascal Paoli, by W.K. esq. 1768.

Poems ludicrous, satirical and moral. 1768, 1770 ('with additions').

Love in the suds, a town eclogue: being the lamentations of Roscius for the loss of his Nyky. 1772 (5 edns, some with additional matter, both as above and as A letter to David Garrick esq from William Kenrick LlD).
A letter to David Garrick esq, occasioned by his having moved the Court of King's Bench against the publisher of Love in the suds. 1772.
A whipping for the Welch parson: being a comment upon the Rev Mr Evan Lloyd's epistle to David Garrick esq. 1773. Anon.
The duellist. C CG 20 Nov 1773. 1773 (3 edns), Dublin 1774; Larpent ms.
Introduction to the school of Shakespeare. [1774].
The London review of English and foreign literature. 10 vols 1775–9. Ed and largely written by Kenrick.
The lady of the manor. CO CG 23 Nov 1778. 1778 (3 edns), Dublin 1779; Larpent ms.
The spendthrift: or a Christmas gambol. F 21 Dec 1778. Larpent ms.
Also pamphlets on divorce, mechanics and Christian evidences, an English dictionary, an account of Robert Lloyd prefixed to Lloyd's Poetical works, *1774, and trns of Gesner, Rousseau, Voltaire, Buffon and Millot.*

CHARLOTTE LENNOX
1730–1804

§ 1

Poems on several occasions, written by a young lady. 1747.
The life of Harriot Stuart, written by herself. 2 vols 1751. Anon. A novel.
The female Quixote: or the adventures of Arabella. 2 vols 1752 (anon), 1752 ('corrected'), Dublin 1752, 1 vol [1752?] (abridged as Entertaining history of the female Don Quixote, 2 vols Dublin 1763, London 1783, [1799]; ed M. Dalziel, Oxford 1970.
Shakespear illustrated: or the novels and histories, on which the plays of Shakespear are founded, collected and translated. 3 vols 1753–4.
Henrietta. 2 vols 1758, Dublin 1758, London 1761 ('corrected'), 1787.
Philander: a dramatic pastoral. Unacted. 1757, Dublin 1758.
The lady's museum. 11 nos 1 March 1760–1 Jan 1761. 2 vols 1760–1. Ed and mainly written by Mrs Lennox.
Sophia. 2 vols 1762. A novel.
The history of the Marquis of Lussan and Isabella. Dublin 1764.
The sister. C CG 18 Feb 1769. 1769, 1769; Larpent ms. Dramatized from Henrietta, above.
Old city manners, altered from the original Eastward Hoe. C DL 9 Nov 1775. 1775; Larpent ms.
Euphemia. 4 vols 1790. A novel.

§ 2

Small, M. R. Charlotte Ramsay Lennox: an eighteenth-century lady of letters. New Haven 1935.
Maynadier, G. H. The first American novelist? Cambridge Mass 1940.

CHARLES MACKLIN
1699?–1797

Collections

The man of the world; Love à la mode. 1793. Subscription edn, organized by Arthur Murphy.
Plays. Dublin 1793.

§ 1

The case of Charles Macklin, comedian. 1743.
Mr Macklin's reply to Mr Garrick's answer. 1743.
Henry the Seventh: or the Popish impostor. T DL 18 Jan 1746. 1746.
A will and no will: or a bone for the lawyers. C DL 23 April 1746. Larpent ms; ed J. B. Kern, Los Angeles 1967 (Augustan Reprint Soc).
The new play criticiz'd: or the plague of envy. F DL 24 March 1747. Larpent ms; ed J. B. Kern, Los Angeles 1967 (Augustan Reprint Soc).
Covent Garden theatre: or Pasquin turn'd Drawcansir, censor of Great Britain. Bsq CG 8 April 1752. Larpent ms; ed J. B. Kern, Los Angeles 1965 (facs) (Augustan Reprint Soc).
Epistle from Tully in the shades to Orator M—n in Covent Garden. 1755.
Love à la mode. F DL 12 Dec 1759. [Dublin?] 1784 (pirated), Dublin 1785, 1785, London 1786, 1793 (authorized), Dublin 1793.
The true born Irishman: or the Irish fine lady. C Crow Street Dublin 14 May 1762. Dublin 1793; Larpent ms (for CG performance 28 Nov 1767 as The Irish fine lady).
An apology for the conduct of Mr Charles Macklin, comedian. 1773.
The genuine arguments of the Council why an information should not be exhibited against Thomas Leigh [et al] for a conspiracy to deprive Charles Macklin of his livelihood. 1774.
Riot and conspiracy: the trial of Thomas Leigh and others for conspiring to ruin in his profession Charles Macklin. [1775].
The man of the world. C CG 10 May 1781. Dublin 1785 (pirated), London 1786, Dublin 1791, London 1793 (authorized), Dublin 1793; Larpent ms; ed D. MacMillan, Los Angeles 1951 (Augustan Reprint Soc).

ARTHUR MURPHY
1727–1805

Collections

Works. 7 vols 1786.
The way to keep him and five other plays by Murphy. Ed J. P. Emery, New York 1956.
New essays. Ed A. Sherbo, East Lansing 1963.

§ 1

The Gray's Inn Journal, by Charles Ranger. 2 vols 1756, Dublin 1756. 104 nos originally issued weekly in 52 nos 29 Sept 1753–21 Sept 1754.
The apprentice. F DL 2 Jan 1756. 1756, 1756, Dublin 1756, London 1764, Belfast 1773.
The Englishman from Paris. F DL 3 April 1756. Ed S. Trefman, Los Angeles 1969 (Augustan Reprint Soc).
The upholsterer: or what news? F DL 30 March 1758. 1758, 1760, 1763, 1765, 1769 ('with alterations and additions'), Newry 1786, London 1793; Larpent ms.
The orphan of China. T DL 21 April 1759. 1759, 1759, Dublin 1759, 1761, London 1772, Dublin 1787; Larpent ms. Based on the play by Voltaire, who pbd A letter to the author of the Orphan of China, 1759.
The desert island: a dramatic poem in three acts. DL 24 Jan 1760. 1760, Dublin 1760, London 1762, 1786.
A letter to M. de Voltaire on the Desert island. 1760.
A poetical epistle to Samuel Johnson. 1760.
The way to keep him. C DL 24 Jan 1760. 1760, 1760, Dublin 1760, London 1761 (4th edn, enlarged from 3 to 5 acts, as performed DL 10 Jan 1761, and with song by Garrick), Dublin 1765, London 1765, 1770, 1770, 1785; Larpent ms; ed J. P. Emery, New York 1956.
All in the wrong. C DL 15 June 1761. 1761, Dublin 1762,

Cork 1765, Dublin 1765, London 1775, 1787, Cork 1795; Larpent ms.

The old maid. F DL 2 July 1761; 1761, 1761, [1761], Dublin 1762, Belfast 1769.

The citizen. F DL 2 July 1761. 1763, Dublin 1763, London 1766, 1770, Dublin 1774, London 1784.

An ode to the Naiads of Fleet Ditch. 1761. A reply to Churchill's Rosciad.

The examiner. 1761. A reply to Murphiad: a mock heroic poem by Philim Maculloch, 1761.

A letter from a Right Honourable Person [the elder Pitt] and the answer to it [by William Beckford] translated into verse. 1761. Anon. Also attributed to Philip Francis.

A letter from the anonymous author of the Letters versified to the anonymous writer of the Monitor. 1761. Anon. Also attributed to Philip Francis.

An essay on the life and genius of Henry Fielding. In Works of Fielding vol 1, 1762.

The auditor. 43 nos 15 July 1762–16 May 1763.

No one's enemy but his own. C CG 9 Jan 1764. 1764, Dublin 1764; Larpent ms.

What we must all come to. F CG 9 Jan 1764. 1764 ('as it was intended to be acted'), [1776] (as Three weeks after marriage: or what we must all come to, as revived CG 30 March 1776), 1776, [1778]; Larpent ms.

The choice. C DL 23 March 1765. In Works vol 1, 1786, Larpent ms.

The school for guardians. C CG 10 Jan 1767. 1767; Larpent ms.

Zenobia. T DL 27 Feb 1768. 1768 (4 edns), Dublin 1784; Larpent ms.

The Grecian daughter. T DL 26 Feb 1772. 1772, 1772, Dublin 1774, London 1776, 1777, 1787, 1792, 1796; Larpent ms.

Alzuma. T CG 23 Feb 1773. 1773 (3 edns), 1774; Larpent ms.

News from Parnassus: a prelude. CG 23 Sept 1776. In Works vol 4, 1786; Larpent ms.

Know your own mind. C CG 22 Feb 1777. 1778, 1787, [1800]; Larpent ms.

Seventeen hundred and ninety-one: a poem in imitation of the thirteenth satire of Juvenal. 1791.

An essay on the life and genius of Samuel Johnson. 1792.

The works of Tacitus with notes, supplements etc. 4 vols 1793, 8 vols 1811, 2 vols 1813.

The rival sisters, adapted for theatrical representation. T King's Haymarket 18 March 1793. 1793, 1793, Dublin 1793; Larpent ms; first pbd in Works vol 7, 1786.

The history of Catiline's conspiracy; with the four orations of Cicero, by George Frederick Sydney. 1795.

Arminius. T Unacted. 1798, [1800] (as Arminius: or the champion of liberty).

The bees: a poem from the fourteenth book of Vaniere's Praedium rusticum. 1799.

The life of David Garrick. 2 vols 1801, Dublin 1801.

The works of Sallust translated. 1807.

Hamlet with alterations: a tragedy in three acts. Bsq Unacted. In J. Foot, Life of Murphy, 1811. Satirizing Garrick; dated 15 Dec 1772.

The game of chess: a poem translated from the Latin [of Vida]. Amsterdam 1876.

§ 2

Emery, J. P. Murphy: an eminent English dramatist of the eighteenth century. Philadelphia 1946.

Dunbar, H. H. The dramatic career of Murphy. New York 1946.

JOHN O'KEEFFE
1747–1833
Collections

Dramatic works. 4 vols 1798.

§ 1

The she gallant: or square toes outwitted. F Smock Alley Dublin 14 Jan 1767. Dublin [1767], London 1767.

Tony Lumpkin in town. F New Hay 2 July 1778. 1780 (authorized), Dublin 1780.

The son-in-law: a musical farce. New Hay 14 Aug 1779. Dublin 1783, 1788; Larpent ms.

The dead alive: a musical farce. New Hay 16 June 1781. Dublin 1783, Belfast 1784; Larpent ms (as Edward and Caroline: or the dead alive).

The agreeable surprise. CO New Hay 3 Sept 1781. Newry 1783, Dublin 1784, 1785, 1786, 1787, 1792; Larpent ms.

The banditti: or love's labyrinth. CO CG 28 Nov 1781. 1781 (songs only); Larpent ms.

The positive man. F CG 16 March 1782. 1798 (in O'Keeffe's works vol 2), 1800; Larpent ms.

Harlequin Teague: or the giant's causeway. Pant New Hay 17 Aug 1782. 1782 (songs only); Larpent ms.

The castle of Andalusia. CO CG 2 Nov 1782. Dublin 1783 ('with additional songs by Sig Tenducci'), 1788, 1794, London 1794 (authorized); Larpent ms.

Lord Mayor's Day: or a flight from Lapland. Pant CG 25 Nov 1782. 1782 (songs only); Larpent ms.

The maid the mistress: a burletta. CG 15 Feb 1783. 1783 (songs only); Larpent ms (as The servant mistress).

The Shamrock: or St Patrick's Day. C Crowe Street Dublin 15 April 1777. Larpent ms (for CG performance 7 March 1783, as The Shamrock, or anniversary of St Patrick: a pastoral romance).

The young Quaker. C New Hay 26 July 1783. Dublin 1784, 1784, 1788; Larpent ms.

The birth-day, or the Prince of Arragon: a dramatick piece with songs. New Hay 12 Aug 1783. Dublin 1783 (authorized); Larpent ms.

The poor soldier. CO CG 4 Nov 1783. Dublin 1785 ('a new edition corrected'), 1786, 1788, London 1798 (in O'Keeffe's works vol 1); 1800; Larpent ms.

Friar Bacon: or Harlequin's adventures in Lilliput, Brobdinnag etc. Pant CG 23 Dec 1783. [1784] (music only); Larpent ms.

Peeping Tom of Coventry. CO New Hay 6 Sept 1784. Dublin 1785, 1786, 1787, 1792, Coventry 1815; Larpent ms.

Fontainebleau: or our way to France. CO CG 16 Nov 1784. Dublin 1785, 1787, 1790, London 1798 (in O'Keeffe's works 2); Larpent ms.

The blacksmith of Antwerp: a musical farce. CG 7 Feb 1785. In O'Keeffe's works vol 2, 1798; Larpent ms.

A beggar on horseback: an operatic farce. New Hay 16 June 1785. In O'Keeffe's works vol 3, 1798; Larpent ms.

Omai: or a trip around the world. Pant CG 20 Dec 1785. 1785 (songs and synopsis); Larpent ms.

Patrick in Prussia: or love in a camp. CO CG 17 Feb 1786. Dublin 1786 ('from the author's original manuscript'), 1792, London 1798 (in O'Keeffe's works vol 4 as Love in a camp), 1800; Larpent ms.

The siege of Curzola. CO New Hay 12 Aug 1786. 1786 (songs only); Larpent ms.

The man milliner: an operatic farce. CG 27 Jan 1787. In O'Keeffe's works vol 4; Larpent ms.

The farmer. CO CG 31 Oct 1787. Dublin 1788, 1789, 1792, London 1798 (in O'Keeffe's works vol 4); 1800.

Tantara Rara rogues all: an afterpiece. CG 1 March 1788. 1798 (in O'Keeffe's works vol 3); Larpent ms.

The prisoner at large. F New Hay 2 July 1788. 1788 (authorized), Dublin 1789, 1792, London 1800.

The Highland reel. CO CG 6 Nov 1788. Dublin 1789, 1790, [1791], London 1798 (in O'Keeffe's works vol 4); 1800.

Aladdin: or the wonderful lamp. Pant CG 26 Dec 1788. Larpent ms.

The toy: or the life of a day. C CG 3 Feb 1789. 1798 (in

O'Keeffe's works vol 3); Larpent ms (as The toy: or Hampton Court frolics).

The faro table. C CG 4 April 1789. Larpent ms. An alteration of Mrs Centlivre, Gamester.

The little hunch-back: or a frolic in Bagdad. F CG 14 April 1789. 1789; Larpent ms.

Le grenadier: a musical play, intended to have been performed at the Haymarket. 1789, 1798 (in O'Keeffe's works vol 1). Prohibited.

The Czar Peter. CO CG 8 March 1790. 1798 (in O'Keeffe's works vol 3); Larpent ms.

Modern antiques: or the merry mourners. F CG 14 March 1791. Dublin 1792, 1792, London 1798 (in O'Keeffe's works vol 1); 1800; Larpent ms (as The merry musicians).

Wild oats: or the strolling gentleman. C Dublin 1791. Dublin 1792, 1794, London 1794 (authorized), 1806; Larpent ms.

Sprigs of laurel. CO CG 11 May 1793. 1793 (authorized), 1804; Larpent ms (as Sprigs of laurel or royal example).

The London hermit: or rambles in Dorsetshire. C New Hay 29 June 1793. 1793 (authorized, 3 edns), Dublin 1794, London 1798, Larpent ms.

The world in a village. C CG 23 Nov 1793. 1793 (authorized), Larpent ms.

Jenny's whim: or the roasted emperor. F Unacted. Larpent ms. Advertised for New Hay 1 Sept 1794 but prohibited.

Oatlands or the transfer of the laurel: a poem. 1795.

Life's vagaries. C CG 19 March 1795. 1795 (authorized), 1795, 1810; Larpent ms.

The Irish mimic, or Blunders at Brighton: a musical piece. CG 23 April 1795. 1795 (authorized), 1797.

Merry Sherwood: or Harlequin forrester. Pant CG 21 Dec 1795. 1795 (songs only); Larpent ms (as The merry forester).

The lie of the day. C CG 9 March 1796. 1798 (in O'Keeffe's works vol 3); 1800; A revision of Toy, above.

The Wicklow gold mines: or the lad of the hills. CO CG 13 April 1796. Dublin 1814; Larpent ms.

The doldrum: or 1803. F CG 23 April 1796. 1798 (in O'Keeffe's works vol 4), Larpent ms (as The sleeper: or AD 1803).

Alfred, or the magic banner: a drama. New Hay 22 June 1796. Dublin 1796, London 1798 (in O'Keeffe's works vol 4), Larpent ms (as The magick banner: or two wives in a house).

The Wicklow Mountains. CO CG 17 Oct 1796. Dublin 1797, London 1798 (in O'Keeffe's works vol 2). A revision of Wicklow gold mines, above.

Our wooden walls, or all to St Paul's: an interlude. CG 19 Dec 1797. Larpent ms.

The eleventh of June or the Daggerwoods at Dunstable. F DL 5 June 1798. Larpent ms.

Nosegay of weeds: or new servants in old places. F DL 6 June 1798. Larpent ms.

Recollections of the life of John O'Keeffe, written by himself. 2 vols 1826.

A father's legacy to his daughter: being the poetical works of the late John O'Keeffe edited by Adelaide O'Keeffe. 1834.

4. THE NOVEL

I. GENERAL WORKS

(1) BIBLIOGRAPHIES

Esdaile, A. A list of English tales and prose romances printed before 1740. 1912 (Bibl Soc).

Block, A. The English novel 1740–1850: a catalogue including prose romances, short stories and translations of foreign fiction. 1939, 1961 (rev).

Black, F. G. The epistolary novel in the late eighteenth century: a descriptive and bibliographical study. Eugene Oregon 1940.

Summers, M. A Gothic bibliography. [1941].

Gove, P. B. The imaginary voyage in prose fiction: a history of its criticism and a guide to its study with an annotated check-list of 215 imaginary voyages from 1700 to 1800. New York 1941.

Mish, C. C. English prose fiction 1600–1700: a chronological checklist. Charlottesville 1952, 1967 (rev).

Wiles, R. M. Serial publication in England before 1750. Cambridge 1957.

(2) HISTORIES AND STUDIES

Barbauld, A. L. On the origin and progress of novel writing. In British novelists vol 1, 1810.

Scott, W. The lives of the novelists. 10 vols 1821–4.

Green, T. H. Estimate of the value and influence of works of fiction in modern times. 1862; rptd in his Works vol 3, ed R. L. Nettleship 1888.

Baker, E. A. The history of the English novel vol 3: The later romances and the establishment of realism. 1930; vol 4: Intellectual realism from Richardson to Sterne, 1930; vol 5: The novel of sentiment and the Gothic romance, 1934.

Tompkins, J. M. S. The popular novel in England 1770–1800. 1932, 1962.

Boyce, B. (ed). Prefaces to fiction. Los Angeles 1952 (Augustan Reprint Soc).

Watt, I. The rise of the novel: studies in Defoe, Richardson and Fielding. 1957.

Mayo, R. D. The English novel in the magazines 1740–1815. Evanston 1962.

Day, R. A. Told in letters. Ann Arbor 1966.

Parker, A. A. Literature and the delinquent: the picaresque novel in Spain and Europe 1599–1763. Edinburgh 1967. On Defoe, Smollett.

Richetti, J. J. Popular fiction before Richardson: narrative patterns 1700–39. 1969.

II. THE PRINCIPAL NOVELISTS

JOHN BUNYAN
1628–88

Bibliographies

Harrison, F. M. A bibliography of the works of Bunyan. 1932 (Bibl Soc).

Collections

The works of that eminent servant of Christ, Mr John Bunyan. Ed Charles Doe, with prefatory epistle by E. Chandler and J. Wilson 1692. Vol 1 only pbd.

Works with a preface by George Whitefield, including the Divine emblems and other works not collected in 1692. 2 vols 1767–8.

Grace abounding and the Pilgrim's progress. Ed R. Sharrock, Oxford 1966 (OSA).

Miscellaneous works. Ed R. Sharrock et al, Oxford 1978–.

§ I

Some gospel-truths opened according to the Scriptures. London and Newport Pagnell 1656.

A vindication of the book called some gospel-truths opened. London and Newport Pagnell 1657.

A few sighs from Hell: or the groans of a damned soul. London (and Newport Pagnell?) 1658, London [1666?], [1672], 1674, 1675, nd (6th edn), [1686?], 1692, 1700, 1702, 1707 etc.

The doctrine of the law and grace unfolded. London and Newport Pagnell 1659, London 1685, 1701, 1708 etc.

Profitable meditations fitted to mans different condition. (1661?]; ed G. Offor 1862.

I will pray with the spirit, and I will pray with the understanding also. 1663 (2nd edn), nd (3rd edn), 1685, 1692; rptd 1818 from 2nd edn; tr Welsh, 1790. Also in Works 1692, above.

Christian behaviour: or the fruits of true Christianity. [1663], 1680, [1690?].

A mapp shewing the order and causes of salvation and damnation. [1664?], 1691 (broadside). Also in Works 1692, above.

One thing is needful: or serious meditations upon the four last things. [1665?] (no known copy), 1688 (3rd edn).

The holy city: or the new Jerusalem. 1665 (2 imprints), 1669.

Prison meditations. 1665 (broadside), 1688 (with One thing is needful).

The resurrection of the dead. [1665?].

Grace abounding to the chief of sinners: or a brief and faithful relation of the exceeding mercy of God in Christ to his poor servant John Bunyan. 1666, nd (3rd edn, 'corrected and much enlarged'), probably 1672, 1680, 1688, 1692, 1695, Glasgow 1697, London 1701, Edinburgh 1707, 1716 etc; ed E. Venables, Oxford 1879; rev M. Peacock, Oxford 1900; ed J. Brown 1888, Cambridge 1907 (from 1688); ed A. Smellie 1897; ed R. Sharrock, Oxford 1962.

A confession of my faith and a reason of my practice. 1672.

A Christian dialogue. [1672?]. No known copy.

A new and useful confordance to the Holy Bible. [1672?]. No known copy; advertised in 1672.

A defence of the doctrine of justification by faith in Jesus Christ. 1672, 1673.

Differences in judgment about water-baptism. 1673.

The barren fig-tree: or the doom and downfall of the fruitless professor. 1673, 1688, 1692, 1695.

Peaceable principles and true: or a brief answer to Mr D'Anvers and Mr Paul's books. [1674]. No known copy; answered by John Denne in 1674.

Light for them that sit in darkness. 1675.

Instruction for the ignorant. 1675, 1728 (6th edn).

Saved by grace: or a discourse of the grace of God. [1676?]. No known copy.

The strait gate: or great difficulty of going to heaven. 1676.

The pilgrim's progress from this world to that which is to come, delivered under the similitude of a dream wherein is discovered, the manner of his setting out, his dangerous journey, and safe arrival at the desired countrey. 1678, 1678, 1679, 1680 (2 issues), 1680 (5th edn), 1682 (called 'fifth edn', 2 issues), 1681 (6th edn), Boston 1681, London 1682 (also called 'sixth edn'), 1681, 1682, 1683 (9th edn), 1684 (also called 'ninth edn'), 1685, 1688 etc; ed R. Southey 1830; ed G. Offor 1847, 1856; ed C. Kingsley 1860; ed E. Venables, Oxford 1866, 1879 (with Grace abounding, rev M. Peacock 1900); ed J. Brown 1887, 1895, Cambridge 1907; ed C. H. Firth 1898; ed G. K. Chesterton 1908; ed C. Whibley 1926; N. Douglas 1928 (facs of 1st edn); ed J. B. Wharey, Oxford 1928, rev R. Sharrock, Oxford 1960, corrected 1968.

Come and welcome, to Jesus Christ. 1678, 1684, 1685 (3rd edn), 1686 (also called 'third edn'), 1688, 1690, 1691, 1694, 1697 (8th edn), 1700 (8th–9th edns), 1702, 1707, 1715, 1719.

A treatise of the fear of God. 1679

The life and death of Mr Badman presented to the world in a familiar dialogue between Mr Wiseman, and Mr Attentive. 1680, 1685, 1688 ('second edn'), 1698, [1734?]; ed J. Froude 1900; ed J. Brown, Cambridge 1905; ed G. B. Harrison 1928.

The holy war made by Shaddai upon Diabolus for the regaining of the metropolis of the world: or the losing and taking again of the town of Mansoul. 1682, 1684, 1696, [1700?]; ed J. Brown 1887, Cambridge 1905; ed M. Peacock, Oxford 1892 (with Heavenly footman); ed J. F. Forrest, Toronto 1967.

The greatness of the soul and unspeakableness of the loss thereof. 1683, 1691, 1717, 1728, 1730.

A case of conscience resolved. 1683.

A holy life, the beauty of Christianity. 1684, 1689.

Seasonable counsel: or advice to sufferers. 1684.

The pilgrim's progress from this world to that which is to come: the second part, delivered under the similitude of a dream wherein is set forth the manner of the setting out of Christian's wife and children, their dangerous journey and safe arrival at the desired country. 1684, 1685, 1686, 1687, 1690, 1693, 1696; ed J. Wesley 1743 (abridged); ed G. Offor 1847; ed E. Venables, Oxford 1866; ed J. Brown 1887, Cambridge 1907; ed C. H. Firth 1898; ed J. B. Wharey, Oxford 1928, rev R. Sharrock, Oxford 1960, corrected 1968, 1966 (OSA).

A caution to stir up to watch against sin. [1684]. Broadside.

A discourse upon the pharisee and the publicane. 1685, 1704 (3rd edn), [1704] (5th edn), 1703 (also called 'fifth edn').

Questions about the nature and perpetuity of the seventh-day-sabbath. 1685.

A book for boys and girls: or country rhimes for children. 1686, 1701 (subtitled Or temporal things spiritualized), 1724 (9th edn; this and subsequent edns as Divine emblems: or temporal things spiritualized), 1732, 1757; ed J. Brown 1889 (facs of 1686); ed E. S. Buchanan, New York 1928.

Good news for the vilest of men. 1688, 1689 (as The Jerusalem sinner saved), 1691, 1697 ('third edn'), 1700, 1715, 1728.

The advocateship of Jesus Christ clearly explained and largely improved. 1688 (2 issues, 2nd as The work of Jesus Christ as an advocate), 1703 etc.

A discourse of the building, nature, excellency and government of the house of God. 1688.

The water of life. 1688, 1756 etc.

Solomon's temple spiritualiz'd: or gospel light fetcht out of the temple at Jerusalem. 1688, 1691, 1698, 1706, 1707.

The acceptable sacrifice. 1689, 1691, 1698, 1702, 1718.

Mr John Bunyan's last sermon. 1689, [1708?].

The following works were first pbd in Works, 1692, *above:*

An exposition of the first ten chapters of Genesis;

Of justification by imputed righteousness;

Paul's departure and crown;

Of the Trinity and a Christian;

Of the law and a Christian;

Israel's hope encouraged;

The desire of the righteous granted;

The saint's knowledge of Christ's love;

Of the house of the forest of Lebanon;

Of Antichrist and his ruine.

The heavenly footman. 1698, 1700, Edinburgh 1702, London 1708, 1724 etc; ed M. Peacock, Oxford 1892; ed H. A. Talon, God's knotty log, New York and Cleveland 1961.

A relation of the imprisonment of Mr John Bunyan. 1765; rptd in subsequent edns of Grace abounding.

§ 2

Southey, R. Life of Bunyan. In his edn of 1830.

Macaulay, T. B. John Bunyan. Edinburgh Rev 51 1830, Encyclopaedia britannica 1854. Review of Southey's Life, above.

Froude, J. A. Bunyan. 1880 (EML).

Brown, J. Bunyan: his life, times and work. 1885 etc; rev F. M. Harrison 1928.

Sharrock, R. Bunyan and the English emblem writers. RES 21 1945.

— Spiritual autobiography in the Pilgrim's progress. RES 24 1948.

— John Bunyan. 1954.

— The pilgrim's progress. 1966.

Talon, H. A. Bunyan: l'homme et l'œuvre. Paris 1948; tr 1951.

DANIEL DEFOE

1660–1731

Bibliographies

Moore, J. R. A checklist of the writings of Defoe. Bloomington 1960, 1962 (rev), Hamden Conn 1971 (rev).

Collections

A collection of the writings of the author of the True-born Englishman. 1703. Collected by Defoe, though he claimed it was pirated.

A true collection of the writings of the author of the True born English-man, corrected by himself. 1703, 1705 ('corrected and enlarg'd by himself'). Vol 2 as A second volume of the writings of the author of the True-born Englishman, 1705. Both vols reissued as A true collection etc, [1710], [1713], [1721] (as The genuine works of Mr Daniel D'Foe) (with 'a compleat key to the whole work').

Novels. Ed W. Scott 12 vols Edinburgh 1810.

Novels and miscellaneous works, with prefaces attributed to Sir Walter Scott. 20 vols Oxford 1840-1.

Novels and selected writings. 14 vols Oxford 1927-8.

A journal of the plague year and other pieces. Ed A. W. Secord, New York 1935.

The best of Defoe's Review: an anthology. Ed W. L. Payne, New York 1951.

[Selection]. Ed J. T. Boulton 1965.

Robinson Crusoe and other writings. Ed J. Sutherland, Boston 1968.

Selected writings. Ed J. T. Boulton, Cambridge 1975.

§ I

A letter to a Dissenter from his friend at the Hague, concerning the penal laws and the test. [1688]. Probably by Defoe.

Reflections upon the late great revolution, written by a lay-hand in the country. 1689. Probably by Defoe.

The advantages of the present settlement, and the great danger of a relapse. 1689. Probably by Defoe.

An account of the late horrid conspiracy to depose their present Majesties K. William and Q. Mary, to bring in the French and the late King James, and ruine the city of London, with a relation of the miraculous discovery thereof, 1691. Probably by Defoe.

A new discovery of an old intreague: a satyr level'd at treachery and ambition, calculated to the nativity of the Rapparee plott, and the modesty of the Jacobite clergy. 1691; rptd in A true collection, 1705 and in M. E. Campbell, Defoe's first poem, Bloomington 1938.

To the Athenian Society. In C. Gildon, History of the Athenian Society, [1692?]; rptd by J. Dunton in successive edns of The Athenian oracle.

A dialogue betwixt Whig and Tory. 1693, 1710. Probably by Defoe.

The Englishman's choice, and true interest, in a vigorous prosecution of the war against France; and serving K. William and Q. Mary, and acknowledging their right. 1694. Almost certainly by Defoe.

Some seasonable queries on the third head, viz: a general naturalization. 1697? Probably by Defoe.

The character of the late Dr Samuel Annesley, by way of elegy; with a preface. 1697; rptd in A true collection, 1703.

Some reflections on a pamphlet lately publish'd entituled An argument shewing that a standing army is inconsistent with a free government, and absolutely destructive to the Constitution of the English monarchy. 1697, 1697. Reply to J. Trenchard.

An essay upon projects. 1697; reissued as Essays upon several projects, 1702.

An enquiry into the occasional conformity of Dissenters, in cases of preferment, with a preface to the Lord Mayor, occasioned by his carrying the sword to a conventicle. 1697 (for 1698), Dublin 1698, 1701 (for 1700) (with preface to Mr How); rptd in A true collection, 1703; and in G. M. Trevelyan, Select documents for Queen Anne's reign, Cambridge 1929.

An argument shewing that a standing army, with consent of Parliament, is not inconsistent with a free government. 1698; rptd in A true collection, 1703.

A brief reply to the History of standing armies in England, with some account of the authors. 1698, 1698. A reply to J. Trenchard and W. Moyle.

Some queries concerning the disbanding of the army. 1698, 1698. Perhaps by Defoe.

The poor man's plea for a reformation of manners and suppressing immorality in the nation. 1698, 1698, 1700; rptd in Collection, 1703 and in A true collection, 1703.

The interests of the several princes and states of Europe consider'd, with respect to the succession of the crown of Spain, and the titles of the several pretenders thereto examin'd. 1698.

Lex talionis: or an enquiry into the most proper ways to prevent the persecution of the Protestants in France. 1698; rptd in Collection, 1703.

An encomium upon the Parliament (1699). In Poems on affairs of State vol 2, 1703. Perhaps by Defoe.

The pacificator: a poem. 1700; rptd in A true collection vol 2, 1705.

The two great questions consider'd: I. what the French King will do, with respect to the Spanish monarchy; II. what measures the English ought to take. 1700, 1700, 1700, 1700; rptd in A true collection, 1703.

The two great questions further considered, with some reply to the remarks. 1700; rptd in A true collection, 1703 .

Reasons humbly offer'd for a law to enact the castration of popish ecclesiastics. 1700. Perhaps by Defoe.

The six distinguishing characters of a Parliament-man, address'd to the good people of England. 1700 (for 1701); rptd in A true collection, 1703.

The danger of the Protestant religion consider'd, from the present prospect of a religious war in Europe. 1701; rptd in A true collection, 1703.

The true-born Englishman: a satyr. 1700 (for 1701). Preface added and text rev, 9th edn 1701; rptd in Collection, 1703; rptd in A true collection, 1703; further revisions adapting the poem to the reign of George I, 1716; frequently rptd in contemporary miscellanies; ed A. C. Guthkelch, E & S 4 1913.

The succession to the crown of England, considered. 1701.

The free-holders plea against stock-jobbing elections of parliament men. 1701, 1701 (with addns); rptd in A true collection, 1703.

A letter to Mr How, by way of reply to his considerations of the preface to An enquiry into the occasional conformity of Dissenters, by the author of the said Preface and Enquiry. 1701; rptd in Collection, 1703, and in A true collection, 1703.

The livery man's reasons, why he did not give his vote for a certain gentleman either to be Lord Mayor: or Parliament man for the city of London. 1701.

The villainy of stock-jobbers detected, and the causes of the late run upon the bank and bankers discovered and considered. 1701, 1701; rptd in A true collection, 1703.

The apparent danger of an invasion, briefly represented in a letter to a Minister of State, by a Kentish gentleman. 1701. Perhaps by Defoe.

The present state of England and the Protestant interest. 1701. Perhaps by Defoe.

[Legion's memorial]. [1701]; rptd in Somers tracts vol 11, 1814, and in An English garner, ed E. Arber vol 7, 1883.

Ye true-born Englishmen proceed [first line of first stanza]. [1701]. Known by a variety of titles, but most commonly as The ballad.

The history of the Kentish petition. 1701, Edinburgh 1701; rptd in Somers tracts vol 11, 1814, and in An English garner, ed E. Arber vol 7, 1883.

The present state of Jacobitism considered, in two querys: 1, What measures the French King will take with respect to the person and title of the pretended Prince of Wales; 2, What the Jacobites in England ought to do on the same account. 1701. Preface signed D.F.

An argument, shewing that the Prince of Wales, tho' a Protestant, has no just pretensions to the crown of England. 1701.

Reasons against a war with France: or an argument shewing that the French King's owning the Prince of Wales as King of England, Scotland and Ireland is no sufficient ground of a war. 1701; rptd in A true collection, 1703.

Legion's new paper: being a second memorial to the gentlemen of a late House of Commons, with Legion's humble address to his Majesty. 1702 (for 1701). Also as Legion's second memorial; rptd in Somers tracts vol 11, 1814.

The original power of the collective body of the people of

England, examined and asserted. 1702 (for 1701); rptd in A true collection, 1703.

The mock-mourners: a satyr, by way of elegy on King William. 1702; Edinburgh 1703; rptd in Collection, 1703; and in A true collection, 1703.

Reformation of manners: a satyr. 1702, 1702; rptd in Collection, 1703; rptd in A true collection, 1703.

A new test of the Church of England's loyalty: or Whiggish loyalty and church loyalty compar'd. 1702, 1702, [Edinburgh] 1703; rptd in Collection, 1703, and in A true collection, 1703; 1715 (as A defence of Mr Withers' History of resistance); in Somers tracts vol 9, 1813.

Good advice to the ladies: shewing that as the world goes, and is like to go, the best way is for them to keep un-married, by the author of the True born Englishman. 1702, 1705, 1709, 1727, 1728 (as A timely caution).

The Spanish descent: a poem, by the author of the True-born Englishman. 1702, 1703; rptd in Collection, 1703; and in A true collection, 1703.

An enquiry into occasional conformity, shewing that the Dissenters are no way concern'd in it, by the author of the preface to Mr Howe. 1702; rptd in Collection, 1703, and in A true collection, 1703; reissued 1703, 1704 (as An enquiry into the occasional conformity bill).

The opinion of a known Dissenter on the bill for preventing occasional conformity. 1703 (for 1702?).

The shortest way with the Dissenters: or proposals for the establishment of the Church. 1702; rptd in Collection, 1703, and in A true collection, 1703; rptd in English garner, ed E. Arber vol 7, 1883.

A brief explanation of a late pamphlet, entituled the Shortest way with the Dissenters. [1703]; rptd in Collection, 1703; in A true collection, 1703; and in G. M. Trevelyan, Select documents for Queen Anne's reign, Cambridge 1929.

A dialogue between a Dissenter and the observator, con-cerning the Shortest way with Dissenters. 1703; rptd in Collection, 1703.

King William's affection to the Church of England examin'd. 1703 (5 edns).

More reformation: a satyr upon himself, by the author of the True born English-man. 1703; rptd in A true collection vol 2, 1705.

The shortest way to peace and union, by the author of the Shortest way with the Dissenters. 1703, 1703; rptd in A true collection, 1703, 1704.

A hymn to the pillory. 1703 (3 edns), [1703?], [1703?], 1708, [1721?], [1748]; rptd in A true collection vol 2, 1705.

The sincerity of the Dissenters vindicated, from the scandal of occasional conformity, with some considerations on a late book entitul'd Moderation a vertue [by J. Owen]. 1703.

A hymn to the funeral sermon. 1703 (3 edns).

The case of Dissenters as affected by the late bill proposed in Parliament for preventing occasional conformity. 1703; rptd in Somers tracts vol 12, 1814.

An enquiry into the case of Mr Asgil's general translations shewing that 'tis not a nearer way to heaven than the grave, by the author of the True born English-man. 1704 (for 1703).

A challenge of peace, address'd to the whole nation, with an enquiry into ways and means for bringing it to pass. 1703; rptd in A true collection vol 2, 1705.

Some remarks on the first chapter in Dr Davenant's Essays. 1704 (for 1703), 1704 (as The reasonableness of appeals to the people).

Peace without union, by way of reply, to Sir H[umphrey] M[ackworth']s Peace at home. 1703 (4 edns); rptd with preface in A true collection vol 2, 1705.

The Dissenters answer to the High-Church challenge. 1704; rptd in A true collection vol 2, 1705.

An essay on the regulation of the press. 1704; ed J. R. Moore, Oxford 1948.

A serious inquiry into this grand question, whether a law to prevent the occasional conformity of Dissenters, would not be inconsistent with the Act of Toleration, and a breach of the Queen's promise. 1704; rptd in A true collection vol 2, 1705.

The paral[l]el: or persecution of Protestants the shortest way to prevent the growth of popery in Ireland. Dublin 1705 (for 1704?); rptd in A true collection vol 2, 1705.

The lay-man's sermon upon the late storm, held forth at an honest coffee-house-conventicle. 1704.

Royal religion: being some enquiry after the piety of princes, with remarks on a book entituled A form of prayers us'd by King William. 1704, 1704; rptd in A true collection vol 2, 1705.

Moderation maintain'd, in defence of a compassionate enquiry into the causes of the Civil War etc in a sermon preached the thirty-first of January, at Aldgate-Church by White Kennet. 1704.

Legion's humble address to the Lords. [1704]; rptd in Legion's humble address to the Lords answered para-graph by paragraph, [1704].

The Christianity of the High-Church consider'd, dedicated to a noble peer. 1704.

More short-ways with the Dissenters. 1704; rptd in A true collection vol 2, 1705.

The address. [1704]; rptd in Poems on affairs of State vol 4, 1707. Perhaps by Defoe.

The Dissenter[s] misrepresented and represented. [1704]; rptd in A true collection vol 2, 1705.

A new test of the Church of England's honesty. 1704, Edinburgh 1705; rptd in A true collection vol 2, 1705.

The storm: or a collection of the most remarkable casual-ties and disasters which happen'd in the late dreadful tempest, both by sea and land. 1704.

An elegy on the author of the True-born English-man, with an essay on the late storm, by the author of the Hymn to the pillory. 1704, 1704 (as The live man's elegy), Dublin 1704, 1708; rptd in A true collection vol 2, 1705.

A true state of the difference between Sir George Rook Knt and William Colepeper esq. Part 1, 1704. Probably partly by Defoe.

A hymn to victory. 1704 (4 edns), [Edinburgh?] 1704; rptd in A true collection vol 2, 1705.

The Protestant Jesuite unmask'd, in answer to the two parts of Cassandra, wherein the author and his libels are laid open, with my service to Mr Lesley. 1704.

Giving alms no charity, and employing the poor a grievance to the nation. 1704; rptd in A true collection vol 2, 1705; rptd in A select collection of scarce and valuable economic tracts, ed J. R. McCulloch 1859.

Queries upon the bill against occasional conformity. [1704].

The double welcome: a poem to the Duke of Marlbro. 1705, 1705; rptd in A true collection vol 2, 1705.

Persecution anatomiz'd: or an answer to the following questions [4 questions on the High Church and Dis-senters]. 1705.

The consolidator: or memoirs of sundry transactions from the world in the moon, translated from the lunar langu-age, by the author of the True-born English man. 1705, 1705. Extracts from Consolidator, perhaps pirated, perhaps abridged by Defoe to reach a wider audience, were pbd under the following titles: A journey to the world in the moon, [1705]; A letter from the man in the moon, [1705]; A second, and more stragne voyage to the world in the moon, [1705].

The experiment, or the shortest way with the Dissenters exemplified: being the case of Mr Abraham Gill, a Dissenting Minister in the Isle of Ely. 1705, 1707 (for 1706?) (as The honesty and sincerity of those worthy English gentlemen, commonly called High-Church men).

A hint to the Blackwell-hall factors: being the true state of the case between Mr Samuel Weatherhead, Blackwell-hall factor and Mr John Hellier, merchant. 1705. Perhaps by Defoe.

Advice to all parties, by the author of the True-born Englishman. 1705, 1705.

The dyet of Poland: a satyr. 1705, 1705, Dublin 1705; rptd in The dyet of Poland consider'd paragraph by paragraph, 1705.

The ballance: or a new test of the High-Fliers of all sides. 1705.

The High-Church legion, or the memorial examin'd: being a new test of moderation as 'tis recomended to all that love the Church of England and the Constitution. 1705.

Party-tyranny: or an Occasional Bill in miniature, as now practised in Carolina humbly offered to the consideration of both Houses of Parliament. 1705.

An answer to the L[or]d H[aver]sham's speech, by Daniel D'Foe. 1705; rptd Review 24 Nov 1705.

Declaration without doors. [1705].

A hymn to peace, occasion'd by the two Houses joining in one address to the Queen, by the author of the True-born English-man. 1706, 1706, [1706?], 1709.

A reply to a pamphlet entituled the L[or]d H[aversham]'s vindication of his speech etc, by the author of the Review. 1706.

The case of Protestant Dissenters in Carolina, shewing how a law to prevent occasional conformity there, has ended in the total subversion of the Constitution in church and state, recommended to the serious consideration of all that are true friends to our present establishment. 1706.

Remarks on the bill to prevent frauds committed by bankrupts, with observations on the effect it may have upon trade. 1706.

Remarks on the letter to the author of the State-memorial. 1706. Defence of J. Toland and attack on W. Stephens.

An essay at removing national prejudices against a union with Scotland, to be continued during the treaty here. Part I, 1706, [Edinburgh] 1706.

An essay on the great battle at Ramellies, by the author of the Review. 1706; rptd Review 21 May 1706.

Jure divino: a satyr in twelve books, by the author of the True-born-Englishman. 1706 (4 edns).

An essay at removing national prejudices against a union with Scotland, to be continued during the treaty here. Part II, 1706, [Edinburgh] 1706.

Preface to De Laune's plea for the Non-conformists. 1706 (9 edns), 1709 (as Dr Sacheverell's recantation), 1720.

Daniel Defoe's hymn for the thanksgiving. 1706; rptd Review 27 June 1706.

A true relation of the apparition of one Mrs Veal. 1706, 1707, 1710; rptd in C. Drelincourt, The Christian's defence against the fears of death, 1706 (over 20 edns before 1800).

An essay, at removing national prejudices against a union with England. Part III, by the author of the two first, [Edinburgh] 1706.

A letter from Mr Reason, to the high and mighty prince the mob. [Edinburgh 1706].

An answer to my Lord Beilhaven's speech, by an English gentleman. [Edinburgh?] 1706.

The vision: a poem. [Edinburgh 1706] (3 edns), 1706.

A fourth essay, at removing national prejudices; with some reply to Mr H[o]dges and some other authors, who have printed their objections against an union with England. [Edinburgh] 1706.

Observations on the fifth article of The treaty of union, humbly offered to the consideration of the Parliament, relating to foreign ships. [Edinburgh 1706]. Probably by Defoe.

Considerations in relation to trade considered, and a short view of our present trade and taxes, compared with what these taxes may amount to after the union etc reviewed. [Edinburgh] 1706.

A seasonable warning or the Pope and King of France unmasked. [Edinburgh] 1706.

A reply to the Scots answer, to the British vision (by Lord Beilhaven). [Edinburgh 1706] (3 edns).

Caledonia: a poem in honour of Scotland, and the Scots nation, in three parts. Edinburgh 1706, 1706, London 1707, Dublin 1707, London 1748.

The state of the excise after the union, compared with what it is now. [Edinburgh] 1706. Perhaps by Defoe.

The state of the excise etc vindicated from the remarks of the author of the Short view etc, wherein other escapes of that author are likewise taken notice of. [Edinburgh 1706]. Perhaps by Defoe.

A short letter to the Glasgow-men. [Edinburgh 1706]; rptd Review 2 Jan 1707.

The rabbler convicted: or a friendly advice to all turbulent and factious persons, from one of their own number. [Edinburgh 1706].

The advantages of Scotland by an incorporate union with England, compar'd with these of a coalition with the Dutch, or league with France, in answer to a pamphlet call'd the Advantages of the act of security etc. 1706.

A letter concerning trade, from several Scots-gentlemen that are merchants in England, to their country-men that are merchants in Scotland. [Edinburgh 1706]. Probably by Defoe.

An enquiry into the disposal of the equivalent. [Edinburgh 1706].

A Scots poem: or a new-years gift, from a native of the universe, to his fellow-animals in Albania. Edinburgh 1707.

A fifth essay, at removing national prejudices; with a reply to some authors, who have printed their objections against an union with England. [Edinburgh?] 1607 (for 1707).

Two great questions considered: being a sixth essay at removing national prejudices against the union. [Edinburgh] 1707.

The dissenters in England vindicated from some reflections in a late pamphlet entitled Lawful prejudices [by J. Webster]. [Edinburgh 1707].

Passion and prejudice, the support of one another, and both destructive to the happiness of this nation, in church and state; being a reply to the vindicator of Mr W[ebste]r's Lawful prejudices. Edinburgh 1707.

Proposals for printing by subscription a compleat history of the Union, by the author of the True-born-Englishman. [1707].

A discourse upon an union of the two Kingdoms of England and Scotland. 1707. Perhaps by Defoe.

Queries upon the foregoing act. In The copy of an act lately pass'd in Carolina. [1707].

Remarks upon the Lord Haversham's speech in the House of Peers, Feb 15 1707. [Edinburgh 1707]. Probably by Defoe.

A short view of the present state of the Protestant religion in Britain, as it is now profest in the Episcopal Church in England, the Presbyterian Church in Scotland, and the Dissenters in both. Edinburgh 1707, London 1707 (as The Dissenters vindicated: or a short view).

The true-born Britain, written by the author of the True-born Englishman. 1707. Perhaps by Defoe.

A voice from the south: or an address from some Protestant Dissenters in England to the Kirk of Scotland. [Edinburgh 1707]; rptd Review 10, 15 May 1707.

A modest vindication of the present ministry; from the reflections publish'd against them in a late paper entitled the Lord Haversham's speech. 1707.

The trade of Britain stated: being the substance of two papers published in London on occasion of the importation of wine and brandy from North-Britain. [Edinburgh 1707]; rptd from Review 10, 12 June 1707.

An historical account of the bitter sufferings, and melancholly circumstances of the Episcopal Church in Scotland, under the barbarous usage and bloody persecution of the Presbyterian Church government. Edinburgh 1707, 1707 (as Presbyterian persecution examined).

De Foe's answer to Dyer's scandalous news letter. [Edinburgh 1707].

Dyers news examined as to his Sweddish memorial against the Review. [Edinburgh 1707].

Reflections on the prohibition act, wherein the necessity, usefulness and value of that law are evinced and demonstrated. 1708.

A memorial to the nobility of Scotland, who are to assemble in order to choose the sitting peers for the Parliament of Great Britain. Edinburgh 1708. Probably by Defoe.

Scotland in danger: or a serious enquiry into the dangers which Scotland has been in, or may be in since the Union; with some humble proposals for the remedy. [1708]. Probably by Defoe.

An answer to a paper concerning Mr De Foe, against his History of the Union. Edinburgh 1708.

The Scot's narrative examin'd: or the case of the Episcopal ministers in Scotland stated. 1709.

A brief history of the poor Palatine refugees, lately arrived in England. 1709, Dublin 1709; ed J. R. Moore, Los Angeles 1964 (Augustan Reprint Soc).

The history of the Union of Great Britain. Edinburgh 1709, London 1711, 1712 (both as A collection of original papers and material transactions concerning the Union between England and Scotland), 1786 (with appendix of original papers), Dublin 1799 (selection).

Parson Plaxton of Barwick. [1709]; ed S. Peterson, HLQ 19 1955.

A letter to Mr Bisset, eldest brother of the Collegiate Church of St Catherines; in answer to his remarks on Dr Sacheverell's sermon. 1709.

A letter from Captain Tom to the mobb, now rais'd for Dr Sacheverel. [1710].

A reproof to Mr Clark, and a brief vindication of Mr De Foe. [Edinburgh 1710].

Advertisement from Daniel De Foe, to Mr Clark. [Edinburgh 1710?].

A speech without doors. 1710.

The age of wonders: to the tune of Chivy chase. 1710 (3 edns), Edinburgh 1710. Attributed by J. R. Moore, but doubtful.

Greenshields out of prison and toleration settled in Scotland: or the case of Mr Greenshields, farther examin'd. 1710.

A vindication of Dr Henry Sacheverell, by D. D'F. esq: or otherwise etc. [1710].

Instructions from Rome, in favour of the Pretender, inscrib'd to the most elevated Don Sacheverellio, and his brother Don Higginisco. [1710].

The recorder of B[anbu]ry's speech to Dr Sach[eve]rell. 1710. Attributed by J. R. Moore.

The Ban[bur]y apes: or the monkeys chattering to the magpye, in a letter to a friend in London. [1710] (4 edns).

A collection of the several addresses in the late King James's time: concerning the conception and birth of the pretended Prince of Wales. [1710].

Dr Sacheverell's disappointment at Worcester: being a true account of his cold reception there, in a letter from a gentleman in that city to his friend in London. 1710. Attributed by J. R. Moore.

A new map of the laborious and painful travels of our blessed High Church apostle: giving a true account of the many strange, miraculous cures and wonders that he has perform'd both on dumb and blind persons throughout the countreys wheresoever he went. 1710. Probably by Defoe.

High-Church miracles: or modern inconsistencies. 1710 (3 edns). Perhaps by Defoe.

A short historical account of the contrivances and conspiracies of the men of Dr Sacheverell's principles, in the late reigns. [1710]. Probably by Defoe.

Seldom comes a better, or a tale of a lady and her servants: qui capit ille facit. 1710. Perhaps by Defoe.

A letter from a Dissenter in the city of a Dissenter in the country, advising him to a quiet and peaceable behaviour

in this present conjuncture. 1710. Attributed by J. R. Moore, but doubtful.

An essay upon publick credit. 1710 (3 edns), 1797; rptd in Somers tracts vol 13, 1815; and in A select collection of tracts on the national debt, ed J. R. McCulloch 1857.

A new test of the sence of the nation: being a modest comparison between the addresses to the late King James, and those to her present Majesty. 1710.

A letter from a gentleman at the Court of St Germains, to one of his friends in England: containing a memorial about methods for setting the Pretender on the throne of Great Britain. 1710. Perhaps Defoe but also ascribed to Maynwaring.

A condoling letter to the Tattler: on account of the misfortunes of Isaac Bickerstaff esq, a prisoner in the [——] on suspicion of debt. [1710].

Queries to the new hereditary right-men. 1710. Probably by Defoe.

An essay upon loans, by the author of the Essay upon credit. 1710; rptd in Somers tracts vol 13, 1815.

A word against a new election: that the people of England may see the happy difference between English liberty and French slavery; and may consider well before they make the exchange. 1710.

A supplement to the faults on both sides: containing the compleat history of the proceedings of a party ever since the Revolution; in a familiar dialogue between Steddy and Turn-Round, two displac'd officers of State. 1710 (5 edns). Also as Faults on both sides: the second part.

The British visions. [Newcastle 1710], London 1710.

Atalantis Major, printed in Olreeky, the chief city of the north part of Atalantis Major. 1711 (for 1710).

R[ogue]'s on both sides, in which are the characters of some R[ogue]'s not yet describ'd; with a true description of an old Whig, and a modern Whig; an old Tory, and a modern Tory; High-flyer: or motly; as also of a Minister of State. 1711.

A short narrative of the life and actions of his Grace John D. of Marlborough, from the beginning of the Revolution to this present time, by an old officer in the army. 1711.

Counter queries. [1711?].

The Quaker's sermon: or a holding-forth concerning Barabbas. 1711. Perhaps by Defoe.

Captain Tom's remembrance to his old friends the mob of London, Westminster, Southwark and Wapping. [1711]. Probably by Defoe.

A seasonable caution to the general assembly, in a letter from a member of Parliament of North-Britain to a minister in Scotland, occasioned by the House of Lords reversing the sentence of Mr Greenshiels. 1711.

A spectators address to the Whigs, on the occasion of the stabbing Mr Harley. 1711. Probably by Defoe.

The secret history of the October Club, from its original to this time, by a member. 1711, 1711; pt 2, 1711.

The succession of Spain consider'd: or a view of the several interests of the princes and powers of Europe, as they respect the succession of Spain and the Empire. 1711. Probably by Defoe.

Eleven opinions about Mr H[arle]y, with observations. 1711.

The re-representation: or a modest search after the great plunderers of the nation. 1711. Perhaps by Defoe.

The representation examined: being remarks on the state of religion in England. 1711, Edinburgh 1711. Perhaps by Defoe.

Reasons for a peace: or the war at an end. 1711.

An essay upon the trade to Africa. 1711.

The Scotch medal decipher'd, and the new hereditary-right men display'd: or remarks on the late proceedings of the faculty of advocates at Edinburgh, upon receiving the Pretender's medal. 1711. Probably by Defoe.

A speech for Mr D[unda]sse Younger of Arnistown, if he should be impeach'd of h[igh] t[reaso]n for what he said and did about the Pretender's medal, lately sent to the Faculty of Advocates at Edinburgh. 1711.

A true account of the design and advantages of the South-Sea trade; with answers to all the objections rais'd against it; a list of all the commodities proper for that trade, and the progress of the subscription towards the South-Sea Company. 1711.

An essay on the South-Sea trade, by the author of the Review. 1712 (for 1711).

The true state of the case between the government and the creditors of the Navy etc, as it relates to the South-Sea trade, and the justice of the transactions on either side impartially enquired into. 1711.

Reasons why this nation ought to put a speedy end to this expensive war; with a brief essay, at the probable conditions on which the peace now negotiating, may be founded. 1711 (3 edns), Edinburgh 1711.

Reasons why a party among us, and also among the Confederates, are obstinately bent against a treaty of peace with the French at this time, by the author of the Reasons for putting an end to this expensive war. 1711 (3 edns).

Armageddon: or the necessity of carrying on the war, if such a peace cannot be obtained as may render Europe safe, and trade secure. [1711] (3 edns).

The ballance of Europe: or an enquiry into the respective dangers of giving the Spanish monarchy to the Emperour as well as to King Phillip, with the consequences that may be expected from either. 1711.

An essay at a plain exposition of that difficult phrase a good peace, by the author of the Review. 1711.

The felonious treaty: or an enquiry into the reasons which moved his late Majesty King William of glorious memory, to enter into a treaty at two several times with the King of France for the partition of the Spanish monarchy, by the author of the Review. 1711.

An essay on the history of parties, and persecution in Britain: beginning with a brief account of the Test-Act and an historical enquiry into the reasons, the original and the consequences of the occasional conformity of Dissenters. 1711.

A defence of the Allies and the late ministry: or remarks on the Tories new idol [Swift]. 1712.

A justification of the Dutch from several late scandalous reflections: in which is shewn the absolute necessity of preserving a strict and inviolable friendship betwixt Great-Britain and the States-General; with the fatal consequences that must attend a war with Holland. 1712.

No queen, or no general: an argument, proving the necessity her Majesty was in, as well for the safety of her person as of her authority, to displace the D[uke] of M[arl]borough. 1712, 1712.

The conduct of parties in England, more especially of those Whigs who now appear against the new Ministry and a treaty for peace. 1712.

Peace or poverty: being a serious vindication of her Majesty and her Ministers consenting to a treaty for a general peace, shewing the reasonableness, and even necessity, there was for such a procedure. 1712. Probably by Defoe.

The case of the poor skippers and keel-men of Newcastle. [1712?]. Probably by Defoe.

A farther case relating to the poor keel-men of Newcastle. [1712]. Probably by Defoe.

The history of the Jacobite clubs; with the grounds of their hopes from the p[resen]t m[inistr]y; as also a caveat against the Pretender. 1712. Perhaps by Defoe.

Imperial gratitude, drawn from a modest view of the conduct of the Emperor Ch[arl]es VI and the King of Spain Ch[arl]es III; with observations on the difference etc: being a farther view of the deficiencies of our confederates. 1712. Probably by Defoe.

The Highland visions, or the Scots new prophecy: declaring in twelve visions what strange things shall come to pass in the year 1712. 1712.

Plain English, with remarks and advice to some men who need not be nam'd. 1712. Perhaps by Defoe.

Wise as serpents: being an enquiry into the present circumstances of the Dissenters, and what measures they ought to take in order to disappoint the designs of their enemies. 1712.

The present state of the parties in Great Britain: particularly an enquiry into the state of the Dissenters in England, and the Presbyterians in Scotland. 1712.

Reasons against fighting: being an enquiry into this great debate, whether it is safe for her Majesty, or her ministry, to venture an engagement with the French, considering the present behaviour of the Allies. 1712.

The present negotiations of peace vindicated from the imputation of trifling. 1712.

The validity of the renunciations of former powers enquired into, and the present renunciation of the Duke of Anjou impartially considered. 1712.

An enquiry into the danger and consequences of a war with the Dutch. 1712.

A further search into the conduct of the Allies and the late Ministry as to peace and war; containing also a reply to the several letters and memorials of the States-General, with a vindication of the British Parliament in their late resolves and address relating to the deficiences of the Dutch. 1712. Some copies as A farther search.

The justice and necessity of a war with Holland, in case the Dutch do not come into her Majesty's measures, stated and examined. 1712.

An enquiry into the real interest of princes in the persons of their ambassadors. 1712.

A seasonable warning and caution against the insinuations of Papists and Jacobites in favour of the Pretender: being a letter from an Englishman at the Court of Hannover. 1712.

Hannibal at the gates: or the progress of Jacobitism, with the present danger of the Pretender. 1712, 1714 (rev).

A strict enquiry into the circumstances of a late duel, with some account of the persons concern'd on both sides. 1713. On Hamilton and Mohun.

Reasons against the succession of the House of Hanover, with an enquiry how far the abdication of King James, supposing it to be legal, ought to affect the person of the Pretender. 1713 (4 edns).

Not[tingh]am politicks examin'd: being an answer to a pamphlet lately publish'd intitul'd Observations upon the state of the nation. 1713. Probably by Defoe.

The second-sighted Highlander, or predictions and foretold events, especially about the peace, by the famous Scots Highlander: being ten new visions for the year 1713. 1713.

And what if the Pretender should come? or some considerations of the advantages and real consequences of the Pretender's possessing the Crown of Great-Britain. 1713.

An answer to a question that no body thinks of, viz But what if the Queen should die? 1713.

An essay on the Treaty of Commerce with France. 1713, 1713.

An account of the abolishing of duels in France: being extracts out of the edicts of the Kings, the regulations of the Marshals, and the records of the Parliaments of France, with the resolutions of the Archbishops, Bishops and the clergy there, in relation to that matter. 1713.

Union and no union: being an enquiry into the grievances of the Scots, and how far they are right or wrong, who alledge that the union is dissolved. 1713.

Considerations upon the Eighth and Ninth Articles of the Treaty of Commerce and Navigation, now publish'd by authority, with some enquiries into the damages that may accrue to the English trade from them. 1713.

Some thoughts upon the subject of commerce with France, by the author of the Review. 1713.

A general history of trade, and especially consider'd as it respects the British commerce. 4 pts 1713.

The honour and prerogative of the Queen's Majesty vindicated and defended against the unexampled insolence of the author of the Guardian, in a letter from a country Whig to Mr Steele. 1713, 1713. Probably by Defoe.

Memoirs of Count Tariff etc. 1713.

A brief account of the present state of the African trade. 1713.

Reasons concerning the immediate demolishing of Dunkirk: being a serious enquiry into the state and condition of that affair. 1713. Probably by Defoe.

A letter from a member of the House of Commons to his friends in the country, relating to the Bill of Commerce, with a true copy of the Bill, and an exact list of all those who voted for and against engrossing it. 1713, 1713. Probably by Defoe.

Whigs turn'd Tories, and Hanoverian-Tories, from their avow'd principles, prov'd Whigs: or each side in the other mistaken. 1713.

A view of the real dangers of the succession, from the peace with France: being a sober enquiry into the securities proposed in the Articles of Peace, and whether they are such as the nation ought to be satisfy'd with or no. 1713, 1714 (as A view of the real danger of the Protestant succession), Dublin 1714.

A letter to the Dissenters. 1713, 1714 (with new preface).

Proposals for imploying the poor in and about the city of London, without any charge to the publick. 1713.

A letter to the Whigs, expostulating with them upon their present conduct. 1714.

Memoirs of John Duke of Melfort: being an account of the secret intrigues of the Chevalier de S. George, particularly relating to the present times. 1714, 1714.

The Scots nation and union vindicated; from the reflections cast on them, in an infamous libel, entitl'd the Publick spirit of the Whigs etc. 1714.

Reasons for im[peaching] the L[or]d H[igh] T[reasure]r, and some others of the p[resent] m[inistry]. [1714].

A letter to Mr Steele, occasion'd by his letter to a member of Parliament, concerning the bill for preventing the growth of schism, by a member of the Church of England. 1714. Probably by Defoe.

The remedy worse than the disease: or reasons against passing the bill for preventing the growth of schism. 1714.

The weakest go to the wall, or the Dissenters sacrific'd by all parties. 1714.

A brief survey of the legal liberties of the Dissenters, and how far the bill now depending consists with preserving the toleration inviolably, wherein the present bill is publish'd; and also the Toleration Act at large, that they may be compar'd with one another. 1714, Edinburgh 1714.

The Schism act explain'd: wherein some methods are laid down how the Dissenters may teach their schools and academies as usual, without incurring the penalties of the said act. 1714.

The secret history of the white staff: being an account of affairs under the conduct of some late Ministers, and of what might probably have happened if her Majesty had not died. 1714 (4 edns); pt II, 1714 (3 edns), Dublin 1714; pt III, 1715. The 3 pts were subsequently included in one pamphlet.

Advice to the people of Great Britain, with respect to two important points of their future conduct: I, What they ought to expect from the King; II, How they ought to behave by him. 1714, Dublin 1714.

A secret history of one year. 1714; rptd in Somers tracts vol 13, 1815.

Tories and Tory principles ruinous to both prince and people: being a specimen of the inconsistency of their pretended principles and real practices. 1714. Probably by Defoe.

Impeachment, or no impeachment: or an enquiry how far the impeachment of certain persons, at the present juncture, would be consistent with honour and justice. 1714. Probably by Defoe.

The Bristol riot. 1714. Perhaps by Defoe.

The pernicious consequences of the clergy's intermedling with affairs of state, with reasons humbly offer'd for passing a bill to incapacitate them from the like practice for the future. [1714?].

A full and impartial account of the late disorders in Bristol, to which is added the compleat tryals of the rioters before Mr Justice Powys, Mr Justice Tracey and Mr Baron Price. 1714. Perhaps by Defoe.

The secret history of the secret history of the white staff, purse and mitre. 1715.

Strike while the iron's hot: or now is the time to be happy, humbly propos'd upon his Majesty's late most gracious injunction. 1715.

Memoirs of the conduct of her late Majesty and her last Ministry, relating to the separate peace with France, by the Right Honourable the Countess of ——. 1715.

Treason detected, in an answer to that traiterous and malicious libel, entitled English advice to the freeholders of England humbly offer'd to the consideration of all those freeholders who have been poyson'd with that malignant pamphlet. 1715, 1715.

The immorality of the priesthood. 1715. Also pbd without preface as The justice and necessity of restraining the clergy in their preaching. Probably by Oldmixon.

The secret history of state intrigues in the management of the scepter, in the late reign. 1715. Also pbd as The secret history of the scepter.

The candidate: being a detection of bribery and corruption as it is just now in practice all over Great Britain, in order to make members of Parliament, humbly recommended to all those who are now keeping Christmas at the expence of their representatives; they that will buy, will sell. 1715.

A reply to a traiterous libel entituled English advice to the freeholders of Great Britain. 1715.

The Protestant jubilee: a thanksgiving sermon on that doubly remarkable day the 20 of January, appointed for celebrating the praises of God, for our wonderful deliverance, by the happy accession of his most gracious Majesty King George to the throne of Great Britain, when we were just at the brink of ruin. 1714 (for 1715).

A letter to a merry young gentleman intituled Tho. Burnet esq, in answer to one writ by him to the right honourable the Earl of Halifax: by which it plainly appears, the said Squire was not awake when he writ the said letter. 1715 (3 edns). Sometimes attributed to W. Oldisworth.

Burnet and Bradbury: or the confederacy of the press and pulpit for the blood of the last ministry. 1715, 1715.

A view of the present management of the Court of France, and what new measures they are like to take. 1715.

The fears of the Pretender turn'd into the fears of debauchery, propos'd, without ceremony, to the consideration of the lords spiritual and temporal; with a hint to Richard Steele esq. 1715 (3 edns).

A friendly epistle by way of reproof from one of the people called Quakers, to Thomas Bradbury, a dealer in many words. 1715 (6 edns).

Reflections upon Sacheverell's sermons of January 20 and 31 1715: a sermon preach'd January 11 1714/5, by Henry Sacheverell DD Rector of St Andrew's Holborn. 1715. Remarks, preface and postscript by Defoe.

An appeal to honour and justice, tho' it be of his worst enemies, by Daniel De Foe: being a true account of his conduct in publick affairs. 1715; rptd in English garner, ed E. Arber vol 7, 1883.

Some reasons offered by the late ministry in defence of their administration. 1715. Probably by Defoe.

The family instructor, in three parts, with a recommendatory letter by the Reverend Mr S. Wright. Newcastle 1715, London 1715 (corrected by the author), 1720 (8th edn), 1725 (10th edn), 1766 (16th edn) etc; vol 2, in two parts, 1718, 1727 (3rd edn), 1766 (8th edn); rptd 5 pts Bungay 1816. The 2 vols were often sold together. *See also* A new family instructor, 1727, below.

A sharp rebuke from one of the people called Quakers to Henry Sacheverell, the high-priest of Andrew's Holbourn, by the same friend that wrote to Thomas Bradbury. 1715.

An apology for the army, in a short essay on fortitude etc, written by an officer. 1715.

The second-sighted Highlander: being four visions of the eclypse, and something of what may follow. 1715.

Some methods to supply the defects of the late peace without entring into a new war. [1715].

A remonstrance from some country Whigs to a member of a secret committee. 1715. Probably by Defoe.

The happiness of the Hanover succession, illustrated from the conduct of the late administration, wherein their designs are farther expos'd, and publick justice demanded upon the betrayers of our Constitution. 1715. Perhaps by Defoe.

An attempt towards a coalition of English Protestants, from the weakness of the pretensions of the several parties, for being either better Christians, or better subjects, upon any principles wherein they differ; to which is added reasons for restraining the licentiousness of the pulpit and press. 1715.

A seasonable expostulation with, and friendly reproof unto James Butler who, by the men of this world, is stil'd Duke of O[rmon]d, relating to the tumults of the people, by the same friend that wrote to Thomas Bradbury, the dealer in many words, and Henry Sacheverell, the high-priest of St Andrew's Holbourn. 1715.

His Majesty's obligations to the Whigs plainly proved, shewing that he can neither with safety, reason or gratitude depart from them. 1715. Probably by Defoe.

A brief history of the pacific campaign in Flanders anno 1712, and of the fatal cessation of arms. 1715.

Some considerations on the danger of the Church from her own clergy, humbly offer'd to the lower-house of Convocation. 1715.

A letter from a gentleman of the church of England, to all the high-flyers of Great Britain. [London 1715], Dublin 1716.

An humble address to our soveraign lord the people. 1715.

The history of the wars, of his present Majesty Charles XII, King of Sweden. 1715, 1720 (with A continuation to the time of his death).

An account of the conduct of Robert Earl of Oxford. 1715, 1717 (as Memoirs of some transactions during the late Ministry of Robert E. of Oxford).

A hymn to the mob. 1715.

Hanover or Rome: shewing the absolute necessity of assisting his Majesty. 1715, Dublin 1715.

An account of the great and generous actions of James Butler (late Duke of Ormond), dedicated to the famous University of Oxford. [1715].

A view of the Scots rebellion; with some enquiry what we have to fear from them? 1715.

The traiterous and foolish manifesto of the Scots rebels, examin'd and expos'd paragraph by paragraph. 1715.

Bold advice: or proposals for the entire rooting out of Jacobitism in Great Britain, address'd to the present M[inistr]y. 1715.

An address to the people of England, shewing the unworthiness of their behaviour to King George. 1715. Perhaps by Defoe.

A trumpet blown in the North, and sounded in the ears of John Eriskine, call'd by the men of the world Duke of Mar, by a ministring friend of the people call'd Quakers. 1716 (for 1715).

A letter from one clergy-man to another, upon the subject of the rebellion. 1716 (for 1715). Probably by Defoe.

A conference with a Jacobite, wherein the clergy of the Church of England are vindicated from the charge of hypocrisy and perjury, in praying for the King, and taking the oaths of allegiance and abjuration. 1716. Probably by Defoe.

Proper lessons for the Tories, to be read throughout the year: but more particularly upon June 10, the birth-day of the Pretender, alias the fugitive hero. 1716. Sometimes as Proper lessons written by a Quaker.

Some account of the two nights court at Greenwich, wherein may be seen the reason, rise and progress of the late unnatural rebellion, against his sacred Majesty King George and his government. 1716.

The case of the Protestant Dissenters in England, fairly stated, humbly inscrib'd to all true lovers of religion, liberty and their country. 1716. Perhaps by Defoe.

The address of the Episcopal clergy of the Diocese of Aberdeen, to the Pretender, with remarks upon the said address. [1716]. Attributed by J. R. Moore.

The address of the magistrates and Town Council of Aberdeen, to the Pretender, with remarks upon the said address. [1716]. Attributed by J. R. Moore.

Some thoughts of an honest Tory in the country, upon the late dispositions of some people to revolt. 1716.

The conduct of some people, about pleading guilty, with some reasons why it was not thought proper to shew mercy to some who desir'd it. 1716.

An account of the proceedings against the rebels, and other prisoners, tried before the Lord Chief Justice Jefferies, and other judges, in the West of England in 1685 for taking arms under the Duke of Monmouth. 1716 (3 edns).

The proceedings of the government against the rebels, compared with the persecutions of the late reigns. [1716].

Remarks on the speech of James late Earl of Derwentwater, beheaded on Tower-Hill for high-treason, February 24, 1715/16. 1716. Perhaps by Defoe.

An essay upon buying and selling of speeches in a letter to a worshipfull Justice of the Peace, being also a member of a certain worshipfull society of speech-makers. 1716.

Some considerations on a law for triennial Parliaments, with an enquiry 1, Whether there may not be a time when it is necessary to suspend the execution, even of such laws as are most essential to the liberties of the people?; 11, Whether this is such a time or no? 1716, 1716, Edinburgh 1716, Dublin 1716.

The Triennial Act impartially stated. 1716. Ascribed by Boyer in Political State April 1716; denied by Defoe, Mercurius Politicus July 1717.

Arguments about the alteration of triennial elections of Parliament, in a letter to a friend in the country. 1716. Unlike Defoe's style, but claimed by him in Mercurius Politicus July 1717.

The ill consequences of repealing the Triennial Act in a letter to Mr Sh[ippe]n. 1716. Probably by Defoe.

A dialogue between a Whig and a Jacobite, upon the subject of the late rebellion and the execution of the rebel-lords etc, occasion'd by the phaenomenon in the skie, March 6 1715–1716. 1716. Probably by Defoe.

A true account of the proceedings at Perth; the debates in the street council there; with the reasons and causes of the suddain finishing and breaking up of the rebellion, written by a rebel. 1716, 1716, Edinburgh [1716] (abstract); rptd in Spottiswoode miscellany vol 2, 1845 (attributed to the Master of Sinclair).

Remarks on the speeches of William Paul Clerk, and John Hall of Otterburn esq, executed at Tyburn for rebellion, the 13th of July 1716. 1716 (3 edns).

The annals of King George, year the second: being a faithful history of the affairs of Great Britain for the year MDCCXVI, containing also a full and complete history of the rebellion. 1717 (for 1716). Vol 2 as The annals of King George, but the general history of Europe during that time, 1718 (for 1717). Written in part and ed Defoe.

The layman's vindication of the Church of England, as well against Mr Howell's charge of schism, as against Dr Bennett's pretended answer to it. 1716.

Secret memoirs of the new treaty of alliance with France, in which some of the first steps in that remarkable affair are discovered, with some characters of persons. 1716, Dublin 1716.

Secret memoirs of a treasonable conference at S[omerset] House, for deposing the present Ministry and making a new turn at Court. 1717, 1717.

Some national grievances considered in a letter to R[obert] W[alpole]. 1717. Perhaps by Defoe.

The danger of Court differences: or the unhappy effects of a motley ministry, occasion'd by the report of changes at Court. 1717.

The quarrel of the school-boys at Athens, as lately acted at a school near Westminster. 1717.

Faction in power: or the mischiefs and dangers of a High-Church magistracy. 1717. Probably by Defoe.

An impartial enquiry into the conduct of the Right Honourable Charles Lord Viscount T[ownshend]. 1717.

An argument proving that the design of employing and enobling foreigners is a treasonable conspiracy against the Constitution, dangerous to the Kingdom, an affront to the nobility of Scotland in particular and dishonourable to the peerage of Britain in general. 1717.

An account of the Swedish and Jacobite plot, with a vindication of our government from the horrid aspersions of its enemies. 1717. Probably by Defoe.

A curious little oration deliver'd by Father Andrew. 1717, 1717.

An expostulatory letter, to the B[ishop] of B[angor] concerning a book lately publish'd by his Lordship entitul'd A preservative against the principles and practices of the Nonjurors etc. [1717].

Fair payment no spunge: or some considerations on the unreasonableness of refusing to receive back money lent on publick securities, and the necessity of setting the nation free from the insupportable burthen of debt and taxes. 1717.

What if the Swedes should come? with some thoughts about keeping the army on foot, whether they come or not. 1717.

The question fairly stated, whether now is not the time to do justice to the friends of the government as well as to its enemies? 1717.

Christianity no creature of the state: or if it be made one, reasons why it should be abolish'd, by the author of the Case of the Protestant Dissenters in England. 1717. Perhaps by Defoe.

The danger and consequences of disobliging the clergy consider'd, as it relates to making a law for regulating the universities, and repealing some laws which concern the Dissenters. 1717.

Reasons for a royal visitation, occasion'd by the present great defection of the clergy from the government. 1717. Probably by Defoe.

Memoirs of the Church of Scotland, in four periods, with an appendix of some transactions since the union. 1717, 1734.

A farther argument against ennobling foreigners, in answer to the two parts of the state anatomy; with a short account of the anatomizer. 1717.

The conduct of Robert Walpole esq, from the beginning of the reign of her late Majesty Queen Anne to the present time. 1717.

The report reported: or the weakness and injustice of the proceedings of the convocation in their censure of the Ld Bp of Bangor examin'd and expos'd. 1717, 1717. Probably by Defoe.

A short view of the conduct of the King of Sweden. [1717].

A general pardon consider'd, in its circumstances and consequences, particularly relating to the exceptions said to be now in debate, and to the reason why it came out no sooner. 1717. Probably by Defoe.

Observation on the Bishop's answer to Dr Snape, by a lover of truth. 1717.

A vindication of Dr Snape, in answer to several libels lately publish'd against him. [1717]. Probably by Defoe.

A reply to the remarks upon the Lord Bishop of Bangor's treatment of the clergy and convocation, said to be written by Dr Sherlock. 1717.

Minutes of the negotiations of Monsr Mesnager at the Court of England towards the close of the last reign. 1717.

Memoirs of some transactions during the late Ministry of Robert E. of Oxford. 1717.

A declaration of truth to Benjamin Hoadly, one of the high priests of the land, and of the degree whom men call Bishops, by a ministring friend, who writ to Tho. Bradbury, a dealer in many words. 1717.

A history of the clemency of our English monarchs, from the Reformation, down to the present time, with some comparisons. 1717. Probably by Defoe.

The conduct of Christians made the sport of infidels, in a letter from a Turkish merchant at Amsterdam to the Grand Mufti at Constantinople, on occasion of some of our national follies, but especially the late scandalous quarrel among the clergy. 1717.

The old Whig and modern Whig revived, in the present divisions at Court: or the difference betwixt acting upon principle and interest exemplified by some of our present patriots. 1717. Probably by Defoe.

A letter to Andrew Snape, occasion'd by the strife that lately appeared among the people call'd, clergy-men, by the author of the Declaration of truth. 1717.

The case of the war in Italy stated: being a serious enquiry how far Great-Britain is engaged to concern it self in the quarrel between the Emperor and the King of Spain. 1718 (for 1717).

Considerations on the present state of affairs in Great-Britain. 1718, 1718 (as The juncture: or considerations on his Majesty's speech).

The defection farther consider'd, wherein the resigners, as some would have them stil'd, are really deserters. 1718, 1718.

Some persons vindicated against the author of the Defection etc [Tindal], and that writer convicted of malice and falsehood R[obert] W[alpole] esq. 1718.

Memoirs of the life and eminent conduct of that learned and reverend divine Daniel Williams DD. 1718.

Mr de la Pillonniere's vindication: being an answer to the two schoolmasters, and their boys tittle tattle, wherein the dispute between Dr Snape and Mr Pillonniere is set in a true light, by the author of the Lay-man's vindication. 1718.

A brief answer to a long libel: being an examination of a heap of scandal, published by the author of the scourge, entituled the Danger of the Church's establishment, from the insolence of Protestant Dissenters. 1718. Perhaps by Defoe.

A letter from the Jesuists to Father de la Pillonniere, in answer to the letter sent to them by that Father, and published by Dr Snape in his Vindication etc. 1718.

A golden mine of treasure open'd for the Dutch, by a lover of Britain. 1718. Probably by Defoe.

Miserere cleri, or the factions of the Church: being a short view of the pernicious consequences of the clergy intermedling with affairs of State. [1718], 1718.

Some reasons why it could not be expected the government wou'd permit the speech or paper of James Shepheard, which he delivered at the place of execution, to be printed. 1718. Probably by Defoe.

The Jacobites detected, in the methods they made use of

to draw young men into an association against his Majesty King George. 1718. Perhaps by Defoe.

Dr Sherlock's vindication of the Test Act examin'd, and the false foundations of it exposed, in answer to so much of his book against the Bishop of Bangor, as relates to the Protestant Dissenters. 1718. Perhaps by Defoe.

A brief comment upon his Majesty's speech: being reasons for strengthening the Church of England by taking off the penal laws against Dissenters, by one called a Low-Church-Man. 1718. Perhaps by Defoe.

A vindication of the press: or an essay on the usefulness of writing, on criticism, and the qualification of authors. 1718; ed O. C. Williams, Los Angeles 1951 (Augustan Reprint Soc).

A letter from some Protestant dissenting laymen, in the behalf of that whole body, to their friends of the British Parliament, concerning their treatment under the present administration. 1718. Probably by Defoe.

Memoirs of publick transactions in the life and ministry of his Grace the D. of Shrewsbury. 1718.

A letter from Paris, giving an account of the death of the late Queen Dowager, and of her disowning the Pretender to be her son, with some observations. 1718. Probably by Defoe.

A history of the last session of the present Parliament, with a correct list of both Houses. 1718.

A letter to the author of the Flying-post, in answer to a most malicious false story of his from Edinburgh; and to a celebrated deistical letter of his from the Grecian coffee-house. 1718.

A continuation of Letters written by a Turkish spy at Paris. 1718.

The history of the reign of King George, from the death of her late Majesty Queen Anne, to the first of August 1718, collected from the most authentick vouchers, to be continued yearly. 1719 (for 1718).

The memoirs of Majr Alexander Ramkins, a High-land-officer, now in prison at Avignon: being an account of several remarkable adventures during about twenty eight years service in Scotland, Germany, Italy, Flanders and Ireland. 1719 (for 1718).

A friendly rebuke to one Parson Benjamin [Hoadly]; particularly relating to his quarreling with his own church, and vindicating the Dissenters. 1719.

Observations and remarks upon the declaration of war against Spain, and upon the manifesto publish'd in the name of the King of France, explaining the said declaration. 1719. Probably by Defoe.

Merry Andrew's epistle to his old master Benjamin, a mountebank at Bangor-Bridge, on the River Dee, near Wales. 1719. Perhaps by Defoe.

The life and strange surprizing adventures of Robinson Crusoe, of York, mariner, written by himself. 1719 (4 edns), 1720, 1722 etc; ed A. Dobson 1883 (facs); ed J. D. Crowley, Oxford 1972.

A letter to the Dissenters. 1719.

The anatomy of exchange-alley: or a system of stock-jobbing, proving that scandalous trade, as it is now carry'd on, to be knavish in its private practice, and treason in its publick, by a jobber. 1719, 1719; rptd J. Francis in Chronicles and characters of the stock exchange, 1849.

Some account of the life and most remarkable actions of George Henry Baron de Goertz, Privy-Counsellor and Chief Minister of State, to the late King of Sweden. 1719.

The just complaint of the poor weavers truly represented. 1719.

The farther adventures of Robinson Crusoe: being the second and last part of his life. 1719, 1719, 1722.

A brief state of the question, between the printed and painted callicoes and the woollen and silk manufacture, as far as it relates to the wearing and using of printed and painted callicoes in Great-Britain. 1719, 1719, 1720.

Charity still a Christian virtue: or an impartial account of

the tryal and conviction of the Reverend Mr Hendley for preaching a charity-sermon at Chisselhurst. 1719.

The dumb philosopher: or Great Britain's wonder, containing 1: A faithful and very surprizing account how Dickory Cronke, a tinner's son in the county of Cornwal, was born dumb, and continued so for 58 years; and how some days before he died, he came to his speech. 1719, 1719.

[The petition of Dorothy Distaff etc to Mrs Rebecca Woollpack]. [1719?]; rptd in Mercurius Politicus Dec 1719.

The king of pirates: being an account of the famous enterprises of Captain Avery, the mock King of Madagascar, with his rambles and piracies; wherein all the sham accounts formerly publish'd of him, are detected. 1720 (for 1719), 1720.

An historical account of the voyages and adventures of Sir Walter Raleigh, with the discoveries and conquests he made for the crown of England. 1719 (for 1720).

The chimera: or the French way of paying national debts laid open. 1720.

The case of the fair traders, humbly represented to the honourable the House of Commons: being a clear view and state of clandestine trade, as now carry'd on in Great Britain. [1720]. Attributed by J. R. Moore.

The trade to India critically and calmly consider'd, and prov'd to be destructive to the general trade of Great Britain as well as to the woollen and silk manufacturers in particular. 1720.

The case fairly stated between the Turky Company and the Italian merchants, by a merchant. 1720, 1720.

The compleat art of painting: a poem translated from the French of M. du Fresnoy, by D.F. gent. 1720. Defoe's initials and one of his publishers, but few other signs of his hand.

A letter to the author of the Independent Whig, wherein the merits of the clergy are consider'd, the good vindicated, and the bad expos'd. 1720. Perhaps by Defoe.

The history of the life and adventures of Mr Duncan Campbell, a gentleman who, tho' deaf and dumb, writes down any stranger's name at first sight; with their future contingencies of fortune. 1720, 1720, 1732, 1739, 1748; 1728 (as The supernatural philosopher by William Bond). Always attributed to Defoe, perhaps in part or entirely by Bond.

Memoirs of a Cavalier: or a military journal of the wars in Germany, and the wars in England, from the year 1632 to the year 1648. [1720], Edinburgh 1759, 1766, 1788; ed J. T. Boulton, Oxford 1972.

The life, adventures and pyracies of the famous Captain Singleton. 1720, 1721, 1737, 1768, 1810, 1887 etc, 1800 (abridged); ed S. K. Kumar, Oxford 1973.

Serious reflections during the life and surprising adventures of Robinson Crusoe, with his vision of the angelick world. 1720.

The South-Sea scheme examin'd; and the reasonableness thereof demonstrated. 1720 (3 edns). Probably by Defoe.

A true state of the contracts relating to the third money-subscription taken by the South-Sea Company. 1721.

A vindication of the honour and justice of Parliament against a most scandalous libel entituled the Speech of John A[islabie] esq. [1721].

Brief observations on trade and manufactures; and particularly of our mines and metals and the hard-ware works. 1721.

Some account of the life of Sir Charles Sedley by an eminent hand. Prefixed to vol 1 of Works of Sir Charles Sedley, 1722 (for 1721).

The case of Mr Law, truly stated, in answer to a pamphlet, entitul'd A letter to Mr Law. 1721.

A collection of miscellany letters, selected out of Mist's weekly journal. 4 vols 1722, 1722, 1727, 1727. Defoe contributed to and probably edited this work.

The fortunes and misfortunes of the famous Moll Flanders, written from her own memorandums. 1721 (for 1722),

1722, 1722 (rev), 1723, 1740, 1741, 1759 etc; 1723 (abridged, with added ch), 1730 (as Fortune's fickle distribution) (with continuation of the lives of her husband and governess), 1776 (as The history of Laetitia Atkins); chap-books c. 1750, c. 1760, c. 1770 etc; ed H. Davis, Oxford 1961 (WC) (from 1721); ed G. A. Starr, Oxford 1971.

Due preparations for the plague as well for soul as body: being some seasonable thoughts upon the visible approach of the present dreadful contagion in France. 1722.

Religious courtship: being historical discourses, on the necessity of marrying religious husbands and wives only. 1722, 1729, 1734, 1735, 1737 etc, 1789 ('21st edn'), 1797 etc.

A journal of the plague year: being observations or memorials of the most remarkable occurrences, as well publick as private, which happened in London during the last great visitation in 1665. 1722, 1754 (as The history of the great plague in London), 1832, 1832?, 1835, 1840, 1863 etc; 1795 (abridged), 1824, 1886 etc; ed L. A. Landa, Oxford 1969.

A brief debate upon the dissolving the late Parliament. 1722.

An impartial history of the life and actions of Peter Alexowitz, the present Czar of Muscovy, from his birth down to this present time, written by a British officer in the service of the Czar. 1723 (for 1722), 1725 (with addns, as A true, authentick and impartial history of the Czar).

The history and remarkable life of the truly honourable Col Jacque, commonly call'd Col Jack. 1723 (for 1722), 1723, 1724, 1738, 1810 etc; 1809 (abridged), 1813; ed S. H. Monk, Oxford 1965.

A memorial to the clergy of the Church of England, relating to their conduct since the Revolution; together with some advice to them upon the present state of affairs, by a clergyman. 1723. Probably by Defoe.

The fortunate mistress: or a history of the life and vast variety of fortunes of Mademoiselle de Beleau, afterwards call'd the Countess de Wintselsheim, in Germany, being the person known by the name of the lady Roxana, in the time of King Charles II. [1724], [1745?], 1750 (with anon continuation partly from E. Hayward's British recluse), 1755, 1923; ed W. Cather, New York 1924; ed R. B. Johnson [1926]; ed J. Jack, Oxford 1964.

The great law of subordination consider'd; or the insolence and unsufferable behaviour of servants in England duly enquir'd into, in ten familiar letters. 1724, 1726 (reissued as The behaviour of servants in England inquired into).

A general history of the robberies and murders of the most notorious pyrates, and also their policies, discipline and government, from their first rise and settlement in the island of Providence, in 1717, to the present year 1724, by Captain Charles Johnson. 1724, 1724, 1725 (reissued with addns), 1726 etc; Dublin 1727 (abridged); ed P. Gosse 1925; Vol 2 as The history of the pyrates, 1728, 1729; ed A. L. Hayward 1926. A fictional section excerpted as Of Captain Mission, ed M. E. Novak, Los Angeles 1961 (Augustan Reprint Soc.)

A tour thro' the whole island of Great Britain, divided into circuits or journies: giving a particular and diverting account of whatever is curious and worth observation, by a gentleman. [Vol 1] 1724; vol 2, 1725; vol 3, 1727 (for 1726); 3 vols 1738 (rev S. Richardson?), 4 vols 1742, 1748, 1753, 1761–2, 1769, 1778; ed G. D. H. Cole 2 vols 1927; ed P. Rogers 1971 (Pelican)(abridged).

The royal progress: or a historical view of the journeys or progresses, which several great princes have made to visit their dominions. 1724.

[Letter about the King's intended progress]. Rptd in Political State, ed A. Boyer, June 1724.

A narrative of the proceedings in France, for discovering and detecting the murderers of the English gentlemen, September 21 1723, near Calais, translated from the French. 1724, 1724, 1725.

A narrative of all the robberies, escapes etc of John Sheppard: giving an exact description of the manner of his wonderful escape from the castle in Newgate, written by himself during his confinement. 1724 (8 edns); ed H. Bleackley as Jack Sheppard, [1933].

Some farther account of the original disputes in Ireland, about farthings and halfpence, in a discourse with a Quaker of Dublin. 1724.

The history of the remarkable life of John Sheppard, containing a particular account of his many robberies and escapes. [1724] (3 edns), [1724?]; ed H. Bleackley as Jack Sheppard, [1933].

A new voyage round the world, by a course never sailed before. 1725 (for 1724), 3 vols 1787, 2 vols Edinburgh 1810.

An epistle from Jack Sheppard to the late L[or]d C[hance]l-l[o]r of E[nglan]d, who when Sheppard was try'd, sent for him to the Chancery Bar. [1725]. Perhaps by Defoe.

The life of Jonathan Wild, from his birth to his death, containing his rise and progress in roguery, by H.D. late clerk to Justice R——. 1725, 1725.

Every-body's business is no-body's business: or private abuses, publick grievances; exemplified in the pride, insolence and exorbitant wages of our women-servants, footmen etc, by Andrew Moreton esq. 1725 (5 edns, 5th edn with a preface).

The true and genuine account of the life and actions of the late Jonathan Wild, not made up of fiction and fable, but taken from his own mouth. 1725; ed W. Follett, New York 1926 (with Fielding's novel).

An account of the conduct and proceedings of the late John Gow alias Smith, Captain of the late pirates. [1725]; ed J. R. Russell 1890.

The complete English tradesman, in familiar letters; directing him in all the several parts and progressions of trade. 1726 (for 1725), Dublin 1726, 1727 (for 1726) (with suppl; suppl issued separately, dated 1727), 1732; vol 2, 1727 (as The compleat English tradesman). Both vols 1732, 1738, 1745, Edinburgh 1839 (with notes).

A general history of discoveries and improvements, in useful arts, particularly in the great branches of commerce, navigation and plantation, in all parts of the known world. 4 monthly pts Oct 1725–Jan 1726; 1727 (for 1726) (bound together as The history of the principal discoveries and improvements, in the several arts and sciences).

A brief case of the distillers, and of the distilling trade in England, shewing how far it is the interest of England to encourage the said trade. 1726.

A brief historical account of the lives of the six notorious street-robbers, executed at Kingston, viz William Blewet, Edward Bunworth, Emanuel Dickenson, Thomas Berry, John Higges and John Legee. 1726.

An essay upon literature: or an enquiry into the antiquity and original of letters; proving that the two tables, written by the finger of God in Mount Sinai, was the first writing in the world. 1726.

The political history of the Devil, as well ancient as modern: in two parts. 1726, 1727 (with new preface), 1734 etc.

Unparallel'd cruelty: or the tryal of Captain Jeane of Bristol, who was convicted at the Old Bailey for the murder of his cabbin-boy. 1726.

The friendly daemon, or the generous apparition: being a true narrative of a miraculous cure, newly perform'd upon that famous deaf and dumb gentleman Dr Duncan Campbell, by a familiar spirit that appear'd to him in a white surplice, like a cathedral singing boy. 1726.

The four years voyages of Capt George Roberts: being a series of uncommon events, which befell him in a voyage to the islands of the Canaries, Cape de Verde and Barbadoes, from whence he was bound to the coast of Guiney. 1726.

Mere nature delineated, or a body without a soul: being observations upon the young forester lately brought to town from Germany; also a brief dissertation upon the usefulness and necessity of fools, whether political or natural. 1726.

Some considerations upon street-walkers, with a proposal for lessening the present number of them, in two letters to a Member of Parliament. [1726].

The Protestant monastery: or a complaint against the brutality of the present age, particularly the pertness and insolence of our youth to aged persons, by Andrew Moreton esq. 1727 (for 1726), 1731 (for 1730) (with new preface and postscript as Chickens feed capons: or a dissertation on the pertness of our youth in general) (4 edns).

A system of magick, or a history of the black art: being an historical account of mankind's most early dealing with the Devil; and how the acquaintance on both sides first began. 1727 (for 1726), 1728, 1729, 1731.

The evident approach of a war, and something of the necessity of it, in order to establish peace and preserve trade. 1727, 1727.

Conjugal lewdness: or matrimonial whoredom. 1727 (reissued as A treatise concerning the use and abuse of the marriage bed); ed M. E. Novak, Gainesville 1967.

The evident advantages to Great Britain and its allies from the approaching war, especially in matters of trade. 1727.

A brief deduction of the original, progress and immense greatness of the British woolen manufacture. 1727.

An essay on the history and reality of apparitions. 1727, 1728 (as The secrets of the invisible world disclos'd: or an universal history of apparitions), 1729, 1735, 1738, 1740 etc.

A new family instructor, in familiar discourses between a father and his children, on the most essential points of the Christian religion, in two parts, with a poem upon the divine nature of Jesus Christ, in blank verse, by the author of the Family instructor. 1727, 1742.

Parochial tyranny: or the house-keeper's complaint against the insupportable exactions, and partial assessments of select vestries etc, by Andrew Moreton esq. [1727].

Some considerations on the reasonableness and necessity of encreasing and encouraging the seamen, founded on the gracious expressions, in their favour, contain'd in his Majesty's speech from the throne. 1728.

Augusta triumphans: or the way to make London the most flourishing city in the universe. 1728, 1731 (for 1730) (rev as The generous projector: or a friendly proposal to prevent murder and other enormous abuses).

A plan of the English commerce: being a compleat prospect of the trade of this nation, as well the home trade as the foreign, in three parts. 1728, 1730 (with appendix on foreign trade).

The memoirs of an English officer who serv'd in the Dutch war in 1672, to the peace of Utrecht in 1713, by Capt George Carleton. 1728, 1740 (as A true and genuine history of the last two wars), 1743 (as The memoirs of Cap George Carleton); ed W. Scott 1808. Probably largely by a real G. Carleton.

Atlas maritimus and commercialis: or a general view of the world, so far as it relates to trade and navigation; describing all the coasts, ports, harbours and noted rivers, according to the latest discoveries and most exact observations. 1728.

An impartial account of the late famous siege of Gibraltar; to which are added most accurate plans of the town, and of the approaches and camp of the Spaniards, with many remarkable transactions never made publick before, by an officer. 1728.

Second thoughts are best: or a further improvement of a late scheme to prevent street robberies; by which our streets will be so strongly guarded, and so gloriously illuminated, that any part of London will be as safe and pleasant at midnight as at noonday; and burglary totally impracticable, by Andrew Moreton esq. 1729 (for 1728).

Street-robberies consider'd: the reason of their being so frequent, with probable means to prevent 'em, written

by a converted thief; to which is prefix'd some memoirs of his life. [1728].

Reasons for a war, in order to establish the tranquillity and commerce of Europe. 1729.

The unreasonableness and ill consequences of imprisoning the body for debt, prov'd from the laws of God and nature, human policy and interest, address'd to a noble lord. 1729.

An humble proposal to the people of England, for the encrease of their trade, and encouragement of their manufactures; whether the present uncertainty of affairs issues in peace or war, by the author of the Compleat tradesman. 1729.

An enquiry into the pretensions of Spain to Gibraltar, together with a copy of a letter (said to be sent) to his Catholick Majesty. 1729, 1729.

Some objections humbly offered to the consideration of the hon House of Commons, relating to the present intended relief of prisoners. 1729.

The advantages of peace and commerce; with some remarks on the East-India trade. 1729.

Madagascar: or Robert Drury's journal, during fifteen years captivity on that island, written by himself, digested into order, and now publish'd at the request of his friends. 1729, 1731, 1743, 1750 etc. Edited and written in part by Defoe.

A brief state of the inland or home trade of England, and of the oppressions it suffers and the dangers which threaten it from the invasion of hawkers, pedlars and clandestine traders of all sorts. 1730.

The perjur'd Free Mason detected, and yet the honour and antiquity of the Society of Free Masons preserv'd and defended, by a Free Mason. 1730.

An effectual scheme for the immediate preventing of street robberies, and suppressing all other disorders of the night. 1731 (for 1730).

The compleat English gentleman. Ed K. D. Bülbring 1890.

Of royall educacion: a fragmentary treatise. Ed K. D. Bülbring 1895.

The meditations (1681). Ed G. H. Healey, Cummington Mass 1946.

Periodicals

For Review and Manufacturer, Defoe probably wrote almost every line; for the journals of Mist and Applebee, he was only an occasional contributor and editor.

A review of the affairs of France: and of all Europe. 9 vols 19 Feb 1704–11 June 1713; ed A. W. Secord 22 vols New York 1938; Index by W. L. Payne, New York 1948.

The London post. 25 Sept 1704?–8 June 1705. Defoe's hand is not evident until 6 Dec 1704.

The Edinburgh courant. 24 Sept 1708–July 1709 (and perhaps for a period after 15 May 1710).

The London post-man. 1706–8. Occasional contributions.

The Newcastle gazette: or northern courant. Dec 1710. Some connection with Defoe.

The Scots postman. 27 Oct–end of 1710.

The observator. 19 July–11 Oct 1710.

Mercator: or commerce retrieved. 26 May 1713–20 July 1714.

The monitor. 22 April–21 Aug 1714.

The flying post: and medley. 27 July–21 Aug 1714.

The flying post. Occasional contributions? *See* [Two letters to the author of the flying-post], rptd in Political State, ed A. Boyer, Aug 1724.

Mercurius politicus. May 1716–Oct 1720.

[Dormer's news letter. June 1716–Aug 1718?]. Suppositious title and dates for a journal Defoe edited at this time.

The weekly-journal: or Saturday's evening post. (Mist's weekly-journal). c. Feb 1717–24 Oct 1724.

The weekly journal: being an auxiliary packet to the Saturday's post. 25 Sept–23 Oct 1717.
Mercurius britannicus. Jan 1718–March 1719.
The White-Hall evening post. 18 Sept 1718–c. 14 Oct 1720.
The daily post. 3 Oct 1719–c. 27 April 1725.
The manufacturer. 30 Oct–17 Feb 1720.
The commentator. 1 Jan–16 Sept 1720.
The original weekly journal (later called Applebee's original weekly journal). 25 June 1720–14 May 1726 (and occasionally after).
The director. 5 Oct 1720–16 Jan 1721. In part and perhaps wholly by Defoe.
The citizen. 18 Sept–17 Nov 1727. Perhaps Defoe.
The universal spectator and weekly journal. 12 Oct 1728.
Fog's weekly journal. 11 Jan 1729.
The political state of Great-Britain. Dec 1729–Oct 1730.

Letters

Letters. Ed G. H. Healey, Oxford 1955.

§ 2

For early criticism see Defoe: the critical heritage, ed P. Rogers 1973.
Gildon, C. The life and surprising adventures of D— D— F—. 1719; ed P. Dottin as Robinson Crusoe examin'd and criticis'd, 1923.
Rousseau, J.–J. In his Emile, Amsterdam 1762. On Crusoe.
Chalmers, G. Life of Defoe. 1785, 1790 (first separate edn with author's name and bibliography); also prefixed to his edn of Defoe's History of the Union, 1786.
Scott, W. In his Miscellaneous works vol 4, Edinburgh 1827.
Wilson, W. Memoirs of the life and times of Defoe. 3 vols 1830. With contributions by C. Lamb.
Stephen, L. Defoe's novels. In his Hours in a library ser 1, 1874. Rptd from Cornhill Mag 1868.
Woolf, V. In her Common reader, 1925.
—— Robinson Crusoe. In her Second common reader, 1932.
Sutherland, J. R. Defoe. 1937, 1954 (rev).
—— Defoe. 1954 (Br Council pamphlet).
—— The relation of Defoe's fiction to his non-fictional writings. In Imagined worlds, ed M. Mack and I. Gregor 1968.
—— Defoe: a critical study. Oxford 1971.
Moore, J. R. Defoe in the pillory and other studies. Bloomington 1939.
—— Defoe: citizen of the modern world. Chicago 1958.
Payne, W. L. Mr Review: Defoe as author of the Review. New York 1947.
Watt, I. The naming of characters in Defoe, Richardson and Fielding. RES 25 1949.
—— Robinson Crusoe as myth. EC 1951.
—— Defoe as novelist. In A Pelican guide to English literature vol 4, ed B. Ford 1954.
—— In his Rise of the novel, 1957.
—— Serious reflections on the Rise of the novel. Novel 1 1968.
Baine, R. M. Defoe and the supernatural. Athens Georgia 1968.
Novak, M.E. Economics and the fiction of Defoe. Berkeley 1962.
—— Defoe and the nature of man. Oxford 1963.
Starr, G. A. Defoe and spiritual autobiography. Princeton 1965.
Ellis, F. H. (ed). Twentieth-century interpretations of Robinson Crusoe. Englewood Cliffs NJ 1969.
Richetti, J. J. Defoe's narratives. Oxford 1975.
Earle, P. The world of Defoe. 1976.

SAMUEL RICHARDSON
1689–1761

Bibliographies

Sale, W. M. Richardson: a bibliographical record of his literary career with historical notes. New Haven 1936.

Collections

The works, with a sketch of life and writings by E. Mangin. 19 vols 1811.
The novels; to which is prefixed a memoir of the life of the author [by Sir Walter Scott]. 3 vols 1824 (Ballantyne's Novelist's Lib vols 6–8).
The novels. 18 vols Oxford 1929–31.

§ 1

The apprentice's vade mecum. 1734 (for 1733).
A seasonable examination of the pleas and pretensions of the proprietors of, and subscribers to, play-houses, erected in defiance of the royal licence. 1735.
Aesop's fables. 1740 (for 1739), [1747?], [1753].
The negotiations of Sir Thomas Roe, in his embassy to the Ottoman Porte. 1740. Co-edited by Richardson, the dedication signed by him.
Pamela: or virtue rewarded. 2 vols 1741 (for 1740), 1741 (4 edns); vols 3 and 4 (Pamela in her exalted condition), 1742 (for 1741); 4 vols 1742, [1746?], 1754, 1762 (for 1761), 1767, 1772, 1801 (14th edn); abridged [1769?], Edinburgh 1817. Introduction to Pamela, ed S. W. Baker, Los Angeles 1954 (Augustan Reprint Soc).
Letters written to and for particular friends, directing the requisite style and forms to be observed in writing familiar letters. 1741, 1742, 1746, 1750, 1752, 1755; ed B. W. Downs 1928 (as Familiar letters on important occasions).
A tour thro' the whole island of Great Britain [by Defoe]; with very great additions, improvements and corrections [by Richardson]. 4 vols 1742, 1748, 1753, 1761–2.
Clarissa: or the history of a young lady. 7 vols 1748 (for 1747–8), 1749, 8 vols ('in which many passages and some letters are restored from the original manuscripts'), 1751, 1751, 1759, 1764, 1768, 1774, 1784; abridged [1769?]; ed G. Sherburn, Boston 1962.
Clarissa: preface, hints of prefaces, and postscript, ed R. Brissenden, Los Angeles 1964 (Augustan Reprint Soc).
The history of Sir Charles Grandison. 7 vols 1754, 1754, 6 vols 1754, 1762, 1766, 1770, 1776, 1781, 1783, 1796, 1810; abridged [1769?]; ed G. Saintsbury 1895; J. Harris 3 vols Oxford 1972.
The case of Samuel Richardson of London, printer. 1753.
Letter to a lady, who was solicitous for an additional volume to the history of Sir Charles Grandison. 1754.
An address to the public, on the treatment which the editor of the history of Sir Charles Grandison has met with. 1754.
A collection of the moral and instructive sentiments contained in the histories of Pamela, Clarissa and Sir Charles Grandison. 1755.
The paths of virtue delineated: or the history in miniature of the celebrated Pamela, Clarissa Harlowe and Sir Charles Grandison, familiarized and adapted to the capacities of youth. 1756, 1773, 1813 (as Beauties of Richardson).
Six original letters upon duelling. Candid Rev & Literary Repository 1 1765.

Letters

The correspondence of Richardson, selected from the original manuscripts, to which are prefixed a biographical account of the author and observations on the writings. Ed A. L. Barbauld 6 vols 1804.

Selected letters. Ed J. Carroll, Oxford 1964.
The Richardson-Stinstra correspondence and Stinstra's prefaces to Clarissa. Ed W. Slattery 1969.

§ 2

Critical remarks on Sir Charles Grandison, Clarissa and Pamela, by a lover of virtue. 1754; ed A. D. McKillop, Los Angeles 1950 (Augustan Reprint Soc).
Diderot, D. Eloge de Richardson. Journal Etranger Jan 1762.
Hazlitt, W. On the English novelists. In his Lectures on the English comic writers, 1819.
Stephen, L. Richardson's novels. In his Hours in a library ser 1, 1874.
Dobson, A. Samuel Richardson. 1902 (EML)
McKillop, A. D. Richardson, printer and novelist. Chapel Hill 1936.
—— In his Early masters of English fiction, Lawrence Kansas 1956.
Watt, I. The naming of characters in Defoe, Richardson and Fielding. RES 25 1949.
—— In his Rise of the novel, 1957.
—— In The novelist as innovator, ed W. Allen 1965.
Kermode, J. F. Richardson and Fielding. Cambridge Jnl Nov 1950.
Day, R. A. Told in letters: epistolary fiction before Richardson. Ann Arbor 1966.
Eaves, T. C. D. and B. D. Kimpel. Richardson: a biography. Oxford 1971.
Kinkead-Weekes, M. Richardson: dramatic novelist. 1973.
Doody, M. A. A natural passion. Oxford 1974.

HENRY FIELDING

1707–54

Collections

Miscellanies. 3 vols 1743; ed H. K. Miller, Oxford 1972– (Wesleyan edn).
Dramatick works. 2 vols [1745], 3 vols 1755 (with addns).
Works, with the life of the author [by Arthur Murphy]. 4 vols 1762, 8 vols 1762, 12 vols 1766, 8 vols 1771, 12 vols 1771 etc, 1783 (vol 4 adds The fathers: or the good-natured man) etc.
Novels. Ed W. Scott 1821 (Ballantyne's Novelist's Lib).
Complete works. Ed W. E. Henley 16 vols 1903, New York 1967.
Works. Ed G. Saintsbury 12 vols [1926] (Navarre Soc). Illustr G. Cruikshank. The novels only.
Fielding's novels. 10 vols Oxford 1926 (Shakespeare Head edn).
Works. Ed W. B. Coley et al, Oxford and Middletown Conn 1967– (Wesleyan edn). In progress.

§ 1

The masquerade: a poem, inscribed to C[oun]t H[ei]d-[eg]g[e]r, by Lemuel Gulliver, poet laureat to the King of Lilliput. 1728, 1731 (with the Grub-street opera, dedication added); ed C. E. Jones, Liverpool 1960 (in his edn of Female husband and other writings).
Love in several masques: a comedy. (Drury Lane 16 Feb 1728). 1728.
The Temple beau: a comedy. (Goodman's Fields 26 Jan 1730). 1730.
The author's farce; and the pleasures of the town, written by Scriblerus Secundus. (Haymarket 30 March 1730). 1730 (2 printings), 1730, 1750 (text of rev version performed in 1734); ed C. B. Woods, Lincoln Nebraska 1966.
Tom Thumb: a tragedy. (Haymarket 24 April 1730). 1730, 1730 ('written by Scriblerus Secundus', rev), 1730, 1731 (rev as The tragedy of tragedies: or the life and death of Tom Thumb the Great, with the annotations of H. Scriblerus Secundus (Haymarket 24 March

1731), 1737, 1751 etc; ed J. T. Hillhouse, New Haven 1918; ed J. Hampden 1925.
Rape upon rape, or the justice caught in his own trap: a comedy. (Haymarket 23 June 1730). 1730, 1730 (as The coffee-house politician).
A dialogue between a beau's head and his heels, taken from their mouth as they were spoke at St James's Coffee-house. 1731 (in The musical miscellany: being a collection of choice songs and lyrications vol 6).
The letter-writers, or a new way to keep a wife at home: a farce, written by Scriblerus Secundus. (Haymarket 24 March 1731). 1731, 1750.
Epilogue to Lewis Theobald's Orestes. (Lincoln's-Inn Fields 3 April 1731). 1731.
The Welsh opera: or the grey mare the better horse, written by Scriblerus Secundus. (Haymarket 22 April 1731). [1731], 1731 (rev as The genuine Grub-street opera), 1731 (as The Grub-street opera; to which is added The masquerade: a poem, printed in 1728); ed E. V. Roberts, Lincoln Nebraska 1968.
The lottery: a farce. (Drury Lane 1 Jan 1732). 1732, 1732, 1732, 1733, 1748 etc.
Epilogue to Charles Bodens' The modish couple. (Drury Lane 10 Jan 1732). 1732.
The modern husband: a comedy. (Drury Lane 14 Feb 1732). 1732, 1732.
The Covent-Garden tragedy. (Drury Lane 1 June 1732). 1732, 1754 etc.
The old debauchees: a comedy. (Drury Lane 1 June 1732). 1732, 1732, 1745 (as The debauchees: or the Jesuit caught), 1746, 1750.
The mock doctor, or the dumb lady cur'd: a comedy done from Molière. (Drury Lane 23 June 1732). 1732, 1732 (rev), 1734, 1742, 1753 etc; ed J. Hampden [1931]. From Molière, Le médecin malgré lui.
Epilogue to Charles Johnson's Caelia: or the perjur'd lover. (Drury Lane 11 Dec 1732). 1733 (for 1732).
The miser: a comedy taken from Plautus and Molière. (Drury Lane 17 Feb 1733). 1733, 1744, 1754 etc. From Plautus, Aulularia, and Molière, L'avare.
[Deborah: or a wife for you all]. (Drury Lane 6 April 1733). Never pbd. See E. V. Roberts, BNYPL Nov 1962.
The intriguing chambermaid: a comedy of two acts, taken from the French of Regnard. (Drury Lane 15 Jan 1734). 1734, 1750. From Regnard, Le retour imprévu.
Don Quixote in England: a comedy. (Haymarket 5 April 1734). 1734, 1754 etc.
An old man taught wisdom, or the virgin unmask'd: a farce. (Drury Lane 6 Jan 1735). 1735, 1735 (with fewer songs), 1742, 1749 etc.
The universal gallant, or the different husbands: a comedy. (Drury Lane 10 Feb 1735). 1735.
Pasquin, a dramatick satire on the times: being the rehearsal of two plays, viz a comedy call'd the Election; and a tragedy call'd the Life and death of Common-Sense. (Haymarket 5 March 1736). 1736, 1737, 1740, 1754.
Tumble-down Dick, or Phaeton in the suds: a dramatick entertainment of walking, in serious and foolish characters, interlarded with burlesque, grotesque, comick interludes call'd Harlequin a pick-pocket, invented by the ingenious Monsieur Sans Esprit; the musick compos'd by the harmonious Signior Warblerini, and the scenes painted by the prodigious Mynheer Van Bottom-Flat. (Haymarket 29 April 1736). 1736, 1744.
Prologue to George Lillo's Fatal curiosity. (Haymarket 27 May 1736). 1737.
Eurydice, a farce: as it was d-mned at the Theatre-Royal in Drury-Lane. (Drury Lane 19 Feb 1737, as Eurydice: or the devil hen-peck'd). 1743 (in Miscellanies vol 2).
The historical register for the year 1736; to which is added a very merry tragedy called Eurydice hiss'd: or a word to the wise. (Haymarket 21 March 1737, Historical register; 13 April 1737, Eurydice hiss'd). [1737],

[1737] (rev), 1741, 1744; ed W. W. Appleton, Lincoln Nebraska 1967.

Letter signed 'Pasquin'. Common Sense 21 May 1737; rptd in London Mag May 1737; Common Sense vol 1 1738.

The military history of Charles XII, King of Sweden, by M. Gustavus Alderfeld, translated into English. 3 vols 1740.

Of true greatness: an epistle to the Right Honourable George Dodington esq. 1741, 1743 (in Miscellanies vol 1).

ΤΗΣ ΟΜΗΡΟΥ VEPNON-ΙΑΔΟΣ, ΡΑΨΩιΔΙΑῆ ΓΡΑΜΜΑ Α΄: the Vernon-iad, done into English from the original Greek of Homer, lately found at Constantinople, with notes in usum etc, book the first. 1741.

An apology for the life of Mrs Shamela Andrews, by Mr Conny Keyber. 1741, 1741; ed R. B. Johnson 1926; ed B. W. Downs, Cambridge 1930; ed S. W. Baker, Berkeley 1953; ed I. Watt, Los Angeles 1956 (Augustan Reprint Soc); ed M. C. Battestin, Boston 1961 (with Joseph Andrews, below).

The opposition: a vision. 1742 (for 1741).

The history of the adventures of Joseph Andrews and of his friend Mr Abraham Adams, written in imitation of the manner of Cervantes, author of Don Quixote. 2 vols 1742, 1742 ('revised and corrected with alterations and additions by the author'), 1743 (illustr J. Hulett), 1749 (for 1748), 1751 etc; illustr G. Cruikshank 1832 (Novelist's Lib); illustr 'Phiz' 1857; ed G. Saintsbury 1902; ed I. Ehrenpreis, New York 1960; ed M. C. Battestin, Boston 1961 (with Shamela, above); ed A. R. Humphreys 1963 (EL); ed I. Watt, New York 1966; ed M. C. Battestin, Oxford and Middletown Conn 1967 (Wesleyan edn, textual preface by F. T. Bowers); ed D. Brooks, Oxford 1970.

A full vindication of the Dutchess Dowager of Marlborough, both with regard to the account lately published by her Grace and to her character in general. 1742, 1742.

Miss Lucy in town, a sequel to the virgin unmasqued: a farce, with songs. (Drury Lane 6 May 1742). 1742 etc. A collaboration with Garrick? See C. B. Woods, PQ 41 1962.

Plutus, the god of riches: a comedy translated from the original Greek of Aristophanes, with large notes explanatory and critical. 1742. With W. Young.

Some papers proper to be read before the Royal Society concerning the Terrestrial Chrysipus, Golden-Foot or Guinea, collected by Petrus Gualterus, but not published till after his death. 1743, 1743 (in Miscellanies vol 1, postscript added).

The wedding-day: a comedy. (Drury Lane 17 Feb 1743). 1743, 1743 (in Miscellanies vol 2).

A journey from this world to the next. 1743 (in Miscellanies vol 2).

The life of Mr Jonathan Wild the Great. 1743 (in Miscellanies vol 3), 1754 ('with considerable corrections and additions'); illustr 'Phiz' 1840; ed G. Saintsbury [1932] (EL) (with Journal of a voyage to Lisbon).

Preface to Sarah Fielding's Adventures of David Simple. Vol 1, 1744 (2nd edn).

An attempt towards a natural history of the Hanover rat. 1744.

The charge to the jury: or the sum of the evidence on the trial of A.B.C.D. and E.F. all M. D. for the death of one Robert at Orfud before Sir Asculapius Dosem. 1745.

The history of the present rebellion in Scotland, taken from the relation of James Macpherson, who was an eyewitness of the whole. 1745, 1745; ed I. K. Fletcher, Newport 1934.

A serious address to the poeple of Great Britain, in which the certain consequences of the present rebellion are fully demonstrated. 1745 (2 printings), 1745 ('corrected').

A dialogue between the devil, the Pope and the Pretender. 1745.

The female husband: or the surprising history of Mrs Mary, alias Mr George Hamilton, taken from her own mouth since her confinement. 1746; ed C. E. Jones, Liverpool 1960.

Ovid's Art of love paraphrased and adapted to the present time, with notes and a most correct edition of the original, book 1. 1747, Dublin 1759 (as The lover's assistant); ed C. E. Jones, Los Angeles 1961 (Augustan Reprint Soc).

Preface and letters 40–44 of Sarah Fielding's Familiar letters between the principal characters in David Simple and some others. 2 vols 1747.

A dialogue between a gentleman of London, agent for two Court candidates, and an honest alderman of the Country Party, earnestly address'd to the electors of Great Britain. 1747, 1747.

A proper answer to a late scurrilous libel, entitled An apology for the conduct of a late celebrated second-rate minister, by the author of the Jacobite's journal. 1747, 1748.

The history of Tom Jones, a foundling. 6 vols 1749, 1749, 4 vols 1749 (rev), 1750 (for 1749) (rev); illustr Rowlandson, Edinburgh 1805; illustr G. Cruikshank 1831; ed G. Sherburn, New York 1950 (Modern Lib); ed R. P. C. Mutter 1966 (Penguin); ed A. Sherbo, New York 1967.

A charge delivered to the Grand Jury at the sessions of the peace held for the City and Liberty of Westminster etc on Thursday the 29th of June 1749. 1749.

A true state of the case of Bosavern Penlez, who suffered on account of the late riot in the Strand. 1749.

An enquiry into the causes of the late increase of robbers etc with some proposals for remedying this growing evil. 1751, 1751.

Amelia. 4 vols 1752 (for 1751), 1762 (rev, in Murphy's edn of Fielding's Works) etc; illustr G. Cruikshank 1832; illustr 'Phiz' 1857; ed G. Saintsbury 1930 (EL).

A plan of the Universal Register office. 1752 (for 1751), 1753 etc. With John Fielding.

Examples of the interposition of Providence in the detection and punishment of murder, with an introduction and conclusion, both written by Henry Fielding esq. 1752 etc.

A proposal for making an effectual provision for the poor, for amending their morals and for rendering them useful members of the society. 1753.

A clear state of the case of Elizabeth Canning, who hath sworn that she was robbed and almost starved to death for which one Mary Squires now lies under sentence of death. 1753, 1753, 1754.

The journal of a voyage to Lisbon (with A fragment of a comment on L. Bolingbroke's essays). 1755 (edited text, really 2nd edn), 1755 (original text, really 1st edn) etc; ed A. Dobson 1892, 1907 (WC).

Plain truth. 1758 (in J. Dodsley's Collection of poems in six volumes by several hands vol 5).

A treatise on the office of constable. 1761 (in Sir John Fielding's Extracts from such of the penal laws as particularly relate to the peace and good order of this metropolis).

The fathers, or the good-natur'd man: a comedy. (Drury Lane 30 Nov 1778). 1778. Originally written by Fielding c. 1737.

An original song written on the first appearance of The beggars opera [1728]. 1788 (in Country magazine for the years 1786 and 1787, Salisbury and London 1788).

Periodicals

The champion: or the British Mercury, by Capt Hercules Vinegar of Hockley in the Hole. 15 Nov 1739–June 1741 (with James Ralph); rptd 2 vols 1741 (essays of 15 Nov 1739–19 June 1740 only), 1743, 1766.

The true patriot: and the history of our own times. 5 Nov 1745–17 June 1746; ed M. A. Locke, University Alabama 1964 (facs).

The Jacobite's journal, by John Trott Plaid esq. 5 Dec 1747–5 Nov 1748.

The Covent-Garden journal, by Sir Alexander Drawcansir, Knt Censor of Great Britain. 4 Jan–25 Nov 1752; ed G. E. Jensen, New Haven 1915.

§ 2

For early criticism see Fielding: the critical heritage, *ed R. Paulson and T. Lockwood 1969.*

Murphy, A. An essay on the life and genius of Henry Fielding esq. 1762. Prefixed to his edn of Fielding's Works.

Hazlitt, W. In his Lectures on the English comic writers, 1819. Lecture 6 a revision of essay in Edinburgh Rev 24 1815.

Scott, W. In his Lives of the novelists, 1825. Rptd from essay in Ballantyne's Novelist's Lib 1821.

Stephen, L. In his History of English thought in the eighteenth century vol 2, 1876.
—— Fielding's novels. Cornhill Mag Feb 1877; rptd in his Hours in a library 3rd ser, 1879.

Cross, W. L. The history of Fielding. 3 vols New Haven 1918.

Digeon, A. Les romans de Fielding. Paris 1923; tr 1925.

Sherburn, G. Fielding's Amelia: an interpretation. ELH 3 1936.
—— Fielding's social outlook. PQ 35 1956.

Greene, G. Fielding and Sterne. In From Anne to Victoria: essays by various hands, ed B. Dobrée 1937; rptd in his Lost childhood, 1951.

'Alain' (E. Chartier). En lisant Fielding. Nouvelle Revue Française March 1939.

Renwick, W. L. Comic epic in prose. E & S 32 1946.

Watt, I. P. The naming of characters in Defoe, Richardson and Fielding. RES 25 1949.
—— In his Rise of the novel, 1957. *See also* his Serious reflections on the Rise of the novel, Novel 1 1968.

Crane, R. S. The plot of Tom Jones. Jnl of General Education 4 1950; rev as The concept of plot and the plot of Tom Jones in Critics and criticism ancient and modern, ed Crane, Chicago 1952.

Kermode, F. Richardson and Fielding. Cambridge Jnl Nov 1950.

Booth, W. C. The self-conscious narrator in comic fiction before Tristram Shandy. PMLA 67 1952.
—— 'Fielding' in Tom Jones. In his Rhetoric of fiction, Chicago 1961.

Butt, J. Fielding. 1954 (Br Council pamphlet), 1959 (rev).

Murry, J. M. In defence of Fielding. In his Unprofessional essays, 1956.

'West, Rebecca' (C. I. Andrews). The great optimist. In her Court and the castle, 1957.

Empson, W. Tom Jones. Kenyon Rev 20 1958. Reply by C. J. Rawson, N & Q Nov 1959.

Battestin, M. C. The moral basis of Fielding's art: a study of Joseph Andrews. Middletown Conn 1959.
—— (ed). Tom Jones: a collection of critical essays. Englewood Cliffs NJ 1968.

Miller, H. K. Essays on Fielding's Miscellanies: a commentary on volume one. Princeton 1961.

Paulson, R. (ed). Fielding: a collection of critical essays. Englewood Cliffs NJ 1962.
—— Fielding the satirist; the anti-romanticist; the novelist. In his Satire and the novel in eighteenth-century England, New Haven 1967.

Wright, A. Fielding: mask and feast. 1965.

Rawson, C. J. Fielding and the Augusten ideal under stress. 1972.

Harrison, B. Fielding's Tom Jones. 1975.

LAURENCE STERNE
1713–68

The mss of A sentimental journey vol 1 *and of* Journal to Eliza *are in BM; and* Pierpont Morgan Library, New York *has his* Letter-book *and* Fragment in the manner of Rabelais.

Bibliographies etc

A catalogue of a collection of books, among which are included the entire library of the late Sterne, which will begin to be sold on Tuesday, August 23 1768, by J. Todd and H. Sotheran. [York 1768]; ed C. Whibley 1930 (facs).

Collections

Works. 5 vols 1769, 1773, 1774; ed G. Saintsbury 6 vols 1894 (illustr E. J. Wheeler); ed W. L. Cross 12 vols New York 1904; ed Cross 12 vols Cambridge Mass 1906 (illustr) (Jenson Soc); 7 vols Oxford 1926–7 (Shakespeare Head edn).

A sentimental journey, with selections from the journals, sermons and correspondence. Ed W. L. Cross, New York 1926, 1942.

A sentimental journey; Journal to Eliza. Ed G. Saintsbury 1926 (EL); ed D. George [1960] (EL).

Memoirs; The life and opinions of Tristram Shandy; A sentimental journey; Selected sermons and letters. Ed D. Grant 1950 (Reynard Lib).

A sentimental journey; Journal to Eliza; A political romance. Ed I. Jack, Oxford 1968.

§ 1

Various contributions to newspapers (see L. P. Curtis, The politicks of Sterne, Oxford 1929), *of which the following are known in separate printings:*

A paragraph taken from the York-Courant, June 9th 1741. Broadside.

To the Rev Mr James Scott at Leeds. [1741]. Broadside.

Query upon query: being an answer to J.S.'s letter printed in the York-Courant, October 20. York 1741; also in York Courant 27 Oct 1741, Daily Gazetteer 28 Oct 1741, Leeds Mercury 3 Nov 1741.

An answer to J.S.'s letter, address'd to a freeholder of the county of York. [1741]. Broadside; also in York Courant 10 Nov 1741.

The unknown world: verses. GM July 1743; rptd Scots Mag July 1743, Ladies Mag 10 Aug 1751.

Dialogue ('How imperfect the joys of the soul'). In Joseph Baildon's Collection of new songs sung at Ranelagh, [c. 1765] and The laurel: a collection of English songs bk 2 (New Musical Mag no 93) [c. 1785].

On a lady's sporting a somerset. 4-line epigram attributed to Sterne in Muse's mirrour, 2 vols 1778.

The dream, to Mr Cook. Ptd as Fragment inédit by P. Stapfer, Sterne: sa personne et ses ouvrages, Paris 1870.

Sermons

The case of Elijah and the widow of Zerephath. York 1747.

The abuses of conscience. York 1750.

The sermons of Mr Yorick. Vols 1–2, [1760], 1760 (2nd and 3rd edns), Dublin 1760, London 1761 (4th edn), 1 vol Dublin 1761, London 1763 (5th edn vol 1), 1764 (5th edn vol 2, 6th edn vols 1–2), 1765 (7th edn), [1766?] ('new edn'), 1 vol Dublin 1766 ('3rd edn'), London 1767 (8th edn), 1768 (9th edn).

3 sermons rptd in The practical preacher, 1762; 2 in The English preacher, 1773.

A political romance addressed to —— —— esq of York. York 1759 (rptd W. L. Cross, Club of Odd Volumes, Boston 1914), London 1769. Rptd in collections as The history of a good warm watch-coat.

The life and opinions of Tristram Shandy, gentleman.
Vols 1–2, [York] 1760, London 1760 (3 edns), 1 vol (2
pts) Dublin 1760 ('3rd edn'), London 1763 (5th edn),
1767 (6th edn); vols 3–4, 1761, 1761, 1 vol (2 pts) Dublin 1761; vols 5–6, 1762, 1767 (2nd edn, 3 settings of vol
5); vols 7–8, 1765, 1765; vol 9, 1767, Dublin 1767; vols
1–4, 1 vol Dublin 1761, 1765 ('2nd edn'); vols 5–8, 1 vol
Dublin '1765'; vols 1–9, 3 vols '1760'–67.
Vol 1, 1768 (7th edn); vols 3–4, 1768 ('new edn'); vol 2,
1769 (7th edn); vols 3–4, 6, 1769 ('new edn'); vols
1–9, 2 vols 1769, 6 vols 1770 (vols 1–2 8th edn); ed W. L.
Cross 4 vols New York 1904; ed G. Saintsbury 1914
(EL); ed Cross, New York 1925; ed J. A. Work, New
York 1940 (with commentary); ed S. H. Monk, New
York 1950; ed A. D. McKillop 1962; ed I. Watt, Boston
1965; ed G. Petrie, introd by C. Ricks 1967 (Penguin).
A sentimental journey through France and Italy, by Mr
Yorick. 2 vols 1768 (3 edns), Dublin 1768, 1768; ed V.
Woolf, Oxford 1928 (WC); ed G. Petrie, introd by A.
Alvarez 1967 (Penguin); ed G. D. Stout, Berkeley 1967.

Letters

Letters from Yorick to Eliza. 1773, Philadelphia 1773,
London 1775 (6 edns of which 3 are 'a new edn').
Sterne's Letters to his friends on various occasions, to which
is added his History of a watch coat. 1775, 1775, Dublin
1775. 12 letters, of which 8 are fabrications presumably
by William Combe.
Letters of the late Rev Mr L. Sterne to his most intimate
friends, with a fragment in the manner of Rabelais; to
which are prefix'd memoirs of his life and family written by
himself, published by his daughter Mrs Medalle. 3 vols
1775, 1776, 1 vol (3 pts) Dublin 1776.
Letters from Yorick to Eliza, Letters on various occasions.
Dublin 1776, Altenburg 1776; Letters from Yorick to
Eliza, Letters on various occasions, Letters to his most
intimate friends, 1790; Letters from Yorick to Eliza,
Letters on various occasions, Letters to his most intimate friends, An appendix of xxxii letters, i.e. Original
letters of the late Rev Mr L. Sterne, 1788.
Letters. Ed L. P. Curtis, Oxford 1935, 1965.

§2

For early criticism see Sterne: the critical heritage, *ed A. B.
Howes 1974.*
Ferriar, J. Illustrations of Sterne. 1798, 2 vols 1812.
Scott, W. Prefatory memoir to Sterne. Ballantyne's
Novelist's Lib 5 1823; rptd in his Lives of the novelists,
ed A. Dobson 1906 (WC).
Bagehot, W. Sterne and Thackeray. Nat Rev 18 1864;
rptd in his Collected works, ed N. St John Stevas vol 2,
1965.
Fitzgerald, P. The life of Sterne. 2 vols 1864, 1896; rptd
by W. L. Cross in Works of Sterne, New York 1904.
Stephen, L. Sterne. Cornhill Mag July 1880; rptd in his
Hours in a library vol 3, 1892.
Cross, W. L. The life and times of Sterne. New York
1909, 2 vols New Haven 1925, 1 vol 1929 (rev with
addns).
Woolf, V. Sterne. TLS 12 Aug 1909; rptd in her Granite
and rainbow, 1958 (with Eliza and Sterne).
'Melville, Lewis' (L. S. Benjamin). The life and letters of
Sterne. 2 vols 1910.
Greene, G. Fielding and Sterne. In From Anne to
Victoria, ed B. Dobrée 1937; rptd in his Lost childhood,
1951.
Booth, W. C. The self-conscious narrator in comic fiction
before Tristram Shandy. PMLA 67 1952.
— In his Rhetoric of fiction, Chicago 1961.
Mendilow, A. A. In his Time and the novel, 1952.
Traugott, J. Tristram Shandy's world: Sterne's philo-
sophical rhetoric. Berkeley 1954.

— (ed). Sterne: a collection of critical essays. New York
1968.
Fluchère, H. Sterne: de l'homme à l'oeuvre. Paris 1961;
tr and abridged as Sterne from Tristram to Yorick, Ox-
ford 1965.
Tuveson, E. Locke and Sterne. In Reason and the
imagination: studies in the history of ideas 1600–1800,
ed J. A. Mazzeo, New York 1962.
Stedmond, J. M. The comic art of Sterne. Toronto 1967.
Cash, A. H. and J. M. Stedmond (ed). The winged skull:
papers from the Sterne bicentenary conference. Kent
Ohio 1971.
Cash, A. H. Sterne: the early and middle years. 1975.
Conrad, P. Shandyism. Oxford 1978.

TOBIAS GEORGE SMOLLETT
1721–71

§1

The tears of Scotland. In The land of cakes, c. 1746; in
Thrush, 1749; in Craftsman, c. 1750; in Mitre and
Crown, 1750, and in The Union, ed T. Warton 1753,
1759, 1766. In A collection of the most esteemed pieces
of poetry, 1767; and The beauties of English poesy, ed
O. Goldsmith 1767.
Advice: a satire. 1746, 1748 (with Reproof, below).
Reproof: a satire. 1747, 1748 (with Advice).
The adventures of Roderick Random. 2 vols 1748, 1748
(frontispieces by F. Hayman and C. Grignion), Dublin
1748–9, London 1750, 1752, 1754, Dublin 1755,
London 1762, 1760, 1763, 1764, 1766, Dublin 1768,
London 1769, 1770; ed H. W. Hodges [1927] (EL);
Oxford [1930] (WC); ed P.-G. Boucé, Oxford 1979.
The regicide, or James the First of Scotland: a tragedy.
1749 (by subscription), 1749, Dublin 1749.
The adventures of Peregrine Pickle, in which are included
Memoirs of a lady of quality. 4 vols 1751, 3 vols Dublin
1751, 4 vols 1758 (rev); ed J. L. Clifford, Oxford 1964.
An essay on the external use of water in a letter to Dr ****,
with particular remarks upon the present method of
using the mineral waters at Bath in Somersetshire and a
plan for rendering them more safe, agreeable and
efficacious. 1752, 1767, 1770; ed C. E. Jones, Baltimore 1935.
The adventures of Ferdinand Count Fathom. 2 vols 1753
(ptd for W. Johnston), 1753 (pirated?; ptd for T.
Johnson), Dublin 1753, London 1760, 1771, Dublin
1772; ed D. Grant, Oxford 1971.
The reprisal, or the tars of Old England: a comedy of two
acts. 1757 ('printed for R. Baldwin'), 1757 (pirated?;
'printed for Paul Vaillant'), Dublin 1757, London
1761, Belfast 1767, London 1774, 1776.
The life and adventures of Sir Launcelot Greaves. Br Mag
Jan 1760–Dec 1761 (serially); 2 vols 1762, 1 vol Dublin
1762, 1763, 1769, 1783, Cork 1767, 2 vols 1774; ed D.
Evans, Oxford 1973.
The history and adventures of an atom. 2 vols 1749 (for
1769), Dublin 1769.
A complete history of England, deduced from the descent
of Julius Caesar to the Treaty of Aix la Chapelle 1748:
containing the transactions of one thousand eight hundred and three years. 4 vols 1757–8, 11 vols 1758–60 etc.
Often rptd as a continuation of Hume's History.
Continuation of the Complete history of England. 4 vols
1760–1; vol 5, 1765.
Travels through France and Italy: containing observations
on character, customs, religion, government, police,
commerce, arts and antiquities, with a particular
description of the town, territory and climate of Nice; to
which is added a register of the weather, kept during a
residence of eighteen months in that city. 2 vols 1766,
1766, Dublin 1766, 1772, London 1767, 1769, 1778;
ed W. F. Mavor (in General collection of voyages

and travels vol 17, 1813); ed T. Seccombe, Oxford [1907] (WC); ed O. Sitwell [1949].

The expedition of Humphry Clinker. 3 vols 1771 (vol 1, '1671') (several issues), 2 vols Dublin 1771, 3 vols 1772, 2 vols Dublin 1774, London 1779, 3 vols 1681 (for 1781), 2 vols Dublin 1781, 3 vols 1683 (for 1783), 2 vols 1784, Dublin 1784, 1785, London 1685 (for 1785), 1785; Novelist's Mag 19 1785 (illustr E. F. Burney); 2 vols 1788, Edinburgh 1788, Leith 1788, Dublin 1790, 3 vols 1792, 1793 (illustr T. Rowlandson), Dublin 1793, London 1793; ed L. Rice-Oxley, Oxford [1925] (WC); ed V. S. Pritchett 1954; ed L. M. Knapp, Oxford 1966; ed A. Ross [1967] (Penguin); ed A. Parreaux 1968.

Ode to independence. Glasgow 1773, London 1774; Pennsylvania Mag July 1776; Glasgow 1794; in Poetry original and selected, Glasgow 1796.

Translations

The adventures of Gil Blas of Santillane. 4 vols 1748 (no known copy), 1749, 1750, Dublin 1759, 1767, London 1761, 1764, 1766, 1768, Edinburgh 1771, 1773.

The history and adventures of the renowned Don Quixote, translated from the Spanish of Miguel De Cervantes Saavedra. 2 vols 1755 (illustr Francis Hayman), 4 vols 1761 (corrected), 1765, Dublin 1765, London 1770.

The works of M. de Voltaire, translated from the French, with notes, historical and critical, by Dr Smollet and others. 38 vols 1761–74, 39 vols 1761–74 etc; Arouet edition, 22 vols 1927 (rev with additional trns by W. F. Fleming).

The adventures of Telemachus, the son of Ulysses, translated from the French of Messire François Salignac de la Mothe-Fenelon, Archbishop of Cambray. 2 vols 1776, Dublin 1777, 1793, London 1786, 1787, 1792.

Periodicals

Monthly Review 1751–2. For Smollett's contributions, see B. C. Nangle, The Monthly Review first series 1749–89: indexes of contributors and articles, Oxford 1934.

Critical Review: or Annals of Literature, by a Society of Gentlemen. Jan–Feb 1756–Dec 1790. Smollett was doubtless editor-in-chief and contributed many reviews until 1763, and a few after.

British Magazine: or Monthly Repository for Gentlemen and Ladies. 8 vols Jan 1760–Dec 1767. Vols 1–2 contain the first pbn of Launcelot Greaves.

Briton. 29 May 1762–12 Feb 1763.

Letters

Letters. Ed E. S. Noyes, Cambridge, Mass 1926; ed L. M. Knapp, Oxford 1970.

§ 2

Hazlitt, W. In his Lectures on the English comic writers, 1819.

Scott, W. A memoir of the life of Smollett. Prefixed to Novels of Smollett in Ballantyne's Novelist's Lib vol 2, 1821.

'Melville, Lewis' (L. S. Benjamin). The life and letters of Smollett. [1926].

Martz, L. L. The later career of Smollett. New Haven 1942.

Kahrl, G. M. Smollett: traveler-novelist. Chicago [1945].

Knapp, L. M. Smollett: doctor of men and manners. Princeton 1949.

—— Smollett's self-portrait in the expedition of Humphry Clinker. In The age of Johnson: essays presented to C. B. Tinker, New Haven 1949.

Boucé, P.-G. The novels of Smollett. 1976.

Grant, D. Smollett: a study in style. Manchester 1977.

FRANCES BURNEY, later D'ARBLAY
1752–1840

§ 1

Evelina: or the history of a young lady's entrance into the world. 3 vols 1778, 1779 (3 edns), 2 vols Dublin 1779, 1780, 3 vols 1783, 1784, 2 vols Dublin 1784, 3 vols Dresden 1788, 2 vols 1791, 1793, 1794, 1798, 1801, 1808, 1810, 1814 (with biographical sketch), 1815 etc; ed F. D. Mackinnon, Oxford 1930; ed E. A. Bloom, Oxford 1968.

Cecilia: or memoirs of an heiress. 5 vols 1782, 1783, 3 vols Dublin 1783, 5 vols 1784, 3 vols Dublin 1784, 5 vols 1786, Dresden 1790, 1791; 3 vols Dublin 1795, 5 vols 1796, 1802 (8th edn), Birmingham 1809, 3 vols 1810 etc; ed R. B. Johnson 3 vols 1893.

Brief reflections relative to the emigrant French clergy. 1793.

Camilla: or a picture of youth. 5 vols 1796, 3 vols Dublin 1796, 5 vols 1802, 3 vols 1840; ed E. A. and L. D. Bloom, Oxford 1972.

The wanderer: or female difficulties. 5 vols 1814.

Memoirs of Dr Burney. 3 vols 1832.

Edwy and Elgiva. Ed M. J. Benkovitz, Hamden Conn 1957.

Letters, Diaries etc

The diary and letters of Madame d'Arblay 1778–1840. Ed C. Barrett 7 vols 1842–6 (2 issues of vols 1–2), 1854, 4 vols 1876, 1891; ed W. C. Ward 3 vols 1890–1; ed C. Barrett and A. Dobson 6 vols 1904–5; ed C. B. Tinker 1912 (as Dr Johnson and Fanny Burney); Journals and letters [1791–1840], ed Joyce Hemlow et al, Oxford 1969–.

The early diary of Frances Burney 1768–78. Ed A. R. Ellis 2 vols 1889, 1907 (rev), 1913.

The Queeney letters: being letters addressed to Hester Maria Thrale by Dr Johnson, Fanny Burney and Mrs Thrale-Piozzi. Ed Marquis of Lansdowne 1934. 18 letters by Fanny Burney.

§ 2

Macaulay, T. B. Edinburgh Rev 75 1843. A review of Diary and letters.

Dobson, A. Fanny Burney. 1903 (EML).

Johnson, R. B. Fanny Burney and the Burneys. 1926.

Cecil, D. Fanny Burney's novels. In Essays on the eighteenth century presented to David Nichol Smith, Oxford 1945.

—— In his Poets and story-tellers, 1949.

Edwards, A. Fanny Burney: a biography. 1948.

Scholes, P. A. The great Dr Burney: his life, his travels, his works, his family and his friends. 2 vols 1948.

Hemlow, J. The history of Fanny Burney. Oxford 1958.

—— Dr Johnson and the young Burneys. In New light on Dr Johnson, ed F. W. Hilles, New Haven 1959.

—— Letters and journals of Fanny Burney: establishing the text. In Editing eighteenth-century texts, ed D. I. B. Smith, Toronto 1968.

Gérin, W. The young Fanny Burney: a biography. 1961.

Lonsdale, R. H. Dr Charles Burney: a literary biography. Oxford 1965.

WILLIAM BECKFORD
1760–1844

Bibliographies

Chapman, G. and J. Hodgkin. A bibliography of Beckford of Fonthill. 1930.

§ 1
Vathek

In French

Vathek. Lausanne 1787 (for 1786), 1791 (as Les caprices et les malheurs du calife Vathek), Paris 1787 (rev as Vathek: conte arabe), 1815 (final revision), nd [1828?]; ed S. Mallarmé, Paris 1876 (from Paris 1787, with a few misreadings), 1893 (rev); ed G. Chapman (from Paris 1787); ed J. B. Brunius, Paris 1948 (from Paris 1787); ed E. Giddey, Lausanne 1962 (from Paris 1787).

In English

An Arabian tale, from an unpublished manuscript, with notes critical and explanatory. 1786 (tr Samuel Henley, unauthorized from unknown French ms), 1809, 1816 ('revised and corrected'), Philadelphia 1816, London 1823 ('revised and corrected'); ed R. B. Johnson 1922; Vathek: a new translation by H. B. Grimsditch 1929 (text as 1815 edn), 1953 (with new introd); ed R. H. Lonsdale, Oxford 1970 (text of 1816, with original notes).

Episodes of Vathek

The episodes of Vathek. Tr F. T. Marzials 1912 (includes French text); [1922] (English trn only, in Abbey Classics); Vathek with the episodes of Vathek, ed G. Chapman 2 vols 1929 (French text only); Vathek et les épisodes, ed J. B. Brunius, Paris 1948.

Other Works

Biographical memoirs of extraordinary painters. 1780, 1824, 1834.
Dreams, waking thoughts and incidents, in a series of letters, from various parts of Europe. 1783 (suppressed by Beckford except for 6 copies); ed G. T. Bettany 1891 (with Vathek); ed G. Chapman 1928 (The travel diaries vol 1).
Modern novel writing: or the elegant enthusiast; and interesting emotions of Arabella Bloomville: a rhapsodical romance; interspersed with poetry, by the Right Hon Lady Harriet Marlow. 2 vols 1796.
Azemia: a descriptive and sentimental novel, interspersed with pieces of poetry, by Jaquetta Agneta Mariana Jenks. 2 vols 1797, 1798; Arnold et la belle musulmane, Paris 1808 (French trn).
The story of Al Raoui: a tale from the Arabic. 1799 (with German version and a few poems), 1799.
A dialogue in the shades. [1819], 1821.
Epitaphs, some of which have appeared in the Literary Gazette of March and April 1823. [1825].
Italy; with sketches of Spain and Portugal, by the author of Vathek. 2 vols 1834, 1834 (rev), Paris 1834, Philadelphia 1834, 2 vols 1835, 1 vol 1840 (with Recollections of an excursion); ed G. T. Bettany 1891 (with Vathek); ed G. Chapman 1928 (The travel diaries vol 2).
Recollections of an excursion to the monasteries of Alcobaça and Batalha. 1835, Philadelphia 1835, London 1840 (rev) (with Italy); ed G. T. Bettany 1891 (with Vathek); ed G. Chapman 1928 (The travel diaries vol 2); ed A. Parreaux, Paris 1956 (from 1840, with French trn).
The vision; Liber veritatis. Ed G. Chapman 1930.

Letters, Diaries etc

Journal in Portugal and Spain 1787-8. Ed B. Alexander 1954.
Life at Fonthill 1807-22, from the correspondence of Beckford. Tr (mostly from the Italian) and ed B. Alexander 1957.
1794 journal. Ed B. Alexander, New Haven 1960 (in Beckford of Fonthill).

§ 2

Parreaux, A. Le Portugal dans l'oeuvre de Beckford. Paris 1935.
— Beckford: auteur de Vathek. Paris 1960.
Chapman, G. Beckford. 1937, 1952.
Alexander, B. England's wealthiest son. 1962.

III. MINOR FICTION

Newcastle, Margaret Cavendish, Duchess of. CCXI sociable letters. 1664, 1718. Primitive letter-fiction depicting domestic life. See D. Grant, Margaret the first, 1956.
Head, Richard and Francis Kirkman. The English rogue described in the life of Meriton Latroon. 4 pts 1665-80, 1 vol 1693, 1697 (4th edn). Many edns to 1786; ed M. Shinagel, Boston 1961 (Head's pt only). See S. Gibson, A bibliography of Kirkman, Oxford 1950. Sensational patchwork; many sources.
Newcastle, Margaret Cavendish, Duchess of. The description of a new world called the blazing world. 1666, 1668.
Nevile, Henry. The isle of pines. 1668, 1668 (with 2nd pt), 1704; ed W. C. Ford, Boston 1920; pt 1, 1930 (EL). Narrator populates deserted island with progeny, founds commonwealth; see G. Bullough, Polygamy among the reformers, in Renaissance and modern essays presented to V. de S. Pinto, 1966.
Boyle, Roger, Earl of Orrery. Parthenissa. 1669 (last pt; others appeared 1651-6), 1676 (complete); other edns in 18th century. Preface ed C. Davies, Los Angeles 1953 (Augustan Reprint Soc). Lengthy imitation of Greek and French romances; see K. Lynch, Roger Boyle, Knoxville 1965.

Kirkman, Francis. The counterfeit lady unveiled. 1673, 1679; ed S. Peterson, Garden City NY 1961.
— The unlucky citizen; with several choice novels. 1673. Autobiography mixed with fiction; London life.
Head, Richard. The western wonder: or O Brazeel, an inchanted island discovered. 1674, 1675 (as O-Brazile); ed I. M. Westcott, Los Angeles 1958 (Augustan Reprint Soc).
The right pleasant and variable tragical history of Fortunatus. 1676, 1679; other versions and abridgments to 1700; ed C. C. Mish in Short fiction of the seventeenth century, New York 1963. First datable prose version of popular folk tale of marvels, of German origin.
Five love-letters from a nun to a cavalier. 1678; at least 12 edns by 1716. Tr Sir Roger L'Estrange; rptd N. Würzbach in The novel in letters, 1969. Widely influential for epistolary fiction. Probably by G. J. L. de Guilleragues.
Behn, Aphra. Love letters between a nobleman and his sister. 3 pts 1683-7 (pt 3, as Amours of Philander and Sylvia); at least 16 edns by 1765; rptd in N. Würzbach, The novel in letters, 1969 (pt 1).
Dunton, John. The informer's doom: or an amazing and seasonable letter from Utopia, directed to the man in the moon. 1683.

—— The pilgrim's guide from the cradle to his death-bed, with his glorious passage from thence to the new Jerusalem. 1684. Allegory in manner of Bunyan.

[Reynolds, John?]. Delightful and ingenious novels: being choice and excellent stories of amours tragical and comical. 1685, 1685, 1686, 1686. 6–8 tales of love and intrigue, with middle-class characters; *see* C. Morgan, The rise of the novel of manners, New York 1911.

Boyle, Robert, Earl of Orrery. The martyrdom of Theodora and of Didymus. 1687, 1703. Historical and psychological romance. Preface ed C. Davies, Los Angeles 1953 (Augustan Reprint Soc).

Behn, Apha. The fair jilt. 1688, 1688 (in Three histories), 1696 (in Histories and novels, below); ed M. Summers in Works of Aphra Behn, 1915, New York 1967.

—— Oroonoko: or the royal slave. 1688, 1696.

—— The history of the nun: or the fair vowbreaker. 1689, 1696 (in Histories and novels.

—— The lucky mistake. 1689, 1696 (in Histories and novels.

Dunton, John. A voyage round the world: the rare adventures of Don Kainophilus. 1691. Eccentric novel; anticipates Sterne.

Congreve, William, Incognita: or love and duty reconcil'd. 1692, 1700; 5 edns by 1730; 1930 (EL); ed A. N. Jeffares 1966. See I. Simon, Early theories of prose fiction: Congreve and Fielding; A. Williams, Congreve's Incognita and the contrivances of Providence; both in Imagined worlds, ed M. Mack and I. Gregor 1968.

Settle, Elkanah. The notorious impostor. 1692; ed S. Peterson, Los Angeles 1958 (Augustan Reprint Soc) (with Settle, Diego redivivus). Rogue biography; the confidence-man William Morrell.

Trotter, Catherine. Olinda's adventures. 1693 (in Letters of love, gallantry and several occasions), 1718, 1724 (in Familiar letters of love); ed R. A. Day, Los Angeles 1969 (Augustan Reprint Soc). Excellent domestic novel in letters.

Settle, Elkanah. The complete memoirs of the life of that notorious impostor Will Morrell. 1694, 1698; ed S. Peterson in The counterfeit lady unveiled, Garden City NY 1961; *see* S. Peterson, William Morrell and late seventeenth-century fiction, PQ 42 1963. Rogue biography.

Behn, Aphra. The histories and novels [reprints Oroonoko, The fair jilt, Agnes de Castro, The lover's watch, The lucky mistake [see above]; adds Mrs Behn's letters and fictional biography]. 1696, 1697 (with The King of Bantam, The nun, The black lady); at least 10 edns by 1751.

Manley, Mary de la Riviere. Letters written by Mrs Manley, to which is added a letter from a suppos'd nun in Portugal. 1696, 1713, 1725 (as A stage-coach journey to Exeter), 1735 (in Mr Pope's literary correspondence).

Behn, Aphra. The unfortunate bride: or the blind lady a beauty; The unfortunate happy lady; The wandring beauty. 1698 (as separate pamphlets?), 1700 (bound into Histories, novels and translations); ed M. Summers in Works of Aphra Behn, 1915, New York 1967.

Ward, Edward. The London spy. 18 pts, 2 vols 1698–1700, 1 vol 1700; 7 or more edns by 1724; ed K. Fenwick 1955. *See* H. W. Troyer, Ned Ward of Grubstreet, Cambridge Mass 1946. Lively account of rambles through London's districts.

Winstanley, William. The Essex champion: or the famous history of Sir Billy of Billerecay. 1699 (an earlier edn, perhaps 1690). The adventures of an English Quixote, bemused by romances.

Behn, Aphra. The dumb virgin; The unhappy mistake. 1700 (in Histories, novels and translations: also separately?).

Brown, Thomas. Amusements serious and comical, calculated for the meridian of London. 1700; at least 10 edns by 1760; ed A. L. Hayward 1927; *see* B. Boyce,

Tom Brown of facetious memory, Cambridge Mass 1939. Uses ingénu device for social satire.

Ward, Edward, et al. A pacquet from Will's. 1701, 1705 (in Works of Voiture vol 2), 1724 (in Familiar letters of love). Miscellany of narrative letters, humorous and satirical.

The adventures of Lindamira, a lady of quality. 1702, 1703, 1713 (as The lover's secretary) etc; ed B. Boyce, Minneapolis 1949. Epistolary domestic novel of excellent quality; ascription to Thomas Brown unjustified.

Manley, Mary Delariviere. The secret history of Queen Zarah and the Zarazians. 1705; 5 edns by 1749. Sensational account of Sarah, Duchess of Marlborough. Preface ed B. Boyce, Los Angeles 1952 (Augustan Reprint Soc).

Galland, Antoine. The Arabian nights entertainments: consisting of one thousand and one stories. 1706; 8 edns listed by 1736; numerous edns through century in 3–12 vols. Pts 1–6 of French version had appeared by 1704, the remainder by 1717.

Manley, Mary Delariviere. The lady's pacquet of letters, taken from her by a French privateer in her passage to Holland. 1707, 1708. Pt 1, ptd with d'Aulnoy, Memoirs of the Court of England; Pt 2, ptd with d'Aulnoy, History of the Earl of Warwick, 1711 (complete, 41 letters, as Court intrigues). Epistolary fiction of several varieties, excellent technique; *see* P. B. Anderson, Delariviere Manley's prose fiction, PQ 13 1934. Letter 33 ed N. Würzbach in The novel in letters, 1969.

Gildon, Charles. The golden spy: or a political journal of the British nights entertainments. 2 vols 1709–10, 1 vol [1724?]. Inanimate spy; gold piece explores many social levels; early example of popular genre.

Manley, Mary Delariviere. Secret memoirs and manners of several persons of quality of both sexes from the new Atalantis. 1709; at least 7 edns by 1736. Alleged secrets of numerous contemporary notables; the archetypal scandal novel; highly popular.

[Cibber, Colley?]. The secret history of Arlus and Odolphus, ministers of state to the Empress of Grandinsula. 1710 (3 edns). Thinly-veiled political satire, pro-Harley, anti-Godolphin. One of several similar works in a controversy using the same names.

Manley, Mary Delariviere. Memoirs of Europe, towards the close of the eighth century. 1710, 1711 etc, 1720 (with New Atalantis as Secret memoirs); 7th edn by 1736. Continuation of scandal-chronicle of contemporary personages.

Oldmixon, John. The secret history of Europe. 1712; 4 edns by 1724. Secret history with Whig bias.

A new voyage to the island of fools, representing the policy, government and present state of the Stultitians. 1713, 1715. Ramble through London; satire of manners. Attributed to Edward Ward; resembles his manner in London spy.

Smith, Alexander. The history of the lives and robberies of the most noted highway-men. 1713; 6 edns by 1720 (2–3 vols); 1734 (with Charles Johnson, General history of the pyrates); ed A. L. Hayward, New York 1926. Collection of short rogue biographies, male and female; lively and often obscene; highly popular.

[Walpole, Sir Robert?]. The present state of fairy-land. 1713. Anti-Tory propaganda in form of a letter to Louis XIV from an English squire; replies to attack on Walpole, The Testimonies of several citizens of Fickleborough. *See* J. H. Plumb, Sir Robert Walpole, 1956.

Hamilton, Anthony. Memoirs of the life of the Count de Grammont. 1714, 1719; at least 4 edns by 1760. Tr Abel Boyer; ed and tr N. Deakin 1965.

Manley, Mary Delariviere. The adventures of Rivella. 1714, 1717, 1725. Lively fictionalized autobiography; secret history, scandal.

The double captive: or chains upon chains. 1718; ed N. Würzbach in The novel in letters, 1969. Epistolary tale, ostensibly by prisoner in Newgate; realistic pictures of prison life.

Hearne, Mary. The lover's week: or the six days adventures of Philander and Amaryllis. 1718, 1718, 1720 (in Honour the victory and love the prize), 1724 (serialized in Original London Post), 1726; ed N. Würzbach in The novel in letters, 1969. Epistolary autobiographical tale; excellent characterization.

Barker, Jane. The entertaining novels of Mrs Jane Barker. 1719; 3 edns by 1736; 1750. Consists of Exilius, Bosvil and Galesia.

Gildon, Charles. The post-man robb'd of his mail: or the packet broke open. 1719. Epistolary miscellany containing psychological novel, The lover's sighs.

Haywood, Eliza. Love in excess: or the fatal enquiry. 1719; at least 9 edns by 1750. Sensationally popular; melodramatic romance of passion and intrigue.

Hearne, Mary. The female deserters. 1719, 1720 (with The lover's week; see 1718, above), 1731 (in A collection of curious novels). Sequel to The lover's week; inserted histories.

A select collection of novels in six volumes. 1720, 1725, 1729 (with 9 novels added); 6 edns by 1740. Ed Samuel Croxall; 26 titles, mostly trns, of best and most popular short fiction of previous century; authors include Cervantes, Machiavelli, Mme de La Fayette, Lesage, Brémond, Scarron, Saint-Réal, Alemán, Mlle de La Roche-Guilhem, Fénelon; Huet's essay on romances in vol 1.

Gildon, Charles. Miscellanea aurea: or the golden medley. 1720. Epistolary miscellany, moral in tone; contains 2 utopian imaginary voyages and a psychological novel in letters.

Manley, Mary Delariviere. The power of love, in seven novels. 1720, 1741. Free adaptations from Bandello, perhaps from versions in Painter, Palace of pleasure.

Aubin, Penelope. The life of Madam de Beaumont, a French lady. 1721, 1728; several other edns; c. 1770 (as Belinda). Adventure, romance, religion; see R. B. Dooley, Penelope Aubin: forgotten Catholic novelist, Renascence 11 1959.

—— The strange adventures of the Count de Vinevil and his family. 1721, 1728 etc, 1739 (in A collection of entertaining histories and novels). Sensational adventures; Turkish setting.

—— The life and amorous adventures of Lucinda, an English lady. 1722, 1739. Autobiography; heroine captured by Barbary pirates.

—— The noble slaves: or the lives and adventures of two lords and two ladies. 1722, 1729; numerous edns through century. Similar in plot to Lucinda, above.

Haywood, Eliza. The British recluse: or the secret history of Cleomira, suppos'd dead. 1722; 4 edns by 1732. Imitation of Mrs Aubin's romances.

Aubin, Penelope. The life of Charlotta Du Pont. 1723, 1733; 6 edns by 1800. Abduction and adventure in North and South America.

Blackamore, Arthur. Luck at last: or the happy unfortunate. 1723, 1737 (as The distress'd fair); ed W. H. McBurney, in Four before Richardson, Lincoln Nebraska 1963. Decorous and domestic; heroine disguised as servant.

Haywood, Eliza. Idalia: or the unfortunate mistress. 1723; 4 edns by 1732. The Haywood formula established; amorous misadventures.

—— Lasselia: or the self-abandon'd. 1723; 4 edns by 1732.

—— The fatal secret: or constancy in distress. 1724; 4 edns by 1732. Novel of passion; melodramatic psychology.

—— The masqueraders: or fatal curiosity. 1724; 6 edns by 1732. Intrigue in high life.

—— A spy upon the conjurer. 1724-5 (several issues). Secret history, largely epistolary, of Duncan Campbell, a famous soothsayer of the period.

—— The works of Mrs Eliza Haywood. 1724; 8 novels, together with poems and plays, rptd in 4 vols.

—— Bath-intrigues. 1725 (3 edns), 1727 (in Secret histories). Lively epistolary scandal chronicle.

—— Fantomina: or love in a maze. 1725, 1732 (in Secret histories). Clever story of amorous stratagems.

—— Memoirs of a certain island adjacent to the kingdom of Utopia. 1725, 1726. Scandal chronicle of politics and amours in high life, in manner of New Atalantis, with key.

—— Secret histories, novels and poems. 4 vols 1725; 4 edns by 1742. Reissue of 11 novels.

Aubin, Penelope. The life and adventures of the lady Lucy. 1726, 1728, 1739 (in collection). Separated spouses, fantastic adventures; historical matter involving Irish rebellion under James II.

Barker, Jane. The lining for the patch-work screen. 1726. Tales as a sequel.

Haywood, Eliza. The city jilt: or the alderman turn'd beau. 1726 (3 edns), 1727 (in Secret histories).

—— The mercenary lover: or the unfortunate heiresses. 1726, 1726, 1728. Primitive psychological novel.

—— Cleomelia: or the generous mistress. 1727, 1727. Passion, adventure, intrigue.

—— The fruitless enquiry. 1727; 5 edns by 1800. Stories linked by framework of a quest for happiness.

—— Letters from the palace of fame. 1727 (also in Secret histories). Epistolary scandal chronicle of political figures.

—— Love in its variety. 1727. 6 novels, said to be trns from Bandello; more probably original or very freely adapted.

—— The perplex'd Dutchess, or treachery rewarded: being some memoirs of the Court of Malfy. 1727, 1727, 1728. No connection with Webster's play; intrigues of a scheming parvenue.

—— Philidore and Placentia: or l'amour trop delicat. 1727; ed W. M. McBurney in Four before Richardson, Lincoln Nebraska 1963. Highflown tale of love and adventure.

—— The secret history of the present intrigues of the Court of Caramania. 1727, 1727. Love and politics at the English Court; a key-novel.

Rowe, Elizabeth. Friendship in death. 3 pts 1728-32; at least 18 edns by 1800. Letters from the dead to the living device for pious instruction; see H. S. Hughes, Elizabeth Rowe and the Countess of Hertford, PMLA 49 1944; J. J. Richetti, Mrs Elizabeth Rowe: the novel as polemic, PMLA 82 1967.

—— The agreeable Caledonian: or memoirs of signiora di Morella, a Roman lady. 2 pts 1728, 1729, 1 vol 1768 (as Clementina). Intrigues and adventures in Italy; heroine abducted from convent.

—— Letters moral and entertaining. 3 pts 1729-33.

Haywood, Eliza. Love-letters on all occasions lately passed between persons of distinction. 1730. Collection ranging in scope from single narrative letters to short letter novels.

Madden, Samuel. Memoirs of the twentieth century: being original letters of state under George the Sixth. 1733, 1763 (as The reign of George VI); ed C. Oman 1899. Satire against George II and Court; 6 vols projected, suppressed after vol 1.

Lyttelton, George, Baron. Letters from a Persian in England to his friend at Ispahan. 1735 (4 edns); spurious continuation in same year, as The Persian letters continued; at least 11 edns by 1800. Influential; much imitated; foreign commentator on English institutions derived from Montesquieu, Lettres persanes.

Haywood, Eliza. Adventures of Eovaai, Princess of Ijaveo. 1736, 1741 (as The unfortunate Princess). Pretended trn; secret history and satire attacking Walpole.

Mottley, John. Joe Miller's jests: or the wit's vademecum. 1739 (3 edns); many further edns and versions; ed R. Hutchinson, New York 1963. The classic jestbook of the period; some anecdotes approach short fiction.

Lyttelton, George, Baron. The Court-secret: a melancholy truth. 1741 (5 edns); 2 more by 1743. Pseudo-oriental scandal chronicle.

Collyer, Mary. The virtuous orphan: or the life of Marianne. 1742; ed W. H. McBurney and M. F. Shugrue, Carbondale 1965; 1746 (with changes as The life and adventures of Indiana). Very free adaptations of Marivaux, Vie de Marianne.

Fielding, Sarah. The adventures of David Simple. 3 vols 1744-53, 1744 (1-2 rev Henry Fielding), 5 vols Dublin 1761; 3 more edns by 1792; ed M. Kelsall, Oxford 1969.

Haywood, Eliza. The fortunate foundlings: being the genuine history of Colonel M—rs and his sister Madam Du P—y. 1744; 4 edns by 1761. Distresses in the manner of Marivaux; moral. Another version, The happy orphans, 1759; 3 edns by 1770, is a trn by Edward Kimber of a French version with addns by Crébillon.

Fielding, Sarah. Familiar letters between the characters in David Simple. 1747, 1752. A sequel.

Cleland, John. Memoirs of a woman of pleasure. 2 vols 1748-9, 1750 (a reworking); numerous surreptitious edns; ed P. C. Quennell 1963. See J. Hollander, The old last act, Encounter Oct 1963; D. Foxon, Libertine literature in England 1660-1745, 1965. Epistolary-autobiographical; the classic of English pornography.

Haywood, Eliza. Life's progress through the passions: or the adventures of Natura. 1748. Education of the heart by a series of encounters.

The history of Charlotte Summers, the fortunate parish girl. 1749, 1750 (corrected), Dublin 1753 etc. Popular and esteemed; female Tom Jones as heroine; sentimental; introduces Lady Bountiful.

Fielding, Sarah. The governess, or the little female academy: being the history of Mrs Teachum and her nine girls. 1749; at least 7 edns by 1800; ed J. E. Gray, Oxford 1968. Didactic; advocates educational ideas of Locke.

Lennox, Charlotte. The life of Harriot Stewart, written by herself. 1750, 1751. Uses skeleton of Clarissa plot; autobiographical; troubled love; American scenes. See G. H. Maynadier, The first American novelist?, Cambridge Mass 1940.

Cleland, John. Memoirs of a coxcomb: or the history of Sir William Delamere. 1751, 1782, New York 1963. Fictional autobiography; amorous adventures.

Coventry, Francis. The history of Pompey the little: or the life and adventures of a lap-dog. 1751; at least 10 edns by 1800; rptd 1926; preface ed C. E. Jones, Los Angeles 1957 (Augustan Reprint Soc); ed R. A. Day, Oxford 1974.

Haywood, Eliza. The history of miss Betsy Thoughtless. 1751, Dublin 1751; at least 8 edns by 1800. Girl matures, learns prudence; Haywood's best work.

Lennox, Charlotte. The female Quixote: or the adventures of Arabella. 1752, Dublin 1752 (and an abridgment), 1783; 7 edns by 1800; ed M. Dalziel, Oxford 1969. Heroine bedazzled by reading romances.

Haywood, Eliza. The history of Jenny and Jemmy Jessamy. 1753, Dublin 1753, London 1769, 1785 (Novelists' Mag). Hero escapes wiles of pretended innocent; she becomes debauched.

Amory, Thomas. Memoirs: containing the lives of several ladies of Great Britain. 1755, 1769 (as Memoirs of several ladies). Didactic, uneven, idiosyncratic; fantasy voyage with female paragons.

—— The life of John Buncle. 2 vols 1756-66, 4 vols 1770; ed E. A. Baker 1904. Eccentric, extravagant narrator; much admired; pioneer in romantic description of landscape.

Fielding, Sarah. The lives of Cleopatra and Octavia. 1757, 1758; ed R. B. Johnson 1928. Moralizing hybrid of history and fiction.

Griffith, Elizabeth, and Richard. A series of genuine letters between Henry and Frances. 6 vols 1757-70 (several edns), 1786. Borderline fiction; letters fictionalized; extreme delicacy of feeling emphasized; see J. M. S. Tompkins, The polite marriage, Cambridge 1938.

Fielding, Sarah. The history of the Countess of Dellwyn. 1759.

—— The history of Ophelia. 1760, 1785, 1787. Sufferings of orphan; pioneering use of Gothic elements; epistolary.

Johnstone, Charles. Chrysal: or the adventures of a guinea. 4 vols 1760-5; perhaps 20 edns by 1800; ed E. A. Baker 1908. Immense success; gold coin as spy; satire of manners, politics; depicts many famous contemporaries in all walks of life.

—— The reverie: or a flight to the paradise of fools. 1762; at least 6 edns by 1800. Political satire; attacks Bute, other prominent political figures.

Langhorne, John. Solyman and Almena: an oriental tale. 1762; 5 edns by 1800. Sentimental, moralistic; descriptions of Eastern scenery.

Leland, Thomas. Longsword, Earl of Salisbury. 1762, Dublin 1766; ed J. C. Stephens jr, New York 1957. Called first English historical novel; actually pre-Gothic, sentimental.

Lennox, Charlotte. Sophia. 1762. Sense and sensibility theme.

Brooke, Frances. The history of lady Julia Mandeville. 1763; 10 edns by 1792; ed E. P. Poole 1930. Highly regarded; sentimental; tragic conclusion.

Brooke, Henry. The fool of quality: or the history of Henry, Earl of Moreland. 5 vols 1765-70; ed E. A. Baker 1906.

Cleland, John. The surprises of love, exemplified in the romance of a day. 1765.

Walpole, Horace. The castle of Otranto: a Gothic story. 1765; ed W. S. Lewis, Oxford 1964. See col 635, below.

Goldsmith, Oliver. The vicar of Wakefield. 2 vols 1766. See col 607, below.

Mackenzie, Henry. The man of feeling. Edinburgh and Dublin 1771, 1771; at least 9 edns by 1800; ed B. Vickers, Oxford 1967.

Graves, Richard. The spiritual Quixote: or the summer's ramble of Mr Geoffrey Wildgoose. 1773; at least 6 edns by 1800; ed C. R. Tracy, Oxford 1967. Dilemmas of idealism exemplified; satire on Methodists.

Mackenzie, Henry. The man of the world. 1773, 1773, 1783, 1787.

—— Julia de Roubigné. 1777; at least 8 edns by 1800. Epistolary; pre-Gothic.

Reeve, Clara. The champion of virtue: a Gothic story. Colchester 1777; later titled The old English baron; at least 10 edns by 1800; ed J. Trainer, Oxford 1967. Sentiment and terror; supernatural; didactic emphasis.

—— [Castle Connor, c. 1787]. Ms lost; ptd as Fatherless Fanny, 1819.

Croft, Sir Herbert. Love and madness: a story too true, in a series of letters. 1780; 4 edns by 1786. Based on Hackman's murder of Martha Ray, mistress of Earl of Sandwich; digressions on Chatterton and Werther.

Holcroft, Thomas. Alwyn: or the gentleman comedian. 1780. Episodes include autobiography in fictional form.

Bage, Robert. Mount Henneth. 1782, 1788. Philosophical novel; pictures community dedicated to benevolence; histories of its members.

Day, Thomas. The history of Sandford and Merton. 3 vols 1783-9; 7 edns by 1795. Classic improving work for children; see S. H. Scott, The exemplary Mr Day, New York 1935.

Bage, Robert. Barham Downs. 1784, 1788.

Godwin, William. Imogen: a pastoral romance from the ancient British. 2 vols 1784; ed J. W. Marken, New York 1963 (with several studies).

—— Italian letters: or the history of the Count de St

Julian. 1783 (anon); ed B. R. Pollin, Lincoln Nebraska 1965.

Moore, John. Zeluco: various views of human nature. 1786.

Reeve, Clara. The exiles: or memoirs of the Count de Cronstadt. 1788, 1789, Dublin 1789.

Smith, Charlotte. Emmeline: or the orphan of the castle. 1788, 1789 (3rd edn). Gothic; mistreated heroine. *See* F. M. A. Hilbish, Charlotte Smith: poet and novelist, Philadelphia 1941; A. D. McKillop, Charlotte Smith's letters, HLQ 15 1952.

Radcliffe, Ann. The castles of Athlin and Dunbayne: a Highland story. 1789, 1793, 1793, 1799.

Smith, Charlotte. Ethelinde: or the recluse of the lake. 1789, 1790, Dublin 1790.

Radcliffe, Ann. A Sicilian romance. 1790.

Inchbald, Elizabeth. A simple story. 1791, Dublin 1791; 4th edn 1799; ed J. M. S. Tompkins, Oxford 1967.

Radcliffe, Ann. The romance of the forest. 1791; at least 10 edns by 1800.

Bage, Robert. Man as he is. 1792, 1796.

Holcroft, Thomas. Anna St Ives. 7 vols 1792, 1800. Epistolary; includes journals; set in French Revolution.

Smith, Charlotte. The old manor house. 1793, Dublin 1793; ed A. H. Ehrenpreis, Oxford 1969.

Godwin, William. Things as they are: or the adventures of Caleb Williams. 1794, 1797 (3rd edn); ed G. Sherburn, New York 1960. *See col 616, below*.

Holcroft, Thomas. The adventures of Hugh Trevor. 6 vols 1794–7; 1–3 rptd 1794, Dublin 1795; 4–6, 1797.

Radcliffe, Ann. The mysteries of Udolpho. 1794, 1794, 1795, Dublin 1800; ed B. Dobrée, Oxford 1966.

Lewis, Matthew Gregory. The monk. 1795, 1796, 1796, Dublin 1796, London 1797 etc; ed L. F. Peck, New York 1952.

Bage, Robert. Hermsprong: or man as he is not. 1796, 1799; ed V. Wilkins 1951.

Radcliffe, Ann. The Italian. 1797, 1811 (3rd edn); ed F. Garber, Oxford 1968.

Godwin, Mary Wollstonecraft. The wrongs of woman: or Maria. 1798 (incomplete; in Posthumous works), Philadelphia 1799 (as Maria).

Surr, Thomas Skinner. George Barnwell: a novel. 1798, Dublin 1798. Lillo's character translated to genteel high life.

The natural son. 1799. Novel-version of play by Diderot; incest threatened but averted.

Charlton, Mary. Rosella: or modern occurrences. 1799, Dublin 1800. Reacts against sensibility, Gothicism.

Godwin, William. St Leon: a tale of the sixteenth century. 1799, 1800, Dublin 1800.

Reeve, Clara. Destination: or memoirs of a private family. 1799, Dublin 1800.

Moore, John. Mordaunt: being sketches of life, character and manners in various countries. 1800, Dublin 1800; ed W. L. Renwick, Oxford 1965.

5. PROSE

I. ESSAYISTS AND PAMPHLETEERS

SIR ROGER L'ESTRANGE
1616–1704

§ I

To a gentleman, a member of the House of Commons. 1646 (8 July).

L'Estrange his appeale from the Court Martiall to the Parliament. 1647 (April).

L'Estrange his vindication to Kent. 1649.

The liberty of the imprisoned royalist. [1649]. Anon; verse.

The fanatique powder-plot. 1660 (24 March). Anon.

Peace to the nation. [Feb 1660]. Anon.

Let me speake too? or eleven queries. 1659.

No blinde guides, in answer to Milton's Brief notes upon a late sermon. 1660 (20 April).

Physician cure thyself: or an answer to Eye-salve for the English army. 1660 (23 April).

Sir Politique uncased: or a sober answer to A letter intercepted. [1660?]. Anon.

L'Estrange his apology; with a short view of some late and remarkable transactions. 1660.

An appeal in the case of the late King's party. 1660. Anon.

A plea for a limited monarchy. 1660. Anon. Rptd Harleian miscellany vol 1, 1744, 1808.

A caveat to the cavaliers, dedicated to the author [James Howell] of A cordial for the cavaliers. 1661 (4 edns).

A modest plea for the caveat, and the author of it. 1661 (Aug), 1661, 1662.

Interest mistaken: or the holy cheat. 1661, 1661, 1662, 1662, 1682 (as The holy cheat).

The relaps'd apostate: or notes upon a petition for peace. 1661 (Nov) ('1641'), 1661, 1681.

To the Right Hon Edward Earl of Clarendon, Lord High Chancellor. 1661 (3 Dec).

State divinity: or a supplement to the Relaps'd apostate. 1661 (4 Dec).

A memento directed to all those that truly reverence the memory of King Charles the Martyr: the first part. 1662 (April), 1682 (omits last 3 chs; as A memento treating of the rise, progress and remedies of sedition).

Truth and loyalty vindicated, from the reproches and clamours of Mr Edward Bagshaw. 1662 (7 June).

The visitation: or long look'd-for comes at last. 1662. Anon.

A whipp, a whipp for the schismatical animadverter [Bagshaw] upon the Bishop of Worcester's letter. 1662 (Feb), 1662.

Toleration discuss'd. 1663, 1670, 1673 ('enlarged'), 1681.

Considerations and proposals in order to the regulation of the press, together with diverse instances of treasonous and seditious pamphlets. 1663 (3 June).

The intelligencer, published for the satisfaction and information of the people, with privilege. 31 Aug 1663–29 Jan 1666. A weekly, pbd on Monday.

The newes, published for the satisfaction and information of the people, with privilege. 3 Sept 1663–29 Jan 1666. Originally a distinct weekly periodical, pbd on Thursday, but from 1664 a Thursday suppl to Intelligencer, above, with numbering and pagination continuous throughout both papers.

Publick intelligence, with sole privilege. No 1 (all issued), 28 Nov 1665.

Publick advertisements (with privilege). No 1 (all issued?), 25 June 1666.

The visions of Quevedo, made English. 1667, 1668 (3rd edn), 1708 (10th edn) etc; rptd 1904, Fontwell 1963.

A guide to eternity. 1672 (anon), 1680, 1680, 1688, 1694, 1709, 1712, 1722; ed J. W. Stanbridge 1900. From the Latin of Cardinal J. Bona.

A discourse of the fishery. 1674, 1695.

The city mercury. 1675. Licensed, and possibly ed L'Estrange.

The parallel: or an account of the growth of knavery under the pretended fears of arbitrary government and popery. 1677. Also issued as An account of the growth of knavery, with a parallel betwixt the reformers of 1677 and those of 1641, 1678, 1679, 1681, 1681.

A treatise of wool and cattel. 1677.

A register of the nativity of the present Christian princes. 1678.

Tyranny and popery lording it over King and people. 1678 (anon), 1680, 1681.

The gentleman 'pothecary: a true story done out of the French. 1678, 1726.

Five love letters from a nun to a cavalier, from the French. 1678, 1686, 1693, 1701.

Seneca's Morals by way of abstract. 1678, 1682, 1693 (5th edn), 1696, 1699, 1702, 1711, 1718, 1722, 1729 etc.

The history of the plot: or a brief and historical account of the charge and defence of Edward Coleman esq [and 16 others], by authority. 1679 (anon), 1680.

An answer to The appeal [by Charles Blount] from the country to the city. 1679, 1681, 1684.

The case put, concerning the succession of his Royal Highness the Duke of York. 1679 (anon), 1679 ('enlarged'), 1680.

The reformed Catholique: or the true Protestant. 1679, 1679 ('corrected').

The free-born subject: or the Englishman's birthright. 1679 (anon), 1680, 1681.

Citt and Bumpkin, in a dialogue over a pot of ale, concerning matters of religion and government. 1680 (anon, 4 edns), 1681; ed B. J. Rahn, Los Angeles 1965 (Augustan Reprint Soc).

Citt and Bumpkin, the second part: or a learned discourse upon swearing and lying, and other laudable qualities tending to a thorow reformation. 1680 (3 edns), 1681.

A seasonable memorial in some historical notes upon the liberties of the presse and pulpit. 1680, 1681 (3rd edn).

A further discovery of the plot. 1680 (3 edns), 1681.

L'Estrange's narrative of the plot, set forth for the edification of his Majesty's liege people. 1680 (3 edns).

The casuist uncas'd in a dialogue betwixt Richard and Baxter, with a moderator between them for quietnesse sake. 1680, 1680, 1681.

Discovery upon discovery, in a defence of Dr Oates against B.W.'s libellous vindication of him. 1680, 1680.

A letter to Miles Prance. 1680.

L'Estrange's case in a civil dialogue between 'Zekiel and Ephraim. 1680, 1680 ('with additions').

A short answer to a whole litter of libels. 1680. Some copies have 'libellers'.

To the Rev Dr Thomas Ken. 1680 (1 Feb).

The committee: or popery in masquerade. 1680, 1681. Verse 'explanation' of an engraving.

A compendious history of the most remarkable passages of the last fourteen years. 1680. Anon.

Goodman country to his worship the City of London. 1680. Anon.

The presbyterian sham. 1680.

The state and interest of the nation, with respect to the Duke of York. 1680.

Twenty select colloquies out of Erasmus Roterodamus. 1680, 1689 (adds 2 colloquies), 1699 (with 7 further colloquies tr Thomas Brown), 1711, 1725.

Tully's Offices. 1680, 1681, 1684, 1688, 1699, 1720 etc; rptd 1900 (Temple Classics).

The character of a papist in masquerade, in answer to the Character of a popish successor. 1681.

A reply to the second part of the Character of a popish successor. 1681.

L'Estrange his appeal humbly submitted to the King's most excellent Majesty and the Three Estates. 1681.

L'Estrange no papist, in answer to a libel entituled L'Estrange a papist. 1681, 1685.

An apology for the protestants, done out of French into English. 1681.

Machiavil's advice to his son, newly translated. 1681. Anon; verse.

Seven Portuguese letters. 1681. Tr L'Estrange.

The Observator in question and answer. 13 April 1681– 9 March 1687.

The dissenter's sayings, in requital for L'Estrange's sayings: published in their own words, for the information of the people. 1681 (3 edns), 1683.

Dissenters sayings: the second part, dedicated to the Grand-Jury of London, August 29 1681. 1681, 1681.

Notes upon Stephen College, grounded principally upon his own declarations and confessions. 1681, 1681.

The reformation reformed: or a short history of new-fashioned Christians. 1681.

A word concerning libels and libellers, humbly presented to the Right Hon Sir John Moor, Lord-Mayor of London. 1681, 1681.

The shammer shamm'd, in a plain discovery. 1681.

A letter out of Scotland. 1681. Anon ('R.L.').

A new dialogue between some body and no body: or the Observator observed. 1681.

Dialogue upon dialogue: or L'Estrange no papist nor jesuite, but the dog Towzer. 1681. By 'Philo-Anglicus'; L'Estrange?

The account clear'd, in answer to a libel intituled A true account from Chichester. 1682.

The apostate protestant, a letter to a friend. 1682 (July). Anon.

Remarks on the growth and progress of non-conformity. 1682. Anon.

Reflections upon two scurrilous libels called Speculum crapegownorum. 1682. Anon.

A sermon prepared to be preach'd. 1682.

Considerations upon a printed sheet entituled the Speech of the late Lord Russel to the sheriffs; together with the paper delivered by him to them on July 21 1683. 1683. Anon; rptd 1882 (Clarendon Historical Soc).

The lawyer outlaw'd. 1683, 1683.

Theosebia: or the churches advocate. 1683.

The whore's rhetorick, calculated to the meridian of London. 1683. Anon; by L'Estrange?

Five love letters written by a cavalier. 1683, 1694.

The observator defended, by the author of the Observator. 1685.

An answer to a letter [by Halifax] to a dissenter, upon occasion of his Majestie's late gracious declaration of indulgence. 1687.

A brief history of the times. 3 pts 1687–8.

A reply to the reasons of the Oxford clergy against addressing. [c. 1687]; rptd W. Scott in Somers tracts vol 9, 1809.

Two cases submitted to consideration. 1687, 1709.

Notice to the reader. In Fairfax's Tasso, 1687.

The Spanish Decameron: or ten novels made English.

1687, [1700], 1712, 1720. 5 novels by Cervantes and 5 by A. del Castillo Solorzano.

Heraclitus ridens redivivus: or a dialogue between Harry [Henry Care] and Roger [L'Estrange] concerning the times. Oxford 1688.

A dialogue between Sir R.L. and T.O.D. [Oates]. 1689.

Some queries concerning the election of members for the ensuing Parliament. 1690. Reply by James Harrington with similar title.

The fables of Aesop and other eminent mythologists, with morals and reflexions. 1692, 1694, 1704. This was followed by Fables and storyes moralized: being a second part of the fables of Aesop, 1699; rptd 2 vols 1703, 1708, 1714, 1715, 1724, 1730, 1738.

Terence's comedies made English. 1694, 1698, 1705, 1718, 1724, 1733, 1741. 'By several hands', including L'Estrange.

The works of Flavius Josephus. 1702, 1708 (abridged), 1709, 1725 (4th edn) etc.

A poem upon imprisonment, written by Sir Roger L'Estrange, when in Newgate, in the days of Oliver Cromwell's usurpation. 1705.

Key to Hudibras. In Samuel Butler, Posthumous works, 1715.

The Spanish pole-cat: or the adventures of Seniora Rufina. 1717, 1727 (as Spanish amusements). From the Spanish of A. del Castillo Solorzano; begun by L'Estrange and completed by J. Ozell.

§ 2

Kitchin, G. L'Estrange: a contribution to the history of the press in the seventeenth century. 1923.

SIR WILLIAM TEMPLE
1628–99
Collections

Works. 2 vols 1720, 1731, 1740, 1750.

Essays on ancient and modern learning and on poetry. Ed J. E. Spingarn, Oxford 1909.

Early essays and romances, with the life and character by his sister Lady Giffard. Ed G. C. Moore Smith, Oxford 1930.

Five miscellaneous essays. Ed S. H. Monk, Ann Arbor 1963.

§ 1

Upon the death of Mrs Catherine Philips. 1664. Anon; verse.

Lettre d'un marchand de Londres a son amy a Amsterdam. [1666]. Anon.

Poems by Sir W.T. [1670?] (priv ptd). A copy with ms corrections by the author in BM.

An essay upon the advancement of trade in Ireland. Dublin [1673].

Observations upon the United Provinces of the Netherlands. 1673, 1673, 1676, 1680, 1690, 1693, 1696, 1705, Edinburgh 1747; ed G. N. Clark, Cambridge 1932, Oxford 1972.

Miscellanea: the first part. 1680, 1681 ('augmented'), 1691, 1693, 1697, 1705.

Miscellanea: the second part. 1690, 1690, 1692 ('augmented'), 1696, 1705.

Miscellanea: the third part, published by Jonathan Swift. 1701.

An essay upon the original and nature of government. In Miscellanea pt 1, 1680; ed R. C. Steensma, Los Angeles 1964 (Augustan Reprint Soc).

Memoirs of what past in Christendom, from the war begun in 1672 to the peace concluded 1679. 1692, 1692, 1693, 1694, 1700, 1709.

An essay upon taxes. 1693.

An answer to a scurrilous pamphlet, lately printed, in-

tituled A letter from Monsieur de Cros to the Lord —.
1693. Anon.

An introduction to the history of England. 1659, 1699
('corrected'), 1708.

The temple of death. 1695 (2nd edn). Verse.

Memoirs: part III, from the peace concluded 1679 to the
time of the author's retirement from publick business,
publish'd [with preface] by Jonathan Swift. 1709, 1709.

Letters

Letters written by Sir William Temple during his being
Ambassador at the Hague to the Earl of Arlington and
Sir John Trevor. 1699.

Letters written by Sir W. Temple Bart and other ministers
of State, published by Jonathan Swift. 2 vols 1700.

Letters to the King, the Prince of Orange: being the third
and last volume, published by Jonathan Swift. 1703.
Continuation of above.

Select letters to the Prince of Orange, King Charles the IId
and the Earl of Arlington; to which is added an Essay
upon the state and settlement of Ireland. 1701.

[Osborne, Dorothy, afterwards Lady Temple]. Letters
from Dorothy Osborne to Sir William Temple. Ed
E. A. Parry, Edinburgh 1888, 1888, 1903 (rev), [1914];
ed G. C. Moore Smith, Oxford 1928.

§ 2

Courtenay, T. P. Memoirs of the life, works and correspondence of Temple. 2 vols 1836. Reviewed by T. B.
Macaulay, Edinburgh Rev 68 1838.

Douglas, D. C. In his English scholars 1660–1730, 1939,
1951 (rev).

Woodbridge, H. E. Temple: the man and his work. New
York 1940.

Ehrenpreis, I. In his Jonathan Swift vol 1, 1962.

GEORGE SAVILE,
1st MARQUIS OF HALIFAX
1633–95
Collections

Foxcroft, H. C. The life and letters of Halifax, with a new
edition of his works. 2 vols 1898.

Complete works. Ed W. Raleigh, Oxford 1912.

Works. Ed J. P. Kenyon 1969 (Pelican).

§ 1

Observations upon a late libel. [1681 ?]; ed H. Macdonald,
Cambridge 1940.

A letter to a dissenter upon occasion of his Majesties late
gracious declaration of indulgence, by T.W. 1687 (6
edns); 1689 (in Fourteen papers); rptd W. Scott in
Somers tracts vol 9, 1813.

A letter from a clergyman in the city to his friend in the
country, containing his reasons for not reading the
Declaration. [1688]. Anon.

The character of a trimmer, by the Honourable Sir
W[illiam] C[oventry]. 1688, 1689, 1689, 1689 ('by Mss
H.'), 1697, 1699. Circulated in ms 1685.

The anatomy of an equivalent. 1688, 1689 (in Fourteen
papers), 1706.

The lady's new-year gift: or advice to a daughter. 1688,
1688 ('corrected'), 1688, Edinburgh 1688, London
1692, 1696, 1699, 1701, 1707, 1734 (11th edn) etc; ed B.
Dobrée 1927.

Maxims [33] found amongst the papers of the Great
Almanzor. 1693.

A rough draft of a new model at sea. 1694; rptd A. F.
Pollard 1897 (in Political pamphlets).

Some cautions to those who are to chuse members to serve
in Parliament. 1695, 1695, 1701, 1734; rptd A. F.
Pollard 1897 (with above).

Miscellanies. 1700, 1704, 1717. Includes Advice to a
daughter; Character of a trimmer etc.

A character of King Charles the Second, and political,
moral and miscellaneous thoughts and reflections. 1750,
Dublin 1750.

Letters

Savile correspondence. Ed W. D. Cooper 1858 (Camden
Soc).

Some unpublished letters of Savile to Gilbert Burnet. Ed
D. L. Poole, EHR 26 1911.

The Rochester-Savile letters 1671–80. Ed J. H. Wilson,
Columbus 1941. Includes 14 letters to Rochester.

§ 2

Foxcroft, H. C. The life and letters of Halifax. 2 vols 1898,
1 vol Cambridge 1946 (rev as A character of the trimmer).

James, D. G. In his Life of reason, 1949.

JOHN DENNIS
1657–1734
Collections

Critical works. Ed E. N. Hooker 2 vols Baltimore 1939–43.

§ 1

Poems in burlesque. 1692.

Poems and letters upon several occasions. 1692.

The passion of Byblis. 1692. Tr from Ovid.

The impartial critick: or some observations upon A short
view of tragedy, written by Mr Rymer. 1693; rptd in
Critical essays of the seventeenth century vol 3, ed J. E.
Spingarn, Oxford 1909.

Miscellanies in verse and prose. 1693, 1697 (as Miscellany
poems, with Passion of Byblis, above).

The court of death: a pindarique poem, to the memory of
Queen Mary. 1695, 1695.

Remarks on a book entitul'd Prince Arthur. 1696. On
Blackmore.

The nuptials of Britain's genius and fame: a pindarick
poem on the peace. 1697.

A plot and no plot: a comedy. (Drury Lane, 8 May 1697).
[1697].

The annals and history of Cornelius Tacitus. 1698. Vol 3.
The 5th bk was tr Dennis. Other translators included
Dryden, William Bromley and John Potenger.

The usefulness of the stage. 1698. A reply to Jeremy
Collier.

[The seamen's case]. [1698–9].

Rinaldo and Armida: a tragedy. (Lincoln's Inn Fields, c.
Nov 1698). 1699.

Iphigenia: a tragedy. (Lincoln's Inn Fields, Dec 1699).
1700.

The advancement and reformation of modern poetry: a
critical discourse in two parts. 1701.

The comical gallant, or the amours of Sir John Falstaffe: a
comedy. (Drury Lane, 1702). 1702. An adaptation of
Merry wives.

The danger of priestcraft to religion and government. 1702.

An essay on the navy. 1702, 1702.

A large account of the taste in poetry and the causes of the
degeneracy of it. Prefixed to The comical gallant, 1702;
rptd in Critical essays 1700–25, ed W. H. Durham, New
Haven 1915.

The monument: a poem to the memory of William the
Third. 1702.

A proposal for putting a speedy end to the war. 1703.

Britannia triumphans. 1704.

Liberty asserted: a tragedy. (Lincoln's Inn Fields, 24 Feb 1704). 1704.

The person of quality's answer to Mr Collier's letter. 1704.

The grounds of criticism in poetry, contain'd in some new discoveries never made before. 1704; rptd in Critical essays 1700–25, ed W. H. Durham, New Haven 1915.

Gibraltar, or the Spanish adventure: a comedy. (Drury Lane, 16 Feb 1705). 1705.

The battle of Ramillia. 1706.

An essay on the operas after the Italian manner. 1706.

Orpheus and Eurydice: a masque. (Unacted). 1707.

Appius and Virginia: a tragedy. (Drury Lane, 5 Feb 1709). [1709].

An essay upon publick spirit: being a satyr in prose upon the manners and luxury of the times. 1711.

Reflections critical and satyrical upon a late rhapsody, call'd An essay upon criticism. [1711]; rptd in Critical essays 1700–25, ed W. H. Durham, New Haven 1915.

An essay upon the genius and writings of Shakespear. 1712.

Remarks upon Cato: a tragedy. 1713.

A poem upon the death of Queen Anne and the accession of King George. 1714.

Priestcraft distinguish'd from Christianity. 1715.

A true character of Mr Pope and his writings. 1716 (anon), 1717.

Remarks upon Mr Pope's translation of Homer, with two letters concerning Windsor Forest and the Temple of fame. 1717.

Select works. 2 vols 1718, 1718–21 (with Coriolanus).

The characters and conduct of Sir John Edgar and his three deputy governors. 1720. Attacks Steele and the Drury Lane management.

The characters and conduct of Sir John Edgar, in a third and fourth letter. 1720.

The invader of his country, or the fatal resentment: a tragedy. (Drury Lane, 11 Nov 1719). An adaptation of Coriolanus.

A defense of Sir Fopling Flutter. 1722.

Julius Caesar acquitted and his murderers condemn'd. 1722.

A short essay towards an English prosody. In J. Greenwood, Essay towards a practical English grammar, 1722 (2nd edn).

Remarks on a play call'd the Conscious lovers: a comedy. 1723.

Vice and luxury public mischiefs: or remarks on a book intitul'd the Fable of the bees. 1724.

The stage defended from scripture, reason, experience and the common sense of mankind. 1726. A reply to Law.

Miscellaneous tracts in two volumes. Vol 1 (all pbd), 1727. Proposals for printing by subscription were issued [1721].

The faith and duties of Christians. [1728?]. Tr from T. Burnet's Latin.

Remarks on Mr Pope's Rape of the lock, in several letters to a friend; with a preface. 1728.

Remarks upon several passages in the preliminaries to the Dunciad, and in Pope's preface to his translation of Homer's Iliad. 1729.

A treatise concerning the state of departed souls. 1733, 1739. From T. Burnet's Latin.

Letters

Letters upon several occasions. 1696 (to and from Dennis, Dryden, Wycherley, Congreve et al, with trns from Voiture; ed Dennis), 1700 (in Voiture's Familiar and courtly letters pt 2), 1705 (in Works of Voiture vol 1).

Original letters, familiar, moral and critical. 2 vols 1721.

§ 2

Paul, H. G. Dennis: his life and criticism. New York 1911.

THOMAS BROWN
1663–1704
Collections

A collection of miscellany poems, letters etc. 1699, 1699, 1700 (with addns).

A collection of all the dialogues. 1704. Includes the unpbd Democratici Vapulantes.

Works. 2 vols 1707 (3rd vol added later, dated 1708 but advertised Sept 1707), 3 vols 1708, 1709, 4 vols 1711–12, 1715 (vols 1–2 described as 4th edn, vols 3–4 as 3rd edn).

Remains, collected from scarce papers and original manuscripts. 1720. Also issued dated 1718 and 1721.

§ 1

The reasons of Mr Bays changing his religion, considered in a dialogue between Crites, Eugenius and Mr Bays. 1688 (anon), 1691 (with addns).

The weesils: a satirical fable. 1691. Anon; verse. Satire on William Sherlock.

The late converts exposed, or the reasons of Mr Bays's changing his religion: part the second. 1690. Anon.

The reasons of Mr Joseph Hains the player's conversion and reconversion: being the third and last part of the dialogue of Mr Bays. 1690 (anon), 1691.

The reasons of the new convert's taking the oaths to the present government. 1691. Anon.

Wit for money: or poet stutter. 1691. Anon. Satire, probably by Brown, on D'Urfey's comedy Love for money.

Novus reformator vapulans: or the Welch Levite tossed in a blanket. 1691 (anon), 1691.

The London Mercury [later Lacedemonian Mercury]. 32 nos 1 Feb–30 May 1692.

Memoirs of the Court of Spain done into English by T. Brown. 1692, 1701.

Familiar letters written by the Earl of Rochester. 2 vols 1697, 1699, 1705. Vol 1 ed Brown.

Erasmus, D., Seven new colloquies translated out of Erasmus Roterodamus, as also the life of Erasmus. 1699.

Commendatory verses, on the author [Blackmore] of the two Arthurs, and the Satyr against wit; by some of his particular friends. 1700, 1702 (with addns). Dedication and several poems by Brown.

A description of Mr D[ryde]n's funeral: a poem. 1700 (anon), 1700, 1700.

The infallible astrologer: or Mr Silvester Partridge's prophesies. 18 nos 16 Oct–24 Feb 1701. Anon. Brown wrote nos 1–11 and Ned Ward nos 12–18. Selections entitled A comical view of London and Westminster rptd, with authors named, in A legacy for the ladies, 1705.

Scarron, P., The whole comical works of Monsr Scarron, translated by Mr Brown and others. 1700, 1703, 1727, 1892.

Laconics: or new maxims of state and conversation. 1701 (anon), 1705. Mainly by Brown.

Advice to the Kentish long-tails, by the wise-men of Gotham. 1701. Anon; rptd as Brown's in Buckingham's works vol 2, 1705.

The adventures of Lindamira, written with her own hand. 1702, 1703, 1713 (as The lover's secretary), 1734, Dublin 1745, 1751. Ed Brown.

A dissertation upon the Mona of Caesar and Tacitus. In William Sacheverell, An account of the Isle of Man, 1702; rptd 1859 (Manx Soc).

Letters from the dead to the living. 3 pts 1702–3, 1707, 1708. Only signed portions by Brown. Pt 2 first pbd in Certamen epistolare, 1703, as Suppl to 2nd pt.

Miscellanea aulica: or a collection of state-treatises. 1702.

Certamen epistolare: or viii letters between an attorney and a dead person. 1703. With other letters. Certamen epistolare had already appeared in Brown's trn of Select epistles or letters out of Cicero, 1702.

The mourning poet. 1703.

The miscellaneous works of the Duke of Buckingham. 2 vols 1704, 1705, 1715. Ed Brown, with a memoir of Buckingham.

The dying thoughts and last reflections, in a letter to a friend. 1704.

The stage-beaux toss'd in a blanket: or hypocrisie alamode, expos'd in a true picture of Jerry [Jeremy Collier]. 1704. Anon.

A legacy for the ladies: or characters of the women of the age, by T. Brown; with a comical view of London and Westminster: or the merry quack, in two parts, the first part by Mr Tho Brown; the second part by Mr Edw Ward [with a character of Brown by Dr Drake]. 1705.

The works of Monsieur Voiture, made English by John Dryden, T. Brown etc. 1705.

Petronius Arbiter, T., The satirical works made English by Mr Wilson, Mr Brown and several others. 1708, 1713, 1899.

Azarias: a sermon held forth in a Quakers meeting. 1710.

Erasmus, Twenty two select colloquies; to which are added seven more dialogues, with the life of the author by Mr T. Brown. 1711.

Lucian, The works translated from the Greek by several eminent hands. 4 vols 1711, 1745.

§ 2

Boyce, B. Brown of facetious memory. Cambridge Mass 1939.

WILLIAM KING
1662–1712

Collections

Remains. 1732, 1734 (as Posthumous works), 1739. Ed Joseph Browne.

Original works. 3 vols 1776. Ed with detailed memoir by John Nichols, assisted by Isaac Reed.

Poetical works, with the life of the author. 2 vols Edinburgh 1781.

§ 1

Reflections upon Mons Varillas's History of heresy. 1688. With Edward Hannes.

An answer to a book which will be publish'd next week, upon Dr Sherlock's book, in vindication of the Trinity. 1693. Anon.

Animadversions on a pretended account of Danmark. 1694. Anon.

A journey to London in the year 1698, after the ingenious method of that made by Dr Martin Lister to Paris in the same year, written originally in French by Monsieur Sorbière. 1698 (anon), 1700 ('corrected'), 1700; ed K. N. Colvile, A miscellany of the Wits, 1920.

Dialogues of the dead, relating to the present controversy concerning the Epistles of Phalaris. 1699 (anon); ed K. N. Colvile, with above.

The furmetary: a very innocent and harmless poem in three cantos. 1699. Anon.

The transactioneer, with some of his philosophical fancies, in two dialogues. 1700. Anon; satire on Sir Hans Sloane.

Mully of the Mountown: a poem. 1702 (for 1704) ('by the author of the Tale of a tub'), 1704.

The fairy feast. 1704 ('by the author of the Tale of a tub, and the Mully of Mountown').

Some remarks on the Tale of a tub; to which are annexed Molly of Mountown and Orpheus and Eurydice [The fairy feast]. 1704. Anon. This is the only complete and authorized edn of these 2 poems.

Miscellanies in prose and verse. 2 vols [1707?].

The art of cookery, in imitation of Horace's Art of poetry, with some letters to Dr Lister and others. [1708], [1708] (both anon), 1708 (unauthorized edn of Art of cookery alone), 1709.

The art of love, in imitation of Ovid, with a preface containing the life of Ovid. [1709], [1709].

Useful transactions in philosophy and other sorts of learning, for the months of January [–September], 1709. 3 pts 1709. Anon.

The present state of physick in the island of Cajamai, to the members of the R.S. No 1 (all pbd), [1709?].

A friendly letter from honest Tom Boggy to the Rev Mr G[oddard]. 1710. Anon.

A second letter to Mr Goddard. 1710. Anon.

A vindication of the Rev Dr Henry Sacheverell. [1711]. With Charles Lambe.

Mr B[isset]'s recantation. 1711. Anon.

An answer to a second scandalous book that Mr B[isse]t is now writing. 1711. Anon.

An historical account of the heathen gods and heroes. [1711], [1711], 1727 (4th edn), 1731, 1761; rptd 1965.

Nandé, G., Political considerations upon refin'd politicks, translated by Dr King. 1711.

Rufinus: or an historical essay on the favourite ministry under Theodosius the Great and his son Arcadius. 1712. Anon; an attack on Marlborough.

Britain's Palladium: or my Lord Bolingbroke's welcome from France. 1712.

Useful miscellanies: containing 1, A preface; 2, The tragicomedy of Joan of Hedington, in imitation of Shakespeare; 3, Some account of Horace his behaviour in Cambridge. Pt 1 (all pbd), 1712.

The northern Atalantis: or York spy, the whole interspersed with poetical amusements, among which is Apple-pye, or instructions to Nelly: a poem written by Dr W. King. 1713; rptd [1893?].

The Persian and the Turkish tales, compleat, translated into French by M. Pétis de la Croix and now into English by Dr King. 1714, 1718.

[Hall, Joseph]. A fragment of Joseph Hall's Mundus alter et idem, translated by Dr W. King. 1885 (in Henry Morley, Ideal Commonwealth).

§ 2

Johnson, S. In his Lives of the English poets, 1779–81.

Horne, C. J. The Phalaris controversy: King versus Bentley. RES 22 1946.

CHARLES GILDON
1665–1724

The history of the Athenian society. [1691]; rptd with revisions in The Athenian oracle vol 4, 1710, 1728.

Nuncius infernalis: or a new account from below. 1692. Anon. With preface by D'Urfey. Both dialogues rptd in Works of Tom Brown, 1715, 1719, and 2nd in the 1730 and 1749 edns.

Dacier, A., An essay upon satyr. Tr Gildon in Miscellany poems, 1692.

Miscellany poems upon several occasions. 1692. Ed Gildon.

The post-boy rob'd of his mail: or the pacquet broke open. 1692. Signed C.G.

The second volume of the post-boy robb'd of his mail: or the pacquet broke open. 1693. Signed C.G.

The oracles of reason. 1693. By Gildon, Charles Blount et al.

Chorus poetarum: or poems on several occasions. 1694, 1696 (as Poems on several occasions), 1698 (as Poetical remains of the Duke of Buckingham, Mrs Behn and others). Ed Gildon.

Miscellaneous letters and essays on several subjects in prose and verse. 1694, 1697 (as Letters and essays). Ed and partly written by Gildon; 2 essays rptd in Critical essays 1700–25, ed W. H. Durham, New Haven 1915, and a short letter in Critical essays of the seventeenth century vol 3, ed J. E. Spingarn, Oxford 1909.

The miscellaneous works of Charles Blount. 1695. Ed Gildon.

The younger brother, or the amorous jilt: a comedy. (Drury Lane, 1696). 1696. By Aphra Behn; rewritten and pbd by Gildon.

The histories and novels of the late ingenious Mrs Behn. 1696, 1697 (3rd edn), 1700, 1705, 1718, 2 vols 1722, 1735. Ed Gildon.

Familiar letters written by the Earl of Rochester. 2 vols 1697, vol 1, 1697, 2 vols 1699, 1705. Vol 2 ed Gildon.

The Roman bride's revenge: a tragedy. (Drury Lane, 1697). 1697. Anon.

Phaeton, or the fatal divorce: a tragedy. (Drury Lane, 1698). 1698. Anon.

The lives and characters of the English dramatick poets. 1699, nd. Anon. Revision and continuation of Langbaine's Account.

Measure for measure, or beauty the best advocate: a comedy. (Lincoln's Inn Fields, 1699). 1700. Anon. An adaptation of Shakespeare.

Love's victim, or the Queen of Wales: a tragedy. (Lincoln's Inn Fields, 1701). 1701. Anon.

A new miscellany of original poems, on several occasions. 1701. Anon. Ed Gildon.

A comparison between the two stages. 1702 (anon); ed S. B. Wells, Princeton 1942.

Examen miscellaneum, consisting of verse and prose. 1702. Anon. Ed Gildon.

The patriot, or the Italian conspiracy: a tragedy. (Drury Lane, 1703). 1703. Anon; an adaptation of Lee's Lucius Junius Brutus.

Ovid Britannicus: or love epistles in imitation of Ovid. 1703. By David Craufurd, ed Gildon.

The deist's manual. 1705.

A letter from the Princess Sophia to the Archbishop of Canterbury, with another from Hanover. 1706 (anon), 1706, [1706?], 1714. Rptd by Gildon from a continental edn.

A review of her Royal Highness the Princess Sophia's letter to the Lord Archbishop of Canterbury: or a Jacobite plot against the Protestant succession discover'd. [1706].

Threnodia Virginea, or the apotheosis: a poem. 1708. Signed C.G.

Libertas triumphans. 1708. Poem on Marlborough's victory.

The new metamorphosis, or the pleasant transformation: being the Golden Ass of Lucius Apuleius of Medaura, the second edition. 2 vols 1709 (anon), 1724, 1821. First edn c. 1708?

The golden spy: or a political journal of the British nights entertainments of war and peace, and love and politics. 1709. Anon. Attempted serial pbn abandoned after 2 nos 1710; rptd in vol 2 of The new metamorphosis, 1724.

An essay on the art, rise and progress of the stage in Greece, Rome and England: remarks on the plays of Shakespear; remarks on the poems of Shakespear. Included in the vol of Shakespear's poems pbd by Curll in 1710 as suppl to Rowe's Works of Shakespear, pbd by Tonson; rptd 1714, 1725, Dublin 1726, 1728, in various edns of Shakespeare.

The life of Mr Thomas Betterton. 1710. Also issued anon, and with The amorous widow: a comedy, written by Mr Betterton, 2 vols 1710.

Plutarch's Lives. 1710, 1713, 1718. Abridged by Gildon from the Dryden version.

A grammar of the English tongue. 1711 (anon), 1712 ('improved'), 1714, nd (6th edn). Known as Brightland's Grammar from the publisher. Preface by Steele.

The works of Lucian. 4 vols 1711. Gildon translated 2 dialogues in vol 2.

A new rehearsal: or Bays the younger. 1714. Anon; an attack on Rowe and Pope.

Trojan tales. 1714. Anon. Advertised 1724; another edn?

Canons, or the vision: a poem. 1717.

The complete art of poetry. 2 vols 1718. Vol 1 contains specimens of Shakespear's beauties; vol 2 other poets' Beauties. Vol 1, pt 2, is rptd in Critical essays 1700–25, ed W. H. Durham, New Haven 1915.

Memoirs of the life of William Wycherley esq. 1718. Anon.

The post-man robb'd of his mail: or the packet broke open. 1719. Anon.

The life and strange surprizing adventures of Mr D[aniel] DeF[oe]. 1719 (anon), 1719, Dublin 1719; rptd P. Dottin 1923 (with an essay on Gildon's life).

Miscellanea aurea: or the golden medley. 1720. Also issued anon. Ed Gildon.

A new project for the regulation of the stage. 1720, 1720. With Dennis.

All for the better: or the world turn'd upside down. 1720.

The battle of the authors. 1720.

The laws of poetry, as laid down by the Duke of Buckinghamshire, the Earl of Roscommon and by the Lord Lansdowne. 1721.

Milesian tales: or instructive novels for the happy conduct of life, written by Mrs Butler. 1727. Ed Gildon. Reissued 1735 as Irish tales.

JOHN ARBUTHNOT
1667–1735
Collections

Miscellaneous works. 2 vols Glasgow 1751, 1751 (with addns), 1770 (with a short life of Arbuthnot).

Aitken, G. A. The life and works of Arbuthnot. Oxford 1892.

§ I

Of the laws of chance. 1692. Anon; trn of Huygens, De ratiociniis in ludo aleae.

Theses medicae de secretione animali, pro gradu doctoratus in medicina consequendo. [St Andrews] 1696.

An examination of Dr Woodward's account of the deluge, by J.A. MD; with a letter to the author concerning an abstract of Agostino Scilla's book on the same subject, by W.W. FRS. 1697, 1741 (as A philosophico-critical history of the deluge, by Dr Arbuthnot and Dr Wotton).

An essay on the usefulness of mathematical learning, in a letter from a gentleman in the city to his friend in Oxford. Oxford 1701, 1721, 1745. Anon.

Tables of the Grecian, Roman and Jewish measures, weights and coins, reduc'd to the English standard. [1705], 1707, 1709.

A sermon preach'd to the people at the Mercat Cross of Edinburgh on the subject of the Union. [Edinburgh] 1706 (anon), Dublin [1706], [Edinburgh? 1707?], 1707, 1707, [1745?].

An argument for Divine Providence, taken from the constant regularity observed in the births of both sexes. Philosophical Trans of Royal Soc 27 1710.

Law is a bottomless-pit. 1712 (6 March; 5 further edns 1712, all anon), Edinburgh 1712.

John Bull in his senses: being the second part of Law is a bottomless-pit. 1712 (18 March; 3 further edns 1712, all anon), Edinburgh 1712.

John Bull still in his sense: being the third part of Law is a bottomless-pit. 1712 (17 April; 3 further edns 1712, all anon), Edinburgh 1712.

An appendix to John Bull still in his senses: or Law is a bottomless-pit. 1712 (9 May; 3 further edns 1712, all anon), Edinburgh 1712.

Lewis Baboon turned honest and John Bull politician: being the fourth part of Law is a bottomless-pit. 1712 (31 July; one further edn 1712, both anon), Edinburgh 1712.

The history of John Bull [the above 5 pamphlets collected]. Edinburgh 1712 (anon), 1727 (in The Pope-Swift Miscellanies in prose and verse vol 2), Glasgow 1766; ed E. Arber 1883 (English garner vol 6); ed K. N. Colvile, A miscellany of Wits 1920; ed H. Teerink, Amsterdam 1925; ed A. W. Bower and R. A. Erickson, Oxford 1976.

Proposals for printing a very curious discourse, in two volumes in quarto, entitled ΨΕΥΔΟΛΟΓΙΑ ΠΟΛΙΤΙΚΗ or a treatise of the art of political lying. 1712 (anon), 1712, Edinburgh 1746; ed A. F. Pollard 1897 (in Political pamphlets).

Concerning the peace. In L. M. Beattie, John Arbuthnot, Cambridge Mass 1935.

Three hours after marriage: a comedy. 1717. Gay was assisted by Pope and Arbuthnot.

Annus mirabilis, by Abraham Gunter, Philomath. 1722 (21 Dec).

Reasons humbly offer'd by the company of upholders, against part of the Bill, for the better receiving drugs. 1724. Anon.

It cannot rain but it pours: or London strow'd with rarities. 1726. Anon. Begun by Arbuthnot, completed by another.

The Craftsman 1726-7. Contributions by Arbuthnot.

Miscellanies in prose and verse. 4 vols 1727-32. Preface signed by Swift and Pope. Vol 2 contains The history of John Bull and The art of political lying; vol 3 The humble petition of the colliers, An essay concerning the origin of the sciences, It cannot rain but it pours.

Tables of ancient coins, weights and measures, explain'd and exemplify'd in several dissertations. 1727 (anon), 1754 (with Appendix, containing Observations on Dr Arbuthnot's Dissertation by Benjamin Langwith).

Oratio anniversaria Harvaeana. 1727.

The Dunciad, variorum; with prolegomena of Scriblerus. 1729. Contributions by Arbuthnot.

Virgilius restauratus. In Dunciad variorum, above.

A brief account of Mr John Ginglicutt's treatise concerning the altercation or scolding of the Ancients. 1731 (Feb). Anon.

An essay concerning the nature of aliments, and the choice of them, according to the different constitutions of human bodies. 2 vols 1731, Dublin 1731, London 1731-2 (with Practical rules of diet, also sold separately), 1735-6, 1751, 1756.

An epitaph on Francis Chartres. London Mag April 1732; GM April 1732.

An essay of the learned Martinus Scriblerus concerning the origin of species. In Miscellanies vol 3, 1732.

An essay concerning the effects of air on human bodies. 1733, 1751, 1756, 1851.

A supplement to Dr Swift's and Mr Pope's works, now first collected into one volume. Dublin 1739. Contains The history of John Bull; Proposals for printing the Art of political lying; The humble petition of the colliers; Reasons humbly offer'd by the upholders; Annus mirabilis; An essay concerning the origin of sciences; Virgilius restauratus; It cannot rain but it pours; Epitaph of Fr—s Ch—is; and other pieces attributed to Arbuthnot.

Miscellanies by Dr Arbuthnot. Dublin 1746. Contains the above pieces, etc.

ΓΝΩΘΙ ΣΕΑΥΤΟΝ, know yourself: poem. 1734. Anon; rptd in Dodsley's Collection of poems by several hands vol 1, 1748.

Memoirs of the extraordinary life, works and discoveries of Martinus Scriblerus. In Works of Pope in prose vol 2, 1741; rptd Dublin 1741 as 'by Mr Pope'.

Miscellanies in prose and verse, by Dr Arbuthnot: a new edition corrected. Glasgow 1766.

A burlesque of Pope's Lines sung by Durastanti. Annual Register 18 1775.

§2

Aitken, G. A. The life and works of Arbuthnot. Oxford 1892.

Teerink, H. (ed). The history of John Bull, with an investigation into its composition, publication and authorship. Amsterdam 1925.

Beattie, L. M. Arbuthnot: mathematician and satirist. Cambridge Mass 1935.

Memoirs of Martinus Scriblerus. Ed C. Kerby-Miller, New Haven 1950.

Steeves, E. L. (ed). The art of sinking in poetry; with bibliographical notes on the last volume of the Swift-Pope Miscellanies by R. H. Griffith and Steeves. New York 1952.

JONATHAN SWIFT
1667–1745

The principal ms collections are in BM, Victoria & Albert Museum, Trinity College Cambridge, Trinity College Dublin, Pierpont Morgan Library, New York, Houghton Library at Harvard and Huntington Library, San Marino Cal.

Bibliographies etc

Teerink, H. A bibliography of the writings in prose and verse of Swift. Hague 1937, Philadelphia 1963 (rev H. Teerink, ed A. H. Scouten).

Landa, L. A. and J. E. Tobin. Swift: a list of critical studies published from 1895 to 1945. New York 1945.

Stathis, J. A bibliography of Swift studies 1945-65. Nashville 1967.

Shinagel, M. A concordance to the poems of Swift. Ithaca 1972.

Collections

The works of J.S., DD, DSPD. 4 vols Dublin 1735 (8°), 1735 (12°), 6 vols Dublin 1738, 8 vols Dublin 1746, 11 vols Dublin 1763 (8°), 20 vols Dublin 1772. Pbd by Faulkner.

The works of Jonathan Swift DD, Dean of St Patrick's, Dublin, accurately revised. 6 vols 1755 (4°), 12 vols 1755 (8°). Ed J. Hawkesworth for Bathurst in opposition to Faulkner's Dublin edns. The 4° edn was completed by 8 additional vols 1764-79 (including the letters) and the 8° edn by 13 vols. Also pbd 27 vols in 18°.

The works of Jonathan Swift DD, Dean of St Patrick's, Dublin: containing additional letters, tracts and poems, not hitherto published; with notes and a life of the author. Ed Sir W. Scott 19 vols Edinburgh 1814, 1824.

Prose works. Ed H. Davis 14 vols Oxford 1939-68.

Miscellanies

Miscellanies in prose and verse. 1711, 1713. Pbd by Morphew. Contains 25 early pieces.

Miscellanies by Dr Jonathan Swift. 1711. Unauthorized; pbd by Curll.

Miscellanies written by Jonathan Swift DD, Dean of St Patrick's, Dublin. 1722 (4th edn, also issued without the general title-page).

Miscellanea never before published. 2 vols 1727. Unauthorized Curll pbn.

Miscellanies in prose and verse. 3 vols 1727. Called First, Second and Last volume. Variously rptd 3 vols (8° and 12°), 1728-33. Pbd by Motte, with pieces by Pope, Gay, Arbuthnot et al.

Miscellanies in prose and verse. 4 vols Dublin 1728-35.

Miscellanies: the third volume. 1732, 1732, 1733, 1736, 1738. Pbd by Motte and Gilliver. Prose and verse by Swift, Pope, Arbuthnot and Gay.

The Drapier's miscellany. Dublin 1733 (3 edns).

Miscellanies: consisting chiefly of original pieces in prose and verse, by D—n S—t, never before published in this

Kingdom; Dublin printed, London reprinted. 1734, 1734. Unauthorized. Not wholly by Swift.

Miscellanies in prose and verse: volume the fifth. 1735. Pbd by C. Davis. Supplements the 4 vols 1727–32, above, by adding pieces from Faulkner's edn of the works.

A collection of poems etc omitted in the fifth volume of miscellanies. 1735. A separately issued supplement, intended to be bound up with the previous item.

Miscellanies. 6 vols 1736. With slight variations contains the matter of 5 vols 1727–32–35, above.

Miscellanies in prose and verse by Dr Swift. Vol VII [and VIII] 1742. Pbd by Cooper. Intended as a supplement to Miscellanies, 6 vols 1736.

Miscellanies in four volumes by Dr Swift, Dr Arbuthnot, Mr Pope and Mr Gay: the fourth edition corrected. 1742. Pbd by C. Bathurst, and based on the earlier Motte Miscellanies. Extended to 13 vols of varying combinations of edns and dates 1742–53.

The sermons of Dr J. Swift, to which is prefixed the author's life; together with his Prayer for Stella, his Thoughts on and Project for the advancement of religion. 2 vols [1790?].

The Drapier's letters to the people of Ireland. Ed H. Davis, Oxford 1935, 1965 (with rev bibliography).

Poems

The poetical works of J.S., DD, DSPD, reprinted from the second Dublin edition. 1736.

Poems. Ed H. Williams 3 vols Oxford 1937, 1958.

Poetical works. Ed H. Davis, Oxford 1967 (OSA).

Selections

Gulliver's travels and selected writings in prose and verse. Ed J. Hayward 1934 (Nonesuch Press), 1949 (corrected).

Gulliver's travels and other writings. Ed L. A. Landa, Cambridge Mass 1960.

§ 1

Supplement to the fifth volume of the Athenian gazette. 1691–2. Contains a letter from Swift and his Ode to the Athenian Society.

Letters written by Sir W. Temple Bart and other Ministers of State, published by Jonathan Swift, domestick chaplain to his Excellency the Earl of Berkeley. 2 vols 1700. The dedication to William III and publisher's epistle to the reader in vol I are by Swift.

Miscellanea: the third part, by the late Sir William Temple Bar, published by Jonathan Swift AM, prebendary of St Patrick's, Dublin. 1701. The Publisher to the reader is by Swift.

A discourse of the contests and dissensions between the nobles and the commons in Athens and Rome. 1701; ed F. H. Ellis, Oxford 1967.

Letters to the King, the Prince of Orange, the chief ministers of State and other persons by Sir W. Temple Bart: being the third and last volume, published by Jonathan Swift DD. 1703. The Preface is by Swift.

A tale of a tub, written for the universal improvement of mankind; to which is added An account of a battel between the antient and modern books in St James's Library. 1704 (3 edns), 1705. Includes The battel of the books and A discourse concerning the mechanical operation of the spirit.

A tale of a tub: the fifth edition, with the author's apology and explanatory notes, by W. W—tt—n BD and others. 1710. Contains the Apology, the footnotes and 8 plates for the first time. The unsigned footnotes are by Swift.

An apology for the tale of a tub. 1711. A suppl to earlier edns.

A tale of a tub. 1724, 1727, 1733, 1739, 1743, (reissued 1751), 1747, 1751 (as vol I of Works, 14 vols), 1755 etc.

A tale of a tub. 1734. Pirated, and set from the edn of 1720, with a bookseller's advertisement and some additional notes.

Dublin edns: 1705 (4th edn), 1726 (7th edn), 1741 (8th edn). Also Edinburgh 1750, Glasgow 1753. Ed A. Guthkelch and D. N. Smith, Oxford 1920, 1958; ed Guthkelch 1902 (as The battle of the books, with selections from the literature of the Phalaris controversy).

Predictions for the year 1708: wherein the month and day of the month are set down, the persons named and the great actions and events of next year particularly related, as they will come to pass, written to prevent the people of England from being further impos'd on by vulgar almanack-makers, by Isaac Bickerstaff esq. 1708 (and several pirated edns under the same title, or as Esquire Bickerstaff's most strange and wonderful predictions for the year 1708).

The accomplishment of the first of Mr Bickerstaff's predictions: being an account of the death of Mr Partridge, the almanack-maker, upon the 29th inst, in a letter to a person of honour. 1708.

An elegy on Mr Patrige, the almanack-maker, who died on the 29th of this instant March 1708. 1708, Edinburgh 1708. Broadside.

A vindication of Isaac Bickerstaff esq against what is objected to him by Mr Partridge, by the said Isaac Bickerstaff esq. 1709.

A famous prediction of Merlin, the British wizard: written above a thousand years ago and relating to this present year, with explanatory notes by T. N. Philomath. 1709, 1708 (for 1709; pirated), Edinburgh 1709, 1740.

A project for the advancement of religion, and the reformation of manners, by a person of quality. 1709, 1709, Edinburgh 1709.

A letter from a Member of the House of Commons in Ireland, to a Member of the House of Commons in England, concerning the sacramental test. 1709, Dublin 1709.

The tatler, by Isaac Bickerstaff esq. 1709–11. No 230 and nos 5 and 20 in Harrison's continuation by Swift. For other nos attributed wholly or in part, *see* Davis, Prose works vol 2.

Memoirs: part III, from the peace concluded 1679 to the time of the author's retirement from publick business, by Sir William Temple Baronet, publish'd by Jonathan Swift DD. 1709, 1709. The Preface is by Swift.

Baucis and Philemon, imitated from Ovid. 1709. No place; 4 leaves.

Baucis and Philemon: a poem; together with Mrs Harris's earnest petition, by the author of the Tale of a tub; as also an Ode upon solitude by the Earl of Roscommon. 1708 (for 1709), 1709, 1710. Pbd by Hills. Baucis and Philemon was also included, together with Mrs Biddy Floyd, in Poetical miscellanies: the sixth part, 1709, pbd by Tonson.

A meditation upon a broom-stick, and somewhat beside, of the same author's. 1710, 1710.

The examiner. 1710. Swift's principal contributions are in vol I.

The examiners for the year 1711; to which is prefix'd A letter to the examiner. 1712.

A short character of his Ex T.E. of W[harton]. L.L. of I——; with an account of some smaller facts. 1711 (3 edns), 1711 (without title-page), [1715?] (with omissions and alterations), nd, nd.

Some remarks upon a pamphlet entitl'd A letter to the seven Lords of the committee appointed to examine Gregg, by the author of the Examiner. 1711, Dublin 1711.

A new journey to Paris; together with some secret transactions between the Fr—h K—g and an Eng— gentleman, by the Sieur du Baudrier, translated from the French. 1711 (3 edns).

The W—ds—r prophecy. 1711 (3 broadside edns).

The conduct of the allies, and of the late ministry, in beginning and carrying on the present war. 1712 (for 1711; 5 edns), 1712-13, Edinburgh 1712, Dublin 1712.

A fable of the widow and her cat. 1711 (for 1712), 1712, 1712, Dublin 1712. Broadsides and half sheet. Partly by Swift.

The fable of Midas. 1711 (for 1712). Half sheet.

Some advice humbly offer'd to the members of the October Club in a letter from a person of honour. 1712, 1712, Dublin 1712.

Some remarks on the barrier treaty between her Majesty and the States-General by the author of the Conduct of the allies. 1712, 1712, Edinburgh 1712, Dublin 1712, 1712.

A proposal for correcting, improving and ascertaining the English tongue, in a letter to the most honourable Robert Earl of Oxford and Mortimer, Lord High Treasurer of Great Britain. 1712, 1712.

Some reasons to prove that no person is obliged by his principles as a Whig to oppose Her Majesty or her present Ministry, in a letter to a Whig-Lord. 1712, Dublin 1712.

T——nd's invitation to Dismal, to dine with the Calves-head Club. 1712 (broadside, no place), [Edinburgh?] 1712.

A hue and cry after Dismal: being a full and true account, how a Whig Lord was taken at Dunkirk, in the habit of a chimney-sweeper, and carryed before General Hill. 1712 (broadside), 1712 (as Dunkirk to be let with a hue and cry after Dismal).

Peace and Dunkirk: being an excellent new song upon the surrender of Dunkirk to General Hill. 1712. Broadside.

Dunkirk still in the hands of the French. 1712. Mentioned by Swift, Journal to Stella, 17 July 1712, and advertised in Examiner of that date. No known copy.

A letter from the pretender to a Whig-Lord. 1712. Broadside.

A letter of thanks from my Lord W**** n to the Lord Bp of S. Asaph. 1712, 1712.

Remarks on the Bp of S. Asaph's Preface. Examiner 24 July 1712.

An appendix to the Conduct of the allies; and Remarks on the Barrier Treaty. Examiner 16 Jan 1713.

Mr C—n's discourse of free-thinking, put into plain English, by way of abstract, for the use of the poor, by a friend of the author. 1713.

A complete refutation of the falsehoods alleged against Erasmus Lewis esq. Examiner 2 Feb 1713.

The address of the House of Lords to the Queen. 10 April 1713. Ptd in Journals of the House of Lords, 11 April 1713.

Part of the seventh epistle of the first book of Horace imitated, and address'd to a noble peer. 1713 (3 edns), Dublin 1713.

The importance of the Guardian considered, in a second letter to the bailiff of Stockbridge, by a friend of Mr St—le. 1713.

A preface to the B—p of S—r—m's introduction, to the third volume of the history of the reformation of the Church of England, by Gregory Misosarum. 1713, 1713, Dublin 1714.

The first ode of the second book of Horace paraphras'd, and address'd to Richard St—le esq. 1713 (for 1714), 1714, Dublin 1714.

The publick spirit of the Whigs, set forth in their generous encouragement of the author of the Crisis; with some observations on the Seasonableness, candor, erudition and style of that treatise. 1714. Pbd 23 Feb 1714. At least 7 further edns, London and Dublin, in the same year. A long passage offensive to the Scots Lords was expunged after 1st issue. Copies of the 1st and 2nd edns occur censored and uncensored.

Letters, poems and tales: amorous, satyrical and gallant, which passed between several persons of distinction.

1718. Contains A decree for concluding the treaty between Dr Swift and Mrs Long.

The works of Sir William Temple, Bart, in two volumes. 1720. Prefaces etc by Swift.

An elegy on the much lamented death of Mr Demar, the famous rich man, who died the 6th of this inst July, 1720. [Dublin] [1720], [1720]. Broadside.

A proposal for the universal use of Irish manufacture, in cloaths and furniture of houses etc, utterly rejecting and renouncing every thing wearable that comes from England. Dublin 1720.

A letter from a lay-patron to a gentleman, designing for holy orders. Dublin 1720, London 1721 (as A letter to a young gentleman, lately enter'd into holy orders, by a person of quality), 1721.

Epilogue to be spoke at the Theatre-Royal this present Saturday being April the 1st, in the behalf of the distressed weavers. Dublin [1721] (broadside), Dublin [1721] (as An epilogue, as it was spoke by Mr Griffith at the Theatre-Royal on Saturday the first of April in behalf of the distressed weavers). Ptd on the verso of A prologue spoke by Mr Elrington.

The bubble: a poem. 1721, Dublin 1721; rptd in Miscellanies: the last volume, 1727, as The South Sea.

Subscribers to the bank plac'd according to their order and quality, with notes and queries. Dublin [1721]. Probably by Swift.

The run upon the bankers. [Dublin 1720?]. No known copy, but a Cork broadside of 1721 was probably rptd from a Dublin issue.

The wonderful wonder of wonders. [Dublin 1721?], 1722 (amplified as Being an accurate description of the birth, education, manner of living, religion, politicks, learning etc of mine a—se, by Dr Sw—ft). Probably by Swift. Rptd as his in Miscellanies: the third volume, 1732, and in Faulkner's edn of Works, 1735.

The wonder of all the wonders that ever the world wondered at. [Dublin 1721?], 1722. Probably by Swift. Rptd as his in Miscellanies: the third volume, 1732, and in Faulkner's edn of Works, 1735.

The bank thrown down. Dublin 1721, 1721. Broadside.

The last speech and dying words of Ebenezer Elliston, who is to be executed this second day of May 1722: publish'd at his desire for the common good. Dublin [1722].

The first of April: a poem, inscribed to Mrs E.C. [1723?]

Some arguments against enlarging the power of Bishops in letting of leases, with remarks on some queries lately published. Dublin 1723.

A letter to the shop-keepers, tradesmen, farmers and common-people of Ireland, concerning the brass half-pence coined by Mr Woods, with a design to have them pass in this kingdom, by M. B. Drapier. Dublin [1724] (folio and 2 8° edns), [Limerick 1724].

A letter to Mr Harding the printer, upon occasion of a paragraph in his news-paper of Aug 1st relating to Mr Woods's half-pence, by M. B. Drapier. Dublin [1724], [1724], Limerick [1724] (as An answer to Mr Wood's proposal).

Some observations upon a paper call'd The Report of the committee of the most honourable the Privy-Council in England, relating to Wood's half-pence, by M. B. Drapier. Dublin [1724] (at least 3 edns).

A letter to the whole people of Ireland, by M. B. Drapier. Dublin [1724], [1724].

Seasonable advice: since a bill is preparing for the Grand-Jury to find against the printer of the Drapier's last letter, there are several things to be considered before they determine upon it. [Dublin] 1724. Broadside.

An extract out of a book entituled An exact collection of the debates of the House of Commons held at Westminster, October 21 1680. Pag 150. [Dublin 1724].

His Grace's answer to Jonathan. Dublin 1724. Broadside.

To his Grace the Arch-bishop of Dublin: a poem. Dublin [1724]. Broadside.

An excellent new song upon his Grace our good Lord Archbishop of Dublin, by honest Jo, one of his Grace's farmers in Fingal. Dublin 1724. Broadside.

Prometheus, a poem. Dublin 1724. Broadside.

A letter to the Right Honourable the Lord Viscount Molesworth, by M. B. Drapier, author of the letter to the shop-keepers etc. Dublin·[1724].

Fraud detected, or the Hibernian patriot: containing all the Drapier's letters to the people of Ireland on Wood's coinage etc. Dublin 1725.

The birth of manly virtue, from Callimachus. Dublin 1725 (folio and 8°).

A riddle by Dr S—t to my Lady Carteret. [Dublin 1725]. Broadside. Followed by Answered by Dr S—g.

Cadenus and Vanessa: a poem. 1726.

Travels into several remote nations of the world, in four parts, by Lemuel Gulliver, first a surgeon, and then a captain of several ships. Vol 1, 1726.

Travels into several remote nations of the world, by Captain Lemuel Gulliver, pt III: A voyage to Laputa, Balnibarbi, Glubbdubdrib, Luggnagg and Japan; pt IV: A voyage to the Houyhnhnms. 1726.

Travels into several remote nations. 2 vols 1726 (vol II The second edition), 1726 (no indication of edn), 1727 (12°, reissued 1731), 1727 (8°, vol II The second edition, corrected), 1 vol 1742 (4th edn), 1747 (5th edn), 2 vols 1748, 1751 (5th edn, distinct from 1747 edn), 1 vol 1751 (12°), 1751 (6th edn), 1755 (4° and 8°, both rev Hawkesworth in opposition to the text of Faulkner's Dublin edns), 2 vols 1757, 1760, 1765, 1766, 1767, 1768, 1777; ed T. Sheridan 1784.

Travels into several remote nations. Dublin 1726, 1727, 2 vols in 1 1727, 1 vol 1735 (8°, as vol III of Works, and embodying important textual revision), 1735 (12°, as vol III of Works), 1738, 1743, 1752, 1756, 1759 (with textual changes in mistaken deference to the Preface to Bathurst's 1755 edn), 1763, 1772.

Modern annotated edns: G. A. Aitken 1896 (Temple Classics); H. Williams 1926; A. E. Case, New York 1938; P. Dixon and J. Chalker 1967 (Penguin); P. Turner, Oxford 1970.

A short view of the state of Ireland. Dublin 1727-8, [1728]; rptd, with preface by Sheridan, as Intelligencer no 15.

An answer to a paper called A memorial of the poor inhabitants, tradesmen and labourers of the Kingdom of Ireland, by the author of the short view of the state of Ireland. Dublin 1728.

The intelligencer. Numb 1, Saturday May 11, to be continued weekly. Dublin 1728. 20 nos. By Swift and Sheridan. Pbd as vol, 1729 (19 nos), 1730 (20 nos). No 19 was separately rptd as A letter from the Revd J.S. DSPD to a country gentleman in the north of Ireland, printed in the year 1736.

A modest proposal for preventing the children of poor people from being a burthen to·their parents or the country, and for making them beneficial to the publick. Dublin 1729, London 1729, Dublin 1730, London 1730 (3 edns).

The journal of a Dublin lady, in a letter to a person of quality. Dublin [1729], 1729, London 1740 (as The journal of a modern lady). Also half sheet edn of later date. Rptd 1730, 1731, 1743, in 2nd–4th edns of The metamorphosis of the town.

On Paddy's character of the Intelligencer. [Dublin 1729?]. Broadside.

A panegyric on the Reverend Dean Swift. [Dublin] 1729–30, London 1730.

An apology for the Lady C—R—T on her inviting Dean S—F—T to dinner. [Dublin?] 1730.

Lady A—S—N weary of the Dean. [Dublin?] 1730. Broadside.

An epistle to his Excellency John Lord Carteret, Lord Lieutenant of Ireland. Dublin [1730] (folio and 8°).

An epistle upon an epistle from a certain doctor to a certain great Lord: being a Christmas-box for D. D—ny. Dublin 1730.

An epistle to his Excellency John Lord Carteret, Lord Lieutenant of Ireland; to which is added An epistle upon an epistle: being a Christmas-box for Doctor D—ny. Dublin 1730.

A libel on D—D— and a certain great Lord. [Dublin] 1730, 1730, London 1730 (4 edns), 1730 (as A satire on Dr D—NY, by Dr Sw—T).

To Doctor D—l—y on the libels writ against him. London printed and Dublin reprinted in the year 1730. Dublin 1730. The imprint is deliberately misleading. The first printing was in Dublin.

An answer to Dr D—y's fable of the pheasant and the lark. [Dublin?] 1730.

A vindication of his Excellency the Lord C—T, from the charge of favouring none but Tories, High-Churchmen and Jacobites, by the Reverend Dr S—T. 1730, Dublin 1730.

Horace, book I ode XIV, paraphrased and inscribed to Ir—d. [Dublin] 1930 (for 1730).

Traulus: the first part, in a dialogue between Tom and Robin. [Dublin] 1730, 1730.

Traulus: the second part. [Dublin] 1730.

The Hibernian patriot: being a collection of the Drapier's letters to the people of Ireland, concerning Mr Wood's brass half-pence, printed at Dublin. London reprinted 1730. A reprint of Fraud detected, 1725, above, with slight alterations.

Memoirs of Capt John Creichton, written by himself. 1731, Glasgow 1768. The Advertisement to the reader is by Swift.

Helter skelter: or the hue and cry after the attornies, going to ride the circuit. [Dublin 1730, 1731]. Broadside.

The place of the damn'd, by J.S., DD, DSPD. [Dublin] 1731. Broadside.

A soldier and a scholar: or the lady's judgment upon those two characters in the persons of Captain— and D—n S—T. 1732 (pbd Jan by Roberts), 1732 (reissued as 2nd edn), 1732 (3rd edn, reissued as 4th edn), Dublin 1732 (as The grand question debated: whether Hamilton's bawn should be turn'd into a barrack, or a malthouse; according to the London edition, with notes). Last edn adds a paraphrase of Horace, bk I ode XIV.

Considerations upon two bills sent down from the R— H— the H— of L— to the h—ble H— of C— relating to the clergy of I*****D. 1732, 1732 (as Considerations upon two bills, by the Rev Dr Swift DSPD; to which is added A proposal for an Act of Parliament to pay off the debt of the nation, by A— P—, esq).

An examination of certain abuses, corruptions and enormities in the city of Dublin. Dublin 1732, London 1732 (as City cries instrumental and vocal: or an examination of certain abuses, corruptions and enormities in London and Dublin).

The lady's dressing room; to which is added A poem on cutting down the old thorn at Market Hill, by the Rev Dr S—T. 1732, 1732, Dublin 1732 (3 edns).

The advantages propos'd by repealing the sacramental test, impartially considered. Dublin 1732, London 1732 (To which is added Remarks on a pamphlet intitled The nature and consequences of the sacramental test consider'd).

Quæries wrote by Dr J. Swift in the year 1732, very proper to be read (at this time) by every member of the established Church. [Dublin? 1732]. Half sheet. Advantages, above, and Quæries were rptd in The dispute adjusted (by Gibson, Bishop of London), 1733.

An elegy on Dicky and Dolly. Dublin 1732.

An answer to a late scandalous poem, wherein the author most audaciously presumes to compare a cloud to a woman. Dublin 1733. With T. Sheridan, A new simile for the ladies.

Some considerations humbly offered to the Right Honourable the Lord-Mayor, the Court of Aldermen and

Common Council of the honourable City of Dublin, in the choice of a recorder. [Dublin] 1733. Half sheet.

Advice to the freemen of the city of Dublin. [Dublin] 1733. Broadside.

The life and genuine character of Doctor Swift, written by himself. 1733 (folio and 8°), Dublin 1733, 1739 (rev and extended as Verses on the death of Doctor Swift).

A serious and useful scheme to make an hospital for incurables of universal benefit to all his Majesty's subjects; to which is added A petition of the footmen in and about Dublin, by a celebrated author in Ireland. 1733, Dublin 1733, 1733, 1734. Only the Petition is by Swift. A serious and useful scheme is probably by M. Pilkington.

The Presbyterians plea of merit in order to take off the test impartially examined. Dublin 1733, London [1733?], [1733?].

On poetry: a rapsody. 1733, [1734?], Dublin 1734.

Reasons humbly offered to the Parliament of Ireland for repealing the sacramental test etc in favour of the Catholics, otherwise called Roman Catholics, and by their ill-willers Papists, written in the year 1733. [1734?].

Some reasons against the bill for settling the tyth of hemp, flax etc by a modus. Dublin 1724 (for 1734).

An epistle to a lady who desired the author to make verses on her, in the heroick stile; also a poem occasion'd by reading Dr Young's Satires called The universal passion. Dublin, printed and re-printed at London. 1734.

Poems on several occasions [by Mary Barber]. 1734, 1735, 1736. Contains a commendatory letter by Swift to John, Earl of Orrery.

A beautiful young nymph going to bed, written for the honour of the fair sex; to which are added Strephon and Chloe; and Cassinus and Peter. Dublin printed, London reprinted. 1734.

The Rev Dean Swift's reasons against lowering the gold and silver coin. Ptd on verso of title of Reasons why we should not lower the coins now current in this Kingdom, Dublin [1736].

A proposal for giving badges to the beggars in all the parishes of Dublin, by the Dean of St Patrick's. Dublin 1737, London 1737.

Some thoughts on the tillage of Ireland. 1737, Dublin 1738. By Alexander M'Aulay. Prefatory letter by Swift.

An imitation of the sixth satire of the second book of Horace: the first part done in the year 1714 by Dr Swift; the latter part now first added, and never before printed. 1738. Completed by Pope.

The beasts confession to the priest on observing how most men mistake their own talents, written in the year 1732. Dublin 1738, 1738, London 1738 (3 edns).

A complete collection of genteel and ingenious conversation, according to the most polite mode and method now used at court, and in the best companies of England, in three dialogues, by Simon Wagstaff esq. 1738, Dublin 1738; ed E. Partridge, New York 1963.

Verses on the death of Dr Swift, written by himself Nov 1731. 1739 (5 folio edns), London (for Edinburgh?) 1739 (8°), Dublin 1739 (5 edns), London (for Edinburgh?) 1741, Dublin 1741.

Some free thoughts upon the present state of affairs, written in the year 1714. Dublin 1741, 1741, London 1741, 1741.

Three sermons, I: On mutual subjection; I: On conscience; III: On the Trinity, by the Reverend Dr Swift, Dean of St Patrick's. 1744, 1744 (with a 4th sermon, The difficulty of knowing one's self, added [not by Swift?]), Dublin 1744, 1760 (as Four sermons).

Directions to servants in general; and in particular to the butler, cook, by the Reverend Dr Swift DSPD. 1745, 1746, 1749, Dublin 1745, 1746; tr German, 1748.

The story of the injured lady: being a true picture of Scotch perfidy, Irish poverty and English partiality, with letters and poems never before printed, by the Rev Dr Swift DSPD. 1746, Dublin 1749.

The last will and testament of Jonathan Swift DD. Dublin printed, London reprinted 1746.

A true copy of the late Rev Dr Jonathan Swift's will, taken from, and compar'd with, the original. [Dublin? 1746?], London 1746, Dublin 1747.

Brotherly love: a sermon, preached in St Patrick's Church on December 1st 1717, by Dr Jonathan Swift, Dean of St Patrick's, Dublin. Dublin 1754, London 1754.

The history of the four last years of the Queen, by the late Jonathan Swift DD, DSPD. 1758, Dublin 1758 (as vol 9 of Works, and as The history of the last session of Parliament, and of the Peace of Utrecht, written at Windsor in the year 1713).

An enquiry into the behavior of the Queen's last Ministry. Ed I. Ehrenpreis, Bloomington 1956. First pbd 1765 in vol 8 of Hawkesworth's 4° edn of Works.

Letters

Letters to and from Dr J. Swift DSPD from the year 1714 to 1738. Dublin 1741. Pbd by Faulkner; also issued as vol VII of his edn of Works.

Dean Swift's literary correspondence, for twenty-four years from 1714 to 1738. 1741. Curll. Follows above with some variations.

Letters written by the late Jonathan Swift DD, Dean of St Patrick's, Dublin; and several of his friends. Ed J. Hawkesworth 1766, 1766, 1767, 1768, 1769; ed Hawkesworth and D. Swift 6 vols 1768-9. Part of Hawkesworth's edn of Works, 1755-79. Letters 1 and 41-65 of the Journal to Stella were first pbd by Hawkesworth in Works, vol 10, 1766. Letters 2-40 were first pbd by D. Swift in Works vol 12 1768. The best modern annotated edns of the Journal to Stella are G. A. Aitken 1901; H. Williams 2 vols Oxford 1948.

Unpublished letters of Dean Swift. Ed G. B. Hill 1899.

The correspondence of Swift, with an introduction by J. H. Bernard. Ed F. E. Ball 6 vols 1910-14.

The letters of Swift to Charles Ford. Ed D. N. Smith, Oxford 1935.

The correspondence of Swift. Ed H. Williams 5 vols Oxford 1963-5.

§ 2

For early criticism see Swift: the critical heritage, *ed K. Williams 1970.*

Orrery, Earl of. Remarks on the life and writings of Swift. 1752. Reply by P. Delany, Observations upon Lord Orrery's Remarks, 1754.

Hawkesworth, J. Life of Swift. 1755, Dublin 1755.

Johnson, S. In his Lives of the poets, 1779-81.

Sheridan, T. Life of Swift. 1784.

Scott, W. Memoirs of Swift. 1814.

Spence, J. In his Anecdotes, observations and characters, ed S. W. Singer 1820; ed J. Osborn 2 vols Oxford 1966.

Stephen, L. Swift. 1882 (EML).

Williams, H. Dean Swift's library. 1932.

— Swift, Hawkesworth and the Journal to Stella. In Essays on the eighteenth century presented to David Nichol Smith, Oxford 1945.

— Swift's early biographers. In Pope and his contemporaries: essays presented to George Sherburn, Oxford 1949.

— The text of Gulliver's travels. Cambridge 1952.

Woolf, V. Swift's Journal to Stella. In her Second common reader, 1932.

Leavis, F. R. The irony of Swift. Scrutiny 2 1934; rptd in his Determinations, 1934; and in his Common pursuit, 1952.

Jones, R. F. Ancients and moderns: a study of the background of the Battle of the books. St Louis 1936.

— The satire of Swift. New York 1947.

Quintana, R. The mind and art of Swift. New York 1936, 1953 (with additional notes and bibliography).
—— Swift: an introduction. 1955.
Davis, H. The conciseness of Swift. In Essays on the eighteenth century presented to David Nichol Smith, Oxford 1945.
Nicolson, M. H. Voyages to the moon. New York 1948.
'Orwell, George' (E. Blair). Politics vs literature: an examination of Gulliver's travels. In his Shooting an elephant and other essays, 1950.
Landa, L. A. Swift and the Church of Ireland. Oxford 1954.
Price, M. Swift's rhetorical art. New Haven 1953.
—— Swift: order and obligation. In his To the palace of wisdom, New York 1964.
Murry, J. M. Swift: a critical biography. 1954.
Monk, S. H. The pride of Lemuel Gulliver. Sewanee Rev 63 1955; rptd in Eighteenth-century English literature: modern essays in criticism, ed J. L. Clifford, New York 1959.
Ehrenpreis, I. The personality of Swift. Cambridge Mass 1958.
—— Swift: the man, his works, and the age. 3 vols 1962-.
—— Swift and the comedy of evil. In The world of Swift, ed B. Vickers, Oxford 1968.
Williams, K. M. Swift and the age of compromise. Lawrence Kansas 1958.
—— Jonathan Swift. 1968.
Crane, R. S. The rationale of the fourth voyage. In Swift: Gulliver's travels, New York 1961.
—— The Houyhnhnms, the Yahoos and the history of ideas. In Reason and the imagination: studies in the history of ideas 1600–1800, ed J. A. Mazzeo, New York 1962.
Rogers, P. Swift and the idea of authority. In The world of Swift, ed B. Vickers, Oxford 1968.
Donoghue, D. Swift: a critical introduction. Cambridge 1969.
Rawson, C. J. Swift. 1971.
—— Gulliver and the gentle reader. 1973.
Probyn, C. T. The art of Swift. 1978.
Steele, P. Swift: preacher and jester. Oxford 1978.

EDWARD WARD
1667–1731

Most of Ward's works were anon or 'by the author of the London Spy'.

Collections

The writings of the author of the London-Spy. 4 vols 1703–9.

§ 1

The school of politicks: or the humours of a coffee-house. 1690, 1691 (enlarged).
The poet's ramble after riches: or a night's transactions upon the road burlesqu'd. 1691, 1692, 1698, 1699, 1700, 1701, 1720, Dublin 1724.
The miracles perform'd by money. 1692.
Female policy detected: or the arts of a designing woman laid open. 1695, 1702, 1704, 1712, 1716, [1720], 1749, 1755, 1828, Baltimore 1830, Glasgow 1835. Authorship later denied by Ward.
Ecclesia et factio: a dialogue between Bow-steeple dragon and the Exchange grasshopper. 1698.

The London Spy. 18 monthly pts 1698–1700. Pts 1–2, 1700 (3rd edn).
The London-Spy compleat in eighteen-parts, by the author of the Trip to Jamaica. 1703, 1704 (enlarged), 1706 (3rd edn, as The London-Spy compleat in eighteen parts: the first volume of the author's writings), 1709, 1718, 1753 ('revis'd'); ed K. Fenwick 1955.
O raree-show, o pretty-show: or the city feast. 1698.
Sot's paradise: or the humours of a Derby ale-house, with a satyr upon the ale. 1698, 1699, 1700.
A trip to Jamaica, with a true character of the people and the island, by the author of Sot's paradise. 1698 (3 edns), 1699 (3 edns), 1700, 1702; New York 1933 (facs).
The cockpit combat: or the baiting of the tiger. 1699.
The Dutch-guards farewel to England. 1699. A broadside.
A hue and cry after a man-midwife. 1699.
A frolick to the horn-fair with a walk from cuckold's point thro' Deptford and Greenwich. 1699, 1700, 1702, 1704.
The insinuating bawd and the repenting harlot. 1699, 1700, 1755, 1758.
Modern religion and ancient loyalty: a dialogue. 1699.
A trip to New-England, with a character of the country and people, both English and Indians. 1699; New York 1933 (facs).
A walk to Islington, with a description of New Tunbridge Wells and Sadler's musick-house. 1699, 1701.
The weekly comedy as it is dayly acted at most coffee houses. 10 weekly nos 10 May–12 July 1699. Re-issued, with general title and Epilogue, 1699, as The humours of a coffee-house: a comedy.
The world bewitched: a dialogue between two astrologers and the author. 1699.
The dancing school with the adventures of the Easter holydays. 1700.
The English nun: or a comical description of a nunnery. [1700].
The reformer exposing the vices of the age in several characters. 1700.
The grand mistake: or all men happy if they please. [1700?].
Labour in vain: or what signifies little or nothing. 1700.
Laugh and be fat, or an antidote against melancholy. 1700, 1733, 1741 (12th edn), 1761.
The metamorphosed beau: or the intrigues of Ludgate. 1700, 1703.
The pleasures of single life or the miseries of matrimony. [1700?], 1709.
The rambling rakes: or London libertines. 1700.
A step to the Bath, with a character of the place. 1700, 1700.
A step to stir-bitch-fair, with remarks upon the University of Cambridge. 1700.
The infallible astrologer: or Mr Silvester Partridge's prophesies. 18 weekly nos 16 Oct 1700–24 Feb 1701. Tom Brown wrote nos 1–11, Ward nos 12–18. Selections entitled A comical view of London and Westminster were rptd in A legacy for the ladies, 1705.
The wealthy shop-keeper: or the charitable citizen, a poem. 1700, 1702 (rev as The character of a covetous citizen).
Aesop at Paris: his life and letters. 1701.
Battle without bloodshed: or martial discipline buffoon'd by the city train-bands. 1701.
A collection of the writings hitherto extant of Mr Edward Ward. 1701 (13 folio works with general title), 1702 (with addns).
The revels of the gods: or a ramble thro' the heavens. 1701.
Three nights adventures or accidental intrigues. 1701.

Bribery and simony: or a satyr against the corrupt use of money. 1703.

A journey to Hell: or a visit paid to the Devil. 3 pts 1700–5; pt 1, 1700; rptd later as The infernal vision.

The rise and fall of madam coming sir. 1703.

Female dialogues: or ladies conversations, by the author of the London spy. 1704.

The secret history of the Calves-head Clubb: or the republican unmasqu'd. 1703 (3 edns), 1704, 1705, Dublin 1705, 1706 ('with large improvements'), 1707, 1709, 1713 (as The Whig's unmasked: being the secret history of the Calf's head Club), 1714, 1721; rptd in Harleian Miscellany vol 6, 1744.

All men mad: or England a great Bedlam. 1704.

The dissenting hypocrite: or occasional conformist. 1704.

Helter skelter: or the devil upon two sticks. 1704.

The libertine's choice: or the mistaken happiness of the fool in fashion. 1704, 1709.

Fair shell but a rotten kernel: or a bitter nut for a facetious monkey. 1705.

Honesty in distress, but relieved by no party. 1705, 1708 (3 edns), 1710, 1725.

Hudibras redivivus: or a burlesque poem on the times. 24 pts 1705–7, 2 vols 1707, 1708, 1710 ('with an apology and some other improvements throughout the whole; to which is added the Rambling fuddle caps: or a tavern struggle for a kiss'), 1715.

A legacy for the ladies, or characters of the women of the age, by T. Brown, with a comical view of London and Westminster: or the merry quack, in two parts; the first part by Mr Tho Brown; the second part by Mr Edw Ward. 1705.

A pacquet from Will's. In Works of Monsieur Voiture: second edition vol 2, 1705. 4 letters by Ward.

A satyr against wine, with a poem in praise of small beer. 1705.

A trip to Germany: or the poet turn'd carbineer. 1705.

The barbecue-feast: or the three pigs of Peckham, broil'd under an apple-tree. 1706.

The rambling fuddle-caps: or a tavern struggle for a kiss. 1706, 1709.

Mars stript of his armour: or the army display'd in all its true colours. 1707, 1708, 1709, [1710], 1765, 1779.

The humours of a coffee-house: a comedy. 7 nos 25 June–6 Aug 1707.

The London Terraefilius: or the satyrical reformer. 6 pts 1707–8.

The weekly comedy: or the humours of a coffee-house. 24 nos 13 Aug 1707–22 Jan 1708.

The wooden world dissected in the character of a ship of war. 1707, 1708, 1709, 1711, 1749, 1756, 1760, 1801, Chatham 1807, 1929.

The forgiving husband and adultress wife: or a seasonable present to the unhappy pair in Fenchurch-street. 1708, [1710].

Marriage-dialogues: or a poetical peep into the state of matrimony. 1708, 1709, 1710 (as Matrimony unmask'd), 2 vols 1710 (expanded as Nuptial dialogues and debates), 1723, 1737, 1759.

The modern world disrob'd: or both sexes stript of their pretended vertue. 1708, [1710] (as Adam and Eve stripped of their furbelows) (partly verse), 1714.

The satyrical works of Titus Petronius Arbiter. 3 pts 1708.

The wars of the elements: or a description of a sea storm. 1708, 1709, 1709, 1730.

The history of the London clubs: or the citizen's pastime. Pt 1, 1709, 1711; The second part of the London clubs, [1720?]; 2 pts 1709, 1709, 1710 (as The secret history of clubs), 1745 (enlarged to 31 clubs, as A compleat and humorous account of all the remarkable clubs and societies in the cities of London and Westminster), 1756; rptd 1896 (from original edns).

The diverting works of the famous Miguel de Cervantes. 1710. Introd by Ward.

Vulvus britannicus: or the British Hudibras, in fifteen cantos, the five parts compleat in one volume. 1710, 1710, 1711.

Wine and wisdom, or the tipling philosophers: a lyrick poem. 1710, 1710, 1719, Dublin 1751.

The life and notable adventures of that renown'd knight Don Quixote de la Mancha translated into Hudibrastic verse. 2 vols 1711–12, Edinburgh 1804.

The poetical entertainer: or tales, satyrs, dialogues etc serious and comical. 5 nos 1712.

The quack-vintners: or a satyr against bad wine. 1712.

The history of the Grand Rebellion: containing the most remarkable transactions from the beginning of the reign of King Charles I to the happy restoration. 3 vols 1713–15.

The field spy: or the walking observator. 1714.

The Hudibrastic brewer: or a preposterous union between malt and meter. 1714, 1727. Included in A collection of historical and state poems, 1717.

The mourning prophet: or faction revived by the death of Queen Anne. 1714.

The republican procession, or the tumultuous cavalcade: a merry poem. 1714, 1714 (enlarged), 1727 ('to which is added An answer by the same author'), 1730.

The Lord Whiglove's elegy, with a pious epitaph upon the late Bishop of Addlebury. 1715.

St Paul's church: or the protestant ambulators. 1716.

British wonders: or a poetical description of the several prodigies and most remarkable accidents that have happened in Britain since the death of Queen Anne. 1717, 1717.

A collection of the best English poetry, by several hands. 1717.

A seasonable sketch of an Oxford reformation. 1717. Tr from J. Allibone's Latin.

The Tory Quaker: or Aminadab's new vision in the fields. 1717.

The vanity of upstarts. [1717]. A poem.

The delights of the bottle: or the complete vintner; to which is added a South Sea song. 1720, 1720, 1721, 1721, 1743.

A south-sea ballad: or merry remarks upon exchange-alley bubbles. Mercurius Politicus Sept 1720.

The merry travellers, or a trip upon ten-toes, from Moorfields up to Bromley: an humorous poem, intended as the wandering spy. Pt 1, 1721, [1722], 1723 (as The wandering spy or the merry travellers), 1724; The wandering spy: or the merry travellers, pt 2, 1722; The wandering spy: or the merry observator, 6 pts 1724.

The northern cuckold: or the garden house intrigue. 1721, 1721.

The parish gutt'lers: or the humours of a select vestry. 1722, 1732.

The dancing devils, or the roaring dragon: a dumb farce. 1724.

The amorous bugbears: or the humours of a masquerade. 1725.

The batchelor's estimate of the expenses of a married life. [1725], 1729, [1729], [1730]. By Ward?

News from Madrid: the Spanish beauty or the tragi-comical revenge. 1726.

Apollo's maggot in his cups, or the whimsical creation of a little satirical poet: a lyrick ode. 1729.

Durgen: or a plain satyr upon a pompous satirist, inscribed to those gentlemen misrepresented in the Dunciad. 1729, 1742 (as The cudgel: or a crab-tree lecture).

A fidler's fling at roguery. 1730.

To the Right Honourable Humphrey Parsons: a congratulatory poem. 1730.

Five travel scripts commonly attributed to Ward. Ed H. W. Troyer, New York 1933 (facs).

§ 2

Troyer, H. W. Ned Ward of Grubstreet. Cambridge Mass 1946.

BERNARD MANDEVILLE
1670–1733

§ 1

Bernardi à Mandeville de medicina oratio scholastica. Rotterdam 1685.

Disputatio philosophica de brutorum operationibus. Leyden 1689.

Some fables after the easie and familiar method of Monsieur de la Fontaine. 1703, 1704 (with addns, as Æsop dress'd: or a collection of fables writ in familiar verse); ed J. S. Shea, Los Angeles 1966 (Augustan Reprint Soc).

The pamphleteers: a satyr. 1703. Anon.

Typhons, or the wars between the gods and giants: a burlesque poem in imitation of the comical Mons Scarron. 1704.

The grumbling hive: or knaves turn'd honest. 1705, 1705, 1714 (in The fable of the bees pt 1); rptd Boston 1811.

The virgin unmask'd: or female dialogues betwixt an elderly maiden lady and her niece. 1709, 1714 (as The mysteries of virginity), 1724, 1731, 1742, 1757.

Lucinda-Artesia papers [32]. Female Tatler 2 Nov 1709–31 March 1710.

A treatise of the hypochondriack and hysterick passions, vulgarly call'd the hypo in men and vapours in women. 1711, 1711, 1715, 1730 (enlarged as A treatise of the hypochondriack and hysterick diseases in three dialogues), 1730.

Wishes to a godson, with other miscellany poems. 1712.

The fable of the bees: or private vices, publick benefits. Pt 1, 1714, 1714, 1723 (much enlarged), 1724 (rev and slightly enlarged), 1725, 1728, 1729, 1732; pt 2, 1729, 1730, 1730; pts 1–2, [1734?], Edinburgh 1755, 'London 1734', Edinburgh 1772, London 1795, 1795, 1806; ed F. B. Kaye 2 vols Oxford 1924; ed I. Primer, New York 1962; ed P. Harth 1970 (Penguin).

The mischiefs that ought justly to be apprehended from a Whig-government. 1714, [1715?] (advertised Jan 1715 as Non-resistance an useless doctrine in just reigns). Probably by Mandeville.

Free thoughts on religion, the Church and national happiness. 1720, 1721, 1723, 1729 (rev and enlarged), [1733?].

[Vindication of Fable of the bees]. London Jnl 10 Aug 1723; 1723 (with other documents), 1724 etc (in Fable, above).

A modest defence of publick stews: or an essay upon whoring as it is now practis'd in these kingdoms. 1724, 1725, 1740, 1740.

An enquiry into the causes of the frequent executions at Tyburn. 1725. Originally pbd in British Jnl Feb–April 1725; ed M. R. Zirker, Los Angeles 1964 (Augustan Reprint Soc).

Remarks upon two late presentments of the Grand-Jury of the county of Middlesex. 1729. Probably by Mandeville.

An enquiry into the origin of honour, and the usefulness of Christianity in war. 1732.

A letter to Dion [Berkeley], occasion'd by his book call'd Alciphron: or the minute philosopher. 1732; ed J. Viner, Los Angeles 1953 (Augustan Reprint Soc); ed B. Dobrée, Liverpool 1954.

The divine instinct recommended to men, translated from the French [of B. L. de Muralt by B. de Mandeville]. 1751, 1781.

§ 2

Dennis, John. Vice and luxury publick mischiefs. 1724.

Law, William. Remarks upon a late book entitul'd the Fable of the bees. 1724.

Hutcheson, Francis. An inquiry into the original of our ideas of beauty and virtue. 1725.

—— Reflections upon laughter, and remarks upon the Fable of the bees.

Berkeley, George. Alciphron: or the minute philosopher. 1732.

Stephen, L. Mandeville's Fable of the bees. In his Essays on freethinking and plainspeaking, 1873.

—— History of English thought in the eighteenth century. 2 vols 1876, 1881, 1902.

Monro, H. The ambivalence of Mandeville. Oxford 1975.

JOSEPH ADDISON
1672–1719

Wheeler, W. The Spectator: a digest-index. 1892, 1897 (as A concordance).

Collections

Works. Ed T. Tickell 4 vols 1721, Dublin 1722–3, London 1730.

Miscellaneous works, in verse and prose. 3 vols 1726; ed A. C. Guthkelch 2 vols 1914.

§ 1

Examen poeticum: being the third part of miscellany poems. Ed J. Dryden 1693, 1716. Includes Addison's poem To Mr Dryden.

Nova philosophia veteri praeferenda. In Theatri oxoniensis encaenia: sive comitia philologica 1693 celebrata, Oxford 1693; rptd in The altar of love: consisting of poems and other miscellanies, 1727; tr as An oration in defense of the new philosophy in W. Gardiner, English version of Fontenelle's Plurality of worlds, 1728, 1737, 1757, 1769, 1783.

The annual miscellany for the year 1694: being the fourth part of miscellany poems. Ed J. Dryden 1694, 1716. Includes A translation of all Virgil's fourth Georgick, except the story of Aristaeus; A song for St Cecilia's day at Oxford (rptd in Cupid's bee-hive: or the sting of love, translated from Bonefonius, by several hands, with some original poems 1721); The story of Salmacis and Hermaphroditus, from the fourth book of Ovid's Metamorphoses [omitted from the 1716 edn, but rptd with alterations in the trn of Ovid, ed S. Garth 1717]; An account of the greatest English poets, to Mr H.S., April 3 1694.

A poem to his Majesty, presented to the Lord Keeper. 1695, 1716 (in Miscellany poems).

An essay on Virgil's Georgics. In The works of Virgil, translated by Mr Dryden, 1697 etc.

Examen poeticum duplex: sive musarum anglicanarum delectus alter. 1698. Contains unauthorized versions of 7 Latin poems by Addison: Barometri descriptio; ΠΥΓΜΑΙΟ–ΓΕΡΑΝΟΜΑΧΙΑ: sive praelium inter pygmaeos et grues commissum: Resurrectio delineata ad altare Col Magd Oxon [English trn by N. Amhurst pbd separately 1718]; Sphaeristerium; Ad medicum et poetam ingeniosum (rptd in Musarum anglicanarum analecta vol 2, Oxford 1699 as Ad D. D. Hannes, insignissimum medicum et poetam); Machinae gesticulantes: anglice A puppet-show; Ad insignissimum virum D. Tho. Burnettum, Sacrae theoriae telluris autorem.

Musarum anglicanarum analecta: sive poemata quaedam, melioris notae, seu hactenus inedita, seu sparsim edita. 2 vols Oxford 1699. Vol 2, ed Addison, contains the 7 Latin peoms ptd in 1698, above, with considerable alterations; also Pax Gulielmi auspiciis Europae reddita 1697. The dedication to vol 2 is signed by Addison. The lines Ad D. Tho. Burnettum are rptd in The sacred theory of the earth, translated from Burnet's Latin, 1719.

Poetical miscellanies: the fifth part. Ed J. Dryden [and N. Rowe] 1704, 1716. Contains Addison's A letter from Italy, 1703; Milton's stile imitated, in a translation of a story out of the third Æneid; two stories, with notes, translated from Book II of Ovid's Metamorphoses, and nine stories, with notes, translated from Book III. The 1716 edn excludes all but Milton's stile imitated.

The campaign: a poem to his Grace the Duke of Marlborough. 1705 (3 edns), Edinburgh 1705, 1708 (with Latin trn), 1710, 1713, 1713, Dublin 1713, 1725 etc. Also rptd in Poetical miscellanies pt 6, 1716 (2nd edn).

Remarks on several parts of Italy etc in the years 1701, 1702, 1703. 1705, 1718 (rev).

The tender husband. 1705 etc. By Steele. Prologue by Addison.

The British enchanters: or no magick like love. 1706 etc. By George Granville. Epilogue by Addison.

The Muses Mercury. 1707. The Feb issue contains Addison's Horace ode 3, bk 3, rptd with alterations in Poetical miscellanies: the sixth part, ed N. Rowe 1709, 1716; the March issue contains the prologue and epilogue to Rosamond.

Rosamond: an opera, humbly inscrib'd to her Grace the Dutchess of Marlborough. 1707, 1707, 1713.

The present state of the war and the necessity of an augmentation considered. 1708.

Phaedra and Hippolitus. 1709 etc. By Edmund Smith. Prologue by Addison.

The tatler, by Isaac Bickerstaff esq. 271 nos (12 April 1709–2 Jan 1711). About 42 nos by Addison alone, 20 by Addison and Steele. For reprints and selections see under Steele, below.

The Whig examiner. 5 nos (14 Sept–12 Oct 1710). All 5 nos by Addison; rptd in The medleys for the year 1711, to which are prefixed the five Whig-examiners, 1712.

The spectator. 555 nos (1 March 1711–6 Dec 1712); nos 556–635 (18 June–20 Dec 1714); 8 vols 8° and 12° 1712–15 (vols 1–4, 1712; vols 5–7, 1713; vol 8, 1715 [vol 3, 8° and vol 4, 12° are dated 1713]); 1713–4, 1714, 1718, 1720, 1723, 1724 (16 vols), 1726, 1729, 1729, 1733, 1738–9 (12th edn) etc; ed J. Nichols 8 vols 12° 1788, 1788, 8 vols 8° 1789; ed G. Gregory Smith 8 vols 1897–8, 1907 (EL); ed G. A. Aitken 8 vols 1898, 1905; ed D. F. Bond 5 vols Oxford 1965.

The guardian. 175 nos (12 March–1 Oct 1713). 53 nos by Addison. For reprints see under Steele, below.

Cato: a tragedy, as it is acted at the Theatre-Royal in Drury-Lane, by Mr Addison. 1713 (8 authorized edns), Dublin 1713, Hague 1713, Edinburgh 1713, London 1721 (10th edn), 1722, 1725 (11th edn), 1730, Dublin 1732, London 1733 (13th edn), 1734, 1735.

The late tryal and conviction of Count Tariff. 1713, 1714.

The lover, by Marmaduke Myrtle gent. 40 nos (25 Feb–27 May 1714). Nos 10, 39 by Addison. For reprints see under Steele, below.

The free-holder: or political essays. 55 nos (23 Dec 1715–29 June 1716); 1 vol 1716 (12° and 8°), Dublin 1716, London 1723, 1729, 1732, 1739, 1744, 1751. Entirely by Addison.

The drummer, or the haunted-house: a comedy, as it is acted at the Theatre-Royal in Drury-Lane. 1716 (anon, with brief preface by Steele), 1716 ('2nd edn'), 1722 (2nd edn, 'with a preface by Sir Richard Steele, in an epistle dedicatory to Mr Congreve, occasioned by Mr Tickell's preface to the four volumes of Mr Addison's

works'), 1722 (3rd edn), Hague [1725?], Dublin 1725, London 1733 (4th edn), Dublin 1734, London 1735, Glasgow 1749, London 1751, Glasgow 1751, London 1759, 1765.

Epilogue spoken at the Censorium on the King's birthday. In Steele's Town-talk no 4, 6 Jan 1716.

Poetical miscellanies pt 5, 1716 (2nd edn). Includes Verses written for the toasting-glasses of the Kit-Kat Club in the year 1703; Lady Manchester, by Mr Addison.

To her Royal Highness the Princess of Wales, with the tragedy of Cato, Nov 1714; To Sir Godfrey Kneller, on his picture of the King. 1716, 1716 (4th edn); rptd in Cato, 1716 etc.

Ovid's Metamorphoses translated. Ed S. Garth 1717 etc. Contains Addison's trns of 19 stories from Books 2–4, including the 12 already ptd in Dryden's Miscellanies, and notes.

A dissertation upon the most celebrated Roman poets, written originally in Latin by Joseph Addison esq, made English by Christopher Hayes. 1718 (Latin and English texts); rptd in Poems on several occasions, 1719, 1721, 1736, below.

The resurrection: a poem written by Mr Addison. 1718 (3rd edn), 1728 (6th edn). Rptd from Resurrectio delineata ad altare col Magd Oxon, with English translation by Nicholas Amhurst.

Poems on several occasions, with a dissertation upon the Roman poets, by Mr Addison. 1719, 1719. Addison's 8 Latin poems, rptd with English trns.

The old Whig. 2 nos 19 March, 2 April 1719; 1 vol 1720 (3rd edn); ed J. Nichols 1789.

Dialogues upon the usefulness of ancient medals, especially in relation to the Latin and Greek poets. Probably written 1703–5. First pbd in Tickell's edn of Works vol 1, 1721.

Miscellanies in verse and prose, written by the Right Honourable Joseph Addison esq. 1725.

The Christian poet: a miscellany of divine poems, all written by the late Mr Secretary Addison, with memoirs of Mr Addison's life and writings. 1728. Reprints Amhurst's trn of Addison's Resurrectio and the 5 poems from Spectator.

The evidences of the Christian religion. 1730, 1733, 1742. First pbd in Tickell's edn of Works vol 4, 1721.

A discourse on antient and modern learning. 1734, 1739 (9th edn).

Some portions of essays contributed to the Spectator by Mr Joseph Addison, now first printed from his ms notebook. Ed J. D. C[ampbell], Glasgow 1864 (facs).

A fragment [on friendship] by Addison [BM Add ms 33, 441]. Ed R. P. Bond, RES 5 1929.

Selections from essays (see also under Steele, *below*)

Maxims, observations and reflections, moral, political and divine, by Mr Addison. [Ed C. Beckingham] 2 pts 1719, 1720; 1 vol 1737.

Notes upon the twelve books of Paradise lost, collected from the Spectator, written by Mr Addison. 1719, 1731, 1738 etc; ed E. Arber 1868, 1895; ed A. S. Cook, Boston 1892; ed H. Morley 1889.

Selections from Addison's papers contributed to the Spectator. Ed T. Arnold, Oxford 1875.

Essays. Ed J. G. Frazer 2 vols 1915.

Critical essays from the Spectator. Ed D. F. Bond, Oxford 1970.

Letters

Letters. Ed W. Graham, Oxford 1941.

§ 2

G[ay], J[ohn]. The present state of wit. 1711; ed E. Arber in An English garner vol 6, 1877; ed D. F. Bond, Los Angeles 1947 (Augustan Reprint Soc).

Dennis, J. Remarks upon Cato: a tragedy. 1713.

Johnson, S. In his Lives of the English poets, 1779–81.

Spence, J. In his Observations, anecdotes and characters, ed S. W. Singer 1820; ed J. M. Osborn 2 vols Oxford 1966.

Macaulay, T. B. The life and writings of Addison. Edinburgh Rev 78 1843.

Courthope, W. J. Addison. 1884 (EML).

Frazer, J. G. Sir Roger de Coverley and other literary pieces. 1920.

Dobrée, B. In his Essays in biography 1680–1726, Oxford 1925.

Graham, W. In his Beginnings of English literary periodicals 1665–1715, 1926.

Lewis, C. S. In Essays on the eighteenth century presented to David Nichol Smith, Oxford 1945.

Smithers, P. The life of Addison. Oxford 1954, 1968 (rev).

SIR RICHARD STEELE
1672–1729

Collections

Political writings. 1715.

Dramatick works. 1723. The 3 early comedies.

Dramatick works. [1733?], 1734, 1736.

Dramatic works. Ed G. A. Aitken 1894, 1903 (Mermaid Ser). The 4 comedies and fragments of 2 plays.

Tracts and pamphlets. Ed R. Blanchard, Baltimore 1944.

Occasional verse. Ed R. Blanchard, Oxford 1952.

Steele's periodical journalism 1714–16. Ed R. Blanchard, Oxford 1959.

Plays. Ed S. S. Kenny, Oxford 1970.

§ I

The procession: a poem on her Majesty's funeral, by a gentleman of the army. 1695; rptd in Poetical miscellanies, 1714.

Commendatory verses on the author of the Two Arthurs and the Satyr against wit. 1700. Includes To the mirror of British knighthood [a satire on Sir Richard Blackmore] by Steele. Rptd in Works of Mr Thomas Brown vol 4, 1711.

The Christian hero: an argument proving that no principles but those of religion are sufficient to make a great man. 1701, 1701 ('with additions'), 1710, 1711, 1711, 1712 etc; ed R. Blanchard, Oxford 1932.

A new collection of poems on several occasions. Ed C. Gildon 1701, 1701 (another issue as A new miscellany of original poems). Includes To Mr Congreve, occasion'd by the Way of the world. Rptd in Abel Boyer's Letters of wit, politicks and morality, 1701, and Congreve's Collected works vol 2, 1710.

The funeral, or grief à-la-mode: a comedy, as it is acted at the Theatre Royal in Drury-Lane. 1702, 1710, 1712, 1717, 1721, 1723, Dublin 1725, London 1730 (6th edn).

The lying lover, or the ladies friendship: a comedy, as it is acted at the Theatre Royal by her Majesty's servants. 1704, 1712, 1717, 1723, Dublin 1725, London 1732 (5th edn) etc.

The diverting post no 2 (4 Nov 1704). Contains Steele's Imitation of the sixth ode of Horace apply'd to his Grace the Duke of Marlborough. Rptd in Oxford and Cambridge miscellany poems, ed E. Fenton 1708 etc.

The tender husband, or the accomplish'd fools: a comedy, as it is acted at the Theatre-Royal in Drury-Lane. 1705, 1711, 1712, 1717, 1723, Dublin 1725, London 1731 (5th edn) etc; ed C. Winton, Lincoln Nebraska 1967.

The mistake. 1706. By Vanbrugh. Prologue by Steele.

The Muses Mercury. 1707. Jan issue contains To a young lady who had marry'd an old man; Feb contains Song; both by Steele.

The tatler, by Isaac Bickerstaff esq. 271 nos (12 April 1709–2 Jan 1710/11), 1710 (nos 1–100 a piracy), 4 vols (8° and 12°) 1710–11, 1712, 1713, 1716, 1720 etc; ed G. A. Aitken 4 vols 1898–9. About 188 nos by Steele alone, 20 by Steele and Addison.

The medley. 1710–11. Part of no 23 (5 March 1711) by Steele; rptd in Tracts and pamphlets, ed R. Blanchard, Baltimore 1944.

The spectator. 555 nos (1 March 1711–6 Dec 1712), nos 556–653 (18 June–20 Dec 1714). Steele contributed 251 papers to first ser, none to second. For reprints see under Addison, above.

The distrest mother. 1712. By Ambrose Philips. Prologue by Steele.

The Englishman's thanks to the Duke of Marlborough. 1712.

The guardian. 175 nos (12 March–1 Oct 1713), 2 vols 1714 (8° and 12°), 1723, 1726, 1729 etc; ed J. Nichols 2 vols 1789, 1797. 82 nos by Steele.

The Englishman.

The Englishman: being the sequel of the Guardian. 56 nos (6 Oct 1713–11 Feb 1714); 1714 (8° and 12°), Dublin 1713 (40 nos), London [1723?].

The Englishman: being the close of the paper so called [no 57, 15 Feb 1714]; with an epistle concerning the Whiggs, Tories and new converts. 1714 (3 edns), Dublin 1714.

The Englishman: second series. 38 nos (11 July–21 Nov 1715); 1716, 1737. Ed R. Blanchard, Oxford 1955 (complete).

Cato. 1713 (7th edn). By Addison; verses to Addison prefixed.

A letter to Sir M. W[arton] concerning occasional peers. 1713.

The importance of Dunkirk consider'd in defence of the Guardian of August the 7th. 1713 (4 edns), 1730.

The crisis; with some seasonable remarks on the danger of a Popish successor. 1714 [pbd 19 Jan; some copies dated 1713 (Old Style)], 1714 (8°, pirated edn), Edinburgh 1714, Dublin 1714; ed H. Morley 1886 (Famous pamphlets).

The French faith represented in the present state of Dunkirk. 1714.

The ladies library. 3 vols 1714, 1722 (3rd edn), 1732 etc. Ed Steele.

A letter to a Member of Parliament concerning the bill for preventing the growth of schism. 1714, 1714, Dublin 1714, Edinburgh 1714.

The lover, written in imitation of the Tatler by Marmaduke Myrtle gent. 40 nos (25 Feb–27 May 1714).

Mr Steele's apology for himself and his writings, occasioned by his expulsion from the House of Commons. 1714.

Mr Steele's speech upon the proposal of Sir Thomas Hanmer for Speaker. 1714.

Poetical miscellanies, consisting of original poems and translations. 1714, 1727. Ed Steele.

The reader. 9 nos (22 April–10 May 1714).

The Romish ecclesiastical history of late years. 1714 (with and without cancelled leaf F8). Partly by Steele.

An account of the state of the Roman-Catholick religion throughout the world, written for the use of Pope Innocent XI by Monsignor Cerri, now first translated. 1715, 1716. Partly by Steele.

A letter from the Earl of Mar to the King. 1715, Edinburgh 1715, Glasgow 1715; ed J. Nichols 1790. Rptd in Somers Tracts vol 4, 1751, and at end of some copies of Englishman vol 2, 1716, 1737.

Town-talk, in a letter to a lady in the country. 9 nos (17 Dec 1715–13 Feb 1716).

The British subject's answer to the Pretender's declaration. 1716. Single-sheet folio. Also as Town-talk no 5 (13 Jan 1716). Rptd in Somers Tracts vol 4, 1751.

Chit-chat, in a letter to a lady in the country, by Humphrey

Philroye. 3 nos (March 1716). 2 nos extant: no 2 (10 March), no 3 (16 March).

The tea table. 3 nos (Feb–March 1716). No known copy. The Lover, the Reader, Town-talk and Chit-chat. Ed R. Blanchard, Oxford 1959 (as Steele's periodical journalism 1714–16).

A letter to a Member etc concerning the condemn'd Lords. 1716; ed J. Nichols 1789, 1790.

Sir Richard Steele's speech for repealing of the Triennial Act and his reasons for the Septennial Bill. 1716, Dublin 1716; ed J. Nichols 1789, 1790.

Sir Richard Steele's account of Mr Desagulier's new-invented chimneys. 1716.

The Drummer [by Addison]. 1716 (with preface by Steele), 1722 (2nd edn, with preface and dedication to Congreve by Steele).

Lucius. 1717. By Mrs Manley. Prologue by Steele. Rptd, enlarged, in Theatre no 10 (2 Feb 1720).

An account of the fish pool, by Sir Richard Steele and Mr Joseph Gillmore. 1718; ed J. Nichols 1789, 1790.

The antidote, in a letter to the Free-thinker. 1719.

The antidote no 2. In a letter to the Free-thinker, 1719.

The joint and humble address of the Tories and Whiggs, concerning the intended Bill of Peerage. 1719.

A letter to the Earl of O——d concerning the bill of Peerage. 1719 (3 edns); ed J. Nichols 1789, 1790; rptd in The orphan revived: or Powell's weekly journal, 2 Jan 1720.

The plebeian, by a member of the House of Commons. 4 nos (March–April 1719), 1 vol 1719 (6th edn); ed J. Nichols 1789, 1790; ed R. Hurd 1856 (Addison's works vol 5).

The spinster, in defence of the woollen manufactures. No 1 1719.

The crisis of property. 1720, 1720; ed J. Nichols 1791.

A nation a family, being the sequel of the crisis of property: or a plan for the improvement of the South-Sea proposal. 1720; ed J. Nichols 1791.

The state of the case between the Lord-Chamberlain and the governor of the Royal Company of Comedians. 1720, 1720; ed J. Nichols 1791.

The theatre. 1720. Includes in no 10 (2 Feb) Prologue intended for All for love reviv'd; in no 13 (13 Feb) Prologue intended for the players at Hampton Court.

The theatre, by Sir John Edgar. 28 nos (2 Jan–5 April 1720); ed J. Nichols 1791; ed J. Loftis, Oxford 1962.

A prologue to the town [by L. Welsted], with an Epilogue [by Steele]. 1721; rptd in Welsted's Works, 1787.

The conscious lovers: a comedy, as it is acted at the Theatre Royal in Drury-Lane. 1723 (3 issues), Dublin 1725 etc, London 1730, 1733 (4th edn), 1735.

Pasquin. [1722–4]. Nos 46, 51 (9, 26 July 1723) by Steele.

The school of action, and the gentleman. Unacted fragments. Pbd by J. Nichols in Epistolary correspondence, 1809; and by G. A. Aitken in Dramatic works, 1894, 1903.

Letters

Correspondence. Ed R. Blanchard, Oxford 1941, 1968 (with appendix of addns).

§ 2

See also under Addison, above.

Dobson, A. Richard Steele. 1886.

Aitken, G. A. Richard Steele. 2 vols 1889.

The theatre (1720), by 'Sir John Falstaffe'. Ed J. Loftis, Los Angeles 1948 (Augustan Reprint Soc). Nos 16–18, 20–6, a continuation of the 15 nos of Anti-theatre, also by 'Sir John Falstaffe', written in opposition to Steele's periodical Theatre.

HENRY ST JOHN, 1st VISCOUNT BOLINGBROKE
1678–1751
Collections

Works. Ed D. Mallet 5 vols 1754, 1777.

Historical writings. Ed I. Kramnick, Chicago 1972.

§ 1

A letter to the Examiner. 1710, 1710 (both anon), Edinburgh 1710; rptd in Somers tracts, ed W. Scott vol 13, 1815, and in J. Swift, The examiner, ed H. J. Davis, Oxford 1940.

Examiner 3 Aug 1710–26 July 1714. Contributions by Bolingbroke.

Considerations upon the Secret history of the White Staff. [1714]. Anon; sometimes attributed to Bolingbroke.

A copy of my Lord Bolingbroke's letter to my Lord —, Dover, March 27 1715. 1715, 1715 (as A true copy of a letter from Dover), Edinburgh [1715] (as A letter of my Lord Bolingbrokes to his friend at London); rptd in Somers tracts, ed W. Scott vol 13, 1815.

The representation of the Lord Viscount Bolingbroke. 1715, 1715.

The craftsman, by Caleb Danvers. 5 Dec 1726–c. 1747.

The occasional writer. 1727, 1727 (both anon), Edinburgh 1727.

The occasional writer no 2. 1727, 1727 (both anon), Edinburgh 1727.

The occasional writer no 3. 1727.

Observations on the public affairs of Great-Britain, in a letter from W. Raleigh to Caleb D'Anvers. 1729 (2nd edn). Anon; sometimes attributed to Bolingbroke.

The craftsman extraordinary: containing an answer to the Defence of the Enquiry into the reasons of the conduct of Great Britain, in a letter to the Craftsman by John Trot, yeoman, publish'd by Caleb D'Anvers esq. 1729.

A letter to Caleb D'Anvers esq concerning the state of affairs in Europe as published in the Craftsman, January 4 1728–9, by John Trott, yeoman. 1730, Anon; rptd from Craftsman, above.

The case of Dunkirk faithfully stated and impartially considered, by a member of the House of Commons. 1730 (3 edns). Anon.

The monumental inscription on the column at Blenheim-House. 1731. Anon; first pbd in Craftsman, above.

A final answer to the Remarks on the Craftsman's vindication. 1731 (anon), 1731 (8th edn).

The freeholder's political catechism. 1733 (anon), Dublin 1733, [place?] 1757, New London 1769, London 1774. Rptd from Craftsman, above.

The craftsman extraordinary: or the late dissertation on parties continued. 1733. Anon; rptd from Craftsman, above.

A dissertation on parties, in several letters to Caleb D'Anvers. 1735, 1735 (so-called 2nd and 3rd edns, anon), Dublin 1735, London 1739 (5th edn), 1743, 1749, Dublin 1749 ('10th' edn), London 1754 (8th edn), 1771, 1775, 1786. Rptd from Craftsman.

The famous dedication to the pamphlet entitled A dissertation upon parties. [1735] (anon).

Letters to a young nobleman on the study and use of history. 1738. Priv ptd by Pope at Bolingbroke's direction; unique copy in Harvard Library.

The idea of a patriot king. [c. 1740?], [c. 1740?] (both anon); rptd in Letters on the spirit of patriotism, below. On the relation between the 3 known copies, see G. Barber, Library 5th ser 19 1964.

Remarks on the history of England from the minutes of Humphrey Oldcastle esq. 1743, Dublin 1743, London 1747, Dublin 1752, London 1754, [1780?], Basle 1794, 1795. Rptd from Craftsman, above.

A collection of political tracts. 1748, 1748 (both anon), Dublin 1748, London 1769, 1775, 1788.

Good Queen Anne vindicated, by the author of the Dissertation upon parties. 1748. Sometimes attributed to Bolingbroke.

Letters on the spirit of patriotism; on the idea of a patriot king; and on the state of the parties at the accession of King George the First. 1749 (anon), Dublin 1749, Philadelphia 1749, London 1750, 1752, 1767 ('new edition'), 1775, 1783, 1831; ed A. Hassall, Oxford 1917, 1926.

The last will and testament of the late Right Honourable Henry St John, Lord Viscount Bolingbroke. 1752, Dublin 1752.

Letters on the study and use of history. Ed D. Mallet 2 vols 1752, 1 vol 1752 ('corrected'), 2 vols Dublin [1752], 1 vol 1770, Edinburgh 1777, 1779, Basle 1788, London 1791, 1792, Paris 1808, London 1870, [1881], 1889?, 1932 (Letters 6–8 only).

Reflections concerning innate moral principles, written in French by the late Lord Bolingbroke and translated into English. 1752. Advertisement attributes to Bolingbroke.

A letter to Sir William Windham II: Some reflections on the present state of the nation; III: A letter to Mr Pope. 1753, 1753, Dublin 1753, London 1787, 1889.

A tract of the late Viscount Bolingbroke, illustrated with notes and adapted to the present times, with an appendix containing some remarks on the conduct of a late court-martial. [1759?]. Rptd from Craftsman no 371 in connection with death of Admiral Byng.

§ 2

[Warburton, W.] A letter to the editor of the Letters on the spirit of patriotism etc, occasioned by the editor's advertisement. 1749.
—— A view of Lord Bolingbroke's philosophy: four letters. 1754.

Hassall, A. Life of Viscount Bolingbroke. 1889, Oxford 1915 (rev).

Sichel, W. Bolingbroke and his times. 1901.
—— A sequel. 1902. With bibliography and selection of letters.

Petrie, C. Bolingbroke. 1937.

Butterfield, H. Bolingbroke and Machiavelli. In his Statecraft of Machiavelli, 1940.

James, D. G. In his Life of reason: Hobbes, Locke, Bolingbroke, 1949.

Kramnick, I. Bolingbroke and his circle. Cambridge Mass 1968.

SAMUEL JOHNSON
1709–84

Mss of the whole of Irene *and of the Welsh and French diaries are in BM, as well as notes for the* Life of Pope, *others of which are in Victoria & Albert. The collection of Mrs Donald Hyde includes parts of* London *and* Irene, *the* Vanity of human wishes, *the* Life of Rowe. *The complete ms of the* Life of Pope *is in the Pierpont Morgan Library, New York. Prayers and diaries are at Pembroke College, Oxford; various minor mss are in BM, Bodley, Rylands Library Manchester, Yale, Harvard and Huntington.*

Bibliographies

Courtney, W. P. and D. N. Smith. A bibliography of Johnson. Oxford 1915, 1925 (with facs), 1968.

Chapman, R. W. and A. T. Hazen. Johnsonian bibliography: a supplement to Courtney. Proc Oxford Bibl Soc 5 1939.

Clifford, J. L. Johnsonian studies 1887–1950: a survey and bibliography. Minneapolis 1951.

—— and D. J. Greene. Johnson: a survey and bibliography of critical studies. Minneapolis 1971.

Fleeman, J. D. Preliminary handlist of manuscripts and documents by Johnson. Oxford 1967 (Oxford Bibl Soc).

Collections

Works, together with his Life, and notes on his Lives of the poets, by Sir John Hawkins. 11 vols 1787. Hawkins wrote the Life in vol 1 and annotated the Lives in vols 2–4; the remainder is virtually unedited. Vols 12–13 (Debates), [ed George Chalmers] 1787; vol 14 (Miscellaneous pieces) [ed Isaac Reed] 1788, 1792; vol 15 (Miscellaneous pieces) [ed George Gleig] 1789.

Works: a new edition in twelve volumes, with an essay on his life and genius by Arthur Murphy. 1792 (vols 13–14 a reissue of Debates, 1787).

Works. Ed A. T. Hazen et al, New Haven 1958–.

Early biographical writings. Ed J. D. Fleeman, Farnborough 1973 (facs).

Poems

Poetical works. [Ed G. Kearsley] 1785, 1785, 1789 (enlarged).

Poems. Ed D. N. Smith and E. L. McAdam, Oxford 1941, 1951, 1962 (rev), 1974 (rev J. D. Fleeman).

The Yale edition of the works vol 6: Poems. Ed E. L. McAdam and G. Milne, New Haven 1964.

Complete English poems. Ed J. D. Fleeman 1971 (Penguin).

Selections

Johnson on Shakespeare. Ed W. Raleigh, Oxford 1908, 1925 (corrected).

Prose and poetry. Ed R. W. Chapman, Oxford 1922 (WC).

Prefaces and dedications. Ed A. T. Hazen, New Haven 1937.

Prose and poetry. Ed M. Wilson 1950 (Reynard Lib), 1967 (rev).

Selections. Ed R. W. Chapman, Oxford 1955.

Johnson on Shakespeare. Ed W. K. Wimsatt, New York 1960.

Selected writings. Ed R. T. Davies 1965.

Political writings. Ed J. P. Hardy 1968.

Johnson as critic. Ed J. Wain 1973.

§ I

A voyage to Abyssinia, by Father Jerome Lobo, a Portuguese Jesuit, with a continuation of the history of Abyssinia down to the beginning of the eighteenth century, and fifteen dissertations by Mr Legrand, from the French. 1735, 1735, 1789 (to which are added various other tracts by the same author; sometimes known as Works vol 15 and with half-title to that effect; *see* above); rptd J. Pinkerton in A general collection of voyages and travels vol 15, 1814; ed H. Morley 1886.

London: a poem in imitation of the third satire of Juvenal. 1738 (3 edns), 1738 ('2nd edn'), Dublin 1738, London 1739, 1750; rptd in Dodsley's collection of poems vol 1, 1748 etc; as Two satires by Samuel Johnson AM Oxford, 1759; ed T. S. Eliot 1930 (with Vanity, below).

Marmor Norfolciense: or an essay on an ancient prophetical inscription, in monkish rhyme, lately discover'd near Lynn in Norfolk, by Probus Britanicus. 1739, 1775 (with notes and a dedication to Samuel Johnson LlD by Tribunus [i.e. Francis Webb, DNB]) 1820 (from 1739).

A compleat vindication of the licensers of the stage from the malicious and scandalous aspersions of Mr Brooke, author of Gustavus Vasa, with a proposal for making the office of licenser more extensive and effectual, by an impartial hand. 1739.

A commentary on Mr Pope's Principles of morality: or essay on man, by Mons Crousaz. 1739, 1742. Tr and annotated by Johnson.

The life of Admiral Blake. 1740. Rptd from GM June 1740. Added to Life of Savage, 1767 etc.

An account of the life of Mr Richard Savage, son of the

Earl Rivers. 1744, 1748, 1767 (with additional lives), 1769, 1777; ed C. Tracy, Oxford 1970.

The works of Richard Savage esq, with an account of the author, by Samuel Johnson LlD. Vol 1, 1775, 1777, Dublin 1777, 1822; Bell's British poets 1780, 1791, 1807; in Poetical works of Richard Savage, 1795, 1801, New York 1805, London 1806, 1807. Rev and included in Johnson's Lives of the poets, below.

An account of the life of John Philip Barretier, who was master of five languages at the age of nine years. 1744. A conflation of GM Dec 1740, Feb 1741, May 1742.

Miscellaneous observations on the tragedy of Macbeth, with remarks on Sir T. H[anmer]'s edition of Shakespear; to which is affix'd Proposals for a new edition of Shakespear with a specimen. 1745. The Proposals are ptd on a half-sheet folio folded into 4 and inserted at the conclusion.

A sermon preached before the sons of the clergy, second of May 1745, by the Honourable and Reverend Henry Hervey Aston AM. [1745]; ed J. L. Clifford, Los Angeles 1955 (Augustan Reprint Soc).

The plan of a dictionary of the English language, addressed to the Right Honourable Philip Dormer, Earl of Chesterfield, one of his Majesty's Principal Secretaries of State. 1747, 1755; rptd in Harrison's edn of Dictionary, 1786.

Prologue and epilogue, spoken at the opening of the Theatre in Drury-Lane. 1747 ('printed by E. Cave'), 1747 ('printed by W. Webb'); ed A. Dobson and A. S. W. Rosenbach, New York 1902 (facs of Cave); ed R. W. Chapman, Oxford 1924 (facs of Webb). Prologue rptd GM Oct 1747, and collected poems. The Epilogue was by Garrick.

The vanity of human wishes: the tenth satire of Juvenal, imitated by Samuel Johnson. 1749, 1750 (5th edn); ed W. Hoskins 1851; ed J. P. Fleming 1876; ed E. J. Payne, Oxford 1876; ed F. Ryland 1893; Oxford 1927 (facs); Los Angeles 1950 (Augustan Reprint Soc); rptd in Dodsley's collection vol 4, 1755 etc as Two satires, Oxford 1759 (with London); ed T. S. Eliot 1930 (with London).

Irene: a tragedy, as it is acted at the Theatre Royal in Drury-Lane. 1749, Dublin 1749, 8° 1754, 1781.

The rambler, price 2d: to be continued on Tuesdays and Saturdays. No 1 (20 March 1750)–no 208 (14 March 1752); 2 vols 1751 (with Contents & mottoes 1753), 8 vols Edinburgh 1750–2; vols 1–4 Edinburgh 1751–3 (superintended by James Elphinstone and originally sold in penny nos); 6 vols 1752 (2 issues), Dublin 1752, 4 vols 1756 (rev), 1761, 1763, 1767, 1771, Edinburgh 1772, 1776, London 1779, Edinburgh 1781, London 1783, 1784, Dublin 1785; in Harrison's British classicks vol 1, 1785, 1792, 1795, 1796; 1789, 1791, 2 vols 1791.

A new prologue spoken by Mr Garrick, Thursday April 5 1750 at the representation of Comus for the benefit of Mrs Elizabeth Foster, Milton's grand-daughter, and only surviving descendant. 1750, Oxford 1925 (facs), Edinburgh 1750; GM April 1750.

A dictionary of the English language, in which the words are deduced from their originals and illustrated in their different significations by examples from the best writers; to which are prefixed a history of the language and an English grammar, by Samuel Johnson AM. 2 vols 1755, New York 1967 (facs); 1755–6 (in weekly nos at sixpence); 2 vols 1765, 1773 (rev 4th edn), Dublin 1775, 1777, London 1784, 1785 (also issued in weekly nos), 1785 (based on revision of 1773).

A dictionary of the English language abstracted from the folio edition. 2 vols 1756, Dublin 1758, London 1760, Dublin 1764, London 1766, Dublin 1768, London 1770, 1773, 1778, 1778, 1783, 1786, 1 vol 1790.

The Prince of Abissinia: a tale. 2 vols 1759, 1759 (rev), Dublin 1759, London, 1760, 1766; The history of Rasselas, Prince of Abissinia: an Asiatic tale, Philadel-

phia 1768, London 1775, Dublin 1777, 1783; ed R. W. Chapman 1927; ed G. Tillotson and B. Jenkins, Oxford 1971; ed G. B. Hill, Oxford 1887.

The idler. 104 nos (nos 2–105, 15 April 1758–5 April 1760) in Universal Chron or Weekly Gazette; ed W. J. Bate and J. M. Bullitt, New Haven 1963.

The plays of William Shakespeare, with the corrections and illustrations of various commentators; to which are added notes by Sam Johnson. 8 vols 1765, 1765 (an offprint of the Preface was taken from this 2nd edn), 10 vols Dublin 1766, 8 vols 1768, 12 pts Dublin 1771, 10 vols 1773 ('To which are added notes by Samuel Johnson and George Steevens, with an appendix'); 10 vols 1778 ('revised and augmented'; Supplement, ed E. Malone 2 vols 1780), 1785 ('revised and augmented by the editor of Dodsley's collection of old plays', i.e. Isaac Reed); 1793.

Mr Johnson's preface to his edition of Shakespear's plays. 1765. From the 2nd edn of 1765; distinguished from 1st in that the Preface is paginated. A similar separate issue of the Preface was made from the 1785 edn in 1788; rptd in Eighteenth-century essays on Shakespeare, ed D. N. Smith 1903; Johnson on Shakespeare, ed W. Raleigh, Oxford 1908.

The false alarm. 1770, Dublin 1770, London 1770 (3 edns).

Thoughts on the late transactions respecting Falkland's Islands. 1771, 1771, Dublin 1771, New York 1771, London 1948.

The patriot, addressed to the electors of Great Britain. 1774, 1774, 1775, Dublin 1775, 1790.

Taxation no tyranny: an answer to the resolutions and address of the American Congress. 1775, 1775 (3 edns).

The preceding 4 pieces collected and rev in one vol as Political tracts, 1775, Dublin 1777; ed J. P. Hardy 1967.

A journey to the Western Islands of Scotland. 1775, 1775 (no cancels, and a leaf of only 6 errata), Dublin 1775 (3 edns pbd by Leathley, Walker and Williams), London 1775; ed R. W. Chapman, Oxford 1924 (with Boswell's Tour), 1930 (corrected) (OSA).

Prefaces, biographical and critical, to the works of the English poets, by Samuel Johnson. 10 vols 1779–81 (vols 1–4, 1779); rptd 1 vol Dublin 1779, London 1780, 1781; vols 5–6, 1781; rptd Dublin as vols 2–3, 1781 (as The lives of the English poets, and a criticism of their works); 4 vols 1781 (as The lives of the most eminent English poets, with critical observations on their works), 1783 (rev), 6 vols 1790 (as Prefaces), 1790–1, 1793, 1794; ed G. B. Hill 3 vols Oxford 1905, 2 vols Oxford 1906 (WC).

The principal additions and corrections in the third edition of Dr Johnson's Lives of the poets, collected to complete the second edition (compiled by John Nichols). 1783.

Prayers and meditations, composed by Samuel Johnson LlD, and published from his manuscripts, by George Strahan. 1785, Dublin 1785, London 1785 (with additional prayers), 1796 (with additional prayer); ed G. B. Hill in Johnsonian Miscellanies vol 1, Oxford 1897, 1967; ed D. and M. Hyde with E. L. McAdam in Diaries, prayers and annals, New Haven 1958.

Debates in Parliament, by Samuel Johnson LlD. 2 vols 1787 (rptd from GM 1740–3, and pbd as supplementary vols to Sir John Hawkins's edn of Works, 1787.

A diary of a journey into North Wales in the year 1774, by Samuel Johnson LlD. Ed R. Duppa 1816 (variant states). Included in Life 5 and in Diaries, prayers and annals, New Haven 1958; ms in BM.

Dr Johnson and Mrs Thrale, including Mrs Thrale's unpublished Journal of the Welsh tour made in 1774, by A. M. Broadley, with an introductory essay by Thomas Seccombe. 1910.

The French journals of Mrs Thrale and Dr Johnson. Ed M. Tyson and H. Guppy, Manchester 1932.

Letters

Letters to and from the late Samuel Johnson LlD; to which are added some poems never before printed, published from the original mss in her possession by Hester Lynch Piozzi. 2 vols 1788, Dublin 1788.

Letters of Samuel Johnson LlD. Ed G. B. Hill 2 vols Oxford 1892, New York 1892; [additional letters] in Johnsonian miscellanies, ed Hill vol 2, Oxford 1897.

Selected letters. Ed R. W. Chapman, Oxford 1925 (WC), 1951 (rev).

The letters of Johnson, with Mrs Thrale's genuine letters to him. Ed R. W. Chapman 3 vols Oxford 1952.

§ 2

For early criticism see Johnson: the critical heritage, *ed J. T. Boulton 1971.*

For Boswell's Life of Johnson etc 1791, *the standard edn is* ed G. B. Hill, rev L. F. Powell 6 vols Oxford 1934–64.

Boswell, James. The journal of a tour to the Hebrides with Samuel Johnson LlD. 1785.

Piozzi, Hester Lynch (Mrs Thrale). Anecdotes of the late Samuel Johnson LlD during the last twenty years of his life. 1786 (4 edns), Dublin 1786, London 1822, 1826, 1831, 1835, 1856, 1887, 1888. In Johnsoniana, ed R. Napier 1884, 1892; in Johnsonian miscellanies, ed G. B. Hill 1897, 1967; ed S. C. Roberts, Cambridge 1925, 1932; ed A. Sherbo, Oxford 1974 (with W. Shaw, Memoirs).

Hawkins, Sir John. The life of Johnson. 1787, 1787 (rev), Dublin 1787. Also issued as vol 1 in Works, 1787; ed B. H. Davis 1961 (abridged).

Reynolds, Sir Joshua. Johnson and Garrick. 1816 (priv ptd); ed R. B. Johnson 1927; ed F. W. Hilles, New York 1952.

[Macaulay, T. B.]. Essay on Boswell's Life, ed J. W. Croker. Edinburgh Rev 54 1831.

—— Life of Johnson. In Encyclopaedia britannica vol 12, 1856 (8th edn); ed D. Nichol Smith, Edinburgh 1900; ed C. N. Greenough, New York 1912.

Carlyle, T. Essay on Boswell's Life. Fraser's Mag May 1832.

Stephen, L. Samuel Johnson. 1878 (EML).

Raleigh, W. Six essays on Johnson. Oxford 1910, 1927.

Wimsatt, W. K. The prose style of Johnson. New Haven 1941.

—— Philosophic words: a study of style and meaning in the Rambler and Dictionary of Johnson. New Haven 1948.

Thraliana: the diary of Mrs Thrale 1776–1809. Ed K. C. Balderston 2 vols Oxford 1942, 1952 (corrected).

Krutch, J. W. Samuel Johnson. New York 1944.

Starnes, D. T. and G. E. Noyes. The English dictionary from Cawdrey to Johnson. Chapel Hill 1946.

Leavis, F. R. Johnson and Augustanism; Johnson as poet. Both in his Common pursuit, 1952.

Chapman, R. W. Johnsonian and other essays. Oxford 1953.

Bate, W. J. The achievement of Johnson. New York 1955.
—— Samuel Johnson. New York 1977.

Clifford, J. L. Young Samuel Johnson. 1955, New York 1955 (as Young Sam Johnson).

Kolb, G. J. Dr Johnson's Dictionary. Chicago 1955.

Eliot, T. S. In his On poetry and poets, 1957.

Hilles, F. W. (ed). New light on Johnson: essays. New Haven 1959.

Gray, J. Johnson's sermons: a study. Oxford 1972.

Wain, John. Samuel Johnson. 1974.

Edinger, W. Johnson and poetic style. Chicago 1977.

RICHARD GRAVES
1715–1804

§ 1

The festoon: a collection of epigrams, ancient and modern, with an essay on that species of composition. 1766 (for 1765) (anon), 1767 (expanded), nd (4th edn).

The spiritual Quixote, or the summer's ramble of Mr Geoffrey Wildgoose: a comic romance. 3 vols 1773 (anon), 1774, 2 vols Dublin 1774, 3 vols 1783 ('with corrections and additions by the author'), 1792, 2 vols 1808, 1810 (vols 32–3 of British Novelists), 1816 (Walker's Br Classics), Providence 1816, London 1926; ed C. Tracy, Oxford 1967.

The love of order: a poetical essay in three cantos. 1773. Anon.

The progress of gallantry: a poetical essay in three cantos. 1774. Anon.

Galateo: or a treatise on politeness and delicacy of manners, from the Italian of Monsig Giovanni De La Casa. 1774. Anon.

Euphrosyne: or amusements on the road of life, by the author of the Spiritual Quixote. 2 vols 1776–80 (vol 1 rptd 1780), 1783 (adds Pieces written for the Poetical Society at Bath-Easton).

Columella, or the distressed anchoret: a colloquial tale, by the editor of the Spiritual Quixote. 2 vols 1779.

The sorrows of Werter: a German story. 2 vols 1779, 1780, 1782, 1 vol 1785, 1786 (adapted), 2 vols 1794. Tr D. Matthus? from a French version of Goethe's Werther.

Eugenius: or anecdotes of the golden vale, an embellished narrative of real facts. 2 vols 1785 (anon), 1786.

Lucubrations: consisting of essays, reveries etc in prose and verse, by the late Peter of Pontefract. 1786.

A letter from a father to his son at the university relative to a late address to young students etc. Oxford 1787.

Recollections of some particulars in the life of the late William Shenstone esq in a series of letters from an intimate friend of his to —— —— esq FRS [William Seward]. 1788. P. 195 signed R.G.

The rout: or a sketch of modern life, from an academic in the metropolis to his friend in the country. 1789. Anon.

The heir apparent: or the life of Commodus, translated from the Greek of Herodian. 1789. Anon.

Plexippus: or the aspiring plebeian. 2 vols 1790. Anon.

The meditations of the Emperor Marcus Aurelius Antonius: a new translation, with a life, notes etc. Bath 1792, Stourport 1811, Halifax 1826, 1905.

Hiero on the condition of royalty: a conversation from the Greek of Xenophon, by the translator of Antoninus's Meditations. Bath 1793.

The reveries of solitude: consisting of essays in prose, a new translation of the Muscipula, and original pieces in verse, by the editor of Columella, Eugenius etc. Bath 1793.

The coalition, or the opera rehears'd: a comedy in three acts by the editor of the Spiritual Quixote. Bath 1814 (for 1794).

The farmer's son: a moral tale inscribed to Mrs Hannah More by the Rev P.P.M.A. Bath 1795.

Sermons; to which is added A letter from a father to his son at the university. Bath 1799.

Senilities: or solitary amusements in prose and verse, with a cursory disquisition on the future condition of the sexes, by the editor of the Reveries of solitude etc. 1801.

The invalid; with the obvious means of enjoying health and a long life, by a nonagenarian, editor of the Spiritual Quixote etc. 1804.

The triflers: consisting of trifling essays, trifling anecdotes and a few poetical trifles, by an adept in the art of trifling; to which is added the Rout, corrected by the author, also the Farmer's son. 1805, 1806.

Shenstone's Miscellany 1759–63. Ed I. A. Gordon, Oxford 1953. Contains some epigrams by Graves.

§ 2

Hill, C. J. The literary career of Graves. Northampton Mass 1934. With bibliography.

SIR JOSHUA REYNOLDS
1723–92

Collections

Works, containing his Discourses, Idlers, A journey to Flanders and Holland (now first published) and his commentary on du Fresnoy's Art of painting, printed from his revised copies [with] an account of the life and writings of the author. Ed E. Malone 2 vols 1797, 3 vols 1798 ('corrected').

§ 1

A discourse, delivered at the opening of the Royal Academy, January 2 1769, by the President. 1769.

A discourse delivered to the students of the Royal Academy on the distribution of the prizes, December 11 1769, by the President. 1769.

The first 2 discourses were followed by 13 more, with titles like 2nd above: 3rd discourse, 1771 (2 states); 4th, 1772, 1772; 5th, 1773, 1773; 6th, 1775; 7th, 1777; 8th, 1779; 9th and 10th (together), 1781; 11th, 1783; 12th, 1785; 13th, 1787; 14th, 1789; 15th, 1791.

Seven discourses delivered in the Royal Academy by the President. 1778; ed H. Morley 1888.

The [15] discourses of Reynolds. 2 vols 1820, 1 vol Boston 1821, London 1837; ed R. Fry 1905; ed A. Dobson, Oxford 1907 (WC); ed E. Olson, Chicago [1945] (with trn of Longinus, On the sublime); ed R. R. Wark, New Haven 1975.

The art of painting of Charles Alphonse du Fresnoy: translated into English verse by William Mason MA, with annotations by Reynolds verse by William Mason MA, with annotations by Reynolds. York 1783, Dublin 1783.

Johnson and Garrick. 1816 (priv ptd); ed R. B. Johnson 1927.

Characters of the most celebrated painters of Italy. 1816.

Notes and observations on pictures. Ed W. Cotton 1859. Letters from Johnson, Malone, Boswell et al, with transcript of Reynolds' account book.

Letters. Ed F. W. Hilles, Cambridge 1929.

Portraits by Reynolds. Ed F. W. Hilles, New York 1952 (Private papers of Boswell, vol 3).

Journey from London to Brentford, now first published. In D. Hudson, Reynolds: a personal study, 1958.

§ 2

Blake's annotated copy of Malone's edn of Reynolds's Works, 1798 is in BM: the marginalia are ptd in Complete writings of William Blake, *ed G. L. Keynes 1957.*

Northcote, J. Memoirs of Reynolds. 1813; Supplement, 1815; 2 vols 1818.

Leslie, C. R. and T. Taylor. The life and times of Reynolds. 2 vols 1865.

Hilles, F. W. The literary career of Reynolds. Cambridge 1936.

— Sir Joshua's prose. In The age of Johnson: essays presented to C. B. Tinker, New Haven 1949.

Waterhouse, E. K. Reynolds. 1941.

Gombrich, E. H. Reynolds's theory and practice of imitation. Burlington Mag 80 1942.

Burke, J. Hogarth and Reynolds: a contrast in English art theory. Oxford 1943.

'JUNIUS'
probably SIR PHILIP FRANCIS
1740–1818

For an account of the controversy surrounding the identity of Junius, along with new evidence in support of Francis, see A. Ellegård, A statistical method for determining authorship: the Junius Letters, Stockholm 1962; and Who was Junius? Stockholm 1962.

The first of the Letters of Junius *appeared in* Woodfall's Public Advertiser *in London, 21 Jan 1769. Further letters appeared irregularly until 21 Jan 1772. The series attracted enough attention to make it profitable for various booksellers to bring out edns of the* Letters *before the series was concluded. At least 16 of these unauthorized partial edns were pbd before the end of 1771. In 1772, with Junius's authorization, Woodfall pbd the first complete edn with a dedication and preface by the author. Frequent edns of this authorized version were issued by various publishers in England, Scotland, Ireland and America between 1772 and 1812. This version contained 69 letters, of which 42 bear the signature of Junius.*

§ 1

Incomplete Early Editions of Letters

The political contest [pt 1]: containing a series of letters between Junius and Sir William Draper; also the whole of Junius's letters to his Grace the D— of G—, brought into one point of view [ptd for F. Newbery]. [1769] (3 edns), Dublin 1769 ('3rd' edn, including letters from pts 1–2, with 3 new letters, making total of 24; ptd for J. Potts). Contains 14 letters, the last dated 8 July 1769.

The political contest [pt 2]: being a continuation of Junius's letters from the 8th of July last to the present time. [1769]. Contains 7 later letters, ending with that of 25 Sept 1769.

Two letters from Junius to the D— of G—; to which is added a letter from Junius, containing an address supposed to have been made to a great personage, taken from the Public Advertiser. 1769.

Junius's supposed address to a great personage. [Dec 1769 or early 1770].

A collection of the letters of Atticus, Lucius, Junius and others. 1769, 1769 ('a new edition continued to the end of October 1769'), 1769 (as preceding but with addns of Modestus's answer to Letter 30, and Letters 32–3).

A complete collection of Junius's letters with those of Sir William Draper. 1770 (4? issues, each adding further material, the first with 29 letters, the last with 33).

The letters of Junius [ptd for J. Wheble]. 1770, 1770, 1771.

Letters of Junius [ptd for J. Wheble]. 2 vols 1770–4. The first vol is closely associated with the preceding item.

The political contest: containing Junius's letter to the K— and Modestus's answer. Dublin 1770.

Two remarkable letters of Junius and the Freeholder, addressed to the K—. 1770. Only known copy owned by Library Company of Philadelphia.

The state of the nation as represented to a certain great personage by Junius and the Freeholder. 1770.

The letters of Junius. 2 vols 1771–2. Ptd for J. Wheble: contains dedication and all the letters except the first 7 of Philo Junius.

The letters of Junius. 1771. Ptd for W. Morison.

The genuine letters of Junius; to which are prefixed anecdotes of the author. 1771, 1771. Contains 50 letters; Burke is presumed to be the author.

Complete Editions

Junius: stat nominis umbra, printed for Henry Sampson
Woodfall. 2 vols 1772 (2 issues: first lacks table of
contents and index, which appear in 2nd), nd (2nd edn
closely resembling preceding, but with table of contents
and index, Dublin 1772, 1772, London 1775, 1771 (for
after 1775), 1 vol 1779, 1783, 2 vols 1783, 1 vol 1784,
1786, 1787, Dublin 1787, 1788, 1788, 1789, 1791,
Philadelphia 1791, 2 vols 1792 (3 edns), 1 vol Edinburgh
1793, London 1794, 2 vols 1794, 1 vol Philadelphia 1795,
Basle 1795, London, 1796 (3 edns), 2 vols 1796 (with 16
portraits), 1797 (with portraits), 1 vol 1797 (5 edns), 2
vols 1797 (with 21 portraits), 1797 ('new and complete'),
1 vol Huddersfield 1798, London 1798, 2 vols 1798 (with
10 portraits), 1799 (with 21 portraits), 1800 (with 10
portraits), 1801 (with 16 portraits), 1801 (21 portraits).
The letters of Junius: stat nominis umbra, with notes and
illustrations, historical, political, biographical and
critical. Ed R. Heron [2 vols 1801?], 1802, 1804,
Boston 1804, Philadelphia 1804, New York 1804. A
good edn, used by later editors for its notes. Attributes
authorship to Dunning.
The letters of Junius: prodesse civibus. 1806.
The letters of Junius complete, [with a] prefatory enquiry
respecting the real author of John Almon. 2 vols 1806.
Attributes authorship to Hugh Boyd.
Junius: including letters by the same writer under other
signatures (now first collected); to which are added his
confidential correspondence with Mr Wilkes, and his
private letters addressed to Mr H. S. Woodfall. 3 vols
1812. Introductory essays by Mason Good. It is
improbable that Junius wrote any of the miscellaneous
essays in vol 3.
Letters of Junius; with preliminary dissertation and
copious notes by Atticus Secundus. Edinburgh 1822.
The editor, John McDiarmid, argues for Francis as
author.
The letters of Junius. 2 vols Paris 1822. Contains essay
by J. W. Lake favouring the authorship of Francis.
Junius: a new and enlarged edition, with new evidence as
to authorship. Ed J. Wade 1850 etc. 3rd edn of Mason
Good's edn of 1812, above. Wade's revision was
frequently rptd, and was part of Bohn's Lib. Wade
argues for Francis's authorship.
The letters of Junius. Ed C. W. Everett 1927. Argues for
Lord Shelburne's authorship.
Letters to Junius. Ed J. Cannon, Oxford 1978.

Writings by Francis

*Francis was an extensive minor writer. His work includes
letters to newspapers, pamphlets and the ptd versions of his
parliamentary speeches. Many of these pieces are uncertainly
attributed to him.*
A state of the British authority in Bengal under the
government of Mr Hastings. 1780. Anon.
A short account of the resignation of Warren Hastings.
1781. Anon.
Extract of an original letter from Calcutta relative to the
administration of Sir E. Impey. 1781. Anon; attributed
to Francis.
Original minutes of the Governor General and Council of
Fort William on the appointment of Sir E. Impey to be
Judge of the Sudder Duauny Adawlet. 1781. Ed
Francis?
Original minutes of the Governor-General and Council of
Fort William on the settlement and collection of the
revenues of Bengal. 1782. Anon.
State of India, in two letters from Warren Hastings esq to
the Court of Directors, and one from the Nabob Asuful
Dowla, Subadar of Owde, to which are added a series of
explanatory facts and remarks. 1782. Ed Francis.
Ninth report from the Select Committee appointed to take
into consideration the state of the administration of

justice in the provinces of Bengal. 1783. Drawn up in
part by Francis?
Speech [on the East India Company] in the House of
Commons, July 2 1784. 1784.
Two speeches in the House of Commons on the original
East-India Bill and on the amended Bill, on the 16th
and 26th of July 1784. 1784.
A letter from Warren Hastings esq with remarks. 1786.
Anon; sometimes attributed to Francis.
Speech in the House of Commons, 7 March 1786 [on the
affairs of the East India Company]. 1786, 1786.
Observations on the defence made by Warren Hastings.
1787. Anon.
Answer of P. Francis esq to the charge brought against Sir
J. Clavering, Colonel G. Monson and Mr Francis at the
Bar of the House of Commons on 4 February 1788 by
Sir E. Impey. 1788.
Draught of a resolution and plan intended to be proposed
to the Society of Friends of the People. [1792?]. Anon.
Heads of Mr F.'s speech in the House of Commons on the
7th of May 1793, on Mr Grey's notion for a reform in
Parliament. 1793.
Letter from Mr F. to Lord North [on the government of
India]. [1793?].
Mr Francis's speech on the order of the day for the second
reading of the Bill for preventing bribery at Stockbridge
election. [1793].
The speech of Mr F. on the tenth of April in favour of a
radical reform with observations by Merlin. 1793.
Proceedings in the House of Commons on the slave trade
and state of the negroes in the West India islands. 1796.
The question as it stood in March 1798. 1798. Anon.
Mr F.'s speeches on the affairs of India delivered in the
House of Commons on the 29th of July 1803. 1803.
Speeches in the House of Commons on the war against the
Marhattas. 1805.
Mr F.'s speech in the House of Commons, 28 May 1806,
against the exemption of foreign property in the funds
from the duty on income. 1806.
A letter from P.F. to Lord Viscount Howick on the state
of the East India Company. 1807, 1807.
Reflections on the abundance of peper in circulation and
the scarcity of specie. 1810, 1810.
Letter to Earl Grey [occasioned by the blockade of the
ports of Norway by the English fleet]. Pamphleteer 4
1813; 1814, 1814.
Plan of a reform in the election of the House of Commons,
adopted by the Society of the Friends of the People in
1795; with a new introduction and other documents,
republished. Pamphleteer 9 1813; 1817. Anon.
A letter missive from Sir P.F. to Lord Holland [on Irish
politics]. 1816, 1816.
Memoirs of Francis, with his correspondence and journals.
Ed J. Parkes and H. Merivale 2 vols 1867.
The Francis letters, by Sir Philip Francis and other
members of the family. Ed B. Francis and E. Keary 2
vols [1901].

§ 2

Thicknesse, P. Junius discovered. 1789. Attributes
authorship to John Horne Tooke.
Macaulay, T. B. Warren Hastings. Edinburgh Rev
Oct 1841; rptd in his Collected essays, 1843. Attributes
authorship to Francis.
Lecky, W. E. H. In his History of England in the eight-
eenth century vol 3, 1887 (3rd edn). Attributes author-
ship to Francis.
Boulton, J. T. The letters of Junius. Durham Univ Jnl
54 1962; rev in his Language of politics in the age of
Wilkes and Burke, 1963.
Ellegård, A. A statistical method for determining author-
ship: the Junius letters 1769–72. Stockholm 1962
(Gothenburg Stud in Eng 13).
—— Who was Junius? Stockholm 1962. Attributes
authorship to Francis.

EDMUND BURKE
1729-97

Many letters and photostats of letters are in Sheffield City Lib.

Bibliographies

Copeland, T. W. and M. S. Smith. A checklist of the correspondence of Burke. Cambridge 1955 (Index Soc).
Todd, W. B. A bibliography of Burke. 1964 (Soho Bibliographies).

Collections

Works. Ed F. Laurence and W. King 8 vols 1792–1827 (4°; vols 1–4 ed Laurence, vols 5–8 ed King), 8 vols 1801 (8°), 16 vols 1803–27.
Speeches in the House of Commons, and in Westminster-Hall. 4 vols 1816.
Select works. Ed E. J. Payne 3 vols Oxford 1874–8.
Letters, speeches, and tracts on Irish affairs. Ed M. Arnold 1881.
Selected writings and speeches. Ed P. J. Stanlis, Garden City NY 1963.

§ 1

The reformer. Dublin 1747–8. Ed Burke. Unique ser at Pearse St Library, Dublin; ed A. P. I. Samuels in his Early life of Burke, Cambridge 1923.
A vindication of natural society in a letter to Lord ****, by a late noble writer. 1756 (anon), 1757 (with new preface).
An account of the European settlements in America. 2 vols 1757, 1758. Burke revised and contributed to this work, written by his kinsman William Burke.
A philosophical enquiry into the origin of our ideas of the sublime and beautiful. 1757 (anon), 1759 (adds Introductory discourse concerning taste); ed J. T. Boulton 1958.
An essay towards an abridgment of the English history [1757]. [1812].
The annual register. 1759–88. Burke edited this annual till 1766 and probably contributed in later years. Some of the historical surveys were rptd in 1761 as A complete history of the present war, and in later compilations.
A short account of a late short administration. 1766.
Observations on a late state of the nation. 1769, 1769.
Thoughts on the cause of the present discontents. 1770 (4 edns).
Burke's speech [13 Oct]. Bristol 1774.
To the gentlemen of Bristol [13 Oct]. Bristol 1774.
To the gentlemen of Bristol [3 Nov]. Bristol 1774.
Speech to the electors [3 Nov]. Bristol 1774.
To the gentlemen of Bristol [16 Nov]. Bristol 1774. Unique copy at Bristol Central Library.
Burke's speeches at his arrival at Bristol. 1774, 1775.
Speech on American taxation April 19 1774. 1775.
The speech on moving his resolutions for conciliation with the colonies March 22 1775. 1775 (3 edns).
The letters of Valens. 1777. With occasional contributions by Burke.
A letter to John Farr and John Harris, the sheriffs of Bristol, on the affairs of America [3 April]. Bristol 1777, London 1777 (3 edns).
Two letters to gentlemen in the City of Bristol on Ireland. [23 April, 2 May 1778]. 1778.
An authentic copy of the trial of Keppel. 1779; rev as Proceedings of the court-martial of Keppel, 1779. Burke prepared the formal defence.
Substance of the speeches made in the House of Commons on Wednesday 15 December 1779. 1779.
The Yorkshire question. 1780. Apparently with Burke's assistance.
Speech on presenting to the House of Commons 11th of February 1780 a plan of public oeconomy. 1780. Pirated edn, followed by the authentic sequence: Speech on presenting to the House of Commons the 11th of February 1780 a plan for the oeconomical reformation of the civil and other establishments, 1780 (4 edns).
A letter from Burke in vindication of his conduct with regard to the affairs of Ireland. Dublin 1780, London 1780.
To the gentlemen of Bristol [1 Sept]. Bristol 1780.
To the gentlemen of Bristol [6 Sept]. Bristol 1780.
Bristol, 9th Sept [speech beginning 'I decline the election']. Bristol 1780.
To the gentlemen of Bristol [9 Sept]. Bristol 1780.
Speech at the Guildhall in Bristol upon his parliamentary conduct [6 Sept]. 1780.
Heads of objections to Paul Benfield [of the East India Company with] Benfield's answers. [1780].
Report[s] from the Select Committee [on India]. 1782–3. Burke was sole author of reports 9 and 11, and doubtless assisted in the preparation of others.
Letter to a peer of Ireland [Kenmare] on the penal laws [21 Feb]. 1782; ed H. C. Clifford 1824.
Burke's speech on the 1st December 1783 upon the question for the Speaker's leaving the chair, in order for the House to resolve itself into a committee on Mr Fox's East India Bill [1 Dec 1783]. 1784.
A representation to his Majesty, moved in the House of Commons and seconded by William Windham, June 14. 1784.
Burke's speech, on the motion made for papers relative to the Nabob of Arcot's debts. 1785.
Articles of charge of high crimes and misdemeanours, against Warren Hastings, late Governor-General of Bengal, presented to the House of Commons on the 4th day of April [–5th day of May] 1786. 1786.
Articles of impeachment against Warren Hastings. 1787, 1787.
A letter to Philip Francis. 1788.
Substance of the speech in debates upon the Army Estimates. 1790 (3 edns).
Reflections on the Revolution in France, and on the proceedings in certain societies in London relative to that event. 1790 (7 edns); ed E. J. Payne 1875; ed T. H. D. Mahoney 1955; ed W. B. Todd, New York 1959 (from 7th edn); ed C. C. O'Brien 1969 (Pelican).
Lettre à un membre de l'Assemblée Nationale de France. [Paris] 1791; rev and tr 1791.
Two letters on the French Revolution. 1791.
An appeal from the new to the old Whigs, in consequence of some late discussions in Parliament relative to the Reflections on the French Revolution. 1791 (4 edns).
Lettre à l'Archevêque d'Aix. [Paris? 1791].
Lettre to [Rivarol] sur les affaires de France. [Paris? 1791].
Traduction d'un article [from Evening Mail 19 Sept as Case of the suffering clergy of France]. [Paris?] 1792.
Burke's speech in Westminster-Hall 18th and 19th of February 1788. 1792.
J. P. Brissot to his constituents. 1794 (3 edns). Burke supplied the preface and assisted in translating an earlier French edn.
Report from the committee of the House of Commons on the trial of Warren Hastings. 1794.
Substance of the speech in answer to certain observations in the report of the Committee of Managers [of the impeachment of Warren Hastings], representing that report to have been a libel on the judges. 1794, 1794.
A letter to a noble Lord on the attacks made upon him and his pension in the House of Lords by the Duke of Bedford and the Earl of Lauderdale. 1796 (14 edns).
Thoughts on the prospect of a regicide peace. 796. Pirated edn followed by the authentic series: Two letters addressed to a member of the present Parliament on the proposals for peace with the regicide directory of

France, 1796–[1800] (13 edns). A third letter on the proposals for peace with France, 1797. 4th letter, written before all the others (Xmas 1795) was not pbd until 1812, when it was included in vol 5 of Laurence and King's 4° edn of Works.

A letter to the Duke of Portland. 1797. Pirated edn followed by the authentic series: Two letters on the conduct of our domestick parties, 1797 (3 edns). Consists of Letter to the Duke of Portland on the conduct of the minority, 1793; Letter concerning Lord Fitzwilliam, 1795.

[Address to the King]. Monthly Mag July 1797.

Three memorials on French affairs written 1791, 1792 and 1793. 1797 (3 edns).

Thoughts and details on scarcity. 1800. Written 1795.

The Catholic claims. Dublin 1807, London 1807.

Speech of the late Burke on reform in the House of Commons, 1782; with extracts from the speech of the late W. Windham on Mr Curwen's reform bill 1809. 1831.

Speech in opening the impeachment of Warren Hastings 15 Feb 1788. Ed E. A. Bond 1859.

Letters and Notebooks

Epistolary correspondence of Burke and French Laurence. 1827.

Correspondence 1744–97. Ed Earl Fitzwilliam and R. Bourke 4 vols 1844.

Correspondence of Burke and William Windham. Ed J. P. Gilson 1910 (Roxburghe Club).

A note-book [1750–6]. Ed H. V. F. Somerset, Cambridge 1957.

Correspondence. Ed T. W. Copeland et al 10 vols Cambridge 1958–77.

See also A. P. I. Samuels, *below*.

§ 2

Mackintosh, J. Vindiciae gallicae: defence of the French Revolution against Burke. 1791, Dublin 1791, London 1837.

Paine, T. Rights of man: being an answer to Mr Burke's attack on the French Revolution. 2 pts 1791–2 etc.

Priestley, J. Letters to Burke occasioned by his Reflections on the French Revolution. 1791.

Prior, J. Memoir of the life and character of Burke. 1812, 1854 (5th edn), 1967.

Morley, J. Burke: an historical study. 1867.

—— Edmund Burke. 1879 (EML), 1923.

Samuels, A. P. I. The early life, correspondence and writings of Burke. Cambridge 1923. Prints for the first time much of Burke's early writings.

Copeland, T. W. Our eminent friend Edmund Burke: six essays. New Haven 1949.

Magnus, P. Burke: a life. 1939.

Young, G. M. An essay by Burke. TLS 3 Aug 1940. Reply by P. Magnus 10 Aug 1940.

—— In his Today and yesterday, 1948.

Barker, E. Burke and his Bristol constituency; Burke on the French Revolution. In his Essays on government, Oxford 1945.

Fasnacht, G. E. Lord Acton on nationality and Socialism (with an appendix on Burke based on the Acton mss). Oxford 1949.

Hoffman, R. J. S. Burke, New York agent. Philadelphia 1956. Includes some 200 unpbd letters to and from Burke.

Stanlis, P. J. Burke and the natural law. Ann Arbor 1958.

—— (ed). The relevance of Burke. New York 1964.

—— (ed). Burke, the Enlightenment and the modern world. Detroit 1967.

Boulton, J. T. In his Language of politics in the age of Wilkes and Burke, 1963.

Courtney, C. P. Montesquieu and Burke. Oxford 1963.

Kirk, R. Burke: a genius reconsidered. New Rochelle NY 1967.

Wilkins, B. T. The problem of Burke's political philosophy. Oxford 1967.

OLIVER GOLDSMITH
1730?–74

Bibliographies etc

Balderston, K. C. A census of the manuscripts of Goldsmith. New York 1926.

Paden, W. D. and C. K. Hyder. A concordance to the poems of Goldsmith. Lawrence Kansas 1940.

Collections

Miscellaneous works: a new edition. 4 vols 1801, 1806, 6 vols 1809, 4 vols Boston 1809, London 1812, Glasgow 1816, London 1820, 1821, 6 vols 1823. On the history of this edn *see* K. C. Balderston, The history and sources of Percy's Memoir of Goldsmith, Cambridge 1926.

New essays. Ed R. S. Crane, Chicago 1927. Prints 18 new ascriptions; nos 1 and 13 are doubtful.

Selected works. Ed R. Garnett 1950 (Reynard Lib).

Collected works. Ed A. Friedman 5 vols Oxford 1966.

§ 1

The monthly review: or literary journal. 1757, 1758, 1763.

The memoirs of a Protestant, condemned to the galleys of France for his religion. 2 vols 1758 (9 March), Dublin 1765; ed A. Dobson 1895. Tr Goldsmith from the French of J. Marteilhe.

The critical review: or annals of literature. 1759, 1760, 1763.

An enquiry into the present state of polite learning in Europe. 1759 (4 April), 1774 (30 July, rev).

The bee. Nos i–viii, 6 Oct–24 Nov 1759. Reissued in book form 1759 (15 Dec), reissued c. 1800 with new title-page, new edn 1819.

The busy body. 1759.

The weekly magazine: or gentleman and lady's polite companion. 1759, 1760.

The royal magazine: or gentleman's monthly companion. 1759, 1760.

The public ledger. 1760, 1761.

Chinese letters. 119 essays pbd between 24 Jan 1760 and 14 Aug 1761; rptd as Citizen of the world, 1762.

The British magazine: or monthly repository. 1760.

The lady's magazine: or polite companion for the fair sex. 1760, 1761.

Lloyd's evening post and British chronicle. 1762.

The mystery revealed: containing a series of transactions and authentic testimonials respecting the supposed Cock-Lane ghost. 1762 (23 Feb), misdated 1742; rptd Westport Conn 1928.

The citizen of the world: or letters from a Chinese philosopher residing in London to his friends in the East. 2 vols 1762 (1 May), Dublin 1762, 1769, London 1774 (1 July, called 3rd edn), Dublin 1775, London 1776; ed A. Dobson 1891, 1893, 1900.

Plutarch's Lives, abridged from the original Greek, illustrated with notes and reflections. 7 vols 1762 (beginning of each month May–Nov). Goldsmith prepared vols 1–4 but was unable to complete 5.

The life of Richard Nash of Bath esq, extracted principally from his original papers. 1762 (14 Oct), 1762 (9 Dec), Dublin 1762.

A new and accurate system of natural history, by R. Brookes. 6 vols 1763–4 (beginning of each month Aug

1763–Jan 1764), 1772. Goldsmith wrote Preface and Introductions to vols 1–4.

A general history of the world from the creation to the present time, by W. Guthrie, J. Gray and others. 12 vols and index vol 1764–7. Goldsmith wrote Preface to vol 1, pbd 2 April 1764.

An history of England in a series of letters from a nobleman to his son. 2 vols 1764 (26 June), Dublin 1767, London 1769, 1770, 1771, 1772, 1774, 1776, 1780, 1783.

A complete English grammar on a new plan, by C. Wiseman. 1764. Goldsmith wrote Preface.

An history of the lives, actions, travels, sufferings and deaths of the most eminent martyrs and primitive fathers of the Church. 1764 (26 Dec).

The traveller: or a prospect of society. 1765 (19 Dec 1764), 1765 (14 March), 1765, 1765 (6 Aug), 1768 (25 Feb), 1770 (6th edn corrected 29 June), 1770 (8 Dec), 1770, 1774, 1778, 1786; ed G. B. Hill, Oxford 1888; ed W. B. Todd as A prospect of society, Cambridge 1954, Charlottesville 1956. A set, now in BM, of uncorrected proof-sheets of lines 73–92 and 103–400 of first edn of the poem was discovered by and ed B. Dobell as A prospect of society: being the earliest form ·of the Traveller, 1902. For an explanation of these proof-sheets see W. B. Todd, SB 7 1955; L. W. Hanson, Library 5th ser 10 1955; Todd 11 1956.

The geography and history of England, in two parts; the second contains A concise history of England: or the revolutions of the British constitution. 1765 (23 March).

Essays by Mr Goldsmith. 1765 (with engraved title-page, 4 June), 1765 (with ptd title-page, probably a piracy; see A. Friedman, SB 5 1953), 1766 (2nd edn as Essays by Oliver Goldsmith, with 2 additional essays), Dublin 1767, 1772, Altenburgh 1774, London 1775, 1775, 1783, 1789, Dublin 1793, London 1799.

Edwin and Angelina: a ballad by Mr Goldsmith, printed for the amusement of the Countess of Northumberland. [1765], Philadelphia 1964 (facs). Rptd in Vicar of Wakefield, 1766, and in Poems for young ladies, 1767.

The Vicar of Wakefield: a tale. 2 vols 1766 (27 March), 1766 (31 May), 1766 (27 Aug), 1766 (pirated edn), Cork 1766, Dublin 1766, 1767, 1767, London 1768, Berlin 1769, London 1770 (4th edn 9 Dec 1769), 1770, Philadelphia 1772, London 1773 (5th edn 2 April 1774), 1774, Berlin 1776, London 1777, 1778, 1779 (6th edn); ed H. James, New York 1900; ed C. E. Doble, Oxford 1909; ed O. Doughty 1928; ed A. Friedman, Oxford 1974.

A concise history of philosophy and philosophers, by M. Formey. 1766 (24 June). Tr Goldsmith.

Poems for young ladies in three parts: devotional, moral and entertaining. 1767 (15 Dec 1766), 1770 (a reissue), 1785.

The beauties of English poesy, selected by Oliver Goldsmith. 2 vols 1767 (6 April), Dublin 1771.

St James's Chron 23–5 July 1767. Signed letter by Goldsmith answering the charge that he had taken Edwin and Angelina from a ballad by Percy.

Essay on friendship. In H. Kelly's Babler: containing a careful selection from essays in Owen's weekly chronicle, 1767.

The good natur'd man: a comedy. 1768, Dublin 1768, 1770, 1784, London 1792, 1797, [1807]. Produced at Covent Garden 29 Jan 1768.

The present state of the British Empire in Europe, America, Africa and Asia. 1768 (13 May).

The sister: a comedy, by Mrs Charlotte Lennox. 1769 (3 March). Produced at Covent Garden 18 Feb 1769. Goldsmith wrote the epilogue.

The Roman history, from the foundation of the city of Rome to the destruction of the Western Empire. 2 vols 1769 (18 May), Dublin 1769, London 1770, Dublin 1771, 1773, 1775–6, London 1775, 1781.

The deserted village. 4° edns: 1770 (26 May), 1927 (facs),

New York 1934 (facs), 1770 (2nd–6th edns 6, 13, 28 June, 8 Aug, 4 Oct), 1772, 1775, 1779, 1783, Springfield Mass 1783, London [1784], 1786 (14th edn). 12° edns: 1770 (4 edns, some thought to antedate the 1st 4°, but all piracies), 1777, [1783], Dublin 1784. 8° edns: Dublin 1770, 1770, Philadelphia 1771, Altenburgh 1773, London 1775, [1784] (3 edns), Providence RI 1784. 18° edn: Manchester 1793.

Poems on several occasions, written by Dr Thomas Parnell; to which is prefixed the Life of Dr Parnell, written by Dr Goldsmith. 1770 (19 June), 1772, 1773, Dublin 1773. Separate edn of Life of Thomas Parnell, 1770 (5 July); rptd in Davies's Miscellaneous and fugitive pieces vol 3, 1774; rptd abridged in Poems by Goldsmith and Parnell, ed I. Reed 1795.

A dissertation upon parties, by Henry St John, Lord Viscount Bolingbroke; to which is prefixed the Life of the author [by Goldsmith]. 9th edn 1771 (1 Dec 1770), 1775 (10th edn), 1786. Life issued separately as Life of Henry St John, Lord Viscount Bolingbroke, 1770 (4 Dec); rptd in Davies's edn of Bolingbroke's Works, 1774, and in Davies's Miscellaneous and fugitive pieces vol 3, 1774.

The history of England, from the earliest times to the death of George II. 4 vols 1771 (6 Aug), 1774 (17 Dec, corrected), 1784 (4th edn), 1786, 1787, Dublin 1789, London 1790, 1794, Dublin 1796, London 1800, 1805, Bungay 1807 (for c. 1815), London 1815, 1819 (11th edn with continuation to 1815), 1823 (with continuation to 1820) etc.

Zobeide: a tragedy. 1771 (19 Dec), 1772, 1774. By J. Cradock. Produced at Covent Garden 11 Dec 1771. Goldsmith wrote the prologue.

Threnodia augustalis: sacred to the memory of the Princess Dowager of Wales. 1772 (20 Feb).

Dr Goldsmith's Roman history, abridged by himself for the use of schools. 1772 (1 Dec), Dublin 1773, 1781, London 1786 (4th edn), 1790.

The Westminster magazine. 1773.

She stoops to conquer, or the mistakes of a night: a comedy. 1773 (25 March), 1773 (2nd–5th edns); ed A. Friedman, Oxford 1968. Produced at Covent Garden 15 March 1773. 2 epilogues by Goldsmith intended for the play ptd in Miscellaneous works, 1801.

The daily advertiser. 31 March 1773.

Epilogue spoken by Mr Lee Lewes in the character of Harlequin at his benefit, May 7 1773. London Chron 28–30 April 1774; Poetical and dramatic works, 1780.

The grumbler: a farce. Performed once at Covent Garden 8 May 1773. One scene ptd by Prior, Miscellaneous works, 1837. Ed from Larpent ms by A. I. P. Wood, Cambridge Mass 1931. An adaptation of Sir Charles Sedley's trn of Brueys's Le grondeur.

Retaliation: a poem. 1774 (19 April), 1774 (2nd–7th edns; the 2nd issue of 4th edn adds Postscript probably not by Goldsmith); 1776, 1777.

The Grecian history, from the earliest state to the death of Alexander the Great. 2 vols 1774 (14 June), Dublin 1774, London 1785, 1796, 1798, 1800.

An history of the earth and animated nature. 8 vols 1774 (1 July), 1774 (probably ptd much later and misdated to deceive buyers), Dublin 1776–7, London 1779. For Goldsmith's original plan of the work, see Critical Rev 38 1774, rptd by C. E. Jones, N & Q 21 Sept 1946.

An abridgement of the history of England from the invasion of Julius Caesar to the death of George II. 1774 (23 Sept), 1777, Dublin 1779, 1789, London 1793 (7th edn), Philadelphia 1795, London 1796.

The comic romance of Monsieur Scarron, translated by Oliver Goldsmith. 2 vols 1775, Dublin nd.

The haunch of venison: a poetical epistle to Lord Clare. 1776, 1776 (with 'additions and corrections'), Dublin 1776. Written in 1770 or 1771. Ms in New York Public Lib.

A survey of experimental philosophy, considered in its present state of improvement. 2 vols 1776.

The captivity: an oratorio. In Miscellaneous works vol 2, 1820; 1836 (separately). 2 of the songs first pbd in Haunch of venison, 1776, above.

The political view of the result of the present war with America upon Great Britain, France, Prussia, Germany and Holland. In Miscellaneous works, ed Prior 1837 as Preface and introduction to the history of the Seven Years' War. Written c. 1760–1. The ms is in the Huntington Lib.

Letters

Collected letters. Ed K. C. Balderston, Cambridge 1928.

Private papers of James Boswell from Malahide Castle. Ed G. Scott and F. A. Pottle. Vols 8–9, New York 1930. 2 letters not available to Miss Balderston, above.

Seitz, R. W. Goldsmith to Sir William Chambers. TLS 26 Sept 1936. 2 letters of 1773.

Balderston, K. C. New Goldsmith letters. Yale Univ Lib Gazette 39 1964. 2 letters of 1766 to John Bindley.

§ 2

For early criticism see Goldsmith: the critical heritage, *ed G. S. Rousseau 1973.*

Percy, T. Memoirs of Dr Goldsmith (chiefly from his own mouth, 1773). 28 April. Frequently called the Percy Memorandum. Ed K. C. Balderston in The history and sources of Percy's Memoir of Goldsmith, Cambridge 1926.

[Malone, E.] The life of Goldsmith. In Poems and plays, Dublin 1777, London 1780; Poetical and dramatic works, 1780; Miscellaneous works, Perth 1792 etc. A

Piozzi, H. L. In her Anecdotes of the late Samuel Johnson, 1786.

—— In her Autobiography, letters and literary remains of Mrs Piozzi, ed A. Hayward 2 vols 1861 (2nd edn).

—— In her Thraliana, ed K. C. Balderston 2 vols Oxford 1942, 1951 (corrected).

Hawkins, J. In his Life of Samuel Johnson, 1787.

Boswell, James. In his Life of Samuel Johnson, 2 vols 1791.

[Reed, I.] Life of Goldsmith. In Poems by Goldsmith and Parnell, 1795. A revision with some new material of the life by Malone, above.

[Percy, T. et al]. The life of Goldsmith. In Miscellaneous works of Goldsmith vol 1, 1801. Usually called Percy Memoir. *See* K. C. Balderston, History and sources of Percy's Memoir of Goldsmith, Cambridge 1926.

Prior, J. The life of Goldsmith from a variety of original sources. 2 vols 1837.

Irving, W. The life of Goldsmith, with selections from his writings. 1844, 1850 (rev and enlarged as Goldsmith: a biography).

Forster, J. The life and adventures of Goldsmith. 1848, 2 vols 1854 (with notes as The life and times of Goldsmith).

[Woolf, V.] Oliver Goldsmith. TLS 1 March 1934; rptd in her Captain's death bed, 1950.

Quintana, R. Goldsmith: a Georgian study. New York [1967].

Hopkins, R. H. The true genius of Goldsmith. Baltimore [1969].

Sells, A. L. Goldsmith: his life and works. 1974.

Ginger, J. The notable man. 1977.

JAMES BOSWELL
1740–95
Bibliographies

Pottle, F. A. The literary career of James Boswell esq:

being the bibliographical materials for a life of Boswell. Oxford 1929, 1966.

—— and M. S. The private papers of Boswell from Malahide Castle in the collection of Lt-Col R. H. Isham: a catalogue. New York 1931.

Abbott, C. C. A catalogue of papers relating to Boswell, Johnson and Sir William Forbes found at Fettercairn House. Oxford 1936.

Chapman, R. W. (ed). The Johnson-Boswell correspondence. Appendix B vol 3 of Letters of Samuel Johnson, 3 vols Oxford 1952. A calendar of Boswell's side of the correspondence.

§ 1

A view of the Edinburgh theatre during the summer season 1759, by a society of gentlemen. 1760.

Observations good or bad stupid or clever serious or jocular on Squire Foote's dramatic entertainment intitled the Minor, by a genius. Edinburgh 1760, London 1761.

An elegy on the death of an amiable young lady, with an epistle from Menalcas to Lycidas [i.e. Lycidas to Menalcas]; to which are prefixed three critical recommendatory letters. Edinburgh 1761; rptd in Caledoniad vol 1, 1775.

An ode to tragedy, by a gentleman of Scotland. Edinburgh 1661 (for 1761).

A collection of original poems by Scotch gentlemen. Vol 2, Edinburgh 1762.

The cub at Newmarket: a tale. 1762.

Critical strictures on the new tragedy of Elvira written by Mr David Malloch. 1763; ed F. A. Pottle, Los Angeles 1952 (Augustan Reprint Soc). By Boswell, Andrew Erskine and George Dempster.

Disputatio juridica de supellectile legata quam publicae disquisitioni subjicit Jacobus Boswell ad diem 26 Julii. Edinburgh 1766.

The Douglas cause. [Edinburgh 1767]. 2 pp. on one side of a quarter sheet.

Dorando: a Spanish tale. 1767, 1767, Edinburgh 1767, London 1930.

The essence of the Douglas cause, to which is subjoined Some observations on a pamphlet lately published, intitled Considerations on the Douglas cause. 1767 (issued also with the same title-page but without Observations, which were not by Boswell), 1767 (imprint London but probably a Scots piracy); latter reissued 1769, probably at Edinburgh, with Observations on the Douglas cause in general, by Francis Douglas.

Letters of the Right Hon Lady Jane Douglas with several other important pieces of private correspondence. 1767. Boswell may not have been the sole editor.

An account of Corsica; The journal of a tour to that island, and memoirs of Pascal Paoli, by James Boswell esq. Glasgow 1768, London 1768, 1769, Dublin 1768, 1768, 1769. About half the book rptd in Universal Mag Feb-Aug 1768. Abridgement of Account 1794. Journal of a tour, ed G. B. Hill 1879 (with Letters between the Hon Andrew Erskine and James Boswell esq); ed S. C. Roberts, Cambridge 1923; ed 'Morchard Bishop' 1951; ed F. Brady and F. A. Pottle in Boswell on the Grand Tour: Italy, Corsica and France, 1955.

British essays in favour of the brave Corsicans by several hands, collected and published by James Boswell esq 1769 (for Dec 1768). The known authors besides Boswell were Sir John Dick, Edward Dilly and Gen Oglethorpe; Boswell's own marked copy at Johnson Birthplace, Lichfield.

Verses in the character of a Corsican at Shakespeare's jubilee at Stratford-upon-Avon, by James Boswell esq. [Stratford] 6 Sept 1769; Birmingham 7 Sept 1769. Folio half-sheet ptd on one side.

The works of Shakespear. 8 vols Edinburgh 1771, 1771

(for 1773 or later). The dedication to Garrick in vol 1 is by Boswell.

Reflections on the late alarming bankruptcies in Scotland. Edinburgh 1772.

The decision of the Court of Session upon the question of literary property in the cause John Hinton of London bookseller against Alexander Donaldson and John Wood booksellers in Edinburgh and James Meurose bookseller in Kilmarnock, published by James Boswell esq, advocate. Edinburgh 1774, 1774.

The mournful case of poor misfortunate and unhappy John Reid now lying under sentence of death in the Tollbooth of Edinburgh, taken from his own mouth on Wednesday night the 7th of September 1774, being the day fixed for his execution. [Edinburgh 10 Sept 1774]. Folio half-sheet ptd on one side. Journ 7, 14 Sept 1774.

The patriotic Chamberlain: an excellent new song for Midsummer Day 1776. [June 1776]. Long narrow strip ptd on one side. 8 stanzas and refrain urging the liverymen of London to vote for John Wilkes for Chamberlain.

St Cecilia: or the lady's and gentleman's harmonious companion. [Ed Charles Wilson], Edinburgh 1779. Contains Boswell's song The Court of Session garland: to the tune of Logan water, pts 1 and 2, 10 stanzas each. Rptd with slight variations in Robert Chambers, Traditions of Edinburgh, 1825 etc.

To the printer of the Public Advertiser. Letter signed 'Tantalus', 6 April. [c. 8 April 1779].

A letter to Robert Macqueen, Lord Braxfield on his promotion to be one of the judges of the High Court of Justiciary. Edinburgh 1780.

An excellent new war song, the words adapted to Mr Muschet's quick march for the Edinburgh Defensive Band. [Edinburgh 16 July 1782].

A letter to the people of Scotland on the present state of the nation, by James Boswell esq. Edinburgh 1783, London 1784, 1784 (anon, as A letter to the people on the present state of the nation).

A letter to the people of Scotland on the alarming attempt to infringe the Articles of Union and introduce a most pernicious innovation by diminishing the number of the Lords of Session, by James Boswell esq. 1785.

For the Public Advertiser: Mr Boswell's answer to a letter to this paper signed An Ayrshireman. [Signed] James Boswell, Upper Seymour-street, Portman-square, no 1, 25 July 1785. [c. 27 July 1785]. Offprint of Boswell's letter to Public Advertiser 27 July 1785.

Opinion of English counsel on the bill for diminishing the number of the Lords of Session in Scotland, sent to Mr Boswell by Capel Lofft esq of Lincoln's Inn. [Probably London c. 27 Aug 1785].

The journal of a tour to the Hebrides with Samuel Johnson LlD, by James Boswell esq: containing some poetical pieces by Dr Johnson relative to the tour and never before published. 1785, 1785, Dublin 1785, London 1786, 1807, New York and Boston 1810; ed J. W. Croker in his Life of Johnson, 1831, 1835, 1848; ed R. Carruthers 1852; ed G. B. Hill in his edn of Life of Johnson, Oxford 1887, rev L. F. Powell, Oxford 1950, 1964; ed R. W. Chapman in his edn of Johnson's Journey, Oxford 1924; ed F. A. Pottle and C. H. Bennett 1936 (from ms), rev Pottle, New York 1961, London 1963; ed L. F. Powell 1955 (EL).

Two new songs: Houses shut up, or Rowland in the dumps; Rowland deceived, a Carlisle song. [Probably Carlisle c. 12 Dec 1786].

December 12. 1786: To Rowland Stephenson esq banker in London and candidate for Carlisle, the address and remonstrance of independent old freemen. [Carlisle c. 12 Dec 1786]. Folio leaf ptd on one side.

Grand committee, Bluebell, Carlisle 13 Dec 1786. Modest proposals for chairing Mr Rowland Stepenson in case he shall lose his election. [Carlisle c. 13 Dec 1786]. Folio leaf ptd on one side.

Case of chairing: opinion of James Boswell esq of the Inner Temple barrister at law . . . [signed] James Boswell. [Carlisle c. 15 Dec 1786]. Folio leaf ptd on one side.

Ring lost: lost on Wednesday evening 30th of April. . . . [London 1 May 1788]. Small handbill ptd on one side.

Ode by Dr Samuel Johnson to Mrs Thrale upon their supposed approaching nuptials. 1784. Actually pbd a few days after 9 May 1788.

Small paper book lost: lost out of a gentleman's pocket on Monday the 2nd of November . . . [London c. 3 Nov 1789]. Small handbill ptd on one side.

William Pitt the grocer of London: an excellent new ballad written by James Boswell esq and sung by him at Guildhall on Lord Mayor's Day 1790. c. 11 Nov 1790.

No abolition of slavery: or the universal empire of love, a poem. [16 April] 1791.

The celebrated letter from Samuel Johnson LlD to Philip Dormer Stanhope, Earl of Chesterfield, now first published by James Boswell esq. 1790. Actually pbd 12 May 1791.

A conversation between his most sacred Majesty George III and Samuel Johnson LlD illustrated with observations by James Boswell esq. 1790. Actually pbd 12 May 1791.

The life of Samuel Johnson LlD: comprehending an account of his studies and numerous works, a series of his correspondence and conversations with many eminent persons, and various original pieces of his composition never before published, the whole exhibiting a view of literature and literary men in Great Britain for near half a century during which he flourished, by James Boswell esq. 2 vols 1791, 3 vols Dublin 1792, London 1793 ('revised and augmented'); ed Edmond Malone 4 vols 1799 ('revised and augmented'); ed J. W. Croker 5 vols 1831 (with Tour); rev J. Wright 10 vols 1835 (with Tour); ed J. W. Croker 1848 (with Tour); ed P. Fitzgerald 3 vols 1874 (with Tour), 1888 (with A bibliography of Life by H. R. Tedder); ed A. Napier 5 vols 1884 (with Tour) 6 vols 1884; ed G. B. Hill 6 vols Oxford 1887 (with Tour); rev L. F. Powell 6 vols Oxford 1934–50, 1964; ed R. Ingpen 2 vols 1970 (illustr), 3 vols Bath 1925; ed S. C. Roberts 2 vols 1949 (EL); ed R. W. Chapman, with introd by C. B. Tinker, Oxford 1953 (OSA), 1970 (rev J. D. Fleeman).

Song for the glorious 26th of June: being the anniversary of Mr Alderman [William] Curtis's election as one of the Members of Parliament for the City of London, by James Boswell esq [26 June 1792]. Folio leaf ptd on both sides.

Proposals for publishing a new and improved edition of Shakespeare illustrated by Charlotte Lennox. [c. Feb 1793]. Folio leaf ptd on one side.

It is impossible for me an enthusiastic Tory. [c. 17 May 1793]. Single leaf ptd on one side, 11-line paragraph in italic type. For Advertisement of the 2nd edn of Life of Johnson but removed before printing because of the sharp remonstrance of Malone.

The principal corrections and additions to the first edition of Mr Boswell's Life of Dr Johnson. 1793.

Song to an Irish air, by the late James Boswell esq. Edinburgh 1802. P. 17 of Songs chiefly in the Scottish dialect, by Alexander Boswell. Also in Alexander Boswell's Songs, etc 1803 and the Poetical works of Sir Alexander Boswell, ed R. H. Smith 1871.

The laird of Glenlee. Glasgow 1803. Pp. 24–6 of A collection of songs and poems by Isabel Pagan. There is a copy of the song in the Mansfield ms. See F. Miller, The Mansfield manuscript, Dumfries 1935.

The Justiciary garland: being the form of trial before a criminal court. Edinburgh 1813. Pp. 140–4 of Carminum rariorum macaronicorum delectus: editio altera emendata et aucta, ed A. Duncan. Rptd in various edns of James Maidment's Court of Session garland.

Songs in the Justiciary opera composed fifty years ago by C[rosbie], M[aclaurin] and B[oswell]. Auchinleck 1816. Ed and largely composed by Alexander Boswell.

[Song on the Earl of Cassillis and the Misses Cooper]. Edinburgh 1839. In J. Johnson (ed), The Scottish musical museum, 1839.

Remarks on the Journey to the western islands of Scotland. 1848. Pp. 825–6 of J. W. Croker's 3rd edn of Life of Johnson, ptd from a ms in the hand of Boswell's clerk, John Lawrie, then in the Anderdon collection; a few insertions in this ms are in Boswell's hand.

Specimen of Parliament: a poem. 1891. In P. Fitzgerald's Life of Boswell 1.82, from Boswell's ms among Wilkes papers in BM. Also (2 stanzas only) in Letters of Boswell, ed C. B. Tinker, Oxford 1924, 2.519.

[Proof-sheets of the Life]. Boston 1894. Extracts in G. B. Hill, Boswell's proof-sheets, Atlantic Monthly Nov 1894, rptd in G. Whale and J. Sargeaunt (ed), Johnson Club papers by various hands, 1899. Much fuller text by R. W. Chapman, London Mercury Nov–Dec 1926, rptd in D. N. Smith et al, Johnson and Boswell revised, Oxford 1928.

Song to Lord Kames. 1925. Ptd by F. A. Pottle from Bodleian Douce ms 193 in Three new legal ballads by Boswell, Juridical Rev 37 1925. Dated 1766 in ms.

The bl[aeph]lum: S[cots song]. New York 1952. Ptd in L. de la Torre, The heir of Douglas, pp. 211–12. A Douglas cause ballad composed May 1767.

Letters between the Hon Andrew Erskine and James Boswell esq. 1763; ed G. B. Hill 1879 (with Journal of a tour to Corsica); in Letters of Boswell to Temple 1857, 1908 (selected).

Boswelliana. 1856 (Miscellanies of Philobiblon Soc vol 2 no 15). A small selection ed R. M. Milnes, later Lord Houghton, from Boswell's ms then in his possession; rptd as Thoughts on family and friends, by James Boswell, Bookman's Jnl May 1925.

Boswelliana: folium reservatum. 1856. 8 pp. ed R. M. Milnes for private distribution. Other anecdotes, mainly coarse, from Boswell's ms.

Letters of Boswell addressed to the Rev W. J. Temple, now first published from the original mss. [Ed Philip Francis] 1857 (for 1856); ed T. Seccombe 1908.

Boswelliana: the commonplace book of Boswell. Ed C. Rogers 1874 (Grampian Club). A much fuller pbn than Milnes's, above, but not quite complete.

[Boswell's note-book 1776–7]. 1893. Ptd in Collection of autograph letters and historical documents formed by Alfred Morison, 2nd ser 1; ed R. B. Adam [1919]. The R. B. Adam Library, Oxford 1929 2.51 ff; ptd in Catalogue of the Johnsonian collection of R. B. Adam, Buffalo 1921; ed R. W. Chapman, Oxford 1925 (with corresponding passages from Life on opposite pages).

[Boswell's consultation book]. Edinburgh 1922. Extracts in T. B. Simpson, Boswell as an advocate, Juridical Rev 34 1922. Ms in the National Library of Scotland.

Letters of Boswell. Ed C. B. Tinker 2 vols Oxford 1924. The first and only collected edn.

Poetical epistle to Tristram Shandy. 1925. Portions of Bodleian Library Douce ms 193 quoted in F. A. Pottle, Bozzy and Yorick, Blackwood's Mag March 1925.

[Verse letter to Lady Mackintosh]. New York 1925. Ptd from Bodleian Library Douce ms 193 in F. A. Pottle, Bozzy was a bold young blade, New York Times Book Rev 23 Aug 1925.

Private papers of Boswell from Malahide Castle in the collection of Lt-Col R. H. Isham. Ed G. Scott (vols 1–6) and F. A. Pottle (vols 7–18) Mt Vernon 1928–34 (priv ptd). Index by F. A. Pottle, Joseph Foladare, J. P. Kirby et al, Oxford 1937.

The Yale editions of the private papers of Boswell. Ed F. W. Hilles, H. W. Liebert, F. A. Pottle, E. C. Aswell, Edward Kuhn, F. E. Taylor 1950–. 2 edns are projected, the 'trade' and the 'research', consisting in all of more than 30 vols. Of the 'trade' edn the following have appeared:

Boswell's London journal 1762–3. Ed F. A. Pottle 1950, 1951 (enlarged de luxe edn, reset, with Journal of my jaunt harvest 1762 and additional illustrations).

Boswell in Holland 1763–4. Ed F. A. Pottle, New York 1952, 1963, London 1952, 1952 (de luxe impression with additional illustrations).

Portraits by Sir Joshua Reynolds. Ed F. W. Hilles, New York 1952, London 1952. Includes new Boswell-Reynolds letters and a biographical note by Boswell on Reynolds.

Boswell on the Grand Tour: Germany and Switzerland 1764. Ed F. A. Pottle, New York 1953, 1963, London 1953, 1953 (de luxe impression with additional illustrations).

Boswell on the Grand Tour: Italy, Corsica and France. Ed F. Brady and F. A. Pottle, New York 1955, London 1955, 1956 (de luxe impression with additional illustrations).

Boswell in search of a wife 1766–9. Ed F. Brady and F. A. Pottle, New York 1956, London 1957, 1957 (de luxe impression with additional illustrations).

Boswell for the defence 1769–74. Ed W. K. Wimsatt and F. A. Pottle, New York 1959, 1963, London 1960, 1960 (de luxe impression with additional illustrations).

Boswell's journal of a tour to the Hebrides with Samuel Johnson LlD 1773. Ed F. A. Pottle and C. H. Bennett, New York 1961 (from ms), London 1963. New impression of plates of 1936, as above under Journal of a tour to the Hebrides, with new introd and additional notes by Pottle.

Boswell: the ominous years 1774–6. Ed C. Ryskamp and F. A. Pottle 1963.

Boswell in extremes 1776–8. Ed C. McC. Weis and F. A. Pottle 1970.

Of the research edn the following have appeared:

The correspondence of Boswell and John Johnston of Grange. Ed R. S. Walker 1966.

The correspondence of Boswell relating to the making of the Life of Johnson. Ed M. Waingrow 1969.

Printed Legal Papers

Perhaps as many as 200 of Boswell's ptd legal papers have survived; see W. H. Bond and D. E. Whitten, Boswell's Court of Session papers: a preliminary checklist, in Eighteenth-century studies in memory of Donald F. Hyde, New York 1970, for bibliography of 80 titles in the Yale, Hyde and Harvard collections. The Signet Library, Edinburgh has 66 titles (catalogue also at Yale), about half not in Bond-Whitten. Occasional examples are in most other Boswell collections, public and private. The Session Papers in the Advocates' Library, Edinburgh (the largest single collection) have not been searched for papers by Boswell.

Contributions to Periodicals

Boswell was a voluminous contributor of signed and unsigned articles to newspapers and magazines. But failing the recovery of marked files or of lists kept by himself, much of his pbn will always remain untraced. Apart from the difficulty of assembling complete files of the newspapers to which he contributed and the time required to search them systematically, his practice of writing on both sides of questions and in many dramatic modes makes complete recovery difficult. His own marked and partially indexed file of the London Chron 1767–75, now at Yale, provides a large and trustworthy specimen of his methods. His journal identifies many of his anonymous or pseudonymous periodical paragraphs. Finally, several collections of newspapers and newspaper cuttings among the Boswell papers at Yale, some of them labelled (Paragraphs relative to my Life of Dr Johnson, Newspaper paragraphs by myself or relating to me etc) *furnish valuable but tantalizingly inexplicit information of his dealings with the periodical press, especially in his later years.*

§ 2

Hawkins, L. M. Memoirs. 3 vols 1822–4. Extracts in Croker's Boswell 1831, 1835 (rptd in Johnsoniana 1836); in Johnsonian miscellanies, ed G. B. Hill 2 vols Oxford 1897; selections as Gossip about Dr Johnson and others, ed F. H. Skrine 1926.

Macaulay, T. B. Edinburgh Rev 54 1831.

Carlyle, T. Biography: Boswell's Life of Johnson. Fraser's Mag April–May 1832.

Fitzgerald, P. Croker's Boswell and Boswell. 1880.

—— Life of Boswell. 2 vols 1891.

Chapman, R. W. Johnson, Boswell and Mrs Piozzi. Oxford 1929.

—— Two centuries of Johnsonian scholarship. Glasgow 1945.

—— Johnsonian and other essays and reviews. Oxford 1953.

Pottle, F. A. The power of memory in Boswell and Scott. In Essays on the eighteenth century presented to David Nichol Smith, Oxford 1945.

—— The life of Boswell. Yale Rev 35 1946.

—— James Boswell, journalist. In The age of Johnson: essays presented to C. B. Tinker, New Haven 1949.

—— Boswell's university education. In Johnson, Boswell and their circle: essays presented to L. F. Powell, Oxford 1965.

—— Boswell: the earlier years. 1966.

Wimsatt, W. K. Boswell: the man and the journal. Yale Rev 49 1959; rptd in his Hateful contraries, 1965.

Bronson, B. H. Boswell's Boswell. In his Johnson and Boswell: three essays, Berkeley 1944.

Jack, I. Two biographers: Lockhart and Boswell. In Johnson, Boswell and their circle: essays presented to L. F. Powell, Oxford 1965.

Lascelles, M. Notions and facts: Johnson and Boswell on their travels. Ibid.

WILLIAM GODWIN
1756–1836

Bibliographies

Pollin, B. R. Godwin criticism: a synoptic bibliography. Toronto 1967.

§ 1

The history of the life of William Pitt, Earl of Chatham. 1783, 1783 (both anon), Dublin 1783, 1783; rptd in New annual register for the year 1783, 1784.

A defence of the Rockingham party, in their late coalition with Lord North. 1783 (anon); ed B. R. Pollin, Gainesville 1966 (in Four early pamphlets).

An account of the seminary that will be opened on Monday the fourth day of August at Epsom in Surrey. 1783 (anon); ed Pollin, with above.

Italian letters: or the history of the Count de St Julian. 1783; ed B. R. Pollin, Lincoln Nebraska 1965. Only known copy of 1783 in Bristol Public Lib.

The herald of literature. 1784 (anon); ed B. R. Pollin, Gainesville 1967 (in Four early pamphlets).

Sketches of history in six sermons. 1784 (anon), 2 vols Alexandria Virginia 1801, 1802.

Damon and Delia. 1784? No known copy.

Imogen: a pastoral romance. 2 vols 1784. 2 known copies; *see* BNYPL Jan–June 1963 and col 556, above.

Instructions to a statesman, humbly inscribed to the Earl Temple. 1784 (anon); ed B. R. Pollin, Gainesville 1966 (in Four early pamphlets).

History of the internal affairs of the United Provinces.

1787. Anon. Attributed to Godwin by J. W. Marken, PQ 45 1966.

An enquiry concerning the principles of political justice, and its influence on general virtue and happiness. 2 vols 1793, Dublin 1793, London 1796 ('corrected'), New York nd, London 1842; ed F. E. L. Priestley 3 vols Toronto 1946 (facs of 3rd edn with variant readings from 1st–2nd).

Cursory strictures on the charge delivered by Lord Chief Justice Eyre to the Grand Jury, Oct 2 1794. 1794. Anon. Rptd from Morning Chron 21 Oct 1794; attributed to Godwin by B. R. Pollin.

A reply to an answer to Cursory strictures by the author of Cursory stricutures. 1794. Attributed to Godwin by Pollin.

Things as they are: or the adventures of Caleb Williams. 3 vols 1794, 2 vols Dublin 1795, 3 vols 1796 (2nd edn 'corrected'), 1797, 2 vols Philadelphia 1802, 3 vols 1816, 2 vols Philadelphia 1818, 1 vol 1824, 1826, 3 vols 1830, 1 vol 1831, 2 vols New York 1831, 1832, 1 vol New York 1838, Edinburgh 1839, London 1849, 1853, 1903, [1904]; ed V. Wyck Brooks, New York 1936; ed G. Sherburn, New York 1960; ed D. McCracken, Oxford 1970 (from ms). A play entitled The iron chest, founded on Caleb Williams by George Colman jr, was first acted at Drury Lane in 1796; *col 499, above.*

Considerations on Lord Grenville's and Mr Pitt's Bills concerning treasonable and seditious practices. [1795]. Anon.

The enquirer: reflections on education, manners and literature. 1797, Dublin 1797, Edinburgh and London 1823.

Memoirs of the life of Simon, Lord Lovat. 1797. Tr Godwin.

Memoirs of the author of a vindication of the rights of woman. 1798, 1798 ('corrected'), Dublin 1798, Philadelphia 1799, 1802, 1804; ed W. C. Durrant 1927 (with addns); ed J. M. Murry 1930.

Posthumous works of the author of a vindication of the rights of women. 4 vols in 2 1798. Godwin was the anon editor.

St Leon: a tale of the sixteenth century. 4 vols 1799, 1800, 2 vols Dublin 1800, Alexandria Virginia 1801, 1802, 4 vols 1816, 1 vol 1831.

Antonio: a tragedy in five acts. 1800, New York 1806.

Thoughts occasioned by Dr Parr's spital sermon. 1801.

Life of Geoffrey Chaucer the early English poet, including memoirs of John of Gaunt, Duke of Lancaster. 2 vols 1803, 4 vols 1804.

Fables ancient and modern adapted for the use of children. 1805, 1821 (9th edn). By 'Edward Baldwin'.

Fleetwood: or the new man of feeling. 3 vols 1805, 2 vols New York 1805, Alexandria Virginia 1805, 1 vol 1832 (vol 22 of Standard Authors, 'revised with a new preface'), 1849, 1853.

The looking glass: a true history of the early years of an artist. 1805, 1885 (facs). By 'Theophilus Marcliffe'.

The history of England. 1806 etc. By 'Edward Baldwin'.

The life of Lady Jane Grey and of Guildford Dudley her husband. 1806, 1809, 1815, 1824. By 'Theophilus Marcliffe'.

Faulkener: a tragedy. 1807.

Essay on sepulchres. 1809, New York 1809.

The lives of Edward and John Philips, nephews and pupils of Milton. 1815.

Letters of Verax to the editors of the Morning Chronicle on the question of a war to be commenced for the purpose of putting an end to the possession of the supreme power in France by Napoleon Buonaparte. 1815. Anon.

Mandeville: a tale of the seventeenth century in England. 3 vols Edinburgh and London 1817, 2 vols New York 1818, Philadelphia 1818.

Letter of advice to a young American. 1818.

Of population: an answer to Mr Malthus's essay. 1820.

Valperga: a novel by Mary Shelley. 1823. Rev and pbd by Godwin.

History of the commonwealth of England from its commencement to the Restoration of Charles the Second. 4 vols 1824–8.

Cloudesley: a tale. 3 vols 1830, 1830, 2 vols New York 1830.

Thoughts on man, his nature, productions and discoveries. 1831.

Deloraine. 3 vols 1833, 2 vols Philadelphia 1833.

Lives of the necromancers. 1834, New York 1835, 1847, London 1876, New York 1876.

The moral effects of aristocracy. [1835?] (with W. Hazlitt, The spirit of monarchy).

An essay on trades and professions. Manchester 1842. Rptd from Enquirer II.v.

Essays never before published. Ed C. K. Paul 1873.

The elopement of Percy Bysshe Shelley and Mary Wollstonecraft Godwin, as narrated by William Godwin. Ed H. Buxton Forman 1911, [Boston] 1912 (both priv ptd).

Uncollected writings 1785–1822. Ed J. Marken and B. R. Pollin, Gainesville 1968.

Godwin and Mary: letters of Godwin and Mary Wollstonecraft. Ed R. M. Wardle, Lawrence Kansas 1966.

Godwin also pbd other children's books and elementary historical works by 'Edward Baldwin'.

§ 2

Malthus, T. An essay on the principle of population, with remarks on the speculations of Mr Godwin, Mr Condorcet and other writers. 1798 etc.

Scott, W. Godwin's Fleetwood. Edinburgh Rev 6 1805; rptd in his Miscellaneous prose works vol 18, 1835.

Shelley, P. B. (signed 'E.K.'). Remarks on Mandeville and Mr Godwin. Examiner 28 Dec 1817; rptd in his Prose works, ed R. H. Shepherd 2 vols 1888.

Lockhart, J. G. (signed 'T'). Remarks on Godwin's new novel Mandeville. Blackwood's Mag Dec 1817; rptd in Lockhart's literary criticism, ed M. C. Hildyard, Oxford 1931.

Hazlitt, W. In his Spirit of the age, 1825.

—— Mr Godwin. Edinburgh Rev April 1830.

Paul, C. K. Godwin: his friends and contemporaries. 2 vols 1876.

Stephen, L. William Godwin. Fortnightly Rev Oct 1876.

—— Godwin and Shelley. Cornhill Mag March 1879.

—— Godwin's novels. Nat Rev Feb 1902; rptd in Studies of a biographer: 2nd ser vol 3, 1902.

Brailsford, H. N. Shelley, Godwin and their circle. [1913] (Home Univ Lib).

Woodcock, G. Godwin: a biographical study. 1946.

Monro, D. H. Godwin's moral philosophy. 1953.

Cameron, K. N. (ed). Shelley and his circle 1773–1872. 2 vols Cambridge Mass 1961.

MARY WOLLSTONECRAFT, Mrs WILLIAM GODWIN
1759–97
Collections

Posthumous works. Ed W. Godwin 4 vols 1798. Vols 1–2, The wrongs of woman; vols 3–4, Letters and miscellanies.

§ 1

Thoughts on the education of daughters. 1787.

Mary: a fiction. 1788 (anon), [1790?]; ed G. Kelly, Oxford 1976 (with The wrongs of woman, 1798).

Original stories from real life. 1788, 1791 (illustr William Blake); ed E. V. Lucas, Oxford 1906.

Of the importance of religious opinions, translated from the French. 1788, 1791. Trn of J. Necker, De l'importance des opinions religieuses.

A vindication of the rights of men in a letter to Edmund Burke. 1790, 1790; ed E. L. Nicholes, Gainesville 1960.

Elements of morality for the use of children, translated from the German of C. G. Salzmann. 2 vols 1790, 1793, 3 vols 1791, 1792, Baltimore 1811, Edinburgh 1821.

A vindication of the rights of woman. Vol 1 (all pbd), 1792, Dublin 1793; ed E. R. Pennell 1892.

The emigrants. 1793, Dublin 1794; ed R. R. Hare, Gainesville 1964. Normally attributed to Gilbert Imlay before Hare's edn.

An historical and moral view of the origin and progress of the French Revolution. Vol 1 (all pbd), 1794.

Letters

Letters written during a short residence in Sweden, Norway and Denmark. 1796; ed H. Morley 1889.

Mary Wollstonecraft: letters to Imlay. Ed C. K. Paul 1879 (with prefatory memoir).

Love letters to Gilbert Imlay. Ed R. Ingpen 1908 (with prefatory memoir).

Four new letters of Mary Wollstonecraft and Helen Maria Williams. Ed B. P. Kurtz and C. C. Autrey, Berkeley 1937.

Godwin and Mary: letters of William Godwin and Mary Wollstonecraft. Ed R. M. Wardle, Lawrence Kansas 1966.

§ 2

Godwin, W. Memoirs of the author of a Vindication of the rights of woman. 1798 etc, 1927, 1928.

Linford, M. Mary Wollstonecraft 1759–1797. 1925.

James, H. R. Mary Wollstonecraft: a sketch. Oxford 1932.

Woolf, V. Four figures 3: Mary Wollstonecraft. In her Second common reader, 1932.

Wardle, R. M. Mary Wollstonecraft. Lawrence Kansas 1952.

II. LETTERS, DIARIES, AUTOBIOGRAPHIES AND MEMOIRS

The order is chronological, based on the opening date of each entry rather than dates of pbn or composition. Cross-references for letter-writers and diarists whose works are listed elsewhere are inserted according to date of birth.

GENERAL SOURCES

Arniston memoirs 1371–1830. Ed G. W. T. Ormond, Edinburgh 1887.

Harcourt papers [15th century–1837]. Ed E. W. Harcourt 13 vols Oxford 1876–1903.

Manchester, William Montagu, Duke of (ed). Court and society from Elizabeth to Anne [Montagu family papers and letters c. 1500–1708]. 2 vols 1864.

Sitwell, Sir George (ed). Letters of the Sitwells and

Sacheverells [c. 1600–c. 1800]. 2 vols Scarborough 1900–1.

Hatton correspondence [1601–1704]. Ed E. M. Thompson 1878 (Camden Soc).

Browne, Sir Thomas (1605–82). *See col 341, above.*

Jackson, Charles (ed). Yorkshire diaries and autobiographies [1608–1766]. 2 vols 1877, 1886 (Surtees Soc).

Bramston, Sir John (1611–1700). Autobiography. Ed Lord Braybrooke 1845 (Camden Soc).

Herbert correspondence: the sixteenth- and seventeenth-century letters of the Herberts of Chirbury [1613–90]. Ed W. J. Smith, Cardiff 1963.

Baxter, Richard (1615–91). *See col 305, above.*

Josselin, Rev Ralph. Diary and autobiography [1616–83]. Ed E. Hockliffe 1908 (Royal Historical Soc).

Ashmole, Elias (1617–92). Memoirs. 1717; ed R. T. Gunther, Oxford 1927.

Blundell, William. Cavalier: letters to his friends 1620–98. Ed M. Blundell 1933.

Evelyn, John (1620–1706). *See col 629, below.*

Martindale, Adam (1623–86). Life, by himself. Ed R. Parkinson 1845 (Chetham Soc).

Culloden papers [letters 1625–1748]. Ed D. Forbes 1815; More Culloden papers [1626–1747], ed D. Warrand, Inverness 4 vols 1923–30.

Fanshawe, Lady Anne (1625–80). Memoirs. Ed N. H. Nicolas 1829; ed H. C. Fanshawe 1907.

Warwick, Mary Rich, Countess of (1625–78). Autobiography. Ed T. C. Croker 1848 (Percy Soc).

Barnes, Ambrose, sometime Alderman of Newcastle-upon-Tyne (1627–1710). Memoirs. Ed W. H. D. Longstaffe 1867 (Surtees Soc).

Lister, Joseph (1627–1709). Autobiography. Ed T. Wright 1842.

Newcome, Rev Henry (1627–95). Autobiography. Ed R. Parkinson 2 pts 1852 (Chetham Soc).

Ingram, Bruce (ed). Three sea journals of Stuart times [1628, 1659–91, 1701–5]. 1936.

Thornton, Alice. Autobiography [1629–69]. 1875 (Surtees Soc).

Heywood, Rev Oliver (1630–1702). Autobiography and diaries. Ed J. H. Turner 4 vols Brighouse 1882–5.

Wood, Anthony à. Life and times 1632–95 [diaries etc]. Ed A. Clark 5 vols 1891–1907 (Oxford Historical Soc).

Worthington, Dr John. Diary and correspondence [1632–71]. Ed J. Crossley and R. C. Christie 3 pts 1847–86 (Chetham Soc).

Pepys, Samuel (1633–1703). *See col 631, below.*

Reresby, Sir John. Memoirs [1634–89]. 1734; ed J. J. Cartwright 1875; ed A. Browning 1936 (with selected letters).

Ellwood, Thomas (1639–1713). History of life. 1714; rptd 1906 etc.

Hodgson, John C. (ed). Six North Country diaries [1639–1796]. 1910 (Surtees Soc).

Thomson, Gladys. Life in a noble household 1641–1700. 1937. Letters etc of William Russell, Duke of Bedford.

Conway letters 1642–84. Ed M. H. Nicolson, New Haven 1930.

Hothams, Chronicles of the [1642–1778]. Ed A. M. W. Stirling 2 vols 1918.

Manners family correspondence [1642–1771]. Duke of Rutland mss vol 2 1889 (Historical Manuscripts Commission).

Harley papers 1643–1785 [including letters to Duchess of Portland 1735–85]. Marquis of Bath mss vol i 1904 (Historical Manuscripts Commission).

Stukeley, Rev William. Family memoirs [letters and diaries 1643–1764]. 3 vols 1882–7 (Surtees Soc).

Bohun, Edmund (1645–99). Diary and autobiography. Ed S. W. Rix, Beccles Suffolk 1853.

Verney, Lady (Frances Parthenope and Margaret). Memoirs of the Verney family [1645–96]. 4 vols 1892–9.

Ward, Rev John. Diary [1648–79]. Ed C. Severn 1839.

Fox, George. Journal [1650–75]. Ed N. Penney 2 vols Cambridge 1911. *See col 659, below.*

Henry, Rev Philip. Diaries and letters [1650–93]. Ed M. H. Lee 1882.

Taswell, William. Autobiography and anecdotes 1651–82. Ed G. P. Elliott 1853 (Camden Soc Miscellany 2).

North, Roger (1653–1734). *See col 681, below.*

Moore, Rev Giles. Extracts from journal and account book [1655–79]. Ed R. W. Blencowe 1847 (Sussex Archaeological Collections).

Ailesbury, Thomas Bruce, Earl of (1656–1741). Memoirs. Ed W. E. Buckley 2 vols 1890 (Roxburghe Club).

Chesterfield, Philip Stanhope, Earl of. Letters [1656–89]. 1829.

Crisp, Stephen. Correspondence 1657–92. Ed C. Fell-Smith 1892.

Haddock family correspondence 1657–1719. Ed E. M. Thompson 1881 (Camden Soc).

Rugg, Thomas. Diurnal 1659–61. Ed W. L. Sachse 1961.

Defoe, Daniel (1660–1731). *See col 514, above.*

Newton, Evelyn, Lady. Lyme letters 1660–1760. 1925.

Newcome, Rev Henry. Diary 1661–3. Ed T. Heywood 1849 (Chetham Soc).

Savile, Henry. Correspondence [1661–89]. Ed W. D. Cooper 1858 (Camden Soc).

Atterbury, Francis, Bishop of Rochester (1662–1732). *See col 649, below.*

Bentley, Dr Richard (1662–1742). *See col 725, below.*

Cromartie, Earls of. Correspondence [1662–1774]. Ed W. Fraser 2 vols Edinburgh 1876.

Lawrence, William. Diary 1662–81. Ed G. E. Aylmer, Beaminster Dorset 1961.

Dunlop family papers: letters and journals 1663–1889. Ed J. G. Dunlop 1953.

Graham, John M. Annals and correspondence of the Viscount and the 1st and 2nd Earls of Stair [1663–1747]. 2 vols 1875.

Lowe, Roger, of Aston-in-Makerfield Lancs. Diary 1663–74. Ed W. L. Sachse, New Haven 1938.

Giffard, Martha, Lady. Life and correspondence [1664–1722]. Ed J. G. Longe 1911.

Prior, Matthew (1664–1721). *See col 395, above.*

Lauder, Sir John. Journals [1665–76]. Ed D. Crawford, Edinburgh 1900 (Scottish Historical Soc).

Milward, John, MP for Derbyshire. Diary 1666–8. Ed C. Robbins, Cambridge 1938.

Whiston, William (1667–1752). Memoirs. 1749.

Swift, Jonathan (1667–1745). *See col 572, above.*

Yonge, James, Plymouth surgeon. Journal [1667–1708]. Ed F. N. L. Poynter 1963.

Russell, Rachel, Lady. Letters [1670–1723]. Ed Lord John Russell 2 vols 1853.

Brockbank, Rev Thomas. Diary and letter-book 1671–1709. Ed R. T. Lomax 1930 (Chetham Soc).

Calamy, Edmund (1671–?1731). An historical account of my own life. Ed J. T. Rutt 2 vols 1829.

Cibber, Colley (1671–1757). *See col 477, above.*

Drake, Capt Peter. Amiable renegade: memoirs 1671–1753. Ed S. A. Burrell 1960.

Freke, Elizabeth. Diary [1671–1714]. Ed M. Carberry, Cork 1913.

Jolly, Rev Thomas. Notebook 1671–93. Ed H. Fishwick 1894 (Chetham Soc).

De la Pryme, Abraham. Diary [1671–1704]. Ed C. Jackson 1870 (Surtees Soc).

Addison, Joseph (1672–1719). *See col 586, above.*

Hooke, Robert. Diary 1672–80. Ed H. W. Robinson and W. Adams 1935.

Steele, Sir Richard (1672–1729). *See col 589, above.*

Prideaux, Humphrey. Letters to John Ellis 1674–1722. Ed E. M. Thompson 1875 (Camden Soc).

Thoresby, Ralph. Diary and correspondence [1674–1724]. Ed J. Hunter 4 vols 1830–2.

Teonge, Henry, chaplain in HM's navy. Diary [1675–9]. Ed G. E. Manwaring 1927.

Clarendon, Henry Hyde, Earl of. Correspondence [1676–1705]. Ed S. W. Singer 2 vols 1828.

Jeaffreson, Christopher. A young squire of the 17th century from his papers 1676–86. Ed J. C. Jeaffreson 2 vols 1878.

Petty, Sir William. Correspondence with Sir Robert Southwell 1676–87. Ed Marquis of Lansdowne 1928.

Lake, Rev Edward. Diary [1677–8]. Ed G. P. Elliott 1847 (Camden Soc).

Bolingbroke, Henry St John, Viscount (1678–1751). *See col 592, above.*

Hearne, Thomas (1678–1735). Remains: reliquiae Hearnianae, compiled by Dr John Bliss. 2 vols 1857; rev J. Buchanan-Brown 1966.

Pinney, John. Letters 1679–99. Ed G. F. Nuttall, Oxford 1939.

'Psalmanazar, George' (1679?–1763). Memoirs. 1764.

Sidney, Algernon. Letters to Henry Savile [1679–82]. Dublin 1742.

Romney, Henry Sidney, Earl of. Diary with letters [1679–89]. Ed R. W. Blencowe 2 vols 1843.

Warner, Rebecca (ed). Original letters from Baxter, Prior, Bolingbroke, Pope, Cheyne, Johnson and others [1679–1780]. 1817.

Newdigate, Sir Richard. Cavalier and puritan [diary 1680–1706]. Ed Lady Newdigate-Newdegate 1901.

Bristol, John Hervey, Earl of. Letter books 1681–1750. 3 vols Wells 1894.

Burrell, Timothy, barrister-at-law. Journal and account book [1683–1717]. Ed R. W. Blencowe 1850 (Sussex Archaeological Collections).

Erskine, John. Journal 1683–7. Ed W. Macleod, Edinburgh 1893 (Scottish Historical Soc).

Nicolson, William, Bishop of Carlisle. Letters [1683–1727]. Ed J. Nichols 2 vols 1809.

—— Diary [1684–1725]. 1901–5, 1937, 1947 (Trans Cumberland & Westmorland Antiquarian & Archaeological Soc new ser 1–5, 35, 47).

Morris, Claver. Diary of a West Country physician 1684–1726. Ed E. Hobhouse 1934.

Woodforde papers and diaries [1684–90, 1785–6, 1792]. Ed D. H. Woodforde 1932.

Berkeley, George (1685–1753). *See col 735, below.*

Gay, John (1685–1732). *See col 398, above.*

Marchmont papers 1685–1750. Ed G. Rose 3 vols 1831.

Prior, Matthew. Letters 1685–1721. In Marquis of Bath mss 3 1908 (Historical Manuscripts Commission).

Cartwright, Thomas, Bishop of Chester. Diary [1686–7]. 1843 (Camden Soc).

Ellis, John. Correspondence 1686–8. Ed G. J. W. Agar-Ellis 2 vols 1829.

Lapthorne, Richard. Portledge papers 1687–97 [letters to Richard Coffin]. Ed R. J. Kerr and I. C. Duncan 1928.

Bristol, John Hervey, Earl of. Diary 1688–1742. Wells 1894.

Macleod, Sgt Donald (1688–1791). Memoirs. 1791; ed J. G. Fyffe 1933.

Pope, Alexander (1688–1744). *See col 399, above.*

Spence, Joseph. Observations, anecdotes and characters of books and men [c. 1688–c. 1758]. Ed S. W. Singer 1820; ed J. M. Osborn 2 vols Oxford 1966.

Davies, Rev Rowland. Journal [1689–90]. Ed R. Caulfield 1857 (Camden Soc).

Molesworth correspondence [1689–1744]. Vol 8, 1913 (Historical Manuscripts Commission).

Montagu, Lady Mary Wortley (1689–1762). *See col 632, below.*

Richardson, Samuel (1689–1761). *See col 538, above.*

Norris papers [c. 1690–1708]. Ed T. Heywood 1846 (Chetham Soc).

Gordon, James. Diary 1692–1710. Ed G. D. Henderson and H. H. Porter, Aberdeen 1949.

Gent, Thomas. Life of Gent, by himself [1693–1746]. Ed J. Hunter 1832.

Chesterfield, Philip Dormer Stanhope, Earl of (1694–1773). *See col 633, below.*

Coke, Thomas. Correspondence [1694–1726]. In Earl Cowper manuscripts vols 2–3, 1888–9 (Historical Manuscripts Commission).

Carlisle, Charles and Henry Howard, Earls of. Letters and papers [1695–1758]. In Earl of Carlisle Manuscripts 1897 (Historical Manuscripts Commission).

Stirling, Anna. Annals of a Yorkshire house [Spencer-Stanhope family correspondence 1696–1804]. 2 vols 1911.

Verney letters [1696–1799]. Ed Margaret, Lady Verney 2 vols 1930.

Richards, John. Diary [extracts 1697–1701]. Retrospective Rev new ser 1 1853.

Pitt family correspondence [1698–1779]. In Fortescue manuscripts vol 1, 1892 (Historical Manuscripts Commission).

Cremer, Capt John (Ramblin' Jack). Journal [1700–68]. Ed R. R. Bellamy 1936.

Delany, Mary (1700–88). *See col 640, below.*

Oxford, Robert and Edward Harley, Earls of. Correspondence [1700–40]. In Duke of Portland manuscripts vols 4–6, 1897–1901 (Historical Manuscripts Commission).

March, Charles Henry Gordon-Lennox, Earl of. A Duke and his friends: life and letters [1701–50] of 2nd Duke of Richmond. 2 vols 1911.

Wodrow, Rev Robert. Analecta [diary etc 1701–31]. 3 vols Edinburgh 1842–3 (Maitland Club).

Blundell, Nicholas. Diary and letter book 1702–28. Ed M. Blundell, Liverpool 1952.

Marlborough, Sarah Churchill, Duchess of. Private correspondence [1703–38]. 2 vols 1838.

Wesley, John (1703–91). *See col 655, below.*

Banks family letters and papers 1704–60. Ed J. W. F. Hill 1952 (Lincoln Record Soc).

Davenant, Charles. Letters [1704–14]. Ed G. Davies and M. Scofield, HLQ 4 1941.

Isham, Sir Justinian. Diaries 1704–35. Ed H. I. Longden, Trans Royal Historical Soc 3rd ser 1 1907.

Argyll, John Campbell, Duke of (ed). Intimate society letters of the 18th century [1705–1843]. 2 vols 1910.

Cowper, William, Earl. Private diary [1705–14]. Ed E. C. Hawtrey 1833 (Roxburghe Club).

Hearne, Thomas. Collections [diary etc 1705–35]. Ed C. E. Doble, D. W. Rannie and H. E. Salter 11 vols 1885–1921 (Oxford Historical Soc).

Wentworth papers [correspondence 1705–39]. Ed J. J. Cartwright 1883.

Hanmer, Thomas, Speaker of House of Commons. Correspondence [1706–44]. Ed H. E. Bunbury 1838.

Chandos, James Brydges, Duke of. Letters to Bolingbroke [1707–30]. Ed G. Davies and M. Tinling, Huntington Lib Bull 9 1936.

Charke, Charlotte. Life, by herself [c. 1709–55]. 1755, 1927.

Johnson, Samuel (1709–84). *See col 593, above.*

Lyttelton, George, Lord (1709–73). *See col 418, above.*

Marlborough, Sarah Churchill, Duchess of. Letters [1710–26]. 1875.

Stratford, Dr William. Letters to Edward Harley, Earl of Oxford [1710–29]. In Duke of Portland manuscripts vol 7, 1901 (Historical Manuscripts Commission).

Hume, David (1711–76). *See col 743, below.*

Burnet, Thomas. Letters to George Duckett 1712–22. Ed D. N. Smith, Oxford 1914 (Roxburghe Club).

Pilkington, Laetitia (1712–50). Memoirs. 1748; ed J. Isaacs 1928.

Suffolk, Henrietta Howard, Countess of. Correspondence 1712–67. Ed J. W. Croker 2 vols 1824.

Northampton, Elizabeth Compton, Countess of. Correspondence [1713–37]. In Townshend manuscripts, 1887 (Historical Manuscripts Commission).

Sterne, Laurence (1713–68). *See col 544, above.*

Ailesbury, Charles Bruce, Earl of. Correspondence 1714–36 (Historical Manuscripts Commission 15th report vol 7 1898).

Cowper, Mary, Countess. Diary 1714–20. Ed S. Cowper 1865.

Marchant, Thomas. Diary [1714–28]. Ed E. Turner 1873 (Sussex Archaeological Collections).

Shenstone, William (1714–63). *See col 412, above.*

Sundon, Charlotte, Viscountess. Memoirs [letters 1714–36]. Ed A. T. Thomson 2 vols 1847.

Hertford, Frances Seymour, Countess of. The gentle Hertford: her life and letters [selected letters 1715–54]. Ed H. S. Hughes, New York 1940.

Ryder, Dudley. Diary [1715–16]. Ed W. Matthews 1939.

Gray, Thomas (1716–71). *See col 425, above.*

Ilchester, Giles Fox-Strangways, Earl of. Henry Fox, 1st Lord Holland [letters etc 1716–74]. 2 vols 1920.

Carter, Elizabeth (1717–1806). *See col 637, below.*

Dodington, George Bubb. Correspondence [1717–62]. In M. Eyre-Matcham manuscripts, vol 6 1909 (Historical Manuscripts Commission).

Garrick, David (1717–79). *See col 487, above.*

Walpole, Horace, Earl of Orford (1717–97). *See col 634, below.*

Stuart papers at Windsor [1718–49]. Ed A. and H. Tayler 1939.

Aspinall-Oglander, Cecil. Admiral's wife: life and letters of Hon Mrs Edward Boscawen 1719–61. 1940.

Montagu, Elizabeth (1720–1800). *See col 639, below.*

Osborn, Sarah Byng. Political and social letters 1721–71. Ed E. F. D. Osborn 1890; ed J. McClelland, Stanford 1930.

Peake, Richard Brinsley. Memoirs of the Colman family [letters 1721–1828]. 2 vols 1841.

Smollett, Tobias (1721–71). *See col 546, above.*

Byrom, John. Journal [1722–44] and literary remains. Ed R. Parkinson 4 pts 1854–7 (Chetham Soc).

Carlyle, Dr Alexander (1722–1805). Autobiography. Ed J. H. Burton 1860, 1910.

Hutton, William (1723–1815). Life: autobiography finished by Catherine Hutton. 1816.

Huntingdon, Theophilus Hastings and Francis Hastings, Earls of. Correspondence 1724–86. In R. Rawdon Hastings manuscripts 3, 1934 (Historical Manuscripts Commission).

Varley, Charles (1725?–95). The unfortunate husbandman. Ed D. Clarke 1964. An autobiography.

Walkden, Rev Peter. Diary [extracts 1725, 1729, 1730]. Ed W. Dobson, Preston 1866.

Hervey, John, Lord. Lord Hervey and his friends 1726–38 [letters]. Ed Earl of Ilchester 1950.

—— Memoirs of the reign of George II [1727–37]. Ed J. W. Croker 2 vols 1848; ed R. Sedgwick 3 vols 1931.

Chapone, Hester (1727–1801). *See col 640, below.*

Burke, Edmund (1729–97). *See col 603, above.*

Percy, Thomas (1729–1811). *See col 709, below.*

Pyle, Rev Edmund. Memoirs of a royal chaplain 1729–63. Ed A. Hartshorne 1905. Letters to Samuel Kerrich.

St Clair, Rev Patrick. Country neighbourhood [letters to Ashe Windham 1729–41]. Ed R. W. Ketton-Cremer 1951.

Wyndham, Maud. Chronicles of the 18th century [Lyttleton family correspondence 1729–60]. 2 vols 1924.

Egmont, John Perceval, Earl of. Diary 1730–47. In Earl of Egmont manuscript, 3 vols 1920–3 (Historical Manuscripts Commission).

Goldsmith, Oliver (1730?–74). *See col 606, above.*

Cowper, William (1731–1800). *See col 431, above.*

Cumberland, Richard (1732–1811). *See col 493, above.*

Marlborough, Sarah Churchill, Duchess of. Letters of a grandmother 1732–5. Ed G. S. Thomson 1943.

Wedlake, J. H. (ed). Eighteenth-century Quaker love-letters [1732–55]. N & Q 13 March 1937.

Priestley, Dr Joseph. Memoirs [1733–95]. 1806.

Roberts, B. Dew. Mr William Bulkeley and the pirate: a Welsh diarist of the 18th century [1734–60]. Oxford 1936.

Purefoy letters 1735–53. Ed G. Eland 2 vols 1931.

Trusler, Rev John (1735–1820). Memoirs. Bath 1806.

Somerset, Frances Seymour, Duchess of. Select letters between the Duchess of Somerset, Lady Luxborough, William Shenstone and others [1736–72]. Ed T. Hull 2 vols 1778.

Stockdale, Percival (1736–1811). Memoirs. 2 vols 1809.

Gibbon, Edward (1737–94). *See col 693, below.*

Watson, Richard, Bishop of Llandaff (1737–1816). Anecdotes of the life. 1817.

Hertford, Frances Seymour, Countess of. Correspondence with Henrietta Louisa, Countess of Pomfret 1738–41. Ed W. Bingley 3 vols 1805.

Miller, Sanderson. An 18th-century correspondence. Ed L. Dickins and M. Stanton, New York 1910. Letters from Deane Swift, Pitt, the Lytteltons, the Grenvilles et al 1738–79.

Luxborough, Henrietta, Lady. Letters to William Shenstone [1739–56]. Ed J. Hodgetts 1775.

Wilkinson, Tate (1739–1803). Memoirs. 4 vols York 1790.

Boswell, James (1740–95). *See col 609, above.*

Jesse, John Heneage. George Selwyn and his contemporaries [letters 1740–70]. 4 vols 1843–4.

Reynolds, Sir Joshua. Letters [1740–91]. Ed F. W. Hilles, Cambridge 1929.

Young, Edward. Letters to the Duchess of Portland [1740–65]. In Marquis of Bath manuscripts 1, 1904 (Historical Manuscripts Commission).

Somerville, Thomas. Memoirs [1741–1814]. Edinburgh 1861.

Thrale, Hester Lynch, later Piozzi (1741–1821). *See col 638, below.*

Young, Arthur (1741–1820). Autobiography. Ed M. Betham-Edwards 1898.

Cradock, Joseph. Literary and miscellaneous memoirs [1742–c. 1800]. 4 vols 1826.

Hervey, Mary, Lady. Letters 1742–68. Ed J. W. Croker 1821.

Jones, Thomas (1742–1803). Memoirs. 1951 (Walpole Soc).

Russell, Col Charles. Correspondence 1742–54. In Frankland-Russell-Astley manuscripts 1900 (Historical Manuscripts Commission).

Brasbridge, Joseph (1743–1832). Fruits of experience. 1824.

Cappe, Catharine (1744–1821). Memoirs. 1822.

Edgeworth, Richard Lovell (1744–1817). Memoirs. 2 vols 1820. Completed by his daughter Maria.

Charlemont, James Caulfield, Earl of. Letters and memoirs 1745–99. In Charlemont manuscripts vols 1–2, 1891–4 (Historical Manuscripts Commission).

Harriott, John (1745–1817). Struggles through life. 3 vols 1815.

Holcroft, Thomas (1745–1809). *See col 501, above.*

MacDonald, John. Memoirs of an 18th-century footman [1745–79]. Ed J. Beresford 1927.

Malmesbury, James Harris, Earl of. Letters [1745–1820]. Ed 3rd Earl of Malmesbury 2 vols 1870.

More, Hannah (1745–1833). *See col 640, below.*

Cowper, Spencer, Dean of Durham. Letters [1746–74]. Ed E. Hughes 1956 (Surtees Soc).

Hervey, Augustus. Journal of a Captain in the Royal Navy 1746–59. Ed D. Erskine 1953.

Lackington, James. Memoirs [1746–91]. 1791, 1810 (13th edn enlarged).

Coke, Lady Jane. Letters to Mrs Eyre 1747–58. Ed A. Rathborne 1899.

Hurd, Richard. Correspondence with William Mason 1747–94. Ed L. Whibley, Cambridge 1932.

Seward, Anna (1747–1809). *See col 452, above.*

Williamson letters 1748–65. Ed F. J. Manning, Streatley 1954 (Bedfordshire Historical Record Soc).

Dodington, George Bubb. Diary [1749–61]. Ed H. P. Wyndham 1784; ed J. Carswell and L. A. Dralle, Oxford 1965.

Hickey, William. Memoirs 1749–1809. Ed A. Spencer 4 vols 1913–25.

Butler, Charles (1750–1832). Reminiscences. 2 vols 1822, 1827.

Craven, Elizabeth, Baroness, later Margravine of Anspach (1750–1828). Memoirs. 2 vols 1826, 1914.

Norton, John and sons, merchants of London and Virginia. Papers from their counting house [letters etc 1750–95]. Ed F. N. Mason, Richmond Virginia 1937.

Baker, John. Diary [1751–79]. Ed P. C. Yorke 1931.

Knyveton, John. Diary of a surgeon 1751–2. Ed E. Gray, New York 1937.

Minto, Gilbert Elliot, Earl of. Life and letters 1751–1806. Ed Countess of Minto 3 vols 1874.

Pierce, Eliza. Letters 1751–75. Ed V. Macdonald 1927.

Sheridan, Richard Brinsley (1751–1816). *See col 495, above.*

Burney, Frances, later D'Arblay (1752–1840). *See col 548, above.*

Leinster, Emily Fitzgerald, Duchess of. Correspondence [1752–69]. Ed B. Fitzgerald, Dublin 1954 (Irish Manuscripts Commission).

Northumberland, Elizabeth Percy, Duchess of. Diaries of a Duchess [1752–74]. Ed J. Greig 1926.

Ritson, Joseph (1752–1803). *See col 714, below.*

Shackleton, Richard and Elizabeth. Memoirs and letters [1752–92]. Ed M. Leadbeater 1822.

Benenden letters 1753–1821. Ed C. F. Hardy 1901.

Bewick, Thomas (1753–1828). Memoir by himself. Newcastle-on-Tyne 1862.

Childe-Pemberton, William S. The Earl Bishop. 2 vols 1924. Letters of Frederick Hervey, Earl of Bristol 1753–1803.

Lennox, Lord George. Letters and papers 1753–98. In Earl Bathurst manuscripts, 1923 (Historical Manuscripts Commission).

Chatham, William Pitt, Earl of. Love letters [1754]. Ed E. A. Edwards 1926.

Crabbe, Rev George (1754–1832). *See col 436, above.*

Dickinson, John. A Pennsylvania farmer at the Court of King George: London letters 1754–6. Pennsylvania Mag of History & Biography 86 1962.

Francis letters [Sir Philip Francis and others 1754–1818]. Ed B. Francis and E. Keary 2 vols 1901.

Turner, Thomas. Diary of a tradesman [1754–65]. Ed F. M. Turner 1925; ed D. K. Worcester, New Haven 1948.

Waldegrave, James, Earl. Memoirs 1754–8. 1821.

Wilkes, John. Correspondence [1754–98]. Ed J. Almon 5 vols 1805.

Bray, William. Diary [extracts 1756–1800]. Ed F. E. Bray 1938 (Surrey Archaeological Collections).

Coke, Lady Mary. Letters and journals [1756–79]. Ed J. A. Home 4 vols Edinburgh 1889–96.

Dempster, George. Letters to Sir Adam Fergusson 1756–1813. Ed J. Fergusson 1934.

Gifford, William (1756–1826). Autobiography. In J. Nichols, Illustrations of the literary history of the 18th century vol 6, 1831.

Granger, Rev James. Letters [1756–83]. Ed J. P. Malcolm 1805.

Hamilton, Mary (afterwards Mrs John Dickenson). At Court and at home [letters and diaries 1756–1816]. Ed E. and F. Anson 1925.

Knight, Cornelia (1756–1837). Autobiography. 2 vols 1861.

Knyveton, John. Surgeon's mate [diary 1756–62]. Ed E. Gray 1942.

Lewin letters: correspondence and diaries of an English family 1756–1884. Ed T. H. Lewin 2 vols 1910.

Powys, Caroline. Passages from diaries 1756–1808. Ed E. J. Climenson 1899.

Raper, Elizabeth. Receipt book [journal 1756–70]. Ed B. Grant 1924.

Blake, William (1757–1827). *See col 437, above.*

Gainsborough, Thomas. Letters [1757–88]. Ed M. Woodall, Ipswich 1963.

Romilly, Sir Samuel (1757–1818). Memoirs. 3 vols 1840.

Taylor, John (1757–1832). Records of my life. 2 vols 1832.

Telford, Thomas (1757–1834). Life, by himself. 1838.

Palmerston, Henry Temple, Viscount. Portrait of a Whig peer [letters and journals 1758–1801]. Ed B. Connell 1957.

Robinson, Mary ('Perdita') (1758–1800). Memoirs. Ed M. E. Robinson 4 vols 1801, 1 vol 1930.

Woodforde, Rev James. Diary of a country parson 1758–1802. Ed J. B. Beresford 5 vols 1924–31.

Brietzcke, Charles. Diary 1759–65. Ed E. Hailey, N & Q 28 April 1951–. Completed Nov 1964 (65 pts).

Burns, Robert (1759–96). *See col 756, below.*

Fife, James, Lord. Lord Fife and his factor. Correspondence [1759–1809]. Ed A. and H. Tayler 1925.

Angelo, Henry C. W. [1760–1839]. Reminiscences. 2 vols 1828–30; ed H. L. Smith 2 vols 1904.

Barrington, Jonah (1760–1834). Personal sketches of his own times. 2 vols 1827, 3 vols 1830–2.

Hawkins, Laetitia M. (1760–1835). Memoirs, anecdotes, facts and opinions. 2 vols 1824.

Jenkinson papers 1760–6. Ed N. S. Jucker 1949.

Aspinall-Oglander, Cecil. Admiral's widow: life and letters of Hon Mrs Edward Boscawen 1761–1805. 1942.

Cornwallis, Sir William. Correspondence 1761–1818. In Wykeham-Martin manuscripts, 1909 (Historical Manuscripts Commission).

Lennox, Lady Sarah. Life and letters [1761–1817]. Ed Countess of Ilchester and Lord Stavordale 2 vols 1901.

Papendiek, Charlotte. Court and private life in the time of Queen Charlotte: journals [1761–92]. Ed V. D. Broughton 2 vols 1887.

Twining, Rev Thomas. Recreations and studies of a country clergyman [letters and diary 1761–1803]. Ed R. Twining 1882.

Cobbett, William (1762–1835). *See col 1007, below.*

Howard, John. Correspondence [1762–89]. Ed J. Field 1855.

Wilkes, John. Correspondence with Charles Churchill [1762–4]. Ed E. H. Weatherly, New York 1954.

Berry papers. Correspondence of Mary and Agnes Berry [1763–1852]. Ed L. Melville 1914.

Warner, Richard (1763–1857). Literary recollections. 2 vols 1830.

Gray, Almyra. Papers and diaries of a York family 1764–1839. 1927.

Mendoza, Daniel (1764–1836). Memoirs. 1816; ed P. D. Magriel 1951.

Reynolds, Frederick (1764–1841). Life and times, by himself. 2 vols 1826.

Cole, Rev William. Blecheley diary [1765–7]. Ed F. G. Stokes 1931.

Heber, Mary. Dear Miss Heber. Ed F. Bamford 1936. Letters to Miss Heber 1765–1806.

Olson, Alison G. The radical Duke: career and correspondence of Charles Lennox, 3rd Duke of Richmond [1765–1804]. 1961.

Eliot, Lady Harriot. Letters 1766–86. Ed C. Headlam, Edinburgh 1914.

Brown, James B. Memoirs of John Howard the philanthropist [diary and letters 1767–89]. 1818.

Edgeworth, Maria (1767–1849). *See col 875, below.*

Malmesbury, James Harris, Earl of. Diaries and correspondence [1767–1809]. Ed 3rd Earl of Malmesbury 4 vols 1844.

Neville, Sylas. Diary 1767–88. Ed B. Cozens-Hardy, Oxford 1950.

The Noels and the Milbankes [letters 1767–92]. Ed M. Elwin 1967.

Selwyn, George. Letters [1767–90]. In Earl of Carlisle manuscripts, 1897 (Historical Manuscripts Commission).
—— Letters [1767–90] and life. Ed E. S. Roscoe and H. Clergue 1899.

Hoare, Prince. Memoirs of Granville Sharp [letters 1769–1807]. 1820, 2 vols 1828.

Johnson, Samuel. Sir Joshua's nephew: letters by a young man to his sisters 1769–79. Ed S. M. Radcliffe 1930.

Beresford, John. Correspondence illustrative of the last 30 years of the Irish Parliament [1770–1804]. Ed W. Beresford 2 vols 1854.

Herbert, Dorothea. Retrospections [1770–89]. 2 vols 1929–30.

Cumberland, Richard Dennison and George. Letters 1771–84. Ed C. Black 1912.

Manners family correspondence [1771–87]. In Duke of Rutland manuscripts vol 3, 1894 (Historical Manuscripts Commission).

Owen, Robert (1771–1858). Life. 2 vols 1857–8; ed M. Beer 1920.

Pepys, Sir William W. A later Pepys: correspondence [1771–1825]. Ed A. C. C. Gaussen 2 vols 1904.

Sandwich, John Montagu, Earl of. Private papers 1771–82. Ed G. R. Barnes and J. H. Owen 4 vols 1932–8.

Bessborough, Henrietta Ponsonby, Countess of. Lady Bessborough and her family circle [letters 1772–1828]. Ed Earl of Bessborough and A. Aspinall 1940.

Black, Clementina. The Linleys of Bath [correspondence 1772–1830]. 1926.

Windham, William. Early life and diaries [1772–83]. Ed R. W. Ketton-Cremer 1930.

Wraxall, Sir Nathaniel. Historical and posthumous memoirs 1772–84. Ed H. B. Wheatley 5 vols 1884.

Devonshire, Georgiana Cavendish, Duchess of. Extracts from correspondence [1773–1811]. Ed Earl of Bessborough 1955.

Whalley, Dr Thomas Sedgewick. Journals and correspondence [1773–1828]. Ed H. Wickham 2 vols 1863.

Hamilton, Caroline. The Hamwood papers of the ladies of Llangollen and Caroline Hamilton [letters and diaries 1774–1831]. Ed 'Mrs G. H. Bell' (J. Travers) 1930.

Yeoman, John. Diary of visits to London [1774, 1777]. Ed M. Yearsley 1935.

Bute, John Stuart, Earl of. A Prime Minister and his son [correspondence 1775–1800]. Ed E. S. Wortley 1925.

Curwen, Samuel. Journal and letters [1775–84]. Ed G. A. Ward 1842.

Lichtenberg, Georg Christoph. Briefe aus seinem englischen Freundeskreis [letters in English 1775–99]. Ed H. Hecht, Göttingen 1925.

Pinkerton, John. Literary correspondence [1775–1815]. 2 vols 1830.

Windham papers. Life and correspondence of William Windham [1775–1810]. [Ed L. Melville] 2 vols 1913.

Drennan letters [correspondence between William Drennan and Samuel and Martha McTier 1776–1819]. Ed D. A. Chart, Belfast 1931.

Holroyd, Maria Josepha (later Lady Stanley of Alderley). Girlhood [letters 1776–96]. Ed J. H. Adeane 1896.

Knight, William A. Lord Monboddo and some of his contemporaries [letters 1776–92]. 1900.

Newdigate, Sir Roger and Lady. The Cheverels of Cheverel Manor [letters 1776–1800]. Ed Lady Newdigate-Newdegate 1898.

Devonshire, Georgiana and Elizabeth Cavendish, Duchesses of. The two Duchesses: family correspondence 1777–1859. Ed V. Foster 1898.

Elers, George (1777–1842). Memoirs. Ed Lord Monson and G. L. Gower 1903.

Jerningham, Edward, and his friends: a series of 18th-century letters [c. 1777–1801]. Ed L. Bettany 1919.

Jones, Rev William. Diary 1777–1821. Ed O. F. Christie 1929.

Stirling, Anna. Coke of Norfolk and his friends [letters 1777–1837 of Thomas William Coke, later Earl of Leicester]. 2 vols 1907, 1 vol 1912.

Barnard family letters 1778–1824. Ed A. Powell 1928.

Stuart, Lady Louisa. Gleanings from an old portfolio [correspondence 1778–1813]. Ed G. Clark, Edinburgh 3 vols 1895–8.
—— Letters [1778–1834]. Ed R. B. Johnson 1926.

Twining family papers [letters and journals 1778–1844]. Ed R. Twining 1887.

Crisp, Samuel. Burford papers: letters to his sister [1779?–85]. Ed W. H. Hutton 1905.

Frampton, Mary. Journal 1779–1846. Ed H. G. Mundy 1885.

Ailesbury, Thomas Brudenell Bruce, Earl of. Letters and diary 1780–95. 1898 (Historical Manuscripts Commission 15th report vol 7).

Jerningham letters 1780–1843. Ed E. Castle 2 vols 1896.

Pembroke, Henry Herbert, Earl of. Pembroke papers: Letters and diaries 1780–94. Ed Lord Herbert 1950.

Temple, Rev William Johnston. Diaries 1780–96. Ed L. Bettany, Oxford 1929.

Dyott, William. Diary [1781–1845]. Ed R. W. Jeffrey 2 vols 1917.

Granville, Granville Leveson-Gower, Earl. Private correspondence 1781–1821. Ed Castalia, Countess Granville 2 vols 1916.

Greville, Col Robert Fulke. Diaries [1781–4]. Ed F. M. Bladon 1930.

Sinclair, John. Correspondence [c. 1781–1830]. 2 vols 1831.

Torrington, John Byng, Viscount. Diaries [1781–94]. Ed C. B. Andrews 4 vols 1934–8.

Wedgwood, Josiah. Correspondence 1781–94. Ed Lady Farrer 1906.

Auckland, William Eden, Baron. Journal and correspondence [1782–1814]. Ed G. Hogge 4 vols 1860–2.

Heber, Rev Reginald. The Heber letters 1782–1832. Ed R. H. Cholmondeley 1950.

Stuart, Dorothy M. Dearest Bess: the life and times of Lady Elizabeth Foster, afterwards Duchess of Devonshire [1782–1824]. 1955.

Wilberforce, William. Private papers [letters etc 1782–1832]. Ed A. M. Wilberforce 1897.
—— Correspondence [1783–1833]. Ed R. I. and S. Wilberforce 2 vols 1840.
—— Life, by his sons [letters 1783–1833]. 1838.

Berry, Mary. Journals and correspondence [1783–1852]. Ed T. Lewis 3 vols 1865.

Windham, William. Diary 1784–1810. Ed H. Baring 1866.

Nelson, Horatio, Lord. Letters to his wife and other documents 1785–1831. Ed G. P. B. Naish 1958.

Bower, Anna Catherina. Diaries and correspondence [1787–99]. 1903.

Bamford, Samuel. Early days [autobiography 1788–1815]. 1849; ed W. H. Chaloner 1967.

Fitzherbert, Mrs Maria. Letters [1788–1837]. Ed S. Leslie 1940.

Harcourt, Lady Mary. Mrs Harcourt's diary [of the Court of George III 1789–91]. 1872 (Philobiblon Soc).

More, Martha. Mendip annals [journals 1789–1800]. Ed A. Roberts 1859.

Wynne diaries 1789–1820. Ed A. Fremantle 3 vols Oxford 1935–40.

Holland, Elizabeth Fox, Lady. Journal 1791–1811. Ed Earl of Ilchester 2 vols 1908.

Stevens, Rev William Bagshaw. Journal [1792–9]. Ed E. Galbraith, Oxford 1965.

Creevey, Thomas. Creevey papers 1793–1838. Ed H. Maxwell 2 vols 1904.

Farington, Joseph. Diary [1793–1821]. Ed J. Greig 8 vols 1923–8.

Glenbervie, Douglas Sylvester, Lord. Diaries [1793–1819]. Ed F. Bickley 2 vols 1928.

—— Journals [1793–1815]. Ed W. Sichel 1910.

Colchester, Charles Abbot, Lord. Diary and correspondence [1794–1829]. Ed 2nd Lord Colchester 3 vols 1861.

Dunlap, William. Memoirs of George Frederick Cooke [diaries and letters 1794–1809]. 2 vols 1813.

Paget papers [correspondence of Sir Arthur Paget 1794–1807]. Ed A. B. Paget 2 vols 1896.

Cavendish, Lady Harriet. Harry-O: letters 1796–1809. Ed G. L. Gower and I. Palmer 1940.

Wynn, Frances Williams. Diaries of a lady of quality 1797–1844. Ed A. Hayward 1864.

JOHN EVELYN
1620–1706

The ms of the diary is in the possession of the Evelyn family, on deposit in Bodley. A body of unpbd mss remains, mainly at Christ Church, Oxford.

Bibliographies

Keynes, G. L. Evelyn: a study in bibliophily and a bibliography of his writings. Cambridge 1937, Oxford 1968 (with addns).

Collections

Miscellaneous writings. Ed W. Upcott 1825.

§ I

The state of France, by J.E. 1652.

A character of England. 1659, 1659 (both anon), 1659 (anon, as A character of England: with reflections upon Gallus castratus). Original version rptd, with omissions and alterations, as A journey to England, 1700; and complete in Somers tracts 7 1812; and in Harleian Miscellany vol 10, 1813.

An apology for the royal party. 1659 (anon); ed G. L. Keynes, Los Angeles 1951 (Augustan Reprint Soc).

The late news or message from Bruxels unmasked. 1660. Anon.

A panegyric to Charles the Second. 1661; ed G. L. Keynes with An apology, above.

A poem upon his Majestie's coronation. 1661. Anon; attribution doubtful.

Fumifugium. 1661 (2 issues), 1772 etc.

Tyrannus: or the mode. 1661 (preface signed 'J.E.'); ed J. L. Nevinson, Oxford 1951 (Luttrell Soc).

Sculptura. 1662, 1755 (with Evelyn's addns and corrections and an anon life of Evelyn) etc; ed C. F. Bell, Oxford 1906 (with unpbd 2nd part, mainly a trn of part of A. Bosse, Traicté des manieres de graver, Paris 1645).

Sylva: or a discourse of forest trees; to which is annexed Pomona, also Kalendarium hortense. 1664, 1670 (expanded). Further edns, successively expanded, and with further pieces annexed, 1679, 1706 (as Silva); the last rptd 1729. Silva (alone), ed A. Hunter, York 1776 (annotated rpt of edn of 1706 or 1729, with variations and omissions); 1786, 1801, 1812, 1825.

Kalendarium hortense. 1664 (appended to Sylva, above, 1st edn). Not issued separately. Besides the folio edns of Sylva, above, there were 9 octavo edns 1666–1706.

The English vineyard vindicated, by John Rose. 1666 (anon; for proof of authorship *see* Keynes), 1669 (with an addn by Evelyn; appended to the French gardiner, 1669), 1672, 1675, 1691.

Publick employment and an active life prefer'd to solitude. 1667.

The history of the three late famous impostors. 1669 (dedication signed 'J.E.'), 1739.

Navigation and commerce. 1674.

A philosophical discourse of earth. 1676; rptd with Sylva, 1678, 1706 (as Terra etc).

Numismata. 1697.

Acetaria. 1699, New York 1937 (facs), 1706. Also appended to Silva, 1706, 1729.

Memoirs of John Evelyn. Ed W. Bray 2 vols 1818. An improved text, also by Bray, was pbd in 2 vols 1819. The 3rd edn, 5 vols 1827, reproduced the 2nd. The 4th edn, ed J. Forster 4 vols 1850–2, included variant passages. The only edn with important notes, before that of 1955, is by A. Dobson 3 vols 1906, rptd 1 vol 1908 (Globe edn). None of the texts before 1955 was complete or reliable.

The diary of John Evelyn. Ed E. S. de Beer 6 vols Oxford 1955. Definitive edn and full text.

The diary of John Evelyn. Ed E. S. de Beer, Oxford 1959 (OSA). Almost all the text, with a few footnotes selected from 1955 edn.

Selections from the Diary

Voyage de Lister à Paris en MDCXCVIII; on y a joint des extraits des ouvrages d'Evelyn relatifs à ses voyages en France. Ed E. de Sermizelles et al, Paris 1873 (Société des Bibliophiles François).

Evelyn in Naples 1645. Ed H. Maynard Smith, Oxford 1914.

The early life and education of Evelyn. Ed H. Maynard Smith, Oxford 1920.

Other selections, apart from Levis, below, possess no critical value.

Translations

Of liberty and servitude. 1649. Anon; dedicated to George Evelyn. From French of F. de la Mothe le Vayer.

An essay on the first book of T. Lucretius Carus De rerum natura. 1656. Text and trn with Animadversions.

The French gardiner. 1658 (dedication signed 'J.E.'), 1669 (with The English vineyard vindicated), 1672, 1675, 1691. From N. de Bonnefons.

The golden book of St John Chrysostom. 1659.

Instructions concerning erecting of a library. 1661. From French of Gabriel Naudé.

A parallel of the antient architecture with the modern, with Leon Baptista Alberti's Treatise of statues. 1664, 1707 (with expanded version of the Account of architects), 1723 (with Sir H. Wotton, The elements of architecture), 1733. Tr from French of Roland Fréart, Sieur de Chambray.

Μυστήριον τῆς 'Ανομίας: that is another part of the Mystery of Jesuitism, together with the Imaginary heresy. 1664. Anon; tr from French of A. Arnauld and P. Nicole.

The pernicious consequences of the new heresie of the Jesuites. 1666. Anon; tr from French of P. Nicole.

An idea of the perfection of painting. 1668. Tr from French of Roland Fréart.

The compleat gard'ner. 1693. Tr from French of la Quintinye. F. E. Budd, RES 14 1938, also ascribes to Evelyn the trn of The manner of ordering fruit-trees, 1660.

Posthumous Works

The following works were not intended for pbn:

The life of Mrs Godolphin. Ed Bishop Wilberforce 1847, 1848, 1848, 1864; ed E. W. Harcourt 1888; [ed I. Gollancz?] 1904; ed H. Sampson, Oxford 1939.

The history of religion. Ed R. M. Evanson 2 vols 1850.

[Londinium redivivum. 1666]; ed E. S. de Beer, Oxford 1938.

Memoires for my grand-son. Ed G. L. Keynes 1926.

Directions for the gardiner at Says-Court. Ed G. L. Keynes 1932.

A devotionarie book of John Evelyn. Ed W. Frere 1936.

Letters

A selection from his correspondence was pbd with the diary in the edns of 1818, 1819, 1827, 1850–2 and 1859. The fullest collections are in those of 1850–2 and 1859. Many of his letters are also in the various vols of Pepys's and Bentley's pbd correspondence, and elsewhere.

§ 2

Evelyn, H. The history of the Evelyn family. 1915.
Levis, H. C. Extracts from the diaries and correspondence of Evelyn and Pepys relating to engraving. 1915.
Ponsonby, A. John Evelyn. 1933.
Hiscock, W. G. Evelyn and Mrs Godolphin. 1951.
—— Evelyn and his family circle. 1955.
de Beer, E. S. John Evelyn FRS. Notes & Records of Royal Soc 15 1960.

SAMUEL PEPYS
1633–1703

The ms of the diary etc is in the Pepys Library, Magdalene College Cambridge.

Bibliographies etc

A descriptive catalogue of the naval manuscripts in the Pepysian Library. Ed J. R. Tanner 4 vols 1903–23 (Navy Records Soc).
Historical Manuscripts Commission. Report on the Pepys mss preserved at Magdalene College Cambridge. Ed E. K. Purnell 1911.
Bibliotheca Pepysiana: a descriptive catalogue of the library. Pt 1, 'Sea' mss, ed J. R. Tanner 1914; pt 2, Early printed books to 1558, ed E. Gordon Duff 1914; pt 3, Mediaeval mss, ed M. R. James 1923; pt 4, Short-hand books, ed W. J. Carlton 1940.

§ 1

Memoires relating to the state of the Royal Navy for ten years, determin'd December 1688. 1690; ed J. R. Tanner, Oxford 1906 (as Pepys' Memoires of the Royal Navy 1679–1688).
Mr Pepys upon the state of Christ-Hospital. 1698–9; ed R. Kirk, Philadelphia 1935.
An account of the preservation of King Charles II after the battle of Worcester. Ed Sir D. Dalrymple 1766; ed W. Matthews 1966 (as Charles II's escape from Worcester); ed R. Ollard 1966 (as The escape of Charles II after the battle of Worcester). Dictated by the King to Pepys in 1680; often rptd.
The following list does not include abridgements or selections from the diary. For the general reader, the abridgement by O. F. Morshead, 1926, is the best; for the student of history, that by J. P. Kenyon, 1963.
Memoirs 1659 [1660] to 1669, and a selection from his private correspondence. Ed Richard Lord Braybrooke 2 vols 1825, 1828, 5 vols 1828, 1848–9 (as Diary, 'considerably enlarged') 1851, 4 vols 1854 ('revised and corrected'), 1854, 1858 etc. From a transcription of the original ms, mostly in shorthand, by John Smith. About one-quarter of Diary was ptd in 1825; two-fifths in 1848–9 etc.
Diary and correspondence. Ed Mynors Bright 6 vols 1875–9. From Bright's transcription, about four-fifths of Diary.
Diary. Ed H. B. Wheatley 10 vols 1893–9. From Bright's transcription, above, with alterations; about nine-tenths of ms.
Naval minutes. Ed J. R. Tanner 1926 (Navy Records Soc).
The Tangier papers of Pepys [1683–4]. Ed E. Chappell 1935 (Navy Records Soc).
Diary. Ed R. Latham and W. Matthews 11 vols 1970–; The illustrated Pepys, ed Latham 1978.

Letters

Selections from Pepys's correspondence are included in edns

of Diary by Braybrooke and Bright, above, and in edn by Dalrymple of An account of the preservation of King Charles II. *For summaries of his official and other correspondence, see* Calendars of state papers domestic, ed M. A. Everett Green et al, 1660–79, 1684–7; Catalogi codicum manuscriptorum bibliothecae Bodleianae, pt 5 fascicules 1–2, Rawlinson mss, ed W. D. Macray 1862, 1878; A descriptive catalogue of the naval manuscripts in the Pepysian Library, ed J. R. Tanner 4 vols 1903–23 (Navy Records Soc); *and the following Reports of the Historical Mss Commission: 8th (Appendix 1 section 1, Trinity House mss), 1881; 11th (Appendix pt 5, Dartmouth mss), 1887; 15th (Appendix pt 1, Dartmouth mss vol 3), 1896; 15th (Appendix pt 2, J. Eliot Hodgkin mss) 1897; Downshire mss vol 1, 1924; Hastings mss vol 2, 1930.*
Smith, John. The life, journals and correspondence. 2 vols 1841.
Private correspondence 1679–1703. Ed J. R. Tanner 2 vols 1929; Further correspondence 1662–79, ed Tanner 1929.
Letters and the second diary. Ed R. G. Howarth 1932.
Shorthand letters. Ed E. Chappell, Cambridge 1933.
Letters of Pepys and his family circle. Ed H. T. Heath, Oxford 1955.

The Pepys Library

A Pepysian garland. Ed H. E. Rollins, Cambridge 1922. Black-letter broadside ballads 1595–1639, chiefly from Pepys's collection.
The Pepys ballads. Ed H. E. Rollins 8 vols Cambridge Mass 1929–32. With A Pepysian garland, above, reproduces about one-third of Pepys's collection 1534–1703. About another third is in Roxburghe ballads, ed W. Chappell and J. W. Ebsworth, Hertford 1883–95, and in Bagford ballads, ed Ebsworth, Hertford 1876–8. See L. M. Goldstein, The Pepys ballads, Library 5th ser 21 1966.

§ 2

[Scott, Sir W.] Pepys's Memoirs. Quart Rev 33 1826.
Wheatley, H. B. Pepys and the world he lived in. 1880.
Stevenson, R. L. In his Familiar studies, [1882].
Pepys, W. C. Genealogy of the Pepys family. 1887, 1952 (with addns).
Tanner, J. R. Pepys and the Popish Plot. EHR 3 1892.
—— Pepys and the Royal Navy. Cambridge 1920.
—— Mr Pepys. 1925.
—— Pepys and the Trinity House. EHR 44 1929.
Firth, C. H. The early life of Pepys. Macmillan's Mag Nov 1893.
Lubbock, P. Samuel Pepys. 1909.
Ponsonby, A. Samuel Pepys. 1928 (EML).
Bryant, A. Pepys: the man in the making. Cambridge 1933; The years of peril, Cambridge 1935; The saviour of the navy, Cambridge 1938. Unfinished.
Wilson, J. H. The private life of Mr Pepys. 1960.
Emden, C. S. Pepys himself. Oxford 1963.
Nicolson, M. H. Pepys' diary and the new science. Charlottesville 1965.
Ollard, R. Pepys: a biography. 1974.

LADY MARY WORTLEY MONTAGU, née PIERREPOINT
1689–1762

§ 1

Court poems. 1716. 3 town eclogues, misdated 1706.
Verses address'd to the imitator of Horace. 1733. On Pope.
An elegy to a young lady in the manner of Ovid [by James Hammond] with an answer, by a lady, author of the Verses to the imitator of Horace. 1733.
The Dean's provocation for writing the lady's dressing-room. 1734. On Swift.

The nonsense of common-sense 1737–8; ed R. Halsband, Evanston 1947. 9 periodical essays.

Six town eclogues with some other poems. 1747.

Letters of Rt Hon Lady M—y W—y M—e written during her travels. 3 vols 1763 etc.

An additional volume to the letters. 1767. Spurious except for one letter to the Abbé Conti published 1719, 2 prose pieces and some verse.

Poetical works. [Ed I. Reed] 1768.

Works, including her correspondence, poems and essays. Ed J. Dallaway 5 vols 1803, 1805 (5th edn) (with letters to Mrs Hewet).

Original letters to Sir James and Lady Frances Steuart. [Ed J. Dunlop], Greenock 1818.

Letters and works. Ed Lord Wharncliffe 3 vols 1837 (with Introductory anecdotes by Lady Louisa Stuart); ed W. M. Thomas 2 vols 1861 (3rd edn), 1893, 1887 (rev).

Letters. Ed R. B. Johnson 1906 (EL).

Complete letters. Ed R. Halsband 3 vols Oxford 1965–7.

Selected letters. Ed R. Halsband 1970.

Essays and poems, and Simplicity: a comedy. Ed R. Halsband and I. Grunby, Oxford 1977.

§ 2

Hunt, Leigh. Lady Mary Wortley Montagu. Westminster Rev 27 1837; rptd in his Men, women and books 2 vols 1847.

'Paston, George' (E. M. Symonds). Lady Mary Wortley Montagu and her times. 1907.

'Melville, Lewis' (L. S. Benjamin). Life and letters of Lady Mary Wortley Montagu. 1925.

Tillotson, G. Lady Mary Wortley Montagu and Pope's Elegy to the memory of an unfortunate lady. RES 12 1936.

Halsband, R. Life of Lady Mary Wortley Montagu. Oxford 1956, New York 1960 (corrected).

—— Lady Mary Wortley Montagu as letter-writer. PMLA 80 1965; rptd in The familiar letter in the 18th century, ed H. Anderson, P. Daghlian and I. Ehrenpreis, Lawrence Kansas 1966.

PHILIP DORMER STANHOPE, 4th EARL OF CHESTERFIELD
1694–1773

Bibliographies

Gulick, S. L. A Chesterfield bibliography to 1800. PBSA 29 1935.

§ 1

The art of pleasing: in a series of letters to Master Stanhope [later 5th Earl of Chesterfield]. Edinburgh Mag 1–2 1774. 14 letters; rptd in several periodicals, in some edns of Letters to his son, in Miscellaneous works vol 3, and separately 1783, Dublin 1783.

Letters to his son Philip Stanhope, together with several other pieces on various subjects, published by Mrs Eugenia Stanhope. 2 vols 1774, Dublin 1774, 4 vols 1774, Dublin 1776 (adds The art of pleasing), London 1787 (incorporates letters from Supplement), Paris 1789, London 1800 (11th edn), 6 vols Vienna 1800; ed C. Strachey and A. Calthrop 2 vols 1901.

Miscellaneous works: consisting of letters to his friends, never before printed, and various other articles; to which are prefixed Memoirs of his life, by M. Maty. Ed J. O. Justamond 2 vols 1777, 1778 (with 'appendix, containing sixteen characters of great personages' and the letters to Faulkner etc), 3 vols Dublin 1777 (adds letters to Faulkner etc, but not the characters), 4 vols 1779.

Letters to Alderman George Faulkner, Dr Madden, Mr Sexton, Mr Derrick and the Earl of Arran. 1777.

Characters of eminent personages of his own time. 1777 (7 characters), 1778 (16 characters and letters to Faulkner etc).

Miscellaneous works: consisting of letters, political tracts and poems: volume 3 completing edition begun by M. Maty, collected by B. W[ay]. 1778.

Letters from a celebrated nobleman to his heir [later 5th Earl of Chesterfield]. 1783. 14 letters, previously ptd as The art of pleasing, not included.

Supplement to the Letters to his son. 1787, Dublin 1787.

Letters to Arthur Charles Stanhope relative to the education of his Lordship's godson. 1817 (44 letters); rptd as appendix to Chesterfield's letters to his godson, ed Lord Carnarvon 1890.

Letters. Ed Lord Mahon 5 vols 1845–53. Vols 1–2, Letters on education and characters; vols 3–4, Political and miscellaneous letters; vol 5, Miscellanies.

The wit and wisdom of Chesterfield. Ed W. Ernst-Browning 1875. A selection, including poems.

Letters to his godson and successor. Ed Earl of Carnarvon, Oxford 1890, 1890 (adding the 44 letters to A. C. Stanhope). From ms.

Chesterfield's worldly wisdom. Ed G. B. Hill, Oxford 1891. A selection.

Letters to Lord Huntingdon (46). Ed A. F. Steuart 1923 (from ms).

Letters to his son and others. Ed R. K. Root 1929 (EL).

Letters. Selected by P. M. Jones, Oxford 1929 (WC).

Private correspondence of Chesterfield and Newcastle 1744–6. Ed R. Lodge 1930 (Camden Soc). 40 letters by Chesterfield.

Letters. Ed B. Dobrée 6 vols 1932 (most complete edn).

Letters and other pieces. Ed R. P. Bond, New York 1935. A selection.

Unpublished letters of Chesterfield. Ed S. L. Gulick, Berkeley 1937. 25 to his godson and one to Deyverdun.

Five unpublished letters [to the Earl of Bute]. Ed C. Price, Life & Letters 59 1948.

§ 2

Sainte-Beuve, C. A. Lettres de Lord Chesterfield à son fils. In his Causeries du lundi vol 2, Paris 1850.

Strachey, L. Lady Mary Wortley Montagu and Lord Chesterfield. In his Characters and commentaries, 1933.

Gulick, S. L. The publication of Chesterfield's letters to his son. PMLA 51 1936.

—— Johnson, Chesterfield and Boswell. In The age of Johnson: essays presented to C. B. Tinker, New Haven 1949.

HORACE WALPOLE, 4th EARL OF ORFORD
1717–97

The most important collection of mss is in the W. S. Lewis Library at Farmington, Conn.

Bibliographies

Hazen, A. T. Bibliography of the Strawberry Hill Press. New Haven 1942, Folkestone 1973 (with addns).

—— Bibliography of Walpole. New Haven 1948.

—— Catalogue of Walpole's library. 3 vols New Haven 1969.

Collections

Fugitive pieces in verse and prose. Strawberry Hill 1758.

Fugitive pieces in verse and prose. 2 vols Strawberry Hill 1770. A partial collection, ptd but not pbd.

Works. Ed Mary Berry under the name of her father Robert Berry 5 vols 1798. Vol 6, Letters to Montagu and Cole, ed John Martin 1818; vol 7–8, Memoires of

the last ten years of the reign of George II, ed Lord
Holland 2 vols 1822; vol 9, Letters to Lord Hertford,
ed J. W. Croker 1825.

Walpole's fugitive verses. Ed W. S. Lewis, New York
1931.

§ 1

The lesson for the day. 1742. At least 5 edns; also
imitations.

The beauties. 1746.

Epilogue to Tamerlane. 1746.

Aedes Walpolianae. 1747, 1752, 1767.

A letter to the Whigs. 1747, 1748.

A second and third letter to the Whigs. 1748.

Three letters to the Whigs. 1748.

The original speech of Sir William Stanhope. 1748,
Dublin 1748.

The speech of Richard White-Liver. 1748.

A letter from Xo Ho. [1757] (5 numbered edns).

A catalogue of the royal and noble authors of England. 2
vols Strawberry Hill 1758, London 1759, Dublin 1759,
Edinburgh 1792, 1 vol London (also Edinburgh) 1796;
ed T. Park 5 vols 1806, New York 1967.

A dialogue between two great ladies. 1760.

Catalogue of pictures and drawings in the Holbein
Chamber. Strawberry Hill 1760.

Catalogues of the pictures of the Duke of Devonshire etc.
Strawberry Hill 1760.

Anecdotes of painting in England (and A catalogue of
engravers). 4 vols Strawberry Hill 1762–3, 1765; vol 4
of Anecdotes, Strawberry Hill 1771 but pbd 1780; 5
vols 1782, 1786; Catalogue of engravers, 1794; ed J.
Dallaway 5 vols 1826–8; ed R. N. Wornum 3 vols 1849,
1862, 1876, 1879, 1888. Vol 5 of Anecdotes, compiled
from Walpole's Books of materials by F. W. Hilles and
P. B. Daghlian, New Haven 1937.

The opposition to the late Minister vindicated. 1763.
Probably by Walpole.

A counter-address to the public. 1764 (4 edns).

The magpie and her brood. Strawberry Hill 1764.

The castle of Otranto. 1765, 1765, Dublin 1765, 1765,
London 1766, 1782, 1786, 1791, Parma 1791, London
1793, 1793, Berlin 1794, London 1796, 1800; ed W.
Scott 1811 etc; ed M. Summers 1924; ed O. Doughty
1929; ed W. S. Lewis, Oxford 1964, 1969.

An account of the giants lately discovered. 1766.

Historic doubts on Richard III. 1768, 1768, Dublin 1768,
London 1822; ed P. M. Kendall, New York 1965 (with
More's History).

The mysterious mother. Strawberry Hill 1768, London
1781, Dublin 1791, London 1791, 1796.

Reply to Dean Milles. Strawberry Hill [1770]. 6 copies ptd.

A description of the villa of Horace Walpole. Strawberry
Hill 1774, 1784, London 1842, 1965.

A letter to the editor of the Miscellanies of Thomas
Chatterton. Strawberry Hill 1779.

Essay on modern gardening [in English and French].
Strawberry Hill 1785, Paris? [c. 1790]; rptd L. Buddy,
Canton Pa 1904; ed W. S. Lewis, New York 1931;
rptd in I. W. U. Chase, Walpole gardenist, Princeton
1943. First ptd by Walpole in vol 4 of Anecdotes, above.

Hieroglyphic tales. Strawberry Hill 1785 (7 copies ptd),
Newcastle 1822, London 1926.

Postscript to the royal and noble authors. Strawberry Hill
1786.

Notes to the portraits at Woburn Abbey. 1800.

Letters, Diaries etc

Letters to George Montagu. 1818, 1819, 1834 (reissue).

Letters to William Cole. 1818, 1824 (reissue).

Private correspondence. 4 vols 1820, 3 vols 1837.

Letters to the Earl of Hertford. 1825.

Letters to Sir Horace Mann. Ed Lord Dover 3 vols 1833,

1833, 2 vols New York 1833; Concluding ser, 4 vols
1843–4, 2 vols Philadelphia 1844.

Letters. Ed J. Wright 6 vols 1840, Philadelphia 1842,
London 1846.

Short notes of the life of Horace Walpole. Ptd with his
letters to Mann, 1844; rptd by Cunningham and Mrs
Toynbee, and (from original ms) in the Yale edn vol 13,
below.

Letters to the Countess of Ossory. Ed R. Vernon Smith
2 vols 1848, 1848, 3 vols 1903.

Correspondence with Mason. Ed J. Mitford 2 vols 1851.

Letters. Ed P. Cunningham 9 vols 1857 etc.

Some unpublished letters. Ed S. Walpole 1902.

Letters. Ed Mrs P. Toynbee 16 vols Oxford 1903–5;
Supplementary vols ed P. Toynbee 3 vols 1918–25.

Correspondence of Gray, Walpole, West and Ashton. Ed
P. Toynbee 2 vols Oxford 1915.

The Yale ed of Walpole's correspondence. Ed W. S.
Lewis et al 31 vols New Haven 1937–67. 50 or more
vols projected.

A selection of the letters. Ed W. S. Lewis 2 vols New
York 1926. Many other selections have been made,
including a one-vol selection by W. S. Lewis 1951.

Reminiscences written for Mary and Agnes Berry. 1805
(priv ptd), 1818, 1819, 1819, Boston 1820, London
1830; ed P. Toynbee, Oxford 1924.

Memoires of the last ten years of the reign of George II.
Ed Lord Holland 2 vols 1822 (also issued as vols 7–8 of
Works), 3 vols 1846, 1847; rptd New York 1968.

Memoirs of George III. Ed D. Le Marchant 4 vols 1845,
Philadelphia 1845, London 1851; ed G. F. R. Barker
1894; rptd New York 1968.

Journal of George III. Ed J. Doran 2 vols 1859; rptd as
Last journals, 1910.

Memoirs and portraits. Ed M. J. C. Hodgart 1963, New
York 1963 (rev).

§ 2

Walpoliana. Ed J. Pinkerton 2 vols [1799], 1800.

Letters of the Marquise du Deffand to Walpole. Ed Mary
Berry 4 vols 1810, Paris 1811, 1812, 1824; ed Mrs P.
Toynbee 3 vols 1912.

Macaulay, T. B. Horace Walpole. Edinburgh Rev 1833.

Sainte-Beuve, C. A. Lettres de la Marquise du Deffand.
In his Causeries du lundi, Paris 1850.

Stephen, L. Horace Walpole. Cornhill Mag June 1872.

Seeley, L. B. Walpole and his world. 2 vols 1884, 1895.

Dobson, A. Walpole: a memoir. New York 1890, London
1893; ed P. Toynbee 1927.

Strachey, L. Walpole and Mme du Deffand. In his Books
and characters, 1922.

—— In his Characters and commentaries, 1933.

Toynbee, P. (ed). Satirical poems by Mason, with notes
by Walpole. Oxford 1926.

—— Strawberry Hill accounts. Oxford 1927.

—— Walpole's memoir of the poet Gray. MLR 27 1932.

Lewis, W. S. (ed). A commonplace book of Walpole's.
1927 (priv ptd).

—— Anecdotes told me by Lady Denbigh. 1932 (priv ptd).

—— Walpole's letter from Mme de Sévigné. 1933 (priv
ptd).

—— Memoranda Walpoliana. 1937 (priv ptd).

—— Select observations assembled by Walpole. 1937 (priv
ptd).

—— Notes by Walpole on several characters of Shakespeare. 1940 (priv ptd).

'Melville, Lewis' (L. S. Benjamin). Horace Walpole.
[1930].

Lewis, W. S. Collector's progress. New York 1951.

—— Horace Walpole, antiquary. In Essays presented to
Sir L. Namier, 1956.

—— Walpole's library. Cambridge 1958.

—— Horace Walpole. New York [1960].

Ketton-Cremer, R. W. Walpole: a biography. 1940, 1946
(rev).

GILBERT WHITE
1720–93
Bibliographies
Martin, E. A. A bibliography of White; with a biography and a descriptive account of the village of Selborne. [1897], 1934 (rev.)

Collections
Writings. Ed H. J. Massingham 2 vols 1938 (Nonesuch Press). Incomplete; includes Natural history, Antiquities (selected), parts of A naturalist's calendar, the poems and selected private letters.

§ 1
The natural history and antiquities of Selborne, in the county of Southampton; with engravings and an appendix. 1789; ed J. W[hite] 2 vols 1802 (with next item, as The works in natural history of the late Gilbert White); ed J.W[hite] 1813 (adds poems and notes by John Mitford); ed W. Jardine, Edinburgh 1829; ed J. Rennie 1833; ed T. Brown, Edinburgh 1833; ed E. Blyth 1836; ed E. T. Bennett 1837, 1875 (rev J. E. Harting); ed W. Jardine and E. Jesse 1851; ed F. Buckland 2 vols 1876; ed T. Bell 2 vols 1877; ed C. G. Davies [1879]; ed L. C. Miall and W. W. Fowler 1901; ed R. Kearton 1902; ed G. Allen 1902; Oxford 1902 (WC); ed B. C. A. Windle [1906] (EL). Some edns omit Antiquities.
A naturalist's calendar with observations in various branches of natural history. Ed J. Aikin 1795. Rptd, in whole or part, in most edns of Natural history, above.
The antiquities of Selborne. Ed W. S. Scott 1950. With bibliography.

Letters, Diaries etc
The life and letters of White. Ed R. Holt-White 2 vols 1901.
Journals. Ed W. Johnson 1931.

§ 2
Scott, W. S. White of Selborne. 1950.
Lockley, R. M. Gilbert White. 1954.
Emden, C. S. White in his village. 1956.

THE BLUESTOCKINGS

Hawkins, L. M. Anecdotes, biographical sketches and memoirs. Vol 1 (all pbd), 1822.
—— Memoirs, Anecdotes, facts and opinions. 2 vols 1824.
Elwood, A. K. Memoirs of the literary ladies of England from the commencement of the last century. 2 vols 1843.
Gaussen, A. C. C. A later Pepys: the correspondence of Sir W. W. Pepys 1758–1825 with Mrs Chapone, Mrs Hartley, Mrs Montagu, Hannah More, William Franks, Sir James Macdonald, Major Rennell, Sir N. Wraxall and others. 2 vols 1904.
Tinker, C. B. The salon and English letters. 1915.
Reynolds, M. The learned lady in England 1650–1760. Boston 1920.
Anson, E. and F. Mary Hamilton at Court and at home, from letters and diaries 1756 to 1816. 1925.
Johnson, R. B. Bluestocking letters. 1926. A selection.
Tenbury letters. Ed E. H. Fellowes and E. Pine 1943. A selection.
MacCarthy, B. G. Women writers: their contribution to the English novel 1621–1818. 2 vols Cork 1944–7.
Scott, W. S. The bluestocking ladies. 1947.
Halsband, R. Ladies of letters in the eighteenth century. Los Angeles 1969.

ELIZABETH CARTER
1717–1806
§ 1
Poems upon particular occasions. 1738.
An examination of Mr Pope's Essay on man, translated from the French of M. Crousaz. 1739.
Sir Isaac Newton's Philosophy explain'd for the use of ladies, translated from the Italian of Sig Algarotti. 2 vols 1739 etc.
All the works of Epictetus, which are now extant: consisting of his Discourses preserved by Arrian in 4 books, the Enchiridion and Fragments, translated from the original Greek. 1758 etc; ed W. H. D. Rouse 1910.
Poems on several occasions. 1762 etc.
A series of letters between Mrs Elizabeth Carter and Miss Catherine Talbot 1741–70; to which are added letters from Mrs Elizabeth Carter to Mrs Vesey 1763–87. Ed M. Pennington 4 vols 1809.
Letters from Mrs Elizabeth Carter to Mrs Montagu 1755–1800. Ed M. Pennington 3 vols 1817.

§ 2
Pennington, M. Memoirs of the life of Mrs Elizabeth Carter, with a new edition of her Poems; to which are added some miscellaneous essays in prose, together with her notes on the Bible and answers to objections concerning the Christian religion. 2 vols 1807 etc.
Gaussen, A. C. C. A woman of wit and wisdom: a memoir of Elizabeth Carter. 1906.
Dobson, A. The learned Mrs Carter. In his Later essays, 1921.

HESTER LYNCH THRALE,
later PIOZZI, née SALUSBURY
1741–1821

§ 1
The three warnings. In Anna Williams, Miscellanies in prose and verse, 1766; Kidderminster 1792 (separately); Lady's Poetical Mag 1 1781.
Florence miscellany. Florence 1785. Preface and 9 poems by Mrs Piozzi.
Anecdotes of the late Samuel Johnson LlD in the last 20 years of his life. 1786; ed G. B. Hill (in Johnsonian miscellanies vol 1, 1897); ed S. C. Roberts, Cambridge 1925; ed A. Sherbo, Oxford 1974 (with W. Shaw, Memoirs).
Letters to and from Samuel Johnson; to which are added some poems never before printed. 2 vols 1788.
Observations and reflections made in the course of a journey through France, Italy and Germany. 2 vols 1789; ed H. Barrows, Ann Arbor 1967.
British synonymy: or an attempt at regulating the choice of words in familiar conversation. 2 vols 1794.
Three warnings to John Bull. 1798.
Retrospection: or a review of the most striking and important events, characters, situations and their consequences which the last 1800 years have presented to the view of mankind. 2 vols 1801.
Three dialogues. Ed M. Zamick, Bull John Rylands Lib 16 1932.

Letters, Diaries etc
Love letters of Mrs Piozzi, written when she was 80, to W. A. Conway. 1843. But see P. Merritt under §2, below.
Autobiography, letters and literary remains of Mrs Piozzi.

Ed A. Hayward 2 vols 1861, 1861 (enlarged); ed J. H. Lobban 1910 (as Dr Johnson's Mrs Thrale).

Dr Johnson and Mrs Thrale, including Mrs Thrale's unpublished Journal of the Welsh tour in 1774: correspondence of the Streatham coterie, with introductory essay by T. Seccombe. Ed A. M. Broadley 1910.

Intimate letters of Hester Lynch Piozzi and Penelope Pennington 1788–1821. Ed O. G. Knapp 1914.

Unpublished manuscripts, papers and letters of Dr Johnson, Mrs Thrale and their friends, in the John Rylands library. Ed M. Tyson, Bull John Rylands Lib 15 1931. Extracts from letters and journals.

French journals of Mrs Thrale and Dr Johnson. Ed M. Tyson and H. Guppy, Manchester 1932.

Johnson and Queeney: letters from Dr Johnson to Queeney Thrale. Ed Marquis of Lansdowne 1932.

Queeney letters to Hester Maria Thrale by Dr Johnson, Fanny Burney and Mrs Thrale-Piozzi. Ed Marquis of Lansdowne 1934.

Thraliana: the diary of Mrs Thrale 1776–1809. Ed K. C. Balderston 2 vols Oxford 1942, 1951 (corrected).

Letters of Samuel Johnson, with Mrs Thrale's genuine letters to him. Ed R. W. Chapman 3 vols Oxford 1952.

Hyde, M. The Thrales of Streatham Park. Cambridge Mass 1977.

§ 2

Merritt, P. Piozzi marginalia: comprising extracts from mss and annotations. Cambridge Mass 1925.

—— The true story of the so-called love-letters of Mrs Piozzi. Cambridge Mass 1927.

Boswell's Life of Johnson with marginal comments from 2 copies annotated by Hester Piozzi. Ed E. G. Fletcher 3 vols 1938.

Clifford, J. L. Hester Lynch Piozzi. Oxford 1941, 1952 (corrected), 1968 (with bibliography).

—— Mrs Piozzi's letters. In Essays on the eighteenth century presented to David Nichol Smith, Oxford 1945.

Chapman, R. W. Mrs Piozzi's omissions from Johnson's letters to Thrales. RES 22 1946.

—— Mrs Thrale's letters to Johnson published by Mrs Piozzi in 1788. RES 24 1948.

ELIZABETH MONTAGU, née ROBINSON
1720–1800

§ 1

An essay on the writings and genius of Shakespear. 1769 etc, 1777 (including the 3 Dialogues 26–8, which Mrs Montagu contributed to Lyttelton's Dialogues of the dead, 1760).

Letters of Mrs Elizabeth Montagu, with some of the letters of her correspondents. Ed M. Montagu 4 vols 1809–13.

Letters to the Duchess of Portland [1740–80]. In Marquis of Bath mss 1–2, 1904, 1907 (Historical Manuscripts Commission).

Climenson, E. J. Elizabeth Montagu, the Queen of the Blue-stockings: her correspondence from 1720 [1732]–1761. 2 vols 1906.

Blunt, R. Mrs Montagu, 'Queen of the Blues': her letters and friendships from 1762–1800. 2 vols 1923.

§ 2

Doran, J. A lady of the last century, illustrated in her unpublished letters, with a chapter on blue-stockings. 1873.

Huchon, R. Mrs Montagu. 1906.

Hornbeak, K. G. New light on Mrs Montagu. In The age of Johnson: essays presented to C. B. Tinker, New Haven 1949.

CATHERINE TALBOT
1721–70

The works of the late Mrs Catherine Talbot. 1772, 1809 (7th edn, 'with additional papers, together with notes and illustrations, and some account of her life by M. Pennington'), 1819 (9th edn).

Reflections on the seven days of the week. 1770 etc.

Essays on various subjects. 2 vols 1772.

For letters see Elizabeth Carter, above.

HESTER CHAPONE, née MULSO
1727–1801

§ 1

Letters on the improvement of the mind, addressed to a young lady. 2 vols 1773 etc, 1 vol 1806 ('with the life of the author').

Miscellanies in prose and verse [including The story of Fidelia, Adventurer 77–9]. 1775 etc.

A letter to a new-married lady. 1777 etc.

Works. 2 vols Dublin 1786, 4 vols 1807.

Posthumous works: containing her correspondence with Mr Richardson; a series of letters to Mrs Elizabeth Carter; and some fugitive pieces never before published; together with an account of her life and character, drawn up by her own family. 2 vols 1807, 1808.

§ 2

Cole, J. Memoirs of Mrs Chapone, from various authentic sources. 1839.

MARY DELANY, née GRANVILLE
1700–88

Letters to Mrs Frances Hamilton 1779–88. 1820.

Autobiography and correspondence of Mary Granville, Mrs Delany. Ed Lady Llanover 6 vols 1861–2.

'Paston, George' (E. M. Symonds). Mrs Delany: a memoir. 1900. Abridged from above, with new material.

HANNAH MORE
1745–1833

Bibliographies

Green, E. Bibliotheca Somersetensis. 3 vols Taunton 1902.

Collections

Works. 8 vols 1801, 19 vols 1818–19, 11 vols 1830 (rev), 6 vols 1833–4.

Poems. 1816, 1829. With prose pieces Village politics and The white slave trade.

§ 1

A search after happiness: a pastoral drama by a young lady. Bristol [1766?], 1773, London 1796 (11th edn, with alterations). At end of 1st edn are Prologue to Hamlet, 1765, and Prologue to King Lear, not included in collections.

The inflexible captive: a tragedy. Bristol 1774, 1777.

Sir Eldred of the bower and the Bleeding rock: two legendary tales. 1776, 1778.

Essays on various subjects, principally designed for young ladies. 1777, 1791 (5th edn).

Ode to Dragon, Mr Garrick's house-dog at Hampton. 1777, 1778.

Percy: a tragedy. 1778 etc (prologue and epilogue by Garrick).

The fatal falsehood: a tragedy. 1779, 1780.

Sacred dramas, chiefly intended for young persons; to which is added Sensibility: a poem. 1782 etc.

Florio, a tale for fine gentlemen and fine ladies; and the Bas bleu, or conversation: two poems. 1786, 1787.

Slavery: a poem. 1788.

Thoughts on the importance of the manners of the great to general society. 1788, 1788 (with postscript), 1792 (8th edn).

Bishop Bonner's ghost. Strawberry Hill 1789.

An estimate of the religion of the fashionable world. 1791, 1793 (5th edn).

Remarks on the speech of M. Dupont, made in the National Convention of France, on the subjects of religion and education. 1793.

Village politics, by Will Chip. 1793.

Questions and answers for the Mendip and Sunday schools. 1795.

Cheap repository tracts. 1795–8. See Stories, below.

Strictures on the modern system of female education. 2 vols 1799 etc.

Hints towards forming the character of a young princess. 2 vols 1805.

Coelebs in search of a wife. 2 vols 1808 etc.

Practical piety. 2 vols 1811 etc.

Christian morals. 2 vols 1813 etc.

An essay on the character and practical writings of St Paul. 2 vols 1815 etc.

Stories for the middle ranks of society, and tales for the common people. 2 vols 1818. Rptd from Cheap repository tracts, above.

Moral sketches of prevailing opinions and manners. 1819, 1819 (rev), 1820 (6th edn with new preface).

The twelfth of August: or the feast of freedom. 1819, 1827 (as The feast of freedom: or the abolition of domestic slavery in Ceylon).

Bible rhymes on the names of all the books of the old and new testaments. 1821, 1822 (with addns).

The spirit of prayer, selected from published volumes. 1825 etc.

Letters, Diaries etc

Letters to Zachary Macaulay, containing notices of Lord Macaulay's youth. Ed A. Roberts 1860.

Letters, selected. Ed R. B. Johnson 1925.

§ 2

Roberts, W. Memoirs of the life and correspondence of Mrs Hannah More. 4 vols 1834. Includes letters from Mrs Montagu, Mrs Boscawen and Mrs Vesey.

Yonge, C. M. Hannah More. Boston 1888.

Hopkins, M. A. Hannah More and her circle. New York 1947.

Jones, M. G. Hannah More. Cambridge 1952.

III. RELIGION

A. THE RESTORATION DIVINES 1660–1700

General Studies

Baxter, Richard. Reliquiae Baxterianae: or Mr Richard Baxter's narrative of the most memorable passages of his life and times. 1696.

Calamy, Edmund. An abridgment of Mr Baxter's History of his life and times; with an account of many ministers who were ejected at the Restoration. 1702, 2 vols 1713–27; rev S. Palmer 2 vols 1775, 1778, 3 vols 1802–3.

Pattison, M. Tendencies of religious thought in England. In Essays and reviews, 1860, and in his Essays vol 2, Oxford 1889.

Hunt, J. Religious thought in England to the end of the 18th century. 3 vols 1870–3.

Tulloch, J. Rational theology and Christian philosophy in England in the 17th century. 2 vols Edinburgh 1872.

The classic preachers of the English Church. Ed J. E. Kempe 2 sers 1877–8. On Barrow, South, Beveridge, Wilson, Butler, Tillotson et al.

Powicke, F. J. A life of Richard Baxter. 1924.

—— The Cambridge Platonists. 1926.

—— The Rev Richard Baxter: under the cross 1662–91. 1927.

Jones, R. F. The attack on pulpit eloquence in the Restoration. JEGP 30 1931; rptd in his Seventeenth century, Stanford 1951.

Mitchell, W. F. English pulpit oratory from Andrewes to Tillotson. 1932. With select bibliography.

Sykes, N. The Church of England and non-episcopal churches in the 16th and 17th centuries. 1948.

—— Old priest and new presbyter. Cambridge 1956.

—— From Sheldon to Secker: aspects of English Church history. Cambridge 1959.

McAdoo, H. R. The structure of Caroline moral theology. 1949.

—— The spirit of Anglicanism: a survey of Anglican theological method in the 17th century. New York 1965.

Cragg, G. R. From Puritanism to the age of reason: a study of changes in religious thought within the Church of England 1660–1700. Cambridge 1950, 1966.

—— The Church and the age of reason 1648–1789. 1960 (Pelican).

Simon, I. Three Restoration divines: Barrow, South and Tillotson, selected sermons. Vol 1, Paris 1967.

JOSEPH ALLEINE
1634–68
§ 1

A call to Archippus: or an humble and earnest petition to some ejected ministers. 1664.

An alarme to unconverted sinners. 2 pts 1672, 1673 (with prefaces by R. Baxter and R. Alleine), 1678, 1695, 1703 etc, 1879.

A sure guide to heaven [i.e. Pt 1 of An alarme to unconverted sinners, above]. 1675, 1688, 1689, 1691, 1700 etc.

Remaines. [Ed R. Alleine] 1674.

§ 2

Alleine, Theodosia. The life and death of Alleine [with introd by R. Baxter]. 1672, 1673, 1677, 1822, 1832, 1838.

Stanford, C. Alleine: his companions and times. [1861].

RICHARD ALLEINE
1611–81

Godly fear. 1664, 1674. Sermons.
The world conquered. 1668. Sermons.
A rebuke to backsliders and a spur for loiterers. 1677, 1684. Sermons.
Vindiciae pietatis: or a vindication of godliness. 1663, 1664, 3 pts 1663–6.
The godly man's portion [pt 2 of Vindiciae pietatis]. 1663, 1671.
Heaven opened [pt 3 of Vindiciae pietatis]. 1665, 1666.

RICHARD ALLESTREE
1619–81

Collections

Eighteen sermons. 1669.
Forty sermons whereof twenty-one are now first published. 2 pts Oxford 1684. With biographical sketch by John Fell.

§ 1

A paraphrase and annotations upon the epistles of St Paul [with A. Woodhead and O. Walker as co-authors]. 1675, 1702, 1708.
The whole duty of man. 1658, 2 pts 1659, 1660, 1664, 1668, 1670 etc. Anon; many anon continuations.

ISAAC BARROW
1630–77

Collections

Works. Ed J. Tillotson, with memoir by Abraham Hill 4 vols 1683–7, 3 vols 1700 (English works only), 1716, 1722, 1741, 6 vols 1751, Oxford 1818, 5 vols 1820–1, 8 vols Oxford 1830, 7 vols 1830–1, 3 vols Edinburgh 1841–2 (with life by J. Hamilton).
Theological works. Ed A. Napier 9 vols Cambridge 1859. Life by W. Whewell prefixed to vol 9.
Sermons preached upon several occasions. [Ed J. Tillotson] 1678, 1679, 1680.
Several sermons against evil speaking. [Ed J. Tillotson] 1678, 1678, 1682.
Of the love of God and our neighbour in several sermons. [Ed J. Tillotson] 1680.
Of contentment, patience and resignation to the will of God. [Ed J. Tillotson] 1685. Sermons.
Practical discourses upon the consideration of our latter end. [Ed J. Tillotson] 1694.
Sermons selected from the works of Barrow. 2 vols Oxford 1798–1810.
[Twenty-one sermons]. Ed Ch. Wordsworth in Christian institutes vol 2, 1837.
[Selected sermons]. Ed J. Brogden in Illustrations of the liturgy and ritual vol 2, 1842.
[Selected sermons]. Ed I. Simon in Three Restoration divines: Barrow, South and Tillotson vol 1, Paris 1967.

§ 1

The duty and reward of bounty to the poor. 1671, 1677, 1680. A sermon.
A sermon upon the Passion. 1677, 1678, 1682.
A treatise of the Pope's supremacy, to which is added A discourse concerning the unity of the Church. Ed J. Tillotson 1680.

A brief exposition of the Lord's prayer and the decalogue; with the doctrine of the sacraments. Ed J. Tillotson 1681.
A brief exposition on the Creed, the Lord's prayer and Ten Commandments, with the doctrine of the sacraments. 1697.
A defence of the Trinity. 1697. A sermon.
Also mathematical works.

§ 2

Osmond, P. H. Barrow: his life and times. 1944.
Simon, I. Tillotson's Barrow. E Studies 45 1964.

WILLIAM BATES
1625–99

Collections

Works. 1700, 1723, 4 vols 1815.
Sermons upon death and eternal judgment. 1683.
The danger of prosperity. 1685. Sermons.
Sermons preached on several occasions. 1693.
Sermons on forgiveness. 1696.

§ 1

The harmony of divine attributes. 1674, 1697 (4th edn).
Considerations on the existence of God and of the immortality of the soul. 1676, 2 vols 1677.
The four last things. 1691, 1691.
Spiritual perfection. 1699.

WILLIAM BEVERIDGE
1637–1708

Collections

Works, containing all his sermons [ed T. Gregory] with an account of his life and writings [by J. Kimber]. 2 vols 1720, 1729, 6 vols Oxford 1817–18.
Works, with a memoir and a critical examination of the writings. Ed T. H. Horne 9 vols 1824.
Theological works. [Ed J. Bliss] 12 vols Oxford 1842–8 (Lib of Anglo-Catholic Theology vols 11–12).

§ 1

Codex canonum ecclesiae primitivae vindicatus ac illustratus. 1678.
The great necessity and advantage of publick prayers and frequent communion. 1708, 1750 (9th edn).
Private thoughts upon religion digested into twelve articles. 1709, 1720 (10th edn).

GEORGE BULL
1634–1710

Collections

G. Bulli opera omnia. Ed J. E. Grabe 6 pts 1703, 1 vol 1721 (enlarged); tr 2 vols 1725, 3 vols Oxford 1851–5.
Works, collected and revised by E. Burton. 7 vols Oxford 1827, 6 vols 1846. Includes Nelson's Life.
Some important points of primitive Christianity maintained in several sermons. Ed R. Bull, with life by R. Nelson 4 vols 1713, 1714, 3 vols Oxford 1816.

§ 1

Harmonia apostolica. 1669–70; tr T. Wilkinson 1801 (abridged), Oxford 1842, London 1844.
Examen censurae [of Harmonia apostolica]. 1676; tr Oxford 1843.

Apologia pro harmonica. 1676.
Defensio fidei Nicaenae. Oxford 1685, 1688; tr 2 vols Oxford 1851–2.
Judicium ecclesiae catholicae [de divinitate Christi]. Oxford 1694, Amsterdam 1696; tr T. Rankin 1719, 1825.
A vindication of the Church of England. 1719.

§ 2

Nelson, R. The life of Bull, with the history of those controversies in which he was engaged. 1714.
Teale, W. H. Lives of English divines: George Bull. 1846.

JOHN EACHARD
1636?–97
Collections

Works. Ed with a life by F. Davies 3 vols 1774–3.

§ 1

The grounds and occasions of the contempt of the clergy and religion enquired into. 1670 (anon, at least 3 edns), 3 pts 1672 (8th edn, adds Some observations on the answer thereto, 6th edn, and Mr Hobbs's state of nature considered, 4th edn), 1685, 1698–6, 1705 (as Dr Eachard's works), 1712 (with Five letters), 2 vols 1772 (rev); ed E. Arber in An English garner vol 7, 1903.
Some observations upon the answer [by John Bramhall] to An enquiry into the grounds and occasions of contempt of the clergy. 1671 (anon, 3 edns), 1672, 1705 (7th edn).
Mr Hobbs's state of nature considered; to which are added Five letters. 1672 (anon, 3 edns), 1685, 1696; ed P. Ure, Liverpool 1958.
Some opinions of Mr Hobbs considered in a second dialogue. 1673. Anon.
A free and impartial inquiry into the causes of that esteem and honour that the nonconforming preachers are generally held in with their followers. 1673. Anon.

JOHN FELL
1625–86

The interest of England stated. 1659; ed F. Maseres in Select tracts pt 2, 1815.
Life of Dr Allestree. Prefixed to Forty sermons, Oxford 1684.
Life of Dr Henry Hammond. 1661, 1662 etc; ed C. Wordsworth in Ecclesiastical biography vol 5, 1818.
Seasonable advice to Protestants, shewing the necessity of maintaining the established religion in opposition to Popery. 1688.
S. Cypriani opera. Oxford 1682, 1691. Ed Fell.
For The whole duty of man *see under Allestree, above.*

GEORGE HICKES
1642–1715
Collections

Sermons on various subjects. 2 vols 1713.
Posthumous discourses. Ed N. Spinckes 1726.
Thirteen sermons on practical subjects. Ed N. Spinckes 1741.

§ 1

An apologetical vindication of the Church of England. 1687 (anon), 1706 (rev).
The harmony of divinity and law [on non-resistance]. 1684.

Institutiones grammaticae Anglo-Saxonicae et Mœso-Gothicae. 3 pts Oxford 1689–88, 1 vol 1703.
The doctrine of passive obedience and jure divino disproved. 1689.
An apology for the new separation. 1691.
Linguarum vett. septentrionalium thesaurus grammatico-criticus et archaeologicus. 2 vols Oxford 1703–5.
The constitution of the Catholick Church and the nature and consequences of schism. 1716.
Two treatises on the Christian priesthood. 1707, 2 vols 1711 (3rd edn enlarged), 1715 (with suppl); ed J. Barrow 3 vols Oxford 1847–8 (Lib of Anglo-Catholic Theology).
See also col 723, below.

THOMAS KEN
1637–1711
Collections

[Poetical] works, published from original manuscripts. Ed W. Hawkins 4 vols 1721.
Poems, devotional and didactic. Ed J.R. 1835.
Prose works, with some of his letters and his life by W. Hawkins. Ed J. T. Round 1838.
Prose works, now first collected and edited with a biographical notice by W. Benham. 1889.

§ 1

A manual of prayers for the use of scholars of Winchester College. 1674, 1736 (25th edn).
The practice of divine love. 1685.
An exposition of the Church catechism. 1685, 1686, 1696, 1703.
Occasional prayers; A paraphrase on the Creed; A paraphrase on the Lord's prayer. 1708.
A crown of glory, the reward of the righteous: being meditations upon the vicissitude of all sublunary enjoyments. 1725.

§ 2

Hawkins, W. Life of Ken. 1713; rptd in Ken, Prose works, 1838.
Bowles, W. L. Life of Ken. 2 vols 1830.
Plumptre, E. H. Life of Ken. 2 vols 1888, 1890 (rev).
Rice, H. A. L. Ken, Bishop and non-juror. 1958.
Cowley, P. Ken, Bishop of Bath and Wells 1685–91. 1961.

SAMUEL PARKER
1640–88

A free and impartial censure of the Platonick philosophy. Oxford 1666, 1667.
An account of the nature and extent of the divine dominion of goodness. Oxford 1666.
Tentamina physico-theologica de Deo. 1665.
A discourse of ecclesiastical politie. 1670.
A defence and continuation of the ecclesiastical politie. 1671.
Disputationes de Deo et providentia divina. 1678, 1714.
A demonstration of the divine authority of the law of nature and of the Christian religion. 2 pts 1681.
The case of the Church of England. 1681.
An account of the government of the Church for the first six hundred years. 1683.
Religion and loyalty. 2 pts 1684–5.
Reasons for abrogating the tests imposed upon all members of Parliament. 1688, 1688, Edinburgh 1688.
A discourse sent to the late King James to persuade him to embrace the Protestant religion. 1690.
Reverendi Patris, S. Parker, de rebus sui temporis commentariorum libri quatuor. 1726; tr T. Newlin as

History of his own time, 1727, 1728 ('with remarks upon each book, and an impartial account of Parker's life and his conversion from Presbytery to Popery'), 1730 (as Bishop Parker's History: or the Tories chronicle from the restauration of King Charles II to the year 1680).

WILLIAM SHERLOCK
1641?–1707
Collections
Sermons. 2 vols 1719, 1755 (4th edn).

§ 1
A discourse concerning the knowledge of Jesus Christ. 1674, 1674.
A discourse about Church unity: being a defence of Dr Stillingfleet. 1681 (anon); Continuation, 1682 (anon).
The case of resistance to the supreme powers. 1684, 1690.
A short summary of the principal controversies between the Church of England and the Church of Rome. 1687.
A preservative against Popery. 1688 (5 edns).
A letter to a member of the Convention. 1688.
A vindication of some Protestant principles of Church-unity from the charge of agreement with the Church of Rome. 1688, 1688.
A practical discourse concerning death. 1689, 1735 (22nd edn).
Proposals of terms of union between the Church and dissenters. 1689.
A vindication of the doctrine of the Trinity. 1690, 1694 (3rd edn).
A practical discourse concerning a future judgment. 1692, 1692, 1739 (11th edn).
The present state of the Socinian controversy. 1698.
For Sherlock's writings on the Socinian argument see DNB.

ROBERT SOUTH
1634–1716
Collections
[Five] sermons preached upon several occasions. Oxford 1679.
Twelve sermons. [Vol 1], 1692; vol 2, 1694; vols 1–2, 1697; vol 3, 1698; vols 1–3, 1704; vols 1–4, 1715, 1718, 1722; vols 5–6, 1717; vols 1–6, 1727, 1737.
Five additional volumes of sermons first printed from the author's manuscripts. 1744.
Sermons preached upon several occasions. 7 vols Oxford 1823, 5 vols Oxford 1842, 4 vols 1843, 2 vols 1840–65.

§ 1
Musica incantans. Oxford 1655, 1667; tr 1700. A Latin poem.
Interest deposed and truth restored, in two sermons. Oxford 1660, 1668.
Posthumous works [including Memoirs]. 1717, 1721 (as Memoirs of Dr South).
Opera posthuma latina. 1717.
Animadversions upon Dr Sherlock's Vindication of the doctrine of the Trinity. 1693. Anon.
Tritheism charged upon Dr Sherlock's new notion of the Trinity. 1695. Anon.
A short history of Valentinus Gentilis the tritheist, translated into English for the use of Dr Sherlock. 1696. Anon.
Decreti oxoniensis vindicatio. 1696. Anon.

§ 2
Memoirs of the life of Dr South. 1717 (in Posthumous works), 1721.

Sutherland, J. R. Robert South. REL 1 1960.
Simon, I. In her Three Restoration divines: Barrow, South and Tillotson, Paris 1967.

EDWARD STILLINGFLEET
1635–99
Collections
Works, with his life [by R. Bentley]. 6 vols 1707–10.
Sermons preached on several occasions. 4 vols 1696–1701.
Sermons preached on several occasions. 1673.
Six sermons. 1669.
Miscellaneous discourses on several occasions. Ed J. Stillingfleet 1735.

§ 1
Irenicum. 1659, 1661, 1662, 1662, 1681.
Origines sacrae: or a rational account of the grounds of the Christian faith. 1662, 1663, 1666, 1675, 1702 (7th edn).
A rational account of the grounds of the Protestant religion: being a vindication of Archbishop Laud's relation of a conference between himself and J. Fisher, a Jesuit. 1664, 1665, 1681.
A letter to a deist. 1677.
Several conferences between a Romish priest, a fanatic chaplain and a divine of the Church of England. 1679.
The mischief of separation. 1680 (4 edns).
The unreasonableness of separation. 1681, 1682.
Origines britannicae: or the antiquities of the British Church. 1685; ed T. P. Pantin 2 vols Oxford 1842.
The doctrines and practices of the Church of Rome truly represented. 1686 (3 edns).
The doctrine of the Trinity and transubstantiation compared. 2 pts 1687.
A discourse concerning the doctrine of Christ's satisfaction. 2 pts 1696–1700, 3 pts 1697–1700.
A discourse in vindication of the doctrine of the Trinity. 1696, 1697.
The Bishop of Worcester's answer to Mr Locke's letter. 1697.
The Bishop of Worcester's answer to Mr Locke's second letter. 1698.
A discourse concerning the unreasonableness of a new separation on account of the oaths. 1705.

§ 2
Nankivell, J. W. H. Stillingfleet, Bishop of Worcester. Worcester 1946.

THOMAS TENISON
1636–1715
§ 1
The creed of Mr Hobbes examined. 1670, 1671.
Baconiana. 1678.
A discourse of idolatry. 1678.
A discourse concerning a guide in matters of faith. 1683. Anon.
A true account of the conference held about religion between Andrew Pulton and Thomas Tenison. 1687 (4 edns).
Difference betwixt the Protestant and Socinian methods. 1687.
Notes of the Church as laid down by Cardinal Bellarmine examined and confuted. 1688.
A discourse concerning the ecclesiastical commission opened in the Jerusalem chamber. 1689.

§2

Memoirs of the life and times of Tenison, late Archbishop of Canterbury. [1715] (3 edns).

Carpenter, E. Tenison: his life and times. 1948.

JOHN TILLOTSON
1630–94
Collections

Works, containing fifty-four sermons and the Rule of faith. 1696, 1735 (10th edn).

[Two hundred sermons]. Ed R. Barker 14 vols 1695–1704, 2 vols 1712, 1735 (5th edn). From 1717 the Works include 254 sermons and the Rule of faith.

Works. Ed T. Birch 3 vols 1752, 10 vols 1820. Includes a life, also issued separately, and 255 sermons.

Sermons preached upon several occasions. 1671, 1673, 1678; vol 2, 1678; vols 1–2, 1679, 1685, 1688, 1694.

Sermons and discourses [vol 3]. 1686, 1687, 1691, 1694.

Sermons concerning the divinity and incarnation of our Saviour. 1693.

Sermons preached upon several occasions, vol 4. 1694.

Six sermons. 1694.

[Selected] sermons. Ed G. W. Weldon 1886.

The golden book of Tillotson. Ed J. Moffat 1926. Extracts.

§1

About 30 sermons pbd separately by himself; many more after his death.

The morning exercise at Cripplegate. In Samuel Annesley, The morning exercise at Cripplegate, 1661. Anon.

The wisdom of being religious. 1664.

The rule of faith. 1666, 1676, 1688.

§2

H[utchinson], F. The life of Tillotson compiled from the minutes of [Edward] Young. 1717.

Birch, Thomas. Life. 1752.

Sykes, N. The sermons of Archbishop Tillotson. Theology 58 1955.

Simon, I. In her Three Restoration divines: Barrow, South and Tillotson, Paris 1967.

B. THE EIGHTEENTH-CENTURY DIVINES

General Studies

Stephen, L. History of English thought in the 18th century. 2 vols 1876, 1927 (rev).

Woodforde, J. The diary of a country parson. Ed J. Beresford 5 vols 1924–31, 2 vols 1968.

Sykes, N. Edmund Gibson, Bishop of London. Oxford 1926.

—— Church and State in England in the 18th century. Cambridge 1934.

—— Archbishop Wake and the Whig party 1716–23. Cambridge Historical Jnl 3 1945.

Crane, R. S. Anglican apologetics and the idea of progress 1699–1745. MP 31 1934; rptd in his Idea of the humanities and other essays vol 2, Chicago 1967.

Cragg, G. R. From Puritanism to the Age of Reason. Cambridge 1950.

—— Reason and authority in the eighteenth century. Cambridge 1964.

Knox, R. A. Enthusiasm. Oxford 1950.

Raven, C. E. Natural religion and Christian theology. 2 vols Cambridge 1953.

Best, G. F. A. Temporal pillars: Queen Anne's bounty, the Ecclesiastical Commissioners and the Church of England. Cambridge 1964.

Davies, R. and G. Rupp (ed). A history of the Methodist Church in Great Britain. Vol 1, 1965.

Curtis, L. P. Anglican moods of the eighteenth century. Hamden Conn 1966.

FRANCIS ATTERBURY
1662–1732
Collections

The epistolary correspondence, visitation charges, speeches and miscellanies, with historical notes. Ed J. Nichols 5 vols 1783–90, 1789–98 (as Miscellaneous works).

Fourteen sermons preached on several occasions; together with a large vindication of the doctrine contained in the sermon preached at the funeral of Thomas Burnet. 1708.

Sermons and discourses on several subjects and occasions. Vols 1–2, 1723, 1726, 1730; vols 3–4, ed T. Moore 1734; 4 vols 1735, 1737, 1740.

§1

A letter to a Convocation man concerning the rights, powers and privileges of that body. 1697.

A discourse occasioned by the death of Lady Cutts. 1698.

The rights, powers and privileges of an English Convocation stated and vindicated. 1700, 1701.

The power of the Lower House of Convocation to adjourn itself vindicated. 1701.

A letter [A second, A third letter] to a clergyman in the country concerning the choice of members for Convocation. 3 vols 1701–2.

The case of the schedule stated. 1702.

The parliamentary original and rights of the Lower House of Convocation cleared. 1702.

A faithful account of some transactions in the last three sessions of the present Convocation. 4 pts 1702–5.

The mitre and the crown: or a real distinction between them. 1711.

English advice, to the freeholders of England. 1714.

Letters

Letters of Pope to Atterbury when in the Tower of London. Ed J. Nichols 1859.

Williams, R. F. Memoirs and correspondence of Fr Atterbury. 2 vols 1869.

Letters of Canon W. Stratford. In Portland mss vol 7, 1901 (Historical Mss Commission).

§2

Beeching, H. C. Francis Atterbury. 1909.

SAMUEL CLARKE
1675–1729
Collections

Works. 4 vols 1738. With Life by B. Hoadly.

Sermons. Ed J. Clarke, with life by B. Hoadly 10 vols 1730–1, 2 vols Dublin 1734, 11 vols 1749 (7th edn), 8 vols 1756.

Six sermons. 1718.

Seventeen sermons. 1724.

Eighteen sermons. 1734.

Forty sermons. Ed S. Clapham 1806.

§ I

Three practical essays on baptism, confirmation, repentance. 1699.
A paraphrase on the four Evangelists. 2 vols 1701-2, 1 vol 1714 etc.
A demonstration of the being and attributes of God. 1705, 1706 (corrected); abridged by G. Burnet in A defence of natural and revealed religion vol 2, 1737.
A discourse concerning the unchangeable obligations of natural religion and the truth of the Christian revelation [8 sermons]. 1706; rptd in A collection of theological tracts vol 4, 1785, 1791.
The scripture-doctrine of the Trinity. 1712, 1732 (3rd edn).
An exposition of the Church catechism. 1729, 1730.
For Clarke's philosophical works see col 737, below.

EDMUND GIBSON
1669-1748

A short state of some present questions in Convocation. 1700.
The right of the Archbishop of Canterbury to prorogue the whole of Convocation. 1701.
Synodus anglicana: or the constitution and proceedings of an English Convocation. 1672 (for 1702).
The pretended independence of the Lower House of Convocation. 1703.
Family devotions. 1705, 1750 (18th edn).
Three charges to the clergy of his diocese. 3 vols 1717-42.
Three pastoral letters occasioned by some late writings in favour of infidelity. 3 vols 1728-31, 1732, 1735 (7th edn).
A preservative against Popery, in several discourses. 1738.
Pastoral letter against lukewarmness on the one hand and enthusiasm on the other. 1739, 1741, 1748.
Observations upon the conduct and behaviour of a certain sect usually distinguished by the name of Methodists. 1740, 1744.
Pastoral letter occasioned by the present dangers and exciting to serious reformation of life and manners. 1745.
For Gibson's historical works see col 691, below.

BENJAMIN HOADLY
1676-1761

Collections

Works. Ed J. Hoadly 3 vols 1773. With a life and a list of the tracts relating to the Bangorian controversy.
Sixteen sermons. 1754.
Twenty sermons. 1755.

§ I

A letter to Mr Fleetwood occasioned by his Essay on miracles. 1702.
A letter to a clergyman concerning the votes of the Bishops. 1703.
The reasonableness of conforming to the Church of England. 1703, 1712.
A persuasive to lay-conformity: or the reasonableness of constant communion with the Church of England. 1704.
A defence of the reasonableness of conformity. 1705.

The measures of submission to the civil magistrate considered. 1706, 1708, 1710, 1718.
A defence of episcopal ordinations. 1707.
The happiness of the present establishment and the unhappiness of absolute monarchy: a sermon. 1708.
The original and institution of civil government discussed. 1710.
The thoughts of an honest Tory upon the present proceedings of that party. 1710.
A serious enquiry into the present state of the Church of England: or the danger to the Church from the rashness of the clergy. 1711.
Several discourses concerning the terms of acceptance with God. 1711.
A preservative against the principles and practices of the non-jurors both in Church and State. 1716.
The nature of the Kingdom or Church of Christ. 1717. A sermon.
The common rights of subjects defended, and the nature of the sacramental test considered. 1718, 1719.
An answer to the representation drawn up by the committee of the Lower House of Convocation. 1718.
A plain account of the nature and end of the sacrament of the Lord's Supper. 1735, 1751, 1761, 1767, 1772. Anon.

Letters

The correspondence of J. Hughes and Hoadly. 1773.

§ 2

Sykes, N. Benjamin Hoadly, Bishop of Bangor. In The social and political ideas of some English thinkers of the Augustan age, ed F. J. C. Hearnshaw 1928.

RICHARD HURD
1720-1808
Collections

Works. 8 vols 1811.
Moral and political dialogues. 1759, 1760; 3 vols 1765, 1771, 1776, 1788 (with Letters on chivalry).
Sermons preached at Lincoln's Inn between 1765 and 1776. 3 vols 1776-80, 1785.

§ I

The mischiefs of enthusiasm and bigotry. 1752. A sermon.
An introduction to the study of the prophecies concerning the Christian Church. 1772, 1772, 1773, 1776, 1788; ed E. Bickersteth 1839. 12 sermons.
A charge to the clergy of Lichfield and Coventry. 1776.
For Hurd's literary criticism see col 720, below.

Letters

The correspondence of Hurd and William Mason; and Letters of Hurd to Thomas Gray. Ed E. H. Pearce and L. Whibley, Cambridge 1932.
Nankivell, J. Extracts from the destroyed letters of Hurd to William Mason. MLR 45 1950.

§ 2

Kilvert, F. Memoirs of the life and writings of Bishop Hurd. 1860.
Evans, A. W. Warburton and the Warburtonians. Oxford 1932.

WHITE KENNETT
1660–1728

§ 1

A dialogue between two friends [a Jacobite and a Williamite], occasioned by the late Revolution. 1689.

An occasional letter on the subject of English convocations. 1701.

Ecclesiastical synods and parliamentary convocations in the Church of England. 1701.

The present state of Convocation. 1702.

The case of impropriations and of the augmentation of vicarages and other insufficient cures. 1704.

The Christian scholar. 1708, 1710 (5th edn).

A vindication of the Church and clergy of England. 1709.

A true answer to Dr Sacheverell's sermon. 1709.

Bibliothecae americanae primordia. 1713.

Monitions and advices delivered to the clergy of the diocese of Peterborough at the primary visitation. 2 pts 1720.

An historical account of the discipline and jurisdiction of the Church of England. 1730 (2nd edn).

§ 2

[Sharpe, J.] Short remarks on some passages in the life of Dr Kennett. 1730.

[Newton, W.] The life of White Kennett, with some original letters. 1730.

Bennett, G. V. White Kennett, Bishop of Peterborough: a study in the political and ecclesiastical history of the early eighteenth century. 1957.

JOHN NEWTON
1725–1807

Collections

Works. 6 vols 1808, 12 vols 1821, Edinburgh 1827 (with a memoir by R. Cecil), 1830, 1834, 1836, London 1839 (with a life by R. Cecil), Edinburgh 1840.

Sermons preached in the parish church of Olney. 1767.

Letters, sermons and a review of ecclesiastical history. Edinburgh 1780, 1787.

§ 1

An authentic narrative of some particulars in the life of [Newton] in a series of letters to Mr Haweis. 1764, 1765, 1775, 1792, 1799.

A review of ecclesiastical history. 1770.

Apologia: four letters to a minister of an independent Church. 1784.

Messiah: fifty discourses on the scriptural passages which form the subject of the Oratorio. 2 vols 1786.

See also under William Cowper, col 431, above.

Letters

Cardiphonia. 1781. A selection from his religious correspondence.

Letters to a wife. 2 vols 1793.

Forty-one letters on religious subjects. 1807, 1813, 1825, 1830, 1831.

Sixty-eight letters to a clergyman and his family [1791–1801]. 1845.

One hundred and twenty-nine letters from Newton to the Rev William Bull [1773–1805]. 1847.

Letters. 1960.

§ 2

Callis, J. Newton: sailor, preacher, pastor and poet. 1908.

Martin, B. The ancient mariner and the authentic narrative. 1949.

—— Newton: a biography. 1950.

—— Newton and the slave trade. 1961.

THOMAS SECKER
1693–1768

Collections

Works. Ed B. Porteus and G. Stinton 6 vols Dublin 1775, 4 vols 1792, 6 vols 1825.

§ 1

Fourteen sermons on several occasions. 1766, 1771.

Lectures on the catechism of the Church of England. 2 vols 1769, 1771, 1777, 1791, 1799, 1814, 1824 etc.

Sermons on severals ubjects. Ed B. Porteus and G. Stinton 7 vols 1770–71. With a life.

Eight charges to the clergy of Oxford and Canterbury. Ed B. Porteus and G. Stinton 1769.

§ 2

Porteus, B. A review of the life and character of Archbishop Secker. 1773.

Sykes, N. In his From Sheldon to Secker, Cambridge 1959.

THOMAS SHERLOCK
1678–1761

Collections

Works. Ed T. S. Hughes 5 vols 1830. With a life.

Discourses preached at the Temple church. 4 vols 1754–8, 1755, 1755–8, 1756–64, Edinburgh 1770, 5 vols 1772–5 (with a life), 1797.

§ 1

Remarks upon the late Bishop of Bangor's [B. Hoadly's] treatment of the clergy and Convocations. 1717. Anon.

A vindication of the Corporation and Test Acts. 1718.

The proceedings of the Vice-Chancellor and University of Cambridge against Dr Bentley, stated and vindicated. 1719.

The use and intent of prophecy in the several ages of the world. 1725. Sermons.

The trial of the witnesses of the resurrection of Jesus. 1729 etc, 1800 (16th edn).

A letter to the clergy and people of London and Westminster on occasion of the late earthquakes. 1750.

§ 2

Carpenter, E. Thomas Sherlock. 1936.

AUGUSTUS MONTAGUE TOPLADY
1740–78

Collections

Sermons and essays. 1793.

Works, with a memoir by W. Row. 1794, 6 vols 1825, 1828, 1841, 1853.

Hymns and sacred poems. 1860. With a life.

§ 1

Poems on sacred subjects. 1759.

A letter to Mr Wesley. 1770.

More work for Mr Wesley. 1772.

Historic proof of the doctrinal Calvinism of the Church of England. 2 vols 1774.

The Church of England vindicated from the charge of Arminianism. 1779.

The scheme of Christian and philosophical necessity asserted, in opposition to Mr Wesley's tract. 1775.
Psalms and hymns for public and private worship. 1776 etc.
The Rev Mr Toplady's dying avowal of his religious sentiments. 1778.

§2

Wright, T. Augustus M. Toplady. 1912.
Wilkins, H. J. An enquiry concerning Toplady and his hymn Rock of ages. Bristol 1938.
Howell, A. C. Toplady and Quarles' Emblems. SP 57 1960.

HENRY VENN
1725–97
§1

Sermons. 1759.
The compleat duty of man. 1763, 1807 (9th edn).
Examination of Dr Priestley's Free addresses on the Lord's Supper. 1769.
A token of respect to the memory of the Rev George Whitefield. 1770. A funeral sermon.
Mistakes in religion exposed. 1774, 1807.
Memoirs of Sir John Barnard. 1776, 1807, 1825.

§2

Venn, J. and H. The life and a selection from the letters of the Rev Henry Venn. 1834, 1835, 1836.
Loane, M. L. Henry Venn, Fellow of Queen's College. In his Cambridge and the evangelical succession, 1952.

CHARLES WESLEY
1707–88
Collections

Hymns and sacred poems. 2 vols Bristol 1749.
Sermons, with a memoir. Ed S. Wesley 1816.
Representative verse. Ed F. Baker 1962.

§1

An epistle to the Rev Mr John Wesley. 1755.
An epistle to the Rev Mr George Whitefield. 1755.
An elegy on the late Rev George Whitefield. 1771.
Journal. Ed T. Jackson 2 vols 1849.
The early journal 1736–9. Ed J. Telford 1909.

§2

Jackson, T. Life and correspondence of Charles Wesley. 2 vols 1841.
— Memoirs of the Rev Charles Wesley. 1848.
Colquhoun, F. Charles Wesley. 1947.
Baker, F. Charles Wesley as revealed in his letters. 1948.
— Charles Wesley's verse. 1964.
Gill, F. C. Charles Wesley the first Methodist. 1964.
Myers, E. Singer of a thousand songs: a life of Charles Wesley. New York 1965.
See also under John Wesley, below.

JOHN WESLEY
1703–91
Bibliographies etc

Green, R. Bibliography of the works of John and Charles Wesley. 1896, 1906.

Collections

Works. 32 vols Bristol 1771–4; ed T. Jackson 14 vols 1829–31; 15 vols 1856–62 (with a life by J. Beecham) (11th edn); 14 vols 1872, rptd Grand Rapids Michigan 1958–9.
[44] Sermons on several occasions. 4 vols Bristol 1746–60, 1 vol 1944.
Sermons on several occasions. 9 vols 1788–1800; ed T. Jackson 2 vols 1825.
Standard sermons. Ed E. H. Sugden 1921.
A collection of psalms and hymns. Charlestown 1737.
The poetical works of John and Charles Wesley. 13 vols 1868–72.
Works. Ed F. Baker et al, Oxford 1975–.

§1

For the sermons, many of which were pbd singly, see Collections, *above.*
A dialogue between a predestinarian and his friend. Bristol 1742 (3rd edn).
An earnest appeal to men of reason and religion. Bristol 1743 (2nd edn).
A farther appeal. 1745.
Advice to the people called Methodists. 1745.
A second dialogue between an antinomian and his friend. 1745.
The principles of a Methodist. Bristol 1746.
Primitive physick: or an easy and natural method of curing most diseases. Bristol 1747, Nottingham 1805 (26th edn); ed W. H. Paynter, Plymouth 1958.
The character of a Methodist. Bristol 1747, 1802 (13th edn), 1950.
A letter to a person lately joined with the people called Quakers. 1748.
A plain account of the people called Methodists. Bristol 1749, 1795 (9th edn), 1951.
A short address to the inhabitants of Ireland. Dublin 1749.
The nature, design and general rules of the United Societies. 1750 (6th edn).
Serious thoughts upon the perseverance of saints. 1751.
Popery calmly considered. 1752, 1814 (9th edn).
Serious thoughts occasioned by the late earthquake at Lisbon. Bristol 1755 (2nd edn).
Queries humbly proposed to Count Zinzendorff. 1755.
An address to the clergy. 1756.
The doctrine of original sin. Bristol 1757.
A preservative against unsettled notions in religion. Bristol 1758.
A blow at the root: or Christ stabbed in the house of his friends. 1762.
Thoughts on the imputed righteousness of Christ. Dublin 1762.
A survey of the wisdom of God in the Creation. 2 vols Bristol 1763.
The complete English dictionary. Bristol 1764.
Explanatory notes upon the Old Testament. Bristol 1765.
The witness of the Spirit. Bristol 1767.
A plain account of Christian perfection as believed and taught by John Wesley from 1725 to 1765. Bristol 1770 (3rd edn), 1797 (8th edn).
Free thoughts on the present state of public affairs. 1770. Anon.
Minutes of several conversations between the Rev Messieurs John and Charles Wesley, and others. 1770.
Thoughts upon slavery. 1774.
A calm address to our American colonies. Bristol 1775 etc.
A concise history of England. 4 vols 1776.
Some observations on liberty. Edinburgh 1776.
A serious address to the people of England. 1778.
Reflections on the rise and progress of the American rebellion. 1780.
A concise ecclesiastical history. 4 vols 1781. Anon.

A short account of the life and death of the Rev J. Fletcher. 1786.
Serious considerations concerning the doctrine of election and reprobation. 1790.
The Scripture doctrine concerning predestination. 1797.
Prayers. Ed F. C. Gill 1951; ed C. E. Vulliamy 1954; ed J. A. Kay 1958.

Letters, Diaries etc

Journal. 21 pts [1739]–91, 4 vols 1827; ed F. W. Macdonald 1906; ed N. Curnock 8 vols 1909–16; 4 vols 1922–30. Selection ed H. Martin 1955.
Letters. Ed J. Telford 1931, 1956; Selections, ed F. C. Gill 1956.

§2

Hampson, J. Memoirs of John Wesley. 3 vols Sunderland 1791.
Coke, T. and H. Moore. Life of John Wesley. 1792, 2 vols 1824–5.
Whitehead, J. Life of John and Charles Wesley. 2 vols 1793–6.
Southey, R. Life of Wesley. 2 vols 1820, 1846 (with Coleridge's notes).
Stevens, A. A history of Methodism. 3 vols 1860–70, 1863–5 (rev).
Birrell, A. John Wesley. 1938.
Green, V. H. H. The young Mr Wesley. 1961, 1964.
Marshall, D. John Wesley. Oxford 1965.

GEORGE WHITEFIELD
1714–70

Bibliographies

Austin, R. Bibliography of the works of Whitefield. Burnley [1916].

Collections

Works. Ed J. Gillies 6 vols 1771–2.
Hymns for social worship. 1753 etc, 1794 (35th edn), 1799 (rev and enlarged), 1821 (9th edn); ed W. Chapman 1836 etc.
Nine sermons. 1742; Five sermons, 1747; Six sermons, 1750; Ten sermons, 1760; Twelve sermons, 1771 (2nd edn); Twenty-three sermons, 1770.

§1

A short account of God's dealings with George Whitefield. 1740; A full account, 1747; A further account, 1747.
A letter to John Wesley in answer to his sermon on free grace. 1740.
Three letters [1–2 concerning Archbishop Tillotson; 3 to the inhabitants of Maryland]. Philadelphia 1740.
Observations on some fatal mistakes in [William Warburton's] The doctrine of grace. 1743.

A letter to the remaining disconsolate inhabitants of Lisbon. 1755.

Letters, Diaries etc

A journal of a voyage from London to Savannah. 2 pts 1738, 1740.
A continuation of the Rev Mr Whitefield's journal. 1739, 1741.
A further continuation. 1741.
Journals. Ed W. Wale 1905; ed I. Murray 1960, 1962 (complete).
A select collection of letters. 3 vols 1772.

§2

Philip, R. Life and times of George Whitefield. 1837.
Smith, G. T. The times and character of Whitefield. 1854.
Andrews, J. R. Whitefield: a light rising in obscurity. 1864, 1930 (7th edn).
Gledstone, J. P. Life and travels of Whitefield. 1871.
—— George Whitefield, field-preacher. 1900.
Tyerman, L. Life of Whitefield. 2 vols 1876–7. With bibliography.
Loane, M. Oxford and the evangelical succession. 1950.
Henry, S. C. Whitefield, wayfaring witness. New York 1957.

THOMAS WILSON
1663–1755

Collections

Works, with a life. Ed C. Cruttwell 2 vols Bath 1781, 8 vols Bath 1782–89, 1797–1808, 3 vols 1785; ed J. Keble 7 vols Oxford 1847–63 (Lib of Anglo-Catholic Theology).
Sermons. 1791, 4 vols 1795–6.
Thirty-three sermons. 2 vols 1823, 1825–7 etc.

§1

The principles and duties of Christianity in English and Manks. 1707, 1738 (6th edn).
The many advantages of a good language to any nation. 1724.
A short and plain instruction for the better understanding of the Lord's Supper. 1733 etc, 1819 (38th edn). The same work, in English and Manx, Whitehaven 1777.
The knowledge and practice of Christianity made easy: or an essay towards an instruction for the Indians. 1740, 1802 (17th edn).
The sacra privata: or private meditations and prayers. Ed C. Cruttwell, Bath 1781 etc.
Parochialia. Bath 1788 etc.
Diaries 1731–7 and 1750. Ed C. L. S. Linnell 1964.

C. THE EARLY QUAKERS

The library of the Friends House, London, contains the most comprehensive collection of Quaker books and mss, notably the Swarthmore mss, mainly unpbd. Joseph Smith, Descriptive catalogue of Friends' books, 3 vols with supplement (pbd 1867, but kept up to date) may be consulted there. See also his Bibliotheca antiquakeriana, 1873. The unpbd Swarthmore mss form a collection of about 1,400 original seventeenth-century letters, papers etc. For a bibliography of the letters in this collection see G. F. Nuttall, Early Quaker letters from the Swarthmore mss to 1660, calendared, indexed and annotated, 1952 (unpbd but available at Friends House and in a few American libraries).

General Studies

Penn, William. A brief account of the rise and progress of the people called Quakers. 1694. Introd to Fox's Journal, but also pbd separately.
Croese, G. The general history of the Quakers. 1696.

Sewel, William. The history of the Quakers. 1722.
Besse, J. A collection of the sufferings of the people called Quakers from 1650 to 1689. 1753.

Gough, J. A history of the people called Quakers. 4 vols Dublin 1789–90.

Clarkson, T. A portraiture of Quakerism. 3 vols 1806.

Rowntree, J. S. Quakerism past and present. 1859.

—— An inquiry into the truthfulness of Lord Macaulay's portraiture of George Fox. York 1861.

Janney, S. M. History of the religious society of Friends, from its rise to the year 1828. 4 vols Philadelphia 1861–70.

Penney, N. The first publishers of truth: early records of the introduction of Quakerism into the counties of England and Wales. 1907.

—— Extracts from State Papers relating to Friends 1654–72. 1910–11.

Braithwaite, W. C. The beginnings of Quakerism 1647–1660. 1912; rev H. J. Cadbury, Cambridge 1955.

—— The second period of Quakerism 1660–1725. 1919; rev H. J. Cadbury, Cambridge 1961.

Wright, L. M. The literary life of the early Friends 1650–1725. 1932.

Dalglish, D. N. People called Quakers. Oxford 1938.

Cadbury, H. J. (ed). The Swarthmore documents in America. 1940. 28 early Quaker letters now in USA.

—— Quakerism and early Christianity. 1957.

Sykes, N. The Quakers: a new look at their place in society. 1958.

GEORGE FOX
1624–91
Collections

Gospel truth demonstrated in a collection of doctrinal books given forth by Fox. 1706.

Works. Philadelphia 1831.

§ I

A declaration against all Popery. 1655.

The great misery of the great whore unfolded. 1659.

A battle-door for teachers and professors to learn singular and plural: you to many, and thou to one. 1660. By Fox, John Stubbs, Benjamin Furly.

Truth's triumph in the eternal power over the dark inventions of fallen man. 1661.

An answer to the arguments of the Jews. 1661.

The ancient simplicity as it was once witnessed unto. 1661.

Christ's light the only antidote to overcome and expel the poison of Satan's greatest temptations. 1662.

Three general epistles to be read in all the congregations of the righteous. 1664.

The arraignment of Popery. 1667.

Some principles of the elect people of God, scornfully called Quakers. 1671.

A looking-glass for the Jews. 1674.

Christian liberty commended. 1675.

Cain against Abel, representing New England's hierarchy. 1675.

The Christian judges so-called. 1676.

Concerning revelation, prophecy, measures and rule, and the inspiration and sufficiency of the spirit. 1676.

Concerning the true baptism and the false. 1676.

The beginning of tythes in the Law, and ending of tythes in the Gospel. 1676.

Concerning Christ, the spiritual and holy head over his holy Church. 1677.

Christ's parable of Dives and Lazarus. 1677.

What election and reprobation is clearly discovered. 1679.

Concerning the living God of truth. 1680.

The devil was and is the old informer against the righteous. 1682.

An encouragement for all to trust in the Lord. 1682.

Selection from the epistles. Ed S. Tuke 1825, 1848.

Fox's teaching of the indwelling presence of Christ. Selly Oak 1935. Quotations from Journal, below.

A day-book of counsel and comfort from the epistles of Fox. Ed L. V. Hodgkin 1937.

Fox's Book of miracles. Ed H. J. Cadbury, Cambridge 1948.

Letters, Diaries etc

A journal: or historical account of the life, travels, sufferings, Christian experiences and labours of love in the work of the ministry of Fox. 1694. Rev Thomas Ellwood; preface by William Penn. Called vol 1 of Journal.

A collection of epistles, letters and testimonials. 1698. Preface by George Whitehead. Called vol 2 of Journal.

A journal [i.e. vols 1–2]. 1709, 1765 etc; ed N. Penney 2 vols 1901–2; ed Penney, introd by T. E. Harvey 2 vols 1911; abridged Penney, introd by R. M. Jones 1924; ed J. L. Nickalls, introd by G. F. Nuttall, epilogue by H. J. Cadbury, Cambridge 1952 (with bibliography of mss and edns).

Autobiography, from the Journal. Ed H. S. Newman 1886; ed R. M. Jones, Philadelphia 1903.

A short journal and itinerary journal of Fox, now first published. Ed N. Penney, Cambridge 1925.

WILLIAM PENN
1644–1718
Collections

A collection of the works of Penn; to which is prefixed a Journal of his life, with many original letters. Ed J. Besse 2 vols 1726.

Select works; to which is prefixed a Journal. Ed J. Fathergill 1771, 5 vols 1782, 3 vols 1825.

The peace of Europe; The fruits of solitude and other writings. Ed J. V. Cheney 1906.

Selections from the works. Ed I. Sharpless 1909.

§ I

Sandy foundation shaken. 1668.

Innocency with her open face. 1669.

No cross, no crown. 1669 etc; ed J. D. Hilton 1902; ed N. Penney 1930.

The great case of liberty of conscience. 1670.

The people's ancient and just liberties asserted. 1670 etc.

A seasonable caveat against Popery. 1670.

A serious apology for the principles and practices of the people called Quakers. 1671. With G. Whitehead.

The spirit of truth vindicated. 1672.

The new witnesses proved old heretics. 1672. Against Muggleton.

The Christian Quaker and his divine testimony vindicated. 2 pts 1674–3, 1699. Pt 1 by Penn, pt 2 by G. Whitehead.

The continued cry of the oppressed for justice. 1675.

A treatise of oaths. 1675. With R. Richardson.

An address to Protestants upon the present conjunction. 1679, 1692.

A brief account of the province of Pennsylvania. 1681. Facs in Mass Historical Soc, Americana ser 115 1924.

A brief examination and state of liberty spiritual. 1681.

The frame of Government of the province of Pennsylvania. 1682; ed M. G. Brumbaugh and J. S. Walton, Philadelphia 1898.

A brief description of Pennsylvania. 1683.

A further account of the province of Pennsylvania and its improvements. 1685.

A persuasive to moderation to Church dissenters. 1686; in California State Library, Suto Branch, occasional papers, English ser 6 pt 4 1940.

A letter upon the subject of penal laws and tests. 1687; A second letter, 1687; A third letter, 1687.

Good advice to the Church of England, Roman Catholic and Protestant dissenter. 1687. Against penal laws and tests.

The reasonableness of toleration. 1687.

The speech of William Penn to his Majesty upon the delivering the Quakers' address [after the declaration of indulgence]. 1687.

The great and popular objection against the repeal of the penal laws and tests. 1688.

Three letters on the abolishment of the penal laws and tests. 1688.

A key to discern the difference between the Quakers and their adversaries. 1693.

Some fruits of solitude. 1693 etc; ed E. Gosse 1900; ed J. Clifford 1905; ed J. V. Cheney 1906.

An account of [his] travels in Holland and Germany anno 1677. 1694 etc; ed J. Barclay 1835.

A brief account of the rise and progress and the people called Quakers. 1694. First pbd as Preface to Fox's Journal, 1694.

A call to Christendom. 1695 (2nd edn).

Primitive Christianity revived. 1696, Dublin 1702, 1779 (5th edn).

Fruits of a father's love: being advice to his children. 1726, 1780 (8th edn).

The harmony of divine and heavenly doctrines. 1723 (2nd edn). By Penn, G. Whitehead et al.

An essay towards the present and future peace of Europe. Ed J. B. Braithwaite, Gloucester 1915.

Letters, Journal

My Irish journal 1669–70. Ed I. Grub 1952.

Letters from Penn to Charles II. Philadelphia 1826 (Historical Soc of Pennsylvania, Memoirs vol 1 pt 2).

Inedited letters. Philadelphia 1826 (Memoirs vol 2 pt 2).

Correspondence between Penn and J. Logan and others. Ed E. Armstrong, Philadelphia 1826 (Memoirs vols 9–10).

ISAAC PENINGTON
1616–79
Collections

The works of the long-mournful and sorely distressed Isaac Penington. 2 pts 1680–1, 2 vols 1761, 4 vols 1784, New York 1861–3.

§ I

A touchstone or trial of faith. 1648.

The great and soule troubler of the times: or a glimpse of the heart of man. 1649.

The fundamental right, safety and liberty of the people. 1651.

The life of a Christian. 1653.

Divine essays. 1654.

The scattered sheep sought after. 1659, 1665.

The new covenant of the gospel distinguished from the old covenant of the law. 1660.

The great question concerning the lawfulness or unlawfulness of swearing. 1661.

Concerning the sum and substance of our religion, who are called Quakers. 1667.

Of the Church in its first and pure state, in its declining state, in its declined state and in its recovery. 1668.

The holy truth and people defended. 1672.

Naked truth. 1674.

The flesh and blood of Christ, with a brief account concerning the people called Quakers. 1675.

Letters

Letters to his relations and friends. Ed J. Kendall 1796.

Letters, the greater part not published before. Ed J. Barclay 1828, 1844 (3rd edn).

ROBERT BARCLAY
1648–90
Collections

Truth triumphant through the spiritual warfare: Christian labours and writings of Barclay. 1692. Collected works, with preface by William Penn.

§ I

A catechism and confession of faith. 1673, 1803 (8th edn).

Theses theologicae. Ed B. Furly 2 pts Rotterdam 1674, 1675; tr 1711.

Theologiae verae Christianae apologia. Amsterdam 1676; tr as An apology for the true Christian divinity, Aberdeen 1678 etc; ed W. Allen 1837 (selections).

Quakerism confirmed: or a vindication of the chief doctrines and principles of the people called Quakers. 1676. With George Keith.

The anarchy of the Ranters and other libertines. 1676.

Universal love considered and established upon its right foundation. 1677.

Apology vindicated. 1679.

Barclay in brief: a condensation of Apology for the true Christian divinity. Ed E. P. Mather, Pendle Hill Pa 1941.

Reliquiae Barclaianae. Ed D. Barclay 1870.

THOMAS ELLWOOD
1639–1713
Collections

A collection of poems on various subjects. [1710–30 ?].

§ I

A seasonable dissuasive from persecution. 1683.

Rogero-mastix: a rod for William Rogers. 1685. Verse.

Sacred history: or the historical part of the Holy Scriptures. 1705–9, 1794 (5th edn).

The glorious brightness of the gospel day. 1707.

Davideis: a sacred poem. 1712 etc; ed W. Fischer, Heidelberg 1936.

The history of the life of Ellwood written by his own hand. Ed J. W[yeth] 1714, 1714, 1765, 1791; ed C. G. Crump 1900; ed S. Graveson 1906.

See col. 390, above.

D. THE MYSTICS

General Studies

Fox, George. A journal: or historical account of the life, travels and sufferings of George Fox. 1694; ed N. Penney and T. E. Harvey 2 vols 1911; ed J. L. Nickalls, Cambridge 1952.

Baxter, Richard. Reliquiae Baxterianae: or Mr Richard Baxter's narrative of the most memorable passages of his life and times. 1696.

Woodward, J. An account of the rise and progress of the religious societies. 1701 (3rd edn).

Southey, R. The life of Wesley, with notes by S. T. Coleridge. 2 vols 1846.

Marsden, J. B. History of Christian Churches and sects. 2 vols 1856.

Pattison, M. Tendencies of religious thought in England. In Essays and reviews, 1860, and Essays by Mark Pattison vol 2, Oxford 1889.

Blunt, J. H. Dictionary of sects, heresies, ecclesiastical parties and schools of religious thought. 1874.

Barclay, R. The inner life of the religious societies of the Commonwealth. 1876.

Stephen, L. History of English thought in the 18th century. 2 vols 1876, 1927 (rev).

Overton, J. H. and C. J. Abbey. The English Church in the 18th century. 2 vols 1878.

Vaughan, R. A. Hours with the mystics. 2 vols 1880.

Abbey, C. J. The English Church and its Bishops 1700–1800. 2 vols 1887.

Julian, J. A dictionary of hymnology 1892, 1907 (rev).

Skeats, H. S. A history of the Free Churches of England. 1894.

Inge, W. R. Christian mysticism. 1899.

—— Studies of English mystics. 1906.

Jones, R. M. Studies in mystical religion. 1909.

Underhill, E. Mysticism. 1911, 1930 (rev).

—— The mystics of the Church. [1925].

Bullett, G. The English mystics. 1950.

Langton, E. History of the Moravian Church. 1956.

WILLIAM LAW
1686–1761

Collections

Works. 9 vols 1753–76; ed G. B. Moreton 9 vols Brockenhurst 1892–3 (priv ptd) (with memoir).

Liberal and mystical writings. Ed W. S. Palmer and W. P. Du Bosc 1908.

Selected mystical writings. Ed with twenty-four essays in the mystical theology of William Law and Jacob Boehme by S. Hobhouse 1938, 1948 (rev).

The pocket William Law. Ed A. W. Hopkinson 1950. Abridged edn of Christian perfection, An appeal to all that doubt, and The spirit of prayer.

§1

A sermon preached at Hazelingfield 7 July 1713. 1713. Not collected.

The Bishop of Bangor's late sermon and his letter to Dr Snape in defence of it, answered. 1717 etc, 1721 (8th edn).

A second letter to the Bishop of Bangor. 1717.

A reply to the Bishop of Bangor's answer to the representation of the committee of Convocation. 1719.

Three letters to the Bishop of Bangor 1717–19. 1753; ed J. O. Nash and C. Gore as Law's Defence of Church principles, 1893.

Remarks upon the Fable of the bees. 1724, 1725, 1726 etc; ed F. D. Maurice, Cambridge 1844.

The absolute unlawfulness of the stage-entertainments fully demonstrated. 1726 etc, 1759 (4th edn).

A practical treatise of Christian perfection. 1726 etc; ed L. H. M. Soulsby 1901; ed J. J. Trebeck 1902; abridged by J. Wesley as The nature and design of Christianity, 1740 etc.

A serious call to a devout and holy life. 1728 etc, 1772 (10th edn); ed J. H. Overton 1898; ed C. Bigg 1899, 1906; ed N. Sykes 1955. Many selections.

The case of reason: or natural religion fairly stated in answer to [M. Tindal's] Christianity as old as the creation. 1731, 1755, 1757.

A demonstration of the errors of [Bishop Hoadly's] A plain account of the nature and end of the sacrament of the Lord's Supper. 1737 etc, 1757 (4th edn).

The grounds and reasons of Christian regeneration. 1739, 1750 (3rd edn).

An answer to Dr Trapp's Discourse of the folly, sin and danger of being righteous overmuch. 1740.

An appeal to all that doubt or disbelieve the truths of the gospel; to which are added Some animadversions upon Dr Trapp's late reply. 1740, 1742.

The spirit of prayer: or the soul rising out of the vanity of time into the riches of eternity. 2 pts 1749–50.

The way to divine knowledge. 1752.

The spirit of love: being an appendix to the Spirit of prayer. 2 pts 1752–4.

Reflections on a favourite amusement [i.e. the theatre]. 1756.

A short but sufficient confutation of Dr Warburton's Projected defence (as he calls it) of Christianity in his Divine legation of Moses. 1757.

Of justification by faith and works: a dialogue between a Methodist and a Churchman. 1760.

A humble, earnest and affectionate address to the clergy. 1761.

Letters

A collection of letters. Ed T. Law and G.W. 1760. Includes a tract called Christian piety freed from the many delusions of modern enthusiasts, by Philalethes, 1756 (2nd edn).

Letters to a lady inclined to enter into the communion of the Church of Rome. 1779. Written 1731–2 to Miss Dodwell, daughter of Henry Dodwell the nonjuror.

The divine indwelling: selection from the letters of Law. Ed A. Murray 1897.

The spirit in life: a selection from the letters of Law. Ed M. M. Schofield 1917.

§2

Wesley, John. A letter to Mr Law, occasioned by some of his late writings. 1756.

[Langcake, Thomas]. A serious and affectionate address to all orders of men, in which are recommended the works of Law. Bath 1781. Includes 3 letters written by Law in 1749, 1750 and 1753.

Stephen, L. William Law. 3 vols 1877–81.

Overton, J. H. Law: nonjuror and mystic. 1881.

Gem, S. H. Law on Christian practice and on Christian mysticism. Oxford 1905.

—— The mysticism of Law. 1914.

Hobhouse, S. Law and eighteenth-century Quakerism, including some unpublished letters and fragments of Law and John Byrom. 1927.

Green, J. B. John Wesley and Law. 1945.

Baker, E. W. A herald of the evangelical revival: a critical enquiry into the relation of Law to John Wesley and the beginnings of Methodism. 1948.

Hopkinson, A. W. About Law: a running commentary on his works. 1948.

Talon, H. Law: a study in literary craftsmanship. 1948.

Grainger, M. Law and the life of the spirit. 1950.

JOHN BYROM
1692–1763

Collections

Miscellaneous poems. 2 vols Manchester 1773; ed J. Nichols, Leeds 1814 (with a life).

Poems. Ed A. W. Ward 3 vols Manchester 1894–5, 1912 (Chetham Soc).

§1

A pastoral. Spectator 6 Oct 1714.

A review of the proceedings against Dr Bentley. 1719.
An epistle to a gentleman of the Temple. 1749.
Enthusiasm: a poetical essay. 1751.
Letter to Mr Comberbach in defence of rhyme. 1755.
Seasonably alarming and humiliating truths in a metrical version of some passages from the works of William Law. 1774. Collected by F. Okely.

Letters

Private journals and literary remains. Ed R. Parkinson 4 vols Manchester 1854–7 (Chetham Soc).
Journal, letters etc 1730–1. Manchester 1882.
Selections from his journals and papers. Ed H. Talon 1950. Contains Memoir and select bibliography.

§2

A catalogue of the library of the late John Byrom. 1848.

Contains a valuable list of contemporary and earlier mystical and theological books, tracts and pamphlets.
Hoole, E. Byrom and the Wesleys. 1864.
Stephen, L. In his Studies of a biographer vol 1, 1898.
Hobhouse, S. William Law and eighteenth-century Quakerism, including some letters and fragments of William Law and Byrom. 1927.
Thomson, W. H. Christians awake written by John Byrom. Manchester [1948].
—— Previously unpublished Byromania relating to Byrom. Manchester 1954.
—— Byrom's birthplace, Manchester. Manchester 1955.
—— Byrom deeds and wills in the possession of W. H. Thomson BA; with notes on omissions and duplicates. Manchester 1956.
—— The Thomson-Byrom collection. Bull John Rylands Lib 46 1963.

E. DISSENT

Congregational, Baptist, Presbyterian and Unitarian writers. For the Quakers see above. For Restoration Nonconformists see also under A. Restoration Divines, *above.*

JOHN BUNYAN

See col 511, above.

DANIEL DEFOE
1660–1731

An enquiry into the occasional conformity of Dissenters, in cases of preferment. 1697 etc.
The shortest way with the Dissenters. 1702.
For other works by Defoe see col 514, above.

PHILIP DODDRIDGE
1702–51

Collections

Works. Ed E. Williams and E. Parsons, with memoirs of the life, character and writings of Doddridge, by J. Orton. 10 vols Leeds 1802–25, 5 vols 1803–4.
Hymns founded on various texts in the Holy Scripture. Ed J. Orton, Shrewsbury 1755, 1793 (7th edn); ed J. Humphreys 1839 (as Scriptural hymns) (with addns).
A course of lectures on pneumatology, ethics and divinity. Ed S. Clark 1763, 1776, 1794.
Sermons on various subjects. Ed J. D. Humphreys 4 vols 1826.
Ten sermons on the power and grace of Christ. 1736.
Sermons to young persons. 1737 (2nd edn).
Practical discourses on regeneration. 2 pts 1741–2 etc, 1799 (6th edn).
Three sermons on the evidence of the Gospel. 1752.

§I

Free thoughts on the most probable means of reviving the dissenting interest. 1730.
The absurdity and iniquity of persecutions for conscience sake. 1736.
An answer to Christianity not founded on argument etc. In Three letters to the author [H. Dodwell], 3 pts 1743.
Of the evidences of Christianity. 1743.
The rise and progress of religion in the soul. 1745 etc, 1807 (15th edn).

Letters and Diaries

Correspondence and diary. Ed J. D. Humphreys 5 vols 1829–31.

Devotional letters and sacramental mediations, with lectures on preaching. 1832.

§2

Orton, J. Memoirs of the life, character and writings of Doddridge. Shrewsbury 1766.
Stoughton, J. Doddridge: his life and labours. 1851.
Nuttall, G. F. (ed). Doddridge: his contribution to English religion. 1951.
—— Richard Baxter and Doddridge. 1951.
—— Richard Baxter and Doddridge: a study in a tradition. Oxford 1952.

ISAAC WATTS
1674–1748

Collections

Works. Ed D. Jennings and P. Doddridge 6 vols 1753; ed E. Parson 7 vols Leeds 1800; ed G. Burder 6 vols 1810–11, 9 vols Leeds 1812–13.
Sermons on various subjects. 3 vols 1721–7 etc, 1772 (9th edn).

§I

An essay against uncharitableness. 1707.
A guide to prayer. 1715, 1753 (10th edn).
The art of reading and writing English. 1721.
The Christian doctrine of the Trinity. 1722.
Death and heaven: or the last enemy conquered and separate spirits made perfect. 1722 etc, 1822 (15th edn).
Three dissertations relating to the Christian doctrine of the Trinity. 1724.
Logic. 1725.
The knowledge of the heavens and the earth made easy: or the first principles of astronomy and geography. 1726.
A defense against the temptation of self-murder. 1726.
An essay towards the encouragement of charity schools. 1728.
A caveat against infidelity. 1729.
Catechisms: or instructions in the principles of the Christian religion and the history of Scripture for children and youth. 1730.
Philosophical essays on various subjects; with some remarks on Mr Locke's Essay concerning human understanding. 1733.
Reliquiae juveniles: miscellaneous thoughts in prose and verse. 1734, 1766 (5th edn).
The redeemer and the sanctifier. 1736.

Humility represented in the character of St Paul. 1737.

A new essay on civil power in things sacred. 1739.

The doctrine of the passions explained and improved. 1739 (3rd edn).

Faith and practice represented in 54 sermons preached in 1733 by Isaac Watts, D. Neal, J. Guyse, S. Price, D. Jennings and J. Hubbard. 2 vols 1739 (2nd edn).

The improvement of the mind: or a supplement to the art of logic. 1741.

The world to come: or discourses on the joys and sorrows of departed souls. 2 vols 1745.

Useful and important questions concerning Jesus, the Son of God. 1746.

The glory of Christ as God-man displayed in three discourses. 1746.

Evangelical discourses on several subjects. 1747.

The rational foundation of a Christian Church, and the terms of Christian communion. 1747.

Discourses on the love of God and its influence on all passions. 1760 (4th edn).

A treatise on the education of children and youth. 1769 (2nd edn).

§2

Davis, A. P. Watts: his life and works, with a bibliography. New York 1943.
See also col 424, above.

EDMUND CALAMY
1671–1732

An abridgement of Mr Baxter's History of his life and times. 1702, 2 vols 1713 (with continuation till 1711).

An account of the ministers, lecturers etc ejected in 1660 [ch 9 of Abridgement]. 1713.

A continuation of the account. 2 vols 1727.

The Nonconformists' memorial [Abridgement and Continuation of the account, above, condensed by S. Palmer]. 2 vols 1775, 3 vols 1802–3.

A defence of moderate nonconformity. 3 vols 1703–5.

Sermons on the inspiration of the holy writings. 1710.

Thirteen sermons concerning the doctrine of the Trinity, with four sermons on John v 7. 1719.

Memoirs of the life of John Howe. 1724.

A letter to a divine in Germany: giving a brief account of the Protestant Dissenters in England. 1736.

A historical account of my own life, with some reflections on the times I have lived in 1671–1731. Ed J. T. Rutt 2 vols 1829.

GEORGE WHITEFIELD

See col 657, above.

IV. HISTORY

A. RESTORATION HISTORIANS 1660–1700

SIR WILLIAM DUGDALE
1605–86

Bibliographies

Maddison, F. et al. Dugdale 1605–86: a list of his printed works. Warwick 1953. Includes mss.

§1

A full relation of the passages concerning the late treaty begun at Uxbridge 1644. Oxford 1645 (anon); rptd in A short view of the late troubles, 1681.

Monasticon anglicanum. 3 vols 1655–73. Vols 1–2 bear names of Dodsworth and Dugdale, vol 3 that of Dugdale alone. Vol 1, 1682 (rev). Tr J. Caley, H. Ellis, B. Bandinel 6 vols in 8 1817–30 (much enlarged), 1846. Tr and abridged by J. W[right] 1693, [J. Stevens] 1718; 2-vol continuation to Stevens's abridgement as The history of the antient abbeys, monasteries, hospitals, cathedral and collegiate churches, 1722; The appendix, containing charters, grants and other original writings, 1723.

The antiquities of Warwickshire illustrated. 1656; ed W. Thomas 2 vols 1730 (enlarged), Coventry 1765, (abridged) 1817, [c. 1830].

The history of St Paul's Cathedral. 1658; ed E. Maynard 1716 (enlarged); H. Ellis 1818 (enlarged); rptd in Stowe's Survey of London, 1753.

The history of imbanking and drayning of divers fenns and marshes. 1662; rev C. N. Cole 1772.

Origines juridiciales: or historical memorials of the English laws, courts of justice, forms of tryall etc, with a chronologie of the Lord Chancellors and Keepers of the Great Seal etc. 1666, 1671 (enlarged), 1680 (en-

larged); abridged by E. Cooke as Chronica juridicialia, 1685, 1739.

The baronage of England: or an historical account of our English nobility. 3 vols in 2 1675–6.

A short view of the late troubles in England. Oxford 1681, 1681 (both anon); rptd in The good old cause: the English revolution of 1640–60, ed C. Hill and E. Dell 1949 (extracts).

The antient usage in bearing of such ensigns of honour as are commonly call'd arms; with a catalogue of the present nobility. Oxford 1682, 1682; ed T. C. Banks 1811.

A perfect copy of all summons of the nobility to the great councils and parliaments of this realm. 1685.

The life of Sir William Dugdale. 1713. Also in Biographia collectanea 1713, and found with separate pagination in some copies of Miscellanies on several curious subjects [ed R. Rawlinson] 1714; rptd with The history of St Paul's, 1716, 1818; in Dallaway's Inquiries into the origin and progress of the science of heraldry in England, 1793; in his Heraldic miscellanies, [1793?]; in Hamper, under Letters, below, and in W. West, The history, topography and directory of Warwickshire, Birmingham 1830.

Some account of Wolverhampton. In S. Erdeswicke, A survey of Staffordshire, [ed R. Rawlinson?] 1717.

Directions for the search of records and making use of them, in order to an historical discourse of the antiquities of Staffordshire. In J. Ives, Select papers chiefly relating to English antiquities, 1773.

Visitations. Lancashire, 1851 (fragment) (Chetham Soc 24), ed F. R. Raines 1872–3 (Chetham Soc 84–5, 88); Derbyshire, ed J. Rogers, Middle Hill 1854, 1879 (index priv ptd F. A. Crisp 1887); Staffordshire, ed J. Rogers, Middle Hill 1854, ed H. S. Grazebrook 1885 (William Salt Archaeological Soc vol 5 pt 2), on which is based Staffordshire pedigrees ed G. J. Armytage and W. H. Rylands 1912 (Pbns Harleian Soc 62); Yorkshire, ed R. D[avies] 1859 (Pbns Surtees Soc 36) (index priv ptd G. J. Armytage 1872), ed with addns J. W. Clay in Genealogist new ser 9–33 1893–1917, and in 3 vols Exeter 1899–1917 (see Yorks Archaeological & Topographical Assoc Record Ser 9 1890); Durham, ed J. Foster 1887 (priv ptd), on which is based Durham monuments, Newcastle 1925 (Pbns Newcastle Records Committee 5); Cumberland and Westmorland, ed J. Foster, Carlisle [1891]; Northumberland, ed Foster, Newcastle [1891], 1924 (reshaped as Northumbrian monuments) (Pbns Newcastle Records Committee 4); Cheshire, ed A. Adams 1941 (Pbns Harleian Soc 93).

Notes of the Warwickshire inquisitions 1512, 1518, 1549. In The domesday of inclosures 1517–18, ed I. S. Leadam vol 2, 1897 (Royal Historical Soc).

Dugdale also edited and contributed to vol 2 of H. Spelman, Concilia, decreta, leges etc in re ecclesiarum orbis britannici, 1664, *and edited* Spelman, Glossarium archaiologicum, 1664. *Collaboration with W. Somner in his* Dictionarium saxonico-latino-anglicum, 1659, *has also been suggested (see Maddison, above, no 27).* A. Collins, Proceedings, precedents and arguments concerning baronies by writ, 1734 *is based in part on Dugdale's collections.*

The life, diary and correspondence. Ed W. Hamper 1827; The diary for 1656, ed F. Madan, Athenaeum 3 Nov 1888. *See also* Maddison, *above*, pp. 63–7.

§2

Douglas, D. C. Dugdale: the grand plagiary. History Dec 1935; rev as The grand plagiary in his English scholars 1660–1730, 1939, 1951 (rev).

Cronne, H. A. The study and use of charters by English scholars in the seventeenth century: Sir Henry Spelman and Dugdale. In English historical scholarship in the sixteenth and seventeenth centuries, ed L. Fox, Oxford 1956 (Dugdale Soc).

EDWARD HYDE,
1st EARL OF CLARENDON
1609–74

Collections

An appendix to the History of the grand rebellion: consisting of some valuable pieces written by Clarendon. 1724. Contains A full answer; The difference and disparity; extracts from parliamentary speeches 1660–2; The petition and address; Two letters to the Duke and Duchess of York; with a life. Rptd as vol 1 of A collection of several valuable pieces of Clarendon, 2 vols 1727 (vol 2 reprints the History of the rebellion in Ireland).

A collection of several tracts of the Earl of Clarendon. 1727. Contains A discourse by way of vindication of my self from the charge of high-treason; Reflections upon several Christian duties, divine and moral, by way of essays. Rptd as A compleat collection of tracts, 1747, and as Miscellaneous works of Clarendon, 1751 (2nd edn).

Characters of eminent men in the reigns of Charles I and II from the works of Clarendon. Ed E. T[urner] 1793.

Selections from the History of the rebellion and the Life by himself. Ed G. Huehns, Oxford 1955 (WC), 1978 (with foreword by H. R. Trevor-Roper).

§1

Mr Hides argument before the Lords [against the Council of the North]. 1641; rptd in Historical collections, ed J. Rushworth vol 4, 1721.

Mr Hyde's speech at a conference betweene both Houses, July 6 1641, at the impeachments against Lord Daven-

port etc. 1641; rptd in Historical collections, ed J. Rushworth vol 4, 1721; in Somers tracts, ed W. Scott vol 4, 1810.

Two speeches made in the House of Peers on Munday 19 Dec [1642] for and against accommodation, by the Earl of Pembroke [and] Lord Brooke. 1642, 1642; rptd in Somers tracts, ed W. Scott vol 6, 1811. Owned by Clarendon in his Life.

Transcendent and multiplied rebellion and treason discovered by the laws of the land. 1645. Anon.

An answer to a pamphlet entit'led A declaration of the Commons of England expressing their reasons and grounds of passing the late resolutions touching no further addresse to be made to the King. 1648, 1648 (both anon); enlarged as A full answer to an infamous and trayterous pamphlet entituled [etc], 1648; rptd in An appendix to the history of the grand rebellion, 1724; and in A collection of several valuable pieces, 1727; tr Latin, 1649.

The difference and disparity between the estates and conditions of George Duke of Buckingham and Robert Earl of Essex. In H. Wootton, Reliquiae Wottonianae, 1651. Ascribed to Clarendon in 1672 and 1685 edns of Reliquiae, pbd separately as The characters of Robert Earl of Essex and George Duke of Buckingham, 1706; rptd in An appendix to the History of the grand rebellion, 1724; and in A collection of several valuable pieces vol 1, 1727.

A letter from a true and lawfull Member of Parliament [i.e. Clarendon] to one of his Highness councell upon occasion of the last declaration 31 Oct 1655. 1656. Anon.

A collection of orders used in Chancery. 1661.

His Majesties speech, together with the Lord Chancellors [i.e. Clarendon's to Parliament] 13 Sept 1660. 1660. Other official parliamentary speeches dated 29 Dec 1660, 8, 10 May 1661, 19 May 1662 (rptd in Somers tracts, ed W. Scott vol 7, 1812), 10 Oct 1665, pbd with similar titles in year of delivery, that of 10 Oct 1665 at Oxford.

Second thoughts: or the case of a limited toleration, stated according to the present exigence of affairs in Church and State. [1671] (anon), [1689?].

Animadversions upon a book intituled Fanaticism fanatically imputed to the catholick church, by Dr Stillingfleet, and the imputation refuted by S. C[ressy]. 1673 (anon), 1674, 1685.

A brief view and survey of the dangerous and pernicious errors to Church and State in Mr Hobbes's book entitled Leviathan. [Oxford] 1676, 1676.

Two letters: one to the Duke of York, the other to the Dutchess, occasioned by her embracing the Roman Catholick religion. [1680?]; rptd in State tracts, 1689, 1693; An appendix to the History of the grand rebellion, 1724; in A collection of several valuable pieces vol 1, 1727; in Harleian miscellany, ed T. Park vol 3, 1809.

To the Right Honourable the Lords Spiritual and Temporal in Parliament assembled: the humble petition and address of Clarendon. [1667?]; rptd as News from Dunkirk-house: or Clarendon's farewell to England Dec 3 1667, [1667?]; rptd in State tracts, 1693; separately as The petition and address to the House of Lords in answer to the charge of the House of Commons against his Lordship, 1715; in An appendix to the History of the grand rebellion, 1724; in A collection of several valuable pieces vol 1, 1727; in Harleian miscellany, ed T. Park vol 5, 1810; in Somers tracts, ed W. Scott vol 8, 1812.

The history of the rebellion and civil wars in England, begun in the year 1641. 3 vols Oxford 1702–4 (folio), 1705–6 (8°), 1707, 1707 (folio), 1712 (8°), 1717, Dublin 1719 (folio), Oxford 1720–1 (8°), 1731–2, 1 vol 1732 (folio), 12 vols Basle 1798 (8°), 3 vols Oxford 1807, 1816 (4°), 1819 (8°), 8 vols 1826, (8°), 6 vols Boston 1827, 7 vols Oxford 1839 (12°), 1 vol 1839 (8°), 1843, 7 vols 1849; ed W. D. Macray 6 vols Oxford 1888. The edns of 1816, 1826, 1849 contain The history of the rebellion in

Ireland; 1826, 1827, 1849 contain Warburton's notes; 1843 contains Clarendon's autobiography. The Lord Clarendon's history of the grand rebellion compleated, 1717 (2nd edn), Dublin 1720 contains portraits, maps and other illustrative material.

The history of the rebellion and civil wars in Ireland. Dublin 1719–20, London 1720, 1721; rptd as A collection of several valuable pieces of Clarendon vol 2, 1727, and in 1816, 1826, 1849 edns of The history of the rebellion in England, above.

An appendix to the history of the grand rebellion. 1724. *See* Collections, *above.*

A collection of several valuable pieces. 2 vols 1727. *See* Collections, An appendix etc, *above.*

The life of Clarendon written by himself. Oxford 1759, 3 vols Oxford 1759, Dublin 1759, 2 vols Oxford 1760, 3 vols Oxford 1761, 2 vols Oxford 1817, 3 vols Oxford 1827, 2 vols Oxford 1857; rptd in 1843 edn of The history of the rebellion in England, above. Contains life to 1660, continuation to 1667.

Religion and policy and the countenance and assistance each should give to the other. 2 vols Oxford 1811.

Letters

Evelyn, J. Memoirs, to which is subjoined correspondence between Clarendon and Sir Richard Browne. Ed W. Bray vol 5, 1827.

Lister, T. H. Life and administration of Clarendon vol 3. 1837.

Notes which passed at meetings of the Privy Council between Charles II and Clarendon 1660–7, together with a few letters. Ed W. D. Macray 1896 (Roxburghe Club).

§ 2

The proceedings in the House of Commons touching the impeachment of Clarendon 1667. 1700.

State papers collected by Clarendon containing the material from which his History of the rebellion was composed. 3 vols Oxford 1767–86. Vols 1–2 ed R. Scrope, vol 3 ed T. Monkhouse.

Lister, T. H. Life and administration of Clarendon. 3 vols 1837–8.

Calendar of the Clarendon state papers. 4 vols Oxford 1872–1932. Vol 1 ed O. Ogle and W. H. Bliss, vols 2–3 W. D. Macray, vol 4 ed F. J. Routledge.

Ranke, L. von. In his History of England in the seventeenth century vol 6, tr Oxford 1875.

Stephen, J. F. Clarendon's History of the rebellion. In his Horae sabbaticae ser 1, 1892.

Draft by Hyde of a declaration on the murder of Charles I, to be issued by Charles II in 1649, with a note by S. R. Gardiner. EHR 8 1893.

Firth, C. H. Clarendon's History of the rebellion: 1, the original History; 2, the life of himself; 3, the history of the rebellion. EHR 19 1904.

—— Clarendon as statesman, historian and Chancellor of the University. Oxford 1909.

Craik, H. Life of Clarendon. 2 vols 1911.

Feiling, K. A letter of Clarendon during the elections of 1661. EHR 42 1927.

—— Clarendon and the act of uniformity 1662–3. EHR 44 1929.

Rowse, A. L. Clarendon's Life. In his English spirit, 1944.

Wormald, B. H. G. How Hyde became a royalist. Cambridge Historical Jnl 8 1945.

—— Clarendon: politics, history and religion 1640–60. Cambridge 1951.

Knights, L. C. Reflections on Clarendon's History of the rebellion. Scrutiny 15 1948; rptd in his Further explorations, 1965.

Trevor-Roper, H. R. The copyright in Clarendon's works. TLS 17 Feb 1950. *See* 3–10 March, 7 July 1950.

—— Clarendon and the great rebellion. In his Historical essays, 1957.

—— Three historians: 1, Clarendon. Listener 30 Sept 1965.

—— Clarendon and the practice of history. In Milton and Clarendon, Los Angeles 1965.

Hill, C. Clarendon and the civil war. History Today Oct 1953; rptd in his Puritanism and revolution, 1958.

Wedgwood, C. V. Some contemporary accounts of the civil war. Trans Royal Soc of Lit 26 1953. On Clarendon's methods of portraiture.

JOHN AUBREY
1626–97

Selections

Brief lives and other selected writings. Ed A. Powell 1949.
Brief lives. Ed O. L. Dick 1949, 1950, 1958 (rev).

§ 1

Queries in order to the description of Britannia. [1673].
Proposals for printing Monumenta britannica. [1693].
Miscellanies: i, Day-fatality; ii, Local-fatality; iii, Ostenta; iv, Omens; v, Dreams etc, collected by Aubrey. 1696, 1721 (best edn, enlarged, with a life), 1784, 1857, 1890.
The natural history and antiquities of the county of Surrey. [Ed R. Rawlinson] 5 vols 1718–19.
Lives of eminent men. [Ed P. Bliss] in Letters written by eminent persons in the seventeenth and eighteenth centuries, [ed J. Walker] vol 2, 1813; Brief lives, ed A. Clark 2 vols Oxford 1898 (bowdlerized, but fullest edn). *See under* Selections, *above.*
The natural history of Wiltshire. Ed J. Britton 1847 (Wiltshire Topographical Soc).
Wiltshire: the topographical collections of Aubrey. Ed J. E. Jackson 1862 (Wiltshire Archaeological & Natural History Soc). The part relating to North Wilts priv ptd in 2 pts by Sir Thomas Phillipps as Aubrey's collections for Wilts, 1821, Middle Hill 1838. The introd originally ptd in Miscellanies on several curious subjects, [ed R. Rawlinson] 1714, 1718 (2nd edn, as Introduction towards a natural history of Wiltshire, with other curious miscellanies).
Remaines of gentilisme and Judaisme. Ed J. Britten 1881 (Pbns Folk-lore Soc 4).

Letters

Memoir of Aubrey. Ed J. Britton 1845 (Wilts Topographical Soc). Extracts.

§ 2

Powell, A. Aubrey and his friends. 1948, 1963 (rev).
Young, G. M. The man who noticed. In his Last essays, 1950.
Auden, W. H. New Yorker 15 Feb 1958. Review of Brief lives, ed Dick.
Hunter, M. Aubrey and the realm of learning. 1975.

ANTHONY à WOOD
1632–95

Bibliographies

Huddesford, W. Catalogus librorum manuscriptorum Antonii a Wood: a catalogue of the manuscript collections in the Ashmolean Museum. Oxford 1761; rptd by Sir Thomas Phillipps, Middle Hill 1824. *See* introd to Life and times, ed A. Clark vol 1, Oxford 1861.

§ 1

Historia et antiquitates universitatis oxoniensis [tr Latin

by R. Peers and R. Reeve]. 2 vols Oxford 1674. The original English version first pbd in pts by J. Gutch 1786–96: The history and antiquities of the colleges and halls in the University of Oxford, with a continuation to the present time, Oxford 1786, 1790 (with Fasti oxonienses, separate title-page and pagination, as an appendix); The history and antiquities of the University of Oxford, 2 vols in 3 Oxford 1792–6.

Athenae oxonienses: an exact history of all the writers and Bishops who have had their education in the University of Oxford from 1500 to 1690; to which are added the Fasti or annals of the University. 2 vols 1691–2 (anon), 1721 (rev and enlarged); ed P. Bliss 5 vols 1813–20 (enlarged with continuation). Of a new edn planned by Ecclesiastical History Soc only one vol was issued, containing Wood's autobiography, ed P. Bliss 1848. See The libel issu'd out of the Chancellor's Court of the University of Oxford against Mr Anthony à Wood, by the Earl of Clarendon, with Mr Wood's answer, and the sentence given after the tryal, begun March 3 1692/3 finish'd July 29 1693, [Oxford 1693?] (anon), rptd in Miscellanies on several curious subjects, [ed R. Rawlinson] 1714.

Life 1632–72 written by himself. In Thomae Caii vindiciae antiquitatis academiae Oxoniensis, ed T. Hearne vol 2, Oxford 1730. Continued to his death in The lives of John Leland, Thomas Hearne and Anthony à Wood, ed W. Huddesford vol 2, Oxford 1772, rptd in Athenae, ed Bliss vol 1, 1813, and in vol 1 of projected edn of Athenae, 1848. Fullest edn as The life and times of Anthony Wood 1632–95, ed A. Clark 5 vols Oxford 1891–1900 (Pbns Oxford Historical Soc 19, 21, 26, 30, 40); abridged L. Powys 1932, Oxford 1961 (WC). Huddesford's edn and both of Bliss's contain additional material from Wood's ms collections; Clark's edn integrates the autobiography with all other relevant material in a single chronological sequence.

Modius salium: a collection of such pieces of humour as prevail'd at Oxford in the time of Mr Anthony à Wood. Oxford 1751.

Survey of the antiquities of the city of Oxford. Ed A. Clark 3 vols Oxford 1889–99 (Pbns Oxford Historical Soc 15, 17, 37). Extracts pbd as Some notes relating to the history of Oxford in Liber niger scaccarii, ed T. Hearne vol 2, Oxford 1728, 1771. An inaccurate edn as The ancient and present state of the city of Oxford, ed J. Peshall 1773 (with addns).

Parochial collections [of Wood and R. Rawlinson]. Ed F. N. Davis 3 vols Oxford 1920–9 (Oxfordshire Record Soc).

Wood also edited Γνωστὸν τοῦ Θεοῦ, καὶ Γνωστὸν τοῦ Χριστοῦ *by* [his brother] Edward Wood, Oxford 1656, 1674.

§2

[Wood, Thomas]. A vindication of the historiographer of the University of Oxford from the reproaches of the Bishop of Salisbury etc, by E.D. 1693.

[Rawlinson, R]. The life of Anthony à Wood. [1711].

Gibson, S. and M. A. An index to Rawlinson's collections c. 1700–50 for a new edition of Wood's Athenae oxonienses. Proc Oxford Bibl Soc 1 1925.

Benham, A. R. The so-called anonymous or earliest life of Milton. ELH 6 1939. Reply by E. S. Parsons with rejoinder by Benham 9 1942. See TLS 13 Sept, 11 Oct, 27 Dec 1957; W. R. Parker, Wood's life of Milton: its sources and significance, PBSA 52 1958.

GILBERT BURNET
1643–1715
Collections

The collections of 1685, 1689 (A second collection) and 1703 are apparently reissues of remainders bound up together. The following is a selective list. For full details see Clarke and Foxcroft's Life pp. 553–4.

A collection of several tracts and discourses written in the years 1677–85. 1685. Contains A vindication of the ordinations of the Church of England; A letter written upon the discovery of the late plot; The unreasonableness and impiety of Popery; A relation of the barbarous and bloody massacre in 1572; A decree made at Rome the second of March 1679 etc. Reissued as vol 1 of Collection, 3 vols 1704, below.

Dr Burnet's tracts. 2 vols 1689. Vol 1 contains Animadversions on Reflections upon travels; Three letters concerning the present state of Italy; vol 2 contains Burnet's trn of A relation of the death of the primitive persecutors by Lactantius; Answers to Varillas (Reflections on Mr Varillas's History, A defence of the Reflections, A continuation of Reflections etc).

A second collection of several tracts and discourses written in the years 1686–9. 1689. Contains A letter containing some remarks on two papers writ by Charles II; Reasons against repealing the acts of Parliament concerning the test; Some reflections on his Majesty's proclamation for a toleration in Scotland; A letter containing some reflections on his Majesty's declaration for liberty of conscience etc. Reissued as vol 2 Collection, 3 vols 1704, below.

A third collection of several tracts and discourses written in the years 1690 to 1703. 1703. Contains Injunctions for the archdeacons of the diocese of Sarum; A sermon preached before the Queen at Whitehall 16 July 1690; A sermon preached at the funeral of Anne Lady Brooke 19 February 1690/1 etc. Reissued as vol 3 of Collection, 3 vols 1704, below.

A collection of several tracts and discourses written in the years 1677 to 1704. 3 vols 1704. Remainders of Collections of 1685, 1689, 1703 reissued.

A collection of speeches, prefaces, letters etc, with a description of Geneva and Holland. 1713. Contains Accounts of Geneva and Holland; Extract on revision of liturgy from visitation charge 1704; Character of Tillotson etc.

§1

Burnet pbd many sermons and many polemical and apologetic works, generally omitted in the following list. For full details see Foxcroft's Appendix.

A discourse on the memory of Sir Robert Fletcher of Saltoun. Edinburgh 1665. Anon.

The memoires of the lives and actions of James and William, Dukes of Hamilton; in which an account is given of the rise and progress of the civil wars of Scotland. 1677, Oxford 1852. Originally pbd as vol 2 of Spottiswoode's History of the Church and State of Scotland, 1677.

The history of the reformation of the Church of England. 3 vols 1679, 1681, 1715. Other edns: vol 1, 1681; vols 1–2 1683; vol 3, 1715, 1715, 1753; 3 vols Dublin 1730–3 (complete); 6 vols in 3 Oxford 1816, 1820, 1825, 4 vols Oxford 1829; ed N. Pocock 7 vols Oxford 1865 (best edn). Abridgements of vols 1–2 1682; of vol 3 (issued with 5th edn of abridgement of vols 1–2 1719) 1719; 1728 (6th edn of abridgement of vols 1–2, 2nd edn of abridgement of vol 3), Oxford 1808.

Reflections on Mr Varillas's History of the revolutions that have happened in Europe in matters of religion, and more particularly in his ninth book that relates to England. 'Amsterdam' (London?) 1686, rptd 1689 separately and in Tracts vol 2.

A defence of the Reflections on Mr Varillas's History of heresies: being a reply to his answer. Amsterdam 1687; rptd in Tracts vol 2, 1689.

A continuation of Reflections on Mr Varillas's History of heresies, particularly his third and fourth tomes. Amsterdam 1687; rptd in Tracts vol 2, 1689.

Reflections on the relation of the English reformation [by Obadiah Walker], lately printed at Oxford: part I. Amsterdam 1688; Reflections on the Oxford Theses relating to the English Reformation, part II, Amsterdam 1688 (anon); rptd together, 1689; reissued in A second collection of tracts, 1689.

A letter to Mr Thevenot containing a censure of M. le Grand's History of K. Henry the eighth's divorce. 1688, 1688 (with addns); rptd in Tracts vol 2, 1689; reissued in A second collection of tracts, 1689.

A censure of M. de Meaux [i.e. Bossuet's] History of the variations of the Protestant churches; together with some further reflections on M le Grand. [Amsterdam?] 1688; pbd with A letter to Thevenot, 1689; rptd in Tracts vol 2, 1689; reissued in A second collection of tracts, 1689.

A letter writ by the Bishop of Salisbury to the Bishop of Coventry and Litchfield concerning a book by Anthony Harmer [i.e. Henry Wharton]. 1693; reissued in A third collection of tracts, 1703. Burnet's reply to [H. Wharton's] A specimen of some errors in The history of the Reformation by Anthony Harmer, 1693.

Some passages of the life and death of John [Wilmot] Earl of Rochester. 1680, Dublin 1681, London 1692, 1700–1, 1724, Glasgow 1752 etc. Abridged as The libertine overthrown: or a mirror for atheists, [1690?]; as A mirror for atheists, 1693.

The life and death of Sir Matthew Hale. 1682 (3 edns), 1700.

The history of the rights of princes in the disposing of ecclesiastical benefices and church-lands. 1682.

An answer to the animadversions on the History of the rights of princes. 1682; reissued in A collection of several tracts etc, 1685. Burnet's reply to [T. Comber's] Animadversions on Burnet's History of the rights of princes etc, 1682.

Utopia written in Latin by Sir Thomas More, translated into English. 1684. Anon.

The life of William Bedell, Bishop of Kilmore. 1685 (anon), 1692.

A letter written to Dr Burnet, giving an account of Cardinal Pool's secret powers. 1685 (anon); reissued in A collection of several tracts etc, 1685; rptd in Harleian miscellany, et T. Park vol 7, 1811.

Some letters containing an account of what seemed most remarkable in Switzerland, Italy etc, written to T.H.R.B. [i.e. The Honourable Robert Boyle]. Amsterdam 1686, 1687 (6 edns) etc.

A relation of the death of the primitive persecutors, written originally in Latin by L. C. F. Lactantius, english'd by G. Burnet; to which he hath made a large preface concerning persecution. Amsterdam 1687; rptd in Tracts vol 2, 1689, rptd as God's judgements upon tyrants, 1715 (2nd edn). Part of Burnet's preface, with anti-Catholicism removed, pbd as The case of compulsion in matters of religion, 1688, the full preface as The Bishop of Salisbury's new preface to his pastoral care considered, [1713?] (2nd edn).

Supplement to Dr Burnet's letters written by a nobleman of Italy and communicated to the author. Rotterdam 1687, 1689.

Three letters concerning the present state of Italy: a supplement to Dr Burnet's letters. 1688, 1688 (both anon); rptd in Tracts vol 1, 1689.

Animadversions upon the Reflections upon Dr Burnet's travels. [Amsterdam?] 1688; rptd in Tracts vol 1, 1689.

A discourse of the pastoral care. 1692, 1692, 1713 (with addns), 1713.

An essay on the memory of the late Queen. 1695, Edinburgh 1695, Dublin 1695, 1696.

An introduction to the third volume of the History of the reformation of the Church of England. 1713, 1714.

A character of Gilbert, Bishop of Sarum with a true copy of his last will and testament: containing 1, his profession of faith; 2, his charitable benefactions; 3, an account of the History of his life and times, with directions for the publication of that and other manuscripts etc. 1715 (3 edns), 1717 (omitting the Character), 1728 (in Lives and last wills of eminent persons).

Bishop Burnet's history of his own times. Vol 1, 1724, Dublin 1724, 3 vols Hague 1725, 1725; abridged T. Stackhouse 1724; vol 2, 1734, 3 vols Hague 1734, Dublin 1734, 3 vols 1734; ed R. Flexman 4 vols 1753 (complete); ed M. J. Routh 7 vols Oxford 1823, 6 vols Oxford 1833 (enlarged); ed O. Airy, Oxford 1897 (vols 1–2); abridged 1874, 1906 (EL).

A supplement to Burnet's History of my own times, derived from his memoirs etc. Ed H. C. Foxcroft, Oxford 1902.

Certain papers of Robert Burnet [and] Burnet. Ed H. C. Foxcroft, Edinburgh 1904 (Pbns Scottish History Soc).

Thoughts on education. 1761; ed J. Clarke, Aberdeen 1914.

Letters

For a list of extant letters see Appendix III to Clarke and Foxcroft's Life, below.

Some unpublished letters of Burnet [to George Savile, Lord Halifax]. 1907 (Camden Soc 3rd ser 13).

§2

Le Clerc, J. The life of Dr Burnet, with his character, and an account of his writings. Tr 1715.

Sewell, G. An essay towards a true account of the life and character of the late Bishop of Salisbury, in remarks upon, and collections from his own writings. 1715.

[Burnet, T.]. A character of the right reverend father in God, Gilbert Lord Bishop of Sarum. 1715 (2nd edn).

Clarke, T. E. S. and H. C. Foxcroft. A life of Burnet. Cambridge 1907.

Foxcroft, H. C. An early revision of Burnet's Memoirs of the Dukes of Hamilton. EHR 24 1909.

Whibley, C. In his Political portraits [1st ser], 1917.

Firth, C. H. Burnet as an historian. First pbd as introd to Clarke and Foxcroft, Life, 1907, above; rptd in his Essays historical and literary, Oxford 1938.

Gooch, G. P. Burnet and the Stuart kings; Burnet and William III. In his Courts and cabinets, 1944.

MINOR HISTORICAL WRITERS 1660–1700

Historians

SIR PAUL RYCAUT or RICAUT

1628–1700

The capitulations and articles of peace betweene the King of England and the Sultan of the Ottoman Empire, as now lately in the city of Adrianople in 1661 amplified. Constantinople 1663.

The present state of the Ottoman Empire. 1667, 1668, 1670 (3rd edn), 1675, 1682 (5th edn, enlarged), 1686; rptd in Knolles, Turkish history vol 2, 1687 (6th edn); abridged J. Savage in Turkish history vol 2, 1701.

The present state of the Greek and Armenian churches. 1679.

The history of the Turkish Empire from 1623 to 1677. 1680; rptd in Knolles, Turkish history vol 2, 1687 (6th edn); abridged J. Savage in Turkish history vol 2, 1701. A continuation of Knolles.

The lives of the Popes [tr from Latin of B. Planta], continued from 1471 to present time. 1685, 1688.

The history of the Turks, beginning with 1679 until the end of 1698, 1699. 1700; abridged J. Savage in Turkish history vol 2, 1701.

Rycaut's diplomatic letters from Hamburgh 1692. Middle Hill [1841 ?] (priv ptd by Sir Thomas Phillipps).

GEORGE MACKENZIE, VISCOUNT TARBAT, EARL OF CROMARTY
1630–1714

A memorial for his Highness the Prince of Orange in relation to the affairs of Scotland. 1689. With Sir George Mackenzie. Anon.

A vindication of Robert III, King of Scotland, from the imputation of bastardy. Edinburgh 1695, 1713.

Several proposals conducing to a further union of Britain. 1711. Anon.

An historical account of the conspiracies by the Earls of Gowry and Robert Logan of Restalrig against James VI. Edinburgh 1713.

A vindication of the Historical account of the conspiracies against James VI. Edinburgh 1714.

The genealogie of the Mackenzies, preceeding the year mdclxi, wreattin in the year mdclxix. [Ed J. W. Mackenzie], Edinburgh 1829. Anon.

History of the family of Mackenzie. In W. Fraser, Earls of Cromartie vol 2, 1876.

SIR GEORGE MACKENZIE
1636–91
Collections

Essays upon several moral subjects. 1713. With a life.

Works. [Ed with a life by T. Ruddiman] 2 vols Edinburgh 1716–22.

§1

Aretina: or the serious romance. Edinburgh 1660, London 1661, [1661]. Anon.

Religio stoici. Edinburgh 1663, 1663, London 1663, Edinburgh 1665, 1665 (anon); as The religious stoic, Edinburgh 1685, London 1693.

A moral essay, preferring solitude to publick employment. Edinburgh [1665] (anon), 1666, London 1685, 1693.

Moral gallantry; [and] A moral paradox. Edinburgh 1667, London 1669, 1669, 1685, 1821.

Pleadings in some remarkable cases before the supreme courts of Scotland since the year 1661. Edinburgh 1672, 1673 (anon), 1704.

Observations against dispositions made in defraud of creditors. Edinburgh 1675, 1698; rptd in The laws and customes of Scotland in matters criminal, 1699 below.

The laws and customes of Scotland in matters criminal. Edinburgh 1678, 1699.

Observations upon the laws and customs of nations as to precedency; [and] The science of herauldry treated as a part of the civil law. Edinburgh 1680; Observations rptd in J. Guillim, Display of heraldry, 1724 (6th edn).

Idea eloquentiae forensis hodiernae. Edinburgh 1681.

A vindication of his Majesties government and judicatures in Scotland. Edinburgh 1683, London 1683. Anon.

The institutions of the law of Scotland. Edinburgh 1684, 1688 (enlarged), London 1694, Edinburgh 1699, 1706, 1719, 1723, 1730, 1758.

Jus regium: or the just and solid foundations of monarchy; [and] That the lawful successor cannot be debarr'd from succeeding to the crown. Edinburgh 1684, 1684, London 1684, 1684.

A defence of the antiquity of the royal line of Scotland. Edinburgh 1685, London 1685, 1685.

The antiquity of the royal line of Scotland farther cleared and defended. 1686.

Observations on the Acts of Parliament made by James I [and his successors]. Edinburgh 1686, 1687.

A letter from the nobility, barons and Commons of Scotland in 1320 directed to Pope Iohn. Edinburgh 1689, 1700, 1703, 1745; rptd in Harleian miscellany vol 1, ed T. Park 1808; in Somers tracts vol 11, ed W. Scott 1814; in Miscellanea scotica vol 3, Glasgow [1820].

Oratio inauguralis. 1689; rptd in Catalogus librorum [of Advocates' Library], Edinburgh 1692.

A memorial for his Highness the Prince of Orange in relation to the affairs of Scotland. 1689. Anon. With George Mackenzie, Viscount Tarbat and Earl of Cromarty.

Reason: an essay. 1690, 1695; tr Latin, 1690, 1691, 1700.

The moral history of frugality. 1691, Edinburgh 1691.

A vindication of the government in Scotland during the reign of Charles II. 1691, Edinburgh 1712.

Caelia's country-house and closet: a poem. In A choice collection of comic and serious Scots poems pt 2, ed J. Watson, Edinburgh 1709, Glasgow 1869; rptd separately [1715?].

Memoirs of the affairs of Scotland from the restoration of King Charles II. Edinburgh 1821 (priv ptd).

§2

Lang, A. Mackenzie: his life and times. 1909.

de Beer, E. S. The letters from Mackenzie to Evelyn. N & Q 5 June 1937.

Loudon, J. H. Mackenzie's speech at the formal opening of the Advocates' Library Edinburgh, 15 March 1689. Trans Edinburgh Bibl Soc 2 1945.

ROBERT KNOX
1641?–1720
Selections

Robert Knox in the Kandyan Kingdom. Ed E. F. C. Ludowyk, Oxford 1948.

§1

An historical relation of Ceylon. 1681; rptd J. Harris in Navigantium bibliotheca vol 2, 1705; rptd [R. Fellowes] as appendix to History of Ceylon by Philalethes, 1817, 1818; ed E. Arber in An English garner vol 1, 1877; ed J. Ryan, Glasgow 1911 (enlarged).

§2

Moore, J. R. Defoe's sources for Robert Drury's Journal. Bloomington [1943]. Ch 3 on Defoe's use of Knox.

Williams, H. With Knox in Ceylon. 1964.

JAMES WELLWOOD or WELWOOD
1652–1727

A vindication of the present great revolution in England. 1689.

An answer to the late King James's declaration. 1689, 1693; rptd in A collection of state tracts vol 2, 1706.

Memoirs of the most material transactions in England for the last hundred years preceding the Revolution in 1688. 1700 (2nd–3rd edns), 1710; ed F. Maseres 1820.

Biographers and Autobiographers

SAMUEL CLARKE

1599–1683

The marrow of ecclesiastical historie, contained in the lives of the Fathers and other learned men and famous divines. 1650, 1654, 1675 (both enlarged).

A generall martyrologie from the creation to our present times. 1651, 1657, 1660, 1677 (3rd edn, with Lives of thirty-two English divines, below).

A martyrologie: containing all the persecutions which have befallen the Church of England to the end of Queen Maries reign, with the lives of ten English divines. 1652, 1677; rptd in A generall martyrologie, 1677 (3rd edn enlarged).

England's remembrancer: containing a true and full narrative of those two never to be forgotten deliverances, the one from the Spanish invasion, the other from the hellish Powder plot. 1657, 1671 (as A true and full narrative), 1676, 1677, 1679. Other edns as pt 2 of Historians guide, below.

The lives of two and twenty English divines. 1660, 1662.

A collection of the lives of ten eminent divines. 1662.

The lives of thirty-two English divines. 1677.

The historians guide: 1, A chronology of the world from the Creation; 2, England's remembrancer. 1676 (anon), 1679, 1688, 1690, 1701.

The history of the glorious life, reign and death of the illustrious Queen Elizabeth. 1682, 1683.

The lives of sundry eminent persons in this later age: 1, Divines; 2, Nobility and gentry; to which is added his own life. 1683.

LORD DENZIL HOLLES

1599–1680

The grand question concerning the judicature of the House of Peers. 1669. Anon.

A true relation of the unjust accusation of certain French gentlemen. 1671.

The case stated concerning the judicature of the House of Peers in the point of appeals. 1675. Anon.

The case stated of the jurisdiction of the House of Lords in the point of appeals. 1675. Anon.

The case stated of the jurisdiction of the House of Lords in the point of impositions. 1676. Anon.

The Lord Holles his vindication of himself. 1676.

A letter of a gentleman to his friend, shewing that the Bishops are not to be judges in Parliament in cases capital. 1679 (anon), 1679.

Lord Hollis his remains: being a second letter to a friend, concerning the judicature of the Bishops in Parliament. 1682.

Memoirs from 1641 to 1648. 1699; rptd in Select tracts, ed F. Maseres 1815.

THOMAS FAIRFAX, 1st BARON FAIRFAX

1612–71

A short memorial of the northern actions in which I was engaged; Short memorials of some things to be cleared during my command. [Ed B. Fairfax] 1699, Leeds 1776; rptd in Antiquarian repertory vol 3, ed E. Lodge 1808; in Somers tracts vol 5, ed W. Scott 1811; in Select tracts, ed F. Maseres 1815; in An English garner vol 8, ed E. Arber 1896; in Stuart tracts, ed C. H. Firth 1903.

Letters

Epistolary curiosities: unpublished letters illustrative of the Herbert family from Fairfax. Pt 1, ed R. W[arner], Bath 1818.

The Fairfax correspondence: memoirs of the reign of Charles I. Ed G. W. Johnson 2 vols 1848; in Memorials of the Civil War: the correspondence of the Fairfax family, ed R. Bell 2 vols 1849.

EDMUND LUDLOW

1617?–92

Memoirs. 3 vols Vivay [London?] 1698–9, London 1721–0, Edinburgh 1751, 1 vol 1751, 1771; ed C. H. Firth 2 vols Oxford 1894 (with letters).

LUCY HUTCHINSON

b. 1620

Memoirs of the life of Colonel Hutchinson; to which is prefixed the life of Mrs Hutchinson, written by herself. Ed J. Hutchinson 1806, 1808, 2 vols 1810; ed C. H. Firth 2 vols 1885 (with Hutchinson's letters), 1906 (rev); ed H. Child 1904; [1908], 1965 (EL); ed J. Sutherland, Oxford 1973.

ELIAS ASHMOLE

1617–92

The institution, laws and ceremonies of the Order of the Garter. 1672, 1693, 1715 (abridged with continuation by T. Walker as The history of the Order of the Garter).

Memoirs drawn up by himself by way of a diary. 1717 (with letters); [ed T. Davies] 1774 (with William Lilly, History of his life and times, an autobiography); ed R. T. Gunther, Oxford 1927; in Autobiographical and historical notes etc, ed C. H. Josten 5 vols Oxford 1966. Josten's edn integrates all autobiographical material, from whatever source, in a chronological sequence.

The antiquities of Berkshire. 3 vols 1719, 1723, 1 vol Reading 1736.

Autobiographical and historical notes, his correspondence etc. Ed C. H. Josten 5 vols Oxford 1966. See above.

DAVID LLOYD

1635–92

Modern policy compleated: or the publick actions and councels of General Monck, 1639 to 1660. 1660.

ΕΙΚΟΝ ΒΑΣΙΛΙΚΗ: or the true pourtraiture of his sacred Majestie Charls II. 1660 (anon), 1660; tr Dutch, 1661.

The states-men and favourites of England since the Reformation. 1665, 1670 (enlarged as State worthies), 1679; ed C. Whitworth 2 vols 1766 (enlarged).

Memoires of the lives of those personages that suffered for the Protestant religion, and allegiance to their soveraign from 1637 to 1660, continued to 1666. 1668, 1677.

B. EARLY EIGHTEENTH-CENTURY HISTORIANS 1700–50

JOHN STRYPE
1643–1737

Collections

Historical and biographical works. 19 vols Oxford 1812–24; Index [by R. F. Laurence], 2 vols Oxford 1828.

§1

Memorials of Thomas Cranmer. 1694, 2 vols Oxford 1812 (enlarged), 3 vols 1848–54 (Ecclesiastical History Soc); ed P. E. Barnes 2 vols 1853.

The life of the learned Sir Thomas Smith, principal Secretary of State to King Edward the Sixth and Queen Elizabeth. 1698, Oxford 1820.

Historical collections of the life and acts of John Aylmer, Bishop of London. 1701, Oxford 1821.

The life of the learned Sir John Cheke, Secretary of State to Edward VI. 1705, Oxford 1821.

Annals of the Reformation and establishment of religion, and other occurrences in the Church of England, during the first twelve years of Queen Elizabeth's reign. 1709 (vol 1 only), 4 vols 1725–31 (much enlarged), 1735–7, Oxford 1824.

The history of the life and acts of Edmund Grindal, Bishop of London and Archbishop of York and Canterbury in the reign of Q. Elizabeth. 1710, Oxford 1821.

The life and acts of Matthew Parker, Archbishop of Canterbury in the reign of Queen Elizabeth. 1711, 3 vols Oxford 1821.

The life and acts of John Whitgift, Archbishop of Canterbury in the reign of Queen Elizabeth. 1718, 3 vols Oxford 1822.

Ecclesiastical memorials, relating chiefly to religion and the Reformation of it under Henry VIII, Edward VI and Mary. 3 vols 1721, 1733 (with new vol 1), Oxford 1822 (enlarged).

Strype also edited and extended J. Stow, Survey of the cities of London and Westminster, *with a life of* Stow, 2 vols 1720, 1754–5 (*much enlarged*).

ROGER NORTH
1653–1734

Collections

The lives of the Norths. Ed H. Roscoe 3 vols 1826 (Francis, Dudley and John); ed A. Jessopp 3 vols 1890 (with R. North's autobiography and [letters). *See below.*

North on music: a selection of his essays written c. 1695–1728. Ed J. Wilson 1959.

§1

A discourse on fish and fish-ponds. 1713 (anon), 1714, 1715.

Examen: or an enquiry into the credit and veracity of a pretended complete history; together with some memoirs, all tending to vindicate Charles II. [Ed M. North] 1740; pp. 329–41 rptd as A discourse on the English constitution in The scholar armed vol 1, 1795, 1800 (slightly amended).

The life of Francis North, Baron Guildford. [Ed M. North] 1742, 2 vols 1808, 1 vol [1939] (abridged). *See Collections, above.*

The life of Sir Dudley North and of Dr John North. 1744. *See Collections, above.*

A discourse of the poor. [Ed M. North] 1753.

A discourse on the study of the laws. 1824.

Memoirs of musick. Ed E. F. Rimbault 1846.

Autobiography. Ed A. Jessopp 1887 (priv ptd). *See Collections, above.*

The musicall gramarian. Ed H. Andrews, Oxford [1925].

Letters

Lives of the Norths vol 3. Ed A. Jessop 1890.

§2

Birrell, A. North's autobiography. In his Collected essays and addresses 1880–1920 vol 1, 1922.

Gore, F. C. A seventeenth-century barrister. Quart Rev 260 1933.

Carver, G. North and his brothers. In his Alms for oblivion, Milwaukee 1946.

Birrell, T. A. North and political morality in the later Stuart period. Scrutiny 17 1950.

Letwin, W. The authorship of Sir Dudley North's Discourses on trade. Economica new ser 18 1951. Ascribed to North.

Ketton-Cremer, R. W. North. E & S new ser 12 1959.

Clifford, J. L. North and the art of biography. In Restoration and eighteenth-century literature: essays in honor of A. D. McKillop, Chicago 1963.

THOMAS MADOX
1666–1727

Formulare anglicanum: or a collection of ancient charters and instruments of divers kinds, from the Norman Conquest to the end of the reign of Henry VIII. 1702.

The history and antiquities of the Exchequer of the kings of England, from the Norman Conquest to the end of the reign of Edward II. 1711, 2 vols 1769 (with index).

Firma burgi: or an historical essay concerning the cities towns and buroughs of England. 1726.

Baronia anglica: an history of land-honors and baronies, and of tenure in rapite. 1736 (with index to the History of the Exchequer), 1741.

THOMAS HEARNE
1678–1735

Collections

Works. 4 vols 1810. Contains chronicles of Robert of Gloucester (vols 1–2) and Peter Langtoft (vols 3–4). *See below.*

§1

Reliquiae Bodleianae: or some genuine remains of Sir Thomas Bodley. 1703.

C. Plinii Caecilii secundi epistolae et panegyricus. Oxford 1703.

Eutropii breviarum historiae romanae. Oxford 1703, Leyden 1729, 1762, 1793.

Ductor historicus: or a short system of universal history, and an introduction to the study of it. 2 vols 1705–4 (vol 2 written, vol 1 ed Hearne); Hearne had no hand in the edns of 1714, 1723, 1724.

M. Juniani Justini historiarum ex Trogo Pompeio libri xliv. Oxford 1705.

T. Livii Patavini historiarum ab urbe condita libri qui supersunt. 6 vols Oxford 1708.

A letter containing an account of some antiquities between Windsor and Oxford. Monthly Miscellany Nov 1708–Jan 1709 (pirated); rptd 1725.

The life of Aelfred the Great by Sir John Spelman. Oxford 1709 (enlarged).

The itinerary of John Leland the antiquary. 9 vols Oxford 1710–12, 1744–5, 1768–9.

Henrici Dodwelli de Parma equestri Woodwardiana dissertatio. Oxford 1713. Includes Collegiorum scholarumque publicarum academiae oxoniensis topographica delineatio, per T. Nelum, which is rptd in Elizabethan Oxford, ed C. Plummer, Oxford 1887 (Pbns Oxford Historical Soc).

Joannis Lelandi antiquarii de rebus britannicis collectanea. 6 vols Oxford [1715], London 1770, 1774.

Acta apostolorum graeco-latine, litteris majusculis, e codice Laudiano. Oxford 1715.

Joannis Rossi antiquarii Warwicensis historia regum Angliae. Oxford 1716, 1745.

Titi Livii Foro-Juliensis vita Henrici quinti, regis Angliae. Oxford 1716.

Aluredi Beverlacensis annales. Oxford 1716.

Guilielmi Roperi vita D. Thomae Mori lingua anglicana contexta. [Oxford] 1716.

Guilielmi Camdeni annales rerum anglicarum et hibernicarum regnante Elizabetha. 3 vols [Oxford] 1717.

Guilielmi Neubrigensis historia sive chronica rerum anglicarum. 3 vols Oxford 1719.

Thomae Sprotti chronica. Oxford 1719.

A collection of curious discourses written by eminent antiquaries upon several heads in our English antiquities. Oxford 1720, 2 vols 1771 (enlarged).

Textus Roffensis. Oxford 1720.

Roberti de Avesbury historia de mirabilibus gestis Edvardi III. Oxford 1720.

Johannis de Fordun Scotichronicon. 5 vols Oxford 1722.

The history and antiquities of Glastonbury [by R. Rawlinson]. Oxford 1722.

Hemingi chartularium ecclesiae Wigorniensis. 2 vols Oxford 1723.

Robert of Gloucester's chronicle. 2 vols Oxford 1724, 1810.

Peter Langtoft's chronicle, improv'd by Robert of Brunne. 2 vols Oxford 1725, 1810.

Joannis Glastoniensis chronica: sive historia de rebus glastoniensibus. 2 vols Oxford 1726.

Adami de Domerham historia de rebus gestis glastoniensibus. 2 vols Oxford 1727.

Thomae de Elmham vita et gesta Henrici quinti. Oxford 1727.

Liber niger scaccarii. 2 vols Oxford 1728, 1771.

Historia vitae et regni Ricardi II, a monacho quodam de Evesham consignata. Oxford 1729.

Johannis de Trokelow annales Edvardi II. Oxford 1729.

Thomae Caii vindiciae antiquitatis academiae oxoniensis. 2 vols Oxford 1730.

Walteri Hemingford historia de rebus gestis Edvardi I, Edvardi II et Edvardi III. 2 vols Oxford 1731.

A vindication of those who take the oath of allegiance to his present Majestie. 1731. Unauthorized by Hearne.

Duo rerum anglicarum scriptores veteres: viz Thomas Otterbourne et Johannes Whethamstede. 2 vols Oxford 1732.

Chronicon: sive annales prioratus de Dunstaple. 2 vols Oxford 1733.

Benedictus abbas Petroburgensis de vita et gestis Henrici II et Ricardi I. 2 vols Oxford 1735.

Autobiography. In Lives of John Leland, Hearne and Anthony à Wood, [ed W. Huddesford] 2 vols Oxford 1772 (enlarged).

Letters and Diaries

An account of my journey to Whaddon-hall in Bucks 1716; An account of Hearne's journey to Reading and Silchester 1714. In Letters written by eminent persons in the seventeenth and eighteenth centuries [ed J. Walker] vol 2, 1813. Extracts.

Reliquiae Hearnianae: the remains of Hearne. Ed P. Bliss 2 vols Oxford 1857, 3 vols 1869 (enlarged); rev J. Buchanan-Brown 1966. Selections.

Remarks and collections of Hearne. Ed C. E. Doble et al 11 vols Oxford 1885–1921 (Pbns Oxford Historical Soc).

§2

Bibliotheca Hearneiana. [Ed B. Botfield] 1848 (priv ptd); ed P. Bliss in Reliquiae Hearnianae vol 3, 1869 (2nd edn).

Douglas, D. C. Portrait of Hearne. In his English scholars 1660–1730, 1939, 1951 (rev).

RICHARD RAWLINSON

1690–1755

The life of Mr Anthony à Wood. [1711]. Anon.

Miscellanies on several curious subjects. [Ed Rawlinson] 1714.

A full and impartial account of the Oxford-riots in a letter from a member of the University [signed Philoxon]. 1715.

The history and antiquities of the cathedral church of Rochester. 1717. Anon.

The history and antiquities of the city and cathedral-church of Hereford. 1717. Anon.

A survey of Staffordshire, by S. Erdeswicke. 1717. Ed Rawlinson?

Petri Abaelardi et Heloissae epistolae. 1718.

Some memoirs of the life of Elias Ashmole. In Ashmole, Antiquities of Berkshire vol 1, 1719.

The natural history and antiquities of the county of Surrey, by John Aubrey. 5 vols 1719. Ed Rawlinson.

The history and antiquities of the cathedral-church of Salisbury, and the abbey-church of Bath. 1719 (anon), 1723.

The English topographer: or an historical account of all the pieces relating to the antiquities, natural history or topographical description of any part of England. 1720. Anon.

The history and antiquities of Glastonbury. Ed T. Hearne, Oxford 1722.

A new method of studying history, originally written in French by M. Lenglet du Fresnoy. 2 vols 1728. Tr Rawlinson.

The history of Sir John Perrott, Lord Lieutenant of Ireland. 1728. Ed Rawlinson.

The deed of trust and will of R. Rawlinson of St John Baptist College, Oxford; containing his endowment of an Anglo-Saxon lecture to the College and University. 1755.

Monmouthshire, a small specimen of the many mistakes in Dugdale's Baronage: reprint of a scarce and curious pamphlet addressed to Hearne. Ed C. Heath, Monmouth 1801.

A short historical account of the life and designs of Thomas Bray DD. In T. Bray: his life and selected works, ed B. C. Steiner, Baltimore 1901 (Pbns Maryland Historical Soc).

Parochial collections [of Wood and Rawlinson]. Ed F. N. Davis 3 vols Oxford 1920–9 (Oxfordshire Record Soc).

THOMAS BIRCH

1705–66

A general dictionary historical and critical, in which a new and accurate translation of that of Mr Bayle is included, by John Peter Bernard, Birch etc. 10 vols 1734–41. Ed Birch, who also wrote the 618 new biographies signed T and H.

An historical and critical account of the life and writings of Mr John Milton. In A complete collection of the historical, political and miscellaneous works of John Milton, 2 vols 1738, 1 vol 1753.

The life of Mr William Chillingworth. In Works of William Chillingworth, 3 vols Oxford 1738 (9th edn), London 1742 (10th edn).

The complete works of Francis Bacon; to which is prefixed a new life of the author. 4 vols 1740. Ed Birch.

A collection of the state papers of John Thurloe, to which is prefixed the life of Thurloe. 7 vols 1742. Ed Birch.

An account of the life and writings of Ralph Cudworth. In Cudworth, The true intellectual system of the universe, 1743 (2nd edn), rptd in Cudworth's Works vol 1, 1829.

Lives and characters. In J. Houbraken and G. Vertue, Heads of illustrious persons of Great Britain, 2 vols 1743–51, 1747–52, 1 vol 1756, 1813.

The life of the Hon Robert Boyle. 1744; in Boyle's Works vol 1, 1744, 1772.

An inquiry into the share which Charles I had in the transactions of the Earl of Glamorgan for bringing over a body of Irish rebels to assist that King in 1645 and 1646. 1747 (anon), 1756 (enlarged).

An historical view of the negociations between the Courts of England, France and Brussels 1592–1617; to which is added A relation of the state of France drawn up by Sir George Carew in 1609. 1749.

The life of Mrs Catharine Cockburn. In her Works, 2 vols 1751.

The life of Mr Edmund Spenser. In The Faerie Queene, 3 vols 1751.

Memoirs of the reign of Queen Elizabeth from 1581 till her death. 2 vols 1754.

The life of Dufresnoy. In [J.] Wills, De arte graphica: or the art of painting, translated from the Latin of C. A. Dufresnoy, 1754.

The history of the Royal Society of London. 4 vols 1756–7.

The life of Henry Prince of Wales, eldest son of James I. 1760, Dublin 1760.

Letters between Colonel R. Hammond and the Committee of Lords and Commons at Derby House relating to Charles I while he was confined in Carisbrooke Castle. 1764.

An account of the life of John Ward, Professor of Rhetoric in Gresham College. 1766.

The Court and times of James the First, illustrated by authentic and confidential letters. 2 vols 1848. Transcribed by Birch, ed R. F. Williams.

The Court and times of Charles the First, including memoirs of the mission in England of the Capuchin friars in the service of Queen Henrietta Maria. 2 vols 1848. Transcribed by Birch, ed R. F. Williams.

The life of Sir Walter Ralegh. In Ralegh's Works, 2 vols 1751; rptd in Ralegh's Works vol 1, Oxford 1829.

The life of John Tillotson, Archbishop of Canterbury. 1752, 1753 (enlarged); in Tillotson's Works vol 1, 1752, 1820.

MINOR HISTORICAL WRITERS 1700–1750

Historians

THOMAS RYMER
1641–1713

Collections

Critical works. Ed C. A. Zimansky, New Haven 1956.

§1

Reflections on Aristotle's treatise of poesie, by R. Rapin. 1674 (anon), 1694; in Whole critical works of Monsieur Rapin vol 2, 1706, 1716, 1731; preface in Critical works of Rymer, ed C. A. Zimansky, New Haven 1956. Tr Rymer, with a preface.

The tragedies of the last age. 1678 (for 1677), 1692; in Critical works, ed C. A. Zimansky, New Haven 1956.

Edgar, or the English monarch: an heroick tragedy. 1678, 1691, 1693.

A general draught and prospect of government in Europe, shewing the antiquity, power, decay of parliaments. 1681 (anon), 1689, 1714, 1714, 1715, 1715; rptd (with misattribution to Algernon Sydney) as A general view of government in Europe, in J. Ralph, Of the use and abuse of parliaments vol 1, 1744, and in Sidney's Works, ed J. Robertson 1772.

Historia ecclesiastica carmine elegiaco concinnata, authore Thoma Hobbio Malmesburiensi. 1688 (anon); tr as A true ecclesiastical history, from Moses to the time of Martin Luther, 1722. Preface by Rymer.

Poems on several occasions; with Valentinian: a tragedy, written by John late Earl of Rochester. 1691 (anon), 1696, 1705, 1710, 1714, 1732; in Critical works, ed C. A. Zimansky, New Haven 1956. Preface by Rymer.

A short view of tragedy. 1692; in Critical works, ed C. A. Zimansky, New Haven 1956. See J. Dennis, The impartial critick: or some observations upon A short view of tragedy, 1693.

Letters to the Bishop of Carlisle, occasioned by some passages in his late book of the Scotch Library: letter I. 1702 (anon); letter II, [1703?] (anon); letter III, 1706 (anon).

Foedera, conventiones, literae et cujuscunque generis acta publica, inter reges Angliae etc. 17 vols 1704–1617 (for 1717) (vols 16–17 by R. Sanderson), on period 1101–1625; ed G. Holmes 20 vols 1727–35 (enlarged) (vols 15–20 by Sanderson); 10 vols Hague 1739–45 (enlarged); ed A. Clarke, J. Caley, F. Holbrooke 4 vols 1816–69 (incomplete). Syllabus of the Foedera by T. D. Hardy, 3 vols 1869–85. Calendar in English, with index in vol 3.

§2

Stoll, E. E. Oedipus and Othello: Corneille, Rymer and Voltaire. Revue Anglo-américaine 12 1935; rptd in Shakespeare and other masters, Cambridge Mass 1940.

Walcott, F. G. John Dryden's answer to Rymer's The tragedies of the last age. PQ 15 1936.

Douglas, D. C. Rymer and Madox. In his English scholars 1660–1730, 1939, 1951 (rev).

Leech, C. Rymer on Othello. In his Shakespeare's tragedies and other studies in seventeenth-century drama, 1950.

Watson, G. In his Literary critics, 1962 (Pelican), 1964 (rev).

—— Dryden's first answer to Rymer. RES new ser 14 1963.

HUMPHREY PRIDEAUX
1648–1724

§1

The true nature of imposture fully display'd in the life of Mahomet. 1697, 1697, 1708 (4th edn), 1723 (8th edn), Dublin 1730.

The Old and New Testament connected in the history of the Jews. 2 vols 1716–18, 1749 (11th edn), 4 vols 1808, 1815 (17th edn), 2 vols 1839, 1845; ed J. T. Wheeler 1858.

Letters

The life of Prideaux with several tracts and letters. 1748.

Letters to John Ellis 1674–1722. Ed E. M. Thompson 1875 (Camden Soc).

§2

The life of Prideaux with several tracts and letters. 1748.
Ketton-Cremer, R. W. In his Norfolk assembly, 1957.

JEREMY COLLIER
1650–1726

Collier's attacks upon the theatre and the literature and scholarship arising from them are not included here; see col 459 above.

Miscellanies. 1694–5 (pts 1–2); 1697 (enlarged as Essays upon several moral subjects); 1705–9 (pts 3–4).
The great historical, geographical, genealogical and poetical dictionary, collected from historians, especially L. Morery. 2 vols 1701 (2nd edn, enlarged to 1688); Supplement, 1705 (continuation to 1705); Appendix, 1721.
An ecclesiastical history of Great Britain, chiefly of England, with a brief account of the affairs of religion in Ireland. 2 vols 1708–14; ed F. Barham 9 vols 1840–1; ed T. Lathbury 9 vols 1852.

WHITE KENNETT
1660–1728

The life of Mr Somner. In W. Somner, A treatise of the Roman ports and forts in Kent, Oxford 1693; rptd in W. Somner, A treatise of gavelkind, 1726 (2nd edn).
Parochial antiquities attempted in the history of Ambrosden, Burcester and other adjacent parts in the counties of Oxford and Bucks. Oxford 1695; ed B. Bandinel 2 vols 1818 (much enlarged).
Ecclesiastical synods and parliamentary convocations in the Church of England historically stated, and justly vindicated from the misrepresentations of Mr Atterbury. 1701.
The case of impropriations and of the augumentation of vicarages and other insufficient cures, stated by history and law, with an appendix of records and memorials. 1704.
The history of England from the commencement of the reign of Charles I to the end of the reign of William III. In A complete history of England; with the lives of all the Kings and Queens thereof to the death of William III vol 3, 1706, 1719.
Memoirs of the family of Cavendish. 1708, Dublin 1737 (enlarged); ed J. Nichols 1797 (enlarged).
A memorial to Protestants on the fifth of November; containing a more full discovery of some particulars relating to the happy deliverance of James I anno 1605. 1713.
A register and chronicle ecclesiastical and civil, from the restauration of Charles II. Vol 1, 1728 (all pbd).
An historical account of the discipline and jurisdiction of the Church of England. 1730 (2nd edn).

LAURENCE ECHARD
1670?–1730

An exact description of Ireland. 1691.
A most compleat compendium of geography. 1691, 1691, 1693, 1697, 1713 (8th edn).
The gazetteer's or newsman's interpreter: being a geographical index of all the considerable cities etc in Europe. 1692, 1693, 1695, 1744 (16th edn).

The Roman history, from the building of the city to the perfect settlement of the Empire by Augustus. 1695, 1696, 1697, 1699; vol 2, from Augustus to Constantine, 1698, 1699; 2 vols 1699 (4th edn).
A general ecclesiastical history from the nativity of Constantine. 1702, 2 vols 1712 (3rd edn), 1 vol 1719 (5th edn), 2 vols 1729 (7th edn).
The history of England, from the first entrance of Julius Caesar to the end of the reign of James the First. 1707. Vols 2–3, To the establishment of William and Mary, 1718; complete work 2 vols 1720 (enlarged); Appendix, 1720 (addns etc). *See* The conduct of the Earl of Nottingham: being a continuation by several hands of Echard's History of England etc, ed W. A. Aiken, New Haven 1941.
The history of the Revolution and the establishment of England in 1688. 1725, Dublin 1725.

JOHN OLDMIXON
1673?–1742

Poems on several occasions, written in imitation of the manner of Anacreon etc. 1696.
An idyll on the peace. 1697. Anon.
Thyrsis: a pastoral. In P. A. Motteux, The novelty, 1697.
Amintas: a pastoral, made English out of Italian from the Aminta of Tasso. 1698.
A poem humbly addresst to the Earl of Portland on his Lordships return from his embassy in France. 1698.
Reflections on the stage and Mr Collyer's Defence of the Short view. 1699.
The grove, or love's paradice: an opera. 1700.
A funerall idyll, sacred to the glorious memory of K. William III. 1702.
The governour of Cyprus: a tragedy. 1703.
Amores britannici: espistles historical and gallant, in English heroic verse. 2 vols 1703.
A pastoral poem on the victories at Schellenburgh and Blenheim, with a large preface shewing the antiquity and dignity of pastoral poetry. 1704.
Life of Blake. In Lives English and foreign including the history of England and other nations of Europe from 1550 to 1690 vol 2, 1704.
Iberia liberata: a poem occasion'd by the success of her Majesties arms in Catalonia, Valencia etc. 1706.
A complete history of England, with the lives of all the kings and queens thereof to the death of William III. 3 vols 1706, 1719. Ed Oldmixon, who also added new lives in vol 1.
The Muses Mercury: or the monthly miscellany. Jan 1707–Jan 1708. Ed and partly written by Oldmixon.
The British Empire in America. 2 vols 1708, 1741 (rev).
The history of addresses. 2 vols 1709–11; vol 1, 1710 (2nd edn). Anon.
The medley. 5 Oct 1710–6 August 1711; 1711 (collected). A weekly periodical, ed and largely written by Oldmixon.
A letter to the seven Lords of the committee appointed to examine Gregg. 1711 (anon); rptd in Prose works of Swift vol 3, ed H. Davis et al, Oxford 1950.
Remarks upon remarks: or the barrier-treaty and the succession vindicated. 1711. Anon.
Letters and negotiations of the Count D'Estrades translated by several hands. 3 vols 1711. Partly tr Oldmixon.
The history of Dr Sacheverell faithfully transcribed from the Paris-gazette with remarks comical and political. 1711. Anon.
Reflections on Dr Swift's letter to the Earl of Oxford about the English tongue. [1712] (anon); ed L. A. Landa, Ann Arbor 1948 (Augustan Reprint Soc).
The Dutch barrier our's: or the interest of England and Holland inseparable. 1712, 1712. Anon.
A defence of Mr Maccartney, by a friend. 1712. Anon.
Dejanira to Hercules. In Ovid's epistles, translated by

several hands, 1712 (8th edn), 1716, 1720, 1725, 1729, 1736, 1748, 1761, 1768, 1775, 1795.

The secret history of Europe. 4 vols 1712–15. Anon.

The life and history of Belisarius and a parallel between him and a modern heroe [Marlborough]. 1713. Anon.

Poems and translations by several hands; to which is added the Hospital of fools: a dialogue by the late William Walsh. 1714, 1714 (as Original poems and translations). Ed Oldmixon.

The dedication for the Latin edition of Lucretius, written in the year 1711 by Dr Garth, now made English by Mr Oldmixon. 1714.

Arcana gallica: or the secret history of France for the last century. 1714. Anon.

The false steps of the ministry after the revolution, with some reflections on the license of the pulpit and press. 1714; rptd in Somers tracts vol 3, 1748. Anon.

The Court of Atalantis: containing a four years history of that famous island, intermixt with fables and epistles, by several hands. 1714, 1717 (for 1716) (as Court tales: or a history of the amours of the present nobility), 1720, 1732 (for 1731). Ed Oldmixon.

Memoirs of North-Britain, in which it is proved that the Scots nation have always been zealous in the defence of the Protestant religion and liberty. 1715. Anon.

Memoirs of the life of the most noble Thomas late Marquis of Wharton. 1715. Anon.

The life and posthumous works of Arthur Maynwaring. 1715. Anon.

Nixon's Cheshire prophecy at large, 1715?, 1719 (6th edn), 1740 (7th edn), 1744 (13th edn). Anon.

The Catholick poet [Pope], or Protestant Barnaby's [Lintott] sorrowful lamentation: an excellent new ballad. 1716. Anon.

Memoirs of the life of John Lord Somers, with a large introduction in vindication of the modern biography. 1716. Anon.

Memoirs of Ireland from the Restoration to the present times. 1716. Anon.

The critical history of England, ecclesiastical and civil, wherein the errors of the monkish writers, and others before the Reformation are expos'd and corrected, as are also the deficiency and partiality of later historians; and particular notice is taken of the History of the Grand Rebellion and Echard's History of England to which are added remarks on some objections made to Bishop Burnet's History of his times. Vol 1, 1724, 1725, 1726, 1728, 1730 (all with addns); vol 2, Containing an examen of Mr Echard's History of the reigns of Henry VIII etc, 1726, 1730. Anon.

A review of Dr Zachary Grey's Defence of our ancient and modern historians. 1725; reissued with subsequent edns of the Critical history vol 1, above. Anon.

Clarendon and Whitlock compar'd; to which is added a comparison between the History of the Rebellion and other histories of the Civil War. 1727, 1737. Anon.

An essay on criticism, as it regards design, thought and expression. 1728; issued with the Critical history vol 1, above, 1728, 1730; ed R. J. Madden, Los Angeles 1964 (Augustan Reprint Soc).

The arts of logick and rhetorick. 1728. Anon.

The history of England, during the reigns of the royal house of Stuart, wherein the errors of late histories are discover'd and corrected. 1730 (for 1729). Anon.

Mr Oldmixon's reply to the late Bishop Atterbury's Vindication of Bishop Smallridge, Dr Aldrich and himself. 1732.

The history of England during the reigns of William and Mary, Anne, George I: being the sequel of the reigns of the Stuarts. 1735.

The history of England during the reigns of Henry VIII, Edward VI, Mary, Elizabeth. 1739.

The history and life of Robert Blake. [1741]. Anon.

Memoirs of the press, historical and political from 1710 to 1740. 1742.

CONYERS MIDDLETON
1683–1750

Collections

Miscellaneous works. 4 vols 1752, 5 vols 1755.

§1

A dissertation concerning the origin of printing in England. Cambridge 1735; rptd in W. Bowyer and J. Nichols, The origin of printing, 1776–81 (2nd edn).

The history of the life of Cicero. 2 vols 1741, 3 vols 1741, 2 vols Dublin 1741, 3 vols 1755 (5th edn).

The epistles of Cicero to Brutus, and of Brutus to Cicero, with English notes [and a] prefatory dissertation. 1743.

A treatise on the Roman Senate. 1747; ed T. Knowles 1778.

A free inquiry into miraculous powers in the Christian Church. 1749.

Letters

Stuart, D. M. Some unpublished letters of John, Lord Hervey and Middleton. English 2 1938.

Horace Walpole's correspondence with Sir David Dalrymple, Middleton et al. Ed W. S. Lewis et al, New Haven 1952 (vol 15 of Yale edn of Walpole's correspondence).

JOHN, 2nd BARON HERVEY
1696–1743

Collections

The laurel: poetical works of Collins, Dr Johnson, Pomfret, Hammond and Hervey. [1808].

Poetical works of Hammond and Hervey. Ed G.D. 1818.

§1

Observations on the writings of the Craftsman [Bolingbroke's letters on English history]. 1730 (anon); sequel, 1730 (anon).

Farther observations on the writings of the Craftsman. 1730 (anon). Reply to An answer to a late pamphlet entitled Observations on the writings of the Craftsman, 1731.

Remarks on the Craftsman's vindication of his two honble patrons [Bolingbroke and W. Pulteney] in his paper of May 22, 1731. 1731 (7 edns). Anon. Sometimes ascribed to William Arnall; see DNB.

An epistle from a nobleman [Hervey] to a Doctor of Divinity. 1733 (anon); ed W. P. Jones, Los Angeles 1960 (Augustan Reprint Soc).

Letters between Hervey and Dr Middleton concerning the Roman Senate. Ed T. Knowles 1778.

Memoirs of the reign of George the Second. Ed J. W. Croker 2 vols 1848, 3 vols 1884 (with a life of Hervey); ed R. Sedgwick 3 vols 1931 (as Some materials towards memoirs of the reign of George II), 1 vol 1952 (abridged), 1963 (rev).

Letters

Stuart, D. M. Some unpublished letters of Hervey and Dr Conyers Middleton. English 2 1938.

Hervey and his friends 1726–38. Ed Earl of Ilchester 1950. Extracts. See TLS 15 Dec 1950, 19–26 Jan, 2 Feb 1951.

§2

Namier, L. B. The Memoirs of Hervey. In his In the margin of history, 1939; rptd in Crossroads of power: collected essays vol 2, 1962.

Gooch, G. P. Hervey and Queen Caroline; Hervey and George II. In his Courts and cabinets, 1944.

Quennell, P. C. In his Singular preference, 1952.
Connolly, C. In his Previous convictions, 1963.

Antiquaries
EDMUND GIBSON
1669–1748

§1

Chronicon saxonicum, ex mss codicibus nunc primum integrum edidit. Oxford 1692.
Camden's Britannia newly translated into English, with large additions and improvements. 1695, 2 vols 1722, 1753, 1772.
Reliquiae Spelmannianae: posthumous works of Sir Henry Spelman. Oxford 1698; rptd in Spelman, English works, 1723, below. Ed Gibson.
Synodus anglicana: or the constitution and proceedings of an English Convocation, shown from the acts and registers thereof, to be agreeable to an episcopal church. 1672 (for 1702), 1730 (as A compleat history of convocations from 1356 to 1689); ed E. Cardwell, Oxford 1854.
Codex juris ecclesiastici anglicani: or the statutes, constitutions, canons, rubricks and articles of the Church of England, methodically digested under their proper heads. 2 vols 1713, Oxford 1761.
The English works of Sir H. Spelman, together with his posthumous works. 1723, 1727. Ed Gibson.
For Gibson's religious writings see col 651, above.

Letters

Original letters of eminent literary men. Ed H. Ellis 1843 (Camden Soc).
Griffiths, G. M. Eight letters from Gibson to Bishop [Humphrey] Humphreys 1707–9. Jnl of Nat Lib of Wales 10 1958.

§2

Sykes, N. Gibson, Bishop of London: a study in politics and religion in the eighteenth century. Oxford 1926.
—— Gibson and Sir Robert Walpole. EHR 44 1929.

WILLIAM STUKELEY
1687–1765

§1

An account of a Roman temple near Graham's Dike in Scotland. [1720].

Of the Roman amphitheater at Dorchester. [1723]; ed A. M. Broadley, Weymouth [1913] (priv ptd), 1925.
Itinerarium curiosum: or an account of the antiquitys and remarkable curiositys in nature or art, observed in travels thro Great Britain. 1724 (Centuria 1); 2 vols 1776 (complete and much enlarged).
Palaeographia sacra: or discourses on monuments of antiquity that relate to sacred history. 1736.
Stonehenge: a temple restor'd to the British druids. 1740.
Abury: a temple of the British druids, with some others, described. 1743.
Palaeographia britannica: or discourses on antiquities in Britain. 1743–52 (nos 1–3), Cambridge 1795.
An account of Richard of Cirencester, with his antient map of Roman Brittain and the itinerary thereof. 1757.
The medallic history of Carausius, Emperor in Brittain. 2 vols 1757–9.
Memoirs of Isaac Newton's life 1752. Ed A. H. White 1936.

Letters and Diaries

The family memoirs of Stukeley, and the antiquarian and other correspondence of Stukeley, R. and S. Gale etc. [Ed W. C. Lukis] 3 vols Newcastle 1882–7 (Pbns of Surtees Soc). Autobiography, diary, letters etc.

§2

Piggott, S. Stukeley: an eighteenth-century antiquary. Oxford 1950.

HARLEIAN MISCELLANY

The Harleian miscellany: a collection of scarce, curious and entertaining pamphlets and tracts in the late Earl of Oxford's library. [Ed W. Oldys] 8 vols 1744–6; ed T. Park, index by T. H. Horne, 10 vols 1808–13.

SOMERS TRACTS

A collection of scarce and valuable tracts, selected from an infinite number in the Royal, Cotton, Sion and other publick as well as private libraries, particularly that of the late Lord Sommers. 4 vols 1748; Second collection, 4 vols 1750; Third collection, 4 vols 1751; Fourth, 4 vols 1751–2; ed W. Scott 13 vols 1809–15.

C. LATE EIGHTEENTH-CENTURY HISTORIANS 1750–1800

WILLIAM ROBERTSON
1721–93

Collections

Historical works, with an account of his life and writings by G. Gleig. 6 vols Edinburgh 1813.
Works, to which is prefixed an account of his life and writings by Dugald Stewart. 12 vols 1817, 1822.
Works, with a sketch of his life and writings by R. A. Davenport. 11 vols Chiswick 1824, 8 vols Oxford 1825.

§1

The situation of the world at the time of Christ's appearance, and its connexion with the success of his religion, considered: a sermon. Edinburgh 1755, London 1759, 1775 (5th edn), Edinburgh 1791, 1818.
The history of Scotland during the reigns of Queen Mary and of King James VI till his accession to the Crown of England, with a review of the Scotch history previous to that period and an appendix containing original papers. 2 vols 1759, 1759, 1760, 1761, 1762, 1769, 1771, Dublin 1772, London 1776, 1787 (11th edn 'corrected'), 1791, Edinburgh 1791, London 1794 (14th edn, 'with the author's last emendations and additions'), 3 vols 1797, Glasgow 1800, London 1802 (16th edn, with account of the life and writings of the author by Dugald Stewart).
Memorial relating to the University of Edinburgh. 1768. Anon.
The history of the reign of the Emperor Charles V, with a view of the progress of society in Europe from the subversion of the Roman Empire to the beginning of the sixteenth century. 3 vols 1769, Dublin 1769, Philadelphia 1770, 4 vols 1774, 1777 ('new edition, with corrections'), 1782, 1787, 1792 (7th edn), 1796, 1798, 1802, Edinburgh 1805, London 1806, 1809, 1812, Philadelphia 1812, Glasgow 1817, New York 1840, 2 vols 1857 ('with an account of the Emperor's life after his abdication by W. H. Prescott').

A new geographical and historical grammar by Thomas Salmon, with great amendments and improvements by Mr Robertson. 1772.

The history of America. 2 vols 1777, Dublin 1777, London 1778, 1780, 1783, 1787, Vienna 1787, London 1788 (5th edn 'with corrections'), Basle 1790, London 1792, 1796, 1796 (bks 9–10 containing the History of Virginia to the year 1688 and the History of New England to the year 1652, ed W. Robertson the younger), 3 vols 1800–1, 4 vols 1800 (9th edn 'in which is included the post-humous volume, containing the History of Virginia and of New England').

An historical disquisition concerning the knowledge which the ancients had of India. 1791, Basle 1792, Philadelphia 1792, London 1794 (2nd edn, 'with the author's last corrections and additions').

Letters

Horace Walpole's correspondence with Robertson. Ed W. S. Lewis, C. H. Bennett and A. G. Hoover, New Haven 1952 (vol 15 of Yale edn of Walpole's correspondence).

EDWARD GIBBON
1737–94

Bibliographies etc

Keynes, G. L. The library of Gibbon: a catalogue of his books. 1940.

Norton, J. E. A bibliography of the works of Gibbon. Oxford 1940.

§I

Essai sur l'étude de la littérature. 1761, Paris 1761, 1762, Geneva? 1762 (with indexes), Dublin 1777; tr 1764 ('presumably not written by Becket (publisher) himself but by some professional translator') (Norton). Miscellaneous works, 1837, contains what is said to be an entirely new version; rptd in The life of Edward Gibbon, Paris 1840.

Mémoires littéraires de la Grande Bretagne, pour l'an 1767. 1768, Leyden 1768 (the London edn with cancel title-page); Pour l'an 1768, 1769 (vol 2). Written by Gibbon and Deyverdun; Gibbon in later life professed to be unable to separate his work from Deyverdun's. 2 articles from vol 2, Doutes historiques par Mr Horace Walpole and Réflexions sur les Doutes historiques par Mr D. Hume, and rptd in Miscellaneous works vol 3, 1814.

Critical observations on the sixth book of the Aeneid. 1770 (anon), 1794.

The history of the decline and fall of the Roman Empire. 4°: Vol 1, chs 1–16, 1776 (17 Feb), 1776 (3 June), 1777 (May 'revised'; see Bury's edn, vol 1, pp. 506–9, for Gibbon's alterations), 1781, 1782; vols 2, chs 17–26; 3, chs 27–38; 1781 (with portrait after Reynolds and 2 maps (parts of Europe and Asia adjacent to Constantinople; eastern part of the Empire) in vol 2, and map of western part of the Empire in vol 3), 1781 (for 1782) (without portrait; new title-pages), 1787; vols 1–3, 3 vols 1789, chs 39–47; 5, chs 48–57; 6, chs 58–71, 1788 (8 May).

8°: 6 vols 1783 (reprint of vols 1–3 4°), 1788; 6 vols 1790 (reprint of vols 4–6 4°); 12 vols 1791–2, 1797, 1802. London copyright edns. Dublin edns: 2 vols 1776 (reprint of vol 1 4°), 1777, 6 vols 1781 (reprint of vols 1–3 4°), 1788 (reprint of vols 4–6 4°), 1789 (reprint of vols 1–3 4°). Basle edns: 13 vols 1787–9 (reprint of vols 1–6 4°), 7 vols 1789 (reprint of vols 1–3 4°).

Later edns

Ed H. H. Milman (with maps and notes by F. P. G. Guizot from the French trn of 1812) 12 vols 1838–9, 6

vols 1846, 8 vols 1854–5 (with additional notes by William Smith and 14 maps); ed H. G. Bohn (with notes by Guizot, F. A. W. Wenck, C. G. Schreiter and G. H. Hugo) 7 vols 1853–5 etc; ed J. B. Bury (with introd, notes, appendices and maps) 7 vols 1896–1900, 1909–14 (illustr O. M. Dalton and with bibliography of edns, trns and selections from the Decline and fall by H. M. Beatty, vol 7, pp. 348–64, 7 vols 1903–4 (WC), 6 vols [1910] (EL), 7 vols 1926–9 (rev text and with 'important additions to Gibbon's notes with a view to bringing the information up to the level of modern historical scholarship').

Abridgements

2 vols 1789; ed Bowdler 5 vols 1826; ed M. K. Graham 1940 (priv ptd); ed D. M. Low 1960; ed J. Sloan 2 vols New York 1962; ed M. Hadas 1962; ed H. R. Trevor-Roper 1963 (with other selected writings); ed R. Price 1967.

A vindication of some passages in the fifteenth and sixteenth chapters of the History of the decline and fall of the Roman Empire. 1779, 1779 (rev), Dublin 1779; rptd in Gibbon's Miscellaneous works vol 2 1796, vol 4 1814, vol 5 Basle 1796–7.

Mémoire justificatif pour servir de réponse à l'exposé etc de la cour de France. 1779 (anon), 1779 (with the Exposé des motifs de la conduite du roi de France); tr 1779. A French and English version of Mémoire justificatif and Exposé pbd 1780. Mémoire rptd in S. N. H. Linguet, Annales politiques, civiles et littéraires vol 7, 1779; and in Gibbon, Miscellaneous works vol 2, 1796, vol 4 Basle 1796–7, vol 5 London 1814.

Copy of the answer transmitted to the Marquis d'Almovodar by the Lord Viscount Weymouth, July 13 1779. French version rev Gibbon.

Miscellaneous works of Edward Gibbon esquire, with memoirs of his life and writings composed by himself; illustrated from his letters with occasional notes and narrative by John [Holroyd] Lord Sheffield. 2 vols 1796, 3 vols Dublin 1796 (with notice of Mme de Sévery), 7 vols Basle 1796–7, 5 vols 1814 ('with considerable additions'), 1815 (with additional matter of 1814 edn, rptd to be uniform as vol 3 with 1796 edn), 1837 (with new trn of Essai sur l'étude de la littérature), New York 1837.

The Antiquities of the House of Brunswick *was pbd separately in one vol in 1814; there were also separate edns of the Memoirs, below.*

Memoirs. 2 vols 1827, 1830, 1 vol [1831]?; ed H. Milman 1839, Paris 1840; ed J. Murray 1896 ('printed verbatim from hitherto unpublished mss, with an introduction by the Earl of Sheffield'). This vol contains the 6 drafts of Gibbon's autobiography from which the first Lord Sheffield contructed his texts of the memoirs for his edns of Miscellaneous works, 1796 and 1814. Ed O. F. Emerson, Boston 1898; ed G. Birkbeck Hill 1900 (a conflation of 1796 and 1814 edns, with preface, notes, 68 excursuses and index); ed J. B. Bury, Oxford (WC) 1907; ed O. Smeaton 1911 (EL); ed G. A. Bonnard 1966 (from ms, as Memoirs of my life).

English essays. Ed P. B. Craddock, Oxford 1972 (from ms).

Letters and Journals

Private letters of Edward Gibbon 1753–94. Ed R. E. Prothero 2 vols 1896.

Gibbon's journal to January 28th 1763; My journal I, II and III, and Ephemerides with introductory essays by D. M. Low. 1929.

Le journal de Gibbon à Lausanne 17 août 1763–19 avril 1764. Ed G. A. Bonnard, Lausanne 1945.

Miscellanea Gibboniana. Ed G. R. de Beer, G. A. Bonnard and L. Junod, Lausanne 1952.

Letters. Ed J. E. Norton 3 vols 1956.

Gibbon's journey from Geneva to Rome: his journal from 20 April to 2 October 1764. Ed G. A. Bonnard 1961.

§2

Sainte-Beuve, C.-A. In his Causeries du lundi vol 8, Paris 1855.
Bagehot, W. In his Estimates of some Englishmen and Scotchmen, 1858.
Young, G. M. Gibbon. 1932, 1948 (with introd).
McCloy, S. T. Gibbon's antagonism to Christianity. 1933.
Dawson, C. Edward Gibbon. Proc Br Acad 20 1934.
Mowat, R. B. Gibbon. 1936.
Low, D. M. Edward Gibbon. 1937.
Hill, M. C. The Sheffield edition of Gibbon's Autobiography. RES 14 1938.
Bonnard, G. A. Essai sur l'étude de la littérature as judged by contemporary reviews and Gibbon himself. E Studies 32 1951.
—— Le journal de Gibbon à Lausanne. Paris 1955.
de Beer, G. R. Gibbon and his world. 1968.
Wedgwood, C. V. Edward Gibbon. 1955.
—— In her Truth and opinion, 1960.
Bond, H. L. The literary art of Gibbon. Oxford 1960.
Momigliano, A. In his Studies in historiography, 1966.

JOHN NICHOLS
1745–1826

Nichols was primarily an editor and compiler. There are typescript copies of a bibliography by A. H. Smith in London and Leicester Univ libraries.

Verses on the coronation of their late Majesties King George II and Queen Caroline. 1761. By W. Bowyer and Nichols.
The buds of Parnassus: a collection of original poems. 1763, 1764?
Islington: a poem. 1763.
The laurel-wreath: being a collection of original miscellaneous poems by W. P[erfect]. 1766. Nichols contributed to this collection.
The amours of Lais: or the misfortunes of love. 1766. Conclusion by Nichols.
The origin of printing, in two essays: I, The substance of Dr Middleton's dissertation on the origin of printing in England; II, Mr Meerman's account of the first invention of the art. 1774, 1776 ('with improvements'); suppl 1781. Ed Bowyer and Nichols.
The works of Jonathan Swift. Vol 9 (4°), vol 17 (large 8°), vol 18 (12°), 1775. Includes index to previous vols of this edn by Hawkesworth.
A supplement to Dr Swift's works: being a collection of miscellanies in prose and verse, by the Dean, Dr Delany, Dr Sheridan and others, with explanatory notes. Vols 24–5 (large 8°), 1776–9, vols 25–7 (small 8°), vol 14 (4°), vols 25–7 (12°), 1779.
The original works of William King, with historical notes, and memoirs of the author. 3 vols 1776.
Anecdotes, biographical and literary, of the late Mr William Bowyer, printer. 1778 (anon; priv ptd), 1782 (greatly enlarged as Biographical and literary anecdotes of William Bowyer).
A dissertation upon English typographical founders and founderies by E. R. Mores. 1778 (for 1779); ed D. B. Updike, New York 1924 (Grolier Club); ed H. Carter and C. Ricks, Oxford 1961. With appendix signed J.N.
The gentleman's magazine. 1778–92 (jointly with D. Henry), 1792–1826.
Six old plays on which Shakespeare founded his Measure for measure etc. 2 vols 1779. Comedy of Errors, Shrew, King John, Henry IV, Henry V, Lear.
The history of the royal abbey of Bec by J. Bourget, translated from the French. 1779. Ed A. C. Ducarel assisted by Nichols.

Some account of the alien priories. 2 vols 1779, 1786. By A. C. Ducarel and J. Warburton; ed Ducarel, R. Gough, Nichols et al.
Anecdotes of Mr Hogarth. [1780?] (priv ptd), 1781 (enlarged as Biographical anecdotes of William Hogarth) 1782, 1785, 3 vols 1808–17 (enlarged as The genuine works of William Hogarth by John Nichols and George Steevens), 1822 (as The works of William Hogarth, from the original plates restored by James Heath, to which is prefixed, a biographical essay on the genius and productions of Hogarth, and explanations of the subjects of the plates by John Nichols), 2 vols 1833.
Bibliotheca topographica britannica. 8 vols 1780–90. Ed Nichols; contributions by Nichols listed separately under date below.
A collection of all the wills of the Kings and Queens of England. 1780.
A select collection of poems. 8 vols 1780–4.
Biographical memoirs of William Ged, including a particular account of his progress in the art of block-printing. 1781, Newcastle 1819.
The history and antiquities of Hinckley, in the county of Leicester. Bibliotheca topographica britannica no 7, 1782 (in vol 7 1790), 1813 (from The history and antiquities of the county of Leicester).
Critical conjectures and observations on the New Testament by W. Bowyer. 1782 (3rd edn), 1812 (4th edn).
The epistolary correspondence of Francis Atterbury, with historical notes. 4 vols 1783–7, 5 vols 1789–98 (as Miscellaneous works).
Novum testamentum graecum [ed W. Bowyer]; editio secunda cura Johannis Nichols [assisted by H. Owen]. 1783.
The principal additions and corrections in the third edition of Dr Johnson's Lives of the poets, collected to complete the second edition. [1783]. Compiled by Nichols.
A new and general biographical dictionary. 12 vols 1784 ('a new edition, greatly enlarged and improved'). With R. Heathcote.
Miscellaneous tracts by the late William Bowyer and several of his learned friends, collected and illustrated with occasional notes. 1785.
The plays of William Shakespeare, accurately printed from the text of Mr Malone's edition, with select explanatory notes. 7 vols 1786–90.
The Tatler: the lucubrations of Isaac Bickerstaff, with notes. 6 vols 1786. Ed J. Calder and Nichols from notes of T. Percy.
The epistolary correspondence of Sir Richard Steele, with literary and historical anecdotes. 2 vols 1787, 1809.
The history and antiquities of Aston Flamvile and Burbach, with an appendix to the history of Hinckley. Bibliotheca topographica britannica no 43, 1787 (in vol 7 1790).
The works of Leonard Welsted, with historical notes and biographical memoirs of the author. 1787.
The history and antiquities of Canonbury-House at Islington. Bibliotheca topographica britannica no 49, 1788 (in vol 2 1790).
The progresses and public processions of Queen Elizabeth. 3 vols and pt 1 of vol 4 1788–1821, 3 vols 1823. With R. Gough.
The Lover, by Marmaduke Myrtle gent, to which is added the Reader; with notes and illustrations. 1789.
The Lover and Reader: to which are prefixed the Whig-Examiner and a selection from the Medley. 1789.
The Town talk, the Fish pool, the Plebeian, the Old Whig, the Spinster etc, with notes and illustrations. 1789, 1790.
Collections towards the history and antiquities of the town and county of Leicester. 2 pts Bibliotheca topographica britannica nos 50–1, 1790 (in vols 7–8 1790).
The antiquaries museum by Jacob Schnebbelie. 1791. Ed Nichols and R. Gough.
Miscellaneous antiquities (in continuation of the Bibliotheca topographica britannica). Nos 1–6, 1791–7.

The Theatre by Sir R. Steele; to which are added the Anti-Theatre etc, illustrated with literary and historical anecdotes. 1791.

The history and antiquities of the county of Leicester. 4 vols in 8 1795–1815.

Illustrations of the manners and expences of antient times in England, with explanatory notes. 1797.

The plays of William Shakespeare, accurately printed from the text of Mr Steevens's last edition, with a selection of the most important notes. 8 vols 1797.

A sermon preached at the funeral of William Duke of Devonshire, with some memoirs of the family of Cavendish, by White Kennett. 1797 ('the second edition, with additions by the author, and by the editor').

A list of the members of the Society of Antiquaries of London, from 1717 to 1796, arranged in chronological and alphabetical order. 1798. Anon. Compiled by R. Gough and Nichols.

A comment upon part of the fifth journey of Antoninus through Britain. 1800, 1819.

An historical account of Beauchief Abbey by S. Pegge. 1801.

The works of Jonathan Swift. 19 vols 1801, 24 vols 1803, 19 vols 1808. Sheridan's edn, 'corrected and revised' by Nichols. Malone assisted Nichols with the 1808 edn.

Anecdotes of the English language by S. Pegge. 1803, 1814.

Brief memoirs of John Nichols. 1804.

Curialia: or an historical account of the Royal Household etc etc, pts 4 and 5 by Samuel Pegge. 1806.

Anonymiana, compiled by [S. Pegge], published from the ms. 1809, 1818.

Biographical memoirs of Richard Gough. GM March–April 1809; rptd 1809.

Letters on various subjects to and from William Nicolson. 2 vols 1809.

Biographical anecdotes of Richard Gough. 1810. Extracted from Literary anecdotes of the eighteenth century.

A catalogue of the library of Richard Gough. [1810]. With a biographical preface by Nichols.

The history of the worthies of England by T. Fuller, with a few explanatory notes. 2 vols 1811.

Literary anecdotes of the eighteenth century: comprizing memoirs of William Bowyer and many of his learned friends. 9 vols 1812–16. Vol 7: pt 1, 1813, index to vols 1–6; pt 2, 1816, index to vols 8–9.

The battle of Bosworth Field by W. Hutton. 1813 (2nd edn, with addns).

Some account of the Abbey Church of St Alban. 1813. With Gough.

Illustrations of the literary history of the eighteenth century. 8 vols 1817–58. J. B. Nichols continued this work after Nichols's death.

Curialia miscellanea: or anecdotes of old times by Samuel Pegge. 1818.

The miscellaneous works of George Hardinge. 3 vols 1818.

Poems, Latin, Greek and English, by George Hardinge. 1818.

Two music speeches at Cambridge by Roger Long and John Taylor, [with] memoirs. 1819.

A prefatory introduction, descriptive of the rise and progress of the [Gentleman's] Magazine, with anecdotes of the projector. In general index to GM 1787–1818, vol 3 1821; rptd as The rise and progress of the Gentleman's Magazine, 1821.

Four sermons: 1, by John Taylor, 1745; 2, by Dr Taylor, 1757; 3, by Bishop Lowth, 1758; 4, by Bishop Hayter, 1750. 1822.

The progresses, processions, and magnificent festivities, of King James the First. 3 vols in 4 1828.

Birth-day odes, and other domestic poems. 1827.

Minor lives: a collection of biographies. Ed E. L. Hart, Cambridge Mass 1971.

MINOR HISTORICAL WRITERS 1750–1800

GEORGE CHALMERS
1742–1825

Political annals of the present united colonies, from their settlement to the peace of 1763: book 1. 1780.

An introduction to the history of the revolt of the colonies. Vol 1 ptd and cancelled, [1782]; rptd 2 vols Boston 1845.

An estimate of the comparative strength of Britain during the present and four preceding reigns, and of the losses of her trade from every war since the Revolution. 1782, 1786, 1794 (corrected and improved).

Opinions on interesting subjects of public law and commercial policy; arising from American independence. 1784, 1785 ('corrected').

The life of Daniel De Foe. 1785 (anon), 1786, 1790.

Historical tracts by Sir John Davies, [with] a new life of the author. 1786.

A collection of treaties between Great Britain and other powers. 2 vols 1790.

Life of Thomas Pain, by Francis Oldys AM of the University of Pennsylvania [Chalmers]. 1791 (3 edns), 1792 (5th edn 'enlarged'), 1793 (10th edn).

The life of Thomas Ruddiman. 1794.

Parliamentary portraits; to which is prefixed A review of the present administration. 2 vols 1795.

A vindication of the privilege of the people in respect of the constitutional right of free discussion. 1796. Anon.

Life of Sir David Lyndsay. In Chalmers's edn of Lindsay's poetical works, 3 vols 1806.

Caledonia: or an account of North Britain. 3 vols 1807–24, 8 vols Paisley 1887–1902.

Opinions of eminent lawyers on various points of English jurisprudence, chiefly concerning the colonies, fisheries and commerce of Great Britain, collected and digested from the originals in the Board of Trade and other depositories. 1814.

Comparative views of the state of Great Britain and Ireland before the war; as it is since the peace. 1817.

The life of Mary, Queen of Scots. 2 vols 1818.

The poetic remains of some of the Scotish kings. 1824. Ed Chalmers.

A detection of the love-letters attributed in Hugh Campbell's work to Mary Queen of Scots, wherein his plagiarisms are proved and his fictions fixed. 1825. Anon.

Chalmers pbd a number of pamphlets. See also col 721, below.

SIR DAVID DALRYMPLE, LORD HAILES
1726–92

Memorials and letters relating to the history of Britain in the reign of James I. Glasgow 1762, 1766 ('corrected').

Memorials and letters relating to the history of Britain in the reign of Charles I. Glasgow 1766.

The secret correspondence of Sir R. Cecil with James VI. Edinburgh 1766. Ed Dalrymple.

Remarks on the history of Scotland. Edinburgh 1773.

Annals of Scotland, from Malcolm III to Robert I. Edinburgh 1776, 1779 ('continued to the accession of the House of Stewart'), 3 vols Edinburgh 1797 ('to which are added several tracts relative to the history'), 1819 (3rd edn).

See also col 761, below.

Letters

Horace Walpole's correspondence with Dalrymple. Ed W. S. Lewis, C. H. Bennett and A. G. Hoover, New Haven 1952 (vol 15 of Yale edn of Walpole's correspondence).

The correspondence of Thomas Percy and Dalrymple. Ed A. F. Falconer, Baton Rouge 1954.

SIR JOHN DALRYMPLE
1726–1810

An essay towards a general history of feudal property in Great Britain. 1757, 1759 (4th edn, 'corrected and enlarged').

Memoirs of Great Britain and Ireland, from the dissolution of the last Parliament of Charles II until the sea-battle off La Hogue. 2 pts Edinburgh 1771, Dublin 1771, London 1771; vol 2 (appendixes to vol 1), 3 pts 1773, 1773; vol 1 (for 3) ('From the battle off La Hogue till the capture of the French and Spanish fleets at Vigo'), 2 pts Edinburgh 1788; [complete work], 3 vols 1790.

RICHARD GOUGH
1735–1809
§1

The history of Carausius: or an examination of what has been advanced on that subject by Genebrier and Stukeley. 1762. Anon.

Anecdotes of British topography: or an historical account of what has been done for illustrating the topographical antiquities of Great Britain and Ireland. 1768 (anon), 2 vols 1780 (as British topography).

Archaeologia I. 1770. Anon introd containing an historical account of the origin and establishment of Society of Antiquaries.

A catalogue of the coins of Canute, King of Denmark and England. 1777. Anon.

The history of the town of Thetford, in the counties of Norfolk and Suffolk. 1779. Ed Gough from collections of T. Martin.

Observations on the round towers in Ireland and Scotland. 1779.

Catalogue of Sarum and York Missals. [1780]. Anon.

Bibliotheca topographica britannica. Ed J. Nichols 8 vols 1780–90. Gough's contributions include memoir of the author in no 1 (Edward Rowe Mores's History of Tunstall); nos 2, 20, Reliquiae Galeanae: account of the Gentlemen's Society at Spalding; no 3, Preface to William Orem's Description of the Chanonry in old Aberdeen (anon); nos 4, 19, Memoirs of Sir John Hawkwood (anon); nos 11, 22, The history of Croyland; no 31, A short genealogical view of the family of Oliver Cromwell (preface signed R.G.).

A comparative view of the antient monuments of India, particularly those in the island of Salset near Bombay. 1785. Preface signed R.G.

Sepulchral monuments in Great Britain applied to illustrate the history of families, manners, habits and arts, at the different periods from the Norman Conquest to the seventeenth century. 2 vols 1786–96.

Britannia by William Camden, translated and enlarged by the latest discoveries. 3 vols 1789, 4 vols 1806.

The life of Sir John Falstolff by W. Oldys. [1793]. Ed Gough.

An account of a missal executed for John Duke of Bedford. 1794. Dedication signed R.G.

The history and antiquities of Dorset by John Hutchins. 4 vols 1796–1815 (2nd edn). Ed Gough and J.B. Nichols.

The parochial history of Castor and its dependencies, [with] an account of Marham and several other places. In Kennet Gibson, A comment upon part of the fifth journey of Antoninus through Britain, 1800, 1819 ('corrected and enlarged').

The history and antiquities of Pleshy in the county of Essex. 1803. Preface signed R.G.

Coins of the Seleucidae, Kings of Syria. 1803. Anon.

Description of the Beauchamp Chapel, adjoining to the church of St Mary at Warwick. 1804 (anon), 1809.

Some account of the Abbey church of St Alban. 1813.

§2

Nichols, J. Biographical memoirs of Gough, extracted from the Gentleman's Magazine for March and April 1809. [1809].

—— Biographical anecdotes of Gough, extracted from Literary anecdotes of the eighteenth century. 1810.

A catalogue of the books relating to British topography, bequeathed to the Bodleian library in 1799 by Gough. Oxford 1814.

JAMES MACPHERSON
1736–96

An introduction to the history of Great Britain and Ireland. Dublin 1771, London 1772 (enlarged), 1773, 1781.

The history of Great Britain from the Restoration to the accession of the House of Hanover. 2 vols 1775, 1776.

Original papers: containing the secret history of Great Britain, [1660–1714]; to which are prefixed extracts from the life of James II, as written by himself. 2 vols 1775, 1776.

For Macpherson's Ossianic and other writings, see col 434 above.

JOHN PINKERTON
1758–1826

Rimes. 1781, 1782.

An essay on medals. 1784 (anon), 2 vols 1789, 1808.

A dissertation on the origin and progress of the Scythians or Goths. 1787.

Vitae antiquae sanctorum qui habitaverunt in Scotia. 1789; rev and enlarged by W. M. Metcalfe 2 vols Paisley 1889.

An enquiry into the history of Scotland preceding the reign of Malcolm III or the year 1056. 2 vols 1789, Edinburgh 1814.

The medallic history of England to the Revolution. 1790 (anon), 1802.

Iconographia scotica: or portraits of illustrious persons of Scotland with biographical notices. 1797.

The history of Scotland from the accession of the House of Stuart to that of Mary. 2 vols 1797.

The Scotish gallery: or portraits of eminent persons of Scotland, with brief accounts of the characters represented. 1799.

A general collection of voyages and travels. 17 vols 1808–14. Ed Pinkerton.

Literary correspondence. 2 vols 1830.

See also col 716, below.

V. LITERARY STUDIES

(1) GENERAL STUDIES

Nichol Smith, D. Eighteenth-century essays on Shake-speare. Glasgow 1903, Oxford 1963 (rev).
—— Shakespeare in the 18th century. Oxford 1928.
Brinkley, R. F. Arthurian legend in the 17th century. Baltimore 1932.
McKerrow, R. B. The treatment of Shakespeare's text by his earlier editors 1709-68. Proc Br Acad 19 1933; rptd in Studies in Shakespeare, ed P. Alexander, Oxford 1964.
Ford, H. L. Shakespeare 1700-40. Oxford 1935.
Black, M. W. and M. A. Shaaber. Shakespeare's seven-teenth-century editors 1632-85. New York 1937.
Read, A. W. Suggestions for an academy in England in the latter half of the eighteenth century. MP 36 1938.
Tuve, R. Ancients, moderns and Saxons. ELH 6 1939.

Douglas, D. C. English scholars 1660-1730. 1939, 1951 (rev).
Wellek, R. The rise of English literary history. Chapel Hill 1941.
Jones, E. Geoffrey of Monmouth 1640-1800. Berkeley 1944.
Wasserman, E. R. Elizabethan poetry in the eighteenth century. Urbana 1947.
—— Elizabethan poetry in the eighteenth century. Urbana 1947.
Kliger, S. The Goths in England. Cambridge Mass 1952.
Friedman, A. B. The ballad revival: studies in the influ-ence of popular on sophisticated poetry. Chicago 1961.
Johnston, A. Enchanted ground: the study of medieval romance in the eighteenth century. 1964.

(2) MAJOR SCHOLARS

GERARD LANGBAINE the younger
1656–92

An exact catalogue of all the comedies that were ever printed or published, till this present year 1680. Oxford 1680.
The hunter: a discourse of horsemanship. Oxford 1686, 1697.
Momus triumphans: or the plagiaries of the English stage expos'd in a catalogue of all the comedies, tragi-comedies [etc]. 1688, 1688 (as A new catalogue of English plays).
An account of the English dramatick poets. Oxford 1691. Essay on Dryden rptd in Critical essays of the seven-teenth century vol 3, ed J. E. Spingarn, Oxford 1909.
The lives and characters of the English dramatick poets; also an account of all the plays ever yet printed in the English tongue, [first] begun by Langbaine, improv'd and continued [by Charles Gildon]. 1698. Also issued nd and 1699.

ZACHARY GREY
1688–1766

[Butler, Samuel]. Hudibras, in three parts; with large annotations and a preface. 2 vols Cambridge 1744 (vol 2 London), 3 vols Glasgow 1753, 2 vols 1764, 3 vols Edinburgh 1770, London 1770, Edinburgh 1779 etc.
An answer to certain passages in Mr W[arburton]'s preface to his edition of Shakespear, together with some remarks on the many errors and false criticisms in the work itself. 1748. Anon. Perhaps by Grey.
Remarks upon a late edition of Shakespeare [Warburton's], with a defence of Sir Thomas Hanmer. [1747?], 1752 (as Examination of a late edition etc).
Critical, historical and explanatory notes upon Hudibras, by way of supplement to the two editions published in the years 1744 and 1745; [with] a dissertation on burles-que poetry by M. Bacon and a translation of part of the first canto of the first book into Latin doggerel. 1752.
Critical, historical, and explanatory notes on Shakespeare; with emendations of the text and metre. 2 vols 1754.

Miscellaneous Works

A defence of our antient and modern historians against the frivolous cavils of a late pretender to critical history [John Oldmixon]; in two parts. 1725.

In answer to J. Oldmixon, A review of Grey's defence of our ancient and modern historians. 1725.
An attempt towards the character of the royall martyr King Charles I. 1738.
A word or two of advice to William Warburton. 1746.
A free and familiar letter to that great refiner of Pope and Shakespeare, William Warburton. 1750.
A chronological and historical account of the most memor-able earthquakes from the beginning of the Christian period to the present year 1750. 2 pts Cambridge 1750, 1756.
Fragmentum est pars rei fractae. 1751. On disputes at Cambridge University.
Masters, R. Memoirs of the life and writings of Thomas Baker BD, from the papers of Grey. Cambridge 1784.
Grey contributed at least 15 tracts to theological controversies as well as assisting Peter Whalley in his edn of Ben Jonson, and Francis Peck in Desiderata curiosa.

LEWIS THEOBALD
1688–1744

For Theobald's dramatic writings see col 486, above.

§ 1

A Pindarick ode on the Union. 1707.
The mausoleum: a poem sacred to the memory of Queen Anne. 1714.
The cave of poverty: a poem, written in imitation of Shakespeare. [1714?].
A complete key to the last new farce, the what d'ye call it [by Gay]; to which is prefix'd a hypercritical preface on the nature of burlesque. 1715. Anon. Attributed by Pope to Theobald and Benjamin Griffin.
The censor. 1717. A collection of 96 papers by Theobald et al which appeared 3 times per week, 11 April–17 June 1715, 1 Jan–1 June 1717.
Memoirs of Sir Walter Raleigh. 1719 (3 edns).
The grove: or a collection of original poems. 1721, 1732 (as A miscellany of original poems).
Miscellaneous observations upon authors, ancient and modern. 2 vols 1731-2. By John Jortin, with papers by Theobald.
An epistle humbly addressed to the Rt Hon John, Earl of Orrery. [1732]. In appendix to Eustace Budgell, Memoirs of the late Earl of Orrery, 1732, 1732, 1737.

Translations

The life and character of Marcus Portius Cato collected from Plutarch, Lucan, Sallust, Lucius Florus and other authors, designed for the readers of Cato: a tragedy. 1713, 1713 (2nd edn enlarged).

Plato's dialogue of the immortality of the soul [Phaedo], translated. 1713.

Electra: a tragedy, translated from Sophocles, with notes. 1714; rptd in Bell's British theatre vol 16, 1777.

Plutus, or the world's idol: a comedy, translated from the Greek of Aristophanes. 1715.

The clouds: a comedy, translated from the Greek of Aristophanes. 1715.

Monsieur[Jean]Le Clerc's observations upon Mr Addison's travels through Italy, done from the French. 1715.

Oedipus, King of Thebes: a tragedy, translated from Sophocles, with notes. 1715.

A translation of book 1 of the Odyssey, with notes. 1716.

The history of the loves of Antiochus and Stratonice, in which are interspers'd some accounts relating to Greece and Syria. 1717.

The grove: or a collection of original poems. 1721.

Scholarly Works

Shakespeare restored: or a specimen of the many errors as well committed as unamended by Mr Pope, in his late edition of this poet. 1726, 1740.

The posthumous works of William Wycherley, in prose and verse, faithfully publish'd from his original manuscripts by Mr Theobald; to which are prefixed, some memoirs of Wycherley's life by Major Pack. 1728. Pope pbd a vol 2 in 1729.

A miscellany on taste. 1732. Reprints Theobald's letter to the Daily Jnl 17 April 1729, Mr Pope's taste of Shakespeare.

The works of Shakespeare, collated with the oldest copies, and corrected, with notes, explanatory and critical. 7 vols 1734, Dublin 1739, 8 vols 1740, 1752, 1757, 1762, 1767, 12 vols 1772, 8 vols 1773, 12 vols [1777?]. Preface rptd in Eighteenth-century essays on Shakespeare, ed D. Nichol Smith, Glasgow 1903, and ed H. G. Dick, Los Angeles 1949 (Augustan Reprint Soc).

The works of Beaumont and Fletcher, with notes critical and explanatory by Messrs Theobald, Seward and Sympson. 10 vols 1750. Theobald was responsible for vol 1 and parts of vols 2–3.

§2

Jones, R. F. Theobald: his contribution to English scholarship, with some unpublished letters. New York 1919.

WILLIAM OLDYS
1696–1761

A vindication of the Lord Chancellor Bacon, from the aspersion of injustice cast upon him by Mr Wraynham. 1725. Pbd by Oldys from anon ms.

A collection of epigrams; to which is prefix'd a critical dissertation on this species of poetry. 1727, 1735, 2 vols 1736 (enlarged). The dissertation is said to be by Oldys.

A dissertation upon pamphlets and the undertaking of Phoenix britannicus to revive the most excellent among them. 1731; rptd in J. Morgan, Phoenix britannicus, 1732 and in J. Nichols, Literary anecdotes vol 4, 1812.

A short view of the long life and raigne of Henry the Third, King of England, presented to King James by Sir Robt Cotton, but not printed till 1627. In Phoenix britannicus, 1732.

The polite correspondence, or rational amusement: being a series of letters, philosophical, poetical, historical, critical, amorous, moral and satyrical. [c. 1735]. By Thomas Campbell. Bk 5 attributed to Oldys.

Life of Sir Walter Raleigh. Prefixed to W. Raleigh, History of the world, 2 vols 1736; Life rptd 1740; prefixed to Works of Raleigh, 8 vols Oxford 1829.

The British librarian, exhibiting a compendious review or abstract of our most scarce, useful and valuable books. 1737, 1738.

Life of Sir John Fastolff. In Birch's General dictionary vol 5, 1737. Oldys also wrote several other lives for this compilation, but they cannot be identified.

The Muses library. 1737, 1738 (some copies as The historical and poetical medley), 1741. By Elizabeth Cooper assisted by Oldys.

Memoirs of Mrs Anne Oldfield. 1741. Attributed to Oldys.

Catalogus bibliothecae Harleianae. 5 vols 1743. By Samuel Johnson, M. Maittaire and Oldys.

The Harleian miscellany: or a collection of scarce, curious and entertaining tracts and pamphlets found in the late Earl of Oxford's library, interspersed with historical, political and critical notes. 8 vols 1744–6. Ed Oldys. Rptd 10 vols 1808–13 ed Thomas Park.

A complete and exact catalogue of pamphlets in the Harleian miscellany. 1746. At end of Harleian miscellany. Rptd in vol 10 of Park's edn, 1813.

A short view of the life and writings of Dr Thomas Moffet. Prefixed to Moffet, Health's improvement, 1746.

Biographia britannica. Vol 1, 1747. Lives signed G: George Abbot, Robert Abbot, Thomas Adams, William Alexander, (Earl of Stirling), Charles Aleyn, Edward Alleyn, William Ames, John Atherton, Peter Bates.

An historical essay on the life and writings of Michael Drayton. Prefixed to The works of Michael Drayton, now first collected into one volume, 1748, 4 vols 1753.

Biographia britannica. Vol 2, 1748. John Bradford, William Bulleyn, William Caxton.

Biographia britannica. Vol 3, 1750. Michael Drayton, Sir George Etherege, George Farquhar, Sir John Fastolff, Thomas Fuller, Sir William Gascoigne.

Biographia britannica. Vol 4, 1752. Fulke Greville (Lord Brooke), Richard Hakluyt, Wenceslaus Hollar.

Observations on the cure of William Taylor, the blind boy of Ightham, in Kent. In A specimen of some cures performed by John Taylor, 2 pts 1753.

Biographia britannica. Vol 5, 1760. Life of Thomas May.

Some account of the life and writings of Charles Cotton esq, in a letter to the editor of the Complete angler. In Sir John Hawkins' edn, 1760.

The life of Dr George Abbot, Lord Archbishop of Canterbury. Guildford 1777. Rptd from Biographia britannica vol 1, 1747.

Oldys also contributed papers to Universal Spectator 1728–31. *He left many notes in ms which were used for the second edn of* Biographia britannica. *Anecdotes of Shakespeare from Oldys' mss were pbd by Steevens in his 1778 edn, and frequently rptd.*

JOHN JORTIN
1698–1770

Miscellaneous observations upon authors, ancient and modern. 2 vols 1731–2. Ed Jortin.

Remarks on Spenser's poems. 1734.

Letter concerning the music of the Ancients. In Charles Avison, An essay on musical expression, 1753 (2nd edn), 1775.

The life of Erasmus. 2 vols 1758–60, 3 vols 1808.

Tracts, philological, critical and miscellaneous. 2 vols 1790. Ed Rogers Jortin, with memoir. Includes Remarks on Spenser, remarks on Milton, critical remarks on modern authors (Pope, Swift etc).

Jortin also pbd sermons. For his works on ecclesiastical history see DNB.

JOSEPH SPENCE
1699–1768

An essay on Pope's Odyssey, in which some particular beauties and blemishes of that work are considered. 2 pts Oxford 1726–7, 1737, 1747.

A full and authentick account of Stephen Duck, the Wiltshire poet, in a letter to a Member of Parliament. 1731; rptd with Duck's Poems on several occasions, 1736, 1737, 1738, and with The beautiful works of Stephen Duck, 1753, and abridged in GM June 1736.

Some account of the Lord Buckhurst [Thomas Sackville]. The tragedy of Gorboduc, written by Thomas Sackville, 1736.

Polymetis: or an enquiry concerning the agreement between the works of the Roman poets and the remains of the antient artists, in ten books. 1747, 1755, 1774; tr German, 1773–6. Abridged by Nicholas Tindal, 1764.

An apology for the late Mr Pope. 1749. Attributed by Wright, under §2, below.

Crito: or a dialogue on beauty, by Sir Harry Beaumont [Spence]. 1752, 1752; rptd in Dodsley's Fugitive pieces vol 1, 1761, 1762, 1765, 1771.

A particular account of the Emperor of China's gardens near Pekin, in a letter from J. D. Attiret, translated from the French by Sir Harry Beaumont. 1752; rptd in Dodsley's Fugitive pieces vol 1, 1761, 1762, 1765, 1771.

The works of Virgil in Latin and English, with several new observations by Mr Holdsworth, Mr Spence and others. 4 vols 1753, 1 vol 1763 (English only), 4 vols 1778 (Latin and English).

Moralities: or essays, letters, fables and translations, by Sir Harry Beaumont. 1753.

An account of the life, character and poems of Mr Blacklock, student of philosophy in the University of Edinburgh. 1754, 1756 (rev and prefixed to 2nd edn of Blacklock's poems).

A parallel, in the manner of Plutarch, between a most celebrated man of Florence, and one, scarce ever heard of, in England. Strawberry Hill 1758, 1759; rptd in Dodsley's Fugitive pieces vol 2, 1761, 1765, 1771.

Remarks and dissertations on Virgil, with some other classical observations, by the late Mr [Edward] Holdsworth, published, with several notes and additional remarks, by Mr Spence. 1768.

The first three stanzas of the twenty-fourth canto of Dante's Inferno, made into a song, in imitation of the Earl of Surrey's stile. Museum 1746; rptd in Nichols's Select collection vol 8, 1782.

Observations, anecdotes and characters of books and men, arranged with notes by the late Edmond Malone. 1820; ed J. M. Osborn 2 vols Oxford 1966.

Anecdotes, observations and characters of books and men, with notes and a life of the author, by Samuel Weller Singer. 1820, 1858; ed J. Underhill 1890 (selection); ed B. Dobrée 1964.

Quelques remarques hist sur les poètes anglois. Ed J. M. Osborn. In his First history of English poetry, in Pope and his contemporaries: essays presented to George Sherburn, Oxford 1949.

THOMAS BIRCH
1705–66

A general dictionary historical and critical, in which a new and accurate translation of that of Mr Bayle is included, by John Peter Bernard, Tho. Birch, John Lockman and other hands. 10 vols 1734–41. Ed Birch, who also wrote the 618 new biographies signed T and H.

A complete collection of the historical, political and miscellaneous works of Milton, with an historical and critical account of the life and writings of the author. 2 vols 1738, 1 vol 1753.

The complete works of Francis Bacon, with several additional pieces never before printed; to which is prefixed a new life of the author by Mr [David] Mallet. 4 vols 1740. Ed Birch.

The heads of illustrious persons of Great Britain, engraven by Houbraken and Vertue, with their lives and characters. 2 vols 1743–51, 1747–52, 1 vol 1756, 1813.

The Faerie Queene, by Edmund Spenser, with an exact collation of the two original editions; to which are now added a new life of the author, and also a glossary. 3 vols 1751.

The works of Sir Walter Raleigh Kt, political, commercial and philosophical, together with his letters and poems; to which is prefix'd a new account of his life by Thomas Birch. 2 vols 1751. Life rptd with Ralegh's Works, Oxford 1829.

Letters, speeches, charges, advices etc of Francis Bacon, now first published by Thomas Birch. 1763.

For Birch's historical work see col 684, above.

JOHN UPTON
1707–60

Miscellaneous observations upon authors, ancient and modern. 2 vols 1731–2. By Jortin. Vol 2 contains the following papers by Upton: On Hesychius; on Theocritus.

Critical observations on Shakespeare. 1746, Dublin 1747, 1748 (rev with preface on Warburton's edn).

A new canto of Spenser's Fairy Queen. 1747.

A letter concerning a new edition of Spenser's Faerie Queene, to Gilbert West. [1751].

Spenser's Faerie Queene: a new edition with a glossary, and notes explanatory and critical. 2 vols 1758.

Remarks on the action and history of the Faerie Queene. In H. J. Todd's edn of Spenser vol 2, 1805.

SAMUEL JOHNSON
1709–84

Miscellaneous observations on the tragedy of Macbeth, with remarks on Sir T[homas] H[anmer]'s edition of Shakespear; to which is affix'd proposals for a new edition of Shakespear, with a specimen. 1745.

Life of the Earl of Roscommon [with notes]. GM May 1748. Enlarged, with the notes incorporated in the text, in Lives of the poets, below.

Christian morals, with a life of the author by Johnson. 1756, 1761; ed S. C. Roberts, Cambridge 1927. By Sir Thomas Browne. Johnson added notes to those of John Jeffery.

Proposals for printing, by subscription, the dramatick works of William Shakespeare, corrected and illustrated by Johnson. 1756 etc.

The English works of Roger Ascham, with notes and observations [by James Bennet], and the author's life. 1761, 1765.

The plays of William Shakespeare, with the corrections and illustrations of various commentators, to which are added notes by Johnson. 8 vols 1765, 10 vols Dublin 1766, 8 vols 1768. For later edns *see* under George Steevens, below.

Prefaces, biographical and critical, to the works of the English poets. 10 vols 1779–81, 3 vols Dublin 1779–81 (without poems, as Lives of the English poets), 4 vols 1781 (rev as Lives of the most eminent English poets), 1783, 6 vols 1790–1 (with additional lives by Isaac Reed).

Annotations by Johnson and George Steevens and various commentators upon the Merchant of Venice written by Will Shakespeare. 1787.

Annotations by Sam Johnson and Geo Steevens, and the various commentators, upon King Henry V, written by Will Shakspere. 1787.

Johnson's prefaces and dedications. Ed A. T. Hazen, New Haven 1937.

Johnson on Shakespeare Ed A. Sherbo 2 vols New Haven 1968.

See also col 593, above.

EDWARD CAPELL
1713–81

Antony and Cleopatra: an historical play, fitted for the stage by abridging only. 1758. By Capell and David Garrick.

Prolusions: or select pieces of antient poetry, offer'd as specimens of the integrity that should be found in the editions of worthy authors. 1760. Anon.

Mr William Shakespeare his comedies, histories and tragedies, set out by himself in quarto, or by the players his fellows in folio. 10 vols [1767–8].

The works of Shakespear adorned with sculptures. Oxford 6 vols 1770–1. Sir Thomas Hanmer's second edn, with various readings of Theobald and Capell.

The plays of Shakespeare, from the text of Dr Samuel Johnson, with the prefaces, notes etc of Rowe, Pope, Theobald, Hanmer, Warburton, Johnson, and select notes from many other critics; also the introduction of the last editor, Mr Capell, and a table shewing his various readings. 7 vols Dublin 1771.

Notes and various readings to Shakespeare: part 1; with a general glossary. [1774].

Catalogue of Mr Capell's Shakespeariana, presented by him to Trinity College Cambridge. 1779 (priv ptd); ed W. W. Greg, Cambridge 1903. Transcribed and ptd by George Steevens.

Notes and various readings to Shakespeare. 3 vols 1779–83.

The poems of William Shakespeare, with Mr Capell's history of the origin of Shakespeare's fables, to which is added a glossary. [1798].

SIR JOHN HAWKINS
1719–89
§1

The complete angler: or contemplative man's recreation, in two parts, by Izaac Walton and Charles Cotton; to which are now prefixed the lives of the authors. 1760, 1775, 1784, 1792, 1797, 1808, 1815, 1822, 1825, 1826; ed J. E. Harting 2 vols 1893. Ed Hawkins; the life of Cotton is by William Oldys.

The life of Samuel Johnson. 1787, 1787, Dublin 1787, London 1797 (as vol 1 of Hawkins' edn of Works of Johnson). Extracts rptd in Johnsonian miscellanies, ed G. B. Hill vol 2 Oxford 1897; abridged and ed B. H. Davis 1961.

The works of Samuel Johnson, together with his life, and notes on his lives of the poets. 15 vols 1787–9. Notes frequently rptd in part.

Annotations illustrative of the plays of Shakespeare. 2 vols 1819. Some by Hawkins.

The life of Samuel Johnson [by Boswell]; to which are added anecdotes by Hawkins. 5 vols 1835.

Miscellaneous Works

Observations on the state of the highways, and on the laws for amending and keeping them in repair, with a draught of a bill. 1763.

A charge to the grand jury of Middlesex delivered the eighth of January 1770. 1770.

Principles and power of harmony. 1771.

A general history of the science and practice of music. 5 vols 1776, 3 vols 1853 ('with the author's posthumous notes'). *See also* A dictionary of musicians: comprising the most important contents of the works of Sir John Hawkins, 1827 (anon).

Of the practice of bidding prayers, with an ancient form of such bidding, as also a form of cursing, communicated July 1779 [to Soc of Antiquaries]. [1779].

A charge to the grand jury of Middlesex delivered the eleventh of September 1780. 1780.

A dissertation on the armorial ensigns of the county of Middlesex and of the abbey and city of Westminster. 1780.

§2

Scholes, P. A. The life and activities of Hawkins. Oxford 1953.

Davis, B. H. Johnson before Boswell: a study of Hawkins' life of Samuel Johnson. New Haven 1960.

THOMAS WARTON the younger
1728–90

For Warton's other works see col 453, above.

§1

The Union: or select Scots and English poems. Edinburgh 1753, 1753, London 1759, Dublin 1761, London 1766, Oxford 1796. Ed Warton.

Observations on the Faerie Queene of Spenser. 1754, 2 vols 1762, 1807.

The life and literary remains of Ralph Bathurst MD, Dean of Wells. 1761.

The Oxford sausage: or select poetical pieces, written by the most celebrated wits of the University of Oxford. 1764, Dublin 1766, Oxford 1772, 1777, 1804, London 1814, 1815 etc. Ed Warton.

The life of Sir Thomas Pope, founder of Trinity College. 1772, 1780, 1784.

The history of English poetry, from the close of the eleventh to the commencement of the eighteenth century; to which are prefixed two dissertations: 1, on the origin of romantic fiction in Europe; 2, on the introduction of learning into England. Vol 1, 1774; vol 2, 1778; vol 3 (containing a dissertation on the Gesta Romanorum), 1778. 2nd edn of vol 1, 1775; new edn of vol 3, 1781; vol 4 (unfinished; only 88 pages) nd; ed R. Price 4 vols 1824 (complete); ed R. Taylor 3 vols 1840; ed W. C. Hazlitt 4 vols 1871; rptd (from edns of '1778 and 1781') 1870, 1872, 1875. An index by T. Fillingham, 1806.

Milton, John. Poems upon several occasions, English, Italian and Latin, with translations; with notes and illustrations by Warton. 1785, 1791 (rev and enlarged; appendix, containing remarks on the Greek verses of Milton, by Charles Burney jr).

A history of English poetry: an unpublished continuation by Warton. Ed R. M. Baine, Los Angeles 1953 (Augustan Reprint Soc).

An enquiry into the authenticity of the poems attributed to T. Rowley [i.e. Chatterton]. 1782, 1782.

Correspondence of Thomas Percy and Warton. Ed M. G. Robinson and L. Dennis, Baton Rouge 1951.

§2

[Ritson, J.] Observations on the three first volumes of the history of English poetry, in a letter to the author. 1782.

Ker, W. P. Thomas Warton. Proc Br Acad 4 1909–10; rptd in his Collected essays, 1925.

Nichol Smith, D. Warton's history of English poetry.
Proc Br Acad 15 1929.
Wellek, R. In his Rise of English literary history, Chapel
Hill 1941.
Johnston, A. In his Enchanted ground, 1964.

THOMAS PERCY
1729–1811

O Nancy will you go with me. In Dodsley's Collection of
poems vol 6, 1758.
Hau Kiou Choaan, or the pleasing history: a translation
from the Chinese; to which are added the argument or
story of a Chinese poetry, with notes. 4 vols 1761.
Miscellaneous pieces relating to the Chinese. 2 vols 1762.
The matrons: six short histories. 1772 (for 1762?). Ed
and in part tr Percy.
Five pieces of Runic poetry translated from the Islandic
language. 1763.
The Song of Solomon newly translated from the original
Hebrew; with a commentary and annotations. 1764.
Reliques of ancient English poetry. 3 vols 1765, 1767,
1775; [nominally] ed his nephew T. Percy (really by
Percy himself) 1794, 1812; ed G. Gilfillan 3 vols
Edinburgh 1855; ed H. B. Wheatley 3 vols 1876–7, 1891;
ed M. M. A. Schröer 2 vols Berlin 1893.
A letter describing the ride to Hulme Abbey. 1765.
A key to the New Testament. 1766 etc.
The household books of the Earl of Northumberland in
1512. 1768, 1770, 1827. Ed Percy.
A sermon. [1769]. On John xiii. 35.
Northern antiquities: or a description of the manners,
customs, religion and laws of the ancient Danes, with a
translation of the Edda and other pieces from the
ancient Islandic tongue. 2 vols 1770, Edinburgh 1809.
Tr from Mallet's Introduction à l'histoire de Danne-
marc, with additional notes, and Goranson's Latin
version of the Edda.
The hermit of Warkworth: a Northumberland ballad.
1771, 1771, 1772, 1775 etc.
On some large fossil horns. Archaeology 7 1785.
A sermon. Dublin 1790. On Proverbs xxvii. 6.
An essay on the origin of the English stage, particularly
on the historical plays of Shakespeare. 1793.
Memoir of Goldsmith. In Goldsmith's Miscellaneous
works vol 1, 1801.
Bishop Percy's folio ms. Ed J. W. Hales and F. J.
Furnivall 3 vols 1867, 1868; ed I. Gollancz 4 vols 1905.
Life of Percy by John Pinkerton prefixed to vol 1.
Ancient songs, chiefly on Moorish subjects, translated
from the Spanish by Thomas Percy, with a preface by
D. Nichol Smith. Oxford 1932.

Letters

Letters from Thomas Percy, John Callander, David Herd
and others to George Paton. Edinburgh 1830.
Correspondence. In J. Nichols, Illustrations of the
literary history of the eighteenth century vols 6–8,
1817–58.
The Percy letters. Ed D. Nichol Smith and C. Brooks.
Baton Rouge and New Haven 1944–.
The correspondence of Percy and Edmond Malone. Ed
A. Tillotson, Baton Rouge 1944.
The correspondence of Percy and Richard Farmer. Ed
C. Brooks, Baton Rouge 1946.
The correspondence of Percy and Thomas Warton. Ed
M. G. Robinson and L. Dennis, Baton Rouge
1951.
The correspondence of Percy and David Dalrymple,
Lord Hailes. Ed A. F. Falconer, Baton Rouge
1954.
The correspondence of Percy and Evan Evans. Ed A.
Lewis, Baton Rouge 1957.
The correspondence of Percy and George Paton. Ed
A. F. Falconer, New Haven 1961.

THOMAS TYRWHITT
1730–86

Proceedings and debates in the House of Commons in
1620, 1621. 2 vols Oxford 1766.
Observations and conjectures upon some passages of
Shakespeare. Oxford 1766.
Elsynge, Henry, The manner of holding parliaments in
England, corrected and enlarged from the author's
original manuscript. 1768. Ed Tyrwhitt.
The Canterbury tales of Chaucer; to which are added an
essay upon his language and versification: an introductory discourse, and notes. 5 vols 1775–8, 2 vols Oxford
1798, 5 vols 1822, 1830 etc.
Poems, supposed to have been written at Bristol, by
Thomas Rowley and others in the 15th century, now
first published; to which are added a preface, an introductory account of the pieces and a glossary. 1777,
1777, 1778 (with an appendix containing some observations upon the language of these poems, tending to
prove that they were written by Thomas Chatterton),
1782, 1794 (without appendix, ed J. Miller); ed M. E.
Hare, Oxford 1911.
A vindication of the appendix to the poems called Rowley's.
1782. For the literature of the Rowley controversy, see
col 435, above.
Tyrwhitt also contributed to Steevens' Shakespeare 1778,
and to Reed's Steevens' Shakespeare 1785.

Miscellaneous Works

An epistle to Florio, at Oxford. 1749; rptd in Crypt Dec
1829; GM Dec 1835.
The eighth Isthmian of Pindar [translated into] English
[by Tyrwhitt]. In Translations in verse, Oxford 1752.
Musgrave, S., Exercitationum in Euripidem libri duo.
Leyden 1762. Tyrwhitt gave Musgrave notes.
Observations on the inscriptions upon three ancient
marbles said to have been brought from Smyrna, and now
in the British Museum, in a letter from Tyrwhitt to
Matthew Duane, read at the Society of Antiquaries
July 9 1772. Archaeologia 3 1772.
Fragmenta duo Plutarchi from Harley 5612. 1773. Ed
Tyrwhitt.
Dissertatio de Babrio, fabularum Aesopearum scriptore,
inseruntur fabulae quaedam Aesopeae; accedunt Babrii
fragmenta. 1776, 1781, Erlangen 1785 (with addns and
a preface by T. C. Harles), Erlangen 1810.
Notae in Orpheum de lapidibus. 1781, Leipzig 1805.
Dawes, R., Miscellanea critica. Ed T. Burgess 1781.
Pp. 344–491 for Tyrwhitt's contributions.
Musgrave, S., Two dissertations: 1, On the Grecian
mythology; 2, An examination of Sir Isaac Newton's
objections to the chronology of the Olympiads. 1782.
Ed Tyrwhitt.
Conjecturae in Strabonem. 1783; ed T. C. Harles,
Erlangen 1788.
Cleaver, W., De rhythmo Graecorum liber singularis, in
usum juventutis coll. aen. nas. olim conscriptus, et
nunc demum in lucem editus. Oxford 1789. Contains
Tyrwhitt's observations and corrections.
Toup, J., Emendationes in Suidam et Hesychium et alios
lexicographos. 4 vols Oxford 1790. Ed Richard Porson.
Contains Notae breves in Toupii emendationes in
Suidam; authore T. Tyrwhitt.
Aristotelis De poetica liber, gr et lat; lectionem constituit,
animaduersionibus illustravit Tyrwhitt. Oxford 1794,
1794, 1806, 1817, 1827.
Brunck, R. F. P., Tragoediae septem [of Sophocles] ex
editione R. F. P. Brunck. 2 vols Oxford 1808. Brunck
used notes by Tyrwhitt.
Conjecturae in Aeschylum, Euripidem et Aristophanem;
accedunt epistolae diversorum ad Tyrwhittum. Oxford
1822.

Monk, J. H., Euripides Alcestis, cum delectis adnotationibus, potissimum J. H. Monkii, accedunt emendationes G. Hermanii. Leipzig 1824. With notes from Tyrwhitt.

RICHARD FARMER
1735–97

An essay on the learning of Shakespeare. Cambridge 1767, 1767, 1789, 1821. Also included in edns of Shakespeare by Steevens, Reed, Malone and James Boswell jr. Rptd in Eighteenth-century essays on Shakespeare, ed D. Nichol Smith, Glasgow 1903.
The correspondence of Thomas Percy and Farmer. Ed C. Brooks, Baton Rouge 1946.

GEORGE STEEVENS
1736–1800

Twenty of the plays of Shakespeare collated with different copies and publish'd from the originals. 4 vols 1766.
The plays of William Shakespeare, with notes by Samuel Johnson and George Steevens. 10 vols 1773, 1778; ed I. Reed 10 vols 1785, 15 vols 1793, 21 vols 1803, 21 vols 1813. Detached pieces of criticism appended to the Johnson-Steevens edns of Shakespeare, 1778, 1785, 1793.
Six old plays on which Shakespeare founded his Measure for measure, Comedy of errors, The taming of the shrew, King John, King Henry 4 and King Henry 5, King Lear. 2 vols 1779. Selected by Steevens; John Nichols prepared them for the press.
Catalogue of Mr Capell's Shakesperiana, presented by him to Trinity College Cambridge. 1779 (priv ptd). Transcribed and ptd by Steevens.
Annotations by Sam Johnson and Geo Steevens, and the various commentators, upon King Henry 5, written by Will Shakspere. 1787.
Annotations by Samuel Johnson and George Steevens and various commentators upon the Merchant of Venice, written by Will Shakespeare. 1787.
Shakspeare. 1794. Account by Steevens, under the assumed signature of William Richardson, printseller, of a pretended portrait of Shakespeare, proposals for engraving a print from it, and an eulogy upon it.

Miscellaneous Works

Biographical anecdotes of Hogarth. 1781. With John Nichols.
Johnsoniana. European Mag Jan 1785; rptd in Johnsonian miscellanies vol 2, ed G. B. Hill, Oxford 1897.
Fenn, Sir John. Original letters written during the reigns of Henry 6, Edward 4, Edward 5, Richard 3 and Henry 7, with notes. Vols 1–2, 1787, 1787. Contains contributions by Steevens.
Genuine works of William Hogarth, illustrated with biographical anecdotes, a chronological catalogue and commentary, by John Nichols and George Steevens. 3 vols 1808–17. Steevens also contributed to Johnson's Lives of the poets, Dodsley's Annual register, Reed's Biographia dramatica, Sayer's Caricatures, Critical Rev, St James's Chron, Public Advertiser, Morning Post, General Evening Post, GM etc.

EDMOND MALONE
1741–1812

§ I

Goldsmith, Oliver, Poems and plays; [with] the life of the author. 2 vols Dublin 1777, London 1780 (as Poetical and dramatic works of Goldsmith, now first collected, with an account of the life and writings of the author).
An attempt to ascertain the order in which the plays attributed to Shakespeare were written. In Steevens's edn of Shakespeare vol 1, 1778; subsequently in the variorum Shakespeares.
The tragicall hystory of Romeus and Juliet. 1780. Tr Arthur Brooke from Matteo Bandello; ed Malone from 1562 edn.
A supplement to the edition of Shakespeare published in 1778 by Johnson and Steevens: containing additional observations, with the genuine poems of the same author and seven plays which have been ascribed to him, with notes by the editor and others. 2 vols 1780.
Remarks on two new publications on Rowley's poems. GM Dec 1781. Concluded in suppl for the year 1781; expanded and rptd as Cursory observations on the poems attributed to Thomas Rowley, 1782, 1782; ed J. M. Kuist, Los Angeles 1966 (Augustan Reprint Soc).
Baker, D. E., Biographia dramatica. 2 vols 1782. Ed I. Reed, but most of the 'additions and corrections' were supplied by Malone.
A second appendix to Mr Malone's supplement to the last edition of the plays of Shakespeare. 1783 (priv ptd).
The journal of a tour to the Hebrides with Samuel Johnson LlD by James Boswell esq. 1785. Malone revised first edn and supervised 2nd.
A dissertation on the three parts of King Henry 6. 1787; rptd in his edns of Shakespeare, 1790, 1794, 1821.
Jephson, Robert, The Count of Narbonne. 1787 (2nd edn corrected). Ed Malone.
The plays and poems of William Shakespeare. 10 vols in 11 1790, 16 vols Dublin 1794. Contains: An essay on the chronological order of Shakespeare's plays; An essay relative to Shakespeare and Jonson; A dissertation on the 3 parts of King Henry 6; An historical account of the English stage; The tragical hystory of Romeo and Juliet.
The plays of William Shakespeare, accurately printed from the text of Mr Malone's edition; with select explanatory notes [by John Nichols]. 7 vols 1790.
Caveat against the booksellers respecting an edition of Shakespeare, attributed to Malone. 1790?
Prospectus of a new edition of Shakespeare's plays and poems. 1792.
A letter to Dr Richard Farmer, relative to the edition of Shakespeare published in 1790, and some late criticisms [by Joseph Ritson] on that work. 1792, 1792.
Roman portraits: a poem by Robert Jephson. 1794. Ed Malone.
The biographical mirrour. 3 vols 1795–8. Engravings by Silvester Harding; 25 lives by Malone and all corrected by him.
Proposals [for a new edition of Shakespeare]. 1795.
An inquiry into the authenticity of certain papers attributed to Shakespeare, Queen Elizabeth and Henry, Earl of Southampton. 1796.
Works of Sir Joshua Reynolds, with an account of his life and writings. 2 vols 1797, 3 vols 1798, 1809, 1819.
Boswell, James, The Life of Samuel Johnson. Malone greatly assisted Boswell in preparation of the first edn; also edited and contributed notes to the 3rd edn, 4 vols 1799, 4th 1804, 5th 1807, 6th 1811.
The critical and miscellaneous prose works of John Dryden, with notes and illustrations, and an account of the life and writings of the author. 3 vols in 4 1800.
Hamilton, W. G., Parliamentary logick; to which are subjoined two speeches, delivered in the House of Commons of Ireland, and other pieces, with an appendix containing considerations on the corn laws by Samuel Johnson. 1808. Ed with a memoir of Hamilton by Malone.
An account of the incidents from which the title and part of the story of Shakespeare's Tempest were derived, and its true date ascertained. 1808 (priv ptd).

A biographical memoir of William Windham. GM June 1810; rptd with enlargements 1810.

Spence, Joseph, Observations, anecdotes and characters of books and men, arranged with notes by the late Edmond Malone esq. 1820.

[Boswell, J., jr.], The plays and poems of William Shakespeare, with a life of the poet and an enlarged history of the stage, by the late Edmond Malone, with a new glossarial index. 21 vols 1821.

Correspondence of Thomas Percy and Malone. Ed A. Tillotson, Baton Rouge 1944.

§2

[Ritson, J.] Cursory criticisms on the edition of Shakespeare published by Malone. 1792.

Ireland, S. Mr Ireland's vindication of his conduct, respecting the publication of the supposed Shakespeare mss: being a preface or introduction to a reply to the critical labours of Mr Malone in his Enquiry into the authenticity of certain papers etc. 1796.

—— An investigation of Mr Malone's claim to the character of scholar, or critic: being an examination of his inquiry into the authenticity of the Shakespeare manuscript. [1798]. By Thomas Caldecott.

Boswell, J., jr. Memoirs and character of Edmond Malone esq. GM June 1813; rptd priv 1814; prefixed to Boswell's edn of Malone's Shakespeare, 1821; prefixed to Catalogue of early English poetry etc, below, 1836.

Catalogue of early English poetry and works illustrating the British drama collected by Malone and now preserved in the Bodleian Library. Oxford 1836. With Boswell's memoir of Malone.

Prior, J. Life of Malone, editor of Shakespeare; with selections from his ms anecdotes. 1860.

Halliwell[-Phillipps], J. O. A hand-list of the early English literature preserved in the Malone collection in the Bodleian Library, selected from the printed catalogue of that collection. 1860.

Original letters from Malone, the editor of Shakespeare, to John Jordan, the poet. Ed J. O. Halliwell[-Phillipps] 1864 (priv ptd).

The correspondence of Malone with J. Davenport, Vicar of Stratford-on-Avon [on Shakespeare's family]. Ed J. O. Halliwell [-Phillipps] 1864 (priv ptd).

Greg, W. W. Editors at work and play. RES 2 1926.

Osborn, J. M. Dr Johnson on the sanctity of an author's text. PMLA 50 1935. As reported by Malone.

—— Malone: scholar-collector. Library 5th ser 19 1964.

—— Malone and Dr Johnson. In Boswell, Johnson and their circle, ed M. Lascelles, Oxford 1965.

Nichol Smith, D. Malone. HLQ 3 1940.

ISAAC REED
1742–1807

Poetical works of the Right Hon Lady M[ar]y W[ortle]y M[ontagu]. 1768. Ed Reed.

Musae Seatonianae: a complete collection of the Cambridge prize poems, from the first institution of that premium by Thomas Seaton, in 1750, to the present time. 1772. Ed Reed.

[Nichols, J.], The original works of William King LlD. 3 vols 1776. Reed assisted Nichols.

Historical memoirs of the life and writings of the late W. Dodd LlD. 1777, 1777.

The repository: a select collection of fugitive pieces of wit and humour, in verse and prose, by the most eminent writers. 4 vols 1777–83, 1790. Ed Reed.

Middleton, Thomas, A tragi-comodie called the Witch. 1778. Rptd by Reed.

Young, Edward, The works of the author of the Night thoughts; to which is prefixed an account of the life of the author. 6 vols 1778–9. Reed edited vol 6.

Nichols, J., A supplement to Dr Swift's works. 3 vols 1779. Reed assisted Nichols.

Dodsley, R., A select collection of old plays: second edition, corrected, with notes [by Reed]. 12 vols 1780. J. Payne Collier's edn 12 vols 1825–7, rptd Reed's notes with addns from his mss.

Dodd, W., Thoughts in prison. 1781. Ed Reed.

Nichols, J., Biographical and literary anecdotes of William Bowyer, and of his learned friends: containing an incidental view of the progress of literature in this Kingdom from the beginning of the present century to 1777. 1782. Reed assisted Nichols.

Dodsley, R., A collection of poems by several hands, with notes [by Reed]. 6 vols 1782.

Baker, D. E., Biographia dramatica, or a companion to the playhouse: a new edition [by Reed]. 2 vols 1782; ed S. Jones 1812.

Pearch, G., A collection of poems, by several hands. 4 vols 1783. Reed wrote biographical notices for this edn.

The plays of William Shakespeare, with the corrections and illustrations of various commentators; to which are added notes by S. Johnson and G. Steevens: the third edition. 10 vols 1785.

The plays of William Shakespeare. 15 vols 1793, 23 vols Basle 1779–1802, 21 vols 1803, 1813.

Johnson, Samuel, The works of the English poets, with prefaces biographical and critical. 75 vols 1790. For this edn Reed wrote biographical notices of John Armstrong, James Cawthorn, Charles Churchill, John Cunningham, William Falconer, Oliver Goldsmith, Matthew Green, Soame Jenyns, Dr Johnson, John Langhorne, Edward Moore, Paul Whitehead and William Whitehead. The life of Goldsmith was rptd in Poems by Goldsmith and Parnell, 1795.

Seward, W., Biographiana. 2 vols 1799. Reed wrote Life of Dr Farmer, pp. 578–98.

The Reed diaries 1762–1804. Ed C. E. Jones, Berkeley 1946.

Reed also contributed to Westminster Mag, European Mag and GM, and to the various pbns of John Nichols.

JOHN NICHOLS
1745–1826

See col 695, above.

JOSEPH RITSON
1752–1803

§1

Observations on the three first volumes of the history of English poetry [by Thomas Warton] in a letter to the author. 1782.

Remarks, critical and illustrative, on the text and notes of the last edition of Shakespeare. 1783. Contains, at end, proposals for publishing Shakespeare's plays in 8 vols.

A select collection of English songs. 3 vols 1783; ed T. Park 3 vols 1813. Contains an historical essay on national song.

The bishoprick garland, or Durham minstrel: being a choice collection of excellent songs relating to the above county. Stockton 1784, Newcastle 1792.

Gammer Gurton's garland, or the nursery parnassus: a choice collection of pretty songs and verses, for the amusement of all little good children who can neither read nor run. Stockton [1784], London 1809, 1810, Glasgow 1866, Stockton nd, nd.

The Spartan manual, or tablet of morality: being a genuine collection of the apophthegms, maxims and precepts of the philosophers and other celebrated characters of antiquity. 1785.

The quip modest: or a few words by way of supplement to remarks, critical and illustrative, on the text and notes of the last edition of Shakespeare [i.e. Johnson's and Steevens's, 1778], occasioned by the republication of that edition by [Isaac Reed]. 1788 (cancelled), 1788.

The Yorkshire garland: being a curious collection of old and new songs concerning that famous county. Pt 1 (all pbd), York 1788.

Ancient songs, from the time of King Henry the 3rd to the Revolution. 1790, 3 vols 1829; ed W. C. Hazlitt 1877. Contains Observations on the ancient English minstrels: a dissertation on the songs and music of the ancient English.

Pieces of ancient popular poetry, 1791, 1833; ed E. Goldsmid, Edinburgh 1884.

The North-country chorister: an unparalleled variety of excellent songs collected and published together, for general amusement, by a bishoprick ballad singer. Durham 1792, 1802.

Cursory criticisms on the edition of Shakespeare published by Edmond Malone. 1792.

The Northumberland garland, or Newcastle nightingale: a matchless collection of famous songs. Newcastle 1793. Ed Ritson; first edn of Northumberland garland was in 1768.

The English anthology. 3 vols 1793-4.

Scotish song. 2 vols 1794, 1866. A collection of Scotch songs, with the airs, and an historical essay.

Poems on interesting events in the reign of Edward 3 written in the year 1352 by Laurence Minot, with a preface, dissertation, notes and a glossary. 1795, 1825.

Robin Hood: a collection of all the ancient poems, songs and ballads now extant relative to that outlaw; to which are prefixed historical anecdotes of his life. 2 vols 1795, 1 vol 1820, 1832, 1853, 1862, 1884, 1885.

Ancient English metrical romances. 3 vols 1802.

Bibliographia poetica: a catalogue of English poets, of the 12th, 13th, 14th, 15th and 16th centurys, with a short account of their works. 1802. Joseph Haslewood made collections for a new edn. Addns and alterations were pbd in Sir Egerton Brydges, Censura literaria, 1805.

Dido: a tragedy as it was performed at the Theatre Royal in Drury-Lane, with universal applause, by Joseph Reed. 1808. Ptd in 1792; Ritson contributed notes and supervised the printing.

Northern garlands. 1810, Edinburgh 1887-8. The Bishoprick garland, the Yorkshire garland, the Northumberland garland and the north-country chorister, rptd by Joseph Haslewood.

The Caledonian Muse: a chronological selection of Scotish poetry from the earliest times. 1821. Ptd 1785.

Warton, Thomas, The history of English poetry: new edition carefully revised, with numerous additional notes by the late Mr Ritson [et al]. 4 vols 1824, 3 vols 1840.

The life of King Arthur. Ed J. Frank 1825.

Fairy tales, now first collected; to which are prefixed 2 dissertations: 1, On pygmies; 2, on fairies. 1831, 1875 (preface by W. C. Hazlitt).

Miscellaneous Works

Verses addressed to the ladies of Stockton. In the Newcastle miscellany, 1772; rptd Newcastle nd and in Haslewood, Account of Ritson, 1824.

The office of a Lord High Steward of England. 1776.

Tables, shewing the descent of the crown of England. 1778 (priv ptd), 1783.

The Stockton jubilee: or Shakespeare in all his glory. Newcastle 1781.

A digest of the proceedings of the Court Leet of the manor and liberty of the Savoy. 1789, 1809, 1816.

The jurisdiction of the Court Leet. 1791, 1809, 1816.

The office of Constable. 1791, 1815.

Law tracts. 1794. Reprints first edns of A digest of the proceedings of the Court Leet of the Manor and liberty of the Savoy; The jurisdiction of the Court Leet; and The office of constable.

An essay on abstinence from animal food as a moral duty. 1802.

Practical points: or maxims in conveyancing, drawn from the daily experience of a late eminent conveyancer [R. Bradley]; to which are added, critical observations on the various and essential parts of a deed, by the late Joseph Ritson. 1804, 1820, 1825.

The office of bailiff of a liberty. Ed J. Frank 1811.

Memoirs of the Celts or Gauls. Ed J. Frank 1827.

Annals of the Caledonians, Picts and Scots; and of Strathclyde, Cumberland, Galloway, and Murray. Ed J. Frank 2 vols Edinburgh 1828.

The letters of Ritson, edited chiefly from originals in the possession of his nephew [Joseph Frank]; to which is prefixed a memoir of the author by Sir H. Nicolas. Ed J. Frank 2 vols 1833.

§2

Malone, E. A letter to Dr Farmer, relative to the edition of Shakespeare published in 1790, and some later criticisms [by Ritson] on that work. 1792, 1792.

Haslewood, J. Some account of the life and publications of Ritson. 1824.

Letters to Mr George Paton [from Ritson], to which is added a Critique by John Pinkerton upon Ritson's Scottish songs. Edinburgh 1829.

Burd, H. A. Ritson: a critical biography. Urbana 1916. Appendix C is a bibliography of the pbd and unpbd works of Ritson.

Ker, W. P. Ritson. 1922 (Modern Humanities Research Assoc); rptd in his Collected essays, 1925.

Bronson, B. H. Ritson, scholar-at-arms. 2 vols Berkeley 1938. With bibliography.

Johnston, A. In his Enchanted ground, 1964.

JOHN PINKERTON
1758–1826

Craigmillar castle: an elegy. Edinburgh 1776.

Rimes. 1781, 1782.

Scottish tragic ballads. 1781, 1783 (enlarged as vol 1 of Select Scotish ballads). Contains Dissertations, On the oral tradition in poetry, and On the tragic ballad.

Two dithyrambic odes. 1782.

Tales, in verse. 1782.

Other juvenile poems, by the author of Rimes. [London?] nd. Contains the Two dithyrambic odes.

Select Scotish ballads. 2 vols 1783. Vol 1, Ballads in the tragic style, 2nd edn enlarged; vol 2, Ballads of the comic kind.

Letters of literature, by R. Heron. 1785.

The treasury of wit: being a methodical selection of about twelve hundred of the best apophthegms and jests, by H. Bennet. 2 vols 1786.

Ancient Scotish poems never before in print, but now published from the ms collections of Sir R. Maitland: comprising pieces written from about 1420 till 1586, with large notes and a glossary; prefixed are an Essay on the origin of Scotish poetry, a list of all the Scotish poets; [and] an appendix is added containing an account of the contents of the Maitland and Bannatyne mss. 2 vols 1786.

A new tale of a tub. 1790.

Barbour, James, The Bruce: or the history of Robert I King of Scotland; in Scottish verse: the first genuine edition, published from a ms dated 1489, with notes and a glossary. 3 vols 1790.

Scotish poems, reprinted from scarce editions. 3 vols 1792.

Walpoliana. 2 vols [1799]. Rptd from Monthly Mag.

Miscellaneous Works

An essay on medals. 1784, 1789, 1808.
A dissertation on the origin and progress of the Scythians or Goths. 1787.
[A series of 12] letters to the people of Great Britain, on the cultivation of their national history. GM Feb (suppl) 1788.
An enquiry into the history of Scotland, preceding the year 1056. 2 vols 1789, 1795, 1814.
Vitae antiquae sanctorum qui habitaverunt in ea parte Britanniae nunc vocata Scotia, cum variis lectionibus et notis. 1789, 2 vols Paisley 1889 (rev and enlarged by W. M. Metcalfe).
The medallic history of England to the Revolution. 1790, 1802.
Iconographia scotica: or portraits of illustrious persons of Scotland, with short biographical notices. 1797.
The history of Scotland from the accession of the House of Stuart to that of Mary. 2 vols 1797.
The Scotish gallery: or portraits of eminent persons of Scotland, with brief accounts of the characters represented, and an introduction on the rise and progress of painting in Scotland. 1799.

An historical dissertation on the Gowrie conspiracy. In Malcolm Laing, History of Scotland, 2 vols 1800, 4 vols 1804.
Modern geography. 2 vols 1802, 3 vols 1807, 2 vols 1817; abridged 1803, 1806; tr French, 1811.
Critique on the Complaynt of Scotland. Critical Rev May 1802; rptd in Critiques by David Herd and others on the new edition of the Complaynt of Scotland, Edinburgh 1829.
Esquisse d'une nouvelle classification de minéralogie etc, traduit de l'anglais par H. J. Jansen. Paris 1803.
Recollections of Paris in the years 1802–5. 2 vols 1806.
A general collection of voyages and travels in all parts of the world. 17 vols 1807–14. Early Australian voyages rptd from Pinkerton in Cassell's Nat Lib, 1886.
Petralogy: a treatise on rocks. 2 vols 1811.
Turner, D. The literary correspondence of Pinkerton, now first printed from the originals. 2 vols 1830.
Walpole's correspondence with Chatterton, Lort, Pinkerton [etc]. Ed W. S. Lewis, A. D. Wallace and R. M. Williams, New Haven 1952 (vol 16 of Yale edn of Walpole's correspondence).

(3) MINOR SCHOLARS

THOMAS RYMER
1641–1713

The tragedies of the last age. 1678, 1692. For Dryden's replies, see cols 381, 384, above.
A short view of tragedy, its original, excellency and corruption, with some reflections on Shakespeare, and other practitioners for the stage. 1692. Selection rptd in Critical essays of the 17th century vol 2, ed J. E. Spingarn, Oxford 1908.
Critical works. Ed C. A. Zimansky, New Haven 1956.

RICHARD BENTLEY
1662–1742

Milton's Paradise lost: a new edition. 1732.
Milton restor'd and Bentley depos'd: containing i, Some observations on Dr Bentley's preface; ii, his various readings and notes on Paradise lost etc. 1732.
A review of the text of Milton's Paradise lost, in which the chief of Dr Bentley's emendations are consider'd etc. 1732, 1733.
A friendly letter to Dr Bentley, occasion'd by his new edition of Paradise lost etc. 1732, 1732.
See col 725, below.

CHARLES GILDON
1665–1724

The lives and characters of the English dramatick poets; also an account of all the plays that were ever yet printed in the English tongue, first begun by Mr Langbaine, improv'd and continued. 1699. Anon.

NICHOLAS ROWE
1674–1718

The works of Mr William Shakespear, revis'd and corrected, with an account of the life and writings of the author. 6 vols 1709 (a 7th vol including the poems and critical essays, by Charles Gildon, followed in 1710,

rptd in 1714 edn), 1710, 9 vols 1714. Life of Shakespeare rptd in Pope's version in most 18th-century edns of Shakespeare; the original version rptd in 18th-century essays on Shakespeare, ed D. Nichol Smith, Glasgow 1903; in Materials for the life of Shakespeare, ed P. Butler, Chapel Hill 1930, and ed S. H. Monk, Los Angeles 1948 (Augustan Reprint Soc).

THOMAS RUDDIMAN
1674–1757

Virgil's Aeneis, translated into Scottish verse by the famous Gawin Douglas Bishop of Dunkeld. Edinburgh 1710. Ed Ruddiman, who compiled the glossary; contains a Life of Douglas by Bishop John Sage.
The works of William Drummond of Hawthornden: consisting of those which were formerly printed, and those which were design'd for the press, now published from the author's original copies. Edinburgh 1711. Ed Ruddiman, with an introd and life of Drummond by Bishop Sage.
Buchanan, George, Opera omnia, curante Thoma Ruddimanno. 2 vols Edinburgh 1715, Leyden 1725 (cum indicibus rerum memorabilium, et praefatione Petri Burmanni).
—— Paraphrasis Psalmorum Davidis poetica, ex optimis codicibus summo studio recognita et castigata a Thoma Ruddimanno; praemissa est accuratior quam antehac carminum explicatio; accessere duae ejusdem Geo Buchanini tragoediae Jephthes et Baptistes. Edinburgh 1716.

SIR THOMAS HANMER
1677–1746

Some remarks on the tragedy of Hamlet, Prince of Denmark, written by Mr William Shakespeare. 1736; ed C. D. Thorpe, Los Angeles 1947 (Augustan Reprint Soc). Evidence against attributing this to Hanmer is provided by C. D. Thorpe, MLN 49 1934.
The works of Shakespear, carefully revised and corrected. Oxford 6 vols 1743–4, 1744–6, London 1745, 9 vols 1747, 1748, 1750–1, 1760; ed T. Hawkins 6 vols Oxford 1770–1.

THOMAS HEARNE
1678–1735

Robert of Gloucester's chronicle. 2 vols Oxford 1724. With a glossary and some remarks on Chaucer and his writings, vol 2 pp. 596–606.

Peter Langtoft's chronicle (as illustrated and improv'd by Robert of Brunne) from the death of Cadwalader to the end of K. Edward the First's reign, transcribed and now first publish'd, from a ms in the Inner-Temple Library. 2 vols Oxford 1725, 1810. Vol 2 has a ME glossary. *See col 682, above.*

ELIJAH FENTON
1683–1730

Paradise lost: a poem written in twelve books by John Milton, 12th edn; to which is prefix'd an account of his life, 1725. With note on Milton's verse, and full index, with occasional textual notes; Fenton's life was frequently rptd.

Waller, Edmund, Works in verse and prose, published by Mr Fenton. 1729, 1730, 1744, 1752, 1772. With 88 pp. of Observations. *See col 416, above.*

ALEXANDER POPE
1688–1744

The works of Shakespeare, collated and corrected. 6 vols 1725 (7th vol of poems ed George Sewell, above, 1725), 8 vols Dublin 1726, 10 vols Dublin 1728, 9 vols 1728 (vol 9 contains Pericles and the spurious plays), 10 vols 1728 (vol 10 Poems), 9 vols 1731 (plays only), 8 vols 1734–6 (plays only), 9 vols 1635 (for 1735).

Shakespeare, William, The tempest, collated and corrected by the former editions by Mr Pope. Dublin 1725.

Scheme for a history of English poetry. In O. Ruffhead, Life of Pope, 1769.

WILLIAM WARBURTON
1698–1779

The works of Shakespear: the genuine text (collated with all the former editions and then corrected and emended), with a comment and notes, by Pope and Warburton. 8 vols 1747, Dublin 1747 (plays only).

Warburton also contributed notes to Theobald's edn of Shakespeare and Zachary Grey's edn of Hudibras, and a dissertation on the origin of books of chivalry to C. Jervas' trn of Don Quixote, 2 vols 1742.

ROBERT DODSLEY
1703–64

A select collection of old plays. 12 vols 1744; ed I. Reed 12 vols 1780; ed J. P. Collier 12 vols 1825–7; ed W. C. Hazlitt 15 vols 1874–6.

THOMAS NEWTON
1704–82

Paradise lost: new edition, with notes of various authors. 2 vols 1749, 1750, 1754, 1 vol Birmingham 1758 (text only), 1758, 1759, 2 vols 1760, 1763, 1770, 1777 (with Fenton's life of Milton), 1778, 1790, 3 vols 1795, 2 vols 1796 (with Johnson's criticism).

Paradise regain'd, to which is added Samson Agonistes and poems upon several occasions: new edition with notes. 2 vols 1752, 1753, 1760, 1766, 1 vol 1773, 1777, 2 vols 1785.

DAVID HUME
1711–76

History of Great Britain. Edinburgh 1754. Ch 6 on the reign of James I has a section (pp. 136–41) on learning and the arts.

THOMAS GRAY
1716–71

Copy of an original letter from Gray to T. Warton on the History of English poetry, communicated by a gentleman of Oxford. GM Feb 1783. Outlining Gray's own scheme.

Matthias, T. J. Works of Gray. 2 vols 1814. Prints extracts from Gray's commonplace book.

Martin, R. Chronologie de la vie et de l'oeuvre de Gray. Toulouse 1931. Prints extracts from Gray's commonplace book.

HUGH BLAIR
1718–1800

The works of Shakespear, in which the beauties observed by Pope, Warburton and Dodd are pointed out. 8 vols Edinburgh 1753, London 1753, Edinburgh 1761, 1769, 1769, 1771, London [1771 ?] (plays only).

A critical dissertation on the poems of Ossian. 1763, 1765, etc.

RICHARD HURD
1720–1808

Letters on chivalry and romance. 1762; rptd and expanded in Moral and political dialogues, 3 vols 1765; ed E. J. Morley 1911; ed H. Trowbridge, Los Angeles 1963 (Augustan Reprint Soc). Letters 8–12 rptd in vol 2 of Todd's edn of Spenser 1805.

Moral and political dialogues. 1759, 1760, 3 vols 1765, 1771, 1776, 1788.

Select works of Cowley. 2 vols 1772, 1772, 1777.

Hurd left material for the annotated edn of Addison 6 vols 1811.

CHARLOTTE LENNOX
1730–1804

Shakespear illustrated: or the novels and histories on which the plays of Shakespear are founded, corrected and translated from the original authors, with critical remarks. 3 vols 1753–4. With Dr Johnson.

JOSEPH WARTON
1722–1800

The adventurer. Nos 93, 97, 113, 116, 122. 2 vols 1752–4. Remarks on Tempest and King Lear.

Sidney, Sir Philip, Defense of poesie. 1787.

The works of Pope. 9 vols 1797. Warton also contributed to John Nichols, Select collection of poems, 8 vols 1780–2 and notes to Nichols' edn of Swift, as well as to the 1811 edn of Dryden ed Todd.

SIR DAVID DALRYMPLE, LORD HAILES
1726–92

Ancient Scottish poems, published from the ms of George Bannatyne 1568. Edinburgh 1770, London 1770. Ed Dalrymple.
Sketch of the life of John Barclay, author of Argenis. [Edinburgh 1786].
Horace Walpole's correspondence with Dalrymple. Ed W. S. Lewis et al, New Haven 1952.
Correspondence of Thomas Percy and Dalrymple. Ed A. F. Falconer, Baton Rouge 1954.

THOMAS HAWKINS
1729–72

The origin of the English drama, illustrated in its various species by specimens from our earliest writers, with notes by Hawkins. 3 vols Oxford 1773.
Hawkins also edited the 2nd edn of Hanmer's Shakespeare, 6 vols Oxford 1770–1.

GEORGE COLMAN the elder
1732–94

Critical reflections on the old English dramatick writers, intended as a preface to the works of Massinger, addressed to David Garrick. 1761; rptd in J. M. Mason's edn of Massinger, 1779.
The dramatic works of Beaumont and Fletcher, collated with all the former editions and corrected; with notes critical and explanatory by various commentators. 10 vols 1778; rptd 1811, with Jonson's dramatic works from Whalley's edn.

JAMES BEATTIE
1735–1803

Dissertations moral and critical [on fable and romance, pp. 501–74, is an historical sketch of fiction]. 1783, 2 vols Dublin 1783, London 1786.
Beattie's London diary 1773. Ed R. S. Walker, Aberdeen 1946.
Beattie's day book 1773–98. Ed R. S. Walker, Aberdeen 1948.

THOMAS ZOUCH
1737–1815

Walton, Izaak, Love and truth, in two modest and peaceable letters concerning the distempers of the present times; written from a quiet and conformable citizen of London to two busie and factious shopkeepers in Coventry: a new edition, with notes and a preface. York 1795. Also added to Zouch's edn of Walton's Lives, 1817.
——The lives of Dr John Donne; Sir Henry Wotton; Mr Richard Hooker; Mr George Herbert; and Dr Robert Sanderson, with notes and the life of the author. York 1796, 2 vols Oxford 1805, York 1807, 1817 (contains Zouch's edn of Walton's Love and truth), New York 1846–8, Boston 1860. Life of Walton separately pbd 1823, 1825.
Memoir of Sir Philip Sidney. York 1808, 1809.

GEORGE CHALMERS
1742–1825

The life of De Foe. 1785, 1786, 1790.
The life of Thomas Ruddiman. 1794.

An apology for the believers in the Shakspear-papers which were exhibited in Norfolk-street. 1797.
A supplemental apology for the believers in the Shakspeare-papers. 1799. Contains section on the chronology of Shakspeare's dramas.
Ramsay, Allan, Poems, with a life. 1800, 1851.
Lyndsay, David, Poetical works, with a life. 3 vols. 1806.
Another account of the incidents from which the title and part of the story of Shakspeare's Tempest was derived. 1815. A reply to Malone.
Henryson, Robert, Robene and Makyne and the Testament of Cresseid. 1824. Ed Chalmers.

WILLIAM HAYLEY
1745–1820

The poetical works of Milton, with a life of the author. 3 vols 1794–7.
The life of Milton in three parts; to which are added conjectures on the origin of Paradise lost. 1796, Dublin 1797, Basle 1799, 1810. Appendix contains extracts from the Adamo of Andreini etc.

GEORGE ELLIS
1753–1815

Specimens of the early English poets, 1790, 3 vols 1801 ('to which is prefixed an historical sketch of the rise and progress of the English poetry and language'), 1803, 1811, 1845, 1851.
Fabliaux or tales, selected and translated in English verse [by G. L. Way]. Vol 1, 1796, 1800; vol 2, 1800; 3 vols 1815. Introd and notes by Ellis.
Specimens of early English metrical romances. 3 vols 1805, Edinburgh 1811, 1847.
Diary of William Windham 1749–1810. Ed Mrs H. Baring 1866. Preface by Ellis.
Ellis also contributed to the Rolliad *and the* Anti-Jacobin, *and to* Edinburgh Rev *and* Quart Rev.

HENRY HARINGTON
1755–91

Nugae antiquae: being a miscellaneous collection of original papers by Sir John Harington and others, with an original plate of the Princess Elizabeth. 2 vols 1769–75, 3 vols 1779 (enlarged), 1792; ed T. Park 2 vols 1804.

FRANCIS DOUCE
1757–1834

The dance of death, painted by J. Holbein and engraved by W. Hollar: contains the daunce of Machabree, wherein is lively expressed the State of Manne, made by Dan John Lydgate, monke of St Edmunds Bury; the whole edited by Douce. 1794, 1804, 1833, 1849.
Dissertation on the life and writings of Mary, an Anglo-Norman poetess of the 13th century, by M. de la Rue, communicated by Douce. [1797]. Rptd from Archaeologia 13 1800, read 12 Jan 1797.
Illustrations of Shakespeare and of ancient manners. 2 vols 1807.
Judicium, a pageant, with introduction and glossary by F.D. 1822.
The metrical life of St Robert. 1824. Introd by Douce.
Douce assisted in the revision of the catalogue of Harley mss 1808–12 and in the catalogue of Lansdowne mss 1819. His notes were incorporated in other men's works, especially Price's edn of Warton's History of English poetry, *4 vols 1824.*

WALTER WHITER
1758–1832

A specimen of a commentary on Shakespeare: containing i, Notes on As you like it; ii, An attempt to explain and illustrate various passages, on a new principle of criticism, derived from Mr Locke's doctrine of the association of ideas. 1794; ed R. Over and M. Bell 1967.

HENRY JOHN TODD
1763–1845

Milton, John, Comus: a mask, with notes by various commentators. Canterbury 1798.
—— Poetical works, with the principal notes of various commentators. 6 vols 1801, 1809, 1826.
Spenser, Edmund, Works, with the notes of various commentators. 8 vols 1805.
Illustrations of the lives and writings of Gower and Chaucer. 1810.

(4) OLD ENGLISH SCHOLARSHIP

General Works

Turner, Sharon. History of the Anglo-Saxons. 4 vols 1799–1805, 2 vols 1807, 3 vols 1839 (as vols 1–3 of Turner's History of England, 12 vols 1839), 1852. Bk 9 is on OE literature.
Seaton, E. Literary relations of England and Scandinavia. Oxford 1935.
Tuve, R. Ancients, Moderns and Saxons. ELH 6 1939.
Douglas, D. C. English scholars 1660–1730. 1939, 1951 (rev).
Wellek, R. The rise of English literary history. Chapel Hill 1941, New York 1966 (rev). Ch 4, The study of early literature.
Evans, J. The history of the Society of Antiquaries. 1956.

Major Scholars
FRANCISCUS JUNIUS the younger
1589–1677

Caedmonis monachi paraphrasis poetica Genesios ac praecipuarum sacrae paginae historiarum. Amsterdam 1655.
Quatuor D. N. Jesu Christi Evangeliorum versiones perantiquae duae, Gothica scil. et Anglo-Saxonica. Dordrecht 1665, Amsterdam 1684. By Junius in collaboration with Thomas Marshall.

SIR THOMAS BROWNE
1605–82

Of languages and particularly of the Saxon tongue. Tract 8 of Certain miscellany tracts, 1684.

GEORGE HICKES
1642–1715

Institutiones grammaticae anglo-saxonicae et moeso-gothicae. Oxford 1689. Contains Runolph Jonas's Icelandic grammar, a catalogue of northern books, and Edward Bernard's Etymologicon britannicum.
[A Latin version of Aelfric's Anglo-Saxon preface to the Heptateuch]. In Henry Wharton, Auctarium historiae dogmaticae Jacobi Useeri Armachani de scripturis et sacris vernaculis, 1690, pp. 377–86.
Linguarum vett. septentrionalium thesaurus grammatico-criticus et archaeologicus. 2 vols Oxford 1703–5.
Wotton, W. Linguarum vett. septentrionalium thesauri grammatico-critici et archaeologi, auctore G. Hickesio, conspectus brevis. 1708. Attributed to Wotton but planned by Hickes, who also supplied the notes. Tr Maurice Shelton 1735, 1737.
Grammatico anglo-saxonica ex Hickesiano linguarum septentrionalium thesauro excerpta [by Edward Thwaites]. Oxford 1711.
Hickes also wrote some 25 tracts and many prefaces; there are 3 vols of his collected sermons.

EDWARD THWAITES
1667–1711

Heptateuchus, Liber Job et Evangelium Nicodemi, anglo-saxonice; Historiae Judith fragmentum, dano-saxonice. Oxford 1698.
Benson, T. Vocabularium anglo-saxonicum. Oxford 1701. Thwaites was responsible for much of the work.
Notae in anglo-saxonum nummos. 1708. Also appended to Wotton's Conspectus of Hickes's Thesaurus and Shelton's trn, above.
Grammatica anglo-saxonica ex Hickesiano linguarum septentrionalium thesauro excerpta. Oxford 1711.

HUMFREY WANLEY
1672–1726

Librorum vett. septentrionalium, qui in Angliae bibliothecis extant, nec non multorum vett. codd. septentrionalium alibi extantium Catalogus historico-criticus. In Hickes's Thesaurus, 1705. Tr Latin by Edward Thwaites.
The diary of Humfrey Wanley 1715–26. Ed C. E. Wright and R. C. Wright 2 vols 1966 (Bibl Soc).
Wanley also assisted Tanner in his Notitia monastica; Nicolson in his English historical library and Chamberlayne in his State of England. He supplied much of the material for Edward Bernard's Catalogi librorum mss Angliae et Hiberniae in unum collecti, Oxford 1697.

WILLIAM ELSTOB
1673–1715

Hormesta Pauli Orosii quam olim patrio sermone donavit Aelfredus Magnus. Oxford 1699. Title and 2 leaves only ptd.
Sermo lupi ad Anglos. Oxford 1701; rptd in Hickes's Thesaurus vol 2, 1705.
Of the offices of the daily and nightly hours of prayer. OE text tr Elstob as appendix to Several letters which passed between Dr Geo. Hickes and a Popish priest, 1705.
[Latin version of the OE homily on the birthday of St Gregory]. In his sister's edn of that work, 1709, below.
Offices of devotion used in the Anglo-Saxon church, with an English translation and notes. In Hickes, Controversial discourses, 1715, 1727.

THOMAS HEARNE
1678–1735

For Hearne's miscellaneous works, see col 682, above.

Joannis Lelandi antiquarii de rebus Britannicus collectanae. 6 vols Oxford [1715], London 1770, 1774. Vol 5 contains Saxon dictionary.

Libri saxonici qui ad manus Joannis Joscelini venerunt. In his edn of Robert of Avesbury, 1720.

Textus Roffensis. Oxford 1720.

Hemingi chartularium ecclesiae Wigorniensis. 2 vols Oxford 1723.

Johannis confratris et monachi Glastoniensis chronica: sive historia de rebus glastoniensibus. Oxford 1726. Battle of Maldon ptd as appendix.

ELIZABETH ELSTOB
1683–1756

An English-Saxon homily on the birthday of St Gregory, anciently used in the English-Saxon church. 1709; rptd as An Anglo-Saxon homily, London and Leicester 1839. William Elstob also contributed material.

Some testimonies of learned men in favour of the intended edition of the Saxon homilies, concerning the learning of the author of those homilies; and the advantages to be hoped for from an edition of them. 1713.

The English-Saxon homilies of Aelfric, Arch-bishop of Canterbury. Oxford 1715. Only 2 pp. ptd.

The rudiments of grammar for the English-Saxon tongue, first given in English; with an apology for the study of northern antiquities. 1715.

An apology for the study of northern antiquities. Ed C. Peake, Los Angeles 1956 (Augustan Reprint Soc).

VI. CLASSICAL STUDIES

RICHARD BENTLEY
1662–1742

Bibliographies

Bartholomew, A. T. Bentley: a bibliography of his works, with introduction by J. W. Clark. Cambridge 1908.

Collections

Works. Ed A. Dyce 3 vols 1836–8. Incomplete.

Correspondence. Ed C. Wordsworth 2 vols 1842.

Pol, E. H. Some letters of Bentley. Leyden 1959.

§1

Epistola ad Joannem Millium [on Malalas]. Appendix to Mill's edn of the Historia chronica of Malalas, Oxford 1691.

The folly of atheism. 1692 (Boyle Lecture 1).

Matter and motion cannot think. 1692 (Boyle Lecture 2).

A confutation of atheism from the structure and origin of humane bodies. 3 pts 1692 (Boyle Lectures 3–5).

A confutation of atheism from the origin and frame of the world. 3 pts 1692–3 (Boyle Lectures 6–8).

Sermons on the confutation of atheism. 1699, 1724, 1735, 1809.

Of Revelation and the Messias. 1696. A sermon.

Callimachi fragmenta a Richardo Bentleio collecta; R. Bentleii Animadversiones in nonnulla hymnorum Callimachi loca. In edn by J. G. Graevius, Utrecht 1697.

A proposal for building a Royal Library. 1697; rptd in A. T. Bartholomew and J. W. Clark, Bibliography of Bentley, Cambridge 1908.

Dissertation upon the Epistles of Phalaris, Themistocles, Socrates, Euripides and others; and the Fables of Aesop. Ptd with the 2nd edn of W. Wotton, Reflections upon ancient and modern learning, 1697.

A dissertation upon the Epistles of Phalaris; with an answer to the objections of the Hon C. Boyle. 1699, 1777, 1816, 1817, 1874, 1883.

Emendationes ad Ciceronis Tusculanas. Ptd in edn by J. Davies, Cambridge 1709.

Emendationes in Menandri et Philemonis reliquias ex nupera editione Joannis Clerici, auctore Phileleuthero Lipsiensi. Utrecht 1710, Cambridge 1713.

The present state of Trinity College in Cambridge, in a letter from Dr Bentley to the Bishop of Ely, published by a gentleman of the Temple. 1710, 1710.

Q. Horatius Flaccus ex recensione et cum notis R. Bentleii. Cambridge 1711, Amsterdam 1713, 1728.

Q. Horatius Flaccus ad nuperam Richardi Bentleii editionem accurate expressus; notas addidit Thomas Bentleius. Cambridge 1713.

Remarks upon a late discourse of free-thinking [by Anthony Collins], in a letter to F[rancis] H[are] DD, by Phileleutherus Lipsiensis. 1713.

A sermon upon Popery. Cambridge 1715.

A sermon preached before King George. 1717.

Two letters to Dr Bentley concerning his intended edition of the Greek Testament; together with the doctor's answer. 1717.

Proposals for printing a new edition of the Greek Testament. [1720].

Dr Bentley's proposals for printing a new edition of the Greek Testament; with a full answer to all the remarks [of Middleton]. 1721.

Publii Terentii comoediae, Phaedri fabulae Aesopiae, Publii Syri et aliorum veterum sententiae, ex recensione R. Bentleii. Cambridge 1726, Amsterdam 1727.

The case of Trinity College in Cambridge; whether the Crown or the Bishop of Ely be the General Visitor. 1729.

Milton's Paradise lost: a new edition by R[ichard] B[entley]. 1732.

M. Manilii astronomicon, ex recensione R. Bentleii. 1739.

M. Annaei Lucani Pharsalia cum notis Hugonis Grotii et R. Bentleii. Ed R. Cumberland, Strawberry Hill 1760.

§2

Temple, Sir William. Upon ancient and modern learning. In Miscellanea pt 2, 1690. Extols the writings of Phalaris and Aesop.

Wotton, William. Reflections upon ancient and modern learning, 1694. Answer to Temple.

Dr Bentley's Dissertations on the Epistles of Phalaris and the Fables of Aesop, examin'd by the Hon C. Boyle. 1698. Mainly by Francis Atterbury.

Middleton, Conyers. Remarks upon the proposals for printing a new edition of the Greek Testament. 1721; Some farther remarks, 1721.

Newton, Sir Isaac. Four letters [to Bentley], containing some arguments in proof of a Deity. 1756. Written 1692–3 for Bentley to use in his Boyle Lectures.

Monk, J. H. Life of Bentley. 1830, 2 vols 1833 (enlarged).

De Quincey, Thomas. Essay on Bentley written as review of Monk's Life. Blackwood's Mag Sept–Oct 1830; rptd in Works vol 7, 1854 etc.

Jebb, R. C. Bentley. 1882, 1902 (EML).

Mackail, J. W. Bentley's Milton. Proc Br Acad 11 1924; rptd in his Studies in humanism, 1938.

Empson, W. Milton and Bentley. In his Some versions of pastoral, 1935.

Garrod, H. W. Phalaris and Phalarism. In Seventeenth-century studies presented to Sir Herbert Grierson, Oxford 1938.

Fox, A. John Mill and Bentley: a study of the textual criticism of the New Testament. Oxford 1954.

White, R. J. Dr Bentley: a study in academic scarlet. 1965.

RICHARD PORSON
1759–1808

Papers in the Library of Trinity College Cambridge, arranged by H. R. Luard in 1859 and bound in 4 vols, contain (1) the originals of many of the letters ptd in the correspondence; (2) transcripts of Photius; (3) transcripts of the Medea and the Phoenissæ; (4) notes on ancient authors, including a collation of the Aldine Æschylus. Also Adversaria in most of the 274 books, formerly belonging to Porson, now in the Library of Trinity College Cambridge; and unpbd letters in the libraries of Edinburgh Univ and Magdalen College Oxford.

Editions

Ξενοφωντος Κυρου 'Αναβασις βιβλια έπτα, recognovit T. Hutchinson. 1786. Notes, pp. 41–59, and preface.

Publii Virgili Maronis opera varietate lectionis et perpetua adnotatione illustrata a C. G. Heyne; accedit index uberrimus: editio tertia auctior. 4 vols 1793. Preface by Porson.

Æschyli tragœdiæ septem, cum versione latina. 2 vols Glasgow, London, Oxford 1794 (ptd) and 1806 (pbd). Anon.

Αἱ του Αἰσχυλου τραγωδιαι έπτα. Glasgow 1795. Pirated.

Εὐριπιδου 'Εκαβη: Euripidis Hecuba, ad fidem manuscriptorum emendata. 1797.

Εὐριπιδου 'Ορεστης: Euripidis Orestes ad fidem manuscriptorum emendata et brevibus notis emendationum potissimum rationes reddentibus instructa. 1798.

Εὐριπιδου Φοινισσαι: Euripidis Phœnissæ ad fidem manuscriptorum emendata et brevibus notis emendationum potissimum rationes reddentibus instructa. 1799.

Εὐριπιδου Μηδεια: Euripidis Medea ad fidem manuscriptorum emendata et brevibus notis emendationum potissimum rationes reddentibus instructa. Cambridge 1801.

'Ομηρου 'Ιλιας και 'Οδυσσεια. 4 vols Oxford 1800–1. Ed T. Grenville, Porson, W. Cleaver et al, with Porson's collation of the Harleian ms of the Odyssey.

Euripidis tragœdiæ priores quatuor ['Εκαβη, 'Ορεστης, Φοινισσαι, Μηδεια] edidit R. Porson; recensuit suasque notulas subjecit J. Scholefield. Cambridge 1826.

Literary Remains

R. Porsoni adversaria: notae et emendationes in poetas graecos, quas ex schedis manuscriptis Porsoni apud Collegium S.S. Trinitatis Cantabrigiæ repositis deprompserunt et ordinarunt J. H. Monk, C. J. Blomfield. Cambridge 1812.

Tracts and miscellaneous criticisms, collected and arranged by Thomas Kidd. 1815.

Ricardi Porsoni notæ in Aristophanem, quibus Plutum comœdiam partim ex ejusdem recensione partim e manuscriptis emendatam et variis lectionibus instructam præmisit, et collationum appendicem adjecit Petrus Paulus Dobree. 3 pts Cambridge 1820.

Notes on Pausanias appended to T. Gaisford's Lectiones Platonicæ. 1820.

Φωτιου Λεξεων συναγωγη: e codice Galeano descripsit R. Porsonus. 2 pts Cambridge 1822.

Correspondence. Ed H. R. Luard, Cambridge 1867. 68 letters.

§2

Clarke, M. L. Porson: a biographical essay. Cambridge 1937.

—— In his Greek studies in England 1700–1830, Cambridge 1945.

Page, D. L. Richard Porson 1759–1808. Proc Br Acad 45 1960.

THOMAS CREECH
1659–1700

T. Lucretius Carus his six books De natura rerum, done into English verse. 1682.

The odes, satyrs and epistles of Horace, done into English. 1684.

Idylliums of Theocritus done into English. 1684.

T. Lucretii Cari de rerum natura libri vi, quibus interpretationem et notas addidit T. Creech. 1695.

The five books of M. Manilius done into English verse. 1697.

CONYERS MIDDLETON
1683–1750

Miscellaneous works. 4 vols 1752, 5 vols 1755.
For Middleton's separate pbns see col 690, above.

SAMUEL PARR
1747–1825
Collections

Works, with memoirs of his life and writings, and a selection from his correspondence, by J. Johnstone. 8 vols 1828.

§1

A discourse on education and on the plans pursued in charity schools, for the charity schools in Norwich. 1786.

G. Bellendeni de statu libri tres: editio secunda longe emendatior [by S. Parr]. 2 pts 1787–8.

A spital sermon preached upon Easter Tuesday, April 15 1800; to which are added notes. 1801.

Characters of the late Charles James Fox, selected and in part written by Philopatris Varvicensis. 2 vols 1809.

A letter to Dr Milner, occasioned by some passages contained in his book entitled The end of religious controversy. Ed J. Lynes 1825.

§2

Field, W. Memoirs of the life, writings and opinions of Parr. 2 vols 1828.

Barker, E. H. Parriana: or notices of the Rev S. Parr, collected from various sources, printed and manuscript, and in part written by E. H. Barker. 2 vols 1828–9.

Derry, W. Dr Parr: a portrait of the Whig Dr Johnson. Oxford 1966.

JOSEPH SPENCE
1699–1768

Polymetis: or an enquiry concerning the agreement between the works of the Roman poets and the remains of the antient artists. 1747.
See col 705, above.

THOMAS TWINING
1735-1804

Aristotle's treatise on poetry, translated with notes and two dissertations. 1789; ed H. Hamilton, Dublin 1851.

Recreations and studies of a country clergyman of the eighteenth century: being selections from the correspondence of Twining. 1882.

THOMAS TYRWHITT
1730-86

Περι λιθων: poema Orpheo a quibusdam adscriptum, græce et latine, ex editione J. M. Gesneri; recensuit notasque adjecit T. Tyrwhitt; simul prodit auctarium Dissertationis de Babrio [with the Dissertation, both by Tyrwhitt]. 2 pts 1776- 81.

Conjecturæ in Strabonem, edit Amstel 1707. [1783].

Isaei oratio de Meneclis hereditate. 1785.

Aristotelis De poetica liber: textum recensuit, versionem refinxit et animadversionibus illustravit T. Tyrwhitt. Oxford 1794. Only 30 copies ptd. Greek and Latin.

Conjecturae in Aeschylum, Euripidem, et Aristophanem. Oxford 1822.

For Tyrwhitt's other writings see col 710, above.

GILBERT WAKEFIELD
1756-1801

Silva critica: sive in auctores sacros profanosque commentarius philologus (accedunt tres hymni Orphici e codicibus mss nunc primum in lucem dati). 5 vols Cambridge 1789-95.

Memoirs, written by himself. 1792; [ed J. T. Rutt and A. Wainewright] 2 vols 1804.

Q. Horatii Flacci quæ supersunt, recensuit et notulis instruxit G. Wakefield. 2 vols 1794.

Tragœdiarum delectus: Hercules furens, Alcestis, Euripideae, Philoctetes, Sophoclea: et Eumenides, Æschylea) in scholarum usum edidit et illustravit G. Wakefield. 2 vols 1794.

Animadversiones ad Æschyli tres priores tragœdias. Jena 1794-9.

Βιωνος και Μοσχου τα λειψανα: illustrabat et emendabat G. Wakefield. 1795.

T. Lucretii Cari de rerum natura libros sex. 3 vols 1796-7, 4 vols Glasgow 1813.

Publii Virgilii Maronis opera: emendabat et notulis illustrabat G. Wakefield. 1796.

In Euripidis Hecubam, Londini nuper publicatum [by R. Porson] diatribe extemporalis. 1797.

Select essays of Dion Chrysostom translated into English from the Greek; with notes, critical and illustrative. 1800.

Noctes Carcerariae: sive de legibus metricis poetarum graecorum qui versibus hexametris scripserunt, disputatio. 1801.

Correspondence with C. J. Fox, chiefly on subjects of classical literature. 1813.

VII. PHILOSOPHY

GENERAL STUDIES

Leland, J. A view of the principal Deistical writers. 3 vols 1754-6.

Pattison, M. Tendencies of religious thought in England 1688-1750. In Essays and reviews, 1860; rptd in Pattison, Essays vol 2, Oxford 1889.

Stephen, L. A history of English thought in the eighteenth century. 2 vols 1876.

Green, T. H. In his Works, ed R. L. Nettleship vols 1-2, 1885-6. On Hume, Locke, Berkeley et al.

Selby-Bigge, L. A. British moralists: being selections from writers, principally of the eighteenth-century period. 2 vols Oxford 1897.

Powicke, F. J. The Cambridge Platonists. 1926.

Cassirer, E. Die Philosophie der Aufklärung. Tübingen 1932; tr Princeton 1951.

—— Die Platonische Renaissance in England und die Schule von Cambridge. Leipzig 1932; tr Edinburgh 1953.

Willey, B. The seventeenth-century background. 1934.

—— The eighteenth-century background. 1940.

Cragg, G. R. From Puritanism to the Age of Reason. Cambridge 1950.

—— Reason and authority in the eighteenth century. Cambridge 1964.

Bethell, S. L. The cultural revolution of the seventeenth century. 1951.

Jones, R. F. et al. The seventeenth century: studies in the history of English thought and literature from Bacon to Pope. Stanford 1951.

British empirical philosophers: Locke, Berkeley, Hume, Reid and J. S. Mill. Ed A. J. Ayer and R. Winch 1952.

Kliger, S. The Goths in England: a study in seventeenth- and eighteenth-century thought. Cambridge 1952.

Røstvig, M. S. The happy man: studies in the metamorphoses of a classical ideal 1600-1760. 2 vols Oslo 1954-8, 1971 (rev).

Simon, I. 'Pride of reason' in the Restoration and earlier eighteenth century. Brussels 1959.

Reason and the imagination: studies in the history of ideas 1600-1800. Ed J. A. Mazzeo, New York 1962.

The English mind: studies in the English moralists presented to Basil Willey. Ed H. S. Davies and G. Watson, Cambridge 1964.

A. LOCKE AND HIS CONTEMPORARIES

JOHN LOCKE
1632-1704

Bibliographies etc

Long, P. A summary catalogue of the Lovelace Collection of the papers of Locke in the Bodleian Library. Oxford 1959.

Harrison, J. and P. Laslett. The library of Locke. Oxford 1965, 1971.

Collections

Posthumous works. 1706.

Remains. 1714.

Works. 3 vols 1714, 1722, 1727, 1740, 1751, 1759.

A collection of several pieces of Mr Locke, published by P. Des Maizeaux under the direction of Mr Anthony Collins. 1720, 1739.

Educational writings. Ed J. W. Adamson, Cambridge 1912, 1922 (rev); ed J. L. Axtell, Cambridge 1968.

The second treatise of civil government and A letter concerning toleration. Ed J. W. Gough, Oxford 1946, 1956, 1966 (both rev).
Locke on politics, religion and education. Ed M. Cranston, New York 1965.
Clarendon edition of the works. Ed P. H. Nidditch 30 vols Oxford 1975–.
The Locke reader. Ed J. W. Yolton, Cambridge 1977.

§ 1

A poem in Latin and in English dedicated to Cromwell. In Musarum oxoniensium ᾿ελαιοφορία, Oxford 1654.
On the marriage of King Charles II with the Infanta of Portugal. In Domiduca oxoniensis: sive musae academicae, Oxford 1662. A poem.
In Tractatum de febribus D. D. Sydenham, praxin medicam apud Londinenses mira solertia æque ac fælicitate exercentis. In T. Sydenham, Methodus curandi febres, 1668 (2nd edn). A poem.
Méthode nouvelle de dresser des recueils. Bibliothèque Universelle et Historique July 1686; tr 1706.
Essai philosophique concernant l'entendement. Bibliothèque Universelle et Historique Jan 1688.
An essay concerning humane understanding. 1690, 1694 (with large addns), 1695, 1700, 1706, 2 vols 1716, 1729; ed A. C. Fraser 2 vols Oxford 1894, New York 1959; ed A. S. Pringle-Pattison, Oxford 1924 (abridged); ed P. H. Nidditch, Oxford 1975, 1978 (without Glossary and with new introd).
An essay concerning the understanding, knowledge, opinion and assent. Ed B. Rand, Cambridge Mass 1931.
An early draft of Locke's Essay, together with excerpts from his journals. Ed R. I. Aaron and J. Gibb, Oxford 1936.
A letter to the Right Reverend Edward Ld Bishop of Worcester, concerning some passages relating to Mr Locke's Essay of humane understanding. 1697.
Mr Locke's reply to the Right Reverend the Lord Bishop of Worcester's Answer to his Letter, concerning some passages relating to Mr Locke's Essay. 1697.
Mr Locke's reply to the Right Reverend the Lord Bishop of Worcester's Answer to his second letter. 1699.
Epistola de tolerantia ad clarissimum virum TARPTOLA. Gouda 1689; tr W. Popple 1689, 1690; ed H. Morley 1889; ed M. Montuori, Hague 1963 (Latin and English); ed R. Klibansky, tr J. W. Gough, Oxford 1968 (Latin and English).
A second letter concerning toleration. 1690.
A third letter for toleration. 1692. Part of a Fourth letter for toleration appeared in Posthumous works, 1706, above.
Scritti editi e inediti sulla tolleranza. Ed C. A. Viano, Turin 1961.
Two treatises of government. 1690, 1694, 1698; ed P. Laslett, Cambridge 1960, 1967 (rev).
Social contract: essays by Locke, Hume and Rousseau. Ed E. Barker 1947. Second treatise of government.
Some considerations of the consequences of the lowering of interest and raising the value of money. 1692, 1696.
Further considerations concerning raising the value of money. 1695.
Short observations on a printed paper, intituled For encouraging the coinage of silver money in England, and after for keeping it there. 1695.
Several papers relating to money, interest and trade &c. 1696.
Some thoughts concerning education. 1693, 1695 (3rd enlarged edn), 1699, 1705; ed R. H. Quick, Cambridge 1880; ed P. Gay, New York 1964.
The reasonableness of Christianity as delivered in the Scriptures. 1695, 1696.
A vindication of the Reasonableness of Christianity etc, from Mr Edwards's Reflections. 1695.

A second vindication of the Reasonableness of Christianity etc. 1697.
A paraphrase and notes on the Epistle of St Paul to the Galatians. 1705.
Some thoughts on the conduct of the understanding in the search of truth. 1762; ed T. Fowler, Oxford 1881, 1901 (rev).
Essays on the law of nature: the Latin text with a translation. Ed W. von Leyden, Oxford 1954.
Two tracts on government. Ed P. Abrams, Cambridge 1967. Written 1660.

Letters, Diaries etc

Some familiar letters between Mr Locke and several of his friends. 1708.
The correspondence of Locke and Edward Clarke. Ed B. Rand, Oxford 1927.
Locke's travels in France 1675–9, as related in his journals, correspondence and other papers. Ed J. Lough, Cambridge 1953.
Correspondence. Ed E. S. de Beer 8 vols Oxford 1976–.

§ 2

Leibnitz, G. W. von. Nouveaux essais sur l'entendement humain. In his Œuvres philosophiques, ed R. E. Raspe, Amsterdam 1765.
Cousin, V. La philosophie de Locke. Paris 1819.
King, P. The life of Locke. 1829, 2 vols 1830, 1 vol 1858 (Bohn's Lib) (as The life and letters of Locke).
Fox-Bourne, H. R. The life of Locke. 2 vols 1876.
Fraser, A. C. Locke. 1890.
Alexander, S. Locke. 1908.
Ryle, G. Locke on the human understanding. Oxford 1933.
Aaron, R. I. John Locke. Oxford 1937, 1955 (rev).
James, D. G. The life of reason: Hobbes, Locke and Bolingbroke. 1949.
Cranston, M. Locke: a biography. 1957.
—— Locke. 1961 (Br Council pamphlet).
Gough, J. W. Locke's political philosophy: eight studies. Oxford 1950.
O'Connor, D. J. John Locke. 1952 (Penguin).
Tuveson, E. L. The imagination as a means of grace: Locke and the aesthetics of romanticism. Berkeley 1960.
Locke and Berkeley: a collection of critical essays. Ed C. B. Martin and D. M. Armstrong 1968.
Locke, problems and perspectives: a collection of new essays. Ed J. W. Yolton, Cambridge 1969.
Yolton, J. W. Locke and the compass of human understanding. Cambridge 1970.

Other Philosophical Writers 1660–1700

CHARLES BLOUNT
1654–93

Anima mundi. 1679.
Great is Diana of the Ephesians. 1690.
The two first books of Philostratus concerning the life of Apollonius Tyaneus. 1680.
Miscellaneous works. 1695. Preface by C. Gildon.

THOMAS BURNET
1635?–1715

Telluris theoria sacra. 2 vols 1681–9.
The theory of the earth. 2 vols 1684–90; ed B. Willey 1965. An enlarged and rev version of above.
Remarks upon an Essay concerning humane understanding. 1697; Second remarks, 1697; Third remarks, 1699.

JOSEPH GLANVILL
1636–80

§1

The vanity of dogmatizing. 1661, 1665 (rev as Scepsis scientifica); ed J. Owen 1885; ed M. E. Prior, New York 1931 (facs).
Lux orientalis. 1662, 1665, 1687 (with George Rust, Defence of truth).
Plus ultra: or the progress and advancement of knowledge since the days of Aristotle. 1668; ed J. I. Cope, Gainesville 1958 (facs).
Λόγου θρησκεία: or a seasonable recommendation and defence of reason in the affairs of religion against infidelity. 1670.
Philosophia pia: or a discourse of the religious temper of the experimental philosophy which is profest by the Royal Society. 1671.
Essays on several important subjects. 1676.
An essay concerning preaching, written for the direction of a young divine. 1678, 1703.
A seasonable defence of preaching, and the plain way of it. 1678.
Saducismus triumphatus. 1681, 1682, 1689, 1726 ('with some account of Mr Glanvill's life and writings'); ed C. O. Parsons, Gainesville 1966 (facs).
Some discourses, sermons and remains. 1681. Preface by A. Horneck.

§2

Popkin, R. H. Glanvill: a precursor of Hume. JHI 14 1953.
Cope, J. I. Glanvill: Anglican apologist. St Louis 1956.

JOHN NORRIS
1657–1711

Poems. 1684; rptd in A collection of miscellanies below.
A collection of miscellanies. Oxford 1687, 1692, 1699, 1706.
The theory and regulation of love: a moral essay, to which are added Letters philosophical and moral between the author and Dr Henry More. 1688, 1694.
Christian blessedness; to which is added Reflections upon a late Essay concerning the human understanding. 1690, 1692.
Cursory reflections upon a book call'd An essay concerning human understanding. 1690; ed G. D. McEwen, Los Angeles 1961 (Augustan Reprint Soc) (facs).
Practical discourses upon several divine subjects. 4 vols 1691–8.
Letters concerning the love of God. 1695.
An account of reason and faith in relation to the mysteries of Christianity. 1697.
An essay towards the theory of the ideal or intelligible world, desig'd for two parts. 2 vols 1701–4.
A philosophical discourse concerning the natural immortality of the soul. 1708.
Poems. Ed A. B. Grosart 1871.

SIR DUDLEY NORTH
1641–91

Discourses upon trade. 1691, Edinburgh 1822; ed J. R. McCulloch 1856, Cambridge 1954.
Considerations upon the East India trade. 1701; ed J. R. McCulloch 1856, Cambridge 1954.

SIR WILLIAM PETTY
1632–87

§1

Reflections upon some persons and things in Ireland. 1660.
A treatise of taxes and contributions. 1662, 1667, 1679, 1685.
The discourse made concerning the use of duplicate proportion. 1674.
An essay concerning the multiplication of mankind. 1682, 1686.
Another essay in political arithmetick. 1683.
The fourth part of the present state of England. 1683.
Observations upon the Dublin-bills of morality. 1683.
Deux essays d'arithmétique politique. 1686.
Two essays in political arithmetick. 1687.
Cinq essays sur l'arithmétique politique. 1687.
Five essays in political arithmetick. 1687.
Political arithmetick. 1690, 1691.
The political anatomy of Ireland; to which is added Verbum sapienti. 1691.
Sir William Petty's quantulumcunque concerning money. 1695.
Several essays in political arithmetick. 1699.
Economic writings. Ed C. H. Hull 2 vols Cambridge 1899.

§2

Bevan, W. L. Sir William Petty. Baltimore 1894.
Fitzmaurice, E. Life of Petty. 1895.
Strauss, E. Petty: portrait of a genius. 1954.

JOHN RAY
1627–1705
Bibliographies
Keynes, G. L. Ray: a bibliography. Oxford 1951.

§1

Historia generalis plantarum. 3 vols 1686–1704.
The wisdom of God manifested in the Creation. 1691.
Synopsis methodica animalium. 1693.
Philosophical letters. 1718.

§2

Raven, C. E. Ray, naturalist. Cambridge 1942.

SIR RICHARD TEMPLE
1634–97

An essay upon taxes, calculated for the present juncture of affairs in England. 1693.
Some short remarks upon Mr Lock's book, in answer to Mr Lounds. 1696.

WILLIAM WAKE
1657–1737

§1

Sermons. 1690.
The genuine epistles of the Apostolic Fathers, translated with discussions. 1693.
Principles of the Christian religion. 1699.
The state of the Church and clergy of England. 1703.

§2

Sykes, N. Wake, Archbishop of Canterbury. 2 vols Cambridge 1957.

B. BERKELEY AND HIS CONTEMPORARIES

GEORGE BERKELEY
1685–1753

Bibliographies

Jessop, T. E. A bibliography of Berkeley, with an inventory of Berkeley's manuscript remains by A. A. Luce. Oxford 1934.
Keynes, G. L. A bibliography of Berkeley. Oxford 1976.

Collections

Works, to which is added a life and several letters to T. Prior, Dean Gervais and Mr Pope. [Ed T. Stock] 2 vols Dublin 1784, 3 vols 1820, 1837.
Works, including many of his writings hitherto unpublished, with prefaces, annotations, his life and letters, and an account of his philosophy. Ed A. C. Fraser 4 vols Oxford 1871, 1901 (rev).
Works. Ed A. A. Luce and T. E. Jessop 9 vols Edinburgh 1948–57. Includes all Berkeley's known letters.
Philosophical writings, selected. Ed T. E. Jessop 1952.
The principles of human knowledge, with three dialogues between Hylas and Philonous [abridged]. Ed A. J. Ayer and R. Winch 1952.

§ 1

Arithmetica absque algebra aut Euclide demonstrata. Dublin 1707.
Miscellanea mathematica. Dublin 1707 (in Arithmetica, above).
An essay towards a new theory of vision. Dublin 1709, London 1709 (adds appendix). Rptd with rev text but without appendix in Alciphron vol 2, 1732, below.
A treatise concerning the principles of human knowledge. Pt 1 (all pbd), Dublin 1710, London 1734 (rev text with Three dialogues, below); ed P. Wheelwright, New York 1935; ed T. E. Jessop 1937 (1710 texts with variants of 1734); ed G. J. Warnock 1962 (with Three dialogues).
Passive obedience: or the Christian doctrine of not resisting the Supreme Power, proved and vindicated upon the principles of the law of nature. 1712, 1712, 1713 (rev).
Three dialogues between Hylas and Philonous. 1713, 1725, 1734 (with Principles of human knowledge); ed G. J. Warnock 1962.
Advice to the Tories who have taken the oaths. 1715.
De motu: sive de motus principio et natura, et de causa communicationis motum. 1721; rptd in A miscellany, 1752, below.
An essay towards preventing the ruin of Great Britain. 1721; rptd in A miscellany, 1752, below.
A proposal for the better supplying of churches in our foreign plantations, and for converting the savage Americans to Christianity, by a college to be erected in the Summer Islands, otherwise called the Isles of Bermudas. 1725, 1731; rptd in A miscellany, 1752, below.
A sermon preached before the incorporated Society for the Propagation of the Gospel in foreign parts. 1732; rptd in A miscellany, 1752, below.
Alciphron: or the minute philosopher, in seven dialogues. 2 vols 1732, 1732, Dublin 1732, London 1752 (omits Theory of vision, below), 1752 (rev, omitting Theory of vision), 1767.
The theory of vision: or visual language, shewing the immediate presence and providence of a Deity, vindicated and explained. 1733.
The analyst: or a discourse addressed to an infidel mathematician. 1734, Dublin 1734, 1754.
A defence of free-thinking in mathematics. 1735, Dublin 1735.

Reasons for not replying to Mr Walton's Full answer in a letter to PTP. Dublin 1735.
The querist: containing several queries proposed to the consideration of the public. 3 pts Dublin 1735–7, London 1735–7, 1750 (rev, adding A word to the wise), Glasgow 1751; rptd in A miscellany, 1752, below; ed J. M. Hone, Dublin 1936.
A letter on the project of a national bank. 1737.
A discourse addressed to magistrates and men in authority. Dublin 1732, London 1736, 1738, Dublin 1738.
A chain of philosophical reflexions and inquiries concerning the virtues of tar water. 1744, 1744 (rev as Siris: a chain etc), Dublin 1744, London 1744, 1744, 1746, 1747, 1748.
A letter to T[homas] P[rior] esq, containing some farther remarks on the virtues of tar-water. Dublin 1744, London 1744.
Two letters, the one to Thomas Prior esq concerning the usefulness of tar-water in the plague; the other to the Rev Dr Hales, on the benefit of tar-water in fevers. Dublin 1747, London 1747.
A word to the wise: or an exhortation to the Roman Catholic clergy of Ireland. Dublin 1749, Boston 1750, 1752; rptd in The querist, 1750, Glasgow 1751, and in A miscellany, 1752, below.
Maxims concerning patriotism, by a lady. Dublin 1750; rptd in A miscellany, 1752, below.
A miscellany, containing several tracts on various subjects. 1752, Dublin 1752. Includes, in addition to works already ptd, Farther thoughts on tar water, and Verses on the prospect of planting arts and learning in America.
The Irish patriot: or queries upon queries. Ed J. M. Hone, TLS 13 March, 3 April 1930.
Commonplace book. First pbd in Works, ed A. C. Fraser vol 4, 1871; ed G. A. Johnson 1930; ed A. A. Luce as Philosophical commentaries, Edinburgh 1944 (rev).

§ 2

Fraser, A. C. Berkeley. 1881.
—— Berkeley and spiritual realism. 1908.
Hone, J. M. and M. M. Rossi. Bishop Berkeley: his life, writings and philosophy. 1934.
Luce, A. A. Berkeley and Malebranche. Oxford 1934.
—— The life of Berkeley, Bishop of Cloyne. Edinburgh 1949.
Davie, D. A. Berkeley's style in Siris. Cambridge Jnl April 1951.
—— Berkeley and the style of dialogue. In The English mind, ed H. S. Davies and G. Watson, Cambridge 1964.
Warnock, G. J. Berkeley. 1953 (Pelican).
Wisdom, J. O. The unconscious origin of Berkeley's philosophy. 1953.
Ritchie, A. D. Berkeley's Siris: the philosophy of the great chain of being and the alchemical theory. Proc Brit Acad 40 1954.
—— Berkeley's Siris. 1955.
Jessop, T. E. George Berkeley. 1959.

Other Philosophical Writers 1700–50

RICHARD BENTLEY
1662–1742

The folly and unreasonableness of atheism, in eight sermons [Boyle lectures 1692]. 1693, 1699, Cambridge 1724, 1735 [adds 3 sermons], Oxford 1809.
Remarks upon a late Discourse of free-thinking [by A. Collins], by Phileleutherus Lipsiensis. 1713.
See col 725, above.

JOSEPH BUTLER
1692–1752
Collections
Works. Ed W. E. Gladstone 2 vols Oxford 1896.
Works. Ed J. H. Bernard 2 vols 1900.

§ 1
Fifteen sermons preached at the Chapel of the Rolls Court. 1726, 1729 (with Preface), 1736, 1749 (adds Six sermons preached on public occasions), 1765, 2 vols Glasgow 1769 etc; ed W. R. Matthews 1914 (adds Dissertation on virtue from Analogy, below).
The analogy of religion, natural and revealed, to the constitution and course of nature. 1736, 1736 (corrected), 1740, Glasgow 1754, 1765, Aberdeen 1775; ed S. Halifax 1788; ed H. Morley 1884; ed R. Bayne 1906; ed W. E. Gladstone, Oxford 1907 (WC).
Six sermons preached upon public occasions. 1739, 1740, 1741, 1747, 1748.
A charge delivered to the clergy at the visitation of Durham. 1871.

§ 2
Mackintosh, J. On the progress of ethical philosophy chiefly during the seventeenth and eighteenth centuries. 1830, 1872 (rev).
Gladstone, W. E. Studies subsidiary to the works of Bishop Butler. Oxford 1896.
Broad, C. D. In his Five types of ethical theory, 1930.
Mossner, E. C. Bishop Butler and the Age of Reason. New York 1936.
Duncan-Jones, A. Butler's moral philosophy. 1952 (Pelican).

SAMUEL CLARKE
1675–1729
Collections
Works, with a preface giving some account of the life, writings and character of the author, by Benjamin Hoadly. 4 vols 1738.
Sermons. Ed John Clarke 10 vols 1730–1.

§ 1
Some reflections on that part of a book [by J. Toland] called Amyntor: or a defence of Milton's life, which relates to the writings of the primitive Fathers and the canon of the New Testament. 1699.
Three practical essays on baptism, confirmation, repentance. 1699.
A paraphrase on the four Evangelists. 2 vols 1701–2.
A demonstration of the being and attributes of God, more particularly in answer to Mr Hobbs, Spinoza and their followers. 1705, 1706, 1716 (adds correspondence with Joseph Butler), 1719, 1725 (adds Discourse concerning prophecies), 1732, 1739.
A letter to Mr Dodwell, wherein all the arguments in his Epistolary discourse are particularly answered. 1706.
The scripture-doctrine of the Trinity. 1712.
A collection of papers which passed between the late learned Mr Leibnitz and Dr Clarke (to which are added remarks upon a book [by Anthony Collins] entitled A philosophical enquiry concerning human liberty). 1717; ed H. G. Alexander, Manchester 1956.
Jacobi Rohaulti physica, latine vertit, recensuit et uberioribus jam annotationibus, ex illustrissimi Isaaci Newtoni philosophia maximam partem hastis, amplificavit et ornavit S. Clarke. 1718; tr 2 vols 1735.
A discourse concerning the connexion of the prophecies in the Old Testament, and the application of them to Christ. 1725, 1725.

A letter to Benjamin Hoadly FRS occasioned by the controversy relating to the proportion of velocity and force in bodies in motion. 1728.
See also col 650, above.

JAMES HERVEY
1714–58
Collections
The works of the late Reverend James Hervey, with a particular account of the life of the author. 6 vols Edinburgh 1769, Newcastle 1789, 1792, 7 vols 1797, 6 vols Pontefract 1805, Edinburgh 1834.
Sermons and miscellaneous tracts. 1764, 1784–92, Glasgow 1790.

§ 1
Meditations among the tombs, in a letter to a lady. 1746.
Meditations and contemplations [vol 1 contains Meditations among the tombs]. 2 vols 1748, 1748; 26 edns to 1792.
Remarks on Lord Bolingbroke's Letters on the study and use of history. 1752, Dublin 1752.
Theron and Aspasio: or a series of dialogues and letters upon the most important and interesting subjects. 3 vols 1755, 1755, 1767, 2 vols 1772, 3 vols 1789.
Dialogues between Theron and Aspasio, by J.H.; together with his Letters to Mr John Wesley in vindication thereof. Ed W. Hervey 3 vols Pontefract 1805, 2 vols 1808.

Letters
A collection of the letters of J.H., to which is prefixed an account of his life and death. 2 vols 1760, Dublin 1760, London 1784.
The life of J.H.; to which is added a collection of his letters. Berwick 1770, 1772.
Letters illustrative of the author's character, never before published, by J.H. [Ed J. Burgess] 1811.

FRANCIS HUTCHESON
1695–1747
An inquiry into the original of our ideas of beauty and virtue, in two treatises. 1725 (anon), 1726 (rev), 1726, 1729, Glasgow 1738, 1753.
An essay on the nature and conduct of the passions and affections, with illustrations on the moral sense. 1728, Dublin 1728, London 1730, 1742, Dublin 1751, 1756.
De naturali hominum socialitate oratio inauguralis. Glasgow 1730, 1756.
Considerations on patronages. 1735, Glasgow 1774.
Letters between the late Mr Gilbert Burnet and Mr Hutchinson concerning the true foundation of virtue or moral goodness. 1735, Glasgow 1772. First ptd in London Jnl 1728 as Letters between 'Philanthropus' and 'Philaretus'. With the title Letters concerning the true goodness between Mr Gilbert Burnet and Mr Francis Hutcheson and including 6 articles in Dublin Jnl 1725–6, later ptd in Reflections upon laughter, 1750, below.
Metaphysicae synopsis: ontologiam et pneumatologiam complecteus. Glasgow 1742, 1744, 1749, 1756, Strasbourg 1772. Anon.
Philosophiae moralis institutio compendiaria. Glasgow 1742, Rotterdam 1745, Glasgow 1745, 1755, Dublin 1787; tr Glasgow 1747, 1753.
The meditations of M. Aurelius Antoninus. Glasgow 1742, 1749, 1752, 1764. Anon.
Reflections upon laughter, and remarks upon the Fable of the bees. Glasgow 1750; rptd as Thoughts on laughter and observations on bees, Glasgow 1758. First ptd as 6 articles in Dublin Jnl 1725–6, signed 'Philomeides' and 'P.M.'.

A system of moral philosophy, in three books, to which is prefixed some account of the life, writings and character of the author. 2 vols Glasgow and London 1755.
Logicae compendium. Glasgow 1759, 1764, 1778, 1787.

ANTHONY ASHLEY COOPER, 3rd EARL OF SHAFTESBURY
1671–1713

§ 1

Select sermons of Dr [Benjamin] Whichcot. 1698. Ed Shaftesbury, with preface.
An inquiry concerning virtue in two discourses. 1699 (unauthorized), 1711 (rev).
A letter concerning enthusiasm. 1708; ed A.-L. Leroy, Paris 1930.
Sensus communis: an essay on the freedom of wit and humour. 1709.
Soliloquy: or advice to an author. 1710.
Characteristicks of men, manners, opinions, times. 3 vols 1711, 1711, 1714 (rev), 1723, 1727, 1732, 1733, 1737, 1743, 4 vols Glasgow 1758; ed W. M. Hatch 1870; ed J. M. Robertson 2 vols 1900, New York 1964 (with new introd by S. Grean).
A notion of the historical draught: or tablature of the judgment of Hercules. 1712 (Fr trn), 1713. Included in 1714 edn of Characteristicks, above.
Second characters: or the language of forms. Ed B. Rand, Cambridge 1914. Contains the Judgment of Hercules and A letter concerning design (ptd in 1732 edn of Characteristicks, above), which Shaftesbury intended as part of a separate work, together with The picture of Cebes and Plastics.

Letters

Several letters written by a noble Lord to a young man at the university. 1716.
Letters from the Right Honourable the late Earl of Shaftesbury to Robert Molesworth esq. Ed J. Toland 1721.
Original letters of Locke, Algernon Sidney and Shaftesbury. Ed T. Forster 1830.
The life, unpublished letters and philosophical regimen of Shaftesbury. Ed B. Rand 1900.

§ 2

Brown, J. Essays on the Characteristics. 1751, 1752, Dublin 1752, 1764.
Brett, R. L. The third Earl of Shaftesbury. 1951.

MATTHEW TINDAL
1657–1733

An essay concerning the law of nations and the rights of sovereigns. 1693, 1694 (with An account of what was said at the Council-board).
Essay concerning obedience to the supreme powers. 1694.
A letter to the clergy of both universities concerning the Trinity. 1694.
An essay concerning the power of the magistrates and the rights of mankind in matters of religion. 1697.
The liberty of the press. 1698.
Reasons against restraining the press. 1704.
The rights of the Christian Church asserted against the Romish and all other priests who claim an independent power over it, with a preface. 1706, 1706, 1707.
A defence of the rights of the Christian Church. 1707, 1709; A second defence, 1708.
Four discourses on obedience, laws of nations, power of the magistrate and liberty of the press. 1709.

New High Church turned old Presbyterian. 1709, 1710.
High-Church catechism. 1710.
The merciful judgements of the High Church triumphant. 1710.
The Jacobitism, perjury and Popery of High-Church priests. 1710.
The nation vindicated from the aspersions cast on it. 1711.
The defection considered, and the designs of those who divided the friends of government set in a true light. 1717 (4 edns), 1718.
Destruction a certain consequence of division. 1717.
The judgement of Dr Prideaux concerning the murder of Julius Caesar. 1721.
A defence of our present happy establishment. 1722.
Enquiry into the causes of our present disaffection. 1722.
An address to the inhabitants of London and Westminster. 1729, 1730 (rev); A second address, 1730, 1730.
Christianity as old as the Creation: or the Gospel a republication of the religion of nature. 1730, 1730, 1731.

JOHN TOLAND
1670–1722
Collections

A collection of several pieces. 2 vols 1726 (with Life by Des Maizeaux), 1747, 1 vol 1814.

§ 1

The danger of mercenary parliaments. [1695], 1722, 1810 (in Harleian Miscellany vol 9); ed W. H. Dunham and S. Pargellis in Complaint and reform in England 1436–1714, New York 1938.
Christianity not mysterious. 1696, 1696, 1702 (with Apology for Mr Toland).
The life of John Milton. 1698, 1699.
Amyntor: or a defence of Milton's Life. 1699.
Memoirs of Denzil, Lord Holles. 1699. Ed with a preface by Toland.
Clito: a poem on the force of eloquence. 1700.
The Oceana of James Harrington with his Life prefix'd, by J. Toland. 1700, 1737, 1758.
The art of governing by parties. 1701.
Propositions for uniting the two East India companies. 1701.
Anglia libera. 1701.
Paradoxes of state. 1702.
Vindicius liberius: or Mr Toland's defence of himself against Convocation. 1702.
Letters to Serena. 1704.
An account of the courts of Prussia and Hanover. 1705, 1706.
The memorial of the state of England. 1705.
Adeisidæmon and Origines judaicae. Hague 1709.
Lettre d'un Anglois à un Hollandois au sujet du Docteur Sacheverell. 1710.
The description of Epsom. 1711.
A letter against Popery. 1712.
Her Majesty's reasons for creating the electoral Prince of Hanover a Peer of the Realm. 1712.
An appeal to honest people against wicked priests. [1710], 1712.
Cicero illustratus: dissertatio philologico-critica. 1712.
Dunkirk, or Dover: or the Queen's honour. 1713, 1713.
The art of restoring: or the piety and probity of General Monk. 1714.
Reasons for naturalising the Jews in Great Britain and Ireland. 1713, 1714.
The grand mystery laid open. 1714.
The state anatomy of Great Britain. 1717 (8 edns).
The second part of the state anatomy. 1717, 1717, 1718.
Nazarenus: or Jewish, Gentile and Mahometan Christianity. 1718.
The destiny of Rome. 1718.

Pantheisticon: sive formula celebrandæ sodalitatis Socra-
ticæ. 1720; tr 1751.

Tetradymus. 1720.

A critical history of the Celtic religion and learning.
[1740], 1814.

Hypatia: or the history of a most learned lady. 1753.

WILLIAM WARBURTON
1698–1779

Collections

Works. Ed R. Hurd 7 vols 1788, 12 vols 1811.

§ 1

Miscellaneous translations, in prose and verse from Roman
poets, orators and historians. 1724; rptd in Tracts by
Warburton and a Warburtonian, 1789, below.

A critical and philosophical inquiry into the causes of
prodigies and miracles, as related by historians, in two
parts. 1727; rptd in Tracts by Warburton and a
Warburtonian, 1789, below.

An apology for Sir Robert Sutton. 1733.

The alliance between Church and State: or the necessity
and equity of an established religion and a test-law
demonstrated, from the essence and end of civil society,
upon the fundamental principles of the law of nature
and nations, in three parts. 1736, 1741, 1748, 1766 etc.

The divine legation of Moses demonstrated on the principles of a religious Deist, in six books. 2 vols 1738–41,
1742, 1755, 1765 (first complete edn of 6 bks).

A vindication of the author of the divine legation of Moses.
1738.

Faith's working by charity to Christian edification: a
sermon preach'd in the diocese of Lincoln. 1738.

A vindication of Mr Pope's Essay on man, from the misrepresentations of Mr de Crousaz, professor of philosophy and mathematicks in the university of Lausanne,
in six letters. 1740; A seventh letter, which finishes the
vindication of Mr Pope's Essay on man, from Lausanne,
1740. *See* Commentary, *below.*

The nature, extent and right improvement of Christian
liberty: a sermon preached at Maidstone. 1741.

A critical and philosophical commentary on Mr Pope's
Essay on man, in which is contain'd A vindication of the
said Essay from the misrepresentations of Mr De
Resnel, the French translator, and of Mr De Crousaz,
professor of philosophy and mathematics in the Academy of Lausanne, the commentator. 1742. Rev and
enlarged version of Vindication, above.

A sermon preached at the Abbey-Church at Bath.
1742.

Remarks on several occasional reflections, in answer to the
Rev Dr Middleton, Dr Pococke, the Master of the
Charter House, Dr Richard Grey and others. 1744.

Remarks on several occasional reflections, in answer to the
Reverend Doctors Stebbing and Sykes. 1745.

A faithful portrait of Popery: a sermon preached at St
James's church, Westminster. 1745.

A sermon occasioned by the present unnatural rebellion,
preached in Mr Allen's chapel at Prior-Park, near Bath.
1745.

The nature of national offences truly stated: a sermon
preached on the general Fast day. 1746.

An apologetical dedication to the Reverend Dr Henry
Stebbing in answer to his censure and misrepresentations of the sermon preached on the general Fast day.
1746.

The works of Shakespear in eight volumes, with a comment and notes, critical and explanatory, by Mr Pope
and Mr Warburton. 8 vols 1747.

A sermon preach'd on the Thanksgiving appointed to be
observed the ninth of October. 1746.

A letter from an author to a Member of Parliament concerning literary property. 1748.

A letter to the editor of the Letters on the spirit of patriotism, the idea of a patriot-king and the state of the parties.
1749.

Julian: or a discourse concerning the earthquake and fiery
eruption which defeated that emperor's attempt to re-
build the Temple at Jerusalem. 1750, 1751.

The works of Alexander Pope esq, in nine volumes complete, together with the commentaries and notes of Mr
Warburton. 9 vols 1751.

The principles of natural and revealed religion occasionally
opened and explained. 2 vols 1753–4.

A view of Lord Bolingbroke's philosophy in four letters to
a friend. 3 vols 1754–5.

A sermon preached before his Grace Charles Duke of
Marlborough at the parish-church of St Andrew,
Holborn. [1755].

Natural and civil events the instruments of God's moral
government: a sermon preached at Lincoln's-Inn chapel.
1756.

Remarks on Mr David Hume's Essay on the natural
history of religion. 1757.

A sermon preached in the Abbey Church, Westminster.
1760.

A rational account of the nature and end of the sacrament
of the Lord's Supper. 1761.

The doctrine of grace: or the office and operations of the
Holy Spirit vindicated from the insults of infidelity and
the abuses of fanaticism. 2 vols 1763 (3 edns).

A sermon preached before the incorporated Society for the
Propagation of the Gospel in foreign parts. 1766.

A sermon preached at St Lawrence Jewry. 1767.

Sermons and discourses on various subjects and occasions.
1767.

Tracts by Warburton and a Warburtonian not admitted
into the collections of their respective works. [Ed
S. Parr] 1789.

A selection from the unpublished papers. Ed F. Kilvert
1841.

Letters

Letters of a late eminent prelate to one of his friends. Ed
R. Hurd, Kidderminster [1808].

Letters from the Reverend Dr Warburton, Bishop of
Gloucester to the Hon Charles Yorke, from 1752 to
1770. 1812 (priv ptd by Lord Hardwicke).

§ 2

Law, W. A short but sufficient confutation of the Rev Dr
Warburton's projected defence of Christianity in his
Divine legation of Moses. 1757.

[Lowth, R.] A letter to the Right Reverend author of the
Divine legation of Moses. 1765.

Figgis, J. N. In Typical English churchmen, ed W. E.
Collins 1902.

Evans, A. W. Warburton and the Warburtonians. Oxford
1932.

WILLIAM WOLLASTON
1660–1724

§ 1

The religion of nature delineated. 1722, 1724, 1725, 1726,
1731, 1738, 1750.

§ 2

Clarke, J. An examination of the notion of moral good and
evil advanced in a late book entitled The religion of
nature delineated. 1725.

Thompson, C. G. The ethics of Wollaston. 1922.

C. HUME, ADAM SMITH, BENTHAM AND THEIR CONTEMPORARIES

DAVID HUME
1711–76

The principal collection of mss is in the Royal Society, Edinburgh; for details see E. C. Mossner, Life of Hume, Edinburgh 1954, 1972 (rev).

Bibliographies

Todd, W. B. A bibliography of Hume. 1972.

Collections

Philosophical works. Ed T. H. Green and T. H. Grose 4 vols 1874–5.
Hume: philosophical historian. Ed D. F. Norton and R. H. Popkin, Indianapolis 1965.
Hume's ethical writings. Ed A. MacIntyre, New York 1965.

§ I

A treatise of human nature: book I, Of the understanding; book II, Of the passions. 2 vols 1739; Book III, Of morals, with an appendix, 1740; [bks 1–3] 2 vols 1817; ed L. A. Selby-Bigge, Oxford 1888, 1978 (rev P. H. Nidditch).
An abstract of a Treatise of human nature 1740. Ed J. M. Keynes and P. Sraffa, Cambridge 1938.
Essays moral and political. Edinburgh 1741, 1742; vol II, Edinburgh 1742; 1743 (both vols), 1748 (with Three essays, below, thereafter in Essays and treatises, below). Essays moral and political; Of the original contract. Ed E. Barker in his Social contract, Oxford [1946] (WC).
A letter from a gentleman to his friend containing some observations on religion and morality. Edinburgh 1745 (anon). Unique copy in Nat Lib of Scotland ed E. C. Mossner and J. V. Price, Edinburgh 1967.
Three essays moral and political, never before published. 1748.
Philosophical essays concerning human understanding. 1748, 1750, 1751; rptd in Essays and treatises, below.
A true account of the behaviour and conduct of Archibald Stewart. 1748 (anon); rptd in J. V. Price, The ironic Hume, Austin 1965.
An enquiry concerning the principles of morals. 1751; rptd in Essays and treatises, below.
The petition of the Bellmen. [1751] (anon); rptd in A Scotch haggis, Edinburgh 1822. Copy of 1751 in Bodley.
Political discourses. Edinburgh 1752, 1752, 1754; rptd in Essays and treatises, below.
Scotticisms. [1752]. Anon. Often included in edns of the Essays, below.
Essays and treatises on several subjects. 4 vols 1753–6. Vol 1, Essays moral and political, 1753 (4th edn); vol 2, Philosophical essays, 1756 (3rd edn); vol 3, Enquiry concerning morals, 1753 (2nd edn); vol 4, Political discourses, 1754 (3rd edn), 1758 (order changed, and Philosophical essays concerning human understanding now called Enquiry concerning human understanding), 4 vols 1760 (with material from Four dissertations), 2 vols 1764, 1767, 1768, 4 vols 1770, 2 vols 1772, 1777 (with author's last corrections); ed L. A. Selby-Bigge, Oxford 1894, 1902 (with Comparative table for treatise and enquiries), 1975 (rev P. H. Nidditch).
An inquiry concerning human understanding. Ed C. W. Hendel, New York 1955; ed R. Kirk, Chicago 1956; ed E. C. Mossner, New York 1963 (with other essays).
History of Great Britain. Vol I ('containing the Reigns of James I and Charles I'), Edinburgh 1754.
Vol II ('containing the Commonwealth, and the Reigns of Charles II and James II'), 1757 (for 1756).

History of England under the house of Tudor. 2 vols 1759.
History of England from the invasion of Julius Caesar to the accession of Henry VII. 2 vols 1762.
History of England. Vols 5–6, 1762. A new edn of the Stuarts, with title-pages altered to bring them into line with other vols.
History of England from the invasion of Julius Caesar to the Revolution in 1688. 8 vols 1763, 1767, 1770, 1773, 1778 (with author's last corrections, My own life and Adam Smith's letter to Strahan).
Four dissertations. 1757; rptd in Essays and treatises, 1760 etc. The natural history of religion, Of the passions, Of tragedy, Of the standard of taste.
The natural history of religion. Ed H. E. Root 1956.
Exposé succinct de la contestation entre Hume et Rousseau. Tr and ed J.-B. A. Suard 1766 (3 edns); tr 1766.
Two essays [Of suicide, Of the immortality of the soul]. 1777 (anon), 1783. These essays, at first intended for Four dissertations, were withdrawn in proof.
The life, written by himself, and letter from Adam Smith to Wm Strahan. 1777, 1777/. Included in most edns of the Essays and History after 1778.
Dialogues concerning natural religion. 1779, 1779; ed N. K. Smith, Oxford 1935. Also rptd in many edns of Essays and treatises.
Hume as literary patron: a suppressed review of Robert Henry's History of Great Britain 1773. Ed E. C. Mossner, MP 39 1942.
An historical essay on chivalry and modern honour. Ed E. C. Mossner, MP 45 1947. First complete text of Hume's earliest extant essay.
Early memoranda 1729–40: the complete text. Ed E. C. Mossner, JHI 9 1948.

Letters

Letters. Ed J. Y. T. Greig 2 vols Oxford 1932.
New letters. Ed R. Klibansky and E. C. Mossner, Oxford 1954.

§ 2

Huxley, T. H. Hume. 1878 (EML).
Hendel, C. W. Studies in the philosophy of Hume. 1925, 1963 (rev).
Laird, J. Hume's philosophy of human nature. 1933.
Mossner, E. C. The life of Hume. Edinburgh 1954, 1972 (rev).
Price, H. H. Hume's theory of the external world. Oxford 1940.
— The permanent significance of Hume's philosophy. Philosophy 15 1940.
Smith, N. K. The philosophy of Hume. 1941, 1960.
Passmore, J. A. Hume's intentions. Cambridge 1952.
Flew, A. Hume's philosophy of belief: a study of his first inquiry. 1961.
Broad, C. D. Hume's doctrine of space. Proc Br Acad 47 1961.
Hume: a symposium by Stuart Hampshire and others. Ed D. F. Pears 1963.
Forbes, D. Hume's philosophical politics. Cambridge 1975.
Hume: bicentenary papers. Ed G. P. Morice, Edinburgh 1977.

ADAM SMITH
1723–90

Collections

Works. 5 vols 1811–12.
Early writings. Ed J. R. Lindgren, New York 1967.

The Glasgow edition of the works and correspondence. Ed D. D. Raphael et al, Oxford 1976–.

§ 1

The theory of moral sentiments. 1759, 1761, 1767 (adds a Dissertation on the origin of languages), 1774, 1781, 1790.

An inquiry into the nature and causes of the wealth of nations. 2 vols 1776, 1778, 3 vols 1784, 1786, 1789, 1791; ed J. R. McCulloch 1828; ed J. E. T. Rogers 1869; ed J. S. Nicholson 1884; ed E. Cannan 1904, 1920; Additions and corrections to the first and second editions. [1778?].

Essays on philosophical subjects; to which is prefixed an account of the life and writings of the author, by Dugald Stewart. 1795.

Lectures on justice, police, revenue and arms reported by a student in 1763. Ed E. Cannan, Oxford 1896.

Lectures on rhetoric and belles lettres reported by a student in 1762–3. Ed J. M. Lothian 1963.

§ 2

Stewart, D. Biographical memoir of Smith. Trans Royal Soc of Edinburgh 1793; rptd separately with memoirs by William Robertson and Thomas Reid, 1811, and in Stewart's Works vol 10, 1858.

Bagehot, W. In his Economic studies, 1880.

—— In his Biographical studies, 1881.

Hirst, F. W. Adam Smith. 1904 (EML).

Scott, W. R. Adam Smith. Proc Br Acad 10 1923.

—— Smith as student and professor; with unpublished documents. Glasgow 1937.

—— A manuscript criticism of the Wealth of nations in 1776 by Hugh Blair. Economic History 3 1938.

—— Studies relating to Smith during the last fifty years. Proc Br Acad 26 1940.

Forbes, D. Scientific Whiggism: Smith and John Millar. Cambridge Jnl Aug 1954.

Fay, C. R. Burke and Smith. Belfast 1956.

—— Smith and the Scotland of his day. Cambridge 1956.

Lothian, J. M. Smith as a critic of Shakespeare. In Papers mainly Shakespearian, ed G. I. Duthie 1966.

Macfie, A. L. The individual in society: papers on Smith. 1967.

Essays on Adam Smith. Ed A. S. Skinner and T. Wilson, Oxford 1975.

O'Brien, D. P. The classical economists. Oxford 1975.

JEREMY BENTHAM
1748–1832

Bentham's mss, largely unpbd, are in University College, London (catalogue by T. Whittaker, 1892) and in BM.

Collections

Works. Ed J. Bowring 11 vols 1838–43. Vols 10–11 contain a life of Bentham and an index to his works.

A fragment on government: an introduction to the principles of morals and legislation. Ed W. Harrison, Oxford 1948.

Economic writings: critical edition based on his printed works and unprinted manuscripts. Ed W. Stark 3 vols 1952–4.

Collected works. Ed J. H. Burns et al 1968–.

§ 1

A fragment on government: being an examination of what is delivered on the subject of government in William Blackstone's Commentaries, with a preface. 1776, 1822 (3rd edn); ed F. C. Montague 1891.

View of the Hard Labour Bill. 1778.

Defence of usury. 1787, 1790, 1816.

An introduction to the principles of morals and legislation. 1789, 1823, Oxford 1879.

The limits of jurisprudence defined: being part two of An introduction. Ed C. W. Everett, New York 1945.

The panopticon: or inspection house. 1791. Written 1787.

A protest against law taxes. 1795.

Poor laws and pauper management. In Arthur Young's Annals, Sept 1797 and later.

The panopticon versus New South Wales. 1802.

Traités de législation civile et pénale. Tr E. Dumont 3 vols 1802, 1820; tr 1864, 1876, ed C. K. Ogden 1931.

A plea for the constitution. 1803.

Scotch reform, with a summary view of a plan for a judicatory. 1808, 1811.

Théorie des peines et des récompenses. Tr E. Dumont 2 vols 1811, Paris 1818, 1825; part 2 tr 1825, part 1 1830. Written c. 1775.

A table of the springs of action, printed 1815. [Ed James Mill] 1817.

Chrestomathia. 1816.

Swear not at all. 1817. Written 1813.

Tactique des assemblées délibérantes et traité des sophismes politiques. Tr E. Dumont 1816.

Catechism of parliamentary reform. Pamphleteer Jan 1817. Written 1809.

Papers upon codification and public instruction. 1817. Written 1811–15.

Church of Englandism and its catechism examined. 1818.

Radical reform bill, with explanations. Pamphleteer Dec 1819.

Elements of the art of packing as applied to special juries. 1821. Written 1809.

Three tracts relating to Spanish and Portuguese affairs. 1821.

On the liberty of the press. 1821. Addressed to Spain.

The analysis of the influence of natural religion upon the temporal happiness of mankind, by Philip Beauchamp. [Ed G. Grote] 1822.

Traité des preuves judiciaire et de la codification. Tr E. Dumont 1823.

Traité des preuves judiciaires. Tr E. Dumont 1823; tr 1825.

De l'organisation judiciaire et de la codification. Tr E. Dumont 1823.

Not Paul but Jesus, by Gamaliel Smith. 1823.

Codification proposals. 1823.

Book of fallacies. [Ed P. Bingham] 1824; ed H. A. Larrabee, Baltimore 1952.

The rationale of evidence. [Ed J. S. Mill] 5 vols 1827.

Constitutional code for the use of all nations and all governments professing liberal opinions. Vol 1 (all pbd separately), 1830.

Official aptitude maximised—expense minimised. 1831. A collection of papers written in 1810 and after.

Deontology or science of morality. [Ed J. Bowring] 2 vols 1834.

§ 2

Mill, J. S. London & Westminster Rev Aug 1838; rptd in his Dissertations and discussions vol 1, 1859, and in Mill on Bentham and Coleridge, ed F. R. Leavis 1950.

Sidgwick, H. Fortnightly Rev May 1877; rptd in his Miscellaneous essays and addresses, 1904.

Halévy, E. In his La formation du radicalisme philosophique en Angleterre, 3 vols Paris 1901–4; tr 1928.

Dicey, A. V. In his Law and public opinion in England, 1905.

Pringle-Pattison, A. S. In his Philosophical Radicals and other essays, 1907.

Everett, C. W. The education of Bentham. New York 1931.

Ogden, C. K. Bentham's theory of fictions. 1932.

Baumgardt, D. Bentham and the ethics of today, with

Bentham manuscripts hitherto unpublished. Princeton 1952.

Hart, H. L. A. Bentham. Proc Br Acad 48 1962.

Letwin, S. R. The pursuit of certainty: Hume, Bentham, Mill, Beatrice Webb. Cambridge 1965.

Robbins, L. C. Bentham in the twentieth century. 1965.

Other Philosophical Writers 1750–1800

ADAM FERGUSON
1723–1816

Of natural philosophy. [Edinburgh c. 1760].

Analysis of pneumatics and moral philosophy. Edinburgh 1766.

An essay on the history of civil society. Edinburgh 1767, Dublin 1767, London 1768, 1769, 1773 (rev); ed D. Forbes, Edinburgh 1966.

Institutes of moral philosophy. Edinburgh 1769, 1773, 1785.

The history of the progress and termination of the Roman Republic. 3 vols 1783.

Remarks on a pamphlet by [Richard] Price. 1776.

Principles of moral and political science. 2 vols Edinburgh 1792. *See also col 763, below.*

DAVID HARTLEY
1705–57

Conjecturae quaedam de sensu motu et idearum generatione. 1746; tr R. E. A. Palmer, Los Angeles 1959.

Observations on man, his frame, his duty and his expectations. 2 vols 1749, 1791 (with a sketch of the author's life, and notes and additions translated from the German of H. A. Pistorius), 3 vols 1801 (with addns by Joseph Priestley).

HENRY HOME, LORD KAMES
1696–1782
§ 1

Essays on the principles of morality and natural religion. Edinburgh 1751, London 1758, 1779.

Objections against the Essays on morality and natural religion examined. Edinburgh 1756.

Introduction to the art of thinking. Edinburgh 1761, 1764, 1775.

Elements of criticism. 3 vols Edinburgh 1762, 1763 (enlarged), 2 vols Edinburgh 1769, 1785 (rev and enlarged), 1788, 1796 etc.

Sketches of the history of man. 2 vols Edinburgh 1774.

§ 2

Tytler, A. F. Memoirs of the life and writings of Home. 2 vols Edinburgh 1807.

Randall, H. W. The critical theory of Kames. Northampton Mass 1944.

JAMES BURNETT, LORD MONBODDO
1714–99
§ 1

Of the origin and progress of language. 6 vols Edinburgh 1773–92.

Antient metaphysics: or the science of universals. 6 vols Edinburgh 1779–99.

§ 2

Knight, W. Lord Monboddo and some of his contemporaries. 1900.

Lovejoy, A. O. Monboddo and Rousseau. MP 30 1933; rptd in his Essays in the history of ideas, Baltimore 1948.

THOMAS PAINE
1737–1809
Collections

Works. 1792.

Political works. 2 vols 1817.

Miscellaneous letters and essays. 1819.

Writings. Ed M. D. Conway 4 vols New York 1894–6.

Complete writings. Ed P. S. Foner 2 vols New York 1945.

§ 1

Common sense. 1776 (5 edns), 1791, Philadelphia 1791, London 1792.

Letter addressed to the Abbé Raynal on the affairs of North America. 1782, Boston 1782, London 1795.

Rights of man: being an answer to Burke's attack on the French Revolution. 2 pts 1791–2 (at least 9 edns); ed H. B. Bonner 1907; ed G. J. Holyoake 1915 (EL).

The age of reason: being an investigation of true and fabulous theology. 2 pts Paris 1794–London 1795 etc; ed M. D. Conway, New York 1896; ed J. M. Robertson 1905.

Dissertation on the first-principles of government. 1795 (4 edns).

§ 2

Conway, M. D. The life of Paine. 2 vols New York 1892.

Copeland, T. W. Burke, Paine and Jefferson. In his Our eminent friend Edmund Burke, New Haven 1949.

Boulton, J. T. Paine and the vulgar style. EC 12 1962; rev in his Language of politics in the age of Wilkes and Burke, 1963.

The Burke-Paine controversy: texts and criticism. Ed R. B. Browne, New York 1963.

WILLIAM PALEY
1743–1805
Collections

Works. 7 vols 1825.

§ 1

The principles of moral and political philosophy. 1785; ed R. Whateley 1859; ed A. Bain nd (Moral philosophy only).

Horae Paulinae: or the truth of the scripture history of St Paul evinced. 1790.

A view of the evidences of Christianity. 1794.

Natural theology: or evidences of the existence and attributes of the Deity collected from the appearances of nature. 1802; ed Lord Brougham and C. Bell 1836.

RICHARD PRICE
1723–91

A review of the principal questions and difficulties in morals. 1758, 1769, 1787; ed D. D. Raphael, Oxford 1948.

Observations on reversionary payments. 1771, 1783 (4th edn).

An appeal to the public on the subject of the national debt. 1772.

Observations on the nature of civil liberty, the principles of government and the justice and policy of the war with America. 1776; Additional observations, 1777.

The general introduction and supplement to the two tracts on civil liberty. 1778.

A free discussion of the doctrines of materialism and philosophical necessity. 1778–80.
An essay on the population of England. 1780.
A discourse on the love of our country. 1789.

JOSEPH PRIESTLEY
1733–1804

Bibliographies

Crook, R. E. A bibliography of Priestley 1733–1804. 1966.

Collections

Theological and miscellaneous works. Ed J. T. Rutt 25 vols 1817–32.
Writings on philosophy, science and politics. Ed J. A. Passmore, New York 1965.

§ 1

The history and present state of electricity. 1767.
An essay on the first principles of government. 1768, 1771.
A free address to protestant dissenters as such. 1769.
Institutes of natural and revealed theology. 3 vols 1772–4.
Experiments and observations on different kinds of air. 6 vols 1774–86.
An examination of Reid's Inquiry, Beattie's Essay and Oswald's Appeal to common sense. 1774.
Hartley's Theory of the human mind on the principle of the association of ideas. 1775.
Disquisitions relating to matter and spirit. 1777, 1782.
A course of lectures on oratory and criticism 1777; ed V. M. Bevilacqua and K. Murphy, Carbondale 1965.
The doctrine of philosophical necessity illustrated. 1777.
A free discussion on the doctrines of materialism etc. 1778.
Observations on the importance of the American Revolution. 1784.

§ 2

Holt, A. Life of Priestley. Oxford 1931.
Park, M. C. Priestley and the problem of pantisocracy. Philadelphia 1947.
Gibbs, F. W. Priestley: adventures in science and champion of truth. 1965.

THOMAS REID
1710–96

Collections

Works. Ed G. N. Wright 2 vols 1843.
Works. Ed W. Hamilton 2 vols Edinburgh 1846, 1852, 1854, 1858, 1863 (with addns).

§ 1

An essay on quantity. Philosophical Trans of Royal Soc 1748.
An inquiry into the human mind on the principles of common sense. Edinburgh 1763, 1765, 1785.
A brief account of Aristotle's logic. In Lord Kames, Sketches of the history of man vol 2, 1774.
Essays on the intellectual powers of man. Edinburgh 1785; ed A. D. Woozley 1941 (abridged); ed A. J. Ayer and R. Winch in British empirical philosophers, 1952 (excerpts).
Essays on the active powers of man. Edinburgh 1785.
Philosophical orations delivered at graduation ceremonies in King's College, Aberdeen 1753, 1756, 1759, 1762. Ed W. R. Humphries, Aberdeen 1937.

§ 2

Priestley, Joseph. An examination of Reid's Inquiry into the human mind, Beattie's Essay on truth and Oswald's Appeal to common sense. 1774.
Stewart, Dugald. Biographical memoirs of Adam Smith, William Robertson and Reid. Edinburgh 1811; rptd in his Works vol 10, 1858, and in Reid's Works, 1846.
Fraser, A. C. Thomas Reid. 1898.

DUGALD STEWART
1753–1828

Collections

Works. 7 vols Cambridge 1829.
Collected works. Ed W. Hamilton 11 vols Edinburgh 1854–8.

§ 1

Elements of the philosophy of the human mind. 3 vols 1792–1827, 1842.
Outlines of moral philosophy. Edinburgh 1793 etc.
Philosophical essays. Edinburgh 1810.
Biographical memoirs of Adam Smith, of W. Robertson and of T. Reid. Edinburgh 1811; rptd in his Works vol 10, 1858 and in Reid's Works vol 1, ed W. Hamilton 1846.
Some account of a boy born blind. Edinburgh [1815].
A general view of the progress of metaphysical, ethical and political philosophy. In Encyclopaedia britannica supplementary dissertation, 2 pts 1816–21.
The philosophy of the active and moral powers. Edinburgh 1828.

JOHN HORNE TOOKE
1736–1812

Ἔπεα πτερόεντα: or the diversions of Purley. 2 vols 1786–1805; ed R. Taylor 2 vols 1829.
Review of the constitution. 1791.
Proceedings on trial of Tooke for high treason. 2 vols 1795.

ARTHUR YOUNG
1741–1820

On the war in North America. 1758.
Reflections on the present state of affairs at home and abroad. 1759.
A farmer's letters to the people of England. 2 vols 1768.
A six weeks' tour through the southern counties of England and Wales. 1768, 1769 (enlarged), 1772.
A six months' tour through the north of England. 4 vols 1771.
The farmer's tour through the east of England. 4 vols 1770–1.
A course of experimental agriculture. 1770.
The farmer's calendar. 1771.
Political arithmetic. 1774.
Tour in Ireland. 2 vols 1780.
Travels during the years 1787, 1788, 1789, and 1790 undertaken with a view of ascertaining the cultivation, wealth, resources and national prosperity of the Kingdom of France. 2 vols Bury St Edmunds 1792–4; ed M. Betham-Edwards 1889 (3rd edn); ed C. Maxwell, Cambridge 1929.
The example of France a warning to England. 1793 etc.
Autobiography. Ed M. Betham-Edwards 1898.

6. SCOTTISH LITERATURE

I. GENERAL INTRODUCTION

BIBLIOGRAPHIES

Aldis, H. G. A list of books printed in Scotland before 1700, including those printed furth of the realm for Scottish booksellers, with brief notes on the printers and stationers. Pbns of Edinburgh Bibl Soc 6 1904.

Terry, C. S. A catalogue of the publications of Scottish historical and kindred clubs and societies, and of the volumes relative to Scottish history issued by his Majesty's Stationery Office 1780–1908. Glasgow 1909; continuation by C. Matheson, 1908–27, Aberdeen 1928.

Jessop, T. E. A bibliography of David Hume and of Scottish philosophy from Francis Hutcheson to Lord Balfour. 1938.

Gaskell, P. A bibliography of the Foulis Press. 1964.

DICTIONARIES

Jamieson, J. An etymological dictionary of the Scottish tongue. 5 vols Paisley 1875–87.

Craigie, W. A. and A. J. Aitken. A dictionary of the older Scottish tongue from the twelfth century to the end of the seventeenth. Chicago 1931–. Incomplete.

Grant, W. and D. D. Murison. The Scottish national dictionary. Edinburgh 1931–. 'Containing all the Scottish words known to be in use or to have been in use since ca. 1700'; incomplete.

LITERARY HISTORIES

Millar, J. H. A literary history of Scotland. 1903.

—— Scottish prose of the seventeenth and eighteenth centuries. Glasgow 1912.

Mackenzie, A. M. An historical survey of Scottish literature to 1714. 1933.

Power, W. Literature and oatmeal. 1935.

Speirs, J. The Scots literary tradition. 1940, 1962 (enlarged).

Wittig, K. The Scottish tradition in literature. Edinburgh 1958.

Craig, D. Scottish literature and the Scottish people 1680–1830. 1961.

MISCELLANEOUS STUDIES

Graham, H. G. The social life of Scotland in the eighteenth century. 2 vols 1899, 1900 (rev), 1 vol 1901 (2 issues, rev), 1906, 1928.

Newbigging, T. The Scottish Jacobites and their songs and music. 1899, 1907.

Couper, W. J. The Edinburgh periodical press 1642–1800. 2 vols Stirling 1908.

Craigie, W. A. et al. The Scottish tongue. 1924.

Fyfe, J. G. (ed). Scottish diaries and memoirs 1550–1746. Stirling [1927].

—— Scottish diaries and memoirs 1746–1843. Stirling 1942.

Anderson, D. The Bible in seventeenth-century Scottish life and literature. 1936.

Mackenzie, A. M. Scotland in modern times 1720–1939. 1941.

——(ed). Scottish pageant 1625–1707, 1707–1802. Edinburgh 1949, 1950. 2 pts of a 4-vol anthology of prose and poetry.

Joyce, M. Edinburgh: the golden age 1769–1832. 1951.

Daiches, D. The paradox of Scottish culture: the eighteenth-century experience. Oxford 1964.

Trevor-Roper, H. R. The Scottish Enlightenment. Stud in Voltaire & Eighteenth Century 58 1967.

Young, D. Scotland and Edinburgh in the eighteenth century. Ibid.

II. POETRY AND DRAMA

A. COLLECTIONS

[Watson, J.] A choice collection of comic and serious Scots poems both ancient and modern. 3 pts Edinburgh 1706–11, 1711, 1 vol Glasgow 1869.

Ramsay, A. The tea-table miscellany. 4 vols Edinburgh 1723–37.

—— The ever green: being a collection of Scots poems wrote by the ingenious before 1600. 2 vols Edinburgh 1724. For subsequent edns see under Ramsay, below.

Johnson, J. The Scots musical museum. 6 vols Edinburgh 1787–1803; ed W. Stenhouse, D. Laing and C. K. Sharpe 6 vols Edinburgh 1838 (with copious notes), 4 vols Edinburgh 1853 (with new addns), 2 vols Hatboro Pa 1962.

Thomson, G. A select collection of original Scotish airs, also suitable English verses in addition to such of the songs as are written in the Scottish dialect. 6 vols 1793–1825.

[Ritson, J.] Scotish songs. 2 vols 1794 (with lengthy Historical essay on Scotish song), 1 vol 1866 (without essay), 2 vols Glasgow 1869 (with essay).

— The Caledonian Muse: a chronological selection of Scotish poetry from the earliest times. 1821 (ptd in 1785).

Burns, R. (son of poet). The Caledonian musical museum. 3 vols 1809–11.

Hogg, J. The Jacobite relics of Scotland. 2 vols Edinburgh 1819–21, Paisley 1874.

[Laing, D.] Various pieces of fugitive Scotish poetry. 2 vols Edinburgh 1825–53. Type facs of 90 Scottish poems pbd 1600–1707.

Chambers, R. The popular rhymes of Scotland, with illustrations chiefly collected from oral sources. Edinburgh 1826.

— The Scottish songs. 2 vols Edinburgh 1829–32.

— Songs of Scotland prior to Burns. Edinburgh 1862, 1890.

'MacDiarmid, Hugh' (C. M. Grieve). The golden treasury of Scottish poetry. 1940, 1941, 1946, 1948.

Fergusson, J. The green garden: a new collection of Scottish poetry. Edinburgh 1946. To Burns.

Oliver, J. W. and J. C. Smith. A Scots anthology. Edinburgh 1949.

MacQueen, J. and T. Scott. The Oxford book of Scottish verse. Oxford 1966.

B. GENERAL STUDIES

Irving, D. The lives of the Scottish poets, with dissertations on the literary history of Scotland. 2 vols Edinburgh 1804, 1810, London 1810.

— The history of Scottish poetry. Ed J. A. Carlyle, Edinburgh 1861.

Douglas, G. Scottish poetry: Drummond of Hawthornden to Fergusson. Glasgow 1911.

Kinsley, J. (ed). Scottish poetry: a critical survey. 1955.

Crawford, T. Scottish popular ballads and lyrics of the eighteenth and nineteenth centuries: some preliminary conclusions. Studies in Scottish Lit 1 1964.

C. INDIVIDUAL WRITERS

ALLAN RAMSAY
1686–1758
Collections

Poems. Edinburgh 1720 (made up of various pamphlets, some reprints, previously issued separately by Ramsay; contents of individual copies varies considerably, and pagination is not always continuous; no copy of postulated first issue is known; of the 7 known issues 5 probably appeared in 1720, one in 1721, one in 1722), 1723 (2 issues, one issued in 1724), 1727 ('4th edn', 3 issues, one, though dated 1727, is actually of 1728, one of 1732; no copy of 1727 issue known); vol 2, Edinburgh 1729 (designed as a companion vol for 1727 edn).

Poems. Edinburgh 1721. Subscribers' edn, ptd by Ruddiman.

Miscellaneous works of that celebrated Scotch poet Allan Ramsay. Dublin 1724. Contains the Tea-Table miscellany.

Poems. 2 vols Edinburgh 1728 (vol 1 a re-issue of the 1721 edn), 2 vols 1731, 1 vol Dublin 1733, 2 vols 1751.

Poems: a new edition corrected and enlarged. Ed with life by G. Chalmers and remarks on his poems by Lord Woodhouselee 2 vols 1800, 1 vol 1805, 2 vols Leith 1814, Paisley 1877, 3 vols 1848 (with addns).

Poems: epistles, fables, satires, elegies and lyrics, from the edition [of] 1721–8. Ed H. H. Wood, Edinburgh 1940.

Works. Ed B. Martin, J. W. Oliver et al 5 vols Edinburgh 1951–.

§ 1

A poem to the memory of the famous Archibald Pitcairn MD. Edinburgh [1713]. Anon; no known copy.

On this great eclipse: a poem by A.R. Edinburgh 1715. Single sheet.

The battel, or morning interview: an heroi-comical poem. Edinburgh 1716 (anon), 1719 (signed, as The morning interview), 1720, 1721, 1724, 1731.

Christ's kirk on the green in two cantos. Edinburgh 1718, [Edinburgh 1718?] (2 signed broadsides), 1718 (in three cantos), 1720, 1722; and A collection of other humorous poems in the Scottish dialect, Edinburgh 1763; [Christ's Kirk only], Glasgow 1768, 1786, 1794, 1799. Canto 1 by James I of Scotland (suppositious), cantos 2–3 by Ramsay.

Edinburgh's address to the country. [Edinburgh 1718?] (anon); rptd with The morning interview, 1719 etc, above.

Elegies on Maggy Johnston, John Cowper and Lucky Wood. Edinburgh 1718 (2nd edn 'corrected and amended'); with Lucky Spence's last advice [Edinburgh 1719?], [Edinburgh 1720?]. No known copy of first edn.

Elegy on Lucky Wood. [Edinburgh 1718?]. Anon broadside.

Lucky Spence's last advice. [Edinburgh 1718?] (anon), [Glasgow?] nd (as Elegy on the death of an auld bawd or bawdy-house keeper), [Edinburgh?] nd (broadside).

The scriblers lash'd. Edinburgh 1718 (anon), 1718 (signed), 1720, 1721, 1723, 1728.

Tartana or the plaid. Edinburgh 1718, 1719, 1720 (Scottish version of 1719 edn), 1721, 1724, 1732, [Edinburgh 1720?] (as To the most beautiful Scots ladies, this poem on the plaid is humbly dedicated).

Content: a poem. Edinburgh 1719, 1719, London 1720, Edinburgh 1721, 1723, 1728.

An epistle to W— H— [William Hamilton] on the receiving the compliment of a barrel of Loch-fyne herrings from him. [Edinburgh 1720?]. Anon.

Familiar epistles between W— H— and A— R—. [Edinburgh 1719] (3 anon edns), [1720?].

Richy and Sandy: a pastoral on the death of Mr Joseph Addison. [Edinburgh 1719?] (2 edns); also in Pope, Eloisa to Abelard, 1720 (2nd edn).

Bessy Bell and Mary Gray. [Edinburgh 1720?] (anon, single sheet), [Edinburgh?] nd (as a broadside with The young laird and Edinburgh Katie).

Edinburgh's salutation to the most Honourable My Lord Marquess of Carnarvon. [Edinburgh 1720].

Grubstreet nae satyre, in answer to Bagpipes no musick. [Edinburgh c. 1720?]. Anon broadside.

To Mr Law. Edinburgh 1720, [Oxford 1924] (facs).

An ode with a pastoral recitative on the marriage of the Rt Hon James Earl of Wemyss and Mrs Janet Charteris. [Edinburgh 1720].

Patie and Roger: a pastoral inscribed to Josiah Burchet esq, Secretary of the Admiralty. [Edinburgh 1720] (anon), London 1720 (signed).

A poem on the South Sea by Mr Alexander Ramsay, to which is prefixed a familiar epistle to Anthony Hammond. 1720, 1720 (as Wealth, or the woody, with Ramsay's name correct), [Edinburgh 1720?], [Edinburgh 1720?] (without the epistle to Hammond), London 1720.

Prologue spoke by one of the young gentlemen who, for their improvement and diversion, acted the Orphan, and Cheats of Scapin, the last night of the year 1719. [Edinburgh 1720]. Single sheet; anon.

The prospect of plenty: a poem on the North-Sea fishery. 1720, [Edinburgh 1720] (2 edns) (as To the Royal Burrows of Scotland).

The young laird and Edinburgh Katie. [Edinburgh 1720?] (2 poems signed A.R.), [Edinburgh?] nd (as a broadside with Bessy Bell and Mary Gray).

An elegy on Patie Birnie. [Edinburgh 1721]. Broadside signed A.R.

The rise and fall of stocks 1720: an epistle to the Right Honourable My Lord Ramsay; [with] the satyr's comick project. Edinburgh 1721. Anon.

Robert, Richy and Sandy: a pastoral on the death of Matthew Prior esq. 1721.

Fables and tales. Edinburgh 1722 (15 pieces), 1722 (18 pieces, 2 edns), Edinburgh 1730 (as Collection of thirty fables).

Fy gar rub her o're wi strae: an Italian canzone (of seven hundred years standing) imitated in braid Scots. [Edinburgh? c. 1722]. A broadside, 2 issues, one unsigned, one signed A.R. Part of this poem appeared as To the Ph—: an ode, 1721. The poem was rptd in the Tea-table miscellany.

A tale of three bonnets. [Edinburgh?] 1722 (anon), Glasgow 1785, 1787, 1791, 1792, 1795, 1807, Stirling nd (2 edns), Edinburgh 1793 (as The ancient history of three bonnets), Falkirk 1820 (as Duniwhistle's testament: or a diverting tale of three bonnets).

Translation of the Aeneid x 693-6. Br Jnl 9 March 1723.

The fair assembly: a poem. Edinburgh 1723.

Jenny and Meggy, a pastoral: being a sequel to Patie and Roger. Edinburgh 1723.

The nuptials: a masque on the marriage of his Grace James Duke of Hamilton and Lady Anne Cochran. Edinburgh 1723, London 1723.

Health: a poem. Edinburgh 1724 (3 edns containing 22, 48 and 80 pp. respectively), 1730 (with addns).

The monk and the miller's wife: or all parties pleas'd. [Edinburgh 1724], Glasgow 1779.

Mouldy-Mowdiwart: or the last speech of a wretched miser. [Edinburgh 1724].

An ode sacred to the memory of her Grace Anne Dutchess of Hamilton. Br Jnl 14 Nov 1724. In a letter from Ramsay denying the accuracy of an earlier version twice pbd in the same journal—3 Oct 1724, 24 Oct 1724. The spurious version contains 9 stanzas; Ramsay's contains 16.

The poetick sermon: to R— Y— [Robert Yarde] esq. [Edinburgh 1724].

On pride: an epistle to —. [Edinburgh 1724].

On the Royal Company of Archers marching under the command of his Grace Duke of Hamilton Aug 4 1724. [Edinburgh 1724]; also in Poems in English and Latin, 1726, below.

On seeing the archers diverting themselves at the butts and rovers. [Edinburgh 1724]; also in Poems in English and Latin 1726, below.

The gentle shepherd: a Scots pastoral comedy. Edinburgh 1725, 1726, Dublin 1727, Edinburgh 1729, London 1730 (copy in Nat Lib of Scotland), Edinburgh 1734, Glasgow 1743, 1745, 1747, Belfast 1748, Glasgow 1750, [New York 1750? – no known copy], Glasgow 1752, London 1752, Edinburgh 1753, Aberdeen 1754, Belfast 1755, Edinburgh 1755, 1758 (no known copy), Glasgow 1758, London 1758.

Works edited by Ramsay

Tea-table miscellany

This collection was issued one vol at a time, and individual vols were rptd as the need arose in order to make complete sets available for sale.

The tea-table miscellany [vol 1]. Edinburgh 1723 (only known copy in Yale Lib), 1724 (only known copy in Huntington Lib), 1727, 1732 (6th edn, only known copy in Yale Lib).

Vol 2. Edinburgh 1726 (Nat Lib of Scotland has microfilm of presumed unique copy), 1735 (only known copy in Yale Lib).

Vols 1–2 as A new miscellany of Scots sangs. 1727. Anon, pirated.

Vol 3. Edinburgh 1727.

3 vols Dublin 1729 (pagination continues throughout vols), [Edinburgh 1729] (no known copy).

1 vol 1730. Includes contents of vols 1–3.

3 vols 1733, Dublin 1733, Dublin 1734 (3 vols in one).

Vol 4. [Edinburgh 1737] (no known copy).

4 vols 1740 (pagination continues), 1750 (pagination continues), Glasgow 1753 (copy in Mitchell Lib).

Ever green

Musick for Allan Ramsay's Collection of Scots songs, set by Alexr Stuart. 6 pts [Edinburgh 1724]. Contains music only to 69 songs.

The ever green: being a collection of Scots poems wrote by the ingenious before sixteen hundred. 2 vols Edinburgh 1724, 1761, Glasgow 1824, 1874, 1875, 1876.

Scots proverbs

A collection of Scots proverbs, more complete and correct than any heretofore published. Edinburgh 1737 (2,522 proverbs), 1750, 1797 (to which are added A tale of three bonnets and Verses on the Bannatyne manuscript.)

A collection of above nine hundred Scots proverbs. Glasgow 1781.

A collection of Scots proverbs. Glasgow 1785.

Aphorisms of wisdom: or a complete collection of the most celebrated proverbs in the English, Scotch, French, Spanish, Italian and other languages, ancient and modern, collected and digested by Thomas Fuller; to which is added Ramsay's collection of Scottish proverbs, new edition. Glasgow 1814, London 1819 (as Gnomologia).

§2

Smeaton, W. H. O. Allan Ramsay. Edinburgh [1896] (Famous Scots ser).

—— Allan Ramsay and the Gentle shepherd. [c. 1905].

Mackail, J. W. Allan Ramsay and the Romantic revival. E & S 10 1924.

Chapman, R. W. Allan Ramsay's Poems 1720. RES 3 1927.

Gibson, A. New light on Ramsay. Edinburgh 1927.

Martin, B. Allan Ramsay. Cambridge Mass 1931.

ROBERT BURNS
1759–96

Bibliographies etc

Reid, J. H. A complete word and phrase concordance to the poems and songs of Burns. Glasgow 1889, New York 1967.

[Hepburn, A. G., A. Hunter and D. R. Younger]. Catalogue of Burns collection in the Mitchell Library. Glasgow 1959.

Egerer, J. W. A bibliography of Burns. Edinburgh 1964.

Roy, G. R. Robert Burns. Columbia SC 1966. Supplements Egerer, 1964, above.

Collections

The works, with an account of his life and a criticism on his writings. [Ed J. Currie] 4 vols Liverpool 1800.

Works. Ed Ettrick Shepherd [James Hogg] and William Motherwell 5 vols Glasgow 1834–6.

Works, with his life by Allan Cunningham. 8 vols 1834.

Poetry. Ed W. E. Henley and T. F. Henderson 4 vols

Edinburgh 1896–7, 1901, New York 1905, London nd.

Complete poetical works. Ed J. L. Robertson 3 vols Oxford 1896 (Oxford Miniature edn), 1 vol 1904, 1906, 1908, 1910, 1912, 1913, 1916, 1917, 1921, 1923, 1926, 1928, 1936, 1939, 1942, 1945, 1948, 1951, 1958, 1960 (OSA).

Poems and songs. Ed J. Kinsley 3 vols Oxford 1968, 1 vol Oxford 1969 (OSA).

§ I

Poems chiefly in the Scottish dialect. Kilmarnock 1786.

Poems chiefly in the Scottish dialect. Edinburgh 1787 (enlarged; 2 issues with many textual differences, known as the 'skinking' (earlier) and 'stinking' edn, the text of the earlier being the more accurate), London 1787, Belfast 1787, Dublin 1787.

The calf, The unco calf's answer, Virtue—to a mountain bard, and The de'il's answer to his vera worthy frien' R. Burns. [Scotland 1787]. Chap-book; only the first poem by Burns.

The Scots musical museum. Ed James Johnson 6 vols Edinburgh [1787, 1788, 1790, 1792, 1796, 1803]; vols 1–5 re-issued with vol 6; with notes by W. Stenhouse [completed by C. K. Sharpe and D. Laing] 6 vols Edinburgh 1838, 4 vols 1853; ed H. G. Farmer 2 vols Hatboro Pa 1962. Burns was the virtual editor of vols 2–5 and contributed 177 of the 600 songs, as well as collecting many others.

Here Stewarts once in triumph reign'd. In J. Maxwell, Animadversions on some poets and poetasters of the present age especially R—t B—s and J—n L—k, Paisley 1788. Copy in Mitchell Lib.

Poems chiefly in the Scottish dialect. Philadelphia 1788; to which are added Scots poems from R. Ferguson, New York 1788, Belfast 1789, Dublin 1789.

To the author ('Auld nibor, I'm three times, doubly, o'er'). In D. Sillar, Poems, Kilmarnock 1789.

The Ayrshire garland: an excellent new song. [Dumfries 1789?]. Broadside first appearance of 13 stanzas of Kirk's alarm.

The prayer of Holy Willie, a canting, hypocritical, Kirk elder. [Scotland?] 1789. First pbn of this poem; copy in Birthplace Museum, Alloway.

Poems chiefly in the Scottish dialect. Belfast 1790, Dublin 1790.

The kirk's alarm [2 new stanzas]. In A. Tait, Poems and songs. [Paisley?] 1790 (with 3 scurrilous poems on Burns).

Tam O'Shanter. In F. Grose, The antiquities of Scotland vol 2, 1791. First book pbn of this poem, which was written for the work.

The whistle: a poem. [Dumfries? 1791?]. Chapbook; first pbn of this poem.

Address to the shade of Thomson. In D. S. Erskine (Earl of Buchan), Essays on the lives and writings of Fletcher of Saltoun and the poet Thomson, 1792. Burns sent the poem on declining an invitation to attend a ceremony in honour of Thomson.

Poems chiefly in the Scottish dialect. 2 vols Edinburgh 1793 (enlarged), Belfast 1793, Edinburgh 1794.

A select collection of original Scotish airs. Ed G. Thomson 5 vols 1793–1818; various combinations re-issued 1801, 1804, 1809?, 1811?, 1815, 1817, 1822–3, 1825, 1826, 1828, 1831, 1838. First pbn of 59 songs written or altered by Burns for this work; also reprints several songs by Burns. A 6th vol without songs by Burns was pbd 1825.

O my love's like a red, red rose. In A selection of Scots songs harmonized by P. Urbani vol 2, Edinburgh [1794]. First pbn.

An address to the deil, with the answer by J. Lauderdale. Near Wigton 1795. Chapbook; Burns poem rptd from 1786 vol.

Address to the people of Scotland respecting Francis

Grose, the British antiquarian; to which are added verses on seeing the ruins of an ancient magnificent structure. [Glasgow? c. 1795]. Only the first poem is by Burns.

Fy, let us a' to K[irkcudbright]. [Scotland c. 1795–6] (broadside); rptd [c. 1820].

Wha will buy my troggin? [Scotland c. 1795–6]. A broadside; copy in Birthplace Museum, Alloway.

Wham will we send to London Town. [Scotland c. 1795–6]. A broadside.

Poetry: original and selected. 4 vols Glasgow [1795?–8]. Pbd by Brash & Reid in 99 penny nos before being gathered into vols, contains 21 poems by Burns. Individual nos were re-issued, and odd vols made up at least till 1805.

An unco' mornfu tale; to which is added the Antiquarian ['Hear land o' cakes']. Glasgow 1796 (Stewart & Meikle chapbook).

Poems chiefly in the Scottish dialect. 2 vols Edinburgh 1797, 1798, 2 vols in 1 Philadelphia 1798.

Elegy on the year eighty-eight. Edinburgh 1799. Chapbook, also includes Burns's Written at Dalcardoch ('When death's dark stream'), and Written on a window of the Inn at Carron ('We can na here'). Copy in Nat Lib of Scotland.

The bonny lass of Ballochmyle. In Polyhumnia no 18, Glasgow [1799]. A ser of 20 chapbooks issued 1798–9.

The jolly-beggars: a cantata. Glasgow [1799] (Stewart & Meikle chapbooks).

The kirk's alarm: a satire; A letter to a taylor, The deil's awa' wi' the exciseman and An unco' mournfu' tale. Glasgow [1799] (Stewart & Meikle chapbook).

Holy Willie's prayer, Letter to John Goudie and six favourite songs by Burns. Glasgow [1799] (Stewart & Meikle chapbook).

Extempore verses on dining with Lord Daer, accompanied with a prose letter to a friend. Glasgow [1799] (Stewart & Meikle chapbook).

The inventory. Glasgow [1799] (Stewart & Meikle chapbook).

The henpeck'd husband, Address to his illegitimate child, An epigram and On a bank of flowers. Glasgow [1799] (Stewart & Meikle chapbook).

[7 poems by Burns]. In the passage of Mount St Gothard, by the Duchess of Devonshire, Glasgow [1799] (Stewart & Meikle chapbook). Another poem, Shelah O'Neil, is here incorrectly attributed to Burns. Rptd as The poetical miscellany: containing posthumous poems, songs, epitaphs and epigrams, by Burns, Glasgow 1800 (copy in Nat Lib of Scotland).

Poems chiefly in the Scottish dialect; to which are added Scots poems selected from the works of R. Ferguson. New York 1799. The sheets of the New York 1788 edn with new title-page.

Poems chiefly in the Scottish dialect. 2 vols Belfast 1800, Edinburgh 1800, Berwick 1801 (4 issues), Edinburgh 1801, 1 vol Glasgow 1801 (ptd by T. Duncan), Glasgow 1801 (ptd by Chapman & Lang, 5 issues), Montrose 1801.

The answer ('Guidwife: I mind it weel'). In Elizabeth Scot, Alonzo and Cora, with other original poems. 1801. First printing of poem.

Poems ascribed to Burns, the Ayrshire bard, not contained in any edition of his works hitherto published. Glasgow 1801 (several variants) rptd in part in Miscellanea Perthensis, Perth 1801, London 1802 (as The picnic).

Holy Willie's prayer and epitaph. Edinburgh 1801.

Poems chifley in the Scottish dialect. 2 vols Paisley 1801–2.

The merry diversions of Halloween. Stirling 1802.

Poems chiefly in the Scottish dialect. 2 vols Edinburgh 1802, Belfast 1803, Dublin 1803 (2 edns, one with Heron's Life), 1 vol 1803 (3 issues).

Reliques of Burns: consisting chiefly of original letters, poems and critical observations on Scottish songs. Ed R. H. Cromek 1808 (nearly all copies have cancelled leaves (AA6–8), Wellesley College Lib has copy with original leaves), Philadelphia 1809, London 1813, 1814, 1817.

Poems, letters etc ascribed to Burns. 1809. Includes Poems ascribed to Burns, 1801 and Letters addressed to Clarinda, 1802.

Poems chiefly in the Scottish dialect. Baltimore 1812.

Poems chiefly Scottish. 2 vols Perth 1813 (vol 1 was also issued separately).

Poems chiefly in the Scottish dialect. Baltimore 1815, Edinburgh [1816] (also issued with Belfast and Dublin imprints), London 1824, 1824.

Songs chiefly in the Scottish dialect. 1824

Poems chiefly in the Scottish dialect. Ed W. Scott Douglas, Kilmarnock 1877.

Single Poems

Cotter's Saturday night
In Roach's beauties of the poets, 1795, Belfast 1797.

Jolly beggars
Glasgow [1799], [1800]; in The poetical miscellany, Glasgow 1800.

Tam O'Shanter
In F. Grose, The antiquities of Scotland vol 2, 1791 (first book pbn; Burns wrote the poem for Grose), Glasgow [1795 or 1796] (in Brash & Reid chap-books, at least 6 issues), [1801], Ayr 1802 (in Four funny tales).

Many of Burns's Poems and songs were included in the numerous chap-books and song books of the early and mid nineteenth century.

Merry Muses
The title was used indiscriminately in connection with Burns's name, although much of the material pbd was not by him.

The merry Muses of Caledonia: a collection of favourite Scots songs, ancient and modern, selected for the use of the Crochallan Fencibles. 1799; ed G. Legman, New Hyde Park NY 1965 (type facs, with bibliography from Cunningham ms etc).

The merry Muses of Caledonia. Ed J. Barke and S. G. Smith, with prefatory note by J. DeL. Ferguson, Edinburgh 1959.

Letters and Diaries

Letters addressed to Clarinda [Agnes M'Lehose]. Glasgow 1802, 1802 (25 letters from Burns to Clarinda, 3 other letters by Burns).

Letters addressed to Clarinda and others. 1812.

Prose works. Newcastle 1816.

Letters and correspondence. 2 vols 1817.

Burns's common place book [1783–5]. Edinburgh 1872; ed J. C. Ewing and D. Cook, Glasgow 1938 (facs); ed D. Daiches 1965.

Burns and Mrs Dunlop correspondence, now published in full for the first time, with elucidations by W. Wallace. 1898, 2 vols New York 1898 (fuller text).

Journal of a tour in the Highlands made in 1787. Ed J. C. Ewing 1927 (facs).

Letters. Ed R. B. Johnson 1928. A selection.

Letters. Ed J. DeL. Ferguson 2 vols Oxford 1931.

Journal of the Border tour. Ed DeL. Ferguson in Burns, his associates and contemporaries, ed R. T. Fitzhugh, Chapel Hill 1943. First pbd, inaccurately, by A. Cunningham in 1834.

Selected letters. Ed J. DeL. Ferguson, Oxford 1953 (WC).

§ 2

For early criticism see Burns: the critical heritage, *ed D. A. Low 1974.*

[Currie, J.] Life of Burns. Vol 1 of Works of Burns, 4 vols Liverpool 1800; 1826 (separately), Edinburgh 1838 (extended by R. Chambers).

[Lockhart, J. G.] Burns's dinner; Edinburgh Review on Burns. In his Peter's letters to his kinsfolk vol 1, 1819.

—— Life of Burns. Edinburgh 1828, 1828, 1830 (3rd edn corrected), New York 1831, London 1838, 1847, [1871]; with additional notes by W. S. Douglas 1846, 1892, 1905, 2 vols Liverpool 1914 (to which is added an essay by W. Raleigh); ed J. H. Ingram 1889, 1890; ed J. M. Sloan 1904; ed E. Rhys [1907], 1933, 1959 (EL).

Carswell, C. The life of Burns. 1930, 1951.

—— Robert Burns. 1933.

'Hugh MacDiarmid' (C. M. Grieve). The Burns cult. In his At the sign of the thistle: a collection of essays, [1934].

—— Burns today and tomorrow. Edinburgh 1959.

Ferguson, J. DeL. Pride and passion: Burns. New York 1939, 1964.

Dewar, R. In Essays on the eighteenth century presented to David Nichol Smith, Oxford 1945.

—— Burns and the Burns tradition. In Scottish poetry: a critical survey, ed J. Kinsley 1955.

Montgomerie, W. (ed). Burns: essays by six contemporary writers. Glasgow 1947.

Daiches, D. Robert Burns. New York 1950, London 1950, 1952, 1966 (rev).

—— Robert Burns. 1957 (Br Council pamphlet).

—— The identity of Burns. In Restoration and eighteenth-century literature: essays in honor of A. D. McKillop, Chicago 1963; rptd in his More literary essays, 1968.

Critical essays on Burns. Ed D. A. Low 1975.

ROBERT FERGUSSON
1750–74
Collections

Poems. Edinburgh 1773.

Poems on various subjects. Edinburgh 1779 (pt 2 of 1773, above), 1782 (with poetry from 1773 and 1779).

Poetical works. Ed D. Irving, Glasgow 1800, Edinburgh 1805 (with a short life, unsigned), 1806; [ed A. Peterkin] 1807, 1807, Greenock 1810; ed J. Bannington 1809; ed M. P. McDiarmid 2 vols Edinburgh 1954–6 (STS).

§ 1

No repose can I discover. In G. F. Tenducci's adaptation of G. Rush's opera The royal shepherd, 1769. Probably Fergusson's first appearance in print.

By Heaven's displeasure the wretch thus is thrown; What doubts oppress my wounded heart; O where shall I wander my lover to find. In Artaxerxes: an English opera as it is performed at the Theatre-Royal Edinburgh, with music composed by T. A. Arne; with the addition of three favourite Scots airs, the words by Mr R. Fergusson, Edinburgh 1769. Libretto tr from Metastasio's Artaserse.

To Andrew Gray. Perth Mag of Knowledge & Pleasure 2 July 1773. In answer to a poem by Gray 11 June 1773. Gray answered 17 Sept. With 3 poems from Weekly Mag.

Auld Reekie. Edinburgh 1773.

Poem to the memory of John Cunningham. Edinburgh 1773.

Verses on visiting Dumfries. Dumfries Weekly Mag 26 Sept 1773.

The Edinburgh buck. A burlesque pbd as an epilogue to Garrick's Bucks have at ye all, Edinburgh [1783?].

On night. In Arthur Masson, A collection of prose and verse, Perth 1792.

The ghaists: a kail-yard eclogue. Paisley 1796. First pbd in Ruddiman's Weekly Mag.

The farmer's ingle. Glasgow [1798?]. 3 24 Brash & Reid chap-books.

The daft days: The King's birth-day in Edinburgh; and Braid claith. Edinburgh 1808.

Cape song. In Songs from David Herd's manuscripts, ed H. Hecht, Edinburgh 1904.

Unpublished poems. Ed W. E. Gillis, Edinburgh 1955.

62 of Fergusson's poems were first pbd in Ruddiman's Weekly Mag 1771–3.

§ 2

Irving, D. The life of Fergusson. Glasgow 1799; enlarged

in Lives of Scotish authors: viz Fergusson, Falconer and Russell, Edinburgh 1801.

— In his Lives of the Scottish poets vol 2, Edinburgh 1804, 1810.

Sommers, T. Life of Fergusson. Edinburgh 1803.

Grosart, A. B. Robert Fergusson. Edinburgh [1898].

Smith, S. G. (ed). Fergusson: essays by various hands to commemorate the bicentenary of his birth. Edinburgh 1952.

MacLaine, A. H. Robert Fergusson. New York 1965.

III. PROSE

SIR DAVID DALRYMPLE, LORD HAILES
1726–92

Sacred poems: or a collection of translations or paraphrases from the Holy Scriptures, by various authors. Edinburgh 1751. Ed Dalrymple.

Edom of Gordon: an ancient Scottish poem. Glasgow 1755. Ed Dalrymple.

British songs sacred to love and virtue. Edinburgh 1756. Ed Dalrymple.

John Smith, Select discourses. Edinburgh 1756. Ed Dalrymple.

Memorials and letters relating to the history of Britain in the reign of James the First: published from the originals. Glasgow 1762, 1766 (corrected and enlarged).

A specimen of a book entitled Ane compendious booke of godly and spiritual sangs. Edinburgh 1765. A selection from John Wedderburn, Ane compendious booke of godly and spirituall songs, Edinburgh 1621, commonly called The gude and godlie ballatis. Ed Dalrymple.

Memorials and letters relating to the history of Britain in the reign of Charles the First, published from the originals. Glasgow 1766.

An examination of some of the arguments for the high antiquity of Regiam majestatem, and an enquiry into the authenticity of Leges Malcolmi. Edinburgh 1769.

Historical memorials concerning the provincial councils of the Scottish clergy. Edinburgh 1769.

Ancient Scottish poems published from the ms of George Bannatyne MDLXVIII. Edinburgh 1770, London 1770 (for 1815). Ed Dalrymple.

Remarks on the history of Scotland. Edinburgh 1773.

Annals of Scotland from Malcolm III to Robert I. 2 vols Edinburgh 1776–9, 3 vols Edinburgh 1797 (enlarged), 1819.

Miscellaneous remarks on the Enquiry into the evidence against Mary Queen of Scots. 1784. On work by William Tytler.

Sketch of the life of John Barclay, author of Argenis. [Edinburgh 1786?].

Davidis Humei, Scoti, summi apud suos philosophi, de vita sua acta, liber singularis. [Edinburgh] 1787.

Sketch of the life of Mark Alexander Boyd. [Edinburgh 1787].

Sketch of the life of Sir James Ramsay, a general officer in the armies of Gustavus Adolphus King of Sweden. [Edinburgh 1787].

The little freeholder: a dramatic entertainment in two acts. 1790. Anon.

Tracts relative to the history and antiquities of Scotland. Edinburgh 1800. Reissue of 5 tracts.

Of the eminent heathen writers, from Seneca to Marcus Antonius. In John Brown, Theological tracts, 3 vols Edinburgh 1853.

Correspondence of Thomas Percy and Dalrymple. Ed A. F. Falconer, Baton Rouge 1954 (vol 4 of Percy letters).

Dalrymple also edited and translated historical and legal works; see cols 698, 721 above

JOHN MILLAR, Professor of Law, University of Glasgow
1735–1801

§ 1

Observations concerning the distinction of ranks in society. 1771, Dublin 1771, London 1773 (2nd edn enlarged), 1779 (title varies), Edinburgh 1806 (corrected with life of author by J. Craig).

An historical view of the English government from the settlement of the Saxons in Britain to the accession of the House of Stewart. 1787, Dublin 1789, London 1790 (2nd edn).

An historical view of the English government from the settlement of the Saxons in Britain to the Revolution in 1688; to which are subjoined some dissertations connected with the history of the government from the Revolution to the present time. 4 vols 1803, 1812.

§ 2

Lehmann, W. C. Millar: his life and thought and his contributions to sociological analysis. Cambridge 1960.

HUGH BLAIR
1718–1800
Collections

Lectures on rhetoric and belles lettres. 2 vols 1783, 3 vols Dublin 1783, 1 vol Philadelphia 1784, 3 vols 1785 (rev); ed H. F. Harding 2 vols Carbondale 1965.

Essays on rhetoric. 1784 (2nd edn), Dublin 1784, London 1785, 1787, Boston 1793, Philadelphia 1793 etc. Abridgements of lectures.

Sermons. Vols pbd separately as follows: 1, Edinburgh 1777 (20 other edns before 1801); 2, 1780 (17 other edns before 1801); 3, 1790 (9 other edns before 1801); 4, 1794 (5 other edns before 1801); 5, with a life by J. Finlayson, 1801 (available separately, or with vols 1–4 as first collected edn; frequently rptd). Single sermons were also frequently pbd in anthologies and separately.

§ 1

A poem sacred to the memory of the Rev Mr James Smith. Edinburgh 1736.

Dissertatio philosophica inauguralis, de fundamentis & obligatione legis naturae. Edinburgh 1739.

The wrath of man praising God: a sermon. Edinburgh 1746.
The importance of religious knowledge to the happiness of mankind: a sermon. Edinburgh 1750; rptd in The Scotch preacher vol 1, Edinburgh [1775], 1789.
Observations upon a pamphlet entitled An analysis on the moral and religious sentiments contained in the writings of Sapho [Henry Home] and David Hume. Edinburgh 1755. Anon.
Objections against the essays on morality and natural religion [by Henry Home, Lord Kames] examined. Edinburgh 1756. By Blair, assisted by George Wishart, Robert Hamilton and Robert Wallace.
A critical dissertation on the poems of Ossian. 1763 (limited to a discussion of Fingal), 1765 (enlarged to include Temora), Dublin 1765, Hanover 1765. Anon; frequently rptd in edns of Ossian.
Heads of the lectures on rhetoric and belles lettres. Edinburgh 1767, 1771, 1777.
The compassion and beneficience of the deity: a sermon. Edinburgh 1796.

ADAM FERGUSON LID
1723–1816

The morality of stage-plays seriously considered. Edinburgh 1757. Anon.
The history of the proceedings in the case of Margaret, commonly called Peg, only lawful sister to John Bull esq. 1761, 1761. An anon tract on the militia question.
An essay on the history of civil society. Edinburgh 1767, Dublin 1767, London 1768, 1773 (rev), Basle 1789 etc; ed D. Forbes, Edinburgh 1966.

Institutes of moral philosophy. Edinburgh 1769, 1773, 1785.
The history of the progress and termination of the Roman republic. 3 vols 1783, 5 vols Edinburgh 1799 (rev) etc.
Principles of moral and political science. 2 vols Edinburgh 1792.
Also sermons including one in Gaelic to the First Highland Regiment of Foot, preached Dec 1745, tr Ferguson and pbd 1746. See col. 747, above.

HENRY HOME, LORD KAMES
1696–1782
Collections

Memoirs of the life and writings of Home. Ed A. F. Tytler 2 vols Edinburgh 1807; suppl 1809; 3 vols 1814.

§ I

Essays upon several subjects concerning British antiquities. Edinburgh 1747, London 1749, Edinburgh 1763 (with addns), 1797.
Essays on the principles of morality and natural religion. Edinburgh 1751, London 1758.
Introduction to the art of thinking. Edinburgh 1761, 1764, 1775, 1789, 1810, New York 1818. Anon.
Elements of criticism. 3 vols Edinburgh 1762, 1763, 2 vols Edinburgh 1765, 1769, Dublin 1772, Edinburgh 1774, 1785 (with last corrections and addns).
Sketches of the history of man. 2 vols Edinburgh 1774, Dublin 1775, 4 vols Edinburgh 1778, 1788.
Critical observations on the poems of Ossian. In The poems of Ossian, 2 vols Edinburgh 1797.

Part III
1800–1900

1. INTRODUCTION

(1) BIBLIOGRAPHIES

Sadleir, M. Excursions in Victorian bibliography. 1922. 1st edns of Trollope, Marryat, Disraeli, Wilkie Collins, Reade, Whyte-Melville, Mrs Gaskell.

Bernbaum, E. Guide through the romantic movement. New York 1930, 1954 (rev and enlarged).

Templeman, W. D. et al. Victorian bibliography for 1932. MP 30 1933 (continued annually in MP till 1956); Bibliographies of studies in Victorian literature 1932–44, ed Templeman, Urbana 1945 (collected); Bibliographies of studies in Victorian literature 1945–54, ed A. Wright, Urbana 1956 (collected). *See* Townsend, below.

Brussel, I. R. Anglo-American first editions 1826–1900: describing first editions of English authors whose books were published in America before their publication in England. 1935.

Kunitz, S. J. and H. Haycraft. British authors of the nineteenth century. New York 1936. An encyclopaedia with brief bibliographies.

Graham, W. et al. The romantic movement: a current selective and critical bibliography for 1936. ELH 4 1937 (continued annually in ELH till 1949, in PQ 1950–64 and in Eng Lang Notes 1965–).

Raysor, T. M. et al. The English romantic poets: a review of research. New York 1950, 1956 (rev).

Ray, G. N., C. J. Weber and J. W. Carter. Nineteenth-century English books: some problems in bibliography. Urbana 1952.

Townsend, F. G. et al. Recent publications: a selected list.

Victorian News Letter no 1 1952 (continued quarterly).

— et al. Victorian bibliography for 1957. Victorian Stud 1 1958. Continued annually.

Faverty, F. E. et al. The Victorian poets: a guide to research. Cambridge Mass 1956, 1968 (rev).

Houtchens, C. W. and L. H. The English romantic poets and essayists: a review of research and criticism. New York 1957, 1966 (rev).

Altick, R. D. and W. R. Matthews. Guide to dissertations in Victorian literature 1886–1958. Urbana 1960.

Tobias, R. C. The year's work in Victorian poetry 1962. Victorian Poetry 1– 1963–. Continued annually.

Stevenson, L. Victorian fiction: a guide to research. Cambridge Mass 1964.

Fredeman, W. E. Pre-Raphaelitism: a bibliocritical study. Cambridge Mass 1965.

Houghton, W. E. The Wellesley index to Victorian periodicals 1824–1900. Toronto 1966–.

Ward, W. S. A bibliography of literary reviews in British periodicals 1798–1820. 2 vols New York 1972.

DeLaura, D. J. Victorian prose: a guide to research. New York 1973.

Wolff, M., J. S. North and D. Deering. The Waterloo directory of Victorian periodicals 1824–1900: phase 1. Waterloo Ont 1976.

Brown, L. M. and I. R. Christie. Bibliography of British history 1789–1851. Oxford 1977.

(2) LITERARY HISTORIES AND SURVEYS

Saintsbury, G. A history of nineteenth-century literature 1780–1895. 1896.

Batho, E. C. and B. Dobrée. The Victorians and after 1830–1914. New York 1938, 1951 (rev).

Young, G. M. The age of Tennyson. Proc Br Acad 25 1939.

Chew, S. C. The nineteenth century and after. In A literary history of England, ed A. C. Baugh, New York 1948.

Ford, B. (ed). The Pelican guide to English literature, vol 5: From Blake to Byron. 1957; vol 6: From Dickens to Hardy, 1958.

Renwick, W. L. English literature 1789–1815. Oxford 1963 (OHEL); I. Jack, English literature 1815–32, Oxford 1963 (OHEL).

Watson, G. The English ideology. 1973.

Tillotson, G. A view of Victorian literature. Oxford 1977.

2. POETRY

I. EARLY NINETEENTH-CENTURY POETRY

SAMUEL ROGERS
1763–1855

Collections

Italy; The pleasures of memory; Human life, and other poems. [1845].
Poetical works. 1856; ed E. Bell 1875 (Aldine).

§1

An ode to superstition, with some other poems. 1786. Anon.
The pleasures of memory: a poem in two parts. 1792 (4 edns), 1793, 1794 (illustr T. Stothard), 1806 (15th edn).
An epistle to a friend, with other poems. 1798, 1798.
Verses written in Westminster Abbey after the funeral of Charles James Fox. [1806].
The voyage of Columbus: a poem. 1810, [1812].
Miscellaneous poems. 1812. With E. C. Knight et al.
Poems. 1812, 1814, 1816, 1820, 1822, [1833], 1834 (illustr J. M. W. Turner and T. Stothard), 2 vols 1836, 1838 1839, 1840; ed S. Sharpe 1860.
Jacqueline: a poem. 1814, 1814 (both with Byron's Lara).
Human life: a poem. 1819, Cambridge Mass 1820; tr Italian, 1820.
Italy, a poem: part the first. 1822, 1823; part the second, 1828; [both parts] 1830 (illustr J. M. W. Turner and T. Stothard), 1838.
Recollections of the table-talk of Samuel Rogers, with a memoir [by A. Dyce]. 1856 (3 edns), 1887; ed 'Morchard Bishop' (O. Stonor) 1952.
Recollections. [Ed W. Sharpe] 1859, 1859.
Reminiscences and Table-talk, collected by G. H. Powell. 1903.
Italian journal. Ed J. R. Hale 1956.

§2

Jeffrey, F. Edinburgh Rev 31 1819. Review of Human life.
Barbier, C. P. Rogers and William Gilpin: their friendship and correspondence. Oxford 1959.
Hale, J. R. Rogers the perfectionist. HLQ 25 1961.

WILLIAM WORDSWORTH
1770–1850

Bibliographies etc

Catalogue of the varied and valuable historical, poetical, theological and miscellaneous library of the late venerated poet-laureate. Preston [1859]; rptd in Trans Wordsworth Soc no 6 [1884?].
Cooper, L. A concordance to the poems of Wordsworth. 1911.
Wise, T. J. A bibliography of the writings in prose and verse of Wordsworth. 1916 (priv ptd).
Healey, G. H. The Cornell Wordsworth collection: a catalogue of books and manuscripts. Ithaca 1957.

Collections

Poems: including Lyrical ballads, and the miscellaneous pieces of the author, with additional poems, a new preface and a supplementary essay. 2 vols 1815.

The miscellaneous poems. 4 vols 1820.
The poetical works: new edition. 4 vols 1832.
The poetical works: new edition. 6 vols 1836 [vols 1–2] –1837 [vols 3–6], 1840 (with variations), 1841, 1843. Poems chiefly of early and late years was issued in 1842 with an alternative title-page to form vol 7.
The sonnets of William Wordsworth, collected in one volume, with a few additional ones, now first published. 1838.
Poems, chiefly of early and late years, including the Borderers: a tragedy, by William Wordsworth. 1842.
The poems of William Wordsworth, DCL, poet laureate: a new edition. 1845, 1847, 1849 etc. Prelude added after 1850.
The poetical works of William Wordsworth, DCL, poet laureate, honorary member of the Royal Society of Edinburgh, and of the Royal Irish Academy. 7 vols 1846, 1849. Similar to the edn of 1836–7 etc, but with the Poems chiefly of early and late years (1842) distributed.
The poetical works of William Wordsworth, DCL, poet laureate: new edition. 6 vols 1849 [vols 1–2]–1850 [vols 3–6].
The poetical works of William Wordsworth. 6 vols 1857, 1864, 1865, 1869, 1870 (centenary edn), 1874, 1881, 1882. Includes Fenwick notes.
The poetical works. Ed W. M. Rossetti 1870, 1871. Based on one-vol edn of 1845, with Prelude.
The poetical works. Ed T. Hutchinson, Oxford 1895. Basis of OSA edn, frequently rptd; rev edn, ed E. de Selincourt 1936. Also 5 vols 1895.
The poetical works. Ed W. Knight 8 vols 1896.
The poems. Ed N. C. Smith 3 vols 1908.
The poetical works. Ed E. de Selincourt and H. Darbishire 5 vols Oxford 1940–9; rev edn of vols 1–4, 1952–8. The standard edn.
The Cornell Wordsworth. Ed S. M. Parrish and M. L. Reed, Ithaca 1975–. The longer poems.

Prose Works

Prose works. Ed W. Knight 2 vols 1896.
Prose works. Ed W. J. B. Owen and J. W. Smyser 3 vols Oxford 1974.

Selections

Poems of Wordsworth. Ed M. Arnold 1879. With Arnold's introd; frequently rptd.
Wordsworth's literary criticism. Ed N. C. Smith, Oxford 1905.
Poetry and prose. Ed W. M. Merchant 1955 (Reynard Lib).
Literary criticism. Ed W. J. B. Owen 1974.

§1

An evening walk: an epistle in verse, addressed to a young lady from the lakes of the north of England, by W. Wordsworth BA of St John's, Cambridge. 1793.
Descriptive sketches in verse, taken during a pedestrian tour in the Italian, Grison, Swiss and Savoyard Alps, by W. Wordsworth BA of St John's, Cambridge. 1793.
Lyrical ballads, with a few other poems. 1798 (2 issues, the first with imprint 'Bristol: printed by Biggs and Cottle, for T. N. Longman, Paternoster-Row, London.'; the second with imprint 'London: printed for J. & A. Arch, Gracechurch-Street'); ed W. J. B. Owen, Oxford 1967.

Lyrical ballads, with other poems, in two volumes, by W. Wordsworth. 2 vols 1800; ed R. L. Brett and A. R. Jones 1963.

Lyrical ballads, with pastoral and other poems, in two volumes, by W. Wordsworth. 2 vols 1802, 1805 (new edn called the fourth on the title-pages); ed G. Sampson, The lyrical ballads 1798–1805, 1903.

Lyrical ballads, with other poems: in two volumes, by W. Wordsworth. Philadelphia 1802. 2 issues.

Wordsworth's preface to Lyrical ballads. Ed W. J. B. Owen, Copenhagen 1957.

Poems in two volumes, by William Wordsworth, author of the Lyrical ballads. 2 vols 1807; ed H. Darbishire 1914, 1952 (rev).

Concerning the relations of Great Britain, Spain and Portugal to each other, and to the common enemy, at this crisis: and specifically as affected by the convention of Cintra: the whole brought to the test of those principles, by which alone the independence and freedom of nations can be preserved or recovered. 1809; ed A. V. Dicey, Oxford 1915; ed R. J. White, in Political tracts of Wordsworth, Coleridge and Shelley, Cambridge 1953 (with omissions).

Essay upon epitaphs. Friend 25 (22 Feb 1810); rptd as a note to the Excursion bk 5 in 1814 and in subsequent edns. The first essay of 3. The second and third were first pbd in Grosart's edn of the Prose works, 1876.

The excursion, being a portion of the Recluse: a poem, by William Wordsworth. 1814. Rptd 1820, and as a vol of Poetical works, 1827, 1832, 1836–7, 1849–50.

The white doe of Rylstone: or the fate of the Nortons, a poem by William Wordsworth. 1815 (with The force of prayer: or the founding of Bolton priory); ed A. P. Comparetti, Ithaca 1940.

Thanksgiving ode, January 18, 1816, with other short pieces, chiefly referring to recent public events, by William Wordsworth. 1816. Includes various odes and sonnets later collected in Poems dedicated to national independence and liberty, and some other poems.

Peter Bell: a tale in verse, by William Wordsworth. 1819, 1819. Contains also Sonnets suggested by Mr W. Westall's views of the caves &c in Yorkshire, previously pbd in Blackwood's Mag Jan 1819; later collected in the group Miscellaneous sonnets.

The waggoner: a poem, to which are added sonnets, by William Wordsworth. 1819. Contains 12 sonnets later collected in the group Miscellaneous sonnets.

The river Duddon: a series of sonnets; Vaudracour and Julia; and other poems, to which is annexed A topographical description of the country of the lakes in the north of England, by William Wordsworth. 1820. Also includes Dion, Artegal and Elidure, The prioress's tale, and about 30 shorter poems.

A description of the scenery of the lakes in the north of England: third edition (now first published separately) with additions, and illustrative remarks upon the scenery of the Alps, by William Wordsworth. 1822, 1823 ('fourth'), 1835 ('fifth'); ed E. de Selincourt 1906; ed W. M. Merchant 1951. The 'first' and 'second' edns are Wordsworth's Introduction to Joseph Wilkinson, Select views in Cumberland, Westmoreland and Lancashire, 1810; and The river Duddon, 1820, pp. 213–321.

Ecclesiastical sketches by William Wordsworth. 1822; ed A. F. Potts, New Haven 1922 (as The ecclesiastical sonnets).

Memorials of a tour on the Continent 1820. 1822.

Yarrow revisited, and other poems. 1835, 1836, 1839, Boston and New York 1835, Boston 1836.

Grace Darling. Carlisle [1843] (priv ptd), Newcastle [1843].

Verses composed at the request of Jane Wallas Penfold by William Wordsworth esq, poet laureate. [1843]. Unique copy, BM Ashley 5140. Contains Fair lady! can I sing of flowers.

Kendal and Windermere railway: two letters re-printed from the Morning Post, revised with additions. Kendal 1845. Priv ptd, followed by London issue with imprints of Whittaker and Moxon as well as the Kendal imprint.

Ode performed in the Senate-House, Cambridge, on the sixth of July MDCCCXLVIII, at the first commencement after the installation of His Royal Highness the Prince Albert, Chancellor of the University. Cambridge 1847. 4 leaves ptd by Univ Press.

The prelude, or growth of a poet's mind; an autobiographical poem, by William Wordsworth. 1850, New York and Philadelphia 1850; ed E. de Selincourt, Oxford 1926, 1959 (rev H. Darbishire); text of 1805, ed de Selincourt, Oxford 1933, 1970 (rev S. Gill); Prelude: a parallel text, ed J. C. Maxwell 1971 (Penguin) (1805 and 1850 texts); Prelude 1798–9, ed S. Parrish, Ithaca 1977.

The recluse. 1889; ed B. Darlington, Ithaca 1977 (as Home at Grasmere, from ms).

A letter to the Bishop of L[l]andaff on the extraordinary avowal of his political principles contained in the appendix to his late sermon: by a republican [1793]. Substantial ms fragment first ptd in Grosart's edn of the Prose works 1876; Grosart's text unreliable.

Essay on morals [1798?]. Ms fragment first ptd in full by G. L. Little, REL 2 1961.

Letters, Diaries etc

Memorials of Coleorton: being letters from Coleridge, Wordsworth and his sister, Southey and Sir Walter Scott to Sir George and Lady Beaumont of Coleorton, Leicestershire, 1803 to 1834. Ed W. Knight 2 vols Edinburgh 1887.

Letters from the Lake poets, Coleridge, Wordsworth, Southey, to Daniel Stuart, editor of the Morning Post and the Courier 1800–38. 1889 (priv ptd).

Letters of the Wordsworth family from 1787 to 1855. Ed W. Knight 3 vols 1907.

The correspondence of Henry Crabb Robinson with the Wordsworth circle (1808–66). Ed E. J. Morley 2 vols Oxford 1927.

The early letters of William and Dorothy Wordsworth. Ed E. de Selincourt, Oxford 1935, 1967 (rev C. L. Shaver).

The letters of William and Dorothy Wordsworth: the middle years. Ed E. de Selincourt 2 vols Oxford 1937, 1969–70 (rev M. Moorman and A. G. Hill).

The letters of William and Dorothy Wordsworth: the later years. Ed E. de Selincourt 3 vols Oxford 1939.

The letters of Wordsworth, selected. Ed P. Wayne, Oxford 1954 (WC).

The letters of Sara Hutchinson from 1800 to 1835. Ed K. Coburn 1954.

Letters of Mary Wordsworth 1800–55. Ed M. E. Burton, Oxford 1958.

Journals of Dorothy Wordsworth. Ed W. Knight 2 vols 1897, 1 vol 1930; ed E. de Selincourt 2 vols 1941, 1952; ed H. Darbishire, Oxford 1958 (WC); ed M. Moorman, Oxford 1971.

Henry Crabb Robinson on books and their writers. Ed E. J. Morley 3 vols 1938.

Wordsworth's pocket notebook. Ed G. H. Healey, Ithaca 1942.

§2

Jeffrey, F. Southey's Thalaba. Edinburgh Rev 1 1802.
—— Wordsworth's Poems in two volumes. Edinburgh Rev 11 1807.
—— The excursion. Edinburgh Rev 24 1814.
—— The white doe of Rylstone. Edinburgh Rev 25 1815.
Hazlitt, W. The excursion. Examiner 21, 28 Aug, 2 Oct 1814.

—— In his Lectures on the English poets, 1818.
—— My first acquaintance with poets. Liberal 3 1823.
—— In his Spirit of the age: or contemporary portraits, 1825.
Lamb, C. The excursion. Quart Rev 12 1814.
Coleridge, S. T. In his Biographia literaria, 1817.
De Quincey, T. Lake reminiscences from 1807 to 1830. Tait's Mag Jan–Feb, April 1839.
—— Recollections of Grasmere. Tait's Mag Sept 1839.
—— On Wordsworth's poetry. Tait's Mag Sept 1845.
—— In his Recollections of the Lakes and the Lake poets, Coleridge, Wordsworth and Southey, Edinburgh 1863.
Wordsworth, C. Memoirs of William Wordsworth. 1851.
Clough, A. H. Lecture on the poetry of Wordsworth. In his Poems and prose remains, 1869.
Pater, W. Wordsworth. Fortnightly Rev April 1874; rptd in his Appreciations, 1889.
Stephen, L. Wordsworth's ethics. Cornhill Mag Aug 1876; rptd in Hours in a library: third series, 1879.
Knight, W. A. (ed). Transactions of the Wordsworth Society. 1882–7. Includes reprint of sale catalogue of Wordsworth's library (1859) and H. D. Rawnsley, Reminiscences of Wordsworth among the peasantry of Westmoreland.
Rawnsley, H. D. Literary associations of the English Lakes. Glasgow 1894.
Legouis, E. La jeunesse de Wordsworth 1770–98. Paris 1896; tr 1897 (as The early life of Wordsworth 1770–98).
—— Wordsworth and Annette Vallon. 1922.
—— Wordsworth in a new light. Cambridge Mass 1923.
Raleigh, W. Wordsworth. 1903.
Bradley, A. C. English poetry and German philosophy in the age of Wordsworth. Manchester 1909.
—— In his Oxford lectures on poetry, 1909.
de Selincourt, E. In his English poets and the national ideal, Oxford 1915.
—— The hitherto unpublished preface to Wordsworth's Borderers. Nineteenth Century Nov 1926; rptd in his Oxford lectures on poetry, Oxford 1934.
—— Dorothy Wordsworth. Oxford 1933.
—— The early Wordsworth; Wordsworth and his daughter's marriage; The interplay of literature and science during the last three centuries. In his Wordsworth and other studies, Oxford 1947.
Harper, G. M. Wordsworth: his life, works and influence. 1916, 1929 (rev).
Dicey, A. V. The statesmanship of Wordsworth. Oxford 1917.
Garrod, H. W. Wordsworth. Oxford 1923, 1927 (rev).
—— In his Profession of poetry and other lectures, Oxford 1929. On the Lucy poems.
Havens, R. D. The mind of a poet: a study of Wordsworth's thought with particular reference to the Prelude. Baltimore 1941.
Darbishire, H. The poet Wordsworth. Oxford 1950.
Empson, W. Sense in the Prelude. Kenyon Rev 13 1951; rptd in his Structure of complex words, 1952.
Davie, D. Diction and invention. In his Purity of diction in English verse, 1952.
—— Syntax in the blank verse of Wordsworth's Prelude. In his Articulate energy, 1955.
Abrams, M. H. In his Mirror and the lamp, New York 1953.
Bateson, F. W. Wordsworth: a re-interpretation. 1954, 1956 (rev).
Hartman, G. H. The unmediated vision: an interpretation of Wordsworth, Hopkins, Rilke and Valéry. New Haven 1954.
—— Wordsworth's poetry 1787–1814. New Haven 1964.
Jones, J. The egotistical sublime: a history of Wordsworth's imagination. 1954.
Moorman, M. Wordsworth, a biography: the early years 1770–1803. Oxford 1957, 1968 (corrected); The later years 1803–50, Oxford 1965.
Davies, H. S. Wordsworth and the empirical philosophers.

In The English mind, ed Davies and G. Watson, Cambridge 1964.
—— A new poem by Wordsworth. EC 15 1965. On A slumber did my spirit seal. Reply by R. F. Storch, ibid; J. Wordsworth and G. W. Ruoff 16 1966.
Salvesen, C. The landscape of memory: a study of Wordsworth's poetry. 1965.
Welsford, E. Salisbury Plain: a study in the development of Wordsworth's mind and art. Oxford 1966.
Drabble, M. Wordsworth. 1966.
Rader, M. M. Wordsworth: a philosophical approach. Oxford 1967.
Reed, M. L. Wordsworth: the chronology of the early years 1770–1799. Cambridge Mass 1967.
Woodring, C. R. Wordsworth. Cambridge Mass 1968.
Owen, W. J. B. Wordsworth as critic. Toronto 1969.
Wordsworth, J. The music of humanity: a critical study of Wordsworth's Ruined cottage. 1969.
Parrish, S. M. The art of the Lyrical ballads. Cambridge Mass 1973.

SAMUEL TAYLOR COLERIDGE
1772–1834

By far the most important collection of mss and of annotated and association books is in the BM; the complementary collection, for many years preserved intact by the Coleridge family, is in the Victoria College Library, Toronto.

Bibliographies etc

Wise, T. J. A bibliography of the writings in prose and verse of Coleridge. 1913 (priv ptd); Supplement: Coleridgeana, 1919.
Logan, E. A concordance to the poetry of Coleridge. Saint Mary-of-the-Woods Indiana 1940.
Raysor, T. M. In English romantic poets: a review of research, ed Raysor, New York 1950, 1956 (rev).
Healey, G. H. The Cornell Wordsworth collection. Ithaca 1957. Includes Coleridge material.

Collections

Poetical works 3 vols 1834. The last issued during Coleridge's lifetime, reissued 1835, 1836, 1837, 1840, 1844.
Complete works, with an introductory essay upon his philosophical and theological opinions. Ed W. G. T. Shedd 7 vols New York 1853, 1871, 1875, 1884.
Select poetry and prose. Ed S. Potter 1933, 1950 (with some marginalia added), 1962 (Nonesuch).
The political thought of Coleridge. Ed R. J. White 1938.
The portable Coleridge. Ed I. A. Richards, New York 1950, 1961.
Poems. Ed J. B. Beer 1963 (EL), 1974 (with new introd).
Collected works of Coleridge. Ed K. Coburn et al, c. 24 vols London and Princeton 1969–.

§ 1

The fall of Robespierre: an historic drama. Cambridge 1794. Act 1 by Coleridge, acts 2–3 by Southey.
A moral and political lecture delivered at Bristol. Bristol [1795]; expanded in Conciones, below; in Collected works: Lectures 1795.
The plot discovered. Bristol 1795; rptd in Conciones, below; in Collected works: Lectures 1795.
Conciones ad populum: or addresses to the people. [Bristol] 1795. In Collected works: Lectures 1795.
The plot discovered: or an address to the people, against ministerial treason. Bristol 1795. In Collected works: Lectures 1795.
    Lectures 1795: on politics and religion. Ed L. Patton and J. P. Mann 1971 (Collected works). Includes Conciones ad populum, The plot discovered, A moral and political lecture etc.

Ode on the departing year. Bristol 1796.

Poems on various subjects. London and Bristol 1796 (ptd in Bristol).

[Sonnets from various authors.] [1796] (priv ptd). 4 sonnets and prefatory essay on the sonnet by Coleridge, 24 sonnets by Bowles, Lamb, Lloyd, Southey et al. Prefatory essay rptd variously in Poems 1797. *For existing marked copies see* G. Whalley, TLS 23 Nov 1956.

The watchman. 10 nos Bristol 1796. Advertised 'to be published every eighth day'; issued 1 March–13 May 1796. Prospectus rptd by J. D. Campbell, Athenaeum 9 Dec 1893. Coleridge's contributions rptd in pt in Essays on his own times, ed S. Coleridge 1853.

The watchman. Ed L. Patton 1970 (Collected works).

Poems by S. T. Coleridge, second edition, to which are now added poems by Charles Lamb and Charles Lloyd. Bristol and London 1797 (ptd in Bristol). Includes much of Poems 1796, above, but substantially a new book.

Fears in solitude, written in 1798 during the alarm of an invasion; to which are added France: an ode; and Frost at midnight. 1798, [1812] (another edn, perhaps rptd from the Poetical Register 7 1812).

Lyrical ballads, with a few other poems [by W. Wordsworth and S. T. Coleridge]. [Bristol? and] London 1798 (ptd in Bristol). Lewti cancelled in proof and Coleridge's Nightingale substituted. *See* D. F. Foxon, The printing of Lyrical ballads 1798, Library 5th ser 9 1954. *See under Wordsworth, cols 772–3, above. For separate edns of the* Ancient mariner, *see below.*
2 vols 1800 (with Coleridge's poem Love), 1802 (with omission of Coleridge's Dungeon), 1805.
The most recent critical edns are ed R. L. Brett and A. R. Jones 1963 (text of 1798 with the additional 1800 poems and prefaces, with introd, notes and appendixes); ed W. J. B. Owen, Oxford 1967 (text of 1798).
The Ancient Mariner. The rime of the ancyent marinere. In Lyrical ballads, 1798; The rime of the ancient mariner, in Lyrical ballads, 1800 (extensively rev), 1802, 1805; in Sibylline leaves, 1817 (with marginal gloss); in Poetical works, 1828, 1829, 1834 (with minor successive revisions). *See* J. L. Lowes, The road to Xanadu, Boston 1927, 1930 (rev).

Wallenstein: a drama in two parts translated from the German of Frederic Schiller. 1800. The Piccolomini (5 acts) and The death of Wallenstein (5 acts).

Poems: third edition. 1803. Omits poems by Lamb and Lloyd; a fresh selection and arrangement supervised by Lamb.

The friend: a literary, moral and political weekly paper, excluding personal and party politics and the events of the day. 28 nos Penrith 1809–10. Nos 1–27, with supernumerary no between 20 and 21, issued 1 June 1809–15 March 1810. Includes contributions by Wordsworth et al, but almost entirely Coleridge's composition. Rptd in Collected works.
1812. Re-issue with supplementary matter.
3 vols 1818. A new edn, carefully rev and with extensive addns.
3 vols 1837, 1844. Ed H. N. Coleridge. With the author's last corrections, an appendix and a synoptical table of the contents of the work by H. N. Coleridge.
The friend. Ed B. E. Rooke 2 vols 1969 (Collected works). Reprints complete texts of 1818 and 1809–10.

Remorse: a tragedy in five acts. 1813 (3 edns), 1884. Prologue by C. Lamb.

Christabel; Kubla Khan: a vision; The pains of sleep. 1816 (3 edns).

The statesman's manual, or the Bible the best guide to political skill and foresight: a lay sermon addressed to the higher classes of society, with an appendix containing comments and essays connected with the study of the inspired writings. 1816. Referred to as first Lay sermon. Ed R. J. White, Lay sermons, 1972 (Collected works).

Biographia literaria: or biographical sketches of my literary life and opinions. 2 vols 1817; ed H. N. Coleridge and Sara Coleridge 2 vols 1847 (with long introd and biographical suppl); ed J. Shawcross 2 vols Oxford 1907 (with the aesthetic essays; text oscillates between 1817 and 1847); ed G. Watson 1956, 1960, 1965 (with addn) (EL) (excludes Satyrane's letters and the critique of Bertram; text of 1817).

Blessed are ye that sow beside all waters: a lay sermon addressed to the higher and middle classes on the existing distresses and discontents. 1817. Second Lay sermon.

Sibylline leaves: a collection of poems. 1817. First collective edn, assembled in 1815 omitting contents of the 1816 Christabel vol.

Zapolya: a Christmas tale in two parts; the prelude entitled The usurper's fortune and the sequel entitled The usurper's fate. 1817.

[On method.] General introd to Encyclopaedia metropolitana, 1818 (also separate offprint, 1818); ed A. D. Snyder 1934 (with ms fragments, detailed introd and notes).

Aids to reflection in the formation of a manly character, on the several grounds of prudence, morality and religion, illustrated by select passages from our elder divines, especially from Archbishop Leighton. 1825, New York 1829, London 1831, 1836; ed H. N. Coleridge 1839 (4th edn with author's last corrections), 2 vols 1843 (with preliminary essay by J. H. Green and appendixes), 1848; ed D. Coleridge 1854, 1856; ed T. Fenby, Liverpool 1873, 1883. Edinburgh 1896, 1905 (with copious index and trns of Greek and Latin quotations).

The poetical works, including the dramas of Wallenstein, Remorse and Zapolya. 3 vols 1828, 1829, with a few addns. Guide text for Poetical works, ed J. D. Campbell 1893.

On the constitution of the Church and State according to the idea of each, with aids toward a right judgment on the late Catholic bill. 1830. Ed H. N. Coleridge 1839, 1852; rptd with the 2 Lay sermons in 1839 and after 1852.

The devil's walk: a poem, edited with a biographical memoir and notes by Professor Porson [i.e. Coleridge and Southey]. Ed H. W. Montagu 1830, 1830 (with engravings on wood by Bonner and Slader after R. Cruikshank); 1830, 1830 (with names of Coleridge and Southey in place of Porson's on the title-page). Rptd in I. Cruikshank, Facetiae, 2 vols 1831. Originally composed by Coleridge and Southey in 1799, ptd anon in Morning Post 6 Sept 1799 as The devil's thoughts; amplified by Southey in 1827 without Coleridge's collaboration.

The poetical works. 3 vols 1834. Probably prepared and arranged by H. N. Coleridge. 66 uncollected pieces added to Poetical works 1829 with some rearrangement. Rptd 1835, 1836, 1840, 1844 (as Poetical and dramatic works). Guide text for Complete poetical works, ed E. H. Coleridge 2 vols 1912.

Confessions of an inquiring spirit. Ed H. N. Coleridge 1840, 1849, 1853, 1863 (with some miscellaneous pieces and introd by J. H. Green); ed H. N. Coleridge 1884 etc (Bohn's Lib) (with Aids to reflection, 1886 (with miscellaneous essays from Friend); ed H. S. Stanford 1957 (with J. H. Green's introd).

The poems. Ed Sara Coleridge 1844, 1848.

Hints toward the formation of a more comprehensive theory of life. Ed S. B. Watson 1848; ed T. Ashe 1885 (in Miscellanies, aesthetic and literary).

Essays on his own times, forming a second series of the

Friend. Ed Sara Coleridge 3 vols 1850. Newspaper and periodical articles mostly from Watchman, Morning Post and Courier, and a number of topical and epigrammatic poems.

The poems: a new edition. Ed Derwent and Sara Coleridge. 1852 etc (in later edns associated with Dramatic works 1852, below); Leipzig 1852 (Tauchnitz edn with biographical memoir by F. Freiligrath); in Complete works, ed W. G. T. Shedd, New York 1853 etc; 3 vols Boston 1854, 1863 etc (with addns); 1870 (with introductory essay by Derwent Coleridge, and the 1798 text of the Ancient mariner and a few new poems in an appendix).

The dramatic works. Ed Derwent Coleridge 1852 etc.

The poetical words. Ed J. D. Campbell 1893 etc. The biographical introd was issued separately 1894 as Coleridge: a narrative of the events of his life.

The complete poetical works, including poems and versions of poems now published for the first time. Ed E. H. Coleridge 2 vols Oxford 1912, 1957, 1962, 1966; 1 vol Oxford 1912 (OSA) (omitting dramatic writings and bibliographical matter). Text based on Poetical works 1834, above.

The philosophical lectures, hitherto unpublished. Ed K. Coburn 1949. The text, primarily based on a shorthand transcript taken at the lectures, is reconstructed by use of notebooks, marginalia and pbd works.

Letters, Notebooks, Marginalia and Fragments

Omniana: or horae otiosiores. Ed R. Southey 2 vols 1812 (Coleridge's contributions identified in the contents by asterisks); ed T. Ashe 1884 (Bohn's Lib) (with Table-talk, below).

Specimens of the table-talk of the late Samuel Taylor Coleridge. Ed H. N. Coleridge 2 vols 1835, 1836 (corrected), 1851; ed H. Morley 1874, 1884 (with Ancient mariner, Christabel, Kubla Khan); ed T. Ashe in Table talk and Omniana, 1884 etc (with additional table-talk from Allsop's Recollections and unpbd ms matter).

The literary remains. Ed H. N. Coleridge 4 vols 1836–9.

Allsop, T. Letters, conversations and recollections of Coleridge. 2 vols 1836, 1858, 1864 (omitting prefaces of 1st and 2nd edns).

Notes and lectures upon Shakespeare and some of the old poets and dramatists, with other literary remains. Ed Mrs H. N. Coleridge 2 vols 1849. Rptd from Literary remains vols 1–2, above, with a few addns.

Notes on English divines. Ed Derwent Coleridge 2 vols 1853. Marginalia rptd from Literary remains vols 3–4, above.

Notes theological, political and miscellaneous. Ed Derwent Coleridge 1853. Marginalia, about one-third from Literary remains, the rest unpbd.

Seven lectures on Shakespeare and Milton by the late S. T. Coleridge. Ed J. P. Collier 1856.

Osorio: a tragedy, as originally written in 1797. [Ed R. H. Shepherd] [1873]. Early and unpbd version of Remorse collated with the pbd text.

Knight, W. G. Memorials of Coleorton: being letters from Coleridge, Wordsworth and his sister, Southey and Sir Walter Scott to Sir George and Lady Beaumont of Coleorton Leicestershire 1803–34. 2 vols Edinburgh 1887.

Anima poetae, from the unpublished notebooks of Coleridge. Ed E. H. Coleridge 1895.

Letters. Ed E. H. Coleridge 2 vols 1895.

Notizbuch aus den Jahren 1795–8. Ed A. L. Brandl, Archiv 97 1896. Edn of Gutch memorandum book.

Haney, J. L. A bibliography of Coleridge. Philadelphia 1903. Ch 10 lists 341 titles of annotated and marked books, including works by Coleridge.

—— The marginalia of Coleridge. In Schelling anniversary papers, ed J. L. Haney, New York 1923.

—— Coleridge the commentator. In Coleridge studies, ed E. Blunden and E. L. Griggs 1934.

Letters hitherto uncollected. Ed W. F. Prideaux 1913 (priv ptd).

Snyder, A. D. Books borrowed by Coleridge from the library of the University of Göttingen 1799. MP 25 1928.

—— Coleridge on logic and learning, with selections from the unpublished manuscripts. New Haven 1929. Includes selections from philosophical notebooks.

Coleridge's Shakespearean criticism. Ed T. M. Raysor 2 vols Cambridge Mass 1930, London 1960 (EL) (rev).

Unpublished letters, including certain letters republished from original sources. Ed E. L. Griggs 2 vols 1932.

Coleridge's miscellaneous criticism. Ed T. M. Raysor, Cambridge Mass 1936.

Brinkley, R. F. (ed). Coleridge on the seventeenth century. Durham NC 1955.

Coburn, K. Inquiring spirit: a new presentation of Coleridge from his published and unpublished prose writings. 1951. Includes excerpts from notebooks and marginalia, about one-third unpbd.

Collected letters. Ed E. L. Griggs 6 vols Oxford 1956–71.

Notebooks. Ed K. Coburn 4 vols New York 1957–61. 11 vols (including index) are projected. See her Coleridge's quest for self-knowledge, Listener 8 Sept 1949.

Coleridge on Shakespeare: the lectures 1811–12. Ed R. A. Foakes 1971.

§2

Lamb, C. Recollections of Christ's Hospital. GM June 1813 (2 pts, signed); rptd in his Works, below.

—— Christ's Hospital five and thirty years ago. London Mag Nov 1820; rptd in his Essays of Elia, 1823.

—— The two races of men. London Mag Dec 1820; rptd in his Essays of Elia.

——[On the death of Coleridge]. In Charles Lamb: his last words on Coleridge, New Monthly Mag Feb 1835. Lamb's ms note of 21 Nov 1834, perhaps his last composition; rptd in his Works, below.

—— In his Works, ed E. V. Lucas 6 vols 1912.

—— In Letters of Charles and Mary Lamb, ed E. V. Lucas 3 vols 1935.

[Hazlitt, W.] Mr Coleridge and Mr Southey. Examiner 6 April 1817.

Hazlitt, W. On the living poets: Coleridge. In his Lectures on the English poets, 1818.

—— Coleridge's Lay sermon and Statesman's manual. In his Political essays, with sketches of public characters, 1819.

—— My first acquaintance with poets. Liberal April 1823.

—— Mr Coleridge. In his Spirit of the age, 1825.

—— In his Complete works, ed P. P. Howe 21 vols 1930–4.

Peacock, T. L. Melincourt. 3 vols 1817. Coleridge satirized as Moley Mystic.

—— Nightmare Abbey. 1818. Coleridge satirized as Mr Flosky.

—— Crotchet Castle. 1831. Coleridge satirized as Mr Skionar.

Hunt, L. Coleridge: sketches of the living poets no 4. Examiner 21 Oct 1821.

—— Mr Coleridge, Lord Byron and some of his contemporaries. 1828.

—— In his Autobiography, with reminiscences of friends and contemporaries, 3 vols 1850.

—— In his Imagination and fancy, 1883.

De Quincey, T. Samuel Taylor Coleridge. Tait's Mag Sept–Nov 1834, Jan 1835.

—— Coleridge and opium eating. Blackwood's Mag Jan 1845. On Gillman's Life.

—— In his Collected writings: new and enlarged edition, ed D. Masson 14 vols Edinburgh 1889–90.
—— Conversation and Coleridge. Ed A. H. Japp 2 vols 1891.
Cottle, J. Early recollections, chiefly relating to the late Coleridge during his long residence in Bristol. 2 vols 1837–9, 1 vol 1847 (rev and enlarged as Reminiscences of Coleridge and R. Southey).
Gillman, J. The life of Coleridge. Vol 1, 1838. All pbd.
Mill, J. S. Coleridge. London & Westminster Rev 5 1840; rptd in his Dissertations and discussions vol i, 1859; ed F. R. Leavis 1950 (in Mill on Bentham and Coleridge).
Maurice, F. D. The kingdom of Christ. 1842 (2nd edn). *See also his* Life told in his own letters, 2 vols 1884.
Carlyle, T. In his Life of John Sterling, 1851. Pt 1, ch 8.
Emerson, R. W. A visit to Coleridge. In his English traits, 1856, Boston 1891.
Rogers, S. In Recollections of the table talk, 1856.
Robinson, H. C. Diary, reminiscences and correspondence. Ed T. Sadler 3 vols 1869, 2 vols 1872.
—— Blake, Coleridge, Wordsworth, Lamb etc: being selections from the remains of Henry Crabb Robinson. Ed E. J. Morley, Manchester 1922.
—— Correspondence with the Wordsworth circle. Ed E. J. Morley 2 vols Oxford 1927.
—— On books and their writers. Ed E. J. Morley 3 vols 1938.
Pater, W. H. In his Appreciations, 1890.
—— Coleridge's writings. 1910.
Campbell, J. D. Coleridge: a narrative of the events of his life. 1894; ed L. Stephen 1896. A biographical introd to his edn of Poetical works, 1893.
Lowes, J. L. The road to Xanadu. Boston 1927, 1930 (rev).
Blunden, E. In his Leigh Hunt's Examiner examined, [1928].
—— Coleridge the less. In his Votive tablets, 1931. On the value of annotations and fragments by Coleridge and his son Hartley.
—— Coleridge and Christ's Hospital. In Coleridge studies, ed Blunden and E. L. Griggs 1934.
Bradley, A. C. Coleridge's use of light and colour. In his A miscellany, 1929.
Griggs, E. L. Hartley Coleridge, his life and work. 1929.
—— An early defense of Christabel. In Wordsworth and Coleridge: studies in honor of G. M. Harper, ed Griggs, Princeton 1939.
—— Coleridge fille: a biography of Sara Coleridge. Oxford 1940.
—— Wordsworth through Coleridge's eyes. In Wordsworth centenary studies, ed G. T. Dunklin, Princeton 1951, Hamden Conn 1963.
de Selincourt, E. In his Dorothy Wordsworth: a biography, Oxford 1933.
Eliot, T. S. Wordsworth and Coleridge. In his Use of poetry and use of criticism, 1933.
Abrams, M. H. The milk of paradise: the effect of opium visions on the works of De Quincey, Crabbe, Francis Thompson and Coleridge. Cambridge Mass 1934.
—— In his Mirror and the lamp, New York 1953.
—— The correspondent breeze: a romantic metaphor. Kenyon Rev 19 1957; rev in English romantic poets: modern essays in criticism, ed Abrams, New York 1960.
—— Structure and style in the greater romantic lyrics. In From sensibility to romanticism: essays presented to F. A. Pottle, New York 1965.
Coleridge studies by several hands on the hundredth anniversary of his death. Ed E. Blunden and E. L. Griggs 1934.
Richards, I. A. Coleridge on imagination. 1934, 1950 (rev), Bloomington 1960 (with preface by K. Coburn),

London 1962. Reply by F. R. Leavis, Scrutiny 3 1935.
Willey, B. In his Eighteenth-century background, 1934.
—— Coleridge on imagination and fancy. Proc Br Acad 32 1946.
—— In his Nineteenth-century studies: Coleridge to Matthew Arnold, 1949.
Potter, S. Coleridge and STC. 1935.
Lovejoy, A. O. Coleridge and Kant's two worlds. ELH 7 1940; rptd in his Essays in the history of ideas, Baltimore 1948.
Woolf, V. The man at the gate; Sara Coleridge. New Statesman 19–26 Oct 1940; rptd in her Death of the moth, 1942.
Burke, K. The Ancient mariner. In his Philosophy of literary form, New York 1941.
Knight, G. W. Coleridge's Divine comedy. In his Starlit dome, Oxford 1941; rptd in English romantic poets, ed M. H. Abrams, New York 1960.
Leavis, F. R. Coleridge in criticism. Scrutiny 9 1941; rptd in Importance of Scrutiny, ed E. Bentley, New York 1948.
Whalley, G. The Mariner and the albatross. UTQ 16 1947.
—— Coleridge and Southey in Bristol 1795. RES new ser 1 1950.
—— The integrity of Biographia literaria. E & S new ser 6 1953.
—— Two views of imagination [Kant's and Coleridge's]. In his Poetic process, 1953.
—— Coleridge and Sara Hutchinson and the Asra poems. 1955.
—— Preface to Lyrical ballads: a portent. UTQ 25 1956.
—— Coleridge's debt to Charles Lamb. E & S 11 1958.
—— Portrait of a bibliophile: 7, Coleridge. Book Collector 10 1961.
—— Coleridge unlabyrinthed. UTQ 32 1963.
Read, H. Coleridge as critic. Sewanee Rev 1948; rptd in his Lectures in criticism, New York 1949 and in his True voice of feeling, 1953.
—— The notion of organic form: Coleridge. In his True voice of feeling, 1953.
Tillyard, E. M. W. Coleridge: the Ancient mariner 1798. In his Five poems 1470–1870, 1948.
Brett, R. L. Coleridge's theory of the imagination. E & S 2 1949.
—— In his Reason and imagination, Oxford 1960.
Fogle, R. H. The dejection of Coleridge's Ode. ELH 17 1950.
—— The idea of Coleridge's criticism. Berkeley 1962.
Davie, D. A. Coleridge and improvised diction. In his Purity of diction in English verse, 1952.
—— In his Articulate energy, 1955. On function of syntax in Dejection and Lime tree bower.
House, H. Coleridge. 1953 (Clark Lectures).
Jordan, J. E. De Quincey on Wordsworth's theory of diction. PMLA 68 1953.
Margoliouth, H. M. Wordsworth and Coleridge: dates in May and June 1798. N & Q Aug 1953.
—— Wordsworth and Coleridge 1795–1834. Oxford 1953 (Home Univ Lib).
Raine, K. Coleridge. 1953 (Br Council pamphlet).
—— Traditional symbolism in Kubla Khan. Sewanee Rev 72 1964.
Watson, G. 'Imagination' and 'fancy'. EC 3 1953.
—— Coleridge the poet. 1966.
Hough, G. In his Romantic poets, 1953.
—— Coleridge and the Victorians. In The English mind: studies in the English moralists presented to Basil Willey, Cambridge 1964.
Hutchinson, S. The letters of Sara Hutchinson 1800–35. Ed K. Coburn, 1954.
Beer, J. Coleridge the visionary. 1959.
Erdman, D. V. Coleridge, Wordsworth and the Wedgwood fund. BNYPL Sept–Oct 1956.

—— Immoral acts of a library cormorant: the extent of Coleridge's contributions to the Critical Review. BNYPL Sept, Nov 1959.

Salingar, L. G. Coleridge: poet and philosopher. In Pelican guide to English literature vol 5: from Blake to Byron, ed B. Ford 1958.

Williams, R. In his Culture and society 1780–1950, 1958, 1961 (rev).

Woodring, C. R. Politics in the poetry of Coleridge. Madison 1961.

Empson, W. The Ancient mariner. CQ 6 1964.

Appleyard, J. A. Coleridge's philosophy of literature. Cambridge Mass 1965.

Coburn, K. (ed). Coleridge: a collection of critical essays. Englewood Cliffs NJ 1967.

McFarland, T. Coleridge and the pantheistic tradition. Oxford 1969.

Jackson, J. R. de J. (ed). Coleridge: the critical heritage. 1970.

Barfield, O. What Coleridge thought. 1972.

Willey, B. Samuel Taylor Coleridge. 1972.

ROBERT SOUTHEY
1774–1843
Bibliographies

Curry, K. Southey's contributions to the Annual Review. Bull of Bibliography 16 1939.

—— The contributors to the Annual Anthology. PBSA 42 1948.

—— In The English romantic poets and essayists: a review of research and criticism, ed C. W. and L. H. Houtchens, New York 1957, 1966 (rev).

—— The published letters of Southey: a checklist. BNYPL March 1967.

Shine, H. and H. C. The Quarterly Review under Gifford. Chapel Hill 1949. Identifies Southey's articles 1809–24.

Collections

The poetical works of Southey, collected by himself. 10 vols 1837–8, New York 1839. Each vol has a separate preface by Southey.

§ 1

The fall of Robespierre: an historic drama. Cambridge 1794. Coleridge wrote Act 1, Southey Acts 2 and 3.

Poems: containing The retrospect, odes, elegies, sonnets etc by Robert Lovell and Southey. Bath 1795.

Joan of Arc: an epic poem. Bristol 1796, 2 vols Bristol 1798 (rev), 1 vol Boston 1798, 2 vols 1806 (rev), 1812 (rev), 1817, 1 vol 1853.

Poems. Bristol 1797 (for 1796), 1797 (rev), Boston 1799; vol 2, Bristol 1799; 2 vols 1800, 1801, 1806–8.

Letters written during a short residence in Spain and Portugal, with some account of Spanish and Portugueze poetry. Bristol 1797, 1799, 2 vols 1808 (enlarged as Letters written during a journey in Spain, and a short residence in Portugal).

On the French revolution, by Mr Necker, translated from the French. 2 vols 1797. Vol 2 by Southey.

The annual anthology. 2 vols Bristol 1799–1800. Anon, ed and partly written by Southey.

Thalaba the destroyer. 2 vols 1801, 1809, Boston 1812, London 1814, 1821, 1 vol 1846, 1853, 1856, 1860.

Madoc: a poem, in two parts. 1805, 2 vols Boston 1806, London 1807, 1812, 1815, 1825, 1 vol 1853.

Metrical tales and other poems. 1805, Boston 1811. Poems rptd from Annual Anthology 1799–1800.

Letters from England, by Don Manuel Alvarez Espriella, translated from the Spanish. 3 vols 1807 (anon),

2 vols Boston 1807 (anon), 3 vols 1808 (anon), 2 vols New York 1808 (anon), 3 vols 1814, 2 vols Philadelphia 1818, New York 1836; ed J. Simmons 1951.

The remains of Henry Kirke White: with an account of his life. 2 vols 1807, 1811 (5th edn 'corrected'), Philadelphia 1811, London 1813, New York 1815, London 1816, 1819, 1821; vol 3, 1822.

Chronicle of the Cid, from the Spanish. 1808, 1846, Lowell Mass 1846, London 1868, 1883; ed R. Markham, New York 1883; ed V. S. Pritchett, New York 1958.

The curse of Kehama. 1810, 2 vols New York 1811, London 1812, 1818, 1 vol 1853; ed H. Morley 1886.

History of Brazil. Pt 1 1810, 1822; pt 2 1817; pt 3 1819.

The history of Europe [in Edinburgh Annual Register for 1808–11]. Vols 1–4 Edinburgh 1810–13. Anon.

Omniana: or horae otiosores. 2 vols 1812. Anon; 45 contributions by Coleridge, 201 by Southey.

The origin, nature and object of the new system of education. 1812. Anon.

An exposure of the misrepresentations and calumnies in Mr Marsh's review of Sir George Barlow's administration at Madras, by the relations of Sir George Barlow. 1813. Anon.

The life of Nelson. 2 vols 1813, New York 1813, London 1814 (rev), 1825, 1 vol 1830 (rev) etc (at least 30 edns by 1900); ed A. D. Power 1903; ed H. B. Butler, Oxford 1911; ed G. A. R. Callender 1922; ed H. Newbolt 1925; ed E. R. H. Harvey 1953; ed K. Fenwick 1956; ed C. Oman 1962 (EL).

Roderick: the last of the Goths. 1814, 2 vols 1815, 1815, 1 vol Philadelphia 1815, 2 vols 1816, 1818, 1826, 1 vol 1891.

Odes to His Royal Highness the Prince Regent, His Imperial Majesty the Emperor of Russia and His Majesty the King of Prussia. 1814.

Carmen triumphale, for the commencement of the year 1814. Rptd with the Odes, above, 1821.

A summary of the life of Arthur Duke of Wellington, from the period of his first achievements in India to his invasion of France and the decisive battle of Waterloo. Dublin 1816. Anon; rptd from Quart Rev 13 1815. Copy in Nat Lib of Ireland.

The poet's pilgrimage to Waterloo. 1816 (12 large paper copies also issued), 1816, New York 1816, Boston 1816.

The lay of the laureate: carmen nuptiale. 1816. On the marriage of the Princess Charlotte.

Wat Tyler: a dramatic poem. 1817 (many pirated edns), Newcastle [1820?], London [1820?], [1825?], Newcastle [1830?], London [1835?], Boston 1850.

A letter to William Smith esq MP. 1817 (4 edns). On the Wat Tyler controversy.

The byrth, lyf and actes of King Arthur, with an introduction and notes. 2 vols 1817.

The life of Wesley, and the rise and progress of Methodism. 2 vols 1820, 1820, New York 1820; ed C. C. Southey 1846 (embodying notes by Coleridge and Remarks on Wesley by A. Knox), New York 1847, London 1858, 1 vol 1864; ed J. A. Atkinson 1889; ed M. H. Fitzgerald 2 vols Oxford 1925.

A vision of judgement. 1821, 1822 (as The two visions: or Byron v. Southey: containing The vision of Judgement by Dr Southey LL D; also another Vision of judgement, by Lord Byron), New York 1823 (with Byron's travesty), London 1824 (with Byron). Both poems ed E. M. Earl 1929; ed R. E. Roberts, Harrow Weald 1932.

The expedition of Orsua and the crimes of Aguirre. 1821, Philadelphia 1821. Rptd slightly rev from Edinburgh Annual Register vol 3 pt 2.

Life of John Duke of Marlborough. 1822. Anon; abridged from Quart Rev 23 1820.

History of the Peninsular War. Vol 1 1823, vol 2 1827, vol 3 1832; rptd 6 vols, vols 1–4 1828, vols 5–6 1837.

The book of the church. 2 vols 1824, 1824, 1825, Boston 1825, 1 vol 1837, 1841, 1848, 1859, 1869 (with notes from Vindiciae ecclesiae anglicanae, below), [1885].

A tale of Paraguay. 1825, Boston 1827, London 1828.

Vindiciae ecclesiae anglicanae: letters to Charles Butler esq, comprising Essays on the Romish religion and vindicating the Book of the church. 1826.

All for love; and The pilgrim to Compostella. 1829, Paris 1829.

Sir Thomas More: or colloquies on the progress and prospects of society. 2 vols 1829, 1831, 1 vol 1887.

The pilgrim's progress: with a life of John Bunyan. 1830, Boston 1832, New York 1837, London 1839, 1844, New York 1846, London 1847, 1881.

The devil's walk: a poem by Professor Porson. 1830, 1830, 1830 (as by Coleridge and Southey), 1830. By Coleridge and Southey. Originally ptd as The devil's thoughts, Morning Post 6 Sept 1799, and expanded by Southey alone in 1827.

Essays, moral and political, now first collected. 2 vols 1832.

Lives of the British admirals, with an introductory view of the naval history of England. Vol 1 1833, Philadelphia 1835 (as The naval history of England), London 1839; vol 2 1833; vol 3 1834, 1848; vol 4 1837; vol 5 1840 (continued by R. Bell); ed D. Hannay 1895 (as English seamen), 1904.

The doctor. Vols 1–2 1834, 1835; vol 3 1834; vol 4 1837; vol 5 1838 (all anon); vols 6–7 ed J. W. Warter 1847. Vols 1–3 rptd in 2 vols New York 1836, 1860; vols 1–7 ed J. W. Warter 1 vol 1848, 1849, 1853, 1856, New York 1856, London 1862, 1864, 1865, New York 1872; abridged by R. B. Johnson [1898]; by M. H. Fitzgerald 1930.

Horae lyricae: poems by Isaac Watts, with a memoir of the author. 1834, 1837, Boston 1854.

The works of William Cowper, with a life of the author. 15 vols 1835–7, 8 vols 1853–5. Life of Cowper rptd Boston 1858.

The life of the Rev Andrew Bell, comprising the history of the rise and progress of the system of mutual tuition. 3 vols 1844. Southey wrote vol 1, C. C. Southey vols 2–3.

Select biographies: Cromwell and Bunyan. 1844.

Robin Hood: a fragment by the late Robert Southey and Caroline Southey, with other fragments and poems. Edinburgh 1847.

Southey's common place book. Ed J. W. Warter 4 sers 1849–50.

Journal of a tour in the Netherlands in the autumn of 1815. 1902, Boston 1902; ed W. R. Nicoll 1903.

Journal of a tour in Scotland in 1819. Ed C. H. Herford 1929.

Journals of a residence in Portugal 1800–1, and a visit to France 1838. Ed A. Cabral, Oxford 1960.

Letters

Southey, C. C. The life and correspondence of the late Robert Southey. 6 vols 1849–50.

Selections from the letters of Southey. Ed J. W. Warter 4 vols 1856.

The correspondence of Southey with Caroline Bowles; to which are added correspondence with Shelley, and Southey's dreams. Ed E. Dowden, Dublin 1881.

Letters of Southey: a selection. Ed M. H. Fitzgerald, Oxford 1912 (WC).

New letters of Southey. Ed K. Curry 2 vols New York 1965. *For fuller list see* K. Curry, The published letters of Southey: a checklist, BNYPL March 1967.

§2

[Jeffrey, F.] Southey's Thalaba. Edinburgh Rev 1 1802; rptd (in part) in Famous reviews, ed R. B. Johnson 1914.

Hazlitt, W. In his Political essays with sketches of public characters, 1819.

— In his Spirit of the age, 1825.

Byron, G. G. The vision of judgment. Liberal 1 1822.

Macaulay, T. B. Southey's Colloquies. Edinburgh Rev 50 1830; rptd in Critical and historical essays vol 1, 1843.

Cottle, J. In his Early recollections, 2 vols 1837, 1 vol 1847 (rev as Reminiscences of Coleridge and Southey).

De Quincey, T. In his Lake reminiscences from 1807 to 1830, no 4: Wordsworth and Southey. Tait's Mag 6 1839; rptd in De Quincey's Works, ed D. Masson, vol 2 Edinburgh 1889; and in Reminiscences of the English Lake poets, ed J. E. Jordan 1961 (EL).

Catalogue of the valuable library of the late Robert Southey esq. [1844].

Robinson, H. C. In his Diary, reminiscences and correspondence, ed T. Sadler 3 vols 1869, 2 vols Boston 1869, London 1872.

— In his Correspondence with the Wordsworth circle, ed E. J. Morley 2 vols Oxford 1927.

— In his On books and their writers, ed E. J. Morley 3 vols 1938.

Dowden, E. Southey. 1874 (EML).

Saintsbury, G. In his Essays in English literature ser 2, 1895. Essay on Southey rptd in his Collected essays and papers vol 1, 1923.

Stephen, L. Southey's letters. In his Studies of a biographer vol 4, 1902.

Simmons, J. Southey. 1945.

Whalley, G. The Bristol Library borrowings of Southey and Coleridge 1793–8. Library 5th ser 4 1949.

— Coleridge and Southey in Bristol 1795. RES new ser 1 1950.

— Coleridge, Southey and Joan of Arc. N & Q Feb 1954.

Carnall, G. D. Southey and his age: the development of a conservative mind. Oxford 1960.

— Robert Southey. 1964 (Br Council pamphlet).

Raimond, J. Southey: l'homme et son temps. Paris 1968.

Madden, L. (ed). Southey: the critical heritage. 1973.

Curry, K. Southey. 1975.

THOMAS CAMPBELL
1777–1844
Bibliographies

Jordan, H. H. In English romantic poets and essayists: a review of research and criticism, ed C. W. and L. H. Houtchens, New York 1957, 1966 (rev).

Collections

Poetical works; biographical sketch by 'a gentleman of New York' (Washington Irving). 2 vols Albany 1810; ed J. L. Robertson, Oxford 1907.

§1

The wounded hussar. Glasgow 1799, Stirling [1800], Newcastle nd, Birmingham nd, London nd. A chapbook.

The pleasures of hope, with other poems. Edinburgh 1799, Glasgow 1800 (4th edn 'corrected and enlarged'), Edinburgh 1801, 1802, 1804 (7th edn), London 1803 (also designated 7th edn 'corrected and enlarged').

Gertrude of Wyoming: a Pennsylvanian tale, and other poems. 1809, 1810, 1810, 1812, 1814, 1816, 1819, 1821, 1825, New York 1809; ed H. M. Fitzgibbon, Oxford 1889, 1891.

Miscellaneous poems. 1824.

Theodric: a domestic tale, and other poems. 1824, 1824, Philadelphia 1825, Paris 1825.

Inaugural discourse on being installed Lord Rector of the University of Glasgow. Glasgow 1827.

Poland: a poem; Lines on the view from St Leonard's. 1831, 1831.

The life of Mrs Siddons. 2 vols 1834, 1 vol New York 1834, London 1839.

Letters from the south. 2 vols 1837, 1842 (as The journal of a residence in Algiers).

The life of Petrarch. 2 vols London 1841, 1843. Abridged in The sonnets, Triumphs and other poems of Petrarch, 1859 (Bohn).

The pilgrim of Glencoe, and other poems. 1842.

§2

Jeffrey, F. Edinburgh Rev 14 1809. On Gertrude of Wyoming.

Bowles, W. L. Letters to Mr T. Campbell as far as regards poetical criticism. Pamphleteer 20 1822.

Hazlitt, W. In his Spirit of the age, 1825.

Beattie, W. Life and letters of Campbell. 3 vols 1849, 1850.

Redding, C. Literary reminiscences and memoirs of Campbell. 2 vols 1860.

THOMAS MOORE
1779–1852

Bibliographies

Jordan, H. H. In English romantic poets and essayists: a review of research, ed C. W. and L. H. Houtchens, New York 1957, 1966 (rev).

Collections

Works. 6 vols Paris 1819; The poetical works, collected by himself, 10 vols 1840–1, 1853, 1 vol Paris 1841, 1842 ('collected and arranged by himself'), 3 vols 1841 ('collected by the author'); ed F. J. Child 6 vols Boston 1856; ed W. M. Rossetti, illustr T. Seccombe, [1870]; ed A. D. Godley, Oxford 1910; ed W. M. Rossetti 1911.

Prose and verse, humorous, satirical and sentimental, ed R. H. Shepherd 1878; Poetical works, ed J. Dorrian 1888; ed J. R. Tutin [1892]; ed C. L. Falkiner 1903; Lyrics and satires, ed S. O'Faolain, Dublin 1929.

§1

Odes of Anacreon, translated into English verse, with notes. 1800, 2 vols 1802, 1803, 1804, 1805, 1806, 1810.

The poetical works of the late Thomas Little esq. 1801, 1802, 1803, 1804, 1804, 1805, 1806 (8th edn), 1808.

Moore sometimes composed or adapted music for his own lyrical poems. Some early examples are : O lady fair! a ballad for three voices, 1802, 1802, [1804]; When time who steals our years away: a ballad, 1802; Good night, a ballad, 1803; Songs and glees, 1805; A Canadian boat song, arranged for three voices, 1805. *He also collaborated with Michael Kelly to compose* The gypsy prince: a comic opera in thee acts, 1801, *of which little more than the music survives.*

Epistles, odes and other poems. 1806, 2 vols 1807.

Corruption and Intolerance: two poems with notes, addressed to an Englishman by an Irishman. 1801, 1809.

A selection of Irish melodies, with symphonies and accompaniments by Sir John Stevenson and characteristic words by Moore. 10 pts and suppl 1808 (pts 1–2), 1810, 1811, 1813, 1815, 1818, 1821, 1824, 1834 (pt 10 and suppl). Stevenson was the composer for the first seven parts only, to 1818.

The sceptic: a philosophical satire, by the author of Corruption and Intolerance. 1809.

A melologue upon national music. London and Dublin [1810].

A letter to the Roman Catholics of Dublin. 1810, Dublin 1810 (2nd edn).

MP, or the blue-stocking: a comic opera in three acts, by Anacreon Moore. 1811, New York 1812.

Intercepted letters: or the two penny post bag, by Thomas Brown the younger. 1813 (at least 11 edns).

Lines on the death of —— [R. B. Sheridan] from the Morning Chronicle of August 5 1816. 1816.

Sacred songs. No 1, 1816; no 2, 1824.

Lalla Rookh: an oriental romance. 1817 (6 edns), 1818 (at least 3 edns); illustr R. Westall 1840, 1842, 1844; illustr by eminent artists 1846; illustr J. Tenniel, 1861.

The Fudge family in Paris, edited by Thomas Brown the younger. 1818 (at least 9 edns).

National airs. 6 nos 1818–27.

Tom Crib's memorial to congress, with preface, notes and appendix, by one of the fancy. 1819 (4 edns)

Irish melodies, with an appendix containing the original advertisements and the prefatory letter on music. 1821 (first authorized edn of words only), 1822 (at least 3 edns), 1825 (6th edn), 1827 (8th edn), 1832 (10th), 1824 (with National airs), 1846 (with other poems).

The loves of the angels: a poem. 1823 (4 edns), 1823 (5th edn) (as The loves of the angels: an eastern romance); rev text and notes to make 'machinery and allusions entirely Mahometan', 1824, 1826, Philadelphia 1823, Paris 1823, 1823, 1843, New York [1844].

Fables for the holy alliance; Rhymes for the road, by Thomas Brown the younger. 1823.

Memoirs of Captain Rock, the celebrated Irish chieftain, with some account of his ancestors, written by himself. 1824 (at least 5 edns), Paris 1824.

Memoirs of the life of the Right Honourable Richard Brinsley Sheridan. 1825, 1825, 2 vols 1825, 1826, 1827 (new preface).

Evenings in Greece: first [second] evening (with music). [1827], [1835], New York 1844.

The epicurean: a tale. 1827 (4 edns), 1828, 1864; illustr J. M. W. Turner, 1839 (with Alciphron).

Odes upon cash, corn, Catholics and other matters, selected from the columns of the Times journal. 1828, Philadelphia 1828, Paris 1829.

Letters and journals of Lord Byron, with notices of his life. 2 vols 1830, 1831, 1833.

The life and death of Lord Edward Fitzgerald. 2 vols 1831, 1 vol Paris 1831, 1835; ed M. MacDermott 1897; abridged as The life and times etc, Dublin 1909 (Irish Lib).

The summer fete: a poem with songs [and music]. 1831, Paris 1832, 1833, Philadelphia 1833.

Travels of an Irish gentleman in search of a religion, with notes and illustrations by the editor of Captain Rock's memoirs. 2 vols 1833, 1 vol Paris 1833.

The Fudges in England: being a sequel to the Fudge family in Paris, by Thomas Brown the younger. 1835, 1835, Paris 1835, 1835.

The history of Ireland. 4 vols 1835–46 (in D. Lardner, The cabinet encyclopaedia), Paris 1835–46, 2 vols Philadelphia 1843–6.

Alciphron: a poem. Illustr J. M. W. Turner 1839, Paris 1840.

Letters, Diaries etc

Memoirs, journal and correspondence of Moore. Ed Lord John Russell 8 vols 1853–6; abridged by Russell 1860.

Notes from the letters of Moore to his music publisher, James Power (the publication of which were suppressed in London). Ed T. C. Croker, New York [1854].

'Thomas Moore' anecdotes: being anecdotes, bon-mots and epigrams from the journal. Ed W. Harrison 1899 (2nd edn).

Tom Moore's diary: a selection. Ed J. B. Priestley, Cambridge 1925.

Letters of Moore. Ed W. S. Dowden 2 vols Oxford 1964.

Journal 1818–41. Ed P. C. Quennell, New York 1964. Selection.

§2

Jeffrey, F. Edinburgh Rev 8 1806. Review of Epistles, odes and other poems, and the cause of Moore's duel with Jeffrey.
—— Edinburgh Rev 57 1817. On Lalla Rookh.
—— Edinburgh Rev 89 1826. On Memoirs of Sheridan.
Hazlitt, W. Yellow Dwarf 25 April 1818.
—— In his Spirit of the age, 1825.
—— On the jealousy and the spleen of party. In his Plain speaker, 1826.
Smith, S. Edinburgh Rev 81 1824. On Memoirs of Captain Rock.
Gwynn, S. Thomas Moore. 1905 (EML).
Jones, H. M. The harp that once: a chronicle of the life of Moore. New York 1937.
Strong, L. A. G. The minstrel boy: a portrait of Tom Moore. 1937.
Birley, R. R. Lalla Rookh. In his Sunk without trace: some forgotten masterpieces reconsidered, 1962 (Clark Lectures).
Coburn, K. Who killed Christabel? TLS 20 May 1965. Attributes review to Moore.

JAMES HOGG
1770–1835

Hogg mss are scattered, but significant collections are available at the Nat Library of Scotland and at Yale Univ Library.

Collections

Poetical works. 4 vols Edinburgh 1822.
Tales and sketches. 6 vols Glasgow 1837, London 1852.
Poetical works. 5 vols Glasgow 1838–40, 1852.
Works. Ed T. Thomson 2 vols Glasgow 1865–6. Vol 2 contains Autobiography, originally the anon Memoir, in The mountain bard, 1869, 1872.
Selected poems. Ed J. C. Hadden, Glasgow 1893; ed W. Wallace 1903.
Works, letters and manuscripts. Ed R. B. Adam, Buffalo 1930 (priv ptd).
Selected poems. Ed J. W. Oliver, Edinburgh 1940.
Selected poems. Ed D. S. Mack, Oxford 1971.

§1

Scottish pastorals, poems, songs etc. Edinburgh 1801.
The mountain bard: consisting of ballads and songs, founded on facts and legendary tales. Edinburgh 1807 (with the autobiographical Memoir of the life of James Hogg), 1821 (3rd edn 'greatly enlarged'), 1839 (with The forest minstrel, below), Glasgow 1840.
The shepherd's guide: being a practical treatise on the diseases of sheep. Edinburgh 1807.
The spy. 52 nos Edinburgh 1810–11. Ed and largely written by Hogg.
The forest minstrel: a selection of songs. 1810, Philadelphia 1816.
The Queen's wake: a legendary poem. Edinburgh 1813 (re-issued as 2nd edn), 1814 (re-issued 1815), Boston 1815, Edinburgh 1819, 1819, 1842, [1867]; Selections, 1879.
The hunting of Badlewe: a dramatic tale. Edinburgh 1814.
A selection of German Hebrew melodies. [1815?].
The pilgrims of the sun. Edinburgh 1815, Philadelphia 1816.
The Ettricke garland: being two excellent new songs. Edinburgh 1815. One song by Hogg; the other by Scott.
The poetic mirror: or the living bards of Britain. 1816, 1817; ed T. E. Welby 1929.
Mador of the moor. Edinburgh 1816.
Dramatic tales. 2 vols Edinburgh 1817.
The long pack: a Northumbrian tale. Newcastle 1817,

1818, Glasgow [1840?], [1850?]; ed G. Richardson, Newcastle 1877 etc.
The Brownie of Bodsbeck and other tales. 2 vols Edinburgh 1818; ed G. Lewis, Selkirk 1903.
A border garland. Edinburgh [1819?], nd (as The border garland).
The Jacobite relics of Scotland. 2 sers Edinburgh 1819–21, 1 vol Paisley 1874.
Winter evening tales. 2 vols Edinburgh 1820, 1 vol Glasgow 1821 (selected), 1824.
The three perils of man, or war, women and witchcraft: a border romance. 3 vols Edinburgh 1822, 1837 (as The siege of Roxburgh, in Tales and sketches).
The royal jubilee: a Scottish mask. Edinburgh 1822.
The three perils of woman, or love, leasing and jealousy: a series of domestic Scottish tales. 3 vols Edinburgh 1823.
The private memoirs and confessions of a justified sinner, written by himself. 1824 (anon), 1828 (as The suicide's grave), 1837 (rptd with alterations as Confessions of a fanatic, in Tales and sketches), 1895 (as The suicide's grave); ed T. E. Welby 1924; ed A. Gide 1947; ed J. Carey, Oxford 1969.
Queen Hynde. 1825.
Select and rare Scottish melodies. [1829].
The shepherd's calendar. 2 vols Edinburgh 1829.
Critical remarks on the psalms of David. Edinburgh 1830. With W. Tennant.
Songs now first collected. Edinburgh 1831, 1855, [1912].
Altrive tales collected among the peasantry of Scotland, and from foreign adventurers. Vol 1 (all pbd), 1832.
A queer book. Edinburgh 1832.
A series of lay sermons on good principles and good breeding. 1834.
The domestic manner·and private life of Sir Walter Scott. Glasgow 1834, New York 1834 (as Familiar anecdotes of Sir Walter Scott), Edinburgh 1882; ed J. E. H. Thomson, Stirling 1909; ed D. S. Mack, Edinburgh 1972 (with Memoirs).
The works of Robert Burns. 5 vols Glasgow 1834–6 etc (vol 5 contains Hogg's Memoir of Burns), 1847, 1848, 1851, 4 vols 1895. Ed with William Motherwell.
Tales of the wars of Montrose. 3 vols 1835.
A tour in the Highlands in 1803: letters by Hogg to Scott. Paisley 1888.
Kilmeny. 1905, 1911.

§2

Wordsworth, W. Extempore effusion on the death of the Ettrick shepherd. Athenaeum 30 Nov 1835.
Garden, Mrs. Memorials of Hogg. Paisley [1885], 1887, 1893.
Saintsbury, G. In his Essays in English literature 1780–1860, 1890.
Stephenson, H. T. The Ettrick shepherd: a biography. Bloomington 1922.
Batho, E. C. The Ettrick shepherd. Cambridge 1927.
Carswell, D. Sir Walter. 1930. On Scott, Hogg, Lockhart, Joanna Baillie.
Strout, A. L. The life and letters of Hogg, vol 1: 1770–1825. Lubbock Texas 1946.
Simpson, L. Hogg: a critical study. 1962.

GEORGE GORDON BYRON,
6th BARON BYRON
1788–1824

Bibliographies etc

Chew, S. C. Byron in England. New York 1924. The fullest list of Byroniana.
—— In English romantic poets: a review of research, ed T. M. Raysor, New York 1950, 1956 (rev).

Wise, T. J. A Byron library. 1928 (priv ptd).
—— A bibliography of the writings in verse and prose of Lord Byron. 2 vols 1932–3 (priv ptd). The fullest discussion of the issues of the first edns. *See* J. Carter, TLS 27 April, 4 May 1933.
Pratt, W. W. Byron and his circle: a calendar of manuscripts in the University of Texas Library. Austin 1948.
Young, I. D. A concordance to the poetry of Byron. 4 vols Austin 1975.

Collections

The poetical works of Lord Byron. 2 vols Philadelphia 1813, Boston 1814, 3 vols New York 1815, Philadelphia 1815, 2 vols 1815, 4 vols 1815, 1815, 3 vols Philadelphia 1816, 5 vols 1817, New York 1817, Philadelphia 1817, 6 vols 1818; vol 7, 1819, vol 8, 1820; 6 vols Paris 1818, Zwickau 1818–19, 13 vols Leipzig 1818–22, 3 vols 1819, 6 vols Paris 1819, 7 vols Brussels 1819, 4 vols New York 1820, 5 vols 1821, Paris 1821, 16 vols Paris 1822–4 (with life by J. W. Lake), 4 vols 1823, 12 vols Paris 1823, 1823–4 (with life by Sir Cosmo Gordon), 8 vols Philadelphia 1824; vols 5–7, 1824; 30 vols Zwickau 1824–5, 6 vols 1825, 7 vols Paris 1825 (with life by J. W. Lake), 8 vols New York 1825, Philadelphia 1825, 33 vols Zwickau 1825–38, 13 vols Paris 1826, 1826 (with life by Lake), Frankfurt 1826, 6 vols 1827, Paris 1827 (with life by Lake), 4 vols 1828, Paris 1828 (with life by Lake), Frankfurt 1828, 6 vols 1829, 4 vols 1829, 2 vols Philadelphia 1829, 1829, 1829, Frankfurt 1829, 4 vols 1830, 1 vol Paris 1830, Brussels 1830, 6 vols 1831, 1831, Paris 1831 (with abridged life by Lake), Philadelphia 1831 (with life by Lake), 4 vols Paris 1832; The works of Lord Byron, with his letters and journals, and his life by Thomas Moore [ed John Wright] 17 vols 1832–3; 13 vols 1898–1904 (A new revised and enlarged edition: poetry, ed E. H. Coleridge, 7 vols; Letters and journals, ed R. E. Prothero 6 vols), 1904 (Poetical works); [ed E. H. Coleridge] 1905.
Poetical works. Oxford 1896, 1904, 1945 (OSA), 1970 (rev J. D. Jump, with addns).
Selections from poetry, letters and journals. Ed P. C. Quennell 1950 (Nonesuch Lib).
Selected prose. Ed P. Gunn 1972 (Penguin).

§ I

In this section and the following the word 'proof' is used to indicate that the work is known to have been put in type, whether a copy is now extant or not. The word 'counterfeit' is used to indicate edns indistinguishable by normal methods of bibliographical description. Of Byron's earlier works many such were produced for commercial purposes before 1820.

Fugitive pieces. [Newark 1806] (anon); (priv ptd); ed H. Buxton Forman 1886 (facs) ed M. Kessel, New York 1933 (facs).
Poems on various occasions. Newark 1807 (priv ptd). Contains 50 pieces of which 12 are new. Anon.
Hours of idleness: a series of poems, original and translated. Newark 1807 (one counterfeit of larger size—*see* Athenaeum 28 May 1898; T. M. B[lagg], Newark as a publishing town, Newark 1898, pp. 20–35; T. J. Wise, Bibliography vol 1 pp. 9–10), 1822, Glasgow 1825. Contains 39 pieces of which 12 are new.
Poems original and translated: second edition. Newark 1808. Contains 39 pieces of which 5 are new. One counterfeit (*see* Texas exhibition, 1924, pp. 93–7). Rptd as Hours of idleness, Paris 1819, London 1820 (4 edns), Paris 1820, 1822.
The British bards. [Newark 1808] (proof in BM). Largely incorporated in the next entry.
English bards and Scotch reviewers: a satire. [1809] (anon) (2 variants, 3 counterfeits), 1809 ('with considerable additions and alterations'), 1810 (8 counterfeits),

Philadelphia 1811, 1810 (4th edn), (one counterfeit), 1811 (4th edn) (6 counterfeits), Boston 1814; ed J. Murray 1936 (Roxburghe Club) (facs of a copy with Byron's ms notes); 1816 ('with additions'), New York 1817, Paris 1818, 1819, Brussels 1819, Geneva 1820, London 1821, Paris 1821, London 1823, 1823, Glasgow 1824, 1825, London 1825, 1826, 1827, 1827.
Hints from Horace. 1811 (proof in BM). Extracts were pbd by R. C. Dallas in 1824 and by T. Moore in 1830; the full text was first pbd in the 6-vol edn of Works, 1831, vol 5 pp. 273–327.
Childe Harold's pilgrimage: a romaunt [cantos 1–2]. 1812 (5 edns), Philadelphia 1812, 1813 (6th edn), 1814 (7th–8th edns), 1815 (10th edn), Philadelphia 1816 (3rd Amer edn), 1819 (11th edn).
Childe Harold's pilgrimage, canto the third. 1816 (3 issues), Boston 1817, Philadelphia 1817.
Childe Harold's pilgrimage, canto the fourth. 1818 (7 states), New York 1818, 1818, Philadelphia 1818 (with other poems).
Childe Harold's pilgrimage [cantos 1–4]. 2 vols 1819, Leipzig 1820, 1 vol 1825, 2 vols Paris 1825, 1 vol 1826, 1827, Paris 1827, 2 vols Brussels 1829; ed A. H. Thompson, Cambridge 1913; ed D. Frew 1918; [cantos iii–iv] ed B. J. Hayes [1932].
Euthanasia. [1812] (proof). First pbd in the 2nd (first 8vo) edn of Childe Harold (cantos i–ii), 1812.
The curse of Minerva. 1812 (priv ptd) (anon), Philadelphia [=London?] 1815, Paris 1818, 1818, 1820, 1821. A slightly different text was first pbd in New Monthly Mag April 1815, as The malediction of Minerva: or the Athenian marble market and rptd under the original title by William Hone in the 8th edn of Poems on his domestic circumstances, 1816.
Waltz: an apostrophic hymn, by Horace Hornem esq. 1813, 1821, 1821, Paris 1821, London 1826.
The Giaour: a fragment of a Turkish tale. 1813, 1813 ('with some additions'), 1813 ('with considerable additions'), Boston 1813, Philadelphia 1813, 1813 (5th edn) ('with considerable additions'), 1813 (6th edn), 1813 (7th edn) ('with some additions'), 1814 (9th–12th edns), 1815 (13th–14th edns), 1825.
The bride of Abydos: a Turkish tale. 1813 (2 issues), 1813 (2nd–5th edns), 1814 (6th–10th edns), Boston 1814, Philadelphia 1814, 1818 (11th edn).
The corsair: a tale. 1814 (3 issues), 1814 (2nd–7th edns), New York 1814, Philadelphia 1814, Boston 1814, Baltimore 1814, 1815 (8th–9th edns), 1818 (10th edn), 1825; ed J. W. Lake, Paris 1830.
Ode to Napoleon Buonaparte. 1814 (anon), 1814 (anon) (2nd–9th edns), Boston 1814, New York 1814, Philadelphia 1814, London 1815 (11th edn), 1816 (12th edn), 1818 (13th edn).
Lara: a tale; Jacqueline: a tale. 1814 (anon, 2 issues; Jacqueline is by Samuel Rogers), 1814 (anon) (2nd–3rd edns), Boston 1814 (anon), 1814 (4th edn, 1st separate and acknowledged edn), New York 1814, 1817 (5th edn).
Hebrew melodies ancient and modern with appropriate symphonies and accompaniments by I. Braham and I. Nathan, the poetry written expressly for the work by Lord Byron. 2 pts [1815], 1 vol 1815 (poetry without the music; 2 issues), Boston 1815, New York 1815, Philadelphia 1815, London 1823, 1825, 1829 (with addns in Fugitive pieces and reminiscences of Lord Byron by I. Nathan); ed T. L. Ashton 1972.
The siege of Corinth: a poem; Parisina: a poem. 1816 (anon), 1816 (2nd–3rd edn) (anon), New York 1816, 1818 (4th edn), 1824, 1826.
The siege of Corinth [alone]. 1824, Paris 1835, Lüneburg 1854, London 1879.
Poems. (John Murray) 1816 (2 issues), 1816 (2nd edn).
The prisoner of Chillon and other poems. 1816 (2 issues), Lausanne 1818, 1822, London 1824.
Monody on the death of the Right Honourable R. B.

Sheridan. 1816 (anon) (2 issues), 1817, 1818.

The lament of Tasso. 1817, 1817 (2nd–5th edns), New York 1817, 1818 (6th edn).

Manfred: a dramatic poem. 1817 (3 issues), 1817 (2nd edn), Philadelphia 1817, New York 1817, 1817, London 1824, 1825, Brussels [c. 1830], London 1863 (as Manfred: a choral tragedy in 3 acts).

Beppo: a Venetian story. 1818 (anon), 1818 (2nd–7th edns), Boston 1818, New York 1818, Paris 1821, London 1825.

Additional stanzas to the first, second and third editions of Beppo. [1818] (single sheet). These were first added to the 4th edn; the 5th edn was the first to bear Byron's name.

Mazeppa: a poem. 1819 (2 issues), Paris 1819, Boston 1819, Paris 1822, London 1824.

Don Juan [cantos 1–2]. 1819 (anon), 1819 (2 more edns), Paris 1819, Philadelphia 1819, London 1820 (3 edns), Paris 1821, London 1822, 1823.

Don Juan: cantos 3, 4 and 5. 1821 (anon), 1821 (4 more edns), Paris 1821, New York 1821, 1822 (rev) (5th edn).

Don Juan: cantos 6, 7 and 8. 1823 (anon), 1823 (2 more edns), Paris 1823, Philadelphia 1823, London 1825.

Don Juan: cantos 9, 10 and 11. 1823 (anon), 1823, Paris 1823, Philadelphia 1823.

Don Juan: cantos 12, 13 and 14. 1823 (anon), 1823 (2 more edns), Paris 1824, New York 1824.

Don Juan: cantos 15 and 16. 1824 (anon), 1824 (2 more edns), Paris 1824.

Dedication to Jon Juan. 1833.

Don Juan [cantos 1–5]. 1822 (4 edns), 1823, 1823, 1824, [1826?]; [Cantos 5–11], 1823; [cantos 1–16], 2 vols 1826, 1826 (3 edns), 1827, 1827, 2 vols 1828, 1828, 1832; ed E. H. Coleridge 1906; ed L. I. Bredvold, New York 1935; ed P. C. Quennell 1949; ed T. G. Steffan and W. W. Pratt 4 vols Austin 1957 (variorum), 1971 (rev), 1 vol 1973 (Penguin).

The beauties of Don Juan. 2 vols 1828.

A letter to [John Murray] on the Rev W. L. Bowles' strictures on the life and writings of Pope. 1821 (2 issues), 1821 (2nd–3rd edns), Paris 1821.

Observations upon Observations: a second letter to John Murray esq on the Rev W. L. Bowles' strictures on the life and writings of Pope. 1821 (proof; no copy extant). First pbd in Works of Lord Byron, ed John Wright vol 6, 1932.

The Irish avatar. [1821] (priv ptd). The only copy known is in BM (Ashley Library). See Athenaeum 26 June 1909. First pbd by Thomas Medwin in his Conversations of Lord Byron, 1824.

Marino Faliero, Doge of Venice: an historical tragedy in five acts, with notes; The prophecy of Dante: a poem. 1821 (2 issues), 1821 (2nd edn), 1823 (3rd edn).

The prophecy of Dante [alone]. Paris 1821, Philadelphia 1821, London 1825.

Sardanapalus: a tragedy; The two Foscari: a tragedy; Cain: a mystery. 1821, Boston 1822.

Sardanapalus [alone]. Paris 1822, New York 1822, London 1823, [c. 1825], 1829, Arnsberg 1849, London [1853] (adapted for representation by Charles Kean).

The two Foscari [alone]. Paris 1822, New York 1822.

Cain [alone]. 1822 (6 edns), Paris 1822, New York 1822, London 1824; ed T. G. Steffan, Austin 1969.

Heaven and earth. [1821] (proof; no copy extant), Paris 1823 (anon), London 1824 (anon), 1825, [c.1825]. First pbd in Liberal no 2 1823.

The vision of judgement. Paris 1822, London 1822 (with Southey's Vision of judgement, as The two visions), New York 1823, London 1824 (anon), [c. 1830] (anon); ed E. M. Earl 1929; ed F. B. Pinion 1958. First pbd in Liberal no 1 1822.

The age of bronze: or carmen seculare et annus haud mirabilis. 1823 (anon), 1823 (2nd–3rd edns), Paris 1823, New York 1823, London 1824, 1825.

The island: or Christian and his comrades. 1823, 1823

(2nd–3rd edns), Paris 1823, New York 1823, London 1826, 1826.

Werner: a tragedy. 1823 (2 issues), Paris 1823, Philadelphia 1823.

The deformed transformed: a drama. 1824 (2 variants), 1824 (2nd–3rd edns), Paris 1824, Philadelphia 1824.

The parliamentary speeches of Lord Byron, printed from copies prepared by his Lordship for publication. 1824.

A political ode. 1880. I.e. An ode to the framers of the Frame Bill. First pbd in Morning Chron 2 March 1812.

A version of Ossian's address to the sun. Cambridge Mass [1898] (priv ptd); rptd Atlantic Monthly Dec 1898.

Letters and Journals

Correspondence of Lord Byron with a friend, including letters to his mother written from Portugal, Spain, Greece and the shores of the Mediterranean in 1809, 1810 and 1811. Ed R. C. Dallas [1824] (suppressed before pbn), 3 vols Paris 1825, 2 vols Philadelphia 1825.

Letters and journals of Lord Byron, with notices of his life by Thomas Moore. 2 vols 1830, New York [1830], 1 vol Paris 1831, 3 vols 1832, 1833, 1 vol 1837, 1847 (as The life of Lord Byron with his letters and journals), 1850, 1860 (as The life, letters and journals of Lord Byron), 1875.

The works of Lord Byron. Vol 1: letters, 1804–13 Ed W. E. Henley 1897. No more pbd.

The works of Lord Byron: letters and journals. Ed R. E. Prothero [Baron Ernle] 6 vols 1898–1904.

Lord Byron's correspondence, chiefly with Lady Melbourne, Mr Hobhouse, the Hon Douglas Kinnaird and P. B. Shelley. 2 vols 1922.

The Ravenna journal, mainly compiled at Ravenna in 1821. Ed Lord Ernle [R. E. Prothero] 1928 (First Editions Club) (priv ptd).

Origo, I. The last attachment. 1949, 1962. 139 Italian letters.

Quennell, P. C. A self portrait: letters and diaries. 2 vols 1950. 56 unpbd letters and 36 first pbd in full.

Cline, C. L. Byron, Shelley and their Pisan circle. Cambridge Mass 1952. 29 letters.

Selected letters. Ed J. Barzun, New York 1953.

Lovell, E. J. His very self and voice: collected conversations of Lord Byron. New York 1954.

Letters and journals. Ed L. A. Marchand 7 vols 1973–. First complete edn.

Pieces First Published in Periodicals and in Books by Other Writers

Hobhouse, J. C. Imitations and translations from the ancient and modern classics. 1809. Pp. 185–230. 9 poems.

[Review of Gell's Geography of Ithaca]. Monthly Rev Aug 1811.

An ode to the framers of the Frame Bill. Morning Chron 2 March 1812; rptd separately as A political ode, 1880.

Stanzas on a lady weeping. Morning Chron 7 March 1812; rptd in Corsair, 1814 (2nd edn).

Address spoken at the opening of Drury Lane Theatre. Morning Chron 12 Oct 1912; rptd in Genuine rejected addresses, presented to the committee of management for Drury Lane Theatre, preceded by that written by Lord Byron, 1812.

Napoleon's farewell. Examiner 30 July 1815; rptd in Poems, 1816.

'We do not curse thee, Waterloo'. Morning Chron 15 March 1816; rptd in Poems, 1816.

[Translations from the Armenian: the epistle of the Corinthians to St Paul etc]. A grammar, Armenian and English, by Yarouthiun Augerean. Venice 1819, 1832, 1873.

'Maid of Athens, ere we part'. In H. W. Williams, Travels in Italy, Greece and the Ionian Isles, Edinburgh 1820. Vol 2, p. 290. *See* TLS 10 Dec 1931.

The vision of judgement; Letter to my grandmother's review; Epigrams on Lord Castlereagh. Liberal no 1, 15 Oct 1822.

Heaven and earth: a mystery; 'Aegle, beauty and poet'; translation from Martial; 'Why how now, Saucy Tom?'. Liberal no 2, 1 Jan 1823.

The blues: a literary eclogue. Liberal no 3, 26 April 1823.

Morgante Maggiore di Messer Luigi Pulci. Liberal no 4, 30 July 1823.

Foscolo, Ugo. In his Essays on Petrarch, 1823. Pp. 215–17.

On this day I complete my 36th year. Morning Chron 29 Oct 1824.

Remember thee (1st edn only); Stanzas to the Po; The Irish Avatar. In T. Medwin, Conversations of Lord Byron at Pisa, 1824 (3 edns).

[Stanzas omitted from Childe Harold, canto 2]. In R. C. Dallas, Recollections of the life of Lord Byron, 1824.

Verses written in compliance with a lady's request to contribute to her album. Casket 1829.

Lines on hearing that Lady Byron was ill. New Monthly Mag Aug 1832; rptd with the next 2 entries in M. Gardiner, Countess of Blessington, Conversations of Lord Byron, 1834.

Newstead Abbey. In J. T. Hodgson, Memoir of the Rev Francis Hodgson vol 2, 1878. P. 187.

Last words on Greece. Murray's Mag Feb 1887.

'I watched thee when the foe was at our side'. Ibid.

Pratt, W. W. Byron at Southwell. Austin 1948.

—— An Italian notebook of Lord Byron. SE 28 1949.

—— 'To these ladies': an unpublished poem by Byron. Ed W. Pafford, Keats-Shelley Jnl 1 1952.

§2

Hobhouse, J. C. (Baron Broughton). A journey through Albania and other provinces of Turkey. 1813, 2 vols 1813, 1855 (as Travels in Albania).

—— Lord Byron's residence in Greece. Westminster Rev 2 1824.

—— [Review of Dallas's Recollections and Medwin's Conversations]. Westminster Rev 3 1824.

—— Italy: remarks made in several visits from 1816 to 1854. 2 vols 1859.

—— Recollections of a long life. 5 vols 1865 (priv ptd) (reviewed in Edinburgh Rev 133 1871), 6 vols 1909–11.

—— Contemporary account of the separation of Lord and Lady Byron, also of the destruction of Lord Byron's memoirs. 1870 (priv ptd); rptd in Recollections of a long life, 2nd edn vol 2.

A narrative of the circumstances which attended the separation of Lord and Lady Byron. 1816.

A catalogue of books the property of a nobleman [Byron] about to leave England, which will be sold by auction by [Robert H. Evans]. 5 April [1816].

[Beyle, M. H.] Rome, Naples et Florence en 1817 par M. de Stendhal. Paris 1817; tr 1818.

—— Lord Byron en Italie et en France. Revue de Paris March 1830; rptd in his Racine et Shakespeare, Paris 1854; tr as Reminiscences of Lord Byron in Italy, Mirror of Lit 17–24 April 1830.

Hazlitt, W. In his Lectures on the English poets, 1818.

—— In his Spirit of the age, 1825.

Medwin, T. Journal of the conversations of Lord Byron at Pisa. 1824 (3 edns).

Dallas, R. C. Recollections of the life of Lord Byron 1808–14. 1824.

Lake, J. W. The life of Lord Byron. Paris 1826, Frankfurt 1827. First pbd in Galignani's edn of the Works of Lord Byron, Paris 1822.

Catalogue of the library of the late Lord Byron, which will be sold at auction by R. H. Evans, 16 July 1827. Ed

G. H. Doane, [Lincoln Nebraska] 1929 (priv ptd).

Hunt, J. H. L. Lord Byron and some of his contemporaries. 1828, 2 vols 1828.

—— Autobiography. 3 vols 1850, 1 vol 1860 (rev); ed R. Ingpen 2 vols 1903.

Moore, T. Letters and journals of Lord Byron, with notices of his life. 2 vols 1830, New York [1830], 1 vol Paris 1831, 3 vols 1832, 1833, 1 vol 1837, 1847, 1850, 6 vols 1851, 1 vol 1860, 1875.

Galt, J. The life of Lord Byron. 1830, [1908].

Blessington, Countess of. Conversations of Lord Byron. 1834, 1893 (rev); ed E. J. Lovell, Princeton 1969.

Trelawny, E. J. Recollections of the last days of Shelley and Byron. 1858; ed E. Dowden 1906; ed J. E. Morpurgo 1952, New York 1961.

—— Records of Shelley, Byron and the author. 2 vols 1878, 1 vol 1887, 1905.

—— The relations of P. B. Shelley with his two wives and a comment on the character of Lord Byron. 1920 (priv ptd).

—— The relations of Lord Byron and Augusta Leigh. 1920 (priv ptd).

Guiccioli, Teresa, Countess of (Mme de Boissy). Lord Byron jugé par les témoins de sa vie. Paris 1868; tr 1869, New York 1869.

Stowe, H. B. The true story of Lady Byron's married life. Macmillan's Mag Sept 1869.

—— Lady Byron vindicated: a history of the Byron controversy.

Arnold, M. In his Essays in Criticism ser 2, 1888. Rptd from The poetry of Byron, 1881.

Ker, W. P. Byron: an Oxford lecture. Criterion 2 1923; rptd in his Collected essays vol i, 1925.

Byron the poet: essays by Viscount Haldane, A. T. Quiller-Couch, H. J. C. Grierson, William Archer, Marie Corelli etc. Ed W. A. Briscoe 1924.

Garrod, H. W. Byron. Oxford 1924.

Nicolson, H. Byron: the last journey. 1924, 1934, 1940 (rev and enlarged), 1948.

—— The poetry of Byron. 1943.

Quennell, P. C. Byron. 1934.

—— Byron, the years of fame. 1935, 1967.

—— Byron in Italy. 1941, 1951.

Origo, I. Allegra. 1935.

—— The last attachment. 1949, 1962.

Eliot, T. S. In From Anne to Victoria, ed B. Dobrée 1937.

Wilson Knight, G. The two eternities. In his Burning oracle, 1939.

—— Byron: Christian virtues. 1953.

—— Byron's dramatic prose. Nottingham 1953.

—— Lord Byron's marriage. 1957.

—— Byron and Shakespeare. 1966.

Stoll, E. E. Heroes and villains: Shakespeare, Middleton, Byron, Dickens. RES 18 1942.

Pinto, V. de S. Byron and liberty. Nottingham 1944.

Bewley, M. The colloquial mode of Byron. Scrutiny 16 1949.

Straumann, H. Byron and Switzerland. Nottingham 1949.

Vincent, E. R. Byron, Hobhouse and Foscolo. Cambridge 1949.

Butler, E. M. Goethe and Byron. Nottingham 1950.

James, D. G. Byron and Shelley. Nottingham 1951.

Read, H. Byron. 1951.

Cline, C. L. Byron, Shelley and their Pisan circle. Cambridge Mass 1952.

Robson, W. W. Byron as poet. Proc Br Acad 43 1957; rptd in his Critical essays, 1966.

Marchand, L. A. Byron: a biography. 3 vols New York 1958.

—— Byron's poetry: a critical introduction. Boston 1965.

—— Byron: a portrait. 1971.

Melchiori, G. Byron and Italy. Nottingham 1958.

West, P. Byron and the spoiler's art. New York 1960.

—— (ed). Byron: a collection of critical essays. Englewood Cliffs NJ 1963.

Moore, D. L. The late Lord Byron. 1961. On his reputation.

—— Lord Byron: account rendered. 1974.

Thorsley, P. L. The Byronic hero: types and prototypes. Minneapolis 1962.

Rutherford, A. Byron: a critical study. 1962.

—— (ed). Byron: the critical heritage. 1970.

Dobrée, B. Byron's dramas. Nottingham 1962.

Auden, W. H. Don Juan. In his Dyer's hand, 1963.

Joseph, M. K. Byron the poet. 1964.

Gleckner, R. F. Byron and the ruins of paradise. Baltimore 1967.

Barton, A. Byron and the mythology of fact. Nottingham 1968.

McGann, J. J. Fiery dust: Byron's poetic development. Chicago 1969.

PERCY BYSSHE SHELLEY
1792–1822

Mss of most of Shelley's verse and prose of 1817–22 have survived and are scattered in public and private collections throughout Britain and America. The principal collections are located in: (1) Bodley: 22 notebooks and boxes, including substantial parts in Shelley's or Mary Shelley's hand of Laon and Cythna, Rosalind and Helen, Julian and Maddalo, Prometheus unbound, Peter Bell III, Swellfoot, Sensitive plant, Epipsychidion, Witch of Atlas, Adonais, Hellas, Charles I, Triumph of life, trns from Euripides, Goethe and Calderón, Speculations on morals and metaphysics, Coliseum, On manners of the antients, Essay on Christianity, Defence of poetry; microfilms of this collection are at Duke University. (2) Huntington Library: 3 notebooks (see Note books of Shelley, ed H. B. Forman, Boston 1911, below) including drafts of Mask of anarchy, Vision of the sea, Cyprian, Una favola: 3 poems in Mary Shelley's hand, and Hellas in E. Williams's hand. (3) Houghton Library Harvard Univ: a fair-copy notebook, and 7 poems. (4) Pforzheimer Library: the Esdaile notebook of early poems, over 30 other poems and fragments, and A philosophical view of reform. (5) BM: Masque of anarchy (Wise ms) and 12 minor poems and fragments; transcripts at Duke University. (6) Pierpont Morgan Library: Julian and Maddalo, and 4 other poems. (7) Library of Congress: Mask of anarchy (Hunt ms) and minor prose. (8) Eton College Library: 6 poems and fragments. The letters are also widely scattered (see F. L. Jones, Letters, 1964, below).

Bibliographies

Forman, H. B. The Shelley library, i: Shelley's own books, pamphlets and broadsides; posthumous separate issues; and posthumous books wholly or mainly by him. 1886 (Shelley Soc). No pt 2 pbd.

Ellis, F. S. An alphabetical table of contents to Shelley's poetical works. 1888 (Shelley Soc).

—— A lexical concordance to the poetical works of Shelley. 1892 (also in 2 vols), Tokyo 1963 (with appendix by T. Saito).

Wise, T. J. A Shelley library. 1924 (priv ptd).

Ricci, S. de. A bibliography of Shelley's letters, published and unpublished. Paris 1927 (priv ptd).

Weaver, B. In English Romantic poets: a review of research, ed T. M. Raysor, New York 1950, 1956 (rev).

The Keats-Shelley journal. New York 1952–. Contains annual bibliography.

Cameron, K. N. (ed). The Carl H. Pforzheimer library: Shelley and his circle 1773–1822. 6 vols Cambridge Mass 1961–73. Catalogue, full texts and commentary.

Collections

The poetical works. Ed M. W. Shelley 4 vols 1839 (prints Queen Mab with omissions), 1 vol 1840 (en-graved title-page dated 1839; adds Swellfoot, Peter Bell III, and Queen Mab complete).

The works. Ed M. W. Shelley 1847, 1854. Comprises Poetical works, above, and Essays and letters from abroad, with separate pagination.

The poetical works: including various additional pieces from ms and other sources, the text carefully revised, with notes and a memoir by W. M. Rossetti. 2 vols 1870, 1 vol [1870] (unannotated edn), 3 vols 1878 (rev).

The poetical works. Ed H. B. Forman 4 vols 1876–7, 1882 (with notes by M. W. Shelley), 2 vols 1882 (without notes), 1886, 1892, 5 vols 1892 (Aldine).

The prose works. Ed H. B. Forman 4 vols 1880.

Complete poetical works. Ed T. Hutchinson, Oxford 1904 (OSA), 1970 (rev G. M. Matthews).

Complete poetical works. Ed N. Rogers 4 vols Oxford 1972–.

§1

Zastrozzi: a romance by P.B.S. 1810, 1839; ed P. Hartnoll 1955 (priv ptd); ed E. Chesser 1965.

Original poetry by Victor and Cazire [P.B. and Elizabeth Shelley]. Worthing 1810; ed R. Garnett 1898; ed S. J. Looker in his Shelley, Trelawny and Henley, Worthing 1950 (photofacs).

Posthumous fragments of Margaret Nicholson: being poems found amongst the papers of that noted female who attempted the life of the king in 1786. Ed John Fitzvictor, Oxford 1810; ed H. B. Forman [1877] (priv ptd). Ed Shelley.

St Irvyne or the Rosicrucian: a romance, by a gentleman of the University of Oxford. 1811 (reissue dated 1822), 1840.

The necessity of atheism [anon, by T. J. Hogg and Shelley]. Worthing [1811], London 1906; ed S. J. Looker in his Shelley, Trelawny and Henley, Worthing 1950 (photofacs); ed E. Chesser 1965.

A poetical essay on the existing state of things, by a gentleman of the University of Oxford. [1811]. No known copy.

An address to the Irish people. Dublin 1812; ed T. J. Wise 1886 (Shelley Soc), 1890.

Proposals for an association of those philanthropists, who convinced of the inadequacy of the moral and political state of Ireland to produce benefits which are nevertheless attainable, are willing to unite to accomplish its regeneration. Dublin [1812].

Declaration of rights. [Dublin 1812]. 2 copies of this anon broadside are in the Public Record Office. Rptd in Republican 24 Sept 1819, in Philobiblon Soc Miscellany 12 1868–9, and in Fifty major documents of the nineteenth century, ed L. L. Snyder, Princeton 1955.

The Devil's walk: a ballad. [Barnstaple? 1812]. Pbd as anon broadside; one copy in Public Records Office, one at Univ of Texas. Rptd by W. M. Rossetti, Fortnightly Rev 1 Jan 1871.

A letter to Lord Ellenborough. [1812] (priv ptd), (one copy in Bodley); [ed J. M. Wheeler] 1883; ed T. J. Wise 1887, (Shelley Soc) 1894.

A vindication of natural diet: being one in a series of notes to Queen Mab, a philosophical poem. 1813; [ed H. S. Salt and W. E. A. Axon] 1884; 1884 (Shelley Soc), 1886, 1922.

Queen Mab: a philosophical poem, with notes. 1813 (priv ptd). Numerous unauthorized edns 1821–57, including 1821 (Clark's edn, some copies bowdlerized), 1821 (Benbow's, with false New York imprint), 1822 (Carlile's, some copies without the notes), 1823, 1826, 1829 (Brooks's), 1830 (S. Hunt's bowdlerized edn), New York 1831, London 1847 (Watson's).

A refutation of deism, in a dialogue. 1814 (anon); rptd in Theological Inquirer March–April 1815.

[Review of] Hogg's Memoirs of Prince Haimatoff. Critical Rev 6 1814 (anon); ed T. J. Wise 1886, 1886 (rev)

(Shelley Soc); rptd in Memoirs of Prince Haimatoff, ed S. Scott 1952 (Folio Soc).

Alastor: or the spirit of solitude, and other poems. 1816; ed H. B. Forman 1876 (priv ptd); ed B. Dobell 1885, 1887 (Shelley Soc).

A proposal for putting reform to the vote throughout the kingdom, by the Hermit of Marlow. 1817; ed H. B. Forman 1887 (facs of holograph ms) (Shelley Soc).

An address to the people on the death of Princess Charlotte, by the Hermit of Marlow. [1817], [1843?] ('facsimile reprint', but no copy known of supposed 1817 edn; ptd from a ms?), Edinburgh 1883 (priv ptd).

Remarks on 'Mandeville' and Mr Godwin, by E.K. ['Elfin Knight', i.e. Shelley]. Examiner 28 Dec 1817; rptd by Medwin, Athenaeum 27 Oct 1832.

History of a six weeks' tour through a part of France, Switzerland, Germany and Holland; with letters descriptive of a sail round the Lake of Geneva, and of the glaciers of Chamouni [by Shelley and M. W. Shelley]. 1817 (anon; reissued 1829); ed C. I. Elton 1894 (abridged).

Laon and Cythna, or the revolution of the golden city: a vision of the nineteenth century in the stanza of Spenser. 1818. Suppressed, rev and reissued as The revolt of Islam: a poem in twelve cantos, 1818 (a few copies dated 1817; reissued 1829).

Rosalind and Helen: a modern eclogue; with other poems. 1819; ed H. B. Forman 1876 (priv ptd); ed H. B. Forman 1888 (Shelley Soc).

The Cenci: a tragedy in five acts. 1819 (ptd in Italy), 1821, 1827 (Benbow's unauthorized edn); ed A. and H. B. Forman 1886 (Shelley Soc).

Prometheus unbound: a lyrical drama in four acts, with other poems. 1820; ed L. J. Zillman, Seattle 1959.

Oedipus tyrannus or Swellfoot the tyrant: a tragedy in two acts, translated from the original Doric. 1820 (anon; edn suppressed); ed H. B. Forman [1876], [1884].

Epipsychidion: verses addressed to the noble and unfortunate Lady Emilia V—— now imprisoned in the convent of ——. 1821 (anon, withdrawn); ed H. B. Forman 1876 (priv ptd); ed R. A. Potts 1887 (Shelley Soc) (introd by S. A. Brooke).

Adonais: an elegy on the death of John Keats, author of Endymion, Hyperion etc. Pisa 1821, Cambridge 1829; [ed H. B. Forman 1877] (priv ptd); ed T. J. Wise 1886, 1886, 1887 (rev) (Shelley Soc); ed W. M. Rossetti, Oxford 1890; ed W. M. Rossetti, rev A. O. Prickard 1903, 1904 (facs).

Hellas: a lyrical drama. 1822; ed T. J. Wise 1886, 1886, 1887 (Shelley Soc).

Poetical pieces by the late Percy Bysshe Shelley: containing Prometheus unmasked, a lyrical drama, with other poems; Hellas: a lyrical drama; The Cenci: a tragedy in five acts; Rosalind and Helen: with other poems. 1823. A reissue of the first edns (second edn of Cenci) with a new title-page; some copies omit Hellas.

Posthumous poems. [Ed M. W. Shelley] 1824. Suppressed.

The masque of anarchy: a poem now first published, with a preface by Leigh Hunt. 1832, 1842; ed H. B. Forman 1887 (Shelley Soc) (photofacs of the holograph ('Wise') ms); ed T. J. Wise 1892 (facs of 1832 edn) (Shelley Soc).

The Shelley papers: memoir by T. Medwin and original poems and papers by Shelley. 1833, 1844. Original material rptd from Athenaeum 28 July, 11, 25 Aug, 1–29 Sept, 20–7 Oct, 10–24 Nov, 8 Dec (by T. F. Kelsall) 1832, 20 April 1833; adds one spurious poem.

Essays, letters from abroad, translations and fragments. Ed M. W. Shelley 2 vols 1840, Philadelphia 1840, London 1841, 1 vol 1845, 2 vols 1852, 1856. First pbn of A defence of poetry.

Shelley memorials, from authentic sources; to which is added An essay on Christianity. Ed Lady Shelley [and R. Garnett] 1859, 1859, Boston 1859, London 1862 ('2nd edn'), 1875 ('3rd edn').

Relics of Shelley. Ed R. Garnett 1862.

The daemon of the world: the first part as published in 1816 with Alastor; the second part deciphered and now printed from his manuscript revision and interpolations in the newly discovered copy of Queen Mab. Ed H. B. Forman 1876 (priv ptd).

To the Nile; and Shelley fragments. St James Mag March 1876. Pt of Essay on Christianity.

Notes on sculptures in Rome and Florence together with a Lucianic fragment and a criticism on Peacock's poem Rhododaphne. Ed H. B. Forman 1879 (priv ptd) (from ms).

[Fragment of a satire on satire]. Ed E. Dowden in his Correspondence of Robert Southey with Caroline Bowles, 1881.

The wandering Jew [or The victim of the eternal avenger]. Ed B. Dobell 1887 (Shelley Soc). Text conflated from extracts in Edinburgh Literary Jnl 20, 27 June, 4 July, 26 Dec 1829 and from text 'in a complete state' in Fraser's Mag July 1831.

An examination of the Shelley manuscripts in the Bodleian Library, by C. D. Locock. Oxford 1903. New and corrected texts.

Shelley's prose in the Bodleian manuscripts. Ed A. H. Koszul, Oxford 1910.

Note books of Shelley, from the originals in the library of W. K. Bixby [now in Huntington Lib], deciphered, transcribed and edited, with a full commentary, by H. Buxton Forman. 3 vols Boston 1911 (priv ptd).

A philosophical view of reform. Ed T. W. Rolleston, Oxford 1920; ed W. E. Peck 1930 (priv ptd); ed R. J. White in his Political tracts of Wordsworth, Coleridge and Shelley, Cambridge 1953.

New fragments by Shelley. Ed E. Gosse, TLS 24 Feb 1921. Verses from mss now at Eton College.

Inédits italiens de Shelley. [Ed] A. Koszul, Revue de Littérature Comparée 2 1922.

[Prose fragment on the resettlement of the Jews]. Ed T. Saito, in The Shelley memorial volume by members of the English Club, Imperial University of Tokyo, Tokyo 1923. With photofacs of ms, which was probably destroyed in 1945–6.

The celandine. Ed W. E. Peck, Boston Herald 21 Dec 1925; ed E. H. Blakeney, Winchester 1927 (priv ptd).

An unpublished ballad by Shelley ['Young parson Richards']. Ed W. E. Peck, PQ 5 1926; ed Peck, Iowa City 1926 (priv ptd).

The Shelley notebook in the Harvard Library. Ed G. E. Woodberry, Cambridge Mass 1929 (photofacs).

On the vegetable system of diet. Ed R. Ingpen 1929 (priv ptd); rptd in his Verse and prose from the mss, 1934, below; 1940, 1947.

Plato's Banquet translated from the Greek: a discourse on the manners of the antient Greeks relative to the subject of love; also A preface to the Banquet. Ed R. Ingpen 1931 (priv ptd) (from ms). See Shelley's translations from Plato, below.

Verse and prose from the manuscripts of Shelley. Ed J. C. E. Shelley-Rolls and R. Ingpen 1934 (priv ptd).

Sadak the wanderer: an unknown Shelley poem. Ed D. Cook, TLS 16 May 1936. Rptd from Keepsake 1828.

A Shelley letter. Ed E. H. Blakeney, Winchester 1936 (priv ptd). Verse letter to Fergus Graham.

[Verses from Claire Clairmont's journal]. In N. I. White, Shelley vol 2, New York 1940; ed L. Robertson, MLR 47 1953.

[Translation from Aristotle, Ethics IX viii]. In Shelley at Oxford, ed W. S. Scott 1944 (priv ptd).

Unpublished fragments by Shelley and Mary. Ed F. L. Jones, SP 45 1948. On miracles and the game laws.

Shelley's translations from Plato: a critical edition. Ed J. A. Notopoulos in his Platonism of Shelley: a study of Platonism and the poetic mind, Durham NC 1949. Includes unpbd material.

[A midsummer night's dream poem]. Ed N. Rogers in his Shelley at work, Oxford 1956, 1967 (rev).

[Italian version of Ode to liberty]. Ibid.

Music, when soft voices die. Ed I. Massey, JEGP 59 1960.

A new text of Shelley's scene for Tasso. Ed G. M. Matthews, Keats-Shelley Memorial Bull 11 1960.

The triumph of life: a new text. Ed G. M. Matthews, Studia Neophilologica 32 1960.

The triumph of life apocrypha. Ed G. M. Matthews, TLS 5 Aug 1960.

[An incitement to Satan]. Ed G. M. Matthews, Stand 5 1960. A poem.

[The pursued and the pursuer]. Ed G. M. Matthews, ibid. A poem.

Shelley and Dante: an essay in textual criticism. J. L. de Palacio, Revue de Littérature Comparée 35 1961. New text of Shelley's trn of Dante's Convito.

Shelley traducteur de Dante: le chant xxviii du Purgatoire. Ed J. L. de Palacio, Revue de Littérature Comparée 36 1962. Commentary in French.

Time: an unpublished sequel. Ed I. Massey, Stud in Romanticism 2 1962.

The Esdaile notebook: a volume of early poems. Ed K. N. Cameron, New York 1964, London 1964 (rev); ed N. Rogers as The Esdaile poems, Oxford 1966.

Reiman, D. H. Shelley's The triumph of life: a critical study based on a text newly edited from the Bodleian ms. Urbana 1965.

New texts of Shelley's Plato. Ed J. A. Notopoulos, Keats-Shelley Jnl 15 1966.

Letters

Prose works. Ed H. B. Forman 4 vols 1880. The first

Letters to William Godwin. Ed T. J. Wise 2 vols 1891 (priv ptd).

Letters to Leigh Hunt. Ed T. J. Wise 2 vols 1894 (priv ptd).

Letters to T. J. Hogg. Ed T. J. Wise with notes by W. M. Rossetti and H. B. Forman 1897 (priv ptd).

Letters. Ed R. Ingpen 2 vols 1909, 1912 (adds 5 letters), 1914 (rev) (Bohn's Lib).

The Shelley correspondence in the Bodleian Library. Ed R. H. Hill, Oxford 1926.

Complete works: correspondence. Ed R. Ingpen 1926. Vols 8–10 of the Julian edn.

Letters, selected by R. B. Johnson. 1929.

Shelley's lost letters to Harriet. Ed L. Hotson 1930.

New Shelley letters. Ed W. S. Scott 1948.

Shelley and his circle 1773–1822. Ed K. N. Cameron, D. Reiman et al 6 vols Cambridge Mass 1961–73.

Letters. Ed F. L. Jones 2 vols Oxford 1964. First complete edn.

§2

Medwin, T. Journal of the conversations of Lord Byron, noted during a residence with his Lordship at Pisa in the years 1821 and 1822. 1824 (3 edns).

—— The Shelley papers: memoir of Shelley. 1833, 1844.

—— Life of Shelley. 2 vols 1847; ed H. B. Forman Oxford 1913 ('from a copy copiously amended and extended by the author').

Hunt, L. Lord Byron and some of his contemporaries. 1828, 2 vols 1828 (rev), 3 vols Paris 1828.

—— In his Autobiography, 3 vols 1850.

—— In his Correspondence, ed [T. Hunt] 2 vols 1862.

Moore, T. In his Letters and journals of Lord Byron, with notices of his life, 2 vols 1830, 1875 (rev).

Lewes, G. H. Shelley. Westminster Rev 35 1841; partly rptd in his Literary criticism, ed A. R. Kaminsky, Lincoln Nebraska 1964.

Browning, R. In Letters of Shelley, 1852. The letters were forged and the edn suppressed. Browning's introd ed W. T. Harden, 1888 (Shelley Soc); ed R. Garnett 1903, Boston 1911; ed H. F. B. Brett-Smith, Oxford 1921, 1923.

Bagehot, W. In his Estimates of some Englishmen and Scotchmen, 1858; rptd in his Literary studies vol 1, ed R. H. Hutton, 1879 and in his Collected works vol 1, ed N. St John-Stevas 1965.

Hogg, T. J. Life of Shelley. 2 vols 1858; ed E. Dowden 1906.

—— Shelley at Oxford. Ed R. A. Streatfeild 1904. Chs 3, 5–8 of his Life, above.

Peacock, T. L. Memoirs of Shelley. Fraser's Mag June 1858, Jan, March 1860, March 1862; ed H. F. B. Brett-Smith, Oxford 1909; rptd in his Works, ed Brett-Smith and C. E. Jones vol 8, 1934.

—— On the portraits of Shelley. 1911.

Trelawny, E. J. Recollections of the last days of Shelley and Byron. 1858, Boston 1858; ed E. Dowden 1906, Oxford 1923, 1931; ed J. E. Morpurgo, 1952 (Folio Soc) ('with additions from contemporary sources').

—— Records of Shelley, Byron and the author. 2 vols 1878, 1 vol 1887, [1905].

—— Letters. Ed H. B. Forman, Oxford 1910.

Symonds, J. A. Shelley. 1878, 1887 (rev), 1902, 1925 (EML).

Stephen, L. Godwin and Shelley. Cornhill Mag March 1879; rptd in his Hours in a library ser 3, 1879.

Dowden, E. Life of Shelley. 2 vols 1886, 1 vol 1896 (rev and abridged); ed H. Read 1951.

Arnold, M. In his Essays in criticism: second series, 1888.

Yeats, W. B. The philosophy of Shelley's poetry [1900]. In his Ideas of good and evil, 1903; rptd in his Essays and introductions, 1961.

—— Prometheus unbound. Spectator 17 March 1933; rptd in his Essays 1931 to 1936, Dublin 1937, and in his Essays and introductions, 1961.

Bradley, A. C. Notes on passages in Shelley. MLR 1 1906.

—— Shelley's view of poetry [1904]. In his Oxford lectures on poetry, 1909.

—— Shelley and Arnold's critique; Odours and flowers in the poetry of Shelley; Coleridge-echoes in Shelley's poems. In his A miscellany, 1929.

Hughes, A. M. D. Shelley's Zastrozzi and St Irvyne. MLR 7 1912.

—— The theology of Shelley. Proc Br Acad 24 1939.

—— The nascent mind of Shelley. Oxford 1947.

—— Alastor: or the spirit of solitude. MLR 43 1948.

—— The triumph of life. Keats-Shelley Memorial Bull 16 1965.

Brailsford, H. N. Shelley, Godwin and their circle. [1913], Oxford 1951 (rev).

Santayana, G. Shelley: or the poetic value of revolutionary principles. In his Winds of doctrine, 1913; rptd in his Essays in literary criticism, ed I. Singer, New York 1956.

White, N. I. Shelley's Swellfoot the tyrant in relation to contemporary political satire. PMLA 36 1921.

—— The unextinguished hearth: Shelley and his contemporary critics. Durham NC 1938.

—— Shelley. 2 vols New York 1940, London 1947 (rev).

—— Portrait of Shelley. New York 1945 (abridged from Shelley, 1940, above).

—— F. L. Jones and K. N. Cameron. An examination of the Shelley legend. Philadelphia 1951.

Gordon, G. S. Shelley and the oppressors of mankind. Proc Br Acad 10 1922; rptd in Selected modern English essays 2nd ser, Oxford 1932 (WC), and in his Discipline of letters, Oxford 1946.

Blunden, E. Shelley and Keats as they struck their contemporaries. 1925.

—— Shelley: a life story. 1946.

Eliot, T. S. Shelley and Keats. In his Use of poetry and use of criticism, 1933.

Hoffman, H. L. An Odyssey of the soul: Shelley's Alastor. New York 1933.

Jones, F. L. The revision of Laon and Cythna. JEGP 32 1933.
— Hogg and the Necessity of atheism. PMLA 52 1937.
— (ed). The letters of Mary Wollstonecraft Shelley. 2 vols Norman Oklahoma 1944.
— (ed). Mary Shelley's journal. Norman Oklahoma 1947.
— Shelley's On life. PMLA 62 1947.
— (ed). Maria Gisborne and Edward E. Williams, Shelley's friends: their journals and letters. Norman Oklahoma 1951.
Leavis, F. R. Revaluations viii: Shelley. Scrutiny 4 1935; rptd in his Revaluation, 1936, and in Critiques and essays in criticism 1920–48, ed R. W. Stallman, New York 1949.
Origo, I. Allegra. 1935.
Read, H. In defence of Shelley and other essays. 1936; rev in his True voice of feeling, 1953.
Lewis, C. S. Shelley, Dryden and Mr Eliot. In his Rehabilitations and other essays, Oxford 1939.
Woolf, V. 'Not one of us'. In her Death of the moth and other essays, 1942.
Scott, W. S. (ed). The Athenians: being correspondence between T. J. Hogg, T. L. Peacock, Leigh Hunt, Shelley and others. 1943 (priv ptd).
— (ed). Harriet and Mary: being the relations between Shelley, Harriet Shelley, Mary Shelley and T. J. Hogg. 1944 (priv ptd).
— (ed). Shelley at Oxford: the early correspondence of Shelley with T. J. Hogg, together with letters of Mary Shelley and T.L. Peacock and a hitherto unpublished prose fragment by Shelley. 1944 (priv ptd).
James. D. G. Purgatory blind. In his Romantic comedy, Oxford 1948.
— Byron and Shelley. Nottingham 1951.
Rogers, N. Keats, Shelley and Rome: an illustrated miscellany. 1949.
— The Shelley-Rolls gift to the Bodleian. TLS 27 July–10 Aug 1949.
— Shelley at work: a critical inquiry. Oxford 1956, 1967 (rev).
Cline, C. L. Byron, Shelley and their Pisan circle. Cambridge Mass 1952.
Davie, D. A. Shelley's urbanity. In his Purity of diction in English verse, 1952; rptd in English Romantic poets: modern essays in criticism, ed M. H. Abrams, New York 1960. Addn, New Statesman 27 Nov 1964.
Abrams, M. H. In his Mirror and the lamp: romantic theory and the critical tradition, New York 1953.
House, H. In his All in due time, 1955.
Matthews, G. M. A volcano's voice in Shelley. ELH 24 1957.
— Comments on recent Shelley studies. REL 2 1961.
— Shelley and Jane Williams. RES new ser 12 1961.
— On Shelley's The triumph of life. Studia Neophilologica 34 1962.
— Julian and Maddalo: the draft and the meaning. Studia Neophilologica 35 1963.
Wasserman, E. R. Shelley: a critical reading. Baltimore 1971.
Chernaik, J. The lyrics of Shelley. Cleveland 1972.
Cameron, K. N. (ed). Shelley: the golden years. Cambridge Mass 1974.
Barcus, J. E. (ed). Shelley: the critical heritage. 1975.

JOHN KEATS

1795–1821

The largest collection of mss is in the Houghton Library at Harvard, though the BM and the Pierpont Morgan Library New York also have important collections. Mss are described in the introd to Poetical works, *ed H. W. Garrod, Oxford 1939, 1958 (rev), and in the appendix to C. L. Finney, The evolution of Keats' poetry, Cambridge Mass 1936, New York 1963 (rev).*

Bibliographies etc

Baldwin, D. L., L. N. Broughton et al. A concordance of the poems of Keats. Washington 1917, Gloucester Mass 1963.
MacGillivray, J. R. A bibliography and reference guide, with an essay on Keats' reputation. Toronto 1949.
Thorpe, C. D. In English romantic poets: a review of research, ed T. M. Raysor, New York 1950, 1956 (rev).
Keats-Shelley journal. 1952–. Contains annual bibliography. Bibliographies to June 1962 rptd as Keats, Shelley, Byron, Hunt and their circles: a bibliography, Lincoln Nebraska 1964.

Collections

Poetical works, chronologically arranged; memoir by Lord Houghton. 1876.
Poetical works and other writings, now first brought together. Ed H. B. Forman 4 vols 1883, 1889 (rev) (Library edn); Poetry and prose, 1890 (suppl vol).
Poetical works. Ed H. B. Forman 1884.
Poems. Ed G. T. Drury, introd by R. Bridges 2 vols 1896, London and New York 1896, nd (ML).
Complete works. Ed H. B. Forman 5 vols Glasgow 1900–1, 1921–4, New York [1900–1].
Poetical works. Ed W. S. Scott, London and New York 1902, 1903; rev G. Sampson, New York 1903.
Poems. Introd by L. Binyon, notes by J. Masefield 1903.
Poems. Ed E. de Selincourt 1905, 1906 (rev).
Poetical works. Ed H. B. Forman, Oxford 1906 etc (OSA).
Poems, arranged in chronological order with a preface by S. Colvin. 2 vols 1915, 1924, 1928.
Poems and verses. Ed J. M. Murry 2 vols 1930, 1 vol New York 1949.
Poetical works. Ed H. W. Garrod Oxford 1939, 1958 (rev with J. Jones). The definitive edn; full critical apparatus.
Poetical works. Ed H. W. Garrod, Oxford 1956 (OSA).
The odes and their earliest known manuscripts. Ed R. Gittings 1970 (with facs).
Poems. Ed M. Allott 1970.
Complete poems. Ed J. Barnard 1973 (Pelican).
Poems. Ed J. Stillinger 1978.

§1

Poems. 1817, 1927 (photo facs), New York 1934 (photo facs).
Endymion: a poetic romance. 1818.
Lamia, Isabella, the Eve of St. Agnes and other poems. 1820; ed M. Robertson, Oxford 1909 (type facs).
Another version of Keats's Hyperion. Rptd by R. M. Milnes from his contribution to Miscellanies of the Philobiblon Society 3 1856–7 (first pbn of The fall of Hyperion: a dream).
Keatsii Hyperionis libri tres. Ed C. Merivale, Cambridge and London 1863 (English with Latin trn; bks 1–2 first pbd 1862); ed J. Hoops, Berlin 1899; Hyperion: a facsimile of Keats's autograph manuscript of The fall of Hyperion, a dream, ed E. de Selincourt, Oxford 1905.
Contributions to periodicals. Only first pbns are listed:
Examiner (ed Leigh Hunt). To Solitude, 5 May 1816; On first looking into Chapman's Homer, 1 Dec 1816; To Kosciusko, 16 Feb 1817; After dark vapours, 23 Feb 1817; Haydon: forgive me, On seeing the Elgin marbles, 9 March 1817; On The floure and the lefe, 16 March 1817; [review of J. H. Reynolds, Peter Bell: a lyrical ballad], 25 April 1819; Lines written in the Highlands, 14 July 1822.
Champion. On the sea, 17 Aug 1817; [dramatic reviews], 21, 28 Dec 1817, 4 Jan 1818. Review of 28 Dec perhaps by J. H. Reynolds; see L. M. Jones, Keats-Shelley Jnl 3 1954.
The literary pocket-book. Ed Leigh Hunt 1819. The human seasons, To Ailsa rock.

Annals of the fine arts. Ode to a nightingale, July 1819; Ode on a Grecian urn, Dec 1819?

Indicator (ed Leigh Hunt). La belle dame sans merci, 10 May 1820; A dream, after reading Dante's episode of Paolo and Francesca, 28 June 1820; The cap and bells [part only], 23 Aug 1820.

The gem: a literary annual (ed Thomas Hood). On a picture of Leander, 1829.

London literary gazette. In a drear-nighted December, 19 Sept 1829.

The comic annual, by Thomas Hood. To a cat, 1830.

Western messenger. Ode to Apollo ('God of the golden bow'), June 1836.

Ladies' companion. Fame like a wayward girl, 'Hither, hither, love', 'Tis the witching hour of night, Aug 1837.

Portsmouth and Devonport weekly journal. To the Nile, 19 July 1838; Written upon the top of Ben Nevis, 6 Sept; Staffa, 20 Sept; Bright star, 27 Sept; The day is gone, 4 Oct; To sleep, 11 Oct; Shed no tear, 18 Oct; Ah! woe is me, 25 Oct; On sitting down to read King Lear once again, 8 Nov; On seeing a lock of Milton's hair, 15 Nov; Old Meg, 22 Nov.

Hood's magazine and comic miscellany. To a lady seen for a few moments at Vauxhall, vol 2 1844; Hush, hush, tread softly, vol 3 1845.

Milnes, R. M. Life, letters and literary remains. 1848. Many poems and letters first pbd here.

Letters, Diaries etc

Life, letters and literary remains. Ed R. M. Milnes 2 vols 1848. See §2, below.

Letters to Fanny Brawne. Ed H. B. Forman 1878, 1889 (rev and enlarged).

Letters of Keats to his family and friends. Ed S. Colvin 1891, 1891, 1918 (rev), 1921, 1925, 1928. Letters to Fanny Brawne omitted.

Letters: complete revised edition. Ed H. B. Forman 1895.

The letters. Ed M. B. Forman 2 vols Oxford 1931, 1 vol Oxford 1935, 1947, 1952 (rev).

The Keats circle: letters and papers 1816–78. Ed H. E. Rollins 2 vols Cambridge Mass 1948.

Selected letters. Ed L. Trilling, New York 1951.

Letters. Ed F. Page, Oxford 1954 (WC); ed R. Gittings, Oxford 1970. Selections.

More letters and poems of the Keats circle. Ed H. E. Rollins, Cambridge Mass 1955.

The letters of Keats 1814–21. Ed H. E. Rollins 2 vols Cambridge Mass 1958. The definitive edn.

§2

Poems, 1817. Champion 9 March 1817 (J. H. Reynolds); European Mag May 1817 (G. F. Mathew); Examiner 1, 6 June, 13 July 1817 (L. Hunt).

Endymion, 1818. Quart Rev 19 1818 (J. W. Croker); Br Critic June 1818; Blackwood's Mag Aug 1818 (J. G. Lockhart); London Mag April 1820; Edinburgh Rev 34 1820 (F. Jeffrey on the Endymion and Lamia vols); Scots Mag Aug 1820.

Lamia, Isabella, The eve of St Agnes and other poems, 1820. Monthly Rev July 1820; New Times 19 July 1820 (C. Lamb); Indicator 2, 9 Aug 1820 (L. Hunt); London Mag Aug 1820; New Monthly Mag Sept 1820; Br Critic Sept 1820; London Mag Sept 1820; Scots Mag Oct 1820.

Shelley, P. B. Adonais. Pisa 1821, Cambridge 1829.

Hunt, L. Lord Byron and some of his contemporaries. 1828.

—— In his Autobiography, with reminiscences of friends and contemporaries, 3 vols 1853.

Milnes, R. M. Life, letters and literary remains of Keats. 2 vols 1848, New York 1848, 1 vol 1867; ed R. Lynd 1927 (EL); Oxford 1931 (WC).

De Quincey, T. In his Essays on the poets and other English writers, Boston 1853.

Arnold, M. Keats. In The English poets, ed T. H. Ward 4 vols 1880; rptd in his Essays in criticism: second series, 1888.

Rossetti, W. M. Life of Keats. 1887.

Colvin, S. Keats. 1887 (EML).

Bridges, R. Keats: a critical essay. 1895.

—— A critical introduction to Keats. Oxford 1929.

Bradley, A. C. The letters of Keats. In his Oxford lectures on poetry, 1909.

Murry, J. M. Keats and Shakespeare: a study of Keats's poetic life from 1816 to 1820. 1925.

—— Studies in Keats. 1930, 1939 (rev and enlarged as Studies in Keats, new and old), 1949 (rev and 're-arranged' as The mystery of Keats), 1955 ('4th edn rev and enlarged' as Keats).

Blunden, E. Shelley and Keats as they struck their contemporaries. 1925.

—— Keats's publisher: a memoir of John Taylor. 1936.

—— John Keats. 1950, 1954 (rev) (Br Council pamphlet).

Garrod, H. W. Keats. Oxford 1926, 1939 (rev).

Ridley, M. R. Keats' craftsmanship: a study in poetic development. Oxford 1933, New York 1962.

Eliot, T. S. In his Use of poetry and use of criticism, 1933.

Bush, D. In his Mythology and the romantic tradition in English poetry, Cambridge Mass 1937.

—— Keats. New York 1966.

Bate, W. J. Negative capability: the intuitive approach in Keats. Cambridge Mass 1939.

—— The stylistic development of Keats. New York 1945.

—— John Keats. Cambridge Mass 1963.

Ford, G. H. Keats and the Victorians. New Haven 1944.

Brooks, C. History without footnotes: an account of Keats' urn. Sewanee Rev 52 1944; rptd in his Well wrought urn, New York 1947.

Rollins, H. E. Fanny Keats: biographical notes. PMLA 59 1944.

—— Keats' reputation in America to 1848. Cambridge Mass 1946.

—— The Keats circle: letters and papers 1816–78. 2 vols Cambridge Mass 1948.

—— More letters and poems of the Keats circle. Cambridge Mass 1955.

Holloway, J. The odes of Keats. Cambridge Jnl April 1952; rptd in his Charted mirror, 1960.

Muir, K. The meaning of Hyperion. EC 2 1952.

—— (ed). Keats: a reassessment. Liverpool 1958.

Trilling, L. The poet as hero: Keats in his letters. In his Opposing self, New York 1955.

Blackstone, B. The consecrated urn: an interpretation of Keats in terms of growth and form. 1959.

Bayley, J. Keats and reality. Proc Br Acad 48 1962.

Laski, M. The language of the nightingale ode. E & S 29 1966.

Jack, I. Keats on the mirror of art. Oxford 1967.

Matthews, G. M. (ed). Keats: the critical heritage. 1971.

Ricks, C. Keats and embarrassment. Oxford 1974.

Stillinger, J. The text of Keats's poems. Cambridge Mass 1974.

JOHN CLARE
1793–1864

Mss by or concerning Clare, some unpbd, are in Peterborough Natural Historical Society Museum; Northampton City Library; BM (letters to Clare); and Pierpont Morgan Library, New York. These collections represent his literary life except 1837–41. Poems written at Northampton Asylum, after 1837, are mostly known in transcripts.

Bibliographies

[Powell, D.] Catalogue of the Clare Collection in the Northampton Public Library. Northampton 1965.

Collections

Poems. Ed J. W. Tibble 2 vols 1935.
Prose. Ed J. W. and A. Tibble 1951.
Letters. Ed J. W. and A. Tibble 1951.

Selections

Clare: poems chiefly from manuscript. Ed E. Blunden and A. Porter 1920.
Madrigals and chronicles: newly found poems by Clare. Ed E. Blunden 1924.
Poems of Clare's madness. Ed G. Grigson 1949.
Selected poems. Ed G. Grigson 1950 (ML).
Selected poems. Ed J. Reeves 1954.
Unpublished poems. Ed E. Robinson and G. Summerfield, Listener 20 March 1962.
Later poems. Ed E. Robinson and G. Summerfield, Manchester 1964.
Selected poems. Ed J. W. and A. Tibble 1965 (EL).
Selected poems and prose. Ed E. Robinson and G. Summerfield, Oxford 1967.

§ 1

Proposals for publishing a collection of trifles in verse. Market Deeping 1817.
Poems descriptive of rural life and scenery. 1820 (3 edns), 1821.
The village minstrel. 2 vols 1821, 1823.
The shepherd's calendar. 1827; ed E. Robinson and G. Summerfield, Oxford 1964 (from mss).
Prospectus: The midsummer cushion. Helpston 1832.
The rural muse. 1835.
Sketches in the life of Clare written by himself. Ed E. Blunden 1930.

§ 2

De Quincey, T. In his Literary reminiscences, Tait's Mag Dec 1840.
Tibble, J. W. and A. Clare: a life. 1932.
—— Clare: his life and poetry. 1956.
Lamb, C. and M. In their Letters, ed E. V. Lucas 3 vols 1935.
Heath-Stubbs, J. Clare and the peasant tradition. Penguin New Writing 32 1937; rptd in his Darkling plain, 1950.
Murry, J. M. In his Clare and other studies, 1950.
Barrell, J. The idea of landscape and the sense of place 1730–1840. Cambridge 1972.
Storey, M. (ed). Clare: the critical heritage. 1973.
Storey, M. The poetry of Clare. 1974.

THOMAS HOOD
1799–1845

Collections

Poems [serious]. 2 vols 1846, 1846, 1851 (4th edn), 1853 (6th edn), 1857 (9th edn), 1858, 1859 etc.
Poems of wit and humour [excluding those in Hood's Own]. 1847, 1849, 1851, 1856 (7th edn), 1860 (9th edn).
Hood's gems. 1861.
Works comic and serious, in prose and verse. Ed with notes by his son [T. Hood jr]. 7 vols 1862–3.
The serious poems. Ed S. Lucas with preface by T. H. the younger [1867], 1870; 2 vols 1876 (with Comic poems, below), 1886; illustr H. G. Fell 1901.
The comic poems. Ed S. Lucas with preface by T. H. the

younger [1867], 2 vols 1876 (with Serious poems), 1885.
Works. Ed his son and daughter [F. F. Broderip]. 10 vols 1869–73 (illustr), 11 vols 1882–4.
Early poems and sketches. Ed his daughter 1869.
[Select poems]. Ed J. B. Payne, illustr G. Doré 1870.
Poetical works. Ed W. M. Rossetti, illustr G. Doré 2 sers [1871–5], [1880].
Poems. Ed A. Ainger 2 vols 1897.
Poems. Ed W. Jerrold, Oxford 1906 (WC).
Selected poems. Ed J. Clubbe, Cambridge Mass 1970.

§ 1

Odes and addresses to great people. 1825 (anon), 1825, 1826. With J. H. Reynolds.
Whims and oddities in prose and verse. 1st ser, 1826, 1829 (4th edn); 2nd ser, 1827, 1829 etc.
National tales. 2 vols 1827.
The plea of the midsummer fairies, Hero and Leander, Lycus the centaur and other poems. 1827.
The Epping hunt. Illustr Cruikshank 1829, 1830, 1889.
The dream of Eugene Aram. Gem 1829; illustr W. Harvey 1831, 1832.
Tylney hall: a novel. 3 vols 1834, 1840, 1857, [1878].
Hood's own: or laughter from year to year [illustr; contains Literary reminiscences]. 1839, 1855; second ser, with preface by his son 1861; [1882] (both sers).
Up the Rhine. 1840, 1840, Frankfrut 1840, New York 1852.
The loves of Sally Brown and Ben the carpenter. [1840?]. A song, 4to, single sheet.
The song of the shirt. Punch Xmas 1843.
Whimsicalities: a periodical gathering, with illustrations by Leech. 2 vols 1844, 1870 (enlarged), [1878].
Lamia: a romance. In W. Jerdan, Autobiography vol 1, 1852. A poem, written c. 1827.
The headlong career and woful ending of precocious piggy. Ed F. F. Broderip, illustr T. H. jr 1859 [1858], [1880].
Fairy land, by the late Thomas and Jane Hood. Ed F. F. Broderip 1861 (for 1860).
Sonnet written in a volume of Shakespeare. Keats-Shelley Jnl 13 1964.

Periodicals edited by Hood

The gem: a literary annual. 1829. Vol 1 only.
The comic annual. 11 vols 1830–42. Literary contributions mainly by Hood. No vol issued 1840–1.
The new monthly magazine. 1841–3.
Hood's magazine. 1–3 1844–5.
The following contain contributions by Hood:
The London magazine. July 1821–July 1823. Ed John Taylor, with Hood as assistant and contributor.
Sporting, with literary contributions by Hood et al. Ed 'Nimrod' (C. J. Apperley) 1838.
The children in the wood. 1865. Preface by Hood.

Letters

Letters of Hood from the Dilke papers in the British Museum. Ed L. A. Marchand, New Brunswick 1945.
Whitley A. Hood and Dickens: some new letters. HLQ 14 1951.
Letters. Ed P. F. Morgan, Edinburgh 1973.

§ 2

Horne, R. H. In his A new spirit of the age vol 2, 1844.
[Broderip, F. F. and T. Hood jr]. Memorials of Hood collected by his daughter, with a preface and notes by his son. 2 vols 1860.
Saintsbury, G. In his Essays in English literature 1780–1860 ser 2, 1895.

Jerrold, W. Hood: his life and times. 1907.
—— Hood and Charles Lamb: the story of a friendship. 1930. Includes reprint of Literary reminiscences.

Blunden, E. Hood's literary reminiscences. In his Votive tablets, 1931.
—— The poet Hood. REL 1 1960.

II. MINOR POETRY 1800–1835

RICHARD HARRIS BARHAM
1788–1845

§ 1

Verses spoken at St Paul's School. 1807. Copy in Bodley.
Baldwin, or a miser's heir: a serio-comic tale, by an old bachelor. 2 vols 1820. In prose.
The Ingoldsby legends: or mirth and marvels, by Thomas Ingoldsby esquire. Illustr G. Cruikshank, J. Leech and J. Tenniel 3 sers 1840–7 (many reissues); ser 3, ed R. H. D. Barham 1847 (with memoir); Philadelphia 1860; ed E. A. Bond 3 vols 1894; illustr A. Rackham 1898, 1907 (rev); ed J. B. Atlay 2 vols 1903; selections ed H. Newbolt [1910], ed J. Tanfield and G. Boas 1951. Many other selections and edns of single legends. First ptd in Bentley's Monthly Miscellany and New Monthly Mag from 1837.
Some account of my cousin Nicholas. 3 vols 1841, 1 vol 1846, 1856. A novel rptd from Blackwood's Mag 1834.
Personal reminiscences by Barham, Harness and Hodder. Ed R. H. Stoddard, New York 1875.
The Ingoldsby lyrics, by Thomas Ingoldsby, edited by his son. 1881. Partly from The Ingoldsby legends, partly from other sources.
The Garrick Club: notices of one hundred and thirty-five of its former members. [New York?] 1896 (priv ptd).

Letters

Barham, R. H. D. The life and letters of Barham. 2 vols 1870, 1 vol 1880, 1899.

§ 2

Horne, R. H. In his A new spirit of the age, 1844.
Saintsbury, G. Three humourists: Hook, Barham, Maginn. In his Essays in English literature 1780–1860 ser 2, 1895.

ROBERT BLOOMFIELD
1766–1823

Collections

The poems of Bloomfield [i.e. The farmer's boy and Rural tales]. Burlington NJ 1803, Wilmington Delaware 1803 (as The farmer's boy; Rural tales etc).
The poems of Bloomfield. 2 vols 1809. With prefaces by Bloomfield.
Collected poems. 2 vols 1817.

§ 1

The farmer's boy: a rural poem. Ed C. Lofft 1800 (3 edns), 1801, New York 1801, Philadelphia 1801, Leipzig 1801, Baltimore 1803, New York 1803 (5th Amer edn), Paris 1804, London 1827 (15th Br edn).
Rural tales, ballads and songs. 1802, 1802, New York 1802, London 1803, Leipzig 1803, Paris 1804, London 1806, 1826 (10th edn).
Good tidings, or news from the farm: a poem. 1804.
Wild flowers: or pastoral and local poetry. 1806, Philadelphia 1806, London 1809, 1816, 1819, 1826.

Nature's music: consisting of extracts from several authors, in honour of the harp of Aeolus. 1808.
The banks of Wye: a poem. 1811, Philadelphia 1812, London 1813, 1823.
The history of little Davy's new hat. 1815, 1817, Paris 1818, London 1824; ed W. Bloomfield 1878.
May day with the muses. 1822, 1822.
Hazelwood-hall: a village drama. 1823. In prose.
The remains of Bloomfield. [Ed J. Weston] 2 vols 1824.
Selections from the correspondence of Bloomfield. Ed W. H. Hart 1870.

§ 2

Views in Suffolk, Norfolk and Northamptonshire, illustrative of the works of Robert Bloomfield. 1806, 1818. With memoir by E. W. Brayley.

SIR JOHN BOWRING
1792–1872

Observations on the state of religion and literature in Spain. 1819.
Specimens of the Russian poets; with preliminary remarks and biographical notices. 1820, Boston 1822, 2 pts 1821–3 (enlarged).
Matins and vespers: with hymns and occasional devotional pieces. 1823, 1824 (enlarged), 1841 ('altered and enlarged'), 1851, Boston 1853, London 1895.
Batavian anthology: or specimens of the Dutch poets; with remarks on the poetical literature and language of the Netherlands, to the end of the seventeenth century. 1824. With H. S. Van Dyk.
Peter Schlemihl: from the German of La Motte Fouqué [i.e. of Chamisso]. Illustr G. Cruikshank 1824, 1861 (3rd edn); illustr G. Browne 1910.
Ancient poetry and romances of Spain: selected and translated. 1824.
Hymns. 1825.
Servian popular poetry translated. 1827.
Specimens of the Polish poets, with notes and observations on the literature of Poland. 1827.
Sketch of the language and literature of Holland: being a sequel to his Batavian anthology. Amsterdam 1829.
Poetry of the Magyars, preceded by a sketch of the language and literature of Hungary and Transylvania. 1830.
Cheskian anthology: being a history of the poetical literature of Bohemia; with translated specimens. 1832.
Minor morals for young people, illustrated in tales and travels, with engravings by G. Cruikshank and W. Heath. 3 pts 1834–9.
Manuscript of the Queen's Court: a collection of old Bohemian lyrics—epic songs, with other ancient Bohemian poems. Prague 1843.
The kingdom and people of Siam: with a narrative of a mission to that country in 1855. 2 vols 1857.
A visit to the Philippine Islands. 1859.
Ode to the Deity, translated from the Russian of [G.R.] Derzhavin. [Brighton? 1861].
Translations from A. [i.e. S.] Petöfi, the Magyar poet. 1866.
Hwa tsien ki, the flowery scroll: a Chinese novel. 1868.
A memorial volume of sacred poetry: to which is prefixed a memoir of the author, by Lady Bowring. 1873.

Autobiographical recollections; with a brief memoir by L. B. Bowring. 1877.
Bowring edited Westminster Rev 1824–36, and Bentham's Collected works 1838–43.

BARBARINA BRAND (née WILMOT), Baroness DACRE
1768–1854

Ina: a tragedy. 1815 (3 edns). Verse.
Le canzoni di Petrarca. [1815?] (priv ptd). With trns.
Due canzoni del Petrarca. Rome 1818 (priv ptd). With trns.
[Due canzoni del Petrarca.] Naples 1819 (priv ptd). With trns.
Dramas, translations and occasional poems. 2 vols 1821 (priv ptd). Includes Ina and the trns from Petrarch; the latter were rptd in Ugo Foscolo, Essays on Petrarch, 1823.
Translations from the Italian. 1836 (priv ptd).
Frogs and bulls: a Lilliputian piece in three acts. 1838.

HENRY FRANCIS CARY
1775–1844

§ 1

An irregular ode to General Elliott. Birmingham [1788].
Sonnets and odes. 1788.
Ode to General Kosciusko. 1797.
The Inferno of Dante: with a translation in blank verse, notes and a life of the author. 2 vols 1805–6.
The vision: or Hell, Purgatory and Paradise of Dante, translated. 3 vols 1814, 1819, 2 vols Philadelphia 1822, 3 vols 1831, 1 vol 1844 etc; illustr G. Doré 2 vols 1866; ed P. Toynbee 1900–2; ed E. Gardner 1908 (EL); illustr J. Flaxman 1910 (with Botticelli drawings and the Italian text), 1928.
The birds of Aristophanes, translated. 1824.
Pindar in English verse. 1833.
Lives of English poets, from Johnson to Kirke White. 1846. Rptd from London Mag Aug 1821–Dec 1824.
The early French poets: notices and translations. 1846; ed T. E. Welby [without French texts] 1923, New York 1925. Rptd from London Mag Nov 1821–April 1824.
Cary edited the poetical works of Pope and Cowper, 1839, and of Milton, Thomson and Young, 1841.

§ 2

[Foscolo, U.] Dante. Edinburgh Rev 29 1818. Sir J. Mackintosh and Samuel Rogers assisted Foscolo.
Cary, H. Memoir of the Rev H. F. Cary. 2 vols 1847.
Toynbee, P. In his Dante in English literature from Chaucer to Cary, 2 vols 1909.
King, R. W. The translator of Dante: the life, work, and friendships of Cary. 1925.

HARTLEY COLERIDGE
1796–1849
Collections

Poems, with a memoir by his brother [Derwent Coleridge]. 2 vols 1851, 1851.
Complete poetical works. Ed R. Colles [1908] (ML).

§ 1

Poems. Vol 1 (all pbd), Leeds 1833, 1833 (as Poems, songs and sonnets).

Biographia borealis: or lives of distinguished northerns. Leeds 1833, London 1836 (as The worthies of Yorkshire and Lancashire); [ed D. Coleridge] 3 vols 1852 (as Lives of northern worthies).
Lives of illustrious worthies of Yorkshire. Hull 1835. Part of the Biographia borealis, above, reissued with new title-page.
The dramatic works of Massinger and Ford, with an introduction by H. Coleridge. 1840, 1848, 1851.
Essays and marginalia. [Ed D. Coleridge] 2 vols 1851.
Ascham, R., The scholemaster, with memoir by H. Coleridge. 1884. Rptd from Biographia, above.
Essays on parties in poetry and on the character of Hamlet. Ed J. Drinkwater, Oxford 1925, New York 1925.
New poems, including a selection from his published poetry. Ed E. L. Griggs 1942.
Letters of Hartley Coleridge. Ed G. E. and E. L. Griggs, Oxford 1936.

§ 2

Horne, R. H. In his A new spirit of the age, 1844.
Bagehot, W. In his Literary studies, 1879.
Griggs, E. L. Hartley Coleridge: his life and work. 1929.
Blunden, E. Coleridge the less. In his Votive tablets, 1931.
Hartman, H. Hartley Coleridge, poet's son and poet. 1931.

GEORGE DARLEY
1795–1846
Collections

Selections from the poems of Darley. Ed R. A. Streatfeild 1904.
Complete poetical works. Ed R. Colles [1908] (ML).

§ 1

The errors of ecstasie: a dramatic poem, with other pieces. 1822.
The labours of idleness: or seven nights entertainments, by Guy Penseval. 1826, 1829 (as vol 2 of The new sketch book). Prose sketches.
Essays and sketches by the late R. Ayton, with a memoir [by Darley?]. 1825.
A system of popular geometry. 1826, 1844 (5th edn).
A system of popular algebra. 1827, 1836 (3rd edn).
A system of popular trigonometry. 1827, 1835.
Sylvia, or the May queen: a lyrical drama. 1827; ed J. H. Ingram 1892.
The geometrical companion. 1828, 1841.
The sorrows of hope. In The anniversary, ed A. Cunningham 1828.
The new sketch book, by Geoffrey Crayon jun. 2 vols 1829. Vol 2 consists of the unused sheets of Labours of idleness, above.
Familiar astronomy. 1830.
Nepenthe. 1835 (priv ptd); ed R. A. Streatfeild 1897.
Syren songs. In The tribute, ed Lord Northampton 1837.
Thomas à Becket: a dramatic chronicle. 1840.
The works of Beaumont and Fletcher, with an introduction by G. Darley. 2 vols 1840.
Ethelstan, or the battle of Brunanburh: a dramatic chronicle. 1841.
Poems of the late George Darley, a memorial volume printed for private circulation. Liverpool [1889].

Letters

Abbott, C. C. The life and letters of Darley, poet and critic. Oxford 1928, 1967.
—— Further letters of Darley. Durham Univ Jnl 33 1940.
Darley contributed to London Mag Dec 1822–March 1825, including 6 letters to the dramatists of the day, signed 'John Lacy'; The characteristic of the present age of poetry,

April 1824; *and some lyrics and 'dramaticles'; to Athenaeum 1834–46 (reviews and articles on literature and fine art, and some lyrics); to Bentley's Miscellany 1844 (short stories and poems); and to Illuminated Mag 1844 (short stories and poems).*

§2

Blunden, E. Darley and his latest biographer [C. C. Abbott]. TLS 14 Feb 1929; rptd in his Votive tablets, 1931.

Greene, G. George Darley: London Mercury March 1929; rptd in his Lost childhood and other essays, 1951.

Bridges, R. In his Collected essays, papers vol 5, Oxford 1931. Written 1906.

Heath-Stubbs, J. In his Darkling plain: a study of the later fortunes of romanticism in English poetry from Darley to W. B. Yeats, 1950.

EBENEZER ELLIOTT
1781–1849

Collections

[Poetical works] vol 1: The splendid village, Corn Law rhymes and other poems, 1834; vol 2: The village patriarch, Love and other poems, 1834; vol 3: Kerhonah, The vernal walk, Win hill and other poems, 1835. Reissued as The poetical works of Ebenezer Elliott, 3 vols 1844.

The poetical works. Edinburgh 1840.

The poems. Ed R. W. Griswold, Philadelphia 1844, New York 1850. Includes poems not found in other edns.

The poetical works. Ed E. Elliott 2 vols 1876.

§1

The vernal walk. Cambridge 1801, 1802. Anon.

The soldier and other poems, by Britannicus. Harlow 1810.

Night: a descriptive poem. 1818. Anon.

Peter Faultless to his brother Simon; Tales of night, in rhyme, and other poems, by the author of Night. Edinburgh 1820.

Love: a poem; The giaour: a satirical poem. 1823, 1823, 1831.

Scotch nationality: a vision. 1824, Sheffield 1875 (priv ptd).

The village patriarch: a poem. 1829, 1831.

Corn Law rhymes: the ranter. Sheffield 1830, 1831 (enlarged), 1831, 1904 (selection).

The splendid village: Corn Law rhymes, and other poems. 1833. Reissued 1834 as vol 1 of [Poetical works], above.

More verse and prose by the Cornlaw rhymer. 2 vols 1850. Contains review by Southey.

§2

Carlyle, T. Corn Law rhymes. Edinburgh Rev 55 1832; rptd in his Critical and miscellaneous essays, 1839.

Watkins, J. The life, poetry and letters of Ebenezer Elliott. 1850. Includes autobiographical fragment.

'Searle, January' (G. S. Phillips). The life, character and genius of Ebenezer Elliott. 1850, 1852.

Briggs, A. Ebenezer Elliott, the Corn Law rhymer. Cambridge Jnl 3 1950.

REGINALD HEBER
1783–1826

Collections

Poetical works. 1841, Philadelphia 1841, London 1842, 1852 (with poems by F. Hemans and A. Radcliffe),

1854, [1878]. With poetical works of George Herbert [1861], [1881].

§1

A sense of honour: a prize essay. Oxford 1805, 1836.

Palestine: a prize poem. Oxford 1803 (priv ptd), 1807, London 1809, Oxford 1810, Philadelphia 1828 (with other poems), London 1843 (with other poems). Set to music by W. Crotch, 1812, Oxford 1827 as Palestine: a sacred oratorio. First pbd in Poetical register for 1802, 1803.

Europe: lines on the present war. 1809, 1809.

Poems and translations. 1812, 1829, Liverpool 1841.

The whole works of Jeremy Taylor. Ed Heber 1822. With life.

Hymns, written and adapted to the weekly church service of the year. [Ed A. Heber] 1827, 1828 (4th edn), 1834 (10th edn), 1849 (12th edn), 1867.

Select portions of psalms and hymns, with some compositions of a late distinguished prelate [i.e. Heber]. Welshpool 1827.

Narrative of a journey through India 1824–5. [Ed A. Heber] 2 vols 1828, 3 vols 1828 (2nd and 3rd edns), 1829 (4th edn), Philadelphia 2 vols 1829, London 2 vols 1844, 1846, 1849, 1873.

Sermons preached in England. [Ed A. Heber] 1829, 1829.

Sermons preached in India. [Ed A. Heber] 1829.

Sermons on the lessons, the Gospel or the Epistle, for every Sunday in the year. 3 vols 1837, 2 vols 1838 (3rd edn).

The lay of the purple falcon: a metrical romance [by R. Heber and R. Curzon, Baron Zouche]. 1847.

Blue-beard: a serio-comic oriental romance in one act. 1868, [1874]. Verse.

A number of sermons and charges were also pbd separately. Some hymns were first pbd in Christian Observer 1811–16.

The Heber letters 1782–1832. Ed R. H. Cholmondeley 1950. Includes 17 letters from R. Heber.

§2

Heber, A. The life of Heber, by his widow. 2 vols 1830, 1 vol Boston 1861 (abridged as The life and writings, ed J. W. B.). Includes letters, unpbd poems and prose.

Taylor, T. Memoirs of the life and writings of Heber. 1835, 1836 (3rd edn).

Smith, G. Bishop Heber: poet and missionary. 1895.

FELICIA DOROTHEA HEMANS,
née BROWNE
1793–1835

Collections

The league of the Alps; The siege of Valencia; The vespers of Palermo; and other poems. Ed A. Norton, Boston 1826.

Poetical works of Mrs Felicia Hemans. 2 vols New York 1828, Philadelphia 1832, 1 vol Philadelphia 1836, 1836, 1842 (with critical preface and memoir), 1845, 1854.

The works of Mrs Hemans. Ed (with memoir) by her sister [H. Hughes] 7 vols Edinburgh 1839, Philadelphia 1840 (with An essay on her genius by L. H. Sigourney), 8 vols New York 1845, 2 vols New York 1847, 1 vol Edinburgh 1849 etc (chronologically arranged); ed W. M. Rossetti [1873], Oxford 1914.

§1

Poems. Liverpool 1808.

England and Spain: or valour and patriotism. 1808. Verse.

The domestic affections, and other poems. 1812.

The restoration of the works of art to Italy. Oxford 1816, 1816. Verse.

Modern Greece: a poem. 1817, 1821.
Translations from Camoens and other poets. Oxford 1818.
Tales and historic scenes in verse. 1819, 1824.
Wallace's invocation to Bruce: a poem. Edinburgh 1819.
The sceptic. 1820, 1821 (with the following). Verse.
Stanzas to the memory of the late King. 1820, 1821 (with
    The sceptic, above).
Dartmoor: a poem. 1821.
Welsh melodies. 1822.
The vespers of Palermo. 1823, [1877?]. Verse tragedy.
The siege of Valencia: a dramatick poem; The last
    Constantine, with other poems. 1823.
The forest sanctuary, and other poems. 1825, Boston
    1827, Edinburgh 1829 (enlarged).
Lays of many lands. 1825.
Hymns on the works of nature for the use of children.
    Boston 1827, 1833.
Records of woman, with other poems. 1828.
Songs of the affections, with other poems. Edinburgh
    1830, Philadelphia 1860, 1873.
Hymns for childhood. Dublin 1834, 1839.
National lyrics and songs for music. Dublin 1834, 1836.
Scenes and hymns of life, with other religious poems.
    Edinburgh 1834.
Poetical remains. Edinburgh 1836. With memoir by Δ,
    i.e. D. M. Moir.
Early blossoms of spring, with a life of the authoress.
    1840. Juvenile poems.

SAMUEL WILLIAM
HENRY IRELAND
1777–1835

§ 1

Miscellaneous papers and legal instruments under the
    hand and seal of William Shakespeare. Ed S. Ireland 1796.
An authentic account of the Shaksperian manuscripts.
    1796.
Vortigern: an historical tragedy; and Henry the Second:
    an historical drama, supposed to be written by the
    author of Vortigern. 2 pts 1799. Vortigern was rptd
    1832 with facs of portions of the forged ms.
Ballads in imitation of the antient. 1801.
Mutius Scaevola: or the Roman patriot, an historical
    drama. 1801.
A ballade, wrotten on the feastynge and merrimentes of
    Easter Maunday, laste paste, by Paul Persius, a learnedd
    clerke. 1802.
Rhapsodies. 1803.
The angler: a didactic poem. 1804.
The confessions of William Henry Ireland: containing
    the particulars of his fabrication of the Shakspeare
    manuscripts; together with anecdotes and opinions of
    many distinguished persons. 1805; ed R. G. White,
    New York 1874. An expansion of An authentic account,
    above.
Effusions of love from Chatelar to Mary, Queen of
    Scotland: interspersed with songs, sonnets and notes
    explanatory, by the translator. 1805, 1808.
All the blocks! or an antidote to 'all the talents': a
    satirical poem. 1807.
Stultifera navis: or the modern ship of fools. 1807.
The fisher boy: a poem. 1808.
The sailor boy: a poem. 1809, 1822.
Neglected genius: a poem, illustrating the untimely and
    unfortunate fate of many British poets, containing
    imitations of their different styles. 1812.
Chalcographimania: or the portrait-collector and print-
    seller's chronicle, a humourous poem. 1814.
Jack Junk: or the sailor's cruise on shore. 1814.
Scribbleomania: or the printer's devil's polichronicon.
    1815.
The maid of Orleans. 1822. From Voltaire.

*Ireland also pbd several novels and romances and much
miscellaneous hackwork. Many of his writings were anon
or pseudonymous.*

§ 2

Ingleby, C. M. The Shakspeare fabrications [of J. P.
    Collier]; with an appendix on the authorship of the
    Ireland forgeries. 1859.
Mair, J. The fourth forger. 1938.
Muir, P. H. The Ireland Shakespeare forgeries. Book
    Collector 1 1952.
Grebanier, B. The great Shakespeare forgery. New York
    1965. With bibliography.

CHARLES LLOYD
1775–1839

§ 1

Poems on various subjects. Carlisle 1795.
Poems on the death of Priscilla Farmer, by her grandson.
    1796.
Poems by S. T. Coleridge: second edition; to which are
    now added poems by Charles Lamb and Charles Lloyd.
    Bristol 1797. 28 poems by Lloyd.
Blank verse, by Charles Lloyd and Charles Lamb. 1798.
Edmund Oliver. 2 vols Bristol 1798. A novel.
A letter to the Anti-Jacobin reviewers. Birmingham 1799.
    On Edmund Oliver.
Lines suggested by the fast appointed on Wednesday,
    February 27, 1799. Birmingham 1799.
The tragedies of Vittorio Alfieri, translated. 3 vols 1815.
Nugae canorae: poems—third edition, with additions.
    1819. Mainly new poems.
Isabel: a tale. 2 vols 1820. Prose.
Desultory thoughts in London; Titus and Gisippus, with
    other poems. 1821.
Memoirs of the life and writings of Vittorio Alfieri. 1821.
Poetical essays on the character of Pope as a poet and
    moralist. 1821.
The Duke d'Ormond: a tragedy; and Beritola: a tale.
    1822. Verse.
Poems. 1823.
The Lloyd–Manning letters. Ed F. L. Beaty, Bloomington
    1957.

§ 2

[Lamb, C.] Nugae canorae: poems by Charles Lloyd.
    Examiner 24–25 Oct 1819; rptd in his Works, ed T.
    Hutchinson vol 1, 1908.
De Quincey, T. Reminiscences of Charles Lloyd. Tait's
    Mag 7 1840; rptd in his Collected writings, ed D.
    Masson vol 2, Edinburgh 1889.
Lucas, E. V. Charles Lamb and the Lloyds. 1898.

BRYAN WALLER PROCTER
('BARRY CORNWALL')
1787–1874

Dramatic scenes, and other poems. 1819, 1820, 1857
    (enlarged, and illustr Birket Foster, Tenniel et al).
A Sicilian story, and other poems. 1820, 1820, 1821.
Marcian Colonna: an Italian tale, with three dramatic
    scenes, and other poems. 1820.
Mirandola: a tragedy. 1821, 1821. Verse.
The flood of Thessaly, The girl of Provence, and other
    poems. 1823.
Effigies poeticae: or the portraits of the British poets.
    1824.
English songs. 1832, 1844 (new edn), Boston 1844,
    London 1851 (enlarged).

The life of Edmund Kean. 2 vols 1835.
The works of Ben Johnson, with a memoir [by Procter]. 1838.
The works of Shakspere, with a memoir and essay on his genius [by Procter]. 3 vols 1843, 2 vols 1853, 1857-9, 3 vols 1875-80.
Essays and tales in prose. 2 vols Boston 1853.
Selections from Robert Browning. 1863. Ed Procter and J. Forster.
Charles Lamb: a memoir. 1866, Boston 1866; rptd in Essays of Elia, with a memoir of Lamb, 1879.
Procter: an autobiographical fragment. Ed C. Patmore 1877; ed R. W. Armour, Boston 1936 (selected as The literary recollections of Barry Cornwall).

JOHN HAMILTON REYNOLDS
1796-1852

Collections

Poetry and prose. Ed G. L. Marsh, Oxford 1928. A selection, with detailed biographical introd.
Selected prose. Ed L. M. Jones, Cambridge Mass 1966. With bibliography.

§1

Safie: an eastern tale. 1814.
The Eden of imagination: a poem. 1814.
An ode. 1815. Anon.
The naiad: a tale, with other poems. 1816. Anon.
Peter Bell: a lyrical ballad. 1819 (3 edns). Signed W.W.; an anticipatory parody of Wordsworth's poem.
Benjamin the waggoner, a ryghte merrie and conceitede tale in verse: a fragment. 1819. Anon; a further burlesque of Wordsworth, possibly by Reynolds.
The fancy: a selection from the poetical remains of the late Peter Corcoran, of Gray's Inn, student-at-law, with a brief memoir of his life. 1820; ed J. Masefield [1905].
The garden of Florence and other poems. 1821.
The press, or literary chit-chat: a satire. 1822.
Odes and addresses to great people. 1825 (anon), 1826 (3rd edn). With Thomas Hood.
One, two, three, four, five, by advertisement: a musical entertainment in one act. In J. Cumberland, British theatre vol 31 1829 (anon). Acted 1819.
Confounded foreigners: a farce in one act. [1838].

Letters

Rollins, H. E. The Keats circle. 2 vols Cambridge Mass 1948. Includes 21 letters by Reynolds.

HORATIO (HORACE) SMITH
1779-1849
and
JAMES SMITH
1775-1839

§1

Rejected addresses: or the new theatrum poetarum. 1812 (anon), 1812 (rev), 1813 (9th edn), 1813 (15th edn), 1833 (18th edn 'carefully revised'), 1847 (21st edn); ed P. Cunningham 1851; ed E. Sargent, New York 1871 (with memoirs); ed P. Fitzgerald 1890; ed A. D. Godley 1904; ed A. Boyle 1929 (with bibliography).

Horace in London: consisting of imitations of the first two books of the odes of Horace. 1813, 1813, Boston 1813, London 1815 (4th edn). Rptd from Monthly Mirror.
Also poems, novels etc of Horace Smith alone, together with his edn of James Smith's Comic miscellanies in prose and verse, 2 vols 1840, 1841.

§2

[Jeffrey, F.] Rejected addresses. Edinburgh Rev 20 1812.
Beavan, A. H. James and Horace Smith. 1899.
Blunden, E. The Rejected addresses. In his Votive tablets, 1931.

JOHN THELWALL
1764-1834

Poems on various subjects: vol 1 consisting of tales 2 vols 1787.
A speech in rhyme. 1788.
The peripatetic. 1793.
John Gilpin's ghost, or the warning voice of King Chanticleer: an historical ballad dedicated to the treason-hunters of Oakham. 1795.
Poems written in close confinement in the Tower and Newgate upon a charge of treason. 1795.
Poems chiefly written in retirement—The fairy of the lake: a dramatic romance; Effusions of relative and social feeling; and specimens of The hope of Albion, or Edwin of Northumbria: an epic poem; with memoir of the life of the author and notes and illustrations of runic mythology. Hereford 1801, [1805?].
The daughter of adoption: a tale of modern times, by John Beaufort [i.e. Thelwall]. 4 vols 1801.
The black bowl, Feb 3 1208, or tears of Eboracum: an old monkish legend. York 1802.
The trident of Albion: an epic effusion. Liverpool 1805.
Monody on the Right Hon Charles James Fox. 1806, 1806.
The poetical recreations of the Champion, and his literary correspondents; with a selection of essays, literary and critical, which have appeared in the Champion newspaper. 1822. Ed Thelwall; includes 12 poems by Lamb.

HENRY KIRKE WHITE
1785-1806

Collections

The remains of Kirke White, with an account of his life by Robert Southey. Vols 1-2, 1807, 1811 (5th edn 'corrected'); vol 3, 1822. The contents of vol 3 were included in the 10th and later edns, 2 vols 1823, 1 vol 1825 etc; ed R. A. 4 vols 1825; 1 vol 1825 (with a life), 1828; Glasgow 1828 (with a memoir).

§1

Clifton grove: a sketch in verse, with other poems. 1803.
[Uncollected poems and prose, ed T. O. Mabbott]. N & Q 7 Sept 1940, 13 Jan 1945, 15 June, 2 Nov 1946, 4 Sept 1948.

Letters

Mabbott, T. O. Letters of Kirke White. N & Q 16 Nov 1946.

III. MID-NINETEENTH-CENTURY POETRY

THOMAS LOVELL BEDDOES
1803–49

Collections

Poems posthumous and collected. 2 vols 1851. Vol 1 includes memoir by T. F. Kelsall; vol 2 Death's jest-book, 1850; in 1 vol without Jest-book as Poems by the late Thomas Lovell Beddoes, author of Death's jest-book, with a memoir, 1851.
Poetical works. Ed E. Gosse 2 vols 1890. Memoir rptd in Gosse, Critical kit-kats, 1896.
Complete works. Ed E. Gosse 2 vols 1928, 1 vol 1928 (75 copies).
Works. Ed H. W. Donner, Oxford 1935.
An anthology. Ed F. L. Lucas, Cambridge 1932. Introd rptd in Lucas, Studies French and English, 1934.
Plays and poems. Ed H. W. Donner 1950 (ML).

§ 1

The improvisatore, in three fyttes, with other poems. Oxford 1821.
The brides' tragedy. 1822.
Death's jest-book: or the fool's tragedy. 1850. Anon.
Letters. Ed E. Gosse 1894.

§ 2

Monthly Rev Jan 1823; Album May 1823; GM Oct 1823; G. Darley, London Mag Dec 1823, May 1824; J. Wilson, Blackwood's Mag Dec 1823. Reviews of Brides' tragedy.
Strachey, L. The last Elizabethan. New Quart 1 1907; rptd in his Books and characters, 1922.
Blunden, E. Beddoes and his contemporaries. TLS 13 Dec 1928; rptd in his Votive tablets, 1931.
Donner, H. W. The Browning Box: or the life and works of Beddoes as reflected in letters by his friends and admirers. Oxford 1935.
—— Beddoes: the making of a poet. Oxford 1935.
Heath-Stubbs, J. Penguin New Writing 23 1945; rptd in his Darkling plain, 1950.

WINTHROP MACKWORTH PRAED
1802–39

Collections

Poems, with a memoir by Derwent Coleridge. 2 vols 1864.
Essays, collected and arranged by G. Young. 1887 (Morley's Univ Lib).
Political and occasional poems. Ed G. Young 1888.
Selected poems. Ed K. Allott 1953 (ML).

§ 1

Carmen graecum numismate annuo dignatum 1822 (Pyramides Aegyptiacae). [Cambridge 1822].
Epigrammata numismate annuo dignata 1822 (Nugae seria ducunt in mala). [Cambridge 1822].
Carmen graecum numismate annuo dignatum 1823. In obitum T. F. Middleton, Episcopi Calcuttensis, [Cambridge 1823].
Lillian: a fairy tale. 1823. Verse.
Australasia: a poem which obtained the Chancellor's Medal. Cambridge 1823.
Athens: a poem which obtained the Chancellor's Medal. Cambridge 1824. Rptd with the preceding in Cambridge prize poems, 1828 (4th edn).

Epigrammata numismate annuo dignata 1824 (Scribimus indocti doctique). [Cambridge 1824].
The ascent of Elijah: a poem. Cambridge 1831.
Intercepted letters about the Infirmary Bazaar. Nd. 4 leaflets of 4 pp. each, in verse and ptd on light green paper.
Speech in committee on the Reform Bill, on moving an amendment. 1832.
Trash dedicated without respect to J. Halse esq MP. Penzance 1833.
Political poems. 1835 (priv ptd).
Every-day characters. 1896. First pbd in New Monthly Mag 1828–32 and in Literary Souvenir 1831.
Letters of Praed. Etoniana 1 July 1941–28 Dec 1943. 67 letters dating from Praed's Eton days.

Contributions to Periodicals

The Etonian. 2 vols 1821. Ed and largely written by Praed and W. Blunt, Oct 1820–Aug 1821.
Knight's Quarterly Magazine. 1823–4.
The Brazen Head. 1826. 4 nos only; written and ed by Praed, C. Knight and J. B. B. St Leger.
Praed also contributed to Morning Chron *1823–5,* Albion *1830–2,* Morning Post *1832–4,* Times *and other papers, and to* Literary Souvenir, *ed A. A. Watts 1825 and other poetical annuals.*

§ 2

Saintsbury, G. In his Essays in English literature 1780–1860, 1890.
Hudson, D. A poet in Parliament. 1939.
—— W. M. Praed. N & Q 3 Jan 1942. Addns to his biography.
Allott, K. The text of Praed's poems. N & Q March 1953.
Paden, W. D. Twenty new poems attributed to Tennyson, Praed and Landor: pt 1. Victorian Stud 4 1961.

ALFRED, 1st BARON TENNYSON
1809–92

Tennyson's notebooks are in Trinity College Cambridge (those inherited by his son Hallam) and at Harvard (those inherited by the children of his son Lionel). The Tennyson Research Centre at Lincoln holds a ms of In memoriam. *Other mss are widely scattered. In the 1830's his poems circulated in ms among his friends; hence such transcriptions as the Heath ms in the Fitzwilliam Museum Cambridge.*

Bibliographies etc

W[ise], T. J. A bibliography of the writings of Tennyson. 2 vols 1908 (priv ptd).
Baker, A. E. A concordance to the poetical and dramatic works of Tennyson. 1914, New York 1966; Supplement, 1931 (The devil and the lady).
—— A Tennyson dictionary. [1916].
Baum, P. F. In The Victorian poets: a guide to research, ed F. E. Faverty, Cambridge Mass 1956, 1968 (rev E. D. H. Johnson).
Campbell, N. Tennyson at Lincoln: a catalogue. 3 vols Lincoln 1971–.

Collections

Collected edns began to appear in 1870; see Wise, Bibliography, above.
The canonical text appears in the Eversley edition, ed Hallam Tennyson with annotations by the poet 9 vols 1907–8, 1 vol 1913; American Eversley edition 6 vols New York 1908.
Among the numerous other collected edns pbd since 1902, see
Poems, Oxford 1912, 1953 (with the plays) (OSA);
Poems, ed C. Ricks 1969.

§1

Tennyson required 2 successive proofs for Poems chiefly lyrical, 1830, *and later more;* Poems, 1842 *and* The Princess, 1847 *were often rev, largely on proofs. He had* In memoriam, 1850 *ptd in a preliminary version and distributed copies to friends, to be recalled or destroyed; incompletely rev, the setting of type was unexpectedly used in several early edns, with successive corrections and revisions by the poet. After 1855 he again commonly used unpbd preliminary versions, each ptd in a few copies and lent to advisers for eventual recall or destruction; single examples survive, used by the poet in revision and later given to trusted friends. The gradual discovery of these practices encouraged forgers to provide numerous 'priv ptd edns' for the rare book market; see W. B. Todd (ed), T. J. Wise centenary studies, Austin 1959 pp. 111–13.*

Poems by two brothers. Ptd Louth 1827; ed Hallam Tennyson 1893 (adds 4 poems by Alfred from the ms and Timbuctoo). With Charles Tennyson; Frederick contributed 4 poems. *See* C. Ricks for 2 additional poems by Alfred in the ms (from copies of 1893), Victorian Poetry 3 1965.

Prolusiones academicae. Cambridge 1829. Includes Timbuctoo; priv distributed offprint of Timbuctoo, Cambridge 1829.

Poems, chiefly lyrical. 1830, 1842 (partly rptd and rev).

Poems. 1833 (for 1832). Partly rptd and rev in 1842.

The lover's tale [withdrawn from Poems, 1833]. 1833 (for 1832) (priv circulated edn of c. 12 copies), [1868] (proofs only, rev), 1879 (rev). Piracy by R. H. Shepherd [1870], 1875. Forgery of first piracy '1870' [c. 1890].

[Early poems, suppressed in 1842. Ed J. D. Campbell] 1862; ed J. C. Thomson (with Timbuctoo and The lover's tale of 1833) in The Avon Booklet vol i nos 3–6 1903 and as Suppressed poems 1830–62, Warwick 1904, 1910.

Poems. 2 vols 1842, 1843, 1845, 1846, 1 vol 1848, 1850, 1851, 1853 (some edns rev with addns); partly illustr Millais, Holman Hunt and Rossetti 1857; ed J. C. Collins 1900 (with suppressed poems); ed A. M. D. Hughes, Oxford 1914 (with suppressed poems).

The Princess. 1847, 1850 (rev), 1851 (rev), 1853 (rev); illustr Maclise 1860; ed J. C. Collins 1902 (with In memoriam and Maud).

In memoriam. 1850 (3 edns), 1851, 1851, 1855, 1856 etc. Anon till 1870. Within the sequence occasional revision; additional poem in 4th edn, another inserted in 1870. Preceded by unpbd preliminary version [1850]. Poem ed J. C. Collins, above (with variants).

Ode on the death of the Duke of Wellington. 1852, 1853 (rev).

Maud and other poems. 1855, 1855, 1856 (rev), 1857, 1858, 1859 (rev) etc. Within the sequence occasional revision. No unpbd preliminary version known. Preceded by The charge of the Light Brigade, 1855 (priv ptd) (1,000 copies for soldiers in the Crimea). Maud ed J. C. Collins, above (with variants).

[Stanzas on the marriage of the Princess Royal]. [1858] (priv ptd for Court use). One example known; stanzas pbd in Memoir, 1897.

Idylls of the King. 1859, 1859 etc. Preceded by unpbd preliminary versions called Enid and Nimuë (2 of 1857); The true and the false (1859). Enlarged edns 1862, 1869 (for 1870), 1873, 1889. *See* below, The holy grail; Gareth and Lynette; the last idyll pbd in Tiresias and other poems, 1885. Edn of 1862 preceded by Dedication [1862] (priv ptd).

Enoch Arden and other poems. 1864 etc; illustr Arthur Hughes 1866.

A selection from the work of Tennyson. 1865 (Moxon's Miniature Poets), 1870. Includes 5 unpbd poems and 2 versions of poems not pbd elsewhere etc.

The Holy Grail and other poems. 1870 (for 1869). Preceded by unpbd (and undated) preliminary versions of

The birth of Arthur; The Holy Grail; Sir Pelleas; The death of Arthur; and Property (i.e. The northern farmer, new style). Also preceded by The victim. Canford Manor, 1867 (priv ptd) (folio; proofs in 8vo).

The window or the songs of the wrens: words written for music by Tennyson, the music by Arthur Sullivan. 1871 (for 1870). Preceded by The window: or the loves of the wrens. Canford Manor 1867 (priv ptd); piracy by R. H. Shepherd '1867' (for 1870).

Gareth and Lynette. 1872. Preceded by unpbd (and undated) preliminary versions of The last tournament; Gareth and Lineth.

Queen Mary. 1875, 1875.

Harold. 1877 (for 1876).

Ballads and other poems. 1880.

Hands all round, a national song: the music arranged and edited by C. Villiers Stanford. [1882].

The cup and the falcon. 1884. Preceded by unpbd preliminary version of 1882.

Becket. 1884, 1893 (acting edn).

Tiresias and other poems. 1885. Preceded by Early spring, 1883 (copyright edn); To HRH Princess Beatrice, 1885 (priv ptd for Court use).

Gordon boys' morning and evening hymns: the words edited by Lord Tennyson, the music by Lady Tennyson, edited by Dr Bridge. 1885.

Locksley Hall sixty years after. 1886.

Demeter and other poems. 1889. Preceded by The throstle, 1889 (copyright edn).

The foresters. 1892, 1892. Preceded by unpbd version, [1881?].

The death of Oenone, Akbar's dream and other poems. 1892. Preceded by The silent voices 1892 (copyright edn). Edn of The silent voices with music by J. F. Bridge 1892. Vol includes Riflemen form!, previously pbd [in earlier version] only in newspapers of 1859.

Tennyson's patriotic poems. 1914. Includes A call to arms [also called Arm, arm, arm!—'Oh, where is he, the simple fool'], previously pbd anon in newspapers of 1852; ed C. Ricks MP 62 1964.

The devil and the lady. Ed C. Tennyson 1930, Bloomington 1964 (facs).

Unpublished early poems. Ed C. Tennyson 1931, Bloomington 1964 (facs, with above).

Hallam Tennyson, Materials for a life of A.T., 1896 (priv ptd), *his* Memoir, 1897, *the annotations in the* Eversley *editions, and his memoir in the one-vol* Eversley *edition, 1913, all contain poems not pbd elsewhere. The Christ of Ammergau, which Tennyson dictated extempore to Knowles in 1870, was pbd from Knowles's papers,* Twentieth Century Jan 1955. *A few early poems remain in ms.*

§2

For further reviews of Tennyson's pbd vols see E. F. Shannon jr, Tennyson and the reviewers 1827–51, Cambridge Mass 1952 *and his* The critical reception of Maud, PMLA 68 1953; *for later reviews see bibliography in* W. M. Dixon, A Tennyson primer, 1901 (rev).

[Mill, J. S.] London Rev i 1835. On Poems 1833.

M[ilnes], R. M. (Baron Houghton). Westminster Rev 38 1842. On Poems 1842.

Horne, R. H. [and E. Barrett]. In Horne, A new spirit of the age, 1844.

[Kingsley, C.] Tennyson. Fraser's Mag Sept 1850. On In memoriam.

[Gladstone, W. E.] Tennyson's poems. Quart Rev 106 1859. On Idylls of the King.

—— Locksley Hall and the Jubilee. Nineteenth Century Jan 1887.

Arnold, M. In his On translating Homer: last words, 1862. On Tennyson's style.

Bagehot, W. Wordsworth, Tennyson and Browning: or pure, ornate and grotesque art in English poetry. Nat

Rev Nov 1864; rptd in his Literary studies, ed R. H. Hutton 1879.

Hutton, R. H. Tennyson. Macmillan's Mag Dec 1872; rptd in his Literary essays, 1888.
—— Tennyson's poem on Despair (1881); Locksley Hall in youth and age (1886); rptd in his Criticisms on contemporary thought and thinkers, 1894.

Tennyson, H. Materials for a life of A.T., collected for my children. 1896 (priv ptd).
—— Alfred Lord Tennyson: a memoir. 1897.
—— (ed). Tennyson and his friends. 1911.

Dixon, W. M. A primer of Tennyson, with a critical essay. 1896, 1901 (rev).

Beeching, H. C. In memoriam, with an analysis and notes. 1899, 1923.

Bradley, A. C. A commentary on In memoriam. 1901, 1902 (rev), 1930 (rev).
—— The reaction against Tennyson (1914). In his A miscellany, 1929.

Lang, A. Alfred Tennyson. 1901.

Benson, A. C. Alfred Tennyson. 1904.

Ker, W. P. Tennyson: Leslie Stephen lecture 1909. 1909; rptd in his Collected essays, ed C. Whibley 1925.

Browning, R. An opinion on the writings of Tennyson. 1920 (priv ptd). In a letter of 1870.

Nicolson, H. Tennyson: some aspects of his life, character and poetry. 1923, New York 1962 (with Afterword dated 1960).

Eliot, T. S. In memoriam. Introd to Poems of Tennyson, Edinburgh 1936; rptd in his Essays ancient and modern, 1936.
—— The voice of his time. Listener 12 Feb 1942. On In memoriam.

Young, G. M. The age of Tennyson. Proc Br Acad 25 1939; rptd in Critical essays, ed J. Killham 1960.

Paden, W. D. Tennyson in Egypt. Lawrence Kansas 1942.

Shannon, E. F., jr. Tennyson and the reviewers 1830–42. PMLA 58 1943; included in his Tennyson and the reviewers 1827–51, Cambridge Mass 1952.

Auden, W. H. Introduction. In A selection from the poems of Tennyson, New York 1944.

Hough, G. The natural theology of In memoriam. RES 23 1947; rptd in his Selected essays, Cambridge 1978.

Tennyson, C. B. L. Alfred Tennyson. 1949.
—— Six Tennyson essays. 1954.

Killham, J. Tennyson and the Princess: reflections of an age. 1958.
—— Maud: the function of the imagery. In Critical essays, below.
—— (ed). Critical essays on the poetry of Tennyson. 1960.

Rader, R. W. Tennyson's Maud: the biographical genesis. Berkeley 1963.

Tillotson, K. Tennyson's serial poem. In her Mid-Victorian studies, Oxford 1965. On Idylls of the King.

Jump, J. D. (ed). Tennyson: the critical heritage. 1967.

Sinfield, A. The language of Tennyson's In memoriam. Oxford 1971.

Ricks, C. Tennyson. 1972.

ELIZABETH BARRETT BROWNING
1806–61

Diaries, memo books, ms poems, and nearly a thousand letters are in the Wellesley College Library. Most of Mrs Browning's letters to her sisters are in the Berg Collection of the New York Public Library and the collection of A. A. Houghton, New York City. Important ms materials are in the BM, Huntington Library, Folger Library, Pierpont Morgan Library, libraries of Baylor, Harvard and Yale universities and the universities of Illinois and Texas.

Bibliographies

Wise, T. J. Bibliography of the writings of Elizabeth Barrett Browning. 1918.
—— A Browning library. 1929.

Broughton, L. N., C. S. Northup and R. B. Pearsall. In their Robert Browning: a bibliography, Ithaca 1953.

Barnes, W. A bibliography of Elizabeth Barrett Browning. Austin 1967.

Collections

Poems. 2 vols 1844, New York 1844 (as A drama of exile and other poems); ed Robert Browning 1887.

Poems: new edition. 2 vols 1850. Enlarged as Poems, 3 vols 1856, 1862, 4 vols 1864.

Poetical works. 5 vols 1866, 2 vols New York 1871, 1877 ('corrected by the last London edition'), 6 vols 1899 etc.

Poetical works. Oxford 1904 (OSA).

Complete poetical works. Ed L. Whiting 2 vols New York York 1919.

§ 1

For a list of about a hundred periodical contributions, see G. B. Taplin, PBSA 44 1950.

The battle of Marathon: a poem. 1820; ed H. B. Forman 1891 (facs).

Essay on mind, with other poems. 1826.

Prometheus bound, translated from the Greek of Aeschylus; and miscellaneous poems. 1833.

The Seraphim and other poems. 1838.

Queen Annelida and false Arcite. In The poems of Chaucer modernized, 1841.

A new spirit of the age. 2 vols 1844. With R. H. Horne. Articles on Landor and Milnes, and parts of other articles, are by E. B. B. An essay on Carlyle rptd in Nicoll and Wise, Literary anecdotes, 1896.

Sonnets [or] Sonnets from the Portuguese. In Poems, 1850 etc; often rptd separately. Earliest independent edn Boston 1886. A famous edn dated Reading, 1847, is a forgery by T. J. Wise. Annotated edn, ed F. E. Ratchford and D. Fulton, New York 1950.

Casa Guidi windows: a poem. 1851.

The cry of the children. In Two poems, 1854. The second poem is by Robert Browning.

Aurora Leigh. 1857 (3 edns), 1859, 1860 (rev), 1882 (17th edn), New York 1857 etc; ed A. C. Swinburne 1898; ed H. B. Forman 1899 (Temple Classics).

Poems before congress. 1860, New York 1860 (as Napoleon III in Italy and other poems).

Last poems. 1862.

The Greek Christian poets and the English poets. 1863. First pbd as articles in Athenaeum 1842.

Psyche apocalypte: a lyrical drama. St James Mag Feb 1876; 1876 (separately). A drama 'projected' by E. B. B. and R. H. Horne.

Epistle to a canary. Ed T. J. Wise 1913.

The enchantress, and other poems. Ed T. J. Wise 1913.

Deila: a tale. Ed T. J. Wise 1913.

New poems by Robert and Elizabeth Barrett Browning. Ed F. G. Kenyon 1914.

The poet's enchiridion. Ed H. B. Forman, Boston 1914. Contains 3 items of juvenilia.

Hitherto unpublished poems and stories, with an unedited autobiography. Ed H. B. Forman 2 vols Boston 1914 (pamphlets).

Letters and Papers

Kenyon, F. G. Letters of Elizabeth Barrett Browning. 2 vols 1897.

Letters of Robert Browning and Elizabeth Barrett Browning 1845–6. 2 vols 1899, New York 1899; ed E. Kintner 2 vols Oxford 1969.

Wise, T. J. Letters of Elizabeth Barrett Browning to Robert Browning and other correspondents. 1916.

Miller, B. Elizabeth Barrett to Miss Mitford: unpublished letters. 1954.

Invisible friends. Ed W. P. Pope, Cambridge Mass 1972. Letters to B. R. Haydon 1842-5.

§2

Clarke, I. C. Elizabeth Barrett Browning: a portrait. 1929.

Woolf, V. In her Common reader: second series, 1932.

—— Flush: a dog. 1933.

Hewlett, D. Elizabeth Barrett Browning. 1953.

Taplin, G. B. Life of Elizabeth Barrett Browning. 1957.

Tompkins, J. M. S. Aurora Leigh. 1961 (Fawcett lecture).

Hayter, A. Mrs Browning: a poet's work and its setting. 1962.

—— Elizabeth Barrett Browning. 1965 (Br Council pamphlet).

ROBERT BROWNING
1812–89

Some noteworthy collections of ms material relating to Browning are in the Balliol College Library, Bodley, the BM, the Victoria and Albert Museum; in the Keats-Shelley House in Rome and the Biblioteca Nazionale in Florence; in libraries at the universities of Chicago, Illinois and Texas, and at Baylor University, Wellesley College and Yale; and in the Huntington Library, the Pierpont Morgan Library, and the Berg Collection of the New York Public Library.

Bibliographies etc

Orr, A. A handbook to the works of Browning. 1885. Discusses the whole canon in classified groups, as authorized and partly supervised by Browning.

Wise, T. J. A complete bibliography of Browning. 1897.

—— A Browning library. 1929.

Cook, A. K. A commentary upon Browning's The ring and the book. Oxford 1920, New York 1966.

Broughton, L. N. and B. F. Stelter. A concordance to the poems of Browning, 2 vols 1924-5, 4 vols New York 1970.

Broughton, L. N., C. S. Northup and R. B. Pearsall. Browning: a bibliography 1830-1950. Ithaca 1953.

DeVane, W. C. A Browning handbook. Ithaca 1935, New York 1955 (rev).

Honan, P. In The Victorian poets: a guide to research, ed F. E. Faverty, Cambridge Mass 1956, 1968 (rev).

Kelley, P. and R. Hudson. The Brownings' correspondence: a checklist. New York 1978.

Collections

Poems: a new edition. 2 vols 1849.

Poetical works: third edition. 3 vols 1863.

Poetical works: fourth edition. 3 vols 1865.

Poetical works. 6 vols 1868.

Poetical works. 17 vols 1888-94. Fourth and complete edition, with closing vols ed by E. Berdoe.

Poetical works. 1904 etc. An edn begun by Grant Richards and continued in WC, Oxford edn etc; as Poetical works complete from 1833 to 1868 and shorter poems thereafter, Oxford 1941.

Works. Ed F. G. Kenyon 10 vols 1912. Centenary edn.

Selected poems, ed W. C. DeVane, New York 1949; Poetry and prose, ed S. Nowell-Smith 1950.

Complete works. Ed R. A. King et al, Athens Ohio 1969–.

Poetical works 1833-64. Ed I. Jack, Oxford 1970 (OSA).

§1

Pauline: a fragment of a confession. 1833; ed T. J. Wise 1886; ed N. H. Wallis 1931 (comparing states of the text).

Paracelsus. 1835; ed G. Lowes Dickinson 1899 (Temple Classics); ed M. L. Lee and K. B. Locock 1909.

Johannes Agricola. Monthly Repository Jan 1836.

Porphyria. Ibid.

Contributions to the Life of Strafford by J. Forster. In Lives of statesmen, 1836; ed C. H. Firth and F. J. Furnivall 1892.

Strafford: an historical tragedy. 1837; ed E. H. Hickey 1884; ed A. Wilson 1901; ed H. B. George, Oxford 1908.

Sordello. 1840; ed H. Buxton Forman 1902; ed A. J. Whyte 1913.

Pippa passes (Bells and pomegranates no 1). 1841. Often rptd, e.g. illustr L. L. Brooke 1898; illustr M. Armstrong, New York 1903; ed A. Symons 1906; ed A. L. Irvine 1924; ed E. A. Parker 1927.

King Victor and King Charles (Bells and pomegranates no ii). 1842.

Dramatic lyrics (Bells and pomegranates no iii). 1842; ed J. O. Beatty and J. W. Bowyer, New York 1931 (facs).

Tasso and Chatterton [essay]. Foreign Quart Rev 29 1842 (anon); ed D. Smalley, Cambridge Mass 1948.

The return of the Druses: a tragedy in five acts (Bells and pomegranates no iv). 1843.

A blot in the 'scutcheon: a tragedy in five acts (Bells and pomegranates no v). 1843.

A blot in the 'scutcheon: a tragedy in three acts (Bells and pomegranates no v). 1843, [1846] ('second edition').

Colombe's birthday: a play in five acts (Bells and pomegranates no vi). 1844.

Claret and tokay. Hood's Mag June 1844.

The laboratory (Ancien Régime). Ibid.

Garden fancies (The flower's name, and Sibrandus Schafnaburgensis). Hood's Mag July 1844.

Dramatic romances and lyrics (Bells and pomegranates no vii). 1845, 1897; illustr C. Ricketts 1899; illustr E. F. Brickdale, New York 1909.

The tomb at San Praxed's. Hood's Mag March 1845.

The flight of the Duchess: part first. Hood's Mag April 1845.

Luria and A soul's tragedy (Bells and pomegranates no viii). 1846.

Christmas eve and Easter day. 1850, 1900, 1907; ed O. Smeaton 1918.

Shelley [essay]. In the [spurious] Letters of Percy Bysshe Shelley, 1852; ed F. J. Furnivall 1881 (Browning Soc), 1888 (Shelley Soc), Bibelot 1902; ed H. F. B. Brett-Smith, Oxford 1921 (with Shelley, Defence; Peacock, Four ages of poetry).

The twins. In Two poems (the other by Elizabeth Barrett Browning), 1854.

Men and women. 2 vols 1855, 1 vol Boston 1856, 1863, 1866, 1869; ed H. B. Forman 1899; 2 vols Westminster 1899; illustr H. Osprovat 1903; ed B. Worsfold 1904; 1908; Oxford 1910; ed G. E. Hadow, Oxford 1911, 1920 (facs); ed F. B. Pinion 1963; ed P. Turner, Oxford 1972.

Ben Karshook's wisdom. Keepsake 1856.

May and death. Ibid.

Dramatis personae. 1864, 1864 ('second edn'); ed M. Edwardes 1906 (Temple Classics); 1910; ed J. O. Beatty and J. W. Bowyer, New York 1931 (facs).

Gold hair: a legend of Pornic. Atlantic Monthly May 1864.

Prospice. Atlantic Monthly June 1864.

Under the cliff (from James Lee). Ibid.

The ring and the book: in four volumes. Vols 1-2 1868, vols 3-4 1869; 2 vols Boston 1869, 4 vols 1872 ('second edn'), '2 vols in 1' Boston 1883, 3 vols 1889; ed C. Porter and H. A. Clarke 1897; ed E. Dowden 1912; ed A. K. Cook, Oxford 1940; ed W. Sypher, New York 1961.

Balaustion's adventure, including a transcript from Euripides. 1871, Boston 1871, London 1872 ('second edn'), 1881; ed E. A. Parker 1928.

Prince Hohenstiel-Schwangau, saviour of society. 1871.

Hervé Riel. Cornhill Mag March 1871.

Fifine at the fair. 1872.

Red Cotton night-cap country: or turf and towers. 1873, Boston 1873.

Aristophanes' apology, including a transcript from Euripides: being the last adventures of Balaustion. 1875, Boston 1875.

The inn album. New York Times 14, 21, 28 Nov 1875; London 1875, Boston 1876.

Pacchiarotto and how he worked in distemper; with other poems. 1876, Boston 1877.

The Agamemnon of Aeschylus, transcribed by Browning. 1877.

La Saisiaz, and The two poets of Croisic. 1878.

Dramatic idyls. 1879, 1882 ('second edn').

Dramatic idyls: second series. 1880.

Jocoseria. 1883, Boston 1883, London 1883 ('second edn'), 1884 ('third edn').

Sonnet on Goldoni. Pall Mall Gazette 8 Dec 1883.

Helen's tower. Pall Mall Gazette 28 Dec 1883.

Ferishtah's fancies. 1884, Boston 1885, London 1885 (2nd edn), 1885 (3rd edn).

Sonnet on Rawden Brown. Century Mag Feb 1884.

The founder of the feast. World 16 April 1884.

The names ('Shakespeare, to that name's sounding'). In Shakesperian Show book (for an Albert Hall bazaar), 1884; Pall Mall Gazette 29 May 1884.

Sonnet: why I am a Liberal. In Why I am a Liberal, ed A. Reid 1885.

Parleyings with certain people of importance in their day, to wit: Bernard de Mandeville, Daniel Bartoli, Christopher Smart, George Bubb Dodington, Francis Furini, Gerard de Lairesse, and Charles Avison; introduced by a dialogue between Apollo and the Fates; concluded by another between John Fust and his friends. 1887, Boston 1887.

Jubilee memorial lines. Pall Mall Gazette Dec 1887.

The isle's enchantress (on F. Moscheles' painting). Pall Mall Gazette 26 March 1889.

To Edward FitzGerald. Athenaeum 13 July 1889.

Asolando: fancies and facts. 1890, 1890, 1893 (10th edn), Boston 1890.

New poems. Ed F. G. Kenyon 1913.

Letters and Accounts

Wise, T. J. Letters from Browning to various correspondents. 2 vols 1895. First of a series of pamphlets ed Wise, each containing a few letters.

Browning, R. B. (ed). Letters of Browning and Elizabeth Barrett Browning 1845-6. 2 vols 1899. See col 824, above.

Donner, H. W. The Browning box. Oxford 1935. Letters to T. L. Beddoes.

§2

Bagehot, W. Wordsworth, Tennyson and Browning: or pure, ornate and grotesque art in English poetry. Nat Rev 18 1864; rptd in his Literary studies, ed R. H. Hutton 2 vols 1879.

Nettleship, J. T. Essays on Browning's poetry. 1868, 1890 (enlarged as Essays and thoughts).

James, H. On a drama of Mr Browning. Nation (New York) 20 Jan 1876. The inn album.

—— The novel in the Ring and the book. Trans of Royal Soc of Lit 31 1912.

Furnivall, F. J. (ed). The [London] Browning Society's papers. 13 pts 1881-91.

Symons, A. An introduction to the study of Browning. 1886 (including a Reprint of discarded prefaces to some of Mr Browning's works), 1906 (enlarged).

Orr, A. Life and letters of Browning. 1891, 2 vols Boston 1891 (enlarged).

Pigou, A. C. Browning as a religious teacher. Cambridge 1901.

Chesterton, G. K. Robert Browning. 1903 (EML).

Dowden, E. Robert Browning. 1904.

Griffin, W. H. and H. C. Minchin. The life of Browning, with notices of his writings, his family and his friends. 1910.

Pound, E. In his Instigations, New York 1920. Against Browning's trns from the Greek.

DeVane, W. C. jr. The landscape of Childe Roland. PMLA 40 1925.

—— Browning's Parleyings with certain people: the autobiography of a mind. New Haven 1927.

—— Sordello's story retold. SP 27 1930.

—— The virgin and the dragon. Yale Rev 37 1947.

Gest, J. M. The Old Yellow Book: source of Browning's The ring and the book. Boston 1925. New trns, annotated.

Raymond, W. O. The infinite moment and other essays in Browning. Toronto 1950.

Miller, B. Browning: a portrait. 1952.

Drew, P. (ed). Browning: a collection of critical essays. 1966.

—— The poetry of Browning. 1970.

Blackburn, T. Robert Browning. 1967.

Ward, M. Browning and his world. 1968.

Litzinger, B. and D. Smalley (ed). Browning: the critical heritage. 1970.

Jack, I. Browning's major poetry. Oxford 1973.

Armstrong, I. (ed). Robert Browning. 1974.

Irvine, W. and P. Honan. The book, the ring and the poet: a biography. 1975.

ARTHUR HUGH CLOUGH
1819-61

The mss of most of Clough's poetry, prose and correspondence are in Bodley; others are in the Houghton Library, Harvard.

Bibliographies

Houghton, W. E. The prose works of Clough: a checklist and calendar, with some unpublished passages. BNYPL 1960; rev in Gollin, Houghton and Timko, below.

Gollin, R. M., W. E. Houghton and M. Timko. Clough: a descriptive catalogue. BNYPL Jan–March 1967. Contains unpbd verse and a full list of comment on Clough; rev New York 1967.

Collections

Poems. 1862 (with memoir by F. T. Palgrave), 1863 (slightly rev, with some additional poems), [1906] (ML).

Letters and remains. [Ed Mrs Clough] 1865 (priv ptd). Includes some unpbd poems.

Poems and prose remains. Ed Mrs Clough [and J. A. Symonds]. 2 vols 1869 (with memoir by Mrs Clough).

Poems. Ed H. S. Milford. 1910.

Poems. Ed H. F. Lowry, A. L. P. Norrington and F. L. Mulhauser, Oxford 1951, 1974 (with addns).

Selected prose works. Ed B. B. Trawick, Tuscaloosa 1964. Many unpbd essays and lectures.

Poems. Ed A. L. P. Norrington, Oxford 1968 (OSA).

§1

Clough contributed perhaps 24 poems and 13 essays to the Rugby Mag 2 vols 1835-7.

The bothie of Toper-na-fuosich. Oxford 1848, Cambridge Mass 1849.

Ambarvalia. 1849 (with poems by T. Burbidge), 1850 (without Burbidge's poems), 1853.

Last words: Napoleon and Wellington. Fraser's Mag Feb 1853.

Oxford University Commission. North Amer Rev April 1853.

Recent English poetry. North Amer Rev July 1853.

Recent social theories. Ibid.

Amours de voyage. Atlantic Monthly Feb–May 1858.

Poems and ballads of Goethe. Fraser's Mag June 1859.

Plutarch's lives: the translation called Dryden's corrected from the Greek and revised [with a preface] by Clough. 5 vols Boston 1859; ed E. Rhys 3 vols 1910 (EL).

Greek history from Themistocles to Alexander in a series of lives from Plutarch: revised and arranged. 1860.

Letters

Emerson-Clough letters. Ed H. F. Lowry and R. L. Rusk, Cleveland Ohio 1934; rptd in Correspondence of Emerson and Carlyle, ed J. Slater, New York 1964.

Correspondence. Ed F. L. Mulhauser 2 vols Oxford 1957. Vol 2 contains a 'catalogue of all known letters'.

§2

Emerson, R. W. The Bothie. Mass Quart Rev 2 1849; rptd in his Uncollected writings, New York 1912.

[Kingsley, C.] The Bothie. Fraser's Mag Jan 1849.

Bagehot, W. Mr Clough's poems. Nat Rev 13 1862; rptd in his Literary studies vol 2, 1879.

Sidgwick, H. The poems and prose remains of Clough. Westminster Rev 92 1869; rptd in his Miscellaneous essays and addresses, 1904.

Garrod, H. W. In his Poetry and the criticism of life, Oxford 1931.

Lowry, H. F. Introductory. In his edn of Letters of Arnold to Clough, Oxford 1932.

Tillotson, K. Rugby 1850: Arnold, Clough, Walrond and In memoriam. RES new ser 4 1953; rptd in her Mid-Victorian studies, 1965, with G. Tillotson, Clough's Bothie; Clough: thought and action.

Chorley, K. Clough: the uncommitted mind. Oxford 1962.

Houghton, W. E. The poetry of Clough: an essay in revaluation. New Haven 1963.

Cockshut, A. O. J. Clough: the real doubter. In his Unbelievers, 1964.

Thorpe, M. (ed). Clough: the critical heritage. 1972.

MATTHEW ARNOLD
1822–88

Bibliographies etc

Smart, T. B. The bibliography of Arnold. 1892, 1904 (rev and expanded in Works vol 15).

Parrish, S. M. A concordance to the poems of Arnold. Ithaca 1959.

Wilkins, C. T. The English reputation of Arnold 1840–77. Ann Arbor 1959. With extensive list of reviews.

Brooks, R. L. Arnold's poetry 1849–55: an account of the contemporary criticism and its influence. Ann Arbor 1960.

Collections

Essays in criticism [first series]. Boston 1865, 1866 etc. Includes On translating Homer, A French Eton.

Poems: a new and complete edition. Boston 1856.

Poems. 2 vols 1869.

Poems: new and complete edition. 2 vols 1877, New York 1878 (rev), London 1881 (new edn), New York 1883.

Selected poems. 1878, 1878, 1880 etc, New York 1878. Chosen by Arnold.

Passages from the prose writings. 1880; ed W. E. Buckler, New York 1963. Chosen by Arnold.

Works. 15 vols 1903–4 (Deluxe edn). Includes Letters, ed G. W. E. Russell.

Poems 1840–67. Ed H. S. M[ilford], Oxford 1909 (introd by A. T. Quiller-Couch); ed G. St Quintin, Oxford 1926; with addns as Poetical works, Oxford 1942, 1945 (OSA).

Essays, including Essays in criticism 1865, On translating Homer, with F. W. Newman's reply and five other essays now for the first time collected. Oxford 1914 (OSA).

The portable Arnold. Ed L. Trilling, New York 1949.

Poetical works. Ed C. B. Tinker and H. F. Lowry, Oxford 1950 (OSA). Arnold's arrangement.

Poetry and prose. Ed J. Bryson 1954 (Reynard Lib).

Complete prose works. Ed R. H. Super, Ann Arbor 1960–.

Poems. Ed K. Allott 1965.

§1

Alaric at Rome: a prize poem. Rugby 1840.

Cromwell: a prize poem. Oxford 1843; rptd 1863, 1891 and in Oxford prize poems, Oxford 1846.

The strayed reveller and other poems, by A. 1849.

Empedocles on Etna and other poems, by A. 1852.

Poems: a new edition. 1853 (with critical preface), 1854, 1857 (both rev).

Poems: second series. 1855.

Merope: a tragedy. 1858.

England and the Italian question. 1859; ed M. M. Bevington, Durham NC 1953 (with F. Stephen's reply).

The popular education of France, with notices of that of Holland and Switzerland. 1861.

On translating Homer: three lectures. 1861; On translating Homer: last words, 1862; New York 1883 (both texts, with On the study of Celtic literature), London 1896 (popular edn); ed W. H. D. Rouse 1905.

The twice-revised code: reprinted from Fraser's Magazine. 1862.

A French Eton: or middle class education and the State. 1864, 1892 (with Schools and universities in France).

Essays in criticism [ser 1]. 1865, 1869, 1875, New York 1883, London 1884, Leipzig 1887; ed G. K. Chesterton 1906 (EL), ed K. Allott 1964; ed W. Raleigh 1912.

On the study of Celtic literature. 1867, New York 1883 (with On translating Homer), London 1891 (popular edn); ed E. Rhys 1910 (EL).

New poems. 1867, Boston 1867, London 1868.

Schools and universities on the Continent. 1868. Previously issued in Schools Inquiry Commission report. Partly rptd in his Higher schools and universities in Germany, 1874, 1882, and in A French Eton, to which is added Schools and universities in France, 1892.

Culture and anarchy: an essay in political and social criticism. 1869, 1875, 1882, New York 1883 (with Friendship's garland), London 1889 (popular edn); ed J. D. Wilson, Cambridge 1932.

St Paul and Protestantism; with an introduction on Puritanism and the Church of England. 1870, 1870, 1875, New York 1883 (with Last essays on church and religion), London 1887 (popular edn).

Friendship's garland: being the conversations, letters and opinions of the late Arminius Baron von Thunder-ten-Tronckh collected and edited with a dedicatory letter to Adolescens Leo Esq of the Daily Telegraph. 1871, New York 1883 (with Culture and anarchy), London 1897, 1903 (popular edn).

Literature and dogma: an essay towards a better apprehension of the Bible. 1873 (3 edns), New York 1873, Boston 1873, London 1874 ('fourth edn'), 1876 ('fifth edn'), New York 1876, 1877, 1883, London 1883 (popular edn).

A Bible-reading for schools: the great prophecy of Israel's restoration (Isaiah chs 40–66) arranged and edited for young learners. 1872.

Isaiah 40–66, with the shorter prophecies allied to it, arranged and edited with notes. 1875.

God and the Bible: a review of objections to Literature and dogma. 1875, Boston 1876, New York 1879, 1883, London 1884 (popular edn).

Last essays on Church and religion. 1877, New York 1883 (with St Paul and Protestantism), London 1903 (popular edn).

The six chief lives from Johnson's Lives of the poets, with

Macaulay's Life of Johnson edited with a preface. 1878 etc, 1886 (4th edn with notes), 1889.

Mixed essays. 1879, 1880, New York 1880, 1883 (with Irish essays), London 1903 (popular edn).

Poems of Wordsworth chosen and edited. 1879, 1879 (with addns), 1880 etc.

On the study of poetry: general introduction; Thomas Gray: critical introduction; John Keats: critical introduction. In English poets, ed T. H. Ward 1880; rptd in Essays in criticism: second series, 1888.

Letters, speeches and tracts on Irish affairs by E. Burke, collected and arranged. 1881.

Poetry of Byron, chosen and arranged. 1881.

Irish essays and others. 1882, New York 1883 (with Mixed essays), London 1891 (popular edn).

Isaiah of Jerusalem in the authorised English version, with an introduction, corrections and notes. 1883.

Discourses in America. 1885, New York 1889; ed F. R. Tomlinson, New York 1924.

Education Department: special report on certain points connected with elementary education in Germany, Switzerland and France. 1886, 1888 (with new prefatory note).

General Grant: an estimate. Boston 1887; ed J. Y. Simon, Carbondale 1966 (with Mark Twain's rejoinder). Rptd from Murray's Mag Jan–Feb 1887.

Schools. In The reign of Queen Victoria, ed T. H. Ward 1887.

Essays in criticism: second series. 1888 (posthumous edn with prefatory note by Lord Coleridge); ed K. Allott 1964 (EL).

Civilization in the United States: first and last impressions of America. Boston 1888.

Reports on elementary schools 1852–82. Ed F. Sandford 1889; ed F. S. Marvin 1908.

On Home Rule for Ireland: two letters to the Times. 1891 (priv ptd). With prefatory note by T. B. Smart.

Arnold's notebooks, with a preface by [Eleanor Arnold] Wodehouse. 1902; ed H. F. Lowry, K. Young and W. H. Dunn 1952; Arnold's diaries: the unpublished items transcribed and ed W. B. Guthrie, Ann Arbor 1959.

Arnold as dramatic critic: a reprint of articles signed 'An old playgoer' contributed by him to the Pall Mall Gazette. Ed C. K. Shorter 1903 (priv ptd); Letters of an old playgoer, ed B. Matthews, New York 1919.

Essays in criticism: third series. Ed E. J. O'Brien, Boston 1910.

Thoughts on education chosen from the writings of Arnold. Ed L. Huxley 1912.

Five uncollected essays. Ed K. Allott, Liverpool 1953.

Essays, letters and reviews. Ed F. Neiman, Cambridge Mass 1960.

Letters and Papers

An extensive collection of originals and photographs has been assembled at the Alderman Library, Univ of Virginia.

Russell, G. W. E. Letters of Arnold 1848–88. 2 vols 1895.

Lowry, H. F. The letters of Arnold to Arthur Hugh Clough. Oxford 1932.

Davis, A. K. Arnold's letters: a descriptive checklist. Charlottesville 1968.

§2

['Eliot, George']. Arnold's poems. Westminster Rev 64 1855.

[James, H.] Arnold's Essays in criticism. North Amer Rev 101 1865; rptd in his Views and reviews, Boston 1908.
—— Matthew Arnold. English Illustr Mag Jan 1884; rptd in his Literary reviews and essays, New York 1957.

Sidgwick, H. The prophet of culture. Macmillan's Mag Aug 1867; rptd in Eclectic Mag Oct 1867 and in his Miscellaneous essays and addresses, 1904.

Mallock, W. H. The new republic: or culture, faith and

philosophy in an English country house. Belgravia June–Dec 1876; 1877, 1878; ed J. M. Patrick, Gainesville 1950.

Housman, A. E. Introductory lecture, University College, London. 1892, 1933 (both priv ptd), Cambridge 1937; rptd in Selected prose, below.
—— Appendix. In his Selected prose, ed J. Carter, Cambridge 1961. 3 pages from an unpbd paper of c. 1891.

Stephen, L. Matthew Arnold. Nat Rev Dec 1893; rptd in his Studies of a biographer, 1898.

Saintsbury, G. In his Corrected impressions, 1895.
—— Matthew Arnold. Edinburgh 1899.

Russell, G. W. E. Matthew Arnold. 1904.

Brown, E. K. The critic as xenophobe: Arnold and the international mind. Sewanee Rev 38 1930.
—— Studies in the text of Arnold's prose works. Paris 1935.
—— Arnold: a study in conflict. Chicago 1948.

Bradley, A. C. Shelley and Arnold's critique of his poetry. In his A miscellany, 1931.

Blunden, E. In Great Victorians, ed H. J. and H. Massingham 1932.

Chambers, E. K. Matthew Arnold. Proc Br Acad 18 1932; rptd in his Sheaf of studies, Oxford 1942.
—— Arnold: a study. Oxford 1947, New York 1964.

Leavis, F. R. Arnold as critic. Scrutiny 7 1939.

Trilling, L. Matthew Arnold. New York 1939, 1949, 1955 (rev).

Tinker, C. B. and H. F. Lowry. The poetry of Arnold: a commentary. Oxford 1940.

Tillotson, G. Arnold: the critic and the advocate. Essays by Divers Hands new ser 20 1943.
—— Arnold and eighteenth-century poetry. In Essays on the eighteenth century presented to David Nichol Smith, Oxford 1945.
—— Arnold and Pater: critics historical, aesthetic and otherwise. E & S new ser 3 1950. All three rptd in his Criticism and the nineteenth century, 1951.
—— Arnold in our time; Arnold, the lecturer and journalist. Both in his Mid-Victorian studies, 1965.

Tillotson, K. Arnold and Johnson. RES new ser 1 1950.
—— 'Yes: in the sea of life.' RES new ser 3 1952; rptd in her Mid-Victorian studies, 1965.
—— Rugby 1850: Arnold, Clough, Walrond and In memoriam. RES new ser 4 1953; addn by A. L. P. Norrington, ibid; rptd with above.
—— Arnold and Carlyle. Proc Br Acad 42 1956; rptd in her Mid-Victorian Studies, 1965.

Holloway, J. Arnold and the modern dilemma. EC 1 1951; rptd in his Charted mirror, 1960.
—— In his Victorian sage, 1953.

Allott, K. Pater and Arnold. EC 2 1952.
—— Matthew Arnold. 1955.

Eells, J. S. The touchstones of Arnold. New York 1955.

Culler, A. D. Imaginative reason: the poetry of Arnold. New Haven 1966.

Watson, G. Arnold and the Victorian mind. REL 8 1967; rev in his Politics and literature in modern Britain, 1977.

Bush, D. Arnold: a survey of his poetry and prose. 1971.

Allott, K. Matthew Arnold. 1975.

EDWARD FitzGERALD
1809–83

Bibliographies

Prideaux, W. F. Notes for a bibliography of FitzGerald. 1901.

Collections (including letters)

Letters and literary remains. Ed W. A. Wright 3 vols 1889.

Letters. Ed W. A. Wright 2 vols 1894.

Letters and literary remains. Ed W. A. Wright 7 vols 1902–3. Absorbs collections above.

Letters of FitzGerald. Ed J. M. Cohen 1960.

Selected works. Ed J. Richardson 1962 (Reynard Lib).

§1

Memoir of Bernard Barton. In Selections from the poems and letters of Barton, ed L. Barton 1849.

Euphranor: a dialogue on youth. 1851, 1855 (rev), [1882] (rev, priv ptd, as Euphranor: a May-Day conversation at Cambridge, 'Tis forty years since'); ed F. Chapman 1906 (from 1851 text).

Polonius: a collection of wise saws and modern instances. 1852, 1854; ed S. S. Allen 1905.

Six dramas of Calderón freely translated. 1853, 1854; ed H. Oelsner 1903, [1928] (EL).

Salámán and Absál: an allegory translated from the Persian of Jámí. 1856 (anon), 1871 (rev, priv ptd), 1879 (rev, with 4th edn of the Rubáiyát, below), Leigh-on-Sea 1946.

Rubáiyát of Omar Khayyám, the astronomer-poet of Persia, translated into English verse. 1859 (anon), 1868 (rev, anon), 1872 (rev, anon), 1879 (rev, anon, with the Salámán and Absál of Jámí, above); ed N. H. Dole 2 vols Boston 1896 (includes French and German versions, with voluminous critical material), 1898 (enlarged), 1 vol Philadelphia 1898 (text of 4th and 1st edns); ed F. H. Evans 1914 (variorum text); ed A. J. Arberry 1959 (as The romance of the Rubáiyát: text of 1st edn with introduction, notes and bibliography); ed C. J. Weber, Waterville Maine 1959 (critical text with bibliography).

  Tutin, J. R. A concordance to FitzGerald's translation of the Rubáiyát. 1900.

The mighty magician and Such stuff as dreams are made of: two plays translated from Calderón. 1865 (priv ptd).

Agamemnon: a tragedy taken from Aeschylus. [1869] (priv ptd), London 1876.

Readings in Crabbe's Tales of the Hall. [1879] (priv ptd), 1882, 1883 (with enlarged introd).

The downfall and death of King Oedipus: a drama in two parts, chiefly taken from the Oedipus Tyrannus and Colonaeus of Sophocles. 2 pts 1880–1 (priv ptd).

The two Generals: I, Lucius Aemilius Paullus; II, Sir Charles Napier. nd. 2 poems, priv ptd.

Occasional verses. 1891 (priv ptd).

Eight dramas of Calderón, freely translated. 1906. Consists of Six dramas, 1853, and The mighty magician and Such stuff as dreams, 1865, above.

Dictionary of Madame de Sévigné. Ed M. E. FitzGerald 2 vols 1914.

A FitzGerald medley. Ed C. Ganz 1933.

§2

Jackson, H. FitzGerald and Omar Khayyám: an essay and a bibliography. 1899.

Wright, T. The life of FitzGerald. 2 vols 1904.

Benson, A. C. Edward FitzGerald. 1905 (EML).

Terhune, A. M. The life of FitzGerald. 1947.

COVENTRY KERSEY DIGHTON PATMORE
1823–96

Bibliographies

Stevenson, L. In Victorian poets: a guide to research, ed F. E. Faverty, Cambridge Mass 1956, 1968 (rev).

Collections

Poems. 4 vols [1879]. Vol 1: Amelia, Tamerton Church-tower etc; vol 2: The angel in the house; vol 3: The victories of love; vol 4: The unknown Eros (42 odes).

Poems: collective edition. 2 vols 1886, 1886, 1887 (3rd edn) (with selections from the poems of Henry Patmore).

Works: new uniform edition. 5 vols 1897, 1907.

Poems. Ed F. Page, Oxford 1949 (OSA).

§1

Poems. 1844.

Tamerton church-tower and other poems. 1853 (Pickering), 1854 (Parker) (rev).

The angel in the house: the betrothal. 1854, Boston 1856. Anon.

[The angel in the house]: the espousals. 1856, Boston 1856. Anon.

The angel in the house: bks i–ii The betrothal, The espousals. 2 vols in 1 1854–6 (Parker), 1858 (2nd edn, Parker), 1860 (3rd edn?, Parker), 2 vols 1863.

Faithful for ever. 1860, Boston 1861, London 1866.

The victories of love. Macmillan's Mag Sept–Nov 1861; Boston 1862, 1863 (Macmillan), 1878 (4th edn) (Bell), 1888 (rev with Faithful for ever).

Odes: not published. [1868]. Anon; rptd T. Connolly, Boston 1936.

The unknown Eros and other odes. 1877 (odes i–xxxi) (anon), 1878 (odes i–xlvi) (signed), 1890 (3rd edn, rev).

Amelia. 1878 (priv ptd black letter edn).

Amelia, Tamerton church-tower etc; with prefatory study on English metrical law. 1878.

Saint Bernard on the love of God. Tr M. C. and C. Patmore 1881, 1884.

Hastings, Lewes, Rye and the Sussex marshes. 1887.

Principle in art. 1889, 1890 (2nd edn), 1898 (rev and rearranged). Rptd from St James's Gazette.

Religio poetae. 1893, 1898 (rev and rearranged). Rptd from Fortnightly Rev, Edinburgh Rev etc.

The rod, the root and the flower. 1895, 1907 (2nd edn, rev), 1923; ed D. Patmore 1950.

The wedding sermon. [1911].

Principle in art and other essays. 1912.

Principle in art, Religio poetae and other essays. 1913.

Courage in politics. Ed F. Page 1921.

Seven unpublished poems to Alice Meynell. 1922 (priv ptd).

Essay on English metrical law: a critical edition with a commentary by M. A. Roth. Washington 1961.

Further letters of Gerard Manley Hopkins, including his correspondence with Patmore. Ed C. C. Abbott, Oxford 1938, 1956 (rev and enlarged). With nearly 30 letters from Patmore to Hopkins.

§2

De Vere, A. The angel in the house. Edinburgh Rev 107 1858; rptd in his Essays chiefly literary and ethical, 1889.

Champneys, B. Memoirs and correspondence of Patmore. 2 vols 1900, 1901.

Gosse, E. Patmore. 1905.

Burdett, O. The idea of Patmore. Oxford 1921.

Page, F. Patmore: a study in poetry. Oxford 1933.

Patmore, D. Portrait of my family. 1935.

—— The life and times of Patmore. 1949.

Oliver, E. J. Patmore. New York 1956.

Reid, J. C. The mind and art of Patmore. 1957.

DANTE GABRIEL ROSSETTI
1828–82

Bibliographies

Rossetti, W. M. Bibliography of the works of Rossetti. 1905.

—— Rossetti: classified lists of his writings with the dates. 1906 (priv ptd).

Fredeman, W. E. In his Pre-Raphaelitism: a biblio-critical study, Cambridge Mass 1965 (sections 22–34).

Collections

Collected works. Ed W. M. Rossetti 2 vols 1886.

Poems of Rossetti, with illustrations from his own pictures and designs. Ed W. M. Rossetti 2 vols 1904. First authorized restoration of Nuptial sleep to House of life; several poems added.

Works. Ed W. M. Rossetti 1911. The standard edn.

Poems and translations 1850–70. Oxford 1913 (OSA).

Poems, ballads and sonnets. Ed P. F. Baum, New York 1937.

Poems. Ed O. Doughty 1957.

§1

The first pbd poem, the sonnet This is the Blessed Mary, pre-elect, *appeared in the catalogue of the Free Exhibition, 1849.* The blessed damozel, Hand and soul, *and 11 other pieces, mostly sonnets, were pbd in the 4 nos of* Germ, Jan–April 1850. Sister Helen *appeared in the English edn of the* Düsseldorf artists' album, ed M. Howitt, Leipzig 1854; The burden of Nineveh, *the 2nd version of* The blessed damozel, *and* The staff and the scrip *were included in* Oxford and Cambridge Mag nos 8, 11–12 1856, *rptd with many changes in* Crayon 1858 *and* New Path [Blessed damozel *only*] 1863; *3 sonnets on pictures first appeared in* W. M. Rossetti *and* A. C. Swinburne, Notes on the Royal Academy exhibition, 1868 (pt 2). *Rossetti also contributed substantial portions to* A. Gilchrist, Life of Blake, 1863.

Sir Hugh the Heron: a legendary tale in four parts, by Gabriel Rossetti Junior. 1843 (priv ptd by G. Polidori).

The early Italian poets from Ciullo d'Alcamo to Dante Alighieri (1100–1200–1300) in the original metres, together with Dante's Vita nuova. 1861, 1874 (rev and re-arranged as Dante and his circle).

Of life, love, and death: sixteen sonnets. Fortnightly Rev March 1869.

Hand and soul. 1869 (priv ptd).

Poems. 1870 (4 edns), 1871, 1872. First appearance of House of life. 2 priv printings (1869, 1870) preceded this vol.

The stealthy school of criticism. Athenaeum 16 Dec 1871. A reply to Buchanan, below.

Poems: a new edition. 1881. A revision of Poems 1870, with 4 new poems and 3 trns, omitting House of life and 3 other sonnets.

Ballads and sonnets. 1881, 1881, 1882, 1882. House of life expanded to 101 sonnets, Nuptial sleep dropped.

Lenore, by G. Bürger. Ed W. M. Rossetti 1900. Tr Rossetti.

Henry the leper [by Hartmann von Aue], paraphrased by Rossetti. Ed W. P. Trent 2 vols Boston 1905.

The house of life: a sonnet sequence. Ed P. F. Baum, Cambridge Mass 1928.

Rossetti: an analytical list of manuscripts in the Duke University Library, with hitherto unpublished verse and prose. Ed P. F. Baum, Durham NC 1931.

The blessed damozel: the unpublished manuscript, texts and collation. Ed P. F. Baum, Chapel Hill 1937.

Rossetti's Sister Helen. Ed J. C. Troxell, New Haven 1939.

Jan Van Hunks. Ed J. R. Wahl, New York 1952. 2 earlier edns ed T. Watts-Dunton (1912), and M. Bell (1929).

The Kelmscott love sonnets. Ed J. R. Wahl, Cape Town 1954. From House of life mss in Bodley.

Letters

Dante Gabriel Rossetti: his family letters, with a memoir. Ed W. M. Rossetti 2 vols 1895. 317 letters in vol 2.

Letters of Rossetti to William Allingham 1854–70. Ed G. B. Hill 1897.

Some early correspondence of Rossetti. In Preraphaelite diaries and letters, ed W. M. Rossetti 1900.

Rossetti papers 1862–70. Ed W. M. Rossetti 1903.

Letters of Rossetti to his publisher F. S. Ellis. Ed O. Doughty 1928.

Three Rossettis: unpublished letters to and from Dante Gabriel, Christina, William. Ed J. C. Troxell, Cambridge Mass 1937.

Rossetti's letters to Fanny Cornforth. Ed P. F. Baum, Baltimore 1940.

Letters of Dante Gabriel Rossetti. Ed O. Doughty and J. R. Wahl 5 vols Oxford 1965–.

Rossetti and Jane Morris: their correspondence. Ed J. Bryson, Oxford 1975.

§2

Buchanan, R. In his Fleshly school of poetry and other phenomena of the day, 1872. Expanded from article by 'Thomas Maitland' in Contemporary Rev Oct 1871.

Swinburne, A. C. In his Essays and studies, 1875.

Caine, T. H. Recollections of Rossetti. 1882, 1908 (rev in My story), 1928 (rev).

Sharp, W. Rossetti: a record and a study. 1882.

Knight, J. Life of Rossetti. 1887.

Pater, W. In his Appreciations, 1889.

Rossetti, W. M. Rossetti as designer and writer. 1889.

—— The PRB journal 1849–53. Ed W. D. Fredeman, Oxford 1974.

Hueffer, F. M. [Ford]. Rossetti: a critical essay on his art. 1902.

Dunn, H. T. Recollections of Rossetti and his circle. 1904.

Benson, A. C. Rossetti. 1904 (EML).

Hunt, W. H. Pre-Raphaelitism and the Pre-Raphaelite Brotherhood. 2 vols 1905, 1913 (2nd edn, rev M. E. Holman Hunt).

Waugh, E. Rossetti: his life and works. 1928.

Gaunt, W. The Pre-Raphaelite tragedy. 1942, 1943 (as The Pre-Raphaelite dream).

Doughty, O. A Victorian romantic: Rossetti. 1949, 1960.

Hough, G. Rossetti and the PRB. In his Last Romantics, 1949.

Fleming, G. H. Rossetti and the Pre-Raphaelite Brotherhood. 1967.

CHRISTINA GEORGINA ROSSETTI
1830–94

Collections

Poetical works. Ed W. M. Rossetti 1904 etc (with memoir).

§1

Many of Christina Rossetti's poems and prose works first appeared in periodicals and in anthologies before being incorporated, frequently with significant revisions, into later volumes. A few have never been rptd.

Verses by Christina G. Rossetti, dedicated to her mother. 1847 (priv ptd by G. Polidori); ed J. D. Symon 1906 (Eragny Press). Contains poem To my mother on the anniversary of her birth, April 27 1842, originally pbd as a single sheet by G. Polidori [1842], her earliest ptd poem.

Goblin market and other poems, with 2 designs by DGR. 1862, 1865; illustr L. Housman 1893.

The prince's progress and other poems, with 2 designs by DGR. 1866; rptd with Goblin market as Poems, Boston 1866.

Commonplace and other short stories. 1870.

Sing-song: a nursery rhyme book, with 120 illustrations by A. Hughes. 1872, 1878, 1893 (new and enlarged edn with 5 additional poems).

Annus Domini: a prayer for each day of the year, founded on a text of Holy Scripture. 1874.

Speaking likenesses, with pictures thereof by A. Hughes. 1874.

Goblin market, The prince's progress and other poems: new edition with 4 designs by DGR. 1875, Boston 1876, 1882 (as Poems), London 1879, 1884, 1888. With 37 new poems. *See below* Poems 1890.

Seek and find: a double series of short studies of the Benedicite. 1879.

A pageant and other poems. 1881.

Called to be Saints: the Minor Festivals devotionally studied. 1881. With 13 poems.

Letter and spirit: notes on the Commandments. 1883.

Time flies: a reading diary. 1885. With 130 poems.

Poems: new and enlarged edition, with 4 designs by DGR. 1890, 1890, 1891, 1892, 1894, 1895, 1916. Rptd from Goblin market etc, 1875, together with A pageant 1881, and 13 new poems.

The face of the deep: a devotional commentary on the Apocalypse. 1892. Prose with over 200 poems and verse fragments, many rptd in Reflected lights, ed W. Jay 1900.

Verses reprinted from Called to be saints, Time flies and The face of the deep. 1893. With some alterations and addns.

New poems, hitherto unpublished and uncollected. Ed W. M. Rossetti 1896.

The Rossetti birthday book. Ed Olivia Rossetti [Agresti] 1896.

Maude: a story for girls. Ed W. M. Rossetti 1897. Written in 1850.

Familiar correspondence newly translated from the Italian of Christina G. Rossetti. Stanford Dingley 1962. A trn of her imaginary correspondence pbd in The Bouquet Culled from Marylebone Gardens 1851–2.

Letters

Rossetti papers 1862–70. Ed W. M. Rossetti 1903.

Family letters of Christina Rossetti. Ed W. M. Rossetti 1908.

Troxell, J. C. Three Rossettis: unpublished letters to and from Dante Gabriel, Christina, William. Cambridge Mass 1937.

§2

Birkhead, E. Christina Rossetti and her poetry. 1930.

Sanders, M. F. The life of Christina Rossetti. [1930].

Stuart, D. M. Christina Rossetti. 1930 (EML).

Shove, F. Christina Rossetti. Cambridge 1931.

Thomas, E. W. Christina Rossetti. New York 1931.

Packer, L. M. Christina Rossetti. Berkeley 1963.

Battiscombe, G. Christina Rossetti. 1965 (Br Council pamphlet).

IV. MINOR POETRY 1835–1870

WILLIAM ALLINGHAM
1824–89

Collections

[Works]. 6 vols 1890.

Sixteen poems, selected by W. B. Yeats. Dundrum 1905.

Poems. Ed H. Allingham 1912.

§1

Poems. 1850, Boston 1861 (enlarged).

Day and night songs. 1854, 1855 (rev and enlarged as The music master, a love story, and two series of day and night songs), 1884 (rearranged and enlarged).

Peace and war. 1854. An ode rptd from Daily News, and not rptd in later vols.

Nightingale valley: a collection of the choicest lyrics and short poems, edited by 'Giraldus'. 1860, 1862 (signed).

The ballad book. Ed W. Allingham et al 1864, 1865.

Laurence Bloomfield in Ireland: a modern poem. 1864, 1869 (adds a preface and subtitle: or the new landlord), 1888. An early version appeared in Fraser's Mag.

Fifty modern poems. 1865.

In fairyland. 1870 (for 1869), 1875.

Rambles by 'Patricius Walker'. 1873, 1893 (as vols 1–2 of Varieties in prose). Essays on England and Ireland.

Songs, ballads and stories. 1877.

Evil May-day. 1882. An argumentative poem on the relation of religion to dogma and science.

Ashby Manor: a play in two acts. [1883]; rptd in Thought and word, 1890, below.

The fairies: a child's song. 1883, 1912 (as Up the airy mountain). Rptd from Day and night songs, above.

Blackberries picked off many bushes, by 'D. Pollex and others', put in a basket by W. Allingham. 1884, 1890.

Irish songs and poems. 1887, 1890, 1901.

Rhymes for the young folk. [1887], New York [1915], 1930 (as Robin red breast and other verses).

Flower pieces and other poems. 1888. Includes Day and night songs, above. Opening section priv ptd as Flower pieces [1886?].

Life and phantasy. 1889.

Thought and word. 1890. Poems, including Ashby Manor, above.

Varieties in prose. 3 vols 1893.

A diary. Ed H. Allingham and D. Radford 1907.

By the way: verses, fragments and notes arranged by H. Allingham. 1912, New York 1912.

Letters from William Allingham to Robert and Elizabeth Barrett Browning. [1914].

§2

Letters of D. G. Rossetti to Allingham 1845–70. Ed G. B. Hill 1897.

Letters to W. Allingham. Ed H. Allingham and E. B. Williams 1911.

WILLIAM EDMONDSTOUNE AYTOUN
1813–65

Collections

Poems. Ed F. Page, Oxford 1921.

Stories and verse. Ed W. L. Renwick, Edinburgh 1964.

§1

Poland, Homer and other poems. 1832. Anon.

The life and times of Richard the first, King of England. 1840.

The book of ballads, edited by 'Bon Gaultier'. 1845, 1849 (enlarged), 1903 (16th edn). With T. Martin.

Lays of the Scottish cavaliers and other poems. 1849, 1849 (adds appendix on Macaulay, also issued separately), 1853 (6th edn); ed H. Morley 1891. Lays often rptd separately, numerous selections also rptd for school use.
Firmilian, or the student of Badajoz: a spasmodic tragedy by 'T. Percy Jones'. Edinburgh 1854, New York 1854.
Bothwell: a poem in six parts. 1856, Boston 1856, Edinburgh 1858 (3rd edn rev).
The Glenmutchkin railway. 1858. A short story rptd from Blackwood's Mag in Tales from Blackwood vol 1 1858.
The ballads of Scotland. 2 vols Edinburgh 1858, 1859 (rev and enlarged), 1870 (4th edn rev and enlarged). Ed Aytoun.
Poems and ballads of Goethe. 1859, 1860 (rev and enlarged), 1877. Tr with R. Martin.
Norman Sinclair: a novel. 3 vols 1861.
Nuptial ode on the marriage of the Prince of Wales. 1863.
The burial march of Dundee and the island of the Scots. Ed W. K. Leask 1897.
Endymion: or a family party of Olympus. In Ixion in heaven and Endymion: Disraeli's skit and Aytoun's burlesque. Ed E. Partridge 1927. Written in 1842.

§2

Martin, T. Memoir of Aytoun. 1867.
Frykberg, E. Aytoun, pioneer professor of English at Edinburgh. Gothenburg 1963.

WILLIAM BARNES
1801-86

Collections

Poems of rural life in the Dorset dialect. 1879, 1883.
Select poems chosen and edited with a preface and glossarial notes by T. Hardy. 1908.
Selected poems. Ed G. Grigson 1950 (ML).
Poems. Ed B. Jones 1962. First collected edn.

§1

Poetical pieces. Dorchester 1820.
Orra: a Lapland tale. Dorchester 1822.
An etymological glossary. Shaftesbury 1829.
A catechism of government in general, and of England in particular. Shaftesbury 1833.
The mnemonic manual. 1833.
A few words on the advantages of a more common adoption of the mathematics as a branch of education. 1834.
A mathematical investigation of the principle of hanging doors, gates, swing bridges and other heavy bodies. Dorchester 1835.
An arithmetical and commercial dictionary. 1840.
An investigation of the laws of case in language, exhibited in a system of natural cases. 1840.
A pronouncing dictionary of geographical names. 1841.
The elements of English grammar, with a set of questions and exercises. 1842.
The elements of linear perspective and the projection of shadows. 1842.
Exercises in practical science. Dorchester 1844.
Sabbath lays: six sacred songs. 1844.
Poems of rural life in the Dorset dialect, with a dissertation and glossary. 1844, 1847 (enlarged), 1862, 1866.
Poems, partly of rural life (in national English). 1846.
Humilis domis: some thoughts on the abodes, life and social conditions of the poor. [1849?] (priv ptd)
Se gefylsta (the helper): an Anglo-Saxon delectus, serving as a first class-book of the language. 1849, 1866.
A philological grammar, grounded upon English. 1854.

Notes on ancient Britain and the Britons. 1858.
Views of labour and gold. 1859.
Hwomely rhymes: a second collection of poems in the Dorset dialect. 1859, 1863 (as Poems of rural life in the Dorset dialect: second selection).
The song of Solomon in the Dorset dialect. 1859 (priv ptd).
Tiw: or, a view of the roots and stems of the English as a Teutonic tongue. [1861].
Poems of rural life in the Dorset dialect: third collection. 1862, 1869.
A grammar and glossary of the Dorset dialect, with the history, outspreadings and bearings of south-western English. 1864, 1886 (rev).
A guide to Dorchester. Dorchester 1864.
Early England and the Saxon English, with some notes on the fatherstock of the Saxon English, the Frisians. 1869.
Poems of rural life in common English. 1868, Boston 1868, 1869.
An outline of English speech-craft. 1878.
An outline of rede-craft (logic), with English wording. 1880.
A glossary of the Dorset dialect, with a grammar of its word shapening and wording. 1886.
Barnes was also a voluminous contributor to GM, Hone's Year Book, Retrospective Rev, Macmillan's Mag.

§2

Hardy, T. Obituary. Athenaeum 16 Oct 1886; rptd in L. Johnson, The art of Thomas Hardy, 1894.
Baxter, L. The life of Barnes by his daughter. 1887.
Forster, E. M. Homage to Barnes. New Statesman 9 Dec 1939; rptd in his Two cheers for democracy, 1951.
Grigson, G. In his Harp of Aeolus, 1948.
Heath-Stubbs, J. In his Darkling plain, 1950.
Dugdale, G. Barnes of Dorset. 1953.
Levy, W. T. Barnes: the man and the poems. Dorchester 1960.
Larkin, P. William Barnes. Listener 16 Aug 1962.

THOMAS EDWARD BROWN
1830-97

Collections

Collected poems. Ed H. F. Brown, H. G. Dakyns and W. E. Henley 1900, 1901 (with introd by W. E. Henley).
Poems. Ed A. T. Quiller-Couch 2 vols Liverpool 1952. Reprint of Collected poems 1900, above, with additional poem The Manx Library.

§1

The student's guide to the school of litterae fictitiae, commonly called novel-literature. 1855.
Betsy Lee: a fo'c'sle yarn. 1873 (anon), 1881 (enlarged as Fo'c'sle yarns, including Betsy Lee and other poems).
The doctor and other poems. 1887. In 1891 unsold sheets were divided into 2 vols as Kitty of the Serragh Vane and The doctor.
The Manx witch and other poems. 1889, New York 1889.
Old John and other poems. 1893, New York 1893.
Letters. Ed S. T. Irwin 2 vols 1900, 1900. With memoir.

SARA COLERIDGE
1802-52

§1

Account of the Abipones, translated from the Latin of M. Dobrizhöffer. 3 vols 1821.

The right joyous and pleasant history of the feats, gests and prowesses of the Chevalier Bayard, translated from the French. 2 vols 1825, 1 vol [1906].

Pretty lessons in verse for good children. 1834, 1845 (4th edn), 1853, 1875, 1927.

Phantasmion. 1837 (anon); ed Lord Coleridge 1874. A fairy tale with lyrics.

§2

Memoir and letters of Sara Coleridge. Ed E. Coleridge 2 vols 1873, 1 vol New York 1874.

Sara Coleridge and Henry Reed. Ed L. N. Broughton, Ithaca 1937. Includes Reed's memoir of Sara Coleridge and her letters to Read.

Griggs, E. L. Coleridge fille: a biography of Sara Coleridge. Oxford 1940.

Woolf, V. In her Death of the moth and other essays, 1942.

SYDNEY THOMPSON DOBELL
1824–74

The Roman: a dramatic poem by Sydney Yendys. 1850, 1852.

Balder: part the first. 1853, 1854 (adds preface). Pt 2 never completed; fragments are ptd in Thoughts on art, philosophy and religion, below.

Sonnets on the war. 1855. With Alexander Smith.

America. [1869]. 2 sonnets written in 1855.

England in time of war. 1856. Poems.

Love, to a little girl. 1863. In verse.

Of parliamentary reform: a letter to a politician. 1865.

Thoughts on art, philosophy and religion. Ed J. Nichol 1876. Selected from unpbd works of Dobell.

Life and letters. Ed E. J[olly] 2 vols 1878.

FREDERICK WILLIAM FABER
1814–63
§1

The knights of St John. 1836. Newdigate prize poem.

The Cherwell water-lily and other poems. 1840.

The Styrian lake and other poems. 1842, [1907].

Sir Lancelot: a poem. 1844, 1857.

The rosary and other poems. 1845.

Hymns. Derby 1848, 1849 (enlarged as Jesus and Mary: or Catholic hymns), 1852 (enlarged), 1854 (enlarged as The oratory hymn book), 1861 (complete edn with 150 hymns).

Ethel's book: or tales of the angels. 1858, 1887, 1901. New York [1907]. Stories for children.

The first Christmas: the infant Jesus. 1889. Verses.

Faber also pbd numerous sermons and religious tracts, as well as contributing 9 lives to The lives of the English saints, 1844–5.

§2

Bowden, J. E. The life and letters of Faber. 1869, [1888].

Faber, G. C. In his Oxford apostles, 1933.

Cassidy, J. F. The life of Father Faber. 1946.

RICHARD HENRY (or HENGIST) HORNE
1803–84
§1

Exposition of the false medium and barriers excluding men of genius from the public. 1833. Anon.

The spirit of peers and people: a nation tragi-comedy. 1834.

Cosmo de'Medici: an historical tragedy. 1837, 1875 (with added poems). In verse.

The death of Marlowe: a tragedy in one act. 1837, 1870 (5th edn). Chiefly in verse; rptd in Works of Marlowe, ed A. H. Bullen vol 3, 1885.

The life of Van Amburgh the brute tamer, with anecdotes of his pupils, by Ephraim Watts. [1838].

Gregory VII: a tragedy in one act. 1840, 1849 (3rd edn).

The history of Napoleon. 2 vols 1841, 1 vol 1879.

Poems of Chaucer, modernized. 1841. By various writers. Horne contributed the introd and 3 tales.

Orion: an epic poem in three books. 1843 (3 edns), Melbourne 1854 (adds preface), London 1872 (9th and definitive edn); ed E. Partridge 1928 (with introd on Horne's life and work).

A new spirit of the age, edited [and largely written] by Horne. 2 vols 1844, 1 vol 1844; ed W. Jerrold, Oxford 1907 (WC).

Ballad romances. 1846.

The good-natured bear: a story for children of all ages. 1846, 1856, [1878].

Memoirs of a London doll, written by herself. Ed 'Mrs Fairstar' 1846, Boston 1852, London 1855, New York 1922 (introd by C. W. Hart), London 1923.

Judas Iscariot: a miracle play, with other poems. 1848; rptd in Bible tragedies, [1891].

The poor artist: or seven eye-sights and one object. 1850, 1871 (adds preliminary essay on vision).

Memoir of the Emperor Napoleon. [1850?].

The dreamer and the worker: a story of the present time. 2 vols 1851.

Australian facts and prospects, to which is prefixed the author's Australian autobiography. 1859.

Prometheus the fire bringer: a drama in verse. Edinburgh 1864, Melbourne 1866.

The two Georges: a dialogue of the dead. Melbourne [1865?]. In verse.

The south-sea sisters: a lyric masque. Melbourne [1866]. With trns into French and German verse.

Galatea secunda: an odaic cantata. Melbourne 1867.

Parting legacy of R. H. Horne to Australia (John Ferncliff: an Australian narrative poem). Melbourne [1868].

The great peace-maker: a sub-marine dialogue. 1872 (priv ptd), 1872. Poem, rptd from Household Words.

Ode to the Mikado of Japan. 1873.

Psyche apocalypté: a lyric drama. 1876. Drafts and correspondences between Horne and his co-author E. B. Browning, with connecting narrative by Horne.

Letters of Elizabeth Barrett Browning addressed to Horne. Ed S. R. T. Mayer 2 vols 1877. Connecting narrative by Horne.

The history of duelling in all countries, translated from the French of Coustard de Massi, with introductions and concluding chapter by 'Sir L. O'Trigger'. [1880].

King Nihil's round table: or the regicide's symposium. 1881. A dramatic scene.

Bible tragedies: John the Baptist, or the valour of the soul; Rahman, the apocryphal book of Job's wife; Judas Iscariot, a mystery. [1881]. In prose and verse.

The last words of Cleanthes: a poem. [1883].

Sithron the star-stricken, translated by Salem ben Uzäir. 1883. Written in English by Horne.

King Penguin: a legend of the south sea isles. Ed F. M. Fox, New York 1925.

Horne edited Monthly Repository of Theology & General Lit 1836–7.

§2

Dickens, C. Notes and comments on certain writings by Horne. 1920 (priv ptd). 6 letters from Dickens to Horne.

Letters from A. C. Swinburne to Horne. 1920 (priv ptd).

Mineka, F. E. The dissidence of dissent: the Monthly Repository 1806-38. Chapel Hill 1944.
Pearl, C. Always morning: the life of 'Orion' Horne. Melbourne 1960.

FRANCES ANNE KEMBLE, later BUTLER
1809-93

§1

Francis the first: an historical drama. 1832 (7 edns), New York 1833. In verse.
Journal. 2 vols 1835, 1 vol Brussels 1835 (as Journal of a residence in America).
The star of Seville. 1837, New York 1837. A play.
Poems. Philadelphia 1844, Boston 1859.
Poems. 1844. Contents similar to US edn, above, but arranged differently; later edns follow the US edn.
A year of consolation. 2 vols 1847. Travels in Italy.
Journal of a residence on a Georgian plantation in 1838-9. 1863. Extracts on slavery were rptd by emancipation groups.
Plays: An English tragedy, Mary Stuart (translated from the German of Schiller), Mademoiselle de Belle Isle (translated from the French of Dumas). 1863.
Poems. 1866. Mostly new.
Record of a girlhood: an autobiography. 3 vols 1878, 1879.
Notes upon some of Shakespeare's plays. 1882. Includes On the stage, ed G. Arliss, New York 1926.
Records of later life. 3 vols 1882.
Adventures of John Timothy Homespun in Switzerland: a play stolen from the French of Tartarin de Tarascon. 1889.
Far away and long ago. 1889. A novel.
Further records 1848-83. 2 vols 1890. Letters as a sequel to Record of a girlhood and Records of later life.

§2

James, H. In his Essays in London and elsewhere, New York 1893.
Letters of Edward FitzGerald to Fanny Kemble 1871-83. Ed W. A. Wright 1895.
Pope-Hennessy, U. In her Three English women in America, 1929.
Bobbé, D. Fanny Kemble. New York 1931.
Driver, L. S. Fanny Kemble. Chapel Hill 1933.
Armstrong, M. Fanny Kemble: a passionate Victorian. 1936.

EDWARD LEAR
1812-88

Collections

Complete nonsense. Ed H. Jackson 1947.
Journals: a selection. Ed H. van Thal 1952.
Lear in the original: drawings and limericks. Ed H. W. Liebert, New York 1975.

§1

Views in Rome and its environs. 1841. First of 7 travel-journals 1841-70.
A book of nonsense. 1846 (anon), 1861 (enlarged), 1863 (enlarged), 1870.
Illustrated excursions in Italy. 1846.
Journals of a landscape painter in Albania, Illyria etc. 1851.
Journals of a landscape painter in S. Calabria. 1852; ed P. C. Quennell 1964.
A book of nonsense and more nonsense. 1862.

Views of the seven Ionian islands. 1863.
Journal of a landscape painter in Corsica. 1870, 1966.
Nonsense songs, stories, botany and alphabets. 1871; ed E. Strachey 1894 (with addns).
More nonsense pictures, rhymes, botany etc. 1872.
Laughable lyrics: a fourth book of nonsense poems, songs, botany, music etc. 1877.
Letters. Ed Lady Strachey 1907; Later letters, ed Lady Strachey 1911.
Queery Leary nonsense. 1911. Compiled by Lady Strachey, with introd by Earl of Cromer and some new material.
A tour in Sicily May-July 1847. Ed G. Proby 1938.
Indian journal, from the diary 1873-5. Ed R. Murphy 1953.
Teapots and quails, and other new nonsenses. Ed A. Davidson and P. Hofer, Cambridge Mass 1953. Unpbd fragments.

§2

Davidson, A. Edward Lear. 1938.
Sewell, E. In her Field of nonsense. 1952.
Noakes, V. Lear: the life of a wanderer. 1968.
Kelen, E. Mr Nonsense. 1974.

RICHARD MONCKTON MILNES, 1st BARON HOUGHTON
1809-85

Collections

Memorials of many scenes: poems, legendary and historical. 2 vols 1844.
Selections from the poetical works. 1863.
A selection from the works. 1867. Poems.
Poetical works. 2 vols 1876. Includes songs pbd as flysheets and not mentioned separately below.

§1

The influence of Homer. Cambridge 1829. A prize essay.
Memorials of a tour in some parts of Greece, chiefly poetical. 1834.
Memorials of a residence on the Continent, and historical poems. 1838.
Poems of many years. 1838 (priv ptd), 1840 (for general circulation), 1846.
Poetry for the people, and other poems. 1840.
Palm leaves. 1844. Poems written during and about a tour in the East.
The life, letters and literary remains of John Keats. 2 vols 1848; ed R. Lynd 1927 (EL), Oxford 1931 (WC). Also pbd, in an abridged form, with Keats's poetical works, 1854 etc.
Miscellanies of the Philobiblon Society. 15 vols 1853-84. Ed Milnes, with numerous contributions by him.
Good night and good morning: a ballad. 1859.
Monographs: personal and social. 1873.

Letters and Papers

Reid, T. W. The life, letters and friendships of Milnes. 2 vols 1890.
Fischer, W. Die Briefe Milnes. Heidelberg 1922.

§2

Pope-Hennessy, J. Monckton Milnes. 2 vols 1950-2.

FRANCIS WILLIAM NEWMAN
1805-97

§1

Lectures on logic. 1838.

History of the Hebrew monarchy. 1847.
The soul: her sorrows and her aspirations. 1849. Prose.
Phases of faith. 1850, 1907. Prose.
Regal Rome. 1852. Prose.
The odes of Horace translated. 1853.
The Iliad of Homer translated. 1856.
Theism, doctrinal and practical. 1858.
Homeric translation in theory and practice. 1861. A reply to Arnold; rptd in Essays by Matthew Arnold, Oxford 1914.
Translations of English poetry into Latin verse. 1868.
The cure of the great social evils. 1869.
Miscellanies: chiefly addresses. 3 vols 1869–89.
Anthropomorphism. Ramsgate 1870.
Europe of the near future. 1871.
A dictionary of modern Arabic. 1871.
On the historical depravation of Christianity. 1873.
Hebrew theism: the common basis of Judaism, Christianity and Mohammedism. 1874.
The two theisms. 1874.
Ancient sacrifice. 1874.
Religion not history. 1877.
Life after death? 1886, 1887.
Reminiscences of two exiles. 1888.
Kabai vocabulary. 1887.
Contributions chiefly to the early history of the late Cardinal Newman. 1891.
Hebrew Jesus. Nottingham 1895.

§2

Arnold, M. On translating Homer. 1861.
—— On translating Homer: last words. 1862.
Robbins, W. The Newman brothers. 1966.

FRANCIS TURNER PALGRAVE
1824–97
§1

Preciosa: a tale. 1852.
Idyls and songs. 1854.
The passionate pilgrim: or Eros and Anteros. 1858.
The golden treasury. 1861, 1862, 1878, 1884, 1891 (rev and enlarged), 1896 etc; Second series, 1897. Often rptd.
Essays on art. 1866.
Hymns. 1867, 1868 (enlarged).
Lyrical poems. 1871.
The children's treasury of English song. 2 pts 1875, 1876 (as The children's treasury of lyrical song).
The visions of England, 1880 (priv ptd), 1881 (for general circulation), 1886, 1889, 1891.
The captive child. [1880?]. A poem.
Ode for the twentieth of June 1887. [1887]. Oxford 1887 (as Ode for the twenty-first of June 1887).
The treasury of sacred song. Oxford 1889.
Amenophis and other poems. 1892. Includes all the earlier poems Palgrave wished to preserve.
Prothalamion. [1893] (priv ptd).
Landscape in poetry, from Homer to Tennyson. 1897.
[Miscellaneous essays]. 4 vols [1847–97]. Presented to BM.
Palgrave also pbd numerous edns and selections of the poets.

§2

Palgrave, G. F. Palgrave: his journals and memories of his life. 1899.
Horne, C. J. Palgrave's Golden treasury. E Studies 2 1949.

ADELAIDE ANNE PROCTER
1825–64

Legends and lyrics. 2 vols 1858–61; 1866 (with addns and

introd by C. Dickens), 1895 (with addns), 1906 (EL) (omits introd by Dickens). Most of the poems first appeared in Household Words, and many were later rptd separately.
A chaplet of verses. 1862, 1868 (3rd edn).
The Victoria regia. Ed A. A. Procter 1861.

SIR HENRY TAYLOR
1800–86

Isaac Comnenus. 1827, 1845 (adds Edwin the fair), 1852, 1875. Verse tragedy.
Philip van Artevelde: a dramatic romance. 2 vols 1834, 1 vol 1844 (3rd edn), 1846, 1852 (6th edn), 1872.
The statesman. 1836; ed H. J. Laski, Cambridge 1927; ed L. Silberman 1957.
Edwin the fair: an historical drama. 1842; rptd in Isaac Comnenus, 1845, above. In verse.
The eve of the conquest and other poems. 1847; rptd in A Sicilian summer, 1875, below.
Notes from life in six essays. 1847, 1848, Boston 1853 (7 essays), London 1854. Prose.
Notes from books in four essays. 1849. Chiefly from Quart Rev; 2 essays on Wordsworth.
The virgin widow: a play. 1850, 1875 (as A Sicilian summer). Chiefly in verse.
St Clement's eve: a play. 1862. In verse.
Crime considered. 1869. A letter to Gladstone on the criminal code.
A Sicilian summer: with The eve of the conquest and minor poems. 1875.
Autobiography 1800–75. 1877 (priv ptd), 2 vols 1885.
Correspondence. Ed E. Dowden 1888.

CHARLES TENNYSON, afterwards TURNER
1808–79

Selections

Collected sonnets, old and new. 1880, 1898. With preface by Hallam Tennyson, and introd by J. Spedding.
Charles Tennyson. [1931].

§1

Poems by two brothers. 1827, 1893 (with addns). With Alfred and Frederick Tennyson. *See also col 821, above.*
Sonnets and fugitive pieces. Cambridge 1830.
Sonnets 1864.
Small tableaux. 1868.
Sonnets, lyrics and translations. 1873.

§2

S[hepherd], R. H. Tennysoniana: notes bibliographical and critical on early poems of Alfred and Charles Tennyson. 1866–[75].
Nicolson, H. Tennyson's two brothers. Cambridge 1947.

FREDERICK TENNYSON
1807–98

§1

Poems by two brothers. 1827, 1893 (with addns). With Alfred and Charles Tennyson. *See col 821, above.*
ΑΙΓΥΠΤΟΣ: carmen Graecum numismate annuo dignatum et in curia Cantabrigiensi recitatum comitiis maximis AD MDCCCXXVIII. In Prolusiones academicae, Cambridge 1828.
Days and hours. 1854.

The isles of Greece; Sappho and Alcaeus. 1890.
Daphne and other poems. 1891.
Poems of the day and year. 1895.

§2

Rawnsley, H. D. Memories of the Tennysons. Glasgow 1912.
Letters to Frederick Tennyson. Ed H. J. Schonfield 1930.
Nicolson, H. Tennyson's two brothers. Cambridge 1947.
Fall, C. An index of the letters from papers of Frederick Tennyson. SE 36 1957.

MARTIN FARQUHAR TUPPER
1810-89

§1

Sacra poesis. 1832.
Geraldine: a sequel to Coleridge's Christabel, with other poems. 1838.
Proverbial philosophy: a book of thoughts and arguments, originally treated. 1838; 4 sers [1876?] (complete).
A modern pyramid to commemorate a septuagint of worthies. 1839. A sonnet and an essay on each of 70 famous men.
A thousand lines now first offered to the world we live in 1845.
Hactenus. 1848.
The loving ballad to Brother Jonathan. [1848].

King Alfred's poems turned into English metres. 1850.
Farley Heath. Guildford 1850.
Ballads for the times. 1850, 1851, 1852 (rev).
Half a dozen no-popery ballads. [1851].
A hymn for all nations. 1851.
A dirge for Wellington. 1852.
Half a dozen ballads for Australian emigrants. 1853.
A batch of war ballads. 1854.
A dozen ballads for the times about Church abuses. 1854.
A dozen ballads for the times about white slavery. 1854.
Lyrics of the heart and mind. 1855, 1855.
A missionary ballad. [1855?].
Alfred: a patriotic play. Westminster 1858 (priv ptd).
Martin Tupper on rifle-clubs. 1859.
Three hundred sonnets. 1860.
Plan of the ritualistic campaign. [1865?] (priv ptd), 1868 (as The anti-ritualistic satire).
Our Canadian dominion: half a dozen ballads about a King for Canada. 1868.
Twenty-one Protestant ballads published in the Rock. 1868.
A creed etcetera. 1870.
Fifty of the Protestant ballads. 1874.
Washington: a drama in five acts. 1876.
Autobiography. 1886. Prose.

§2

Hudson, D. Tupper: his rise and fall. 1949.

V. LATE NINETEENTH-CENTURY POETRY

WILLIAM MORRIS
1834-96

Collections

The collected works of Morris, with introductions by May Morris. 24 vols 1910-15, New York 1966.
The defence of Guenevere, the Life and death of Jason, and other poems. Oxford 1914 (WC).
Prose and poetry 1856-70. Oxford 1920 (OSA).
Stories in prose, stories in verse, shorter poems, lectures, and essays: centenary edition. Ed G. D. H. Cole 1934.
Morris: artist, writer, Socialist. Ed May Morris 2 vols Oxford 1936, New York 1966. A suppl to the Collected works, above.
Selected writings and designs. Ed A. Briggs 1962 (Pelican).

§1

The defence of Guenevere and other poems. 1858, 1875, 1892 (Kelmscott Press).
The life and death of Jason: a poem. 1867, 1868 (for Dec 1867) (2nd edn rev), 1868, 1869, 1872 (5th-7th edn), 1882 (rev), 1895 (Kelmscott Press).
The earthly paradise: a poem. 3 (or 4) vols 1868-70. Vol 1 (pts 1-2), (March-Aug) 1868 (edns 1-4), 2 vols 1870 (for 1869), pt 3 (Sept-Nov) 1870 (for 1869) (3 edns); pt 4 (Dec-Feb) 1870, 1870, 1871 (3rd edn); [completed work], 10 vols 1872 (popular edn), 5 vols 1886 (popular edn), 1890 (rev), 8 vols 1896 (Kelmscott Press).
The lovers of Gudrun. Boston 1870. Excerpt from Earthly paradise.
Love is enough or the freeing of Pharamond: a morality. 1873 (for 1872), 1873, 1889, 1898 (Kelmscott Press).
The story of Sigurd the Volsung, and the fall of the Niblungs. 1877 (for 1876) (3 edns), 1887, 1898 (Kelmscott Press).

The decorative arts, their relation to modern life and progress: an address delivered before the Trades' Guild of Learning. [1878]; rptd as The lesser arts in Hopes and fears for art, below.
Address delivered in the Town Hall. Birmingham [1879]; rptd as The art of the people in Hopes and fears for art, 1882.
Labour and pleasure versus labour and sorrow: an address. Birmingham [1880]; rptd as The beauty of life in Hopes and fears for art, 1882, below.
The Wedgwood Institute: reports of the Schools of Science & Art for the year 1880-1, with the address delivered by Morris. Burslem 1881; rptd in Lectures, below, as Art and the beauty of the earth.
Hopes and fears for art: five lectures delivered in Birmingham, London and Nottingham 1878-81. 1882, 1883.
Lectures on art delivered in support of the Society for the Protection of Ancient Buildings. 1882. Morris' 2 lectures are The history of pattern design, 1879 and The lesser arts of life, 1882 (as Some of the minor arts of life).
A summary of the principles of Socialism written for the Democratic Federation by H. M. Hyndman and Morris. 1884, 1884, 1896.
Textile fabrics: a lecture. 1884. Delivered at International Health Exhibition.
Art and Socialism: a lecture; and Watchman, what of the night? 1884 (Leek Bijou Reprints, no 7). Subtitled The aims and ideals of the English Socialists of to-day.
Chants for Socialists, no 1: The day is coming. [1884].
The voice of toil, All for the cause: two chants for Socialists. [1884].
The God of the poor. [1884].
Chants for Socialists. 1885, 1885 (adds Down among the dead men), 1892.
The manifesto of the Socialist League. 1885, 1885 (new edn annotated by Morris and E. B. Bax).

Socialists at play: prologue spoken at the entertainment of the Socialist League. 1885.

The Socialist League: constitution and rules adopted at the General Conference. 1885.

Address to Trades' Unions (The Socialist platform—no 1). 1885. Ed with E. B. Bax.

Useful work v. useless toil (The Socialist platform—no 2). 1885, 1893.

For whom shall we vote? addressed to the working-men electors of Great Britain. [1885].

What Socialists want (Socialist League—Hammersmith Branch—no 11). [1885].

The labour question from the Socialist standpoint (Claims of labour lectures—no 5). Edinburgh 1886; rptd in The claims of labour, Edinburgh 1886. Same as True and false society, below.

A short account of the Commune of Paris (The Socialist platform—no 4). 1886. With E. B. Bax and V. Dave.

Socialism. [1886].

The pilgrims of hope. 1886. An unauthorized reprint from Commonweal by H. B. Forman.

The aims of art. 1887.

The tables turned, or Nupkins awakened: a Socialist interlude. 1887.

Alfred Linnell, killed in Trafalgar Square, Nov 20 1887: a death song. [1887]. Sold for the benefit of Linnell's orphans, with a memorial design by Walter Crane.

The principles of Socialism made plain; and Objections, methods and quack remedies for poverty considered, by F. Fairman. 1888. With preface by Morris.

True and false society (The Socialist platform—no 6). 1888, 1893. Same as Labour question, above.

The Socialist platform written by several hands for the Socialist League, together with the Manifesto and Chants for Socialists by Morris. 1888, 1890 (enlarged to include Monopoly).

Signs of change: seven lectures delivered on various occasions. 1888, 1902.

A dream of John Ball and A King's lesson. 1888, 1892 (Kelmscott Press). Rptd from Commonweal, illustr E. Burne-Jones. A King's lesson separately rptd Aberdeen 1891.

A tale of the house of the Wolfings and all the kindreds of the Mark, written in prose and verse. 1889.

The roots of the mountains wherein is told somewhat of the lives of the men of Burgdale, their friends, their neighbours, their foemen and their fellows in arms. 1890.

Monopoly: or how labour is robbed (The Socialist platform—no 7). 1890, 1891, 1893, 1898.

News from nowhere, or an epoch of rest: being some chapters from a utopian romance. Boston 1890 (uncorrected and unauthorized 'author's edition' from Commonweal text), London 1891 (in 3 different states), 1892 (Kelmscott Press).

The legend of the briar rose: a series of pictures painted by E. Burne-Jones. 1890. With 4 quatrains by Morris.

Statement of principles of the Hammersmith Socialist Society. [1890]. Anon.

Poems by the way. 1891 (Kelmscott Press), 1891 (Chiswick Press).

The Socialist ideal of art. 1891.

The story of the glittering plain which has been also called the land of living men or the acre of the undying. 1891 (Kelmscott Press), 1891 (regular edn, Reeves & Turner), 1894 (Kelmscott Press, rptd with 23 pictures by Walter Crane).

Address on the collection of paintings of the English Pre-Raphaelite school. Birmingham 1891.

Under an elm-tree: or thoughts in the country-side. Aberdeen 1891.

Manifesto of English Socialists. 1893. Anon, written conjointly with H. M. Hyndman and G. B. Shaw.

The reward of labour: a dialogue. [1893].

Concerning Westminster Abbey. [1893]. Anon.

Socialism: its growth and outcome. 1893. With E. B. Bax.

Help for the miners: the deeper meaning of the struggle. [1893].

Gothic architecture: a lecture for the Arts and Crafts Exhibition Society. 1893 (Kelmscott Press).

Arts and crafts essays by members of the Arts and Crafts Exhibition Society. 1893, 1894. With a preface and three essays by Morris: Textiles, Printing (with Emery Walker), Of dyeing as an art.

The wood beyond the world. 1894 (Kelmscott Press), 1895 (regular edn).

The why I ams: Why I am a Communist [with L. S. Bevington's Why I am an expropriationist]. 1894.

Child Christopher and Goldilind the Fair. 2 vols 1895 (Kelmscott Press).

Gossip about an old house on the upper Thames. Birmingham 1895.

The well at the world's end: a tale. 2 vols 1896 (Kelmscott Press), 1896 (ordinary edn ptd Chiswick Press).

Of the external coverings of roofs. [1896].

How I became a Socialist; with some account of his [Morris's] connection with the Social-Democratic Federation by H. M. Hyndman. 1896.

Some German woodcuts of the fifteenth century. Ed S. C. Cockerell 1897 (Kelmscott Press). Reprints partial text of Morris' lecture of 1892, The woodcuts of Gothic books.

The water of the wondrous isles. 1897 (Kelmscott Press, pbd posthumously), 1897.

The sundering flood. 1897 (Kelmscott Press, pbd posthumously), 1898.

A note by Morris on his aims in founding the Kelmscott Press, together with a short description of the press by S. C. Cockerell and an annotated list of the books printed thereat. 1898 (Kelmscott Press).

[Lectures printed at Chiswick Press in Golden type of Kelmscott Press, published by Longmans:] Address delivered at the distribution of prizes to students of the Birmingham Mnicipal School of Art on 21 Feb 1894, 1898; Art and the beauty of the earth, 1899; Some hints on pattern-designing, 1899; Architecture and history, and Westminster Abbey, 1900; Art and its producers, and The arts and crafts of today, 1901.

Architecture, industry and wealth: collected papers. 1902.

The ideal book. New York 1902, 1907, London 1957. Lecture delivered in 1893.

Communism (Fabian Tract no 113). 1903.

The revolt of Ghent. [1911]. Lecture delivered in 1888.

Morris and his Praise of wine. Los Angeles 1958 (priv ptd).

Mr Morris on art matters. 1961. Lecture delivered in 1882 as The progress of decorative art in England.

Translations

Grettis Saga: the story of Grettir the strong. 1869. Tr from the Icelandic by Morris and E. Magnússon.

Völsunga Saga: the story of the Volsungs and Niblungs with certain songs from the Elder Edda. 1870; ed H. Sparling 1888, New York 1965. Tr from the Icelandic Morris and Magnússon.

Three northern love stories and other tales. 1875. Tr Morris and Magnússon.

The Aeneids of Virgil done into English verse. 1876 (for 1875).

The Odyssey of Homer done into English verse. 2 vols 1887.

The Saga library. 5 vols 1891–5. Tr from the Icelandic by Morris and Magnússon.

The order of knighthood. In The order of Chivalry, 1893 (Kelmscott Press).

The tale of King Florus and the Fair Jehane. 1893 (Kelmscott Press).

Of the friendship of Amis and Amile. 1894 (Kelmscott Press).

The tale of the Emperor Coustans and of Over Sea. 1894 (Kelmscott Press).

Old French romances. 1896. Rptd from above 3 items.

The tale of Beowulf, sometime King of the folk of the Weder Geats. 1895 (Kelmscott Press). Tr Morris and A. J. Wyatt.

Letters

Letters of Morris to his family and friends. Ed P. Henderson 1950.

Unpublished letters of Morris. Ed R. P. Arnot 1951.

§2

Swinburne, A. C. In his Essays and studies, 1875.

Pater, W. Aesthetic poetry. In his Appreciations, 1889.

Mackail, J. W. The life of Morris. 2 vols 1899.

Yeats, W. B. The happiest of the poets. In his Ideas of good and evil, 1903.

Jackson, H. Morris: craftsman-Socialist. 1908, 1926 (rev with 4 new chs).

Noyes, A. Morris. 1908 (EML).

Drinkwater, J. Morris: a critical study. 1912.

Shaw, G. B. Morris as I knew him. New York 1936, London 1966.

Lewis, C. S. In his Rehabilitations and other essays, Oxford 1939.

Hough, G. In his Last Romantics, 1949.

Henderson, P. William Morris. 1952, 1964 (rev) (Br Council pamphlet).

Thompson, E. P. Morris: romantic to revolutionary. 1955, 1961.

Arnot, R. P. Morris: the man and the myth. 1964.

Henderson, P. Morris: his life, work and friends. 1967.

Thompson, P. R. The work of Morris. 1967.

Faulkner, P. (ed). Morris: the critical heritage. 1973.

ALGERNON CHARLES SWINBURNE
1837–1909

Bibliographies

Wise, T. J. A bibliography of the writings of Swinburne. 2 vols 1919–20 (priv ptd), 1927 (rev) (vol 20 in Complete works, Bonchurch edn).

—— A Swinburne library. 1925 (priv ptd).

Hyder, C. K. Swinburne's literary career and fame. Durham NC 1933.

—— In The Victorian poets: a review of research, ed F. E. Faverty, Cambridge Mass 1956, 1968 (rev).

Collections

Poems. 6 vols 1904 (with Atalanta and Erechtheus).

A selection. Ed. E. Sitwell 1960.

Poems. Ed. B. Dobrée 1961.

Swinburne as critic. Ed C. K. Hyder 1973.

§1

The Queen-Mother; Rosamond. 1860, 1860 (for 1865, Moxon's reissue), 1866 (Hotten's reissue), 1868 etc.

Pilgrimage of pleasure. In Mary Gordon's Children of the chapel, 1864, 1875, 1910.

Atalanta in Calydon. 1865, 1865, 1866, 1868, 1875 etc, Oxford 1930 (facs).

Chastelard. 1865, 1866 (Hotten's reissue), 1868, 1878 etc.

Poems and ballads. 1866, 1866 (Hotten's reissue), 1866.

Notes on poems and reviews. 1866, 1866.

Byron. 1866.

An appeal to England. 1867.

A song of Italy. 1867, 1868.

Notes on the Royal Academy exhibition. 1868.

William Blake. 1868 (for 1867), 1868, 1906.

Siena. 1868.

Christabel and the poems of Coleridge. 1869.

Ode on the French Republic. 1870.

Songs before sunrise. 1871, 1874 etc.

Bothwell, Act one [an early version]. 1871 (priv ptd).

Under the microscope. 1872.

Le tombeau de Théophile Gautier. 1873.

Bothwell. 1874, 1874, 1882 etc.

George Chapman. 1875.

Songs of two nations. 1875, 1893.

Essays and studies. 1875, 1876, 1888 etc.

Note on the Muscovite crusade. 1876.

Erechtheus. 1876, 1876, 1887, 1896 etc.

Lesbia Brandon. 1877 (galleys); ed R. Hughes 1952; ed E. Wilson, New York 1962.

Note on Charlotte Brontë. 1877, 1877, 1894.

Poems and ballads: second series. 1878, 1878, 1880 etc.

A study of Shakespeare. 1880, 1880, 1895, 1902 etc.

Songs of the springtides. 1880, 1880, 1891, 1902.

Specimens of modern poets: the heptalogia. 1880.

Studies in song. 1880, 1896, 1907.

Mary Stuart. 1881, 1898, 1909.

Tristram of Lyonesse and other poems. 1882, 1882, 1884, 1892 etc.

A century of roundels. 1883, 1883, 1892 etc.

A midsummer holiday and other poems. 1884, 1884, 1889.

Marino Faliero. 1885, 1907.

A study of Victor Hugo. 1886, 1909.

Miscellanies. 1886, 1895, 1911.

The commonweal: a song for unionists. 1886 (rptd from Times 1 July 1886), 1889 (pirated). Rptd in Gathered songs (a forgery with a fraudulent imprint and the date July 1887) and in A channel passage and other poems, 1904.

Cleopatra. 1886–7 or –8 (priv ptd). A forgery, fraudulently dated 1866, but nonetheless the first separate printing.

A word for the Navy. 1887 (priv ptd) (Redway edn).

Locrine. 1887, 1896.

Thomas Middleton. 1887. Introd to Mermaid edn.

The jubilee. [1888–90?] (priv ptd). A forgery, with a fraudulent imprint and the date (not proved false) June 1887. The poem was pbd in Nineteenth Century June 1887 and rptd (as The commonweal) in Poems and ballads: third series, pbd 4 April 1889.

The question. [1888–90?] (priv ptd). A forgery, with a fraudulent imprint and the date (not proved false) May 1887. The poem was ptd in Daily Telegraph 29 April 1887 and rptd in A channel passage and other poems, 1904.

Dead love. [1888?] (priv ptd: a forgery, fraulently dated 1864), [1904?] (a counterfeit of the forgery). Rptd in A pilgrimage of pleasure, Boston 1913 and in Bonchurch edn vol 17.

The Whippingham papers. 1888 (priv ptd). About half the vol, including 2 poems, Arthur's flogging and Reginald's flogging, and one piece in prose, A boy's first flogging at Birchminster, is Swinburne's.

Poems and ballads: third series. 1889, 1889, 1892, etc.

A study of Ben Jonson. 1889.

Gathered songs. [1888–90?] (priv ptd). A forgery, with a fraudulent imprint and the date (not proved false) July 1887; 3 of the 4 poems pbd in Poems and ballads: third series, 4 April 1889.

A sequence of sonnets on the death of Robert Browning. 1890 (priv ptd; pirated).

Robert Herrick. 1891. Introd to ML edn.

The sisters. 1892.

The ballad of Bulgarie. 1893 (priv ptd; pirated).

Grace Darling. 1893 (priv ptd; pirated).

Astrophel and other poems. 1894, 1894.

Studies in prose and poetry. 1894, 1897, 1906, 1915.

The devil's due. [1896?] (priv ptd). A forgery, fraudulently dated 1875.

The tale of Balen. 1896.

Robert Burns. Edinburgh 1896 (priv ptd; pirated).

Aurora Leigh. 1898. Introd to Mrs Browning's poem.
A channel passage. 1899.
Rosamund, Queen of the Lombards. 1899, 1900.
Love's cross-currents: a year's letters. Portland Maine
1901, 1905, 1906; ed E. Wilson, New York 1962; ed
F. J. Sypher, New York 1976. A novel.
Percy Bysshe Shelley. Philadelphia 1903. Also in
Chambers's cyclopaedia of English literature, 1903.
A channel passage and other poems. 1904, 1904, 1904.
The Duke of Gandia. 1908.
The age of Shakespeare. 1909.
Lord Soulis. 1909 (priv ptd).
In the twilight. 1909 (priv ptd).
To W.T.W.D. 1909 (priv ptd).
Lord Scales. 1909 (priv ptd).
M. Prudhomme at the international exhibition. 1909
(priv ptd).
Of liberty and loyalty. 1909 (priv ptd).
The saviour of society. 1909 (priv ptd).
The marriage of Monna Lisa. 1909 (priv ptd).
The portrait. 1909 (priv ptd).
The chronicle of Queen Fredegonde. 1909 (priv ptd).
Burd Margaret. 1909 (priv ptd).
The worm of Spindlestonheugh. 1909 (priv ptd).
Border ballads. 1909 (priv ptd).
Ode to Mazzini. 1909 (priv ptd).
The ballad of truthful Charles and other poems. 1910
(priv ptd).
A criminal case. 1910 (priv ptd).
The ballade of Villon and Fat Madge. 1910 (priv ptd).
A record of friendship. 1910 (priv ptd).
Blest and The centenary of Shelley. 1912 (priv ptd).
Border ballads. Boston 1912 (priv ptd).
Les fleurs du mal and other studies. 1913 (priv ptd).
The cannibal catechism. 1913 (priv ptd).
Charles Dickens. 1913.
A pilgrimage of pleasure, essays and studies. Boston 1913.
A study of Les misérables. 1914 (priv ptd). The first and
fifth essays are not by Swinburne.
Pericles and other studies. 1914 (priv ptd).
Thomas Nabbes. 1914 (priv ptd).
Christopher Marlowe in relation to Greene, Peele and
Lodge. 1914 (priv ptd).
Théophile. 1915 (priv ptd).
Lady Maisie's bairn and other poems. 1915 (priv ptd).
Félicien Cossu. 1915 (priv ptd).
Ernest Clouët. 1916 (priv ptd).
A vision of bags. 1916 (priv ptd).
Poems from Villon and other fragments. 1916 (priv ptd).
The death of Sir John Franklin. 1916 (priv ptd).
The triumph of Gloriana. 1916 (priv ptd).
Poetical fragments. 1916 (priv ptd).
Weareiswa'. 1917 (priv ptd).
Posthumous poems. Ed. E. Gosse and T. J. Wise 1917.
Rondeaux parisiens. 1917 (priv ptd).
The character and opinions of Dr Johnson. 1918 (priv
ptd).
The Italian mother and other poems. 1918 (priv ptd).
The ride from Milan. 1918 (priv ptd).
The two knights and other poems. 1918 (priv ptd).
A lay of lilies and other poems. 1918 (priv ptd).
Queen Yseult. 1918 (priv ptd).
Undergraduate sonnets. 1918 (priv ptd).
Lancelot, the death of Rudel and other poems. 1918
(priv ptd).
Contemporaries of Shakespeare. Ed. E. Gosse and T. J.
Wise 1919.
Shakespeare. Oxford 1919.
The queen's tragedy. 1919 (priv ptd).
French lyrics. 1919 (priv ptd).
Ballads of the English border. Ed. W. A. MacInnes 1925.
Swinburne's Hyperion and other poems. Ed. G. Lafour-
cade 1928.
Lucretia Borgia: the chronicle of Tebaldeo Tebaldei.
Ed. R. Hughes 1942.

Columbus, with a note by J. S. Mayfield. Jacksonville
Fla 1944 (priv ptd).
Pasiphaë. Ed. R. Hughes 1950.
New writings by Swinburne. Ed. C. Y. Lang, Syracuse
NY 1964.

Letters
All the genuine letters listed here were included in The
Swinburne letters, ed Lang 1959-62, *below.*

Letters to T. J. Wise, 1909; Letters on Chapman, 1909;
Letters to J. C. Collins, 1910; Letters on Morris, Omar
Khayyám etc, 1910; Letters to A. H. Bullen, 1910;
Letters to Purnell and others, 1910; Letters concerning
Poe, 1910; Letters to Gosse, 5 ser 1910-11; Letters to
Stedman, 1912; Letters to Burton and others, 1912;
Letters to Henry Taylor, 1912; Letters to Locker-
Lampson and others, 1912; Letters to the press, 1912;
Letters to Lytton, 1913; Letters to Locker, 1913; Letters
to Mallarmé, 1913; Letters to Morley, 1914; Letters to
Dowden, 1914; Letters to Milnes and others, 1915;
Letters to Lady Trevelyan, 1916; Letters to Nichol,
1917; Letters to Hugo, 1917. All priv ptd.
The letters of Swinburne. Ed E. Gosse and T. J. Wise
2 vols 1918. Rptd, rev and enlarged in vol 18 of
Bonchurch edn, above.
The Swinburne letters. Ed. C. Y. Lang 6 vols New
Haven 1959-62.

§2
Rossetti, W. M. Swinburne's Poems and ballads. 1866.
Wilde, O. Pall Mall Gazette 27 June 1889. Review of
Poems and ballads: third series; rptd in his Reviews,
vol 2 1910.
Mackail, J. W. Swinburne. Oxford 1909; rptd in his
Studies of English poets, 1926.
Gosse, E. Life. 1917; rptd in Bonchurch edn, vol 19
(rev).
—— Swinburne. 1925.
Eliot, T. S. Swinburne as critic; Swinburne as poet. In
his Sacred wood, 1920.
Grierson, H. J. C. Byron: Arnold and Swinburne. Proc
Br Acad 9 1921; rptd in his Background of English
literature, 1925.
—— Swinburne. 1953.
Nicolson, H. Swinburne and Baudelaire. Trans Royal Soc
of Lit 6 1926; Oxford 1930 (rev).
—— Swinburne. 1926.
Chew, S. C. Swinburne. Boston 1929.
Hyder, C. K. Swinburne's literary career and fame.
Durham NC 1931.
Tillyard, E. M. W. In his Five poems 1470-1870, 1948.
On Hertha.
Bowra, C. M. Atalanta in Calydon. In his Romantic imagi-
nation, Cambridge Mass 1949; Essays by Divers Hands
25 1950.
Hare, H. Swinburne: a biographical approach. 1949.
Peters, R. L. The crowns of Apollo: Swinburne's prin-
ciples of literature and art. Detroit 1965.
Tillotson, G. In his Mid-Victorian studies, 1965.
McGann, J. J. Swinburne: an experiment in criticism.
Chicago 1972.
Henderson, P. Swinburne. 1974.

JAMES THOMSON ('B.V.')
1834-82

*In 1952 Bodley obtained Bertram Dobell's collection of mss
relating to Thomson, containing holograph poems, notebooks, diaries, letters by and to him, other writings and
memoranda. The BM contains drafts for two-thirds of the
City of dreadful night, 3 other notebooks, and corrected
proofs. A ms of this poem is also in the Pierpont Morgan
Library, New York.*

Collections

Poetical works. Ed B. Dobell 2 vols 1895. With memoir by
B. Dobell.
The city of dreadful night [and a selection of poems]. Ed
B. Dobell 1910.
The city of dreadful night and other poems. Ed E.
Blunden 1932.

§1

A commission of inquiry on royalty etc. 1876.
The story of a famous old Jewish firm. 1876.
The devil in the Church of England and The one thing.
1876.
The pilgrimage to Saint Nicotine. Liverpool 1878.
The city of dreadful night and other poems. 1880. The
City of dreadful night first pbd in Nat Reformer 22
March–17 May 1874.
Vane's story, Weddah and Om-el-Bonain and other poems.
1881 (for 1880).
Essays and fantasies. 1881.
The story of the famous old Jewish firm and other pieces
in prose and rime. 1884 (priv ptd).
Satires and profanities. Ed G. W. Foote 1884.
A voice from the Nile and other poems. 1884. With
memoir by B. Dobell.
Shelley; a poem: with other writings relating to Shelley,
by the late James Thomson (B.V.); to which is added an
essay on the poetry of William Blake by the same author.
1884 (priv ptd). Preface by B. Dobell.
Biographical and critical studies. Ed B. Dobell 1896.
Essays, dialogues and thoughts of Giacomo Leopardi.
[1905]. Tr, with a memoir of Leopardi, by Thomson;
introd by B. Dobell.
Thomson on George Meredith. 1909 (priv ptd).
Walt Whitman: the man and the poet. Ed B. Dobell 1910.
Poems and some letters of Thomson. Ed A. Ridler 1963.

§2

Salt, H. S. The life of Thomson. 1889, 1898, 1914 (rev).
Dobell, B. The laureate of pessimism. 1910.
Walker, I. B. Thomson: a critical study. Ithaca 1950.
Schaefer, W. D. The two cities of dreadful night. PMLA
77 1962.
—— Thomson: beyond 'the City'. 1966.
Vachot, C. James Thomson. Paris 1964.

GERARD MANLEY HOPKINS
1844–89

The mss in Campion Hall Oxford are listed in Journals and
papers, ed H. House, *below, appendix 4; others are in the
possession of Bodley and of Lord Bridges.*

Bibliographies etc

Pick, J. In The Victorian poets: a guide to research, ed
F. E. Faverty, Cambridge Mass 1956, 1968 (rev).
Borrello, A. A concordance of the poetry in English.
Metuchen NJ 1969.
Dunne, T. Hopkins: a comprehensive bibliography.
Oxford 1976.

Collections

Poems. Ed R. Bridges, Oxford 1918.
Poems: second edition, with additional poems. Ed
C. Williams, Oxford 1930; ed W. H. Gardner, Oxford
1948 (3rd edn rev and enlarged); ed Gardner and N. H.
Mackenzie, Oxford 1967 (4th edn rev and enlarged).
Letters of Hopkins to Robert Bridges; Correspondence of
Hopkins and Richard Watson Dixon. Ed C. C. Abbott
2 vols Oxford 1935.

Further letters of Hopkins. Ed C. C. Abbott, Oxford 1938,
1956 (rev and enlarged). Letters to and from Coventry
Patmore et al.
Note-books and papers of Hopkins. Ed H. House, Oxford
1937; 2nd edn rev and enlarged in 2 vols as:
Journals and papers of Hopkins. Ed H. House, com-
pleted by G. Storey, Oxford 1959.
Sermons and devotional writings of Hopkins. Ed C.
Devlin, Oxford 1959.
A selection of poems and prose. Ed W. H. Gardner 1953
(Penguin), 1966 (rev and enlarged).
Selected poems and prose. Ed G. Storey, Oxford 1967.

§1

Winter with the gulf stream. Once a Week 14 Feb 1863.
Barnfloor and winepress. Union Rev 3 1865.
Songs from Shakespeare in Latin: 'Full fathom five thy
father lies'. Irish Monthly Nov 1886; 'Come unto
these yellow sands', Feb 1887.
Poets and poetry of the century. Ed A. H. Miles vol 8
[1893]. Includes texts and extracts of 11 poems, with
introd by R. Bridges.
Lyra sacra. Ed H. C. Beeching 1895. Includes 5 poems.
Rosa mystica. Irish Monthly May 1898.
Carmina Mariana. Ed O. Shipley 1902. Includes 2 poems.
The spirit of man. Ed R. Bridges 1916. Includes texts and
extracts of 6 poems.
A vision of the mermaids: facsimile edition of full text
dated Christmas 1862. Oxford 1929.
Early poems and extracts from the notebooks and papers.
[Ed H. House], Criterion 15 1935.
St Thecla (an unpublished poem). Studies 45 1956.
Jesu dulcis memoria. Month Oct 1947. Trn by Hopkins.

§2

Riding, L. and R. Graves. In their A survey of modernist
poetry, 1927.
Empson, W. In his Seven types of ambiguity, 1930, 1947
(rev).
Read, H. Hopkins. Criterion April 1931.
—— The poetry of Hopkins. In English critical essays:
twentieth century, ed P. M. Jones, Oxford 1933 (WC);
rptd in his Defence of Shelley and other essays, 1936
and in his Collected essays in literary criticism, 1938.
Bridges, R. In his Three friends [memoirs of D. M.
Dolben, R. W. Dixon and H. Bradley], Oxford 1932.
Leavis, F. R. In his New bearings in English poetry,
1932, 1950 (enlarged).
—— The letters of Hopkins. Scrutiny 4 1935.
—— Hopkins. Scrutiny 12 1944; rptd as Metaphysical
isolation in The Kenyon critics, New York 1945. Both
articles rptd in his Common pursuit, 1952.
de Selincourt, E. In his Oxford lectures on poetry,
Oxford 1934.
Eliot, T. S. In his After strange gods, 1934.
Lewis, C. D. In his A hope for poetry, Oxford 1934.
Gardner, W. H. The wreck of the Deutschland. E & S 21
1935.
—— A note on Hopkins and Duns Scotus. Scrutiny 5 1936.
—— The religious problem in Hopkins. Scrutiny 6 1937.
—— Hopkins: a study of poetic idiosyncrasy in relation to
poetic tradition. 2 vols 1944–9, 1948 (vol 1 rev).
House, H. A note on Hopkins's religious life. New Verse
14 1935.
—— Hopkins: poet-priest. Listener 22 June 1944; rptd in
his All in due time, 1955.
Brooks, C. (ed). Hopkins. Kenyon Rev 6 1944 (2 Hopkins
issues); rptd in The Kenyon critics, below.
Kenyon critics. Hopkins. New York 1945.
Weyand, N. (ed). Immortal diamond: studies in Hopkins.
New York 1949.
Winters, Y. The poetry of Hopkins. Hudson Rev 1–2
1949; rptd in his Function of criticism, Denver 1957.

Davie, D. A. Hopkins, the decadent critic. Cambridge Jnl Sept 1951; rptd in his Purity of diction in English verse, 1952.
Bergonzi, B. Gerard Manley Hopkins. 1977.

ROBERT SEYMOUR BRIDGES
1844–1930

Bibliographies
McKay, G. L. A bibliography of Bridges. New York 1933.

Collections
Poetical works. 6 vols 1898–1905.
Poetical works excluding the eight dramas, Oxford 1912, 1936 (enlarged) (OSA), 1953 (with Testament of beauty).

§ I

Poems. 1873; second series 1879 (anon); third series, 1880, Oxford 1884 (H. Daniel) (anon); Shorter poems, 1890 (4 bks in 1 vol), bk 5, Oxford 1893 (H. Daniel), 1894 (rev), 1896 (rev); ed M. M. Bridges, Oxford 1931 (enlarged).
Carmen elegiacum. 1876, 1877 (rev).
The growth of love. 1876, Oxford 1889 (H. Daniel) (rev and enlarged), 1890.
Prometheus the firegiver. Oxford 1883 (H. Daniel), London 1884 (rev).
Nero: an historical tragedy, part 1. 1885; part 2, [1894].
Eros and Psyche. 1885, 1894 (rev).
The feast of Bacchus. Oxford 1889 (H. Daniel), 1894 (rev).
Plays. 1890; Eight plays, 1894.
Eden: an oratorio. 1891 (with music by C. V. Stanford).
The humours of the Court and other poems. 1893.
Milton's prosody. Oxford 1893, 1894, 1901 (enlarged), 1921 (with further addns).
John Keats: a critical essay. 1895 (priv ptd); rptd in Poems of John Keats, ed G. T. Drury 1896; and in Poetical works of John Keats, ed L. Binyon [1916] (rev).
Invocation to music: an ode in honour of Henry Purcell. 1895 (with music by C. H. H. Parry), 1896 (rev as Ode for the bicentenary commemoration of Henry Purcell, with other poems and a preface on the musical setting of poetry. Ode rptd in Later poems, 1912, below; other poems in New poems in Poetical works, above, 1899.
A song of darkness and light. 1898 (with music by C. H. H. Parry); rptd as A hymn of nature in Later poems, 1912, below.
A practical discourse on hymn-singing. Oxford 1901.
Now in wintry delights. Oxford 1903; rptd in Poems in classical prosody, 1912, below.
Peace ode written on the conclusion of the Three years' war. Oxford 1903; rptd in Poems in classical prosody, 1912, below.
Demeter: a masque. Oxford 1905; rptd in Poetical works, 1912, above.
Eton memorial ode. [1908] (with music by C. H. H. Parry); rptd in Later poems, 1912, below.
About hymns. Chilswell 1911.
Sonnet xliv of Michelangelo Buonarroti, translated for Andrew Lang. 1912 (priv ptd).
Later poems and Poems in classical prosody. In Poetical works, Oxford 1912, above.
Poems written in the year mcmxiii. 1914 (priv ptd); rptd in October and other poems, 1920, below.
Ode on the tercentenary of the commemoration of Shakespeare. 1916 (priv ptd); rptd in Shakespeare's England, Oxford 1916 and TLS 6 July 1916.
The chivalry of the sea: naval ode. 1916 (with music by C. H. H. Parry); rptd in October and other poems, 1920, below.
An address to the Swindon branch of the Workers' Educational Association. Oxford 1916.

Ibant obscuri: an experiment in the classical hexameter. Oxford 1916.
The necessity of poetry. Oxford 1918.
Britannia victrix. Oxford 1918; rptd in Times 25 Nov 1918 and New verse, 1925, below.
October and other poems with occasional verses on the war. 1920, Oxford 1929.
Poor Poll. 1923 (priv ptd); rptd in New verse, 1925, below.
The tapestry. 1925 (priv ptd).
New verse written in 1921 with the other poems of that year and a few earlier pieces. Oxford 1925, 1926 (rev).
Henry Bradley: a memoir. Oxford 1926; rptd in Collected papers of H. Bradley, Oxford 1928, and in Three friends, 1932.
The testament of beauty: a poem in four books. 5 pts [1927–29] (priv ptd), 1 vol Oxford 1929 (rev), 1930 ('final corrections').
Poetry: the first of the broadcast national lectures. 1929.
Three friends: memoirs of Digby Mackworth Dolben, Richard Watson Dixon, Henry Bradley. Oxford 1932.

Letters and Papers
Although Bridges's letters to Gerard Manley Hopkins were destroyed by Bridges, his letters to members of Hopkins's family 1889–1929 are in Bodley, most of them unpbd.

Collected essays, papers etc. 30 pts Oxford 1927–36.
The letters of G. M. Hopkins to Bridges. Ed C. C. Abbott, Oxford 1935; Further letters of Hopkins, ed C. C. Abbott, Oxford 1956 includes one from Bridges.
Correspondence of Bridges and Henry Bradley 1900–23. Oxford 1940.
Bridges also edited the Yattendon hymnal, Oxford 1895–9, 1920; Yattendon hymns, Oxford 1897 (for 1898); Hymns from the Yattendon hymnal, Oxford 1899; The small hymn book, 1899, 1914, 1920; Yattendon four-part chants, [1897] (priv ptd); Last poems of R. W. Dixon, Oxford 1905; Poems by R. W. Dixon, with a memoir, 1909; The poems of D. M. Dolben, with memoir, Oxford 1911, 1915 (rev); Society for Pure English [tracts], Oxford 1913–29; The spirit of man, 1916; Poems of G. M. Hopkins, Oxford 1918; The Chilswell book of English poetry, 1924; Selections from the letters of W. Raleigh, 1928 (introd by Bridges); The collected papers of H. Bradley, with a memoir, Oxford 1928.

§ 2

Smith, L. P. Bridges. SPE tract no 35 1931. Includes E. Daryush on Bridges's work on the English language.
Smith, N. C. Notes on the Testament of beauty. Oxford 1931, 1932 (rev), 1940 (rev).
Gordon, G. S. Bridges. Cambridge 1932, 1946 (Rede lecture).
—— Hopkins and Bridges. In his Discipline of letters, Oxford 1947.
Nowell-Smith, S. Bridges' classical prosody: new verses and variants. TLS 28 Aug 1943.
—— A poet in Walton street. In Essays presented to Humphrey Milford, Oxford 1948.
—— Bridges's debt to Hopkins. TLS 12 May 1961.
Thompson, E. Bridges 1844–1930. Oxford 1944.
Sparrow, J. Robert Bridges. 1962 (Br Council pamphlet).

FRANCIS THOMPSON
1859–1907

The largest collection of Thompson mss, notebooks, letters and vols is in the Boston College Library, Mass.

Collections
Selected poems. Ed W. Meynell 1908.

Works. Ed W. Meynell 1913.
Poems. Ed T. L. Connolly, New York 1932, 1941 (rev).
Poems. Ed W. Meynell, Oxford 1937 (OSA), 1955.
Poems. 1946. Collected edn with a bibliography of 1st printings to 1913.
Literary criticisms newly discovered and collected. Ed T. L. Connolly, New York 1948.

§ 1

The life and labours of Saint John Baptist de la Salle. 1891, 1911 (preface by W. Meynell).
The child set in the midst. Ed W. Meynell 1892. Contains 4 poems by Thompson.
Poems. 1893.
Sister songs: an offering to two sisters. 1895. Also priv ptd as Songs wing to wing: an offering to two sisters, 1895.
New poems. 1897.
Victorian ode for Jubilee Day. 1897 (priv ptd).
Little Jesus. [1897] (priv ptd), 1920.
Health and holiness. 1905. Introd by G. Tyrell.
Ode to English martyrs. 1906 (priv ptd).
Eyes of youth. [1909]. Foreword by G. K. Chesterton. Contains 4 early poems by Thompson.
Shelley. 1909. Introd by G. Wyndham.
Saint Ignatius Loyola. Ed J. H. Pollen [1909] (preface by W. Meynell), 1951 (introd by H. Kelly).
Uncollected verses. 1917 (priv ptd).
The mistress of vision. Sussex 1918, London 1966.
Youthful verses. Preston 1928 (priv ptd).
The man has wings: new poems and plays. Ed T. L. Connolly, New York 1957.
The real Robert Louis Stevenson and other critical essays. Ed T. L. Connolly, New York 1959.

§ 2

Meynell, E. The life of Thompson. 1913, 1926 (5th edn rev and condensed).
Connolly, T. L. An account of books and mss of Thompson. Boston 1937.
—— Thompson: in his paths—a vist to persons and places associated with the poet. Milwaukee 1944.
Meynell, V. Thompson and Wilfrid Meynell: a memoir. 1952.
Reid, J. C. Thompson: man and poet. 1959.
Butter, P. H. Thompson. 1961.
—— Thompson. REL 2 1961.
Thomson, P. van K. Thompson: a critical biography. New York 1961.

ALFRED EDWARD HOUSMAN
1859–1936

The Library of Congress Washington has the substantial remains of the ms notebooks Housman used for composing, correcting and polishing from c. 1890, together with a number of fair copies. The library of Trinity College Cambridge has the ms printer's copy (lacking one poem) of A Shropshire lad, *and the Fitzwilliam Museum the ms copy of* Last poems *from which the printer's copy was typed, lacking 5 poems.*

Bibliographies etc.

Hyder, C. K. A concordance to the poems of Housman. Lawrence Kansas 1940.
Carter, J. and J. Sparrow. Housman: an annotated handlist. 1952.

Collections

Collected poems. 1939, 1960 (rev, with note on text by J. Carter).
Selected prose. Ed J. Carter, Cambridge 1961, 1962 (corrected).

Collected poems. Ed J. Carter, New York 1965. Authorized and complete. *See* W. White, PBSA 60 1966.

§ 1

Introductory lecture delivered in University College London. Cambridge 1892 (priv ptd), 1933 (priv ptd), 1937.
A Shropshire lad. 1896; Jubilee edition, ed C. J. Weber, Waterville Maine 1946 (with bibliography).
Last poems. 1922.
Fragment of a Greek tragedy. Amherst 1925 (priv ptd).
Nine essays by Arthur Platt. Cambridge 1927. With preface by Housman.
The name and nature of poetry. Cambridge 1933.
Three poems: the parallelogram, the amphisbaena, the crocodile. 1935 (priv ptd); ed W. White, Los Angeles 1941.
More poems. [Ed L. Housman] 1936.
Additional poems. In L. Housman, A.E.H.: some poems, some letters and a personal memoir, 1937.
A meeting with the Royal Family. Los Angeles 1941.
The manuscript poems. Ed T. B. Haber, Minneapolis 1955.
Housman's Cambridge inaugural [1911]. TLS 9 May 1968; ed J. Carter, Cambridge 1969 (as The confines of criticism).

Letters and Papers

Housman, L. In his A.E.H.: some poems, some letters and a personal memoir, 1937.
Richards, G. In his Housman 1897–1936, Oxford 1941.
Letters from Housman to E. H. Blakeney. Winchester 1941 (priv ptd).
B[lakeney], E. H. A.E.H. W.W. Winchester 1944 (priv ptd). Pamphlet on Sir William Watson, with one letter.
Thirty Housman letters to Witter Bynner. Ed T. B. Haber, New York 1957.
White, W. Housman to Joseph Ishill: five unpublished letters. Berkeley Heights NJ 1959 (priv ptd).
Also critical editions of Manilius (1903–30), Juvenal (1905) and Lucan (1926).
Classical papers. Ed J. Diggle and F. R. D. Goodyear 3 vols Cambridge 1972.

§ 2

Archer, W. Housman. Fortnightly Rev 1 Aug 1898; rptd in his Poets of the younger generation, 1902.
Tinker, C. B. Housman's poetry. Yale Rev 25 1935; rptd in his Essays in retrospect, New Haven 1948.
Gow, A. S. F. Housman: a sketch together with a list of his writings and indexes to his classical papers. Cambridge 1936.
Pound, E. Mr Housman at little Bethel. Criterion 13 1934; rptd in his Polite essays, 1936.
Housman, L. A.E.H.: some poems, some letters and a personal memoir. 1937.
Carter, J. On collecting Housman. Colophon new ser 3 1938; rptd in his Books and book-collectors, 1956.
—— A poem of Housman. TLS 5–12 June 1943.
—— The Housman mss in the Library of Congress. Book Collector 4 1955.
—— The text of Housman's poems. TLS 15 June 1956.
—— and J. W. Scott. Housman: catalogue of an exhibition on the centenary of his birth. 1959.
Chambers, R. W. Philologists at University College. In his Man's unconquerable mind, 1939.
Garrod, H. W. Housman 1939. E & S 25 1939.
Richards, G. Housman 1897–1936. Oxford 1941.
Ricks, C. The nature of Housman's poetry. EC 14 1964.
—— (ed). Housman: a collection of critical essays. Englewood Cliffs NJ 1968.

VI. MINOR POETRY 1870–1900

SIR EDWIN ARNOLD
1832–1904

Collections

Poetical works. 8 vols 1888.
The Arnold poetry reader: selections, with memoir and notes by E. L. Arnold. 1920.

§ 1

The feast of Belshazzar: a prize poem. Oxford 1852.
Poems, narrative and lyrical. Oxford 1853.
Griselda: a tragedy, and other poems. 1856.
The wreck of the northern belle: a poem. Hastings 1857.
Education in India: a letter from the ex-principal of an Indian government college to his appointed successor. 1860.
The Marquis of Dalhousie's administration of British India. 2 vols 1862–5.
The poets of Greece. 1869.
A simple transliteral grammar of the Turkish language with dialogues and vocabulary. 1877.
The light of Asia, or the great renunciation. 1879; ed E. D. Ross 1926.
Poems. Boston 1880.
Indian poetry. 1881.
Pearls of the faith: or Islam's rosary. 1883.
The secret of death, with some collected poems. 1885.
India revisited. 1886.
Death—and afterwards. 1887.
Lotus and jewel. 1887.
With Sa'di in the garden: or the book of love. 1888.
In my lady's praise: being poems, old and new, written in the honour of Fanny, Lady Arnold, and now collected for her memory. 1889.
The light of the world, or the great consummation: a poem. 1891.
Seas and lands. 1891.
Japonica. 1892.
Potiphar's wife and other poems. 1892.
Adzuma, or the Japanese wife: a play in four acts. 1893.
Wandering words. 1894.
The tenth muse and other poems. 1895.
East and west. 1896.
Victoria, Queen and Empresss: the sixty years. 1896.
The Queen's justice: a true story of Indian village life. 1899.
The voyage of Ithobal: a poem. 1901.

ALFRED AUSTIN
1835–1913

§ 1

Randolph: a poem in two cantos. 1854, 1877 (recast as Leszco the bastard: a tale of Polish grief).
Five years of it: a novel. 2 vols 1858.
The season: a satire. 1861, 1861 (rev with preface), 1869 (rev).
The human tragedy: a poem. 1862 (withdrawn), 1876 (rev), 1889 (rev), 1889 (rev with preface On the position and prospects of poetry), 1891 (omits preface).
An artist's proof: a novel. 3 vols 1864.
Won by a head: a novel. 3 vols 1866.
A vindication of Lord Byron. 1869. Reply to Mrs Stowe.
The poetry of the period. 1870.
The golden age: a satire in verse. 1871.
Interludes. 1872.
Madonna's child. 1873. Incorporated as Act 2 in The human tragedy, 1876.

Rome or death! a poem. 1873. Forms Act 3 of The human tragedy. 1876.
The tower of babel: a poetical drama. 1874.
Savonarola: a tragedy. 1881.
Soliloquies in song. 1882.
At the gate of the convent, and other poems. 1885.
Prince Lucifer. 1887, 1887 (adds essay on The end and limits of objective poetry), 1891 (omits essay).
Love's widowhood, and other poems. 1889.
Lyrical poems. 1891.
Narrative poems. 1891.
Fortunatus the pessimist: a dramatic poem. 1892.
The garden that I love. 2 ser 1894–1907.
In Veronica's garden. 1895.
England's darling. 1896, 1901 (as Alfred the Great, England's darling).
The conversion of Winckelmann, and other poems. 1897.
Victoria: June 20 1837, June 20 1897. 1897.
Lamia's winter quarters. 1898. A story.
Songs of England. 1898, 1900, 1900, 1900 (all enlarged).
Spring and autumn in Ireland. 1900.
Polyphemus. 1901.
A tale of true love, and other poems. 1902.
Haunts of ancient peace. 1902. A story.
Flodden field: a tragedy. 1903.
The poet's diary, edited by Lamia. 1904.
The door of humility: a poem. 1906.
Sacred and profane love, and other poems. 1908.
The bridling of Pegasus. 1910. 9 essays on poetry and poets.
Autobiography. 2 vols 1911.

§ 2

Crowell, N. B. Austin: Victorian. Albuquerque 1953.

AUBREY VINCENT BEARDSLEY
1872–98

Bibliographies

Gallatin, A. E. Beardsley's drawings. 1903.
—— Beardsley: catalogue of drawings and bibliography. New York 1945.
—— and A. D. Wainwright. Catalogue of the Beardsley collection in Princeton University Library. Princeton 1952.

Collections

The best of Beardsley. Ed R. A. Walker 1948.
A Beardsley miscellany. Ed R. A. Walker 1949.

§ 1

Under the hill and other essays in prose and verse. 1904. Rptd from Yellow Book and Savoy.
Last letters, with an introductory note by J. Gray. 1904.
The story of Venus and Tannhäuser: a romantic novel. 1907 (priv ptd; original, unexpurgated version of Under the hill, above), New York 1967 (with introd by P. J. Gillette).
Letters from Beardsley to Leonard Smithers. Ed R. A. Walker 1937.

§ 2

Symons, A. Beardsley. 1897, 1905 (rev and enlarged).
Ross, R. Beardsley. 1909, New York 1967.
Ross, M. (ed). Robert Ross: friend of friends. 1952.
Weintraub, S. Beardsley. New York 1967.

ROBERT LAURENCE BINYON
1869–1943
Collections

Selected poems. 1926.
A Binyon anthology. 1927.
Collected poems. 2 vols 1931.

§I

Four poems. In Primavera: poems by Binyon, S. Phillips, M. Ghose and A. S. Cripps, 1890.
Lyric poems. 1894.
Poems. Oxford 1895.
Dutch etchers of the seventeenth century. 1895.
London visions. 1896 (bk 1), 1896 (12 poems, of which 5 rptd from Pall Mall Gazette and Poems 1895), 1899 (bk 2), 1908 (collected edn, rptd from Poems 1895, above, and from Porphyrion and other poems, below, adding new poems).
The praise of life: poems. 1896.
The supper: a lyrical scene. 1897 (priv ptd).
John Crone and John Sell Cotman. 1897.
Porphyrion and other poems. 1898.
Western Flanders: a medley of things seen, considered and imagined. 1899.
Thomas Girtin: his life and works: an essay. 1900.
Odes. 1901, 1913 (rearranged and rev).
The death of Adam and other poems. 1903.
Dream come true. 1905.
Penthesilea: a poem. 1905.
Paris and Œnone. 1906.
Attila: a tragedy. 1907.
England and other poems. 1909.
Augeries. 1913.
The winnowing-fan: poems on the great war. 1914.
The anvil and other poems. 1916.
The cause: poems of war. [1917?].
The new world: poems. 1918.
English poetry in its relation to painting and the other arts. 1918 (Br Acad).
Poetry and modern life. 1918.
The four years: war poems collected and newly augmented. 1919.
Six poems on Bruges. 1919.
The secret: sixty poems. 1920.
Arthur: a tragedy. 1923.
Ayuli: a play in three acts and an epilogue. Oxford 1923.
The sirens: an ode. 1924, 1925.
Little poems from the Japanese, rendered into English verse. Leeds 1925 (priv ptd).
The wonder night. 1927.
Boadicea: a play in eight scenes. 1927.
Sophro the wise: a play for children. 1927.
The idols: an ode. 1928.
Three short plays: Godstow nunnery, Love in the desert, Memnon. 1930. In verse.
Landscape in English art and poetry. Tokyo 1930, 1931.
Akbar. 1932, 1939.
English water-colours. 1933, 1944.
The Inferno of Dante, translated into English verse. 1933.
Three poems. Derby 1934.
The case of Christopher Smart. 1934 (Eng Assoc).
The young king. 1935.
Brief candles. 1938.
The Purgatorio of Dante, translated into English triple rhyme. 1938.
Art and freedom. Oxford 1939 (Romanes lecture).
The north start and other poems. 1941.
The ruins. Horizon 6 1942. Early versions of poems included in The burning of the leaves.
The Paradiso of Dante, translated into English triple rhyme. 1943.
British Museum diversion: a play for puppets. Horizon 10 1944.

The burning of the leaves and other poems. Ed C. M. Binyon 1944.
The madness of Merlin. Ed G. Bottomley 1947.

WILFRID SCAWEN BLUNT
1840–1922
Collections

The poetry of Blunt, selected and arranged by W. E. Henley and G. Wyndham. 1898.
Poetical works. 2 vols 1914.

§I

Sonnets and songs by Proteus. 1875.
Proteus and Amadeus: a correspondence. Ed A. de Vere 1878. Between Blunt and W. Meynell on religion and philosophy.
The love sonnets of Proteus. 1880.
The future of Islam. 1882.
The wind and the whirlwind. 1883. Poem on Britain in Egypt.
Ideas about India. 1885.
In vinculis. 1889.
A new pilgrimage and other poems. 1889.
The celebrated romance of the stealing of the mare. 1892, 1930. Tr from Arabic by A. Blunt, done into verse by Blunt.
Esther, love lyrics and Natalia's resurrection. 1892, Boston 1895 (as Esther and The love sonnets of Proteus).
The love lyrics and songs of Proteus. 1892 (Kelmscott Press). Rptd from 1875 and 1880 edns, above, but in full texts with additional sonnets.
Griselda. 1893.
Satan absolved, a Victorian mystery: a poem. 1899.
Mu'allakāt: the seven golden odes. 1903. Done into English verse.
Atrocities of justice under British rule in Egypt. 1906, 1907 (with new preface).
The secret history of the English occupation of Egypt: being a personal narrative of events. 1907, 1907 (with special appendices).
India under Ripon: a private diary. 1909.
Gordon of Khartoum: being a personal narrative of events. 1911.
The land war in Ireland. 1912.
My diaries. 2 vols 1919–20, 1922 (with preface by Lady Gregory).

CHARLES STUART CALVERLEY,
earlier BLAYDS
1831–84
Collections

Complete works, with a biographical notice by W. J Sendall. 1901.
Verses, translations and fly leaves. 1904.
Verses and translations. Ed O. Seaman 1905.

§I

Verses and translations. 1862, 1865 (3rd edn rev), 1871 (4th edn rev).
Translations into English and Latin. Cambridge 1866, 1885 (rev).
Theocritus translated into English verse. Cambridge 1869, 1883 (rev).
Fly leaves. Cambridge 1872, 1885 (as Verses and fly leaves).
The literary remains with a memoir by W. J. Sendall. 1885.
The eclogues of Virgil, translated into English verse. Ed M. Hadas, New York 1960.

§2

Thompson, F. Calverley. Academy 13 July 1901; rptd in his Literary criticism, ed T. L. Connolly, New York 1948.

Babington, P. L. Browning and Calverley, or poem and parody: a elucidation. 1925.

Ince, R. B. Calverley and some Cambridge wits of the nineteenth century. 1929.

JOHN DAVIDSON
1857–1909

Bibliographies

Lester, J. A., jr. Davidson: a Grub street bibliography. Charlottesville 1958.

Collections

Selected poems. 1905.

Poems and ballads. Ed R. Macleod 1959.

A selection of his poems. Ed M. Lindsay, preface by T. S. Eliot, with an essay by H. McDiarmid 1961.

§1

Diabolus amans: a dramatic poem. Glasgow 1885.

The north wall. Glasgow 1885. A novel.

Bruce. Glasgow 1886. A verse play.

Smith: a tragedy. Glasgow 1888.

Plays. Greenock 1889 (An unhistorical pastoral, A romantic farce, Scaramouch in Naxos), 1894 (adds Bruce and Smith, frontispiece by A. Beardsley).

Perpervid: the career of Ninian Jamieson. 1890.

The great men and a practical novelist. 1891. Collection of tales.

Laura Ruthven's widowhood: a novel. 1892. With C. J. Wills.

Persian letters. 1892. Trn of Montesquieu.

Fleet street eclogues. 2 sers 1893–6.

Sentences and paragraphs. 1893. Essays and epigrams.

Ballads and songs. 1894.

A random itinerary. 1894.

Baptist lake: a novel. 1894.

A full and true account of the wonderful mission of Earl Lavender. 1895. A satirical novel.

St George's day: a Fleet street eclogue. New York 1895. Included in Fleet street eclogues ser 2, above.

Miss Armstrong's and other circumstances. 1896. A collection of tales.

For the crown. 1896. Trn of Coppée.

New ballads. 1897.

Godfrida. 1898. A dramatic work.

The last ballad and other poems. 1899.

Self's the man: a tragi-comedy. 1901.

The testament of a vivisector. 1901.

The testament of a man forbid. 1901.

The testament of an empire-builder. 1902.

A rosary. 1903. Essays.

The knight of the maypole. 1903. A comedy in prose and verse.

A rosary. 1903. A play.

The testament of a Prime Minister. 1904.

A queen's romance. 1904. Trn of Hugo, Ruy Blas.

The theatrocrat: a tragic play of church and state. 1905.

Holiday and other poems, with a note on poetry. 1906.

God and Mammon. 1907. Pt 1 The triumph of Mammon, pt 2 Mammon and his message, pt 3 not completed.

The testament of John Davidson. 1908.

Fleet street and other poems. 1909.

Seventeen poems. 1925.

§2

Turner, P. Davidson: the novels of a poet. Cambridge Jnl 5 1952.

Macleod, R. D. Davidson: a study in personality. 1957.

Townsend, J. B. Davidson: poet of Armageddon. New Haven 1961.

RICHARD WATSON DIXON
1833–1900

Selections

Poems: a selection, with a memoir by R. Bridges. 1909.

§1

The close of the tenth century of the Christian era. Oxford 1858. Prize essay.

Christ's company and other poems. 1861.

Historical odes and other poems. 1864.

Essay on the maintenance of the Church of England as an established church. 1874.

The life of James Dixon DD. 1874.

The history of the Church of England from the abolition of the Roman jurisdiction. 6 vols 1878–1902.

The monastic comperta, so far as they regard the religious houses of Cumberland and Westmorland. Kendal 1879.

Mano: a poetical history in four books. 1883, 1891 (rev).

Odes and eclogues. Oxford 1884 (priv ptd).

Lyrical poems. Oxford 1887 (priv ptd).

The story of Eudocia and her brothers. Oxford 1888 (priv ptd).

Songs and odes. Ed R. Bridges 1896.

Mackail, J. W. The life of William Morris. Vol. 1 1899. Dixon contributed reminiscences.

The last poems. Ed R. Bridges 1905.

The correspondence of Gerard Manley Hopkins and Dixon. Ed C. C. Abbott, Oxford 1935.

§2

Bridges, R. Three friends: memoirs of Dolben, Dixon and Bradley. Oxford 1932.

Sambrook, J. A poet hidden: the life of Dixon. 1962.

DIGBY MACKWORTH DOLBEN
1848–67

Poems. Ed R. Bridges 1911 (with memoir and letters), 1915 (rev and enlarged). Memoir rptd in Three friends: memoirs of Dolben, Dixon and Bradley, Oxford 1932.

CHARLES MONTAGU DOUGHTY
1843–1926

§1

On the Jöstedal-Brai glaciers in Norway. 1866. A geological paper.

Documents épigraphiques recueillis dans le nord de l'Arabie. Paris 1884. Introd by E. Renan.

Travels in Arabia deserta. 2 vols Cambridge 1888, London 1921 (new preface and introd by T. E. Lawrence). Abridged as Wanderings, below.

Under arms. 1900.

The dawn in Britain. 6 vols 1906; ed B. Fairley 1935 (selected passages); 1943.

Adam cast forth. 1908. Sacred drama in 5 songs.

Wanderings in Arabia. Ed E. Garnett 2 vols 1908. Abridgement of Travels in Arabia deserta, above.

The cliffs. 1909. A verse play.

The clouds. 1912. Poetic drama.

The titans. 1916.

Mansoul: or the riddle of the world. 1920, 1922 (rev).

Hogarth's Arabia. 1922 (priv ptd).

Passages from Arabia deserta. Ed E. Garnett 1931.

§2

Fairley, B. Doughty: a critical study. 1927.
Hogarth, D. G. The life of Doughty. 1928.
Treneer, A. Doughty: a study of his prose and verse. 1935.

LORD ALFRED DOUGLAS
1870–1945
Collections
Collected poems. 1919.
Complete poems, including the light verse. 1928.

§1

Salome. 1894. Trn from Wilde's French.
Poems (Poèmes). Paris 1896. In French and English.
Tails with a twist. 1898.
The city of the soul. 1899.
The Duke of Berwick. 1899, 1925.
The placid pug and other rhymes. 1906.
The Pongo papers and the Duke of Berwick. 1907.
Sonnets. 1909, 1935, 1943 (with addns).
Oscar Wilde and myself. 1914.
The Rossiad. Galashiels [1916?]. A lampoon.
In excelsis. 1924. Sonnet sequence.
Nine poems. 1926 (priv ptd).
The autobiography of Douglas. 1929.
The true history of Shakespeare's sonnets. 1933.
Lyrics. 1935.
Without apology. 1938.
Oscar Wilde: a summing up. 1940; ed D. Hudson.
The principles of peotry: an address delivered before the Royal Society of Literature 1943.

§2

Braybrooke, P. Douglas: his life and work. 1931.
Freeman, W. The life of Douglas. 1948.
Stopes, M. C. Douglas: his poetry and personality. 1949.

ERNEST CHRISTOPHER DOWSON
1867–1900
Collections
Poems, with a memoir by A. Symons. 1905.
Poetical works. Ed D. Flower 1934, 1967. Includes 40 unpbd poems.
Poems. Ed M. Longaker, Philadelphia 1962.

§1

The book of the Rhymers' Club. 1892. Contains 6 poems by Dowson; The second book 1894 contains 6 more poems.
A comedy of masks: a novel. 3 vols 1893, 1896. With A. Moore.
Dilemmas: stories and studies in sentiment. 1895.
Verses. 1896.
The Pierrot of the minute: a dramatic phantasy in one act. 1897, 1923 (Grolier Club).
Adrian Rome. 1899. With A. Moore.
Decorations in verse and prose. 1899.
Stories. Ed M. Longaker, Philadelphia 1947.
Letters. Ed D. Flower and H. Maas 1967.

§2

Plarr, V. Dowson 1888–1897: reminiscences, unpublished letters and marginalia. 1914.
Orage, A. R. In his Readers and writers, 1922.

Longaker, M. Dowson. Philadelphia 1944, 1967 (with addns).
Swann, T. B. Dowson. New York 1964.

WILLIAM ERNEST HENLEY
1849–1903
Collections
Collected plays. 1892 (3 plays), 1896 (complete edn).
Works. 7 vols 1908, 5 vols 1921.
Henley. 1931. Selected poems.

§1

Deacon Brodie. 1880 (priv ptd), 1888 (finished version). A play, with R. L. Stevenson.
Admiral Guinea. 1884. A play, with R. L. Stevenson.
Beau Austin. 1884. A play, with R. L. Stevenson.
Macaire. 1885. A play, with R. L. Stevenson.
Mephisto: a new and original travestie by Byron M'Guiness. 1887.
A book of verses. 1888.
Pictures at play by two art-critics. 1888. With Andrew Lang.
Views and reviews: essays in appreciation: literature. 1890.
The song of the sword and other verses. 1892.
London voluntaries and other verses. 1893.
Dictionary of slang and its analogues. 1894–1904. With J. S. Farmer.
Burns: life, genius, achievement: an essay. Edinburgh 1898.
London types. 1898. Quatorzains, illustr W. Nicholson.
Poems. 1898.
Hawthorn and lavender: songs and madrigals. 1899, 1901 (with other verses).
For England's sake: verses and songs in time of war. 1900.
Views and reviews: essays in appreciation: art. 1902.
A song of speed. 1903.
Twenty-five new poems: a centenary discovery. Ed W. M. Parker, Poetry Rev 40 1949.
Henley also edited anthologies of verse and prose, and works of Blunt, Burns, Byron, Fielding, Shakespeare and Smollett.
Some letters of Henley. Ed V. Payen-Payne 1933.

§2

Williamson, K. Henley: a memoir. 1930.
'Connell, John' (J. H. Robertson). Henley. 1949.

LAURENCE HOUSMAN
1865–1959
Collections
Selected poems. 1908.
Little plays of St Francis. 3 vols 1935. Complete edn.
Collected poems. 1937.
The golden sovereign. 1937. Collection of plays.
Happy and glorious: a dramatic biography. 1945. Selectien of Queen Victoria plays.
Back words and fore words: an author's year-book 1893–1945. 1945.

§1

A farm in fairyland. 1894.
The house of joy. [1895]. Fairy tales.
Green arras. 1895. Poems.
All-fellows: seven legends of lower redemption, with insets in verse. 1896.
God and their makers. 1897.

The field of clover. 1898. Tales.
Spikenard: a book of devotional love-poems. 1898.
The story of the seven young goslings. [1899].
Rue. 1899. Poems.
The little land, with songs from its four rivers. 1899.
An Englishwoman's love-letters. 1900.
The love concealed. 1928.
Four plays of St Clare. 1934.
Victoria Regina: a dramatic biography. 1934.
The unexpected years. 1937, New York 1936. Auto-biography.
A.E.H.: some poems, some letters and a personal memoir. 1937.
Hop-o'-me-heart: a grown-up fairy tale. Flansham 1938.
What next? provocative tales of faith and morals. 1938.
The preparation of peace. 1940.
Gracious majesty. 1941.
Palestine plays. 1942.
Samuel the king-maker: a play in four acts. 1944.
Cynthia. 1947. Poems.
Strange ends and discoveries: tales of this world and the next. 1948.
Old testament plays. 1950.
The family honour: a comedy in four acts. 1950.
The kind and the foolish: short tales of myth, magic and miracle. 1952.

LIONEL PIGOT JOHNSON
1867–1902

Collections

Twenty-one poems, selected by W. B. Yeats. Dundrum 1904.
Selections from the poems, including some now collected for the first time, with a prefatory memoir [by C. K. Shorter]. 1908.
Poetical works, with an introduction by Ezra Pound. 1915.
The complete poems. Ed I. Fletcher 1953.

§ I

The book of the Rhymers' Club. 1892. Contains 6 poems by Johnson; Second book, 1894 contains 6 more.
The Gordon riots. 1893 (Catholic Truth Soc).
Bits of old Chelsea. 1894.
The art of Thomas Hardy. 1894 (with bibliography by J. Lane), 1923.
Poems. 1895.
Ireland and other poems. 1897.
Poetry and Ireland: [2] essays by W. B. Yeats and Johnson. Dundrum 1908.
Post liminium: essays and critical papers. Ed T. Whittemore 1911.
Some Winchester letters. 1919.
Reviews and critical papers. Ed R. Shafer 1921.
Seven new poems. Ed I. Fletcher, Poetry Rev 41 1950.
Fifteen new poems. Poetry Rev 43 1952.

EDWARD ROBERT BULWER LYTTON, 1st EARL OF LYTTON, 'OWEN MEREDITH'
1831–91

Collections

Poetical works. 2 vols 1867.

§ I

Clytemnestra, the Earl's return, the artist and other poems. 1855.
The wanderer. 1857, 1893 (rev, adds preface, discards pseudonym).

Lucile. 1860, 1893 (3rd edn, adds preface). A novel in verse.
Tannhäuser: or the battle of the bards, by Neville Temple and Edward Trevor. 1861. Really by Julian Fane and Lytton.
Serbski pesme or national songs of Servia. 1861; ed G. H. Powell 1918. Free versions of Serbian songs and ballads.
The ring of Amasis, from the papers of a German physician (Dr N—). 2 vols 1863, 1890 (shortened and recast in form of a novel).
Chronicles and characters. 2 vols 1868. 'An attempt at a poetic history of the education of man.'
Orval: or the fool of time and other imitations and para-phrases. 1869. Founded on the Infernal comedy by Krazinski. Many Serbski pesme rptd in appendix.
Julian Fane: a memoir. 1871.
Fables in song. 2 vols Edinburgh 1874.
King Poppy: a story without end. 1875 (priv ptd), 1892 (rev). A narrative poem.
The life, letters and literary remains of Edward Bulwer, Lord Lytton. 2 vols 1883. On his novelist father.
Glenaveril, or the metamorphoses: a poem in six books. 2 vols 1885.
After paradise: or legends of exile with other poems. 1887.
Marah. 1892. Preface by E. L. [Edith Lady Lytton].

Letters

Personal and literary letters. Ed Lady B. Balfour 2 vols 1906.
Letters of Owen Meredith to Robert and Elizabeth Barrett Browning. Ed A. B. and J. L. Harlan, Waco Texas 1937.

ALICE MEYNELL, née THOMPSON
1847–1922

Collections

Poems: collected edition. 1913.
Essays. 1914.
The poems: complete edition. 1923; ed F. Page 1940, Oxford 1940 (OSA).
Prose and poetry: centenary volume. Ed F. Page, V. Meynell, O. Sowerby and F. Maynell, with an introd by V. Sackville-West. 1947.

§ I

Poems. 1893.
The colour of life and other essays. 1896.
Other poems. 1896 (priv ptd).
The children. 1897. Essays.
London impressions. 1898.
The spirit of place and other essays. 1899.
John Ruskin: a biography. 1900.
Later poems. 1902, 1914 (as Shepherdess and other poems, 2 poems omitted).
Children of old masters. 1903.
Ceres' runaway and other essays. 1909.
Mary, the mother of Jesus: an essay. 1912.
Francis Thompson, by E. Meynell. 1913. Contains letters and articles by Alice Meynell.
Childhood 1913.
Ten poems 1913–5. 1915.
Poems on the war. 1916.
A father of women and other poems. 1917.
Hearts of controversy. [1917].
Second person singular and other essays. Oxford 1921.
Last poems. 1923.
The wares of Autolycus: selected literary essays. Ed P. M. Fraser, Oxford 1965.

SIR HENRY JOHN NEWBOLT
1862–1937
Collections

Collected poems 1897–1907. 1910.
Prose and poetry, selected by the author. 1920.
Selected poems. Ed J. Betjeman 1940.

§ 1

A fair death. 1882. Anon.
Taken from the enemy: a novel. 1892.
Mordred: a tragedy. 1895.
Admirals all and other verses. 1897 etc, New York 1898.
The island race. 1898. Poems.
The sailing of the long ships and other poems. 1902.
The year of Trafalgar. 1905. Prose.
The old country: a romance. 1906.
Clifton chapel and other school poems. 1908.
Songs of memory and hope. 1909.
The new June. 1909. Fiction.
The Twymans: a tale of youth. Edinburgh 1911.
Poems new and old. 1912.
Drake's drum and other songs of the sea. 1914.
Aladore. Edinburgh 1914. Fiction.
The book of the blue sea. 1914. Prose.
The war and the nations. 1915.
The book of the thin red line. 1915.
Tales of the great war. 1916.
A new study of English poetry. 1917.
The book of the happy warrior. 1917. Prose.
St George's day and other poems. 1918.
Submarine and anti-submarine. 1918. Prose.
The book of the long trail. 1919. Prose.
Poetry and time. 1919 (Warton lecture).
The book of good hunting. 1920. Prose.
A naval history of the war 1914–18. 5 vols 1920–31.
The book of the Grenvilles. 1921.
Days to remember. 1923. On the European war, with J. Buchan.
Studies green and gray. 1926. Criticism.
The linnet's nest. 1927. Poetry.
A child is born. 1931. Poetry.
My world as in my time. 1932. Prose.
A perpetual memory and other poems, with brief memoirs by W. de la Mare and F. Furse. 1939.
The later life and letters of Newbolt. Ed M. Newbolt 1942. Vol 2 of My world as in my time.

JAMES KENNETH STEPHEN
1859–92

Lapsus calami. Cambridge 1891, 1891 (3rd edn, with omissions and addns).
Quo musa tendis? Cambridge 1891.
Lapsus calami and other verses, with introduction by H. Stephen. 1896.

ARTHUR SYMONS
1865–1945

An introduction to the study of Browning. 1886, 1906 (rev and enlarged).
Days and nights. 1889, 1924 (with original notice by William Pater).
Silhouettes. 1892, 1896 (rev).
London nights. 1895, 1897 (rev).
Amoris victima. 1897.
Studies in two literatures. 1897.

Aubrey Beardsley. 1898, 1905 (rev), 1948.
The symbolist movement in literature. 1899.
Images of good and evil. 1899.
The loom of dreams. 1901 (priv ptd).
Cities. 1903. Prose.
Plays, acting and music. 1903, 1909 (rev). Prose.
Studies in prose and verse. 1904. Rptd partly from Studies in two literatures, above.
Spiritual adventures. 1905. Prose sketches.
A book of twenty songs. 1905.
The fool of the world and other poems. 1906.
Studies in seven arts. 1906. Prose.
Cities of Italy. 1907.
Great acting in English. 1907 (priv ptd).
William Blake. 1907.
London: a book of aspects. 1909 (priv ptd). Prose.
The romantic movement in English poetry. 1909.
Dante Gabriel Rossetti. 1910.
Knave of hearts 1894–1908. 1913.
Figures of seven centuries. 1916. Prose.
Tragedies. 1916. The death of Agrippa, Cleopatra in Judaea, The harvesters.
Tristran and Iseult. 1917. Play.
Cities and sea-coasts and islands. 1917. Prose.
Colour studies in Paris. 1918. Prose.
The toy cart. 1919. Play.
Cesare Borgia, Iseult of Brittany, The toy cart. New York 1920. Plays.
Charles Baudelaire. 1920. Prose.
Studies in Elizabethan drama. 1920. Rptd with addns from Studies in two literatures, above.
Lesbia and other poems. New York 1920.
Love's cruelty. 1923.
Dramatis personae. Indianapolis 1923, 1925 (corrected). Prose.
The Café Royal and other essays. 1923.
From Catullus, chiefly concerning Lesbia. 1924. Latin and English poems.
Notes on Joseph Conrad with some unpublished letters. 1925.
Studies in modern painters. New York 1925.
Eleonora Dusa. 1926.
Parisian nights. 1926. Essays.
A study of Thomas Hardy. 1927.
Studies in strange souls. 1929. Rossetti and Swinburne.
From Toulouse-Lautrec to Rodin with some personal impressions. 1929.
Confessions: a study in pathology. New York 1930.
A study of Oscar Wilde. 1930.
Mes souvenirs. Chapelle-Réanville 1931. In English prose.
Wanderings. 1931. Prose.
Jezebel Mort and other poems. 1931.
A study of Walter Pater. 1932.

SIR WILLIAM WATSON
1858–1935

Autograph letters and mss of Watson are in Bodley.

The prince's quest and other poems. 1880, 1892.
Epigrams of art, life and nature. Liverpool 1884.
Wordsworth's grave and other poems. 1890, 1892 (as Poems, adds 26 poems).
Lachrymae musarum. 1892 (priv ptd), 1892 (adds poems). Verses on the death of Tennyson.
Shelley's centenary. 1892 (priv ptd).
The eloping angels: a caprice. 1893.
Excursions in criticism: being some prose recreations of a rhymer. 1893.
Odes and other poems. 1894.
The father of the forest and other poems. 1895.
Ode for the centenary of the death of Burns. 1895.

The purple east: a series of sonnets on England's desertion
  of Armenia. 1896.
The hope of the world and other poems. 1898.
New poems. Greenfield Mass 1902, 1909.
For England: poems written during estrangement. 1904.
Sable and purple with other poems. 1910.
The heralds of the dawn. 1912. A play.
The muse in exile. 1913.

The man who saw and other poems arising out of the war.
  1917.
Retrogression and other poems. 1917.
Pencraft: a plea for the older ways. 1917. Prose.
The superhuman antagonists and other poems. 1919.
Ireland arisen. 1921.
Ireland unfreed. 1921.
Poems brief and new. 1925.

3. THE NOVEL

I. GENERAL WORKS

(1) BIBLIOGRAPHIES ETC

Block, A. The English novel 1740–1850: a catalogue. 1939, 1961 (rev).

Summers, M. A Gothic bibliography. [1941].

Carter, J. and M. Sadleir. Victorian fiction. Cambridge 1947.

Sadleir, M. XIX century fiction: a bibliographical record. 2 vols 1951.

Leclaire, L. A general analytical bibliography of the regional novelists of the British Isles 1800–1950. Paris 1954.

Stevenson, L. (ed). Victorian fiction: a guide to research. Cambridge Mass 1964.

(2) HISTORIES AND STUDIES

Lanier, W. S. The English novel. New York 1883.

Besant, W. The art of fiction. 1884. Reply by James, below.

James, H. The art of fiction. In his Partial portraits, 1888; rptd in his House of fiction, ed L. Edel 1957.

—— The new novel. In his Notes on novelists, 1914; rptd in James and H. G. Wells, ed L. Edel and G. N. Ray 1958.

Saintsbury, G. Names in fiction. Macmillan's Mag Dec 1888.

—— The present state of the English novel. In his Miscellaneous essays, 1892.

—— The historical novel. Macmillan's Mag Aug–Oct 1894; rptd in his Essays, 1895.

—— Novels of university life. Macmillan's Mag March 1898.

—— The English novel. 1913.

Cazamian, L. Le roman social en Angleterre 1830–50. Paris 1904.

Baker, E. A. History in fiction. 2 vols 1907.

—— The history of the English novel. 9 vols 1924–38 (vols 5–9).

Priestley, J. B. The English comic characters. 1925.

—— The English novel. 1927.

Quiller-Couch, A. T. Dickens and other Victorians. Cambridge 1925.

Forster, E. M. Aspects of the novel. 1927 (Clark lectures).

Muir, E. The structure of the novel. 1928.

Ford, F. M. The English novel. 1930.

Leavis, Q. D. Fiction and the reading public. 1932.

Cecil, D. Early Victorian novelists. 1934, 1964 (rev).

Lukács, G. Der historische Roman. Berlin 1937; tr 1962.

Summers, M. The Gothic quest. 1938.

Daiches, D. The novel and the modern world. 1940, 1960 (rev).

Leavis, F. R. The great tradition. 1948. On George Eliot, Henry James, Conrad, Dickens.

Mendilow, A. A. Time and the novel. 1951.

Leclaire, L. Le roman régionaliste dans les Iles Britanniques 1800–1950. Paris 1954.

Tillotson, K. Novels of the eighteen-forties. Oxford 1954.

—— The tale and the teller. In her Mid-Victorian studies, 1965.

Thomson, P. The Victorian heroine. 1956.

Dalziel, M. Popular fiction a hundred years ago. 1957.

Allott, M. (ed). Novelists on the novel. 1959.

Freeman, W. Dictionary of fictional characters. 1965.

Graham, K. English criticism of the novel 1865–1900. Oxford 1965.

Hardy, B. The appropriate form: an essay on the novel. 1965.

Harvey, W. J. Character and the novel. 1965.

Tillotson, G. and K. Mid-Victorian studies. 1965. On Charlotte Yonge, Trollope, George Eliot et al.

Lodge, D. Language of fiction: essays in criticism and verbal analysis of the English novel. 1966. On key words in Jane Eyre, Hard times, Tess.

Marcus, S. The other Victorians: a study of sexuality and pornography in mid-nineteenth-century England. New York 1966.

II. THE EARLY NINETEENTH-CENTURY NOVEL

MARIA EDGEWORTH
1768–1849

Bibliographies

Slade, B. C. Maria Edgeworth 1767–1849: a bibliographical tribute. 1937.

Collections

Tales and miscellaneous pieces. 14 vols 1825.

Tales and novels. 18 vols 1832–3, 1848, 1857.

§1

Letters for literary ladies, to which is added An essay on the noble science of self-justification. 1795 (anon), 1799 (signed), 1805, Georgetown 1810, London 1814.

The parent's assistant: or stories for children. 3 vols 1796 (anon; no known copy), 1796 (adds Barring out), 6 vols 1800 (signed; adds 8 new stories and omits 3 transferred to Early lessons); ed A. T. Ritchie 1897.

Practical education. 2 vols 1798, 3 vols 1801, 2 vols New York 1801, London 1808, 1811 (as Essays on practical education), 1815.

Castle Rackrent, an Hibernian tale: taken from facts, and from the manners of the Irish squires, before the year 1782. 1800, 1800, Dublin 1800 (all anon), London 1801 (signed), Dublin 1802 (3rd edn); ed G. Watson, Oxford 1964.

[Early lessons]. Harry and Lucy, part i: being the first part of Early lessons, by the author of the Parent's assistant. 1801 (by R. L. Edgeworth and Mrs Honora Edgeworth; substantially a reprint of Practical education: or the history of Harry and Lucy, vol 2 (anon), ptd but never (?) pbd 1780); pt ii, 1801 (by R. L. Edgeworth); Rosamond, pt i, 1801 (containing The purple jar from Parent's assistant and 2 other stories); pt ii, 1801 (3 stories); pt iii, 1801 (The rabbit); Frank, pts i–iv, 1801; The little dog Trusty, The orange man, and The cherry orchard: being the tenth part of Early lessons [first 2 stories from Parent's assistant], 1801–2 (2 issues); [complete work] 10 vols 1803 (no known copies of pts i, ii, iv–vi), 7 vols Philadelphia 1804–8, 10 vols 1809, 2 vols 1813.

Moral tales for young people (including Mademoiselle Panache transferred from Parent's assistant). 5 vols 1801, 3 vols 1802, 1806, 1809 (5th edn).

Belinda. 3 vols 1801, 2 vols Dublin 1801, 3 vols 1802, 2 vols Dublin 1802; ed A. L. Barbauld 1810 (Br Novelist ser) (with Modern Griselda, below; major alterations in latter part of story), 3 vols 1811; ed A. T. Ritchie 1896.

Essay on Irish bulls. 1802, 1803, Philadelphia 1803, New York 1803 (2 edns), London 1808. Essay on Irish humour; with R. L. Edgeworth.

Popular tales. 3 vols 1804, 2 vols Philadelphia 1804, 3 vols 1805, 1807, 1811; ed A. T. Ritchie 1895.

The modern Griselda: a tale. 1805, 1805; ed A. L. Barbauld 1810 (Br Novelist ser) (with Belinda).

Leonora. 2 vols 1806, New York 1806, London 1815.

Essays on professional education, by R. L. (and Maria) Edgeworth. 1809, 1812.

Tales of fashionable life. Vols 1–3 (Ennui, Almeria, Madame de Fleury, The dun, Manoeuvring), 1809 (3 edns).

Patronage. 4 vols 1814, 1814, 3 vols Philadelphia 1814, 4 vols 1815 (in the 1825 collected edn, above, there were substantial alterations, including rewriting of the last vol).

Continuation of Early lessons. 2 vols 1814, 1815. From 1821 pbd as vols 3–4 of Early lessons, above. Continuation of Harry and Lucy, Frank, Rosamond, the first with R. L. Edgeworth.

Harrington: a tale; and Ormond: a tale. 3 vols 1817, 1817; ed A. T. Ritchie 1895.

Memoirs of Richard Lovell Edgeworth esq. 2 vols 1820, 1821, 1 vol 1844 (abridged); ed B. L. Tollemache 1896 (selection). Vol 1 by R. L. Edgeworth, vol 2 by Maria Edgeworth.

Rosamond: a sequel to Early lessons. 2 vols 1821.

Frank: a sequel to Frank in Early lessons. 3 vols 1822.

Harry and Lucy concluded: being the last part of Early lessons. 4 vols 1825, Boston 1825, London 1827.

Helen: a tale. 3 vols 1834; ed A. T. Ritchie 1896.

The most unfortunate day of my life: being a hitherto unpublished story, together with the Purple jar and other stories. 1931.

Letters and Papers

Many unpbd letters are now in the National Library of Ireland, Dublin. Letters to Swiss correspondents are in the Bibliothèque Publique et Universitaire, Geneva.

A memoir of Maria Edgeworth, with a selection from her letters by the late Mrs [Frances] Edgeworth. 3 vols 1867 (priv ptd).

Correspondence of Ricardo with Maria Edgeworth. Economic Jnl 17 1907.

Butler, H. J. and H. E. The black book of Edgeworthstown and other Edgeworth memories 1585–1817. 1927.

—— Sir Walter Scott and Maria Edgeworth: some unpublished letters. MLR 23 1928.

Chosen letters. Ed F. V. Barry 1931.

Butler, R. F. Maria Edgeworth and Sir Walter Scott: unpublished letters 1823. RES new ser 9 1958.

Letters from England 1813–44. Ed C. Colvin, Oxford 1971.

§2

Woolf, V. The lives of the obscure: the Taylors and the Edgeworths. In her Common reader, 1925.

Newby, P. H. Maria Edgeworth. 1950.

Davie, D. A. In his Heyday of Sir Walter Scott, 1961.

Butler, M. Maria Edgeworth: a literary biography. Oxford 1972.

SIR WALTER SCOTT
1771–1832

Almost all mss by or relating to Scott are now in public libraries. The Pierpont Morgan Library, New York, has the largest single collection of Scott's own works, including the Journal, Lady of the lake, Rokeby, Bridal of Triermain, Lord of the Isles, Guy Mannering, Antiquary, Old Mortality, Black dwarf, Ivanhoe, Monastery, Peveril of the Peak, Quentin Durward, St Ronan's Well, Woodstock, Anne of Geierstein, the first ser of Tales of a grandfather, the Life of Napoleon and Doom of Devorgoil. The National Library of Scotland, Edinburgh, owns Marmion, Heart of Midlothian, Redgauntlet and minor works. Harold the Dauntless is in the Huntington Library. The BM has Kenilworth and Tapestried chamber. Fortunes of Nigel and Count Robert of Paris are in King's School, Canterbury. Bride of Lammermoor, and memoirs of Goldsmith, Johnson and part of Sterne are in the Signet Library, Edinburgh. The Siege of Malta is in the New York Public Library. Harvard has the Life of Swift. The largest collection of mss relating to Scott is in the National Library of Scotland. It contains the Abbotsford Collection acquired in 1931–2 and the Walpole Collection of about 6,000 letters to Scott purchased from Abbotsford by Sir Hugh Walpole.

Bibliographies

Corson, J. C. A bibliography of Scott: a classified and annotated list of books and articles relating to his life and works 1797–1940. Edinburgh 1943.

§1

The chase, and William and Helen: two ballads from the German of Gottfried Augustus Bürger. Edinburgh 1796.

Goetz of Berlichingen, with the iron hand: a tragedy, translated from the German of Goethé. 1799.

The eve of Saint John: a Border ballad. Kelso 1800.

The lay of the last minstrel. 1805, 1805, 1806 (3 edns).

Ballads and lyrical pieces. Edinburgh 1806, 1806, 1810.

Marmion: a tale of Flodden Field. Edinburgh 1808 (4 edns), 1810, 1810.

The lady of the lake: a poem. Edinburgh 1810 (8 edns).

The vision of Don Roderick: a poem. Edinburgh 1811 (priv ptd), 1811, 1811, 1815.

Rokeby: a poem. Edinburgh 1813 (5 edns), 1815, 1821.

The bridal of Triermain: or the vale of St John, in three cantos. Edinburgh 1813 (3 edns), 1814, 1817.

Waverley: or 'tis sixty years since. 3 vols Edinburgh 1814 (4 edns), 1815, 1816, 1817, 1821. The first of the novels, all anon.

Guy Mannering: or the astrologer, by the author of Waverley. 3 vols Edinburgh 1815, 1815, 1817, 1820.

The Lord of the Isles: a poem. Edinburgh 1815 (5 edns).

The field of Waterloo: a poem. Edinburgh 1815 (3 edns).

The antiquary, by the author of Waverley. 3 vols Edinburgh 1816, 1816, 1818 (5th edn).

Tales of my landlord, collected and arranged by Jedediah Cleishbotham [The black dwarf; Old Mortality]. 4 vols Edinburgh 1816, 1817, 1817, 1818, 1819, 1819.

Harold the dauntless: a poem. Edinburgh 1817.

Rob Roy, by the author of Waverley. 3 vols Edinburgh 1818 (for 1817), 1818 (3 edns).

Tales of my landlord: second series [The Heart of Mid-Lothian]. 4 vols Edinburgh 1818 (4 edns).

Tales of my landlord: third series [The bride of Lammermoor and A legend of Montrose]. 4 vols Edinburgh 1819 (3 edns).

Ivanhoe: a romance, by the author of Waverley. 3 vols Edinburgh 1820 (for 1819), 1820, 1821.

The monastery: a romance, by the author of Waverley. 3 vols Edinburgh 1820, 1820.

The abbot, by the author of Waverley. 3 vols Edinburgh 1820.

Kenilworth: a romance, by the author of Waverley. Edinburgh 1821, 1821.

The pirate, by the author of Waverley. 3 vols Edinburgh 1822 (for 1821), 1822.

The fortunes of Nigel, by the author of Waverley. 3 vols Edinburgh 1822 (3 edns).

Halidon Hill: a dramatic sketch. Edinburgh 1822, 1822.

Peveril of the Peak, by the author of Waverley. 4 vols Edinburgh 1822 (for 1823), 1823.

Quentin Durward, by the author of Waverley. 3 vols Edinburgh 1823, 1823.

St Ronan's Well, by the author of Waverley. 3 vols Edinburgh 1824 (for 1823), 1824.

Redgauntlet: a tale of the eighteenth century, by the author of Waverley. 3 vols Edinburgh 1824.

Tales of the Crusaders, second series, by the author of Waverley [The betrothed; The talisman]. 4 vols Edinburgh 1825.

Woodstock: or the cavalier, by the author of Waverley. 3 vols Edinburgh 1826.

Chronicles of the Canongate [first series: Croftangry's introds; The Highland widow; The two drovers; The surgeon's daughter]. 2 vols Edinburgh 1827, 1828.

Chronicles of the Canongate, second series, by the author of Waverley [Croftangry's introd; The fair maid of Perth]. 3 vols Edinburgh 1828, 1828.

Anne of Geierstein: or the maiden of the mist, by the author of Waverley. 3 vols Edinburgh 1829.

Tales of my landlord, fourth series [Count Robert of Paris and Castle Dangerous]. 4 vols Edinburgh 1832 (for 1831).

The siege of Malta. Ed D. E. Sultana 1976 (from ms). The last novel.

Miscellaneous Prose Works

Miscellaneous prose works. 6 vols Edinburgh 1827.

Miscellaneous prose works. Ed J. G. Lockhart 28 vols Edinburgh 1834-6.

Jane Austen's Emma. Quart Rev 14 1816.

Remarks on Frankenstein: or the modern Prometheus: a novel by Mrs Shelley. Blackwood's Mag March 1818.

Romance. In Encyclopaedia Britannica, suppl to 4th-6th edns, vol 6, pt 1, 1824. 19 May 1824.

Lord Byron. Edinburgh Weekly Jnl 19 May 1824.

Lives of the novelists. 2 vols Paris 1825. Pirated from Ballantyne's novelist's library. See Edited works, below.

Pepys's Memoirs. Quart Rev 33 1826.

The life of Napoleon Buonaparte. 9 vols Edinburgh 1827.

Tales of a grandfather: being stories taken from Scottish history. 3 vols Edinburgh 1828 (for 1827), 1828 (4 edns), 1829, 1829.

Tales of a grandfather, being stories taken from Scottish history: second series. 3 vols Edinburgh 1829 (for 1828).

Tales of a grandfather, being stories taken from the history of Scotland: third series. 3 vols Edinburgh 1830 (for 1829).

The history of Scotland. 2 vols 1830 (for 1829-30).

Letters on demonology and witchcraft. 1830, 1831.

Tales of a grandfather, being stories taken from the history of France: fourth series. 3 vols 1831 (for 1830).

Private letters of the seventeenth century. Scribner's Mag 14 1893 (in part); ed D. Grant, Oxford 1948 (complete).

Letters and Journal

Journal 1825-32. Ed D. Douglas 2 vols Edinburgh 1890, Edinburgh 1939-46, 1 vol Edinburgh 1950; ed W. E. K. Anderson, Oxford 1972.

Familiar letters. Ed D. Douglas 2 vols Edinburgh 1894.

Partington, W. The private letter-books of Scott. 1930, New York 1930.

—— Sir Walter's post-bag: more stories and sidelights from his unpublished letter-books. 1932.

The letters of Scott. Ed H. J. C. Grierson 12 vols 1932-7. No index.

Tait, J. G. The missing tenth of Scott's journal. Edinburgh 1936.

—— Scott's journal and its editor. Edinburgh 1938.

The correspondence of Scott and Charles Robert Maturin. Ed F. E. Ratchford and W. H. McCarthy, Austin 1937.

Edited Works

Minstrelsy of the Scottish Border. 2 vols Kelso 1802, 3 vols Edinburgh 1803, 1806, 1810, 1812; ed T. F. Henderson 4 vols Edinburgh 1902, 1932.

Sir Tristrem: a metrical romance by Thomas of Ercildoune. Edinburgh 1804, 1806, 1811, 1819, Paris 1837.

The works of John Dryden. 18 vols 1808, 1821; rev G. Saintsbury 18 vols Edinburgh 1882-93.

Memoirs of Capt George Carleton. Edinburgh 1808, 1809 (4th edn).

The life of Edward Lord Herbert of Cherbury, written by himself. Edinburgh 1809. Attributed to Scott.

A collection of scarce and valuable tracts. 13 vols 1809-15. 'Somers tracts.'

English minstrelsy. 2 vols Edinburgh 1810.

Memoirs of Count Grammont, by Anthony Hamilton. 2 vols 1811.

The Castle of Otranto, by Horace Walpole. Edinburgh 1811.

Secret history of the court of King James the First. 2 vols Edinburgh 1811.

The works of Jonathan Swift. 19 vols Edinburgh 1814, 1824.

Ballantyne's novelist's library. 10 vols 1821-4.

§2

[Jeffrey, F.] Scott's Lay of the last minstrel. Edinburgh Rev 6 1805; rptd in his Contributions to the Edinburgh Review vol 2, 1844.

—— Scott's Marmion. Edinburgh Rev 12 1808.

—— Scott's Lady of the lake. Edinburgh Rev 16 1810; rptd ibid vol 2.

—— Waverley. Edinburgh Rev 24 1815; rptd ibid vol 3.

—— Tales of my landlord. Edinburgh Rev 28 1817; rptd ibid vol 3.

—— Rob Roy. Edinburgh Rev 29 1818; rptd ibid vol 3.

—— Ivanhoe. Edinburgh Rev 33 1820; rptd ibid vol 3.

—— Nigel. Edinburgh Rev 37 1822; rptd ibid vol 3.

[Hazlitt, W.] The pirate. London Mag Jan 1822; rptd in his Works vol 11, 1904.

—— Peveril of the Peak. London Mag Feb 1823; rptd in his Works vol 11, 1904.

—— In his Spirit of the age, 1825.

[Senior, N. W.] Novels by the author of Waverley. Quart Rev 26 1822; rptd in his Essays on fiction, 1864.

Hogg, J. Familiar anecdotes of Scott. New York 1834; rptd as Domestic manners and private life of Scott, Glasgow 1834.

Lockhart, J. G. Memoirs of the life of Scott. 7 vols Edinburgh 1837–8, 10 vols Edinburgh 1839 etc; ed A. W. Pollard 5 vols 1900 (adds material from the Narrative, below).

[Bagehot, W.] The Waverley novels. Nat Rev 6 1858; rptd in his Literary studies, 1879.

Cornish, S. W. The Waverley manual: a handbook of the chief characters. Edinburgh 1871.

[Stephen, L.] Some words about Scott. Cornhill Mag Sept 1871; rptd in his Hours in a library 1st ser, 1874.

Hutton, R. H. Sir Walter Scott. 1878 (EML).

Swinburne, A. C. The journal of Scott 1825–32. Fortnightly Rev May 1891; rptd in his Studies in prose and poetry, 1894.

Saintsbury, G. Scott and Dumas. Macmillan's Mag Sept 1894; rptd in his Essays in English literature: second series, 1895.

—— Sir Walter Scott. Edinburgh 1897.

Lang, A. Sir Walter Scott. 1906.

—— Scott and the Border minstrelsy. 1910.

Ker, W. P. Sir Walter Scott. Anglo-French Rev 2 1919; rptd in his Collected essays vol 1, 1925.

—— Scott's Scotland. [1922]; rptd in his Collected essays vol 1, 1925.

Buchan, J. The man and the book: Scott. 1925.

—— Sir Walter Scott. 1932.

Grierson, H. J. C. Scott and Carlyle. E & S 13 1928; rptd in his Essays and addresses, 1940.

—— Sir Walter Scott Bart: a new life. 1938.

Carswell, D. Sir Walter: a four-part study in biography. 1930, Garden City NY 1930 (as Scott and his circle).

Pope-Hennessy, U. The Laird of Abbotsford. 1932.

—— Scott in his works. Essays by Divers Hands new ser 12 1933.

—— Sir Walter Scott. 1948.

Hillhouse, J. T. The Waverley novels and their critics. Minneapolis 1936.

Muir, E. Scott and Scotland. 1936.

Trevelyan, G. M. Influence of Scott on history. In his Autobiography and other essays, 1949.

Young, G. M. Scott and history. In Edinburgh University, Sir Walter Scott lectures, Edinburgh 1950; also Essays by Divers Hands new ser 25 1950.

Daiches, D. Scott's achievement as a novelist. Nineteenth-Century Fiction 6 1952; rptd in his Literary essays, Edinburgh 1956.

Forbes, D. The rationalism of Scott. Cambridge Jnl April 1954.

Pearson, H. Scott: his life and personality. 1954.

Tillyard, E. M. W. Scott's linguistic vagaries. Etudes Anglaises 11 1958; rptd in his Essays literary and educational, 1962.

Davie, D. A. The heyday of Scott. 1961.

—— The poetry of Scott. Proc Br Acad 47 1961.

Raleigh, J. H. What Scott meant to the Victorians. Victorian Stud 7 1964.

Crawford, T. Scott. Edinburgh 1965 (Writers & Critics).

Cockshut, A. O. J. The achievement of Scott. 1969.

Johnson, E. Scott: the great unknown. 2 vols 1970.

Hayden, J. O. (ed). Scott: the critical heritage. 1970.

Lascelles, M. In her Notions and facts, Oxford 1972.

Oman, C. The wizard of the north. 1973.

JANE AUSTEN

1775–1817

Bibliographies

Keynes, G. L. Jane Austen: a bibliography. 1929.

Chapman, R. W. Jane Austen: a critical bibliography. Oxford 1953, 1955 (corrected).

Collections

Novels by Miss Jane Austen. 5 vols 1833, 1837, 1856, 1866, 1869, 6 vols (vol vi: the 1871 Memoir) 1878–9.

Oxford edition. Ed R. W. Chapman 5 vols Oxford 1923, 6 vols (vol vi: Minor works) 1954, 5 vols 1966–9.

§ 1

Volume the first. Ed R. W. Chapman, Oxford 1933.

Love and freindship. Ed G. K. Chesterton 1922; ed B. C. Southam, Oxford 1963 (as Volume the second, Jane Austen's title).

Volume the third. Ed R. W. Chapman, Oxford 1951.

The 3 ms notebooks contain transcripts of virtually all the juvenilia c. 1787–93, entered and corrected until c. 1809.

Lady Susan. Ed J. E. Austen-Leigh 1871 (in Memoir); ed R. W. Chapman, Oxford 1925. Composed c. 1793–4, with addn c. 1805.

The Watsons. Ed J. E. Austen-Leigh 1871 (in Memoir); ed R. W. Chapman, Oxford 1927. Fragment of c. 17,500 words, written c. 1804–5.

Minor works. Ed R. W. Chapman, Oxford 1954, 1968. Vol vi of Works; collected edn of juvenilia, early works, verse and the ms fragments (rev B.C. Southam).

Sense and sensibility. 3 vols 1811, 1813 (corrected); ed D. Cecil, Oxford 1931 (WC); ed Q. D. Leavis 1958 (with Lady Susan and The Watsons); ed I. Watt, New York 1961; ed M. M. Lascelles 1962; ed C. Lamont, Oxford 1970. Originally written in letters c. 1795 as Elinor and Marianne; re-writing as Sense and sensibility begun Nov 1797, rev 1809–10, pbd anon c. Nov 1811.

Pride and prejudice. 3 vols 1813, 1813, 2 vols 1817; ed G. Saintsbury 1894; ed R. W. Chapman, Oxford 1929 (WC); ed B. A. Booth, New York 1963; ed M. M. Lascelles 1963. Originally written, perhaps in letters, Oct 1796 to Aug 1797 as First impressions rev 1809–10, 1811, 1812, pbd anon Jan 1813 2nd edn Nov 1813.

Mansfield Park. 3 vols 1814, 1816 (corrected); ed M. M. Lascelles, Oxford 1929 (WC); ed Q. D. Leavis 1957; ed M. M. Lascelles 1963; ed J. Lucas, Oxford 1970. Written Feb 1811 to June 1813, pbd anon May 1814, 2nd edn Feb 1816.

Emma. 3 vols 1816; ed E. V. Lucas, Oxford 1907 (WC); ed L. Trilling, Boston 1957; ed M. M. Lascelles 1964. Written 21 Jan 1814 to March 1815, pbd anon Dec 1815.

Northanger Abbey and Persuasion. 4 vols 1818; ed M. M. Lascelles 1962; ed D. Lodge, Oxford 1971. Pbd Dec 1817 with a biographical notice by Henry Austen.

Northanger Abbey. Ed M. Sadleir, Oxford 1930 (WC). Originally written c. 1798–9 as Susan, re-written by 1803, rev as Catherine 1816–17.

Persuasion. Ed F. Reid, Oxford 1930 (WC); ed D. W. Harding 1965 (with Memoir); ed J. Davie, Oxford 1971. Written 8 Aug 1815 to Aug 1816.

Two chapters of Persuasion. Ed R. W. Chapman, Oxford 1926 (250 copies with ms facs). First draft of chs 10 and 11 in vol 2, written 8 to 16 July 1816. Ch 10 first ptd in 1871 Memoir.

Plan of a novel according to hints from various quarters. Ed J. E. Austen-Leigh 1871 (in Memoir, altered and reduced); ed R. W. Chapman, Oxford 1926. Probably written early 1816. The 1926 edn includes Jane Austen's transcript of opinions of Mansfield Park and Emma, and notes on dates of composition and profits from several of the novels.

Sanditon. Ed J. E. Austen-Leigh 1871 (in Memoir, extracts amounting to one-sixth); ed R. W. Chapman, Oxford 1925 (250 copies with ms facs); ed R. B. Johnson 1934 (with Lady Susan and The Watsons); ed B. C. Southam, Oxford 1975 (ms facs). A fragment of c. 24,000 words written 17 Jan to 18 March 1817.

Letters

Austen-Leigh, J. E. A memoir of Jane Austen. 1870, 1871 (enlarged with extracts from letters).

Austen-Leigh, W. and R. A. Jane Austen: her life and letters. 1913. Includes extensive quotations from unpbd letters.

Five letters from Jane Austen to her niece Fanny Knight. Ed R. W. Chapman, Oxford 1924 (facs).
Jane Austen's letters. Ed R. W. Chapman 2 vols or 1 Oxford 1932, 1 vol Oxford 1952 (with corrections and addns, including notes and indexes to the literary works).
Letters of Jane Austen 1796–1817. Ed R. W. Chapman, Oxford 1955 (WC). Selection.

§2

[Scott, W.] Quart Rev 14 1815. Review of Emma.
[Lewes, G. H.] Recent novels. Fraser's Mag Dec 1847.
—— The lady novelists. Westminster Rev 58 1852.
—— The novels of Jane Austen. Blackwood's Mag July 1859.
Austen-Leigh, J. E. A memoir of Jane Austen. 1870, 1871 (enlarged), Boston 1892 (as Lady Susan, The Watsons); ed R. W. Chapman, Oxford 1926 (text of 1871, omitting extracts from juvenilia, minor works and fragments); ed D. W. Harding 1965 (1871 text, omitting extracts etc, with Persuasion).
Austen-Leigh, W. In his Augustus Austen-Leigh, 1906.
—— and R. A. Jane Austen: her life and letters. 1913.
Bradley, A. C. Jane Austen. E & S 2 1911; rptd in his A miscellany, 1929.
[Chapman, R. W.] Jane Austen's methods. TLS 9 Feb 1922.
Chapman, R. W. Jane Austen and her publishers. London Mercury Aug 1930.
—— Jane Austen's library. Book Collectors' Quart 11 1933.
—— Jane Austen's text. TLS 13 Feb 1937.
—— Jane Austen: facts and problems. Oxford 1948, 1950 (corrected).
Woolf, V. In her Common reader, 1925.
—— In her Granite and rainbow, 1958.
Sadleir, M. The Northanger novels. Oxford 1927.
Cecil, D. Jane Austen. 1935.
Lascelles, M. Some characteristics of Jane Austen's style. E & S 22 1937.
—— Jane Austen and her art. Oxford, 1939, 1941 (corrected).
Harding, D. W. Regulated hatred: an aspect of the work of Jane Austen. Scrutiny 8 1940.
Leavis, Q. D. A critical theory of Jane Austen's writings. Scrutiny 10 1942, 12 1944.
Woolf, L. The economic determinism of Jane Austen. New Statesman 18 July 1942.
Brower, R. A. The controlling hand: Jane Austen and Pride and prejudice. Scrutiny 13 1945.
—— In his Fields of light, New York 1951.
Muir, E. In his Essays on literature and society, 1949.
Wilson, E. A long talk about Jane Austen. In his Classics and commercials, New York 1950.
Trilling, L. A portrait of Western man. Listener 11 June 1953.
—— Mansfield Park. Partisan Rev 21 1954; rptd in his Opposing self, New York 1955; rev as Jane Austen and Mansfield Park in Pelican guide to English literature, ed B. Ford vol 5, 1957.
—— Emma. Encounter June 1957.
Bowen, E. Persuasion. London Mag April 1957.
Southam, B. C. The manuscript of Volume the first. Library 5th ser 17 1962.
—— Mrs Leavis and Miss Austen: the 'critical theory' reconsidered. Nineteenth-Century Fiction 17 1963.
—— Jane Austen. TLS 30 Nov 1962. Replies.
—— Jane Austen's literary manuscripts. Oxford 1964.
—— (ed). Jane Austen: critical essays. 1968.
—— (ed). Jane Austen: the critical heritage. 1973.
Jane Austen: a collection of critical essays. Ed I. Watt, Englewood Cliffs NJ 1963.
Craik, W. A. Jane Austen: the six novels. 1965.
Litz, A. W. Jane Austen: a study of her artistic development. 1965.

Ryle, G. Jane Austen and the moralists. Oxford Rev 1 1966.
Crane, R. S. Persuasion. In his Idea of the humanities vol 2, Chicago 1967.
Lerner, L. The truthtellers: Jane Austen, George Eliot, D. H. Lawrence. 1967.
Poirier, R. In his A world elsewhere, New York 1967.
Phillipps, K. C. Jane Austen's English. 1970.
Butler, M. Jane Austen and the war of ideas. Oxford 1975.

THOMAS LOVE PEACOCK
1785–1866
Collections

Headlong Hall, Nightmare Abbey, Maid Marian and Crotchet Castle. Vol 57 of Bentley's Standard novel ser 1837, 1849. All rev, with new preface.
[Works]. Ed H. Cole 3 vols 1875. With preface by Baron Houghton, biographical notice by Edith Nicolls.
[Works]. The Halliford edition. Ed H. F. B. Brett-Smith and C. E. Jones 10 vols 1924–34.
Novels. Ed D. Garnett 1948, 2 vols 1963 (corrected).

§1

Palmyra and other poems. 1806, 1812 (below, extensively rev), 1817.
The genius of the Thames: a lyrical poem in two parts. 1810, 1812 (below, rev), 1817.
The genius of the Thames, Palmyra and other poems. 1812, 1817.
The philosophy of melancholy: a poem in four parts, with a mythological ode. 1812.
Sir Hornbook, or Childe Launcelot's expedition: a grammatico-allegorical ballad. [1813], 1814, 1815, 1815. Anon.
Sir Proteus: a satirical ballad, by P. M. O'Donovan esq. 1814. Anon.
Headlong Hall. 1816 (anon), Philadelphia 1816, London 1816 (rev), 1823 (rev), 1837 (slightly rev) (Bentley's Standard Novels), London 1856 (first signed edn); ed R. Garnett 1908 (EL); Oxford 1929 (WC); ed P. Yarker 1961 (EL).
Melincourt, by the author of Headlong Hall. 3 vols 1817, 2 vols Philadelphia 1817, 1 vol 1856 (with new preface).
Nightmare Abbey, by the author of Headlong Hall. 1818, Philadelphia 1819, and C. E. Jones 1923; 1837 (Bentley's Standard Novels) (rev; all subsequent edns except 1923 follow rev text), 1849, New York 1845, 1850 (with Headlong Hall), London 1856; ed R. Garnett 1908 (EL); Oxford 1929 (WC); ed A. Hodge, introd by J. B. Priestley 1947 (with Crotchet Castle); ed J.-J. Mayoux, Paris 1936 (with Misfortunes of Elphin) (with French trn); ed P. Yarker 1961 (EL).
The four ages of poetry. Ollier's Literary Miscellany no 1 (only issue) 1820 (anon), [Belfast 1863] (priv ptd) (anon); ed R. Garnett 1891 (with Calidore etc); ed A. S. Cook, Boston 1891 (with Shelley's Defence); ed H. F. B. Brett-Smith 1921 (with Shelley's Defence and Browning's Essay on Shelley), 1923 (corrected); ed J. E. Jordan, Indianapolis 1965 (with Shelley's Defence).
Maid Marian, by the author of Headlong Hall. 1822; 1837 (Bentley's Standard Novels) (rev), 1849, 1856 (with Crotchet Castle); ed G. Saintsbury 1959 (with Crotchet Castle).
The misfortunes of Elphin, by the author of Headlong Hall. 1829; ed R. W. Chapman, Oxford 1924 (WC) (with Crotchet Castle).
Crotchet Castle, by the author of Headlong Hall. 1831; 1837 (Bentley's Standard Novels) (rev), 1849; 1856 (with Maid Marian); ed R. W. Chapman, Oxford 1924 (WC) (with Misfortunes of Elphin); ed A. Hodge, introd by J. B. Priestley 1947 (with Nightmare Abbey).

Report from the select committee on steam navigation to India: appendix. 1834.

Paper money lyrics, and other poems. 1837 (priv ptd).

Memoirs of Percy Bysshe Shelley. Fraser's Mag June 1858–March 1862; ed H. F. B. Brett-Smith 1909.

Gryll Grange, by the author of Headlong Hall. Fraser's Mag April–Dec 1860; 1861 (rev), 1947 (Penguin).

Letters and Papers

Letters to Edward Hookham and Percy B. Shelley, with fragments of unpublished manuscripts. Ed R. Garnett, Boston 1910.

Halliford edition vol 8. Ed H. F. B. Brett-Smith and C. E. Jones 1934.

New Shelley letters. Ed W. S. Scott 1948.

§2

Saintsbury, G. Thomas Love Peacock. Macmillan's Mag April 1886; rptd in his Essays in English literature 1780–1860, 1890.

Freeman, A. M. Peacock: a critical study. 1911.

Van Doren, C. The life of Peacock. 1911.

Priestley, J. B. In his English comic characters, 1925. On Prince Seithenyn in Misfortunes of Elphin.

—— Thomas Love Peacock. 1927 (EML), 1966 (with preface by J. I. M. Stewart).

Mayoux, J.-J. Un épicurien anglais: Peacock. Paris 1932.

House, H. The works of Peacock. Listener 8 Dec 1949.

Nicholes, E. L. In Shelley and his circle vol i, Cambridge Mass 1961. Introd and commentary in letters and papers 1792–1809.

Stewart, J. I. M. Thomas Love Peacock. 1963 (Br Council pamphlet).

Felton, F. Thomas Love Peacock. 1973.

Butler, M. Peacock displayed. 1979.

FREDERICK MARRYAT
1792–1848
Collections

Works. 2 vols Philadelphia 1836.

Novels: the King's own edition. Ed W. L. Courtney 24 vols 1896–9.

Novels. Ed R. B. Johnson 24 vols 1896–8, 26 vols 1929–30.

§1

A code of signals for the use of vessels employed in the merchant service. 1817, 1837 (rev), 1841 (last edn rev Marryat).

A suggestion for the abolition of the present system of impressment in the naval service. 1822.

The naval officer: or scenes and adventures in the life of Frank Mildmay. 3 vols 1829, 1 vol 1836, 1839 etc, Paris 1840, London [1873] (with memoir by Florence Marryat).

The King's own. 3 vols 1830, 1 vol Paris 1834, 3 vols 1836, 1 vol 1838 etc; 1874 (with memoir by Florence Marryat); ed R. B. Johnson 1912.

Newton Forster: or the merchant service. 3 vols 1832, 1 vol Paris 1834, London 1838 etc; illustr E. J. Sullivan, ed D. Hannay 1897.

Peter Simple. 3 vols Philadelphia 1833–4, London 1834, 1 vol Paris 1834; ed R. B. Johnson 1907; ed M. Sadleir 2 vols 1929.

Jacob Faithful. 3 vols Philadelphia 1834, London 1834, 1834, 1 vol Paris 1834, 3 vols 1835; ed G. Saintsbury 2 vols 1928.

The Pacha of many tales. 3 vols 1835, 1835, 1 vol 1838.

The diary of a blasé. Philadelphia 1836.

The pirate and the Three cutters, with illustrations by C. Stanfield. 1836, New York 1836 (as Stories of the sea), 2 vols Philadelphia 1836, 1 vol Paris 1836, 15 pts 1845, 1861 (with a memoir) etc.

Japhet in search of a father. 4 pts New York 1835–6, 3 vols 1836, 1836, 1 vol Paris 1836, London 1838 etc.

Mr Midshipman Easy. 3 vols 1836, 1 vol Paris 1836, London 1838 etc; ed O. Warner 1954.

Snarleyyow: or the dog fiend. 3 vols 1837, 1 vol Philadelphia 1837, Paris 1837, London 1847 (as The dog fiend) etc.

The phantom ship. 3 vols 1839, 1 vol Paris 1839, London 1847 etc; ed W. C. Russell 1906; ed M. W. Disher 1948.

A diary in America, with remarks on its institutions. 2 pts 6 vols 1839, Philadelphia 1839–40; ed J. Zanger 1960 (with bibliography); ed S. W. Jackman, New York 1963 (abridged).

Poor Jack. 12 monthly pts illustr C. Stanfield 1840, 1 vol 1840.

Olla podrida. 3 vols 1840, 1 vol Paris 1840, 3 vols 1842, 1 vol 1849 etc.

Masterman Ready: or the wreck of the Pacific, written for young people. 3 vols 1841–2, 1 vol Paris 1842, London 1845 etc; ed D. Hannay 1901.

Joseph Rushbrook: or the poacher. 3 vols 1841, 1 vol Paris 1841, London 1846 (as The poacher) etc.

Percival Keene. 3 vols 1842, 1 vol Paris 1842, London 1848, 1857 (with memoir) etc.

Narrative of the travels and adventures of Monsieur Violet in California, Sonora and Western Texas. 3 vols 1843, 1 vol 1843 (as Travels and romantic adventures of Monsieur Violet among the Snake Indians), 1849 etc.

The settlers in Canada, written for young people. 2 vols 1844 etc; ed O. Warner 1956.

The mission: or scenes in Africa. 2 vols 1845.

The privateer's-man one hundred years ago. 2 vols 1846, 1 vol Paris 1846.

The children of the New Forest. 2 vols 1847; illustr Frank Marryat 1849, 1850 etc. Planned for part-issue. Pt 1 only issued April 1847.

The little savage. 2 vols 1848–9 (pbd posthumously by Frank S. Marryat who completed the work from ch 3 of vol 2), 1853

Valerie: an autobiography. 2 vols 1849 etc. Finished by another hand and pbd posthumously.

Marryat owned and edited Metropolitan Mag *1832–6 and contributed 2 papers on* Novels and novel writing, Nov 1832, Oct 1834. *In 1836 he sponsored an anon novel by his sub-editor Edward Howard,* Rattlin the reefer. *This and Howard's other novels,* The old Commodore, Outward bound, Jack ashore, Sir Henry Morgan the buccaneer, *were often attributed to Marryat.*

§2

Marryat, Florence. Life and letters of Marryat. 2 vols 1872.

Hannay, D. Life of Frederick Marryat. 1889.

Conrad, J. Tales of the sea. Outlook 1898; rptd in his Notes on life and letters, 1924.

Lloyd, C. Captain Marryat and the old navy. 1939.

Woolf, V. The captain's death bed. In her Captain's death bed and other essays, 1950.

Warner, O. Captain Marryat: a rediscovery. 1953.

III. MINOR FICTION 1800–1835

SUSAN EDMONSTONE FERRIER
1782–1854

Collections

Miss Ferrier's novels. 2 vols London and New York 1873–4.
Miss Ferrier's novels. London and Edinburgh 6 vols 1882.
Novels. Ed R. B. Johnson, illustr N. Erichsen 6 vols 1894.
Works. Ed Lady M. Sackville 4 vols 1928. Vol 4 consists of Doyle's Memoir, below.

§ 1

Marriage: a novel. 3 vols 1818 (anon), 1819, 2 vols Edinburgh 1826, 1 vol 1831, 1841, 1847, 1856 (rev), [1873], [1878], New York 1882, 2 vols Boston 1893; ed Earl of Iddesleigh (with biographical preface by A. Goodrich-Freer) 2 vols 1902; ed R. B. Johnson 1928 (EL); ed H. Foltinek, Oxford 1971.
The inheritance, by the author of Marriage. 3 vols 1824, 1825, 1 vol 1831, 1841, 1847, 1857 (rev), [1873], [1878], 2 vols Boston 1893; ed Earl of Iddesleigh (with biographical preface by A. Goodrich-Freer) 2 vols 1903.
Destiny: or the chief's daughter, by the author of Marriage and the Inheritance. 3 vols Edinburgh 1831, 1 vol 1841 (rev), 1856, [1873], [1878], 2 vols Boston 1893.

§ 2

Memoir and correspondence of Susan Ferrier 1782–1854. Ed J. A. Doyle 1898, 1929.
Grant, A. Susan Ferrier of Edinburgh: a biography. Denver 1957.
Parker, W. M. Susan Ferrier and John Galt. 1965.

JOHN GALT
1779–1839

Booth, B. A. A bibliography of Galt. Bull of Bibliography 16 1936.

Collections

Works. Ed D. S. Meldrum and S. R. Crockett, illustr J. Wallace 10 vols Edinburgh and Boston 1895.
Novels. Ed Δ [D. M. Moir] 4 vols 1907.
Works. Ed D. S. Meldrum and W. Roughead, illustr C. E. Brock 8 vols Edinburgh 1936.

§ 1

The battle of Largs: a Gothic poem with several miscellaneous pieces. 1804. Anon.
Cursory reflections on political and commercial topics as connected with the Regent's accession to royal authority. 1812.
Voyages and travels in the years 1809, 1810 and 1811, containing statistical, commercial and miscellaneous observations on Gibraltar, Sardinia, Sicily, Malta, Serigo and Turkey. 1812.
The life and administration of Cardinal Wolsey. 1812, 1817, Edinburgh 1824; ed W. Hazlitt 1846.
The tragedies of Maddelen, Agamemnon, Lady Macbeth, Antonia and Clytemnestra. 1812, 1812.
Letters from the Levant. 1813.
The new British theatre, edited by John Galt. 4 vols 1814–15. Contains several of Galt's own dramas.
The Majolo: a tale. 2 vols 1816. Anon.
Life and studies of Benjamin West. 2 pts 1816–20, 1 vol Philadelphia 1816, 1817, London 1817, 1820; ed N. Wright, Gainesville 1960.
The crusade: a poem. 1816.

The earthquake: a tale. 3 vols Edinburgh 1820 (anon), 2 vols New York 1821.
The wandering Jew: or the travels and observations of Hareach the prolonged, by the Rev T. Clark [J. Galt]. 1820, [1820] (rev as The travels and observations of Hareach, the wandering Jew).
All the voyages round the world, by Samuel Prior. 1820, New York 1843. 'Samuel Prior' was another of Galt's pseudonyms.
A tour of Europe and Asia, by Rev T. Clark [Galt]. 2 vols 1820.
George the Third, his Court and family. 2 vols 1820, 1824.
Pictures historical and biographical, drawn from English, Scottish and Irish history. 2 vols 1821, 1824.
The Ayrshire legatees: or the Pringle family. Edinburgh 1821 (anon), 1823 (with Gathering of the West, below); ed F. Beaumont [1930].
Annals of the parish: or the chronicle of Dalmailing during the ministry of the Rev Micah Balwhidder. Edinburgh 1821 (anon), 1822, 1841 (with Ayrshire legatees, above), 1844 etc; ed G. S. Gordon 1908; ed J. Kinsley, Oxford 1967.
Sir Andrew Wylie, of that ilk. 3 vols Edinburgh 1822, 1822, 2 vols New York 1822, London 1841.
The Provost. Edinburgh 1822 (anon), 1822, New York 1822, Edinburgh 1842 (with The steamboat and The omen), 1850.
The steamboat. Edinburgh 1822, New York 1823; rptd with Provost and Omen, Edinburgh 1842, 1850, 1869; ed I. A. Gordon, Oxford 1973.
The gathering of the West: or We've come to see the King. Edinburgh 1823 (anon, with Ayrshire legatees); ed B. A. Booth, Baltimore 1939.
The entail: or the lairds of Grippy. 3 vols Edinburgh 1823, ed Δ [D. M. Moir]. New York 1823, London 1842, 1850, 2 vols Boston 1896; ed J. Ayscough, Oxford 1913 (WC).
Ringan Gilhaize: or the Covenanters. 3 vols Edinburgh 1823 (anon).
Glenfell: or Macdonalds and Campbells. Edinburgh [1823].
The spaewife: a tale of the Scottish chronicles. 3 vols Edinburgh 1823.
Rothelan: a romance of the English histories. 3 vols Edinburgh 1824, 2 vols New York 1825.
The bachelor's wife: a selection of curious and interesting extracts. Edinburgh 1824. Essays.
The omen. Edinburgh 1825 (anon); rptd with Provost and Steamboat, 1842, New York 1844 (in The omnibus of modern romance), 1850, 1869.
The last of the lairds: or the life and opinions of Malachi Mailings esq of Auldbiggings. Edinburgh 1826; ed I. A. Gordon 1976. The final chs were written by D. M. Moir.
Lawrie Todd: or the settlers in the woods. 3 vols 1830, 1830, 2 vols New York 1830, 1832; ed G. Thorburn 1845, 1849 (rev).
Southennan. 3 vols 1830, 2 vols New York 1830.
The life of Lord Byron. 1830, 1830.
The lives of the players. 2 vols 1831, Boston 1831, 1 vol 1886.
Bogle Corbet: or the emigrants. 3 vols [1831].
The member: an autobiography. 1832, 1833 (with The Radical, below, as The reform); ed I. A. Gordon, Edinburgh 1975.
The Radical: an autobiography. 1832, 1833 (with The member, above, as The reform).
The Canadas as they at present commend themselves to the enterprise of emigrants, colonists and capitalists, compiled and condensed from original documents furnished by John Galt, by Andrew Picken. 1832.
Stanley Buxton: or the schoolfellows. 3 vols 1832.
Poems. 1833.
Eben Erskine: or the traveller. 3 vols 1833.

The stolen child: a tale of the town. 1833, Philadelphia 1833.
Stories of the study. 3 vols 1833.
The Ouranoulogos: or the celestial volume. Illustr J. Martin 1833.
Autobiography. 2 vols Edinburgh 1833.
The literary life and miscellanies. 3 vols 1834.
Efforts, by an invalid. Greenock 1835, London 1835. Verse.
A contribution to the Greenock calamity fund. Greenock 1835. Verse.
The demon of destiny and other poems. Greenock 1839.
The Howdie and other tales. Ed W. Roughead, Edinburgh 1923.
A rich man and other stories. Ed W. Roughead 1925.
Poems. Ed G. H. Needler, Toronto 1954.

§2

Jeffrey, F. Secondary Scottish novels. Edinburgh Rev 39 1823.
Millar, J. H. The novels of Galt. Ed W. Bates [1873].
Aberdein, J. W. John Galt. Oxford 1936.
Lyell, F. H. A study of the novels of Galt. Princeton 1942.
Parker, W. M. New Galt letters. TLS 6 June 1942.
—— Susan Ferrier and Galt. 1965.
Needler, G. H. Galt's dramas. 1945.
Pritchett, V. S. A Scottish documentary. In his Living novel, 1946.
Hamilton, T. W. John Galt. 1947.
Brownlie, W. M. Galt: social historian. 1952.
Gordon, I. A. Galt: the life of a writer. Edinburgh 1972.

THEODORE EDWARD HOOK
1788–1841

§1

The man of sorrow, by Alfred Allendale. 3 vols 1808, 1 vol 1842 (as Ned Musgrave: or the most unfortunate man in the world), 1854.
Facts illustrative of the treatment of Napoleon Buonaparte in Saint Helena. 1819 (anon), 1910 (in C. K. Shorter, Napoleon in his own defence).
Tentamen: or an essay towards the history of Whittington, by Vicesimus Blinkinsop. 1820, 1821. A satire on Sir Matthew Wood, the partisan of Queen Caroline.
Sayings and doings: a series of sketches from life. 3 sers 9 vols 1824–8.
Maxwell, by the author of Sayings and doings. 3 vols 1830, 1 vol 1849, 1854 (rev), [1878].
Love and pride, by the author of Sayings and doings. 3 vols 1833, Philadelphia 1834, 1842 (as The widow and the Marquess: or love and pride), 1868.
The parson's daughter, by the author of Sayings and doings. 3 vols 1833, Philadelphia 1833, 1835 (rev and corrected), 1847, 1867, 1872.
Gilbert Gurney, by the author of Sayings and doings. 3 vols 1836, Paris 1836, London 1841, 1850.
Jack Brag, by the author of Sayings and doings. 3 vols 1837, Paris 1837, London 1839, 1847, 1850, 1872, 1884.
Gurney married: a sequel to Gilbert Gurney, by the author of Sayings and doings. 3 vols 1838, 1839.
Births, deaths and marriages, by the author of Sayings and doings. 3 vols 1839, 2 vols Philadelphia 1839, London 1842 (as All in the wrong: or births, deaths and marriages), [1863] (as All in the wrong).
Precepts and practice. Illustr Phiz 3 vols 1840, 1857.
Fathers and sons: a novel. 3 vols 1842.
Peregrine Bunce, or settled at last: a novel. 3 vols 1842, 1 vol 1857.
Ned Musgrave, or the most unfortunate man in the world: a comic novel. Nd, 1854. First pbd as The man of sorrow, 1808.

The Ramsbottom letters. 1872, [1874] (as The Ramsbottom papers, complete and unabridged).
1841, as well as the following novels: A. Dumas, Pascal Bruno, 1837; J. T. J. Hewlett, Peter Priggins, 3 vols 1841; The Parish Clerk, 3 vols 1841; and H. M. G. Smythies, Cousin Geoffrey: the old bachelor, 3 vols 1840. He was editor of John Bull from 1820 to 1841, and of New Monthly Mag & Humourist from vol 49 to 62.

§2

Lockhart, J. G. Blackwood's Mag Feb 1825. Review of Sayings and doings.
—— Hook: a sketch. 1852 (3 edns), 1853.
Horne, R. H. In his A new spirit of the age vol 2, 1844.
Barham, R. H. D. The life and remains of Hook. 2 vols 1849, 1853 (rev and corrected), 1877 (rev).
Brightfield, M. F. Hook and his novels. Cambridge Mass 1928.

GEORGE PAYNE RAINSFORD JAMES
1799–1860

Collections

Works, revised and corrected by the author, with an introductory preface. 21 vols 1844–9.

§1

The ruined city: a poem. 1828 (priv ptd), 1829 (with Adra: or the Peruvians).
Richelieu: a tale of France. 3 vols 1829, 1831; ed R. Dircks 1909 (EL).
Darnley: or the field of the cloth of gold. 3 vols 1830.
De l'Orme, by the author of Richelieu and Darnley. 3 vols 1830, 1 vol 1836, 1837 (rev), 1854, 1856.
The history of chivalry. 1830.
Philip Augustus: or the brothers in arms, by the author of Darnley, De l'Orme etc. 3 vols 1831.
Memoirs of great commanders. 3 vols 1832 2 vols Boston 1835; illustr Phiz [or rather E. Corbould] 1858.
Henry Masterton: or the adventures of a young cavalier, by the author of Richelieu, Darnley etc. 3 vols 1832.
The string of pearls, by the author of Darnley etc. 2 vols 1832, 1 vol 1849. Tales.
Delaware, or the ruined family: a tale. 3 vols Edinburgh 1833, 1 vol 1848 (as Thirty years since: or the ruined family), 1855, 1865.
Mary of Burgundy: or the revolt of Ghent, by the author of Darnley. 3 vols 1833.
The life and adventures of John Marston Hall, by the author of Darnley. 3 vols 1834, 1 vol 1851.
The gipsey: a tale, by the author of Richelieu. 3 vols 1835.
My aunt Pontypool. 3 vols 1835, 1 vol 1857.
One in a thousand: or the days of Henri Quatre, by the author of the Gipsey. 3 vols 1835.
The desultory man, by the author of Richelieu. 3 vols 1836.
A history of the life of Edward the Black Prince and of various events connected therewith. 2 vols 1836.
Attila: a romance, by the author of the Gipsey. 3 vols 1837.
The robber: a tale by the author of Richelieu. 3 vols 1838.
Henry of Guise: or the states of Blois. 3 vols 1839.
The Huguenot: a tale of the French Protestants, by the author of the Gipsey. 3 vols 1839.
Charles Tyrrell: or the bitter blood. 2 vols 1839.
The gentleman of the old school: a tale. 3 vols 1839.
The King's highway: a novel. 3 vols 1840.
The man at arms, or Henry de Cerons: a romance. 1840.
Corse de Leon, or the brigand: a romance. 3 vols 1841.
Bertrand de la Croix: or the siege of Rhodes. 1841.

The ancient regime: a tale. 3 vols 1841, 1 vol 1850 (as Castlenau).
The Jacquerie, or the lady and the page: an historical romance. 3 vols 1841.
Morley Ernstein: or the tenants of the heart. 3 vols 1842.
The commissioner: or de lunatico inquirendo. Illustr Phiz 1843 (anon), Dublin 1843.
Forest days: a romance of old times. 3 vols 1843.
The false heir. 3 vols 1843, 1 vol 1853.
Eva St Clair and other collected tales. 2 vols 1843.
Agincourt: a romance. 3 vols 1844.
Arabella Stuart: a romance from English history. 3 vols 1844.
Rose d'Albret: or troublous times. 3 vols 1844.
Arrah Neil: or times of old. 3 vols 1845.
The smuggler: a tale. 3 vols 1845.
Beauchamp: or the error. 3 vols 1848.
The stepmother: or evil doings. 1845 (priv ptd), 3 vols 1846.
Heidelberg: a romance. 3 vols 1846.
The castle of Ehrenstein, its lords spiritual and temporal, its inhabitants earthly and unearthly. 3 vols 1847.
A whim and its consequences. 3 vols 1847 (anon), 1850.
The convict: a tale. 3 vols 1847.
Russell: a tale of the reign of Charles II. 3 vols 1847.
Margaret Graham: a tale founded on facts. 2 vols 1848.
Sir Theodore Broughton: or laurel water. 3 vols 1848.
The forgery: or best intentions. 3 vols 1849.
John Jones's tales for little John Joneses. 2 vols 1849.
The woodman: a romance of the times of Richard III. 3 vols 1849.
The old oak chest: a tale of domestic life. 3 vols 1850.
Henry Smeaton: a Jacobite story of the reign of George I. 3 vols 1851.
The fate: a tale of stirring times. 3 vols 1851.
Remorse and other tales. New York 1852.
Revenge: a novel. 3 vols 1852.
Adrian, or the clouds of the mind: a romance. 2 vols 1852. With M. B. Field.
Pequinillo: a tale. 3 vols 1852.
Agnes Sorel: an historical romance. 3 vols 1853.
A life of vicissitudes: a story of revolutionary times. New York 1852, 3 vols 1853 (as The vicissitudes of a life: a novel).
Ticonderoga, or the black eagle: a tale of times not long past. 3 vols 1854, 1 vol New York 1854, London 1859 (as The black eagle: or Ticonderoga).
Prince Life: a story for my boy. 1856.
The old dominion, or the Southampton massacre: a novel. 3 vols 1856, 1 vol New York 1856, London 1858.
Leonora d'Orco: a historical romance. 3 vols 1857.
Lord Montagu's page: a historical romance. 3 vols 1858.
The cavalier: an historical novel. Philadelphia 1859, 2 vols 1854 (as Bernard Marsh: a novel).
The man in black: an historical novel of the days of Queen Anne. Philadelphia 1860.

§ 2

Horne, R. H. In his A new spirit of the age vol 1, 1844.
Ellis, S. M. The solitary horseman: or the life and adventures of James. 1927.

MATTHEW GREGORY LEWIS
1775-1818

§ 1

The monk: a romance. 3 vols 1796, 1796, 2 vols Dublin 1796, Waterford '1796' (watermarked 1818), 3 vols 1797, 2 vols Dublin 1797, 3 vols 1798 (expurgated as Ambrosio: or the monk, rptd New York 1830); ed E. A. Baker 1907; ed L. F. Peck, New York 1952.
Village virtues: a dramatic satire. 1796.

The minister: a tragedy translated from the German of Schiller. 1797.
The Castle spectre: a drama. 1798 (7 edns).
Rolla, or the Peruvian hero: a tragedy translated from the German of Kotzebue. 1799 (4 edns).
Tales of terror. Kelso 1799 (reissued as An apology for tales of terror). Includes 4 ballads by Lewis with others by Scott and Southey.
The love of gain: a poem imitated from Juvenal. 1799.
Alonzo the brave and fair Imogine: a ballad [from Monk]. 1797 (in Poetry original and selected vol 2).
The East Indian: a comedy. 1800, 1800, Dublin 1800 (as Rivers: or the East Indian). Adapted as an opera, 1818.
Adelmorn the outlaw: a romantic drama. 1801, 1801.
Songs in Adelmorn the outlaw. 1801.
Alfonso, King of Castile: a tragedy. 1801, 1802.
Tales of wonder, written and collected by M. G. Lewis. 2 vols 1801.
The bravo of Venice: a romance translated from the German [of J. H. D. Zschokke]. 1805.
Feudal tyrants, or the Counts of Carlsheim and Sargans: a romance, taken from the German. 4 vols 1806, 1807.
Romantic tales. 4 vols 1808, 1838, 1848.
Venoni, or the novice of St Mark's: a drama. 1809.
Monody on the death of Sir John Moore. 1809.
Poems. 1812.
The isle of devils: a historical tale [in verse] founded on an anecdote in the annals of Portugal. Kingston Jamaica 1827, 1912.
Crazy Jane [by Lewis, with other songs]. Waterford [1830?] (anon), Manchester [1835?].
Journal of a West India proprietor kept during a residence in the island of Jamaica. 1834, 1845 (as Journal of a residence among the negroes in the West Indies), 1861; ed M. Wilson 1929.

§ 2

[Baron-Wilson, M.] The life and correspondence of Lewis, with many pieces never before published. 2 vols 1839.
Parreaux, A. The publication of the Monk. Paris 1960.
Peck, L. F. A life of Lewis. Cambridge Mass 1961.

CHARLES ROBERT MATURIN
1782-1824

Fatal revenge: or the family of Montorio, by Dennis Jasper Murphy. 3 vols 1807, 4 vols 1824, 1 vol 1841.
The wild Irish boy, by the author of Montorio. 3 vols 1808, 2 vols New York 1808, 1814, 1839.
The Milesian chief: a romance by the author of Montorio and the Wild Irish boy. 4 vols 1812.
Bertram, or the Castle of St Aldobrand: a tragedy. 1816 (7 edns), 1817, 1817, 1827, 1829.
Manuel: a tragedy in five acts by the author of Bertram. 1817, 1817.
Women, or pour et contre: a tale by the author of Bertram etc. 3 vols Edinburgh 1818.
Fredolfo: a tragedy in five acts. 1819.
Sermons. 1819, 1821.
Melmoth the wanderer: a tale by the author of Bertram. 4 vols Edinburgh 1820, 1821, 3 vols 1892 (with memoir and bibliography); ed W. F. Axton, Lincoln Nebraska 1961.
The Albigenses: a romance by the author of Bertram etc. 4 vols 1824, 3 vols Philadelphia 1824.
Five sermons on the errors of the Roman Catholic Church. 1824, 1826.
Leixlip Castle. 3 vols 1825.
The universe: a poem, 1821, *which bears Maturin's name, was really by James Wills.*

MARY RUSSELL MITFORD
1787-1855

Collections

Works, prose and verse. Philadelphia 1841.
Dramatic works. 2 vols 1854.

§ 1

Poems. 1810, 1811 (with addns).
Christina, the maid of the South Seas: a poem. 1811.
Blanche of Castile. 1812.
Watlington Hill: a poem. 1812.
Narrative poems on the female character. Vol 1, 1813. No more pbd.
Julian: a tragedy in five acts. 1823, 1823, 1823, 1829.
Our village: sketches of rural character and scenery. 5 vols 1824-32, 2 vols 1852, 1 vol 1862 (as Children of the village), 1881 (as Village tales and sketches; illustr F. Barnard et al 1889 (selection); ed E. Rhys 1891 (selection); ed A. T. Ritchie 1893 (selection); ed E. Gollancz 1900 (selection).
Foscari: a tragedy. 1826, 1827 etc.
Foscari and Julian: tragedies. 1827.
Dramatic scenes, sonnets and other poems. 1827.
Rienzi: a tragedy. 1828, 1828, 1828 etc.
Mary, Queen of Scots: a scene in English verse. 1831.
Belford Regis: or sketches of a country town. 3 vols 1835.
Country stories 1837, 1850; illustr G. Morrow 1895.
Recollections of a literary life: or books, places and people. 3 vols 1852, 1859, 1 vol 1883 (as Recollections and selections from my favourite poets and prose writers).
Atherton and other tales. 3 vols 1854, 1 vol Boston 1854.
The life of Mary Russell Mitford in a selection from her letters. Ed A. G. L'Estrange 3 vols 1870.
Letters to C. Boner. 1871, 1876.
The letters of Mary Russell Mitford: second series. Ed H. F. Chorley 2 vols 1872; ed R. B. Johnson [1925].
The friendships of Mary Russell Mitford in letters from her literary correspondents. Ed A. G. L'Estrange 2 vols 1882, 1 vol New York 1882.
Correspondence with C. Boner and J. Ruskin. Ed E. Lee [1914], Chicago [1915].
Stories of village and town life: or word pictures of old England. Ed J. P. Briscoe and E. M. P. Knight 1915.

§ 2

Woolf, V. In her Common reader, 1925.
Astin, M. Mary Russell Mitford: her circle and her books. 1930.
Watson, V. G. M. R. Mitford. 1949.
Duncan-Jones, C. M. Miss Mitford and Mr Harness: records of a friendship. 1954.
Miller, B. (ed). Elizabeth Barrett to Miss Mitford: unpublished letters. 1954.

JAMES JUSTINIAN MORIER
1780-1849

Journey through Persia, Armenia and Asia Minor to Constantinople 1808-9.
Second journey through Persia, Armenia and Asia Minor to Constantinople 1810-16, 1818.
The adventures of Hajji Baba of Ispahan. 3 vols 1824, 1824 (with preface), 1 vol 1835 (rev); ed C. W. Stewart, Oxford 1923 (WC); ed R. D. Altick, New York [1954].
The adventures of Hajji Baba of Ispahan in England. 2 vols 1828, 1 vol 1835 (rev), 1850; ed L. S. Jast 1942.
Zohrab the hostage, by the author of Hajji Baba. 3 vols 1832, 1832, 1833 (rev with notes).

Ayesha: the maid of Kars, by the author of Zohrab. 3 vols 1834, 1834.
Abel Allnutt: a novel. 3 vols 1837.
An oriental tale, by the author of Hajji Baba. [1839].
The adventures of Tom Spicer, who advertised for a wife: a poem. 1840 (priv ptd).
The Mirza. 3 vols 1841.
Misselmah: a Persian tale. Brighton 1847.
Martin Toutrond: a Frenchman in London in 1831. 1849 (anon), 1849 (signed), 1852. Written in French by Morier and translated by himself.

AMELIA OPIE,
née ALDERSON
1769-1853

§ 1

The dangers of coquetry: a novel. 2 vols [1790] (anon).
The father and daughter: a tale in prose, with an epistle from the maid of Corinth to her lover, and other poetical pieces. 1801 (2nd edn), 1804 (4th edn).
Poems. 1802, 1803, 1804, 1806, 1808, 1811.
Adeline Mowbray, or the mother and daughter: a tale. 3 vols 1804, 1805, 2 vols 1844 (with The welcome home and The Quaker and The young man of the world).
Simple tales. 4 vols 1806, 1806, 1815 (4th edn).
The warrior's return and other poems. 1808.
Temper, or domestic scenes: a tale. 3 vols 1812, 4 vols 1813.
Tales of real life. 3 vols 1813, 1816 (3rd edn).
Valentine's Eve. 3 vols 1816, 1816.
New tales. 4 vols 1818, 1819 (3rd edn).
Tales of the heart. 4 vols 1820.
Madeline: a tale. 2 vols 1822.
Illustrations of lying, in all its branches. 2 vols 1825.
Tales of the Pemberton family, for the use of children. 1825, 1826.
The black man's lament: or how to make sugar. 1826. Verse.
Detraction displayed. 1828.
A wife's duty: a tale. 1828, 1847.
Happy faces: or benevolence and selfishness; and The revenge. 1830. Tales.
Lays for the dead. 1834, 1840.
The ruffian boy; and After the ball: or the two Sir Williams. 1858.

§ 2

Brightwell, C. L. Memorials of the life of Amelia Opie, from her letters, diaries and other manuscripts. Norwich 1854, 1854.
—— Memoir of Amelia Opie. 1855.
[Ritchie, Lady]. Mrs Opie. Cornhill Mag Oct 1883; rptd in her A book of sibyls, 1883.
Macgregor, M. E. Amelia Alderson Opie, worldling and Friend. Northampton Mass 1933. With a bibliography.
Menzies-Wilson, J. and H. Lloyd. Amelia: the tale of a plain Friend. Oxford 1937.

SYDNEY OWENSON,
afterwards LADY MORGAN
1776-1859

§ 1

Poems. Dublin 1801.
St Clair: or the heiress of Desmond, by S. O. Dublin 1803, 2 vols Stockdale 1812 (corrected and greatly enlarged).
Twelve original Hibernian melodies. [1805].
The novice of St Dominick. 4 vols 1805, 1806, 1808, 1823.
The wild Irish girl. 3 vols 1806.

The lay of an Irish harp: or metrical fragments. 1807.
Patriotic sketches of Ireland written in Connaught. 2 vols
1807, 1 vol Baltimore 1809.
Woman: or Ida of Athens. 4 vols 1809.
The missionary: an Indian tale. 3 vols 1811 (4 edns), 1859
(extensively rev as Luxima, the prophetess: a tale of
India).
O'Donnel: a national tale. 3 vols 1814, 1814, 1815, 1835,
1 vol 1835 (rev).
France. 2 vols 1817, 1817.
Florence Macarthy: an Irish tale. 4 vols 1818, 1818, 1819.
Italy. 2 vols 1821, 3 vols 1821 (text differs in part).
Letters to the reviewers of Italy. 1821.
Absenteeism. 1825.
The O'Briens and the O'Flahertys: a national tale. 4 vols
1827, 1827, 1827, 1828.
France in 1829–30. 2 vols 1830.
Dramatic scenes from real life. 2 vols 1833, New York 1833.
The book without a name. 2 vols 1841. With Sir T. C.
Morgan.
The Princess: or the Beguine. 3 vols 1835.
Woman and her master. 2 vols 1840, Philadelphia 1840.
Letter to Cardinal Wiseman. 1851.
Passages in my autobiography. 1859, New York 1859.
Memoirs: autobiography, diaries and correspondence.
Ed W. H. Dixon 1862, 1863, 1 vol 1863.
Both France *and* Italy *aroused considerable controversy, to
which Lady Morgan replied.*

§2

Fitzpatrick, W. J. The friends, foes and adventures of
Lady Morgan. Dublin 1859, 1860 (enlarged as Lady
Morgan: her career literary and personal etc).
Stevenson, L. The wild Irish girl: the life of Sydney
Owenson, Lady Morgan. 1936.

ANN RADCLIFFE,
née WARD
1764–1823

§1

The Castles of Athlin and Dunbayne: a Highland story.
1789, 1793, 1793.
A Sicilian romance. 2 vols 1790, 1792, 1796, 1809, 1818.
The romance of the forest, interspersed with some pieces
of poetry. 3 vols 1791 (anon), 1792, 1794, 1795, 1796;
ed D. M. Rose 1904.
The mysteries of Udolpho: a romance, interspersed with
some pieces of poetry. 4 vols 1794, 1794; ed B. Dobrée,
Oxford 1966.
A journey made in the summer of 1794 through Holland
and the western frontier of Germany. 1795.
The Italian, or the confessional of the black penitents: a
romance. 3 vols 1797, 1797; ed F. Garber, Oxford
1968.
Gaston de Blondeville, or the Court of Henry III keeping
festival in Ardenne: a romance; St Alban's abbey: a
metrical tale; with some poetical pieces, [and] a memoir
of the author [by W. Radcliffe?] with extracts from her
journals. 4 vols 1826, 2 vols 1834, 1839.

§2

Lang, A. Mrs Radcliffe's novels. In his Adventures
among books, 1905.
Summers, M. A great mistress of romance: Ann Radcliffe.
Trans Royal Soc of Lit [1917]; rptd in his Essays in
petto, 1928.
MacIntyre, C. F. Ann Radcliffe in relation to her time.
New Haven 1920.
Wieten, A. S. S. Mrs Radcliffe: her relation towards

romanticism. Amsterdam 1926. Appendix on false
attributions.
Tompkins, J. M. S. In her Popular novel in England
1770–1800, 1932. Ch 8 and Appendix 3.
Ruff, W. Ann Radcliffe: or the hand of taste. In The age
of Johnson: essays presented to C. B. Tinker, New
Haven 1949.
Grant, A. Ann Radcliffe. Denver 1952.

MARY WOLLSTONECRAFT
SHELLEY, née GODWIN
1797–1851

§1

History of a six weeks' tour through a part of France,
Switzerland, Germany and Holland. 1817. Anon. With
her husband Percy Bysshe Shelley.
Frankenstein: or the modern Prometheus. 3 vols 1818
(anon), 2 vols 1823, 1 vol 1831 (rev); ed H. Bloom, New
York 1965; ed M. K. Joseph, Oxford 1969.
Valperga: or the life and adventures of Castruccio Prince
of Lucca, by the author of Frankenstein. 3 vols 1823.
The last man, by the author of Frankenstein. 3 vols 1826,
1826; ed H. J. Luke, Lincoln Nebraska 1965.
The fortunes of Perkin Warbeck: a romance, by the
author of Frankenstein. 3 vols 1830, 1830 ('revised,
corrected and illustrated with a new introduction by the
author'), 1857.
Lodore, by the author of Frankenstein. 3 vols 1835.
Falkner: a novel, by the author of Frankenstein. 3 vols
1837.
Rambles in Germany and Italy in 1840, 1842 and 1843.
2 vols 1844.
The choice: a poem on Shelley's death. Ed H. B. Forman
1876 (priv ptd).
The heir of Mandolfo [a tale]. Appleton's Jnl Jan 1877;
ed R. D. Spector, New York 1963 (in Seven masterpieces of Gothic horror).
Shelley and Mary: a collection of letters and documents of
a biographical character in the possession of Sir Percy
and Lady Shelley. 3 vols 1882 (priv ptd).
Letters, mostly unpublished. Ed H. H. Harper, Boston
1918.
Proserpine and Midas: mythological dramas. Ed A.
Koszul 1922.
Harriet and Mary: being the relations between P. B.,
Harriet and Mary Shelley and T. J. Hogg as shown in
letters between them. Ed W. S. Scott 1944.
Letters. Ed F. L. Jones 2 vols Norman Oklahoma 1944.
Journal. Ed F. L. Jones, Norman Oklahoma 1947.
Eight letters. Ed E. Nitchie, Keats-Shelley Memorial
Bull 3 1950.
My best Mary: selected letters. Ed M. Spark and D.
Stanford 1953.
Mary Shelley to Maria Gisborne: new letters 1818–22.
Ed F. L. Jones, SP 52 1955.
Mathilda. Ed E. Nitchie, Chapel Hill 1959.
The last man. Ed H. J. Luke, Lincoln Nebraska 1965.
Collected tales and stories. Ed C. E. Robinson, Baltimore
1976.
Mary Shelley edited Shelley's Poems, *1839. In 1824 she
brought out his* Posthumous poems *and in 1840 his*
Essays, letters from abroad, translations and fragments.

§2

Marshall, F. A. The life and letters of Mary Wollstonecraft Shelley. 2 vols 1889.
'Grylls, R. G.' (Lady Mander). Mary Shelley. 1938.
Spark, M. Child of light: a reassessment of Mary Shelley.
1951.
—— Mary Shelley: a prophetic novelist. Listener 22 Feb
1951.

Norman, S. Mary Shelley 1797–1851. Fortnightly Rev Feb 1951.
Nitchie, E. Mary Shelley: author of Frankenstein. New Brunswick 1953.

FRANCES TROLLOPE,
née MILTON
1780–1863

§ 1

Domestic manners of the Americans. Illustr A. Hervieu 2 vols 1832 (4 edns); ed M. Sadleir 1927; ed D. Smalley, illustr Hervieu, New York 1949.
The refugee in America: a novel. 3 vols 1832, 2 vols New York 1833.
The Abbess: a romance. 3 vols 1833.
Belgium and Western Germany in 1833. 2 vols 1834, Paris 1834.
Tremordyn cliff. 3 vols 1835.
Paris and the Parisians in 1835. 2 vols 1836.
The life and adventures of Jonathan Jefferson Whitlaw: or scenes on the Mississippi. Illustr A. Hervieu 3 vols 1836, 1836, [1857] (as Lynch law).
The vicar of Wrexhill. Illustr A. Hervieu 3 vols 1837.
A romance of Vienna. 3 vols 1838.
Vienna and the Austrians, with some account of a journey through Swabia, Bavaria, the Tyrol and the Salzbourg. Illustr A. Hervieu 2 vols Paris 1838.
The widow Barnaby. 3 vols 1839, 1 vol 1840, 1856.
The life and adventures of Michael Armstrong, the factory boy. 3 vols 1840.
One fault: a novel. 3 vols 1840, 1858.
The widow married: a sequel to the Widow Barnaby. Illustr R. W. Buss 3 vols 1840.
Charles Chesterfield: or the adventures of a youth of genius. Illustr Phiz 3 vols 1841, 1846.
The ward of Thorpe Combe. 3 vols 1842.
The blue belles of England. 3 vols 1842.
A visit to Italy. 2 vols 1842.

The Barnabys in America: or adventures of the widow wedded. Illustr Leech 3 vols 1843, [1859] (as Adventures of the Barnabys in America).
Hargrave: or the adventures of a man of fashion. 3 vols 1843.
Jessie Phillips: a tale of the present day. Illustr Leech 3 vols 1843, 1844.
The Laurringtons: or superior people. 3 vols 1844.
Young love: a novel. 3 vols 1844.
The attractive man: a novel. 3 vols 1846.
The Robertses on their travels. 3 vols 1846.
Travels and travellers: a series of sketches. 2 vols 1846.
Father Eustace: a tale of the Jesuits. 3 vols 1847.
The three cousins: a novel. 3 vols 1847, [1858].
Town and country: a novel. 3 vols 1848, [1857] (as The days of the Regency).
The young Countess: or love and jealousy. 3 vols 1848, 1 vol 1860 (as Love and jealousy).
The lottery of marriage: a novel. 3 vols 1849, 1 vol [1860].
The old world and the new: a novel. 3 vols 1849.
Petticoat government: a novel. 3 vols 1850.
Mrs Mathews, or family mysteries: a novel. 3 vols 1851.
Second love, or beauty and intellect: a novel. 3 vols 1851.
Uncle Walter: a novel. 3 vols 1852.
The young heiress: a novel. 3 vols 1853, 1864.
The life and adventures of a clever woman, illustrated with occasional extracts from her diary. 3 vols 1854.
Gertrude: or family pride. 3 vols 1855, 1864.
Fashionable life: or Paris and London. 3 vols 1856.

§ 2

Trollope, F. E. Frances Trollope: her life and literary works from George III to Victoria. 2 vols 1895.
Sadleir, M. Trollope: a commentary. 1927. Appendix.
Pope-Hennessy, U. In her Three English women in America, 1929.
Stebbins, L. P. and R. P. The Trollopes: the chronicle of a writing family. 1946.
Bigland, E. The indomitable Mrs Trollope. 1953.

IV. THE MID-NINETEENTH-CENTURY NOVEL

BENJAMIN DISRAELI,
1st EARL OF BEACONSFIELD
1804-81

Bibliographies

Dahl, C. In Victorian fiction: a guide to research, ed L. Stevenson, Cambridge Mass 1964.

Collections

Novels and tales. 10 vols 1870–1. With preface.
Novels and tales: Hughenden edition. 11 vols 1881.
Works: Empire and Earls edition. Ed E. Gosse with biographical preface by R. Arnot 20 vols 1904–5.
Novels and tales: Bradenham edition. Ed P. Guedella 12 vols 1926–7.

§ 1

Rumpel Stiltskin: a dramatic spectacle, by 'B. D.' and 'W. G. M.' [Disraeli, W. G. Meredith]. 1823 (priv ptd); ed M. Sadleir, Glasgow 1952.
The modern Aesop. 2 weekly pts Star Chamber 24–31 May 1826; ed M. Sadleir 1928 (with the Dunciad of to-day, here attributed to Disraeli, 2 weekly pts, from Star Chamber 10–17 May 1826).

Vivian Grey. Vols 1–2 1826, vols 3–5 1827; 1 vol 1853 (with preface); ed L. Woolf 2 vols 1904. Key to Vivian Grey, 1827 (10th edn).
The young Duke, by the author of Vivian Grey. 3 vols 1831, 1 vol 1853, 1888; ed L. Wolf 1905; ed W. S. Northcote 1906.
The voyage of Captain Popanilla, by the author of Vivian Grey. 1828; ed W. S. Northcote 1906.
Contarini Fleming: a psychological autobiography. 4 vols 1832, 1834, 3 vols 1846, 1 vol 1853, 1888; ed W. S. Northcote 1905.
The wondrous tale of Alroy and the Rise of Iskander. 4 vols 1832, 1834, 3 vols 1846, 1853, [1888]; ed W. S. Northcote 1906. Alroy rptd separately, 1888.
The revolutionary epick. 2 vols 1834, 1864 (rev); ed W. D. Adams 1904.
Henrietta Temple: a love story. 3 vols 1837, 1 vol 1853, [1888]; ed W. S. Northcote 1906.
Venetia. 3 vols 1837, 1853, 2 vols 1858, [1888]; ed W. S. Northcote 1905.
The tragedy of Count Alarcos, by the author of Vivian Grey. 1839, 1853 (with Ixion); ed W. S. Northcote 1906 (with Alroy, above).
Coningsby: or the new generation. 3 vols 1844, 1844; ed 'André Maurois', Oxford 1931 (WC); ed W. Allen 1948.

Sybil: or the two nations. 3 vols 1845, 1 vol Paris 1845, London 1853, 1882, [1888]; ed H. D. Traill 1895; ed W. S. Northcote 1905; ed W. Sichel, Oxford 1925 (WC).

Tancred: or the new crusade. 3 vols 1847; ed W. S. Northcote 1905.

Ixion in Heaven; The infernal marriage; Popanilla; Count Alarcos. 1853; ed W. S. Northcote 1906. Ixion 2 monthly pts New Monthly Mag Dec 1832–Jan 1833; rptd separately 1925, 1927 (with W. E. Aytoun, Endymion); Infernal marriage 2 monthly pts New Monthly Mag July–Aug 1834; rptd separately, 1929.

Lothair. 3 vols 1870 (7 edns), 1877, 1908; ed V. Bogdanor, Oxford 1975.

Endymion, by the author of Lothair. 3 vols 1880, 1 vol New York 1880, London 1881, New York 1881 (with key to the characters).

Tales and sketches. Ed J. L. Robertson 1891.

Unfinished novel [no title]. 3 pts Times 20–3 Jan 1905; rptd in W. F. Monypenny and G. E. Buckle, The life of Disraeli, 6 vols 1910–20, below.

Political Writings and Speeches

England and France: or a cure for the ministerial Gallomania. 1832.

What is he? 1833, 1833 (rev); ed F. Hitchman [1884] (with Vindication of the English Constitution).

The crisis examined. 1834.

Vindication of the English Constitution in a letter to a noble and learned lord. 1835; ed F. Hitchman [1884] (with What is he?); ed F. A. Hyndman [1895].

The letters of Runnymede, The spirit of Whiggism. 1836; ed F. Bickley 1923; ed W. Hutcheon 1913. Letters of Runnymede first pbd in Times Jan–May 1836; 1836 (priv ptd); ed F. Hitchman 1885.

Lord George Bentinck: a political biography. 1852 (4 edns), 1858, 1872 (8th edn rev); ed C. Whibley 1905.

Selected speeches. Ed T. E. Kebbel 2 vols 1882.

Whigs and Whiggism: political writings. Ed W. Hutcheon 1913.

Letters

Home letters 1830–1. Ed R. Disraeli 1885, 1885, 1887 (below).

Correspondence with his sister. Ed R. Disraeli 1886; rptd with above, 1887 (as Lord Beaconsfield's letters 1830–52); ed A. Birrell 1928.

Letters of Disraeli to Lady Bradford and Lady Chesterfield. Ed Marquis of Zetland 2 vols 1929.

Letters to Frances Anne, Marchioness of Londonderry 1837–61. 1938.

§2

Francis, G. H. Disraeli: a critical biography. 1852.

MacGilchrist, J. Life of Disraeli. [1868].

Stephen, L. Disraeli's novels. In his Hours in a Library ser 2, 1876.

Monypenny, W. F. and G. E. Buckle. The life of Disraeli. 6 vols 1910–20, 2 vols 1929 (rev).

Somervell, D. C. Disraeli and Gladstone. 1925.

'Maurois, André' (E. S. W. Herzog). La vie de Disraeli. Paris 1927; tr 1928.

Pritchett, V. S. In his Living novel, 1946.

Smith, S. M. Willenhall and Wodgate: Disraeli's use of Blue Book evidence. RES new ser 13 1962.

—— Mr Disraeli's readers: letters written to Disraeli and his wife by nineteenth-century readers of Sybil. Nottingham 1966.

Blake, R. Disraeli. 1966.

—— Disraeli's political novels. History Today 16 1966.

CHARLES DICKENS
1812–70

Most of the mss of Dickens's works are in the Forster Collection at the Victoria and Albert Museum, London; a small quantity, including a few leaves of Pickwick, *in BM; the ms of* Great Expectations *in Wisbech Museum; and that of* Our mutual friend *in Pierpont Morgan Library, New York.*

Bibliographies etc

Pierce, G. A. The Dickens dictionary: a key to the characters and principal incidents in the tales of Dickens. Boston 1872; 1880, 1894 (with addns by W. A. Wheeler), 1926, New York 1965 (rev).

Victoria and Albert Museum, South Kensington. A catalogue of the printed books bequeathed by John Forster. 1888.

—— A catalogue of the paintings, manuscripts, autograph letters, pamphlets etc, bequeathed by Forster. 1893.

Eckel, J. C. The first editions of the writings of Dickens: a bibliography. 1913, 1932 (rev and enlarged).

Nisbet, A. In Victorian fiction: a guide to research, ed L. Stevenson, Cambridge Mass 1964.

Dickens studies: a journal of modern research and criticism. Boston 1965 —. In progress.

Hardwick, M. and M. The Dickens companion. 1965.

Collections

Editions published by Chapman & Hall

The works of Charles Dickens. 17 vols 1847–67; 1st ser 1847–52 also issued in weekly and monthly pts. The first systematic re-issue, known as the 'first cheap edition'. Frontispiece illustrations only. Contains some new prefaces.

Library edition. 22 vols 1858–9. Frontispiece illustrations only. Includes Reprinted pieces 1858, from Household Words. Dedicated to John Forster. Re-issued in 30 vols (including later works) 1861–74, with new title-pages and illustrations.

The People's edition. 25 vols 1865–7. A re-issue of the Cheap edition, excluding prefaces etc.

Charles Dickens edition. 21 vols 1867–[75]. Mainly rptd from foregoing, with slight addns and revisions by Dickens, including the addn of running headlines and some new prefaces. This is the text most often rptd.

Household edition. 22 vols [1871–9]; issued in monthly pts. With new illustrations by F. Barnard, J. Mahoney et al. Includes Forster's Life of Dickens.

Illustrated library edition. 30 vols 1873–6.

Gadshill edition. Introds, general essay and notes by A. Lang 36 vols 1897–[1908]. Contains all the original illustrations, with many additional ones. Vols 35–6, Miscellaneous papers (not previously collected), ed B. W. Matz 1908. Rptd in edn de luxe 38 vols 1903–[8], with Forster's Life of Dickens, 2 vols, added.

Oxford India paper Dickens. 17 vols 1901–2. With Henry Frowde (afterwards Humphrey Milford). Copyright text, on thin paper, with the original illustrations. Forster's Life added 1907.

Biographical edition. Ed A. Waugh 19 vols 1902–3. With the original illustrations. Includes Collected papers (prefaces and minor works). Miscellaneous papers, ed B. W. Matz, as additional volume 1908.

Other Editions

Everyman's library. 22 vols [1906–21]. Introds to Barnaby Rudge and A tale of two cities by W. Jerrold, to remainder by G. K. Chesterton.

Charles Dickens library. Ed J. A. Hammerton 18 vols [1910]. 1200 illustrations in all, including the original ones and 500 specially drawn by Harry Furniss.

Waverley edition. 30 vols 1913–18. With character-study

illustrations by Charles Pears and coloured versions of F. Barnard's illustrations. Introds by G. B. Shaw, W. de Morgan, J. Galsworthy, A. C. Benson, H. Caine et al.

The Nonesuch Dickens. Ed A. Waugh, H. Walpole, W. Dexter and T. Hatton. 23 vols 1937–8. Text from Charles Dickens edn, 1867–75.

The New Oxford illustrated Dickens. 21 vols Oxford 1947–58.

The Clarendon Dickens. Ed. J. Butt and K. Tillotson, Oxford 1966– .

§ I

All Dickens's novels were first pbd serially; and reviews, imitations, parodies, dramatizations etc often appeared before the work was complete.

Sketches by Boz

Sketches by 'Boz' illustrative of every-day life and every-day people. Illustr George Cruikshank 2 vols 1836; The second series, 1836.

Sketches by 'Boz' [both sers]. 20 monthly pts Nov 1837–June 1839 (variants) with 40 illustrations by Cruikshank, 13 of them new; 1839, with new preface (the monthly pts in 1 vol; known as the first 8vo edn; variants).

Pickwick Papers

The posthumous papers of the Pickwick Club containing a faithful record of the perambulations, perils, travels, adventures and sporting transactions of the corresponding members, edited by Boz. 20 (as 19) monthly pts, April 1836 to Nov 1837 except June 1837; illustr Robert Seymour, d. April 1836 (pts 1–2); Robert W. Buss (pt 3); Hablot Knight Browne ('Phiz') for remainder; 1 vol 1837 (Buss's illustrations omitted).

Oliver Twist

Oliver Twist: or, the parish boy's progress, by 'Boz'. 3 vols 1838, 1838 (by Charles Dickens), 1839 (by Charles Dickens, 2nd edn), 1840 (by 'Boz'), 1841 (by Charles Dickens, 3rd edn, with author's introd). All illustr G. Cruikshank. In 24 monthly instalments, Bentley's Miscellany Feb 1837–April 1839 (except June and Oct 1837 and Sept 1838). 2 vols Philadelphia 1839 [1838] unillustr, 1 vol 1839 (illustr G. Cruikshank): these Philadelphia edns are unique texts, partly based on proofs of Bentley's Miscellany before Dickens's corrections.

The adventures of Oliver Twist: or the parish boy's progress. New edition, revised and corrected. In 10 monthly pts and 1 vol 1846 (illustr and new cover by G. Cruikshank); cheap edn 1850 (and in 19 weekly pts, 5 monthly pts, Dec 1849–April 1850; with new preface by Dickens and frontispiece by G. Cruikshank); Charles Dickens edn 1867 (with rev preface); ed K. Tillotson, Oxford 1966.

Greene, G. The young Dickens. In his Lost childhood, 1951, rptd from his edn, 1950.

Auden, W. H. Huck and Oliver. Listener 1 Oct 1953.

Pritchett, V. S. In his Books in general, 1953.

House, H. An introduction to Oliver Twist. In his All in due time, 1955.

Tillotson, K. Oliver Twist. E & S new ser 12 1959.

—— Oliver Twist in three volumes. Library 5th ser 18 1963.

Bayley, J. In Dickens and the twentieth century, ed J. Gross and G. Pearson 1962.

Hollingsworth, K. The Newgate novel 1830–47. Detroit 1963.

Nicholas Nickleby

The life and adventures of Nicholas Nickleby, containing a faithful account of the fortunes, misfortunes, uprisings, downfallings and complete career of the Nickleby family, edited by 'Boz', with illustrations by 'Phiz'. Title on wrapper. On title-page, The life and adventures of Nicholas Nickleby, by Charles Dickens. 20 (as 19) monthly pts (with variants) April 1838 to Oct 1839; 1 vol Oct 1839 (with preface, and portrait of Dickens by Daniel Maclise, as The life and adventures of Nicholas Nickleby), Philadelphia 1839, cheap edn 1848 (and in 30 weekly pts, 8 monthly pts, Oct 1847–May 1848; with new preface, and frontispiece from painting by T. Webster), 1867 (Charles Dickens edn); ed A. Waugh 1953.

Nicholas Nickleby at the Yorkshire School: a reading in four chapters. [1861?] (priv ptd), nd (rev and 'in three chapters'), both rptd ('in four chapters').

Master Humphrey's Clock, Old Curiosity Shop, Barnaby Rudge

Master Humphrey's clock, by 'Boz', with illustrations by G. Cattermole and H. K. Browne. 88 weekly pts and 20 monthly nos from 4 April 1840; 3 vols 1840–1 ('by Charles Dickens') with preface to each vol, that to vol 3 being the preface to Barnaby Rudge; ed F. T. Marzials [1891] (with other early pieces). The Old Curiosity Shop pbd 25 April 1840 to 6 Feb 1841; Barnaby Rudge 13 Feb to 27 Nov 1841. The 'Clock' setting was not retained when the 2 long stories were pbd as separate works.

The old curiosity shop. 1841 (with the original illustrations; first separate edn; ptd from the stereotype plates of the Clock, vols 1–2, and retaining their pagination, but adding some matter on short pages), 4 extra illustrations by H. K. Browne issued separately; cheap edn 1848 (and in 20 weekly pts, 5 monthly pts June–Oct 1848; with new preface and Frontispiece by G. Cattermole).

Barnaby Rudge: a tale of the riots of 'eighty. 1841 (with the original illustrations; first separate edn; ptd from the stereotype plates of the Clock, vols 2–3, and retaining their pagination), cheap edn 1849 (and in 24 weekly pts, 6 monthly pts, Nov 1848–April 1849; 4 extra illustrations by H. K. Browne issued separately).

Martin Chuzzlewit

The life and adventures of Martin Chuzzlewit, his relatives, friends and enemies: comprising all his wills and his ways, with an historical record of what he did, and what he didn't; showing, moreover, who inherited the family plate, who came in for the silver spoons, and who for the wooden ladles: the whole forming a complete key to the House of Chuzzlewit, edited by 'Boz', with illustrations by 'Phiz'. [Title on wrapper. On title-page and for vol issue, The life and adventures of Martin Chuzzlewit, by Charles Dickens.] 20 (as 19) monthly pts, Jan 1843 to July 1844 (with variants); 1 vol 1844 (with preface), cheap edn 1849 (and in 32 weekly pts, 8 monthly pts, May–Nov 1849; with new preface, and frontispiece by F. Stone), 1867 (Charles Dickens edn, with rev preface); ed K. Hayens 1953; ed M. Mudrick, New York 1965.

Dombey and Son

Dealings with the firm of Dombey and Son wholesale, retail and for exportation, with illustrations by H. K. Browne. [Title on wrapper. On title-page and for vol issue, Dombey and Son.] 20 (as 19) monthly pts, Oct 1846 to April 1848 (with variants), 1 vol 1848 (with preface), New York 1847 [1846–8], Philadelphia 1848, 1858 (cheap edn), 2 vols 1865 (with new frontispiece), 1867 (Charles Dickens edn, with new preface); ed A. Pryce-Jones, New York 1964; ed A. Horsman, Oxford 1973. After Martin Chuzzlewit, Dickens for a time transferred his new works from Chapman & Hall to Bradbury & Evans. But Chapman & Hall pbd 12 separate extra illustrations to Dombey and Son, by 'Phiz' 2 pts 1848.

The story of little Dombey [a reading]. [1858] (priv ptd), 1858, 1862, nd, Boston 1868.

Butt, J. and K. Tillotson. Dickens at work on Dombey and Son. E & S new ser 4 1951.

Tillotson, K. A lost sentence in Dombey and Son. Dickensian 47 1951. See D. S. Bland 52 1956.

— In her Novels of the eighteen-forties, Oxford 1954.

Leavis, F. R. Sewanee Rev 70 1962.

David Copperfield

The personal history, adventures, experiences and observations of David Copperfield the younger, of Blunderstone Rookery, (which he never meant to be published on any account), with illustrations by H. K. Browne. [Title on wrapper. On title-page and for vol issue, The personal history of David Copperfield.] 20 (as 19) monthly pts, May 1849 to Nov 1850 (with variants); 1 vol 1850 (with preface), 2 vols New York 1850, 1 vol 1858 (Cheap edn, with new preface), 1867 (Charles Dickens edn, with rev preface); ed E. Kibblewhite, Oxford 1916; ed F. M. Ford, A. Meynell et al, Bath 1922; ed H. S. Hughes 2 vols Garden City NY 1936; ed and abridged W. S. Maugham, Philadelphia 1948; ed E. K. Brown, New York 1950; ed and tr S. Monod 2 vols Paris 1956; ed G. H. Ford, Boston 1958; ed E. Johnson, New York 1962; ed T. Blount 1966.

David Copperfield: a reading in five chapters. nd (priv ptd), Boston 1868, 1921 (reprint of first edn, with a note by J. H. Stonehouse summarizing the Maria Beadnell correspondence and the relation between David Copperfield and Dickens's own life).

Joyce, J. Ulysses. Paris 1922. Parody in Oxen of the Sun episode.

Woolf, V. David Copperfield. Nation (London) 22 Aug 1925; rptd in her Moment and other essays, 1947.

Jones, J. In Dickens and the twentieth century, ed J. Gross and G. Pearson 1962.

Bleak House

Bleak House, with illustrations by H. K. Browne. 20 (as 19) monthly pts, March 1852 to Sept 1853 (slight variants); 1 vol 1853 (with preface), 1858 (Cheap edn), 1868 (Charles Dickens edn, with rev preface); ed R. B Johnson 1953; ed M. D. Zabel, Boston 1956; ed G. Tillotson, New York 1964.

Zabel, M. D. The undivided imagination. In his Craft and character in modern fiction, New York 1957.

Harvey, W. J. In Dickens and the twentieth century, ed J. Gross and G. Pearson 1962.

Hard Times

Hard times, for these times. 1854. No illustrations. Not issued in pts, but pbd weekly in Household Words 1 April to 12 Aug 1854. 1862 (illustr F. Walker), 1865 (Cheap edn), 1868 (Charles Dickens edn). Ed G. B. Shaw 1912; ed J. Richardson 1954 (EL); ed W. W. Watt, New York 1958; ed J. H. Middendorf, New York 1960; ed C. Shapiro, New York 1961; ed R. D. Spector, New York 1964; ed G. H. Ford and S. Monod, New York 1966; ed R. Williams, New York 1966.

Ruskin, J. In his Unto this last, Cornhill Mag Aug 1860.

Leavis, F. R. Hard times: an analytic note. In his Great tradition, 1948.

Fielding, K. J. Dickens and the Department of practical art. MLR 48 1953.

— The battle for Preston. Dickensian 50 1954.

— Mill and Gradgrind. Nineteenth-Century Fiction 11 1957.

Holloway, J. In Dickens and the twentieth century, ed J. Gross and G. Pearson 1962.

Carnall, G. D. Dickens, Mrs Gaskell and the Preston strike. Victorian Stud 8 1964.

Lodge, D. The rhetoric of Hard times. In his Language of fiction, 1966.

Little Dorrit

Little Dorrit, with illustrations by H. K. Browne. 20 (as 19) monthly pts, Dec 1855 to June 1857 (variants); 1 vol 1857 (with preface), 1861 (Cheap edn), 1868 (Charles Dickens edn, with rev preface; ed H. P. Sucksmith, Oxford 1978.

Shaw, G. B. Dickens and Little Dorrit. Dickensian 4 1908.

Booth, B. A. Trollope and Little Dorrit. Trollopian 2 1948.

Trilling, L. Kenyon Rev 15 1953; also introd to New Oxford illustrated edn 1953, and in his Opposing self, New York 1955.

Leavis, Q .D. A note on literary indebtedness: Dickens, George Eliot, Henry James. Hudson Rev 8 1955.

Butt, J. The topicality of Little Dorrit. UTQ 29 1959.

Wain, J. In Dickens and the twentieth century, ed J. Gross and G. Pearson 1962.

Reid, J. C. Dickens: Little Dorrit. 1967.

A Tale of Two Cities

A tale of two cities, with illustrations by H. K. Browne. Appeared simultaneously in All the Year Round 30 April to 26 Nov 1859, and in 8 (as 7) monthly pts, June to Dec 1859. 1 vol 1859 (with preface). Variants. Philadelphia [1859] from advance proofs. 1864 (Cheap edn), 1868 (Charles Dickens edn). Ed E. Wagenknecht, New York 1950; ed E. Johnson, New York 1957; ed M. D. Zabel, New York 1958; ed S. Marcus, New York 1962; ed P. Pickrel, Boston 1962.

The Bastille prisoner: a reading. [1861?] (priv ptd). Arranged by Dickens, but never used. Not rptd.

Zabel, M. D. The revolutionary fate. In his Craft and character in modern fiction, New York 1957.

Gross, J. In Dickens and the twentieth century, ed J. Gross and G. Pearson 1962.

Elliott, R. W. V. Dickens: A tale of two cities. 1966.

Great Expectations

Great expectations. Pbd weekly in All the Year Round 1 Dec 1860 to 3 Aug 1861. 3 vols 1861 (variants). No issue in pts, no illustrations. New York [1860], Philadelphia [1861], from advance proofs. 1862 (illustr M. Stone), 1863 (Cheap edn), 1868 (Charles Dickens edn). Ed G. B. Shaw 1937 (limited edn), 1947; ed E. Davis, New York 1948; ed K. Hayens 1953; ed and tr S. Monod, Paris 1959; ed A. Wilson, New York 1963; ed L. Crompton, Indianapolis 1964; ed A. Calder 1965; ed R. D. McMaster, Toronto 1965. See Forster's Life, bk 9 ch 3, for original ending.

Great expectations: a drama, in three stages. Founded on, and compiled from, the story of that name, by Charles Dickens. 1861 (priv ptd). A copyrighting device.

Great expectations: a reading, in three stages. [1861?] (priv ptd). Arranged by Dickens, but never used. Not rptd.

Shaw, G. B. Introduction (1937); rptd in A book of prefaces, ed Van Wyck Brooks et al, New York 1949.

Butt, J. Dickens's plan for the conclusion of Great expectations. Dickensian 45 1949.

House, H. GBS on Great expectations. In his All in due time, 1955.

Fielding, K. J. The critical autonomy of Great expectations. REL 2 1961.

Ricks, C. In Dickens and the twentieth century, ed J. Gross and G. Pearson 1962.

Hardy, B. Food and ceremony in Great expectations. EC 13 1963.

Our Mutual Friend

Our mutual friend. With illustrations by Marcus Stone. 20 (as 19) monthly pts, May 1864 to Nov 1865; 2 vols Feb and Nov 1865 (with 'Postscript in lieu of a preface'), 1 vol 1865; 1867 (Cheap edn), 1868 (Charles Dickens edn). Ed M. Engel, New York 1960; ed J. H. Miller, New York 1964.

The Mystery of Edwin Drood

The mystery of Edwin Drood. With twelve illustrations by S. L. Fildes, and a portrait. In 6 monthly pts, April–Sept 1870 (Dickens's death in June 1870 having cut short the announced 12 pts); 1 vol 1870; Boston 1870 (from advance proofs); [1875] (Charles Dickens edn). Ed V. Starrett, New York 1941; ed 'Michael Innes' (J. I. M. Stewart) 1952; ed C. D. Lewis 1957; ed M. Cardwell, Oxford 1972. Forster prints a cancelled ch, How Mr Sapsea ceased to be a member of the Eight Club (Life, bk 11 ch 2).
Pritchett, V. S. In his Living novel, 1946.
Ford, G. H. Dickens's notebook and Edwin Drood. Nineteenth-Century Fiction 6 1952.
Cockshut, A. O. J. In Dickens and the twentieth century, ed J. Gross and G. Pearson 1962.

Christmas Books

Christmas books. 1852 (Cheap edn of Works: in 17 weekly pts, 4 monthly pts, June–Sept 1852). Frontispiece by J. Leech. Collects the 5 books, with a preface. 1859 (Library edn); 1868 (Charles Dickens edn, with rev preface); 1878; ed C. Shorter, illustr C. Green and L. Rossi, 5 pts [1912]. First collected New York 1849 (without Haunted man).
A Christmas carol, in prose: being a ghost story of Christmas, with illustrations by John Leech. 1843.
A Christmas carol. Ed facs (from original ms) F. G. Kitton 1890, 1897 (without introd), 1906; ed facs (from original edn) G. K. Chesterton and B. W. Matz 1922; E. Johnson, New York 1956.
A Christmas carol: reading edition. 1858, nd, rev Boston 1868.

The chimes: a goblin story of some bells that rang an old year out and a new year in. 1845 (for 1844). Illustr Daniel Maclise, John Leech, Richard Doyle and Clarkson Stanfield. Slight variants. Illustr John Leech and F. Barnard, New York 1887; illustr Arthur Rackham, introd E. Wagenknecht 1931 (priv ptd).
The chimes: reading edition. 1858, [1868?] (rev and priv ptd with Sikes and Nancy, from Oliver Twist).

The cricket on the hearth: a fairy tale of home. 1846 (for 1845). Illustr Daniel Maclise, John Leech, Richard Doyle, Clarkson Stanfield and Edwin Landseer. Rptd from stereotype plates, 1887; illustr John Leech and Frederick Barnard 1887; introd Henry Morley 1887, 1904; illustr Hugh Thomson, introd W. de la Mare 1933 (priv ptd).
The cricket on the hearth: reading edition. 1858 nd.

The battle of life: a love story. 1846. Dickens's name on ptd title-page, not on engraved. Illustr Daniel Maclise, John Leech, Richard Doyle and Clarkson Stanfield.

The haunted man and the ghost's bargain: a fancy for Christmas time. 1848. Illustr John Leech, Clarkson Stanfield, John Tenniel and F. Stone.

Periodicals Edited by Dickens

Dickens contributed many items to his periodicals and, particularly over his weeklies (in which almost all contributions were unsigned), accepted responsibility for the tenor as well as the quality of whatever he published; so he often silently rewrote or otherwise amended his colleagues' work. Many stories and essays by other contributors were rptd, especially in America, as his work. See B. W. Matz, Writings wrongly attributed to Dickens, Chambers's Jnl 16 Aug 1924, rptd in Dickensian 21 1925, though Matz's list is incomplete.

Bentley's Miscellany. Monthly from Jan 1837. Dickens was its first editor and resigned Feb 1839. Contents included Oliver Twist and sundry shorter items, mostly signed.
  Prospectus for Bentley's Miscellany. Ptd from Dickens's ms. Appendix D: Letters of Dickens, ed M. House and G. Storey vol 1, Oxford 1965.
Daily News. From 21 Jan 1846. Dickens was its first editor and resigned 9 Feb 1846. Contents included his Travelling letters, rptd as Pictures from Italy.
Household Words. Weekly, 30 March 1850 to 28 May 1859, when it was incorporated into All the Year Round. Also in monthly pts and 19 half-yearly vols. Cheap edn, 19 vols 1868–73; ed H. Stone 2 vols 1969. Contents included A child's history of England, Hard times, Christmas stories and numerous unsigned essays.
All the Year Round. Weekly from 30 April 1859. Also in monthly pts and half-yearly vols. Edited by Dickens until his death, and by Charles Dickens jr thereafter; incorporated 1895 in the revived Household Words. Bound, 20 vols 1859–68 (with General index, 1868); new ser 1868–88. Contents included A tale of two cities, The uncommercial traveller, Great expectations, Christmas stories and some unsigned essays.
Novels and tales reprinted from Household Words, conducted by Charles Dickens. 11 vols Leipzig 1856–9 (Tauchnitz).

Letters and Speeches

Speeches literary and social by Dickens, now first collected, with chapters on Dickens as a letter writer, poet and public reader. [Ed R. H. Shepherd] 1870; rev and with a bibliography as The speeches of Dickens 1841–70, 1884; with introd by B. Darwin [1937].
The letters of Dickens. edited by his sister-in-law [Georgina Hogarth] and his eldest daughter [Mamie (Mary) Dickens]. 3 vols 1880–2, 2 vols 1882, 1 vol 1893; with Letters to Wilkie Collins, 2 vols 1908 (National edn of Works).
The letters of Dickens. Ed W. Dexter 3 vols 1938 (Nonesuch).
The speeches of Dickens. Ed K. J. Fielding, Oxford 1960.
The Pilgrim edition of the letters of Dickens. Ed M. House and G. Storey, Oxford 1965–. First complete edn.
Hans Christian Andersen's correspondence. Ed F. Crawford [1891]. Letters to and from Dickens.
Letters of Dickens to Wilkie Collins 1851–70, selected by Miss G. Hogarth. Ed L. Hutton 1892.
Dickens as editor: letters written by him to William Henry Wills, his sub-editor. Ed R. C. Lehmann 1912.
Letters to Mark Lemon. Ed T. J. Wise 1917 (priv ptd).
The unpublished letters of Dickens to Mark Lemon. Ed W. Dexter 1927.
Clark, C. Dickens and his Jewish characters. 1918.
—— The story of a great friendship: Dickens and Clarkson Stanfield, with seven unpublished letters. 1918.
The letters of Dickens to the Baroness Burdett-Coutts. Ed C. C. Osborne 1931. Selection with narrative.

Dickens to his oldest friend: the letters of a lifetime. Ed W. Dexter 1932.

Dickens's letters to Charles Lever. Ed F. V. Livingston, introd by H. E. Rollins, Cambridge Mass 1933.

Mr and Mrs Charles Dickens: his letters to her. Ed W. Dexter 1934.

The love romance of Dickens, told in his letters to Maria Beadnell (Mrs Winter). Ed W. Dexter 1936.

House, H. A new edition of Dickens's letters. Listener 18 Oct 1951; rptd in his All in due time, 1955.

Johnson, E. The heart of Dickens. New York 1952, London 1953 (as Letters from Dickens to Angela Burdett Coutts 1841–65).

Selected letters. Ed F. W. Dupee, New York 1960.

The public readings. Ed P. Collins, Oxford 1975.

§2

Biographies

Forster, J. The life of Dickens. 3 vols 1872–4 (revisions in successive edns of each vol), 2 vols 1876 (Library edn), 1879 (illustr); rev and abridged G. Gissing 1903; Memorial edn, ed B. W. Matz 2 vols 1911 (500 portraits, facs etc); ed G. K. Chesterton 2 vols 1927 (EL) (rev); ed A. J. Hoppé 2 vols 1966; ed J. W. T. Ley 1928 (notes embody much new matter).

Ward, A. W. Charles Dickens. 1882 (EML).

Dickens, M. Charles Dickens, by his eldest daughter. 1885, 1911.

—— My father as I recall him. [1897].

Marzials, F. T. Life of Dickens. 1887.

Kitton, F. G. Dickens by pen and pencil, including anecdotes and reminiscences collected by his friends and companions. 1890. Supplement 1890; additional illustrations 1891.

—— Dickens: his life, writings and personality. 2 vols Edinburgh [1902].

Matz, B. W. Dickens: the story of his life and writings. [1902].

Pope-Hennessy, U. Dickens. 1945.

Pearson, H. Dickens: his character, comedy and career. 1949.

Johnson, E. Dickens: his tragedy and triumph. 2 vols New York 1952, 1 vol New York 1977 (rev and abridged).

MacKenzie, N. and J. Dickens: a life. Oxford 1979.

Special Periods and Aspects

Ley, J. W. T. The Dickens circle: a narrative of the novelist's friendships. 1918.

Carlton, W. J. Dickens, shorthand writer. 1926.

Darwin, B. The Dickens advertiser: a collection of the advertisements in the original parts of novels by Dickens. 1930. A narrative and criticism with facs.

Critical Studies

Gissing, G. Dickens: a critical study. 1898, 1903 (rev, in Imperial edn of the Works).

Chesterton, G. K. Charles Dickens. 1906; rptd as Dickens: a critical study, New York 1911 and as Dickens: the last of the great men, introd by A. Woollcott, New York 1942.

—— Appreciations and criticisms of the works of Dickens. 1911; rptd as Criticisms and appreciations of the works of Dickens, 1933. Collects introds to EL.

House, H. The Dickens world. Oxford 1941, 1942 (corrected).

'Alain' (E. Chartier). En lisant Dickens. Paris 1945.

Fielding, K. J. Dickens: a survey. 1953, 1960 (rev), 1963 (rev) (Br Council pamphlet).

—— Dickens: a critical introduction. 1958, 1965 (rev and enlarged).

Monod, S. Dickens romancier. Paris 1953; tr and rev Norman Oklahoma 1968.

Ford, G. H. Dickens and his readers: aspects of novel-criticism since 1836. Princeton 1955.

Butt, J. and K. Tillotson. Dickens at work. 1957.

Miller, J. H. Dickens: the world of his novels. Cambridge Mass 1958.

Cockshut, A. O. J. The imagination of Dickens. 1961.

Ford, G. H. and L. Lane jr (ed). The Dickens critics. Ithaca 1961. Anthology with introd and bibliography.

Collins, P. Dickens and crime. 1962, 1963 (rev).

—— Dickens and education. 1963, 1964 (rev).

—— (ed). Dickens: the critical heritage. 1971.

Gross, J. and G. Pearson (ed). Dickens and the twentieth century. 1962.

Garis, R. The Dickens theatre: a reassessment of the novels. Oxford 1965.

Leavis, F. R. and Q .D. Dickens the novelist. 1970.

Carey, J. The violent effigy. 1973.

GEORGE HENRY BORROW
1803–81

Borrow's mss are chiefly in Norwich Public Library and in the Romany Collection of the Brotherton Library at Leeds University.

Bibliographies

Wise, T. J. A bibliography of the writings in prose and verse of Borrow. 1914.

Collections

The works: Norwich edition. Ed C. K. Shorter 16 vols 1923–4. Includes unpbd ms material.

§1

The Zincali: or an account of the gypsies of Spain, with an original collection of their songs and poetry, and a copious dictionary of their language. 2 vols 1841, 1843, 1843, 1846, 1870, 1882, 1888, 1893, 1901 (definitive edn); ed H. Walpole 1936; ed W. Starkie 1961 (EL).

The Bible in Spain: or the journeys, adventures and imprisonments of an Englishman, in an attempt to circulate the Scriptures in the Peninsula. 3 vols 1843 (6 edns), 1896 (18th edn) etc; ed E. Thomas 1906 (EL); Oxford 1906 (WC).

Lavengro: the scholar, the gypsy, the priest. 3 vols 1851, 1872, 1888, 1896; ed T. Watts[-Dunton] 1893; ed W. I. Knapp 1900; ed F. H. Groome 2 vols 1901; 1904 (WC); ed I. Seccombe 1906 (EL); ed W. Starkie 1961 (EL).

The Romany Rye: a sequel to Lavengro. 2 vols 1857, 1858, 1872, 1888, 1896; ed T. Watts[-Dunton] [1900]; [ed W. I. Knapp] 1900; ed J. Sampson 1903; 1906 (EL); 1906 (WC); ed W. Starkie 1949.

The Welsh and their literature. Quart Rev 109 1861.

Wild Wales: its people, language and scenery. 3 vols 1862, 1865, 1888, 1896, 1901 (authoritative edn); 1906 (EL); Oxford 1920 (WC).

Romano Lavo-Lil: word-book of the Romany, or English gypsy language; with many pieces in gypsy, illustrative of the way of speaking and thinking of the English gypsies; with specimens of their poetry and an account of certain gypsies or places inhabited by them, and of various things relating to gypsy life in England. 1874, 1888, 1905, 1907, 1908, 1919.

Letters to the British and Foreign Bible Society. Ed T. H. Darlow 1911.

Letters to his wife Mary Borrow. 1913 (priv ptd).

Letters to his mother Ann Borrow, and to other correspondents. 1913 (priv ptd).

A supplementary chapter to the Bible in Spain, inspired by Ford's Hand-book for travellers in Spain. 1913 (priv ptd).

Wild Wales: suppressed chapters. Ed H. G. Wright, Welsh Outlook 9–10 1922–3.

Celtic bards, chiefs and kings. Ed H. G. Wright 1928. Probably written 1857–60.

§2

Stephen, L. In his Hours in a Library: third series, 1881.

Saintsbury, G. George Borrow. Macmillan's Mag Jan 1886; rptd in his Essays in English literature 1780–1860, 1890.

Johnson, L. O rare George Borrow. Outlook 1 April 1899; rptd in his Post liminium, 1911.

Thomas, E. Borrow: the man and his books. 1912.

Jenkins, H. Life of Borrow, compiled from unpublished official documents, his works, correspondence etc. 1912.

Shorter, C. K. Borrow and his circle: wherein may be found many hitherto unpublished letters of Borrow and his friends. 1913.

—— The life of Borrow. [1920].

Fréchet, R. Borrow: vagabond, polyglotte, agent biblique, écrivain. Paris 1956.

Meyers, R. R. George Borrow. New York 1966.

WILLIAM MAKEPEACE THACKERAY
1811–63

Bibliographies

Shepherd, R. H. The bibliography of Thackeray. 1881, 1887 (rev and enlarged in his edn of Sultan Stork and other stories).

Gordan, J. D. Thackeray. BNYPL May 1947. Catalogue of Berg collection.

Stevenson, L. In Victorian fiction: a guide to research, ed Stevenson, Cambridge Mass 1964.

Collections

Works. Library edition 22 vols 1867–9 (2 more vols 1885–6); Cheaper illustrated edition 24 vols 1877–9; De luxe edition 26 vols 1878–86 (with memoir by L. Stephen).

Prose works. Ed W. Jerrold 30 vols 1901–3.

Works. Ed 'Lewis Melville' (from vol 8) 20 vols 1901–7, 1911 (rptd from first edns and including much new matter); London edition 13 vols 1903 (topographical introds by J. McVicar in vols 1–12; vol 13 is Melville's Life of Thackeray, first pbd 2 vols 1899); Oxford edition 17 vols 1908 (introds by G. Saintsbury).

§1

Flore et Zéphyr: ballet mythologique par Théophile Wagstaff. 1836. 9 lithographed plates; no text.

The Yellowplush correspondence. Fraser's Mag Nov 1837–July 1838; Philadelphia 1838, New York 1852 (as The Yellowplush papers).

Some passages in the life of Major Gahagan. New Monthly Mag Feb 1838–Feb 1839; Philadelphia 1839 (as Reminiscences of Major Gahagan).

An essay on the genius of George Cruikshank. Westminster Rev June 1840; 1840; ed W. E. Church 1884.

The Paris sketch book, by Mr Titmarsh. 2 vols 1840, New York 1852.

Comic tales and sketches, edited and illustrated by Mr Michael Angelo Titmarsh. 2 vols 1841. Vol 1 contains The Yellowplush papers.

The second funeral of Napoleon, in three letters to Miss Smith of London; and The chronicle of the drum, by Mr M. A. Titmarsh. 1841.

The Irish sketch-book, by Mr M. A. Titmarsh. 2 vols 1843, 1 vol New York [1843], 2 vols 1845, 1 vol 1857.

The luck of Barry Lyndon: a romance of the last century. Fraser's Mag Jan-Dec 1844; 2 vols New York 1852–3, 1 vol 1856 (rev, with omissions, as The memoirs of Barry Lyndon esq).

Jeames's diary. Punch 2 Aug 1845–7 Feb 1846; New York 1846.

Notes of a journey from Cornhill to Grand Cairo, by way of Lisbon, Athens, Constantinople and Jerusalem, performed in the steamers of the Peninsular and Oriental Company, by Mr M. A. Titmarsh. 1846, 1846 (with postscript signed W. M. T.), New York 1846.

The snobs of England, by one of themselves. Punch 28 Feb 1846–27 Feb 1847; 1848 (as The book of snobs, omitting chs 17–23), New York 1852 (complete), London 1855; ed G. K. Chesterton 1911.

Vanity Fair: pen and pencil sketches of English society. 20 monthly pts Jan 1847–July 1848; Vanity Fair: a novel without a hero, 1848, 1848, 1853 (rev), 1863 (rev); ed J. W. Beach, New York 1950; ed G. H. Ford, New York 1958; ed G. and K. Tillotson 1963.

Mrs Perkins's ball, by Mr M. A. Titmarsh. 1847 (3 edns), 1898 (facs).

The history of Samuel Titmarsh and the great Hoggarty diamond. Frasers's Mag Sept-Dec 1841; New York 1848 (as The great Hoggarty diamond), London 1849 (with original title), 1857.

'Our street', by Mr M. A. Titmarsh. 1848, 1848.

The history of Pendennis: his fortunes and misfortunes, his friends and his greatest enemy. 24 monthly pts Nov 1848–Dec 1850; 2 vols 1849–50, 1850, 1 vol 1856, 1863 (rev).

Doctor Birch and his young friends, by Mr M. A. Titmarsh. 1849, New York 1853.

Miscellanies: prose and verse. 2 vols Leipzig 1849–51. Vol 1 contains The great Hoggarty diamond, The book of snobs; vol 2 The Kickleburys abroad, A legend of the Rhine, Rebecca and Rowena, The second funeral of Napoleon, The chronicle of the drum.

The Kickleburys on the Rhine, by Mr M. A. Titmarsh. 1850, 1851 (with Preface being an essay on thunder and small beer), Frankfurt 1851, New York 1851, London 1866.

Stubbs's calendar: or the fatal boots. New York 1850.

Rebecca and Rowena: a romance upon romance, by Mr M. A. Titmarsh. 1850, Paris 1850. Revision of Proposals for a continuation of Ivanhoe, Fraser's Mag Aug-Sept 1846.

The history of Henry Esmond esq, a colonel in the service of Her Majesty Q. Anne, written by himself. 3 vols 1852, 1853, 1 vol 1858 (rev); ed G. N. Ray, New York 1950.

The confessions of Fitz-Boodle; and some passages in the life of Major Gahagan. New York 1852.

A shabby genteel story and other tales. New York 1852, 1853, 1853 (enlarged). Contains also The professor, The Bedford Row conspiracy, A little dinner at Timmins's (from Punch 27 May–29 July 1848).

Men's wives. Fraser's Mag March–Nov 1843; New York 1852.

Jeames's diary, A legend of the Rhine and Rebecca and Rowena. New York 1853.

Mr Brown's letters to a young man about town; with the Proser and other papers. Punch 1845, 1848–51; New York 1853.

Punch's prize novelists, The fat contributor and Travels in London. Punch 1844–5, 1847–8, 1850; New York 1853. Contains also Going to see a man hanged, from Fraser's Mag Aug 1840.

The English humourists of the eighteenth century: a series of lectures delivered in England, Scotland and the United States of America. 1853, 1853 (rev), 1858; ed W. L. Phelps, New York 1900.

The Newcomes: memoirs of a most respectable family, edited by Arthur Pendennis esqre. 24 monthly pts Oct 1853–Aug 1855; Harper's Mag Nov 1853–Oct 1855; 2 vols 1854–5, 1 vol 1860, 1863 (rev).

The rose and the ring, or the history of Prince Giglio and Prince Bulbo: a fireside pantomime for great and small children, by Mr M. A. Titmarsh. 1855 (for 1854), 1855, 1855, New York 1855, London 1866; ed G. N. Ray, New York 1947 (ms facs).

Miscellanies: prose and verse. 4 vols 1855–7, 1861, 1865.

Christmas books. 1857. Contains Mrs Perkins's ball, 'Our street', Doctor Birch and his young friends.

The Virginians: a tale of the last century. 24 monthly pts Nov 1857–Sept 1859; Harper's Mag Dec 1857–Nov 1859; 2 vols 1858–9, 1 vol 1863 (rev); ed G. Saintsbury and J. L. Robertson 1911.

The four Georges: sketches of manners, morals, court and town life. Cornhill Mag July–Oct 1860; Harper's Mag Aug–Nov 1860; New York 1860, 1860, London 1861, Leipzig 1861; ed G. Meredith and T. Bayne 1903.

Lovel the widower. Cornhill Mag Jan–June 1860; Harper's Mag Feb–July 1860; New York 1860, London 1861 (rev).

The adventures of Philip on his way through the world, shewing who robbed him, who helped him, and who passed him by. Cornhill Mag Jan 1861–Aug 1862; Harper's Mag Feb 1861–Sept 1862; 3 vols 1862.

Roundabout papers. Cornhill Mag Jan 1860–Feb 1863; 1863, New York 1863; ed J. E. Wells, New York 1925 (from ms).

Denis Duval. Cornhill Mag March–June 1864; Harper's Mag April–Aug 1864; New York 1864, London 1867.

Early and late papers hitherto uncollected. Ed J. T. Fields, Boston 1867.

Miscellanies vol 5. Boston 1870. Contains Catherine (from Fraser's Mag May 1839–Feb 1840), Christmas books, Ballads etc.

The orphan of Pimlico and other sketches, fragments and drawings. 1876. Notes by A. I. Thackeray.

Sultan Stork and other stories and sketches (1829–44), now first collected [by R. H. Shepherd]. 1887.

Loose sketches, an eastern adventure etc. 1894.

The hitherto unidentified contributions of W. M. Thackeray to Punch, with a complete authoritative bibliography from 1845 to 1848. Ed M. H. Spielmann 1899.

Mr Thackeray's writings in the National Standard and the Constitutional. Ed W. T. Spencer 1899.

Stray papers: being stories, reviews, verses, and sketches 1821–47. Ed 'Lewis Melville' 1901. Subtitle should read 1829–51.

The new sketch book: being essays now first collected from the Foreign Quarterly Review. Ed R. S. Garnett 1906.

Thackeray's contributions to the Morning Chronicle. Ed G. N. Ray, Urbana 1955.

Letters

Some family letters of Thackeray, together with recollections by his kinswoman B. W. Cornish. 1911.

Unpublished letters. Ed C. K. Shorter 1916 (priv ptd).

Thackeray and Edward FitzGerald, a literary friendship: unpublished letters and verses by Thackeray. Ed C. K. Shorter 1916 (priv ptd). Introd by Lady Ritchie.

Letters of Anne Thackeray Ritchie, with forty-two additional letters from her father. Ed H. Ritchie 1924.

The letters and private papers of Thackeray. Ed G. N. Ray 4 vols Cambridge Mass 1945–6.

§2

Bagehot, W. Sterne and Thackeray. Nat Rev April 1864; rptd in his Literary studies, 1879.

Dickens, C. In memoriam W. M. T. Cornhill Mag Feb 1864.

Hannay, J. A brief memoir of the late Mr Thackeray. Edinburgh 1864.

— Studies on Thackeray. 1869.

Senior, N. W. In his Essays on fiction, 1864.

Trollope, A. Thackeray. 1879 (EML).

Saintsbury, G. In his Corrected impressions, 1895.

— A consideration of Thackeray. Oxford 1931. Introds rptd from Oxford edn of Thackeray's works.

'Melville, Lewis' (L. S. Benjamin). The life of Thackeray. 2 vols 1899.

— Thackeray: a biography. 2 vols 1910, 1 vol 1927 (without bibliography).

Stevenson, L. Vanity Fair and Lady Morgan. PMLA 48 1933.

Greig, J. Y. T. Thackeray: a reconsideration. Oxford 1950.

Tillotson, G. Thackeray the novelist. Cambridge 1954.

— and D. Hawes (ed). Thackeray: the critical heritage. 1968.

Tillotson, K. Vanity Fair. In her Novels of the eighteen-forties, Oxford 1954.

Talon, H. A. Time and memory in Henry Esmond. RES new ser 13 1962.

— Thackeray's Vanity Fair revisited: fiction as truth. In Of books and humankind, ed J. Butt 1964.

Dyson, A. E. Vanity Fair: an irony against heroes. CQ 6 1964; rptd in his Crazy fabric, 1965.

Sutherland, J. Thackeray at work. 1973.

THE BRONTËS

Bibliographies

Wood, B. A bibliography of the works of the Brontë family. 1895 (Brontë Soc); Supplement, 1897.

Wise, T. J. A bibliography of the writings in prose and verse of the Brontë family. 1917 (priv ptd).

— A Brontë library: a catalogue of printed books, manuscripts and autograph letters by the members of the Brontë family. 1929 (priv ptd).

Christian, M. G. In Victorian fiction: a guide to research, ed L. Stevenson, Cambridge Mass 1964.

Collections and Composite Works

Poems by Currer, Ellis and Acton Bell. 1846, 1848, Philadelphia 1848, London 1860 (with the Professor, Emma).

The life [by Mrs Gaskell] and works of Charlotte Brontë and her sisters. 7 vols 1872–3.

The life [by Mrs Gaskell] and works of Charlotte Brontë and her sisters: Haworth edition. Ed Mrs H. Ward and C. K. Shorter 7 vols 1899–1900.

The novels and poems of Charlotte, Emily and Anne Brontë. 7 vols 1901–7 (WC). General introd by T. Watts-Dunton prefixed to the Professor.

Poems by Charlotte, Emily and Anne Brontë now for the first time printed. New York 1902.

The Shakespeare Head Brontë. Ed T. J. Wise and J. A. Symington 19 vols Oxford 1932–8.

The Clarendon edition of the novels. Ed I. and J. Jack, Oxford 1969–.

§1

CHARLOTTE BRONTË, later NICHOLLS

1816–55

Jane Eyre: an autobiography, edited by Currer Bell. 3 vols 1847, 1848 (with dedication and preface), 1848, 1 vol New York 1848, London 1850, 2 vols Leipzig 1850, 1 vol 1857, 1858 etc; ed C. K. Shorter [1889]; ed M. Lane [1957] (EL); ed M. Schorer, Boston 1959;

ed Q.D. Leavis 1966 (Penguin); ed M. Smith, Oxford 1973.

Shirley: a tale, by Currer Bell. 3 vols 1849, 2 vols Leipzig 1849, 1 vol New York 1850, London 1852, 1857, 1860, 1862 etc; ed M. Sinclair [1908] (EL).

Villette, by Currer Bell. 3 vols 1853, 1 vol Leipzig 1853, New York 1853, London 1855, 1857, 1858, 1860, 1861, 1866, 1867 etc; ed M. Sinclair [1908] (EL); ed M. Lane [1957] (EL).

The professor: a tale, by Currer Bell. 2 vols 1857 (with preface by A.B. Nicholls), 1 vol New York 1857, London 1860 (with Emma and poems by Currer, Ellis and Acton Bell), 1860, 1862 etc; ed M. Sinclair [1910] (EL).

Emma. Cornhill Mag April 1860; 1860 (with Professor). Fragment.

The story of the Brontës, their home, haunts, friends and works: part second—Charlotte's letters. Bradford 1889. Letters to Ellen Nussey; ptd but not pbd.

The adventures of Ernest Alembert: a fairy tale. Ed T. J. Wise 1896 (priv ptd).

The Moores. Ed W. R. Nicoll 1902 (with Jane Eyre). Fragment.

Richard Cœur de Lion and Blondel: a poem. Ed C. K. Shorter 1912 (priv ptd).

The love letters of Charlotte Brontë to Constantin Heger. Ed M. H. Spielmann, Times 29 July 1913; 1914 (priv ptd).

Letters recounting the deaths of Emily, Anne and Branwell Brontë by Charlotte Brontë; to which are added letters signed 'Currer Bell' and 'C. B. Nicholls.' 1913 (priv ptd).

Saul and other poems. 1913 (priv ptd).

Lament befitting these times of night. Ed G. E. MacLean, Cornhill Mag Aug 1916; 1916 (priv ptd).

Unpublished essays in novel writing by Charlotte Brontë. Ed G. E. MacLean 1916.

The violet: a poem written at the age of fourteen. Ed C. K. Shorter [1916] (priv ptd).

The Red Cross Knight and other poems. 1917 (priv ptd).

The Swiss emigrant's return and other poems. 1917 (priv ptd).

The four wishes: a fairy tale. Ed C. K. Shorter 1918 (priv ptd).

Latest gleanings: being a series of unpublished poems from early manuscripts. Ed C. K. Shorter 1918 (priv ptd).

Napoleon and the spectre: a ghost story. 1919 (priv ptd).

Thackeray and Charlotte Brontë: being some hitherto unpublished letters by Charlotte Brontë. 1919 (priv ptd).

Darius Codomannus: a poem written at the age of eighteen years. 1920 (priv ptd).

The complete poems of Charlotte Brontë. Ed C. K. Shorter and C. W. Hatfield 1923.

The twelve adventurers and other stories. [Ed C. W. Hatfield 1925].

The spell: an extravaganza. Ed G. E. MacLean, Oxford 1931.

Legends of Angria: compiled from the early writings of Charlotte Brontë. Ed F. E. Ratchford and W. C. De Vane, New Haven 1933.

Five novelettes. Ed W. Gérin 1971 (from ms).

EMILY JANE BRONTË
1818–48

Wuthering Heights: a novel, by Ellis Bell. 2 vols 1847 (with vol 3, Agnes Grey: a novel by Acton Bell, i.e. Anne Brontë), 1 vol New York 1848, London 1850 (with Agnes Grey; rev edn with biographical notice of the authors, a selection from their literary remains and a preface by Currer Bell), 1851, Leipzig 1851, London 1858 etc; ed H. W. Garrod, Oxford 1930 (WC); ed R. A. Gettmann, New York 1950; ed V. S. Pritchett, Boston [1956]; ed T. C. Moser, New York 1962; ed

W. M. Sale, New York 1963; ed H. Marsden and I. Jack, Oxford 1976.

Poems of Emily Brontë. Ed A. Symons 1906.

The complete works of Emily Brontë. Ed C. K. Shorter and W. R. Nicoll 2 vols 1910–11.

The complete poems of Emily Jane Brontë. Ed C. K. Shorter and C. W. Hatfield [1923].

Two poems: Love's rebuke, Remembrance. Ed F. E. Ratchford, Austin 1934 (priv ptd).

Gondal poems, now first published from the manuscript in the British Museum. Ed H. Brown and J. Mott, Oxford 1938.

The complete poems. Ed C. W. Hatfield, New York 1941.

Five essays written in French by Emily Jane Brontë. Tr L. W. Nagel, ed F. E. Ratchford, Austin 1948.

The complete poems. Ed P. Henderson 1951.

Gondal's Queen: a novel in verse. Ed F. E. Ratchford, Austin 1955.

ANNE BRONTË
1820–49

Agnes Grey. [See Emily Brontë, above]; Philadelphia 1850, London 1858 (with Wuthering Heights).

The tenant of Wildfell Hall, by Acton Bell. 3 vols 1848 (reissued as 2nd edn with new preface), 1 vol New York 1848, London 1854, 1859, 1867 etc; ed M. Sinclair [1914] (EL)

Self-communion: a poem. Ed T. J. Wise 1900 (priv ptd).

Dreams and other poems. 1917 (priv ptd).

The complete poems of Anne Brontë. Ed C. K. Shorter and C. W. Hatfield [1920].

§2

[Lewes, G. H.] Fraser's Mag Dec 1847. On Jane Eyre.
—— Edinburgh Rev 91 1850. On Shirley.
Gaskell, E. C. The life of Charlotte Brontë. 2 vols 1857.
Stephen, L. Charlotte Brontë. Cornhill Mag Dec 1877; rptd in his Hours in a library ser 3, 1879.
Swinburne, A. C. A note on Charlotte Brontë. 1877.
—— Emily Brontë. In his Miscellanies, 1886.
Shorter, C. K. Charlotte Brontë and her circle. 1896, [1914] (rev as The Brontës and their circle).
—— Charlotte Brontë and her sisters. 1905.
—— The Brontës: life and letters. 2 vols 1908.
Woolf, V. Jane Eyre and Wuthering Heights. In her Common reader, 1925.
Ratchford, F. E. Charlotte Brontë's Angrian cycle of stories. PMLA 43 1928.
—— The Brontës' web of dreams. Yale Rev 21 1931.
—— The Brontës' web of childhood. New York 1941.
Wise, T. J. and J. A. Symington. The Brontës: their lives, friendships and correspondence. 4 vols Oxford 1932.
Tinker, C. B. The poetry of the Brontës. In his Essays in retrospect, New Haven 1948.
Hanson, L. and E. M. The four Brontës. 1949, Hamden Conn 1967 (rev).
Schorer, M. Fiction and the matrix of analogy. Kenyon Rev 11 1949. On Wuthering Heights.
Lane, M. The Brontë story: a reconsideration of Mrs Gaskell's Life of Charlotte Brontë. 1953.
Spark, M. and D. Stanford. Emily Brontë: her life and work. 1953.
Tillotson, K. Jane Eyre. In her Novels of the eighteen-forties, Oxford 1954.
Gérin, W. Anne Brontë. 1959, 1976.
—— Branwell Brontë. 1961.
—— Charlotte Brontë. 1966.
—— Emily Brontë, Oxford 1971.
Lock, J. and W. T. Dixon. A man of sorrows. 1965. On Rev Patrick Brontë.
Allott, M. (ed). The Brontës: the critical heritage. 1973.

ELIZABETH CLEGHORN GASKELL, née STEVENSON

1810–65

Mrs Gaskell's mss are gathered chiefly in Leeds in the Brotherton Library of the University; in Manchester in the Arts Library of the University, the John Rylands Library and the Manchester Central Library; in London in the archives of John Murray Ltd; in USA in the Parrish Collection at Princeton University, the Symington Collection at Rutgers University and the Berg Collection in New York Public Library. Some 60 letters by Mrs Gaskell are in the possession of her great-granddaughter, Mrs Trevor Jones.

Bibliographies

Barry, J. D. In Victorian fiction: a guide to research, ed L. Stevenson, Cambridge Mass 1964.

Collections

The works: Knutsford edition. Ed A. W. Ward 8 vols 1906.

The novels and tales. Ed C. K. Shorter 11 vols Oxford 1906–19 (WC).

§1

Sketches among the poor, no 1: Poem written with her husband. Blackwood's Mag Jan 1837; rptd in Knutsford edn vol 1, WC edn vol 10, above.

Account of Clopton Hall, Warwickshire. In W. Howitt, Visits to remarkable places, 1840; rptd WC edn vol 10, above.

Life in Manchester, by Cotton Mather Mills esq. 2 pts W. Howitt's Jnl of Lit & Popular Progress 1, 3 1847; 8 Manchester 1848. Contains Libbie Marsh's three eras, rptd 1850, 1855; The sexton's hero, rptd 1865; Christmas storms and sunshine, rptd 1865.

Mary Barton: a tale of Manchester life. 2 vols 1848 (anon), 1849, 1849, Leipzig 1849, 1 vol 1854 (includes 2 lectures by W. Gaskell on the Lancashire dialect), 1861, New York 1864, London 1865, 1866, 1867, 1869 etc; ed T. Seccombe 1911 (EL); ed L. Cooper 1947; ed M. F. Brightfield 1958.

The moorland cottage, by the author of Mary Barton. 1850 (illustr Birket Foster), 1898 (with Cranford).

Bran: poem. Household Words 22 Oct 1853; rptd WC edn vol 10, above.

The scholar's story. Household Words 25 Dec 1853; rptd WC edn vol 10, above. W. Gaskell's trn of the Breton ballad of the Vicomte de la Villemarque, with introd by Mrs Gaskell.

Ruth: a novel, by the author of Mary Barton. 3 vols 1853, 1855, 2 vols [1857], 1 vol [1861], 1867 (8th edn), [1895].

Cranford, by the author of Mary Barton, Ruth etc. 22 weekly pts Household Words 13 Dec 1851–21 May 1853; 1853, New York 1853, London 1855, 1858, 1858, 1864 (illustr); ed A. T. Ritchie 1891; ed W. R. Nicoll 1898 (with The moorland cottage, above); ed E. V. Lucas 1899 etc; ed E. Rhys 1906 (EL); ed G. A. Payne 1914; ed A. Thirkell 1951; ed D. Ascoli 1952, 1954 (EL); ed E. P. Watson, Oxford 1972.

Lizzie Leigh and other tales. 1855, 1865, 1871, 1871 etc.

Hand and heart and Bessy's troubles at home, by the author of Mary Barton. 1855.

North and South, by the author of Mary Barton, Ruth, Cranford etc. 22 weekly pts Household Words 2 Sept 1854–27 Jan 1855; 2 vols 1855, 1 vol 1855, 1859 (4th edn); ed E. A. Chadwick 1914 (EL); ed E. Bowen 1951; ed A. Easson, Oxford 1973.

A Christmas carol: poem. Household Words 27 Dec 1856.

The life of Charlotte Brontë. 2 vols 1857, 1857, 1857 (rev and corrected); ed C. K. Shorter 1900; ed T. Scott and B. Willett 1901, [1905]; ed M. Sinclair 1908 (EL); ed M. Lane 1947.

Maria Vaughan, by the author of the Lamplighter (Maria S. Cummins). Preface by Mrs Haskell. 1857.

My Lady Ludlow. 14 weekly pts Household Words 19 June–25 Sept 1858; New York 1859, 1861. *See* Round the sofa, below.

Round the sofa. 1859, 1859, 1861 (as My Lady Ludlow and other tales included in Round the sofa), 1866.

Right at last and other tales. 1860, New York 1860, London 1867.

Lois the witch and other tales. Leipzig 1861.

A dark night's work. 9 weekly pts All the Year Round 24 Jan–21 March 1863; 1863 (illustr G. du Maurier), New York 1863, Leipzig 1863, London 1864.

Sylvia's lovers. 3 vols 1863 (illustr G. du Maurier), 2 vols Leipzig 1863, New York 1863, London 1870, 1 vol 1904 etc; ed T. Seccombe 1910, 1914 (EL); ed A. Pollard 1964.

The cage at Cranford. All the Year Round 28 Nov 1863; rptd WC edn, above.

Robert Gould Shaw. Macmillan's Mag Dec 1863.

Cousin Phillis: a tale. 4 monthly pts Cornhill Mag Nov 1863–Feb 1864; New York 1864, London 1865.

Cousin Phillis and other tales. 1865 (illustr G. du Maurier); ed T. Seccombe 1908, 1912 (EL).

The grey woman and other tales. 1865 (illustr G. du Maurier), 1871, 1871.

Wives and daughters: an every-day story. 18 monthly pts Cornhill Mag Aug 1864–Jan 1866 (last pt completed by F. Greenwood); 2 vols 1866 (illustr G. du Maurier); ed T. Seccombe 1912; ed R. Lehmann 1948.

Letters and Diaries

Letters on Charlotte Brontë. 1916 (priv ptd).

'My diary': the early years of my daughter Marianne. 1923 (priv ptd). Written 10 March 1835–28 Oct 1838.

Letters of Mrs Gaskell and C. E. Norton 1855–65. Ed J. Whitehill, Oxford 1932.

Letters. Ed J. A. V. Chappie and A. Pollard, Manchester 1966.

§2

James, H. Wives and daughters. Nation (New York) 2 1866; rptd in his Notes and reviews, 1921.

Dickens, C. In his Letters, ed G. Hogarth and M. E. Dickens 3 vols 1880–2.

— In his Letters to Wilkie Collins, ed L. Hutton 1892.

Shorter, C. K. In his Charlotte Brontë and her circle, 1896.

Sanders, G. de W. Elizabeth Gaskell. New Haven 1929.

Hopkins, A. B. Elizabeth Gaskell: her life and work. 1952.

Tillotson, K. Mary Barton. In her Novels of the eighteen-forties, Oxford 1954.

Kovalev, Y. V. In his Literature of Chartism, Moscow 1956; tr Victorian Stud 2 1958.

Williams, R. The industrial novels. In his Culture and society 1780–1950, 1958. On Mary Barton.

Allott, M. Elizabeth Gaskell. 1960 (Br Council pamphlet).

Pollard, A. Mrs Gaskell. Bull John Rylands Lib 43 1961.

— Mrs Gaskell: novelist and biographer. Manchester 1965.

— Mrs Gaskell's Life of Charlotte Brontë. Bull John Rylands Lib 47 1965.

Carnall, G. D. Dickens, Mrs Gaskell and the Preston Strike. Victorian Stud 8 1964.

Gross, J. Mrs Gaskell. Listener 11 March 1965; rptd in The novelist as innovator, ed W. Allen 1965.

Wright, E. Mrs Gaskell: the basis for reassessment. Oxford 1965.

Craik, W. A. Elizabeth Gaskell and the English provincial novel. 1975.

Gérin, W. Elizabeth Gaskell: a biography. Oxford 1976.

CHARLES READE
1814–84

Bibliographies

Burns, W. In Victorian fiction: a guide to research, ed L. Stevenson, Cambridge Mass 1964.

§ 1

Peregrine Pickle. [1851] (priv ptd).

The ladies' battle, or un duel en amour: a comedy in three acts. [1851], Boston [1855], London 1877 (rev).

Angelo: a tragedy in four acts. [1851].

The lost husband: a drama in four acts. [1852], 1872.

Gold! a drama in five acts. [1853], 1899.

Peg Woffington: a novel. 1853, Boston 1855, London 1857, 1868, [1872], 1899, [1901] etc.

Christie Johnstone: a novel. 1853, 1854, Boston 1855, London 1857, 1868, 1872 etc.

The courier of Lyons, or the attack upon the mail: a drama in four acts. 1854, Cambridge 1895 (as The Lyons mail).

The King's rival: a drama in five acts by Tom Taylor and Reade. 1854.

Masks and faces, or before and behind the curtain: a comedy in two acts by Tom Taylor and Reade. 1854.

Two loves and a life: a drama in four acts by Tom Taylor and Reade. 1854.

It is never too late to mend: a matter of fact romance. 3 vols 1856, 1856, 2 vols Boston 1856, Leipzig 1856, 1 vol 1857, 1868, [1872], 1893, 1900 etc.

Poverty and pride: a drama in five acts. 1856.

The course of true love never did run smooth. 1857, 1868, [1873]. Contains The bloomer; Art: a dramatic tale; Clouds and sunshine, above.

The hypochondriac: adapted to the English stage from the Malade imaginaire of Molière. 1857.

Propria quae maribus: a jeu d'esprit; and The box tunnel: a fact. Bentley's Miscellany Nov 1853; Boston 1857. Propria pro maribus is the same story as The bloomer, above.

White lies: a story. London Jnl 11 July–5 Dec 1857; 3 vols 1857, 1 vol Boston 1858, London 1868 1872 (as Double marriage: or white lies).

Cream. 1858, [1873]. Contains Jack of all trades: a matter-of-fact romance (Harper's Mag Dec 1857–May 1858), The autobiography of a thief.

A good fight and other tales. New York 1859; A good fight, ed A. Lang 1910. A good fight, Once a Week 2 July–1 Oct 1859, was expanded into The cloister and the hearth, below.

It is never too late to mend: proofs of its prison revelations. 1859. Pamphlet.

'Love me little, love me long'. 2 vols 1859, New York 1859, Leipzig 1859, London 1868, [1873].

The eighth commandment. 1860.

Monopoly versus property. 1860. Pamphlet.

The cloister and the hearth: a tale of the Middle Ages. 4 vols 1861, 1861 (rev), 1 vol New York 1861, London 1862; ed W. Besant 4 vols 1894; ed A. C. Swinburne 1905 (EL); ed C. B. Wheeler 1915 etc.

Hard cash: a matter-of-fact romance. All the Year Round 28 March– 26 Dec 1863 (as Very hard cash); 3 vols 1863, 1864, 1 vol New York 1864, 1 vol 1868, [1872].

It's never too late to mend: a drama in four acts. [1865]; [1873]; ed L. Rives, Toulouse 1940.

Griffith Gaunt: or jealousy. Argosy Dec 1865–Nov 1866, 3 vols 1866, 1 vol Boston 1866, 3 vols 1867, 1868 (5th edn), 1869, [1872].

Dora: a pastoral drama in three acts. [1867].

The double marriage: a drama in five acts by August Maquet and Reade. [1867].

Foul play, by Dion Boucicault and Reade. Once a Week 4 Jan–20 June 1868; 3 vols 1868, 1 vol Boston 1868, London 1869, [1873], 1927.

Put yourself in his place. Cornhill Mag March 1869–July 1870; 3 vols 1870, 1 vol New York 1870, London 1871, 1876.

Foul play: a drama in four acts by Dion Boucicault and Reade. [1871?], 1883 (rev as Foul play: a drama in a prologue and five acts by Reade).

Rachel the reaper: a rustic drama in three acts. 1871.

A terrible temptation: a story of the day. Cassell's Mag April–Sept 1871; 3 vols 1871, 1 vol Boston 1871, London [1882].

To the editor of the Daily Globe, Toronto: a reply to criticism. 1871. Pamphlet.

Kate Peyton, or jealousy: a drama in a prologue and four acts. 1872, 1883 (rev).

The legal vocabulary. 1872. Pamphlet.

The wandering heir. Graphic Dec 1872; Toronto 1872, Boston, New York, 1873, London, 1882, 1905, 1924.

Cremona violins: four letters reprinted from the Pall Mall Gazette [19–31 Aug 1872]. Gloucester 1873.

A simpleton: a story of the day. London Soc Aug 1872–Sept 1873; 3 vols 1873, 1 vol New York 1873.

A hero and a martyr: a true and accurate account of the heroic feats and sad calamity of James Lambert. 1874, New York 1875.

Trade malice: a personal narrative; and The wandering heir: a matter of fact romance. 1875.

The jilt: a novel. Belgravia March–June 1877, New York 1877.

A woman hater. Blackwood's Mag June 1876–June 1877; 3 vols 1877, 1 vol New York 1877.

Golden crowns: Sunday stories. Manchester [1877].

The coming man: letters contributed to Harper's Weekly. New York 1878.

Dora: or the history of a play. 1878. Pamphlet.

The well-born workman: or a man of the day. 1878. Play adapted from Put yourself in his place, above.

Single heart and double face: a matter-of-fact romance. Life 8 June–7 Sept 1882; New York 1882, London 1884.

The countess and the dancer, or high life in Vienna: a comedy drama in four acts. 1883.

Love and money: an original drama in prologue and four acts by Reade and Henry Pettitt. 1883.

Readiana: comments on current events. 1883, New York 1884.

Good stories of man and other animals. 1884, New York 1884.

The jilt and other stories. 1884.

A perilous secret. Temple Bar Sept 1884–May 1885; 2 vols 1884, 1 vol New York 1884, London 1885, 1891.

Nance Oldfield: a comedy in one act. [1884?] (priv ptd).

The picture. Harper's Mag March–April 1884; New York 1884.

Bible characters. 1888.

Androgynism: or woman playing at man. English Rev Aug–Sept 1911. From an unpbd ms.

§ 2

Archer, W. In his English dramatists, 1882.

Besant, W. The novels of Reade. GM April 1882.

Swinburne, A. C. Reade. Nineteenth Century Oct 1884; rptd in his Miscellanies, [1886].

Reade, C. L. and C. Reade, dramatist, novelist, journalist: a memoir. 2 vols 1887.

Quiller-Couch, A. T. In his Adventures in criticism, 1896.

Coleman, J. Reade as I knew him. 1903.

Phillips, W. C. Dickens, Reade and Collins: sensation novelists. New York 1919.

Elwin, M. Reade: a biography. 1931.

'Orwell, George'. Books in general. New Statesman 17 Aug 1940.

Smith, S. M. Realism in the drama of Reade. English 12 1958.

—— Propaganda and hard facts in Reade's didactic novels. Nottingham Renaissance & Modern Stud 4 1960.

ANTHONY TROLLOPE
1815–82

Bibliographies etc

Sadleir, M. Trollope: a bibliography. 1928, 1934 (rev), 1964.

Gerould, W. G. and J. T. A guide to Trollope. Princeton 1948.

Smalley, D. In Victorian fiction: a guide to research, ed L. Stevenson, Cambridge 1964.

Collections

Chronicles of Barsetshire. 8 vols 1878; The Barchester novels: Shakespeare head edition, ed M. Sadleir 14 vols Oxford 1929; The Oxford illustrated Trollope, ed M. Sadleir and F. Page 15 vols Oxford 1948–54 (unfinished). 36 of the works have been issued Oxford 1907–(WC).

§ I

The Macdermotts of Ballycloran. 3 vols 1847, 1848, 1 vol 1859, 1865, 1866.

The Kellys and the O'Kellys, or landlords and tenants: a tale of Irish life. 3 vols 1848, 1 vol 1859, 1865 (5th edn), 1866, Oxford 1929 (WC).

La Vendée: an historical romance. 3 vols 1850, 1 vol [1875].

The Warden. 1855, 1858, 1859, Leipzig 1859, New York 1862, London 1866, 1870, Oxford 1918 (WC).

Barchester Towers. 3 vols 1857, 1 vol 1858, 1866, 1870, Oxford 1918 (WC).

The three clerks: a novel. 3 vols 1858, 1 vol 1859, 1860, 1865, 1878, 1907 (WC).

Doctor Thorne: a novel. 3 vols 1858, 1858, 1 vol 1859, New York 1859, London 1865, Oxford 1926 (WC).

The Bertrams: a novel. 3 vols 1859, 1 vol 1860, 1861, 1866, [1904].

The West Indies and the Spanish Main. 1859, 1860, 1861, 1862, 1869.

Castle Richmond: a novel. 3 vols 1860, 1 vol 1860, 1866.

Framley Parsonage. Cornhill Mag Jan 1860–April 1861; 3 vols 1861, 1 vol 1861, 1869, 1872, 1879, Oxford 1926 (WC).

The Civil Service as a profession. 1861 (priv ptd). A lecture.

Tales of all countries. 1861; second series, 1863; [both sers] 1864, 1866, Oxford 1931 (WC).

Orley Farm. 20 monthly pts March 1861–Oct 1862; 2 vols 1862, 1 vol 1868, 1871, Oxford 1935 (WC).

The struggles of Brown, Jones and Robinson, by one of the firm. Cornhill Mag Aug 1861–March 1862; New York 1862, London 1870.

North America. 2 vols 1862, 1862, 1864, 1 vol 1866; ed D. Smalley and B. A. Booth, New York 1951.

The present condition of the northern states of the American Union. [1862?] (priv ptd). A lecture.

Rachel Ray: a novel. 2 vols 1863, 1 vol 1864, 1866, Oxford 1924 (WC).

The small house at Allington. Cornhill Mag Sept 1862–April 1864; 2 vols 1864, 1 vol 1864, 1869, 1872, 1877, 1879, Oxford 1938 (WC).

Can you forgive her? 20 monthly pts Jan 1864–Aug 1865; 2 vols 1864, 1865, 1 vol 1866, 1868, 1869, 1871, 1873, Oxford 1938 (WC).

Hunting sketches. Pall Mall Gazette 9 Feb–20 March 1865; 1865, 1866; ed J. Boyd 1934; ed L. Edwards 1952.

Miss Mackenzie. 2 vols 1865, 1 vol 1866, [1876], Oxford 1924 (WC).

The Belton estate. Fortnightly Rev 15 May 1865–1 Jan 1866; 3 vols 1866 (3 edns), 1 vol 1866, 1868, Oxford 1923 (WC).

Travelling sketches. Pall Mall Gazette 3 Aug–6 Sept 1865; 1866.

Clergymen of the Church of England. Pall Mall Gazette 20 Nov 1865–25 Jan 1866; 1866.

The Claverings. Cornhill Mag Feb 1866–May 1867; New York 1866 (?), 2 vols 1867, 1 vol 1871, 1872, Oxford 1924 (WC).

Nina Balatka: the story of a maiden of Prague. Blackwood's Mag July 1866–Jan 1867 (anon); 2 vols 1867, 1 vol 1879, Oxford 1946 (WC) (with Linda Tressel).

The last chronicle of Barset. 32 weekly pts 1 Dec–6 July 1867; 2 vols 1867, 3 vols Leipzig 1867, 1 vol 1869, 1872, 1879, Oxford 1932 (WC).

Lotta Schmidt and other stories. 1867, 1870, 1882.

Linda Tressel. Blackwood's Mag Oct 1867–May 1868 (anon); 2 vols 1868, 1879, Oxford 1946 (WC) (with Nina Balatka).

Higher education for women. [1868] (priv ptd). A lecture.

Phineas Finn: the Irish Member. St Paul's Mag Oct 1867–May 1869; 2 vols 1869, 1 vol 1870, 1871, Oxford 1937 (WC).

He knew he was right. 32 weekly pts 17 Oct 1868–22 May 1869; 2 vols 1869, 1 vol 1870, 1871, Oxford 1948 (WC).

Did he steal it? a comedy in three acts. 1869 (priv ptd); ed R. H. Taylor, Princeton 1952.

The vicar of Bullhampton. 11 monthly pts July 1869–May 1870; 1870, 1 vol 1871, 1875, Oxford 1924 (WC).

An editor's tales. St Paul's Mag Oct 1869–May 1870; 1870, 1871, 1873, 1876.

On English prose fiction as a rational amusement. [1870] (priv ptd). A lecture.

The commentaries of Caesar. 1870, New York 1872.

Sir Harry Hotspur of Humblethwaite. Macmillan's Mag May–Dec 1870; 1871, Oxford 1928 (WC).

Ralph the heir. 19 monthly pts Jan 1870–July 1871 (supplement to St Paul's Mag); 3 vols 1871, 1 vol 1871, 1872, 1878, Oxford 1939 (WC).

The Golden Lion of Granpere. Good Words Jan–Aug 1872; 1872, 1873, 1873, 1885, Oxford 1947 (WC).

The Eustace diamonds. Fortnightly Rev July 1871–Feb 1873; New York 1872, 3 vols 1873 (for 1872), 1 vol 1875, Oxford 1930 (WC).

Australia and New Zealand. 2 vols 1873, 7 pts Melbourne 1873, 4 pts 1874, 2 vols 1876.

Lady Anna. Fortnightly Rev April 1873–April 1874; 2 vols Leipzig 1873, London 1874, 1 vol London 1875, Oxford 1936 (WC).

Phineas redux. Graphic 19 July 1873–10 Jan 1874; 2 vols 1874, 1 vol 1874, 1875, Oxford 1937 (WC).

Harry Heathcote of Gangoil: a tale of Australian bush life. Graphic 25 Dec 1873; 1874, 1874, 1963.

The way we live now. 20 monthly pts Feb 1874–Sept 1875; 2 vols 1875, 1876, 1 vol 1879, Oxford 1941 (WC).

The Prime Minister. 8 monthly pts Nov 1875–June 1876; 4 vols 1876, 1 vol 1877, 1878, Oxford 1938 (WC).

The American Senator. Temple Bar May 1876–July 1877; 3 vols 1877, 1 vol 1877, 1878, 1886, Oxford 1931 (WC).

Christmas at Thompson Hall. Graphic 25 Dec 1876; New York 1877, London 1885.

Is he Popenjoy? a novel. All the Year Round 13 Oct 1877–13 July 1878; 3 vols 1878, 1879, Oxford 1944 (WC).

Iceland. Fortnightly Rev Aug 1878; 1878 (priv ptd).

How the 'mastiffs' went to Iceland. 1878 (priv ptd).

South Africa. 2 vols 1878, 1 vol 1879 (rev and abridged); ed P. Haworth 1938 (abridged).

The lady of Launay. Light 6 April–11 May 1878; New York 1878.

An eye for an eye. Whitehall Rev 24 Aug 1878–1 Feb 1879; 2 vols 1879, 1 vol 1879 (rev).

John Caldigate. Blackwood's Mag April 1878–June 1879; 3 vols 1879, 1 vol 1880, 1885, Oxford 1946 (WC).

Cousin Henry: a novel. Manchester Weekly Times Suppl 8 March–24 May 1879; 2 vols 1879, 1 vol 1880, Oxford 1929 (WC).

Thackeray. 1879 (EML).

The Duke's children: a novel. All the Year Round 4 Oct

1879–24 July 1880; 3 vols 1880, 1 vol 1880, Oxford 1938 (WC).

The life of Cicero. 2 vols 1880.

Dr Wortle's school: a novel. Blackwood's Mag May–Dec 1880; 2 vols 1881, 1 vol Oxford 1928 (WC).

Ayala's angel. 3 vols 1881, 1 vol 1882, 1884, Oxford 1929 (WC).

Why Frau Frohmann raised her prices, and other stories. 1882.

The fixed period: a novel. Blackwood's Mag Oct 1881–March 1882; 2 vols 1882.

Lord Palmerston. 1882 (Eng Political Leaders ser).

Marion Fay: a novel. Graphic 3 Dec 1881–3 June 1882; 3 vols 1882.

Kept in the dark: a novel. Good Words May–Dec 1882; 2 vols 1882.

Not if I know it. Life Dec 1882; New York 1883.

The two heroines of Plumplington. Good Words Dec 1882; New York 1882; ed J. Hampden 1953.

Mr Scarborough's family. All the Year Round 27 May 1882–16 June 1883; 3 vols 1883, 1 vol 1883, Oxford 1947 (WC).

The Landleaguers. Life 16 Nov 1882–4 Oct 1883; 3 vols 1883, 1 vol 1884.

An autobiography. 2 vols 1883; ed M. Sadleir, Oxford 1923 (WC); ed B. A. Booth, Berkeley 1947; ed F. Page, Oxford 1950; ed J. B. Priestley 1962.

Alice Dugdale and other stories. Leipzig 1883.

La mère bauche and other stories. Leipzig 1883.

The mistletoe bough and other stories. Leipzig 1883.

An old man's love. 2 vols Edinburgh 1884, 1 vol Oxford 1936 (WC).

The noble jilt: a comedy. Ed M. Sadleir 1923 (500 copies).

London tradesmen. Pall Mall Gazette 10 July–7 Sept 1880; ed M. Sadleir 1927.

Four lectures. Ed M. L. Parrish 1938.

The tireless traveller: twenty letters to the Liverpool Mercury 1875. Ed B. A. Booth, Cambridge 1941.

Letters. Ed B. A. Booth, Oxford 1951.

The New Zealander. Ed N. J. Hall, Oxford 1972. Written 1855–6.

§ 2

[Hutton, R. H.] Spectator 11 Oct 1862. Review of Orley Farm.

—— Spectator 9 April 1864. Review of Small house at Allington.

—— Spectator 12 June 1869. Review of He knew he was right.

James, H. Anthony Trollope. Century Mag July 1883; rptd in his Partial portraits, 1888, and in his House of fiction, ed L. Edel 1957.

—— In his Notes and reviews, Cambridge Mass 1921.

Bryce, J. In his Studies in contemporary biography, 1903.

Sadleir, M. A guide to Trollope. Nineteenth Century April 1922.

—— Trollope and his publishers. Library 4th ser 5 1924.

—— Trollope: a commentary. 1927, 1945 (rev).

Walpole, H. Anthony Trollope. 1928 (EML).

Booth, B. A. Trollope and the Pall Mall Gazette. Nineteenth-Century Fiction 4 1950.

—— Trollope on Scott. Nineteenth-Century Fiction 5 1951.

—— Trollope on the novel. In Essays dedicated to L. B. Campbell, Berkeley 1950.

—— Trollope and the Royal Literary Fund. Nineteenth-Century Fiction 7 1953.

—— Trollope: aspects of his life and work. Bloomington 1958.

—— Orley Farm: artistry manqué. In From Jane Austen to Joseph Conrad, ed R. C. Rathburn and M. Steinmann, Minneapolis 1958.

Chapman, R. W. The text of Trollope. TLS 25 Jan, 22 March 1941.

—— Trollope's American Senator. TLS 21 June 1941.

—— Trollopian criticism. TLS 5, 26 July 1941.

—— Trollope's autobiography. N & Q 1 Nov 1941.

—— The text of Trollope's autobiography. RES 17 1941.

—— The text of Trollope's novels. Ibid.

—— The text of Phineas redux. RES 17–8 1941–2.

—— The text of Ayala's angel. MP 39 1942.

—— The text of Phineas Finn. TLS 25 March 1944.

—— The text of Barchester Towers. TLS 30 Aug 1947.

—— Personal names in Trollope's political novels. In Essays presented to Sir Humphrey Milford, Oxford 1948.

—— Trollope on Emma and the Monk: unpublished notes. Nineteenth-Century Fiction 4 1950.

Stebbins, L. P. and R. P. The Trollopes: the chronicle of a writing family. 1945.

The Trollopian. Ed B. A. Booth, Los Angeles 1945–49. Title changed in 1949 to Nineteenth-Century Fiction.

Bowen, E. Trollope: a new judgment. Oxford 1946.

Tinker, C. B. Trollope. Yale Rev new ser 36 1947; rptd in his Essays in retrospect, New York 1948.

Briggs, A. Trollope, Bagehot and the English constitution. Cambridge Jnl March 1952; rptd in his Victorian people, 1954.

Cockshut, A. O. J. Trollope: a critical study. 1955.

Mizener, A. Trollope: the Palliser novels. In From Jane Austen to Joseph Conrad, ed R. C. Rathburn and M. Steinmann, Minneapolis 1958.

Davies, H. S. Trollope. 1960 (Br Council pamphlet).

—— Trollope and his style. REL 1 1960.

Hewitt, M. Trollope: historian and sociologist. Br Jnl of Sociology 14 1963. On the place of women.

Tillotson, G. Trollope's style. In his Mid-Victorian studies, 1965.

Smalley, D. (ed). Trollope: the critical heritage. 1969.

Snow, C. P. Trollope. 1975.

GEORGE MEREDITH
1828–1909
Bibliographies

Esdaile, A. J. K. Bibliography of the writings in prose and verse of Meredith. 1907.

Forman, M. B. A bibliography of the writings in prose and verse of Meredith. 1922.

—— Meredithiana: being a supplement to the bibliography of Meredith. 1924.

Stevenson, L. In Victorian poets: a guide to research, ed F. E. Faverty, Cambridge Mass 1956, 1968 (rev).

Cline, C. L. In Victorian fiction: a guide to research, ed L. Stevenson, Cambridge Mass 1964.

Collie, M. Meredith: a bibliography. 1974.

Collections
Novels

Collected edition. 12 vols 1885–95.

Library edition, Revised edition [or] New Popular edition. 18 vols 1897–8. Celt and Saxon added 1910; texts rev Meredith.

Edition de luxe. 39 vols 1896–1912. Includes Miscellaneous prose, bibliography by A. Esdaile.

Poems

Poetical works. Ed G. M. Trevelyan 1912.

§ 1

Poems. 1851, New York 1898, London 1909, New York 1909 (adds Poems from Modern love, Scattered poems).

The shaving of Shagpat: an Arabian entertainment. 1856 (for 1855), 1865, 1872, 1912; ed F. M. Meynell, illustr H. Guilbeau, New York 1955.

Farina: a legend of Cologne. 1857, 1865, 1868, 1898 (with Short stories).

The ordeal of Richard Feverel: a history of father and son. 3 vols 1859, 2 vols 1875, 1 vol 1878 (rev), 1890, 1899, 1901; ed F. W. Chandler, New York 1917; ed R. Sencourt 1935; ed N. Kelvin, New York 1961.

Evan Harrington: or he would be a gentleman. New York 1860 (mag version), 3 vols 1861, 1 vol 1866, 1885; ed G. F. Reynolds, New York 1922.

Modern love, and Poems of the English roadside, with Poems and ballads. 1862; ed E. Cavazza, Portland Maine 1891, Boston 1892 (rev), London 1892 (adds The sage enamoured, The honest lady); ed R. le Gallienne, New York 1909; ed C. Day Lewis 1948.

The cruise of the Alabama and the Sumter: from the private journals and other papers of Commander R. Semmes. 1864. Introductory and concluding chs by Meredith.

Emilia in England. 3 vols 1864, 1 vol 1886 (as Sandra Belloni).

Rhoda Fleming: a story. 3 vols 1865.

Vittoria. 3 vols 1867 (for 1866).

The adventures of Harry Richmond. 3 vols 1871, 1871.

Beauchamp's career. 3 vols 1876 (for 1875), 2 vols 1876; ed G. M. Young, Oxford 1950.

The house on the beach: a realistic tale. New York 1877, 1878, London 1894 (adds The tale of Chloe, The case of General Ople and Lady Camper), 1898 (rev in Short stories).

The egoist: a comedy in narrative. 3 vols 1879, New York 1879, 1 vol 1880, 1880, 1890; ed W. C. Brownell, New York 1901; The egoist arranged for the stage, ed A. Sutro 1920 (priv ptd); The egoist, ed Lord Dunsany, Oxford 1947 (WC); ed L. Stevenson, Boston 1958; ed A. Wilson, New York 1963.

The tragic comedians: a study in a well-known story, enlarged from the Fortnightly Review. 2 vols 1880, 1881, 1 vol 1881, 1881; ed C. K. Shorter 1891 (rev), 1946 (Penguin).

Poems and lyrics of the joy of earth. 1883.

Diana of the crossways: a novel, considerably enlarged from the Fortnightly Review. 3 vols 1885, 1885, 1885, 1 vol New York 1885 (incomplete mag version); ed A. Symons, New York [1930?]. 26 chs only ptd in Fortnightly Rev 1884.

Ballads and poems of tragic life. 1887, Boston 1887, London 1894, 1897.

A reading of earth. 1888, Boston 1888, London 1895, New York and London 1901.

Jump-to-glory Jane: a poem. 1889 (priv ptd); illustr L. Housman 1892.

The case of General Ople and Lady Camper. New York 1890, 1891, 1894 (adds The tale of Chloe, The house on the beach), 1900. First pbd 1877 in New Quart Mag.

The tale of Chloe: an episode in the history of Beau Beamish. New York 1890, 1891, London 1894 (adds The house on the beach, The case of General Ople and Lady Camper), New York 1898 (in Short stories, below). First pbd in New Quart Mag 1879.

One of our conquerors. 3 vols 1891 (3 edns).

Poems: The empty purse, with Odes to the comic spirit, to youth in memory and verses. 1892, 1895.

Lord Ormont and his Aminta: a novel. 3 vols 1894.

The tale of Chloe and other stories. 1894, 1895.

The amazing marriage. 2 vols 1895.

On the idea of comedy and the uses of the comic spirit: a lecture delivered at the London Institute, February 1st 1877. 1897, New York 1897; ed L. Cooper, Ithaca 1956. First pbd in New Quart Mag 1877.

Selected poems. 1897. Meredith's selection.

Odes in contribution to the song of French history. 1898.

Poems. 2 vols New York and London 1898. A collection.

Short stories: The tale of Chloe. The house on the beach, Farina, The case of General Ople and Lady Camper. New York 1898.

A reading of life, with other poems. 1901.

Twenty poems. 1909. Collected from Household Words, some repudiated by Meredith's son.

Last poems. 1909.

Poems written in early youth (published in 1851), Poems from Modern love (first edition) and Scattered poems. 1909, New York 1909.

Milton. 1909. A poem on the tercentenary.

Celt and Saxon. 1910, New York 1910.

Letters

Letters, collected and edited by his son [W. M. Meredith]. 2 vols 1912.

Letters to E. Clodd and C. K. Shorter. 1913 (priv ptd).

Letters to R. H. Horne. Cape Town 1919 (priv ptd).

Letters to A. C. Swinburne and T. Watts-Dunton. Cape Town 1922 (priv ptd).

Letters to Alice Meynell, with annotations thereto. 1923.

Letters to various correspondents. Pretoria 1924 (priv ptd).

Collected letters. Ed C. L. Cline 3 vols Oxford 1970.

§2

Stevenson, R. L. Books which have influenced me. In his Essays in the art of writing, 1905.

Trevelyan, G. M. Optimism and Mr Meredith: a reply. Independent Rev 6 1905.

—— The poetry and philosophy of Meredith. 1906.

—— In his Clio: a muse, and other essays, 1913.

Barrie, J. M. George Meredith. 1909.

Chesterton, G. K. The moral philosophy of Meredith. Contemporary Rev July 1909.

Hammerton, J. A. Meredith in anecdote and criticism. 1909, Edinburgh 1911 (rev).

Beach, J. W. The comic spirit of Meredith. 1911.

Priestley, J. B. George Meredith. 1926 (EML).

Hardy, T. GM: a reminiscence. Nineteenth Century Feb 1928.

Woolf, V. The novels of Meredith. In her Common reader: second series, 1928.

—— Meredith revisited. In her Granite and rainbow, 1958.

Everett, E. M. In his Party of humanity: the Fortnightly Review and its contributors 1865–74, Chapel Hill 1939.

Chambers, E. K. Meredith's Modern love; Meredith's nature poetry. In his Sheaf of studies, Oxford 1942.

Sassoon, S. George Meredith. 1948.

Sitwell, O. The novels of Meredith and some notes on the English novel. Oxford 1948.

Tinker, C. B. Meredith's poetry. In his Essays in retrospect, New Haven 1948.

Gettmann, R. A. Meredith as publisher's reader. JEGP 48 1949.

Stevenson, L. The ordeal of Meredith. 1954.

Bartlett, P. Meredith: early manuscript poems in the Berg Collection. BNYPL Aug 1957.

—— The novels of Meredith. REL 3 1962.

—— George Meredith. 1963 (Br Council pamphlet).

Beerbohm, M. Hethway speaking. In his Mainly on the air, 1957 (enlarged). Meredith's conversation reported by a Chelsea neighbour.

Haight, G. S. Meredith and the Westminster Review. MLR 53 1958.

Beer, G. Meredith: a change of masks. 1970.

Pritchett, V. S. Meredith and English comedy. 1970.

Williams, I. (ed). Meredith: the critical heritage. 1971.

Fletcher, I. (ed). Meredith now: some critical essays. 1971.

'GEORGE ELIOT',
MARY ANN EVANS,
later CROSS
1819–80

The ms Scenes of clerical life *is in the Pierpont Morgan Library, New York; the mss of all other major works are in the BM. The largest collection of letters is in Yale Univ Library. The diary for 1879 is in the Berg Collection; other journals and diaries are at Yale. Yale also has several notebooks, including the 'Quarry' for Felix Holt; the Quarry for Romola is at Princeton; Harvard has the main Middlemarch Quarry, though 2 other Middlemarch notebooks are in the Folger Library.*

Bibliographies etc

Mudge, I. G. and M. E. Sears. A George Eliot dictionary. New York 1924.
Harvey, W. J. In Victorian fiction, ed L. Stevenson, Cambridge Mass 1964.

Collections

Novels: illustrated edition. 6 vols 1867–[78].
Works: cabinet edition. 24 vols 1878–[85].
Novels: cheap edition. 6 vols 1881.

§1

The life of Jesus critically examined, by David Friedrich Strauss, translated from the fourth German edition. 3 vols 1846, 1 vol 1892, New York 1855. Begun by Mrs Charles Hennell and completed anon by Eliot.
The essence of Christianity, by Ludwig Feuerbach, translated from the second German edition by Marian Evans. 1854, New York 1857, 1957.
Scenes of clerical life. 2 vols Edinburgh 1858, 1859, 1860, 1863 (with Silas Marner), 1868 etc, New York 1858; ed A. Mattheson, Oxford 1909 (WC); ed W. W. Fowler and E. Limouzin 1916; ed A. M. Macmillan 1924. First pbd in Blackwood's Mag: The sad fortunes of the Rev Amos Barton, Jan–Feb 1857; Mr Gilfil's love story, March–June 1857; Janet's repentance, July–Nov 1857.
Adam Bede. 3 vols Edinburgh 1859 (7 edns), 1862 (10th edn), New York 1859; ed G. S. Haight, New York 1949; ed G. Bullett 1953; ed M. H. Goldberg, New York 1956.
The mill on the Floss. 3 vols Edinburgh 1860, 2 vols Edinburgh 1860, 1 vol Edinburgh 1861 (corrected), 1862 (5th edn); ed G. S. Haight, Boston 1961.
Silas Marner: the weaver of Raveloe. Edinburgh 1861 (7 edns), 1864 (with Scenes of clerical life), 1868 etc; ed K. M. Lobb 1958.
Romola. 3 vols 1863, 1865 (illustr), 2 vols 1880 etc, 1 vol New York 1863; ed V. Meynell, Oxford 1929 (WC). First pbd, illustr Leighton, Cornhill Mag July 1862–Aug 1863.
Brother Jacob. Cornhill Mag July 1864; rptd with Silas Marner in Works, 1878, above.
Felix Holt the radical. 3 vols Edinburgh 1866, 2 vols Edinburgh 1866; ed V. Meynell, Oxford 1913 (WC).
Address to working men, by Felix Holt. Blackwood's Mag Jan 1868.
The Spanish gypsy: a poem. Edinburgh 1868 (3 edns), 1875 (5th edn), Boston 1868.
Agatha. 1869 (priv ptd). First pbd in Atlantic Monthly 1869. 2nd edn a forgery? *See* J. Carter and H. G. Pollard, An enquiry into the nature of certain nineteenth-century pamphlets, 1934.

Brother and sister: sonnets by Marian Lewes. 1869 (priv ptd). A forgery? *See* Agatha, above.
How Lisa loved the King. Boston 1869, 1883. First pbd in Blackwood's Mag May 1869.
Amgart. Macmillan's Mag July 1871.
Middlemarch: a study of provincial life. 4 vols Edinburgh 1872, 1873, 1 vol 1874 (corrected); ed R. M. Hewit, Oxford 1947 (WC); ed G. S. Haight, Boston 1956; ed Q. Anderson 1963; ed F. Kermode 1964; ed W. J. Harvey 1965 (Penguin). First pbd in 8 bks, Dec 1871–Dec 1872.
The legend of Jubal and other poems. Edinburgh 1874. The legend of Jubal first pbd Macmillan's Mag May 1870.
Daniel Deronda. 4 vols Edinburgh 1876, 1877, 1 vol 1877, New York 1876; ed F. R. Leavis, New York 1961; ed E. L. Jones 2 vols 1964 (EL); ed B. Hardy 1967 (Penguin). First pbd in 8 bks Jan–Sept 1876.
A college breakfast party. Macmillan's Mag July 1878.
Impressions of Theophrastus Such. Edinburgh 1879.
Essays and leaves from a note-book. Ed C. L. Lewes, Edinburgh 1884, New York 1884.
Early essays. 1919 (priv ptd). Not rptd from mss, as the preface claims, but from cuttings of George Eliot's contributions to the Coventry Herald exhibited in 1919.
Essays. Ed T. Pinney 1963.

Letters

George Eliot's life as related in her letters and journals, arranged and edited by her husband J. W. Cross. 3 vols Edinburgh 1885.
The George Eliot letters. Ed G. S. Haight 7 vols New Haven 1954–6. First complete edn.

§2

James, H. The novels of George Eliot. Atlantic Monthly Oct 1866.
—— Galaxy 15 1873. On Middlemarch.
—— The life of George Eliot. Atlantic Monthly May 1885.
Hutton, R. H. In his Essays theological and literary, 2 vols 1871.
—— In his Essays on some of the modern guides of English thought in matters of faith, 1887.
Stephen, L. George Eliot. 1902 (EML).
Woolf, V. In her Common reader, 1925.
Haight, G. S. George Eliot and John Chapman; with Chapman's diaries. New Haven 1940.
—— (ed). A century of George Eliot criticism. Boston 1965.
—— George Eliot: a biography. Oxford 1968.
Bennett, J. George Eliot: her mind and art. 1948.
Leavis, F. R. In his Great tradition, 1948.
Willey, B. In his Nineteenth-century studies, Coleridge to Matthew Arnold, 1949.
Hanson, L. and E. Marian Evans and George Eliot. 1952.
House, H. Qualities of George Eliot's unbelief. In his All in due time, 1955.
Hardy, B. The novels of George Eliot. 1959.
—— (ed). Middlemarch. 1967.
Thale, J. The novels of George Eliot. New York 1959.
Harvey, W. J. The art of George Eliot. 1961.
Tillotson, G. and K. The George Eliot letters. In their Mid-Victorian studies, 1965.
Lerner, L. and J. Holmstrom (ed). George Eliot and her readers: a selection of contemporary reviews. 1966.
Carroll, D. (ed). George Eliot: the critical heritage. 1971.

V. MINOR FICTION 1835–1870

WILLIAM HARRISON AINSWORTH
1805–82

Bibliographies

Locke, H. A bibliographical catalogue of the published novels and ballads of Ainsworth. 1925.

Collections

Works. 14 vols 1850–1.
Collected works. 16 vols 1875, 31 vols 1878–80, 12 vols 1923.
There is no complete edn of Ainsworth's writings.

§ 1

Poems by Cheviot Tichburn. 1822.
Monody on the death of John Philip Kemble. Manchester 1823.
December tales. 1823.
The Boeotian. Manchester 1824.
The works of Cheviot Tichburn. Manchester 1825.
A summer evening tale. 1825.
Consideration on the best means of affording immediate relief to the operative classes in the manufacturing districts. 1826.
Letters from cockney lands. 1826, 1827.
Sir John Chiverton: a romance. 1826. Anon; in collaboration with J. P. Aston.
Rookwood: a romance. 3 vols 1834 (anon), 1834, 1835.
Crichton. 3 vols 1837, Paris 1837, 1849 (rev).
Jack Sheppard: a romance. 1839, 15 weekly pts 1840, 1 vol 1840, 1854, 1856, 1862, 1865, 1884 etc. First pbd in Bentley's Miscellany 1839–40.
The Tower of London. 13 monthly pts 1840; 1 vol 1840, 1842, 1842, 1843, 1844, 1845, 1853, 1854, 1878, 1882 etc.
Guy Fawkes, or the gunpowder treason: an historical romance. 3 vols 1841, 1857, 1878, 1884, 1891. First pbd in Bentley's Miscellany Jan 1840–Nov 1841.
Old Saint Paul's: a tale of the Plague and the Fire. 12 monthly pts 1841; 3 vols 1841, 1847, 1855, 1857, 1884, 1891 etc. First pbd in Sunday Times Jan–Dec 1841.
The miser's daughter: a tale. 3 vols 1842, 1843, 1848, 1855, 1879, 1886, 1892. First pbd in Ainsworth's Mag 1842.
Modern chivalry: or a new Orlando Furioso. 2 vols 1843. With Catherine Gore.
Windsor castle: an historical romance. 3 vols 1843, 1843, 11 pts 1843–4, 1 vol 1844, 1847, 1853, 1878, 1884, 1891 etc. First pbd in Ainsworth's Mag 1842–3.
Saint James's, or the Court of Queen Anne: an historical romance. 3 vols 1844, 1846, 1853, 1879, 1889. First pbd in Ainsworth's Mag 1884.
James the Second, or the revolution of 1688: an historical romance. 3 vols 1848, 1854, 1890.
The Lancashire witches: a novel. 1849 (priv ptd), 3 vols 1849 (as The Lancashire witches: a romance of Pendle forest), 1854, 1878, 1884. First pbd in Sunday Times 1848.
Life and adventures of Mervyn Clitheroe. 12 monthly pts Dec 1851–March 1852, Dec 1857–June 1858; 1 vol 1858 (as Mervyn Clitheroe).
The Star Chamber: an historical romance. 2 vols 1854, 1857, 1861, 1879, 1889, 1892. First pbd in Home Companion 1853.
The flitch of bacon: or the custom of Dunmow. 1854, 1855, 1874, 1879, 1889, 1892. First pbd in New Monthly Mag 1853–4.
Ballads: romantic, fantastical and humorous. 1855, [1872] (with memoir of Ainsworth by J. Crossley, and adding The combat of the thirty). Rptd from the novels.

The spendthrift: a tale. 1857, 1879, 1889, 1892. First pbd in Bentley's Miscellany 1855–7.
The combat of the thirty, from a Breton lay of the fourteenth century. 1859.
Ovingdean Grange: a tale of the South Downs. 1860, 1879, 1891. First pbd in Bentley's Miscellany 1859–60.
The Constable of the Tower: an historical romance. 3 vols 1861, 1880, 1906. First pbd in Bentley's Miscellany 1861.
The Lord Mayor of London: or city life in the last century. 3 vols 1862, 1880, 1906. First pbd in Bentley's Miscellany 1862.
Cardinal Pole or the days of Philip and Mary: an historical romance. 3 vols 1863, 1864, 1881 etc. First pbd in Bentley's Miscellany 1862–3.
John Law the projector. 3 vols 1864, 1866, 1881. First pbd in Bentley's Miscellany 1863–4.
The Spanish match: or Charles Stuart at Madrid. 3 vols 1865, 1865, 1880, 1894. First published in Bentley's Mag 1864–5 as The house of seven chimneys.
Auriol: or the elixir of life. 1865 (with The old London merchant, and A night's adventure in Rome–2 short stories), [1875], 1875, 1881, 1890, 1892. First pbd in Ainsworth's Mag and New Monthly Mag 1844–6.
The Constable de Bourbon. 3 vols 1866, 1880. First pbd in Bentley's Miscellany 1865–6.
Old Court: a novel. 3 vols 1867; 1880. First pbd in Bentley's Miscellany 1866–7.
Myddleton Pomfret: a novel. 3 vols 1868, 1881. First pbd in Bentley's Miscellany 1867–8.
Hilary St Ives: a novel. 3 vols 1870, 1881. First pbd in New Monthly Mag 1869.
The South Sea Bubble: a tale of the year 1720. [1871], 1902. First pbd in Bow Bells 1868.
Talbot Harland. 1871. First pbd in Bow Bells 1870.
Tower Hill. [1871]. First pbd in Bow Bells 1871.
Boscobel, or the Royal Oak: a tale of the year 1651. 3 vols 1872, 1874, 1875, 1879, 1889. First pbd in New Monthly Mag 1872.
The good old times: the story of the Manchester rebels of '45. 3 vols 1873, 1874 (as The Manchester rebels of the fatal '45), 1880, 1884, 1890, 1893.
Merry England: or nobles and serfs. 3 vols 1874, [1875]. First pbd in Bow Bells 1874.
The goldsmith's wife: a tale. 3 vols 1875, [1875]. First pbd in Bow Bells 1874.
Preston Fight, or the insurrection of 1715: a tale. 3 vols 1875, 1879.
Chetwynd Calverley: a tale. 3 vols 1876, [1877]. First pbd in Bow Bells 1876.
The leaguer of Lathom: a tale of the Civil War in Lancashire. 3 vols 1876, 1880.
The fall of Somerset. 3 vols 1877, [1878]. First pbd in Bow Bells 1877–8.
Beatrice Tyldesley. 3 vols 1878, [1879]. First pbd in Bow Bells 1878.
Beau Nash: or Bath in the eighteenth century. 3 vols [1879], 1880, 1881, 1889.
Stanley Brereton. 3 vols [1881], 1882, 1884. First pbd in Bolton Weekly Jnl 1881.
Ainsworth edited Bentley's Miscellany from March 1840, and from 1842 began the pbn of Ainsworth's Magazine which lasted until 1853, when he bought The New Monthly Magazine.

§ 2

Evans, J. The early life of Ainsworth. 1882.
Axon, W. E. A. Ainsworth: a memoir. 1902.
Ellis, S. M. Ainsworth and his friends. 2 vols 1911.
Hollingsworth, K. In his Newgate novel 1830–47, Detroit 1963.

'CUTHBERT BEDE', EDWARD BRADLEY
1827–89

The adventures of Mr Verdant Green, an Oxford freshman. 1853.

The further adventures of Mr Verdant Green. 1854.

Mr Verdant Green married and done for: being the third and concluding part of the Adventures of Mr Verdant Green, an Oxford freshman. 1857. The 3 pts have been frequently rptd together as Mr Verdant Green, with illustrations by the author.

Motley: prose and verse, grave and gay, with illustrations by the author. 1855.

Love's provocations: being extracts taken in the most unmanly and unmannerly manner from the diary of Miss Polly C——; illustrations by the author. 1855.

Photographic pleasures popularly portrayed with pen and pencil. 1855.

Medley. [1856].

Tales of college life. 1856, 1862 (as College life).

Nearer and dearer, a tale of out school: a novelette illustrated by the author. 1857.

Fairy fables, with illustrations by Alfred Crowquill. 1858.

Funny figures, by A. Funnyman. 1858. 'One shilling plain: two shillings coloured,' the latter with 24 coloured pictures.

Happy hours at Wynford Grange: a story for children, with coloured illustrations. 1859.

Glencreggan: or a highland home in Cantire. 2 vols 1861.

Our new rector: or the village of Norton, edited by Cuthbert Bede. 1861.

The curate of Cranston; with other prose and verse. 1862.

A tour in tartan-land. 1863.

The visitor's handbook to Rosslyn and Hawthornden. 1864.

The white wife; with other stories, supernatural, romantic, legendary, collected and illustrated by Cuthbert Bede. 1865.

The rook's garden: essays and sketches. 1865.

Mattins and muttons, or the Beauty of Brighton: a love story. 2 vols 1866.

Round the peat fire at Glenbrechy, with illustrations by the author. Xmas no of Once a Week 1869.

Little Mr Bouncer and his friend Verdant Green, with illustrations by the author. 1873.

RICHARD DODDRIDGE BLACKMORE
1825–1900

§ 1

Poems by Melanter. 1854.

Epullia [and other poems]. 1854.

The bugle of the Black Sea: or the British in the East, by Melanter. 1855.

The fate of Franklin. 1860.

The farm and fruit of old: a translation in verse of the first and second Georgics of Virgil, by a market-gardener. 1862.

Clara Vaughan: a novel. 3 vols 1864, 1872 (rev).

Cradock Nowell: a tale of the New Forest. 3 vols 1866, 1873 (rev). First pbd in Macmillan's Mag May 1865–Aug 1866.

Lorna Doone: a romance of Exmoor. 3 vols 1869, 1873 (6th edn); ed H. S. Ward, New York 1908; ed H. Warren, Oxford 1914 (WC); ed R. O. Morris 1920.

The Georgics of Virgil, translated. 1871; ed R. S. Conway 1932.

The maid of Sker. 3 vols Edinburgh 1872, 1873. First pbd in Blackwood's Mag Aug 1871–July 1872.

Alice Lorraine; a tale of the South Downs. 3 vols 1875, 1876 (6th edn rev). First pbd in Blackwood's Mag March 1874–April 1875.

Cripps the carrier: a woodland tale. 3 vols 1876, 1877.

Erema: or my father's sin. 3 vols 1877, 1878. First pbd in Cornhill Mag Nov 1876–Nov 1877.

Figaro at Hastings, St Leonards, with illustrations by the author. 1877.

Mary Anerley: a Yorkshire tale. 3 vols 1880, 1881. First pbd in Fraser's Mag July 1879–Sept 1880.

Christowell: a Dartmoor tale. 3 vols 1882, 1882. First pbd in Good Words Jan–Dec 1881.

The remarkable history of Sir Thomas Upmore Bart MP, formerly known as 'Tommy Upmore'. 2 vols 1884, 1884, 1885.

Humour, wit and satire: containing i Book of beauty; ii Motley; iii Medley, with numerous illustrations by the author. 1885.

Fotheringay and Mary Queen of Scots: being an account, historical and descriptive, of Fotheringay Castle, the last prison of Mary Queen of Scots and the scene of her trial and execution, with illustrations by the author. 1886. First pbd in Leisure Hour 1865.

Springhaven: a tale of the great war. 3 vols 1887. First pbd in Harper's Mag April 1886–April 1887.

Betrothal ring of Mary Queen of Scots 1565. 1887.

Kit and Kitty: a story of west Middlesex. 3 vols 1890.

Perlycross: a tale of the western hills. 3 vols 1894.

Fringilla: a tale in verse. 1895.

Tales from the telling house. 1896.

Dariel: a romance of Surrey. 1897.

Argyll's highlands: or MacCailein Mor and the Lords of Lorne; with traditional tales. Ed J. Mackay, Glasgow 1902.

§ 2

Burris, Q. G. Blackmore: his life and novels. Urbana 1930.

Dunn, W. H. Blackmore: the author of Lorna Doone. 1956.

Budd, K. The last Victorian: Blackmore and his novels. 1960.

EDWARD GEORGE EARLE LYTTON BULWER-LYTTON, 1st BARON LYTTON
1803–73

Bibliographies

Dahl, C. In Victorian fiction, ed L. Stevenson, Cambridge Mass 1964.

Collections

Novels. 10 vols 1840.

Dramatic works. 1841.

Novels. 41 vols 1859–62, 22 vols 1877–8 (Library edn).

Poetical works. 1859, 1865, 1873.

Novels and romances. 43 vols 1864, 23 vols 1867. 1868.

Speeches, with memoir by his son. 2 vols 1874.

§ 1

Ismael: an oriental tale, with other poems. 1820.

Delmour: or the tale of sylphid, and other peoms. 1823. Anon.

Weeds and wild flowers, by E.G.L.B. Paris 1826 (priv ptd).

Falkland. 1827, 2 vols Paris 1833, [1876] etc.

O'Neill: or the rebel. 1827, Paris 1829.

Pelham: or the adventures of a gentleman. 3 vols 1828.

The disowned. 4 vols 1828, 3 vols 1829, 1831, 2 vols 1835.

Devereux: a tale. 3 vols 1829, 1831, 1836, 1839, 1841.
Paul Clifford. 3 vols 1830, 1835.
The Siamese twins: a satirical tale of the times. 1831.
Eugene Aram. 3 vols 1832.
Asmodeus at large. 1833, Philadelphia 1833.
England and the English. 2 vols 1833, 1834. (3rd edn with new preface.)
Godolphin. 3 vols 1833 (anon), 1850, 1854, 1860, 1862.
A letter to a late Cabinet Minister on the present crisis. [1834] (20 edns).
The last days of Pompeii. 3 vols 1834, 1835 ('revised and corrected'); ed E. Johnson, New York 1956.
The pilgrims of the Rhine. 1834.
Rienzi, the last of the Tribunes. 3 vols 1835.
The student: a series of papers. 2 vols 1835, 1840.
Literary remains of William Hazlitt, with thoughts on his genius and writings. 2 vols 1836.
The Duchess de la Vallière. 1836.
Athens: its rise and fall. 2 vols 1837, 1874, 2 vols nd.
Ernest Maltravers, 3 vols 1837, 1851, 1854.
Leila: or the siege of Granada. 1838, 1847, 9 pts 1850 (as Leila and Calderon the courtier).
Alice: or the mysteries. 3 vols 1838, 1852, 1854, 1860.
Richelieu: or the conspiracy. 1839, 1850, 1873.
The sea captain, or the birthright: a drama. 1839.
Money: a comedy. 1840, 1848, 1851, 1873, 1874.
Night and morning. 3 vols 1841, 1851, 1854, 2 vols 1876.
Eva, the ill-omened marriage and other poems. 1842.
Zanoni. 3 vols 1842, 1 vol 1845, 1853, 1856.
The last of the Barons. 3 vols 1843, 1850, 1854, 1860, 1874, 1878, 1884, [1888] etc; ed F. C. Romilly 1913.
Poems and ballads of Schiller. 2 vols 1844, 1852, 1859, 1870, 1877.
Confessions of a water patient, in a letter to W. Harrison Ainsworth. 1846.
Lucretia: or children of the night. 3 vols 1846, 2 vols Leipzig 1846, 1 vol 1847, 1853, 1855, 1860, 2 vols 1863.
The new Timon. 1846.
A word to the public. 1847.
Harold, the last of the Saxon kings. 3 vols 1848, 1848, 1853, 1855, 1866; ed G. L. Gomme [1906].
King Arthur: an epic poem. 3 pts 1848–9, 2 vols 1849, 1870 (rev), [1888].
The Caxtons: a family picture. 3 vols 1849, 2 vols 1849, 1853, 1854, 1855, 1874. First pbd anon in Blackwood's Mag.
Letters to John Bull esquire. 1851.
Not so bad as we seem, or many sides to a character: a comedy. 1851, 1853.
'My novel', by Pisistratus Caxton: or varieties in English life. Paris 1852, 4 vols 1853, 1854, 1856, 1861, 2 vols Paris [1861], London 1892. First pbd in Blackwood's Mag.
The haunted and the haunters. 1857, 1905 etc.
Speech on the representation of the people bill, delivered in the House of Commons, March 22nd 1859. 1859.
What will he do with it? by Pisistratus Caxton. 4 vols 1859, 1860. First pbd in Blackwood's Mag.
St Stephen's: a poem. 1860. First pbd in Blackwood's Mag.
The new Reform Bill: speech delivered in the House of Commons, revised and corrected by the author. 1860.
A strange story. 2 vols 1862 (3 edns), 1863 (rev), 1864, 1865, 1875. First pbd in Blackwood's Mag.
Caxtoniana. 2 vols 1863, 1875.
The boatman by Pisistratus Caxton. 1864. First pbd in All the Year Round.
The lost tales of Miletus. 1866, 1870.
The rightful heir. 1868, Leipzig 1869.
The odes and epodes of Horace: a metrical translation into English. 1869, 1872, [1887], 1894.
Walpole: or every man has his price. 1869.
The coming race. 1871 (anon), 1872, 1873, 1874, 1875, 1886.

Kenelm Chillingly: his adventures and opinions. 3 vols 1873, 1874, 1875, [1876], 1878, 1892, 1904 etc.
The Parisians. 4 vols 1873, Edinburgh [1873], 2 vols 1876, 1878, [1890], 1892. First pbd in Blackwood's Mag.
Pamphlets and sketches. 1875.
Quarterly essays. 1875.
Pausanias the Spartan. 1876. An unfinished historical romance ed Lytton's son.
New Monthly Mag 33–48 *was ed Lytton and contains many articles, poems and sketches from his pen.*

§2

Horne, R. H. In his A new spirit of the age vol 2, 1844.
Senior, N. W. In his Essays on fiction, 1864.
Jowett, B. Lord Lytton: the man and the author; to which is attached a biography by M. Marsden. 1873.
Cooper, T. Lord Lytton: a biography. 1873.
'Lytton, Lady'. A blighted life. 1880. Authorship denied by Rosina Bulwer-Lytton.
The life, letters and literary remains, edited by his son. 2 vols 1883.
Letters of the late Edward Bulwer, Lord Lytton, to his wife, published in vindication of her memory. Ed L. Devey 1884.
Escott, T. H. S. Edward Bulwer, first Baron Lytton of Knebworth. 1910.
Frost, W. A. Bulwer Lytton: errors of his biographers. 1913.
Lytton, V. A. G. R. B. The life of Lytton, by his grandson. 2 vols 1913.
—— Bulwer-Lytton. 1948.
Sadleir, M. Bulwer, a panorama: i, Edward and Rosina 1803–36. 1931.
Rosa, M. W. The Silver Fork School: novels of fashion preceding Vanity Fair. New York 1936.

WILLIAM WILKIE COLLINS
1824–89

Bibliographies

Parrish, M. L. Wilkie Collins and Charles Reade. 1940.
Ashley, R. In Victorian fiction, ed L. Stevenson, Cambridge Mass 1964.

§1

Memoirs of the life of William Collins RA; with selections from his journals and correspondence. 2 vols 1848.
Antonina, or the fall of Rome: a romance of the fifth century. 3 vols 1850.
Rambles beyond railways: or notes in Cornwall taken a-foot. 1851, 1961 (adds The cruise of the Tomtit, first pbd in Household Words 1855).
Mr Wray's cash box, or the mask and the mystery: a Christmas sketch. 1852.
Basil: a story of modern life. 3 vols 1852, 1862 (preface and text much rev).
Hide and seek. 3 vols 1854.
After dark. 2 vols 1856. 6 stories.
The dead secret. 2 vols 1857.
The Queen of Hearts. 3 vols 1859. 10 stories.
The woman in white. 3 vols 1860, 1861 (contains correction of all dates in latter part of Marion Halcombe's diary in consequence of criticism in Times); ed H. P. Sucksmith, Oxford 1975. First pbd in All the Year Round from 26 Nov 1859.
A message from the sea: a drama in three acts. 1861. With Dickens.
No name. 3 vols 1862. First pbd in All the Year Round from 15 March 1862.
No name: a drama in five acts. 1863. *See below.*
My miscellanies. 2 vols 1863. Various articles and sketches, all first pbd in Household Words.

Armadale. 2 vols 1866. First pbd in Cornhill Mag and
 Harper's Mag 1864–5.
Armadale: a drama in three acts. 1866.
The frozen deep: a drama in three acts. 1866 (ptd, never
 pbd).
No thoroughfare: a drama in five acts. 1867. With
 Dickens. Also issued 1867 with a different text from
 Act iv scene 3 to end.
The moonstone: a romance. 3 vols 1868. First pbd in All
 the Year Round from 4 Jan 1868.
Black and white: a love story in three acts. 1869. With
 Charles Fechter.
Man and wife: a novel. 3 vols 1870.
No name: a drama in four acts. 1870. A different text
 from that pbd in 1863, above.
The woman in white: a drama in prologue and four acts.
 1871.
Poor Miss Finch: a novel. 3 vols 1872.
The new Magdalen: a dramatic story in a prologue and
 three acts. 1873.
Miss or Mrs? and other stories in outline. 1873.
The frozen deep and other stories: readings and writings
 in America. 2 vols 1874.
The law and the lady: a novel. 3 vols 1875.
Miss Gwilt: a drama in five acts. 1875 (ptd, never pbd).
The two destinies: a romance. 2 vols 1876.
The moonstone: a dramatic story in three acts. 1877 (priv
 ptd).
The haunted hotel: a mystery of modern Venice, to which
 is added My Lady's money. 2 vols 1879.
A rogue's life: from his birth to his marriage. 1879.
The fallen leaves: first series. 3 vols 1879. Not successful;
 sequel never written.
Considerations on the copyright question addressed to an
 American friend. 1880.
Jezebel's daughter. 3 vols 1880. Book version of play,
 The red vial.
The black robe. 3 vols 1881.
Heart and science: a story of the present time. 3 vols 1883.
I say no. 3 vols 1884.
The evil genius: a domestic story. 3 vols 1886. Ch i also
 pbd separately under same title, Bolton 1885.
The guilty river. 1886 (Arrowsmith's Annual).
Little novels. 3 vols 1887.
The legacy of Cain. 3 vols 1889.
Blind love. 3 vols 1890. Preface by Sir Walter Besant.
 First pbd in Illustr London Mag 1889. By Collins up
 to the end of the 18th weekly pt.
The lazy tour of two idle apprentices; No thoroughfare;
 The perils of certain English prisoners. 1890. With
 Dickens.

§ 2

Forster, J. In his Life of Charles Dickens, 3 vols 1872–4.
Dickens, C. In his Letters, ed G. Hogarth and M. Dickens
 3 vols 1880–2; Pilgrim edition, ed M. House and G.
 Storey, Oxford 1965– .
—— Letters to Wilkie Collins 1851–70. Ed G. Hogarth
 1892.
Phillips, W. C. Dickens, Reade and Collins: sensation
 novelists. New York 1919.
Eliot, T. S. Wilkie Collins and Dickens. In his Selected
 essays, 1932.
Booth, B. A. Collins and the art of fiction. Nineteenth-
 Century Fiction 6 1952.
Robinson, K. Wilkie Collins: a biography. 1951.
Davis, N. P. The life of Wilkie Collins. Urbana 1956.
Page, N. (ed). Collins: the critical heritage. 1974.

THOMAS HUGHES
1822–96

§ I

History of the Working Tailor's Association. [1850].
 Tracts on Christian Socialism 11.
A lecture on the shop system, especially as it bears upon
 the females engaged in it, delivered at Reading. 1852.
Tom Brown's school days, by an old boy. Cambridge
 1857 (3 edns); ed V. Rendall 1904; ed F. Sidgwick 1913.
The scouring of the white horse: or the long vacation
 ramble of a London clerk, illustrated by Richard Doyle.
 1859, 1859, 1889 (with The ashen faggot; a tale for
 Christmas) etc.
Tom Brown at Oxford, by the author of Tom Brown's
 schooldays. 3 vols Cambridge 1861, 1864, 1865, 1869.
Tracts for priests and people, no 1: Religio laici. Cam-
 bridge 1861 (4 edns). Afterwards included in Tracts
 for priests and people, ser i.
The struggle for Kansas. Appended to J. M. Ludlow, A
 sketch of the history of the United States, Cambridge
 1862.
The cause of freedom: which is its champion in America,
 the North or the South? [1863].
A layman's faith. 1868.
Alfred the Great. 3 pts 1869, [1871], 1873, 1874, 1877.
Memoir of a brother. 1873, 1873.
The old Church: what shall we do with it? 1878.
The manliness of Christ. 1879, 1880, 1907.
Memoir of Daniel MacMillan. 1882, 1882 (corrected), 1883.
Life and times of Peter Cooper. 1886 (priv ptd).
James Fraser, second Bishop of Manchester: a memoir
 1818–35. 1887, 1888, 1889.
David Livingstone. 1889, 1889.
Co-operative faith and practice: an address. [1890].
Vacation rambles. 1895.
Early memories for the children. 1899 (priv ptd).
Fragments of autobiography. Ed H. C. Shelley, Cornhill
 Mag March–May 1925.
Some letters of Hughes. Economic Rev 24 1914.

§ 2

Selfe, S. Chapters from the history of Rugby School.
 1910.
Mack, E. C. and W. H. G. Armytage. Hughes: the life
 of the author of Tom Brown's school days. 1953.

GERALDINE ENSOR JEWSBURY
1812–80

§ I

Zoe: the history of two lives. 3 vols 1845.
The half-sisters: a tale. 2 vols 1848.
Marian Withers. 3 vols 1851.
The history of an adopted child. 1853.
Constance Herbert. 3 vols 1855.
The sorrows of gentility. 2 vols 1856.
Angelo: or the pine forest in the Alps. 1856.
A selection from the letters of Geraldine Jewsbury to Jane
 Welsh Carlyle. Ed Mrs A. Ireland 1892.

§ 2

[Woolf, V.] Geraldine and Jane. TLS 28 Feb 1929.
Howe, S. Geraldine Jewsbury: her life and errors. 1935.

CHARLES KINGSLEY
1819-75

Bibliographies

Barry, J. D. In Victorian fiction: a guide to research, ed L. Stevenson, Cambridge Mass 1964.

§1

The saint's tragedy. 1848, 1859, 1861.

On English composition; On English literature. In Introductory lectures delivered at Queen's College London, 1849.

Twenty-five village sermons. 1849, 1857, 1861 (with other sermons, as Town and country sermons).

Alton Locke, tailor and poet: an autobiography. 2 vols 1850 (anon), 1852, 1856 (with preface addressed to the working men of Great Britain), 1862 (with a new preface To the undergraduates of Cambridge), 1875, 1876 (with a prefatory memoir by Thomas Hughes).

Cheap clothes and nasty, by Parson Lot. 1850, 1851.

The application of associative principles and methods to agriculture: a lecture. 1851.

Yeast: a problem. 1851 (anon), 1859 (4th edn, with a new preface), 1867, 1875. First pbd Fraser's Mag July–Dec 1848.

Who are the friends of order? 1852.

Phaethon: or loose thoughts for loose thinkers. Cambridge 1852, 1854, 1859.

Sermons on national subjects. 1852, 1872 (as The King of the Earth, and other sermons preached in a village church), 1873.

Hypatia: or new foes with an old face. 2 vols 1853, 1 vol 1856, 1863, 1874. First pbd in Fraser's Mag Jan 1852–April 1853.

Alexandria and her schools. Cambridge 1854.

Sermons on national subjects: second series. 1854, 2 vols 1872, 1880.

Who causes pestilence? 1854.

Glaucus: or the wonders of the shore. Cambridge 1855, 1856 (3rd edn, corrected and enlarged), 1859 (enlarged). First pbd in North Br Rev Nov 1854.

Sermons for the times. 1855, 1858, 1872, 1878.

Sermons for sailors. [1855], 1885 (as Sea sermons).

The country parish: a lecture. In Lectures to ladies on practical subjects, Cambridge 1855, 1857.

Westward Ho! or the voyages and adventures of Sir Amyas Leigh, Knight. 3 vols Cambridge 1855, 1855, 1861, 1865, 1869, 1873; ed L. A. G. Strong 1953; ed J. A. Williamson 1955.

The heroes: or Greek fairy tales for my children, with 8 illustrations by the author. Cambridge 1856.

Two years ago: a novel. 3 vols Cambridge 1857.

Andromeda and other poems. 1858, 1862.

Miscellanies reprinted chiefly from Fraser's Magazine and the North British Review. 2 vols 1859.

The good news of God: sermons. 1859.

The limits of exact science as applied to history: inaugural lecture. Cambridge 1860.

The Gospel of the Pentateuch: a set of parish sermons. 1863, 1864, 1872, 1878, 1881.

The water-babies: a fairy tale for a land-baby. 1863, 1869, 1871, 1872.

Hints to stammerers, by a minute philosopher. 1864. Also issued as The irrationale of speech.

The Roman and the Teuton: a series of lectures delivered before the University of Cambridge. Cambridge 1864; ed F. M. Müller 1875, 1879.

Mr Kingsley and Dr Newman: a correspondence on the question whether Dr Newman teaches that truth is no virtue. 1864.

'What, then, does Dr Newman mean?': a reply to a pamphlet lately published by Dr Newman. 1864; ed W. Ward, Oxford 1913 (with Newman's Apologia).

David: four sermons delivered before the University of Cambridge. 1865, 1874 (5 sermons).

American notes: letters from a lecture tour 1874. Ed R. B. Martin, Princeton 1958.

Hereward the Wake: 'last of the English'. 2 vols 1866, 1867; ed L. A. G. Strong 1954. First pbd in Good Words Jan–Dec 1865.

Three lectures delivered at the Royal Institution on the Ancien Régime before the French Revolution. 1867.

The water of life and other sermons. 1868, 1872, 1881.

Discipline and other sermons. 1868, 1872, 1881.

The hermits. 3 pts [1868], 1 vol 1878, 1880.

Madam How and Lady Why: or first lessons in earth-lore for children. 1870, 1872. First pbd in Good Words for the Young Nov 1868–Oct 1869.

At last: a Christmas in the West Indies, with illustrations. 2 vols 1871, 1872, 1880, 1889, 1910.

Poems: collected edition. 1872, 1878 (enlarged), 1879, 1880 (enlarged as vol i of Works), 2 vols 1884 (enlarged).

Town geology. 1872, 1879.

Plays and Puritans, and other historical essays. 1873, 1880.

Prose idylls, new and old. 1873, 1880, 1889.

Westminster sermons. 1874, 1877.

Health and education. 1874.

Lectures delivered in America in 1874. 1875.

Letters to young men on betting and gambling. 1877.

True words for brave men. 1878, 1879, 1914.

All Saints Day and other sermons. Ed W. Harrison 1878.

Historical lectures and essays. 1880 (Works vol 17), 1889.

Sanitary and social lectures and essays. 1880 (Works vol 17), 1889.

Literary and general lectures and essays. 1880 (Works vol 20).

Scientific lectures and essays. 1885 (Works vol 19).

From death to life: fragments of teaching to a village congregation, with letters on the life after death, edited by his wife. 1887.

Words of advice to schoolboys, collected from hitherto unpublished notes and letters. Ed E. F. Johns 1912.

The tutor's story, by the late Charles Kingsley, revised and completed by his daughter 'Lucas Malet'. 1916, 1920. This story, of which c. 150 foolscap pages were left in ms by Kingsley, seems to have been written about 1863.

American notes: letters from a lecture tour 1874. Ed R. B. Martin, Princeton 1958.

§2

James, H. Life and letters of Charles Kingsley. Nation (New York) 24 1876.

Charles Kingsley: his letters and memories of his life, edited by his wife. 2 vols 1877 etc. Rptd as vols 1–4 of Life and works, 1901–2. Abridged 2 vols 1879 (for 1878).

Stephen, L. In his Hours in a library ser 3, 1879.

Marriott, J. A. R. Charles Kingsley, novelist. 1892.

Baldwin, S. E. Charles Kingsley. Ithaca 1934.

Thorp, M. F. Charles Kingsley. Princeton 1937.

Kendall, G. Kingsley and his ideas. 1947.

Pope-Hennessy, U. Canon Charles Kingsley. 1948.

Martin, R. B. The dust of combat: a life of Charles Kingsley. 1960.

HENRY KINGSLEY
1830-76

The recollections of Geoffrey Hamlyn. 3 vols 1859, 1860, 1872, 1885, [1891] (with memoir by C. K. Shorter), 1909 etc, Oxford 1924 (WC).

Ravenshoe. 3 vols 1861, 1862, 1864, 1872, 1875, Oxford 1925 (WC).

Austin Elliott. 2 vols 1863 (3 edns), 1866, 1872, Oxford 1932 (WC).

The Hillyars and the Burtons: a story of two families. 3 vols 1865, 1866.
Leighton Court: a country house story. 2 vols 1866, 1867.
Silcote of Silcotes. 3 vols 1867, 1869.
Mademoiselle Mathilde. 3 vols 1868, 1870, 1885. First pbd in GM.
Stretton. 3 vols 1869, 1870, 1879, 1885.
Tales of old travel re-narrated. 1869, 1871.
The boy in grey and other stories and sketches. 1871.
Hetty and other stories. 1871, 1885.
The lost child. 1871.
Old Margaret and other stories. 2 vols 1871, 1872.
Valentin: a French boy's story of Sedan. 2 vols 1872, [1874] (rev), 1885.
Hornby Mills and other stories. 2 vols 1872, 1873, 1885.
Oakshott Castle, by Mr Granby Dixon, edited by Henry Kingsley. 3 vols 1873, 1878. 'Granby Dixon' was Kingley's pseudonym.
Reginald Hetherege. 3 vols 1874, 1875.
Number seventeen. 2 vols 1875, 1876, 1879.
Fireside studies. 2 vols 1876.
The Grange garden: a romance. 3 vols 1876.
The mystery of the island. 1877.

JOSEPH SHERIDAN LE FANU
1814–73
§ 1

The cook and anchor: being a chronicle of old Dublin city. 3 vols Dublin 1845 (anon), 1873 (as Morley Court); ed B. S. Le Fanu [1895].
The fortunes of Colonel Torlogh O'Brien. Dublin 1847 (anon), 1855, nd, 1896.
Ghost stories and tales of mystery. Dublin 1851.
The house by the church-yard. 3 vols 1863, 1866.
Wylder's hand: a novel. 3 vols 1864, [1870], [1903].
Uncle Silas: a tale of Bartram-Haugh. 3 vols 1864, 1865, 1 vol 1865; ed E. Bowen 1946.
Guy Deverell. 3 vols 1865, 1 vol 1866, [1869].
All in the dark. 2 vols 1866, [1869].
The tenants of Malory: a novel. 3 vols 1867, [1872].
A lost name. 3 vols 1868.
Haunted lives: a novel. 3 vols 1868.
The Wyvern mystery: a novel. 3 vols 1869, 1889, [1904].
Checkmate. 3 vols 1871.
The rose and the key. 3 vols 1871.
Chronicles of Golden Friars. 3 vols 1871.
In a glass darkly. 3 vols 1872, 1884, 1923, 1929.
Willing to die. 3 vols 1873, [1895?].
The Purcell papers, with a memoir by Alfred Perceval Graves. 3 vols 1880.
The watcher and other weird stories. [1894].
The evil guest. [1895].
Poems. Ed A. P. Graves 1896.
Madam Crowl's ghost and other tales of mystery. Ed M. R. James 1923.
Le Fanu joined the staff of the Dublin Univ Mag in 1837 and many of his tales and novels were originally pbd there. He was editor and proprietor 1869–72.

§ 2

Ellis, S. M. Wilkie Collins, Le Fanu and others. 1931.
Pritchett, V. S. An Irish ghost. In his Living novel, 1946.
Browne, N. Sheridan Le Fanu. 1951.

CHARLES JAMES LEVER
1806–72
Collections

The military novels, illustrated by George Cruikshank and 'Phiz'. 9 vols nd.

Works. 34 vols 1876–8. Harry Lorrequer edn.
Novels, edited by his daughter [Julia Kate Neville]. 37 vols 1897–9.

§ 1

The confessions of Harry Lorrequer. Dublin 1839, 1845, 1882, 1884; ed 'Lewis Melville' (L. S. Benjamin) [1907] (EL).
Diary and notes of Horace Templeton, late Secretary of Legation. Philadelphia [1840?], 2 vols 1848, [1878].
Charles O'Malley, the Irish dragoon, edited by Harry Lorrequer. 2 vols Dublin 1841, London 1842, 1845.
Our Mess. 3 vols Dublin 1843–4, 1857, 1876, 1885.
Arthur O'Leary: his wanderings and ponderings in many lands. 3 vols 1844, 1845, 1 vol 1856 (as Adventures of Arthur O'Leary), 1877, 1886.
St Patrick's Eve. 1845, 1871 (with A rent in the cloud etc).
Nuts and nutcrackers. 1845.
Tales of the trains. 1845.
The O'Donoghue: a tale of Ireland fifty years ago. Dublin 1845, 1858, 1868, 1876.
The Knight of Gwynne: a tale of the time of the Union. 1847, 1858, 1867, 1877, 1889.
The Martins of Gro' Martin. 1847, 1856, 1856, 1878.
Confessions of Con Cregan, the Irish Gil Blas. 2 vols [1849], 1854, 1876, 1891.
Roland Cashel. 1850, 1858, 1864.
The Daltons: or three roads in life. 2 vols 1850–2, 1859.
Maurice Tiernay: the soldier of fortune. 1852, [1855], 2 vols 1861, 1878.
The Dodd family abroad. 2 vols 1852–4, 1859, 1877.
Sir Jasper Carew: his life and experiences. [1855], 1878.
The fortunes of Glencore. 3 vols 1857, 1878.
Davenport Dunn: or the man of the day. 1859.
One of them. 1861, 1877.
A day's ride. 2 vols 1863, 1878.
Barrington. 1863, 2 vols Leipzig 1863, 1 vol 1878.
Cornelius O'Dowd upon men, women and other things in general. 3 sers 1864–5, 1 vol 1874. First pbd in Blackwood's Mag.
Luttrell of Arran. 1865, 1877.
A rent in a cloud. [1865], 1878 (with St Patrick's Eve etc).
Tony Butler. 3 vols Edinburgh 1865, 1878.
Sir Brook Fossbrooke. 3 vols 1866, 1867, 1878.
The Bramleighs of Bishop's Folly. 3 vols 1868, 1877.
Paul Gosslett's confessions in law and the Civil Service. 1868, 1924. First pbd in Saint Paul's Mag.
That boy of Norcott's. 1869, 1878 (with A rent in a cloud, above, etc).
Lord Kilgobbin: a tale of Ireland in our own time. 3 vols 1872, 1877, 1906.
Gerald Fitzgerald the Chevalier. 1899. First pbd in Dublin Univ Mag; rptd 27 years after Lever's death.
Lever edited Dublin Univ Mag 1835–72 and from 1835 was also a regular contributer to Blackwood's Mag.

§ 2

Fitzpatrick, W. J. Life of Lever. 2 vols 1879.
Downey, E. Lever: life in his letters. 2 vols 1906.
Stevenson, L. Dr Quicksilver. 1939.

GEORGE MacDONALD
1824–1905
Collections

Works of fancy and imagination. 10 vols 1871.
MacDonald: an anthology. Ed C. S. Lewis 1946.

§ 1

Within and without: a poem. 1855.
Poems. 1857.

Phantastes: a faerie romance for men and women. 1858.
David Elginbrod. 3 vols 1863.
Adela Cathcart. 3 vols 1864.
The portent: a story of the inner vision of the Highlanders commonly called the second sight. 1864.
Alec Forbes of Howglen. 3 vols 1865.
Annals of a quiet neighbourhood. 3 vols 1867.
Dealings with the fairies. 1867.
The disciple and other poems. 1867.
Unspoken sermons. 3 sers 1867–89.
Guild Court. 3 vols 1868.
Robert Falconer. 3 vols 1868.
The seaboard parish. 3 vols 1868.
The miracles of Our Lord. 1870.
At the back of the north wind. 1871 (for 1870).
Ranald Bannerman's boyhood. 1871.
The Princess and the goblin. 1872 (for 1871).
The Vicar's daughter. 3 vols 1872.
Wilfred Cumbermede. 3 vols 1872.
Gutta Percha Willie: the working genius. 1873.
England's Antiphon. 1874.
Malcolm. 3 vols 1875.
The wise woman: a parable. 1875, 1895 (as The lost Princess: or the wise woman); ed E. Yates 1965.
Thomas Wingfold, curate. 3 vols 1876.
St George and St Michael. 3 vols 1876.
The Marquis of Lossie. 3 vols 1877.
Sir Gibbie. 3 vols 1879.
Paul Faber, surgeon. 3 vols 1879.
A book of strife, in the form of the diary of an old soul. 1880, 1909, 1913.
Mary Marston. 3 vols 1881.
Castle Warlock: a homely romance. 3 vols 1882.
Orts. 1882, 1893 (enlarged as A dish of orts).
Weighed and wanting. 3 vols 1882.
The gifts of the child Christ and other tales. 2 vols 1882. Later pbd as Stephen Archer and other tales, nd.
Donal Grant. 3 vols 1883.
The Princess and Curdie. 1883 (for 1882).
What's mine's mine. 3 vols 1886.
Home again: a tale. 1887.
The elect lady. 1888.
A rough shaking: a tale. 1890.
The light Princess and other fairy stories. 1890.
There and back. 3 vols 1891.
The flight of the shadow. 1891.
The hope of the Gospel. 1892.
Heather and snow. 2 vols 1893.
Poetical works. 2 vols 1893.
Lilith: a romance. 1895.
Rampolli: growths from a long-planted root, being translations chiefly from the German, along with a year's diary of an old soul. 1897. Poems.
Salted with fire: a tale. 1897.

§2

Johnson, J. MacDonald: a biography and critical appreciation. 1906.
MacDonald, G. MacDonald and his wife, with an introduction by G. K. Chesterton. 1924.
Fremantle, A. The visionary novels of MacDonald. New York 1954.
Wolff, R. L. The golden key: a study of the fiction of MacDonald. New Haven 1961.

HARRIET MARTINEAU
1802–76

Bibliographies

Rivlin, J. B. Harriet Martineau: a bibliography of the separately printed books. BNYPL May–July, Oct 1946–Jan 1947.

§1

Devotional exercises for the use of young persons. 1823, 1832 (enlarged as Devotional exercises, to which is added a guide to the study of the scriptures).
Addresses with prayers and original hymns for the use of families, by a lady. 1826.
Essential faith of the universal Church deduced from the sacred records. 1831.
Five years of youth: or sense and sentiment. 1831.
Illustrations of political economy. 9 vols 1832–4.
The Faith as unfolded by many prophets: an essay addressed to the disciples of Mohammed. 1832.
Providence as manifested through Israel. 1832.
Poor laws and paupers illustrated. 4 pts 1833–4.
Illustrations of taxation. 1834.
Miscellanies. 2 vols [Boston] 1836.
Society in America. 3 vols 1837.
A retrospect of western travel. 3 vols 1838.
Deerbrook: a novel. 3 vols 1839.
Guides to service. [1839?].
The martyr age of the United States of America. 1840.
The hour and the man: an historical romance. 3 vols 1841.
The playfellow: a series of tales. 4 vols 1841.
The rioters. nd; 1842 (unauthorized). A short story.
Life in the sick-room: or essays by an invalid. 1844.
Dawn Island: a tale. Manchester 1845. Pbd on behalf of the Anti-Corn Law League.
Forest and game-law tales. 3 vols 1845–6.
Letters on Mesmerism. 1845.
The billow and the rock. 1846.
The land we live in. 1847. With Charles Knight.
Eastern life, past and present. 3 vols 1848.
Household education. 1849.
History of England during the Thirty Years' Peace 1816–46. 2 vols 1849–50, 1855 (rev as History of the peace 1816–46), 4 vols [1877–8].
Two letters on cow-keeping. [1850?].
Letters on the laws of man's nature and development. 1851. With H. G. Atkinson.
Introduction to the history of the peace from 1800 to 1815. 1851, 1878.
Half a century of the British Empire: a history of the Kingdom and the people from 1800 to 1850. Pt 1 (all pbd), [1851].
Merdhen, the manor and the eyrie, and old landmarks and old laws. 1852.
Letters from Ireland. 1853.
The positive philosophy of August Comte freely translated and condensed. 2 vols 1853.
Complete guides to the Lakes. 1854.
Guide to Windermere, with tours to the neighbouring lakes and other interesting places. Windermere [1854].
The factory controversy: a warning against meddling legislation. Manchester 1855.
A history of the American compromises. 1856.
Corporate traditions and national rights: local dues on shipping. [1857].
Guide to Keswick and its environs. Windermere [1857].
Suggestions towards the future government of India. 1858.
Endowed schools of Ireland. 1859.
England and her soldiers. 1859.
Survey of the Lake District. 1860.
Health, husbandry and handicraft. 1861.
Biographical sketches. 1869, 1877 (enlarged and with autobiographical sketch).
Harriet Martineau's autobiography, with memorials by Maria Weston Chapman. 3 vols 1877.
The Hampdens: an historiette. 1880 (illustr J. E. Millais).

Harriet Martineau also wrote over 1,600 articles for Daily News 1851–66, as well as contributing to Edinburgh Rev from 1859.

§2

[Lockhart, J. G.] Illustrations of political economy nos 1–12. Quart Rev 49 1833. An attack.
Horne, R. H. In his A new spirit of the age vol 2, 1844.
Wheatley, V. The life and work of Harriet Martineau. 1957.
Webb, R. K. Harriet Martineau: a radical Victorian. 1960.

AUGUSTUS SEPTIMUS MAYHEW
1826–75

The greatest plague of life: adventures of a lady in search of a good servant, illustrated by George Cruikshank. [1847]. With his brother Henry Mayhew.
The good genius that turned everything into gold, or the Queen Bee and the magic dress: a Christmas fairytale. 1847. With Henry Mayhew.
Whom to marry and how to get married, illustrated by George Cruikshank. [1848]. With Henry Mayhew.
The image of his father: or one boy is more trouble than a dozen girls, illustrated by 'Phiz'. 1848. With Henry Mayhew.
The magic of kindness: or the wondrous story of the good Huan, illustrated by George Cruikshank and Kenny Meadows. [1849], [1869] (illust Walter Crane). With Henry Mayhew.
Living for appearances: a tale. 1855. With Henry Mayhew.
Kitty Lamere or a dark page in London life: a tale. 1855.
Paved with gold, or the romance and reality of London streets: an unfashionable novel, illustrated by H. K. Browne. 1858.
The finest girl in Bloomsbury: a serio-comic tale of ambitious love. 1861.
Blow hot—blow cold: a love story. 1862.
Faces for fortunes. 3 vols 1865.
The comic almanack. 1870 etc. With Henry Mayhew.

DINAH MARIA MULOCK,
later CRAIK
1826–87

The Ogilvies: a novel. 3 vols 1849, 1875.
Cola Monti: or the story of a genius. [1849], [1866] (rev).
Olive. 3 vols 1850.
The head of the family. 3 vols 1851.
Alice Learmont: a fairy tale. 1852, 1884 (rev).
Bread upon the waters: a governess's life. 1852.
Avillion and other tales. 3 vols 1853.
Agatha's husband: a novel. 3 vols 1853.
A hero: Philip's book. 1853.
John Halifax, gentleman. 3 vols 1856.
Nothing new: tales. 1857.
A woman's thoughts about women. 1858.
A life for a life. 3 vols 1859.
Poems. [1859].
Romantic tales. 1859.
Domestic stories. [1859?].
Our year: a child's book. 1860.
Studies from life. 1861.
Mistress and maid. 2 vols 1863.
The fairy book. 1863.
Christian's mistake. 1865.
A New Year's gift for sick children. 1865.
Home thoughts and home scenes. 1865.
A noble life. 2 vols 1866.
How to win love, or Rhoda's lesson: a story for the young. [1866?].
Two marriages. 2 vols 1867.
The woman's kingdom. 3 vols 1869.
A brave lady. 3 vols 1870.

The unkind word and other stories. 2 vols 1870.
Fair France: impressions of a traveller. 1871.
Little Sunshine's holiday. 1871.
Hannah. 2 vols 1872.
Is it true? tales curious and wonderful. 1872.
The adventures of a Brownie. 1872.
My mother and I. 1874.
Sermons out of church. 1875.
The little lame Prince. 1875.
Will Denbigh, nobleman. 1877.
The laurel bush. 1877.
Young Mrs Jardine. 3 vols 1879.
Children's poetry. 1881.
His little mother and other tales. 1881.
Thirty years: poems new and old. 1881, 1888 (as Poems by the author of John Halifax, gentleman).
Plain speaking. 1882.
An unsentimental journey through Cornwall. 1884.
Miss Tommy. 1884.
About money and other things. 1886.
King Arthur—not a love story. 1886.
Work for the idle hands [in Ireland]. 1886.
An unknown country. 1887.
Fifty golden years: incidents in the Queen's reign. [1887].
Concerning men and other papers. 1888.

THOMAS MAYNE REID
1818–83
§1

The Rifle Rangers: or adventures of an officer in southern Mexico. 2 vols 1850, 1853, [1857], [1871], 1891 etc.
The scalp hunters: or romantic adventures in northern Mexico. 3 vols 1851, 1852, [1886], 1892 etc.
English Family Robinson. 1851.
The desert home: or the adventures of a lost family in the wilderness. 1852, [1884].
The boy hunters: or adventures in search of a white buffalo. 1852, [1884], [1892].
The young voyagers: or the boy hunters in the north. [1853], [1884], Paris [1877].
The forest exiles: or the perils of a Peruvian family amid the wilds of the Amazon. [1854].
The white chief: a legend of northern Mexico. 3 vols 1855, [1871].
The hunter's feast: or conversations around the camp fire. [1855], [1860], [1871].
The quadroon: or a lover's adventures in Louisiana. 3 vols 1856, Paris 1858.
The bush boys: or the adventures of a Cape farmer and his family in the wild karoos of southern Africa. 1856.
The young jägers: or a narrative of hunting adventures in southern Africa. 1857, 1884, Paris 1859.
The plant hunters: or adventures among the Himalaya mountains. 1857, Paris 1859, [1884], [1892].
The war trail: or the hunt of the wild horse. 1857.
Ran away to sea. 1858, 1884.
Oceola the Seminole. New York 1858, 3 vols 1859.
The boy tar: or a voyage in the dark. 1859.
Bruin: or the great bear hunt. 1860, Paris 1863, [1884].
Odd people: being a popular description of singular races of men. 1860, Paris 1862, [1884].
Quadrupeds, what they are, and where found: a book of zoology for boys. [1860], 1867.
The wild huntress. 3 vols 1861, 1865, 1871, Paris [1875], [1890].
The maroon: a novel. 3 vols 1862, [1864], Paris [1874], [1891].
Croquet. 1863, 1865, 1866, New York 1869.
The tiger hunter. 1863.
Garibaldi rebuked by one of his best friends: being a letter addressed to him by Captain Mayne Reid. 1864.

The cliff climbers: or the lone home in the Himalayas. [1864], Paris 1865, [1872], [1888].

Ocean waifs. 1864, [1871].

The white gauntlet: a romance. 3 vols [1864], [1865].

Lost Lenore. 3 vols 1864, 1865, [1872], [1888], [1908]. Pbd under the pseudonym 'Charles Beach'.

The boy slaves. [1865], Paris [1869], London [1872].

The headless horseman: a strange tale of Texas. 2 vols 1866, [1868], [1874], [1888].

Afloat in the forest. 1866, [1868].

The bandolero: or a marriage among the mountains. 1866, [1867] (as The mountain marriage: or the Bandolero).

The guerilla chief and other tales. 1867, [1871], [1891].

The giraffe hunters. 3 vols 1867, [1868], Paris [1869].

The child wife: a tale of the two worlds. 3 vols 1868, 1888.

The fatal cord: a tale of backwood retribution. [1869], [1872] (with The falcon rover).

The yellow chief: a romance of the Rocky Mountains. [1870].

The castaways: a story of adventure in the wilds of Borneo. 1870, Paris [1872].

The white squaw and the yellow chief. 2 pts [1871].

The lone ranche: a tale of the Staked Plain. 2 vols 1871.

A zigzag journey through Mexico. [1872].

The finger of fate: a romance. 2 vols 1872, Paris 1873.

The death shot: a romance of forest and prairie. 3 vols 1873, 1884.

Gaspar the gaucho: a tale of the Gran Chaco. Paris [1874].

The half blood. 1875.

The flag of distress: a story of the South Sea. 3 vols 1876.

Gwen Wynn: a romance of the Wye. 3 vols 1877, 1889.

The Queen of the lakes: a romance of the Mexican valley. 1879.

The free lances: a romance of the Mexican valley. 3 vols 1881, [1888].

The chase of Leviathan: or adventures in the ocean. Paris 1882, 1885.

Love's martyr: a tragedy. Perth [1884].

The lost mountain: a tale of Sonora. Paris [1883], 1884.

The land of fire: a tale of adventure. [1884], Paris 1885.

The Vee Boers: a tale of adventure in Southern Africa. Paris [1884], London [1885], [1907].

The pierced heart and other stories. [1885].

The Star of Empire: a romance. 1886, [1888].

No quarter. 3 vols 1888.

The naturalist in Siluria. 1889.

A dashing dragoon: the Murat of the American army (Philip Kearny). New York 1913.

§ 2

Reid, E. Mayne Reid: a memoir of his life. 1890.
—— Captain Mayne Reid: his life and adventures. 1900.

GEORGE AUGUSTUS HENRY SALA
1828–96

The Great Exhibition. 1850.

A journey due north: being notes of a residence in Russia in the summer of 1856. 1858.

Grand national, historical and chivalric pantomime, ye belle alliance: or harlequin good humour and ye Field of ye Clothe of Golde. [1856]. Verse.

How I tamed Mrs Cruiser, by Benedict Cruiser, illustrated by 'Phiz'. 1858.

Gaslight and daylight; with some London scenes they shine upon. 1859.

Twice round the clock: or the hours of the day and night in London. [1859].

Lady Chesterfield's letters to her daughter. 1860.

Looking at life: or thoughts and things. 1860.

Make your game, or the adventures of the stout gentleman, the slim gentleman and the man with the iron chest: a narrative of the Rhine and thereabouts. 1860.

The Baddington peerage, who won and who wore it: a story of the best and worst society, illustrated by 'Phiz'. 3 vols 1860.

Dutch pictures, with some sketches in the Flemish manner. 1861, 1883 (with Pictures done with a quill).

Accepted addresses. 1862.

The seven sons of Mammon. 3 vols 1862.

The ship chandler and other tales. 1862.

The two prima donnas; the dumb door porter. 1862.

Breakfast in bed, or philosophy between the sheets: a series of indigestible discourses. 1863.

The perfidy of Captain Slyboots and other tales. 1863.

The strange adventures of Captain Dangerous. 3 vols 1863.

After breakfast: or pictures done with a quill. 2 vols 1864.

Quite alone. 3 vols 1864.

Robson [the actor]: a sketch. 1864.

My diary in America in the midst of war. 2 vols 1865.

A trip to Barbary by a roundabout route. 1866.

William Hogarth: essays on the man, the work and the time. 1866.

From Waterloo to the Peninsula: four months' hard labour in Belgium, Holland, Germany, Spain. 2 vols 1867.

Banter. 1868.

The complete correspondence and works of Charles Lamb, with an essay on his life and genius by Sala. Vol 1 (all pbd), 1868.

The battle of the safes: or British invincibles versus Yankee ironclads. 1868.

Notes and sketches of the Paris Exhibition. 1868.

Rome and Venice. 1869.

Wat Tyler MP. 1869. An 'operatic extravaganza'.

Charles Dickens: an essay. [1870].

The late MD—and other tales. [1870].

Papers humorous and pathetic: being selections from the works of Sala, revised and abridged by the author for public reading. 1872.

Under the sun: essays mainly written in hot countries. 1872.

The story of the Count de Chambord: a trilogy. 1873.

India and the Prince of Wales. [1875].

Paris herself again in 1878–9. 2 vols 1879.

The hats of humanity historically, humorously and aesthetically considered. [1880].

America revisited. 2 vols 1882.

Living London: echoes re-echoed. 1883.

Stories with a vengeance. [1883]. With others.

Dead men tell no tales, but live men do: nine stories. [1884].

Echoes of the year 1883. [1884].

A journey due south. 1885.

Mrs General Mucklestrap's four tall daughters. [1887].

Right round the world. [1887].

Dublin Whiskey: an essay. [1888].

Not a friend in the world and other stories. [1890].

London up to date. 1894.

Things I have seen and people I have known. 2 vols 1894.

Brighton as I have known it. 1895.

The life and adventures of Sala. 2 vols 1895.

The thorough good cook: a series of chats on the culinary art and nine hundred recipes. [1895].

Margaret Foster: a dream within a dream. 1897.

Paris herself again. Ed P. H. P. Perry 1948.

Sala also edited Temple Bar 1860–6.

ROBERT SMITH SURTEES
1803–64

The horseman's manual: being a treatise on soundness, the law of warranty and generally on the laws relating to horses. 1831.

Jorrocks' jaunts and jollities: or the hunting, racing, driving, sailing, eating, eccentric and extravagant exploits of that renowned sporting citizen, Mr John Jorrocks of St Botolph Lane and Great Coram Street; with illustrations by Phiz. 1838, 1839, 1843, 1869 (rev and enlarged; illustr Henry Alken).

Handley Cross, or the spa hunt: a sporting tale. 3 vols 1843 (no illustrations), 17 monthly pts March 1853–Oct 1854; expanded as Handley Cross: or Mr Jorrocks's hunt; illustr John Leech 1854, 1888 (new illustrations).

Hillingdon Hall, or the cockney squire: a tale of country life. 3 vols 1845, 1888 (with coloured illustrations) etc.

The analysis of the hunting field: being a series of sketches of the principal characters that compose one; the whole forming a slight souvenir of the season 1845–6. 1845 (anon; illustr Henry Alken), 1869 etc.

Hawbuck Grange: or the sporting adventures of Thomas Scott esq. 1847 (illustr 'Phiz'), [1888], 1891, 1892 etc.

Mr Sponge's sporting tour. 13 monthly pts 1853 (illustr John Leech), 1853, [1888], 1892, 1893 (as Soapey Sponge's sporting tour) etc.

Ask Mamma: or the richest commoner in England. 13 monthly pts 1858 (illustr John Leech), 1858.

Plain or ringlets? 13 monthly pts 1860 (illustr John Leech), 1860.

Mr Romford's hounds. 12 monthly pts 1865 (illustr John Leech and 'Phiz'), 1865 (as Mr Facey Romford's hounds).

Surtees also helped to found New Sporting Magazine, which he edited 1831–6.

CHARLOTTE MARY YONGE
1823–1901

Bibliographies

Laski, M. and K. Tillotson. In A chaplet for Charlotte Yonge, ed G. Battiscombe and M. Laski 1965.

Collections

Novels and tales: new edition. 40 vols 1879–99.

§ 1

Le Château de Melville: ou recréations du cabinet d'étude. 1839.

Abbeychurch: or self-control and self-conceit. 1844. 1872.

Scenes and characters: or eighteen months at Beechcroft. 1847.

Kings of England: a history for young children. 1848.

Harriet and her sister. [1848?].

Henrietta's wish: or domineering a tale. 1850.

Kenneth: or the rearguard of the Grand Army. 1850.

Langley School. 1850.

Landmarks of history. 3 vols 1852–7.

The two guardians: or home in this world. 1852, 1861.

The heir of Redclyffe. 2 vols 1853, 1854, 1868 (17th edn); ed A. Meynell 1909 (EL); ed C. Haldane 1965.

The herb of the field. 1853, 1887.

The castle builders: or the deferred confirmation. 1854.

Heartsease: or the brother's wife. 1854, 1862.

The little Duke: or Richard the fearless. 1854, 1857, 1891; ed E. Mason 1910 (EL).

The history of the life and death of the good Knight Sir Thomas Thumb. 1855, 1859.

The Lances of Lynwood. 1855, 1857, 1894 (abridged); ed L. M. Crump 1911 (EL).

The railroad children. 1855.

Ben Sylvester's word. 1856.

The daisy chain. 2 vols 1856, 1868 (9th edn) etc.

Leonard the Lionheart. 1856.

Dynevor Terrace. 2 vols 1857, 1858, 1860.

The instructive picture book: lessons from the vegetable world. 1857.

The Christmas mummers. 1858.

Friarswood post office. 1860.

Hopes and fears: or scenes from the life of a spinster. 2 vols 1860, 1861.

The mice at play. 1860.

The strayed falcon. 1860.

The pigeon pie. 1860, 1861.

The Stokesley secret. 1861, 1862, 1892 (with Countess Kate).

The young stepmother: or a chronicle of mistakes. 1861.

Biographies of good women. 2 sers 1862–5.

The Chosen People: a compendium of sacred and Church history for school children. 1862.

Countess Kate. 1862.

The sea spleenwort and other stories. 1862.

A history of Christian names. 2 vols 1863, 1884.

The apple of discord: a play. 1864.

A book of golden deeds of all times and all lands. 1864.

Historical dramas. 1864.

The trial: more links of the daisy chain 1864, 1868 (4th edn), 2 vols 1870.

The Wars of Wapsburgh. 1864.

The clever woman of the family. 2 vols 1865, 1867.

The dove in the eagle's nest. 2 vols 1866, 1 vol 1870; ed E. Hall 1908 (EL).

The Prince and the page: a story of the last Crusade. 1865.

The Danvers papers: an invention. 1867.

The six cushions. 1867.

Cameos from English history. 9 vols 1868–99.

The chaplet of pearls: or the white and black Ribaumont. 1868.

New ground: Kaffirland. 1868.

The pupils of St John the Divine. 1868.

A book of worthies, gathered from the old histories and now written out anew. 1869.

Keynotes of the first lessons for every day in the year. 1869.

The seal: or the inward spiritual grace of confirmation. 1869.

The caged lion. 1870.

A storehouse of stories. 2 sers 1870–2. Ed C. M. Yonge.

Little Lucy's wonderful globe. 1871.

Musings over the Christian year and Lyra innocentium, together with a few gleanings of recollections of the Rev J. Keble, gathered by several friends. 1871.

A parallel history of France and England, consisting of outlines and dates. 1871.

Pioneers and founders: or recent works in the mission field. 1871.

Scripture readings for schools, with comments. 5 vols 1871–9.

P's and Q's: or the question of putting upon. 1872.

Questions on the Prayer-book. 1872.

Life of John Coleridge Patterson, missionary Bishop to the Melanesian Islands. 2 vols 1873, 1878 (6th edn).

The pillars of the house: under wode, under rode. 4 vols 1873, 2 vols 1875.

Lady Hester: or Ursula's narrative. 1874.

My young Alcides: a faded photograph. 1875.

Eighteen centuries of beginnings of Church history. 1876.

The three brides. 1876.

Womankind. 1877.

The disturbing element: or chronicles of the Bluebell Society. 1878.

The story of the Christians and Moors of Spain. 1878.

Burnt out: a story for mothers' meetings. 1879, 1880.

Magnum bonum: or Mother Carey's brood. 1879.

Bye-words: a collection of tales new and old. 1880.

Love and life: an old story in eighteenth-century costume. 1880.

Verses on the gospel for Sundays and holy days. 1880.

Aunt Charlotte's evenings at home with the poets. 1881.

Frank's debt. 1881, 1882.

How to teach the New Testament. 1881.

Lads and lasses of Langley. 1881. 5 stories.

Practical work in Sunday schools. 1881.

Questions on the Psalms. 1881.
Wolf. 1881.
Given to hospitality. 1882.
Historical ballads. 2 pts 1882–3.
Langley little ones: six stories. 1882.
Pickle and his page boy, or unlooked for: a story. 1882.
Sowing and sewing: a Sexagesima story. 1882.
Talks about the laws we live under: or at Langley night-school. 1882.
Unknown to history: a story of the captivity of Mary of Scotland. 2 vols 1882, 1884.
Aunt Charlotte's stories of American history. 1883. With J. H. Hastings Weld.
English Church history, adapted for use in day and Sunday schools. 1883.
Landmarks of recent history 1770–1883. 1883.
Langley adventures. 1884.
The miz maze, or the Winkworth puzzle: a story in letters by nine authors. 1883.
Stray pearls: memoirs of Margaret de Ribaumont, Viscountess of Bellaise. 1883.
The armourer's 'prentices. 1884.
Higher reading-book for schools, colleges and general use. 1885.
Nuttie's father. 1885.
Pixie lawn. In Please tell me a tale: short original stories for children, 1885.
The two sides of the shield. 1885.
Astray: a tale of a country town. 1886.
Chantry house. 2 vols 1886, 1887.
Just one tale more. 1886. With others.
The little rick-burners. 1886.
A modern Telemachus. 1886.
Teachings on the catechism: for the little ones. 1886.
The Victorian half-century: a jubilee book. 1886.
Under the storm: or steadfast's charge. 1887.
What books to lend and what to give. 1887.
Beechcroft at Rockstone. 1888.
Hannah More. 1888.
Nurse's memories. 1888.
Our new mistress: or changes at Brookfield Earl. 1888.
Preparation of prayer-book lessons. 1888.
The cunning woman's grandson: a tale of Cheddar a hundred years ago. 1889.
Neigh-bour's fare. In Stories jolly. 1889.
The parent's power: address to the conference of the Mother's Union. 1889.
A reputed changeling: or three seventh years two centuries ago. 1889.
Life of HRH the Prince Consort. 1890.
More bywords. 1890.
The slaves of Sabinns: Jew and Gentile. 1890.
The constable's tower: or the times of Magna Charta. 1891.
Old times at Otterbourne. 1891.

Simple stories relating to English history. 1891.
Twelve stories from early English history. 1891.
Twenty stories and biographies from 1066 to 1485. 1891.
Two penniless princesses. 1891.
Westminster historical reading books. 2 vols 1891–2.
The cross roads: or a choice in life. 1892.
The Hanoverian period, with biographies of leading persons. 1892.
The Stewart period, with biographies of leading persons. 1892.
That stick. 1892.
The Tudor period, with biographies of leading persons. 1892.
Chimes for the mothers: a reading for each week in the year. 1893.
The girl's little book. 1893.
Grisly Grisell, or the laidly lady of Whitburn: a tale of the Wars of the Roses. 1893.
The strolling players: a harmony of contrasts. 1893. With C. Coleridge.
The treasures in the marches. 1893.
The cook and the captive: or Attalus the hostage. 1894.
The rubies of St Lo. 1894.
The story of Easter. 1894.
The Carbonels. 1895.
The long vacation. 1895.
The release: or Caroline's French kindred. 1896.
The wardship of Steepcombe. 1896.
The pilgrimage of the Ben Beriah. 1897.
Founded on paper: or uphill and downhill between the two jubilees. 1898.
John Keble's parishes: a history of Hursley and Otterbourne. 1898.
The patriots of Palestine: a story of the Maccabees. 1898.
The herd boy and his hermit. 1900.
The making of a missionary: or day dreams in earnest. 1900.
Modern broods: or developments unlooked for. 1900.
Reasons why I am a Catholic, and not a Roman Catholic. 1901.

§2

Coleridge, C. R. Charlotte Mary Yonge: her life and letters. 1903.
Battiscombe, G. Charlotte Mary Yonge: the story of an uneventful life. 1943.
Battiscombe, G. and M. Laski (ed). A chaplet for Charlotte Yonge. 1965.
Mare, M. and A. C. Percival. Victorian best-seller: the world of Charlotte Yonge. 1947.
Tillotson, K. The heir of Redclyffe. In her Mid-Victorian studies, 1965.

VI. THE LATE NINETEENTH-CENTURY NOVEL

'LEWIS CARROLL', CHARLES LUTWIDGE DODGSON
1832–98

Bibliographies
Williams, S. H. and F. Madan. A handbook of the literature of the Rev C. L. Dodgson. Oxford 1931. Addns by F. Madan, Oxford 1935; see Green, below.

Green, R. L. The Carroll handbook. Oxford 1962, 1970. Based on Williams and Madan, above.

Collections
No collection is absolutely complete, mathematical works and various juvenilia being excluded.

Collected verse. Ed J. F. McDermott, New York 1929.
Complete works. Ed A. Woollcott, New York 1939.

The annotated Alice. Ed M. Gardner 1960.
Works. Ed R. L. Green 1965.

§1

The following books and pamphlets, generally accepted as by Dodgson, bear his name, his pseudonym or other pseudonyms, or are anon. See also col 1121, below.

The fifth book of Euclid treated algebraically. Oxford 1858, 1868 (rev).
Rules for court circular. Oxford 1860, 1862.
A syllabus of plane algebraical geometry, part 1. Oxford 1860.
Notes on the first two books of Euclid. Oxford 1860.
The formulae of plane trigonometry. Oxford 1861.
Notes on the first part of algebra. Oxford 1861.
Endowment of the Greek professorship. Oxford 1861.
An index to In memoriam. 1862.
The enunciations of the propositions of Euclid, bks I and II. Oxford 1863, 1873 (rev).
Croquet castles for five players. [Oxford 1863].
Examination statute. [Oxford 1864].
A guide to the mathematical student, part 1. Oxford 1864.
American telegrams. [Oxford] 1865.
The new method of evaluation as applied to π. [Oxford] 1865.
The dynamics of a parti-cle. Oxford 1865.
Alice's adventures in Wonderland. 1865, New York 1866, London 1866, 1886, 1897 (both rev); ed M. Gardner, New York 1960; ed R. L. Green, Oxford 1971 (with Through the looking-glass, below).
Castle-croquet for four players. [Oxford] 1866.
The elections to the Hebdomadal Council. Oxford 1866.
Condensation of determinants. 1866.
The deserted Parks. Oxford 1867.
An elementary treatise on determinants. 1867.
Bruno's revenge. Aunt Judy's Mag 4 1867; ed J. Drinkwater 1924.
The offer of the Clarendon trustees. Oxford 1868.
Phantasmagoria and other poems. 1869.
The Guildford gazette extraordinary. [Guildford] 1869.
Songs from Alice's adventures in Wonderland 1870. With addns.
To all child readers of Alice's adventures in Wonderland. [Oxford] 1871.
Through the looking-glass, and what Alice found there. 1872 (for 1871), 1897 (rev).
The new belfry of Christ Church, Oxford. Oxford 1872.
The vision of the three T's. Oxford 1873.
A discussion of the various methods of procedure in conducting elections. Oxford 1873.
The blank cheque: a fable. Oxford 1874.
Notes by an Oxford chiel. Oxford 1874.
Suggestions as to the best method of taking votes. Oxford 1874.
Euclid, book V, proved algebraically. Oxford 1874.
Vivisection as a sign of the times. Pall Mall Gazette 12 Feb 1875; nd (no known copy).
Some popular fallacies about vivisection. Oxford 1875 (priv ptd).
Euclid books I, II edited. Oxford 1875, 1882 (rev).
Song for Puss in boots. Brighton 1876 (no known copy).
A method of taking votes on more than two issues. [Oxford] 1876.
The hunting of the snark: an agony in eight fits. 1876.
An Easter greeting to every child who loves Alice. [Oxford] 1876.
Fame's penny-trumpet. [Oxford] 1876.
Word-links: a game for two players. Oxford 1878.
Euclid and his modern rivals. 1879, 1885 (rev); Supplement, 1885.
Doublets: a word-puzzle. 1879, 1880.
Lanrick: a game for two players. Oxford 1881.
Dreamland. [Oxford 1882].
Mischmasch: a word-game. [Oxford] 1882.

Lawn tennis tournaments: the true method of assigning prizes. 1883.
Rhyme? and reason? 1883.
Christmas greetings: from a fairy to a child. [1884].
Twelve months in a curatorship. Oxford 1884; Supplement, Postscript, Oxford 1884.
The principles of parliamentary representation. 1884; Supplement, 1885.
The profits of authorship. 1884 (no known copy).
A tangled tale. 1885.
Three years in a curatorship. Oxford 1886.
Suggestions as to the elections of proctors. Oxford 1886.
The game of logic. 1886, 1887.
Alice's adventures underground. 1886; ed M. Gardner, New York 1965.
Curiosa mathematica, part 1: a new theory of parallels. 1888.
The nursery Alice. 1889; ed M. Gardner, New York 1966.
Sylvie and Bruno. 1889.
Circular billiards, for two players. [Oxford 1890].
Eight or nine wise words about letter-writing. Oxford 1890.
A postal problem. [Oxford?] 1891; Supplement, 1891.
Curiosissima curatoria. Oxford 1892.
Syzygies and Lanrick: a word-puzzle and a game. 1893.
Curiosa mathematica, part II: pillow-problems. 1893.
Sylvie and Bruno concluded. 1893.
A disputed point in logic. [Oxford] 1894. 5 papers.
What the tortoise said to Achilles. 1894.
Symbolic logic, part 1: elementary. 1896 (3 edns), 1897.
Resident women-students. Oxford 1896.
Three sunsets and other poems. 1898.
The Lewis Carroll picture book. 1899, New York 1961 (as Diversions and digressions).
The story of Sylvie and Bruno. Ed E. H. Dodgson 1904.
Feeding the mind. 1907.
Some rare Carrolliana. 1924 (priv ptd).
Novelty and romancement. Boston 1925.
Further nonsense verse and prose. Ed L. Reed 1926.
A Christmas Carroll. Edinburgh 1930 (priv ptd).
To M.A.B. Edinburgh 1931 (priv ptd).
For the Train. Ed H. J. Schonfield 1932. Contributions to Train 1856–7.
The rectory umbrella and Mischmasch. Ed F. Milner 1932.
How the boots got left behind. 1943 (priv ptd).
Fugitive pieces by Carroll. Ed R. L. Green, TLS 31 July 1953.
Useful and instructive poetry [1845]. Ed D. Hudson 1956.
Mathematical recreations of Carroll. New York 1958.

Letters, Diaries etc

The life and letters of Carroll by S. D. Collingwood. 1898.
The Carroll picture book. Ed S. D. Collingwood 1899.
Six letters by Carroll. Ed W. Partington 1924 (priv ptd).
Tour in 1867. Philadelphia 1928; ed J. F. McDermott, New York 1935 (as The Russian journal).
A selection from the letters of Carroll to his child-friends. Ed E. M. Hatch 1933.
Diaries. Ed R. L. Green 2 vols 1953.

§2

Collingwood, S. D. The life and letters of Carroll. 1898.
Reed, L. The life of Carroll. 1932.
Chesterton, G. K. Lewis Carroll. New York Times 1932; in his A handful of authors, 1953.
Empson, W. In his Some versions of pastoral, 1935.
Green, R. L. The story of Carroll. 1949.
—— Lewis Carroll. 1960.
Gernsheim, H. Lewis Carroll, photographer. 1949, 1951 (rev).

Wilson, E. Lewis Carroll: an estimate. In his Shores of light, New York 1952.

Sewell, E. In her Field of nonsense, 1952.

Hudson, D. Lewis Carroll. 1954.

—— Lewis Carroll. 1958 (Br Council pamphlet).

Weaver, W. Alice in many tongues. Madison 1964.

Phillips, R. (ed). Aspects of Alice 1865–1971. 1972.

THOMAS HARDY
1840–1928

Bibliographies etc

Purdy, R. L. Hardy: a bibliographical study. Oxford 1954, 1968 (rev).

Stevenson, L. In The Victorian poets: a guide to research, ed F. E. Faverty, Cambridge Mass 1956, 1968 (rev).

Fayen, G. S. In Victorian fiction: a guide to research, ed L. Stevenson, Cambridge Mass 1964.

Collections

Wessex novels. 16 vols 1895–6.

[Works]: Wessex edition. 24 vols 1912–31; rptd in part as Autograph edition, 20 vols New York 1915; Anniversary edition, 21 vols 1920.

[Works]: Mellstock edition [de luxe]. 37 vols 1919–20.

Selected poems. 1916, 1921, 1929 (rev and enlarged as Chosen poems).

Collected poems. 1919, 1923, 1928, 1930.

Short stories. 1928.

Selected poems. Ed G. M. Young 1940.

Hardy's love poems. Ed C. J. Weber 1963.

Complete poems. Ed J. Gibson 1976.

§ 1

Desperate remedies: a novel. 3 vols 1871 (anon), 1 vol New York 1874 (rev), London 1889 ('new edition' with Prefatory note), 1892 ('popular edition'), 1896 (rev, with addn to Prefatory note), 1912 (rev, with further addn to Prefatory note), 1920.

Under the greenwood tree: a rural painting of the Dutch school. 2 vols 1872, 1 vol 1873, New York 1873, London 1876 (illustr R. Knight), 1878, 1891, 1896 (rev, with preface), 1912 (rev, with further preface), 1920.

A pair of blue eyes: a novel. 3 vols 1873, 1 vol New York 1873, London 1877, 1895 (rev, with preface), 1912 (rev, with Postscript), 1920 (rev). First pbd Tinsleys' Mag Sept 1872–July 1873, Semi-weekly New York Tribune 26 Sept–16 Dec 1873.

Far from the madding crowd. 2 vols 1874 (illustr H. Paterson [Allingham]), 1 vol New York 1874, 2 vols 1875 (rev), 1 vol 1877, 1895 (with preface), 1902 (rev), 1912, 1919. First pbd anon in Cornhill Mag Jan–Dec 1874, Every Saturday 31 Jan–24 Oct 1874, Littell's Living Age 31 Jan 1874–9 Jan 1875, Eclectic Mag March 1874–Feb 1875, Semi-weekly New York Tribune 26 June–15 Dec 1874. Dramatization (by Hardy and J. Comyns Carr), Prince of Wales Theatre Liverpool, 27 Feb 1882.

The hand of Ethelberta: a comedy in chapters. 2 vols 1876 (illustr G. Du Maurier), 1 vol New York 1876, London 1877, 1895 (rev, with preface), 1912 (rev, with Postscript), 1920. First pbd Cornhill Mag July 1875–May 1876, New York Times 20 June 1875–9 April 1876.

The return of the native. 3 vols 1878, 1 vol New York 1878, London 1880, 1884, 1895 (rev, with preface), 1912 (rev, with Postscript), 1920. First pbd Belgravia Jan–Dec 1878 (illustr A. Hopkins), Harper's New Monthly Mag Feb 1878–Jan 1879.

Fellow-townsmen. New York 1880, London 1888 (rev for Wessex tales). First pbd New Quart Mag new ser 2 1880, Harper's Weekly 17 April–15 May 1880.

The trumpet-major: a tale. 3 vols 1880, 1 vol New York 1880, London 1881, 1895 (rev, with preface), 1912, 1920. First pbd Good Words Jan–Dec 1880, Demorest's Monthly Mag Jan 1880–Jan 1881. Notes in Personal notebooks, 1978.

A Laodicean: a novel. New York 1881, 3 vols 1881 (rev), 1 vol 1882, 1896 (rev, with preface), 1912 (rev, with Postscript), 1920. First pbd Harper's New Monthly Mag (European edn) Dec 1880–Dec 1881 (illustr G. Du Maurier) and in Amer edn Jan 1881–Jan 1882.

Two on a tower: a romance. 3 vols 1882, 1 vol New York 1882, 3 vols 1883 (rev), 1 vol 1883 (rev), 1895 (rev, with preface), 1912 (rev, with addn to preface), 1920. First pbd Atlantic Monthly May–Dec 1882.

The romantic adventures of a milkmaid: a novel. New York [1883], London 1913 (rev for A changed man). First pbd Graphic 25 June 1883, Harper's Weekly 23 June–4 Aug 1883.

The Mayor of Casterbridge: the life and death of a man of character. 2 vols 1886, 1 vol New York 1886, London 1895 (rev, with preface), 1912 (rev, with addn to preface), 1920; ed R. B. Heilman, Boston 1962. First pbd Graphic and Harper's Weekly 2 Jan–15 May 1886.

The woodlanders. 3 vols 1887, 1 vol New York 1887, London 1887, 1895 (rev, with preface), 1912 (rev, with Postscript), 1920. First pbd Macmillan's Mag May 1886–April 1887, Harper's Bazar 15 May 1886–9 April 1887.

Wessex tales: strange, lively, and commonplace. 2 vols 1888, 1 vol New York 1888, London 1889, 1896 (with preface; adds An imaginative woman), 1912 (with addn to preface; omits An imaginative woman), 1920 (with addn to preface). Includes The three strangers (first pbd Longman's Mag March 1883, Harper's Weekly 3–10 March 1883); The withered arm (Blackwood's Mag Jan 1888); Fellow-townsmen (see above, 1880); Interlopers at the Knap (Eng Illustr Mag May 1884); The distracted preacher (New Quart Mag new ser 1 1879 and Harper's Weekly 19 April–17 May 1879).

A group of noble dames. 1891, New York 1891, London 1896 (with preface), 1912, 1920.

Tess of the d'Urbervilles: a pure woman faithfully presented. 3 vols 1891, 1892 (rev), 1 vol New York 1892 (illustr), London 1892 (with preface), 1895 (rev, with additional preface), 1912 (rev, note to prefaces, 'General preface to the novels and poems'), 1919, 1926; ed W. E. Buckler, Boston 1960; ed S. Elledge New York 1965 (with critical essays). First pbd, omitting some chs, in Graphic 4 July–26 Dec 1891 (illustr H. von Herkomer et al) in Nat Observer (Edinburgh) 14 Nov 1891, ch 14 in Fortnightly Rev May 1891), in Harper's Bazar 18 July–26 Dec 1891 (ch 4 in Eclectic Mag June 1891); rptd complete in John O'London's Weekly 24 Oct 1895–10 July 1926; dramatized 1894–5, produced New York 2 March 1897 (rev L. Stoddard); produced Dorchester 1924, London 1925, 1929 (rev Hardy).

The three wayfarers: a pastoral play in one act. New York 1893, New York and London 1930 (rev, illustr), Dorchester 1935, New York 1943 (facs). Dramatized from The three strangers, Wessex tales; produced Terry's 3 June 1893.

Life's little ironies: a set of tales with some colloquial sketches entitled A few crusted characters. 1894, New York 1894, London 1896 (with preface), 1912 (rev, omits preface, adds Prefatory note), 1920.

The spectre of the real, by Hardy and Florence Henniker. To-day 17 Nov 1894; rptd in Scarlet and grey: stories of soldiers and others by Florence Henniker, 1896.

Jude the obscure. 1896 (for 1895) (with preface), New York 1896 (for 1895), 1912 (rev, with Postscript), 1920; ed A. Alvarez, New York 1961; ed I. Howe, Boston 1965. First pbd abridged and modified as The simpletons, then as Hearts insurgent in Harper's New Monthly Mag Dec 1894–Nov 1895 (illustr W. Hatherell).

The well-beloved: a sketch of a temperament. 1897 (with preface). New York 1897, London 1912 (rev), 1920. First pbd as The pursuit of the well-beloved in Illustr London News and Harper's Bazar 1 Oct–17 Dec 1892.

Wessex poems and other verses, with thirty illustrations by the author. 1898, New York 1899, London 1912, 1920.

Poems of the past and the present. 1902 (for 1901), 1902 (rev), 1912, 1920.

The dynasts: a drama of the Napoleonic wars. Pt 1, 1903 (for 1904), 1904 (rev); pt 2, 1905 (for 1906); pt 3, 1908, 1910; The dynasts, 1 vol 1910, 1913, 1920, 3 vols 1927; ed J. Wain 1965; Prologue and epilogue, 1914. Abridged version produced by H. Granville-Barker 25 Nov 1914–30 Jan 1915.

Select poems of William Barnes, chosen and edited with a preface and glossorial notes. 1908, 1922 (for 1921), 1933.

Time's laughingstocks and other verses. 1909, 1910, 1913, 1915, 1920.

A changed man, The waiting supper and other tales. 1913, 1920.

Satires of circumstance: lyrics and reveries with miscellaneous pieces. 1914, 1915, 1919, 1920.

Moments of vision and miscellaneous verses. 1917, 1919, 1920.

The play of Saint George. Cambridge 1921 (priv ptd), New York 1928 (with modernized version by R. S. Loomis).

Late lyrics and earlier with many other verses. 1922, 1926.

The famous tragedy of the Queen of Cornwall. 1923, 1924 (rev), 1926.

Human shows, far phantasies: songs and trifles. 1925, New York 1925, 1931.

Life and art: essays, notes and letters. Ed E. Brennecke, New York 1925 (unauthorized).

Winter words in various moods and metres. 1928, New York 1928, 1931. Partially serialized Daily Telegraph 19 March–26 Sept 1928.

Hardy, F. E. The early life of Hardy 1840–91. 1928, New York 1928; The later years of Hardy 1892–1928, 1930, New York 1930. Collected 1962, New York 1962. Both mainly by Hardy, and dictated to his second wife. Omissions in Personal notebooks, 1978.

An indiscretion in the life of an heiress. 1934 (priv ptd); ed C. J. Weber, Baltimore 1935. First pbd Harper's Weekly 29 June–27 July 1878, New Quart Mag 1878 (rev); a reworking of The poor man and the lady, Hardy's first novel, now lost. See R. L. Purdy, above.

Our exploits at West Poley. 1952. First pbd Household (Boston) Nov 1892–April 1893.

Hardy, E. Some unpublished poems of Hardy. London Mag Jan 1956.

—— Hardy: plots for five unpublished stories. London Mag Nov 1958.

—— An unpublished poem by Hardy. TLS 2 June 1966. Facs of A Victorian rehearsal.

Hardy's personal writings: prefaces, literary opinions, reminiscences. Ed H. Orel, Lawrence Kansas 1966.

Letters and Notebooks

Letters of Hardy [at Colby]. Ed C. J. Weber, Waterville Maine 1954.

Hardy's notebooks and some letters from Julia Augusta Martin. Ed E. Hardy 1955.

'Dearest Emmie': Hardy's letters to his first wife. Ed C. J. Weber, New York 1963.

The architectural notebook. Ed C. Beatty, Dorchester 1966. Foreword by J. Summerson.

One rare fair woman: Hardy's letters to Florence Henniker 1893–1922. Ed E. Hardy and F. B. Pinion 1972.

Personal notebooks [1867–1927]. Ed R. H. Taylor 1978.

§2

Abercrombie, L. Hardy: a critical study. 1912, New York 1927 (abridged).

Symons, A. A study of Hardy. 1927.

Woolf, V. The novels of Hardy. In her Common reader ser 2, 1932.

—— Half of Hardy. In her Captain's death bed and other essays, 1950.

Lawrence, D. H. Study of Hardy. In his Phoenix, 1936.

Weber, C. J. Chronology in Hardy's novels. PMLA 53 1938.

—— Hardy of Wessex: his life and literary career. New York 1940, Hamden Conn 1962, 1965 (rev).

—— The manuscript of Hardy's Two on a tower. PBSA 40 1946. Reply by R. C. Schweik 60 1966.

—— Hardy in America: a study of Hardy and his American readers. Waterville Maine 1946.

—— Hardy and the lady from Madison Square. Waterville Maine 1952.

Rutland, W. R. Hardy: a study of his writings and their background. Oxford 1938.

Southern Rev 6 1940. Hardy centennial issue.

Blunden, E. Thomas Hardy. 1942.

Cecil, D. Hardy the novelist. 1943.

Southworth, J. G. The poetry of Hardy. New York 1947.

Stewart, J. I. M. The integrity of Hardy. E & S new ser 1 1948.

—— In his Eight modern writers, Oxford 1963 (OHEL).

Lewis, C. D. The lyrical poetry of Hardy. Proc Br Acad 37 1951.

Brown, D. Thomas Hardy. 1954, 1961 (rev).

—— The Mayor of Casterbridge. 1962.

Hardy, E. Hardy: a critical biography. 1954.

Holloway, J. Hardy's major fiction. In From Jane Austen to Joseph Conrad, ed R. Rathburn and M. Steinmann, Minneapolis 1958; rptd in his Charted mirror, 1960.

—— Tess and the awkward age. In his Charted mirror, 1960.

Hardy, Emma. Some recollections, together with some relevant poems by Hardy. Ed E. Hardy and R. Gittings, Oxford 1961.

Hardy: a collection of critical essays. Ed A. J. Guerard, New York 1963.

Williams, R. Thomas Hardy. CQ 6 1964.

Hardy and his readers. Ed L. Lerner and J. Holmstrom 1968.

Bailey, J. O. The poetry of Hardy. Chapel Hill 1970.

Cox, R. G. (ed). Hardy: the critical heritage. 1970.

Davie, D. A. Hardy and British poetry. 1973.

Gittings, R. Young Hardy. 1975; The older Hardy, 1978.

Bayley, J. An essay on Hardy. Cambridge 1978.

HENRY JAMES
1843–1916

Bibliographies

Phillips, L. A bibliography of the writings of James. Boston 1906, New York 1930 (rev).

Edel, L. and D. H. Laurence. A bibliography of James. 1957, 1961 (rev) (Soho Bibliographies).

Collections

[Novels and tales]. 14 vols 1883, 1886–7.

Novels and tales: New York edition. 26 vols New York 1907–18, 1961–5, 24 vols 1908–9, 1913.

Uniform tales. 14 vols 1915–20, 7 vols Boston 1917–18.

Novels and stories. Ed P. Lubbock 35 vols 1921–3.

The art of the novel: critical prefaces [to New York edn, above]. Ed R. P. Blackmur, New York 1934.

American novels and stories. Ed F. O. Matthiessen, New York 1947.

Complete plays. Ed L. Edel, Philadelphia 1949, London 1949.

Complete tales. Ed L. Edel 12 vols 1962-5, Philadelphia 1962-5. First book pbn.

Tales. Ed M. Aziz 8 vols Oxford 1973-. First pbd versions.

§ I

James was an inveterate reviser, freely revising not only from serial to book, but from one edn to the next, and even from one impression to the next within a single edn.

A passionate pilgrim, and other tales. Boston 1875. A passionate pilgrim; The last of the Valerii; Eugene Pickering; The madonna of the future; The romance of certain old clothes; Madame de Mauves.

Transatlantic sketches. Boston 1875, Leipzig 1883 (rev as Foreign parts).

Roderick Hudson. Boston 1876 (for 1875), 3 vols 1879 (rev), 1 vol 1880, Boston 1882 (rev), London 1888; ed L. Edel, New York 1960. First pbd in Atlantic Monthly Jan–Dec 1875.

The American. Boston 1877, London [1877] (unauthorized), 1879, [c. 1888], 1894 (unauthorized); ed R. G. Dennis 1975 (facs of 1908 revision). First pbd in Atlantic Monthly June 1876–May 1877. Dramatic version, 1891 (2 impressions, priv ptd); acted at Opera Comique, London, 26 Sept 1891.

French poets and novelists. 1878, Leipzig 1883 (rev), London 1884 (rev); ed L. Edel, New York 1964.

Watch and ward. Boston 1878; ed L. Edel 1960. First pbd in Atlantic Monthly Aug–Dec 1871.

The Europeans. 2 vols 1878, Boston 1879 (for 1878), London 1879; ed E. Sackville-West 1952; ed L. Edel 1967 (with Washington Square, below). First pbd in Atlantic Monthly July–Oct 1878.

Daisy Miller. New York 1879 (for 1878), 2 vols 1879 (with An international episode and Four meetings), 1 vol 1880, New York 1883 (with An international episode, The diary of a man of fifty and A bundle of letters), London 1888, New York 1892 (with An international episode), 1900. First pbd in Cornhill Mag June–July 1878. Dramatic version, 1882 (priv ptd), Boston 1883. First pbd in Atlantic Monthly April–June 1883.

An international episode. New York 1879, 2 vols 1879 (with Daisy Miller and Four meetings), 1 vol 1880, New York 1883 (with Daisy Miller, The diary of a man of fifty, and A bundle of letters), New York 1892 (with Daisy Miller), New York 1902. First pbd in Cornhill Mag Dec 1878–Jan 1879.

The madonna of the future and other tales. 2 vols 1879, 1 vol 1880, 1888. Vol 1: The madonna of the future; Longstaff's marriage; Madame de Mauves; vol 2: Eugene Pickering; The diary of a man of fifty; Benvolio.

Confidence. 2 vols 1880 (for 1879), Boston 1880, 1 vol 1880, 1881, 1882, Boston 1891; ed H. Ruhm, New York 1962 (from ms). First pbd in Scribner's Monthly Aug 1879–Jan 1880.

Hawthorne. 1879, New York 1880, London 1883, 1887, 1902 (EML); ed W. M. Sale jr, Ithaca 1956.

A bundle of letters. Boston [1880], New York [1880], (both unauthorized), New York 1880 (with The diary of a man of fifty), 1883 (with Daisy Miller, An international episode, and The diary of a man of fifty). First pbd in Parisian 18 Dec 1879.

Washington Square. New York 1881 (for 1880), 2 vols 1881, 1 vol 1881, 1889; ed L. Edel 1967 (with Europeans, above). First pbd in Cornhill Mag July–Nov 1880 and in Harper's New Monthly Mag July–Dec 1880.

The portrait of a lady. 3 vols 1881, 1 vol Boston 1882 (for 1881), London 1882; ed G. Greene, Oxford 1947 (WC); ed L. Edel, Boston 1956. First pbd in Macmillan's

Mag Oct 1880–Nov 1881 and in Atlantic Monthly Nov 1880–Dec 1881.

The point of view. 1882 (priv ptd).

The siege of London, The pension Beaurepas, and The point of view. Boston 1883, Leipzig 1884 (rev). A passionate pilgrim replaced The pension Beaurepas in the Leipzig edn.

Portraits of places. 1883, Boston 1884.

A little tour in France. Boston 1885 (for 1884), 1900, London 1900, Boston 1907, 1914. First pbd as En province in Atlantic Monthly July–Nov 1883, Feb, April–May 1884.

Tales of three cities. Boston 1884, London 1884. The impressions of a cousin; Lady Barberina; A New England winter.

The art of fiction. Boston 1885 (for 1884), 1887 (for 1888?), 1889. Pbd with Walter Besant's essay of same title; rptd in The house of fiction, ed L. Edel 1957.

The author of Beltraffio. Boston 1885. The author of Beltraffio; Pandora; Georgina's reasons; The path of duty; Four meetings.

Stories revived. 3 vols 1885, 2 vols 1885.

The Bostonians. 3 vols 1886, New York 1886, 1 vol 1886; ed P. Rahv, New York 1945; ed L. Trilling 1952; ed I. Howe, New York 1956 (Modern Lib); ed L. Edel 1967. First pbd in Century Mag Feb 1885–Feb 1886.

The Princess Casamassima. 3 vols 1886, New York 1886, 1 vol 1887, 1888; ed L. Trilling 2 vols New York 1948. First pbd in Atlantic Monthly Sept 1885–Oct 1886.

Partial portraits. 1888, New York 1888, London 1894.

The reverberator. 2 vols 1888, New York 1888, 1 vol 1888; ed S. Nowell-Smith 1949. First pbd in Macmillan's Mag Feb–July 1888.

The Aspern papers; Louisa Pallant; The modern warning. 2 vols 1888, New York 1888, 1 vol 1890. Aspern papers first pbd in Atlantic Monthly March–May 1888.

A London life; The Patagonia; The liar; Mrs Temperly. 2 vols 1889, New York 1889, 1 vol 1889.

The tragic muse. 2 vols Boston 1890, 3 vols 1890, 1 vol 1891; ed L. Edel, New York 1960; ed R. P. Blackmur, New York 1961. First pbd in Atlantic Monthly Jan 1889–May 1890.

Daudet, A., Port Tarascon. New York 1891 (for 1890), London 1891 (for 1890). Tr James. First pbd in Harper's New Monthly Mag June–Nov 1890.

The lesson of the master; The marriages; The pupil; Brooksmith; The solution; Sir Edmund Orme. New York 1892, London 1892.

The real thing, and other tales. New York 1893, London 1893. The real thing; Sir Dominick Ferrand; Nona Vincent; The Chaperon; Greville Fane.

Picture and text. New York 1893.

The private life; The wheel of time; Lord Beaupré; The visits; Collaboration; Owen Wingrave. 1893, 2 vols New York 1893.

Essays in London and elsewhere. 1893, New York 1893.

Theatricals. New York 1894, London 1895. Tenants; Disengaged (acted Hudson Theatre, New York, 11 March 1909).

Guy Domville. 1894 (priv ptd). Acted St James's Theatre, 5 Jan 1895.

Theatricals: second series. 1894, New York 1894. The album; The reprobate (acted Royal Court Theatre, 14 Dec 1919).

Terminations. 1895, New York 1895. The death of the lion; The Coxon fund; The middle years; The altar of the dead.

Embarrassments. 1896, New York 1896, London 1897. The figure in the carpet; Glasses; The next time; The way it came.

The other house. 2 vols 1896, New York 1896, 1 vol 1897;

ed L. Edel 1948. First pbd in Illustr London News 4 July–26 Sept 1896.

The spoils of Poynton. 1897, New York 1897; ed L. Edel 1967. First pbd as The old things in Atlantic Monthly April–Oct 1896.

What Maisie knew. 1898 (for 1897), Chicago 1897. First pbd in Chapbook 15 Jan–1 Aug 1897 and in New Rev Feb–Sept 1897 (rev and abridged).

John Delavoy. New York 1897 (priv ptd).

In the cage. 1898, Chicago 1898, New York 1906; ed M. D. Zabel 1958.

The two magics: The turn of the screw; Covering end. 1898, New York 1898. Turn of the screw first pbd in Collier's Weekly 26 Jan–2 April 1898.

The awkward age. 1899, New York 1899; ed L. Edel 1967. First pbd in Harper's Weekly 1 Oct 1897–8 Jan 1899.

The soft side. 1900, New York 1900. The great good place; 'Europe'; Paste; The real right thing; The great condition; The tree of knowledge; The abasement of the Northmores; The given case; John Delavoy; The third person; Maud-Evelyn; Miss Gunton of Pough-keepsie.

The sacred fount. New York 1901, London 1901; ed L. Edel, New York 1953, London 1959 (rev).

The wings of the dove. 2 vols New York 1902, London 1902; ed H. Read 1948; ed R. P. Blackmur, New York 1958.

The better sort. 1903, New York 1903. Broken wings; The Beldonald Holbein; The two faces; The tone of time; The special type; Mrs Medwin; Flickerbridge; The story in it; The beast in the jungle; The birthplace; The papers.

The ambassadors. 1903, New York 1903; ed L. Edel, Boston 1960; ed S. P. Rosenbaum, New York 1966. First pbd in North Amer Rev Jan–Dec 1903.

William Wetmore Story and his friends. 2 vols Edinburgh 1903, 2 vols Boston 1903.

The golden bowl. 2 vols New York 1904, London [1905]; ed R. P. Blackmur, New York 1952.

The question of our speech; The lesson of Balzac. Boston 1905. 2 lectures.

English hours. 1905, Boston 1905, 1914.

The American scene. 1907, New York 1907; ed W. H. Auden, New York 1946.

Views and reviews. Ed L. Phillips, Boston 1908.

Julia Bride. New York 1909.

Italian hours. 1909, Boston 1909.

The finer grain. New York 1910, London 1910. The velvet glove; Mora Montravers; A round of visits; Crapy Cornelia; The bench of desolation.

The outcry. [1911], New York 1911.

A small boy and others. New York 1913, London 1913. An autobiography continued in Notes of a son and brother and Middle years, below; collected as Autobiography, ed F. W. Dupee 1956.

The American volunteer motor-ambulance corps in France. 1914.

Notes of a son and brother. New York 1914, London 1914.

Notes on novelists. 1914, New York 1914.

The question of the mind. [1915].

Pictures and other passages from James. Ed R. Head 1916, New York [1917].

The ivory tower. [1917], New York 1917; Notes for the Ivory tower, New York [1947].

The sense of the past. [1917], New York 1917.

The middle years. [Ed P. Lubbock] [1917], New York 1917.

Gabrielle de Bergerac. New York 1918.

Within the rim. [1919].

Travelling companions. New York 1919. Travelling companions; The sweetheart of M. Briseux; Professor Fargo; At Isella; Guest's confession; Adina; De Grey: a romance.

A landscape painter. New York 1919 (for 1920). A landscape painter; Poor Richard; A day of days; A most extraordinary case.

Refugees in Chelsea. [1920] (priv ptd).

Master Eustace. New York 1920. Master Eustace; Longstaff's marriage; Théodolinde; A light man; Benvolio.

The scenic art. Ed A. Wade, New Brunswick 1948.

Daumier, caricaturist. [1954].

The American essays. Ed L. Edel, New York 1956.

The future of the novel: essays on the art of fiction. Ed L. Edel, New York 1956, London 1957 (with variations, as The house of fiction).

The painter's eye: notes and essays on the pictorial arts. Ed J. L. Sweeney 1956.

Parisian sketches. Ed L. Edel and I. D. Lind, New York 1957.

Letters and Papers

Letters to an editor [Clement Shorter]. 1916 (priv ptd).

Letters. Ed P. Lubbock 2 vols 1920, New York 1920.

'A most unholy trade': being letters on the drama. Cambridge Mass 1923 (priv ptd).

Three letters to Joseph Conrad. 1926 (priv ptd).

Letters to A. C. Benson and Auguste Monod. 1930.

Notebooks. Ed F. O. Matthiessen and K. B. Murdock, New York 1947.

James and Robert Louis Stevenson: a record of friendship and criticism. Ed J. A. Smith 1948.

Selected letters. Ed L. Edel, New York 1955.

James and H. G. Wells: a record of their friendship. Ed L. Edel and G. N. Ray 1958.

Letters. Ed. L. Edel 1974–.

§2

Howells, W. D. James's Passionate pilgrim and other tales. Atlantic Monthly April 1875; Henry James jr, Century Nov 1882; Editor's study, Harper's New Monthly Mag Oct 1888; Mr Henry James's later work, North Amer Rev Jan 1903. All rptd in Discovery of a genius, ed A. Mordell, New York 1961.

Conrad, J. James: an appreciation. North Amer Rev Jan 1905; rptd in his Notes on life and letters, 1921.

Hueffer, F. M. James: a critical study. 1913.

'West, Rebecca' (C. I. Andrews). Henry James. 1916.

Beach, J. W. The method of James. New Haven 1918, Philadelphia 1954 (enlarged).

Pound, E. In his Instigations, New York 1920; rptd in his Make it new, New Haven 1935.

Brooks, V. W. The pilgrimage of James. New York 1925.

Roberts, M. James's criticism. Cambridge Mass 1929.

Gide, A. Henry James. Yale Rev 19 1930.

Edel, L. James: les années dramatiques. Paris 1931.

—— The prefaces of James. Paris 1931.

—— James: the untried years 1843–70. 1953; The conquest of London 1870–81, 1962; The middle years 1882–95, Philadelphia 1962.

Greene, G. In his Contemporary essays, 1933; rptd with addns in his Lost childhood, 1951.

Matthiessen, F. O. In his American renaissance, New York 1941.

—— James: the major phase. New York 1944.

Dupee, F. W. (ed). The question of James: a collection of critical essays. New York 1945.

—— Henry James. New York 1951, Garden City NY 1956 (rev and enlarged).

Nowell-Smith, S. (ed). The legend of the master. 1947.

Leavis, F. R. In his Great tradition, 1948.

Bewley, M. In his Complex fate, 1952.

Anderson, Q. The American James. New Brunswick 1957.

Jefferson, D. W. Henry James. Edinburgh 1960 (Writers & Critics).

—— James and the modern reader. Edinburgh 1964.

Poirier, R. The comic sense of James: a study of the early novels. 1960.

Cargill, O. The novels of James. New York 1961.

Krook, D. The ordeal of consciousness in James. Cambridge 1962.
Putt, S. G. A reader's guide to James. 1966.
James: a collection of critical essays. Ed L. Edel, Englewood Cliffs NJ 1963.
Stewart, J. I. M. In his Eight modern writers, Oxford 1963 (OHEL vol 12).
Gard, R. (ed). James: the critical heritage. 1968.

GEORGE ROBERT GISSING
1857–1903

The main sources of material are the Huntington Library, which possesses the mss of Born in exile, The crown of life, Denzil Quarrier, Eve's ransom, In the year of jubilee, The nether world, Thyrza, The whirlpool; the Berg Collection, New York Public Library, which has the mss of Demos, The emancipated, New Grub Street, Will Warburton, as well as Gissing's diary, commonplace book and letters, particularly those to Gabrielle Fleury Gissing; the Yale Library, which contains the letters to Bertz and much family correspondence; the Carl H. Pforzheimer Library, which has a miscellaneous collection; and the Univ of Texas, which holds the ms of Workers in the dawn. Many items of current interest will be found in the Gissing Newsletter 1965–.

Bibliographies

Korg, J. In Victorian fiction: a guide to research, ed L. Stevenson, Cambridge Mass 1964.

§ 1

Notes on Social Democracy. Pall Mall Gazette 9, 11 Sept 1880; The new censorship of literature, 15 Dec 1884; Why I don't write plays, 10 Sept 1892.
Workers in the dawn: a novel. 3 vols 1880; ed R. Shafer 2 vols New York 1935.
The unclassed: a novel. 3 vols 1884, 1895 (rev).
Isabel Clarendon. 2 vols 1886.
Demos: a story. 1886, 1890, 1897.
Thyrza: a tale. 3 vols 1887, 1891, 1895, 1927.
A life's morning. 3 vols 1888, New York 1888, London 1914, 1928, 1938; ed W. Plomer 1947.
The nether world: a novel. 3 vols 1889.
The emancipated: a novel. 3 vols 1890, 1893.
New Grub Street: a novel. 3 vols 1891, 1892, 1907; ed G. W. Stonier 1958 (WC); ed I. Howe 1963.
Denzil Quarrier: a novel. 1892, 1911.
Born in exile: a novel. 3 vols 1892, 1907.
The odd women. 3 vols 1893, New York 1893, London 1907.
In the year of jubilee. 3 vols 1894.
Eve's ransom. 1895, New York 1895, London 1911, 1929.
The paying guest. 1895, New York 1895.
Sleeping fires. 1895, New York 1895, London 1927.
The whirlpool. 1897, New York 1897, London 1911.
Human odds and ends: stories and sketches. 1898, 1911.
The town traveller. 1898, New York 1898, Toronto 1899.
Charles Dickens: a critical study. 1898, 1902 (with topographical notes by F. G. Kitton).
The crown of life. 1899, 1927, New York 1899.
The Rochester edition of the works of Charles Dickens. 6 vols (all pbd) 1900–1. Introds by Gissing, notes by F. G. Kitton.
By the Ionian sea: notes of a ramble in southern Italy. 1901, 1905, 1917; ed V. Woolf 1933.
Our friend the charlatan. 1901, New York 1901.
Forster's life of Dickens, abridged and revised. 1903.
The private papers of Henry Ryecroft. 1903.
Veranilda: a romance. 1904, 1905, Oxford 1929 (WC).
Will Warburton: a romance of real life. 1905, Oxford 1929 (WC).

The house of cobwebs and other stories. 1906, New York 1915 (preface by T. Seccombe).
An heiress on condition. Philadelphia 1923.
Sins of the fathers and other tales. Chicago 1924. 4 short stories.
Critical studies of the works of Charles Dickens. Ed T. Scott, New York 1924. Introds to the Rochester edn, including 3 unpbd.
The immortal Dickens. 1925.
A victim of circumstance and other stories. 1927.
A Yorkshire lass. New York 1928 (priv ptd).
Selections, autobiographical and imaginative, from the works of Gissing, with biographical and critical notes by his son [A. C. Gissing]. Ed V. Woolf 1929.
Hope in vain. [Winchester] 1930 (priv ptd). A poem.
Autobiographical notes, with comments on Tennyson and Huxley. In Three letters to Edward Clodd, Edinburgh 1930 (priv ptd).
Brownie, now first reprinted from the Chicago Tribune, together with six other stories attributed to [Gissing]. Ed G. E. Hastings, V. Starrett and T. O. Mabbott, New York 1931.
Stories and sketches published for the first time in book form. Ed A. C. Gissing 1938.

Letters and Papers

Letters to Edward Clodd. 1914 (priv ptd).
Letters to an editor [C. K. Shorter]. 1915 (priv ptd).
Letters to members of his family. Ed A. and E. Gissing 1927.
The letters of Gissing to Eduard Bertz 1887–1903. Ed A. C. Young, New Brunswick 1961.
Gissing and H. G. Wells: their friendship and correspondence. Ed R. A. Gettmann, Urbana 1961.
Gissing's commonplace book. Ed J. Korg, New York 1962.
The letters of Gissing to Gabrielle Fleury Gissing. Ed P. Coustillas, New York 1965.
Henry Hick's recollections, together with Gissing's letters to Hick. 1973.
Letters to Edward Clodd. 1973.

§ 2

Wells, H. G. The novels of Mr Gissing. Contemporary Rev Aug 1897.
Roberts, M. The private life of Henry Maitland. 1912, 1923 (rev); ed 'Morchard Bishop' 1958. Biography disguised as a novel.
Swinnerton, F. Gissing: a critical study. 1912.
James, H. The English novel and the work of Gissing. In his Notes on novelists, 1914.
Woolf, V. In her Common reader ser 2, 1932.
Leavis, Q. D. Gissing and the English novel. Scrutiny 7 1938.
Murry, J. M. In his Katherine Mansfield and other literary studies, 1959.
Ward, A. C. Gissing. 1959.
'Orwell, George' (E. Blair). George Gissing. London Mag June 1960.
Korg, J. Gissing: a critical biography. Seattle 1963.
Davis, O. H. Gissing: a study in literary leanings. 1966.
Coustillas, P. and C. Partridge (ed). Gissing: the critical heritage. 1973.
Poole, A. Gissing in context. 1975.

ROBERT LOUIS STEVENSON
1850–94

The great depository of Stevenson material is the Edwin J. Beinecke Collection at Yale, which contains 1,000 letters by Stevenson and 2,000 to and about him, as well as a large group of mss, including the Amateur emigrant, *most of* Catriona, Ebb tide, Wrong box, Body snatcher, *and part of* An inland voyage, St Ives *and* Weir of Hermiston. *The Huntington Library possesses most of* Kidnapped, Beach of Falesá, St Ives, *the* Silverado squatters *diary, the* South Seas journal, *and the* Cévennes journal. *The Pierpont Morgan Library has* Dr Jekyll and Mr Hyde *and a draft of* Weir of Hermiston; *the Widener Library at Harvard has a late version of* Catriona; *and the Princeton Library has a draft of* St Ives. *The Mitchell Library at Sydney has* In the South Seas. *2 important groups of letters, to Mrs Sitwell and to W. E. Henley, are held by the National Library of Scotland.*

Bibliographies

Prideaux, W. F. A bibliography of the works of Stevenson. 1903, 1917 (rev F. V. Livingston).
McKay, G. L. The Stevenson library of E. J. Beinecke. 6 vols New Haven 1951–64.

Collections

Vailima edition. Ed L. Osbourne and F. Van de G. Stevenson 26 vols 1922–3.
Collected poems. Ed J. A. Smith 1950, 1971 (with addns).

§ I

The Pentland rising. Edinburgh 1866 (priv ptd), [1925].
The charity bazaar. Edinburgh [not before 1871] (priv ptd); Westport Conn 1929.
An appeal to the clergy. Edinburgh 1875.
An inland voyage. 1878, 1881, 1887.
Edinburgh: picturesque notes, with etchings. 1879.
Travels with a donkey in the Cévennes. 1879, 1887.
Deacon Brodie, or the double life: a melodrama founded on facts in four acts and ten tableaux. Edinburgh 1880 (priv ptd), 1888 (rev, priv ptd). With W. E. Henley.
Virginibus puerisque and other papers. 1881, 1887.
Familiar studies of men and books. 1882.
New Arabian nights. 2 vols 1882.
The Silverado squatters: sketches from a Californian mountain. 1883.
Treasure Island. 1883, 1884, 1885, Boston 1884, 1885, New York 1886 (3 edns).
Admiral Guinea: a melodrama in four acts. Edinburgh 1884 (priv ptd). With W. E. Henley.
Beau Austin: a play in four acts. Edinburgh 1884 (priv ptd). With W. E. Henley.
A child's garden of verses. 1885, 1895, New York 1885, 1895. 39 of the 64 poems priv ptd in 1883 as Penny whistles, including 9 poems omitted from A child's garden; these 9 poems were priv ptd by L. S. Livingston in 1912 as Verses by RLS.
More new Arabian nights: the dynamiter. 1885. Except for Zero's tale of the explosive bomb, largely the work of Fanny Stevenson.
Prince Otto: a romance. 1885.
Macaire: a melodramatic farce in three acts. Edinburgh 1885 (priv ptd). With W. E. Henley.
Strange case of Dr Jekyll and Mr Hyde. 1886.
Kidnapped: being memoirs of the adventures of David Balfour in the year 1751; how he was kidnapped and castaway; his sufferings in a desert isle; his journey in the wild highlands; his acquaintance with Alan Breck Stewart and other notorious Highland Jacobites; with all that he suffered at the hands of his uncle, Ebenezer Balfour of Shaws, falsely so-called: written by himself

and now set forth by Robert Louis Stevenson. 1886.
The merry men and other tales and fables. 1887.
Underwoods. 1887, New York 1887, 1905. 38 poems in English, 16 in Scots.
Memoirs and portraits. 1887, New York 1887, 1905. 16 essays, including Some college memories and Thomas Stevenson, mainly rptd from Cornhill Mag and Longman's Mag.
Thomas Stevenson, civil engineer. 1887 (priv ptd).
Ticonderoga. Edinburgh 1887 (priv ptd). First pbd in Scribner's Mag Dec 1887; rptd in Ballads, 1890.
The hanging judge: a drama in three acts and six tableaux. Edinburgh 1887 (priv ptd); ed E. Gosse 1914 (priv ptd). With Fanny Stevenson.
The misadventures of John Nicholson: a Christmas story. New York 1887, 1887, 1893. Piratically rptd from Yule-Tide: Cassell's Christmas annual for 1887.
The papers of H. Fleeming Jenkin; with a memoir by R. L. Stevenson. 2 vols 1887. Memoir rptd alone, New York 1887, London 1912.
The black arrow: a tale of the two roses. 1888, 1891.
The master of Ballantrae: a winter's tale. 1889. This edn was preceded by a small priv ptd edn in 1888 to establish copyright.
The wrong box. 1889, 1892, 1895, New York 1889, 1890. With Lloyd Osbourne.
Ballads. 1890, New York 1890.
Father Damien: an open letter to the Reverend Dr Hyde of Honolulu. 1890, 1901, 1909, 1910, Sydney 1890. This edn was preceded by a priv ptd edn at Sydney and a second at Edinburgh.
Across the plains, with other memories and essays. 1892.
A footnote to history: eight years of trouble in Samoa. 1892, New York 1892.
Three plays: Deacon Brodie, Beau Austin, Admiral Guinea. 1892, New York 1892.
The wrecker. 1892, 1899, New York 1892. With Lloyd Osbourne.
Island nights entertainments: consisting of The beach of Falesá, The bottle imp, The isle of voices. 1893, 1902, 1904, New York 1893.
War in Samoa. 1893 (priv ptd).
Catriona: a sequel to Kidnapped, being memoirs of the further adventures of David Balfour at home and abroad in which are set forth his misfortunes anent the Appin murder; his troubles with Lord Advocate Grant; captivity on the Bass Rock; journey into Holland and France; and singular relations with James More Drummond or MacGregor, a son of the notorious Rob Roy, and his daughter Catriona, written by himself, and now set forth by Robert Louis Stevenson. 1893.
The ebb-tide: a trio and a quartette. Chicago 1894, London 1894. With Lloyd Osbourne.
The body-snatcher. New York 1895.
The amateur emigrant from the Clyde to Sandy Hook. Chicago 1895, New York 1902.
Weir of Hermiston: an unfinished romance. 1896. The first printing in book form is that of a copyright edn, Chicago 1896.
A mountain town in France: a fragment. New York 1896.
Songs of travel and other verses. 1896.
St Ives: being the adventures of a French prisoner in England. 1897. 30 chs by Stevenson, the remainder by A. T. Quiller-Couch.
Three short poems. 1898 (priv ptd), Chicago 1902.
RLS Teuila. New York 1899 (priv ptd). 20 poems.
In the South Seas. New York 1896, 1908, London 1900. 15 of the 35 letters priv ptd in 1890 as The South Seas: a record of three cruises; the letters first pbd in the Sun (New York) 1891.
The morality of the profession of letters. New York 1899.

A Stevenson medley. Ed S. Colvin 1899. Includes the Davos-Platz booklets, mainly ptd from the original blocks.
Essays and criticisms. Boston 1903.
Prayers written at Vailima, with an introduction by Mrs Stevenson. 1905.
Tales and fantasies. 1905.
Essays of travel. 1905.
Essays in the art of writing. 1905.
Records of a family of engineers. 1912.
Memoirs of himself. Philadelphia 1912 (priv ptd).
The poems and ballads of Stevenson: complete edition. New York 1913.
Political fragments. [1915] (priv ptd).
The waif woman. 1916.
On the choice of a profession. 1916.
An ode of Horace: book ii, ode iii—experiments in three metres. [1916] (priv ptd).
Poems hitherto unpublished. Ed G. S. Hellman 2 vols Boston 1916 (Bibliophile Soc).
New poems and variant readings. 1918.
Poems hitherto unpublished. Ed G. S. Hellman and W. P. Trent, Boston 1921 (Bibliophile Soc).
Hitherto unpublished prose writings. Ed H. H. Harper, Boston 1921 (Bibliophile Soc).
Confessions of a unionist: an unpublished talk on things current, written in 1888. Ed F. V. L[ivingston], Cambridge Mass 1921.
The manuscripts of Stevenson's Records of a family of engineers: the unfinished chapters. Chicago 1930.
Silverado journal. Ed J. E. Jordan, San Francisco 1954.
From Scotland to Silverado. Ed J. D. Hart, Cambridge Mass 1966. First complete texts of Amateur emigrant and Silverado squatters, with unpbd essay, Simoneau's at Monterey.

Letters and Papers

Vailima letters: being correspondence addressed by Stevenson to Sidney Colvin, November 1890–October 1894. 1895.
The letters of Stevenson to his family and friends, selected. Ed S. Colvin 2 vols 1899, 4 vols 1911 (enlarged).
Some letters by Stevenson. Ed H. Townsend, New York 1902. 5 letters to A. T. Haddon 1879–84.
Letters to an editor. [1914] (priv ptd). To C. K. Shorter.
Letters to Charles Baxter. [1914] (priv ptd).
Some letters of Stevenson. Ed L. Osbourne 1914.
Henry James and Stevenson: a record of friendship and criticism. Ed J. A. Smith 1948. Chiefly letters.
RLS: Stevenson's letters to Charles Baxter. Ed De Lancey Ferguson and M. Waingrow, New Haven 1956.

§2

James, H. In his Partial portraits, 1888.
—— In his Notes on novelists, 1914.
Raleigh, W. Robert Louis Stevenson. 1895.
Hammerton, J. A. Stevensoniana. 1903, 1907, 1910 (rev).
Pinero, A. W. Stevenson the dramatist: a lecture. 1903; ed C. Hamilton, New York 1914.
Strong, I. and L. Osbourne. Memories of Vailima. 1903.
Stevenson, M. I. Letters from Samoa. 1906.
—— Stevenson's baby book: being a record of the sayings and doings of RLS. San Francisco 1922.
Swinnerton, F. Stevenson: a critical study. 1914.
Osbourne, L. An intimate portrait of RLS. New York 1924.
Chesterton, G. K. Robert Louis Stevenson. 1927.
Garrod, H. W. The poetry of Stevenson. In his Profession of poetry, Oxford 1929.
—— The poetry of Stevenson. In Essays presented to Sir Humphrey Milford, Oxford 1948.
Daiches, D. Stevenson. New York 1946.
—— Stevenson and the art of fiction. New York 1951.

Greene, G. From feathers to iron. In his Lost childhood and other essays, 1951.
Stevenson, Fanny. Our Samoan adventure. Ed C. Neider, New York 1955. A diary.
Aldington, R. Portrait of a rebel: the life and work of Stevenson. 1957.
McKay, G. L. Some notes on Stevenson, his finances, and his agents and publishers. New Haven 1958.
Pope-Hennessy, J. Robert Louis Stevenson. 1974.

GEORGE MOORE
1852–1933
Bibliographies

Korg, J. In Victorian fiction: a guide to research, ed L. Stevenson, Cambridge Mass 1964.

Collections

Works: Carra edition. 21 vols 1922–4; Uniform edition, 20 vols 1924–33; Ebury edition, 20 vols 1936–8.

§1

Flowers of passion. 1878 (for 1877). Poems.
Martin Luther: a tragedy in five acts. 1879. Verse; with Bernard Lopez.
Pagan poems. 1881.
A modern lover. 3 vols 1883, 1 vol 1885 (rev), New York 1890. Rewritten in 1917 as Lewis Seymour and some women.
A mummer's wife. 1885 (for 1884), 1886 (for 1885) (rev), 1918 (rev), New York 1889 (as An actor's wife), 1903, 1917 (rev).
Literature at nurse: or circulating morals. 1885. Pamphlet on the selection of books at Mudie's Library.
A drama in muslin: a realistic novel. 1886, 1915 (largely rewritten as Muslin), New York 1915.
A mere accident. 1887, 1895 (rewritten as John Norton in Celibates).
Parnell and his island. 1887. Sketches.
Confessions of a young man. 1888, 1889 (rev), 1904 (rev), 1917 (rev), 1926 (expanded), New York 1888, 1917 (rev).
Spring days: a realistic novel—a prelude to Don Juan. 1888, 1912 (rev with preface), New York 1891 (as Shifting love), 1912.
Mike Fletcher: a novel. 1889, New York 1890.
Impressions and opinions. 1891, 1913 (rev).
Vain fortune. [1891], 1895 (rev), New York 1892, 1892 (rev).
Modern painting. 1893, 1897 (for 1896) (enlarged), New York 1893, 1898 (enlarged), 1923 (with article from Impressions and opinions).
The strike at Arlingford: a play in three acts. 1893, New York 1894.
Esther Waters: a novel. 1894, 1899 (rev), 1920 (rev), 1926 (rev), Chicago 1894, 1899 (rev), New York 1894, 1899, 1901, 1917, 1921 (rev); ed G. Hough, Oxford 1964 (WC). Dramatized 1913, Boston 1913.
Celibates. 1895, New York 1895, 1915.
Evelyn Innes. 1898, 1898 (rev), 1901 (rev), 1908 (rev), New York 1898; tr German, 1905.
The bending of the bough: a comedy in five acts. 1900, 1900 (rev), New York 1900.
Sister Theresa. 1901, 1909 (rev), [1928] (entirely rewritten).
The untilled field. 1903, 1914 (rev), 1926 (rev), 1931 (rev), New York 1903, Leipzig 1903 (rev). Short stories.
The lake. 1905, 1905 (rev), 1921 (rev), New York 1906, Leipzig 1906 (rev).
Memoirs of my dead life. 1906, 1907, 1915 (expanded), 1921 (rev and enlarged), Leipzig 1906 (rev), New York 1907 (for 1906), 1920 (rev).

Reminiscences of the impressionist painters. Dublin 1906.

The apostle: a drama in three acts. Dublin 1911, Boston 1911, London 1923. Rewritten as The passing of the Essenes, 1930.

'Hail and farewell': a trilogy. London and New York 3 vols 1911–14, 2 vols 1925. Pt 1, Ave; Pt 2, Salve; Pt 3, Vale.

Elizabeth Cooper: a comedy in three acts. Dublin 1913, Boston 1913. Rewritten as The coming of Gabrielle, 1920.

The brook Kerith: a Syrian story. 1916, 1916 (rev), 1921 (rev), 1927, 1929, 1952, New York 1916, 1916 (rev), 1923 (rev).

Lewis Seymour and some women. 1917, New York 1917, 1922. A rewriting of A modern lover, above.

A story-teller's holiday. London and New York 1918 (priv ptd), 2 vols 1928 (rev with additional tales).

Avowals. 1919 (priv ptd), 1921 (rev), New York 1919 (priv ptd).

The coming of Gabrielle: a comedy. 1920 (priv ptd), New York 1921 (priv ptd), Leipzig 1922 (rev).

Héloïse and Abélard. 2 vols 1921 (priv ptd), 1 vol 1925, New York 1921, 1923 (rev), 1932. Some 'fragments' i.e. addns and corrections, were priv ptd New York 1921 and later edns.

In single strictness. 1922 (priv ptd), 1927 (as Celibate lives), New York 1922, 1923 (rev), 1927 (as Celibate lives).

Conversations in Ebury Street. 1924, 1930 (rev).

Peronnik the fool. New York 1924 (with Daphnis and Chloe), Mt Vernon NY 1926 (separately), Chapelle-Réanville France 1928 (rev), London 1933, 1933 (with Daphnis and Chloe).

The pastoral lives of Daphnis and Chloe, done into English from Longus. 1924, 1927, 1933 (with Peronnik, above), 1954, New York 1924 (with Peronnik), 1934.

Pure poetry: an anthology. 1924, New York 1924.

Ulick and Soracha. 1926, New York 1926. Incorporated in A story-teller's holiday, 1928.

The making of an immortal: a play in one act. New York 1927.

A flood. New York 1930.

The passing of the Essenes: a drama in three acts. 1930, 1931 (rev), New York 1930. A revision of The apostle, above.

Aphrodite in Aulis. 1930, 1931 (rev), New York 1930, 1931 (rev).

The talking pine. Paris 1931, Tempe Arizona 1948.

A communication to my friends. 1933 (used as new preface for Uniform and subsequent editions of A mummer's wife).

Letters

Moore versus Harris. Detroit 1921, Chicago 1925.

Letters to Edouard Dujardin 1866–1922. New York 1929. From the French, tr 'John Eglinton' (W. K. Magee).

Letters to Lady Cunard 1895–1933. Ed R. Hart-Davis 1957.

Moore in transition: letters to T. Fisher Unwin and Lena Milman [1888–1906]. Ed H. E. Gerber, Detroit 1968.

§2

Archer, W. Conversation with Mr Moore. Critic July 1901; rptd in his Real conversations, 1904.

Beerbohm, M. In his Christmas garland, 1912. A parody.
—— In his Mainly on the air, 1957 (enlarged). A broadcast of 1950, first pbd in Atlantic Monthly Dec 1950.

Ransom, J. C. A man without a country. Sewanee Rev 33 1925.
—— In his World's body, New York 1938.

'Mansfield, Katherine'. Esther Waters revisited. In her Novels and novelists, 1930.

Ford, F. M. Contrasts: memories of John Galsworthy

and Moore. Atlantic Monthly May 1933; rptd in his It was a nightingale, Philadelphia 1933.

Hone, J. M. The life of Moore. 1936.

Yeats, W. B. In his Dramatis personae, 1936.

Woolf, V. In her Death of the moth, 1942.

Cunard, N. GM: memories of Moore. 1957.

Hough, G. Moore and the novel. REL 1 1960; rptd in his Image and experience, 1960.
—— Moore and the nineties. In Edwardians and late Victorians, ed R. Ellmann, New York 1960; rptd in his Image and experience, 1960.

Noel, J. C. George Moore. Paris 1966.

RUDYARD KIPLING
1865–1936

Bibliographies

Livingston, F. V. Bibliography of the works of Kipling. New York 1927; Supplement, 1938.

Stewart, J. McG. Kipling: a bibliographical catalogue. Ed A. W. Yeats, Toronto 1959.

Collections

Collected Works

Outward bound edition. 36 vols New York 1897–1937.

Sussex edition. 35 vols 1937–9.

Burwash edition. 28 vols 1941.
Sussex and Burwash are the only edns containing all acknowledged and authorized works, and are identical in contents. Cited as SBE, below.

Selections

Soldier tales. 1896, New York 1896 (as Soldier stories).

The Kipling reader. 1900, 1901 (rev), 1908, 1925 (as Selected stories).

A choice of Kipling's prose. Ed W. S. Maugham 1952.

Verse

Kipling's verse: inclusive edition 1885–1918. 3 vols 1919, New York 1919 (omits Mowgli's song at the Council Rock), 1921 (adds Philadelphia, When 'Omer smote 'is bloomin' lyre), London 1921 (omits Great heart, adds 12 poems rptd from periodicals), 1927 (adds verses from Debits and credits, 7 rptd from periodicals and A song of the desert), 3 vols 1929 (adds 6 poems to The muse among the motors), 1933 (adds verses from Brazilian sketches, Limits and renewals, and 10 rptd from periodicals etc).

Kipling's verse: definitive edition. 1940, New York 1940. Omits early and miscellaneous verse rptd only in SBE.

A choice of Kipling's verse. Ed T. S. Eliot 1941.

§1

Schoolboy lyrics. Lahore 1881 (c. 50 copies priv ptd). Rptd in SBE except The night before.

Echoes, by two writers. Lahore 1884. 32 poems by Kipling, 7 by his sister.

Quartette, by four Anglo-Indian writers. Lahore 1885. Prose and verse by Kipling, his sister and parents. 2 stories by Kipling subsequently rptd; for 2 stories and 5 poems, no authorized reprint.

Departmental ditties and other verses. Lahore 1886, Calcutta 1886 (with 5 new poems), Calcutta 1888 (with 10 new poems), 1890 (10 new poems), 1891 (with glossary), 1898 (Edition de luxe), 1899 (rev) etc.

Plain tales from the hills. Calcutta 1888 (40 stories, 32 rptd from Civil & Military Gazette), 1890 (rev), New York 1890 (with letter from Kipling), New York 1899 (pirated, adds The last relief, only collected in SBE), New York 1899 (adds Bitters neat and Haunted subalterns, also collected in SBE with biographical introd by C. E. Norton), 1899 (rev).

Soldiers three. Allahabad 1888, 1890 (rev). 7 stories, 6 rptd from Week's News.

The story of the Gadsbys. Allahabad 1888, 1890 (rev). 8 scenes, 6 rptd from Week's News.

In black and white. Allahabad 1888, 1890 (rev). 8 stories, 7 rptd from Week's News.

Under the deodars. Allahabad 1888, 1890 (rev). 6 stories, 5 rptd from Week's News.

The phantom rickshaw and other tales. Allahabad 1888, 1890 (rev). 4 stories rptd from Quartette and Week's News.

Wee Willie Winkie and other child stories. Allahabad 1888 (for 1889), 1890 (rev). 4 stories, 3 rptd from Week's News.

Departmental ditties, barrack-room ballads and other verses. New York 1890. Ballads and other verses rptd from Scots Observer and Eng Illustr Mag.

The courting of Dinah Shadd and other stories. New York 1890, 1890. With essay by A. Lang. 6 stories rptd from magazines; 2nd edn substitutes Badalia Herodsfoot for Krishna Mulvaney.

The light that failed. New York 1890 (with happy ending as ptd in Lippincott's Mag, 12 chs), New York 1890 (unhappy ending, 14 chs), 1891 (15 chs, dedicatory poem and preface), 1898 (rev).

The city of dreadful night and other sketches. Allahabad 1890 (suppressed). 18 stories and sketches from Civil & Military Gazette and Pioneer; 4 not in SBE.

The city of dreadful night and other places. Allahabad 1891 (suppressed), 1891. 11 sketches rptd from Pioneer.

The Smith administration. Allahabad 1891 (suppressed). 20 articles rptd from Civil & Military Gazette and Pioneer.

Letters of marque. Allahabad 1891 (suppressed), 1891 (vol 1 suppressed). 19 articles rptd from Pioneer.

American notes. New York 1891. Piratical reprint from Pioneer.

Mine own people. New York 1891. With essay by H. James. 12 stories, 6 rptd from Courting of Dinah Shadd.

Life's handicap: being stories of mine own people. 1891, New York 1891. All stories from Mine own people except A conference of the powers, plus 17 stories, all but 3 rptd from periodicals.

The Naulahka: a story of West and East. 1892, New York 1892. Rptd from Century Mag. In collaboration with Wolcott Balestier.

Barrack-room ballads and other verses. 1892 (all but 8 poems rptd from books and periodicals), New York 1892, 1893 (as Ballads and barrack-room ballads, with 4 new poems from periodicals); The complete barrack-room ballads, ed C. Carrington 1973.

Many inventions. 1893. 14 stories (9 rptd from periodicals) and 2 poems.

The jungle book 1894 (7 stories rptd from periodicals, 7 poems), New York 1894 (with variants), London 1899 (rev).

The second jungle book. 1895 (8 stories rptd from periodicals, and 8 poems), New York 1895 (textual variants), London 1895 (rev). The two jungle books, 1924, stories rearranged.

Out of India. New York 1895. City of dreadful night and other places, Letters of marque, rptd without authority.

Soldiers three; The story of the Gadsbys; In black and white. New York 1895. Rev, 2 new stories from Civil and Military Gazette, not in English edn of 1895 or until SBE.

Wee Willie Winkie; Under the deodars; The phantom 'rickshaw. New York 1895. Rev, 2 new stories from Civil & Military Gazette, not in English edn of 1895 or until SBE.

The seven seas. 1896. 47 poems, 13 here first pbd.

The Kipling birthday book. 1896. Many quotations from verses in Civil & Military Gazette not otherwise rptd.

'Captains courageous': a story of the Grand Banks. 1897 (serialized in McClure's Mag and Pearson's Mag), New York 1897 (slight textual variants); ed J. de L. Ferguson, New York 1959.

An almanac of twelve sports. 1898. Verses to drawings by W. Nicholson.

The day's work. 1898. 12 stories rptd from periodicals; The brushwood boy rptd separately New York 1899, 1907, London 1907; The Maltese cat, London, and New York 1936.

A fleet in being: notes of two trips with the Channel Squadron. 1898 (rptd from Times, Morning Post, World).

Recessional and other poems. 1899. Unauthorized reprint of 4 poems from periodicals.

Stalky & Co. 1899 (9 stories rptd from magazines; The complete Stalky & Co., 1929, adds 5 stories, 4 previously collected in other vols, one from magazine); ed S. Marcus, New York 1962.

From sea to sea. New York 1899, 1900. Rev versions of Letters of marque, City of dreadful night, Smith administration, American notes etc.

With number three; Surgical and medical, and new poems. Santiago 1900. Unauthorized collection from periodicals etc; all items in SBE.

Kim. 1901 (serialized in McClure's Mag and Cassell's Mag), New York 1962 (preface by J. I. M. Stewart), New York 1962 (preface by C. E. Carrington), New York 1962 (preface by A. L. Rowse).

Just so stories for little children. 1902 (12 stories, 11 rptd from periodicals, and 9 poems); [Just so song book 1903, music by E. German]; New York 1903 (Outward bound edition vol 20, includes The tabu tale rptd from periodicals otherwise only collected in SBE); The Just so stories painting books, 1922–3.

The five nations. 1903. 54 poems, 28 of them unpbd.

Traffics and discoveries. 1904. 11 stories rptd from periodicals, 11 poems.

Puck of Pook's Hill. 1906 (11 stories rptd from Strand Mag; 16 poems), New York 1906 (small textual variants); All the Puck stories [with Rewards and fairies], 1935.

Letters to the family: notes on a recent trip to Canada. Toronto 1908. 8 articles rptd from newspapers, later included in Letters of travel; 7 poems later included in Songs from books and Verse.

Actions and reactions. 1909 (8 stories rptd from periodicals; 8 poems), New York 1909 (slight textual variants).

Abaft the funnel. New York 1909 (pirated), New York 1909 (authorized). 30 stories and sketches and one poem from Indian newspapers. No English edn until SBE.

Rewards and fairies. 1910, New York 1910 (textual variants), London 1926 (school edn, rev). 11 stories, (9 from periodicals), 23 poems.

A history of England. 1911, 1930 (rev). By C. R. L. Fletcher; 23 poems by Kipling, rptd in various verse collections and SBE.

Songs from books. New York 1912, Toronto 1912, London 1913 (with many addns). Poems from prose vols, many expanded.

The new army in training. 1915. 6 articles rptd, much rev, from Daily Telegraph.

France at war. 1915. 6 articles rptd from newspapers.

Fringes of the Fleet. 1915. 6 articles rptd from newspapers, and 6 poems.

Tales of 'the trade'. 1916. 3 articles rptd from Times.

Sea warfare. 1916. Fringes of the Fleet, Tales of 'the trade', Destroyers at Jutland, rptd from newspapers; one poem.

The war in the mountains. 1917, New York 1917; tr Italian, 1917. 5 newspaper articles. In SBE.

A diversity of creatures. 1917. 14 stories (12 rptd from periodicals), 14 poems.

The eyes of Asia. New York 1918. 4 articles rptd from newspapers. No English edn until SBE.

To fighting Americans. Paris [1918]. 2 speeches rptd from newspapers. Not in SBE.

The graves of the fallen. 1919, 1928 (rev as War graves of the Empire). Much is by Kipling; only one epitaph from it in SBE.

The years between. 1919 (46 poems, 12 new, rest rptd from periodicals etc), 1919. Bombay, Seven seas edns vol 25 add The muse among the motors, 20 parodies all in SBE.

Letters of travel (1892–1913). 1920. From tideway to tideway, Letters to the family, Egypt of the magicians rptd from periodicals, 1920 (Sussex edn vol 24 adds Brazilian sketches, 7 articles rptd from Morning Post pbd separately New York 1940).

The Irish Guards in the Great War. 2 vols 1923, New York 1923. Only rptd in SBE.

Land and sea tales for Scouts and Guides. 1923. One story, 8 poems new; 10 stories rptd.

Debits and credits. 1926. 14 stories rptd from magazines, 21 poems, 2 of them rptd.

A book of words. 1928. 31 speeches; 6 added in SBE.

Thy servant a dog. 1930 (3 stories, 2 rptd from Cassell's Mag), 1938 (as Thy servant a dog and other dog stories; adds 2 stories and 2 poems not previously collected).

Limits and renewals. 1932. 14 stories (11 rptd from magazines), 19 poems (one rptd).

Souvenirs of France. 1933. Sketches rptd.

Something of myself for my friends known and unknown. 1937. Serialized in Morning Post, New York Times, Civil & Military Gazette.

Letters

Letters from Kipling to Guy Paget 1919–36. 1936 (12 copies, priv ptd).

Cohen, M. N. Kipling to Rider Haggard: the record of a friendship. 1965.

§ 2

Young, W. A. A dictionary of the characters and scenes in the stories and poems of Kipling 1886–1911. 1911, 1921 (rev); rev J. H. McGrivring 1967 (as A Kipling dictionary).

Dobrée, B. Rudyard Kipling. Criterion 6 1927; rptd in his Lamp and the lute, Oxford 1929 and in Gilbert, below, 1965.

—— Rudyard Kipling. 1951.
—— Kipling: realist and fabulist. 1967.

Wilson, E. The Kipling that nobody read. Atlantic Monthly Feb 1941; rptd in his Wound and the bow, Boston 1941, in Rutherford 1964 and in Gilbert 1965, below.

'Orwell George', (E. Blair). Rudyard Kipling. Horizon Feb 1942; rptd in his Critical essays, 1946, and in Rutherford 1964 and in Gilbert 1965, below.

Trilling, L. Mr Eliot's Kipling. Nation (New York) 16 Oct 1943; rptd in Rutherford 1964 and Gilbert 1965, below.

Auden, W. H. The poet of encirclement. New Republic 25 Oct 1943.

McLuhan, H. M. Kipling and Forster. Sewanee Rev 52 1944.

Lewis, C. S. Kipling's world. In Literature and life, 1948 (Eng Assoc), Kipling Jnl 25 1958; rptd in his They asked for a paper, 1962 and in Gilbert, below, 1965.

Trevelyan, G. M. In his Layman's love of letters, 1954.

Carrington, C. E. Kipling: his life and work. 1955.

Eliot, T. S. In praise of Kipling. In his On poetry and poets, 1957. Rev preface to A choice of Kipling's verse, 1941.

—— Rudyard Kipling. Mercure de France Jan 1959; rev in Kipling Jnl 26 1959, rptd Gilbert, below, 1965.

Tompkins, J. M. S. The art of Kipling. 1959, 1965 (rev).

Stewart, J. I. M. In his Eight modern writers, Oxford 1963 (OHEL vol 12).

—— Rudyard Kipling. New York 1966, London 1967.

Bodelsen, C. A. Aspects of Kipling's art. Manchester 1964.

Rutherford, A. (ed). Kipling's mind and art. Edinburgh 1964. 5 rptd essays of 1940–60 and 6 new.

Gilbert, E. L. (ed). Kipling and the critics. New York 1965, London 1965. 14 rptd essays of 1891–1962, one new.

—— The good Kipling. Manchester 1972.

Green, R. L. Kipling and the children. 1965.

—— (ed). Kipling Jnl: centenary no Dec 1965.

—— (ed). Kipling: the critical heritage. 1971.

Henn, T. R. Kipling. 1967.

Sandison, A. The wheel of Empire. 1967.

VII. MINOR FICTION 1870–1900

'F. ANSTEY', THOMAS ANSTEY GUTHRIE

1856–1934

Bibliographies

Turner, M. J. A bibliography of the works of F. Anstey (Thomas Anstey Guthrie). 1931 (priv ptd).

Collections

Humour and fantasy. 1931. Includes Vice versa; The tinted Venus; A fallen idol; The brass bottle; The talking horse; Salted almonds.

§ 1

Vice versa: or a lesson to fathers. 1882, 1883 (rev), 1894 (with addns).

The giant's robe. 1884.

The black poodle and other tales. 1884.

The tinted Venus. Bristol 1885.

A fallen idol. 1886.

Burglar Bill and other pieces. [1888], [1892] (enlarged as The young reciter); ed C. L. Graves 1931 (with Mr Punch's model music-hall songs and dramas, below).

The pariah. 3 vols 1889.

Voces populi. 2 sers 1890–2. From Punch.

Tourmalin's time cheques. Bristol 1891, 1905 (as The time bargain: or Tourmalin's time cheques).

The travelling companions. 1892, 1908 (rev).

Mr Punch's model music-hall songs and dramas. 1892.

The talking horse and other tales. 1892.

Mr Punch's pocket Ibsen. 1893, 1895 (enlarged).

The man from Blankley's and other sketches, 1893. From Punch.

Under the rose: a story in scenes [from Punch]. [1894].

Lyre and lancet: a story in scenes. 1895.

The statement of Stella Maberley. 1896.

Puppets at large: scenes and subjects from Mr Punch's show. 1897.

Baboo Jabberjee BA. 1897. From Punch.

Love among the lions. 1898. From Idler Mag.
Paleface and Redskin, and other stories for boys and girls. [1898].
The brass bottle. 1900. From Strand Mag.
A Bayard from Bengal. 1902. From Punch.
Only toys! 1903. From Strand Mag.
Salted almonds and other tales. 1906.
In brief authority. 1915.
Percy and others: sketches, mainly reproduced from Punch. 1915.
The last load: stories and essays. 1925.
Four Molière comedies, freely adapted. 1931.
Three Molière plays, freely adapted. 1933.
A long retrospect. Oxford 1936.

SIR WALTER BESANT
1836–1901

Studies in early French poetry. 1868.
Jerusalem: the city of Herod and Saladin. 1871. With E. H. Palmer.
The French humourists. 1873.
Constantinople. 1879. With W. J. Brodribb.
Gaspard de Coligny. 1879.
Rabelais. 1879.
The revolt of man. 1882.
All sorts and conditions of men. 3 vols 1882.
All in a garden fair. 3 vols 1883.
The captain's room. 3 vols 1883.
The life and achievements of E. H. Palmer. 1883.
Life in an hospital: an East End chapter. [1883].
Readings in Rabelais. 1883.
The art of fiction: a lecture. 1884.
Dorothy Forster. 3 vols 1884.
Uncle Jack [etc]. 1885. 5 tales.
Children of Gibeon. 3 vols 1886.
Twenty-one years' work 1865–86. 1886 (Palestine Exploration Fund), 1895 (with addns).
Katherine Regina. Bristol [1887].
The world went very well then. 3 vols 1887.
Herr Paulus. 3 vols 1888.
The inner house. Bristol 1888.
The eulogy of Richard Jefferies. 1888.
Fifty years ago. 1888.
The doubts of Dives. Bristol [1889]; rptd in Verbena camellia stephanotis, below, 1892.
The bell of St Paul's. 3 vols 1889.
For faith and freedom. 3 vols 1889.
To call her mine, etc. 1889.
Armorel of Lyonesse. 3 vols 1890.
Captain Cook. 1890.
The demoniac. Bristol [1890].
The holy rose, etc. 1890.
St Katherine's by the Tower. 3 vols 1891.
Verbena camellia stephanotis etc. 1892. The doubts of Dives and 2 short stories.
The ivory gate. 3 vols 1892.
London. 1892.
The history of London. 1893.
The Society of Authors. 1893.
The rebel Queen. 3 vols 1893.
Beyond the dreams of avarice. 1895.
In deacon's orders, etc. 1895.
Westminster. 1895.
The charm and other drawing room plays. 1896. With W. Pollock.
The city of refuge. 3 vols 1896.
The master craftsman. 2 vols 1896.
A fountain sealed. 1897.
The rise of the Empire. [1897].
Alfred: a lecture. 1898.
The changeling. 1898.
The orange girl. 1899.

The pen and the book. 1899.
South London. 1899.
The fourth generation. 1900.
East London. 1901.
The Lady of Lynn. 1901.
The story of King Alfred. 1901.
Autobiography. 1902.
A five year's tryst and other stories. 1902.
London in the eighteenth century. 1902.
No other way. 1902.
The survey of London. 10 vols 1902–12. Ed Besant.
London in the time of the Stuarts. 1903.
As we are and as we may be. 1903. Essays.
Essays and historiettes. 1903.
The Thames. 1903.
London in the time of the Tudors. 1904.
Mediaeval London. 2 vols 1906.
Early London: Prehistoric, Roman, Saxon and Norman. 1908.
London in the nineteenth century. 1909.
London south of the Thames. 1912.

RHODA BROUGHTON
1840–1920

Not wisely, but too well. 3 vols 1867.
Cometh up as a flower. 2 vols 1867.
Red as a rose is she. 3 vols 1870.
'Goodbye, sweetheart': a tale. 3 vols 1872.
Nancy: a novel. 3 vols 1873.
Tales for Christmas Eve. 1873, 1879 (as Twilight stories).
Joan: a tale. 3 vols 1876.
Second thoughts. 2 vols 1880.
Belinda. 3 vols 1883.
Doctor Cupid: a novel. 3 vols 1886.
Alas!: a novel. 3 vols 1890.
A widower indeed. 1891. With E. Bisland.
Mrs Bligh: a novel. 1892.
A beginner. 1894.
Scylla or Charybdis?: a novel. 1895.
Dear Faustina. 1897.
The game and the candle. 1899.
Foes in law. 1900.
Lavinia. 1902.
A waif's progress. 1905.
Mamma. 1908.
Thr Devil and the deep sea. 1910.
Between two stools. [1912].
Concerning a vow. [1914].
A thorn in the flesh. 1917 (3rd edn).
A fool in her folly. [1920]. With an appreciation by Mrs Belloc Lowndes.

SIR THOMAS HENRY HALL CAINE
1853–1931

§ 1

Richard III and Macbeth: a dramatic study. 1877.
Recollections of D. G. Rossetti. 1882, 1929 (rev).
Cobwebs of criticism. 1883.
The shadow of a crime. 3 vols 1885.
The Deemster. 3 vols 1887.
A son of Hagar. 3 vols 1887.
Life of Coleridge. 1887.
The bondman: a new saga. 3 vols 1890.
The little Manx nation. 1891.
The scapegoat. 2 vols 1891.
Capt'n Davy's honeymoon and other stories. 1893.
The Manxman. 1894.
The Christian. 1897.
The Eternal City. 1901.

The prodigal son. 1904.
My story. 1908.
The white prophet. 2 vols 1909.
The woman thou gavest me. 1913.
King Albert's book. 1914. Ed Hall Caine.
The drama of 365 days: scenes in the Great War. 1915.
The master of man. 1921.
The woman of Knockaloe. 1923.
Life of Christ. 1938.

§2

Kenyon, C. F. Hall Caine: the man and the novelist. 1901.
MacCarthy, D. In his Portraits, 1931.

MARIE CORELLI
1864–1924

§1

A romance of two worlds. 2 vols 1886.
Vendetta, or the story of one forgotten: a novel. 3 vols 1886.
Thelma: a society novel. 3 vols 1887.
Ardath: the story of a dead self. 3 vols 1889.
My wonderful wife: a study in smoke. 1889.
Wormwood: a drama of Paris. 3 vols 1890.
The silver domino. 1892. Anon.
The soul of Lilith. 3 vols 1892.
Barabbas: a dream of the world's tragedy. 3 vols [1893].
The sorrows of Satan, or the strange experiences of one Geoffrey Tempest, millionaire: a romance. 1895.
The murder of Delicia. 1896.
The mighty atom. 1896.
Cameos: short stories. 1896.
Zisha: the problem of a wicked soul. 1897.
Jane: a social incident. 1897.
Boy: a sketch. 1900.
The master Christian. 1900.
God's good man: a simple love story. 1904.
The strange visitation of Josiah McNason: a Christmas ghost story. 1904.
Free opinions freely expressed on certain phases of modern social life and conduct. 1905.
The treasure of heaven: a romance of riches. 1906.
Woman or suffragette? a question of national choice. 1907.
Holy orders. 1908.
The devil's motor. 1910.
The life everlasting: a reality of romance. 1911.
Innocent, her fancy and his fact: a novel. 1914.
Eyes of the sea. 1917.
The young Diana: an experience of the future. 1918.
My little bit. 1919.
The love of long ago, and other stories. 1920.
The secret power. 1921.
Love and the philosopher. 1923.
Open confession to a man from a woman. 1925.
Poems. Ed B. Vyver 1925.

§2

Bullock, G. Marie Corelli: the life and death of a best-seller. 1940.
Sadleir, M. The camel's back: or the last tribulation of a Victorian publisher. In Essays presented to Sir Humphrey Milford, Oxford 1948.
Bigland, E. Marie Corelli: the woman and the legend. 1953.
Scott, W. S. Marie Corelli: the story of a friendship. 1955.

SIR ARTHUR CONAN DOYLE
1859–1930
Collections

Works: the author's edition. 12 vols 1903. Incomplete.
The principal works of fiction. 20 vols 1913.
Collected poems. 1922.
The Conan Doyle historical romances. 2 vols 1931–2.
The annotated Sherlock Holmes. Ed W. S. Baring-Gould 2 vols 1968.

§1

A study in scarlet. In Beeton's Christmas annual: twenty-eighth season, [1887]; 1888.
The mystery of Cloomber. 1889.
Micah Clarke. 1889.
Mysteries and adventures. 1889, 1893 (as The gully of Bluemansdyke and other stories).
The sign of four. 1890.
The captain of the polestar and other tales. 1890.
The firm of Girdlestone. 1890.
The white company. 3 vols 1891.
The doings of Raffles Haw. 1892.
The great shadow. 1892.
Beyond the city. New York 1892.
The adventures of Sherlock Holmes. 1892.
The refugees. 3 vols 1893.
Jane Annie. 1893. A comic opera, with J. M. Barrie.
The memoirs of Sherlock Holmes. 1894.
Round the red lamp: being facts and fancies of medical life. 1894.
The parasite. 1894.
The Stark Munro letters. 1895.
The exploits of Brigadier Gerard. 1896.
Rodney Stone. 1896.
Uncle Bernac: a memory of the Empire. 1897.
Songs of action. 1898.
The tragedy of the Korosko. 1898.
A duet with an occasional chorus. 1899.
The great Boer War. 1900.
The green flag and other stories of war and sport. 1900.
The hound of the Baskervilles. 1902.
The war in South Africa: its cause and conduct. 1902.
Adventures of Gerard. 1903.
The return of Sherlock Holmes.
Sir Nigel. 1906.
Through the magic door. 1907.
Round the fire stories. 1908.
The crime of the Congo. 1909.
The last galley. 1911.
Songs of the road. 1911.
The lost world. 1912.
The poison belt. 1913.
The German war: sidelights and reflections. 1914.
The valley of fear. 1915.
The British campaign in France and Flanders. 6 vols 1916–9.
A visit to three fronts. 1916.
His last bow. 1917.
Danger! and other stories. 1918.
The new revelation: or what is spiritualism? 1918.
The Guards came through, and other poems. 1919.
The vital message. 1919.
The wanderings of a spiritualist. 1921.
The case for spirit photography. 1922.
The coming of the fairies. 1922.
Our American adventure. 1923.
Three of them. 1923.
Memories and adventures. 1924.
Our second American adventure. 1924.
The spiritualist's reader. 1924.
The history of spiritualism. 2 vols 1926.
The land of mist. 1926.

The case-book of Sherlock Holmes. 1927.
Pheneas speaks. 1927.
The Maracot Deep and other stories. 1929.
Our African winter. 1929.
The adventure of the blue carbuncle. Ed E. W. Smith, New York 1948.

§2

Knox, R. In his Essays in satire, 1928.
Roberts, S. C. Doctor Watson. 1931.
—— Holmes and Watson: a miscellany. Oxford 1953.
Pearson, H. Conan Doyle: his life and art. 1943, 1961 (rev).
Sayers, D. In her Unpopular opinions, 1946.
Carr, J. D. The life of Conan Doyle. 1948.
Kenner, H. Baker Street to Eccles Street: the Odyssey of a myth. Hudson Rev 1 1949.
Isherwood, C. In his Exhumations, 1966.
Pearsall, R. Conan Doyle: a biographical solution. 1977.

JULIANA HORATIA EWING, née GATTY
1841–85
Collections

Uniform edition. 18 vols 1894–6.
Jackanapes, Daddy Darwin's dovecot, and the Story of a short life. 1916 (EL).
Mrs Overtheway's remembrances and other stories. 1916 (EL).

§1

Melchior's dream and other tales. 1862. Ed Mrs Gatty.
Mrs Overtheway remembrances. 1869.
The Brownies and other tales. 1870.
A flat iron for a farthing. 1872.
Lob-lie-by-the-fire: or the luck of Lingborough and other tales. 1874.
Six to sixteen. 1875.
Jan of the windmill. 1876.
A great emergency and other tales. 1877.
We and the world. 1880.
Old fashioned fairy tales. 1882.
Brothers of pity and other tales. 1882.
Blue and red. 1883.
Jackanapes. 1884.
Daddy Darwin's dovecot. 1884.
The story of a short life. 1885.
Mary's meadow. 1886.
Dandelion clocks and other tales. 1887.
The peace egg: a Christmas mumming play. 1887.
Snapdragon and old Father Christmas. 1888.
Verses for children. 3 vols 1888.

§2

Gatty (later Eden), H. K. F. Juliana Horatia Ewing and her books. 1885 (in Uniform edition, above).
Maxwell, C. Mrs Gatty and Mrs Ewing. 1949.
Laski, M. Mrs Ewing, Mrs Molesworth and Mrs Hodgson Burnett. 1951.
Avery, G. Mrs Ewing. 1961.

'MICHAEL FAIRLESS', MARGARET FAIRLESS BARBER
1869–1901

The gathering of Brother Bilarius. 1901.
The roadmender and other papers. 1902; ed N. E. Dowson 1926 (with addns).
The child king: four Christmas writings. 1902.

The grey brethren and other fragments in prose and verse. 1905.
Stories told to children. Ed 'M. E. Dowson' (W. S. Palmer) 1914.

JOHN MEADE FALKNER
1858–1932

Handbook for travellers in Oxfordshire. 1894.
The lost Stradivarius. 1895, Oxford 1954 (WC).
Moonfleet. 1898.
A history of Oxfordshire. 1899.
Handbook for Berkshire. 1902.
The nebuly coat. 1903, Oxford 1954 (WC).
Bath in history and social tradition. 1918.
Poems. 1933.

FREDERIC WILLIAM FARRAR
1831–1903

Eric, or little by little: a tale of Roslyn School. Edinburgh 1858.
Julian Home: a tale of college life. Edinburgh 1859.
St Winifred's: or the world of school. 1862.
The three Homes: a tale for fathers and sons. 1873 (under the pseudonym 'F.T.L.'), 1896 (signed).
Darkness and dawn, or scenes in the days of Nero: an historic tale. 2 vols 1891.
Gathering clouds: a tale of the days of St Chrysostom. 2 vols 1895.
Allegories. 1898.

KENNETH GRAHAME
1859–1932
§1

Pagan papers. 1894, 1898 (rev).
The golden age. 1895.
The headswoman. 1898. Story.
Dream days. 1899 (for 1898).
The wind in the willows. 1908; ed A. A. Milne, New York 1940.
Bertie's escapade. 1949.

§2

Chalmers, P. R. Life, letters and unpublished writings of Grahame. 1933.
Grahame, Mrs E. First whisper of the Wind in the willows. 1944.
Green, P. Grahame: a biography. 1959.
Graham, E. Kenneth Grahame. 1963.

SIR HENRY RIDER HAGGARD
1856–1925
Bibliographies

McKay, G. L. A bibliography of the writings of Rider Haggard. 1930.
Scott, J. E. A bibliography of the works of Rider Haggard. 1947.

§1

Cetywayo and his white neighbours. 1882, 1888 (with addns).
Dawn. 3 vols 1884.
The witch's head. 3 vols 1885.

King Solomon's mines. 1885; ed R. L. Green 1955.
She. 1887.
Jess. 1887.
Allan Quatermain. 1887.
A tale of three lions. New York 1887.
Mr Meeson's will. 1888.
Maiwa's revenge: or the war of the little hand. 1888.
My fellow laborer and the Wreck of the 'Copeland'. New York 1888.
Colonel Quaritch VC. 3 vols 1888.
Cleopatra. 1889.
Allan's wife and other tales. 1889.
Beatrice. 1890.
The world's desire. 1890. With Andrew Lang.
Eric Brighteyes. 1891.
Nada the lily. 1892.
Montezuma's daughter. 1893.
The people of the mist. 1894.
Church and State. 1895.
Joan Haste. 1895.
Heart of the world. New York 1895, London 1896.
The wizard. Bristol 1896.
Dr Therne. 1898.
A farmer's year. 1899.
The last Boer War. 1899. Rptd from Cetywayo, above.
Swallow. 1899.
Black heart and white heart, and other stories. 1900.
Lysbeth. 1901.
A winter pilgrimage. 1901.
Rural England. 2 vols 1902.
Pearl Maiden. 1903.
Stella Fregelius. 1904.
The brethren. 1904.
Ayesha: the return of She. 1905.
A gardener's year. 1905.
Report on Salvation Army colonies. 1905, 1905 (rev as The poor and the land).
The way of the spirit. 1906.
Benita. 1906.
Fair Margaret. 1907.
The ghost kings. 1908.
The yellow god. New York 1908, London 1909.
The lady of Blossholme. 1909.
Morning star. 1910.
Queen Sheba's ring. 1910.
The Mahatma and the hare. 1911.
Red eve. 1911.
Rural Denmark. 1911.
Marie. 1912.
Child of storm. 1913.
A call to arms. 1914 (priv ptd).
The wanderer's necklace. 1914.
The holy flower. 1915.
The ivory child. 1916.
Finished. 1917.
Love eternal. 1918.
Moon of Israel. 1918.
When the world shook. 1919.
The ancient Allan. 1920.
Smith and the Pharaohs, and other tales. Bristol 1920.
She and Allan. 1921.
The virgin of the sun. 1922.
Wisdom's daughter. 1923.
Heu-Heu. 1924.
Queen of the dawn. 1925.
The days of my life. 2 vols 1926.
Treasure of the lake. 1926.
Allan and the ice gods. 1927.
Mary of Marion Isle. 1929.
Belshazzar. 1930.

§2

Greene, G. Books in general. New Statesman 14 July 1951.
Haggard, L. R. The cloak that I left: a biography. 1951.

Cohen, M. Rider Haggard: his life and works. 1960.
—— Rudyard Kipling to Rider Haggard: the record of a friendship. 1965.

GEORGE ALFRED HENTY
1832–1902

§1

Out of the pampas: or the young settlers. 1871 (for 1870).
The young franc-tireurs. 1872.
Facing death. 1883.
Under Drake's flag. 1883.
With Clive in India. 1884.
True to the old flag. 1885.
With Wolfe in Canada. 1887.
The cat of Bubastes. 1889.
Redskin and cowboy. 1892.
In Greek waters. 1893.
Beric the Briton. 1893.
On the Irrawaddy. 1897.
With Buller in Natal. 1901.
With Roberts to Pretoria. 1902.
With Kitchener in the Sudan. 1903.
With the Allies to Pekin. 1904.
Also 75 other story-books for young people.

§2

Fenn, G. M. Henty: the story of an active life. 1907.
Thompson, J. C. The boys' Dumas: Henty. Cheadle 1975.

'ANTHONY HOPE',
SIR ANTHONY HOPE HAWKINS
1863–1933

§1

A man of mark. 1890.
Father Stafford. 1891.
Mr Witt's widow. 1892.
A change of air. 1893.
Half a hero. 2 vols 1893.
Sport Royal and other stories. 1893.
The Dolly dialogues. 1894.
The god in the car. 2 vols 1894.
The indiscretion of the Duchess. 1894.
The prisoner of Zenda. 1894; ed R. L. Green 1966 (EL) (with Rupert, below).
The chronicle of Count Antonio. 1895.
Comedies of courtship. 1896.
The heart of Princess Osra and other stories. 1896.
Phroso. 1897.
Rupert of Hentzau: being a sequel to a story by the same writer entitled the Prisoner of Zenda. Bristol [1898].
Simon Dale. 1898.
The King's mirror. 1899.
Quisanté. 1900.
Tristram of Blent. 1901.
The intrusions of Peggy. 1902.
Double harness. 1904.
A servant of the public. 1905.
Sophy of Kravonia. 1906.
Tales of two people. 1907.
The great Miss Driver. 1908.
Dialogue. 1909 (Eng Assoc lecture).
Second string. 1910.
Mrs Maxon protests. 1911.
A young man's year. 1915.
Captain Dieppe. 1918.
Beaumaroy home from the wars. 1919.
Lucinda. 1920.
Little tiger. 1925.
Memories and notes. [1927].

§2

Mallet, C. Anthony Hope and his books: being the authorized life of Sir Anthony Hope Hawkins. 1935.

Putt, S. G. The prisoner of the prisoner of Zenda: Hope and the novel of society. EC 6 1956.

WILLIAM HENRY HUDSON
1841–1922
Bibliographies

Wilson, G. F. A bibliography of the writings of Hudson. 1922.

Collections

Collected works. 24 vols 1922–3.
A Hudson anthology, arranged by Edward Garnett. 1924.
Works: uniform edition. 1951–.

§1

The purple land that England lost: travels and adventures in the Banda Oriental, South America. 2 vols 1885.
A crystal age. 1887 (anon), 1906 (with signed preface).
Ralph Herne. Youth 12 1888. Hudson's first story; not separately rptd, but included in Collected works, 1922–3, above.
Fan: the story of a young girl's life. 3 vols 1892. Pbd under the pseudonym 'Henry Harford'.
The naturalist in La Plata. 1892.
Birds in a village. 1893, [1920] (with Poems of birds by various writers).
Idle days in Patagonia. 1893.
British birds. 1895.
Birds in London. 1898.
Nature in Downland. 1900.
Birds and man. 1901.
El Ombú [and other tales]. 1902, 1909 (as South American sketches).
Hampshire days. 1903.
Green mansions: a romance of the tropical forest. 1904.
A little boy lost. 1905.
The land's end: a naturalist's impressions in West Cornwall. 1908.
Afoot in England. 1909.
A shepherd's life: impressions of the South Wiltshire downs. 1910.
Adventures among birds. 1913.
Far away and long ago: a history of my early life. 1918, 1931 (rev).
Birds in town and village. 1919.
The book of a naturalist. [1919].
Birds of La Plata. 2 vols 1920.
Dead man's plack, and An old thorn. 1920.
A traveller in little things. 1921.
A hind in Richmond Park. Ed M. Roberts 1922.
Rare, vanishing and lost British birds. 1923. Compiled from Hudson's notes by L. Gardiner.
153 letters. Ed E. Garnett 1923, 1925 (as Letters from W. H. Hudson to Edward Garnett).
Men, books and birds, with notes, some letters, and an introduction by Morley Roberts. 1925.

§2

Hamilton, E. W. H. Hudson. 1946.
Liandrat, F. Hudson, naturaliste: sa vie et son oeuvre. Lyons 1946.
West, H. F. Hudson's reading. 1947.
Haymaker, R. E. From pampas to hedgerows and downs: a study of Hudson. New York 1954.

RICHARD JEFFERIES
1848–87
Collections

Jefferies: selections of his work. Ed H. Williamson 1937.
Works: uniform edition. Ed H. C. Warren 6 vols 1948–9.

§1

Jack Bass, Emperor of England. Swindon 1873.
Reporting, editing and authorship. Swindon [1873].
The scarlet shawl: a novel. 1874.
Restless human hearts. 3 vols 1875.
The world's end. 3 vols 1877.
The gamekeeper at home. 1878.
Wild life in a southern county. 1879.
The amateur poacher. 1879.
Green Ferne Farm. 1880.
Hodge and his masters. 2 vols 1880.
Round about a great estate. 1880.
Wood magic: a fable. 2 vols 1880.
Bevis: the story of a boy. 3 vols 1882; ed E. V. Lucas 1904.
Nature near London. 1883.
The story of my heart: my autobiography. 1883.
The dewy morn: a novel. 2 vols 1884.
The life of the fields. 1884.
Red deer. 1884.
After London: or wild England, I: The relapse into barbarism; II: Wild England. 2 pts 1885.
The open air. 1885.
Amaryllis at the fair: a novel. 1887.
Field and hedgerow: being the last essays of Jefferies, collected by his widow. 1889.
The toilers of the field. 1892.
The early fiction of Jefferies. Ed G. Toplis 1896.
T. T. T. Wells. 1896. An early romance.
The hills and the vale. Ed E. Thomas 1909.
Hodge and his masters. Ed H. Williamson 1937.
The nature diaries and notebooks. Ed S. J. Looker, Billericay 1941.
Jefferies' countryside: nature essays. Ed S. J. Looker 1944.
Chronicles of the hedges and other essays. Ed S. J. Looker 1948.
Field and hedgerow. Ed S. J. Looker 1948.
The gamekeeper at home. Ed C. H. Warren 1948.
Field and farm: essays now first collected. Ed S. J. Looker 1957.

§2

Besant, W. The eulogy of Jefferies. 1888.
Salt, H. S. Jefferies: a study. 1894.
Symons, A. In his Studies in two literatures, 1897.
Thomas, E. Jefferies: his life and work. 1909.
Arkell, R. Richard Jefferies. 1933.
—— Jefferies and his countryside: biography of a countryman. 1947.
Keith, W. J. Jefferies: a critical study. 1966.

JEROME KLAPKA JEROME
1859–1927

§1

Idle thoughts of an idle fellow. 1886.
On the stage and off. 1888.
Stageland. 1889.
Three men in a boat (to say nothing of the dog). Bristol 1889.
Diary of a pilgrimage (and six essays). Bristol 1891.
Told after supper. 1891.

Novel notes. 1893. Rptd from Idler.
John Ingerfield and other stories. 1894.
Sketches in lavender, blue and green. 1897.
The second thoughts of an idle fellow. 1898.
Three men on the bummel. 1900.
The observations of Henry. 1901.
Paul Kelver. 1902.
Tea-table talk. 1903.
Tommy and Co. 1904.
Idle ideas in 1905. 1905.
The passing of the third floor back, and other stories. 1907. Dramatized, 1910.
The angel and the author and others. 1908.
They and I. 1909.
Malvina of Brittany. 1916.
All roads lead to Calvary. 1919.
Anthony John. 1923.
A miscellany of sense and nonsense from the writings of Jerome, selected by the author. 1923.
My life and times. 1926.

§ 2

Walkley, A. B. In his Playhouse impressions, 1892.
Moss, A. Jerome: his life and works. 1929.

RICHARD LE GALLIENNE
1866–1947

§ 1

My lady's sonnets. [Liverpool] 1887 (priv ptd).
Volumes in folio. 1889. Poems.
George Meredith: some characteristics. 1890.
The student and the body-snatcher. [1890]. With R. K. Leather.
The book-bills of Narcissus: an account rendered. [Derby] 1891, 1895 (3rd edn, rev).
English poems. 1892.
A fellowship in song. [Rugby 1893]. With Alfred Hayes and Norman Gale.
The religion of a literary man. 1893.
Young lives. 1893.
Limited editions: a prose fancy; together with Confessio Amantis: a sonnet. 1893 (priv ptd).
Bits of old Chelsea. 1894. With Lionel Johnson.
Prose fancies. 2 sers 1894–6.
Robert Louis Stevenson and other poems. 1895.
The quest of the golden girl. 1896.
Retrospective reviews. 2 vols 1896.
If I were God. 1897.
Rubáiyát of Omar Khayyám: a paraphrase. 1897.
The romance of Zion Chapel. 1898.
The worshipper of the image. 1899.
Sleeping beauty and other prose fancies. 1900.
The beautiful lie of Rome. 1900.
Rudyard Kipling: a criticism. 1900.
Travles in England. 1900.
The life romantic. 1901.
Perseus and Andromeda: the story retold. New York 1903.
Odes from the Divan of Hafiz freely rendered. 1903.
An old country house. 1903.
The burial of Romeo and Juliet. 1904.
How to get the best out of books. 1904.
Romances of old France. New York 1905.
Omar repentant. 1908. Poems.
Painted shadows. 1908.
Little dinners with the Sphinx and other prose fancies. 1909.
Attitudes and avowals. 1910.
New poems. 1910.
Orestes: a tragedy. New York 1910.
The loves of the poets. New York 1911.
October vagabonds. 1911.

The maker of rainbows, and other fairy-tales and fables. 1912.
The lonely dancer and other poems. 1914.
The highway to happiness. 1914.
Vanishing roads and other essays. 1915.
The silk-hat soldier and other poems. 1915.
Pieces of eight. 1918.
The junk man and other poems. New York 1920.
A jongleur strayed. New York 1922.
Old love stories retold. 1924.
The romantic Nineties. 1926; ed H. M. Hyde 1952.
There was a ship. [New York] 1930.

§ 2

Archer, W. In his Poets of the younger generation, 1902.
Whittington-Egan, R. and G. Smerdon. The quest of the golden boy: the life and letters of Le Gallienne. 1960.

WILLIAM HURRELL MALLOCK
1849–1923
Bibliographies

Nickerson, C. C. A bibliography of the novels of Mallock. Eng Fiction in Transition 6 1963.

§ 1

Poems. 1867 (priv ptd).
The parting of the ways: a poetic epistle. 1867.
The Isthmus of Suez. Oxford 1871.
Everyman his own poet: or the inspired singer's recipe book. Oxford 1872. Anon.
The new republic: or culture, faith and philosophy in an English country house. 2 vols 1877; ed J. M. Patrick, Gainesville 1950.
Lucretius. 1878.
The new Paul and Virginia: or Positivism on an island. 1878.
Is life worth living? 1879.
Poems. 1880.
A romance of the nineteenth century. 2 vols 1881.
Social equality: a short study in a missing science. 1882.
Atheism and the value of life: five studies in contemporary literature. 1884.
Property and progress: or a brief enquiry into contemporary social agitation in England. 1884. A reply to H. George, Progress and poverty.
The landlords and the national income. 1884.
The old order changes: a novel. 3 vols 1886.
In an enchanted island: or a winter retreat in Cyprus. 1889.
A human document: a novel. 3 vols 1892.
Labour and the popular welfare. 1893, 1894 (with Appendix).
Verses. 1893. Partly rptd from the 1880 collection, above.
The heart of life: a novel. 3 vols 1895.
Studies of contemporary superstition. 1895.
The individualist: a novel. 1899.
Doctrine and doctrinal disruption: being an examination of the intellectual position of the Church of England. 1900.
Lucretius on life and death. 1900. A very free adaptation of Lucretius in the metre of FitzGerald, Omar Khayyám.
The fiscal dispute made easy: or a key to the principles involved in the opposite policies. 1903.
Religion as a credible doctrine. 1903.
The veil of the temple: or from night to twilight. 1904.
The reconstruction of belief. 1905.
A critical examination of Socialism. New York 1907.
An immortal soul. 1908.
The limits of pure democracy. 1918, 1924 (abridged as Democracy.

Capital, war and wages: three questions in outline. 1918.
Memoirs of life and literature. 1920.

§ 2

Shaw, G. B. Socialism and superior brains: a reply to
  Mr Mallock. 1909.
Woodring, C. R. Notes on Mallock's The new republic.
  Nineteenth-Century Fiction 6 1952.
Nickerson, C. C. Mallock's contributions to the Miscel-
  lany. Victorian Stud 6 1962.
—— The novels of Mallock. Eng Fiction in Transition
  6 1963.
Tucker, A. V. Mallock and late Victorian Conservatism.
  UTQ 31 1962.

MARY LOUISA MOLESWORTH
née STEWART
1839–1921

§ 1

Tell me a story. 1875.
Carrots: just a little boy. 1876.
The cuckoo clock. 1877.
The tapestry room. 1879.
A Christmas child. 1880.
The adventures of Herr Baby. 1881.
Hoodie. 1882.
Two little waifs. 1883.
Christmas tree land. 1884.
Us: an old fashioned story. 1885.
Four winds farm. 1887 (for 1886).
The children of the castle. 1890.
Nurse Heatherdale's story. 1891.
The carved lions. 1895; ed G. Avery 1960; ed R. L. Green
  1964.
The house that grew. 1900.
Peterkin. 1902.
The story of a year. 1910.
Fairies afield. 1911.
Fairy stories. Ed R. L. Green 1957.

§ 2

Green, R. L. Mrs Molesworth. 1961.

ARTHUR MORRISON
1863–1945

§ 1

The shadows around us. 1891.
Martin Hewitt: investigator. 1894.
Tales of mean streets. 1894.
Chronicles of Martin Hewitt. 1895.
Zig-zags at the zoo. 1895.
A child of the Jago. 1896.
Hewitt: third series. 1896.
The Dorrington deed box. 1897.
To London town. 1899.
Cunning Murrell. 1900.
The hole in the wall. 1902.
The red triangle. 1903.
The green eye of Goona. 1904.
Divers vanities. 1905.
Green ginger. 1909.
The painters of Japan. 2 vols 1911.
Short stories of to-day and yesterday. 1929.
Fiddle O'Dreams. 1933.

§ 2

Pritchett, V. S. In his Living novel, 1947.
Bell, J. A study of Morrison. E & S new ser 5 1952.
Brome, V. In his Four realist novelists, 1965.

'OUIDA', MARIE LOUISE
de la RAMÉE
1839–1908

§ 1

Held in bondage. 3 vols 1863.
Strathmore. 3 vols 1865.
Chandos. 1866.
Under two flags. 3 vols 1867.
Cecil Castlemaine's gage and other novelettes. 1867.
Idalia. 3 vols 1867.
Tricotrin. 2 vols 1869.
Puck. 3 vols 1870.
Folle Farine. 3 vols 1871.
A dog of Flanders and other stories. 1872.
Pascarel. 3 vols 1873.
Two little wooden shoes. 1874.
Signa. 3 vols 1875.
In a winter city. 1876.
Ariadne: the story of a dream. 3 vols 1877.
Friendship. 3 vols 1878.
Moths. 3 vols 1880.
Pipistrello and other stories. 1880.
A village commune. 2 vols 1881.
In Maremma. 3 vols 1882.
Bimbi: stories for children. 1882.
Frescoes: dramatic sketches. 1883.
Wanda. 3 vols 1883.
Princess Napraxine. 3 vols 1884.
A rainy June. [1885].
Othmar. 3 vols 1885.
Don Gesualdo. 1886.
A house party. 1887.
Guilderoy. 3 vols 1889.
Ruffino etc. 1890.
Syrlin. 3 vols 1890.
Santa Barbara. 1891. Tales.
The tower of Taddeo. 3 vols 1892.
The new priesthood: a protest against vivisection. 1893.
Two offenders and other tales. 1894.
The silver Christ, and A lemon tree. 1894.
Toxin. 1895.
Views and opinions. 1895. Essays.
Le Selve and other tales. 1896.
An altruist. 1897.
The Massarenes. 1897.
La Strega and other stories. 1899.
Critical studies. 1900.
The waters of Edera. 1900.
Street dust and other stories. 1901.
Helianthus. 1908. Unfinished.

§ 2

Beerbohm, M. In his More, 1899.
Lee, E. Ouida: a memoir. 1914.
Bigland, E. Ouida: the passionate Victorian. 1950.

'Q', SIR ARTHUR THOMAS
QUILLER-COUCH
1863–1944
Collections

Selected stories by Q chosen by the author. [1921].
The Duchy edition of tales and romances. 30 vols 1928.

Collected poems. 1929.
'Q' anthology. Ed F. Brittain 1948.

§ 1

Athens: a poem. [Bodmin] 1881.
Dead man's rock. 1887.
The astonishing history of Troy Town. 1888.
The splendid spur. 1889.
Noughts and crosses: stories. 1891.
I saw three ships, and other winter's tales. 1892.
The blue pavillions. 1892.
The Warwickshire Avon. 1892.
The delectable Duchy: stories. 1893.
Green bays: verses and parodies. 1893.
Fairy tales, far and near. 1895.
Wandering heath: stories. 1895.
Adventures in criticism. 1896.
Ia. 1896.
Poems and ballads. 1896.
St Ives, by Robert Louis Stevenson. 1898. Completed
    from ch 31 by Quiller-Couch.
The ship of stars. 1899.
Old fires and profitable ghosts: stories. 1900.
The laird's luck and other fireside tales. 1901.
The Westcotes. 1902.
The white wolf and other fireside tales. 1902.
The adventures of Harry Revel. 1903.
Two sides of the face: tales. 1903.
The collaborators: or the comedy that wrote itself. 1903.
Hetty Wesley. 1903.
Fort Amity. 1904.
Shakespeare's Christmas and other stories. 1905.
Shining ferry. 1905.
From a Cornish window. 1906.
Sir John Constantine. 1906.
The Mayor of Troy. 1906.
Major Vigoureux. 1907.
Poison Island. 1907.
Merry-garden and other stories. 1907.
True Tilda. 1909.
Corporal Sam and other stories. 1910.
Lady Good for Nothing. 1910.
Brother Copas. 1911.
Hocken and Hunken. 1912.
The vigil of Venus and other poems. 1912.
In powder and crinoline: old fairy tales retold. [1913].
News from the Duchy. 1913.
Poetry. 1914.
Nicky-Nan, reservist. 1915.
On the art of writing. Cambridge 1916.
Memoir of A. J. Butler. 1917.
Mortallone and Aunt Trinidad: tales of the Spanish Main.
    1917.
Foe-Farrell. 1918.
Shakespeare's workmanship. 1918.
Studies in literature. 3 sers Cambridge 1918–29.
On the art of reading. Cambridge 1920.
Charles Dickens and other Victorians. Cambridge 1925.
The age of Chaucer. 1926.
A lecture on lectures. 1927.
The poet as citizen and other papers. Cambridge 1934.
Memories and opinions: an unfinished autobiography.
    Ed S. C. Roberts, Cambridge 1944.

Editions

The Oxford book of English verse 1250–1900. Oxford
    1900.
The Oxford book of ballads. Oxford 1910.
The roll call of honour. 1912.
The Oxford book of Victorian verse. Oxford 1912.
The King's treasuries of literature. 1920–.
The works of Shakespeare. Cambridge 1921—(New
    Cambridge edn). The comedies were edited by Quiller-

Couch and J. D. Wilson, the tragedies and histories by
Wilson alone.
The Oxford book of English prose. Oxford 1925.

§ 2

Archer, W. In his Poets of the younger generation, 1902.
Brittain, F. Quiller-Couch: a biographical study of
    'Q'. Cambridge 1947.

'MARK RUTHERFORD',
WILLIAM HALE WHITE
1831–1913

Bibliographies

Nowell-Smith, S. Mark Rutherford: a bibliography of
    the first editions. 1930.

§ 1

The autobiography of Mark Rutherford, dissenting
    minister. 1881. A novel.
Mark Rutherford's deliverance: being the second part of
    his autobiography. 1885, 1888 (rev and expanded with
    the Autobiography, above); ed B. Willey, Leicester
    1969.
The revolution in Tanner's Lane. 1887.
Miriam's schooling and other papers. 1890.
Catharine Furze. 2 vols 1893.
Clara Hopgood. 1896.
Pages from a journal, with other papers. 1900, 1910
    (expanded), Oxford 1930 (WC).
More pages from a journal. 1910.
Last pages from a journal. Ed D. V. White 1915.
The early life of Mark Rutherford (W. Hale White), by
    himself. 1913. Preface by White's son. An auto-
    biography.
Letters to three friends. Ed D. V. White 1924.

§ 2

Murry, J. M. The religion of Mark Rutherford. In his
    To the unknown God, 1924.
Stone, W. H. Religion and art of White. Stanford 1954.
MacLean, C. M. Mark Rutherford: a biography of
    W. H. White. 1955.
Stock, I. William Hale White (Mark Rutherford). 1956.

OLIVE SCHREINER
1865–1920

§ 1

The story of an African farm: a novel. 2 vols 1883. First
    pbd under the pseudonym 'Ralph Iron'.
Dreams. 1891.
Dream life and real life: tales by Ralph Iron. 1893.
The political situation in Cape Colony. 1896. With
    S. C. Schreiner.
Trooper Peter Halket of Mashonaland. 1897.
An English-South African's view of the situation: words
    in season. 1899.
Closer union: a letter on the South African Union and the
    principles of government. 1909.
Woman and labour. 1911.
Thoughts on South Africa. 1923.
The letters of Olive Schreiner. Ed S. C. Schreiner 1924.
From man to man: or perhaps only. 1926.
Undine. 1928. With introd by S. C. Schreiner.

§ 2

Schreiner, S. C. The life of Olive Schreiner. 1924.
Gregg, L. Memories of Olive Schreiner. 1957.

JOSEPH HENRY SHORTHOUSE
1834-1903
Collections

Collected edition of the novels. 6 vols 1891-4.

§ 1

John Inglesant: a romance. Birmingham 1880 (priv ptd), 2 vols 1881, 1881, 1882 (10 edns), 1 vol 1883 (3 edns) etc; ed M. Ramsey 1961 (abridged as John Inglesant in England).
The little schoolmaster Mark: a spiritual romance. 2 pts 1883-4.
Sir Percival: a story of the past and present. 1886.
A teacher of the violin and other tales. 1888.
The Countess Eve. 1888.
Blanche, Lady Falaise: a tale. 1891.
The life and letters of Shorthouse, edited by his wife [Sarah]. 2 vols 1905. Contains Literary remains.
Shorthouse also pbd a paper On the Platonism of Wordsworth, 1882, *and wrote introds to* George Herbert, The Temple *and to several devotional works.*

§ 2

Acton, J. E. D. C., Baron. In his Letters to Mary Gladstone, 1904. Contains a discussion of Shorthouse's historical point of view.
Polak, M. The historical, philosophical and religious aspects of John Inglesant. Oxford 1934.
Anson, H. The Church in nineteenth-century fiction: Shorthouse. Listener 4 May 1939.

ANNE ISABELLA THACKERAY, later LADY RITCHIE
1837-1923

§ 1

The story of Elizabeth. 1863, 1895 (with Two hours and From an island).
The village on the cliff. 1867.
Five old friends; and a young prince. 1868.
To Esther and other sketches. 1869.
Old Kensington. 1873.
Bluebeard's keys and other stories. 1874.
Toilers and spinsters and other essays. 1874.
Madame de Sévigné. 1881.
Miss Angel. 1875.
Miss Williamson's divagations. 1881.
A book of sibyls: Mrs Barbauld, Mrs Opie, Miss Edgeworth, Miss Austen. 1883.
Mrs Dymond. 1885.
Jack Frost's little prisoners. 1887.
Records of Tennyson, Ruskin and Robert and Elizabeth Browning. 1892.
Lord Tennyson and his friends. 1893.
Chapters from some memoirs. 1894.
Blackstick papers. 1908.
A discourse on modern sibyls. 1913 (Eng Assoc lecture).
From the porch. 1913. Essays.
From friend to friend, edited by Emily Ritchie. 1919. Reminiscences and a short story, Binnie.
Letters of Anne Thackeray Ritchie. Ed H. Ritchie 1924.
Lady Ritchie also edited or contributed introds to works by Thackeray, Mary Russell Mitford, Mrs Gaskell, Maria Edgeworth etc.

§ 2

Woolf, V. The enchanted organ: Anne Thackeray. In her Moment and other essays, 1948.

Fuller, H. T. and V. Hammersley. Thackeray's daughter: some reminiscences of Anne Thackeray Ritchie. 1952.

MRS HUMPHRY WARD, i.e. MARY AUGUSTA WARD, née ARNOLD
1851-1920
Collections

Writings, with introductions by the author. 16 vols 1911-12 (Westmorland edn).

§ 1

Milly and Olly: or a holiday among the mountains. 1881.
Miss Bretherton. 1884.
Amiel's Journal in time, translated with introduction and notes. 2 vols 1885.
Robert Elsmere. 3 vols 1888 (3 edns).
The history of David Grieve. 3 vols 1892 (6 edns, the 6th with a prefatory letter answering criticisms).
Marcella. 3 vols 1894.
The story of Bessie Costrell. 1895.
Sir George Tressady. 1896.
Helbeck of Bannisdale. 1898.
Eleanor. 1900.
Lady Rose's daughter. 1903.
The marriage of William Ashe. 1905.
Fenwick's career. 1906.
Play-time of the poor. 1906. Rptd from Times.
Diana Mallory. 1908.
Daphne: or marriage à la mode. 1909.
Canadian born. 1910.
Letters to my neighbours on the present election. 1910.
The case of Richard Meynell. 1911.
The mating of Lydia. 1913.
The Coryston family. 1913.
Delia Blanchflower. 1915.
Eltham House. 1915.
A great success. 1916.
Lady Connie. 1916.
'Missing'. 1917.
The war and Elizabeth. 1918.
A writer's recollections. 1918.
Cousin Philip. 1919.
Fields of victory: the journey through the battlefields of France. 1919.
Harvest. 1920, 1929 (as Love's harvest).

§ 2

Gwynn, S. L. Mrs Humphry Ward. 1917.
Trevelyan, J. P. Life of Mrs Humphry Ward. 1923.
Willey, B. How Robert Elsmere struck some contemporaries. E & S new ser 10 1957.
Laski, M. Words from Robert Elsmere. N & Q June 1961. Addns by R. L. Green, Oct 1961.

ISRAEL ZANGWILL
1864-1926
Bibliographies

Peterson, A. Zangwill: a selected bibliography. Bull of Bibliography 23 1961.

Collections

Works. 14 vols 1925.

§ 1

The Premier and the painter. 1888. With Louis Cowen.
The bachelor's club. 1891.
The big bow mystery. 1892.
Children of the Ghetto. 3 vols 1892.
The old maid's club. 1892.

Ghetto tragedies. 1893.
Merely Mary Ann. 1893.
The King of Schnorrers: grotesques and fantasies. 1894.
Joseph the dreamer. 1895.
The master. 1895.
Without prejudice: reprinted articles. 1896.
The celibates' club. 1898.
Dreamers of the ghetto. 1898.
'They that walk in darkness'. 1899.
The mantle of Elijah. 1900.
Blind children. 1903. Poems.
The grey wig: stories and novelettes. 1903.
Ghetto comedies. 1907.

Italian fantasies. 1910.
The war god: a tragedy. 1911.
The next religion. 1912. A play.
The melting pot: a drama. 1914.
The war for the world. 1916.
Jinny the carrier. 1919.
The voice of Jerusalem. 1920.

§ 2

Feftwich, J. Zangwill: a biography. New York 1957.
Wohlgelernter, M. Zangwill: a study. 1964.

4. DRAMA

I. GENERAL WORKS

Mss of plays submitted to the Lord Chamberlain in the first quarter of the century are in the Larpent Collection in the Huntington Library; those of plays submitted during the second quarter of the century have now been deposited by the Lord Chamberlain in the BM. See below, D. MacMillan (1939) *and* British Museum (1964).

(1) BIBLIOGRAPHIES ETC

Lowe, R. W. A bibliographical account of English theatrical literature. 1888.

Parker, J. Who's who in the theatre. 1912, 1967 (rev F. Gaye). Contains lists of casts and long 'runs'.

Firkins, I. T. E. Index to plays 1800–1926. New York 1927; Supplement to Index to plays 1800–1926, New York 1935.

MacMillan, D. Catalogue of the Larpent plays in the Huntington Library. San Marino 1939. Corrections and addns by E. Pearce, HLQ 6 1943.

Loewenberg, A. A bibliography of the theatre of the British Isles excluding London. 1950.

British Museum. Plays submitted to the Lord Chamberlain 1824–51: catalogue of additions to the manuscripts. 1964.

Arnott, J. F. and J. W. Robinson. English theatrical literature 1559–1900: a bibliography. 1969.

(2) GENERAL HISTORIES

Dickens, C. The amusements of the people. Household Words 30 March, 30 April 1850. A vivid picture of the early Victorian cheap theatres in London; see Great expectations chs 31, 47 and, for its provincial parallel, Nicholas Nickleby chs 20–5, 29, 48.

—— The guild of literature and art. Household Words 10 May 1851.

Cunliffe, J. W. Modern English playwrights: a short history of the English drama from 1825. New York 1927.

Downer, A. S. Players and painted-stage: nineteenth-century acting. PMLA 61 1946.

Nicoll, A. A history of English drama 1660–1900. Vol IV: Early nineteenth-century drama 1800–1850, Cambridge 1955; vol V: Late nineteenth-century drama 1850–1900, Cambridge 1959 (both rev).

Rowell, G. The Victorian theatre: a survey. Oxford 1956.

(3) CRITICISM

Archer, W. English dramatists of today. 1882.

—— About the theatre. 1886.

—— The theatrical 'World'. 5 vols 1893–7.

—— Study and stage: a yearbook of criticism. 1899.

—— Play-making. 1912, 1913, 1926, 1930.

—— The old drama and the new. 1923.

Shaw, G. B. The quintessence of Ibsenism. 1891, 1913 (rev).

—— Dramatic opinions and essays. 2 vols 1907.

—— Our theatres in the nineties. 3 vols 1932.

Beerbohm, M. Around theatres. 2 vols 1924, New York 1930, London 1953.

(4) COLLECTIONS

The London theatre: a collection of the most celebrated dramatic pieces. Ed T. J. Dibdin 26 vols 1815–18.

The new English drama. Ed W. Oxberry 20 vols 1818–23. Contains 100 plays, each with separate title-page.

[John] Duncombe's new acting drama. 12 nos [one play each] 1821–5.

[Thomas] Dolby's British theatre. 12 vols 1823–5. Contains 84 plays, each with separate title-page. Continued as Cumberland, below.

The British drama: a collection of the most esteemed tragedies, comedies, operas and farces in the English language. 2 vols 1824–6, Philadelphia 1837–8.

The London stage: a collection of the most reputed tragedies, comedies, operas, melo-dramas, farces and interludes. 4 vols [1824–7].

[John] Duncombe's British theatre. 67 vols [1828–52].

[John] Cumberland's British theatre; with remarks biographical and critical [by 'D.G.', George Daniel]. 48 vols 1826–[61]. Contains 398 plays.

[T.H.] Lacy's acting edition of plays, dramas, extravaganzas, farces etc. 165 vols [1849–1917]. In progress; pbd as single plays.

The British drama, illustrated. 12 vols 1864–72.

Moses, M. J. (ed). Representative British drama, Victorian and modern. Boston 1918.

Rowell, G. (ed). Nineteenth-century plays. Oxford 1953 (WC).

Brings, L. M. (ed). Gay nineties melodramas. Minneapolis 1963.

Booth, M. (ed). Hiss the villain: six English and American melodramas. 1964.

For further titles see C. J. Stratman, A bibliography of British dramatic periodicals, 1962; *and* J. F. Arnott and J. W. Robinson, English theatrical literature 1559–1900: a bibliography, 1969.

II. THE EARLY NINETEENTH-CENTURY DRAMA
1800–35

For abbreviations see cols 461–2, above.

CHARLES DANCE
1794–1863

A match in the dark. F. (Olym 21 Feb 1833). 1836; Dicks standard plays 852.

The Beulah spa. C. (Olym 18 Nov 1833). 1833; Dicks 446.

Pleasant dreams. F. (CG 24 May 1834). 1834; Lacy 80; Dicks 590.

The Bengal tiger. Ba. (Olym 18 Dec 1837).

Naval engagements. Ba. (Olym 3 May 1838). Ed B. N. Webster 4; Dicks 351.

Delicate ground: or Paris in 1793. C. (Lyc 27 Nov 1849). Dicks 1008.

A morning call. C. (DL 17 March 1851). [1847]; Lacy 22.

Marriage a lottery. F. (Str 20 May 1858); Lacy 36.

See also Nicoll 4, pp. 288–9, 578–9; 5, pp. 335.

CHARLES ISAAC MUNGO DIBDIN
known as CHARLES DIBDIN
1768–1833

§ 1

Wizard's wake: or harlequin's regeneration. [1803].

The little gipsies. [1804].

Harlequin and the water kelpe. 1806.

Mirth and metre: consisting of poems, serious, humorous and satirical. 1807.

The wild man: or the water pageant. 1809, 1814.

The council of ten: or the lake of the grotto. 1811.

The farmer's wife. 1814.

My spouse and I. 1815, 1816.

Young Arthur, or the child of mystery: a metrical romance. 1819.

Life in London: or the day and night adventures of Logic, Tom and Jerry. 1821.

Comic tales and lyrical fancies: including the Chessiad, a mock heroic in five cantos; and the wreath of love in four cantos. 1825.

History and illustrations of the London theatres: comprising an account of the origin and progress of the drama in England. 1826.

Dibdin was enormously productive. Most of his pieces were pantomimes, operatic farces and melodramas.

§ 2

Memoirs of Charles Dibdin the younger. Ed G. Speaight 1955.

THOMAS JOHN DIBDIN
1771–1841

The mouth of the Nile, or the glorious first of August: a musical entertainment. 1798.

The Jew and the doctor. 1800, 1809 (in Mrs Inchbald's Collection of farces, vol 2).

Il Bondocani: or the caliph robber. 1801, 1801 (songs and choruses).

Valentine and Orson. 1804.

The cabinet. Dublin 1802 (pirated), 1805, New York 1809, 1810, 1811; 1802, 1803 (songs and duets).

Two faces under a hood. [1807], 1807 (songs and duets).

Harlequin harper: or a jump from Japan. 1813.

A metrical history of England: or recollections in rhyme of some of the most prominent features in our national chronology. 2 vols 1813.

Ivanhoe: or the Jew's daughter. 1820.

The fate of Calais. 1820, nd.

The reminiscences of Thomas Dibdin. 2 vols 1827, 1837.

Thomas Dibdin's penny trumpet. 1832. A periodical of which only 4 nos appeared.

Bunyan's Pilgrim's progress metrically condensed. 1834.

Dibdin also wrote many songs, and several collections were pbd.

CHARLES KEMBLE
1775–1854

The point of honour. 1800, 1801, 1805.

The wanderer: or the rights of hospitality. 1808, [1809].

Plot and counterplot: or the portrait of Michael Cervantes. 1808, 1812.

Kemble (afterwards Butler), F. A. Record of a girlhood: an autobiography. 3 vols 1878.

—— Records of later life. 3 vols 1882.

JAMES SHERIDAN KNOWLES
1784–1862

§ 1

The Welch harper: a ballad. 1796.

Fugitive pieces. 1810.

Caius Gracchus. Glasgow 1823.

Virginius: or the liberation of Rome. 1820, 1820, 1823 (5th edn).

William Tell. 1825.

The beggar's daughter of Bethnal Green. 1828.

The hunchback. 1832, 1832, 1836.

The wife: a tale of Mantua. 1833 (6 edns). Charles Lamb wrote a prologue and an epilogue to the play.

The love-chase. 1837.

Fortescue: a novel. 1846 (priv ptd), 3 vols 1847.

George Lovell: a novel. 3 vols 1847.

The rock of Rome: or the arch heresy. 1849.

The idol demolished by its own priest: an answer to Cardinal Wiseman's lectures on transubstantiation. Edinburgh 1851.

The gospel attributed to Matthew is the record of the whole original apostlehood. 1855.

Lectures on dramatic literature etc: lectures on oratory, gesture and poetry; to which is added a correspondence with four clergymen in defence of the stage. Ed S. W. Abbott and F. Harvey 2 vols 1873 (priv ptd).

Lectures on dramatic literature: Macbeth. 1875.

Tales and novelettes. Rev and ed F. Harvey 1874 (priv ptd).

§ 2

Hazlitt, W. In his Spirit of the age, 1825.

Knowles, R. B. The life of Knowles. Rev and ed F. Harvey 1872 (priv ptd).

Meeks, L. H. Knowles and the theatre of his time. Bloomington 1933. With bibliography.

SIR THOMAS NOON TALFOURD
1795–1854
Collections

Tragedies; to which are added a few sonnets and verses. 1844, 1852 (11th edn).

§ 1

Poems on various subjects. 1811.

The Athenian captive. 1838.

Ion, T. [1835] (priv ptd), [1835] (priv ptd, with a few sonnets), 1836 (3 edns), 1837 (4 edns).

The letters of Charles Lamb, with a sketch of his life by T. N. Talfourd. 1837.

Speech delivered in the House of Commons on moving for leave to bring in a Bill to consolidate the law relating to copyright and to extend the term of its duration. 1837.

Glencoe: or the fate of the Macdonalds. 1839 (priv ptd), 1840.

Three speeches in favour of a measure for an extension of copyright. 1840.

Speech for the defendant in the prosecution of the Queen v. Moxon for the publication of Shelley's works. 1841.

Recollections of a first visit to the Alps, in August and September 1841. [1842?] (priv ptd).

Vacation rambles and thoughts. 2 vols 1845, 1851.

Supplement to Vacation rambles. 1854.

Final memorials of Charles Lamb, consisting chiefly of his letters not before published. 1848, 1850.

The Castilian. 1853.

III. THE MID-NINETEENTH-CENTURY DRAMA

THOMAS WILLIAM ROBERTSON
1829–1871
Collections

Principal dramatic works, with a memoir by his son [T. W. S. Robertson]. 2 vols 1889.

§ 1

David Garrick: a love story. 1865. A novel.

Caste. Ed M. J. Moses, Boston 1918; ed M. Slater 1951.

Home. New York [1879].

School. Philadelphia 1903.

My Lady Clara. New York [1875?].

§ 2

Pemberton, T. E. The life and writings of Robertson. 1893.

Savin, M. Robertson: his plays and stagecraft. Providence 1950.

GILBERT ABBOT À BECKETT
1811–56

§ 1

Scenes from the rejected comedies, by some of the competitors for the prize of £500 offered by Mr B. Webster. 1844.

The comic Blackstone. 1844, 1846 (illustr G. Cruikshank).

The quizziology of the British drama. 1846.

The comic history of England, with coloured etchings and woodcuts by John Leech. 2 vols 1847–8, 1894.

The comic history of Rome, illustrated by John Leech. 1852, [1897].

À Beckett is supposed to have written '50 or 60' pieces.

§ 2

À Beckett, A. W. The à Becketts of Punch: memories of father and sons. 1903.

DIONYSIUS LARDNER BOUCICAULT
1822–90
Collections

Forbidden fruit and other plays. Ed A. Nicoll and F. T. Clark, Princeton 1940.

Krause, D. (ed). The Dolmen Boucicault; with an essay by the editor on the theatre of Dion Boucicault and the complete authentic texts of Boucicault's three Irish plays. 1964.

§ 1

London assurance. 1841, 1841.

Old heads and young hearts. [1845], [1845].

The knight of Arva. New York [1868?].

The Corsican brothers. [1852].

Arrah-na-Pogue: or the Wicklow wedding. [1865].

The art of acting. New York 1926.

§ 2

Walsh, T. The career of Dion Boucicault. [1915].

Duggan, G. C. The stage Irishman. Dublin 1937.

DOUGLAS WILLIAM JERROLD
1803–57
Collections

Writings. 8 vols 1851–4.

Works, with an introductory memoir by his son W. B. Jerrold. 4 vols 1863–4.

§ 1

The rent day. 1832.

Beau Nash, the king of Bath. 1834.

Men of character. 3 vols 1838.

Heads of the people, drawn by Kenny Meadows, described by Douglas Jerrold [et al]. 2 vols 1840–1.

Punch's letters to his son. 1843.
The story of a feather. 1844.
Time works wonders. 1845.
Punch's complete letter writer. 1845.
The chronicles of Clovernook; with some account of the
    hermit of Bellyfulle. 1846.
Mrs Caudle's curtain lectures. 1846 etc.; ed W. Jerrold
    1907 (WC).
A man made of money. 1849.
Cakes and ale. 1852. Tales and essays.
The Brownrigg papers. Ed B. Jerrold 1860.
Other times: being Liberal leaders contributed to Lloyd's
    Weekly Newspaper by Douglas and Blanchard Jerrold.
    1868.
The barber's chair: and the hedgehog letters. Ed B.
    Jerrold 1874.

§ 2

Jerrold, W. B. The life and remains of Jerrold. 1859.
Stirling, J. H. Jerrold, Tennyson and Macaulay. Edin-
    burgh 1868.
Jerrold, W. Jerrold and Punch. 1910.
—— Jerrold: dramatist and wit. 2 vols [1914].

TOM TAYLOR
1817–80

*There is a large collection of Taylor mss in the British
Theatre Museum.*

§ I

Masks and faces: or before and behind the curtain. 1854.
    With C. Reade. Played also as Peg Woffington.
Our American cousin. 1869.
The fool's revenge. New York [1863?].
Birket Foster's pictures of English landscape; with
    pictures in words by Tom Taylor. 1863 (for 1862).
Life and times of Sir Joshua Reynolds, commenced by
    C. R. Leslie, continued by Tom Taylor. 2 vols 1865.
The theatre in England: some of its shortcomings and
    possibilities. 1871.
Storm at midnight, and other poems. Ed J. H. Burn,
    Mintlaw 1893.
Taylor edited Punch *from 1874 until his death in 1880.
Besides the above works, he edited* C. R. Leslie, Auto-
biographical recollections, 1860; B. R. Haydon, Life,
1853.

§ 2

Tolles, W. Taylor and the Victorian Drama. New York
    1940.

IV. THE LATE NINETEENTH-CENTURY DRAMA

SIR WILLIAM SCHWENCK GILBERT
1836–1911

Bibliographies etc

Searle, T. A bibliography of Gilbert, with bibliographical
    adventures in the Gilbert and Sullivan operas; introduc-
    tion by R. E. Swartwout. [1931] (priv ptd), 1931
    (as Gilbert: a topsy-turvy adventure).
Dunn, G. E. A Gilbert and Sullivan dictionary. 1936.

Collections

Original plays. Ser 1, 1876; ser 2, [1881] etc; ser 3, 1895;
    ser 4, 1911, 1920 (enlarged).
The Savoy operas: being the complete text of the Gilbert
    and Sullivan operas. 1926.

§ I

The 'Bab' ballads: much sound and little sense, with
    illustrations by the author. 1869, 1870.
More 'Bab' ballads; with illustrations by the author.
    [1873].
The 'Bab' ballads and more 'Bab' ballads: much sound
    and little sense; with illustrations by the author. [1874];
    ed J. Ellis, Cambridge Mass 1970. Complete.

Trial by jury: a novel original dramatic cantata. 1875,
    1888 (full score), [1898] (with Sorcerer). With Arthur
    Sullivan.
The sorcerer: an entirely original modern comic opera.
    [1877], [1884?].
HMS Pinafore, or the lass that loved a sailor: an entirely
    original nautical comic opera. [1878], New York 1879.
    With Sullivan.
The pirates of Penzance, or the slave of duty: an entirely
    original comic opera. [1887?]. With Sullivan.
An entirely new and original aesthetic opera, in two acts,
    entitled Patience: or Bunthorne's bride! [1881]. With
    Sullivan.
An entirely original fairy opera in two acts, entitled
    Iolanthe: or the peer and the peri. [1885]. With
    Sullivan.
A respectful operatic per-version of Tennyson's Princess
    in two acts, entitled Princess Ida: or Castle Adamant.
    [1884]. With Sullivan.
An entirely new and original Japanese opera in two acts,
    entitled the Mikado: or the town of Titipu. [1885].
    With Sullivan.
An entirely original supernatural opera in two acts,
    entitled Ruddygore: or the witch's curse! [1887].
    Spelling of title altered to Ruddigore 4 days after
    production. With Sullivan.
A new and original opera in two acts, entitled the Yeomen

of the Guard: or the merryman and his maid. [1888]. With Arthur Sullivan.

An entirely original comic opera in two acts, entitled the Gondoliers: or the King of Barataria. [1889]. With Sullivan.

Songs of a Savoyard, illustrated by the author. 1890. Lyrics from the operas performed at the Savoy Theatre.

Foggerty's fairy and other tales. 1890.

The Grand Duke, or the statutory duel: a comic opera. 1896.

The Bab ballads, with which are included Songs of a Savoyard; with 350 illustrations by the author. 1898.

Lost Bab ballads: collected and illustrated by T. Searle. 1932.

§2

Archer, W. In his English dramatists of today, 1882.

Fitzgerald, P. H. The Savoy opera and the Savoyards. 1894.

Goldberg, A. Gilbert, a study in modern satire: handbook on Gilbert and the Gilbert and Sullivan operas. Boston [1913].

— The story of Gilbert and Sullivan. 1929.

Cellier, F. A. and C. Bridgeman. Gilbert, Sullivan and D'Oyly Carte: reminiscences of the Savoy and the Savoyards. 1914, 1927.

Dark, S. and R. Grey. Gilbert: his life and letters. 1923.

Godwin, A. H. Gilbert and Sullivan: a critical appreciation of the Savoy operas; with an introduction by G. K. Chesterton. 1926.

Pearson, H. Gilbert and Sullivan: a biography. 1935, 1947 (rev).

— Gilbert: his life and strife. 1957.

Darlington, W. A. The world of Gilbert and Sullivan. New York 1950.

Moore, F. L. (ed). The handbook of Gilbert and Sullivan. 1962.

HENRY ARTHUR JONES
1851–1929

Collections

Representative plays. Ed C. Hamilton 4 vols 1926.

§1

Saints and sinners. 1891.

The middleman. [1907].

Judah. New York 1894.

The dancing girl: a drama. [1907].

The crusaders: an original comedy of modern London life. 1893.

The bauble shop. [1893].

The tempter: a tragedy in verse. [1893] (priv ptd), 1898.

The masqueraders. [1894] (priv ptd), 1899.

The case of rebellious Susan. 1894 (priv ptd), 1897.

The triumph of the Philistines: a comedy. 1895 (priv ptd), 1899.

Grace Mary. [1895] (priv ptd); rptd in The theatre of ideas, 1915.

The renascence of the English drama: essays, lectures and fragments relating to the modern English stage 1883–94. 1895.

Michael and his lost angel. [1896] (priv ptd), 1896.

The rogue's comedy. [1896] (priv ptd), 1898.

The physician. [1897] (priv ptd), 1899.

The liars: an original comedy. [1897] (priv ptd), New York 1901.

The manoeuvres of Jane: an original comedy. [1898] (priv ptd), 1904.

Carnac Sahib. 1899 (priv ptd), 1899.

The lackey's carnival. 1900 (priv ptd).

Mrs Dane's defence. [1900] (priv ptd), 1905.

The Princess's nose: a comedy. [1902] (priv ptd).

Chance the idol. [1902] (priv ptd).

James the fogey. [1902] (priv ptd).

Whitewashing Julia: a comedy. [1903] (priv ptd), 1905.

Joseph entangled: a comedy. [1904] (priv ptd), [1906].

The chevaleer: a comedy. [1904] (priv ptd), [1905 ?].

The heroic Stubbs: a comedy. [1906] (priv ptd).

The hypocrites. [1907] (priv ptd), [1908].

The evangelist: a tragi-comedy. [1908 ?] (as The Galilean's victory).

Dolly reforming herself: a comedy. [1908] (priv ptd), [1913].

The knife. [New York 1909 ?].

Fall in, rookies. [1910] (priv ptd).

We can't be as bad as all that. New York 1910 (priv ptd).

The ogre. [1911 ?].

Lydia Gilmore. [1912 ?].

Mary goes first: a comedy. 1913.

The foundations of a national drama: a collection of lectures, essays and speeches, delivered and written in the years 1896–1912. 1913

The goal. [1919 ?] (priv ptd); in The theatre of ideas, 1915.

The lie. New York 1915, London 1923.

The theatre of ideas: a burlesque allegory; and three one-act plays: The goal; Her tongue; Grace Mary. 1915.

The pacifists: a parable. [1917 ?] (priv ptd).

Patriotism and popular education. 1919, 1919.

My dear Wells: a manual for the haters of England; being a series of letters upon Bolshevism, collectivism, internationalism and the distribution of wealth, addressed to Mr H. G. Wells. 1921, 1922.

What is capital? an inquiry into the meaning of the words 'capital' and 'labour'. 1925.

§2

Walkley, A. B. In his Playhouse impressions, 1892.

— In his Drama and life, 1907.

Archer, W. In his Old drama and the new, 1923.

Jones, D. A. The life and letters of Jones. 1930.

Cordell, R. A. Jones and the modern drama. 1932.

SIR ARTHUR WING PINERO
1855–1934

Collections

The social plays of Pinero. Ed C. Hamilton 4 vols New York 1917–22.

§1

The squire: an original comedy. [1905].

The rocket: an original comedy. [1905].

In chancery: an original fantastic comedy. [1905].

The magistrate: a farce. 1892.

The schoolmistress: a farce. 1894.

The hobby-horse: a comedy. 1892.

Dandy Dick: a farce. 1893.

Sweet Lavender: a domestic drama. 1893.

The weaker sex: a comedy. 1894.

The profligate. 1892.

The Cabinet Minister: a farce. 1892.

Lady Bountiful: a story of years. 1892.

The Times: a comedy. 1891.

The Amazons: a farcical romance. 1895.

The second Mrs Tanqueray. 1895.

The notorious Mrs Ebbsmith: a drama. 1895.

The benefit of the doubt: a comedy. 1896.

The Princess and the butterfly, or the fantastics: a comedy. 1898.

Trelawny of the 'Wells': a comedietta. New York 1898, London 1899.

The gay Lord Quex. 1900.

Iris. 1902.

Robert Louis Stevenson the dramatist: a lecture. 1903,

1909 (in Critic 42), New York 1914 (with introd and biographical appendix by C. Hamilton).
Letty. 1904.
A wife without a smile: a comedy in disguise. 1905.
His house in order. 1909.
The thunderbolt. 1909.
Mid-channel. 1910.
Preserving Mr Panmure: a comic play. 1912.
The 'mind the paint' girl: a comedy. 1913.
Browning as a dramatist. Trans Royal Soc of Lit 31 1912.
The big drum: a comedy. 1915.
The freaks, an idyll of suburbia: a comedy. 1922.
The enchanted cottage: a fable. 1922.
Dr Harmer's holidays: a contrast in nine scenes. 1930. Pbd with Child man: a sedate farce (unacted) in Two plays, 1930 (with preface).
Collected letters [1873–1933]. Ed J. P. Wearing, Minneapolis 1974.

§2

Archer, W. In his English dramatists of to-day, 1882.
—— In his Old drama and the new, 1923.
Moore, G. In his Impressions and opinions, 1913.
Mason, A. E. W. Sir George Alexander and the St James's Theatre. 1935.
Boas, F. S. In his From Richardson to Pinero, 1936.
Dunkel, W. D. Pinero: a critical biography with letters. Chicago [1941], London 1943.

GEORGE BERNARD SHAW
1856–1950

Bibliographies etc
Broad, C. L. and V. M. Dictionary to the plays and novels of Shaw, with bibliography of his works and of the literature concerning him; with a record of the principal Shavian play productions. 1929.

Collections
Plays pleasant and unpleasant. 2 vols 1898.
Three plays for Puritans: The Devil's disciple, Caesar and Cleopatra and Captain Brassbound's conversion. 1901.
Dramatic opinions and essays, with an apology; containing as well a word on the dramatic opinions and essays of Shaw by James Huneker. 2 vols New York 1906, 1906 (with preface), London 1907. Selected from Saturday Rev 5 Jan 1895–21 May 1898.
Works. 33 vols 1930–8. First 30 vols issued as Ayot St Lawrence edn, New York 1930–2. (Limited collected edn).
Standard edition. 34 vols 1931–51.
Complete plays. 1931, 1934, 1938, 1950, 1952, 1965.
Prefaces. 1934.
Plays and players: selected essays. Ed A. C. Ward 1952.
Shaw on theatre. Ed E. J. West, New York 1958, 1959 (rev by D. H. Laurence), London 1959.
Platform and pulpit. Ed D. H. Laurence, New York 1961, London 1962.
Shaw on Shakespeare. Ed E. Wilson, New York 1961, London [1962].
GBS on music. 1962.
Collected plays with their prefaces. Ed D. H. Laurence 7 vols 1970–4.

§1

Cashel Byron's profession: a novel. 1886, [1889] (rev), 1901 (newly rev as Novels of his nonage, no 4). First pbd in To-day 1885–6; dramatized as The admirable Bashville.
An unsocial Socialist. 1887. First pbd in To-day 1884.
Fabian essays in Socialism. 1889. Ed Shaw.
The quintessence of Ibsenism. 1891, 1913 (completed to the death of Ibsen).

Widowers' houses. 1893, 1898 (rev in Plays pleasant and unpleasant).
Arms and the man. (Avenue 21 April 1894). 1898 (in Plays pleasant).
Candida. 1898 (in Plays pleasant).
The Devil's disciple. 1901 (in Three plays for Puritans).
The man of destiny. 1898 (in Plays pleasant).
The perfect Wagnerite: a commentary on the Ring of the Niblungs. 1898, 1902 (with new preface), 1913 (new preface), 1923 (new preface).
Mrs Warren's profession. 1898 (in Plays unpleasant), 1903 (Stage Soc edn with author's apology; apology alone, with introd by J. Corbin, The tyranny of police and press, New York 1905).
The philanderer. 1898 (in Plays unpleasant).
Caesar and Cleopatra. 1901 (in Three plays for Puritans).
Fabianism and the Empire: a manifesto. 1900. Ed Shaw.
Love among the artists. Chicago 1900, London 1914.
Man and superman: a comedy and a philosophy. 1903 (includes Epistle dedicatory, The revolutionist's handbook, and Maxims for revolutionists), New York 1904 (with textual variations), London 1911 (with new foreword).
The common sense of municipal trading. 1904, 1908 (with new preface).
How he lied to her husband. 1907 (with John Bull's other island).
John Bull's other island. 1907 (with Major Barbara, and How he lied to her husband), 1912 (with new prefatory material).
Passion, poison and petrification, or the fatal gazogene: a tragedy. [1905]. First pbd in Harry Furniss's Christmas Annual 1905, 1926 (in Translations and tomfooleries).
The irrational knot: being the second novel of his nonage. 1905.
Major Barbara. 1907 (with John Bull's other island), 1945 (film version).
The doctor's dilemma. 1911 (with Getting married and The shewing-up of Blanco Posnet).
The sanity of art: an exposure of the current nonsense about artists being degenerate. 1908. A criticism of Max Nordau, Entartung; rev and rptd from Liberty, New York 1895.
Getting married. 1911 (with The doctor's dilemma).
Socialism and superior brains: a reply to Mr [W. H.] Mallock. 1909.
Press cuttings: a topical sketch compiled from the editorial and correspondence columns of the daily papers. 1909.
The shewing-up of Blanco Posnet. 1909, 1911 (with The doctor's dilemma).
Misalliance. 1914 (with A treatise on parents and children, The dark lady of the sonnets, and Fanny's first play).
The dark lady of the sonnets. 1914 (in Misalliance).
Fanny's first play. 1914 (in Misalliance).
Overruled. 1916 (in Androcles and the lion).
Androcles and the lion. 1916 (with Over-ruled and Pygmalion), [1962] (Shaw alphabet edn).
Great Catherine. 1919 (in Heartbreak House).
The music cure. 1926 (in Translations and tomfooleries).
Common sense about the War. Suppl to New Statesman 14 Nov 1914, 1931 (in What I really wrote about the War).
The Inca of Perusalem. 1919 (in Heartbreak House).
Augustus does his bit. 1919 (in Heartbreak House).
O'Flaherty VC. 1919 (in Heartbreak House).
How to settle the Irish question. Dublin 1917.
Annajanska, the Bolshevik Empress. 1919 (in Heartbreak House).
Peace Conference hints. 1919.
Heartbreak House. 1919.
Ruskin's politics. 1921.
Back to Methuselah: a metabiological pentateuch. 1921 (with preface on Creative evolution as the creed of the twentieth century), 1945 (rev with a postscript).

Jitta's atonement, adapted from the German of S. Trebitsch. 1926 (in Translations and tomfooleries).

Saint Joan: a chronicle play in six scenes and an epilogue. 1924.

Table-talk of GBS: conversations on things in general between Shaw and his biographer, by Archibald Henderson. 1925.

Do we agree? a debate between G. K. Chesterton and Shaw with Hilaire Belloc in the chair. [1928].

The intelligent woman's guide to Socialism and Capitalism. 1928, 1929 (with new introd); 1937 (with two new chapters on Fascism and Sovietism).

The apple cart: a political extravaganza. 1930.

Bernard Shaw and Karl Marx: a symposium 1884-9. New York 1930. Articles on Marx by Shaw and controversy between Shaw and P. H. Wicksteed, ed R. W. Ellis.

Immaturity. 1930 (in Limited collected edn), 1931 (in Standard edn).

Doctors' delusions. 1931 (in Limited collected edn), 1932 (rev in Standard edn).

What I really wrote about the War. 1931.

The adventures of the black girl in her search for God. 1932.

Short stories, scraps and shavings. 1932 (in Limited collected edn).

Too true to be good. 1934 (with Village wooing and On the rocks.

The future of political science in America: a lecture. New York 1933, London 1933 (as The political madhouse in America and nearer home).

On the rocks. 1934 (in Too true to be good).

Village wooing. 1934 (in Too true to be good).

The six of Calais. 1936.

The simpleton of the Unexpected Isles. 1935, 1936 (in Standard edn).

William Morris as I knew him. New York 1936. First pbd as preface to M. Morris, William Morris: artist, writer, Socialist, 1936.

The millionairess. 1936.

Cymbeline refinished. 1946 (in Geneva, below).

Geneva. 1939, 1946 (in Standard edn, with Cymbeline refinished and Good King Charles).

In good King Charles's golden days. 1939, 1946 (in Geneva, above).

Everybody's political what's what? 1944.

Buoyant billions. 1949, 1951 (in Standard edn, with Farfetched fables and Shakes versus Shaw).

Sixteen self sketches. 1949 (in Standard edn).

Farfetched fables. 1950 (with Buoyant billions).

Rhyming picture guide to Ayot Saint Lawrence. Luton 1950.

My dear Dorothea: a practical system of moral education for females; with a note by Stephen Winsten. 1956.

An unfinished novel. Ed S. Weintraub 1958.

The rationalization of Russia. Ed H. M. Geduld, Bloomington [1964].

Letters

Letters to Miss Alma Murray. Edinburgh 1927; More letters to Miss Alma Murray, Edinburgh 1932.

Ellen Terry and Shaw: a correspondence. 1931.

Florence Farr, Shaw and W. B. Yeats letters. Ed C. Bax, Dublin 1941, New York 1942, London 1946.

Correspondence between Shaw and Mrs Patrick Campbell. Ed A. Dent 1952.

Advice to a young critic and other letters [to R. Golding Bright]. Ed E. J. West, New York [1955].

Letters to Granville-Barker. Ed C. B. Purdom, New York 1957, London 1957.

To a young actress: the letters of Shaw to Molly Tompkins. Ed P. Tompkins, New York [1960], London [1961].

Collected letters. Ed D. H. Laurence 1965-.

§2

Mencken, H. L. Shaw: his plays. Boston 1905.

Jackson, H. Shaw. 1907.

Chesterton, G. K. Shaw. 1909, New York 1909, 1935 (with new ch), New York 1950.

Henderson, A. Shaw: his life and works. 1911.
—— Shaw: man of the century. New York 1956.

Duffin, H. C. The quintessence of Shaw. 1920, 1939 (expanded).

Harris, F. Frank Harris on Shaw: an unauthorised biography based on first hand information, with a postscript by Shaw. 1931.

Pearson, H. Shaw: his life and personality. 1942, 1961.
—— GBS: a postscript. New York 1950, London 1951.

Irvine, W. The universe of GBS. New York 1949.

MacCarthy, D. Shaw. 1951, New York 1951 (as Shaw's plays in review).

Ervine, St J. Shaw: his life, work and friends. 1956.

Meisel, M. Shaw and the nineteenth-century theatre. Princeton 1963.

Kaufmann, R. J. (ed). Shaw: a collection of critical essays. Englewood Cliffs NJ [1965].

Chappelow, A. Shaw: 'the chucker-out'. 1969.

Evans, T. F. (ed). Shaw: the critical heritage. 1976.

OSCAR FINGALL O'FLAHERTIE WILLS WILDE
1854-1900

Bibliographies

'Mason, Stuart' (C. S. Millard). Bibliography of Wilde. 1908 (priv ptd), [1914]; ed T. d'A. Smith 1967.

Collections

[Works]. 14 vols 1908.

[Works. Ed R. B. Ross]. 12 vols (with 2 suppl vols) 1908.

Selected writings. Ed R. Ellmann, Oxford 1961.

Complete works. Ed P. Drake, introd by V. Holland 1966.

The artist as critic: critical writings. Ed R. Ellmann 1970.

§1

Poems. 1881 (3 edns).

The happy Prince and other tales, illustrated by Walter Crane and Jacomb Hood. 1888, 1888, 1889.

The Duchess of Padua: a tragedy of the xvi century, written in Paris in the xix century. [New York 1883] (priv ptd), 1907 (prefatory letter by R. B. Ross).

The picture of Dorian Gray. [1891], 1895; ed I. Murray, Oxford 1974.

Intentions. 1891, 1894.

Lord Arthur Savile's crime, and other stories. 1891.

Lady Windermere's fan: a play about a good woman. 1893, 1893.

A woman of no importance. 1894, New York 1894.

An ideal husband. 1899, [1914].

The importance of being earnest: a trivial comedy for serious people. 1899; ed S. A. Dickson, New York 1956 (from ms); ed V. Holland 1957 (longest version, from ms).

The soul of man. 1895 (priv ptd), 1912 (as The soul of man under Socialism; with preface by R. B. Ross).

Salomé: drame en un acte. Paris 1893; tr Lord Alfred B. Douglas 1894 (illustr Aubrey Beardsley).

The ballad of Reading Gaol, by C.3.3. 1898 (6 edns).

De profundis. 1905 (with preface by R. B. Ross), 1907 etc, New York 1908, [1909] (with 80 pp. of new matter); ed V. Holland 1949.

The suppressed portion of De profundis now for the first time published by his literary executor, Robert

Ross. New York 1913 (priv ptd). Fuller text of whole work in Letters, ed Hart-Davis, 1962, below.

A Florentine tragedy. Written 1893–4; ms lost; first pbd in first collected edn of the works, 1908, with opening scene by T. Sturge Moore, replacing one lost.

Letters

After Reading: letters to Robert Ross. 1921.
After Berneval: letters to Robert Ross. 1922.
Letters to the Sphinx (Ada Leverson); with reminiscences of the author by Ada Leverson. 1930.
Letters. Ed R. Hart-Davis 1962.
Selected letters. Ed R. Hart-Davis, Oxford 1977.

§2

Gide, A. Wilde. In his Prétextes: réflexions critiques sur quelques points de littérature et de morale, Paris 1903, 1910 (as Wilde: In memoriam (souvenirs), le De profundis); tr 'Stuart Mason' (C. S. Millard) 1905 (with introd, notes and bibliography).
—— Wilde. 1951. Tr with addns.
The trial of Wilde, from the shorthand reports. 1906.
Ransome, A. Wilde: a critical study. 1912.
Douglas, Lord A. Wilde and myself. 1914.
—— Wilde: a summing-up. 1940, 1962.
Harris, F. Wilde: his life and confessions, together with memories of Wilde, by Bernard Shaw. 2 vols New York 1918; ed G. B. Shaw 1938.
Symons, A. A study of Wilde. 1930.
Pearson, H. The life of Wilde. 1946.
Hyde, H. M. (ed). The trials of Wilde. 1948.
—— Wilde: the aftermath. 1963.
—— Oscar Wilde. 1976.
Ervine, St J. Wilde. 1951.
Holland, V. Son of Wilde. 1954.
—— Wilde: a pictorial biography. Oxford 1960.
Mercier, V. The fate of Wilde. 1955.
Auden, W. H. An improbable life. New Yorker 9 March 1963. On Letters, ed Hart-Davis, 1962.
Beckson, K. (ed). Wilde: the critical heritage. 1970.

SIR JAMES MATTHEW BARRIE
1860–1937

Collections

Uniform edition of the plays. 12 vols 1918–38.
Plays. 1928.
Plays. Ed A. E. Wilson 1942. Definitive edn.

§1

Caught napping. 1883 (priv ptd).
Better dead. 1888 (for 1887), 1888, New York [1890] (with My Lady Nicotine, below).
Auld licht idylls. 1888, 1895, 1898 (11th edn).
When a man's single: a tale of literary life. 1888.
An Edinburgh eleven: pencil portraits from college life. 1889, New York 1892.
A window in Thrums. 1889, 1892, 1898 (16th edn).
Richard Savage. 1891 (priv ptd). With H. B. Marriott Watson.
My Lady Nicotine. 1890, New York 1896.
Ibsen's ghost: or Toole up-to-date. 1939 (priv ptd).
The little minister. 3 vols 1891, 1891, New York 1891.
Walker, London: a farcical comedy.
A holiday in bed, and other sketches; with a short biographical sketch of the author. New York 1892. Unauthorized collection of contributions to periodicals.
Jane Annie, or the good conduct prize: a new and original English comic opera. 1893. With A. Conan Doyle.

A lady's shoe. New York [1893] (unauthorized 1st edn, with The inconsiderate waiter), London 1894 (in Miss Parson's adventure by W. C. Russell, and other stories by other writers), New York 1898.
Two of them. New York [1893]. Unauthorized collection of contributions to periodicals.
An Auld Licht manse, and other sketches. New York [1893]. Unauthorized collection.
A Tillyloss scandal. New York [1893], [1893], 1894, 1915? Unauthorized collection.
A powerful drug; and other stories. New York [1893]. Unauthorized collection.
Scotland's lament: a poem on the death of Robert Louis Stevenson, December 3rd 1894. 1895 (priv ptd).
Margaret Ogilvy; by her son J. M. Barrie. 1896
Sentimental Tommy: the story of his boyhood. 1896.
Jess. Boston [1898]. Unauthorized collection of the first 16 stories in A window in Thrums.
Life in a country manse. New York 1899. Unauthorized.
Tommy and Grizel. 1900.
Quality Street. 1913.
The Admirable Crichton. 1914.
The little white bird. 1902.
Peter Pan in Kensington Gardens; from The little white bird; with drawings by Arthur Rackham. 1906.
When Wendy grew up: an afterthought. 1957.
George Meredith. 1909, Chicago 1910 (as Neither Dorking nor the Abbey).
Peter and Wendy. 1911, New York 1911, London 1915, 1921 (as Peter Pan and Wendy).
Der Tag. [1914].
Shakespear's legacy. [1916] (priv ptd).
Who was Sarah Findlay? by Mark Twain; with a suggested solution of the mystery by Barrie. 1917 (priv ptd).
The truth about the Russian dancers. New York 1962.
Shall we join the ladies? In The black mask, ed C. Asquith 1927.
Courage: the Rectorial Address delivered at St Andrews University, May 3rd 1922. [1922], [1922].
Neil and Tintinnabulum. In The flying carpet, ed C. Asquith 1925.
The entrancing life: speech at Edinburgh. 1930.
The Greenwood hat. 1930 (priv ptd), 1937.
Farewell, Miss Julie Logan. 1932 (in uniform edn).
For Dear Brutus, Mary Rose, Peter Pan, The boy David, What every woman knows, *and other plays first pbd in uniform edn; for* Pantaloon, The twelve-pound look, Rosalind, *and* The will, *first pbd in* Half hours; *for* The old lady shows her medals, *first pbd in* Echoes of the War; *for* Old friends, Half an hour *and* Seven women *first pbd in* Plays, 1928; *for* The professor's love story *and* Little Mary *first pbd in* Plays, 1942; *see under collections. The following have not been pbd:* The adored one (D of Y 4 Sept 1913) *as* Legend of Leonora (Empire, New York 5 Jan 1914); Rosy rapture: or the pride of the beauty chorus (D of Y 22 March 1915).
Letters. Ed V. Meynell 1942.

§2

Hammerton, J. A. Barrie and his books: biographical and critical studies. 1900.
—— Barrie: the story of a genius. 1929.
Darton, F. J. H. Barrie. 1929.
Darlington, W. A. Barrie. 1938.
Mackail, D. The story of JMB. 1941. The authorized biography.
Asquith, C. In her Haply I may remember, 1950.
—— Portrait of Barrie. 1954.
Green, R. L. Fifty years of Peter Pan. 1954. Includes Scenario for a silent film of Peter Pan.
—— Barrie. 1960.

For Synge, Yeats and the other Anglo-Irish dramatists of the Nineties and after, see col 1161, below.

5. PROSE

I. EARLY NINETEENTH-CENTURY PROSE

WILLIAM COBBETT
1763–1835

Cobbett's mss and correspondence are widely scattered both in Britain and the USA. The notable collection in Nuffield College Oxford, listed by M. L. Pearl in typescripts in the possession of Nuffield and Bodley, includes many mss of pbd articles written for his periodicals and numerous items of unpbd material such as correspondence, fragments of diaries and family papers.

Bibliographies

Pearl, M. L. Cobbett: a bibliographical account of his life and times. Oxford 1953.

Collections

The works of Peter Porcupine. Philadelphia 1795, 1796.
Porcupine's works. 12 vols 1801. Hostile selections, 1807–32.
Life and adventures of Peter Porcupine. Ed G. D. H. Cole 1927. Autobiographical selections to 1800.
The progress of a ploughboy. Ed W. Reitzel 1933, 1947 (rev as The autobiography of Cobbett).
The opinions of Cobbett. Ed G. D. H. and M. Cole 1944. Selections from Political register 1802–35.

§ 1

Observations on the emigration of Dr Priestley. Philadelphia 1794, 1794 (author and publisher anon), New York 1794, London 1794 (3 edns), [Liverpool?] 1794, Birmingham 1794, Philadelphia 1795 ('3rd edn' naming publisher with Story of a farmer's bull, Address), 1795, 1796 ('4th edn' naming Peter Porcupine as author), 1796, London 1798, Philadelphia 1798.
A bone to gnaw for the Democrats, part 1. Philadelphia 1795 (3 edns; anon in 1st), 1796 ('4th edn' by 'Peter Porcupine'), 1797 ('3rd edn' pbd by Cobbett); part 2, 1795, 1795, 1797, 1797; pts 1–2, 1797 (with A rod for the backs of the critics by 'Humphrey Hedgehog') [J. Gifford]).
A kick for a bite, by Peter Porcupine. Philadelphia 1795, 1796.
Le tuteur anglais. Philadelphia 1795, Paris 1801.
A little plain English, by Peter Porcupine. Philadelphia 1795, Boston 1795, London 1795, Philadelphia 1796.
Summary of the law of nations. Philadelphia 1795, London 1802 (as A compendium of the law of nations), 1829 ('4th edn'). By G. F. von Martens; tr Cobbett.
A new year's gift to the Democrats, by Peter Porcupine. Philadelphia 1796, 1796, 1798.
A prospect from the Congress gallery, by Peter Porcupine. Philadelphia 1796, 1796. Continued as monthly periodical The political censor 1796–7.
The bloody buoy, by Peter Porcupine. Philadelphia 1796, 1796, Reading Pa 1797 (German trn as Die Blut-Fahne); (facs and English trans of extracts of this trn, Description of an old book, ed J. A. Donahoe, Wilmington [c. 1958]); London [1796], Cambridge 1797 (as Annals of blood by an American), London 1798 ('4th', '7th', '10th', '11th' edns), Paradise Pa 1823 ('2nd' edn), Philadelphia 1823 ('3rd' edn).

The political censor. Philadelphia 1796–7. A monthly periodical, ed Cobbett, nos 2–9, a continuation of A prospect from the Congress gallery and continued as Porcupine's gazette.
The scare-crow, by Peter Porcupine. Philadelphia 1796, 1797. Rptd from Political censor, 1796, above.
The life and adventures of Peter Porcupine, by Peter Porcupine. Philadelphia 1796, 1796, 1797, London 1797, Glasgow 1797, 1798, London 1809 ('2nd edn'), rev as The life of William Cobbett, 1809, 1816 ('2nd', '7th', '8th', '9th' edns); ed G. D. H. Cole 1927 ('with other records of his early career').
An answer to Paine's Rights of man. Philadelphia 1796. By H. Mackenzie, above. Ed Cobbett with A letter to John Swanwick.
The life of Thomas Paine, by 'Peter Porcupine'. [1796?], 1797, 1797 (as Cobbett's review of the life). Hostile edns, Sunderland 1819, Durham 1819.
The gros mousqueton diplomatique: or diplomatic blunderbuss. Philadelphia 1796. By P. A. Adet, tr and ed Cobbett, rptd from Political censor, 1796, above.
The history of Jacobinism. 2 vols Philadelphia 1796 (with appendix), 1796 (as History of the American Jacobins), Edinburgh 1797, London 1798 (with appendix). By W. Playfair, ed Cobbett with his own appendix, History of the American Jacobins.
A letter to the infamous Tom Paine, by Peter Porcupine. Philadelphia 1796, London 1797, Glasgow 1797, Edinburgh 1797, [1798?]. Rptd from Political censor, 1796, above.
A letter from Edmund Burke. Philadelphia 1796. By Burke; ed Cobbett, with preface.
Observations on the debates of the American Congress by Peter Porcupine. [Philadelphia 1797?], London 1797. Rptd from Political censor, 1796, above.
Porcupine's gazette and United States daily advertiser (daily evening periodical, ed Cobbett, Philadelphia, 4 March 1797–28 Aug 1799, title changed to Porcupine's gazette 24 April 1799; weekly, Bustleton, 6 Sept 1799–11 Oct 1799 and 19–26 Oct 1799; New York, final no, 13 Jan 1800; another tri-weekly edn, Philadelphia, 3 March 1798–28 Aug 1799, title changed to The country porcupine 30 April 1798).
A view of the war with France. Philadelphia 1797. By T. Erskine et al, ed Cobbett as 'Peter Porcupine', with 'dedication' and 'appendix'.
The anti-Gallican. Philadelphia 1797. By 'A citizen of New England', 'Leonidas', 'Philo-Leonidas', 'Ascanius', 'Impartial'; brief dedication by Cobbett and pbd by him.
An answer to Paine's letter to Washington. Philadelphia 1798. By P. Kennedy; brief 'advertisement' by 'P.P.' (Cobbett) and pbd by him.
The democratic judge, by 'Peter Porcupine'. Philadelphia 1798; pbd in England as The republican judge, 1798 (3 edns).
Observations on the dispute between the United States and France. Philadelphia 1798. By R. G. Harper et al, ed Cobbett with 'preface' and appendix; '3rd' American edn pbd and ed Cobbett.
Detection of a conspiracy, by 'Peter Porcupine'. Philadelphia 1798, London 1799, Dublin 1799.
Detection of Bache, by 'Peter Porcupine'. Philadelphia

1798. Broadside, rptd from Porcupine's Gazette 20 June 1798, above.

French arrogance, by 'Peter Porcupine'. Philadelphia 1798, New York 1915 (in Magazine of History, no 44).

Remarks on the insidious letter [The antidote], by Peter Porcupine. Philadelphia 1798. Broadside, rptd from Porcupine's Gazette July 1798, above.

Democratic principles illustrated by example, by Peter Porcupine. 2 pts (pt 1 extracted from pt 2 of A bone to gnaw 1795, pt 2 extracted from The bloody buoy, 1796), Dublin [1797-]1798, London 1798 ('2nd'-'11th' edns), Aberdeen 1798 ('7th' edn), Edinburgh 1798 ('7th' edn), Birmingham [1798] (shortened [unauthorized?] rev pt 1 as Read and reflect: a faint picture of the horrors).

The cannibal's progress. 1798, Philadelphia 1798 (as Introductory address to the people of America), 1798 (rev as A warning to Britons), 1801 (as The cannibal's progress, with an introductory address to the subjects of the British Empire), 1803. Tr A. Aufrere, ed Cobbett with 'introductory address'.

Remarks on the explanation by Dr Priestley, by Peter Porcupine. 1799 (rptd from Porcupine's Gazette Sept 1798-Jan 1799).

The trial of republicanism. Philadelphia 1799 (no known copy), London 1801 (with postscript).

Proposals for publishing Porcupine's works. [Philadelphia] 1799.

The rush-light. Fortnightly periodical, ed 'Peter Porcupine'; New York 15 Feb-30 April 1800 nos 1-5; London, 30 Aug 1800 no 6-repbd as An address to the people of England [Philadelphia? 1800?]; nos 1-4 repbd as The American rush-light, 1800. The republican rush-light 30 Aug 1800 no 7 is a forgery.

History of the campaigns of Suworow. New York 1800. Tr J. F. Anthing, ed and pbd Cobbett with additional trn, A history of his Italian campaign, by Cobbett.

Cobbett's advice. [1800]. Broadside, rev and repbd as Prospectus of the Porcupine, 1800.

The porcupine. Daily periodical, ed Cobbett, 30 Oct 1800-31 Dec 1801, nos 1-3 (another edn); from no 299 as The porcupine and anti-Gallican monitor; from 1 Jan 1802 absorbed by True Briton.

A collection of facts, including letters to Lord Hawkesbury. 1801, Philadelphia 1802. Rptd mainly from Porcupine, 1801, above.

Letters to Addington 1802.

Letters to Lord Hawkesbury and Addington. 1802, 1802. Rptd mainly from A collection of facts, 1801, and from Letters to Addington, 1802, above.

Cobbett's political register. Weekly periodical, ed Cobbett as Cobbett's annual register, Jan 1802-Dec 1803; as Cobbett's weekly political register 7 Jan 1804-5 April 1817 (none issued in England 12 April-5 July 1817, but twice weekly edn 12 Sept 1810-22 June 1811); Cobbett's weekly political pamphlet, July-Dec 1817; Cobbett's weekly political register Jan 1818-7 April 1821 (none issued 21 March, 2 May, 27 June-15 Aug, 17 Oct-14 Nov 1818, 29 May-7 Aug, 16 Oct, 20-27 Nov 1819, or 26 Feb-18 March 1820); as Cobbett's weekly register, 14 April-Dec 1827; Cobbett's weekly political register, Jan 1828-12 Sept 1835 (no 11); extracts 1830-2 pbd as Cobbett's two-penny trash, 1831, 1832; [from 20 June 1835 (no 12) ed W. Cobbett jr]; as Renewal of Cobbett's Register, Jan 1836 (unnumbered) and 20 Feb 1836 ('no 2'). Many pamphlet reprints of articles in Political register were issued, particularly after 1810.

Letter to Lord Auckland on the Post Office. 1802. Rptd from Political Register 27 Nov 1802.

A treatise on fruit trees (by W. Forsyth, ed Cobbett with introd and notes, 'adapting . . . the treatise to . . . America'), Philadelphia 1802, New York, 1802 Albany 1803, Philadelphia 1803 (by 'an American farmer', as An epitome of Mr Forsyth's treatise).

Narrative of the taking of the invincible standard. 1803. Rptd from Political Register 25 Dec 1803.

The empire of Germany. 1803. By J. G. Peltier, tr Cobbett with a trn of a memoir by Peltier rptd from Political Register 1802.

Four letters to the Chancellor of the Exchequer. 1803. Rptd from Political Register 9, 16, 23, 30 April 1803.

Important considerations for the people of this Kingdom. 1803 etc. Anon. Rptd from Political Register 30 July 1803.

The political Proteus: R. B. Sheridan. 1804. Rptd largely from Political Register 1803.

Cobbett's parliamentary debates. 1804-. Ed Cobbett with J. Wright till 1811; then by Wright only. From 1813 (vol 24) as The parliamentary debates; supplemented by Cobbett's parliamentary history, similarly edited, 36 vols 1806-20, which also passed out of his hands in 1812 and is entitled The parliamentary history from vol 13. The parliamentary debates became Hansard's parliamentary debates in 1818 and eventually the present Hansard.

Cobbett's spirit of the public journals. Weekly periodical ed Cobbett 2 Jan-26 Dec 1804; 1 vol 1805.

Cobbett's complete collection of state trials. 33 vols 1800-26. Cobbett with J. Wright and T. B. Howell until 1811; then by T. B. Howell; from 1812 dissociated from Cobbett as Howell's state trials.

Cobbett's remarks on Burdett's letter. 1809. Rptd from Political Register 24 March 1810.

An essay on sheep. 1811, New Haven 1813. By R. R. Livingston, ed Cobbett from first edn, New York 1809 with his preface and notes.

Three letters to the electors of Bristol. Bath 1812. Rptd from Political Register 4 July, 1, 15 Aug 1812.

Letters to the Prince Regent. 1812. No known copy. Rptd from Political Register 1812.

Letter to the inhabitants of Southampton on the Corn Bill. 1814. Rptd from Political Register 4 June 1814.

Five letters to Lord Sheffield. 1815. Rptd from Political Register 26 Aug 1815.

Letters on the late war between the United States and Great Britain. New York 1815. One letter rptd as An address to the clergy of Massachusetts, Boston 1815, 1815, taken from Political Register 10 Dec 1814. Rptd, except for one letter, from Political Register 1811-15.

Paper against gold. 2 vols 1815, 15 pts 1817 (24 Feb-29 March) and 1 vol, 1821 and 1822 ('4th' edn) (accompanied by separately pbd Preliminary part of Paper against gold, 1821), 1828 (omits last 3 of a total of 32 articles or 'letters'), New York 1834, Manchester 1841 ('condensed' by M. Chappelsmith), London 1841 (no known copy), New York 1846. Paper against gold rptd from Political Register 1810-5; Preliminary part of Paper against gold rptd from Political Register 1803-6.

Cobbett's American political register 1816-7. See Cobbett's Political Register, above.

[Address] To the journeymen and labourers. Manchester 1816. Rptd from Political Register 2 Nov 1816 and also issued as unstamped Political Register by Cobbett in London.

A letter addressed to Mr Jabet of Birmingham. Coventry 1816. Rptd from Political Register 9 Nov 1816.

Our anti-neutral conduct reviewed. [New York 1817]. Rptd mainly from American Political Register 1817.

Cobbett's new year's gift to old George Rose. Nottingham 1817. Rptd from Political Register 4 Jan 1817.

Mr Cobbett's taking leave of his countrymen. 1817. Rptd from Political Register 5 April 1817.

Cobbett's address to the Americans. [1817].

Mr Cobbett's address to his countrymen. [1817].

[Long Island prophecies] Cobbett's too long petition: Letter to Tierney; Letter to the Regent. 1822 (5 issues including caption title Long Island prophecies). Rptd from Political Register 7 Feb, 1 July 1818, 30 Oct 1819.

A year's residence in the United States of America. New York 1818–19, London 1818–19, 1818–19, Belfast 1818–19, London 1822 ('3rd' edn), 1822, 1828 (another '3rd' edn), 1922, Carbondale and Fontwell [1964].

A grammar of the English language. New York 1818, London '1819' (for 1818), 1819 (3 edns), 1820 ('4th' edn), 1823 (with additional 'six lessons').

The trial of Miss Tocker. New York 1818, Boston 1818. Ed Cobbett with 'letter' and 'address'.

Correspondence between Cobbett, Tipper and Burdett. 1819.

A full report of a public meeting [with a speech by Cobbett]. 1819.

Cobbett's evening post. Daily periodical, ed Cobbett, 29 Jan–1 April 1820.

Cobbett's parliamentary register. Weekly periodical, ed Cobbett, 6 May–Dec 1820.

A letter from the Queen to the King [by 'Queen Caroline', actually by Cobbett]. 1820, Philadelphia 1821 ('5th edn') etc. Rptd from Political Register 19 Aug 1820.

An answer to the speech of the Attorney-General against the Queen. 1820. Rptd from Political Register 26 Aug 1820.

The Queen's answer to the letter from the King. 1821, Philadelphia 1821. Rptd from Political Register 27 Jan 1821.

Cobbett's sermons. 12 monthly pts 1821–2 (nos 1–3 as Cobbett's monthly religious tracts, nos 4–12 as Cobbett's monthly sermons), 1822 ('stereotype' edn), 1823, (Andover ptd) as Twelve Sermons 1828, New York (as Thirteen sermons with 'address', an additional sermon, and Good Friday, which was also pbd separately, London 1830), 1834, Philadelphia [183?], New York 1846.

The American gardener. 1821, Baltimore 1823, 1829 (rev as The English gardener).

Cottage economy. 7 monthly pts Aug 1821–March 1822 etc; 1822, 1823 ('new' edn), 1824 ('6th' edn); ed G. K. Chesterton 1926.

The farmer's friend. 1822. Rptd from Political Register 15 Dec 1821, 5 Jan 1822.

[Proceedings at the dinner:] Cobbett's warnings to Norfolk farmers. 1822. Rptd from Political Register 29 Dec 1821, 5 Jan 1822.

American slave trade. 1822. By J. Torrey jr, ed Cobbett with preface from 1st Amer edn, Portraiture of domestic slavery, Philadelphia 1822.

The farmer's wife's friend. 1822. Rptd from Political Register 23 March 1822.

The statesman. Daily evening periodical 1806–24, incorporated in the Globe and traveller, 1824, part owned by Cobbett March 1822–May 1823, when he wrote articles for it, some rptd in Cobbett's collective commentaries 1822, below.

The horse hoeing husbandry. 1822, 1829. Ed Cobbett with introd from A specimen etc by J. Tull, 1731.

Reduction no robbery. 1822. Rptd from Political Register 22 June 1822.

Cobbett's collective commentaries. 1822. Mainly rptd from Statesman 1822, above.

Mr Cobbett's publications. A descriptive catalogue frequently rptd from Political Register and advertisements in Cobbett's books 1822–4; later versions as List of Mr Cobbett's publications, c. 1824; List of Mr Cobbett's books 1828–32, 1834, 1842; and The Cobbett library, 1830, 1835.

The Norfolk yeoman's gazette. Weekly periodical, ed Cobbett, Norwich 8 Feb–3 May 1823.

To Lord Suffield. 1823. Rptd from Political Register 1 Feb 1823.

A French grammar. 1824, Paris 1825, London 1829.

A history of the Protestant Reformation in England and Ireland. 16 nos 1824–6, many nos rptd and bound together.

Gold for ever. 1825; rptd in Political Register 10 Sept 1825.

Big O and Sir Glory. 1825. Rptd from Political Register 24 Sept 1825.

Cobbett at the King's cottage [1826]. Rptd from Political Register 5 Aug 1826.

Cobbett's poor man's friend. 4 nos Aug–Nov 1826. Hostile imitation; The poor man's friend, 1826. No 5 Oct 1827, nos 2–4, pbd as 'new' edn Oct 1830, 1833 (rev as Cobbett's poor man's friend) (in Cottage economy, below), 1826, 1829, [1830], ('new' edn), [1832], [1836–184?].

Catalogue of American trees. 1827. Rptd from Political Register 8 Dec 1827.

Elements of the Roman history. 1828, 1829 (rev as An abridged history of the Emperors, 1829). By J. H. Sievrac, tr Cobbett.

The woodlands. 7 nos Dec 1825–March 1828, 1 vol 1825 (for 1828).

Noble nonsense. [1828]. Rptd from Political Register 3 May 1828.

The English gardener. 1829 (for 1828) (2 edns), 1833, 1838, 1845. Rev from American gardener, above.

Usury. 1828, 1834, 1856. By J. O'Callaghan, ed Cobbett from 1st edn New York 1824, with dedication.

Facts for the men of Kent. [1828]. Rptd from Political Register 25 Oct 1828.

A letter to the Pope. 1828. Rptd from Political Register 15 Nov 1828.

A treatise on Cobbett's corn. 1828, 1831 ('with an addition').

The emigrant's guide. 1829, 1830, 1830.

Mr Cobbett's lecture. 5 pts 1829–30. 5 lectures; third lecture also pbd Birmingham [1830] as broadside, A summary report.

Report of lecture-speech, Halifax. Halifax 1830, 1830.

Three lectures, Sheffield. Sheffield 1830.

Mr Cobbett's address to the tax-payers. [1830]. Rptd from Political Register 10 April 1830, with addns.

Good Friday. 1830; rptd in Thirteen sermons, New York 1834, below, and in Political Register 9 March 1833.

Rural rides. 1830, 1830. Rptd from Political Register 1821–6; later edns from Political Register 1821–34; rptd 1833 (as Cobbett's tour in Scotland and the northern counties of England in 1832); ed J. P. Cobbett 1853; ed G. D. H. and M. Cole 1930 (with addns not previously rptd from Political Register); ed G. Woodcock 1967 (Penguin) (on Southern counties).

Cobbett's exposure of the pretended friends of the blacks. 1830. Rptd from Political Register 26 June 1830.

French Revolution: an address to the people of Paris. Birmingham 1830. Rptd from Political Register 21 Aug 1830.

Advice to young men. 14 pts June 1829–Sept 1830; 1 vol London ('Andover' ptd '1829') (for 1830) (2 edns), 'London 1829' (for 1830).

Eleven lectures on the French and Belgian revolutions. 11 pts Sept–Oct 1830; 1 vol 1830.

A letter to the king. [1830].

History of George the Fourth. ? pts 1830–4; 2 vols 1830–4, 2 vols 1834; rptd in Political Register 1830–4.

Cobbett's plan of parliamentary reform. 1830. Rptd from Political Register 30 Oct 1930.

Surplus population. [1831?], [1835?]. A play, rptd from Political Register 28 May 1831 and Cobbett's twopenny trash June 1831.

Cobbett's twopenny trash. 24 pts July 1830–July 1832; 2 vols 1831–2, 1832. One pt (Tithes) tr Welsh, 1831 (no known copy). Rptd from Political Register 1830–2, except for vol 1 nos 1–6 and vol 2 nos 4, 10; Cobbett's penny trash, nos 1–3; no 1, also issued as Cobbett's genuine twopenny trash, is a hostile imitation.

A spelling book. 1831, 1831, 1832, 1834, 1845 ('9th' edn).

Cobbett's letter on the abolition of tithes. Dublin

[1831?]. Rptd from Political Register 10 Sept 1831. Rptd as Mr Cobbett's propositions, Manchester 1831.

Cobbett's Manchester lectures. 1832.

A geographical dictionary. 1832. Ed Cobbett et al.

Mansell & Co's report of the important discussion held in Birmingham. Birmingham [1832], [1832]. Ed anon, not by Cobbett.

Extracts from Cobbett's register, and Mr Cobbett's remarks. Birmingham [1832].

Mr Cobbett's answer to Mr Stanley's manifesto. [1833], [1833]. Rptd from Political Register 29 Dec 1832.

Cobbett's poor man's friend. [1833]. Rev from Poor man's friend, 1826–7, above; rptd from Political Register 5 Jan 1833.

The speeches of W. Cobbett MP. 2 nos 1833. Rptd from True Sun 1833.

The flash in the pan. 1833. Rptd from Political Register 18–25 May 1833.

Cobbett's magazine. Monthly periodical Feb 1833–March 1834; title changed to Saturday magazine, April 1834. Ed J. M. and J. P. Cobbett with some articles by Cobbett.

Disgraceful squandering of the public money. Glasgow 1833. Rptd from Political Register 15 June 1831.

The curse of paper money. 1833. By W. M. Gouge, ed Cobbett with preface and introd rptd from Political Register 20 July 1833, the rest from Philadelphia 1823 edn.

A new French and English dictionary. 1833.

Popay the police spy. 1833. Rptd from Political Register 17 Aug 1833.

Four letters to Worsley. 1834. Rptd from Political Register 31 Aug–19 Oct 1833.

Rights of industry 1833. By Cobbett and J. Fielden. Rptd from Political Register 14 Dec 1833.

Mr Cobbett's speech for an abolition of the malt tax. 1834. Rptd from Political Register 22 March 1834.

Life of Andrew Jackson. 1834, New York 1834, 1834, Baltimore 1834. Ed Cobbett from the Life by J. H. Eaton, Philadelphia 1824.

Get gold! get gold! Leeds 1834. Rptd from Political Register 16 Aug 1834.

[Five] Letters to the Earl of Radnor. 1834. Rptd from Political Register 9, 23 Aug, 20 Sept, 18, 25 Oct 1834.

Three lectures on Ireland. Dublin 1834. First lecture in another version in Political Register 4 Oct 1834.

Cobbett's legacy to labourers. 1834 (for 1835), 1835, 1835, New York 1835, 1844, London 1872. Dedication rptd as A letter to Peel, 1836, below.

The malt tax. 1835. Rptd from Political Register 24 March 1835.

Cobbett's legacy to parsons. 1835 (6 edns), New York 1835, 1844, 1860, London 1868, 1869, Croydon 1876 (as There being no gospel for tithes), London 1947.

Cobbett's legacy to Peel. 1836. Rptd from Political Register 24 Jan–18 April 1835.

Doom of the tithes. 1836. Introd by Cobbett to a trn from a Spanish work Historia y origen di las rentas Iglesia, 1793.

Cobbett's reasons for war against Russia. 1854. Ed anon; extracts rptd from Political Register 1822, 1826, 1829, 1833, 1834.

Mr Cobbett's remarks on our Indian empire. 1857. By Cobbett and J. Fielden, ed anon; extracts rptd from Political Register 1804–22.

A history of the last hundred days of English freedom. 1921. By Cobbett, ed J. L. Hammond; rptd from Political Register 26 July–18 Oct 1817.

Letters

Cobbett's 'letters' were mostly part of his polemical and political writings, not always despatched to those to whom they were 'addressed' but ptd for the first time in his periodicals, above.

Cole ,G. D. H. Letters from Cobbett to Edward Thornton 1797–1800. Oxford 1937.

Pearl, M. L. Cobbett at Botley, Cobbett and his men, Cobbett and his family, Cobbett and the 'Chop-sticks'. Countryman 153–4 1951, 157 1953.

§2

Hazlitt, W. Character of Cobbett. In his Table talk vol i, 1821 and Spirit of the age, 1825 (2nd edn).

Carlyle, E. I. Cobbett: a study of his life. 1904.

Cole, G. D. H. The life of Cobbett. 1924, 1927, 1947 (rev).

Chesterton, G. K. William Cobbett. [1925].

Clark, M. E. Peter Porcupine in America. Philadelphia 1939.

Pemberton, W. B. William Cobbett. 1949.

Chaloner, W. H. Cobbett and Manchester: the first election address. Manchester Guardian 16 May 1955.

Osborne, J. W. Cobbett: his thought and his times. New Brunswick 1966.

Sambrook, J. William Cobbett. 1973.

WALTER SAVAGE LANDOR
1775–1864
Bibliographies

Wise, T. J. and S. Wheeler. A bibliography of the writings in prose and verse of Landor. 1919.

Wise, T. J. A Landor library. 1928 (priv ptd).

Super, R. H. The publication of Landor's works. 1954.

—— In The English romantic poets and essayists: a review of research and criticism, ed C. W. and L. H. Houtchens, New York 1957, 1966 (rev).

Collections

Gebir, Count Julian and other poems. 1831.

The works of Landor. 2 vols 1846, 1853, 1868, 1895.

The works and life of Landor. Ed J. Forster 8 vols 1876.

The complete works: prose. Ed T. E. Welby 12 vols 1927–31; Poetry, ed S. Wheeler 4 vols 1933–6; 3 vols Oxford 1937.

§1

Poems. 1795.

Moral epistle respectfully dedicated to Earl Stanhope. 1795.

To the burgesses of Warwick. [Warwick 1797]; ed R. H. Super, Oxford 1949 (Luttrell Soc).

Gebir: a poem in seven books. 1798, Oxford 1803; Gebirus poema, Oxford 1803 (Latin trn by Landor).

Poems from the Arabic and Persian with notes by the author of Gebir. Warwick 1800 (first issue, with French preface); Warwick and London 1800 (second issue), 1927 (facs).

Poetry by the author of Gebir. Warwick 1800 (first issue, with An address to the fellows of Trinity College Oxford, Postscript to Gebir etc), 1802 (second issue).

Iambi incerto auctore. [Oxford? 1802?].

Simonidea. Bath [1806].

Three letters written in Spain to D. Francisco Riguelme [Riquelme]. 1809.

Ode ad Gustavum regem; ode ad Gustavum exulem. 1810.

Count Julian: a tragedy. 1812.

Commentary on memoirs of Mr Fox. 1812 (ptd but not pbd); rptd as Charles James Fox: a commentary on his life and character, ed S. Wheeler 1907.

Letters addressed to Lord Liverpool and the Parliament on the preliminaries of peace by Calvus. 1814.

Letter from Mr Landor to Mr Jervis. Bath 1814, Gloucester Jnl 23 May 1814.

Idyllia nova quinque heroum atque heroidum. Oxford 1815.

Sponsalia Polyxenae. Pistoia 1819.

Idyllia heroica decem librum phaleuciorum unum. Pisa 1820.

Poche osservazioni sullo stato attuale di que' popoli che vogliono governarsi per mezzo delle rappresentanze. [Naples?] 1821.

Imaginary conversations of literary men and statesmen. Vols 1–2 1824, 1826; vol 3 1828; vols 4–5 1829; 5 vols Boston 1882, London 1883; ed E. de Selincourt, Oxford 1915 (WC); ed T. E. Welby, Oxford 1934 (introd by C. Williams, notes by F. A. Cavenagh and A. C. Ward).

Citation and examination of William Shakspeare before the worshipful Sir Thomas Lucy Knight touching deer stealing, to which is added a conference of Master Edmund Spenser, a gentleman of note, with the Earl of Essex touching the state of Ireland. 1834, 1891; ed H. W. Mabie, New York [1891].

Pericles and Aspasia. 2 vols 1836, Philadelphia 1839, 1 vol Boston 1871; ed C. G. Crump 2 vols 1890 (Temple Lib); ed H. Ellis [1892]; ed G. R. Dennis 1903.

The letters of a conservative, in which are shown the only means of saving what is left of the English Church. 1836.

Terry Hogan: an eclogue. 1836. Anon, probably Landor's.

A satire on satirists and admonition to detractors. 1836.

Literary hours by various friends. Ed J. Ablett, Liverpool 1837 (priv ptd). Contains prose and verse by Landor.

The pentameron and pentalogia. 1837, Boston 1888 (with Citation and examination of Shakspeare, minor prose pieces and criticisms); ed H. Ellis 1889; ed D. Pettoello, Turin 1954.

Andrea of Hungary and Giovanna of Naples. 1839.

Fra Rupert. 1840.

To Robert Browning. [1845].

The hellenics enlarged and completed. 1847; The hellenics, comprising heroic idyls &c, Edinburgh 1859 (enlarged); The hellenics and Gebir, ed A. Symons 1907 (Temple Classics).

The Italics of Landor. 1848.

Savagius Landor Lamartino. [Bath? 1848].

Imaginary conversation of King Carlo-Alberto and the Duchess Belgioioso on the affairs and prospects of Italy. [1848].

Carmen ad heroinam. [Bath? 1848].

Epistola ad Pium IX pontificem. [Bath? 1849].

Epistola ad Romanos. [Bath? 1849].

Ad Cossuthum et Bemum. [Bath? 1849].

Statement of occurrences at Llanbedr. Bath [1849].

Popery, British and foreign. 1851, Boston 1851.

On Kossuth's voyage to America. [Birmingham? 1851].

Tyrannicide, published for the benefit of the Hungarians in America. [Bath 1851].

Imaginary conversations of Greeks and Romans. 1853; Epicurus Leontion and Ternissa [1896].

The last fruit off an old tree. 1853.

Letters of an American mainly on Russia and revolution. 1854.

Antony and Octavius: scenes for the study. 1856.

Letter from Landor to R. W. Emerson. Bath [1856]; rptd with Emerson's paper on Landor from Dial, ed S. A. Jones, Cleveland 1895.

Landor and the Honorable Mrs Yescombe. [Bath 1857].

Mr Landor threatened. Bath [1857], [1857].

Dry sticks fagoted by Landor. Edinburgh 1858.

Mr Landor's remarks on a suit preferred against him at the summer assizes in Taunton 1858. 1859.

Savonarola e il priore di San Marco. Florence 1860.

Heroic idyls with additional poems. 1863.

An address to the Fellows of Trinity College Oxford on the alarm of invasion. 1917 (priv ptd).

Garibaldi and the President of the Sicilian Senate (an Imaginary conversation). 1917 (priv ptd).

A modern Greek idyl. 1917 (priv ptd).

To Elizabeth Barrett Browning and other verses. 1917 (priv ptd).

Letters and Papers

Wheeler, S. Letters and other unpublished writings of Landor. 1897.

—— Letters of Landor private and public. 1899.

Minchin, H. C. Landor: last days, letters and conversations. 1934.

Super, R. H. Landor's letters to Wordsworth and Coleridge. MP 55 1958.

§2

[Southey, R.] Critical Rev Sept 1799. Review of Gebir.

—— Annual Rev 1 1803. Review of Poetry 1802.

—— Quart Rev 8 1812. Review of Count Julian.

Horne, R. H. In his New spirit of the age, 1844. Written chiefly by Elizabeth Barrett.

Forster, J. Landor: a biography. 2 vols 1869.

Stephen, L. Landor's Imaginary conversations. Cornhill Mag Dec 1878; rptd in his Hours in a library, 1879.

Colvin, S. Landor. 1881 (EML).

Swinburne, A. C. Landor. Encyclopaedia britannica 1882 (9th edn); rptd in his Miscellanies, 1886.

Browning, R. Some records of Landor. Ed by T. J. Wise 1919 (priv ptd). 3 letters to I. Blagden.

de Selincourt, E. Classicism and romanticism in the poetry of Landor. In England und die Antike, ed F. Saxl, Berlin 1932.

—— Landor's prose. In his Wordsworthian and other studies, Oxford 1947.

Richards, I. A. Fifteen lines from Landor. Criterion 12 1933; rptd in his Speculative instruments, 1955. Reply by C. Mauron 12 1933.

Super, R. H. Landor: a biography. New York 1954, London 1957.

Elwin, M. Savage Landor. New York 1941, 1958 (rev and enlarged as Landor: a replevin).

Leavis, F. R. Landor and the seasoned epicure. Scrutiny 11 1943.

Chambers, E. K. Some notes on Landor. RES 20 1944.

Davie, D. A. The shorter poems of Landor. EC 1 1951; rptd in his Purity of diction in English verse, 1952. Replies by W. J. Harvey and Davie 2 1952.

Vitoux, P. L'oeuvre de Landor. Paris 1964.

Pinsky, R. Landor's poetry. Chicago 1968.

LEIGH HUNT
1784–1859

The most noteworthy collection of Hunt mss is the Brewer Collection at the State Univ of Iowa, Iowa City: over 100 literary mss and more than 650 letters from Hunt. Bodleian MS Eng Poet e 38 is a notebook containing unptd draft poems by Hunt.

Collections

Poetical works. 3 vols 1819.

Poetical works. Ed his son Thornton Hunt. 1860.

In 1870 Smith, Elder pbd a uniform reprint in 7 vols of some of Hunt's prose works. There has been no full collected edn of the prose, though substantial parts have been completed.

Poetical works. Ed H. S. Milford, Oxford 1923.

Essays. Ed J. B. Priestley 1929 (EL). A selection.

Dramatic criticism 1808–31. Ed L. H. and C. W. Houtchens, New York 1950.

Literary criticism. Ed L. H. and C. W. Houtchens, with an essay, Leigh Hunt as man of letters, by C. D. Thorpe, New York 1956.

Political and occasional essays. Ed L. H. and C. W. Houtchens, with an essay, Leigh Hunt as political essayist, by C. R. Woodring, New York 1962.

§1

Juvenilia written between the ages of twelve and sixteen. 1801, 1801, 1802, 1803.

Critical essays on the performers of the London theatres. 1807.

An attempt to shew the folly and danger of Methodism. 1809.

The reformist's answer to the article entitled State of parties in the last Edinburgh Review (no 30). 1810.

The Prince of Wales v the Examiner: a full report of the trial of John and Leigh Hunt, to which are added observations on the trial by the editor of the Examiner. 1812.

The feast of the poets with notes, and other pieces. 1814 (2 issues, different imprints), 1815 ('amended and enlarged').

The descent of liberty: a mask. 1815, 1816.

The story of Rimini. 1816, 1817, 1819, Boston 1844.

Musical copyright: Whitaker versus Hume; to which are subjoined observations on the defence made by Sergeant Joy, by Leigh Hunt. 1816.

The round table: a collection of essays. 1817. The round table in Examiner was principally by Hazlitt: but of the 52 papers collected in vol form 10 are by Hunt.

Foliage: or poems original and translated. 1818.

Hero and Leander, and Bacchus and Ariadne. 1819.

Amyntas: a tale of the woods. 1820. Tr from Tasso; dedicated to Keats.

The months descriptive of the successive beauties of the year. 1821; ed W. Andrews 1897; ed R. H. Bath 1929.

Ultra-Crepidarius: a satire on William Gifford. 1823.

Bacchus in Tuscany, translated from the Italian of F. Redi. 1825.

Lord Byron and some of his contemporaries. 1828, 2 vols 1828, 3 vols Paris 1828 (with addns). The Autobiography, 1850, below, was partly a reconstruction of this work.

Sir Ralph Esher: or adventures of a gentleman of the Court of Charles II. 3 vols 1832 (anon), 1850 (4th edn, with preface). A novel; some copies dated 1830.

Christianism: or belief and unbelief reconciled. 1832. Expanded for general circulation into The religion of the heart, 1853, below.

The indicator and the companion: a miscellany for the fields and the fireside. 2 vols 1834, 1840, 1845. Hunt's selections from the periodicals named.

Captain sword and captain pen. 1835, 1839, 1849 (with new preface).

A legend of Florence: a play. 1840, 1840 (with added preface); rptd in G. H. Lewes, Modern British dramatists, 1867.

The seer: or common-places refreshed. 2 pts 1840-1, 1850.

Heads of the people drawn by Kenny Meadows, with original essays. 1840. Hunt's contributions are The monthly nurse and The omnibus conductor.

Notice of the late Mr Egerton Webbe. 1840.

The poems of Geoffrey Chaucer modernized. 1841. Ed R. H. Horne and Hunt, who modernized the Tales of the Squire and the Friar.

The palfrey: a love-story of old times. 1842.

Imagination and fancy; with an essay in answer to the question What is poetry? 1844, 1845, 1846, 1852, 1883; ed E. Gosse 1907.

Wit and humour, with an illustrative essay. 1846, 1846.

Stories from the Italian poets. 2 vols 1846, 1854. An excerpt entitled Dante's Divine comedy: the book and its story, 1903.

Men, women and books. 2 vols 1847, 1852.

A jar of honey from Mount Hybla. 1848, 1852.

The town: its memorable characters and events. 2 vols 1848, 1859; ed A. Dobson, Oxford 1907 (WC).

The autobiography. 3 vols 1850, 1860 ('revised by the author; with further revision, and introduction by his eldest son'); ed R. Ingpen 2 vols New York 1903; ed

E. Blunden, Oxford 1928 (WC); ed J. E. Morpurgo 1949; ed from the ms in the Brewer Collection by S. F. Fogle as Leigh Hunt's Autobiography: the earliest sketches, Gainesville 1959.

Table talk. 1851.

The religion of the heart. 1853. *See* Christianism, *above*.

The old court suburb: or memorials of Kensington. 2 vols 1855, 1855 (enlarged), 1860; ed A. Dobson 2 vols 1902.

Stories in verse now first collected. 1855.

A saunter through the West End. 1861.

A day by the fire; and other papers hitherto uncollected. Ed J. E. Babson 1870.

The wishing-cap papers, now first collected [by J. E. Babson]. Boston 1873.

Ballads of Robin Hood. Ed L. A. Brewer, Cedar Rapids Iowa 1922.

The love of books. Ed L. A. and E. T. Brewer, Cedar Rapids Iowa 1923. Rptd from Hunt's My books.

Marginalia. Ed L. A. Brewer, Cedar Rapids Iowa 1926.

Musical evenings or selections, vocal and instrumental. Ed D. R. Cheney, Columbia Missouri 1964.

Hunt on eight sonnets of Dante. Ed D. Rhodes, Iowa City 1965.

Periodicals

No register has yet been made of Hunt's very numerous and often anon contributions to periodicals other than those which he edited.

The examiner: a Sunday paper. 1808-21. Hunt's editorial work ended in 1821, but he contributed until 1825.

The reflector: a quarterly magazine. 1810-11. Re-issued as Reflector: a collection of essays, 2 vols 1812.

The literary pocket-book: or companion for the lover of nature and art. 1818-22 (for 1819-23).

The indicator. 76 nos Wednesday 13 Oct 1819-21 March 1821; 2 vols in 1 1822.

The liberal: verse and prose from the south. 1822-3 (4 nos, 2 vols); rptd New York 1967.

The literary examiner. 1823. Probably ed John Hunt.

The companion. 9 Jan 1828-23 July 1828 (nos 1-28); rptd New York 1967.

The chat of the week. 28 June 1930-28 Aug 1830.

The tatler: a daily journal of literature and the stage. 4 Sept 1830-13 Feb 1832.

Leigh Hunt's London journal. 2 vols 2 April 1834-26 Dec 1835; rptd New York 1967.

The monthly repository. July 1837-April 1838. *See* F. E. Mineka. The dissidence of dissent, Chapel Hill 1944.

Leigh Hunt's journal. 7 Dec 1850-29 March 1851. Weekly.

Letters

Correspondence. Ed his eldest son 2 vols 1862.

My Hunt library: the holograph letters. Ed L. A. Brewer, Iowa City 1938.

§2

Keats, J. In his Poems, 1817.

Shelley, P. B. The Cenci. 1821. Dedication.

—— Letters to Hunt. Ed T. J. Wise 2 vols 1894.

Hazlitt, W. In his Spirit of the age, 1825.

Haydon, B. R. In his Autobiography and journals, 3 vols 1853.

Dickens, C. In his Bleak house, 1853. The character Harold Skimpole.

Moore, T. In his Memoirs, journals and correspondence vol 8, 1856.

Saintsbury, G. In his Essays in English literature 1780-1860, 1890.

Blunden, E. Hunt's Examiner examined. 1928.

—— Hunt: a biography. 1930, New York 1930 (as Hunt and his circle).

Munby, A. N. L. Letters to Hunt from his son Vincent. 1934.
Landré, L. Leigh Hunt. 2 vols Paris 1935–6.
MacCarthy, D. In his Humanities, 1953.

CHARLES LAMB
1775–1834

Bibliographies

Barnett, G. L. and S. M. Tave. In English romantic poets and essayists: a review of research and criticism, ed C. W. and L. H. Houtchens, New York 1957, 1966 (rev).

Collections

Works. 2 vols 1818.
Works. [Ed T. N. Talfourd] 1840 (includes Letters with a sketch of his life), 2 vols New York 1852, 4 vols 1850 (vols 1–2 new edns of Letters and Final memorials).
Works. Ed E. V. Lucas 7 vols 1903–5, 6 vols 1912 (includes rev edn of Letters in 2 vols but omits Dramatic specimens).
Works. Ed T. Hutchinson 2 vols Oxford [1908] (OSA).
Lamb's criticism: a selection. Ed E. M. W. Tillyard, Cambridge 1923.

§ 1

Poems on various subjects by S. T. Coleridge. 1796. Includes 4 sonnets by Lamb.
[Sonnets by various authors. Ed S. T. Coleridge] Bristol 1796 (priv ptd). Includes 4 sonnets by Lamb.
Poems by S. T. Coleridge, second edition, to which are now added poems by Lamb and Charles Lloyd. Bristol 1797.
Blank verse by Charles Lloyd and Lamb. 1798.
A tale of Rosamund Gray and old blind Margaret. Birmingham 1798, London 1798, 1835 (with Recollections of Christ's Hospital); ed R. B. Johnson 1928.
John Woodvil: a tragedy; to which are added Fragments of Burton. 1802.
The king and queen of hearts. 1805 (anon), 1806, 1808, 1809; ed E. V. Lucas 1902 (facs).
Tales from Shakespear, designed for the use of young persons. 2 vols 1807, 1809, 1810, Philadelphia 1813 (unauthorized), London 1816, 1822, 1 vol 1831; ed F. J. Furnivall 2 vols 1901; 1906 (EL); ed G. Tillotson 1962 (EL); ed J. C. Trewin 1964 (Nonesuch Lib). Some of the tales were issued separately as well as in pairs and tetrads. Mary Lamb's name first appeared on the title-page in 1838 (6th edn).
Adventures of Ulysses. 1808, 1819, 1827; ed A. Lang 1890; ed E. A. Gardner, Cambridge 1921.
Specimens of English dramatic poets who lived about the time of Shakespeare, with notes. 1808, 1813, 2 vols 1835, 1 vol 1854 (with added extracts from the Garrick plays); ed I. Gollancz 2 vols 1893; ed J. D. Campbell 1907.
Mrs Leicester's school: or the history of several young ladies related by themselves. 1809 (anon), 1809, 1810, Georgetown DC 1811, London 1814, 1828 (10th edn).
Poetry for children, entirely original, by the author of Mrs Leicester's school. 2 vols 1809 (anon), 1 vol Boston 1812, New Haven 1820; ed R. H. Shepherd 1872; ed A. W. T[uer] 2 vols 1892 (facs).
Beauty and the beast, or a rough outside with a gentle heart: a poetical version of an ancient tale. [1811] (anon), 1813, 1825; ed R. H. Shepherd 1886; ed A. Lang [1887].
Prince Dorus, or flattery put out of countenance: a poetical version of an ancient tale. 1811 (anon), 1818; ed A. W. T[uer] 1889; ed J. P. Briscoe, [Nottingham] 1896.
Mr H: or beware a bad name. Philadelphia 1813, 1825.

The poetical recreations of the Champion. 1822. Ed and pbd by J. Thelwall with many contributions by Lamb.
Elia: essays which have appeared under that signature in the London Magazine. 1823 (anon), 1823. See end-note, below.
Elia: second series. Philadelphia 1828. Anon and unauthorized.
Album verses. 1830.
Satan in search of a wife, with the whole process of his courtship and marriage, and who danced at the wedding, by an eyewitness. 1831. Anon.
The last essays of Elia: being a sequel to essays published under that name. 1833. Anon.
Elia. 2 vols 1835. Moxon's first collected edn of both sers.
Essays of Elia [both sers]; to which are added Letters, and Rosamund: a tale. Paris 1835. Unauthorized.
Recollections of Christ's Hospital. 1835 (with Rosamund Gray and other pieces).
Eliana: being the hitherto uncollected writings. [Ed J. E. Babson] 1864.
Mary and C. Lamb: poems, letters and remains. Ed W. C. Hazlitt 1874.
The following later edns may be noted among the innumerable reprints of the essays of Elia: both sers ed N. L. Hallward and S. C. Hill 2 vols 1895–1900; 1901 (WC); 1906 (EL); ed A. H. Thompson 2 vols Cambridge 1913; ed W. Macdonald 2 vols 1929 (introd by R. Lynd); 2 vols Newtown 1929–30 (Gregynog Press); ed M. Elwin 1952. First ser ed O. C. Williams, Oxford 1911. Second ser ed F. Page, Oxford 1929 (introd by E. Blunden).

Letters and Papers

Letters of Lamb, with a sketch of his life. Ed T. N. Talfourd 2 vols 1837.
Final memorials of Lamb, consisting chiefly of his letters not before published, with sketches of some of his companions. Ed T. N. Talfourd 2 vols 1848.
Letters. Ed W. C. Hazlitt 2 vols 1886.
Hazlitt, W. C. The Lambs: their lives, their friends and their correspondence. 1897.
— Lamb and Hazlitt: further letters and records. 1900.
The letters of Lamb to which are added those of his sister Mary Lamb. Ed E. V. Lucas 3 vols 1935.
Letters of Charles and Mary Lamb. Ed E. W. Marrs, Ithaca 1976–.

§ 2

Hazlitt, W. In his Table-talk 2 vols 1821–2; The spirit of the age, 1825; The plain speaker, 2 vols 1826. Rptd in Complete works, ed P. P. Howe vols 8, 11–12 1930–4.
[Patmore, P. G.] Personal recollections of the late C. Lamb, with original letters. Court Mag March–April, Dec 1835.
— My friends and acquaintance. 3 vols 1854.
De Quincey, T. In his Collected writings, ed D. Masson vols 3, 5 Edinburgh 1889–90.
Pater, W. In his Appreciations, 1889.
Lucas, E. V. Bernard Barton and his friends. 1893.
— The life of Lamb. 2 vols 1905, 1910 (5th edn), 1921 (rev). The standard life.
Blunden, E. Leigh Hunt's Examiner examined. 1928.
— Lamb and his contemporaries. Cambridge 1933.
— Lamb: his life recorded by his contemporaries. 1934.
— Elia and Christ's Hospital. E & S 22 1936.
— Lamb. 1954.
Orage, A. R. The danger of the whimsical. In his Selected essays and critical writings, ed H. Read and D. Saurat 1935.
Whalley, G. Coleridge's debt to Lamb. E & S new ser 11 1958.

WILLIAM HAZLITT
1778–1830

Bibliographies

Keynes, G. L. Bibliography of Hazlitt. 1931.
Schneider, E. W. In English romantic poets and essayists: a review of research and criticism, ed C. W. and L. H. Houtchens, New York 1957, 1966 (rev).

Collections

The 12 vols ed Hazlitt's son 1838–58, under §1, below, were part of a projected collected edn that was to include all the ptd works with addns from ms and other sources. The 7 vols ed W. C. Hazlitt 1869–86, under §1, below, represent part of a similar project.

The collected works. Ed A. R. Waller and A. Glover 13 vols 1902–6. Introd by W. E. Henley.
The complete works. Ed P. P. Howe 21 vols 1930–4.
Selected essays. Ed G. L. Keynes 1930 (Nonesuch Lib).

§1

An essay on the principles of human action: being an argument in favour of the natural disinterestedness of the human mind, to which are added some remarks on the systems of Hartley and Helvetius. 1805 (anon); ed W. Hazlitt jun [1835–6] (with additional essay on abstract ideas).
Free thoughts on public affairs: or advice to a patriot in a letter addressed to a member of the old opposition. 1806 (anon); ed W. C. Hazlitt 1886 (with Spirit of the age, Letter to William Gifford).
An abridgement of the Light of nature pursued, by Abraham Tucker. 1807. Anon.
The eloquence of the British senate: or select specimens from the speeches of the most distinguished parliamentary speakers from the beginning of the reign of Charles I to the present time, with notes. 2 vols 1807 (anon), 1808, Brooklyn 1809–10, London 1812.
A reply to the Essay on population by the Rev T. R. Malthus, in a series of letters. 1807 (anon), New York 1967. Letters 1–3 first pbd in Cobbett's Political Register 14 March, 16–23 May 1807.
A new and improved grammar of the English tongue for the use of schools; to which is added a New guide to the English tongue [by Godwin]. 1810. Rptd only in Complete works, ed P. P. Howe, above. Outline of English grammar, 1810, is an abridgement by Godwin.
Memoirs of the late Thomas Holcroft, written by himself and continued to the time of his death [by Hazlitt]. 3 vols 1816, 1852 (abridged); ed E. Colby 2 vols 1925; Oxford 1926 (WC).
The round table: a collection of essays on literature, men and manners. 2 vols Edinburgh 1817 (includes 12 essays by Leigh Hunt); ed W. Hazlitt jun 1841 (retains Hunt's essays, omits 12 by Hazlitt, adds 3 uncollected essays from Liberal 1882–3); 1869 (omits Hunt's essays with one exception and a few of Hazlitt's); ed W. C. Hazlitt 1871 (Hazlitt's essays only, with Northcote's conversations, Characteristics); 1936 (EL) (with Characters of Shakespear's plays).
Characters of Shakespear's plays. 1817, 1818, Boston 1818; ed W. Hazlitt jun 1838, 1848, 1854; New York 1845; ed W. C. Hazlitt 1869 (with Lectures on the dramatic literature of the age of Elizabeth); 1903 (with Lectures on English poets); 1905; 1906 (EL) (with Round table, rptd 1936); ed J. H. Lobban, Cambridge 1908; Oxford 1916 (WC); ed C. Morgan 1948 (as Liber amoris and dramatic criticisms, introd rptd in his Writer and his world, 1960).
A view of the English stage: or a series of dramatic criticisms. 1818, 1821; ed W. Hazlitt jun 1851 (selection pbd as Criticisms and dramatic essays of the

English stage); ed W. Archer and R. W. Lowe 1895 (as Dramatic essays), New York 1957 (as Hazlitt on theatre); ed W. S. Jackson 1906 (text from original articles, with 3 uncollected contributions from Examiner).
Lectures on the English poets, delivered at the Surrey Institution. 1818, Philadelphia 1818, London 1819; ed W. Hazlitt jun 1841 (further matter in 4 appendixes); ed W. C. Hazlitt 1869 (with Lectures on English comic writers); 1903 (with Characters of Shakespear's plays); 1908; 1910 (EL) (with Spirit of the Age); Oxford 1924 (WC); Oxford 1929.
A letter to William Gifford esq. 1819, 1820; ed W. C. Hazlitt 1886 (with Spirit of the age, Free thoughts). First draft in Examiner 15 June 1818.
Lectures on the English comic writers, delivered at the Surry Institution. 1819, Philadelphia 1819; ed W. Hazlitt jun 1841 (expanded, mainly from prefaces originally contributed to Oxberry's New English drama 1818–9); ed W. C. Hazlitt 1869 (with Lectures on English poets); ed A. Dobson 1900; ed R. B. Johnson, Oxford 1907 (WC); ed W. E. Henley 1910 (EL) (with essays from New Monthly Mag and Monthly Mag); ed A. Johnson 1965.
Political essays, with sketches of public characters. 1819, 1822. Mainly rptd from articles in various periodicals 1813–18, but including extracts from the Eloquence of the British senate, Reply to Malthus.
Lectures chiefly on the dramatic literature of the age of Elizabeth, delivered at the Surry Institution. 1820, 1821; ed W. Hazlitt jun 1840; New York 1845; ed W. C. Hazlitt 1869 (with Characters of Shakespear's plays).
Table-talk: or original essays. 2 vols 1821–2, 1824, Paris 1825, New York 1845–6 (Hazlitt's selection from Table-talk 1821–2, with essays later collected in Plain speaker, below); ed W. Hazlitt jun 2 vols 1845–6 (based like all succeeding edns on first edn); ed W. C. Hazlitt 1869; 1901 (WC); 1908 (EL).
Liber amoris: or the new Pygmalion. 1823 (anon), 1884; ed R. Le Gallienne 1893; ed (with much additional matter) R. Le Gallienne [and W. C. Hazlitt] 1894 (priv ptd); 1907; Portland Maine 1908; ed C. Morgan 1948 (as Liber amoris and dramatic criticisms).
Characteristics, in the manner of Rochefoucault's Maxims. 1823 (anon); ed R. H. Horne 1837, 1927; ed W. C. Hazlitt 1871 (with Round table, Northcote's conversations).
Sketches of the principal picture-galleries in England, with a criticism on Marriage à-la-mode. 1824 (anon); ed W. Hazlitt jun 1843 (as part of Criticisms on art ser 1). Originally contributed to London Mag 1822–3. Hogarth essay rptd from Round table 1817.
Select British poets: or new elegant extracts from Chaucer to the present time, with critical remarks. 1824 (withdrawn owing to infringements of copyright in the contemporary section), 1825 (omitting copyright matter, as Select poets of Great Britain).
The spirit of the age: or contemporary portraits. 1825, 1825 (anon) (2nd edn enlarges Coleridge, adds Cobbett from Table-talk), Paris 1825 (re-arranged, omitting Moore and Irving, adds Canning and Knowles); ed W. Hazlitt jun 1858; ed E. C. Hazlitt 1886 (with Letter to William Gifford, Free thoughts); [selection] ed R. B. Johnson 1893; Oxford 1904 (WC); 1910 (EL) (with Lectures on English poets). Partly rptd from London Mag and New Monthly Mag.
The plain speaker: opinions on books, men and things. 2 vols 1826 (anon); ed W. Hazlitt jun 2 vols 1851–2; ed W. C. Hazlitt 1870; 1928 (EL).
Notes of a journey through France and Italy. 1826, Philadelphia 1833.
The life of Napoleon Buonaparte. 4 vols 1828–30 (vols 1–2 re-issued 1830), 3 vols New York 1847–8; rev W. Hazlitt jun 4 vols 1852; 6 vols Paris and Boston 1895 (Napoleon Soc); 6 vols [1910] (Grolier Soc).
Conversations of James Northcote esq RA 1830; ed

W. C. Hazlitt 1871 (with Round table, Characteristics); ed E. Gosse 1894; ed F. Swinnerton 1949. Rptd from New Monthly Mag Aug 1826–March 1827, London Weekly Rev 1829, Atlas March–Nov 1829, Court Jnl 1830.

Literary remains of the late William Hazlitt, with a notice of his life by his son, and thoughts on his genius and writings by E. L. Bulwer esq MP and Mr Sergeant Talfourd MP. 2 vols 1836, 1 vol New York 1836. 22 essays mainly rptd from periodicals.

Sketches and essays, now first collected by his son. 1839, 1852 (as Men and manners); ed W. C. Hazlitt 1872 (with Winterslow); 1902 (WC). 18 essays rptd from periodicals.

Criticisms on art, and sketches of the picture galleries of England. Ed W. Hazlitt jun 2 sers 1843–4; ed W. C. Hazlitt 1873 (expanded as Essays on the fine arts).

Winterslow: essays and characters written there, collected by his son. 1850; ed W. C. Hazlitt 1872 (with Sketches and essays); 1902 (WC). Partly rptd from Literary remains, but mainly from periodicals.

A reply to Z. Ed C. Whibley 1923. Unpbd reply to article signed 'Z' in Blackwood's Mag Aug 1818.

New writings by Hazlitt. Ed P. P. Howe 2 sers 1925–7. Articles rptd from periodicals and Oxberry's New English drama 1818–9.

Hazlitt in the workshop: the manuscript of the Fight, transcribed with collation, notes and commentary. Ed S. C. Wilcox, Baltimore 1943.

Letters and Papers

Hazlitt, W. C. Memoirs of Hazlitt, with portions of his correspondence. 2 vols 1867.
—— Lamb and Hazlitt: further letters and records. 1900.

§2

Stephen, L. In his Hours in a library ser 2, 1876.
De Quincey, T. In his Collected writings, ed D. Masson vols 3, 5, 9, 11 Edinburgh 1889–90.
Saintsbury, G. In his Essays in English literature 1780–1860 ser 1, 1890.
Birrell, A. Hazlitt. 1902 (EML).
Howe, P. P. Hazlitt and Liber amoris. Fortnightly Rev Feb 1916.
—— Life of Hazlitt. 1922, 1928 (rev); ed F. Swinnerton 1947.
Garrod, H. W. The place of Hazlitt in English criticism. In his Profession of poetry and other lectures, Oxford 1929.
Woolf, V. In her Common reader ser 2, 1932.
Schneider, E. W. The aesthetics of Hazlitt. Philadelphia 1933, 1952.
Pearson, H. The fool of love. 1934.
Maclean, C. M. Born under Saturn: a biography. 1943.
Priestley, J. B. Hazlitt. 1960.
Baker, H. Hazlitt. Cambridge Mass 1962.
Park, R. Hazlitt and the spirit of the age. Oxford 1971.

THOMAS DE QUINCEY
1785–1859
Bibliographies

Jordan, J. E. In English romantic poets and essayists: a review of research and criticism, ed C. W. and L. H. Houtchens, New York 1957, 1966 (rev).

Collections

Writings. 24 vols Boston 1851–9, 22 vols in 11 Boston 1873. Ed J. T. Fields, with the consent of De Quincey.
Selections grave and gay, from writings, published and unpublished, of De Quincey, revised and arranged by himself. 14 vols Edinburgh 1853–60.

Collected writings: new and enlarged edn by David Masson. 14 vols Edinburgh 1889–90.
Posthumous works, edited from original mss with introductions and notes by A. H. Japp. 2 vols 1891–3.
Literary criticism. Ed H. Darbishire, Oxford 1909; De Quincey as critic, ed J. E. Jordan 1973.
New essays: his contributions to the Edinburgh Saturday Post and the Edinburgh Evening Post 1827–8. Ed S. M. Tave, Princeton 1966.

§1

Concerning the relations of Great Britain, Spain and Portugal, as affected by the convention of Cintra, by Wordsworth, appendix on the letters of Sir J. Moore by De Quincey. 1809.
Confessions of an English opium eater. London Mag Sept–Oct 1821, Sept 1822 (appendix); 1822, 1823, Edinburgh 1856 (greatly enlarged); ed R. Garnett 1885; ed E. Sackville-West 1950 (from 1st edn with selections from Autobiography); ed M. Elwin 1956 (both edns with Suspiria); ed J. E. Jordan 1960 (EL).
Encyclopaedia britannica. 7th edn 1827–42. Articles on Goethe, 1835; Pope, 1837–8; Schiller, 1838; Shakespeare, 1838.
The logic of political economy. Edinburgh 1844.
China. 1857. Rev from articles in Titan, with preface and addns.
The wider hope: essays on future punishment, with a paper on the supposed scriptural expression for eternity. 1890.
Dr Johnson and Lord Chesterfield. New York 1945 (priv ptd).
Recollections of the Lake poets. Ed E. Sackville-West 1948; ed D. Wright 1970 (Penguin). Rev text supplemented from Tait's Mag 1839–40.
Reminiscences of the English Lake poets. Ed J. E. Jordan 1961 (EL). Rev text with notes on 1839–40 mag text.

Letters and Papers

De Quincey memorials: being letters and other records here first published, with communications from Coleridge, the Wordsworths, Hannah More, Professor Wilson and others. Ed A. H. Japp 2 vols 1891.
A diary of De Quincey 1803, here reproduced in replica as well as in print from the original manuscript. Ed H. A. Eaton [1927].
De Quincey at work: as seen in one hundred and thirty new and newly edited letters. Ed W. H. Bonner, Buffalo 1936.
De Quincey to Wordsworth: a biography of a relationship, with the letters of De Quincey to the Wordsworth family. Ed J. E. Jordan, Berkeley 1962.

§2

Cottle, J. In his Early recollections, 2 vols 1837–9.
Masson, D. In his Essays biographical and critical, 1856.
—— De Quincey. 1881 (EML).
Stephen, L. In his Hours in a library, 1874.
'Page, H. A.' (A. H. Japp). De Quincey: his life and writings; with unpublished correspondence. 2 vols 1877, 1 vol 1890 (rev with omissions and addns).
Carlyle, T. In his Reminiscences, ed. J. A. Froude 2 vols 1881.
Saintsbury, G. In his Essays in English literature 1780–1860, 1890.
Hogg, J. De Quincey and his friends: personal recollections, souvenirs and anecdotes. 1895.
Woolf, V. In her Common reader ser 2, 1932.
Abrams, M. H. The milk of paradise: the effect of opium visions on the works of De Quincey, Crabbe, Francis Thompson and Coleridge. Cambridge Mass 1934.
Eaton, H. A. De Quincey: a biography. Oxford 1936.

Sackville-West, E. A flame in sunlight: the life and work of De Quincey. 1936, 1974.

Jordan, J. E. De Quincey's dramaturgic criticism. ELH 18 1951.

—— De Quincey: literary critic. Berkeley 1952.

—— De Quincey on Wordsworth's theory of diction. PMLA 68 1953.

—— De Quincey to Wordsworth: a biography of a relationship. Berkeley 1962.

Jack, I. De Quincey revises his Confessions. PMLA 72 1957.

Carnall, G. D. De Quincey on the knocking at the gate. REL 2 1961.

Davies, H. S. Thomas De Quincey. 1964 (Br Council pamphlet).

Moreux, F. De Quincey: la vie–l'homme–l'œuvre. Paris 1964.

Goldman, A. The mine and the mint: sources for the writings of De Quincey. Carbondale 1965.

THOMAS CARLYLE
1795–1881

Bibliographies

Dyer, I. W. A bibliography of Carlyle's writings and ana. Portland Maine 1928.

Moore, C. In English romantic poets and essayists, ed C. W. and L. H. Houtchens, New York 1966 (rev).

Collections

Centenary edition. Ed H. D. Traill 30 vols 1896–9, New York 1896–1901. The fullest collection.

Carlyle: an anthology. Ed G. M. Trevelyan 1953.

Selected works, reminiscences and letters. Ed J. Symons 1955 (Reynard Lib).

§ 1

Goethe's Faust. New Edinburgh Rev 2 1822; ed R. Garnett, Pbns of Eng Goethe Soc 4 1888.

Schiller's life and writings. London Mag Oct 1823, Jan, July-Sept 1824; rptd as The life of Schiller, 1825, 1845.

Wilhelm Meister's apprenticeship: a novel from the German of Goethe. 3 vols Edinburgh 1824 (anon), 1839; ed E. Dowden 1890; ed N. H. Dole, Boston 1901.

Jean Paul Friedrich Richter. Edinburgh Rev 46 1827.

State of German literature. Ibid.

German romance: specimens of its chief authors with biographical and critical notices, by the translator of Wilhelm Meister, and the author of the life of Schiller. 4 vols Edinburgh 1827.

Life and writings of Werner. Foreign Rev 1 1828.

Goethe's Helena. Ibid.

Goethe. Foreign Rev 2 1828.

Life of Heyne. Ibid.

Burns. Edinburgh Rev 48 1828.

German playwrights. Foreign Rev 3 1829.

Voltaire. Ibid.

Signs of the times. Edinburgh Rev 49 1829.

Novalis. Foreign Rev 4 1829.

Jean Paul Friedrich Richter again. Foreign Rev 5 1830.

Jean Paul Richter's review of Madame de Staël's De l'Allemagne. Fraser's Mag Feb, May 1830.

Cui bono? and four fables by Pilpay Junior. Fraser's Mag Sept 1830.

Thoughts on history. Fraser's Mag Nov 1830.

Luther's Psalm. Fraser's Mag Jan 1831.

Peter Nimmo: a rhapsody. Fraser's Mag Feb 1831.

The Beetle. Ibid.

Taylor's historic survey of German poetry. Edinburgh Rev 53 1831.

Schiller. Fraser's Mag March 1831.

The sower's song. Fraser's Mag April 1831.

The Niebelungenlied. Westminster Rev 15 1831.

Tragedy of the night-moth. Fraser's Mag Aug 1831.

German literature of the fourteenth and fifteenth centuries. Foreign Quart Rev 8 1831.

Characteristics. Edinburgh Rev 54 1831.

Faust's curse. Athenaeum 7 Jan 1832.

Schiller, Goethe and Madame de Staël, and Goethe's portrait. Fraser's Mag March 1832.

Biography. Fraser's Mag April 1832.

Boswell's Life of Johnson. Fraser's Mag May 1832.

Death of Goethe. New Monthly Mag June 1832.

Corn Law rhymes. Edinburgh Rev 55 1832.

Goethe's works. Foreign Quart Rev 10 1832.

The tale, by Goethe. Fraser's Mag Oct 1832.

Novelle, by Goethe. Fraser's Mag Nov 1832.

Diderot. Foreign Quart Rev 11 1833.

Quae cogitavit on history again. Fraser's Mag May 1833.

Count Cagliostro. Fraser's Mag July-Aug 1833.

Sartor resartus. Fraser's Mag Nov 1833–Aug 1834. Pbd separately with subtitle The life and opinions of Herr Teufelsdröckh in three books, with preface by R. W. Emerson, Boston 1836, London 1838, 1841, 1849; ed E. Dowden 1896; ed C. F. Harrold, New York 1937.

Death of Edward Irving. Fraser's Mag Jan 1835.

Mirabeau. Westminster Rev 26 1837.

The diamond necklace. Fraser's Mag Jan-Feb 1837.

Parliamentary history of the French Revolution. Westminster Rev 27 1837.

The French Revolution: a history. 3 vols 1837, 1839, 1848; ed J. H. Rose 3 vols 1902; ed C. F. Harrold, New York 1937.

Lectures on German literature. May 1837. Not pbd; see Spectator 6 May 1837 for concise report.

Sir Walter Scott. Westminster Rev 28 1838.

Varnhagen von Ense's memoirs. Westminster Rev 32 1828.

Critical and miscellaneous essays. 4 vols Boston 1838, New York 1839, London 1839, 5 vols 1840, 4 vols 1847, 1857. Contains most contributions to periodicals to 1838.

Appeal for London Library. Examiner 27 Jan 1839.

Petition on the Copyright Bill. Examiner 7 April 1839.

[Six lectures on revolutions in modern Europe. May 1839. Not pbd.]

On the sinking of the Vengeur. Fraser's Mag July 1839.

Chartism. 1840 (for 1839), Boston 1840, 1842.

On heroes, hero-worship, and the heroic in history: six lectures delivered in May 1840. 1841, 1842, 1846; ed A. MacMechan, Boston 1901; ed J. C. Adams, Boston 1907; ed P. C. Parr 1910; ed H. M. Buller 2 vols 1926.

Preface to Emerson's essays. Boston 1841, London 1841.

Baillie the Covenanter. Westminster Rev 37 1842.

Dr Francia. Foreign Quart Rev 31 1843.

Past and present. 1843, Boston 1843, London 1845; ed O. Smeaton 1902 (Temple Classics); ed F. Harrison [1903]; ed A. M. D. Hughes, Oxford 1921; ed E. Rhys nd (with Emerson's review) (EL); ed R. D. Altick, Boston 1965.

On the opening of Mazzini's letters. Times 19 June 1844.

An election to the Long Parliament. Fraser's Mag Oct 1844.

Oliver Cromwell's letters and speeches, with elucidations. 2 vols 1845, New York 1845, 3 vols 1846 (enlarged), 4 vols 1850; ed S. C. Lomas 1904; ed W. A. Shaw [1907] (EL); ed E. Sanderson, New York [1924] (abridged).

Thirty-five unpublished letters of Oliver Cromwell. Fraser's Mag Dec 1847.

Louis Philippe. Examiner 4 March 1848.

Repeal of the Union. Examiner 29 April 1848.

Legislation for Ireland. Examiner 13 May 1848.

Ireland and the British Chief Governor; Irish regiments of the new era. Spectator 13 May 1848.

Death of Charles Buller. Examiner 2 Dec 1848.

Indian meal. Fraser's Mag May 1849.

Ireland and Sir Robert Peel. Spectator 14 April 1849.

Trees of liberty, from Mr Bramble's unpublished Arboretum Hibernicum. Nation (Dublin) 1 Dec 1849.

Occasional discourse on the nigger question. Fraser's Mag Dec 1849; 1853 (separately).

Latter-day pamphlets. 1850, New York 1850, London 1855, 1858. 8 pamphlets.

Two hundred and fifty years ago: a fragment about duels. Leigh Hunt's Jnl 7, 21 Dec 1850, 11 Jan 1851.

Life of John Sterling. 1851, 1852; ed W. H. White 1907 (WC).

The opera. Keepsake 1852.

The Prinzenraub. Westminster Rev 63 1855.

Suggestions for a national exhibition of Scottish portraits. Proc Soc of Antiquaries of Scotland 1 1855.

The history of Friedrich II of Prussia, called Frederick the Great. 6 vols 1858–65, 13 vols Leipzig 1858–65, 6 vols New York 1858–64, 1863–71, 7 vols 1869, 10 vols 1872–3; ed C. Ransome, New York 1892 (abridged); ed E. Sanderson 1909 (abridged); ed A. M. D. Hughes, Oxford 1916 (abridged).

Inspector Braidwood. Times 2 July 1861.

Memoranda concerning Mr Leigh Hunt. Macmillan's Mag July 1862.

Ilias (Americana) in nuce: the American Iliad in a nutshell. Macmillan's Mag Aug 1863.

Inaugural address at Edinburgh, April 2nd 1866, on the choice of books, with a memoir of Carlyle by J. C. Hotten. 1866, 1869 ('with a new life of the author').

Shooting Niagara: and after? Macmillan's Mag Aug 1867.

Reminiscences of Sir William Hamilton. In Memoir of Sir William Hamilton, 1868.

On the French–German war. Times 18 Nov 1870.

Early Kings of Norway. Fraser's Mag Jan–March 1875; rptd with An essay on the portraits of John Knox, 1875.

On the Eastern question. Times 28 Nov 1876.

On the crisis. Times 5 May 1877. On Disraeli's foreign policy.

Last words of Carlyle on trades-unions, promoterism and the signs of the times. Ed J. C. Aitken, Edinburgh 1882.

Wotton Reinfred. New Rev Jan–March 1892; rptd in Last words, 1892, below. An unfinished philosophical novel.

Last words of Carlyle: Wotton Reinfred, a romance; Excursion (futile enough) to Paris; Letters. 1892, New York 1892 (with introd on Wotton Reinfred).

Lectures on the history of literature, delivered April to July 1838. Ed J. R. Greene 1892; ed R. P. Karkaria, Bombay 1892.

Historical sketches of notable persons and events in the reigns of James I and Charles I. Ed A. Carlyle 1898. Written 1842–3.

Carlyle's unfinished history of German literature. Ed H. Shine, Lexington Kentucky 1951.

Letters and Journals

About two-thirds of the ms letters are in the National Library of Scotland; other large holdings are owned by the Marquess of Northampton (Ashburton letters), the descendants of Alexander Carlyle in Canada, the Victoria and Albert Museum, the John Rylands Library, Harvard, Yale, the Huntington Library, New York Public Library, Trinity College Cambridge, Carlyle's House Chelsea, the Pierpont Morgan Library, the Univ of Edinburgh, the BM, the Goethe-Schiller Archiv Weimar, and the Arched House Ecclefechan. Both Carlyles kept journals, from which Froude and other biographers have quoted.

Reminiscences. Ed J. A. Froude 2 vols 1881; ed C. E. Norton 2 vols 1887, 1932 (EL).

Shepherd, R. H. Memoirs of Carlyle. 2 vols 1881.

Letters and memorials of Jane Welsh Carlyle. Ed J. A. Froude 3 vols 1883.

The correspondence of Carlyle and Ralph Waldo Emerson. Ed C. E. Norton, Boston 1883, 1883, Boston 1886 (with addns), 1888; ed J. Slater, New York 1964 (with addns and notes).

Early letters of Carlyle 1814–26. Ed C. E. Norton 2 vols 1886, 2 vols in 1 1886.

Correspondence between Goethe and Carlyle. Ed C. E. Norton 1887.

Early letters of Carlyle 1826–36. Ed C. E. Norton 2 vols 1888, 2 vols in 1 1889.

Early letters of Jane Welsh Carlyle. Ed D. G. Ritchie 1889.

Conversations with Carlyle. By C. G. Duffy 1892.

Two note books of Carlyle from 23 March 1822 to 16 May 1832. Ed C. E. Norton, New York 1898.

New letters and memorials of Jane Welsh Carlyle. Ed A. Carlyle 2 vols 1903.

New letters of Carlyle. Ed A. Carlyle 2 vols 1904.

Unpublished letters of Carlyle. Ed F. Harrison 1907.

Love letters of Carlyle and Jane Welsh. Ed A. Carlyle 2 vols 1909.

[Letters to Ruskin]. In Works of John Ruskin, ed E. T. Cook and A. D. O. Wedderburn 36–37 1909.

Letters to William Allingham. 1911.

Correspondence between Carlyle and Browning. Ed A. Carlyle, Cornhill Mag May 1915.

Letters of Carlyle to John Stuart Mill, John Sterling and Robert Browning. Ed A. Carlyle 1923.

Jane Welsh Carlyle: letters to her family 1839–63. Ed L. Huxley 1924.

New letters of Carlyle to Eckermann. Ed W. A. Speck, Yale Rev 15 1926.

Jane Welsh Carlyle: a new selection of her letters. Ed T. Bliss 1950.

Letters of Carlyle to William Graham. Ed J. Graham jr, Princeton 1950.

Carlyle: letters to his wife. Ed T. Bliss 1953.

[Carlyle's letters to Clough]. Correspondence of A. H. Clough. Ed F. L. Mulhauser 2 vols Oxford 1957.

Collected letters of Thomas and Jane Welsh Carlyle. Ed C. R. Sanders et al, Durham NC 1971–.

§ 2

Sterling, J. On the writings of Carlyle. Westminster Rev 33 1839; rptd in his Essays and tales, 1848.

Mazzini, J. On the History of the French Revolution. Morning Chron 1840; On the genius and tendency of the writings of Carlyle, Br & Foreign Rev 16 1844. Both rptd in Life and writings of Mazzini vol 4, 1867.

Taine, H. A. L'idéalisme anglais: étude sur Carlyle. Paris 1864.

Stephen, L. [Review of Carlyle's essay on Scott]. In his Hours in a library ser 1, 1874.

Froude, J. A. Carlyle: a history of the first forty years of his life 1795–1835. 2 vols 1882.

—— Carlyle: a history of his life in London 1834–81. 2 vols 1884.

Hutton, R. H. In his Essays on some of the modern guides to English thought in matters of faith, 1887.

—— In his Criticisms on contemporary thought and thinkers, 1894.

Wilson, D. A. Life of Carlyle. 6 vols 1923–34.

Neff, E. E. Carlyle and Mill: mystic and utilitarian. New York 1924.

—— Carlyle. 1932.

Grierson, H. J. C. Scott and Carlyle. E & S 13 1928.

—— Carlyle and Hitler [1931]. In his Essays and addresses, 1940.

—— Thomas Carlyle. Proc Br Acad 26 1940.

Shine, H. Carlyle and the German philosophy problem during the year 1826–7. PMLA 50 1935.

—— Carlyle's fusion of poetry, history and religion by 1834. Chapel Hill 1937.

—— Carlyle and the St-Simonians: the concept of historical periodicity. Baltimore 1941.
—— Carlyle's early reading to 1834. Lexington Kentucky 1953.
Hanson, L. and E. Necessary evil: the life of Jane Welsh Carlyle. 1952.

Tillotson, K. In her Novels of the eighteen-forties, Oxford 1954.
Tennyson, G. B. Sartor called Resartus. Princeton 1965.
Seigel, J. P. (ed). Carlyle: the critical heritage. 1971.
Fielding, K. J. and R. L. Tarr (ed). Carlyle past and present. 1976.

II. MINOR PROSE 1800–1835

SIR SAMUEL EGERTON BRYDGES
1762–1837

§ 1

Sonnets and other poems, with a versification of the six bards of Ossian. 1785 (anon), 1785 (signed and expanded), 1795, 1807 (further expanded as Poems).
The topographer: containing a variety of original articles, illustrative of the local history and antiquities of England. 4 vols 1789–91. With Lawrence Stebbing Shaw.
Topographical miscellanies. 1792.
Mary de Clifford: a story; interspersed with many poems. 1792 (anon), 1800.
Verses on the late unanimous resolutions to support the Constitution [with] some other poems. Canterbury 1794.
Arthur Fitz Albini: a novel. 2 vols 1798, 1799, 1810.
Le Forester: a novel. 3 vols 1802.
Censura literaria: containing titles, abstracts and opinions of old English books, with original disquisitions, articles of biography and other literary antiquities. 10 vols 1805–9, 1815 (articles re-arranged chronologically).
The British bibliographer. 4 vols 1810–4.
The sylvan wanderer: consisting of a series of moral, sentimental and critical essays. 4 pts Lee Priory 1813–21 (priv ptd).
The ruminator: containing a series of moral, critical and sentimental essays. 2 vols 1813.
Occasional poems, written in the year 1811. Lee Priory 1814 (priv ptd).
Select poems. Lee Priory 1814 (priv ptd).
Bertram: a poetical tale. Lee Priory 1814 (priv ptd), 1816.
Restituta: or titles, extracts and characters of old books in English literature revived. 4 vols 1814–16.
Excerpta Tudoriana: or extracts from Elizabethan literature, with a critical preface. 2 vols Lee Priory 1814–18 (priv ptd).
Archaica: containing a reprint of scarce old English tracts, with prefaces, critical and biographical. 2 vols 1815 (priv ptd).
Desultoria: or comments of a South-Briton on books and men. Lee Priory 1815 (priv ptd).
Lord Brokenhurst: or a fragment of winter leaves. Geneva 1819; rptd in his Tragic tales, 1820.
Coningsby. Paris 1819; rptd in his Tragic tales, 1820.
Sir Ralph Willoughby: an historical tale of the sixteenth century. Florence 1820.
Res literariae: bibliographical and critical. 3 nos Naples, Rome, Geneva 1820–2.
The hall of Hellingsley: a tale. 3 vols 1821.
Odo, Count of Lingen: a poetical tale in six cantos. Geneva 1824, Paris 1826.
Gnomica: detached thoughts, sententious, axiomatic, moral and critical. Geneva 1824.
Letters on the character and poetical genius of Lord Byron. 1824.

An impartial portrait of Lord Byron as a poet and a man. Paris 1825.
Recollections of foreign travel on life, literature and self-knowledge. 2 vols 1825.
Modern aristocracy: or the bard's reception. Geneva 1831. Poem on Byron.
The lake of Geneva: a poem moral and descriptive. 2 vols Geneva 1832.
Imaginative biography. 2 vols 1834.
The autobiography, times, opinions and contemporaries of Sir Egerton Brydges. 2 vols 1834.
Moral axioms in single couplets for the use of the young. 1837.
Human fate, and an address to the poets Wordsworth and Southey: poems. Great Totham 1846 (priv ptd).

§ 2

Woodworth, M. K. The literary career of Brydges. Oxford 1935.

CHARLES COWDEN CLARKE
1787–1877

§ 1

Readings in natural philosophy: or a popular display of the wonders of nature etc. 1828.
Tales from Chaucer in prose: designed chiefly for the use of young persons. 1833, 1870 (carefully rev).
Adam the gardener. 1834. A boys' book.
The riches of Chaucer. 1835, 1870.
Carmina minima. 1859.
Shakespeare characters: chiefly those subordinate. 1863.
Molière-characters. Edinburgh 1865.
On the comic writers of England. GM April-Dec 1871.

§ 2

Altick, R. D. The Cowden Clarkes. New York 1948.

HENRY NELSON COLERIDGE
1798–1843

Six months in the West Indies in 1825. 1826 (anon), 1832, 1841 (both with addns); tr Dutch, 1826.
Introductions to the study of the Greek classic poets. Pt 1 (all pbd), 1830, 1834. On Homer.
Specimens of the table-talk of the late Samuel Taylor Coleridge. 2 vols 1835, 1836 (with slight alterations), 1851 etc.
For H. N. Coleridge's edns of his uncle's Literary remains, Aids to reflection, Confessions of an inquiring spirit, Biographia literaria *etc, see under S. T. Coleridge, col 778, above.*

JOHN WILSON CROKER
1780–1857

§ I

Familiar epistles on the state of the Irish stage. Dublin 1804 (anon), 1804 (with addn); ed W. Donaldson 1875.
An intercepted letter from Canton. Dublin 1804. A satire on Dublin society.
The amazoniad, or figure and fashion: a scuffle in high life. 2 pts Dublin 1806. Anon; a satirical poem.
A sketch of the state of Ireland. 1808. Anon.
The battles of Talavera. Dublin 1809, 1812 (9th edn, as Talavera; to which are added other poems).
A key to the orders in council. 1812. Anon.
The letters on the subject of the naval war with America. 1813.
A letter on the fittest style and situation for the Wellington testimonial about to be erected in Dublin. 1815.
Stories for children from the history of England. 1817.
Keats's Endymion. Quart Rev 19 1818.
Substance of the speech in the House of Commons on the Roman Catholic question. 1819.
An answer to O'Meara's Napoleon in exile. New York 1823. Rptd from Quart Rev.
Progressive geography for children. 1828.
Poems by Alfred Tennyson. Quart Rev 49 1833.
The life of Samuel Johnson LlD by James Boswell. 5 vols 1831, 1835, 1848 ('thoroughly revised with much additional matter').
Speech on the reform question. 1831.
Speech on the question that 'The reform bill do pass'. 1831.
Resolutions moved by Mr Croker on the report of the reform bill. 1832.
Johnsoniana: or supplement to Boswell. 2 vols 1835, 1859 (with much new material).
Memoirs of the reign of George the second by John, Lord Hervey. 2 vols 1848.
Robespierre. 1835. Rptd from Quart Rev 54 1835.
Macaulay's History of England. Quart Rev 84 1849.
History of the guillotine. 1853. Rev from Quart Rev.
Correspondence with the Right Honourable Lord John Russell on some passages of Moore's diary; with a postscript by Mr Croker explanatory of Mr Moore's acquaintance and correspondence with him. 1854.
Essays on the early period of the French Revolution. 1857.
An essay towards a new edition of Pope's works. 1871 (priv ptd).
The Croker papers: the correspondence and diaries of Croker. Ed L. J. Jennings 3 vols 1884 (with memoir), 1885 (rev).
The Croker papers 1808–57. Ed B. Pool 1967.

§ 2

Macaulay, T. B. The life of Johnson. Edinburgh Rev 54 1831; rptd in his Critical and historical essays contributed to the Edinburgh Review, 3 vols 1843.
Brightfield, M. F. Croker. Berkeley 1940.
de Beer, E. S. Macaulay and Croker: the reviewer of Croker's Boswell. RES new ser 10 1959.

CHARLES WENTWORTH DILKE
1789–1864

Old English plays: being a selection from the early dramatic writers. 6 vols 1814–15. Ed Dilke to supplement Dodsley's collection.
The papers of a critic: selected from the writings of Dilke, with a biographical sketch by his grandson, Sir Charles Wentworth Dilke. 2 vols 1875.
Dilke was for many years editor of Athenaeum *and contributed regularly 1848–64; his best earlier writing was for* Retrospective Rev 1820–5.

ISAAC D'ISRAELI
1766–1848

Collections

Miscellanies of literature. 1840, [1882–3] (monthly pts), [1884], [1886].
Works. Ed B. Disraeli 7 vols 1858–9 (with memoir).

§ I

A defence of poetry. 1790, 1791.
Curiosities of literature: consisting of anecdotes, characters, sketches and dissertations literary, critical and historical. Ser 1, 1791, 3 vols 1793–1817 (with addns), 5 vols 1823; ser 2, 3 vols 1834 (containing the Secret histories); both sers 6 vols 1834, 3 vols 1849 (with memoir by B. Disraeli), 1858, 1866, 1881; ed E. V. Mitchell 1932 (abridged); ed E. Bleiler 1964 (abridged).
A dissertation on anecdotes. 1793, 1801 (with Literary miscellanies).
Domestic anecdotes of the French nation. 1794, 1800.
An essay on the manners and genius of the literary character. 1795, 1818 (rev and enlarged as The literary character), 2 vols 1822 (rev and enlarged), 1828 (rev and enlarged), 1 vol 1840 (rev as part of Miscellanies of literature); ed B. Disraeli 1927.
Miscellanies: or literary recreations. 1796, 1801 (as Literary miscellanies; adds The dissertation on anecdotes).
Vaurien: or sketches of the times. 2 vols 1797.
Mejnoun and Leila: the Arabian Petrarch and Laura. 1797, 1799 (adds Love and humility, The lovers, and a Poetical essay on romance), 1801 (adds The daughter).
Romances. 1799 (Mejnoun and Leila, Love and humility, The lovers), 1801 (adds The daughter), 1803, 1807 (omits The daughter).
The loves of Mejnoun and Leila. 1800.
Narrative poems. 1803.
Flim-flams! or the life and errors of my uncle, and the amours of my aunt! with an illuminating index! 3 vols 1805, 1806 (rev and enlarged).
Despotism: or the fall of the Jesuits. 2 vols 1811.
Calamities of authors: including some inquiries respecting their moral and literary characters. 2 vols 1812; ed B. Disraeli 1859, [1881].
Quarrels of authors: or some memoirs for our literary history. 3 vols 1814; ed B. Disraeli [1881] (with Calamities of authors).
Inquiry into the literary and political character of James I. 1816.
Psyche. [1823?].
Commentaries on the life and reign of Charles the First, King of England. 5 vols 1828–31; ed B. Disraeli 2 vols 1851 (rev).
Eliot, Hampden and Pym. 1832.
Genius of Judaism. 1833.
Amenities of literature: consisting of sketches and characters of English literature. 2 vols 1841, 1 vol 1842, [1884].

§ 2

Disraeli, B. The life and writings of Mr Disraeli by his son. Prefixed to Curiosities of literature, 1849.
Monypenny, W. F. and G. E. Buckle. The life of Benjamin Disraeli. 2 vols 1929 (rev). Vol 1 has a ch on Isaac D'Israeli.

THOMAS ERSKINE,
1st BARON ERSKINE
1750–1823

Collections

Speeches at the bar, on subjects connected with the liberty

of the press. 4 vols 1810, 1812, Georgetown 1813, 4 vols 1813–16, 1847 (with prefatory memoir by Lord Brougham), 2 vols 1870 (with memoir by E. Walford).

§ 1

Plain thoughts of a plain man addressed to the common sense of the people of Great Britain. 1797.

A view of the causes and consequences of the present war with France. 1797 (35 edns).

Cruelty to animals: the speech of Lord Erskine in the House of Peers on the second reading of the bill for preventing malicious and wanton cruelty to animals. 1809, 1824.

Armata: a fragment. 1817 (anon, 4 edns); The second part of Armata, 1817 (3 edns). A political romance.

A short defence of the Whigs against the imputations attempted to be cast upon them during the late election for Westminster. 1819, 1819.

A letter to An elector of Westminster, author of A reply to the short defence of the Whigs. 1819.

The defences of the Whigs. 1819. Rptd from 2 preceding.

The farmer's vision, by E. 1819 (priv ptd).

A letter to the Earl of Liverpool on the subject of the Greeks. 1822 (2nd edn).

The poetical works; with a biographical memoir. 1823.

Age of reason: Erskine's defence of the cause of Newton, Boyle, Locke, Hale and Milton, versus T. Paine. [1831].

Erskine's opinion of Paine's Age of reason. [1831].

§ 2

Fraser, J. A. L. Erskine. Cambridge 1932.

BASIL HALL
1788–1844

Account of a voyage of discovery to the west coast of Corea and the Great Loo-Choo Island; with an appendix and a vocabulary of the Loo-Choo language by H. I. Clifford. 1818, 1820 (with plates), Edinburgh 1826, 1840 (with an interview with Napoleon Bonaparte at St Helena).

Extracts from a journal written on the coasts of Chili, Peru and Mexico, in the years 1820, 1821, 1822. 2 vols 1823, Edinburgh 1824, 1825 (4th edn); tr Portuguese, 1906; Spanish, 1920.

Hall's voyages. 4 vols Edinburgh 1826–7.

Travels in North America in the years 1827 and 1828. 3 vols Edinburgh 1829, 2 vols Philadelphia 1829; tr French, [1841?].

Fragments of voyages and travels. Ser 1, 3 vols 1831; ser 2, 3 vols Edinburgh 1832; ser 3, 3 vols Edinburgh 1833, 1834; tr French, 1858. Autobiographical sketches from this work were separately pbd as The midshipman and The lieutenant and commander, 1862.

Schloss Hainfeld: or a winter in Lower Styria. Edinburgh 1836, 1836.

Patchwork. 3 vols 1841.

Voyages and travels. 1895. With biographical preface.

Travels in India, Ceylon and Borneo, selected and edited with biographical introduction by H. G. Rawlinson. 1931.

JULIUS CHARLES HARE
1795–1855

La Motte Fouqué's Sintram and his companions. 1820.

Guesses at truth, by two brothers. Ser 1, 1827, 1838 (with addns), 1840 (rev); ser 2, 1848 (title-page states '2nd edn with large addns', but preface explains that '2nd edn'

means that part of ser 1 is included); both sers, 1866, 1871 (with memoir of J. C. Hare by E. H. Plumptre), 1905. With A. W. Hare, until his death; essays, epigrams etc.

Niebuhr's The History of Rome. 3 vols 1828–42. Vols 1–2 by Hare and Connop Thirlwall.

A vindication of Niebuhr's History of Rome. Cambridge 1829.

The old man of the mountain; The lovecharm; and Pietro of Abano: tales from the German of Tieck. 1831.

The victory of faith and other sermons. Cambridge 1840; ed E. H. Plumptre 1874.

The mission of the Comforter and other sermons, with notes. 2 vols 1846, Cambridge 1850 (rev); ed E. H. Plumptre 1876. Vindication of Luther ptd separately, 1855.

Schiller's poems. 1847. Tr with some poems by Goethe.

Memoir of John Sterling. Prefixed to Essays and tales of John Sterling, collected and ed Hare 2 vols 1848.

Thou shalt not bear false witness against thy neighbour: a letter to the editor of the English Review, with a letter from Professor Maurice to the author. 1849.

The life of Luther in forty-eight historical engravings by G. Koenig. 1855. Text by Hare, continued by S. Winkworth.

Charges to the clergy of the archdeaconry of Lewes 1840–54. 3 vols 1856.

Fragments of two essays in English philology. Ed J. E. B. Mayor 1873.

BENJAMIN ROBERT HAYDON
1786–1846

§ 1

The judgment of connoisseurs upon works of art compared with that of professional men, in reference more particularly to the Elgin Marbles. 1816.

New churches considered with respect to the opportunities they afford for the encouragement of painting. 1818.

Some enquiry into the causes which have obstructed the advance of historical painting for the last seventy years in England. 1829.

On academies of art (more particularly the Royal Academy) and their pernicious effect on the genius of Europe: lecture xiii. 1839.

Thoughts on the relative value of fresco and oil painting, as applied to the architectural decorations of the Houses of Parliament. 1842.

Letters, Diaries etc

The life of Haydon, from his autobiography and journals. Ed T. Taylor 3 vols 1853, 1853 (with additional appendix and index by W. R. S. Ralston); ed A. Huxley 2 vols 1926; ed A. P. D. Penrose 1927; ed E. Blunden, Oxford 1927 (WC); ed M. Elwin 1950.

Correspondence and table-talk: with a memoir by his son F. W. Haydon; with fascimile illustrations from his journals. 2 vols 1876.

The diary of Haydon. Ed W. B. Pope 5 vols Cambridge Mass 1960–3.

§ 2

Woolf, V. The genius of Haydon. Nation 18 Dec 1926; rptd in her Moment and other essays, 1947.

George, E. The life and death of Haydon. Oxford 1948.

Hayter, A. In her Sultry month, 1964.

WILLIAM HOWITT
1792-1879

§1

A poet's thoughts at the interment of Lord Byron. 1824.
The book of the seasons: or the calendar of nature. 1831.
A popular history of priestcraft in all ages and nations. 1833, 1834 (4th edn, enlarged), [1834] (abridged).
Pantika: or traditions of the most ancient times. 2 vols 1835.
Colonization and Christianity: a popular history of the treatment of the natives by the Europeans in all their colonies. 1838.
The rural life of England. 2 vols 1838.
The boy's country-book: being the real life of a country boy. 1839.
Visits to remarkable places, old halls, battlefields and scenes illustrative of striking passages in English history and poetry. 1840; ser 2 'chiefly in the counties of Durham and Northumberland', 1842.
The student-life of Germany, by Dr Cornelius. 1841.
The rural and domestic life of Germany; with characteristic sketches of its cities and scenery, collected in a general tour, and during a residence in the country in 1840, 41 and 42. 1842.
German experiences, addressed to the English, both stayers at home and goers abroad. 1844.
The life and adventures of Jack of the mill, commonly called Lord Othmill: a fire-side story. 2 vols 1844.
Homes and haunts of the eminent British poets. 2 vols 1847, 1857 (3rd edn).
The hall and the hamlet: or scenes and characters of country life. 2 vols 1848.
The year-book of the country: or the field, the forest and the fireside. 1850.
Madam Dorrington of the dene. 3 vols 1851.
A boy's adventures in the wilds of Australia: or Herbert's note-book. 1854.
Land, labour and gold: or two years in Victoria; with visits to Sydney and Van Diemen's Land. 2 vols 1855.
Cassell's illustrated history of England: the text to Edward I by J. F. Smith and [thence] by W. Howitt. 8 vols [1856]-64.
Tallangetta, the squatter's home: a story of Australian life. 2 vols 1857.
The man of the people. 3 vols 1860.
The history of the supernatural in all ages and nations, and in all churches, christian and pagan, demonstrating a universal faith. 2 vols 1863.
The history of discovery in Australia, Tasmania and New Zealand from the earliest date to the present day. 1865.
Woodburn Grange: a story of English country life. 3 vols 1867.
The northern heights of London: or historical associations of Hampstead, Highgate, Muswell Hill, Hornsey and Islington. 1869.
The mad war-planet and other poems. 1871.
The religion of Rome described by a Roman. 1873.

§2

Woodring, C. R. Victorian samplers: William and Mary Howitt. Lawrence Kansas 1952.
Lee, A. Laurels and rosemary: the life of William and Mary Howitt. Oxford 1955.

FRANCIS, LORD JEFFREY
1773-1850

§1

Observations on Mr Thelwall's letter to the editor of the Edinburgh Review. 1804.

Wordsworth's Poems. Edinburgh Rev 11 1807.
A summary view of the rights and claims of the Roman Catholics of Ireland. Edinburgh 1808.
Byron's Childe Harold. Edinburgh Rev 19 1812; Scott's Waverley, 24 1814; Byron's poetry, 27 1816; Keats's Poems, 34 1820; Byron's tragedies, 36 1822.
Essay on beauty. Rptd from Edinburgh Rev with addns in Encyclopaedia Britannica supplement, 1824, 1841; rptd in Contributions to the Edinburgh Rev vol 1, 1844.
Combinations of workmen: a speech. Edinburgh 1825.
Corrected report of the speech of the Lord Advocate of Scotland upon the motion of Lord John Russell, in the House of Commons, for reform of Parliament. 1831.
Eulogium of James Watt. 1839.
Contributions to the Edinburgh Review. 4 vols 1844, 3 vols 1846, Philadelphia 1848, 1 vol 1853.
Peter and his enemies. Edinburgh 1859 (2nd edn). A story exposing abuses in the law.
Jeffrey's literary criticism. Ed D. N. Smith 1910. With list of Jeffrey's articles in Edinburgh Rev.
Contemporary reviews of romantic poetry. Ed J. Wain 1953.
For full list of his contributions to Edinburgh Rev *see* Wellesley Index to Victorian periodicals vol 1, Toronto 1966.
The letters of Jeffrey to Ugo Foscolo. Ed J. Purves, Edinburgh 1934.

§2

Cockburn, H. T. Life of Jeffrey; with a selection from his correspondence. 2 vols Edinburgh 1852.
Greig, J. A. Jeffrey of the Edinburgh Review. 1948.
Clive, J. Scotch reviewers: the Edinburgh Review 1802-15. Cambridge Mass 1957.

MARY ANN LAMB
1764-1847

Helen. Poem, pbd with Charles Lamb, John Woodvil, 1802.
Tales from Shakespear, designed for the use of young persons. 2 vols 1807 (for 1806), 1809; ed F. J. Furnivall 2 vols 1901. With Charles Lamb; Mary's name did not appear on the title-page of 1st edn.
Mrs Leicester's school: or the history of several young ladies, related by themselves. 1807 (anon), 1809, 1825 (9th edn), 1827; ed A. Ainger 1885 (with other writings) With Charles Lamb.
See also under Charles Lamb, col 1019, above.

JOHN GIBSON LOCKHART
1794-1854

Peter's letters to his kinsfolk, by Peter Morris the odontist. 3 vols Edinburgh 1819, 1 vol 1952 (abridged). Assisted by 'Christopher North' (J. Wilson).
Valerius: a Roman story. 3 vols Edinburgh 1821 (anon), 1 vol 1842 (rev).
Some passages in the life of Mr Adam Blair, minister of the gospel at Cross Meikle: a novel. Edinburgh 1822 (anon), 1843 (with Matthew Wald); ed D. Craig, Edinburgh 1963.
Reginald Dalton: a story of English university life. 3 vols Edinburgh 1823, 1 vol 1842, [1880].
Ancient Spanish ballads, historical and romantics: translated with notes. Edinburgh 1823, 1841 (rev), New York 1856 (rev with memoir), 1870.
The history of Matthew Wald: a novel. Edinburgh 1824 (anon), 1843 (with Adam Blair).
Janus: or the Edinburgh literary almanack. Edinburgh 1826. With John Wilson.
Life of Robert Burns. Edinburgh 1828; ed W. S. Douglas 1882, 1890 (rev J. H. Ingram); ed E. Rhys 1907 (EL); ed J. Kinsley 1959 (EL).

The history of Napoleon Buonaparte. 1829 (anon), 2 vols New York 1843, London 1867, 1878 (abridged by W. Tegg), Edinburgh 1885 (abridged), London 1889, 1906 (EL); ed J. H. Rose, Oxford 1916.

The history of the late war: including sketches of Buonaparte, Nelson and Wellington: for children. 1832.

Memoirs of the life of Sir Walter Scott Bart. 7 vols Edinburgh 1837–8, 10 vols Edinburgh 1839, 1902–3 (with addns from Narrative, below), 2 vols 1848 (rev and abridged as Narrative of the life of Sir Walter Scott); ed O. L. Reid 1914 (abridged).

The Ballantyne-humbug handled. Edinburgh 1839. Reply to criticisms of the Life of Scott made by James Ballantyne's trustees and son.

The noctes ambrosianae of Blackwood. 4 vols Philadelphia 1843, Edinburgh 1863; ed R. S. Mackenzie 5 vols New York 1866, 1 vol 1904 (abridged). First pbd in Blackwood's Mag 1822–35. Mainly by John Wilson; but Lockhart wrote several of the earlier papers.

Theodore Hook: a sketch. 1953.

Lockhart's literary criticism: with introduction and bibliography by M. C. Hildyard. Oxford 1931.

John Bull's letter to Lord Byron (1821). Ed A. L. Strout, Norman Oklahoma 1947.

THOMAS ROBERT MALTHUS
1766–1834
§ 1

An essay on the principle of population. 1798, 1803, 2 vols 1806, 1807, 3 vols 1817 (5th edn with addns), 2 vols 1826, 1 vol 1872; ed G. T. Bettany 1890, 2 vols [1914] (EL), 1926.

An investigation of the cause of the present high price of provisions. 1800, 1800.

A letter to Samuel Whitbread on his proposed Bill for the Amendment of the Poor Laws. 1807, 1807.

Observations on the effect of the Corn Laws on the agriculture and general wealth of the country. 1814.

An inquiry into the nature and progress of rent. 1815; ed J. H. Hollander 1903.

The grounds of an opinion on the policy of restricting the importation of foreign corn. 1815.

Statements respecting the East India College. 1817.

Principles of political economy. 1820; ed E. Maltby 1836 (with addns), 1936, Oxford 1951.

Godwin on Malthus. Edinburgh Rev 35 1821.

The measure of value stated and illustrated, with an application of it to the alterations in the value of English currency since 1790. 1823.

Definitions in political economy. 1827, 1853 (with addns by J. Cazenove), New York 1954.

Letters and Diaries

For Malthus's correspondence with Nassau Senior see Senior, Two lectures on population, 1829; *and with Ricardo, see* Ricardo, Works vols 6–9, ed P. Sraffa, Cambridge 1952.

Travel diaries. Ed P. James, Cambridge 1966.

§ 2

Hazlitt, W. A reply to the Essay on population by Malthus. 1807; in his Collected works. ed P. P. Howe vol 1, 1930.

—— An examination of Malthus's doctrines. In his Political essays, 1819; in his Collected works vol 7, 1932.

—— In his Spirit of the age, 1825; in his Collected works vol 11, 1932.

Godwin, W. Of population: an answer to Malthus's Essay. 1820.

De Quincey, T. Malthus on population. London Mag Oct 1823; in his Collected writings, ed D. Masson, vol 9 1897.

Stephen, L. In his English Utilitarians vol 2, 1900.

Ricardo, D. Notes on Malthus's Principles of political economy. Ed J. H. Hollander and T. E. Gregory, Baltimore 1928.

Keynes, J. M. In his Essays in biography, 1933.

Smith, K. The Malthusian controversy. 1951.

Glass, D. V. (ed). Introduction to Malthus. 1953.

MacCleary, G. F. The Malthusian population theory. 1953.

Meek, R. L. (ed). Marx and Engels on Malthus. 1953.

Boner, H. A. Hungry generations: the nineteenth-century case against Malthusianism. 1955.

ROBERT OWEN
1771–1858
Collections

A new view of society and other writings. Ed G. D. H. Cole 1927 (EL).

§ 1

A statement regarding the New Lanark establishment. 1812.

A new view of society: or essays on the principle of the formation of human character. 1813, 1816, 1817, New York 1825, Edinburgh 1826; abridged L. D. Abbott 1946.

Observations on the effect of the manufacturing system. 1815, 1817, 1818.

An address to the inhabitants of New Lanark at the opening of the New Institution established for the formation of character. 1816 (2nd edn), 1817.

Peace on earth: development of the plan for the relief of the poor and the emancipation of mankind. [1817].

Two memorials on behalf of the working classes: the first presented to the governments of Europe and America, the second to the Allied Powers assembled at Aix-la-Chapelle. 1818.

Lectures on an entire new state of society: comprehending an analysis of British society relative to the production and distribution of wealth. [1820?].

Report to the county of Lanark of a plan for relieving public distress and removing discontent by giving employment to the poor and working classes. Glasgow 1821, London 1832.

An exploration of the cause of the distress which pervades the civilised parts of the world and of the means whereby it may be removed. 1823.

Discourses on a new system of society as delivered in the Hall of Representatives of the United States. Louisville 1825.

Address at a public meeting in Philadelphia, to which is added an exposition of the pecuniary transactions between [Owen] and W. McClure. Philadelphia 1827.

Memorial to the Mexican Republic. Philadelphia 1827.

Debate on the evidences of Christianity between Owen and A. Campbell. Ed A. Campbell 2 vols Bethany Va 1829, London 1839.

Six lectures on charity at New Lanark. 1833–4.

Lectures on the marriages of the priesthood of the old immoral world. Leeds 1835.

The book of the new moral world concerning the rational system of society. Pt 1, 1836, Glasgow 1837.

Public discussion between Owen and J. H. Roebuck. Manchester 1837, 1837.

A development of the origin and effects of moral good and of the principles and practices of moral good. Manchester 1838.

The marriage system of the new world. Leeds 1838.

Six lectures delivered in Manchester previously to the discussion between Owen and J. H. Roebuck. Manchester [1839].

The catechism of the new moral world. Manchester [1840?].

Manifesto of Owen. 1840, 1841 (8th edn).
An outline of the rational system of society. Manchester [1840?], Leeds 1840 (6th edn).
Social hymns. 1840, 1841.
The social Bible, being an outline of the rational system of society. [1840?].
The signs of the times: or the approach of the millennium. 1841 (2nd edn).
An address to the Socialists on the present position of the rational system of society, May 1841. 1841.
Lectures on the rational system of society versus Socialism as explained by the Bishop of Exeter and others. 1841.
What is Socialism? discussion between Owen and J. Brindley. 1841.
A development of the principles and plans on which to establish home colonies. 1841.
Address to the ministers of all religions, 21 Dec 1845. Philadelphia 1845.
On the employment of children in manufactories. [New Lanark 1848].
The revolution in the mind and practice of the human race. 1849; A supplement, 1849.
Letters on education. 1849.
The future of the human race. 1853, 1854.
Address to the human race on his eighty-fourth birthday. 1854.
The new existence of man upon the earth. 8 pts 1854–5.
Address in St Martin's Hall on 1 Jan 1855. 1855.
Tracts on the coming millennium. 1855.
Papers sent to the National Association for Promoting Social Sciences at its first meeting, 1857. [1857].
Life written by himself; with selections from his writings and correspondence. Vol 1 (2 pts), 1857–8; ed M. Beer 1920.

§2

Jones, L. Life, times and labour of Owen. 2 vols 1889–90.
Davies, R. E. Life of Owen. 1907.
Cole, G. D. H. Owen. 1925.
—— Life of Owen. 1930; ed M. Cole 1965 (3rd edn).
—— Owen and Owenism. In his Persons and periods, 1938.
Davies, A. T. Owen 1771–1858: pioneer social reformer and philanthropist. 1948.
Cole, M. Owen of New Lanark. 1953.
House, H. New Lanark. In his All in due time, 1955.

HENRY JOHN TEMPLE,
3rd VISCOUNT PALMERSTON
1784–1865

§1

The new Whig guide. 1819, 1824. By Palmerston and others; edited by 'E'.
Speech in the House of Commons on 1 June 1829, upon the motion of Sir J. Macintosh respecting the relations of England with Portugal. [1829].
Speech in the House of Commons on 16 February 1842, on Lord John Russell's motion against a sliding scale of duties on the importation of foreign corn. 1842.
Speech to the electors of Tiverton 31 July 1847. 1847.
Speech in the House of Commons on 25 June 1850, on Mr Roebuck's motion on the foreign policy of the government. 1850.
Opinions and policy of Viscount Palmerston; with a memoir by G. H. Francis. 1852.
Selections from [Palmerston's] diaries and correspondence. In H. L. E. Bulwer, Life, 5 vols 1871–6.
Selection from private journals of tours in France in 1815 and 1818. 1871.
The Palmerston papers: Gladstone and Palmerston—

being the correspondence of Lord Palmerston with Mr Gladstone 1851–65. Ed P. Guedalla 1928.
Regina v. Palmerston: the correspondence between Queen Victoria and her Prime Minister 1837–65. Ed B. Connell 1962.

§2

[Francis, G. H.] The oratory of Lord Palmerston. Fraser's Mag March 1846.
Bulwer, H. L. E. The life of Palmerston. 5 vols 1871–6.
Trollope, A. Lord Palmerston. 1882.
Bell, H. C. F. Lord Palmerston. 2 vols 1936.
Pemberton, N. W. B. Lord Palmerston. 1954.

FRANCIS PLACE
1771–1854

The mystery of the sinking fund explained. 1821.
Illustrations and proofs of the principle of population. 1822; ed N. E. Himes 1930.
On the law of libel. 1823.
Observations on Mr Huskisson's speech on the laws relating to combinations of workmen. [1825].
An essay on the state of the country in respect to the condition and conduct of the husbandry labourers and to the consequences likely to result therefrom. [1831].
A letter to a Minister of State respecting taxes on knowledge. [1831], 3rd ed 1835.
Improvement of the working people: drunkenness—education etc. 1834.
Observations on a pamphlet relating to the Corn Laws. [1840].

DAVID RICARDO
1772–1823

Collections

Collected works. Ed J. R. McCulloch 1846.
Works and correspondence. Ed P. Sraffa and M. H. Dobb 11 vols Cambridge 1951–73. Letters in vols 5–9.

§1

Three letters on the price of gold, contributed to the Morning Chronicle. 1809; ed J. H. Hollander, Baltimore 1903.
The high price of bullion. 1810, 1810 (3rd edn) (with addns), 1811 (4th edn) (corrected).
Reply to Mr Bosanquet's Practical observations on the Report of the Bullion Committee. 1811.
An essay on the influence of a low price of corn on the profits of stock. 1815.
Proposals for an economical and secure currency. 1816.
On the principles of political economy and taxation. 1817, Georgetown DC 1819; ed E. C. K. Gonner 1891, [1911] (EL).
On protection to agriculture. 1822.
Plan for the establishment of a national bank. 1824.
Letters to T. R. Malthus 1810–23. Ed J. Bonar, Oxford 1887.
Letters to J. R. McCulloch 1816–23. Ed J. H. Hollander, New York 1895.
Letters to H. Trower and others 1811–23. Ed J. Bonar and J. H. Hollander, Oxford 1899.
Correspondence with Maria Edgeworth. Economic Jnl 17 1907.
Notes on Malthus's Principles of political economy. Ed J. H. Hollander and T. E. Gregory, Oxford 1928.
Minor papers on the currency question 1809–23. Ed J. H. Hollander, Baltimore 1932.

HENRY CRABB ROBINSON
1775–1867

§ 1

Strictures [by T. Clarkson] on a Life of W. Wilberforce by the Rev W. Wilberforce and the Rev S. Wilberforce; with a correspondence between Lord Brougham and Mr Clarkson; also a supplement. 1838. Ed Robinson.

Exposure of misrepresentations contained in the preface to the correspondence of William Wilberforce. 1840.

The diary, reminiscences and correspondence of Crabb Robinson. Ed T. Sadler 3 vols 1869, 2 vols 1872 (with Augustus De Morgan's Recollections of Robinson).

Blake, Coleridge, Wordsworth etc: being selections from the remains of Crabb Robinson. Ed E. J. Morley, Manchester 1922.

The correspondence of Crabb Robinson with the Wordsworth circle 1808–66. Ed E. J. Morley 2 vols Oxford 1927.

Crabb Robinson in Germany 1800–5: extracts from his correspondence. Ed E. J. Morley, Oxford 1929.

Crabb Robinson on books and their writers. Ed E. J. Morley 3 vols 1938.

§ 2

Bagehot, W. In his Literary studies vol 2, 1879.

Morley, E. J. The life and times of Crabb Robinson. 1935.

Elliott, I. Index to the Crabb Robinson letters in Dr Williams's Library. 1960.

NASSAU WILLIAM SENIOR
1790–1864

An introductory lecture on political economy delivered before the University of Oxford, 6 Dec 1826. 1827.

Three lectures on the transmission of the precious metals from country to country and the mercantile theory of wealth. 1828, [1931].

Two lectures on population; to which is added a correspondence between the author and the Rev T. R. Malthus. 1829.

Three lectures on the cost of obtaining money and on some effects of private and government paper money. 1830, [1931].

Three lectures on the rate of wages. 1830.

Three lectures on the value of money. 1830, 1931.

A letter to Lord Howick on a legal provision for the Irish poor: commutation of tithes and a provision for the Irish Roman Catholic clergy. 1831.

Statement of the provision for the poor and of the condition of the labouring classes in a considerable portion of America and Europe. 1835.

An outline of the science of political economy. 1836, 1938.

Letters on the Factory Act as it affects the cotton manufacture. 1837, 1844.

Remarks on the opposition to the Poor Law Amendment Bill. 1841.

Four introductory lectures on political economy delivered before the University of Oxford. 1852.

A journal kept in Turkey and Greece in the autumn of 1857 and the beginning of 1858. 1859.

Resolutions and heads of report [on elementary education]. 1860.

Suggestions on popular education. 1861.

American slavery: a reprint of an article on Uncle Tom's cabin. [1862].

Address on education. 1863.

Biographical sketches. 1863.

Essays on fiction. 1864.

Historical and philosophical essays. [Ed M. C. M. Senior] 1865.

Journals, conversations and essays relating to Ireland. 2 vols 1868.

Journals kept in France and Italy from 1848 to 1852. Ed M. C. M. Simpson, formerly Senior 2 vols 1871.

Conversations with Thiers, Guizot and other distinguished persons during the Second Empire. Ed M. C. M. Simpson 2 vols 1878.

Conversations with distinguished persons during the Second Empire from 1860 to 1863. Ed M. C. M. Simpson 2 vols 1880.

Conversations and journals in Egypt and Malta. Ed M. C. M. Simpson 2 vols 1882.

Industrial efficiency and social economy. Ed S. L. Levy [1929].

SYDNEY SMITH
1771–1845

Collections

Works. 4 vols 1839–40, 1839–40, 3 vols 1840.

The letters of Peter Plymley, with other selected writings, sermons and speeches. Ed G. C. Heseltine 1929.

Selected writings. Ed W. H. Auden, New York 1956.

Selected letters. Ed N. C. Smith, Oxford 1956 (WC).

§ 1

Six sermons. Edinburgh 1800, 2 vols 1801 (enlarged).

Elementary sketches of moral philosophy. 1804, 1805, 1806 (priv ptd), 1850 (public issue). Lectures at the Royal Institution 1804–6.

The letters of Peter Plymley on the subject of the Catholics to my brother Abraham who lives in the country. 1807–8, 1808 (the 9 letters collected); ed H. Morley 1886 (with Selected essays); ed G. C. Heseltine 1929 (with other selected writings).

A sermon upon the conduct to be observed by the Established Church towards Catholics and other dissenters. 1807.

Catholic claims: a speech. 1825.

A sermon on religious charity. York 1825.

A letter to the electors upon the Catholic question. York 1826.

Mr Dyson's speech to the freeholders on reform. 1831. 'Dyson' was Smith.

Speech at the Taunton reform meeting. [1831].

The new reign: the duties of Queen Victoria—a sermon. 1837.

A letter to Archdeacon Singleton on the ecclesiastical commission. 1837.

A letter to Lord John Russell on the Church bills. 1838.

Second letter to Archdeacon Singleton: being the third of the cathedral letters. 1838.

Third letter to Archdeacon Singleton. 1839.

Ballot. 1839. Against the secret ballot.

Letters on American debts. 1844 (2nd edn).

A fragment on the Irish Roman Catholic Church. 1845 (7 edns).

Essays 1802–[27]. 2 vols 1874–80.

Essays social and political 1802–25. [1874], [1877] (adds Essays from Edinburgh Rev and Letters of Peter Plymley, with a brief memoir by S. O. Beeton).

Letters. Ed N. C. Smith 2 vols Oxford 1953.

§ 2

Russell, G. W. E. Sydney Smith. 1905 (EML).

Pearson, H. The Smith of Smiths. 1934.

Auden, W. H. Portrait of a Whig. Eng Miscellany (Rome) 3 1952; rev as introd to Selected writings, above, and in his Forewords and afterwords, 1973.

JOHN STERLING
1806–44

§ 1

Thoughts on the foreign policy of England by Jacob Sternwall. 1827.
FitzGeorge: a novel. 3 vols 1832. Anon.
Arthur Coningsby: a novel. 3 vols 1833. Anon.
Poems. 1839.
The election: a poem in seven books. 1841. Anon.
Strafford: a tragedy. 1843.
Essays and tales: collected and edited with a memoir of his life by Julius Charles Hare. 2 vols 1848.

Letters

Letters to a friend [William Coningham]. Brighton [1848] (priv ptd), 1851 (as Twelve letters), Bath [1872].
A correspondence between Sterling and Ralph Waldo Emerson. Ed E. W. Emerson, Boston 1897.

§ 2

Carlyle, T. The life of Sterling. 1851, 1852; ed W. H. White, Oxford 1907 (WC).
Tuell, A. K. Sterling: a representative Victorian. New York 1941.

EDWARD JOHN TRELAWNY
1792–1881

The adventures of a younger son. 3 vols 1831, 1 vol 1835, 1848; ed E. Garnett 1890; ed H. N. Brailsford 2 vols 1914; ed E. C. Mayne, Oxford 1925 (WC).
Recollections of the last days of Shelley and Byron. 1858, 2 vols 1878 (with addns, as Records of Shelley, Byron and the author); ed E. Dowden 1906; ed J. E. Morpurgo 1952.
The relations of Percy Bysshe Shelley with his two wives Harriet and Mary, and a comment on the character of Lady Byron. 1920 (priv ptd).

Letters

Letters. Ed H. Buxton Forman 1910.
The relations of Lord Byron and Augusta Leigh. 1920 (priv ptd). 4 letters.

JOHN WILSON,
'CHRISTOPHER NORTH'
1785–1854
Collections

The works of Professor Wilson of the University of Edinburgh. Ed his son-in-law Professor Ferrier 12 vols Edinburgh 1855–8.

§ 1

The isle of palms and other poems. Edinburgh 1812.
The magic mirror, addressed to Walter Scott esq. Edinburgh 1812.
The city of the plague and other poems. Edinburgh 1816.
Translation from an ancient Chaldee manuscript, from no vii of Blackwood's Magazine. [Edinburgh 1817].
Lights and shadows of Scottish life: a selection from the papers of the late Arthur Austin. Edinburgh 1822.
Little Hannah Lee: a winter's story. 1823. From Lights and shadows, above.
The trials of Margaret Lyndsay, by the author of Lights

and shadows of Scottish life. Edinburgh 1823, 1854.
The foresters, by the author of Lights and shadows of Scottish life and the Trials of Margaret Lyndsay. Edinburgh 1825, 1852.
Poems: a new edition. 2 vols 1825.
Janus: or the Edinburgh literary almanack. Edinburgh 1826. With Lockhart.
Some illustrations of Mr McCullogh's Principles of political economy by Mordecai Mullion, private secretary to Christopher North. Edinburgh 1826.
The land of Burns: a series of landscapes and portraits, illustrative of the life and writings of the Scottish poet. 2 vols Glasgow 1840.
Blind Allan: a tale. [?1840], [Falkirk? 1850?]. From Lights and shadows, above.
The recreations of Christopher North. 3 vols Edinburgh 1842.
The Noctes ambrosianae of Blackwood. 4 vols Philadelphia 1843, Edinburgh 1863; ed R. S. Mackenzie 5 vols New York 1866 (best edn), 4 vols 1868, 1 vol 1904. Mainly by Wilson. Selections: ed J. Skelton, Edinburgh 1876; ed J. S. Moncrieff and J. H. Millar 1904.
The poetical works. Edinburgh 1865, 1874.
Tales: Lights and shadows, Margaret Lyndsay, The foresters. Edinburgh 1865.
Essays critical and imaginative. 4 vols Edinburgh 1866.
Letters from the Lakes. Ambleside 1889.
Lakeland poems. Ed W. Bailey-Kempling, Ambleside 1902.
Contemporary reviews of romantic poetry. Ed J. Wain 1953.

§ 2

Lockhart, J. G. Peter's letters to his kinsfolk. 3 vols Edinburgh 1819.
Saintsbury, G. In his Essays in English literature 1780–1860, 1890.
Swann, E. Christopher North (John Wilson). Edinburgh 1934.

DOROTHY WORDSWORTH
1771–1855

§ 1

George and Sarah Green: a narrative by Dorothy Wordsworth. Ed E. de Selincourt, Oxford 1936.
The poetry of Dorothy Wordsworth, edited from the journals by H. Eigerman. New York 1940.

Letters and Diaries

Recollections of a tour made in Scotland AD 1803. Ed J. C. Shairp, Edinburgh 1874, 1874, 1894.
Letters to Sir George and Lady Beaumont. In W. Knight, Memorials of Coleorton, 2 vols 1887.
Journals of Dorothy Wordsworth. Ed W. Knight 2 vols 1897; ed E. de Selincourt 2 vols Oxford 1941; ed H. Darbishire, Oxford 1958 (WC); ed M. Moorman, Oxford 1971.
Letters of the Wordsworth family from 1787 to 1855, collected by W. Knight. 3 vols 1907.
The letters of William and Dorothy Wordsworth. Ed E. de Selincourt 6 vols Oxford 1935–9, 1967– (rev).
Home at Grasmere: extracts and poems. Ed C. Clark 1960 (Pelican).

§ 2

The section on William Wordsworth, col 771 above, should also be consulted.
Maclean, C. M. Dorothy and William Wordsworth. 1927.
—— Dorothy Wordsworth: the early years. 1932.
de Selincourt, E. Dorothy Wordsworth: a biography. Oxford 1933.

III. MID-NINETEENTH-CENTURY PROSE

JOHN HENRY NEWMAN
1801–90

Collections
[Collected works]. 36 vols 1868–81.
Sermons and discourses 1825–39. Ed C. F. Harrold, New York 1949; Sermons and discourses 1839–57, ed Harrold, New York 1949.
Prose and poetry. Ed G. Tillotson 1957 (Reynard Lib).

§ I

The Arians of the fourth century: their doctrine, temper and conduct, chiefly as exhibited in the councils of the Church, between AD 325 and AD 381. 1833; ed G. H. Forbes 1854; 1871 (rev), 1876 (rev).
Tracts for the times, by members of the University of Oxford. [Ed Newman] 6 vols 1833–41. 90 tracts were issued anon between 9 Sept 1833 (3 tracts) and 27 Feb 1841 (no 90).
Parochial sermons. 3 vols 1834–6, 6 vols (2–3 are of the 2nd edn) 1834–42; ed W. J. Copeland 8 vols 1868 (including Plain sermons by contributors to the Tracts for the times, vol 5, as Parochial and Plain sermons). Selection from the First four volumes of parochial sermons, 1841. Selection adapted to the seasons of the ecclesiastical year from the Parochial and plain sermons, ed W. J. Copeland 1870.
The restoration of suffragan bishops recommended, as a means of effecting a more equal distribution of episcopal duties, as contemplated by His Majesty's recent Ecclesiastical Commission. 1833; rptd in The via media of the Anglican Church vol 2, 1877 etc, below.
Elucidations of Dr Hampden's theological statements. Oxford 1836. Signed J. H. N.
Make ventures for Christ's sake: a sermon. Oxford 1836 (anon); 1839 etc (in Parochial sermons, vol 4, below).
Lectures on the prophetical office of the Church, viewed relatively to Romanism and popular Protestantism. 1837; rptd, with additional matter, in The via media of the Anglican Church vol 1, 1877 etc, below.
A letter to the Rev Godfrey Faussett DD, Margaret Professor of Divinity, on certain points of faith and practice. Oxford 1838; rptd in The via media of the Anglican Church vol 2, 1877 etc, below.
Lectures on justification. 1838, 1840, 1874 (as Lectures on the doctrine of justification), 1885, 1890, 1892.
The Church of the Fathers. Dublin [1839] (anon), London 1840 (anon), 1842, 1857, 1868, 1872 (in Historical sketches vol 3; material omitted from the 1857 and 1868 edns rptd rev in Historical sketches vol 2, below).
The Tamworth reading room: letters on an address delivered by Sir Robert Peel Bart MP on the establishment of a reading room at Tamworth, by Catholicus, originally published in the Times, and since revised and corrected by the author. 1841; rptd in Discussions and arguments, 1872, below; Washington 1946.
A letter addressed to the Rev R. W. Jelf DD, Canon of Christ Church, in explanation of no 90 in the series called the Tracts for the times, by the author. Oxford 1841 (3 edns), 1877 (in The via media of the Anglican Church vol 2, 1877 etc, below). Signed J. H. N.
A letter to the Right Reverend Father in God, Richard [Bagot], Lord Bishop of Oxford, on occasion of no 90 in the series called the Tracts for the times. 1841, 1877 (in The via media of the Anglican Church vol 2, below).
An essay on the miracles recorded in the ecclesiastical history of the early ages. In Fleury's Ecclesiastical history, 1842; Oxford 1843, 1870 (in Two essays on Scripture miracles and on ecclesiastical), 1870, 1873 (in

Two essays on Biblical and ecclesiastical miracles), 1881.
Sermons, bearing on subjects of the day. 1843, 1844; ed W. J. Copeland 1869, 1873, 1879, 1885.
Sermons, chiefly on the theory of religious belief, preached before the University of Oxford. 1843, 1844, 1872 (as Fifteen sermons preached before the University of Oxford), 1880, 1884.
Plain sermons by contributors to the Tracts for the times. 1843 (vol 5 (anon) by Newman), 1868 etc (in Parochial and plain sermons).
The Cistercian saints of England, [continued as] Lives of the English saints. 4 vols 1–2 1844–5 ed Newman, who wrote the prose portions of St Bettelin, St Edilwald and St Gundleas; ed A. W. Hutton 6 vols 1900–1.
An essay on the development of Christian doctrine. 1845, 1846, 1878, 1885, 1890, 1894; ed C. F. Harrold, New York 1949 (with appendix on Newman's textual changes by O. I. Schreiber); ed G. Weigel 1960.
Loss and gain. 1848 (anon), 1853 (signed; with subtitle The story of a convert), Dublin 1853, London 1858, 1874, 1881; ed M. Trevor 1962. A novel.
Discourses addressed to mixed congregations. 1849, 1850, 1880, 1881, 1886, 1891, 1892.
Lectures on certain difficulties felt by Anglicans in submitting to the Catholic Church. 1850, 1850, Dublin 1857 (rev), London 1872 (as Difficulties felt by Anglicans in Catholic teaching considered I, In twelve lectures addressed to the party of the religious movement in 1833; II, In a letter addressed to the Rev E. B. Pusey &c), 1876 (as Certain difficulties felt by Anglicans in Catholic teaching considered in a letter addressed to the Rev E. B. Pusey and in a letter addressed to the Duke of Norfolk &c), 2 vols 1876–9, 1885 (as Difficulties felt by Anglicans in Catholic teaching), 1891, 1894 (as Certain difficulties felt by Anglicans in Catholic teaching considered).
Christ upon the waters: a sermon preached on occasion of the establishment of the Catholic hierarchy in this country. Birmingham 1850 (3 edns) [1852], London 1857 etc (in Sermons preached on various occasions, below), Birmingham [1898].
Lectures on the present position of Catholics in England, addressed to the Brothers of the Oratory. 1851, 1851, Birmingham 1851 (as Lectures on Catholicism in England), Dublin nd (as Lectures on Catholicism in England), 1872.
Discourses on the scope and nature of university education, addressed to the Catholics of Dublin. Dublin 1852, London 1859 (rev and altered, and with new titles to several of the discourses, as The scope and nature of university education), 1873 (with some titles of discourses again altered, and with addn of 10 pieces pbd in 1859 as Lectures and essays on university subjects, as The idea of a university defined and illustrated, I: In nine discourses addressed to the Catholics of Dublin; II: In occasional lectures and essays addressed to the members of the Catholic University), 1875, 1885, 1889, 1891, 1893, 1896 (2 discourses only, in My campaign in Ireland), 1898 (as The idea of a university etc), 1902; ed A. R. Waller 1903; ed W. Ward 1915 (EL; as On the scope and nature of university education), 1923 (as The idea of a university defined and illustrated etc); ed C. F. Harrold, New York 1947 (as The idea of a university defined and illustrated); 1955 (EL; as On the scope and nature of university education); ed M. J. Svaglic, New York 1960 (as The idea of a university defined and illustrated); ed I. T. Ker, Oxford 1976.
The second spring: a sermon preached in the synod of Oscott, on Tuesday July 13th 1852. 1852, 1857 etc (in Sermons preached on various occasions, below); ed F. P. Donnolly, New York 1911.
Verses on religious subjects. Dublin 1853. Anon. Most

of the poems in this collection are rptd in Verses on various occasions, 1868 etc, below.

Lectures on the history of the Turks in its relation to Christianity, by the author of Loss and gain. Dublin 1854 (anon), 1872 etc (in Historical sketches vol 2).

Callista: a sketch of the third century. 1856 (anon). A novel.

The office and work of universities [articles rptd from Catholic Univ Gazette]. 1856, 1859, 1872 etc (as The rise and progress of universities, in Historical sketches vol 2); ed G. Sampson [1902] (as University sketches); ed C. F. Harrold 1948 (selection of 8 of the 20 articles, in Essays and sketches vol 2); ed M. Tierney, Dublin 1952 (as University sketches).

Sermons preached on various occasions. 1857, 1870, 1874.

Lectures and essays on university subjects. 1859, 1873 etc (as pt 2 of The idea of a university defined and illustrated). See also under Discourses on the scope and nature of university education, above.

Mr Kingsley and Dr Newman: a correspondence on the question whether Dr Newman teaches that truth is no virtue? 1864, 1913, 1931 (both with Apologia pro vita sua).

Apologia pro vita sua: being a reply to a pamphlet [by Charles Kingsley] entitled What, then, does Dr Newman mean? 7 pts, with appendix issued on successive Thursdays 21 April to 2 June 1864; the appendix pbd a fortnight later. Pts 1–2 and appendix were omitted by Newman from later edns. 1864, 1865 (as History of my religious opinions), 1865 (as Apologia pro vita sua: being a reply to a pamphlet entitled What, then, does Dr Newman mean?), 1865, 1865, 1869 (as History of my religious opinions), 1873 (as Apologia pro vita sua: being a history of his religious opinions), 1878, 1879, 1882 (as A history of his religious opinions), 1885 (as Apologia pro vita sua: history of his religious opinions), 1887 (as Apologia pro vita sua: being a history of his religious opinions), 1890; ed W. Ward, Oxford 1913 (the 2 versions of 1864 and 1865, preceded by Newman's and Kingsley's pamphlets); ed C. F. Harrold, New York 1947; ed A. D. Culler, New York 1956; ed B. Willey, Oxford 1964 (WC); ed M. J. Svaglic, Oxford 1967.

The dream of Gerontius. Month May–June 1865, 1866 (dedication signed J. H. N.), 1868 etc (in Verses on various occasions, below).

A letter to the Rev E. B. Pusey DD on his recent Eirenicon. 1866 (3 edns), 1872 etc (in Difficulties felt by Anglicans in Catholic teaching).

The Pope and the revolution: a sermon preached in the Oratory Church Birmingham on Sunday October 7 1866. 1866, 1870 etc (in Sermons preached on various occasions, below).

Verses on various occasions. 1868 (dedication signed J. H. N.), 1869, 1874, 1880, 1883, 1888, 1890.

An essay in aid of a grammar of assent. 1870, 1870, 1874, 1881, 1885, 1891, 1892; ed C. F. Harrold, New York 1947; ed D. Gilson 1955.

Two essays on Scripture miracles and on ecclesiastical. 1870, 1873 (as Two essays on Biblical and on ecclesiastical miracles), 1881, 1885, 1890, 1890.

Essays critical and historical. 2 vols 1872, 1877, 1885.

Historical sketches [i.e. The office and work of universities, 1856, rptd as The rise and progress of universities; Lectures on the history of the Turks, 1854; Personal and literary character of Cicero, 1824; Apollonius of Tyana, 1824; Primitive Christianity (from the 1840 and 1842 edns of The Church of the Fathers); The Church of the Fathers (text of 1857 and 1868 edns) and various shorter pieces]. 3 vols 1872–3, 1873, 1876, 1878–81, 1891.

Discussions and arguments on various subjects. 1872.

Prologue to the Andria of Terence. 1882 (ptd for priv circulation). Copy of this work, written in 1820, in BM.

Orate pro anima Jacobi Roberti Hope Scott [a sermon]. [1873] (advertisement and text signed J. H. N.), 1874

etc (as In the world but not of the world, in Sermons on various occasions, above).

The idea of a university. 1873 etc. See also above, Discourses on the scope and nature of university education.

Tracts theological and ecclesiastical. 1874.

A letter addressed to his Grace the Duke of Norfolk on occasion of Mr Gladstone's recent expostulations. 1875, 1875 (with Postscript on Mr Gladstone's Vaticanism), 1875 (4th edn, with Postscript), New York 1875, London 1876 etc (appended to Certain difficulties felt by Anglicans in Catholic teaching, above); ed A. S. Ryan, Notre Dame 1962 (in Newman and Gladstone).

The via media of the Anglican Church, illustrated in lectures, letters, and tracts written between 1830 and 1841; with a preface and notes. 2 vols 1877, 1885, 1891.

Two sermons preached in the Church of S Aloysius, Oxford on Trinity Sunday 1880. [Oxford 1880] (priv ptd).

What is of obligation for a Catholic to believe concerning the inspiration of the canonical scriptures: being a postscript to an article in the February no of the Nineteenth Century Review in answer to Professor Healy. [1884], 1890 (as Further illustrations, in Stray essays on controversial points variously illustrated).

Stray essays on controversial points variously illustrated. Birmingham 1890 (priv ptd). Reprints What is of obligation for a Catholic to believe, 1884 and 2 other periodical articles.

Meditations and devotions. Ed W. P. Neville 1893; ed M. Trevor 1964.

My campaign in Ireland, part I: Catholic University reports and other papers. Ed W. P. Neville, Aberdeen 1896 (priv ptd).

Sermon notes 1849–78. Ed Fathers of the Birmingham Oratory 1913.

Autobiographical writings. Ed H. Tristram 1956.

Faith and prejudice and other unpublished sermons. Ed C. S. Dessain, New York 1956, London 1957 (as Catholic sermons).

On consulting the faithful in matters of doctrine. Ed J. Coulson 1961.

Theological papers. Ed J. D. Holmes, Oxford 1975.

Works Edited, Translated, or with Contributions by Newman

Elements of logic, by R. Whately. 1826. Newman had a large share in the composition.

Tracts for the times, by members of the University of Oxford. 6 vols 1833–41. Ed Newman.

Lyra apostolica. Derby 1836. Most of the poems by Newman, but not all, were included in Verses on various occasions, 1868 etc. The hymn known as Lead, kindly light was first pbd anon in Br Mag, 1 Feb 1834.

A library of the Fathers of the Holy Catholic Church, anterior to the division of the East and West. Ed J. Keble, Newman, E. B. Pusey and [1843–57] C. Marriott. 48 vols Oxford 1838–85. Newman translated and annotated Select treatises of S Athanasius in controversy with the Arians, 2 vols 1842–4, 1881; also contributed prefaces to the following volumes in A library of the Fathers: S Cyril's Catechetical lectures, 1838; S Cyprian's treatises, 1839; S Chrysostom on Galatians and Ephesians, 1840; and S Athanasius's historical tracts, 1843.

Remains of the late Rev R. H. Froude. 4 vols 1838–9. Ed. Newman and J. Keble.

The devotions of Bishop [Lancelot] Andrewes. 2 pts Oxford 1842–4. Pt i tr from the Greek and arranged by Newman; pt 2 tr from the Latin by J. M. Neale. Pt i had appeared in 1840 as no 88 of Tracts for the times, above. Rptd Oxford 1867; ed and rev E. Venables 1883.

The Cistercian saints of England [continued as Lives of the English saints. Newman, the projector and, in the case of the first 2 vols, the editor of the ser, was the author of the Lives of the hermit SS Gundleus, Edel-

wald and Bettelin (prose portion).] 14 vols 1844-5; ed
A. W. Hutton 6 vols 1900-1.

Maxims of the kingdom of heaven. 1860, 1867, 1873
(enlarged and re-arranged), 1887. A collection of
passages from the Scriptures with a preface by Newman.

Letters

Letters and correspondence of Newman during his life in
the English Church; with a brief autobiography. Ed
A. Mozley 2 vols 1891.

Ward, W. P. The life of Newman based on his private
journals and correspondence. 2 vols 1912.

Correspondence of Newman with John Keble and others
1839-45. Ed at Birmingham Oratory [by J. Bacchus]
1917.

Selections from the correspondence of the first Lord
Acton, vol i: Correspondence with Cardinal Newman,
Lady Blennerhassett, W. E. Gladstone and others. Ed
J. N. Figgis and R. V. Laurence 1917.

Letters of Newman: a selection. Ed D. Stanford and
M. Spark. 1957.

The letters and diaries of Newman. Ed C. S. Dessain et
al, Edinburgh (later Oxford) 1961-.

Newman family letters. Ed D. Mozley 1962.

§ 2

Newman, F. W. In his Phases of faith, 1850.

—— Contributions chiefly to the early history of Cardinal
Newman. 1891.

Kingsley, C. Mr Kingsley and Dr Newman: a correspondence on the question whether Dr Newman teaches
that truth is no virtue? 1864.

—— 'What, then, does Dr Newman mean?' a reply to a
pamphlet lately published by Dr Newman. 1864.

Froude, J. A. Father Newman on the Grammar of assent.
In his Short studies on great subjects ser 2, 1871.

—— In his Short studies on great subjects ser 4, 1883.

Hutton, R. H. In his Essays on some of the modern guides
of English thought in matters of faith. 1887.

—— Cardinal Newman. 1891.

Ward, W. P. The life and times of Cardinal Newman. 2
vols 1897.

—— The life of Newman based on his private journals and
correspondence. 2 vols 1912, 1913, 2 vols in 1 1927.

Meynell, W. Newman: the founder of modern Anglicanism and a Cardinal of the Roman Church. 1890,
1907 (rev).

Faber, G. C. In his Oxford apostles: a character study of
the Oxford Movement, 1933.

Young, G. M. In his Daylight and champagne, 1937.

—— Newman again. In his Last essays, 1950.

Harrold, C. F. Newman: an expository and critical study
of his mind, thought and art. New York 1945.

Houghton, W. E. The art of Newman's Apologia. New
Haven 1945.

Culler, A. D. The imperial intellect: a study of Newman's
educational ideal. New Haven 1955.

Trevor, M. Newman: light in winter. 1962; Newman:
the pillar of the cloud, 1962. A biography.

Tillotson, G. In his Mid-Victorian studies, 1965. 3
articles.

Vargish, T. Newman: the contemplation of mind.
Oxford 1970.

JOHN RUSKIN
1819-1900

Bibliographies

Wise, T. J. and J. P. Smart. A bibliography of the
writings in prose and verse of Ruskin. 19 pts 1889-93
(priv ptd), 2 vols 1964.

Cook, E. T. and A. D. O. Wedderburn. The works of
Ruskin: library edition, vol 38: Bibliography. 1912.

Carter, J. and H. G. Pollard. An enquiry into the nature of
certain nineteenth-century pamphlets. 1934. 8 of the
pamphlets discussed are by Ruskin.

Collections

Collected works. 15 vols New York 1861-3.

Collected works. 11 vols 1871-80.

The poems of Ruskin: now first collected from original
manuscript and printed sources, and edited in chronological order, with notes, biographical and critical, by
W. G. Collingwood. 2 vols Orpington 1891.

The works of Ruskin: library edition. Ed E. T. Cook and
A. D. O. Wedderburn 39 vols 1902-12.

The lamp of beauty. Ed J. Evans 1959.

Ruskin today. Ed K. Clark 1964.

§ 1

Modern painters: their superiority in the art of landscape
painting to all the ancient masters proved by examples of
the true, the beautiful, and the intellectual, from the
works of modern artists, especially those of J. M. W.
Turner, by a graduate of Oxford. 1843, 1844 (with new
preface), 1846 (with new preface), New York 1847,
London 1848, 1851 (with Ruskin's name for the first
time), 1857, 1867; vol 2, 1846 (anon), 1848, 1851 (with
Ruskin's name for the first time), 1856, 1869, 2 vols
Orpington 1883 (rev and rearranged), New York 1883,
Orpington 1885, 1888, 1891; vol 3, 1856, 1867; vol 4,
1856, 1868; vol 5, 1860; 5 vols New York 1865, London
1873 (Autograph edn), New York 1876, 1882, 2 vols
New York 1884, 5 vols 1885, Orpington 1888, New
York 1889, Orpington 1892, 2 vols Boston 1894, 5 vols
New York 1894, Orpington 1897, 1898 etc; ed L. Cust
5 vols 1907 (EL; text from 1st edns).

Frondes agrestes: readings in Modern painters.
Orpington 1875.

The seven lamps of architecture, with illustrations drawn
and etched by the author. 1849, New York 1849,
London 1855, New York 1876, Orpington 1880, New
York 1880, Orpington 1883, New York 1884, 1885, 1885,
Orpington 1886, New York 1889, Orpington 1890, 1891,
1894, 1895, 1897, 1898, 1899; ed R. Sturgie, New York
1899, 1900 (9 edns) etc; ed S. Image 1907 (text EL from
1st edn); ed A. Meynell 1910 (text from 1st edn).

The King of the Golden River, or the black brothers: a
legend of Styria. Illustr Richard Doyle 1851 (3 edns),
1856, Boston 1856 (in Curious stories), London 1859,
New York 1860, London 1863, 1867, Boston 1875 (in
Little Classics. ed. R. Johnson, vol 10), Boston 1876,
New York 1876, Orpington 1882, New York 1882,
London 1885, 1885, Boston 1885, Orpington 1886, 1888,
New York 1888, 1888, Boston 1888, New York 1890,
1890, Orpington 1892, New York 1895, Boston 1895,
1899, New York 1899, 1900 etc, 1907 (EL); ed E. A.
Noble, New York 1930; ed A. B. Allen 1946.

The stones of Venice, vol 1; The foundations, with
illustrations drawn by the author. 1851, 1858; vol 2:
The sea stories, with illustrations drawn by the author.
1853, 1867; vol 3: The Fall, with illustrations drawn by
the author. 1853, 1867. 3 vols New York 1865; London
1874; Orpington 1886, 1898, 1900 etc; ed L. M.
Phillipps 3 vols 1907 (EL).

Notes on the construction of sheepfolds. 1851, 1851,
Orpington 1875, New York 1876, Orpington 1879.
Rptd in On the old road vol 2, 1885.

Pre-Raphaelitism, by the author of Modern painters. 1851,
1862 (with Ruskin's name), New York 1876 (with other
essays by Ruskin); 1891; ed W. M. Rossetti, Boston
1899; ed L. Binyon 1907 (EL) (with other essays by
Ruskin). Also rptd in On the old road vol 1, 1885.

Giotto and his works in Padua: being an explanatory notice
of the series of woodcuts executed for the Arundel

Society after the frescoes in the Arena Chapel. 1854. Really 3 pts 1853, 1854, 1860, bound up as 1 vol 1877, New York 1890, Orpington 1900, 1905.

Lectures on architecture and painting delivered at Edinburgh in November 1853, with illustrations drawn by the author. 1854, New York 1854, London 1855, New York 1885, Orpington 1891; ed C. E. Norton, New York 1892; Orpington 1899, London 1902 etc, 1907 (EL) (with other essays by Ruskin).

The opening of the Crystal Palace considered in some of its relations to the prospects of art. 1854; rptd in On the old road vol 1, 1885.

Notes on some of the principal pictures exhibited in the rooms of the Royal Academy, 1855. 1855, 1855 (anon), 1855 (with suppl), 1907 (EL) (with other essays by Ruskin). Modern painters vol 2 (2nd edn) had included as Addenda: Notes on pictures exhibited in the Royal Academy, 1848.

The harbours of England, engraved by Thomas Lupton, from original drawings made expressly for the work by J. M. W. Turner, with illustrative text by J. Ruskin. 1856, [1857?], [1859?], 1872, 1877; [ed T. J. Wise] Orpington 1895, London 1900 etc.

Notes on the Turner Gallery at Marlborough House, 1856. 1857 (5 edns, 4th adds Preface, 5th rev), [1907] (EL) (with other essays).

The elements of drawing in three letters to beginners, illustrated by the author. 1857, New York 1857, London 1857 (adds Appendix), 1859, 1860, 1861, New York 1876, London 1887, 1892, Orpington 1892, 1895, 1898, 1900 etc, London 1907 (EL) (with The elements of perspective).

The political economy of art: being the substance (with additions) of two lectures delivered at Manchester, July 10th and 13th 1857. 1857, 1867, 1868, New York 1876; ed O. Lodge 1907 (EL) (with Unto this last); ed C. F. G. Masterman 1907.

Cambridge School of Art: Mr Ruskin's inaugural address, delivered at Cambridge, Oct 29 1858. Cambridge 1858, Orpington 1879. Also ptd in Cambridge School of Art, inaugural soirée, Cambridge 1858.

The Oxford Museum, by Henry W. Acland and John Ruskin. 1859, 1860, 1866, (omitting Ruskin's contributions) 1867, 1893 (adds new Preface by Ruskin). Ruskin's original contributions are rptd in Arrows of the chace vol 1, 1880.

The unity of art, delivered at the annual meeting of the Manchester School of Art, Feb 22nd 1859. Manchester 1859. Largely rptd in The two paths, 1859, below.

The two paths: being lectures on art, and its application, to decoration and manufacture, delivered in 1858-9. 1859, Orpington 1884, 1887, New York 1889, London 1891, 1896, 1898, 1900 etc; ed G. Wallas 1907; ed O. Lodge 1907 (EL) (with other Ruskin essays).

The elements of perspective arranged for the use of schools, and intended to be read in connexion with the first three books of Euclid. 1859, 1876, 1907 (EL) (with The elements of drawing), 1910 (rev).

'Unto this last': four essays on the first principles of political economy. 1862, New York 1866, London 1876, Orpington 1877, 1882, 1884, New York 1855, Orpington 1887, 1888, 1890, 1892, 1893, 1895, 1896, 1898, 1899, 1900 etc; ed J. A. Hobson 1907; ed O. Lodge 1907 (EL) (with The political economy of art and Munera pulveris); ed J. D. C. Monfries and G. E. Hollingsworth 1931.

Sesame and lilies: two lectures delivered at Manchester in 1864: 1, Of kings' treasuries 2, Of queens' gardens. 1865, New York 1865, London 1865 (adds Preface), 1866, 1867, Orpington 1882 (with new Preface), 1884, New York 1884, 1885, Orpington 1886, 1887, 1888, New York 1888, Chicago 1889, Orpington 1889, 1890, 1891, New York 1891, 1892, Philadelphia 1892, Orpington 1892, London 1894, 1896, 1897, 1898, 1898,

New York 1898, London 1900, 1900, New York 1900 (10 edns), Cambridge Mass 1900 etc; ed O. Lodge 1907 (EL) (with The two paths etc). Also rev and enlarged with new Preface and a third lecture, The mystery of life and its arts as Collected works vol 1, Keston 1871; rptd in this form New York 1876, Orpington 1876, 1880, New York 1880, Orpington 1883, 1887, New York 1889, 1890, Orpington 1893, 1894, 1895, New York 1895, 1896, 1897, Toronto 1897, 1898, New York 1898, London 1898, 1898, 1899, 1900, New York 1900 (4 edns), Portland Maine 1900 etc; ed A. H. Bates, New York 1909; ed S. Wragge [1920]; ed J. W. Bartram 1925; ed G. E. Hollingsworth 1932.

An inquiry into some of the conditions at present affecting the study of architecture in our schools. New York 1865, 1866, 1876.

The ethics of the dust: ten lectures to little housewives on the elements of crystallisation. 1866, New York 1866, 1876, Orpington 1877 (with new Preface), 1883, New York 1885, Orpington 1886, 1888, New York 1889, 1890, Orpington 1890, New York 1891, Orpington 1892, Philadelphia 1893, Orpington 1894 (adds index), 1896, 1898, 1900 etc; ed G. Rhys 1908 (EL); ed R. O. Morris 1914.

The crown of wild olive: three lectures on work, traffic and war. 1866 (3 edns), New York 1866, 1876, Orpington 1882 (vol 6 of Collected works; rev and adding both a 4th lecture, The future of England and Notes on the political economy of Russia), New York 1885, Orpington 1886, 1889, New York 1889, 1890, 1890, Orpington 1890, New York 1891, Orpington 1892, 1894 (adds index), 1895, 1897; ed J. C. Saul and D. M. Duncan, Toronto 1897; London 1898, 1899, 1900, New York 1900 (14 edns), Boston 1900, Philadelphia 1900, Chicago 1900 etc; ed C. Bax 1907 (EL); ed W. F. Melton, New York 1919 (with The queen of the air).

Time and tide by Weare and Tyne: twenty-five letters to a working man of Sunderland on the laws of work. 1867, 1867, New York 1868, 1876, 1884, 1885, Orpington 1886, 1891, New York 1891, London 1894 (with index), 1897, 1899, 1900 etc, 1910 (EL) (with other Ruskin essays).

First notes on the general principles of employment for the destitute and criminal classes. 1868 (priv ptd), 1868 (enlarged with 'First' omitted from title). Rptd with further addns in The queen of the air, 1869.

The queen of the air: being a study of the Greek myths of cloud and storm. 1869, 1869, New York 1869, 1876, 1885, 1885, Orpington 1887, New York 1889, London 1890, New York 1891, London 1892, 1895 (adds index). Rptd in part from the preceding item and from passages in The Cestus of Aglaia, below.

Lectures on art delivered before the University of Oxford in Hilary Term 1870. Oxford 1870, New York 1870, Oxford 1875, New York 1876, Oxford 1880, New York 1885, Orpington 1887 (rev), New York 1889, Orpington 1890, New York 1891, Orpington 1891, 1894 (with index).

Fors clavigera: letters to the workmen and labourers of Great Britain. 8 vols 1871-84, New York 1876 (vols 1-5); New York 1880, 1884 (vols 1-7); New York 1886 (vols 1-8); 3 vols New York 1890, 4 vols New York 1891, 8 vols New York 1899.

Munera pulveris: six essays on the elements of political economy. Keston 1872 (= Collected works vol 2), New York 1873, Orpington 1880, New York 1885, Orpington 1886, New York 1889, 1891, Orpington 1894, 1898, 1899 etc, 1907 (EL) (with The political economy of art and Unto this last).

Aratra pentelici: six lectures on the elements of sculpture. Keston 1872 (= Collected works, vol 3), New York 1876, 1876, Orpington 1879, New York 1885, Orpington 1890 (adds next item).

The relation between Michael Angelo and Tintoret: seventh of the course of lectures on sculpture delivered at Oxford 1870–1. Keston 1872, Orpington 1879, 1887. Rptd in 1890 and subsequent edns of Aratra pentelici.

The eagle's nest: ten lectures on the relation of natural science to art, given before the University of Oxford in Lent Term 1872. Keston 1872 (= Collected works, vol 4), New York 1876, Orpington 1880, New York 1885, 1886, Orpington 1887, 1891, New York 1891, 1892, Orpington 1894 (adds index).

The sepulchral monuments of Italy: monuments of the Cavalli family in the Church of Santa Anastasia, Verona. 1872 (Arundel Soc). Rptd in On the old road vol 1, 1885.

Love's meinie: lectures on Greek and English birds, given before the University of Oxford. Lecture 1: The robin, Keston 1873; Lecture 2: The swallow, Keston 1873; Lecture 3: The dabchicks, Orpington 1881. Lectures 1–2, New York 1876, Orpington 1883, 1892. Collected edns: Orpington 1881, New York 1885, Orpington 1893, 1897 (adds index) etc. Lecture 4 (The chough) first pbd in Collected works, ed E. T. Cook and A. D. O. Wedderburn, vol 25.

The poetry of architecture: or the architecture of the nations of Europe considered in its association with natural scenery and national character. New York 1873, 1876, 1890, Orpington 1893 (1st authorized edn).

Ariadne Florentina: six lectures on wood and metal engraving, with appendix, given before the University of Oxford in Michaelmas Term 1872. Orpington 1876 (= Collected works vol 7), New York 1876, Orpington 1890, New York 1891 etc. Originally issued in 7 pts: pts 1–2, 1873; pts 3–4, 1874; pts 5–7, 1875.

Val D'Arno: ten lectures on the Tuscan art directly antecedent to the Florentine Year of Victories, given before the University of Oxford in Michaelmas Term 1874. Orpington 1874 (= Collected works vol 8), 1882, New York 1885, 1886, Orpington 1890, New York 1891, London 1900 (with index) etc.

Mornings in Florence: being simple studies of Christian art, for English travellers. 6 pts Orpington 1876–7, 1881–3, 1889–92 (pt 1 rptd 1894), Orpington 1885, New York 1886, Orpington 1889, 1894 (adds index).

Proserpina: studies of wayside flowers, while the air was yet pure among the Alps, and in the Scotland and England which my father knew. Vol 1 (all collected): Orpington 1879, 1882, 1883, New York 1885, 1886. Originally

Deucalion: collected studies of the lapse of waves and life of stones. Vol 1 (all collected), Orpington 1879, 1882, New York 1885, 1886, 1889, Orpington 1891, Boston 1900.

Letters to the Times on the principal Pre-Raphaelite pictures in the Exhibition of 1854, from the author of Modern painters. 1876 (priv ptd). Originally pbd in Times 5, 25 May 1854; rptd in Arrows of the chace vol 1, 1880, and 'A. G. Crawford' (i.e. A. G. Wise), Notes on the pictures of Mr Holman Hunt exhibited at the rooms of the Fine Art Society, 1886.

Guide to the principal pictures in the Academy of Fine Arts at Venice, arranged for English travellers. 2 pts Venice 1877, Orpington 1882–3, London 1891 (rev).

Notes by Mr Ruskin on his drawings by the late J. M. W. Turner, exhibited at the Fine Arts Society's Galleries, March 1878; also an appendix containing a list of the engraved works of J. M. W. Turner exhibited at the same time. [1878], [1878], 1878 (with Addenda and Epilogue) (4 edns), 1878 (rev with appendix by W. Kingsley), 1878; 1878 (with 2nd pt On his own handiwork illustrative of Turner), 1878 (pt 2 rev) (4 edns).

St Mark's rest: the history of Venice, written for the help of the few travellers who still care for her monuments. New York 1879, Orpington 1884 (1st complete and authorized collection), New York 1884, 1885, 1886, 1889, Orpington 1894.

The laws of Fiesole: a familiar treatise on the elementary principles and practice of drawing and painting, as determined by the Tuscan masters, arranged for the use

of schools. Vol 1 (all pbd), Orpington 1879, New York 1879, Orpington 1882, 1890, Boston 1900 etc.

Notes on Samuel Prout and William Hunt, illustrated by a loan collection of drawings, exhibited at the Fine Art Society's Galleries. 1789–80 (4 edns), 1880.

Circular respecting memorial studies of St Mark's Venice, now in progress under Mr Ruskin's direction. 1879, 1879 (adds postscript), 1880.

Letters addressed by Prof Ruskin to the clergy on the Lord's Prayer and the Church. Ed F. A. Malleson 1879 (priv ptd), [1880] (adds Replies from clergy and laity, and an epilogue by Mr Ruskin), 1883, 1896 (rev and with additional letters).

Arrows of the chace: being a collection of scattered letters published chiefly in the daily newspapers 1840–1880, and now edited by an Oxford pupil [A. D. O. Wedderburn] with a preface by the author. 2 vols Orpington 1880, New York 1881, 1890.

The art of England: lectures given in Oxford. Orpington 1884, New York 1883–4, 1885, 1885, 1886, Orpington 1887, New York 1889, 1892, Orpington 1898, 1898 (with The pleasures of England), 1900 etc.

The pleasures of England: lectures given in Oxford. Orpington 1884, New York 1885 (pts 1–3), 1885 (complete), Orpington 1898 (with The art of England)

The storm cloud of the nineteenth century: two lectures delivered at the London Institution, Feb 4 & 11 1884. 2 pts Orpington 1884, New York 1884, London 1885.

On the old road: a collection of miscellaneous essays, pamphlets &c &c published 1834–85. [Ed A. D. O. Wedderburn] 2 vols Orpington 1885, 3 vols Orpington 1899 (rev) etc.

Praeterita: outlines of scenes and thoughts perhaps worthy of memory in my past life, volume 1. Orpington 1886, 1886, New York 1886, 1886, 1889, 3 vols New York 1890 (with vol 2), New York 1892, Orpington 1899, 1900. Largely from Fors clavigera, above. Originally issued in 12 pts: pts 1–7 1885, pts 8–12 1886, rptd New York 1885–6.

Praeterita: volume 2. Orpington 1887, New York 1889, 3 vols New York 1890 (with vol 1), 1892, Orpington 1899, 1900. Originally issued in 12 pts: pts 13–20 1886, pts 21–24 1887, New York 1886–7.

Praeterita: volume 3. 4 pts Orpington 1888–9, New York 1888–9, Orpington 1900 (with index and Dilecta, below), 1900. Pts 25–6 1888, pts 27–8 1889.

> Praeterita. Ed K. Clark 1949. Abridged. See also S. E. Brown, The unpublished passages in the ms of Ruskin's autobiography, Victorian Newsletter no 16 1959.

Dilecta: correspondence, diary notes and extracts from books, illustrating Praeterita. 3 pts Orpington 1886–1900. Pt 2 1887, pt 3 first issued with reprint of pts 1–2 and Praeterita vol 3 1900.

Hortus inclusus: messages from the wood to the garden, sent in happy days to the sister ladies of the Thwaite, Coniston [Mary and Susie Beever]. [Ed A. Fleming] Orpington 1887, New York 1887, Orpington 1888, New York 1892 (with In montibus sanctis and Coeli enarrant) etc.

Ruskiniana, part 1: Letters published in, and collected from various sources, and mostly reprinted in Igdrasil, 1890. [Ed A. D. O. Wedderburn] 1890 (priv ptd).

Ruskiniana, part 2: lectures and addresses reported in the press, but not reprinted in collected works. [Ed A. D. O. Wedderburn] 1892 (priv ptd).

Verona and other lectures. [Ed W. G. Collingwood], Orpington 1894.

Comments on Ruskin on the Divina commedia, compiled by G. P. Huntington, with an introduction by C. E. Norton. Boston 1903.

The Cestus of Aglaia. Orpington 1905; ed C. Bax 1907 (EL).

Letters and Diaries

There is a long list of Ruskin's private letters and notebooks in Collected works, ed Cook and Wedderburn, vol 38.

Letters upon subjects of general interest from Ruskin to various correspondents. Ed T. J. Wise 1892 (priv ptd).

Stray letters from Prof Ruskin to a London bibliophile [F. S. Ellis]. Ed T. J. Wise 1892 (priv ptd).

Letters from Ruskin to William Ward. Ed T. J. Wise 2 vols 1892 (priv ptd), Boston 1922 (with a biography of Ward by William C. Ward, introd by A. M. Brook).

Letters on art and literature. Ed T. J. Wise 1894 (priv ptd).

Letters to Ernest Chesneau. Ed T. J. Wise 1894 (priv ptd).

Letters addressed to a college friend [Edward Clayton] 1840–5. Orpington 1894, New York 1894.

Letters to Rev F. J. Faunthorpe. Ed T. J. Wise 1894 (priv ptd).

Letters to Rev F. A. Malleson. Ed T. J. Wise 1896 (priv ptd).

Letters to F. J. Furnivall. Ed T. J. Wise 1897 (priv ptd). (Sydney) 3 Feb 1900.

Letters to M G & H G [Mary and Hellen Gladstone]. Edinburgh 1903 (priv ptd), New York 1903.

The letters of Ruskin to C. E. Norton. [Ed C. E. Norton] 2 vols Boston 1903.

Letters to Bernard Quaritch 1867–88. Ed C. Q. Wrentmore 1938.

The gulf of years: letters to Kathleen Olander. Ed R. Unwin [1953].

Ruskin's letters from Venice 1851–2. Ed J. L. Bradley, New Haven 1955.

The diaries of Ruskin. Ed J. Evans and J. H. Whitehouse 3 vols Oxford 1956–9.

Spence, M. Dearest Mama Talbot. 1966. Letters to Mrs Talbot 1874–89.

The Brentwood diary [1876–84]. Ed H. G. Viljoen, New Haven 1971.

Ruskin in Italy: letters to his parents 1845. Ed H. I. Shapiro, Oxford 1972.

§2

Collingwood, W. G. Ruskin: a biographical outline. 1889.
—— The art teaching of Ruskin. 1891.
—— The life and work of Ruskin. 2 vols 1893, 1900 (with biographical addns, as The life of Ruskin).
Cook, E. T. Studies in Ruskin. Orpington 1890.
—— The life of Ruskin. 1911.
Benson, A. C. Ruskin: a study in personality. 1911.
Proust, M. Pastiches et mélanges. Paris 1919.
Shaw, G. B. Ruskin's politics. 1921.
Collingwood, R. G. Ruskin's philosophy. 1922.
Clark, K. The Gothic Revival. 1929.
—— Ruskin at Oxford. Oxford 1947.
Quennell, P. C. Ruskin: the portrait of a prophet. 1949.
Hough, G. In his Last Romantics, 1949.
Bell, Q. Ruskin. Edinburgh 1963 (Writers & Critics).
Lutyens, M. Effie in Venice. 1965.
—— Millais and the Ruskins. 1967.

CHARLES ROBERT DARWIN
1809–82

The chief ms collection is in the Cambridge Univ Library, including the unpbd ms of Natural selection, *an abstract of which is* On the origin of species, *below. Important collections of unpbd letters are in the American Philosophical Association, Philadelphia and in BM.*

Bibliographies

Handlist of Darwin papers at the University Library Cambridge. Cambridge 1960.

Freeman, R. B. The works of Darwin: an annotated bibliographical handlist. 1965.

§1

The zoology of the voyage of HMS Beagle, under the command of Captain Fitzroy RN, during the years 1832 to 1836, edited and superintended by Charles Darwin. 5 pts 1838–43.

Journal of researches into the geology and natural history of the various countries visited by HMS Beagle. 1839 (issued separately, and as vol 3: Journal and remarks, of The narrative of the voyages of HM Ships Adventure and Beagle, ed R. Fitzroy), 1840, 1845 (rev as Journal of researches into the natural history and geology), 1847, 1852, 1860 (with addns), 1870, 1872, 1873, 1876, 1879.

The structure and distribution of coral reefs, being the first part of the geology of the voyage of the Beagle. 1842.

Geological observations on the volcanic islands, being the second part of the geology of the voyage of the Beagle. 1844, New York 1896 (with third part).

Geological observations on South America, being the third part of the geology of the voyage of the Beagle. 1846.

Geology. In A manual of scientific enquiry prepared for the use of Her Majesty's Navy and adapted for travellers in general, ed J. F. W. Herschel, 1849, 1851, 1859, 1871, 1886; rev and rptd separately as Geology, 1849; as Manual of geology, 1859.

A monograph of the sub-class cirripedia. 2 vols 1851–4, 1 vol 1965.

A monograph of the fossil lepadidae. 2 vols 1851–4.

On the tendency of species to form varieties, and on the perpetuation of varieties and species by natural means of selection, by Charles Darwin and Alfred Wallace, communicated by Sir Charles Lyell and J. D. Hooker. Jnl of Linnean Soc, Zoology 3 1858; 1858 (offprint); rptd in Evolution by natural selection, ed G. de Beer, Cambridge 1958.

On the origin of species by natural selection. 1859, 1901, 1902, 1906, 1910, 1950, Cambridge Mass 1964; 1860 (2nd edn rev), 1861 (3rd edn rev), 1866 (4th edn rev), 1869 (5th edn rev), 1872 (as The origin of species) (6th edn rev), 1873, 1875, 1876 (with slight changes), 1878, 1880, 1882 etc; New York 1860 (with notes not in 2nd English edn), 1868, 1870 etc; A variorum text, ed M. Peckham, Philadelphia 1959; tr German, 1860 (with first form of Historical sketch, rev and expanded in 3rd English edn).

On the various contrivances by which British and foreign orchids are fertilised by insects. 1862, 1877 (rev as The various contrivances), 1882 etc, New York 1877, 1884.

On the movements and habits of climbing plants. Jnl of Linnean Soc 9 1865, 1865 (offprint), 1875 (rev, much enlarged, and pbd separately), 1876, 1882 etc.

The variation of animals and plants under domestication. 2 vols 1868, 1875 (rev), 1882 etc, New York 1878, 1890.

The descent of man, and selection in relation to sex. 2 vols 1871, 1871 (3 rev issues), 1874 (2nd edn rev), 1875 (rev), 1877 (rev), 1879, 1881, 1882 etc, New York 1871.

The expression of the emotions in man and animals. 1872, 1873, 1890 (with addns) etc, New York 1873, 1896, 1899; ed M. Mead, New York 1955.

Insectivorous plants. 1875, 1876, 1888 (2nd edn rev by F. Darwin) etc, New York 1875 etc.

The effects of cross and self fertilisation in the vegetable kingdom. 1876, 1878 (2nd edn rev), 1891 etc, New York 1877, 1892.

The different forms of flowers on plants of the same species. 1877, 1880 etc, New York 1877.

The life of Erasmus Darwin. In E. Krause, Erasmus Darwin, tr from German by W. S. Dallas, 1879, 1887.

The power of movement in plants, assisted by Francis Darwin, 1880, 1882, New York 1881.

The formation of vegetable mould, through the action of

worms with observations on their habits. 1881, 1881 (rev), 1882 (rev), 1883 (corrected by F. Darwin) etc, New York 1882 etc.

Essay on instinct. In G. J. Romanes, Mental evolution in animals, 1883, 1885, New York 1883. A ch from unpbd Natural selection, above.

The foundations of the Origin of species: two essays written in 1842 and 1844. Ed F. Darwin 1909; rptd in Evolution by natural selection, above.

Letters, Diaries, Notebooks and Autobiography

The life and letters of Darwin, including an autobiographical chapter. Ed F. Darwin 3 vols 1887, 1887 (3 rev edns), 1888, New York 1888, 1891. Autobiography ed G. de Beer, Oxford 1974 (with T. H. Huxley's).

Darwin: his life told in an autobiographical chapter, and in a selected series of his published letters. Ed F. Darwin 2 vols 1892, 1902 etc, New York 1888, 1896, 1958.

More letters. Ed F. Darwin and A. C. Seward 2 vols 1903.

Emma Darwin, wife of Charles Darwin; a century of family letters. Ed H. E. Litchfield 2 vols Cambridge 1904 (priv ptd), 1915 (rev).

The complete correspondence between Wallace and Darwin 1857–81. In Alfred Russell Wallace, Letters and reminiscences, ed J. Marchant 2 vols 1916.

The autobiography of Darwin. 1929, 1931, 1937; ed N. Barlow 1958 ('with original omissions restored'); ed G. de Beer, Oxford 1974 (with T. H. Huxley's).

Diary of the voyage of HMS Beagle. Ed N. Barlow, Cambridge 1933.

Darwin and the voyage of the Beagle. Ed N. Barlow 1945.

Darwin and Henslowe: letters 1831–60. Ed N. Barlow 1967.

§2

Butler, S. Evolution old and new. 1879.
—— Unconscious memory. 1880.
—— Luck or cunning as the main means of organic modification? [1886].

Huxley, T. H. Darwiniana. 1893. Collects reviews and essays. 1859–88.

Stevenson, L. Darwin among the poets. Chicago 1932.

'West, Geoffrey' (G. H. Wells). Darwin: the fragmentary man. 1937.

Irvine, W. Apes, angels and Victorians: a joint biography of Darwin and Huxley. 1955.

de Beer, G. Darwin: lecture on a master mind. Oxford 1958.
—— Charles Darwin. Proc Br Acad 44 1959.
—— Darwin: evolution by natural selection. 1963.

Ellegård, A. Darwin and the general reader: the reception of Darwin's theory of evolution in the British periodical press 1859–72. Stockholm 1958.

Huxley, J. S. et al. A book that shook the world: anniversary essays on Darwin's Origin of species. Pittsburgh 1958.
—— and H. B. D. Kettlewell. Darwin and his world. 1965.

Passmore, J. Darwin's impact on British metaphysics. Victorian Stud 3 1959.

Peckham, M. Darwinism and Darwinisticism. Ibid.

Willey, B. Darwin and Butler: two versions of evolution. 1960.

Wichler, G. Darwin: the founder of the theory of evolution and natural selection. Oxford 1961.

Himmelfarb, G. Darwin and the Darwinian revolution. 1959.

Hyman, S. F. In his Tangled bank, New York 1962.

WALTER BAGEHOT
1826–77

Collections

The works and life. Ed E. I. Barrington 10 vols 1915.
Collected works. Ed N. St John-Stevas 8 vols 1965–.

§1

Estimates of some Englishmen and Scotchmen. 1858.

Parliamentary reform: an essay reprinted, with considerable additions, from the National Review. 1859.

The history of the unreformed Parliament and its lessons: an essay reprinted from the National Review. 1860.

Memoir of the Rt Hon J. Wilson 1861.

Count your enemies and economise your expenditure. 1862.

The English constitution, reprinted from the Fortnightly Review. 1867, 1872 (adds one ch); ed A. J. Balfour, Oxford 1928 (WC); ed R. H. S. Crossman 1964 (with bibliography on government and politics).

A practical plan for assimilating the English and American money, reprinted from the Economist with additions. 1869.

Physics and politics: or thoughts on the application of the principles of 'natural selection' and 'inheritance' to political society. 1872; ed J. Barzun, New York 1948.

Lombard Street: a description of the money market. 1873; ed E. Johnstone 1892 (brought up to date); ed H. Withers 1910; ed A. W. Wright 1915 (notes rev); ed F. C. Genovese, Homewood Ill 1962.

Some articles on the depreciation of silver and on topics connected with it, reprinted from the Economist. 1877.

Literary studies. Ed R. H. Hutton 2 vols 1879 (with memoir), 3 vols 1895, 1906 (re-issue of vol 3 with addns); ed G. Sampson 2 vols 1906 (EL). Rptd in part from Estimates, above.

Economic studies. Ed R. H. Hutton 1880.

Biographical studies. Ed R. H. Hutton 1881, 1907 (adds index).

Essays on parliamentary reform. 1883.

The postulates of English political economy: student's edition with a preface by A. Marshall. 1885. Rptd from Economic studies, above.

Estimations in criticism. Ed C. Lennox 2 vols 1908. Rptd from Literary studies, above.

The love-letters of Bagehot and Eliza Wilson. Ed E. I. Barrington 1933.

§2

Hutton, R. H. In his Criticisms on contemporary thought and thinkers, 2 vols 1894.

Stephen, L. In his Studies of a biographer vol 3, 1902.

Irvine, W. Walter Bagehot. New York 1939.

Young, G. M. Victorian psychology. TLS 25 Jan 1936.
—— The greatest Victorian: the case for Bagehot. Spectator 18 June and 2 July 1937; rptd in his Today and yesterday, 1948.

Briggs, A. Trollope, Bagehot and the English constitution. Cambridge Jnl March 1952; rptd in his Victorian people, 1954.

St John-Stevas, N. Walter Bagehot. 1959.

Buchan, A. The spare Chancellor: the life of Bagehot. 1959.

Sisson, C. H. The case of Bagehot. 1972.

IV. MINOR PROSE 1835-1870

ROBERT CHAMBERS
1802-71

§ 1

Illustrations of the author of Waverley: being notices and anecdotes of real characters, scenes and incidents supposed to be described in his works. Edinburgh 1822, 1825 (enlarged).

Traditions of Edinburgh. 4 vols Edinburgh 1828, 1869 (rev); ed C. E. S. Chambers 1912.

Walks in Edinburgh. Edinburgh 1825, 1829 ('with an improved plan, and a view of the city'). A sequel to Traditions of Edinburgh, above.

Notices of the most remarkable fires in Edinburgh from 1385 to 1824. Edinburgh 1825.

Popular rhymes of Scotland; with illustrations, collected from tradition. Edinburgh 1826, 1840 (rev with addns).

History of the rebellion in Scotland in 1745, 1746. 2 vols Edinburgh 1827, 1840 (greatly enlarged), 1869 (with appendix).

The picture of Scotland. 2 vols Edinburgh 1827.

History of the rebellions in Scotland under the Marquis of Montrose and others, from 1638 till 1660. 2 vols Edinburgh 1828.

History of the rebellions in Scotland, under the Viscount of Dundee and the Earl of Mar, in 1689 and 1715. Edinburgh 1829.

The life of King James the First. 2 vols Edinburgh 1830.

Life of Sir Walter Scott. Edinburgh 1832; rev W. Chambers 1871, 1894 (rev with addns).

A biographical dictionary of eminent Scotsmen. 4 vols Glasgow 1832-5, 5 vols Glasgow 1855 (rev with supplemental vol by T. Thomson), 3 vols 1870 (rev T. Thomson), 1875 (with suppl).

Reekiana: or minor antiquities of Edinburgh. Edinburgh 1833.

Poems. Edinburgh 1835 (priv ptd).

English language and literature. Edinburgh 1836.

The life of Robert Burns with a criticism of his writings. Edinburgh 1838. By James Currie. Expanded by Chambers.

The poetical works of Robert Burns; to which are now added notes illustrating historical, personal and local allusions. Edinburgh 1838.

The prose works of Robert Burns; with the notes of Currie and Cromek, and many by the present editor. Edinburgh 1839.

Vestiges of the natural history of Creation. 1844 (anon), 1884 (12th edn, introd by A. Ireland), 1887 (introd by H. Morley).

Cyclopaedia of English literature. 2 vols Edinburgh 1844.

Explanations: a sequel to Vestiges by the author of that work. 1845.

Ancient sea-margins, as memorials of changes in the relative level of sea and land. Edinburgh 1848.

The history of Scotland. 2 vols 1849.

Tracings of the North of Europe. 1851 (priv ptd).

Life and works of Robert Burns. 4 vols 1851.

Tracings of Iceland and the Faröe Islands. 1856.

Domestic annals of Scotland from the Reformation to the Revolution. 2 vols Edinburgh 1858, 1 vol Edinburgh 1885 (abridged).

Edinburgh papers. 5 pts Edinburgh 1859-61, 1861.

Sketch of the history of the Edinburgh Theatre Royal. Edinburgh 1859 (priv ptd).

Domestic annals of Scotland from the Revolution to the Rebellion of 1745. 1861.

The book of days: a miscellany of popular antiquities. 2 vols 1862-4.

Smollett: his life and a selection of his writings. 1867.

The Threiplands of Fingask: a family memoir. 1880.

§ 2

Chambers, W. Memoir of Robert Chambers with autobiographical reminiscences of William Chambers. Edinburgh 1872, 1884 (enlarged).

Turnbull, A. William and Robert Chambers. Edinburgh [1946], [1963] (rev).

ENEAS SWEETLAND DALLAS
1828-79

Poetics: an essay on poetry. 1852.

The gay science. 2 vols 1866.

The Stowe-Byron controversy: a complete résumé of all that has been written and said upon the subject, together with an impartial review of the merits of the case. [1869].

Kettner's Book of the table: a manual of cookery. 1877.

Dallas also edited an abridgement of Richardson's Clarissa, *1868. He was editor of* Once a Week, *1868, and on the staff of the* Times.

JOHN FORSTER
1812-76

The life and adventures of Oliver Goldsmith. 1848, 2 vols 1854 (enlarged as The life and times of Goldsmith); ed R. Ingpen 1903 (abridged).

Daniel De Foe and Charles Churchill. 2 vols 1855. Rptd from Edinburgh Rev; later included in Historical and biographical essays, vol 2, below.

Historical and biographical essays. 2 vols 1858, 1860 (with rev and enlarged edn of vol 2).

The arrest of the five members by Charles the First: a chapter of history re-written. 1860.

The debates on the Grand Remonstrance, November and December 1641; with an introductory essay on English freedom under the Plantagenet and Tudor sovereigns. 1860. Rptd with addns from Historical and biographical essays, vol 1, above.

Walter Savage Landor: a biography. 2 vols 1869, 1876 (rev and abridged as vol 1 of The works of Landor).

The life of Charles Dickens. 3 vols 1872-4; ed G. Gissing 1903 (rev and abridged); ed G. K. Chesterton 2 vols 1927 (EL); ed J. W. T. Ley [1928] (rev).

The life of Jonathan Swift. Vol 1 (all pbd), 1875. Completed by Sir H. Craik.

Dramatic essays by John Forster and G. H. Lewes. Ed W. Archer and R. W. Lowe 1896.

SIR FRANCIS GALTON
1822-1911

The telotype: a printing electric telegraph. 1850.

The narrative of an explorer in tropical South Africa. 1853, 1889 (with biographical introd).

The art of travel: or shifts and contrivances available in wild countries. 1855, 1856, 1860 (both rev and enlarged), 1867, 1872.

Meteorographica or methods of mapping the weather. 1863.

Hereditary genius: an enquiry into its laws and consequences. 1869, 1914, 1950.

English men of science: their nature and nurture. 1874.

Inquiries into human faculty and its development. 1883, [1907] (EL).

Life history album 1884, 1902 (re-arranged). Ed Galton.

Record of family faculties. 1884.

Natural inheritance. 1889.

Finger prints. 1892. Supplementary ch on decipherment pbd separately 1893.

Fingerprint directories. 1895.

Index to achievements of near kinsfolk of some Fellows of the Royal Society. [1904].

Eugenics: its definition, scope and aims. 1905, 1906.

Probability, the foundation of eugenics. Oxford 1907.

Galton also edited a ser of Vacation tourists and notes of travel, 1860–3.

GEORGE GILFILLAN
1813–78

A gallery of literary portraits. Ser 1, Edinburgh 1845; ser 2, Edinburgh 1850; ser 3, Edinburgh 1854; 2 vols Edinburgh 1856–7 (complete); ed (in part) W. R. Nicoll [1909] (EL).

The connection between science, literature and religion: a lecture. 1849.

The bards of the Bible. Edinburgh 1851.

The martyrs, heroes and bards of the Scottish Covenant. 1852.

Library edition of poets of Britain. 48 vols 1853–60. Ed Gilfillan, with short memoirs and notes.

The history of a man, edited [in fact written] by Gilfillan. 1856. Autobiography.

Christianity and our era: a book for the times. Edinburgh 1857.

Alpha and omega: or a series of scripture studies. 2 vols 1860.

Specimens, with memoirs, of the less-known British poets. 3 vols Edinburgh 1860.

Remoter stars in the church sky: being a gallery of uncelebrated divines. 1867.

Night: a poem. 1867.

Modern Christian heroes: a gallery of protesting and reforming men. 1869.

The life of Sir Walter Scott. Edinburgh 1870.

The life of the Rev W. Anderson. 1873.

Life of Burns. In the Works of Burns: national edition, 1878.

Sketches literary and theological. Ed F. Henderson, Edinburgh 1881.

Watson, R. A. and E. S. Gilfillan: letters and journals, with memoir. 1892. Includes list of his contributions to periodicals and his introductory essays.

WILLIAM EWART GLADSTONE
1809–98
§ 1

The State in its relations with the Church. 1838, 1841 (rev and enlarged).

Church principles considered in their results. 1840.

A manual of prayers from the liturgy, arranged for family use. 1845.

Studies on Homer and the Homeric age. 3 vols Oxford 1858.

Speeches on parliamentary reform in 1866; with an appendix. 1866.

A chapter of autobiography. 1868.

Juventus mundi: the gods and men of the heroic age. 1869.

Speeches on great questions of the day. 1870.

Rome and the newest fashions in religion: three tracts— the Vatican decrees; Vaticanism; Speeches of the Pope. 1875.

Homeric synchronism: an enquiry into the time and place of Homer. 1876.

Bulgarian horrors and the question of the East. 1876.

The Church of England and ritualism. [1876].

Gleanings of past years 1843–78. 7 vols 1879.

Speeches of the Rt Hon W. E. Gladstone; with a sketch of his life. Ed H. W. Lucy 1885.

Speeches on the Irish question in 1886; with an appendix containing the full text of the Government of Ireland and the Sale and Purchase of Land Bills of 1886. [Ed P. W. Clayden], Edinburgh 1886.

Landmarks of Homeric study; together with an essay on the points of contact between the Assyrian tablets and the Homeric text. 1890.

The impregnable rock of Holy Scripture. 1890, 1892 (rev).

The speeches and public addresses of the Right Hon W. E. Gladstone MP; with notes and introductions. Ed A. W. Hutton and H. J. Cohen 2 vols 1892. This edn was projected in 10 vols, but only 2 appeared.

The odes of Horace. 1894, 1895.

The psalter; with a concordance and other auxiliary matter. 1895.

On the condition of man in a future life. 3 pts 1896.

Studies subsidiary to the works of Bishop Butler: additional volume uniform with the works. 1896.

Later gleanings, theological and ecclesiastical. 1897.

Gladstone's speeches: descriptive index and bibliography by A. T. Bassett; with a preface by Viscount Bryce OM and introductions to the selected speeches by Herbert Paul. 1916.

Two hymns translated into Latin verse by Gladstone. Winchester 1951.

Essay on public speaking. Ed L. D. Reid, Quart Jnl of Speech 39 1953.

For Gladstone's reviews see Wellesley index to Victorian periodicals, Toronto 1966–.

Letters and Diaries

Correspondence on church and religion. Ed D. C. Lathbury 2 vols 1910.

The Queen and Mr Gladstone. Ed P. Guedalla 1933.

Gladstone to his wife. Ed A. T. Bassett 1936.

The political correspondence of Mr Gladstone and Lord Granville 1868–76. Ed A. Ramm 1952.

§ 2

Russell, G. W. E. Gladstone. 1891, 1913 (EL).

Morley, J. The life of Gladstone. 3 vols 1903; ed C. F. G. Masterman [1927] (abridged).

Young, G. M. Mr Gladstone. Oxford 1944 (Romanes Lecture); rptd in his Today and yesterday, 1948.

Vidler, A. R. The orb and the cross: a normative study in the relations of Church and State with reference to Gladstone's early writings. 1945.

Hammond, J. L. and M. R. D. Foot. Gladstone and Liberalism. 1952.

Magnus, P. Gladstone: a biography. 1954.

Myres, J. L. Homer and his critics. Ed D. Gray 1958.

SIR GEORGE GROVE
1820–1900

Beethoven's nine symphonies: analytical essays, with a preface by G. Henschel. Boston 1884, London 1896 (rev as Beethoven and his nine symphonies).

A dictionary of music and musicians AD 1450–1880, by eminent writers. Ed Grove 4 vols 1879–89; ed J. A. F. Maitland 4 vols 1900, 5 vols 1904–10; ed N. C. Colles 6 vols 1927–40; ed E. Blom 9 vols 1954; American supplement, ed W. S. Pratt and C. N. Boyd, Philadelphia 1920.

A short history of cheap music as exemplified in the records of the house of Novello, Ewer & Co, with especial reference to the first fifty years of the reign of Queen Victoria; with portraits, and a preface by Grove. 1887.

Beethoven, Schubert, Mendelssohn. Ed E. Blom 1951.

Grove's wide literary activities included the writing of a large portion of Sir William Smith's Dictionary of the Bible, 1860–3, other biblical works and a primer of geography. He edited various works on music, and was for some years editor of Macmillan's Mag.

ARTHUR HENRY HALLAM
1811–33
Collections

Remains, in verse and prose. 1834 (priv ptd). Ed with a prefatory memoir by Henry Hallam.

Writings. Ed T. H. V. Motter, New York 1943.

§ I

Timbuctoo. [Cambridge 1829] (priv ptd).

Adonais: an elegy on the death of John Keats, author of Endymion, Hyperion etc, by Percy B. Shelley. Cambridge 1829.

Poems by A. H. Hallam esq. [1830] (priv ptd).

Essay on the philosophical writings of Cicero. Cambridge 1832 (priv ptd).

Oration on the influence of Italian works of imagination on the same class of compositions in England, delivered in Trinity College Chapel, December 16 1831. Cambridge 1832 (priv ptd).

Some unpublished poems. Ed C. Tennyson and F. T. Baker, Victorian Poetry 3 1965.

RICHARD HOLT HUTTON
1826–97
Selections

Aspects of religious and scientific thought. Ed E. M. Roscoe 1899. Selection from contributions to Spectator.

Brief literary criticisms selected from the Spectator. Ed E. M. Roscoe 1906.

§ I

The incarnation and principles of evidence. [1862].

The relative value of studies and accomplishments in the education of women. 1862.

Studies in parliament. 1866.

The political character of the working class. 1867.

Essays theological and literary. 2 vols 1871. *See col 1131, below.*

Sir Walter Scott. 1878 (EML).

Essays on some of the modern guides of English thought in matters of faith. 1887.

Cardinal Newman. 1891.

Criticisms on contemporary thought and thinkers. 2 vols 1894.

DAVID MASSON
1822–1907

College-education and self-education: a lecture. [1854].

Essays biographical and critical, chiefly on English poets. Cambridge 1856.

British novelists and their styles: being a critical sketch of the history of British prose fiction. Cambridge 1859.

The life of John Milton, narrated in connexion with the

political, ecclesiastical and literary history of his time. 7 vols 1859–94, 1881–96 (rev edn of vols 1–3).

Recent British philosophy. Cambridge 1865, London 1877 (adds ch).

The state of learning in Scotland: a lecture. Edinburgh 1866.

University teaching for women. Edinburgh 1868. In Introductory lectures of the second series of lectures in Shandwick Place, 1868.

Drummond of Hawthornden: the story of his life and writings. 1873.

Chatterton: a story of the year 1770. 1874, 1899 (rev and enlarged). Rptd from Essays biographical and critical, above.

The three devils: Luther's, Milton's and Goethe's. 1874. 5 essays rptd from Essays biographical and critical, above, with How literature may illustrate history.

Wordsworth, Shelley, Keats and other essays. 1874.

De Quincey. 1881, 1885 (rev) (EML).

Oliver Goldsmith. Memoir prefixed to Vicar of Wakefield, 1883.

Carlyle personally and in his writings: two lectures. 1885.

Edinburgh sketches and memories. 1892.

Milton. In In the footsteps of the poets, [1893].

James Melvin, rector of the grammar school of Aberdeen: a sketch. Aberdeen 1895.

Memories of London in the 'forties: arranged and annotated by Flora Masson. Edinburgh 1908.

Memories of two cities, Edinburgh and Aberdeen. Ed F. Masson, Edinburgh 1911.

Shakespeare personally. Ed R. Masson 1914. Lectures delivered 1865–95 at Edinburgh University.

JOHN FREDERICK DENISON MAURICE
1805–72

Eustace Conway, or the brother and sister: a novel. 3 vols 1834. Anon.

The Kingdom of Christ: or hints on the principles, ordinances and constitution of the Catholic Church. 3 vols 1838. *See col 1132, below.*

Moral and metaphysical philosophy. 1845, 2 vols 1872. A section of Encyclopaedia metropolitana, ed E. Smedley. Later expanded into 4 separate works: Ancient philosophy, 1850; Philosophy of the first six centuries, 1853; Mediaeval philosophy, 1857; Modern philosophy, 1862.

The religions of the world, and their relation to Christianity. 1847 (Boyle Lectures), 1848 (rev).

Theological essays. Cambridge 1853, 1853 (with addns), London 1871; ed E. F. Carpenter 1958.

Sermons. 6 vols [1857–9], 1860.

The workman and the franchise: chapters from English history on the representation and education of the people. 1866.

The conscience: lectures on casuistry. 1868, 1872.

Social morality: twenty-one lectures. 1869.

The friendship of books and other lectures. Ed T. Hughes 1874.

HENRY MAYHEW
1812–87
Selections

The street trader's lot. 1851; ed S. Rubenstein 1947 (with introd by M. D. George).

Mayhew's London. Ed P. C. Quennell 1949, 1951.

London's underworld. Ed P. C. Quennell 1950. Selections from London labour and the London poor vol 4.

Mayhew's characters. Ed P. C. Quennell 1951.

§1

The wandering minstrel. 1834?, Philadelphia 1836, London 1850, Boston 1856, [1880] (with Intrigue), [1897] (with The tradesman's ball). A one-act farce.

But, however–. 1838, 1843, [1883]. A one-act farce. With Henry Baylis.

What to make and how to teach it. Pt 1 1842. No more pbd.

The Prince of Wales's library: no 1—the primer. 1844.

The greatest plague of life: or the adventures of a lady in search of a servant. Illustr G. Cruikshank [1847], [1892]. With his brother Augustus Mayhew.

The good genius. 1847, 1879, New York 1890. Fairy tale. With Augustus Mayhew.

Whom to marry. [1848], 1854, 1872. With Augustus Mayhew.

The image of his father. Illustr 'Phiz' 1848, 1850, 1859. With Augustus Mayhew.

The magic of kindness. Illustr G. Cruikshank and K. Meadows [1848], [1869], Manchester [1879]. With Augustus Mayhew.

Acting charades. [1850], [1852].

London labour and the London poor. Nos 1–63. Vol 1 and pts of vols 2–3, 1851; expanded as 4 vols 1861–2; 4th vol only 1864. Some of the material first appeared as Labour and the poor, Morning Chron 1849–50; ed E. P. Thompson and E. Yeo 1971 (selected as The unknown Mayhew).

1851: or the adventures of Mr and Mrs Sandboys. 1851. With John Binny.

Home is home, be it never so homely. In Meliora, ed Earl of Shrewsbury 1852.

The story of the peasant-boy philosopher. 1854, 1855, New York 1856, London 1857.

Living for appearances. 1855. With Augustus Mayhew.

The wonders of science: or young Humphry Davy. 1855, 1856, New York 1856.

The Rhine and its picturesque scenery. Illustr B. Foster 1856, 1860 (as The lower Rhine).

The great world of London. Pts 1–9 [1856]. Completed by John Binny as The criminal prisons of London and scenes of prison life, 1862.

The upper Rhine. Illustr B. Foster 1858.

Young Benjamin Franklin: or the right road through life. 1861, New York 1862, London [1870].

The boyhood of Martin Luther. 1863, [1879].

German life and manners as seen in Saxony at the present day. 2 vols 1864, 1 vol 1865.

The shops and companies of London and the trades and manufactories of Great Britain. Pts 1–7 [1865].

London characters. Illustr W. S. Gilbert et al [1870], 1874, 1881. With others.

The comic almanack. 2 vols 1871. With Augustus Mayhew, Thackeray et al. Collection of earlier writings.

Report concerning the trade and hours of closing usual among the unlicensed victualling establishments at certain so-called 'Working Men's Clubs'. 1871.

HENRY MORLEY
1822–94

The dream of the Lilybell: tales and poems, with translations of the Hymns to night from the German of Novalis and Jean Paul's Death of an angel. 1845.

How to make home unhealthy. 1850. Anon. Rptd from Examiner; afterwards included in Early papers and some memories, 1891.

A defence of ignorance. 1851. A satirical essay on education.

Palissy the potter. 2 vols 1852.

The life of Geronimo Cardano of Milan, physician. 2 vols 1854.

Cornelius Agrippa von Nettesheim. 2 vols 1856.

Gossip. 1857. Tales, papers and verses rptd from Household Words.

Memoirs of Bartholomew Fair. 1859.

Fables and fairy tales. 1860.

Oberon's horn: a book of fairy tales. 1861.

English writers. Vol 1, 1864 (subsequently divided into 2 half vols); vol 2, 1867 (half vol only; 2nd half never pbd, and all 3 half vols allowed to go out of print). Vols 1–11, 1887–1895. 20 vols intended, but Morley only lived to write 10, vol 11 being completed by W. Hall Griffin.

The journal of a London playgoer from 1851 to 1866. 1866.

Fairy tales. 1867, [1877] (as The chicken market and other fairy tales). Tales previously pbd in Fables and fairy tales and Oberon's horn, above.

Tables of English literature. 1870, 1870 (with index).

Clement Marot and other studies. 2 vols 1871.

A first sketch of English literature. [1873], 1886 (enlarged).

Cassell's library of English literature. 5 vols 1875–1881.

University College London 1827–78: a lecture. 1878.

An account of the new north wing and recent additions to University College London. 1881. Anon.

Of English literature in the reign of Victoria, with a glance at the past. Leipzig 1881.

Morley's universal library. 6 vols 1883–1888. 1891. Every vol with critical and biographical introd, by Morley.

Candide, by F. A. M. de Voltaire. 1884; [1922]. Trn by Morley; originally ptd with Johnson's Rasselas as Morley's Universal Library vol 19, above.

Cassell's national library. 213 vols 1886–92. A wide selection from the English classics with introd to each vol by Morley.

The Carisbrooke library. 14 vols 1889–92. Ed Morley.

Memoir of Thomas Sadler. [1891].

Early papers and some memories. 1891.

MARK PATTISON
1813–84

§1

The lives of the English saints. Ed J. H. Newman 4 vols 1844–5; rev A. W. Hutton 6 vols 1901. Pattison contributed anon lives of Stephen Langton and St Edmund.

Oxford studies. In Oxford essays, 1855. On university reform.

Report on elementary education in Protestant Germany. 1859. Contained in the Report of the Assistant Commissioners on the state of popular education in Continental Europe vol 4, 1861.

Tendencies of religious thought in England 1688–1750. In Essays and reviews, 1860; enlarged in Essays, 1889, below.

Suggestions on academical organisation, with special reference to Oxford. Edinburgh 1868.

Isaac Casaubon 1559–1614. 1875; ed H. Nettleship, Oxford 1892 (with index).

Review of the situation. In Essays on the endowment of research, 1876.

Milton. 1879, 1880 (rev) (EML).

Memoirs. Ed Mrs Pattison 1885.

Essays. Ed H. Nettleship 2 vols Oxford 1889, London [1908] (5 essays omitted).

The Estiennes: a biographical essay, illustrated with original leaves from books printed by the three greatest members of that distinguished family. San Francisco 1949.

§2

Green, V. H. H. Oxford common room: a study of Lincoln College and Pattison. 1957.

Sparrow, J. Pattison and the idea of a university. Cambridge 1967.

AUGUSTUS WELBY NORTHMORE PUGIN
1812-52

Gothic furniture in the style of the 15th century, designed and etched by A. W. N. Pugin. 1835.
Contrasts: or a parallel between the noble edifices of the fourteenth and fifteenth centuries and similar buildings of the present day, shewing the present decay of taste. 1836.
An apology for a work entitled Contrasts: being a defence of the assertions advanced in that publication, against the various attacks lately made upon it. Birmingham 1837.
The true principles of pointed or Christian architecture. 1841.
An apology for the revival of Christian architecture in England. 1843.
The present state of ecclesiastical architecture in England, re-published from the Dublin Review. 1843.
Glossary of ecclesiastical ornament and costume compiled and illustrated from ancient authorities and examples. 1844; rev B. Smith 1868.
Some remarks on the articles which have recently appeared in the Rambler relative to ecclesiastical architecture and decoration. 1850.
A treatise on chancel screens and rood lofts, their antiquity, use and symbolic signification; illustrated with figures. 1851.

WILLIAM MICHAEL ROSSETTI
1829-1919

The germ: thoughts towards nature in poetry, literature and art. 4 nos 1850. Ed W. M. Rossetti; he pbd a facs, rptd in 1901.
Swinburne's poems and ballads: a criticism. 1866.
Fine art, chiefly contemporary: notices re-printed. 1867.
Notes on the Royal Academy exhibition. 1868. With A. C. Swinburne.
Lives of famous poets. 1878.
Memoir of Percy Bysshe Shelley, with new preface. 1886. Rptd from Rossetti's edn of Shelley, 1870.
Life of John Keats. 1887.
Dante Gabriel Rossetti as designer and writer. 1889.
D. G. Rossetti: his family letters, with a memoir. 2 vols 1895.

Ruskin; Rossetti; Preraphaelitism; papers 1854 to 1862. 1899.
Preraphaelite diaries and letters. 1900; The PRB journal 1849-53, ed W. D. Fredeman, Oxford 1974.
Rossetti papers 1862-70. 1903.
Some reminiscences. 2 vols 1906.
Democratic sonnets. 2 vols 1907.
Dante and his convito: a study with translations. 1910.

Letters etc

Letters about Shelley interchanged by Edward Dowden, Richard Garnett and Wm Michael Rossetti. Ed R. S. Garnett 1917.
Letters of William Michael Rossetti concerning Whitman, Blake and Shelley to Anne and Herbert Gilchrist. Ed C. Gohdes and P. F. Baum, Durham NC 1934.
Three Rossettis: unpublished letters to and from Dante Gabriel, Christina, William. Ed J. C. Troxell, Cambridge Mass 1937.
The Rossetti–Macmillan letters. Ed L. M. Packer, Berkeley 1963.
Diary 1870-3. Ed O. Bornand, Oxford 1977.

JAMES SPEDDING
1808-81

Evenings with a reviewer, or a free and particular examination of Mr Macaulay's article on Lord Bacon, in a series of dialogues. 2 vols 1848 (priv ptd), 1881 (with prefatory notice by G. S. Venables).
Companion to the railway edition of Lord Campbell's Life of Bacon, by a railway reader. 1853.
The works of Francis Bacon. Ed Spedding, R. L. Ellis and D. D. Heath 7 vols 1857-9.
The letters and the life of Francis Bacon, set forth in chronological order, with a commentary. 7 vols 1861-72.
Publishers and authors. 1867.
A conference of pleasure, composed about 1592 by Francis Bacon. 1870. Ed Spedding.
An account of the life and times of Francis Bacon. 2 vols Boston 1878.
Reviews and discussions, literary, political and historical, not relating to Bacon. 1879.
Studies in English history by James Gairdner and James Spedding. Edinburgh 1881.
Charles Tennyson, afterwards Turner. In Turner's Collected sonnets, old and new, 1898.

V. LATE NINETEENTH-CENTURY PROSE

SIR LESLIE STEPHEN
1832-1904

§1

The poll degree from a third point of view. 1863.
Sketches from Cambridge, by a don. 1865; ed G. M. Trevelyan, Oxford 1932.
The Times on the American war: an historical study by L. S. 1865.
The playground of Europe. 1871, 1894 (rev); ed H. E. G. Tyndale, Oxford 1936.
Essays on freethinking and plainspeaking. 1873, 1905 (with introductory essays by J. Bryce and H. Paul).
Hours in a library. 3 sers 1874-9, 1892 (with addns), 4 vols 1907 (with addns).

History of English thought in the eighteenth century. 2 vols 1876.
Samuel Johnson. 1878 (EML).
Alexander Pope. 1880 (EML).
The science of ethics. 1882.
Swift. 1882 (EML).
The dictionary of national biography. 21 vols 1885-1909. Editor 1882-91; contributed 378 articles.
Life of Henry Fawcett. 1885.
An agnostic's apology, and other essays. 1893.
The life of Sir James Fitzjames Stephen. 1895.
Social rights and duties. 2 vols 1896.
Studies of a biographer. 4 vols 1898-1902.
The English Utilitarians. 3 vols 1900, 1950 (rptd by London School of Economics).
George Eliot. 1902 (EML).
Robert Louis Stevenson: an essay. 1902.

English literature and society in the eighteenth century. 1904.

Hobbes. 1904 (EML).

Some early impressions. 1924.

Stephen edited Alpine Jnl 1868–72 *and* Cornhill Mag 1871–82.

Mausoleum book. Ed A. Bell, Oxford 1977 (from ms).

§2

Maitland, F. W. Life and letters of Stephen. 1906.

Woolf, V. Stephen: the philosopher at home. Times 28 Nov 1932.

—— In her Captain's death bed and other essays, 1950.

—— My father: Leslie Stephen. Atlantic Monthly March 1950.

MacCarthy, D. Leslie Stephen. Cambridge 1937 (Leslie Stephen lecture).

Leavis, Q. D. Stephen: Cambridge critic. Scrutiny 7 1939.

Wilson, J. D. Stephen and Matthew Arnold as critics of Wordsworth. Cambridge 1939.

Annan, N. G. Stephen: his thought and character in relation to his time. 1951.

—— The intellectual aristocracy. In Studies in social history: a tribute to G. M. Trevelyan, 1955.

SAMUEL BUTLER
1835–1902

Bibliographies

Hoppé, A. J. A bibliography of the writings of Butler and of writings about him, with some letters from Butler to F. G. Fleay now first published. [1925].

Harkness, S. B. The career of Butler: a bibliography. 1955.

Collections

The Shrewsbury edition of the works. Ed H. F. Jones and A. T. Bartholomew 20 vols 1923–6.

The essential Butler. Ed G. D. H. Cole 1950, 1961 (rev).

§1

A first year in Canterbury settlement. 1863; ed R. A. Streatfeild 1914 (with other early essays).

The evidence for the resurrection of Jesus Christ, as given by the four evangelists, critically examined. 1865. Anon.

Erewhon: or over the range. 1872 (anon), 1872 (rev and corrected), 1901 (rev); ed F. N. Hackett, New York 1917; ed L. Mumford, New York 1927; ed H. M. Tomlinson, New York 1931; ed A. Huxley, New York 1934; ed D. McCarthy 1960; ed K. Amis, New York 1961.

The fair haven: a work in defence of the miraculous element in our Lord's ministry upon earth, both as against rationalistic impugners and certain orthodox defenders, by the late J. P. Owen, edited by W. B. Owen, with a memoir of the author. 1873; ed R. A. Streatfeild 1913; ed A. T. Bartholomew 1929; ed G. Bullett 1938.

Life and habit: an essay after a completer view of evolution. 1878; ed R. A. Streatfeild 1910 (with addns).

Evolution, old and new: or the theories of Buffon, Dr Erasmus Darwin and Lamarck, as compared with that of Mr Charles Darwin. 1879, 1882 (with appendix and index); ed R. A. Streatfeild 1911.

Unconscious memory: a comparison between the theory of Dr Ewald Hering, professor of physiology at Prague, and the philosophy of the unconscious of Dr Edward von Hartmann; with translations from these authors. 1880; [ed R. A. Streatfeild] 1910 (with introd by M. Hartog).

Alps and sanctuaries of Piedmont and the Canton Ticino.

1882; ed R. A. Streatfeild 1913 (with author's revisions and index, and introd).

Selections from previous works, with remarks on Mr G. J. Romanes' Mental evolution in animals, and A psalm of Montreal. 1884.

Luck or cunning as the main means of organic modification? an attempt to throw additional light upon the late Mr Charles Darwin's theory of natural selection. 1887; ed H. F. Jones 1920.

Ex voto: an account of the Sacro Monte or New Jerusalem at Varallo-Sesia, with some notice of Tabachetti's remaining work at the sanctuary of Crea. 1888, 1889 (rev and enlarged).

A lecture on the humour of Homer, January 30th 1892; reprinted with preface and additional matter from the Eagle. Cambridge 1892.

The life and letters of Dr Samuel Butler, headmaster of Shrewsbury School 1798–1836, and afterwards Bishop of Lichfield. 2 vols 1896.

The authoress of the Odyssey, where and when she wrote, who she was, the use she made of the Iliad, and how the poem grew under her hands. 1897; ed H. F. Jones 1922.

The Iliad of Homer, rendered into English prose. 1898; ed L. R. Loomis, New York 1942.

Shakespeare's sonnets reconsidered, and in part re-arranged, with introductory chapters by Butler. 1899.

The Odyssey, rendered into English prose. 1900; ed L. R. Loomis, New York 1942.

Erewhon revisited twenty years later, both by the original discoverer of the country and by his son. 1901; ed G. M. Acklom, New York 1920.

The way of all flesh. [Ed R. A. Streatfeild] 1903; ed W. L. Phelps, New York 1916; ed T. Dreiser, New York 1936; ed G. B. Shaw 1936; ed R. A. Gettmann, New York 1948; ed W. Y. Tindall, New York 1950; ed M. D. Zabel, New York 1950; ed D. F. Howard, Boston 1964 (complete, as Ernest Pontifex). Written 1873–84.

Essays on life, art and science. Ed R. A. Streatfeild 1904.

The humour of Homer, and other essays. Ed R. A. Streatfeild 1913. With a biographical sketch by H. F. Jones.

Hesiod's works and days: a translation. 1924.

Letters and Notebooks

Note-books: selections. Ed H. F. Jones 1912; Selections, ed A. T. Bartholomew 1930.

Butleriana. 1932 (Nonesuch). Compiled mainly from previously unpbd portions of the note-books by A. T. Bartholomew.

Further extracts from the note-books. Ed A. T. Bartholomew 1934.

Letters between Butler and Miss E. M. A. Savage. Ed G. L. Keynes and B. Hill 1935.

Butler's notebooks: selections. Ed G. L. Keynes and B. Hill 1951.

Correspondence of Butler with his sister May. Ed D. F. Howard, Berkeley 1962.

The family letters of Butler 1841–86. Ed A. Silver, Stanford 1962.

§2

Streatfeild, R. A. Butler: a critical study. 1902.

—— Butler: records and memorials. 1903.

Jones, H. F. Diary of a journey through North Italy to Sicily. 1904.

—— Charles Darwin and Butler: a step towards reconciliation. 1911.

—— Butler: a memoir. 2 vols 1919.

—— and A. T. Bartholomew. The Butler collection at St John's College Cambridge. Cambridge 1921.

Muggeridge, M. The earnest atheist: a study of Butler. 1936.

Cole, G. D. H. Butler and the Way of all flesh. 1947.

Furbank, P. N. Samuel Butler. Cambridge 1948.
Greene, G. In his Lost childhood and other essays, 1951.
Henderson, P. Butler: the incarnate bachelor. 1953.
Willey, B. Darwin and Butler: two versions of evolution. 1960.

WALTER HORATIO PATER
1839–94

Bodley has the ms of Pascal; *King's School Canterbury has* Diaphaneitè, *and Mr John Sparrow the ms of the unpbd chs of* Gaston de Latour, *as well as the ms of* Demeter and Persephone. *There are many further mss at Harvard; the letters are scattered.*

§1

Studies in the history of the Renaissance. 1873, 1877 (rev, omitting Conclusion and including The school of Giorgione as The Renaissance: studies in art and poetry), 1888 (Conclusion restored with changes); ed K. Clark 1961.
Marius the Epicurean: his sensations and ideas. 2 vols 1885, 1888 (with changes), 1892 (with extensive changes); ed J. C. Squire 2 vols 1929.
Imaginary portraits. 1887; ed E. J. Brzenk, New York 1962 (including An English poet).
Appreciations: with an essay on style. 1889, 1890 (Aesthetic poetry replaced by review of Feuillet, La morte).
Plato and Platonism: a series of lectures. 1893.
An imaginary portrait (The child in the house). Oxford 1894. Pbd as separate vol after earlier appearance in Macmillan's Mag; rptd in Miscellaneous studies, below.
Greek studies: a series of essays, prepared for the press by C. L. Shadwell. 1895.
Miscellaneous studies: a series of essays, prepared for the press by C. L. Shadwell. 1895.

Gaston de Latour: an unfinished romance, prepared for the press by C. L. Shadwell. 1896.
Essays from the Guardian. 1896 (priv ptd); [ed T. B. Mosher?], Portland Maine 1897; 1901 (uniform with Works, above).
Uncollected essays. [Ed T. B. Mosher?], Portland Maine 1903.
Sketches and reviews. New York 1919.
Letters. Ed L. Evans, Oxford 1970.

§2

Benson, A. C. Walter Pater. 1906 (EML).
Wright, T. The life of Pater. 2 vols 1907.
Thomas, E. Pater: a critical study. 1913.
Yeats, W. B. In his Autobiographies, 1926.
—— Introduction. In his Oxford book of modern verse, Oxford 1936.
Du Bos, C. Sur Marius l'Epicurien de Pater. In his Approximations, Paris 1930.
Eliot, T. S. The place of Pater. In The eighteen-eighties, ed de la Mare, Cambridge 1930; rptd as Arnold and Pater, Bookman (New York) Sept 1930 and in his Selected essays, 1932.
Tillotson, G. Pater, Mr Rose and the Conclusion of the Renaissance. E & S 32 1946.
—— Arnold and Pater: critics historical, aesthetic and otherwise. E & S new ser 3 1950. Both rptd with changes in his Criticism and the nineteenth century, 1951.
Hough, G. In his Last Romantics, 1949.
Allott, K. Pater and Arnold. EC 2 1952.
Cecil, D. Pater: the scholar-artist. 1955; rptd in his Fine art of reading, 1957.
Wellek, R. Pater's literary theory and criticism. Victorian Stud 1 1957; rptd in his A history of modern criticism 1750–1950 vol 3, 1958.
d'Hangest, G. Pater: l'homme et l'œuvre. 2 vols Paris 1961. With bibliography.
Ward, A. Pater: the idea in nature. 1966.

VI. MINOR PROSE 1870–1900

WILLIAM ARCHER
1856–1924

The fashionable tragedian: a criticism. Edinburgh 1877. An essay on Henry Irving, with R. W. Lowe.
English analyses of the French plays represented at the Gaiety Theatre London, June and July 1879. 1879.
English dramatists of today. 1882.
Henry Irving, actor and manager: a critical study. [1883].
About the theatre: essays and studies. 1886.
The drama 1837–87. In The reign of Queen Victoria, ed T. H. Ward vol 2, 1887.
Masks or faces? a study in the psychology of acting. 1888.
William Charles Macready. 1890.
The theatrical 'world'. 5 vols 1893–7.
Study and stage: a year-book of criticism. 1899.
America to-day: observations and reflections. 1900.
Poets of the younger generation. 1902.
Real conversations. 1904. Dialogues with Pinero, Hardy, Stephen Phillips, George Moore, Gilbert et al.
A national theatre: scheme and estimates. 1907. With Sir H. Granville-Barker.
Some common objections. 3 pts 1908–9. On simplified spelling.

Through Afro-America: an English reading of the race problem. 1910.
The life, trial and death of Francisco Ferrer. 1911.
The great analysis: a plea for a rational world-order, with an introd by Gilbert Murray. 1912. Anon.
Play-making: a manual of craftsmanship. 1912.
Art and the commonweal: delivered at South Place Institute on February 23 1912. 1912.
The playhouse. In Shakespeare's England vol 2, Oxford 1916. With W. J. Lawrence.
God and Mr Wells: a critical examination of God, the invisible King. 1917.
War is war, or the Germans in Belgium: a drama of 1914. New York 1919.
The green goddess: a play in four acts. New York 1921.
The old drama and the new: an essay in re-valuation. 1923.
William Archer as rationalist: a collection of his heterodox writings. Ed J. M. Robertson 1925.
Three plays; with a personal note by Bernard Shaw. 1927. Includes Martha Washington, Beatriz Juana, Lidia.
Archer translated into prose all Ibsen's more important plays, occasionally in collaboration with Charles Archer or Edmund Gosse, 1888–1913, as well as plays by Hauptmann and Maeterlinck.

ARTHUR CHRISTOPHER BENSON
1862–1925

Memoirs of Arthur Hamilton BA of Trinity College Cambridge, by 'Christopher Carr'. 1886.
William Laud, sometime Archbishop of Canterbury. 1887.
Men of might: studies of great characters. 1892, 1921. With H. F. W. Tatham.
Le cahier jaune. Eton 1892 (priv ptd).
Poems. 1893.
Lyrics. 1895.
The professor. Eton 1895 (priv ptd).
Thomas Gray. Eton 1895 (priv ptd).
Genealogy of the family of Benson, with biographical and illustrative notes. Eton 1895 (priv ptd).
Babylonica. Eton 1895.
Essays. 1896.
Monnow: an ode. Eton 1896.
Lord Vyet and other poems. 1897.
Ode in memory of the Rt Honble William Ewart Gladstone. Eton 1898 (priv ptd).
Fasti Etonenses: a biographical history of Eton selected from the lives of celebrated Etonians. Eton 1899.
The life of Edward White Benson, sometime Archbishop of Canterbury. 2 vols 1899, 1 vol 1901 (abridged).
The professor and other poems. 1900.
Coronation ode, set to music by E. Elgar: book of words, with analytical notes by Joseph Bennett. 1902.
Ode to Japan. 1902 (priv ptd).
The schoolmaster: a commentary upon the aims and methods of an assistant-master in a public school. 1902.
The myrtle bough: a vale. Eton 1903 (priv ptd).
The hill of trouble and other stories. 1903.
The house of quiet: an autobiography. 1904. Anon.
Alfred Tennyson. 1904.
Rossetti. 1904 (EML).
Edward FitzGerald. 1905 (EML).
The thread of gold, by the author of the House of quiet. 1905.
The isles of sunset. 1905. Stories.
Peace and other poems. 1905.
Walter Pater. 1906 (EML).
The Upton letters, by T. B. 1905, 1906 (with new preface)
From a college window. 1906.
The gate of death: a diary. 1906. Anon.
The altar fire. 1907.
Beside still waters. 1907.
At large. 1908.
Poems. 1909.
The silent isle. 1910.
The leaves of the tree: studies in biography. 1911.
Ruskin: a study in personality. 1911.
Paul the minstrel and other stories: reprinted from the Hill of trouble and the Isles of sunset. 1911.
The child of the dawn. 1912.
Thy rod and thy staff. 1912.
Along the road. 1913.
Joyous gard. 1913.
Watersprings. 1913.
Where no fear was: a book about fear. 1914.
The orchard pavilion. 1914.
Hugh: memoirs of a brother. 1915. On Robert Hugh Benson.
Escape and other essays. 1915.
Father Payne. 1915. Anon.
Life and letters of Maggie Benson. 1917.
Cambridge essays on education. Cambridge 1917. Ed Benson, his own contribution being The training of the imagination.
The reed of Pan: English renderings of Greek epigrams (from the Greek Anthology) and lyrics. 1922.
The trefoil: Wellington College, Lincoln and Truro. 1923. On the early life of Archbishop Benson.

Magdalene College Cambridge: a little view of its buildings and history. Cambridge 1923.
Memories and friends. 1924.
Chris Gascoyne: an experiment in solitude, from the diaries of John Trevor. 1924.
The house of Menerdue. 1925.
Basil Netherby. [1926].
The canon. 1926.
Rambles and reflections. 1926.
Cressage. 1927.

Letters and Diaries

Meanwhile: a packet of war letters, by H. L. G. [A. C. Benson], with a foreword by K. W. 1916.
Extracts from the letters of Dr A. C. Benson to M. E. A[llen]. 1926.
Diary. Ed P. Lubbock [1926].

AUGUSTINE BIRRELL
1850–1933

Obiter dicta. Ser 1, 1884 (anon and priv ptd); ser 2, 1887; 2 sers, 1910.
The life of Charlotte Brontë. 1887.
Res judicatae. 1892.
Essays about men, women and books. 1894.
The duties and liabilities of trustees: six lectures. 1896.
Four lectures on the law of employers' liability at home and abroad. 1897.
The ideal university: a lecture. [1898].
Sir Frank Lockwood: a biographical sketch. 1898.
Seven lectures on the law and history of copyright in books. 1899.
Miscellanies. 1901.
William Hazlitt. 1902 (EML).
Emerson: a lecture. 1903.
In the name of the Bodleian and other essays. 1905.
Andrew Marvell. 1905 (EML).
Mr Balfour's parliament: a speech. [1905].
The Lords and the Education Bill: a speech. 1906.
On a dictum of Mr Disraeli's and other matters: an address. 1912.
A rogue's memoirs. 1912.
John Wesley, his times and work. Ch 2 in Letters of John Wesley, ed G. Eayrs 1915.
Frederick Locker-Lampson. 1920.
More obiter dicta. 1924.
Some early recollections of Liverpool. Liverpool 1924.
Et cetera. 1930.
Things past redress. [1937]. Autobiographical.

STOPFORD AUGUSTUS BROOKE
1832–1916

The life and letters of the Rev F. W. Robertson. 1865.
Theology in the English poets. 1874, [1910] (EL).
English literature. 1876, 1896 (rev), 1901 (with chs on English literature 1832–92, and on American literature by G. R. Carpenter), 1924 (with new ch on Literature since 1832 by G. Sampson).
Milton. 1879.
Riquet of the tuft. 1880. A play.
Notes on the Liber studiorum of J. M. W. Turner, with illustrations. 1885.
The inaugural address to the Shelley Society. 1886 (priv ptd); rptd in Studies in poetry, 1907, below.
Poems. Edinburgh 1888.
Dove Cottage: Wordsworth's home from 1800–8. 1890.
The history of early English literature: being the history

of English poetry from its beginning to the accession of King Alfred. 2 vols 1892.

The development of theology as illustrated in English poetry from 1780–1830. 1893.

The need and use of getting Irish literature into the English tongue: an address. 1893.

Tennyson: his art and relation to modern life. 1894.

English literature from the beginning to the Norman Conquest. New York 1898.

Religion in literature and religion in life: two lectures. 1900.

King Alfred as educator of his people and man of letters. 1901.

The poetry of Robert Browning. 1902.

On ten plays of Shakespeare. 1905.

The sea-charm of Venice. 1907.

Studies in poetry. 1907.

A study of Clough, Arnold, Rossetti and Morris. 1908.

EDWARD CARPENTER
1844–1929

Narcissus and other poems. 1873.

Moses: a drama in five acts. [1875], 1909, 1910 (rev as The promised land).

Towards democracy. Pt 1, Manchester 1883; 2 pts, Manchester 1885; 3 pts, London 1892; pt 4 (Who shall command the heart?) 1902; 4 pts, 1905.

England's ideal and other papers on social subjects. 1887.

Civilization: its cause and cure, and other essays. 1889, 1921 (enlarged).

From Adam's Peak to Elephanta: sketches in Ceylon and India. 1892, 1903 (enlarged), 1910 (rev), 1911 (4 chs pbd separately as A visit to a gnani).

Sex-love: and its place in a free society. Manchester 1894.

Woman and her place in a free society. Manchester 1894.

Marriage in a free society. Manchester 1894.

Homogenic love: and its place in a free society. Manchester 1894 (priv ptd).

St George and the dragon. Manchester 1895. A children's play.

Love's coming-of-age: a series of papers on the relations of the sexes. Manchester 1896, London 1902, 1906 (enlarged), [1914] (omits Note on preventive checks).

An unknown people. 1897. On the intermediate sex.

Angels' wings: a series of essays on art and its relation to life. 1898.

The story of Eros and Psyche from Apuleius and the first book of the Iliad of Homer done into English verse. 1900, 1923 (as Eros and Psyche together with some early verses). Eros and Psyche is in prose. The early poems are rptd from Narcissus, 1873, above.

The art of creation: essays on the self and its powers. 1904, 1907 (enlarged).

Prisons, police and punishment: an inquiry into the causes and treatment of crime and criminals. 1905.

Days with Walt Whitman; with some notes on his life and work. 1906.

The intermediate sex: a study of some transitional types of men and women. 1908.

Sketches from life in town and country, and some verses. 1908.

The drama of love and death: a study of human evolution and transfiguration. 1912.

Intermediate types among primitive folk: a study in social evolution. 1914.

The healing of nations and the hidden sources of their strife. 1915.

My days and dreams: being autobiographical notes. 1916.

Towards industrial freedom. 1917.

Pagan and Christian creeds: their origin and meaning. 1920.

Some friends of Walt Whitman. 1924.

The psychology of the poet Shelley. 1925. With George Barnefield.

JOHN CHURTON COLLINS
1848–1908

Sir Joshua Reynolds as a portrait painter. 1874.

Bolingbroke; and Voltaire in England. 1886.

Illustrations of Tennyson. 1891.

The study of English literature: a plea for its recognition and organization at the universities. 1891.

Jonathan Swift: a biographical and critical study. 1893.

Essays and studies. 1895.

Ephemera critica: or plain truths about current literature. 1901.

Studies in Shakespeare. 1904.

Studies in poetry and criticism. 1905.

Voltaire, Montesquieu and Rousseau in England. 1908.

Greek influence on English poetry. Ed M. Macmillan 1910.

Posthumous essays. Ed L. Churton Collins 1912. Shakespeare, Johnson, Burke, Arnold, Browning etc.

Collins also pbd edns of Sidney, Greene, Lord Herbert, Milton, Dryden, Pope, Tennyson, Arnold et al.

SIR SIDNEY COLVIN
1845–1927

§ 1

E. J. Poynter; Albert Moore; E. Burne-Jones; Simeon Solomon; Frederick Walker; Ford Madox Brown. In English painters of the present day, 1871.

Millais; George Mason; Thomas Armstrong; G. H. Boughton. In English artists of the present day, 1872.

Children in Italian and English design. 1872.

A selection from occasional writings on fine art. 1873 (priv ptd).

Landor. 1881 (EML).

Keats. 1887 (EML).

Engravings and engravers in England 1545–1695: a critical and historical essay. 1905.

On concentration and suggestion in poetry. 1905 (Eng Assoc pamphlet).

John Keats: his life and poetry, his friends, critics and after-fame. 1917.

Memories and notes of persons and places. 1921.

§ 2

Stevenson, R. L. In his Vailima letters, 1895. Letters written by Stevenson to Colvin, Nov 1890–Oct 1894.

Lucas, E. V. The Colvins and their friends. 1928.

WILLIAM JOHN COURTHOPE
1842–1917

Poems by Novus Homo. Oxford 1865.

Ludibria lunae, or the wars of the women and the gods: an allegorical burlesque. 1869.

The paradise of birds: an old extravaganza in modern dress. Edinburgh 1870.

Joseph Addison. 1884 (EML).

The liberal movement in English literature. 1885.

The life of Pope. 1889. Vol 5 of The works of Pope, completed by Courthope.

A history of English poetry. 6 vols 1895–1910.

Liberty and authority in matters of taste: an inaugural lecture. 1896; rptd in Life in poetry: law in taste, 1901, below.

The longest reign: an ode on the completion of the sixtieth year of the reign of Her Majesty Queen Victoria. Oxford 1897.

Life in poetry: law in taste. 1901. Lectures delivered while Professor of Poetry at Oxford.

The revolution in English poetry and fiction. 1907. In The Cambridge Modern History vol 10, Cambridge 1902.

A consideration of Macaulay's comparison of Dante and Milton. Proc Br Acad 3 1908.

The poetry of Spenser. CHEL vol 3 1909.

The connexion between ancient and modern romance. [1911] (Br Acad lecture).

Selections from the epigrams of M. Valerius Martialis: translated or imitated in English verse. 1914.

The country town and other poems; with a memoir by A. O. Prickard. 1920.

HENRY AUSTIN DOBSON
1840–1921

Collections

Collected poems. 1897, 1902 (adds selection from Carmina votiva, 1901), 1909 (enlarged), 1913 (adds 27 pieces), Oxford 1923 (Oxford Poets).

Complete poetical works. Ed A. T. A. Dobson, Oxford 1923.

Selected poems. Oxford 1924 (WC).

What is virtually a collected edn of the essays is formed by the WC reprints, 9 vols Oxford 1923–6.

§ I

Vignettes in rhyme. 1873, 1874 (with omissions and addns).

The civil service handbook of English literature. 1874, 1880 (rev and extended).

Proverbs in porcelain. 1877, 1878 (enlarged), 1893 (as Proverbs in porcelain, to which is added Au revoir, the latter rptd from At the sign of the lyre; only retains the 6 proverbs from 1877 edn).

Hogarth. 1879.

Vignettes in rhyme and other verses. New York 1880, London 1883 (with addns and omissions as Old world idylls), 1906 (with further notes).

Fielding. 1883 (EML).

Thomas Bewick and his pupils. 1884.

At the sign of the lyre. 1885, New York 1885 (with addns and omissions), London 1889 (with further addns and omissions).

Richard Steele. 1886.

Life of Oliver Goldsmith. 1888.

Poems on several occasions. 2 vols 1889, 1895 (rev and adds 12 poems).

The sundial: a poem. New York 1890.

Four Frenchwomen. 1890, Oxford 1923 (WC).

Horace Walpole. 1890; rev P. Toynbee, Oxford 1927.

William Hogarth. 1891, 1898 (enlarged); ed W. Armstrong 1902, 1907 (enlarged).

Eighteenth century vignettes. Ser 1, 1892, 1897 (At Leicester Fields added); ser 2, 1894; ser 3, 1896.

The ballad of Beau Brocade and other poems of the xviiith century. 1892.

The story of Rosina and other verses. 1895.

Miscellanies. Ser 1, New York 1898, London 1899 (with addns, and omissions, as A paladin of philanthropy), Oxford 1925 (WC); ser 2, 1901.

Carmina votiva and other occasional verses. 1901 (priv ptd).

Samuel Richardson. 1902 (EML).

Side-walk studies. 1902, Oxford 1924 (WC).

Fanny Burney. 1903 (EML).

De libris: prose and verse. 1908, 1911 (adds 2 essays).

Old Kensington Palace and other papers. 1910, Oxford 1926 (WC).

At Prior Park and other papers. 1912, Oxford 1925 (WC).

Rosalba's journal and other papers. 1915, Oxford 1926 (WC).

A bookman's budget. Oxford 1917. A collection of extracts from the works of English prose writers.

Later essays 1917–20. Oxford 1921.

Three unpublished poems. 1930 (priv ptd).

EDWARD DOWDEN
1843–1913

Mr Tennyson and Mr Browning. 1863.

Shakespeare: a critical study of his mind and art. 1875.

Poems. 1876; [ed E. D. Dowden] 2 vols 1914 (with addns).

Studies in literature 1789–1877. 1878.

Southey. 1879. (EML).

The life of Percy Bysshe Shelley. 2 vols 1886, 1 vol 1896.

Transcripts and studies. 1888.

New studies in literature. 1895.

The French Revolution and English literature: lectures. 1897.

A history of French literature. 1897.

Literary criticism in France. In Studies in European literature: being the Taylorian Lectures 1889–99, Oxford 1900.

Puritan and Anglican: studies in literature. 1900.

Robert Browning. 1904; 1915 (EL).

Michel de Montaigne. 1905.

Milton in the eighteenth century 1701–50. Proc Br Acad 3 [1909].

Essays modern and Elizabethan. 1910.

Letters

Fragments from old letters: E. D. to E. D. W. 1869–92. 1914.

Letters of Dowden and his correspondents. [Ed E. D. and H. M. Dowden] 1914.

Letters about Shelley interchanged by Dowden, Robert Garnett and Wm Michael Rossetti. Ed R. S. Garnett 1917.

HENRY HAVELOCK ELLIS
1859–1939

§ I

The new spirit. 1890, 1892 (with new preface). Essays.

The criminal. 1890, 1901 (rev and enlarged).

The nationalisation of health. 1892.

Man and woman: a study of human secondary sexual characters. 1894, 1904 (rev and enlarged), [1914] (rev), 1934 (rev).

Sexual inversion. 2 vols 1897–1924. Originally vol 1 of Studies in the psychology of sex, with an appendix by J. A. Symonds. Later issued as vol 2 of that series, without Symonds' contribution.

Affirmations. 1898, 1915 (with new preface).

The evolution of modesty. 1899. Later issued as vol 1 of Studies in the psychology of sex.

The nineteenth century: a dialogue in Utopia. 1900.

Analysis of the sexual impulse. Philadelphia 1903. Later issued as vol 3 of Studies in the psychology of sex.

A study of British genius. 1904, 1927 (rev and enlarged).

Studies in the psychology of sex. 7 vols Philadelphia 1905–28.

The soul of Spain. 1908, 1937 (with new preface).

The problems of race degeneration. 1911.

The world of dreams. 1911, 1926 (new edn).

The task of social hygiene. 1912.

Impressions and comments. 3 sers 1914–24, 1 vol Boston 1931 (as Fountain of life).

Essays in war-time. 1916.

The philosophy of conflict and other essays in war-time. 1919.

Little essays of love and virtue. 1922.

Kanga Creek: an Australian idyll. Waltham St Lawrence 1922, [New York] 1935.

The dance of life. 1923.

Sonnets, with folk songs from the Spanish. Waltham St Lawrence 1925.

More essays of love and virtue. 1931. The two vols of Essays of love and virtue, above, were combined and enlarged as On life and sex, Garden City NY 1937, London 1945.

Concerning Jude the Obscure. 1931.

The colour-sense in literature. 1931.

The revaluation of obscenity. Paris 1931.

Views and reviews: a selection of uncollected articles 1884–1932. 2 vols 1932.

Psychology of sex: a manual for students. 1933.

Chapman, with illustrative passages. 1934.

My confessional: questions of our day. 1934.

From Rousseau to Proust. 1936.

Questions of our day. 1936.

My life: the autobiography. Boston 1939.

From Marlowe to Shaw: studies 1576–1936. In English literature, ed 'John Gawsworth' 1950.

The genius of Europe. Ed F. Delisle 1950.

From 1887 to 1889 Ellis edited the Mermaid series of old dramatists, and from 1889 to 1914 the Contemporary science series. He also edited a number of literary texts, including Heine's prose, Ibsen's plays and Vasari's Lives of Italian painters. He wrote numerous pamphlets, particularly on sexual psychology.

§2

Peterson, H. Ellis, philosopher of love. 1928.

Calder-Marshall, A. Havelock Ellis. 1959.

Collis, J. S. An artist of life: a study of the life and work of Ellis. 1959.

RICHARD GARNETT
1835–1906

Primula: a book of lyrics. 1858 (anon), 1859 (signed, as Io in Egypt and other poems), 1893 (rev with addns as Poems).

Poems from the German. 1862.

Idylls and epigrams, chiefly from the Greek anthology. 1869, 1892 (as A chaplet from the Greek anthology).

Richmond on the Thames. 1870.

Carlyle. 1887.

Shelley and Lord Beaconsfield. 1887 (priv ptd).

Emerson. 1888.

The twilight of the gods and other tales. 1888, 1903 (augmented). Cynical apologues.

Milton. 1890.

Iphigenia in Delphi. 1890. A play; also includes Homer's Shield of Achilles and other trns from the Greek.

The soul and the stars, by A. G. Trent. 1893, 1903 (expanded).

The age of Dryden. 1895.

William Blake: painter and poet. 1895.

One hundred and twenty-four sonnets from Dante, Petrarch and Camoens. 1896.

History of Italian literature. 1897.

Edward Gibbon Wakefield. 1898.

Essays in librarianship and bibliography. 1899.

Essays of an ex-librarian. 1901.

The queen and other poems. 1901.

English literature: an illustrated record by Richard Garnett and Edmund Gosse. 4 vols 1903–4. Vols 1–2 by Garnett.

Tennyson. 1903. With G. K. Chesterton.

Coleridge. 1904.

William Shakespeare, pedagogue and poacher. 1905. A play.

De flagello myrteo. 1905. Anon; aphorisms.

William Johnson Fox. 1910. Completed by Edward Garnett.

Letters about Shelley interchanged by Edward Dowden, Garnett and Wm Michael Rossetti. Ed R. S. Garnett 1917.

Garnett also pbd several tracts on library problems; he was keeper of BM printed books 1890–9. He contributed many articles to DNB and other composite works.

SIR EDMUND WILLIAM GOSSE
1849–1928

Madrigals, songs and sonnets. 1870. 32 by Gosse.

On viol and flute. 1873, 1890 (33 poems from the original edn and 36 poems drawn from other vols including New poems, 1879).

The ethical condition of the early Scandinavian peoples. [1874].

King Erik. 1876, 1893 (with introductory essay by Theodore Watts [-Dunton]). A tragedy in verse.

The unknown lover. 1878. A play for private performance with an essay on the Chamber drama in England.

New poems. 1879.

Studies in the literature of Northern Europe. 1879.

Gray. 1882, 1889 (rev) (EML).

Cecil Lawson: a memoir. 1883.

Lawrence Alma Tadema. 1883.

Seventeenth-century studies: a contribution to the history of English poetry. 1883.

A critical essay on the life and works of George Tinworth. 1883.

Notes on the pictures and drawings of Mr Alfred W. Hunt. 1884.

Firdausi in exile and other poems. 1885.

The masque of painters. 1885 (priv ptd).

From Shakespeare to Pope. Cambridge 1885.

Raleigh. 1886.

The life of William Congreve. 1888, 1924 (rev and enlarged).

A history of eighteenth-century literature 1660–1780. 1889.

Robert Browning: personalia. Boston 1890.

The life of Philip Henry Gosse. 1890.

Northern studies. 1890.

Gossip in a library. 1891.

Wolcott Balestier: a portrait sketch. 1892 (priv ptd).

The secret of Narcisse: a romance. 1892.

Questions at issue. 1893.

In russet and silver. 1894.

The Jacobean poets. 1894.

Critical kit-kats. 1896.

Short histories of the literature of the world. 15 vols 1897–1915. Vol 3 on modern English literature entirely by Gosse, who was also general editor.

A short history of modern English literature. 1898, 1924 (with 2 further chs).

The life and letters of John Donne. 2 vols 1899.

Hypolympia, or the gods in the island: an ironic fantasy. 1901.

English literature: an illustrated record. 4 vols 1903–4. Vol 1 by Richard Garnett; vol 2 by Garnett and Gosse; vols 3–4 by Gosse.

The challenge of the Brontës. 1903 (priv ptd).

Jeremy Taylor. 1903 (EML).

British portrait painters and engravers of the eighteenth

century—Kneller to Reynolds; with an introductory essay and biographical notes. 2 vols 1905.

Coventry Patmore. 1905.

French profiles. 1905.

Sir Thomas Browne. 1905 (EML).

Father and son: a study of two temperaments. 1907.

Ibsen. 1907.

Scandinavia 1815–70; Dano-Norwegian literature 1815–65. 1908. In The Cambridge modern history vol 11, 1902.

Biographical notes on the writings of Robert Louis Stevenson. 1908 (priv ptd).

Catalogue of the library of the House of Lords. 1908 (priv ptd).

Swinburne: personal recollections. 1909 (priv ptd).

The autumn garden. 1909.

Two visits to Denmark, 1872, 1874. 1911.

Portraits and sketches. 1912.

Browning's centenary. 1912. Addresses by Gosse, Arthur Pinero and Henry James.

The future of English poetry. 1913.

Lady Dorothy Nevill: an open letter. 1913 (priv ptd).

Sir Alfred East. 1914.

Two pioneers of Romanticism: Joseph and Thomas Warton. [1915].

Catherine Trotter: the precursor of the Blue-stockings. 1916 (priv ptd).

Inter Arma: being essays written in time of war. 1916.

The life of Algernon Charles Swinburne. 1917.

Lord Cromer as a man of letters. 1917 (priv ptd).

The novels of Benjamin Disraeli. 1918 (priv ptd).

Three French moralists, and the gallantry of France. 1918. On La Rochefoucauld, La Bruyère, Vauvenargues.

A catalogue of the works of A. C. Swinburne in the library of Gosse. 1919 (priv ptd).

Some diversions of a man of letters. 1919.

The first draft of Swinburne's Anactoria. Cambridge [1919] (priv ptd). A short critical essay.

Some literary aspects of France in the war. 1919 (priv ptd).

Malherbe and the classical reaction in the seventeenth century. Oxford 1920. A lecture.

Books on the table. New York 1921; More books on the table, 1923.

The continuity of literature: an address. 1922.

Byways round Helicon. 1922.

Aspects and impressions. 1922.

Swinburne: an essay written in 1875 and now first printed. Edinburgh 1925 (priv ptd).

Tallement des Réaux or the art of miniature biography: the Zaharoff lecture. Oxford 1925.

Silhouettes. 1925.

Leaves and fruit. 1927.

AUGUSTUS JOHN CUTHBERT HARE
1834–1903

A handbook for travellers in Berks, Bucks and Oxfordshire. 1860.

A winter in Mentone. [1862].

A handbook for travellers to Durham and Northumberland. 1864.

Walks in Rome. 2 vols 1871, 1 vol 1925 (22nd edn).

Memorials of a quiet life. 3 vols 1872–6. Memoir of Maria Hare.

Wanderings in Spain. 1873.

Days near Rome. 2 vols 1875.

Cities of Northern and Central Italy. 3 vols 1876.

Walks in London. 2 vols 1878.

Life and letters of Frances, Baroness Bunsen. 2 vols 1879.

Cities of Southern Italy and Sicily. 1883.

Florence. 1884, 1925 (9th edn).

Venice. 1884.

Cities of Central Italy. 2 vols 1884.

Cities of Northern Italy. 2 vols 1884.

Sketches in Holland and Scandinavia. 1885.

Studies in Russia. 1885.

Days near Paris. 1887.

Paris. 1887.

North eastern France. 1890.

South eastern France. 1890.

South western France. 1890.

The story of two noble lives: Charlotte Countess Canning and Louisa Marchioness of Waterford. 3 vols 1893.

The life and letters of Maria Edgeworth. 2 vols 1894.

Sussex. 1894.

Biographical sketches. 1895.

The Gurneys of Earlham. 2 vols 1895.

North western France. 1895.

The story of my life. 6 vols 1896–1900. Abridged below.

The Rivieras. 1896.

Shropshire. 1898.

The years with mother. Ed M. Barnes 1952. Abridged from vols 1–3 of Story of my life, above.

In my solitary life. Ed M. Barnes 1953. Abridged from vols 4–6 of The story of my life, above.

FREDERIC HARRISON
1831–1923

Order and progress. 2 pts 1875. Political essays.

The present and the future. 1880.

The choice of books and other literary pieces. 1886.

Oliver Cromwell. 1888.

Annals of an old manor house, Sutton Place, Guildford. 1893, 1899 (abridged).

The meaning of history and other historical pieces. 1894.

Studies in early Victorian literature. 1895.

William the Silent. 1897.

Tennyson, Ruskin, Mill and other literary estimates. 1899.

Byzantine history in the early Middle Ages. 1900.

George Washington and other American addresses. 1901.

John Ruskin. 1902 (EML).

Theophano: the crusade of the tenth century: a romantic monograph. 1904.

Chatham. 1905.

Memories and thoughts: men-books-cities-art. 1906.

Nicephorus: a tragedy of new Rome. 1906. A verse drama on the same subject as Theophano, above.

Carlyle and the London Library: account of its foundation. 1907.

The philosophy of common sense. 1907.

The creed of a layman: apologia pro fide mea. 1907.

National and social problems. 1908.

Realities and ideals social, political, literary and artistic. 1908.

My alpine jubilee 1851–1907. 1908.

Autobiographic memoirs. 2 vols 1911.

Among my books: centenaries, reviews, memoirs. 1912.

The positive evolution of religion. 1913.

The German peril. [1915].

On society. 1918.

Obiter scripta 1918. 1919.

On jurisprudence and the conflict of laws. 1919.

Novissima verba: last words 1920. 1921.

De senectute: more last words. 1923.

See also col 1122, below.

WILLIAM PATON KER
1855–1923

Bibliographies

Pafford, J. H. P. Ker 1855–1923: a bibliography. 1950.

§ 1

Epic and romance: essays on mediaeval literature. 1897, 1908.
The dark ages. Edinburgh 1904; ed B. I. Evans 1955.
Essays on mediaeval literature. 1905.
English literature: mediaeval. [1912] (Home Univ Lib).
The art of poetry: seven lectures 1920–2. Oxford 1923.
Collected essays. Ed C. Whibley 2 vols 1925.
Form and style in poetry: lectures and notes. Ed R. W. Chambers 1928.
On modern literature: lectures and addresses. Ed T. Spencer and J. R. Sutherland, Oxford 1955.
Ker also edited Dryden's essays, Berners's Froissart, and some other English and French classics.

§ 2

Chambers, R. W. Ker. Proc Br Acad 11 1925.
—— Philologists at University College London. In his Man's unconquerable mind, 1939.
Evans, B. I. Ker as a critic of literature. Glasgow 1955.

ANDREW LANG

1844–1912

§ 1

Ballads and lyrics of old France; with other poems. 1872, 1907.
Mythology and fairy tales. Fortnightly Rev May 1873. 'The first full refutation of Max Müller's mythological system'.
Aristotle's politics. 1877. With W. E. Bolland.
The Odyssey of Homer, book vi. 1877 (priv ptd).
Specimens of a translation of Theocritus. 1879 (priv ptd).
The Odyssey of Homer, done into English prose by S. H. Butcher and Lang. 1879, 1887, 1924, 1930.
Oxford: brief historical and descriptive notes. 1880, 1890, 1906, 1916.
Theocritus, Bion and Moschus rendered into English prose, with an introductory essay. 1880, 1889, 1922.
xxii ballades in blue china. 1880.
xxii and x: xxxii ballades in blue china. 1881, 1888 (with addns).
The library. 1881, 1892.
Notes on a collection of pictures by J. E. Millais. 1881.
The black thief: a play. 1882 (priv ptd).
Helen of Troy. 1882, 1883, 1913.
The Iliad of Homer, done into English prose by Lang, Walter Leaf and Ernest Myers. 1883, 1914.
Custom and myth. 1884, 1885 (rev), 1893, 1898, 1904.
Much darker days, by 'A huge longway'. 1884, 1885 (rev). Parodies Hugh Conway, Dark days.
The princess Nobody: a tale of fairy land. [1884].
'That very Mab'. 1885 (anon). With May Kendall.
Rhymes à la mode. 1885.
The politics of Aristotle: introductory essays. 1886.
In the wrong paradise, and other stories. 1886.
The mark of Cain. Bristol 1886.
Letters to dead authors. 1886, 1893 (with addns), 1906 (with addns).
Books and bookmen. 1886, New York 1886, London 1892, 1912.
Myth, ritual and religion. 2 vols 1887, 1899 (rev).
Aucassin and Nicolete. 1887, 1896, 1898, 1902, 1904, 1905.
Cupid and Psyche. 1887.
Beauty and the beast. 1887.
He, by the authors of It, King Solomon's wives and Bess. 1887. With W. H. Pollock.
Grass of Parnassus: rhymes old and new. 1888, 1892 (with addns).
The gold of Fairnilee. Bristol 1888.

Pictures at play or dialogues of the galleries: by two art-critics. 1888. With W. E. Henley.
Prince Prigio. Bristol 1889.
Letters on literature. 1889, 1892.
Lost leaders. 1889.
Old friends: essays in epistolary parody. 1890, 1892.
The world's desire. 1890, 1894, [1907], 1916. With Sir H. Rider Haggard.
How to fail in literature: a lecture. 1890.
Life, letters and diaries of Sir Stafford Northcote, first Earl of Iddesleigh. 2 vols Edinburgh 1890.
Angling sketches. 1891, 1895.
Essays in little. 1891.
Prince Ricardo of Pantouflia. Bristol [1893], 1932 (with Prince Prigio as Chronicles of Pantouflia).
Kirk's secret commonwealth. 1893.
The tercentenary of Izaak Walton. 1893 (priv ptd).
Homer and the epic. 1893.
St Andrews. 1893; ed G. H. Bushnell, St Andrews 1951.
Ban and arrière ban: a rally of fugitive rhymes. 1894.
Robert F. Murray: his poems; with a memoir by Lang. 1894.
Cock Lane and common-sense. 1894, 1896.
The voices of Jeanne d'Arc. 1895 (priv ptd).
My own fairy book. Bristol 1895. Collected fairy tales.
A monk of Fife. 1896.
The life and letters of J. G. Lockhart. 2 vols 1897.
Modern mythology: a reply to Max Müller. 1897.
The book of dreams and ghosts. 1897, 1899.
Pickle the spy: or the incognito of Prince Charles. 1897.
The making of religion. 1898, 1900.
The companions of Pickle. 1898.
Parson Kelly. New York 1899, London 1900. With A.E.W. Mason.
The Homeric hymns: a new prose translation and essays. 1899.
Prince Charles Edward. 1900.
A history of Scotland from the Roman occupation. 4 vols Edinburgh 1900–7.
Notes and names in books. Chicago 1900 (priv ptd).
The mystery of Mary Stuart. 1901, 1901, 1904 (rev).
Alfred Tennyson. Edinburgh 1901.
Magic and religion. 1901.
Adventures among books. Cleveland 1901 (priv ptd).
The young Ruthven. 1902 (priv ptd ballad).
The disentanglers. 1902.
James VI and the Gowrie mystery. 1902.
Hugo, Victor, Notre-Dame of Paris, with a critical introduction. 1902, 1924.
Social origins, by Lang; Primal Law, by J. J. Atkinson. 1903.
The valet's tragedy, and other studies. 1903.
The story of the golden fleece. 1903.
Historical mysteries. 1904, [1911].
New collected rhymes. 1905.
The puzzle of Dickens's last plot. 1905.
The secret of the totem. 1905.
Adventures among books. 1905.
The Clyde mystery: a study in forgeries and folklore. Glasgow 1905.
John Knox and the reformation. 1905.
Homer and his age. 1906.
Sir Walter Scott. 1906.
The story of Joan of Arc. [1906].
Portraits and jewels of Mary Stuart. 1906.
Tales of a fairy court. [1907].
The origins of religion and other essays. 1908.
The maid of France: the life and death of Jeanne d'Arc. 1908, 1913, 1922. A reply to Anatole France, Vie de Jeanne d'Arc, 1908.
The origin of terms of human relationship. [1909].
Sir George Mackenzie, King's Advocate: his life and times. 1909.
The world of Homer. 1910.
Sir Walter Scott and the Border minstrelsy. 1910.

Method in the study of totemism. Glasgow 1911.
A short history of Scotland. Edinburgh 1911.
Ode on a distant memory of Jane Eyre. [1912].
Shakespeare, Bacon and the great unknown. 1912.
History of English literature from Beowulf to Swinburne. 1912, 1912 (rev), 1913.
The Annesley case. 1912.
Highways and byways in the Border. 1913. With J. Lang.
Bibliomania. 1914 (priv ptd).
The new Pygmalion. 1962 (priv ptd). Poems.

Lang edited and introduced many English and other classics. He also pbd a series of fairy books consisting of re-tellings of traditional tales. He was one of the founders of the Soc for Psychical Research.

§2

Gordon, G. S. Obituary. TLS 5 Sept 1912 (anon); rptd in his Lives of authors, 1950.
—— Lang: Lang lecture. Oxford 1928; rptd in his Discipline of letters, Oxford 1949.
Beerbohm, M. Two glimpses of Lang. Life & Letters June 1929.
Buchan, J. Lang and the Border: Lang lecture. Oxford 1933.
Grierson, H. J. C. Lang, Lockhart and biography: Lang lecture. Oxford 1935.
Green, R. L. Lang: a critical biography with a short-title bibliography of the works of Lang. Leicester 1946.
—— Lang. 1962.
Tolkien, J. R. R. On fairy-stories. In Essays presented to Charles Williams, Oxford 1947. Lang lecture for 1938, expanded; rptd in his Tree and leaf, 1964.
Murray, G. Lang the poet. Oxford 1948. Lang lecture.
Webster, A. B. (ed). Concerning Lang: being the Lang lectures delivered before the University of St Andrews 1927–37. Oxford 1949.

'VERNON LEE', VIOLET PAGET
1856–1935

Collections
A Vernon Lee anthology. Ed I. C. Willis 1929.

§1

Studies of the eighteenth century in Italy. 1880.
Tuscan fairy tales. [1880]. Ed Vernon Lee.
Belcaro: being essays on sundry aesthetical questions. [1883].
The prince of the hundred soups: a puppet-show in narrative, edited [i.e. written] with an introduction by Vernon Lee. 1883. Illustr S. Birch.
Ottilie: an eighteenth-century idyl. 1883.
Miss Brown: a novel. 3 vols 1884.
The Countess of Albany. 1884.
Euphorion: being studies of the antique and the mediaeval in the Renaissance. 2 vols 1884, 1 vol 1885 (rev).
Baldwin: being dialogues on views and aspirations. 1886.
A phantom lover: a fantastic story. Edinburgh 1886.
Juvenilia: being a second series of essays on sundry aesthetical questions. 2 vols 1887.
Hauntings: fantastic stories. 1890.
Vanitas: polite stories. 1892, 1911 (adds A frivolous conversion).
Althea: a second book of dialogues on aspirations and duties. 1894.
Renaissance fancies and studies: being a sequel to Euphorion. 1895.
Limbo and other essays. 1897, 1908 (adds Ariadne in Mantua).
Genius loci: notes on places. 1899.

Ariadne in Mantua: a romance in five acts. Oxford 1903.
Penelope Brandling: a tale of the Welsh coast in the eighteenth century. 1903.
Hortus vitae: essays on the gardening of life. 1904.
Pope Jacynth and other fantastic tales. 1904, 1956.
The enchanted woods and other essays on the genius of places. 1905.
The spirit of Rome: leaves from a diary. 1906.
Sister Benvenuta and the Christ child: an eighteenth century legend. 1906.
The sentimental traveller: notes on places. 1908.
Gospels of anarchy and other contemporary studies. 1908.
Laurus nobilis: chapters on art and life. 1909.
Vital lies: studies of some varieties of recent obscurantism. 2 vols 1912.
Beauty and ugliness, and other studies in psychological aesthetics. 1912. With C. A. Thomson.
The beautiful: an introduction to psychological aesthetics. 1913.
The tower of the mirrors and other essays on the spirit of places. 1914.
Louis Norbert: a two-fold romance. 1914.
The ballet of the nations: a present-day morality. 1915.
Satan the waster: a philosophic war trilogy. 1920.
The handling of words and other studies in literary psychology. 1923.
The golden keys and other essays on the genius loci. 1925.
Proteus: or the future of intelligence. 1925.
The poet's eye. 1926.
For Maurice: five unlikely stories. 1927.
Music and its lovers: an empirical study of emotion and imaginative responses to music. [Ed I. C. Willis] 1932.
The snake lady and other stories. [Ed H. Gregory], New York 1954.
Supernatural tales: excursions into fantasy. [Ed I. C. Willis] 1955.
Vernon Lee's letters. [Ed I. C. Willis] 1937.

§2

Gunn, P. Vernon Lee, Violet Paget 1856–1935. 1964.

JOHN MORLEY, VISCOUNT MORLEY
1838–1923

§1

Modern characteristics. 1865. Anon; essays.
Studies in conduct. 1867. Anon; essays.
Edmund Burke: a historical study. 1867.
Critical miscellanies. 2 sers 1871–7; 3 vols 1886 (with addns and omissions); ser 4, 1908.
Voltaire. 1872, 1872 (rev).
Rousseau. 2 vols 1873.
The struggle for national education. 1873.
On compromise. 1874, 1886.
Diderot and the encyclopaedists. 2 vols 1878.
Edmund Burke. 1879, 1923 (rev) (EML).
The life of Richard Cobden. 2 vols 1881, 1 vol 1882 (abridged).
Emerson: an essay. New York 1884.
Walpole. 1889.
Studies in literature. 1890.
Machiavelli: the Romanes lecture. 1897.
Oliver Cromwell. 1900.
The life of William Ewart Gladstone. 3 vols 1903, 1 vol 1927 (abridged, with preface by C. F. G. Masterman).
Free trade v protection. 1904.
Literary essays. 1906.
Speeches on Indian affairs: with an appreciation. Madras 1908, 1917 (rev and enlarged).

Indian speeches 1907–8. 1909.
Science and literature. [Oxford] 1911 (priv ptd).
Notes on politics and history: a university address. 1913.
Recollections. 2 vols 1917.
Memorandum on resignation—August 1914; with an introduction by F. W. Hirst. 1928.
Morley also pbd several lectures, tracts and single speeches. He was general editor of the original EML ser and of Fortnightly Rev 1867–82.

§2

Hirst, F. W. Early life and letters of Morley. 2 vols 1927.
—— Richard Cobden and Morley. 1941.
Everett, E. M. The party of humanity: the Fortnightly Review and its contributors 1865–74. Chapel Hill 1939.
Scott, J. W. R. The life and death of a newspaper: Morley, W. T. Stead and other editors of the Pall Mall Gazette. 1952.
Das, M. N. India under Morley and Minto. [1964].

SIR WALTER ALEXANDER RALEIGH
1861–1922

The English novel: being a short sketch of its history from the earliest times to the appearance of Waverley. 1891.
Robert Louis Stevenson. 1895.
Style. 1897.
Milton. 1900.
Wordsworth. 1903.
The English voyages of the sixteenth century. In Hakluyt's Voyages vol 12, 1905.
Shakespeare. 1907, 1950 (EML).
Six essays on Johnson. Oxford 1910.
Romance: two lectures. Princeton 1916.
Shakespeare's England: an account of the life and manners of his age. 2 vols Oxford 1916. Planned by Raleigh, and the section The age of Elizabeth written by him.
England and the war: being sundry addresses delivered during the war. 1918.
The war in the air: being the story of the part played in the Great War by the Royal Air Force. Vol 1 Oxford 1922.
Laughter from a cloud. 1923. Humorous sketches and poems.
Some authors: a collection of literary essays 1896–1916. 1923.
On writing and writers: being extracts from his note-books, selected and edited by George Gordon. 1926.
The letters of Raleigh 1789–1922. Ed Lady Raleigh 2 vols 1926, 1928 (enlarged).
A selection from the letters of Raleigh 1880–1922. Ed Lady Raleigh 1928. Including some letters not previously pbd.

JOHN MACKINNON ROBERTSON
1856–1933

Walt Whitman, poet and democrat. Edinburgh 1884.
The religion of Shakespeare: two discourses. [1887].
Essays towards a critical method. 1889.
Modern humanists. 1891.
Buckle and his critics: a study in sociology. 1895.
The Saxon and the Celt: a study in sociology. 1897.
New essays towards a critical method. 1897.
Montaigne and Shakespeare. 1897, 1909 (adds 2 essays on the Originality and Learning of Shakespeare).
The dynamics of religion: an essay in English culture history. 1897, 1926 (rev). Originally pbd under pseudonym of M. W. Wiseman.

Miscellanies. 1898.
Patriotism and empire. 1899.
A short history of free thought, ancient and modern. 1899, 2 vols 1906 (rewritten and greatly enlarged), 1915 (rev and expanded).
Christianity and mythology. 1900, 1910 (expanded).
Studies in religious fallacy. 1900.
Letters on reasoning. 1902, 1905 (rev), [1935] (abridged).
A short history of Christianity. 1902, 1913 (rev), 1931 (condensed).
Criticisms. 2 vols 1902–3.
Browning and Tennyson as teachers: two studies. 1903.
Essays in ethics. 1903.
Pagan christs: studies in comparative hierology. 1903, 1911 (rev and expanded).
Studies in practical politics. 1903.
Essays in sociology. 2 vols 1904.
What to read: suggestions for the better utilisation of public libraries. 1904.
Rudyard Kipling: a criticism. Madras [1905].
Did Shakespeare write Titus Andronicus? a study in Elizabethan literature. 1905, 1924 (rev and expanded as Introduction to the study of the Shakespeare canon).
Pioneer humanists. 1907.
The evolution of states: an introduction to English politics. 1912.
The meaning of Liberalism. 1912, 1925 (rev and enlarged).
Rationalism. 1912, 1945 (abridged).
The Baconian heresy: a confutation. 1913.
Elizabethan literature. 1914.
The historical Jesus: a survey of positions. 1916.
The Jesus problem: a re-statement of the myth theory. 1917.
The problem of the Merry wives of Windsor. [1918].
The economics of progress. 1918.
Bolingbroke and Walpole. 1919.
The problem of Hamlet. 1919.
Free trade. 1919.
A short history of morals. 1920.
Charles Bradlaugh. 1920. Based on the chs contributed to H. B. Bonner, Memoir of her father, 2 vols 1894.
Voltaire. 1922.
The Shakespeare canon. 5 vols 1922–32.
Croce as Shakespearean critic. 1922.
Hamlet once more. 1923.
Explorations. 1923.
Ernest Renan. 1924.
Gibbon. 1925.
Mr Shaw and the Maid. [1925].
Spoken essays. 1925.
The problems of the Shakespeare sonnets. 1926.
Modern humanists reconsidered. 1927.
Jesus and Judas: a textual and historical investigation. 1927.
A history of free thought in the nineteenth century. 1929, 2 vols 1936 (rev).
The genuine in Shakespeare: a conspectus. 1930.
Literary detection: a symposium on Macbeth. 1931.
The state of Shakespeare study: a critical conspectus. 1931.
Marlowe: a conspectus. 1931.
Electoral justice: a survey of the theory and practice of electoral representation. [1931].

GEORGE EDWARD BATEMAN SAINTSBURY
1845–1933

A primer of French literature. Oxford 1880, 1884 (rev), 1891 (rev), 1896 (rev), 1912 (rev), 1925 (with suppl).
Dryden. 1881 (EML).
A short history of French literature. Oxford 1882, 1897 (rev).

A history of Elizabethan literature. 1887.
Essays in English literature 1780–1860. 2 sers 1890–5.
Essays on French novelists. 1891.
The Earl of Derby. 1892.
Miscellaneous essays. 1892.
Corrected impressions. 1895.
A history of nineteenth-century literature 1780–1895. 1896.
The flourishing of romance and the rise of allegory. Edinburgh 1897.
Sir Walter Scott. [1897].
A short history of English literature. 1898.
Matthew Arnold. 1899.
The history of criticism and literary taste in Europe. 3 vols Edinburgh 1900–4.
The earlier Renaissance. Edinburgh 1901.
Loci critici. Boston 1903. An anthology of criticism.
Minor poets of the Caroline period. 3 vols Oxford 1905–21.
A history of English prosody from the twelfth century to the present day. 3 vols 1906–10.
The later nineteenth century. Edinburgh 1907.
A historical manual of English prosody. 1910.
A history of English criticism: being the English chapters of A history of criticism and literary taste in Europe, revised, adapted and supplemented. Edinburgh 1911, 1949.
A history of English prose rhythm. 1912.
The English novel. 1913.
The peace of the Augustans. 1916, Oxford 1946 (WC).
A history of the French novel to the close of the nineteenth century. 2 vols 1917–9.
Notes on a cellar-book. 1920.
A letter book. 1922.
A scrap book. 1922.
A second scrap book. 1923.
The collected essays and papers 1875–1920. 4 vols 1923–4.
A last scrap book. 1924.
A consideration of Thackeray. 1931.
Prefaces and essays. Ed O. Elton 1933.
Shakespeare. Cambridge 1934. Rptd from CHEL vol 5 1910.
Muir, A. et al (ed). Saintsbury: the memorial volume— a new collection of his essays and papers: memoir by A. B. Webster; personal portraits by O. Elton, H. J. C. Grierson, J. W. Oliver and J. Purves. 1945.
A last vintage: essays and papers. 1950.

THEODORE WATTS-DUNTON, earlier WATTS
1832–1914

The coming of love and other poems. 1898, 1899 (includes Rhona Boswell's story in title and adds long prefatory note), 1906 (rev and enlarged).
Aylwin: a novel. 1899, [1900] (adds further introd), 1901 (with 2 appendixes).
Charlotte Brontë. Introd to vol 6 of Novels and poems of Charlotte, Emily and Anne Brontë, 1901 (WC).
The Rhodes memorial at Oxford: the work of Cecil Rhodes—a sonnet sequence. [1907].
Rossetti and Charles Wells: a reminiscence of Kelmscott Manor. In Joseph and his brethren by Charles Wells, Oxford 1908 (WC).
Vesprie towers: a novel. 1916.
Old familiar faces. 1916.
Poetry and the renascence of wonder: with a preface by Thomas Hake. 1916.

CHARLES WHIBLEY
1859–1930

The cathedrals of England and Wales. 1888.
A book of scoundrels. 1897.
Studies in frankness. 1898.
The pageantry of life. 1900. Essays.
Musings without method: a record of 1900–1 by Annalist. 1902.
William Makepeace Thackeray. 1903.
Literary portraits. 1904.
William Pitt. 1906.
American sketches. 1908.
The letters of an Englishman. 2 vols 1911–12.
Essays in biography. 1913.
Political portraits. 2 sers 1917–23.
Literary studies. 1919.
Lord John Manners and his friends. 2 vols 1925.
Whibley also edited or introduced some 30 English, French and Latin classics. He was general editor of Tudor translations ser 2 1924–30.

VII. HISTORY

General Studies

Gooch, G. P. History and historians in the nineteenth century. 1913, 1952 (rev, with introd).
Butterfield, H. The Whig interpretation of history. 1931.
—— Man on his past: the study of the history of historical scholarship. Cambridge 1955.
Thompson, J. W. and B. J. Holm. A history of historical writing. 2 vols New York 1942.
Neff, E. E. The poetry of history: the contribution of literature and literary scholarship to the writing of history since Voltaire. New York 1947.
Wedgwood, C. V. Literature and the historian. 1956.

HENRY HALLAM
1777–1859

§ I

View of the state of Europe during the Middle Ages. 2 vols 1818, 3 vols 1819, 4 vols Philadelphia 1821, 2 vols Paris 1835, 3 vols 1837 (7th edn), 2 vols Paris 1840, London 1846 (9th edn), 3 vols 1853, 1855; ed W. Smith, New York 1871, 1880; ed G. L. Burr 2 vols New York 1899; ed A. R. Marsh, New York 1900 (as History of Europe during the Middle Ages).
The constitutional history of England from the accession of Henry VII to the death of George I. 2 vols 1827, 3 vols 1829, Boston 1829, London 1832, 2 vols 1846 (5th edn), 3 vols 1854 (7th edn), 1855, 1866 (11th edn);

ed W. Smith, New York 1896; ed J. H. Morgan 3 vols 1912, 1930 (EL).

Survey of the principal repositories of the public records: extracted from the proceedings of the commissioners on the public records. 1833. With R. H. Inglis.

Memoir of A. H. Hallam. In Remains in verse and prose of A. H. Hallam, 1834 (priv ptd), 1862, Boston 1863.

Introduction to the literature of Europe in the fifteenth, sixteenth and seventeenth centuries. 4 vols 1837–9, Paris 1839, 2 vols New York 1841, 3 vols 1854.

§2

Southey, R. Hallam's Europe during the Middle Ages. Quart Rev 30 1818; rptd in his Essays moral and political, 1832.

Macaulay, T. B. Hallam's Constitutional history. Edinburgh Rev 48 1828; rptd in his Critical and historical essays, 1843.

Bond, W. H. Henry Hallam, the Times newspaper and Halliwell case. Library 5th ser 18 1963.

HENRY HART MILMAN
1791–1868

Fazio: a tragedy. Oxford 1815, 1816, London 1818 (4 edns), 1821 (with the Belvidere Apollo etc).

Samor: lord of the bright city. 1818, 1818, New York 1818.

The fall of Jerusalem: a dramatic poem. 1820, 1820, New York 1820, London 1821, 1822, 1853.

The martyr of Antioch: a dramatic poem. 1822.

Belshazzar: a dramatic poem. 1822, Boston 1822.

Anne Boleyn: a dramatic poem. 1826.

The character and conduct of the apostles. Oxford 1827.

The history of the Jews. 3 vols 1829 (anon), 1830, New York 1832, 1841, London 1843, 1863, New York 1864, London 1866 (4th edn); ed A. P. Hayes, Philadelphia 1871; 3 vols 1878, 1880, 1892; ed G. H. Jones 2 vols 1909, 1923, 1930 (EL).

Poetical works of Milman, Bowles, Wilson and Barry Cornwall. Paris 1829.

Nala and Damayanti and other poems, translated from the Sanscrit. Oxford 1835, 1860, 1914; Nala (only) rev M. Williams, Oxford 1879.

The history of the decline and fall of the Roman empire, by Edward Gibbon. 12 vols 1838–9. Ed Milman.

The life of Edward Gibbon with selections from his correspondence. 1839, 1840. Ed Milman.

The history of Christianity from the birth of Christ to the abolition of paganism in the Roman Empire. 3 vols 1840, New York 1841, London 1863 (rev).

History of Latin Christianity, including that of the Popes to Nicolas V. 6 vols 1854–5, 1857, 9 vols 1864.

Life of Thomas à Becket. New York 1860.

Memoir of Lord Macaulay. 1862, 1862, 1862 (in Macaulay's History of England vol 8).

The Agamemnon of Aeschylus and the Bacchanals of Euripides. 1865; Bacchanals (only), 1888, rptd in The plays of Euripides, ed V. R. Reynolds 2 vols 1906, 1911, 1934 (EL). Tr Milman.

Annals of St Paul's Cathedral. Ed A. Milman 1868, 1869.

Savonarola, Erasmus and other essays reprinted from the Quarterly Review. Ed A. Milman 1870.

GEORGE GROTE
1794–1871

§1

Statement of the question of parliamentary reform. 1821.

Analysis of the influence of natural religion on the temporal happiness of mankind, by Philip Beauchamp. 1822, 1875. Based on notes by Jeremy Bentham.

Institutions of ancient Greece. Westminster Rev 5 1826. A critique of W. Mitford, History of Greece.

Essentials of parliamentary reform. 1831, 1873 (in Minor works).

A history of Greece. 12 vols 1845–56, 1854–7 (4th edn), 8 vols 1862, 12 vols 1869; ed A. D. Lindsay 12 vols 1906, 1934 (EL).

Seven letters on the recent politics of Switzerland. 1847, 1876 (with Letter to A. de Tocqueville).

Plato's doctrine respecting the rotation of the earth and Aristotle's comment upon that doctrine. 1860, 1873 (in Minor works).

Plato and the other companions of Sokrates. 3 vols 1865, 1867, 1874, 4 vols 1885, 1888.

Review of the work of Mr J. S. Mill entitled Examination of Sir William Hamilton's philosophy. 1868 (for 1867), 1873 (in Minor works).

Aristotle. Ed A. Bain and G. C. Robertson 2 vols 1872, 1880 (for 1879).

Poems 1815–23. [1872] (priv ptd).

The minor works; with remarks by A. Bain. 1873.

Posthumous papers. 1874 (priv ptd).

Fragments on ethical subjects. Ed A. Bain 1876.

§2

Mill, J. S. Grote's History of Greece. Spectator 4 April 1846, 5 June 1847, 3 March 1849.

—— Grote's History of Greece vols 1–2. Edinburgh Rev 84 1846.

—— Grote's History of Greece vols 9–11. Edinburgh Rev 98 1853; rptd in his Dissertations and discussions, 1868.

Grote, H. The personal life of Grote. 1873.

Stephen, L. In his English Utilitarians, 1900.

Momigliano, A. Grote and the study of Greek history. 1952.

Clarke, M. L. Grote: a biography. 1962.

THOMAS ARNOLD
1795–1842

Thirteen letters on our social condition. 1822.

Sermons. 3 vols 1829–34; rev J. A. Forster 6 vols 1878.

Principles of Church reform. 1833 (3 edns), 1833 (4th edn with postscript); ed A. P. Stanley 1845 (in Miscellaneous works, below); ed M. J. Jackson and J. Rogan 1962.

Introductory lectures on modern history; with the inaugural lecture. Oxford 1842, 1843, New York 1845, London 1849 (4th edn).

The Christian life: its hopes, its fears and its close. Ed M. Arnold 1842, 1845 (3rd edn); ed J. A. Forster 1878 (as vol 5 of Sermons).

Fragment on the Church. 1844.

Sermons chiefly on the interpretation of scripture. Ed M. Arnold 1845; ed J. A. Forster 1878 (as vol 6 of Sermons).

Sermons preached in the chapel of Rugby School; with an address before confirmation. 1845, New York 1846; ed J. A. Forster 1878 (as vol 2 of Sermons).

History of the later Roman commonwealth. 2 vols 1845, Miscellaneous works. Ed A. P. Stanley 1845, New York 1845 (with 9 essays added), London 1858 (2nd edn).

Arnold's travelling journals, with extracts from the Life and letters. Ed A. P. Stanley 1852.

THOMAS BABINGTON MACAULAY
1st BARON MACAULAY
1800–59

The mss of the diary etc are in the library of Trinity College Cambridge, with annotated edns of the classics and the corrected proofs of the Life of Pitt.

Collections

Selections from Macaulay's essays and speeches. 2 vols 1856.
The miscellaneous writings of Lord Macaulay. Ed T. F. Ellis 2 vols 1860, 1 vol 1865, 1871 (with Speeches), 4 vols 1880 (with Poems), 1 vol 1910, 1958 (EL) (with Lays).
Prose and poetry. Ed G. M. Young 1953 (Reynard Lib).

§ 1

Ivry. Knight's Quart Mag 1 1823; rptd in Lays, below.
A speech in the House of Commons, March 2 1831, on a bill to amend the representation of the people in England and Wales. 1831.
The speech of T. B. Macaulay on the second reading of the third Reform Bill, 16 December 1831. 1831.
A speech on the second reading of the East India Bill, 10 July 1833. 1833.
The Armada. Friendship's Offering 1833; rptd in Lays, below.
A Penal Code prepared by the Indian Law Commissioners and published by command of the Governor General of India in Council. Calcutta 1837.
Critical and miscellaneous essays. 3 vols Boston and Philadelphia 1840–1, 5 vols Philadelphia 1841–4. Unauthorized.
Lays of ancient Rome. 1842, 1846 (7th edn), 1847, 1848 (with Ivry and The Armada); ed G. M. Trevelyan 1928.
Critical and historical essays contributed to the Edinburgh Review. 3 vols 1843, New York 1843, London 1848, 1849 (containing all the essays Macaulay wished to preserve); ed A. J. Grieve 2 vols 1907 (EL), 2 vols Oxford 1913; ed H. Trevor-Roper 1965.
Speech in the House of Commons, February 26 1845, on the proposed duties on sugar. Edinburgh 1845.
Speech in the House of Commons, July 9 1845, on the Bill for the abolition of Scottish university tests. Edinburgh 1845; Government plan of education: speech in the House of Commons, April 19 1847, [1847].
The history of England from the accession of James II. Vols 1–2, 1849, Philadelphia 1849, New York 1850; vols 3–4, 1855; vol 5 ed Lady Trevelyan 1861; 10 vols Leipzig 1849–61; 8 vols 1858–62 (with memoir by H. H. Milman); ed S. A. Allibone 5 vols Philadelphia 1875; ed H. D. Sedgwick 10 vols Boston 1899; ed D. Jerrold 3 vols 1906, 1934 (EL); ed C. H. Firth 6 vols 1913–15; ed T. F. Henderson 5 vols Oxford 1931 (WC).
Inaugural address delivered on his installation as Lord Rector of the University of Glasgow. Glasgow 1849, Edinburgh 1849.
Speeches, parliamentary and miscellaneous. 2 vols 1853, 2 vols New York 1853. Unauthorized.
Speeches corrected by himself. 1854, New York 1854, London 1866; ed W. E. Gladstone 1909, 1924 (EL); ed G. M. Young, Oxford 1935 (WC).
The Indian Civil Service. 1855. A report by Macaulay, Ashburton, Jowett et al.
The Indian education minutes of Lord Macaulay. Ed H. Woodrow, Calcutta 1862.
Hymn by Lord Macaulay: an effort of his early childhood. Ed L. Horton-Smith, Cambridge 1902.
Marginal notes. Ed G. O. Trevelyan 1907.
Essay and speech on Jewish disabilities. Ed I. Abrahams and S. Levy, Edinburgh 1910, 1920.

Lord Macaulay's legislative minutes. Ed C. D. Dharker, Madras 1946.
Letters. Ed T. Pinney, 6 vols Cambridge 1974–81.

§ 2

Bagehot, W. Macaulay. Nat Rev 2 1856; rptd in his Literary studies, ed R. H. Hutton 1879.
Paget, J. The new examen: or an inquiry into the evidence relating to certain passages in Macaulay's history. Edinburgh 1861, 1934; rptd in his Paradoxes and puzzles, Edinburgh 1874.
Trevelyan, G. O. The life and letters of Macaulay. 2 vols 1876, New York 1876 (with appendix, Macaulay on American institutions); ed G. M. Trevelyan 2 vols Oxford 1932 (WC); 1 vol 1959, 2 vols Oxford 1961.
Morley, J. Macaulay. Fortnightly Rev April 1876; rptd in his Critical miscellanies, 1877.
Froude, J. A. Macaulay. Fraser's Mag June 1876.
Gladstone, W. E. Macaulay. Quart Rev 142 1876; rptd in his Gleanings of past years, 1879.
Stephen, L. In his Hours in a library ser 3, 1879.
Davies, H. S. Macaulay's marginalia to Lucretius. In Lucretius, De rerum natura, tr R. C. Trevelyan, Cambridge 1937.
Young, G. M. In his Daylight and champaign, 1937; rptd in his Victorian essays, 1962.
Firth, C. H. A commentary on Macaulay's History of England. Ed G. Davies 1938, 1964.
Geyl, P. Macaulay in his essays. In his From Ranke to Toynbee, Northampton Mass 1952; rptd in his Debates with historians, New York 1955.
Plumb, J. H. Macaulay. UTQ 26 1956; rptd in his Men and places, 1963.
Trevor-Roper, H. R. Macaulay and the Glorious Revolution. In his Men and events, 1957.
Knowles, D. Macaulay 1800–59. Cambridge 1960.
Fraser, G. S. Macaulay's style as an essayist. REL 1 1960.
Clive, J. Macaulay's historical imagination. Ibid.
—— Macaulay: the shaping of the historian. 1973.
Munby, A. N. L. Macaulay's library. Glasgow 1966; rptd in his Essays and papers, 1977.

JAMES ANTHONY FROUDE
1818–94

§ 1

St Neot. In Lives of the English saints, 4 vols 1844–5; ed A. W. Hutton 6 vols 1900–1. Ser suggested by J. H. Newman.
Shadows of the clouds, by Zeta. 1847.
The nemesis of faith. 1848, 1849.
The book of Job. 1854.
Suggestions on the best means of teaching English history. In Oxford essays by members of the University, Oxford 1855.
History of England from the fall of Wolsey to the death of Elizabeth. 12 vols 1856–70 (vols 1–2 rev 1858; vols 1–4, 7–8 rev 1862–4), 2 vols New York 1867–8, 12 vols New York 1869–71, London 1870 (as History of England from the fall of Wolsey to the defeat of the Spanish Armada); ed W. L. Williams 10 vols 1909–12 (EL).
The Edinburgh Review and Mr Froude's History. Fraser's Mag Sept 1858.
The pilgrim: a dialogue on the life and actions of King Henry the eighth, by William Thomas. 1861. Ed Froude.
Short studies on great subjects. 2 vols 1867, New York 1868, London 1872; ed H. Belloc 1915 (EL); Oxford 1924 (WC); Second series, 1871, New York 1872; Third series, 1877, New York 1882; Fourth series, 1883, New York 1883. Collected 3 vols 1877 (with preface), New York 1878, 4 vols 1883.

Inaugural address delivered to the University of St Andrews 19 March 1869. 1869.

The cat's pilgrimage. Edinburgh 1870; ed O. Maurer, New Haven 1949.

Calvinism: an address delivered to the University of St Andrews 17 March 1871. 1871.

The English in Ireland in the eighteenth century. 3 vols 1872–4, New York 1873–4, London 1881.

The life and times of Thomas Becket. New York 1878.

Caesar: a sketch. 1879, New York 1879, London 1880, New York 1884, London 1894.

Science and theology ancient and modern. Toronto 1879, New York 1880 (in Theological unrest: discussions in science and religion).

Bunyan. 1880 (EML), New York 1880, London 1884.

Two lectures on South Africa delivered before the Philosophical Institute. Edinburgh 1880; ed M. Froude 1900.

Thomas Carlyle, Reminiscences. 2 vols 1881. Ed Froude.

Thomas Carlyle: a history of the first forty years of his life 1795–1835. 2 vols 1882, 1882.

Luther: a short biography. 1883, 1884, New York 1884.

Memorials of Jane Welsh Carlyle, prepared for publication by Thomas Carlyle. 3 vols 1883. Ed Froude.

Historical and other sketches. Ed D. H. Wheeler, New York 1883.

Thomas Carlyle: a history of his life in London 1834–81. 2 vols 1884, 1884, New York 1884, London 1890.

Oceana: or England and her colonies. 1886, 1887.

The Knights Templars. New York 1886.

The English in the West Indies: or the bow of Ulysses. 1888, 1900, New York 1900.

Liberty and property: an address to the Liberty and Property Defence. 1888.

The two chiefs of Dunboy: or an Irish romance of the last century. 1889, New York 1889.

Lord Beaconsfield. 1890, New York 1890, London 1905 (9th edn); 1906, 1931 (EL).

The divorce of Catherine of Aragon: being a supplement to the History of England. 1891, New York 1891.

The Spanish story of the Armada and other essays. 1892.

Life and letters of Erasmus. 1893, 1894, New York 1894.

Lectures on the Council of Trent. 1893, 1896.

English seamen in the sixteenth century. 1895, New York 1895, 1901; ed A. A. Froude 1923, 1925.

Selected essays. Ed H. G. Rawlinson 1900.

My relations with Carlyle; together with a letter from the late Sir James Stephen. Ed A. A. Froude and M. Froude 1903.

The dissolution of the monasteries and other essays. 1905.

A siding at a railway station: an allegory. 1905.

Letters of J. A. Froude. Ed R. M. Bennett, Jnl Rutgers Univ Lib 11–12 1947–8, 25–6 1961–2.

§2

[Freeman, E. A.] Saturday Rev 16–30 Jan 1864, 27 Oct, 3, 24 Nov, 1 Dec 1866, 22–9 Jan, 5–12 Feb 1870, 8, 29 Sept 1877. Attacks on Froude's History.

—— Mr Froude's Life and times of Thomas Becket. Contemporary Rev March–April, June 1878. Reply by Froude, A few words on Mr Freeman, Nineteenth Century April 1879. Rejoinder by Freeman, Last words on Mr Froude, Contemporary Rev May 1879.

Wilson, D. A. Mr Froude and Carlyle. 1898.

Stephen, L. In his Studies of a biographer, 1902.

Paul, H. The life of Froude. 1905.

Dunn, W. H. Froude and Carlyle: a study of the Froude–Carlyle controversy. New York 1930.

—— Froude: a biography. 2 vols Oxford 1961–3.

Strachey, L. One of the Victorians. Saturday Rev of Lit 6 Dec 1930; rptd in his Characters and commentaries, 1933.

HENRY THOMAS BUCKLE
1821–62

§1

History of civilization in England. 2 vols 1857–61, 1858–64, 3 vols 1903–4, Oxford 1931 (WC); ed J. M. Robertson 1904, 1925.

The influence of women on the progress of knowledge. Fraser's Mag April 1858.

Mill on liberty. Fraser's Mag May 1859.

A letter to a gentleman respecting Pooley's case. 1859.

Essays; with a biographical sketch of the author. Leipzig 1867, New York 1877.

Miscellaneous and posthumous works. Ed H. Taylor 3 vols 1872, 2 vols New York 1873; ed G. Allen 2 vols 1885 (abridged); ed J. M. Robertson 1904.

§2

[Pattison, M.] Buckle's History. Westminster Rev 68 1857; rptd in his Essays, ed H. Nettleship 1889.

Froude, J. A. The science of history. In his Short studies, 1867.

Stephen, L. An attempted philosophy of history. Fortnightly Rev May 1880.

Robertson, J. M. Buckle and his critics. 1895.

St Aubyn, G. A Victorian eminence: the life and works of Buckle. 1958.

SIR HENRY JAMES
SUMNER MAINE
1822–88

§1

Memoir of Henry Fitzmaurice Hallam. [1851], 1862 (in Remains in verse and prose of A. H. Hallam). With F. Lushington.

Roman law and legal education. 1856 (in Cambridge essays), 1876 (in Village-communities, 3rd edn).

Ancient law: its connection with the early history of society and its relation to modern ideas. 1861, New York 1864, 1885 (10th edn); ed T. W. Dwight, New York 1888; London 1894 (15th edn), 1897 (16th edn); ed F. Pollock 1906, 1907, 1930; ed J. H. Morgan 1917, 1930, 1960 (EL); ed C. K. Allen, Oxford 1931 (WC).

Village-communities in the east and west. 1871, 1876 (3rd edn with lectures, addresses, essays), 1895 (7th edn).

The early history of the property of married women: a lecture. [1873].

Lectures on the early history of institutions. 1875.

The effects of observation of India on modern European thought (Rede lecture 1875). 1875, 1876 (in Village-communities, 3rd edn).

The King in his relation to early civil justice. Proc Royal Inst 9 1882.

Dissertations on early law and custom. 1883, 1890.

Popular government: four essays. 1885.

India. In The reign of Queen Victoria, ed T. H. Ward 1887.

International law (Whewell lectures 1888). 1888.

Minutes 1862–9; with a note on Indian codification. Calcutta 1892.

§2

Mill, J. S. Mr Maine on village communities. Fortnightly Rev May 1871.

Morley, J. Maine on popular government. Fortnightly Rev Feb 1886; rptd in his Oracles on man and government, 1923.

Vinogradoff, P. The teaching of Maine. 1904.
Roach, J. Liberalism and the Victorian intelligentsia. Cambridge Historical Jnl 13 1957.

EDWARD AUGUSTUS FREEMAN
1823–92
§ I

Principles of church restoration. 1846.
Thoughts on the study of history with reference to the proposed changes in the public examinations. Oxford 1849.
A history of architecture. 1849.
Poems: legendary and historical. 1850. With G. W. Cox.
An essay on the origin and development of window tracery in England. Oxford 1851.
The preservation and restoration of ancient monuments. Oxford 1852.
Suggestions with regard to certain proposed changes in the University and colleges of Oxford. Oxford 1854. With F. H. Dickinson.
The history and conquests of the Saracens: six lectures. Oxford 1856, 1876, 1876.
Ancient Greece and mediaeval Italy. In Oxford essays by members of the University, Oxford 1857.
History of federal government: general introduction; history of the Greek federations. 1863; ed J. B. Bury 1893 (as History of federal government in Greece and Italy).
Froude's History of England. Saturday Rev 16–30 Jan 1864, 27 Oct, 3, 24 Nov, 1 Dec 1866, 22–9 Jan, 5–12 Feb 1870, 8, 29 Sept 1877. Anon.
The history of the Norman Conquest of England; its causes and its results. 6 vols Oxford 1867–79, vols 1–3 1870–5 (2nd edn), 6 vols New York 1873–80, vols 1–2 Oxford 1877 (3rd edn).
Old English history for children. 1869, 1881, 1892 (9th edn), 1911 (EL).
Historical essays. 1871, 1896 (5th edn); Historical essays: second series, 1873, 1880, 1889; Historical essays: third series, 1879; Historical essays: fourth series, 1892.
The growth of the English constitution from the earliest times. 1872, 1894, 1898.
General sketch of European history. 1872, 1873 (3rd edn).
The unity of history (Rede lecture 1872). 1872, 1873 (with Comparative politics, below).
The cathedral churches of the old foundation. In Essays on cathedrals, ed J. S. Howson 1872.
Comparative politics. 1873 (with The unity of history, above), 1896.
Disestablishment and disendowment: what are they? 1874, 1885.
History of Europe. 1876, 1877, 1884, New York 1884; ed F. J. C. Hearnshaw 1926.
Historical and architectural sketches, chiefly Italian. 1876.
The eastern question in its historical bearings: an address. Manchester 1876.
The Ottoman power in Europe. 1877, New York 1877.
The Turks in Europe. 1877, New York 1877.
Mr Froude's Life and times of Thomas Becket. Contemporary Rev March–April, June 1878. Reply by Froude, A few words on Mr Freeman, Nineteenth Century April 1879; rejoinder by Freeman, Last words on Mr Froude, Contemporary Rev May 1879.
The origin of the English nation. New York 1879.
How the study of history is let and hindered: an address.
A short history of the Norman Conquest of England. Oxford 1880, 1896, 1901.
Sketches from the subject and neighbour lands of Venice. 1881.
The historical geography of Europe. 2 vols 1881, 1882; ed J. B. Bury 2 vols 1903.
Lectures to American audiences. Philadelphia 1882.

The reign of William Rufus and the accession of Henry the first. 2 vols Oxford 1882.
Some impressions of the United States. 1883.
English towns and districts: addresses and sketches. 1883.
The office of the historical professor: inaugural lecture. 1884, 1886 (with The methods of historical study).
The methods of historical study. 1886.
The chief periods of European history: six lectures with an essay on Greek cities under Roman rule. 1886.
Greater Greece and greater Britain; George Washington the expander of England: two lectures. 1886.
Four Oxford lectures 1887: Fifty years of European history; Teutonic conquest in Gaul and Britain. 1888.
William the Conqueror. 1888, 1894; ed H. Ketcham, New York 1902.
Sketches from French travel. Leipzig 1891.
The history of Sicily from the earliest times. 4 vols Oxford 1891–4. Vol 4 ed A. J. Evans.
Sicily: Phoenician, Greek and Roman. 1892.
The physical and political bases of national unity. In Britannic federation, ed A. S. White 1892.
Studies of travel: Greece, Italy. 2 vols New York [1893].
Sketches of travel in Normandy and Maine. Ed W. H. Hutton 1897.
Western Europe in the fifth century: an aftermath. 1904.
Western Europe in the eighth century and onward: an aftermath. 1904.

§ 2

Green, J. R. Freeman's Norman Conquest. Saturday Rev 13, 27 April 1867, 15–29 Aug 1868, 3–10 Feb 1872; rptd in his Historical studies, 1903.
Stephens, W. R. W. The life and letters of Freeman. 2 vols 1895.
Harrison, F. The historical method of Freeman. Nineteenth Century Nov 1898; rptd in his Tennyson, Ruskin, Mill and other literary estimates, 1899.

SAMUEL RAWSON GARDINER
1829–1902

History of England from the accession of James I to the disgrace of Chief-Justice Coke 1603–16. 2 vols 1863.
Prince Charles and the Spanish marriage 1617–23. 2 vols 1869.
A history of England under the Duke of Buckingham and Charles I 1624–8. 2 vols 1875.
The personal government of Charles I: a history of England from the assassination of the Duke of Buckingham to the declaration of the judges on ship-money 1628–37. 2 vols 1877.
The fall of the monarchy of Charles I 1637–49 [–42]. 2 vols 1882.
History of England from the accession of James I to the outbreak of the Civil War 1603–42. 10 vols 1883–4, 1883–6, 1894–6, 1900–8. A collected edn of the 5 works listed above.
The Thirty Years' War. 1874, 1886 (7th edn).
The first two Stuarts and the Puritan revolution 1603–60. 1876, Boston 1876, New York 1886, London 1888 (8th edn), New York 1890, London 1902 (15th edn).
English history for students. 1881, New York 1881. With J. B. Mullinger.
Introduction to the study of English history. 1881, 1882, 1894, 1903. With J. B. Mullingar.
Outline of English history. 2 vols 1881, 1896, 1901, 1912; ed D. Salmon 1919, 1927.
Illustrated English history. 3 vols 1883, vol 1 1887 (5th edn); vol 3 1902 (continued to 1901), 1912 (continued to 1910).
Historical biographies. 1884, 1906.
An easy history of England. 1887–8.

The constitutional documents of the Puritan revolution 1628–60. Oxford 1889, 1899, 1906, 1958 (3rd edn rev). Ed Gardiner.

A student's history of England from the earliest times to 1885. 3 vols 1890–1, 1892, 1897, 1898, 1899; vol 3 (with continuations) 1902, 1907, 1910, 1920, 1922; ed A. H. Shearer, New York 1906, 1913, 1938, 1939 (as England).

The Tudor period. 1893.

The Stuart period. 1894.

History of the Commonwealth and Protectorate 1649–60. 3 vols 1894–1901, 4 vols 1894–1903. Unfinished at Gardiner's death; completed by C. H. Firth, The last years of the Protectorate, 2 vols 1909.

Cromwell's place in history (Ford lectures 1896). 1897.

What Gunpowder Plot was. 1897.

Oliver Cromwell. 1899, 1901; ed M. Ashley, New York 1962.

Gardiner also edited 17th-century documents for the Camden Soc and contributed to DNB (21 articles) and Encyclopaedia britannica 9th edn (17 articles).

JOHN EMERICH EDWARD DALBERG ACTON, 1st BARON ACTON
1834–1902

§ I

The war of 1870: a lecture. 1871.

The history of freedom in antiquity: an address. Bridgnorth [1877].

The history of freedom in Christianity: an address. Bridgnorth [1877].

A lecture on the study of history. 1895, 1896, 1905, 1906 (in Lectures on modern history), 1911. Acton's inaugural lecture at Cambridge.

Lectures on modern history. Ed J. N. Figgis and R. V. Laurence 1906, 1952, 1956, New York 1959; ed H. R. Trevor-Roper 1961; ed H. Kohn, New York 1961 (as Renaissance to revolution: the rise of the free state).

Historical essays and studies. Ed J. N. Figgis and R. V. Laurence 1907.

The history of freedom and other essays. Ed J. N. Figgis and R. V. Laurence 1907.

Lectures on the French revolution. Ed J. N. Figgis and R. V. Laurence 1910.

Essays on freedom and power. Ed G. Himmelfarb, Boston 1948.

Essays on church and state. Ed D. Woodruff 1952.

Letters

Letters of Lord Acton to Mary, daughter of W. E. Gladstone; with a memoir. Ed H. Paul 1904.

Gasquet, F. A. Lord Acton and his circle. 1906.

Selections from the correspondence of the first Lord Acton. Ed J. N. Figgis and R. V. Laurence 1917.

Correspondence of Lord Acton and Richard Simpson. Ed J. L. Altholz and D. McElrath 3 vols Cambridge 1971–5.

§ 2

Bryce, J. Lord Acton. Proc Br Acad 1 1904.

—— In his Studies in contemporary biography, 1903.

Matthew, D. Acton: the formative years. 1946, 1968 (completed as Lord Acton and his times).

Butterfield, H. Journal of Lord Acton: Rome 1857. Cambridge Historical Jnl 8 1946.

—— Lord Acton. 1948 (Historical Assoc).

—— Acton and the massacre of St Bartholomew. Cambridge Historical Jnl 11 1953.

—— Lord Acton. Cambridge Jnl May 1953.

—— Acton: his training, methods and intellectual system.

In Studies in diplomatic history in honour of G. P. Gooch, 1961.

Fasnacht, G. E. Acton on nationality and Socialism. Oxford 1949.

—— Acton's political philosophy: an analysis. 1952.

Himmelfarb, G. The American revolution in the political philosophy of Lord Acton. Jnl of Modern History 21 1949.

—— Acton: a study in conscience and politics. Chicago 1952.

Kochan, L. Acton on history. 1954.

JOHN RICHARD GREEN
1837–83

Oxford during the last century: being two series of papers published in the Oxford Chronicle and Bucks and Berks Gazette during 1859. Oxford 1859 (anon); ed C. L. Stainer 1901 (as Studies in Oxford history); ed Mrs J. R. Green and K. Norgate 1901 (Green's ser only, in Oxford studies). With G. Roberson.

A short history of the English people. 1874, 1875, 1876, New York 1876, London 1877; ed Mrs J. R. Green (with memoir) 1888; 4 vols 1889–91 (with tables and analysis by C. W. A. Tait); ed Mrs J. R. Green and K. Norgate 4 vols 1892–4 (illustr edn); ed G. B. Adams 2 vols New York 1898; ed A. S. Cook 3 vols New York 1900; 1 vol 1911 (rev), New York 1911, London 1916 (with Epilogue 1815–1914 by Mrs J. R. Green).

Stray studies from England and Italy. 1876; Stray studies: second series, ed Mrs J. R. Green 1903.

History of the English people. 4 vols 1877–80, New York 1878–80, London 1881, 1882, 5 vols New York 1882, 4 vols 1886, 1890, 8 vols 1895–6 (Eversley edn); 4 vols New York 1898 (as England, with suppl by J. Hawthorne).

A short geography of the British islands. 1879, 1884, 1893, 1896 (rev). With Mrs J. R. Green.

The making of England. 1881, 1882, New York 1882, London 1885 (3rd edn), 2 vols 1897, 1900.

The conquest of England. 1883, New York 1883, London 1884, 2 vols 1899 (3rd edn).

Letters of J. R. Green. Ed L. Stephen 1901.

Oxford studies. Ed Mrs J. R. Green and K. Norgate 1901.

Historical studies. Ed Mrs J. R. Green 1903.

WILLIAM EDWARD HARTPOLE LECKY
1838–1903

Friendship and other poems, by Hibernicus. 1859.

The religious tendencies of the age. 1860. Anon.

The leaders of public opinion in Ireland. 1861 (anon), 1871 (rev, omitting Clerical influences), New York 1872, London 1882, 2 vols 1903 (omitting Life of Swift).

On the declining sense of the miraculous. Dublin 1863.

History of the rise and influence of the spirit of rationalism in Europe. 2 vols 1865, 1865, 1866, 1869 (4th edn); ed C. W. Mills, New York 1955.

History of European morals from Augustus to Charlemagne. 2 vols 1869, 1877 (3rd edn), 1886 (7th edn rev); ed C. W. Mills, New York 1955.

A history of England in the eighteenth century. 8 vols 1878–90, New York 1878–90, London 1883–90 (vols 1–2 3rd edn, vols 3–4 2nd edn).

The American revolution: chapters and passages relating to America from History of England in the eighteenth century. Ed J. A. Woodburn, New York 1898.

The French Revolution: chapters from History of England during the eighteenth century. Ed H. E. Bourne, New York 1904, 1928.

Poems. 1891, New York 1891.

The political value of history. Birmingham 1892, London 1892 (rev), 1908 (in Historical and political essays).

The Empire, its value and its growth: an inaugural address. 1893, 1908 (in Historical and political essays).

Speeches and addresses of Edward Henry 16th Earl of Derby. Ed T. H. Sanderson and E. S. Roscoe 2 vols 1894. Memoir by Lecky.

Democracy and liberty. 2 vols 1896, 1896, New York 1896, London 1899 (rev), 1900.

The map of life: conduct and character. 1899.

Historical and political essays. 1908.

MANDELL CREIGHTON
1843–1901

History of Rome. 1875, 1877 (3rd edn), 1884 (10th edn).

The Tudors and the Reformation. 1876, New York 1877.

The age of Elizabeth. 1876.

The shilling history of England: being an introductory volume to Epochs of English history. 1879, New York 1879 (as The half-hour history of England); ed L. Creighton 1904.

A history of the Papacy during the period of the Reformation. 5 vols 1882–94, 1887–94 (rev), 6 vols 1897 (as History of the Papacy from the Great Schism to the sack of Rome), New York 1902–4, London 1919.

Memoir of Sir George Grey. Newcastle-on-Tyne 1884 (priv ptd); ed E. Grey 1901.

Cardinal Wolsey. 1888, 1904; ed H. Ketcham, New York 1903.

Persecution and tolerance (Hulsean lectures 1893–4). 1895.

The early renaissance in England (Rede lecture 1895). Cambridge 1895.

Queen Elizabeth. 1896.

The heritage of the spirit and other sermons. 1896, 1913.

The story of some English shires. 1897, 1898.

Lessons from the cross: addresses. 1898.

The abolition of the Roman jurisdiction. 1899, 1899.

The Church and the nation: charges and addresses. Ed L. Creighton 1901.

Counsels for churchpeople. Ed J. H. Burn 1901.

Historical essays and reviews. Ed L. Creighton 1902, 1902.

Thoughts on education: speeches and sermons. Ed L. Creighton 1902; ed E. A. Knox 1906 (abridged).

Historical lectures and addresses. Ed L. Creighton 1903.

University and other sermons. Ed L. Creighton 1903.

The mind of St Peter and other sermons. Ed L. Creighton 1904.

Counsel for the young: extracts from letters. Ed L. Creighton 1905.

Life of Simon de Montfort. 1905.

The claims of the common life: sermons preached in Merton College chapel 1871–4. 1905.

FREDERIC WILLIAM MAITLAND
1850–1906

Justice and police. 1885.

Why the history of English law is not written: an inaugural lecture. Cambridge 1888.

The history of English law before the time of Edward I. 2 vols Cambridge 1895. With F. Pollock.

Domesday book and beyond: three essays. Cambridge 1897, Boston 1897, Cambridge 1907; ed E. Miller 1960.

Roman canon law in the church of England: six essays. Cambridge 1898.

Township and borough: being the Ford lectures 1897 with notes relating to the history of Cambridge. Cambridge 1898, 1965.

English law and the Renaissance (Rede lecture 1901). Cambridge 1901.

Essays on the teaching of history. Ed W. A. J. Archbold, Cambridge 1901. With H. M. Gwatkin et al.

The life and letters of Leslie Stephen. 1906.

The constitutional history of England. Ed H. A. L. Fisher, Cambridge 1908. Lectures delivered 1887–8.

Equity: also the forms of action at common law. Ed A. H. Chaytor and W. J. Whittaker, Cambridge 1909; Equity, ed J. Brunyate, Cambridge 1936, 1949; Forms of action, ed Chaytor and J. Whittaker, Cambridge 1936.

Collected papers. Ed H. A. L. Fisher 3 vols Cambridge 1911.

A sketch of English legal history. Ed J. F. Colby, New York [1915]. With F. C. Montague.

Selected essays. Ed H. D. Hazeltine, G. Lapsley and P. H. Winfield, Cambridge 1936.

Selected historical essays. Ed H. M. Cam, Cambridge 1957.

Selections from his writings. Ed R. L. Schuyler, Berkeley 1960.

Letters. Ed C. H. S. Fifoot, Cambridge 1965.

Maitland also edited medieval legal documents (chiefly for the Selden Soc) 1884–1907.

SIR JAMES GEORGE FRAZER
1854–1941

Bibliographies

Besterman, T. A bibliography of Frazer. 1934.

§ 1

Totemism. Edinburgh 1887.

The golden bough: a study in comparative religion. 2 vols 1890, New York 1890, 3 vols 1900 (rev), New York 1900, 12 vols 1911–15 (as The golden bough: a study in magic and religion; vols 1–2: The magic art and the evolution of kings, 1911; vol 3: Taboo and the perils of the soul, 1911; vol 4: The dying god, 1911; vols 5–6: Adonis, Attis, Osiris, 1914; vols 7–8: Spirits of the corn and the wild, 1912; vol 9: The scapegoat, 1913; vols 10–11: Balder the beautiful, 1913; vol 12: Bibliography and general index, 1915), 13 vols 1955 (with Aftermath); 1 vol 1922 (abridged); chs 1–7 ed G. M. Trevelyan 1944 (as Magic and religion); ed T. H. Gaster, New York 1959, 1965 (as The new Golden bough).

Leaves from the Golden bough culled by Lady Frazer. 1924.

Pausanias, Description of Greece. 6 vols 1898. Tr and ed Frazer.

The origin of totemism. Fortnightly Rev April–May 1899. Reply by A. Lang, Mr Frazer's theory of totemism, June 1899.

Pausanias and other Greek sketches. 1900, 1917 (as Studies in Greek scenery, legend and history).

Lectures on the early history of the kingship. 1905, 1920 (as The magical origin of kings).

Adonis, Attis, Osiris: studies in the history of oriental religion. 1906, 1907, 1914 (as vols 5–6 of Golden bough, above), New York 1962; Adonis, 1932.

Questions on the customs, beliefs and languages of savages. Cambridge 1907.

The scope of social anthropology. 1908, 1927 (with The devil's advocate, below).

Psyche's task: a discourse concerning the influence of superstitions on the growth of institutions. 1909, 1913, 1920, 1927 (as The devil's advocate: a plea for superstition), 1928.

Totemism and exogamy: a treatise on certain early forms of superstition and society. 4 vols 1910.

The letters of William Cowper. 2 vols 1912. Ed Frazer.

The belief in immortality and the worship of the dead.

Vol 1 (Gifford lectures 1911–12), 1913; vol 2, 1922; vol 3, 1924.
Folk-lore in the Old Testament: studies in comparative religion, legend and law. 3 vols 1918, 1919, 1919, 1 vol 1923 (abridged).
Sir Roger de Coverley and other literary pieces. 1920, 1927 (as The gorgon's head).
Sur Ernest Renan. Paris 1923.
Frazer: selected passages from his works. Ed G. Roth, Paris 1924.
The worship of nature. 1926, New York 1926.
Man, god and immortality: passages chosen by Pierre Sayn from the writings of Frazer, revised and edited by the author. 1927, New York 1927.
Publii Ovidii Nasonis Fastorum libri sex. 5 vols 1929, 1 vol 1931 (Loeb Lib).
Myths of the origin of fire. 1930, 1930, New York 1942.
The growth of Plato's ideal theory. 1930.
Garnered sheaves: essays, addresses and reviews. 1931.
The fear of the dead in primitive religion. 3 vols 1933–6.
Condorcet on the progress of the human mind (Zaharoff lecture 1933). Oxford 1933.
Creation and evolution in primitive cosmogonies, and other pieces. 1935.
Aftermath: a supplement to the Golden bough. 1936, New York 1937, London 1951, 1955 (as vol 12 of Golden bough).
Totemica: a supplement to Totemism and exogamy. 1937.
Greece and Rome: a selection from the works of Frazer. Ed S. G. Owen 1937.
Pasha the pom: the story of a little dog. Philadelphia 1937. With Lady Frazer.
Anthologia anthropologica. Ed R. A. Downie 4 vols 1938, 1939.

§ 2

Downie, R. A. Frazer: the portrait of a scholar. 1940.
— Frazer and the Golden bough. 1970.
Hyman, S. E. The tangled bank: Darwin, Marx, Frazer and Freud as imaginative writers. New York 1962.
Vickery, J. B. The literary impact of the Golden bough. Princeton 1973.

HENRY PETER BROUGHAM,
1st BARON BROUGHAM AND VAUX
1778–1868

The Brougham papers are at Univ College, London.

Collections

Opinions of Lord Brougham on politics, theology, law, science, education &c &c. 1837.
Speeches upon questions relating to public rights. 4 vols Edinburgh 1898, 2 vols Philadelphia 1841.
Works. 11 vols 1855–61, Edinburgh 1872–3.
Contributions to the Edinburgh Review. 3 vols 1856.
Brougham's acts and bills from 1811 to the present time now first collected. Ed J. E. Eardley-Wilmot 1857, 1860 (as Brougham's law reforms).

§ 1

An inquiry into the colonial policy of the European powers. 2 vols Edinburgh 1803.
An inquiry into the state of the nation at the commencement of the present administration. 1806, 1806 (6th edn), 1806 (7th edn rev).
Practical observations upon the education of the people. 1825, 1825 (11th edn), 1825 (17th edn), 1825 (20th edn).
Inaugural discourse on being installed Lord Rector of the University of Glasgow. Glasgow 1825.
Thoughts upon the aristocracy of England, by Isaac Tomkins, Gent. 1835, 1835 (6th edn), 1835 (11th edn).

'We can't afford it!': being thoughts upon the aristocracy of England part 2, by Isaac Tomkins, Gent. 1835, 1835 (4th edn), 1835 (6th edn).
A discourse of natural theology. Brussels 1835, London 1835 (4th edn), Philadelphia 1835.
Dissertations on subjects of science connected with natural theology. 2 vols 1839.
Historical sketches of statesmen who flourished in the time of George III. 2 vols 1839, Philadelphia 1839; Second series, 2 vols 1839, Philadelphia 1839; Third series, 2 vols 1842, Philadelphia 1842; collected 3 vols 1845–53, 2 vols Philadelphia 1854, 3 vols 1855–6, 1856–8.
Sketches of public characters. 2 vols Philadelphia 1839.
Political philosophy. 3 vols 1842–3, 1 vol Paris 1845, 3 vols 1846, 1853, 1855, 1861.
The British constitution. 1844, 1861 (3 edns).
Dialogues on instinct. 1844, Philadelphia 1845.
Albert Lunel: or the chateau of Languedoc. 3 vols 1844 (anon), 1872. A novel.
Lives of men of letters and science in the time of George III. 2 vols 1845–6, 3 vols 1845–7.
Masters and workmen: a tale illustrative of the social and moral condition of the people, by Lord B——. 3 vols 1851. A novel attributed to Brougham.
History of England and France under the house of Lancaster. 1852 (anon), 1855, 1861.
Analytical view of Sir Isaac Newton's Principia. 1855. With E. J. Routh.
Addresses on popular literature. 1858.
Tracts: mathematical and physical. 1860.
The life and times of Lord Brougham written by himself. 3 vols Edinburgh 1871, 1872 (3rd edn).
Brougham and his early friends: letters to James Loch 1798–1809. Ed R. H. M. Buddle-Atkinson and G. A. Jackson, 3 vols Edinburgh 1908 (priv ptd).

§ 2

Bagehot, W. Brougham. Nat Rev 5 1857; rptd in his Biographical studies, 1881.
Aspinall, A. Brougham and the Whig party. Manchester 1927.
Hawes, F. Henry Brougham. 1957.
New, C. W. The life of Brougham to 1830. Oxford 1961.

JAMES BRYCE,
1st VISCOUNT BRYCE OF
DECHMONT
1838–1922

§ 1

The flora of the island of Arran. 1859.
The Holy Roman Empire (Arnold prize essay 1864). Oxford 1864, London 1871 (3rd edn rev), 1886 (8th edn), New York 1886, London 1892, 1896, 1904 (rev), 1906, 1919, New York 1921, London 1922 (enlarged); ed H. Kohn, New York 1961.
Report on the condition of education in Lancashire. 1867.
The academic study of the civil law: an inaugural lecture delivered at Oxford. 1871.
Trans-Caucasia and Ararat: being notes of a vacation tour in the autumn of 1876. 1877, 1877, 1896 (4th edn rev).
The trade marks registration act. 1877.
The predictions of Hamilton and de Tocqueville. Baltimore 1887.
Handbook of home rule: being articles on the Irish question. 1887. Ed Bryce.
The American commonwealth. 3 vols 1888, 2 vols 1888, 1889 (2nd edn rev), 1891, 1893–5 (3rd edn rev) New York 1910 (new edn rev); ed L. M. Hacker 2 vols New York 1959. Selections: ed M. G. Fulton, New York 1918 (as Bryce on American democracy); ed H. S.

Commager, New York 1961 (as Reflections on American institutions).

The migrations of the races of men considered historically. 1893.

Legal studies in the University of Oxford: a valedictory lecture. 1893.

Impressions of South Africa. 1897, New York 1897, London 1898, 1900 (3rd edn).

William Ewart Gladstone: his characteristics as man and statesman. 1898, New York 1898.

Studies in history and jurisprudence. 2 vols Oxford 1901, New York 1901.

Studies in contemporary biography. 1903, 1911, 1927.

The relations between the advanced and the backward races of mankind. Oxford 1903.

Constitutions. New York 1905.

Marriage and divorce. New York 1905.

The hindrances to good citizenship. New Haven 1909.

South America: observations and impressions. 1912, New York 1912, 1913, London 1914 (rev).

University and historical addresses delivered during a residence in the United States. New York 1913.

The ancient Roman Empire and the British Empire in India; the diffusion of Roman and English law throughout the world—two essays. Oxford 1914.

Neutral nations and the war. 1914.

The attitude of Great Britain in the present war. 1916.

Proposals for the prevention of future wars. 1917.

Essays and addresses in war time. New York 1918.

Modern democracies. 2 vols 1921, New York 1921, London 1929, New York 1931.

Canada: an actual democracy. Toronto 1921.

The study of American history. Cambridge 1921, New York 1922.

International relations: eight lectures. New York 1922.

Memories of travel. Ed Lady Bryce 1923, New York 1923.

§2

Freeman, E. A. The Holy Roman Empire. North Br Rev 42 1865; rptd in his Historical essays, 1871.

Fisher, H. A. L. Viscount Bryce. Proc Br Acad 12 1926.
— James Bryce. 2 vols 1927.

Bryce's American commonwealth: fiftieth anniversary. Ed R. C. Brooks, New York 1939. Includes reviews by Acton, Woodrow Wilson et al.

Toynbee, A. J. In his Acquaintances, 1967.

THOMAS CLARKSON
1760–1846

An essay on the slavery and commerce of the human species. 1786, Philadelphia 1786, London 1788.

An essay on the impolicy of the African slave trade. 1788, 1788 (rev).

A portraiture of Quakerism, as taken from a view of the moral education, discipline, peculiar customs, religious principles, political and civil œconomy and character of the Society of Friends. 3 vols 1806, New York 1806, London 1807 (3rd edn), Philadelphia 1808; ed R. Smeal, Glasgow 1869 (as A portraiture of the Christian profession and practice of the Society of Friends).

The history of the rise, progress and accomplishment of the abolition of the African slave-trade. 2 vols 1808, Philadelphia 1808 London 1839.

Memoirs of the private and public life of William Penn. 2 vols 1813, Philadelphia 1813, 1814, Dover New Hampshire 1827; ed W. E. Forster 1849, New York 1849.

An essay on the doctrines and practice of the early Christians as they relate to war. 1817, 1818 (3rd edn), 1824 (7th edn), 1832, 1839, 1844.

The cries of Africa to the inhabitants of Europe. [1822].

Thoughts on the necessity for improving the condition of the slaves in the British colonies with a view to their ultimate emancipation. 1823, 1823 (rev), 1824 (4th edn).

Researches antediluvian, patriarchal and historical. 1836.

Strictures on a life of William Wilberforce; with a correspondence between Lord Brougham and Mr Clarkson. Ed H. C. Robinson 1838.

Henry Christophe and Clarkson: a correspondence. Ed E. L. Griggs and C. H. Prater, Berkeley 1952.

ALBERT VENN DICEY
1835–1922

The Privy Council (Arnold prize essay 1860). Oxford 1860, London 1887.

A treatise on the rules for the selection of parties in an action. 1870; ed J. H. Truman, New York 1876; London, 1886; ed J. B. Moore, New York 1896.

The law of domicil. 1879.

Can English law be taught at the universities? an inaugural lecture (Oxford 1883). 1883.

Lectures introductory to the study of the law of the constitution. 1885, 1889 (3rd edn rev as Introduction to the study of the law of the constitution), 1893, 1897, 1902, 1908, 1915 (8th edn); ed C. S. Wade 1939.

England's case against Home Rule. 1886, 1887 (3rd edn), 1887 (as Why England maintains the union).

Letters on unionist delusions. 1887.

The verdict: a tract on the political significance of the report of the Parnell Commission. 1890.

A leap in the dark: or our new constitution. 1893, 1911.

A digest of the laws of England with reference to the conflict of laws. 1896, Boston 1896, London 1908; ed A. B. Keith 1922 (3rd edn), 1927, 1932; ed J. H. C. Morris 1949 (6th edn as Conflict of laws), 1958.

Lectures on the relation between law and public opinion in England during the nineteenth century. 1905, 1914, 1920, 1924, 1930; ed E. C. S. Wade 1962.

Letters to a friend on votes for women. 1909, 1912.

A fool's paradise: being a constitutionalist's criticism of the Home Rule Bill of 1912. 1913.

The statesmanship of Wordsworth. Oxford 1917.

Thoughts on the union between England and Scotland. 1920. With R. S. Rait.

GEORGE FINLAY
1799–1875

The Hellenic kingdom and the Greek nation. 1836; ed S. G. Howe, Boston 1837.

Remarks on the topography of Oropia and Diacria. Athens 1838.

Greece under the Romans. Edinburgh 1844, 1857; ed V. R. Reynolds 1907, 1927 (EL).

On the site of the Holy Sepulchre. 1847.

The history of Greece from its conquest by the Crusaders to its conquest by the Turks, and of the empire of Trebizond 1204–1461. Edinburgh 1851.

History of the Byzantine and Greek empires 716–1453. 2 vols Edinburgh 1853-4, 1855, 1 vol Edinburgh 1856 (2nd edn: 716–1507); Byzantine empire, ed V. R. Reynolds 1906, 1935 (EL).

The history of Greece under Othoman and Venetian domination. Edinburgh 1856.

History of the Greek revolution. 2 vols Edinburgh 1861.

Objects found in Greece in the collection of G. Finlay. Athens 1869.

A history of Greece from its conquest by the Romans to the present time B.C. 146 to A.D. 1864. Ed H. F. Tozer 7 vols Oxford 1877. Includes Greece under the Romans, Byzantine and Greek empires, and Greece under Othoman and Venetian domination.

ALEXANDER WILLIAM KINGLAKE
1809–91

Eothen: or traces of travel brought home from the East. 1844 (anon), 1844, 1845, New York 1845, 1845, Leipzig 1846, London 1847 (5th edn), 1849, New York 1849, London 1850, 1856, 1859, New York 1859, London 1864, 1878, Edinburgh 1879, New York 1879, 1891; ed J. Bryce, New York 1900; ed W. H. D. Rouse 1901; ed J. C. Hogarth, Oxford 1906; ed A. T. Quiller-Couch 1907; ed H. Spender 1908, 1931, 1954 (EL); illustr F. Brangwyn 1913; ed J. W. Oliver, Edinburgh 1941; ed P. H. Newby 1949, 1952; ed F. Baker 1964.

The invasion of the Crimea: its origin and an account of its progress down to the death of Lord Raglan. Vols 1–2 Edinburgh 1863 (4 edns), 2 vols New York 1863–8, 8 vols Edinburgh 1863–87, 7 vols Leipzig 1863–89, 9 vols Edinburgh 1877–8 (6th edn); ed G. S. Clarke, Edinburgh 1899 (abridged).

JOHN LINGARD
1771–1851

Catholic loyalty vindicated. 1805.
The antiquities of the Anglo-Saxon Church. 2 vols Newcastle 1806, 1810, Philadelphia 1841, 1845 (rev as The history and antiquities of the Anglo-Saxon Church).
Letters on Catholic loyalty. Newcastle 1807.
Observations on the laws and ordinances which exist in foreign states relative to the religious concerns of their Roman Catholic subjects. 1817, 1851.
The history of England from the first invasion by the Romans to the accession of Henry VIII. 3 vols 1819, 8 vols 1819–30 (as History of England from the first invasion by the Romans to the accession of William and Mary in 1688), 14 vols 1825 (3rd edn), 13 vols 1837–9 (rev), 10 vols 1849, 1854 (6th edn with memoir by M. A. Tierney), 11 vols 1912–15 (supplementary vol by H. Belloc); ed H. N. Birt 1903, 1912.
A collection of tracts on several subjects connected with the civil and religious principles of Catholics. 1826.
A new version of the four Gospels with notes critical and explanatory, by a Catholic. 1836, 1846, 1851.

JUSTIN McCARTHY
1830–1912

Con amore: or critical chapters. 1868.
The settlement of the Alabama question. 1871.
Modern leaders: biographical sketches. New York 1872.
Dear Lady Disdain. 1875, 1878, 1887. A novel.
A history of our own times from the accession of Queen Victoria to the Berlin Congress. Vols 1–2 1879, vols 3–4 1880 (as History of our own times from the accession of Queen Victoria to the general election of 1880), 5 vols 1889–97 (with continuation to the Diamond jubilee), 7 vols 1897–1905 (with continuation to the accession of Edward VII); ed G. M. Adam 2 vols New York 1900.
The epoch of reform 1830–50. 1882.
A history of the four Georges. 2 vols 1884, 4 vols 1901 (as A history of the four Georges and of William IV, vols 3–4 completed by J. H. McCarthy), 2 vols 1905.
A short history of our own times. New York 1884, London 1888.
Ireland's cause in England's parliament. Ed J. B. O'Reilly, Boston 1888.

Charing Cross to St Paul's. Illustr J. Pennell 1891, 1893.
Sir Robert Peel. 1891, London 1906 (4th edn).
Pope Leo XIII. 1896, 1899, New York 1899.
The Daily News jubilee: a political and social retrospect. 1896. With J. R. Robinson.
The story of Mr Gladstone's life. 1897, 1898 (rev).
The inner life of the House of Commons, by W. White. 2 vols 1897. Ed McCarthy.
Modern England. 2 vols 1899, New York 1899 (as The story of the people of England in the nineteenth century).
Reminiscences. 2 vols 1899, New York 1899.
English literature in the reign of Queen Victoria. Ed R. Ackermann, Dresden 1899. Selected from History of our own times, above.
The reign of Queen Anne. 2 vols 1902, 1905.
Portraits of the sixties. 1903, New York 1903.
Ireland and her story. 1903.
British political portraits. 1903.
Irish literature. 10 vols Chicago 1904. Ed McCarthy et al.
The story of an Irishman. 1904, New York 1904 (as An Irishman's story). Autobiography.
Irish recollections. 1911.
Our book of memories: letters of McCarthy to Mrs Campbell Praed. 1912.

McCarthy also pbd novels, many in collaboration with Mrs Campbell Praed.

SIR JAMES MACKINTOSH
1765–1832

Vindiciae gallicae. Dublin 1791, London 1791 (rev), 1791 (3rd edn). A reply to Burke's Reflections on the revolution in France.
A discourse on the study of the law of nature and of nations. 1799, Dublin 1799, London 1828, 1835, Edinburgh 1835; ed J. G. Marvin, Boston 1843.
Dissertation on the progress of ethical philosophy chiefly during the seventeenth and eighteenth centuries. 1830 (as suppl to Encyclopaedia britannica 7th edn), Edinburgh 1830 (priv ptd), Philadelphia 1832, 1834; ed W. Whewell, Edinburgh 1836 (as A general view of the progress of ethical philosophy), 1862, 1872 (4th edn).
The history of England. 3 vols 1830–2 (in Cabinet cyclopaedia, ed D. Lardner 1830–40), 3 vols Philadelphia 1830–3, 10 vols 1850 (completed by W. Wallace and R. Bell); ed R. J. Mackintosh 2 vols 1853.
The life of Sir Thomas More. 1831 (in Cabinet cyclopaedia), 1844.
History of the revolution in England in 1688 completed to the settlement of the crown by the editor William Wallace. 1834 (with memoir), Philadelphia 1835; London 1835 (Mackintosh's portion only, as A view of the reign of James II).
Tracts and speeches. 5 pts Edinburgh 1840 (25 copies).
Miscellaneous works. Ed R. J. Mackintosh 3 vols 1846.

SIR THOMAS ERSKINE MAY,
1st BARON FARNBOROUGH
1815–86

The Imperial Parliament. 1840 (anon in Penny cyclopaedia vol 17), 1841 (in Knight's Store of knowledge for all readers).
A treatise on the law, privileges, proceedings and usage of Parliament. 1844, 1851 (rev), 1859 (4th edn), 1868 (6th edn), 1879 (8th edn), 1883; ed R. R. D. Palgrave

and A. B. Carter 1893; ed T. L. Webster and W. E. Grey 1906, 1924 (13th edn); ed G. Campion and T. G. B. Cocks 1950 (15th edn); ed E. Fellowes and T. G. B. Cocks 1957 (16th edn); ed B. Cocks 1965 (17th edn).

Remarks and suggestions with a view to facilitating the dispatch of public business in Parliament. 1849, 1849 (2nd edn).

On the consolidation of the election laws. 1850.

The constitutional history of England since the accession of George III. 2 vols 1861–3, 1863–5, Boston 1862–3, 3 vols 1871, 2 vols New York 1876–7, 3 vols 1878 (6th edn), 1896 (11th edn); ed F. Holland 3 vols 1912.

Democracy in Europe: a history. 2 vols 1877, New York 1878.

The machinery of parliamentary legislation. 1881.

CHARLES MERIVALE
1808–93

History of Rome under the Emperors: the Augustan age. 1843.

A history of the Romans under the Empire. 7 vols 1850–62, 1862, New York 1864–79, 8 vols 1865, 1890.

C. Sallustii Crispi Catilina et Jugurtha. 1852; Jugurtha, 1884; Catilina, 1888. Ed Merivale.

The fall of the Roman Republic: a short history of the last century of the commonwealth. 1853, 1853 (2nd edn). An abridgement of vols 1–3 of History of the Romans, above.

An account of the life and letters of Cicero, by B. R. Abeken. 1854. Tr Merivale.

Keatsii Hyperionis libri tres. Cambridge 1863, 1882 (rev). Tr Merivale.

The conversion of the Roman Empire (Boyle lectures 1864). 1865, 1865, New York 1865.

The conversion of the northern nations (Boyle lectures 1865). 1866, New York 1866.

Homer's Iliad in English rhymed verse. 2 vols 1869.

The contrast between pagan and Christian society: a lecture. 1872, 1880.

A general history of Rome from the foundation of the city to the fall of Augustulus B.C. 753–A.D. 476. 1875, 1875, 1876, 1877, New York 1891; ed C. Puller 1877, New York 1878 (abridged); ed O. Smeaton 2 vols 1910 (as History of Rome to the reign of Trajan), 1928 (EL).

The Roman triumvirates. 1876, 1883 (3rd edn), 1887 (5th edn), New York 1889.

The heathen world and St Paul. 1877.

Four lectures on some epochs of early church history. 1879.

Autobiography and letters. Ed J. A. Merivale, Oxford 1898 (priv ptd), London 1899 (as Autobiography of Merivale with selections from his correspondence).

SIR WILLIAM
FRANCIS PATRICK NAPIER
1785–1860

The art of war. Edinburgh Rev 35 1821.

History of the war in the Peninsula and the south of France from the year 1807 to the year 1814. 6 vols 1828–40, 1851 (rev), 5 vols 1856, New York 1856, 3 vols 1876–82, 6 vols 1882, 1900; ed R. W. O'Byrne 1889; ed W. T. Dobson 1889; ed E. A. Arnold 1905; ed A. T. Quiller-Couch, Oxford 1908; ed M. Fanshawe 1911; ed H. Strang 1913. Abridged by Napier as English battles, below.

A reply to various opponents. 1832 (in History vol 1, 2nd edn), 1833, 1833.

Colonel Napier's justification of his third volume. 1833.

The conquest of Scinde; with some introductory passages in the life of Major-General Sir Charles James Napier. 1845, 1845 (2nd edn).

History of General Sir Charles James Napier's administration of Scinde and campaign in the Cutchee Hills. 1851, 1857, 1858 (3rd edn).

English battles and sieges in the Peninsula. 1852, 1855, 1866, 1904, 1910; ed W. H. D. Rouse 2 vols 1905. Abridgment by Napier of The war in the peninsula, above.

The life and opinions of General Sir Charles James Napier. 4 vols 1857, 1857 (2nd edn).

FREDERICK YORK POWELL
1850–1904

Early England up to the Norman Conquest. 1876, New York 1877, London 1895 (11th edn).

An Icelandic prose reader. Oxford 1879. With G. Vigfússon.

Alfred the Great and William the Conqueror. 1881.

Old stories from British history. 1882, 1885 (3rd edn).

Corpus poeticum boreale: the poetry of the old northern tongues. 2 vols Oxford 1883. Ed and tr with G. Vigfússon.

History of England. 3 vols 1885–90, 1898–1900, 1 vol 1904. With J. M. Mackay and T. F. Tout.

English history by contemporary writers. 1887. Ed Powell.

Sketches from British history. 1888, 1889.

The first nine books of the Danish history of Saxo Grammaticus translated by Oliver Elton. 1894. Ed Powell.

Some words on allegory in England. 1895 (priv ptd); ed E. Clarke and J. Todhunter 1910.

The tale of Thrond of Gate: commonly called Faereyinga saga. 1896. Tr Powell.

XXIV quatrains from Omar. New York 1900. Tr Powell.

Two Oxford historians. Quart Rev 195 1902. With C. H. Firth; on S. R. Gardiner and J. R. Green.

John Ruskin and thoughts on democracy. 1905.

Origines Islandicae: a collection of the more important sagas. 2 vols Oxford 1905. Ed and tr with G. Vigfússon.

Collingwood, W. G. Scandinavian Britain; with chapters introductory to the subject by F. York Powell. 1908.

Elton, O. Powell: his life and a selection from his letters and occasional writings. 2 vols Oxford 1906.

SIR JOHN ROBERT SEELEY
1834–95

The student's guide to the University of Cambridge. Cambridge 1863, 1866; rev R. B. Somerset 1874. Ed Seeley.

Classical studies as an introduction to the moral sciences: an introductory lecture. 1864.

Ecce homo: a survey of the life and work of Jesus Christ. 1866 (for 1865) (anon), 1866 (5th edn), Boston 1866, 1867, London 1867, 1895; ed O. Lodge [1908], 1923 (EL); ed J. E. Odgers 1910.

Lectures and essays. 1870; ed M. Seeley 1895.

Livy, book I. Oxford 1871, 1881 (3rd edn). Ed Seeley.

English lessons for English people. 1871. With E. A. Abbott.

Life and times of Stein: or Germany and Prussia in the Napoleonic age. 3 vols Cambridge 1878.

Natural religion, by the author of Ecce homo. 1882, Boston 1882, London 1891 (3rd edn), 1895.

The expansion of England. 1883, Boston 1883, 1888, 1895, 1898; abridged 1887 (as Our colonial expansion).

A short history of Napoleon the first. 1886.

Roman imperialism and other lectures and essays. Boston 1889.

Goethe reviewed after sixty years. Boston 1893, London 1894, Leipzig 1894.

The growth of British policy: an historical essay. 2 vols Cambridge 1895, 1903, 1 vol Cambridge 1921, 1922. Memoir by G. W. Prothero.

Introduction to political science. Ed H. Sidgwick 1896, 1901.

GOLDWIN SMITH
1823–1910

Oxford university reform. In Oxford essays by members of the University, Oxford 1858.

Lectures on modern history. Oxford 1861, 1865 (as Lectures on the study of history).

Irish history and Irish character. Oxford 1861, 1862.

Rational religion and the rationalistic objections of the Bampton lectures for 1858. Oxford 1861. On H. L. Mansel, Limits of religious thought.

Does the Bible sanction American slavery? Oxford 1863, Cambridge Mass 1863.

The Empire: a series of letters published in the Daily News. Oxford 1863.

England and America: a lecture. Atlantic Monthly Dec 1864; rptd Boston 1865, Manchester 1865.

A letter to a Whig member of the Southern Independence Association. Boston 1864.

A plea for the abolition of tests in the University of Oxford. Oxford 1864.

The civil war in America: an address. 1866.

Three English statesmen: a course of lectures. 1867, New York 1867. On Pym, Cromwell and Pitt.

The reorganization of the University of Oxford. 1868.

The political destiny of Canada. Toronto 1877, 1878.

Cowper. 1880 (EML).

Lectures and essays. Toronto 1881 (priv ptd).

False hopes: or fallacies socialistic and semi-socialistic briefly answered. New York 1883, London 1886.

Life of Jane Austen. 1890.

Loyalty, aristocracy and jingoism: three lectures. Toronto 1891.

Canada and the Canadian question. 1891, Toronto 1891.

A trip to England. Toronto 1891, 1892, 1895.

The moral crusader: William Lloyd Garrison. Toronto 1892, New York 1892.

The United States: an outline of political history 1492–1871. 1893, New York 1893, 1899.

Essays on questions of the day: political and social. New York 1893, 1894 (rev), Boston 1894.

Oxford and her colleges. 1894, New York 1895, 1906.

Shakespeare the man. Toronto 1899, New York 1900.

The United Kingdom: a political history. 2 vols 1899.

Commonwealth or empire? a bystander's view of the question. New York 1902.

In the court of history: an apology for Canadians who were opposed to the South African War. Toronto 1902.

The founder of Christendom. Boston 1903.

My memory of Gladstone. 1904, 1904, Toronto 1904.

Irish history and the Irish question. 1905.

In quest of light. New York 1906.

No refuge but in truth. Toronto 1908, London 1909, New York 1909.

Reminiscences. Ed A. Haultain, New York 1910, 1911.

A selection from Smith's correspondence. Ed A. Haultain 1913, New York 1913.

PHILIP HENRY STANHOPE, 5th EARL STANHOPE
called Viscount Mahon 1821–55
1805–75

The life of Belisarius. 1829, 1848.

History of the war of the succession in Spain. 1832–3, 1836.

Lord John Russell and Mr Macaulay on the French Revolution. 1833.

Letters from the Earl of Peterborough to General Stanhope in Spain. 1834. Ed Stanhope.

History of England from the Peace of Utrecht to the Peace of Aix-la-Chapelle. 7 vols 1836–54, 1839–54 (as History of England from the Peace of Utrecht to the Peace of Versailles 1713–83); ed H. Reed 2 vols New York (as History of England from the Peace of Utrecht to the Peace of Paris); 7 vols 1853–4 (3rd edn rev).

The rise of our Indian Empire. 1838, 1876 (3rd edn). Extracted from History of England, above.

Spain under Charles the second: extracts from the correspondence of the honourable Alexander Stanhope. 1840. Ed Stanhope.

Essai sur la vie du grand Condé. 1842 (priv ptd); tr 1845 (as The life of Louis Prince of Condé), New York 1845.

Correspondence between William Pitt and Charles Duke of Rutland. 1842 (priv ptd), 1890. Ed Stanhope.

The decline of the last Stuarts: extracts from despatches. 1843. Ed Stanhope.

The letters of Philip Dormer Stanhope, Earl of Chesterfield. 5 vols 1845–53. Ed Stanhope.

Historical essays contributed to the Quarterly Review. 1849, 1861. See Joan of Arc, below.

The Forty-Five. 1851, 1851. Extracted from History of England, above.

Secret correspondence connected with Mr Pitt's return to office in 1804. 1852 (priv ptd). Ed Stanhope.

Joan of Arc. 1854. Rptd from Historical essays, above.

Lord Chatham at Chevening 1769. 1855, 1859.

Addresses delivered at Manchester, Leeds and Birmingham. 1856.

Memoirs of Sir Robert Peel. 2 vols 1856–7. Ed Stanhope and E. Cardwell.

Were human sacrifices in use among the Romans? Correspondence between Mr Macaulay, Sir Robert Peel and Lord Mahon. 1860 (priv ptd); ed T. Thayer 1878 (priv ptd) (as Some inquiries concerning human sacrifice among the Romans).

Life of William Pitt. 4 vols 1861–2, 1862, 1867 (3rd edn).

Miscellanies. 1863, 1863 (rev); Second series, 1872.

History of England comprising the reign of Queen Anne until the Peace of Utrecht. 1870, 1870.

Notes of conversation with Louis-Philippe at Claremont. 1873 (priv ptd).

The French retreat from Moscow and other historical essays. 1876.

Notes of conversations with the Duke of Wellington. 1888, 1889 (3rd edn); ed P. Guedalla, Oxford 1938 (WC).

SIR JAMES STEPHEN
1789–1859

Critical and miscellaneous essays. Philadelphia 1843, 1846, 1848, Boston 1854, 1856, New York 1873.

Essays in ecclesiastical biography. 2 vols 1849, 1853 (3rd edn); ed J. F. Stephen 1860, 1872, 1907.

Lectures on the history of France. 2 vols 1851, 1852, 1 vol New York 1852, 1855, 2 vols 1857 (3rd edn rev).

Letters: with biographical notes by his daughter C. E. Stephen. Gloucester 1906 (priv ptd).

SIR JAMES FITZJAMES STEPHEN
1829–94

§ I

The relation of novels to life. In Cambridge essays, 1855.
The characteristics of English criminal law. In Cambridge essays, 1857.
Matthew Arnold and the Italian question. Saturday Rev 13 Aug 1859; ed M. M. Bevington, Durham NC 1953 (with Arnold's England and the Italian question).
Essays by a barrister. 1862. Anon.
Defence of the Rev Rowland Williams. 1862.
A general view of the criminal law of England. 1863.
The definition of murder considered. 1866.
The Indian Evidence Act of 1872. 1872, Calcutta 1904 (as Introduction to the Indian Evidence Act).
Liberty, equality, fraternity. 1873.
A digest of the law of evidence. 1876, 1876, St Louis 1876, London 1877 (3rd edn); ed H. and H. L. Stephen 1899 (5th edn); ed G. E. Beers, Hartford 1901; ed H. L. Stephen and L. F. Sturge 1936 (12 edn).
A digest of the criminal law (crimes and punishments). 1877, St Louis 1877, London 1879, 1883 (3rd edn), 1887; ed H. and H. L. Stephen 1894 (4th edn); ed L. F. Sturge 1947 (8th edn).
A digest of the criminal procedure in indictable offences. 1883. With H. Stephen.
A history of the criminal law of England. 3 vols 1883.
Letters on the Ilbert Bill: reprinted from the Times. 1883.
The story of Nuncomar and the impeachment of Sir Elijah Impey. 2 vols 1885.
The late Mr Carlyle's papers. 1886 (priv ptd). Defends Froude's conduct as Carlyle's literary executor.
Horae sabbaticae. 3 sers 1892.

§ 2

Stephen, L. The life of J. F. Stephen. 1895.
Annan, N. In his Leslie Stephen, 1951.
Radzinowicz, L. In his History of English criminal law, 1956.
—— Stephen and his contribution to the development of criminal law. 1957.
Roach, J. Liberalism and the Victorian intelligentsia. Cambridge Historical Jnl 13 1957.
Cockshut, A. O. J. In his Anglican attitudes, 1959.

WILLIAM STUBBS
1825–1901

§ I

Registrum sacrum anglicanum: an attempt to exhibit the course of episcopal succession in England. Oxford 1858; ed S. E. Holmes, Oxford 1897.
Select charters and other illustrations of English constitutional history. Oxford 1866, 1895 (8th edn); ed H. W. C. Davis, Oxford 1913 (9th edn).
An address delivered by way of inaugural lecture. 1867, Oxford 1867 (rev).
Memorials of St Dunstan. 1874. Ed Stubbs.
The historical works of Gervase of Canterbury. 2 vols 1870–80. Ed Stubbs.
The constitutional history of England in its origin and development. 3 vols Oxford 1874–8, 1877–80, 1896–7, 1926–9; preface, ed C. Morley, Madison NJ 1950 (as Kettel Hall Christmas 1873).
The early Plantagenets. 1876, Boston 1876, London 1886 (5th edn), New York 1887, London 1889, New York 1889, London 1901 (10th edn).
Two lectures on the present state and prospects of historical study. Oxford 1876 (priv ptd).

The mediaeval kingdoms of Cyprus and Armenia: two lectures. Oxford 1878.
Chronicles of the reigns of Edward I and Edward II. 2 vols 1882–3. Ed Stubbs.
Origines celticae. 2 vols 1883. Ed Stubbs and C. Deedes.
An address delivered by way of a last statutory lecture. Oxford 1884.
Seventeen lectures on the study of mediaeval and modern history. Oxford 1886, 1887, 1900.
Wilhelmi Malmesbiriensis de gestis regum Anglorum. 1887. Ed Stubbs.
Ordination addresses. Ed E. E. Holmes 1901.
Historical introductions to the Rolls Series. Ed A. Hassall 1902.
Lectures on European history. Ed A. Hassall 1904.
Letters of Stubbs. Ed W. H. Hutton 1904, 1906 (abridged).
Visitation charges. Ed E. E. Holmes 1904.
Lectures on early English history. Ed A. Hassall 1906.
Germany in the early Middle Ages 476–1250. Ed A. Hassall 1908.
Germany in the later Middle Ages 1200–1500. Ed A. Hassall 1908.
Genealogical history of the family of Bishop Stubbs, compiled by himself. Ed F. Collins 1915.
On convocation. Ed W. H. Hutton 1917.

§ 2

Maitland, F. W. Stubbs: Bishop of Oxford. EHR 16 1901; rptd in his Collected papers, ed H. A. L. Fisher 1911.
Green, J. R. Stubbs's inaugural lecture. In his Stray studies 2nd ser, 1903.
Cam, H. Stubbs seventy years after. Cambridge Historical Jnl 9 1948.
Edwards, J. G. William Stubbs. 1952.

JOHN ADDINGTON SYMONDS
1840–93

§ I

The Escorial: a prize poem. Oxford 1860.
The Renaissance: an essay. Oxford 1863.
The ring and the book. Macmillan's Mag Jan 1869.
Miscellanies, by J. A. Symonds M.D. 1871. Ed Symonds.
An introduction to the study of Dante. 1872, Edinburgh 1890; ed H. F. Brown 1899 (4th edn).
The renaissance of modern Europe: a lecture. 1872.
Studies of the Greek poets. 2 vols 1873–6, New York 1880, London 1893 (3rd edn), 1902, 1920.
Sketches in Italy and Greece. 1874, 1879.
The Renaissance in Italy. 7 vols 1875–86, New York 1881–7, 5 vols 1900; ed A. Pearson 2 vols 1893, 1935 (as A short history of the Renaissance in Italy).
Shelley. 1878 (EML).
Many moods: a volume of verse. 1878.
The sonnets of Michelangelo Buonarroti and Tommaso Campanella. 1878; Michelangelo, New York and London 1950. Tr Symonds.
Sketches and studies in Italy. 1879.
New and old: a volume of verse. 1880, Boston 1880.
Sketches and studies in southern Europe. 2 vols New York 1880.
Animi figura. 1882.
Italian byways. 1883.
A problem in Greek ethics. 1883, 1901, 1908 (all priv ptd), 1928 (in Studies in sexual inversion).
Fragilia labilia. 1884 (priv ptd), Portland Maine 1902.
Vagabunduli libellus. 1884.
Shakspere's predecessors in the English drama. 1884.

Wine, women and song: mediaeval Latin students' songs. 1884. Tr Symonds.

Life of Ben Jonson. 1886.

Sir Philip Sidney. 1886 (EML).

The life of Benvenuto Cellini. 1888; ed J. Pope-Hennessy, New York 1949. Tr Symonds.

Webster and Tourneur. 1888 (Mermaid ser). Ed Symonds.

Essays speculative and suggestive. 2 vols 1890, 1 vol 1894, New York 1894; ed H. F. Brown 1907 (3rd edn).

The memoirs of Count Carlo Gozzi. 2 vols 1890; ed P. Horne, Oxford 1962. Tr Symonds.

A problem in modern ethics. 1891 (priv ptd) (anon), 1896, 1897 (in Sexual inversion by H. Ellis and Symonds), 1928 (in Studies in sexual inversion).

Our life in the Swiss highlands. 1892, 1907. With M. Symonds.

Midnight at Baiae. 1893.

In the key of blue and other prose essays. 1893, 1896 (3rd edn).

The life of Michelangelo Buonarroti. 2 vols 1893, 1893, 1911 (3rd edn).

Walt Whitman: a study. 1893, 1893, 1896, 1906.

Blank verse. Ed H. F. Brown 1894, 1895.

Giovanni Boccaccio as man and author. 1895.

Sketches and studies in Italy and Greece. Ed H. F. Brown 3 vols 1898, 1900. Includes Sketches in Italy and Greece, Sketches and studies in Italy, Italian byways.

Last and first: two essays. New York 1919.

Letters and papers. Ed H. F. Brown 1923.

§2

Brown, H. F. Symonds: a biography. 2 vols 1895.

Harrison, F. J. A. Symonds. 1896.

Symonds, M. Last days of Symonds. 1906.

Brooks, Van W. Symonds: a biographical study. 1914.

Grosskurth, P. M. Symonds: a biography. 1964.

CONNOP THIRLWALL
1797–1875

The history of Rome, by B. G. Niebuhr. 3 vols Cambridge 1828–42, 1847–51 (3rd edn). Vols 1–2 tr Thirlwall and J. C. Hare.

A vindication of Niebuhr's History of Rome from the charges of the Quarterly Review, by J. C. Hare. Cambridge 1829. Postscript by Thirlwall.

A letter to the Rev T. Turton on the admission of Dissenters to academical degrees. Cambridge 1834, 1834 (rev).

A history of Greece. 8 vols 1835–44 (in Cabinet cyclopaedia, ed D. Lardner), 1839–44, 1845–52.

The centre of unity: a sermon. 1850; ed J. E. B. Mayor, Cambridge 1901.

The present state of the relations between science and literature. 1867.

Remains, literary and theological. Ed J. J. S. Perowne 3 vols 1877, 1878.

Essays, speeches and sermons. 1880.

Letters literary and theological. Ed J. J. S. Perowne and L. Stokes 1881.

Letters to a friend. Ed A. P. Stanley 1881.

SIR GEORGE OTTO TREVELYAN
1838–1928

The Cambridge Dionysia: a classic dream by the editor of the Bear. Cambridge 1858.

Horace at the University of Athens: a dramatic sketch. Cambridge 1861 (anon), 1862.

The Pope and his patron. 1862.

The dawk bungalow: or 'Is his appointment pucka?' by H. Broughton. 1863. A comedy.

Letters from a competition wallah. Macmillan's Mag May 1863–May 1864; rptd 1864 (as The competition wallah).

Cawnpore. 1865, 1866, 1886, 1894, 1910.

The ladies in Parliament and other pieces. Cambridge 1869, London 1888.

The life and letters of Lord Macaulay. 2 vols 1876, New York 1876 (with appendix, Macaulay on American institutions), 1877 (rev), 1 vol 1889, 1908 ('enlarged'), 1913; ed G. M. Trevelyan 2 vols Oxford 1932 (WC); 1 vol 1959, 2 vols Oxford 1961.

Selections from the writings of Lord Macaulay. 1876. Ed Trevelyan.

The early history of Charles James Fox. 1880.

The American Revolution. 4 vols London and New York 1899–1907; ed R. B. Morris, New York 1964 (abridged).

Interludes in verse and prose. 1905, 1924.

Marginal notes by Lord Macaulay. 1907. Ed Trevelyan.

George the third and Charles Fox: the concluding part of The American Revolution. 2 vols 1912–14.

SIR SPENCER WALPOLE
1839–1907

The life of Spencer Perceval by his grandson. 2 vols 1874.

A manual of the law of salmon fisheries in England and Wales. 1877.

A history of England from the conclusion of the great war in 1815. 3 vols 1879–80, 5 vols 1879–86 (2nd edn), 6 vols 1890 (rev), 1902–5, 1912.

The electorate and the legislature. 1881, 1892.

Foreign relations. 1882.

The British fish trade. 1883.

The life of Lord John Russell. 2 vols 1889, 1889, 1891.

On parliamentary government in England, by A. Todd. 2 vols 1892. Ed Walpole.

The land of home rule: an essay on the history and constitution of the Isle of Man. 1893.

Some unpublished letters of Horace Walpole. 1902. Ed Walpole.

The history of twenty-five years 1856–1880. 2 vols 1904, 4 vols 1904–8. Vols 3–4 completed by A. C. Lyall.

Studies in biography. 1907, 1907, New York 1907.

Essays political and biographical. Ed F. Holland 1908.

THOMAS WRIGHT
1810–77

The history and topography of the County of Essex. 2 vols 1836.

The history and antiquities of London, Westminster, Southwark and parts adjacent. 5 vols 1837. Vols 1–4 by T. Allen; vol 5 by Wright.

The universities: Le Keux's Memorials of Cambridge; with historical and descriptive accounts by Thomas Wright and H. Longueville Jones. 2 vols 1841–2; ed C. H. Cooper 2 vols Cambridge 1860, 3 vols Cambridge [1880].

The history of Ludlow and its neighbourhood. Ludlow 1852 (for 1841–52).

Biographia britannica literaria: or biography of literary characters of Great Britain and Ireland. Anglo-Saxon period. 1842. Anglo-Norman period, 1846; Introduction also separately pbd as An essay on the state of literature and learning under the Anglo-Saxons, introductory to the Biographia Britannica literaria, 1839.

St Patrick's purgatory: an essay on the legends of Purgatory, Hell and Paradise current during the Middle Ages. 1844.

Essays on subjects connected with the literature, popular superstitions and history of England in the Middle Ages. 2 vols 1846.

England under the House of Hanover: its history during the reigns of the three Georges, illustrated from the caricatures and satires of the day. 2 vols 1848, [1868], 1876 (as Caricature history of the Georges).

The history of Ireland. 3 vols [1848–52].

Narratives of sorcery and magic. 2 vols 1851.

Historical and descriptive account of the caricatures of James Gillray. 1851, [1873] (expanded as The works of James Gillray, with the history of his life and times). With R. H. Evans.

The Celt, the Roman and the Saxon: a history of the early inhabitants of Britain, down to the conversion of the Anglo-Saxons. 1852, 1861 (rev), 1875, 1885.

The history of Scotland. 3 vols [1852–5], [1873–4], 1888.

Wanderings of an antiquary, chiefly upon the traces of the Romans in Britain. 1854.

The history of France. 3 vols [1856–62], 3 vols [1871–2].

Dictionary of obsolete and provincial English. 2 vols 1857.

Guide to the ruins of the Roman city of Uriconium at Wroxeter near Shrewsbury. Shrewsbury 1859, 1859 (as The ruins of the Roman city of Uriconium).

Essays on archaeological subjects and on various questions connected with the Middle Ages. 2 vols 1861.

A history of domestic manners and sentiments in England during the Middle Ages. 1862, 1871 (expanded as The homes of other days).

A history of caricature and grotesque in literature and art. 1865.

Ludlow sketches: a series of papers. Ludlow 1867.

Womankind in Western Europe from the earliest times to the seventeenth century. 1869.

Uriconium: a historical account of the ancient Roman city. 1872.

VIII. PHILOSOPHY

General Studies

Masson, D. Recent British philosophy. 1865.

Hutton, R. H. Criticisms on contemporary thought and thinkers. 2 vols 1894.

Stephen, L. The English Utilitarians. 3 vols 1900.

Halévy, E. La formation du radicalisme philosophique. 3 vols Paris 1901–4; tr 1928, 1952.

Dicey, A. V. Lectures on the relation between law and public opinion in England during the nineteenth century. 1905.

Muirhead, J. H. (ed). Contemporary British philosophy. 2 vols 1924–5.

Somervell, D. C. English thought in the nineteenth century. 1929, 1950.

Plamenatz, J. The English Utilitarians. Oxford 1949, 1958 (rev) (Home Univ Lib).

Houghton, W. E. Victorian anti-intellectualism. JHI 13 1952.

—— The Victorian frame of mind 1830–70. New Haven 1957.

Robbins, L. The theory of economic policy in English classical political economy. 1952.

Holloway, J. The Victorian sage: studies in argument. 1953.

Passmore, J. A hundred years of philosophy. 1957 (with bibliography), 1966 (rev, without bibliography).

Quinton, A. The neglect of Victorian philosophy. Victorian Stud 1 1958.

JOHN AUSTIN
1790–1859

§ 1

The province of jurisprudence determined. 1832.

Centralisation. Edinburgh Rev 85 1847.

A plea for the Constitution. 1859.

Lectures on jurisprudence: or the philosophy of positive law. Ed S. Austin 3 vols 1861–3, 1885 (5th edn).

The province of jurisprudence determined, and The uses of the study of jurisprudence. Ed H. L. A. Hart 1954.

§ 2

Mill, J. S. Austin on jurisprudence. In his Dissertations and discussions vol 3, 1867.

Smith, C. I. Locke and Austin on the idea of morality. JHI 23 1962.

ALEXANDER BAIN
1818–1903

On the applications of science to human health and well-being. 1848.

The senses and the intellect. 1855, 1864 (rev and enlarged), 1868 (enlarged), 1894.

The emotions and the will. 1859, 1865 (rev), 1875 (rev), New York 1876, 1899 (with addns).

On the study of character, including an estimate of phrenology. 1861.

An English grammar. 1863, 1872 (rev as A higher English grammar), 1879 (rev), 1904 (rev and enlarged). Also A first English grammar, with key, 1872, 1882.

The methods of debate: an address delivered to the Aberdeen University Debating Society. Aberdeen 1863.

A letter to Westerton, chairman of Mill's [election] committee. [1865].

English composition and rhetoric. 1866, 1869, 2 vols 1887–8 (enlarged).

Mental and moral science. 1868, 2 vols 1872 (enlarged).

Logic: deductive and inductive. 2 vols 1870, 1873, 1879, New York 1887 (rev).

Mind and body: the theories of their relation. 1873, 1910 (11th edn).

Education as a science. 1879 (7 edns).

James Mill. 1882. Enlarged from Mind 1–2 1876–7.

John Stuart Mill. 1882. Rptd from Mind 4–5 1879–80.

Practical essays. 1884.

On teaching English, with an enquiry into the definition of poetry. 1887. Auxiliary to enlarged edn of English composition and rhetoric, above.

Dissertations on leading philosophical topics. 1903.

Autobiography. Ed W. L. Davidson 1904.

ARTHUR JAMES BALFOUR, 1st EARL OF BALFOUR
1848–1930

§ 1

A defence of philosophic doubt. 1879, 1921.
Handel. [1887?].
The pleasures of reading: inaugural address as Rector of St Andrews University. 1888.
The religion of humanity. Edinburgh 1888.
A fragment on progress: inaugural address as Rector of the University of Glasgow. Edinburgh 1892.
Essays and addresses. Edinburgh 1893, 1905 (3rd edn enlarged).
The foundations of belief. 1895, 1901 (8th edn).
The nineteenth century: inaugural address at Cambridge. Cambridge 1900.
Reflections suggested by the new theory of matter: presidential address to the British Association for the Advancement of Science. 1904.
Decadence. Cambridge 1908.
Questionings on criticism and beauty. 1909, Oxford 1910 (rev as Criticism and beauty).
Francis Bacon. 1913.
Theism and humanism: Gifford lectures. 1915.
Essays speculative and political. 1920.
Theism and thought. [1923].
Familiar beliefs and transcendent reason. 1927.
Chapters of autobiography. Ed Mrs E. Dugdale 1930.

§ 2

Alderson, B. Balfour: the man and his work. 1903.
'Raymond, E. T.' (E. R. Thompson). Balfour: a biography. 1920.
Dugdale, B. E. C. Balfour. 1936.
Young, K. Balfour: the happy life of the politician, Prime Minister, statesman and philosopher. 1963.

BERNARD BOSANQUET
1848–1923

§ 1

Knowledge and reality. 1885.
Introduction to Hegel's philosophy of the fine arts. 1886.
Logic: or the morphology of knowledge. 2 vols Oxford 1888, 1911.
Essays and addresses. 1889, 1899 (3rd edn).
'In darkest England': on the wrong track. 1891.
A history of aesthetic. 1892, 1917 (4th edn).
The civilisation of Christendom and other studies. 1893, 1899 (2nd edn).
Aspects of the social problem. 1895. Ed Bosanquet.
The essentials of logic. 1895.
Companion to Plato's Republic. 1895.
Rousseau's Social contract. 1895.
Psychology of the moral self. 1897.
The philosophical theory of the state. 1899, 1923 (4th edn).
The communication of moral ideas as a function of an ethical society. 1900.
Education of the young in Plato. Cambridge 1900.
The social criterion. 1907.
Truth and coherence. St Andrews 1911.
The principle of individuality and value. 1912.
The value and destiny of the individual. 1913.
The distinction between mind and its objects. Manchester 1913.
Germany in the nineteenth century. Manchester 1915.
Three lectures on aesthetic. 1915, ed R. Ross, Indianapolis 1963.
Social and international ideals. 1917.

Some suggestions in ethics. 1918.
Implication and linear inference. 1920.
What religion is. 1920.
Meeting of extremes in contemporary philosophy. 1921.
Three chapters on the nature of mind. Ed H. Bosanquet 1923.
Science and philosophy and other essays. Ed J. H. Muirhead and R. C. Bosanquet 1927.

§ 2

Bradley, A. C. and R. B. Haldane. Bosanquet. Proc Br Acad 10 1923.
—— Bosanquet. [1924].
Laski, H. J. Bosanquet's theory of the general will (symposium). Proc Aristotelian Soc Suppl 8 1928.
Lindsay, A. D. Bosanquet's theory of the general will (symposium). Ibid.
Muirhead, J. H. (ed). Bosanquet and his friends: letters illustrating sources and development of his philosophical opinions. 1935.

FRANCIS HERBERT BRADLEY
1846–1924

§ 1

The presuppositions of critical history. Oxford 1874.
Ethical studies. Oxford 1876, 1927 (rev), 1959; ed R. G. Ross, New York 1951.
Mr Sedgwick's hedonism. 1877.
The principles of logic. 1883, 1922 (rev edn with commentary and terminal essays), 1958.
Appearance and reality. 1893, 1897 (rev), Oxford 1959.
Essays on truth and reality. Oxford 1914, 1962.
Aphorisms. Oxford 1930.
Collected essays. 2 vols Oxford 1935.

§ 2

Sidgwick, H. Bradley's Ethical studies. Mind 1 1876. Replies by Bradley and Sidgwick 2 1877.
Bosanquet, B. Knowledge and reality. 1885.
Russell, B. Some explanations in reply to Bradley. Mind new ser 19 1910. Reply by Bradley 20 1911.
Broad, C. D. Bradley on truth and reality. Mind new ser 23 1914.
Eliot, T. S. Leibnitz's monads and Bradley's finite centers. Monist 26 1916.
—— Knowledge and experience in the philosophy of Bradley. Ed A. Bolgan 1964. A Harvard PhD thesis, written 1916.
Taylor, A. E. Bradley. Proc Br Acad 11 1925.
—— Mind new ser 34 1925.
Wollheim, R. A. In The revolution in philosophy, ed A. J. Ayer 1956.
—— Bradley. 1959 (Pelican).
Pears, D. F. et al. Metaphysics. In The nature of metaphysics, ed D. F. Pears 1957.

EDWARD CAIRD
1835–1908

§ 1

A critical account of the philosophy of Kant. Glasgow 1877.
The problem of philosophy at the present time. Glasgow 1881.
Hegel. Edinburgh 1883.
The social philosophy and religion of Comte. Glasgow 1885.
The critical philosophy of Kant. 2 vols Glasgow 1889.

Essays on literature and philosophy. 2 vols Glasgow 1892.
Vol 1 rptd as Essays on literature, 1909.
The evolution of religion. 2 vols Glasgow 1893.
Individualism and Socialism. Glasgow 1897.
The evolution of theology in the Greek philosophers.
2 vols Glasgow 1904, 1923.
Lay sermons and addresses. Glasgow 1907.

§ 2

Bosanquet, B. Caird. Proc Br Acad 3 1908.
Jones, H. and J. H. Muirhead. The life and philosophy of
Caird. 1921.

CHARLES LUTWIDGE DODGSON, 'LEWIS CARROLL'
1832–98

See also col 947, above.
The game of logic. 1886, 1887.
A logical paradox. Mind new ser 3 1894. Replies by
A. Sidgwick, W. E. Johnson, ibid; A. Sidgwick, 4
1895; E. E. C. Jones, 'W', 14 1905; A. W. Burks,
I. M. Copi, 59 1950; and A. J. Baker, 64 1955.
What the tortoise said to Achilles. Mind new ser 4 1895.
Replies by W. J. Rees, 60 1951; D. G. Brown, 63 1954.
Symbolic logic, part I: elementary. 1896 (3 edns), 1897.

ALEXANDER CAMPBELL FRASER
1819–1914

Introductory lecture on logic and metaphysics. Edinburgh
1851.
Essays in philosophy. Edinburgh 1856.
Rational philosophy in history and in system. Edinburgh
1858.
Whately and the restoration of the study of logic. Cam-
bridge [1863].
On mental philosophy. Edinburgh 1868.
Life and letters of Berkeley, and an account of his philo-
sophy. Oxford 1871.
Berkeley. Edinburgh 1881.
Locke. Edinburgh 1890.
The philosophy of theism. 2 ser 1895–6, 1899 (rev).
Reid. 1898.
Biographia philosophica. Edinburgh 1904.
Locke as a factor in modern thought. Proc Br Acad 1
1904.
Berkeley and spiritual realism. 1908.

THOMAS HILL GREEN
1836–82

§ 1

Liberal legislation and freedom of contract. Oxford
1881.
Prolegomena to ethics. Ed A. C. Bradley, Oxford 1883,
1907 (5th edn).
The witness of God, and faith: two lay sermons. Ed A. and
C. Toynbee 1883.
Works. Ed R. L. Nettleship 3 vols 1885–8 (with memoir),
1889–90.
An essay on the value and influence of works of fiction.
Ed F. N. Scott, Ann Arbor 1911.

§ 2

Sidgwick, H. Lectures on the ethics of Green, Spencer
and Martineau. 1902.

Bryce, J. In his Studies in contemporary biography,
1903.
Nettleship, R. L. Memoir of Green. 1906.
Muirhead, J. H. The service of the state: four lectures on
the political teaching of Green. 1908.
Richter, M. The politics of conscience: Green and his age.
Cambridge Mass 1964.
Randall, J. H. Green: the development of English thought
from Mill to Bradley. JHI 27 1966.

JOHN GROTE
1813–66

A few notes on a pamphlet by Mr Shilleto entitled
Thucydides or Grote? 1851.
Old studies and new. Cambridge 1856.
Essays and reviews. Cambridge 1862.
Exploratio philosophica. 2 pts Cambridge 1865–1900.
An examination of the Utilitarian philosophy. Ed J. P.
Mayor, Cambridge 1870.
Sermons. Cambridge 1872.
A treatise on the moral ideals. Ed J. P. Mayor, Cam-
bridge 1876.
Plato's utilitarianism: a dialogue by Grote and H. Sidgwick.
Classical Rev 3 1889.

SIR WILLIAM HAMILTON
1788–1856

Works of Reid. 2 vols Edinburgh 1846, 1 vol Edinburgh
1852 (3rd edn), 2 vols Edinburgh 1863 (6th edn).
Ed Hamilton.
Letter to De Morgan on his claim to an independent
rediscovery of a new principle in the theory of syllogism.
1847.
Discussions on philosophy and literature, education and
university reform. 1852, 1853 (enlarged), 1866.
Collected works of Stewart. 11 vols Edinburgh 1854–60.
Ed Hamilton.
Lectures on metaphysics and logic. Ed H. L. Mansel and
J. Veitch 4 vols Edinburgh 1859–60, London 1861–6
(rev).

FREDERIC HARRISON
1831–1923

Order and progress. 2 pts 1875.
Science and humanity: a lay sermon. 1879.
The social factor in psychology. [1879].
The present and the future. 1880.
Politics and a human religion. 1885.
Moral and religious socialism. 1891.
The meaning of history and other historical pieces. 1894.
Tennyson, Ruskin, Mill and other literary estimates. 1899.
Positivism: its position, aims and ideals. 1901.
The religion of duty. Philadelphia 1901.
Herbert Spencer. Oxford 1905.
Collected essays. 4 pts 1907–8.
Autobiographic memoirs. 2 vols 1911.
Among my books: centenaries, reviews, memoirs. 1912.
The positive evolution of religion. 1913.
On society. 1918.
See also col 1082, above.

THOMAS HENRY HUXLEY
1825–95

§ 1

On the educational value of the natural history sciences.
1854.
On races, species and their origin. 1860.

Evidence as to man's place in nature. Edinburgh 1863.
On the methods and results of ethnology. 1865.
Lay sermons, addresses and reviews. 1870.
Critiques and addresses. 1873.
The evidence of the miracle of resurrection. 1876.
American addresses. 1877.
Hume. 1878 (EML).
Science and culture, and other essays. 1881.
The advance of science in the last half-century. New York 1887.
Social diseases and worse remedies. 1891, 1891 (2nd edn).
Essays on some controverted questions. 1892.
Evolution and ethics. 1893, 1893, 1893. With Prolegomena (1894) in Collected essays vol 9, below.
Collected essays. 9 vols 1893-4. Includes an autobiography, ed G. de Beer, Oxford 1974 (with Darwin's).
Scientific memoirs. Ed M. Foster and E. R. Lankester 5 vols 1898-1903.
Religion without revelation. Ed J. Huxley 1957.

§2

Huxley, L. Life and letters of Huxley. 2 vols 1900.
— Huxley. 1920.
Huxley, A. Huxley as a man of letters. 1932.
The Huxley papers: a descriptive catalogue. 1946.
Irvine, W. Apes, angels and Victorians: the story of Darwin, Huxley and evolution. New York 1955.
Bibby, C. Huxley: scientist, humanist and educator. 1959.
Cockshut, A. O. J. Huxley: the scientific sage. In his Unbelievers: English agnostic thought 1840-90, 1964.

WILLIAM STANLEY JEVONS
1835-82

Pure logic: or the science of quality apart from quantity. 1864.
The state in relation to labour. 1866.
The substitution of similars. 1869.
Elementary lessons in logic. 1870, 1884, 1891, 1905, 1957.
The theory of political economy. 1871, 1879 (enlarged), New York 1965 (with bibliography).
Logic. 1872, 1876, 1880, 1889.
The principles of science. 2 vols 1874, New York 1877 (rev).
Primer of logic. 1878.
Studies in deductive logic. 1880, 1896 (3rd edn).
Methods of social reform, and other papers. Ed H. A. Jevons 1883.
Letters and journal ed by his wife. 1886.
Pure logic and other minor works. Ed R. Adamson and H. A. Jevons 1890.
The principles of economics. Ed H. Higgs 1905.

GEORGE HENRY LEWES
1817-78

A biographical history of philosophy. 4 vols 1845-6, 1 vol 1857 (rev), 2 vols 1867 (as History of philosophy), 2 vols 1871 (rev), 2 vols 1880.
The Spanish drama: Lope de Vega and Calderón. 1846.
Ranthorpe. 1847. A novel.
Rose, Blanche and Violet. 3 vols 1848. A novel.
The life of Robespierre. 1849, 1899 (3rd edn).
The noble heart: a tragedy. 1850.
A certain age. 1851; The game of speculation, 1851; A chain of events, 1852; Taking by storm, 1852. Plays.
Comte's philosophy of the sciences. 1853, 1878.
The lawyers. 1853; Stay at home, 1853; Strange history in nine chapters, 1853; Buckstone's adventure with the Polish princess, 1855. Plays.

The life and works of Goethe. 2 vols 1855, 1864, 1873 (abridged), 1875 (3rd edn rev).
Sea-side studies at Ilfracombe, Tenby, the Scilly Isles and Jersey. Edinburgh 1858, 1860.
The physiology of common life. 2 vols 1859-60.
Captain Bland. 1860. A play.
Studies in animal life. 1862.
Aristotle: a chapter from the history of science. 1864.
The foundations of a creed. 2 vols [1873], 1875 (in Problems of life and mind, 1st ser).
Problems of life and mind. 5 vols [1873]-9.
On actors and the art of acting. 1875, New York 1957.
The physical basis of mind. 1877 (in Problems of life and mind, 2nd ser).
The study of psychology. 2 vols 1879 (in Problems of life and mind, 3rd ser).
The principles of success in literature. Ed F. N. Scott 1891; ed T. S. Knowlson [1898].
Dramatic essays reprinted from the Examiner. Ed W. Archer and R. W. Lowe 1894.
Literary criticism. Ed A. R. Kaminsky, Lincoln Nebraska 1964.
GHL's literary receipts *are pbd for the first time from the ms in the Berg Collection, New York Public Library, in* The George Eliot letters vol 7, ed G. S. Haight, New Haven 1956, *and identify some anon articles.*

SIR JAMES MACKINTOSH
1765-1832

Disputatio physiologica inauguralis de actione musculari. Edinburgh 1787.
Vindiciae gallicae. Dublin 1791, London 1791 (rev), 1791, 1837 (new edn).
A discourse on the study of the law of nature and of nations. 1799, 1828, 1835 (enlarged).
Dissertation on the progress of ethical philosophy. Edinburgh 1830; ed W. Whewell, Edinburgh 1836, 1862, 1872.
History of England. 3 vols 1830-2, 10 vols 1850, 2 vols 1853.
History of the revolution in England in 1688, with life by Wallace. 1834.
Tracts and speeches. 5 pts Edinburgh 1840 (25 copies).
Miscellaneous works. Ed R. J. Mackintosh 3 vols 1846.
See also col 1108, above.

JAMES MARTINEAU
1805-1900

The rationale of religious inquiry. 1836, 1844, 1845, 1853, [1908] (as What is Christianity?).
The Christian view of moral evil. 1839.
Introductory lecture on mental and moral philosophy. 1841.
Endeavours after the Christian life. 2 vols 1843-7, 1 vol 1881 (6th edn); ed J. E. Carpenter 1907.
Miscellanies. Ed T. S. King, Boston 1852.
A plea for philosophic studies. 1854.
Essays philosophical and theological. Boston 1866, 2 vols 1868, New York 1879.
The place of mind in nature, and intuition in man. 1872.
Religion as affected by modern materialism. 1874.
Modern materialism in its relations to religion and theology. 1876, New York 1877.
The supposed conflict between efficient and final causation. 1877.
Ideal substitutes for God considered. 1878, 1879 (3rd edn).
The relation between ethics and religion. 1881.
A study of Spinoza. 1882, 1883 (rev).
A study of religion, its sources and contents. 2 vols 1888, 1889 (rev), 1900.
Types of ethical theory. 2 vols Oxford 1885, 1886, 1889, 1891 (enlarged), 1898.

Essays, reviews and addresses. 4 vols 1890–1.
National duties, and other sermons and addresses. Ed
G. and E. Martineau 1903.
Also specifically religious works; see col 1132, below.

JAMES MILL
1773–1836
§1

An essay on the impolicy of a bounty on the exportation of
grain. 1804.
Commerce defended. 1807, 1808.
Schools for all, not schools for Churchmen only. 1812.
Proposals for establishing in the metropolis a day school
for the application of the methods of Bell, Lancaster and
others to the higher branches of education. 1815.
With F. Place.
History of British India. 3 vols 1817, 1820, 6 vols 1826,
9 vols 1840–8 (with notes and continuation by H. H.
Wilson).
An account of the maison de force at Ghent. 1817.
Elements of political economy. 1821, 1824 (rev and
enlarged), 1826 (rev and enlarged).
An essay on government. 1821. *See* Essays on government
etc, below.
Statement of the question of parliamentary reform. 1821.
Essays on government, jurisprudence, liberty of the
press, prisons and prison discipline, colonies (separately
issued 1820), law of nations and education. [1825] (50
copies), [1828]. Rptd from the suppl to 5th edn of
Encyclopaedia britannica, to which he contributed other
articles.
Analysis of the phenomena of the human mind. 2 vols
1829, ed J. S. Mill 1869.
On the ballot. 1830, [1830] (3rd edn).
A fragment on Mackintosh. 1835, 1870.
The principles of toleration. 1837.
Selected economic writings. Ed D. Winch, Edinburgh
1966.

§2

Macaulay, T. B. Mill's Essay on government. Edinburgh
Rev 49 1829.
—— Bentham's defence of Mill. Ibid.
—— Utilitarian theory of government, and the greatest
happiness principle. Edinburgh Rev 50 1829.
Mill, J. S. In E. L. Bulwer, England and the English
vol 2, 1833. Altered by Bulwer.
—— In his Autobiography, 1873.
Bain, A. James Mill. 1882.
Stephen, L. In his English Utilitarians vol 2, 1900.
Forbes, D. James Mill and India. Cambridge Jnl Oct 1951.
Sraffa, P. (ed). Works of David Ricardo, vols 6–9. Cam-
bridge 1952.
Stokes, E. The English Utilitarians and India. Oxford 1959.
Hamburger, J. James Mill and the art of revolution. New
Haven 1963.

JOHN STUART MILL
1806–73
Collections

Collected works. Ed F. E. L. Priestley, F. E. Mineka,
J. M. Robson et al 25 vols Toronto 1963–.
Essays in literature and society. Ed J. B. Schneewind,
New York 1965; Ethical writings, ed Schneewind, New
York 1965.
Literary essays. Ed E. Alexander, Indianapolis 1967.

§1

Jeremy Bentham, Rationale of judicial evidence, 5 vols
1827. Ed Mill, with notes and addns.
A system of logic, ratiocinative and inductive. 2 vols
1843, 1846 (rev; significant alterations also pbd separately as Two chapters of A system of logic), 1851
(rev), 1856 (rev), 1862 (rev), 1865 (rev), 1868 (rev),
1872 (rev).
Essays on some unsettled questions of political economy.
1844, 1874, 1877, 1948.
Remarks on Mr Fitzroy's Bill. 1853.
On liberty. 1859, 1859, 1864, 1869; ed M. Warnock 1962
(with Utilitarianism, below, and Bentham); ed R.
Wollheim, Oxford 1975.
Thoughts on parliamentary reform. 1859, 1859 (with
addns), 1867 (in Dissertations and discussions, below,
vol 3).
Dissertations and discussions. 2 vols 1859, 3 vols 1867.
On Bentham and Coleridge, ed F. R. Leavis 1950.
Considerations on representative government. 1861, 1861
(rev), 1865.
Utilitarianism. 1863, 1864 (rev), 1867 (rev), 1871 (rev).
Auguste Comte and Positivism. 1865, 1866 (rev).
An examination of Hamilton's philosophy. 1865, 1865
(rev), 1867 (rev), 1872 (rev).
Inaugural address at St Andrews. 1867, 1867.
England and Ireland. 1868 (5 edns).
James Mill, Analysis of the phenomena of the human
mind. 2 vols 1869 (2nd edn). Ed Mill, with notes.
The subjection of women. 1869, 1869, 1870; ed R.
Wollheim, Oxford 1975 (with On liberty, above).
Chapters and speeches on the Irish land question. 1870,
1870.
Autobiography. Ed Helen Taylor. 1873, 1873, 1874, 1874,
1879, 1908; ed H. J. Laski, Oxford (WC) 1924 (with
appendix of speeches); ed R. Howson, New York 1924
(from holograph ms); ed J. Stillinger, Boston 1969.
Early draft. Ed J. Stillinger, Urbana 1961.
Three essays on religion. Ed H. Taylor 1874.
Socialism. Chicago 1879; ed W. D. Porter, New York
1891.
The spirit of the age. Ed F. A. von Hayek, Chicago 1942.

Letters etc

Correspondence inédite avec G. d'Eichthal. Ed E.
d'Eichthal, Paris 1898.
Letters. Ed H. S. R. Elliot 2 vols 1910.
Mill's boyhood visit to France 1820–1, a journal and
notebook. Ed A. J. Mill, Toronto 1960.
Earlier letters. Ed F. E. Mineka 2 vols Toronto 1963;
Later letters 1849–73, ed Mineka and D. N. Lindley
4 vols Toronto 1973.

§2

Stephen, J. F. Liberty, equality, fraternity. 1873.
Bain, A. J. S. Mill: a criticism. 1882.
Green, T. H. In his Prolegomena to ethics, ed A. C.
Bradley, Oxford 1883.
—— The logic of Mill. In his Works vol 2, 1886.
Stephen, L. In his English Utilitarians vol 3, 1900.
Neff, E. E. Carlyle and Mill: mystic and utilitarian.
New York 1924, 1926 (2nd edn rev as Carlyle and Mill:
an introduction to Victorian thought).
Britton, K. Mill, the ordeal of an intellectual. Cambridge
Jnl 2 1948.
Hayek, F. A. von. Mill and Harriet Taylor: their friend-
ship and subsequent marriage. Chicago 1951.
Packe, M. St J. Life of Mill. 1954.
Russell, B. Mill. Proc Br Acad 41 1955.
—— In his Portraits from memory, 1956.
Berlin, I. Mill and the ends of life. [1961]; rptd in his
Four essays on liberty, Oxford 1969.

Annan, N. In The English mind, ed H. S. Davies and G. Watson, Cambridge 1964.

Cockshut, A. O. J. Mill, the half-circle. In his Unbelievers: English agnostic thought, 1964.

Schneewind, J. B. (ed). Mill: a collection of critical essays. New York 1968.

Himmelfarb, G. On liberty and liberalism. New York 1974.

Ryan, A. J. S. Mill. 1974.

GEORGE JOHN ROMANES
1848–94

A candid examination of theism. Boston 1878, 1892 (3rd edn). By 'Physicus'.

Darwin. 1882.

The scientific evidences of organic evolution. 1882.

Animal intelligence. New York 1883, London 1886 (4th edn).

Mental evolution in animals. 1883.

Mental evolution in man. 1888.

Poems. 1889.

Darwin and after Darwin. Chicago 3 vols 1892–7.

An examination of Weismannism. 1893.

Mind and motion and monism. 1895.

Thoughts on religion. Ed C. Gore, Chicago 1895, 1897 (3rd edn).

Essays. Ed C. L. Morgan 1897.

Also works on psychology.

ANDREW SETH, from 1898 PRINGLE-PATTISON
1856–1931

The development from Kant to Hegel. 1882.

Essays in philosophical criticism. Ed Seth and R. B. Haldane 1883.

Scottish philosophy: a comparison of the Scottish and German answers to Hume. Edinburgh 1885.

Hegelianism and personality. Edinburgh 1887, 1893.

The present position of the philosophical sciences. Edinburgh 1891.

Two lectures on theism. New York 1897.

Man's place in the cosmos. Edinburgh 1897, 1902 (rev).

The philosophical radicals, and other essays. Edinburgh 1907.

The idea of God in the light of recent philosophy. Aberdeen and Oxford 1917, 1920 (rev).

The idea of immortality. Oxford 1922.

The philosophy of history. [1924].

Haldane. 1930.

Studies in the philosophy of religion. Oxford 1930.

The Balfour lectures on realism. Ed G. F. Barbour, Edinburgh 1933. With memoir.

HENRY SIDGWICK
1838–1900

The ethics of conformity and subscription. 1870.

The methods of ethics. 1874, 1877 (enlarged), 1884 (enlarged), 1907 (7th edn), 1962.

The incoherence of empirical philosophy. [1879].

Principles of political economy. 1883, 1901 (3rd edn), 1924.

The scope and method of economic science. 1885.

Outline of the history of ethics. 1886, 1888, 1892, 1896.

The elements of politics. 1891, 1897 (rev), 1919 (4th edn).

Practical ethics: a collection of addresses and essays. 1898.

The scope and limits of the work of an ethical society; the aims and methods of an ethical society. 1900.

Philosophy: its scope and relations. Ed J. Ward 1902.

Lectures on the ethics of Green, Spencer and Martineau. Ed E. E. C. Jones 1902.

The development of European polity. Ed E. M. Sidgwick 1903, 1920 (3rd edn).

Miscellaneous essays and addresses. Ed E. M. and A. Sidgwick 1904.

Lectures on the philosophy of Kant and other philosophical lectures and essays. Ed J. Ward 1905.

WILLIAM RITCHIE SORLEY
1855–1935

On the ethics of naturalism. Edinburgh 1885, 1904 (rev).

Recent tendencies in ethics. Edinburgh 1904.

Agnosticism: its meanings and claims. 1908.

The moral life and moral worth. Cambridge 1911.

The interpretation of evolution. [1912].

Moral values and the idea of God. Aberdeen and Cambridge 1918.

Spinoza. 1918.

A history of English philosophy. Cambridge 1920, 1965 (as A history of British philosophy to 1900). Based on CHEL.

Value and reality. In Contemporary British philosophy, ed J. H. Muirhead vol 2, 1925.

Tradition. Oxford 1926.

HERBERT SPENCER
1820–1903

§ I

The proper sphere of government. 1843.

Social statics: or the conditions essential to human happiness specified. 1851, New York 1865, London 1876, 1892 (abridged and rev), 1910 (abridged and rev).

A new theory of population. 1852.

Over-legislation. 1854.

Railway morals and railway policy. 1855.

Essays scientific, political and speculative. Ser 1, 1858; ser 2, 1863; as Illustrations of universal progress, New York 1864, 3 vols 1868–74, 1 vol 1875 (new edn), 3 vols 1878 (3rd edn), 2 vols 1883, 3 vols 1885 (4th edn), 1891 (new edn enlarged).

Education: intellectual, moral and physical. 1861, New York 1864, 1883 (new edn).

A system of synthetic philosophy. 10 vols 1860–96, 15 vols New York and London 1900.

The classification of the sciences. 1864, 1870, 1871. Pt 2 rev as Reasons for dissenting from the philosophy of Comte, 1884.

Spontaneous generation and the hypothesis of physiological units. New York 1870.

Recent discussions in science, philosophy and morals. New York 1871.

The study of sociology. 1873, 1874, 1874, 1880 (9th edn).

Descriptive sociology: or groups of sociological facts. 1873–81.

Philosophy of style. New York 1873.

The morals of trade. 1874, 1891.

The data of ethics. 1879.

The man versus the State. 1884, 1885, 1909, 1940, 1950.

The factors of organic evolution. 1887.

From freedom to bondage. 1891.

The inadequacy of natural selection. 1893.

A rejoinder to Weismann. 1893.

Weismannism once more. 1894.

Against the metric system. 1896, 1904 (3rd edn enlarged).

Various fragments. 1897, 1900 (enlarged).

Facts and comments. 1902, 1914.

Autobiography. 2 vols 1904, 1926.

Essays on education and kindred subjects. 1904.

§ 2

Maitland, F. W. Spencer's theory of society. Mind 8 1883.

Green, T. H. Spencer and Lewes: their application of the doctrine of evolution to thought. In his Works vol 1, 1886.

Sidgwick, H. In his Lectures on the ethics of Green, Spencer and Martineau, 1902.

—— In his Philosophy of Kant and other lectures, 1905.

Barker, E. Political thought in England from Spencer to the present day. 1915.

Cockshut, A. O. J. In his Unbelievers, 1964.

THOMAS TAYLOR
1758–1835

Proclus Diadochus: the philosophical and mathematical commentaries translated. 2 vols 1778, 1779.

A dissertation of the Eleusinian and Bacchic mysteries. Amsterdam [1790], 2 pts 1813; ed A. Wilder, New York 1875, 1891 (4th edn).

A vindication of the rights of brutes. 1792.

Plato's works. 5 vols 1804. Tr with F. Sydenham.

Miscellanies in prose and verse. 1805.

Collectanea. 1806.

Aristotle's works translated and illustrated. 10 vols 1806–12.

A dissertation on the philosophy of Aristotle. 1812.

Theoretic arithmetic. 1816.

Elements of a new arithmetical notation. 1823.

Also trns of many other classical works.

JAMES WARD
1843–1925

Naturalism and agnosticism. 2 vols 1899.

The realm of ends: or pluralism and theism. Cambridge 1911, 1912, 1920.

Heredity and memory. Cambridge 1913.

Psychological principles. Cambridge 1918, 1920.

A study of Kant. Cambridge 1922.

Psychology applied to education. Ed G. D. Hicks, Cambridge 1926.

Essays in philosophy. Ed W. R. Sorley and G. F. Stout, with memoir by O. Ward Campbell. Cambridge 1927.

RICHARD WHATELY
1787–1863

Elements of logic. 1826, 1832 (4th edn rev), 1836 (6th edn rev), 1840 (rev), 1844 (rev), 1848 (rev).

Elements of rhetoric. 1828, 1836 (5th edn rev), 1846 (7th edn rev); ed D. Ehninger, Carbondale 1963.

Easy lessons on reasoning. 1843.

Paley's Works. 1859. A lecture.

Miscellaneous lectures and reviews. 1861.

WILLIAM WHEWELL
1794–1866

Boadicea: a poem. Cambridge 1820.

The history of the inductive sciences. 3 vols 1837, 1847 (rev, with suppl, 1857), 1857 (with addns).

On the foundation of morals. Cambridge [1838?].

The philosophy of the inductive sciences founded on their history. 2 vols 1840, 1847 (enlarged), 3 vols 1858 (pt 1 as History of scientific ideas; pt 2 enlarged as Novum organon renovatum).

Two introductory lectures to two courses of lectures on moral philosophy. Cambridge 1841.

On the fundamental antithesis of philosophy. Cambridge 1844.

A letter to Herschel. Cambridge [1844].

The elements of morality, including polity. 2 vols 1845, 1854 (enlarged), 1864 (4th edn enlarged).

Of a liberal education in general. 3 pts 1845–52.

Lectures on systematic morality. 1846.

Of induction, with especial reference to Mill's System of logic. 1849.

Lectures on the history of moral philosophy in England. 1852, Cambridge 1862 (enlarged).

Of the plurality of worlds. 1853, 1854.

On the influence of the history of science upon intellectual education. In Royal Institute of Gt Britain lectures on education, 1855.

On the philosophy of discovery. 1860.

Also works on science, mathematics and education.

IX. RELIGION

A. THE LIBERAL THEOLOGIANS AND THE EVANGELICALS

General Studies

Lecky, W. E. H. History of the rise and influence of the spirit of rationalism in Europe. 2 vols 1865.

Stephen, L. History of English thought in the eighteenth century. 2 vols 1876, 1881 (for 1880), 1902, 1927.

Robertson, J. M. A short history of freethought, ancient and modern. 1899, 2 vols 1906 (rewritten and greatly enlarged), 1915 (rev and expanded), 1936 (as A history of freethought).

Cockshut, A. O. J. Anglican attitudes: a study of Victorian religious controversies. 1959.

—— The unbelievers: English agnostic thought 1840–1890. 1964.

Brown, F. K. Fathers of the Victorians: the age of Wilberforce. Cambridge 1961.

THOMAS ARNOLD
1795–1842

Sermons. 3 vols 1829–34; rev Mrs W. E. Forster 6 vols 1878.

Principles of Church reform. 1833 (3 edns); Postscript to Principles of Church reform, 1833 (in 4th edn).

Life and correspondence. Ed A. P. Stanley 2 vols 1844 (3 edns) etc, 1 vol 1901, 1903 (abridged).

Miscellaneous works. Ed A. P. Stanley 1845. *See col 1092, above.*

REGINALD HEBER
1783–1826

The personality and office of the Christian comforter. 1816.
Life of Bishop Jeremy Taylor. 1822 (in Whole works of Jeremy Taylor), 1828 (in Whole works), 1828 (separately).
Poetical works. 1841 etc.

MATTHEW ARNOLD
1822–88

St Paul and Protestantism. 1870; ed R. H. Super, Ann Arbor 1968.
Literature and dogma. 1873 (3 edns); ed Super (with above).
God and the Bible. 1875, 1884.
Last essays on Church and religion. 1877.
See also col 829, above.

JOHN WILLIAM COLENSO
1814–83

The Pentateuch and Book of Joshua critically examined. 7 pts 1862–79, 1862–4 (rev); pt 1, 1863 (rev); [1863] (extracts), 5 pts 1865, 1865 (preface and part of pt 5 only), 3 pts 1884, 1885.

'GEORGE ELIOT'
1819–80

The life of Jesus critically examined, by D. F. Strauss. 3 vols 1846, 1 vol 1892. Anon trn.
The essence of Christianity, by Ludwig Feuerbach, translated by Marian Evans. 1854.
See col 925, above.

Essays and reviews [by F. Temple, Rowland Williams, Baden Powell, H. B. Wilson, C. W. Goodwin, Mark Pattison, B. Jowett]. 1860, 1861 (3 edns), 1862, 1862, 1865; ed F. H. Hedge, New York 1874.

FREDERIC WILLIAM FARRAR
1831–1903

The life of Christ. 1874, 2 vols 1874, [1876–8] (illustr), [1878] (illustr), 1 vol [1887–89], [1890–1] (illustr), 1894 (illustr); ed W. Lefroy 1903; ed A. F. W. Ingram 1906; 1907, 1913, 1963 (reissue of edn of 1894).
Eternal hope. 1878, 1892 (with new preface).

FENTON JOHN ANTHONY HORT
1828–92

The way, the truth, the life: Hulsean lectures. 1871; ed B. F. Westcott 1893, 1897.
Judaistic Christianity. 1894.
Life and letters. Ed A. F. Hort 2 vols 1896.
The Christian Ecclesia. Ed J. O. F. Murray 1897.

RICHARD HOLT HUTTON
1826–97

Essays theological and literary. 2 vols 1871, 1877 (for 1876) (rev and enlarged), 1888 (Theological essays only), 1895 (Theological essays only).

Essays on some of the modern guides of English thought in matters of faith. 1887.
Aspects of religious and scientific thought. 1899.
See also col 1063, above.

BENJAMIN JOWETT
1817–93

Epistles of St Paul to Thessalonians, Galatians and Romans: translation and commentary with essays and dissertations. 2 vols 1855, 1859; ed L. Campbell 2 vols 1894 (the trn and commentary, 'edited and condensed').

CHARLES KINGSLEY
1819–75

The good news of God: sermons. 1859.
What, then, does Dr Newman mean? 1864 (3 edns); ed W. Ward, Oxford 1913 (in J. H. Newman, Apologia pro vita sua).
Letters and memories of his life, ed by his wife. 2 vols 1877 (3 edns), 1 vol 1879 (for 1878) (abridged), 1883 (abridged).
See also col 935, above.

JAMES MARTINEAU
1805–1900

The rationale of religious inquiry. 1836, 1844, 1845, 1853, [1908] (as What is Christianity?).
Endeavours after the Christian life. 2 sers 1843–7, 1 vol 1867, 1874, 1900, [1907]; ed J. E. Carpenter [1907]. 1907, [1907].
Types of ethical theory. 2 vols Oxford 1885, 1886, 1889, 1891 (enlarged), 1898.
A study of religion. 2 vols 1888, 1889 (rev).
The seat of authority in religion. 1890.
Essays, reviews and addresses. 4 vols 1890–1.
See J. Drummond and C. B. Upton, Life and letters, 2 vols 1902; and J. Estlin Carpenter, Martineau: theologian and teacher, 1905.

JOHN FREDERICK DENISON MAURICE
1805–72

The Kingdom of Christ, by a clergyman of the Church of England. [1837–8], 3 vols 1838, 2 vols 1842, 1883; [1906] (EL); ed A. R. Vidler 2 vols 1958, [1960].
Moral and metaphysical philosophy. 1845, 4 vols 1850–7, 2 vols 1871–2.
The religions of the world. 1847, 1848 (rev).
Theological essays. Cambridge 1853, 1853 (enlarged), 1854 (concluding essay and preface only), London 1871; E. F. Carpenter 1950.
The doctrine of sacrifice. 1854.
The epistles of St John: lectures on Christian ethics. 1857.
The conscience: lectures on casuistry. 1868, 1872.
The friendship of books and other lectures. Ed T. Hughes 1874.
Life of Maurice, chiefly told in his own letters. Ed J. F. Maurice 2 vols 1884.
See col 1064, above.

FRANCIS WILLIAM NEWMAN
1805–97

The soul: her sorrows and her aspirations. 1849, 1852, 1905 (with memoir by C. B. Upton).
Phases of faith. 1850, 1907.
Memoir and letters. Ed I. G. Sieveking 1909.
See col 845, above.

MARK PATTISON
1813–84

Tendencies of religious thought in England 1688–1750. 1860 (in Essays and reviews).
Sermons. 1885.
Memoirs. Ed Mrs Pattison 1885.
Essays, collected by H. Nettleship. 2 vols Oxford 1889, London [1908] (containing 16 of the original 21 essays).
See col 1066, above.

SIR JOHN ROBERT SEELEY
1834–95

Ecce homo. 1866 (for 1865) (anon), 1866, Boston 1866 etc; ed O. Lodge [1908]; ed J. E. Odgers 1910.
Natural religion, by the author of Ecce homo. 1882, 1891, 1895.
See also col 1110, above.

HENRY SIDGWICK
1838–1900

The ethics of conformity and subscription. 1870, 1898 (in Practical ethics).

ARTHUR PENRHYN STANLEY
1815–81

Sermons and essays on the apostolical age. Oxford 1847, 1874, [1890].
Essays, chiefly on questions of Church and State. 1870, 1884.
Christian institutions. 1881, 1882, 1884.
See G. G. Bradley, Recollections, 1883; R. E. Prothero, Life and correspondence, 1893.

JOHN STERLING
1806–44

Essays and tales. Ed J. C. Hare 2 vols 1848. With memoir.
Twelve letters [to William Coningham]. Ed W. Coningham 1851, 1872.
See T. Carlyle, Life of Sterling, 1851, 1852; ed W. H. White, Oxford 1907 (WC).

CONNOP THIRLWALL
1797–1875

Remains, literary and theological. Ed J. J. S. Perowne 3 vols 1877–8.
Letters, literary and theological. Ed J. J. S. Perowne and L. Stokes 1881, 1882.
See J. C. Thirlwall, Connop Thirlwall, 1936.

WILLIAM RALPH INGE
1860–1954

Christian mysticism. 1899, 1912, 1933.
The philosophy of Plotinus. 2 vols 1918, 1923, 1929.
Outspoken essays. 1919; 2nd ser, 2 vols 1919 [22], 1921.
Christian ethics and modern problems. 1930.

ANDREW SETH
from 1898 A. S. PRINGLE-PATTISON
1856–1931

Man's place in the cosmos. Edinburgh 1897, 1902 (rev and enlarged).
The idea of God in the light of recent philosophy. Aberdeen and Oxford 1917, 1920 (rev).
The idea of immortality. Oxford 1922.
See col 1127, above.

JAMES WARD
1843–1925

Naturalism and agnosticism. 2 vols 1899, 1903, 1906, 1 vol 1915.
The realm of ends: or pluralism and theism. Cambridge 1911, 1912, 1920.
See col 1129, above.

MARY AUGUSTA WARD,
née ARNOLD
1851–1920

Robert Elsmere. 3 vols 1888 (3 edns), 1 vol 1899, [1907], 1952.
A writer's recollections. 1918.
See col 988, above.

WILLIAM WILBERFORCE
1759–1833

A practical view of the prevailing religious system of professed Christians. 1797, 1797, 1798, Boston 1803, London 1805, 1817, 1824, 1826 (with introd by D. Wilson), Edinburgh [1854], [1871], London 1888 (with prefatory memoir by W. B.), [1830?] (abridged as Nominal and real Christianity contrasted).
An appeal to the religion, justice and humanity of the inhabitants of the British Empire, in behalf of the negro slaves of the West Indies. 1823, 1823.
See Robert Isaac and Samuel Wilberforce (his sons), Life of William Wilberforce, 5 vols 1838, 1 vol 1843 (abridged).

B. THE OXFORD MOVEMENT AND THE HIGH CHURCHMEN

General Studies

Perceval, A. P. A collection of papers connected with the theological movement of 1833. 1842, 1843.

Palmer, W. A narrative of events connected with the publication of the Tracts for the times. Oxford 1843, 1843, 1843 (with postscript), London 1883 (with introd and supplement to 1883).

Church, R. W. The Oxford Movement: twelve years 1833–45. 1891.

Sparrow Simpson, W. J. The history of the Anglo-Catholic revival from 1845. 1932.

Faber, G. Oxford Apostles: a character study of the Oxford Movement. 1933, 1936, 1954 (Pelican).

Dawson, C. H. The spirit of the Oxford Movement. 1933.

Reckitt, M. B. Maurice to Temple: a century of the social movement in the Church of England. 1947.

Principal Writings

Tracts for the times. Ed J. H. Newman 6 vols 1833–41. 90 tracts were issued anon between 9 Sept 1833 (Three tracts) and 27 Feb 1841 (Tract no 90).

Lyra apostolica. 1836; ed H. S. Holland and H. C. Beeching 1899. Poems originally ptd in Br Mag. Of the 179 pieces, Newman wrote 109, Keble 46.

The library of the Fathers of the Holy Catholic Church, anterior to the division of the East and West. Ed J. Keble, J. H. Newman, E. B. Pusey and [1843–57] C. Marriott, 48 vols 1838–85.

Plain sermons by the contributors to the Tracts for the times. [Ed I. Williams and W. J. Copeland] 10 vols 1839–48.

The library of Anglo-Catholic theology. 88 vols 1841–63. Ed W. J. Copeland 1841–3, W. F. Audland 1843–7, C. L. Cornish 1847–54, J. Barrow 1854–63.

Lives of the English saints. 4 vols 1844–5; ed A. W. Hutton 6 vols 1900–1. Suggested by Newman, but he ceased to be editor after the first 2 Lives.

Village sermons preached at Whatley. [1st ser] 1892; [2nd ser] 1894; [3rd ser] 1897; 1899 (1st ser); 1902 (2nd ser).

Pascal and other sermons. 1895.

The message of peace and other Christmas sermons. 1895, 1896, 1897.

Occasional papers 1846–90. [Ed M. C. Church] 2 vols 1897 (as vols 8–9 in Miscellaneous writings).

RICHARD WILLIAM CHURCH
1815–90

Lives of the English Saints: life of Wulstan. 1844 (anon), 1901.

Essays and reviews, collected from the British Critic and the Christian Remembrancer. 1854.

Sermons preached before the University of Oxford. 1868, 1880 (in The gifts of civilisation), [1913] with preface by the Bishop of London (as The gifts of civilisation).

Life of St Anselm. 1870.

Civilization before and after Christianity: two lectures. 1872, 1880 (in The gifts of civilisation).

On some influences of Christianity upon national character: three lectures. 1873, 1880 (in The gifts of civilisation).

The sacred poetry of early religions: two lectures. 1874, 1880 (in The gifts of civilisation).

The beginning of the Middle Ages. 1877.

Dante: an essay. Christian Remembrancer 1850; 1854 (in Essays and reviews); 1878 (with a trn of De Monarchia by F. J. Church).

Human life and its conditions: sermons preached before the University of Oxford in 1876–8 etc. 1878.

Spenser. 1880 (EML).

Bacon. 1884 (EML).

Discipline of the Christian character. 1885. Sermons.

Advent sermons. 1885, 1886.

[Miscellaneous writings.] 10 vols 1888 (uniform edn).

The Oxford Movement: twelve years 1833–45. 1891.

Cathedral and University sermons. 1892.

AUBREY THOMAS de VERE
1814–1902

Essays, chiefly on poetry. 2 vols 1887.

Essays, chiefly literary and ethical. 1889, New York 1889.

Recollections. New York 1897.

See W. P. Ward, De Vere: a memoir, 1904 and col 1157, below.

DIGBY MACKWORTH DOLBEN
1848–67

Poems. Ed R. Bridges, Oxford 1911 (with a memoir), 1915 (rev and enlarged).

RICHARD HURRELL FROUDE
1803–36

Tracts for the times. Nos 9, 59, 63 and possibly part of 35 1833–5.

Lyra apostolica. 1836 etc. Poems signed β.

Remains: part 1. [Ed J. Keble and J. H. Newman] 2 vols 1838; part 2 [ed J. B. Mozley, preface by J. Keble] 2 vols 1839.

See L. I. Guiney, Hurrell Froude: memoranda and comments, 1904.

JOHN KEBLE
1792–1866

§ I

The Christian year: thoughts in verse for the Sundays and Holydays throughout the year. 1827 (anon), 1827 (anon), 1828, 1829, 1832, 1834, 1835, 1840, 1841, 1848, 1849, 1850, 1858, 1866; ed A. H. Grant [1886]; ed 'Pilgrim' (James Hogg) 1886 (with Collects, and a series of meditations and exhortations selected from the works of H. P. Liddon); introd H. Morley 1887; ed J. C. Sharp [1914], Oxford 1914 (WC), 1914 (with Lyra innocentium and other poems and the sermon National apostasy).

National apostasy considered in a sermon. Oxford 1833, 1847 etc (in Sermons, academical and occasional), 1914 (in The Christian year, Lyra innocentium and other poems etc); ed R. J. E. Boggis, Torquay [1931].

Ode for the Encænia at Oxford. 1834 (anon), 1869 (in Miscellaneous poems).

Tracts for the times. Nos 4, 13, 40, 52, 54, 57, 60, 1834; no 89, 1841.

Lyra apostolica. 1836 etc. 46 poems signed γ.

Primitive tradition recognized in Holy Scripture: a sermon. 1836, 1837, 1837 (with postscript and Tract no 78 as appendix).

The Psalter or Psalms of David in English verse. 1839 (anon), 1840 (anon), 1869, 1904, 1906.

The case of Catholic subscription to the XXXIX articles. 1841 (priv ptd), 1865 (with Tract 90 by J. H. Newman).

Praelectiones poeticae. 1844.

Lyra innocentium: thoughts in verse on Christian children. Oxford 1846 (anon), 1846, 1846, 1851, 1867, 1884; ed W. Lock 1899; illustr B. Handler 1903; [1906], 1914 (with The Christian year and other poems and the sermon National apostasy).
Sermons, academical and occasional. Oxford 1847, 1848.
On Eucharistical adoration. Oxford 1857, 1859, 1867.
Sermons, occasional and parochial. 1868.
Miscellaneous poems. Ed G. Moberly 1869.
Village sermons on the baptismal service. [Ed E. B. Pusey] Oxford 1869 (for 1868).
Letters of spiritual counsel and guidance. Ed R. F. Wilson 1870, 1875 (enlarged); ed B. W. Randolph 1904.
Sermons for the Christian year [with an 'Advertisement' by E. B. P., i.e. E. B. Pusey]. 11 vols Oxford 1875–80.
Occasional papers and reviews. Ed E. B. Pusey, Oxford 1877.
Studia sacra. Ed J.P.N., i.e. J. P. Norris 1877.
Keble's lectures on poetry 1832–41, translated from Latin by E. K. Francis. 2 vols Oxford 1912.

§ 2

Shairp, J. C. Keble. Edinburgh 1866, 1868 (in Studies in poetry and philosophy).
Coleridge, J. T. A memoir of Keble. 1869, 2 vols 1869, 1870 (with corrections and addns).
Yonge, C. M. Musings over the Christian year and Lyra innocentium, together with a few gleanings of recollections of Keble, gathered by several friends. 1871.
Lock, W. Keble: a biography. 1893.
Wood, E. F. L. (Earl of Halifax). John Keble. 1909, 1932.
Battiscombe, G. Keble: a study in limitations. 1963.
Martin, B. W. Keble: priest, professor and poet. 1976.

HENRY EDWARD MANNING
1808–92

The unity of the Church. 1842.
Sermons. 4 vols 1842–50, 1 vol 1844.
Sermons preached before the University of Oxford. 1844.
The temporal mission of the Holy Ghost. 1865, 1866, 1877, 1892.
Sermons on ecclesiastical subjects. 3 vols 1867–73.
Miscellanies. 3 vols 1877–88.

EDWARD BOUVERIE PUSEY
1800–82

Tracts for the times. Nos 18, 66, 67, 68, 69, 70, 77, 81 and possibly 76, 1834–7.
A letter to the Archbishop of Canterbury. Oxford 1842, London 1842, 1843 (with notes).
A letter to the Bishop of London. Oxford 1851, 1851.
Parochial sermons. 3 vols 1852–73.
The doctrine of the Real Presence. 1855.
The Real Presence. 1857.
Sermons preached before the University of Oxford 1859–72. Oxford 1872.
The minor prophets. 1860.
Daniel the prophet: nine lectures. 1864, 1868.
An eirenicon. Pt 1, 1865; pt 2 (1st letter to Dr Newman), 1869; pt 3 (Is healthful reunion impossible?), 1870.
Historical preface to [J. H. Newman's] Tract no 90. 1865, 1866.
Lenten sermons 1858–74. Oxford 1874.
What is of faith as to everlasting punishment? Oxford 1880, 1880, 1880.
Parochial and Cathedral sermons. 1883.
See H. P. Liddon, Life of Pusey, ed J. O. Johnston, R. J. Wilson and W. E. Newbolt 4 vols 1893–7; G. W. E. Russell, Dr Pusey, 1907.

NICHOLAS PATRICK STEPHEN WISEMAN
1802–65

Lectures on the doctrines and practices of the Roman Catholic Church. 1836 (ptd without the author's sanction), 2 vols 1836 (authorized edn as Lectures on the principal doctrines and practices etc), 1851.
High Church claims: or a series of papers on the Oxford controversy. 1841.
Essays on various subjects. 3 vols 1853; ed J. Murphy 1888.
Fabiola: or the Church of the Catacombs. 1855 (anon), [1855], [1896], [1904], [1906]; ed J. R. and A. C. Hagan 1932 (school edn).
Recollections of the last four Popes and of Rome in their times. 1858, [1859] (rev), 1936 (abridged).
See W. Ward, The life and times of Cardinal Wiseman, 2 vols 1897.

X. ENGLISH STUDIES

EDWARD ARBER
1836–1912

English reprints. 30 vols 1868–71.
The first printed English New Testament, translated by William Tyndale, photolithographed from the unique fragment now in the Grenville Collection, British Museum. 1871.
Annotated reprints. 3 vols 1872–5.
A transcript of the Register of the Company of Stationers of London 1554–1640 AD. 5 vols 1875–94 (priv ptd).
An English garner: ingatherings from our history and literature. 8 vols 1877–96; ed and rearranged T. Seccombe 12 vols 1903.
The English scholar's library of old and modern works. 16 vols 1878–84.

An introductory sketch to the Martin Marprelate controversy 1558–90. 1880. No 8 of English scholar's library, above.
The first three English books on America ?1511–55 AD: being chiefly translations, compilations, etc by Richard Eden. Birmingham 1885.
The war library. 2 vols Birmingham 1894.
The story of the Pilgrim Fathers 1606–23 AD as told by themselves, their friends and their enemies. 1897.
British anthologies. 10 vols 1899–1901.
The term catalogues 1668–1709 AD; with a number for Easter term 1711 AD, from the quarterly lists issued by the booksellers. 3 vols 1903–6 (priv ptd).
A Christian library: a popular series of religious literature. 3 vols 1907 (priv ptd).

THOMAS ARNOLD
1823–1900

A manual of English literature, historical and critical; with an appendix on English metres. 1862, 1867 (rev and enlarged), 1873, 1877, 1885, 1888, 1897 (all rev).
Chaucer to Wordsworth: a short history of English literature, from the earliest times to the present day. [1870], 2 vols 1875.
A Catholic dictionary. 1884, 1917, [1928], 1951. With W. E. Addis.

Editions

Select English works of John Wycliff. 3 vols Oxford 1869–71.
Selections from Addison's papers contributed to the Spectator. 1875.
Beowulf: a heroic poem of the eighth century; with translation, notes and appendix. 1876.
Pope, selected poems: the Essay on criticism, the Moral essays, the Dunciad. 1876.
Henrici, Archidiaconi Huntendunensis, Historia Anglorum: the history of the English by Henry, Archdeacon of Huntingdon, from AC 55 to AD 1154. 1879 (Rolls Ser).
Symeonis monachi opera omnia. 2 vols 1882–5 (Rolls Ser).
Clarendon, History of the rebellion, book vi. 1886.
Dryden, An essay of dramatic poesy. 1889, 1903.
Memorials of St Edmund's Abbey. 1890.

WILLIAM BLADES
1824–90

The life and typography of William Caxton, England's first printer. 2 vols 1861–3.
A catalogue of books printed by (or ascribed to the press of) William Caxton. 1865.
A list of medals, jettons, tokens, etc in connection with printers and the art of printing. 1869 (priv ptd).
How to tell a Caxton. 1870.
A list of medals struck by order of the Corporation of London. 1870 (priv ptd).
Typographical notes. [1870] (priv ptd).
Shakspere and typography: being an attempt to show Shakspere's personal connection with, and technical knowledge of, the art of printing. A jeu d'esprit.
Some early type specimen books of England, Holland, France, Italy and Germany 1875.
The biography and typography of William Caxton. 1877. A different work from the Life, above.
The enemies of books. 1880, 1888 (rev and enlarged).
Numismata typographica: or the medallic history of printing, reprinted from the Printers' Register. 1883.
An account of the German morality-play entitled Depositio cornuti typographici; with a rhythmical translation of the German version of 1648. 1885.
Bibliographical miscellanies. 5 pts 1890.
The Pentateuch of printing, with a chapter on Judges, with a memoir of the author, and list of his works, by T. B. Reed. 1891.
Blades also contributed many essays on printing and bibliography; he edited Juliana Berners, Boke of St Albans; The dictes and sayings of the philosophers, Christine Pisan, Moral proverbes.

JAMES BOSWELL
1778–1822

A biographical memoir of the late Edmond Malone. 1814 (priv ptd). Rptd from GM June 1813; reissued in

Catalogue of early English poetry by E. Malone, 1836.
A Roxburghe garland. 1817.
The plays and poems of William Shakespeare comprehending an enlarged history of the stage, by the late E. Malone. 21 vols 1821. The 3rd variorum edn; ed Boswell from Malone's mss.
Boswell also pbd the 6th (rev) edn of his father's Life of Johnson.

JOSEPH BOSWORTH
1789–1876

Grammars and Dictionaries

An introduction to Latin construing. 1821, 1846.
Latin construing. 1821, 1850.
The elements of Anglo-Saxon grammar. 1823.
A compendious grammar of the primitive English or Anglo-Saxon language. 1826.
Græcæ grammatices rudimenta by William Bosworth, with additions by Joseph Bosworth. 1830.
A dictionary of the Anglo-Saxon language. 1838, 4 vols Oxford 1898 (rev partly from Bosworth's mss by T. N. Toller), 1908–1921.
A compendious Anglo-Saxon and English dictionary. 1848, 1881, 1888.

Editions, Translations etc

The origin of the Dutch. 1836.
Scandinavian literature. 1839. Anthology.
The origins of the English, Germanic and Scandinavian languages and nations. 1848.
A literal English translation of King Alfred's Anglo-Saxon version of the Compendious history of the world by Orosius. 1855, 1859.
A description of Europe, and the voyages of Ohthere and Wulfstan, with Anglo-Saxon test and a literal English translation and notes. 1855.
The history of the Lauderdale manuscript of King Alfred's Anglo-Saxon version of Orosius. Oxford 1858.
King Alfred's Anglo-Saxon version of the Compendious history of the world by Orosius, containing facsimile specimens of the Lauderdale and Cotton manuscripts. 1859.
The Gothic and Anglo-Saxon Gospels in parallel columns with the versions of Wycliffe and Tyndale. 1865.

HENRY BRADLEY
1845–1923

The Goths from the earliest times to the end of the Gothic dominion in Spain. 1888.
The making of English. 1904.
Changes in the language to the days of Chaucer. CHEL vol 1 1907.
The misplaced leaf of Piers the plowman. In J. M. Manly, Piers the plowman and its sequence, 1908 (EETS).
The authorship of Piers the plowman. 1910 (EETS).
English place names. 1910 (English Assoc).
On the relations between spoken and written language, with special reference to English. 1914; Proc Br Acad 8 1919.
The numbered sections in Old English poetical mss. 1916; Proc Br Acad 7 1918.
Shakespeare's English. In Shakespeare's England vol 2, 1916.
Sir James Murray 1837–1915. [1919]; Proc Br Acad 8 1919.
On the text of Abbo of Fleury's Quaestiones grammaticales. [1922]; Proc Br Acad 10 1921.
The collected papers, with a memoir by Robert Bridges. Oxford 1928. With bibliography.
The 'Cædmonian' Genesis. E & S 6 1910.

Editions

A new English dictionary on historical principles, founded mainly on the materials collected by the Philological Society, edited by James A. H. Murray, Henry Bradley, William A. Craigie, C. T. Onions. 11 vols Oxford 1884–1933. Bradley was joint editor from 1889, and was responsible for E, F–G, L–M, S–SH, ST, W–WEZZON.

Stratmann, F. H. A Middle-English dictionary: new edition revised by Henry Bradley. Oxford 1894.

Morris, R. Historical outlines of English accidence, revised by L. Kellner with the assistance of Henry Bradley. 1895.

—— Elementary lessons in historical English grammar, revised by Henry Bradley. 1897.

Caxton, W. Dialogues in French and English. 1900 (EETS).

Stevenson, W. Gammer Gurton's Needle, edited with critical essay and notes. In Representative English comedies, ed C. M. Gayley vol 1, New York 1903.

HENRY BRADSHAW
1831–86

Discovery of the long lost Morland mss in the library of the University of Cambridge. In J. H. Todd, The books of the Vaudois, 1865.

The printer of the Historia S Albani. 1868.

The skeleton of Chaucer's Canterbury Tales: an attempt to distinguish the several fragments of the work as left by the author. 1868, [1871].

Notice of a fragment of the fifteen Oes and other prayers printed at Westminster by William Caxton about 1490, 91, preserved in the library of the Baptist College, Bristol. 1877.

Collected papers, comprising 1: Memoranda; 2: Communications read before the Cambridge Antiquarian Society. Ed F. J. H. Jenkinson, Cambridge 1889.

The early collection of canons known as the Hibernensis: two unfinished papers. Ed F. J. H. Jenkinson, Cambridge 1893.

ARTHUR HENRY BULLEN
1857–1920

Anthologies

A Christmas Garland: cards and poems from the fifteenth century to the present time. 1885.

Lyrics from the song-books of the Elizabethan age. 1887; More lyrics from the song-books of the Elizabethan age, 1888; 1889 (selected from the 2 preceding volumes).

Lyrics from the dramatists of the Elizabethan age. 1889.

Musa Proterva: love poems of the Restoration. 1889 (priv ptd).

Speculum amantis: love poems from rare song-books and miscellanies of the seventeenth century. 1889 (priv ptd).

Poems, chiefly lyrical, from romances and prose tracts of the Elizabethan age; with chosen poems of Nicholas Breton. 1890.

Shorter Elizabethan poems. 1903. Part of E. Arber, An English garner.

Some longer Elizabethan poems. 1903. Part of E. Arber, An English garner.

Editions and Reprints

The works of John Day. 7 pts 1881 (priv ptd).

A collection of old English plays. 4 vols 1882–5 (priv ptd).

The English dramatists. 14 vols 1885–7 (priv ptd). Marlowe, 3 vols; Middleton, 8 vols; Marston, 3 vols.

A collection of old English plays: new series. 3 vols 1887–90 (priv ptd).

Robert Burton's The anatomy of melancholy, with introduction. 1893, 1904, 1923.

The works of Francis Beaumont and John Fletcher: variorum edition. Vols 1–4 (all pbd), 1904–12. Bullen was general editor.

Sonnets by William Shakespeare. Stratford-on-Avon 1905, 1921 (rev with memoir of Bullen by H. F. B. Brett-Smith).

The works of William Shakespeare. 10 vols Stratford-on-Avon 1910 (Stratford Town edn).

Bullen also issued edns of Peele, Campion, William Browne, Arden of Feversham, Davison's Poetical Rhapsody, Englands Helicon (1600), a selection from Drayton etc. He contributed largely to DNB and GM which he edited in 1906 and was general editor of ML.

ALEXANDER CHALMERS
1759–1834

A lesson in biography. 1798, Edinburgh 1887 (priv ptd). A parody of Boswell's Life of Samuel Johnson.

The Tatler, with prefaces, historical and biographical. 4 vols 1803.

The British essayists; with prefaces, historical and biographical. 45 vols 1803. With index.

The Spectator. 8 vols 1806.

The Guardian. 2 vols 1806.

Walker's classics. 45 vols 1808–12. Prefaces by Chalmers.

The British gallery of contemporary portraits. 2 vols 1809–16. Many lives by Chalmers.

A history of the Colleges, Halls and public buildings attached to the University of Oxford. 2 vols Oxford 1810.

The works of the English poets from Chaucer to Cowper. 21 vols 1810. A much expanded revision of Dr Johnson's collection, the additional lives all by Chalmers.

The Projector. 3 vols 1811. Periodical essays rptd from GM.

The general biographical dictionary. 32 vols 1812–17. Expanded by Chalmers from A new and general biographical dictionary, rev W. Tooke, R. Nares and W. Beloe 15 vols 1798–1810.

A dictionary of the English language. 1820. Dr Johnson's dictionary abridged.

The life of Martin Luther. 1857.

Chalmers also supervised edns of the following, generally with memoirs of some length: Beattie, Burns, Cruden, Fielding, Gibbon, Johnson, Milton, Paley, Edward Reynolds, Shakespeare.

JOHN PAYNE COLLIER
1789–1883

Trilogy on the emendations of Shakespeare's text contained in Mr Collier's corrected folio, 1632, and employed by recent editors of the poet's works. 3 pts [1814].

Criticisms on the Bar, including strictures on the principal counsel, by Amicus Curiæ. 1819. Anon.

The poetical Decameron, or ten conversations on English poets and poetry, particularly of the reigns of Elizabeth and James I. 2 vols Edinburgh 1820.

The poet's pilgrimage: an allegorical poem. 1822.

Punch and Judy, accompanied by the dialogue of the puppet show, an account of its origin, and of puppet plays in England. 1828, 1870, 1944.

The history of English dramatic poetry to the time of Shakespeare, and annals of the stage to the Restoration. 3 vols 1831, 1879 (rev).

New facts regarding the life of Shakespeare. 1835.

New particulars regarding the works of Shakespeare. 1836.

A catalogue, bibliographical and critical, of early English literature, the property of Lord Francis Egerton. 1837.

Further particulars regarding Shakespeare and his works. 1839.

The Egerton papers: a collection of public and private documents, chiefly illustrative of the times of Elizabeth and James I. 1840.

Reasons for a new edition of Shakespeare's works. 1841, 1842 (expanded).

Memoirs of Edward Alleyn, including some new particulars respecting Shakespeare. 1841 (Shakespeare Soc). Contains some of the forgeries ascribed to Collier.

Memoirs of the principal actors in the plays of Shakespeare. 1846 (Shakespeare Soc).

Notes and emendations to the text of Shakespeare's plays from early mss corrections in a copy of the folio 1632 in the possession of J. P. Collier. 1852, 1853 (with preface).

Reply to Mr N. E. S. Hamilton's Inquiry into the imputed Shakespeare forgeries. 1860.

Illustrations of early English popular literature. 2 vols 1863–4 (priv ptd).

A bibliographical and critical account of the rarest books in the English language. 2 vols 1865.

Illustrations of Old English literature. 3 vols 1866 (priv ptd).

Odds and ends. 1870 (priv ptd).

An old man's diary, forty years ago. 4 pts 1871 (priv ptd).

Collier also made trns from Schiller 1824–5.

Editions

A select collection of old plays. 12 vols 1825–7. Dodsley's collection with additional plays by Collier.

Kynge Johan, by John Bale. 1838.

Patient Grisil, by Henry Chettle. 1841.

The school of abuse, by Stephen Gosson. 1841.

The works of William Shakespeare: the text formed from an entirely new collation of the old editions, with the various readings, notes, a life of the poet, and a history of the early English stage. 8 vols 1842–4.

Shakespeare's library: a collection of the romances [etc] used by Shakespeare. 2 vols [1843], 6 vols 1875 (rev).

Book entries of the stationers' register relating to the drama and popular literature to 1586. 1848–9 (Shakespeare Soc).

The diary of Philip Henslowe, from 1591 to 1609. 1848.

Seven lectures of Shakespeare and Milton by the late S. T. Coleridge. 1856. Collier's own ms notes, at first unjustly suspected to be forged.

Poems by Michael Drayton. 1856.

The works of Edmund Spenser. 5 vols 1862.

The firste (second) part of Churchyard's Chippes, by Thomas Churchyard. [1870].

Foure letters, by Gabriel Harvey. [1870].

Pierces supererogation, by Gabriel Harvey. [1870].

Have with you to Saffron-Walden, by Thomas Nash. [1870].

Epitaphes, epigrams, songs and sonetes, by George Turberville. [1870].

Collier also rptd, generally with introds, many Elizabethan and Stuart rarities (mainly dramatic and poetic), both independently and for the Camden, Percy and Shakespeare Socs and Roxburghe Club, including works by Thomas Heywood, Anthony Munday, and Thomas Wash. The BM possesses a number of books containing Collier's notes and annotations in ms.

THOMAS FROGNALL DIBDIN
1776–1847

Poems. 1797.

An introduction to the knowledge of rare and valuable editions of the Greek and Roman classics. Gloucester 1802, 1804 (enlarged), 2 vols 1808 (rev), 1827 (greatly enlarged).

The Director; a weekly literary journal. 2 vols 1807. Ed Dibdin.

Specimen bibliothecae britannicae. 1808.

The bibliomania or book-madness, in an epistle addressed to Richard Heber. 1809, 1811 (enlarged), 2 pts 1842 (improved), 1876, 1905.

The typographical antiquities of Great Britain. Vols 1–4 (all pbd), 1810–19. A partial revision of Ames.

Bibliography, a poem: book I. [1812].

Bibliotheca Spenceriana: or a descriptive catalogue of the library of Earl Spencer. 4 vols 1814–15.

The bibliographical Decameron. 3 vols 1817.

A bibliographical antiquarian and picturesque tour in France and Germany. 3 vols 1821.

Aedes Althorpianae: or an account of the mansion, books and pictures at Althorp. 2 vols 1822.

A descriptive catalogue of the books lately of the library of the Duke di Cassana Serra and now of the Earl Spencer. 4 vols 1823.

The library companion. 2 vols 1824.

The Sunday library: a selection of sermons from eminent divines. 6 vols 1831.

Bibliophobia: remarks on the present languid state of literature and the book trade, by Mercurius Rusticus. 1832.

Reminiscences of a literary life. 2 pts 1836.

The bibliographical, antiquarian and picturesque tour in the northern counties of England and Scotland. 3 vols 1838.

Cranmer: a novel, by a member of the Roxburghe Club. 3 vols 1839.

Dibdin also pbd reprints of Tudor and Stuart rarities, mainly for the Roxburghe Club, as well as sermons, pamphlets etc.

FRANCIS DOUCE
1757–1834

The dance of death. [1794?] (anon), 1833 (enlarged). Ed Douce with elaborate dissertation.

Illustrations of Shakespeare and of ancient manners, with dissertation on the clowns and fools of Shakespeare. 2 vols 1807.

A catalogue of the Harleian mss in the British Museum. 1808–12. Revised by Douce.

A catalogue of the Lansdowne mss in the British Museum. 1819. With Sir H. Ellis.

Douce also pbd edns of Arnold's Chronicle, 1811; and a few ME texts for the Roxburghe Club. Bodley possesses numerous books annotated by Douce.

ALEXANDER DYCE
1798–1869

Specimens of British poetesses. 1825, 1827.

The poetical works of William Collins. 1827.

The works of George Peele. 3 vols 1828–39.

The works of John Webster. 4 vols 1830, 1857.

The dramatic works of Robert Greene. 2 vols 1831, 1861.

The dramatic works and poems of James Shirley. 6 vols 1833.

Specimens of English sonnets. 1833.

The works of Richard Bentley. 3 vols 1836–8.

The works of Thomas Middleton. 5 vols 1840.

The poetical works of John Skelton. 2 vols 1843, 1856.

The works of Beaumont and Fletcher. 11 vols 1843–6.

The works of Christopher Marlow. 3 vols 1850.

Recollections of the table talk of Samuel Rogers. 1856, 1887, 1903, 1952 (rev).

The works of Shakespeare: the text revised. 6 vols 1857, 9 vols 1864–7 (adds glossary), 1907.

The works of John Ford. 3 vols 1869.

Dyce also pbd the Aldine edns of Akenside, Beattie, Parnell, Pope and Shakespeare's poems, as well as several Elizabethan texts for the Camden, Percy and Shakespeare Socs.

Remarks on Mr J. P. Collier's and Mr Charles Knight's editions of Shakespeare. 1844.
A few notes on Shakespeare with occasional remarks on Mr Collier's copy of the folio 1632. 1858, 1859.

JOHN EARLE
1824–1903

Gloucester fragments, legends of St Swithun and Sancta Maria Aegyptiaca. 1861.
Guide to Bath, ancient and modern. 1864.
Two of the Saxon chronicles parallel. 1865, 1889, 1892.
A book for the beginner in Anglo-Saxon. 1866, 1902.
The philology of the English tongue. 1866, 1892.
Rhymes and reasons: essays by J. E. 1871.
English plant names. 1880.
Anglo-Saxon literature. 1884.
A handbook to the land charters and other Saxonic documents. 1888.
English prose: its elements, history and usage. 1890.
Deeds of Beowulf done into modern prose. 1892.
The Psalter of 1539. 1894.
Bath during British independence. 1895.
A simple grammar of English now in use. 1898.
Alfred as a writer. In Alfred the Great, ed A. Bowker 1899.
The Alfred jewel. 1901.
The place of English in education. In Furnivall miscellany, 1901.

ALEXANDER JOHN ELLIS
1814–90

Phonetics: a familiar system of the principles of that science, by A. J. E. 1844.
The essentials of phonetics. 1848.
An extension of phonography to foreign languages. 1848.
Phonetic spelling familiarly explained, for the use of romanic readers: with numerous examples. 1849.
On early English pronunciation, with especial reference to Shakespeare and Chaucer. 5 pts 1869–89 (Chaucer Soc, Philolog Soc, EETS). Pt 5 a dialect survey of England.
On the sensations of tone as a physiological basis for the theory of music, by Hermann Ludwig von Helmholtz; translated from the third German edition, with additions and notes. 1875, 1885 (rev with addns). 'More than a third consisted of work by Ellis himself'– DNB.
The English, Dionysian and Hellenic pronunciations of Greek. 1876.
An early English hymn to the Virgin, with notes on the Welsh phonetic copy. 1876 (English Dialect Soc).
The history of musical pitch, reprinted with corrections and an appendix, from the Journal of the Society of Arts. 1880.
Ellis also wrote many other papers and books on phonetics, phonography, music, mathematics, philosophy etc, and produced phonetic texts of the Bible, Macbeth, The Tempest, Bunyan's Pilgrim's Progress *etc. He edited* The Fonetic Frend 1849 *and* The Spelling Reformer 1849–50.

HARRY BUXTON FORMAN
1842–1917

Our living poets: an essay in criticism. 1871.
The works of Percy Bysshe Shelley, in verse and prose. 8 vols [1876]–80. Also poems only, 4 vols 1876, and with memoir 5 vols 1892 (Aldine edn).
Letters of John Keats to Fanny Brawne, written in the years 1819 and 1820. 1878, 1889 (rev and enlarged).
The poetical works and other writings of John Keats. 4 vols 1883; supplement, 1890; [poems only] 1884.
The Shelley library: an essay in bibliography. 1886.
The letters of John Keats: complete edition. 1895.
The books of William Morris described, with some account of his doings in literature and in the allied crafts. 1897.
The complete works of John Keats. 5 vols Glasgow 1900–1.
The poetical works of John Keats. Oxford 1906.
Note books of Percy Bysshe Shelley, deciphered, transcribed and edited, with a full commentary. 1911 (Boston Bibliophile Soc).
The life of Percy Bysshe Shelley, by Thomas Medwin, with an introduction and commentary. 1913.
Forman also supervised edns of separate poems by Shelley as well as works by Matthew Arnold, the Brownings et al.

FREDERICK JAMES FURNIVALL
1825–1910

§ I

Editions for the Ballad Society
(founded by Furnivall in 1868)

Ballads from manuscripts. 1868.
Captain Cox: his ballads and books. 1871.
Love poems and humerous ones 1614–19. 1874.

Editions for the Chaucer Society
(founded by Furnivall in 1868)

A six-text print of Chaucer's Canterbury tales in parallel columns. [1868].
The Cambridge ms of Chaucer's Canterbury tales. 1868–79; The Corpus ms, 1868–79; The Ellesmere ms, 1868–79; The Hengwrt ms, 1868–79; The Lansdowne ms, 1868–79; The Petworth ms, 1868–79; The Harleian ms 7,334, 1885; The Cambridge ms Dd 4.24, completed by the Egerton ms 2726, 1901–2.
Essays on Chaucer: his words and works. [1868–94].
Odd texts of Chaucer's minor poems. 1868.
A parallel-text edition of Chaucer's minor poems. [1871]; Trial-forewords, 1871.
Supplementary parallel-texts of Chaucer's minor poems. [1871].
A one-text print of Chaucer's minor poems. [1871].
Originals of some of Chaucer's Canterbury tales. [1872].
Chaucer as valet and squire to Edward III. 1876.
Supplementary Canterbury Tales. 1876.
Animadversions upon the annotacions and corrections of some imperfections of impressions of Chaucers workes reprinted in 1598 sett downe by F. Thynne. 1876.
Autotypes of Chaucer's manuscripts. 1877.
A parallel-text print of Chaucer's Troilus and Criseyde. [1881].
Chaucer's Boecce. 1886.
John Lane's continuation of Chaucer's Squire's tale. 1887.
A one-text print of Chaucer's Troilus and Criseyde. 1894.
The romaunt of the rose. 1911.

Editions for EETS
(founded by Furnivall in 1864)

Arthur: a short sketch of his life and history in English verse. 1864.
Thynne on Speght's Chaucer. 1865. With G. Kingsley.
The Wrights chaste wife, by Adam of Cobsam. 1865.
Political, religious and love poems. 1866, 1903.
The book of quinte essence. 1866.
Hymns to the Virgin and Christ; the Parliament of Devils. 1867.
The staciouns of Rome; and The pilgrim's sea-voyage; with Clene maydenhod. 1867.
The babees book, Aristotle's ABC, Urbanitatis [etc]. 1868.
Caxton's Book of curtesye. 1868.
Queene Elizabethes Achademy [etc], [by Sir H. Gilbert]. 1869.
Awdeley's Fraternitye of vacabondes, Harman's Caveat etc. 1869. With E. Viles.
The fyrste boke of the introduction of knowledge made by A. Borde [etc.]. [1870].
The minor poems of William Lauder. 1870.
A supplicacyon for the beggars, by Simon Fish. 1871.
The history of the Holy Grail, by Henry Lovelich from the French of Sir R. de Borron. 1874–8.
Emblemes and epigrames, by Francis Thynne. 1878.
Adam Davy's 5 dreams about Edward II [etc]. 1878.
The fifty earliest English wills in the Court of Probate 1387–1439. 1882.
The anatomie of the bodie of man, by Vicary. 1888.
The Curial made by maystere A. Charretier, translated by Caxton. 1888.
Caxton's Eneydos. 1890.
Hoccleve's works. 1892–7.
The three king's sons, englisht from the French. 1895.
The English conquest of Ireland AD 1166–85. 1897.
Child-marriages, divorces and ratifications in the diocese of Chester AD 1561–6. 1897.
Lydgate's Deguileville's Pilgrimage of the life of man. 1899–1901.
Robert of Brunne's Handlyng synne. 1901–3.
Minor poems of the Vernon ms. 1901.
The Macro plays. 1904.
The tale of Beryn etc. 1909. With W. G. Stone.
The Gild of St Mary, Lichfield. 1920.

Editions for the New Shakespeare Society
(founded by Furnivall in 1873)

Stafford's Compendious examination of certayne complaints of divers of our countrymen. 1876.
Spalding's A letter on Shakespeare's authorship of the Two noble kinsmen. 1876.
Tell-trothes new-yeares gift etc. 1876.
Harrison's description of England in Shakespere's youth. 1877.
Stubbes's Anatomy of abuses. 1877.
The Digby mysteries. 1882.
A list of all the songs and passages in Shakspere which have been set to music. 1884. With J. Greenhill.
Some 300 fresh allusions to Shakspere. 1886.
Robert Laneham's letter. 1890, 1907.

Editions for the Roxburghe Club

Seynt Graal: or the Sank Ryal, partly in English verse by Henry Lovelich and wholly in French prose by Robiers de Borron. 2 vols 1861–3.
Robert of Brunne's Handlyng Synne, William of Waddington's Le manuel des pechiez. 1862.
La queste del Saint Graal; in the French prose of Walter Map. 1864.
A royal historie of the excellent knight Generides. Hertford 1865.
The boke of nurture, by John Russell; The boke of kervynge, by Wynkyn de Worde; The boke of nurture, by Hugh Rhodes. 2 vols 1866.

Editions of Shakespeare

The Leopold Shakspere, in chronological order, from the text of Prof Delius. [1877].
Double text dallastype Shakespeare. 1895.
The works of William Shakespeare according to the orthography and arrangement of the more authentic quarto and folio versions. 1904 (Old Spelling Shakespeare).
The Century Shakespeare. 40 vols 1908.
Cassell's illustrated Shakespeare. 1913.
Furnivall also edited a number of the plays separately.

Other Editions

Le Morte Arthur, edited from the Harleian ms 2,252 in the British Museum. 1864.
Bishop Percy's folio manuscript: ballads and romances. 1867. With J. W. Hales.
The boke of nurture by H. Rhodes. [1868?].
Mannyng of Brunne, Robert. The story of England AD 1338. 1887 (Rolls Ser).
Lamb's Tales from Shakespeare, with introduction and additions. 1901.
Many other works were written, edited or provided with introds by Furnivall, who founded the Wiclif Soc and the Browning Soc in 1881, and the same year compiled a Browning bibliography. In 1886 he founded the Shelley Soc. He was, as secretary of the Philological Soc, the proposer of the scheme for the New English Dictionary.

§2

An English miscellany presented to Dr Furnivall in honour of his seventy-fifth birthday. Oxford 1901.
Ker, W. P. Memoir. Proc Br Acad 3 1910.
Furnivall: a volume of personal record. 1911.

SIR ISRAEL GOLLANCZ
1863–1930

Pearl: an English poem of the fourteenth century, edited with a modern rendering. 1891, EETS 1923 (with Cleanness, Patience and Sir Gawain).
Cynewulf's Christ, edited with a modern rendering. 1892.
Charles Lamb's Specimens of English dramatic poets, now first edited anew. 1893.
The Exeter book, edited with a translation, notes and introduction. EETS 1895.
The parlement of the thre ages, edited with introduction, notes. 1897.
Hoccleve's works, vol 2: The minor poems in the Ashburnham ms addit 133. EETS 1897.
Marlowe's The tragical history of Doctor Faustus. 1897.
Hamlet in Iceland: being the Icelandic Ambales Saga, edited and translated. 1898.
Otway's Venice preserved. 1899.
Select early English poems. 1913.
A book of homage to Shakespeare. 1916. Gollancz was general editor.
Ich dene: some observations on a ms of the life and feats of arms of Edward Prince of Wales, the Black Prince, a metrical chronicle in French verse by the Herald of Sir John Chandos. 1921.
The Middle Ages in the lineage of English poetry. 1921.
Sir Gawayne and the Greene Knight, re-edited by R. Morris, revised. 1925, 1940.
The sources of Hamlet. 1926.
The Cædmon manuscripts of Anglo-Saxon Biblical poetry, Junius XI in the Bodleian Library. 1927.
Allegory and mysticism in Shakespeare: reports of three lectures. 1931 (priv ptd).
Gollancz was general editor of the following publishers' sers: The Temple Shakespeare, The Temple Classics, The King's Classics, The King's Novels, The Shakespeare Library. For memoir see F. G. Kenyon, Proc Br Acad 18 1932.

ALEXANDER BALLOCH GROSART
1835–99

The Fuller worthies library. 39 vols Edinburgh and Blackburn 1868–76 (priv ptd).

Miscellanies of the Fuller worthies library. 4 vols Blackburn 1870–6 (priv ptd).

Occasional issues of unique and very rare books. 18 vols 1875–83 (priv ptd).

The Chertsey worthies library, edited with memorial-introductions, notes, illustrations and facsimiles. 14 vols [Blackburn] 1876–80 (priv ptd). ˙

Early English poets, edited with memorial-introductions and notes. 9 vols 1876–7 (priv ptd).

The Huth library: or Elizabethan-Jacobean unique or very rare books, largely from the library of Henry Huth, edited with notes, introductions and illustrations. 29 vols 1881–6 (priv ptd).

Grosart also issued The complete works of Edmund Spenser, 9 vols 1882–4 (priv ptd) (*with contributions by E. Dowden, F. T. Palgrave et al*), The complete works of Samuel Daniel, 5 vols 1885–96 (priv ptd), The poetical works of George Herbert, 1891 (Aldine), *edns for Camden Soc, Roxburghe Club and Chetham Soc, and numerous other reprints including a number of 17th-century Puritan divines.*

JAMES ORCHARD HALLIWELL,
later HALLIWELL-PHILLIPPS
1820–89

Shakesperiana: a catalogue of the early editions of Shakespeare's plays and of the commentaries and other publications illustrative of his works. 1841.

A dictionary of archaic and provincial words, obsolete phrases, proverbs and ancient customs from the fourteenth century. 2 vols 1846–7, 6 edns by 1904.

The life of William Shakespeare. 1848.

Contributions to early English literature derived chiefly from rare books and ancient inedited manuscripts from the fifteenth to the seventeenth century. 6 pts 1849.

A new boke about Shakespeare and Stratford-on-Avon. 1850.

Observations on the Shakespeare forgeries at Bridgewater House, illustrative of a facsimile of the spurious letter of H.S. 1853 (priv ptd). On the John Payne Collier controversy.

A brief hand-list of books, manuscripts etc illustrative of the life and writings of Shakespeare, collected between the years 1842 and 1859. 1859 (priv ptd).

A dictionary of old English plays from the earliest times to the close of the seventeenth century. 1860.

A brief hand-list of the records belonging to the Borough of Stratford-on-Avon. 1862 (priv ptd).

A handlist of upwards of a thousand volumes of Shakesperiana added to the three previous collections of a similar kind. 1862 (priv ptd).

A descriptive calendar of the ancient manuscripts and records in the possession of the Corporation of Stratford-on-Avon. 1863 (priv ptd).

Illustrations of the life of Shakespeare in a discursive series of essays. 1874.

New lamps or old? a few additional words respecting the E and the A in the name of our national dramatist. Brighton 1880. Favours the spelling 'Shakespeare'.

Outlines of the life of Shakespeare. Brighton 1881 (priv ptd), 1882 (tripled in size), 2 vols 1887 (7th edn, enlarged). A different work from the Life of Shakespeare, above.

A calendar of the Shakespearean rarities, drawings and engravings, preserved at Hollingbury Copse. 1887 (priv ptd); ed E. E. Baker 1891 (enlarged).

Editions

The voiage and travaile of Sir John Maundevile, kt, reprinted from the edition of 1725. 1839.

The harrowing of Hell: a miracle play, written in the reign of Edward the second, now first published from the original manuscript in the British Museum. 1840.

The first sketch of the Merry wives of Windsor. 1842 (Shakespeare Soc).

The nursery rhymes of England, obtained principally from oral tradition. 1842, 1843 (with addns), 1846 (4th edn, with addns) (Percy Soc).

Private diary of John Dee, and the catalogue of his library of manuscripts. 1842 (Camden Soc).

Nugae poeticae: select pieces of old English popular poetry, illustrating the manners and arts of the fifteenth century. 1844.

The Thornton romances: the early English metrical romances of Perceval, Isumbras, Eglamom and Degrevant, selected from manuscripts at Lincoln and Cambridge. 1844 (Camden Soc).

Letters of the Kings of England, now first collected from the originals. 2 vols 1846.

Morte Arthure: the alliterative romance of the death of King Arthur. 1847.

The poetry of witchcraft illustrated by copies of the plays on the Lancashire witches by Heywood, [Brome] and Shadwell. 1853 (priv ptd).

The works of William Shakespeare: the text formed from a new collation of the early editions; to which are added all the original novels and tales on which the plays are founded, copious archaeological annotations on each play; an essay on the formation of the text; and a life of the poet. 16 vols 1853–65 (150 copies ptd for the editor).

A glossary or collection of words, phrases, names and allusions to customs, proverbs etc which have been thought to require illustration in the works of the English authors, particularly Shakespeare and his contemporaries, by Robert Nares: a new edition, with considerable additions. 2 vols 1859. With Thomas Wright.

A treatyse of a galaunt; with the maryage of the fayre Pusell, the bosse of Byllyngesgate unto London Stone, from the unique edition printed by Wynkyn de Worde. 1860 (priv ptd).

Shakespearian facsimiles: a collection of curious and interesting documents, plans, signatures &c illustrative of the biography of Shakespeare and the history of his family, from the originals chiefly preserved at Stratford-on-Avon, facsimiled by E. W. Ashbee, selected by Halliwell. 1863 (priv ptd).

Those songs and poems from the excessively rare first edition of England's Helicon, 1600, which are connected with the works of Shakespeare. 1865 (25 copies).

Stratford-upon-Avon in the times of the Shakespeares, illustrated by extracts from the Council books of the Corporation, selected especially with reference to the history of the poet's father. 1864–5.

Halliwell edited some 150 works, mainly but not entirely in 17th-century literature, and did much work for the Camden, Percy and Shakespeare Socs. In 1841–2, with Thomas Wright, he edited Archaeologist *and* Jnl of Antiquarian Science, *of which only 10 issues appeared.*

GEORGE BIRKBECK NORMAN HILL
1835–1903

Dr Johnson, his friends and critics. 1878.

The life of Sir Rowland Hill. 2 vols 1880.

Footsteps of Dr Johnson (Scotland). 1890.

Writers and readers. 1892.

Harvard College, by an Oxonian. New York 1894.
Talks about autographs. Boston 1896.
Letters written by a grandfather, selected by Lucy Crump. 1903.
Letters, arranged by Lucy Crump. 1906.

Editions

Boswell's Life of Johnson, including Boswell's Journal of a tour to the Hebrides and Johnson's diary of a journey into North Wales. 6 vols Oxford 1887, 1934.
The history of Rasselas. Oxford 1887.
Wit and wisdom of Samuel Johnson. Oxford 1888.
Letters of David Hume to William Strahan. Oxford 1888.
Goldsmith, The traveller. Oxford 1888.
Select essays of Dr Johnson. 2 vols 1889.
Lord Chesterfield's Worldly wisdom: selections. Oxford 1891.
Letters of Dante Gabriel Rossetti to William Allingham. 1897.
Johnsonian miscellanies. 2 vols Oxford 1897.
Unpublished letters of Dean Swift. 1899.
The memoirs of the life of Edward Gibbon. 1900.
Lives of the English poets, by Samuel Johnson. 3 vols Oxford 1905.

SIR SIDNEY LEE
1859–1926

Stratford-on-Avon, from the earliest times to the death of William Shakespeare. 1885, 1907.
The study of English literature: an address. 1893 (priv ptd).
A life of William Shakespeare. 1898, 1915 (rewritten and enlarged), 1925 (new preface).
Shakespeare's King Henry the Fifth: an account and an estimate. 1900, 1908.
Queen Victoria: a biography. 1902.
Great Englishmen of the sixteenth century. 1904.
Shakespeare and the modern stage, with other essays. 1906.
The French renaissance in England. Oxford 1910.
Principles of biography: the Leslie Stephen lecture. Cambridge 1911.
The place of English literature in the modern university: a lecture. 1913.
King Edward VII: a biography. 2 vols 1925–7.
Elizabethan and other essays. Ed F. S. Boas, Oxford 1929 (with memoir).

Editions

The boke of Duke Huon of Burdeux, by Lord Berners. 4 pts EETS 1882–7.
The autobiography of Edward, Lord Herbert of Cherbury. 1886, 1906.
The dictionary of national biography, vol 27–end of suppl 2 1891–1917. In addition to editing the Dictionary, Lee contributed 820 articles, exclusive of his work in the supplements.
Shakespeare's comedies, histories and tragedies: being a reproduction in facsimile of the first folio edition, with introduction and census of copies. Oxford 1902. Similar facs reprints of Pericles, Sonnets, Venus and Adonis, Lucrece, 1905. Census also pbd separately; Notes and additions to the census, 1906.
Elizabethan sonnets, with an introduction. 2 vols 1904.
Methuen's standard library. 40 vols 1905–6.
The works of William Shakespeare. 20 vols Cambridge Mass 1907–10 (Caxton edn). General introd only by Lee.
The chronicle history of King Leir. 1909. With introd.
Shakespeare's England. 2 vols Oxford 1916. Planned and partly ed Lee.

GEORGE CAMPBELL MACAULAY
1852–1915

Francis Beaumont: a critical study. 1883.
The history of Herodotus, translated. 2 vols 1890.
Poems by Matthew Arnold, selected and edited. 1896, 1928.
The complete works of John Gower, edited from the manuscripts with introductions, notes and glossaries. 4 vols Oxford 1899–1902.
Gower: selections from Confessio amantis. Oxford 1903.
James Thomson. 1908 (EML).

SIR FREDERIC MADDEN
1801–73

The ancient English romance of Havelok the Dane, accompanied by the French text. 1828 (Roxburghe Club).
Privy purse expenses of the Princess Mary, daughter of King Henry the eighth. 1831.
The ancient English romance of William and the Were-wolf. 1832 (Roxburghe Club).
Illuminated ornaments, selected from manuscripts and early printed books from the sixth to the seventeenth centuries, drawn and engraved by H. Shaw; with descriptions by Madden. 1833.
The Olde English versions of the Gesta Romanorum, edited for the first time from manuscripts in the British Museum and University Library, Cambridge. 1838 (Roxburghe Club).
Syr Gawayne: a collection of ancient romance-poems by Scottish and English authors, relating to that celebrated Knight of the Round Table, with an introduction, notes and a glossary. 1839 (Bannatyne Club).
Lazamon's Brut, or chronicle of Britain: a poetical semi-Saxon paraphrase of the Brut of Wace, now first published from the Cottonian manuscripts in the British Museum; accompanied by a literal translation, notes and a grammatical glossary. 3 vols 1847 (Soc of Antiquaries).
The Holy Bible in the earliest English versions made from the Latin Vulgate by John Wycliffe and his followers; edited by the Rev Josiah Forshall and Madden. 4 vols Oxford 1850.
Universal palaeography: or facsimiles of writings of all periods and nations, by J. B. Silvestre; accompanied by an historical and descriptive text by Champollion-Figeac and A. Champollion, translated from the French, and edited, with corrections and notes. 2 vols 1850.
Matthei Parisiensis, Monach Sancti Albani, Historia Anglorum, sive, ut vulgo dicitur, historia minor: item, ejusdem abbreviato chronicorum Angliae. 3 vols 1866–9 (Rolls Ser). To vol 3 is prefaced a life and criticism of Matthew Paris.

Madden was Keeper of mss at the BM from 1837, and produced various guides and catalogues for that department; his other edns included one of Warton's History of English poetry.

RICHARD MORRIS
1833–94

The etymology of local names. Pt 1 (all pbd) 1857.
Historical outlines of English accidence, comprising chapters on the history and development of the language, and on word-formation. 1872; rev H. Bradley 1893.
Elementary lessons in historical English grammar. 1874; rev H. Bradley 1897.
English grammar. 1875.
Notes and queries [on Pali lexicography]. [1887].

Editions

Rolle's Pricke of conscience. 1863.
Early English alliterative poems of the West Midlands dialect of the fourteenth century. EETS 1894, 1934.
Sir Gawayne and the Green Knight: an alliterative romance-poem. EETS 1864, 1925.
The story of Genesis and Exodus: an Early English song. EETS 1865, 1895.
Dan Michel's Ayenbite of Inwyt: or remorse of conscience. EETS 1866.
Specimens of early English AD 1250–AD 1400, with grammatical introduction, notes and glossary. Oxford 1867; rev W. W. Skeat, Oxford 1872.
Old English homilies and homiletic treatises of the twelfth and thirteenth centuries. EETS 2 sers 1868–73.
Chaucer's translation of Boethius's De consolatione philosophiae. EETS 1868, 1886.
Legends of the Holy Rood; symbols of the Passion and crosspoems. In Old English of the eleventh, fourteenth and fifteenth centuries, EETS 1871.
An Old English miscellany: containing a bestiary, Kentish sermons, Proverbs of Alfred, religious poems of the thirteenth century. EETS 1872.
Cursor mundi: the cursur of the world—a Northumbrian poem of the XIVth century in four versions. EETS 6 pts 1874–93.
The Blickling homilies of the tenth century. EETS 3 pts [1874–80].

SIR JAMES AUGUSTUS HENRY MURRAY
1837–1915

Sir David Lindesay's works: the minor poems. EETS 1863.
The complaynt of Scotlande, vyth ane exortatione to the thre estaits to be vigilante in the deffens of their public veil. EETS 1872.
The romance and prophecies of Thomas of Erceldoune, with illustrations from the prophetic literature of the 15th and 16th centuries. EETS 1875.
A new English dictionary on historical principles, founded mainly on materials collected by the Philological Society. 11 vols Oxford 1884–1933, 13 vols Oxford 1933 (a corrected re-issue, with introd, suppl and bibliography, as The Oxford English Dictionary). Murray was chief creator of the NED, though his actual editorial responsibility covered only A–D, H–K, O, P, T.
The Romanes lecture 1900: the evolution of English lexicography. Oxford 1900.

WALTER WILLIAM SKEAT
1835–1912

The vision of William concerning Piers Plowman. EETS 4 pts 1867–85.
The Bruce, by John Barbour. EETS 4 pts 1870–89.
The Holy Gospels in Anglo-Saxon, Northumbrian and Old Mercian versions. 4 pts Cambridge 1871–87.
The poetical works of Thomas Chatterton. 1871, 1891.
Ælfric's Lives of the Saints. EETS 2 pts 1881–1900.
Wulfila's The gospel of Saint Mark. 1882.
Specimens of early English. 3 vols Oxford 1882. With R. Morris.
The Kingis quair. 1884, 1911 (STS).
Twelve facsimiles of old English manuscripts. 1892.
The complete works of Geoffrey Chaucer. 7 vols Oxford 1894–7.
The student's Chaucer. Oxford 1895.
Skeat also edited many other early English texts, mainly for Chaucer Soc, EETS, STS, and English Dialect Soc, which he founded.

Dictionaries and Philological Works

A Mœso-Gothic glossary. 1868.
An etymological dictionary of the English language, arranged on an historical basis. Oxford 1882, 1884 (corrected), 4 edns by 1910.
A concise etymological dictionary of the English language. Oxford 1882, 1886 (rev), 6 edns to 1936.
A concise dictionary of Middle English. 1888. With A. L. Mayhew.
A primer of English etymology. Oxford 1892, 6 edns to 1920.
A student's pastime. Oxford 1896. Articles from N & Q, including Skeats's autobiography.
Notes on English etymology, chiefly reprinted from the transactions of the Philological Society. Oxford 1901.
A primer of classical and English philology. Oxford 1905.
The science of etymology. Oxford 1912.

HENRY SWEET
1845–1912

King Alfred's West-Saxon version of Gregory's Pastoral care. EETS 2 pts 1871–2.
An Anglo-Saxon reader in prose and verse, with grammatical introduction, notes and glossary. Oxford 1876, 8 edns by 1908 (rev Onions).
The Epinal glossary, edited with transliteration. 1883.
King Alfred's Orosius. EETS 1883; [extracts] Oxford 1885.
Ælfric, grammaticus, Abbot of Eynsham: selected homilies. Oxford 1885.
The oldest English texts. EETS 1885
A second Anglo-Saxon reader, archaic and dialectal. Oxford 1887.

Primers and Writings

A history of English sounds. 1874 (English Dialect Soc).
A handbook of phonetics. Oxford 1877.
An Anglo-Saxon primer, with grammar, notes and glossary. Oxford 1882, 8 edns to 1896, 1953 (rev).
First Middle English primer: extracts from the Ancren Riwle and Ormulum. Oxford 1884.
Elementarbuch des gesprochenen Englisch: Grammatik, Texte und Glossen. Oxford 1885; tr Oxford 1890 (as A primer of spoken English).
An Icelandic primer, with grammar, notes and glossary. Oxford 1886.
Second Middle English primer: extracts from Chaucer, with grammar and glossary. Oxford 1886.
A history of English sounds from the earliest period, with full word-lists. Oxford 1888.
A primer of phonetics. Oxford 1890, 4 edns by 1932.
A manual of current shorthand. Oxford 1892.
A new English grammar, logical and historical. 2 pts Oxford 1892–8.
A short historical English grammar. Oxford 1892.
A primer of historical English grammar. Oxford 1893.
First steps in Anglo-Saxon. Oxford 1897.
The student's dictionary of Anglo-Saxon. Oxford 1897.
The practical study of languages. 1899.
The history of language. 1900.
The sounds of English: an introduction to phonetics. Oxford 1908.
Collected papers, arranged by H. C. K. Wyld. Oxford 1913.

WILLIAM ALDIS WRIGHT
1831–1914

Bacon's Essays and Colours of good and evil. 1862.
The works of William Shakespeare. 9 vols Cambridge 1863–6. Vol 1 ed W. G. Clark and J. Glover; vols 2–9 by Clark and Wright.

The works of William Shakespeare. 1864, 1904 (Globe). With W. G. Clark.

The Bible word-book: a glossary of old English Bible words. 1866, 1884 (rev). With J. Eastwood.

Chaucer, The clerk's tale. 1867.

Shakespeare's select plays. 10 vols Oxford 1868–83. With W. G. Clark.

Bacon's Advancement of learning. 1869, 1875, 1880.

The pilgrimage of the lyf of the manhode, from the French of de Deguilleville. 1869 (Roxburghe Club).

Generydes: a romance in seven-line stanzas. EETS 2 pts 1873–8.

The metrical chronicle of Robert of Gloucester. 1887 (Rolls Ser).

Letters and literary remains of Edward FitzGerald. 1889; Letters, 1894; Letters to Fanny Kemble, 1895; Rubáiyát, 1899; Miscellanies, 1900; More letters, 1901.

Facsimile of the manuscript of Milton's minor poems. 1899.

Milton's poetical works. 1903.

Roger Ascham, English works. Cambridge 1904.

The authorised version of the English Bible 1611. Cambridge 1909.

Femina, now first printed from a unique ms in the Library of Trinity College Cambridge. 1909 (Roxburghe Club).

The Hexaplar Psalter: being the Book of Psalms in six English versions. 1911.

Wright also pbd biblical studies and was editor of the Jnl of Philology 1868–1913.

6. ANGLO-IRISH LITERATURE

I. GENERAL WORKS

MacCarthy, D. The poets and dramatists of Ireland. Dublin 1846.

Ryan, W. The Irish literary revival. 1894.

'Eglinton, John' (W. K. Magee). Literary ideals in Ireland. 1899. With W. B. Yeats, AE and W. Larminie.

Gregory, I. A., Lady. Ideals in Ireland. 1901. Contributions by Yeats et al.

— Our Irish theatre: a chapter of autobiography. New York 1913.

Gwynn, S. Irish literature and drama in the English language: a short history. 1936.

The Abbey theatre: lectures delivered during the Abbey theatre festival in Dublin in 1938. Ed L. Robinson 1939. Lectures by the editor et al.

Ellis-Fermor, U. The Irish dramatic movement. 1939, 1954 (rev).

Robinson, L. Pictures in a theatre: a conversation piece. Dublin [1946].

— Ireland's Abbey theatre: a history 1899–1951. [1951].

MacNamara, B. Abbey plays 1899–1948, including the productions of the Irish Literary Theatre. Dublin 1949.

Flanagan, T. The Irish novelists 1800–50. New York 1959.

Mercier, V. The Irish comic tradition. Oxford 1962.

II. POETS

JAMES CLARENCE MANGAN
1803–49

Collections

Poems, original and translated: being a selection from his contributions to Irish periodicals. [Dublin] 1852.

Poems. Ed D. O'Donoghue, Dublin 1903.

Prose writings. Ed D. O'Donoghue, Dublin 1904.

§ 1

Anthologia germanica. 2 vols Dublin 1845. Trns from German.

The poets and poetry of Munster. Dublin 1849 (trns from Irish with Irish texts, ed J. O'Daly), 1850; ser 2 1860, 189–? (Irish texts rev by W. Hennessey and ed C. Meehan).

Romances and ballads of Ireland. Ed H. Ellis, Dublin 1850. With contributions by Mangan.

The tribes of Ireland: a satire by Aenghus O'Daly. Dublin 1852. Irish texts with trn by Mangan.

§ 2

O'Donoghue, D. The life and writings of Mangan. Edinburgh 1897, Chicago 1897.

Joyce, James. James Clarence Mangan. [1930], [1930]; rptd in The critical writings of Joyce, ed E. Mason and R. Ellmann, New York 1959.

AUBREY THOMAS de VERE
1814–1902

Collections

Poems. 1855.

Poetical works. 6 vols 1884–98.

§ 1

The Waldenses, or the fall of Rora: a lyrical sketch, with other poems. Oxford 1842.

The search after Proserpine; Recollections of Greece and other poems. Oxford 1843.

English misrule and Irish deeds: four letters from Ireland addressed to an English Member of Parliament. 1848.

Picturesque sketches in Greece and Turkey. 2 vols 1850.

May carols: or ancilla domini. 1857, New York 1866, London 1870 (with addns), 1881 (with addns).

The sisters, Inisfail and other poems. 1861.

Inisfail: a lyrical chronicle of Ireland. Dublin 1863.

The infant bridal and other poems. 1864, 1876.

The Church settlement of Ireland: or Hibernia pacanda. 1866, 1866.

The Church Establishment in Ireland, illustrated exclusively by Protestant authorities. 1867.

Ireland's church property, and the right use of it. 1867.

Pleas for secularization. 1867.

Reply to certain strictures by Myles O'Reilly Esq. 1868.

Ireland's Church question: five essays. 1868.

Irish odes and other poems. New York 1869.

The legends of Saint Patrick. 1872, 1889, 1905.

Alexander the Great: a dramatic poem. 1874.

St Thomas of Canterbury: a dramatic poem. 1876.

Antar and Zara: an eastern romance; Inisfail and other poems. 1877.

The fall of Rora, The search after Proserpine and other poems. 1877.

Proteus and Amadeus: a correspondence [with W. S. Blunt]. Ed A. T. de Vere 1878.

Legends of the Saxon saints. 1879, 1893.

The children of Lir: an Irish legend. [New York] [1881].

Constitutional and unconstitutional political action. Limerick 1881.

The foray of Queen Maeve, and other legends of Ireland's heroic age. 1882.

Ireland and proportionate representation. Dublin 1885.

Essays, chiefly on poetry. 2 vols 1887.

Legends and records of the Church and the empires. 1887.

Saint Peter's chains, or Rome and the Italian revolution: a series of sonnets. 1888.

Essays, chiefly literary and ethical. 1889, New York 1889.

Medieval records and sonnets. 1893.

Religious problems of the nineteenth century: essays. Ed J. Wenham 1893.

The search after Proserpine and other poems. 1896.

Recollections. New York 1897.

§ 2

Ward, W. P. De Vere: a memoir based on his unpublished diaries and correspondence. 1904.

Reilly, S. De Vere: Victorian observer. Lincoln Nebraska [1953], Dublin [1956].

DOUGLAS HYDE
1860–1949

Beside the fire. 1890.
The love songs of Connacht. Dublin 1893, 1895, Dundrum 1904, Dublin 1963.
The revival of Irish literature: addresses by Hyde and others. 1894.
The last three centuries of Gaelic literature. Dublin 1894.
The three sorrows of story-telling and Ballads of St Columkille. 1895.
The story of early Gaelic literature. 1895.
A literary history of Ireland from the earliest times to the present day. 1899, New York 1899, London 1903.
Irish poetry: an essay in Irish with translation in English. Dublin 1902.
Songs ascribed to [Anthony] Raftery. 1903. Collected and tr Hyde.
The religious songs of Connacht. 2 vols Dublin 1906.
The poor house. 1906. With Lady Gregory.
The twisting of the rope, translated from Irish by Lady Gregory. Dublin nd.
Beside the fire: a collection of Irish Gaelic folk stories. 1910.
Legends of saints and sinners, collected and translated by Hyde. [1915].
Mayo stories told by Thomas Casey, collected, edited and translated by Hyde. Dublin 1939.
Poems from the Irish. Dublin 1963. Introd by M. Gibbon.

KATHARINE TYNAN, later HINKSON
1861–1931

Collections

Twenty one poems, selected by W. B. Yeats. Dundrum 1907.
Collected poems. 1930.
Poems of Katharine Tynan. Dublin 1963. Introd by M. Gibbon.

§ 1

Louise de la Vallière, and other poems. 1885.
Shamrocks. 1887.
A nun, her friends and her order: being a sketch of the life of Mother Xaveria Fallon. 1891.
Ballads and lyrics. 1891.
Irish love-songs, selected by Katharine Tynan. 1892.
Cuckoo songs. 1894.
Miracle plays: Our Lord's coming and childhood. 1895.
An isle in the water. 1895. Stories.
Land of mist and mountain. [1895]. Stories.
The way of a maid. 1895.
A lover's breast-knot. 1896.
An isle in the water. 1896.
Oh, what a plague is love! 1896.
The wind in the trees: a book of country verse. 1898.
The dear Irish girl. 1899.
The handsome Brandons: a story for girls. 1899.
Led by a dream, and other stories. 1899.
A daughter of the fields. 1900.
Poems. 1901.
A girl of Galway. 1902.
Innocencies: a book of verse. 1905.
The rhymed life of St Patrick. 1907.
Experiences. 1908.
Lauds. 1909.
Ireland. 1909.
Peggy the daughter. 1909.
New poems. 1911.
Irish poems. 1913, 1914.
The wild harp: a selection from Irish poetry by Katharine Tynan. 1913.

Twenty-five years: reminiscences. 1913, New York [1913].
The house of the foxes. 1915.
Flower of youth: poems in war-time. 1915.
Countrymen all. 1915.
Lord Edward: a study in romance. 1916.
The holy war. 1916.
The middle years. 1916, Boston 1917.
Book of Irish history. Dublin [1917].
Late songs. 1917.
Kit. 1917.
Kitty at school and college. Dublin [1917?].
Herb O'Grace: poems in war-time. 1918.
The years of the shadow. 1919, Boston 1919.
The man from Australia. [1919].
The wandering years. 1922.
Evensong. Oxford 1922.
Memories. 1924.
Life in the occupied area. [1925].
Twilight songs. Oxford 1927, New York 1927.
The river. 1929.
See W. B. Yeats, Letters to Katharine Tynan, ed R. McHugh, Dublin [1953].

'A.E.' or 'AE',
GEORGE WILLIAM RUSSELL
1867–1935

Most of AE's mss and letters are in the National Library Dublin, the Lilly Library of Indiana Univ and at Colby College, Waterville Maine and Yale Univ. There are notebooks in the County Museum Armagh and the Congressional Library Washington. Letters and rare pamphlets are at Harvard and in the Berg Collection of the New York Public Library.

Collections

Collected poems. 1913, 1919 (enlarged), 1926 (enlarged), 1935 (enlarged).
Selected poems. 1935, New York 1935, London 1951, New York 1951.

§ 1

Homeward: songs by the way. Dublin 1894, 1895, London 1896, Portland Maine 1895 (enlarged).
The future of Ireland and the awakening of the fires. [Dublin 1897].
Ideals in Ireland: priest or hero? Dublin [1897].
The earth breath and other poems. [1897].
Cooperative credit. Dublin [1898], 1898 (in I.A.O.S. Annual report for 1898).
An artist of Gaelic Ireland. [Dublin 1902, 1902, 1902].
The nuts of knowledge: lyrical poems, old and new. Dundrum 1903.
Deirdre: a drama in three acts. Dublin 1903, (rptd from All-Ireland, rev, and from Irish Homestead), 1907, 1922.
The divine vision and other poems. 1904, New York 1904.
Controversy in Ireland: an appeal to Irish journalists. Dublin [1904].
The mask of Apollo, and other stories. Dublin [1905], London [1905].
Some Irish essays. Dublin 1906.
By still waters: lyrical poems old and new. Dundrum 1906.
Ireland and tariff reform, by 'Libra'. Dublin [1909].
The hero in man. [1909], 1910, Bombay [1945].
The renewal of youth. 1911.
Cooperation and nationality: a guide for rural reformers from this to the next generation. Dublin 1912.
The rural community: an address to the American commission of agricultural inquiry. Dublin 1913.
To the masters of Dublin: an open letter. [Dublin 1913]; rptd in 1,000 years of Irish prose, ed V. Mercier and D. H. Greene, New York 1952, 1961.
The tragedy of labour in Dublin. [London 1913].

The Dublin strike. 1913, Dublin [1913]. A speech; rptd in 1,000 years of Irish prose, ed V. Mercier and D. H. Greene, New York 1952, 1961.

Oxford university and the co-operative movement. Oxford 1914.

Ireland, agriculture and the war. Dublin 1915.

Gods of war, with other poems. Dublin 1915 (priv ptd).

Imaginations and reveries, 1915, Dublin 1915.

The national being: some thoughts on an Irish polity, Dublin 1916, 1918, 1918.

Salutation: a poem on the Irish rebellion of 1916. 1917 (priv ptd).

Thoughts for a convention: memorandum on the state of Ireland. 1917, 1917, Dublin 1917, 1917, 1918.

Conscription for Ireland: a warning to England. Dublin [1918].

The candle of vision. 1918, 1918, 1919, 1919, 1919.

Literary imagination. Dublin [1919].

Michael. Dublin 1919 (priv ptd).

A plea for justice, being a demand for a public enquiry into the attacks on co-operative societies in Ireland. Dublin [1920], Dublin [1921] (with addns).

The economics of Ireland and the policy of the British government. New York 1920, 1920, 1921.

Thoughts for British co-operators: being a further demand for a public enquiry into the attacks on co-operative societies in Ireland. Dublin [1921].

The inner and the outer Ireland. Dublin 1921, 1921.

Ireland and the Empire at the court of conscience. Dublin 1921.

Ireland, past and future. 1922.

The interpreters. 1922, New York 1923.

Voices of the stones. 1925, New York 1925, London 1931.

Midsummer Eve. New York 1928.

Dark weeping; with designs by P. Nash. 1929, 1929 (no 19 of Ariel poems).

Enchantment, and other poems. New York 1930.

Vale, and other poems. 1931.

Song and its fountains. 1932, New York 1932.

Verses for friends. Dublin 1932 (priv ptd).

The avatars: a futurist fantasy. 1933, New York 1933.

The house of the Tirans, and other poems. 1934.

The living torch: AE. Ed M. Gibbon 1937.

Letters

Some passages from the letters of AE to W. B. Yeats. Dublin 1936.

AE's letters to Minanlabain. Ed L. Porter, New York 1937.

The letters of AE. Ed A. Denson [1961].

§ 2

'Eglinton, John' (W. K. Magee). A memoir of AE. 1937.

'O'Connor, Frank' (M. O'Donovan). Two friends: Yeats and AE. Yale Rev 29 1939.

O'Faolain, S. AE and W.B. Virginia Quart Rev 15 1939.

Gogarty, O. Mourning becomes Mrs Spendlove. New York 1948.

O'Casey, S. Dublin's glittering guy. In his Inisfallen fare thee well, 1949.

Loftus, R. In his Nationalism in modern Anglo-Irish poetry, Madison 1964.

III. YEATS AND SYNGE

WILLIAM BUTLER YEATS
1865–1939

Most of Yeats's mss and personal papers are in the possession of his family. There are mss and letters in the National Library Dublin, the Berg Collection of the New York Public Library and the Univ of Texas.

Bibliographies etc

Wade, A. A bibliography of the writings of Yeats. 1951, 1958 (rev), 1968 (rev R. K. Alspach).

Parrish, S. M. A concordance to the poems of Yeats. Ithaca 1963.

Cross, K. G. W. and R. T. Dunlop. A bibliography of Yeats criticism 1887–1965. 1971.

Domville, E. A concordance to the plays of Yeats. 2 vols Ithaca 1972.

Collections

Poems. 1895, Boston 1895, London 1899, 1901, 1904, 1908, 1912, 1913, 1927, 1929 (all rev).

The poetical works in two volumes: vol 1 Lyrical poems, 1906; vol 2 Dramatical poems, 1907, 1912 (rev).

The collected works in verse and prose. Stratford-on-Avon 1908.

Poems: second series. Stratford-on-Avon 1909.

Collected edition of the works. 6 vols 1922–6.

The collected poems. New York 1933, London 1933, 1950 (enlarged with author's final corrections).

The collected plays. 1934, New York 1935, (with first pbn of Oedipus at Colonus), London 1952 (enlarged).

The poems of Yeats. 2 vols 1949. Definitive edn with author's final corrections and revisions.

The variorum edition of the poems. Ed P. Allt and R. Alspach, New York 1957.

Poems. Ed A. N. Jeffares 1963 (selection); Selected prose, ed Jeffares 1964; Selected plays, ed Jeffares 1964; selected criticism, ed Jeffares 1964.

Uncollected prose. Ed J. P. Frayn 2 vols 1970–5.

Manuscripts. Ed D. R. Clark et al, Dublin 1972–.

§ 1

Mosada: a dramatic poem, reprinted from the Dublin University Review [June 1886]. Dublin 1886, Dundrum 1943.

The wanderings of Oisin and other poems. 1889, 1892.

Ganconagh. John Sherman and Dhoya. 1891, 1891, 1892, New York [1891]. 'Ganconagh' is Yeats's pseudonym.

The Countess Cathleen and various legends and lyrics. 1892, 1892, Boston 1892.

The Celtic twilight: men and women, dhouls and fairies. 1893, New York 1894, London 1902 (rev and enlarged).

The land of heart's desire. 1894.

The secret rose, with illustrations by J. B. Yeats. 1897.

The tables of the law; The adoration of the magi. 1897 (priv ptd), 1904, Stratford-on-Avon 1914.

The wind among the reeds. 1899.

The shadowy waters. 1900.

Cathleen ni Houlihan. 1902, 1902.

Where there is nothing: a play in five acts. Dublin 1902.

Ideas of good and evil. 1903, 1903.

In the seven woods: being poems chiefly of the Irish heroic age. Dundrum 1903.

The hour glass: a morality. 1903; theatre edn 1907; Dundrum 1914 (a new version, partly in verse and partly in prose rptd from Mask (Florence) April 1913).

The hour-glass and other plays, being volume two of plays for an Irish theatre. New York 1904, London 1904 (entitled The hour-glass, Cathleen ni Houlihan, The pot of broth: being volume two of plays for an Irish theatre), Dublin 1905.

The king's threshold. New York 1904 (priv ptd for J. Quinn), London 1904 (with On Baile's strand), Dublin 1905; theatre edn, Stratford-on-Avon 1911.

On Baile's strand. Dublin 1905, London 1907 (rev).

Stories of Red Hanrahan. Dundrum 1905. Stories from The secret rose, above, rewritten with the help of Lady Gregory.

The pot of broth. 1905, 1911 (rptd from The hour glass and other plays, New York 1904, above).

Poems 1899–1905. 1906.

Deirdre. 1907, Stratford-on-Avon 1911 (rev).

Discoveries: a volume of essays (rev). Dundrum 1907.

The unicorn from the stars and other plays, with Lady Gregory. New York 1908.

The golden helmet. New York 1908 (priv ptd for J. Quinn).

The green helmet and other poems. Dundrum 1910, New York 1911, London 1912 (enlarged).

The green helmet: an heroic farce. Stratford-on-Avon 1911.

Synge and the Ireland of his time, with a note concerning a walk through Connemara with him by Jack Butler Yeats. Dundrum 1911.

Plays for an Irish theatre: Deirdre, The green helmet, On Baile's strand, The king's threshold, The shadowy waters, The hour glass, Cathleen ni Houlihan. 1911.

The Countess Cathleen. 1912 (rev version of the text in vol 3 of Collected works 1908, above), 1924 (with The land of heart's desire).

The cutting of an agate. New York 1912, London 1919 (enlarged).

Stories of Red Hanrahan, the secret rose, rosa alchemica. 1913, New York 1914.

A selection from the love poetry of Yeats. Dundrum 1913.

Poems written in discouragement 1912–13. Dundrum 1913.

Nine poems chosen from the works of Yeats. [New York] 1914 (priv ptd for J. Quinn).

Responsibilities: poems and a play. Dundrum 1914.

Reveries over childhood and youth. Dundrum 1915, New York 1916, London 1916.

Responsibilities and other poems. 1916, New York 1916.

Easter 1916. 1916 (priv ptd for C. Shorter).

The wild swans at Coole, other verses and a play in verse. Dundrum 1917, London 1919 (enlarged).

Per amica silentia lunae. 1918, New York 1918.

Nine poems. 1918 (priv ptd for C. Shorter).

Two plays for dancers. Dundrum 1919. The dreaming of the bones, The only jealousy of Emer.

Michael Robartes and the dancer. Dundrum 1920 (for 1921).

Four plays for dancers. 1921, New York 1921. At the hawk's well, The only jealousy of Emer, The dreaming of the bones, Calvary.

Seven poems and a fragment. Dundrum 1922.

The trembling of the veil. 1922 (priv ptd).

The player queen. 1922.

The cat and the moon and certain poems. Dundrum 1924.

A vision: an explanation of life founded upon the writings of Giraldus and upon certain doctrines attributed to Kusta Ben Luka. 1925 (priv ptd). See below.

October blast. Dundrum 1929.

Stories of Red Hanrahan and The secret rose, illustrated by N. McGuiness. 1927. Text of the 6 Red Hanrahan stories rev with Lady Gregory's help in 1904.

The tower. 1928, New York 1928.

Sophocles' King Oedipus: a version for the modern stage. 1928, New York 1928.

A packet for Ezra Pound. Dundrum 1929.

The winding stair. New York 1929.

Stories of Michael Robartes and his friends: an extract from a record made by his pupils and a play in prose. Dundrum 1931 (for 1932).

Words for music perhaps and other poems. Dundrum 1932.

The winding stair and other poems. 1933, New York 1933.

The words upon the window pane: a play in one act, with notes upon the play and its subject. Dundrum 1934.

Wheels and butterflies. 1934, New York 1935.

The king of the great clock tower: commentaries and poems. Dundrum 1934, New York 1935.

The singing head and the lady. 1934 (priv ptd by F. Prokosch).

A full moon [in March]. 1935.

Dramatis personae. Dundrum 1935.

Poems. Dundrum 1935. 9 poems.

Leda and the swan. Florence. 1935 (priv ptd by F. Prokosch).

Dramatis personae 1896–1902, Estrangement, The death of Synge, The bounty of Sweden. New York 1936, London 1936.

A vision. 1937, New York 1938, 1956 (with author's final corrections), London 1962, 1962. A substantially new version of A vision, 1925, above.

Essays 1931 to 1936. Dundrum 1937.

The herne's egg: a stage play. 1938; tr French, 1950.

The herne's egg and other plays. New York 1938.

New poems. Dundrum 1938.

The autobiography of Yeats, consisting of Reveries over childhood and youth, The trembling of the veil and Dramatis personae. New York 1938. Enlarged as Autobiographies, below.

Last poems and two plays. Dundrum 1939.

On the boiler. Dundrum 1939, Dublin 1939.

Last poems and plays. 1940, New York 1940.

If I were four-and-twenty. Dundrum 1940.

Autobiographies. 1955. Contains Reveries over childhood and youth, The trembling of the veil, Dramatis personae, Estrangement, The death of Synge, The bounty of Sweden.

Essays and introductions. 1961. Contains Ideas of good and evil, The cutting of an agate, later essays and introds.

Explorations. 1962. Essays, introds, articles etc selected by Mrs Yeats.

Mythologies. 1962. Contains The Celtic twilight, The secret rose, Stories of Red Hanrahan, Rosa alchemica, The tables of the law, The adoration of the magi, Per amica silentia lunae.

Letters, Diaries, Speeches etc

Letters

Letters on poetry from Yeats to Dorothy Wellesley. Oxford 1940, New York 1940.

Florence Farr, Bernard Shaw and W. B. Yeats. Ed C. Bax, Dundrum 1941, New York 1942, London 1946.

Some letters from Yeats to John O'Leary and his sister, from originals in the Berg Collection. Ed A. Wade, New York 1953.

Yeats and T. Sturge Moore: their correspondence 1901–37. Ed U. Bridge, Oxford 1953.

Letters to Katharine Tynan. Ed R. McHugh, Dublin 1953, New York 1953.

The letters of Yeats. Ed A. Wade 1954, New York 1955.

Diaries

Four years. Dundrum 1921.

Estrangement: being some fifty thoughts from a diary kept by Yeats in the year nineteen hundred and nine. Dundrum 1926.

The death of Synge, and other passages from an old diary. Dundrum 1928.

Pages from a diary written in nineteen hundred and thirty. Dundrum 1940.

Memoirs: autobiography, first draft journal [1915-17]. Ed D. Donoghue 1972.

Speeches

The bounty of Sweden: a meditation and a lecture delivered before the Royal Swedish Academy. Dundrum 1925.

Reale Accademia d'Italia. The Irish national theatre. Rome 1934. Text of a lecture by Yeats.

Modern poetry. 1936. BBC broadcast of 11 Oct 1936.

A speech [before the Irish Academy of Letters] and two poems. Dublin 1937 (priv ptd).

The Senate speeches of Yeats. Ed D. Pearce, Bloomington 1960.

§2

Moore, G. Hail and farewell: ave. 1911.

Gregory, Lady. Our Irish theatre. 1914.

Reid, F. Yeats: a critical study. 1915.

Hone, J. Yeats: the poet in contemporary Ireland. Dublin 1916.

—— Yeats 1865-1939. 1941. A biography.

Pound, E. In his Pavanes and divisions, New York 1918.

Empson, W. In his Seven types of ambiguity, 1930, 1953 (rev with addns). On Who goes with Fergus.

Williams, C. In his Poetry at present, Oxford 1930.

Wilson, E. In his Axel's castle, New York 1931.

Eliot, T. S. In his After strange gods, 1934.

—— The poetry of Yeats. Southern Rev 7 1941; rptd in The permanence of Yeats, below.

—— In his On poetry and poets, 1957.

Gogarty, O. As I was walking down Sackville Street. 1937.

—— Yeats: a memoir. Dublin 1963. Preface by M. Dillon.

'O'Connor, Frank' (M. F. O'Donovan). Two friends: Yeats and AE. Yale Rev 29 1939.

—— Quarrelling with Yeats: a friendly recollection. Esquire Dec 1964.

Ransom, J. C. Yeats and his symbols. Kenyon Rev 1 1939; rptd in The permanence of Yeats, below.

Auden, W. H. Yeats: master of diction. Saturday Rev of Lit 8 June 1940.

—— In memory of Yeats. In his Collected poetry, New York 1945. A poem.

—— The public vs the late William Butler Yeats. In Partisan reader 1934-44, New York 1946; and in Foundations of modern literary judgement, ed M. Schorer, New York 1948.

—— Yeats as an example. Kenyon Rev 10 1948; rptd in The permanence of Yeats, below.

Blackmur, R. P. The later poetry of Yeats. In his Expense of greatness, New York 1940.

—— Between myth and philosophy: fragments of Yeats. Southern Rev 7 1941.

Scattering branches: tributes to the memory of Yeats. Ed S. Gwynn 1940.

Burke, K. On motivation in Yeats. Southern Rev 7 1941; rptd in The permanence of Yeats, below.

—— The problem of the intrinsic. In his Grammar of motives, New York 1945.

MacNeice, L. The poetry of Yeats. Oxford 1941; ed R. Ellmann 1967.

Southern Review 7 1941: Yeats memorial issue. Contributions from H. Baker, R. P. Blackmur, K. Burke, D. Davidson, T. S. Eliot, H. Gregory, R. Jarrell, L. C. Knights, F. O. Matthiessen, A. Mizener, J. C. Ransom, A. Schwartz, A. Tate, A. Warren, M. D. Zabel.

J. B. Yeats: letters to his son W. B. Yeats and others 1869-1922. Ed J. Hone 1944.

Savage, D. S. In his Personal principle, 1944.

'Orwell, George' (E. Blair). In his Critical essays, 1946.

Ure, P. Towards a mythology: studies in the poetry of Yeats. Liverpool 1946.

—— Yeats the playwright: a commentary on character and design in the major plays. 1963.

—— Yeats. Edinburgh 1963 (Writers & Critics).

—— Yeats and Anglo-Irish literature. Liverpool 1974.

Ellmann, R. Yeats: the man and the masks. New York 1948.

—— The identity of Yeats. Oxford 1954.

—— Eminent domain. New York 1967.

Jeffares, A. N. Yeats: man and poet. 1949. A biography.

—— Yeats: the poems. 1961.

—— The poems of Yeats. 1962.

—— and K. G. W. Cross (ed). In excited reverie. 1965.

—— A commentary on the collected poems of Yeats. 1968; A commentary of the collected plays, 1975 (with A. S. Knowland).

—— (ed). Yeats: the critical heritage. 1977.

Hough, G. In his Last romantics, 1949.

Henn, T. R. The lonely tower: studies in the poetry of Yeats. 1950, 1965 (rev).

The permanence of Yeats: selected criticism. Ed J. Hall and M. Steinmann, New York 1950.

Moore, V. The unicorn: Yeats's search for reality. New York 1954.

Wain, J. Yeats's Among school children. In Interpretations: essays on twelve English poems, ed Wain 1955.

Kermode, F. In his Romantic image, 1957.

Alvarez, A. In his Shaping spirit, 1958.

Wilson, F. A. C. Yeats and tradition. 1958.

Donoghue, D. Yeats and the clean outline. In his Third voice, Princeton 1959.

—— (ed). The integrity of Yeats. Cork 1964.

—— Yeats. 1971.

Yeats: images of a poet. Ed D. Gordon, Manchester 1961.

Bushrui, S. Yeats's verse plays: the revisions 1900-10. Oxford 1965.

Stallworthy, J. Between the lines: Yeats's poetry in the making. Oxford 1963.

—— Vision and revision in Yeats's last poems. Oxford 1969.

Tuohy, F. Yeats. 1976.

EDMUND JOHN MILLINGTON SYNGE

1871-1909

Collections

[Works]. 4 vols Dublin 1910, 5 vols Dublin 1911 (not complete; contains unrev version of act 3 of The well of the saints); ed E. Rhys [1941] (EL) (with unrev version of act 3 of The well of the saints); ed M. MacLiammoir 1958 (EL).

[Plays]. 4 vols Dublin 1911, Dublin and London 1915. London [1932] (contains rev version of act 3 of The well of the saints and other unpbd material), 1 vol Oxford 1962 (WC) (4 plays and The Aran islands), London [1963] (with poems); Two plays (The playboy and Deirdre), Dublin 1911; Four plays (Riders to the sea, The shadow of the glen, The tinker's wedding, The well of the saints), Dublin 1911.

Collected works. Ed R. Skelton et al 5 vols Oxford 1962-.

Plays and poems. Ed T. R. Henn 1963.

§1

In the shadow of the glen: a play in one act. New York 1904 (priv ptd). London 1905 (with Riders to the sea), 1911.

Riders to the sea. 1905 (with In the shadow of the glen), 1911, Oxford 1936 (set to music by R. V. Williams), London 1961 (with The playboy).

The well of the saints. Dublin 1905, London 1905 (with introd by W. B. Yeats), New York 1905 (priv ptd for J. Quinn), Dublin 1907.

The playboy of the western world. Dublin 1907, 1907.

The Aran islands. Dublin 1907 (with drawings by Jack Yeats).

The tinker's wedding. Dublin 1907, 1911 (with Riders to the sea, The shadow of the glen), London 1924 (with Riders to the sea, The shadow of the glen).

Poems and translations. Dundrum 1909 (with preface by W. B. Yeats), New York 1909 (priv ptd for J. Quinn), Dublin 1911, 1911, London 1924, 1950, Oxford 1962. Vol 1 of Collected works, with unpbd verse.

Deirdre of the sorrows. Dundrum 1910, New York 1910 (priv ptd for J. Quinn).

In Wicklow, West Kerry and Connemara. Dublin 1911 (with drawings by Jack Yeats, rptd from vol 4 of Works, Dublin 1910).

With Petrarch: twelve sonnets. Larchmont NY 1928. Prose trns by Synge.

Translations. Ed R. Skelton [Dublin 1961]. Contains unpbd material.

The autobiography of Synge, constructed from the manuscripts by Alan Price with 14 photographs by Synge and an essay on Synge and the photography of his time by P. J. Pocock. Dublin 1965.

§2

Yeats, W. B. Introduction. In his Well of the saints, 1905.

—— Preface. In his Poems and translations, Dundrum 1909.

—— Synge and the Ireland of his time.. 1911.

—— The death of Synge and other passages from an old diary. Dundrum 1928.

Gregory, Lady. Our Irish theatre: a chapter of autobiography. 1914.

Moore, G. Yeats, Lady Gregory and Synge. Eng Rev 16 1914.

—— Hail and farewell: vale. 1914.

Empson, W. In his Seven types of ambiguity, 1930, 1953 (rev). On Deirdre of the sorrows.

Synge, S. Letters to my daughter: memories of Synge. Dublin [1932].

Journal and letters of Stephen MacKenna. Ed E. R. Dodds 1936.

Ellis-Fermor, U. The Irish dramatic movement. 1939, 1954 (rev).

'O'Connor, Frank' (M. F. O'Donovan). In The Abbey theatre, ed L. Robinson 1939. A lecture.

Strong, L. A. G. John Millington Synge. 1941.

Grene, N. Synge: a critical study of the plays. 1975.

IV. DRAMATISTS

ISABELLA AUGUSTA, LADY GREGORY
1852–1932

§1

Mr Gregory's letter box 1813–30. 1898. Ed Lady Gregory.

Ideals in Ireland. 1901. Ed Lady Gregory, with contributions by AE, D. Moran, G. Moore, D. Hyde, S. O'Grady, W. B. Yeats.

Cuchulain of Muirthemine: the story of the men of the Red Branch of Ulster. 1902, New York 1903. With preface and note by W. B. Yeats.

Poets and dreamers: studies and translations from the Irish. Dublin 1903.

Gods and fighting men: the story of the Tuatha de Danaan and of the Fianna of Ireland. 1904.

Kincora. Dublin 1905, 1905, London 1912 (in Irish folk-history plays ser 1).

Spreading the news, The rising of the moon, by Lady Gregory; The poorhouse, by Lady Gregory and Douglas Hyde. Dublin 1906. Spreading the news and Rising of the moon rptd Dublin 1909, London 1923 (in Seven short plays).

A book of saints and wonders put down here according to the old writings and the memory of the people of Ireland. Dundrum 1906.

The unicorn from the stars, and other plays, by W. B. Yeats and Lady Gregory. 1908, 1915. Contains also Cathleen ni Houlihan and The hourglass.

The workhouse ward. Dublin [1909?].

Seven short plays. Dublin 1909, [1911], London [1923], New York [1923?].

The Kiltartan history book. Dublin 1909, London 1926.

The image: a play in three acts. Dublin 1910, London 1922 (with Hanrahan's oath, Shanwalla, The wrens).

The Kiltartan wonder book. Dublin [1910].

The full moon: a comedy in one act. Dublin 1911 (priv ptd).

Irish folk-history plays. 2 vols 1912.

New comedies: The bogie men, The full moon, Coats, Damer's gold, McDonough's wife. 1913; all rptd separately [1923].

Our Irish theatre: a chapter of autobiography. 1913.

The golden apple: a play for Kiltartan children. 1916.

The Kiltartan poetry book: prose translations from the Irish. New York 1919.

Visions and beliefs in the west of Ireland, collected and arranged by Lady Gregory, with two essays and notes by W. B. Yeats. 2 vols 1920.

The dragon: a wonder play in three acts. Dublin 1920, London 1920; rptd in Three wonder plays, [1923].

Hugh Lane's life and achievement, with some account of the Dublin galleries. 1921.

Three wonder plays. [1922]. The dragon, Aristotle's bellows, The jester.

The story brought by Brigit: a passion play in three acts. 1924, 1924.

On the race course. New York [1925]. In One-act plays for stage and study, ser 2, 1926. A rewriting of Lady Gregory's unpbd but produced play Twenty-five, [1926].

Case for the return of Sir Hugh Lane's pictures to Dublin. Dublin 1926.

Three last plays. 1928. Sancho's master, Dave, The would-be gentleman (from Molière).

My first play. 1930. Colman and Guaire.

Coole. Dundrum 1931. With an introductory poem by Yeats.

Journals 1916–30. Ed L. Robinson 1946, New York 1947.

Selected plays. Ed E. Coxhead [1962], New York 1963. Introd by Sean O'Casey.

§2

Moore, G. Yeats, Lady Gregory and Synge. Eng Rev Jan-Feb 1914.

Coxhead, E. Lady Gregory: a literary portrait. 1961, 1966 (rev).

—— J. M. Synge and Lady Gregory. [1962] (Br Council pamphlet).

PADRAIC COLUM
1881–1972

Collections

Collected poems. New York 1932, 1953 (enlarged).
The poet's circuit: collected poems of Ireland. Oxford 1960.

§ I

The land: a play in three acts. Dublin 1905, 1909 (with The fiddler's house, below), 1917 (in Three plays, below); rptd in Plays of the Irish renaissance, ed C. Canfield, New York 1929.
Wild earth: a book of verse. Dublin 1907, New York 1916 (enlarged).
The fiddler's house: a play in three acts. Dublin 1907, 1909 (with The land, above), 1917 (in Three plays, below).
Studies. Dublin 1907.
The miracle of the corn: a miracle play in one act. Dublin 1907 (in Studies, above), 1922 (in Dramatic legends and other poems, below).
Thomas Muskerry: a play in three acts. Dublin 1910, 1917 (in Three plays, below).
Eyes of youth, with S. Leslie and others. [1910].
My Irish year. [1912].
The desert. 1912.
A boy in Eirinn. [1913].
Poems of the Irish revolutionary brotherhood. Ed P. Colum, Boston 1916.
Three plays. Boston 1916, Dublin 1917, 1963. The land, Thomas Muskerry, The fiddler's house.
The King of Ireland's son. 1916.
Mogu, the wanderer, or the desert: a fantastic comedy in three acts. Boston 1917.
The girl who sat by the ashes. New York 1919.
The children of Odin. New York [1920].
The boy apprenticed to an enchanter. New York 1920.
The golden fleece and the heroes who lived before Achilles. New York 1921.
Anthology of Irish verse. New York 1922, [1948] (enlarged). Ed Colum.
Dramatic legends and other poems. New York 1922.
Castle conquer. New York 1923.
At the gateways of the day. New Haven 1924.
The island of the mighty: being the hero stories of Celtic Britain retold from the Mabinogion. New York 1924.
The bright islands. New Haven 1925.
The road round Ireland. New York 1926.
Creatures. New York 1927.
The voyagers: being legends and romances of Atlantic discovery. New York 1927, 1930.
The fountain of youth. New York 1927.
The adventures of Odysseus and the Tale of Troy. New York [1928].
Balloon. New York 1929.
Balloon: a comedy in four acts. New York 1929.
Orpheus: myths of the world. New York 1930.
Cross roads in Ireland. New York 1930.
Old pastures. New York 1930, 1931.
Poems. 1932, New York 1932.
The peep-show man. New York 1932.
A half-day's ride: or estates in Corsica. New York 1932.
The betrayal. In One-act plays of to-day ser 4, ed J. Marriott [1939].
The white sparrow. New York 1933.
The children who followed the piper. New York 1933.
The big tree of Bunlahy: stories of my own countryside. New York 1933.
The boy who knew what the birds said. New York 1934.
The legend of Saint Columba. New York 1935.
The King of Ireland's son. [New York 1916?].
The story of Lowry Maen. New York 1937.
Legends of Hawaii. New Haven and Oxford 1937.

Flower pieces: new poems. Dublin 1938.
The jackdaw. [Dublin 1942].
The frenzied prince: being heroic stories of ancient Ireland. Philadelphia [1943].
Wild earth: poems. Dublin [1950].
The vegetable kingdom. [Bloomington 1954].
A treasury of Irish folklore. New York [1954].
The flying swans. New York [1957].
Our friend James Joyce, with M. Colum. Garden City NY 1958, London 1959.
Irish elegies. Dublin 1958, 1961.
Arthur Griffith. Dublin [1959], New York 1959 (as Ourselves alone: the story of Arthur Griffith and the origin of the Irish Free State, New York [1959]).
Irish elegies. Dublin 1961.
Moytura: a play for dancers. [Dublin 1963].
Three plays. Dublin 1963.

LENNOX ROBINSON
1886–1958

The cross-roads: a play in a prologue and two acts. Dublin [1909].
Two plays: Harvest and The Clancy name. Dublin 1911.
Patriots: a play in three acts. Dublin 1912.
The dreamers: a play in three acts. 1915.
A young man from the south. Dublin 1917.
The lost leader: a play in three acts. Dublin 1918.
Eight short stories. Dublin [1919?].
The whiteheaded boy: a play in three acts. 1920, New York 1921 (introd by E. Blythe).
The round table: a comic tragedy in three acts. 1924, 1928 (in Plays, below).
Crabbed youth and age: a little comedy. 1924, 1928 (in Plays, below).
A golden treasury of Irish verse. Ed L. Robinson 1925.
The white blackbird, and Portrait. Dublin [1926?], 1928 (in Plays, below).
A little anthology of modern Irish verse. Ed L. Robinson, Dublin 1928.
The big house: four scenes in its life. 1928, 1928 (in Plays, below).
Give a dog: a play in three acts. 1928, 1928 (in Plays, below).
Plays. 1928. The round table. Crabbed youth and age, Portrait, The white blackbird, The big house and Give a dog.
Ever the twain. 1930.
The far-off hills: a comedy in three acts. 1931.
Is life worth living? an exaggeration in three acts. 1933, 1939 (in Killycreggs in twilight, and other plays, below), Dublin 1953 (as Drama at Imish). First performed as Drama at Imish.
More plays. 1935. All's over, then? and Church street.
Three homes: Lennox Robinson, Tom Robinson and Nora Dorman. [1938]. An autobiography written with his brother and sister.
The Irish theatre: lectures delivered during the Abbey Theatre Festival held in Dublin in August 1938. Ed L. Robinson 1938.
Killycreggs in twilight, and other plays. 1939.
Curtain up: an autobiography. 1942.
Towards an appreciation of the theatre. Dublin 1945.
Lady Gregory's journals 1916–30. Ed L. Robinson 1946.
Pictures in a theatre: a conversation piece. Dublin [1946].
Ireland's Abbey Theatre: a history 1899–1951. [1951].
Church street: a play. Belfast 1955.
I sometimes think. Dublin [1956].
The Oxford book of Irish verse. Ed D. MacDonagh and L. Robinson, Oxford 1958.

ST JOHN ERVINE
1883–1971

Mixed marriage: a play in four acts. Dublin 1912.
The magnanimous lover: a play in one act. Dublin 1912.
Jane Clegg: a play in three acts. 1914.
Four Irish plays. 1914. Mixed marriage, The critics, Jane Clegg, The Orangemen.
John Ferguson: a play in four acts. Dublin 1915.
Some impressions of my elders. New York 1922, London 1923.
The ship: a play in three acts. 1922.
The lady of Belmont: a play in five acts. 1923.
Mary, Mary, quite contrary: a light comedy in four acts. 1923.
The organized theatre. New York 1924.
Anthony and Anna: a comedy in three acts. 1925, 1936 (rev).
Four one-act plays. 1928.
The first Mrs Fraser. 1929.
People of our class: a comedy. 1936.
Boyd's shop: a comedy. 1936.
Robert's wife: a comedy. 1938.
Friends and relations. 1947.
Private enterprise. 1948.
The Christies. 1949.
My brother Tom. 1952.

EDWARD JOHN MORETON DRAX PLUNKETT, 18th BARON DUNSANY
1878–1957

The gods of Pegāna. 1905, 1911.
Time and the gods. 1906.
The sword of Welleran, and other stories. 1908.
A dreamer's tales. 1910.
The book of wonder: a chronicle of little adventures at the edge of the world. 1912.
Selections from the writings of Lord Dunsany. Dundrum 1912. Preface by W. B. Yeats.
Five plays. 1914.
Fifty-one tales. 1915.
A night at an inn: a play in one act. New York 1916, London 1925, 1917 (in Plays of gods and men).
Tales of wonder. 1916, 1917.
The last book of wonder. Boston [1916].
Plays of gods and men. Dublin 1917, London 1917.
Tales of war. Boston 1918, Dublin [1918].
Nowadays. Boston 1918, 1920.
Tales of three hemispheres. Boston [1919], London 1920.
Unhappy far-off things. 1919.

If: a play in four acts. 1921, 1922.
The chronicles of Rodriguez. [1922], New York 1922 (as Don Rodriguez: chronicles of Shadow Valley).
Plays of near and far. [1922], New York 1923.
The laughter of the gods. [1922].
The compromise of the king of the golden isles. New York 1924.
The King of Elfland's daughter. New York and London 1924.
The amusements of Khan Kharuda. [1925].
The evil kettle. London and New York [1925].
The old King's tale. London and New York [1925].
The charwoman's shadow. New York and London 1926.
The blessing of Pan. New York and London [1927].
Seven modern comedies. [1928].
Fifty poems. London and New York [1929].
The old folk of the centuries: a play. 1930.
The travel tales of Mr Joseph Jorkens. New York 1931.
Lord Adrian: a play in three acts. 1933.
The curse of the wise woman. [1933].
Lord Adrian: a play in three acts. Waltham Saint Lawrence, Berkshire [1933].
Building a sentence. New York [1934?].
Jorkens remembers Africa. New York and London 1934.
If I were dictator: the pronouncements of the Grand Macaroni. [1934].
Mr Jorkens remembers Africa. [1934].
Mr Faithful. 1935.
Up in the hills. [1935].
Mr Faithful: a comedy in three acts. [1935].
My talks with Dean Spanley. [1936], New York 1936.
Rory and Bran. [1936], New York 1937.
My Ireland. [1937], New York 1937, London [1950].
Plays for earth and air. 1937.
Patches of sunlight. [1938]. An autobiography.
Mirage water. [1938].
The story of Mona Sheehy. [1939].
Jorkens has a large whiskey. [1940].
War poems. 1941.
A journey. 1943.
Wandering songs. 1943.
The Donellan lectures 1943. 1945.
Guerilla. 1944.
While the sirens slept. 1944. An autobiography.
A glimpse from a watchtower: a series of essays. 1945.
The sirens wake. 1945.
The year. 1946.
The fourth book of Jorkens. [1947?].
The odes of Horace, translated by Lord Dunsany. [1947].
To awaken Pegasus, and other poems. Oxford [1949].
The man who ate the phoenix. [1949].
The strange journeys of Colonel Polders. [1950].
The last revolution: a novel. [1951].
His fellow men: a novel. [1952].
Jorkens borrows another whiskey. [1954].

Part IV
1900–1950

1. INTRODUCTION

I. GENERAL WORKS

(1) BIBLIOGRAPHIES

Danielson, H. Bibliographies of modern authors. 1921. On Beerbohm, Brooke, de la Mare, Drinkwater, Dunsany, Flecker, Letwidge, Mackenzie, Masefield, Walpole.

Manly, J. M. and E. Rickert. Contemporary British literature: bibliographies and study outlines. New York 1921, 1928 (rev), 1935 (rev F. B. Millett).

The nineteenth century and after. Year's Work in English Stud 1921 (for 1919–20) onwards. Separate ch for The twentieth century from vol 35 1956 (for 1954) onwards.

Batho, E. C. and B. Dobrée. In their The Victorians and after 1830–1914, 1938, 1950 (rev).

Kunitz, S. J. and H. Haycraft. Twentieth-century authors: a biographical dictionary. New York 1942. Suppl by S. Kunitz, 1955. Includes brief bibliographies.

Connolly, C. The modern movement: 100 key books 1880–1950. 1966.

Harmon, M. Modern Irish literature, 1800–1967: a reader's guide. Dublin 1968.

Temple, R. Z. Twentieth-century British literature: a reference guide and bibliography. New York 1968.

Ward, A. C. Longman companion to twentieth-century literature. 1970, 1975 (rev with addns).

(2) LITERARY HISTORIES, SPECIAL STUDIES AND COLLECTIONS OF ESSAYS

Ford, F. M. (formerly Hueffer). The critical attitude. 1911. Essays.

—— Portraits from life: memories and criticisms. New York 1937, London 1938 (as Mightier than the sword). Essays. Conrad, Wells, Lawrence, Galsworthy.

—— Critical writings. Ed F. MacShane, Lincoln Nebraska 1964.

Mair, G. English literature: modern. [1911], 1914 (expanded), 1944 (brought up to 1939 by A. C. Ward).

Scott-James, R. A. Personality in literature. 1913, 1931 (as Personality in literature 1913–31, with additional material).

—— Fifty years of English literature 1900–50. 1951.

Bennett, A. Books and persons: being comments on a past epoch 1908–11. 1917.

Murry, J. M. Aspects of literature. 1920.

—— Katherine Mansfield and other literary portraits. 1949.

Orage, A. R. Readers and writers 1917–21. 1922. Essays.

Huxley, A. On the margin: notes and essays. 1923.

—— Literature and science. 1963.

Grieve, C. M. Contemporary Scottish studies. 1926.

—— (as H. MacDiarmid). Selected essays. Ed D. Glen 1969.

Muir, E. Transition: essays on contemporary literature. 1926.

—— The present age, from 1914. 1939 (Introductions to English Literature 5).

MacCarthy, D. Literary taboos. Life & Letters 1 1928.

—— The bubble reputation. Life & Letters 7 1931.

—— Portraits. 1931. Essays.

—— Criticism. 1932. Essays.

—— Experience. 1935. Essays.

Swinnerton, F. A London bookman. 1928. Essays.

—— The Georgian scene: a literary panorama. New York 1934, London 1935 (as The Georgian literary scene), 1938 (rev), 1950 (rev), 1969 (rev).

Ward, A. C. Twentieth-century literature 1901–25. 1928, 1940 (enlarged to 1940), 1960 (enlarged to 1960).

—— The nineteen-twenties: literature and ideas in the postwar decade. 1930.

'West, Rebecca' (C. I. Andrews). The strange necessity: essays and reviews. 1928.

Dobrée, B. The lamp and the lute: studies in six modern authors. Oxford 1929, 1964 ('seven authors'). Forster, Lawrence, Eliot; adds Durrell in 1964.

Wilson, E. A preface to modern literature. New Republic 20 March 1929.

—— Axel's castle: a study in the imaginative literature of 1870–1930. New York 1931.

—— The triple thinkers: ten essays on literature. New York 1938, 1949 (rev).

—— Europe without Baedeker: sketches among the ruins of Italy, Greece and England. New York 1947.

Krutch, J. W. The modern temper. New York 1930.

Eliot, T. S. After strange gods: a primer of modern heresy. 1934.

Spender, S. The destructive element: a study of modern writers' beliefs. 1935.

—— The new realism: a discussion. 1939.

—— The creative element: a study of vision, despair and orthodoxy among some modern writers. 1953.

—— The struggle of the modern. 1963.

Daiches, D. New literary values: studies in modern literature. Edinburgh 1936.

—— Literary essays. Edinburgh 1956.

—— The present age, after 1920. 1958, Bloomington 1958 (as The present age in British literature).

Forster, E. M. Abinger harvest. 1936. Essays.

Lawrence, D. H. Phoenix: the posthumous papers of D. H. Lawrence. Ed E. McDonald, New York 1936.

—— Selected literary criticism. Ed A. Beal 1955.

Batho, E. and B. Dobrée. The Victorians and after: 1830–1914. 1938 (Introductions to English Literature 4), 1950 (rev).

'Caudwell, Christopher' (C. St J. Sprigg). Studies in a dying culture. 1938.

—— Further studies in a dying culture. Ed E. Rickword 1949. Selections from this and the previous item included in his Concept of freedom, 1965.

Connolly, C. Enemies of promise. 1938, New York 1948 (rev), Garden City NY 1960 (as Enemies of promise and other essays: an autobiography of ideas).

—— The condemned playground: essays 1927–44. 1945.

—— Ideas and places. 1953. Rptd from Horizon.

—— Previous convictions. 1963. Essays. Section on The modern movement.

Lawrence, T. E. Men in print: essays in literary criticism. Ed A. W. Lawrence 1939.

'Orwell, George' (E. A. Blair). Inside the whale, and other essays. 1940.

—— Critical essays. 1946, New York 1946 (as Dickens, Dali and others: studies in popular culture).

—— Shooting an elephant and other essays. 1950.

—— Such, such were the joys. New York [1953]. Essays.

—— Collected essays, journalism and letters. Ed S. Orwell and I. Angus 4 vols 1968.

Beerbohm, M. Mainly on the air. 1946, 1957 (enlarged).

Chew, S. The nineteenth century and after 1879–1939. In A literary history of England, ed A. Baugh, New York 1948, 4 vols 1967 (Chew's section rev R. Altick).

The importance of Scrutiny. Ed E. Bentley, New York 1948.

Beach, J. W. The literature of the nineteenth and early twentieth centuries: 1798 to the First World War. In A history of English literature, ed H. Craig, New York 1950.

Bowen, E. Collected impressions. 1950. Essays.

Brower, R. A. The fields of light: an experiment in critical reading. 1951, New York 1951. On V. Woolf, Forster, Yeats et al.

Greene, G. The lost childhood and other essays. 1951.

Isaacs, J. An assessment of twentieth-century literature. 1951.

Leavis, F. R. The common pursuit. 1952. Essays.

—— (ed). A selection from Scrutiny. 2 vols Cambridge 1968.

Fraser, G. S. The modern writer and his world. 1953, 1964 (rev) (Pelican).

Nott, K. The emperor's clothes. 1953.

—— A soul in the quad. 1969.

Johnstone, J. K. The Bloomsbury group: a study of Forster, Strachey, Woolf and their circle. 1954.

Enright, D. J. The apothecary's shop: essays on literature. 1957.

—— Conspirators and poets. 1966. Essays.

Hoggart, R. The uses of literacy. 1957.

—— Speaking to each other. 2 vols 1970. Essays on society and literature.

Writers at work: the Paris Review interviews. Ser 1–3 New York 1958–67. Ed M. Cowley, A. Kazin.

Hough, G. Image and experience: studies in a literary revolution. 1960.

Symons, J. The thirties: a dream revolved. 1960.

—— Critical occasions. 1966. Essays.

Ford, B. (ed). The modern age. 1961 (Pelican guide to English literature vol 7).

Stewart, J. I. M. Eight modern authors. Oxford 1963 (OHEL). Includes Conrad, Joyce, Lawrence.

Wain, J. Essays on literature and ideas. 1963.

Holloway, J. The colours of clarity: essays on contemporary literature and education. 1964.

Nowell-Smith, S. (ed). Edwardian England 1901–14. Oxford 1964.

Bergonzi, B. Heroes' twilight: a study of the literature of the Great War. 1965.

—— (ed). The twentieth century. 1970 (Sphere history of Lit in the Eng Lang vol 7).

Dyson, A. E. The crazy fabric: essays in irony. 1965. Strachey, Huxley, Waugh, Orwell.

Robson, W. W. Critical essays. 1966.

—— Modern English literature. 1970.

Woolf, V. Collected essays. Ed L. Woolf 4 vols 1966–9.

Alvarez, A. Beyond all this fiddle: essays 1955–67. 1968.

Bell, Q. Bloomsbury. 1968.

Burgess, A. Urgent copy: literary studies. 1968.

Donoghue, D. The ordinary universe: soundings in modern literature. 1968.

Gross, J. The rise and fall of the man of letters: aspects of English literary life since 1800. 1969.

Bradbury, M. and J. McFarlane (ed). Modernism 1890–1930. 1976 (Penguin), Hassocks Sussex 1978.

Watson, G. Politics and literature in modern Britain. 1977.

2. POETRY

I. GENERAL WORKS

(1) HISTORIES AND STUDIES

Archer, W. Poets of the younger generation. 1902.

Hueffer, F. H. M. (afterwards Ford). Modern poetry. In his The critical attitude, 1911.

Pound, E. Prolegomena. Poetry Rev 1 1912.

—— A few dont's by an Imagiste. Poetry 1 1913. Both rptd as A retrospect, in Pavannes and divisions, New York 1918; and as A stray document in Make it new, 1934, below.

—— Make it new: essays. 1934.

—— Polite essays. 1937. Monro, Hueffer (Ford), Eliot etc. Much of this and the above rptd in Literary essays of Pound, ed Eliot 1954.

Flint, F. S. Imagisme. Poetry 1 1913.

—— The history of imagism. Egoist 1 May 1915.

Hulme, T. E. Lecture on modern poetry. [1914]. In M. Roberts, T. E. Hulme, 1938. Rptd in Hulme, Further speculations, ed S. Hynes, Minneapolis 1955.

Eliot, T. S. Reflections on 'vers libre'. New Statesman 3 March 1917. Rptd in his To criticize the critic, 1965.

—— Reflections on contemporary poetry. Egoist 4 1917.

—— Tradition and the individual talent. Egoist 6 1919; rptd in his Sacred wood, 1920.

—— The modern mind. In his The use of poetry and the use of criticism, 1933.

—— In his After strange gods: a primer of modern heresy, 1934.

—— In his On poetry and poets, 1957.

Read, H. Definitions towards a modern theory of poetry. Arts & Letters 3 1918.

—— Form in modern poetry. 1932, 1948 (with prefatory note).

Graves, R. Contemporary techniques of poetry: a political analogy. 1925 (Hogarth Essays 8).

—— Another future of poetry. 1926 (Hogarth Essays 18).

—— The common asphodel. 1949.

—— These be your gods, O Israel! In his The crowning privilege, 1955.

—— In his On poetry: collected talks and essays. Garden City NY 1969. See also L. Riding, below.

Richards, I. A. A background for contemporary poetry. Criterion 3 1925.

—— In his Science and poetry, 1926, 1935 (rev).

—— In his Practical criticism, 1929.

'MacDiarmid, Hugh' (C. M. Grieve). In his A drunk man looks at the thistle, Edinburgh 1926.

Riding, L. and R. Graves. A survey of modernist poetry. 1927.

Riding, L. Contemporaries and snobs. 1928.

—— and R. Graves. A pamphlet against anthologies. 1928.

Bridges, R. Humdrum and harum-scarum: a lecture on free verse. In his Collected essays vol 2, 1928.

Blunden, E. Tradition in poetry. In Tradition and experiment in present-day literature, 1929.

—— War poets 1914–18. 1958, 1964 (rev) (Br Council pamphlet).

Sitwell, E. Experiment in poetry. In Tradition and experiment in present-day literature, 1929.

—— Aspects of modern poetry. 1934.

—— Three eras of modern poetry. In Trio, by O., E. and S. Sitwell, 1938.

—— Lecture on poetry since 1920. Life & Letters 39 1943.

Leavis, F. R. New bearings in English poetry. 1932, 1950 (with Retrospect 1950). On Eliot, Hopkins et al.

'Roberts, Michael' (W. E. Roberts). Introduction to New signatures, ed Roberts 1932.

—— Introduction to New country, ed Roberts 1933.

—— In his A critique of poetry, 1934.

—— Introduction to The Faber book of modern verse, ed Roberts 1936.

—— In his T. E. Hulme, 1938.

Stevenson, L. Darwin among the poets. 1932.

Woolf, V. A letter to a young poet. 1932; rptd in her The death of the moth, 1942.

—— The leaning tower. Folios of New Writing 2 1940. Replies by E. Upward, B. L. Coombes, L. MacNeice and J. Lehmann, 3 1941. On writers of the 1930's.

Housman, A. E. The name and nature of poetry. Cambridge 1933. A lecture.

Bullough, G. The trend of modern poetry. Edinburgh 1934, 1941 (rev), 1949 (rev).

Day Lewis, C. A hope for poetry. Oxford 1934, New York 1935 (in his Collected poems 1929–33 and A hope for poetry), Oxford 1936 (new postscript).

—— Revolutionaries and poetry. Left Rev 1 1935.

—— Poetry today. Left Rev 2 1937.

—— The poetic image. 1947.

Sparrow, J. Sense and poetry. 1934. Anti-modern essays.

Gordon, G. S. Poetry and the moderns: an inaugural lecture. Oxford 1935.

MacNeice, L. Poetry. In The arts today, ed G. Grigson 1935.

—— Subject in modern poetry. E & S 22 1936.

—— Modern poetry: a personal essay. 1938, Oxford 1968 (introd by W. Allen).

Yeats, W. B. Modern poetry. 1936. Broadcast lecture; rptd in his Essays 1931 to 1936, Dublin 1937, and his Essays and introductions, 1961.

—— Introduction to The Oxford book of modern verse, Oxford 1936.

—— Letters on poetry from Yeats to Dorothy Wellesley. 1940.

'Caudwell, Christopher' (C. St J. Sprigg). Illusion and reality: a study of the sources of poetry. 1937.

Daiches, D. Poetry and the modern world: a study of poetry in England between 1900 and 1939. Chicago 1940.

Fraser, G. S. In his The modern writer and his world, 1953, 1964 (rev, Pelican).

—— Vision and rhetoric: studies in modern poetry. 1959.

Tate, A. Modern poets and convention. Amer Rev 8 1937; rptd in his Collected essays, Denver 1959, and Essays of four decades, Chicago 1968.

Savage, D. S. The personal principle: studies in modern poetry. 1944.

Scarfe, F. Auden and after: the liberation of poetry 1930–41. 1942.

Bowra, C. M. The heritage of symbolism. 1943.

—— The background of modern poetry. Oxford 1946. A lecture.

—— The creative experiment. 1949.

—— Poetry and the first World War. Oxford 1961. A lecture; rptd in his In general and particular, 1964.

—— Poetry and politics 1900–60. Cambridge 1966.

Comfort, A. English poetry and the war. Partisan Rev 10 1943.

—— On interpreting the war. Horizon 5 1944. Letter on the role of poets; reply by S. Spender, ibid.

Shapiro, K. Essay on rime. New York 1945. In verse.

—— English prosody and modern poetry. ELH 14 1947. Rptd separately Baltimore 1947.

— Modern poetry as a religion. Amer Scholar 28 1959.

— (ed). Prose keys to modern poetry. New York 1962.

Williams, O. (ed). Comments by the poets. In The war poets, New York 1945.

Miles, J. In her Major adjectives in poetry: from Wyatt to Auden, Univ of Calif Pbns in Eng 12 1946.

— The primary language of poetry in the 1940's. Berkeley 1951.

Winters, Y. In defense of reason. Denver 1947.

Isaacs, J. The assessment of twentieth-century literature. 1951.

— The background of modern poetry. 1951.

Pinto, V. de S. Crisis in English poetry 1880–1940. 1951, 1961 (rev).

Blackmur, R. P. In his Language as gesture: essays in poetry, New York 1952. A selection from this book was pbd as Form and value in modern poetry, New York 1957.

Durrell, L. Key to modern poetry. 1952, Norman Oklahoma 1952 (as A key to modern British poetry).

Saunders, J. W. Poetry in the managerial age. EC 4 1954.

Auden, W. H. On writing poetry today. Listener 30 June 1955.

— Making, knowing and judging. Oxford 1956; rptd in his The dyer's hand, New York 1962, below. A lecture.

— The dyer's hand. New York 1962.

Davie, D. In his Articulate energy: an inquiry into the syntax of English poetry, 1955.

— The poet in the imaginary museum. Listener 11–18 July 1957.

Kermode, F. Romantic image. 1957.

Langbaum, R. In his The poetry of experience: the dramatic monologue in modern literary tradition, New York 1957.

Alvarez, A. The shaping spirit: studies in modern English and American poets. 1958, New York 1958 (as Stewards of excellence). On Yeats, Eliot, Empson, Auden, Lawrence et al.

Cohen, J. M. In his Poetry of this age 1908–58, 1959, 1966 (rev, as Poetry of this age 1908–65).

Beach, J. W. Obsessive images: symbolism in poetry of the 1930's and 1940's. Minneapolis 1960.

Hough, G. Image and experience: studies in a literary revolution. 1960. Partially pbd as Reflections on a literary revolution, Washington 1960. On Imagism.

Jennings, E. Every changing shape. 1961. Includes essays on Hopkins, Muir, Eliot, Gascoyne et al.

Tomlinson, C. Poetry today. In The modern age, Pelican guide to English literature vol 7, ed B. Ford 1961, 1963 (rev).

Cox, C. B. and A. E. Dyson. Modern poetry: studies in practical criticism. 1963.

Hamilton, I. (ed). The modern poet: essays from The Review. 1968. On Empson et al.

Stead, C. K. The new poetic: Yeats to Eliot. 1964.

Ellmann, R. Eminent domain: Yeats among Wilde, Joyce, Pound, Eliot and Auden. New York 1967, 1970 (corrected).

Hollander, J. (ed). Modern poetry: essays in criticism. New York 1968.

(2) ANTHOLOGIES

Sitwell, E. Wheels: an anthology of verse. [First cycle] Oxford 1916, 1917 (2nd edn with preface); second cycle, Oxford 1917; third cycle, Oxford 1919; fourth cycle, 1919; fifth cycle, 1920; sixth cycle, 1921.

Roberts, M. New signatures. 1932.

— New country: prose and poetry by the authors of New signatures. 1933.

— The Faber book of modern verse. 1936, 1951 (with supplement chosen by A. Ridler), 1965 (rev with supplement chosen by D. Hall).

Yeats, W. B. The Oxford book of modern verse 1892–1935. 1936.

Grigson, G. New verse: an anthology. 1939.

— Poetry of the present: an anthology of the thirties and after. 1949.

Spender, S. and J. Lehmann. Poems for Spain. 1939.

Jones, P. M. Modern verse 1900–40. 1940, 1955 (enlarged, as Modern verse 1900–50) (WC).

Ridler, A. The little book of modern verse. 1941. Preface by T. S. Eliot.

Allott, K. The Penguin book of contemporary verse. 1950, 1962 (rev, as The Penguin book of contemporary verse 1918–60).

Lehmann, J. Pleasures of New Writing: an anthology of

poems, stories and other prose pieces from the pages of New Writing. 1952.

New poems 1952–: a PEN anthology. 1952. Continued annually.

Heath-Stubbs, J. Images of tomorrow: an anthology of recent poetry. 1953.

— and D. Wright. The Faber book of twentieth-century verse: an anthology of verse in Britain 1900–50. 1953, 1965 (rev), 1967 (rev).

Reeves, J. The modern poets' world. 1957 (Poetry Bookshelf).

— Georgian poetry. 1962 (Penguin Poets).

Cecil, D. and A. Tate. Modern verse in English. 1958, New York 1958.

Wain, J. Anthology of modern poetry. 1963, 1967 (rev).

Hamilton, I. The poetry of war 1939–1945. 1965.

Wright, D. The mid century: English poetry 1940–1960. 1965 (Penguin).

— Longer contemporary poems. 1966 (Penguin).

MacBeth, G. Poetry 1900 to 1965. [1967].

Cox, C. B. and A. E. Dyson. Poems of this century. 1968.

Larkin, P. The Oxford book of twentieth-century English verse. Oxford 1973.

II. INDIVIDUAL POETS

THOMAS STEARNS ELIOT
1888–1965

There are significant collections of Eliot's mss in Houghton Library, Harvard; in Texas University Library, including an autograph fair copy of The waste land, *made in 1960; in the John Hayward Bequest, King's College Cambridge; and in New York Public Library. This last holds the most important*

collection of Eliot's mss in a public institution. It originates from the collection of John B. Quinn, subsequently sold to the Berg Collection, described by D. Gallup, TLS 7 Nov 1968. It includes the ms and typescript of The waste land, *with comments and deletions by Ezra Pound, a notebook containing* Prufrock *and other poems, and several sequences of loose sheets containing pbd and unpbd poems.*

The holograph and typescripts of Marina *are in Bodley.*

Bibliographies

Gallup, D. Eliot: a bibliography, including contributions to periodicals and foreign translations. 1952, New York [1953], London 1969 (rev and extended).

Collections

Complete poems and plays 1909–50. New York [1952].
Complete poems and plays. 1969.

§1

Poetry

Prufrock and other observations. 1917.
Poems. Richmond 1919 (ptd by L. and V. Woolf). 7 poems, all rptd in next.
Ara vus prec. [1920] (264 copies: correct title Ara vos prec), New York 1920 (as Poems; with a different order of contents and one poem, Hysteria, substituted for Ode). For the text of Gerontion, here first pbd, see W. H. Marshall, The text of Eliot's Gerontion, SB 4 1951.
The waste land. New York 1922, Richmond 1923 (ptd by L. and V. Woolf), London 1961 (for 1962) (ptd at Verona by G. Mardersteig). First pbd in Criterion 1 1922, without notes, subsequently thus in Dial 73 1922. Eliot regarded the 1961 text as standard. See D. H. Woodward, Notes on the publishing history and text of The waste land, PBSA 58 1964. For preliminary discussion of the ms etc including some facsimiles, see D. Gallup TLS 7 Nov 1968.
Poems 1909–1925. 1925, New York [1932]. Collects contents of previous books.
Journey of the Magi. [1927] (Ariel Poems 8), New York 1927 (27 copies for copyright purposes). This and subsequent Ariel Poems were rptd in Collected poems, 1963, below.
A song for Simeon. [1928] (Ariel Poems 16).
Animula. 1929 (Ariel Poems 23).
Ash-Wednesday. 1930, New York 1930.
Anabasis: a poem by St J. Perse with a translation into English by Eliot. 1930, New York 1938 (rev), 1949 (rev and corrected), 1959 (with alterations by the author).
Marina. 1930 (Ariel Poems 29).
Triumphal march. 1931 (Ariel Poems 35).
Sweeney agonistes: fragments of an Aristophanic melodrama. 1932. A short concluding scene was pbd in H. Flanagan, Dynamo, New York [1943], and in C. H. Smith's Eliot's dramatic theory and practice, Princeton 1963.
The builders: song from The rock. [1934]. Music by M. Shaw.
Words for music. [Bryn Mawr Pa] 1934 [for Feb 1935]. 2 poems, New Hampshire, Virginia, pbd in an edn of at least 20 copies by F. Prokosch; rptd in Collected poems, 1936, below.
Two poems. [Cambridge] 1935 (25 copies, ptd for F. Prokosch). 2 poems, Cape Anne, Usk, both rptd in next.
Collected poems 1909–1935. 1936, New York [1936].
Old Possum's book of practical cats. London 1939], London 1940 (illustr N. Bentley), 1953 (with addition of Cat Morgan introduces himself).
The waste land and other poems. 1940, New York [1955]. Selection.
East Coker. 1940 (New Eng Weekly Easter no, suppl [an offprint]), 1940 (pbd Faber).
Burnt Norton. 1941. First pbd in Collected poems, 1936 above.
Later poems 1925–1935. 1941. Selection.
The Dry Salvages. 1941.
Little Gidding. 1942.
Four quartets. New York [1943], London 1944. Burnt Norton; East Coker; The Dry Salvages; Little Gidding.
A practical possum. Cambridge Mass 1947 (80 copies). Single poem, not rptd elsewhere.

Selected poems. 1948 (Penguin Poets), New York [1967] (Harbrace Paperback).
The undergraduate poems of Eliot, published when he was at college in The Harvard Advocate. Cambridge Mass [1949]. An unauthorized edn. These poems appear in the authorized Poems written in early youth, 1950 (below).
Poems written in early youth. Stockholm 1950 (priv ptd, 12 copies), London 1967, New York 1967 (trade edn, with note by Mrs Eliot). Compiled by John Hayward, includes 2 poems not previously pbd and corrected texts of poems in The undergraduate poems, [1949] (above).
Cat Morgan introduces himself. [1951]. Anon. Duplicated, with an issue of Faber Book News. Rptd as broadside, New Haven 1953 (30 copies) and in 1953 edn of Old Possum's book of practical cats, above.
The cultivation of Christmas trees. 1954 (Ariel Poems, new ser), New York [1956].
Collected poems 1909–1962. 1963, New York [1963].

Verse Plays

Sweeney agonistes. 1932. See Poems, above.
The rock: a pageant play written for performance at Sadler's Wells Theatre 28 May–9 June 1934. 1934, New York [1934].
Murder in the cathedral. (Festival of the Friends of Canterbury Cathedral May 1935, Mercury 1 Nov 1935). Canterbury 1935 (acting edn, altered and abbreviated for performance), London 1935, New York [1935], London 1936 (2nd edn with alterations), New York [1936], London 1937 (with further alterations), 1938 (4th edn, with further alterations), New York [1963] (with author's notes for first–fourth edns), 1965 (introd and notes by N. Coghill). The text of the screen version appears in The film of Murder in the cathedral by Eliot and G. Hoellering, 1952, New York [1952].
The family reunion: a play. (Westminster 21 March 1939). 1939, New York [1939].
The cocktail party: a comedy. (Edinburgh Festival 22 Aug 1949, New 3 May 1950). 1950, New York [1950].
The confidential clerk: a play. (Edinburgh Festival 25 Aug 1953, Lyric 16 Sept 1953). 1954, New York [1954].
The elder statesman. (Edinburgh Festival 25 Aug 1958, Cambridge 25 Sept 1958). 1959, New York 1959.
Collected plays. 1962. Excludes The rock.

Other Works

Ezra Pound, his metric and poetry. New York 1917. Anon. Rptd in To criticize the critic, 1965, below.
The sacred wood: essays on poetry and criticism. 1920, New York 1921, London 1928 (with preface by the author), New York 1930.
Homage to John Dryden: three essays on poetry of the seventeenth century. 1924 (Hogarth Essays 4).
Shakespeare and the stoicism of Seneca: an address read before the Shakespeare Association 18th March 1927. 1927.
For Lancelot Andrewes: essays on style and order. 1928, Garden City NY 1929.
Dante. 1929 (The Poets on the Poets 2).
Thoughts after Lambeth. 1931 (Criterion Miscellany 30).
Charles Whibley: a memoir. 1931 (Eng Assoc pamphlet 80).
Selected essays 1917–1932. 1932, New York [1932], London 1934 (with an additional essay), New York [1950] (with 4 essays additional to those in first edn), London 1951 (with these 4 essays added to contents of 1934 edn).
John Dryden the poet, the dramatist, the critic: three essays. New York 1932.
The use of poetry and the use of criticism: studies in the relation of criticism to poetry in England. 1933, Cambridge Mass 1933, London 1964 (with new preface).
After strange gods: a primer of modern heresy. 1934, New York [1934].
Elizabethan essays. 1934. Rptd from Selected essays, 1932, except for John Marston.

Essays ancient & modern. 1936, New York [1936].

The idea of a Christian society. 1939, New York [1940].

Points of view. 1941. Selection by J. Hayward of critical writings.

The classics and the man of letters: the presidential address delivered to the Classical Association on 15 April 1942. 1942. Rptd in To criticize the critic, 1965, below.

The music of poetry: the third W. P. Ker memorial lecture delivered in the University of Glasgow 24 February 1942. Glasgow 1942; rptd in On poetry and poets, 1957, below.

Reunion by destruction: reflections on a scheme for Church union in South India. [1943]. (Council for the Defence of Church Principles pamphlet 7).

What is a classic? an address delivered before the Virgil Society on the 16th October 1944. 1945; rptd in On poetry and poets, 1957, below.

Die Einheit der europäischen Kultur. Berlin 1946. Text in German and English; latter rptd as appendix to Notes towards the definition of culture, 1948, below.

On poetry: an address on the occasion of the twenty-fifth anniversary of Concord Academy. Concord 1947.

Milton. 1947 (Br Acad Annual Lecture on a Master Mind); rptd in On poetry and poets, 1957, below.

A sermon preached in Magdalene College Chapel 7 March 1948. Cambridge 1948.

Notes towards the definition of culture. 1948, New York [1949], London 1962 (with minor alterations).

From Poe to Valéry. New York 1949 (priv ptd); rptd in To criticize the critic, 1965, below.

The aims of poetic drama: the presidential address to the Poets' Theatre Guild. 1949.

Poetry and drama. Cambridge Mass 1951, London 1951 (Theodore Spencer Memorial Lecture); rptd in On poetry and poets, 1957, below.

The value and use of cathedrals in England to-day: an address delivered to the Friends of Chichester Cathedral on June 16th, 1951. Chichester [1952].

An address to the members of the London Library, July 1952. 1952, Providence RI 1953.

Selected prose. Ed J. Hayward 1953 (Penguin).

American literature and the American language: an address delivered at Washington University on June 9 1953. St Louis [1953]; rptd in To criticize the critic, 1965, below.

The three voices of poetry. 1953, New York 1954; rptd in On poetry and poets, 1957, below.

Religious drama: mediaeval and modern. New York 1954. 'Delivered to the Friends of Rochester Cathedral in 1937'.

Gedenkschrift zur Verleihung des Hansischen Goethe-Preises 1954 der gemeinnützigen Stiftung F.V.S. zu Hamburg durch die Universität Hamburg an Thomas Stearns Eliot. [Hamburg 1955]. Consists mainly of Eliot's address Goethe as the sage, in English and German. Rptd in On poetry and poets, 1957, below.

The literature of politics: a lecture. 1955 (Conservative Political Centre pamphlet); rptd in To criticize the critic, 1965, below.

Essays on Elizabethan drama. New York [1956], London 1963 (with preface, as Elizabethan dramatists). Selection from Selected essays, 1951 (3rd edn), above.

The frontiers of criticism: a lecture delivered at the University of Minnesota Williams Arena on April 30 1956. [Minneapolis 1956]. Rptd in next.

On poetry and poets. 1957, New York 1957. Consisting mainly of rptd lectures and introds; substantially unaltered, apart from Poetry and drama.

Christianity and culture. New York [1960]. Reprints The idea of a Christian society and Notes towards the definition of culture.

Geoffrey Faber 1889–1961. 1961 (priv ptd). A memorial address.

George Herbert. 1962 (Br Council pamphlet).

Knowledge and experience in the philosophy of F. H. Bradley. 1964, New York [1964]. Eliot's Harvard PhD thesis, with 2 articles on Leibniz rptd from the Monist. Some copies of a suppressed edn of 1963 survive.

To criticize the critic and other writings. 1965, New York [1965].

Eliot was one of the editors of Harvard Advocate 1909–10, and assistant editor of Egoist 1917–19. From 1922 to 1939 he was editor of Criterion, to which he frequently contributed A commentary. For Eliot and TLS, see T. S. Eliot, Bruce Lyttleton Richmond, TLS 13 Jan 1961.

§2

Aldington, R. The poetry of Eliot. In his Literary studies and reviews, 1924.

—— In his Life for life's sake: a book of reminiscences, New York 1941.

—— Ezra Pound & Eliot: a lecture. 1954.

Ransom, J. C. Waste lands. In Modern essays, ed C. Morley, New York 1925.

—— A cathedralist looks at murder. In his World's body, New York 1928.

—— Eliot: the historical critic. Norfolk Conn [1941].

Richards, I. A. On Mr Eliot's poetry. In his Principles of literary criticism, 1926 (2nd edn).

Dobrée, B. In his Lamp and the lute, Oxford 1929.

Williamson, G. The talent of Eliot. Seattle 1929.

—— A reader's guide to Eliot: a poem-by-poem analysis. New York 1953, 1955 (rev).

Burke, K. The allies of humanism abroad. In The critique of humanism, ed C. H. Grattan, New York 1930.

Williams, C. In his Poetry at present, 1930.

Leavis, F. R. In his New bearings in English poetry, 1932, 1950 (with Retrospect 1950).

—— Eliot's classical standing. In F. R. and Q. D. Leavis, Lectures in America, 1969.

Passmore, J. A. T. S. Eliot. Sydney 1934. Pamphlet.

Sitwell, E. In her Aspects of modern poetry, 1934.

Blackmur, R. P. The dangers of authorship. In his Double agent, New York [1935]. On After strange gods.

—— Eliot: from Ash Wednesday to Murder in the cathedral. Ibid.

—— 'It is later than he thinks'. In his Expense of greatness, New York 1940. On The idea of a Christian society.

Matthiessen, F. O. The achievement of Eliot. Cambridge Mass 1935, 1947 (rev and enlarged), 1958 (rev and enlarged, with ch on Eliot's later work by C. L. Barber).

Spender, S. Eliot in his poetry; Eliot in his criticism. In his Destructive element, 1935.

—— Eliot. 1975.

Preston, R. Four quartets rehearsed: a commentary on Eliot's cycle of poems. New York 1946.

Rajan, B. (ed). Eliot: a study of his writings by several hands. 1947.

Unger, L. (ed). Eliot: a selected critique. New York [1948].

Drew, E. Eliot: the design of his poetry. New York 1949.

Gardner, H. The art of Eliot. 1949.

—— T. S. Eliot and the English poetic tradition. Nottingham 1966 (Byron Foundation Lecture 1965).

—— The composition of Four quartets. 1978.

Smidt, K. Poetry and belief in the work of Eliot. Oslo 1949, London 1961 (rev).

Bradbrook, M. C. T. S. Eliot. 1950, 1960 (rev) (Br Council pamphlet).

Maxwell, D. E. S. The poetry of Eliot. 1952.

Smith, G. Eliot's poetry and plays: a study in sources and meaning. Chicago 1956, 1960 (rev, with ch on The elder statesman).

Braybrooke, N. (ed). T. S. Eliot: a symposium for his seventieth birthday. 1958.

Donoghue, D. In his Third voice: modern British and American verse drama, Princeton 1959.

Kenner, H. The invisible poet: Eliot. New York 1959.

—— (ed). Eliot: a collection of critical essays. Englewood Cliffs NJ [1962].

Hough, G. In his Image and experience: studies in a literary revolution, 1960.

—— In his Selected essays, Cambridge 1978.

Jones, D. E. The plays of Eliot. 1960.

Lucy, S. Eliot and the idea of tradition. 1960.

Watson, G. In his Literary critics: a study of English descriptive criticism, 1962 (Pelican), 1964 (rev).

Frye, N. T. S. Eliot. Edinburgh 1963 (Writers and Critics).

Stead, C. K. In his New poetic, 1964.

Tate, A. (ed). Eliot: the man and his work. New York 1966.

Southam, B. C. A student's guide to the selected poems of Eliot. 1968.

Bergonzi, B. T. S. Eliot. 1972, 1978 (with addns). A biography.

Gordon, L. Eliot's early years. Oxford 1977.

ROBERT VON RANKE GRAVES
b. 1895

The Lockwood Memorial Library (State Univ of New York, Buffalo), the Berg Collection (New York Public Library), the Humanities Research Center of the Univ of Texas (Austin), and the Univ of Southern Illinois (Carbondale) have collections of Graves mss.

Bibliographies

Higginson, F. H. A bibliography of the works of Graves. 1966.

Collections

The crowning privilege: the Clark lectures 1954–5, also various essays on poetry and sixteen new poems. 1955, Garden City NY 1956 (as The crowning privilege: collected essays on poetry; omits the poems and adds 9 essays), London 1959 (Penguin).

5 pens in hand. Garden City NY 1958. Lectures, essays, stories, 'historical anomalies' and poems.

Steps: stories, talks, essays, poems, studies in history. 1958. Much of the material is the same as in 5 pens in hand, above.

Food for centaurs: stories, talks, critical studies, poems. Garden City NY 1960.

Selected poetry and prose, chosen, introduced and annotated by J. Reeves. 1961.

Poetry

Over the brazier. 1916, [1920] (with omissions).

Goliath and David. [1916] (priv ptd, 200 copies). Contents rptd in next.

Fairies and fusiliers. 1917, New York 1918.

Treasure box. [1919] (priv ptd, 200 copies). 10 poems, mostly rptd in The pier-glass, below.

Country sentiment. 1920, New York 1920.

The pier-glass. 1921, New York 1921.

Whipperginny. 1923, New York 1923.

The feather bed. Richmond Surrey 1923 (254 copies).

Mock Beggar Hall. 1924.

John Kemp's wager: a ballad opera. Oxford 1925, New York 1925.

Welchman's hose. 1925.

Poems 1914–26. 1927, Garden City NY 1929.

Poems 1914–27. 1927 (115 copies). Poems 1914–26 with 9 additional poems.

Poems 1929. 1929 (Seizin 3, 225 copies).

Ten poems more. Paris 1930 (200 copies).

Poems 1926–1930. 1931.

To whom else? Deyá 1931 (Seizin 6, 200 copies).

Poems 1930–1933. 1933.

Collected poems. 1938, New York 1938.

No more ghosts: selected poems. 1940. Mainly from preceding.

Work in hand. [By] A. Hodge, N. Cameron, R. Graves. 1942. 18 poems by Graves.

[Thirty-one poems.] [1943] (Augustan Poets). Selection.

Poems 1938–1945. 1946, New York [1946].

Collected poems 1914–1947. 1948.

Poems and satires. 1951.

Poems 1953. 1953.

Collected poems 1955. Garden City NY 1955.

Poems selected by himself. 1957, 1961 (rev and enlarged), 1966 (rev and enlarged) (Penguin Poets).

The poems of Robert Graves chosen by himself. Garden City NY 1958.

Collected poems 1959. 1959.

The penny fiddle: poems for children. 1960, Garden City NY 1961.

More poems. 1961.

Collected poems. Garden City NY 1961.

The more deserving cases: eighteen old poems for reconsideration. [Marlborough] 1962 (400 copies). Pbd Marlborough College Press.

New poems. 1962, Garden City NY 1963.

Man does, woman is. 1964.

Ann at Highwood Hall: poems for children. 1964, Garden City NY 1966.

Love respelt. 1965 (250 copies) Garden City NY 1966. Most rptd in next.

Collected poems, 1965. 1965.

Collected poems, 1966. Garden City NY 1966.

Seventeen poems missing from Love respelt. 1966 (priv ptd, 330 copies).

Colophon to Love respelt. 1967 (priv ptd, 386 copies).

Poems 1965–1968. 1968, Garden City NY 1969.

Beyond giving. 1969 (priv ptd, 536 copies).

Fiction

My head! My head!: being the history of Elisha and the Shunamite woman; with the history of Moses as Elisha related it, and her questions put to him. 1925, New York 1925.

The shout. 1929.

No decency left, by 'Barbara Rich'. 1932. By Graves and Laura Riding.

The real David Copperfield. 1933, New York 1934 (with alterations, as David Copperfield by Dickens condensed).

I, Claudius: from the autobiography of Tiberius Claudius emperor of the Romans. 1934, New York 1934, 2 vols 1941 (Penguin), 1 vol New York 1965 (with introd).

Claudius the god and his wife Messalina. 1934, New York 1935.

'Antigua, penny, puce'. Deyá, London 1936, New York [1937] (as The Antigua stamp).

Count Belisarius. 1938, New York [1938].

Sergeant Lamb of the Ninth. 1940, New York [1940] (as Sergeant Lamb's America).

Proceed, Sergeant Lamb. 1941, New York [1941].

The story of Marie Powell, wife to Mr Milton. 1943, New York 1944 (as Wife to Mr Milton, the story of Marie Powell), London 1954 (Penguin).

The golden fleece. 1944, New York 1945 (as Hercules, my shipmate).

King Jesus. New York 1946, London 1946.

Watch the north wind rise. New York 1949, London 1949 (as Seven days in New Crete).

The islands of unwisdom. Garden City NY 1949, London 1950 (as The isles of unwisdom).

Homer's daughter. 1955, Garden City NY 1955.

¡Catacrok! mostly stories, mostly funny. 1956.

The big green book. [New York] 1962. For children.

The siege and fall of Troy. 1962, Garden City NY 1963.

Collected short stories. Garden City NY 1964, London 1965.

Two wise children. New York [1966], London 1967.

The poor boy who followed his star and [3] children's poems. 1968.

Other Works

On English poetry: being an irregular approach to the psychology of this art, from evidence mainly subjective. New York 1922, London 1922.

The meaning of dreams. 1924.

Poetic unreason and other studies. 1925.

Contemporary techniques of poetry: a political analogy. 1925 (Hogarth Essays 8).

Another future of poetry. 1926. A reply to R. C. Trevelyan, Thamyris: or is there a future for poetry?, 1926.

The English ballad: a short critical survey. 1927, 1957 (rev, as English and Scottish ballads), New York 1957.

Lars Porsena: or the future of swearing and improper language. 1927, New York 1927, London 1936 (rev, as The future of swearing and improper language).

Impenetrability: or the proper habit of English. 1926 (for 1927) (Hogarth Essays 2nd ser 3).

John Skelton, laureate, 1460?-1529. [1927] (Augustan Books of English Poetry). Selection, modernisation of the poems, and editor's note by Graves.

Lawrence and the Arabs. 1927, Garden City NY 1928 (as Lawrence and the Arabian adventure), London 1934 ('concise' edn).

The less familiar nursery rhymes. [1927] (Augustan Books of English Poetry). Selection and foreword by Graves.

A survey of modernist poetry. 1927, Garden City NY 1928. With Laura Riding.

A pamphlet against anthologies. 1928, Garden City NY 1928. With Laura Riding.

Mrs Fisher: or the future of humour. 1928.

Goodbye to all that: an autobiography. 1929, New York [1930], Garden City NY 1957 (rev), London 1957.

But it still goes on: an accumulation. 1930, New York [1931]. Sequel to Goodbye to all that, above.

Old soldiers never die, by Private Frank Richards [rewritten by Graves]. 1933, 1964 (with introd by Graves).

Old soldier sahib, by Private Frank Richards [rewritten by Graves]. 1936, New York [1936] (with introd by Graves), London 1965 (with new foreword by Graves).

T. E. Lawrence to his biographer, Robert Graves: information about himself, in the form of letters, notes and answers to questions edited with a critical commentary [by Graves]. New York 1938, London 1938 [1939], [1963] (as T. E. Lawrence to his biographers Robert Graves and Liddell Hart), Garden City NY 1963.

The long week-end: a social history of Great Britain 1918-1939. 1940, New York 1941. With Alan Hodge.

The reader over your shoulder: a handbook for writers of English prose. 1943, New York 1944, London 1947 (abridged). With Hodge.

The white goddess: a historical grammar of poetic myth. 1948, New York 1948, London 1952 (rev and enlarged), New York 1958, London 1961 (rev and enlarged).

The common asphodel: collected essays on poetry 1922-1949. 1949. With revisions.

Occupation: writer. New York 1950, London 1951. 'A collection of my short stories, plays and miscellaneous essays . . . revised'.

The Nazarene Gospel restored. 1953, Garden City NY 1954, London 1955 (pt 3, text of the Gospel, only). With Joshua Podro.

The Greek myths. 2 vols 1955, Baltimore 1955, 1 vol London 1958 (with rev introd) (Penguin).

Adam's rib and other anomalous elements in the Hebrew creation myth: a new view. 1955, New York 1958.

The crowning privilege. 1955. See Collections, above.

Jesus in Rome: a historical conjecture. 1957. With Podro.

They hanged my saintly Billy. 1957, Garden City NY 1957 (as They hanged my saintly Billy: the life and death of Dr William Palmer).

5 pens in hand. 1958. See Collections, above.

Steps. 1958. See Collections, above.

Food for centaurs. 1960. See Collections, above.

Greek gods and heroes. Garden City NY 1960, London 1961 (as Myths of ancient Greece).

Oxford addresses on poetry. 1962, Garden City NY 1962.

Nine hundred iron chariots. Cambridge Mass 1963 (Arthur Dehon Little memorial lecture). Rptd in Mammon and the black goddess, 1965, below.

Mammon: oration delivered at the London School of Economics and Political Science 6 December 1963. 1964. Rptd in Mammon and the black goddess, 1965, below.

The Hebrew myths: the book of Genesis. Garden City NY 1964, London 1964. With Raphael Patai.

Mammon and the black goddess. 1965, Garden City NY 1965. Lectures and an essay.

Majorca observed. [1965], Garden City NY 1965. With Paul Hogarth.

Poetic craft and principle: lectures and talks. 1967.

The crane bag and other disputed subjects. 1969. Lectures, essays, reviews etc.

Translations

Lucius Apuleius. The transformation of Lucius, otherwise known as the golden ass. 1950 (Penguin Classics), New York 1951.

'Sand, George'. Winter in Majorca, with José Quadrado's refutation of George Sand. 1956, Mallorca 1956.

Lucan. Pharsalia: dramatic episodes of the civil wars. 1956 (Penguin Classics), Baltimore 1957.

Gaius Suetonius Tranquillus. The twelve Caesars. 1957 (Penguin Classics).

Fable of the hawk and the nightingale, translated from Hesiod's Works and days. Lexington Kentucky 1959 (about 110 copies).

The anger of Achilles: Homer's Iliad translated. Garden City NY 1959, London 1960.

The Rubaiyat of Omar Khayaam: a new translation with critical commentaries by Graves and Omar Ali-Shah. 1967, Garden City NY 1968.

§ 2

Muir, E. In his Transition, 1926.

Graves, A. P. To return to all that: an autobiography. 1930. Includes ch on his son Robert.

Williams, C. In his Poetry at present, Oxford 1930.

Trilling, L. A ramble on Graves. In his A gathering of fugitives, Boston 1956.

Davie, D. The toneless voice of Graves. Listener 2 July 1959.

Cohen, J. M. Robert Graves. Edinburgh 1960 (Writers and Critics).

Kirkham, M. The poetry of Graves. 1969.

WYSTAN HUGH AUDEN
1907-73
Bibliographies

Bloomfield, B. C. Auden: a bibliography; the early years through 1955. Charlottesville 1964, 1972 (enlarged).

§ 1
Poetry

Poems. 1928 (priv ptd by Stephen Spender, c. 30 copies), Cincinnati [1964] (photo facs with preface by Spender). Some poems not rptd in later collections.

Poems. [1930] [1933] (with 7 substituted poems).

The orators: an English study. 1932, 1934 (with corrections and excisions), 1966 (further excisions and new preface), New York 1967 (further corrections). Verse and prose.

Poem. [New Haven] 1933 (priv ptd by F. Prokosch, c. 22 copies). Contains Hearing of harvest rotting in the valley; rptd in Look stranger!, 1936, below.

The witnesses. 1933. Single sheet; rptd from Listener, 20 copies.

Poems. New York [1934]. Contains Poems 1933, above, The orators and The dance of death (*see* Plays, below).

Two poems. [New Haven] 1934 (priv ptd by F. Prokosch, c. 22 copies).

Our hunting fathers. [Cambridge] 1935 (priv ptd for F. Prokosch, c. 22 copies); rptd in Look stranger!, 1936, below.

Sonnet. [Cambridge] 1935 (priv ptd for F. Prokosch, c. 22 copies).

Look, stranger! 1936, New York [1937] (as On this island).

Spain. 1937, [Paris] 1937 (in Les poètes du monde défendent le peuple espagnol 5, priv ptd by Nancy Cunard).

Letters from Iceland. 1937, New York [1937], London 1967 (revisions and excisions), New York 1969. With L. MacNeice. Verse and prose.

Nightmail. [1938?]. Single sheet; rptd in Collected shorter poems 1927–1957, 1966 below.

Selected poems. 1938. Selected by the author.

Epithalamion commemorating the marriage of G. A. Borgese and E. Mann. [New York] 1939; rptd in Another time, 1940.

Journey to a war. 1939, New York [1939]. With C. Isherwood. Poems and commentary.

Another time. New York [1940], London 1940.

Some poems. 1940. Selected by the author.

The double man. New York [1941], London 1941 (as New Year letter).

Three songs for St Cecilia's Day. [New York] 1941 (priv ptd, 250 copies); rptd from Harper's Bazaar Dec 1941; rptd in Collected poetry, 1945, below.

For the time being. New York [1944], London 1945.

Collected poetry. New York [1945]. Selection from previous vols with some revision and some uncollected poems.

Litany and anthem for S. Matthew's Day, written for the Church of S. Matthew, Northampton. [Northampton 1946].

The age of anxiety: a baroque eclogue. New York [1947], London [1948].

Collected shorter poems 1930–44. [1950]. Differs from the corresponding sections in Collected poetry [1945], above; there are omissions, changes of title and addns.

Nones. New York [1951], London 1952.

Mountains. 1954 (Ariel poem); rptd in next.

The shield of Achilles. New York [1955], London 1955.

The old man's road. New York 1956. Also separate limited edn, 50 copies.

Reflections in a forest. [Greencastle Ind] 1957. Single sheet; rptd in Homage to Clio, 1960.

Goodbye to the Mezzogiorno: poesia inedita e versione italiana di C. Izzo. Milan 1958; rptd in Homage to Clio, 1960.

W. H. Auden: a selection by the author. 1958 (Penguin Poets), New York 1959 (Modern Library, as The selected poetry of W. H. Auden). With revisions.

Homage to Clio. New York [1960], London 1960.

W. H. Auden: a selection with notes and a critical essay by R. Hoggart. 1961 (Hutchinson English Texts).

The common life. Darmstadt 1964; rptd in About the house, 1965.

About the house. New York [1965], London 1966.

Half-way. Cambridge Mass 1965. Single sheet. 75 copies; rptd in Collected shorter poems 1927–57, 1966.

The cave of making. Darmstadt 1965. Also in About the house, 1965, above.

Collected shorter poems 1927–57. 1966, New York 1967.

But I can't. Cambridge Mass 1966. Single sheet. 12 copies, rptd from Collected poetry, 1945.

Marginalia. Cambridge Mass 1966. 150 copies.

Portraits. Northampton Mass 1966. 20 copies; poems rptd from Collected poetry, 1945.

River profile. Cambridge Mass 1967. c. 50 copies; rptd in City without walls, 1969, below.

Brussels in winter. [New Haven] 1967. Single sheet. 10 copies.

Collected longer poems. 1968, New York 1969. Contains Paid on both sides, Letter to Lord Byron, New Year letter, For the time being, The sea and the mirror, The age of anxiety. Some revisions.

Selected poems. 1968. With revisions.

Two songs. New York 1968. 126 copies; rptd in City without walls, 1969.

City without walls. 1969, New York 1970.

A New Year greeting. [New York 1969].

See also B. C. Bloomfield and E. Mendelson, A poem attributed to Auden [The Platonic blow], Library 5th ser 25 1970.

Christopher Isherwood's Lions and shadows, *1938, in which Auden appears as 'Hugh Weston', contains some early poems by Auden.*

Plays and Libretti

The dance of death. (Westminster 24 Oct 1934). 1933.

The dog beneath the skin: or where is Francis? a play in three acts. (Westminster 12 Jan 1936). 1935, New York 1935. With C. Isherwood.

The ascent of F 6: a tragedy in two acts. (Mercury 26 Feb 1937). 1936, New York 1937 (rev), London 1937 (2nd edn again rev). With C. Isherwood, the verse being by Auden.

No more peace! By E. Toller, lyrics tr Auden. New York 1937, London 1937.

On the frontier: a melodrama in three acts. (Arts Theatre, Cambridge 14 Nov 1938). 1938, New York [1939]. With C. Isherwood.

The dark valley. (Columbia Workshop 2 June 1940). In Best broadcasts of 1939–40, New York [1940].

The rake's progress: opera in three acts. Music by I. Stravinsky, libretto by Auden and C. Kallman. (Venice, 11 Sept 1951). 1951, 1966 (rev).

The magic flute: an opera in two acts. Music by W. A. Mozart, English version after the libretto of Schikaneder and Giesecke by Auden and Kallman. (NBC Television 15 Jan 1956). New York [1956], London 1957.

Don Giovanni: opera in two acts. Music by W. A. Mozart, libretto by L. da Ponte. English version by Auden and Kallman. (NBC Television 10 April 1960). New York [1961].

Elegy for young lovers: opera in three acts by Auden and C. Kallman, music by H. W. Henze. (Stuttgart 20 May 1961). Mainz 1961.

The Bassarids: opera seria with intermezzo in one act based on the Bacchae by Euripides by Auden and C. Kallman. Music by H. W. Henze. (Salzburg 6 Aug 1966). Mainz [1966].

Auden also wrote the libretto for an operetta, Paul Bunyan, *by Britten, performed at Columbia Univ in May 1941 but was later withdrawn by the composer. Another libretto by Auden and Kallman,* Delia or a masque of night *was pbd in Botteghe Oscure 12 1953. Auden collaborated with Brecht in adapting Webster's* Duchess of Malfi *in 1945–6, and translated with Kallman Brecht's* Die sieben Todsünden *(pbd Tulane Drama Rev 6 1961); with J. and T. Stern, Der kaukasische Kreidekreis (pbd in Brecht's* Plays, vol 1 *1960); and with Kallman, Mahagonny (1960, unpbd). He also translated Cocteau's* Les chevaliers de la table ronde *(pbd in Cocteau's*

Infernal machine and other plays, *New York* [*1964*]).
He collaborated on the films Coal face, Night mail, The
way to the sea *and* Londoners *in 1935–9.*

Other Works

Education today—and tomorrow. 1939 (Day to Day
pamphlets 40). With T. C. Worsley
The enchaféd flood: or the romantic iconography of the
sea. New York [1950], London 1951.
Making, knowing and judging: an inaugural lecture de-
livered before the University of Oxford. Oxford 1956;
rptd in next.
The dyer's hand and other essays. New York [1962],
London 1963. Selected critical pieces.
Louis MacNeice: a memorial address delivered at All
Souls Langham Place. [1963] (priv ptd, 250 copies).
Selected essays. 1964. All from The dyer's hand. Two
essays and Postscript rptd as Reading and Writing,
Tokyo 1966.
Secondary worlds. 1968, New York [1969]. First Eliot
lectures at University of Kent.
Worte und Noten. Salzburg 1968. An address.

§ 2

Empson, W. A note on Auden's Paid on both sides.
Experiment 7 1931.
—— Early Auden. Review (Oxford) no 5 1963.
Spender, S. Five notes on Auden's writing. Twentieth
Century (Promethean Soc) 3 1932.
—— In his Destructive element, 1935.
—— The poetic dramas of Auden and Isherwood. New
Writing new ser 1 1938.
—— In his World within world, 1951.
—— Auden and his poetry. Atlantic Monthly 192 1953;
rptd in Auden, ed M. K. Spears 1964.
—— In his Creative element, 1953.
Leavis, F. R. Auden, Bottrall and others. Scrutiny 3 1934.
Review of Poems (1933) and The dance of death.
Isherwood, C. In his Lions and shadows: an education in
the Twenties, 1938. With poems by Auden.
MacNeice, L. In his Modern poetry, 1938.
Southworth, J. G. Auden. Sewanee Rev 46 1938; rptd in
his Sowing the spring, Oxford 1940.
Brooks, C. In his Modern poetry and the tradition, Chapel
Hill 1939; excerpts rptd in Auden, ed M. K. Spears 1964.
—— Auden as a critic. Kenyon Rev 26 1964.
Jarrell, R. Changes of attitude and rhetoric in Auden's
poetry. Southern Rev 7 1941.
—— Freud to Paul: the stages of Auden's ideology. Parti-
san Rev 12 1945; both essays rptd in his Third book of
criticism, New York 1969.
Scarfe, F. Auden and after: the liberation of poetry 1930–
41. 1942.
Savage, D. S. The strange case of Auden. In his Personal
principle, 1944.
Beach, J. W. The poems of Auden and the prose diathesis.
Virginia Quart Rev 25 1949.
—— The making of the Auden canon. Minneapolis 1957.
Hoggart, R. Auden: an introductory essay. 1951.
—— W. H. Auden. 1957, [1962] (rev), [1966] (rev) (Br
Council pamphlet); rptd in his Speaking to each other
vol 2, 1970.
Spears, M. K. Late Auden: the satirist as lunatic clergy-
man. Sewanee Rev 59 1951.
—— The dominant symbols of Auden's poetry. Ibid.
—— Auden in the fifties: rites of homage. Sewanee Rev 69
1961.
—— The poetry of Auden: the disenchanted island. New
York 1963, 1968 (rev).
—— (ed). Auden: a collection of critical essays. Engle-
wood Cliffs NJ 1964. All previously pbd.
Wilson, E. Auden in America. New Statesman 9 June
1956; rptd in Auden, ed M. K. Spears 1964, and in
Wilson's Bit between my teeth, New York 1965.

Robson, W. W. Mr Auden's profession. Twentieth Cen-
tury 161 1957; rptd in his Critical essays, 1966.
Alvarez, A. Auden: poetry and journalism. In his The
shaping spirit, 1958, New York 1958 (as Stewards of
excellence).
Larkin, P. What's become of Wystan? Spectator 15 July
1960.
Fuller, J. A reader's guide to Auden. 1970.
Duchene, F. The case of the helmeted airman. 1972.
Spender, S. (ed). Auden: a tribute. 1975.
Hynes, S. The Auden generation. 1976.

DYLAN MARLAIS THOMAS
1914–53

*The Lockwood Memorial Library, Buffalo, has a collection of
Thomas's letters and mss, including the four notebooks ed
R. N. Maud as* The notebooks of Thomas, *1967 and a prose
notebook.*

Bibliographies etc

Rolph, J. A. Dylan Thomas: a bibliography. 1956.
Williams, R. C. A concordance to the Collected poems of
Thomas. Lincoln Nebraska 1967.

§ 1
Poetry

18 poems. 1934.
Twenty-five poems. 1936.
The map of love: verse and prose. 1939.
The world I breathe. Norfolk Conn 1939. Selection of 40
poems, 11 stories.
New poems. Norfolk Conn [1943] (Poets of the year).
Deaths and entrances: poems. 1946.
Twenty-six poems. 1950, Norfolk Conn 1950. 150 copies,
ptd at Verona by G. Mardersteig. Selection.
In country sleep and other poems. New York [1952].
Collected poems 1934–1952. 1952, New York 1953 [with
Elegy, reconstructed from drafts, with notes by Vernon
Watkins], London 1966 (EL).
The notebooks. Ed R. N. Maud, Norfolk Conn 1967,
London 1968 (as Poet in the making: the notebooks of
Dylan Thomas). Contains text of poems in 4 notebooks
used by Thomas 1930–33 now in Lockwood Memorial
Library, Buffalo; together with 20 poems mainly from
mss in BM.
The colour of saying: an anthology of verse spoken by
Thomas, *ed R. N. Maud and A. T. Davies, was pbd in
1963.*

Other Works

Portrait of the artist as a young dog. 1940, Norfolk Conn
[1940]. Stories.
The doctor and the devils. 1953, [Norfolk Conn] 1953.
Film script based on a story by D. Taylor.
Under Milk Wood: a play for voices. Preface and musical
settings by Daniel Jones. 1954, New York [1954],
London [1958] (acting edn). First pbd in shorter version
as Llareggub: a piece for radio perhaps, in Botteghe
Oscure 9 1952. Final version during the author's life-
time first read publicly, under the sponsorship of the
YM-YWHA Poetry Center, at the Kaufman Auditorium
New York 24 Oct 1953; first broadcast, BBC Third
Programme 25 Jan 1954. First stage production after
a trial week at Newcastle-on-Tyne, at the Lyceum
Theatre Edinburgh 21 Aug 1956 and at the New
Theatre London 20 Sept 1956. For a tentative list of
pbd and unpbd versions, see letter by D. Cleverdon,
TLS 18 July 1968.
Quite early one morning: broadcasts. 1954, New York
[1954] (with addns, omissions and alterations).
Conversation about Christmas. [New York?] 1954 (priv
ptd). First pbd in Picture Post 27 Dec 1947, rptd in
A prospect of the sea, 1955, below.

Adventures in the skin trade and other stories. [New York, 1955]. Title story (unfinished by Thomas) and 20 others some previously uncollected. Title story pbd separately with introd by V. Watkins, 1955.

A prospect of the sea and other stories and prose writings. Ed Daniel Jones 1955. 7 stories rptd from The map of love, 1939, the remainder uncollected.

A child's Christmas in Wales. Norfolk Conn [1955]. Rptd from American edn of Quite early one morning, 1954.

Return journey. In A. Durband (ed), New directions: five one act plays, 1961. Broadcast 15 June 1947.

The beach of Falesá: based on a story by R. L. Stevenson. New York [1963], London 1964. Filmscript.

A film script of Twenty years a-growing, from the story by M. O'Sullivan. 1964.

Me and my bike. 1965, New York [1965], London 1968 (with next, as Two tales). Filmscript.

Rebecca's daughters. 1965. Filmscript.

The doctor and the devils and other scripts. [New York 1966]. Includes Twenty years a-growing, A dream of winter, The Londoner.

Letters
Letters to Vernon Watkins. Ed Watkins 1957, [New York] 1957.

Selected letters of Dylan Thomas. Ed C. Fitzgibbon 1966, [New York 1967].

§2
Sitwell, E. Four new poets. London Mercury 33 1936. Empson, Bottrall, Thomas and Archibald MacLeish.

Berryman, J. The loud hill of Wales. Kenyon Rev 2 1940; rptd in J. C. Ransom (ed), The Kenyon critics, New York 1951.

Scarfe, F. The poetry of Thomas. Horizon 2 1940; rptd in his Auden and after, 1942, and in Brinnin 1960 and Tedlock 1960, below.

Empson, W. How to understand a modern poem. Strand Mag 112 1947. A refusal to mourn the death, by fire, of a child in London.

—— Books in general. [Review of Collected poems and Under Milk Wood]. New Statesman 15 May 1954; rptd in Brinnin 1960 and Cox 1966, below.

Tindall, W. Y. The poetry of Thomas. Amer Scholar 17 1948.

—— Burning and crested song. Amer Scholar 22 1953. Review of Collected poems.

—— A reader's guide to Thomas. New York 1962.

Brinnin, J. M. Dylan Thomas in America: an intimate journal. Boston 1955.

—— (ed). A casebook on Thomas. New York [1960]. A collection of essays, with 10 of Thomas's poems and a bibliography.

Dylan Thomas: memories and appreciations [by] D. Jones, T. Roethke, L. MacNeice, M. Adix, G. Barker. Encounter 2 1954. Rptd in Tedlock 1960, below. (Jones, MacNeice and Adix also rptd in Brinnin 1960, above).

Maud, R. N. Thomas's poetry. EC 4 1954.

—— Obsolete and dialect works as serious puns in Thomas. E Studies 41 1960.

—— Entrances to Thomas' poetry. Pittsburgh 1963.

Stanford, D. Dylan Thomas: a literary study. 1954. Poetry (Chicago) 87 1955.

Thomas, C. In her Leftover life to kill, 1957.

Wain, J. Thomas: a review of his Collected poems. In his Preliminary essays, 1957.

Aiken, C. In his A reviewer's ABC, New York 1958.

Cox, C. B. Thomas's Fern Hill. CQ 1 1959.

—— (ed). Dylan Thomas: a collection of critical essays. Englewood Cliffs NJ [1966].

Tedlock, E. W. (ed). Dylan Thomas—the legend and the poet: a collection of biographical and critical essays. 1960.

Holbrook, D. Metaphor and maturity: T. F. Powys and Thomas. In The modern age (vol 7, Pelican Guide to Eng Lit, ed B. Ford 1961).

—— Llareggub revisited: Thomas and the state of modern poetry. Cambridge 1962, Carbondale [1964] (rev, as Dylan Thomas and poetic dissociation).

Nowottny, W. In her The language poets use, 1962; rptd in Cox 1966, above.

Fitzgibbon, C. The life of Thomas. 1965.

Cleverdon, D. Under Milk Wood. TLS 18 July 1968.

—— The growth of Milk Wood; with the textual variants of Under Milk Wood. 1969.

SIR HAROLD MARIO MITCHELL ACTON
b. 1904
Poetry

Aquarium. 1923.
An Indian ass. 1925.
Five saints and an appendix. 1927.
This chaos. Paris 1930 (priv ptd, 150 copies).

Other Works
Cornelian: a fable. 1928. Short story.
Humdrum. 1928, New York [1929]. Novel.
The last of the Medici [an anon life of Gian Gastone de' Medici]. Tr Acton, introd by N. Douglas, Florence 1930 (priv ptd, 365 copies).
The last Medici. 1932, 1958 (rev), New York 1959. Biography.
Modern Chinese poetry. 1936. With Ch'ên Shih-hsiang.
Famous Chinese plays. Tr and ed L. C. Arlington and Acton, Peiping 1937, New York 1963.
Fêng Mêng-lung. Glue and lacquer: four cautionary tales. Tr Acton and Lee Yi-hsieh 1941 (350 copies), 1947 (as Four cautionary tales).
Peonies and ponies. 1941. Novel.
Memoirs of an aesthete. 1948. Autobiography.

Prince Isidore. 1950. Novel.
The Bourbons of Naples, 1734–1825. 1956, 1957 (rptd with corrections), New York 1958.
Art and ideas in eighteenth-century Italy: lectures given at the Italian Institute 1957–8. Rome 1960. With others.
Florence. [1961], New York 1961. With M. Hürlimann.
The last Bourbons of Naples, 1825–61. 1961, New York 1962.
Old lamps for new. 1965. Novel.
More memoirs of an aesthete. 1970.

KENNETH ALLOTT
1912–74
Poetry

Poems. 1938.
The ventriloquist's doll. [1943].

Other Works
The rhubarb tree. 1937. Novel, with S. Tait.
Jules Verne. [1940], New York 1941. Biography.
The Penguin book of contemporary verse. Ed with introd and notes by Allott 1950, 1962 (rev) (Penguin Poets).
The art of Graham Greene. 1951, New York 1963. With M. Farris.
A room with a view: a play adapted from the novel by E. M. Forster, by S. Tait and Allott. 1951.

Selected poems of W. M. Praed. Ed with introd and commentary by Allott 1953, Cambridge Mass 1953. (ML).

Five uncollected essays of Matthew Arnold. Ed Allott, [Liverpool] 1953, New York 1953 (Liverpool Reprints 9).

Matthew Arnold. 1955 (Br Council pamphlet).

The Pelican book of English prose. General editor: K. Allott. 5 vols 1956.

Browning, R. Selected poems, chosen and ed Allott 1967.

Allott has also edited Arnold's poems for Penguin Poets, *1954,* EL, *1965 and* Longman's Annotated English Poets, *1965.*

GEORGE GRANVILLE BARKER
b. 1913
Poetry

Thirty preliminary poems. 1933.
Poems. 1935.
Calamiterror. 1937.
Elegy on Spain. 1939.
Lament and triumph. 1940.
Selected poems. New York 1941.
Sacred and secular elegies. Norfolk Conn 1943.
Eros in dogma. 1944.
Love poems. New York 1947.
News of the world. 1950.
The true confession of George Barker. 1950, New York 1964, London 1965 (enlarged).
A vision of beasts and gods. 1954.
Collected poems 1930-1955. 1957, New York 1958. Omits The true confession.
Penguin modern poets, 3: Barker, M. Bell, C. Causley. 1962. Selection, 15 poems.
The view from a blind I. 1962.
Collected poems 1930-1965. New York 1965.
Dreams of a summer night. 1966.
The golden chains. 1968.
At Thurgarton Church: a poem with drawings. 1969.
Runes and rhymes and tunes and chimes. 1969.

Other Works

Alanna autumnal. 1933. Novel.
Janus. 1935. Two tales: The documents of death and The Bacchant.
The dead seagull. 1950, New York 1951. Novel.
Two plays. 1958. The seraphina; In the shade of the old apple tree.
Alfred Tennyson. Idylls of the king and a selection of poems, with a foreword by Barker. New York 1961, London 1962.
Essays. 1970.

JULIAN HEWARD BELL
1908-37

Chaffinches. Cambridge 1929.
Cambridge poetry 1929-30. 2 vols 1929-30. 5 poems contributed by Bell.
Winter movement and other poems. 1930.
New signatures. Ed M. Roberts 1932. 3 poems contributed by Bell.
We did not fight: 1914-18 experiences of war resisters. Ed J. Bell 1935.
Poems by Stéphane Mallarmé. Tr R. Fry; ed C. Mauron and J. Bell 1936. Rptd with additional material 1952.
Work for the winter and other poems. 1936.
Essays, poems and letters. Ed Q. Bell 1938. Contributions by J. M. Keynes, D. Garnett, C. Mauron, C. Day Lewis and E. M. Forster.

FRANCIS BERRY
b. 1915

Gospel of fire. 1933.
Snake in the moon. 1936.

The iron Christ: a poem. 1938.
Fall of a tower and other poems. 1943.
Murdock and other poems. 1947.
The galloping centaur: poems 1933-1951. 1952, 1970 (adds Envoy—1968). Omits most of Gospel of fire, 1933.
Herbert Read. 1953, [1961] (rev) (Br Council pamphlet).
Poets' grammar: person, time and mood in poetry. 1958.
Morant Bay and other poems. 1961.
Poetry and the physical voice. 1962, New York 1962.
The Shakespeare inset: word and picture. 1965, New York 1966.
Ghosts of Greenland. 1966.
John Masefield: the narrative poet. 1968. Inaugural lecture, Univ of Sheffield.

SIR JOHN BETJEMAN
b. 1906
Bibliographies

Carter, J. Betjemaniana. Book Collector 9 1960.
Stapleton, R. J. Betjeman: a bibliography. Metuchan NJ 1974.

§1
Poetry

Mount Zion: or in touch with the infinite. [1931].
Continual dew: a little book of bourgeois verse. 1937.
Sir John Piers, by 'Epsilon' [i.e. Betjeman]. Mullingar [1938]. 5 poems, rptd in next.
Old lights for new chancels: verses topographical and amatory. 1940.
New bats in old belfries. 1945.
Slick, but not streamlined: poems and short pieces, selected and with an introduction by W. H. Auden. New York 1947.
Selected poems, chosen, with a preface, by J. Sparrow. 1948.
A few late chrysanthemums. 1954.
Poems in the porch. 1954.
Collected poems, compiled and with an introduction by the Earl of Birkenhead. 1958, Boston 1959, London 1962 (with addns).
[Thirty-one poems]. 1958 (Pocket Poets). Selection with one uncollected poem.
Summoned by bells. 1960, Boston 1960. Verse autobiography.
A ring of bells: poems, introduced and selected by I. Slade. [1962], Boston 1963.
High and low. 1966.

Other Works

Ghastly good taste: or a depressing story of the rise and fall of English architecture. 1933.
Cornwall illustrated in a series of views. Ed Betjeman 1934 (Shell Guides).
Devon. 1936, 1955 (rev by B. Watson) (Shell Guides).
An Oxford University chest: comprising a description of the present state of the town and university of Oxford. 1938.
Antiquarian prejudice. 1939. Lecture on architecture.
Vintage London. 1942.
English cities and small towns. 1943.
John Piper. 1944 (Penguin Modern painters).
Murray's Buckinghamshire architectural guide. Ed Betjeman and J. Piper 1948.
Murray's Berkshire architectural guide. Ed Betjeman and J. Piper 1949.
Studies in the history of Swindon, by Betjeman [et al]. Swindon 1950.
Shropshire. 1951. By J. Piper and Betjeman (Shell Guides).
First and last loves. 1952. Essays on architecture and English towns.

R. S. Thomas. Song at the year's turning: poems 1942–1954. 1955. Introd by Betjeman.

The English town in the last hundred years. Cambridge 1956. Lecture.

English love poems, chosen by Betjeman and G. Taylor. 1957.

Collins guide to English parish churches. Ed Betjeman 1958, New York 1959 (as An American's guide to English parish churches), London 1968 (rev in 2 vols as Collins Pocket guide [etc].).

Altar and pew: Church of England verses. 1959. Selection by Betjeman.

Ground plan to skyline. [By] 'Richard M. Farran' [i.e. Betjeman]. 1960.

A wealth of poetry, selected for the young in heart by W. Hindley with the assistance of Betjeman. Oxford [1963].

Cornwall: a Shell guide. 1964. The work of 1934 completely rewritten.

English churches. 1964. With B. Clarke.

The City of London churches. [1965].

Victorian and Edwardian London from old photographs. 1969.

West Country churches. 1973.

A nip in the air. 1974.

Betjeman was general editor of Shell Guides *first pbd in 1934. He was also editor of* Watergate Children's Classics *from 1947. He contributed a weekly column,* City and suburban, *to* Spectator *from 15 Oct 1954 to Jan 1958.*

§2

Stanford, D. John Betjeman: a study. 1961.

EDMUND CHARLES BLUNDEN
1896–1974

Selections

A selection of his poetry and prose made by K. Hopkins. 1950, New York 1951.

§1
Poetry

Poems, 1913 and 1914. Horsham 1914 (100 copies).

Poems translated from the French: July 1913–January 1914. Horsham 1914 (100 copies).

The barn, with certain other poems. Uckfield 1916 (priv ptd, 50 copies).

The harbingers: poems. Uckfield 1916 (priv ptd, 200 copies).

Pastorals: a book of verses. 1916.

Three poems. Uckfield 1916 (50 copies). Contains The silver bird of Herndyke Mill, Stane Street, The gods of the earth beneath.

The waggoner, and other poems. 1920 (400 copies), New York 1921 (100 copies).

Old homes: a poem. Clare 1922 (priv ptd, 100 copies).

The shepherd, and other poems of peace and war. 1922, New York 1922.

Dead letters. 1923 (50 copies).

To nature: new poems. 1923 (392 copies).

English poems. Preface by Blunden 1925, New York 1926, London 1929 (rev). Most of poems 1921–5 with addns.

Masks of time: a new collection of poems, principally meditative. 1925 (390 copies).

[Twenty-one poems]. [1925] (Augustan Books of Modern Poetry). Selection.

Japanese garland. 1928 (390 copies).

Retreat: new sonnets and poems. 1928, Garden City NY 1928.

Winter nights: a reminiscence. [1928] (Ariel Poem).

Near and far: new poems. 1929, New York 1930.

Poems. Preface by Blunden 1930, New York 1932.

A summer's fancy. 1930 (405 copies).

Constantia and Francis: an autumn evening. Edinburgh 1931 (priv ptd, 200 copies).

In summer: the rotunda of the Bishop of Derry. 1931 (priv ptd, 305 copies).

To Themis: poems on famous trials; with other pieces. 1931 (405 copies).

Halfway house: a miscellany of new poems. 1932, New York 1933.

Choice or chance: new poems. 1934.

Verses to HRH the Duke of Windsor. Oxford 1936 (100 copies).

An elegy, and other poems. 1937.

On several occasions, by 'A Fellow of Merton College'. 1939 (60 copies).

Poems 1930–1940. 1940 (for 1941), New York 1941.

Shells by a stream: new poems. 1944, New York 1945.

After the bombing, and other short poems. 1949, New York 1949.

Eastward: a selection of verses original and translated. Tokyo 1949 (250 copies).

Records of friendship: occasional and epistolary poems written during visits to Kyushu. Fukuoka 1950.

Poems of many years. Preface by Blunden 1957.

A Hong Kong house: poems, 1951–1961. 1962.

Eleven poems. Cambridge 1965.

A selection of the shorter poems. Long Melford [1966].

Poems on Japan, hitherto uncollected and mostly unprinted. Ed T. Saito, [Tokyo] 1967.

The midnight skaters: poems for young readers chosen and introduced by C. Day Lewis. 1968.

A selection from the poems. Long Melford [1969].

Other Works

Poems chiefly from manuscript by John Clare. Ed Blunden and A. Porter [1920] (200 copies), New York 1921.

The appreciation of literary prose: being one of the special courses of the art of life. [1921].

The Bonadventure: a random journal of an Atlantic holiday. 1922, New York 1923.

Christ's Hospital: a retrospect. [1923].

Madrigals and chronicles: being newly found poems by John Clare. Ed Blunden 1924 (398 copies).

A song to David, with other poems, by Christopher Smart. Introd and notes by Blunden 1924.

Shelley and Keats as they struck their contemporaries: notes partly from manuscript sources. Ed Blunden 1925 (390 copies).

The actor: a poem by Robert Lloyd; to which is prefix'd an essay by Blunden. 1926 (270 copies).

Bret Harte: selected poems. Ed Blunden and B. Brady, Tokyo 1926.

Autobiography of Benjamin Robert Haydon. Ed Blunden, Oxford 1927 (WC).

A hundred English poems from the Elizabethan age to the Victorian. Ed Blunden, Tokyo 1927, 1949 (rev).

Lectures in English literature. Tokyo 1927, 1952 (enlarged).

On the poems of Henry Vaughan: characteristics and intimations; with his principal Latin poems carefully translated into English verse. 1927.

The autobiography of Leigh Hunt. Ed Blunden 1928 (WC).

Leigh Hunt's Examiner examined: comprising some account of that celebrated newspaper's contents etc 1808–25. 1928, New York 1928.

Undertones of war. 1928, New York 1929, London 1930 (rev), 1956 (WC) (with new preface), [1965] (with new introd).

Keats' view of poetry, by Takeshi Saito; to which is prefixed an essay on English literature in Japan by Blunden. 1929.

Last essays of Elia, by Charles Lamb. Ed Blunden 1929.

Nature in English literature. 1929, New York 1929 (Hogarth Lectures on Lit).

The poems of William Collins. Ed Blunden 1929, New York 1929.

Shakespeare's significances: a paper read before the Shakespeare Association. 1929, New York 1929.

De bello germanico: a fragment of trench history, written in 1918 by the author of Undertones of war. Hawstead 1930 (275 copies).

Leigh Hunt: a biography. 1930, New York 1930 (as Leigh Hunt and his circle).

The poems of Wilfred Owen. 1931, New York 1931. With memoir by Blunden, also rptd in Owen's Collected poems, 1963.

The rime of the ancient mariner by Samuel Taylor Coleridge. Introd by Blunden, New York 1931.

Sketches in the life of John Clare written by himself, now first published with an introduction, notes and additions by Blunden. 1931, New York 1931.

Tragical consequences, or a disaster at Deal: being an unpublished letter of William Godwin. Preface by Blunden 1931.

Votive tablets: studies chiefly appreciative of English authors and books. 1931 (60 copies), New York 1932. 39 essays rptd with some adjustment from TLS and Times.

The city of dreadful night, and other poems by James Thomson. Introd by Blunden 1932.

The face of England in a series of occasional sketches. 1932, New York 1932. Essays and 8 poems.

Fall in, ghosts: an essay on a battalion reunion. 1932 (50 copies).

Charles Lamb and his contemporaries. Cambridge 1933, New York 1933 (Clark Lectures).

We'll shift our ground: or two on a tour, almost a novel. 1933. With S. Norman.

Charles Lamb: his life recorded by his contemporaries. Compiled by Blunden 1934.

Coleridge: studies by several hands on the hundredth anniversary of his death. Ed Blunden and E. L. Griggs 1934.

The mind's eye: essays. 1934.

Edward Gibbon and his age. Bristol [1935] (Arthur Skemp Memorial Lecture).

Keats's publisher: a memoir of John Taylor 1781–1864. 1936.

Shelley is expelled. In On Shelley, 1938.

English villages. 1941, New York 1941 (Britain in Pictures).

Thomas Hardy. 1941, New York 1942 (EML).

Poems of this war by younger poets. Ed P. Ledward and C. Strang, introd by Blunden, Cambridge 1942.

Romantic poetry and the fine arts. 1942 (Warton Lecture on English Poetry).

Return to husbandry: an annotated list of books dealing with the history, philosophy and craftsmanship of rural England, with four preliminary essays. Ed Blunden 1943.

Cricket country. 1944.

Poems, by C. W. Brodribb. Introd by Blunden 1946.

Shelley: a life story. 1946, New York 1947.

Hymns for the amusement of children by Christopher Smart. Ed Blunden, Oxford 1947 (Luttrell reprints 5).

The life of George Crabbe, by his son. Introd by Blunden 1947.

Shakespeare to Hardy: short studies of characteristic English authors. Tokyo 1948.

Shelley's Defence of poetry. Ed Blunden, Tokyo 1948.

Two lectures on English literature. Osaka 1948. Contains 4 poems.

Addresses on general subjects connected with English literature. Tokyo 1949.

Poetry and science, and other lectures. Osaka 1949.

Sons of light: a series of lectures on English writers. Hosei 1949.

Chaucer to 'B.V.'; with an additional paper on Herman Melville. Tokyo 1950.

Favourite studies in English literature. Tokyo 1950.

Hamlet and other studies. [Tokyo 1950].

Influential books: lectures given at Waseda University in 1948 and 1949. Tokyo 1950.

John Keats. 1950, 1954 (rev), 1966 (rev) (Br Council pamphlet).

Reprinted papers, partly concerning some English romantic poets. Tokyo 1950.

A wanderer in Japan: sketches and reflections in prose and verse. 1950, 1951 (without Japanese trn).

Sketches and reflections; with notes by S. Tomiyama. Tokyo [1951].

Essayists of the romantic period. Ed I. Nishizaki, Tokyo [1952].

Christ's Hospital book. Ed Blunden 1953.

The dede of pittie: dramatic scenes reflecting the history of Christ's Hospital and offered in celebration of the quatercentenary 1953. [1953]. In prose and verse.

Charles Lamb. 1954, 1964 (rev) (Br Council pamphlet).

Poems, by Ivor Gurney, principally selected from unpublished mss, with a memoir by Blunden. 1954.

Selected poems, by Shelley. Ed Blunden 1954.

Selected poems, by Keats. Ed Blunden 1955.

Thomson, J. The castle of indolence. Introd by Blunden, Hong Kong 1956.

Visick, M. The genesis of Wuthering Heights. Introd by Blunden, Hong Kong 1958.

War poets 1914–1918. 1958, 1964 (rev) (Br Council pamphlet).

Three young poets: critical sketches of Byron, Shelley and Keats. Tokyo 1959.

Selected poems of Tennyson. Ed Blunden 1960.

A Wessex worthy: Thomas Russell. Beaminster 1960 (100 copies).

English scientists as men of letters. Hong Kong 1961 (Jubilee Congress Lecture, University of Hong Kong).

Memoir of Thomas Bewick, written by himself 1822–1828. Introd by Blunden 1961.

A Corscombe inhabitant. Beaminster 1963.

Wayside poems of the seventeenth (early eighteenth) century: an anthology gathered by Blunden and B. Mellor. 2 vols Hong Kong 1963–4.

William Crowe 1745–1829. Beaminster 1963.

Guest of Thomas Hardy. Beaminster 1964.

A brief guide to the great Church of the Holy Trinity, Long Melford, Ipswich. 1965, 1966 (rev).

A few not quite forgotten writers? 1967. Eng Assoc Presidential Address.

§2

Bridges, R. The dialectical words in Blunden's poems. Soc for Pure Eng Tract 5 1921.

Williams, C. In his Poetry at present, 1930.

House, H. Shelley II. In his All in due time, 1955. Review of Shelley: a life story.

Willy, M. The poetry of Blunden. English 11 1957.

Hardie, A. M. Edmund Blunden. 1958 (Br Council pamphlet).

Bergonzi, B. In his Heroes' twilight, 1965.

Fraser, G. S. Edmund Blunden. London Mag 6 1966.

Thorpe, M. The poetry of Blunden. E Studies 48 1967.

—— The poetry of Blunden. 1971.

GORDON BOTTOMLEY
1874–1948

Collections

Poems and plays. Ed C. C. Abbott 1953, New York 1953. Poems mainly from Poems of thirty years, 1925.

Poetry and Verse Plays

Many of Bottomley's plays were produced by amateur companies. For details, see his A stage for poetry, *1948 below.*

The mickle drede and other verses. Kendal 1896 (150 copies).

Poems at white-nights: a book of verse. 1899.
The crier by night: a play in one act. 1902.
The gate of Smaragdus. 1904.
Midsummer eve. Flansham 1905 (120 copies).
Chambers of imagery. Ser 1, 1907; ser 2, 1912.
Laodice and Danaë: play in one act. (Lyric, Hammersmith 1930). 1909 (priv ptd; 150 copies), Boston 1916.
The riding to Lithend: a play in one act. (Festival Theatre, Cambridge 1928). Flansham 1909 (120 copies), Portland Maine 1910.
A vision of Giorgione: three variations on Venetian themes. Portland Maine 1910, London 1922 (rev with addns, as A vision of Giorgione: three variations on a Venetian theme). Extract from The gate of Smaragdus, 1904 above.
King Lear's wife: a play in one act. (Birmingham Repertory Theatre Sept 1915; His Majesty's 19 May 1916). New York 1916.
King Lear's wife; The crier by night; The riding to Lithend; Midsummer eve; Laodice and Danaë. 1920, Boston 1921, London 1922 (with a new poem), Boston 1924.
Gruach (Scottish National Theatre Soc, Glasgow March 1923; St Martin's Theatre 1924) and Britain's daughter (Old Vic 1922): two plays. 1921, Boston 1922.
Poems of thirty years. 1925. Selection, with uncollected poems.
Frescoes from buried temples, by J. Guthrie, with poems by G. Bottomley. Flansham 1927.
[Nineteen poems]. [1928] (Augustan Books of Verse). Selection.
A parting and The return. (Oxford Recitations 1928). New York 1928. Short duologues.
Scenes and plays. 1929, New York 1929. A parting; The return; The sisters; The widow; Towie Castle; Ardvorlich's wife; The singing sands.
Festival preludes. 1930 (110 copies).
The Viking's barrow at Littleholme. [Flansham] 1930 (20 copies).
Lyric plays. 1932, New York 1932. Marsaili's weeping; Culbin Sands; The Bower of Wandel; Suilven and the eagle; Kirkconnel Lea; The woman from the Voe.
The acts of Saint Peter: a cathedral festival play. (Exeter Cathedral 27 June 1933). 1933, Boston 1933.
The falconer's daughter. (Scottish Community Drama Festival, Edinburgh 1938). In Twenty-five modern one-act plays, ed J. Bourne 1938; rptd in Choric plays, 1939, as The falconer's lassie.
Choric plays and a comedy. 1939. Fire at Calbart; The falconer's lassie; Dunaverty.
Kate Kennedy: a comedy in three acts. (Pilgrim Players CEMA tour, Spring 1944). 1945.
Maids of Athens. [Dublin] 1945 (50 copies). Verse play.

Other Works

Poems by Isaac Rosenberg. Selected and ed G. Bottomley 1922.
The collected works of Isaac Rosenberg. Ed Bottomley and D. Harding 1937.
Deirdre: drama in four acts in Gaelic and English, adapted from A. Carmichael's Barra story and lay. Inverness 1944.
A note on poetry and the stage. [1944?] (Religious Drama pamphlet).
A stage for poetry: my purposes with my plays. Kendal 1948 (priv ptd).
The collected poems of Isaac Rosenberg. Ed Bottomley and D. Harding 1949, New York 1949.

Letters

Poet and painter: being the correspondence between Bottomley and Paul Nash 1910–46. Ed C. C. Abbott and A. Bertram 1955, New York 1955.

FRANCIS JAMES RONALD BOTTRALL
b. 1906

The loosening and other poems. Cambridge 1931.
Festivals of fire. 1934.
The turning path. 1939.
Farewell and welcome. 1945.
Selected poems, with a preface by Edith Sitwell 1946.
The palisades of fear. 1949.
Adam unparadised. 1954.
Collected poems. Introd by C. Tomlinson [1961]. Selection, with 7 new poems.

RUPERT CHAWNER BROOKE
1887–1915

The principal collections of Brooke's mss are in the Temple Library of Rugby School and in the Library of King's College Cambridge.

Bibliographies

Keynes, G. L. A bibliography of Brooke. 1954, 1959 (rev) (Soho Bibliographies).

§ 1

The Pyramids. Rugby 1904; rptd in Poetical works, 1946, below.
The Bastille: a prize poem recited in Rugby School 24 June 1905. Rugby 1905 [c. 1920]; rptd in Poetical works, 1946, below.
Poems. 1911.
1914 and other poems. 1915, New York 1915 (as 1914 and other poems; limited to 87 copies for copyright purposes). Mostly rptd from periodicals, including many from New Numbers.
Collected poems. New York 1915. Introd by G. E. Woodberry and biographical note by M. Lavington; includes only Poems, 1911, and 1914 and other poems, 1915.
'1914': five sonnets. 1915. Rptd from New Numbers.
War poems. [1915]. According to Keynes 'an unknown number of copies were printed for Lady Desborough'. Contains 5 sonnets rptd from New Numbers Dec 1914 and the fragment The feet that ran with mine have found their goal.
The Old Vicarage Grantchester. 1916. Single poem, which appeared in Basileon 1912, in Poetry Rev 1912, and in 1914 and other poems, 1915 above.
John Webster and the Elizabethan drama. New York 1916, London 1916.
Letters from America. Preface by Henry James, New York 1916, London 1916. Letters originally written to Westminster Gazette as articles.
Poems. [c. 1916]. 6 poems all previously pbd.
Selected poems. 1917. 37 poems.
Collected poems, with a memoir [by E. Marsh]. 1918, 1928 (with 2 more poems, and order of poems made chronological), 1942 (with Marsh named as author of Memoir).
Fragments now first collected, some being hitherto unpublished. Ed R. M. G. Potter, Hartford Conn 1925 (99 copies).
[Twenty-two poems]. [1925] (Augustan Books of Modern Poetry). Selection.
Complete poems. 1932. Contents as in Collected poems 1928, but without the Memoir.
Twenty poems. 1935. Selected by F. Sidgwick.
Two sonnets, with a memoir of W. S. Churchill. 1945. Secretly ptd by the Dutch Resistance; contains Safety, The soldier.
Poetical works. Ed G. L. Keynes 1946. Adds 26 poems to contents of Collected poems 1928.

Democracy and the arts. Preface by G. Keynes 1946 (for Feb 1947). Essay read in Cambridge 1910.
Five poems: Tiare Tahiti, Clouds, The goddess in the wood, Mary and Gabriel, The Chilterns. 1948.
Poems. 1948 (Folio Soc). Illustr Buckland-Wright; contents as Collected poems, 1918.
Poems. Ed G. L. Keynes 1952. Adds 4 poems, in introd, to contents of Collected poems, 1928.
The prose of Rupert Brooke. Ed C. Hassall 1956. Selection from books, articles and unpbd mss.
The letters of Brooke. Ed G. L. Keynes 1968, New York 1968.

§2

Drinkwater, J. Rupert Brooke: an essay. 1916; rptd in his Prose papers, 1917 (corrected).
—— Brooke on John Webster. In his Prose papers, 1917.
de la Mare, W. Brooke and the intellectual imagination: a lecture. 1919.
Moore, T. S. In his Some soldier poets, 1919.
Garrod, H. W. In his Profession of poetry, Oxford 1929.
Hassall, C. Rupert Brooke: a biography. 1964.
Bergonzi, B. In his Heroes' twilight, 1965.

BASIL BUNTING
b. 1900

Redimiculum matellarum. Milan 1930.
Poems: 1950, prefaced by D. Flynn. Galveston Texas [1950].
Loquitur. [1965]. Mostly rptd from Poems: 1950, above, or from periodicals.
The spoils. Newcastle upon Tyne [1965]. First pbd in Poetry (Chicago) 79 1951.
Briggflatts. [1966] (500 copies), 1966 (trade edn).
First book of odes. [1966] (201 copies).
What the chairman told Tom. Cambridge Mass 1967 (226 copies). Single poem.
Collected poems. [1968].
Bunting contributed substantially to Active anthology, *ed Ezra Pound, 1933. See* Agenda 4 1966.

IGNATIUS ROY DUNNACHIE CAMPBELL
1901–57
§1
Poetry

The flaming terrapin. 1924, New York 1924.
The wayzgoose: a South African satire. 1928.
Adamastor: poems. 1930, New York 1931, London 1941 (abridged, as Sons of the Mistral), Cape Town 1950 (with new preface).
The gum trees. 1930 (Ariel Poem).
Poems. Paris 1930 (priv ptd, 200 copies).
[Nineteen poems]. [1931] (Augustan Books of Poetry). Most previously pbd in Adamastor, 2 from Poems, 1930.
Choosing a mast. 1931 (Ariel Poem).
The Georgiad: a satirical fantasy in verse. 1931.
Pomegranates: a poem. 1932.
Flowering reeds: poems. 1933.
Mithraic emblems: poems. 1936.
Flowering rifle: a poem from the battlefield of Spain. 1939.
Talking bronco. 1946, Chicago 1956.
Collected poems. 3 vols 1949–60, Chicago 1959–60. Many poems rev, some previously uncollected. Vol 3, Translations, is a selection, though some are previously unpbd.
Nativity. 1954 (Ariel Poem).
Poems chosen and introduced by Uys Krige. Cape Town 1960.
Selected poetry. Ed J. M. Lalley 1968, Chicago 1968.

Other Works

Taurine Provence. 1932, New York 1932 (with subtitle, The philosophy, technique and religion of the bull-fighter).
Broken record: reminiscences. 1934.
Light on a dark horse: an autobiography 1901–35. 1951, Chicago 1952, London 1969 (foreword by L. Lee).
Lorca: an appreciation of his poetry. Cambridge 1952, New Haven 1952.
Il Paradiso di Dante: an English version by T. W. Ramsey, with a foreword by Campbell. Aldington 1952.
The Mamba's precipice. 1953, New York 1954. For children.
Portugal. 1957, Chicago 1958.

Translations

Helge Krog. Three plays: The copy; Happily every after; The triad. 1934.
The poems of St John of the Cross. 1951.
Poems of Baudelaire: a translation of his Fleurs du mal. 1952, 1960 (as Baudelaire). Selection in Pocket Poets ser.
Eça de Queiroz. Cousin Bazilio. 1953.
Eça de Queiroz. The city and the mountains. 1955.
The classic theatre. Ed E. Bentley, vol 3, Garden City NY 1959. Contains Tirso de Molina's Trickster of Seville and his Guest of stone, and Calderón's Life is a dream, both tr Campbell.
Nostalgia: a collection of poems by J. Paço d'Arcos. Tr with introd by Campbell 1960.
Calderón de la Barca. The surgeon of his honour. Madison 1960.
With W. Plomer, Campbell founded and edited the magazine Voorslag (*Durban*) 1926–7 *and, with R. Lyle,* Catacomb 1949–52.

§2

Lucas, F. L. Turtle and mock terrapin. In his Authors dead and living, 1926; rptd from New Statesman.
Sitwell, E. Roy Campbell. Poetry 92 1958.
Temple, F.-J. [et al]. Hommage à Roy Campbell. Montpellier 1958.
Plomer, W. 'Voorslag' days. London Mag 6 1959.
Graves, R. It ended with a bang. In his Food for centaurs, Garden City NY 1960.
Wright, D. Roy Campbell. 1961 (Br Council pamphlet).

RICHARD THOMAS CHURCH
1893–1972
Poetry

The flood of life and other poems. 1917.
Hurricane and other poems. 1919.
Philip and other poems. Oxford 1923.
The portrait of the abbot: a story in verse. 1926.
The dream and other poems. [1927].
Mood without measure. 1927.
Theme with variations. [1928].
The glance backward: new poems. 1930.
News from the mountain. 1932.
Twelve noon. 1936.
The solitary man and other poems. 1941.
Twentieth-century psalter. 1943.
The lamp. 1946.
Collected poems. 1948.
Selected lyrical poems. 1951.
The prodigal: a play in verse. 1953.
The inheritors: poems 1948–1955. 1957.
[Forty-seven poems.] 1959 (Pocket Poets). Selection with 3 previously uncollected poems.
North of Rome. 1960.
The burning bush: poems 1958–1966. 1967.
Twenty-five lyrical poems from the hand of Richard Church. 1967. Selection.

Other Works

Mary Shelley. 1928, New York 1928.
Oliver's daughter: a tale. 1930.
High summer. 1931, New York 1932. Novel.
The prodigal father. 1933. Novel.
The apple of concord. 1935. Novel.
The porch. 1937, 1961 (with foreword). Pt 1 of trilogy of novels.
An essay in estimation of Dorothy Richardson's Pilgrimage. [1938].
Calling for a spade. 1939. Essays on country themes.
The stronghold. 1939. Pt 2 of trilogy.
Poems and prose, by A. C. Swinburne. Ed Church 1940 (EL).
The room within. 1940. Pt 3 of trilogy.
Eight for immortality. 1941. Essays on contemporary writers.
Plato's mistake. 1941. On the poet in society. Booklet.
A squirrel called Rufus. 1941, Philadelphia 1946. For children.
The sampler. 1942. Novel.
British authors: a twentieth century gallery. 1943, 1948 (rev).
Green tide. 1945. Essays, mainly on country themes.
Kent. 1948. Topography.
Richard Jefferies centenary 1848–1948. Swindon [1948?]. Lecture.
The cave. 1950, New York 1951 (as Five boys in a cave), London 1953 (rev). For children.
Poems for speaking: an anthology, with an essay on reading aloud. 1950.
The growth of the English novel. 1951.
A window on a hill. [1951]. Essays, mainly on country themes.
The nightingale. 1952. Novel.
Dog Toby: a frontier tale. [1953], New York 1958. For children.
A portrait of Canterbury. 1953, 1968 (rev).
Over the bridge: an essay in autobiography. 1955, New York 1956.
The dangerous years. 1956, New York 1958. Novel.
The royal parks of London. 1956. Guide book.
Down river. New York 1957, London 1958. For children.
The golden sovereign: a conclusion to Over the bridge. 1957, New York 1957. Autobiography.
Small moments. 1957, New York 1958. Essays.
A country window: a round of essays. 1958.
The crab-apple tree. 1959. Novel.
The bells of Rye. 1960, New York 1961. For children.
Calm October: essays. 1961.
Prince Albert. 1963. Novel.
The voyage home. 1964, New York 1966. Autobiography.
A look at tradition. 1965 (Eng Assoc presidential address).
A stroll before dark: essays. 1965.
Speaking aloud. 1968.
The white doe. 1968. For children.
Little Miss Moffatt: a confession. 1969. Novel.

AUSTIN CLARKE
1896–1974

§1

Poetry and Verse Plays

The vengeance of Fionn. Dublin 1917.
The fires of Baäl. Dublin 1921.
The sword of the west. Dublin 1921.
The cattledrive in Connaught and other poems. 1925.
The son of learning: a poetic comedy in three acts. (Cambridge Festival Theatre Oct 1927; Abbey, Dublin June 1945). [1927].
Pilgrimage and other poems. 1929, New York 1930.
The flame: a play in one act. (School of Speech Training

and Drama, Edinburgh June 1932; Dublin Verse-Speaking Soc, at the Peacock Theatre 1941). 1930.
Collected poems. Introd by P. Colum 1936.
Night and morning. Dublin 1938.
Sister Eucharia: a play in three scenes. (Gate, Dublin July 1939). Dublin and London 1939.
Black fast: a poetic farce in one act. (Abbey, Dublin Jan 1942). Dublin 1941.
As the crow flies: a lyric play for the air. (Dublin Verse-Speaking Soc, Radio Eireann 6 Feb 1942). Dublin and London 1943.
The straying student. Dublin 1944.
The viscount of Blarney and other plays. Dublin and London 1944.
The second kiss: a light comedy. (Lyric Theatre Company at the Abbey, Dublin July 1946). Dublin and London 1946.
The plot succeeds: a poetic pantomime. (Lyric Theatre Company at the Abbey, Dublin Feb 1950). Dublin 1950.
The moment next to nothing: a play in three acts. (Players' Theatre, Trinity College, Dublin Jan 1958). Dublin 1953.
Ancient lights: poems and satires, first series. Templeogue 1955.
Too great a vine: poems and satires, second series. Templeogue 1957.
The horse-eaters: poems and satires, third series. Dublin 1960.
Later poems. Dublin 1961. Selection from works pbd 1929–60.
Forget-me-not. Dublin 1962.
Collected plays. Dublin 1963.
Flight to Africa and other poems. Dublin 1963.
Poems by Austin Clarke, Tony Connor and Charles Tomlinson. 1964. Selection.
Mnemosyne lay in dust. Dublin 1966.
Old-fashioned pilgrimage and other poems. Dublin 1967.
The echo at Coole and other poems. Dublin 1968.
Two interludes adapted from Cervantes: The student from Salamanca, La cueva de Salamanca; The silent lover, El viejo celoso. Dublin [1968]. The student from Salamanca produced at the Lantern Theatre, Dublin 29 Dec 1966.

Other Works

The bright temptation: a romance. 1932, New York 1932.
The singing-men at Cashel. 1936. Novel.
First visit to England and other memories. Dublin and London 1945.
Poetry in modern Ireland. Dublin 1951, 1962 (rev).
The sun dances at Easter: a romance. 1952.
Twice round the black church: early memories of Ireland and England. 1962.
The poems of Joseph Campbell, edited with an introduction by Clarke. Dublin 1963.
The plays of G. Fitzmaurice; dramatic fantasies. Dublin 1967. Introd by Clarke.
A penny in the clouds: more memories of Ireland and England. 1968.
The Celtic twilight and the nineties. Dublin 1969.

§2

Montague, J. and L. Miller (ed). A tribute to Clarke. Dublin 1966.

ALEXANDER COMFORT
b. 1920

Poetry

France and other poems. [1941]. France rptd in A wreath for the living, 1942.
Three new poets: R. McFadden, Comfort, I. Serraillier. Billericay 1942. 8 poems by Comfort.
A wreath for the living. 1942.

Cities of the plain: a democratic melodrama. 1943. Prose and verse.
Elegies. 1944.
The song of Lazarus. Barnet 1945 (200 copies), New York 1945. Rptd in next.
The signal to engage. 1946.
And all but he departed. 1951.
Haste to the wedding. 1962.

Other Works

The silver river: being the diary of a schoolboy in the South Atlantic, 1936. 1938.
No such liberty. 1941. Novel.
The almond tree: a legend. 1942. Novel.
Into Egypt: a miracle play. Billericay 1942.
Poetry folios. 10 nos. Ed Comfort and P. Wells 1942–6.
New road: new directions in European art and letters. Ed Comfort and J. Bayliss 2 vols Billericay 1943–4.
The power house. 1944, New York 1945. Novel.
Art and social responsibility: lectures on the ideology of romanticism. 1946.
C. F. Ramuz. The triumph of death. Tr A. R. Macdougall and Comfort 1946.
Peace and disobedience. [1946] (Peace News pamphlet).
Letters from an outpost. 1947. 12 stories.
Barbarism and sexual freedom: lectures on the sociology of sex from the standpoint of anarchism. 1948.
First-year physiological technique. 1948.
The novel & our time. 1948.
On this side nothing. 1949, New York 1949. Novel.
The pattern of the future. 1949. 4 broadcast talks.
The right thing to do: a broadcast talk, together with The wrong thing to do: a speech at a Peace Pledge Union meeting. 1949 (Peace News pamphlet).
Authority and delinquency in the modern state: a criminological approach to the problem of power. 1950.
Sexual behaviour in society. 1950, New York 1950, London 1963 (rev, as Sex in society).
Delinquency: a lecture delivered at the Anarchist summer school, London, August 1950. 1951.
A giant's strength. 1952. Novel.
Social responsibility in science and art. 1952 (Peace News pamphlet). Broadcast talk.
The biology of senescence. 1956, New York 1956, London 1964 (rev, as Ageing: the biology of senescence), New York 1964.
Come out to play. 1961. Novel.
Darwin and the naked body: discursive essays on biology and art. 1961, New York 1962.
The process of ageing. New York 1964, London 1965.
Nature and human nature. 1966.
The anxiety makers: some curious preoccupations of the medical profession. 1967.

FRANCES CROFTS CORNFORD
née DARWIN
1886–1960

A collection of mss is in BM.

Poems. Hampstead, Cambridge [1910].
Death and the princess: a morality. Cambridge 1912. Play in prose and verse.
Spring morning. 1915. Illustr G. Raverat.
Autumn midnight. 1923.
Different days. 1928.
Mountains & molehills. Cambridge 1934. Illustr G. Raverat.
Poems from the Russian. Chosen and tr F. Cornford and E. P. Salaman 1943.
Travelling home and other poems. 1948.
Le dur désir de durer, by Paul Eluard, with the translation in English verse by S. Spender and Frances Cornford. Philadelphia, London 1950.

Collected poems. 1954. Selection with some revision, with poems 1948–53 and occasional verses.
On a calm shore. 1960. Designs by C. Cornford.

WILLIAM HENRY DAVIES
1871–1940

§ 1
Poetry

The soul's destroyer and other poems. [1905] (priv ptd, 40 poems), 1907 (abridged, 14 poems).
New poems. 1907, Boston [? 1916–17], London 1922 (rev).
Nature poems and others. 1908, Boston [? 1916–17].
Farewell to poesy and other pieces. 1910, Boston [? 1916–17].
Songs of joy and others. 1911, Boston [? 1916–17].
Foliage: various poems. 1913, Boston [? 1916–17], London 1922 (rev).
The bird of paradise and other poems. 1914.
Child lovers and other poems. 1916.
Collected poems. 1916, New York 1916. 111 selected poems. American edn has 12 additional poems.
Forty new poems. 1918. 42 poems.
Raptures: a book of poems. 1918 (272 copies). Contains 30 poems from Forty new poems.
The song of life and other poems. 1920.
The captive lion and other poems. New Haven 1921. Contains Forty new poems and The song of life.
The hour of magic and other poems. 1922, New York 1922.
Collected poems: second series. 1923, New York 1923. 112 poems selected from New poems, Foliage, Forty new poems, The song of life, The hour of magic.
Selected poems. 1923, New York 1925.
Secrets. 1924, New York 1924.
A poet's alphabet. 1925.
[Thirty poems]. [1925] (Augustan Books of Modern Poetry). Selection.
The song of love. 1926.
A poet's calendar. 1927, New York 1934.
Collected poems. 1928. 431 poems.
Forty-nine poems, selected and illustrated by Jacynth Parsons. 1928, New York 1929.
Moss and feather. [1928] (Ariel Poem).
Selected poems, arranged by E. Garnett, with a foreword by the author. Newtown 1928 (310 copies).
Ambition and other poems. 1929.
In winter. 1931 (priv ptd, 305 signed copies). Short poem.
Poems 1930–1. 1932, New York 1932.
The lovers' song-book. Newtown 1933 (250 copies). Included in Love poems 1935, below.
Poems. 1934, New York 1935. 533 poems from Collected poems, 1928, Ambition, 1929, Poems 1930–1, and including poems from My birds and My garden (*see* below, Other works).
Love poems. 1935, New York 1935. Contains The lovers' song-book, with 20 additional poems.
The birth of song: poems 1935–36. 1936, New York 1936.
The loneliest mountain and other poems. 1939.
Poems 1940. 1940, 1943 (as Collected poems, with introduction by O. Sitwell), New York 1946. 636 poems from Poems 1934, Love poems, The birth of song, The loneliest mountain.
Common joys and other poems. 1941. Selection.
Complete poems, with an introduction by O. Sitwell and a foreword by D. George 1963, Middletown Conn 1965. 749 poems. George was responsible for the addition of 113 poems omitted by Davies from 1943 collection.

Autobiographies

The autobiography of a super-tramp. 1908, New York

1917, London 1920 (with note by Davies and 5 poems from The soul's destroyer). Preface by G. B. Shaw.
Beggars. 1909.
The true traveller. 1912.
A poet's pilgrimage. 1918, New York 1929.
Later days. 1925, New York 1926.
The adventures of Johnny Walker, tramp. 1926. Material from Beggars and The true traveller, with additional material to form a continuous narrative.

Other Works
A weak woman. 1911. Novel.
Nature. 1914, New York 1914.
True travellers: a tramp's opera in three acts. 1923, New York 1923. Prose, with lyrics.
Dancing mad. 1927. Novel.
My birds. 1933, New York 1933. Nature studies, with some poems.
My garden. 1933, New York 1933. Nature studies, with some poems. Rptd with previous 1939.
Collins, W. J. T. The romance of the echoing wood. Newport 1937. Epilogue, Poetry in life and letters, by Davies.

§2
Pound, E. William H. Davies, poet. Poetry (Chicago) 11 1917.
Stonesifer, R. J. Davies: a critical biography. 1963.

CECIL DAY-LEWIS
1904–72
Day-Lewis signed his books 'C. Day Lewis'.

Poetry and Verse Translations
Beechen vigil and other poems. 1925.
Country comets. 1928.
Transitional poem. 1929.
From feathers to iron. 1931.
The magnetic mountain. 1933.
Collected poems 1929–33. 1935, New York [1935] (as Collected poems 1929–33 & A hope for poetry).
A time to dance and other poems. 1935, New York [1936] (as A time to dance: Noah and the waters and other poems; with an essay, Revolution in writing).
Noah and the waters. 1936.
Overtures to death and other poems. 1938.
The georgics of Virgil. 1940. Verse trn.
Poems in wartime. 1940; rptd in Word over all, 1943 below.
Selected poems. 1940.
[Seventeen poems.] [1943] (Augustan Poets). Selection.
Word over all. 1943.
Short is the time: poems 1936–43. New York 1945. Reprints contents of Overtures to death, and Word over all, above.
Valéry, P. The graveyard by the sea. 1946. Verse trn rptd in Poems 1943–47, below.
Collected poems 1929–36. 1948 (for March 1949). Omissions from A time to dance and Noah and the waters, above.
Poems 1943–47. 1948, New York 1948.
Selected poems. 1951, 1969 (rev and expanded) (Penguin Poets). Preface by the author.
The Aeneid of Virgil. 1952, New York [1952]. Verse trn.
An Italian visit. 1953, New York [1953].
Collected poems. 1954. A complete collection from 1929, apart from omissions from A time to dance and Noah and the waters.
Christmas Eve. 1954 (Ariel Poem); rptd in next.
Pegasus and other poems. 1957, New York 1958.
The newborn: D.M.B. 29th April 1957. [1957] (200 copies). Single poem.
The gate and other poems. 1962.

The eclogues of Virgil. 1963, Garden City NY 1964. Verse trn.
Requiem for the living. New York [1964]. Some poems previously pbd in The gate and other poems, 1962, others rptd in next.
The room and other poems. 1965.
The abbey that refused to die. Ballintubber Abbey, Co. Mayo. 1967. Single poem.
Selections from his poetry. Ed P. Dickinson 1967.
A number of Day-Lewis's poems, e.g. Lullaby, 1938, and Madrigal, 1938, were issued by him as greetings cards. Both these were rptd from A time to dance, *1935.*

Fiction
(a) as by C. Day Lewis
Dick Willoughby. Oxford [1933], New York 1938. For children.
The friendly tree. 1936, New York 1937.
Starting point. 1937, New York 1938.
Child of misfortune. 1939.
The Otterbury incident. 1948, New York 1949. For children.

(b) detective fiction as by 'Nicholas Blake'
A question of proof. [1935], New York 1935.
Thou shell of death. [1936], New York 1936 (as Shell of death).
There's trouble brewing. [1937], New York 1937.
The beast must die. [1938], New York 1938.
The smiler with the knife. 1939, New York 1939.
Malice in wonderland. 1940, New York [1940] (as The summer camp mystery).
The case of the abominable snowman. 1941, New York [1941] (as The corpse in the snowman).
Minute for murder. 1947, New York 1948.
Head of a traveller. 1949, New York 1949.
The dreadful hollow. 1953, New York 1953.
The whisper in the gloom. 1954, New York 1954.
A tangled web. 1956, New York 1956.
End of chapter. 1957, New York 1957.
A penknife in my heart. [1958], New York 1959.
The widow's cruise. [1959], New York 1959.
The worm of death. [1961], New York 1961.
The deadly joker. [1963].
The sad variety. [1964], New York 1964.
The morning after death. 1966.
The private wound. 1968.
As 'Nicholas Blake', Day-Lewis contributed an essay, The detective story—why? to H. Haycraft (ed), The art of the mystery story, New York [1947]. He also contributed criticism of the genre to Spectator.

Other Works
A hope for poetry. Oxford 1934, 1936 (with postscript).
Revolution in writing. 1935. Pamphlet.
Imagination and thinking. 1936. With L. S. Stebbing. 2 addresses.
We're not going to do nothing: a reply to Mr Aldous Huxley's pamphlet, 'What are you going to do about it?'. 1936.
Poetry for you: a book for boys and girls on the enjoyment of poetry. Oxford 1944, New York 1947.
The colloquial element in English poetry. Newcastle-upon-Tyne 1947. Lecture.
Enjoying poetry. 1947, 1951 (rev), 1956 (rev) (National Book League Reader's Guide).
The poetic image. 1947, New York 1947 (Clark lectures).
The poet's task: an inaugural lecture. Oxford 1951.
The grand manner. Nottingham [1952] (Byron Foundation lecture).
The lyrical poetry of Thomas Hardy. [1953] (Warton lecture on English poetry 1951).

Notable images of virtue: Emily Brontë, George Meredith, W. B. Yeats. Toronto 1954.
The poet's way of knowledge. Cambridge 1957. Lecture.
The buried day. 1960, New York 1960. Autobiography.
The lyric impulse. 1965, Cambridge Mass 1965 (Charles Eliot Norton lectures).
Thomas Hardy. 1965 (Br Council pamphlet). With R. A. Scott-James.
A need for poetry? Hull 1968. Lecture.

WALTER JOHN DE LA MARE
1873–1956
Selections

Story and rhyme: a selection from the writings of de la Mare, chosen by the author. [1921].
Stories, essays and poems. Ed M. M. Bozman 1938 (EL).
A selection from his writings made by K. Hopkins. 1956.

§ 1
Poetry

Poems. 1906.
The listeners and other poems. 1912, New York 1916.
The old men. [1913]. Broadside. Poem rptd in Motley and other poems, 1918, below.
The sunken garden and other poems. 1917 (270 copies). All but one rptd in next.
Motley and other poems. 1918, New York 1918.
Flora: a book of drawings by P. Bianco, with 27 illustrative poems by de la Mare. [1919]. Copies exist with various matchings of poems and drawings.
Poems 1901 to 1918. 2 vols 1920.
The veil and other poems. 1921, New York 1922. Includes 7 poems from Flora, 1919, above.
Thus her tale. Edinburgh 1923. Poem; rptd in The fleeting and other poems, 1933, below.
A ballad of Christmas. [1924] (100 copies); rptd in The fleeting and other poems, 1933, below.
Before dawn. [1924] (100 copies). Rptd from The veil and other poems, 1921, above.
The hostage. [1925] (100 copies).
St Andrews: two poems specially contributed by Rudyard Kipling & de la Mare. 1926. A memory, by de la Mare, rptd in Poems 1919 to 1934, 1935, below.
[Twenty-nine poems]. [1926] (Augustan Books of Modern Poetry). Selection.
Alone. [1927], New York 1927 (Ariel Poem).
Selected poems. New York [1927].
Stuff and nonsense and so on. 1927, 1946 (with additional poems). Light verse.
The captive and other poems. New York 1928. Contents rptd in The fleeting and other poems, 1933, below.
Self to self. [1928] (Ariel Poem).
A snowdrop. 1929 (Ariel Poem).
News. 1930 (Ariel Poem).
To Lucy. 1931 (Ariel Poem).
The sunken garden and other verses. Birmingham 1931. Selection, with different contents from The sunken garden, 1917, above.
Two poems. 1931 (priv ptd, 100 copies). Contains Come! and The strange spirit.
The fleeting and other poems. 1933, New York 1933. Reprints all the Ariel Poems, 2 rev.
Poems 1919 to 1934. 1935, New York [1936]. Includes contents of The veil, The fleeting, most of Flora, selections from the children's books and 7 new poems.
Poems. 1937 (priv ptd, 40 copies). Contents all rptd in next.
Memory and other poems. 1938, New York [1938].
Two poems, by de la Mare and (but!) Arthur Rogers. Newcastle-upon-Tyne 1938 (priv ptd). In a library, by de la Mare, rptd in Collected poems, [1941].
Haunted. 1939. Broadside. Poem rptd in Inward companion, 1950, below.

Collected poems. New York [1941], London 1942. Contains almost all poems pbd to this year, except those intended primarily for children. 'Very few revisions'. New York edn has one poem more and is arranged differently from London edn.
Time passes and other poems. 1942. Selection by A. Ridler.
The burning-glass and other poems, including The traveller. New York 1945, London 1945 (omits The traveller and Problems).
The traveller. 1946. Text differs from that pbd in New York edn of The burning glass, 1945.
Inward companion. 1950.
Winged chariot. 1951, New York 1951 (as Winged chariot and other poems). New York edn includes contents of preceding.
O lovely England and other poems. 1953.
The winnowing dream. 1954 (Ariel Poem, new ser).
Selected poems, chosen by R. N. Green-Armytage. 1954. Includes selection of children's verse.
The morrow. Bath 1955 (priv ptd, 50 copies). 2 unpbd poems, The morrow and The sun.
Walter de la Mare. Selected by J. Hadfield 1962 (Pocket Poets). Includes children's verse.
A choice of de la Mare's verse. Ed W. H. Auden 1963.
Complete poems. 1969. 'Contains all the poems de la Mare published in book form during his lifetime; also all the uncollected poems that have been found and a selection of unpublished poems.' Intended as 'the definitive text'.

Children's Books in Poetry and Prose
Some of the collections and selections in the previous section contain children's verse.

Songs of childhood, by 'Walter Ramal'. 1902, 1916 (as by de la Mare, with revision), 1923 (enlarged with revision), 1935 (omitting 3 poems), 1942 (with poems as in 1916 edn, but with some poems in text of 1902 edn).
The three mulla-mulgars. 1910, 1935 (as The three royal monkeys).
A child's day: a book of rhymes to pictures by C. and W. Cadby. 1912, New York [1923].
Peacock pie: a book of rhymes. 1913, [1924] (with 10 additional poems).
Crossings: a fairy play, with music by C. A. Gibbs. 1921 (330 copies), New York 1923.
Down-adown-derry: a book of fairy poems. 1922. All but 5 poems previously collected.
Broomsticks & other tales. 1925, New York 1925.
Miss Jemima. Oxford [1925]. Story.
Readings: traditional tales. Oxford 1925–8. 6 bks.
Lucy. Oxford [1927]. Story.
Old Joe. Oxford [1927]. Story.
Told again: traditional tales. Oxford 1927, 1959 (as Tales told again).
Stories from the Bible. 1929. Stories of Joseph, Moses and Samuel and Saul rptd separately 1958–60.
Poems for children. [1930]. Selection from previously pbd vols, together with some poems rptd from periodicals and some previously unpbd.
Silver. Gaylordsville 1930 (priv ptd, 9 copies). Poem rptd from Peacock pie, 1913, above.
The Dutch cheese. New York 1931. Stories, rptd from Broomsticks, 1925, above.
Old rhymes and new, chosen for use in schools. 2 ser 1932. Selection.
The Lord Fish. [1933]. Stories.
Letters from Mr Walter de la Mare to Form Three. Blaydon 1936.
This year, next year. 1937. Poems.
Bells and grass: a book of rhymes. 1941, New York 1942.
Mr Bumps and his monkey. Philadelphia [1942]. Story, first pbd in The Lord Fish, [1933] (as The old lion).
The old lion and other stories. 1942. Selection.
The magic jacket and other stories. 1943. Selection.

Collected rhymes & verses. 1944, New York [1947] (with some changes and 60 more poems, as Rhymes and verses: collected poems for children).

The scarecrow and other stories. 1945. Selection.

The Dutch cheese and other stories. 1946. Apart from the title story, a different selection from that of 1931.

Collected stories for children. 1947.

Jack and the beanstalk. 1951, New York [1959]. This and next 3 items are slightly adapted from the versions pbd in Told again, 1927, above.

Dick Whittington. 1951.

Snow-White. 1952.

Cinderella. 1952.

Selected stories and verses. 1952 (Puffin).

A penny a day. New York 1960. Selection of stories.

Poems. Selected by E. Graham 1962 (Puffin).

Fiction

Henry Brocken: his travels and adventures in the rich, strange, scarce-imaginable regions of romance. 1904, [1924] (rev).

The return. 1910, 1922 (rev), 1945 (rev).

Memoirs of a midget. [1921], New York 1921, London 1933 (without introd).

Lispet, Lispett and Vaine. 1923 (200 copies); rptd in next.

The riddle and other stories. 1923.

Ding dong bell. 1924, New York 1924, London 1936 (with a fourth story).

Two tales: The green-room; The connoisseur. [1925] (250 copies).

The connoisseur and other stories. [1926], New York 1926.

Seaton's aunt. 1927. Rptd from The riddle and other stories, 1923, above.

At first sight: a novel. New York 1928; rptd in next.

On the edge: short stories. 1930.

Seven short stories. 1931. Selection.

The Walter de la Mare omnibus. [1933]. Contains Henry Brocken, The return, Memoirs of a midget.

A froward child. 1934. Story.

The nap and other stories. [1936]. Selection.

The wind blows over. 1936. Stories.

The picnic and other stories. 1941. Selection.

Best stories of Walter de la Mare. 1942. Selection.

The almond tree. 1943. Rptd from The riddle and other stories, 1923, above.

The orgy. 1943. Rptd from On the edge, 1930, above.

The collected tales of Walter de la Mare, chosen and with an introduction by E. Wagenknecht. New York 1950.

A beginning and other stories. 1955.

Ghost stories. 1956.

Some stories. 1962. Selection.

Other Works

M. E. Coleridge: an appreciation. 1907 (about 200 copies).

Rupert Brooke and the intellectual imagination: a lecture. 1919.

Some thoughts on reading. [Bembridge] 1923 (priv ptd, 350 copies). Lecture.

The printing of poetry. Cambridge 1931 (90 copies). Lecture.

Lewis Carroll. 1932. Essay, rptd from The eighteen eighties, ed de la Mare 1930.

Poetry in prose. [1936]. Lecture.

Arthur Thompson: a memoir. [1938] (priv ptd).

Pleasures and speculations. 1940. Essays, lectures etc.

Private view. Ed D. Cecil 1953. Selected reviews.

Works edited by de la Mare

This list is confined mainly to anthologies.

Come hither: a collection of rhymes and poems for the young of all ages. 1923, New York [1923], London 1928 (rev and enlarged), New York [1928].

Desert islands and Robinson Crusoe. 1930, New York 1930, London 1932 (rev). Anthology, with commentary.

Christina Rossetti: poems chosen by de la Mare. Newtown 1930.

The eighteen-eighties: essays by Fellows of the Royal Society of Literature. Cambridge 1930. Ed, with a contribution, Lewis Carroll.

Tom Tiddler's ground. 3 vols [1932], 1 vol [1932], 1961 (with foreword by L. Clark). Verse anthology for children.

Early one morning in the spring: chapters on children and on childhood. 1935, New York 1935. Anthology with commentary.

Animal stories: chosen, arranged and in some part re-written by de la Mare. 1939, New York 1940.

Behold, this dreamer! 1939, New York 1939. Anthology with commentary.

Love. 1943, New York 1946. Anthology with introd.

§2

Aiken, C. In his Scepticisms, New York 1919.

Gosse, E. Fairy in the garden. In his Books on the table, 1921.

Mégroz, R. L. de la Mare: a biographical and critical study. 1924.

Reid, F. de la Mare: a critical study. 1929.

Williams, C. de la Mare. In his Poetry at present, 1930.

Murry, J. M. The poetry of de la Mare. In his Countries of the mind ser 1, 1931.

Chesterton, G. K. Walter de la Mare. Fortnightly Rev new ser 132 1932; rptd in his The common man, 1950.

Atkins, J. de la Mare: an exploration. 1947.

Greene, G. de la Mare's short stories. In his The lost childhood and other essays, 1951.

Hopkins, K. Walter de la Mare. 1953 (Br Council pamphlet).

Sackville-West, V. The personality of de la Mare. Listener 30 April 1953.

—— Walter de la Mare and The traveller. 1953 (Warton lecture on English poetry).

Cecil, D. The prose tales of de la Mare. In his The fine art of reading, [1957].

Clark, L. Walter de la Mare. 1960, 1968 (rev, in Three Bodley Head monographs, ed K. Lines).

Dyson, A. E. de la Mare's Listeners. CQ 2 1960.

McCrosson, D. R. Walter de la Mare. New York 1966.

Bonnerot, L. L'œuvre de de la Mare: une aventure spirituelle. Paris 1969.

PATRIC THOMAS DICKINSON
b. 1914

Poetry and Verse Plays and Translations

The seven days of Jericho. 1944.

Theseus and the Minotaur [a play] and poems. 1946.

Stone in the midst [a play] and poems. 1948.

The sailing race and other poems. 1952.

The scale of things. 1955.

Aristophanes against war: The Acharnians; The peace; Lysistrata. Tr Dickinson 1957.

The world I see. 1960.

Vergil—The Aeneid: a new translation. New York 1961.

A durable fire: a play. 1962.

This cold universe. 1964.

Selected poems. 1968.

Other Works

Soldiers' verse: verses chosen by Dickinson. 1945.

Byron: poems selected and introduced by Dickinson. 1949.

A round of golf courses: a selection of the best eighteen. 1951.

Poems to remember: a book for children. [1958]. Compiled with S. Shannon.

The good minute: an autobiographical study. 1965.

Cecil Day Lewis: selections from his poetry. Ed Dickinson 1967.

Poets' choice: an anthology of English poetry from Spenser to the present day. 1967. With S. Shannon.

Dickinson edited, with S. Shannon, the Personal portraits series, 1950–1.

KEITH CASTELLAIN DOUGLAS
1920–44

Most of Douglas's literary mss are in the BM.

§1
Poetry

Selected poems by J. Hall, K. Douglas, N. Nicholson. 1943.

Collected poems. Ed J. Waller and G. S. Fraser 1951, 1966 (in chronological order, with minor addns and introd by E. Blunden).

Selected poems, edited with introduction by T. Hughes. 1964, New York 1964.

Complete poems. Ed D. Graham, Oxford 1978.

Other Works

Augury: an Oxford miscellany of verse & prose. Ed A. M. Hardie and Douglas, Oxford 1940. Contains a short statement on the nature of poetry by Douglas, rptd in Collected poems, 1951, above.

Alamein to Zem Zem. 1946. War experiences, illustr Douglas; includes poems, rptd in Collected poems 1951, above.

§2

Tambimuttu, M. J. In memory of Douglas. Poetry London ten 1944.

Fraser, G. S. Douglas: a poet of the second world war. Proc Br Acad 42 1956.

Hughes, T. The poetry of Douglas. Listener 21 June 1962.

— The poetry of Douglas. CQ 5 1963.

JOHN DRINKWATER
1882–1937

Poetry

Poems. Birmingham 1903.

The death of Leander and other poems. Birmingham 1906.

Lyrical and other poems. Cranleigh 1908.

Poems of men and hours. 1911.

Poems of love and earth. 1912.

Cromwell, and other poems. 1913.

Lines for the opening of the Birmingham Repertory Theatre. Birmingham 1913 (priv ptd).

Swords and ploughshares. 1915.

June dance. 1916 (priv ptd, 35 copies). Originally pbd in Lyrical and other poems, 1908. Here rev; rptd in Poems: 1908–1914, 1917, below.

Olton pools. 1916.

Poems 1908–1914. 1917, New York 1918.

Tides: a book of poems. 1917 (270 copies), 1917 (unlimited, with 15 additional poems).

Loyalties: a book of poems. 1918 (18 poems; 200 copies, illustr), 1919 (with 23 additional poems).

Poems 1908–1919. Boston 1919. Selection.

Persuasion: twelve sonnets. 1921 (priv ptd, 50 copies); rptd in next.

Seeds of time. 1921, Boston 1922.

Christmas 1922. [1922] (210 copies); rptd in From an unknown isle, 1924, below.

Preludes 1921–1922. 1922, Boston 1923.

Selected poems. 1922.

Collected poems. 3 vols 1923–37.

The atom of God. Sevenoaks 1924 (priv ptd) (Waterden broadsheets 2); rptd in next.

From an unknown isle. 1924.

From the German: verses written from the German poets. 1924.

Missolonghi April 19th 1824–1924. [Athens? 1924]. English poem with Greek trn. Also ptd in From an unknown isle, 1924, above.

Prayer: from the German of Eduard Mörike. 1924 (100 copies). Single poem, rptd from From the German, above.

At Pisa. Pisa [1925] (40 copies). Signed J.D.

New poems. Boston 1925. Contains From an unknown isle and From the German, above.

[Twenty-seven poems]. [1925] (Augustan Books of Modern Poetry). Selection.

An appeal for St George's Hospital in London. [1926] (priv ptd). Rptd from From an unknown isle, 1924, above.

A graduation song for the University of London. 1926.

Persephone. New York 1926. Single poem.

To be spoken with an appeal for funds for the rebuilding of the Shakespeare Memorial Theatre at Stratford-upon-Avon. [1926] (25 copies).

All about me: poems for a child. [1928], Boston 1928.

Poems: selected by the author for the Tauchnitz edition. Leipzig 1928.

Thomas Hardy, June 2nd 1925: his eighty-fifth birthday. 1928 (25 copies). Single poem, rptd from Sunday Times.

Uncle Wat. Roanoke [1928] (125 copies). Single poem; rptd in American vignettes, 1931, below.

More about me: poems for a child. [1929], Boston 1930.

Penelope's trees. Huntingdon 1930 (100 copies). Single poem; rptd in Summer harvest, 1933, below.

American vignettes, 1860–1865. Boston 1931. Rptd in Summer harvest, 1933, below.

Christmas poems. 1931.

Poems for a child: All about me—More about me. [1932].

P.A.D. aetat three, 26. vii. 32. Huntingdon 1932 (50 copies). Rptd in next.

Summer harvest: poems 1924–1933. 1933.

Plays

Cophetua: a play in one act. (Pilgrim Players 18 Nov 1911). 1911.

An English medley. Bournville 1911 (priv ptd). Performed at Bournville 1911. A masque.

Puss in boots: a play in five scenes. [1911].

The pied piper: a tale of Hamelin city. (Bournville 27 June 1912). 1912 (priv ptd). A masque.

The only legend: a masque of the scarlet pierrot. (Bournville 10 July 1913). 1913 (priv ptd).

Rebellion: a play in three acts. (Birmingham Repertory Theatre 2 May 1914). [1914].

Robin Hood and the pedlar. (Bournville 25 June 1914). [1914] (priv ptd). A masque.

The storm: a play in one act. (Birmingham Repertory Theatre 8 May 1915). [Birmingham] 1915.

The god of quiet: a play in one act. (Birmingham Repertory Theatre 7 Oct 1916). [Birmingham] 1916.

X = O: a night of the Trojan war. (Birmingham Repertory Theatre 14 April 1917). Birmingham 1917. Play in one act.

Pawns: three poetic plays. 1917. Contains The storm, The god of quiet and X = O, with foreword. Pbd 1922 with Cophetua, as Pawns and Cophetua.

Abraham Lincoln. (Birmingham Repertory Theatre 12 Oct 1918). 1918, Boston 1919 (introd by A. Bennett).

Oliver Cromwell. (Theatre Royal, Brighton 16 Feb 1921; Haymarket 29 May 1921). 1921, Boston 1921.

Mary Stuart. (Everyman 25 Sept 1922). 1921, New York 1921, London 1922 (rev), Boston 1924.

Robert E. Lee. (Regent 20 June 1923). 1923, Boston 1923.

Collected plays. 2 vols 1925. All plays and masques etc except Puss in boots.

Robert Burns. 1925, Boston 1925.

Bird in hand: a play in three acts. (Birmingham Repertory Theatre 3 Sept 1927; Royalty 18 April 1928). 1927, 1927 (rev), [1930] (French's Acting edn).

John Bull calling: a political parable in one act. (Coliseum 12 Nov 1928). 1928.

Napoleon: the hundred days. (New 18 April 1932). A play by B. Mussolini and G. Forzano, adapted from the Italian for the English stage by Drinkwater.

Midsummer eve: a play primarily intended for wireless. (Broadcast Midsummer eve 1932). 1932.

Laying the devil: a play in three acts. (Playhouse, Liverpool 2 May 1933; Shaftesbury 2 July 1933). 1933.

A man's house: a play in three acts. (Malvern Festival 23 July 1934). 1934, [1935] (French's Acting edn).

Garibaldi: a chronicle play of Italian freedom in ten scenes. 1936.

Other Works

William Morris: a critical study. 1912.

Swinburne: an estimate. 1913, 1924 (with author's note).

The lyric. [1915] (Art and Craft of Letters).

Rupert Brooke: an essay. 1916 (115 copies). First pbd in Contemporary Rev; rptd in Prose papers, 1917, with corrections.

Politics and life. [Birmingham] 1917. Pbd by Birmingham Liberal Association.

Prose papers. 1917.

Lincoln: the world emancipator. Boston 1920.

Cotswold characters. New Haven 1921.

A tribute to the late C. Lovat Fraser. [1921] (priv ptd).

Some contributions to the English anthology, with special reference to the seventeenth century. [1922] (Warton Lecture on English Poetry).

The world and the artist. 1922 (156 copies); rptd in part in The muse in council, 1925.

Claud Lovat Fraser: a memoir. 1923. With A. Rutherston.

The poet and communication. 1923 (Conway Memorial Lecture, 1923).

Victorian poetry. 1923, New York 1924.

Patriotism in literature. 1924, New York [1924].

Robert Burns: an address. Edinburgh 1924; rptd in English edn of The muse in council.

The muse in council. 1925, Boston 1925 (omitting 5 essays in London edn, but adding 9, 5 rptd from Prose papers).

The pilgrim of eternity: Byron—a conflict. 1925, New York 1925.

A book for bookmen: being edited manuscripts & marginalia with essays on several occasions. 1926. Also issued (50 copies) with illustrations.

Mr Charles, king of England. 1926, New York 1926.

Cromwell: a character study. [1927], New York [1927] (as Oliver Cromwell: a character study).

The gentle art of theatre-going. 1927, Boston 1927 (as The art of theatre-going).

Charles James Fox. 1928, New York 1928.

'The other point of view...'. 1928. Oration delivered by Drinkwater at University College, London, Union Society.

The world's Lincoln. New York 1928.

Story-folk. [1929]. 4 booklets for children. With E. Terriss.

Art and the state. Liverpool 1930 (Roscoe Lecture, 1930).

Pepys: his life and character. 1930, Garden City NY 1930.

Inheritance: being the first book of an autobiography. 1931, New York [1931].

The life and adventures of Carl Laemmle. New York 1931, London 1931.

Poetry and dogma. Bristol [1931] (Arthur Skemp Memorial Lecture, 1931).

The stamps of the Confederate States of America 1861–5. [Leicester 1931] (priv ptd). Paper given at Eighteenth Philatelic Congress of Great Britain.

Discovery: being the second book of an autobiography, 1897–1913. 1932.

John Hampden's England. 1933.

Shakespeare. 1933.

This troubled world. New York 1933. 4 essays.

A pageant of England's life presented by her poets, with a running commentary by Drinkwater. 1934.

Speeches in commemoration of William Morris. Walthamstow 1934. By Drinkwater, H. Jackson and H. Laski.

The King's reign: a commentary in prose and picture. 1935. On the reign of George V.

Robinson of England. 1937, New York 1937. Novel.

English poetry: an unfinished history. 1938. Appendix reprints Poetry and dogma and Some contributions to the English anthology.

Books Edited or with Introductions

The way of poetry. [1920], Boston 1922. Anthology for children.

The outline of literature. 26 pts [1923–4], New York 1923–4, 1 vol [1930], New York 1931, London 1940 (rev H. Pollock and C. Nairne), 1950 (rev H. Shipp), 1957 (rev).

An anthology of English verse. [1924], Boston 1924.

The way of prose. 4 bks [1924]. Anthology for children.

The eighteen-sixties: essays by Fellows of the Royal Society of Literature. Cambridge 1932. Ed Drinkwater, who also wrote the introd and an essay, Eneas Sweetland Dallas.

Drinkwater contributed introds to a great many works, particularly to collections of English verse by individual authors.

LAWRENCE GEORGE DURRELL
b. 1912

§1
Poetry

Quaint fragment: poems written between the ages of sixteen and nineteen. 1931 (priv ptd).

Ten poems. 1932.

A ballade of slow decay. [Bournemouth] 1932. Anon. A Christmas card with a poem.

Transition: poems. 1934.

Mass for the old year. [Bournemouth] 1935. A New Year card with a poem.

A private country. 1943.

Premature epitaphs and all. Alexandria 1944. Limited to 6 copies in typescript.

Cities, plains and people. 1946.

The Parthenon: for T. S. Eliot. [Rhodes 1945 or 1946] (priv ptd). A Christmas card.

On seeming to presume. 1948.

A landmark gone. Los Angeles 1949. Limited to 125 copies for L. C. Powell (priv ptd).

Deus loci: a poem. Ischia 1950 (priv ptd, 200 copies).

Private drafts. Nicosia 1955 (priv ptd, 100 copies).

The tree of idleness and other poems. 1955.

Selected poems. 1956, New York 1956, London 1964 (as Selected poems 1935–63). With additional poems.

Collected poems. 1960, New York 1960, London 1968 (rev).

Penguin modern poets, 1: Durrell, E. Jennings, R. S. Thomas. 1962. Selection.

Poetry. New York 1962.

A Persian lady. [Edinburgh] 1963 (6 copies). Broadsheet.

The ikons and other poems. 1966.

Novels

Pied piper of lovers. 1935.

Panic spring: a romance by 'Charles Norden' (i.e. Durrell). 1937, New York 1937.

The black book: an agon. Paris 1938 (Obelisk press, Villa Saurat ser 1), Paris 1059 (Olympia press, with new preface), New York 1960 (with introd by G. Sykes). Extracts pbd in New Directions 4 1939 (as Gracie). Preface to 1959 edn pbd in Two Cities 1 1959 (with slight alterations).

Cefalù: a novel. 1947, 1958 (as The dark labyrinth; with alterations), New York 1962.

Justine: a novel. 1957, New York 1957. 1st vol of Alexandria quartet.

White eagles over Serbia. 1957, New York 1957, London 1961 (abridged by G. A. Verdin). For children.

Balthazar: a novel. 1958, New York 1958. 2nd vol of Alexandria quartet.

Mountolive: a novel. 1958, New York 1959. 3rd vol. Alexandria quartet.

Clea: a novel. 1960, New York 1960. 4th vol.

The Alexandria quartet: Justine, Balthazar, Mountolive, Clea. 1962, New York 1962. Rev, with corrections throughout, deletions from Balthazar and Mountolive, addns to Clea and a new preface by the author.

Tunc. 1968, New York 1968.

Nunquam. 1970, New York 1970.

Other Works

Bromo Bombastes: a fragment from a laconic drama by Gaffer Peeslake. 1933. Limited to 100 copies. A satire on Shaw's Black girl in search of God.

Prospero's cell: a guide to the landscape and manners of the island of Corcyra. 1945, New York 1960 (with Reflections on a marine Venus, below).

Zero and Asylum in the snow. Rhodes 1946 (priv ptd), Berkeley 1947 (as Two excursions into reality).

Sappho: a play in verse. 1950, New York [1958]. First performed in German at Deutsches Schauspielhaus, Hamburg, 2 Nov 1959; first performed in English, Royal Lyceum Theatre, Edinburgh 28 Aug 1961.

Key to modern poetry. 1952, Norman Oklahoma 1952 (as A key to modern British poetry).

Reflections on a marine Venus: a companion to the landscape of Rhodes. 1953, New York 1960 (with Prospero's cell).

Bitter lemons. 1957, New York 1958. On Cyprus.

Esprit de corps: sketches from diplomatic life. 1957, New York 1958 (with 2 additional sketches, La valise and Cry wolf).

Stiff upper lip: life among the diplomats. 1958, New York 1959 (with an additional story, A smircher smirched, but without the sketches, La valise and Cry wolf).

Art and outrage: a correspondence about Henry Miller between A. Perlès and Durrell. 1959, New York 1961.

Briefwechsel über 'Actis'. Hamburg 1961. With G. Gründgens.

Beccafico. Le becfigue. Montpellier 1963 (priv ptd). Limited to 100 copies. With French trn by F.-J. Temple. Essay.

An Irish Faustus: a morality in nine scenes. 1963, New York 1964.

Lawrence Durrell and Henry Miller: a private correspondence. Ed G. Wickes, New York 1963, London 1963.

La descente du Styx. Traduite de l'anglais par F.-J. Temple et suivie du texte original. Montpellier 1964 (priv ptd). Limited to 250 copies.

Acte: a play. 1965, New York 1965. First performed in German at Deutsches Schauspielhaus, Hamburg, Nov 1961.

Sauve qui peut. 1966, New York 1967. Sketches.

Spirit of place. 1969. Essays on travel, ed A. G. Thomas.

Works Translated or with Contributions by Durrell

Proems. 1938. Contains Unckebunck, Five soliloquies upon the tomb, Themes heraldic.

Miller, H. The colossus of Maroussi. San Francisco 1941, London 1942. Appendix contains letter from Durrell.

Tambimuttu, M. J. (ed). Poetry in wartime. 1942. 5 poems.

Moore, N. and D. Newton (ed). Atlantic anthology. 1945. 7 poems.

Personal landscape: an anthology of exile. Compiled by by R. Fedden, T. Tiller, B. Spencer, L. Durrell 1945.

Selection from periodical Personal Landscape, Cairo 1942–5.

The happy rock: a book about Henry Miller. Berkeley 1945. First essay, The happy rock, by Durrell.

Waller, J. and E. de Mauny (ed). Middle East anthology. 1946. 3 poems.

Six poems from the Greek of Sekilianos and Seferis. Rhodes 1946.

Stephanides, T. Climax in Crete. Foreword by Durrell 1946.

Seferis, G. The king of Asine and other poems. Tr from the Greek by B. Spencer, N. Valaoritis, L. Durrell 1948.

Venezis, I. Aeolia. Preface by Durrell 1949.

Rexroth, K. (ed). The new British poets: an anthology. [Norfolk Conn 1949]. 4 poems.

Royidis, E. Pope Joan: a romantic biography. Tr Durrell 1954, 1960 (rev), New York 1961.

Temple, F.-J. [et al]. Hommage à Roy Campbell. Montpellier 1958. 2 contributions by Durrell.

Tremayne, P. Below the tide. Preface by Durrell 1958, Boston 1959. On Cyprus.

The Henry Miller reader. Ed Durrell New York 1959, London 1960 (as The best of Henry Miller).

Tedlock, E. W. (ed). Dylan Thomas: the legend and the poet. 1960. Essay, The shades of Dylan Thomas, by Durrell.

Groddeck, G. The book of the It. Introd by Durrell 1961. Rptd from Horizon 17 1948.

No clue to living. In The writer's dilemma, 1961.

New poems 1963. Ed Durrell 1963. A P.E.N. anthology of contemporary poetry.

Durrell edited, with others, the periodicals The Booster (and its successor, Delta) Paris 1937–9, Personal Landscape, Cairo 1942–5, and the Cyprus Review 1954–5. *He also contributed a column to the* Egyptian Gazette in 1941.

§2

Stanford, D. In his The freedom of poetry, 1947; rptd in The world of Durrell, ed H. T. Moore 1962, below.

Durrell, G. My family and other animals. 1956.

Kermode, F. Durrell and others. In his Puzzles and epiphanies, 1962. Partly rptd from London Mag 5 1958.

—— Fourth dimension. REL 1 1960.

Young, K. A dialogue with Durrell. Encounter Dec 1959.

Dobrée, B. Durrell's Alexandrian series. Sewanee Rev 69 1961; rptd in The world of Durrell, ed H. T. Moore 1962, below.

Manzalaoui, M. Curate's egg: an Alexandrian opinion of Durrell's Quartet. Études Anglaises 15 1962.

Moore, H. T. (ed). The world of Durrell. Carbondale [1962]. 18 essays by various authors and 3 sections (2 interviews and some letters) by Durrell.

Scholes, R. Return to Alexandria: Durrell and the western narrative tradition. Virginia Quart Rev 40 1964.

—— Durrell and the return to Alexandria. In his The fabulators, Oxford 1967.

Unterecker, J. Lawrence Durrell. New York and London 1964 (Columbia Essays on Modern Writers).

Weigel, J. A. Lawrence Durrell. New York [1966].

Modern Fiction Studies 13 1967. Durrell no.

Fraser, G. S. Durrell: a study with a bibliography by A. G. Thomas. 1968.

CLIFFORD DYMENT
b. 1914

Poetry

First day. 1935.

Straight or curly? 1937.

The axe in the wood. 1944.

Selected poems. 1945.

Poems 1935–1948. 1949. Selection with some revision and 16 uncollected poems.

Experiences and places: new poems. 1955.
Collected poems. 1970.

Other Works

Matthew Arnold: an introduction and a selection by Dyment 1948.
Poems by Thomas Hood, selected & introduced by Dyment 1948 [1949?].
Poems by Matthew Arnold, selected and introduced by Dyment 1948.
New poems 1952: a P.E.N. anthology. Ed Dyment [et al] 1952.
C. Day Lewis. 1955, 1963 (rev) (Br Council pamphlet).
The railway game: an early autobiography. 1962.

SIR WILLIAM EMPSON
b. 1906

§1
Poetry

Letter IV. Cambridge 1929.
Poems. [Tokyo?] 1934 (priv ptd). 14 poems.
Poems. 1935.
The gathering storm. 1940.
Collected poems. New York [1949].
Collected poems. 1955. Adds Chinese ballad and The birth of steel: a masque, to [1949].

Criticism

Seven types of ambiguity. 1930, 1947 (rev), 1953 (rev), New York 1955.
Some versions of pastoral. 1935, New York 1938 (as English pastoral poetry), London 1950 (with errata).
Shakespeare survey. [1937] (Survey pamphlets no 2). With George Garrett. Includes The best policy and Timon's dog.
The structure of complex words. 1951, New York 1951.
Milton's God. 1961, Norfolk Conn 1962, London 1964 (rev, corrected, with notes and appendix).

Contributions to Books

Cambridge poetry. 1929. 6 poems by Empson.
Virginia Woolf. In Scrutinies, vol 2, ed E. Rickword 1931.
Science and well-being, by J. B. S. Haldane, put into Basic by Empson. 1935 (Psyche miniatures 77).
The outlook of science, by J. B. S. Haldane, put into Basic by Empson. 1935 (Psyche miniatures 80).
The style of the master. In T. S. Eliot: a symposium. Ed R. March and Tambimuttu 1948.
Emotions in poems. In The Kenyon critics, Cleveland 1951.
The symbolism of Dickens. In Dickens and the twentieth century, ed J. Gross and G. Pearson 1962.
Empson edited the first three numbers of Experiment *(Nov 1928–May 1929), and contributed to subsequent issues.*

§2

Bradbrook, M. C. The criticism of Empson. Scrutiny 2 1933–4.
Mason, H. A. Empson's criticism. Scrutiny 4 1935–6. Review of Some versions of pastoral.
Ransom, J. C. Mr Empson's muddles. Southern Rev 4 1938.
—— I. A. Richards, the psychological critic, and William Empson, his pupil. In his The new criticism, Norfolk Conn [1941].
Richards, I. A. Note on Empson. Furioso 1940.
Burke, K. Exceptional improvisation, exceptional book. In his Philosophy of literary form, Baton Rouge 1941. Review of Some versions of pastoral.
Kenner, H. Son of spiders. Poetry (Chicago) 76 1950.
—— Alice in Empsonland. Hudson Rev 5 1952; rptd in his Gnomon, New York 1958.

Olson, E. Empson, contemporary criticism and poetic diction. MP 47 1950; rptd in Critics and criticism, ed R. S. Crane, Chicago 1952.
Wain, J. Ambiguous gifts: notes on a twentieth-century poet. Penguin New Writing no 40 1950; rptd in his Preliminary essays, 1957.
Hyman, S. E. Empson and categorical criticism. In his The armed vision, New York 1952.
Alvarez, A. A style from despair: Empson. Twentieth Century 1957; rptd in his The shaping spirit, 1958.
Review (Oxford) 6–7 1963. Special no devoted to Empson.
Gill, R. (ed). Empson: the man and his work. 1974.
Gardner, P. and A. The god approached: a commentary on the poems of Empson. 1978.
Norris, C. Empson and the philosophy of literary criticism. 1978.

JAMES ELROY FLECKER
(b. HERMAN ELROY FLECKER)
1884–1915

The corrected typescript of Hassan *is in Bodley, and the ms of* Don Juan *is in Cheltenham Public Library. There is other ms material in BM, Fitzwilliam Museum, Lockwood Memorial Library Buffalo, and British Embassy, Beirut.*

Poetry

The bridge of fire. 1907.
Thirty-six poems. 1910. 20 poems from previous, rev.
Forty-two poems. 1911. Contents of preceding with 6 new poems. Reissued 1924 with The Grecians.
The golden journey to Samarkand. 1913. Preface by author.
The burial in England. 1915 (20 copies). Ptd by Clement Shorter; rptd in Collected poems, 1916, below.
God save the King. 1915 (20 copies). Ptd by Shorter; rptd in Collected poems, 1916.
The old ships. [1915].
Collected poems. Ed with introd by J. C. Squire 1916, New York 1916, London 1935 (with additional introd), 1946 (with textual corrections).
Selected poems. 1918. Introductory note by J.C.S. [i.e. J. C. Squire].
14 poems. 1921. Ptd in Dijon, pbd Poetry Book Shop; 550 copies. Selection.
[Twenty-five poems]. [1931] (Augustan Books of Poetry). Selection.
Unpublished poems and drafts. Ed M. Booth 1971 (priv ptd).

Plays

Hassan: the story of Hassan of Bagdad and how he came to make the golden journey to Samarkand; a play in five acts. (His Majesty's 20 Sept 1923). 1922, New York 1922, London 1923 (introd by J. C. Squire), 1951 (acting edn with textual alterations, introd by B. Dean), 1966 (rev).
Don Juan: a play in three acts. (Three Hundred Club, Court 25 April 1926). 1925, New York 1925. Preface by Hellé Flecker.

Other Works

The best man: Eights' Week, 1906. Oxford 1906. Anon. Miscellany.
The last generation: a story of the future. 1908.
The Grecians: a dialogue on education. 1910, New York 1910. Reissued 1924 with Forty-two poems, above.
The scholar's Italian book: an introduction to the study of the Latin origins of Italian. 1911.
The king of Alsander. 1914, New York 1914. Novel.
Collected prose. 1920. Contains Tales and sketches (9 pieces including The last generation), The Grecians, Critical studies (7 essays).

Letters

The letters of Flecker to F. Savery. Ed H. Flecker 1926 (590 copies).

Some letters from abroad, with a few reminiscences by H. Flecker and an introd by J. C. Squire 1930. Includes most of the letters to Savery.

See J. Sherwood, No golden journey: a biography of Flecker, *1973.*

FRANK STEWART FLINT
1885–1960

Poetry

In the net of the stars. 1909.
Cadences. [1915].
Otherworld: cadences. Preface by Flint 1920.

Other Works

Some modern French poets: a commentary with specimens. 1919 (Monthly Chapbook 4).
The younger French poets. 1920 (Chapbook 17).
Economic equilibrium. [1940?]. Pamphlet.
Paying for war and peace. Southport [1941]. Pamphlet.
Flint's work appeared in the anthologies Des Imagistes, *1914,* Some imagist poets, *1915–17 and* Imagist anthology, *1930. He translated numerous works of biography, history etc; and poems and a play,* Philip II, *by Emile Verhaeren. He was the regular contributor of a* French chronicle *to* Poetry & Drama, *1913–14.*

ROY BROADBENT FULLER
b. 1912

Poetry

Poems. [1940].
The middle of a war. 1942.
A lost season. 1944.
Epitaphs and occasions. 1949.
Counterparts. 1954.
Brutus's orchard. 1957.
Collected poems 1936–61. 1962, Philadelphia 1962. Selection, with unpbd poems.
Buff. 1965, Chester Springs Pa 1965.
New poems. 1968.
Roy Fuller and R. S. Thomas, selected by E. Owen 1968 (Pergamon Poets).
Off course. 1969 (250 copies).
From the joke shop. 1975.

Novels etc

Savage gold: a story of adventure. 1946. For children.
With my little eye: a mystery story for teenagers. 1948, New York 1957.
Fantasy and fugue. 1954, New York 1956.
The second curtain. 1954, New York 1956.
Image of a society. 1956, New York 1957.
The ruined boys. 1959, New York 1959 (as That distant afternoon).
The father's comedy. 1961.
The perfect fool. 1963.
My child, my sister. 1965.
Catspaw. 1966. For children.
Owls and artificers. 1971; Professors and gods, 1973. Oxford lectures.
Fuller has also edited several anthologies, a selection from Byron, and works on the law relating to building societies. He contributed an essay, Poetry: tradition and belief, *to* The craft of letters in England, *ed J. Lehmann, 1956.*

DAVID EMERY GASCOYNE
b. 1916

Poetry and Verse Translations

Roman balcony and other poems. 1932.
A bunch of carrots: twenty poems by B. Péret. Selected and tr by H. Jennings and Gascoyne 1936, 1936 (2nd edn rev, with 2 substituted poems, as Remove your hat).
Man's life is this meat. [1936].
Paul Eluard. Thorns of thunder: selected poems. Ed G. Reavey [1936]. 12 of the poems tr Gascoyne.
Hölderlin's madness. [1938]. Free adaptation, with introd, of poems by Hölderlin, linked with original poems.
Poems 1937–1942. 1943, 1948 (with minor alterations). Includes poems previously uncollected.
A vagrant and other poems. 1950.
Night thoughts. 1956, New York [1956].
Collected poems. Ed R. Skelton 1965.
Collected verse translations. Ed A. Clodd and R. Skelton 1970.

Other Works

Opening day. 1933. Novel.
Conquest of the irrational, by S. Dali. Tr Gascoyne, New York 1935.
A short survey of surrealism. 1935.
What is surrealism? by A. Breton. Tr Gascoyne 1936 (Criterion miscellany 43).
Thomas Carlyle. 1952 (Br Council pamphlet).
Paris journal 1937–9. 1978.

'JOHN GAWSWORTH',
TERENCE IAN FYTTON
ARMSTRONG
1912–71

Confession: verses. 1931 (262 copies pbd by Twyn Barlwm Press).
Fifteen poems: three friends. 1931 (200 copies pbd by Twyn Barlwm Press).
Snowballs. [1931] (Blue Moon Booklets 9). By 'Orpheus Scrannel'.
An unterrestrial pity: being contributions towards a biography of the late Pinchbeck Lyre. Friern Barnet 1931 (250 copies, pbd by Blue Moon Press). By 'Orpheus Scrannel'.
Kingcup: suite sentimentale. 1932 (75 copies pbd by Twyn Barlwm Press), 1932 (rev as Lyrics to Kingcup) (Blue Moon Booklets 11).
Mishka and Madeleine: a poem sequence for Marcia. 1932 (225 copies, pbd by Twyn Barlwm Press).
Poems 1930–1932. 1933.
The flesh of Cypris. 1936 (500 copies).
Poems. 1938. Described as 4th edn of Poems 1930–1932.
New poems. 1939.
The mind of man. 1940.
Marlow Hill. 1941.
Legacy to love: selected poems 1931–1941. 1943. Described in The crimson thorn, 1945, below, as vol 1 of Poetical works.
Quatorze poèmes. [Séte, Algeria 1943] (7 copies). In English.
De Londres à Carthage: poèmes. Tunis [1944] (110 copies). In English.
Out of Africa: fourteen verses, November 1942–July 1943. Italy 1944.
Into Europe: ten verses, September–December 1943. Italy 1944.
The crimson thorn: poems for lovers 1931–1941 (Poetical works vol 2). Calcutta 1945.

In English fields: poems from books 1931–1941 (Poetical works vol 3). Calcutta 1945.

Snow and sand: poems from the Mediterranean 1942–1944 (Poetical works vol 5). Calcutta 1945.

Blow no bugles: poems from two wars 1942–1945 (Poetical works vol 6). Calcutta 1945.

Collected poems. 1948. Selection.

Vol 4 of the Poetical works *with the title* Farewell to youth: last poems 1931–1941 *was announced but apparently never pbd. Gawsworth also pbd single poems in limited edns. Pamphlets containing one or more poems by Gawsworth were pbd, with French or Italian trns by various authors, in Italy in 1944.*

OLIVER ST JOHN GOGARTY
1878–1957
§1
Poetry

Cervantes: tercentenary of Don Quixote. Vice-chancellor's English verse prize, Trinity College, Dublin 1905. [Dublin, 1905?]

The ship and other poems. Dublin 1918.

An offering of swans. Dublin 1923 (300 copies).

Wild apples. Dublin 1928 (50 copies), New York [1929], Dublin 1930 (with addns and omissions and preface by W. B. Yeats) (250 copies).

Selected poems. Forewords by 'A. E.' and H. Reynolds, New York 1933.

Others to adorn. Preface by W. B. Yeats, forewords by 'A. E.' and H. Reynolds 1938.

Elbow room. Dublin 1939 (450 copies). New York 1942.

Perennial. Baltimore 1944, London 1946 [with slightly different contents].

Collected poems. 1951, New York 1954.

Unselected poems. Baltimore 1954.

Gogarty is said by O'Connor (below, §2) to have pbd a volume of verse, Hyperthuleana, *in an edn of 5 copies in 1916.*

Other Works

Blight: the tragedy of Dublin. An exposition in 3 acts, by Alpha and Omega. Dublin 1917. By Gogarty and Joseph O'Connor.

The enchanted trousers: a play in one act. (By 'Gideon Ouseley'.) [Dublin 1919].

A serious thing. By 'Gideon Ouseley'. [Dublin 1919.] Play.

As I was going down Sackville Street: a phantasy in fact. 1937, New York 1937. Reminiscences.

I follow Saint Patrick. 1938, New York [1938]. On the journeys of St Patrick.

Tumbling in the hay. 1939, New York [1939]. Novel.

Going native. New York 1940, London 1941. Sketches.

Mad grandeur. Philadelphia [1941], London 1943. Novel.

Mr Petunia. New York 1945, London 1946. Novel.

Mourning became Mrs Spendlove and other portraits, grave and gay. New York [1948].

James Augustine Joyce. Dallas 1949.

Intimations. New York [1950]. Essays.

Rolling down the lea. 1950. Essays.

It isn't this time of year at all! An unpremeditated autobiography. Garden City NY 1954, London 1954.

Start from somewhere else: an exposition of wit and humor, polite and perilous. Garden City NY 1955.

A week end in the middle of the week and other essays on the bias. Ed B. L. Burman, Garden City NY 1958.

William Butler Yeats: a memoir. Ed M. Dillon, Dublin 1963.

§2

Jeffares, A. N. Oliver St John Gogarty. 1961 (Chatterton lecture).

O'Connor, U. Gogarty: a poet and his times. 1964, New York 1964 (as The times I've seen: Gogarty).

JULIAN HENRY FRANCIS GRENFELL
1888–1915
§1

Into battle. Times 28 May 1915. Included in A crown of amaranth, 1915; The spirit of man, ed R. Bridges 1916, and in many other anthologies; also (with 4 other poems by Grenfell) in Soldier poets, 1916.

§2

Grenfell, E. A. P. (Lady Desborough). Pages from a family journal 1888–1915. [Eton] 1916 (priv ptd). Includes letters from Grenfell.

Meynell, V. Julian Grenfell. [1917].

Bergonzi, B. Brooke, Grenfell, Sorley. In his Heroes' twilight: a study of the literature of the Great War, 1965.

SIR GEORGE ROSTREVOR HAMILTON
1888–1967
Poetry

The search for loveliness and other verses. 1910.

Stars and fishes and other poems, by 'George Rostrevor'. London, New York 1917.

Escape and fantasy, by 'George Rostrevor'. 1918, New York 1919.

Pieces of eight, by 'George Rostrevor'. 1923.

The making. 1926.

Epigrams. 1928.

Light in 6 moods and other poems. 1930.

John Lord, satirist: a satire. 1934.

Unknown lovers and other poems. 1935.

Memoir 1887–1937 and other poems. 1938.

The sober war and other poems of 1939. 1940.

Apollyon and other poems of 1940. 1941.

The trumpeter of Saint George: an engraving by S. Gooden, with verses by G. Rostrevor Hamilton. 1941.

Death in April and other poems. Cambridge 1944, New York 1944.

Selected poems and epigrams. 1945. Includes a few previously uncollected poems.

Crazy Gaunt and other dramatic sketches. 1946. In verse.

The inner room. 1947.

The carved stone: small poems and epigrams. 1952.

The Russian sister and other poems. 1955.

Collected poems and epigrams. 1958. Selection, with some previously uncollected poems.

Landscape of the mind: late poems. 1963.

Other Works

Bergson and future philosophy: an essay on the scope of intelligence, by 'George Rostrevor'. 1921, New York 1921.

The soul of wit: a choice of English verse epigrams. Ed Hamilton 1924, New York 1926.

The Latin portrait: an anthology. Ed Hamilton 1929, New York 1929. Latin verse, with verse trns.

The Greek portrait: an anthology of English verse translations from the Greek poets, Homer to Meleager, with the corresponding Greek text. Ed Hamilton 1934, New York 1934 (425 copies).

Wit's looking-glass: French epigrams, madrigals, etc of all periods, chosen and reflected in English verse by Hamilton. 1934. Some rptd in Selected poems, 1945, above.

Poetry and contemplation: a new preface to poetics. Cambridge 1937, New York 1937.

The world to come. 1939 (I Believe ser).

Landmarks: a book of topographical verse for England and Wales. Ed Hamilton and J. Arlott, Cambridge 1943.

Hero or fool?: a study of Milton's Satan. 1944 (PEN Books).

James Hurnard, a Victorian character: being passages from The setting sun. Ed Hamilton, Cambridge 1946, New York 1946.

The tell-tale article: a critical approach to modern poetry. 1949, New York 1950.

Guides and marshals: an essay on words and imaginative order. 1956.

Walter Savage Landor. 1960 (Br Council pamphlet).

English verse epigram. 1965 (Br Council pamphlet).

Rapids of time: sketches from the past. 1965.

Hamilton edited E & S *1950 and 1956 and* Essays by Divers Hands *1955.*

JOHN FRANCIS ALEXANDER HEATH-STUBBS
b. 1918

Poetry and Verse Translations

Wounded Thammuz. 1942.

Beauty and the beast. 1943.

The divided ways. 1946.

Poems from Giacomo Leopardi. Heath-Stubbs 1946.

The charity of the stars. New York [1949]. Contains some poems from Beauty and the beast, 1943, above, and some previously uncollected poems.

The swarming of the bees. 1950.

Aphrodite's garland: five ancient love poems translated by Heath-Stubbs. Saint Ives 1951.

Hafiz of Shiraz: thirty poems translated by P. Avery and Heath-Stubbs. 1952.

A charm against the toothache. 1954.

Helen in Egypt and other plays [The talking ass and The harrowing of hell]. 1958. Verse and prose.

The triumph of the muse and other poems. 1958.

The blue-fly in his head. 1962.

Selected poems. 1965.

Satires and epigrams. 1968.

Artorius: a heroic poem. 1973 (priv ptd), 1974 (rev).

Other Works

The darkling plain: a study of the later fortunes of romanticism in English poetry from George Darley to W. B. Yeats. 1950.

The forsaken garden: an anthology of poetry 1824–1909. Ed Heath-Stubbs and D. Wright 1950.

Mountains beneath the horizon [poems], by William Bell. Ed with an introd by Heath-Stubbs 1950.

Images of tomorrow: an anthology of recent poetry. Ed Heath-Stubbs 1953.

The Faber book of twentieth-century verse: an anthology of verse in Britain 1900–50. Ed Heath-Stubbs and D. Wright 1953, 1965 (rev), 1967 (rev).

Charles Williams. 1955 (Br Council pamphlet)

Collected plays by Charles Williams, with an introduction by Heath-Stubbs. 1963.

The ode. 1969.

The pastoral. 1969.

The verse satire. 1969.

SIR ALAN PATRICK HERBERT
1890–1971

Herbert was for many years a frequent contributor to Punch and many of the vols of poems and sketches etc below were rptd from it.

Poetry

Poor poems and rotten rhymes. Winchester 1910.

Play hours with Pegasus. Oxford 1912.

Half-hours at Helles. Oxford 1916.

The bomber gipsy and other poems. 1918, 1919 (rev and enlarged).

The wherefore and the why: some new rhymes for old children. 1921.

'Tinker, tailor...': a child's guide to the professions. [1922], Garden City NY 1923.

Laughing Ann and other poems. 1925, Garden City NY 1926.

She-shanties. 1926, Garden City NY 1927.

Plain Jane. 1927, Garden City NY 1927.

Ballads for broadbrows. 1930, Garden City NY 1931.

Wisdom for the wise: being 'Tinker, tailor...' and The wherefore and the why. 1930.

A book of ballads: being the collected light verse of A. P. Herbert. 1931, Garden City NY 1931 (as Ballads for broadbrows and others).

Siren song. 1940, New York 1941.

Let us be gay. 1941.

Let us be glum. 1941.

Bring back the bells. 1943.

A.T.I. 'There is no need for alarm'. 1944.

'Less nonsense'. 1944.

Light the lights. 1945.

Leave my old morale alone. Garden City NY 1948. Collects a number of earlier vols of verse.

'Full enjoyment' and other verses. 1952.

Silver stream: a beautiful tale of hare & hound for young and old. 1962.

Plays and Libretti

Double demon: an absurdity in one act. In Four one-act plays 1923; pbd separately Oxford 1926.

Riverside nights: an entertainment, written and arranged by Herbert and N. Playfair. (Lyric, Hammersmith 10 April 1926). 1926.

Two gentlemen of Soho. (Playhouse, Liverpool 3 Sept 1927). [1927] (French's Acting edn).

Fat King Melon and Princess Caraway: a drama in five scenes. [1927].

La vie parisienne: a comic opera in three acts. (Lyric, Hammersmith 29 April 1929). 1929 (Contemporary British Dramatists). With A. Davies-Adams.

Tantivy Towers: a light opera in three acts. (Lyric, Hammersmith 16 Jan 1931). 1931, Garden City NY 1931.

Helen: a comic opera in three acts, based upon La belle Hélène by H. Meilhac and L. Halévy. English version by Herbert. (Adelphi 30 Jan 1932). 1932.

Derby day: a comic opera in three acts. (Lyric, Hammersmith 24 Feb 1932). 1931.

Big Ben: a light opera in two acts. (Adelphi 17 July 1946). 1946.

Bless the bride: a light opera in two acts. (Adelphi 26 April 1947). [1948] (French's Acting edn).

Come to the ball: or Harlequin—a new libretto for the music of Die Fledermaus by Johann Strauss. 1951. With R. Arkell.

Other Works

Entries which are not annotated or self-explanatory consist of essays or sketches, mainly rptd from Punch.

The secret battle. 1919, New York 1920. Novel.

The house by the river. 1920, New York 1921.

Light articles only. 1921, New York 1921 (as Little rays of moonshine).

The man about town. 1923, Garden City NY 1923.

The old flame. 1925, Garden City NY 1925.

Misleading cases in the Common Law. 1927, New York 1930.

Honeybubble & Co. 1928.
The trials of Topsy. 1928.
Topsy, MP. 1929, Garden City NY 1930 (as Topsy).
More misleading cases. 1930.
The water gipsies. 1930, Garden City NY 1930. Novel.
'No boats on the river', with a technical essay by J. H. O.
  Bunge. 1932. On river transport for London.
Still more misleading cases. 1933.
Holy deadlock. 1934, Garden City NY 1934. Novel.
Mr Pewter: being the text of the broadcast series of talks
  entitled 'Mr Pewter works it out'. 1934. Dialogues on
  topical subjects.
Letter to the electors of Oxford University, General
  Election, November 1935. [1935].
Uncommon law: being sixty-six Misleading cases revised
  and collected in one volume, including ten cases not
  published before. 1935, New York 1936.
What a word! being an account of the principles and pro-
  gress of 'The word war' conducted in Punch. 1935,
  Garden City NY 1936.
Mild and bitter. 1936, Garden City NY 1937.
The ayes have it: the story of the Marriage Bill. 1937, New
  York 1938.
Sip! Swallow! 1937, Garden City NY 1938.
General cargo. 1939, New York 1940.
Let there be liberty. 1940, New York 1940. Speech.
'Well, anyhow...': or, Little talks. 1942. Dialogues on
  topical subjects.
A better sky: or, Name this star. 1944. Astronomy.
The point of Parliament. 1946.
Topsy turvy. 1947.
Mr Gay's London: with extracts from the proceedings at
  the Sessions of the Peace, and Oyer and Terminer for
  the City of London and County of Middlesex in the
  years 1732 and 1733. 1948.
The Topsy omnibus: comprising The trials of Topsy,
  Topsy MP and Topsy turvy. 1949.
The English laugh. 1950. Eng Assoc presidential address
  1950.
Independent member. 1950, Garden City NY 1951.
  Autobiography.
Number nine: or the mind-sweepers. 1951, Garden City
  NY 1952. Novel.
Codd's last case and other misleading cases. 1952, New
  York 1953.
Why Waterloo? 1952, Garden City NY 1953. Novel.
Pools pilot: or, Why not you? 1953. On football pools.
The right to marry. 1954. On divorce.
'No fine on fun': the comical history of the entertainments
  duty. 1957.
Made for man. 1958, Garden City NY 1958. Novel.
I object: letter to the electors of East Harrow. 1959.
Anything but action? a study of the uses and abuses of
  committees of inquiry. 1960.
Look back and laugh. 1960.
'Public lending right': authors, publishers & libraries—a
  preliminary memorandum. 1960 (priv ptd).
Libraries: free-for-all? some issues in political economy
  by R. Harris; The rate for the reading: an appeal to
  Parliament from authors and publishers prepared by
  Herbert. 1962.
Bardot MP? and other modern misleading cases. 1964,
  Garden City NY 1965.
Watch this space (six years of it): an anthology of space
  (fact) 4 October 1957–4 October 1963. 1964. Compiled
  and edited by Herbert; newspaper reports of objects in
  space.
The Thames. [1966].
Wigs at work. 1966 (Penguin). Selection from the vols of
  'misleading cases'.
Sundials old and new: or, Fun with the sun. 1967.
The singing swan: a yachtsman's yarn. 1968. Novel.

RALPH HODGSON
1871–1962

The last blackbird and other lines. 1907, New York 1917.
Eve and other poems. 1913 (priv ptd, At the Sign of
  Flying Fame). Included in Poems, 1917 below.
The bull. 1913 (priv ptd, At the Sign of Flying Fame).
  Included in Poems, 1917.
The song of honour. 1913 (priv ptd). Included in Poems,
  1917.
The mystery and other poems. 1913 (priv ptd). Included
  in Poems, 1917.
Poems. 1917, New York 1917. 25 poems including 15
  from previous Flying Fame pbns.
Hymn to Moloch. 1921; rptd in The skylark, 1958 below.
Silver wedding and other poems. Minerva Ohio 1941.
  Rptd in The skylark, 1958.
The muse and the mastiff. Pt 1, Minerva Ohio 1942 (priv
  ptd). Dramatic poem; rptd in The skylark, 1958.
The mystery. Bethesda Md 1956. Rptd from Poems,
  1917, above.
The skylark and other poems. Ed C. Fenton 1958 (limited
  edn), 1959, New York 1960. Wood engravings by
  Reynolds Stone. Includes all poems pbd by Hodgson
  since Poems 1917, with several pbd before 1917 but not
  included in the collection of that year.
Collected poems. Ed C. Fenton 1961. Includes contents
  of The last blackbird, 1907, Poems, 1917, The skylark,
  1958, and bibliographical note and a note on 2 uncollected poems.
*The following poems were issued as broadsides, plain, coloured
and on Japanese vellum (12 copies) for Flying Fame: A
song, February, The beggar, The birdcatcher, The
gipsy girl, The late, last rook, Playmates. Hodgson also
issued, 1944-51, through Namleda & Co of Philadelphia,
a series of broadsides entitled A flying scroll. They contain
one or more short poems, all of which were rptd in The
skylark, 1958.*

DAVID MICHAEL JONES
1895–1974
Selections

Epoch and artist: selected writings. Ed H. Grisewood
  1959, New York [1959].

§1

In parenthesis. 1937, 1961 (70 copies, with introd by
  T. S. Eliot), New York 1961 (unlimited edn, with the
  Eliot introd), London 1963.
David Jones. With introd by R. Ironside 1949 (Penguin
  Modern Painters).
The anathemata: fragments of an attempted writing. 1952,
  New York 1963.
Agenda 5 1967. David Jones special issue. Contains 6
  poems, of which The wall, The dream of Private Clitus,
  The tutelar of the place, The hunt, together with the
  next 2 separately ptd items, constitute a 'work-in-
  progress'.
The fatigue, c. A.U.C. DCCLXXXIV, tantus labor non
  sit cassus. Cambridge 1965 (priv ptd, 298 copies).
The tribune's visitation. 1969.
An introduction to the Rime of the ancient mariner. 1972.
The sleeping lord and other fragments. 1974.
The Kensington mass. Ed R. Hague 1975 (Agenda edns).

§2

Bergonzi, B. Remythologizing: Jones's In parenthesis. In
  his Heroes' twilight, 1965.
Blamires, D. The ordered world: The anathemata of Jones.
  REL 7 1966; rptd (rev) in next.
Agenda 5 1967. David Jones special issue, with 15 articles.

PATRICK KAVANAGH
1904–1967

Ploughman and other poems. 1936.
The green fool. 1938, New York 1939. Autobiography.
The great hunger. Dublin 1942 (250 copies), London 1966 [with minor changes]. Pt previously pbd as The old peasant in Horizon 5 1942. Single poem.
A soul for sale: poems. 1947.
Tarry Flynn. 1948, New York 1949. Novel.
Recent poems. New York 1958 (25 copies ptd on Peter Kavanagh's hand press).
Come dance with Kitty Stobling and other poems. 1960, Philadelphia 1964.
Collected poems. 1964, New York 1964, London 1972.
Self portrait. Dublin 1964, 1975. Prose.
Collected pruse. 1967.
The green fool. 1971, 1975 (Penguin).
He edited, and with his brother Peter wrote most of, Kavanagh's Weekly; a journal of literature and politics (Dublin), which ran for 13 nos in 1952.

SIDNEY ARTHUR KILWORTH KEYES
1922–43

Eight Oxford poets; selected by M. Meyer and Keyes. 1941. Contains 6 poems by Keyes.
The iron laurel. 1942.
The cruel solstice. 1943.
Collected poems. Ed with a memoir and notes by M. Meyer 1945, New York [1947] (with preface by H. Read).
Minos of Crete: plays and stories. Ed with selections from his notebook and letters and some early unpbd poems by M. Meyer 1948. Also containing The artist in society, rptd from P. Colson, The future of faith, [1942].
J. Guenther, Sidney Keyes, 1967, *contains one unpbd poem. Keyes was joint-editor of* Cherwell *May to June 1941.*

JAMES FALCONER KIRKUP
b. 1918

Poetry and Verse Translations

The cosmic shape: an interpretation of myth and legend, with three poems, by R. Nichols and J. Kirkup. 1946. Includes The glass fable and The sleeper in the earth, poems by Kirkup.
The drowned sailor and other poems. 1947.
The creation. Hull 1951.
The submerged village and other poems. 1951.
A correct compassion and other poems. 1952.
The vision and other poems by Todja Tartschoff. Tr Kirkup and L. Sirombo 1953.
A spring journey and other poems of 1952–3. 1954.
Upon this rock: a dramatic chronicle of Peterborough Cathedral. 1955.
The true mistery of the Nativity. Adapted and tr from the French medieval mystery cycle of A. and S. Gréban 1956.
The descent into the cave and other poems. 1957.
Five German plays. In The classic theatre, ed E. R. Bentley, vol 2, Garden City NY 1959. Contains Schiller's Don Carlos and Kleist's The prince of Homburg, both tr in verse by Kirkup.
Refusal to conform: last and first poems. 1963.
Paper windows: poems from Japan. 1968.
The body servant: poems of exile. 1971.

Other Works

The only child: an autobiography of infancy. 1957.

Sorrow, passions and alarms: an autobiography of childhood. 1959.
The love of others. 1962. Novel.
These horned islands: a journal of Japan. 1962, New York 1962.
Tropic temper: a memoir of Malaya. 1963.
Japan industrial: some impressions of Japanese industries. Osaka 1964.
Tokyo. 1966, South Brunswick NJ 1966.
Bangkok. 1968, South Brunswick NJ 1968.
Filipinescas: travels through the Philippine Islands. 1968.
One man's Russia. 1968.
Shepherding winds: an anthology of poetry from east and west. 1969.
Streets of Asia. 1969.
Kirkup also translated works, mainly novels, from French and German.

EDMUND GEORGE VALPY KNOX
1881–1971
Poetry

The brazen lyre. 1911.
A little loot. 1920. Verse, and sketches in prose.
'Parodies regained'. 1921.
These liberties. 1923. Parodies in verse and prose.
Poems of impudence. 1926, Garden City NY 1927.
A winter sports alphabet: pictures by Joyce Dennys, verses by Evoe. 1926.
I'll tell the world! A guide to the greatness of England, mainly intended for American use. 1927, Garden City NY 1928. Sketches and verse.
Blue feathers. 1929.
Folly calling. 1932.

Other Works

Fiction as she is wrote. 1923, New York 1924. Sketches.
An hour from Victoria and some other excursions. 1924. Sketches.
Fancy now. 1924. Sketches.
Quaint specimens. 1925. Sketches.
Gorgeous times. 1926. Essays and sketches.
It occurs to me. 1926. Sketches.
Awful occasions. 1927. Sketches.
Here's misery! A book of burlesques. 1928.
Wonderful outings. 1928. Sketches.
Mr Punch on the links. Ed Knox 1929, New York 1929.
This other Eden. 1929. Sketches.
Things that annoy me. 1930. Sketches.
Slight irritations. 1931. Sketches.
The mechanism of satire: the Leslie Stephen lecture 10 May 1951. 1951.
Knox contributed to Punch *as 'Evoe', and the contents of most of his books were rptd from it. He edited* Punch *1932–49, and* Methuen's Library of humour *1933–35.*

LAURIE LEE
b. 1914
Poetry and Verse Plays

The sun my monument. 1944, Garden City NY 1947.
The bloom of candles: verse from a poet's year. 1947.
The voyage of Magellan: a dramatic chronicle for radio. 1948.
Peasant's priest: a play. Canterbury [1952]. Pbd for the Festival of the Friends of Canterbury Cathedral.
My many-coated man. 1955, New York 1957.
[Thirty-nine poems]. 1960 (Pocket Poets). Selection.

Other Works

Land at war (The official story of British farming 1939–44). 1945. Anon. Ministry of Information pamphlet.

Vassos the goatherd: a story of Cyprus. 1947. An adaptation by J. Maddison of Lee's notes and script for the film Cyprus is an island.

We made a film in Cyprus. 1947. With R. Keene.

An obstinate exile. Los Angeles 1951 (priv ptd, 101 copies). Rptd from Listener 13 Sept 1951. Lee's reaction as a countryman to London.

A rose for winter: travels in Andalusia. 1955, New York [1956?].

Epstein: a camera study of the sculptor at work by G. Ireland. Introd by Lee 1958.

Cider with Rosie. 1959, New York 1960 (as The edge of day: a boyhood in the west of England).

Man must move: the story of transport. [1960], Garden City NY 1960 (as The wonderful world of transportation), London 1969 (rev and enlarged as The wonderful world of transport). With D. Lambert.

The firstborn. 1964. On his daughter.

As I walked out one midsummer morning. 1969. Autobiography.

I can't stay long. 1975.

RUDOLPH JOHN FREDERICK LEHMANN
b. 1907
Poetry

A garden revisited and other poems. 1931.

The noise of history. 1934.

Forty poems. 1942.

The sphere of glass and other poems. 1944.

The age of the dragon: poems 1930–51. 1951, New York [1952]. Selection, with uncollected poems.

Collected poems 1930–63. 1963. Selection, with uncollected poems.

Christ the hunter. 1965. Prose poems.

Other Works

Prometheus and the Bolsheviks. 1937, New York 1938. Travel.

Ralph Fox. A writer in arms. Ed Lehmann, T. A. Jackson, C. Day Lewis 1937. Introd to The imaginative writer by Lehmann.

Evil was abroad. 1938. Novel.

Down river: a Danubian study. 1939. Travel.

New writing in England. New York 1939 (Critics Group pamphlet).

Poems for Spain. Ed S. Spender and Lehmann 1939.

New writing in Europe. 1940 (Pelican), New York 1940.

Poems from New Writing, 1936–1946. 1946.

Demetrios Capetanakis: a Greek poet in England. 1947.

French stories from New Writing, selected by Lehmann. 1947, New York 1948 (as Modern French stories).

English stories from New Writing. Ed Lehmann 1951, New York 1951 (as Best stories from New Writing).

Edith Sitwell. 1952 (Br Council pamphlet).

The open night. 1952, New York 1952. Essays on literature.

Pleasures of New Writing: an anthology of poems, stories and other prose pieces from the pages of New Writing. Ed Lehmann 1952.

The whispering gallery: autobiography I. 1955, New York 1955.

The Chatto book of modern poetry 1915–55. Ed C. Day Lewis and Lehmann 1956.

The craft of letters in England: a symposium. Ed Lehmann 1956, Boston 1957.

Coming to London. Ed Lehmann 1957. Reminiscences by various writers.

I am my brother: autobiography II. 1960, New York 1960.

Ancestors and friends. 1962. On the author's family, etc.

Selected poems of Edith Sitwell. Chosen with an introd by Lehmann 1965.

The ample proposition: autobiography III. 1966.

A nest of tigers: Edith, Osbert and Sacheverell Sitwell in their times. 1968.

In my own time: memoirs of a literary life. Boston 1969. Reissue in 1 vol of The whispering gallery, I am my brother, and The ample proposition.

Virginia Woolf and her world. 1975.

Lehmann edited New Writing, *1936–9 (continued as* Folios of New Writing, *1940–1, and as* New Writing & Daylight, *1942–6);* Penguin New Writing, *1940–50;* Orpheus: a symposium of the arts, *1948–9;* London Mag, *1954–61. In or about 1928 he issued a set of 10 priv ptd single sheet poems, illustrated with his own wood engravings.*

ALUN LEWIS
1915–44
Poetry

Two poems. Llanllechid [1941] (Caseg broadsheet). Contains Raiders' dawn and Song of innocence.

Raiders' dawn and other poems. 1942.

Ha! Ha! among the trumpets: poems in transit. Foreword by Robert Graves 1945.

Selected poetry and prose, with a biographical introduction by I. Hamilton. 1966. Includes previously uncollected poems.

Other Works

The last inspection. 1942, New York 1943. Short stories.

Letters from India, with a note by Mrs Alun Lewis and a preface by A. L. Rowse, Cardiff 1946. Included in In the green tree, below.

In the green tree, with a preface by A. L. Rowse. 1948 (for 1949). Postscript by Gwyn Jones. Contains Letters from India and 6 uncollected short stories.

'HUGH MACDIARMID', CHRISTOPHER MURRAY GRIEVE
1892–1978
§1
Poetry

Sangschaw. Edinburgh and London 1925.

Penny wheep. Edinburgh and London 1926.

A drunk man looks at the thistle. Edinburgh and London 1926, Glasgow 1953 (with introd by D. Daiches and note by the author), Edinburgh 1956 (rev).

The lucky bag. Edinburgh 1927 (Porpoise Press broadsheet).

To Circumjack Cencrastus: or the curly snake. Edinburgh and London 1930.

First hymn to Lenin and other poems, with an introductory essay by 'AE' (George William Russell). 1931 (450 copies).

O wha's been here afore me, lass. 1931 (Blue Moon poem for Christmas) (100 copies). Rptd from A drunk man looks at the thistle, above.

Tarras. Edinburgh 1932 (20 copies); rptd in next.

Scots unbound and other poems. Stirling 1932 (350 copies).

Second hymn to Lenin. Thakeham Sussex [1932] (100 copies).

Stony limits and other poems. 1934.

Selected poems. 1934 (Macmillan's Contemporary poets).

Second hymn to Lenin and other poems. 1935.

Direadh. Dunfermline [1938] (20 copies).

Speaking for Scotland. 1939 (Lumphen Press broadsheet 3).

Cornish heroic song for Valda Trevlyn. Glasgow [1943]; rptd in A kist of whistles, 1947 below.

Selected poems. Ed R. C. Saunders, Glasgow [1944] (Poetry Scotland).

Poems of the east-west synthesis. 1946.

Speaking for Scotland: selected poems. Introd by Compton Mackenzie, Baltimore 1946 (Distinguished Poets ser). Similar to Selected poems 1934, omitting 2 and adding 3 poems.

A kist of whistles: new poems. Glasgow [1947] (Poetry Scotland).

Selected poems. Ed O. Brown, Glasgow 1954, 1955 (as Poems).

In memoriam James Joyce: from A vision of world language. Glasgow 1955.

Stony limits and Scots unbound and other poems. Edinburgh 1956. Includes poems suppressed in 1934 edn of Stony limits.

The battle continues. Edinburgh 1957.

Three hymns to Lenin. Edinburgh [1957].

The kind of poetry I want. Edinburgh 1961 (300 copies).

Bracken hills in autumn. 1962.

Collected poems. New York 1962, Edinburgh 1962, New York [1967] (with corrigenda and enlarged glossary). Selection, with previously uncollected poems.

Poetry like the hawthorn: from In memoriam James Joyce. Hemel Hempstead 1962.

Poems to paintings by William Johnstone 1933. Edinburgh 1963. Most previously uncollected.

The ministry of water: two poems. Glasgow 1964 (125 copies).

Six vituperative verses. 1964 (priv ptd) (25 copies).

The terrible crystal: a vision of Scotland. Skelmarlie 1964 (55 copies).

The fire of the spirit: two poems. Glasgow 1965 (350 copies).

Whuchulls: a poem. Preston [1966] (100 copies); rptd in next.

A lap of honour. 1967.

On a raised beach: a poem. Preston 1967 (200 copies).

Early lyrics. Ed J. K. Annand, Preston [1968] (350 copies).

A clyack-sheaf. 1969.

Complete poems 1920–76. Ed M. Grieve and W. R. Aitken 2 vols 1978.

Other Works

Northern numbers: being representative selections from certain living Scottish poets. 3 sers Edinburgh and London 1920–2. Ed Grieve, and containing some of his poems. Ser 3 was pbd by him at Montrose.

Annals of the five senses. Montrose 1923, Edinburgh 1930. Poems and 'psychological sketches'.

Contemporary Scottish studies: first series. 1926.

Albyn: or, Scotland and the future. 1927, New York 1927 (Today and Tomorrow ser).

Tenreiro, R. M. de. The handmaid of the Lord. 1930. Anon trn by MacDiarmid.

At the sign of the thistle: a collection of essays. [1934].

Five bits of Miller. 1934 (40 copies). Prose sketch.

Scottish scene: or, the intelligent man's guide to Albyn. 1934. With 'Lewis Grassic Gibbon' (J. L. Mitchell).

MacDonald, A. The Berlinn of Clanranald. Tr from the Scots Gaelic by MacDiarmid, St Andrews 1935 (100 copies).

Scottish eccentrics. 1936.

The islands of Scotland: Hebrides, Orkneys and Shetlands. 1939, New York 1939.

The golden treasury of Scottish poetry. Ed MacDiarmid 1940.

Auntran blads: an outwale o verse, by Douglas Young. Selected by MacDiarmid. Glasgow 1943.

Lucky poet: a self-study in literature and political ideas, being the autobiography of Hugh MacDiarmid (Christopher Murray Grieve). 1943.

Collected poems, by William Soutar. Ed MacDiarmid 1948.

Cunninghame Graham: a centenary study. Glasgow [1952].

Francis George Scott: an essay on the occasion of his seventy-fifth birthday. Edinburgh 1955.

Burns today and tomorrow. Edinburgh 1959.

David Hume, Scotland's greatest son: a transcript of the lecture given at Edinburgh University, April 1961. Edinburgh [1961?].

The man of—almost—independent mind. Edinburgh 1962. On David Hume.

The ugly birds without wings. Edinburgh 1962. Reply to attacks by I. H. Finlay et al.

When the rat-race is over: an essay in honour of the 50th birthday of John Gawsworth. 1962 (40 copies).

Martinson, H. Aniara. Adapted from the Swedish by MacDiarmid and E. M. Schubert. 1963.

Sydney Goodsir Smith. Edinburgh [1963] (135 copies). An address.

The company I've kept. 1966. Autobiography.

Scotland. In Celtic nationalism, 1968.

The uncanny Scot: a selection of prose by MacDiarmid, ed with an introd by K. Buthlay 1968.

MacDiarmid edited the following periodicals: Scottish Chapbook *1922–3*, Scottish Nation *1923*, Northern Rev *1924*, Voice of Scotland *1938–58, and the 5th no (*PEN Congress no) *of* Scottish Art & Letters *1950. He was the 'guest editor' of the 4th and last no of* Poetry Scotland *1949.*

§2

Duval, K. D. and S. G. Smith (ed). Hugh MacDiarmid: a Festschrift. Edinburgh 1962.

Glen, D. Hugh MacDiarmid (Christopher Murray Grieve) and the Scottish renaissance. Edinburgh 1964.

Buthlay, K. Hugh MacDiarmid (C. M. Grieve). Edinburgh 1964 (Writers & Critics).

MacDiarmid and Scottish poetry. Agenda 5–6 1967–8.

FREDERICK LOUIS MACNEICE
1907–63

Some of MacNeice's mss were sold at Sotheby's on 12 Dec 1961. Many mss are now in the Library of the Univ of Texas. See F. G. Stoddard, The Louis MacNeice collection, Lib Chron 8 1968.

Bibliographies

Armitage, C. M. and N. Clark. A bibliography of the works of MacNeice. 1973.

§1
Poetry and Verse Translations

MacNeice edited, with S. Spender, Oxford poetry, 1929. This includes 4 poems by him.

Blind fireworks. 1929.

Poems. 1935, New York [1937].

The Agamemnon of Aeschylus. 1936, New York 1937. Verse trn.

Letters from Iceland. 1937, New York [1937]. Verse and prose. With W. H. Auden.

The earth compels. 1938.

I crossed the Minch. 1938. See Other works, below.

Autumn journal. 1939, New York [1939].

The last ditch. Dublin 1940.

Poems 1925–40. New York [1940].

Selected poems. 1940.

Plant and phantom. 1941.

Springboard: poems 1941–4. 1944, New York 1945.

Holes in the sky: poems 1944–7. 1948, New York 1949.

Collected poems 1925–48. 1949. Selection, with revision of late poems. Omits trns.

Goethe's Faust: parts 1 and 2; an abridged version translated by MacNeice. 1951, New York 1953.

Ten burnt offerings. 1952, New York 1953.

Autumn sequel: a rhetorical poem in xxvi cantos. 1954. Sequel to Autumn journal, 1939, above.

The other wing. 1954 (Ariel Poem); rptd in next.
Visitations. 1957, New York 1958.
Eighty-five poems. 1959, New York 1959. Selection.
Solstices. 1961, New York 1961.
The burning perch. 1963, New York 1963.
Selected poems: selected and introduced by W. H. Auden. 1964.
Collected poems. Ed E. R. Dodds 1966. Excludes juvenilia etc which were omitted from Collected poems, 1949; trns however are included. Omitted poems are listed in appendix.

Plays

The sale of some MacNeice mss at Sotheby's included dupli-cated scripts of unpbd radio and other plays. The BBC archives also hold copies of these.

Out of the picture: a play in two acts. (Group Theatre, at the Westminster 5 Dec 1937). 1937, New York 1938. Verse and prose.
Christopher Columbus: a radio play. (BBC Home Service 12 Oct 1942). 1944 (with introd on radio drama), 1963 (school edn with new introd).
The dark tower and other radio scripts. 1947, 1964 (con-taining The dark tower only). Includes further com-ments on radio drama; The dark tower: a radio parable play (BBC Home Service 1 Jan 1946); Sunbeams in his hat: a study of Tchehov as a man (BBC Home Service 16 July 1944); The nosebag: a Russian folk story (BBC Home Service 13 March 1944); The March Hare saga: 1, The March Hare resigns (BBC Home Service 29 March 1945), 2, Salute to All Fools (BBC Home Service 1 April 1946).
The mad islands (BBC Third Programme 4 April 1962); and The administrator (BBC Third Programme 10 March 1961): two radio plays. 1964.
One for the grave: a modern morality play. (Dublin Theatre Festival, at the Abbey Theatre 1966). 1968.
Persons from Porlock and other plays for radio. Introd by W. H. Auden. 1969. Enter Caesar: a study of the evo-lution and background of the first great dictator of the modern type (BBC Home Service 20 Sept 1946); East of the sun and west of the moon: a Norwegian folk tale (BBC Third Programme 25 July 1959); They met on Good Friday: a sceptical historical romance (BBC Third Programme 8 Dec 1959); Persons from Porlock: the story of a painter (BBC Third Programme 30 Aug 1963).

Other Works

Roundabout way, [by] 'Louis Malone'. 1932. Novel.
Grigson, G. (ed). The arts today. 1935. Contains Poetry, by MacNeice.
Verschoyle, D. (ed). The English novelists. 1936. Sir Thomas Malory, by MacNeice.
I crossed the Minch. 1938. Travel in the Hebrides. Prose, with verse.
Modern poetry: a personal essay. Oxford 1938, 1968 (introd by W. Allen).
Zoo. 1938. On the London Zoo.
The poetry of W. B. Yeats. Oxford 1941, 1967 (introd by R. Ellmann).
Meet the U.S. Army. 1943. Prepared for the Board of Education by the Ministry of Information.
Apuleius The golden ass. Tr W. Adlington; introd by MacNeice 1946.
March, R. and Tambimuttu (ed). T. S. Eliot: a sym-posium. 1948. Contains Eliot and the adolescent, by MacNeice.
The penny that rolled away. New York 1954, London 1956 (as The sixpence that rolled away). For children.
Tedlock, E. (ed). Dylan Thomas: the legend and the poet. 1960. Contribution by MacNeice.
Astrology. 1964, Garden City NY 1964.

The strings are false: an unfinished autobiography. 1965, New York 1966.
Varieties of parable. Cambridge 1965 (Clark lectures 1963).

§2

Scarfe, F. MacNeice: poetry and commonsense. In his Auden and after, 1942.
Matthiessen, F. O. In his The responsibilities of the critic, New York 1952.
Auden, W. H. Louis MacNeice: a memorial address delivered at All Souls Langham Place on 17 October 1963. [1963].
— Louis MacNeice. Encounter 21 1963.
Betjeman, J. MacNeice and Bernard Spencer. London Mag 3 1964.
Connolly, C. In his Previous convictions, 1963.
Press, J. Louis MacNeice. 1965 (Br Council pamphlet).
Hough, G. MacNeice and Auden. CQ 9 1967.
McKinnon, W. T. Apollo's blended dream. 1971.
Brown, T. MacNeice: sceptical vision. Dublin 1975.

CHARLES HENRY MADGE
b. 1912

Poetry
The disappearing castle. 1937.
The father found. 1941.

Other Works
Mass-Observation. With T. Harrisson. Foreword by J. Huxley 1937 (Mass-Observation ser no 1).
May the twelfth: Mass-Observation day-surveys, 1937. 1937. By H. Jennings, Madge et al.
First year's work, 1937–38, by Mass-Observation. Ed Madge and T. Harrisson 1938.
Britain, by Mass-Observation, arranged and written by Madge and T. Harrisson. 1939, New York 1939.
War begins at home, by Mass Observation, ed and arranged by T. Harrisson [and] Madge. 1940.
Industry after the war: who is going to run it? 1943 (Target for Tomorrow ser). By Madge in consultation with D. Tyerman.
War-time pattern of saving and spending. Cambridge 1943, New York 1943 (National Inst of Economic and Social Research Occasional Papers 4).
Pilot guide to the general election. Ed Madge 1945.
Pilot papers: social essays and documents, vol 1. Ed Madge 1945. Continued as a quarterly jnl.
To start you talking: a collection of scripts with introduc-tory sections by Madge and others. 1945.
Survey before development in Thai villages. [New York?] 1957. Pbd by United Nations.
Village meeting places: a pilot enquiry. [Delhi?] 1958. Pbd by Indian Ministry of Information.
Society in the mind: elements of social eidos. 1964, New York 1964 (Society Today and Tomorrow).
Madge edited the Target for Tomorrow ser 1943–5 and the periodical Pilot Papers 1946–7.

JOHN EDWARD MASEFIELD
1878–1967

Bibliographies
Simmons, C. H. A bibliography of Masefield. New York 1930.
Nevinson, H. W. Masefield: an appreciation, together with a bibliography. 1931.

Collections and Selections
Collected works: Wanderer edition. 5 vols 1935–7.

A book of both sorts: selections from the verse and prose of Masefield. 1947.

A book of prose selections. 1950, New York 1950.

§1

Poetry and Plays

Salt-water ballads. 1902, New York 1913.

Ballads. 1903.

The tragedy of Nan and other plays. 1909, New York 1909. Contains The tragedy of Nan (New Royalty 24 May 1908); The Campden wonder (Court Theatre 8 Jan 1907); Mrs Harrison. The tragedy of Nan rptd separately 1911, New York 1921, 1926.

The tragedy of Pompey the great. (Aldwych 4 Dec 1910). 1910, Boston 1910, 1914 (rev), New York 1914.

Ballads and poems. 1910. Ballads, 1903, with addns including poems from Salt-water ballads 1902.

Ballads. 1911. Selection from Ballads, 1903, and Ballads and poems, 1910.

The everlasting mercy. 1911, Portland Maine 1911. Rptd from Eng Rev.

The everlasting mercy and The widow in the bye street. New York 1912. Both rptd from Eng Rev.

The widow in the bye street. 1912.

The story of a round-house and other poems. New York 1912, 1913 (rev). Selection, with 9 poems not previously pbd in book form, including Dauber.

The daffodil fields. New York 1913, London 1913.

Dauber: a poem. 1913.

Philip the King and other poems. 1914, New York 1914.

The faithful: a tragedy in three acts. (Birmingham Rep 4 Dec 1915). 1915, New York 1915.

Good Friday and other poems. New York 1916.

Good Friday. (Garrick 25 Feb 1917). Letchworth 1916, New York 1916 (as Good Friday: a dramatic poem).

Sonnets. New York 1916. 61 sonnets from Good Friday and other poems, 1916.

Sonnets and poems. Letchworth 1916 (200 copies) (46 sonnets from Good Friday and other poems, 1916, with one new sonnet), Lollingdon, Cholsey 1916 (slightly rev collection).

The locked chest; The sweeps of ninety-eight: two plays in prose. Letchworth 1916, New York 1916.

Salt-water poems and ballads. 1916.

The cold Cotswolds. Cambridge 1917. Rptd from Cambridge Mag.

Lollingdon Downs and other poems. New York 1917, London 1917 (as Lollingdon Downs and other poems, with Sonnets; includes poems from Good Friday and other poems, and Sonnets and poems).

Poems of John Masefield, selected by H. S. Canby and others. New York 1917.

Rosas. New York 1918.

The poems and plays of Masefield. 2 vols New York 1918.

A poem and two plays. 1919. Contains Rosas; The locked chest; The sweeps of ninety-eight.

Reynard the fox: or the ghost heath run. New York 1919, London 1919, New York 1920 (illustr C. Moore Park, with introd by Masefield on 'Fox hunting' rptd in Recent prose, 1924, below), London 1921 (illustr G. D. Armour).

Animula. 1920 (priv ptd, 250 copies); rptd in next.

Enslaved and other poems. 1920, New York 1920.

Right Royal. New York 1920, London 1920.

King Cole. 1921, New York 1921.

Esther: a tragedy adapted and partially translated from the French of Jean Racine. 1922. In verse. For U.S. edn, see next.

Esther and Berenice: two plays. New York 1922. In verse.

Berenice: a tragedy translated from the French of Jean Racine. 1922. In verse. For U.S. edn, see preceding.

The dream. [1922], New York 1922 (illustr Judith Masefield).

Melloney Holtspur. 1922, New York 1922, 1923 (as Melloney Holtspur: or the pangs of love). Prose play.

Selected poems. 1922, 1922 (530 copies, containing the unpbd Nireus), New York 1923 (with 6 unpbd poems).

King Cole and other poems. 1923.

The dream and other poems. New York 1923. Same as King Cole and other poems, but omitting King Cole and The eye and the object.

A king's daughter: a tragedy in verse. 1923, New York 1923.

Collected poems. 1923.

The trial of Jesus. (RADA Theatre 28 March 1926). 1925, New York 1925.

Poems. 2 vols New York 1925. Collection.

Verse plays. New York 1925. Collection.

Prose plays. New York 1925. Collection.

Sonnets of good cheer to the Lena Ashwell Players from their well-wisher John Masefield. [1926] (priv ptd). 4 sonnets.

Tristan and Isolt: a play in verse. (Oxford Playhouse May 1923). 1927, New York 1927.

The coming of Christ. 1928, New York 1928. Play in verse.

Midsummer night and other tales in verse. 1928, New York 1928.

Oxford recitations. 1928.

Easter: a play for singers. 1929, New York 1929. In verse.

Poems, complete in one volume. New York 1929.

South and east. 1929, New York 1929. Rptd from Midsummer night, 1928, above.

The Wanderer of Liverpool. 1930, New York 1930. On the voyages of the 'Wanderer' in prose and verse, with A masque of Liverpool, and other poems.

Poems of the Wanderer: the ending. 1930 (priv ptd; 25 copies).

Minnie Maylow's story and other tales and scenes. 1931, New York 1931.

Collected poems. 1932. Enlarged edn of Collected poems, 1923, above.

A tale of Troy. 1932, New York 1932.

End and beginning. 1933, New York 1933. Verse play.

Poems: complete edition, with recent poems. New York 1935.

A letter from Pontus and other verse. 1936, New York 1936.

Lines spoken by Masefield at the Tercentenary of Harvard University. 1937 (150 copies), New York 1937 (150 copies) (as Lines on the tercentenary of Harvard University).

The country scene in poems by Masefield and pictures by E. Seago. [1937], New York [1938].

Selected poems. 1938, New York 1938. Rev edn of Selected poems, 1922, above.

Collected poems. 1938. Enlarged edn of Collected poems, 1932, above.

Tribute to ballet in poems by Masefield and pictures by E. Seago. [1938], New York 1938.

Some verses to some Germans. 1939, New York 1939.

Shopping in Oxford. 1941 (500 copies); rptd in next.

Gautama the enlightened and other verse. 1941, New York 1941.

Natalie Maisie and Pavilastukay: two tales in verse. 1942, New York 1942.

Land workers. 1942, New York 1943.

A generation risen. [1942], New York 1943. Illustr E. Seago.

Wonderings: between one and six years. 1943, New York 1943.

Reynard the fox: a tale in verse, with selected sonnets and lyrics. 1946.

Poems. 1946. Rev edn of Collected poems, 1938, above.

A play of St George. 1948, New York 1948. In verse.

On the hill. 1949, New York 1949.

Selected poems ('new edition'). 1950, New York 1950. A new selection.

In praise of nurses. [1950].

Poems: complete edition with recent poems. New York 1953.

Bluebells and other verse. 1961, New York 1961.

The western Hudson shore. [New York 1962?] (priv ptd).

Old Raiger and other verse. 1964, New York 1965.

Fiction and Other Works

Lyrists of the Restoration from Sir Edward Sherburne to William Congreve. Ed J. and C. Masefield 1905 (Chapbooks no 1).

A mainsail haul. 1905, 1913 (rev and enlarged), New York 1913, London 1954 (with 2 additional pieces), New York 1954. Stories.

Sea life in Nelson's time. 1905, New York 1925.

Essays moral and polite 1660–1714. Ed J. and C. Masefield 1906 (Chapbooks no 2).

On the Spanish Main: or some English forays on the Isthmus of Darien; with a description of the buccaneers and a short account of old-time ships and sailors. 1906, New York 1906.

The poems of Robert Herrick. Ed with biographical introd by Masefield 1906 (Chapbooks no 5).

A sailor's garland. Selected and ed Masefield 1906, New York 1906.

Dampier's voyages. Ed Masefield 2 vols 1906, New York 1907.

Lyrics of Ben Jonson, Beaumont and Fletcher. Ed Masefield 1906 (Chapbooks no 4).

A tarpaulin muster. 1907, New York 1908. Stories.

An English prose miscellany. Ed Masefield 1907 (EL).

Hakluyt's voyages. Ed Masefield [1907] (EL).

Captain Margaret: a romance. 1908, Philadelphia 1908.

Defoe. Selections, ed Masefield 1909, New York 1909.

Multitude and solitude. 1909, New York 1910. Novel.

My faith in woman suffrage. [1910]. Speech.

Martin Hyde, the Duke's messenger. 1910, Boston 1910. Dramatized by Ruth P. Kimball, 1935, Boston 1935. For boys.

A book of discoveries. 1910, New York [1910]. For boys.

Lost endeavour. 1910, New York 1917. Story for boys.

Anson's voyage round the world. Introd by Masefield [1911] (EL).

The street of to-day. 1911, New York 1911. Novel.

William Shakespeare. [1911], New York 1911, London 1954 (rev), New York 1954.

Jim Davis. 1911, New York 1912, Boston 1918 (as The captive of the smugglers). Novel, for boys.

John M. Synge: a few personal recollections, with biographical notes. Churchtown, Dundrum 1915, New York 1915; rptd in The taking of Helen and other prose selections, 1924, below.

Gallipoli. 1916, New York 1916.

Anne Pedersdotter: a drama by H. Wiers-Jenssen. Tr Masefield, Boston 1917.

The old front line: or the beginning of the battle of the Somme. 1917, New York 1917 (as The old front line).

The war and the future. New York 1918, London 1919 (as St George and the dragon). Lectures.

The battle of the Somme. 1919 (268 copies).

John Ruskin. Bembridge 1920 (priv ptd, 150 copies).

A Foundation Day address [at Bembridge School]. Bembridge 1921, (priv ptd, 250 copies).

The taking of Helen. 1923, New York 1924 (750 copies). Novel.

The taking of Helen and other prose selections. New York 1924, London 1924 (as Recent prose), 1932 (rev and enlarged).

Shakespeare and spiritual life. Oxford 1924 (Romanes lecture).

Sard Harker. 1924, New York 1924. Novel.

With the living voice: an address given at the first general meeting of the Scottish Association for the Speaking of Verse. 1925, New York 1925.

Odtaa. 1926, New York 1926. Novel.

The midnight folk. 1927, New York 1927. Novel.

The hawbucks. 1929, New York 1929. Novel.

Speech after receiving the Freedom of the City of Hereford. 1930 (priv ptd).

Speech at a festival in honour of W. B. Yeats. 1930 (priv ptd).

Chaucer. Cambridge 1931, New York 1931 (Leslie Stephen lecture).

Poetry. 1931, New York 1932. Lecture.

The Conway from her foundation to the present day. 1933, New York 1933, London 1953 (rev), New York 1954. On the training ship 'Conway'.

The bird of dawning. 1933, New York 1933 (as The bird of dawning: or the fortunes of the sea). Novel.

The taking of the Gry. 1934, New York 1934. Novel.

The box of delights: or When the wolves were running. 1935, New York 1935. For children.

Victorious Troy: or The hurrying angel. 1935, New York 1935. Novel.

Eggs and Baker: or The days of trial. 1936, New York 1936. Novel.

The square peg: or The gun fella. 1937, New York 1937. Novel.

Dead Ned: the autobiography of a corpse. 1938, New York 1938. Novel.

Live and kicking Ned: a continuation of the tale of dead Ned. 1939, New York 1939.

Basilissa: a tale of the Empress Theodora. 1940, New York 1940.

Some memories of W. B. Yeats. Dublin 1940, New York 1940. Verse and prose.

The nine days wonder: the Operation Dynamo. 1941, New York 1941. On Dunkirk, 1940.

In the mill. 1941, New York 1941. Experiences in a factory.

Conquer: a tale of the Nika rebellion in Byzantium. 1941, New York 1941.

I want! I want! 1944, New York 1945. On books and reading; introd by G. Faber.

New chum. 1944, New York 1945. Experiences on the training ship 'Conway'.

A Macbeth production. 1945, New York 1946.

Thanks before going: notes on some of the original poems of D. G. Rossetti. 1946, New York 1947.

A reply to the toast of Honorary graduands at the University of Sheffield. [1946] (priv ptd).

Thanks before going, with other gratitude for old delights, including A Macbeth production and various papers not before printed. 1947.

Badon parchments. 1947. Novel.

My favourite English poems, gathered and introduced by Masefield. 1950, New York 1950.

The Ledbury scene as I have used it in my verse. Ledbury [1951] (priv ptd, 250 copies). Included in next.

St Katherine of Ledbury and other Ledbury papers. 1951.

So long to learn: chapters of an autobiography. 1952, New York 1952 (as So long to learn).

An Elizabethan theatre in London. 1954 (priv ptd).

Words spoken at the unveiling of the memorials to the poets Keats and Shelley. 1954 (priv ptd).

Words on the anniversary of the birthday of William Blake. 1957.

Grace before ploughing: fragments of autobiography. 1966, New York 1967.

§2

Murry, J. M. The nostalgia of Masefield. In his Aspects of literature, 1920.

Hamilton, W. H. Masefield: a critical study. 1922.

Lucas, F. L. In his Authors dead and living, 1926.

Lowell, A. In her Poetry and poets, 1930.

Thomas, G. John Masefield. 1933.

Highet, G. Poetry and romance: Masefield. In his People, places and books, New York 1953.

Spark, M. John Masefield. 1953.

Graves, R. Robert Graves on Masefield. TLS 22 June 1967.

Berry, F. Masefield: the narrative poet. Sheffield 1968.

Smith, C. B. Masefield: a life. Oxford 1978.

HAROLD EDWARD MONRO
1879–1932

The principal collections of Monro's mss are in the Library of the University of California, Los Angeles, the Maurice Browne Collection, University of Michigan, and in the Edward Marsh Collection, New York Public Library.

§ 1
Poetry

Poems. 1906.

Judas. Cranleigh 1907.

Before dawn: poems and impressions. 1911.

Children of love. 1914.

Trees. 1916. Rptd with alterations in next.

Strange meetings. 1917.

Real property. 1922.

[Sixteen poems.] [1927] (Augustan Books of English Poetry).

The earth for sale. 1928.

The winter solstice. 1928 (Ariel Poem). Drawings by D. Jones.

Elm angel. 1930 (Ariel Poem). Wood engravings by E. Ravilious.

Collected poems. Ed A. Monro, with biographical sketch by F. S. Flint and critical note by T. S. Eliot 1933.

The silent pool and other poems, chosen by A. Monro. 1942.

Other Works

Proposals for a voluntary nobility. Norwich 1907. Anon, with Maurice Browne.

The evolution of the soul. Norwich 1907.

The chronicle of a pilgrimage: Paris to Milan on foot. 1909.

Some contemporary poets: 1920. 1920.

One day awake: a morality. 1922 (Chapbook 32).

Twentieth century poetry: an anthology chosen by Monro. 1929, 1946 (rev and enlarged by A. Monro).

Monro edited Poetry Rev during 1912, Poetry & Drama 1913–14, and Chapbook (originally Monthly chapbook) 1919–25. He founded the Poetry Bookshop in 1913 and directed it until his death, publishing among other books the five volumes of Georgian Poetry. He contributed poems to all of these.

§ 2

Pound, E. Harold Monro. Criterion 11 1932; rptd in his Polite essays, 1937.

Savage, D. S. Monro: a study in integration. In his Personal principle, 1944.

Ross, R. H. In his The Georgian revolt 1910–22, Carbondale 1965.

THOMAS STURGE MOORE
1870–1944

§ 1
Poetry and Verse Plays

Two poems. 1893 (priv ptd). About hope and Mountain shadows.

The vinedresser and other poems. 1899.

Aphrodite against Artemis: a tragedy. 1901.

Absalom: a chronicle play in three acts. 1903.

Danaë: a poem. 1903, New York 1903. First pbd in Dial 1893, here rev, again rev 1920 (*see* below).

The centaur's booty. 1903. Dramatic poem.

The rout of the Amazons. 1903. Dramatic poem.

The gazelles and other poems. 1904.

Pan's prophecy. 1904. Dramatic poem.

To Leda and other odes. 1904.

Theseus, Medea, and lyrics. 1904.

The little school: a posy of rhymes. 1905, New York 1905, London 1917 (enlarged), New York 1920.

Poems. 1906. Reissue of The centaur's booty, The rout of the Amazons, The gazelles, To Leda, and Theseus, Medea and lyrics, in one vol.

Salome; A Florentine tragedy; Vera. By Oscar Wilde. Boston [1908] (vol 6 of Ross edn). Opening scene of A Florentine tragedy by Sturge Moore.

Mariamne. 1911. Play.

A Sicilian idyll; and Judith: a conflict. 1911. 2 plays.

The sea is kind. 1914, Boston 1914. Selection from The vinedresser and The little school, with 21 new poems.

Danaë, Aforetime, Blind Thamyris. 1920.

Tragic mothers: Medea, Niobe, Tyrfing. 1920. 3 plays.

Judas. 1923, Chicago 1924.

Roderigo of Bivar. New York 1925 (500 copies). Play, rptd in Poems, 1931–3, below.

Mystery and tragedy: two dramatic poems [Psyche in Hades, and Daimonassa]. 1930.

Nine poems. Maastricht 1930 (125 copies). Includes 3 previously unpbd poems.

Poems. 4 vols 1931–3. Collected edn. Includes poems previously pbd only in periodicals and some unpbd poems.

Selected poems. Ed M. Sturge Moore 1934.

The unknown known and a dozen odd poems. 1939.

Other Works

The passionate pilgrim and the songs in Shakespeare's plays. Ed Sturge Moore 1896.

The centaur; The bacchante, by M. de Guérin. Tr Sturge Moore 1899.

Shakespeare's sonnets, reprinted from the edition of 1609. (Seen through the press by Sturge Moore) 1899.

Altdorfer. 1900, New York 1901.

The Vale Shakespeare. Ed Sturge Moore 39 vols 1900–3.

Albrecht Altdorfer: a book of 71 woodcuts, with introduction by Sturge Moore London, New York 1902.

Poems from Wordsworth chosen, edited and illustrated by Sturge Moore [1902].

A brief account of the origin of the Eragny Press & a note on the relation of the printed book as a work of art to life. 1903, New York 1904.

Albert Durer. 1905, New York 1905.

Correggio. London, New York 1906.

Art and life. 1910. Essays.

Hark to these three: talk about style. 1915.

Theory and practice: a paper read by Sturge Moore before the members of the Art Students' Union at the School of Art, Leicester, February 5 1916. Leicester 1916.

Some soldier poets. 1919, New York 1920. Essays, mainly rptd from Eng Rev.

The powers of the air. 1920. Prose and verse, rptd in Poems 1931–3 (see Poems, above).

A selection from the poems of Michael Field. Compiled by Sturge Moore 1923.

Ought art to be taught in schools? an address delivered at the Birmingham Central School of Arts & Crafts on 15th March 1923. Birmingham 1926.

Armour for Aphrodite. 1929. Aesthetics.

Watson, E. L. G. The common earth. Introd by Sturge Moore 1932.

Charles Ricketts, R. A.: sixty-five illustrations, introduced by Sturge Moore 1933.

Works and days, from the journal of Michael Field. Ed Sturge Moore and D. C. Sturge Moore 1933.

Poems of Wang Ching-wei, translated by Seyuan Shu. Foreword by Sturge Moore 1938.

Self-portrait, taken from the letters and journals of Charles Ricketts, R.A. collected and compiled by Sturge Moore. Ed C. Lewis 1939.

W. B. Yeats and T. Sturge Moore: their correspondence 1901–37. Ed Ursula Bridge 1953, New York 1953.

Moore was also known as a wood engraver and illustrator: his work decorates the covers of some of his books, and those of W. B. Yeats et al.

§2

Winters, Y. Sturge Moore. Hound & Horn 6 1933. Incorporated in his Primitivism and decadence, New York 1937.

—— The poetry of Moore. Southern Rev 2 1966.

Gwynn, F. L. Sturge Moore and the life of art. Lawrence Kansas 1951.

EDWIN MUIR
1887–1959

Some of Muir's mss materials have been deposited by Mrs Muir in the National Library of Scotland. BM additional ms 52409 consists of a notebook of drafts, various separate drafts of poems, and heavily corrected ptd versions of Chorus of the newly dead, *1926 and* A song *('I was haunted all that day by memories knocking').*

Bibliographies

Mellown, E. W. Bibliography of the writings of Muir. University Alabama [1964], London 1966 (rev).

§1
Poetry

First poems. 1925, New York 1925.

Chorus of the newly dead. 1926.

Six poems. Warlingham 1932 (110 copies). Contents rptd, with changes, in Journeys and places, 1937, below.

Variations on a time theme. 1934.

Journeys and places. 1937.

The narrow place. 1943.

The voyage and other poems. 1946.

The labyrinth. 1949.

Collected poems 1921–51. 1952, New York 1953. Selection, ed. J. C. Hall.

Prometheus. 1954 (Ariel Poem, new ser).

One foot in Eden. 1956, New York 1956. Includes the new poems 1949–51 from Collected poems, 1952, above.

Collected poems 1921–58. Ed Willa Muir and J. C. Hall 1960, 1963 (with alterations and an additional poem), New York 1965 (with preface by T. S. Eliot). Selection, but contains poems omitted from Collected poems 1921–51, above.

Selected poems, with a preface by T. S. Eliot. 1965. Preface by Eliot to this and Collected poems 1921–58, above, rptd from Listener 28 May 1964.

Essays and Criticism

We moderns: enigmas and guesses, by 'Edward Moore'. 1918, New York 1920 (by 'Edwin Muir', with minor alterations). Rptd from New Age.

Latitudes. [1924], New York 1924. 23 essays, mostly rptd from Freeman, New Statesman and Athenaeum.

Transition: essays on contemporary literature. 1926, New York 1926. 12 essays, rptd from Nation (NY) and Nation & Athenaeum.

The structure of the novel. 1928, New York 1929.

Scott and Scotland: the predicament of the Scottish writer. 1936, New York 1938.

The present age, from 1914. 1939, New York 1940 (Introductions to English Lit 5).

The politics of King Lear. Glasgow 1947 (W. P. Ker memorial lecture).

Essays on literature and society. 1949, 1965 (rev and enlarged; 6 new essays), Cambridge Mass 1965.

The estate of poetry. 1962, Cambridge Mass 1962 (Charles Eliot Norton lectures, 1955–6).

Other Works

The marionette. 1927, New York 1927. Novel.

John Knox: portrait of a Calvinist. 1929, New York 1929.

The three brothers. 1931, New York 1931. Novel.

Poor Tom. 1932. Novel.

Scottish journey. 1935.

Social credit and the Labour Party: an appeal. 1935 (Pamphlets on the New Economics 15).

Frost, R. Selected poems. 1936. Introductory essays by Muir et al.

A Franz Kafka miscellany. New York 1940. Contains Franz Kafka by Muir.

The story & the fable: an autobiography. 1940. *See also* An autobiography, 1954, below.

Żyw, A. Poles in uniform: sketches of the Polish army, navy and air force. 1943. Drawings with captions by Muir.

The Scots and their country. [1946].

Poznámka k Franzi Kafkovi. In Franz Kafka a Praha, Prague 1947. Rptd in English in Essays on literature and society, 1949, above.

Marsh, R. and M. J. Tambimuttu (ed). T. S. Eliot: a symposium. 1948. A tribute, by Muir.

Sir Walter Scott lectures 1940–8. Edinburgh 1950.

An autobiography. 1954, New York 1954. First pbd as The story and the fable, 1940; here rev.

Brower, R. A. (ed). On translation. Cambridge Mass 1959. Translating from the German, by Muir.

New poets. Ed Muir 1959.

Selected letters. Ed P. H. Butter 1974.

Muir (with Willa Muir) tr many works by contemporary German authors including Asch, Broch, Feuchtwanger, Hauptmann and Kafka (The castle, *1930, New York 1930;* The Great Wall of China and other pieces, *1933;* The trial, *1937, New York 1937;* America, *1938, Norfolk Conn 1940;* Parables in German and English, *New York 1947;* In the penal settlement, *New York 1948, London 1949*). With J. Lavrin, Muir edited* European Quarterly, *1934–5. With Rosamund Lehmann, C. Day Lewis and D. Kilham Roberts, he edited the periodical* Orion, *vols 1–2 1945. A selection of Muir's letters to Stephen Hudson were pbd in* Encounter 26 1966.

§2

Grieve, C. M. In his Contemporary Scottish studies 1st ser, 1926.

Spender, S. In his Poetry since 1939, 1946.

Hall, J. C. Muir: an introduction. Penguin New Writing 38 1949.

—— Edwin Muir. 1956 (Br Council pamphlet).

Blackmur, R. P. Muir: between the tiger's paws. Kenyon Rev 21 1959.

Hamburger, M. Edwin Muir. Encounter 15 1960.

Holloway, J. The poetry of Muir. Hudson Rev 13 1960–1.

Jennings, E. Muir as poet and allegorist. London Mag 7 1960; rev, in her Every changing shape, 1961.

Gardner, H. Edwin Muir. Cardiff 1961 (W. D. Thomas memorial lecture).

Raine, K. Muir: an appreciation. Texas Quart 4 1961.

Butter, P. H. Edwin Muir. Edinburgh 1962 (Writers & Critics).

—— Edwin Muir: man and poet. Edinburgh 1966.

Morgan, E. Edwin Muir. Review (Oxford) 5 1963.

Muir, Willa. Belonging: a memoir. 1968.

NORMAN CORNTHWAITE NICHOLSON
b. 1914

Poetry and Verse Plays

Selected poems: by J. Hall, K. Douglas, N. Nicholson. 1943.
Five rivers. 1944, New York 1945.
The old man of the mountains: a play in three acts. (Mercury 13 Sept 1945). 1946, 1950 (rev), New York 1950.
Rock face. 1948.
Prophesy to the wind: a play in four scenes and a prologue. (Watergate 7 Aug 1951). 1950.
The pot geranium. 1954.
A match for the devil. (St Mary's Hall, Edinburgh 27 Aug 1953). 1955. Play.
Birth by drowning. (Quarry, Mirfield 9 July 1959). 1960. Play in verse and prose.
Selected poems. 1966.

Other Works

An anthology of religious verse, designed for the times. Ed Nicholson 1942 (Pelican books).
Man & literature: an enquiry into the assumptions as to the nature and purpose of man which underlie much of modern writing. 1943.
The fire of the Lord. 1944, New York 1946. Novel.
The green shore. 1947. Novel.
Cumberland and Westmorland. 1949, New York 1949.
Wordsworth: an introduction and a selection. 1949.
H. G. Wells. 1950, Denver 1950.
Poems by William Cowper, selected and introduced by Nicholson. 1951.
William Cowper. 1951.
The Lakers: the adventures of the first tourists. 1955.
Provincial pleasures. 1959. On life in a small industrial town.
William Cowper. 1960 (Br Council pamphlet).
Portrait of the Lakes. 1963.
Enjoying it all. 1964. Radio talks in ser 'Lift up your hearts'.
The second chance. In Writers on themselves, 1964.
Greater Lakeland. 1969.

ALFRED NOYES
1880–1958

Poetry

The loom of years. 1902.
The flower of Old Japan: a dim strange tale for all ages. 1903, New York 1907 (as The flower of Old Japan and other poems).
Poems. Edinburgh 1904.
The forest of wild thyme: a tale for children under ninety. Edinburgh 1905, 1911 (with alterations).
Drake: an English epic. 2 vols Edinburgh 1906–8, 1 vol New York [1909].
Poems. Introd by H. W. Mabie, New York 1906.
Forty singing seamen and other poems. Edinburgh 1907, New York [1930].
The Golden Hynde and other poems. New York 1908.
The enchanted island and other poems. Edinburgh 1909, New York 1910.
In memory of Swinburne. Cleveland Ohio 1909 (priv ptd, 36 copies).
Collected poems. Vols 1 and 2, Edinburgh 1910, New York 1913 (with different contents), Edinburgh 1928–9 (rev with omissions, and additions including Robin Hood, below). For vols 3 and 4 see 1920, 1927 below.
The prayer for peace. Cleveland Ohio 1911 (priv ptd, 100 copies).

Sherwood or Robin Hood and the three kings: a play. New York 1911, Edinburgh 1926 (with alterations, as Robin Hood).
Tales of the Mermaid Tavern. Edinburgh 1913, New York 1913.
The carol of the fir tree. [1913].
Two Christmas poems. Cleveland Ohio 1913 (priv ptd).
The wine-press: a tale of war. Edinburgh 1913, New York [1913].
The searchlights. [1914]. Single poem.
A tale of Old Japan. Edinburgh 1914. Rptd from Collected poems vol 2 (as The two painters).
The lord of misrule and other poems. New York 1915.
A salute from the fleet and other poems. 1915.
Songs of the trawlers. [1916] (priv ptd, 25 copies).
The avenue of the allies, and Victory. New York 1918.
The new morning. New York [1918].
The elfin artist and other poems. Edinburgh 1920, New York [1920].
Collected poems. Vol 3, Edinburgh 1920, New York 1920 [with different contents].
Selected verse including A victory dance and other poems, old and new. Edinburgh 1921.
The torch-bearers (The watchers of the sky; The book of the earth; The last voyage). 3 vols Edinburgh 1922–30, New York 1922–30, 1 vol London 1937.
Songs of Shadow-of-a-leaf and other poems. Edinburgh 1924.
Princeton, May 1917; The call of the spring. Dansville NY [1925]. With outline, study and explanatory notes by F. R. Signor.
Robin Hood: a play. 1926. See Sherwood, 1911 above.
Dick Turpin's ride and other poems. New York 1927.
Collected poems. Vol 4, Edinburgh 1927.
Ballads and poems. Edinburgh 1928. Selection.
The strong city. [1928].
[Twelve poems]. [1931] (Augustan Books of Poetry). Selection.
Poems: the author's own selection for schools. [1935].
Orchard's Bay. 1939. Contains poems previously unpbd in book form. See Other works, below.
If judgment comes: a poem. New York 1941.
Shadows on the down and other poems. New York [1941], London [1945].
Poems of the new world. Introd by Viscount Halifax, Philadelphia 1942.
Collected poems. Philadelphia 1947, London 1950, 1963 (adding a selection from A letter to Lucian, and four other poems), Port Washington NY 1966 (with 13 additional poems). Selection, excluding The torch-bearers.
Daddy fell into the pond and other poems for children. New York 1952.
A letter to Lucian and other poems. 1956, Philadelphia 1957.
Some single poems were ptd in small edns by E. H. Blakeney at his private press at Winchester. They include The cormorant, *1936,* Youth and memory [verse only], *1937,* Wizards, *1938,* The Assumption: an answer, *1950 and* A Roehampton School song, *1950. Not all were rptd in* Collected poems, *above.*

Other Works

The magic casement: an anthology of fairy poetry. Ed with introd by Noyes [1908], New York 1909.
The minstrelsy of the Scottish border, by Sir Walter Scott. Ed with introd by Noyes. 1908, New York 1913.
William Morris. [1908] (EML).
The temple of beauty: an anthology. Ed Noyes 1910, New York [1911] (as A poet's anthology of poems).
Lamszus, W. The human slaughterhouse. Introd by Noyes, New York 1913.
Rada: a drama of war in one act. New York 1914, London 1915 (as Rada: a Belgian Christmas Eve), New York [1915] (as A Belgian Christmas Eve: being Rada re-

written and enlarged as an Episode of the Great War).
In prose and verse.
A book of Princeton verse, 1916. Ed Noyes, Princeton
1916, London 1916.
Mystery ships: trapping 'U'-boats. 1916.
What is England doing? 1916.
Open boats. Edinburgh 1917, New York [1917]. On war
at sea.
Walking shadows. 1918, New York 1918 (as Walking
shadows: sea tales and others).
Beyond the desert: a tale of Death valley. New York
[1920].
The hidden player. [1924], New York 1924. Tales.
Some aspects of modern poetry. [1924], New York 1924.
New essays and American impressions. New York [1927].
The opalescent parrot. 1929, New York 1929. Essays on
literary and miscellaneous subjects.
The return of the scare-crow. 1929, New York 1929 (as
The sun cure). Novel.
Tennyson. Edinburgh 1932.
The unknown god. 1934, New York 1934, London 1949
(with an epilogue).
Happiness and success, by S. Baldwin, A. Noyes [et al].
1936.
Voltaire. 1936, New York 1936, London 1939 (with new
preface). See M. Ryan, Noyes on Voltaire, Dublin
[1938].
Youth and memory: spoken at the Empire Youth Rally,
18 May 1937. [1937]. In prose and verse.
Orchard's Bay. 1939, New York 1939, London 1955 (as
The incompleat gardener). Essays, with 40 poems unpbd
in book form.
The last man. 1940, New York 1940 (as No other man).
Novel.
Pageant of letters. New York 1940. Literary essays.
The edge of the abyss. Sackville, New Brunswick [1942],
London 1944 (with new preface). Lectures.
The secret of Pooduck Island. New York 1943, London
[1946]. For children.
The golden book of Catholic poetry. Ed Noyes, Phila-
delphia 1946.
Portrait of Horace. 1947, New York 1947 (as Horace:
a portrait).
Two worlds for memory. 1953, Philadelphia 1953. Auto-
biography.
The devil takes a holiday. 1955. Novel.
The accusing ghost: or justice for Casement. 1957, New
York 1957 (as The accusing ghost of Roger Casement).
Noyes edited the Helicon poetry series, *4 vols 1925, and
contributed a general introd to the series and introds to
the individual poets Wordsworth, Tennyson, Longfellow,
Keats.*

'SEUMAS O'SULLIVAN',
JAMES SULLIVAN STARKEY
1879-1958
Poetry

The twilight people. Dublin, London 1905.
Verses sacred and profane. Dublin 1908.
The earth lover and other verses. Dublin 1909.
Lyrics. Portland Maine 1910 (Bibelot 16 no 11).
Poems. Dublin 1912. Selection.
An epilogue to the praise of Angus and other poems.
Dublin, London 1914.
Requiem and other poems. Dublin 1917 (priv ptd, 100
copies). Rptd in next.
The Rosses and other poems. Dublin, London 1918.
The poems of Seumas O'Sullivan. Introd by P. Colum,
Boston 1923.
Common adventures: a book of prose and verse; Nicolas
Flamel: a play in four acts from the French of G. de
Nerval. Dublin 1926 (200 copies).
The lamplighter and other poems. Dublin 1929.

Twenty-five lyrics. Introd by 'A.E.' Flansham 1933 (150
copies). Selection.
At Christmas: verses. Dublin 1934 (priv ptd, 50 copies).
Rptd in Collected poems, 1940, below.
Personal talk: a book of verses. Dublin 1936 (priv ptd, 100
copies). Mostly rptd in Collected poems, 1940, below.
Poems 1930-8. Dublin 1938 (300 copies). Includes
most of At Christmas and Personal talk.
Collected poems. Dublin 1940.
Dublin poems. Foreword by P. Colum, New York 1946.
Translations and transcriptions. Belfast 1950.

Other Works

Impressions: a selection from the note-books of the late
J. H. Orwell. Foreword by O'Sullivan, Dublin 1910.
Mud and purple: pages from the diary of a Dublin man.
Dublin, London 1917.
Facetiae et curiosa: being a selection from the note books
of the late J. H. Orwell, made by his friend Seumas
O'Sullivan. Dublin 1937 (100 copies).
Poems by William Starkey M.D., selected with a preface
by his son James Sullivan Starkey—Seumas O'Sullivan.
Dublin 1938 (priv ptd).
Editor's choice: a little anthology of poems selected from
the Dublin Magazine by O'Sullivan. Dublin 1944.
Essays and recollections. Dublin, Cork 1944.
The rose and the bottle and other essays. Dublin 1946.
O'Sullivan founded and edited the Dublin Mag *1923-58. He
also edited the first two sers of* Tower Press *booklets 1906-8
and the third ser 1938-9 with Austin Clarke.*

WILFRED EDWARD SALTER OWEN
1893-1918

*Most of Owen's mss other than letters and juvenilia are in the
BM.*

Bibliographies

Milne, H. J. M. The poems of Owen. BM Quart 9 1935.
Description of Additional mss 43720 and 43721.
Welland, D. S. R. Owen's manuscripts. TLS 15, 22 June
1956, and subsequent correspondence.
Brown, T. J. English literary autographs xlviii: Owen.
Book Collector 12 1963.
White, W. Wilfred Owen 1893-1918: a bibliography.
Kent Ohio 1967. Rptd from Serif 2 1965. Includes
critical material and reviews.

§1

Poems. With introd by S. Sassoon 1920, New York 1921,
London 1931 (as The poems of Wilfred Owen: a new
edition, including many pieces now first published and
notices of his life and work by E. Blunden), New York
1931.
Thirteen poems. Northampton Mass 1956 (400 copies).
Illustr B. Shahn. Selection.
Collected poems. Ed C. Day Lewis and with a memoir by
E. Blunden 1963, New York 1964. Blunden's memoir
rptd from Poems 1931, above.

Letters

Collected letters. Ed J. Bell and H. Owen 1967.

§2

Spender, S. Poetry and pity. In his The destructive
element, 1935.
Sitwell, O. In his Noble essences, 1950.
Welland, D. S. R. Owen: a critical study. 1960.
Owen, H. Journey from obscurity: Owen 1893-1918: i,
Childhood; ii, Youth; iii, War. 3 vols 1963-5.

Walsh, T. J. (ed). A tribute to Owen. [1964]. Contributors include S. Sassoon, F. Berry and K. Muir.
Bergonzi, B. Rosenberg and Owen. In his Heroes' twilight: a study of the literature of the Great War, 1965.
Stallworthy, J. Wilfred Owen. 1974.

RUTH PITTER
b. 1897

§1

First poems. 1920.
First and second poems 1912–25. Preface by H. Belloc 1927, Garden City NY 1930.
Persephone in Hades. Auch 1931 (100 copies). Single poem.
A mad lady's garland. Preface by H. Belloc 1934, New York [1935].
A trophy of arms: poems 1926–35. Preface by James Stephens [1936], New York 1936. Omits contents of A mad lady's garland.
The spirit watches. [1939], New York 1940.
The rude potato. 1941. Humorous verse on gardening.
Poem. Southampton 1943 (60 copies). Rptd in next.
The bridge: poems 1939–44. 1945, New York 1946 (as The bridge: poems 1939–45).
Ruth Pitter on cats. 1947.
Urania: poems selected from A trophy of arms, The spirit watches and The bridge. 1950.
The ermine: poems 1942–1952. 1953.
Still by choice. 1966.
Poems 1926–66. 1968.

§2

Russell, A. (ed). Ruth Pitter: homage to a poet. 1969.

FRANK TEMPLETON PRINCE
b. 1912

Poetry

Poems. 1938, Norfolk Conn 1938 ([New Directions] Poet of the month).
Soldiers bathing and other poems. 1954.
The stolen heart. San Francisco [1957]. Single poem, rptd in The doors of stone, below.
The doors of stone: poems 1938–62. 1963. Selection.

Other Works

The Italian element in Milton's verse. Oxford 1954, 1962 (corrected).
Milton, Samson agonistes. Ed Prince 1957.
In defence of English: an inaugural lecture. Southampton 1959.
The poems of Shakespeare. Ed Prince 1960 (New Arden).
Sir Thomas Wyatt, by S. Baldi. Tr Prince 1961 (Br Council pamphlet).
Milton, Paradise lost, books I and II. Ed Prince, Oxford 1962.
Shakespeare: the poems. 1963 (Br Council pamphlet).
Milton, Comus and other poems. Ed Prince 1968.

KATHLEEN JESSIE RAINE
b. 1908

Poetry

Stone and flower: poems 1935–43. 1943.
Living in time. 1946.
The pythoness and other poems. 1949, New York 1952.

Selected poems. New York 1952 (250 copies). 38 poems selected with one exception from previous books.
The year one. 1952, New York 1953.
Collected poems. 1956, New York 1957.
Christmas 1960. [1960] (priv ptd). Single poem issued as a greetings card.
The hollow hill and other poems 1960–4. 1965.
Kathleen Raine and Vernon Watkins: selected by E. Owen. 1968 (Pergamon Poets).
Six dreams and other poems. 1968.
The oval portrait and other poems. 1977.

Other Works

William Blake. 1951, 1958 (with addns) (Br Council pamphlet), 1969.
The letters of Samuel Taylor Coleridge. Selected and with an introd by Kathleen Raine 1950 [1952].
Coleridge. 1953 (Br Council pamphlet).
Coleridge, Poems and prose. Selected with an introd by Kathleen Raine. 1957 (Penguin Poets).
Pinto, V. de S. (ed). The divine vision: studies in the poetry and art of William Blake. 1957. Contains The little girl lost and found and The lapsed soul.
Poetry in relation to traditional wisdom. 1958. Lecture.
Blake and England. Cambridge 1960. Lecture.
Defending ancient springs. 1967. Essays on literature.
The written word: a speech. 1967 (210 copies).
Blake and tradition. Princeton 1969, London 1969.
Farewell happy fields. 1973; The lion's mouth, 1977. Autobiography.
Kathleen Raine tr works by Balzac, Paul Foulquié, Denis de Rougemont and Calderón.

HENRY REED
b. 1914

Poetry

A map of Verona: poems. 1946, New York 1947 (as A map of Verona and other poems).

Other Works

The novel since 1939. 1946 (The arts in Britain).
Moby Dick: a play for radio from Herman Melville's novel. 1947.
Perdu and his father, by Paride Rombi, translated from the Italian by Reed. 1954.
Three plays by Ugo Betti: comprising The queen and the rebels, The burnt flower-bed, Summertime. Tr Reed 1956, New York 1958.
Crime on Goat Island, by Ugo Betti. Tr Reed [1960], San Francisco 1961.
Dino Buzzati, Larger than life. Tr Reed 1962.
Honoré de Balzac, Eugénie Grandet: a new translation by Reed, New York 1964.
Natalia Ginzburg, The advertisement—L'inserzione. Tr Reed 1969.

'JAMES REEVES',
JOHN MORRIS REEVES
1909–78

Poetry

The natural need. Deyá Majorca, London 1935. With verse preface by L. Riding.
The imprisoned sea. [1949].
The wandering moon. 1950, New York 1960. For children.
The blackbird in the lilac: poems for children. 1952, New York 1959.

The password and other poems. 1952.

A health to John Patch: a ballad operetta. [1957]. For children.

Prefabulous animiles. 1957, New York 1960. With E. Ardizzone. For children.

The talking skull. 1958.

Collected poems 1929–59. 1960.

Hurdy-gurdy: selected poems. 1961. For children.

Ragged Robin. [1961], New York 1961. For children.

The questioning tiger. 1964.

Selected poems. 1967.

Subsong. 1969.

Other Works

The quality of education. Ed D. Thompson and Reeves 1947.

Mulcaster market: three plays for young players. 1951.

The king who took sunshine: a comedy for children in two acts. 1954.

The critical sense: practical criticism of prose and poetry. 1956.

Pigeons and princesses. 1956, New York 1962 (as pt of Sailor Rumbelow and other stories, below). For children.

The idiom of the people: English traditional verse edited with an introduction and notes from the manuscripts of Cecil J. Sharp. 1958, New York 1958.

Mulbridge Manor. 1958. Novel for children.

Teaching poetry: poetry in class from five to fifteen. 1958.

The personal vision. Poetry Supplement, ed Reeves for the Poetry Book Society. 1959.

Titus in trouble. 1959, New York 1960. Story for children.

The everlasting circle: English traditional verse, ed with an introd and notes from the manuscripts of S. Baring-Gould, H. E. D. Hammond and G. B. Gardiner 1960, New York 1960.

The war 1939–45. Edited by D. Flower and Reeves 1960, New York 1960 (as The taste of courage: the war 1939–1945).

Great English essays, selected and ed Reeves 1961.

Selected poetry and prose of Robert Graves 1961.

A short history of English poetry 1340–1940. 1961, New York 1962.

Georgian poetry, selected and introduced by Reeves. 1962 (Penguin Poets).

Sailor Rumbelow and Britannia. 1962, New York 1962 (with contents of Pigeons and princesses, 1956, as Sailor Rumbelow and other stories). For children.

The peddler's dream and other plays. New York 1963.

The story of Jackie Thimble. New York 1964, London 1965. For children.

The strange light. 1964. Stories for children.

The Cassell book of English poetry 1965, New York 1965.

The pillar-box thieves. 1965. Story for children.

Understanding poetry. 1965.

Rhyming Will. 1967. Story for children.

An anthology of free verse. Oxford 1968.

Homage to Trumbull Stickney: poems selected by Reeves and S. Haldane. 1968.

Reeves also wrote a number of school textbooks, mainly on the appreciation of literature; compiled prose and verse anthologies for children; and wrote versions for children of several well-known literary works and traditional and biblical stories. He edited, with J. Bronowski, the series Songs for sixpence, Cambridge 1929, and several other series, including Poetry Bookshelf, 1951–, and an anthology The modern poets' world. He also edited Unicorn Books, 1960–.

ANNE BARBARA RIDLER, née BRADBY
b. 1912

Poetry and Verse Plays

Poems. 1939.

A dream observed and other poems. [1941] (Poetry London pamphlet).

Cain: a play in two acts. 1943.

The nine bright shiners. 1943.

The shadow factory: a nativity play. (Mercury 19 Dec 1945). 1946.

Henry Bly and other plays (The mask; The missing bridegroom). 1950. The mask and The missing bridegroom produced at the Watergate, 6 March 1951.

The golden bird and other poems. 1951.

The trial of Thomas Cranmer: a play. 1956. Broadcast 21 March 1956; produced in the University Church, Oxford, May 1956.

A matter of life and death. 1959.

Selected poems. New York 1961.

Who is my neighbour? (The Wayfarers, at the Leeds Civic Theatre, Oct 1961), and How bitter the bread. 1963.

Other Works

Shakespeare criticism 1919–35, selected with an introduction by Anne Bradby. Oxford 1936 (WC).

The little book of modern verse, chosen by Anne Ridler. 1941.

Time passes and other poems, by Walter de la Mare, selected and arranged by Anne Ridler. 1942.

Best ghost stories, selected by Anne Ridler. 1945.

The Faber book of modern verse. Ed M. Roberts 1951 (with supplement of new poems chosen by Anne Ridler).

The image of the city and other essays by Charles Williams, selected by Anne Ridler with a critical introduction. 1958.

Charles Williams: selected writings, chosen by Anne Ridler. 1961, Carbondale 1963.

Poems and some letters of James Thomson, edited by Anne Ridler. 1963.

Shakespeare criticism 1935–60, selected with an introduction by Anne Ridler. Oxford 1963 (WC).

Best stories of church and clergy: edited with an introduction by C. Bradby and Anne Ridler. 1966.

Thomas Traherne, Poems, centuries and three thanksgivings, edited by Anne Ridler. 1966.

Olive Willis and Downe House: an adventure in education. 1967.

'MICHAEL ROBERTS', WILLIAM EDWARD ROBERTS
1902–48

Poetry

These our matins. 1930.

Poems. 1936.

Orion marches. 1939.

Collected poems, with an introductory memoir by Janet Roberts [Janet Adam Smith]. 1958. Includes unpbd poems.

Roberts also contributed 5 poems to his anthology New country, 1933, below.

Other Works

New signatures: poems by several hands. 1932.

Elizabethan prose, selected and prefaced by Roberts. 1933.

New country: prose and poetry by the authors of New signatures. 1933. Ed Roberts, with preface, 5 poems

Critique of poetry. 1934.

Newton and the origin of colours. 1934. With E. R. Thomas.

The Faber book of modern verse. Ed Roberts 1936, 1951 (with supplement by A. Ridler), 1965 (rev, with suppl D. Hall).
The modern mind. 1937, New York 1937.
T. E. Hulme. 1938.
The recovery of the west. 1941.
The Faber book of comic verse, compiled by Roberts. 1942.
Belgium and Holland. 1944 (Army Bureau of Current Affairs).
Notes on College history 1840–65. College of St Mark and St John, Chelsea. Ed Roberts 1946.
The estate of man. 1951. Ed Janet Adam Smith, Roberts's widow. Unfinished.

WILLIAM ROBERT RODGERS
1909–69

Awake! and other poems. 1941, New York 1942 (as Awake! and other wartime poems).
The Ulstermen and their country. [1947]. Prose.
Europa and the bull and other poems. 1952, New York 1953.
Ireland in colour: a collection of forty colour photographs, with an introductory text and notes on the illustrations by Rodgers. 1957, New York 1957.

ISAAC ROSENBERG
1890–1918

§ 1

Night and day. [1912].
Youth. 1915.
Moses: a play. 1916. Includes poems.
Poems, selected and ed G. Bottomley, with an introductory memoir by L. Binyon. 1922.
Collected works: poetry, prose, letters and some drawings, edited by G. Bottomley and D. Harding. 1937. Foreword by S. Sassoon. Includes unpbd verse and contributions to periodicals, some posthumous.
Collected poems. Ed G. Bottomley and D. Harding 1949, New York [1949]. Reimpression of Poems section of Collected works, 1937, above; 'revised'.
Collected works. Ed I. Parsons 1979.

§ 2

Lucas, F. L. In his Authors dead & living, 1926.
Harding, D. W. Aspects of the poetry of Rosenberg. Scrutiny 3 1935; rptd in his Experience into words, 1963.
Bergonzi, B. Rosenberg and Owen. In his Heroes' twilight: a study of the literature of the Great War, 1965.

ALAN ROSS
b. 1922

Poetry

Summer thunder. Oxford 1941.
The derelict day: poems in Germany. 1947.
Something of the sea: poems 1942–52. 1954, Boston 1955.
To whom it may concern: poems 1952–7. 1958.
African negatives. 1962.
North from Sicily: poems in Italy 1961–4. 1965.
Poems 1942–67. 1967.

Other Works

Time was away: a notebook in Corsica. 1948.
The forties: a period piece. 1950.
The gulf of pleasure. 1951. Anthology of Naples.

Poetry 1945–1950. 1951 (The Arts in Britain).
The bandit on the billiard table: a journey through Sardinia. 1954, 1960 (rev as South to Sardinia).
Australia 55: a journal of the MCC tour. 1955.
Cape summer, and the Australians in England. 1957.
The onion man. 1959. For children.
The cricketer's companion. Ed Ross 1960.
Danger on Glass Island. 1960. For children.
Through the Caribbean: the MCC tour of the West Indies, 1959–60. 1960.
Australia 63. 1963.
The West Indies at Lord's. 1963.
Stories from the London Magazine. Ed Ross 1964.
The wreck of Moni. 1965. For children.
London Magazine stories 3 (–5). Ed Ross 1968–70.
Ross tr works by P. Diolé, P.-D. Gaisseau, R. Merle and A. Embiricos. He edited London Mag from 1961.

VICTORIA MARY SACKVILLE-WEST
1892–1962

Poetry

Poems of west and east. 1917.
Orchard and vineyard. 1921.
The land. 1926.
King's daughter. 1929, Garden City NY 1930.
Duineser Elegien. Elegies from the castle of Duino, tr from the German of R. M. Rilke by V. Sackville-West and E. Sackville-West. 1931 (238 copies).
Invitation to cast out care. 1931 (Ariel Poem).
Sissinghurst. 1931 (500 copies).
[Twenty-three poems]. [1931] (Augustan Books of Poetry). Selection with previously uncollected poems.
Collected poems, volume one. 1933, Garden City NY 1934. No more pbd.
Solitude: a poem. 1938, New York 1939.
Selected poems. 1941. Selection, with 5 new poems.
The garden. 1946, Garden City NY 1946.

Other Works

Heritage. [1919], New York [1919]. Novel.
The dragon in shallow waters. 1921, New York 1922. Novel.
The heir: a love story. [1922] (priv ptd). Single story, rptd in The heir: a love story, below.
The heir: a love story. 1922, New York 1922. 5 stories.
Knole and the Sackvilles. 1922, New York 1923, London 1958 (rev).
The challenge. New York [1923]. Novel.
The diary of the Lady Anne Clifford, with an introductory note by V. Sackville-West. 1923.
Grey Wethers: a romantic novel. 1923, New York [1923].
Seducers in Ecuador. 1924, New York 1925. Story. Rptd 1944, with Gottfried Künstler (1932).
Passenger to Teheran. 1926, New York 1927. Travel.
Aphra Behn: the incomparable Astrea. 1927, New York 1928.
Twelve days: an account of a journey across the Bakhtiari mountains in south-western Persia. 1928, Garden City NY 1928.
Andrew Marvell. 1929.
Granville-Barker, H. (ed). The eighteen-seventies. Cambridge 1929. Contains The women poets of the seventies.
The Edwardians. 1930, Garden City NY 1930. Novel; dramatized 1960 by R. Gow.
Wellesley D. (ed). The annual: being a selection from the forget-me-nots, keepsakes and other annuals of the nineteenth century. Introd by V. Sackville-West [1930].
All passion spent. 1931, Garden City NY 1931. Novel.
Family history. 1932, Garden City NY 1932. Novel.
Thirty clocks strike the hour and other stories. Garden City NY 1932. 2 stories, The death of noble Godavary

and Gottfried Künstler, also pbd separately in Benn's
New ninepenny novels series, 1932; Gottfried Künstler
rptd 1944 with Seducers in Ecuador (1924).

The dark island. 1934, Garden City NY 1934.

Beginnings, by A. Alington [et al]. 1934. Includes essay
by V. Sackville-West on her beginnings as a writer.

Saint Joan of Arc. 1936, Garden City NY 1936, London
1948 (rev).

Joan of Arc. 1937. New York 1938.

Pepita. 1937, Garden City NY 1937. Biographies of
Josefa Duran y Ortega and Victoria Sackville-West,
Lady Sackville, the author's grandmother and mother.

Some flowers. 1937. Descriptions of garden flowers.

Country notes. 1939, New York 1940.

Country notes in wartime. 1940, New York 1941.

English country houses. 1941 (Britain in Pictures).

Grand canyon. 1942, Garden City NY 1942. Novel.

The eagle and the dove, a study in contrasts: St Teresa of
Avila, St Thérèse of Lisieux. 1943, Garden City NY
1944.

Seducers in Ecuador and Gottfried Künstler. 1944
(Penguin).

The Women's Land Army. 1944.

Another world than this: an anthology, compiled by
V. Sackville-West and H. Nicolson. 1945.

Alice Meynell. Prose and poetry: centenary volume edited
by F. Page [et al] with a biographical & critical introduction by V. Sackville-West. 1947.

Devil at Westease: the story as related by Roger Liddiard.
New York 1947. Detective story.

Nursery rhymes. 1947 (Dropmore essays, 550 copies),
1950 (unlimited edn). Essay.

In your garden. 1951. On gardening.

Hidcote Manor garden, Hidcote Bartrim. 1952.

The Easter party. 1953, Garden City NY 1953. Novel.

In your garden again. 1953.

Walter de la Mare and The traveller. 1953 (Warton lecture
on English poetry).

More for your garden. 1955.

Even more for your garden. 1958.

A joy of gardening: a selection for Americans. Ed H. I.
Popper, New York [1958].

Daughter of France: the life of Anne Marie Louise
d'Orléans duchesse de Montpensier 1627–93, La
Grande Mademoiselle. 1959, Garden City NY 1959.

Faces: profiles of dogs; text, V. Sackville-West; photographs, L. Goehr. [1961].

No signposts in the sea. 1961, Garden City NY 1961.
Novel.

Victoria Sackville-West's garden book: a collection taken
from In your garden, In your garden again, More for
your garden, Even more for your garden, by Philippa
Nicolson. 1968.

Portrait of a marriage, by Nigel Nicolson. 1973. By her
son, based on her diary.

Victoria Sackville-West contributed book reviews to Listener
and Nation *and* Athenaeum. *She also contributed* Country notes *regularly to* New Statesman *1938–41, many
being rptd in* Country notes, *1939 and* Country notes
in wartime, *1940, above. She wrote weekly articles on
gardening for* Observer, *many being rptd in* In your
garden, *1951,* In your garden again, *1953 etc above.*

SIEGFRIED LORAINE SASSOON
1886–1967

Bibliographies

Keynes, G. L. A bibliography of Sassoon. 1962 (Soho
Bibliographies). Includes trns.

§1
Poetry

Poems. 1906 (priv ptd, 50 copies). Anon.

Sonnets and verses. 1909 (priv ptd, 25[?] copies). Anon.

Sonnets. 1909 (priv ptd, 'probably 50 copies, according
to the author' (Keynes)). Anon.

Twelve sonnets. 1911 (priv ptd, 25 copies).

Poems. 1911 (priv ptd, 38 copies).

Melodies. 1912 (priv ptd, 37 copies). Anon.

An ode for music. 1912 (priv ptd, 60 copies).

The daffodil murderer: being the Chantrey Prize Poem, by
'Saul Kain' [i.e. Sassoon]. 1913. Parody of Masefield's
The Everlasting mercy.

Discoveries. 1915 (priv ptd, 65 copies).

Morning-glory. [1916] (priv ptd, 11 copies). Anon.

The Redeemer. Cambridge 1916. Rptd from Cambridge
Mag 2 1913.

To any dead officer. Cambridge 1917. Rptd from Cambridge Mag 6 1917.

The old huntsman, and other poems. 1917, New York
1918.

Four poems. Cambridge 1918. Rptd from Cambridge
Mag 7 1918.

Counter-attack, and other poems. Introd by R. Nichols.
1918, New York 1918.

A literary editor for the new London daily newspaper.
[1919]. Prospectus for Daily Herald, containing 4 poems
rptd from Counter-attack.

Picture-show. Cambridge 1919 (priv ptd), New York
1920 (with 7 additional poems).

The war poems of Siegfried Sassoon. 1919.

Lines written in the Reform Club. 1921.

Recreations. 1923 (priv ptd, 75 copies). Anon.

Lingual exercises for advanced vocabularians, by the
author of Recreations. Cambridge 1925 (priv ptd, 99
copies).

Selected poems. 1925.

[Thirty-two poems]. [1926] (Augustan Books of Modern
Poetry). Selection.

Satirical poems. 1926, New York 1926, London 1933
(with 5 additional poems).

Nativity. [1927] (Ariel Poem).

The heart's journey. New York and London 1927 (limited
edn, anon but with author's autograph signature on
title-page), London 1928 (unlimited edn, with 7 additional poems), New York 1929.

To my mother. [1928] (Ariel Poem).

A suppressed poem. 1919 [i.e. 1929?]. The single poem,
I'd timed my death in action to the minute, pirated from
the first, suppressed edn of Robert Graves' Goodbye to
all that, 1929.

On Chatterton: a sonnet. Winchester 1930 (priv ptd, 14
copies).

In Sicily. [1930] (Ariel Poem).

Poems, by 'Pinchbeck Lyre' [i.e. Sassoon]. 1931.

To the red rose. [1931] (Ariel Poem).

Prehistoric burials. New York [1932].

The road to ruin. 1933.

Vigils, by S.L.S. Bristol 1934 (priv ptd, 272 copies) (22
poems), London 1935 (trade edn, 35 poems), New York
1936.

Rhymed ruminations. 1939 (priv ptd, 75 copies), 1940
(trade edn, with 9 additional poems), New York 1941.

Poems newly selected, 1916–1935. 1940.

[Forty-eight poems]. [1943] (Augustan Poets). Selection.

Collected poems. 1947, New York 1949. Contains The
old huntsman, Counter-attack, Picture-show, Satirical
poems, The heart's journey, The road to ruin, Vigils,
Rhymed ruminations. With addns and omissions.

Common chords. Stanford Dingley 1950 (107 copies).

Emblems of experience. Cambridge 1951 (75 copies).

The tasking. Cambridge 1954 (priv ptd, 100 copies).

An adjustment, by 'S.S.' Royston 1955 (priv ptd, 150
copies). Foreword by P. Gosse.

Sequences. 1956, New York 1957. 62 poems selected
from Common chords, Emblems of experience, The
tasking.

Poems selected by D. Silk. Marlborough 1958 (priv ptd, 150 copies).

Lenten illuminations; Sight sufficient. Cambridge 1958 (35 copies).

The path to peace: selected poems. Worcester 1960 (500 copies). Ptd Stanbrook Abbey Press.

Collected poems 1908–56. 1961. Contains Collected poems 1947, Common chords (omitting 1 poem, adding To my mother), Emblems of experience, The tasking.

An octave: 8 September 1966. Introd by C. Causley 1966 (priv ptd, 350 copies). 8 poems.

Other Works

Orpheus in Dilœryum. 1908. Anon. 'A sort of Masque'.

Hyacinth: an idyll. 1912 (27 copies). A play in prose with 6 pieces in verse.

Amyntas: a mystery. 1912. A short dramatic piece, suppressed by the author. Proof copy in BM.

Memoirs of a fox-hunting man. 1928 (anon), New York 1929 ('by Siegfried Sassoon'), London 1929. Semi-fictional autobiography. *See* also next 2 items.

Memoirs of an infantry officer, by the author of Memoirs of a fox-hunting man. 1930, New York 1930 ('by Siegfried Sassoon'), London 1930.

Sherston's progress. 1936, New York 1936.

The complete memoirs of George Sherston. 1937, Garden City NY 1937 (as The memoirs of George Sherston). Contains Memoirs of a fox-hunting man, Memoirs of an infantry officer, Sherston's progress.

The old century and seven more years. 1938, New York 1939, London 1968 (introd by M. Thorpe). Autobiography to 1907.

On poetry. Bristol 1939. Lecture.

The flower show match, and other pieces. 1941. Selections from Memoirs of a fox-hunting man, Memoirs of an infantry officer, Sherston's progress and The old century.

Early morning long ago. 1941 (priv ptd, 50 copies); rptd in next.

The weald of youth. 1942, New York 1942. Autobiography to 1914.

Siegfried's journey 1916–20. 1945, New York 1946. Autobiography.

Meredith. 1948, New York 1948. Biography.

Something about myself, by Siegfried Sassoon aged eleven. Worcester 1966 (ptd Stanbrook Abbey Press). From the ms entitled More poems.

Letters to a critic [1963–7]. Ed M. Thorpe 1976. *28 letters from Sassoon to Sir Sidney Cockerell are included in* The best of friends, *ed V. Meynell 1956.*

Sassoon was the first literary editor of Daily Herald.

§ 2

Blunden, E. Sassoon's poetry. London Mercury 20 1929; rptd in his The mind's eye, 1934.

Graves, R. Goodbye to all that. 1929, 1957 (rev).

Bergonzi, B. In his Heroes' twilight: a study of the literature of the Great War, 1965.

Thorpe, M. Sassoon: a critical study. Leyden 1966.

Jackson, S. The Sassoons. 1968.

EDWARD BUXTON SHANKS
1892–1953

Songs. 1915.

Poems. 1916.

The queen of China and other poems. 1919, New York 1919.

The island of youth and other poems. [1921].

Fête galante: a dance-dream in one act, after Maurice Baring's story of that name, dramatized and composed by Ethel Smyth. Vienna, New York [1923]. Poetic version by Shanks.

The shadowgraph and other poems. [1925].

Collected poems 1909–25, arranged in six books. [1926]. Contains most previously pbd verse, but excludes The queen of China. Some revisions and addns.

The beggar's ride: a tragedy in six scenes. [1926]. Included in Poems 1939–1952, below.

Poems 1912–32. 1933. Selection, with 18 newly collected poems.

The man from Flanders and other poems. 1940 (priv ptd, 250 copies). Most rptd in next.

The night watch for England and other poems. 1942.

Images from the progress of the seasons. 1947 (450 copies).

Poems 1939–52. 1954. Includes 20 poems from the 2 previous books and others newly collected.

Shanks was the assistant editor of London Mercury *1919–22. He was leader-writer on* Evening Standard *1928–35.*

FREDEGOND SHOVE, née MAITLAND
1889–1949

Dreams and journeys. Oxford 1918.

Daybreak. Richmond, Surrey 1922.

Christina Rossetti: a study. Cambridge 1931.

Poems. Cambridge 1956. Selection of pbd and unpbd work. Foreword by E. Maitland.

DAME EDITH LOUISA SITWELL
1887–1964

Sales of Edith Sitwell's mss were held at Sotheby's on 12 Dec 1961, 19 June 1962 and 11 May 1964. Most are now in the library of the University of Texas.

Bibliographies

Fifoot, R. A bibliography of Edith, O. and S. Sitwell. 1963 (Soho Bibliographies), 1971 (rev).

§ 1
Poetry

The mother and other poems. Oxford 1915.

Twentieth-century harlequinade and other poems, by Edith and O. Sitwell. Oxford 1916. 7 poems.

Clowns' houses. Oxford 1918.

The wooden Pegasus. Oxford 1920.

Façade. 1922 (priv ptd, 150 copies). Concert version for voice and orchestra by William Walton performed Jan 1922.

Bucolic comedies. 1923.

The sleeping beauty. 1924, New York 1924.

Troy Park. 1925, New York 1925.

Poor young people. By Edith, O. and S. Sitwell. 1925 (375 copies). 8 poems by Edith Sitwell.

[Eleven poems]. [1926] (Augustan Books of Modern Poetry). Selection.

Elegy on dead fashion. 1926 (225 copies).

Poem for a Christmas card. [1926] (210 copies).

Rustic elegies. 1927, New York 1927.

Popular song. 1928 (Ariel Poem).

Five poems. 1928 (275 copies). Included in Collected poems, 1930, below.

Gold Coast customs. 1929, Boston 1929.

Collected poems. 1930. Selection with some revision and 2 new poems.

In spring. 1931 (priv ptd, 305 copies).

Jane Barston 1719–46. 1931 (Ariel Poem).

Epithalamium. 1931 (100 copies).

Five variations on a theme. 1933.

Selected poems, with an essay on her own poetry by E. Sitwell. 1936, Boston 1937. Includes 2 previously uncollected poems.

Poems new and old. 1940. Selection, with 2 previously uncollected poems.

Street songs. 1942.

Green song and other poems. 1944, New York [1946].

The weeping babe: motet for soprano solo and mixed choir. [1945]. Music by M. Tippett.

The song of the cold. 1945. Selection, with previously uncollected poems.

The shadow of Cain. 1947.

The song of the cold. New York 1948. Selection with previously uncollected poems, differing greatly from the London edn of 1945, above.

The canticle of the rose: selected poems 1920–47. 1949, New York 1949 (as The canticle of the rose: poems 1917–49; with same contents, but adding Some notes on my own poetry).

Poor men's music. 1950, Denver 1950.

Façade and other poems 1920–1935. 1950. Selection; introd by J. Lindsay.

Selected poems. 1952 (Penguin Poets). Selection, with previously uncollected poems.

Gardeners and astronomers. 1953, New York 1953 (omitting 4 poems; as Gardeners and astronomers: new poems).

Collected poems. New York [1954], London 1957 (with addns). Selection, with previously uncollected and unpbd poems.

[Twenty-three poems]. 1960 (Pocket Poets). Selection.

The outcasts. 1962.

Music and ceremonies. New York [1963]. Contents of The outcasts, 1962, above, with 4 other poems, 3 unpbd.

Selected poems, chosen with an introd by J. Lehmann. 1965.

Edith Sitwell edited and contributed substantially to the 6 'cycles' of Wheels, 1916–21.

Other Works

Children's tales—from the Russian ballet. 1920, [1921 or 1922] (as The Russian ballet gift book).

Poetry and modern poetry. In Yea and nay: a series of lectures and counter-lectures given at the London School of Economics. 1923.

Poetry and criticism. 1925, New York [1926].

Experiment in poetry. In Tradition and experiment in present-day literature: addresses delivered at the City Literary Institute, 1929.

Alexander Pope. 1930, New York 1930.

The pleasures of poetry: a critical anthology. 3 vols 1930–2, New York 1930–2, 1 vol London 1934.

Bath. 1932, New York 1932.

Prose poems from Les illuminations of Arthur Rimbaud. Tr H. Rootham, with an introductory essay by E. Sitwell. 1932.

The English eccentrics. 1933, Boston 1933, New York 1957 (rev and enlarged), London 1958.

Aspects of modern poetry. 1934.

Victoria of England. 1936, Boston 1936.

Sitwell, S. Collected poems, with a long introductory essay by E. Sitwell. 1936.

I live under a black sun. 1937, Garden City NY 1938. Novel.

Three eras of modern poetry. In Trio: dissertations on some aspects of national genius, by O., Edith and S. Sitwell, 1938 (Northcliffe Lectures, Univ of London).

The last party: a radio play. In Twelve modern plays, selected by J. Hampden, 1938.

Edith Sitwell's anthology. 1940. English and French poetry, with introd.

Look! the sun. Ed Edith Sitwell 1941. Anthology of poetry.

English women. 1942 (Britain in Pictures).

A poet's notebook. 1943.

Maiden voyage, by Denton Welch. Foreword by Edith Sitwell 1943, New York 1945.

Planet and glow-worm: a book for the sleepless, compiled by Edith Sitwell. 1944. Anthology of verse and prose.

Fanfare for Elizabeth. New York 1946, London 1946. On the childhood of Elizabeth I.

A notebook on William Shakespeare. 1948, Boston 1961.

A book of the winter, compiled by Edith Sitwell. 1950, New York 1951. Anthology of verse and prose.

A poet's notebook. Boston 1950. Contains A poet's notebook, 1943, above, with omissions and revisions, and A notebook on William Shakespeare, 1948, above, with omissions.

The American genius: an anthology of poetry with some prose. Ed Edith Sitwell 1951.

A book of flowers, compiled by Edith Sitwell. 1952. Anthology, including recipes for cordials, scents etc.

Dylan Thomas: a bibliography, by J. A. Rolph. Foreword by Edith Sitwell 1956.

The Atlantic book of British and American poetry. Boston 1958, London 1959. Ed Edith Sitwell.

Roy Campbell. In Hommage à Roy Campbell, Montpellier 1958.

The collected poems of Roy Campbell. Vol 3, 1960 (with foreword by Edith Sitwell).

Swinburne: a selection. Ed Edith Sitwell 1960, New York 1960.

Comment on Dylan Thomas. In Dylan Thomas: the legend and the poet, ed E. W. Tedlock 1960.

The queens and the hive. 1962, Boston 1962. On Elizabeth I and Mary Tudor, Mary Queen of Scots, Catharine de' Medici.

Taken care of: an autobiography. 1965, New York 1965.

Selected letters. Ed J. Lehmann and D. Parker 1970.

§2

Graves, R. In his Contemporary techniques of poetry, 1925.

Muir, E. Edith Sitwell. Nation 15 April 1925.

—— Miss Edith Sitwell. Nation 18 Sept 1926; rptd in his Transition, 1926.

Vines, S. The three Sitwells. In Scrutinies vol 2, ed E. Rickword 1931.

Reed, H. The poetry of Edith Sitwell. Penguin New Writing no 21 1944; rptd in Writers of to-day, ed D. V. Baker 1946.

Lehmann, J. Edith Sitwell. 1952 (Br Council pamphlet). Rptd as introd to Selected poems, 1965, above.

—— A nest of tigers: Edith, O. and S. Sitwell in their times. 1968.

Connolly, C. In his Previous convictions, 1963.

Pearson, J. Façades: Edith, Osbert and Sacheverell Sitwell. 1978.

SIR FRANCIS OSBERT SACHEVERELL SITWELL
1892–1969

Bibliographies

Fifoot, R. A bibliography of Edith, O. and S. Sitwell, 1963 (Soho Bibliographies), 1971 (rev).

Poetry

Twentieth-century harlequinade and other poems, by Edith and O. Sitwell. Oxford 1916. Includes 2 war poems and The lament of the mole-catcher, by O. Sitwell.

The Winstonburg Line: 3 satires. [1919].

Argonaut and juggernaut. 1919, New York 1920.

At the house of Mrs Kinfoot: consisting of four satires. 1921 (priv ptd, 101 copies). Included in Collected satires and poems, 1931, below.

Out of the flame. 1923, New York 1925.

Poor young people, by Edith, O. and S. Sitwell. 1925 (375 copies). Includes Long winter: 12 songs by O. Sitwell.

Winter the huntsman. [1927]. Rptd from Poor young people, 1925, above.

England reclaimed: a book of eclogues. 1927, Garden City NY 1928. *See* also England reclaimed and other poems, 1949, below.

Miss Mew. Stanford Dingley 1929 (101 copies). 6 poems. Included in next.

Collected satires and poems. 1931.

Three-quarter length portrait of Michael Arlen; with a preface, The history of a portrait, by the author. [1931].

A three-quarter-length portrait of the Viscountess Wimborne. Cambridge 1931 (57 copies).

Mrs Kimber. 1937. 6 poems.

Selected poems, old and new. 1943. Includes 9 previously uncollected poems.

Four songs of the Italian earth. [Pawlet Vermont] 1948 (260 copies); rptd in England reclaimed and other poems, 1949, below.

Demos the emperor: a secular oratorio. 1949.

England reclaimed and other poems. Boston 1949. A different collection from England reclaimed, 1927, above.

Wrack at Tidesend: a book of balnearics, being the second volume of England reclaimed. 1952, New York 1953 (slightly rev).

On the Continent: a book of inquilinics, being the third volume of England reclaimed. 1958.

Poems about people: or England reclaimed. 1965. Collects contents of 3 previous books.

Autobiographies

Left hand, right hand! Boston 1944, London 1945 (as Left hand, right hand! an autobiography: vol 1, The cruel month).

The scarlet tree. Boston 1946, London 1946 (as The scarlet tree: being the second volume of Left hand, right hand! an autobiography).

Great morning! Boston 1947, London 1948 (as Great morning: being the third volume of Left hand, right hand! an autobiography).

Laughter in the next room. Boston 1948, London 1949 (as Laughter in the next room: being the fourth volume of Left hand, right hand! an autobiography).

Noble essences or courteous revelations: being a book of characters and the fifth and last volume of Left hand, right hand! an autobiography. 1950, Boston 1950 (as Noble essences: a book of characters).

Tales my father taught me: an evocation of extravagant episodes. 1962, Boston [1962].

Other Works

Who killed Cock-Robin? remarks on poetry, on criticism, and, as a sad warning, the story of Eunuch Arden. 1921.

Triple fugue. 1924, New York [1925]. Stories.

Discursions on travel, art and life. 1925, New York [1925].

C. R. W. Nevinson. 1925. Signed 'O.S.'.

Before the bombardment. 1926, New York [1926]. Novel.

All at sea: a social tragedy in three acts for first-class passengers only, by O. and S. Sitwell; with a preface entitled A few days in an author's life by O. Sitwell. 1927, Garden City NY 1928.

The people's album of London statues, described by Sitwell, drawn by N. Hamnett. 1928.

The works of Ronald Firbank. Vol 1, 1929 (for Dec 1928). Biographical memoir by Sitwell; rptd, rev, in I. K. Fletcher, Ronald Firbank, 1930, and again (rev) in Firbank's Five novels, 1949.

The man who lost himself. 1929, New York 1930. Novel.

Sober truth: a collection of nineteenth-century episodes, fantastic, grotesque and mysterious, compiled and ed M. Barton and Sitwell. 1930, New York [1930].

Dumb-animal and other stories. 1930, Philadelphia 1931.

Victoriana: a symposium of Victorian wisdom ed and compiled by M. Barton and Sitwell. 1931.

Belshazzar's feast, by William Walton. Text selected and arranged from the Holy Bible by Sitwell. 1931.

Dickens. 1932.

Winters of content: more discursions on travel, art and life. 1932, Philadelphia 1932. *See* also Winters of content and other discursions, 1950, below.

Miracle on Sinai: a satirical novel. 1933, New York [1934], London 1948 (with new preface by the author).

Johnson's England. Ed A. S. Turberville vol 2, Oxford 1933. Contains Taste, by Sitwell and M. Barton.

Brighton. 1935, Boston 1935. With M. Barton.

Penny foolish: a book of tirades and panegyrics. 1935. Miscellaneous essays mainly rptd from Sunday Referee.

Those were the days: panorama with figures. 1938. Novel.

Dickens and the modern novel; The modern novel, its cause and cure. In Trio: dissertations on some aspects of national genius, by O., Edith and S. Sitwell. 1938 (Northcliffe Lectures, Univ of London).

Escape with me! an oriental sketch-book. 1939, New York 1940, London 1948 (with new introd).

Two generations. Ed Sitwell 1940. Reminiscences of Georgiana Caroline Sitwell, afterwards Swinton, and the journal of Florence Alice Sitwell.

Open the door! a volume of stories. 1941, New York 1941.

A place of one's own. 1941. Nouvelle.

Gentle Caesar: a play in three acts. 1942 (for March 1943). With R. J. Minney.

Sing high! sing low! a book of essays. 1944. Mostly rptd, rev, from periodicals.

A letter to my son. 1944. Rptd, rev, from Horizon. On authorship and contemporary life.

The true story of Dick Whittington: a Christmas story for cat-lovers. 1945 (for Feb 1946).

A free house! or the artist as craftsman, being the writings of W. R. Sickert. Ed Sitwell 1947.

Alive—alive oh! and other stories. 1947. Selection from Dumb-animal, 1930, above, and Triple fugue, 1924, above.

The novels of George Meredith and some notes on the English novel. 1947 (Eng Assoc Presidential Address).

Death of a god and other stories. 1949. Mostly rptd from Open the door!, 1941, above; with A place of one's own, 1941, and Staggered holiday.

Sir George Sitwell on the making of gardens. Introd by Sitwell 1949.

Introduction to the catalogue of the Frick collection. [New York] 1949.

Winters of content and other discursions on Mediterranean art and travel. 1950. Contains Winters of content, 1932, chs from Discursions, 1925, and Echoes, a story from Dumb-animal, 1930.

Collected stories. 1953, New York [1953].

The four continents: being more discursions on travel, art and life. 1954, New York [1954].

Fee fi fo fum! a book of fairy stories. 1959.

A place of one's own and other stories. 1961. All rptd from Collected stories, 1953, above.

Pound wise. 1963, Boston, Mass [1963].

§2

Williams, C. In his Poetry at present, 1930.

Vines, S. The three Sitwells. In Scrutinies vol 2, ed E. Rickword 1931.

Fulford, R. Osbert Sitwell. 1951 (Br Council pamphlet).

Lehmann, J. A nest of tigers: Edith, O. and S. Sitwell in their times. 1968.

SIR SACHEVERELL SITWELL
b. 1897

Bibliographies

Fifoot, R. A bibliography of Edith, O. and S. Sitwell. 1963 (Soho Bibliographies), 1971 (rev).

§1
Poetry

The people's palace. Oxford 1918.
Doctor Donne and Gargantua: first canto. 1921 (priv ptd, 101 copies).
The hundred and one harlequins. 1922, New York [1922].
Doctor Donne and Gargantua: canto the second. 1923 (priv ptd, 40 copies).
The parrot. [1923].
The thirteenth Caesar and other poems. 1924, New York 1925.
Poor young people. By Edith, O. and S. Sitwell. 1925 (375 copies). 12 poems by S. Sitwell.
Exalt the eglantine and other poems. 1926 (370 copies).
Doctor Donne and Gargantua: canto the third. Stratford-upon-Avon 1926 (priv ptd, 65 copies).
The cyder feast and other poems. 1927, New York 1927.
[Twenty-five poems.] [1928] (Augustan Books of English Poetry). Selection, adding Two songs, previously unpbd.
Two poems, ten songs. 1929 (275 copies).
Doctor Donne and Gargantua: the first six cantos. 1930.
Canons of giant art: twenty torsos in heroic landscapes. 1933.
Collected poems, with a long introductory essay by Edith Sitwell. 1936. Includes a few previously uncollected or unpbd poems.
Selected poems, with a preface by O. Sitwell. 1948, New York 1948. Includes previously unpbd poems.
48 poems by Sitwell were pbd in Poetry Rev 58 1967.

Other Works

Southern baroque art: a study of painting, architecture and music in Italy and Spain of the 17th and 18th centuries. 1924, New York 1924, London 1927 (for 1928) (with new preface), 1930 (omitting pt 4, Mexico).
Masters of painting: Antoine Watteau. Foreword by Sitwell 1925.
All summer in a day: an autobiographical fantasia. 1926, New York [1926].
German baroque art. 1927, New York 1928.
All at sea: a social tragedy in three acts for first-class passengers only. By O. and S. Sitwell. 1927, Garden City NY 1928.
A book of towers and other buildings of southern Europe: a series of dry-points engraved by R. Wyndham. 1928 (350 copies). Introd and brief descriptions by Sitwell.
The gothick north: a study of mediaeval life, art and thought. 3 vols 1929–30, 1 vol Boston 1929, London 1938.
Beckford and Beckfordism: an essay. 1930 (265 copies).
Far from my home: stories long and short. 1931.
Spanish baroque art, with buildings in Portugal, Mexico and other colonies. 1931.
Mozart. New York 1932, London 1932.
Liszt. 1934, Boston 1934, London 1955 (rev).
Touching the orient: six sketches. 1934.
A background for Domenico Scarlatti 1685–1757. 1935.
Dance of the quick and the dead: an entertainment of the imagination. 1936, Boston 1937. On art and miscellaneous subjects.
Conversation pieces: a survey of English domestic portraits and their painters. 1936, New York 1937.
Narrative pictures: a survey of English genre and its painters. 1937, New York 1938.
La vie parisienne: a tribute to Offenbach. 1937, Boston 1938.
Roumanian journey. 1938, New York 1938.
Edinburgh. 1938, Boston 1938. With F. Bamford.
German baroque sculpture. 1938.
Palladian England; George Cruikshank. In Trio: dissertations on some aspects of national genius, by O., Edith and S. Sitwell. 1938 (Northcliffe Lectures, Univ of London).

The romantic ballet in the lithographs of the time. 1938. With C. W. Beaumont.
Massine: camera studies by G. Anthony, with an appreciation by Sitwell. 1939.
Old fashioned flowers. 1939. Illustr J. Farleigh.
Mauretania: warrior, man and woman. 1940.
Poltergeists: an introduction and examination, followed by chosen instances. 1940, New York 1959.
Sacred and profane love. 1940. Reflections on art, travel and miscellaneous subjects.
Valse des fleurs: a day in St Petersburg and a ball at the Winter Palace in 1868. 1941.
Primitive scenes and festivals. 1942.
The homing of the winds and other passages in prose. 1942. Selection, with a sketch of the Scarborough Sands, previously unpbd.
Splendours and miseries. 1943. On art, music and miscellaneous subjects.
British architects and craftsmen: a survey of taste, design and style during three centuries, 1600 to 1830. 1945, 1946 (rev), New York 1946, London 1947 (rev), 1948 (for 1949) (rev), 1960 (rev).
The hunters and the hunted. 1947, New York 1948. On art, birds, music and miscellaneous subjects.
The Netherlands: a study of some aspects of art, costume and social life. [1948], 1952 (rev).
Morning, noon and night in London. 1948. On lithographs by A. Concanen.
Theatrical figures in porcelain: German 18th century. 1949 (The Masque, 9).
Spain. 1950, 1951 (rev), 1961 (rev).
The sacred rites of pride. In Diversion: twenty-two authors on the lively arts, ed J. Sutro 1950.
Cupid and the Jacaranda. 1952. On art and miscellaneous subjects.
Truffle hunt. 1953. Mainly articles entitled 'People and memories' rptd, rev, from Sunday Times.
Fine bird books 1700–1900. 1953. With H. Buchanan and J. Fisher.
Selected works. Indianapolis [1953]. Selected mainly from works on art and travel.
Portugal and Madeira. 1954.
Album de Redouté, with twenty-five facsimile colour plates from the edition of 1824, and a new Redouté bibliography. 1954. With R. Madol.
Old garden roses. Pt 1, 1955. With J. Russell.
Selected works. 1955. A different selection from that of 1953, above, though similar in scope.
Denmark. 1956, New York [1956].
Great flower books, 1700–1900: a bibliographical record of two centuries of finely-illustrated flower books. 1956. With W. Blunt.
Arabesque and honeycomb. 1957, New York 1958. Travel in Persia etc.
Malta. 1958. With T. Armstrong-Jones.
Austria. 1959, New York 1959. Text by Sitwell, photographs by T. Schneiders.
Journey to the ends of time: vol 1, Lost in the dark wood. 1959, New York 1959. 'The problems and mysteries of life and death'.
Bridge of the brocade sash: travels and observations in Japan. [1959], Cleveland [1960].
Golden wall and mirador: from England to Peru. [1961], Cleveland [1961] (as Golden wall and mirador: travels and observations in Peru).
Great houses of Europe. Ed Sitwell [1961]. Photographs by E. Smith.
The red chapels of Banteai Srei, and temples in Cambodia, India, Siam and Nepal. [1962], New York 1963 (as Great temples of the east: the wonders of Cambodia, India, Siam and Nepal).
Monks, nuns and monasteries. [1965], New York 1965.
Southern baroque revisited. [1967].
Gothic Europe. 1969.

SYDNEY GOODSIR SMITH
b. 1915

Poetry

Skail wind. Edinburgh 1941.
The wanderer and other poems. Edinburgh 1943.
The deevil's waltz. Glasgow 1946.
Selected poems. Edinburgh 1947.
Under the eildon tree: a poem in XXIV elegies. Edinburgh 1948.
The aipple and the hazel. [Edinburgh] 1951.
So late into the night: fifty lyrics 1944–48. 1952.
Cokkils. Edinburgh 1953 (220 copies).
Omens. Edinburgh 1955 (300 copies).
Orpheus and Eurydice: a dramatic poem. Edinburgh 1955.
Figs and thistles. Edinburgh 1959.
The vision of the prodigal son. Edinburgh 1960.
The Wallace: a triumph in five acts. Edinburgh 1960.
Kynd Kittock's land. Edinburgh 1965.
Fifteen poems and a play. Edinburgh 1969.

Other Works

Carotid Cornucopius, caird o the Cannon Gait and voyeur of the Outluik Touer, by Gude Schir Skidderie Smith-ereens. Glasgow 1947, Edinburgh 1964 (rev and enlarged).
A short introduction to Scottish literature. Edinburgh
Robert Fergusson 1750–74: essays by various hands to commemorate the bicentenary of his birth. Ed Goodsir Smith, Edinburgh 1952.
'Robert Garioch': The masque of Edinburgh. Edinburgh 1954.
Gavin Douglas: a selection from his poetry. Edinburgh 1959.
Robert Burns The merry muses of Caledonia. Ed J. Barke and Goodsir Smith, Edinburgh 1959 (priv ptd), New York 1964, London 1965 (with rearrangement of Burns' text).
Hugh MacDiarmid: a festschrift. Ed K. D. Duval and Goodsir Smith, Edinburgh 1962. Includes MacDiarmid's Three hymns to Lenin by Goodsir Smith.
Bannockburn: the story of the battle and its place in Scotland's history. Ed Goodsir Smith, Stirling [1965]. Includes an extract from his The Wallace.
A choice of Burns's poems and songs. Ed Goodsir Smith. 1966.
Goodsir Smith edited Lines Rev Jan 1955 to Summer 1956.

CHARLES HAMILTON SORLEY
1895–1915

Marlborough and other poems. Cambridge 1916, 1916 (rev and enlarged), 1916 (with illustrations in prose), New York 1916, Cambridge 1919 (rearranged, with notes), New York 1919.
[Sixteen poems]. [1931] (Augustan Books of Poetry). Selection.

Letters

Letters from Germany and from the Army. Ed W. R. Sorley, Cambridge 1916 (priv ptd).
The letters of Sorley, with a chapter of biography [by Janet Sorley]. Ed W. R. Sorley, Cambridge 1919, New York 1919.

WILLIAM SOUTAR
1898–1943

There is a collection of Soutar's mss in the National Library of Scotland.

Collections and Selections

Collected poems, ed with introductory essay by 'Hugh MacDiarmid' (C. M. Grieve) 1948. An incomplete collection, but containing unpbd poems.
Poems in Scots and English, selected by W. R. Aitken. [Edinburgh] 1961. Includes unpbd poems.

§1
Poetry

Gleanings by an undergraduate. Paisley [1923]. Anon, preface signed W.S.
Conflict. 1931.
Seeds in the wind: poems in Scots for children. Edinburgh 1933, London 1943 (rev and enlarged).
The solitary way. Edinburgh 1934.
Brief words: one hundred epigrams. Edinburgh 1935.
Poems in Scots. Edinburgh 1935.
A handful of earth. Edinburgh 1936.
Riddles in Scots. 1937.
In the time of tyrants: poems, with an introductory note on pacifist faith and necessity. Perth 1939 (priv ptd, 100 copies).
But the earth abideth: a verse-sequence. 1943.
The expectant silence. 1944.

Autobiographies

Diaries of a dying man. Ed A. Scott, Edinburgh 1954.

§2

'MacDiarmid, Hugh' (C. M. Grieve). William Soutar. Poetry Scotland 2 1945.
Scott, A. Still lite: William Soutar 1898–1943. Edinburgh 1958.

CHARLES BERNARD SPENCER
1909–63

Aegean islands and other poems. 1946, New York 1948.
George Seferis. The king of Asine and other poems. Tr from the Greek by Spencer, N. Valaoritis, L. Durrell 1948.
The twist in the plotting: twenty five poems. Reading 1960 (150 copies). Rptd in With luck lasting, below.
With luck lasting. 1963, Chester Springs Pa 1965.
Collected poems. 1965.
Spencer edited Oxford Poetry 1930 (with S. Spender) and Oxford Poetry 1931 (with R. Goodman), contributing 3 poems to the former and 4 to the latter. He also edited, with L. Durrell and R. Fedden, the periodical Personal Landscape, 1942–5, and the anthology Personal landscape, 1945, compiled from it.

STEPHEN HAROLD SPENDER
b. 1909

§1

Poetry, Plays and Verse Translations

Nine experiments, by S.H.S.: being poems written at the age of eighteen. Hampstead 1928 (30 copies or less), Cincinnati [1964] (rptd in facs).
Twenty poems. Oxford [1930].
Poems. 1933, 1934 (with omissions and many addns), New York 1934.
Vienna. 1934, New York 1935.
Trial of a judge: a tragedy in five acts. (Group Theatre 18 March 1938). 1938, New York 1938.
García Lorca, F. Poems: with English translation by Spender and J. L. Gili. 1939, New York 1939.

Rilke, R. M. Duino elegies: the German text, with an English translation, introduction and commentary by J. B. Leishman and Spender. 1939, New York 1939.
The still centre. 1939.
Selected poems. 1940.
Ruins and visions. 1942, New York 1942.
Selected poems of Federico García Lorca, translated by J. L. Gili and Spender 1943. Selection from Poems, 1939, with alterations.
Spiritual exercises: to Cecil Day Lewis. 1943 (priv ptd, 125 copies); rptd with alterations in next as Spiritual explorations.
Poems of dedication. 1947, New York 1947.
Returning to Vienna 1947: nine sketches. [New York] 1947 (500 copies); rptd with alterations in next.
The edge of being. 1949, New York [1949].
Le dur désir de durer, by Paul Eluard, with the translation in English verse by S. Spender and Frances Cornford. Philadelphia, London 1950.
Rilke, R. M. The life of the Virgin Mary: the German text with an English translation and introd by Spender. 1951, New York 1951.
Sirmione Peninsula. 1954 (Ariel Poem).
Collected poems 1928–1953. 1955, New York [1955]. Selection with extensive revision.
Inscriptions. 1958. 3 short poems ptd in facs of the author's ms.
Schiller's Mary Stuart, translated and adapted by Spender. (Assembly Hall, Edinburgh 2 Sept 1958; Old Vic 17 Sept 1958). 1959.
Selected poems. New York [1964], London 1965 (with slightly different introd). Includes 3 previously uncollected poems.

Other Works

The destructive element: a study of modern writers and beliefs. 1935, Boston 1935.
The burning cactus. 1936. Stories.
Forward from liberalism. 1937, New York [1937].
Danton's death: a play in four acts by George Büchner. Tr Spender and G. Rees 1939.
The new realism: a discussion. 1939.
Pastor Hall: a play in three acts by E. Toller. 1939, New York [1939] (adds Toller and D. Johnston's Blind man's buff). Tr with H. Hunt.
The backward son. 1940. Novel.
Life and the poet. 1942.
Citizens in war—and after. 1945.
European witness. 1946, New York 1946. Impressions of Germany in 1945.
Poetry since 1939. 1946 (The Arts in Britain).
World within world. 1951, New York 1951. Autobiography.
Five tragedies of sex, by F. Wedekind. Tr F. Fawcett and Spender 1952, New York 1952.
Learning laughter. 1952, New York [1953]. On a visit to Israel.
Shelley. 1952 (Br Council pamphlet).
The creative element: a study of vision, despair and orthodoxy among some modern writers. 1953.
The making of a poem. 1955, New York 1962.
Engaged in writing and The fool and the princess. 1958, New York [1958]. 2 short novels.
The imagination of the modern world. Washington 1962. Lectures.
The struggle of the modern. 1963, Berkeley 1963.
Chaos and control in poetry. Washington 1966. Lecture.
Love–hate relations: a study of Anglo-American sensibilities. 1974.
Eliot. 1975.

Principal Works Edited or with Contributions by Spender

Oxford poetry 1929. Oxford 1929. Ed with L. MacNeice; 4 poems by Spender.

Oxford poetry 1930. Oxford 1930. Ed with B. Spencer; 5 poems by Spender.
Poems for Spain. Ed Spender and J. Lehmann 1939. Anthology; introd by Spender.
Jim Braidy: the story of Britain's firemen. By W. Sansom, J. Gordon, S. Spender. 1943.
Botticelli. 1945 (Faber Gallery), New York 1948.
A choice of English romantic poetry. New York 1947.
La Tour du Pin, P. de. The dedicated life in poetry and the correspondence of Laurent de Cayeux. Tr G. S. Fraser with an introd by Spender 1948.
The god that failed: six studies in communism. Ed R. H. S. Crossman 1950. Ch by Spender.
Europe in photographs [by M. Hürlimann]. Commentary by Spender. 1951.
The writer's dilemma: essays first published in the Times Literary Supplement. Introd by Spender 1961.
The concise encyclopedia of English and American poets and poetry. Ed Spender and D. Hall, New York 1963, 1970 (rev).
Ghika. Paintings, drawings, sculpture. 1964, Boston 1965. Texts by Spender and P. Leigh Fermor.
Lowry, M. Under the volcano. Introd by Spender 1967.
Spender was joint-editor of Encounter *1953–67. He contributed to symposia and other collections of essays principally dealing with contemporary literature.*

§2

Young, G. M. Out of the twilight: into the fog. In his Daylight and champaign, 1937. Rptd review of Forward from liberalism, 1937.
Daiches, D. Poetry of the 1930's: II, W. H. Auden and Spender. In his Poetry and the modern world, 1940.
Isherwood, C. In his Christopher and his kind 1929–39, 1977.

SIR JOHN COLLINGS SQUIRE
1884–1958
Poetry

Poems and Baudelaire flowers. 1909.
The three hills and other poems. 1913.
Christmas hymn. 1914 (priv ptd); rptd in next.
The survival of the fittest and other poems. 1916.
Twelve poems. 1916.
The lily of Malud and other poems. 1917.
Poems: first series. 1918, New York 1919. Selection with new poems.
The birds and other poems. 1919, New York 1920.
The moon. [1920], New York 1920.
Poems: second series. New York 1921, London 1922. Collection 1918–21, with new poems.
The rugger match. 1922 (priv ptd, 250 copies). Rptd from previous.
American poems and others. [1923], New York 1923.
A new song of the Bishop of London and the city churches. 1924; rptd in Poems in one volume, 1926, below.
[Eighteen poems]. [1925] (Augustan Books of Modern Poetry). Selection.
Poems in one volume. 1926. Collection including previously unpbd poems.
A face in candlelight and other poems. 1932.
Poems of two wars. 1940.
The symbol. [1940] (priv ptd, 55 copies).
Selected poems. 1948.
Collected poems; with a preface by J. Betjeman. 1959.

Parodies and Humour

Imaginary speeches and other parodies in prose and verse. 1912.
Steps to Parnassus and other parodies and diversions. 1913.
Tricks of the trade. 1917, New York 1917.
Collected parodies. [1921], New York 1922.

The clown of Stratford. Bristol 1926 (priv ptd, 110 copies). Prose play in one act.

Pick-me-up: 13 drawings in colour by I. Fenwick, with rhymed recipes by A. N. Other [i.e. Squire]. 1933.

Weepings and wailings. 1935. Illustr I. Fenwick.

Other Works

Socialism and art. Introd by W. Crane [1907].

William the Silent. 1912.

The gold tree. 1917. Short stories.

Books in general, by 'Solomon Eagle' [i.e. Squire]. [1918], New York 1919. Essays rptd from New Statesman.

Books in general: second series, by 'Solomon Eagle'. [1920], New York 1920. Rptd from New Statesman.

Life and letters. [1920], New York 1920. Essays rptd from Land & Water.

Books in general: third series, by 'Solomon Eagle'. [1921], New York 1922. Rptd from New Statesman.

Books reviewed, by 'Solomon Eagle'. [1922], New York 1923. Rptd from Observer.

Essays at large, by 'Solomon Eagle'. [1922], New York 1923. Rptd mainly from Outlook.

Essays on poetry. [1923], New York 1924.

The Invalids: a chronicle. 1923 (priv ptd). On a cricket club.

The Grub Street nights entertainments. [1924], New York 1924. Short stories.

Life at the Mermaid. [1927]. Short essays, some previously uncollected.

Berkeley Square: a play in three acts, by J. L. Balderston in collaboration with J. C. Squire. [1928] (French's Acting edn), 1929, New York 1929.

Contemporary American authors, by J. C. Squire and associate critics of the London Mercury. Introd by H. S. Canby, New York 1928.

Robin Hood: a farcical romantic pastoral. 1928. With Joan R. Young.

Pride and prejudice: a play in four acts adapted from Jane Austen's novel. 1929. With E. H. Squire.

Sunday mornings. 1930. Articles rptd from Observer.

Speech at the Lewis Carroll centenary exhibition. [1932].

Outside Eden. 1933, New York 1933. Short stories.

Flowers of speech: being lectures in words and forms in literature. 1935. 2 series of broadcast lectures.

Reflections and memories. 1935. Collection of prefaces and sketches.

Shakespeare as a dramatist. 1935.

The hall of the Institute of Chartered Accountants in England and Wales. 1937.

The honeysuckle and the bee: reminiscences. 1937, New York 1937.

Water-music: or a fortnight of bliss. 1939. On a canoe journey.

Squire founded London Mercury *and edited it 1919–34. He was literary editor of* New Statesman *1913–19 (contributing to it as 'Solomon Eagle') and of* Land and Water *1914–20, and contributed weekly articles to* Observer *1921–31. He was general editor of the following series:* English Men of Letters, *1926–30;* English Heritage Ser (*with Viscount Lee of Fareham*) *1929–36.*

JAMES STEPHENS
1882–1950

The largest holding of literary mss is in the Berg and De-Coursey Fales collections of New York Public Library. Stephens' correspondence with his agent, J. B. Pinker, is in the Houghton Library, Harvard University.

Bibliographies

Bramsbäck, B. Stephens: a literary and bibliographical study. Upsala 1959.

Selections

A Stephens reader, selected with introd by L. Frankenberg, preface by P. Colum. New York 1962, London 1962 (as James Stephens: a selection).

§ 1
Poetry

Where the demons grin. Dundrum 1908 (Cuala Press broadside 6). Rptd in Insurrections.

Insurrections. Dublin 1909, New York 1909.

The lonely god and other poems. New York 1909.

The hill of vision. New York 1912, Dublin 1912, London 1922 (12 poems omitted).

Five new poems. 1913. Ptd by A. T. Stevens for Flying Fame.

Songs from the clay. 1915, New York 1915.

The adventures of Seumas Beg; The rocky road to Dublin. 1915, New York 1915 (as The rocky road to Dublin; The adventures of Seumas Beg. 2 sers of poems.

Green branches. Dublin 1916 (500 copies), New York 1916 (500 copies).

Reincarnations. 1918, New York 1918.

Little things and other poems. Freelands Ky 1924 (priv ptd, 200 copies).

A poetry recital. New York 1925, London 1925.

Collected poems. 1926, New York 1926, London 1954 (with later poems added), New York 1954. Selection, with preface by Stephens.

Optimist. Gaylordsville Conn 1929 (83 copies); rptd in Collected poems, 1954.

The outcast. 1929 (Ariel Poem).

Theme and variations. New York 1930. Included with addns in next.

Strict joy. 1931, New York 1931.

Kings and the moon. 1938, New York 1938.

Other Works

The charwoman's daughter. 1912, Boston [1912] (as Mary, Mary; with introd by P. Colum). Novel.

The crock of gold. 1912, Boston [1912], New York 1942 (introd by C. Fadiman). Novel.

Here are ladies. 1913, New York 1913. Stories with 7 poems, 4 of latter rptd in Collected poems, 1954, above.

The demi-gods. 1914, New York 1914. Novel.

The insurrection in Dublin. Dublin 1916, New York 1916.

The poetical works of Thomas MacDonagh. Ed Stephens, 1916, New York [1917?].

Hunger: a Dublin story by 'James Esse' [i.e. Stephens]. Dublin 1918. Included in Etched in moonlight, 1928, below.

Irish fairy tales. 1920, New York 1920.

Deirdre. 1923, New York 1923. Novel.

In the land of youth. 1924, New York 1924. Stories.

Arthur Griffith, journalist and statesman. Dublin [1924?].

Etched in moonlight. 1928, New York 1928. Stories.

On prose and verse. New York 1928. 2 essays. On prose was originally a preface, unpbd, written for French trn of The charwoman's daughter.

Julia Elizabeth: a comedy in one act. New York 1929.

English romantic poets. Ed Stephens, E. L. Beck, R. H. Snow, New York [1933]. Includes essay by Stephens, The poets and poetry of the nineteenth century. Rptd in next.

Victorian and later English poets. Ed Stephens, E. L. Beck, R. H. Snow, New York [1934].

Garrity, D. (ed). Irish stories and tales. New York 1955. Contains A rhinoceros, some ladies, and a horse, by Stephens. According to Bramsbäck, thought to be pt of an unpbd autobiography; rptd in O'Connor, F. (ed), Modern Irish short stories, Oxford 1957 (WC).

James, Seumas & Jacques: unpublished writings of James Stephens, chosen and ed with introd by L. Frankenberg. New York 1964, London 1964. Mainly broadcast talks.

Stephens contributed numerous articles to Sinn Féin, *to* Irish Rev, *of which he was associate editor, and to* New Ireland Rev.

§ 2

'A.E.' (G. W. Russell). Poetry of Stephens. In his Imaginations and reveries, 1915.

Mercier, V. Stephens: his version of pastoral. Irish Writing no 14 1951.

Colby Lib Quart ser 5 no 9 1961. A tribute to Stephens.

Pyle, H. Stephens: his work and an account of his life. 1965.

JULIAN GUSTAVE SYMONS
b. 1912

Poetry

Confusions about X. [1939].
The second man. 1943.

Other Works

An anthology of war poetry, compiled by Symons. 1942 (Pelican), New York 1942.

The immaterial murder case. 1945, New York 1957. Fiction.

A man called Jones. 1947. Fiction.

Bland beginning: a detective story. 1949, New York 1949.

Selected writings of Samuel Johnson. Ed Symons 1949.

A. J. A. Symons: his life and speculations. 1950.

The thirty-first of February: a mystery novel. 1950, New York [1950] (as The 31st of February).

Charles Dickens. 1951, New York [1951].

Thomas Carlyle: the life and ideas of a prophet. 1952, New York 1952.

The broken penny. 1953, New York [1953]. Fiction.

The narrowing circle. 1954, New York [1954]. Fiction.

Carlyle: selected works, reminiscences and letters. Ed Symons 1955.

Horatio Bottomley: a biography. 1955.

The paper chase. 1956, New York [1957] (as Bogue's fortune). Fiction.

The colour of murder. 1957, New York [1957]. Fiction.

The general strike: a historical portrait. 1957.

The gigantic shadow. [1958], New York [1959] (as The pipe dream). Fiction.

The progress of a crime. 1960, New York [1960]. Fiction.

A reasonable doubt: some criminal cases re-examined. 1960.

The thirties: a dream revolved. 1960.

Murder! Murder! 1961. Stories.

The detective story in Britain. 1962 (Br Council pamphlet).

The killing of Francie Lake. [1962], New York [1962] (as The plain man). Fiction.

Buller's campaign. 1963. On the Boer war.

The end of Solomon Grundy. [1964], New York [1964]. Fiction.

The Belting inheritance. [1965], New York [1965]. Fiction.

England's pride: the story of the Gordon relief expedition. 1965.

Francis Quarles investigates. 1965. Stories.

Crime and detection: an illustrated history from 1840. 1966.

Critical occasions. 1966.

The Julian Symons omnibus. 1967. Introd by Symons. The 31st of February, The progress of a crime, The end of Solomon Grundy.

The man who killed himself. [1967], New York [1967]. Fiction.

The man whose dreams came true. 1968, New York [1968]. Fiction.

Essays and biographies, by A. J. A. Symons. Ed Symons 1969.

Symons *founded and edited* Twentieth-Century Verse, *1937–9.*

PHILIP EDWARD THOMAS
1878–1917

The principal collections of poetical mss are in BM, in Bodley, and in Lockwood Lib, Buffalo. Mss of a few poems, some letters and a substantial number of prose works are in New York Public Library.

§ 1

Poetry

Most of the verse pbd by Thomas in his lifetime appeared in anthologies and under the pseudonym 'Edward Eastaway'.

Beautiful Wales, painted by R. Fowler, described by Thomas. 1905. Includes Eluned, by 'Llewelyn the Bard', i.e. Thomas.

This England: an anthology from her writers. Ed Thomas 1915. Includes 2 poems by 'Edward Eastaway', Haymaking and The manor farm.

Six poems, by 'Edward Eastaway'. Flansham [1916] (100 copies; pbd by Pear Tree Press).

An annual of new poetry. 1917. Includes 18 poems by 'Edward Eastaway', 4 previously pbd in Six poems, [1916], above.

Poems by Edward Thomas—'Edward Eastaway'. 1917, New York 1917. 64 poems, including Cock-crow from Six poems, [1916] above.

Last poems. 1918.

Twelve poets: a miscellany of new verse. 1918. 10 poems by Thomas, simultaneously pbd in Last poems, above.

In memoriam: Edward Thomas. 1919. Contains Up in the wind, previously unpbd.

Collected poems. 1920 (containing Poems, 1917 and Last poems, 1918, and one additional poem; foreword by W. de la Mare), New York 1921, London 1928 (with 4 more poems and a few corrections), 1949 (with additional poem, P.H.T.).

[Twenty-four poems]. [1926] (Augustan Books of Modern Poetry). Selection.

Selected poems. Newtown 1927 (275 copies). Introd by E. Garnett contains excerpts from letters.

Two poems. 1927 (85 copies). The lane and The watchers, previously unpbd; rptd in 1928 edn of Collected poems, above.

The trumpet and other poems. 1940. Selection.

[Thirty-three poems]. 1960 (Pocket Poets). Selection by H. Thomas.

Selected poems. Ed R. Skelton 1962.

Selected poems, selected and introduced by R. S. Thomas. 1964.

The green roads: poems for young readers, chosen and introduced by E. Farjeon. 1965, New York 1965 (as The green roads: poems).

Collected poems. Ed R. G. Thomas, Oxford 1978.

Other Works

The woodland life. Edinburgh 1897. Essays and a naturalist's diary.

Horae solitariae. 1902, New York [1902?]. Essays.

Oxford, painted by J. Fulleylove, described by Thomas. 1903, 1922 (rev).

Rose Acre papers. 1904. Essays. *See also* Rose Acre papers, etc, 1910, below.

Beautiful Wales, painted by R. Fowler, described by Thomas. 1905, 1924 (as Wales). Includes Eluned, a poem by Thomas. *See* Poetry above.

The heart of England. 1906.

The pocket book of poems and songs for the open air. 1907, New York 1929. Anthology.

The book of the open air. Ed Thomas 1907-[8]. 12 pts bound in 2 vols entitled British country life in spring and summer, and British country life in autumn and winter.

British butterflies and other insects. Ed Thomas 1908. Rptd from The book of the open air, 1907-8, above.

Some British birds. Ed Thomas 1908. Rptd from The book of the open air, 1907-8, above.

Richard Jefferies: his life and work. 1909.

The south country. 1909, 1932 (with introd by Helen Thomas and woodcuts by E. F. Daglish).

Rest and unrest. 1910, New York 1910. Essays.

Rose Acre papers, including essays from Horae solitariae. 1910. 2 essays from Rose Acre papers, 1904, 12 from Horae solitariae, 1902.

Feminine influence on the poets. 1910, New York 1911.

Windsor Castle, described by Thomas, pictured by E. W. Haslehurst. 1910.

Celtic stories. Oxford 1911.

The Isle of Wight, described by Thomas, pictured by E. W. Haslehurst. 1911.

Light and twilight. 1911. Essays.

Maurice Maeterlinck. 1911.

The tenth muse. [1911], 1917 (with memoir of Thomas by J. Freeman). Based on ch 8 of Feminine influence on the poets, 1910, above.

Algernon Charles Swinburne: a critical study. 1912, New York 1912.

George Borrow: the man and his books. 1912.

Lafcadio Hearn. 1912, Boston 1912.

Norse tales. Oxford 1912.

The Icknield Way. 1913, New York 1913.

The country. 1913.

The happy-go-lucky Morgans. 1913. Autobiographical novel.

Walter Pater: a critical study. 1913.

In pursuit of spring. 1914. On a bicycle journey from London to the Quantocks.

Four-and-twenty blackbirds. 1915, 1965 (foreword by H. Thomas), New York 1966 (as The complete fairy tales of Edward Thomas). Expansions of proverbial phrases for children.

The life of the Duke of Marlborough. 1915.

This England: an anthology from her writers. 1915. Includes 2 of Thomas's own poems. *See* Poetry, above.

The flowers I love: drawings in colour by K. Cameron with an anthology of flower poems selected by Thomas. [1916], New York 1917.

Keats. 1914 (for 1916).

A literary pilgrim in England. 1917, New York 1917.

Cloud Castle and other papers. 1922, New York [1923]. Essays with foreword by W. H. Hudson.

Chosen essays. Newtown 1926 (350 copies). Selection.

Essays of today and yesterday: Thomas. 1926. Selection.

The last sheaf. 1928. Essays rptd from periodicals; foreword by T. Seccombe.

The childhood of Edward Thomas: a fragment of autobiography. 1938. Preface by J. Thomas.

The friend of the blackbird. Flansham 1938 (100 copies, pbd by Pear Tree Press). First pbd in Nation. Rptd from author's corrected copy.

The prose of Edward Thomas, selected by R. Gant. 1948.

Letters to Gordon Bottomley. Ed R. G. Thomas 1968.

§ 2

Moore, T. S. Soldier poets III. Eng Rev 27 1918; rptd in his Some soldier poets, 1919.

In memoriam Edward Thomas. 1919. Contributions by V. Locke Ellis, J. W. Haines, W. H. Davies, Julian Thomas.

Huxley, A. Edward Thomas. Athenaeum 24 Sept 1920; rptd in his On the margin, 1923.

Murry, J. M. In his Aspects of literature, 1920.

T., H. [Helen Thomas]. As it was. 1926, New York 1927. An account by the poet's widow of her life with him.

—— World without end. 1931. Sequel to As it was. Both books pbd together under this title New York 1931, London 1935 (as As it was: world without end).

Eckert, R. P. Edward Thomas: a biography and a bibliography. 1937.

Moore, J. The life and letters of Edward Thomas. 1939.

Coombes, H. The poetry of Edward Thomas. EC 3 1953.

—— Edward Thomas. 1956.

Day Lewis, C. The poetry of Edward Thomas. Essays by Divers Hands 28 1956.

—— Edward Thomas. Stand 4 1960.

Cooke, W. Edward Thomas: a critical biography. 1970.

RONALD STUART THOMAS
b. 1913

Poetry

The stones of the field. Carmarthen 1946.

An acre of land. Newtown [1952].

The minister. Newtown 1953.

Song at the year's turning: poems 1942–1954. Introd by J. Betjeman 1955. Selection, with 19 new poems.

Poetry for supper. 1958, Chester Springs 1961.

Judgement day. 1960. Single poem in facs of author's ms.

Tares. 1961, Chester Springs 1961.

Penguin modern poets, 1: Lawrence Durrell, Elizabeth Jennings, R. S. Thomas. 1962. Selection, 27 poems.

The bread of truth. 1963, Chester Springs 1963.

Pietà. 1966.

Not that he brought flowers. 1968.

Roy Fuller and R. S. Thomas, selected by E. Owen. 1968.

Other Works

The Batsford book of country verse. Ed Thomas 1961.

The Penguin book of religious verse. Ed Thomas 1963.

Selected poems by Edward Thomas. Ed R. S. Thomas 1964.

Words and the poet. Cardiff 1964. Lecture.

A choice of George Herbert's verse. Ed Thomas 1967.

The mountains. New York [1968] (350 copies). Illustr J. Piper.

TERENCE TILLER
b. 1916

Poems. 1941.

The inward animal. 1943.

Unarm, Eros. 1947.

Reading a medal and other poems. 1957.

Confessio amantis, The lover's shrift [by] John Gower; translated into modern English with an introduction by Tiller. 1963 (Penguin Classics).

Chess treasury of the air. Ed Tiller 1966 (Penguin).

Notes for a myth and other poems. 1968.

RUTHVEN TODD
b. 1914

Poetry

Poets of tomorrow, first selection: representing the work of P. Hewett, H. B. Mallalieu, R. Todd, R. Waller. 1939. 12 poems by Todd.

Ten poems. Edinburgh 1940.

Until now. [1942].

The acreage of the heart. Glasgow 1944 (Poetry Scotland).

The planet in my hand. 1944 (priv ptd), 1946.

A mantelpiece of shells. New York 1955.
Garland for the winter solstice: selected poems. 1961, Boston 1962. Some poems previously uncollected.

Other Works

The laughing mulatto: the story of Alexandre Dumas. [1939].
Over the mountain. 1939, New York 1939. Novel.
Life of William Blake, by Alexander Gilchrist. Ed Todd 1942 (EL).
The lost traveller. 1943. Novel.
Tracks in the snow: studies in English science and art. 1946, New York 1947.
A century of British painters, by Richard and Samuel Redgrave. Ed Todd 1947.
A song to David and other poems by Christopher Smart, selected and with an introduction by Todd 1947.
Poems by William Blake, selected and introduced by Todd. 1949.
Loser's choice. New York 1953. Novel.
The tropical fish book. Greenwich Conn 1953.
Trucks, tractors and trailers. New York 1954. For children.
Blake's Dante plates. 1968.
Todd also wrote stories for children, and wrote detective stories as 'R. T. Campbell'.

HENRY TREECE
1911–66

Poetry

38 poems. [1940].
Towards a personal Armageddon. Prairie City Ill 1941.
Invitation and warning. 1942.
Sailing tomorrow's seas: an anthology of new poems by Treece [et al]. Ed M. Lindsay 1944. 3 poems by Treece.
The black seasons. 1945.
Collected poems. New York 1946.
The haunted garden. 1947.
The exiles. 1952.

Novels

The dark island. 1952, New York 1953.
The rebels. 1953.
The golden strangers. 1956, New York 1957, London 1967 (rev).
The great captains. 1956, New York 1956.
Red queen, white queen. 1958, New York 1958.
The master of Badger's Hall. New York 1959, London 1960 (as A fighting man).
Jason. 1961, New York 1961.
Electra. 1963, New York 1963 (as Amber princess).
Oedipus. 1964, New York 1965 (as The eagle king).
The green man. 1966, New York 1966.
Treece also wrote a large number of novels (and a few historical works) for children.

Other Works

The white horseman: prose and verse of the New Apocalypse. Ed J. F. Hendry and Treece 1941.
Wartime harvest: an anthology of prose and verse. Ed S. Schimanski and Treece 1943. Selected from periodical Kingdom Come.
Air Force poetry. Ed J. Pudney and Treece 1944.
Herbert Read: an introduction to his work by various hands. Ed Treece 1944.
A map of hearts: a collection of short stories. Ed S. Schimanski and Treece [1944].
The crown and the sickle: an anthology, compiled by J. F. Hendry and Treece [1945].
How I see Apocalypse. 1946.
I cannot go hunting tomorrow: short stories. 1946.

Leaves in the storm: a book of diaries. Ed with a running commentary by S. Schimanski and Treece 1947.
Selected poems by A. C. Swinburne. Ed with an introd by Treece 1948.
Dylan Thomas: 'dog among the fairies'. 1949, 1956 (rev), New York 1956.
A new romantic anthology. Ed S. Schimanski and Treece 1949.
Carnival king: a play in three acts. 1955.
The Crusades. 1962, New York 1963.
Treece and Schimanski were editors of Transformation *(4 nos 1943–7), a miscellany of prose, poetry and plays. They were also general editors of* Transformation Library *1946–7. They were joint editors of* Kingdom Come *from 1941.*

ARTHUR DAVID WALEY
1889–1966
A collection of Waley's papers is in the Library of Rutgers University, New Brunswick NJ.

Bibliographies

Johns, F. A. A bibliography of Waley. New Brunswick NJ [1968].

§1
Verse Translations

Chinese poems. 1916 (anon, priv ptd, about 50 copies), [1965] (facs with note by F. A. Johns).
A hundred and seventy Chinese poems. 1918, New York 1919, London 1962 (as One hundred and seventy Chinese poems [with new introd]).
More translations from the Chinese. 1919, New York 1919.
Japanese poetry: the 'Uta'. Oxford 1919. Trn of poems from the Manyōshū, the Kokinshū and other minor collections.
The Nō plays of Japan; with letters by O. Sickert. 1921, New York 1922 (with abridged introd and additional plates). Trns in verse and prose.
The temple and other poems. 1923, New York 1923. With an introductory essay on early Chinese poetry.
Poems from the Chinese. [1927] (Augustan Books of English Poetry). Selection.
The soul of China, by R. Wilhelm. 1928, New York 1928. Text tr by J. H. Reece, poems by Waley.
Select Chinese verses. Shanghai 1934. With H. A. Giles. Selected from A hundred and seventy Chinese poems, 1918, with Chinese text.
The book of songs [the Shih Ching]. 1937, Boston 1937, London 1954 (with new preface, textual changes and additional notes), New York 1960.
Translations from the Chinese. New York 1941. Contents of A hundred and seventy Chinese poems (omitting 5 poems) and More translations from the Chinese, (omitting 1 poem) with some corrections.
Folk songs from China. 1943. With Tzu-jen Ku and I. Gass. Music arranged by R. Redman.
Chinese poems, selected from 170 Chinese poems, More translations from the Chinese, The temple and The book of songs [with a few addns]. 1946, 1961 (rev, with new poems).
The great summons, by Ch'u Yuan. Honolulu 1949 (100 copies). Rptd from previous.
77 poems, [by] Alberto de Lacerda. Tr Lacerda and Waley 1955. Portuguese and English texts.
Ballads and stories from Tun-huang: an anthology. 1960, New York 1960. Verse and prose trn.
Waley did not collect all his trns. See Section B in Johns's Bibliography *(above).*

Prose Translations

The tale of Genji [pt 1], by Lady Murasaki. 1925, Boston 1925. Tr from the Japanese.

The sacred tree [The tale of Genji, pt 2]. 1926, Boston 1926.

A wreath of cloud [The tale of Genji, pt 3]. 1927, Boston 1927.

Blue trousers [The tale of Genji, pt 4]. 1928, Boston 1928.

The pillow-book of Sei Shōnagon [selections]. 1928, Boston 1928. Tr from the Japanese.

The lady who loved insects [attributed to Fujiwara no Kanesuke). 1929. Story, included in The real Tripitaka, 1952 (see Oriental studies, below). Tr from the Japanese.

The travels of an alchemist: the journey of the Taoist Ch'ang-Ch'un recorded by Li Chih-Ch'ang. 1931 (Broadway Travellers). Tr from the Chinese with introd by Waley.

The lady of the boat [The tale of Genji, pt 5]. 1932, Boston 1932.

The bridge of dreams: being the second volume of The lady of the boat [The tale of Genji, pt 6]. 1933, Boston 1933.

The tale of Genji: a novel in six parts, by Lady Murasaki. 1935, 2 vols Boston 1935.

The analects of Confucius, translated and annotated by Waley. 1938, New York 1939.

Monkey, by Wu Ch'êng-ên. 1942, New York 1942 (with introd by Hu Shih). Tr from the Chinese.

Conze, E. (ed). Buddhist texts throughout the ages, newly translated. (Pt 4, Texts from China and Japan, by Waley). Oxford 1954.

Oriental Studies etc

Several of the books below contain prose and verse trns.

The poet Li Po, AD 701–762: a paper read before the China Society. 1919.

An index of Chinese artists represented in the Sub-Department of Oriental Prints and Drawings in the British Museum. 1922.

Zen Buddhism and its relation to art. 1922.

An introduction to the study of Chinese painting. 1923, New York 1923. Includes some verse trns.

The originality of Japanese civilization. 1929, Tokyo 1941 (pamphlet).

A catalogue of paintings recovered from Tun-huang by Sir Aurel Stein. 1931.

The way and its power: a study of the Tao Tê Ching and its place in Chinese thought. 1934. With trn of the text.

Three ways of thought in ancient China. 1939, New York 1954 (slightly abridged). On Chuang Tzu, Mencius and the Realist school with extracts from their works.

In the gallery. Zurich 1949 (priv ptd). Story: rptd in The secret history of the Mongols, 1963, below.

The life and times of Po Chü-i 772–846 AD. 1949.

The poetry and career of Li Po 701–762 AD. 1950.

The real Tripitaka and other pieces. 1952, New York 1952.

The nine songs: a study of shamanism in ancient China. 1955, New York 1956. With trns of the poems.

Yuan Mei: eighteenth-century Chinese poet. 1956, New York 1957.

The Opium War through Chinese eyes. 1958, New York 1958.

The secret history of the Mongols and other pieces. 1963, New York 1964. Includes trn of 50 poems from the Manyōshū and Ryōjin Hishō, not previously collected.

Hatto, A. T. (ed). Eos: an enquiry into the theme of lovers' meetings and partings at dawn in poetry. Hague 1965. Chinese and Japanese sections by Waley.

Waley contributed introds to trns from Chinese and to other works, including The works of Ronald Firbank, *1929.*

He edited Year book of oriental art and culture, *1924–5.*

VERNON PHILLIPS WATKINS
1906–67

Most of Watkins' mss are in the BM.

Poetry

Ballad of the Mari Lwyd and other poems. 1941.

The lamp and the veil. 1945.

The lady with the unicorn. 1948.

Selected poems. Norfolk Conn 1948. From first 2 works, above.

The death bell: poems and ballads. 1954, Norfok Conn 1954.

Heinrich Heine, The North Sea, translated by Watkins. 1955.

Cypress and acacia. 1959, Norfolk Conn [1959].

Affinities. 1962, Norfolk Conn 1963.

Selected poems 1930–60. 1967.

Fidelities. 1968.

Kathleen Raine and Vernon Watkins: selected by E. Owen. 1968 (Pergamon Poets).

I that was born in Wales: a new selection from the poems. Ed G. Watkins and R. Pryor, Cardiff 1976.

Selected verse translations. Ed M. Hamburger 1977.

Other Works

Dylan Thomas. Letters to Vernon Watkins. Ed with an introd by Watkins 1957, New York 1957.

Landmarks and voyages: poetry supplement [pbd Poetry Book Soc] Christmas 1957. Ed Watkins 1957.

Richard Hughes. A high wind in Jamaica, with a foreword by Watkins. New York 1961.

DOROTHY VIOLET WELLESLEY, née ASHTON

1889–1956

Early poems. By 'M.A.' [i.e. D. Wellesley]. 1913.

Poems. 1920.

Pride and other poems. 1923.

Lost lane. 1925.

Genesis: an impression. 1926.

Matrix. 1928.

Jupiter and the nun. 1932.

Poems of ten years 1924–1934. 1934. Selection with revisions. Includes previously unpbd poems.

Selections from the poems of Dorothy Wellesley. 1936, New York 1936. Introd by W. B. Yeats; includes a new poem, Fire.

Lost planet and other poems. 1942.

The poets and other poems. Tunbridge Wells 1943.

Desert wells. 1946.

Selected poems. 1949.

Rhymes for middle years. 1954.

Early light: the collected poems of Dorothy Wellesley. 1955. Includes previously unpbd poems.

Letters on poetry from W. B. Yeats to Dorothy Wellesley. 1940, 1964 (with introd by Kathleen Raine). Ed Dorothy Wellesley.

HUMBERT WOLFE
1885–1940

Poetry, Verse Plays and Verse Translations

London sonnets. Oxford 1920.

Shylock reasons with Mr Chesterton, and other poems. Oxford 1920.

Kensington Gardens. 1924, New York [1927].

Lampoons. 1925.

The unknown goddess. 1925, New York [1925] (with 2 new poems), London 1927.

Humoresque. 1926.

News of the devil. 1926, New York 1926.

[Thirty-four poems.] [1926] (Augustan Books of Modern Poetry). Selection.

Cursory rhymes. 1927, Garden City NY 1928.

Others abide. 1927. Verse trns from the Greek Anthology.

Requiem. 1927, New York [1927].

Veni Creator! 1927 (priv ptd); rptd in The uncelestial city, 1930, below.

The blind rose. 1928, Garden City NY 1929.

The silver cat and other poems. New York, London 1928.

Troy. [1928] (Ariel Poem).

Early poems. Oxford 1930, New York 1931. Contains London sonnets and Shylock reasons with Mr Chesterton. With a preface by Wolfe.

Homage to Meleager. New York 1930 (464 signed copies). Verse trns from Greek.

Portrait of Heine. 1930, 1935 (as Selected lyrics of Heine). Trns by Wolfe.

The uncelestial city. 1930, New York 1930.

Snow. 1931.

ABC of the theatre. [1932].

Reverie of policeman: a ballet in three acts. 1933.

Sonnets pour Hélène, by Pierre de Ronsard, with English renderings by Wolfe. 1934, New York 1934.

The fourth of August: a sonnet sequence. 1935.

Stings and wings. 1935.

X at Oberammergau: a poem. 1935.

Cyrano de Bergerac: a translation of Rostand's play. [1937].

Don J. Ewan. 1937.

The silent knight: a romantic comedy in three acts from the Hungarian of Eugene Heltai. 1937.

Out of great tribulation. 1939.

Kensington Gardens in war-time. 1940.

See also A winter miscellany, 1930, *below.*

Other Works

Circular saws. 1923. Short stories.

Labour supply and regulation. Oxford 1923 (Economic and social history of the World War: British ser).

The craft of verse: Oxford poetry essay. New York 1928.

Dialogues and monologues. 1928, New York 1929. On literary topics.

Notes on English verse satire. 1929, New York [1929].

The wall of weeping, by Edmond Fleg. Tr by Wolfe 1929.

Tennyson. 1930.

A winter miscellany [in prose and verse], edited and compiled by Wolfe, to which are added original poems by the editor. 1930, New York 1930.

George Moore. 1931, New York 1932, London 1933 (rev).

Signpost to poetry: an introduction to the study of verse. 1931.

The life of Percy Bysshe Shelley as comprised in The life of Shelley by Thomas Jefferson Hogg, The recollections of Shelley and Byron by Edward John Trelawny, Memoirs of Shelley by Thomas Love Peacock. Ed Wolfe 2 vols 1933.

Now a stranger. 1933. Autobiography.

Romantic and unromantic poetry. Bristol [1933] (Arthur Skemp memorial lecture).

Portraits by inference. 1934. Reminiscences and sketches of contemporaries.

Ronsard and French romantic poetry: the Zaharoff lecture for 1934. Oxford 1935.

P.L.M.: peoples, landfalls, mountains. 1936. Travel in France.

Personalities: a selection from the writings of A. A. Baumann. Ed Wolfe 1936, New York 1936.

The pilgrim's way. 1936. Anthology, chiefly of poetry, selected by Wolfe.

The upward anguish. 1938. Autobiography. Contains The old man of Königsberg, or Kant and re-Kant: a Greats Week pantomime, in verse written in part by Wolfe and pbd separately.

Wolfe edited the second ser of Augustan Books of English Poetry.

ANDREW JOHN YOUNG
1885–1971

§1

Young's first 8 books are described on the title-pages as being 'by A. J. Young'.

Songs of night. [1910].

Cecil Barclay Simpson: a memorial by two friends. Edinburgh 1918. With D. Baillie. Memorial verses by Young.

Boaz and Ruth and other poems. 1920.

The death of Eli and other poems. 1921.

Thirty-one poems. 1922.

The adversary [and Rizpah]. 1923. 2 short verse plays.

The bird-cage. 1926.

The cuckoo clock. [1928].

The new shepherd. 1931.

Winter harvest. 1933.

The white blackbird. 1935.

Collected poems. 1936. Contains Winter harvest and The white blackbird and 17 new poems.

Nicodemus: a mystery, with incidental music by Imogen Holst. 1937. Rptd in Collected poems, 1950, below.

Speak to the earth. 1939.

The green man. 1947.

Collected poems. 1950. Selection, with revisions.

Into Hades. 1952. Rev and rptd in Out of the world and back.

Out of the world and back: Into Hades and A traveller in time. 1958. Two poems.

Quiet as moss: thirty-six poems chosen by L. Clark. 1959, Philadelphia 1963. Selection.

Collected poems, arranged with a bibliographical note by L. Clark. 1960. Collected poems 1950, with 22 addns all previously pbd.

Burning as light: thirty-seven poems chosen by L. Clark. 1967.

The new Poly-Olbion: topographical excursions with an introductory account of the poet's early days. 1967.

Complete poems. Ed L. Clark 1974.

§2

Clark, L. (ed). Andrew Young, prospect of a poet: essays and tributes by fourteen writers. 1957.

Clark, L. Andrew Young. 1964 (Br Council pamphlet). With R. G. Thomas on R. S. Thomas.

3. THE NOVEL

I. HISTORIES AND STUDIES

James, H. The younger generation. TLS 19 March, 2 April 1914. Rptd, extended and rev, as The new novel, in his Notes on novelists, 1914.
—— James and H. G. Wells: a record of their friendship, their debate on the art of fiction, and their quarrel. Ed L. Edel and G. N. Ray 1958.
Woolf, V. Modern novels. TLS 10 April 1919; rptd as Modern fiction, in her Common reader, 1925, and in Modern British fiction, ed M. Schorer 1961, below.
—— Character in fiction. Criterion 2 1924; rptd as Mr Bennett and Mrs Brown, 1924 (as pamphlet), and in her Captain's death bed, 1950.
—— Is fiction an art? New York Herald Tribune 16 Oct 1927. Rptd, rev, as The art of fiction, in her The moment and other essays, 1947.
—— Contemporary writers. Ed J. Guiguet 1965. Uncollected essays from TLS.
Walpole, H. The English novel: some notes on its evolution. Cambridge 1925.
—— et al. Tendencies of the modern novel. 1934.
Muir, E. Transition: essays on contemporary literature. 1926. On Joyce, Lawrence, V. Woolf, S. Hudson, Huxley, Contemporary fiction etc.
—— The structure of the novel. 1928.
—— The decline of the novel. In his Essays on literature and society, 1949, 1965 (rev).
'Mansfield, Katherine' (K. M. Beauchamp). Novels and novelists. Ed J. M. Murry 1930.
Beach, J. W. The twentieth-century novel: studies in technique. New York 1932.
Lawrence, D. H. Why the novel matters. In Phoenix: the posthumous papers, ed. E. D. McDonald 1936.
Connolly, C. The condemned playground: essays 1927–44. 1945.
—— Previous convictions: selected writings of a decade. 1963. On Lawrence, Joyce, Orwell et al.

'Orwell, George' (E. A. Blair). Critical essays. 1946, New York (as Dickens, Dali and others). On Wells, Koestler, Wodehouse etc.
Savage, D. S. The withered branch: six studies in the modern novel. 1950.
Greene, G. The lost childhood and other essays. 1951. Pt 2: Novels and novelists.
Newby, P. H. The novel 1945–50. 1951 (Br Council pamphlet).
Mayoux, J.-J. L'inconscient et la vie intérieure dans le roman anglais 1905–40. Nancy 1952.
Edel, L. The psychological novel 1900–50. Philadelphia 1955, New York 1964 (rev as The modern psychological novel).
Zabel, M. D. Craft and character: texts, method, and vocation in modern fiction. New York 1957. On Conrad, Forster, Ford, G. Greene.
Aiken, C. A reviewer's ABC. New York 1958. On Lawrence, W. Lewis, K. Mansfield.
Writers at work: the Paris Review interviews. Ser 1, ed M. Cowley, New York 1958. On Forster, Cary, O'Connor. Ser 3, ed A. Kazin, New York 1967. On Waugh.
Kermode, J. F. Puzzles and epiphanies: essays and reviews 1958–61. 1962. On Forster, Joyce, Waugh, Greene et al.
—— The house of fiction: interviews with seven English novelists. Partisan Rev 30 1963.
Stewart, J. I. M. Eight modern writers. Oxford 1963 (OHEL). On Conrad, Joyce, Lawrence.
Davie, D. (ed). Russian literature and modern English fiction. Chicago 1965.
Realism, reality and the novel. Novel 2 1969. A symposium.
Bergonzi, B. The situation of the novel. 1970, 1979 (with addns).
Bradbury, M. (ed). The novel today. 1977.

II. INDIVIDUAL NOVELISTS

JOSEPH CONRAD
(JÓZEF TEODOR KONRAD
NAŁECZ KORZENIOWSKI)
1857–1924

The principal collections are at the A.S.W. Rosenbach Foundation, Philadelphia (the bulk of the Conrad mss), Yale Univ (the Keating Conrad Memorial Library), BM (T. J. Wise's Ashley Library). Harvard Univ, Lilly Library Indiana Univ, and the New York Public Library also have collections.

Bibliographies

Wise, T. J. A bibliography of the writings of Conrad 1895–1920. 1920 (priv ptd), 1921 (priv ptd, rev and enlarged), 1964.
—— A Conrad library: a catalogue of printed books, manuscripts and autograph letters. 1928 (priv ptd).
Lohf, K. A. and E. P. Sheehy. Joseph Conrad at midcentury: editions and studies 1895–1955. Minneapolis 1957. Includes trns.

Ehrsam, T. G. A bibliography of Conrad. Metuchen NJ 1969. Primary and secondary material; includes trns.

Collections

Works. Garden City NY 1920–5 (Sun-dial edn, limited to 735 sets), London 1923–8 (Uniform edn). The texts of those vols issued before Conrad's death were rev.
Works. 20 vols 1921–7 (Heinemann, limited to 780 sets). Contents same as the Sun-dial edn, but excludes Tales of hearsay and Last essays. Possibly the last state of the texts rev by Conrad for these collected edns of his works.
Notes on my books. Garden City NY 1921, London 1921, 1937 (ed E. Garnett, as Conrad's prefaces to his works). Reprints prefaces from Sun-dial edn.
Complete short stories. [1933].
Three plays: Laughing Anne, One day more and The secret agent. 1934.

Selections

The Conrad reader. Ed A. J. Hoppé 1946, 1947 (as The Conrad companion).

The portable Conrad. Ed M. D. Zabel, New York 1947, 1976 (rev F. R. Hall).

§1

Prose Fiction

Almayer's folly: a story of an eastern river. 1895, New York 1895.

An outcast of the islands. 1896, New York 1896 (bowdlerized).

The nigger of the 'Narcissus': a tale of the sea. 1897 (7 copies for copyright purposes, with subtitle 'a tale of the forecastle') New York 1897 (as The children of the sea), London 1898 (as The nigger of the 'Narcissus': a tale of the sea), Garden City NY 1914 (with the preface, first pbd in New Rev Dec 1897 and previously suppressed, and with an introd by Conrad 'To my readers in America'), New York 1951 (introd by M. D. Zabel), [1965] (introd by H. M. Jones). First pbd in New Rev Aug–Dec 1897. The preface was ptd separately at Hythe, 1902 (100 copies) and pbd at Garden City NY 1914 (as Joseph Conrad on the art of writing, with 'to my readers in America').

Tales of unrest. New York 1898, London 1898. Karain: a memory; The idiots; An outpost of progress; The return; The lagoon.

Lord Jim: a tale. Edinburgh 1900, New York 1900 (as Lord Jim: a romance), London 1917 (as Lord Jim: a tale; with Author's note), New York 1957 (ed R. D. Heilman), 1958 (introd by W. F. Wright), Boston 1958 (introd by M. D. Zabel). First pbd in Blackwood's Mag Oct 1899–Nov 1900 (as Lord Jim: a sketch).

The inheritors: an extravagant story. New York 1901, London 1901. With F. M. Hueffer [Ford].

Youth: a narrative, and two other stories. Edinburgh 1902, New York 1903, London 1917 (with Author's note); ed M. D. Zabel, Garden City NY 1959. Youth; Heart of darkness; The end of the tether.

Typhoon. New York 1902, London 1912. First pbd in Pall Mall Mag Jan–March 1902 and in Critic (New York) Feb–May 1902.

Typhoon and other stories. 1903, Garden City NY 1923. Typhoon; Amy Foster; Falk: a reminiscence; Tomorrow. The latter 3 stories were pbd in New York 1903 as Falk; Amy Foster; Tomorrow: three stories.

Romance: a novel. 1903, New York 1904. With F. M. Hueffer [Ford]. See Hueffer's note in The nature of a crime, below, for details of the collaboration.

Nostromo: a tale of the seaboard. 1904, New York 1904, London 1918 (with Author's note), New York 1951 (introd by R. P. Warren, rptd in his Selected essays, New York 1958 (Modern Library), 1960 (foreword by F. R. Leavis), 1961 (introd by D. Van Ghent). First pbd in T.P.'s Weekly 29 Jan–7 Oct 1904.

The secret agent: a simple tale. 1907, New York 1907. First pbd (shorter version) in Ridgway's (New York) 6 Oct 1906–12 Jan 1907.

A set of six. 1908, Garden City NY 1915. Gaspar Ruiz; The informer; The brute; An anarchist; The duel (pbd separately New York 1908 as The point of honor: a military tale); Il Conde. Gaspar Ruiz rptd separately with Youth, and with Author's note, 1920.

Under western eyes: a novel. 1911, New York 1911, 1951 (introd by M. D. Zabel, rptd, rev, as Conrad: the threat to the West, in his Craft and character 1957, §2, below), 1963 (rev and expanded introd by Zabel, rptd in Mudrick, [1966], §2, below). First pbd in Eng Rev and North Amer Rev Dec 1910–Oct 1911.

'Twixt land and sea: tales. 1912, New York 1912. A smile of fortune; The secret sharer; Freya of the Seven Isles.

Chance: a tale in two parts. Toronto [1913], London 1913, New York 1914. First pbd in New York Herald 21 Jan–30 June 1912.

Victory: an island tale. Garden City NY 1915, London 1915 (with Author's note). First pbd in Munsey's Mag Feb 1915 and Star (London) 24 Aug–9 Nov 1915. A second Author's note, written 1920, appears in the collected edns of Conrad's Works, above.

Within the tides: tales. 1915, Garden City NY 1916. The planter of Malata; The partner; The inn of the two witches; Because of the dollars.

The shadow-line: a confession. 1917, Garden City NY 1917. First pbd in Eng Rev Sept 1916–March 1917.

The arrow of gold: a story between two notes. Garden City NY 1919, London 1919 (with corrections). First pbd Lloyd's Mag Dec 1918–Feb 1920.

The tale. 1919 (priv ptd by C. K. Shorter, 25 copies); rptd in Tales of hearsay, 1925 below.

Prince Roman. 1920 (priv ptd for Conrad, 25 copies); rptd in Tales of hearsay, 1925, below.

The warrior's soul. 1920 (priv ptd for Conrad, 25 copies); rptd in Tales of hearsay, 1925, below.

The rescue: a romance of the shallows. Garden City NY 1920, London 1920. First pbd in Land and Water 30 Jan–31 July 1919 and in Romance (New York) Nov 1919–May 1920.

The black mate: a story. Edinburgh 1922 (priv ptd, 50 copies); rptd in Tales of hearsay, 1925, below.

The rover. Garden City NY 1923, London 1923.

The nature of a crime. 1924, Garden City NY 1924. With F. M. Hueffer (US edn gives 'F. M. Ford'). Prefaces by Conrad and Hueffer, and appendix, A note on Romance, by Hueffer. First pbd in Eng Rev April–May 1909 as by 'Ignatz von Aschendorf'.

Suspense: a Napoleonic novel. Garden City NY 1925, London 1925 (introd by R. Curle). First pbd in Hutchinson's Mag Feb–Aug 1925 and in Saturday Rev of Lit 27 June–12 Aug 1925.

Tales of hearsay. With preface by R. B. Cunninghame Graham. 1925, Garden City NY 1925. The warrior's soul; Prince Roman; The tale; The black mate.

The sisters. New York 1928. Unfinished; with introd by F. M. Ford.

Other Works

The mirror of the sea: memories and impressions. 1906, New York 1906. The sections called The 'Tremolino' pbd separately New York 1942.

A personal record. 1912 (as Some reminiscences), New York 1912 (as A personal record), London 1916, 1919 (with Author's note). First pbd in Eng Rev Dec 1908 to June 1909 (as Some reminiscences). The Dec 1908 instalment was pbd as a pamphlet in a limited edn, New York 1908, for copyright purposes.

Joseph Conrad on the art of writing. Garden City NY 1914. See The nigger of the 'Narcissus', 1897, Prose Fiction, above.

One day more: a play in one act. (Stage Society 25 June 1905; Birmingham Repertory Th 12 Sept 1918). 1917 (priv ptd by C. K. Shorter, 25 copies), 1919, Garden City NY 1920. Dramatization of Tomorrow, from Typhoon and other stories.

The first news. 1918 (priv ptd by C. K. Shorter, 25 copies). On Poland in 1914. This and all the following articles, essays etc (except London's river) priv ptd as pamphlets 1918–20, were rptd in Notes on life and letters, 1921, below.

'Well done!' 1918 (priv ptd for Shorter, 25 copies). On British seamen.

Anatole France. 1919 (priv ptd for T. J. Wise, 25 copies).

Autocracy and war. 1919 (priv ptd for Wise, 25 copies).

Guy de Maupassant. 1919 (priv ptd for Wise, 25 copies).

Henry James: an appreciation. 1919 (priv ptd for Wise, 25 copies).

The lesson of the collision: a monograph upon the loss of the Empress of Ireland. 1919 (priv ptd for Wise, 25 copies).

London's river. 1919 (priv ptd for Shorter, 25 copies). Rptd from The mirror of the sea.

My return to Cracow. 1919 (priv ptd for Wise, 25 copies).

The North Sea on the eve of war. 1919 (priv ptd for Wise, 25 copies).

The Polish question: a note on the joint protectorate of the western powers and Russia. 1919 (priv ptd by Shorter, 25 copies).

The shock of war: through Germany to Cracow. 1919 (priv ptd for Wise, 25 copies).

Some aspects of the admirable inquiry into the loss of the Titanic. 1919 (priv ptd for Wise, 25 copies).

Some reflections, seamanlike and otherwise, on the loss of the Titanic. 1919 (priv ptd for Wise, 25 copies).

Tales of the sea. 1919 (priv ptd for Wise, 25 copies). On Marryat.

To Poland in war-time: a journey into the east. 1919 (priv ptd for Wise, 25 copies).

Tradition. 1919 (priv ptd for Wise, 25 copies).

Alphonse Daudet. 1920 (priv ptd for Wise, 25 copies).

Anatole France: 'L'île des pingouins'. 1920 (priv ptd for Wise, 25 copies).

Books. 1920 (priv ptd for Wise, 25 copies).

Confidence. 1920 (priv ptd for Wise, 25 copies).

An observer in Malay. 1920 (priv ptd for Wise, 25 copies). Rptd review of Studies in brown humanity, by H. Clifford.

Notes on life and letters. 1921, Garden City NY 1921. With Author's note.

Notes on my books. 1921. See Collections, above.

The secret agent: drama in four acts. (Ambassadors 2 Nov 1922). Canterbury 1921 (priv ptd for Conrad, 52 copies), London 1923 (priv ptd, as The secret agent: a drama in three acts).

Simple cooking precepts for a little house by Jessie Conrad, with preface by Conrad. 1921 (priv ptd, 100 copies). The preface only. This and the following articles, essays etc priv ptd as pamphlets, were rptd in Last essays, 1926, below. This item was rptd as Cookery.

The Dover patrol: a tribute. Canterbury 1922 (priv ptd for Wise, 75 copies).

John Galsworthy: an appreciation. Canterbury 1922 (priv ptd for Wise, 75 copies).

Travel: a preface to Into the East, by R. Curle. 1922 (priv ptd for Curle, 20 copies).

Laughing Anne: a play. 1923. Dramatization of Because of the dollars, from Within the tides.

The Torrens: a personal tribute. 1923 (priv ptd for Wise, 20 copies).

Geography and some explorers. 1924 (priv ptd for Wise, 30 copies).

Laughing Anne and One day more: two plays, with an introduction by John Galsworthy. 1924, Garden City NY 1925. Laughing Anne first pbd 1923, One day more 1917.

'Admiralty paper', written by Joseph Conrad. 1925 (priv ptd for Jerome Kern, 93 copies); rptd in Last essays as The unlighted coast.

Notes by Joseph Conrad written in a set of his first editions in the possession of Richard Curle, with an introduction and explanatory comments [by Curle]. 1925 (priv ptd, 100 copies).

Joseph Conrad's diary of his journey up the valley of the Congo in 1890, with introd and notes by R. Curle. 1926 (priv ptd, 100 copies).

Last essays. Introd by Curle. 1926, Garden City NY 1926.

Winawer, B. The book of Job: a satirical comedy. Tr Conrad 1931.

Letters

Five letters by Conrad written to Edward Noble in 1895. 1925 (priv ptd, 100 copies). With foreword by Noble.

Symons, A. Notes on Conrad, with some unpublished letters. 1925.

Jean-Aubry, G. Conrad: life and letters. 2 vols Garden City NY 1927, London 1927. Contains a selection of about 600 letters, including some translated.

Conrad's letters to his wife. 1927 (priv ptd, 220 copies).

Letters from Conrad 1895–1924. Ed E. Garnett, Indianapolis 1928, London 1928. Contains about 300 letters, mostly not included in Jean-Aubry's Life and letters.

Conrad to a friend: 150 selected letters from Conrad to Richard Curle. Ed Curle 1928, New York 1928 (as Letters: Conrad to Richard Curle), Garden City NY 1928 (as Conrad to a friend). The New York edn has more complete versions.

Joseph Conrad's letters to R. B. Cunninghame Graham. Ed C. T. Watts 1969.

§2

See Conrad: the critical heritage, ed N. Sherry 1973.

Curle, R. H. P. Conrad: a study. 1914.

—— Conrad and his characters: a study of six novels. 1957.

Walpole, H. Joseph Conrad. [1916], 1924 (rev).

Mencken, H. L. In his A book of prefaces, New York 1918. Later printings have revisions.

—— In his Prejudices: fifth series, New York 1926.

Ford, F. M. (formerly Hueffer). To Joseph Conrad. In his English novel from the earliest days to the death of Conrad, Philadelphia 1919.

—— Conrad: a personal remembrance. 1924.

Conrad [Korzeniowski], Jessie. Personal recollections of Conrad. 1924 (priv ptd, 100 copies). Incorporated, rev, in next.

—— Conrad as I knew him. 1926.

—— Conrad and his circle. 1935, Port Washington 1964.

Jean-Aubry, G. Conrad au Congo. Paris 1925; tr 1926.

—— Conrad: life and letters. 2 vols Garden City NY 1927.

—— Vie de Conrad. Paris 1947 (tr as The sea dreamer: a definitive biography of Conrad, 1957).

Symons, A. Notes on Conrad, with some unpublished letters. 1925. Pamphlet.

Crankshaw, E. Conrad: some aspects of the art of the novel. 1936.

Forster, E. M. In his Abinger harvest, 1936.

Gordan, J. D. Conrad: the making of a novelist. Cambridge Mass 1940.

Bradbrook, M. C. Conrad: Poland's English genius. Cambridge 1941.

Guerard, A. J. Joseph Conrad. Norfolk Conn 1947.

—— Conrad the novelist. Cambridge Mass 1958.

Leavis, F. R. The great tradition: George Eliot, James, Conrad. 1948.

Stallman, R. W. Life, art and The secret sharer. In Forms of modern fiction, ed W. V. O'Connor, Minneapolis 1948.

—— (ed). The art of Conrad: a critical symposium. East Lansing 1960.

Greene, G. Remembering Mr Jones; The domestic background. In his The lost childhood and other essays, 1951.

Zabel, M. D. In his Craft and character: texts, method and vocation in modern fiction, New York 1957.

Joseph Conrad Korzeniowski: essays and studies. Warsaw 1958.

Baines, J. Conrad: a critical biography. 1960.

Krzyżanowski, L. (ed). Joseph Conrad: centennial essays. New York 1960.

Karl, F. R. A reader's guide to Conrad. New York 1960.

Stewart, J. I. M. Conrad. In his Eight modern writers, Oxford 1963 (OHEL).

—— Joseph Conrad. 1968.

Tanner, T. Conrad: Lord Jim. 1963.

Watt, I. Conrad: alienation and commitment. In The English mind: studies in the English moralists presented to Basil Willey, Cambridge 1964.

Sherry, N. Conrad's Eastern world. Cambridge 1966; Conrad's Western world, Cambridge 1971.

—— Conrad and his world. 1972.

—— (ed.) Conrad: a commemoration. 1976.

HERBERT GEORGE WELLS
1866–1946

The most important collection of Wells papers is in the Wells Archive at the Univ of Illinois at Urbana.

Bibliographies

Wells, G. H. A bibliography of the works of Wells 1893–1925, with some notes and comments. 1925. Enlarged and rev as The works of Wells 1887–1925: a bibliography, dictionary and subject-index, 1926.

H. G. Wells: a comprehensive bibliography compiled by the H. G. Wells Society. 1966, 1968 (rev).

Collections and Selections

Works: Atlantic edition. 28 vols 1924–7. Texts rev by Wells, special preface by Wells to each vol, also general introd to set.

Works: Essex edition. 24 vols 1926–7.

The door in the wall, and other stories. New York 1911, London 1915 (60 copies from American sheets).

Short stories. 1927, Garden City NY 1929, London 1966 (as The complete short stories).

The scientific romances. Introd by Wells 1933.

Stories of men and women in love. Preface by Wells [1933].

Seven famous novels. Preface by Wells, New York 1934. Contents as in The scientific romances (1933), except for omission of Men like gods.

§1

Prose Fiction

The chronic argonauts. Science Schools Jnl April–June 1888. Story, rptd in Bergonzi, The early Wells, 1961.

Select conversations with an uncle, now extinct, and two other reminiscences. 1895, New York 1895. 12 'conversations' and 2 short stories, A misunderstood artist, and The man with a nose.

The time machine: an invention. 1895, New York 1895 (as by 'H. S. Wells'), [1895] (as by H. G. Wells), 1935 (with preface by Wells). Based on The chronic argonauts.

The wonderful visit. 1895, New York 1895. Dramatized by Wells and St John Ervine for production at St Martin's Theatre, London 10 Feb 1921.

The stolen bacillus, and other incidents. 1895.

The island of Dr Moreau. 1896, New York 1896.

The wheels of chance: a holiday adventure. 1896, New York 1896 (as The wheels of chance: a bicycling idyll). A dramatization, Hoopdriver's holiday, made by Wells 1903–4 was pbd (ed M. Timko) in Eng Lit in Transition 7 1964.

The Plattner story, and others. 1897.

The invisible man: a grotesque romance. 1897, New York 1897 (with epilogue), London 1900, 1953 (with introd by F. Wells), New York 1967 (introd by B. Bergonzi).

Thirty strange stories. New York 1897.

The war of the worlds. 1898, New York 1898.

When the sleeper wakes: a story of the years to come. 1899, New York 1899, London [1910] (rev, with preface by Wells, as The sleeper awakes), 1954 (with introd by M. Belgion).

Tales of space and time. 1900 [1899], New York 1899.

Love and Mr Lewisham. 1900, New York 1900, London 1954 (with introd by F. Wells).

The first men in the moon. 1901, Indianapolis 1901, London 1954 (with introd by F. Wells).

The sea lady: a tissue of moonshine. 1902, New York 1902 (as The sea lady).

Twelve stories and a dream. 1903, New York 1905.

The food of the gods, and how it came to earth. 1904, New York 1904, London 1955 (with introd by R. Seth).

A modern utopia. 1905, New York 1905, Lincoln Nebraska 1967 (with introd by M. R. Hillegas).

Kipps: the story of a simple soul. 1905, New York 1905, London 1952 (with introd by E. Shanks).

In the days of the comet. 1906, New York 1906, London 1954 (with introd by F. Wells).

The war in the air, and particularly how Mr Bert Smallways fared while it lasted. 1908, New York 1908.

Tono-Bungay. New York 1908, London 1909, 1953 (with introd by C. E. M. Joad), Boston 1966 (ed B. Bergonzi).

Ann Veronica: a modern love story. 1909, New York 1909.

The history of Mr Polly. 1910, New York 1910, London 1953 (ed F. Wells), Boston 1960 (ed G. N. Ray).

The new Machiavelli. New York 1910, London 1911.

The country of the blind, and other stories. [1911].

Marriage. 1912, New York 1912.

The passionate friends. 1913, New York 1913, London 1922 (abridged).

The world set free: a story of mankind. 1914, New York 1914, London 1956 (with introd by R. Calder).

The wife of Sir Isaac Harman. 1914, New York 1914.

Boon, the mind of the race, the wild asses of the devil, and the last trump: being a first selection from the literary remains of George Boon, appropriate to the times, prepared for publication by Reginald Bliss with an ambiguous introduction by H. G. Wells. 1915, New York 1915, London 1920 (naming Wells as author).

Bealby: a holiday. 1915, New York 1915.

The research magnificent. 1915, New York 1915.

Mr Britling sees it through. 1916, New York 1916.

The soul of a bishop: a novel—with just a little love in it—about conscience and religion and the real troubles of life. 1917, New York 1917.

Joan and Peter: the story of an education. 1918, New York 1918.

The undying fire: a contemporary novel. [1919], New York 1919.

The secret places of the heart. 1922, New York 1922.

Men like gods. 1923, New York 1923.

The dream. 1924, New York 1924.

Christina Alberta's father. 1925, New York 1925.

The world of William Clissold: a novel at a new angle. 3 vols 1926, 2 vols New York 1926.

Meanwhile: the picture of a lady. 1927, New York 1927.

Mr Blettsworthy on Rampole Island. 1928, Garden City NY 1928.

The king who was a king: the book of a film. 1929, Garden City NY 1929. The film was never made.

The adventures of Tommy. 1929, New York 1967. For children.

The autocracy of Mr Parham: his remarkable adventure in this changing world. 1930, Garden City NY 1930.

The Bulpington of Blup. [1932], New York 1933.

The shape of things to come: the ultimate resolution. 1933, New York 1933. Partly historical.

Things to come: a film story based on the material contained in his history of the future, The shape of things to come. 1935, New York 1935; rptd in Two film stories, 1940.

The croquet player: a story. 1936, New York 1937.

Man who could work miracles: a film story based on the material contained in his short story [In Tales of space and time]. 1936, New York 1936; rptd in Two film stories, 1940.

Star begotten: a biological fantasia. 1937, New York 1937.

Brynhild. 1937, New York 1937.

The Camford visitation. 1937.

The brothers: a story. 1938, New York 1938.

Apropos of Dolores. 1938, New York 1938.

The holy terror. 1939, New York 1939.

Babes in the darkling wood. 1940, New York 1940.

All aboard for Ararat. 1940, New York 1941.

You can't be too careful: a sample of life 1901–51. 1941, New York 1942.

The desert daisy. Ed G. N. Ray, Urbana 1957. Ms (facs) of story written between 1878–80.

The wealth of Mr Waddy: a novel. Ed H. Wilson, Carbondale 1969.

Other Works

Text-book of biology. Introd by G. B. Howes. 2 vols [1893] (University Correspondence College Tutorial ser.) Vol I rev 1894; subsequent revisions by A. M. Davies et al, as Text-book of zoology.

Honours physiography. 1893. With R. A. Gregory.

Certain personal matters: a collection of material, mainly autobiographical. 1898 (for 1897). Humorous essays.

Anticipations of the reaction of mechanical and scientific progress upon human life and thought. 1902 (for 1901), New York 1902, London 1914 (with introd by Wells).

The discovery of the future: a discourse delivered to the Royal Institution on January 24th, 1902. 1902, New York 1913.

Mankind in the making. 1903, New York 1904, London 1914 (with introd by Wells).

The future in America: a search after realities. 1906, New York 1906.

Faults of the Fabian. [1906] (priv ptd for Fabian Soc). Pamphlet.

Reconstruction of the Fabian Society. [1906] (priv ptd). Pamphlet.

Socialism and the family. 1906. Booklet.

The so-called science of sociology. 1907. Pamphlet; rptd in An Englishman looks at the world, 1914, below.

This misery of boots. 1907, Boston 1908. Fabian Soc pamphlet.

Will socialism destroy the home? [1907]. Independent Labour Party pamphlet; rptd in next.

New worlds for old. 1908, New York 1908, London 1917 (rev).

First & last things: a confession of faith and rule of life. 1908, New York 1908, London 1917 (rev, with new preface by Wells), 1929 (definitive edn).

Floor games. 1911, Boston 1912.

The great state: essays in construction. 1912, New York 1912 (as Socialism and the great state). By Wells, Lady Warwick et al.

The labour unrest. 1912. Pamphlet; rptd in An Englishman looks at the world, 1914, below.

War and common sense. 1913. Pamphlet; rptd (as The common sense of warfare) in An Englishman looks at the world, 1914 below.

Liberalism and its party: what are we Liberals to do? [1913]. Nat Unionist Assoc pamphlet.

Little wars: a game for boys from twelve years of age to one hundred and fifty, and for that more intelligent sort of girls who like boys' games and books. 1913, Boston 1913, London 1931 (rev).

An Englishman looks at the world: being a series of unrestrained remarks upon contemporary matters. 1914, New York 1914 (as Social forces in England and America).

The war that will end war. 1914, New York 1914. Collected articles first pbd 7–29 Aug 1914.

The end of the armament rings. New York 1914. World Peace Federation pamphlet. Rptd from previous.

The peace of the world. [1915].

The war of socialism. [1915]. Reprint of 2 chs from The war that will end war, 1914 above.

What is coming? a forecast of things after the war. 1916, New York 1916 (as What is coming? a European forecast).

The elements of reconstruction. Introd by Viscount Milner 1916. 6 letters to the Times, signed D.P.

War and the future: Italy, France and Britain at war. 1917, New York 1917 (as Italy, France and Britain at war).

God the invisible king. 1917, New York 1917.

A reasonable man's peace. 1917. Nat Council of Civil Liberties pamphlet; rptd in next.

In the fourth year: anticipations of a world peace. 1918, New York 1918, 1918 (abridged, as Anticipations of a world peace).

British nationalism and the League of Nations. 1918. League of Nations Union pamphlet.

Memorandum on propaganda policy against Germany. [1918]. In G. Stuart, Secrets of Crewe House, 1920; rptd in The common sense of war and peace, 1940, below.

History is one. [Boston 1919]. Pamphlet.

The outline of history, being a plain history of life and mankind. 1920, New York 1920, and numerous rev edns thereafter both in Britain and USA. First pbd in 24 fortnightly parts Nov 1919–Nov 1920, with footnotes by other writers, many of which do not appear in the book edns.

Russia in the shadows. 1920, New York 1921. Sunday Express articles.

The salvaging of civilisation. 1921, New York 1921.

The new teaching of history: with a reply to some recent criticisms of The outline of history. 1921.

Washington and the hope of peace. [1922], New York 1922 (as Washington and the riddle of peace). Articles rptd from New York World.

What H. G. Wells thinks about The mind in the making. New York 1922, London 1923 (rev, as introd to J. H. Robinson's Mind in the making).

University of London election. [1922]. Electoral letter.

The world, its debts, and the rich men: a speech. 1922. Election address substituted for the previous.

A short history of the world. 1922, New York 1922, and numerous rev edns thereafter.

Socialism and the scientific motive. 1923. Speech.

To the electors of London University general election, 1923, from H. G. Wells, B.Sc., Lond. [1923]. Address.

The Labour ideal of education. 1923. Pamphlet, to accompany preceding item.

A walk along the Thames embankment. 1923. Independent Labour Party booklet. Rptd from pt of ch I of New worlds for old, 1908, above.

The story of a great schoolmaster: being a plain account of the life and ideas of Sanderson of Oundle. 1924, New York 1924.

The P.R. Parliament. [1924]. Proportional Representation Soc pamphlet; rptd in next.

A year of prophesying. 1924, New York 1925. Articles, all previously pbd in journals and newspapers.

A forecast of the world's affairs. 1925. Rptd from These eventful years, by J. L. Garvin et al, 2 vols 1924.

Mr Belloc objects to The outline of history. 1926, New York 1926. See Belloc's Companion to Mr Wells's Outline of history, 1926, and his Mr Belloc still objects to Mr Wells's Outline of history, 1926.

Democracy under revision: a lecture delivered at the Sorbonne. 1927, New York 1927; rptd in The way the world is going, 1928 below.

Playing at peace. 1927. Nat Council for the Prevention of War pamphlet; rptd in The way the world is going, below.

The way the world is going: guesses and forecasts of the years ahead. 1928, Garden City NY 1929.

The open conspiracy: blue prints for a world revolution. 1928, Garden City NY 1928, London 1930 (rev), 1931 (rev, as What are we to do with our lives?).

The common sense of world peace: an address delivered to the Reichstag. 1929; rptd in After democracy, 1932, below.

Imperialism and the open conspiracy. 1929 (Criterion Miscellany 3).

The science of life: a summary of contemporary knowledge about life and its possibilities. 3 vols 1929–30, 1 vol 1931, 9 vols 1934–7 (corrected, as Science of life ser), 1 vol

1938 (rev). First pbd in 31 fortnightly parts. With J. S. Huxley and G. P. Wells.

The way to world peace. 1930. Pamphlet.

The problem of the troublesome collaborator: an account of certain difficulties in an attempt to produce a work in collaboration [The science of work and wealth], and of the intervention of the Society of Authors therein. Woking 1930 (priv ptd, 175 copies).

Settlement of the trouble between Mr Thring [Secretary of the Society of Authors] and Mr Wells: a footnote to The problem of the troublesome collaborator. [1930] (priv ptd).

What are we to do with our lives? 1931. *See* The open conspiracy, 1928, above.

The work, wealth and happiness of mankind. 2 vols Garden City NY 1931, 1 vol London 1932, 1934 (rev), Garden City NY 1936 (as The outline of man's work and wealth).

After democracy: addresses and papers on the present world situation. 1932.

What should be done now? New York 1932. Pamphlet. Rptd from After democracy, above.

Experiment in autobiography: discoveries and conclusions of a very ordinary brain since 1866. 2 vols 1934, New York 1934, London 1966 (without portraits).

Stalin-Wells talk: the verbatim record, and a discussion by G. Bernard Shaw, H. G. Wells, J. M. Keynes, Ernst Toller et al. 1934. Pamphlet.

The new America: the new world. 1935, New York 1935. Impressions.

The anatomy of frustration: a modern synthesis. 1936, New York 1936.

The idea of a world encyclopaedia. 1936. Lecture to the Royal Institution; rptd in World brain, 1938 below.

The informative content of education. 1937. Presidential address to the education section of Br Assoc.

World brain. 1938, Garden City NY 1938. Articles and lectures.

Travels of a republican radical in search of hot water. 1939 (Penguin Special).

The fate of Homo sapiens: an unemotional statement of the things that are happening to him now and of the immediate possibilities confronting him. 1939, New York 1939.

The new world order: whether it is obtainable, how it can be attained, and what sort of world a world at peace will have to be. 1940, New York 1940.

The rights of man: or, what are we fighting for? [1940] (Penguin Special).

The common sense of war and peace: world revolution or war unending? 1940 (Penguin Special).

Two hemispheres or one world? 1940. Pamphlet.

Guide to the new world: a handbook of constructive world revolution. 1941.

The outlook for Homo sapiens: an amalgamation and modernization of two books, The fate of Homo sapiens and The new world order. 1942.

Science and the world-mind. 1942.

Phoenix: a summary of the inescapable conditions of world reorganization. 1942.

A thesis on the quality of illusion in the continuity of individual life of the higher metazoa, with particular reference to the species Homo sapiens. [1942] (priv ptd); rptd in '42 to '44, below. An abridgement pbd in Nature 1 April 1944 was rptd as a pamphlet, The illusion of personality.

The conquest of time, by H. G. Wells: written to replace his First and last things. 1942.

The new rights of man. Girard Kansas 1942. Pamphlet.

Crux ansata: an indictment of the Roman Catholic Church. 1943 (Penguin Special).

The Mosley outrage. 1943. Pamphlet.

'42 to '44: a contemporary memoir upon human behaviour during the crisis of the world revolution. 1944. Essays.

The happy turning: a dream of life. 1945.

Mind at the end of its tether. 1945.

Letters

Edel, L. and G. N. Ray (ed). Henry James and Wells: a record of their friendship, their debate on the art of fiction and their quarrel. Urbana 1958.

Wilson, H. (ed). Arnold Bennett and Wells: a record of a personal and literary friendship. Urbana 1960.

Gettmann, R. A. (ed). Gissing and Wells: their friendship and correspondence. 1961.

§2

See Wells: the critical heritage, *ed P. Parrinder 1972.*

Chesterton, G. K. Wells and the giants. In his Heretics, 1905.

'West, Geoffrey' (G. H. Wells). H. G. Wells: a sketch for a portrait. 1930.

Orage, A. R. The marks of Mr Wells. In his Selected essays and critical writings, 1935.

'Caudwell, Christopher' (C. St J. Sprigg). Wells: a study in utopianism. In his Studies in a dying culture, 1938.

Brome, V. H. G. Wells: a biography. 1951.

Amis, K. Starting points. In his New maps of hell, 1961. On the science-fiction.

Bergonzi, B. The early Wells: a study of the scientific romances. Manchester [1961].

—— (ed). Wells: a collection of critical essays. Englewood Cliffs NJ 1976.

Borges, J. L. The first Wells. In his Other inquisitions, Austin 1964.

Snow, C. P. In his Variety of men, 1966.

ENOCH ARNOLD BENNETT
1867–1931

The chief collections of Bennett mss are in the New York Public Library (Berg Collection), Indiana Univ (The old wives' tale), University College London (C. K. Ogden Collection), The Arnold Bennett Museum (Stoke-on-Trent), Keele Univ. See J. C. Hepburn, Bennett manuscripts and rare books: a list of holdings, Eng Fiction in Transition 1 1958.

Collections and Selections

Minerva edition. 7 vols 1926.

Three plays: The bright island; Cupid and common sense; Sacred and profane love. [1931].

§1
Prose Fiction

A man from the north. 1898, New York 1898.

The Grand Babylon Hotel: a fantasia on modern themes. 1902, New York 1902 (as T. Racksole and daughter), London 1954 (Penguin; introd by F. Swinnerton). First pbd serially in the Golden Penny 2 Feb 1901–.

Anna of the Five Towns: a novel. 1902, New York 1903, London 1954 (Penguin, introd by F. Swinnerton).

The gates of wrath: a melodrama. 1903. First pbd serially in Myra's Jnl 1 Oct 1899–.

Leonora: a novel. 1903, New York 1910.

A great man: a frolic. 1904, New York 1910.

Teresa of Watling Street: a fantasia on modern themes. 1904.

Tales of the Five Towns. 1905.

The loot of cities: being the adventures of a millionaire in search of joy—a fantasia. 1905, [1917] (with additional stories). The 6 stories in 1905 edn first pbd serially in Windsor Mag summer and autumn 1904.

Sacred and profane love: a novel in three episodes. 1905, New York 1911 (rev as The book of Carlotta; with preface by Bennett).

Hugo: a fantasia on modern themes. 1906, New York 1906. First pbd serially in To-day 3 May–19 July 1905.

Whom God hath joined. 1906, New York 1911.

The sinews of war: a romance of London and the sea. [1906], New York 1906 (as Doubloons). With E. Phillpotts. First pbd serially in T.P.'s Weekly 2 March 1906–.

The ghost: a fantasia on modern themes. 1907, Boston 1907.

The grim smile of the Five Towns. 1907.

The city of pleasure: a fantasia on modern themes. 1907, New York 1915. First pbd serially in Staffordshire Sentinel and other provincial newspapers 6 Jan–14 April 1906.

The statue. 1908, New York 1908. With E. Phillpotts.

Buried alive: a tale of three days. 1908, New York 1910.

The old wives' tale: a novel. 1908, New York [1911] (with preface by Bennett), London 1912, 2 vols 1927 (facs from author's ms), Oxford 1941 (Limited Editions Club, introd by F. Swinnerton, preface by Bennett), 1 vol London 1954 (Penguin, introd by F. Swinnerton), 1964 (introd by A. Sillitoe).

The glimpse: an adventure of the soul. 1909, New York 1909.

Helen with the high hand: an idyllic diversion. 1910, New York 1910. First pbd serially (as The miser's niece) in Star, 12 June 1909–.

Clayhanger. 1910, New York 1910, London 1954 (Penguin, introd by F. Swinnerton). First vol of Clayhanger trilogy.

The card: a story of adventure in the Five Towns. 1911, New York 1911 (as Denry the audacious). The first 3 chs issued New York 1911 as The deeds of Denry the audacious, for copyright purposes. First pbd serially in Times Weekly Edition 4 Feb 1910–.

Hilda Lessways. 1911, New York 1911. 2nd vol of Clayhanger trilogy.

The matador of the Five Towns, and other stories. 1912, New York 1912. The contents of the English and American edns are not identical.

The regent: a Five Towns story of adventure in London. 1913, New York 1913 (as The old Adam). Sequel to The card. First pbd serially in London Mag Nov 1912–, and American Mag Dec 1912–.

The price of love: a tale. 1914, New York 1914. First pbd serially in Harper's Mag Dec 1913–.

These twain. New York 1915, London 1916. 3rd vol of Clayhanger trilogy. First pbd serially in Munsey's Mag Sept–Oct 1915.

The lion's share. 1916, New York 1916. First pbd serially in Metropolitan Mag Oct 1915–.

The pretty lady: a novel. 1918, New York 1918, London 1950 (introd by F. Swinnerton).

The roll-call. 1918, New York 1918.

Mr Prohack. 1922, New York 1922. First pbd serially in Delineator July 1921–Jan 1922 and in Westminster Gazette.

Lilian. 1922, New York 1922. First pbd serially in Cassell's Mag July 1922–.

Riceyman Steps: a novel. 1923, New York 1923, London 1954 (Penguin, introd by F. Swinnerton), 1956 (with Elsie and the child, introd by Michael Sadleir), 1964 (introd by A. Sillitoe [same as introd to Old Wives' tale, above]).

Elsie and the child: a tale of Riceyman Steps, and other stories. 1924, New York 1924.

The Clayhanger family. 1925. Contains Clayhanger, Hilda Lessways and These twain.

Lord Raingo. 1926, New York 1926. First pbd serially in Evening Standard 20 Sept 1926–.

The vanguard: a fantasia. New York [1927], London 1928 (as The strange vanguard: a fantasia).

The woman who stole everything, and other stories. 1927, New York 1927.

Accident. New York 1928, London 1929. First pbd serially (as Train de luxe) in Daily Express 16 July 1928–.

'Piccadilly': story of the film. [1929]. First pbd serially

in Film Weekly 22 Oct 1928–.

Elsie and the child. 1929 (limited edn). Short story, first pbd 1924 with other stories.

Imperial Palace. 1930 (1 vol and 2 vols [limited] edns), New York 1930.

The night visitor, and other stories. Garden City NY 1931, London 1931.

Venus rising from the sea. 1931 (350 copies). Short story. See next.

Dream of destiny: an unfinished novel, and Venus rising from the sea [short story]. 1932, New York 1932 (as Stroke of luck, and Dream of destiny: an unfinished novel).

Plays, Libretti etc

Plays are listed in order of production, not of pbn.

Rosalys: a music play for girls in two acts. Libretto by Bennett. (Welsh Girls' School, Ashford Middlesex 27 July 1898). In M. Locherbie-Goff, La jeunesse de Bennett, 1939.

Polite farces for the drawing-room. 1900, New York 1912. Plays: contains The stepmother, A good woman, A question of sex. All reissued separately 1929–30.

Cupid and commonsense: a play in four acts. (Stage Soc, Shaftesbury Theatre 26 Jan 1908). 1909, New York [1910]. Based on Anna of the Five Towns. With preface on The crisis in the theatre.

What the public wants: a play in four acts. (Aldwych 2 May 1909). 1909, New York 1910.

The honeymoon: a comedy in three acts. (Royalty 6 Oct 1911). 1911, New York 1912.

Milestones: a play in three acts. (Royalty 5 March 1912; Liberty, New York 12 Sept 1912). 1912, New York [1912]. With E. Knoblauch [Knoblock].

The great adventure: a play of fancy in four acts. (Kingsway 25 March 1913). 1913, New York [1913]. Based on Buried alive, 1908, above.

A good woman. (Palace 16 Feb 1914, as Rivals for Rosamund). In Polite farces for the drawing-room, 1900, above.

The title: a comedy in three acts. (Royalty 20 July 1918). 1918, New York 1918.

Judith: a play in three acts, founded on the apocryphal book of Judith. (Kingsway 30 April 1919). 1919, New York 1919.

Sacred and profane love: a play in four acts. (Playhouse, Liverpool 15 Sept 1919; Aldwych 10 Nov 1919). 1919, New York 1920. Based on the novel.

Body and soul: a play in four acts. (Playhouse, Liverpool 15 Feb 1922; Regent, Euston Rd 11 Sept 1922). New York 1921, London 1922.

The love match: a play in five scenes. (Strand 21 March 1922). 1922, New York 1922.

Don Juan de Marana: a play in four acts. 1923 (priv ptd).

London life: a play in three acts and nine scenes. (Drury Lane 3 June 1924). 1924, New York 1924. With E. Knoblock.

The bright island. (Aldwych 15 Feb 1925). 1924 (200 copies), New York 1925, London 1926.

Flora. (Rusholme, Manchester 19 Oct 1927). In Five three-act plays, 1933.

Mr Prohack: a comedy in three acts. (Court 16 Nov 1927). 1927. With E. Knoblock; based on the novel.

Judith: an opera in one act. (Covent Garden 25 June 1929). [1929]. Music by E. Goossens; libretto by Bennett.

The snake-charmer. In Eight one-act plays, 1933.

The Ides of March. In One-act plays for stage and study, ser 8, New York 1934. With F. Alcock.

Don Juan de Mañara: opera in four acts. (Covent Garden 24 June 1937). 1935. Vocal score. Libretto by Bennett, music by E. Goossens. Based on Don Juan de Marana, 1923, above.

Other Works

Journalism for women: a practical guide. 1898.

Fame and fiction: an inquiry into certain popularities. 1901, New York 1901.

How to become an author: a practical guide. 1903.

The truth about an author. 1903 (anon), New York 1911 (with preface by Bennett), London 1914. Autobiographical.

Things that interested me: being leaves from a journal. Preface by G. Sturt, Burslem 1906 (priv ptd).

The reasonable life: being hints for men and women. 1907, New York [1911] (expanded, as Mental efficiency and other hints to men and women), London [1912].

Things which have interested me: being leaves from a journal. Preface by A. Hooley 2nd ser, Burslem 1907 (priv ptd, 100 copies).

How to live on 24 hours a day. 1908, 1910 (with preface by Bennett), New York 1910.

The human machine. 1908, New York 1911.

Things which have interested me: 3rd ser, Burslem 1908 (priv ptd, 100 copies). Preface [in French] by M. D. Calvocoressi.

Literary taste: how to form it; with detailed instructions for collecting a complete library of English literature. 1909, New York 1927 (with additional lists by F. Swinnerton), 1938 (Penguin, with a further list by F. Swinnerton).

The present crisis: plain words to plain men. Burslem [1910]. A pamphlet against tariff reform.

The feast of St Friend. 1911, New York 1911, London 1914 (as Friendship and happiness: a plea for the feast of St Friend). Essays.

Those United States. 1912, New York 1912 (as Your United States: impressions of a first visit).

How to be happy. New York [1912]. Pamphlet rptd from Metropolitan Mag and rptd in The plain man and his wife, 1913, below.

Paris nights, and other impressions of places and people. 1913, New York 1913.

The plain man and his wife. [1913], New York [1913], New York 1913 (as Married life), London 1916 (as Marriage: the plain man and his wife).

From the log of the Velsa. New York 1914, London 1920. Travel.

Liberty: a statement of the British case. 1914, New York 1914.

The author's craft. 1914, New York 1914.

Over there: war scenes on the western front. 1915, New York 1915.

Wounded. 1915. Wounded Allies' Relief Committee pamphlet.

The Wounded Allies' Relief Committee: a short account of work done. 1915. Pamphlet.

'Wounded Allies' at the Caledonian Market: the greatest war fair. [1916]. Publicity circular.

Books and persons: being comments on a past epoch 1908–11. 1917, New York 1917. Selected articles from New Age, written by 'Jacob Tonson'; with some revisions.

A national responsibility: future employment of the disabled. Manchester 1917. Pamphlet.

The embargo v. the gun. 1918. League of Free Nations Assoc pamphlet.

Independence and sovereignty. [1918]. League of Nations Union pamphlet.

Self and self-management: essays about existing. 1918, New York 1918.

Thoughts on national kitchens. 1918. Pamphlet.

Our women: chapters on the sex-discord. 1920, New York 1920.

Things that have interested me. 1921, New York 1921. This, and subsequent ser with same title, below, are

distinct from 3 similar titles priv ptd at Burslem 1906–8, above.

Things that have interested me. 2nd ser 1923, New York 1923.

How to make the best of life. [1923], New York 1923. Essays.

Things that have interested me. 3rd ser 1926, New York 1926.

The savour of life: essays in gusto. 1928, Garden City NY 1928.

Mediterranean scenes: Rome—Greece—Constantinople. 1928. Travel.

The religious interregnum. 1929. Pamphlet.

How to live. Garden City NY 1929. Reprints How to live on 24 hours a day; The human machine; Mental efficiency and other hints to men and women; Self and self-management.

Journal, 1929. 1930, New York 1930 (as Journal of things new and old).

The journals of Bennett 1896–1928. Ed N. Flower 3 vols 1932–3, New York 1932–3 (rev, as The journal of Bennett), 1 vol New York 1935. A selection by F. Swinnerton from this and Journal 1929 pbd 1954 (Penguin).

Florentine journal 1st April–25th May 1910. Ed S. Sitwell 1967.

Bennett contributed regularly to Woman *1894–1900 and was editor 1896–1900; to* Academy *1898–1901 (dramatic criticism and reviews); to* New Age *1908–11 as 'Jacob Tonson' on Books and persons; to* John Bull *1922–3 (miscellaneous articles); and* Evening Standard *1926–31 (book reviews). He also contributed to* T.P.'s Weekly *in the early 1900s and to* Daily News *during the 1914–18 war. Many of the pieces were collected in the books listed above.*

Letters

Bennett's letters to his nephew [Richard Bennett], with a preface by F. Swinnerton. New York 1935, London 1936.

Bennett and H. G. Wells: a record of a personal and literary friendship. Ed H. Wilson, Urbana 1960.

Correspondance André Gide—Bennett: vingt ans d'amitié littéraire 1911–31. Ed L. F. Brugmans, Geneva 1964.

Letters. Ed J. G. Hepburn 3 vols 1966–70.

Dorothy Cheston Bennett, Bennett: a portrait done at home *(1935) contains 170 letters from Bennett.*

§2

Woolf, V. Character in fiction. Criterion 2 1924; rptd as Mr Bennett and Mrs Brown, 1924, and in her The captain's death bed, 1950.

Bennett, Mrs A. M. Arnold Bennett. 1925.

—— My Arnold Bennett. 1931.

Muir, E. Scrutinies IV: Bennett. Calendar of Modern Letters June 1925; rptd in Scrutinies, ed E. Rickword 1928.

Orage, A. R. In his Art of reading, New York [1930]. Various comments, rptd from New Age.

Ford, F. M. (formerly Hueffer). In his Return to yesterday, 1931.

Gide, A. Arnold Bennett. Nouvelle Revue Française 36 1931.

'West, Geoffrey' (G. H. Wells). The problem of Bennett. 1932.

Swinnerton, F. In his Georgian scene, New York [1934].

Wells, H. G. In his Experiment in autobiography, 1934.

Sitwell, O. In his Laughter in the next room, Boston 1948.

—— In his Noble essences, 1950.

Wilson, A. Bennett's novels. London Mag 1 1954.

Wain, J. The quality of Bennett. In his Preliminary essays, 1957.

—— Arnold Bennett. New York 1967.

Drabble, M. Bennett: a biography. 1974.

EDWARD MORGAN FORSTER
1879–1970

The ms of Where angels fear to tread *is in BM, and that of* A passage to India *in the Univ of Texas. The other major and most minor mss are at King's College, Cambridge.*

Bibliographies

Kirkpatrick, B. J. A bibliography of Forster. With a foreword by Forster 1965, 1968 (rev) (Soho bibliographies).

Collections and Selections

Uniform edn. 5 vols 1924–6. Novels only: texts as in first edns.
Pocket edn. 8 vols 1947–62.
The collected tales. New York 1947, London [1948] (as Collected short stories). Incorporates The celestial omnibus and The eternal moment; includes a preface by Forster which is slightly rev in the English edn.
The Abinger edition. Ed O. Stallybrass 1972–.

§1
Prose Fiction

Where angels fear to tread. Edinburgh 1905, New York 1920.
The longest journey. Edinburgh 1907, New York 1922, Oxford 1960 (WC) (with introd by Forster).
A room with a view. 1908, New York 1911, London 1951 (as play by S. Tait and K. Allott produced at Arts Theatre Cambridge 6 Feb 1950).
Howards End. 1910, New York 1910 (for 1911) (with unauthorized alterations), London 1919, New York 1921 (with text of first English edn).
The celestial omnibus and other stories. 1911, New York 1923.
The story of the siren. Richmond 1920 (Hogarth Press). Short story, rptd in The eternal moment, below.
A passage to India. 1924, New York 1924, London [1942] (EL) (with foreword and notes by Forster and introd by P. Burra), 1957 (with foreword and notes rev); 1960 (as play by S. R. Rau produced at Oxford Playhouse 19 Jan 1960).
The eternal moment and other stories. 1928, New York [1928].
Maurice: a novel. 1971; ed P. N. Furbank 1975 (Penguin).

Other Works

Alexandria: a history and a guide. Alexandria 1922, 1938 (rev), New York 1961 (with text of first edn and new introd).
Pharos and Pharillon. Richmond 1923 (Hogarth Press), New York 1923. Articles first pbd in the Egyptian Mail and the Athenaeum.
Anonymity: an enquiry. 1925 (Hogarth essays 12). First pbd in Calendar of modern letters 2 1925, rptd in Two cheers for democracy.
Aspects of the novel. 1927, New York 1927.
A letter to Madan Blanchard. 1931 (Hogarth letters 1), New York 1932. Rptd in Two cheers for democracy.
Goldsworthy Lowes Dickinson. 1934, New York 1934. Biography.
Pageant of Abinger: in aid of the Parish Church Preservation Fund. [Abinger 1934]; rptd (as Abinger pageant) in Abinger harvest.
Abinger harvest. 1936, New York 1936, London 1936 (without A flood in the office), New York 1947; London 1940 (with rev prefatory note and without Abinger pageant), 1953 (with original prefatory note and Abinger pageant). Articles and reviews rptd from various journals.

England's pleasant land: a pageant play. Westcott Surrey 1938 (synopsis only), London 1940 (full text).
What I believe. 1939 (Hogarth sixpenny pamphlets 1). First pbd, with some omissions, as Two cheers for democracy, in Nation 16 July 1938; rptd in Two cheers for democracy.
Reading as usual. 1939. Broadcast talk rptd from the Listener 21 Sept 1939.
Nordic twilight. 1940 (Macmillan war pamphlets 3).
Virginia Woolf. Cambridge 1942, New York 1942 (Rede lecture 1941); rptd in Two cheers for democracy.
The development of English prose between 1918 and 1939. Glasgow 1945 (W. P. Ker memorial lecture 1944); rptd (rev) in Two cheers for democracy.
The new disorder. New York 1949. Essay rptd from Horizon 4 1941.
Two cheers for democracy. 1951, New York 1951. Essays, reviews and broadcasts, mostly rptd.
Billy Budd: opera in four acts. Music by B. Britten, libretto by Forster and E. Crozier, adapted from the story by H. Melville. 1951, 1962 (rev).
Desmond MacCarthy. Stanford Dingley 1952. Priv ptd (Mill House Press) 72 copies. Tribute first pbd in Listener 26 June 1952.
Reply to Lord Cohen who had proposed the health of [King's] College at Founder's Feast December 6th 1952. [Cambridge 1952]. Mimeographed.
The hill of Devi, being letters from Dewas State Senior. 1953, New York 1953. Reminiscences of India.
'I assert that there is an alternative in humanism'. 1955. Essay first pbd as a letter in Twentieth Century 157 1955.
Battersea Rise. New York [1955] (priv ptd). The first chapter of Marianne Thornton, slightly condensed. Rptd as Daughter dear, London Mag 3 1956.
Marianne Thornton 1797–1887: a domestic biography. 1956, New York 1956.
Tourism v. thuggism. 1957. Review of Portrait of Greece, by Lord Kinross. Offprint from Listener 17 Jan 1957.
E. K. Bennett—Francis—1887–1958. 1959 (priv ptd). Tribute rptd from Caian 55 1958. 300 copies.
A presidential address to the Cambridge humanists, summer 1959. 1963. Mimeographed, 50 copies. Rptd from Univ Humanist Bull 11 1963.
Letters to Donald Windham. Verona 1975.

§2

Woolf, V. The novels of Forster. Atlantic Monthly 140 1927; rptd in her The death of the moth, 1942.
Dobrée, B. In his The lamp and the lute, Oxford 1929.
Macaulay, R. The writings of Forster. 1938.
Trilling, L. Forster: a study. Norfolk Conn 1943, London 1967 (rev).
Warner, R. E. M. Forster. 1950, 1960 (rev J. Morris) (Br Council pamphlet).
Johnstone, J. K. The Bloomsbury group: a study of Forster, Strachey, V. Woolf and their circle. 1954.
Beer, J. B. The achievement of Forster. 1962.
Crews, F. C. Forster: the perils of humanism. Princeton 1962.
Gransden, K. W. E. M. Forster. Edinburgh 1962 (Writers & Critics), 1970 (rev).
Bradbury, M. (ed). Forster: a collection of critical essays. Englewood Cliffs, NJ 1966.
Stone, W. The cave and the mountain: a study of Forster. Stanford 1966.
Stallybrass, O. (ed). Aspects of Forster. 1969.
Furbank, P. N. Forster: a life. 2 vols 1977–8, 1 vol Oxford 1979.

JAMES AUGUSTINE ALOYSIUS JOYCE
1882–1941

Principal collections are at the BM (Finnegans wake), *New York Public Library, Yale Univ* (*the Slocum Library includes* Dubliners), *National Library of Ireland* (*includes* A portrait of the artist as a young man, *and the Joyce-Léon correspondence*), *the Rosenbach Foundation* (Ulysses), *State Univ of New York at Buffalo, and Cornell and Southern Illinois universities.*

Bibliographies

Slocum, J. J. and H. Cahoon. A bibliography of Joyce 1882–1941. 1953 (Soho Bibliographies).

Deming, R. H. A bibliography of Joyce studies. Lawrence Kansas 1964.

Collections and Selections

Collected poems. New York 1936. Chamber music, Pomes penyeach and Ecce puer.

Eliot, T. S. (ed). Introducing Joyce: a selection from Joyce's prose. 1942.

Levin, H. (ed). The portable Joyce. New York 1947, London 1948 (as The essential Joyce), New York 1949 (as The indispensable Joyce), 1966 (rev, as The portable Joyce).

The critical writings of Joyce. Ed E. Mason and R. Ellmann 1959.

§ I

Et tu Healy! [1891]. No copy known to survive. Verse.

The day of the rabblement. In Two essays, Dublin [1901] (with A forgotten aspect of the university question by F. J. C. Skeffington). Rptd Minneapolis 1957.

The holy office. [Pola 1904 or 1905]. Broadside poem.

Chamber music. 1907, 1918, Boston [1918] (unauthorized), New York 1918, London 1927; ed W. Y. Tindall, New York 1954.

Gas from a burner. Flushing 1912. Broadside poem.

Dubliners. 1914, New York 1916 (English sheets), 1917, London 1926 (with introd by P. Colum), 1967 (corrected text, ed R. Scholes), New York 1967. Stories. Contains The sisters, An encounter, Araby, Eveline, After the race, Two gallants, The boarding house, A little cloud, Counterparts, Clay, A painful case, Ivy Day in the committee room, A mother, Grace, The dead.

A portrait of the artist as a young man. New York 1916. London [1917] (American sheets), [1918], New York 1928 (with introd by H. Gorman), London 1930; ed J. S. Atherton 1964; ed C. G. Anderson, New York 1964, London 1968. First pbd serially in Egoist 1–2 1914–15. *See* also Stephen hero, 1944 below. *See* also The workshop of Daedalus, ed R. Scholes and R. M. Kain, Evanston 1965. A facsimile of the final holograph manuscript, ed H. W. Gabler 2 vols New York 1977.

Exiles: a play in three acts. 1918, New York 1918, Norfolk Conn 1945 (with introd by F. Fergusson), New York 1951 (with previously unpbd notes by Joyce and introd by P. Colum), London 1952. First performed, in German, at the Münchener Theater, Munich 1919; in English, at the Neighborhood Playhouse, New York 19 Feb–22 March 1925, and by the Stage Soc at the Regent Theatre 14–15 Feb 1926.

Ulysses. Paris 1922, London 1922 (Paris ptd), [New York 1929] (unauthorized), 2 vols Hamburg 1932 (rev S. Gilbert at Joyce's request), New York 1934, 1935 (with introd by S. Gilbert), London 1936. 13 episodes, and pt of 14th, pbd in Little Rev March 1918–Dec 1920; some episodes pbd in Egoist 6 1919; 14 episodes rptd unauthorized in Two Worlds Monthly 1–3 1926–7. A

facsimile of the manuscript, ed H. Levin 2 vols New York 1975.

Pomes penyeach. Paris 1927, [Princeton] 1931 (50 copies, for copyright), Cleveland 1931 (priv ptd), London 1932 (Paris ptd), 1933, Oxford [1933] (as The Joyce book, with prologue by J. Stephens, essay by P. Colum and musical settings of each poem), London 1966 (with Ecce puer, The holy office, and Gas from a burner; as Pomes penyeach and other verses).

Work in progress: volume 1. New York 1928 (20 copies, for copyright). Rptd from Transition April–Nov 1927.

Work in progress: parts 11 and 12. [New York 1928] (5 copies, for copyright). Rptd from Transition March 1928.

Anna Livia Plurabelle: fragment of Work in progress. New York 1928 (with introd by P. Colum), London 1930.

Anna Livia Plurabelle: the making of a chapter. Ed F. H. Higginson 1960.

Work in progress: part 13. [New York 1928] (5 copies, for copyright). Rptd from Transition summer 1928.

Work in progress: part 15. [New York 1929] (5 copies, for copyright). Rptd from Transition Feb 1929.

Tales told of Shem and Shaun: three fragments from Work in progress. Paris 1929. Contains The mookse and the gripes, The muddest thick that was ever heard dump, The ondt and the gracehoper. Preface by C. K. Ogden.

Two tales of Shem and Shaun: fragments from Work in progress. 1932. Contains The mookse and the gripes, and The ondt and the gracehoper.

Work in progress: part 18. [New York 1930] (5 copies, for copyright). Rptd from Transition Nov 1929.

Haveth childers everywhere: fragment from Work in progress. New York 1930 (Paris ptd), London 1931.

The mime of Mick, Nick and the maggies: a fragment from Work in progress. Hague 1934.

Storiella as she is syung. 1937 (176 copies). A section of Work in progress.

Finnegans wake. 1939, New York 1939, London 1946 (with list of corrections), New York 1947, London 1950 (incorporating most of the corrections), 1964 (incorporating remainder of corrections), 1966 (abridged by A. Burgess, as A shorter Finnegans wake). Some sections pbd separately from 1928 as Work in progress; *see* above. *See* also J. F. Spoerri, Finnegans wake by Joyce: a check list, Evanston 1953. Corrections of misprints in Finnegans wake was first pbd separately New York 1945. *See* B. O. Hehir and J. M. Dillon, A classical lexicon for Finnegans wake, Berkeley 1977. A first-draft version of Finnegans wake. Ed D. Hayman, Austin 1963.

Pastimes. New York 1941. Facs of a poem in holograph.

Stephen hero: part of the first draft of A portrait of the artist as a young man. Ed T. Spencer 1944, New York 1944 (US edn differs slightly and is regarded by the editor as superior); ed J. J. Slocum and H. Cahoon, New York 1955, 1963 (with addns).

The early Joyce: the book reviews 1902–03. Ed S. Joyce and E. Mason, Colorado Springs 1955.

Epiphanies. Ed O. A. Silverman, Buffalo 1956. *See* also The workshop of Daedalus, ed Scholes and Kain, 1965.

Scribbledehobble: the ur-workbook for Finnegans wake. Ed T. E. Connolly, Evanston 1961.

The cat and the devil. New York 1964, London 1965. Children's story in the form of a letter to Joyce's grandson dated 10 Aug 1936.

Daniel Defoe. Ed and tr J. Prescott, Buffalo Stud 1 1964. Lecture given in Italian in 1912 at the Università Popolare Triestina.

Giacomo Joyce. Ed R. Ellmann, New York 1968, London 1968. With facs. Written about 1914.

Joyce in Padua. Ed L. Berrone, New York 1977.

Letters

A collection of letters between Joyce and P. Léon 1930–40 is deposited in the National Library of Ireland and will not be available till 1991.

Letters of Joyce. 3 vols; vol 1, ed S. Gilbert 1957; vols 2–3, ed R. Ellmann 1966; New York 1966 (with corrections to vol 1).
Selected letters. Ed R. Ellmann 1975.

§2

Reviews are listed and excerpted in Joyce: the critical heritage, *ed R. H. Deming 2 vols 1970.*

Biographical Studies

Gorman, H. Joyce: his first forty years. New York 1924.
—— James Joyce. New York 1940, 1948 (rev).
Pound, E. Past history. Eng Jnl 22 1933; rptd in next.
—— Pound/Joyce: the letters of Pound to Joyce, with Pound's essays on Joyce. Ed F. Read, New York 1967.
Budgen, F. Joyce and the making of Ulysses. New York 1934, London 1934 (corrected), Bloomington 1960 (rev, with next, but without the London edn corrections).
—— Further recollections of Joyce. 1955; rptd (rev) Partisan Rev 23 1956.
Gogarty, O. St J. As I was going down Sackville Street. 1937.
—— Joyce: a portrait of the artist. In his Mourning became Mrs Spendlove, New York 1948.
—— It isn't that time of year at all. Garden City NY 1954.
'Svevo, Italo' (E. Schmitz). James Joyce. Convegno 25 April 1937; tr S. Joyce 1950; rptd with additional material in his Saggi e pagine sparse, 1954.
Joyce, S. Ricordi di Joyce. Letteratura 5 1941. Tr E. Mason, New York 1950 (as Recollections of Joyce by his brother); and tr F. Giovanelli, Hudson Rev 2 1950.
—— My brother's keeper. Ed R. Ellmann, New York 1958.
—— In his Dublin diary, ed G. H. Healy, Ithaca 1962.
—— The meeting of Svevo and Joyce. Udine 1965.
Hutchins, P. Joyce's Dublin. 1950.
—— Joyce's world. 1957.
Ellmann, R. A portrait of the artist as friend. Kenyon Rev 18 1956; also in Eng Institute Essays 1955, New York 1956.
—— Joyce in love. Ithaca 1959.
—— James Joyce. New York 1959.
—— Eminent domain: Yeats among Wilde, Joyce, Pound, Eliot and Auden. New York 1967.
—— Ulysses on the Liffey. 1972.
—— The consciousness of Joyce. 1977.
Colum, M. and P. Our friend Joyce. Garden City NY 1958.
Beach, S. Shakespeare and Company. New York 1959.
Furbank, P. N. Svevo and Joyce. In his Italo Svevo, 1966.
Peake, C. H. Joyce: the citizen and the artist. 1977.

General Studies

Muir, E. In his Transition, 1926.
Lewis, W. An analysis of the mind of Joyce. Enemy 1 1927; rptd in his Time and western man, 1927.
O'Faolain, S. Style and the limitations of speech. Criterion 8 1928.
—— In his Vanishing hero: studies in the novelists of the twenties, 1956.
'West, Rebecca' (C. I. Andrews). In her Strange necessity, 1928.
Connolly, C. The position of Joyce. Life & Letters 2 1929; rptd in his Condemned playground, 1945.
Dujardin, E. Le monologue intérieur: son apparition, ses origines, sa place dans l'oeuvre de Joyce. Paris 1931.
Wilson, E. In his Axel's castle, New York 1931.
Eliot, T. S. In his After strange gods, 1933.

Levin, H. Joyce: a critical introduction. Norfolk Conn 1941, 1960 (rev).
Ellmann, R. Joyce and Yeats. Kenyon Rev 12 1950.
—— The limits of Joyce's naturalism. Sewanee Rev 63 1955.
—— A portrait of the artist as friend. Kenyon Rev 18 1956; rptd in Eng Institute Essays 1955, New York 1956.
Savage, D. S. In his Withered branch, 1950.
Tindall, W. Y. Joyce: his way of interpreting the modern world. New York 1950.
—— Joyce and the hermetic tradition. JHI 15 1954.
—— A reader's guide to Joyce. New York 1959.
McLuhan, H. M. Joyce, Aquinas and the poetic process. Renascence 4 1951; rptd in Joyce's Portrait: criticisms and critiques, ed T. E. Connolly, New York 1962.
—— A survey of Joyce criticism. Ibid.
—— Joyce: trivial and quadrivial. Thought 28 1953.
—— Joyce, Mallarmé and the press. Sewanee Rev 62 1954; rptd, with preceding, in his Interior landscape, ed E. McNamara, New York 1969.
Mayoux, J.-J. L'hérésie de Joyce. Eng Miscellany (Rome) 2 1951.
—— James Joyce. Paris 1965.
Huxley, A. and S. Gilbert. Joyce the artificer: two studies of Joyce's method. 1952.
Edel, L. The psychological novel 1900–50. Philadelphia 1955, 1964 (rev and enlarged).
Smidt, K. Joyce and the cultic use of fiction. Oslo 1955.
Kenner, H. Dublin's Joyce. 1955 (for 1956).
—— Joyce's voices. 1978.
Magalaner, M. and R. M. Kain. Joyce: the man, the work, the reputation. New York 1956.
Magalaner, M. (ed). A Joyce miscellany. New York 1957; second series, Carbondale 1959; third series, 1962.
Magalaner, M. Time of apprenticeship: the fiction of young Joyce. New York 1959.
Stewart, J. I. M. James Joyce. 1957, 1964 (rev) (Br Council pamphlet).
—— In his Eight modern writers, Oxford 1963 (OHEL).
Litz, W. The art of Joyce: method and design in Ulysses and Finnegans wake. 1961.
—— James Joyce. New York 1966.
Goldberg, S. L. James Joyce. Edinburgh 1962 (Writers & Critics).
Burgess, A. Here comes everybody: an introduction to Joyce for the ordinary reader. 1965, New York 1965 (as Re Joyce).
Adams, R. M. Joyce: common sense and beyond. New York 1966.
Gross, J. Joyce, 1971, 1976 (corrected).
Hodgart, M. Joyce: a student's guide. 1978.

ADELINE VIRGINIA WOOLF, née STEPHEN
1882–1941

The Berg Collection of New York Public Library has an important group of ms notebooks. The ms of Mrs Dalloway *is in BM; that of* Orlando *is at Knole.*

Bibliographies

Kirkpatrick, B. J. A bibliography of Virginia Woolf. 1957, 1967 (rev) (Soho Bibliographies).

Collections and Selections

Works: uniform edition. 17 vols 1929–55.
Collected essays. Ed L. Woolf 4 vols 1966–7, New York 1967.

§1
Prose Fiction

The voyage out. 1915, New York 1920 (rev), London 1920 (from American sheets).

Two stories: written and printed by Virginia Woolf and L. S. Woolf. Richmond Surrey 1917 (150 copies). Contains The mark on the wall, by Virginia Woolf, and Three Jews, by Leonard Woolf.

The mark on the wall. Richmond Surrey 1919 (150 copies). First pbd 1917 in Two stories, above; rptd (rev) in Monday or Tuesday, below, and in A haunted house, below.

Kew Gardens. Richmond Surrey 1919 (150 copies). Story; rptd in Monday or Tuesday, below, and in A haunted house, below.

Night and day. 1919, New York 1920.

Monday or Tuesday. Richmond Surrey 1921, New York 1921.

Jacob's room. Richmond Surrey 1922, New York 1923.

Mrs Dalloway. 1925, New York 1925, 1928 (Modern Lib, with introd by V. Woolf).

To the lighthouse. 1927, New York 1927, London 1938 (EL, introd by D. M. Hoare).

Orlando: a biography. New York 1928 (limited edn), London 1928, New York 1960 (Signet Classics, with afterword by E. Bowen).

The waves. 1931, New York 1931.

The years. 1937, New York 1937.

Between the acts. 1941, New York 1941.

A haunted house, and other short stories. 1943 (for 1944), New York 1944. With 6 not previously pbd.

Nurse Lugton's golden thimble. 1966. Children's story.

Other Works

F. M. Dostoevsky. Stavrogin's confession and the plan of The life of a great sinner. Tr S. S. Koteliansky and V. Woolf, Richmond Surrey 1922.

Tolstoi's love letters, with a study on the autobiographical elements in Tolstoy's work by P. Biryukov. Tr S. S. Koteliansky and V. Woolf, Richmond Surrey 1923.

Talks with Tolstoy, by A. B. Goldenveizer. Tr S. S. Koteliansky and V. Woolf, Richmond Surrey 1923.

Mr Bennett and Mrs Brown. 1924 (Hogarth Essays 1). First pbd in Criterion 2 1924 (as Character in fiction); rptd in Hogarth essays, New York 1928, and in The captain's death bed, below.

The common reader. 1925, New York 1925, 1948 (with The common reader: second series, in one vol). Essays. American edns include an additional essay, Lives of the obscure III: Miss Ormerod, which does not appear in the English edns.

A room of one's own. New York 1929 (limited edn), London 1929, New York 1929. Essay.

Street haunting. San Francisco 1930. Essay, first pbd in Yale Rev 1927; rptd in The death of the moth, below.

On being ill. 1930 (250 copies). Essay, first pbd in New Criterion, 1926; rptd in Forum 1926 (as Illness: an unexplored mine). This text rptd in The moment, below.

Beau Brummell. New York 1930. Essay, first pbd in Nation & Athenaeum 1929; rptd in The common reader: second series, below.

A letter to a young poet. 1932 (Hogarth Letters 8). Essay, first pbd in Yale Rev 1932; rptd in The death of the moth, below. See P. Quennell, A letter to Mrs Virginia Woolf (Hogarth Letters 12), 1932.

The common reader: second series. 1932, New York 1932 (as The second common reader), London 1944, New York 1948 (with The common reader: first series, in one vol, as The common reader).

Flush: a biography. 1933, New York 1933. A 'biography' of Elizabeth Barrett Browning's spaniel.

Walter Sickert: a conversation. 1934. Essay, first pbd in Yale Rev 1934 (as A conversation about art); rptd in The captain's death bed, below.

The Roger Fry memorial exhibition: an address. Bristol 1935 (125 copies, not for sale); rptd in The moment, below (as Roger Fry).

Three guineas. 1938, New York 1938. On the part that women can play in the prevention of war.

Reviewing. 1939 (Hogarth Sixpenny pamphlets 4). Essay; rptd in The captain's death bed, below.

Roger Fry: a biography. 1940, New York 1940.

The death of the moth, and other essays. 1942, New York 1942.

The moment, and other essays. 1947, New York 1948.

The captain's death bed, and other essays. New York 1950, London 1950.

Hours in a library. New York [1958]. Essay, first pbd in TLS 30 Nov 1916; rptd in Granite and rainbow, below.

Granite and rainbow: essays. 1958, New York 1958.

Contemporary writers, with a preface by Jean Guiguet. 1965, New York 1966. Essays, mostly rptd from TLS.

Letters and Diaries

A writer's diary: being extracts from the diary of Virginia Woolf. Ed L. Woolf 1953, New York 1954; Diary, ed A. O. Bell 5 vols 1977-(complete).

Virginia Woolf and Lytton Strachey: letters. Ed L. Woolf and J. Strachey 1956, New York 1956.

Letters. Ed. N. Nicolson and J. Trautmann 1975-.

§2

See Virginia Woolf: the critical heritage, ed R. Majumdar and A. McLaurin 1975.

Empson, W. In Scrutinies, ed E. Rickword vol 2, 1931.

Daiches, D. Virginia Woolf. 1942, 1963 (rev).

Forster, E. M. Virginia Woolf. Cambridge 1942 (Rede lecture); rptd in his Two cheers for democracy, 1951.

Mortimer, R. In his Channel packet, 1942.

Bennett, J. Virginia Woolf: her art as a novelist. Cambridge 1945, 1964 (rev).

Auerbach, E. Der braune Strumpf. In his Mimesis, Berne 1946; tr W. R. Trask, Princeton 1953. On To the lighthouse.

Blackstone, B. Virginia Woolf: a commentary. 1949.

—— Virginia Woolf. 1952, 1956 (rev) (Br Council pamphlet).

Savage, D. S. In his Withered branch, 1950.

Brower, R. A. Something central which permeated Virginia Woolf and Mrs Dalloway. In his Fields of light, New York 1951.

Johnstone, J. K. The Bloomsbury group: a study of E. M. Forster, Lytton Strachey, Virginia Woolf and their circle. 1954.

Woolf, L. Sowing: an autobiography of the years 1880–1904. 1960.

—— Growing: an autobiography of the years 1904–11. 1961.

—— Beginning again: an autobiography of the years 1911–18. 1964.

—— Downhill all the way: an autobiography of the years 1919–39. 1967.

—— The journey not the arrival matters: an autobiography of the years 1939–69. 1969.

Guiguet, J. Virginia Woolf et son oeuvre. Paris 1962; tr 1965.

Bell, Q. Virginia Woolf: a biography. 2 vols 1972.

Recollections of Virginia Woolf. Ed J. R. Noble 1972.

DAVID HERBERT LAWRENCE
1885–1930
Bibliographies

McDonald, E. D. A bibliography of the writings of Lawrence. Philadelphia 1925.

Roberts, F. W. A bibliography of Lawrence. 1963 (Soho Bibliographies).

Collections and Selections

The plays of Lawrence. 1933. Contains The widowing of Mrs Holroyd, Touch and go, and David.

The ship of death and other poems. 1933. A selection from Last poems; not the same as the 1941 selection of the same title.

The tales of D. H. Lawrence. 1934. 46 selected stories.

Selected poems. 1934.

The spirit of place: an anthology compiled from the prose of D. H. Lawrence. Ed R. Aldington 1935.

Pornography and so on. 1936. Contains Nettles, Pornography and obscenity, and the introd to The paintings of D. H. Lawrence.

Poems. 2 vols 1939. First collected edn.

The portable Lawrence. Ed Diana Trilling, New York 1947.

Sex, literature and censorship: essays. Ed H. T. Moore, New York [1953], London 1955 (enlarged, with rev introd).

Complete short stories. 3 vols 1955.

Selected literary criticism. Ed A. Beal 1956.

Complete poems. 3 vols 1957.

Complete poems. Ed V. de S. Pinto and F. W. Roberts 2 vols 1964, 1 vol 1977 (Penguin).

Complete plays. 1965.

§1

The white peacock. New York 1911, London 1911, 1950 (Penguin) (with introd by R. Aldington), Carbondale 1966 (preface by H. T. Moore, text from first English printing with restoration of rev passages from first American edn).

The trespasser. 1912, New York 1912.

Love poems, and others. 1913, New York 1913.

Sons and lovers. 1913, New York 1913, 1922 (with introd by J. Macy), 1951 (with introd by M. Schorer), 1962 (introd by A. Kazin, rptd from Partisan Rev 29 1962).

The widowing of Mrs Holroyd: a drama in three acts. (Altrincham Feb 1920 (amateur); Kingsway 13 Dec 1926). Ed E. Bjorkman, New York 1914, London 1914.

The Prussian officer, and other stories. 1914, New York 1916.

The rainbow. 1915 (unexpurgated, suppressed), New York 1915 (expurgated), New York 1924 (unexpurgated), London 1926, 1949 (Penguin, unexpurgated).

Twilight in Italy. 1916, New York 1916 (English sheets), London 1950 (with introd by R. Aldington). Travel sketches.

Amores: poems. [1916], New York 1916.

Look! we have come through! 1917 (expurgated), New York 1918 (English sheets), Marazion 1958 (unexpurgated). Verse.

New poems. 1918, New York 1920.

Bay: a book of poems. 1919.

Touch and go: a play in three acts. 1920, New York 1920. Unperformed.

Women in love. New York 1920 (priv ptd), London [1921], New York 1937 (with Lawrence's Foreword: see below, 1936), London 1951 (with introd by R. Aldington).

The lost girl. 1920, New York 1921, London 1950 (Penguin, with introd by R. Aldington). The first edn has 3 states, involving textual changes; the American 1921 edn has original unaltered text.

Movements in European history, by Lawrence H. Davison [i.e. Lawrence]. 1921, 1925 (illustr, as by D. H. Lawrence), Dublin [1926] (rev). School textbook.

Psychoanalysis and the unconscious. New York 1921, London 1923.

Tortoises. New York 1921. Verse, rptd in Birds, beasts and flowers, below.

Sea and Sardinia. New York 1921, London 1923, 1956 (with introd by R. Aldington). Travel.

Aaron's rod. New York 1922, London 1922, 1950 (Penguin, with introd by R. Aldington).

Fantasia of the unconscious. New York 1922, London 1923 (without epilogue).

England my England, and other stories. New York 1922, London 1924.

The ladybird, The fox, The captain's doll. 1923, New York 1923 (as The captain's doll: three novelettes). The first version of The fox was ed H. T. Moore in his D. H. Lawrence miscellany, Carbondale 1959.

Studies in classic American literature. New York 1923, London 1924 (without foreword), New York 1962 (as The symbolic meaning: the uncollected versions [i.e. the original versions ptd Nov 1918–July 1921 in Eng Rev and in Nation & Athenaeum] of Studies in classic American literature, ed A. Arnold with preface by H. T. Moore).

Kangaroo. 1923, New York 1923, London 1950 (Penguin, with introd by R. Aldington).

Birds, beasts and flowers: poems. New York 1923, London 1923, 1930 (illustr, with prefaces not pbd elsewhere until Phoenix, 1936).

The boy in the bush. 1924, New York 1924. With M. L. Skinner.

Memoirs of the foreign legion by M.M. [Maurice Magnus]. Introd by Lawrence 1924, New York 1925. The introd is a substantial item in its own right (83 pp.).

St Mawr, together with The princess. 1925, New York 1925 (St Mawr only), London 1950 (Penguin, St Mawr together with The virgin and the gipsy, with introd by R. Aldington). Short novel and story.

Reflections on the death of a porcupine, and other essays. Philadelphia 1925, London 1934.

The plumed serpent (Quetzalcoatl). 1926, New York 1926, 1950 (Penguin, with introd by R. Aldington), New York 1950 (with introd by W. Y. Tindall).

David: a play. (Regent 22 May 1927). 1926, New York 1926.

Sun. 1926 (priv ptd, 100 copies), Paris 1928 (unexpurgated, 165 copies). Story; expurgated text rptd in the Woman who rode away.

Glad ghosts. 1926. Story; rptd in The woman who rode away.

Mornings in Mexico. 1927, New York 1927, London 1950 (with introd by R. Aldington). Travel sketches.

Rawdon's roof. 1928 (Woburn Books 7). Story; rptd in Lovely lady, 1932, below.

The woman who rode away, and other stories. 1928, New York 1928 (with extra story, The man who loved islands), London 1950 (Penguin, with introd by R. Aldington; adds A modern lover and Strike-pay but omits The man who loved islands).

Lady Chatterley's lover. [Florence] 1928 (priv ptd), Paris 1929 (priv ptd, with My skirmish with Jolly Roger), London 1932 (expurgated), New York 1932, Hamburg 1933 (unexpurgated, with prefatory note by Frieda Lawrence), New York [1944] (as The first Lady Chatterley, with foreword by Frieda Lawrence and ms report by E. Forbes [first edn of first ms version]), New York [1957] (unexpurgated 1928 text; with introd by M. Schorer, rptd in A propos of Lady Chatterley's lover, 1961 (Penguin), London 1960 (Penguin), 1961 (with introd by R. Hoggart); tr Italian, 1954 (as Le tre Lady Chatterley [i.e. the 3 versions of the novel], with introd by P. Nardi, including the first edn of the 2nd ms version). A description of the 3 versions is given in Schorer's introd.

Collected poems. 2 vols (vol 1, Rhyming poems; vol 2, Unrhyming poems) 1928, New York 1929 (in one vol), London 1932. Preface by Lawrence. Many poems rev and retitled from original appearances; Song of a man who is loved pbd first in this collection.

Sex locked out. 1928 (priv ptd). Article, rptd from Sunday Dispatch, and rptd in Assorted articles, below.

The paintings of D. H. Lawrence. [1929] (priv ptd). Introd by Lawrence.

Pansies: poems. Introd by Lawrence 1929 (expurgated), 1929 (priv ptd, unexpurgated), New York 1929 (expurgated).

My skirmish with Jolly Roger, written as an introduction to and a motivation of the Paris edition of Lady Chatterley's lover. New York 1929, London 1930 (rev, as A propos of Lady Chatterley's lover); rptd in Sex, literature and censorship, Collections above, and in Phoenix II, below.

Pornography and obscenity. 1929 (Criterion Miscellany 5), New York 1930, 1948 (with preface by F. A. Hasratoff); rptd in Sex, literature and censorship, and in Phoenix.

The escaped cock. Paris 1929, London 1931 (as The man who died), New York 1931; rptd (as The man who died) in the Tales of Lawrence, 1934, Collections above.

The life of J. Middleton Murry, by J.C. [Jesus Christ]. 1930 (priv ptd, 50 copies). 5 lines.

Nettles. 1930 (Criterion Miscellany 11). Verse.

Assorted articles. 1930, New York 1930. Mostly from 1928–9.

The virgin and the gipsy. Florence 1930, London 1930, New York 1930; rptd in Tales, 1934, above.

Love among the haystacks and other pieces, with a reminiscence by D. Garnett. 1930, New York 1933 (with extra piece, Christs in the Tirol). Stories and sketches.

Apocalypse. Florence 1931, New York 1931 (with introd by R. Aldington), London 1932.

The triumph of the machine. 1930 (for 1931). Poem; rptd in Last poems, below.

Etruscan places. 1932, New York 1932 (English sheets), London 1950 (Penguin, with introd by R. Aldington). Travel sketches.

Last poems. Ed R. Aldington and G. Orioli, Florence 1932, New York 1933, London 1933.

The lovely lady. 1932 (for 1933), New York 1933. Stories.

We need one another. New York 1933. 2 essays, rptd in Phoenix, below.

A collier's Friday night. (Royal Court 8 Aug 1965). 1934. Play; introd by E. Garnett.

An original poem. 1934 (priv ptd, 100 copies). With note by C. Carswell. 'The wind, the rascal'.

A modern lover. 1934, New York 1934. Stories.

Lawrence's unpublished foreword to Women in love. San Francisco 1936 (103 copies).

Phoenix: the posthumous papers. Ed E. D. McDonald, New York 1936, London 1936. Contains a great deal not previously pbd in book form, and some ms material.

Fire, and other poems, with a foreword by Robinson Jeffers and a note on the poems by Frieda Lawrence. San Francisco 1940. Mostly previously unpbd.

A prelude, by D. H. Lawrence: his first and previously unrecorded work. Thames Ditton 1949 (priv ptd, 160 copies); rptd in Phoenix II, below. Story, rptd from Nottinghamshire Guardian 7 Dec 1907; foreword by P. B. Wadsworth.

Life. St Ives 1954 (250 copies). Essay, first pbd in Eng Rev Feb 1918; rptd in Phoenix, above.

The man who was through with the world: an unfinished story by Lawrence. Ed J. R. Elliot jr, EC 9 1959.

Complete poems. Ed V. de S. Pinto and W. Roberts 2 vols 1964. Poems previously collected, together with uncollected poems from ptd and ms sources, appendices of juvenilia, variants and early drafts; includes all Lawrence's critical introds to his poems.

The paintings of Lawrence, ed M. Levy, with essays by H. T. Moore, J. Lindsay and H. Read. 1964.

Complete plays. 1965, New York 1965.

Phoenix II: uncollected, unpublished and other prose works. Ed F. W. Roberts and H. T. Moore 1968.

Roberts, F. W. Lawrence, the second 'poetic me': some new material. Renaissance & Modern Stud 14 1970. Poems from the Clarke notebook.

Lawrence edited Signature, *with Murry, for 3 nos (Oct–Nov 1915) and made numerous contributions to periodicals, the most important being* Adelphi, Eng Rev *and* Dial.

Translations

All things are possible, by Leo Shestov, authorized translation by S. S. Koteliansky, with a foreword by Lawrence. Tr Lawrence and Koteliansky, 1920.

The gentleman from San Francisco and other stories, by I. A. Bunin, tr S. S. Koteliansky and Leonard Woolf. Richmond 1922. Title story tr by Lawrence and Koteliansky.

Mastro-Don Gesualdo, by Giovanni Verga, tr Lawrence. New York 1923, London 1928 (with introd by Lawrence).

Little novels of Sicily, by Giovanni Verga, tr Lawrence. New York 1925.

Cavalleria rusticana and other stories, by Giovanni Verga, tr and with an introd by Lawrence. 1928.

The story of Doctor Manente, being the tenth and last story from the Suppers of A. F. Grazzini called Il Lasca. Trn and introd by Lawrence, Florence 1929.

The grand inquisitor, by F. M. Dostoevsky, tr S. S. Koteliansky, with introd by Lawrence. Tr Lawrence and Koteliansky 1930 (300 copies).

Letters

Letters. Ed A. Huxley 1932.

Brewster, E. and A. Lawrence: reminiscences and correspondence. 1934.

Letters to Bertrand Russell. Ed H. T. Moore, New York [1948].

Letters, selected by R. Aldington. 1950 (Penguin). Introd by A. Huxley.

Selected letters. Ed Diana Trilling, New York [1958].

Collected letters. Ed H. T. Moore 2 vols New York [1962].

Lawrence in love: letters to Louie Burrows. Ed J. T. Boulton, Nottingham 1968.

Letters from Lawrence to Martin Secker 1911–30. Ed Secker, Iver 1970 (priv ptd, 500 copies).

The quest for Rananim: Lawrence's letters to S. S. Koteliansky 1914–30. Ed G. J. Zytaruk, Montreal 1970.

The Centaur letters. Ed E. D. McDonald, Austin 1970.

Letters to Thomas and Adele Seltzer. Ed G. M. Lacy, Santa Barbara 1976.

Letters. Ed. J. T. Boulton 8 vols Cambridge 1979–.

§2

Douglas, N. Lawrence and Maurice Magnus: a plea for better manners. [Florence] 1924 (priv ptd); rptd in his Experiments, 1925. This refers to Lawrence's introd to Magnus's Foreign legion.

Aldington, R. Lawrence: an indiscretion. Seattle 1927, London 1930 (as D. H. Lawrence).

—— In his Artifex, 1935.

—— Portrait of a genius but... 1950.

Leavis, F. R. D. H. Lawrence. Cambridge 1930; rptd in his For continuity, Cambridge 1933.

—— D. H. Lawrence, novelist. 1955.

—— The necessary opposite, Lawrence. In his English literature in our time and the university, 1969.

—— Thought, words and creativity. 1976.

Murry, J. M. Lawrence: two essays. Cambridge 1930.

—— Son of woman: the story of Lawrence. 1931, 1954 (with new introd, as D. H. Lawrence, son of woman).

—— Reminiscences of Lawrence. 1933.

Potter, S. Lawrence: a first study. 1930.

'West, Rebecca' (C. I. Andrews). D. H. Lawrence. 1930 (pamphlet); rptd in her Ending in earnest, 1931.

Ford, F. M. (formerly Hueffer). In his Return to yesterday, 1931.

Carswell, C. The savage pilgrimage: a narrative of Lawrence. 1932, 1932 (rev). Reply to J. M. Murry, Son of woman, above.

Corke, H. Lawrence and Apocalypse. 1933.

—— Lawrence: the Croydon years. Austin 1965.

Eliot, T. S. In his After strange gods, 1934.

Lawrence, Frieda. Not I, but the wind...Santa Fe, New Mexico 1934 (priv ptd), New York 1934. Includes original material by Lawrence.
— Memoirs and correspondence. Ed E. W. Tedlock 1961.
'E.T.' (Jessie Chambers Wood). Lawrence: a personal record. 1935; ed J. D. Chambers 1965 (includes additional material by J. D. Chambers, Helen Corke, J. A. Bramley and May Holbrook).
Savage, D. S. Lawrence: a study in dissolution. In his Personal principle, 1944.
Nardi, P. La vita di Lawrence. Milan 1947.
Woolf, V. Notes on Lawrence. In her The moment and other essays, 1947.
Bowen, E. In her Collected impressions, 1950.
West, A. D. H. Lawrence. 1950.
Auden, W. H. Heretics. In Literary opinion in America, ed M. D. Zabel, New York 1951; rptd in his Dyer's hand, 1962.
Bynner, W. Journey with genius: recollections and reflections concerning the Lawrences. New York 1951.
Moore, H. T. The life and works of Lawrence. New York 1951, 1964 (rev, as Lawrence: his life and works).
— The intelligent heart: the story of Lawrence. New York 1954, London 1960 (Penguin) (rev) 1974 (as The priest of love), 1976 (Penguin) (rev).
— (ed). A Lawrence miscellany. Carbondale 1959.
— and W. Roberts (ed). Lawrence and his world. 1966.
Young, K. D. H. Lawrence. 1952, 1960 (rev), 1963 (rev) (Br Council pamphlet).
Spilka, M. The love ethic of Lawrence. Bloomington 1955.
— (ed). Lawrence: a collection of critical essays. Englewood Cliffs NJ 1963.
Hough, G. G. The dark sun: a study of Lawrence. 1956.
— Two exiles: Lord Byron and Lawrence. Nottingham 1956. Lecture. Rptd in his Image and experience, 1960.
Russell, B. In his Portraits from memory, 1956.
Nehls, E. (ed). Lawrence: a composite biography. 3 vols Madison 1957-9.
Beal, A. D. H. Lawrence. Edinburgh 1961 (Writers and Critics).
Rolph, C. H. (ed). The trial of Lady Chatterley. 1961 (Penguin).
Sparrow, J. The censor as aedile. In his Independent essays, 1963.
Stewart, J. I. M. In his Eight modern writers, Oxford 1963 (OHEL).
Tedlock, E. W. Lawrence—artist and rebel: a study of Lawrence's fiction. Albuquerque 1963.
— (ed). Lawrence and Sons and lovers: sources and criticism. New York 1965.
Draper, R. P. D. H. Lawrence. New York 1964.
— D. H. Lawrence. 1969 (Profiles in Literature).
— (ed). Lawrence: the critical heritage. 1970.
Gilbert, S. M. Acts of attention: the poems of Lawrence. Ithaca 1972.
Kermode, F. Lawrence. 1973.

GRAHAM GREENE
b. 1904

Collections and Selections

Uniform edition. 1947–. Textual changes from first edns in many cases.
Collected essays. 1969, New York 1969.
Collected edition. 1970–. With prefaces by Greene.
Shades of Greene: the televised stories. 1975.

§1
Prose Fiction

The man within. 1929, Garden City NY 1929, London 1952 (with note by Greene).
The name of action. 1930, Garden City NY 1931.
Rumour at nightfall. 1931, Garden City NY 1932.

Stamboul train: an entertainment. 1932, Garden City NY 1933 (as Orient express).
It's a battlefield. 1934, Garden City NY 1934, New York 1962 (introd by Greene).
England made me. 1935, Garden City NY 1935, New York 1953 (as The shipwrecked).
The basement room, and other stories. 1935. Contains The basement room (retold as The fallen idol in The third man, and The fallen idol, 1950, below), etc.
The bear fell free. 1935 (limited to 285 copies) (Grayson Books). Story.
This gun for hire: an entertainment. Garden City NY 1936, London 1936 (as A gun for sale), Toronto 1942 (as This Gun, Inc).
Brighton rock: an entertainment. New York 1938, London 1938 (with sub-title 'a novel').
The confidential agent: an entertainment. 1939, New York 1939.
The power and the glory. 1940, New York 1940 (as The labyrinthine ways), New York 1946 (as The power and the glory), London 1963 (introd by Greene, rptd from Introductions to three novels, 1962, below).
The Ministry of Fear: an entertainment. 1943, New York 1943.
Nineteen stories. 1947, New York 1949 (omitting The lottery ticket, adding The hint of an explanation). Includes contents of The basement room, 1935, above.
The heart of the matter. 1948, New York 1948.
The third man: an entertainment. New York 1950, London 1950, (with The fallen idol, as The third man, and The fallen idol). The third man was written as a preliminary to the script of the film of the same name. First pbd as story in Amer Mag March 1949. The filmscript with changes by Carol Reed, Orson Welles etc pbd 1969.
The end of the affair. 1951, New York 1951.
Twenty-one stories. 1954, New York 1954. Contents as Nineteen stories, 1947, above, omitting The lottery ticket and The other side of the border, and adding The hint of an explanation, The blue film, Special duties, The destructors.
The quiet American. 1955, New York 1956. First pbd, in Swedish trn, from ms, Stockholm 1955.
Loser takes all: an entertainment. 1955, New York 1957. Pbd as serial in Harper's Mag Oct 1955–Jan 1956.
Our man in Havana. 1958, New York 1958.
A visit to Morin. [1959] (250 copies). First pbd, in French trn, Les Œuvres Libres new ser no 131 1957.
A burnt-out case. 1961, New York 1961. First pbd, in Swedish trn from ms, Stockholm 1960.
A sense of reality. 1963, New York 1963. Stories; contains Under the garden, A visit to Morin, Dream of a strange land, A discovery in the woods.
The comedians. 1966, New York 1966.
May we borrow your husband? and other comedies of the sexual life. 1967, New York 1967.

Other Works

Babbling April. Oxford 1925. Verse.
The old school: essays by divers hands. Ed Greene 1934. Contains The last word, by Greene.
Journey without maps: a travel book. 1936, Garden City NY 1936, London 1948 (rev).
The lawless roads: a Mexican journey. 1939, New York 1939 (as Another Mexico).
British dramatists. 1942 (Britain in Pictures).
The little train, by Dorothy Craigie [i.e. illustr D. Craigie, text by Greene]. [1946], 1957 (as by Greene), New York 1958. For children.
Why do I write?: an exchange of views between Elizabeth Bowen, Greene and V. S. Pritchett. 1948, New York 1948.
The little fire engine. [1950], New York 1953 (as The little red fire engine). For children.
The lost childhood, and other essays. 1951, New York 1952.
For Christmas. 1951 (limited to 12 copies). 7 poems.

The little horse bus. [1952], New York 1954. For children.

The living room: a play in two acts. (Wyndham's 16 April 1953). 1953, New York 1954, London 1955 (introd by P. Glenville). Slight difference between the endings of the English and US edns. First pbd, in Swedish trn from ms, Stockholm 1952.

Essais catholiques. Paris 1953. 6 essays, tr M. Sibon; 3 not previously pbd in English.

The little steamroller: a story of adventure, mystery and detection. [1953], New York 1955. For children.

Nino Caffé. New York [1953]. Essay on the painter Caffé.

The potting shed: a play in three acts. (Bijou, New York 29 Jan 1957; Globe 5 Feb 1958). New York [1957], London 1958, 1959 (French's Acting Edn).

The spy's bedside book: an anthology ed G. Greene and H. Greene. 1957.

The complaisant lover: a comedy. (Globe 18 June 1959). 1959, New York 1960, London [1961] (French's Acting Edn).

In search of a character: two African journals. 1961, New York 1962. Contains Congo journal, containing material used in A burnt-out case, and Convoy to West Africa.

Introductions to three novels. Stockholm 1962. The power and the glory, The heart of the matter, The end of the affair.

The revenge: an autobiographical fragment. 1963 (priv ptd, 300 copies).

Carving a statue: a play. (Haymarket 17 Sept 1964). 1964, New York 1964.

Lord Rochester's monkey. 1974.

Greene has contributed to numerous periodicals, notably reviews for Spectator *(1932–45), London Mercury, Fortnightly Rev, Observer, Time & Tide, Now & Then, Life & Letters, Tablet, New Statesman and Evening Standard. A number of his film criticisms were rptd in Garbo and the night watchman, ed A. Cooke 1937.*

§2

Allott, K. and M. Farris. The art of Greene. 1951.

Wyndham, F. Graham Greene. 1955, 1958 (rev) (Br Council pamphlet).

Atkins, J. A. Graham Greene. 1957, 1966 (rev).

Lewis, R. W. B. Greene: the religious affair. In his Picaresque saint, New York 1959.

Pryce-Jones, D. Graham Greene. Edinburgh 1963 (Writers & Critics), 1973.

Lodge, D. Graham Greene. New York 1966.

RICHARD ALDINGTON
1892–1962

§1

Images 1910–15. [1915], Boston 1916 (as Images old and new), London [1919] (as Images, with additional poems). Verse.

The love poems of Myrrhine and Konallis: a cycle of prose poems. Cleveland 1917 (40 copies), Chicago 1926 (as The love of Myrrhine and Konallis, and other prose poems).

Reverie: a little book of poems for H.D. Cleveland 1917 (50 copies).

Images of desire. 1919. Verse.

Images of war: a book of poems. 1919 (pbd Beaumont Press), 1919 (enlarged, but omitting some of the poems in the Beaumont Press edn, as Images of war).

War and love 1915–18. Boston 1919. Contains most of Images of desire and Images of war.

The Berkshire Kennet. 1923 (50 copies). Poem.

Exile and other poems. 1923.

Literary studies and reviews. 1924.

A fool i' the forest: a phantasmagoria. 1925. Verse.

Voltaire. 1925, 1929 (rev). Biography.

French studies and reviews. 1926, New York 1926.

D. H. Lawrence: an indiscretion. Seattle 1927 (Univ of Washington Chapbooks 6), London 1930 (as D. H. Lawrence). Pamphlet.

Collected poems. New York 1928, 1929, 1933 (as Collected poems 1915–23, omitting A fool i' the forest).

Hark the herald. [Paris 1928]. Poem, rptd in Movietones.

Remy de Gourmont: a modern man of letters. Seattle 1928 (Univ of Washington Chapbooks 13).

Death of a hero. New York 1929, London 1929, Paris 1930 (2 vols, unexpurgated), London 1965.

The eaten heart. Chapelle-Réanville 1929 (200 copies), Poem, rptd in The eaten heart [and other poems], 1933 below.

At all costs. 1930. Story, rptd in Roads to glory.

Balls, and Another book for suppression. 1930 (Blue Moon Booklets 7, 100 copies), Westport Conn 1932 (priv ptd, about 100 copies).

Last straws. Paris 1930. Story, rptd in US edn (only) of Soft answers, below.

Love and the Luxembourg. New York 1930, London 1930 (as A dream in the Luxembourg). Poem.

Two stories: Deserter; The lads of the village. 1930; rptd in Roads to glory, below.

Roads to glory. 1930, Garden City NY 1930. Stories.

The colonel's daughter. 1931, Garden City NY 1931.

Stepping heavenward: a record. Florence 1931, London 1931. Story; rptd in Soft answers.

Movietones, invented and set down 1928–1929. [1932?] (priv ptd, 10 copies). Verse.

Soft answers. 1932, Garden City NY 1932. Stories.

All men are enemies: a romance. 1933, Garden City NY 1933.

The eaten heart [and other poems]. 1933.

The poems of Richard Aldington. Garden City NY 1934.

The squire. 1934 (12 copies). Essay.

Women must work. 1934, Garden City NY 1934.

Artifex: sketches and ideas. 1935, Garden City NY 1936.

Life quest. 1935, Garden City NY 1935. Verse.

D. H. Lawrence: a complete list of his works, together with a critical appreciation [1936?]. Pamphlet, not identical with Aldington's earlier work of same title.

Life of a lady: a play. Garden City NY 1936, London [1936] (with subtitle, A play in three acts). With D. Patmore.

The crystal world. 1937, Garden City NY 1938. Verse.

Very heaven. 1937, Garden City NY 1937.

Seven against Reeves: a comedy-farce. 1938, New York 1938. Fiction.

Rejected guest. New York 1939, London 1939 (with note by Aldington on textual differences between US and English edns).

W. Somerset Maugham: an appreciation. New York 1939. Pamphlet.

Life for life's sake: a book of reminiscences. New York 1941, London 1968.

The Duke: being an account of the life and achievements of Arthur Wellesley, 1st Duke of Wellington. New York 1943, London 1946 (as Wellington, [etc]).

The romance of Casanova. New York 1946, London 1947. Fiction.

Four English portraits 1801–51. 1948.

The complete poems. Introd by Aldington 1948.

Jane Austen. Pasadena 1948. Pamphlet.

The strange life of Charles Waterton 1782–1865. 1949, New York 1949.

Portrait of a genius, but...: the life of D. H. Lawrence. 1950, New York 1950 (as D. H. Lawrence: portrait of a genius, but...).

Ezra Pound and T. S. Eliot: a lecture. Hurst 1954.

Pinorman: personal recollections of Norman Douglas, Pino Orioli and Charles Prentice. 1954.

A. E. Housman and W. B. Yeats: two lectures. Hurst 1955.

Lawrence of Arabia: a biographical enquiry. 1955, Chicago 1955.
Introduction to Mistral. 1956, Carbondale 1960 (with preface by H. T. Moore).
Frauds. 1957. Biography.
Portrait of a rebel: the life and work of Robert Louis Stevenson. 1957.
A letter [to G. W. V. Potocki], and a summary bibliography of Count Potocki's published works. Draguignan [1961].
A tourist's Rome. Draguignan [1961]. Sketch.
Selected critical writings 1928–60. Ed A. Kershaw, Carbondale 1970.

Aldington pbd trns, mostly from the French, and edited anthologies and works by other authors, including some of the last works of D. H. Lawrence.

§ 2

Snow, C. P. Richard Aldington: an appreciation. 1938.
Moore, H. T. Aldington in his last years. Texas Quart 6 1963.
Kershaw, A. and Temple, F.-J. (ed). Aldington: an intimate portrait. Carbondale 1965.
Gates, N. T. The poetry of Aldington. University Park Pa 1974. With uncollected poems.

WALTER ERNEST ALLEN
b. 1911

Innocence is drowned. 1938.
Blind man's ditch. 1939.
Living space. 1940.
The Black Country. 1946. Topography.
Rogue elephant. 1946, New York 1946.
Arnold Bennett. 1948, Denver 1949.
The festive baked-potato cart, and other stories. 1948.
Writers on writing, selected and introduced by W. Allen. 1948, New York 1949 (as The writer on his art), Boston 1958 (as Writers on writing).
Reading a novel. 1949, 1956 (rev), 1963 (rev).
Dead man over all. 1950, New York 1951 (as Square peg).
Joyce Cary. 1953, 1963 (rev) (Br Council pamphlet).
The English novel: a short critical history. 1954, New York 1955.
The novel today. 1955, 1960 (rev) (Br Council pamphlet).
Six great novelists: Defoe, Fielding, Scott, Dickens, Stevenson, Conrad. 1955.
All in a lifetime. 1959, New York 1959 (as Threescore and ten).
George Eliot. New York 1964, London 1965.
Tradition and dream: the English and American novel from the twenties to our time. 1964, New York 1964 (as The modern novel in Britain and the United States).
The urgent West. 1969, New York 1969.

MICHAEL ARLEN
formerly
DIKRAN KUYUMJIAN
1895–1956

The London venture. [1920], New York [1920].
The romantic lady, and other stories. [1921], New York 1921.
'Piracy': a romantic chronicle of these days. [1922], New York [1923].
These charming people. [1923], New York [1924]. Stories.
The green hat: a romance for a few people. [1924], New York [1924], 1925 (acting version).
May Fair (in which are told the last adventures of These charming people). [1925], New York 1925. Stories.

The ace of cads, and other stories. [1927]. Stories from May Fair, above.
Ghost stories. 1927.
The man with the broken nose, and other stories. [1927]. Stories from These charming people, above.
Young men in love. [1927], New York [1927].
The zoo: a comedy in three acts. [1927]. With W. Smith.
Lily Christine: a romance. Garden City NY 1928, London 1929.
Babes in the wood. Garden City NY 1929, London [1930]. Stories.
Men dislike women: a romance. 1931, Garden City NY 1931.
A young man comes to London. [1932]. Story.
Good losers: a play in three acts and a prologue. [1933]. With W. Hackett.
Man's mortality: a story. 1933, Garden City NY 1933.
Hell! said the duchess: a bed-time story. 1934, Garden City NY 1934.
The crooked coronet, and other misrepresentations of the real facts of life. 1937, Garden City NY 1937. Stories.
Flying Dutchman. [1939], New York 1939.

NIGEL MARLIN BALCHIN
1908–70

How to run a bassoon factory: or, business explained. 1934, Boston 1936, London 1950 (with Business for pleasure, and An appreciation of the late Mr Spade by Nigel Balchin). As 'Mark Spade'; humour.
No sky. 1934.
Business for pleasure. 1935, 1950 (with How to run a bassoon factory, and An appreciation of the late Mr Spade by Nigel Balchin, above). As 'Mark Spade'; humour.
Simple life. 1935.
Fun and games: how to win at almost anything. 1936. As 'Mark Spade'; humour.
Income and outcome: a study of personal finance. 1936.
Lightbody on liberty. 1936.
Darkness falls from the air. 1942.
The small back room. 1943, Boston 1945.
Mine own executioner. 1945, Boston 1946.
The aircraft builders: an account of British aircraft production 1939–45. 1947.
Lord, I was afraid. 1947.
The Borgia testament. 1948, Boston 1949.
A sort of traitors. 1949, Boston 1950 (as Who is my neighbour?).
The anatomy of villainy. 1950. Essays.
A way through the wood. 1951, Boston 1951.
Sundry creditors. 1953, Boston 1953 (as Private interests).
Last recollections of my Uncle Charles. 1954, New York 1957. Stories.
The worker in modern industry. 1954. Pamphlet.
The fall of the sparrow. 1955, New York 1956 (as The fall of a sparrow).
Seen dimly before dawn. 1962, New York 1962.
Burnt Njal—the irredeemable crime. In Fatal fascination: a choice of crime, by N. Balchin [et al], 1964, Boston 1965.
In the absence of Mrs Petersen. 1966, New York 1966.
Kings of infinite space. 1967, New York 1968.

MAURICE BARING
1874–1945

Hildesheim: quatre pastiches. Paris 1899, London 1924.
The Black Prince, and other poems. 1903 [1902].
Gaston de Foix and other plays. 1903. In verse. For rev version of the title play, see Gaston de Foix 1913, below.
The story of Forget-me-not and Lily of the valley. [1905] (priv ptd, 25 copies), 1909 (trade edn), 1928 (as Forget-me-not and Lily of the valley). For children.

With the Russians in Manchuria. 1905.
Mahasena. Oxford 1905. Verse play.
Sonnets and short poems. Oxford 1906.
Desiderio. Oxford 1906, 1911 (rev). Verse drama.
A year in Russia. 1907, 1917 (rev, with new preface).
Proserpine: a masque. Oxford 1908. In verse.
Russian essays and stories. 1908.
Orpheus in Mayfair, and other stories and sketches. 1909.
Landmarks in Russian literature. 1910.
Dead letters. 1910, Boston 1910. Imaginary letters, rptd
    from Morning Post.
The glass mender, and other stories. 1910, New York 1911
    (as The blue rose fairy book).
Diminutive dramas. 1911, Boston 1911. Rptd from
    Morning Post.
The Russian people. 1911.
The grey stocking, and other plays. 1911.
Gaston de Foix. Oxford 1913. Text rev from that in
    Gaston de Foix, and other plays, 1903, above.
Letters from the Near East, 1909 and 1912. 1913. Rptd
    from Morning Post and Times.
Lost diaries. 1913, Boston 1913. Rptd from The Eye
    Witness. Fiction.
Palamon and Arcite: a play for puppets. Oxford 1913.
Round the world in any number of days. Boston 1914,
    London 1919.
The mainsprings of Russia. 1914.
An outline of Russian literature. 1915.
English landscape: an anthology compiled by Baring. 1916.
Translations, found in a commonplace book, edited by
    'S.C.' Oxford 1916, London 1918 (as Translations
    ancient and modern by M. Baring, with additional
    material), 1925 (with originals which had in fact been
    written by Ronald Knox et al). Fiction.
In memoriam: Auberon Herbert. Oxford 1917 (priv ptd,
    35 copies), 1917 (trade edn).
Poems 1914-17. 1917, 1920 (with addns, as Poems 1914-
    19).
Manfroy: a play in five acts. 1920 (priv ptd, 25 copies);
    rptd in His Majesty's embassy and other plays, 1923
    below.
R.F.C., H.Q., 1914-18. 1920, 1930 (as Flying Corps
    Headquarters 1914-18).
Passing by. 1921.
The puppet show of memory. 1922, Boston 1922. Auto-
    biography.
Overlooked. 1922, Boston 1922.
His Majesty's embassy and other plays. 1923.
A triangle: passages from three notebooks. 1923.
C. 1924, 2 vols Garden City NY 1924.
Punch and Judy and other essays. 1924, Garden City NY
    1924.
The Oxford book of Russian verse, chosen by M. Baring.
    Oxford 1924.
Half a minute's silence, and other stories. 1925, Garden
    City NY 1926.
Cat's cradle. 1925.
Daphne Adeane. 1926, New York 1927.
Catherine Parr: or Alexander's horse. Lockport Ill 1927.
    From Diminutive dramas.
French literature. 1927. Pamphlet.
Last days of Tsarskoe Selo: being the personal notes and
    memoirs of Count Paul Benckendoff. Tr Baring 1927.
Tinker's leave. 1927, Garden City NY 1928.
Cecil Spencer. 1928 (priv ptd), 1929 (trade edn). Com-
    memorative verse.
Comfortless memory. 1928, Garden City NY 1928 (as
    When they love).
Forget-me-not and Lily of the valley. 1928. See The
    story of Forget-me-not and Lily of the valley, 1905,
    above.
The coat without seam. 1929, New York 1929.
Passing by, and Overlooked. 1929. First pbd separately
    1921 and 1922.
Robert Peckham. 1930, New York 1930.

In my end is my beginning. 1931, New York 1931.
Poems translated from Pushkin by M. Baring. 1931 (priv
    ptd, 50 copies).
Friday's business. 1932, New York 1933.
Lost lectures: or the fruits of experience. 1932, New York
    1932. Essays.
Sarah Bernhardt. 1933, New York 1934.
The lonely land of Dulwich. 1934, New York 1934.
Darby and Joan. 1935, New York 1936.
Have you anything to declare?: a notebook with commen-
    taries. [1936], New York 1937.

*Baring pbd privately pamphlets of verse in small edns, most of
    the contents of which were rptd in* Collected poems, *1925
    and* Poems 1892-1929. *Some of Baring's letters were ptd
    in E. Smyth,* Maurice Baring, *1938 and L. Lovat,*
    Maurice Baring, *1947. With R. A. Leigh and H. Cornish,
    Baring edited and largely wrote* The Cambridge ABC
    *(4 nos, 1894), and with Hilaire Belloc he edited, and
    largely wrote,* The North Street Gazette *(1 no only,
    March 1910). He was also co-editor of the* Russian Rev
    (1912-14).

HERBERT ERNEST BATES
1905-74

Collections and Selections

Thirty tales. 1934.
Country tales: collected short stories. 1940.
Something in the air: stories by Flying Officer 'X'. 1944.
Thirty-one selected tales. 1947.
Works Evensford edition. 1951-.
Selected short stories chosen and introduced by the
    author. 1951.
Twenty tales. 1951.
Selected stories. 1957 (Penguin).
Seven by five: stories by H. E. Bates 1926-61. Preface by
    H. Miller 1963, Boston 1963 (as The best of H. E. Bates).

§I

The last bread: a play in one act. 1926.
The two sisters. 1926, New York 1926.
The seekers. 1926. Stories.
The spring song, and In view of the fact that: two stories.
    1927 (priv ptd, 100 copies), San Francisco 1927 (priv
    ptd, 50 copies).
Day's end, and other stories. 1928.
Song for December. [1928] (priv ptd, 150 copies). Poem.
Seven tales and Alexander. 1929, New York 1930.
Catherine Foster. 1929, New York 1929.
The tree. [1930] (Blue Moon Booklets 3). Story.
The Hessian prisoner. Foreword by E. Garnett 1930
    (Furnivall Books 2). Story
Christmas 1930. [1930] (priv ptd). Poem.
Charlotte's Row. 1931.
Holly and sallow. 1931 (100 copies). Poem.
Mrs Esmond's life. 1931 (priv ptd, 300 copies). Story.
A threshing day. 1931. (300 copies). Story.
The black boxer: tales. 1932.
Sally go round the moon. 1932. Story.
A German idyll. Waltham St Lawrence 1932 (307 copies).
    Story.
The fallow land. 1932, New York 1933.
The story without end, and The country doctor. 1932
    (130 copies).
The house with the apricot, and two other tales. 1933.
The woman who had imagination, and other stories. 1934,
    New York 1934.
Cut and come again: fourteen stories. 1935.
The duet. 1935 (285 copies) (Grayson Books). Story.
Flowers and faces. [Waltham St Lawrence] 1935 (325
    copies). On gardening.
The poacher. 1935, New York 1935.
A house of women. 1936, New York 1936.

Through the woods: the English woodlands—April to April. 1936, New York 1936. Essays.
Down the river. 1937, New York 1937. Essays.
Something short and sweet: stories. 1937.
Spella Ho. 1938, Boston 1938.
The flying goat. 1939. Stories.
My Uncle Silas. 1939.
The beauty of the dead, and other stories. 1940.
The seasons and the gardener: a book for children. Cambridge 1940. Non-fiction.
The beauty of the dead and one other short story (The bridge). 1941 (25 copies).
The modern short story: a critical survey. 1941.
The greatest people in the world, and other stories, by Flying Officer 'X'. 1942, New York 1943 (as There's something in the air). Anon.
In the heart of the country. 1942. Essays.
The bride comes to Evensford. 1943. Story.
Country life. 1943 (Penguin). Notes, rptd from Spectator.
How sleep the brave, and other stories, by Flying Officer 'X'. 1943. Anon.
O more than happy countryman. 1943. Essays.
Fair stood the wind for France. Boston 1944, London 1944.
There's freedom in the air: the official story of the allied air forces from the occupied countries. 1944. Anon.
The day of glory: a play in three acts. 1945.
The cruise of the Breadwinner. 1946, Boston 1947.
The tinkers of Elstow. [1946]. Pamphlet history of an ordnance factory.
Otters and men. [1947]. Essay rptd from Down the river, 1937, above
The purple plain. 1947, Boston 1947.
The bride comes to Evensford, and other tales. 1949.
The country heart. 1949. Rev edn of O more than happy countryman, 1943, above, and In the heart of the country, 1942, above.
Dear life. Boston 1949, London 1950.
The jacaranda tree. 1949, Boston 1949.
Edward Garnett. 1950. Biography.
The scarlet sword. 1950, Boston 1951.
Colonel Julian, and other stories. 1951, Boston 1952.
The country of white clover. 1952. Essays.
The face of England. 1952. Non-fiction.
Love for Lydia. 1952, Boston 1953.
The nature of love: three short novels. 1953, Boston 1954.
The feast of July. 1954, Boston [1954].
The daffodil sky. 1955, Boston 1956. Stories.
The sleepless moon. 1956, Boston [1956].
Death of a huntsman: four short novels. 1957, Boston 1957 (as Summer in Salandar).
Sugar for the horse. 1957. Stories.
The darling buds of May. 1958, Boston 1958.
A breath of French air. 1959, Boston 1959.
The watercress girl, and other stories. 1959, Boston 1960.
An aspidistra in Babylon: four novellas. 1960, Boston 1960 (as The grapes of paradise).
When the green woods laugh. 1960, Boston 1961 (as Hark, hark, the lark).
The day of the tortoise. 1961.
Now sleeps the crimson petal, and other stories. 1961, Boston 1961 (as The enchantress, and other stories).
Achilles the donkey. 1962. Children's story.
A crown of wild myrtle. 1962, New York 1963.
The golden oriole: five novellas. 1962, Boston 1962.
Achilles and Diana. 1963, New York 1963. Children's story.
Oh! to be in England. 1963, New York 1964.
Achilles and the twins. 1964, New York 1965. Children's story.
The fabulous Mrs V. 1964. Stories.
A moment in time. 1964, New York 1964.
The wedding party. 1965. Stories.
The distant horns of summer. 1967.
The four beauties. 1968. Stories.

The white admiral. 1968. Children's story.
The wild cherry tree. 1968. Stories.
The vanished world: an autobiography. 1969–.

ADRIAN HANBURY BELL
b. 1901

Corduroy. 1930. Rptd in Silver ley, below.
Silver Ley. 1931, New York 1931.
The cherry tree. 1932, New York 1932.·
Folly field. 1933.
The balcony. 1934, New York 1936.
Seasons. 1934. Verse.
Poems. 1935 (30 copies).
By-road. 1937.
Men and the fields. 1939, New York 1939. Non-fiction.
The shepherd's farm. 1939.
Apple acre. 1942, 1964 (rev).
Sunrise to sunset. 1944.
The budding morrow. 1946.
The black donkey. 1949.
The flower and the wheel. 1949.
The path by the window. 1952. Stories.
Music in the morning. 1954.
A young man's fancy. 1955, New York 1956.
A Suffolk harvest. 1956. Non-fiction.
The mill house. 1958.
My own master. 1961. Autobiography.
A street in Suffolk. 1964. Non-fiction.

STELLA BENSON
1892–1933

Collections

Poems. 1935. Contains Twenty, and a selection of other poems made by the author.
Collected short stories. 1936.

§I

I pose. 1915, New York 1916.
This is the end. 1917.
Twenty. 1918, New York 1918. Verse.
Living alone. 1919.
Kwan-Yin. San Francisco 1922 (priv ptd, 100 copies). Play.
The poor man. 1922, New York 1923.
Pipers and a dancer. 1924, New York 1924.
The little world. 1925, New York 1926. Travel.
The awakening: a fantasy. San Francisco 1925. Story.
Goodbye, stranger. 1926, New York 1926.
Worlds within worlds. 1928, New York 1929. Travel.
The man who missed the 'bus. 1928. Story.
Come to Eleuthera. [1929?]. Travel, ed and partly written by Stella Benson.
The far-away bride. New York 1930, London 1931 (as Tobit transplanted).
Hope against hope, and other stories. 1931.
Christmas formula, and other stories. 1932.
Mundos: an unfinished novel. 1935.

EDMUND CLERIHEW BENTLEY
1875–1956

Collections

Clerihews complete. [1951].
Trent's case book, with an introduction by B. R. Redman. New York 1953. Contains Trent's last case, Trent's own case, and Trent intervenes.

§1

Biography for beginners. [1905]. As 'E. Clerihew'. Humorous verse.

Trent's last case. [1913], New York 1913 (as The woman in black), London 1929 (rev, as Trent's last case), New York 1930.

Peace year in the City 1918–19; an account of the outstanding events in the City of London during Peace year. 1920 (priv ptd).

More biography. 1929. Humorous verse.

Trent's own case. 1936, New York 1936. With H. W. Allen.

Trent intervenes. 1938, New York 1938. Stories.

Baseless biography. 1939. Humorous verse.

Those days: an autobiography. 1940.

Elephant's work: an enigma. 1950, New York 1950.

PHYLLIS ELEANOR BENTLEY
1894–1977

Pedagomania: or the gentle art of teaching, by 'A Bachelor of Arts'. 1918.

The world's bane, and other stories. 1918.

Environment. 1922, New York 1935.

Cat-in-the-manger. 1923. Sequel to Environment, above.

The partnership. 1928, Boston 1929.

The spinner of the years. 1928, New York [1929].

Carr: being the biography of Philip Joseph Carr, manufacturer. 1929, New York 1933. Fiction.

Sounding brass: a play in one act. Halifax 1930.

Trio. 1930.

Inheritance. 1932, New York 1934.

A modern tragedy. 1934, New York 1934.

The whole of the story. 1935. Stories.

Freedom, farewell! 1936, New York 1936.

Sleep in peace. 1938, New York 1938.

Take courage. 1940, New York 1940 (as The power and the glory).

The English regional novel. 1941.

Manhold. 1941, New York 1941.

Here is America. 1942. Non-fiction.

The rise of Henry Morcar. 1946, New York 1946.

Some observations on the art of narrative. 1946, New York 1947.

The Brontës. 1947, New York 1947.

Colne Valley cloth from the earliest times to the present day. Huddersfield 1947.

Life story. 1948, New York 1948. Fiction.

The Brontë sisters. 1950 (Br Council pamphlet).

Quorum. 1950, New York 1951.

Panorama: tales of the West Riding. 1952, New York 1952.

The house of Moreys: a romance. 1953, New York 1953.

Noble in reason. 1955, New York 1955.

Love and money: seven tales of the West Riding. 1957, New York 1957.

Crescendo. 1958, New York 1958.

Kith and kin: nine tales of family life. 1960, New York 1960.

The young Brontës. [1960], New York [1960].

Committees. 1962 (Collins Nutshell books). Non-fiction.

O dreams, O destinations: an autobiography. 1962, New York 1962.

Enjoy books: reading and collecting. 1964.

Public speaking. 1964 (Collins Nutshell books). Non-fiction.

The adventures of Tom Leigh. 1964, Garden City NY [1964]. For children.

Tales of the West Riding. 1965.

A man of his time. 1966, New York 1966.

Ned Carver in danger. 1967. For children.

Gold pieces. 1968.

The Brontës and their world. 1969, New York 1969.

Ring in the new. 1969.

JOHN DAVYS BERESFORD
1873–1947

The early history of Jacob Stahl. 1911, Boston [1911]. First vol of Stahl trilogy.

The Hampdenshire wonder. 1911, New York [1917] (as The wonder), London 1948 (with introd by W. de la Mare).

A candidate for truth. 1912, New York 1912. 2nd vol of Stahl trilogy.

Goslings. 1913, New York 1913 (as A world of women).

The house in Demetrius Road. 1914, New York [1914].

The compleat angler: a duologue. [1915] (French's Acting edn). With A. S. Craven.

H. G. Wells. 1915.

The invisible event. 1915, New York [1915]. 3rd vol of Stahl trilogy.

The mountains of the moon. 1915.

Poems by two brothers. 1915. With R. Beresford.

These Lynnekers. 1916, New York [1916].

House-mates. 1916 [1917], New York [1917].

W. E. Ford: a biography. [1917], New York [1917]. With K. Richmond; semi-autobiographical fiction.

God's counterpoint. [1918], New York [1918].

Nineteen impressions. 1918. Stories.

The perfect machine. Eng Rev 26 1918. Play, with A. S. Craven.

The Jervaise comedy. [1919], New York 1919.

An imperfect mother. 1920, New York 1920.

Revolution. [1921], New York 1921.

Signs & wonders. Waltham Saint Lawrence 1921, New York 1921. Stories.

The prisoners of Hartling. [1922], New York 1922.

Taken from life. [1922]. Text by Beresford, photographs by E. O. Hoppé. Character sketches.

The imperturbable duchess, and other stories. [1923].

Love's pilgrim. [1923], Indianapolis [1923].

Unity. [1924], Indianapolis [1924].

The monkey-puzzle. [1925], Indianapolis [1925].

That kind of man. [1926], Indianapolis [1926] (as Almost pagan).

The decoy. [1927].

The tapestry. [1927], Indianapolis [1927].

The instrument of destiny: a detective story. [1928], Indianapolis [1928].

All or nothing. [1928], Indianapolis [1928].

Writing aloud. [1928].

Experiment in the novel. In Tradition and experiment in present-day literature: addresses delivered at the City Literary Institute, 1929.

The meeting place, and other stories. 1929.

Real people. [1929].

Love's illusion. 1930, New York 1930.

Seven, Bobsworth. 1930.

An innocent criminal. [1931], New York [1931].

The old people. [1931], New York [1932]. First vol of Three generations trilogy.

The next generation. 1932.

The middle generation. [1932], New York [1933]. 2nd vol of Three generations trilogy.

The inheritor. 1933.

The Camberwell miracle. 1933.

The young people. 1933, New York [1934]. 3rd vol of Three generations trilogy.

The case for faith-healing. 1934.

Peckover. 1934, New York [1935].

On a huge hill. 1935.

Blackthorn winter, and other stories. [1936].

The faithful lovers. [1936], New York [1936].

Cleo. [1937].

The root of the matter: essays by J. D. Beresford [et al]. Ed H. R. L. Sheppard 1937. Human relations, by Beresford.

The unfinished road. [1938].

What I believe. 1938 (I believe: a series of personal statements 1).
Strange rival. 1939.
Snell's folly. [1939].
The idea of God. [1940].
Quiet corner. [1940].
'What dreams may come...' [1941].
A common enemy. [1941].
The benefactor. [1943].
The long view. [1943].
Men in the same boat. [1943]. With E. Wynne-Tyson.
If this were true—. [1944].
The riddle of the tower. [1944]. With E. Wynne-Tyson.
The prisoner. [1946].
The gift. [1947]. With E. Wynne-Tyson.

GERARD HUGH TYRWHITT, later TYRWHITT-WILSON, LORD BERNERS
1883–1950

First childhood. 1934, New York [1934]. Autobiography.
The camel: a tale. 1936.
The girls of Radcliff Hall. [Faringdon] [1937] (priv ptd). By 'Adela Quebec'.
Count Omega. 1941.
Far from the madding war. 1941.
Percy Wallingford and Mr Pidger: two stories. Oxford 1941.
The romance of a nose. 1941.
A distant prospect: a sequel to First childhood. 1945.

'GEORGE A. BIRMINGHAM', JAMES OWEN HANNAY
1865–1950

The seething pot. 1905.
Hyacinth. 1906.
Benedict Kavanagh. 1907.
The northern iron. Dublin 1907, London [1913].
The bad times. 1908.
Spanish gold. 1908, New York 1912.
The search party. 1909.
Lalage's lovers. 1911, New York [1911].
The lighter side of Irish life. 1911. Non-fiction.
The major's niece. 1911.
The Simpkins plot. 1911, New York 1912.
Dr Whitty's patient, and Mrs Challmer's public meeting. New York [1912].
The inviolable sanctuary. 1912, New York 1912 (as Priscilla's spies).
The red hand of Ulster. 1912, New York [1912].
The adventures of Dr Whitty. 1913, New York [1913]. Stories.
General John Regan. 1913, New York [1913]; London 1933 as play.
An intolerable honour, and Hygienic and scientific apparatus. New York [1913].
Irishmen all. 1913. Non-fiction.
Miss Mulhall's lecture, and Dr Whitty's honeymoon. New York [1913].
Connaught to Chicago. 1914, New York 1914 (as From Dublin to Chicago: some notes on a tour in America).
The lost tribes. 1914, New York [1914].
Gossamer. 1915, New York [1915].
Minnie's bishop, and other stories of Ireland. 1915, New York [1915].
The island mystery. 1918, New York [1918].
A padre in France. [1918], New York [1919]. Non-fiction.
An Irishman looks at his world. 1919, New York 1919. Non-fiction.

Our casualty, and other stories. [1919], New York 1919.
Up, the rebels! 1919, New York [1919].
Good conduct. 1920.
Inisheeny. 1920.
Adventurers of the night. New York [1921].
Lady Bountiful. 1921, New York 1922. Stories.
The lost lawyer. 1921.
The great-grandmother. 1922, Indianapolis [1923].
A public scandal, and other stories. [1922].
Found money. 1923, Indianapolis [1923].
King Tommy. [1923], Indianapolis [1924].
Send for Dr O'Grady. [1923].
The Grand Duchess. [1924].
Bindon Parva. 1925, Indianapolis [1925].
The gun-runners. [1925].
A wayfarer in Hungary. 1925, New York 1925. Travel.
Goodly pearls. [1926].
The lady of the abbey. Indianapolis 1926.
The smugglers' cave. [1926], Indianapolis [1927].
Spillikins: a book of essays. 1926.
Fidgets. [1927].
Gold, gore & gehenna. Indianapolis [1927].
Now you tell one: stories of Irish wit and humour. 1927.
Ships and sealing-wax. 1927. Essays.
The runaways. 1928, Indianapolis [1928].
The major's candlesticks. 1929, Indianapolis [1929].
Murder most foul! a gallery of famous criminals. 1929.
The hymn tune mystery. 1930, Indianapolis [1931].
Wild justice. 1930, Indianapolis [1930].
Fed up. 1931, Indianapolis [1931].
Elizabeth and the archdeacon. 1932, Indianapolis [1933].
Irish short stories. Ed G. A. Birmingham 1932.
The silver-gilt standard. 1932.
Angel's adventure. 1933.
Pleasant places. 1934. Autobiography.
Two fools. 1934.
Love or money, and other stories. 1935.
Millicent's corner. 1935.
Daphne's fishing. 1937.
Isaiah. 1937.
Mrs Miller's aunt. 1937.
Magilligan Strand. 1938.
Appeasement. 1939.
God's iron: a life of the prophet Jeremiah. 1939, New York 1956 (as The prophet Jeremiah).
Miss Maitland's spy. 1940.
The search for Susie. 1941.
Over the border. 1942.
Poor Sir Edward. 1943.
Lieutenant Commander. 1944.
Good intentions. 1945.
The Piccadilly lady. 1946.
Golden apple. 1947.
A sea battle. 1948.
Laura's bishop. 1949.
Two scamps. 1950.
Hannay also wrote some theological and devotional works under his own name.

ALGERNON HENRY BLACKWOOD
1869–1951

The empty house, and other ghost stories. 1906, New York 1915.
The listener, and other stories. 1907, New York 1914.
John Silence, physician extraordinary. 1908, New York 1909. Stories.
The education of Uncle Paul. 1909, New York 1910. For children.
Jimbo: a fantasy. 1909, New York 1909.
The human chord. 1910, New York 1910.
The lost valley, and other stories. 1910, New York 1914.
The centaur. 1911, New York 1911.

Pan's garden: a volume of nature stories. 1912, New York 1912.

A prisoner in fairyland: the book that 'Uncle Paul' wrote. 1913, New York 1913. For children.

Incredible adventures. 1914, New York 1914. Stories.

Ten minute stories. 1914, New York 1914.

The extra day. 1915, New York 1915. For children.

Julius Le Vallon: an episode. 1916, New York 1916.

The wave: an Egyptian aftermath. 1916, New York [1916].

Day and night stories. 1917, New York [1917].

The garden of survival. 1918, New York [1918].

Karma: a re-incarnation play in prologue, epilogue and 3 acts. 1918, New York [1918]. With V. A. Pearn.

The promise of air. 1918, New York [1918].

The bright messenger. 1921, New York [1922].

The wolves of God, and other fey stories. 1921, New York [1921]. With W. Wilson.

Episodes before thirty. 1923, New York [1924], London 1934 (as Adventures before thirty). Autobiographical.

Tongues of fire, and other sketches. 1924, New York [1925].

Through the crack: a play in five scenes. [1925]. With V. A. Pearn.

The dance of death, and other tales. 1927, New York 1928.

Sambo and Snitch. Oxford [1927], New York 1927. Children's story.

Mr Cupboard. Oxford [1928]. Children's story.

Dudley & Gilderoy: a nonsense. 1929, New York [1929].

Full circle. 1929. Story.

By underground. Oxford [1930]. Children's story.

The parrot and the—cat! Oxford [1931]. Children's story; from Dudley & Gilderoy, above.

The Italian conjuror. Oxford [1932]. Children's story.

Maria—of England—in the rain. Oxford [1933]. Children's story.

The fruit stoners: being the adventures of Maria among the fruit stoners. 1934, New York 1935.

Sergeant Poppett and Policeman James. Oxford [1934]. Children's story.

The fruit stoners. Oxford [1935]. Children's story, from The fruit stoners, above.

Shocks. 1935, New York [1935]. Stories.

How the circus came to tea. Oxford [1936]. Children's story.

The doll, and one other. Sauk City Wisconsin 1946. Two stories.

PHYLLIS BOTTOME
1884–1963

Life the interpreter. 1902.

The master hope. 1904.

Raw material: some characters and episodes among working lads. 1905.

The imperfect gift. 1907.

Crooked answers. 1911. With H. de L. Brock.

The common chord. 1913.

'Broken music'. 1914, Boston 1914.

The captive. 1915.

Secretly armed. 1916, New York 1916 (as The dark tower).

A certain star. 1917.

The derelict [and other stories]. New York 1917, London 1923.

The second fiddle. New York 1917.

Helen of Troy, and Rose. New York 1918.

A servant of reality. [1919], New York 1919.

The crystal heart. New York 1921.

The kingfisher. 1922, New York [1922]; rptd in The belated reckoning, below.

The victim, and The worm. New York [1923].

The depths of prosperity. [1924]. With Dorothy Thompson.

The perfect wife. New York [1924].

The belated reckoning. New York [1926], London [1927]. Stories.

Old wine. New York [1926], London [1926].

The rat. 1926, New York [1927]. Based on a play by I. Novello and Constance Collier.

The messenger of the gods. New York [1927].

Strange fruit: tales. [1928], Boston 1928.

Tatter'd loving. [1929], Boston 1930.

Windlestraws. [1929], Boston 1929.

Devil's due. Boston 1931, London [1931] (as Wind in his fists).

The advances of Harriet. Boston 1933, London 1933.

Innocence and experience: stories. Boston 1934, London 1935.

Private worlds. Boston 1934, London 1934.

Stella Benson. San Francisco 1934 (priv ptd). Booklet.

Level crossing. New York 1936, London 1936.

The mortal storm. 1937, Boston 1938.

Alfred Adler: a biography. New York [1939], London 1939 (as Alfred Adler: apostle of freedom).

Murder in the bud. 1939, Boston 1939 (as Danger signal).

Heart of a child. 1940, New York [1940] (as The heart of a child).

Masks and faces. 1940, Boston 1940.

Formidable to tyrants. 1941, Boston 1941 (as Mansion House of liberty). England in war-time.

London pride. 1941, Boston 1941.

Within the cup. 1943, Boston 1943 (as Survival).

Austria's contribution towards our new order. 1944. Lecture.

From the life. 1944. Biographical sketches.

Individual countries. 1946. Non-fiction.

The life line. Boston 1946, London 1946.

Search for a soul. 1947, New York 1948. Autobiography.

Fortune's finger: short stories. 1950.

Under the skin. New York [1950], London 1950.

The challenge. 1952. New York 1953. Sequel to Search for a soul, above.

Man and beast. 1953, New York 1954. Stories.

Against whom? 1954, New York 1954 (as The secret stair).

Not in our stars. 1955. Essays.

'Eldorado Jane'. 1956, New York 1957 (as Jane).

Walls of glass. 1958, New York [1958]. Stories.

The goal. 1962, New York [1962]. Autobiography.

ELIZABETH DOROTHEA COLE BOWEN
1899–1973

Collections and Selections

Selected stories. Ed R. Moore 1946.

Collected edition. 1948—.

Early stories. New York 1951. Includes Encounters and Ann Lee's.

Stories. New York 1959. A selection with preface by the author.

§ I

Encounters: stories. 1923, 1949 (with preface by the author).

Ann Lee's & other stories. 1926, New York [1928].

The hotel. 1927, New York 1928.

Joining Charles, and other stories. 1929, New York 1929.

The last September. 1929, New York 1929.

Friends and relations. 1931, New York 1931.

She gave him. In Consequences: a complete story in the manner of the old parlour game in nine chapters each by a different author, Waltham St Lawrence 1932.

To the north. 1932, New York 1933.

The cat jumps, and other stories. [1934].

The house in Paris. 1935, New York 1936.
The death of the heart. 1938, New York 1939.
Look at all those roses: short stories. 1941, New York 1941.
Seven winters. Dublin 1942, London 1943, New York 1962 (with Afterthought, below). Reminiscences of childhood.
Bowen's Court. 1942, New York 1942, 1964 (with addns), London 1964. Family history.
English novelists. 1942 (Britain in pictures).
The demon lover and other stories. 1945, New York 1946 (as Ivy gripped the steps, with preface rptd in Collected impressions, below).
Anthony Trollope: a new judgment. 1946, New York 1946. Play; rptd in Collected impressions, below.
How I write my novels, by Elizabeth Bowen [et al]. 1948. Radio interviews, ed T. Jones.
Why do I write? an exchange of views between Elizabeth Bowen, Graham Greene and V. S. Pritchett. 1948, New York 1948.
The heat of the day. 1949, New York 1949.
Collected impressions. 1950, New York 1950. Essays, reviews and prefaces etc.
The Shelbourne: a centre in Dublin life for more than a century. 1951, New York 1951 (as The Shelbourne hotel).
A world of love. 1955, New York 1955.
A time in Rome. 1960, New York 1960. Travel.
Afterthought: pieces about writing. 1962, New York 1962 (with Seven winters, above).
The little girls. 1964, New York 1964.
A day in the dark and other stories. [1965].
The good tiger. New York [1965]. For children.
Eva Trout, or changing scenes. New York 1968, London 1969.

An unpbd play, Castle Anna, written with John Perry, was first performed in London in 1948. From 1941 Miss Bowen made regular contributions to Tatler *as its permanent book reviewer. During 1954–61 she was on the editorial board of* London Mag. *She edited the* Faber book of modern stories, *1937. The preface to this, and to edns of works by various individual authors, were rptd in* Collected impressions *above.*

§2

Brooke, J. Elizabeth Bowen. 1952 (Br Council pamphlet).
O'Faolain, S. Elizabeth Bowen: or romance does not pay. In his The vanishing hero, 1956.
Heath, W. Elizabeth Bowen: an introduction to her novels. Madison 1961.
Glendinning, V. Elizabeth Bowen: portrait of a writer. 1977.

'ERNEST BRAMAH',
ERNEST BRAMAH SMITH
1868?–1942

Some of Bramah's mss, typescripts, galleys and page-proofs are in the Humanities Research Center of the Univ of Texas.

English farming and why I turned it up. 1894. Autobiographical.
The wallet of Kai Lung. 1900, Boston 1900, London 1923 (with introd by G. Richards). Stories.
The mirror of Kung Ho. 1905, 1929 (with preface by J. C. Squire), New York 1930.
What might have been: the story of a social war. 1907, 1909 (as The secret of the league).
The transmutation of Ling. 1911, New York 1912. Story, first pbd in The wallet of Kai Lung.
Max Carrados. 1914. Detective stories.
Kai Lung's golden hours, with a preface by H. Belloc. 1922, New York 1923. Stories.

The eyes of Max Carrados. 1923, New York 1924. Detective stories.
The specimen case. 1924, New York 1925. Stories.
Max Carrados mysteries. 1927. Detective stories.
The story of Wan and the remarkable shrub, and The story of Ching-kwei and the destinies. New York 1927. Both rptd in Kai Lung unrolls his mat.
Kai Lung unrolls his mat. 1928, New York 1928. Stories.
A guide to the varieties and rarity of English regal copper coins: Charles II–Victoria, 1671–1860. 1929.
A little flutter. 1930.
The moon of much gladness, related by Kai Lung. 1932, New York 1937 (as The return of Kai Lung).
The bravo of London. 1934.
Kai Lung beneath the mulberry tree. 1940. Stories.

JOHN BUCHAN,
1st BARON TWEEDSMUIR
1875–1940

Numerous mss are in the Buchan collection at Queen's University Kingston (Ontario).

Bibliographies

Hanna, A. Buchan: a bibliography. Hamden Conn 1953.

§1

Sir Quixote of the moors: being some account of an episode in the life of the Sieur de Rohaine. 1895, New York 1895.
Scholar gipsies. 1896. Essays.
John Burnet of Barns: a romance. 1898, New York 1898.
Brasenose College. 1898 (College histories: Oxford).
Grey weather: moorland tales of my own people. 1899.
A lost lady of old years: a romance. 1899.
The half-hearted. 1900, Boston 1900.
The watcher by the threshold, and other tales. Edinburgh 1902, New York 1918 (with additional tales).
The African colony: studies in the reconstruction. Edinburgh 1903.
The law relating to the taxation of foreign income. 1905.
A lodge in the wilderness. Edinburgh 1906. Anon.
Some eighteenth-century byways, and other essays. Edinburgh 1908.
Prester John. 1910, New York 1910 (as The great diamond pipe).
Sir Walter Raleigh. 1911, New York 1911. For children.
The moon endureth: tales and fancies. Edinburgh 1912, New York 1912 (omitting several tales).
The marquis of Montrose. 1913, New York [1913].
Andrew Jameson, Lord Ardwall. Edinburgh 1913.
Britain's war by land. [1915] (Oxford pamphlets 1914–15).
Nelson's history of the war. [1915–19] (24 vols), [1921–2] (4 vols, as A history of the Great War), Boston 1922 (8 vols autographed edn, 4 vols standard edn).
The achievement of France. 1915. Articles rptd from Times.
The thirty-nine steps. Edinburgh 1915, New York 1915.
Salute to adventurers. [1915], Boston 1915.
Ordeal by marriage: an eclogue. 1915.
The power-house. Edinburgh 1916, New York [1916].
Greenmantle. 1916, New York 1916.
Poems, Scots and English. 1917, 1936 (rev and enlarged).
Mr Standfast. 1918, New York 1919.
These for remembrance. 1919 (priv ptd). Reminiscences of friends killed in the war.
The island of sheep, by 'Cadmus' and 'Harmonia' [i.e. John and Susan Buchan]. 1919, Boston 1920. Non-fiction: for novel of same title, see 1936.
The battle-honours of Scotland, 1914–18. Glasgow [1919].
The history of the South African forces in France. [1920].

Francis and Riversdale Grenfell: a memoir. 1920.
The path of the king. [1921], New York 1921.
Huntingtower. 1922, New York [1922].
A book of escapes and hurried journeys. 1922, Boston 1923.
The last secrets: the final mysteries of exploration. 1923, Boston 1924.
Midwinter: certain travellers in old England. [1923], New York [1923].
Days to remember: the British empire in the Great War. 1923. With H. Newbolt.
Some notes on Sir Walter Scott. 1924 (Eng Assoc pamphlet).
The three hostages. [1924], Boston 1924.
Lord Minto: a memoir. 1924.
The history of the Royal Scots Fusiliers 1678–1918. 1925.
John Macnab. 1925, Boston 1925.
The man and the book: Sir Walter Scott. 1925.
Two ordeals of democracy. Boston 1925. Lecture, On the American Civil War and the First World War.
The dancing floor. 1926, Boston 1926.
Homilies and recreations. [1926]. Essays.
Witch wood. 1927, Boston 1927.
The Runagates Club. 1928, Boston 1928. Stories.
Montrose. 1928, Boston 1928, Oxford 1957 (WC, with introd by K. Feiling).
The courts of the morning. 1929, Boston 1929.
The causal and the casual in history. Cambridge 1929 (Rede lecture).
The Kirk in Scotland 1560–1929. [1930].
Montrose and leadership. 1930 (Walker Trust lectures on leadership 1).
The revision of dogmas. Ashridge [1930?]. Lecture.
Castle Gay. 1930, Boston 1930.
Lord Rosebery 1847–1930. 1930. Rptd from Proc Br Acad.
The blanket of the dark. 1931, Boston 1931.
The novel and the fairy tale. 1931 (Eng Assoc pamphlet).
Sir Walter Scott. 1932, New York 1932.
The gap in the curtain. 1932, Boston 1932.
Julius Caesar. 1932, New York 1932.
The magic walking-stick. 1932, Boston 1932.
The massacre of Glencoe. 1933, New York 1933.
A prince of the captivity. 1933, Boston 1933.
Andrew Lang and the border. 1933 (Andrew Lang lecture 1932).
The margins of life. 1933 (Birkbeck College foundation oration).
The free fishers. 1934, Boston 1934.
Gordon at Khartoum. 1934.
Oliver Cromwell. 1934, Boston 1934.
The King's grace: 1910–35. 1935, Boston 1935 (as The people's king: George V), London 1936 (with second epilogue).
The house of the four winds. 1935, Boston 1935.
The island of sheep. 1936, Boston 1936 (as The man from the Norlands).
Augustus. 1937, Boston 1937.
Memory hold-the-door. 1940, Boston 1940 (as Pilgrim's way: an essay in recollection). Autobiography. The ch My America was rptd by the British Library of Information, New York 1940.
Comments and characters, ed with an introd by W. F. Gray. 1940. A selection of Buchan's contributions to the Scottish Rev.
Canadian occasions: addresses by Lord Tweedsmuir. Toronto 1940, London 1941.
Sick heart river. 1941, Boston 1941 (as Mountain meadow, with introd by H. Swiggett).
The long traverse. 1941, Boston 1941 (as Lake of gold).

Many more of Buchan's political and other public addresses were pbd separately as pamphlets. Buchan edited The northern muse: an anthology of Scots vernacular poetry *1922, and* The long road to victory *and* Great hours in sport, *the latter two anthologies forming the 2 vols of* John

Buchan's Annual, *1920, 1921. Buchan also edited* The nature of to-day: a new history of the world, *12 vols 1923, 1924. As chief literary adviser and, later, director of Thomas Nelson & Son 1907–29 Buchan edited a number of that publisher's series and encyclopaedias. Buchan was on the staff of* Spectator *1903–6, edited* Scottish Rev *1907–8, wrote the 'Atticus' column in* Sunday Times *1930–5 and a fortnightly article in* Graphic *1930–2.*

§2

'MacDiarmid, Hugh' (C. M. Grieve). John Buchan. Scottish Educational Jnl 19 June 1925; rpts in his Contemporary Scottish studies, 1926.
Greene, G. The last Buchan. Spectator 18 May 1941; rptd in his The lost childhood, 1951.
Buchan, S. et al. Buchan, by his wife and friends. 1947.
Himmelfarb, G. Buchan: an untimely appreciation. Encounter 15 1960.
—— Buchan, the last Victorian. In her Victorian minds, 1968.
Smith, J. A. Buchan: a biography. 1965.
—— Buchan and his world. 1979.

GILBERT CANNAN
1884–1955

Peter Homunculus. 1909, New York 1909.
Devious ways. 1910.
Little brother. 1912.
Four plays: James and John (Haymarket 27 March 1911); Miles Dixon, (Gaiety, Manchester 21 Nov 1910); Mary's wedding (Coronet 6 May 1912); A short way with authors (Cosmopolis 26 May 1913). 1913, Boston [1920] (separately).
The joy of the theatre. 1913.
Round the corner: being the life and death of Francis Christopher Folyat. 1913, New York 1913.
Love. 1914. Non-fiction.
Old Mole: being the surprising adventures in England of Herbert Jocelyn Beenham M A. 1914, New York 1914.
Satire. [1914]. Non-fiction.
Adventurous love, and other verses. 1915.
Samuel Butler: a critical study. 1915.
Windmills: a book of fables. 1915.
Young Earnest: the romance of a bad start in life. 1915, New York 1915.
Mendel: a story of youth. 1916, New York [1916].
Three pretty men. 1916, New York [1916] (as Three sons and a mother).
Everybody's husband. (Birmingham Repertory 14 April 1917). 1917, [1927] (French's Acting edn). Play, rptd in Seven plays, 1923, below.
Freedom, 1917. Non-fiction.
Noel: an epic in ten cantos. 3 pts [1917–18] (only cantos 1–4 pbd), 1922 (as Noel: an epic in seven cantos).
The stucco house. 1917, New York 1918.
Mummery: a tale of three idealists. [1918], New York [1919].
The anatomy of society. 1919. Non-fiction.
Pink roses. 1919, New York [1919].
Time and eternity: a tale of three exiles. 1919, New York 1920.
The release of the soul. 1920. Essay.
Pugs and peacocks. [1921].
Annette and Bennett. [1922], New York 1923.
Sembal. [1922], New York 1924.
Letters from a distance. 1923. Articles rptd from New York Freeman.
Seven plays. 1923. Everybody's husband; The fat kine and the lean; In the park; Someone to whisper to; The same story; Pierrot in hospital; The polite art of conversation.

The house of prophecy. 1924, New York 1924.

Cannan also made a number of trns from the French, including Rolland, Jean Christophe, and Russian and German. He was dramatic critic of the Star 1909–10.

See D. Farr, Cannan: a Georgian prodigy, 1978.

ARTHUR JOYCE LUNEL CARY
1888–1957

The James M. Osborn collection of Cary mss is in the Bodleian Library.

Collections

Carfax edition. 1951–. Reprints of the novels, with a prefatory essay by the author to each novel.
Selected essays. Ed A. G. Bishop 1976.

§1

Verse. Edinburgh 1908. Signed: Arthur Cary.
Aissa saved. 1932, New York [1962].
An American visitor. 1933, New York 1961.
The African witch. 1936, New York 1936.
Castle Corner. 1938, New York 1963.
Power in men. 1939, Seattle 1963 (with introd by H. Adams). Non-fiction.
Mister Johnson. 1939 [1951] (with prefatory essay by Cary rptd in the Carfax edn).
Charley is my darling. 1940, New York 1960.
A house of children. 1941, New York [1956].
The case for African freedom. 1941 (with foreword by 'George Orwell'), 1944 (rev, omitting foreword).
Herself surprised. 1941, New York 1948, 1961 (with critical and biographical material by A. Wright). First bk of a trilogy.
To be a pilgrim. 1942 New York 1949. 2nd bk of a trilogy.
Process of real freedom. 1943. Pamphlet.
The horse's mouth. 1944, New York 1950, London 1957 (rev, with the preface to the Carfax edn and the discarded ch The old strife at Plant's, ed A. Wright), New York 1959 (with introd by A. Wright). 3rd bk of a trilogy.
Marching soldier. 1945. Verse.
The moonlight. 1946, New York 1947.
Britain and West Africa. 1946, 1947 (rev).
The drunken sailor: a ballad-epic. 1947.
A fearful joy. 1949, New York [1950].
Prisoner of grace. 1952, New York 1952. First bk of a trilogy.
Except the Lord. New York 1953, London 1953. 2nd bk of a trilogy.
Not honour more. 1955, New York 1955. 3rd bk of a trilogy.
The old strife at Plant's. Oxford 1956 (priv ptd, 100 copies). A discarded ch from The horse's mouth. Rptd in the 1957 edn of the novel.
Art & reality. Cambridge 1958, New York 1958. Clark lectures, 1956.
First trilogy. New York [1958]. Contains Herself surprised; To be a pilgrim; The horse's mouth. With preface by Cary.
The captive and the free. Introd D. Cecil, ed W. Davin, New York 1959, London 1959.
Spring song and other stories. 1960, New York 1960. With 5 hitherto unpbd stories.
Memoir of the Bobotes. Austin 1960 (introd J. B. Meriwether), London 1964 (foreword by W. Allen). Reminiscences of the First Balkan War.

Cary also pbd, under the pseudonym 'Thomas Joyce', 10 short stories in the Saturday Evening Post, 1920, 3 in Strand Mag 1921 and 1923, and 1 in Hutchinson's Mag 1921. Not rptd in Spring Song 1960.

§2

Allen, W. The horse's mouth. In his Reading a novel, 1949.
— Joyce Cary. 1953, 1963 (rev) (Br Council pamphlet).
Adam International Rev 18 1950. Special Cary issue.
Wright, A. Cary: a preface to his novels. 1958.
— Cary's unpublished work. London Mag 5 1958.
— Cary: fragments of an oeuvre. International Literary Annual 1 1958.
Modern Fiction Stud 9 1963. Special Cary no.
Mahood, M. M. Cary's Africa. 1964.
O'Connor, W. Van. Joyce Cary. New York 1966.
Foster, M. Cary: a biography. Boston 1968.
Wolkenfeld, J. Cary: the developing style. New York 1968.

ROBERT ERSKINE CHILDERS
1870–1922

The riddle of the sands: a record of secret service recently achieved. Ed [i.e. written] Erskine Childers 1903, New York 1915.

Childers also wrote a number of works on military history and Irish politics.

DAME AGATHA MARY CLARISSA CHRISTIE
(afterwards MALLOWAN)
1890–1976

The mysterious affair at Styles: a detective story. 1920.
The secret adversary. 1922, New York 1922.
The murder on the links. 1923, New York 1923.
The man in the brown suit. 1924, New York 1924.
Poirot investigates. 1924, New York 1925. Stories.
The secret of Chimneys. 1925, New York 1925.
The murder of Roger Ackroyd. 1926, New York 1926. Dramatized by M. Morton as Alibi, Prince of Wales 15 May 1928; pbd 1929 (French's Acting edn).
The big four. [1927], New York 1927.
The mystery of the Blue Train. [1928], New York 1928.
Partners in crime. [1929], New York [1929]. Chs 11–22 pbd London 1933 as The Sunningdale mystery. Stories.
The Seven Dials mystery. [1929], New York 1929.
The under dog, by A. Christie, and Blackman's wood, by E. Phillips Oppenheim. [1929], [1936] (as Two thrillers).
Black coffee: a play in three acts. (Embassy 8 Dec 1930; St Martin's 9 April 1931). 1934, [1952] (French's Acting edn).
The murder at the vicarage. [1930], New York 1930. Dramatized by M. Charles and B. Toy, Playhouse 16 Dec 1949; pbd 1950 (French's Acting edn).
The mysterious Mr Quin. 1930, New York 1930. Also pbd as The passing of Mr Quin. Stories.
The Sittaford mystery. 1931, New York 1931 (as The murder at Hazelmoor).
Peril at End House. [1932], New York 1932. Dramatized by A. Ridley, Vaudeville 1 May 1940; pbd [1945] (French's Acting edn).
The thirteen problems. 1932, New York 1933 (as The Tuesday Club murders), London 1953 (as Miss Marple and the thirteen problems) (Penguin). Stories.
The hound of death and other stories. [1933].
Lord Edgware dies. [1933], New York 1933 (as Thirteen at dinner).
The Sunningdale mystery. 1933. *See* Partners in crime, 1929, above.
The Listerdale mystery, and other stories. 1934. The story Philomel cottage, dramatized by F. Vosper as Love from a stranger, Wyndham's 2 Feb 1936; New 31 March 1936; pbd 1936 (French's Acting edn).

Murder in three acts. New York [1934], London [1935] (as Three act tragedy).

Murder on the Orient Express. [1934], New York 1934 (as Murder in the Calais coach).

Parker Pyne investigates. 1934, New York 1934 (as Mr Parker Pyne, detective). Stories.

Why didn't they ask Evans? [1934], New York 1935 (as The boomerang clue).

Death in the clouds. [1935], New York 1935 (as Death in the air).

The ABC murders. [1936], New York 1936.

Cards on the table. [1936], New York 1937.

Murder in Mesopotamia. [1936], New York 1936.

Dead man's mirror. New York 1937. Stories.

Death on the Nile. 1937, New York 1938. Dramatized as Hidden horizon, Wimbledon 9 April 1945, renamed Murder on the Nile, Ambassadors 19 March 1946; pbd 1948 (French's Acting edn).

Dumb witness. [1937], New York 1937 (as Poirot loses a client). Also pbd as Murder at Littlegreen House, and Mystery at Littlegreen House.

Murder in the mews, and other stories. [1937]. Includes stories in Dead man's mirror, above, together with The incredible theft.

Appointment with death. [1938], New York 1938. Dramatized, Piccadilly 31 March 1945; pbd 1956 (French's Acting edn).

Hercule Poirot's Christmas. 1939 (for 1938), New York 1939 (as Murder for Christmas), 1947 (as A holiday for murder).

Murder is easy. [1939], New York 1939 (as Easy to kill).

The regatta mystery, and other stories. New York 1939.

Ten little niggers. [1939], New York 1940 (as And then there were none). Also pbd as Ten little Indians, and The nursery rhyme murders. Dramatized, Wimbledon 20 Sept 1943, St James 17 Nov 1943; pbd 1944 (French's Acting edn).

One, two, buckle my shoe. 1940, New York 1941 (as The patriotic murders).

Sad cypress. [1940], New York 1940.

Evil under the sun. 1941, New York 1941.

N or M? 1941, New York 1941.

The body in the library. 1942, New York 1942.

Five little pigs. 1942, New York 1942 (as Murder in retrospect). Dramatized as Go back for murder, Duchess 23 March 1960; pbd 1960 (French's Acting edn).

The moving finger. New York 1942, London 1943.

Towards zero. 1944, Philadelphia 1944. Also pbd as Come and be hanged. Dramatized by the author and G. Verner, St James's 4 Sept 1956; pbd New York 1957 (Dramatists Play Service), London 1958 (French's Acting edn).

Death comes as the end. 1945.

Sparkling cyanide. 1945, New York 1945 (as Remembered death).

The hollow. 1946, New York 1946 (as Murder after hours). Dramatized, Fortune 7 June 1951; pbd 1952 (French's Acting edn).

A holiday for murder. New York 1947. See Hercule Poirot's Christmas, 1939, above.

The labours of Hercules. 1947, New York 1947. Stories.

Taken at the flood. 1948, New York 1948 (as There is a tide).

The witness for the prosecution, and other stories. New York 1948. Title story dramatized, Winter Garden 28 Oct 1953; pbd in Famous plays of 1954, and separately (French's Acting edn), New York 1954.

Crooked house. 1949, New York 1949.

A murder is announced. 1950, New York 1950.

Three blind mice, and other stories. New York [1950?]. Also pbd as The mousetrap and other stories; title story dramatized as The mousetrap, Ambassadors 25 Nov 1952; pbd 1956 (French's Acting edn).

Blood will tell. New York [1951], London 1952 (as Mrs McGinty's dead), New York 1952.

They came to Baghdad. 1951, New York 1951.

The under dog, and other stories. New York 1951. Title story first pbd 1929.

They do it with mirrors. 1952, New York 1952 (as Murder with mirrors).

After the funeral. 1953, New York 1953 (as Funerals are fatal), London 1963 (wrapper title Murder at the gallop).

Miss Marple and the thirteen problems. 1953. See The thirteen problems, 1932, above.

A pocket full of rye. 1953, New York [1953].

Spider's web: a play in three acts. (Savoy 13 Dec 1954). [1957] (French's Acting edn).

Destination unknown. 1954, New York 1955 (as So many steps to death).

Hickory, dickory, dock. 1955, New York 1955 (as Hickory, dickory, death).

Dead man's folly. [1956], New York 1956.

4.50 from Paddington. 1957, New York 1957 (as What Mrs McGillicuddy saw!), 1961 (as Murder she said).

The unexpected guest. (Duchess 12 Aug 1958). [1958] (French's Acting edn).

Verdict: a play in two acts. (Strand 22 May 1958). 1958, [1958] (French's Acting edn).

Ordeal by innocence. [1958], New York 1959.

Cat among the pigeons. [1959], New York 1960.

The adventures of the Christmas pudding, and a selection of entrées. [1960]. Stories.

Double sin, and other stories. New York 1961.

The pale horse. [1961], New York 1962.

Afternoon at the seaside; The patient; The rats. (Duchess 20 Dec 1962). Three one-act plays; pbd separately [1963] (French's Acting edn).

The mirror crack'd from side to side. [1962], New York [1963] (as The mirror crack'd).

The clocks. [1963].

Murder at the gallop. 1963. See After the funeral, 1953, above.

A Caribbean mystery. 1964.

At Bertrams Hotel. 1965, New York 1966.

Third girl. 1966, New York 1968.

By the pricking of my thumbs. 1968, New York 1968.

Hallowe'en party. 1969.

An autobiography. 1977.

Agatha Christie has also written novels under the pseudonym Mary Westmacott, and books on archaeological experiences in Syria; also stories and poems under the name Agatha Christie Mallowan.

DAME IVY COMPTON-BURNETT
1892–1969

Collected edition. 1948–.

§1

Dolores. Edinburgh 1911.

Pastors and masters: a study. 1925.

Brothers and sisters. 1929, New York [1929].

Men and wives. 1931, New York [1931].

More women than men. 1933, New York 1965 (with A family and a fortune, below).

A house and its head. 1935.

Daughters and sons. 1937, New York 1938.

A family and a fortune. 1939, New York 1965 (with More women than men, above).

Parents and children. 1941.

Elders and betters. 1944.

Manservant and maidservant. 1947, New York 1948 (as Bullivant and the Lambs).

Two worlds and their ways. 1949, New York 1949.

Darkness and day. 1951, New York 1951.

The present and the past. 1953, New York 1953.

Mother and son. 1955, New York 1955.
A father and his fate. 1957, New York 1958.
A heritage and its history. 1959, New York 1960.
The mighty and their fall. 1961, New York 1962.
A god and his gifts. 1963, New York 1964.
The last and the first. 1971.

§2

A conversation between I. Compton-Burnett and M. Jourdain. Orion 1 1945.
Liddell, R. The novels of I. Compton-Burnett. In his A treatise on the novel, 1947.
—— The novels of I. Compton-Burnett. 1955.
Bowen, E. In her Collected impressions, 1950.
Hansford-Johnson, P. Three novelists and the drawing of character: C. P. Snow, J. Cary, Ivy Compton-Burnett. E & S new ser 3 1950.
—— I. Compton-Burnett. 1951 (Br Council pamphlet).

ARCHIBALD JOSEPH CRONIN
b. 1896

Hatter's castle. 1931, Boston 1931.
Three loves. 1932, Boston 1932.
Grand canary. 1933, Boston 1933.
The stars look down. 1935, Boston 1935.
The citadel. 1937, Boston 1937.
Jupiter laughs: a play in three acts. Boston 1940, London 1941.
The keys of the kingdom. Boston 1941, London 1942.
The green years. Boston 1944, London 1945, Boston 1960 (with Shannon's way, below).
Shannon's way. 1948, Boston 1948, 1960 (with The green years, above). Sequel to The green years.
The Spanish gardener. 1950, Boston 1950.
Adventures in two worlds. 1952, New York [1952]. Autobiography.
Beyond this place. 1953, Boston 1953.
Crusader's tomb. 1956, Boston 1956 (as A thing of beauty).
The innkeeper's wife. New York 1958. Story.
The northern light. 1958, Boston 1958.
The Judas tree. 1961, Boston 1961.
A song of sixpence. 1964, Boston 1964.
A pocketful of rye. 1969, Boston 1969.

GEORGE WARWICK DEEPING
1877–1950

Uther & Igraine. 1903, New York 1903.
Love among the ruins. 1904, New York 1904.
The seven streams. 1905.
The slanderers. New York 1905, London 1907.
Bess of the woods. 1906.
A woman's war. 1907.
Bertrand of Brittany. New York 1908, London 1908.
Mad Barbara. 1908, New York 1909.
The red saint. 1909, New York 1940.
The return of the petticoat. 1909, 1913 (rev).
The lame Englishman. 1910.
The rust of Rome. 1910.
Fox farm. 1911, New York [1911], 1933 (as The eyes of love).
Joan of the tower. 1911.
Sincerity. 1912, New York 1912 (as The strong hand), 1932 (as The challenge of love).
The house of spies. 1913, New York 1913.
The white gate. 1913, New York 1914.
The king behind the king. 1914, New York 1914.
The pride of Eve. 1914.

Marriage by conquest. 1915, New York 1915.
Unrest. 1916, New York 1916 (as Bridge of desire).
Martin Valliant. 1917, New York 1917.
Valour. 1918, New York 1934.
Countess Glika, and other stories. 1919.
Second youth. 1919, New York 1932 (as The awakening).
The prophetic marriage. 1920.
The house of adventure. 1921, New York 1922.
Lantern lane. 1921.
Orchards. 1922, New York 1933 (as The captive wife).
Apples of gold. 1923.
The secret sanctuary: or the saving of John Stretton. 1923.
Suvla John. 1924.
Three rooms. 1924.
Sorrell and son. 1925, New York 1926.
Doomsday. 1927, New York 1927.
Kitty. 1927, New York 1927.
Old Pybus. 1928, New York 1928.
Roper's Row. 1929, New York 1929.
Exiles. 1930, New York 1930 (as Exile).
The road. 1931, New York 1931 (as The ten commandments).
Old wine and new. 1932, New York 1932.
Smith. 1932, New York 1932.
The black sheep. 1933, New York 1933.
The captive wife. New York 1933. See Orchards, above.
The eyes of love. New York 1933. See Fox farm, above.
The man on the white horse. 1934, New York 1934.
Seven men came back. 1934, New York 1934.
Sackcloth into silk. 1935, New York 1935 (as The golden cord).
Two in a train, and other stories. 1935.
No hero—this. 1936, New York 1936.
Blind man's year. 1937, New York 1937.
These white hands. New York 1937.
The woman at the door. 1937, New York 1937.
The malice of men. 1938, New York 1938.
Fantasia. 1939, New York 1939 (as Bluewater).
Shabby summer. 1939, New York 1939 (as Folly island).
The man who went back. 1940, New York 1940.
The shield of love. New York 1940.
Corn in Egypt. 1941, New York 1942.
The dark house. 1941, New York 1941.
I live again. 1942, New York 1942.
Slade. 1943, New York 1943.
Mr Gurney and Mr Slade. 1944, New York 1944 (as The cleric's secret).
Reprieve. 1945, New York 1945.
The impudence of youth. 1946, New York 1946.
Laughing house. 1946, New York 1946.
Portrait of a playboy. 1947, New York 1948 (as The playboy).
Paradise Place. 1949.
Old mischief. 1950.
Time to heal. 1952.
Man in chains. 1953.
The old world dies. 1954.
Caroline Terrace. 1955.
The serpent's tooth. 1956.
The sword and the cross. 1957.

'E. M. DELAFIELD',
EDMÉE ELIZABETH MONICA DE LA PASTURE
1890–1943

Zella sees herself. 1917.
The war-workers. 1918, New York 1918.
The pelicans. 1918, New York 1919.
Consequences. [1919], New York 1919.
Tension. [1920], New York 1920.
The heel of Achilles. [1921].

Humbug. [1921], New York 1922.
The optimist. [1922], New York 1922.
A reversion to type. [1923], New York 1923.
Mrs Harter. [1924], New York [1925].
Messalina of the suburbs. [1924] (with stories and a one-act play), 1929 (alone).
The chip and the block. [1925], New York [1926].
Jill. [1926], New York [1927].
The entertainment. [1927], New York [1927]. Stories.
The way things are. [1927], New York [1928].
The suburban young man. [1928].
What is love? 1928, New York 1929 (as First love).
Women are like that: short stories. 1929.
Turn back the leaves. 1930, New York 1930.
Diary of a provincial lady. 1930.
Challenge to Clarissa. 1931, New York [1931] (as House party).
To see ourselves: a domestic comedy in three acts. In Famous plays of 1931, 1931, New York [1932].
Thank heaven fasting. 1932.
The provincial lady goes further. 1932, New York 1933 (as The provincial lady in London).
Gay life. 1933.
General impressions. 1933. Essays.
The glass wall: a play in three acts. 1933.
The provincial lady in America. 1934.
The Bazalgettes. 1935. Anon.
Faster! faster! 1936.
As others hear us: a miscellany. 1937. Stories.
Ladies and gentlemen in Victorian fiction. 1937, New York [1937].
Nothing is safe. 1937 ,New York 1937.
Straw without bricks: I visit Soviet Russia. 1937, New York 1937 (as I visit the Soviets).
When women love. New York 1938, London 1939 (as Three marriages). Stories.
Love has no resurrection, and other stories. 1939.
People you love. [1940]. On the status of the family under Nazism.
The provincial lady in war-time. 1940, New York [1940].
No one now will know. 1941, New York [1944].
Late and soon. 1943, New York 1943.

WILLIAM FREND DE MORGAN
1839–1917

Report on the feasibility of a manufacture of glazed pottery in Egypt. Cairo 1894.
Joseph Vance: an ill-written autobiography. 1906, New York 1906, London 1954 (with introd by A. C. Ward) (WC).
Alice-for-short: a dichronism. New York 1907, London 1907.
Somehow good. 1908, New York 1908.
It can never happen again. 2 vols 1909, 1 vol New York 1909.
An affair of dishonour. 1910, New York 1910.
A likely story. 1911, New York 1911.
When ghost meets ghost. [1914], New York 1914.
The old madhouse. 1919, New York 1919. Completed by Mrs E. de Morgan.
The old man's youth and the young man's old age. 1920, New York 1920. Completed by Mrs E. de Morgan.

NIGEL FORBES DENNIS
b. 1912

Boys and girls come out to play. 1949, Boston 1949 (as A sea change).
Cards of identity. 1955, New York 1955.
Two plays and a preface. [1958], New York [1958].

Contains dramatized version of Cards of identity, and The making of Moo.
August for the people: a play in two acts. [1962].
Dramatic essays. [1962].
Jonathan Swift: a short character. New York 1964, London 1965.
A house in order. [1966], New York 1966.

GEORGE NORMAN DOUGLAS
[DOUGLASS]
1868–1952

Bibliographies

Woolf, C. A bibliography of Douglas. 1954, 1954 (rev) (Soho Bibliographies).

§1
Prose Fiction

Unprofessional tales. 1901. By 'Normyx' (i.e. Douglas and his wife Elsa FitzGibbon).
South wind. 1917, New York 1918, [1925] (with new introd) (Modern Lib), London 1942 (abridged, and with introductory note by Douglas), 1946 (with ch divisions and introductory letter by W. King).
They went. 1920, 1921 (abridged, with introductory letter by Douglas), New York 1921.
In the beginning. Florence 1927 (priv ptd), London 1928 (expurgated), New York 1928 (unexpurgated), London 1953.
The angel of Manfredonia. San Francisco 1929 (225 copies). Story, from Old Calabria, below.
Nerinda, 1901. Florence 1929, New York [1929]. Story rptd (rev) from Unprofessional tales, above.

Other Works

Siren land. 1911, New York 1911, London 1923 (rev), New York 1923, London 1957 (with Fountains in the sand, below), New York 1957. Travel.
Fountains in the sand: rambles among the oases of Tunisia. 1912, New York 1912, London 1944 (rev, Penguin), 1957 (with Siren land, above), New York 1957.
Old Calabria. 1915, Boston 1915, New York 1928 (with introd) (Modern Lib), Oxford 1938 (with new introd) (WC), London 1955 (with introd by J. Davenport), New York 1956.
London street games. 1916, 1931 (rev).
Alone. 1921, New York 1922. On Italy.
Together. 1923, New York 1923. On the Vorarlberg.
D. H. Lawrence and Maurice Magnus: a plea for better manners. [Florence] 1924 (priv ptd); rptd (rev) in Experiments, below (New York and London edns only). Written in connection with Lawrence's introd to Magnus's Memoirs of the Foreign Legion, 1924.
Experiments. [Florence] 1925 (priv ptd), New York 1925, London 1925. Essays.
Birds and beasts of the Greek anthology. Florence 1927 (priv ptd), London 1928 (rev), New York 1929 (with foreword by W. A. Percy).
Some limericks collected for the use of students and ensplendour'd with introduction, geographical index and with notes explanatory and critical by N. Douglas. [Florence] 1928 (priv ptd, 110 copies), [New York] 1928 (priv ptd, 750 copies), London 1969 (as The Norman Douglas limerick book).
How about Europe?: some footnotes on East and West. Florence 1929 (priv ptd), New York 1930 (as Goodbye to western culture), London 1930.
One day. Chapelle-Réauville 1929. On Athens; rptd in Three of them 1930.
Capri: materials for a description of the island. Florence 1930. Collects 8 pamphlets priv ptd 1904–15.
Paneros: some words on aphrodisiacs and the like.

Florence 1930 (priv ptd), London 1931, New York 1932.

Summer islands: Ischia and Ponza. [1931], New York 1931, London 1942 (for 1944) (with introductory letter by Douglas); rptd (with omissions) in Late harvest, 1946, below.

Looking back: an autobiographical excursion. 2 vols 1933, New York [1933], 1 vol 1934.

Late harvest. 1946, 1947 (with addns). Comments on his work, with reprints of essays and reviews.

Footnote on Capri. 1952, New York 1952. Essay, accompanying photographs by Islay Lyons.

Venus in the kitchen: or love's cookery book, by 'Pilaff Bey', ed by N. Douglas, introd by G. Greene. 1952, New York 1953. By Douglas and Orioli.

Douglas contributed frequently to Eng Rev 1909–16, mostly reviews.

§2

Tomlinson, H. M. Norman Douglas. 1931, 1952 (rev).

'MacGillivray, Richard' (R. M. Dawkins). Norman Douglas. Florence 1933, London 1952 (rev, as by R. M. Dawkins).

Fitzgibbon, C. Norman Douglas: a pictorial record. 1953.

Aldington, R. Pinorman: personal recollections of Douglas, Pino Orioli and C. Prentice. 1954.

Cunard, N. Grand man: memories of Douglas. 1954.

Greenlees, I. Norman Douglas. 1957 (Br Council pamphlet).

Lindeman, R. Norman Douglas. New York 1965.

Leary, L. Norman Douglas. New York 1968.

DAME DAPHNE DU MAURIER
b. 1907

The loving spirit. 1931, Garden City NY 1931.

I'll never be young again. 1932, Garden City NY 1932.

The progress of Julius. 1933, Garden City NY 1933.

Gerald: a portrait. 1934, Garden City NY 1935. Biography of Gerald du Maurier.

Jamaica Inn. 1936, Garden City NY 1936.

The du Mauriers. 1937, Garden City NY 1937. Biography.

Rebecca. 1938, New York 1938, London 1940 (as play), New York 1943.

Come wind, come weather. 1940, New York 1941. Stories.

Happy Christmas. New York 1940, London [1943]. Story.

Frenchman's Creek. 1941, Garden City NY 1942.

Consider the lilies. [1943]. Story.

Escort. 1943. Story. Rptd in Nothing hurts for long, and Escort, below.

Hungry hill. 1943, Garden City NY 1943.

Nothing hurts for long, and Escort. 1943. 2 stories.

Spring picture. [1944], New York 1944. Story.

Leading lady. [1945]. Story.

London and Paris. 1945.

The years between: a play in two acts. 1945, Garden City NY 1946.

The king's general. 1946, Garden City NY 1946.

The parasites. 1949, Garden City NY 1950.

September tide: a play in three acts. 1949, Garden City NY 1950.

My cousin Rachel. 1951, Garden City NY 1952.

The apple tree: a short novel and some stories. 1952, Garden City NY 1953 (as Kiss me again, stranger).

Mary Anne. 1954, Garden City NY 1954.

The scapegoat. 1957, Garden City NY 1957.

Breaking point: eight stories. 1959, Garden City NY 1959.

The infernal world of Branwell Brontë. 1960, Garden City NY 1961. Non-fiction.

The glass-blowers. 1963, Garden City NY 1963.

The flight of the falcon. 1965, Garden City NY 1965.

Vanishing Cornwall. 1967.

The house on the strand. 1969, Garden City NY 1969.

ARTHUR ANNESLEY RONALD FIRBANK
1886–1926

Seven of the Valmouth *notebooks are now at the Univ of Texas, Austin, another is in the Berg Collection, New York Public Library and the* Caprice *notebooks are at Harvard.*

Bibliographies

Benkovitz, M. J. A bibliography of Ronald Firbank. 1963 (Soho bibliographies).

Collections and Selections

Works. 6 vols 1929–34, 5 vols New York 1929. Introd by A. Waley, biographical memoir by O. Sitwell. Based on first edns, with minor textual revisions, except for Odette for which 1916 edn was used.

The complete Ronald Firbank. 1961 (preface by A. Powell), Norfolk Conn 1961. Texts as in Works with minor textual corrections, except for texts of Santal and The artificial princess, which are those of the 1st edns.

§1

Odette d'Antrevernes and A study in temperament. 1905. Short stories. 1st story pbd separately 1916 with slight textual revisions (as Odette: a fairy tale for weary people).

Vainglory. 1915, New York [1925] (rev).

Inclinations. 1916.

Odette: a fairy tale for weary people. 1916. See Odette d'Antrevernes above.

Caprice. 1917.

Valmouth: a romantic novel. 1919, 1956 (text as in Works), New York 1956. Unrevised version of ch 8 first pbd in Art & Letters new ser 2 1919 (as Fantasia for orchestra in F sharp minor).

The Princess Zoubaroff: a comedy. 1920. First performed June 1951 at the Watergate Theatre.

Santal. 1921, New York [1955]. Story.

The flower beneath the foot: being a record of the early life of St Laura de Nazianzi and the times in which she lived. 1923, New York [1924] (corrected, with preface by Firbank).

Prancing nigger. New York 1924 (with introd by C. van Vechten), London 1924 (as Sorrow in sunlight, corrected and without the introd), 1931 (as Prancing nigger, with minor revisions i.e. the 1929 Works text). Unrevised version of ch 11 first pbd in Reviewer (Richmond Va) 4 1923 (as A broken orchid).

Concerning the eccentricities of Cardinal Pirelli. 1926.

The artificial princess. Introd by C. Kennard 1934.

A letter from Arthur Ronald Firbank to Madame Albani: written 1902–3 and found amongst her papers after her death. [1934].

The new rythum and other pieces. 1962 (with introd by A. Harris), Norfolk Conn 1963. Contains, in addition to the unfinished title novel, A study in temperament, Lady Appledore's mésalliance, Impression d'automne and a miscellany of unpbd juvenilia.

The wind and the roses. Ed M. Benkovitz 1965.

Far away. Ed M. Benkovitz, Iowa City 1966.

Firbank is often credited with the authorship of Count Fanny's nuptials *1907, but the attribution rests on hearsay. See Benkovitz's bibliography, above.*

§2

Fletcher, I. K. Ronald Firbank. 1930. With personal reminiscences by Lord Berners, V. B. Holland, A. John and O. Sitwell.

Forster, E. M. Ronald Firbank. In his Abinger harvest, 1936.

Connolly, C. Anatomy of dandyism. In his Enemies of promise, 1938.

Sitwell, O. Ronald Firbank. In his Noble essences, 1950.

Brooke, J. Ronald Firbank. 1951.

— Firbank and J. Betjeman. 1962 (Br Council pamphlet).

Benkovitz, M. J. Firbank: a biography. New York 1969.

FORD MADOX FORD
formerly
JOSEPH LEOPOLD FORD
HERMANN MADOX HUEFFER
1873–1939

Collections of Ford mss and letters are in Mrs J. Loewe's private collection (Pasadena), the Brustlein deposit at Princeton Univ, E. Naumburg's private collection (New York), Yale Univ Library and Virginia Univ Library.

Bibliographies

Harvey, D. D. Ford: a bibliography of works and criticism. Princeton 1962.

Collections and Selections

Collected poems. 1914 [1913]. Signed F. M. Hueffer. With a preface by the author.

The Bodley Head Ford Madox Ford. Ed G. Greene 5 vols 1962–71.

Critical writings. Ed F. MacShane, Lincoln Nebraska 1964.

§1

All works before The Marsden case *1923 (except pseudonymous ones) are signed Ford Madox Hueffer.*

Prose Fiction

The brown owl: a fairy story. 1892 [1891], New York 1891.

The feather. 1892, New York 1892. Fairy story.

The shifting of the fire. 1892.

The queen who flew. 1894. Fairy story.

The inheritors: an extravagant story. New York 1901, London 1901. With Joseph Conrad.

Romance: a novel. 1903, New York 1904. With Conrad.

The benefactor: a tale of a small circle. 1905.

The fifth queen and how she came to court. 1906. First of The fifth queen trilogy.

Christina's fairy book. [1906]. Fairy stories.

Privy seal: his last venture. 1907. Second of The fifth queen trilogy.

An English girl: a romance. [1907].

The fifth queen crowned: a romance. 1908. Third of The fifth queen trilogy: dramatisation by Ford and F. N. Connell performed at Kingsway Theatre March 1909.

Mr Apollo: a just possible story. [1908].

The Half moon: a romance of the old world and the new. 1909, New York 1909. Planned as part of a trilogy called The three ships; neither of the other pts pbd.

A call: the tale of two passions. 1910. Rptd from Eng Rev 1909 with addn of an 'Epistolary epilogue'.

The portrait. [1910].

The Simple Life Limited. 1911, New York 1911. Satire, under the pseudonym 'Daniel Chaucer'.

Ladies whose bright eyes: a romance. 1911, New York 1911, Philadelphia 1935 (rev).

The panel: a sheer comedy. 1912, Indianapolis [1913] (rev and expanded as Ring for Nancy).

The new Humpty-Dumpty. 1912, New York 1912. Satire, under the pseudonym of 'Daniel Chaucer'.

Mr Fleight. 1913. Satire.

The young Lovell: a romance. 1913.

The good soldier: a tale of passion. 1915, New York 1915, 1927 (with preface by Ford), London 1928, New York 1951 (with essay by M. Schorer). The first part of this novel appeared, in somewhat different form, in Blast 20 June 1914, as The saddest story.

The Marsden case: a romance. [1923].

Some do not—a novel. [1924], New York 1924, London 1948 (with preface by R. A. Scott-James). First of the Tietjens tetralogy.

The nature of a crime. [1924], New York 1924. With Conrad; originally pbd in Eng Rev 1909.

No more parades. [1925], New York [1925], London 1948 (with same preface by Scott-James as to Some do not). Second of the Tietjens tetralogy.

A man could stand up—a novel. [1926], New York 1926, London 1948 (with Scott-James' preface as in Some do not). Third of the Tietjens tetralogy.

The last post. New York 1928, London 1928 (as Last post), London 1948 (with Scott-James' preface as in Some do not). Fourth of the Tietjens tetralogy.

A little less than gods: a romance. [1928], New York 1928.

When the wicked man. New York [1931], London 1932.

The rash act: a novel. New York 1933, London 1933.

Henry for Hugh: a novel. Philadelphia 1934.

Vive le roy: a novel. Philadelphia 1936, London 1937.

An unpbd novel, That same poor man, *exists in ms in the Brustlein deposit at Princeton.*

Other Writings

The questions at the well, with sundry other verses for notes of music. By 'Fenil Haig' [i.e. Ford]. 1893.

Ford Madox Brown: a record of his life and work. 1896.

Poems for pictures and for notes of music. 1900.

The Cinque Ports: a historical and descriptive record. 1900.

Rossetti: a critical essay on his art. [1902], New York [1902].

The face of the night: a second series of poems for pictures. 1904.

The soul of London: a survey of a modern city. 1905.

Hans Holbein the younger: a critical monograph. [1905], New York [1905].

The heart of the country: a survey of a modern land. 1906.

England and the English: an interpretation. New York 1907. Contains The soul of London, The heart of the country and The spirit of the people.

From inland and other poems. 1907.

The Pre-Raphaelite brotherhood: a critical monograph. [1907], New York [1907].

The spirit of the people: an analysis of the English mind. 1907. Previously pbd in U.S.A. only, in England and the English, above.

Songs from London. 1910. Poems.

Ancient lights and certain new reflections. 1911, New York 1911 (as Memories and impressions: a study in atmospheres). Reminiscences.

The critical attitude. 1911. Essays, originally in Eng Rev.

High Germany: eleven sets of verse. 1911 (for 1912).

This monstrous regiment of women. [1913]. Suffragette pamphlet.

The desirable alien: at home in Germany. 1913. With V. Hunt. Travel.

Henry James: a critical study. 1913 (for 1914).

Antwerp. [1915]. Poem.

When blood is their argument: an analysis of Prussian culture. 1915. Anti-German war propaganda.

Between St Dennis and St George: a sketch of three civilisations. 1915. Anti-German war propaganda.

Zeppelin nights: a London entertainment. 1916 (for 1915). With V. Hunt. Historical sketches.

On heaven, and poems written on active service. 1918.

A house: modern morality play. 1921 (Chapbook 21). Poem.

Thus to revisit: some reminiscences. 1921.

Women and men. Paris 1923. Essays originally pbd in Little Rev.

Mister Bosphorus and the Muses. [1923]. Poem.

Joseph Conrad: a personal remembrance. 1924, Boston 1924.

A mirror to France. [1926]. Impressions.

New poems. New York 1927.

New York is not America. [1927], New York 1927. Impressions.

New York essays. New York 1927. Rptd from various American journals.

The English novel from the earliest days to the death of Conrad. Philadelphia 1929, London 1930.

No enemy: a tale of reconstruction. [New York 1929]. Disguised autobiography.

Return to yesterday (reminiscences 1894–1914). 1931, New York 1932.

The cantos of Ezra Pound: some testimonials by E. Hemingway, Ford, T. S. Eliot, H. Walpole, A. Mac-Leish, J. Joyce et al. New York 1933. Ford was apparently the organizer of the tribute.

It was the nightingale. Philadelphia 1933, London 1934. Reminiscences, from 1918.

Provence: from minstrels to the machine. Philadelphia 1935, London 1938. Impressions.

Great trade route. New York 1937, London 1937. Impressions.

Portraits from life: memories and criticisms. New York 1937, London 1938 (as Mightier than the sword). Most of these essays first pbd in Amer Mercury.

The march of literature from Confucius to modern times. New York 1938, London 1939.

Ford edited the English Review *for 15 months from its foundation in Dec 1908, and also the* Transatlantic Review *for 1924.*

Letters. Ed R. M. Ludwig, Princeton 1965.

§2

Hunt, V. The flurried years. 1926, New York 1926 (rev) (as I have this to say). Reminiscences of Ford.

Goldring, D. The last pre-Raphaelite: the life and writings of Ford. 1948, New York 1949 (as Trained for genius).

Conrad, Jessie. Joseph Conrad and his circle. 1935.

Greene, G. Ford Madox Ford. Spectator 7 July 1939. Obituary essay, rptd in his The lost childhood, 1951.

— Last post? TLS 16 Sept 1965.

Aldington, R. Life for life's sake. New York 1941.

Pound, E. Letters. New York 1950.

Garnett, D. The golden echo. 1953.

Young, K. Ford Madox Ford. 1956 (Br Council pamphlet).

Cassell, R. A. Ford: a study of his novels. Baltimore 1961.

Meixner, J. A. Ford's novels: a critical study. Minneapolis 1962.

MacShane, F. The life and work of Ford. 1964.

Modern Fiction Stud 9 1963.

Mizener, A. The saddest story: a biography of Ford. 1972.

CECIL SCOTT FORESTER
1899–1966

Napoleon and his court. 1924.

The paid piper. 1924.

A pawn among kings. 1924.

Josephine, Napoleon's empress. 1925, New York 1925.

Payment deferred. 1926, Boston 1942.

Love lies dreaming. 1927, Indianapolis [1927].

Victor Emmanuel II and the union of Italy. 1927, New York 1927.

The wonderful week. 1927, Indianapolis [1927] (as One wonderful week).

Louis XIV, King of France and Navarre. 1928.

The shadow of the hawk. 1928, Indianapolis [1928] (as The daughter of the hawk).

Brown on resolution. 1929, New York 1929 (as Single-handed).

Nelson. 1929, Indianapolis [1929] (as Lord Nelson).

The voyage of the Annie Marble. 1929. Travel.

The Annie Marble in Germany. 1930. Travel.

Plain murder. 1930, New York 1954.

Two-and-twenty. 1931, New York 1931.

U97: a play in three acts. 1931.

Death to the French. 1932.

The gun. 1933, Boston 1933.

Nurse Cavell: a play in three acts. 1933. With C. E. Bechhofer Roberts.

The peacemaker. 1934, Boston 1934.

The African Queen. 1935, Boston 1935, New York 1963 (with new foreword by author).

The general. 1936, Boston 1936.

Marionettes at home. 1936. Non-fiction.

The happy return. 1937, Boston 1937 (as Beat to quarters).

Flying colours. 1938, Boston 1939.

A ship of the line. 1938, Boston 1938.

The earthly paradise. 1940, Boston 1940 (as To the Indies).

The captain from Connecticut. 1941, Boston 1941.

Poo-poo and the dragons. 1942, Boston 1942. For children.

The ship. 1943, Boston 1943.

The commodore. 1945, Boston 1945 (as Commodore Hornblower).

Lord Hornblower. 1946, Boston 1946.

The sky and the forest. 1948, Boston 1948.

Mr Midshipman Hornblower. 1950, Boston 1950.

Randall and the river of time. Boston 1950, London 1951.

Lieutenant Hornblower. 1952, Boston 1952.

The Barbary pirates. New York 1953, London 1956. For children.

Hornblower and the Atropos. 1953, Boston 1953.

The adventures of John Wetherell, ed with an introd by Forester. 1953.

The nightmare. 1954, Boston 1954.

The good shepherd. 1955.

The age of fighting sail: the story of the naval war of 1812. Garden City NY 1956, London 1957 (as The naval war of 1812).

Hornblower in the West Indies. 1958, Boston 1958 (as Admiral Hornblower in the West Indies).

Hunting the Bismarck. 1959, Boston 1959 (as The last nine days of the Bismarck). A fictional account.

Hornblower and the Hotspur. 1962, Boston 1962.

The Hornblower companion. 1964, Boston 1964. Contains autobiographical notes.

William Joyce. In Fatal fascination: a choice of crime, by N. Balchin, Forester [et al], 1964, Boston 1965.

Hornblower and the crisis: an unfinished novel. 1967.

Long before forty. 1967, Boston 1968. Autobiography to the age of 31. Contains autobiographical notes rptd from The Hornblower companion, 1964.

The man in the yellow raft. 1969, Boston 1969. Short stories.

JOHN GALSWORTHY
1867–1933

*The Univ of Birmingham Library contains Galsworthy's own
collection of mss (see Catalogue pbd by the Library 1967).
The ms of* The Forsyte Saga *is in the BM.*

Bibliographies
Marrot, H. V. A bibliography of the works of Galsworthy.
1928.

Collections and Selections
Plays. 7 sers 1909–30. Sers 1–6 pbd New York 1909–26.
Works: Manaton edition. 30 vols New York 1922–36,
London 1923–35. Contains prefaces specially written
by the author for this edn, and other prefaces by Ada
Galsworthy.
Works: Grove edition. 26 vols 1927–34.
Collected poems. Ed A. Galsworthy [1934], New York
1934.

§1
Prose Fiction
From the four winds, by John Sinjohn [i.e. Galsworthy].
1897. Stories.
Jocelyn, by John Sinjohn. 1898.
Villa Rubein, by John Sinjohn. 1900, New York 1908 (as
by Galsworthy), London 1909 (rev, with A man of
Devon, below).
A man of Devon, by John Sinjohn. 1901. Stories; rptd
(rev) in 1909 edn of Villa Rubein, above.
The island Pharisees. 1904, 1908 (rev).
The man of property. 1906, New York 1906, [1964]
(Limited Editions Club, introd by E. Waugh); rptd in
The Forsyte saga, 1922, below.
The country house. 1907, New York 1907.
A commentary. 1908, New York 1908. Stories.
Fraternity. 1909, New York 1909.
A motley. 1910, New York 1910. Stories.
The patrician. 1911, New York 1911, [1926] (introd by
B. Perry).
The dark flower. 1913, New York 1913.
The little man, and other satires. New York 1915, London
1915. Stories.
The Freelands. 1915, New York 1915.
Beyond. New York 1917, London 1917, 1923 (rev).
Five tales. New York 1918, London 1918, 1920 (2 vols,
The first and the last; The stoic), New York 1965 (as
The apple tree and other tales). Includes Indian sum-
mer of a Forsyte, rptd in The Forsyte saga, below.
The burning spear: being the adventures of Mr John
Lavender in time of war, recorded by A.R.P—M. 1919,
New York 1923 (as by Galsworthy, with foreword by
him).
Saint's progress. New York 1919, London 1919.
Tatterdemalion. 1920, New York 1920. Stories.
In Chancery. 1920, New York 1920; rptd in The Forsyte
saga, below.
Awakening. New York [1920], London [1920]; rptd in
The Forsyte saga, below.
To let. New York 1921, London 1921; rptd in The
Forsyte saga, below.
The Forsyte saga. New York 1922, London 1922, 1933
(with preface by A. Galsworthy), New York 1933.
Captures. 1923, New York 1923. Stories.
The white monkey. New York 1924, London 1924; rptd
in A modern comedy, 1929, below.
Abracadabra and other satires. 1924. Stories first pbd in
The little man and other satires, above.
The silver spoon. 1926, New York 1926; rptd in A
modern comedy, below.
Two Forsyte interludes: A silent wooing; Passers by.
1927, New York 1938.

Swan song. New York 1928, London 1928; rptd in A
modern comedy, below.
Four Forsyte stories. New York 1929, London 1929.
A modern comedy. 1929, New York 1929. The white
monkey, The silver spoon, Swan song.
On Forsyte 'change. 1930, New York 1930. Stories.
Soames and the flag. 1930, New York 1930.
Maid in waiting. 1931, New York 1931. This and the
next two items rptd in End of the chapter, 1934 below.
Flowering wilderness. 1932, New York 1932.
Over the river. 1933, New York 1933 (as One more
river).
The apple tree. New York 1934. Story, first pbd in Five
tales, 1918.
End of the chapter. New York 1934, London 1935. Maid
in waiting, Flowering wilderness, Over the river.
'Corduroys', by John Sinjohn. Kansas City 1937 (priv
ptd).
The rocks, by John Sinjohn. Kansas City 1937 (priv ptd).
'Nyasha. Kansas City 1939 (priv ptd, 30 copies). Story.

Plays
Plays are listed in order of production, where known.

The silver box: a comedy in three acts. (Royal Court
25 Sept 1906). In Plays ser 1, 1909, Collections, above;
pbd separately New York 1909, London 1910.
Joy: a play on the letter I in three acts. (Savoy 24 Sept
1907). In Plays ser 1, 1909, Collections, above; pbd
separately 1910.
Strife: a drama in three acts. (Duke of York's 9 March
1909). In Plays ser 1, 1909, Collections, above; pbd
separately 1910, New York 1920.
Justice: a tragedy in four acts. (Duke of York's 21 Feb
1910). 1910, New York 1910.
The little dream: an allegory in six scenes. (Gaiety,
Manchester 15 April 1911; Court 28 Oct 1912). New
York 1911, London [1911], [1912] (rev).
The pigeon: a fantasy in three acts. (Royalty 30 Jan 1912).
1912, New York 1912.
The eldest son: a domestic drama in three acts. (Kingsway
25 Nov 1912). 1912, New York 1912.
The fugitive: a play in four acts. (Royal Court 16 Sept
1913). 1913.
The mob: a play in four acts. (Coronet 20 April 1914).
1914, New York 1914.
A bit o' love: a play in three acts. (Kingsway 25 May 1915).
1915, New York 1915.
The foundations: an extravagant play in three acts. (Roy-
alty 26 June 1917). 1920, New York 1920.
The skin game: a tragi-comedy in three acts. (St Martin's
21 April 1920). 1920, New York 1920.
A family man: in three acts. (Comedy 2 June 1921). 1922,
New York 1922.
Six short plays. 1921, New York 1921. Contains The first
and the last; The little man; Hall-marked; Defeat; The
sun; Punch and go.
Loyalties: a drama in three acts. (St Martin's 8 March
1922). 1922.
Defeat: a play in one act. (Everyman 17 April 1922). In
Six short plays, 1921, above.
Windows: a comedy in three acts for idealists and others.
(Royal Court 25 April 1922). 1922, New York 1923.
The forest: a drama in four acts. (St Martin's 6 March
1924). 1924, New York 1924.
Old English: a play in three acts. (Haymarket 21 Oct 1924).
1924, New York 1925.
The show: a drama in three acts. (St Martin's 1 July 1925).
1925, New York 1925.
Punch and go: a comedy. (Everyman 24 May 1926). In
Six short plays, 1921, above.
Escape: an episodic play in a prologue and two parts.
(Ambassadors 12 Aug 1926). 1926. For the discarded
Episode VII, *see* The winter garden, 1935, below.

Exiled: an evolutionary comedy in three acts. (Wyndham's 19 June 1929). 1929.

The roof: a play in seven scenes. (Vaudeville 5 Nov 1929). 1929, New York 1931.

The little man: a farcical morality in three scenes. (Little 19 June 1934). In Six short plays, 1921, above; pbd separately 1924.

The winter garden: four dramatic pieces. 1935. The winter garden; Escape—episode VII; The golden eggs; Similes.

Other Works

A commentary. 1908. Sketches.

A justification of the censorship of plays. 1909. Pamphlet.

Horses in mines. [1910]. Rptd from Times.

A motley. 1910, New York 1910. Essays.

The spirit of punishment. 1910. Rptd, rev, from Daily Chron.

For love of beasts. 1912. Rptd from Pall Mall Gazette.

The inn of tranquillity. New York 1912, London 1912. Essays.

Moods, songs & doggerels. New York 1912, London 1912.

'Gentles, let us rest'. [1913]. Rptd from Nation.

The slaughter of animals for food. [1913]. Rptd from Daily Mail.

Treatment of animals. [1913]. Speech.

Memories. 1914, New York 1914. First pbd in the Inn of tranquillity, 1912.

A sheaf. 1916, New York 1916. Essays.

Your Christmas dinner is served! 1916. Leaflet, issued by the National Committee for Relief in Belgium.

The land: a plea. [1917]. Pamphlet.

Addresses in America. New York 1919, London 1919.

Another sheaf. 1919, New York 1919. Essays.

Five poems. New York 1919 (priv ptd, 10 copies).

To the Cliff-Dwellers [of Chicago]: an address. Chicago 1919 (priv ptd).

The bells of peace. Cambridge 1921. Poem.

International thought. Cambridge 1923. Pamphlet.

Memorable days. 1924 (priv ptd, 60 copies). Pamphlet; autobiographical.

On expression. 1924 (English Assoc presidential address).

Is England done? Hove 1925 (priv ptd, 60 copies). Rptd from Sunday Times.

A talk on playing the game with animals and birds. [1926.]

Verses new and old. 1926, New York [1926].

Castles in Spain & other screeds. 1927, New York 1927. Essays.

The way to prepare peace. 1927 (priv ptd, 20 copies). Rptd from Daily Mirror.

Mr Galsworthy's appeal for the miners. [1928]. Rptd from Manchester Guardian Weekly.

The plight of the miners: a national danger: Mr Galsworthy's suggestions. [1928]. Rptd from Manchester Guardian.

A rambling discourse. 1929. Address to the Associated Societies of Edinburgh University.

Two essays on Conrad. Cincinnati 1930 (priv ptd).

The creation of character in literature. Oxford 1931 (Romanes lecture).

'Literature and life'. Princeton 1931. Lecture.

[Forty poems]. [1932] (Augustan Books of Poetry).

Author and critic. New York 1933. Booklet.

Glimpses & reflections. 1937. Miscellaneous papers.

Address to the PEN Club (Brussels June 1927). Kansas City 1939 (priv ptd, 30 copies).

Letters

Autobiographical letters of Galsworthy: a correspondence with Frank Harris, hitherto unpublished. New York 1933.

Letters from Galsworthy 1900–32. Ed E. Garnett 1934.

Wilson, A. B. Galsworthy's letters to Leon Lion. Hague 1968.

§2

Kaye-Smith, S. John Galsworthy. 1916.

Conrad, J. Galsworthy: an appreciation. Canterbury 1922; rptd in his Last essays, 1926.

Lawrence, D. H. In Scrutinies, ed E. Rickword 1928; rptd in his Phoenix, New York 1936.

Marrot, H. V. A note on Galsworthy, dramatist. 1928.

—— The life and letters of Galsworthy. 1935.

Ford, F. M. (formerly Hueffer). It was the nightingale. 1933. Includes reminiscences of Galsworthy.

Mottram, R. H. John Galsworthy. 1953 (Br Council pamphlet).

—— For some we loved: an intimate portrait of Ada and John Galsworthy. 1956.

Morris, M. My Galsworthy story. 1967. Includes letters.

Sauter, R. Galsworthy the man: an intimate portrait. 1967.

Holloway, D. John Galsworthy. [1968].

DAVID GARNETT
b. 1892

Dope-darling, by Leda Burke [i.e. Garnett]. [1919].

Lady into fox. 1922, New York 1923, London 1928 (with A man in the zoo, below), New York 1966 (with note by author and introd by V. Starrett).

A man in the zoo. 1924, New York 1924, London 1928 (with Lady into fox, above).

The sailor's return. 1925, New York 1925, London 1948 (with Beany-eye, below).

Go she must! 1927, New York 1927.

The old dovecote, and other stories. 1928.

No love. 1929, New York 1929.

The grasshoppers come. 1931, New York [1931].

A rabbit in the air: notes from a diary kept while learning to handle an aeroplane. 1932.

A terrible day. 1932.

Pocahontas: or the nonpareil of Virginia. 1933, New York [1933]. Biography.

Beany-eye. 1935, New York [1935], London 1948 (with The sailor's return, above).

The letters of T. E. Lawrence. Ed Garnett 1938, New York 1939, London 1952 (as Selected letters of T. E. Lawrence).

War in the air: September 1939 to May 1941. 1941, Garden City NY 1941.

The essential T. E. Lawrence, selected by Garnett. 1951, New York 1951.

The golden echo. 1953, New York 1954. Autobiography.

Aspects of love. 1955, New York 1956.

The flowers of the forest. 1955, New York 1956. Autobiography; sequel to The golden echo, above.

A shot in the dark. 1958, Boston 1958.

A net for Venus. 1959.

The familiar faces. 1962, New York 1963. Autobiography: sequel to The flowers of the forest, above.

Two by two: a story of survival. 1963, New York 1964.

Ulterior motives. 1966, New York 1967.

The [T.H.] White/Garnett letters. Ed Garnett 1968, New York 1968.

WILLIAM ALEXANDER GERHARDIE
1895–1977
Gerhardie formerly used the spelling Gerhardi.

Collections

Collected uniform revised edition. 1947–.

§1

Futility: a novel on Russian themes. [1922], New York 1922.

Anton Chehov: a critical study. [1923], New York 1923.
The polyglots. [1925], New York 1925.
A bad end. 1926. Story, rptd in Pretty creatures, below.
Perfectly scandalous: or 'The immortal lady'. 1927, 1929 (as Donna Quixote: or Perfectly scandalous). Play.
The vanity-bag. 1927. Story rptd in Pretty creatures, below.
Pretty creatures. 1927, New York 1927. Stories.
Jazz and Jasper: the story of Adams and Eva. [1928], New York 1928 (as Eva's apples), London 1947 (rev, as My sinful earth).
Pending heaven. 1930, New York 1930.
Memoirs of a polyglot. 1931, New York 1931. Autobiography.
The memoirs of Satan. 1932, Garden City NY 1933. With B. Lunn.
The Casanova fable: a satirical revaluation. 1934. Non-fiction; with 'Hugh Kingsmill'.
Resurrection. 1934, New York [1934].
Meet yourselves as you really are. 1936, 1962 (rev) (Penguin). With Prince Leopold zu Loewenstein.
Of mortal love. 1936.
My wife's the least of it. 1938.
The Romanovs. New York [1939], London 1940. Non-fiction.

STELLA DOROTHEA GIBBONS
b. 1902

The mountain beast and other poems. 1930.
Cold Comfort Farm. 1932.
Bassett. 1934.
The priestess, and other poems. 1934.
Enbury Heath. 1935.
The untidy gnome. 1935. For children.
Miss Linsey and Pa. 1936.
Roaring tower and other short stories. 1937.
The lowland Venus, and other poems. 1938.
Nightingale wood. 1938.
My American: a romance. 1939, New York 1940.
Christmas at Cold Comfort Farm, and other stories. 1940.
The rich house. 1941.
Ticky. 1943.
The bachelor. 1944, New York 1944.
Westwood: or, the gentle powers. 1946, New York 1946 (as The gentle powers).
Conference at Cold Comfort Farm. 1949.
The matchmaker. 1949.
Collected poems. 1950.
The Swiss summer. 1951.
Fort of the bear. 1953.
Beside the pearly water. 1954.
The shadow of a sorcerer. 1955.
Here be dragons. 1956.
White sand and grey sand. [1958].
A pink front door. [1959].
The weather at Tregulla. [1962].
The wolves were in the sledge. 1964.
The charmers. 1965.
Starlight. 1967.
The snow-woman. 1969.

ELINOR SUTHERLAND GLYN
1864–1943

§1

Many of Elinor Glyn's novels were serialized before pbn in book form, notably in Nash's Mag *and* Cosmopolitan.

The visits of Elizabeth. 1900, New York 1901.
Reflections of Ambrosine. 1902, New York 1902 (as The seventh commandment).

The damsel and the sage. 1903, New York 1903.
The vicissitudes of Evangeline. 1905, New York 1905 (as Red hair).
Beyond the rocks. 1906, New York 1906.
Three weeks. 1907, New York 1907.
The sayings of Grandmamma and others. 1908, New York 1908.
Elizabeth visits America. 1909, New York 1909.
His hour. 1910, New York 1910. Some later edns titled When the hour came, or When his hour came.
The reason why. 1911, New York 1911.
Halcyone. 1912, New York 1912. Some American edns titled Love itself.
The contrast, and other stories. 1913.
The sequence 1905–12. 1913, New York 1913 (as Guinevere's lover).
Letters to Caroline. 1914, New York 1914 (as Your affectionate godmother).
The man and the moment. New York 1914, London 1915.
Three things. 1915, New York [1915]. Articles.
The career of Katherine Bush. New York 1916, London 1917.
Destruction. 1918. Non-fiction.
The price of things. [1919], New York 1919 (as Family), Auburn NY 1924 (as The price of things).
Points of view. [1920].
The philosophy of love. [1920]. Articles.
The Elinor Glyn system of writing. 4 vols Auburn NY [1922].
Man and maid—renaissance. 1922, Philadelphia 1922.
The great moment. 1923, Philadelphia 1923.
The philosophy of love. Auburn NY [1923], London [1928] (as Love—what I think of it). Not the same as The philosophy of love, 1920, above.
Six days. 1924, Philadelphia 1924.
Letters from Spain. 1924. Travel.
This passion called love. 1925, Auburn NY [1925].
Love's blindness. 1926, Auburn NY [1926].
The wrinkle book: or how to keep looking young. 1927, New York [1928] (as Eternal youth).
It, and other stories. 1927, New York [1927].
The flirt and the flapper: dialogue. 1930.
Glorious flames. 1932, New York [1933]. Based on the film script for The price of things, above.
Love's hour. 1932, New York [1932].
Saint or satyr? and other stories. 1933, New York [1933] (as Such men are dangerous).
Sooner or later. 1933, New York 1935.
Did she? 1934.
Romantic adventure. 1936, New York 1937. Autobiography.
The third eye. 1940.

Elinor Glyn also wrote a number of film-scripts, most of which were based on her novels and stories.

§2

Bennett, A. In his Books and persons, 1917.
'Glyn, Anthony' (G. L. S. Davson). Elinor Glyn. 1955, 1968 (rev).

KENNETH GRAHAME
1859–1932

§1

Pagan papers. 1894 (for 1893), 1898 (omitting Golden age stories). Essays and stories.
The golden age. 1895, Chicago 1895. Stories, some previously pbd in Pagan papers.
The headswoman. 1898. Story.
Dream days. 1899 (for 1898).

The wind in the willows. 1908, New York 1908, 1940 (with introd by A. A. Milne) (Limited Editions Club). Dramatized by A. A. Milne (as Toad of Toad Hall) 1929, New York 1929.

The Cambridge book of poetry for children. Ed Grahame, Cambridge 1916, New York [1916], Cambridge 1932 (rev), New York [1933].

First whisper of The wind in the willows. Ed E. Grahame 1944, Philadelphia 1945. Unpbd stories.

Bertie's escapade. 1949, Philadelphia 1949. Story rptd from First whisper.

Some unpbd pieces by Grahame, together with some previously uncollected contributions to periodicals, are ptd in P. R. Chalmers, Kenneth Grahame, §2, below.

§2

Chalmers, P. R. Grahame: life, letters and unpublished work. 1933.

Green, P. Grahame: a study of his life, work and times. [1959].

FREDERICK LAWRENCE GREEN
1902–53

Julius Penton. 1934.
On the night of the fire. 1939, New York 1939.
The sound of winter. 1940.
Give us the world. 1941.
Music in the park. 1942.
A song for the angels. 1943.
On the edge of the sea. 1944.
Odd man out. 1945, New York 1947, London 1950 (as film, with R. C. Sherriff, in Three British screenplays, ed R. Manvell).
A flask for the journey. 1946, New York 1948.
A fragment of glass. 1947.
Mist on the waters. 1948, New York 1949.
Clouds in the wind. 1950, New York 1951.
The magician. 1951, New York 1951.
Ambush for the hunter. 1952, New York 1953.

'HENRY GREEN',
HENRY VINCENT YORKE
1905–74

§1

Blindness. 1926, New York [1926].
Living. 1929.
Party going. 1939, New York 1951.
Pack my bag: a self-portrait. 1940.
Caught. 1943, New York 1950.
Loving. 1945, New York 1949.
Back. 1946, New York 1950.
Concluding. 1948, New York 1951.
Nothing. 1950, New York 1950.
Doting. 1952, New York 1952.

§2

Green, H. The art of fiction 20. Paris Rev no 19 [1958]. An interview with T. Southern; rptd in Writers at work: the Paris Review interviews, ser 2 1963.

London Mag 6 1959. Green special no.

Stokes, E. The novels of Green. 1959.

Russell, J. Henry Green: nine novels and an unpacked bag. New Brunswick 1960.

Ryf, R. S. Henry Green. New York 1967.

MARGUERITE RADCLYFFE HALL
1883?–1943

§1

'Twixt earth and stars: poems. 1906.
A sheaf of verses. 1908.
Poems of the past & present. 1910.
Songs of three counties, and other poems. Introd by R. B. Cunninghame-Graham 1913.
The forgotten island. 1915. Verse.
The forge. 1924.
The unlit lamp. 1924, New York 1929.
A Saturday life. 1925, New York 1930.
Adam's breed. 1926, Garden City NY 1926.
The well of loneliness. 1928, Paris 1928, New York [1928] (with commentary by Havelock Ellis), London 1949 (without commentary). The first English edn was withdrawn 22 Aug 1928, but the Paris edn was ptd from stereos of the type.
The master of the house. 1932, New York 1932.
Miss Ogilvy finds herself. 1934, New York [1934]. Stories.
The sixth beatitude. 1936, New York [1936].

§2

'West, Rebecca' (C. I. Andrews). Concerning the censorship. In her Ending in earnest, Garden City NY 1931. On The well of loneliness.

Troubridge, U. V. The life and death of Radclyffe Hall. 1961.

Brittain, V. Radclyffe Hall: a case of obscenity? 1968.

LESLIE POLES HARTLEY
b. 1895

Collections

Eustace and Hilda: a trilogy. 1958, New York 1958. Introd by D. Cecil.

Collected short stories. 1968. Introd by D. Cecil.

§1

Night fears, and other stories. 1924. Mostly rptd from Oxford Chron and Oxford Outlook.

Simonetta Perkins. 1925, New York 1926. Story.
The killing bottle. 1932. Stories.
The shrimp and the anemone. 1944, New York 1945 (as The west window).
The sixth heaven. 1946, New York 1947.
Eustace and Hilda. 1947.
The travelling grave, and other stories. Sauk City 1948, London 1951. Includes various stories rptd from Night fears and The killing bottle.
The boat. 1949, New York 1950.
My fellow devils. 1951.
The go-between. 1953, New York 1954, London 1963 (with introd by Hartley).
The white wand, and other stories. 1954. Includes various stories rptd from Night fears and The killing bottle.
A perfect woman. 1955, New York 1956.
The hireling. 1957, New York 1958.
Facial justice. 1960, Garden City NY 1961.
Two for the river, and other stories. 1961.
The brickfield. 1964.
The betrayal. 1966.
The novelist's responsibility. 1967. Essays.
Poor Clare. 1968.
The love-adept: a variation on a theme. 1969.

§2

Adam International Rev 29 1961. Special Hartley no.

Bloomfield, P. L. P. Hartley. 1962 (Br Council pamphlet). With B. Bergonzi on Anthony Powell.
Bien, P. L. P. Hartley. 1963.

'IAN HAY',
JOHN HAY BEITH
1876–1952
Collections

Writings: Argyll edition. 10 vols Boston 1921.

§1

Plays are listed in order of production, where known; otherwise, of pbn.

'Pip': a romance of youth. 1907, Boston 1917.
'The right stuff': some episodes in the career of a North Briton. 1908, Boston 1910.
A man's man. 1909, Boston 1910.
A safety match. 1911, Boston 1911. Dramatized, Strand 13 Jan 1921, pbd 1927 (French's Acting Edn).
The crimson cocoanut, and other plays (A late delivery; The missing card). Boston 1913. The crimson cocoanut pbd separately 1928 (French's Acting Edn).
Happy-go-lucky. 1913, Boston 1913. Dramatized as Tilly of Bloomsbury, Apollo 10 July 1919, pbd 1922 (French's Acting Edn).
A knight on wheels. 1914, Boston 1914.
The lighter side of school life. 1914, Boston 1915. Articles, rptd from Blackwood's Mag.
The first hundred thousand: being the unofficial chronicle of a unit of 'K(1)' (Kitchener's First Army). 1915, Boston 1916.
Scally: the story of a perfect gentleman. Boston 1915, London 1932. Story, rptd in The lucky number, 1923, below.
Carrying on—after the first hundred thousand. 1917, Boston 1917 (as All in it: K(1) carries on).
Getting together. 1917, Garden City NY 1917. On the US and Great Britain in the European War.
The oppressed English. Garden City NY 1917.
The last million. [1919], Boston 1919. On the US Army.
The willing horse. [1921], Boston 1921.
The happy ending: a play in three acts. (St James's 30 Nov 1922). [1927] (French's Acting Edn).
The lucky number. [1923], Boston 1923. Stories.
The sport of kings: a domestic comedy in three acts. (Savoy 9 Sept 1924). [1926] (French's Acting Edn).
'The Liberry'. Boston 1924.
The shallow end. 1924, Boston 1924. Essays and sketches.
Paid with thanks. [1925], Boston 1925 (as Paid in full).
Half-a-sovereign. [1926], Boston 1926.
The ship of remembrance, Gallipoli–Salonica. [1926].
A damsel in distress: a comedy in three acts. (New 13 Aug 1928). [1930] (French's Acting Edn). With P. G. Wodehouse, adapted from Wodehouse's novel.
A blank cartridge: a farce. [1928] (French's Acting Edn).
Personally or by letter: a little comedy. [1928] (French's Acting Edn).
The poor gentleman. 1928, Boston 1928.
Treasure trove: a fantasy. [1928] (French's Acting Edn).
Baa, baa, black sheep: a farcical comedy in three acts. (New 22 April 1929). [1930] (French's Acting Edn). With P. G. Wodehouse.
The middle watch: a romance of the Navy in three acts. (Shaftesbury 12 Aug 1929). [1931] (French's Acting Edn). As novel 1930, Boston 1930. With S. King-Hall.
A song of sixpence: a Scottish comedy. (Daly's 17 March 1930). [1930] (French's Acting Edn). With G. Bolton.
Leave it to Psmith: a comedy of youth, love and misadventure in three acts. (Shaftesbury 29 Sept 1930).

[1932] (French's Acting Edn). With P. G. Wodehouse.
Mr Faint-heart: a romantic comedy in three acts. (Shaftesbury 20 April 1931). [1931] (French's Acting Edn).
The midshipmaid: a naval manoeuvre in three acts. (Shaftesbury 10 Aug 1931). [1932] (French's Acting Edn). With S. King-Hall. Pbd 1933 as novel, by Hay alone.
Their name liveth: the book of the Scottish National War Memorial. 1931.
Orders are orders: a military diversion in three acts. (Shaftesbury 9 Aug 1932). [1933] (French's Acting Edn). With A. Armstrong.
A present from Margate: a frivolous comedy in three acts. (Shaftesbury 14 Dec 1933). [1934] (French's Acting Edn). With A. E. W. Mason.
Find the lady: a comedietta in one act. [1933] (French's Acting Edn).
The great wall of India. 1933, Boston 1933.
It is quicker to telephone: a comedy in one act. [1933] (French's Acting Edn).
Admirals all: an amphibious adventure in three acts. (Shaftesbury 6 Aug 1934). [1935] (French's Acting Edn). With S. King-Hall.
David and destiny. 1934, Boston 1934.
Lucky dog. 1934.
Right of search: a comedy in one act. [1935] (French's Acting Edn).
Housemaster. 1936, Boston 1937, London [1938] (as play, Apollo 12 Nov 1936) (French's Acting Edn), New York 1938 (as play, with title Bachelor born) (French's Standard Library Edn).
The King's service: an informal history of the British infantry soldier. 1938, 1942 (abridged, as The British infantryman).
Little ladyship: a comedy in three acts. (Kings Glasgow 16 Jan 1939). [1941] (French's Acting Edn). Pbd 1941 as novel.
Stand at ease: stories and memories. 1940.
The battle of Flanders, 1940. 1941.
America comes across. 1942.
The unconquered isle: the story of Malta GC. 1943, New York 1943 (as Malta epic).
A flat and a sharp: a domestic complication in one act. [1944] (French's Acting Edn).
Burglar alarm: a midnight adventure in one act. [1945] (French's Acting Edn).
Peaceful invasion. 1946.
The Post Office went to war. 1946.
Off the record: a naval comedy in three acts. (King's, Edinburgh 17 March 1947; Apollo 3 June 1947). [1949] (French's Acting Edn). With S. King-Hall.
The fourpenny box: a play in one act. [1947] (French's Acting Edn).
Let my people go. 1948. Play.
Arms and the men. 1950. War history.
The Royal Company of Archers 1676–1951. 1951.
The commissioner's bungalow: a play in three acts. [1952] (French's Acting Edn). With J. Smyth.
One hundred years of Army nursing. 1953.

MAURICE HENRY HEWLETT
1861–1923

Earthwork out of Tuscany: being impressions and translations. 1895, 1899 (rev, with new preface), New York 1900, London 1901 (rev). Essays.
A masque of dead Florentines. 1895. Verse.
Songs and meditations. 1896.
The forest lovers. 1898, New York 1898.
Pan and the young shepherd. 1898, 1906 (abridged). Verse play.
Little novels of Italy. 1899, New York 1899.

The life and death of Richard Yea-and-nay. 1900, New York 1900.
New Canterbury tales. 1901, New York 1901.
The queen's quair: or the six years' tragedy. 1904, New York 1904.
The road in Tuscany. 2 vols 1904, New York 1904, 1 vol London 1906. Travel.
Fond adventures: tales of the youth of the world. 1905, New York 1905.
The fool errant: being the memoirs of Francis-Antony Strelley esq, citizen of Lucca. 1905, New York 1905.
The stooping lady. 1907, New York 1907.
The Spanish jade. 1908, New York 1908.
Halfway house: a comedy of degrees. 1908, New York 1908. 1st part of a trilogy.
Letters to Sanchia. 1908 (priv ptd), 1910 (rev, as Letters to Sanchia upon things as they are), New York 1910. Incorporated into Open country, below.
A sacrifice at Prato. Englewood NJ 1908 (80 copies). First pbd in Earthwork out of Tuscany, above.
Artemision: idylls and songs. 1909, New York 1909.
Open country: a comedy with a sting. 1909, New York 1909. 2nd pt of trilogy.
The ruinous face. New York 1909. Story.
Rest harrow: a comedy of resolution. 1910, New York 1910. 3rd pt of trilogy.
The agonists: a trilogy of God and man. 1911, New York 1911. Verse plays.
The birth of Roland. Chicago [1911]. Story.
Brazenhead the great. 1911, New York 1911. One section, The captain of Kent, first pbd in Fond adventures, above, as Brazenhead the great.
The song of Renny. 1911, New York 1911.
Songs of loss. [c. 1911] (priv ptd). Anon.
Mrs Lancelot: a comedy of assumptions. 1912, New York 1912.
Bendish: a study in prodigality. 1913, New York 1913.
Helen redeemed, and other poems. 1913, New York 1913.
Lore of Proserpine. 1913, New York 1913. Essays and stories.
Sing-songs of the war. 1914.
The wreath. 1914 (priv ptd, 25 copies).
The little Iliad. 1915, Philadelphia 1915.
A lovers' tale. 1915, New York 1916.
Frey and his wife. 1916, New York 1916.
Gai saber: tales and songs. 1916, New York 1916. Verse.
Love and Lucy. 1916, New York 1916.
The song of the plow, being the English chronicle. 1916, New York 1916.
The loving history of Peridore and Paravail. [1917]. Verse.
Thorgils of Treadholt. 1917, New York 1917 (as Thorgils).
Gudrid the fair. 1918, New York 1918.
The village wife's lament. 1918, New York 1918. Verse.
The outlaw. 1919, New York 1920.
Flowers in the grass—Wiltshire plainsong. 1920.
In a green shade: a country commentary. 1920.
The light heart. 1920, New York 1920.
Mainwaring. New York 1920, London [1921].
Wiltshire essays. 1921.
Extemporary essays. 1922.
Last essays. 1924.
Letters to which is added A diary in Greece 1914. Ed L. Binyon 1926. With memoir by E. Hewlett.

JAMES HILTON
1900–54

Catherine herself. 1920.
Storm passage. 1922.
The passionate year. 1923, Boston 1924.
The dawn of reckoning. 1925, New York 1937.

The meadows of the moon. 1926, Boston 1927.
Terry. 1927.
The silver flame. 1928.
And now goodbye. 1931, New York 1932.
Murder at school. 1931 (by 'Glen Trevor'), New York 1933 (as Was it murder?), 1935 (as by James Hilton).
Contango. 1932, New York 1932 (as Ill wind).
Rage in heaven. New York 1932.
Knight without armour. 1933, New York 1934 (as Without armor).
Lost horizon. 1933, New York 1933.
Good-bye, Mr Chips. 1934, Boston 1934, London 1938 (as play, with B. Burnham).
We are not alone. 1937, Boston 1937.
To you, Mr Chips. 1938. Stories, with a chapter of autobiography.
Mr Chips looks at the world. [Los Angeles 1939]. Lecture.
Random harvest. 1941, Boston 1941.
The story of Dr Wassell. Boston 1943, London 1944.
So well remembered. Boston 1945, London 1947.
Nothing so strange. Boston 1947, London 1948.
Twilight of the wise. [1949]. Story.
Morning journey. 1951, Boston 1951.
Time and time again. 1953, Boston 1953.

CONSTANCE HOLME
1880–1955

Crump folk going home. 1913, Oxford 1934 (with preface by the author) (WC).
The lonely plough. 1914, Oxford 1931 (with preface by the author) (WC).
The old road from Spain. 1916, Oxford 1932 (with preface by the author) (WC).
Beautiful end. 1918, Oxford 1935 (WC).
The splendid fairing. 1919, Oxford 1933 (WC).
The trumpet in the dust. 1921, Oxford 1933 (WC).
The things which belong—. 1925, Oxford 1934 (WC).
He-who-came? 1930, Oxford 1936 (WC).
Four one-act plays. Kirkby Lonsdale [1932].
'I want!': a fantasy in three acts. In Five three-act plays, 1933.
The wisdom of the simple, and other stories. Oxford 1937 (WC).

WINIFRED HOLTBY
1898–1935

Bibliographies
Handley-Taylor, G. Winifred Holtby: a concise and selected bibliography, together with some letters. 1955.

§1

My garden, and other poems. 1911.
Anderby wold. 1923.
The crowded street. 1924.
The land of green ginger. 1927, New York 1928.
Eutychus, or the future of the pulpit. 1928, New York 1928. Essay.
A new voter's guide to party programmes: political dialogues. 1929.
Poor Caroline. 1931, New York 1931.
Virginia Woolf. 1932.
The astonishing island. 1933, New York 1933. Satire.
Mandoa! Mandoa! a comedy of irrelevance. 1933, New York 1933.
Truth is not sober. 1934, New York 1934. Stories.
Women and a changing civilisation. 1934, New York 1935.
The frozen earth, and other poems. 1935.

South Riding: an English landscape. 1936, 1936 (limited edn with introd by V. Brittain), New York 1936 (with epitaph by V. Brittain). Fiction.

Pavements at Anderby: tales of 'South Riding' and other regions. Ed H. S. Reid and V. Brittain 1937, New York 1938.

Take back your freedom. 1939. Play, with N. Ginsbury.

Letters

Letters to a friend. Ed A. Holtby and J. McWilliam 1937, New York 1938.

Letters. In G. Handley-Taylor, Winifred Holtby, 1955.

Selected letters of Winifred Holtby and Vera Brittain 1930–8. Ed V. Brittain and G. Handley-Taylor 1960.

§2

White, E. E. M. Winifred Holtby as I knew her. [1938].

Brittain, V. Testament of friendship: the story of W. Holtby. 1940.

'STEPHEN HUDSON',
SYDNEY SCHIFF
1868–1944

About 950 letters written to Schiff and his wife Violet are in BM. See M. A. F. Borrie, The Schiff papers, BM Quart 31 1966, and G. D. Painter, Proust's letters to Sydney and Violet Schiff, BM Quart 32 1968.

Concessions. 1913. As Sydney Schiff.
War-time silhouettes. 1916.
Richard Kurt. 1919.
Elinor Colhouse. 1921, New York 1922.
In sight of chaos, by H. Hesse. Tr Hudson, Zürich 1923.
Prince Hempseed. 1923.
Tony. 1924, New York 1924.
Myrtle. 1925, New York 1925.
Richard, Myrtle and I. New York 1926, London 1926, Philadelphia [1962] (ed Violet Schiff, with biographical note and critical essay by T. E. M. Boll).
Céleste and other sketches. 1930.

RICHARD ARTHUR WARREN
HUGHES
1900–76

Gipsy-night, and other poems. Waltham St Lawrence [1922], Chicago 1922 (63 copies).

The sisters' tragedy. Oxford 1922. Play.

The sisters' tragedy, and three other plays. 1924, New York 1924 (as A rabbit and a leg: collected plays), London 1966 (as Plays).

Confessio juvenis: collected poems. 1926.

A moment of time. 1926. Stories.

A high wind in Jamaica. 1929, New York 1929 (as The innocent voyage, with introd by I. Paterson), [1932] (as A high wind in Jamaica) (Modern Lib).

Burial, and The dark child. 1930 (priv ptd, 60 copies). Poem and children's story.

The spider's palace and other stories. 1931, New York 1932. For children.

In hazard: a sea story. 1938, New York 1938, London 1953 (ed and abridged by author), New York 1966 (with new introd by author).

Don't blame me! and other stories. 1940. For children.

The administration of war production. 1955 (History of the Second World War). With J. D. Scott.

The fox in the attic. 1961, New York [1962]. Vol 1 of The human predicament.

Gertrude's child. New York 1966, London 1967; Gertrude and the mermaid, New York 1971. For children.

Plays. 1966.

The wooden shepherdess. 1973. Vol 2 of The human predicament.

RAY CORYTON HUTCHINSON
b. 1907

Thou hast a devil: a fable. 1930.
The answering glory. 1932, New York 1932.
The unforgotten prisoner. 1933, New York 1934.
One light burning. 1935, New York 1935.
Shining scabbard. 1936, New York 1936.
Testament. 1938, New York 1938.
The fire and the wood. 1940, New York [1940].
Interim. 1945, New York 1945. Reminiscences.
Elephant and Castle: a reconstruction. 1949, New York 1949.
Recollection of a journey. 1952, New York 1952 (as Journey with strangers).
The stepmother. 1955, New York [1955].
March the ninth. 1957, New York 1957.
Image of my father. 1961, New York 1962 (as The inheritor).
A child possessed. 1964, New York 1964.
Johanna at daybreak. 1969.

ALDOUS LEONARD HUXLEY
1894–1963

Many Huxley mss are in the Library of the Univ of California at Los Angeles.

Bibliographies

Eschelbach, C. J. and J. L. Shober. Aldous Huxley: a bibliography 1916–59. Berkeley 1961.

Wickes, G. (ed). Aldous Huxley at UCLA: a catalogue of the mss in the Aldous Huxley collection, with the texts of three unpublished letters. Los Angeles 1964.

Collections and Selections

Collected edition. 1946–.
Stories, essays and poems. 1937 (EL).
Collected short stories. 1957, New York 1957.
Collected essays. New York 1959, London 1960. A selection only. Preface by Huxley.

§1

Many of Huxley's books appeared in limited edns as well as trade edns. The first ch of an unfinished novel is in L. A. Huxley, This timeless moment, 1968.

Prose Fiction

Limbo. 1920, New York 1920. Stories.
Crome yellow. 1921, New York 1922.
Mortal coils. 1922, New York 1922. Stories.
Antic hay. 1923, New York 1923.
Little Mexican, and other stories. 1924, New York 1924 (as Young Archimedes).
Those barren leaves. 1925, New York 1925.
Two or three graces, and other stories. 1926, New York 1926.
Point counter point. 1928, Garden City NY 1928, New York 1947 (introd by H. Watts).
Brief candles: stories. 1930, Garden City NY 1930.
Brave new world. 1932, Garden City NY 1932, New York 1946 (with foreword by Huxley) 1950 (introd by C. J. Rolo), 1960 (foreword by Huxley).
Eyeless in Gaza. 1936, New York 1936.
The Gioconda smile. 1938 (Zodiac Books). Story, first pbd in Mortal coils.

After many a summer. 1939, New York 1939 (as After many a summer dies the swan).
Time must have a stop. New York 1944, London 1945.
Ape and essence. New York 1948, London 1949.
The genius and the goddess. 1955, New York 1955.
Island. 1962, New York 1962.
The crows of pearblossom. New York 1967, London [1968]. Children's story.

Other Works

The burning wheel. Oxford 1916. Verse.
Jonah. Oxford 1917 (50 copies). Verse.
The defeat of youth, and other poems. Oxford 1918.
Leda. 1920, New York 1920. Verse.
On the margin: notes and essays. 1923, New York 1923.
The discovery: a comedy in five acts written by Mrs Frances Sheridan, adapted for the modern stage by Huxley. (RADA 4 May 1924). 1924.
Along the road: notes and essays of a tourist. 1925, New York 1925.
Selected poems. Oxford 1925, New York 1925.
Essays new and old. 1926, New York 1927. Some essays rptd from On the margin and Along the road.
Jesting Pilate: the diary of a journey. 1926, New York 1926 (as Jesting Pilate: an intellectual holiday). Travel.
Proper studies. 1927, Garden City NY 1928. Essays.
Arabia infelix, and other poems. New York 1929, London 1929.
Do what you will: essays. 1929, Garden City NY 1929.
Holy face, and other essays. 1929.
Apennine. Gaylordsville 1930 (91 copies). Poem; rptd in The cicadas.
Vulgarity in literature: digressions from a theme. 1930, New York 1966.
Music at night, and other essays. 1931, New York 1931.
The world of light: a comedy in three acts. (Royalty, 30 March 1931). 1931, Garden City NY 1931.
The cicadas, and other poems. 1931, Garden City NY 1931.
The letters of D. H. Lawrence. 1932, New York 1932. Ed Huxley.
Texts and pretexts: an anthology with commentaries. 1932, New York 1933.
T. H. Huxley as a man of letters. [1932] (Huxley memorial lecture); rptd in The olive tree, below.
Beyond the Mexique bay. 1934, New York 1934. Travel.
1935...peace? [1936]. Leaflet for Friends Peace Committee.
The olive tree, and other essays. 1936, New York 1937.
What are you going to do about it?: the case for constructive peace. 1936, New York 1936, London 1936 (as The case for constructive peace). Reply by C. Day Lewis, We're not going to do nothing, 1936.
An encyclopaedia of pacifism. Ed Huxley 1937, New York 1937.
Ends and means: an enquiry into the nature of ideals and into the methods employed for their realization. 1937, New York 1937.
The most agreeable vice. Los Angeles 1938. Essay on reading.
Words and their meanings. Los Angeles [1940] (100 copies).
Grey eminence: a study in religion and politics. 1941, New York 1941. A biography of Father Joseph, Capuchin.
The art of seeing. New York 1942, London 1943.
The perennial philosophy. New York 1945, London 1946. Anthology of mysticism, with commentary.
Science, liberty and peace. New York 1946, London 1947.
The Gioconda smile: a play. (New, 3 June 1948). 1948, New York 1948 (as Mortal coils), London 1949 (French's Acting Edn). Based on Huxley's own story.
Prisons: with the 'Carceri' etchings by Piranesi. [1949], Los Angeles 1949.

Themes and variations. 1950, New York 1950. Essays.
The devils of Loudun. 1952, New York 1952.
Joyce the artificer: two studies of Joyce's method. 1952 (priv ptd, 90 copies). With S. Gilbert.
A day in Windsor. 1953. With J. A. Kings.
The French of Paris. Paris [1953]. Text accompanying photographs by S. H. Roth.
The doors of perception. 1954, New York 1954, London 1959 (with Heaven and hell).
Adonis and the alphabet, and other essays. 1956, New York 1956 (as Tomorrow and tomorrow and tomorrow, and other essays).
Heaven and hell. 1956, New York 1956, London 1959 (with The doors of perception).
Brave new world revisited. New York 1958, London 1959.
Literature and science. 1963, New York 1963.
The politics of ecology: the question of survival. Santa Barbara 1963 (Center for the Study of Democratic Institutions, Occasional paper).
Letters. Ed G. Smith 1969.

§2

Muir, E. In his Transition, 1926.
Bowen, E. Huxley's essays. In her Collected impressions, 1950. On The olive tree.
Brooke, J. Aldous Huxley. 1954, 1958 (rev) (Br Council pamphlet).
Atkins, J. A. Huxley: a literary study. 1956, 1967 (rev).
Aldous Huxley 1894–1963: a memorial volume. Ed J. Huxley 1965.
Bowering, P. Huxley: a study of the major novels. 1968.
Clark, R. W. The Huxleys. 1968.
Huxley, L. A. This timeless moment: a personal view of Huxley. New York 1968.
Meckier, J. Huxley: satire and structure. 1969.
Watts, H. H. Aldous Huxley. New York 1969.
Bedford, S. Huxley: a biography. 2 vols 1973–4.

'MICHAEL INNES',
JOHN INNES MACKINTOSH
STEWART
b. 1906

Death at the President's lodging. 1936, New York 1937 (as Seven suspects).
Hamlet, revenge! 1937, New York 1937.
Lament for a maker. 1938, New York 1938.
Stop press. 1939, New York 1939 (as The spider strikes).
The secret vanguard. 1940, New York 1941.
There came both mist and snow. 1940, New York 1940 (as A comedy of terrors).
Appleby on Ararat. 1941, New York 1941.
The daffodil affair. 1942, New York 1942.
The weight of the evidence. New York 1943, London 1944.
Appleby's end. 1945, New York 1945.
From London far. 1946, New York 1946 (as The unsuspected chasm).
What happened at Hazlewood. 1946, New York 1946.
A night of errors. New York 1947, London 1948.
Character and motive in Shakespeare. 1949, New York 1949. As J. I. M. Stewart.
The journeying boy. [1949], New York 1949 (as The case of the journeying boy).
Three tales of Hamlet. 1950. With R. Heppenstall. Contains The hawk and the handsaw and The mysterious affair at Elsinore, by Innes.
Operation Pax. 1951, New York 1951 (as The paper thunderbolt).
A private view. 1952, New York 1952 (as One-man show).
Christmas at Candleshoe. 1953, New York 1953.
Appleby talking. 1954, New York 1954 (as Dead man's shoes). Stories.

Mark Lambert's supper. 1954. As J. I. M. Stewart.
The guardians. 1955, New York 1957. As J. I. M. Stewart.
The man from the sea. 1955, New York 1955.
Appleby plays chicken. 1956, New York 1957 (as Death on a quiet day).
Appleby talks again. 1956, New York 1957. Stories.
Old Hall, New Hall. 1956, New York 1956 (as A question of queens).
James Joyce. 1957, 1960 (rev) (Br Council pamphlet). As J. I. M. Stewart.
A use of riches. 1957, New York 1957. As J. I. M. Stewart.
The long farewell. 1958, New York 1958.
Hare sitting up. 1959, New York 1959.
The man who wrote detective stories, and other stories. 1959, New York 1959. As J. I. M. Stewart.
The new Sonia Wayward. 1960, New York 1960 (as The case of Sonia Wayward), 1962 (as The last of Sonia Wayward).
The man who won the pools. 1961, New York 1961. As J. I. M. Stewart.
Silence observed. 1961, New York 1961.
A connoisseur's case. 1962, New York 1962 (as The Crabtree affair).
Eight modern writers. Oxford 1963 (OHEL). As J. I. M. Stewart.
The last Tresilians. 1963, New York 1963. As J. I. M. Stewart.
Thomas Love Peacock. 1963 (Br Council pamphlet). As J. I. M. Stewart.
Money from Holme. 1964, New York 1965.
An acre of grass. 1965, New York 1966. As J. I. M. Stewart.
The Aylwins. 1966, New York 1967. As J. I. M. Stewart.
The bloody wood. 1966, New York 1966.
A change of heir. 1966, New York 1966.
Rudyard Kipling. 1966, New York 1966. As J. I. M. Stewart.
Vanderlyn's kingdom. 1967, New York 1968. As J. I. M. Stewart.
Appleby at Allington. 1968.
Joseph Conrad. 1968. As J. I. M. Stewart.
Cucumber sandwiches, and other stories. 1969. As J. I. M. Stewart.
A family affair. 1969.

CHRISTOPHER WILLIAM BRADSHAW ISHERWOOD
b. 1904

Bibliographies

Westby, S. and M. B. Clayton. Isherwood: a bibliography 1923-67. Los Angeles 1968.

§1

All the conspirators. 1928, New York 1958.
The memorial: portrait of a family. 1932, Norfolk Conn 1946.
Mr Norris changes trains. 1935, New York 1935 (as The last of Mr Norris).
The dog beneath the skin: or where is Francis? a play in three acts. (Westminster Theatre 12 Jan 1936). 1935, New York 1935. With W. H. Auden.
The ascent of F6: a tragedy in two acts. (Mercury Theatre 26 Feb 1937). 1936, New York 1937 (rev), London 1937 (2nd edn again rev). With W. H. Auden.
Sally Bowles. 1937. Story.
Lions and shadows: an education in the twenties. 1938, Norfolk Conn 1947. Autobiographical.
On the frontier: a melodrama in three acts. (Arts Theatre, Cambridge 14 Nov 1938). 1938, New York [1939]. With W. H. Auden.

Goodbye to Berlin. 1939, New York 1939. Stories.
Journey to a war. 1939, New York [1939]. Travel in China; with W. H. Auden.
Vedanta for the western world. Ed Isherwood, Hollywood 1945, London 1948.
Prater violet. New York 1945, London 1946.
The Berlin stories. New York 1946, 1954 (with new preface by the author). Contains The last of Mr Norris and Goodbye to Berlin.
The condor and the cows. New York 1948, London 1949. Travel in South America.
Vedanta for modern man. Ed Isherwood, New York 1951, London 1952.
The world in the evening. New York 1954, London 1954.
Down there on a visit. New York 1962, London 1962.
A single man. New York 1964, London 1964.
Ramakrishna and his disciples. New York 1965, London 1965.
Exhumations: stories, articles, verses. New York 1966, London 1966.
A meeting by the river. New York 1967, London 1967.
Kathleen and Frank. 1971. On his parents.
Christopher and his kind 1929-39. 1977.

§2

Spender, S. The poetic dramas of Auden and Isherwood. New Writing new ser 1 1938.
Kermode, F. The interpretation of the times. Encounter 15. 1960; rptd in his Puzzles and epiphanies, 1962. Mainly on The world in the evening and The memorial.
Finney, B. Isherwood: a critical biography. 1979.

See also under W. H. Auden, cols 1193-4, above, for additional items on Isherwood's collaborations with Auden.

WILLIAM WYMARK JACOBS
1863-1943

Plays are listed in order of date of production, where known; otherwise of pbn.

Many cargoes. 1896, New York [1897]. Stories.
The skipper's wooing, and The brown man's servant. 1897, New York [1897]. Stories.
Sea urchins. 1898, New York [1898] (as More cargoes). Stories.
A master of craft. New York [1900], London 1900.
Light freights. 1901, New York 1901. Stories.
At Sunwich Port. 1902, New York 1902.
The lady of the barge, and other stories. New York 1902, London 1902. Includes The monkey's paw; *see next.*
The monkey's paw: a story in three scenes. (Haymarket 6 Oct 1903). [1910] (Lacy's Acting Edn), [1910] (French's Acting Edn). Dramatized by L. N. Parker.
Odd craft. [1903], New York 1903. Stories.
Beauty and the barge: a farce in three acts. (New 30 Aug 1904). [1910] (French's Acting Edn). With L. N. Parker.
Dialstone Lane. 1904, New York 1904.
Captains all. 1905, New York 1905. Stories.
The boatswain's mate: a play in one act. [1907] (Lacy's Acting Edn). With H. C. Sargent.
Short cruises. 1907, New York 1907. Stories.
The changeling: a play in one act. [1908] (Lacy's Acting Edn). With H. C. Sargent.
The ghost of Jerry Bundler. [1908] (Lacy's Acting Edn). Play; with C. Rock.
The grey parrot. [1908] (Lacy's Acting Edn). Play; with C. Rock.
Salthaven. 1908, New York 1908.
Admiral Peters: a comedy in one act. [1909] (Lacy's Acting Edn). With H. Mills.
Sailor's knots. 1909, New York 1909. Stories.
Ship's company. [1911], New York 1911. Stories.

A love passage: a comedy in one act. (Little 3 Feb 1913). [1913] (Lacy's Acting Edn). With P. E. Hubbard.

In the library. (Little 3 Feb 1913). [1913] (Lacy's Acting Edn). Play; with H. C. Sargent.

Night watches. 1914, New York 1914. Stories.

Keeping up appearances: a farce in one act. (Savoy 17 April 1915). [1919] (French's Acting Edn).

The castaways. 1916, New York 1917.

Deep waters. [1919], New York 1919. Stories.

The castaway: a farce in one act. [1924] (French's Acting Edn). With H. C. Sargent.

Establishing relations: a comedy. [1925] (French's Acting Edn).

Sea whispers. [1926], New York 1926. Stories.

The warming pan: a comedy in one act. [1929] (French's Acting Edn).

A distant relative: a comedy in one act. [1930] (French's Acting Edn).

Master mariners. [1930]. Play.

Matrimonial openings: a comedy in one act. [1931] (French's Acting Edn).

Dixon's return: a comedy in one act. [1932] (French's Acting Edn).

Double dealing: a comedy in one act. [1935] (French's Acting Edn).

The last 6 plays were rptd in Six collected one-act plays, *1937.*

MONTAGUE RHODES JAMES
1862–1936

§ 1

Ghost-stories of an antiquary. 1904, New York 1919.

More ghost stories of an antiquary. 1911, New York 1911, London 1959 (as More ghost stories) (Penguin).

A thin ghost, and others. 1919, New York 1920.

The five jars. 1922, New York 1922. Story.

A warning to the curious, and other ghost stories. 1925, New York 1925.

Eton and King's: recollections, mostly trivial 1875–1925. 1926.

Wailing well. Stanford Dingley 1928 (157 copies). Story.

The collected ghost stories. 1931, New York 1931.

James contributed an introd on ghost stories to V. H. Collins, Ghosts and marvels, 1924.

Letters to a friend. Ed G. McBryde 1956.

§ 2

Gaselee, S. Montague Rhodes James. [1937]. Rptd from Proc Br Acad 22 1936.

Lubbock, S. G. A memoir of James. Cambridge 1939.

MARGARET STORM JAMESON
b. 1897

The pot boils. 1919.

The happy highways. 1920, New York 1920.

Modern drama in Europe. [1920].

The clash. 1922, Boston 1922.

Lady Susan and life: an indiscretion. 1923.

The pitiful wife. 1923, New York 1924.

Three kingdoms. 1926, New York 1926.

The lovely ship. 1927, New York 1927. Vol 1 of trilogy, The triumph of time, 1932, below.

Farewell to youth. 1928, New York 1928.

Full circle: a play in one act. Oxford 1928.

The Georgian novel and Mr Robinson. 1929, New York 1929.

The decline of merry England. 1930, Indianapolis [1930].

The voyage home. 1930, New York 1930. Vol 2 of trilogy, The triumph of time, below.

A richer dust... 1931, New York 1931. Vol 3 of trilogy, The triumph of time, below.

The single heart. 1932. Rptd in A day off, 1959, below.

That was yesterday. 1932, New York 1932.

The triumph of time. 1932.

A day off. 1933. Rptd in A day off, 1959, below.

No time like the present. 1933, New York 1933. Autobiography.

Women against men. New York 1933. 3 stories.

Company parade. 1934, New York 1934. Vol 1 of trilogy, The mirror in darkness.

Love in winter. 1935, New York 1935. Vol 2 of trilogy, The mirror in darkness.

The soul of man in an age of leisure. 1935. Pamphlet.

In the second year. 1936, New York 1936.

None turn back. 1936. Vol 3 of trilogy, The mirror in darkness.

Delicate monster. 1937.

The moon is making. 1937, New York 1938.

Here comes a candle. 1938, New York 1939.

The novel in contemporary life. Boston [1938].

Civil journey. 1939. Articles rptd from periodicals.

Farewell night, welcome day. 1939, New York 1939 (as The captain's wife).

Cousin Honoré. 1940, New York 1941.

Europe to let: the memoirs of an obscure man. 1940, New York 1940.

The fort. 1940, New York 1941.

The end of this war. 1941 (PEN books).

Then we shall hear singing: a fantasy in C major. 1942, New York 1942.

Cloudless May. 1943, New York 1944.

The journal of Mary Hervey Russell. 1945, New York 1945.

The other side. 1946, New York 1946.

Before the crossing. 1947, New York 1947.

The black laurel. 1947.

The moment of truth. 1949, New York 1949.

The writer's situation, and other essays. 1950.

The green man. 1952, New York 1953.

The hidden river. 1955, New York 1955, London [1957] (as play by R. and A. Goetz).

The intruder. 1956, New York 1956.

A cup of tea for Mr Thorgill. 1957, New York 1957.

A Ulysses too many. 1958, New York 1958 (as One Ulysses too many).

A day off: two short novels and some stories. 1959.

Last score: or the private life of Sir Richard Ormston. 1961, New York 1961.

Morley Roberts: the last eminent Victorian. 1962. Biography.

The road from the monument. 1962, New York 1962.

A month soon goes. 1963, New York 1963.

The Aristide case. 1964, New York 1964 (as The blind heart).

The early life of Stephen Hind. 1966, New York 1966.

The white crow. 1968, New York 1968.

Journey from the north: autobiography. 1969–.

PAMELA HANSFORD JOHNSON
b. 1912

Symphony for full orchestra. 1934 (Sunday Referee Poets, 1).

This bed thy centre. 1935, New York [1935], London 1961 (with preface by the author).

Blessed above women. 1936, New York [1936].

Here to-day. 1937.

World's end. 1937, New York [1938].

The monument. 1938, New York [1938].

Girdle of Venus. 1939.

Too dear for my possessing. 1940, New York 1940. First vol of trilogy.
The family pattern. 1942.
Winter quarters. 1943, New York 1944.
The Trojan brothers. 1944, New York 1945.
An avenue of stone. 1947, New York 1948. 2nd vol of trilogy.
Thomas Wolfe: a critical study. 1947, New York 1948 (as Hungry Gulliver: an English critical appraisal of Thomas Wolfe), 1963 (as The art of Thomas Wolfe).
A summer to decide. 1948. 3rd vol of trilogy.
The Philistines. 1949.
Corinth House: a play in three acts. [1950], Boston 1950, London 1954 (with an essay on the future of prose-drama).
Family party. [1951]. Play, with C. P. Snow.
Her best foot forward. [1951]. Play, with C. P. Snow.
I. Compton-Burnett. 1951 (Br Council pamphlet).
The pigeon with the silver foot. [1951]. Play, with C. P. Snow.
Spare the rod. [1951]. Play, with C. P. Snow.
The supper dance. [1951]. Play, with C. P. Snow.
To murder Mrs Mortimer. [1951]. Play, with C. P. Snow.
Catherine Carter. 1952, New York 1952.
An impossible marriage. 1954, New York 1955.
The last resort. 1956, New York 1957 (as The sea and the wedding).
Six Proust reconstructions. 1958, Chicago 1958 (as Proust recaptured).
The humbler creation. 1959, New York 1960.
The unspeakable Skipton. 1959, New York 1959.
An error of judgement. 1962, New York [1962].
Night and silence—who is here?: an American comedy. 1963, New York 1963.
Cork Street, next to the hatter's: a novel in bad taste. 1965, New York 1965.
On iniquity: some personal reflections arising out of the Moors murder trial. 1967.
The survival of the fittest. 1968, New York 1968.

Pamela Hansford Johnson contributed an essay, The novel of Marcel Proust *to Proust's* Letters to his mother, *tr and ed G. D. Painter, 1956. She translated, with G. Black, J. Anouilh,* La répétition (*as* The rehearsal) *1961.*

A wedding morn: a story. 1928.
Mrs Adis: a tragedy in one act, with The mock-beggar, a comedy in one act. [1929]. With J. Hampden.
Sin. 1929. Essays.
The village doctor. 1929, New York [1929].
Shepherds in sackcloth. 1930, New York 1930.
The history of Susan Spray, the female preacher. 1931, New York 1931 (as Susan Spray).
Songs late and early. 1931.
The children's summer. 1932, New York 1932 (as Summer holiday).
The ploughman's progress. 1933, New York 1933 (as Gipsy waggon).
Gallybird. 1934, New York 1934.
Superstition corner. 1934, New York 1934, Chicago 1955 (with preface by G. B. Stern).
Selina is older. 1935, New York 1935 (as Selina).
Rose Deeprose. 1936, New York 1936.
Three ways home. 1937, New York 1937. Autobiographical essays.
Dropping the hyphen: a story of a conversion. 1938.
Faithful stranger, and other stories. 1938, New York 1938.
The valiant woman. New York 1938, London 1939.
Ember lane: a winter's tale. 1940, New York [1940].
The hidden son. 1941, New York 1942 (as The secret son).
Talking of Jane Austen. 1943, New York 1944 (as Speaking of Jane Austen). With G. B. Stern.
Tambourine, trumpet and drum. 1943, New York 1943.
Kitchen fugue. 1945, New York 1945. Essays.
The Lardners and the Laurelwoods. New York 1947, London 1948.
The happy tree. New York 1949, London 1950 (as The treasures of the snow).
More about Jane Austen. New York 1949, London 1950 (as More talk of Jane Austen). With G. B. Stern.
Mrs Gailey. 1951, New York 1951.
Quartet in heaven. 1952, New York 1952. Biographical studies.
Weald of Kent and Sussex. 1953. Topography.
The view from the parsonage. 1954, New York 1954.
All the books of my life: a bibliobiography. 1956, New York 1956.

SHEILA KAYE-SMITH
1887–1955

The tramping Methodist. 1908, New York 1922.
Starbrace. 1909, New York 1926.
Spell land: the story of a Sussex farm. 1910, New York 1926.
Isle of thorns. 1913, New York 1924.
Three against the world. 1914, Philadelphia 1914 (as The three furlongers), New York 1929 (as Three against the world).
Willow's forge, and other poems. 1914.
John Galsworthy. 1916, New York 1916. Criticism.
Sussex gorse: the story of a fight. 1916, New York 1916.
The challenge to Sirius. 1917, New York 1918.
Little England. 1918, New York 1919 (as The four roads).
Tamarisk town. 1919, New York [1920].
Green apple harvest. 1920, New York [1921].
Joanna Godden. 1921, New York [1922].
The end of the house of Alard. 1923, New York [1923].
Saints in Sussex. Birmingham 1923, London 1926 (with two plays, The child born at the plough and The shepherd of Lattenden), New York 1927.
Anglo-Catholicism. 1925.
The George and the Crown. 1925, New York [1925].
The mirror of the months. 1925, New York 1931. Essays.
Joanna Godden married, and other stories. 1926, New York 1926.
Iron and smoke. 1928, New York [1928].

ARTHUR KOESTLER
b. 1905

Collections

Danube edition. 1965–. Contains additional prefaces, or postscripts, to the individual works, with occasional textual revision.

§1

Menschenopfer unerhört: Schwarzbuch über Spanien. Paris 1937.
Spanish testament. 1937. Pt 1, an adaptation of Menschenopfer unerhört; pt 2, entitled Dialogue with death. Tr T. and P. Blewitt. German original, Ein spanisches Testament, pbd Zürich 1938. Autobiographical.
The gladiators. Tr E. Simm 1939, New York 1939.
Darkness at noon. Tr D. Hardy 1940, New York 1941, 1961 (with foreword by P. Viereck).
Scum of the earth. 1941, New York 1941, London 1955 (corrected, with preface by Koestler). Autobiographical.
Dialogue with death [pt 2 of Spanish testament, 1937]. 1942, New York 1942, London [1954] (corrected against the original German version, Zürich 1938, with preface by Koestler).
Arrival and departure. 1943, New York 1943.
Twilight bar: an escapade in four acts. 1945, New York 1945. Play.
The yogi and the commissar, and other essays. 1945, New York 1945.

Thieves in the night: chronicle of an experiment. 1946, New York 1946.

What the modern world is doing to the soul of man. In The challenge of our time: a series of essays by Koestler [et al], 1948.

Insight and outlook: an inquiry into the common foundations of science, art and social ethics. 1949, New York 1949.

Promise and fulfilment: Palestine 1917–49. 1949, New York 1949.

The god that failed: six studies in Communism by Koestler [et al]. Ed R. H. S. Crossman 1950, New York 1950.

The age of longing. 1951, New York 1951.

Arrow in the blue: an autobiography. 1952, New York 1952.

The invisible writing: being the second volume of Arrow in the blue. 1954, New York 1954.

The trail of the dinosaur, and other essays. 1955, New York 1955.

Reflections on hanging. 1956, New York 1957.

The sleepwalkers: a history of man's changing vision of the universe. 1959, New York 1959. Pt 4, The watershed [a biography of Johannes Kepler] pbd separately Garden City NY 1960, London 1961.

The lotus and the robot. 1960, New York 1961.

Hanged by the neck: an exposure of capital punishment in England. 1961, Baltimore 1961. With 'C. H. Rolph' (C. R. Hewitt).

Suicide of a nation? an enquiry into the state of Britain today. Ed with introd by Koestler 1963, New York 1964.

The act of creation. 1964, New York 1964. Non-fiction.

The ghost in the machine. 1967, New York 1968. Non-fiction.

Drinkers of infinity: essays 1955–67. 1968, New York 1969.

The case of the midwife toad. 1971.

The heel of Achilles: essays 1968–73. 1974.

The thirteenth tribe. 1976.

From 1934 to 1939, under the pseudonym 'Dr A. Costler', Koestler collaborated in the writing of some French works of popular sexology. See 'Introducing Dr Costler' in The invisible writing, 1954, above.

§2

Mortimer, R. Arthur Koestler. Cornhill Mag 192 1946.

'Orwell, George' (E. A. Blair). In his Critical essays, 1946.

Pritchett, V. S. Arthur Koestler. Horizon 15 1947; rptd (as The art of Arthur Koestler) in his Books in general, 1953.

Atkins, J. Arthur Koestler. 1956.

Howe, I. Malraux, Silone, Koestler. In his Politics and the novel, New York 1957.

Strachey, J. The strangled cry. Encounter 15 1960; rptd in his The strangled cry, 1962. On Darkness at noon.

Calder, J. Chronicles of conscience: a study of Orwell and Koestler. 1968.

Nott, K. Koestler and his critics. Encounter 30 1968.

ROSAMOND NINA LEHMANN
b. 1903

Dusty answer. 1927, New York 1927.

A note in music. 1930, New York [1930].

A letter to a sister. 1931, New York [1932] (Hogarth Letters 3).

Invitation to the waltz. 1932, New York [1932].

The weather in the streets. 1936, New York [1936].

No more music: a play in three acts. [1939], New York 1939.

The ballad and the source. 1944, New York 1945.

The gipsy's baby, and other stories. 1946, New York 1946.

The echoing grove. 1953, New York 1953.

The swan in the evening: fragments of an inner life. 1967, New York 1968.

Rosamond Lehmann was one of the editors of the first 3 vols of Orion: a miscellany, 1945–6. *She also edited, with extensive commentary,* A man seen afar, *by W. T. Pole, 1965.*

ADA LEVERSON
1862–1933

The twelfth hour. 1907.

Love's shadow. 1908.

The limit. 1911, New York 1951.

Tenterhooks. [1912].

Bird of paradise. 1914, New York 1952.

Love at second sight. 1916.

Letters to the Sphinx from Oscar Wilde, with reminiscences of the author by A. Leverson. 1930.

PERCY WYNDHAM LEWIS
1882–1957

The Carlow collection of Lewisiana is at the State Univ of New York, Buffalo. For details of the Lewis collection at Cornell Univ, see W. K. Rose, Wyndham Lewis at Cornell, Ithaca 1961.

§1

Blast: review of the great English vortex. No 1, 1914: no 2, 1915. Ed and largely written by Lewis; no 1 contains the first version of The enemy of the stars, pbd separately (rev) in 1932.

The ideal giant; The code of a herdsman; Cantelman's springmate. [1917] (priv ptd for Little Rev, 50 copies). Play; criticism; story.

Tarr. New York 1918, London 1918, 1928 (rev). Expanded from version serialized in Egoist, April 1916–Nov 1917.

Harold Gilman: an appreciation. 1919. With L. F. Fergusson. Art criticism.

The Caliph's design: architects! where is your vortex? 1919; rptd (rev) in Wyndham Lewis the artist, 1939.

The tyro: a review of the arts of painting, sculpture and design. no 1, 1921; no 2, 1922. Ed Lewis, with contributions by him.

The art of being ruled. 1926, New York 1926.

The enemy: a review of art and literature. Nos 1–2, 1927; no 3, 1929. Ed and largely written by Lewis.

The lion and the fox: the rôle of hero in the plays of Shakespeare. 1927, New York 1927.

Time and western man. 1927, New York [1928] (with new preface). Bk 1 first pbd in Enemy no 1.

The wild body: a soldier of humour and other stories. 1927, New York [1928]. Some stories first pbd in Little Rev.

The Childermass: section 1. 1928, New York 1928, London 1956 (rev) (as bk 1 of The human age, 1955 below).

Paleface: the philosophy of the 'melting pot'. 1929. Part first pbd in Enemy, no 2.

The apes of God. 1930, New York 1932, London 1955 (with introd by Lewis). Part first pbd in Criterion 2 1924.

Satire & fiction: preceded by The history of a rejected review (Have with you to Great Queen Street!), by R. Campbell. 1930. (Enemy pamphlets 1). In defence of The apes of God.

Hitler. 1931. Articles, rptd from Time & Tide 17 Jan–14 Feb 1931.

The diabolical principle and The dithyrambic spectator. 1931. Rptd from Calendar of Modern Letters 1 1925 and Enemy no 3.

Doom of youth. New York 1932, London 1932 (withdrawn). Articles rptd from Time & Tide 13 June–25 July 1931.

Filibusters in Barbary: record of a visit to the Sous. 1932, New York 1932. Rptd from Everyman Oct 29 1931–7 Jan 1932.

Enemy of the stars. 1932. Play, heavily rev from the original text pbd in Blast no 1, with appended essay The physics of the not-self, rptd (rev) from Chapbook no 40, 1925.

Snooty baronet. 1932.

The old gang and the new gang. 1933. Pamphlet to replace the withdrawn English edn of Doom of youth.

Engine-fight talk; The song of the militant romance; If so the man you are; One-way song: Envoi. (Cover and half-title: One-way song). 1933, 1960 (as One-way song, with foreword by T. S. Eliot). Poems.

Men without art. 1934, New York 1964. Essays.

Left wings over Europe: or how to make a war about nothing. 1936.

The roaring queen. 1936 (withdrawn before pbn).

Count your dead: they are alive! or a new war in the making. 1937. Political commentary in fictional form.

The revenge for love. 1937, Chicago 1952.

Blasting and bombardiering. 1937, 1967 (preface by A. Wyndham Lewis with additional chs). Autobiography 1914–26. Reprints parts of Blast, with minor revision.

The Mysterious Mr Bull. 1938. Social criticism.

The Jews: are they human? 1939.

The Hitler cult, and how it will end. 1939.

America, I presume. New York [1940].

The vulgar streak. 1941.

Anglosaxony: a league that works. Toronto [1941]. Pamphlet.

America and cosmic man. 1948, Garden City NY 1949.

Rude assignment: a narrative of my career up-to-date. [1950].

Rotting Hill. 1951, Chicago 1952. Stories.

The writer and the absolute. 1952.

Self condemned. 1954, Chicago 1955. Semi-autobiographical.

The demon of progress in the arts. 1954, Chicago 1955.

The human age: bk 2, Monstre gai; bk 3, Malign fiesta. 2 vols 1955. Bk 1, The Childermass, 1956 (rev from version pbd 1928). The Childermass, adapted by D. G. Bridson, broadcast BBC Third Programme 18 June 1951; Monstre gai and Malign fiesta, adapted by Bridson and Lewis, broadcast 24, 26, 28 May 1955. *See* Bridson in Agenda 7–8 1969–70.

The red priest. 1956.

Letters. Ed W. K. Rose 1963, Norfolk Conn 1964.

The Wyndham Lewis special issue of Agenda 7–8 1969–70 prints excerpts from Hoodopip *and* Joint, *sections of the uncompleted* Man of the world (*see prefatory notes by H. Kenner*). *Lewis also pbd drawings and wrote introds to various art exhibition catalogues.*

§2

Aldington, R. Blast. Egoist 1 1914.

Pound, E. Wyndham Lewis. Egoist 1 1914.

—— Art notes, by 'B. H. Dias' [i.e. E. Pound]: Lewis at the Goupil. New Age 20 Feb 1919; rptd (as The war paintings of Lewis) in Agenda 7–8 1969–70 (Lewis special issue).

—— In his Instigations, 1920; rptd in his Literary essays, 1954.

—— Augment of the novel. New Directions 6 1941; rptd in Agenda 7–8 1969–70.

Eliot, T. S. Tarr. Egoist 5 1918.

—— A note on Monstre gai. Hudson Rev 7 1955.

—— Wyndham Lewis. Hudson Rev 10 1957.

'West, Rebecca' (C. I. Andrews). Tarr. Nation 10 Aug 1918; rptd in Agenda 7–8 1969–70.

Rickword, E. In Scrutinies vol 2, ed E. Rickword 1931.

Leavis, F. R. Mr Eliot, Lewis and Lawrence. Scrutiny 3 1934; rptd in his Common pursuit, 1952.

Twentieth-Century Verse. Wyndham Lewis double no, 6–7 1937.

Grigson, G. A master of our time: a study of Lewis. 1951.

Handley-Read, C. (ed). The art of Wyndham Lewis. 1951. Lewis' pictorial art.

Shenandoah 4 1953. Wyndham Lewis no.

Kenner, H. Wyndham Lewis. Norfolk Conn 1954.

Tomlin, E. W. F. Wyndham Lewis. 1955 (Br Council pamphlet).

Wagner, G. Wyndham Lewis: a portrait of the artist as the enemy. New Haven 1957.

Harrison, J. R. In his Reactionaries, 1966.

Pritchard, W. H. Wyndham Lewis. New York 1968.

Agenda 7–8 1969–70. Wyndham Lewis special issue.

ERIC ROBERT RUSSELL LINKLATER
1899–1974

Collections

The Orkney edition. 1950–.

Stories. 1968, New York 1969.

§1

Poobie. Edinburgh 1925 (Porpoise Press broadsheets). Verse.

Poet's pub. 1929, New York [1930].

White-maa's saga. 1929.

A dragon laughed, and other poems. 1930.

Ben Jonson and King James: biography and portrait. 1931.

Juan in America. 1931, New York [1931].

The men of Ness: a saga of Thorlief Coalbiter's sons. 1932, New York [1933].

The crusader's key. [1933], New York 1933. Story, rptd in God likes them plain, below.

Mary Queen of Scots. 1933, New York 1933.

The devil's in the news: a comedy to be played with occasional music. 1934.

Magnus Merriman. 1934, New York [1934].

The revolution. 1934. 3 stories, rptd in God likes them plain, below.

Robert the Bruce. 1934, New York 1934.

God likes them plain: short stories. 1935.

The lion and the unicorn: or what England has meant to Scotland. 1935.

Ripeness is all. 1935, New York [1935].

Juan in China. 1937, New York [1937].

The sailor's holiday. 1937, New York [1938].

The impregnable women. 1938, New York [1938].

Judas. 1939, New York [1939].

The man on my back: an autobiography. 1941.

The raft, and Socrates asks why: two conversations. 1942.

Crisis in heaven: an Elysian comedy. 1944. Play.

The great ship, and Rabelais replies: two conversations. 1944.

The wind on the moon: a story for children. 1944, New York 1944.

Private Angelo. 1946, New York 1946.

The art of adventure. 1947. Essays.

Sealskin trousers, and other stories. 1947.

The pirates in the deep green sea: a story for children. 1949.

A spell for old bones. 1949, New York 1950.

Love in Albania: a comedy in three acts. [1950].

Mr Byculla. 1950, New York 1951.

Two comedies: Love in Albania, and To meet the MacGregors 1950.

The campaign in Italy. 1951.

Laxdale Hall. 1951, New York 1952.
The Mortimer touch: a farcical comedy. [1952].
Our men in Korea. 1952. Non-fiction.
The house of Gair. 1953, New York 1954.
A year of space: a chapter in autobiography. 1953, New York 1953.
The faithful ally. 1954, New York [1954] (as The sultan and the lady).
The ultimate Viking. 1955, New York 1956. Sweyn Asleifsson and the Icelandic sagas.
The dark of summer. 1956, New York 1957.
A sociable plover, and other stories and conceits. 1957.
Breakspear in Gascony. 1958. Play.
Karina with love. 1958. For children.
Position at noon. 1958, New York 1959 (as My fathers and I).
The merry muse. 1959, New York 1960.
Edinburgh. 1960, New York 1961.
Roll of honour. 1961.
Husband of Delilah. 1962, New York 1963.
A man over forty. 1963.
The murder of Darnley. In Fatal fascination: a choice of crime, by N. Balchin, Linklater [et al], 1964, Boston 1965.
Orkney and Shetland: an historical, geographical, social and scenic survey. 1965.
The prince in the heather. [1965], New York 1966. The escape of the Young Pretender after Culloden.
The conquest of England. 1966, Garden City NY 1966. Non-fiction.
A terrible freedom. 1966.
The survival of Scotland. 1968, New York 1968.

CLARENCE MALCOLM LOWRY
1909–57

Lowry's literary mss are in the library of the Univ of British Columbia, Vancouver.

Ultramarine. 1933, 1963 (rev).
Under the volcano. New York 1947, London 1947, Paris 1949 (French trn, with preface tr from Lowry's notes; this was tr into English by G. Woodcock, Canadian Lit no 9 1961), London 1967 (with foreword by S. Spender).
Hear us, O Lord, from heaven thy dwelling place. Philadelphia 1961, London 1962. Stories.
Dark as the grave wherein my friend is laid. Ed D. Day and M. B. Lowry, New York 1968, London 1969.
Lunar caustic. Ed E. Birney and M. B. Lowry 1968; foreword by C. Knickerbocker. First pbd in Paris Rev no 29 1963.
Selected letters of Lowry. Ed H. Breit and M. B. Lowry, Philadelphia 1965, London 1967.

DAME EMILIE ROSE MACAULAY
1881–1958

Abbots Verney. 1906.
The furnace. 1907.
The secret river. 1909.
The valley captives. 1911, New York 1911.
The lee shore. [1912], New York [1912].
Views and vagabonds. 1912, New York 1912.
The making of a bigot. [1914].
The two blind countries. 1914. Verse.
Non-combatants and others. 1916.
What not: a prophetic comedy. 1918.
Three days. 1919. Verse.
Potterism: a tragi-farcical tract. 1920, New York [1920].
Dangerous ages. 1921, New York [1921].

Mystery at Geneva. [1922], New York 1923.
Told by an idiot. [1923], New York [1923], London 1965 (introd by R. Mortimer).
Orphan island. [1924], New York [1925].
A casual commentary. 1925, New York 1926. Essays.
Catchwords and claptrap. 1926. Essays.
Crewe train. [1926], New York 1926.
[Twenty-two poems]. [1927] (Augustan Books of English Poetry).
Keeping up appearances. [1928], New York 1928 (as Daisy and Daphne).
Staying with relations. 1930, New York [1930].
Some religious elements in English literature. 1931, New York [1931].
They were defeated. 1932, New York 1932 (as The shadow flies).
Going abroad. 1934, New York 1934.
Milton. 1934, New York 1935, London 1957 (rev), New York 1957.
Personal pleasures. 1935, New York 1936.
I would be private. 1937, New York 1937.
An open letter to a non-pacifist. [1937]. Rptd from Time & Tide.
The writings of E. M. Forster. 1938, New York 1938.
And no man's wit. [1940], Boston 1940.
Life among the English. 1942 People in Pictures).
They went to Portugal. 1946. On English visitors.
Fabled shore: from the Pyrenees to Portugal. 1949, New York 1951.
The world my wilderness. 1950, Boston 1950.
Pleasure of ruins. 1953. Non-fiction.
The towers of Trebizond. 1956, New York 1957.

Letters

Letters to a friend 1950–2. Ed C. B. Smith 1961, New York 1962. To J. H. C. Johnson.
Last letters to a friend 1952–8. Ed C. B. Smith 1962, New York 1963. To J. H. C. Johnson.
Letters to a sister. Ed C. B. Smith 1964, New York 1964. To Jean Macaulay. Includes a fragment of a novel, Venice besieged.

ARCHIBALD GORDON MACDONELL
1895–1941

The factory on the cliff. 1928. As 'Neil Gordon'.
The new gun-runners. New York [1928]. As 'Neil Gordon'.
The professor's poison. 1928, New York [1928]. As 'Neil Gordon'.
The seven stabs. 1929, New York 1930. As 'John Cameron'.
The silent murders. 1929, New York 1930. As 'Neil Gordon'.
The Big Ben alibi. 1930. As 'Neil Gordon'.
Murder in Earl's Court. 1931. As 'Neil Gordon'.
Body found stabbed. 1932. As 'John Cameron'.
England, their England. 1933, New York 1933 (with foreword by C. Morley), London 1942 (with preface by J. C. Squire). Non-fiction.
The Shakespeare murders. [1933], New York [1933]. As 'Neil Gordon'.
How like an angel! 1934, New York 1935.
Napoleon and his marshals. 1934, New York 1934.
A visit to America. 1935, New York 1935. Travel.
Lords and masters. 1936, New York 1937.
My Scotland. 1937, New York 1937. Non-fiction.
Autobiography of a cad. 1938. Novel.
Flight from a lady. 1939. Travel, in fictional form.
The Spanish pistol, and other stories. 1939.
What next, baby? or, shall I go to Tanganyika? 1939. Play.
The crew of the Anaconda. 1940.
The fur coat. 1943. Play.

ARTHUR LLEWELYN JONES MACHEN
1863–1947

Bibliographies

Goldstone, A. and W. D. Sweetser. A bibliography of Machen. Austin [1965].

§1

Eleusinia, by a former member of H[ereford] C[athedral] S[chool]. Hereford 1881. Verse.

The anatomy of tobacco: or smoking methodised, divided and considered after a new fashion, by Leolinus Siluriensis. 1884, New York, London 1926 (with introd by Machen).

A chapter from the book called The ingenious gentleman Don Quijote de la Mancha which by some mischance has not till now been printed. [1887]. Pamphlet, rptd (as The priest and the barber) in The shining pyramid, 1923, below. Anon.

The chronicle of Clemendy: or the history of the IX joyous journeys. Carbonnek [i.e. London] 1888, Carbonnek [i.e. New York] 1923 (with introd by Machen), London 1925 (with different introd by Machen), New York 1926. Stories.

Thesaurus incantatus—the enchanted treasure: or the spagyric quest of Beroaldus Cosmopolita, in which is sophically and mystagorically declared the first matter of the stone. [1888]; rptd (as The spagyric quest of Beroaldus Cosmopolitan in The shining pyramid. 1923, below. Anon.

The great god Pan, and The inmost light. 1894, Boston 1894, London [1916] (with introd by Machen and omitting The inmost light). Stories, rptd in The house of souls, 1906, below.

The three impostors: or the transmutations. 1895, Boston 1895, New York 1923 (with introd by Machen and omitting the story The iron maid, but including The red hand, not in first edns). Stories, rptd in The house of souls, 1906, below.

Hieroglyphics. 1902, 1912 (rev), New York 1913, London 1960 (with introd by M. Bishop). 'A note upon ecstasy in literature.'

The house of the hidden light, manifested and set forth in certain letters communicated from a lodge of the adepts by the high fratres Filius Aquarum [Machen] and Elias Aetista [A. E. Waite]. Zion [i.e. London] 1904 (priv ptd).

The house of souls. 1906, New York 1922 (omitting The three impostors and The red hand), 1923 (with introd by Machen), London 1923 (with note by Machen). Stories.

Dr Stiggins: his views and principles. 1906, New York 1925 (with introd by Machen). Satire.

The hill of dreams. 1907, New York 1923 (with introd by Machen), London 1968 (with introd by Lord Dunsany).

The angels of Mons—The bowmen and other legends of the war, with an introduction by the author. 1915, 1915 (rev, with two additional stories), New York 1915 (with contents as in first English edn). Stories.

The great return. 1915.

The terror: a fantasy. 1917, New York [1917] (as The terror: a mystery), London 1927 (rev), New York 1964 (with introd by V. Starrett).

War and the Christian faith. 1918.

The secret glory. [1922], New York 1922.

Far off things. 1922 (100 copies), New York 1922, London [1922] (trade edn); rptd in The autobiography of Machen, 1951.

Things near & far. 1923, New York 1923; rptd in The autobiography of Machen, 1951.

The grande trouvaille: a legend of Pentonville. [1923] (priv ptd). Pamphlet.

The shining pyramid. Chicago 1923. Introd by V. Star-

rett. Stories and essays. Contents differ from 1924 book of same title.

The collector's craft. [1923] (priv ptd). Pamphlet.

Strange roads. (With The gods in spring). 1923, 1924 (with introd by Machen). 2 articles.

Dog and duck. New York 1924, London 1924 (as Dog and duck: a London calendar et cætera). Articles.

The London adventure: or the art of wandering. 1924, New York 1924 (subtitled An essay in wandering).

The glorious mystery, ed V. Starrett. Chicago 1924. Essays and stories.

Precious balms. 1924. Review articles of his own works.

Ornaments in jade. New York 1924. Stories, some previously pbd in The glorious mystery and The shining pyramid (1923).

The shining pyramid. Introd by Machen 1924 (limited edn), 1925, New York 1925. Stories.

A preface to Casanova, Escape from the leads. 1925 (priv ptd, 25 copies); rptd in Machen's trn of Casanova, Escape from the leads, 1925.

The Canning wonder. 1925, New York 1926. On the case of Elizabeth Canning 1753-4.

Dreads and drolls. 1926, New York 1927. Articles.

Notes and queries. 1926. Articles.

Parish of Amersham. [Amersham] 1930. Anon pamphlet.

Tom o' Bedlam and his song. [Glen Rock Pa] 1930.

Beneath the barley: a note on the origins of Eleusinia. 1931 (priv ptd, 25 copies).

In the 'eighties: a reminiscence of the Silurist put down by him. Amersham 1931 (priv ptd, 10 copies), London 1933 (50 copies). Anon pamphlet.

An introduction to John Gawsworth, Above the river. [1931] (priv ptd, 12 copies); rptd in Gawsworth, Above the river, 1931.

The glitter of the brook. Dalton Ga 1932 (priv ptd, 10 copies). Stories.

The rose garden. [Stanford]. 1932 (priv ptd, 50 copies). Story rptd from The glorious mystery, 1924, above.

The green round. 1933.

The cosy room and other stories. 1936. Mostly previously pbd in various collections.

The children of the pool, and other stories. [1936].

The autobiography of Machen, ed with introd by M. Bishop. 1951. Contains Far off things, Things near and far.

Bridles & spurs, with preface by N. Van Patten. Cleveland 1951. Essays, mostly written 1931-4.

A critical essay by Machen: his thoughts on A bookman's diary, by J. A. Hammerton. Lakewood Ohio 1953 (priv ptd, 50 copies).

A receipt for fine prose. [New York] 1956 (priv ptd, 2 copies).

A note on poetry. [Wichita 1959] (priv ptd, 50 copies). Essay first pbd in Wind & Rain 2 1943.

From the London Evening News, with introduction by J. H. S[tewart] jr. Wichita 1959 (priv ptd, 50 copies). 3 articles, first pbd 1921.

An excellent ballad of the armèd man. 1963 (priv ptd, 40 copies). First pbd Poetry Rev 41 1950.

SIR EDWARD MONTAGUE COMPTON MACKENZIE
1883–1972

There is a collection of Mackenzie's mss in Texas Univ Library.

§1

Prose Fiction

The passionate elopement. 1911, New York 1911, London 1953 (with foreword by Mackenzie).

Carnival. 1912, New York 1912, London 1951 (with foreword by Mackenzie).

Sinister Street. 2 vols 1913–14, New York 1913–14 (vol 1 as Youth's encounter, vol 2 as Sinister Street), 1 vol London 1949 (with foreword by Mackenzie).
Guy and Pauline. 1915, New York 1915 (as Plashers Mead), Oxford 1938 (WC, with introd by Mackenzie).
The early life and adventures of Sylvia Scarlett. 1918, New York 1918.
Poor relations. 1919, New York [1919].
Sylvia and Michael: the later adventures of Sylvia Scarlett. 1919, New York 1919.
The vanity girl. 1920, New York [1920].
Rich relatives. 1921, New York [1921].
The altar steps. 1922, New York [1922], London 1956 (with foreword by J. Betjeman).
The parson's progress. 1923, New York [1924]. Sequel to The altar steps.
The seven ages of woman. 1923, New York [1923].
The heavenly ladder. 1924, New York [1924]. Sequel to The parson's progress.
The old men of the sea. 1924, New York 1924, London 1963 (with new preface, as Paradise for sale).
Santa Claus in summer. 1924, New York 1925. For children.
Coral: a sequel to Carnival. 1925, New York [1925].
Fairy gold. 1926, New York [1926].
The life and adventures of Sylvia Scarlett. 1927, 1950 (as The adventures of Sylvia Scarlett, with foreword by Mackenzie). Contains the two Sylvia Scarlett novels.
Mabel in Queer Street. Oxford [1927]. For children.
Rogues and vagabonds. 1927, New York [1927].
Vestal fire. 1927, New York [1927].
Extraordinary women: theme and variations. 1928, Garden City NY 1928, London 1929 (abridged), 1953 (with foreword by Mackenzie).
Extremes meet. 1928, Garden City NY 1928.
The unpleasant visitors. Oxford [1928]. For children.
The adventures of two chairs. Oxford [1929]. For children.
The three couriers. 1929, Garden City NY 1929.
April fools: a farce of manners. 1930, Garden City NY 1930.
The enchanted blanket. Oxford [1930]. For children.
Told. Oxford 1930, New York 1930. Children's stories and verse.
Buttercups and daisies. 1931, Garden City NY 1931 (as For sale).
The conceited doll. Oxford [1931]. For children.
Our street. 1931, Garden City NY 1932.
The fairy in the window-box. Oxford [1932]. For children.
The dining-room battle. Oxford [1933]. For children.
Water on the brain. 1933, Garden City NY 1933.
The darkening green. 1934, Garden City NY 1934.
The enchanted island. Oxford [1934]. For children.
Figure of eight. 1936.
The naughtymobile. Oxford [1936]. For children.
The four winds of love:
    The east wind of love. 1937, New York 1937 (as The east wind).
    The south wind of love. 1937, New York 1937.
    The west wind of love. 1940, New York 1940.
    West to north. 1940, New York 1941.
    The north wind of love: book one. 1944, New York 1945.
    The north wind of love: book two. 1945, New York 1946 (as Again to the north).
The stairs that kept on going down. Oxford [1937]. For children.
The monarch of the glen. 1941, Boston 1951.
The red tapeworm. 1941.
Keep the Home Guard turning. 1943.
Whisky galore. 1947, Boston 1950 (as Tight little island).
Hunting the fairies. 1949.
The rival monster. 1952.
Ben Nevis goes east. 1954.
Thin ice. 1956, New York 1957.
Rockets galore. 1957.
The lunatic republic. 1959.
Mezzotint. [1961].
Paradise for sale. 1963. See above, The old men of the sea, 1924.
Little cat lost. 1965, New York [1965]. For children.
The stolen soprano. 1965.
Paper lives. 1966.
The strongest man on earth. 1968. On Heracles; for children.
The secret island. 1969. For children.

Other Works

Poems. Oxford 1907.
Kensington rhymes. 1912. For children.
Gramophone nights. 1923. With A. Marshall.
Gallipoli memories. 1929, Garden City NY 1930. First vol of war memoirs.
First Athenian memories. 1931. Second vol of war memoirs.
Address delivered in the St Andrew's Hall on January 29th 1932 on the occasion of his installation as Rector [of Glasgow Univ]. Glasgow 1932.
Greek memories. 1932, 1939 (with postscript). 3rd vol of war memoirs.
Prince Charlie: de jure Charles III, King of Scotland, England, France and Ireland. 1932, New York 1933.
Unconsidered trifles. 1932. Essays.
Literature in my time. 1933.
The lost cause: a Jacobite play. 1933.
Reaped and bound. 1933. Essays.
Marathon and Salamis. 1934.
Prince Charlie and his ladies. 1934, New York 1935.
Catholicism and Scotland. 1936.
Pericles. 1937.
The Windsor tapestry. 1938, New York 1938, London 1952 (rptd with index). On the Duke of Windsor.
A musical chair. 1939. Articles rptd from the Gramophone.
Ægean memories. 1940. 4th vol of war memoirs.
Calvary. 1942. Reflections on the war etc. With F. Compton Mackenzie.
Mr Roosevelt. 1943, New York 1944.
Wind of freedom: the history of the invasion of Greece by the Axis Powers 1940–1. 1943.
Dr Benes. 1946.
The vital flame. 1947. On the gas industry.
All over the place. 1948. Travel.
Eastern epic: vol 1, Defence. 1951. On the Indian Army in World War II.
The house of Coalport 1750–1950. 1951. The Coalport China Company.
I took a journey: a tour of National Trust properties. 1951.
The Queen's house: a history of Buckingham Palace. [1953].
The Savoy of London. 1953.
Echoes. 1954. Broadcast talks.
Realms of silver: one hundred years of banking in the East. 1954. The Chartered Bank of India, Australia and China.
My record of music. 1955, New York 1956.
A posy of sweet months. [1955] (priv ptd).
Sublime tobacco. 1957, New York 1958.
Cats' company. [1960], New York [1961].
Greece in my life. 1960.
Catmint. 1961, New York 1962.
On moral courage. 1962, Garden City NY (as Certain aspects of moral courage).
Look at cats. 1963.
My life and times: octave 1–10. 1963–71.
Robert Louis Stevenson. 1968.

Mackenzie founded The Gramophone *in 1923 and edited it for many years.*

§2

Robertson, L. Compton Mackenzie: an appraisal of his literary work. 1954.
Young, K. Compton Mackenzie. 1968 (Br Council pamphlet).

FREDERIC MANNING
1882-1935

The vigil of Brunhild: a narrative poem. 1907.
Scenes and portraits. 1909, New York 1909, London 1930 (rev), New York 1931. Stories.
Poems. 1910.
Eidola. 1917, New York 1918. Verse.
Poetry in prose. In Poetry and prose: three essays by T. S. Eliot, F. Manning, R. Aldington, 1921 (Chapbook 22).
The life of Sir William White. 1923, New York 1923. Biography.
Epicurus's morals, with introductory essay by Manning. 1926.
The middle parts of Fortune: Somme and Ancre 1916. 2 vols 1929, 1930 (abridged) (as Her privates we), New York 1930; ed E. Blunden 1964. The middle parts of Fortune pbd anon; Her privates we pbd as by 'Private 19022'.

OLIVIA MANNING
d. 1980

The wind changes. 1937, New York 1938.
The remarkable expedition: the story of Stanley's rescue of Emin Pasha from equatorial Africa. 1947, Garden City NY 1947 (as The reluctant rescue).
Growing up. 1948. Stories.
Artist among the missing. 1949.
The dreaming shore. 1950. Travel, West coast of Ireland.
School for love. 1951.
A different face: a novel. 1953, New York 1957.
The doves of Venus: a novel. 1955, New York 1956.
My husband Cartwright. 1956. Stories.
The great fortune. 1960, Garden City NY 1961. Vol 1 of The Balkan trilogy.
The spoilt city. 1962, Garden City NY 1962. Vol 2.
Friends and heroes. 1965, Garden City NY 1966. Vol 3.
Extraordinary cats. 1967. Non-fiction.
A romantic hero, and other stories. 1967.
The play room. 1969, New York 1969 (as The Camperlea girls).
The rain forest. 1974.
The danger tree. 1977. Vol 1 of The Levant trilogy.
The battle lost and won. Vol 2.

'KATHERINE MANSFIELD', KATHLEEN MANSFIELD BEAUCHAMP
1888-1923

Bibliographies

Mantz, R. C. The critical bibliography of Katherine Mansfield. Introd by J. M. Murry 1931.

Collections and Selections

Short stories. Ed J. M. Murry, New York 1937.
Collected stories. 1945.
Stories: a selection made by J. M. Murry. New York 1930.
Selected stories. Ed D. M. Davin, Oxford 1953 (WC).
Stories. Ed E. Bowen, New York 1956, London 1957 (as 34 short stories).

§1

In a German pension. [1911], 1926 (introd by J. M. Murry), New York 1926. Stories. Contains The child-who-was-tired, Germans at meat, The baron, The Luft Bad, At Lehmann's, Frau Brechenmacher attends a wedding, The sister of the baroness, Frau Fischer, A birthday, The modern soul, The advanced lady, The swing of the pendulum, A blaze. All previously pbd in New Age except last 3.
Prelude. Richmond Surrey [1918]. Story; rptd in Bliss, and other stories, below.
Je ne parle pas français. Hampstead 1919 (priv ptd). Story; rptd in Bliss, and other stories, below.
Bliss, and other stories. 1920, New York 1921. Contains The wind blows, The little governess, Mr Reginald Peacock's day, Feuille d'album, A dill pickle, Prelude, Bliss, Pictures, Je ne parle pas français, The man without a temperament, Revelations, The escape, Sun and moon, Psychology. All except Psychology previously pbd, either separately or in various periodicals.
The garden-party, and other stories. 1922, New York 1922. Contains Bank Holiday, The young girl, Miss Brill, The lady's maid, The stranger, The life of Ma Parker, The daughters of the late Colonel, Mr and Mrs Dove, An ideal family, Her first ball, The voyage, Marriage à la mode, At the bay, The garden-party, The singing lesson. All except The singing lesson previously pbd in various periodicals.
The dove's nest, and other stories. Ed J. M. Murry 1923, New York 1923. Contains The doll's house, Taking the veil, The fly, Honeymoon, A cup of tea, The canary (all previously pbd in various periodicals); and 15 stories unfinished at the author's death: A married man's story, The dove's nest, Six years after, Daphne, Father and the girls, All serene, A bad idea, A man and his dog, Such a sweet old lady, Honesty, Susannah, Second violin, Mr & Mrs Williams, Weak heart, Widowed.
Poems. 1923, New York 1924, London 1930 (with 2 more poems).
Something childish, and other stories. [1924], New York 1924 (as The little girl, and other stories). Contains The journey to Bruges, A truthful adventure, The woman and the store, How Pearl Button was kidnapped, The little girl, New dresses, Ole Underwood, Pension Séguin, Millie, Violet, Bains turcs, Two tuppenny ones please, Late at night, The black cap, Sixpence, Poison, A suburban fairy tale, Something childish but very natural, The tiredness of Rosabel, See-saw, Carnation, An indiscreet journey, Spring pictures, This flower, The wrong house. All except the last 5 previously pbd in various periodicals.
Reminiscences of Leonid Andreyev by Maxim Gorky. Tr K. Mansfield and S. S. Koteliansky, New York 1928, London [1931].
The aloe. Ed J. M. Murry 1930, New York 1930. The original longer version of Prelude, written in 1916.
Novels and novelists. Ed J. M. Murry 1930. Reprints book reviews from Athenaeum 1919-20.
A fairy story. Stanford 1932 (priv ptd, 25 copies). Issued by Stanford Univ Library.
To Stanislaw Wyspianski. 1938 (priv ptd, 100 copies). Poem dated Jan 1910.
The scrapbook. Ed J.M.M[urry] 1939, New York 1940.

For the unfinished novel Maata, see P. A. Lawlor, The mystery of Maata, Wellington 1946. Katherine Mansfield contributed numerous stories to New Age, and later to the magazines she edited with Murry 1912-15: Rhythm, Blue Rev and Signature.

Letters, Diaries etc

The journal. Ed J. M. Murry 1927, New York 1927, London 1954 (with introd replaced by short preface, and with some textual addns).

The letters. Ed J. M. Murry 2 vols 1928, New York 1929.

Letters to John Middleton Murry 1913–22. Ed Murry 1951, New York 1951. Passages omitted in 1928 edn restored.

Forty-six letters. Adam no 300 1965. Letters to A. E. Rice and to Mr and Mrs S. Schiff.

Letters and journals: a selection. Ed C. K. Stead 1977 (Penguin).

§2

Orage, A. R. Talks with Katherine Mansfield. Century Mag 87 1924; rptd in his Selected essays, 1935.

Woolf, V. A terribly sensitive mind. New York Herald Tribune 19 Sept 1927; rptd in her Granite and rainbow, 1958, and in Collected essays vol 1, 1966. Review of The journal of Katherine Mansfield.

Murry, J. M. Between two worlds: an autobiography. 1935.

—— Katherine Mansfield and other literary portraits. 1949.

Mantz, R. E. and J. M. Murry. The life of Katherine Mansfield. 1933.

Alpers, A. Katherine Mansfield: a biography. New York 1953.

Gordon, I. A. Katherine Mansfield. 1954 (Br Council pamphlet).

ALFRED EDWARD WOODLEY MASON
1865–1948

§1

Blanche de Malétroit: a play in one act founded upon the story by R. L. Stevenson. [1894].

A romance of Wastdale. 1895, New York 1895.

The courtship of Morrice Buckler: a romance. 1896.

Lawrence Clavering. 1897, New York 1897.

The philanderers. 1897, New York 1897.

Miranda of the balcony. 1899, New York 1899.

Parson Kelly. New York 1899, London 1900. With A. Lang.

The watchers (Arrowsmith's Christmas Annual 1899). Bristol 1899, New York 1899.

Clementina. 1901, New York 1901.

Ensign Knightley, and other stories. 1901, New York 1901.

The four feathers. 1902, New York 1902.

The truants. 1904, New York 1904.

The broken road. 1907, New York 1907.

Running water. 1907, New York 1907.

At the Villa Rose. 1910, New York 1910. Dramatized as At the Villa Rose: a play in four acts, [1928].

The clock. New York 1910. Story, rptd in The four corners of the world, below.

Making good. New York 1910. Story.

The turnstile. [1912], New York 1912.

The witness for the defence. 1913, New York 1914. Dramatized as The witness for the defence: a play in four acts, [1913], New York [1913].

Green stockings: a comedy in three acts. [1914], New York [1914].

The affair at the Semiramis Hotel. New York 1917. Story, rptd in The four corners of the world, below.

The four corners of the world. 1917, New York 1917. Stories.

'The episode of the thermometer'. New York 1918. Story.

The Royal Exchange: a note on the occasion of the bi-centenary of the Royal Exchange Assurance. [1920].

The summons. [1920], New York 1920.

The winding stair. [1923], New York 1923.

The house of the arrow. [1924], New York 1924.

No other tiger. 1927, New York 1927.

The prisoner in the opal. [1928], Garden City NY 1928.

The dean's elbow. 1930, Garden City NY 1931.

The three gentlemen. 1932, Garden City NY 1932.

The sapphire. 1933, Garden City NY 1933.

Dilemmas. 1934, Garden City NY 1935. Stories.

A present from Margate: a frivolous comedy in three acts. [1934]. With I. Hay.

Sir George Alexander and the St James' Theatre. 1935, New York 1935.

They wouldn't be chessmen. 1935, Garden City NY 1935.

Fire over England. 1936, Garden City NY 1936.

The drum. 1937, Garden City NY 1937. Story.

Königsmark. 1938, New York 1939.

The secret fear. New York 1940. Story.

The life of Francis Drake. 1941, Garden City NY 1942.

Musk and amber. 1942, Garden City NY 1942.

The house in Lordship Lane. 1946, New York 1946.

§2

Green, R. L. A. E. W. Mason. 1952.

WILLIAM SOMERSET MAUGHAM
1874–1965

Bibliographies

Stott, R. T. The writings of Maugham. 1956, with suppls 1961 and 1964, 1973 (rev as A bibliography of the works of Maugham).

Collections and Selections

Collected edition. 1931–. Prefaces by the author, many titles rev from previous edns. Plays issued in 6 vols 1931–4, under the title Plays by W. Somerset Maugham.

East and west: the collected short stories. Garden City NY 1934, London 1934 (as Altogether). Preface by the author.

The round dozen: a collection of his stories selected by W. Somerset Maugham. [1939].

Quartet: four stories. 1948, New York 1949. The facts of life, The alien corn, The kite, The colonel's lady; with film scripts by R. C. Sherriff.

Trio: stories by Maugham; screen adaptation by Maugham, R. C. Sherriff and Noel Langley. 1950, New York 1950. The verger, Mr Know-all, Sanatorium.

Encore: stories by Maugham; screen adaptation by T. E. B. Clarke, A. Macrae and E. Ambler. 1951. The ant and the grasshopper, Winter cruise, Gigolo and Gigolette.

The complete short stories. 3 vols 1951, 2 vols New York 1952. With prefaces by the author.

Collected plays. 3 vols 1952. First pbd in 6 vols 1931–4.

Selected novels. 3 vols 1953. With prefaces by the author.

The partial view. 1954. Contains The summing up and A writer's notebook, with a new preface.

The travel books. 1955. On A Chinese screen, The gentleman in the parlour, Don Fernando. With new preface.

§1

Prose Fiction

Liza of Lambeth. 1897, New York 1921, London 1930 (with preface by Maugham), 1947 (with expanded preface).

The making of a saint: a romance of medieval Italy. Boston 1898, London 1898.

Orientations: short stories. 1899.

The hero. 1901.

Mrs Craddock. 1902, New York 1920, London 1928 (rev).

The merry-go-round. 1904, New York 1904.

The land of the Blessed Virgin: sketches and impressions in Andalusia. 1905, New York 1920, 1921 (as Andalusia: sketches and impressions).

The bishop's apron: a study in the origins of a great family. 1906. Novel version of the play Loaves and fishes, 1911.
The explorer. 1908 (for 1907), Boston 1908.
The magician. 1908, New York 1909.
Of human bondage. New York 1915, London 1915, New Haven 1938 (introd by T. Dreiser), New York 1956 (Modern Lib edn, introd by R. A. Cordell), 1967 (abridged, introd by Maugham).
The moon and sixpence. 1919, New York [1919], [1941] (with excerpts from author's letters).
The trembling of a leaf: little stories of the South Sea Islands. New York 1921, London 1921, [1928] (as Sadie Thompson and other stories of the South Seas), New York 1932 (as Rain and other stories of the South Sea islands).
On a Chinese screen. New York [1922], London 1922. Travel.
The painted veil. New York 1925, London 1925.
The casuarina tree: six stories. 1926, New York 1926, London [1930] (as The letter: stories of crime).
Ashenden: or the British agent. 1928, New York 1928. Stories.
Cakes and ale: or the skeleton in the cupboard. 1930, New York 1930, 1950 (with preface by Maugham), London 1954.
The gentleman in the parlour: a record of a journey from Rangoon to Haiphong. 1930, Garden City NY 1930.
Six stories written in the first person singular. Garden City NY 1931, London 1931.
The book-bag. Florence 1932. Story, rptd in Ah King.
The narrow corner. 1932, New York 1932.
Ah King: six stories. 1933, Garden City NY 1933.
The judgment seat. 1934. Story, rptd in Cosmopolitans.
Don Fernando: or variations on some Spanish themes. 1935, Garden City NY 1935, London 1950 (rev). Travel and criticism.
Cosmopolitans. Garden City NY 1936, London 1936 (with subtitle, Very short stories).
My South Sea island. Chicago 1936 (50 copies). Travel, rptd from Daily Mail 31 Jan 1922.
Theatre. Garden City NY 1937, London 1937.
The summing up. 1938, Garden City NY 1938.
Christmas holiday. [1939], New York 1939.
Princess September and the nightingale. 1939. Rptd from The gentleman in the parlour, 1930, above.
Books and you. 1940, Garden City NY 1940. Essays rptd from Saturday Evening Post.
France at war. 1940, New York 1940. Essay.
The mixture as before: short stories. 1940, New York 1940, 1947 (as Great stories of love and intrigue).
Strictly personal. Garden City NY 1941, London 1942. Autobiography, previously serialised in Saturday Evening Post 29 March–12 April 1941 (as Novelist's flight from France).
Up at the villa. New York 1941, London 1941. Previously serialised in Red Book Mag as The villa on the hill.
The hour before dawn. Garden City NY 1942.
The unconquered: a short story. New York 1944; rptd (rev) in Creatures of circumstance, 1947, below.
The razor's edge. Garden City NY 1944, London 1944.
Of human bondage, with a digression on the art of fiction: an address. Washington 1946. On the occasion of presenting the original ms to the Library of Congress.
Then and now. 1946, Garden City NY 1946.
Creatures of circumstance: short stories. 1947, Garden City NY 1947.
Catalina: a romance. 1948, Garden City NY 1948. First pbd serially in The Windmill 1948.
Great novelists and their novels: essays on the ten greatest novels of the world and the men and women who wrote them. Philadelphia [1948], London 1954 (rev as Ten novels and their authors), Garden City NY 1955 (rev, as The art of fiction). Essays, originally pbd in Atlantic Monthly 1947–8 except that on Tolstoy.

A writer's notebook. 1949, Garden City NY 1949; rptd in The partial view, 1954.
The writer's point of view. 1951. National Book League lecture.
The vagrant mood: six essays. 1952, Garden City NY 1953.
Points of view. 1958, Garden City NY 1959. Essays.
Purely for my pleasure. 1962, Garden City NY 1963. On his art collection.

Maugham was joint editor, with L. Housman, of the periodical Venture: an annual of art and literature, *2 vols 1903–5.*

Plays
Plays are listed in order of production, not of pbn.

Schiffbrüchig. (Schall und Rauch, Berlin 3 Jan 1902). Not pbd. English version, Marriages are made in heaven: a play in one act, pbd in Venture 1 1903.
A man of honour: a play in four acts. (Stage Soc, at the Imperial 22 Feb 1903). 1903, Chicago [1912]. Also pbd as suppl to Fortnightly Rev March 1903.
Mademoiselle Zampa: a new one-act farce. (Avenue 18 Feb 1904). Not pbd.
Lady Frederick: a comedy in three acts. (Court 26 Oct 1907). 1912, Chicago 1912, London [1947] (French's Acting Edn).
Jack Straw: a farce in three acts. (Vaudeville 26 March 1908). 1912, Chicago 1912.
Mrs Dot: a farce in three acts. (Comedy 27 April 1908). 1912, Chicago 1912.
The explorer: a melodrama in four acts. (Lyric 13 June 1908). 1912, Chicago [1912].
Penelope: a comedy in three acts. (Comedy 9 Jan 1909). 1912, Chicago [1912].
The noble Spaniard: a comedy in three acts, adapted from the French of Grenet-Dancourt. (New Royalty 20 March 1909). 1953 (Evans' Acting Edn).
Smith: a comedy in four acts. (Comedy 30 Sept 1909). 1913, Chicago [1913].
The tenth man: a tragic comedy in three acts. (Globe 24 Feb 1910). 1913, Chicago [1913].
Grace: a play in four acts. (Duke of York's 15 Oct 1910). Pbd as Landed gentry: a comedy in four acts 1913, Chicago [1913].
Loaves and fishes: a comedy in four acts. (Duke of York's 24 Feb 1911). 1924.
The perfect gentleman: an adaptation of Molière's Le bourgeois gentilhomme. (His Majesty's 27 May 1913). Not pbd.
The land of promise: a comedy in four acts. (Lyceum, New York 25 Dec 1913; Duke of York's 26 Feb 1914). 1913, New York 1923.
Caroline: a light comedy in three acts. (New 8 Feb 1916). Pbd 1923 as The unattainable: a farce in three acts.
Our betters: a comedy in three acts. (Hudson, New York 12 March 1917; Globe 12 Sept 1923). 1923, New York 1924.
Love in a cottage. (Globe 26 Jan 1918). In 4 acts; not pbd.
Caesar's wife: a comedy in three acts. (Royalty 27 March 1919). 1922, New York 1923.
Home and beauty: a farce in three acts. (Playhouse 30 Aug 1919; Booth, New York 8 Oct 1919, as Too many husbands). 1923, [1951] (French's Acting Edn).
The unknown: a play in three acts. (Aldwych 9 Aug 1920). 1920, New York 1920.
The circle: a comedy in three acts. (Haymarket 3 March 1921). 1921, New York 1921, London 1948 (French's Acting Edn).
East of Suez: a play in seven scenes. (His Majesty's 2 Sept 1922). 1922, New York 1922.
The camel's back: a new farce in three acts. (Vanderbilt, New York 13 Nov 1923; Playhouse 31 Jan 1924). Not pbd.

The constant wife: a comedy in three acts. (Maxine Elliott, New York 29 Nov 1926; Strand 6 April 1927). New York [1927], London 1927, [1949] (French's Acting Edn).

The letter: a play in three acts. (Playhouse 24 Feb 1927). 1927, New York 1927, London 1949 (French's Acting Edn). Dramatization of the story pbd in the preceding year.

The sacred flame: a play in three acts. (Henry Miller, New York 19 Nov 1928; Playhouse 8 Feb 1929). New York 1928, London 1928, 1948 (French's Acting Edn).

The breadwinner: a comedy in one act. (Vaudeville 30 Sept 1930). 1930, Garden City NY 1931, London 1948 (French's Acting Edn).

For services rendered: a play in three acts. (Globe 1 Nov 1932). 1932, Garden City NY 1933, London [1948] (French's Acting Edn).

Sheppey: a play in three acts. (Wyndham's 14 Sept 1933). 1933, 1948 (French's Acting Edn).

§2

Dottin, P. Maugham et ses romans. Paris 1928.
—— Le théâtre de Maugham. Paris 1937.
Aldington, R. W. Somerset Maugham: an appreciation. New York 1939.
Brophy, J. Somerset Maugham. 1952, 1958 (rev) (Br Council pamphlet).
Jonas, K. W. (ed. The Maugham enigma. New York 1954.
—— The gentleman from Cap Ferrat. New Haven 1956; rptd in his World of Maugham, 1959, below.
—— (ed). The world of Maugham. 1959.
Zabel, M. D. A cool hand. In his Craft and character in modern fiction, New York 1957. On Up at the villa.
Hassall, C. Edward Marsh. 1959. Includes unpbd letters.
Brander, L. Maugham: a guide. Edinburgh 1963.
Kanin, G. Remembering Mr Maugham. Introd by Noel Coward 1966.
Maugham, R. Somerset and all the Maughams. 1966.
Nichols, B. A case of human bondage. 1966. A memoir.
Curtis, A. The pattern of Maugham. 1974.
Raphael, F. Maugham and his world. 1976.

ALAN ALEXANDER MILNE
1882–1956

Fiction, Prose and Verse

Lovers in London. 1905.
The day's play. 1910. Sketches and verse rptd from Punch.
The holiday round. 1912. Sketches rptd from Punch.
Once a week. 1914, New York [1925]. Sketches rptd from Punch.
Happy days. New York [1915]. Sketches rptd from Punch.
Not that it matters. 1919, New York [1920]. Essays.
If I may. 1920, New York [1921]. Essays.
Mr Pim. [1921], New York 1922, London 1929 (as Mr Pim passes by). Based on the play; see below.
The sunny side. 1921, New York 1922. Sketches and verse mainly rptd from Punch.
The Red House mystery. 1922, New York [1922], 1926 (with introd by Milne).
For the luncheon interval: cricket and other verses. 1925.
The ascent of man. 1928.
By way of introduction. 1929, New York [1929]. Prefaces, reviews and essays.
The secret, and other stories. New York 1929.
Those were the days: The day's play; The holiday round; Once a week; The sunny side. 1929. The collected Punch writings, with 'Prelude' by Milne.

When I was very young. 1930, New York 1930. Autobiography, illustr E. H. Shepard.
Two people. 1931, New York 1931.
Four days' wonder. 1933, New York [1933].
Peace with honour: an enquiry into the War Convention. 1934, New York [1934] (with special preface for the American edn), London 1935 (enlarged), New York 1935.
It's too late now: the autobiography of a writer. 1939, New York 1939 (as Autobiography).
Behind the lines. 1940, New York [1940]. Verse.
War with honour. 1940 (Macmillan War pamphlets).
War aims unlimited. 1941. Pamphlet.
Chloe Marr. 1946, New York 1946.
Going abroad? [1947]. Pamphlet on travel.
Birthday party, and other stories. New York 1948, London 1949.
Books for children. 1948 (Nat Book League Reader's Guide).
The Norman church. 1948. Verse.
A table near the band, and other stories. 1950, New York 1950.
Year in, year out. 1952. Monthly calendar of reminiscences, sketches and essays, illustr E. H. Shepard.

Milne was assistant editor of Punch *1906–14.*

Children's Books

Once on a time. 1917, New York 1922.
Make-believe: a children's play in a prologue and three acts, the lyrics by C. E. Burton. (Lyric, Hammersmith 24 Dec 1918). In Second plays, 1921, below (with new prologue and without lyrics); pbd separately 1925 (French's Acting Edn) (with lyrics).
When we were very young. 1924, New York [1924]. Verse.
A gallery of children. 1925, Philadelphia [1925]. Stories.
Winnie-the-Pooh. 1926, New York 1926. Stories.
Now we are six. 1927, New York [1927]. Verse.
The house at Pooh Corner. 1928, New York [1928]. Stories.
Toad of Toad Hall: a play from Grahame's book The wind in the willows. (Lyric 17 Dec 1930). 1929, New York 1929, London [1932] (French's Acting Edn).
Prince Rabbit, and the princess who could not laugh. 1966, New York 1966.

Milne pbd a number of selections of his children's stories and verse under various titles.

Plays

Plays are listed in order of production where known.

Wurzel-Flummery: a comedy in two acts. (New 7 April 1917). [1921] (French's Acting edn). Rev version in one act pbd in First plays, 1919, below, and pbd separately 1922 (French's Acting Edn).
Belinda: an April folly in three acts. (New 8 April 1918). In First plays, 1919, below. Pbd separately 1922 (French's Acting Edn).
The boy comes home: a comedy in one act. (Victoria Palace 9 Sept 1918). In First plays, 1919, below. Pbd separately 1926 (French's Acting Edn).
Make-believe. 1918. *See above*, Children's books.
The Camberley triangle: a comedy in one act. (Coliseum 8 Sept 1919). In Second plays, 1921, below. Pbd separately 1925 (French's Acting Edn).
First plays. 1919, New York 1930. Wurzel-Flummery; The lucky one; The boy comes home; Belinda; The red feathers.
Mr Pim passes by: a comedy in three acts. (Gaiety, Manchester 1 Dec 1919; New 5 Jan 1920). In Second plays, 1921, below. Pbd separately 1921 (French's Acting Edn). For the novel *see* Fiction, etc, above.
The romantic age: a comedy in three acts. (Comedy 18 Oct 1920). In Second plays, 1921, below. Pbd separately 1922 (French's Acting Edn).

The stepmother: a play in one act. (Alhambra 16 Nov 1920). In Second plays, 1921, below. Pbd separately 1921 (French's Acting Edn).

Second plays. 1921. Make-believe; Mr Pim passes by; The Camberley triangle; The romantic age; The stepmother.

The great Broxopp: four chapters in her life—a comedy. (Punch and Judy, New York 14 Nov 1921; St Martin's 6 March 1923). In Three plays, 1922, below.

The truth about Blayds: a comedy in three acts. (Globe 20 Dec 1921). In Three plays, 1922, below. Pbd separately 1923 (French's Acting Edn).

The Dover road: a comedy in three acts. (New Bijou 23 Dec 1921; Haymarket 7 June 1922). In Three plays, 1922, below. Pbd separately 1923 (French's Acting Edn).

The lucky one. (Garrick, New York 20 Nov 1922). In First plays, 1919, above.

Three plays: The Dover road; The truth about Blayds; The Great Broxopp. New York 1922, London 1923.

Success. (Haymarket 21 June 1923; Charles Hopkins, New York 4 March 1931, as Give me yesterday). In Four plays, 1926 below.

The artist: a duologue. [1923].

To have the honour: a comedy in three acts. (Wyndham's 22 April 1924; Lyceum, New York 25 Feb 1929, as To meet the prince). [1925] (French's Acting Edn).

The man in the bowler hat: a terribly exciting affair. (New York Belasco 5 May 1924). [1923] (French's Acting Edn).

Ariadne, or business first: a comedy in three acts. (Garrick, New York 25 Feb 1925; Haymarket 22 April 1925). [1925] (French's Acting Edn).

Portrait of a gentleman in slippers: a comedy in one act. (Liverpool Repertory 4 Sept 1926). In Four plays, 1926, below.

Four plays. 1926. To have the honour; Ariadne; Portrait of a gentleman in slippers; Success.

Miss Marlow at play: a one-act comedy. (Coliseum 11 April 1927). [1936] (French's Acting Edn).

The ivory door: a legend in a prologue and three acts. (Charles Hopkins, New York 18 Oct 1927; Haymarket 17 April 1929). New York 1928, London 1929, [1930] (French's Acting Edn).

The fourth wall: a detective story in three acts. (Haymarket 29 Feb 1928; Charles Hopkins, New York 27 Nov 1928, as The perfect alibi). New York [1929], London [1930] (French's Acting Edn).

Toad of Toad Hall. 1929. See above, Children's books.

Michael and Mary: a play in three acts. (St James's, New York 1 Feb 1930). 1930, [1932] (French's Acting Edn).

Four plays: Michael and Mary; To meet the prince; The perfect alibi; Portrait of a gentleman in slippers. New York 1932.

Other people's lives: a play in three acts. (Wyndhams 11 July 1933). [1935] (French's Acting Edn).

Sarah Simple: a comedy in three acts. (Garrick 4 May 1937). [1939] (French's Acting Edn).

Miss Elizabeth Bennet: a play from Pride and prejudice (People's Palace 3 Feb 1938). 1936.

The ugly duckling: a play in one act. [1941] (French's Acting Edn).

Before the Flood: a play in one act. [1951] (French's Acting Edn).

Milne also wrote the following unpbd plays: Let's all talk about Gerald (*Arts 11 May 1928*); They don't mean any harm (*Charles Hopkins, New York 23 Feb 1932*); Gentleman unknown (*St James's 16 Nov 1928*).

NANCY FREEMAN MITFORD
1904–73

Highland fling. 1931.

Christmas pudding. 1932.

Wigs on the green. 1935.

Pigeon pie: a wartime receipt. 1940, New York 1959.

The pursuit of love. 1945, New York 1946.

Love in a cold climate. 1949, New York 1949.

The Princesse de Cleves [by] Madame de Lafayette. Tr N. Mitford 1950, 1962 (rev) (Penguin).

The blessing. 1951, New York 1951.

The little hut, by A. Roussin, adapted from the French by N. Mitford. 1951.

Madame de Pompadour. 1954, 1968 (rev), New York 1968. Biography.

Noblesse oblige: an enquiry into the identifiable characteristics of the English aristocracy by A. S. C. Ross, N. Mitford [et al]. 1956, New York 1956.

Voltaire in love. 1957, New York 1957. Biography.

Don't tell Alfred. 1960, New York 1961.

The water beetle. 1962, New York [1962]. Essays.

The Sun King. 1966, New York 1966. On Louis XIV.

See H. Acton, Nancy Mitford: a memoir, 1975.

NICHOLAS JOHN TURNEY MONSARRAT
1910–79

Think of to-morrow. [1934].

At first sight. [1935].

The whipping boy. [1937].

This is the schoolroom. 1939, New York 1940.

H.M. Corvette. 1942, Philadelphia 1943. Reminiscences.

East coast corvette. 1943, Philadelphia 1943. Reminiscences.

Corvette command. 1944. Reminiscences.

Leave cancelled. New York 1945; rptd in Depends what you mean by love, 1947, below.

Three corvettes. 1945, 1953 (with rev foreword). Reissue of H.M. Corvette, East coast corvette and Corvette command, above.

H.M. Frigate. 1946. Reminiscences.

Depends what you mean by love. 1947, New York 1948. Stories.

My brother Denys. 1948, New York 1948. Reminiscences.

The cruel sea. 1951, New York 1951.

HMS Marlborough will enter harbour. 1952. First pbd in Depends what you mean by love, 1947, above.

The story of Esther Costello. 1953, New York 1953.

Castle Garac. New York 1955.

The tribe that lost its head. 1956, New York 1956.

The ship that died of shame, and other stories. 1959, New York 1959.

The nylon pirates. 1960, New York 1960.

The white rajah. 1961, New York 1961.

The time before this. 1962, New York 1962. Pt of his Signs of the times ser.

Smith and Jones. 1963, New York 1963. Pt of his Signs of the times ser.

To Stratford with love. Toronto [1963]. On the Stratford, Ontario, Shakespeare Festival.

A fair day's work. 1964, New York 1964. Pt of his Signs of the times ser.

The pillow fight. 1965, New York 1965.

Something to hide. 1965, New York 1966. Pt of the Signs of the times ser.

Life is a four-letter word. 1966–. Autobiography.

Richer than all his tribe. 1968, New York 1969.

CHARLES EDWARD MONTAGUE
1867–1928

§ I

The Manchester stage 1880–1900: criticisms reprinted from the Manchester Guardian. [1900]. By Montague et al.

William Thomas Arnold, journalist and historian. Manchester 1907, New York 1907. With Mrs Humphry Ward.

A hind let loose. 1910.

Dramatic values. 1911, New York 1911, London 1925 (rev), New York 1925. Essays.

The morning's war: a romance. 1913, New York 1913.

The front line. 1916. Pamphlet on 1914–18 war.

The western front; drawings by Muirhead Bone, with text by C. E. Montague. 2 vols 1917.

Notes from Calais base, and pictures of its many activities. 1918. Pamphlet on 1914–18 war.

Disenchantment. 1922, New York 1922. Essays.

Fiery particles. 1923, New York 1923. Stories.

The right place: a book of pleasures. 1924, New York 1924. Essays.

Rough justice. 1926, New York 1926.

Right off the map. 1927, New York 1927.

Action, and other stories. 1928, New York 1929.

A writer's notes on his trade. Introd by H. M. Tomlinson. 1930, New York 1930. Essays.

§ 2

Elton, O. Montague: a memoir. 1929. Contains letters and some uncollected fragments.

CHARLES LANGBRIDGE MORGAN
1894–1958

The gunroom. 1919.

My name is Legion. 1925, New York 1925.

Portrait in a mirror. 1929, New York 1929.

The fountain. 1932, New York 1932.

Epitaph on George Moore. 1935, New York 1935.

Sparkenbroke. 1936, New York 1936.

The flashing stream: a play. (Lyric 1 Sept 1938). 1938 (with an essay, On Singleness of mind), New York 1938, London 1948 (rev).

The voyage. 1940, New York 1940.

The empty room. 1941, New York 1941.

Ode to France. [1942].

Du génie français. Paris 1943. Pamphlet.

The house of Macmillan 1843–1943. 1943, New York 1944.

Reflections in a mirror. First ser 1944, 2nd ser 1946.

The artist in the community. Glasgow 1945 (W. P. Ker memorial lecture).

The judge's story. 1947, New York 1947.

The liberty of thought and the separation of powers: a modern problem considered in the context of Montesquieu. 1948 (Zaharoff lecture).

The river line. 1949, New York 1949. First pbd serially in Woman's Home Companion Sept, Oct 1948 (as Edge of happiness); adapted as a play 1952, New York 1952 (with a preface by the author, On transcending the age of violence); first performed Lyric, Hammersmith 2 Sept 1952, Strand 28 Oct 1952.

A breeze of morning. 1951, New York 1951.

Liberties of the mind. 1951, New York 1951. Essays.

The burning glass: a play. (Royal, Brighton 18 Jan 1954; Apollo 18 Feb 1954). 1953 (with a preface, On power over nature), New York 1953, London 1955 (rev).

Dialogue in novels and plays. Aldington [1954], Philadelphia 1954 (Herman Ould Memorial Lecture).

On learning to write. 1954 (Eng Assoc Presidential Address).

Challenge to Venus. 1957, New York 1957.

The writer and his world: lectures and essays. 1960.

Selected letters. Ed E. Lewis 1967.

LEOPOLD HAMILTON MYERS
1881–1944

§ I

Arvat: a dramatic poem in four acts. 1908.

The Orissers. 1922, New York 1922.

The 'Clio'. 1925, New York 1925.

The near and the far. 1929, New York [1930].

Prince Jali. 1931, New York 1931. Continues The near and the far, above.

The root and the flower. 1935, New York 1935. Contains The near and the far and Prince Jali, both rev, with a new third part, Rajah Amar.

Strange glory. 1936, New York [1936].

The pool of Vishnu. 1940, New York [1940]. Conclusion of The root and the flower, above.

The near and the far: containing The root and the flower and The pool of Vishnu, above. 1940 (Book Soc), 1943, New York 1947, London 1956 (with introd by L. P. Hartley).

§ 2

Harding, D. W. The work of Myers. Scrutiny 3 1934.

Bantock, G. H. Myers: a critical study. 1956.

Simon, I. The novels of Myers. Brussels 1956.

Bottrall, R. L. H. Myers. REL 2 1961.

PERCY HOWARD NEWBY
b. 1918

A journey to the interior. 1945, Garden City NY 1946.

Agents and witnesses. 1947, Garden City NY 1947.

The spirit of Jem. 1947. For children.

Mariner dances. 1948.

The loot runners. 1949. For children.

The snow pasture. 1949.

Maria Edgeworth. 1950, Denver 1950. Criticism.

The young May moon. 1950, New York 1951.

The novel 1945–50. 1951 (Br Council pamphlet).

A season in England. 1951, New York 1952.

A step to silence. 1952.

The retreat. 1953, New York 1953.

The picnic at Sakkara. 1955, New York 1955.

Revolution and roses. 1957, New York 1957.

Ten miles from anywhere and other stories. 1958.

A guest and his going. 1959, New York 1960.

The Barbary light. 1962.

One of the founders. 1965, Philadelphia 1965.

The Third Programme. 1965. Lecture.

Something to answer for. 1968, Philadelphia 1969.

JOHN BEVERLEY NICHOLS
b. 1899

Prelude. 1920.

Patchwork. 1921, New York 1922.

Self. 1922.

25: being a young man's candid recollections of his elders and betters. [1926], New York [1926].

Are they the same at home? 1927, New York [1927]. Impressions.

Crazy pavements. 1927, New York [1927].

The star-spangled manner. 1928, Garden City NY 1928. Autobiography.

Women and children last. 1931, Garden City NY 1931. Non-fiction.

Down the garden path. 1932, Garden City NY [1932]. Non-fiction.

Evensong. 1932, Garden City NY 1932. Adapted as play, with E. Knoblock, 1933.

For adults only. 1932, Garden City NY 1933.

Cry havoc! 1933, Garden City NY 1933. Non-fiction.

Failures: three plays. 1933.

A thatched roof. 1933, Garden City NY [1933]. Non-fiction.

A village in a valley. 1934, Garden City NY 1934. Non-fiction.

Mesmer: a play in three acts. 1935.

The fool hath said. 1936, Garden City NY 1936. Non-fiction.

No place like home. 1936, Garden City NY 1936. Travel.

News of England: or a country without a hero. 1938, New York 1938. Non-fiction.

Green grows the city: the story of a London garden. 1939, New York [1939].

Revue. 1939, New York 1939.

Men do not weep. 1941, New York 1942. Stories.

Verdict on India. 1944, New York 1944. Non-fiction.

The tree that sat down. 1945, 1960 (abridged with The stream that stood still, 1948, below), New York 1966. For children.

The stream that stood still. 1948, 1960 (abridged, with The tree that sat down, 1945, above), New York 1966. For children.

All I could never be: some recollections. 1949, New York 1952.

Shadow of the vine: a play in three acts. 1949.

Yours sincerely. 1949. Essays; with Monica Dickens.

The mountain of magic: a romance for children. 1950.

Uncle Samson. 1950. Travel in USA.

Merry Hall. 1951, New York 1953. Non-fiction.

A pilgrim's progress. 1952. Non-fiction.

Laughter on the stairs. 1953, New York 1954. Non-fiction.

No man's street. 1954, New York 1954.

The moonflower. 1955, New York 1955 (as The moonflower murder).

Death to slow music. 1956, New York 1956.

Sunlight on the lawn. 1956, New York [1956]. Non-fiction.

The rich die hard. 1957, New York 1958.

The sweet and twenties. [1958], New York 1958. Non-fiction.

Cats' ABC. 1960, New York 1960.

Murder by request. 1960, New York 1960.

Beverley Nichols' Cats' XYZ. 1961, New York 1961.

Garden open today. 1963, New York 1963. Non-fiction.

Forty favourite flowers. 1964, New York 1965.

A case of human bondage. 1966, New York 1966. On Somerset Maugham.

Powers that be. 1966, New York 1966. Non-fiction.

The art of flower arrangement. 1967, New York 1967.

Garden open tomorrow. 1968, New York 1969. Non-fiction.

The sun in my eyes: or how not to go round the world. 1969. Travel.

Father figure. 1972.

'FLANN O'BRIEN', BRIAN O'NOLAN
1911–66

At Swim-two-birds. 1939, New York 1951.

An béal boċt: nó, An milleánach. Dublin 1941. As by 'Myles na gCopaleen'.

Faustus Kelly. Dublin 1943. Play, first performed at the Abbey, Dublin 1943.

The hard life: an exegesis of squalor. 1961, New York 1962.

The Dalkey archive. 1964, New York 1965.

The third policeman. 1967, New York 1968.

The best of Myles: a selection from 'Cruiskeen lawn'. Ed K. O'Nolan 1968, New York 1968. Articles written for the Irish Times 1940–66 under pseud 'Myles na gCopaleen'.

O'Brien also wrote an unfinished novel, The great sago saga; *a sketch,* Thirst (*Gate Theatre, Dublin 1942, rewritten for radio and television); and adapted Capek's* Insect play (*1943*).

'FRANK O'CONNOR', MICHAEL FRANCIS O'DONOVAN
1903–66

Guests of the nation. 1931, New York 1931.

The saint and Mary Kate. 1932, New York 1932.

Bones of contention and other stories. 1936, New York 1936.

Three old brothers and other poems. 1936.

The big fellow: a life of Michael Collins. 1937, New York 1937 (as Death in Dublin: Michael Collins and the Irish revolution), Dublin 1965 (rev, as The big fellow: Michael Collins and the Irish revolution).

In the train [1937]. In The genius of the Irish theater, ed S. Barnet et al, New York 1960. Play; with H. Hunt.

Dutch interior. 1940, New York 1940.

Three tales. Dublin 1941 (250 copies).

A picture book. Dublin 1943 (480 copies). Descriptions of Ireland.

Crab apple jelly: stories and tales. 1944, New York 1944.

Towards an appreciation of literature. Dublin 1945.

The art of the theatre. Dublin 1947.

The common chord: stories and tales. 1947, New York 1948.

Irish miles. 1947. Topography.

The road to Stratford. 1948, Cleveland 1960 (rev, as Shakespeare's progress).

Leinster, Munster and Connaught. [1950], New York 1950. Topography.

Traveller's samples: stories and tales. 1951, New York 1951.

The stories of Frank O'Connor. New York 1952, London 1953.

More stories. New York 1954.

The mirror in the roadway: a study of the modern novel. New York 1956, London 1957.

Domestic relations: short stories. 1957, New York 1957.

An only child. 1961, New York 1961. Autobiography.

The lonely voice: a study of the short story. Cleveland 1963, London 1963.

Collection two. 1964. Stories.

The backward look: a survey of Irish literature. 1967.

My father's son. [1968], New York 1969. Autobiography.

Collection three. 1969. Stories.

O'Connor wrote the unpbd plays, The invincibles, Moses' rock (*both with H. Hunt) and* Time's pocket. *He also edited* Modern Irish short stories, *Oxford 1957 (WC), and* A book of Ireland, *1959 (Collins Nat Anthologies).*

SEÁN O'FAOLÁIN
b. 1900

Midsummer madness and other stories. 1932, New York 1932.

The life story of Eamon de Valera. Dublin 1933.
A nest of simple folk. 1933, New York 1934.
Constance Markievicz, or the average revolutionary: a biography. 1934, 1968 (rev).
There's a birdie in the cage. 1935. Story, rptd in A purse of coppers, below. 285 copies.
Bird alone. 1936, New York 1936.
A born genius: a short story. Detroit 1936. Rptd in A purse of coppers, below.
A purse of coppers: short stories. 1937, New York 1938.
King of the beggars: a life of Daniel O'Connell. 1938, New York 1938.
She had to do something: a comedy in three acts. 1938.
De Valera. 1939 (Penguin).
Come back to Erin. 1940, New York 1940.
An Irish journey. 1940, New York 1940. Non-fiction.
The great O'Neill: a biography of Hugh O'Neill, Earl of Tyrone 1550–1616. 1942, New York 1942.
The story of Ireland. 1942, New York 1943 (Britain in Pictures).
The Irish. 1947 (Pelican), New York 1949, London 1969 (rev).
Teresa, and other stories. 1947, New York 1948 (as The man who invented sin).
The short story. 1948, New York 1951.
A summer in Italy. 1949, New York 1950. Non-fiction.
Newman's way. 1952, New York 1952. Biography.
South to Sicily. 1953, New York 1953 (as Autumn in Italy).
The vanishing hero: studies in novelists of the twenties. 1956, Boston 1957.
I remember, I remember. Boston 1961, London 1962. Stories.
Vive-moi! an autobiography. Boston 1964, London 1965.
The heat of the sun: stories and tales. 1966, Boston 1966.

LIAM O'FLAHERTY
b. 1897

Thy neighbour's wife. 1923, New York [1924].
The black soul. 1924.
Spring sowing. 1924. Stories.
The informer. 1925, New York 1925, 1961 (with afterword by D. MacDonagh).
Civil war. 1925 (priv ptd, 100 copies). Story. Rptd in The tent, 1926, below.
The terrorist. 1926 (priv ptd, 100 copies). Story. Rptd in The tent, below.
Darkness: a tragedy in three acts. 1926 (priv ptd, 100 copies).
The tent [and other stories]. 1926.
Mr Gilhooley. 1926, New York [1927].
The child of God. 1926 (priv ptd, 100 copies). Story. Rptd in The mountain tavern, 1929, below.
The life of Tim Healy. 1927, New York [1927].
The fairy-goose, and two other stories. New York 1927, London 1927.
The assassin. 1928, New York [1928].
Red Barbara, and other stories. New York 1928, London 1928.
The mountain tavern, and other stories. 1929, New York [1929].
A tourist's guide to Ireland. [1929].
The house of gold. 1929, New York [1929].
The return of the brute. 1929, New York 1930.
Joseph Conrad: an appreciation. [1930].
Two years. 1930, New York [1930]. Autobiographical.
The ecstasy of Angus. 1931 (priv ptd). Story.
A cure for unemployment. 1931.
I went to Russia. 1931, New York [1931].
The puritan. 1931, New York [1932].
The wild swan, and other stories. Foreword by R. Davies 1932.
Skerrett. 1932, New York 1932.
The martyr. 1933, New York 1933.

Shame the devil. 1934. Autobiographical.
Hollywood cemetery. 1935.
Famine. 1937, New York [1937].
Land. 1946, New York 1946.
Two lovely beasts, and other stories. 1948, New York 1950.
Insurrection. 1950, Boston 1951.
Dúil [Desire]. Dublin 1953. Stories.

CAROLA MARY ANIMA OMAN (LADY LENANTON)
b. 1897

The Menin road and other poems. 1919.
Princess Amelia. 1924, New York 1924.
The road royal. 1924, New York 1924.
King heart. 1926.
Mrs Newdigate's window. 1927, New York 1927. As C. Lenanton.
The holiday. 1928, New York 1928. As C. Lenanton.
Crouchback. [1929], New York 1929.
Miss Barrett's elopement. [1929], New York 1930. As C. Lenanton.
'Fair stood the wind...'. 1930. As C. Lenanton.
Major Grant. [1931], New York 1932.
The empress. 1932, New York 1932.
The best of his family. 1933.
Over the water. 1935.
Prince Charles Edward. 1935 (Great Lives).
Ferry the fearless. 1936. For children.
Henrietta Maria. 1936, New York 1936. Biography.
Johel. 1937, New York 1937. For children, sequel to Ferry the fearless, above.
Robin Hood, the prince of outlaws. 1937, New York 1937. For children.
Elizabeth of Bohemia. 1938, 1964 (rev). Biography.
Alfred, king of the English. 1939, New York 1940. For children.
Baltic spy. [1940]. For children.
Nothing to report. 1940.
Britain against Napoleon. 1942, Garden City NY 1942 (as Napoleon at the Channel).
Somewhere in England. 1943. Non-fiction.
Nelson. Garden City NY 1946, London [1947]. Biography.
Sir John Moore. 1953. Biography.
Lord Nelson. 1954 (Brief Lives).
David Garrick. [1958]. Biography.
Mary of Modena. 1962. Biography.
Ayot Rectory. 1965. Biography of Mary Sneade Brown, based on the ms memoir by her daughter Ellen Olive.
Napoleon's viceroy, Eugène de Beauharnais. 1966. Biography.
The Gascoyne heiress: the life and diaries of Frances Mary Gascoyne-Cecil 1802–39. 1968.

'GEORGE ORWELL', ERIC ARTHUR BLAIR
1903–50

The Orwell Archive at University College London contains letters, mss and unpbd material, and attempts completeness in work pbd by and on Orwell. Other collections of letters are in the Berg Collection, New York Public Library, and the Humanities Research Center, University of Texas.

Collections and Selections

Collected essays. 1961, 1961 (2nd edn) (adds Rudyard Kipling, and Reflections on Gandhi).
Decline of the English murder, and other essays. 1965 (Penguin).

Collected essays, journalism and letters. Ed Sonia Orwell and I. Angus 4 vols 1968, 1970 (Penguin).

§1

Down and out in Paris and London. 1933, New York 1933. Autobiographical.

Burmese days. New York 1934, London 1935 (with slight alterations), 1944 (restoring original text) (Penguin).

A clergyman's daughter. 1935, New York 1936.

Keep the aspidistra flying. 1936, New York 1956.

The road to Wigan pier. 1937, 1937 (Left Book Club edn, with foreword by V. Gollancz), New York 1958 (with Gollancz's foreword), London 1965 (with introd by R. Hoggart).

Homage to Catalonia. 1938, New York 1952 (with introd by L. Trilling).

Coming up for air. 1939, New York 1950.

Inside the whale, and other essays. 1940.

The lion and the unicorn: socialism and the English genius. 1941 (Searchlight Books 1).

Animal farm: a fairy story. 1945, New York 1946, 1956 (with introd by C. M. Woodhouse), London 1960 (with introd by L. Brander).

Critical essays. 1946, New York 1946 (as Dickens, Dali and others: studies in popular culture).

James Burnham and the managerial revolution. 1946. First pbd in Polemic as Second thoughts on James Burnham.

The English people. 1947 (Britain in Pictures).

Politics and the English language. Evansville Indiana 1947. First pbd in Horizon.

British pamphleteers: 1, From the sixteenth century to the French revolution. Ed Orwell and R. Reynolds 1948. Introd by Orwell.

Nineteen eighty-four. 1949, New York 1949, 1961 (with afterword by E. Fromm), 1963 (ed I. Howe, with sources and selected criticism), London 1965 (with introd by S. Spender).

Shooting an elephant, and other essays. 1950, New York 1950.

Such, such were the joys. New York 1953, London 1953 (as England your England, and other essays). The London edn omits 'Such such were the joys' and adds North and south, and Down the mine (both from The road to Wigan pier).

With T. R. Fyvel, Orwell edited a series of 10 Searchlight books 1941-3. He wrote forewords for 2 of them: The end of the 'old school tie', by T. C. Worsley, and The case for African freedom, by J. Cary. He was literary editor of Tribune 1943-5, writing the weekly column 'As I please' (after his resignation irregularly till 1947). He contributed regularly to Adelphi 1930-5, New English Weekly 1935-40, Time & Tide 1936-43, Observer and Manchester Evening News 1943-6. See the chronologies appended to each vol of Collected essays, 1968.

§2

See Orwell: the critical heritage, *ed J. Meyers 1975.*

Connolly, C. A Georgian boyhood. In his Enemies of promise, 1938, New York 1948 (rev).

—— In his Previous convictions, 1963.

Lewis, W. Orwell: or two and two make four. In his The writer and the absolute, 1952.

Trilling, L. Orwell and the politics of truth. Commentary 13 1952; rptd as introd to Homage to Catalonia, 1952, above, and in his Opposing self, New York 1955.

Hopkinson, T. George Orwell. 1953, 1955 (rev), 1962 (rev) (Br Council pamphlet).

Atkins, J. A. Orwell: a literary study. 1954.

Brander, L. George Orwell. 1954.

Hollis, C. A study of Orwell, the man and his works. 1956.

Warburg, F. J. In his An occupation for gentlemen, 1959. Reminiscences of Orwell by his publisher.

Rees, R. Orwell: fugitive from the camp of victory. 1961, Carbondale 1962 (with preface by H. T. Moore).

Thomas, E. M. Orwell. Edinburgh 1965 (Writers & Critics).

Woodcock, G. The crystal spirit: a study of Orwell. Boston 1966, London 1967 (abridged).

Alldritt, K. The making of Orwell: an essay in literary history. 1969.

Gross, M. (ed). The world of Orwell. 1971.

Stansky, P. and W. Abrahams. The unknown Orwell. 1972; Orwell: the transformation, 1979.

Watson, G. In his Politics and literature, 1977.

MERVYN LAURENCE PEAKE
1911–68

Captain Slaughterboard drops anchor. 1939, 1945 (rev), 1967 (rev), New York 1967. Story for children.

Shapes and sounds. [1941]. Verse.

Rhymes without reason. 1944.

The craft of the lead pencil. 1946. Non-fiction.

Titus Groan. 1946, New York 1946 (as Titus Groan: a Gothic novel).

Letters from a lost uncle. 1948. Story for children.

Drawings by Mervyn Peake. 1949 (for Sept 1950).

The glassblowers. 1950. Verse.

Gormenghast. 1950. Sequel to Titus Groan, above.

Mr Pye. 1953.

Figures of speech. 1954. Humorous drawings.

Sometime, never: three tales of imagination by W. Golding, J. Wyndham, M. Peake. 1956. Contains Boy in darkness, by Peake.

Titus alone. 1959. Sequel to Titus Groan and Gormenghast, above.

The rhyme of the flying bomb. 1962.

Poems and drawings. 1965 (150 copies).

A reverie of bone and other poems. 1967 (320 copies).

Peake's progress: selected writings and drawings. Ed M. Gilmore 1978. Poems, stories, etc ed by his widow.

Peake illustrated most of his books. He also illustrated books by other authors. A play, The wit to woo, was produced at the Arts Theatre 12 March 1957.

WILLIAM CHARLES FRANKLYN PLOMER
1903–73

Collections and Selections

Selected poems. 1940.

A choice of ballads. 1960 (priv ptd).

Collected poems. 1960, 1973 (enlarged).

§1

Turbott Wolfe. 1926, New York [1926], London 1965 (with introd by L. van der Post), New York 1965.

I speak of Africa. 1927. Contains 3 short novels: Portraits in the nude, Uda Masondo, Black peril; 7 short stories; 2 plays for puppets.

Notes for poems. 1927.

The family tree. 1929. Verse

Paper houses. 1929, New York 1929, London 1943 (with new introd.). Stories.

Sado. 1931, New York [1932] (as They never came back).

The case is altered. 1932, New York [1932].

The fivefold screen. 1932, New York 1932. Verse.

Cecil Rhodes. 1933, New York 1933.

The child of Queen Victoria, and other stories. 1933.
The invaders. 1934.
Ali the lion: Ali of Tebeleni, pasha of Jannina, 1741–1822. 1936.
Visiting the caves. 1936. Verse.
Double lives: an autobiography. 1943, 1950 (rev), New York 1956 (rev).
Curious relations. By 'William d'Arfey' [A. Butts]. Ed W. Plomer. 1945, New York 1947, London 1968 (as by Plomer and Butts). Stories.
The Dorking thigh and other satires. 1945. Verse.
Four countries. 1949. Stories, some rptd from I speak of Africa, Paper houses, The child of Queen Victoria.
Museum pieces. 1952, New York [1954].
Gloriana: opera in 3 acts. Libretto by W. Plomer. [1953].
A shot in the park. 1955, New York 1955 (as Borderline ballads). Verse.
At home: memoirs. 1958, New York [1958].
Conversation with my younger self. Ewelme 1963 (priv ptd, 25 copies).
Curlew river: a parable for church performance, set to music by B. Britten. 1964. Based on the Japanese No play, Sumidagawa, by Juro Motomasa.
The burning fiery furnace: second parable for church performance, set to music by B. Britten. 1966.
Taste and remember. 1966. Verse.
The prodigal son: third parable for church performance, set to music by B. Britten. 1968.
Autobiography. 1975.
Plomer edited a number of diaries, Japanese lady in Europe, by H. Ichikawa, 1937; Kilvert's diary, 3 vols 1938–40; and A message in code: the diary of Richard Rumbold 1932–60, [1964]. With Roy Campbell he edited the magazine Voorslag, Durban 1926–7.

ANTHONY DYMOKE POWELL
b. 1905

Afternoon men. 1931, Boston 1963.
Venusberg. 1932, New York 1952 (with Agents and patients, below, as Two novels).
From a view to a death. 1933.
Caledonia: a fragment. 1934 (priv ptd). Verse satire.
Agents and patients. 1936, New York 1952 (with Venusberg, above, as Two novels).
What's become of Waring? 1939, Boston 1963.
John Aubrey and his friends. 1948, New York 1948, London 1963 (rev), New York 1963. Non-fiction.
A question of upbringing. 1951, New York 1951. This and the following novels form the Music of time sequence.
A buyer's market. 1952, New York 1953.
The acceptance world. 1955, New York [1955].
At Lady Molly's. 1957, Boston [1957].
Casanova's Chinese restaurant. 1960, Boston 1960.
A dance to the music of time. 1962, Boston 1962. Contains A question of upbringing, A buyer's market and The acceptance world, above.
The kindly ones. 1962, Boston 1962.
A dance to the music of time: second movement. Boston 1964. Contains At Lady Molly's, Casanova's Chinese Restaurant, The kindly ones, above.
The valley of bones. 1964, Boston 1964.
The soldier's art. 1966, Boston 1966.
The military philosophers. 1968, Boston 1969.
Books do furnish a room. 1971.
Temporary kings. 1973.
Hearing secret harmonies. 1975.
To keep the ball rolling: memoirs. 2 vols 1976–8.

Powell edited Barnard letters 1778–1824, 1928; Novels of high society from the Victorian age, 1947; Brief lives and other selected writings by John Aubrey, 1949. He contributed a preface to The complete Ronald Firbank, 1961.

JOHN COWPER POWYS
1872–1963

Bibliographies

Langridge, D. W. Powys: a record of achievement. 1966. Includes contributions to periodicals, reviews of Powys' works and other recording material: also prints lecture-synopses and a number of early poems.

§ I

Odes and other poems. 1896.
Poems. 1899.
The war and culture: a reply to Professor Münsterberg. New York 1914, London 1915 (as The menace of German culture). Reply to Münsterberg's War and America.
Visions and revisions: a book of literary devotions. New York 1915, London 1915, 1955 (with new introd by Powys). Critical essays.
Wood and stone: a romance. New York 1915, London 1917.
Confessions of two brothers: J. C. Powys, Llewellyn (sic) Powys. Rochester NY 1916.
Wolf's-bane: rhymes. New York 1916, London [1916].
One hundred best books, with commentary and an essay on books and reading. New York 1916.
Rodmoor: a romance. New York 1916.
Suspended judgments: essays on books and sensations. New York 1916. Some of these essays were rptd individually from 1923 at Girard Kansas in the Little Blue Book series.
Mandragora: poems. New York 1917.
The complex vision. New York 1920. Philosophy.
Samphire. New York 1922. Verse.
The art of happiness. Girard Kansas [1923]. Differs from 1935 book with same title.
Psychoanalysis and morality. San Francisco 1923.
Ducdame. New York 1925, London 1925.
The religion of a sceptic. New York 1925.
The secret of self development. Girard Kansas 1926. Essay.
The art of forgetting the unpleasant. Girard Kansas 1928. Essays.
Wolf Solent. 2 vols New York 1929, 1 vol London 1929, 1961 (with preface by Powys).
The meaning of culture. New York [1929], London 1930, New York 1939 (enlarged, with introd and conclusions by Powys), London 1940.
Debate! Is modern marriage a failure? New York 1930. With Bertrand Russell.
The owl, the duck, and—Miss Rowe! Miss Rowe! Chicago 1930 (250 copies).
In defence of sensuality. New York 1930, London 1930.
Dorothy M. Richardson. 1931. Expanded from articles in Adelphi 2 1931.
A Glastonbury romance. New York 1932, London 1933, 1955 (with preface by Powys).
A philosophy of solitude. New York 1933, London 1933 (with introd by Powys).
Autobiography. New York 1934, London 1934, 1967 (introd by J. B. Priestley).
Weymouth sands. New York 1934, London 1935 (as Jobber Skald), 1963 (as Weymouth sands). 1935 edn has changes in personal and place-names, restored in 1963.
The art of happiness. New York 1935, London 1935. Differs from 1923 book with same title.
Maiden Castle. New York 1936, London 1937, 1966 (with preface by M. Elwin).
Morwyn: or the vengeance of God. 1937.
The enjoyment of literature. New York 1938, London 1938 (with variations, as The pleasures of literature).
Owen Glendower: an historical novel. 2 vols New York [1940], 1 vol London 1941.

Mortal strife. 1942. Philosophy.

The art of growing old. 1944.

Pair Dadeni: or, 'The cauldron of rebirth'. Carmarthen 1946. Rptd from Wales 6 1946.

Dostoievsky, 1947.

Obstinate Cymric: essays 1935–47. Carmarthen 1947.

Rabelais: his life, the story told by him, selections therefrom newly translated, and an interpretation of his genius and his religion. 1948, New York 1951.

Porius: a romance of the dark ages. 1951, New York 1952.

The inmates. 1952, New York 1952.

In spite of: a philosophy for everyman. 1953, New York 1953.

Atlantis. 1954.

Lucifer: a poem. 1956. Written 1906.

The brazen head. 1956.

Up and out. 1957. Contains Up and out: a mystery tale; The mountains of the moon: a lunar love story.

Homer and the aether. 1959. Adaptation of the Iliad.

All or nothing. 1960.

Letters

Letters to Louis Wilkinson 1935–56. Ed L. Wilkinson 1958.

§2

Knight, G. W. Lawrence, Joyce and Powys. EC 11 1961.

—— The Saturnian quest: a chart of the prose works of Powys. 1964.

Churchill, R. C. The Powys brothers. 1962 (Br Council pamphlet).

REL 1963. J. C. Powys no.

Hopkins, K. The Powys brothers: a biographical appreciation. 1967.

Breckon, R. John Cowper Powys: the solitary giant. 1969.

THEODORE FRANCIS POWYS
1875–1953

Bibliographies

Riley, A. P. A bibliography of Powys. Hastings 1967. Includes trns, contributions to periodicals and anthologies, unpbd material.

§1

Some of Powys' stories were issued in limited edns of a few hundred copies; many stories were previously pbd in periodicals; some were pbd in periodicals and anthologies and have not yet been collected.

An interpretation of Genesis. [1907] (priv ptd, 100 copies), 1929, New York 1929.

The soliloquy of a hermit. New York 1916, London 1918 (as Soliloquies of a hermit), 1926 (rev).

The left leg: containing The left leg, Hester Dominy, Abraham men. 1923, New York 1923. Stories, previously unpbd.

Black bryony. 1923, New York 1923.

Mark only. [1924], New York 1924.

Mr Tasker's gods. 1925, New York 1925.

Mockery Gap. 1925, New York 1925.

A stubborn tree. 1926 (priv ptd, 100 copies). Story.

Innocent birds. 1926, New York 1926.

Feed my swine. 1926 (priv ptd, 100 copies). Story; rptd in The white paternoster, below.

A strong girl, and The bride: two stories. 1926 (priv ptd, 100 copies). A strong girl was previously unpbd; The bride was rptd in The white paternoster, below.

What lack I yet? 1927 (priv ptd, 100 copies), San Francisco 1927 (35 copies). Story, rptd in The white paternoster, below.

Mr Weston's good wine. 1927 (660 copies), New York 1928 (first trade edn), London 1928.

The rival pastors. 1927 (priv ptd, 100 copies). Story, rptd in The white paternoster, below.

The house with the echo: twenty-six stories. 1928, New York 1928.

The dewpond: a story. 1928 (Woburn Books 2). Not previously pbd; rptd in Bottle's path, below.

Fables. New York 1929, London 1929 (750 copies), 1930, 1934 (as No painted plumage). 19 stories not previously pbd.

Christ in the cupboard. 1930 (Blue Moon booklet 5). Story, rptd in The white paternoster, below.

The key of the field. 1930 (Furnival Books 1). With foreword by S. Townsend Warner. Story not previously pbd; rptd in Bottle's path, below.

Kindness in a corner. 1930, New York 1930.

The white paternoster, and other stories. 1930, New York 1931. Some stories not previously pbd.

Uriah on the hill. Cambridge 1930 (Minority pamphlet 2). Story, not previously pbd.

Uncle Dottery: a Christmas story. Bristol 1930. Not previously pbd.

The only penitent. 1931. Story; rptd in Bottle's path, below.

When thou wast naked: a story. Waltham St Lawrence 1931; rptd in Bottle's path, below.

Unclay. 1931, New York 1932.

The tithe barn, and The dove & the eagle. 1932. Stories; The dove and the eagle was rptd in Bottle's path, below.

The two thieves: In good earth, God, The two thieves. 1932, New York 1933. Stories.

Captain Patch: twenty-one stories. 1935. The shut door not previously pbd.

Make thyself many. 1935 (285 copies). Story; rptd in No want of meat, sir!, ed J. Hackney 1936.

Goat Green; or the better gift. 1937. Story; rptd in Bottle's path (as The better gift).

Bottle's path, and other stories. 1946.

Rosie Plum, and other stories. Ed F. Powys 1966, New York 1966.

Come and dine, and Tadnol. Ed A. P. Riley, Hastings 1967. 2 stories not previously pbd.

13 letters to L. C. Powys and Elizabeth Myers are ptd in Theodore: essays on T. F. Powys, ed B. Sewell 1964. Numerous letters are quoted in 'Louis Marlow', Welsh Ambassadors, 1936.

§2

Powys, J. C. In his Autobiography, 1934.

Coombes, H. T. F. Powys. 1960.

Hopkins, K. The second brother: a note on T. F. Powys. REL 4 1963.

—— The Powys brothers: a biographical appreciation. 1967.

Sewell, B. (ed). Theodore: essays on T. F. Powys. Aylesford 1964. Also contains a story by Powys, The useless woman, and a number of letters.

JOHN BOYNTON PRIESTLEY
b. 1894

A substantial collection of Priestley typescripts is in the University of Texas Humanities Research Center.

Collections and Selections

Works. 5 vols 1931–7.

Plays. 3 vols 1948–50, New York 1950–2 (vol 1 as Seven plays).

Essays of five decades. Ed S. Cooper, Boston 1968, London 1969.

§1

The chapman of rhymes. 1918.

Brief diversions: being tales, travesties and epigrams. Cambridge 1922. Many items from Cambridge Rev.

Papers from Lilliput. Cambridge 1922. Essays rptd from various periodicals.

I for one. 1923, New York 1924. Essays rptd from Challenge.

Figures in modern literature. 1924, New York 1924. Essays, mostly rptd from London Mercury.

The English comic characters. 1925, New York 1925. Essays.

George Meredith. 1926 (EML), New York 1926.

Talking. 1926, New York 1926.

Adam in moonshine. 1927, New York 1927.

Benighted. 1927, New York 1928 (as The old dark house).

The English novel. 1927, 1935 (rev).

Open house: a book of essays. 1927, New York 1927. Rptd from Saturday Rev.

Thomas Love Peacock. 1927 (EML), New York 1927, London 1966 (introd by J. I. M. Stewart).

Apes and angels: a book of essays. 1928.

The balconinny, and other essays. 1929, New York 1930. Rptd from Saturday Rev.

English humour. 1929, New York 1929.

Farthing Hall. 1929, Garden City NY 1929. With H. Walpole.

The good companions. 1929, New York 1929. For the dramatization, with E. Knoblock, see Plays, below.

Angel Pavement. 1930, New York 1930.

The town major of Miraucourt. 1930. Story.

Far away. 1932, New York 1932.

Self-selected essays. 1932, New York 1932. More than half previously uncollected.

Albert goes through. 1933, New York 1933. Story.

I'll tell you everything: a frolic. 1933, New York 1933. With G. Bullett.

Wonder hero. 1933, New York 1933.

English journey: being a rambling but truthful account of what one man saw and heard and felt and thought during a journey through England during the autumn of the year 1933. 1934, New York 1934.

They walk in the city: the lovers in the stone forest. 1936, New York 1936.

Midnight on the desert: a chapter of autobiography. 1937, New York 1937.

The doomsday men: an adventure. 1938, New York 1938.

Let the people sing. 1939, New York 1940.

Rain upon Godshill: a further chapter of autobiography. 1939, New York 1939.

Britain speaks. New York 1940. Based on broadcast talks.

Postscripts. 1940. Broadcast talks.

Out of the people. 1941, New York 1941. Politics.

Black-out in Gretley: a story of—and for—wartime. 1942, New York 1942.

Britain at war. New York 1942.

British women go to war. [1943].

Daylight on Saturday: a novel about an aircraft factory. 1943, New York 1943.

Here are your answers. [1944]. Pamphlet.

Manpower. 1944.

Letter to a returning serviceman. 1945. Pamphlet.

Three men in new suits. 1945, New York 1945.

Bright day. 1946, New York 1946, London 1966 (EL) (with new introd by Priestley).

The new citizen. [1946]. Pamphlet.

Russian journey. 1946. Pamphlet.

The secret dream: an essay on Britain, America and Russia. 1946. Based on broadcast talks.

The arts under socialism. 1947.

Jenny Villiers: a story of the theatre. 1947, New York 1947.

Theatre outlook. 1947.

Delight. 1949, New York 1949.

Festival at Farbridge. 1951, New York 1951 (as Festival).

The other place, and other stories of the same sort. 1953, New York [1953].

Low notes on a high level: a frolic. 1954, New York [1954].

The magicians. 1954, New York 1954.

Journey down a rainbow. 1955, New York [1955]. With J. Hawkes. Travel in New Mexico and Texas.

The writer in a changing society. Aldington 1956. Lecture.

The art of the dramatist: a lecture together with appendices and discursive notes. 1957.

Thoughts in the wilderness. 1957, New York [1957].

Topside, or the future of England: a dialogue. 1958.

The story of theatre. [1959], Garden City NY [1959] (as The wonderful world of the theatre); London 1969 (rev), Garden City NY 1969. For children.

Literature and western man. 1960, New York 1960.

William Hazlitt. 1960 (Br Council pamphlet).

Charles Dickens: a pictorial biography. [1961], New York 1962.

Saturn over the water. 1961, Garden City NY 1961.

Margin released: a writer's reminiscences and reflections. 1962, New York [1962].

The shapes of sleep: a topical tale. 1962, Garden City NY 1962.

Man and time. 1964, Garden City NY 1964. Philosophy.

Sir Michael and Sir George: a tale of COMSA and DISCUS and the New Elizabethans. 1964, Boston [1964] (with sub-title: a comedy of the New Elizabethans).

Lost empires: being Richard Herncastle's account of his life on the variety stage. 1965, Boston 1965.

The moments, and other pieces. 1966. Essays.

Salt is leaving. 1966.

It's an old country. 1967, Boston 1967.

All England listened: the wartime broadcasts of Priestley. Ed E. Sevareid, New York 1968.

The image men (Out of town; London end). 2 vols 1968, 1 vol Boston 1969.

Trumpets over the sea: being a rambling and egotistical account of the London Symphony Orchestra's engagement at Daytona Beach, Florida, in July–August 1967. 1968.

The prince of pleasure and his regency 1811–20. 1969, New York 1969.

Plays

Plays are listed in order of production, where known

The good companions: a play in two acts. (His Majesty's 14 May 1931). [1935] (French's Acting Edn). With E. Knoblock: based on the novel, 1929 above.

Dangerous corner: a play in three acts. (Lyric 17 May 1932). 1932, New York 1932, London [1933] (French's Acting Edn).

The roundabout: a comedy in three acts. (Playhouse, Liverpool 14 Dec 1932). [1933] (French's Acting Edn), 1933.

Laburnum Grove: an immoral comedy in three acts. (Duchess 28 Nov 1933). 1934, [1935] (French's Acting Edn).

Eden End: a play in three acts. (Duchess 13 Sept 1934), 1934, [1935] (French's Acting Edn).

Cornelius: a business affair in three transactions. (Duchess 20 March 1935). 1935, [1936] (French's Acting Edn).

Duet in floodlight: a comedy. (Apollo 4 June 1935). 1935.

Bees on the boat deck: a farcical tragedy in two acts. (Lyric 5 May 1936). 1936, [1936] (French's Acting Edn).

Spring tide: a play in three acts. (Duchess 15 July 1936). [1936], [1937] (French's Acting Edn). With G. Billam.

I have been here before: a play in three acts. (Royalty 22 Sept 1937). 1937, New York 1938, London 1939 (French's Acting Edn).

Time and the Conways: a play in three acts. (Duchess 26 Aug 1937). 1937, New York 1938, London 1939 (French's Acting Edn).

People at sea: a play in three acts. (Apollo 24 Nov 1937). 1937, [1938] (French's Acting Edn).
Mystery at Greenfingers: a comedy of detection. 1937. Test piece for News Chron Amateur Dramatic Contest.
Music at night. (Malvern Festival April 1938; Westminster 10 Oct 1939). In Three plays, 1943, below. Pbd separately 1947 (French's Acting Edn).
When we are married: a Yorkshire farcical comedy. (St Martin's 11 Oct 1938). [1938], [1940] (French's Acting Edn).
Johnson over Jordan: the play and all about it—an essay. (New 22 Feb 1939). 1939, New York [1939], [1941] (French's Standard Library Edn, with subtitle, A modern morality play in three acts).
The long mirror. (Playhouse, Oxford March 1940; Gateway 6 Nov 1945). In Three plays, 1943, below. Pbd separately 1947 (French's Acting Edn).
Goodnight children: a comedy of broadcasting. (New 5 Feb 1942). In Three comedies, 1945, below.
They came to a city. (Globe 21 April 1943). In Three plays, 1943, below. Pbd separately 1944 (French's Acting Edn).
Desert highway: a play in two acts and an interlude. (Theatre Royal, Bristol 13 Dec 1943; Playhouse 10 Feb 1944). 1944, [1944] (French's Acting Edn).
Three plays. 1943. Music at night; The long mirror; They came to a city.
How are they at home?: a topical comedy in two acts. (Apollo 4 May 1944). [1945] (French's Acting Edn).
The golden fleece: a comedy in three acts. In Three comedies, 1945, below. Pbd separately 1948 (French's Acting Edn). Performed under the title Bull market at the Bradford Civic Theatre and the Glasgow Citizens Theatre, 1944.
Three comedies. 1945. Goodnight children; The golden fleece; How are they at home?
Jenny Villiers: a play in two acts. (Theatre Royal, Bristol March 1946). Not pbd.
An inspector calls: a play in three acts. (New 1 Oct 1946). 1947, [1948] (French's Acting Edn).
Ever since paradise: an entertainment chiefly referring to love and marriage, in three acts. (New 4 June 1947). [1949] (French's Acting Edn).
The linden tree: a play in two acts and four scenes. (Duchess 15 Aug 1947). 1948, New York 1948, London [1948] (French's Acting Edn).
The Rose and Crown: a play in one act. 1947 (French's Acting Edn).
Home is tomorrow: a play in two acts. (Princes, Bradford 17 Oct 1948; Cambridge 4 Nov 1948). 1949, [1950] (French's Acting Edn).
The high Toby: a play for the toy theatre. [1948].
Summer day's dream: a play in two acts. (Prince's, Bradford 8 Aug 1949; St Martin's 8 Sept 1949). [1950] (French's Acting Edn).
The Olympians: opera in three acts. (Covent Garden 29 Sept 1949). [1950]. Music by Bliss. Vocal score.
Bright shadow: a play of detection in three acts. (Coliseum, Oldham 3 April 1950; Intimate, Palmers Green 10 April 1950). 1950 (French's Acting Edn).
Treasure on Pelican: a play in three acts. (Prince of Wales, Cardiff 4 Feb 1952). 1953 (for 1954) (Evans Plays).
Dragon's mouth: a dramatic quartet in two parts. (Festival, Malvern 13 April 1952; Winter Garden 13 May 1952). 1952, [1953] (French's Acting Edn). With J. Hawkes.
Mother's day: a comedy in one act. [1953] (French's Acting Edn).
Private rooms: a one act comedy in the Viennese style. [1953] (French's Acting Edn).
Try it again: a one act play. [1953] (French's Acting Edn).
The white countess. (Gaiety, Dublin 16 Feb 1954; Saville 24 March 1954). With J. Hawkes. Unpbd.
A glass of bitter: a play in one act. [1954] (French's Acting Edn).

The scandalous affair of Mr Kettle and Mrs Moon: a comedy in three acts. (Pleasure Gardens, Folkestone 22 Aug 1955; Duchess 1 Sept 1955). [1956].
Take the fool away. (Burgtheater, Vienna Feb 1956; Playhouse, Nottingham 28 Sept 1959). Unpbd.
These our actors. (Citizens, Glasgow 1 Oct 1956). Unpbd.
The glass cage: a play in two acts. (Piccadilly 26 April 1957). [1958] (French's Acting Edn).
A severed head: a play in three acts. (Criterion 27 June 1963). With Iris Murdoch; based on her novel of same title.
The pavilion of masks. (Old Vic, Bristol 7 Oct 1963). Unpbd.
Priestley also wrote a number of film scripts.

§2

Brown, I. J. B. Priestley. 1957, 1964 (rev) (Br Council pamphlet).
Evans, G. L. Priestley: the dramatist. 1964.

SIR VICTOR SAWDON PRITCHETT
b. 1900

Marching Spain. 1928. Travel.
Clare Drummer. 1929.
The Spanish virgin and other stories. 1930.
Shirley Sanz. 1932, Boston 1932 (as Elopement into exile).
Nothing like leather. 1935, New York 1935.
Dead man leading. 1937.
You make your own life. 1938. Stories.
In my good books. 1942. Essays.
It may never happen & other stories. 1945, New York 1947.
Build the ships: the official story of the shipyards in wartime. 1946.
The living novel. 1946, New York 1947, 1964 (rev, with contents of The working novelist, below, as The living novel & later appreciations). Essays.
Why do I write?: an exchange of views between Elizabeth Bowen, Graham Greene and V. S. Pritchett. 1948, New York 1948.
Mr Beluncle. 1951, New York 1951.
Books in general. 1953, New York 1953. Essays.
The Spanish temper. 1954, New York 1954. Non-fiction.
Collected stories. 1956.
When my girl comes home. 1961, New York 1961. Stories.
London perceived. [1962], New York 1962. Topography.
The key to my heart: a comedy in three parts. 1963, New York 1964. Stories.
Foreign faces. 1964, New York 1964 (as The offensive traveller). Travel.
New York proclaimed. [1965], New York 1965. Topography.
The working novelist. 1965. Essays.
Dublin: a portrait. 1967. Topography.
A cab at the door: an autobiography. 1968, New York 1968.
Blind love, and other stories. 1969.

Many of Pritchett's stories and essays were first pbd in New Statesman (*of which he was literary editor for two years shortly after World War II*).

BARBARA MARY CRAMPTON PYM
1913–80

Some tame gazelle. 1950.
Excellent women. 1952.
Jane and Prudence. 1953.
Less than angels. 1955, New York 1957.
A glass of blessings. 1958.
No fond return of love. 1961.

ARTHUR MICHELL RANSOME
1884–1967

§ 1

The souls of the streets, and other little papers. 1904.
The stone lady, ten little papers, and two mad stories. 1905.
Pond and stream. [1906].
The child's book of the seasons. [1906].
The things in our garden. [1906].
Highways and byways in fairyland. [1906].
Bohemia in London. 1907, New York 1907, London 1912 (rev).
A history of story-telling: studies in the development of narrative. 1909.
Edgar Allan Poe: a critical study. 1910, New York 1910.
The imp and the elf and the ogre. 1910. Reprints (rev) Pond and stream, The child's book of the seasons, The things in our garden.
The hoofmarks of the faun. 1911. Stories.
Oscar Wilde: a critical study. 1912, 1913 (rev), New York 1913.
Portraits and speculations. 1913.
The elixir of life. 1915.
Old Peter's Russian tales. 1916, New York 1917, London [1938] (with new preface).
Aladdin and his wonderful lamp, in rhyme. [1919].
Six weeks in Russia in 1919. 1919, New York 1919 (as Russia in 1919).
The soldier and death: a Russian folk tale told in English. 1920, New York 1922.
The crisis in Russia. 1921, New York 1921.
'Racundra's' first cruise. 1923, New York 1923. Autobiographical.
The Chinese puzzle. 1927. Non-fiction.
Rod and line: essays, together with Aksakov on fishing. 1929.
Swallows & Amazons. 1930, Philadelphia 1931.
Swallowdale. 1931, Philadelphia 1932.
Peter Duck. 1932, Philadelphia [1933].
Winter holiday. 1933, Philadelphia [1934].
Coot club. 1934, Philadelphia [1935].
Pigeon post. 1936, Philadelphia [1937].
We didn't mean to go to sea. 1937, New York 1938.
Secret water. 1939, New York 1940.
The big six. 1940, New York 1941.
Missee Lee. 1941, New York 1942.
The Picts and the martyrs: or not welcome at all. 1943, New York 1943.
Great Northern? 1947, New York 1948.
Mainly about fishing. 1959.

§ 2

Shelley, H. Arthur Ransome. 1960, 1968 (rev).

FORREST REID
1875–1947

§ 1

The kingdom of twilight. 1904.
The garden god: a tale of two boys. 1905.
The Bracknels: a family chronicle. 1911. See also Denis Bracknel, below.
Following darkness. 1912. See also Peter Waring, below.
The gentle lover: a comedy of middle age. 1913.
At the door of the gate. 1915, Boston 1916.
W. B. Yeats: a critical study. 1915.
The spring song. 1916, Boston 1917.
A garden by the sea: stories and sketches. Dublin and London 1918. Also includes verse.

Pirates of the spring. Dublin and London 1919, Boston 1920.
Pender among the residents. [1922], Boston 1923.
Apostate. 1926, Boston 1926. Autobiography.
Demophon: a traveller's tale. 1927.
Illustrators of the sixties. 1928. On the illustration of books and periodicals.
Walter de la Mare: a critical study. 1929.
Uncle Stephen. 1931.
Brian Westby. 1934.
The retreat: or the machinations of Henry. 1936.
Peter Waring. 1937. A rewritten version of Following darkness, 1912, above.
Private road. 1940. Autobiography.
Retrospective adventures. 1941. Essays and stories.
Notes and impressions. Newcastle Co Down 1942.
Poems from the Greek Anthology. Tr Reid 1943.
Young Tom: or very mixed company. 1944.
The milk of paradise: some thoughts on poetry. 1946.
Denis Bracknel. 1947. A 'completely rewritten' version of The Bracknels, 1911, above.

§ 2

Forster, E. M. In his Abinger harvest, 1936.
—— In his Two cheers for democracy, 1951.
Forrest Reid memorial: addresses [by E. M. Forster, W. de la Mare, S. Gilbert]. 1952.
Burlingham, R. Forrest Reid: a portrait and a study. 1953.
Putt, S. G. Pan in Ulster: Reid. In his Scholars of the heart, 1962.

JEAN RHYS
1894–1979

The left bank and other stories, with a preface by F. M. Ford. 1927.
Postures. 1928, New York 1929 (as Quartet).
After leaving Mr Mackenzie. 1931, New York 1931.
Voyage in the dark. 1934, New York 1935.
Good morning, midnight. 1939.
The wide Sargasso Sea. 1966, New York 1967. With introd by F. Wyndham.
Tigers are better-looking. 1968. Stories.

DOROTHY MILLER RICHARDSON
1873–1957

§ 1

The Quakers past and present. 1914, New York 1914.
Pilgrimage. Originally pbd as separate vols, as follows:
Pointed roofs. 1915, New York 1916. With introd by J. D. Beresford.
Backwater. 1916, New York 1917.
Honeycomb. 1917, New York 1919.
Interim. 1919, New York 1920. Serialized in Little Rev 6–7 1919–20.
The tunnel. 1919, New York 1919.
Deadlock. 1921, New York 1921 (with foreword by W. Follett).
Revolving lights. 1923, New York 1923.
The trap. 1925, New York 1925.
Oberland. 1927, New York 1928.
Dawn's left hand. 1931, New York 1931.
Clear horizon. 1935, New York 1936.
Collected edn, with final section Dimple hill, and with foreword by the author. 4 vols 1938, New York 1938, London 1967 (with introd by W. Allen and a final section, March moonlight, previously unpbd in book form).

John Austen and the inseparables. 1930. Essay on book illustration.

§2

Powys, J. C. Dorothy M. Richardson. 1931.
Edel, L. Dorothy M. Richardson. Modern Fiction Stud 4 1958.
—— In his The modern psychological novel, New York 1964.
Trickett, R. The living dead V: Dorothy Richardson. London Mag 6 1959.
Blake, C. R. Dorothy Richardson. Ann Arbor [1960].
Gregory, H. Dorothy Richardson: an adventure in self-discovery. New York 1967.

FREDERICK WILLIAM SERAFINO AUSTIN LEWIS MARY ROLFE ('BARON CORVO')
1860–1913

Bibliographies

Woolf, C. A bibliography of Frederick Rolfe, Baron Corvo. 1957, 1969 (rev) (Soho Bibliographies).

§1

Tarcissus: the boy martyr of Rome in the Diocletian persecution, by F.W.R. [1880]. Verse.
Stories Toto told me. 1898, New York 1898. First pbd in Yellow Book.
The attack on St Winefride's well: or Holywell gone mad. [1898]. Anon; attributed to Corvo by Woolf.
In his own image. 1901, 1924 (with introd by S. Leslie), New York 1925. Stories.
Chronicles of the House of Borgia. 1901, New York 1901, 1931 (as A history of the Borgias, with introd by S. Leslie).
Hadrian the seventh. 1904, New York 1925, 1953 (with introd by H. Weinstock). Adapted as play, The play of Hadrian the seventh, by P. Luke, 1968, New York 1969.
Don Tarquinio: a kataleptic phantasmatic romance. 1905.
The weird of the wanderer: being the papyrus records of some incidents in one of the previous lives of Mr Nicholas Crabbe here produced by Prospero and Caliban. 1912. With C. H. C. Pirie-Gordon.
The bull against the enemy of the Anglica-race. 1929 (priv ptd, 50 copies). Attack on Northcliffe, rptd in Symons, Quest for Corvo, 1955.
The desire and pursuit of the whole: a romance of modern Venice. 1934 (with introd by A. J. A. Symons), 1953 (with foreword by W. H. Auden), New York 1953.
Hubert's Arthur: being certain curious documents found among the literary remains of Mr N. C., here produced by Prospero and Caliban. Ed A. J. A. Symons 1935.
Three tales of Venice. [1950] (150 copies). First pbd in Blackwood's Mag 1913.
Amico di Sandro: a fragment of a novel. 1951 (priv ptd, 150 copies).
The cardinal prefect of propaganda, and other stories. 1957. Introd by C. Woolf; first pbd in various periodicals. 250 copies.
Nicholas Crabbe: or the one and the many. Ed C. Woolf 1958.
Don Renato: an ideal content. Ed C. Woolf 1963 (200 copies).

Letters

Letters to Grant Richards. Hurst 1952.
Letters to C. H. C. Pirie-Gordon. Ed C. Woolf and epilogue by Pirie-Gordon 1959.
Letters to Leonard Moore. Ed C. Woolf and B. W. Korn, and epilogue by L. Moore 1960.

Letters to R. M. Dawkins. Ed C. Woolf and epilogue by L. M. Ragg 1962.
Without prejudice: one hundred letters to John Lane. Ed C. Woolf 1963 (priv ptd).
The Venice letters; selected. Ed C. Woolf. Art & Lit no 5 1965, 1974.

§2

Lawrence, D. H. Adelphi 3 1925; rptd in his Phoenix, 1936.
Symons, A. J. A. Frederick Baron Corvo. 1927 (Sette of Odd Volumes 81).
—— The quest for Corvo. 1934, 1952 (introd by N. Birkett, memoir by S. Leslie, appendix of Holywell letters), 1955 (preface by J. Symons and 2 appendices).
Greene, G. Spectator 16 Feb 1934; rptd in his Lost childhood, 1951.
Woolf, C. and B. Sewell (ed). Corvo 1860–1960: a collection of essays by various hands. Aylesford 1961 (300 copies), London 1965 (as New quests for Corvo).
Woolf, C. and B. Sewell. The clerk without a benefice: a study of Fr Rolfe Baron Corvo's conversion and vocation. Aylesford 1964.
Johnson, P. H. The fascination of the paranoid personality: Baron Corvo. E & S new ser 16 1963.

EDWARD CHARLES SACKVILLE-WEST
1901–65

Piano quintet. 1925, New York 1925.
The ruin: a Gothic novel. 1926, New York 1927.
The apology of Arthur Rimbaud: a dialogue. 1927. Essay.
Mandrake over the water-carrier. 1928.
Simpson: a life. 1931, New York 1931 London 1951 (rev). Fiction.
The sun in Capricorn: a recital. 1934.
A flame in sunlight: the life and work of Thomas de Quincey. 1936, New Haven Conn 1936 (as Thomas de Quincey).
Graham Sutherland. 1943, 1955 (rev) (Penguin Modern Painters).
The rescue: a melodrama for broadcasting based on Homer's Odyssey. 1945.
And so to bed: an album compiled from his BBC feature by E. Sackville-West. 1947.
Inclinations. 1949. Essays, rptd (rev) from various jnls.

'SAKI', HECTOR HUGH MUNRO
1870–1916

Collections and Selections

Works. 8 vols 1926–7, New York 1927–9.
The short stories of Saki complete, with introduction by C. Morley. New York 1930, [London] 1930.
The novels and plays of Saki. 1933, New York 1933.
Selected stories. 1939.
The best of Saki, with introduction by G. Greene 1950, New York 1961.
The Bodley Head Saki, selected and introduced by J. W. Lambert. 1963, 2 vols [The unbearable Bassington and other stories; Saki: selected from Beasts and super-beasts, and other stories] 1965.

§1

The rise of the Russian empire. 1900.

The Westminster Alice. 1902, 1927 (Works, introd by J. A. Spender), New York 1929. Political satires, rptd from Westminster Gazette.

Reginald. 1904, 1921 (with Reginald in Russia), New York 1921, London 1926 (Works, introd by H. Walpole), New York 1928.

Reginald in Russia and other sketches. 1910, 1921 (with Reginald), New York 1921, London 1926 (Works, introd by H. Walpole), New York 1928. Stories, with playlet The baker's dozen.

The chronicles of Clovis. 1912, New York 1912, London 1926 (Works, introd by A. A. Milne), New York 1927. Stories.

The unbearable Bassington. 1912, New York 1912, London 1926 (Works, introd by M. Baring), New York 1927, London 1947 (with introd by E. Waugh).

When William came: a story of London under the Hohenzollerns. 1914, New York 1914, London 1926 (Works, introd by Lord Charnwood), New York 1929.

Beasts and super-beasts. 1914, New York 1914, London 1926 (Works, introd by H. W. Nevinson), New York 1928. Stories.

The toys of peace, and other papers, with a memoir by R. Reynolds. 1919, New York 1919, London 1926 (Works, introd by G. K. Chesterton), New York 1928. Stories.

The square egg, and other sketches, with three plays; with a biography by his [i.e. Saki's] sister. 1924, 1926 (Works, introd by J. C. Squire), New York 1929.

The miracle-merchant. In One-act plays for stage and study, 8th ser ed Alice Gerstenberg, New York 1934.

§2

Greene, G. The burden of childhood. In his The lost childhood, 1951; rptd from The best of Saki, above.

Hudson, D. A little master. Spectator 30 May 1952. Correspondence followed during June from G. Greene and E. Munro.

Pritchett, V. S. The performing lynx. New Statesman 5 Jan 1957; rptd in his Working novelist, 1965.

Spears, G. J. The satire of Saki. New York [1963].

Gillen, C. H. H. H. Munro—Saki. New York [1969].

WILLIAM SANSOM
1912–76

Selections

Selected short stories, chosen by the author. 1960.

Stories. Ed E. Bowen [1963], Boston 1963.

§1

Jim Braidy: the story of Britain's firemen. 1943. With J. Gordon and S. Spender.

Fireman Flower and other stories. 1944, New York 1945.

Three: stories. 1946, New York 1947.

Westminster in war. 1947. Historical.

The equilibriad. 1948. Story.

Something terrible, something lovely. 1948, New York 1954. Stories.

South: aspects and images from Corsica, Italy and Southern France. 1948, New York 1950. Stories.

The body. 1949, New York 1949.

The passionate north. [1950], New York 1953. Stories.

The face of innocence. 1951, New York 1951.

A touch of the sun. 1952, New York 1958. Stories.

It was really Charlie's castle. 1953. Children's story.

The light that went out. 1953. Children's story.

Pleasures strange and simple. 1953. Essays.

A bed of roses. 1954, New York 1954.

Lord love us. 1954. Stories.

A contest of ladies. 1956, New York 1956.

The loving eye. 1956, New York [1956].

Among the dahlias, and other stories. 1957. Stories.

The cautious heart. 1958, New York 1958.

The icicle and the sun. 1958, New York 1959. Travel in Scandinavia and Finland.

The bay of Naples: introduction and commentaries. 1960, New York 1960. Photographs by K. Otto-Wasow.

Blue skies, brown studies. 1961, Boston 1961. Travel.

The last hours of Sandra Lee. 1961, Boston 1961, London 1964 (as The wild affair).

Away to it all. 1964, New York 1966. Travel.

The ulcerated milkman. 1966, New York 1966. Stories.

Christmas. 1968, New York 1968 (as A book of Christmas).

The Grand Tour today. 1968.

The vertical ladder, and other stories. 1969.

'SAPPER',
HERMAN CYRIL McNEILE
1888–1937

Selections

John Walters. [1927].

Bull-dog Drummond: his four rounds with Carl Peterson. [1929], New York 1930 (as Four rounds of Bull-dog Drummond).

Sapper's war stories, collected in one volume. [1930].

51 stories by Sapper: his one-man omnibus of thrill and adventure. 1934.

§1

The lieutenant and others. 1915. Stories.

Sergeant Michael Cassidy, RE. 1915, New York [1916] (as Michael Cassidy, Sergeant).

Men, women and guns. 1916, New York [1916]. Stories.

No man's land. 1917, New York [1917]. Stories.

The human touch. 1918, New York [1918]. Stories.

Mufti. 1919, New York [1919]. As McNeile.

Bull-dog Drummond. [1920], New York [1920]. As McNeile. As play, adapted by Sapper and G. Du Maurier, London [1925] (French's Acting Edn).

The man in ratcatcher, and other stories. [1921], New York [1921]. As McNeile.

The black gang. [1922], New York [1922]. As McNeile.

The dinner club: stories. [1923], New York [1923]. As McNeile.

Jim Maitland. [1923], New York [1924]. As McNeile.

The third round. [1924], New York 1924, [1924] (as Bull-dog Drummond's third round). As McNeile.

Out of the blue. 1925, New York [1925]. Stories.

The final count. [1926], New York [1926].

Jim Brent. [1926].

Shorty Bill. [1926].

Word of honour. [1926], New York [1926]. Stories.

The saving clause. [1927].

The female of the species. [1928], Garden City NY 1928, New York 1943 (as Bulldog Drummond—and the female of the species).

Temple Tower. 1929, Garden City NY 1929.

The finger of fate. [1930], Garden City NY [1931]. Stories.

Tiny Carteret. [1930], Garden City NY 1930.

The island of terror. 1931.

The return of Bull-dog Drummond. 1932, Garden City NY [1932] (as Bulldog Drummond returns).

Bulldog Drummond strikes back. Garden City NY 1933, London 1934 (as Knock-out).

Ronald Standish. 1933.

When Carruthers laughed. 1934.

Bulldog Drummond at bay. 1935, Garden City NY 1935.

Ask for Ronald Standish. 1936, New York 1936. Stories.

Challenge: a Bulldog Drummond novel. 1937, Garden City 1937.

A number of individual stories were pbd separately in America. After McNeile's death the Bulldog Drummond ser was continued, under the 'Sapper' pseudonym, by Gerard T. Fairlie.

DOROTHY LEIGH SAYERS
1893–1957

Op 1. Oxford 1916, New York 1916. Verse.
Catholic tales and Christian songs. Oxford 1918, New York 1918. Verse.
Whose body? 1923, New York [1923].
Clouds of witness. 1926, New York 1927, 1938 (with The documents in the case).
Unnatural death. 1927, New York 1928 (as The Dawson pedigree), 1938 (with Lord Peter views the body).
Lord Peter views the body. 1928, New York 1929, 1938 (with The Dawson pedigree).
The unpleasantness at the Bellona Club. 1928, New York 1928.
The documents in the case. 1930, New York 1931, 1938 (with Clouds of witness). With 'Robert Eustace' (E. Rawlins).
Strong poison. 1930, New York 1930, 1936 (with Have his carcase).
The five red herrings. 1931, New York 1931 (as Suspicious characters.)
The floating admiral, by certain members of the Detection Club [D. L. Sayers et al]. 1931.
Have his carcase. 1932, New York 1932, 1936 (with Strong poison).
Ask a policeman. [1933]. By A. Berkeley, D. L. Sayers et al.
Hangman's holiday. 1933, New York 1933, 1938 (with Murder must advertise).
Murder must advertise: a detective story. 1933, New York 1933, 1938 (with Hangman's holiday,).
The nine tailors. 1934, New York 1934.
Gaudy night. 1935, New York 1936.
Papers relating to the family of Wimsey. Ed 'Matthew Wimsey' [D. L. Sayers] [c .1935] (priv ptd).
The murder of Julia Wallace. In The anatomy of murder: famous crimes considered by members of the Detection Club, 1936, New York 1937.
Busman's honeymoon: a love story with detective interruptions. 1937, New York [1937]. As play, with M. St C. Byrne, (Comedy 16 Dec 1936); in Famous plays of 1937, 1937.
The zeal of thy house. (Chapter House, Canterbury 12 June 1937; Westminster 29 March 1938). 1937, New York 1937. Verse play.
The greatest drama ever staged. 1938. On Easter.
He that should come: a nativity play in one act. (BBC Radio 25 Dec 1938). 1939.
The devil to pay: being the famous history of John Faustus [etc]: a stage-play. (Chapter House, Canterbury 10 June 1939; His Majesty's 20 July 1939). Canterbury 1939 (Acting Edn for the Festival of the Friends of Canterbury Cathedral), London 1939, New York 1939.
Double death: a murder story, by D. L. Sayers [et al]. 1939.
In the teeth of the evidence, and other stories. 1939, New York 1940.
Strong meat. 1939. Religious tract.
Begin here: a war-time essay. 1940, New York 1941.
Creed or chaos? [1940]. Lecture.
The mind of the maker. 1941, New York 1942. Religious tract.
The mysterious English. 1941 (Macmillan War pamphlets 10).
Why work? 1942. Lecture.
The man born to be king: a play-cycle on the life of Our Lord and Saviour Jesus Christ, written for broadcasting. Presented by the British Broadcasting Corporation Dec 1941–Oct 1942. 1943, New York 1949.

The other six deadly sins. 1943. Lecture.
Even the parrot: exemplary conversations for enlightened children. 1944.
The just vengeance: the Lichfield Festival Play for 1946. (Lichfield Cathedral 15 June 1946). 1946.
Unpopular opinions: twenty-one essays. 1946, New York 1947.
Creed or chaos? and other essays in popular theology. 1947, New York 1949.
The lost tools of learning. 1948. Lecture.
The emperor Constantine: a chronicle. 1951, New York 1951. Play.
Introductory papers on Dante. 1954, New York 1954. Preface by B. Reynolds.
Further papers on Dante. 1957, New York 1957.
The poetry of search and the poetry of statement, and other posthumous essays on literature, religion and language. 1963, New York 1969.
Dorothy Sayers tr Dante's Inferno *and* Purgatorio, *Thomas the Troubadour's* Romance of Tristan, *and* The song of Roland.

'NEVIL SHUTE', NEVIL SHUTE NORWAY
1899–1960

Marazan. 1926.
So disdained. 1928, Boston 1928 (as The mysterious aviator).
Lonely road. 1932, New York 1932.
Ruined city. 1938, New York 1938 (as Kindling).
What happened to the Corbetts. [1939], New York 1939 (as Ordeal).
Landfall: a Channel story. 1940, New York 1940.
An old captivity. 1940, New York 1940.
Pied piper. 1942, New York 1942, London 1956 (abridged).
Pastoral. 1944, New York 1944.
Most secret. 1945, New York 1945.
Vinland the good. 1946, New York 1946. Film-play.
The chequer board. 1947, New York 1947.
No highway. 1948, New York 1948, London 1953 (abridged).
A town like Alice. 1950, New York 1950 (as The legacy).
Round the bend. 1951, New York 1951.
The far country. 1952, New York 1952.
In the wet. 1953, New York 1953.
Slide rule: the autobiography of an engineer. 1954, New York 1954.
Requiem for a Wren. 1955, New York 1955 (as The breaking wave).
Beyond the black stump. 1956, New York 1956.
On the beach. 1957, New York 1957.
The rainbow and the rose. 1958, New York 1958.
Trustee from the toolroom. 1960, New York 1960.
Stephen Morris. 1961, New York 1961.

CHARLES PERCY SNOW, BARON SNOW
1905–80

Death under sail. 1932, New York [1932], London 1959 (rev).
New lives for old. 1933. Anon.
The search. 1934, Indianapolis [1935], London 1958 (rev and abridged).
Richard Aldington: an appreciation. 1938. Pamphlet.
Strangers and brothers. 1940, New York 1958. This and the following novels form the Strangers and brothers sequence.
The light and the dark. 1947, New York [1947].
Time of hope. 1949, New York 1950.
The masters. 1951, New York 1951. Dramatized by R. Millar: see The affair [and other plays], 1964, below.

The new men. 1954, New York 1955. Dramatized by R. Millar: *see* The affair [and other plays], 1964, below.

Homecomings. 1956, New York 1956 (as Homecoming).

The conscience of the rich. 1958, New York 1958.

The two cultures and the scientific revolution. Cambridge 1959 (Rede lecture), 1964 (with A second look), New York 1964. *See* F. R. Leavis, Two cultures? the significance of C. P. Snow, 1962; D. K. Cornelius and E. St Vincent (ed), Cultures in conflict: perspectives on the Snow-Leavis controversy, Chicago [1964].

The affair. 1960, New York 1960. Dramatized by R. Millar: *see* The affair [and other plays], 1964, below.

Science and government. 1961, Cambridge Mass 1961, New York 1963 (with new appendix), London 1963.

Magnanimity. 1962. Rectorial address, University of St Andrews.

A postscript to Science and government. 1962.

Recent thoughts on the two cultures. [1962]. Lecture.

The affair; The new men; The masters: three plays by R. Millar with preface by Snow. 1964.

Corridors of power. 1964, New York 1964.

Variety of men. 1967, New York [1967]. Biographical sketches.

Sleep of reason. [1968], New York 1969.

The state of seige. New York 1969. Lectures.

Last things. 1970. Final novel in Strangers and brothers sequence.

Trollope. 1975.

Snow collaborated in a series of one-act plays with Pamela Hansford Johnson, contributed to Proc Royal Soc 1928–35, and edited Cambridge Library of Modern Science 1938–48.

EDITH ŒNONE SOMERVILLE
1858–1949
and
'MARTIN ROSS'
(VIOLET FLORENCE MARTIN)
1862–1915

Mss described as 'The Somerville and Ross papers' were sold at Sotheby's on 9 July 1968. Some mss of Violet Martin were sold at Sotheby's on 10 Dec 1968. Many were acquired for Queen's Univ Belfast.

Collections and Selections

Collected edition. 7 vols 1910.

The Irish R.M., and his experiences. 1928, 1956 (as The Irish R.M. complete).

§1

An Irish cousin. 2 vols 1889 (as by 'Geilles Herring' and Martin Ross), 1889 (as by 'Viva Graham' and Martin Ross), 1903 (rev, as by Somerville and Ross).

Naboth's vineyard. 1891.

In the vine country. 1893. Travel in France.

Through Connemara in a governess cart, by the authors of An Irish cousin. 1893.

The real Charlotte. 3 vols 1894, 1 vol [1919].

Beggars on horseback: a riding tour in North Wales. 1895. As by Ross and Somerville.

The silver fox. 1898 (as by Ross and Somerville), 1902 (rev), [1919] (as by Somerville and Ross).

Some experiences of an Irish R.M. 1899. Stories.

A Patrick's Day hunt. [1902]. Story by Ross, illustr Somerville.

All on the Irish shore: Irish sketches. 1903.

Slipper's ABC of foxhunting. 1903. Drawings and verse by Somerville.

Some Irish yesterdays. 1906, New York 1906. Essays.

Further experiences of an Irish R.M. 1908, New York 1908. Stories.

Dan Russel the fox: an episode in the life of Miss Rowan. 1911, New York 1912.

The story of the discontented little elephant. 1912, New York 1912. Children's story, by Somerville.

In Mr Knox's country. 1915. Irish R.M. stories.

Irish memories. 1917, New York 1918. Autobiography.

Mount music. 1919, New York 1920.

Stray-aways. 1920. Essays.

An enthusiast. 1921, New York 1921.

Wheel-tracks. 1923.

The big house of Inver. 1925, Garden City NY 1925.

French leave. 1928, Boston 1928.

The States through Irish eyes. Boston 1930, London 1931. By Somerville.

An incorruptible Irishman: being an account of Chief Justice Charles Kendal Bushe and of his wife, Nancy Crampton, and their times 1767–1843. 1932, Boston 1932.

The smile and the tear. 1933, Boston 1933. Essays.

Little Red Riding Hood in Kerry. 1934 (priv ptd, 100 copies). Story, rptd in The sweet cry of hounds, below.

The sweet cry of hounds. 1936, Boston 1937. Stories.

Sarah's youth. 1938.

Records of the Somerville family of Castlehaven and Drishane from 1174 to 1940. Cork 1940 (priv ptd, 200 copies). By E. Œ. Somerville and B. T. Somerville.

Notions in garrison. 1941. Essays.

'Happy days!' essays of sorts. 1946.

Miss Somerville edited the Mark Twain birthday book, 1885, *and* Notes of the horn: hunting verse, old and new, 1934.

§2

Pritchett, V. S. The Irish R.M. In his The living novel, 1946.

Cummins, G. Dr E. Œ. Somerville: a biography. 1952.

Collis, M. Somerville and Ross: a biography. 1968.

Institute of Irish Studies, The Queen's University Belfast. Somerville and Ross: a symposium. Belfast 1969.

ROBERT HOWARD SPRING
1889–1965

Darkie and Co. 1932. For children.

Shabby tiger. 1934, New York [1935].

Rachel Rosing. 1935, New York [1936].

Sampson's circus. 1936. For children.

Book parade. 1938. Essays and reviews.

O Absalom! 1938, New York 1938 (as My son, my son!), London 1957.

Heaven lies about us: a fragment of infancy. 1939, New York 1939. Autobiography.

Tumbledown Dick: all people and no plot. 1939, New York 1940. For children.

All they like sheep. 1940. On German propaganda.

Fame is the spur. 1940, New York 1940.

This war we wage. 1941. Non-fiction, with Herbert Morrison and E. M. Delafield.

In the meantime. 1942. Autobiography.

Hard facts. 1944, New York 1944.

And another thing—. 1946, New York 1946. The author's religious experiences.

Dunkerleys. 1946, New York 1947. Sequel to Hard facts.

There is no armour. 1948, New York [1948].

Christmas honeymoon. [1949].

The houses in between. 1951, New York 1952.

Jinny Morgan: a play in 3 acts. 1952 (acting edn). Rptd in Three plays, below.

A sunset touch. 1953, New York 1953.

Three plays: Jinny Morgan; The gentle assassin; St George at the Dragon. 1953.

These lovers fled away. 1955, New York 1955.

Time and the hour. 1957, New York [1957].

All the day long. 1959, New York 1960.

I met a lady. 1961, New York 1961.

Winds of the day. 1964, New York 1965.

CHRISTINA ELLEN STEAD
b. 1902

The Salzburg tales. 1934, New York 1934.
Seven poor men of Sydney. 1934, New York 1935.
The beauties and furies. 1936, New York 1936.
House of all nations. 1938, New York [1938].
The man who loved children. New York 1940, London 1941, New York 1965 (with introd by R. Jarrell), London 1966.
For love alone. New York 1944, London 1945.
Letty Fox, her luck. New York 1946, London 1947.
A little tea, a little chat. New York 1948.
The people with the dogs. Boston 1952.
Dark places of the heart. New York 1966, London 1967 (as Cotters' England).
The puzzle-headed girl: four novellas. New York 1967.

FRANK ARTHUR SWINNERTON
b. 1884

Collections

The novels: uniform edition. 1934–. With prefatory notes.

§1

The merry heart: a gentle melodrama. 1909, Garden City NY 1929.
The young idea: a comedy of environment. 1910, Garden City NY 1930.
The casement: a diversion. 1911, New York 1927.
George Gissing: a critical study. [1912], New York [1923], London 1924 (with preface by author).
The happy family. 1912, New York [1912].
On the staircase. 1914, New York [1914].
R. L. Stevenson: a critical study. 1914, New York [1923].
The chaste wife. 1916, New York [1917].
Nocturne. 1917, New York [1917], London 1918 (with preface by H. G. Wells), Oxford 1937 (WC, with introd by author).
Shops and houses. 1918, New York [1918].
Women. 1918, New York 1919. Non-fiction. Anon.
September. 1919, New York [1919].
Coquette. 1921, New York [1921].
The three lovers. New York [1922], London 1923.
Young Felix. [1923], New York [1923].
The elder sister. [1925], New York [1925].
Summer storm. [1926], New York [1926].
Tokefield papers. 1927, New York [1927], London 1949 (enlarged, as Tokefield papers old and new). Essays.
A brood of ducklings. [1928], Garden City NY 1928.
A London bookman. 1928. Selection of articles written for New York Bookman.
Sketch of a sinner. Garden City NY 1929, London 1930.
Authors and the book trade. 1932, New York 1932, London 1933 (with new preface).
The Georgian house. Garden City NY 1932, London [1933]. Fiction.
Elizabeth. [1934], Garden City NY 1934.
The Georgian scene: a literary panorama. New York [1934], London 1935 (as The Georgian literary scene), 1938 (EL, rev), 1950 (rev), 1969 (rev).
Swinnerton: an autobiography. Garden City NY 1936, London 1937.
The university of books. 1936. With A. Huxley et al.
An anthology of modern fiction. 1937. Ed Swinnerton.
Harvest comedy: a dramatic chronicle. [1937], Garden City NY 1938.
The reviewing and criticism of books. 1939. Lecture.
The two wives. [1940], New York 1940.
The fortunate lady: a dramatic chronicle. [1941], Garden City NY 1941.
Thankless child. [1942], Garden City NY 1942.

A woman in sunshine. [1944], Garden City NY 1945.
English maiden: parable of a happy life. [1946].
The cats and Rosemary. New York 1948, London 1950.
A faithful company: a winter's tale. [1948].
The doctor's wife comes to stay. [1949].
Arnold Bennett. 1950, 1961 (rev) (Br Council pamphlet).
A flower for Catherine. 1950.
The bookman's London. 1951, Garden City NY 1952.
Londoner's post: letters to Gog and Magog. 1952. Essays.
Master Jim Probity. 1952, Garden City NY 1953 (as An affair of love).
A month in Gordon Square. 1953, Garden City NY 1954.
The Sumner intrigue. 1955, Garden City NY 1955.
The adventures of a manuscript: being the story of The ragged-trousered philanthropists. 1956.
Authors I never met. 1956.
Background with chorus: a footnote to changes in English literary fashion between 1901 and 1917. 1956, New York [1956].
The woman from Sicily. 1957, Garden City NY 1957.
A tigress in Prothero. 1959, Garden City NY 1959 (as A tigress in the village).
The Grace divorce. 1960, Garden City NY 1960.
Death of a highbrow. 1961, Garden City NY 1962.
Figures in the foreground: literary reminiscences 1917–40. 1963, Garden City NY 1964.
Quadrille. 1965, Garden City NY 1965.
A galaxy of fathers. 1966, Garden City NY 1966. Biographies.
Sanctuary. 1966, Garden City NY 1967.
The bright lights. 1968, New York 1968.
Reflections from a village. 1969, Garden City NY 1969.
Swinnerton pbd edns of Arnold Bennett, Literary taste, *1937 and 1938, and a selection from his* Journals, *1954 (Penguin).*

§2

Swinnerton: personal sketches by Arnold Bennett, H. G. Wells, G. M. Overton. New York [1920].

ANGELA MARGARET THIRKELL
1890–1961

Selections

An Angela Thirkell omnibus, with introd by E. Bowen. 1966. Ankle deep; High rising; Wild strawberries.
A second Angela Thirkell omnibus. 1967. August folly; Summer half; Pomfret Towers.
The Brandons, and others. 1968. The Brandons; Before lunch; Cheerfulness breaks in.

§1

Three houses. 1931, New York 1931. Memoirs of childhood.
Ankle deep. 1933, New York 1933.
High rising. 1933, New York 1933.
The demon in the house: stories of Tony Moreland. 1934, New York 1935.
Trooper to the Southern Cross. 1934, 1935 (as What happened on the boat). As 'Leslie Parker'.
Wild strawberries. 1934, New York 1934.
The grateful sparrow, and other stories. 1935, New York 1936. For children, adapted from the German.
O these men, these men! 1935.
August folly. 1936, New York 1937.
The fortunes of Harriette: the surprising career of Harriette Wilson. 1936, New York 1936 (as Tribute for Harriette).
Coronation summer. 1937, New York 1937.
Summer half. 1937, New York 1938.
Pomfret Towers. 1938, New York 1938.
Before lunch. 1939, New York 1940.
The Brandons. 1939, New York 1939.

Cheerfulness breaks in: a Barsetshire war survey. 1940, New York 1941.
Northbridge Rectory. [1941], New York 1942.
Marling Hall. 1942, New York 1942.
Growing up. 1943, New York 1944.
The headmistress. 1944, New York 1945.
Miss Bunting. 1945, New York 1946.
Peace breaks out. 1946, New York 1947.
Private enterprise. 1947, New York 1948.
Love among the ruins. 1948, New York 1948.
The old Bank House. 1949, New York 1949.
County chronicle. 1950, New York 1950.
The duke's daughter. 1951, New York 1951.
Happy returns. 1952, New York 1952 (as Happy return).
Jutland Cottage. 1953, New York 1953.
What did it mean? 1954, New York 1954.
Enter Sir Robert. 1955, New York 1955.
Never too late. 1956, New York 1956.
A double affair. 1957, New York 1957.
Close quarters. 1958, New York 1958.
Love at all ages. 1959, New York 1959.
Three score and ten. 1961. With C. A. Lejeune.

JOHN RONALD REUEL TOLKIEN
1892–1973

§1

Prose Fiction and Verse

Songs for the philologists. 1936 (priv ptd). With E. V. Gordon et al.
The hobbit: or, there and back again. 1937, Boston 1938, London 1951 (rev), Boston 1958, London 1966 (rev), New York 1966.
Farmer Giles of Ham. 1949, Boston 1950.
The lord of the rings: pt 1, The fellowship of the ring, 1954, Boston 1954; pt 2, The two towers, 1954, Boston 1955; pt 3, The return of the king, 1955, Boston 1956. The whole rev, with explanatory matter, London 1966, Boston 1967, 1 vol London 1968.
The adventures of Tom Bombadil and other verses from The red book. 1962, Boston 1963.
Tree and leaf. 1964, Boston 1965. Contains On fairy stories (Andrew Lang lecture, 1938) and Leaf by Niggle [a story].
Smith of Wootton Major. 1967, Boston 1967.

Other Works

A middle English vocabulary, designed for use with Sisam's Fourteenth Century verse & prose. Oxford 1922.
Sir Gawain & the Green Knight. Ed Tolkien and E. V. Gordon, Oxford 1925, 1967 (rev H. Davis).
Beowulf: the monsters and the critics. [1937] (Gollancz memorial lecture 1936).
The English text of the Ancrene Riwle: Ancrene Wisse. Ed Tolkien from ms Corpus Christi College Cambridge 402, 1962 (EETS).
Tolkien also edited, with others, the first 7 Oxford English monographs, 1940–59.

§2

Wilson, E. Oo, those awful orcs. Nation 182 1956; rptd in his The bit between my teeth, New York 1965.
The Tolkien Journal. 1965.
Auden, W. H. Good and evil in The lord of the rings. CQ 10 1968.
Isaacs, N. D. and R. A. Zimbardo (ed). Tolkien and the critics: essays on The lord of the rings. Notre Dame 1968.
Stimpson, C. R. J. R. R. Tolkien. New York 1969.
Foster, R. The complete guide to Middle-Earth. 1971.
Carpenter, H. Tolkien: a biography. 1977.

EDWARD FALAISE UPWARD
b. 1903

§1

The colleagues; Sunday. In New country, ed M. Roberts 1933. Stories.
Sketch for a Marxist interpretation of literature. In The mind in chains, ed C. Day Lewis 1937.
Journey to the border. 1938.
The falling tower. In Folios of new writing, ed J. Lehmann 1941. Essay.
New order. Penguin New Writing 14 1942. Prose-poem.
The railway accident. New Directions 11 1949; rptd in The railway accident and other stories, 1969.
In the thirties. 1962. First pt of a trilogy provisionally titled Poet and party. Part of ch 1 first pbd in London Mag 8 1961.
The rotten elements. 1969. 2nd pt of trilogy.

§2

Isherwood, C. Lions and shadows. 1938. Reminiscences of Upward ('Allen Chalmers').

RICHARD HORATIO EDGAR WALLACE
1875–1932

Bibliographies

Lofts, W. O. G. and D. Adley. The British bibliography of Wallace. 1969.

§1

Plays are listed in order of production, where known.

The mission that failed! a tale of the [Jameson] raid and other poems reprinted from the Owl. Cape Town 1898.
War! and other poems. Cape Town [1900].
Writ in barracks. 1900. Verse.
Unofficial despatches. [1901]. On the Boer war. Rptd from Daily Mail.
The Four Just Men. 1905, Boston [1920].
'Smithy'. 1905.
Angel Esquire. Bristol [1908], New York 1908, Oxford 1966 (rev).
The council of justice. 1908.
Captain Tatham of Tatham Island. 1909, 1916 (as The island of galloping gold), [1926] (as Eve's island).
Smithy abroad: barrack room sketches. 1909.
The duke in the suburbs. 1909.
The nine bears. 1910, New York 1911 (as The other man), Cleveland 1930 (as Silinski: master criminal), London 1964 (as The cheaters).
Sanders of the river. 1911, Garden City NY 1930. Stories.
The people of the river. 1912. Stories.
Private Selby. 1912.
The fourth plague. 1913, Garden City NY 1930.
Grey Timothy. 1913, 1914 (as Pallard the punter).
The river of stars. 1913.
The admirable Carfew. 1914. Stories.
Bosambo of the river. 1914. Stories.
Heroes all: gallant deeds of the war. [1914].
Smithy's friend Nobby. 1914, [1916] (as 'Nobby'). Stories.
The standard history of the war. 4 vols [1914–15].
'Bones': being further adventures in Mr Commissioner Sanders' country. 1915. Stories.
Kitchener's army and the Territorial forces: the full story of a great achievement. 6 pts [1915].
The man who bought London. 1915.
The melody of death. 1915 (anon, as By the author of The four just men), [1928] (as by Wallace).

'1925': the story of a fatal peace. 1915.
'Smithy' and the Hun. 1915. Stories.
War of the nations. Vols 2–11 [1915–19]. Pbd in pts. Vol 1 by W. Le Queux.
The clue of the twisted candle. Boston [1916], London [1918].
A debt discharged. 1916.
The island of galloping gold. 1916. *See* Captain Tatham of Tatham Island, 1909, above.
'Nobby'. [1916]. *See* Smithy's friend Nobby, 1914, above.
The tomb of Ts'in. 1916.
The just men of Cordova. 1917.
Kate plus 10. Boston [1917], London 1919 (as Kate plus ten).
The keepers of the king's peace. 1917. Stories.
The secret house. 1917, Boston [1919].
Down under Donovan. [1918].
Lieutenant Bones. 1918. Stories.
Tam o' the scouts. 1918, Boston [1919], London [1928], (as Tam).
Those folk of Bulboro. 1918.
The adventures of Heine. 1919. Stories.
The fighting scouts. 1919. Stories.
The green rust. 1919, Boston [1920] (as Green rust).
The man who knew. [1919].
The daffodil mystery. 1920, Boston [1921] (as The daffodil murder).
Jack o' judgment. [1920], Boston [1921].
Bones in London. 1921. Stories.
The book of all-power. 1921.
The law of the Four Just Men. [1921]. Stories.
The angel of terror. [1922], Boston [1922].
Captains of souls. Boston [1922], London 1923, 1969 (rev).
The crimson circle. [1922], 1968 (rev).
The flying Fifty-Five. [1922], 1968 (rev).
Mr Justice Maxell. 1922. Also pbd as Take-a-chance Anderson.
Sandi the king-maker. 1922.
The valley of ghosts. 1922, Boston [1923], London 1967 (rev).
Bones of the river. [1923]. Stories.
The books of Bart. [1923].
Chick. 1923. Stories.
The clue of the new pin. [1933], Boston [1923].
The green archer. [1923], Boston [1924], New York 1965 (introd by V. Starrett).
The missing million. 1923, Boston [1925].
The dark eyes of London. 1924, Garden City NY 1929. Also pbd as The croakers.
Double Dan. [1924], Boston [1924] (as Diana of Kara-Kara). As play (Savoy 7 May 1927), unpbd.
Educated Evans. [1924], Oxford 1966 (rev). Stories.
The face in the night. [1924], Garden City NY 1929. Also pbd as The diamond men and The ragged princess.
Flat 2. Garden City NY 1924, London [1927].
Room 13. 1924.
The sinister man. [1924], Boston [1925].
The three oak mystery. 1924.
The black Avons. 4 vols 1925.
Blue hand. 1925, Boston 1926. Also pbd as Beyond recall.
The daughters of the night. [1925].
The fellowship of the frog. 1925.
The gaunt stranger. [1925], [1926] (rev, as The Ringer), Garden City NY 1926, London [1929] (as play, Wyndham's 1 May 1926), [1929] (French's Acting Edn). Also pbd as Police work.
The hairy arm. Boston [1925], London 1926 (as The avenger). Also pbd as The extra girl.
A king by night. 1925, Garden City NY 1926.
The mind of Mr J. G. Reeder. [1925], Garden City NY 1929 (as The murder book of J. G. Reeder). Stories.
The strange countess. [1925], Boston [1926]. Also pbd as The sins of the mother.
Barbara on her own. [1926].

The black abbot. [1926], Garden City NY 1927.
The day of uniting. [1926], Garden City NY 1926.
The door with seven locks. [1926], Garden City NY 1926.
Eve's island. [1926]. *See* Captain Tatham of Tatham Island, 1909, above.
The joker. [1926], Garden City NY [1932] (as The colossus). Also pbd as The Park Lane mystery.
The man from Morocco. 1926, Garden City NY 1930 (as The black). Also pbd as Souls in shadow.
The million-dollar story. [1926].
More educated Evans. [1926]. Stories.
The Northing tramp. [1926], Garden City NY 1929.
Penelope of the 'Polyantha'. [1926].
People: a short autobiography. 1926, Garden City NY 1929, London 1929 (as Edgar Wallace: a short autobiography). Also pbd as Edgar Wallace, by himself.
The Ringer. [1926]. *See* The gaunt stranger, [1925], above.
Sanders. [1926], Garden City NY 1930 (as Mr Commissioner Sanders). Stories.
The square emerald. [1926], Garden City NY 1927 (as The girl from Scotland Yard). Also pbd as The woman.
The terrible people. [1926], Garden City NY 1926. Also pbd as The gallows' hand.
The Three Just Men. [1926], Garden City NY 1929.
We shall see! [1926], Garden City NY 1931 (as The gaolbreakers).
The yellow snake. [1926]. Also pbd as The black tenth.
Big foot. 1927.
The brigand. [1927]. Stories.
The feathered serpent. [1927], Garden City NY 1928. Also pbd as Inspector Wade, and as Inspector Wade and the feathered serpent.
The forger. 1927, Garden City NY 1928 (as The clever one). Also pbd as The counterfeiter.
Good Evans! [1927], [1929] (as The educated man—Good Evans!). Stories.
The hand of power. [1927], New York 1930. Also pbd as The proud sons of Ragusa.
The man who was nobody. 1927.
The mixer. 1927. Stories.
Number six. [1927]. Also pbd as Number six and the Borgia.
The squeaker. [1927], Garden City NY 1928 (as The squealer), London [1929] (as play, The squeaker, Apollo 29 May 1928). Also pbd as The sign of the leopard.
The terror. (Lyceum 11 May 1927). [1929]. Play.
Terror Keep. [1927], Garden City NY 1927.
This England. [1927]. Short pieces rptd from Morning Post.
Again Sanders. [1928], Garden City NY [1931]. Stories.
Again the Three Just Men. [1928], Garden City NY 1931 (as The law of the Three Just Men). Also pbd as Again the Three. Stories.
The double. [1928], Garden City NY 1928. Also pbd as Sinister halls.
Elegant Edward. [1928]. Stories.
The Flying Squad. [1928], Garden City NY 1929, London [1929] (as play, Lyceum 7 June 1928).
The gunner. 1928, Garden City NY 1929 (as Gunman's bluff). Also pbd as Children of the poor.
The man who changed his name. (Apollo 14 March 1928). [1929], Garden City NY 1934. Play.
The orator. [1928]. Stories.
Tam. [1928]. *See* Tam o' the scouts, 1918, above.
The thief in the night. 1928, 1962 (with 5 stories rptd from previous collections).
The twister. 1928, Garden City NY 1929, London 1966 (rev).
Again the Ringer. [1929], Garden City NY [1931] (as The Ringer returns). Stories.
The big four. [1929]. Also pbd as Crooks of society. Stories.
The black. [1929], Garden City NY 1930. Also pbd as Blackmailers I have foiled. Stories. Different from

identical title pbd Garden City NY in same year: *see*
The man from Morocco, 1926, above.
The cat burglar. [1929]. Stories, all rptd in Forty-eight
short stories, 1929.
Circumstantial evidence. [1929]. Stories all rptd in Forty-
eight short stories, 1929.
The educated man—Good Evans! [1929]. *See* Good
Evans!, [1927], above.
Fighting Snub Reilly. [1929]. Stories, all rptd in Forty-
eight short stories, 1929.
For information received. [1929]. Stories.
Four square Jane. [1929]. Also pbd as The fourth square.
The ghost of Down Hill, and The queen of Sheba's belt.
[1929]. Stories.
The golden Hades. 1929. Also pbd as Stamped in gold.
The governor of Chi-Foo. [1929], Cleveland [1933].
Stories, all rptd in Forty-eight short stories, 1929.
The green ribbon. [1929], Garden City NY 1930, London
1969 (rev).
The india-rubber men. [1929], Garden City NY 1930,
London 1969 (rev).
The lady of Little Hell. [1929]. Stories.
The little green man. [1929]. Stories, all rptd in Forty-
eight short stories, 1929.
The lone house mystery. [1929]. Stories.
The murder book of J. G. Reeder. Garden City NY 1929.
See The mind of Mr J. G. Reeder, [1925], above.
Planetoid 127, and The Sweizer pump. 1929. Long stories.
The prison-breakers. [1929]. Stories, all rptd in Forty-
eight short stories, 1929.
Red aces: being three cases of Mr Reeder. [1929], Garden
City NY 1930. Stories.
The reporter. [1929]. Also pbd as Wise Y. Symon. Stories.
The terror. [1929]. *See* also play version, [1927], above.
The black. Garden City NY 1930. *See* The man from
Morocco, 1926, above. Different from The black [1929],
above.
The calendar. 1930, Garden City NY [1931], London
[1932] (as play, Wyndhams 18 Sept 1929) (French's
Acting Edn).
The clue of the silver key. 1930, Garden City NY 1930
(as The silver key).
The iron grip. [1930]. Also pbd as Wireless Bryce.
Stories.
Killer Kay. [1930?]. Stories.
The lady called Nita. [1930?]. Stories.
The lady of Ascot. [1930], 1968 (rev).
Mr Commissioner Sanders. Garden City NY 1930. *See*
Sanders, [1926], above.
The mouthpiece: a play. (Wyndhams 20 Nov 1930).
Unpbd. Pbd as novel, with R. G. Curtis, [1935], New
York [1936].
Mrs William Jones & Bill. [1930?]. Stories.
On the spot: a play. (Wyndhams 2 April 1930). Unpbd.
Pbd as novel, 1931, Garden City NY [1931], London
1969 (rev).
Silinski: master criminal. Cleveland 1930. *See* The nine
bears, 1910, above.
White face. 1930, Garden City NY [1931].
The case of the frightened lady: a play in three acts.
(Wyndhams 18 Aug 1931). [1932] (French's Acting
Edn).
The coat of arms. [1931], Garden City NY [1932] (as The
Arranways mystery), London 1969 (rev).
The devil man. [1931], Garden City [1931]. Also pbd as
Sinister-Street, The life and death of Charles Peace, and
Silver steel.
The gaol-breakers. 1931 *See* We shall see!, [1926], above.
The law of the Three Just Men. Garden City NY [1931].
See Again the Three Just Men, [1928], above.
The man at the Carlton. [1931], Garden City NY [1932].
Also pbd as His devoted squealer, and The mystery of
Mary Grier.
On the spot. 1931. *See* play version, 1930, above.
The colossus. [1932]. *See* The joker, [1926], above.

The frightened lady. 1932, Garden City NY 1933 (as The
mystery of the frightened lady). Based on the play. Also
pbd as Criminal at large.
The green pack: a play in three acts. (Wyndhams 9 Feb
1932). [1933] (French's Acting Edn), Garden City NY
1933.
The guv'nor, and other stories [The man who passed; The
treasure house; The shadow man]. 1932, Garden City
NY [1932] (as Mr Reeder returns). The guv'nor and
The man who passed pbd separately as The guv'nor
[1933]; The treasure house and The shadow men pbd
separately as Mr J. G. Reeder returns [1934], 1965 (rev).
My Hollywood diary. [1932].
Sergeant Sir Peter. 1932, Garden City NY 1933, London
[1962] (as Sergeant Dunn CID). Stories.
The steward. [1932]. Stories.
When the gangs came to London. [1932], Garden City
NY [1932], London 1969 (rev). Also pbd as Scotland
Yard's Yankee Dick, and The gangsters come to
London.
The guv'nor. [1933]. *See* The guv'nor, and other stories,
1932, above.
The last adventure. [1934]. Stories.
Mr J. G. Reeder returns. [1934]. *See* The guv'nor, and
other stories, 1932, above.
The woman from the east, and other stories. [1934].
The mouthpiece. [1935]. With R. Curtis. *See* play ver-
sion, 1930, above.
Sergeant Dunn CID. [1962]. *See* Sergeant Sir Peter,
1932, above.
The undisclosed client. [1963]. Stories, including 9 not
previously pbd in book form.

§2

Wallace, E. V. Edgar Wallace. [1932].
Lane, M. Wallace: the biography of a phenomenon. [1938],
1964 (rev).

SIR HUGH SEYMOUR WALPOLE
1884-1941

*The mss of Rogue Herries, Judith Paris, The fortress,
Vanessa, The bright pavilions and Katherine Christian
are in the Fitz Park Museum, Keswick; those of Joseph
Conrad and The crystal box are in the Hugh Walpole
Collection at King's School Canterbury; that of A silly old
fool is in the BM (Ashley Library), and that of The green
mirror in the Berg Collection, New York Public Library. The
mss of The Duchess of Wrexe, The captives and Wintersmoon are in the Library of Congress, Washington.*

Collections and Selections

Works. Cumberland edition. 30 vols 1934-40. Mostly
reissues of earlier edns, with new prefaces by the author.
A Hugh Walpole anthology, selected by the author. [1921].
The Jeremy stories. 1941. Jeremy, Jeremy and Hamlet,
Jeremy at Crale.

§1

The wooden horse. 1909, New York 1915.
Maradick at forty: a transition. 1910.
Mr Perrin and Mr Traill: a tragi-comedy. 1911, New York
1911 (as The gods and Mr Perrin), London 1935 (with
preface by Walpole).
The prelude to adventure. 1912, New York 1912, Oxford
1938 (WC, with new introd by Walpole).
Fortitude: being a true and faithful account of the educa-
tion of an explorer. 1913, New York [1913], 1930 (with
introd by Walpole).
The Duchess of Wrexe, her decline & death: a romantic
commentary. 1914, New York [1914].
The golden scarecrow. 1915, New York 1915. Stories.
The dark forest. 1916, New York [1916].

Joseph Conrad. [1916], 1924 (rev).
The green mirror: a quiet story. New York [1917], London 1918.
Jeremy. 1919, New York [1919].
The secret city: a novel in three parts. 1919, New York [1919].
The art of James Branch Cabell. New York 1920.
The captives: a novel in four parts. 1920, New York [1920].
The thirteen travellers. [1921], New York [1921]. Stories.
The young enchanted: a romantic story. 1921, New York [1921].
The cathedral. 1922, New York [1922], London 1937 (as play).
Jeremy and Hamlet. 1923, New York [1923].
The crystal box. Glasgow 1924.
The old ladies. 1924, New York [1924]. Dramatized by R. Ackland 1935.
The English novel: some notes on its evolution. Cambridge 1925 (Rede Lecture).
Portrait of a man with red hair: a romantic macabre. 1925, New York [1925]. Dramatized by B. Levy 1928.
Harmer John: an unworldly story. 1926, New York [1926].
Reading: an essay. 1926, New York 1926.
Jeremy at Crale. 1927, New York [1927].
Anthony Trollope. 1928 (EML), New York 1928.
My religious experience. 1928 (Affirmations ser). Booklet.
The silver thorn: a book of stories. 1928, Garden City NY 1928.
Wintersmoon: passages in the lives of two sisters, Janet and Rosalind Grandison. 1928, Garden City NY 1928.
Farthing Hall. 1929, Garden City NY 1929. With J. B. Priestley.
Hans Frost. 1929.
Rogue Herries. 1930, Garden City NY 1930. First vol of the Herries chronicle.
Above the dark circus: an adventure. 1931, Garden City NY 1931 (as Above the dark tumult).
Judith Paris. 1931, Garden City NY 1931. 2nd vol of the Herries chronicle.
The apple trees: four reminiscences. Waltham St Lawrence 1932.
The fortress. 1932, Garden City NY 1932. 3rd vol of the Herries chronicle.
A letter to a modern novelist. 1932 (Hogarth Letters 9).
The Waverley pageant; the best passages from the novels of Sir Walter Scott selected with critical introductions by Walpole. 1932.
All Souls' night: a book of stories. 1933, Garden City NY 1933.
Vanessa. 1933, Garden City NY 1933. 4th vol of the Herries chronicle.
Captain Nicholas: a modern comedy. 1934, Garden City NY 1934.
Extracts from a diary. Glasgow 1934 (priv ptd, 100 copies).
Cathedral carol service. 1934. An episode from The inquisitor, 1935, below.
Claude Houghton: appreciations. 1935. With 'Clemence Dane' (W. Ashton). Non-fiction.
The inquisitor. 1935, Garden City NY 1935.
A prayer for my son. 1936, Garden City NY 1936.
John Cornelius: his life and adventures. 1937, Garden City NY 1937.
Head in green bronze and other stories. 1938, Garden City NY 1938.
The joyful Delaneys. 1938, New York 1938.
The Haxtons: a play in three acts. [1939].
The sea tower: a love story. 1939, New York 1939.
The Herries chronicle: Rogue Herries, Judith Paris, The fortress, Vanessa. 1939.
Roman fountain. 1940, New York 1940. Travel.
The bright pavilions. 1940, New York 1940. 5th vol of the Herries chronicle.
A note by Hugh Walpole on the origins of the Herries chronicle. New York 1940.

The freedom of books. [1940]. Pamphlet.
The blind man's house: a quiet story. 1941, Garden City NY 1941.
Open letter of an optimist. 1941 (Macmillan War pamphlets 9).
The killer and the slain: a strange story. 1942, Garden City NY 1942.
Katherine Christian. Garden City NY 1943, London 1944. 6th vol of the Herries chronicle, unfinished.
Women are motherly. 1943. Non-fiction.
Mr Huffam and other stories. 1948.

§2

Overton, G. M. (ed). Hugh Walpole: appreciations by J. Conrad, A. Bennett and J. Hergesheimer. New York 1923.
Steen, M. Hugh Walpole: a study. 1933.
Hart-Davis, R. Hugh Walpole: a biography. 1952.
Swinnerton, F. A. In his Figures in the foreground, 1963.

REX WARNER
b. 1905

The kite. Oxford 1936, London 1963 (rev). Children's story.
Poems. 1937, New York 1938, London 1945 (rev, as Poems and contradictions), New York 1945.
The wild goose chase. 1937, New York 1937.
The professor. 1938, New York 1939.
The aerodrome: a love story. 1941, New York 1946, London 1966 (with introd by A. Wilson), New York 1966.
Why was I killed?: a dramatic dialogue. 1943, New York 1944 (as Return of the traveller).
English public schools. 1945 (Britain in Pictures).
The cult of power: essays. 1946, New York 1947.
John Milton. 1949, New York 1950.
Men of stones: a melodrama. 1949, Philadelphia 1950.
E. M. Forster. 1950, [1960] (rev) (Br Council pamphlet).
Views of Attica and its surroundings. 1950.
Ashes to ashes: a post-mortem on the 1950-1 Tests. 1951.
Greeks and Trojans. 1951, East Lansing 1953.
Escapade: a tale of Average. 1953.
Eternal Greece. New York 1953, London [1953].
The vengeance of the gods. 1954, East Lansing 1955. Stories adapted from Euripides.
Athens. 1956, New York 1956.
The Greek philosophers. 1958, New York 1958.
The young Caesar. 1960, Boston 1960. Historical novel.
Imperial Caesar. 1960, Boston 1960. Historical novel.
Look at birds. 1962. For children.
Pericles the Athenian. 1963, Boston 1963. Historical novel.
The converts. 1967.
Julius Caesar. 1967. Contains The young Caesar and Imperial Caesar, above.
The stories of the Greeks. 1968. Men and gods; Greeks and Trojans; The vengeance of the gods.
Warner has pbd a number of trns: Euripides, Medea (1944), Hippolytus (1949) and Helen (1951); Aeschylus, Prometheus bound (1947); Xenophon, Anabasis (1948); Thucydides, Peloponnesian war (1954); a selection of stories from Ovid (Men and gods, 1950); 6 Lives of Plutarch (The fall of the Roman republic, 1958); War commentaries of Caesar (1960); St Augustine, Confessions (1963); and from modern Greek, Seferis, Poems (1960) and his On the Greek style (1966).

SYLVIA TOWNSEND WARNER
b. 1893

The espalier. 1925, New York 1925. Verse.
Lolly Willowes: or, the loving huntsman. 1926, New York 1926.
Mr Fortune's maggot. 1927, New York 1927.
The maze: a story to be read aloud. 1928.
Time importuned. 1928, New York 1928. Verse.
Some world far from ours, and 'Stay, Corydon, thou swain'. 1929. Stories.
The true heart. 1929, New York 1929.
Elinor Barley. 1930, Chicago 1930. Story.
A moral ending, and other stories. 1931.
Opus 7. 1931, New York 1931. Verse.
Rainbow. New York 1932. Verse.
The salutation. 1932, New York 1932. Stories.
Whether a dove or a seagull. New York 1933, London 1934. Verse, with V. Ackland.
More joy in heaven, and other stories. 1935.
Summer will show. 1936. New York 1936.
After the death of Don Juan. 1938, New York 1939.
The cat's cradle-book. New York 1940, London 1960. Stories.
A garland of straw, and other stories. 1943, New York 1943.
The museum of cheats, and other stories. 1947, New York 1947.
The corner that held them. 1948.
Somerset. 1949. Topography.
Jane Austen 1775–1817. 1951, 1957 (rev) (Br Council pamphlet).
The flint anchor. 1954, New York 1954.
Winter in the air, and other stories. 1955, New York 1956.
Boxwood: sixteen engravings by R. Stone illustrated in verse by S. T. Warner. 1958 (priv ptd), 1960 (as Boxwood: twenty-one engravings).
A spirit rises. 1962, New York 1962.
Sketches from nature. Wells, London 1963. Reminiscences.
A stranger with a bag, and other stories. 1966, New York 1966 (as Swans on an autumn river).
T. H. White: a biography. 1967, New York 1968.

ALEC WAUGH
(ALEXANDER RABAN WAUGH)
b. 1898

The loom of youth. 1917, New York 1920.
Resentment: poems. 1918.
The prisoners of Mainz. 1919, New York 1919.
Pleasure. 1921.
The lonely unicorn. 1922.
Public school life: boys, parents, masters. [1922].
Roland Whateley. New York 1922.
Myself when young: confessions. 1923, New York 1924.
Card castle. 1924.
Kept: a story of post-war London. 1925, New York [1925].
Love in these days: a modern story. 1926, New York [1927].
On doing what one likes. 1926. Essays.
The last chukka: stories of east and west. 1928.
Nor many waters. 1928.
Portrait of a celibate. Garden City NY 1929.
Three score and ten. 1929, Garden City NY 1930.
The coloured countries. 1930, New York [1930] (as Hot countries), London 1948. Travel.
'Sir', she said. 1930, New York [1930].
'Most women . . .'. 1931, New York [1931]. Non-fiction.
So lovers dream. 1931.
Leap before you look. 1932, New York 1933, London 1934 (rev).
No quarter. 1932.

That American woman. New York [1932].
Thirteen such years. 1932, New York [1932].
Tropic seed. New York [1932].
Playing with fire. 1933.
Wheels within wheels: a story of the crisis. 1933, New York [1933] (as The golden ripple).
The Balliols. 1934, New York [1934].
Pages in woman's life: a group of stories. 1934.
Jill Somerset. 1936, New York [1936].
Eight short stories. 1937.
Going their own ways: a story of modern marriage. 1938, New York [1939].
No truce with time. 1941, New York [1941].
His second war. 1944.
The sunlit Caribbean. 1948, New York 1949 (as The sugar islands), London 1953 (rev, with original title). Travel.
These I would choose: a personal anthology. 1948.
Unclouded summer: a love story. 1948, New York 1948.
The Lipton story: a centennial biography. Garden City NY 1950, London 1951.
Where the clocks strike twice. New York 1951, London 1952 (as Where the clocks chime twice). Travel.
Guy Renton: a London story. New York 1952, London 1953.
Island in the sun. New York 1955, London 1956.
Merchants of wine: being a centenary account of the fortunes of the House of Gilbey. 1957.
The sugar islands: a collection of pieces written about the West Indies between 1928 and 1953. 1958, New York [1959] (as Love and the Caribbean: tales, characters and scenes of the West Indies).
In praise of wine. 1959. Non-fiction.
Fuel for the flame. 1960, New York 1960.
My place in the bazaar. 1961, New York 1961.
The early years of Alec Waugh. 1962, New York 1963.
A family of islands: a history of the West Indies from 1492 to 1898. 1964, Garden City NY 1964.
The mule on the minaret. 1965, New York 1965.
My brother Evelyn, and other profiles. 1967, New York 1968.
Wines and spirits. New York 1968.

EVELYN ARTHUR ST JOHN WAUGH
1903–66

§1

The world to come: a poem in three cantos. 1916 (priv ptd).
PRB: an essay on the Pre-Raphaelite Brotherhood 1847–54. 1926 (priv ptd).
Decline and fall: an illustrated novelette. 1928, Garden City NY 1929, London 1962 (rev, with new preface).
Rossetti: his life and works. 1928, New York 1928; ed J. Bryson 1975.
Labels: a Mediterranean journal. 1930, New York [1930] (as A bachelor abroad: a Mediterranean journal).
Vile bodies. 1930, New York [1930], London 1965 (rev, with new preface).
Remote people. 1931, New York [1932] (as They were still dancing). Travel.
Black mischief. 1932, New York [1932], London 1962 (rev, with new preface).
A handful of dust. 1934, New York [1934], London 1964 (rev, with new preface).
Ninety-two days: the account of a tropical journey through British Guiana and part of Brazil. 1934, New York [1934].
Edmund Campion. 1935, New York 1935, Boston 1946 (rev), London 1947, 1961 (with new material).
Mr Loveday's little outing, and other sad stories. 1936, Boston 1936.
Waugh in Abyssinia. 1936, New York 1936.
Scoop: a novel about journalists. 1938, Boston 1938, London 1964 (rev, with new preface).

Robbery under law: the Mexican object-lesson. 1939, Boston 1939 (as Mexico: an object lesson).

Put out more flags. 1942, Boston 1942, London 1967 (rev with new preface).

Work suspended: two chapters of an unfinished novel. 1942, 1949 (rev as Work Suspended and other stories).

Brideshead revisited: the sacred and profane memories of Captain Charles Ryder. 1945, Boston 1945, London 1960 (rev, with new preface).

When the going was good. 1946, Boston 1947. Travel; selections from Labels, Remote people, Ninety-two days, Waugh in Abyssinia.

Scott-King's modern Europe. 1947, Boston 1949.

Wine in peace and war. 1947.

The loved one: an Anglo-American tragedy. [1948], Boston 1948, London 1965 (rev, with new preface).

A selection from the occasional sermons of the Right Reverend Monsignor R. A. Knox. Ed Waugh 1949.

Helena. 1950, Boston 1950.

Men at arms. 1952, Boston 1952, London 1965 (rev, as pt of Sword of honour, 1965, below).

The holy places. 1952. Essays.

Love among the ruins: a romance of the near future. 1953.

Officers and gentlemen. 1955, Boston 1955, London 1965 (rev, as pt of Sword of honour, 1965, below).

The ordeal of Gilbert Pinfold: a conversation piece. 1957, Boston 1957.

The life of Ronald Knox. 1959.

A tourist in Africa. 1960, Boston 1960. Travel.

Unconditional surrender: the conclusion of Men at arms and Officers and gentlemen. 1961, Boston 1962 (as The end of the battle), London 1965 (rev, as pt of Sword of honour, 1965, below).

Basil Seal rides again: or, the rake's regress. 1963, Boston 1963.

A little learning: the first volume of an autobiography. 1964, Boston 1964.

Sword of honour. 1965, Boston 1965. A recension by the author, into a single narrative, of Men at arms, Officers and gentlemen, and Unconditional surrender, above.

Labels: a Mediterranean journal. Ed K. Amis 1974.

Diaries. Ed M. Davie 1976.

§2

Wilson, E. Never apologize, never explain: the art of Waugh. New Yorker 4 March 1944; rptd in his Classics and commercials, New York 1950.

— Splendors and miseries of Waugh. New Yorker 13 July 1946; rptd in Classics and commercials.

Betjeman, J. Waugh: a critical study. In Living writers, ed G. Phelps 1947.

Hollis, C. Evelyn Waugh. 1954 (Br Council pamphlet).

Bergonzi, B. Evelyn Waugh's gentlemen. CQ 5 1963.

Bradbury, M. Evelyn Waugh. Edinburgh 1964 (Writers & Critics).

Donaldson, F. Waugh: portrait of a country neighbour. 1967.

Evelyn Waugh Newsletter. 1967.

Waugh, A. My brother Evelyn, and other profiles. 1967.

Lodge, D. Evelyn Waugh. New York 1971.

Sykes, C. Evelyn Waugh: a biography. 1975, 1977 (Pelican).

MARY GLADYS WEBB, née MEREDITH
1881–1927

Collections and Selections

Collected works. 7 vols 1928–29, 6 vols New York 1929 (omitting The golden arrow). With introds by various authors. Texts rptd in Sarn edn 7 vols 1937.

The spring of joy: poems, some prose pieces and the

unfinished novel Armour wherein he trusted. 1937, New York 1937. With introds as in Collected works.

The essential Mary Webb, selected and introduced by M. Armstrong. 1949.

Fifty-one poems hitherto unpublished in book form. 1946, New York 1947.

§1

The golden arrow. 1916, New York 1935.

Gone to earth. 1917, New York [1917].

The spring of joy: a little book of healing. 1917.

The house in Dormer Forest. [1920], New York 1921.

Seven for a secret: a love story. 1922, New York [1923].

Precious bane. 1924, New York 1926.

Poems, and The spring of joy. 1928, New York [1929]. Issued as a vol in the Collected works, above.

Armour wherein he trusted: a novel and some stories. 1929, New York [1929].

The Chinese lion. 1937. Story.

§2

Addison, H. Mary Webb: a short study of her life and work. 1931.

Moult, T. Mary Webb: her life and work. 1932.

Wrenn, D. P. H. Goodbye to morning: a biographical study of Mary Webb. Shrewsbury 1964.

MAURICE DENTON WELCH
1914–48

A collection of Welch mss is in the library of the Univ of Texas. The ms of Maiden Voyage *is in the BM.*

Maiden voyage, with a foreword by E. Sitwell. 1943, New York 1945. Autobiography.

In youth is pleasure. 1944, New York 1946.

Brave and cruel, and other stories. 1948.

A voice through a cloud. 1950, [Austin Texas 1966].

A last sheaf. Ed E. Oliver 1951. Stories and poems.

I left my grandfather's house: an account of his first walking tour, with an introduction by H. Roeder. 1958 (priv ptd).

Journals. Ed J. Brooke 1952.

Extracts from his published works. Ed J. Brooke 1963.

DAME 'REBECCA WEST', CICILY ISABEL ANDREWS
b. 1892

Henry James. 1916, New York 1916.

The return of the soldier. 1918, New York 1918. Dramatized by J. van Druten 1928.

The judge. [1922], New York 1922.

The strange necessity: essays and reviews. 1928, Garden City NY 1928.

Harriet Hume: a London fantasy. 1929, Garden City NY 1929.

Lions and lambs: caricatures by Low, with interpretations by 'Lynx' [i.e. Rebecca West]. New York 1929.

D. H. Lawrence. 1930, New York 1930 (275 copies, as Elegy: an in memoriam tribute to D. H. Lawrence).

Arnold Bennett himself. New York [1931]. Pamphlet.

Ending in earnest: a literary log. Garden City NY 1931. Essays rptd from Bookman (NY).

A letter to a grandfather. 1933 (Hogarth Letters).

St Augustine. 1933, New York 1933.

The modern 'Rake's progress': words by Rebecca West, paintings by David Low. 1934. Satire.

The harsh voice: four short novels. 1935, Garden City NY 1935.

The thinking reed. [1936], New York 1936.

Black lamb and grey falcon: the record of a journey through Yugoslavia in 1937. 2 vols New York 1941, London 1942.
The meaning of treason. New York 1947, London 1949, 1952 (rev), New York 1964, London 1965 (rev, Penguin).
A train of powder. 1955, New York 1955. Non-fiction.
The court and the castle: some treatments of a recurrent theme. New Haven 1957, London 1958. Essays.
The fountain overflows. 1957, New York 1957.
The Vassall affair. [1963]. Non-fiction.
The birds fall down. 1966, New York 1966.
McLuhan and the future of literature. 1969. Lecture.
See G. N. Ray, H. G. Wells and Rebecca West, *1974*.

TERENCE HANBURY WHITE
1906–64

§1

The green bay tree: or the wicked man touches wood. Cambridge 1929. Verse.
Loved Helen and other poems. 1929.
Dead Mr Nixon. 1931. With R. McNair Scott.
Darkness at Pemberley. 1932, New York [1933].
First lesson. 1932, New York 1933. As by 'James Aston'.
They winter abroad. 1932, New York 1932. As by 'James Aston'.
Farewell Victoria. 1933, New York 1934.
Earth stopped: or Mr Marx's sporting tour. 1934.
Gone to ground. 1935.
England have my bones. 1936, New York 1936. Essays.
Burke's steerage: or the amateur gentleman's introduction to noble sports and pastimes. [1938].
The sword in the stone. 1938, New York 1939; rptd in The once and future king, 1958, below.
The witch in the wood. New York 1939, London [1940]; rptd (as The queen of air and darkness) in The once and future king, below.
The ill-made knight. New York 1940, London 1941; rptd in The once and future king, below.
Mistress Masham's repose. New York [1946], London 1947.
The elephant and the kangaroo. New York [1947], London 1948.
The age of scandal: an excursion through a minor period. 1950, New York 1950. Non-fiction.
The goshawk. 1951, New York, 1952. Non-fiction.
The scandalmonger. 1952, New York 1952. Non-fiction.
The book of beasts: being a translation from a Latin bestiary made and edited by T. H. White. 1954, New York [1954].
The master: an adventure story. 1957, New York 1957. For children.
The once and future king. 1958, New York 1958. Contains The sword in the stone; The queen of air and darkness; The ill-made knight; The candle in the wind.
The godstone and the blackymor. 1959, New York 1959 (as A western wind). Travel.
Verses. Alderney 1962 (priv ptd, 100 copies).
America at last: the American journal. New York [1965].
The White/Garnett letters. Ed D. Garnett 1968, New York 1968.

§2

Warner, S. T. T. H. White: a biography. 1967.

CHARLES WALTER STANSBY WILLIAMS
1886–1945

Collections and Selections

The image of the city, and other essays. Ed A. Ridler 1958.

Selected writings. Ed A. Ridler 1961.
Collected plays. 1963. With introd by J. Heath-Stubbs.

§1

The silver stair. [1912]. Verse.
Poems of conformity. 1917.
Christian symbolism, by Michal [i.e. Mrs Charles] Williams. 1919. Some passages were by Williams.
Divorce. 1920. Verse.
The moon: a cantata prepared from the airs of Purcell by W. G. Whittaker, the words by C. Williams. [1923].
Windows of night. [1924]. Verse.
The masque of the manuscript. 1927 (priv ptd, 100 copies). Music by H. J. Foss.
An urbanity. [1927?] (priv ptd). Verse.
A myth of Shakespeare. 1928. Verse play.
The masque of perusal. 1929 (priv ptd, 100 copies). Music by H. J. Foss.
Heroes and kings. 1930. Verse.
War in heaven. 1930, New York 1949.
Poetry at present. Oxford 1930.
Many dimensions. 1931, New York 1949.
Three plays. 1931. Contains The witch; The chaste wanton; The rite of the Passion. Also includes some previously pbd verse.
The place of the lion. 1931, New York 1951.
The greater trumps. 1932, New York 1950.
The English poetic mind. Oxford 1932, New York 1963.
Shadows of ecstasy. 1933, New York 1950.
Bacon. 1933.
Reason and beauty in the poetic mind. Oxford 1933.
James I. 1934, 1951 (with introd by D. L. Sayers), New York 1953.
Rochester. 1935.
The rite of the Passion. 1936. First pbd in Three plays, 1931, above.
Queen Elizabeth. 1936.
Cranmer of Canterbury. 1936 (acting edn), 1936 (full text, as Thomas Cranmer of Canterbury). Verse play.
Descent into hell. 1937, New York 1949.
Stories of great names. 1937.
Henry VII. 1937.
He came down from heaven. 1938. Theology.
Taliessin through Logres. 1938. Verse.
The descent of the dove: a short history of the Holy Spirit in the Church. 1939, New York 1939, 1956 (introd W. H. Auden).
Judgement at Chelmsford: a pageant play. 1939.
The way of exchange. 1941. Theological pamphlet.
Religion and love in Dante: the theology of romantic love. [1941]. Pamphlet.
Witchcraft. 1941, New York 1959.
The forgiveness of sins. 1942. Theology.
The figure of Beatrice: a study of Dante. 1943, New York 1961.
The region of the summer stars. 1944. Verse.
All Hallows' Eve. 1945, New York 1948 (introd by T. S. Eliot).
The house of the octopus. 1945. Verse play.
Flecker of Dean Close. 1946.
The figure of Arthur. In Arthurian torso, ed C. S. Lewis, 1948. Verse (fragment).
Seed of Adam, and other plays, with introduction by A. Ridler. 1948. Contains Seed of Adam; The death of Good Fortune; The house by the stable; Grab and Grace.

Williams edited Poems of G. M. Hopkins, *1930 and* Letters of Evelyn Underhill, *1943*.

§2

Lewis, C. S. A sacred poem. Theology 38 1939. On Taliessin through Logres.
— Preface In Essays presented to Williams, ed C. S. Lewis. 1947.

—— Williams and the Arthuriad. In his Arthurian torso, 1948.

Eliot, T. S. The significance of Williams. Listener 19 Dec 1946. Rptd (rev) as introd to All Hallows' Eve, New York, 1948.

Heath-Stubbs, J. Charles Williams. 1955 (Br Council pamphlet).

Conquest, R. The art of the enemy. EC 7 1957. With later comments by various hands.

Sayers, D. L. The poetry of the image in Dante and Williams. In her Further papers on Dante, 1957.

HENRY WILLIAMSON
1895–1977

Prose Fiction

The beautiful years. [1921], 1929 (rev), New York [1929]. Book 1 of The flax of dream sequence.

Dandelion days. [1922], 1930 (rev), New York [1930]. Book 2 of The flax of dream sequence.

The peregrine's saga, and other stories of the country green. [1923], New York [1925] (as Sun brothers).

The dream of fair women: a tale of youth after the Great War. [1924], New York [1924], London 1931 (rev), New York [1931]. Book 3 of The flax of dream sequence.

The old stag. 1926. Stories.

Stumberleap: a story taken from The old stag [1926].

Tarka the otter. 1927, New York 1928.

The pathway. 1928, 1929 (rev), New York [1929]. Bk 4 of The flax of dream sequence.

The patriot's progress: being the vicissitudes of Pte John Bullock. 1930, New York [1930].

The gold falcon; or The haggard of love. 1933 (anon), 1947.

The star-born, with an introduction [i.e. written] by H. Williamson 1933, 1948 (rev). 'Pendant' to The flax of dream sequence.

Salar the salmon. 1935, Boston 1936.

The flax of dream. 1936. 4 novels first pbd separately (here rev). See above.

The Phasian bird. 1948, Boston 1950.

Scribbling lark. 1949.

The dark lantern. 1951, 1962 (rev). This and the following novels form the sequence A chronicle of ancient sunlight.

Donkey boy. 1952, 1962 (rev).

Tales of moorland and estuary. 1953. Stories.

Young Phillip Maddison. 1953, 1962 (rev).

How dear is life. 1954, 1963 (rev).

A fox under my cloak. 1955, 1963 (rev).

The golden virgin. 1957, 1963 (rev).

Love and the loveless. 1958, 1963 (rev).

A test to destruction. 1960, 1964 (rev).

The innocent moon. 1961, 1965 (rev).

It was the nightingale. 1962, 1965 (rev).

The power of the dead. 1963, 1966 (rev).

The phoenix generation. 1965, 1967 (rev).

A solitary war. 1966.

Lucifer before sunrise. 1967.

The gale of the world. 1969.

Other Works

The lone swallows. [1922], New York [1926] (as The lone swallows and other essays of the country green), London 1933 (enlarged, as The lone swallows and other essays of boyhood and youth). Essays.

The Ackymals. San Francisco 1929 (225 copies). Essay, rptd (rev) in The village book, 1930, below.

The linhay on the downs. 1929. Essays.

The wet Flanders plain. [1929], 1929 (rev), New York [1929]. Account of visit to the battlefields.

The village book. 1930, New York [1930]. Essays.

The wild red deer of Exmoor: a digression on the logic and ethics and economics of stag-hunting in England today. 1931. Pamphlet.

The labouring life. 1932, New York [1933] (as As the sun shines). Sequel to The village book, 1930, above.

On foot in Devon: or guidance and gossip, being a monologue in two reels. 1933.

The linhay on the downs, and other adventures in the old and the new world. 1934. Essays.

Devon holiday. 1935. Semi-autobiographical.

Richard Jefferies. Selections. Ed. Williamson 1937.

Goodbye West Country. 1937, Boston 1938. Diary.

The children of Shallowford. 1939, 1959 (rev). Autobiographical.

Genius of friendship: T. E. Lawrence. 1941.

The story of a Norfolk farm. 1941. Autobiographical.

Norfolk life. 1943. With L. R. Haggard.

Life in a Devon village. 1945. This, and the following, compiled from material gathered together in The village book, 1930, above, and The labouring life, 1932, above.

Tales of a Devon village. 1945.

The sun in the sands. 1945. Semi-autobiographical.

A clear water stream. 1958. Essays.

In the woods. Llandeilo 1960. Autobiographical essay.

SIR ANGUS FRANK JOHNSTONE-WILSON
b. 1913

§1

The wrong set, and other stories. 1949, New York 1950.

Such darling dodos, and other stories. 1950, New York 1951.

Emile Zola: an introductory study of his novels. 1952, New York 1952, London 1964 (rev).

Hemlock and after. 1952, New York 1952.

For whom the cloche tolls: a scrap-book of the twenties. 1953. Illustr P. Jullian.

Anglo-Saxon attitudes. 1956, New York 1956.

The mulberry bush: a play in three acts. 1956.

A bit off the map, and other stories. 1957, New York 1957.

The middle age of Mrs Eliot. 1958, New York 1959.

The old men at the zoo. 1961, New York 1961.

The wild garden: or, speaking of writing. 1963, Berkeley 1963.

Late call. 1964, New York 1965.

Tempo: the impact of television on the arts. [1964].

No laughing matter. 1967.

§2

Kermode, F. Mr Wilson's people. Spectator 21 Nov 1958; rptd in his Puzzles and epiphanies, 1962.

Millgate, M. In M. Cowley (ed), Writers and their work: the Paris Review interviews, 1958.

Cockshut, A. O. J. Favoured sons: the moral world of Wilson. EC 9 1959.

Scott-Kilvert, I. Angus Wilson. REL 1 1960.

Cox, C. B. The humanism of Wilson: a study of Hemlock and after. CQ 3 1961.

—— The free spirit: a study of liberal humanism in the novels of George Eliot, H. James, E. M. Forster, Virginia Woolf and Wilson. 1963.

Halio, J. L. Angus Wilson. Edinburgh 1964 (Writers & Critics).

Gransden, K. W. Angus Wilson. 1969 (Br Council pamphlet).

PELHAM GRENVILLE WODEHOUSE
1881–1975

See D. A. Jasen, A bibliography and reader's guide to the first editions of Wodehouse, 1971.

Collections and Selections

Jeeves omnibus. 1931, 1967 (rev with 3 additional stories, as The world of Jeeves).
Mulliner omnibus. 1935, 1972 (rev and enlarged as The world of Mr Mulliner).
Week-end Wodehouse. Ed H. Belloc, 1939, New York 1939.
Autograph edition. 1956–.

§1

Love among the chickens. 1906, New York 1909, London 1921 (rev).
Mike: a public school story. 1909, 1935 (2nd half only, as Enter Psmith), New York 1935, London 1953 (complete and rev in 2 vols as Mike at Wrykyn and Mike and Psmith). Mike and Psmith pbd separately New York 1969.
A gentleman of leisure. 1910, New York 1910 (as The intrusion of Jimmy).
Psmith in the City: a sequel to Mike. 1910.
The little nugget. 1913, New York [1914].
The man upstairs, and other stories. 1914.
Something fresh. 1915, New York 1915 (as Something new).
Psmith, journalist. 1915. Revised version of The prince and Betty, 1912.
Uneasy money. New York 1916, London 1917.
The man with two left feet, and other stories. 1917, New York [1933].
Piccadilly Jim. New York 1917, London [1918].
My man Jeeves. [1919]. Stories.
A damsel in distress. 1920 (for 1919), New York 1919.
Their mutual child. New York 1919, London 1920 (as The coming of Bill).
The little warrior. New York 1920, London 1921 (as Jill the reckless).
The indiscretions of Archie. 1921, New York [1921].
The clicking of Cuthbert. 1922, New York [1924] (as Golf without tears). Stories.
The girl on the boat. 1922, New York [1922] (as Three men and a maid).
The adventures of Sally. 1923 [i.e. 1922], New York [1923] (as Mostly Sally).
The inimitable Jeeves. 1923, New York [1923] (as Jeeves).
Leave it to Psmith. 1924 [i.e. 1923], New York [1924].
Ukridge. 1924, New York [1926] (as He rather enjoyed it). Stories.
Bill the conqueror. 1924, New York [1925].
Carry on, Jeeves! 1925, New York [1927]. Stories, 4 rptd from My man Jeeves, 1919, above.
Sam the sudden. 1925, New York [1925] (as Sam in the suburbs).
The heart of a goof. 1926, New York [1927] (as Divots). Stories.
The small bachelor. 1927, New York [1927].
Meet Mr Mulliner. 1927, Garden City NY 1928. Stories.
Money for nothing. 1928, Garden City NY 1928.
Mr Mulliner speaking. 1929, Garden City NY 1930. Stories.
Summer lightning. 1929, Garden City NY 1929 (as Fish preferred), London 1929 (US printing, as Fish deferred).
Very good, Jeeves! 1930, Garden City NY 1930.
Big money. 1931, Garden City NY 1931.
If I were you. 1931, Garden City NY 1931.
Doctor Sally. 1932.
Hot water. 1932, Garden City NY 1932.
Louder and funnier. 1932. Essays.
Mulliner nights. 1933, Garden City NY 1933. Stories.

Heavy weather. 1933, Boston 1933.
Thank you, Jeeves. 1934, Boston 1934.
Right ho, Jeeves. 1934, Boston 1934 (as Brinkley Manor).
Anything goes: a musical comedy. (Palace 14 June 1935). [1936] (French's Acting Edn). With G. Bolton.
Enter Psmith. 1935. See Mike, 1909, above.
Blandings Castle and elsewhere. 1935, Garden City NY 1935. Stories.
The luck of the Bodkins. 1935, Boston 1936.
Young men in spats. 1936, Garden City NY 1936. Stories.
Laughing gas. 1936, Garden City NY 1936.
Lord Emsworth and others. 1937, Garden City NY 1937 (as The crime wave at Blandings). Stories.
Summer moonshine. Garden City NY 1937, London 1938.
The code of the Woosters. 1938, Garden City NY 1938.
Uncle Fred in the springtime. 1939, Garden City NY 1939.
Eggs, beans and crumpets. 1940, Garden City NY 1940. Stories.
Quick service. 1940, Garden City NY 1940.
Money in the bank. Garden City NY 1942, London [1946].
Joy in the morning. Garden City NY 1946, London [1947].
Full moon. [1947], Garden City NY 1947.
Spring fever. [1948], Garden City NY 1948.
Uncle Dynamite. [1948].
The mating season. [1949], New York 1949.
Nothing serious. [1950], Garden City NY 1951. Stories.
The old reliable. 1951, Garden City NY 1951.
Barmy in wonderland. 1952, Garden City NY 1952 (as Angel cake).
Pigs have wings. 1952, Garden City NY 1952.
Bring on the girls: the improbable story of our life in musical comedy, with pictures to prove it. New York 1953, London 1954. With G. Bolton.
Mike at Wrykyn; Mike and Psmith. 1953. See Mike, 1909, above.
Performing flea: a self-portrait in letters. 1953, 1961 (with the text of Wodehouse's five Berlin broadcasts; Penguin), New York 1962 (as Author! author!). Letters to W. T. Townend, ed Townend.
Ring for Jeeves. 1953, New York 1954 (as The return of Jeeves).
Jeeves and the feudal spirit. 1954, New York 1955 (as Bertie Wooster sees it through).
America, I like you. New York 1956, London 1957 (as Over seventy: an autobiography with digressions).
Come on Jeeves: a farcical comedy in three acts. 1956 (Evans Plays). With G. Bolton.
French leave. 1955 (for 1956), New York 1959.
Something fishy. 1957, New York 1957 (as The butler did it).
Cocktail time. 1958, New York 1958.
A few quick ones. 1959, New York 1959. Stories.
Jeeves in the offing. 1960, New York 1960 (as How right you are, Jeeves).
Ice in the bedroom. 1961, New York 1961.
Service with a smile. New York 1961, London 1962.
Stiff upper lip, Jeeves. 1963, New York 1963.
Frozen assets. 1964, New York 1964 (as Biffen's millions).
The brinkmanship of Galahad Threepwood: a Blandings Castle novel. New York 1965, London 1965 (as Galahad at Blandings).
Plum pie. 1966, New York 1967. Stories.
The purloined paperweight. New York 1967, London 1967 (as Company for Henry).
Do butlers burgle banks? 1968, New York 1968.
A pelican at Blandings. 1969.

For details of Wodehouse's unpbd dramatic, musical comedy and film scripts, see appendices to Usborne, Wodehouse at work, 1961.

§2

'Orwell, George' (E. A. Blair). In defence of Wodehouse. Windmill no 2 1945; rptd in his Critical essays, 1946.

Usborne, R. Wodehouse at work: a study of the books and characters. 1961, 1976 (rev)
French, R. B. D. P. G. Wodehouse. Edinburgh 1966 (Writers & Critics).
Jaggard, G. Wooster's world: a companion to the Wooster–Jeeves cycle of Wodehouse, containing a modicum of honey from the Drones. 1967.
—— Blandings the blest and the blue blood: a companion to the Blandings Castle saga of Wodehouse. 1968.
Jason, D. A. Wodehouse: a portrait of a master. 1975.

'DORNFORD YATES', CECIL WILLIAM MERCER
1885–1960

The brother of Daphne. 1914.
The courts of idleness. 1920.
Anthony Lyveden. 1921.
Berry and Co. 1921, New York 1928.
Jonah and Co. 1922, New York 1927, London 1936 (with prologue and epilogue omitted).
Valerie French. 1923.
And five were foolish. 1924.
As other men are. 1925.
The stolen march. 1926, New York 1933.
Blind corner. [1927], New York 1927.
Perishable goods. 1928, New York 1928.
Blood royal. [1929], New York 1930.
Maiden stakes. 1929.
Fire below. 1930.
Adèle and Co. New York 1931, London [1932].
Safe custody. [1932], New York 1932.
Storm music. 1934, New York 1934.
She fell among thieves. 1935, New York [1935].
And Berry came too. [1936], New York [1936].
She painted her face. 1937, New York 1937.
This publican. 1938, Garden City NY 1938 (as The devil in satin).
Gale warning. 1939, New York 1940.
Shoal water. 1940.
Period stuff. 1942.
An eye for a tooth. 1943, New York 1944.
The house that Berry built. 1945, New York 1945.
Red in the morning. 1946, New York 1946 (as Were death denied).
The Berry scene. 1947, New York [1947].
Cost price. 1949, New York [1949] (as The laughing bacchante).
Lower than vermin. 1950.
As Berry and I were saying. 1952.
Ne'er-do-well. 1954.
Wife apparent. 1956.
B-Berry and I look back. [1958].

FRANCIS BRETT YOUNG
1884–1954
Collections

The works of Francis Brett Young: Severn edition. 1934–.

§1

Undergrowth. 1913, New York 1920. With E. B. Young.
Deep sea. 1914.
Robert Bridges: a critical study. 1914.
The dark tower. 1915, New York 1926.
The iron age. 1916.
Five degrees south. 1917. Verse.
Marching on Tanga: with General Smuts in East Africa. 1917, New York 1918, London 1919 (rev).
The crescent moon. 1918, New York 1919.
Captain Swing: a romantic play of 1830. [1919]. With W. E. Stirling.
Poems 1916–18. [1919], New York 1920.
The young physician. 1919, New York 1920.
The tragic bride. [1920], New York 1921.
The black diamond. [1921], New York 1921.
The red knight. [1921], New York 1922.
Pilgrim's rest. [1922], New York 1923.
Cold harbour. [1924], New York 1925.
Woodsmoke. [1924], New York 1924.
Sea horses. 1925, New York 1925.
Portrait of Clare. 1927, New York 1927 (as Love is enough).
The furnace. 1928, New York 1929. Play; with W. Armstrong.
The key of life. 1928, New York 1928.
My brother Jonathan. 1928, New York 1928.
Black roses. 1929, New York 1929.
Jim Redlake. 1930, New York 1930 (as The Redlakes).
Mr and Mrs Pennington. 1931, New York 1931.
Blood oranges. 1932. Story.
The house under the water. 1932, New York 1932.
The cage bird & other stories. 1933, New York 1933.
This little world. 1934, New York 1934.
White ladies. 1935, New York 1935.
Far forest. 1936, New York 1936.
Portrait of a village. 1937, New York 1938.
They seek a country. 1937, New York 1937.
The Christmas box. [1938].
Dr Bradley remembers. 1938, New York 1938, London 1940 (with preface).
The city of gold. 1939, New York 1939.
Cotswold honey and other stories. 1940, New York 1940 (as The ship surgeon's yarn and other stories).
Mr Lucton's freedom. 1940, New York 1940 (as Happy highway).
A man about the house: an old wives' tale. [1942], New York 1942.
The island. 1944, New York 1946. Verse.
In South Africa. 1952. Travel.
Wistanlow. 1956. Unfinished. Pbd as pt of the Severn edn, above.

§2

Young, J. B. Francis Brett Young: a biography. 1962.

4. DRAMA

I. GENERAL WORKS

(1) BIBLIOGRAPHIES

Green room book: or Who's who on the stage—an annual bibliographical record of the dramatic, musical and variety world. 1906-9. Continued as Who's who in the theatre: a bibliographical record of the contemporary stage, 1912-.

International Theatre Institute. World premieres. Paris 1949-64. Lists details of first productions of plays. Incorporated in World Theatre 1965-.

Theatre world annual. 1949-.

The year's work in the theatre. Ed J. C. Trewin 3 vols 1949-51.

The player's library: the catalogue of the Library of the British Drama League. 1950. Suppls 1-3, 1951-6. Lists contents of anthologies and collected volumes of plays.

The Oxford companion to the theatre. Ed P. Hartnoll 1951, 1957 (rev), 1967 (rev).

Modern Drama. 1960-.

Stratman, C. J. A bibliography of British dramatic periodicals 1720-1960. New York 1962.

Patterson, C. A. (ed). Plays in periodicals: an index to English language scripts in twentieth-century journals. Boston [1971?].

(2) COLLECTIONS OF PLAYS

Collections of plays for school or other amateur production are omitted, as are other popular reprint collections. The contents of anthologies are listed in J. H. Ottemiller, Index to plays in collections. New York 1943, 1964 (enlarged); and in The player's library: the catalogue of the library of the British Drama League.

Marriott, J. W. (ed). Great modern British plays. 1932.

Canfield, C. (ed). Plays of the Irish renaissance 1880-1930. New York 1929.

—— Plays of changing Ireland. New York 1936.

Cordell, R. A. (ed). Representative modern plays. New York 1929.

Famous plays of today [and of 1931-9]. 14 vols 1929-39.

Chandler, F. W. and R. A. Cordell (ed). Twentieth-century plays, British. New York 1934, 1939 (rev), 1941 (rev and enlarged).

Trewin, J. C. (ed). Plays of the year, 1948-9 [etc]. 1949-.

Rowell, G. (ed). Late Victorian plays 1890-1914. Oxford 1968 (WC).

(3) HISTORIES AND STUDIES

Montague, C. E. Dramatic values. 1911, New York 1925 (rev).

Yeats, W. B. The cutting of an agate. New York 1912, London 1919 (enlarged); rptd in his Essays and introductions, 1961.

—— Per amica silentia lunae. 1918; rptd in his Mythologies, 1962.

—— The trembling of the veil. 1922 (priv ptd); rptd in The autobiography of W. B. Yeats, New York 1938.

—— Dramatis personae. Dundrum 1935; rptd in The autobiography of W. B. Yeats, New York 1938.

Agate, J. Buzz! buzz! essays of the theatre. 1918.

—— At half-past eight: essays of the theatre 1921-2. 1923.

—— The contemporary theatre, 1923. 1924.

—— The contemporary theatre 1924.

—— The contemporary theatre, 1925. 1926.

—— The contemporary theatre 1926.

—— A short view of the English stage 1900-26. 1926.

—— The contemporary theatre 1924-7. 4 vols 1928.

—— My theatre talks. 1933.

—— First nights. 1934.

—— More first nights. 1937.

—— The amazing theatre. 1939.

—— The contemporary theatre 1944-5. 1946.

See also his regular contributions to Sunday Times 1923-47.

Eliot, T. S. 'Rhetoric' and poetic drama. 1919; rptd in his Selected essays, 1933.

—— The possibility of a poetic drama. In his Sacred wood, 1920.

—— A dialogue on poetic drama. 1928. Introd to Dryden's Of dramatick poesie; rptd (as A dialogue on dramatic poetry) in his Selected essays, 1933.

—— The aims of poetic drama: presidential address to the

Poets' Theatre Guild. 1949; rptd in his Selected essays, 1951.

—— Poetry and drama. 1951; rptd with an additional note in his On poetry and poets, 1957.

—— The three voices of poetry. 1953; rptd in his On poetry and poets, 1957.

Darlington, W. A. *See* his regular contributions to Daily Telegraph 1920-68, New York Times 1939-60.

—— Through the fourth wall. 1922.

—— Literature in the theatre, and other essays. 1925.

—— The actor and his audience. 1949.

—— Six thousand and one nights: forty years a critic. 1960.

Granville-Barker, H. The exemplary theatre. 1922.

—— On dramatic method: being the Clark lectures for 1930. 1931.

—— The use of the drama. Princeton 1945.

Beerbohm, M. Around theatres 1898-1910. 2 vols 1924, 1 vol 1953.

—— More theatres 1898-1903. 1969.

—— Last theatres. 1970.

Nicoll, A. In his British drama, 1925, 1932 (rev), 1947 (rev), 1962 (rev).

—— The development of the theatre: a study of theatrical art from the beginnings to the present day. 1927, 1937 (rev), 1958 (rev), 1966 (rev).

Trewin, J. C. *See* his regular contributions to Morning Post 1932-7, Observer 1937-53, Illustr London News 1947-8.

—— The English theatre. 1948.

—— Drama 1945-50. 1951.

—— Theatre since 1900. 1951.

—— Dramatists of today. 1953.

—— The gay twenties: a decade of the theatre. 1958.

— The turbulent thirties: a further decade of the theatre. 1960.

O'Casey, S. The flying wasp: a laughing look-over of what has been said about the things of the theatre by the English dramatic critics. 1937.

Ellis-Fermor, U. M. Masters of reality. 1942.

— The frontiers of drama. 1945.

Bentley, E. The playwright as thinker: a study of drama in modern times. New York 1946.

— The modern theatre: a study of dramatists and the drama. 1948.

Speaight, R. Drama since 1939. 1948.

— The Christian theatre. 1960.

Donoghue, D. The third voice: modern British and American verse drama. Princeton 1959.

Tynan, K. Curtains. 1961.

Contemporary theatre. Ed J. R. Brown and B. A. Harris 1962.

Gascoigne, B. Twentieth-century drama. 1962.

Wickham, G. Drama in a world of science. 1962.

Elsom, J. Post-war British theatre. 1976, 1979 (rev).

II. INDIVIDUAL DRAMATISTS

Plays are listed in order of date of production, where known, otherwise of pbn. For theatres, the word 'theatre' has been omitted, except in the case of 'Theatre Royal'. 'Court' refers to the 'Court Theatre', London, even for the period during which it was called 'The Royal Court Theatre'. The abbreviations Lacy, French, Deane, Evans, London Play Co, Dramatists Play Service refer to the acting edns of plays issued by these publishers, and Guild to the acting edns of plays issued by the English Theatre Guild Ltd.

For certain Irish dramatists established early in the century, such as Lennox Robinson, St John Ervine, see col. 1170f., above.

SEAN O'CASEY
1880–1964

Mss notebooks, typescript drafts of plays and prose writings in the Berg Collection, New York Public Library. Important letters are in Cornell Univ and Texas Univ Libraries. Private journals, notebooks, correspondence are in the possession of the dramatist's widow.

Collections and Selections

Collected plays. 4 vols 1949–51, New York 1957–9. Within the gates is extensively rev, The silver tassie, Purple dust and Red roses for me are slightly rev.

Selected plays. New York 1954. With foreword by O'Casey.

Mirror in my house: the autobiographies of Sean O'Casey. 2 vols New York 1956, London 1963 (as Autobiographies).

Five one-act plays. 1958.

Three more plays. 1965, New York 1965.

The O'Casey reader: plays, autobiographies, opinions. Ed B. A. Atkinson 1968, New York 1968.

§I

The sacrifice of Thomas Ashe. Dublin 1918.

The story of Thomas Ashe. Dublin 1918.

Songs of the wren. 2 ser Dublin 1918.

More wren songs. Dublin 1918.

The story of the Irish Citizen Army. By 'P. O Cathasaigh' [i.e. O'Casey]. 1919.

The shadow of a gunman: a tragedy in two acts. (Abbey, Dublin 12 April 1923; Court 27 May 1927). In Two plays, 1925, below. Pbd separately 1932 (French).

Kathleen listens in: a phantasy in one act. (Abbey, Dublin 1 Oct 1923). In Feathers from the green crow, 1962, below.

Juno and the paycock: a tragedy in three acts. (Abbey, Dublin 3 March 1924; Royalty 16 Nov 1925). In Two plays, 1925, below. Pbd separately 1932 (French).

Nannie's night out: a comedy in one act. (Abbey, Dublin 29 Sept 1924). In Feathers from the green crow, 1962, below.

Two plays: Juno and the paycock; The shadow of a gunman. 1925, New York 1925.

The plough and the stars: a tragedy in four acts. (Abbey, Dublin 8 Feb 1926, Fortune 12 May 1926). 1926, New York 1926, London [1932] (French).

The silver tassie: a tragi-comedy in four acts. (Apollo 11 Oct 1929). 1928, New York 1928. Rev stage version in Collected plays vol 2, above.

Within the gates: a play of four scenes in a London park. (Royalty 7 Feb 1934). 1933, New York 1934. Rev stage version in Collected plays vol 2, above.

Windfalls: stories, poems, and plays. 1934, New York 1934. Includes The end of the beginning and A pound on demand.

The end of the beginning: a comedy in one act. (Abbey, Dublin 8 Feb 1937; 'Q' 16 Oct 1939). In Windfalls, 1934, above.

The flying wasp: a laughing look-over of what has been said about the things of the theatre by the English dramatic critics. 1937, New York 1937.

A pound on demand: a sketch in one act. ('Q' 16 Oct 1939). In Windfalls, 1934, above.

I knock at the door: swift glances back at things that made me. 1939, New York 1939. 1st vol of autobiography.

The star turns red. (Unity 12 March 1940). 1940.

Pictures in the hallway. 1942, New York 1942. 2nd vol of autobiography.

Red roses for me: a play in four acts. (Olympia, Dublin 15 March 1943; Embassy 26 Feb 1946). 1942, New York 1943. Rev text in Collected plays vol 3, above; further revision pbd New York 1956 (Dramatists Play Service) and in Three more plays, 1965, above.

Purple dust: a wayward comedy in three acts. (People's Theatre, Newcastle-on-Tyne 16 Dec 1943; Mermaid 15 Aug 1962). 1940, New York [1957] (rev) (Dramatists Play Service).

Drums under the windows. 1945, New York 1946. 3rd vol of autobiography.

Oak leaves and lavender: or, A warld on wallpaper. (Lyric 13 May 1947). 1946, New York 1947.

Cock-a-doodle dandy. (People's Theatre, Newcastle-on-Tyne 10 Dec 1949; Court 17 Sept 1959). 1949.

Inishfallen, fare thee well. 1949, New York 1949. 4th vol of autobiography.

Bedtime story: an Anatole burlesque in one act. (Jugoslav-American Hall, New York 7 May 1952). In Collected plays vol 4, above.

Hall of healing: a sincerious farce in one scene. (Jugoslav-American Hall, New York 7 May 1952; Unity 22 May 1953). In Collected plays vol 3, above.

Time to go: a morality comedy in one act. (Jugoslav-American Hall, New York 7 May 1952; Unity 22 May 1953). In Collected plays vol 4, above.

Rose and crown. 1952, New York 1952. 5th vol of autobiography.

Sunset and evening star. 1954, New York 1954. 6th vol of autobiography.

The bishop's bonfire: a sad play within the tune of a polka. (Gaiety, Dublin 28 Feb 1955, Mermaid 26 July 1961). 1955, New York 1955.

The green crow. New York 1956, London 1957. Essays and stories; London edn includes 2 additional essays.

The drums of father Ned: a mickrocosm of Ireland. (Little Th, Lafayette Ind 25 April 1959; Queen's, Hornchurch 8 Nov 1960; Olympia, Dublin 6 June 1966). 1960, New York 1960.

Behind the green curtains (Univ of Rochester NY 5 Dec 1962; Theater der Stadt, Cottbus 20 Nov 1965), Figuro in the night (Th de Lys, New York 30 Oct 1962), The moon shines on Kylenamoe (Theater de Lys, New York 30 Oct 1962): three plays. 1961, New York 1961.

Feathers from the green crow 1905–25. Ed R. Hogan, Columbia Mo 1962, London 1963. Essays, poems, stories, plays. Includes Kathleen listens in and Nannie's night out.

Under a colored cap: articles merry and mournful with comments and a song. 1963, New York 1963.

Blasts and benedictions: articles and stories. Ed R. Ayling 1967, New York 1967.

Letters. Ed D. Krause 1975–.

§2

Starkie, W. Sean O'Casey. In The Irish theatre, ed L. Robinson 1939.

Robinson, L. (ed). Lady Gregory's journals 1916–30. 1946.

—— Ireland's Abbey Theatre: a history 1899–1951. 1951.

Williams, R. The colour of O'Casey. In his Drama from Ibsen to Eliot, 1952, 1968 (rev, as Drama from Ibsen to Brecht).

Ellis-Fermor, U. In her Irish dramatic movement, 1954 (rev).

Hogan, R. The experiments of O'Casey. New York 1960.

—— In his After the Irish renaissance, Minneapolis 1967.

—— and M. J. O'Neill (ed). Joseph Holloway's Abbey Theatre: a selection from his unpublished journal. Carbondale 1967.

Knight, G. W. The drums of father Ned by O' Casey. Stand 4 1960; rptd in his Christian renaissance, 1962 (rev) (as Ever a fighter: on O'Casey's Drums of father Ned).

Krause, D. O'Casey: the man and his work. 1960.

—— A self-portrait of the artist as a man: O'Casey's letters. Dublin 1968.

Coxhead, E. In her Lady Gregory: a literary portrait, 1961, 1966 (rev).

Edwards, A. C. (ed). The Lady Gregory letters to O'Casey. Modern Drama 8 1965.

Fallon, G. O'Casey: the man I knew. 1965.

McCann, S. (ed). The world of O'Casey. 1966.

'Hugh MacDiarmid' (C. M. Grieve). In his Company I've kept: essays in autobiography, 1966.

Malone, M. The plays of O'Casey. Carbondale 1969.

Krause, D. O'Casey and his world. 1976.

SAMUEL BARCLAY BECKETT
b. 1906

Bibliographies

Federman, R. and J. Fletcher. Beckett: his works and his critics. Berkeley and Los Angeles 1970.

Collections and Selections

Molloy—Malone dies—The unnamable: a trilogy. 1959, Paris 1959, New York 1959.

Krapp's last tape and other dramatic pieces. New York 1960. All that fall; Embers; Act without words 1 and 2.

Poems in English. 1961, New York 1963.

End of day: an entertainment from the works of Beckett. (Gaiety, Dublin 5 Oct 1962; New Arts 16 Oct 1962). 1962. Selections from Waiting for Godot etc.

Dramatische Dichtungen. 2 vols Frankfurt 1963–4. Vol 1 contains plays originally written in French, with Beckett's English trns and German trns by E. Tophoven. Vol 2 contains plays originally written in English, with Beckett's French trns and German trns by E. and E. Tophoven.

A Beckett reader. Ed J. Calder 1967.

Odds and ends: plays and sketches. 1977.

Collected poems in English and French. 1977.

§1

Beckett translated his own works, either alone or in collaboration, from English into French and French into English, and such trns are listed separately, below.

Dante... Bruno, Vico... Joyce. In Our exagmination round his factification for incamination of work in progress, Paris 1929, London 1936, Norfolk Conn 1939 (as An exagmination of J. Joyce: analyses of the Work in progress).

From the only poet to a shining whore. In H. Crowder, Henry—music, Paris 1930.

Whoroscope. Paris 1930; London 1961, New York 1963 (in Poems in English, above).

Casket of pralinen for a daughter of a dissipated mandarin; Hell crane to starling; Text; Yoke of liberty. In The European caravan, ed S. Putnam et al, New York 1931.

Proust. 1931, New York [1957].

More pricks than kicks. 1934.

Echo's bones and other precipitates. Paris 1935; London 1961, New York 1963 (in Poems in English, above).

Murphy. 1938, New York [1957].

Murphy. [Paris] 1947. French trn by Beckett, with A. Péron, of preceding.

Assumption; Malacoda. In Transition workshop, New York 1949.

Malone meurt. [Paris] 1951; English trn, Malone dies, 1956, below.

Molloy. Paris 1951, 1963 (with L'expulsé; introd by B. Pingaud). Adapted for stage as Molloy (L'Atelier, Geneva 1 Nov 1965); English trn, Molloy, 1955, below.

En attendant Godot: pièce en deux actes. (Théâtre de Babylone, Paris 5 Jan 1953). [Paris] 1952, New York 1963 (ed G. Brée and E. Schoenfeld), London 1966 (with introd and notes in English by C. Duckworth), New York 1967; English trn, Waiting for Godot, 1955, below.

L'innommable. [Paris] 1953. English trn, The unnamable, 1958, below.

Watt. Paris 1953, New York 1959, London 1963; French trn, Watt, 1968, below.

Waiting for Godot: a tragicomedy in two acts. (Arts 3 Aug 1955; Criterion 12 Sept 1955). New York [1954], London 1956, [1957] French, 1965 (rev and unexpurgated). Trn by Beckett of En attendant Godot, 1953, above. A mimeographed script of the radio version performed by BBC Third Programme, 27 April 1960, pbd 1960.

Molloy. Paris 1955, New York 1955, London 1959 (with Malone dies and The unnamable; see Collections, above). English trn by P. Bowles, with Beckett, of Molloy, 1951, above.

Nouvelles et Textes pour rien. Paris 1955. English trn, Stories and Texts for nothing, New York, 1967, below. Trns of the following were pbd separately; Texte 3, 1960, below; L'expulsé and La fin, 1963, below.

Malone dies. New York [1956], London 1958. Trn by Beckett of Malone meurt, 1951, above.

All that fall: a play for radio. (BBC Third Programme 13 Jan 1957). 1957, New York 1957. French trn, Tous ceux qui tombent, 1959, below.

Acte sans paroles. (Court 3 April 1957; Studio des Champs Elysées, Paris 26 April 1957). Paris 1957 (with Fin de partie). Music by J. Beckett.

Act without words: a mime for one player. 1958 (with Endgame), New York 1958. English trn, by Beckett, of preceding.

Fin de partie. (Court 3 April 1957; Studio des Champs Elysées, Paris 26 April 1957). Paris 1957 (with Acte sans paroles), London 1970 (ed J. and B. S. Fletcher). English trn, Endgame, 1958, below.

From an abandoned work. (BBC Third Programme 14 Dec 1957). 1958. French trn, D'un ouvrage abandonné, 1967, below.

Endgame: a play in one act. (Cherry Lane Theatre, New York 28 Jan 1958; Court 28 Oct 1958). 1958 (with Act without words), New York 1958. Trn by Beckett of Fin de partie, 1957, above.

Krapp's last tape. (Court 28 Oct 1958). 1959 (with Embers), New York 1960 (in Krapp's last tape and other dramatic pieces; see Collections, above). French trn, La dernière bande, 1960, below.

Bram van Velde. Paris 1958 (with G. Duthuit and J. Putman), Turin and Paris 1961 (rev). Includes Beckett's trns of extracts from Three dialogues (with G. Duthuit), first pbd in Transition Forty-nine 5 1949, and Peintres de l'empêchement, first pbd in Derrière le Miroire 11–12 1948. English trn, Bram van Velde, 1960 below.

The unnamable. New York 1958, London 1959 (with Molloy and Malone dies; see Collections, above). Trn by Beckett of L'innommable, 1953, above.

Embers. (BBC Third Programme 24 June 1959). 1959 (with Krapp's last tape), New York 1960 (in Krapp's last tape and other dramatic pieces; see Collections, above). French trn, Cendres, 1966, below (pbd 1960).

Tous ceux qui tombent. (ORTF, Paris 19 Dec 1959). Paris 1957. Trn by R. Pinget, with Beckett, of All that fall, 1957, above.

Henri Hayden: recent paintings. Foreword by Beckett 1959. Rptd from Les Cahiers d'Art-Documents 22 1955.

Gedichte. Wiesbaden 1959. Contains Echo's bones, and uncollected poems in French, with German trns.

Act without words 2: a mime for two players. (Inst of Contemporary Arts 25 Jan 1960). In Krapp's last tape and other dramatic pieces, New York 1960 (see Collections, above); London 1967 (in Eh Joe and other writings). French trn by Beckett, Acte sans paroles 2: pour deux personnages et un aiguillon, in Dramatische Dichtungen, Frankfurt 1963 (see Collections above). Also pbd in Comédie et actes divers, Paris 1966, below.

La dernière bande. (Théâtre Récamier, Paris 22 March 1960). Paris 1960 (with Cendres). Trn by P. Leyris, with Beckett, of Krapp's last tape, 1958, above; adapted as an opera, Krapp: ou la dernière bande, by M. Mihalovici (TNP, Paris 13 Feb 1961).

Bram van Velde. New York 1960. English trn by Beckett, with O. Classe, of Bram van Velde, 1958, above.

Stories and Texts for nothing, 3. In Great French short stories, ed G. Brée, New York 1960. English trn by A. Bonner, with Beckett, of Texte 3 in Nouvelles et Textes pour rien, 1955, above.

Happy days: a play in two acts. (Cherry Lane Theatre, New York 17 Sept 1961; Court 1 Nov 1962). New York 1961, London 1962. French trn, Oh les beaux jours, 1963, below. Bilingual edition, ed J. Knowlson 1978.

Comment c'est. Paris 1961. English trn, How it is, 1964, below.

Words and music. (BBC Third Programme 13 Nov 1962). 1964 (In Play and two short pieces for radio, 1964, below) New York 1968 (in Cascando and other short dramatic pieces, below). Music by J. Beckett. French trn, Paroles et musique, 1966, below.

Text: Ooftish. In R. Cohn, Beckett: the comic gamut, New Brunswick NJ 1962. Uncollected pieces. Text first pbd New Rev April 1932; Ooftish first pbd Transition no 27 1938.

Play: a play in one act. (Ulmer Theater, Ulm-Donau 14 June 1963 [in German trn, Spiel, by E. Tophoven]; Cherry Lane Theatre, New York 4 Jan 1964; Old Vic 7 April 1964). In Play and two short pieces for radio, 1964, below; New York 1968 (in Cascando and other dramatic pieces, below).

Cascando: pièce radiophonique pour musique et voix. (ORTF, Paris 13 Oct 1963). In Dramatische Dichtungen, Frankfurt 1963 (see Collections, above). Also pbd in Comédie et actes divers, Paris 1966, below. Music by M. Mihalovici. English trn, Cascando, 1964, below.

Oh les beaux jours: pièce en deux actes. (Odéon, Paris 21 Oct 1963). Paris 1963. French trn by Beckett of Happy days, 1961, above.

The end. In Writers in revolt, New York 1963; rptd in Stories and Texts for nothing, New York 1967, below. English trn by R. Seaver, with Beckett, of La fin (in Nouvelles et Textes pour rien), 1955, above.

The expelled. In The existential imagination, ed F. R. Karl and L. Hamalian, Greenwich Conn 1963. English trn by R. Seaver, with Beckett, of L'expulsé (in Nouvelles et Textes pour rien), 1955, above.

Comédie: un acte. (Pavillon de Marsan, Paris 14 June 1964). In Dramatische Dichtungen, Frankfurt 1963 (see Collections, above). Also pbd in Comédie et actes divers, Paris 1966, below. French trn by Beckett of Play, 1963, above, with note on spotlight.

Cascando: a radio piece for music and voice. (BBC Third Programme 28 Oct 1964). In Play and two short pieces for radio, 1964, below; New York 1968 (in Cascando and other short dramatic pieces, below). English trn by Beckett of Cascando, 1963, above.

How it is. [1964], New York 1964. English trn by Beckett of Comment c'est, 1961, above.

Play and two short pieces for radio. 1964. Words and music; Cascando.

Come and go: a dramaticule. (Schiller Theater, Berlin Sept 1965 [in German trn]); Abbey [Peacock] Theatre, Dublin 28 Feb 1968). Frankfurt 1966 (in Beckett: aus einem aufgegebenen Werk und kurze Spiele, [with German trn]), London 1967, New York 1968 (in Cascando and other short dramatic pieces). German trn by H. M. Ehardt pbd separately Stuttgart 1968, with facs of Beckett's ms in English. French trn, Va et vient, 1966, below.

Film. (Venice Biennale 4 Sept 1965). In Eh Joe and other writings, 1967, below; New York 1968 (in Cascando and other short dramatic pieces, below), 1969 (with scenario, illustrations of production shots and essay by the director, A. Schneider).

A tribute to Aldington. In R. Aldington: an intimate portrait, ed A. Kershaw and F.-J. Temple, Carbondale [1965].

Imagination morte imaginez. Paris 1965.

Imagination dead imagine. 1965. Trn by Beckett of preceding.

Va et vient. (Odéon, Paris 28 Feb 1966). In Comédie et actes divers, Paris 1966, below. French trn by Beckett of Come and go, 1965, above.

Cendres: pièce radiophonique en un acte (ORTF, Paris 8 May 1966). Paris 1960 (with La dernière bande). Trn by R. Pinget, with Beckett, of Embers, 1959, above.

Eh Joe: a piece for television. (BBC Television 4 July 1966). In Eh Joe and other writings, 1967, below; New York 1968 (in Cascando and other short dramatic pieces, below). French trn, Dis Joe, 1968, below.

Assez. Paris 1966. English trn, Enough, in No's knife, 1967, below.

Bing. Paris 1966. English trn, Ping, ibid.

Comédie et actes divers. Paris 1966. Va et vient; Cascando; Paroles et musique; Dis Joe; Acte sans paroles 2.

Paroles et musique: pièce radiophonique. Paris 1966. In Comédie et actes divers, Paris 1966, above. French trn by Beckett of Words and music, 1962, above.

Dans le cylindre. Biblio 35 1967. Fragment, from the same 'matrix' as L'issue.

D'un ouvrage abandonné. Paris [1967]. French trn by L. and A. Janvier, with Beckett, of From an abandoned work, 1957, above.

Eh Joe and other writings. 1967. Act without words 2; Film.

No's knife: collected shorter prose 1945–66. 1967. Contains Stories and Texts for nothing (1967, below) and From an abandoned work; Residua of unfinished novels (Enough; Imagination dead imagine; Ping). The following were tr Beckett for this edn: The calmative (from Le calmant, 1955); Enough (from Assez, 1966); Ping (from Bing, 1966).

Stories and Texts for nothing. New York 1967. English trn by Beckett (The end and The expelled with R. Seaver) of Nouvelles et Textes pour rien, 1955 above.

Têtes-mortes. Paris 1967. Contains D'un ouvrage abandonné; Assez; Imagination morte imaginez; Bing.

Cascando and other short dramatic pieces New York 1968. Words and music; Eh Joe; Play; Come and go; Film.

Dis Joe: pièce pour la télévision. (ORTF, Paris 2 Feb 1968). In Comédie et actes divers, Paris 1966, above.

L'issue. Paris 1968. Fragment, from the same 'matrix' as Dans le cylindre, with 6 illustrations by Arikha.

Poèmes. Paris 1968.

Watt. Paris 1968. French trn by L. and A. Janvier, with Beckett, of Watt, 1953, above.

Sans. Paris 1969.

Lessness. 1970. Trn by Beckett of preceding.

Mercier et camier: roman. Paris 1970; tr Beckett 1974.

Pour finir encore et autres foirades. Paris 1976; tr Beckett as For to end yet again and other fizzles, 1976.

Four novellas. 1977.

Six residua. 1978.

§2

Muir, E. Listener 4 July 1934. Review of More pricks than kicks.

—— Listener 16 March 1938. Review of Murphy.

Robbe-Grillet, A. Beckett: auteur dramatique. Critique 9 1953; rptd (rev) in his Pour un nouveau roman, Paris 1963; tr 1965 (as Towards a new novel).

Bentley, E. The talent of Beckett. New Republic 14 May 1956; rptd, with addn, Postscript 1967, in Casebook on Waiting for Godot 1967, below.

—— In his What is theatre, Boston 1956.

—— In his Life of the drama, New York 1964.

Mauriac, C. Beckett. Preuves no 61 1956; rptd (rev) in his L'alittérature contemporaine, Paris 1958 (tr 1959 as The new literature).

O'Casey, S. Not waiting for Godot. Encore 6 1956; rptd in his Blasts and benedictions, ed R. Ayling 1967.

In Letters of James Joyce, ed S. Gilbert and R. Ellmann 3 vols 1957–66.

Brooke-Rose, C. Beckett and the anti-novel. London Mag 5 1958.

Esslin, M. Beckett: the search for the self. In his The theatre of the absurd, New York 1961, London 1968 (rev).

—— In The novelist as philosopher, ed J. Cruikshank 1962. See also Twentieth-century views—Beckett: a collection of critical essays, ed Esslin 1965.

Frye, N. The nightmare life in death. Hudson Rev 13 1960.

Heppenstall, R. In his The fourfold tradition, London 1961.

—— In his The intellectual part, 1963.

Kenner, H. Beckett: a critical study. New York 1961, Berkeley 1968 (rev).

—— Flaubert, Joyce and Beckett: the stoic comedians. Boston [1962].

Tynan, K. In his Curtains, 1961.

—— In his Tynan right and left, 1967.

Fletcher, J. The novels of Beckett. 1964. With bibliography.

—— Beckett's art. 1967.

—— The arrival of Godot. MLR 64 1969.

—— and J. Spurling. Beckett: a study of his plays. 1972.

Coe, R. N. Beckett. Edinburgh 1964 (Writers & Critics).

Tindall, W. Y. Beckett. New York 1964.

Federman, R. Journey to chaos: Beckett's early fiction. Berkeley and Los Angeles 1965.

Twentieth century views—Beckett: a collection of critical essays. Ed M. Esslin, Englewood Cliffs NJ [1965].

Modern Drama 9 1966. Beckett issue, ed R. Cohn.

Beckett at sixty: a festschrift. 1967. Introd by J. Calder.

Casebook on Waiting for Godot: the impact of Beckett's modern classic. Ed R. Cohn, New York 1967.

Hayman, R. Beckett. 1968.

Twentieth century interpretations of Endgame. Ed B. G. Chevigny, Englewood Cliffs NJ 1969.

Alvarez, A. Beckett. 1973.

Kenner, H. A reader's guide to Beckett. 1973.

Mercier, V. Beckett/Beckett. New York 1977.

Bair, D. Beckett: a biography. 1978.

JOE RANDOLPH ACKERLEY
1896–1967

Poems by four authors. Cambridge 1923. J. R. Ackerley, A. Y. Campbell, E. Davidson, F. Kendon.

The prisoners of war: a play in three acts. (Court 5 July 1925). 1925.

Escapers all: being the personal narratives of fifteen escapers from war-time prison camps 1914–18. Ed Ackerley 1932.

Hindoo holiday: an Indian journal. 1932, New York 1932, London 1952 (with addns).

My dog Tulip. 1956.

We think the world of you. 1960, New York 1961. Fiction.

My father and myself. 1968. Autobiography.

ENID BAGNOLD
b. 1889

A diary without dates. 1918, New York 1935. Experience as a VAD.

The sailing ships and other poems. 1918.

The happy foreigner. 1920, New York 1920. Novel.

Serena Blandish: or the difficulty of getting married. By a lady of quality. 1924, New York 1925. Anon. Adapted as a play with title Serena Blandish by S. N. Behrman (Morosco, New York 23 Jan 1929, Gate 13 Sept 1938), New York 1925 (in his Three plays).

Alice and Thomas and Jane. 1930, New York 1931. Adapted as children's play with same title by V. Beringer (Westminster 20 Dec 1933), [1934].

Alexander of Asia. 1935. Trn of Alexandre asiatique by M. L. Bibesco.

'National Velvet'. 1935, New York 1935. Novel. As play (Embassy 20 April 1946), [1946] (in Embassy successes, 2), New York 1961 Dramatists' Play Service. Filmed MGM 1944.

The door of life. New York 1938. Novel. Pts pbd serially as Birth.

The squire. 1938. Novel.

Lottie Dundass: a play in three acts. (Wimbledon 5 Oct 1942, Vaudeville 21 July 1943). 1941, [1944] French (rev, in two acts).

Poor Judas. (Bradford Civic Theatre Nov 1946, Arts 18 July 1951). In Two plays, 1951, Collections above.

The loved and envied. 1951, New York 1951. Novel.

The chalk garden. (Ethel Barrymore Theatre, New York 26 Oct 1955, Haymarket 11 April 1956). 1956, New

York [1956] French, London [1959] (rev). Filmed 1964.
The last joke. (Phoenix 28 Sept 1960). In Four plays, 1970, Collections above.
The Chinese prime minister: a comedy in three acts. (Royale, New York 2 Jan 1964; Arts, Cambridge 26 April 1965 [rev], Globe 20 May 1965). New York 1964 French.
Call me Jacky. (Playhouse, Oxford 27 Feb 1968). In Plays of the year, vol 34, 1968.
Autobiography. 1969.
The following play was not pbd: Gertie (*Plymouth, New York 30 Jan 1952, Q 10 Nov 1953* [as Little idiot]).

CLIFFORD BAX
1886–1963

Twenty Chinese poems paraphrased. 1910, [1916] (rev and enlarged, as Twenty-five Chinese poems).
Poems dramatic and lyrical. 1911.
The poetasters of Ispahan: a comedy in verse. (Little 28 April 1912). In Antique pageantry, 1921 below. Pbd separately Boston 1929.
The masque of the planets. In Orpheus no 17, 1912. Play.
Friendship. 1913, New York 1913. Essay.
The summit. In Orpheus no 21, 1913; rptd 1921 in Antique pageantry, below.
The game of death. In Orpheus no 23, 1913. Play.
Aucassin and Nicolette: a verse play. In Orpheus no 26, 1914; rptd 1921 (in Antique pageantry, below), Boston [1930].
Japanese impromptus. Speen 1914. Verse. With D. Bax.
Square pegs: a rhymed fantasy for two girls. (Edwards Sq, Kensington, 9 Jan 1920). 1920, [1927] French.
A house of words. Oxford 1920. Poems.
Antique pageantry: a book of verse plays. 1921. The poetasters of Ispahan; The apricot tree; The summit; Aucassin and Nicolette.
Old King Cole. 1921, Boston 1922, [1935] French (subtitled: a play for children in three acts).
Shakespeare: a play in five episodes. 1921, [1933] French. With H. F. Rubinstein.
The traveller's tale. Oxford 1921. Poem.
The apricot tree: a play in one act. (Deansgate, Manchester 23 Oct 1922). In Orpheus no 25, 1914; rptd 1921 in Antique pageantry, above.
Prelude & fugue: a play in one act. (Studio plays 1). (Etlinger Theatre School 7 Dec 1922). [1924].
Polite satires. 1922. The unknown hand; The volcanic island; Square pegs.
Midsummer madness: a play for music. (Lyric, Hammersmith 3 July 1924). 1923.
Nocturne in Palermo. 1924. Play.
The rose and the cross: a play in one act. (Studio plays, 2). [1924].
The cloak: a play in one act. (Studio plays 3). [1924], [1954] French.
Up stream: a drama in three acts. (Duke of York's 20 Dec 1925). Oxford 1922, New York 1923.
Inland far: a book of thoughts and impressions. 1925.
Mr Pepys: a ballad-opera. (Everyman 11 Feb 1926; Royalty 9 March 1926). 1926, [1927] French.
Bianca Capello. 1927, New York 1928. Biography.
Many a green isle. 1927. Story.
Socrates: a play in six scenes. (Prince of Wales 23 March 1930). 1930.
The Venetian. (Little 28 Feb 1931). In Valiant ladies, 1931 below. Pbd separately [1934] French.
The immortal lady. (Royalty 9 Oct 1931). In Valiant ladies, 1931 below. Pbd separately 1932 French.
The chronicles of Cupid: being a masque of love throughout the ages. [1931] French. With G. Dearmer.
Valiant ladies: three new plays. 1931, New York 1931.

The Venetian, The rose without a thorn, The immortal lady.
The rose without a thorn: a play in three acts. (Duchess 10 Feb 1932). In Valiant ladies, 1931 above. Pbd separately [1933] French.
Farewell, my muse. 1932, New York 1932. Poems.
Leonardo da Vinci. 1932, New York 1932. Biography.
Pretty witty Nell: an account of Nell Gwynn and her environment. 1932, New York 1933.
Silly Willy. In Twelve short plays, 1932.
That immortal sea: a meditation upon the future of religion and sexual morality. 1933.
April in August: a play in three acts. (Comedy 13 May 1934). [1934] French.
The quaker's cello: a play in one act. [1934] French.
Tragic Nesta: a play in one act. [1934] French.
Ideas and people. 1936. Sketches and articles.
Battles long ago. In Eight one-act plays of 1936, ed W. Armstrong 1937.
The life of the white devil [Vittoria Orsini, Duchess of Bracciano]. 1940.
Evenings in Albany. 1942. Reminiscences.
Hemlock for eight: a radio play. (BBC 30 May 1943). 1946. With L. M. Lion.
Time with a gift of tears: a modern romance. 1943. Novel.
Whither the theatre—? a letter to a young playwright. 1945.
Golden eagle: a drama. (Whitehall 29 Jan 1946). 1946.
The beauty of women. 1946.
The Buddha: a radio version of his life and ideas. (BBC 16 March 1947). 1947.
The play of St Lawrence: a pageant play for production in a church. [1947] French.
Circe: a play in three acts (Q 19 Oct 1948 as A day, a night and a morrow). 1949.
Rosemary for remembrance. 1948. Reminiscences.
Some I knew well. 1951, New York 1952. Biographical sketches.
Who's who in Heaven: a sketch. Meldreth 1954 (limited edn).

'JAMES BRIDIE',
OSBORNE HENRY MAVOR
1888–1951

Some talk of Alexander: a revue with interludes in the antique mode. 1926. Wartime reminiscences.
The sunlight sonata: or, To meet the seven deadly sins. (Lyric, Glasgow 20 March 1928). In The switchback [etc], 1930, below.
The switchback (Birmingham Repertory 9 March 1929; rev version Malvern Festival 8 Aug 1931). In The switchback [etc], 1930, below.
What it is to be young. (Birmingham Repertory 2 Nov 1929, Q 26 April 1937). In Colonel Wotherspoon and other plays, 1934, below.
The anatomist: a lamentable comedy of Knox, Burke and Hare and the West Port murders. (Lyceum, Edinburgh 6 July 1930, Westminster 7 Oct 1931). In The anatomist and other plays, 1931, below.
The girl who did not want to go to Kuala Lumpur. (Lyric, Glasgow Nov 1930). In Colonel Wotherspoon and other plays, 1934, below.
Tobias and the angel: a comedy. (Festival Theatre, Cambridge 20 Nov 1930; Westminster 9 March 1932). In The anatomist and other plays, 1931, below.
The switchback; The pardoner's tale; The sunlight sonata: a comedy; a morality; a farce-morality. 1930.
The dancing bear: a comedy in three acts. (Lyric, Glasgow 24 Feb 1931). In Colonel Wotherspoon and other plays, 1934, below.
The anatomist and other plays: The anatomist; Tobias and the angel; The amazed evangelist. 1931.

The perilous adventure of Sir Bingo Walker of Alpaca Square. 1931. Children's story.

The amazed evangelist: a comedy in one act. (Westminster 12 Dec 1932). In The anatomist and other plays, 1931, above. Pbd separately 1932 (as The amazed evangelist: a nightmare).

Jonah and the whale: a morality in three acts and a prologue. (Westminster 12 Dec 1932; preceded by The amazed evangelist). 1932. A 2nd version broadcast (BBC 22 Feb 1942) as The sign of the prophet Jonah: a play for broadcasting, and pbd, with another version, Jonah 3, in Plays for plain people, 1944, below.

A sleeping clergyman: a play in two acts. (Malvern Festival 29 July 1933, Piccadilly 19 Sept 1933). 1933, New York 1934.

Marriage is no joke: a melodrama. (Globe 6 Feb 1934). 1934.

Colonel Wotherspoon, or the fourth way of greatness: a comedy in three acts. (Lyric, Glasgow 23 March 1934; Arts 24 June 1934). In Colonel Wotherspoon and other plays, 1934, below.

Mary Read: a play in three acts. (His Majesty's 21 Nov 1934). 1935. With C. Gurney.

Colonel Wotherspoon and other plays, with a preface. 1934.

Mr Bridie's alphabet for little Glasgow highbrows. 1934. Satirical essays rptd from Glasgow Herald.

The black eye: a comedy. (Shaftesbury 11 Oct 1935). 1935. With author's note to J. Agate.

Mrs Waterbury's millennium: a play in one act. [1935] French.

Storm in a teacup: an Anglo-Scottish version of Sturm im Wasserglas by Bruno Frank. (Edinburgh 20 Jan 1936; Royalty 5 Feb 1936). 1936.

Susannah and the elders. (Duke of York's 31 Oct 1937). In Susannah and the elders and other plays, 1940, below.

The Scottish character as it was viewed by Scottish authors from Galt to Barrie. Greenock 1937; rptd in Tedious and brief, 1944, below.

The king of nowhere: a play in three acts. (Old Vic 15 March 1938). In The king of nowhere and other plays, 1938, below.

Babes in the wood: a quiet farce. (Embassy 14 June 1938). In The king of nowhere and other plays, 1938, below.

The last trump. (Malvern Festival 5 Aug 1938, Duke of York's 13 Sept 1938). In The king of nowhere and other plays, 1938, below.

The kitchen comedy: a play for broadcasting. (BBC Glasgow Regional 18 Nov 1938). In Susannah and the elders and other plays, 1940, below.

The king of nowhere and other plays. 1938. The king of nowhere; Babes in the wood; The last trump.

The letter-box rattles: a sentimental comedy. [1938].

The golden legend of Shults: a play in three acts. (Perth 24 July 1939). In Susannah and the elders and other plays, 1940, below.

What say they?: a play in two acts. (Malvern Festival 7 Aug 1939). 1939.

One way of living. 1939. Autobiography.

The theatre: a paper read to The Thirteen. [Glasgow 1939]; rptd in Tedious and brief, 1944, below.

Susannah and the elders and other plays, with a preface. 1940. Susannah and the elders; What say they?; The golden legend of Shults; The kitchen comedy.

The niece of the hermit Abraham. (Lyric, Glasgow Aug 1942). Re-titled The dragon and the dove: or How the hermit Abraham fought the devil for his niece: a play in two acts. (Arts 9 March 1943, in double bill with A change for the worse).

Jonah 3: a new version of Jonah and the whale. (Unnamed Society, Manchester Nov 1942). In Plays for plain people, 1944, below.

Holy Isle: a play in three acts. (Arts 11 Dec 1942). In Plays for plain people, 1944, below.

A change for the worse. (Arts 9 March 1943). In Tedious and brief, 1944, below.

Mr Bolfry: a play in four scenes. (Westminster 3 Aug 1943). In Plays for plain people, 1944, below.

It depends what you mean: an improvisation for the Glockenspiel: a play in three acts. (Westminster 12 Oct 1944). 1948.

The Forrigan reel. (Glasgow Citizens' at Athenaeum, Glasgow 25 Dec 1944). The rev version, The Forrigan reel: a ballad opera (Sadler's Wells 24 Oct 1945) pbd 1949 in John Knox and other plays, 1949, below.

Plays for plain people: Lancelot, Holy Isle, Mr Bolfry, Jonah 3, The sign of the prophet Jonah, The dragon and the dove. 1944.

Tedious and brief. 1944. Essays, lectures etc.

Lancelot: a play in two acts. (Glasgow Citizens' 30 Oct 1945). In Plays for plain people, 1944, above.

The British drama. Glasgow 1945.

Dr Angelus: a play in three acts. (Edinburgh, 23 June 1947, Phoenix 30 July 1947). In John Knox and other plays, 1949, below.

John Knox: a play in three acts. (Glasgow Citizens' 18 Aug 1947). In John Knox and other plays, 1949, below.

Daphne Laureola: a play in four acts. (Wyndham's 23 March 1949). 1949.

A small stir: letters on the English. 1949. With M. McLaren.

The Christmas card. [1949]. Story.

John Knox and other plays. 1949.

The queen's comedy: a Homeric fragment. (Lyceum, Edinburgh Festival 21 Aug 1950). 1950.

Mr Gillie: a play. (Glasgow Citizens' 13 Feb 1950; Garrick 9 March 1950). 1950.

The Baikie Charivari: or The seven prophets—a miracle play. (Glasgow Citizens' 6 Oct 1952). 1953.

Meeting at night. (Glasgow Citizens' 17 May 1954). 1956 (rev A. Batty). Introd by J. B. Priestley.

'DENIS CANNAN', DENNIS PULLEIN-THOMPSON
b. 1919

Captain Carvallo. (St James's 9 Aug 1950). [1951] French.

Colombe. (New 13 Dec 1951). 1952. Adapted from a play by Anouilh.

Misery me: a comedy of woe. (Duchess 16 March 1955). [1956] French.

You and your wife. (Bristol Old Vic 28 June 1955). [1956] French.

The power and the glory: a drama in three acts. (Phoenix 5 April 1956). New York [1959] French. Adapted from the novel by Graham Greene. With P. Bost.

Who's your father? a comedy in three acts. (Cambridge 16 Dec 1958). [1959] French.

Cannan's first play, Max (People's Palace, Playgoers Club 10 April 1949) was unpbd. He wrote several unpbd screen plays and radio scripts, including Headlong Hall, adapted from the novel by T. L. Peacock (BBC 30 July 1950), The moth and the star, adapted from Liber amoris by W. Hazlitt (BBC 7 Nov 1950) and The greeting, adapted from O. Sitwell (BBC 16 Nov 1964).

SIR NOËL PIERCE COWARD
1899–1973

Collections and Selections

Collected sketches and lyrics. [1931], New York 1932.

Play parade. 6 vols 1934–62. With introds by the author.

The Noël Coward song book. 1953, New York 1953.

§1

'I'll leave it to you': a light comedy in three acts. (Gaiety, Manchester 3 May 1920; New 21 July 1920). [1920] French.

The young idea: a comedy in three acts. (Prince's Bristol 25 Sept 1922, Savoy 1 Feb 1923). [1924] French, New York 1924.

A withered nosegay. 1922, New York 1922 (as Terribly intimate portraits). Sketches.

Poems by Hernia Whittlebot [Noël Coward], with an appreciation by Coward. [1923]. Parody of Edith Sitwell's poetry.

The vortex: a play in three acts. (Everyman 25 Nov 1924). 1925, New York 1925. Silent film version 1927.

Fallen angels: a comedy in three acts. (Globe 21 April 1925). 1925, 1958 French (rev).

Hay fever: a light comedy in three acts. (Ambassadors 8 June 1925). 1925, New York 1925, London 1927 (rev) French.

Easy virtue: a play in three acts. (Empire, New York, Winter 1925; Opera House, Manchester 31 May 1926; Duke of York's 9 June 1926). 1926, New York 1926. Silent film version 1927.

Chelsea buns, by Hernia Whittlebot. Ed [i.e. written by] N. Coward [1925]. Parody of Edith Sitwell's poetry.

The queen was in the parlour: a romance in three acts. (St Martin's 24 Aug 1926). 1926. Film versions 1927 (silent), 1928 (talking).

The rat trap: a play in four acts. (Everyman 18 Oct 1926). 1924.

'This was a man': a comedy in three acts. (Klaw Theatre, New York 23 Nov 1926). New York 1926, London 1928 (in Home chat; Sirocco; 'This was a man': three plays).

The marquise: a comedy in three acts. (Criterion 16 Feb 1927). 1927.

Home chat. (Duke of York's 25 Oct 1927). 1927.

Sirocco. (Daly's 24 Nov 1927). 1927.

This year of Grace. [C. B. Cochran's 1928 revue]. (Palace, Manchester 28 Feb 1928; Pavilion 22 March 1928). In Play parade vol 2, 1939.

Bitter sweet. (Palace, Manchester 2 July 1929; His Majesty's 18 July 1929). 1929, New York 1929. Film versions 1933, 1941.

Private lives: an intimate comedy in three acts. (King's, Edinburgh 18 Aug 1930; Phoenix 24 Sept 1930). 1930, New York 1931, London [1947] French. Film version 1931.

Cavalcade. (Drury Lane 13 Oct 1931). 1932, New York 1933. Film version 1932.

Words and music: a revue. (Opera House, Manchester 25 Aug 1932; Adelphi 16 Sept 1932). In Play parade vol 2, 1939.

Spangled unicorn: a selection from the works of Albrecht Drausler [et al]. [1932], New York 1933. Parodies.

Design for living: a comedy in three acts. (Hanna Theatre, Cleveland, Ohio 2 Jan 1933; Ethel Barrymore, New York 24 Jan 1933; Theatre Royal, Brighton 16 Jan 1939; Haymarket 25 Jan 1939). 1933, New York 1933. Film version 1933.

Conversation piece: a romantic comedy (His Majesty's, 16 Feb 1934). 1934, New York 1934.

Point Valaine: a play in three acts. (Colonial, Boston 25 Dec 1934; Ethel Barrymore, New York 16 Jan 1935; Playhouse, Liverpool 18 Oct 1944; Embassy 3 Sept 1947). 1935, New York 1935.

To-night at 8.30: plays. 3 vols 1936, New York 1936. Pbd separately (French) 1938.

Present indicative. 1937, New York 1937. Autobiography.

Operette. (Opera House, Manchester 17 Feb 1938; His Majesty's 16 March 1938). 1938.

To step aside: seven short stories. 1939, New York 1939.

Blithe spirit: an improbable farce in three acts. (Opera House, Manchester 16 June 1941; Piccadilly 2 July 1941). New York 1941, London 1942, [1942] French,

New York 1966 (television adaptation by R. Hartung). Film version 1944.

Australia visited, 1940. 1941. Broadcasts.

Present laughter: a light comedy in three acts. (Grand, Blackpool 20 Sept 1942; Haymarket 29 April 1943). 1943, New York 1947, London [1949] French, New York [1949].

This happy breed: a play in three acts. (Grand, Blackpool 21 Sept 1942; Haymarket 30 April 1943). 1943, [1945] French, New York 1947. Film version 1943.

Middle East diary: July to October 1943. 1944, New York 1944.

Pacific 1860: a musical romance. (Drury Lane 19 Dec 1946). In Play parade vol 5, 1958.

'Peace in our time': a play in two acts and eight scenes. (Theatre Royal, Brighton 15 July 1947; Lyric 22 July 1947). 1947, New York 1948, London [1949] French.

The ace of clubs: a musical play in 2 acts. (Palace, Manchester 16 May 1950; Cambridge 7 July 1950). In Play parade vol 6, 1962.

Relative values: a light comedy in three acts. (Theatre Royal, Newcastle 15 Oct 1951; Savoy 28 Nov 1951). 1952, [1954] French.

Star quality. 1951, New York 1951. Stories.

Quadrille: a romantic comedy in three acts. (Opera House, Manchester 15 July 1952; Phoenix 12 Sept 1952). 1952, [1954] French, New York 1955.

After the ball: an operette based on Lady Windermere's fan. (Royal Court, Liverpool 1 March 1954; Globe 10 June 1954). Book of lyrics [1954].

Future indefinite. 1954, New York 1954. Autobiography 1939–45.

South Sea bubble: a comedy in three acts. (Opera House, Manchester 19 March 1956; Lyric 25 April 1956). 1956, [1958] French.

Nude with violin: a light comedy in three acts. (Olympia, Dublin 24 Sept 1956; Globe 7 Nov 1956). 1957, [1958] French.

Waiting in the wings: a play in three acts. (Olympia, Dublin 8 Aug 1960; Duke of York's 7 Sept 1960). 1960, [1960] French.

Pomp and circumstance. 1960, New York 1960. Novel.

Seven stories. Garden City NY 1963.

Pretty Polly Barlow and other stories. 1964, New York 1965 (as Pretty Polly and other stories).

Suite in three keys: A song at twilight; Shadows of the evening; Come into the garden, Maud (all at Queen's 14–25 April 1966). 1966, Garden City NY 1967. Pbd separately 1967 French.

Pretty Polly. (ABC Television 23 July 1966). In Pretty Polly Barlow and other stories, 1964, above. Filmed 1967.

Bon voyage and other stories. 1967, New York 1968 (as Bon Voyage).

Not yet the dodo and other verses. 1967, New York 1968.

Post-mortem: a play in eight scenes. (BBC 2 Television 17 Sept 1968). 1931, New York 1931.

Coward also composed the following unpbd plays, revues and musical plays: The last chapter (*later* Ida collaborates) (*Theatre Royal, Aldershot 20 Aug 1917*) *and* Woman and whisky (*Wimbledon 21 Jan 1918*) [*both with* E. Wynne], Bottles and bones (*Drury Lane 16 May 1921*), The better half: comedy in one act (*Little 31 May 1922*), London calling (*Duke of York's 4 Sept 1923*), *with Ronald Jeans*, On with the dance (*Palace, Manchester 17 March 1925*; *Pavilion 30 April 1925*), Set to music (*Haymarket 4 July 1939*), Star chamber (*BBC Home Service 18 May 1940*), Sigh no more (*Piccadilly 28 Aug 1945*), The kindness of Mrs Redcliffe (*BBC Home Service 2 June 1951*), Sail away (*Broadhurst, New York 3 Oct 1961*; *Hippodrome, Bristol 31 May 1962*; *Savoy 21 June 1962*), Mr and Mrs [*based on* Fumed oak *and* Brief encounter] (*Manchester Repertory 10 Nov 1968*; *Palace 11 Dec 1968*). *He adapted* G. Feydeau, Occupe-toi d'Amélie *as* Look after Lulu (*Royal, Newcastle 20 July 1959; Court 29 July 1959*). *The script of the film,* In which we serve (*1942*) *is unpbd.*

§2

MaccCarthy, D. Maugham and Coward. In his Humanities, 1953.
—— Coward. In his Theatre, 1954.
Mander, R. and J. Mitchenson. Theatrical companion to Coward: a pictorial record of the first performances of the theatrical works, with an appreciation of Coward's work in the theatre by T. Rattigan. [1957].
Levin, M. Noel Coward. New York 1968.
Morley, S. A talent to amuse: a biography of Coward. 1969.
Lesley, C. The life of Coward. 1976.

'CLEMENCE DANE',
WINIFRED ASHTON
1888–1965

Collections

Recapture: a Clemence Dane omnibus. 1932.
Collected plays. 1961–.

§1

Regiment of women. 1917, New York 1917. Novel.
First the blade: a comedy of growth. 1918, New York 1918. Novel.
Legend. 1919, New York 1920. Novel.
A bill of divorcement: a play in three acts. (St Martin's 14 March 1921). 1921, New York 1921.
Will Shakespeare: an invention in four acts. (Shaftesbury 17 Nov 1921). 1921, [1951] French.
The way things happen: a story in three acts. (Broad Street, Newark NJ 24 Dec 1923; Ambassadors 2 Feb 1924). 1924. Based on Legend, 1919 above.
Shivering shocks: or the hiding place—a play for boys. [1923] French.
Wandering stars, together with The lover. 1924, New York 1924. Stories.
Naboth's vineyard: a stage piece. 1925.
Granite: a tragedy. (Ambassadors 15 June 1926). 1926, [1949] French.
The woman's side. 1926. New York 1927. Feminist essays.
Mariners. (Plymouth, New York 4 March 1927; Wyndham's 29 April 1929). 1927, New York 1927.
The dearly beloved of Benjamin Cobb: a tale. 1927.
Mr Fox: a play for boys. [1927] French.
A traveller returns: a play in one act. [1927] French.
Adam's opera: the text of a play, set to music by R. Addinsell. (Old Vic 3 Dec 1928). 1928, New York 1929.
The Babyons: a family chronicle. 1928. 4 vols New York 1928.
The king waits: a tale. 1929.
Tradition and Hugh Walpole. New York 1929, London 1930.
Broome stages. 1931, New York 1931. Novel.
Wild Decembers: a play in three acts. (Apollo 26 May 1933), 1932, New York 1933, [1934] French. A Brontë play.
Come of age: a play in music [by R. Addinsell] and verse. (Maxine Elliott, New York Jan 1934). 1933, New York 1934. About Thomas Chatterton.
Moonlight is silver: a play in three acts. (Queen's 19 Sept 1934). 1934.
Fate cries out: nine tales. 1935, New York 1935.
The moon is feminine. 1938, New York 1938. Novel.
The arrogant history of White Ben. 1939, New York 1939. Novel.

Cousin Muriel: a play in three acts. (Globe 7 March 1940). 1940.
The saviours: seven [radio] plays on one theme. (BBC Home Service 24 Nov 1940 to 11 Nov 1941). 1942, New York 1942.
Trafalgar Day 1940. 1940, New York 1941. Poem.
The golden reign of Queen Elizabeth. (Theatre Royal, York 21 Jan 1941). [1941] French.
Alice's adventures in wonderland and through the looking-glass dramatised, with music by R. Addinsell. (Scala 24 Dec 1943). [1948] French; 1951.
The lion and the unicorn: a play in three acts. 1943.
He brings great news: a story. 1944, New York 1945.
Call home the heart: a play. (St James's 10 April 1947). 1947.
The flower girls. 1954, New York 1955. Novel.
Scandal at Coventry. (BBC 17 March 1958). In Collected plays vol 1, 1961, above.
Eighty in the shade: a play in three acts. (Royal, Newcastle 24 Nov 1958; Globe 8 Jan 1959). 1959, [1960] French.
Till time shall end: a play in two acts. (BBC Television 30 Nov 1958). In Collected plays vol 1, 1961, above.
Approaches to drama. 1961. Address.
The godson: a [Shakespearean] fantasy. 1964.
London has a garden. 1964. On Covent Garden.

WILLIAM DOUGLAS-HOME
b. 1912

Selections

Plays. 1958.

§1

Home truths. 1939. Verse.
'Now Barabbas...' (Bolton's 11 Feb 1947; Vaudeville 7 March 1947). 1947. Screenplay: Warner Brothers 1949.
The Chiltern Hundreds: a comedy in three acts. (Vaudeville 26 Aug 1947). [1949] French. Screen play: Two cities 1949.
Master of Arts: a farcical comedy in three acts. (Royal, Brighton 20 June 1949; Strand 1 Sept 1949). [1950] French.
The thistle and the rose. (Bolton's 6 Sept 1949; Vaudeville 15 May 1951). In The plays of W. D. Home, 1958.
The bad Samaritan. (New, Bromley 2 Sept 1952; Criterion 24 June 1953, with Prologue and Epilogue omitted). 1954 Evans. Original version in The plays of W. D. Home, 1958.
The manor of Northstead: a comedy in three acts. (Duchess 28 April 1954). [1956] French.
Half-term report: an autobiography. 1954.
The reluctant debutante: a play in three acts. (Cambridge 24 May 1955; Henry Miller, New York 10 Oct 1956). 1956 Evans, [1957] French. Screen play: MGM 1958.
The iron duchess: a play in two acts. (Royal, Brighton 25 Feb 1957; Cambridge 14 March 1957). 1958 Evans.
Aunt Edwina: a comedy. (Devonshire Park, Eastbourne 14 Sept 1959; Fortune 3 Nov 1959). [1960] French.
The bad soldier Smith. (Westminster 14 June 1961). 1962.
The reluctant peer: a comedy in three acts. (Duchess 15 Jan 1964). [1965] Evans.
A friend indeed: a comedy. (Windsor Repertory 8 Sept 1965; Cambridge 27 April 1966). [1966] French.
The secretary bird: a comedy. (Opera House, Manchester 9 Sept 1968; Savoy 16 Oct 1968). [1969] French.
The bishop and the actress. [1969] French.

RONALD FREDERICK HENRY DUNCAN
b. 1914

The dull ass's hoof: three plays. [1940], New York 1940.
Postcards to Pulcinella. [1941]. Verse.
This way to the tomb: a masque and anti-masque. (Mercury 11 Oct 1945). 1946, New York 1967.
The rape of Lucretia: a libretto [for Britten's opera from Obey's play, Le viol de Lucrèce]. (Glyndebourne 12 July 1946). [1946]; 1948 (with other material, as The rape of Lucretia: a symposium by B. Britten, R. Duncan and others); 1953 (introd Earl of Harewood).
Stratton: a play in two acts and five scenes. (Theatre Royal, Brighton 31 Oct 1949; Mercury 30 May 1950). 1950.
Our Lady's tumbler. (Salisbury Cathedral 5 June 1950; St Thomas, Regent St 25 April 1955). 1951.
The mongrel and other poems. 1950.
The last Adam: a story. 1952.
Don Juan: a play in verse. (Palace, Bideford 13 July 1953; BBC Home Service 13 Feb 1956; Court 15 May 1956). 1954.
The death of Satan: a comedy. (Palace, Bideford 5 Aug 1954; Court 15 May 1956). 1955.
The catalyst: a comedy in two acts. (Arts 25 March 1958). 1964.
Abélard & Héloïse: a correspondence for the stage in two acts. (Arts Theatre Club 24 Oct 1960). 1961.
Judas. 1960. Poems.
The solitudes: poems. 1960.
Saint Spiv. 1961. Novel.
All men are islands: an autobiography. 1964.
O-B-A-F-G [etc]: a play in one act for stereophonic sound. 1964.
How to make enemies. 1969. Autobiography.
The perfect mistress and other stories. 1969.
Unpopular poems. 1969.
All men are islands: an autobiography. 1964.
Collected plays. 1971.
Jan's Journal, *1949*; The blue fox, *1951*, *New York 1952*; Jan at The blue fox, *1952*, *were articles and stories on country themes rptd from the Evening Standard. Also on country subjects were* The journal of a husbandman, *1944*; Home-made home, *1947*; Tobacco cultivation in England, *1951*; Where I live [*Devonshire*], *1953*; *and* A guide to Devon and Cornwall, *1966*.
*He translated and adapted the following works of foreign dramatists :*The eagle has two heads [*Cocteau*] (*Lyric, Hammersmith 4 Sept 1946; Haymarket 12 Feb 1947*), *1948, New York 1948*; The typewriter [*Cocteau*], (*Watergate 14 Nov 1950*), *1950*; A man named Judas [*P. Bost and C. A. Puget*], (*Devon Festival 7 Aug 1956*); The cardinal [*H. Bratt*], (*Arts, Cambridge 18 Feb 1957*); The Apollo de Bellac [*Giraudoux*], *1958*; The rabbit race [*M. Walser*], (*Edinburgh Festival 19 Aug 1963*); and The Trojan women [*Sartre*], *1967*.

CHRISTOPHER FRY
b. 1907

Bibliographies
Schear, B. L. and E. G. Prater. A bibliography on Fry. Tulane Drama Rev 4 1960.

Selections
Three plays: The firstborn; Thor, with angels; A sleep of prisoners. 1960, New York [1961]. The text of The firstborn is revised.
Plays. A phoenix too frequent; Thor, with angels; The lady's not for burning. 1969.

1

The boy with a cart—Cuthman, Saint of Sussex: a play. (Colman's Hatch, Sussex 1937; BBC Third Programme 15 March 1948; Lyric, Hammersmith 19 Jan 1950). 1939, Boston 1939, London 1945 (rev), New York 1951.
A phoenix too frequent: a comedy. (Mercury 25 April 1946). 1946, New York 1950, 1953 Dramatists' Play Service, London 1959.
The firstborn: a play in three acts. (BBC Third Programme 3 Sept 1947; Gateway, Edinburgh 6 Sept 1948; Winter Garden 29 Jan 1952). Cambridge 1946, New York 1947, London 1952 (rev), New York [1958] Dramatists' Play Service.
The lady's not for burning: a comedy in verse in three acts. (Arts 10 March 1948; Globe 11 May 1949). 1949, 1950 (rev), New York 1950, 1953 Dramatists' Play Service, London 1958 (rev), New York [1960].
Thor, with angels: a play. (Chapter House, Canterbury 19 June 1948; Lyric, Hammersmith 27 Sept 1951). Canterbury 1948 (acting edn), London 1949, New York [1953] Dramatists' Play Service.
Ring round the moon: a charade with music. (Royal, Brighton 9 Jan 1950; Globe 26 Jan 1950). 1950, New York [1952] Dramatists' Play Service. Trn of J. Anouilh, L'invitation au château.
Venus observed: a play. (St James's 18 Jan 1950). 1950, New York 1953 Dramatists' Play Service.
A sleep of prisoners: a play. (University Church, Oxford 23 April 1951; St Thomas's, Regent Street 15 May 1951). 1951, New York [1953] Dramatists' Play Service.
An experience of critics; and The approach to dramatic criticism by W. A. Darlington et al. Ed K. Webb 1952, New York 1952.
The dark is light enough: a winter comedy. (Lyceum, Edinburgh 22 Feb 1954; Aldwych 30 April 1954). 1954, New York [1957] Dramatists' Play Service.
The lark. (Lyric, Hammersmith 11 May 1955). 1955, [1965] French, New York [1956], [1957] Dramatists' Play Service. Trn of J. Anouilh, L'alouette.
Tiger at the gates. (Apollo 2 June 1955). 1955, New York [1956] French. Trn of J. Giraudoux, La guerre de Troie n'aura pas lieu.
Duel of angels. (Theatre Royal, Newcastle 3 March 1958; BBC Third Programme 14 Aug 1964). 1958, New York [1961] Dramatists' Play Service. Trn of J. Giraudoux, Pour Lucrèce.
Judith: a tragedy in three acts. (Her Majesty's 20 June 1962). In J. Giraudoux, Plays vol 1, tr Fry, 1963.
Curtmantle: a play. (Lyceum, Edinburgh 4 Sept 1962; Aldwych 9 Oct 1962). 1961, New York 1961, London 1965 (rev).
The following plays have not been pbd : Youth and the Peregrines (*Pump Room, Tunbridge Wells 1 May 1934*); Thursday's child (*Albert Hall 1 June 1939*); Siege: The tower (*Tewkesbury Festival 22 June 1939*); The tall hill (*BBC Home Service 22 Oct 1948*); The open door [*a dramatized life of Dr Barnardo*]; Rhineland journey (*BBC Home Service 14 Nov 1948*) *and* She shall have music (*Savoy 1951*). *He wrote extra lyrics for the film of* The Beggar's opera (*1953*) *and script for the film of* Ben Hur.

2

Stanford, D. Christopher Fry: an appreciation. 1951.
—— Christopher Fry. 1954, 1962 (rev) (Br Council pamphlet).
Donoghue, D. Fry's theatre of words. In his Third voice, Princeton 1959.

HARLEY GRANVILLE-BARKER
1877–1946

Typescripts and mss are held at the BM and elsewhere.

Collections
Collected plays. 1967– (Watergate edn). Foreword by J. B. Priestley; introd by I. Brown.

§1

The marrying of Ann Leete: a comedy in four acts. (Royalty 26 Jan 1902). 1909, Boston 1916.
Prunella: or love in a Dutch garden. (Court 23 Dec 1904). 1906, New York 1906, London 1930 (rev). With L. Housman.
Scheme and estimates for a National Theatre. 1904 (priv ptd), 1907 (as A National Theatre: schemes & estimates), New York 1908. With W. Archer. Completely rewritten by Barker alone as A National Theatre, 1930.
The Voysey inheritance: a play in five acts. (Court 7 Nov 1905). 1909, 1913 (rev), Boston 1916, London 1938 (rev), 1967 (with introd by E. R. Wood).
Waste: a tragedy in four acts. (Imperial 24 Nov 1907). 1909, Boston 1916, London 1927 (rev).
Three plays: The marrying of Ann Leete; The Voysey inheritance; Waste. 1909, New York 1909, London 1913 (with rev text of The Voysey Inheritance).
The Madras House: a comedy in four acts. (Duke of York's 9 March 1910). 1911, New York 1911, London 1925 (rev).
Rococo: a farce in one act. (Little 3 Oct 1911; Glasgow Repertory 20 Nov 1911). In Rococo, 1917 below; pbd separately 1925.
The harlequinade: an excursion. (St James's 25 Oct 1913). 1918, Boston 1918. With D. C. Calthrop.
Souls on Fifth. Boston 1916. Short story.
Vote by ballot. (Court 16 Dec 1917). In Rococo, 1917 below; pbd separately 1925.
Farewell to the theatre. In Rococo 1917 below; pbd separately 1925.
Rococo; Vote by ballot; Farewell to the theatre. 1917, Boston 1917 (as Three short plays).
The exemplary theatre. 1922, Boston 1922.
Prefaces to the Players' Shakespeare. 7 vols 1923–7 (limited edn). Pbd separately as follows: Macbeth 1923, Merchant of Venice 1923, Cymbeline 1923, Midsummer nights dream 1924, Loves labours lost 1924, Julius Caesar 1926, King Lear 1927.
The secret life: a play in three acts. 1923, Boston 1923.
From Henry V to Hamlet. Br Acad Proc 1925, rev in Aspects of Shakespeare, ed J. W. Mackail, Oxford 1933.
Prefaces to Shakespeare. 5 ser 1927–47, 2 vols Princeton 1946–7 (rev), London 1958, 4 vols 1963 (with foreword and notes by M. St C. Byrne). Based on Barker's prefaces to the plays included in The players' Shakespeare, 7 vols 1923–7, with prefaces to Romeo and Juliet, Antony and Cleopatra, Hamlet, Othello and Coriolanus.
His Majesty: a play in four acts. 1928, Boston 1929.
A National Theatre. 1930. *See* Schemes and estimates for a National Theatre, 1904, above.
On dramatic method. 1931, New York 1956. (Clark lectures 1930).
Associating with Shakespeare. 1932. Address to Shakespeare Association.
The study of drama. Cambridge 1934. Lecture.
On poetry in drama: the Romanes lecture. 1937.
The perennial Shakespeare. 1937. Broadcast lecture.
Quality. 1938. (Eng Assoc presidential address).
The use of drama. Princeton 1945, London 1946 (rev). Based on the Trask lectures, Princeton 1944.

Barker wrote the following unpbd plays; The family of the Oldroyds; The weather-hen (*Terry's 29 June 1899*); *and* Our visitor to 'work-a-day' (*all 3 in collaboration with B. Thomas*); Agnes Colander; A miracle (*Terry's 23 March 1907*); The wicked man (*a fragment*) (*all by Barker alone*); *Schnitzler's* Das Märchen (*adapted with C. E. Wheeler*); *Adelphi Play Soc 28 Jan 1912*); *and* The pied piper (*with L. Housman*). *He adapted plays by A. Schnitzler, S. Guitry and J. Romains, and with his wife, Helen Granville-Barker, he adapted 5 plays of G. Martínez Sierra and 8 by S. and J. Álvarez Quintero. Barker wrote an account of the Red Cross in France, 1916, and edited* The eighteen-seventies: essays by Fellows of the Royal Society of Literature, *1929*, A companion to Shakespeare studies, *1934* (*with G. B. Harrison*), *and* The locked book: an anthology, *1936*.

§2

Archer, W. The Vedrenne-Barker season 1904–5: a record and a commentary. [1905].
—— In his The old drama and the new, 1923.
MacCarthy, D. The Court Theatre 1904–7: a commentary and criticism. 1907. With reprint of programmes.
—— In his Theatre, 1954.
Walkley, A. B. In his Drama and life, 1907.
Pearson, H. In his Modern men and mummers, 1921.
—— In his The last actor-managers, 1950.
Beerbohm, M. In his Around theatres, 1924.
Shaw, G. B. Barker: some particulars. Drama new ser 3 1946; rptd in Shaw on theatre, ed E. J. West, New York 1958.
—— Letters to Barker. Ed C. B. Purdom 1956.
Downer, A. S. Sewanee Rev 55 1947.
Purdom, C. B. Barker: man of the theatre, dramatist and scholar. 1955. Includes list of Barker's acting roles, productions and writings.
Wilson, J. D. Memories of Barker and two of his friends. In Elizabethan and Jacobean studies presented to F. P. Wilson, Oxford 1959.
Morgan, M. M. A drama of political man: a study in the plays of Barker. 1961.

CHRISTOPHER VERNON HASSALL
1912–63

Glamorous night: a romantic play with music by I. Novello, lyrics by Hassall. (Drury Lane 2 May 1935). 1938 (vocal score), [1939] French.
Poems of two years. 1935.
Careless rapture: a musical play by I. Novello, lyrics by Hassall. (Drury Lane 11 Sept 1936). 1936 (vocal score).
Devil's dyke, with Compliment and satire. 1936. Verse.
Christ's comet—the story of a thirty years' journey that began and ended on the same day: a play in three acts. (Canterbury Cathedral 25 June 1938; BBC Third Programme 25 Dec 1946). 1937, New York [1938], London 1958 (rev, in 2 acts with preface).
Penthesperon. [1938]. Verse.
The dancing years: a musical play by I. Novello, lyrics by Hassall. (Drury Lane 23 March 1939). 1939 (vocal score), [1953] French.
Crisis. 1939. Verse.
S.O.S.... 'Ludlow'. 1940. Verse.
Notes on the verse drama. 1948 (The Masque no 6).
The timeless quest: Stephen Haggard. 1948.
King's rhapsody: a musical romance by I. Novello, with lyrics by Hassall. (Palace 15 Sept 1949). 1949 (vocal score), [1955] French.
The slow night and other poems 1940–8. 1949.
The rainbow: a tale of Dunkirk, set to music by T. Wood. [1951] (vocal score).

Voices of night: a cantata by F. Reizenstein, text composed and arranged by Hassall. (BBC Third Programme 21 June 1952). [1952] (vocal score).

The player king. (Royal Court, Liverpool 18 Aug 1952, Edinburgh Festival 26 Aug 1952; BBC Home Service 22 Nov 1954). 1953.

Words by request: a selection of occasional pieces in verse and prose. 1952.

Out of the whirlwind: a play for Westminster Abbey. (10 June 1953). 1953.

Eddie Marsh: sketches for a composite literary portrait. 1953. With D. Mathews.

Salutation, by E. Rubbra, words by Hassall. 1953 (vocal score).

Troilus and Cressida: opera in three acts by W. Walton, libretto by Hassall. (Covent Garden 3 Dec 1954). 1954.

The red leaf: poems. 1957.

Genesis: an oratorio by F. Reizenstein, text by Hassall. [1958] (vocal score).

Edward Marsh, patron of the arts: a biography. 1959, New York 1959 (as A biography of Edward Marsh).

Tobias and the angel: an opera in two acts, libretto by Hassall, music by A. Bliss. (BBC Television 19 May 1960). 1962.

Bell Harry and other poems. 1963, New York 1964.

Mary of Magdala: a cantata by A. Bliss, text by Hassall. 1963 (vocal score).

Poems for children, with drawings by D. A. H. Morgan. 1963.

Valley of Song: a musical romance in three acts by I. Novello, lyrics by Hassall, book by P. Park. (Grand, Blackpool 2 March 1964; Toynbee Hall 4 March 1965). [1964] (acting edn).

Ambrosia and small beer: the record of a correspondence [with E. Marsh]. 1964, New York 1965.

Rupert Brooke: a biography. 1964, New York 1964.

WILLIAM
STEPHEN RICHARD KING-HALL,
BARON KING-HALL
1893–1966

Verses from the Grand Fleet, by 'Etienne (Lt. R.N.)' [i.e. S. King-Hall]. 1917.

Strange tales from the Fleet, by 'Etienne'. 1919.

The romantic adventure. 1926. Novel.

The uncharted sea. 1926. Novel.

The middle watch: a romance of the Navy in three acts. (Shaftesbury 12 Aug 1929). [1931] French. With 'Ian Hay' (J. H. Beith). Screen plays: British International 1930, Associated British 1940.

B.J. One: a play in one act. (Globe 9 April 1930). [1930] French (3rd act only). Full text in Three plays and a plaything, 1933, below.

The midshipmaid: a naval manoeuvre in three acts. (Shaftesbury 10 Aug 1931). [1932] French. With 'Ian Hay' (J. H. Beith). Screen play: Gaumont British 1937.

Post-war pirate. 1931. Novel.

Bunga-Bunga. 1932, New York [1933]. Novel.

Three plays and a plaything: 1, The Republican-princess: a satirical farce in three acts; 2, The second generation; 3, B.J. One; 4, Posterity. 1933.

Admirals all: an amphibious adventure in three acts. (Shaftesbury 6 Aug 1934). [1935] French. With 'Ian Hay' (J. H. Beith).

Off the record: a naval comedy in three acts. (King's, Edinburgh 17 March 1947; Apollo 3 June 1947). [1949] French. With 'Ian Hay' (J. H. Beith). Screen play: Renown Pictures, 1957, as Carry on Admiral.

Number 10 Downing Street: a political play in two acts and five scenes. (Bolton's 10 May 1949). [1948].

King-Hall was a prolific writer on political and naval affairs, broadcaster and founder of the King-Hall News Letter Service *(1936) and the* Hansard Society *(1944).*

'FREDERICK LONSDALE',
LIONEL FREDERICK LEONARD
1881–1954

Aren't we all?: a comedy in three acts. (Globe, New York 10 April 1923). New York [1924], London [1925], French [1935]. Screen plays: 1925 (as A kiss in the dark) and 1932.

Spring cleaning: a comedy in three acts. (Adelphi, Chicago 9 Sept 1923; Eltinge, New York 9 Nov 1923; St Martin's 29 Jan 1925). [1925], [1930] French. Screen play 1924 (as The fast set).

The fake: a play in three acts. (Apollo 13 March 1924). [1927] French.

The street singer: a musical play in three acts. (Lyric 27 June 1924). [1929] French. Lyrics by P. Greenbank, music by H. Fraser-Simson.

The last of Mrs Cheyney: a comedy in three acts. (St James's 22 Sept 1925). [1925], [1929] French. Novelized by D. G. Herriot 1930. Screen plays: 1929, 1937, 1951 (as The law and the lady).

On approval: a comedy in three acts. (Gaiety, New York 18 Oct 1926; Fortune 19 April 1927). [1927], [1928] French (rev). Screen play 1945.

The high road: a comedy in three acts. (Shaftesbury 7 Sept 1927). [1927], [1928] French. Screen play 1930 (as The lady of scandal).

Canaries sometimes sing: a comedy in three acts. (Globe 21 Oct 1929). [1930], New York 1930, London [1931] French.

Once is enough: a comedy in three acts. (Henry Miller, New York 15 Feb 1938). New York [1938] French. Revived as Half a loaf (Royal, Windsor 4 July 1948) and as Let them eat cake (Cambridge 6 May 1959). Pbd as Let them eat cake in Plays of the year 1958–59 [1961] Evans.

Another love story: a play in two acts. (Fulton, New York 12 Oct 1943; BBC Home 23 April 1944; Phoenix 13 Dec 1944). [1948] Guild.

The way things go: a comedy in two acts. (Phoenix 2 Mar 1950). [1951] French.

Much of Lonsdale's work remained unpbd.

MICHEÁL MACLIAMMÓIR
1899–1978

Fairy nights. Dublin 1922. Short stories: text in English and Irish.

Diarmuid and Grainne. (Gaelic, Galway 27 Aug 1928, Irish version; Peacock, Dublin 10 Sept 1928, English version). Galway 1935.

Lá agus oidhche. Dublin 1929. Short stories and sketches in Irish.

Where stars walk: a fantasy. (Gaiety, Dublin 19 Feb 1940; Embassy 16 Dec 1947). Dublin 1962.

Ill met by moonlight: a play in three acts. (Gaiety, Dublin 5 April 1946; Vaudeville 5 Feb 1947). Dublin 1954.

All for Hecuba: an Irish theatrical autobiography. 1946, Dublin 1961 (rev), 1967 (rev).

Oidhche Bhealtaine. (Abbey 22 March 1949). Dublin 1932. In Irish.

Theatre in Ireland. Dublin 1950, 1964 (rev).

Put money in thy purse: the diary of the film [by Orson Welles] of 'Othello'. 1952.

The importance of being Oscar. (Dublin Festival 18 Sept 1960; Apollo 31 Oct 1960). Dublin 1963. A dramatic recital on the life and work of Oscar Wilde.

Two lights on actors. 1960.

Each actor on his ass. 1961. Diary of German and Egyptian tours.

Bláth agus Taibhse (Flower and ghost). 1965. Verse. In Irish.

An Oscar of no importance: being an account of the author's adventures with his one-man show about Wilde, The importance of being Oscar. 1968.

IVOR NOVELLO
(formerly DAVID IVOR DAVIES)
1893–1951

§1

The truth game: a light comedy in three acts. (Globe 5 Oct 1928; Ethel Barrymore, New York 29 Dec 1930). [1929] French. Screen play 1932 (as But the flesh is weak).

Symphony in two flats: a play in three acts. (New 14 Oct 1929; Shubert, New York 16 Sept 1930; screen play 1931). In I lived with you [etc], 1932, below.

I lived with you: a comedy in three acts. (Prince of Wales's 23 March 1932; screen play 1935). In I lived with you [etc], 1932, below.

Party. (Arts 19 May 1932). In I lived with you [etc], 1932, below.

I lived with you; Party; Symphony in two flats. Introd by E. Marsh 1932.

Fresh fields: a comedy in three acts. (Criterion 5 Jan 1933). [1934] French, New York 1936.

Proscenium: a play in three acts. (Globe 14 June 1933). [1934] French.

Glamorous night: a romantic play with music. (Drury Lane 2 May 1935). Lyrics by C. Hassall. [1938] (vocal score), [1939] French.

Full house: a light comedy in three acts. (Haymarket 21 Aug 1935). [1936] French.

Careless rapture: a musical play. (Drury Lane 11 Sept 1936). Lyrics by C. Hassall. 1936 (vocal score).

Comedienne: a comedy in three acts. (Haymarket 16 June 1938). [1938] French.

The dancing years: a musical play. (Drury Lane 23 March 1939). Lyrics by C. Hassall. [1939] (vocal score), [1953] French.

Perchance to dream: a musical play. (Hippodrome 21 April 1945). 1945 (vocal score), [1953] French.

We proudly present: a comedy in two acts and a prologue. (Duke of York's 2 May 1947). [1947] French.

King's rhapsody: a musical romance. (Palace, Manchester 25 Aug 1949; Palace, London 15 Sept 1949). Lyrics by C. Hassall. 1949 (vocal score), [1955] French.

§2

Macqueen-Pope, W. J. Ivor: the story of an achievement. 1951, 1954 (rev).

Noble, P. Ivor Novello: man of the theatre. 1951.

SIR TERENCE MERVYN RATTIGAN
1911–77

Collections

Collected plays. 1953–. With preface to each vol by the author.

§1

First episode. (Q 11 Sept 1933). With P. Heimann.

French without tears: a play in three acts. (Criterion 6 Nov 1936). 1937, [1937] French, New York 1938.

After the dance: a play in three acts. (St James's 21 June 1939). 1939.

Follow my leader. (Apollo 16 June 1940). With A. Maurice.

Grey farm. (1940). Unpbd. With H. Bolitho.

Flare path: a play in three acts. (Apollo 13 Aug 1942). 1942, [1943] French.

While the sun shines: a comedy. (Globe 24 Dec 1943). 1944, New York [1945] French, London [1946] French.

Love in idleness. (Lyric 20 Dec 1944). 1945, [1947] French, New York [1949] French (as O mistress mine: a comedy in three acts).

The Winslow boy. (Lyric 23 May 1946). 1946, New York 1946 Dramatists' Play Service, London [1948] French.

Playbill: comprising The Browning version and Harlequinade. (Royal Court, Liverpool 26 July 1948; Phoenix 8 Sept 1948). [1949]. Also pbd separately in French edns 1949.

Adventure story: a play in three acts. (Royal, Brighton 11 Jan 1949; St James's 17 March 1949). 1950, [1950] French.

Who is Sylvia? a light comedy. (Arts, Cambridge 9 Oct 1950; Criterion 24 Oct 1950). 1951, [1951] Evans.

The deep blue sea. (Royal, Brighton 4 Feb 1952; Duchess 6 March 1952). 1952, New York 1953, London [1954] French.

The sleeping prince. (Opera, Manchester 28 Sept 1953; Phoenix 5 Nov 1953). 1954, [1956] French, New York 1957.

Separate tables—two plays: Table by the window; Table number seven. (Royal Court, Liverpool 23 Aug 1954; St James's 22 Sept 1954). 1955, [1957] French, New York 1957.

The prince and the showgirl: the script for the film. New York 1957.

Variation on a theme. (Opera, Manchester 31 March 1958; Globe 8 May 1958). 1958.

Ross: a dramatic portrait. (Royal Court, Liverpool 29 April 1960; Haymarket 12 May 1960). 1960, New York 1962, London [1962] French.

Man and boy. (Royal, Brighton 19 Aug 1963; Queens 4 Sept 1963). New York [1963] French, London 1964.

A bequest to the nation. (Haymarket 23 Sept 1970). Unpbd.

Rattigan has also written a musical and a number of film scripts.

ROBERT CEDRIC SHERRIFF
1896–1975

Journey's end: a play in three acts. (Apollo 10 Dec 1928). 1929, New York 1929, London [1931] French. As novel 1930, with V. Bartlett.

Badger's green: a play in three acts. (Prince of Wales's 12 June 1930). 1930, [1934] French, 1962 (rev).

The fortnight in September: a novel. 1931, New York 1932.

Two hearts doubled: a playlet. [1935] French.

St Helena: a play in twelve scenes. (Old Vic 4 Feb 1936). 1934, New York 1935, London [1937] French. With J. de Casalis.

Greengates. 1936, New York 1936. Novel.

The Hopkins manuscript. 1939, New York 1939, London 1958 (rev, as The cataclysm). Novel.

Chedworth: a novel. New York 1944.

Miss Mabel: a play in three acts. (Royal, Brighton 21 Sept 1948; Duchess 23 Nov 1948). 1949, [1949] French.

Another year: a novel. 1948, New York 1948.

Quartet: stories by W. S. Maugham, screen plays by Sherriff. 1948, Garden City NY 1949.

The Hopkins manuscript. (BBC Light Programme 5, 6 Oct 1949). With E. J. King-Bull.

Home at seven: a play in three acts. (Royal, Brighton

6 Feb 1950; Wyndham's 7 March 1950). 1950, New York 1950, London [1951] French.

Odd man out: a screen play. In Three British screen plays, ed R. Manvell 1950. With F. L. Green.

Trio: stories by W. S. Maugham, screen adaptation by Maugham, Sherriff and N. Langley. 1950, Garden City NY 1950.

The white carnation: a play in two acts. (Royal, Brighton 5 Jan 1953; Globe 20 March 1953). 1953, [1954] French.

King John's treasure: an adventure story. 1954, New York 1954. For children.

The long sunset: a play in three acts. (BBC Home Service 23 April 1955; Repertory, Birmingham 30 Aug 1955; Mermaid 7 Nov 1961). In Plays of the year vol 12, 1955. Pbd separately 1956, 1958 French.

The telescope. (BBC Light programme 31 Oct 1956; Guildford 13 May 1957). [1957] French; [1958].

The colonel's lady: screenplay from a story by W. S. Maugham. In A college treasury, ed P. A. Jorgensen and F. P. Schroyer, New York [1956].

A shred of evidence. (Royal, Brighton 28 March 1960; Duchess 27 April 1960). [1961] French. Also pbd in Plays of the year 1960, 1961.

The wells of St Mary's. 1962. Novel.

No leading lady: an autobiography. 1968.

Sherriff also wrote other unpbd plays for stage, radio and television, and screenplays based on other writers' works.

DODIE SMITH
(DOROTHY GLADYS SMITH)
b. 1896

Autumn crocus: a play in three acts. (Lyric 6 April 1931). 1931, [1933] French. As by 'C. L. Anthony'.

Service: a play in three acts. (Wyndham's 12 Oct 1932). 1932, [1937] French. As by 'C. L. Anthony'.

Touch wood: a play in three acts. (Haymarket 16 May 1934). 1934, [1935] French. As by 'C. L. Anthony'.

Call it a day: a comedy in three acts. (Globe 30 Oct 1935). 1936, [1937] French.

Bonnet over the windmill: a play in three acts. (New 8 Sept 1937). 1937.

Dear Octopus: a comedy in three acts. (Queen's 14 Sept 1938). 1938, [1939] French.

Lovers and friends: a play in three acts. (Plymouth, New York 29 Nov 1943). New York [1947].

Letter from Paris: a comedy. (Royal, Brighton 10 Aug 1952; Aldwych 10 Oct 1952). 1954. Adapted from The reverberator by H. James.

I capture the castle: a romantic comedy. (Grand, Blackpool 19 Jan 1954; Aldwych 4 March 1954). [1954] French. Adapted from her novel.

Amateur means lover. (Playhouse, Liverpool 12 Sept 1961). [1962] French.

Dodie Smith also wrote an unpbd play and pbd several novels and books for children.

ALFRED SUTRO
1863–1933

Aglavaine and Selysette. 1897. From the French of Maeterlinck.

Carrots. (Theatre Royal, Dublin 18 Oct 1900; Prince of Wales, Kensington 21 Nov 1900; Garrick 22 April 1902). 1904 Lacy. Adapted from Poil de carotte by J. Renard.

The cave of illusion: a play in four acts. 1900.

A marriage has been arranged—a duologue: a comedy in one act. (Haymarket 6 May 1902). 1904 Lacy, New York 1904.

Monna Vanna. (Bijou, Bayswater 19 June 1902; Queen's 21 July 1914). 1904. From the French of Maeterlinck.

Alladine and Palomides; The death of Tintagiles. (St George's Hall 22 July 1902). 1899. From the French of Maeterlinck.

Women in love: eight studies in sentiment. 1902.

The walls of Jericho: a play in four acts. (Garrick 31 Oct 1904). [1906].

A maker of men: a duologue. (St James's 27 Jan 1905). In Women in love, 1902 above. Also pbd separately 1905 (Lacy).

Mollentrave on women: a comedy in three acts. (St James's 13 Feb 1905). 1905.

The correct thing. (Drury Lane 27 June 1905). In Women in love, 1902 above. Also pbd separately 1905 (Lacy).

The perfect lover: a play in four acts. (Imperial 14 Oct 1905). New York [1921].

A game of chess: a duologue. In Women in love, 1902, above. Also pbd separately 1905 (Lacy).

The salt of life. In Women in love, 1902 above. Also pbd separately 1905 (Lacy).

The fascinating Mr Vanderveldt: a comedy in four acts. (Garrick 26 April 1906). [1906].

Ella's apology: a duologue. (Bloomsbury Hall 8 Nov 1906). In Women in love, 1902 above. Also pbd separately 1905 (Lacy).

The open door: a duologue. [1906] Lacy, New York 1912.

The price of money. New York 1906.

John Glayde's honour: a new and original play in four acts. (St James's 8 March 1907). [1907].

Mr Steinmann's corner. (His Majesty's 4 June 1907). In Women in love, 1902 above. Also pbd separately 1905 (Lacy).

The barrier: a new and original play in four acts. (Comedy 10 Oct 1907). 1907 (priv ptd), [1921].

The man on the kerb: a duologue. (Aldwych 24 March 1908). [1908] Lacy.

The gutter of time: a duologue. (Eastbourne pier 3 Aug 1908). In Women in love, 1902, above. Also pbd separately 1905 (Lacy).

The builder of bridges: a play in four acts. (St James's 11 Nov 1908). 1909.

The bracelet: a play in one act. (Lyceum New York 15 March 1910; Repertory, Liverpool 26 Feb 1912). [1912] Lacy, New York [1912] French.

The perplexed husband: a comedy in four acts. (Wyndham's 12 Sept 1911). 1913.

The man in the stalls. (Palace 6 Oct 1911). [1911] Lacy, New York [1911] French.

The firescreen: a comedy in four acts. (Garrick 7 Feb 1912). [1912].

Five little plays: The man in the stalls; A marriage has been arranged; The man on the kerb; The open door; The bracelet. 1912, New York 1913.

The two virtues: a comedy in four acts. (St James's 5 March 1914). 1914.

Freedom: a play in three acts. 1914.

Rude Min and Christine: a comedy in three acts. (As The two Miss Farndons, Gaiety, Manchester 21 May 1917; as Uncle Anyhow, Haymarket 1 May 1918). 1915, [1919] French.

The marriage...will not take place: a play in one act. (Coliseum 13 Aug 1917). [1917] French.

The egoist. 1919. From Meredith's novel.

The choice: a play in four acts. (Wyndham's 8 Sept 1919). [1920].

The laughing lady: a comedy in three acts. (Globe 17 Nov 1922). 1922.

The great well: a play in four acts. (New 19 Dec 1922). [1922].

Far above rubies: a comedy in three acts. (Comedy 27 March 1924). 1924.

A man with a heart: a play in four acts. (Wyndham's 14 March 1925). 1925.

The desperate lovers: a frivolous comedy in three acts. (Comedy 28 Jan 1927). 1927.

Living together: a play in four acts. (Wyndham's 29 Jan 1929). 1929.

The blackmailing lady: a play in one act. [1929] French.

Celebrities and simple souls. 1933. Autobiographical reminiscences.

He also pbd short stories, and trns from the prose works of Maeterlinck.

BEN TRAVERS
b. 1886

A cuckoo in the nest: a play in three acts. (Court, Liverpool 13 July 1925; Aldwych 25 July 1925). [1938]. From his own novel pbd 1922.

Rookery nook: a farce in three acts. (Aldwych 30 June 1926). [1930]. From his own novel pbd 1923.

Thark: a farce in three acts. (King's, Southsea 27 June 1927; Aldwych 4 July 1927). [1932].

Plunder: a farce in three acts. (Aldwych 26 June 1928). [1931].

A cup of kindness: a farce in three acts. (Aldwych 7 May 1929). [1934].

Turkey time: a farce in three acts. (Aldwych 26 May 1931). [1934].

Dirty work. (Aldwych 7 March 1932). 1932.

O mistress mine. (St James's 11 Dec 1936). [1956] French (rev, as Nun's veiling).

Banana ridge: a comedy in three acts. (Strand 27 April 1938). [1939].

She follows me about: a comedy in three acts. (Royal, Birmingham 14 June 1943; Garrick 15 Oct 1943). [1945] French.

Outrageous fortune: a farce in three acts. (Winter Garden 13 Nov 1947). [1948] French.

Wild horses: a farcical comedy in three acts. (Opera, Manchester 18 Aug 1952; Aldwych 6 Nov 1952). [1953] French.

Vale of laughter: an autobiography. 1957.

Travers has also pbd short stories and selections of humorous writing.

PETER ALEXANDER USTINOV
b. 1921

House of regrets: a tragi-comedy in three acts. (Arts 6 Oct 1942). 1943.

Beyond: a play in one act. (Arts 17 March 1943). [1944] Guild.

Blow your own trumpet. (Playhouse, Liverpool 26 July 1943; Playhouse 11 Aug 1943). In Plays about people, 1950, below.

The Banbury nose: a play in four acts. (Wyndham's 6 Sept 1944). 1945.

The tragedy of good intentions. (Playhouse, Liverpool 5 Oct 1945). In Plays about people, 1950 below.

The indifferent shepherd. (Criterion 5 Feb 1948). Ibid.

Plays about people. 1950.

The love of four colonels: a play in three acts. (Alexandra, Birmingham 26 March 1951; Wyndham's 23 May 1951). [1951] Guild, New York 1953 Dramatists Play Service.

The moment of truth: a play in four acts. (Royal, Nottingham 15 Oct 1951; Adelphi 21 Nov 1951). [1953] Guild.

No sign of the dove. (Grand, Leeds 19 Oct 1953; Savoy 3 Dec 1953). In Five plays, 1965.

Romanoff and Juliet: a comedy in three acts. (Opera, Manchester 2 April 1956; Piccadilly 11 May 1956). [1957] Guild, New York 1958.

Photo-finish: an adventure in biography in three acts. (Gaiety, Dublin 26 March 1962; Saville 25 April 1962). 1962, [1963] Guild, Boston 1963.

The unknown soldier and his wife. (Chichester Festival 22 May 1968). New York 1967, London 1968.

Dear me. 1977. Autobiography.

JOHN WILLIAM VAN DRUTEN
1901–57

Young Woodley: a play in three acts. (Belmont, New York 2 Oct 1925; Hollis St, Boston 5 Oct 1925). New York 1926, London 1928, [1930] French (rev), New York 1930.

Diversion: a play in three acts. (Lyceum, Rochester NY Aug 1927; Forty-ninth Street, New York 11 Jan 1928; Arts 26 Sept 1928). 1928, [1933] French.

The return of the soldier: a play in three acts. (Playhouse 12 June 1928). 1928. Adapted from novel by Rebecca West.

After all: a play in three acts. (Apollo 5 May 1929). 1929, New York 1931, London [1933] French.

Young Woodley. 1929, New York 1929. Novel based on his play.

A woman on her way. 1930, New York 1931. Novel.

London wall: a comedy in three acts. (Duke of York's 1 May 1931). 1931, [1932] French.

There's always Juliet: a comedy in three acts. (Apollo 12 Oct 1931). 1931, [1932] French.

Hollywood holiday: an extravagant comedy in three episodes. (New 15 Oct 1931). 1931. With B. Levy.

Somebody knows. (St Martin's 12 May 1932). 1932, [1935] French.

Behold we live. (St James's 16 Aug 1932). 1932, [1935] French.

The distaff side: a play in three acts. (Apollo 5 Sept 1933). 1933, New York 1934, London [1934] French.

Flowers of the forest: a play in three acts. (Whitehall 20 Nov 1934). 1934, New York 1936.

Most of the game: a light comedy in three acts. (Cort, New York 1 Oct 1935). New York 1936.

And then you wish. 1936, Boston 1937. Novel.

Gertie Maude: a play in three acts. (St Martin's 17 Aug 1937). 1937.

The way to the present: a personal record. 1938.

Leave her to heaven: a play in three acts. (Longacre, New York Feb 1940). New York 1941.

Old acquaintance: a comedy in three acts. (Morosco, New York 23 Dec 1940; Apollo 18 Dec 1941). New York 1941, London 1943, [1946] French.

The damask cheek: a comedy in three acts. (Playhouse, New York Oct 1942; Repertory, Birmingham 17 Feb 1948; Lyric, Hammersmith 2 Feb 1949). New York 1943, London [1949] French. With L. Morris.

The voice of the turtle: a comedy in three acts. (Shubert, New Haven Conn 4 Dec 1943; Morosco, New York 8 Dec 1943; Piccadilly 9 July 1947). New York [1944] Dramatists Play Service.

I remember mama: a play in two acts. (Music Box, New York 19 Oct 1944; Aldwych 2 March 1948). New York 1945, London [1948] French, New York 1952 (rev) Dramatists Play Service. Adapted from Mama's bank account by K. Forbes.

The mermaids singing: play in three acts. (Shubert, New Haven Conn 8 Nov 1945; Empire, New York 28 Nov 1945). New York [1946] Dramatists Play Service.

The druid circle: a play in three acts. (Morosco New York 22 Oct 1947). New York [1948] Dramatists Play Service.

Make way for Lucia: comedy in three acts. (Cort, New York 22 Dec 1948). New York [1949] Dramatists Play Service. Based on the novels of E. F. Benson.

Bell, book and candle: a comedy. (Shubert, New Haven Conn 25 Oct 1950; Ethel Barrymore, New York 14 Nov

1950; Royal Court, Liverpool 13 Sept 1954; Phoenix 5 Oct 1954). New York 1951, London [1956] French.

I am a camera: a play in three acts. (Empire, New York 28 Nov 1951; Theatre Royal, Brighton 1 March 1954; New 12 March 1954). New York [1952], London 1954. Adapted from the Berlin stories of Christopher Isherwood.

I've got sixpence: a play in two acts. (Ethel Barrymore, New York 2 Dec 1952). New York [1953] Dramatists Play Service. With a preface by the author.

Playwright at work. New York 1953, London 1953. Record of Van Druten's methods as a dramatist.

The vicarious years. 1955, New York 1957. Novel.

Widening circle. 1957, New York 1957. An autobiography.

GEORGE EMLYN WILLIAMS
b. 1905

Collections

The collected plays. 1961–, New York 1961–.

§1

Vigil. (O.U.D.S., Oxford Nov 1925). In The second book of one-act plays, 1954.

A murder has been arranged: a ghost story in three acts. (Strand 9 Nov 1930). 1930.

The late Christopher Bean: a comedy. (St James's 16 May 1933). 1933. Adapted from S. Howard's version of Prenez garde à la peinture! by R. Fauchois.

Vessels departing. (Embassy 3 July 1933). Unpbd.

Spring 1600: a comedy in three acts. (Shaftesbury 21 Jan 1934; rev version Lyric, Hammersmith 6 Dec 1945). 1946.

Josephine. (His Majesty's 25 Sept 1934). Adapted from H. Bahr. Unpbd.

Night must fall: a play in three acts. (Duchess 31 May 1935). 1935.

He was born gay: a romance in three acts. (Queen's 26 May 1937). 1937.

The corn is green: a comedy in three acts. (Duchess 20 Sept 1938). [1938], New York 1941, 1945 (rev) Dramatists Play Service.

The light of heart: a play in three acts. (Apollo 21 Feb 1940). 1940.

The morning star: a play in three acts. (Globe 10 Dec 1941). 1942.

A month in the country: a comedy. (St James's 11 Feb 1943). 1943. Adapted from Turgenev.

The druid's rest: a comedy in three acts. (St Martin's 26 Jan 1944). 1944.

The wind of heaven: a play in six scenes. (St James's 12 April 1945). 1945.

Thinking aloud: a dramatic sketch. (Stage Door Canteen July 1945). [1946] French.

Pepper and sand: a duologue. (BBC 14 July 1947). [1948].

Trespass: a ghost story in six scenes. (Globe 16 July 1947). Unpbd.

Accolade: a play in six scenes. (Aldwych 6 Sept 1950). 1951 Deane.

Someone waiting: a play in three acts. (Royal Court, Liverpool 14 Sept 1953; Globe 25 Nov 1953). 1954, New York 1956 Dramatists Play Service.

Readings from Dickens. [1953]. Adaptations.

Beth: a play in four scenes. (Royal, Brighton 10 Feb 1958; Apollo 20 March 1958). 1959.

George: an early autobiography. 1961, New York 1962.

Beyond belief: a chronicle of murder and its detection. 1967.

Emlyn: an early autobiography 1927-35. 1973.

Williams has also written a number of filmscripts.

§2

'Findlater, Richard' (K. B. F. Bain). Emlyn Williams: an illustrated study of his work, with a list of his appearances on stage and screen [and of his plays]. 1957.

5. PROSE

I. CRITICS AND LITERARY SCHOLARS, ESSAYISTS AND HUMOURISTS

GENERAL STUDIES

Potter, S. The muse in chains. 1937.

Ransom, J. C. The new criticism. Norfolk Conn 1941.

Hyman, S. E. The armed vision: a study in the methods of modern literary criticism. New York 1948.

Wellek, R. and A. Warren. Theory of literature. New York 1949, 1956 (rev), London 1963 (rev) (Peregrine).

Crane, R. S. The languages of contemporary criticism. In his Languages of criticism and the structure of poetry, Toronto 1953.

Tillyard, E. M. W. The muse unchained: an intimate account of the revolution in English studies at Cambridge. [1958].

Holloway, J. The critical intimidation; The new and the newer critics; The new establishment in criticism. In his Charted mirror, 1960.

Leavis, F. R. Scrutiny: a retrospect. Scrutiny 20 1963.
—— (ed). A selection from Scrutiny. 2 vols Cambridge 1968.

Palmer, D. J. The rise of English studies: an account of the study of English language and literature from its origin to the making of the Oxford English school. Hull 1965.

Wimsatt, W. K. Horses of wrath: recent critical lessons. In his Hateful contraries, [Lexington Kentucky] 1965.

Casey, J. P. The language of criticism. 1966.

Gross, J. The rise and fall of the man of letters: aspects of English life since 1800. 1969.

Carpenter, H. The inklings: C. S. Lewis, Tolkien, Charles Williams and their friends. 1978.

LASCELLES ABERCROMBIE
1881–1938

An extensive collection of mss is held in the Brotherton Library, Univ of Leeds; one of the mss of The sale of St Thomas, Act 1, *and those of* The staircase, The Olympians *and the first act of an unfinished, untitled play are in Bodley.*

Prose

Thomas Hardy: a critical study. 1912, New York 1927.

Speculative dialogues. 1913.

Poetry and contemporary speech. 1914 (Eng Assoc pamphlet).

The epic. [1914] (Art and Craft of Letters).

An essay towards a theory of art. 1922.

Principles of English prosody, pt 1: the elements. 1923. A 'systematic conspectus of versification' was projected as a sequel but not pbd.

The theory of poetry. 1924, New York [1926] (with different preface).

The idea of great poetry. 1925.

Romanticism. 1926, New York 1963.

Progress in literature: the Leslie Stephen lecture. Cambridge 1929.

A plea for the liberty of interpreting. 1930.

Colloquial language in literature. [Oxford] 1931 (Soc for Pure Eng Tract 36). With other essays by O. Jespersen, C. T. Onions, H. W. Fowler.

Tennyson. In Revaluations: studies in biography, by L. Abercrombie [et al], 1931.

Principles of literary criticism. In An outline of modern knowledge, ed W. Rose 1931; rptd separately (without synopsis) 1932 (Outline Ser), New York 1961.

Poetry: its music and meaning. 1932.

The art of Wordsworth. 1952, New York 1952. Lectures, ed with preface by R. Abercrombie.

A number of Abercrombie's other academic lectures were pbd separately.

Poetry, Verse Plays

Interludes and poems. 1908, New York 1908, London 1928 (2 poems slightly rev).

Mary and the bramble. Much Marcle 1910 (priv ptd).

The sale of Saint Thomas. Dymock 1911 (priv ptd). One act, rptd in The sale of Saint Thomas in six acts, 1930, below. Included in Georgian poetry, 1911–12, 1912.

Emblems of love, designed in several discourses. 1912, New York 1912.

Deborah: a play in three acts. (Josca's Little Theatre, Oxford 27 April 1964; first act only). 1913, New York 1913, London 1923 (slightly rev).

The adder. (Liverpool Repertory 3 March 1913; Birmingham Repertory 17 May 1913). In Four short plays, 1922, below.

New numbers. Vol 1, nos 1–4. Dymock 1914. By W. W. Gibson, Brooke, Drinkwater and Abercrombie.

Four short plays. 1922.

Phoenix: tragicomedy in three acts. (St Martin's 20 Jan 1924). 1923.

Twelve idyls and other poems. 1928.

Poems. 1930.

The sale of Saint Thomas in six acts. 1930. Act 1 first pbd 1911.

Lyrics and unfinished poems. [Newtown] 1940 (175 copies). Note on Abercrombie's poetry by W. Gibson.

Vision and love. [1966] (priv ptd, 28 copies). 9 previously unpbd poems.

Abercrombie contributed to Georgian Poetry 1911–12, 1913–15, 1918–19 and 1920–2, he compiled (with a preface and note) New English poems: a miscellany, 1931; he contributed a number of prefaces and introds to other works. He held a staff post on the Liverpool Daily Courier 1908–9, contributing leading articles and reviews till 1912; he also contributed reviews to Manchester Guardian 1910–14 and contributed to many other periodicals and jnls.

JAMES EVERSHED AGATE
1877–1947

L. of C. (Lines of communication): being the letters of a temporary officer in the Army Service Corps. 1917. First pbd (in part) in Manchester Guardian.

Buzz, buzz!: essays of the theatre. [1918]. First pbd in Manchester Guardian, Manchester Playgoer.

Responsibility. 1919, New York [1920], London 1943 (rev). Novel.

Alarums and excursions. 1922, New York 1922. Essays on the contemporary theatre.

At half-past eight: essays of the theatre 1921–2. 1923, New York 1924. First pbd in Saturday Rev.

Fantasies and impromptus. [1923]. Essays.

Blessed are the rich: episodes in the life of Oliver Sheldon. 1924, 1944 (rev). Novel.

The contemporary theatre 1923–6. 4 vols 1924–7. Dramatic criticisms mainly first pbd in Saturday Rev, Sunday Times.

On an English screen. 1924. Essays.

White horse and red lion: essays in gusto. [1924].

Agate's folly: a pleasaunce. 1925. Essays.

The common touch. 1926. Essays.

A short view of the English stage 1900–26. 1926 (Today Lib).

Playgoing. 1927, New York 1927.

Gemel in London. 1928, 1945 (rev). Novel.

Rachel [Elisabeth Rachel Félix]. 1928, New York 1928.

Their hour upon the stage. Cambridge 1930. Essays on the London stage, 1925–9.

The English dramatic critics: an anthology, 1660–1932. Ed Agate 1932, New York 1958.

My theatre talks. 1933. Broadcasts 1925–32.

First nights. 1934. Dramatic criticisms first pbd in Sunday Times 1930–4.

Ego (Ego 2–9): the autobiography of Agate. 9 pts 1935–48, 3 vols 1945–9 (abridged, as A shorter ego). Ego 8 and 9 pbd with introd and notes by J. Barzun (as The later ego) New York 1951.

Kingdoms for horses. 1936. Essays.

More first nights. 1937. Dramatic criticisms first pbd in Sunday Times 1934–7.

Bad manners. 1938. Essays.

The amazing theatre. 1939. Dramatic criticisms first pbd in Sunday Times 1937–9.

Speak for England: an anthology of prose and poetry for the forces. Ed Agate [1939].

Express and admirable: the breakfast table talk of Agate. [1941]. First pbd in Daily Express.

Thursdays and Fridays. [1941], New York 1941. Book reviews first pbd in Daily Express and dramatic criticisms first pbd in John O'London's Weekly.

Brief chronicles: a survey of the plays of Shakespeare and the Elizabethans in actual performance. 1943. Rptd from The contemporary theatre, 1924–7; More first nights, 1937; The amazing theatre, 1939.

These were actors: extracts from a newspaper cutting book 1811–33. [Compiled by J. Saint Aubyn]. [1943], New York [1943]. Selected and annotated by Agate.

Lewis, D. B Wyndham. Take it to bed, selected, with a preface, by Agate. [1944]. Articles first pbd in Tatler, Tatler-Bystander.

Noblesse oblige: another letter to another son. 1944. Reply to O. Sitwell's Letter to my son, 1944.

Red letter nights: a survey of the post-Elizabethan drama in actual performance on the London stage 1921–43. 1944. Rptd from The contemporary theatre, 1924–7; More first nights, 1937; The amazing theatre, 1939.

Immoment toys: a survey of light entertainment on the London stage, 1920–43. 1945.

Around cinemas. 1946; ser 2, 1948.

The contemporary theatre, 1944 and 1945. 1946. Dramatic criticisms first pbd in Sunday Times.

Oscar Wilde and the theatre. [1947] (The masque 3).

Those were the nights. Ed Agate [1947], New York [1947]. Extracts from 2 collections of newspaper cuttings of dramatic criticisms 1887–1906.

Thus to revisit. 1947. Essays 1917–42.

Words I have lived with: a personal choice. Ed Agate [1949], New York [1949]. Anthology of prose and verse.

Agate was dramatic critic in succession to Daily Dispatch, Manchester Guardian, Saturday Rev, Sunday Times, BBC.

ARTHUR OWEN BARFIELD
b. 1898

The silver trumpet. 1925, Grand Rapids [1968]. Children's story.

History in English words. 1926, 1933 (rev), 1954 (rev), Grand Rapids 1967.

Poetic diction: a study in meaning. 1928, 1952 (rev), New York 1964 (introd by H. Nemerov).

Romanticism comes of age. 1944, 1966 (rev), Middletown Conn [1967].

Poetic diction and legal fiction. In Essays presented to Charles Williams, by Barfield [et al], Oxford 1947.

This ever diverse pair, by 'G. A. L Burgeon' [i.e. Barfield], with introd by W. de la Mare. 1950. Legal anecdotes.

Saving the appearances: a study in idolatry. 1957, New York [1965].

Worlds apart: a dialogue of the 1960's. 1963, Middletown Conn [1963].

Unancestral voice. 1965, Middletown Conn 1965. Imaginary philosophical discussions.

Gibb, J. (ed). Light on C. S. Lewis, by O. Barfield [et al]. Introd by Barfield 1965, New York 1965.

Speaker's meaning. Middletown Conn 1967.

Mark vs Tristram: correspondence between C. S. Lewis and Barfield. Ed W. Hooper, Cambridge Mass 1967 (126 copies).

What Coleridge thought. 1972.

Barfield has also tr or edited a number of the works of Rudolf Steiner and Hermann Poppelbaum for the Anthroposophical Soc.

FREDERICK NOEL WILSE BATESON
1901–78

English comic drama 1700–50. Oxford 1929, New York 1963.

English poetry and the English language: an experiment in literary history. Oxford 1934, New York 1961 (rev).

The Cambridge bibliography of English literature. Ed Bateson 4 vols Cambridge 1940, New York 1941.

Mixed farming and muddled thinking: an analysis of current agricultural policy; a report of an inquiry organised by Viscount Astor and B. S. Rowntree. [1946]. Anon.

Towards a Socialist agriculture: studies by a group of Fabians. Ed Bateson 1946.

English poetry: a critical introduction. 1950, 1966 (rev), New York 1966.

Pope, A. Epistles to several persons; Moral essays. Ed Bateson 1951, 1961 (rev) (Twickenham edn of the poems of Pope vol 3 pt 2).

Wordsworth: a re-interpretation. 1954, 1956 (rev).

A guide to English literature. New York 1965, London 1965 (rev), 1967 (rev). General essays and critical bibliographies.

Brill: a short history. [Oxford] 1966.

Bateson was agricultural correspondent of Observer, New Statesman *1944–8; general editor of* Longman's *annotated English poets 1965–; and founder of and editor and frequent contributor to* EC *1951–.*

SIR HENRY MAXIMILIAN BEERBOHM
1872–1956

Bibliographies

Gallatin, A. E. and L. M. Oliver. A bibliography of the works of Beerbohm. 1952 (Soho Bibliographies).

Riewald, J. G. Beerbohm, man and writer: a critical analysis with a brief life and a bibliography. Hague 1953.

Collections and Selections

Works. 10 vols 1922–8. Sometimes known as 'Harlequin' edn. Texts of 1st edns with minor revisions. Beerbohm contributed a general preface to vol 1, notes to vols 5–7 and 10 and an Epistle dedicatory to E. G. Craig to vol 8.

The incomparable Max: a selection, introduced by S. C. Roberts. 1962, New York 1962.

Max in verse: rhymes and parodies, collected and annotated by J. G. Riewald. Foreword by S. N. Behrman, Brattleboro Vermont 1963, London 1964 (omits foreword etc).

§1

Works of Max Beerbohm. New York 1896, London 1896 (adds Bibliography by J. Lane). Essays; rptd 1930 with More, 1899, below, as Works and More.

The happy hypocrite: a fairy tale for tired men. New York 1897, London 1897 (Bodley Booklets 1), 1918 (with note by Beerbohm); rptd in A variety of things, 1928, below. Dramatized by Beerbohm (unpbd) as one-act play (Royalty, Dec 1890) and as a 3 act play (His Majesty's, April 1936) with words by C. Dane (unpbd).

More. 1899, New York 1899. Essays. Rptd 1930 with Works, 1896, above, as Works and More.

Yet again. 1909, New York 1910. Essays.

Zuleika Dobson: or an Oxford love story. [1911], New York 1911, London 1947 (adds frontispiece and note by Beerbohm).

A Christmas garland, woven by Beerbohm. 1912, New York 1912, London 1950 (adds Postscript and All roads, a hitherto unpbd parody on Maurice Baring). Parodies.

Seven men. 1919, New York 1920 (adds Appendix and 5 plates with letterpress by Beerbohm), London 1950 (enlarged as Seven men and two others), Oxford 1966 (WC) (with introd by Lord D. Cecil). Stories.

And even now. 1920, New York 1921. Essays.

Around theatres. 2 vols 1924 (Collected works), New York 1930 (with note by Beerbohm), 1 vol London 1953, New York 1954. 153 slightly rev items of dramatic criticism first pbd in Saturday Rev 1898–1910.

A variety of things. 1928 (Collected works 10), New York 1928 (expands Note and omits A note on the Einstein theory and The happy hypocrite). Miscellany.

Lytton Strachey: the Rede lecture. Cambridge 1943, New York 1943; rptd in 1957 edn of Mainly on the air.

William Rothenstein: an address delivered at the memorial service held at St Martin-in-the-Fields, 6 March 1945. 1945 (priv ptd, 100 copies).

Mainly on the air. 1946, New York 1947 (for 1946), London 1957 (enlarged). Broadcast talks and other pieces, mainly first pbd in Listener.

More theatres 1898–1903. Ed R. Hart-Davis. 1969. This and the next reprint the dramatic criticism in Saturday Rev excluded from Around theatres, 1924, above.

Last theatres 1904–1910. 1970.

Caricatures

Caricatures of twenty-five gentlemen. 1896.

The poets' corner. 1904, New York 1904, London 1943 (King Penguin) (introd by J. Rothenstein; adds 4 plates from Rossetti and his circle). 20 caricatures.

A book of caricatures. 1907. 48 caricatures.

Cartoons: 'The second childhood of John Bull'. [1911]. 15 cartoons.

Fifty caricatures. 1913, New York 1913.

A survey. 1921, New York 1922 (for 1921). 51 caricatures (limited edn has 52).

Rossetti and his circle. 1922, New York 1922. 22 caricatures.

Things new and old. 1923, New York 1923. 49 caricatures (limited edn has 50).

Observations. 1925, New York 1925. 51 caricatures (limited edn has 52).

Heroes and heroines of Bitter Sweet. [1931]. 5 drawings of members of cast of Noel Coward's Bitter sweet, 1929, with introductory note by Beerbohm in facsimile.

Max's nineties: drawings 1892–9. 1958, Philadelphia 1958. Introd by O. Lancaster.

Caricatures by Max from the collection of the Ashmolean Museum. [Oxford 1958].

Letters

Letters to Reggie Turner. Ed R. Hart-Davis 1964, Philadelphia 1965 (for 1964).

§2

Rothenstein, W. Beardsley and Max; The Beerbohms and Gordon Craig. In his Men and memories 1872–1900, 1931.

Wilson, E. Analysis of Beerbohm. New Yorker 1 May 1948; rptd in his Classics and commercials, New York 1950.

—— Meetings with Beerbohm. Encounter 21 1963; rptd in his Bit between my teeth, 1965 (as A miscellany of Beerbohm).

Riewald, J. G. Beerbohm, man and writer. Hague 1953.

Roberts, S. C. In his Dr Johnson and others, Cambridge 1958.

—— Max Beerbohm. Essays by Divers Hands 30 1960.

Behrmann, S. N. Conversation with Max. 1960, New York 1960 (as Portrait of Max).

Cecil, D. Max: a biography. 1964.

ARTHUR CLIVE HEWARD BELL
1881–1964

Art. 1914, New York 1914.

Peace at once. Manchester [1915]. Pamphlet.

Ad familiares. 1917 (priv ptd). Verse.

Pot-boilers. 1918. Rptd reviews.

Poems. Richmond Surrey 1921.

Since Cézanne. 1922, New York 1922. Essays.

The legend of Monte della Sibilla; or le paradis de la Reine Sibille. Richmond Surrey 1923. Verse.

On British freedom. 1923, New York 1923.

Landmarks in nineteenth-century painting. 1927, New York 1927.

Civilization: an essay. 1928, New York 1928.

Proust. 1928, New York 1929.

An account of French painting. 1931, New York 1932.

Enjoying pictures: meditations in the National Gallery and elsewhere. 1934, New York 1934.

Modern French painting: the Cone Collection. Baltimore 1951. Address.

Old friends: personal recollections. 1956, New York 1957 (for 1956).

JOSEPH HILAIRE PIERRE RENÉ BELLOC
1870–1953

Bibliographies

Cahill, P. The English first editions of Belloc: a chronological catalogue. 1953.

Collections and Selections

The bad child's book of beasts; together with More beasts for worse children and Cautionary tales. [1923], New York 1930.

Hilaire Belloc. 1935 (Methuen's Lib of Humour). Prose and verse selected by E. V. Knox.

Stories, essays and poems. 1938 (introd by A. G. Mac-donnell), 1957 (enlarged, introd by J. B. Morton) (EL).

Cautionary verses: the collected humorous poems. 1939, 1940 (Album edn, with original pictures; omits The modern traveller), New York 1941.

Selected cautionary verses. 1950, 1964 (rev). Selected from Album edn, above.

An anthology of his prose and verse, selected by W. N. Roughead. 1951.

Songs of the south country. 1951.

The verse of Belloc. Ed W. N. Roughead 1954, 1970 (slightly rev) (as Complete verse).

Selected essays. Ed with introd by J. B. Morton 1958, Baltimore 1959. A different selection from 1948, above.

Prefaces written for fellow authors. Ed J. A. De Chantigny, Chicago 1971.

§I

Miscellaneous Prose

CTS = Catholic Truth Soc pamphlets and leaflets.

Lambkin's remains, by H.B. Oxford 1900, London 1920 (with The aftermath, below). Undergraduate satire.

The aftermath: or gleanings from a busy life, called upon the outer cover, for purposes of sale, Caliban's guide to letters, by H. B. 1903, New York 1903, London 1920 (with Lambkin's remains, above). Humorous sketches.

The great inquiry—only authorised version—faithfully reported by H.B. [1903]. Political satire, illustr G. K. Chesterton.

Avril: being essays on the poetry of the French Renaissance. 1904, New York 1904.

An open letter on the decay of faith. [1906].

Hills and the sea. 1906, New York 1906. Essays.

The Catholic Church and historical truth. Preston 1908 (Catholic Evidence Lectures 3).

On nothing and kindred subjects. 1908. Essays.

An examination of socialism. [1908] (CTS).

On everything. 1909, New York 1910.

The Church and socialism. [1909] (CTS).

The Ferrer case. [1910] (CTS). On the trial and execution of Francesco Ferrer y Guardia.

On anything. 1910, New York 1910. Essays.

On something. 1910. Essays.

The party system. 1911. With C. Chesterton.

Socialism and the servile state: a debate between Belloc and J. Ramsay Macdonald. 1911.

First and last. 1911. Essays.

The servile state. 1912, 1913 (with new preface), 1927 (with new preface), New York [1946] (introd by C. Gauss).

This and that and the other. 1912, New York 1912. Essays.

Anti-Catholic history: how it is written. 1914 (CTS). An examination of J. B. Bury, A history of freedom of thought, 1913.

Three essays. Portland Maine 1914. Contains On sacramental things, On rest, On coming to an end.

At the sign of the lion and other essays from the books of Belloc. Portland Maine 1916. Adds title essay and The autumn and the fall of leaves to contents of preceding.

The free press. 1918.

Religion and civil liberty. 1918 (CTS). On an article by Hypatia Bradlaugh entitled Christianity versus liberty.

The Catholic Church and the principle of private property. 1920 (CTS).

The House of Commons and monarchy. 1920.

Pascal's Provincial letters. 1921 (CTS).

Catholic social reform versus socialism. 1922 (CTS).

The Jews. 1922, Boston 1937 (with new introductory ch). *See* W. R. Inge, The Jews, [1922].

On. 1923, New York [1923]. Essays.

The contrast. 1923, New York 1924. On Europeans and Americans.

Economics for Helen. 1924, New York 1924, 1925 (as Economics for young people).

England and the Faith. [1925] (CTS).

Short talks with the dead and others. 1926. Essays.

Mrs Markham's new history of England. 1926. Satire on contemporary institutions.

A companion to Mr Wells's Outline of history. 1926, [1929] (rev). *See* H. G. Wells, Mr Belloc objects to the Outline of history, 1926.

Mr Belloc still objects to Mr Wells's Outline of history. 1926, San Francisco 1927.

A conversation with an angel and other essays. 1928, New York 1929.

Survivals and new arrivals. 1929, New York 1929. Apologetics.

World conflict. Horsham 1930 (priv ptd) (anon), London 1951 (CTS) (as by Belloc).

A conversation with a cat and others. 1931, New York 1931. Essays.

On translation: the Taylorian lecture. Oxford 1931.

Essays of a Catholic layman in England. 1931, New York 1931 (as Essays of a Catholic).

Nine nines: or novenas from a Chinese litany of odd numbers. Oxford 1931. Rptd from Short talks with the dead and others, above.

Usury. [1931]. Pamphlet rptd (rev) from Essays of a Catholic layman, above.

The question and the answer. New York [1932], London 1938. Apologetics.

Milton. 1935, Philadelphia 1935.

An essay on the restoration of property. 1936, New York 1936 (as The restoration of property). Distributist League pamphlet.

An essay on the nature of contemporary England. 1937, New York 1937.

The issue. [1937], New York [1937]. Apologetics. Pamphlet.

The case of Dr Coulton. 1938. Reply to G. G. Coulton, Divorce, Mr Belloc and the Daily Telegraph, 1937.

The Catholic and the war. 1940. Pamphlet.

On the place of Chesterton in English letters. 1940, New York 1940.

The silence of the sea and other essays. New York 1940, London 1941.

Places. New York 1941, London 1942. Essays.

One thing and another: a miscellany from his uncollected essays. Ed P. Cahill 1955.

Advice. 1960. Introd by E. Waugh. Advice to Bridget Grant on wine and food.

History and Biography

Danton: a study. 1899, New York 1899, London 1928 (rev with new preface), New York 1928.

Robespierre: a study. 1901, New York 1901, London 1927 (with new introd), New York 1928.

The eye-witness. 1908.

Marie Antoinette. 1909, New York 1909.

The French Revolution. [1911], New York [1911].

British battles. 6 vols 1911–13, 1 vol Bristol 1931 (rev, as Six British battles).

Warfare in England. [1912], New York [1912].

A general sketch of the European war. 2 vols 1915 (subtitled The first phase) and 1916 (subtitled The second phase), New York 1915–16 (as The elements of the Great War).

The two maps of Europe and some other aspects of the Great War. 1915.

The last days of the French monarchy. 1916.

The second year of the war. 1916.

Europe and the Faith. 1920, New York 1920, London 1962 (introd by D. Woodruff).

The campaign of 1812 and the Retreat from Moscow. [1924], New York 1926 (as Napoleon's campaign of 1812 and the Retreat from Moscow).

A history of England. 4 vols [B.C. 55–A.D. 1612] 1925–31, New York 1925–32, vol 1 [to 1066] (corrected, with new preface) London 1926. 3 further vols not pbd.
Miniatures of French history. [1925], New York 1926.
The Catholic Church and history. 1926, New York 1926 (Calvert ser).
Oliver Cromwell. 1927.
James the Second. 1928, Philadelphia 1928.
How the Reformation happened. 1928, New York 1928.
Joan of Arc. 1929, New York 1949.
Richelieu: a study. Philadelphia 1929, London 1930.
Wolsey. 1930, Philadelphia 1930.
Cranmer. 1931, Philadelphia 1931.
Napoleon. 1932, Philadelphia 1932.
The tactics and strategy of the great Duke of Marlborough. Bristol 1933.
William the Conqueror. 1933, New York 1934.
Beckett. 1933 (CTS).
Charles the First, King of England. 1933, Philadelphia 1933.
Cromwell. 1934, Philadelphia 1934.
A shorter history of England. 1934, New York 1934.
The battle ground. 1936, Philadelphia 1936. History of Syria to 1187.
Characters of the Reformation. 1936, New York 1936.
The Crusade: the world's debate. 1937, Milwaukee [1937] (as The Crusades: the world's debate). On the military aspect of the Crusades.
The crisis of our civilization. 1937, New York [1937] (as The crisis of civilization).
The great heresies. 1938, New York 1938.
Monarchy: a study of Louis XIV. 1938, New York 1938 (as Louis XIV).
Charles II: the last rally. New York 1939, London 1940 (as The last rally: a story of Charles II).
Elizabethan commentary. 1942, New York 1942 (as Elizabeth, creature of circumstance).

Travel and Topography

Paris. 1900.
The path to Rome. 1902, New York 1902. Illustr Belloc.
The old road [the Pilgrim's Way]. 1904, New York 1923.
Esto perpetua: Algerian studies and impressions. 1906.
Sussex, painted by William Ball. 1906 (anon), 1936 (as The county of Sussex, 'virtually rewritten').
The historic Thames. 1907.
The Pyrenees. 1909, 1923 (rev), 1928 (with new preface).
The four men: a farrago. [1912]. On Sussex.
The river of London. 1912.
The Stane Street: a monograph. 1913.
The road. Manchester 1923, New York 1925.
The cruise of the Nona. 1925, Boston 1925, London 1955 (introd by Lord Stanley of Alderley), Westminster Md 1955.
Towns of destiny. New York 1927, London 1928 (as Many cities).
Return to the Baltic. 1938.

Poetry and Verse

Verses and sonnets. 1896. Withdrawn by Belloc.
The bad child's book of beasts: verses by H.B., pictures by B.T.B. [Basil Blackwood]. Oxford [1896], New York 1923.
More beasts—for worse children, by H.B.; pictures by B.T.B. [1897], New York 1923.
The modern traveller, by H.B. and [with illustrations by] B.T.B. 1898.
A moral alphabet, by H.B., with illustrations by B.B. 1899.
Cautionary tales for children: designed for the admonition of children between the ages of eight and fourteen years; pictures by B.T.B. [1908].
Verses. 1910, New York 1916 (introd by J. Kilmer).
More peers; pictures by B.T.B. [1911], New York 1924.
You wear the morning like your dress: song, the words and music by Belloc. [1913]. Text from Verses, above.

Sonnets and verse. 1923, 1938 (enlarged), New York 1939 (enlarged with biographical introd by R. Jebb), London 1954, 1958 (as Collected verse, with introd by R. Knox).
Hilaire Belloc. [1925] (Augustan Books of Modern Poetry). Nineteen poems.
The chanty of the Nona: poem and drawings by Belloc. [1928] (Ariel Poem). Rptd (rev) from Sonnets and verse, above.
New cautionary tales; pictures by N. Bentley. 1930, New York 1931.
Tarantella: song, words and music by Belloc. 1930. Text from Sonnets and verse, above.
The praise of wine: an heroic poem. 1931 (priv ptd), 1932 (as An heroic poem in praise of wine) (100 copies), [Long Crendon] 1933 (priv ptd) (as In praise of wine). Rptd in Sonnets and verse, above, 1938 edn.
Ladies and gentlemen: for adults only and mature at that; pictures by N. Bentley. 1932.

Fiction

Emmanuel Burden, merchant. [1904], New York 1904.
Mr Clutterbuck's election. 1908.
A change in the Cabinet. 1909.
Pongo and the bull. 1910.
The Girondin. 1911.
The green overcoat. Bristol 1912, New York 1912.
[Rehmatt-Allah, in Arabic script]: that is, The mercy of Allah. 1922, New York 1922.
Mr Petre: a novel. 1925, New York 1925.
The emerald of Catherine the Great. 1926, New York 1926.
The haunted house. 1927, New York 1928.
But soft—we are observed! 1928, New York 1929 (as Shadowed!).
Belinda: a tale of affection in youth and age. 1928, New York 1929.
The missing masterpiece. 1929, New York 1929.
The man who made gold. 1930, New York [1931].
The postmaster-general. 1932, Philadelphia 1932.
The hedge and the horse. 1936.

Letters

Letters from Belloc. Ed R. Speaight [1958], New York 1958.

§2

Woodruff, J. D. (ed). For Belloc: essays in honour of his 72nd birthday. 1942.
Hamilton, R. Hilaire Belloc: an introduction to his spirit and work. 1945.
Haynes, R. Hilaire Belloc. 1953, 1958 (rev) (Br Council pamphlet).
Speaight, R. W. The life of Belloc. 1957.
Brome, V. Dr Coulton versus Belloc; Belloc versus Wells. In his Six studies in quarrelling, 1958.
Knox, R. A. Belloc's verse. In his Literary distractions, 1958.
Bergonzi, B. Chesterton and/or Belloc. CQ 1 1959.

HENRY STANLEY BENNETT
1889–1972

Bibliographies

Brewer, D. S. A list of his writings presented to Bennett on his eightieth birthday. Cambridge 1969.

§1

The Pastons and their England: studies in an age of transition. Cambridge 1922, 1932 (rev).
England from Chaucer to Caxton. 1928.

Life on the English manor: a study in peasant conditions 1150–1400. Cambridge 1937, New York 1937.

Chaucer and the fifteenth century. Oxford 1947 (OHEL 2 pt 1); rptd with corrections 1948, 1954, 1958.

English books and readers, 1475 to 1557: being a study in the history of the book trade from Caxton to the incorporation of the Stationers' Company. Cambridge 1952, 1969.

Six medieval men and women. Cambridge 1955, New York 1962.

English books and readers, 1558 to 1603: being a study in the history of the book trade in the reign of Elizabeth I. Cambridge 1965.

SIR CECIL MAURICE BOWRA
1898–1971

Pindar. Pythian odes, translated by H. T. Wade-Gery and C. M. Bowra. 1928; rptd, with corrections, in The odes of Pindar, 1969, below.

Tradition and design in the Iliad. Oxford 1930.

Ancient Greek literature. 1933, New York 1959, London 1967 (rev).

Greek lyric poetry from Alcman to Simonides. Oxford 1936, 1961 (rev).

Early Greek elegists. 1938, Cambridge Mass 1938.

The Oxford book of Greek verse in translation. Oxford 1938, 1943 (as From the Greek, abridged). Ed Bowra, with T. F. Higham.

A book of Russian verse, translated into English by various hands. 1943. Ed, with trns, by Bowra.

The heritage of symbolism. 1943, New York 1961.

Sophoclean tragedy. Oxford 1944, 1945 (corrected).

From Virgil to Milton. 1945.

A second book of Russian verse, translated into English by various hands. 1948. Ed, with trns, by Bowra.

The creative experiment. 1949, New York 1958. On certain aspects of European poetry since 1910.

The Romantic imagination. Cambridge Mass 1949, London 1950.

Heroic poetry. 1952.

Problems in Greek poetry. Oxford 1953.

Inspiration and poetry. 1955, Folcroft Pa 1969. Essays, including single lectures previously pbd separately.

The Greek experience. 1957, New York [1957].

Primitive song. [1962], Cleveland 1962.

In general and particular. 1964, Cleveland 1964. Essays, including single lectures previously pbd separately.

Pindar. Oxford 1964.

Landmarks in Greek literature. [1966], Cleveland 1966.

Memories 1898–1939. [1966], Cambridge Mass 1967.

Poetry and politics 1900–60. Cambridge 1966.

The odes of Pindar, translated with an introduction by Bowra. 1969 (Penguin), Baltimore 1969.

MURIEL CLARA BRADBROOK
b. 1909

Elizabethan stage conditions: a study of their place in the interpretation of Shakespeare's plays. Cambridge 1932, Hamden Conn 1962 (with additional preface).

Themes and conventions of Elizabethan tragedy. Cambridge 1935.

The school of night: a study in the literary relationships of Sir Walter Ralegh. Cambridge 1936, New York 1965.

Andrew Marvell. Cambridge 1940. With M. G. Lloyd Thomas.

Joseph Conrad: Poland's English genius. Cambridge 1941, New York 1965.

Ibsen the Norwegian: a revaluation. 1946, 1966 (rev), Hamden Conn 1966.

T. S. Eliot. 1950, New York 1950, London 1951 (rev), 1955 (rev), 1958 (rev), 1960 (rev), 1963 (rev), 1968 (rev) (Br Council pamphlet).

Shakespeare and Elizabethan poetry: a study of his earlier work in relation to the poetry of the time. 1951, New York 1952, London 1964 (for 1965) (with new preface).

The growth and structure of Elizabethan comedy. 1955, Berkeley 1956, London 1973.

Sir Thomas Malory. 1958, New York 1958 London 1965 (rev) (Br Council pamphlet).

The rise of the common player: a study of actor and society in Shakespeare's England. 1962, Cambridge Mass 1962.

English dramatic form: a history of its development. 1965, New York 1965.

Shakespeare the craftsman. 1969, New York 1969.

'That infidel place': a short history of Girton College 1869–1969. 1969.

Malcolm Lowry. Cambridge 1974.

The living monument: Shakespeare and the theatre of his time. Cambridge 1976.

ANDREW CECIL BRADLEY
1851–1935

§1

A commentary on Tennyson's In memoriam. 1901, 1902 (rev), 1910 (rev), 1930 (rev), Hamden Conn 1966.

Shakespearean tragedy: lectures on Hamlet, Othello, King Lear, Macbeth. 1904, Cleveland 1961.

Oxford lectures on poetry. 1909, 1909 (corrected), New York 1959, London 1965 (introd by M. R. Ridley).

A miscellany. 1929, Freeport NY 1969.

Ideals of religion: Gifford lectures 1907. 1940.

Bradley edited T. H. Green's Prolegomena to ethics, Oxford 1883, and (with G. R. Benson) R. L. Nettleship's Philosophical lectures and remains 2 vols 1897.

§2

Knights, L. C. In his How many children had Lady Macbeth?: an essay in the theory and practice of Shakespeare criticism, Cambridge 1933.

Mackail, J. W. Bradley. Proc Br Acad 21 1935.

Murry, J. M. In his Katherine Mansfield and other literary portraits, 1949.

Hunter, G. K. Bradley's Shakespearian tragedy. E & S new ser 21 1968.

GERALD BRENAN
(EDWARD FITZGERALD BRENAN)
b. 1894

Jack Robinson: a picaresque novel, by 'George Beaton' [i.e. Brenan]. 1933.

Doctor Partridge's almanack for 1935 collected and set forth by 'George Beaton'. 1934. Fiction.

The Spanish labyrinth: an account of the social and political background of the Civil War. Cambridge 1943, 1950 (corrected).

Spanish scene. 1946 (Current Affairs pamphlet).

The face of Spain. 1950, New York 1951.

The literature of the Spanish people. Cambridge 1951, 1953 (rev), New York 1965.

South from Granada. 1957, New York 1957.

A holiday by the sea. 1961, New York 1961. Fiction.

A life of one's own: childhood and youth. 1962, New York 1962.

The lighthouse always says yes. 1966. Fiction.

St John of the Cross: his life and poetry. Cambridge 1973.

Personal record 1920–72. 1974

'CHRISTOPHER CAUDWELL', CHRISTOPHER ST JOHN SPRIGG
1907–37

The airship: its design, history, operation and future. [1931].

British airways, by C. St J. Sprigg. [1934], New York 1934 (Discovery Books 1). For boys.

Great flights, by C. St J. Sprigg. 1935, New York 1935 (Nelsonian Lib 35). For boys.

This my hand. 1936. Novel.

Illusion and reality: a study of the sources of poetry. 1937, 1946 (with biographical note by G.T. [i.e. G. Thomson], and index), New York 1947.

'Let's learn to fly!', by C. St J. Sprigg. 1937.

Studies in a dying culture. Introd by J. Strachey, 1938, New York 1938, 1958 (with Further studies, 1959), 1963 (with biographical note by G. Thomson).

The crisis in physics. Ed H. Levy 1939, New York 1951.

Poems. 1939. With biographical note.

Further studies in a dying culture. Ed E. Rickword 1949, New York 1949, 1958 (with Studies, 1938).

Caudwell also wrote 7 detective novels as C. St J. Sprigg and a number of unpbd short stories; he founded an aeronautical publishing house; he was the founder and editor of Technical Engineering; *he edited the jnl* Br Malaya, *and, with an introd, an anthology* Uncanny stories, *1936.*

LORD EDWARD CHRISTIAN DAVID GASCOYNE CECIL
b. 1902

The stricken deer: or the life of Cowper. 1929, Indianapolis [1930].

Early Victorian novelists: essays in revaluation. 1934, Indianapolis [1935], Chicago 1958 (as Victorian novelists: essays in revaluation, with a new foreword).

The young Melbourne and the story of his marriage with Caroline Lamb. 1939, Indianapolis [1939], New York 1943 (foreword by C. Van Doren).

The Oxford book of Christian verse. Oxford 1940. Ed Cecil.

The English poets. 1941 (Britain in Pictures).

Hardy the novelist: an essay in criticism. 1943, Indianapolis 1946.

Two quiet lives: Dorothy Osborne, Thomas Gray. 1948, Indianapolis [1948].

Poets and story-tellers: a book of critical essays. 1949, New York 1949. Includes lectures previously pbd separately.

Lord M: or the later life of Lord Melbourne. 1954. Includes a brief selection from The young Melbourne, 1939.

The fine art of reading and other literary studies. 1957, Indianapolis 1957.

Max: a biography. 1964, Boston 1965.

Visionary and dreamer: two poetic painters, Samuel Palmer and Edward Burne-Jones. 1969, Princeton 1970.

The Cecils of Hatfield House. 1973.

A portrait of Jane Austen. 1978.

HECTOR MUNRO CHADWICK
1870–1947

The cult of Othin: an essay in the ancient religion of the North. 1899.

Studies on Anglo-Saxon institutions. Cambridge 1905.

The origin of the English nation. Cambridge 1907.

Early national poetry. In CHEL vol 1, Cambridge 1907.

The heroic age. Cambridge 1912.

The growth of literature. Cambridge 1932–40. With N. K. Chadwick.

The study of Anglo-Saxon. Cambridge 1941, 1955 (rev N. K. Chadwick).

The nationalities of Europe and the growth of national ideologies. Cambridge 1945.

Early Scotland: the Picts, the Scots and the Welsh of southern Scotland. Cambridge 1949.

SIR EDMUND KERCHEVER CHAMBERS
1866–1954

The mediæval stage. 2 vols Oxford 1903.

Notes on the history of the Revels office under the Tudors. 1906, New York 1967.

Early English lyrics amorous, divine, moral and trivial. Ed Chambers and F. Sidgwick 1907, New York 1967.

Aurelian Townshend's Poems and masks. Ed Chambers, Oxford 1912 (Tudor and Stuart Lib).

The Elizabethan stage. 4 vols Oxford 1923, 1961 (rev).

Shakespeare: a survey. 1925.

Arthur of Britain. 1927, Cambridge 1964 (with supplementary bibliography by B. F. Roberts), New York 1967.

William Shakespeare: a study of facts and problems. 2 vols Oxford 1930.

The Oxford book of sixteenth-century verse. Ed Chambers, Oxford 1932, 1961 (corrected).

The English folk-play. Oxford 1933, New York 1964.

Sir Thomas Wyatt and some collected studies. 1933, New York 1965.

Sir Henry Lee: an Elizabethan portrait. Oxford 1936.

Samuel Taylor Coleridge: a biographical study. Oxford 1938, 1963 (corrected).

A sheaf of studies. 1942, Freeport NY 1969.

Shakespearean gleanings. 1944, Folcroft Pa 1969.

English literature at the close of the Middle Ages. Oxford 1945, 1947 (corrected) (OHEL 2 pt 2).

Sources for a biography of Shakespeare. Oxford 1946.

Matthew Arnold: a study. Oxford 1947, New York 1964.

Chambers edited the Red Letter Shakespeare 1904–8 and, with C. H. Herford, A. D. Innes et al, the Warwick Shakespeare 1893 onwards; he was the first President of the Malone Soc and edited, sometimes with W. W. Greg et al, a number of dramatic records.

RAYMOND WILSON CHAMBERS
1874–1942

Widsith: a study in Old English heroic legend. Cambridge 1912, New York 1965.

Beowulf, with the Finnsburg fragment. Ed A. J. Wyatt, rev R. W. Chambers, Cambridge 1914, 1920 (rptd with 3 pages of additional notes), 1932 (rev), 1959 (with a suppl by C. L. Wrenn).

Beowulf: an introduction to the study of the poem, with a discussion of the stories of Offa and Finn. Cambridge 1921, 1932 (rev and enlarged), 1959 (suppl by C. L. Wrenn).

The teaching of English in the universities of England. Oxford 1922 (Eng Assoc pamphlet 53).

On the continuity of English prose from Alfred to More and his school: an extract from the introduction to N. Harpsfield's Life and death of Sir Thomas More. Ed E. V. Hitchcock and Chambers 1932 (EETS).

Thomas More. 1935, New York 1935.

The place of Sir Thomas More in English literature and history . 1937, New York 1964.

Man's unconquerable mind. 1939.

ROBERT WILLIAM CHAPMAN
1881–1960

The portrait of a scholar and other essays written in Macedonia 1916–18. 1920, Freeport NY 1968.

Some account of the Oxford University Press 1468–1921. Oxford 1922. Anon.

—— 1468–1926. Oxford 1926. Anon.

Boswell's revises of the Life of Johnson. In Johnson and Boswell revised by themselves and others: three essays by D. Nichol Smith, R. W. Chapman and L. F. Powell, Oxford 1928.

Cancels. 1930 (Bibliographia ser).

Jane Austen: facts and problems. Oxford 1948, 1961 (corrected).

The sense of the past. In Book collecting: four broadcast talks by R. W. Chapman [et al], Cambridge 1951.

Jane Austen: a critical bibliography. Oxford 1953, 1955 (corrected).

Johnsonian and other essays and reviews. Oxford 1953.

Chapman edited Johnson, Jane Austen etc and wrote a number of tracts for the Soc for Pure English.

GILBERT KEITH CHESTERTON
1874–1936

An extensive collection of mss, letters, notebooks etc is held by Dorothy Collins, Chesterton's literary executrix; other collections include the Robert John Bayer Chesterton Collection, John Carroll Univ, Cleveland Ohio, and that of J. B. Shaw, Tulsa Oklahoma; some mss of juvenilia are held in the library of St Paul's School.

Bibliographies

Sullivan, J. J. Chesterton: a bibliography. 1958.

—— Chesterton continued: a bibliographical supplement together with some uncollected prose and verse. 1968.

Collections and Selections

The Father Brown stories. 1929, New York [1935] (as The Father Brown omnibus), London 1947 (adds The scandal of Father Brown), New York 1951 (as The Father Brown omnibus; adds The vampire of the village).

Stories, essays and poems. 1935, 1957 (introd by M. Ward) (EL).

A G. K. Chesterton omnibus.

Father Brown: selected stories. Ed R. Knox, Oxford 1955 (WC).

An anthology, selected with an introduction by D. B. Wyndham Lewis. Oxford 1957 (WC).

Chesterton: a selection from his non-fictional prose, selected by W. H. Auden. 1970.

§1

The defendant. 1901, New York 1902, London 1903 (adds In defence of a new edition). Essays.

Twelve types. 1902, New York 1903 (as Varied types; adds 7 further essays).

Robert Browning. 1903 (EML), New York 1903.

Heretics. 1905, New York 1905. Essays.

Charles Dickens. 1906, New York, 1906 (as Charles Dickens: a critical study), 1942 (as Charles Dickens, the last of the great men; enlarged, foreword by A. Woollcott), 1965 (introd by S. Marcus).

All things considered. 1908, New York 1908. Essays.

Orthodoxy. 1909 (for 1908), New York 1908 (with preface by Chesterton).

George Bernard Shaw. 1910 (for 1909), New York 1909, London 1935 (with new ch), New York 1950.

Tremendous trifles. 1909, New York 1909. Essays.

What's wrong with the world. 1910, New York 1910.

Alarms and discursions. 1910, New York 1911 (adds The fading fireworks). Essays.

William Blake. [1910].

Appreciations and criticisms of the works of Dickens. 1911, 1933 (as Criticisms and appreciations of the works of Dickens), New York 1966 (with original title). First pbd as introds to Dickens' works in EL.

A miscellany of men. 1912, New York 1912 (adds Preface and The suffragist). Essays.

The Victorian age in literature. [1913], New York [1913], Notre Dame 1962 (foreword by A. Ryan).

The barbarism of Berlin. 1914.

Letters to an old Garibaldian. 1915.

The appetite of tyranny. New York 1915. Contains The barbarism of Berlin and Letters to an old Garibaldian, above.

The crimes of England. 1915, New York 1916.

A short history of England. 1917, New York 1917, London 1924 (with new foreword).

Utopia of usurers and other essays. New York 1917.

Irish impressions. [1919], New York 1920.

The superstition of divorce. 1920, New York 1920.

The uses of diversity. 1920, New York 1921. Essays.

The new Jerusalem. [1920], New York [1921]. Travel.

Eugenics and other evils. 1922. Essays.

What I saw in America. 1922, New York 1922, 1968 (introd by G. H. Knoles).

Fancies versus fads. 1923, New York 1923. Essays.

St Francis of Assisi. [1923], New York [1924].

The end of the Roman road: a pageant of wayfarers. 1924.

The superstition of the sceptic; with a correspondence between the author and G. G. Coulton. Cambridge 1925.

The everlasting man. [1925], New York 1925.

William Cobbett. [1925].

The outline of sanity. 1926, New York 1927. Essays on Distributism.

The Catholic Church and conversion. New York 1926, London 1926 (for 1927) (Calvert ser), 1960 (adds 2 essays).

Culture and the coming peril. 1927.

Robert Louis Stevenson. [1927], New York 1928.

Generally speaking. 1928, New York 1929. Essays.

The thing. 1929, New York 1930 (adds Why I am a Catholic). Essays.

The resurrection of Rome. [1930], New York 1930 (omits 2 appendices).

Come to think of it. 1930, New York 1931. Essays.

All is grist. 1931, New York 1932. Essays.

Chaucer. 1932, New York [1932].

Sidelights on new London and Newer York and other essays. 1932, New York 1932.

All I survey. 1933, New York 1933. Essays.

St Thomas Aquinas. 1933, New York 1933.

Avowals and denials. 1934, New York 1935. Essays.

G.K.'s: a miscellany of the first 500 issues of G.K.'s Weekly. 1934. Introd, many contributions in prose and verse and illustrations.

The well and the shadows. 1935, New York 1935. Essays.

Chesterton explains the English. [1935] (Br Council pamphlet).

As I was saying. 1936, New York 1936. Essays.

Autobiography. 1936, New York 1936, London 1969 (introd A. Burgess).

The coloured lands, illustrated by the author. 1938, New York 1938. Introd by M. Ward. Prose, verse and drawings, much hitherto unpbd, including juvenilia.

The end of the armistice. 1940, New York 1940. Essays, ed F. J. Sheed.

The common man. 1950, New York 1950. Essays.

A handful of authors. Ed D. Collins 1953, New York 1953. Essays first pbd 1901–35.

The glass walking-stick and other essays from Illustrated London News 1905–36. Ed D. Collins 1955.

Lunacy and letters. Ed D. Collins 1958, New York 1958. Essays from Daily News 1901–11.

The spice of life and other essays. Ed D. Collins, Beaconsfield 1964, Philadelphia 1966. Essays contributed to various books and jnls.

Fiction

The Napoleon of Notting Hill. 1904, New York 1904.

The club of queer trades. 1905 (illustr Chesterton), New York 1905 (illustr W. E. Mears). Stories.

The man who was Thursday: a nightmare. 1908, New York 1908.

The ball and the cross. New York 1909, London 1910 (rev).

The innocence of Father Brown. 1911, New York 1911. Stories.

Manalive. 1912, New York 1912.

The flying inn. 1914, New York 1914. Songs rptd (with 1 addn) as Wine, water and song, 1915.

The wisdom of Father Brown. 1914, New York 1915. Stories.

The man who knew too much and other stories. 1922, New York 1922 (omits last 3 stories).

Tales of the long bow. 1925, New York 1925.

The incredulity of Father Brown. 1926, New York 1926. Stories.

The return of Don Quixote. 1927, New York 1927.

The secret of Father Brown. 1927, New York 1927. Stories.

The sword of wood: a story. 1928.

The poet and the lunatics: episodes in the life of Gabriel Gale. 1929, New York [1929].

Four faultless felons. 1930, New York 1930. Stories.

The scandal of Father Brown. 1935, New York 1935. Stories.

The paradoxes of Mr Pond. [1937], New York 1937. Stories.

Verse and Plays

Greybeards at play—literature and art for old gentlemen: rhymes and sketches. 1900.

The wild knight and other poems. 1900, 1905 (adds Prefatory note), 1914 (adds 3 poems).

The ballad of the white horse. 1911, New York 1911.

Magic: a fantastic comedy. (Little Theatre 7 Nov 1913). [1913], York 1913.

Poems. 1915, New York 1915.

Wine, water and song. 1915. Verses first pbd in The flying inn, 1914, with one addition.

Old King Cole. [1920]. Text of the rhyme with versions parodying Tennyson, Yeats, Whitman, Browning.

The ballad of St Barbara and other verses. 1922, New York 1923.

The queen of seven swords. 1926. Poems.

Gloria in profundis. [1927] (Ariel Poem).

The judgement of Dr Johnson: a comedy. (Arts Theatre Club 20 Jan 1932). 1927, New York 1928.

Ubi ecclesia. 1929 (Ariel Poem).

Lepanto. New York 1929. Rptd from Poems, 1915, above.

The grave of Arthur. 1930 (Ariel Poem).

The turkey and the Turk. Ditchling 1930 (St Dominic's Press, 100 copies). Dramatic poem.

The surprise. (Hull Univ Dramatic Soc 5 June 1953). 1952, New York 1953. Preface by D. L. Sayers.

Many of Chesterton's letters and much unpbd prose, verse and some drawings are contained in M. Ward, Gilbert Keith Chesterton, New York 1943, and Return to Chesterton, 1952.

§2

[Chesterton, C.] Chesterton: a criticism. 1908.

Braybrooke, P. Gilbert Keith Chesterton. 1922, 1926 (enlarged).

—— The wisdom of Chesterton. 1929.

—— I remember Chesterton. [1938].

Evans, M. G. K. Chesterton. Cambridge 1938.

Belloc, H. On the place of Chesterton in English letters. 1940.

Ward, M. Gilbert Keith Chesterton. New York 1943.

—— Return to Chesterton. 1952.

Kenner, H. Paradox in Chesterton. 1948.

Hollis, C. G. K. Chesterton. 1950, 1954 (rev bibliography), 1964 (rev bibliography) (Br Council pamphlet).

—— The mind of Chesterton. 1970.

Brome, V. Chesterton versus Bernard Shaw. In his Six studies in quarrelling, 1958.

Bergonzi, B. Chesterton and/or Belloc. CQ 1 1959.

Robson, W. W. Chesterton's Father Brown stories. Southern Rev new ser 5 1969.

Barker, D. Chesterton: a biography. 1973.

Boyd, I. The novels of Chesterton. 1975.

KENNETH MACKENZIE CLARK, BARON CLARK
b. 1903

The gothic revival: an essay in the history of taste. 1928, 1950 (rev and enlarged), 1962 (rev), New York 1962.

A commemorative catalogue of the Exhibition of Italian art held in the Royal Academy 1930. Ed Lord Balniel and Clark 2 vols 1931.

A catalogue of the drawings of Leonardo da Vinci in the collection of His Majesty the King at Windsor Castle. 2 vols Cambridge 1935, New York 1935, 3 vols London 1968–9 (rev, with C. Pedretti).

One hundred details from pictures in the National Gallery. 1938. Plates with introd and notes.

Fry, R. E. Last lectures. Ed Clark, Cambridge 1939.

Leonardo da Vinci: an account of his development as an artist. Cambridge 1939, New York 1939, Cambridge 1952 (rev), London 1958 (rev).

Landscape into art. 1949, New York 1950 (as Landscape painting), London 1956 (corrected), Boston 1961.

Piero della Francesca. 1951, New York 1951, London 1969 (rev). Monograph with plates.

The nude: a study of ideal art. 1956, New York 1956.

Looking at pictures. [1960], New York 1960. With plates.

Pater, W. H. The Renaissance: studies in art and poetry, to which is added the essay on Raphael from Miscellaneous studies. Ed Clark 1961 (Fontana Lib).

Ruskin today: chosen and annotated by Clark. [1964], New York 1965.

Rembrandt and the Italian Renaissance. 1966, New York 1966.

A failure of nerve: Italian painting 1520–35. Oxford 1967.

Civilisation: a personal view. 1969, New York 1969.

CYRIL VERNON CONNOLLY
1903–74

The rock pool. Paris 1936 (Obelisk Press), New York 1936, London 1947 (adds Postscript). Novel.

Enemies of promise. 1938, Boston 1939, New York 1948 (rev with introd), Garden City NY 1960 (as Enemies of promise and other essays: an autobiography of ideas). With an autobiographical section, A Georgian boyhood.

Horizon stories. Ed Connolly 1943, New York [1946]. 18 stories (American edn 20 stories) rptd from Horizon.

The unquiet grave: a word cycle, by 'Palinurus' [i.e. C. Connolly]. 1944, 1945 (rev), New York 1945, London 1951 (rev with introd), 1967 (rev with new introd).

'Vercors' (Jean Bruller). Put out the light: a translation of Le silence de la mer. 1944, New York 1944 (as The silence of the sea). Tr Connolly.

The condemned playground: essays 1927–44. 1945, New York 1946.

The missing diplomats. 1952 (for 1953). On Burgess and Maclean.

The golden Horizon. Ed Connolly 1953, New York [1955]. Miscellany rptd from Horizon.

Ideas and places. 1953, New York 1953. Selection of editorial comments from Horizon.

Les pavillons: French pavilions of the eighteenth century. New York 1962, London 1962. With J. Zerbe.

[James] Bond strikes camp. 1963 (priv ptd, 50 copies). Story, rptd in next.

Previous convictions. 1963, New York 1963. Articles mainly rptd from Sunday Times.

The modern movement: one hundred key books from England, France and America 1880–1950, 1965, New York 1966.

Jarry, A. The Ubu plays. Tr Connolly and S. W. Taylor 1968.

The evening colonnade. 1973.

A romantic friendship: letters to Noel Blakiston. 1975.

Connolly founded and edited Horizon *1940–50; he was literary editor of* Observer *1942–3 and contributed weekly to* Sunday Times.

FRANCIS MACDONALD CORNFORD
1874–1943

The Cambridge classical course: an essay in anticipation of further reform. Cambridge 1903.

Thucydides mythistoricus. 1907.

Microcosmographia academica: being a guide for the young academic politician. Cambridge 1908 (anon), Chicago 1945.

From religion to philosophy: a study in the origins of western speculation. 1912, New York 1912.

The origin of Attic comedy. 1914; ed T. H. Gaster, New York 1961.

Before and after Socrates. Cambridge 1932.

The unwritten philosophy and other essays. Ed W. K. C. Guthrie, Cambridge 1950.

Principium sapientiae: the origins of Greek philosophical thought. Ed W. K. C. Guthrie, Cambridge 1952.

Among his best known work are the series of trns of Aristotle's Physics (*with P. H. Wicksteed*) *1929, Plato's* Theaetetus *and Sophist 1935, his* Timaeus *1937, his* Parmenides *1939 and his* Republic *1941.*

EDWARD HENRY GORDON CRAIG
1872–1966

The Gordon Craig Collection, Bibliothèque de l'Arsenal, Paris, includes unpbd mss; books and documents relating to Craig are held by the Br Inst Library, Florence.

§1

The art of the theatre, together with an introduction. 1905.

On the art of the theatre. 1911, Chicago 1911, London 1912 (with new notes), Chicago 1912, London 1924 (with new preface), Boston 1924, London 1957 (with new illustrations).

School for the art of the theatre. [1911]. Booklet.

A living theatre—the Gordon Craig School—The Arena Goldoni—The Mask: setting forth the aims and objects of the movement and showing by many illustrations the city of Florence, the Arena. Florence 1913.

Towards a new theatre: forty designs for stage scenes, with critical notes by the inventor. 1913.

The theatre—advancing. Boston 1919, London 1921 (adds foreword).

Puppets and poets. 1921 (Monthly Chapbook no 20).

Scene, with a foreword and an introductory poem by J. Masefield, 1923. Stage designs.

Nothing: or the bookplate, with a handlist (of bookplates designed by Craig) by E. Carrick. 1924 (280 copies), 1925.

Woodcuts and some words. Introd by C. Dodgson 1924, Boston 1925.

Books and theatres. 1925.

Henry Irving. 1930, New York 1930.

A production: being thirty-two collotype plates of designs projected or realised for The pretenders of Henrik Ibsen and produced at the Royal Theatre, Copenhagen, 1926. 1930 (605 copies).

Ellen Terry and her secret self. 1931, New York [1932]. With Annex: a plea for G.B.S. on the publication of the correspondence of Ellen Terry and Shaw and on Shaws' preface to that publication.

On eight pages from The story of the theatre, by Glenn Hughes, with some fourteen notes by E. G. Craig. Seattle 1931 (Univ of Washington Quartos no 2). Booklet.

Index to the story of my days: some memoirs 1872–1907. 1957, New York 1957.

Extracts from a diary: woodcuts. [1962]. With a record of Craig's radio talks 1951–7; pbd on his 90th birthday.

Craig also pbd a number of other pamphlets containing designs for the theatre, portfolios of etchings, models and reprints of items first ptd in the periodicals he edited.

§2

Terry, E. A. In her Story of my life, 1908, 1933 (rev).

Leeper, J. Craig: designs for the theatre. 1948 (King Penguin). With chronology by Penguin.

Valogne, C. Gordon Craig. Paris 1953.

Craig, E. A. Gordon Craig: the story of his life. 1968.

SIR WILLIAM ALEXANDER CRAIGIE
1867–1957

A new English dictionary on historical principles, founded mainly on the materials collected by the Philological Society, edited by J. A. H. Murray, H. Bradley, W. A. Craigie, C. T. Onions. 11 vols Oxford 1884–1933, 13 vols Oxford 1933 (corrected re-issue, with introd, suppl and bibliography, as The Oxford English Dictionary).

A primer of Burns. 1896.

Scandinavian folk-lore: selected and translated by W. A. Craigie. Paisley and London 1896.

The religion of ancient Scandinavia. 1906.

The Icelandic sagas. Cambridge 1913, New York 1913.

The Oxford book of Scandinavian verse, xviith century-xxth century, chosen by E. Gosse and W. A. Craigie. Oxford 1925.

A dictionary of the older Scottish tongue, from the twelfth century to the end of the seventeenth. Ed Craigie, Chicago, London 1931 onwards. From pt 17 onwards ed A. J. Aitken.

The northern element in English literature. Toronto [1933].

A dictionary of American English, on historical principles, edited by Sir William Craigie, with the collaboration of J. R. Hulbert, G. Watson [et al]. 4 vols Chicago 1936–44, London 1938–44.

Sýnisbók íslenzkra rímna (Specimens of the Icelandic metrical romances). 3 vols Edinburgh and Reykjavík 1952 [1953].

Craigie also edited a number of works for the STS. He wrote tracts for the Soc for Pure English, and compiled a number of *Anglo-Saxon, Modern English, Scandinavian and Icelandic readers, and textbooks on English spelling and phonetics.*

ALEISTER CROWLEY
(EDWARD ALEXANDER CROWLEY)
1875–1947

The G. J. Yorke Collection of Crowley mss is in the Warburg Institute, Univ of London. Other Crowley mss are in the Univ of Texas Humanities Research Center.

§I

Crowley's works were issued under a large number of pseudonyms, many of which appear in the entries below; a number of works were issued by the Soc for the Propagation of Religious Truth and by the 'OTO' ('Ordo Templi Orientis').

Aceldama, a place to bury strangers in: a philosophical poem, by a gentleman of the University of Cambridge. 1898 (priv ptd).

Jephthah: a tragedy, by a gentleman of the University of Cambridge (Aleister Crowley). 1898 (priv ptd, 25 copies). Verse.

Jezebel and other tragic poems, by Count Vladimir Svareff [i.e. Crowley]. 1898 (priv ptd).

The poem: a little drama in four scenes. 1898 (priv ptd, 10 copies). An advance edn of pt of Jephthah and other mysteries, 1899, below.

Songs of the spirit. 1898.

The tale of Archais: a romance in verse, by a gentleman of the University of Cambridge. 1898.

White stains: the literary remains of George Archibald Bishop, a neuropath of the Second Empire. [Amsterdam] 1898 (100 copies only; many destroyed by HM Customs in 1924). Erotic verse.

An appeal to the American Republic. 1899. Verse.

The honourable adulterers: a tragedy by A.E.C. 1899 (priv ptd, 5 copies). An advance edn of pt of Jephthah and other mysteries, below. Verse.

Jephthah and other mysteries, lyrical and dramatic. 1899.

Carmen saeculare, by St E. A. of M. and S. 1901 (priv ptd, 50 copies), 1901 (trade edn).

The mother's tragedy and other poems. 1901 (priv ptd, 500 copies), Foyers 1907.

The soul of Osiris: a history. 1901. Verse.

Tannhäuser: a story of all times. 1902.

Ahab and other poems, with an introduction and epilogue by Count Vladimir Svareff. 1903 (priv ptd).

Alice: an adultery [and other poems]. 1903 (priv ptd) (with essay by G. F. Kelly), Foyers 1905 (without essay).

[Berashith, in Hebrew characters]: an essay in ontology with some remarks on ceremonial magic, by Abhavananda. [Paris 1903] (priv ptd).

The god-eater: a tragedy of satire. 1903. Verse.

The star and the garter. 1903. Verse.

Summa spes. 1903. Poem.

The Argonauts. Foyers 1904. Verse drama.

The book of the Goetia of Solomon the King, translated into the English tongue by a dead hand [i.e. S. L. MacGregor Mathers]. Foyers 1904.

In residence: the don's guide to Cambridge. Cambridge 1904. Verse.

Snowdrops from a curate's garden, 1881 AD. Paris [c. 1904] (100 copies; many destroyed by HM Customs in 1924). Erotic verse.

The sword of song, called by Christians The book of the beast. Benares 1904. Verse. *See* G. K. Chesterton, Mr Crowley and the creeds and the creed of Mr Chesterton, [1904], Chesterton's review with Crowley's reply.

Why Jesus wept: a study of society and of the grace of God. 1904 (priv ptd), Foyers 1904.

Oracles: the biography of an art, unpublished fragments of the work of Crowley with explanatory notes by R. P. Lester and the author. Foyers 1905. Verse.

Orpheus: a lyrical legend. 2 vols Foyers 1905. Verse.

Rosa mundi: a poem by H. D. Carr, with an original composition by Auguste Rodin. 1905.

Gargoyles: being strangely wrought images of life and death. Foyers 1906. Verse.

Konx om pax: essays in light. Foyers 1907, New York 1907. Magical.

Rodin in rime: seven lithographs by Clot from the watercolours of Auguste Rodin, with a chaplet of verse by Aleister Crowley. 1907 (priv ptd).

Rosa coeli: a poem, by H. D. Carr, with an original composition by Auguste Rodin. 1907.

Rosa inferni: a poem, by H. D. Carr, with an original composition by Auguste Rodin. 1907.

Amphora. 1908 (anon, priv ptd), 1909 (anon, withdrawn), 1912 (as Hail Mary; without the Epilogue). Verse.

Alexandra. [Paris 1909]. Poem. The whole stock is said to have been destroyed by HM Customs.

Clouds without water. Edited from a private ms by the Rev C. Verey. 1909 (priv ptd). Verse.

777: vel prolegomena symbolica ad systemam scepticomysticae viae explicandae, fundamentum hieroglyphicum sanctissimorum scientiae summae. 1909, [1956] (rev and enlarged). Magical.

Bagh-I-Muattar, translated from a rare Indian ms by the late Major Lutiy and another. The scented garden of Abdullah the satirist of Shiraz. 1910 (priv ptd, 200 copies; the bulk of the edn was destroyed by HM Customs in 1924 on the ground of obscenity). Erotica.

Rosa decidua. [1910] (priv ptd, 20 copies). Verse.

[The Holy Book] vol 1, Liber LXI vel causae—Liber cordis cincti serpente vel LXV sub figura ADNI; vol 2, Liber liberi vel lapis lazuli; vol 3, Liber L vel legis. 3 vols [n.p., c. 1909]. Magical. Vol 3 reissued Tunis 1926 as AL, liber legis, London 1938 (as The book of the law).

The winged beetle. 1910 (priv ptd). Verse.

The world's tragedy. Paris 1910 (priv ptd). Verse.

Hail Mary. 1911. *See* Amphora, 1908, above.

The high history of good Sir Palamedes, the Saracen knight, and of his following of the Questing Beast, by Aleister Crowley. 1912. Verse.

Household gods: a comedy. Pallanza 1912 (priv ptd). Verse.

Mortadello, or the angel of Venice: a comedy. 1912. Verse drama.

Baudelaire, C. Little poems in prose. Tr Aleister Crowley 1913, Paris 1928. ('With several added versions of the Epilogue by various hands [i.e. Crowley]').

Book Four, by Frater Perdurabo [Crowley] and Soror Virakam [Mary d'Este Sturges]. 2 vols 1913 Magical.

Liber CCCXXXIII: the book of lies which is also falsely called Breaks, the wanderings or falsifications of the one thought of Frater Perdurabo, which thought is itself untrue. 1913, Ilfracombe 1962 (as The book of lies [etc], with an additional commentary to each chapter). Magical.

The writing on the ground, by E.G.O. [1913] (priv ptd). Poem, A slim gilt soul, and a paper on Lord Alfred Douglas.

Chicago May: a love poem. [New York] 1914 (priv ptd).

The giant's thumb. New York 1915. Verse; never issued; only a set of page proofs survives.

The diary of a drug fiend. [1922], New York 1923.

Songs for Italy: No 1, Tyrol. [Tunis] 1923 (single sheet), [London] 1923.

Magick in theory and practice, by the Master Therion. Paris 1929, London 1929.

Moonchild: a prologue. 1929. Novel.

The spirit of solitude: an autohagiography, subsequently re-antichristened The confessions of Aleister Crowley.

Vols 1–2, 1929 (vols 3–6 not pbd), 1 vol 1969 (as The confessions of Aleister Crowley: an autobiography, ed J. Symonds and K. Grant; 'this is the text of all six volumes, after some redundancies have been removed').

The stratagem and other stories. 1930.

The heart of the master, by Khaled Khan. 1938 (priv ptd). Magical.

Little essays toward truth. 1938 (priv ptd). Magical.

Liber XXI [inscription in Chinese] Khing Kang King: the classic of purity first written down by me [Chinese characters] in the Episode of the Dynasty of Wu and now made into a rime by me, Aleister Crowley. [1939]. 100 copies.

Temperance: a tract for the times. 1939 (priv ptd, 100 copies). Verse.

Thumbs up!: a pentagram—a pantacle to win the war. [1941] (priv ptd, 100 copies), New York 1942 (as Thumbs up!: five poems).

The fun of the fair—Nijni Novgorod, 1913 e.v. Barstow Cal and London 1942. Verse.

The city of God: a rhapsody. 1943.

Olla: an anthology of sixty years of song. 1946.

Magick without tears. Hampton NJ 1954. Magical.

'Eliphas Levi' (A. L. Constant). The key of the mysteries, translated from the French. 1959.

Crowley edited and largely wrote The Equinox: the official organ of the A∴A∴— the review of scientific illuminism, vol 1–vol 3, no 5, 1909–44; vol 2 and vol 3, no 2, *were not pbd.*

§2

Cammell, C. R. Aleister Crowley: the man, the mage, the poet. 1951.

Symonds, J. The great beast: the life of Crowley. New York 1951.

—— The magic of Crowley. 1958.

'Louis Marlow' (L. U. Wilkinson). In his Seven friends, 1953.

DAVID DAICHES
b. 1912

The novel and the modern world. Chicago 1939, 1960 (rev with new chs on Lawrence and Conrad), Cambridge 1960.

Poetry and the modern world: a study of poetry in England between 1900 and 1939. Chicago 1940.

The King James version of the English Bible. Chicago 1941, Hamden Conn 1968.

Virginia Woolf. Norfolk Conn 1942, London 1945, New York 1963 (rev).

Robert Louis Stevenson. Norfolk Conn 1947, Glasgow 1947.

A study of literature for readers and critics. Ithaca NY 1948, London 1968 (with textual changes).

Robert Burns. New York 1950, London 1952, New York 1966 (with textual changes), London 1966.

Willa Cather: a critical introduction. Ithaca NY [1951].

Two worlds: an Edinburgh Jewish childhood. New York 1956, London 1957.

Critical approaches to literature. Englewood Cliffs NJ 1956, London 1956.

Literary essays. Edinburgh 1956, Chicago 1957 (with preface), Edinburgh 1966 (corrected).

Milton. 1957, 1959 (rev), New York 1966.

Robert Burns. 1957 (Br Council pamphlet).

The present age: after 1920. 1958 (Introd to Eng Lit); rptd as The present age in British literature, Bloomington Indiana 1958.

Two studies: the poetry of Dylan Thomas; Walt Whitman, impressionist poet. 1958 (priv ptd, 70 copies).

A critical history of English literature. 2 vols New York 1960, London 1960, New York 1970 (with new concluding chs), London 1970.

The idea of a new university: an experiment in Sussex. Ed Daiches 1964, 1970 (with new concluding ch).

The paradox of Scottish culture: the eighteenth-century experience. 1964.

More literary essays. Edinburgh 1968, Chicago 1968.

Scotch whisky: its past and present. 1969. New York 1969.

Some late Victorian attitudes. 1969.

A third world. Brighton 1971.

Was. 1975.

ERNEST DE SELINCOURT
1870–1943

English poets and the national ideal: four lectures. 1915.

The study of poetry. 1918. Pamphlet.

Dorothy Wordsworth: a biography. Oxford 1933.

Oxford lectures on poetry. Oxford 1934, Freeport NY 1967.

Wordsworthian and other studies. Oxford 1947, New York 1964. Includes individual lectures previously pbd separately.

Also edns of Spenser, Wordsworth etc.

OLIVER ELTON
1861–1945

An introduction to Michael Drayton. Manchester 1895, London 1905 (rev and enlarged with a new bibliography) (as Michael Drayton: a critical study), New York 1966.

The Augustan ages. Edinburgh 1899 (Periods of European Literature 8), New York 1899.

The Manchester stage 1880–1900. [1900]. Criticisms, with introd, rptd from Manchester Guardian. With W. T. Arnold, A. N. Monkhouse, C. E. Montague.

Frederick York Powell: a life and a selection from his letters and occasional writings. 2 vols Oxford 1906.

Modern studies. 1907, Freeport NY [1967]. Includes lectures previously pbd separately.

A survey of English literature 1780–1830. 2 vols 1912; 1830–80, 2 vols 1920, New York 1920. The chs on Scott, Wordsworth, Shelley, Tennyson and Matthew Arnold, The Brownings, Dickens and Thackeray were pbd separately (rev) 1924.

A sheaf of papers. Liverpool 1922. Includes lectures previously pbd separately.

A survey of English literature 1730–80. 2 vols 1928, New York 1928.

C. E. Montague: a memoir. 1929, Garden City NY 1929.

The English muse: a sketch. 1933.

Essays and addresses. 1939, Freeport NY 1969.

Elton also pbd a number of class-room edns of Shakespeare's plays and Milton's early poems 1889–1903.

HENRY WATSON FOWLER
1858–1933

More popular fallacies. 1904. By 'Quillet'.

The King's English. Oxford 1906, 1906 (with new examples), 1930 (rev). With F. G. Fowler.

Si mihi—! 1907 (by 'Egomet'), 1929 (as If wishes were horses, by H. W. Fowler). Essays.

Between boy and man: being lectures to sixth-form boys. 1908. By 'Quilibet'.

The concise Oxford dictionary of current English. Oxford 1911, 1929 (rev), 1934 (rev, with H. G. Le Mesurier), 1951 (rev E. McIntosh), 1964 (rev E. McIntosh, etymologies rev G. W. S. Friedrichsen). First edn with F. G. Fowler.

The pocket Oxford dictionary of current English. Oxford 1924, 1934 (rev, with H. G. Le Mesurier), 1939 (rev H. G. Le Mesurier), 1942 (rev H. G. Le Mesurier and E. McIntosh), 1969 (rev E. McIntosh, etymologies rev G. W. S. Friedrichsen). First edn with F. G. Fowler.

A dictionary of modern English usage. Oxford 1926, 1965 (rev E. Gowers), New York 1965.

—— Find it in Fowler: an alphabetical index to the rev edn of Modern English usage, by J. A. Greenwood. Princeton 1969.

Some comparative values. Oxford 1929. Essays.

Rhymes of Darby to Joan. 1931.

Fowler also wrote several Soc for Pure English Tracts *and he contributed to the* Shorter Oxford English dictionary, 2 vols 1933.

ROGER ELIOT FRY
1866–1934

§ I

Giovanni Bellini. 1899.

Reynolds, J. Discourses. Introds and notes by Fry 1905.

Exhibition of Venetian painting of the eighteenth century. Introd, Venice in the eighteenth century, by Fry 1911.

Dürer, A. Records of journeys to Venice and the Low Countries. Ed Fry, Boston 1913.

The new movement in art: exhibition of representative works selected and arranged by Fry. Birmingham [1917]. Catalogue.

Catalogue of an exhibition of Florentine painting before 1500. 1919. Preface, The art of Florence, by Fry.

Vision and design. 1920, New York 1924, London 1925 (rev).

A sampler of Castile. Richmond Surrey 1923. Impressions of Spain.

The artist and psycho-analysis. 1924 (Hogarth Essays).

The significance of Chinese art. In Chinese art: an introductory review by Fry et al, 1925 (Burlington Mag monographs), 1935 (rev), 1946 (rev), New York [1946–7].

Art and commerce. 1926 (Hogarth Essays).

English handwriting by R[obert] B[ridges], with facsimile plates and artistic and palaeographical criticisms by Fry and E. A. Lowe. Oxford 1926–7 (SPE Tracts).

Transformations: critical and speculative essays on art. 1926, Garden City NY 1956.

Cézanne: a study of his development. 1927, New York 1952.

Flemish art: a critical survey. 1927, New York 1927.

Mauron, C. The nature of beauty in art and literature. Trn and preface by Fry 1927 (Hogarth Essays).

Painting. In Georgian art, 1760–1820: an introductory review by Fry et al, 1929 (Burlington Mag monographs).

Henri-Matisse. Paris 1930, London [1930], 1935 (with different plates).

Russian icon painting from a Western-European point of view. In Masterpieces of Russian painting, ed M. Farbman 1930. Text by Fry et al.

The arts of painting and sculpture. 1932.

Characteristics of French art. 1932.

Art-history as an academic study. Cambridge 1933, Folcroft Pa 1969. Lecture.

Reflections on British painting. 1934, Freeport NY 1969.

Mauron, C. Aesthetics and psychology. Tr Fry and K. John 1935.

Mallarmé, S. Poems. Tr Fry 1936, New York [1951] (with commentaries by C. Mauron).

Last lectures. Cambridge 1939, New York 1939. Introd by K. Clark; includes one previously pbd lecture.

§ 2

Woolf, V. The Roger Fry Memorial Exhibition: an address. 1935; rptd in her The moment and other essays, 1947, and in Collected essays vol 4, 1967.

—— Roger Fry: a biography. 1940.

Hough, G. Ruskin and Fry: two aesthetic theories. Cambridge Jnl 1 1947.

MacCarthy, D. In his Memories, 1953.

Johnstone, J. K. Bloomsbury aesthetics. In his Bloomsbury group, 1954.

Bell, Q. Roger Fry. Leeds 1964. Lecture.

HEATHCOTE WILLIAM GARROD
1878–1960

The religion of all good men and other studies in Christian ethics. 1906, New York 1906 (replacing fifth essay with a new one).

The Oxford book of Latin verse. Ed Garrod, Oxford 1912.

Oxford poems. 1912.

A book of Latin verse. Oxford 1915. Based on The Oxford book of Latin verse, above.

Worms and epitaphs. Oxford 1919. Poems.

Wordsworth: lectures and essays. Oxford 1923, 1927 (enlarged).

Coleridge: poetry and prose. Ed Garrod, Oxford 1925.

Keats. Oxford 1926, 1939 (corrected).

Collins. Oxford 1928, Folcroft Pa 1969.

Merton muniments. Ed with P. S. Allen, Oxford 1928.

The profession of poetry and other lectures. Oxford 1929, Freeport NY 1967. Mainly lectures given as Professor of Poetry, Oxford 1923–8.

Ancient painted glass in Merton College, Oxford. 1931.

Poetry and the criticism of life. Cambridge Mass 1931, London 1931.

The study of poetry. Oxford 1936.

The poetical works of John Keats. Ed Garrod, Oxford 1939, 1958 (rev) (Oxford English Texts). Text also used in OSA edn 1956.

Epigrams. Oxford 1946.

John Donne: poetry and prose. Ed Garrod, Oxford 1946.

Scholarship: its meaning and value. Cambridge 1946.

Genius loci and other essays. Oxford 1950.

The study of good letters. Ed J. Jones, Oxford 1963. Essays, including single lectures previously pbd separately. *See* Jones, Proc Br Acad 48 1963.

ARTHUR ERIC ROWTON GILL
1882–1940

The Eric Gill Collection at the William Andrews Clark Memorial Library, Univ of California, Los Angeles, contains ms material, including diaries and autobiography.

Bibliographies

Gill, E. R. Bibliography of Gill. 1953.

—— The inscriptional work of Gill: an inventory. 1964.

§ I

Serving at Mass: being instructions and directions for laymen as to the manner of serving at Low Mass. Ditchling 1916 (S. Dominic's Press). Compiled chiefly from J. Baldeschi.

Essential perfection. [Ditchling 1917] (S. Dominic's Press); rptd (rev) in Art-nonsense, 1929, below.

Slavery and freedom. [Ditchling 1917] (S. Dominic's Press); rptd in Art-nonsense, 1929, below.

The restoration of the monarchy. Ditchling 1917 (S. Dominic's Press). With D. Pepler.

Sculpture: an essay. Ditchling 1918 (S. Dominic's Press); rptd (rev, as Stone-carving) in Sculpture: an essay on stone-cutting, 1924, and (further rev) in Art-nonsense, 1929, below. 400 copies.

Birth control. Ditchling 1919 (S. Dominic's Press)

Dress: being an essay in masculine vanity and an exposure of the un-Christian apparel favoured by females. Ditchling 1921 (S. Dominic's Press); rptd (rev) in Art-nonsense, 1929, below.

Songs without clothes: being a dissertation on the Song of Solomon and such-like songs. Ditchling 1921 (S. Dominic's Press); rptd (rev) in Art-nonsense, 1929, below. 240 copies.

War memorial. Ditchling 1923 (S. Dominic's Press); rptd (rev) in Art-nonsense, 1929, below.

Sculpture: an essay on stone-cutting, with a preface about God. Ditchling 1924 (S. Dominic's Press); both pieces rptd (rev) in Art-nonsense, 1929, below.

Wood-engravings: a selection. Ditchling 1924 (S. Dominic's Press), New York 1924. Unauthorized.

Id quod visum placet: a practical test of the beautiful. Waltham St Lawrence 1926 (Golden Cockerel Press); rptd (rev) in Art-nonsense, 1929, below. 150 copies.

Architecture and sculpture. Manchester [1927]; rptd (rev) in Art-nonsense, 1929, below.

Art and love. Bristol 1927 (for 1928) (Golden Cockerel Press); rptd (rev) in Art-nonsense, 1929, below. 260 copies.

Christianity and art. Capel-y-ffin 1927 (for 1928); rptd (rev) in Art-nonsense, 1929, below. 200 copies.

Art and prudence: an essay. Waltham St Lawrence 1928; rptd (rev) in Beauty looks after herself, 1933, below.

The future of sculpture. 1928 (priv ptd); rptd in Art-nonsense, 1929, below. 55 copies.

Art and manufacture. [1929]; rptd (rev, as Art and industrialism) in Beauty looks after herself, 1933, below.

Art-nonsense and other essays. 1929.

Engravings: a selection representative of his work to the end of 1927 with a chronological list of engravings and a preface by the artist. Bristol 1929.

Clothes: an essay upon the nature and significance of the natural and artificial integuments worn by men and women. 1931.

Clothing without cloth: an essay on the nude. Waltham St Lawrence [1931]; rptd in In a strange land, 1944, below.

An essay on typography. 1931, 1936 (rev, adds But why lettering?) (Hague and Gill).

Sculpture and the living model. 1932 (Hague and Gill); rptd in Beauty looks after herself, 1933, below.

Beauty looks after herself: essays. 1933.

Unemployment. 1933 (Hague and Gill).

Art and a changing civilization. 1934, 1946 (as Art), New York 1950.

Engravings 1928–33. 1934 (Hague and Gill). 133 wood-engravings. 400 copies.

John Ruskin. In To the memory of John Ruskin, Cambridge 1934; rptd in In a strange land, 1944, below.

The Lord's song: a sermon. 1934; rptd in In a strange land, 1944, below.

Money and morals. 1934, 1937 (adds Unemployment, first pbd 1933). Illustr D. Tegetmeier.

A specimen of three book types designed by Gill: Joanna, Joanna italic, Perpetua. High Wycombe 1934 (priv ptd) (Hague and Gill).

Work and leisure. 1935. Lectures.

The necessity of belief: an enquiry into the nature of human certainty, the causes of scepticism and the grounds of morality, and a justification of the doctrine that the end is the beginning. 1936.

Sculpture on machine-made buildings. [Birmingham] 1937. Lecture; rptd in In a strange land, 1944, below.

Trousers and the most precious ornament. High Wycombe 1937 (Hague and Gill).

Work and property. 1937 (Hague and Gill). Illustr D. Tegetmeier.

And who wants peace? 1938 (Hague and Gill) (Pax pamphlets 1); rptd in It all goes together, 1944, below.

Twenty-five nudes, engraved with an introduction. 1938 (Hague and Gill).

Unholy Trinity. 1938. Illustr D. Tegetmeier. 11 essays.

Work and culture. Newport RI 1938 (John Stevens pamphlets). Lecture. 400 copies.

Sacred and secular in art and industry. 1939, Newport RI 1939. Lecture; rptd in Sacred & secular &c, 1940, and in Last essays, 1942, below. 400 copies.

Social justice and the stations of the Cross. 1939 (Hague and Gill), Wilkes-Barre Pa [1940?], Union Village NJ 1944 (as The stations of the Cross).

Social principles and directions, extracted from the three Papal Encyclicals: Rerum novarum, Quadragesimo anno, Divini redemptoris, arranged according to subject matter. Compiled E. Gill, High Wycombe 1939, 1940 (rev).

All that England stands for. [1940]. Pamphlet.

Autobiography. 1940, New York 1941.

Christianity and the machine age. 1940, New York 1940.

Drawings from life. 1940 (Hague and Gill). 36 drawings with introd by Gill.

The human person and society. 1940 (Hague, Gill and Davey); rptd in In a strange land, 1944, below.

Sacred & secular &c. 1940 (Hague, Gill and Davey).

Last essays. Introd by M. Gill 1942; rptd with next as Essays, 1947. The earlier New York edn, 1944, is entitled It all goes together, and substitutes Who wants peace? (1938) for A diary in Ireland (from In a strange land, 1944, below).

In a strange land: essays. 1944.

First nudes. Introd by J. Rothenstein 1954. Plates.

The Procrustean bed. Philadelphia 1957.

Letters and Diaries

Letters. Ed W. Shewring 1947, New York 1948.

From the Palestine diary of Gill. 1949 (Hague and Gill), 1953 (as From the Jerusalem diary of Gill).

§2

Lawrence, D. H. Gill's 'Art nonsense'. Book-Collector's Quart 12 1933; rptd in his Phoenix, 1936.

Greene, G. In his Lost childhood and other essays, 1951.

Heppenstall, R. Four absentees. 1960. Reminiscences of Gill, Orwell, Dylan Thomas and J. M. Murry.

Speaight, R. The life of Gill. 1966.

The life and works of Gill: papers by C. Gill, B. Warde and D. Kindersley. Los Angeles 1968.

SIR WALTER WILSON GREG
1875–1959

Bibliographies

Francis, F. C. A list of Greg's writings. 1945. Suppl 1945–59, by D. F. McKenzie, Library 5th ser 15 1960.

Collections

Collected papers. Ed J. C. Maxwell, Oxford 1966.

§1

A list of English plays written before 1643 and printed before 1700. 1900.

Verses, by 'W.W.G.' Cambridge 1900 (for 1901).

A list of masques, pageants &c, supplementary to A list of English plays. 1902.

Catalogue of the books presented by Edward Capell to the library of Trinity College in Cambridge. Cambridge 1903.

Pastoral poetry and pastoral drama: a literary inquiry with special reference to the pre-Restoration stage in England. 1906, New York 1959.

A descriptive catalogue of the early editions of the works of Shakespeare preserved in the library of Eton College. Oxford 1909.

Bibliographical and textual problems of the English Miracle cycles. 1914. Lectures.

Two Elizabethan stage abridgements: The battle of Alcazar and Orlando furioso: an essay in critical bibliography. Oxford 1923 (another issue as Malone Soc extra vol 1923).

Shakespeare's hand in the play of Sir Thomas More. Cambridge 1923. Papers by Greg et al.

1623-1923: studies in the First Folio, written for the Shakespeare Assoc by Greg [et al]. 1924.

The calculus of variants: an essay on textual criticism. Oxford 1927.

Dramatic documents from the Elizabethan playhouses: stage plots, actors' parts, prompt books. 2 vols Oxford 1931. Commentary, reproductions and transcripts.

A bibliography of the English printed drama to the Restoration. 4 vols 1939 (for 1940)-59 (Bibl Soc).

The variants in the first quarto of King Lear: a bibliographical and critical inquiry. 1940 (Suppl to Trans Bibl Soc 15).

The editorial problem in Shakespeare: a survey of the foundations of the text. Oxford 1942, 1951 (with new preface and additional notes), 1954 (for 1955) (slightly rev). Lectures.

The Shakespeare first folio: its bibliographical and textual history. Oxford 1955.

Some aspects and problems of London publishing between 1550 and 1650. Oxford 1956. Lectures.

Biographical notes 1877-1947. Oxford 1960 (priv ptd, 100 copies).

Licensers for the press &c to 1640: a biographical index based mainly on Arber's Transcript of the registers of the Company of Stationers. Oxford 1962 (Oxford Bibl Soc Pbns).

A companion to Arber: being a calendar of documents in Edward Arber's Transcript of the registers of the Company of Stationers of London 1554-1640, with text and calendar of supplementary documents. Oxford 1967.

Editions

Henslowe, P. Diary. 2 vols 1904-08.
— Papers: being documents supplementary to Henslowe's Diary. 1907.

Lodge, T. Rosalynde: being the original of Shakespeare's As you like it. 1907, 1931 (corrected) (Shakespeare Lib).

Facsimiles of twelve early English manuscripts in the library of Trinity College, Cambridge. Oxford 1913.

The assumption of the Virgin: a miracle play from the N-town cycle. Oxford 1915.

English literary autographs 1550-1650, selected for reproduction and edited. 4 pts Oxford 1925-32.

Records of the Court of the Stationers' Company 1576 to 1602 from Register B. 1930. With E. Boswell.

The play of Antichrist from the Chester cycle. Oxford 1935.

Marlowe, C. Doctor Faustus 1604-16: parallel texts. Oxford 1950.
— The tragical history of the life and death of Dr Faustus: a conjectural reconstruction. Oxford 1950.

Jonson, B. Masque of gipsies, in the Burley, Belvoir and Windsor versions: an attempt at reconstruction. 1952.

Respublica: an interlude for Christmas 1553, attributed to Nicholas Udall. Re-edited by W. W. Greg 1952 (for 1953) (EETS original ser 226).

Greg edited (sometimes with W. Bang) a number of plays in the ser Materialien zur Kunde des älteren englischen Dramas; at A. W. Pollard's suggestion he founded the Malone Soc, was General Editor of the Malone Soc reprints 1906-39 and Collections 1907-31 and was President of the Soc 1939-59; he edited or assisted in the editing of most of the Soc's pbns; he was editor of the Shakespeare Assoc's Shakespeare Quarto Facsimiles 1-12, 1939-59; he was President of the Bibl Soc 1930-2; he contributed the articles on R. B. McKerrow and A. W. Pollard to DNB.

§2

Wilson, F. P. Shakespeare and the 'new bibliography'. In The Bibliographical Society 1892-1942: studies in retrospect, 1945. Rev H. Gardner, Oxford 1970.

— Sir W. W. Greg. Proc Br Acad 45 1960.

Greg, 9 July 1875-4 March 1959. Library 5th ser 14 1959.

SIR HERBERT JOHN CLIFFORD GRIERSON
1866-1960

Bibliographies

A list of Grierson's publications 1906-37. In Seventeenth-century studies presented to Sir Herbert Grierson, Oxford 1938.

§1

The first half of the seventeenth century. Edinburgh 1906, New York 1906 (Periods of European Literature 7).

The English Parnassus: an anthology of longer poems. Ed with M. Dixon, Oxford 1909.

The poems of John Donne. 2 vols Oxford 1912 (with commentary), 1 vol London 1929 (without commentary) (OSA).

Metaphysical lyrics & poems of the seventeenth century: Donne to Butler. Ed Grierson, Oxford 1921.

The background of English literature and other collected essays & addresses. 1925, New York 1960 (for 1961).

The poems of Milton: English, Latin, Greek and Italian. Ed Grierson 2 vols 1925.

Cross currents in English literature of the XVIIth century. 1929, New York 1958 (with additional preface) (as Cross-currents in 17th-century English literature, etc).

The letters of Scott. Ed Grierson 12 vols 1932-7.

Sir Walter Scott: broadcast lectures to the young. Edinburgh 1932.

Sir Walter Scott today: some retrospective essays and studies. Ed Grierson 1932.

The Oxford book of seventeenth-century verse. Ed with G. Bullough, Oxford 1934.

Milton and Wordsworth, poets and prophets: a study of their reactions to political events. Cambridge 1937, New York 1937.

Sir Walter Scott, Bart: a new life, supplementary to, and corrective of, Lockhart's biography. 1938, New York 1938.

Essays and addresses. 1940.

The English Bible. 1943 (Britain in Pictures).

A critical history of English poetry. 1944, New York 1946, London 1947 (rev). With J. C. Smith.

Rhetoric and English composition. Edinburgh 1944, 1945 (rev).

The personal note: or first and last words from prefaces, introductions, dedications, epilogues. Ed with S. Wason 1946.

GEOFFREY EDWARD HARVEY GRIGSON
b. 1905

New verse: an anthology. 1939. Poems which appeared in the first 30 nos of New verse, ed Grigson 1933-9.

Several observations: thirty five poems. [1939].

Henry Moore. 1943 (Penguin Modern Painters). Plates, with introd by Grigson; introd rptd in The harp of Aeolus, 1947, below.

Under the cliff and other poems. 1943.

The Isles of Scilly and other poems. 1946.

The mint: a miscellany of literature, art and criticism. Ed G. Grigson 2 vols 1946-8.

The harp of Aeolus and other essays on art, literature and nature. 1947.

Samuel Palmer: the visionary years. 1947.

An English farmhouse and its neighbourhood. 1948.

Places of the mind. 1949. Topography.

Poems of John Clare's madness. Ed Grigson 1949.

Poetry of the present: an anthology of the thirties and after, compiled and introduced by G. Grigson. 1949.

Clare, J. Selected poems. Ed Grigson 1950 (ML).

The crest on the silver: an autobiography. 1950.

Flowers of the meadow. 1950.

Selected poems of William Barnes 1800-66. Ed Grigson 1950 (ML).

The Victorians: an anthology chosen by G. Grigson. 1950.

Essays from the air. 1951. Broadcast talks.

A master of our time: a study of Wyndham Lewis. 1951.

Gerard Manley Hopkins. 1955, New York 1955, London 1958 (rev bibliography) (Br Council pamphlet); rptd in Poems and poets, 1969, below.

The Shell guide to flowers of the countryside, painted by E. and R. Hilder, chosen and described by G. Grigson. [1955] (Shell Nature Studies); rptd in the Shell nature book, 1964, below.

The Shell guide to wild life, painted by J. Leigh-Pemberton; text by G. Grigson. 1959 (Shell Nature Studies); rptd in the Shell nature book, 1964, below.

English excursions. 1960.

Samuel Palmer's Valley of vision. 1960. Plates with a selection of Palmer's writings, introd and notes by Grigson.

Christopher Smart. 1961 (Br Council pamphlet); rptd in Poems and poets, 1969, below.

Poets in their pride. 1962, New York 1964. Essays on 10 English poets with selections and portraits.

The Shell country book. 1962.

The collected poems 1924-62. 1963.

The Shell nature book. 1964. New edn of 4 vols pbd 1955-9 as Shell nature studies, with 'Birds and beasts' by J. Fisher.

The Shell country alphabet. 1966.

The English year: from diaries and letters. 1967.

A skull in Salop and other poems. 1967, Chester Springs [1967].

Ingestion of ice-cream, and other poems. 1969.

Poems and poets. 1969, Chester Springs 1969. Essays.

Angles and circles and other poems. 1974.

The contrary views. 1974.

The goddess of love. 1976.

Grigson was also general editor of the About Britain guides, *13 vols 1951, and wrote the text of nos 1 and 2,* West country *and* Wessex; *he compiled selections from the poems of Coleridge, Crabbe and Dryden in the ser* Crown Classics *and other selections of Hardy and William Morris.*

JAMES THOMAS FRANK HARRIS
1856-1931

§1

Elder Conklin and other stories. New York 1894, London 1895 (for 1894).

Montes the matador, and other stories. 1900, New York 1910.

The bomb. 1908, New York 1909, Chicago 1963 (introd by J. Dos Passos). Novel.

The man Shakespeare and his tragic life story. 1909, New York 1909.

Shakespeare and his love: a play in four acts and an epilogue. 1910.

The women of Shakespeare. 1911. Mainly on theory that Mary Fitton was 'Dark Lady' of the Sonnets.

Unpath'd waters. 1913, New York 1913. Stories.

Great days. 1914 (for 1913), New York 1914. Novel.

The yellow ticket, and other stories. 1914.

Contemporary portraits. Ser 1-4, 4 vols New York 1915-23, London 1915-24.

England or Germany? New York 1915.

The veils of Isis, and other stories. New York [1915].

Love in youth. New York [1916]. Novel.

Oscar Wilde: his life and confessions. 2 vols New York 1916, 1918 (with Memories of Oscar Wilde by Bernard Shaw), 1 vol 1930 (including hitherto unpbd confession by Lord Alfred Douglas and Memories by Shaw), London 1938 (as Oscar Wilde, preface by Shaw), [East Lansing] 1959 (with Memories by Shaw and introductory note by L. Blair), [New York] 1960 (with note by L. Blair, Memories by Shaw and Oscar's last drop, a letter from R. Ross).

A mad love: the strange story of a musician. New York 1920.

My life and loves. Vols 1-4 only, Paris 1922-7 (priv ptd) (vols 2-4 are entitled My life; vol 2 has imprint Nice, the author, Imprimerie niçoise, vols 3-4 Comiez, Nice, the author; vols 3-4 have several chs inserted after original printing), 5 vols ed J. F. Gallagher, New York 1963, London 1964 (vol 5 based on Harris' final typescript in Humanities Research Center, Univ of Texas). 5th vol pbd Paris 1958 is not authentic.

Undream'd of shores. 1924, New York [1924]. Stories.

New preface to The life and confessions of Oscar Wilde, by F. Harris and Lord Alfred Douglas. 1925; rptd in New York 1930 edn of Wilde, above.

Joan la Romée: a drama. Nice [1926] (priv ptd), New York 1926, London [1926].

Latest contemporary portraits. New York [1927].

Confessional: a volume of intimate portraits, sketches and studies. New York [1930].

My reminiscences as a cowboy. New York 1930, London 1930 (as On the trail: my reminiscences as a cowboy; with slight textual changes and omission of last ch). Largely written by F. Scully.

Pantopia. New York [1930] (priv ptd, Panurge Press). Novel based on his short story, Temple to the forgotten dead.

Frank Harris on Bernard Shaw: an unauthorized biography based on first hand information, with a postscript by Mr Shaw. 1931, Garden City NY [1931] (as Bernard Shaw: an unauthorized biography).

Mr and Mrs Daventry: a play in four acts based on the scenario by Oscar Wilde. (Royalty Theatre 25 Oct 1900). Ed H. M. Hyde 1956.

Letters

Moore versus Harris: an intimate correspondence between George Moore and Harris. Ed. G. Bruno, Chicago 1925 (priv ptd).

Harris to Bennett: fifty-eight letters 1908–10. Merion Station 1936 (priv ptd, 99 copies).
Harris edited Evening News *1882–6;* Fortnightly Rev *1886–94;* Saturday Rev *1894–8;* Candid Friend *1901–2;* Vanity Fair *1907–10;* Hearth & Home *1911–12;* Modern Society *1913–14;* Pearson's Mag *1916–22;* View of Truth *1927–8.*

§ 2

Roth, S. The private life of Harris. New York 1931.
Tobin, A. I. and E. Gertz. Harris—a study in black and white: an authorized biography. Chicago 1931.
'Hugh Kingsmill' (H. K. Lunn). Frank Harris. 1932.
Murry, J. M. In his Between two worlds: an autobiography, 1935. Reminiscences.
Sherard, R. H. Shaw, Harris and Wilde. 1937.
Scully, F. J. X. In his Rogue's gallery, Hollywood 1943.
Root, E. M. Frank Harris: a biography. New York 1947.
Brome, V. Frank Harris. 1959.

JANE ELLEN HARRISON
1850–1928

§ 1

Myths of the Odyssey in art and literature. 1882 (for 1881).
Introductory studies in Greek art. 1885.
Prolegomena to the study of Greek religion. Cambridge 1903, 1908 (corrected), New York 1960. With critical appendix on the Orphic tablets by G. Murray.
The religion of ancient Greece. 1905.
Primitive Athens as described by Thucydides. Cambridge 1906.
Heresy and humanity. Cambridge 1911. Lecture.
Themis: a study of the social origins of Greek religion, with an excursus on the ritual forms preserved in Greek tragedy by G. Murray and a chapter on the origin of the Olympic games by F. M. Cornford. Cambridge 1912, 1927 (rev and enlarged), Cleveland 1962.
'Homo sum': being a letter to an Anti-suffragist from an anthropologist. [1913]; rptd in Alpha and omega, 1915.
Unanimism: a study in conversion and some contemporary French poets. Cambridge 1913; rptd in Alpha and omega, 1915.
Ancient art and ritual. [1914], New York [1914].
Peace with patriotism. Cambridge 1915. Pamphlet; rptd in Alpha and omega, 1915, below.
Alpha and omega. 1915. Essays.
Russia and the Russian verb: a contribution to the psychology of the Russian people. Cambridge 1915. Pamphlet.
Aspects, aorists and the Classical Tripos. Cambridge 1919.
Epilegomena to the study of Greek religion. Cambridge 1921, New Hyde Park NY 1962.
Mythology. Boston [1924], London [1925].
Reminiscences of a student's life. 1925.
Myths of Greece and Rome. 1927, Garden City NY 1928.

§ 2

Murray, G. Jane Ellen Harrison: an address. Cambridge 1928.
Stewart, J. G. Jane Ellen Harrison: a portrait from letters. [1959].

JOHN DAVY HAYWARD
1905–65

Collected works of John Wilmot, Earl of Rochester. Ed Hayward 1926.

Donne, J. Complete poetry and selected prose. Ed Hayward 1920 (Nonesuch).
The letters of Saint Evremond. Ed Hayward 1930.
Nineteenth-century poetry: an anthology chosen by Hayward. 1932.
Charles II. 1933.
Swift, J. Gulliver's travels and selected writings in prose and verse. Ed Hayward 1934 (Nonesuch).
Love's Helicon: or the progress of love described in English verse, arranged and edited by Hayward. 1940.
English poetry: a catalogue of first and early editions of works of the English poets from Chaucer to the present day exhibited by the National Book League, compiled by Hayward. 1947, 1950 (illustr).
Prose literature since 1939. 1947 (Br Council pamphlet).
Book collecting: four broadcast talks. Cambridge 1950 (for 1951). By Hayward et al.
Eliot, T. S. Selected prose. Ed Hayward 1953 (Pelican).
The Sterling Library: a catalogue. Cambridge 1954 (priv ptd). Compiled by M. B. C. Canney and ed Hayward.
The Penguin book of English verse. Ed Hayward 1956, 1958 (enlarged as The Faber book of English verse).
The Oxford book of nineteenth-century English verse. Ed Hayward, Oxford 1964.
Hayward was editorial director of Book Collector *1952–65, editor of* Soho Bibliographies *and editorial adviser to the* Cresset Press, *editing the* Cresset Library.

ARTHUR HUMPHRY HOUSE
1908–55

The Dickens world. 1941, 1942 (rev).
Coleridge. 1953, Philadelphia 1965.
All in due time: the collected essays and broadcast talks. 1955.
Aristotle's Poetics: a course of eight lectures. Ed C. Hardie 1956.
House also edited The note-books and papers of Gerard Manley Hopkins (*1937*). *His projected edn of Dickens's letters has been continued by M. House and G. Storey.*

THOMAS ERNEST HULME
1883–1917

§ 1

The complete poetical works. New Age 23 Jan 1912; rptd as an appendix to Ezra Pound, Ripostes, 1912 etc, with a prefatory note by Pound. Also rptd in Hulme, Speculations, 1924, below.
Bergson, H. L. An introduction to metaphysics. New York 1912, London 1913. Authorised trn by Hulme.
Sorel, G. Reflections on violence. New York 1914, London 1916 (with introd and bibliography by Hulme), 1925 (omitting introd), Glencoe Ill [1950] (trn corrected by J. Roth, introd by E. A. Shils). Authorized trn by Hulme. Hulme's introd rptd in Speculations, 1924, below.
Poem, abbreviated [?by Ezra Pound] from the conversation of Mr T.E.H.: trenches—St Eloi. In Catholic anthology 1914–1915 [ed Pound], 1915; rptd in Pound, Umbra, 1920.
Fragments, from the note-book of T. E. Hulme who was killed in the war. New Age 6 Oct 1921; rptd in Further speculations, 1955, below. Verse fragments.
Speculations: essays on humanism and the philosophy of art. Ed H. Read [with some assistance from A. R. Orage] 1924 [1923], New York 1924, London 1936 (corrected).
Notes on language and style. Ed H. Read, Seattle 1929. First pbd in Criterion 3 1925; a larger selection from Hulme's mss ptd in next.

Three poems; A lecture on modern poetry; Notes on language and style. In 'Michael Roberts', T. E. Hulme, 1938, below. Rptd in next. Includes ms version of A city sunset, first pbd in For Christmas MDCCCCVIII, [1909], above.

Further speculations. Ed S. Hynes, Minneapolis [1955]. Mainly rptd from New Age and Cambridge Mag. Diary from the trenches first pbd here.

§2

Lewis, P. W. 'Hulme of original sin'. In his Blasting & bombardiering, 1937.
'Michael Roberts' (W. E. Roberts). T. E. Hulme. 1938.
Kermode, J. F. In his Romantic image, 1957.
Jones, A. R. The life and opinions of Hulme. 1960.

HOLBROOK JACKSON
1874–1948

Edward FitzGerald and Omar Khayyám: an essay and a bibliography 1899.
The eternal now: a quatrain sequence and other verses. 1900.
Everychild: a book of verses for children, compiled by Jackson. Leeds [1905]. Includes poems by Jackson.
Bernard Shaw. 1907, Philadelphia 1907, London 1909 (with new preface).
Great English novelists. [1908], Freeport NY 1967.
William Morris: craftsman-socialist. 1908, 1926 (rev and enlarged).
The Caradoc Press. Edinburgh 1909. Rptd from Book-lover's Mag 8 1909.
Platitudes in the making: precepts and advices for gentle-folk. New York 1910, London 1911.
Great soldiers, by 'George Henry Hart' [i.e. Jackson]. [1911].
Romance and reality: essays and studies. 1911, New York 1912.
All manner of folk: interpretations and studies. 1912.
The eighteen nineties: a review of art and ideas at the close of the nineteenth century. 1913, New York 1914; ed C. Campos, Hassocks 1976 (illustr).
Southward ho! and other essays. [1914] (Wayfarer's Lib), Freeport NY 1968. Selected from Romance and reality and All manner of folk, above, (rev) with 4 new essays.
Brown, F. S. Contingent ditties and other soldier songs of the Great War. Ed Jackson 1915.
Occasions: a volume of essays. 1922, Freeport NY 1969.
A brief survey of printing history and practice. 1923. With S. Morison.
End papers: adventures among ideas and personalities. By 'Bernard Lintot' [i.e. Jackson]. 1923.
The anatomy of bibliomania. 2 vols 1930-1 (48 copies), New York 1931, 1 vol London 1932 (rev).
Burton, R. The anatomy of melancholy. Ed Jackson 3 vols 1932 (EL).
A catalogue for typophiles, preceded by an essay on typophily by H. Jackson. [1932]. Essay rptd as a separate booklet [1945].
The fear of books. 1932, New York 1932.
William Caxton: an essay. 1933 (100 copies, nos 1-68 accompanied by an original Caxton leaf).
Maxims of books and reading. 1934 (400 copies). Booklet; rptd in The reading of books, below.
William Morris and the arts & crafts. Berkeley Heights 1934 (160 copies).
A cross-section of English printing: the Curwen Press 1918-34. 1935 (75 copies).
The Double Crown Club—early history: fifteenth dinner address delivered by the President, Holbrook Jackson. Edinburgh 1935 (100 copies).
On the printing of books. New York [1937?] (150 copies).

On the use of books. New York [1937?].
The printing of books. 1938, New York 1939. Essays, some previously pbd separately.
The story of Don Vincente. 1939 (Corvinus Press, 60 copies).
The aesthetics of printing: an essay. [1940?].
Bookman's holiday: a recreation for booklovers, designed by Jackson. 1945, New York 1947 (as Bookman's pleasure: a recreation for booklovers). Anthology.
Typophily. [1945]. Rptd from A catalogue for typophiles, 1932, above.
The reading of books. 1946, New York 1947.
The complete nonsense of Edward Lear. Ed Jackson 1947.
Morris, W. On art and socialism: essays and lectures. Ed Jackson 1947.
Dreamers of dreams: the rise and fall of 19th-century idealism. 1948, New York [1949?].
Pleasures of reading. 1948 (Nat Book League Reader's Guide).

Jackson edited New Age *May–Dec 1907 (jointly with A. R. Orage) and* The Beau, *1910; he was acting editor of* T.P.'s Mag *1911–12 and* T.P.,s Weekly *1911–14 and edited the latter 1914–16; he founded* Today *and edited it 1917–23.*

DAVID GWILYM JAMES
1905–68

Scepticism and poetry: an essay on the poetic imagination. 1937, New York 1960.
The Romantic comedy. 1948. On the English Romantic movement.
The life of reason: Hobbes, Locke, Bolingbroke. 1949, New York 1949. Vol 1 of a series entitled The English Augustans. No more pbd.
The dream of learning: an essay on The advancement of learning, Hamlet and King Lear. Oxford 1951.
The universities and the theatre. Ed James 1952 (Colston papers vol 4).
Matthew Arnold and the decline of English Romanticism. Oxford 1961.
The dream of Prospero. Oxford 1967. On The tempest.

SIR GEOFFREY LANGDON KEYNES
b. 1887

Bibliography of the works of Dr John Donne, Dean of St Paul's. Cambridge 1914, 1932 (rev), 1958 (rev), Oxford 1973 (rev).
A handlist of the works of John Evelyn. Cambridge 1916 (priv ptd).
A bibliography of William Blake. New York 1921.
A bibliography of Sir Thomas Browne. Cambridge 1924, Oxford 1968 (rev).
William Pickering, publisher: a memoir and a handlist of his editions. 1924.
A bibliography of the writings of William Harvey 1628-1928. Cambridge 1928, 1953 (rev, as A bibliography of the writings of Dr William Harvey 1578-1657).
Jane Austen: a bibliography. 1929.
Bibliography of William Hazlitt. 1931.
The Honourable Robert Boyle: a handlist of his works. 1932 (priv ptd).
John Evelyn: a study in bibliophily and a bibliography of his writings. Cambridge 1937, New York 1937 (Grolier Club), Oxford 1968 (rev).
The library of Edward Gibbon: a catalogue of his books. 1940.
John Ray FRS: a handlist of his works. Cambridge 1944 (priv ptd).
Blake studies: notes on his life and works in seventeen chapters. 1949, Oxford 1971 (with addns).

John Ray: a bibliography. 1951, Amsterdam 1976 (with addns).

William Blake's illuminated books: a census. New York 1953. With E. Wolf. Rev edn of section of Keynes' bibliography of Blake, 1921.

A bibliography of Rupert Brooke. 1954, 1959 (rev) (Soho Bibliographies).

Engravings by William Blake—the separate plates: a catalogue raisonné. Dublin 1956.

William Blake's illustrations to the Bible. [Clairvaux] 1957 (506 copies). A catalogue compiled by Keynes.

A bibliography of Dr Robert Hooke. Oxford 1960.

A bibliography of Siegfried Sassoon. 1962 (Soho Bibliographies).

Dr Timothie Bright 1550–1615: a survey of his life with a bibliography of his writings. 1962.

Bibliotheca bibliographici: a catalogue of the library formed by Geoffrey Keynes. 1964.

A study of the illuminated books of William Blake, poet, printer, prophet. Paris 1964 (525 copies), New York 1964, London 1965.

The life of William Harvey. Oxford 1966.

Henry James in Cambridge. Cambridge 1967.

A bibliography of George Berkeley. Oxford 1976 (Soho Bibliographies).

Also edns of Donne, Browne, Blake etc.

'HUGH KINGSMILL', HUGH KINGSMILL LUNN
1889–1949

§ 1

The will to love by H. K. Lunn. 1919. Fiction.

The dawn's delay. 1924. 3 short novels.

Blondel. 1927. Fiction.

Matthew Arnold. 1928, New York 1928.

After Puritanism 1850–1900. 1929.

The return of William Shakespeare. [1929], Indianapolis [1929]. Fiction.

Behind both lines. 1930. War-time reminiscences.

Frank Harris. 1932, New York [1932].

Samuel Johnson. [1933], New York 1934.

The Casanova fable: a satirical revaluation. 1934. With W. A. Gerhardie.

The sentimental journey: a life of Charles Dickens. 1934, New York 1935.

Skye high: the record of a tour through Scotland in the wake of Johnson and Boswell. 1937, New York 1938. With H. Pearson.

D. H. Lawrence. 1938, New York [1938] (as The life of D. H. Lawrence).

The fall. 1940. Fiction.

This blessed plot. 1942. Travel in England and Ireland. With H. Pearson.

The poisoned crown. 1944.

Talking of Dick Whittington. 1947. Travel in southern England. With H. Pearson.

The progress of a biographer. 1949. Collected literary criticism.

Kingsmill edited the following anthologies: Invective and abuse; The worst of love; The English genius; Parents & children; Courage; Made on earth: a panorama of marriage; What they said at the time; The high hill of the muses. *He edited* Johnson without Boswell: a contemporary portrait of Johnson, *and pbd 3 books of parodies (one with M. Muggeridge). He was literary editor of* Punch *1939–45 and of* New Eng Rev *1945–9.*

§ 2

Holroyd, M. Kingsmill: a critical biography. 1964.

GEORGE WILSON KNIGHT
b. 1897

Myth and miracle: an essay on the mystic symbolism of Shakespeare. [1929], Folcroft Pa 1969. Rptd with additional notes in The crown of life, 1947, below.

The wheel of fire: essays in interpretation of Shakespeare's sombre tragedies. 1930, 1949 (rev with 3 new essays), New York 1949, London 1954 (corrected). Introd by T. S. Eliot.

The imperial theme: further interpretations of Shakespeare's tragedies, including the Roman plays. 1931, 1951 (with new preface), 1954 [1955] (corrected), New York 1961.

The Shakespearian tempest. 1932, 1953 (with new preface and a chart of Shakespeare's dramatic universe).

The Christian renaissance, with interpretations of Dante, Shakespeare and Goethe and a note on T. S. Eliot. Toronto 1933, London 1962 (rev with 'new discussions of Oscar Wilde and the Gospel of Thomas', and omitting note on T. S. Eliot), New York 1962.

Shakespeare and Tolstoy. 1934 (English Assoc pamphlet); rptd as Tolstoy's attack on Shakespeare in the Wheel of fire, 1949 edn, above.

Atlantic crossing: an autobiographical design. 1936.

Principles of Shakespearian production, with especial reference to the tragedies. 1936, 1949 (with new preface), 1964 (rev, with addns, as Shakespearian production, with especial reference to the tragedies), Evanston 1964.

The burning oracle: studies in the poetry of action. 1939.

This sceptred isle: Shakespeare's message for England at war. Oxford 1940, Folcroft Pa 1969. Booklet.

The starlit dome: studies in the poetry of vision. 1941, 1959 (corrected, with an introd by W. F. J. Knight and an appendix on spiritualism and poetry), New York 1960.

Chariot of wrath: the message of John Milton to democracy at war. 1942; rptd (abridged) in Poets of action, 1968, below.

The olive and the sword: a study of England's Shakespeare. 1944; rptd (abridged) as This sceptred isle in The sovereign flower, 1958, below.

The dynasty of Stowe. 1945. On Stowe and Stowe School, in part autobiographical.

Hiroshima: on prophecy and the sun-bomb. 1946.

The crown of life: essays in interpretation of Shakespeare's final plays. 1947, 1952 (corrected), 1958 (corrected), New York 1964.

Christ and Nietzsche: an essay in poetic wisdom. 1948.

Lord Byron: Christian virtues. 1952, New York 1953.

The last of the Incas: a play on the conquest of Peru. Leeds 1954.

Laureate of peace: on the genius of Alexander Pope. 1954, New York 1955, 1965 (corrected as The poetry of Pope, laureate of peace).

The mutual flame: on Shakespeare's Sonnets and The phoenix and the turtle. 1955.

Lord Byron's marriage: the evidence of asterisks. 1957, New York 1957.

The sovereign flower: on Shakespeare as the poet of royalism, together with related essays and indexes to earlier volumes [on Shakespeare]. 1958, New York 1958.

The golden labyrinth: a study of British drama. 1962, New York 1962.

Ibsen. Edinburgh 1962, New York 1963 (as Henrik Ibsen) (Writers and Critics).

The saturnian quest: a chart of the prose works of John Cowper Powys. 1964 (for 1965), New York 1964.

Byron and Shakespeare. 1966, New York 1966.

Shakespeare and religion: essays of forty years. 1967, New York 1967.

Gold-dust, with other poetry. 1968, New York [1968].

Poets of action: incorporating essays from The burning oracle. 1968.

Neglected powers: essays on nineteenth and twentieth century literature. 1971.

Jackson Knight: a biography. Oxford 1975.

LIONEL CHARLES KNIGHTS
b. 1906

How many children had Lady Macbeth?: an essay in the theory and practice of Shakespeare criticism. Cambridge 1933; rptd (rev) in Explorations, 1946, below.

Drama and society in the age of Jonson. 1937, New York 1951.

Explorations: essays in criticism, mainly on the literature of the seventeenth century. 1946, New York 1947.

Some Shakespearean themes. 1959, Stanford 1960.

An approach to Hamlet. 1960, Stanford 1961.

Metaphor and symbol. Ed L. C. Knights and B. Cottle 1960 (Colston papers vol 12). Knights' paper Idea and symbol: some hints from Coleridge rptd in Further explorations, 1965, below.

William Shakespeare: the histories, Richard III, King John, Richard II, Henry V. 1962, 1965 (rev) (Br Council pamphlet).

Further explorations. 1965, Stanford 1965.

Public voices. 1971.

Explorations 3. 1976.

Knights was on the editorial board of Scrutiny *1932–53 and a frequent contributor.*

SIR OSBERT LANCASTER
b. 1908

Except for Our sovereigns, *all Lancaster's books are illustr by the author.*

Our sovereigns: from Alfred to Edward VIII. 1936, 1937 (to George VI).

Progress at Pelvis Bay. 1936. Satirical essay in architectural history.

Pillar to post: the pocket lamp of architecture. 1938, New York 1939, London 1956 (enlarged).

Homes sweet homes. 1939, 1953 (enlarged, as Home sweet homes). Interior decoration.

Classical landscape with figures. 1947, Boston 1949, London 1975 (with addn). Travel in Greece.

The Saracen's head: or the reluctant crusader. 1948, Boston 1949. Children's tale.

Drayneflete revealed. 1949, Boston 1950 (as There'll always be a Drayneflete). Satirical essay in architectural history.

Façades and faces. 1950.

All done from memory. 1953, Boston 1953. Autobiography.

Here, of all places. Boston 1958, London [1959].

A cartoon history of architecture. Introd by J. Coolidge, Boston 1964. Parts of this book originally pbd in Pillar to post, Homes sweet homes, and Here, of all places, above.

With an eye to the future. 1967, Boston 1967. Autobiography.

Sailing to Byzantium: an architectural companion. 1969, Boston 1969.

Lancaster has been cartoonist with Daily Express *since 1939, publishing selections of the cartoons beginning with* Pocket cartoons, *1940.*

JAMES LAVER
1899–1975

His last Sebastian, and other poems. 1922.

Portraits in oil and vinegar: studies of contemporary English artists. 1925.

The young man dances, and other poems. 1925.

A stitch in time: or pride prevents a fall. 1927. Poem.

English costume of the nineteenth century. 1929.

A history of British and American etching. 1929.

Love's progress: or the education of Araminta. 1929. Poem.

Macrocosmos: a poem. 1929.

Vera Willoughby, illustrator of books: an appreciation. 1929. Pamphlet.

A complete catalogue of the etchings and dry-points of Arthur Briscoe. 1930.

Whistler. 1930, New York 1930, London 1951 (rev).

English costume of the eighteenth century. 1931, New York 1958.

Nymph errant. 1932, New York 1932. Fiction.

Wesley. 1932, New York 1933.

Background for Venus. 1934, New York 1935. Fiction.

Winter wedding: a decoration. [1934]. Poem.

The laburnum tree and other stories. 1935; rptd in 24 short stories by Graham Greene, Laver and S. T. Warner, [1939].

Panic among Puritans. 1936, New York [1936]. Fiction.

'Vulgar society': the romantic career of James Tissot 1836–1902. 1936.

French painting and the nineteenth century. 1937.

Taste and fashion from the French Revolution until to-day. 1937, 1945 (rev, with ch on fashion and the Second World War).

Nostradamus: or the future foretold. 1942 [1941]. Biography.

A letter to a girl on the future of clothes. 1946. Pamphlet.

Hatchards of Piccadilly 1797–1947. 1947.

Style in costume. 1949.

Dress 1950.

Drama: its costume and décor. 1951.

Clothes. 1952, New York 1953.

The first decadent: being the strange life of J. K. Huysmans. 1954, New York 1955.

Oscar Wilde. 1954 (Br Council pamphlet).

Costume. 1963, New York 1964.

Museum piece: or the education of an iconographer. 1963, Boston 1964. Autobiography.

Costume in the theatre. 1964, New York 1965.

Women's dress in the Jazz Age. 1964.

The age of optimism: manners and morals 1848–1914. [1966], New York [1966] (as Manners and morals in the age of optimism 1848–1914).

Victoriana. [1966], New York 1967. Art history.

Dandies. 1968.

A concise history of costume. 1969, New York 1969.

Modesty in dress: an inquiry into the fundamentals of fashion. 1969, Boston 1969.

FRANK RAYMOND LEAVIS
1895–1978

Selections

The importance of Scrutiny: selections from Scrutiny, a quarterly review 1932–48. Ed E. Bentley, New York 1948.

A selection from Scrutiny, compiled by Leavis. 2 vols Cambridge 1968.

§1

Mass civilization and minority culture. Cambridge 1930 (Minority pamphlet 1); rptd in For continuity, 1933, and in Education and the university, 1948, below.

D. H. Lawrence. Cambridge 1930 (Minority pamphlet 6); rptd in For continuity, 1933, below.

New bearings in English poetry: a study of the contemporary situation. 1932, 1950 (adds Retrospect 1950), New York 1950, London 1954 (with textual changes).

How to teach reading: a primer for Ezra Pound. Cambridge 1932; rptd in Education and the university, 1943, below.

For continuity. Cambridge 1933, Freeport NY 1968. Essays, mainly first pbd in Scrutiny or as Minority pamphlets.

Culture and environment: the training of critical awareness. 1933, 1934 (with textual changes). With D. Thompson.

Towards standards of criticism: selections from The calendar of modern letters 1925–7, chosen and with an introduction by Leavis. 1933.

Determinations: critical essays. Ed Leavis 1934.

Revaluation: tradition and development in English poetry. 1936, New York 1947, London 1964 (with textual changes).

Education and the university: a sketch for an 'English school'. 1943, 1948 (adds Mass civilization and minority culture), New York 1948.

The great tradition: George Eliot, Henry James, Joseph Conrad. 1948, New York 1948, London 1960 (with textual changes).

Mill on Bentham and Coleridge. 1950, New York 1951. With introd by Leavis.

The common pursuit. 1952, New York 1952, London 1962 (with textual changes).

D. H. Lawrence, novelist. 1955, New York 1956, London 1957 (with textual changes), 1962 (with textual changes).

Two cultures?: the significance of C. P. Snow; Richmond lecture 1962. New York 1963 (with a new preface for the American reader).

Scrutiny: a retrospect. Cambridge 1963; also ptd in Scrutiny (reissue) 20 1963.

Anna Karenina and other essays. 1967, New York [1967].

English literature in our time and the university. 1969 (Clark lectures).

Lectures in America. 1969, New York 1969. With Q. D. Leavis.

Dickens the novelist. 1970. With Q. D. Leavis.

Nor shall my sword. 1972.

Letters in criticism. Ed J. Tasker 1974.

Thought, words and creativity: act and thought in Lawrence. 1976.

Editor of Scrutiny *1932–53.*

§2

Trilling, L. The moral tradition. New Yorker 24 Sept 1949; rptd in his Gathering of fugitives, Boston 1956 (as Leavis and the moral tradition).

—— Science, literature and culture: a comment on the Leavis–Snow controversy. Commentary 33 1962; rptd in his Beyond culture: essays on life and literature, New York 1965 (as The Leavis–Snow controversy).

Lerner, L. D. The life and death of Scrutiny. London Mag 2 1955.

JAMES BLAIR LEISHMAN
1902–63

The metaphysical poets: Donne, Herbert, Vaughan, Traherne. Oxford 1934, New York 1963.

The monarch of wit: an analytical and comparative study of the poetry of John Donne. 1951.

Themes and variations in Shakespeare's sonnets. 1961.

The art of Marvell's poetry. 1966, New York 1968.

Milton's minor poems. Ed G. Tillotson 1969.

Leishman was a translator, especially of Rilke (the Duino elegies, with S. Spender), also of Hölderlin and Horace. He edited the Three Parnassus plays 1598–1601, 1949.

CLIVE STAPLES LEWIS
1898–1963

The ms of The Screwtape letters, *1942, is held in the Berg Collection, New York Public Library. Other mss in Bodley.*

§1

Dymer, by 'Clive Hamilton'. 1926, New York 1926, London 1950 (as by C. S. Lewis, with a preface), New York 1950; rptd in Narrative poems, 1969, below.

The pilgrim's regress: an allegorical apology for Christianity, reason and Romanticism. 1933, 1943 (rev with a preface on Romanticism), New York 1944.

The allegory of love: a study in medieval tradition. 1936, New York 1936, London 1938 (corrected).

Out of the silent planet. 1938, New York 1949. Vol 1 of trilogy.

Rehabilitations and other essays. 1939, New York 1939.

The personal heresy: a controversy [between] E. M. W. Tillyard and Lewis. 1939, New York 1939.

The problem of pain. 1940 New York 1944.

The Screwtape letters. 1942, New York 1944, London 1961 (enlarged, with a new preface) (as The Screwtape letters and Screwtape proposes a toast), New York 1962. Preface and Screwtape proposes a toast rptd in Screwtape proposes a toast and other pieces, 1965, below.

A preface to Paradise lost. 1942, New York 1942. Lectures.

Broadcast talks: reprinted with some alterations from two series of broadcast talks (Right and wrong: a clue to the meaning of the universe and What Christians believe) given in 1941 and 1942. 1942, New York 1943 (as The case for Christianity); rptd (rev) in Mere Christianity, 1952, below.

Christian behaviour: a further series of broadcast talks. 1943, New York 1943. Rev versions of broadcast talks with 4 additional essays; rptd (rev) in Mere Christianity, 1952, below.

Perelandra. 1943, New York 1944, London 1953 (as Voyage to Venus). Vol 2 of trilogy.

The abolition of man: or reflections on education with special reference to the teaching of English in the upper forms of schools. 1943, New York 1947. Lectures.

Beyond personality: the Christian idea of God. 1944, New York 1945. Rev versions of broadcast talks; rptd (rev) in Mere Christianity, 1952, below.

That hideous strength: a modern fairy-tale for grown-ups. 1945, New York 1946, London 1955 (abridged by Lewis, with a new preface). Vol 3 of trilogy.

George MacDonald: an anthology. Ed Lewis 1946. Preface rptd (abridged) in G. MacDonald, Phantastes and Lilith, 1962.

The great divorce: a dream. 1945 (for 1946), New York 1946 (as The great divorce).

Miracles: a preliminary study. 1947, New York 1947, 1958 (abridged), London 1960 (ch 3 rev).

Arthurian torso: The figure of Arthur by Charles Williams and a commentary on the Arthurian poems of Charles Williams by Lewis. 1948, New York 1948.

Transposition and other addresses. 1949, New York 1949 (as The weight of glory and other addresses).

The lion, the witch and the wardrobe: a story for children. 1950, New York 1950.

Prince Caspian: the return to Narnia. 1951, New York 1951. Sequel to above.

Mere Christianity: a revised and amplified edition, with a new introduction, of the three books Broadcast talks, Christian behaviour and Beyond personality. 1952, New York 1952, London 1970 (new and enlarged).

The voyage of the Dawn Treader. 1952, New York 1952. For children.

The silver chair. 1953, New York 1953. For children.

The horse and his boy. 1954, New York 1954. For children.

English literature in the sixteenth century, excluding drama: the completion of the Clark lectures 1944. Oxford 1954 (OHEL 3).

The magician's nephew. 1955, New York 1955. For children.

Surprised by joy: the shape of my early life. 1955, New York 1956.

The last battle: a story for children. 1956, New York 1956.

Till we have faces: a myth retold. 1956, New York 1957.

Reflections on the Psalms. 1958, New York 1958.

Shall we lose God in outer space? 1959; rptd in The world's last night and other essays, 1960, below, as Religion and rocketry.

The four loves. 1960, New York 1960.

Studies in words. Cambridge 1960, 1967 (enlarged).

The world's last night and other essays. New York [1960].

A grief observed, by 'N. W. Clerk' [i.e. C. S. Lewis]. 1961, Greenwich Conn 1963, London 1964 (as by C. S. Lewis).

An experiment in criticism. Cambridge 1961.

They asked for a paper: papers and addresses. 1962.

Letters to Malcolm, chiefly on prayer. 1964, New York 1964. Chs 15–17 first priv ptd New York [1963] (as Beyond the bright blur).

The discarded image: an introduction to medieval and Renaissance literature. Cambridge 1964.

Poems. Ed W. Hooper 1964, New York 1965.

Screwtape proposes a toast and other pieces. 1965.

Of other worlds: essays and stories. Ed W. Hooper 1966. Includes essays on fiction, especially children's and science fiction

Studies in medieval and Renaissance literature, collected by W. Hooper. Cambridge 1966.

Christian reflections. Ed W. Hooper 1967.

Spenser's images of life. Ed A. D. S. Fowler. Cambridge 1967.

Selected literary essays. Ed W. Hooper, Cambridge 1969.

Selected narrative poems. Ed W. Hooper 1969. Dymer; Launcelot; The nameless isle; The queen of Drum.

Undeceptions: essays on theology and ethics. Ed W. Hooper 1971.

Letters

Letters. Ed W. H. Lewis 1966, New York 1966.

Letters to an American lady. Ed C. S. Kilby, Grand Rapids 1967.

Mark vs. Tristram: correspondence between Lewis and O. Barfield. Ed W. Hooper, Cambridge Mass 1967 (126 copies).

§2

Gardner, H. L. C. S. Lewis. Proc Br Acad 61 1965.

Gibb, J. (ed). Light on Lewis. 1965.

Patterns of love and courtesy: essays in memory of Lewis. Ed J. Lawlor 1966.

Robson, W. W. The romanticism of Lewis. In his Critical essays, 1966.

Green, R. L. and W. Hooper. Lewis: a biography. 1974.

Carpenter, H. In his Inklings, 1978.

PERCY LUBBOCK
1879–1965

Elizabeth Barrett Browning in her letters. 1906.

Samuel Pepys. 1909.

James, H. The middle years. [1917], New York 1917. Ed Lubbock.

—— The letters of Henry James. 2 vols 1920, New York 1920. Ed Lubbock.

The craft of fiction. 1921, New York 1929.

George Calderon: a sketch from memory. 1921.

Earlham. 1922, New York 1922. Childhood reminiscences.

Roman pictures. 1923, New York 1923. Novel.

The region cloud. 1925, New York 1925. Novel.

The diary of A. C. Benson. [1926], New York 1926. Ed Lubbock.

Mary Cholmondeley: a sketch from memory. 1928.

Shades of Eton. 1929. Reminiscences.

Portrait of Edith Wharton. 1947, New York 1947.

EDWARD VERRALL LUCAS
1868–1938

Bernard Barton and his friends: a record of quiet lives. 1893.

Domesticities: a little book of household impressions. 1900. Essays.

The works of Charles and Mary Lamb. 7 vols 1903–5. Ed Lucas.

Highways and byways in Sussex. 1904, 1935 (rev). Reissued 1937 in 3 vols: West Sussex; Mid-Sussex; East Sussex.

The life of Charles Lamb. 2 vols 1905, New York 1905, 1 vol London 1907 (rev and corrected), 2 vols 1921 (rev and corrected).

A wanderer in Holland. 1905, New York 1905, London 1923 (rev), New York 1924, London 1929 (rev).

Fireside and sunshine. 1906. Essays.

Listener's lure: an oblique narration. 1906, New York 1906 (as Listener's lure: a Kensington comedy).

A wanderer in London. 1906, 1913 (rev), New York 1918, London 1923 (rev), New York 1924, London 1926 (rev), 1931 (rev); rptd in E. V. Lucas, London, 1926, below.

Character and comedy. 1907, New York 1907. Essays.

A swan and her friends. 1907. An account of the life and times of Anna Seward, the 'Swan of Lichfield'.

Over Bemerton's: an easy-going chronicle. 1908, New York 1908.

One day and another. 1909, New York 1909. Essays.

A wanderer in Paris. 1909, New York 1909, London 1911 (rev), 1922 (rev), New York 1924, London 1928 (rev), 1952 (rev by A. Lucas).

Mr Ingleside. 1910, New York 1910. Fiction.

Old lamps for new. 1911, New York 1911. Essays.

London lavender. 1912, New York 1912. Fiction.

A wanderer in Florence. 1912, New York 1912, London 1923 (rev), New York 1924, London 1928 (rev).

Loiterer's harvest: a book of essays. 1913, New York 1913.

Landmarks. 1914, New York 1914. Fiction.

A wanderer in Venice. 1914, New York 1914, London 1923 (rev), New York 1924.

Cloud and silver. 1916, New York 1916. Essays and sketches.

London revisited. 1916, New York [1916] (as More wanderings in London), London 1926 (rev); rptd in E. V. Lucas' London, 1926, below.

Variety Lane. 1916. Essays and sketches.

The vermilion box. 1916, New York [1916]. Fiction.

A Boswell of Baghdad with diversions. 1917, New York 1917. Essays.

Outposts of mercy: the record of a visit to various units of the British Red Cross in Italy. 1917.

'Twixt eagle and dove. 1918. Essays.

Mixed vintages: a blend of essays old and new. 1919.

The phantom journal and other essays and diversions. 1919.

Specially selected: a choice of essays. 1920.

Verena in the midst: a kind of a story. 1920, New York [1920].

Edwin Austen Abbey: the record on his life and work. 2 vols 1921.

Rose and rose. 1921, New York 1921. Fiction.

Roving east and roving west. 1921, New York [1921].

Urbanities: essays new and old. 1921.

Genevra's money. 1922, New York 1923. Fiction.

Giving and receiving: essays and fantasies. 1922, New York 1922.

Vermeer of Delft. 1922.

You know what people are. 1922 Sketches.

Advisory Ben: a story. 1923, New York 1924, London 1932 (rev and enlarged).

Luck of the year: essays, fantasies and stories. 1923, New York [1923].

Encounters and diversions. 1924. Essays.

John Constable the painter. 1924.

Little books on great masters [of painting]. 8 vols 1924-6, New York 1924-6.

The same star: a comedy in three acts. 1924.

Introducing London. 1925.

Zigzags in France and various essays. 1925.

Events and embroideries. 1926, New York 1927. Essays.

E. V. Lucas's London: being A wanderer in London and London revisited in one volume, rearranged with new matter. 1926.

A wanderer in Rome. 1926, New York [1926], London 1930 (rev), Philadelphia 1932, London 1951 (rev).

A fronded isle and other essays. 1927.

The more I see of men: stray essays on dogs. 1927.

The Colvins and their friends. 1928.

Introducing Paris. 1928.

Out of a clear sky: essays and fantasies about birds. 1928; rptd in Animals all, 1934, below.

A rover I would be: essays and fantasies. 1928.

If dogs could write: a second canine miscellany. 1929, Philadelphia 1930.

Turning things over: essays and fantasies. 1929, New York 1929.

Vermeer the magical. 1929. Based on a lecture.

Windfall's eve: an entertainment. 1929, Philadelphia 1930. Fiction.

'—And such small deer'. 1930, Philadelphia 1931; rptd in Animals all, 1934, below.

Down the sky: an entertainment. 1930, Philadelphia 1930.

Traveller's luck: essays and fantasies. 1930.

The barber's clock: a conversation piece. 1931, Philadelphia 1932.

French leaves. 1931. Short essays on French subjects.

Visibility good: essays and excursions. 1931, Philadelphia 1931.

At the sign of the dove. 1932. Essays.

Lemon Verbena and other essays. 1932, Philadelphia 1932.

Reading, writing and remembering: a literary record. 1932, New York 1932.

English leaves. 1933, Philadelphia 1933. Essays.

Saunterer's rewards. 1933. Philadelphia 1934.

Animals all: being '—And such small deer' and Out of a clear sky. 1934.

At the shrine of St Charles: stray papers on Lamb brought together for the centenary of his death in 1834. 1934, New York 1934.

The letters of Charles Lamb to which are added those of his sister, Mary Lamb. 3 vols 1935, 2 vols 1945 (rev and abridged by G. Pocock). Ed Lucas.

The old contemporaries. 1935. Reminiscences.

Pleasure trove. 1935, Philadelphia 1935. Essays and sketches.

London afresh. 1936, Philadelphia [1937].

Only the other day: a volume of essays. 1936.

All of a piece: new essays. 1937, New York 1937.

Adventures and misgivings. 1938.

FRANK LAURENCE LUCAS
1894–1967

Seneca and Elizabethan tragedy. Cambridge 1922, New York 1966.

Euripides and his influence. Boston Mass [1923], London [1924].

Authors dead and living. 1926, New York 1926. Essays.

The river flows. 1926, New York 1926. Novel.

The complete works of John Webster. Ed Lucas 4 vols 1927, New York 1937. The texts of The white devil and The Duchess of Malfi (rev) rptd separately 1958, New York 1959.

Tragedy in relation to Aristotle's Poetics. 1927, New York [1928], London 1957 (rev and enlarged, as Tragedy: serious drama in relation to Aristotle's Poetics), New York 1958.

Time and memory. 1929 (Hogarth Living Poets).

The art of dying: an anthology. Ed F. Birrell and Lucas 1930.

Cécile. 1930, New York [1930]. Novel.

Eight Victorian poets. Cambridge 1930, 1940 (enlarged, as Ten Victorian poets), Hamden Conn 1966.

Marionettes. Cambridge 1930, New York 1930. Verse.

Ariadne. Cambridge 1932 (500 copies). Verse.

Poets in brief. 4 vols Cambridge 1932-3. Anthologies of Tennyson, Beddoes, D. G. Rossetti, Crabbe.

The wild tulip. 1932. Novel.

The bear dances. 1933. Play.

From Olympus to the Styx. 1934. With P. D. Lucas. Travel book on Greece.

Mauron, M. Mount Peacock: or progress in Provence. Cambridge 1934, New York 1935. Tr Lucas.

Studies French and English. 1934, Freeport NY 1969. Essays.

The awakening of Balthazar. 1935. Verse.

Four plays. Cambridge 1935, New York 1935.

Poems, 1935. Cambridge 1935, New York 1935.

The decline and fall of the Romantic ideal. Cambridge 1936, New York 1936.

The Golden Cockerel Greek anthology: a selection, edited with English verse translations by Lucas. [1937] (206 copies). 100 poems rptd in A Greek garland, 1939, below.

The woman clothed with the sun and other stories. 1937, New York 1938.

The delights of dictatorship. Cambridge 1938. Pamphlet.

Doctor Dido. 1938. Novel.

Journal under the terror 1938. 1938.

A Greek garland: a selection from the Palatine anthology, with translations into English verse by Lucas. 1939.

Messene redeemed. 1940, New York 1940. Verse play.

Critical thoughts in critical days. 1942 (PEN books).

Gilgamesh, King of Erech. 1948 (500 copies). Poems.

Greek poetry for everyman. 1951, New York 1951, London 1966 (as Greek poetry) (EL). Tr Lucas.

Literature and psychology. 1951, New York 1957 (rev).

From many times and lands. 1953. Verse.

Greek drama for everyman. 1954, New York 1954, London 1967 (corrected), (as Greek drama for the common reader), New York [1967] (as Greek tragedy and comedy). Chosen and tr by Lucas.

Style. New York 1955.

Tennyson. 1957, New York 1957, London 1961 (rev) (Br Council pamphlet).

The search for good sense: four eighteenth-century characters: Johnson, Chesterfield, Boswell, Goldsmith. 1958, New York 1958.

The art of living, four eighteenth-century minds: Hume, Horace Walpole, Burke, Benjamin Franklin. 1959, New York 1959.

The greatest problem, and other essays. 1960, New York 1961.

The drama of Ibsen and Strindberg. 1962, New York 1962.

The drama of Chekhov, Synge, Yeats and Pirandello. 1963.

The English agent: a tale of the Peninsular War. 1969.

Lucas pbd a number of other trns from the classics: Euripides (Medea, *1923*); Pervigilium Veneris (*1939*), *Catullus* (*three poems, 1942*), *Homer* (The Homeric Hymn to Aphrodite, *1948, selections from* The Odyssey, *1948, and from* The Iliad, *1950*), *Musaeus* (Hero and Leander, *1949*).

ROBERT WILSON LYND
1879–1949

The mantle of the emperor. 1906. With L. L. D. Black. Novel.

The Orangemen and the nation. Belfast 1907. Pamphlet.

Irish and English: portraits and impressions. 1908.

Home life in Ireland. 1909.

The ethics of Sinn Fein. Limerick 1910. Pamphlet.

Rambles in Ireland. 1912, Boston 1912. Illustr J. B. Yeats.

The book of this and that. 1915. Essays.

If the Germans conquered England and other essays. Dublin 1917.

Ireland a nation. 1919, New York 1920.

Old and new masters. 1919. Literary essays.

The art of letters. 1920, New York 1921. Literary essays.

The murders in Ireland: who began it. 1920. Pamphlet.

The passion of labour. 1920, Freeport NY 1969. Essays on socialism mainly rptd from New Statesman.

The pleasures of ignorance. 1921. Essays.

Books and authors. [1922], New York 1923. Essays.

Solomon in all his glory. 1922, New York 1923. Essays.

The sporting life and other trifles. 1922, New York 1922. Essays.

The blue lion and other essays. 1923, New York 1923.

The peal of bells. 1924, New York 1925. Essays.

The money box. 1925, New York 1926. Essays.

The little angel: a book of essays. 1926.

The orange tree: a volume of essays. 1926.

The green man. 1928. Essays.

It's a fine world. 1930. Essays.

Rain, rain, go to Spain. 1931. Essays.

The cockleshell. 1933. Essays.

Both sides of the road. 1934. Essays.

I tremble to think. 1936. Essays.

In defence of pink. 1937. Essays.

Modern poetry: chosen by Lynd. 1939, New York 1939.

Searchlights and nightingales. 1939. Essays.

Life's little oddities. 1941. Essays.

Things one hears. 1945. Essays.

Lynd contributed regularly to Daily News (*afterwards* News Chronicle) *from 1908 until he retired, as literary editor, in 1947 and to* New Statesman, *first anonymously, then under his own name and finally for many years under the pseudonym* 'Y.Y.'; *for a number of years he was* 'John O'London' *of* John O'London's Weekly.

SIR DESMOND MACCARTHY
1877–1952

The Court Theatre 1904–7: a commentary and criticism, with an appendix containing reprinted programmes of the 'Vedrenne–Barker performances'. 1907, Coral Gables Florida [1966] (ed S. Weintraub).

Lady John Russell: a memoir, with a selection from her diaries and correspondence. Ed MacCarthy and Agatha Russell 1910, New York 1911.

Romains, J. The death of a nobody. Tr MacCarthy and S. Waterlow 1914.

Remnants. 1918. Miscellaneous essays.

Ellen Melicent Cobden: a portrait. 1920 (priv ptd, 50 copies).

Ben Kedim: a record of Eastern travel, by Aubrey Herbert. Ed MacCarthy 1924.

Portraits. 1, 1931, New York 1931. No more pbd.

Criticism. 1932, New York [1932]. Essays.

H.H.A.: letters of the Earl of Oxford and Asquith to a friend. Ed MacCarthy 2 vols 1933–4.

William Somerset Maugham, 'the English Maupassant': an appreciation, with a bibliography. 1934; rptd in Memories, 1953.

Experience. 1935 (100 copies), Freeport NY 1968. Miscellaneous essays mainly rptd from New Statesman.

The European tradition in literature from 1600 onwards. In European civilization, its origin and development, vol 6, ed E. Eyre 1937.

Leslie Stephen. Cambridge 1937. Lecture; rptd in Memories, 1953.

Drama. 1940, New York 1940. Dramatic criticism. Some essays rptd in Theatre, 1954.

Shaw. 1951, New York 1951 (as Shaw's plays in review).

Humanities. Ed D. Cecil, 1953, New York 1954.

Memories. 1953, New York 1953. Forewords by R. Mortimer and C. Connolly.

Theatre. 1954, New York 1955. Essays.

MacCarthy also edited and contributed to New Quart, Eye Witness (*later* New Witness) *and* Life & Letters; *he was literary editor and later dramatic critic of* New Statesman, *and from 1928 until his death contributed weekly to* Sunday Times.

JOHN WILLIAM MACKAIL
1859–1945

Mensae secundae: verses written in Balliol College. Oxford 1879. With H. C. Beeching and J. B. B. Nichols.

The masque of B-ll-l. Oxford 1881 (broadsheet, 25 copies); ed W. G. Hiscock, 1939 (as The Balliol rhymes, enlarged). Verse caricatures by Mackail, Beeching, Nichols et al.

Love in idleness. 1883. Verse. With Beeching and Nichols.

The Aeneid of Virgil. 1885, 1908 (rev). Tr Mackail.

The Eclogues and Georgics of Virgil. 1889, New York 1915. Tr Mackail.

Select epigrams from the Greek Anthology. 1890, 1906 (rev), 1911 (rev). Ed and tr Mackail.

Love's looking glass. 1891. Verse. With Beeching and Nichols.

Biblia innocentium: being the story of God's chosen people, written anew for children. 2 pts 1892–1901.

Latin literature. 1895, New York 1895, 1962 (ed with introd by H. C. Schnur).

Homer, Odysseus in Phaeacia. 1896, Portland 1897. Verse trn of Odyssey bk 6.

The life of William Morris. 2 vols 1899, 1 vol Oxford 1950 (introd by S. Cockerell) (WC), 2 vols New York 1968.

Homer, The Odyssey. 3 vols 1903–10, 1 vol Oxford 1932. Verse trn by Mackail.

The hundred best poems—lyrical—in the Latin language, selected by J. W. Mackail. 1905, 1906 (corrected).

The springs of Helicon: a study of the progress of English poetry from Chaucer to Milton. 1909, New York 1909.

Lectures on Greek poetry. 1910, 1926 (rev), New York 1966.

Lectures on poetry. 1911, Freeport NY 1967.

Pervigilium Veneris—The eve of St Venus. In Catullus, Tibullus and Pervigilium Veneris, 1912. Tr Mackail (Loeb Classical Lib).

Russia's gift to the world. 1915, 1917 (rev).

The case for Latin in secondary schools. 1922. Pamphlet.

Virgil and his meaning to the world of today. Boston Mass [1922], London 1923.

Literature. In The legacy of Rome, ed C. Bailey, Oxford 1923.

Classical studies. 1925, Freeport NY 1968.

James Leigh Strachan-Davidson, Master of Balliol: a memoir. Oxford 1925.

Life and letters of George Wyndham. 2 vols [1925]. With Guy Wyndham.

Studies of English poets. 1926, Freeport NY 1968.

The approach to Shakespeare. Oxford 1930.

Virgil, The Aeneid. Oxford 1930. Ed Mackail.

Studies in humanism. 1938, Freeport NY 1969.

RONALD BRUNLEES MCKERROW
1872–1940

§1

Printers and publishers' devices in England and Scotland 1485–1640. 1913 (Bibl Soc).

Notes on bibliographical evidence for literary students and editors of English works of the sixteenth and seventeenth centuries. 1914. Pamphlet rptd from Trans Bibl Soc 12 1893; subsequently the basis of An introduction to bibliography for literary students, 1927, below.

Booksellers, printers and the stationers' trade. In Shakespeare's England vol 2, Oxford 1916.

A note on the teaching of English language and literature, with some suggestions. 1921 (Eng Assoc pamphlet).

A dictionary of the printers and booksellers who were at work in England, Scotland and Ireland from 1668 to 1725, by H. R. Plomer, with the help of McKerrow [et al]. Ed A. Esdaile 1922.

An introduction to bibliography for literary students. Oxford 1927, 1928 (corrected).

Title-page borders used in England and Scotland 1485–1640. 1932 (Bibl Soc). With F. S. Ferguson, who pbd a list of addns in 1936.

The treatment of Shakespeare's text by his earlier editors 1709–68. Proc Br Acad 19 1933. Lecture.

Prolegomena for the Oxford Shakespeare: a study in editorial method. Oxford 1939.

The typescript of McKerrow's unpbd Sandars Lectures, The relationship of English printed books to authors' manuscripts, is held by Cambridge Univ Library.

Editions

Dekker, T. The gull's horn-book. 1904.

The works of Thomas Nashe, edited from the original texts. 5 vols 1904–10, Oxford 1958 (with corrections and supplementary notes by F. P. Wilson).

A dictionary of printers and booksellers in England, Scotland and Ireland, and of foreign printers of English books 1557–1640, by H. G. Aldis [et al]. 1910. Ed McKerrow.

Greg, W. W. English literary autographs 1550–1650, selected and edited by W. W. Greg in collaboration with McKerrow [et al]. 4 pts Oxford 1925–32.

McKerrow helped to found the Malone Soc in 1906 and edited or assisted in editing 5 plays for Malone Soc

Reprints *1907–11; he edited* Library *1934–7* (in 1937 with F. C. Francis); *he founded* RES *in 1925 and edited it 1925–39.*

§2

Greg, W. W. R. B. McKerrow. Proc Br Acad 26 1940.
— McKerrow's Prolegomena reconsidered. RES 17 1941.
— Prolegomena: on editing Shakespeare, a criticism and expansion of the principles laid down in McKerrow's Prolegomena for the Oxford Shakespeare. In his Editorial problem in Shakespeare, Oxford 1942, 1951 (corrected).

Bowers, F. T. McKerrow's editorial principles for Shakespeare reconsidered. Shakespeare Quart 6 1955.

GEORGE GILBERT AIMÉ MURRAY
1866–1957

After his death Murray's papers were deposited in Bodley.

Collections

The plays of Euripides, translated into rhyming verse with explanatory notes. 2 vols 1911, Newtown 1931 (Gregynog Press, 500 copies), New York 1931, 1 vol London 1954 (as Collected plays of Euripides).

Aeschylus. The Oresteia, translated into English rhyming verse. 1928, 1946 (rev). With introd and notes.

Complete plays of Aeschylus, translated into English rhyming verse with commentaries and notes. 1952.

Humanist essays. 1964, New York 1964.

§1

A history of ancient Greek literature. 1897, New York 1897, Chicago 1956 (as The literature of ancient Greece).

Andromache: a play in three acts. 1900, Portland Maine 1913 (450 copies), London 1914 (corrected).

Carlyon Sahib: a drama in four acts. 1900.

Euripides [The Hippolytus and Bacchae together with The frogs of Aristophanes], translated into English rhyming verse by Murray. 1902.

Euripidis Fabulae: recognovit brevique adnotatione critica instruxit Gilbertus Murray. 3 vols Oxford 1902–9.

The Electra of Euripides, translated into English rhyming verse with explanatory notes. 1905, New York 1915 (with The Trojan women and The Medea).

The Trojan women of Euripides, translated into English rhyming verse with explanatory notes. 1905, New York 1915 (with The Medea and The Electra).

The Medea of Euripides, translated into English rhyming verse with explanatory notes. 1906, New York 1906, 1915 (with The Trojan women and The Electra).

The rise of the Greek epic. Oxford 1907, 1911 (rev and enlarged), 1924 (rev and enlarged), New York 1961.

Anthropology in the Greek epic tradition outside Homer. In Anthropology and the classics: six lectures by Murray [et al], ed R. R. Marett, Oxford 1908.

The Iphigenia in Tauris of Euripides, translated into English rhyming verse with explanatory notes. 1910, New York 1910.

Oedipus King of Thebes, by Sophocles, translated into English rhyming verse with explanatory notes. 1910, New York 1910.

The story of Nefrekepta from a demotic papyrus, put into verse by Murray. Oxford 1911.

Four stages of Greek religion: studies based on a course of lectures delivered at Columbia University. New York 1912, London 1912, Oxford 1925 (enlarged as Five stages of Greek religion).

Greek and English tragedy: a contrast. In English literature and the classics, by Murray [et al], ed G. S. Gordon, Oxford 1912.

Harrison, J. E. Themis: a study of the social origins of

Greek religion, with an excursus on the ritual forms preserved in Greek tragedy by Murray. Cambridge 1912, 1927 (rev and enlarged), Cleveland 1962.

Euripides and his age. [1913], New York 1913, London 1946 (rev), New York 1946, London 1965 (introd by H. D. F. Kitto), New York 1965.

The Rhesus of Euripides, translated into English rhyming verse with explanatory notes. 1913, New York 1913.

The Alcestis of Euripides, translated into English rhyming verse with explanatory notes. 1915, New York 1915.

The foreign policy of Sir Edward Grey 1906–15. Oxford 1915. *See* B. Russell, The policy of the Entente 1904–14: a reply to Murray, Manchester [1916].

Faith, war and policy: lectures and essays. Boston 1917, London 1918 (with new preface).

Aeschylus' Agamemnon, translated into English rhyming verse with explanatory notes. 1920, New York 1920.

Essays and addresses. 1921, Boston 1922 (as Tradition and progress).

The problem of foreign policy. 1921, Boston 1921.

The value of Greece to the future of the world. In The legacy of Greece: essays by Murray [et al], ed R. W. Livingstone, Oxford 1921.

The Choëphoroe—Libation bearers—of Aeschylus, translated into English rhyming verse. 1923, New York 1923.

Toynbee, A. J. (ed). Greek historical thought from Homer to the age of Heraclitus, with two pieces [from the Iliad and from Antigone] newly translated by Gilbert Murray. 1924, Boston 1950.

The Eumenides—The furies—of Aeschylus, translated into English rhyming verse. 1925, New York 1925.

Five stages of Greek religion. Oxford 1925.

The classical tradition in poetry: the Charles Eliot Norton lectures 1926. 1927, Cambridge Mass 1927.

The ordeal of this generation: the war, the League and the future. 1929, New York 1929.

Aeschylus' Suppliant women: Supplices, translated into English rhyming verse with introduction and notes. 1930, New York 1930.

The Oxford book of Greek verse, chosen by Murray [et al]. Oxford 1930. Murray also contributed 25 poems to the Oxford book of Greek verse in translation, ed T. F. Higham and C. M. Bowra, Oxford 1938.

Aeschylus' Prometheus bound, translated into English rhyming verse with introduction and notes. 1931, New York 1931.

Aristophanes: a study. Oxford 1933, New York 1933.

Aeschylus' Seven against Thebes, translated into English rhyming verse with introduction and notes. 1935, New York 1935.

Aeschyli Septem quae supersunt tragoediae, recensuit Gilbertus Murray. Oxford 1937, 1955 (rev).

Liberality and civilization. 1938, New York 1938.

Aeschylus' The Persians—Persae—translated into English rhyming verse with preface and notes. 1939, New York 1939.

Aeschylus: the creator of tragedy. Oxford 1940.

Stoic, Christian and humanist. 1940, Boston 1950 (with a new preface), London 1950. Essays.

Sophocles' Antigone, translated into English rhyming verse with introduction and notes. 1941, New York 1941.

The rape of the locks: the Perikeiromenê of Menander, the fragments translated and the gaps conjecturally filled in. 1942, New York 1945 (with The arbitration).

Classical humanism. In Humanism (three BBC talks), by Murray [et al]. [1944].

The arbitration: the Epitrepontes of Menander, the fragments translated and the gaps conjecturally filled in by Murray. 1945, New York 1945 (with The rape of the locks).

Greek studies. Oxford 1946.

The wife of Heracles: being Sophocles' play The Trachinian women, translated into English verse with explanatory notes. 1947, New York 1948.

From the League to UN. 1948. Includes addresses etc previously pbd separately.

Sophocles' Oedipus at Colonus, translated into English rhyming verse with introduction and notes. 1948, New York 1948.

Aristophanes' The birds, translated into English verse with introduction and notes. 1950, New York 1950.

Croce as a European. In Benedetto Croce: a commemoration, by Murray [et al]. 1953.

Hellenism and the modern world: six talks on the Radio-Diffusion Française and the BBC. 1953, Boston 1954.

Euripides, Ion, translated into English rhyming verse with explanatory notes. 1954, New York 1954.

Aristophanes, The knights, translated into English rhyming verse with introduction and notes. 1956.

An unfinished autobiography, with contributions by his friends. Ed J. Smith and A. Toynbee 1960.

Murray also wrote many booklets and pamphlets on the Great War, Liberalism and the League of Nations. With H. A. L. Fisher he was editor of Home Univ Lib.

§2

Eliot, T. S. Euripides and Gilbert Murray: a performance at the Holborn Empire. Art & Letters 3 1920; rptd in his Sacred wood, 1920 (as Euripides and Professor Murray).

Thomson, J. A. K. and A. J. Toynbee (ed). Essays in honour of Murray. 1936.

Thomson, J. A. K. Gilbert Murray. Proc Br Acad 43 1958.

Gilbert Murray: an unfinished autobiography, with contributions by his friends. Ed J. Smith and A. Toynbee 1960.

JOHN MIDDLETON MURRY
1889–1957

Selections

Selected criticism 1916–57, chosen and introduced by R. Rees. 1960, New York 1960.

§1

Fyodor Dostoevsky: a critical study. 1916, New York 1916.

Still life. 1916, New York 1922. Novel.

Poems: 1917–18. Hampstead 1918 (120 copies).

The critic in judgment: or, Belshazzar of Baronscourt. Richmond Surrey [1919]. Verse.

Aspects of literature. 1920, New York 1921. Essays.

Cinnamon and Angelica: a play. 1920, [1941] (rev), New York 1941. Verse.

The evolution of an intellectual. 1920, New York 1920, London 1927 (one essay replaced by 2 others).

Poems: 1916–20. [1921].

Countries of the mind: essays in literary criticism. [1922], New York 1922, London 1931 (rev, with 2 additional essays, as Countries of the mind [etc] first ser), 1937 (rev, with 2nd ser, 1931 below).

The problem of style. 1922, New York 1922.

The things we are. 1922, New York 1922, [1930] (introd by D. B. Leary). Novel.

Pencillings: little essays on literature. [1923], New York 1925.

Discoveries: essays in literary criticism. [1924], 1930 (3 essays replaced by 4 others).

The necessity of art, by Murry [et al]. 1924, New York 1924. Murry's essay, Literature and religion, rptd in his To the unknown God, 1924.

To the unknown God: essays towards a religion. 1924, New York 1930.

The voyage. 1924. Novel.

Wrap me up in my Aubusson carpet. New York 1924 (500 copies).

Keats and Shakespeare: a study of Keats' poetic life from 1816 to 1820. 1925, New York 1925.

The life of Jesus. 1926, New York 1926 (as Jesus: man of genius).

Things to come: essays. 1928, New York 1928, London 1938 (with new ch On love: human and divine).

God: being an introduction to the science of metabiology. 1929, New York 1929.

D. H. Lawrence: two essays. Cambridge 1930 (Minority pamphlets 4). First pbd in New Adelphi, rptd in Reminiscences of D. H. Lawrence, 1933.

The poems and verses of John Keats, edited and arranged in chronological order by Murry. 2 vols 1930 (765 copies), New York 1930, 1 vol London 1949 (rev).

Studies in Keats. 1930, New York 1930, London 1939, New York 1939 (with 3 additional essays, as Studies in Keats, new and old), 1949 (extensively rev, as The mystery of Keats), New York 1949, London 1955 (rev with 3 additional essays, as Keats), New York 1955.

Countries of the mind: essays in literary criticism, 2nd ser. 1931, 1937 (with first ser, rev, 1931, above).

Son of woman: the story of D. H. Lawrence. 1931, New York [1931], London 1954 (with new introd, as D. H. Lawrence, son of woman).

Blake, W. Visions of the daughters of Albion; reproduced in facsimile, with a note by Murry. 1932, New York 1932.

The fallacy of economics. 1932 (Criterion miscellany).

The necessity of Communism. 1932, New York 1933.

The life of Katherine Mansfield, by Ruth E. Mantz. 1933, Toronto 1933. Introd, rev and last ch by Murry.

Reminiscences of D. H. Lawrence. 1933, New York [1933].

William Blake. 1933, Toronto 1933, New York 1964.

Between two worlds: an autobiography. 1935, New York [1936] (as The autobiography of Murry: between two worlds).

Marxism. 1935, New York 1935.

Shakespeare. 1936, New York [1936], London 1954 [1955] (with new preface).

The necessity of pacifism. 1937, Toronto 1937.

Heaven—and earth. 1938, New York [1938] (adds To the American reader) (as Heroes of thought).

The pledge of peace. 1938.

The defence of democracy. 1939, Toronto 1939.

The price of leadership. 1939, New York [1939].

Adam and Eve: an essay towards a new and better society. 1944.

The challenge of Schweitzer. 1948.

The free society. 1948.

Looking before and after: a collection of essays. 1948.

Katherine Mansfield and other literary portraits. 1949.

John Clare and other studies. 1950, New York 1950.

Community farm. 1952, New York 1952.

Jonathan Swift: a critical biography. 1954, New York 1955.

Swift. 1955, New York 1955, London 1961 (rev) (Br Council pamphlet).

Unprofessional essays. 1956, Fairlawn NJ 1956.

Love, freedom and society. 1957, Toronto 1957.

Katherine Mansfield and other literary studies, with a foreword by T. S. Eliot. 1959, Chester Springs Pa 1959.

Not as the scribes: lay sermons 1959, New York 1960.

For the various works of Katherine Mansfield edited by Murry see Katherine Mansfield, col 1381, above. Murry founded Adelphi (became New Adelphi) in 1923 and edited and contributed to it 1923–48; he also edited and contributed to Rhythm (became Blue Rev) 1911–13; Signature (3 nos) 1915; Daily Rev of the Foreign Press (War Office); Athenaeum 1919–21; Wanderer 1933–4; Peace News 1940–6; he contributed regularly to

Westminster Gazette, TLS, Nation, Aryan Path *and* London Mag.

§2

Lea, F. A. The life of Murry. 1959.

Murry, M. M. To keep faith. 1959. Memoir of his last years.

Griffin, E. G. John Middleton Murry. New York 1969.

ERNEST NEWMAN
1868–1959

Gluck and the opera: a study in musical history. 1895.

A study of Wagner. 1899, New York 1899.

Wagner. [1904].

Musical studies. 1905.

Elgar. 1906, New York 1906.

Hugo Wolf. 1907, New York 1966 (introd by W. Legge).

Richard Strauss. 1908.

Wagner as man and artist. 1914, New York 1914.

A musical motley. 1919, New York 1919, 1925 (rev). Essays.

The piano-player and its music. 1920.

A musical critic's holiday. 1925, New York 1925.

The stories of the great operas. 15 pts [1927], 3 vols New York 1928–30, 1935 (in 1 vol, as Stories of the great operas and their composers).

The unconscious Beethoven. 1927, New York 1927.

Fact and fiction about Wagner. 1931, New York 1931.

The life of Richard Wagner. 4 vols 1933–47, New York 1933–46.

The man Liszt: a study of the tragi-comedy of a soul divided against itself. 1934, New York 1935.

More stories of famous operas. New York 1943.

Opera nights. 1943.

Wagner nights. 1949, New York 1949 (as The Wagner operas).

More opera nights. 1954, New York 1955 (for 1954) (as Seventeen famous operas).

From the world of music: essays from the Sunday Times. 1956, New York 1957. Selected by F. Aprahamian.

Great operas, the definitive treatment of their histories, stories and music. New York 1958. Rptd from More stories of famous operas, and Seventeen famous operas, above.

More essays from the world of music: essays from the Sunday Times. 1958, New York 1958.

Testament of music: essays and papers. Ed H. van Thal 1962, New York 1963.

Formerly William Roberts; also used the pseudonym Hugh M. Cecil. Newman was a prolific translator; he edited Handbooks for Musicians 1914–22 and was general editor of the New Library of Music from 1907. In 1905 he was music critic of Manchester Guardian; from 1906–19 of Birmingham Post, from 1920–58 of Sunday Times.

JOHN RAMSAY
ALLARDYCE NICOLL
1894–1976

William Blake and his poetry. 1922.

Dryden and his poetry. 1923, New York 1967.

A history of Restoration drama 1660–1700. Cambridge 1923, 1928 (rev), 1940 (rev), 1952 (rev, with notes, as vol 1 of A history of English drama, 1952–9, below).

An introduction to dramatic theory. 1923, 1931 (rev and enlarged as The theory of drama), New York 1931.

British drama: an historical survey from the beginnings to the present time. 1925, New York [1925], London 1932 (rev), 1947 (rev), New York [195–?], London 1962 (rev), New York [1963].

A history of early eighteenth-century drama 1700–1750. Cambridge 1925, 1927 (with addns), 1952 (rev, with notes, as vol 2 of A history of English drama, 1952–9, below).

The development of the theatre. 1927, New York 1927, London 1937 (rev), New York 1937, 1946 (rev and enlarged), London 1948, 1958 (rev), New York 1958, London 1966 (rev), New York 1967.

A history of late eighteenth-century drama 1750–1800. Cambridge 1927, 1952 (with notes, as vol 3 of A history of English drama, 1952–9, below).

Studies in Shakespeare. 1927, New York [1928].

The English stage. 1928.

A history of early nineteenth-century drama 1800–1850. 2 vols Cambridge 1930, 1 vol 1955 (rev, with supplementary notes, as vol 4 of A history of English drama, 1952–9, below).

Masks, mimes and miracles: studies in the popular theatre. 1931, New York 1931.

The English theatre: a short history. 1936.

Film and theatre. New York [1936], London [1936].

Stuart masques and the Renaissance stage. 1937, New York 1938.

A history of late nineteenth-century drama 1850–1900. 2 vols Cambridge 1946, 1 vol 1959 (with notes, as vol 5 of A history of English drama, 1952–9, below).

World drama from Æschylus to Anouilh. 1949, New York [1950?].

A history of English drama 1660–1900. 6 vols Cambridge 1952–9. For earlier edns of vols 1–5, see above.

Shakespeare. 1952, New York 1952 (as Shakespeare: an introduction).

The theatre and dramatic theory. 1962, New York 1962.

The world of Harlequin: a critical study of the commedia dell'arte. Cambridge 1963.

English drama: a modern viewpoint. 1968, New York 1968.

Nicoll also edited Holinshed's Chronicle (*1927*), *the works of* Tourneur [*1929*], Chapman's Homer (*1957*), *plays by* Sharpham (*1926*) *and* Boucicault (*1940*), *and several anthologies. He was editor of* Shakespeare Survey (*1948–65*).

CHARLES KAY OGDEN
1889–1957

Militarism versus feminism. 1915. Anon.

The foundations of aesthetics. 1922, New York 1948. With I. A. Richards and J. Wood.

L. Wittgenstein, Tractatus. 1922. Tr Ogden. *See also his* Letters to Ogden, ed G. H. von Wright, Oxford 1973.

The meaning of meaning: a study of the influence of language upon thought and of the science of symbolism. 1923, 1927 (rev), 1930 (rev), 1936 (rev), 1944 (rev), New York 1956. With I. A. Richards.

The philosophy of As if, by H. Vaihinger. Tr Ogden 1924.

The meaning of psychology. New York 1926.

The ABC of psychology. 1929.

Basic English: a general introduction with rules and grammar. 1930.

The Basic vocabulary: a statistical analysis, with special reference to substitution and translation. 1930.

Basic English applied–science. 1931.

Brighter Basic: examples of Basic English for young persons of taste and feeling. 1931.

Debabelization, with a survey of contemporary opinion on the problem of a universal language. 1931.

The theory of legislation, by J. Bentham. Ed Ogden 1931.

The ABC of Basic English, in Basic. 1932.

The Basic dictionary: being the 7,500 most useful words with their equivalent in Basic English. 1932.

The Basic words: a detailed account of their uses. 1932, 1964 (rev).

Bentham's Theory of fictions. Ed Ogden 1932.

Jeremy Bentham 1832–2032. 1932.

Opposition: a linguistic and psychological analysis. 1932, Bloomington 1967.

Basic by examples. 1933.

The system of Basic English. New York 1934, New York 1968 (rev E. C. Graham as Basic English: international second language).

Basic English versus the artificial languages. 1935.

Basic step by step. 1935.

The three signs and other American stories put into Basic English. Ed Ogden 1935.

The general Basic English dictionary: giving more than 40,000 senses of over 20,000 words in Basic English. Ed Ogden 1940, New York 1942.

Basic for science. 1942.

Ogden also pbd Basic English textbooks for foreign students and prepared Basic English edns of certain works, e.g. stories from the Bible. He founded and edited Cambridge Mag *1912–22, contributed to* Basic News, *and was general editor of the* International Library of Psychology, Philosophy and Scientific Method, *and other ser.*

ALFRED RICHARD ORAGE
1873–1934
Selections

Selected essays and critical writings. Ed H. Read and D. Saurat 1935, Freeport NY 1967.

§1

Friedrich Nietzsche: the Dionysian spirit of the age. Edinburgh 1906 (Spirit of the age ser), Chicago 1911.

Consciousness: animal, human and superhuman. 1907.

Nietzsche in outline and aphorism. Edinburgh 1907, Chicago 1910. Selection ed Orage.

Hobson, S. G. National Guilds: an enquiry into the wage system and the way out. Ed Orage 1914, New York 1914. Anon. Mainly first pbd in New Age 1912–13.

An alphabet of economics. 1917.

An Englishman talks it out with an Irishman. Dublin 1918, London 1918. Pamphlet.

Douglas, C. H. Credit-power and democracy, with a commentary on the included scheme by A. R. Orage. 1920, 1934 (rev and enlarged).

Readers and writers 1917–21, by 'R.H.C.'—A. R. Orage. 1922, New York 1922. Essays first pbd in New Age.

The art of reading. New York [1930]. Essays mostly first pbd under the initials R.H.C. in New Age.

Politicians and the public service. Ed Orage 1934.

Social credit: broadcast, 1934; and The fear of leisure: an address, 1935. 1935 (Pamphlets on the New Economics 5).

Political and economic writings from New English Weekly 1932–4, with a preliminary section from New Age 1912. Ed M. Butchart 1936, Freeport NY 1967.

The active mind: adventures in awareness. 1954, New York 1954.

Essays and aphorisms. 1954. With biographical note by S. C. Nott; rptd 1957 with On love, 1932, above (as On love, with some aphorisms and other essays).

Orage contributed introds and prefaces to other works. He edited New Age *1907–22 (jointly with Holbrook Jackson May–Dec 1907). He founded* New English Weekly *and edited it 1932–4.*

§2

New English Weekly 15 Nov 1934.

Eliot, T. S. A commentary [on the death of Orage].
Criterion 14 1935.
Pound, E. In the wounds—memoriam A. R. Orage.
Criterion 14 1935; rptd (condensed) in his Impact:
essays on ignorance and the decline of American civiliza-
tion, 1960.
Hastings, B. The old 'New Age': Orage and others. 1936.
Mairet, P. A. R. Orage: a memoir. 1936 (introd by G. K.
Chesterton), New Hyde Park NY 1966 (with a Re-
introduction, omits Chesterton's introd).
Selver, P. Orage and the 'New Age' circle: reminiscences
and reflections. 1959.
Martin, W. The New Age under Orage: chapters in
English cultural history. Manchester [1967].

ERIC HONEYWOOD PARTRIDGE
1894–1979

A critical medley: essays, studies and notes in English,
French and comparative literature. Paris 1926.
Songs and slang of the British soldier 1914–18. 1930, 1930
(rev and enlarged), 1931 (rev and enlarged). With J.
Brophy; further revision, by Brophy, pbd 1965 (as The
long trail: what the British soldier sang and said in the
Great War of 1914–18).
Slang today and yesterday. 1933, New York 1934, London
1935 (rev), 1950 (rev), New York 1950, London [1960]
(rev), New York 1960, London 1971 (rev).
Words, words, words! 1933. Essays.
Name this child: a dictionary of English and American
Christian names. 1936, 1938 (rev and enlarged), 1951
(rev and enlarged), 1959 (abridged).
A dictionary of slang and unconventional English. 1937,
New York 1937; suppl 1938. Frequently rev and
enlarged.
The world of words: an introduction to language in general
and to English and American in particular. 1938, New
York 1939, London 1948 (rev).
A dictionary of clichés with an introductory essay. 1940,
New York 1940, London 1950 (rev).
Usage and abusage: a guide to good English. New York
and London 1942, London 1947 (rev), New York 1949
(as A dictionary of effective speech), London 1957 (rev
and enlarged), 1965 (rev and enlarged). A shortened and
simplified version pbd 1954 (as The concise usage and
abusage: a modern guide to good English).
A dictionary of RAF slang. 1945.
Shakespeare's bawdy: a literary and psychological essay
and a comprehensive glossary. 1947, New York 1948,
London 1955 (rev), New York 1955, London 1968 (rev
and enlarged).
A dictionary of Forces' slang 1939–45. Ed Partridge et al
1948.
Words at war, words at peace: essays on language in
general and particular words. 1948.
A dictionary of the underworld, British and American.
1949, New York 1950, London 1961 (with addenda),
New York 1961, London 1968 (much enlarged).
English: a course for human beings. 1949.
Name into word: proper nouns that have become common
property—a discursive dictionary. 1949, New York
1950 (rev and enlarged).
Here, there and everywhere: essays upon language.
1950.
British and American English since 1900. 1951, New
York 1951, London 1951 (corrected). With J. W. Clark.
Chamber of horrors: a glossary of official jargon both
English and American, by 'Vigilans' [i.e. Partridge].
1952. With introd by Partridge.
From Sanskrit to Brazil: vignettes and essays upon
languages. 1952.
You have a point there: a guide to punctuation and its
allies. 1953.

What's the meaning?: a book for younger people. 1956.
A first book of quotations. Ed Partridge 1958, 1964 (rev,
as A book of essential quotations).
Origins: a short etymological dictionary of modern English.
1958, New York 1958, London 1959 (rev and enlarged),
New York 1959, London 1961 (rev), London 1966 (rev).
A charm of words: essays and papers on language. 1960,
New York 1961.
Comic alphabets: their origin, development, nature. 1961,
New York 1967.
Smaller slang dictionary. 1961, New York 1961, London
1964 (corrections and addns).
The gentle art of lexicography, as pursued and experienced
by an addict. 1963, New York 1963.

SIR NIKOLAUS BERNHARD
LEON PEVSNER
b. 1902

Pioneers of the modern movement from William Morris to
Walter Gropius. 1936, New York 1949 (rev, as Pioneers
of modern design), London 1960 (rev and partly re-
written) (Penguin), 1964 (corrected).
An enquiry into industrial art in England. Cambridge
1937.
Academies of art past and present. Cambridge 1940, New
York 1940.
An outline of European architecture. 1942 (Pelican), New
York 1948. With frequent subsequent revisions.
The leaves of Southwell. 1945 (King Penguin).
High Victorian design: a study of the exhibits of 1851.
1951.
The buildings of England. 1951– (Penguin). Some vols
with collaborators.
The Englishness of English art. 1955, 1956 (rev and
enlarged), New York 1956.
Christopher Wren 1632–1723. Milan 1958, New York
1960. In Italian, tr E. Labò.
The Penguin dictionary of architecture. 1966. With J.
Fleming and H. Honour.
The sources of modern architecture and design. [1968],
New York 1968.
Studies in art, architecture and design: vol 1, From man-
nerism to romanticism; vol 2, Victorian and after. 2 vols
1968. Includes items previously pbd separately.
Some architectural writers of the nineteenth century.
Oxford 1972.
A history of building types. 1976.
Pevsner edited Pelican history of art *1953 onwards and was
art editor of* Penguin Books.

ALFRED WILLIAM POLLARD
1859–1944

Last words on the history of the title-page, with notes on
some colophons and twenty seven fac-similes of title-
pages. 1891 (250 copies).
Chaucer. 1893, 1926 (corrected), 1931 (rewritten and
enlarged), New York 1969.
Early illustrated books: a history of the decoration and
illustration of books in the 15th and 16th centuries.
1893 (Books About Books), New York 1968.
Old picture books, with other essays on bookish subjects.
1902.
Books in the house: an essay on private libraries and collections for young and old. Indianapolis 1904 (510 copies),
London 1907.
An essay on colophons, with specimens and translations.
Chicago 1905 (255 copies).
Shakespeare folios and quartos: a study in the bibliography
of Shakespeare's plays 1594–1685. 1909.

Fine books. 1912 (Connoisseur's Lib), New York 1964.

A census of Shakespeare's plays in quarto 1594–1709. New Haven 1916, London 1916. With H. C. Bartlett.

Shakespeare's fight with the pirates and the problems of the transmission of his text. 1917, Cambridge 1920 (rev with an introd) (Shakespeare Problems). Lectures.

St Catherine of Siena. 1919.

The foundations of Shakespeare's text. [1923]. Lecture.

Shakespeare's hand in the play of Sir Thomas More: papers by Pollard [et al]. Cambridge 1923.

A short-title catalogue of books printed in England, Scotland and Ireland and of English books printed abroad, 1475–1640. 1926. With G. R. Redgrave.

Cobden-Sanderson and the Doves Press. 1929 (priv ptd).

Shakespeare's text. In A companion to Shakespeare studies, ed H. G. Barker and G. B. Harrison, Cambridge 1934.

My first fifty years. In G. Murphy, A select bibliography of the works of Pollard, Oxford 1938.

Pollard also edited Library *1903–34*, Chaucer's *Canterbury* tales *etc.*

STEPHEN MEREDITH POTTER
1900–69

The young man. 1929. Novel.

D. H. Lawrence: a first study. 1930.

Coleridge and S.T.C. 1935, New York 1965.

The muse in chains: a study in education. 1937.

The theory and practice of gamesmanship: or the art of winning games without actually cheating. 1947, New York 1948.

Some notes on lifemanship: with a summary of recent researches in gamesmanship. 1950, New York 1951.

One-upmanship: being some account of the activities and teaching of the Lifemanship Correspondence College of one-upness and gameslifemastery. 1952, New York 1952.

Sense of humour. 1954, New York 1954. Anthology.

Potter on America. 1956, New York 1957.

Supermanship: or how to continue to stay top without actually falling apart. 1958, New York 1959.

The magic number: the story of '57'. 1959. History of H. J. Heinz & Co Ltd.

Steps to immaturity. 1959. Autobiography.

Squawky: the adventures of a clasperchoice. New York 1964, London [1965]. For children.

Anti-woo: the lifeman's improved primer for non-lovers (the first lifemanship guide). 1965, New York 1965.

The complete golf gamesmanship. 1968, New York 1968 (as Golfmanship).

Potter also edited selections from Coleridge; *and Sara Coleridge's letters to Thomas Poole, pbd as* Minnow among tritons, *1934.*

LLEWELYN POWYS
1884–1939

Confessions of two brothers, J. C. Powys, Llewellyn [sic] Powys. Rochester NY 1916. Includes extracts from Powys' diaries with commentary by J. C. Powys.

Ebony and ivory. New York 1923 (preface by T. Dreiser), London 1923 (preface by E. Shanks), 1939 (rev) (Penguin), 1960 (introd by L. Wilkinson). Stories and sketches of life in East Africa.

Thirteen worthies. New York 1923 (preface by V. W. Brooks), London 1924. Essays.

Black laughter. New York [1924], London 1925, 1953 (foreword by N. Farson).

Honey and gall. Girard Kansas [1924]. Essays.

Cup-bearers of wine and hellebore. Girard Kansas [1924]. Essays on writers.

Skin for skin. New York [1925], London 1926 (900 copies), 1948 (with The verdict of Bridlegoose, 1926). Autobiography.

The verdict of Bridlegoose. New York [1926], London 1927 (900 copies), 1948 (with Skin for skin, 1925). Autobiography.

Henry Hudson. 1927, New York 1928. Biography.

The cradle of God. New York [1929], London 1929, 1949 (introd by E. Carr). Jewish development in Biblical times.

Apples be ripe. New York [1930], London 1930. Novel.

The pathetic fallacy: a study of Christianity. 1930, Philadelphia [1930] (as An hour on Christianity).

Impassioned clay. New York 1931, London 1931. Philosophical essay.

A pagan's pilgrimage. New York [1931], London 1931. A journey to Palestine.

The life and times of Anthony à Wood, abridged from A. Clark's edition and with an introduction by L. Powys. 1932.

Now that the gods are dead. New York 1932 (400 copies), London 1949 (with Glory of life, 1934). Philosophical essay.

Glory of life. 1934 (277 copies; Golden Cockerel press, wood engravings by R. Gibbings), 1949 (with Now that the gods are dead, 1932). Philosophical essay.

Earth memories. 1934. Essays on country life; rptd in Earth memories, New York 1938.

Damnable opinions. 1935.

Dorset essays. 1935. 18 essays rptd in Earth memories, New York 1938.

The twelve months. 1936. Essays.

Somerset essays. 1937.

Rats in the sacristy. 1937. Essays on writers.

Love and death: an imaginary autobiography. 1939, New York [1941].

A baker's dozen. Herrin Ill [1939] (493 copies), London 1941 (introd by J. C. Powys). Essays.

Swiss essays. 1947.

Letters

Letters. Ed L. Wilkinson 1943.

Advice to a young poet. 1949; ed R. L. Blackmore, Rutherford NJ 1969. Letters to K. Hopkins.

SIR HERBERT EDWARD READ
1893–1968

Mss in the Herbert Read Archive at the Univ of Victoria.

Collections

Selected writings: poetry and criticism, with foreword by Allan Tate. 1963, New York 1964. With some new material.

Collected poems. 1966, New York 1966.

§1
Prose

English pottery. 1924 (75 copies). With B. Rackham.

In retreat. 1925 (Hogarth essays). Experiences of the British Fifth Army, March 1918; rptd in Annals of innocence and experience, 1946 edn, below.

English stained glass. 1926, New York 1926.

Reason and Romanticism: essays in literary criticism. 1926, New York 1963.

English prose style. 1928, New York [1928], London 1952 (rev), New York [1952].

Phases of English poetry. 1928 (Hogarth lectures on literature ser), New York [1929], London 1950 (rev and enlarged), Norfolk Conn 1950.

The sense of glory: essays in criticism. Cambridge 1929, New York 1967.

Staffordshire pottery figures. 1929.

Ambush. 1930 (Criterion Miscellany). Autobiographical sketches and a poem, partly rptd in Annals of innocence and experience, 1940, below.

Julien Benda and the New Humanism. Seattle 1930.

Wordsworth: the Clark lectures. 1930, New York [1931], London 1949 (rev).

The place of art in a university: an inaugural lecture. Edinburgh 1931; rptd in The meaning of art, below.

The meaning of art. 1931, New York 1932 (as The anatomy of art; adds The place of art in a university, above), London 1936 (rev and enlarged), 1949 (rev and enlarged) (Pelican), 1951 (rev and enlarged), New York 1951, London 1968 (rev).

Form in modern poetry. 1932.

Art now: an introduction to the theory of modern painting and sculpture. 1933, 1936 (rev), New York 1937, London 1948 (rev and enlarged), New York [1948?], London 1960 [1961] (rev and enlarged), New York 1960 [1961].

The innocent eye. 1933. Recollections of childhood; rptd in Annals of innocence and experience, 1940, and in The contrary experience, 1963, below.

Art and industry: the principles of industrial design. 1934, 1944 (rev and enlarged), 1953 (rev), New York 1954, London 1956 [1957] (rev), Bloomington 1961, London 1966 (with rev introd).

Essential communism. 1935; rptd in Poetry and anarchism, 1938, and in Anarchy and order, 1954, below.

In defence of Shelley and other essays. 1936, Freeport NY 1968.

Art and society. 1937, New York 1937, London 1945 (rev with new appendix: William Hogarth), 1956 [1957] (corrected), New York 1966, London 1967 (with new preface).

Collected essays in literary criticism. 1938, 1951 (corrected), New York 1956 (as The nature of literature).

Poetry and anarchism. 1938; rptd in Anarchy and order, 1954, below.

Annals of innocence and experience. 1940, 1946 (rev and enlarged to include In retreat, 1925, above), New York 1947 (as The innocent eye). A substantial part rptd in The contrary experience, 1963, below.

The philosophy of anarchism. 1940. Pamphlet; rptd in Anarchy and order, 1954, below.

To hell with culture: democratic values are new values. 1941. Pamphlet; rptd in The politics of the unpolitical, 1943, and in To hell with culture and other essays, 1963, below.

Education through art. 1943, New York [1945], London 1958 (rev), New York [1958].

The politics of the unpolitical. 1943. Essays, mostly rptd in To hell with culture, and other essays, 1963, below.

The education of free men. 1944. Pamphlet; rptd in Education for peace, 1949, below.

A coat of many colours: occasional essays. 1945, 1956 (rev), New York 1956. On literature and art.

The grass roots of art: four lectures on social aspects of art in an industrial age. New York 1947 [1946], London 1947 (without subtitle, adds The future of art in an industrial civilisation [1943]), 1955 (with subtitle, rev and enlarged), New York 1955.

Education for peace. New York 1949, London 1950. Papers.

Art and the evolution of man. 1951. Lecture.

Byron. 1951 (Br Council pamphlet); rptd in The true voice of feeling, 1953, below.

Contemporary British art. 1951 (Pelican), 1964 (for 1965) (rev), Baltimore 1964.

The philosophy of modern art: collected essays. 1952, New York 1953.

The true voice of feeling: studies in English romantic poetry. 1953, New York 1953.

Anarchy and order: essays in politics. 1954.

Icon and idea: the function of art in the development of human consciousness. Cambridge Mass 1955, London 1955 (Charles Eliot Norton lectures).

The art of sculpture: the A. W. Mellon lectures in the fine arts 1954. New York 1956, London 1956.

The significance of children's art; Art as a symbolic language. Vancouver 1957. 2 lectures, the 2nd rptd in The forms of things unknown, 1960, below.

The tenth muse: essays in criticism. 1957, New York 1958. On literature, philosophy and art.

A concise history of modern painting. 1959, New York 1959, London 1968 (rev), New York [1968].

The forms of things unknown: essays towards an aesthetic philosophy. 1960, New York 1960.

Truth is more sacred: a critical exchange on modern literature between Edward Dahlberg and Herbert Read. 1961, New York [1961?].

A letter to a young painter [and other essays]. [1962], New York 1962.

The contrary experience: autobiographies. 1963, New York 1963. Includes previously unpbd material.

To hell with culture, and other essays on art and society. 1963, New York 1963.

Art and education. Melbourne 1964. Essays.

A concise history of modern sculpture. [1964], New York 1964.

Henry Moore: a study of his life and work. [1965], New York 1966.

The origins of form in art. [1965], New York 1965. Essays.

The redemption of the robot: my encounter with education through art. New York 1966.

T. S. E[liot]: a memoir. [Middletown Conn] 1966.

Art and alienation: the role of the artist in society. [1967], New York 1967. Essays.

Poetry and experience. 1967, New York 1967. Essays.

The cult of sincerity. 1968, New York 1968. Essays.

Essays in literary criticism: particular studies. 1969. Originally pbd as pt 2 of the 1951 edn of Collected essays in literary criticism, 1938, above.

Read frequently contributed introds, notes etc to books of reproductions, exhibition catalogues etc of work by contemporary artists; he also contributed, chs, introds etc to symposia and to surveys of art and literature.

Verse, Novel and Plays

Songs of chaos. 1915.

Auguries of life and death. 1919 (priv ptd). Poem in memory of Charles Read, killed in action 1918.

Eclogues: a book of poems. 1919.

Naked warriors. 1919. Poems, and a sketch.

Mutations of the Phœnix. Richmond Surrey 1923. Poems.

Collected poems 1913–25. 1926 (56 copies).

The end of a war. 1933. Poem.

The green child: a romance. 1935, 1947 (introd by Graham Greene), New York 1948 (introd by K. Rexroth).

Poems 1914–34. 1935, New York 1935. Poems 1913–25 with omissions and some 30 new poems; some revisions.

Thirty-five poems. 1940. Selected from the previous, with addns.

A world within a war. 1943 (50 copies). Poem, rptd in next.

A world within a war: poems. 1944, New York 1945.

Collected poems. 1946, Norfolk Conn 1951, London 1953 (corrected). Omits some early poems; with slight revisions.

Aristotle's mother: an argument in Athens; Thieves of mercy. In Imaginary conversations: eight radio scripts by Read [et al], ed R. Heppenstall 1948.

Moon's farm, and poems mostly elegiac. 1955, New York 1956. Title piece a dramatic dialogue for radio broadcast 21 Jan 1951.

The parliament of women: a drama in three acts. Hemingford Grey 1960 [1961] (100 copies). In prose and verse.
Lord Byron at the opera: a play for broadcasting. North Harrow 1963; broadcast 11 March 1953.

Principal Works Edited by Read

Hulme, T. E. Speculations: essays on humanism and the philosophy of art. 1924 [1923], New York 1924, London 1936 (corrected). Ed with A. R. Orage.
Worringer, W. R. Form in Gothic: authorized translation. 1927, New York 1964.
Hulme, T. E. Notes on language and style. Seattle 1929.
The London book of English prose. 1931, New York 1931 (as The anthology of English prose), London 1949 (rev, as The London book of English prose). With B. Dobrée.
The English vision (the English ideal as expressed by representative Englishmen): an anthology. 1933.
Unit I: the modern movement in English architecture, painting and sculpture. 1934.
Orage, A. R. Selected essays and critical writings. 1935. With D. Saurat.
Surrealism. 1936. Essays by various authors.
The knapsack: a pocket-book of prose and verse. 1939.
Kropotkin: selections from his writings. 1942.
The practice of design. 1946. Essays by various authors.
The London book of English verse. 1949, New York 1949, London 1952 (rev). With B. Dobrée.
Nash, P. Outline: an autobiography, and other writings. 1949.
The collected works of C. J. Jung. New York 1953–, London 1953–. With M. Fordham, G. Adler.
This way delight: a book of poetry for the young. New York 1956, London 1957.
Read also edited Burlington Mag *1933–9*, E & S *vol 21 1936, the* English master painter series *1940–, and the* Acanthus history of sculpture *1960–.*

§2

Burke, K. The calling of the tune. Kenyon Rev 1 1939. Largely an essay-review of Poetry and anarchism, 1938; rptd in his The philosophy of literary form, [Baton Rouge] 1941.
Greene, G. Read. Horizon 3 1941; rptd in his Lost childhood, 1951 and Collected essays, 1969. On Annals of innocence and experience, 1940.
Treece, H. (ed). Read: an introduction to his work by various hands. 1944.
'George Orwell' (E. A. Blair). [Review of A coat of many colours]. Poetry Quart Winter 1945; rptd in his Collected essays, vol 4 1968.
Berry, F. Herbert Read. 1953, 1961 (rev) (Br Council pamphlet).
Tate, A. In his Essays of four decades, Chicago [1968].
Herbert Read: a memorial symposium. Ed R. Skelton 1970. Originally pbd as Jan 1969 number of Malahat Rev.

IVOR ARMSTRONG RICHARDS
1893–1979

§1

The foundations of aesthetics. 1922, New York 1948. With C. K. Ogden and J. Wood.
The meaning of meaning: a study of the influence of language upon thought and of the science of symbolism. 1923, 1927 (rev), 1930 (rev), 1936 (rev), 1944 (rev), New York 1956. With C. K. Ogden.
Principles of literary criticism. 1924, New York 1925 (1924), London 1926 (with 2 new appendices).
Science and poetry. 1926, 1935 (rev and enlarged).

Practical criticism: a study of literary judgment. 1929, 1930 (corrected), New York 1950.
Mencius on the mind: experiments in multiple definition. 1932, New York 1932. With passages from Mencius in Chinese and English.
Basic rules of reason. 1933. Basic English.
Coleridge on imagination. 1934, New York 1950, London 1962 (with a new foreword).
Basic in teaching: East and West. 1935. Basic English.
The philosophy of rhetoric. New York 1936, London 1936.
Interpretation in teaching. [1938], New York [1938].
How to read a page. New York 1942, London 1943).
Basic English and its uses. 1943, New York 1943.
Learning Basic English: a practical handbook for English-speaking people. New York 1945. With C. M. Gibson.
The pocket book of Basic English: a self-teaching way into English with directions in Spanish, French, Italian, Portuguese and German. New York 1945, 1946 (rev), 1952 (with C. M. Gibson as English through pictures).
Nations and peace. New York 1947. Basic English.
The Republic of Plato: a version in simplified English. 1948.
The wrath of Achilles: The Iliad of Homer shortened and in a new translation by. New York 1950, London 1951.
Speculative instruments. 1955, Chicago 1955. Essays on interpretation and language.
First steps in reading English: a first book for readers to be. New York 1957. With C. M. Gibson.
Goodbye earth, and other poems. New York 1958, London 1958 [1959].
The screens, and other poems. New York 1960, London 1960 [1961]. Includes an essay, the Future of poetry, rptd in So much nearer, 1968, below.
Tomorrow morning, Faustus!: an infernal comedy. New York 1962, London 1962.
Why so, Socrates?: a dramatic version of Plato's dialogues, Euthyphro, Apology, Crito, Phaedo. Cambridge 1964.
Plato's Republic. Ed and tr Richards, Cambridge 1966.
So much nearer: essays towards a world English. New York 1968.
Internal colloquies: poems and plays. 1972.
Beyond. 1974.
Poetries: a collection of essays. Ed T. Eaton, Hague 1974.
Complementarities: uncollected essays. Ed J. P. Russo, Manchester 1977.

§2

Russell, B. The meaning of meaning. Dial 81 1926.
Eliot, T. S. Literature, science and dogma. Dial 82 1927. On Science and poetry, 1926.
—— The modern mind. In his Use of poetry and the use of criticism, 1933.
Harding, D. W. Evaluations 1: Richards. Scrutiny 1 1933; rptd in Determinations, 1934.
Leavis, F. R. Richards, Bentham and Coleridge. Scrutiny 3 1935; reply by W. Empson, 4 1935.
Ransom, J. C. The psychologist looks at poetry. Virginia Quart Rev 11 1935; rptd in his World's body, New York 1938.
—— In his New criticism, Norfolk Conn [1941].
Hyman, S. E. Richards and the criticism of interpretation. In his Armed vision, New York 1948.
Crane, R. S. Richards on the art of interpretation. Ethics 59 1949; rptd in Critics and criticism, ed Crane, Chicago 1952.
Wellek, R. On rereading Richards. Southern Rev 3 1967.
Brower, R. (ed). Richards: essays in his honor. New York 1973.

LLOYD LOGAN PEARSALL SMITH
1865–1946

§ 1

The youth of Parnassus and other stories. 1895, New York [1895], Oxford 1909 (as The youth of Parnassus and other stories of Oxford life).

Trivia: printed from the papers of Anthony Woodhouse esq by [i.e. written by] Pearsall Smith. 1902 (priv ptd, 300 copies), Garden City NY 1917 (rev), London 1918.

The life and letters of Sir Henry Wotton. 2 vols Oxford 1907.

Sonnets. [1908?] (priv ptd, 50? copies). Most rptd in next.

Songs and sonnets. 1909.

The English language. [1912], New York [1912], London 1952 (for 1953) (with epilogue by R. W. Chapman).

Donne's sermons: selected passages with essay. Oxford 1919.

More trivia. New York 1921, London 1922.

Words and idioms: studies in the English language. 1925.

The prospects of literature. 1927.

Afterthoughts. 1931, New York [1931]. Aphorisms.

On reading Shakespeare. 1933, New York [1933].

Reperusals and re-collections. 1936, Freeport NY 1968.

Unforgotten years. 1938, Boston 1939. Reminiscences.

Milton and his modern critics. 1940, Boston 1941.

A religious rebel: the letters of 'H.W.S.', Mrs Pearsall Smith. Ed her son, 1949 (for 1952).

A portrait of Logan Pearsall Smith, drawn from his letters and diaries and introduced by J. Russell. 1950.

Pearsall Smith assisted Robert Bridges and others to found the Society for Pure English 1913, and he contributed several Tracts. With Bernard Berenson he edited Golden Urn *3 issues Fiesole 1897–8 (priv ptd). He compiled a number of anthologies, including* A treasury of English aphorisms, *1928.*

§ 2

Gathorne-Hardy, R. Recollections of Pearsall Smith. 1949.

Connolly, C. In his Ideas and places, 1953.

MacCarthy, D. In his Memories, 1953.

ENID MARY STARKIE
1897–1970

Baudelaire. [1933], New York 1933, London 1957 (rewritten), Norfolk Conn 1958, London 1971 (Pelican). Biography.

Arthur Rimbaud in Abyssinia. Oxford 1937, Paris 1938 (as Rimbaud en Abyssinie, with new unpbd material).

Arthur Rimbaud. 1938, 1947 (rev), New York 1947, London 1961 (rev), New York 1962.

A lady's child. 1941. Autobiography.

Pétrus Borel en Algérie: sa carrière comme inspecteur de la colonisation. Oxford 1950.

André Gide. Cambridge 1953 (for 1954), New Haven Conn 1954.

Petrus Borel, the lycanthrope: his life and times. 1954, Norfolk Conn 1954.

From Gautier to Eliot: the influence of France on English literature 1851–1939. 1960.

Flaubert: the making of the master. [1967], New York; Flaubert the master, 1971.

Enid Starkie also edited Baudelaire, Les fleurs du mal, *1942. See J. Richardson,* Enid Starkie, *1973.*

ADRIAN DURHAM STOKES
1902–72

The thread of Ariadne. 1925.

Sunrise in the West: a modern interpretation of past and present. [1926].

The Quattro Cento—a different conception of the Italian renaissance: part 1, Florence and Verona. 1932.

Stones of Rimini. 1934.

To-night the ballet. 1934, New York [1935].

Russian ballets. 1935, New York [1936].

Colour and form. 1937.

Venice: an aspect of art. 1945.

Inside out: an essay in the psychology and aesthetic appeal of space. 1947. Autobiographical.

Art and science: a study of Alberti, Piero della Francesca and Giorgione. 1949.

Smooth and rough. 1951. Autobiographical.

Michelangelo: a study in the nature of art. 1955, New York 1956.

Greek culture and the ego: a psycho-analytic survey of an aspect of Greek civilization and of art. 1958.

Three essays on the painting of our time. 1961.

Painting and the inner world. 1963.

The invitation in art. 1965.

Venice. 1965.

Reflections on the nude. 1967.

The image in form: selected writings. Ed R. Wollheim 1972 (Pelican).

Critical writings. Ed L. Gowing 3 vols 1978.

GEOFFREY TILLOTSON
1905–69

On the poetry of Pope. Oxford 1938.

The rape of the lock and other poems. 1940, 1954 (rev), 1962 (rev) (Twickenham edn of the Poems of Pope, vol 2). Ed Tillotson.

Essays in criticism and research. Cambridge 1942, Hamden Conn 1967 (with new preface).

Criticism and the nineteenth century. 1951, Hamden Conn 1967. Essays.

Thackeray the novelist. Cambridge 1954, London 1963 (corrected).

Pope and human nature. Oxford 1958.

Augustan studies. 1961. Chs 1–4 rptd (corrected) as Augustan poetic diction, 1964.

Mid-Victorian studies. With K. Tillotson 1965.

KATHLEEN MARY TILLOTSON
b. 1906

Novels of the eighteen-forties. Oxford 1954, 1956 (corrected).

Dickens at work. 1957. With John Butt.

The tale and the teller. 1959; rptd in Mid-Victorian studies, 1965 (with essays by herself and her husband Geoffrey).

Also editor of Drayton's Works *vol 5 (1941) (with B. H. Newdigate); the Clarendon Dickens (Oliver Twist 1966) and the Pilgrim edn of Dickens's letters.*

EUSTACE MANDEVILLE WETENHALL TILLYARD
1889–1962

The poetry of Sir Thomas Wyatt: a selection and a study. 1929.

Milton. 1930, 1966 (rev, with preface by P. B. Tillyard), New York 1967.
Poetry direct and oblique. 1934, 1945 (rev).
The Miltonic setting past and present. Cambridge 1938, New York 1949.
Shakespeare's last plays. 1938, New York 1964.
The personal heresy: a controversy. 1939. On poetry and the poet; with C. S. Lewis.
The Elizabethan world picture. 1943, New York 1944.
Shakespeare's history plays. 1944, New York 1946.
Five poems 1470–1870. 1948, 1955 (as Poetry and its background: illustrated by five poems 1470–1870).
Shakespeare's problem plays. Toronto 1949, London 1950.
Studies in Milton. 1951.
The English Renaissance: fact or fiction? 1952, Baltimore 1952.
Milton. 1952, 1959 (rev) (Br Council pamphlet).
The English epic and its background. 1954, New York 1954.
The Metaphysicals and Milton. 1956.
The epic strain in the English novel. 1958, Fair Lawn NJ 1958.
The muse unchained: an intimate account of the revolution in English studies at Cambridge. [1958].
Some mythical elements in English literature. 1961, New York 1962 (as Myth and the English mind).
Essays: literary and educational. 1962, New York 1962.
Shakespeare's early comedies. Ed S. Tillyard 1965, New York 1965.

SIR DONALD FRANCIS TOVEY
1875–1940

Essays in musical analysis. 3 pts [1902].
A companion to Beethoven's pianoforte sonatas: complete analyses. 1931.
A companion to The art of fugue—Die Kunst der Fuge—J. S. Bach. 1931.
Essays in musical analysis. 6 vols 1935–9. Some English symphonists: a selection from Essays in musical analysis pbd 1941.
A musician talks. 2 vols 1941.
Beethoven. Ed H. Foss 1944.
Essays in musical analysis: chamber music. Ed H. Foss 1944.
Musical articles from the Encyclopaedia Britannica. Ed H. Foss 1944.
Essays and lectures on music. Ed H. Foss 1949, New York 1949.
The forms of music. New York 1956, London 1957. Essays, mostly from Encyclopaedia Britannica.

HELEN JANE WADDELL
1889–1965

Lyrics from the Chinese. 1913, New York 1935. Verse, based on J. Legge's prose trn of the Shih Ching.
The spoiled Buddha: a play in two acts. Dublin and London 1919.
The fairy ring (ten books of fairy tales for standards I–III) 10 pts 1921. Anon; texts simplified by another hand. Selection (with some additional unpbd tales), ed E. Colwell, restoring the original texts, pbd 1969 as The princess Splendour and other stories.
The wandering scholars. 1927, 1932 (rev and enlarged), 1934 (rev), New York 1934.
Mediaeval Latin lyrics. 1929, 1933 (rev), New York [1949]. Anthology, with trns and biographical notes.
The Abbé Prévost: a play in a prologue and three acts. Bungay [1931] (priv ptd), 1933 (Raven Miscellany).

The history of Chevalier des Grieux and of Manon Lescaut by the Abbé Prévost d'Exiles. Translated by H. Waddell, with an introduction by G. Saintsbury. 1931, New York 1931.
Peter Abelard: a novel. 1933, New York [1933].
Beasts and saints: translations by H. Waddell. 1934, New York [1934]. Extracts from mediaeval lives of saints.
The desert fathers: translations from the Latin with an introduction by H. Waddell. 1936, Ann Arbor 1957.
Poetry in the Dark Ages. Glasgow 1948, New York [1958]. W. P. Ker Memorial Lecture.

ERNEST WEEKLEY
1865–1954

The romance of words. 1912, 1913 (rev and enlarged), 1961 (introd by I. Brown), New York 1961.
The romance of names. 1914, 1922 (rev).
Surnames. 1916, New York 1927.
An etymological dictionary of modern English. 1921.
A concise etymological dictionary of modern English. 1924, New York 1924, London 1952 (rev), New York 1952. An abridgement of An etymological dictionary of modern English, 1921, above.
Words ancient and modern. 1926, New York 1926.
More words ancient and modern. 1927.
The English language. 1928, New York 1929, London 1952 (rev and enlarged with a ch on the history of American English by J. W. Clark).
Collins' essential English dictionary. [1929], [1934] (as The new essential English dictionary), [1939], (rev, as The modern English dictionary).
Adjectives—and other words. 1930.
Saxo Grammaticus: or first aid for the best seller. 1930, New York [1931] (as Cruelty to words: or first aid for the best seller).
Words and names. 1932.
Jack and Jill: a study in our Christian names. 1934, New York 1940.
Something about words. 1935.
Words ancient and modern. 1946, New York 1965. Selections, rev and extended, from Words ancient and modern, 1926, and More words ancient and modern, 1927, above.

BASIL WILLEY
1897–1978

The seventeenth-century background. 1934, New York 1950.
The eighteenth-century background. 1940, New York 1941.
Nineteenth-century studies: Coleridge to Matthew Arnold. 1949, New York 1949.
Christianity past and present. Cambridge 1952.
More nineteenth-century studies: a group of honest doubters. 1956, New York 1956.
Darwin and Butler: two versions of evolution. 1960, New York 1960.
The English moralists. 1964, New York 1964.
Spots of time: a retrospect of the years 1897–1920. 1965, New York 1965.
Cambridge and other memories 1920–53. 1968, New York 1969.
Religion to-day. 1969.

FRANK PERCY WILSON
1889–1963

The plague in Shakespeare's London. Oxford 1927.
Elizabethan and Jacobean. Oxford 1945.
Marlowe and the early Shakespeare. Oxford 1953.
Seventeenth-century prose: five lectures. Berkeley 1960.
The proverbial wisdom of Shakespeare. Cambridge 1961; rptd in Shakespearian and other studies, Oxford 1969, below.
The English drama 1485–1585. Ed G. K. Hunter, Oxford 1969 (OHEL).
Shakespearian and other studies. Ed Helen Gardner, Oxford 1969.
Shakespeare and the new bibliography. Ed Helen Gardner, Oxford 1970.
Also edns, notably Plague pamphlets *(Oxford 1925), a revision of R. B. McKerrow's* Nashe *(Oxford 1958) and the 3rd edn of the* Oxford dictionary of English proverbs *(Oxford 1970). Wilson was general editor with B. Dobrée of OHEL. See* Elizabethan and Jacobean studies presented to F. P. Wilson in honour of his seventieth birthday, *ed H. Davis and Helen Gardner, Oxford 1959.*

JOHN DOVER WILSON
1881–1969

John Lyly. Cambridge 1905. Harness Prize essay.
The Marprelate controversy. In CHEL vol 3, Cambridge 1909.
The puritan attack upon the stage. In CHEL vol 6, Cambridge 1910.
Martin Marprelate and Shakespeare's Fluellen: a new theory of the authorship of the Marprelate tracts. 1912.
The copy for Hamlet 1603, and the Hamlet transcript 1593. 1918.
Bibliographical links between the three pages [believed to be in Shakespeare's handwriting] and the Good Quartos. In Shakespeare's hand in the play of Sir Thomas More, ed A. W. Pollard, Cambridge 1923.
The task of Heminge and Condell. In Studies in the First Folio, written for the Shakespeare Association, 1924.
The essential Shakespeare: a biographical adventure. Cambridge 1932.
The manuscript of Shakespeare's Hamlet and the problem of its transmission: an essay in critical bibliography. 2 vols Cambridge 1934, New York 1934.
What happens in Hamlet. Cambridge 1935, New York 1935.
The fortunes of Falstaff. Cambridge 1943, New York 1944.
Shakespeare histories at Stratford 1951. 1952, New York 1952. With T. C. Worsley.
Shakespeare's happy comedies. 1962, Evanston Ill 1962.
An introduction to the sonnets of Shakespeare for historians and others. Cambridge 1963.
Milestones on the Dover Road. 1969. Autobiography.

Editions

Life in Shakespeare's England: a book of Elizabethan prose. Cambridge 1911, 1944 (rev) (Pelican). Abridged for children 1939 (as Through Elizabethan eyes).
The new Shakespeare. 39 vols Cambridge 1921–66. Ed with A. Quiller-Couch (to 1931), and (later) with G. I. Duthie, J. C. Maxwell and A. Walker. Wilson edited most of the plays. Known as 'New Cambridge' edn.
Arnold, M. Culture and anarchy. Cambridge 1932, 1935 (corrected) (Landmarks in the History of Education ser).
Dover Wilson pbd much on education, largely wrote the Board of Education report, The teaching of English in England, *1921, and pbd some Workers' Educational Assoc pamphlets. He edited* Cambridge *anthologies, 1910–32 (with W. T.*

Young), Shakespeare problems, *1920–53 (to 1944 with A. W. Pollard), and* Landmarks in the history of education, *1931–5.*

THOMAS JAMES WISE
1859–1937

Wise's unpbd correspondence with Gosse is in the Brotherton Library, Univ of Leeds; a virtually complete collection of his forged pamphlets, with other material relating to him, is held by the Wrenn Library, Univ of Texas.

§ 1

Verses. 1882 (priv ptd, 35 copies).
A complete bibliography of the writings in prose and verse of John Ruskin, with a list of the more important Ruskiniana. Ed Wise 2 vols 1893 (for 1889–93). With J. P. Smart.
The Ashley Library: a list of books printed for private circulation by T. J. Wise. 1893 (priv ptd). Other lists ptd in 1895 and 1897.
A reference catalogue of British and foreign autographs and manuscripts. 1893–8. Pts 1–7 ed Wise.
Spenser's Faerie Queene. Ed Wise 6 vols 1894–7.
Literary anecdotes of the nineteenth century. Ed Wise 2 vols 1895–6. With W. R. Nicoll.
A complete bibliography of the writings in prose and verse of Robert Browning. 1897 (priv ptd, 50 copies).
The Ashley Library: a catalogue of books, manuscripts and autograph letters, collected by Wise. 1901 (priv ptd, 20 copies).
The Ashley Library: a catalogue of printed books, manuscripts and autograph letters, collected by Wise. 2 vols 1905–8 (priv ptd, 12 sets).
A bibliography of the writings of Alfred, Lord Tennyson. 2 vols 1908 (priv ptd, 110 sets).
A bibliography of the writings in prose and verse of Samuel Taylor Coleridge. (Coleridgeiana: a supplement). 2 vols 1913–19 (500 sets).
A bibliography of the writings in prose and verse of George Henry Borrow. 1914 (priv ptd, 100 copies).
A bibliography of the writings in prose and verse of William Wordsworth. 1916 (priv ptd, 100 copies).
A bibliography of the writings in prose and verse of the members of the Brontë family. 1917 (priv ptd, 100 copies).
Swinburne, A. C. The posthumous poems. Ed Wise 1917. With E. Gosse.
A bibliography of the writings in prose and verse of Elizabeth Barrett Browning. 1918 (priv ptd, 100 copies).
The letters of Swinburne. Ed Wise 2 vols 1918. With E. Gosse.
A bibliography of the writings in prose and verse of Algernon Charles Swinburne. 2 vols 1919–20 (priv ptd, 125 sets). A rev version was pbd in Wise's edn of The complete works of Swinburne, 1925–7, below.
A bibliography of the writings in prose and verse of Walter Savage Landor. 1919. With S. Wheeler.
A bibliography of the writings of Joseph Conrad 1895–1920. 1920 (priv ptd, 150 copies), 1921 (rev and enlarged) (priv ptd, 170 copies).
The Ashley Library: a catalogue of printed books, manuscripts and autograph letters, collected by T. J. Wise. 11 vols 1922–36 (priv ptd, 200 sets).
A Shelley library: a catalogue of printed books, manuscripts and autograph letters by Shelley, Harriet Shelley and Mary Wollstonecraft Shelley. 1924 (priv ptd, 180 copies).
A Swinburne library: a catalogue of printed books, manuscripts and autograph letters collected by Wise. 1925 (priv ptd, 200 copies).
The complete works of Swinburne. Ed Wise 20 vols 1925–7 (Bonchurch edn). With E. Gosse.
Two Lake Poets: a catalogue of printed books, manuscripts

and autograph letters by Wordsworth and Coleridge collected by Wise. 1927 (priv ptd, 160 copies).

A Byron library: a catalogue of printed books, manuscripts and autograph letters collected by Wise. 1928 (priv ptd, 230 copies).

A Conrad library: a catalogue of printed books, manuscripts and autograph letters collected by Wise. 1928 (priv ptd, 205 copies).

A Landor library: a catalogue of printed books, manuscripts and autograph letters collected by Wise. 1928 (priv ptd, 195 copies). Introd by S. Wheeler.

A Brontë library: a catalogue of printed books, manuscripts and autograph letters by the members of the Brontë family, collected by Wise. 1929 (priv ptd, 150 copies).

A Browning library: a catalogue of printed books, manuscripts and autograph letters by Robert and Elizabeth Barrett Browning, collected by Wise. 1929 (priv ptd, 190 copies).

A Dryden library: a catalogue of printed books, manuscripts and autograph letters collected by Wise. 1930 (priv ptd, 160 copies).

A Pope library: a catalogue of plays, poems and prose writings, collected by Wise. 1931 (priv ptd, 160 copies).

The Shakespeare Head Brontë. Ed Wise 19 vols Oxford 1931–8. With J. A. Symington.

A bibliography of the writings in verse and prose of Byron. 2 vols 1932–3 (priv ptd, 180 sets).

Letters of Robert Browning collected by Wise, edited with an introduction and notes by T. L. Hood. New Haven 1933, London 1933.

Letters

Letters of Wise to John Henry Wrenn: a further inquiry into the guilt of certain nineteenth-century forgers. Ed F. E. Ratchford, New York 1944.

Between the lines: letters and memoranda interchanged by H. B. Forman and Wise, with a foreword by C. H. Pforzheimer and an introductory essay and notes by F. E. Ratchford. Austin 1945. Implicating Forman in the Wise forgeries.

§ 2

Carter, J. and G. Pollard. An enquiry into the nature of certain 19th-century pamphlets. 1934.

—— Working papers for a second edition of An enquiry into the nature of certain nineteenth century pamphlets. Oxford 1967–.

Carter, J. T. J. Wise. Spectator 21 May 1937; corrected in his Books and book-collectors, 1956.

—— Wise and his forgeries. Atlantic Monthly 175 1945; rptd ibid.

—— Wise after the event. Bookseller 5 Sept 1964; rptd ibid.

Partington, W. Forging ahead: the true story of the upward progress of Wise. New York [1939], London [1946] (enlarged, as T. J. Wise in the original cloth).

Foxon, D. F. Wise and the pre-Restoration drama: a study in theft and sophistication. 1959 (Trans Bibl Soc, suppl 19).

Todd, W. B. (ed). Wise centenary studies: essays by J. Carter, G. Pollard, W. B. Todd. Austin [1959].

HENRY CECIL KENNEDY WYLD
1870–1945

The historical study of the mother tongue: an introduction to philological method. 1906, New York 1906.

The growth of English: an elementary account of the present form of our language and its development. 1907, New York 1907.

The teaching of reading in training colleges. 1908.

Elementary lessons in English grammar. Oxford 1909.

The place names of Lancashire: their origin and history. 1911. With T. O. Hirst.

Collected papers of Henry Sweet. Ed Wyld, Oxford 1913.

A short history of English. 1914, 1927 (rev), New York 1927.

A history of modern colloquial English. 1920, 1921 (rev), Oxford 1936 (with addns), New York 1937.

Studies in English rhymes from Surrey to Pope: a chapter in the history of English. 1923, New York 1965.

The universal dictionary of the English language. Ed H. C. Wyld. [1931–2], New York 1932.

Some aspects of the diction of English poetry. Oxford 1933.

The best English: a claim for the superiority of Received Standard English. Oxford 1934. SPE tract.

Little and Ives complete standard universal dictionary. Ed Wyld and E. Partridge, New York 1957 (also as Little and Ives Webster dictionary).

II. HISTORIANS, AUTOBIOGRAPHERS, WRITERS ON POLITICS, SOCIETY, ECONOMICS ETC

SIR ERNEST BARKER
1874–1960

The political thought of Plato and Aristotle. 1906, New York 1906.

Italy and the west 410–476. In Cambridge medieval history vol 1, Cambridge 1911.

The Dominican order and Convocation. Oxford 1913.

Nietzsche and Treitschke: the worship of power in modern Germany. Oxford 1914.

Why we are at war: Great Britain's case, by members of the Oxford Faculty of Modern History [Barker et al]. Oxford 1914, 1914 (rev and enlarged).

Mothers and sons in war time, and other pieces. 1915, 1917 (rev and enlarged), 1918 (enlarged). Rptd from The Times.

Political thought in England from Herbert Spencer to the present day. [1915], 1928 (rev as Political thought in England 1848 to 1914).

The submerged nationalities of the German empire. Oxford 1915.

Ireland in the last fifty years 1866–1916. Oxford 1917, 1919 (enlarged).

Greek political theory: Plato and his predecessors. 1918, New York [1960]. Rev and enlarged edn of The political thought of Plato and Aristotle 1906, above.

Linguistic oppression in the German empire. 1918, New York 1918.

The future government of India and the Indian civil service. Ed Barker 1919.

The crusades. 1923.

Greek political thought and theory in the fourth century. In Cambridge ancient history vol 6, Cambridge 1927.

National character and the factors in its formation. 1927, 1948 (rev).

Church, state and study: essays. 1930, Michigan 1957 (as Church, state and education; with a new preface).

Burke and Bristol: a study of the relations between Burke and his constituency during the years 1774–80. Bristol 1931. Lectures.

The citizen's choice. Cambridge 1937. Essays.

Oliver Cromwell and the English people. Cambridge 1937.

The values of life: essays on the circles and centres of duty. 1939.

British statesmen. 1941 (Britain in Pictures).

The ideas and ideals of the British Empire. Cambridge 1941, New York 1969.

Britain and the British people. 1942, 1955 (rev).

Reflections on government. 1942. New York 1958.

The development of public services in Western Europe 1660–1930. 1944, Hamden Conn 1966.

British constitutional monarchy [1945], 1950 (rev), New York 1950 (Br Information ser), London 1952 (rev), 1955 (rev). Pamphlet.

Essays on government. Oxford 1945, 1951 (rev and enlarged).

The politics of Aristotle. Tr Barker, Oxford 1946, New York 1958.

The character of England. Ed Barker, Oxford 1947.

Reflections on leisure: adapted from broadcast talks originally composed for Persia. [1947].

Father of the man: memories of Cheshire, Lancashire and Oxford 1874–98. [1948].

Traditions of civility: eight essays. Cambridge 1948, Hamden Conn 1967.

Principles of social and political theory. Oxford 1951.

Age and youth: memories of three universities; and Father of the Man. 1953.

W. P. Ker, a scholar. Cambridge 1953. Rptd from Times.

The European inheritance. Ed Barker et al 3 vols Oxford 1954.

From Alexander to Constantine: passages and documents illustrating the history of social and political ideas, 336 BC–AD 337. Tr with introd, notes and essays by Barker, Oxford 1956.

Social and political thought in Byzantium, from Justinian I to the last Palaeologus; Passages from Byzantine writers and documents. Tr with introd and notes by Barker, Oxford 1957.

SIR ISAIAH BERLIN
b. 1909

Karl Marx: his life and environment. 1939, 1948 (bibliography rev), New York 1959, London 1960 (corrected), 1963 (rev), New York [1963].

The hedgehog and the fox: an essay on Tolstoy's view of history. 1953, New York 1953.

A marvellous decade [Russian literature 1838–48]. Encounter 1955–6.

Mr Churchill in 1940. [1964], Boston 1964. Rptd essay-review of Churchill, Gathering storm.

Four essays on liberty. 1969.

Vico and Herder. 1976.

Selected writings. Ed H. Hardy 4 vols 1978–. Essays.

Berlin tr Turgenev, First love 1950.

WILLIAM HENRY BEVERIDGE, 1ST BARON BEVERIDGE
1879–1963

Unemployment: a problem of industry. 1909, 1912 (with additional appendices), 1930 (with substantial new section, as Unemployment: a problem of industry 1909 and 1930).

The public service in war and peace. 1920.

Insurance for all and everything. [1924]. Rptd from Daily News.

British food control. 1928, New Haven 1928.

Causes and cures of unemployment. 1931.

Tariffs: the case examined. 1931. By a committee of economists with Beveridge as chairman.

Changes in family life. 1932.

Planning under Socialism, and other addresses. 1936.

Prices and wages in England, from the twelfth to the nineteenth century. Vol 1, 1939. By Beveridge et al.

Social insurance and allied services. 2 pts 1942. Report presented to Parliament Nov 1942 ('Beveridge Report'). Abridged as Social insurance and allied services: the Beveridge report in brief, 1942. *See* G. D. H. Cole, Beveridge explained, 1942.

The pillars of security and other war-time essays and addresses. 1943, New York 1943.

Full employment in a free society: a report. 1944, New York 1945, London 1953 (with new preface).

The price of peace. 1945, New York 1945.

Why I am a Liberal. [1945].

India called them. 1947. Biography of his parents.

Voluntary action: a report on methods of social advance. 1948, New York 1948.

Antipodes notebook. 1949. With J. Beveridge.

The evidence for voluntary action. 1949. Ed Beveridge with A. F. Wells.

The London School of Economics and the University of London. In The Webbs and their work, ed M. Cole 1949.

On and off the platform: under the Southern Cross. Wellington, 1949. With J. Beveridge.

Power and influence. 1953, New York 1955. Autobiography; with bibliography.

A defence of free learning. 1959.

The London School of Economics and its problems 1919–37. 1960.

SIR DENIS WILLIAM BROGAN
1900–74

The American political system. 1933, New York 1933 (as Government of the people), London 1943 (new preface), New York 1944 (new preface), London 1947 (rev preface).

Proudhon. 1934.

Abraham Lincoln. 1935, New York 1963.

The development of modern France 1870–1939. 1940, New York 1940 (as France under the Republic), London 1967 (rev).

Is innocence enough?: some reflections on foreign affairs. 1941.

Politics and law in the United States. Cambridge 1941.

USA: an outline of the country, its people and institutions. Oxford 1941.

The English people: impressions and observations. 1943, New York 1943.

The American problem. 1944.

The free state: some considerations on its practical value. 1945, New York 1945.

French personalities and problems. 1946, New York 1947.

American themes. 1948, New York 1949. Articles from periodicals.

The era of Franklin D. Roosevelt: a chronicle of the New Deal and global war. New Haven 1950, London 1952 (as Roosevelt and the New Deal).

The price of revolution. 1951, New York [1951].

An introduction to American politics. 1954, New York 1954 (as Politics in America), 1969 (rev).

The American character. New York 1956.

The French nation from Napoleon to Pétain 1814–1940. 1957, New York 1957.

America in the modern world. New Brunswick 1960, London 1960 (for 1961).
Political patterns in today's world. 1963, New York 1963. With D. V. Verney.
American aspects. 1964, New York 1964.
Worlds in conflict. 1967, New York 1967.
Also a novel, Stop on the green light, 1950 (*under the pseudonym Maurice Barrington*).

SIR ARTHUR WYNNE MORGAN BRYANT
b. 1899

The spirit of conservatism. 1929.
King Charles II. 1931, 1955 (rev).
Macaulay. 1932, New York 1933.
Samuel Pepys: the man in the making. Cambridge 1933.
The England of Charles II. 1934, 1960 (as Restoration England).
The national character. 1934. Broadcast talks.
Samuel Pepys: the years of peril. Cambridge 1935.
The American ideal. 1936. Biographical essays.
George V. 1936.
Stanley Baldwin: a tribute. [1937], New York [1937].
Humanity in politics. [1938]. Essays.
Samuel Pepys: the saviour of the navy. Cambridge 1938.
English saga 1840–1940. 1940, New York [1941] (as Pageant of England 1840–1940).
Unfinished victory. 1940. On Germany 1918–33.
The years of endurance 1793–1812. 1942, New York 1942, London 1975 (illustr).
Years of victory 1802–12. 1944, New York 1945.
Historian's holiday. 1946, 1951 (enlarged). Essays.
The age of elegance 1812–22. 1950, New York 1951.
The story of England: [vol 1] makers of the realm. 1953, Boston 1954, London 1961 (illustrated edn), New York 1962 (as Makers of England: vol 1 of an historical trilogy entitled Atlantic saga).
The turn of the tide 1939–43: a study based on the diaries and autobiographical notes of Viscount Alanbrooke. 1957, New York 1957.
Triumph in the West 1943–6: based on the diaries and autobiographical notes of Viscount Alanbrooke. 1959, New York 1959.
The story of England: [vol 2] the age of chivalry. 1963, New York 1964.
The fire and the rose. 1965, New York 1966, London 1972 (rev). Narrative of 9 decisive events in English history.
The medieval foundation. 1966, New York 1967 (as The medieval foundation of England).
Protestant island. 1967, New York 1967.
The lion and the unicorn. 1969.
Nelson. 1970.
Jackets of green. 1972. On rifle brigade.
The Great Duke. 1971. On Wellington.

JOHN BAGNELL BURY
1861–1927

A history of the later Roman Empire from Arcadius to Irene, 395 AD to 800 AD. 2 vols 1889.
The students' Roman Empire. 1893, New York [190?].
The history of the decline and fall of the Roman Empire by E. Gibbon. Ed Bury. 7 vols 1896–1900, 1909–14 (rev), 3 vols New York 1946.
A history of Greece to the death of Alexander the Great. 1900, 2 vols 1902 (rev), 1 vol 1913 (rev), New York 1937, London 1951 (rev by R. Meiggs). An abridgment, History of Greece for beginners, was pbd 1903, New York 1907 (as A student's history of Greece).
The Ottoman conquest. In The Cambridge modern history vol 1, Cambridge 1902.

The life of Saint Patrick and his place in history. 1905.
Russia 1462–1682. In The Cambridge modern history vol 5, Cambridge 1908.
The ancient Greek historians. 1909, New York 1909.
The imperial administrative system in the ninth century, with a revised text of the Kletorologion of Philotheos. 1911, New York [1958].
A history of the Eastern Roman Empire from the fall of Irene to the accession of Basil I, AD 802–67. 1912, Ann Arbor 1958.
A history of freedom of thought. [1913], New York [1913], London 1952 (epilogue by H. J. Blackham). *See also* H. Belloc, Anti-Catholic history: how it is written, 1914.
The idea of progress: an inquiry into its origin and growth. 1920, New York 1932 (introd by C. A. Beard).
The Hellenistic age and the history of civilization. In The Hellenistic age: aspects of Hellenistic civilization treated by Bury et al, Cambridge 1923.
History of the later Roman Empire from the death of Theodosius I to the death of Justinian, AD 395 to AD 565. 2 vols 1923, New York 1958.
The Achaeans and the Trojan war; Homer; Greek literature from the eighth century to the Persian wars; The age of illumination; Dionysius of Syracuse. In Cambridge ancient history vols 2, 4–6, ed Bury et al, Cambridge 1924, 1926–7.
The invasion of Europe by the barbarians. 1928, New York 1963.
History of the Papacy in the 19th century 1864–78. Ed R. H. Murray 1930, New York 1964 (augmented edn by F. C. Grant).
Selected essays. Ed H. Temperley, Cambridge 1930. Includes lectures previously pbd separately.

SIR HERBERT BUTTERFIELD
1900–79

The historical novel: an essay. Cambridge 1924.
The peace tactics of Napoleon 1806–8. Cambridge 1929.
The Whig interpretation of history. 1931, New York 1951.
Napoleon. 1939, 1940 (rev), New York 1956.
The statecraft of Machiavelli. 1940, New York 1956.
The Englishman and his history. Cambridge 1944.
Lord Acton. 1948 (Historical Assoc pamphlet).
Christianity and history. 1949, New York 1950.
George III, Lord North and the people 1779–80. 1949, New York 1968.
The origins of modern science 1300–1800. 1949, New York 1951, London 1957 (rev), New York 1957.
Christianity in European history. 1951.
History and human relations. 1951, New York 1952.
Liberty in the modern world. Toronto 1952.
Christianity, diplomacy and war. 1953, New York 1953.
Man on his past: the study of the history of historical scholarship. Cambridge 1955, Boston 1960 (with new preface).
George III and the historians. 1957, New York 1959 (rev).
International conflict in the twentieth century: a Christian view. 1960, New York 1960.
The universities and education today. 1962.
Diplomatic investigations: essays in the theory of international politics. 1966, Cambridge Mass 1966. Ed Butterfield, with M. Wight; contributions by Butterfield.
Butterfield also edited Cambridge Historical Jnl *1938–52.*
See The diversity of history: essays in honour of Butterfield, *ed J. H. Elliott et al, 1970.*

EDWARD HALLETT CARR
b. 1892

Dostoevsky. 1931, Boston 1931. Biography.
The romantic exiles. 1933, New York 1933. Portraits of nineteenth-century political exiles from Russia.

Karl Marx: a study in fanaticism. 1934.

International relations since the peace treaties. 1937, 1940 (enlarged), 1947 (as International relations between the two world wars 1919–39), New York 1966.

Michael Bakunin. 1937, New York 1961. **Biography.**

Britain: a study of foreign policy from the Versailles Treaty to the outbreak of war. 1939.

Propaganda in international politics. Oxford 1939, New York 1939. Pamphlet.

The twenty years' crisis 1919–39: an introduction to the study of international relations. 1939, New York 1964.

The future of international government. 1941. Pamphlet; with S. de Madariaga.

The future of nations: independence or interdependence? 1941.

Conditions of peace. 1942, New York 1942.

Nationalism and after. 1945, New York 1945.

The Soviet impact on the western world. 1946, New York 1947.

International relations between the two world wars 1919–39. 1947.

A history of Soviet Russia. 14 vols 1950–78, New York 1951–78.

Studies in revolution. 1950, 1962 (with corrections), New York 1964.

German–Soviet relations between the two world wars 1919–39. Baltimore 1951, London 1952.

The new society. 1951, Boston 1957 (with new preface).

What is history? 1961, New York 1962.

1917: before and after. 1969, New York 1969 (as The October Revolution: before and after).

Carr edited the series Ambassadors at large: studies in the foreign policies of the leading powers. *He was assistant editor of* The Times 1941–6.

See Essays in honour of Carr, ed C. Abramsky 1974.

SIR WINSTON LEONARD SPENCER CHURCHILL
1874–1965

The Chartwell Trust Archives are now housed in Bodley.

Bibliographies

Woods, F. A bibliography of the works of Churchill. 1963, 1967 (rev), 1975 (rev). Includes trns, and books on Churchill.

§1

The story of the Malakand Field Force: an episode of the frontier war. 1898, 1899 (rev, with new preface).

The river war: an historical account of the reconquest of the Soudan. Ed F. Rhodes 2 vols 1899, 1 vol 1902 (rev, with new preface and additional ch), 1933 (with new introd).

Savrola: a tale of the revolution in Laurania. New York 1900, London 1900, New York 1956 (with new foreword).

London to Ladysmith via Pretoria. 1900.

Ian Hamilton's march: together with extracts from the diary of Lieutenant H. Frankland, a prisoner of war at Pretoria. 1900. Continuation of above. These, and the Story of the Malakand Field Force and the River war, reissued, abridged, 1962 (as Frontiers and wars).

Mr Brodrick's army. 1903. Speeches on the Army Scheme of 1901.

Lord Randolph Churchill. 2 vols 1906, 1 vol 1907, [1952] (enlarged with new introd).

For free trade: a collection of speeches. 1906.

For Liberalism and free trade: principal speeches during the campaign in Dundee, May 1908. Dundee 1908. Pamphlet.

My African journey. 1908, New York 1909.

Liberalism and the social problem. 1909, New York 1910. Speeches; introd by H. W. Massingham.

The people's rights, selected from his Lancashire and other recent speeches. [1910].

The world crisis. 5 vols in 6, 1923–31, New York 1923–31, 1 vol London 1931 (abridged and rev with additional ch on The battle of the Marne), New York 1931, 3 vols London [1933–4] (as The Great War, abridged edn pbd in parts with new foreword dated 1933), 1 vol 1933 (priv ptd) (as Sandhurst edition of The world crisis, abridged and rev), 2 vols 1939 (enlarged with new foreword dated 1938).

Parliamentary government and the economic problem: the Romanes lecture. Oxford 1930; rptd in Thoughts and adventures, 1932, below.

My early life: a roving commission. 1930, New York 1930 (as A roving commission: my early life; preface enlarged for American readers), 1939 (introd by D. Thompson).

India: speeches and an introduction. 1931.

Thoughts and adventures. 1932, New York 1932 (as Amid these storms: thoughts and adventures). Preface by E. Marsh.

Marlborough: his life and times. 4 vols 1933–8 (vol 1 rev 1934), 6 vols New York 1933–8, 2 vols London 1947, 1 vol New York [1968] (abridged with introd by H. S. Commager).

Great contemporaries. 1937, New York 1937, London 1938 (rev and enlarged), 1943 (omitting chs on Trotsky and Roosevelt).

Arms and the covenant: speeches, compiled by R. S. Churchill. [1938], New York 1938 (as While England slept: a survey of world affairs 1932–8).

Step by step 1936–9. 1939, New York [1939]. Collected newspaper articles.

Addresses delivered in the year nineteen hundred and forty to the people of Great Britain, of France and to the members of the English House of Commons. San Francisco 1940 (250 copies).

Broadcast addresses to the people of Great Britain, Italy, Poland, Russia and the United States. San Francisco 1941 (250 copies).

Into battle: speeches, compiled by R. S. Churchill. 1941, New York [1941] (as Blood, sweat and tears).

The unrelenting struggle: war speeches compiled by C. Eade. 1942, Boston 1942.

The end of the beginning: war speeches 1942, compiled by C. Eade. 1943, Boston 1943.

Onwards to victory: war speeches 1943, compiled by C. Eade. 1944, Boston 1944.

The dawn of liberation: war speeches 1944, compiled by C. Eade. 1945, Boston 1945.

Victory: war speeches 1945, compiled by C. Eade. 1946, Boston 1946.

Secret session speeches, compiled by C. Eade. 1946, New York 1946.

The Second World War. 6 vols Boston 1948–53, London 1948–54, [1955] ('Chartwell' rev edn), 1 vol 1959 (as Memoirs of the Second World War: an abridgement [by D. Kelly] with an epilogue by the author on the post war years), Boston 1959, 2 vols New York 1959 (as The Second World War: extracts from Kelly's abridgement), 12 vols London 1964 (illustr).

The sinews of peace: post-war speeches. Ed R. S. Churchill 1948, Boston 1949.

Painting as a pastime. 1948, New York 1950. Reproductions of paintings by Churchill, with text rptd from Hobbies and Painting as a pastime in Thoughts and adventures, 1932, above.

Europe unite: speeches 1947 and 1948. Ed R. S. Churchill 1950, Boston 1950.

In the balance: speeches 1949 and 1950. Ed R. S. Churchill 1951, Boston 1952.

The war speeches, compiled by C. Eade. 3 vols 1952, Boston 1953. Contains addns to and omissions from the 7 vols pbd 1941–6.

Stemming the tide: speeches 1951 and 1952. Ed R. S. Churchill 1953, Boston 1954 (for 1953).

A history of the English-speaking peoples. 4 vols 1956–8, New York 1956–8, London 1958 ('Chartwell' edn, illustr), 1 vol 1964 (as The island race, abridged by T. Baker), New York 1964, 1965 (abridged by H. S. Commager).

The unwritten alliance: speeches 1953 to 1959. Ed R. S. Churchill 1961.

Complete speeches 1897–1963. Ed R. R. James, New York 1974.

Collected essays. Ed M. Wolff 4 vols 1976.

§2

Keynes, J. M. Churchill on the war; Churchill on the peace. In his Essays in biography, 1933.

Rowse, A. L. Churchill and English history. In his English spirit, 1944.

— The later Churchills. 1958.

— Churchill as historian. HLQ 25 1962.

Berlin, I. Churchill and F. D. Roosevelt. Cornhill Mag 164 1949; Atlantic Monthly 184 1949. Pbd separately 1964 (as Mr Churchill in 1940).

Cowles, V. Churchill: the era and the man. 1953.

Bonham Carter, V. Churchill as I knew him. 1965.

Churchill, R. S. and M. Gilbert. Winston S. Churchill. 1966–.

Ashley, M. Churchill as historian. 1968.

James, R. R. Churchill: a study in failure 1900–39. 1970, 1973 (Pelican).

Pelling, H. Winston Churchill. 1974.

SIR JOHN HAROLD CLAPHAM
1873–1946

Economic change. In Cambridge modern history vol 10, Cambridge 1907.

The woollen and worsted industries. 1907.

Great Britain and free trade 1841–52. In Cambridge modern history vol 11, Cambridge 1909.

The Abbé Sieyès: an essay in the politics of the French Revolution. 1912.

The economic development of France and Germany 1815–1914. Cambridge 1921.

Pitt's first decade 1782–92. In Cambridge history of British foreign policy vol 1, Cambridge 1922.

Zollverein negotiations. In Cambridge history of British foreign policy vol 2, Cambridge 1923.

An economic history of modern Britain. 3 vols Cambridge 1926–38, vol 1 1930 (rev), 3 vols 1950–2 (vol 1 with corrections).

Commerce and industry in the Middle Ages. In Cambridge medieval history vol 6, Cambridge 1929.

The study of economic history. Cambridge 1929. Inaugural lecture.

The Bank of England: a history. 2 vols Cambridge 1944.

A concise economic history of Britain from the earliest times to 1750. Ed J. Saltmarsh, Cambridge 1949.

Clapham was the first editor of Cambridge Studies in Economic History, *and with Eileen Power was editor of the* Cambridge economic history of Europe.

GEORGE DOUGLAS HOWARD COLE
1889–1959

The world of labour: a discussion of the present and future of trade unionism. 1913, 1915 (rev), 1919 (new introd).

Labour in war time. 1915.

Self-government in industry. 1917, 1920 (rev). Rptd in pt from New Age and other periodicals.

Trade unionism on the railways: its history and problems. 1917. With R. Page Arnot.

Labour in the Commonwealth: a book for the younger generation. [1918], New York 1920.

The payment of wages: a study in payment by results under the wage-system. [1918], 1928 (rev).

Chaos and order in industry. 1920.

Guild socialism re-stated. 1920.

Social theory. 1920, New York 1920, London 1921 (rev).

The future of local government. 1921.

Guild socialism: a plan for economic democracy. New York 1921.

Labour in the coal-mining industry 1914–21. Oxford 1923.

Out of work: an introduction to the study of unemployment. 1923, New York 1923.

Trade unionism and munitions. Oxford 1923.

Workshop organisation. Oxford 1923.

The life of William Cobbett. [1924], 1947 (rev).

Organised labour: an introduction to trade unionism. 1924.

Robert Owen. 1925, 1930 (as The life of Robert Owen).

A short history of the British working class movement 1789–1925(–7). 3 vols 1925–7, 1932 (new foreword), 1937 (with supplementary ch to 1937), 1948 (rev and continued to 1947).

The next ten years in British social and economic policy. 1929.

Politics and literature. 1929, New York 1929.

Gold, credit and employment: four essays for laymen. 1930, New York 1931.

British trade and industry, past and future. 1932.

Economic tracts for the times. 1932.

The intelligent man's guide through world chaos. 1932, New York 1932 (as A guide through world chaos).

Modern theories and forms of industrial organisation. 1932.

Theories and forms of political organisation. 1932.

The intelligent man's review of Europe today. 1933, New York 1933. With M. Cole.

What everybody wants to know about money: a planned outline of monetary problems, by nine economists from Oxford. 1933, New York 1933. Planned and edited by Cole.

What is this socialism?: letters to a young inquirer. 1933.

A guide to modern politics. 1934, New York 1934. With M. Cole.

Some relations between political and economic theory. 1934.

Studies in world economics. 1934, Freeport, New York 1967.

What Marx really meant. 1934, New York 1934.

Principles of economic planning. 1935, New York 1935 (as Economic planning).

The simple case for socialism. 1935.

The condition of Britain. 1937. With M. Cole.

The People's Front. 1937.

Practical economics: or studies in economic planning. 1937 (Pelican)

The common people 1746–1938. 1938, 1946 (enlarged, brought up to date), 1956 (corrected) (Pelican), New York 1939 (as The British common people 1746–1938), 1947 (as The British people 1746–1946). With R. W. Postgate.

The machinery of socialist planning. 1938.

Persons and periods: studies. 1938, 1945 (shorter version) (Pelican), New York 1967. Articles etc from the 30's.

Socialism in evolution. 1938 (Pelican).

British trade-unionism to-day. 1939, 1953 (rev, as An introduction to trade unionism), New York 1955.

Plan for democratic Britain. [1939].

War aims. 1939.

British working class politics 1832–1914. 1941.

Chartist portraits. 1941, 1965 (for 1964) (introd by A. Briggs), New York 1964.

Europe, Russia and the future. 1941, New York 1942.

Great Britain in the post-war world. 1942.

Fabian socialism. 1943.

The means to full employment. 1943.

A century of co-operation. 1944. History of the Co-operative Movement.

Money: its present and future. 1944, 1947 (rev), 1954 (rev, as Money, trade and investment).

Building and planning. 1945.

The intelligent man's guide to the post-war world. 1947.

Local and regional government. 1947.

Samuel Butler and The way of all flesh. 1947, Denver 1948 (as Samuel Butler).

A history of the Labour Party from 1914. 1948.

The meaning of Marxism. 1948, Ann Arbor 1964. Largely based on What Marx really meant, 1934, above.

World in transition. New York 1949. Based on The intelligent man's guide to the post-war world, 1947, above.

Essays in social theory. 1950. Articles from the 40's.

Socialist economics. 1950.

The British Co-operative movement in a socialist society: a report written for the Fabian Society. 1951.

Introduction to economic history 1750–1950. 1952.

A history of socialist thought. 5 vols 1953–60, New York 1953–60.

Attempts at General Union: a study in British trade union history 1818–34. 1953.

Studies in class structure. 1955.

The post-war condition of Britain. 1956, New York 1957 (for 1956).

The case for industrial partnership. 1957.

Cole also pbd a large number of pamphlets, Fabian tracts, study outlines etc. He edited Cobbett, *Hutchinson's University Library, Library of Social Studies, Oxford Studies in Economics, Nuffield College Social Reconstruction Survey (with A. D. Lindsay) etc. He also edited* Guildsman *Sept 1919–Aug 1923 (it became* Guild Socialist *in July 1921), and* New Standards *Oct 1923–Oct 1924. He has also written 2 vols of poetry,* New beginnings *and* The record, *1914, and* The crooked world, *1933; a novel,* The Brooklyn murder, *1923, and further numerous detective stories with Margaret Postgate, afterwards Cole.*

ALFRED DUFF COOPER, 1ST VISCOUNT NORWICH
1890–1954

Talleyrand. 1932, New York 1932.

Haig. 2 vols 1935–6, Garden City NY 1936.

The Second World War: first phase. 1939, New York 1939. Speeches and articles, with connecting narrative.

David. 1943, New York 1943. Biography of David, King of Israel.

Sergeant Shakespeare. 1949, New York 1950. Biography.

Translations and verses. 1949.

Operation heartbreak: a story. 1950, New York 1951.

Old men forget: the autobiography. 1953, New York 1954.

GEORGE GORDON COULTON
1858–1947

Father Rhine. [1899]. An account of a summer tour, illustr by the author.

Public Schools and the public needs. 1901.

Medieval studies. 20 nos separately pbd 1905–31.

Popular Romanist Church history. [1905].

Friar's lantern. 1906. A novel.

From St Francis to Dante: a translation of all that is of primary interest in the Chronicle of the Franciscan Salimben 1221–88. 1906, 1907 (rev and enlarged), New York [1968].

Chaucer and his England. 1908, 1910 (corrected, with 2nd preface in reply to review by G. K. Chesterton), 1921 (corrected with note), 1927 (with new preface), 1963 (with new bibliography by T. W. Craik).

A medieval garner: human documents from the four centuries preceding the Reformation. Ed Coulton 1910, 4 vols Cambridge 1928–30 (rev, as Life in the Middle Ages), 1 vol 1930.

Social life in Britain from the Conquest to the Reformation. Cambridge 1918, New York 1918, Cambridge 1919 (with index).

Christ, St Francis and to-day. Cambridge 1919.

Five centuries of religion. 4 vols Cambridge 1923–50. Vol 1 rptd 1929 (corrected).

A Victorian schoolmaster: Henry Hart of Sedburgh. 1923.

The medieval village. Cambridge 1925.

Chesterton, G. K. The superstition of the sceptic, with a correspondence between the author and Coulton. Cambridge 1925.

Art and the Reformation. Oxford 1928, Hamden Conn 1969.

The Black Death. 1929 (for 1928), New York 1929 (for 1930).

The Inquisition. 1929, New York 1929.

Crusades, commerce and adventure. 1930.

The medieval scene: an informal introduction to the Middle Ages. Cambridge 1930.

Reservation and catholicity: a discussion between A. H. Villiers and Coulton on the Bishop of Gloucester's text: Reservation is, in every sense of the word, a Catholic custom. Oxford 1930.

Romanism and truth. 2 vols 1930–1, Milwaukee 1930–1.

In defence of the Reformation: three lectures, with discussions. 1931. Infallibility; Persecution; The Reformation.

Papal infallibility. 1932, Milwaukee 1932.

Two saints: St Bernard & St Francis. Cambridge 1932. Chs from vols 1–2 of Five centuries of religion, above.

Scottish abbeys and social life. Cambridge 1933.

H. W. Fowler. Oxford 1934 (SPE tract 43).

Divorce, Mr Belloc and the Daily Telegraph. Taunton 1937, 1937 (rev). See H. Belloc, The case of Dr Coulton, 1938.

Sectarian history. Taunton 1937. A defence of H. C. Lea.

Inquisition and liberty. 1938, Gloucester Mass 1969.

Medieval panorama: the English scene from Conquest to Reformation. Cambridge 1938, New York 1938.

Europe's apprenticeship: a survey of medieval Latin, with examples. 1940.

Studies in medieval thought. 1940, New York 1965 (for 1966).

Fourscore years: an autobiography. Cambridge 1943, 1944 (corrected), New York 1944.

Is the Catholic Church anti-social?: a debate between Coulton and A. Lunn. 1946.

Early drawings and etchings. Cambridge [1948]. 22 drawings etc.

Coulton wrote a number of other controversial pamphlets and also a large number of pamphlets advocating compulsory military service. He edited a number of school text books; the series Cambridge Studies in Medieval Life and Thought, *18 vols Cambridge 1920–50; and, with Eileen Power, the series* Broadway Medieval Library, *10 vols 1928–31.*

GOLDSWORTHY LOWES DICKINSON
1862–1932

From king to king: the tragedy of the puritan revolution. 1891, New York 1907 (rev). Dialogues on historical figures, 1632–62.

Revolution and reaction in modern France. 1892, 1927 (rev with new preface and conclusion).

The development of parliament during the nineteenth century. 1895.

The Greek view of life. 1896, 1909 (rev with new preface), 1957 (with preface by E. M. Forster), Ann Arbor 1958.

Poems. 1896 (priv ptd). Anon.

Letters from John Chinaman. 1901 (anon), New York 1903 (as Letters from a Chinese official: being an Eastern view of Western civilization, with a new introduction; anon), London 1907 (as by Dickinson), New York 1932 (as Hands off China!: the letters of a Chinese official; anon), London 1946 (introd by E. M. Forster).

The meaning of good: a dialogue. Glasgow 1901, New York 1906.

A modern symposium. 1905, New York 1905, London 1962 (introd by E. M. Forster), New York 1962, 1963 (introd, The uses of Dickinson, by L. Filler).

Religion: a criticism and a forecast. 1905, New York 1905.

Justice and liberty: a political dialogue. 1908, New York 1908.

A wild rose and other poems. 1910 (priv ptd).

Religion and immortality. 1911, Boston 1911. Essays, with one previously pbd lecture.

Appearances: being notes of travel. 1914, Garden City NY 1914.

An essay on the civilizations of India, China and Japan. 1914.

The European anarchy. 1916, New York 1916.

The choice before us. 1917, New York 1917.

Causes of international war. 1920, New York 1920.

The Magic Flute: a fantasia. 1920.

War: its nature, cause and cure. 1923.

The international anarchy 1904–14. 1926, New York [1926], London 1937 (foreword by A. Salter).

After two thousand years: a dialogue between Plato and a modern young man. 1930, New York [1931].

Points of view: a series of broadcast addresses. 1930, Freeport NY [1969]. By Dickinson et al.

John McT. E. McTaggart. Cambridge 1931.

Plato and his dialogues. 1931, New York [1932].

Dickinson also wrote a number of pamphlets on the First World War and the League of Nations and wrote introds to similar pamphlets by others; he edited The Swarthmore International Handbooks, *8 vols 1920–1 and, with H. O. Meredith,* The Temple Greek and Latin Classics, *6 vols 1906–7.*

SIR ROBERT CHARLES KIRKWOOD ENSOR
1877–1958

Modern poems. 1903.

Modern socialism: as set forth by socialists in their speeches, writings and programmes. Ed Ensor 1904, 1907 (rev and enlarged), 1910 (rev and enlarged).

Belgium. [1915], New York 1915.

Odes, and other poems. 1917.

Catherine: a romantic poem; with a preface on narrative poetry. 1921.

Columbus: a historical poem. 1925.

Courts & judges in France, Germany and England. 1933.

England 1870–1914. Oxford 1936 (Oxford History of England 14).

Herr Hitler's self-disclosure in Mein Kampf. Oxford 1939, New York 1939. Pamphlet.

Who Hitler is. 1939, New York 1939. Pamphlet.

Hedge leaves. 1942. Verse.

A miniature history of the war, down to the liberation of Paris. 1944, New York 1945, London 1945 (enlarged, to the end of the war in Europe).

The uphill war, Sept 1939–Nov 1942. 1944. Pamphlet.

Ensor was leader-writer for Manchester Guardian *1902–4,* Daily News *1909–11, and chief leader-writer for* Daily Chron *1912–30. He contributed weekly articles on foreign affairs to* Sunday Times *under pen-name Scrutator 1940–53.*

EDWARD EVAN EVANS-PRITCHARD
1902–73

Witchcraft, oracles and magic among the Azande. Oxford 1937.

The Nuer: a description of the modes of livelihood and political institutions of a Nilotic people. Oxford 1940.

The political system of the Anuak of the Anglo-Egyptian Sudan. 1940.

Some aspects of marriage and the family among the Nuer. Livingstone, Northern Rhodesia 1945.

The Sanusi of Cyrenaica. Oxford 1949.

Kinship and marriage among the Nuer. Oxford 1951.

Social anthropology. 1951, Glencoe Ill 1952. Broadcast lectures.

Nuer religion. Oxford 1956.

Essays in social anthropology. 1962, New York 1963.

The position of women in primitive societies and other essays in social anthropology. 1965, New York 1965.

Theories of primitive religion. Oxford 1965.

Evans-Pritchard is a general editor of Oxford Monographs on Social Anthropology *(1963–) and also the* Oxford Library of African Literature *(1964–) for which he edited a collection of folk-tales,* The Zande trickster *(1967).*

SIR KEITH GRAHAME FEILING
1884–1977

Toryism: a political dialogue. 1913.

A history of the Tory party 1640–1714. Oxford 1924, 1959 (corrected).

England under the Tudors and Stuarts. [1927].

British foreign policy 1660–72. 1930.

Sketches in nineteenth-century biography. 1930.

What is conservatism? 1930 (Criterion miscellany).

The second Tory party 1714–1832. 1938.

The life of Neville Chamberlain. 1946.

A history of England from the coming of the English to 1918. 1950, New York 1951.

Warren Hastings. 1954, Hamden Conn 1967.

In Christ Church hall. 1960, New York 1960. Essays.

See Essays in British history presented to Feiling, *ed H. R. Trevor-Roper 1964.*

SIR CHARLES HARDING FIRTH
1857–1936

Oliver Cromwell and the rule of the Puritans in England. 1900, New York 1900, Oxford 1953 (introd by G. M. Young) (WC), London 1962 (introd P. H. Hardacre).

Cromwell's army. 1902, 1912 (illustr, corrected, with new preface), 1921 (corrected, new preface).

A plea for the historical teaching of history: an inaugural lecture. Oxford 1904.

The last years of the Protectorate 1656–8. 2 vols 1909, New York 1964.

The House of Lords during the Civil War. 1910.
Historical novels. 1922 (Historical Assoc leaflet).
Modern languages at Oxford 1724–1929. Oxford 1929.
A commentary on Macaulay's History of England. Ed
G. Davies 1938, New York [1965].
Essays, historical & literary. Ed G. Davies, Oxford 1938.
The regimental history of Cromwell's army. 2 vols Oxford
1940. With G. Davies.

Principal Works Edited by Firth

Hutchinson, Mrs L. Memoirs of the life of Colonel
Hutchinson. 2 vols 1885, 1906 (rev).
Cavendish, M. The life of William Cavendish, Duke of
Newcastle. 1886, 1906 (rev).
The Clarke papers: selections from the papers of William
Clarke, secretary to the Council of the Army 1647–9, and
to General Monck and the commanders of the army in
Scotland 1651–60. 4 vols 1891–1901 (Camden Soc new
ser 49, 54, 61–2), New York 1965.
The memoirs of Edward Ludlow 1625–72. 2 vols Oxford
1894.
Scotland and the Commonwealth: letters and papers
relating to the military government of Scotland 1651–3.
Edinburgh 1895 (Scottish History Soc Pbns 18).
The journal of Joachim Hane 1653–4. Oxford 1896.
Scotland and the Protectorate: letters and papers relating
to the military government of Scotland 1654–9. Edin-
burgh 1899 (Scottish Historical Soc Pbns 31).
The narrative of General Venables, with an appendix of
papers relating to the expedition to the West Indies and
the conquest of Jamaica 1654–5. 1900.
Naval songs and ballads. 1908 (Navy Records Soc Pbns
33). Selection.
Acts and ordinances of the Interregnum 1642–60. 3 vols
1911. With R. S. Rait.
Macaulay, T. B. The history of England. 6 vols 1913–15,
New York 1968.
An American garland: being a collection of ballads relating
to America 1563–1759. Oxford 1915, Detroit 1969.

HERBERT ALBERT LAURENS
FISHER
1865–1940

The medieval empire. 2 vols 1898, New York 1898.
Studies in Napoleonic statesmanship: Germany. Oxford
1903, New York 1968.
Brumaire; The Codes; The French dependencies, 1800–
14; The first Restoration, 1814–15; St Helena. In The
Cambridge Modern History, vols 8–9, Cambridge 1904–
6.
The history of England from the accession of Henry VII
to the death of Henry VIII 1485–1547. 1906, New York
1969.
Bonapartism. Oxford 1908.
Frederick William Maitland: a biographical sketch. Cam-
bridge 1910.
The republican tradition in Europe. 1911, New York
1911.
Napoleon. [1913], New York [1913].
Educational reform: speeches. Oxford 1918.
Studies in history and politics. Oxford 1920, New York 1967.
The common weal. Oxford 1924, New York 1968.
James Bryce. 2 vols 1927, New York 1927.
Paul Vinogradoff: a memoir. Oxford 1927; rptd in Col-
lected papers of Vinogradoff vol 1, Oxford 1928.
Our new religion. 1929, New York 1930. On Christian
Science.
If Napoleon had escaped to America. In If it had hap-
pened otherwise, ed J. C. Squire 1931.
A history of Europe. 3 vols 1935, Boston 1935, 1936, 1 vol
London 1936, 3 vols 1938 (rev and enlarged), Boston
1939, 2 vols London 1943, 1952 (as A history of Europe

from the earliest times to 1713; A history of Europe from
the beginning of the 18th century to 1937).
Pages from the past. 1939, New York 1969.
The background and issues of the war. Oxford 1940.
An unfinished autobiography. 1940.

GEORGE PEABODY GOOCH
1873–1968

History of English democratic ideas in the seventeenth
century. Cambridge 1898, New York 1912, Cambridge
1927 (as English democratic ideas in the seventeenth
century, with notes and appendices by H. J. Laski), New
York [1959].
Europe and the French Revolution; Great Britain and
Ireland 1792–1815 (1832–41); The growth of historical
science. In The Cambridge Modern History, vols 8, 9,
10, 12, Cambridge 1904–10.
History of our time 1885–1911. [1911], New York [1911],
London 1946 (as History of our time 1885–1914).
History and historians in the nineteenth century. 1913,
New York 1949, London 1952 (rev), Boston 1959.
Political thought in England from Bacon to Halifax. 1915.
Germany and the French revolution. 1920, New York
1966.
Life of Lord Courtney. 1920.
History of modern Europe 1878–1919. 1923, New York
1923.
Germany. 1925.
Recent revelations of European diplomacy. 1927; en-
larged successively 1928, 1930, 1940.
Studies in modern history. 1931.
Before the war: studies in diplomacy. 2 vols 1936, 1938.
Studies in diplomacy and statecraft. 1942.
Courts and cabinets. 1944, New York 1946. Biographical
studies.
Frederick the Great: the ruler, the writer, the man. 1947,
New York 1947.
Studies in German history. 1948.
Maria Theresa, and other studies. 1951, Hamden Conn
1965.
Catherine the Great, and other studies. 1954, Hamden
Conn 1966.
Louis XV: the monarchy in decline. 1956.
Under six reigns. 1958. Autobiography.
The Second Empire. 1960.
French profiles: prophets and pioneers. 1961.
Historical surveys and portraits. 1966, New York 1966.

PHILIP GUEDALLA
1889–1944

Collections and Selections

Collected essays. 4 vols [1927].
Uniform edition of the works. 5 vols 1937–8.

§1

The partition of Europe: a text-book of European history
1715–1815. Oxford 1914.
Supers and supermen: studies in politics, history and
letters. 1920, New York 1924.
The second Empire: Bonapartism, the Prince, the President, the Emperor. 1922, New York 1922, London 1932
(rev).
Masters and men: essays. 1923, New York 1923.
A gallery. 1924, New York 1924. Studies mainly of contemporary authors and politicians.
Independence day: a sketch book. 1926, New York 1926
(as Fathers of the Revolution).
Palmerston. 1926, New York 1927.

Conquistador: American fantasia. 1927, New York 1928.
Bonnet and shawl: an album. [1928], New York 1930. Biographical sketches of six women of the 19th century.
The Duke [of Wellington]. 1931, New York 1931 (as Wellington).
Argentine tango. 1932, New York 1933.
The Hundred Days. 1934, New York [1934].
The hundred years [1837–1936]. 1936, New York 1937.
The hundredth year [1930]. 1939, New York 1939.
Mr Churchill: a portrait. 1941, New York [1942].
The two marshals: Bazaine, Pétain. 1943, New York [1943].
Middle East 1940–2: a study in air power. 1944.

LUCY BARBARA HAMMOND
1873–1961
and
JOHN LAWRENCE LE BRETON HAMMOND
1872–1949

The village labourer 1760–1832: a study in the government of England before the Reform Bill. 1911.
The town labourer 1760–1832: the new civilization. 1917.
The skilled labourer 1760–1832. 1919.
Lord Shaftesbury. 1923, New York 1924.
The rise of modern industry. 1925, New York 1926, London 1937 (rev and enlarged).
The age of the Chartists 1832–54: a study of discontent. 1930, Hamden Conn 1962.
James Stansfeld: a Victorian champion of sex equality. 1932.
The bleak age: based on The age of the Chartists. 1934, 1947 (rev) (Pelican).

FRIEDRICH AUGUST VON HAYEK
b. 1899

Prices and production. 1931, 1935 (rev and enlarged), New York 1967.
Monetary nationalism and international stability. 1937, New York 1964.
Profits, interest and investment, and other essays on the theory of industrial fluctuations. 1939.
The pure theory of capital. 1941.
The road to serfdom. 1944, Chicago 1944, 1956 (with foreword by Hayek).
Individualism and economic order. 1949, Chicago 1957.
John Stuart Mill and Harriet Taylor: their correspondence and subsequent marriage. Ed Hayek 1951, Chicago 1951.
The counter-revolution of science: studies on the abuse of reason. Glencoe Ill [1952].
The sensory order: an inquiry into the foundations of theoretical psychology. 1952, Chicago 1952.
The political ideal of the rule of law. Cairo 1955.
The constitution of liberty. Chicago 1960, London 1960.
Studies in philosophy, politics and economics. 1967, Chicago 1967.
Law, legislation and liberty. 1973–.
See Essays on Hayek, ed. F. Machlup 1977.

RICHARD HOPE HILLARY
1919–43

The last enemy. 1942, New York 1942 (as Falling through space), London 1943 (foreword by E. Linklater).

LEONARD TRELAWNY HOBHOUSE
1864–1929

The Labour movement. 1893, New York 1912 (rev), London 1913. Preface by R. B. Haldane.
The theory of knowledge: a contribution to some problems of logic and metaphysics. 1896, [1921] (with new preface).
Mind in evolution. 1901, 1915 (rev), 1926 (with 2 new appendices).
Democracy and reaction. 1904.
Lord Hobhouse: a memoir. 1905. With J. L. Le B. Hammond.
Morals in evolution: a study in comparative ethics. 2 vols 1906, 1 vol 1915 (rev), New York 1915, London 1951 (introd by M. Ginsberg).
Liberalism. [1911], New York 1911, 1964 (introd by A. P. Grimes).
Social evolution and political theory. New York 1911. Lectures.
Development and purpose: an essay towards a philosophy of evolution. 1913, 1927 (rev and partly rewritten).
The historical evolution of property in fact and in idea. In Property—its duties and rights: essays by various writers, 1913, New York 1922.
The material culture and social institutions of the simpler peoples: an essay in correlation. 1915 (Univ of London Monographs on Sociology). With G. C. Wheeler and M. Ginsberg.
The world in conflict. 1915.
Questions of war and peace. 1916.
Principles of sociology. 4 vols 1918–24, vols 1–3 New York 1918–22.
Hobhouse was closely associated with Manchester Guardian *from 1897 until the end of his life, contributing frequently 1915–25; he edited* Sociological Rev *1903–5, and was political editor of* Tribune *1906–7; with E. A. Westermarck he edited* Univ of London Monographs on Sociology, *from 1913.*
See S. Collini, Liberalism and sociology, *Cambridge 1979.*

JOHN ATKINSON HOBSON
1858–1940

The physiology of industry: being an exposure of certain fallacies in existing theories of economics. 1889, New York 1956. With A. F. Mummery.
Problems of poverty: an inquiry into the industrial condition of the poor. 1891.
The evolution of modern capitalism: a study of machine production. 1894, 1906 (rev), 1917 (rev), 1926 (rev).
Co-operative labour upon the land and other papers: the report of a conference. Ed Hobson 1895.
The problem of the unemployed: an enquiry and an economic policy. 1896.
John Ruskin: social reformer. 1898, Boston 1898.
The economics of distribution. 1900.
The war in South Africa: its causes and effects. 1900, New York 1969.
The psychology of jingoism. 1901.
The social problem: life and work. 1901.
Imperialism: a study. 1902, New York 1902, London 1905 (rev), 1938 (rev), Ann Arbor 1965 (introd by P. Siegelman).
International trade: an application of economic theory. 1904, New York 1966.
Canada today. 1906.
The fruits of American protection: the effects of the Dingley Tariff upon the industries of the country and especially upon the well being of the people. 1907.
The crisis of Liberalism: new issues of democracy. 1909.

The industrial system: an inquiry into earned and un-
earned income. 1909, 1910 (rev), New York 1969
(introd by A. L. Bekenstein).
A modern outlook: studies of English and American ten-
dencies. 1910. Rptd from Nation.
An economic interpretation of investment. [1911].
The science of wealth. [1911], New York [1911], London
1934 (rev), 1950 (rev by R. F. Harrod).
Gold, prices and wages, with an examination of the quan-
tity theory. 1913.
Traffic in treason: a study of political parties. 1914.
Work and wealth: a human valuation. 1914, New York
1914, London 1933 (rev).
Towards international government. 1915.
The new protectionism. 1916, New York 1916.
Democracy after the war. 1917.
Richard Cobden: the international man. 1918, New York
1919, London 1968 (introd by N. Masterman).
Taxation in the new state. 1919.
The morals of economic internationalism. Boston 1920.
Problems of a new world. 1921.
The economics of unemployment. 1922, 1931 (rev).
Incentives in the new industrial order. 1922.
Free-thought in the social sciences. 1926.
The living wage: a report. 1926. With H. N. Brailsford,
A. C. Jones.
Notes on law and order. 1926 (Hogarth Essays).
The conditions of industrial peace. 1927.
Wealth and life: a study in values. 1929, Boston [1929] (as
Economics and ethics: a study in social values).
Rationalization and unemployment: an economic dilemma.
1930.
God and mammon: the relations of religion and economics.
1931, New York 1931.
L. T. Hobhouse: his life and work. 1931. With M. Gins-
berg.
Poverty in plenty: the ethics of income. 1931, New York
1931.
The recording angel: a report from earth. 1932.
Democracy and a changing civilization. 1934.
Veblen. 1936, New York 1937.
Property and improperty. 1937.
Confessions of an economic heretic. 1938.

JOHN MAYNARD KEYNES,
1ST BARON KEYNES
1883–1946

Collections
Collected writings. 1971– (Royal Economic Soc).

§1

Indian currency and finance. 1913.
The economic consequences of the peace. 1919, New York
1920.
Mr Lloyd George's general election. 1920. Pamphlet,
extracted from preceding.
A treatise on probability. 1921.
A revision of the treaty: being a sequel to The economic
consequences of the peace. 1922, New York 1922.
A tract on monetary reform. 1923, New York 1924 (as
Monetary reform).
Alfred Marshall 1842–1924: a memoir. [1924]; rptd in
Essays in biography, 1933, below.
The economic consequences of Mr Churchill. 1925, New
York [1925] (as The economic consequences of sterling
parity); rptd, in part, in Essays in persuasion, 1931,
below.
A short view of Russia. 1925 (Hogarth Essays); rptd in
Essays in persuasion, 1931, below.
The end of laissez-faire. 1926. Pamphlet, based on lec-

tures; rptd, in part, in Essays in persuasion, 1931,
below.
Official papers by Alfred Marshall. Ed Keynes 1926.
Can Lloyd George do it?: an examination of the Liberal
pledge [to reduce unemployment]. 1929. Pamphlet,
with H. D. Henderson.
A treatise on money. 2 vols 1930, New York 1930.
Essays in persuasion. 1931, New York 1932.
The world's economic crisis and the way of escape. 1932.
By Keynes et al.
Essays in biography. 1933, New York 1933, London 1951
(with 3 new essays, ed G. Keynes), New York 1951.
The means to prosperity. 1933, New York [1933], Buffalo
1959 (bibliography by S. E. Harris). Pamphlet.
The general theory of employment, interest and money.
1936, New York 1936.
Hume, D. An abstract of A treatise of human nature,
1740: a pamphlet hitherto unknown. Ed Keynes and
P. Sraffa, Cambridge 1938.
How to pay for the war: a radical plan for the Chancellor of
the Exchequer. 1940, New York [1940]. Pamphlet.
The balance of payments of the United States. [1946].
Two memoirs: Dr Melchior, a defeated enemy; and My
early beliefs. 1949, New York 1949.
The Arts Council: its policy and hopes. [1951].
Keynes edited Economic Jnl 1912–45, *and, with others,*
Cambridge Economic Handbooks *from 1922.*

§2

Rowse, A. L. Socialism and Mr Keynes. Nineteenth
Century 119 1932; rptd in his End of an epoch, 1947.
—— Mr Keynes and the Labour movement. 1936.
Munby, A. N. L. Keynes and his books. TLS 19 Oct 1946.
Pigou, A. C. J. M. Keynes. Proc Br Acad 32 1946.
—— Keynes's 'General theory': a retrospective view.
1950.
Harris, S. E. (ed). The new economics: Keynes's influence
on theory and public policy. New York 1947.
—— Keynes: economist and policy maker. New York
1955.
Klein, L. R. The Keynesian revolution. New York 1947,
[1966] (rev).
Keynes 1883–1946: a memoir prepared by direction of the
Council of King's College. Cambridge 1949.
Leavis, F. R. Keynes, Lawrence and Cambridge. Scru-
tiny 16 1949; rptd in his Common pursuit, 1952.
Keynes, F. A. In her Gathering up the threads: a study in
family biography, Cambridge 1950.
Harrod, R. F. The life of Keynes. 1951, 1972 (Pelican).
Russell, B. Portraits from memory II: Keynes and
Strachey. Listener 17 July 1952.
Garnett, D. Keynes, Strachey and Virginia Woolf in 1917.
London Mag 2 1955.
Bell, C. In his Old friends: personal recollections, 1956.
Stewart, M. Keynes and after. 1967 (Pelican).
Moggridge, D. E. (ed). Keynes. 1974.
Keynes, M. (ed). Essays on Keynes. Cambridge 1975.

DAVID KNOWLES
(MICHAEL CLIVE KNOWLES)
1896–1974

The English mystics. 1927.
The Benedictines. 1929, New York 1930 (with introd by
J. H. Diman), Saint Leo Fla 1962 (with introd by M. R.
Bowman).
The monastic order in England: a history from the times of
St Dunstan to the Fourth Lateran Council. Cambridge
1940, 1963 (with additional bibliography and notes).
The religious houses of medieval England. 1940. A cata-
logue; *see also* Medieval religious houses 1953, below.
The religious orders in England. 3 vols Cambridge 1948–

59, 1 vol Cambridge 1976 (vol 3 abridged as Bare ruined choirs).

The episcopal colleagues of Archbishop Thomas Becket. Cambridge 1951.

The monastic constitutions of Lanfranc. Tr with introd and notes by Knowles 1951.

Monastic sites from the air. Cambridge 1952 (Cambridge Air Surveys 1). With J. K. S. St Joseph.

Medieval religious houses: England and Wales. 1953. With R. N. Hadcock. An expanded version of The religious houses of medieval England, 1940, above.

Charterhouse: the medieval foundation in the light of recent discoveries. 1954. With W. F. Grimes.

The English mystical tradition. [1960], New York 1961.

The evolution of medieval thought. 1962, Baltimore 1962.

Saints and scholars: twenty-five medieval portraits. Cambridge 1962.

Great historical enterprises [and] Problems in monastic history. [1963].

The historian and character and other essays. Ed C. N. L. Brooke and G. Constable, Cambridge 1963.

From Pachomius to Ignatius: a study in the constitutional history of the religious orders. Oxford 1966.

The nature of mysticism. New York 1966 London 1967 (as What is mysticism?).

The Middle Ages. New York [1968], London 1969. With D. Obolensky.

Christian monasticism. 1969, New York 1969.

Thomas Becket. 1970.

Knowles edited Downside Rev *1930–4; the new series of* Cambridge studies in medieval life and thought *1951–; and was one of the general editors of* Cambridge air surveys *1952–.*

HAROLD JOSEPH LASKI
1893–1950

§1

Studies in the problem of sovereignty. 1917, New Haven 1917.

Authority in the modern state. New Haven 1919.

Political thought in England from Locke to Bentham. [1920], New York [1920].

The foundations of sovereignty and other essays. New York 1921, London [1922].

Karl Marx: an essay. [1922] (Fabian pamphlet), New York 1933 (as Karl Marx: an essay, with the Communist Manifesto; introd by N. Thomas).

The state in the new social order. 1922 (Fabian tract); rptd in Studies in law and politics, 1932.

The position of parties and the right of dissolution. 1924 (Fabian tract).

A grammar of politics. 1925, 1930 (with additional notes), New Haven 1931, London 1934 (with new preface), 1937 (with a new ch), New Haven 1938.

The problem of a Second Chamber. 1925 (Fabian tract); rptd in Studies in law and politics, 1932, below.

Socialism and freedom. 1925 (Fabian tract).

On the study of politics. 1926. Lecture; rptd in The danger of being a gentleman, 1939, below.

Communism. 1927, New York [1927].

The Trades Disputes and Trade Unions Bill. [1927]. With E. J. P. Benn. Pamphlet.

The British cabinet: a study of its personnel 1801–1924. 1928 (Fabian tract); rptd in Studies in law and politics, 1932, below.

The recovery of citizenship. 1928. Pamphlet; rptd in The dangers of obedience, 1930, below.

The dangers of obedience and other essays. 1930, New York 1930.

Liberty in the modern state. 1930, New York 1930, London 1937 (with new introd), 1948 (rev), New York 1949.

The socialist tradition in the French Revolution. 1930. Fabian lecture; rptd in Studies in law and politics, 1932, below.

Justice and the law. 1930. Lecture rptd in Studies in law and politics, 1932, below.

The decline of parliamentary government, discussed by Laski [and] J. Redlich. New York 1931. Pamphlet.

The limitations of the expert. 1931 (Fabian tract).

Politics. Philadelphia 1931, London 1931 (as An introduction to politics), 1951 (for 1952) (ed M. Wight).

The crisis and the Constitution: 1931 and after. 1932 (Fabian pamphlet).

Nationalism and the future of civilization. 1932. Lecture; rptd in The danger of being a gentleman, 1939, below.

Studies in law and politics. 1932, New Haven 1932.

Democracy in crisis. 1933, Chapel Hill 1933. Lectures.

The Labour Party and the constitution. 1933. Pamphlet.

The present position of representative democracy. In Where stands Socialism today? 1933 (Fabian lectures, by Laski et al).

The Roosevelt experiment. 1933. Pamphlet.

Law and justice in Soviet Russia. 1935. Pamphlet; rptd in The danger of being a gentleman, 1939, below.

The state in theory and practice. 1935, New York 1935.

The rise of European liberalism: an essay in interpretation. 1936, New York 1936 (as The rise of liberalism: the philosophy of a business civilization).

The spirit of co-operation. Manchester [1936]. Lecture.

Parliamentary government in England: a commentary. 1938, New York 1938.

The danger of being a gentleman and other essays. 1939, New York 1940.

Introduction to contemporary politics: selected lectures given at the University of Washington. Ed F. G. Wilson, Seattle 1939.

The Labour Party, the war and the future. 1939. Pamphlet.

The prospects of democratic government. Williamsburg Virginia 1939. Lecture.

The American Presidency: an interpretation. 1940, New York [1940].

The decline of liberalism. 1940. Lecture.

Government in wartime. In Where stands democracy?: a collection of essays by members of the Fabian Society, by Laski [et al], 1940.

Is this an imperialist war? 1940. Pamphlet.

Political offences and the death penalty. 1940. Lecture.

The rights of man. 1940. Pamphlet.

Where do we go from here?: an essay in interpretation. 1940, New York 1940.

The economic revolution. [1941]. Pamphlet. By Laski et al.

The freedom of the press in wartime. 1941. Pamphlet.

The Germans—are they human?: a reply to Sir Robert Vansittart [i.e. to his Black record, 1941]. 1941. Pamphlet.

The need for a European revolution. In Programme for victory: a collection of essays prepared for the Fabian Society, by Laski [et al], 1941.

The strategy of freedom: an open letter to American youth. New York 1941, London 1942 (as The strategy of freedom: an open letter to students, especially American).

London, Washington, Moscow: partners in peace? [1943]. Pamphlet.

Marx and today. [1943]. Fabian pamphlet.

Reflections on the revolution of our time. 1943, New York 1943.

Faith, reason and civilization: an essay in historical analysis. 1944, New York 1944.

The secret battalion: an examination of the Communist attitude to the Labour Party. [1946]. Pamphlet.

Edmund Burke: an address delivered on the occasion of the bi-centenary of the foundation of Burke's Club. Dublin 1947.

Russia and the West: policy for Britain. [1947]. Pamphlet.

The Webbs and Soviet Communism. 1947. Lecture.

The American democracy: a commentary and an interpretation. New York 1948, London 1949.

Communist Manifesto—socialist landmark: a new appreciation written for the Labour Party, together with the original texts and prefaces. 1948.

Efficiency in government. In The road to recovery: Fabian lectures, 1947, by Laski [et al], ed D. P. T. Jay 1948.

Socialism as internationalism. 1949. Fabian lecture.

Trade unions in the new society. New York 1949, London 1950.

Reflections on the Constitution: the House of Commons, the Cabinet, the Civil Service. Manchester 1951.

The dilemma of our times: an historical essay. 1952. Ed R. T. Clark; unfinished supplement to Faith, reason and civilization, 1944.

Holmes–Laski letters: the correspondence of Mr Justice Holmes and Laski 1916–35. Ed M. De W. Howe 2 vols Cambridge Mass 1953, London 1953.

§2

Martin, K. Harold Laski 1893–1950: a biographical memoir. 1953.

Zylstra, B. From pluralism to collectivism: the development of Laski's political thought. Assen 1968.

THOMAS EDWARD LAWRENCE
1888–1935

A most important collection of papers relating to Lawrence has been placed in Bodley by his executors, under embargo until AD 2000. Bodley also holds a ms of Seven pillars of wisdom. The BM holds the ms of Lawrence's trn of the Odyssey, an early draft of The mint, and several minor mss. The Public Record office holds important wartime reports, and documents related to his later service. The Kilgour Collection in the Houghton Library, Harvard Univ, contains a ms of The mint, the unpbd draft abridgement of Seven pillars of wisdom made by Lawrence and Edward Garnett in 1922, and minor mss. The T. E. Lawrence Collection, Univ of Texas, contains an early ms abridgement of Seven Pillars of wisdom and minor mss.

Selections
The essential Lawrence. Ed D. Garnett 1951, New York 1951.

§1

As an RAF recruit in 1922 Lawrence used the name J. H. Ross; he changed it in 1923 to T. E. Shaw, and legalized this by deed poll in 1927. All posthumous edns use the name T. E. Lawrence.

Seven pillars of wisdom: a triumph. Oxford 1922 (8 copies priv ptd from ms now in Bodley by Oxford Times, 5 of which with holograph corrections and addns circulated; complete set of sheets later used for the unpbd Garnett–Lawrence abridgement held by Harvard Univ), London 1924 (anon; small priv printing of rev Introduction, i.e. chs 1–8 of the book, which includes 1st ch later suppressed), 1925 (Introduction, i.e. chs 1–7 of the book, further rev with G. B. Shaw, together with prefatory letter signed T. E. Shaw; 100 copies, priv ptd), 1926 (1922 text completely rev and abridged, with new prefatory note signed TES; 202 copies, priv ptd; holograph signed note on collation distinguishes 170 complete copies from 32 lacking some illustrations), New York 1926 (22 [= 24] copies), London 1935 (trade edn; 5 passages omitted; preface by A. W. Lawrence which includes Some notes on the writing of the Seven pillars of wisdom by T. E. Shaw, 1927, below), 1935 (by T. E. Lawrence; limited edn of 750 copies with additional facs and coloured plates not included in trade edn), 1935 (priv ptd, 60 copies as above, but in trade binding and lacking one facs); New York 1935 (trade and limited edns, as London edns), London 1940 (this and all subsequent UK edns include original 1st ch, suppressed 1944, as 'introductory chapter', and addn to the preface by A. W. Lawrence). The 'suppressed introductory chapter' also pbd in Oriental assembly, 1939, below.

Revolt in the desert, by T. E. Lawrence. 1927 (limited edn, 315 copies, and trade edn), New York 1927 (limited edn, 250 copies, and trade edn; with anon introd). Abridgement by Lawrence of Seven pillars of wisdom.

Some notes on the writing of the Seven pillars of wisdom by T. E. Shaw. 1927 (priv ptd, 200 copies); rptd in Seven pillars of wisdom, 1935 edn, above).

The Odyssey of Homer. 1932 (530 copies; anon trn, but some presentation copies signed 'T. E. Shaw'), New York 1932 (limited edn, 34 copies, and trade edns; signed 'T. E. Shaw'), 1934 (introd by J. Finley), London 1935 (without Finley introd, which reappears in later issues of this edn), New York 1940 (limited edn, 2500 copies, without Finley introd), Oxford 1955 (introd by M. Bowra) (WC).

Crusader castles: vol 1, The thesis. 1936 (1000 copies, Golden Cockerel Press; foreword by A. W. Lawrence). Also 75 copies 'not part of the first edition'.

The mint: notes made in the RAF Depot between August and December 1922, and at Cadet College in 1925 by 352087 A/C Ross, regrouped and copied in 1927 and 1928 at Aircraft Depot, Karachi. Garden City NY 1936 (50 copies ptd from text of ms now held by Harvard), London 1955 (rev; limited edn of 2000 copies unexpurgated; trade edn expurgated; as The mint: a day-book of the RAF Depot between August and December 1922, with later notes, prefatory note by A. W. Lawrence), Garden City NY 1955 (limited edn of 1000 copies, and trade edn), both unexpurgated and retaining the 1936 form of the title).

The diary, MCMXI. 1937 (203 copies, Corvinus Press), Garden City NY 1937 (small printing for copyright purposes only). With notes by A. W. Lawrence, poem by W. G. Lawrence, and 3 letters from T. E. Lawrence to his mother. The diary rptd in Oriental Assembly, below; the poem and letters rptd in The home letters, below.

An essay on Flecker. 1937 (32 copies, Corvinus Press), Garden City NY 1937 (small printing for copyright purposes only). The ms text rptd in facs in Men in print, below (30 copies only); the text, rev by A. W. Lawrence, rptd in Men in print, below (all copies).

Two Arabic folk tales. 1937 (31 copies, Corvinus Press).

Oriental assembly. Ed A. W. Lawrence, with photographs by the author, 1939, New York 1940, 1947 (corrected). Miscellaneous writings.

Secret despatches from Arabia. Foreword by A. W. Lawrence. [1939] (Golden Cockerel Press). Mainly rptd from Arab Bull (Cairo) 1916–18. 30 copies include facs of 3 chs in Bodleian ms of Seven pillars of wisdom (ptd in the Oxford 1922 edn).

Men in print: essays in literary criticism. 1940 (500 copies, Golden Cockerel Press). Introd by A. W. Lawrence; 30 copies include facs of ms of An essay on Flecker, above.

Evolution of a revolt: early postwar writings. Ed S. and R. Weintraub, University Park Pa 1968. Reprints articles in periodicals.

Letters
Letters from T. E. Shaw to Bruce Rogers. New York 1933 (priv ptd, 200 copies). Concerning Lawrence's trn of Homer's Odyssey.

More letters from T. E. Shaw to Bruce Rogers. New York 1936 (priv ptd, 300 copies).

A letter from T. E. Lawrence to his mother. 1936 ('24' [= 30] copies, Corvinus Press); rptd in The home letters, below.

Letters from T. E. Shaw to Viscount Carlow. 1936 (17 copies, Corvinus Press); 2 letters rptd in The letters, 1938, below.

Crusader castles: vol 2, The letters. 1936 (1,000 copies and 35 copies 'not part of the first edn'; see Chanticleer: a bibliography of the Golden Cockerel Press, 1936); Garden City NY 1937 (small printing for copyright purposes). Preface by Mrs Lawrence.

Letters. Ed D. Garnett 1938, Garden City NY 1939, London 1964 (corrected, foreword by B. H. Liddell Hart).

T. E. Lawrence to his biographer Robert Graves: information about himself in the form of letters, notes and answers to questions, edited with a critical commentary [by Graves]; T. E. Lawrence to his biographer Liddell Hart: information about himself in the form of letters, notes, answers to questions and conversations. [Ed Liddell Hart]. 2 vols New York 1938 (1000 sets, of which 500 distributed in London 1938 with different binding and title-page), 1 vol London 1963, New York 1963.

Eight letters from TEL [to Harley Granville Barker]. 1939 (priv ptd, 50 copies).

Smith, C. S. The golden reign: the story of my friendship with Lawrence of Arabia. 1940.

Williamson, H. Genius of friendship: Lawrence. 1941.

Shaw-Ede: Lawrence's letters to H. S. Ede 1927–35. Foreword and running commentary by H. S. Ede, 1942 (500 copies, Golden Cockerel Press; 30 copies contain facs of some of the letters).

Selected letters of Lawrence. Ed D. Garnett 1941 (Reprint Soc). Includes some letters not in 1938, above.

The home letters of Lawrence and his brothers. Oxford 1954 (introd by Winston Churchill), New York 1954. Transcribed and ed M. R. Lawrence.

§2

Graves, R. Lawrence and the Arabs. 1927, New York 1928 (as Lawrence and the Arabian adventure), London 1934 (concise edn). Authorized by Lawrence.

Liddell Hart, B. H. Lawrence in Arabia and after. 1934, New York 1934 (as Colonel Lawrence: the man behind the legend), London 1935 (enlarged). Authorized by Lawrence.

Lawrence, A. W. (ed). T. E. Lawrence by his friends. 1937, 1954 (abridged), New York 1963 (with article by W. H. Auden).

— Letters to T. E. Lawrence. 1962, 1962 (corrected).

Aldington, R. Lawrence l'imposteur. Paris 1954; tr (rev) London 1955, 1969 (introd by C. Sykes).

Payne, R. Lawrence of Arabia: a triumph. New York 1962, London 1965 (rev).

Knightley, P. and C. Simpson. The secret lives of Lawrence of Arabia. 1969.

SIR BASIL HENRY
LIDDELL HART
1895–1970

The framework of a science of infantry tactics. [1921], 1923 (rev and enlarged, as A science of infantry tactics simplified), 1926 (rev and enlarged).

Paris: or the future of war. 1925, New York [1925].

A greater than Napoleon: Scipio Africanus. Edinburgh 1926.

The remaking of modern armies. 1927.

Reputations. 1928, Boston 1928 (as Reputations, ten years after). Sketches of military commanders in the European war.

The decisive wars of history: a study in strategy. 1929, Boston 1929, London 1941 (as The strategy of indirect approach), [1943] (as The way to win wars), 1946 (enlarged, as The strategy of indirect approach), 1954 (rev and further enlarged, as Strategy: the indirect approach), New York 1954 (as Strategy), London 1967 (rev and further enlarged, as Strategy: the indirect approach), New York 1967 (as Strategy).

Sherman: soldier, realist, American. New York 1929, London 1930 (as Sherman: the genius of the Civil War), [1959] (original title).

The real war 1914–18. 1930, Boston 1930, London 1934 (enlarged, as A history of the world war 1914–18), Boston 1935, London 1970 (as History of the First World War).

Foch: the man of Orleans. 1931, Boston 1932, 2 vols London 1937.

The British way in warfare. 1932, 1935 (rev and enlarged, as When Britain goes to war: adaptability and mobility).

The future of infantry. 1933, Harrisburg Pa [1936].

The ghost of Napoleon. 1933. A history of military thought from the 18th to the 20th century.

'T. E. Lawrence', in Arabia and after. 1934, New York 1934 (as Colonel Lawrence: the man behind the legend), London 1935 (enlarged, original title), New York 1935 (as Colonel Lawrence: etc), 1937 (enlarged, as The man behind the legend: Colonel Lawrence).

The war in outline 1914–18. 1936, New York [1936].

Europe in arms. 1937, New York [1937].

T. E. Lawrence to his biographer Liddell Hart. 1938, New York 1938, London [1963] (with T. E. Lawrence to his biographer R. Graves), Garden City NY 1963. Ed B. H. L. Hart.

Through the fog of war. 1938, New York [1938]. On military aspects of the European war 1914–18.

The defence of Britain. 1939, New York 1939.

Dynamic defence. 1940.

The current of war. [1941].

This expanding war. 1942.

Thoughts on war. 1944.

Why don't we learn from history? 1944. Enlarged version of a lecture, We learn from history that we do not learn from history, pbd 1938.

The revolution in warfare. 1946, New Haven 1947.

The other side of the hill: Germany's generals, their rise and fall, with their own account of military events 1939–45. 1948, New York 1948 (as The German generals talk).

Defence of the west. 1950, New York 1950.

The letters of Private Wheeler 1809–28. Ed B. H. L. Hart 1951.

The Rommel papers. Ed B. H. L. Hart 1953, New York 1953.

The Soviet army. Ed B. H. L. Hart 1956, New York 1956 (as The Red Army).

The tanks: the history of the Royal Tank regiment and its predecessors. 2 vols 1959, New York 1959.

Deterrent or defence: a fresh look at the West's military position. 1960, New York 1960.

Memoirs. 2 vols 1965, New York 1965–66 (as The Liddell Hart memoirs).

[Churchill]: the military strategist. In Churchill revised, by A. J. P. Taylor [and others], New York 1969, London 1969 (as Churchill: four faces and the man).

History of the Second World War. 1970.

Liddell Hart was military correspondent of Daily Telegraph *1925–35, and of* Times *1935–9. He was military editor of* Encyclopaedia Britannica *14th edn 1929. He compiled various infantry training manuals. He edited* Small arms training *1924, and the series* The next war, *6 vols 1938.*

SIR RICHARD WINN LIVINGSTONE
1880–1960

The Greek genius and its meaning to us. Oxford 1912.
A defence of classical education. 1916.
Greek ideals and modern life. Oxford 1935, Cambridge Mass 1935.
The future in education. Cambridge 1941. Rptd with next, 1954, as On education.
Education for a world adrift. Cambridge 1943.
Some tasks for education. 1946.
Education and the spirit of the age. Oxford 1952.
The rainbow bridge and other essays in education. 1959, Toronto 1961.
Livingstone edited The legacy of Greece: essays, *Oxford 1921*; The mission of Greece: some Greek views of life in the Roman world, *Oxford 1928*; The Clarendon Latin and Greek ser, *and, with J. T. Shepherd*, Classical Rev *1920–2. He also translated and edited Plato and Thucydides.*

BRONISŁAW KASPAR MALINOWSKI
1884–1942

The family among the Australian Aborigines: a sociological study. 1913, New York 1963.
Argonauts of the Western Pacific: an account of native enterprise and adventure in the archipelagoes of Melanesian New Guinea. 1922, New York 1953.
Crime and custom in savage society. 1926, New York 1926.
Myth in primitive psychology. 1926 New York [1926].
The father in primitive psychology. 1927, New York [1927].
Sex and repression in savage society. 1927, New York 1955.
The sexual life of savages in North-Western Melanesia. 1929, New York [1929], London 1932 (with special foreword).
Essays presented to C. G. Seligman. Ed B. Malinowski [et al] 1934.
Coral gardens and their magic: a study of the methods of tilling the soil and of agricultural rites in the Trobriand Islands. 2 vols 1935, Bloomington 1965.
Freedom and civilisation. New York [1944]. Ed A. V. Malinowska.
A scientific theory of culture, and other essays. Chapel Hill 1944.
The dynamics of culture change: an inquiry into race relations in Africa. Ed P. M. Kaberry, New Haven 1945.
Magic, science and religion, and other essays. Ed R. Redfield, Boston Mass 1948.
Marriage, past and present: a debate between Robert Briffault and Malinowski. Ed M. F. Ashley Montagu, Boston Mass 1956.
Sex, culture and myth. New York 1962, London 1963.
A diary in the strictest sense of the term. 1967, New York 1967. Tr N. Guterman.

SIR LEWIS BERNSTEIN NAMIER
1888–1960

Collections

Collected essays. 2 vols (vol 1, Vanished supremacies; vol 2, Crossroads of power) 1958, New York 1958, London 1962, New York 1963. Vol 2 includes the first 3 Ford lectures, 1934, hitherto unpbd.

§1

Germany and Eastern Europe. Ed H. A. L. Fisher 1915.

The structure of politics at the accession of George III. 2 vols 1929, 1957 (rev).
England in the age of the American revolution. 1930, 1961 (rev Lady Namier and J. Brooke).
Skyscrapers and other essays. 1931.
In the margin of history. 1939. Essays.
Conflicts: studies in contemporary history. 1942.
1848: the revolution of the intellectuals. 1946.
Facing East. 1947, New York 1948. Essays, mainly on East European history.
Diplomatic prelude 1938–9. 1948.
Europe in decay: a study in disintegration 1936–40. 1950, Gloucester Mass 1963. Essays.
Avenues of history. 1952. Essays.
In the Nazi era. 1952. Essays.
Personalities and powers. 1955.
Vanished supremacies: essays on European history 1812–1918 (Collected essays 1). 1958, New York 1958.
Crossroads of power: essays on eighteenth-century England (Collected essays 2). 1962, New York 1963.
Charles Townshend. 1964. Completed by J. Brooke.
The history of Parliament: the House of Commons 1754–90. 3 vols 1964. Completed by J. Brooke.
Namier wrote pamphlets for the Czech National Alliance (1917) and several letters to the press on Zionist subjects were rptd. He was general editor of the series Studies in modern history, *and* England in the age of the American revolution.

§2

Butterfield, H. George III and the Namier school. In his George III and the historians, 1957.
Sutherland, L. S. Namier. Proc Br Acad 48 1962.
Berlin, I. Namier: a personal impression. In A century of conflict 1850–1950: essays for A. J. P. Taylor, ed M. Gilbert, 1966.
Plumb, J. H. Atomic historian. New Statesman 1 Aug 1969.
Namier, J. Namier: a biography. 1971. By his widow.

SIR JOHN ERNEST NEALE
1890–1975

Queen Elizabeth. 1934, New York [1934], London 1952 (corrected, as Queen Elizabeth I), New York 1957.
The age of Catherine de Medici. 1943, New York 1959.
The Elizabethan House of Commons. 1949, New Haven 1950, London 1963 (rev, Penguin).
Elizabeth I and her parliaments 1559–1581. 1953, New York 1966.
Elizabeth I and her parliaments 1584–1601. 1957.
Essays in Elizabethan history. 1958, New York 1959.
The age of Catherine de Medici and [a selection from] Essays in Elizabethan History. 1963.

SIR HAROLD GEORGE NICOLSON
1886–1968

Paul Verlaine. [1921], Boston 1921.
Sweet waters: a novel. 1921.
Tennyson: aspects of his life, character and poetry. 1923, Boston 1925.
Byron: the last journey, April 1923–April 1824. 1924, Boston 1934, London 1940 (with supplementary ch), 1948 (with new preface).
Swinburne. 1926 (EML), New York 1926.
The development of English biography. 1927, New York [1928].
Some people. 1927, Boston 1927, New York 1957 (with introd).
Sir Arthur Nicolson, Bart, first Lord Carnock: a study in the old diplomacy. 1930, Boston 1930 (as Portrait of a diplomatist, New York 1939.

People and things: wireless talks. 1931.

Public faces: a novel. 1932, Boston 1933.

Peacemaking 1919. 1933, Boston 1933, London 1944 (with new introd).

Curzon: the last phase 1919–25, a study in post-war diplomacy. 1934, Boston 1934.

Dwight Morrow. 1935, New York [1935].

In search of the past: vol 1, Helen's tower [a biography of the Marquis of Dufferin]; vol 2, The desire to please: a story of Hamilton Rowan and the United Irishmen. 2 vols 1937–43, New York [1938–43].

Small talk. 1937, New York [1937].

Diplomacy. 1939, New York [1939], London 1950 (rev), 1963 (rev).

Marginal comment: January 6–August 4 1939. 1939.

Why Britain is at war. 1939 (Penguin Special).

Friday mornings 1941–4. 1944.

The Congress of Vienna: a study in allied unity 1812–22. 1946, New York 1946.

The English sense of humour. 1946; rptd in The English sense of humour and other essays, 1956.

Comments 1944–8. 1948.

Benjamin Constant. 1949, New York 1949.

King George the Fifth: his life and reign. 1952, New York 1953.

The evolution of diplomatic method. 1954, New York 1962 (as The evolution of diplomacy) (Chichele lectures).

Good behaviour: being a study of certain types of civility. 1955, New York 1956, Boston 1960 (with new introd).

Journey to Java. 1957, New York 1958.

Sainte-Beuve. 1957, New York 1957. Biography.

The age of reason 1700–89. 1960, New York 1961 (as The age of reason: the eighteenth century).

Monarchy. [1962], New York 1962 (as Kings, courts and monarchy).

Letters and Diaries

Diaries and letters. Ed N. Nicolson 3 vols 1966–8, New York 1966–8.

Nicolson also pbd addresses and pamphlets on political, international and current affairs. With V. M. Sackville-West (afterwards Nicolson) he edited an anthology, Another world than this, 1945.

SIR CHARLES WILLIAM CHADWICK OMAN
1860–1946

A history of Greece from the earliest times to the Macedonian conquest. 1890, 1891 (rev).

Warwick the Kingmaker. 1891.

The Byzantine empire. 1892, New York 1892.

Europe 476–918. 1893, 1898 (as The dark ages, 476–918).

The Oxford manuals of English history. Ed C. W. C. Oman 7 vols 1894–1910.

A history of England. [1895], 1919 (rev), New York 1955.

England and the Hundred Years' War. 1898, New York 1898. Vol 3 of Oxford manuals, above.

A history of the art of war: the Middle Ages, from the fourth to the fourteenth century. 1898, 2 vols 1924 (rev, as A history of the art of war in the Middle Ages), Boston 1924, New York 1959 (rev).

England in the nineteenth century. 1899, New York 1899, London 1902 (rev), 1920 (rev).

The reign of George VI 1900–25: a forecast written in the year 1763. Ed C. W. C. Oman 1899.

A history of the Peninsular war. 7 vols Oxford 1902–30.

Seven Roman statesmen of the later Republic. 1902.

A history of England. Ed C. W. C. Oman 8 vols 1904–34.

The great revolt of 1381. Oxford 1906, 1969 (new introd and notes by E. B. Fryde).

The history of England from the accession of Richard II to the death of Richard III 1377–1485. 1906.

The Peninsular war, 1808–14; The hundred days, 1815; In Cambridge modern history vol 9, Cambridge 1907.

England before the Norman Conquest. 1910, New York 1910, London 1929 (rev), 1938 (rev).

Wellington's army 1809–14. 1912, New York 1912.

The outbreak of the war of 1914–18: a narrative based mainly on British official documents. 1919.

The unfortunate Colonel Despard and other studies. 1922.

Castles. 1926.

Studies in the Napoleonic wars. 1929, New York 1930.

The coinage of England. Oxford 1931.

Things I have seen. 1933.

The art of war in the fifteenth century. In Cambridge medieval history vol 8, Cambridge 1936.

The sixteenth century. 1936. Essays.

A history of the art of war in the sixteenth century. 1937, New York 1937.

The text of the second betting book of All Souls' College, 1873–1919, ed C. Oman, Oxford 1938 (priv ptd).

On the writing of history. 1939, New York 1939.

Memories of Victorian Oxford and of some early years. 1941.

The Lyons mail: being an account of the crime of April 27, 1796. 1945.

ALBERT FREDERICK POLLARD
1869–1948

Henry VIII. 1902, 1905 (rev and enlarged), New York 1966 (introd A. G. Dickens), London 1970 (introd J. E. Neale).

Tudor tracts 1532–88. 1903. Ed Pollard Garner ser).

Thomas Cranmer and the English Reformation 1489–1556. 1904, New York [1905].

The conflict of creeds and parties in Germany; National opposition to Rome in Germany; The reformation under Edward VI; Religious war in Germany; Social revolution and Catholic reaction in Germany. In Cambridge modern history vol 2, Cambridge 1903.

Factors in modern history. 1907, 1926 (enlarged and corrected), 1932 (enlarged), Boston 1960.

The British empire: its past, its present and its future. Ed Pollard 1909.

The history of England from the accession of Edward VI to the death of Elizabeth 1547–1603. 1915, New York 1969. (Political History of England, ed W. Hunt and R. L. Poole vol 6).

On the educational value of the study of history. 1911 (Historical Assoc pamphlet).

The history of England: a study in political evolution [1912], New York [1912].

The reign of Henry VII from contemporary sources. Ed Pollard 3 pts 1913–14, New York 1967.

The war—its history and its morals: a lecture. 1915.

The Commonwealth at war. 1917. Essays.

The League of Nations: an historical argument. Oxford 1918.

The League of Nations in history. 1918. Pamphlet.

The evolution of Parliament. 1920, 1926 (rev), New York 1964.

A short history of the Great War. 1920.

Factors in American history. Cambridge 1925, New York 1925.

Wolsey. 1929, 1953 (corrected, with additional notes), 1965 (introd by G. R. Elton), New York 1966 (as Wolsey: church and state in sixteenth century England; introd by A. G. Dickens).

Pollard was an assistant editor of DNB 1893–1901, and contributed to it. He edited History 1916–22, Bull of Historical Research 1923–9.

SIR KARL RAIMUND POPPER
b. 1902

§1

The open society and its enemies. 2 vols 1945, 1 vol Princeton 1950 (rev, enlarged), 2 vols London 1952 (rev, enlarged), 1957 (rev with addn), 1962 (rev and new addn), 1966 (rev).
The poverty of historicism. 1957, Boston 1957, London 1960 (rev).
The logic of scientific discovery. 1959, New York 1959, London 1960 (rev), New York 1961 (rev), London 1968 (rev). Originally pbd as Logik der Forschung, Vienna 1935 (for 1934).
Conjectures and refutations: the growth of scientific knowledge. 1963, New York 1963, London 1969 (rev). Essays and lectures.
Objective knowledge: an evolutionary approach. Oxford 1972.
The self and its brain. Berlin 1977. With J. C. Eccles.

§2

Rhees, R. The open society and its enemies. Mind 56 1947.
Ryle, G. The open society and its enemies. Ibid.
The critical approach to science and philosophy: in honor of Popper. Ed M. Bunge, New York 1964.
Bambrough, R. (ed). Plato, Popper and politics: some contributions to modern controversy. Cambridge 1967.
Cornforth, M. The open philosophy and the open society: a reply to Popper's refutations of Marxism. 1968.

SIR FREDERICK MAURICE POWICKE
1879–1963

The loss of Normandy 1189–1204: studies in the history of the Angevin empire. Manchester 1913, 1961 (rev).
Bismark and the origin of the German empire. 1914.
Stephen Langton. Oxford 1928, New York 1965.
England: Richard I and John; The reigns of Philip Augustus and Louis VIII of France. In Cambridge medieval history vol 6, Cambridge 1929.
The medieval books of Merton College. Oxford 1931.
Medieval England 1066–1485. 1931.
The Christian life in the Middle Ages and other essays. Oxford 1935.
The Reformation in England. In European civilisation: its origin and development vol 4, ed E. Eyre 1936. Pbd separately 1941 (as The Reformation in England).
History, freedom and religion. 1938.
King Henry III and the Lord Edward: the community of the realm in the thirteenth century. 2 vols Oxford 1947.
Three lectures given in the hall of Balliol College. Oxford 1947.
Ways of medieval life and thought: essays and addresses. [1950], New York 1964.
The life of Ailred of Rievaulx, by Walter Daniel. 1950. Tr with introd by Powicke.
The thirteenth century 1216–1307. Oxford 1953, 1954 (corrected), 1962 (rev) (Oxford History of England 4).
Modern historians and the study of history: essays and papers. 1955. Includes items previously pbd separately.
Councils and synods with other documents relating to the English church 1205–1313. Ed Powicke and C. R. Cheney 2 vols 1964.
Powicke edited Oxford Historical ser 1932–50 (with G. N. Clark and C. R. Cruttwell).

LIONEL CHARLES ROBBINS, BARON ROBBINS
b. 1898

Wages: an introductory analysis of the wage system under modern capitalism. [1926].
An essay on the nature and significance of economic science. 1932, 1935 (rev, extended).
The Great Depression. 1934.
Economic planning and international order. 1937.
The economic basis of class conflict, and other essays in political economy. 1939.
The economic causes of war. 1939, New York 1968.
The economic problem in peace and war. 1947.
The theory of economic policy in English classical political economy. 1952.
The economist in the twentieth century, and other lectures in political economy. 1954, New York 1954.
Robert Torrens and the evolution of classical economics. 1958, New York 1958.
Politics and economics: papers on political economy. 1963, New York 1963.
The university in the modern world, and other papers on higher education. 1966, New York 1966.
The theory of economic development in the history of economic thought. 1968.
The evolution of modern economic theory. 1970.
Autobiography of an economist. 1971.
Money, trade and international relations. 1971.
Political economy past and present. 1976.
Robbins was chairman of the Committee on Higher Education, 1963 (the 'Robbins Report'). With A. Plant he edited Studies in economics and commerce *from 1933.*
See Essays in honour of Lord Robbins, *ed M. Peston and B. Corry 1972.*

BENJAMIN SEEBOHM ROWNTREE
1871–1954

Poverty: a study in town life. 1901, 1902 (enlarged), 1922 (new preface).
Betting and gaming: a national evil. Ed Rowntree 1905. By Rowntree et al.
Land and labour: lessons from Belgium. 1910.
Unemployment: a social study. 1911. With B. Lasker.
How the labourer lives: a study of the rural labour problem. [1913]. With M. Kendall.
Lectures on housing. Manchester 1914. With A. C. Pigou.
The way to industrial peace and the problem of unemployment. 1914.
The human needs of labour. [1919], 1937 (rewritten).
The human factor in business. 1921, 1925 (rev), 1938 (largely rewritten).
Poverty and progress: a second social survey of York. 1941.
Portrait of a city's housing: being the results of a detailed survey in the city of York 1935–9. Ed R. L. Reiss 1945.
English life and leisure: a social study. 1951. With G. R. Lavers.
Poverty and the welfare state: a third social survey of York dealing only with economic questions. 1951. With G. R. Lavers.

ALFRED LESLIE ROWSE
b. 1903

On history: a study of present tendencies. 1927, New York [1928] (as Science and history: a new view of history).
Politics and the younger generation. 1931.

Queen Elizabeth and her subjects. 1935. With G. B. Harrison.

Mr Keynes and the Labour Movement. 1936.

Sir Richard Grenville of the Revenge: an Elizabethan hero. 1937, Boston, 1937.

Poems of a decade 1931–41. 1941.

Tudor Cornwall: portrait of a society. 1941, 1969 (corrected, with new preface), New York 1969.

A Cornish childhood. 1942, New York 1947. Autobiography.

The spirit of English history. 1943, New York 1945.

The English spirit: essays in history and literature. 1944, 1966 (rev), New York 1967.

Poems chiefly Cornish. 1944.

West-country stories. 1945.

Poems of deliverance. 1946.

The use of history. 1946, New York 1948, London 1963 (rev), New York 1963 (Teach Yourself History Lib).

The end of an epoch: reflections on contemporary history. 1947.

The west in English history. 1949.

The Elizabethan age: vol 1, The England of Elizabeth: the structure of society; 1950, New York 1951; vol 2, The expansion of Elizabethan England, 1955, New York 1955.

The English past: evocations of persons and places. 1951, New York 1952, London 1965 (as Times, persons, places: essays in literature).

An Elizabethan garland. 1953, New York 1953. Essays.

The early Churchills: an English family. 1956, New York 1956.

The later Churchills. 1958, New York 1958 (as The Churchills from the death of Marlborough to the present).

The Elizabethans and America. 1959, New York 1959.

Poems partly American. 1959.

St Austell: church, town, parish. St Austell 1960.

All Souls and appeasement: a contribution to contemporary history. 1961, New York 1961 (as Appeasement: a study in political decline 1933–9).

Ralegh and the Throckmortons. 1962, New York 1962 (as Sir Walter Ralegh, his family and private life).

William Shakespeare: a biography. 1963, New York 1963, London 1967 (rev).

Christopher Marlowe: a biography. 1964, New York 1965.

Shakespeare's sonnets. Ed Rowse, 1964, New York 1964.

Shakespeare's Southampton, patron of Virginia. 1965, New York 1965.

Bosworth Field and the wars of the Roses. 1966, New York 1966 (as Bosworth Field: from medieval to Tudor England).

The Churchills: the story of a family. 1966, New York [1966]. Abridged edn of The early Churchills, 1956, and The later Churchills, 1958, above.

Cornish stories. 1967.

Poems of Cornwall and America. 1967.

A Cornish anthology, chosen by A. L. Rowse. 1968.

The Cornish in America. 1969, New York 1969 (as The cousin Jacks: the Cornish in America).

Shakespeare the man. 1973, 1973 (rev).

Jonathan Swift. 1975.

Simon Forman. 1974, 1976 (as The case books of Forman).

SIR JAMES COCHRAN STEVENSON RUNCIMAN
b. 1903

The emperor Romanus Lecapenus and his reign. Cambridge 1929.

A history of the first Bulgarian empire. 1930.

Byzantine civilisation. 1933, New York 1956 (abridged), 1959 (complete).

The medieval Manichee: a study of the Christian Dualist heresy. Cambridge 1947, New York 1961.

A history of the crusades. 3 vols Cambridge 1951–4.

The eastern schism: a study of the papacy and the eastern churches during the XIth and XIIth centuries. Oxford 1955.

The Sicilian Vespers: a history of the Mediterranean world in the later thirteenth century. Cambridge 1958, Baltimore 1960.

The white rajahs: a history of Sarawak from 1841 to 1946. Cambridge 1960.

The fall of Constantinople 1453. Cambridge 1965.

The Great Church in captivity: a study of the Patriarchate of Constantinople from the eve of the Turkish conquest to the Greek War of Independence. Cambridge 1968.

The last Byzantine renaissance. Cambridge 1970.

The Byzantine theocracy. 1977.

A Cornishman at Oxford. 1965; A Cornishman abroad, 1976. Autobiography.

SIR RONALD HENRY AMHERST STORRS
1881–1955

A chronology of Cyprus. Nicosia 1930.

Orientations. 1937, New York 1937 (as The memoirs of Sir Ronald Storrs). Pt rptd 1940 as Lawrence of Arabia, Zionism and Palestine (Penguin).

A record of the war: the first quarter, September–November 1939; the second quarter, December 1939–February 1940. 2 vols 1940. Remaining 22 vols of this work by P. Graves.

Dunlop in war and peace. [1946].

Ad Pyrrham: a polyglot collection of translations of Horace's Ode to Pyrrha. 1950. Introd by Storrs.

Storrs also pbd articles on the arts in Near East *from 1926 into the 30's; he was special correspondent for* Sunday Times *from Portugal and Persia 1942–3.*

GILES LYTTON STRACHEY
1880–1932

Mss of Eminent Victorians, Queen Victoria *and* Elizabeth and Essex *are in the BM, Univ of Texas and Duke Univ respectively.*

Collections

The collected works. Ed J. Strachey 6 vols 1948.

§1

Prolusiones academicae. Cambridge 1902.

Euphrosyne: a collection of verse. Cambridge 1905.

Landmarks in French literature. 1912, New York 1912.

Eminent Victorians: Cardinal Manning; Florence Nightingale; Dr Arnold; General Gordon. 1918, New York 1918. Rptd with Queen Victoria, below, as Five Victorians 1942. Florence Nightingale rptd separately 1938.

Queen Victoria. 1921, New York 1921. Rptd with Eminent Victorians, above as Five Victorians, 1942.

Books and characters, French and English. 1922, New York 1922.

Pope: the Leslie Stephen lecture for 1925. Cambridge 1925; rptd in Characters and commentaries, 1933.

Elizabeth and Essex: a tragic history. 1928, New York 1928.

Portraits in miniature and other essays. 1931, New York 1931.

Characters and commentaries. 1933, New York 1933. Ed with preface by J. Strachey.

Virginia Woolf and Lytton Strachey: letters. Ed L. Woolf and J. Strachey 1956, New York 1956.

Spectatorial essays: [ed] with a preface by J. Strachey. 1964, New York 1965. Selected book and theatre reviews appearing in Spectator 1904–14.

§ 2

Huxley, A. The author of Eminent Victorians. Vanity Fair 19 Sept 1922; rptd in his On the margin, 1923.
Muir, E. Contemporary writers 1: Strachey. Nation Athenaeum 25 April 1925; rptd in his Transition, 1926.
Woolf, L. Strachey. New Statesman 30 Jan 1932. Obituary.
—— Cambridge. In his Sowing, 1960.
Wilson, E. Strachey. New Republic 2 Sept 1932; rptd in his The shores of light, New York 1952.
Woolf, V. The art of biography. Atlantic Monthly 163 1939; rptd in her Death of the moth, 1942, and Collected essays, vol 4 1968.
Beerbohm, M. Lytton Strachey. Cambridge 1943.
Trevor-Roper, H. Books in general—the Collected works of Strachey. New Statesman 12 Feb 1949; rptd as Strachey as historian, in his Historical essays, 1957.
Sanders, C. R. The Strachey family 1588–1932: their writings and literary associations. Durham NC 1953.
—— Strachey: his mind and art. New Haven 1957.
Johnstone, J. K. The Bloomsbury Group: a study of E. M. Forster, Strachey, Virginia Woolf and their circle. 1954.
Garnett, D. Keynes, Strachey and Virginia Woolf in 1917. London Mag 2 1955.
Scott-James, R. A. Lytton Strachey. 1955 (Br Council pamphlet).
Holroyd, M. Lytton Strachey: a critical biography. 2 vols 1967–8.

ALPHONSE JAMES ALBERT SYMONS
1900–41

§ 1

Emin, the governor of Equatoria. 1928, 1950 (as Emin, governor of Equatoria).
An episode in the life of the queen of Sheba. 1929 (priv ptd, 150 copies).
H. M. Stanley. 1933, New York 1933.
Rolfe, F. ('Baron Corvo'). The desire and the pursuit of the whole: a romance of modern Venice. Ed Symons 1934.
The quest for Corvo: an experiment in biography. 1934, New York 1934, London 1952 (introds by N. Birkett and S. Leslie), 1955 (introd by J. Symons), East Lansing 1955.
Rolfe, F. ('Baron Corvo') and C. Gordon. Hubert's Arthur: being certain curious documents found among the literary remains of Mr. N. C. Ed Symons, 1935.
Symons edited Book-Collector's Quart *1930–4* (*with D. Flower*).

§ 2

Symons, J. A. J. A. Symons: his life and speculations. 1950.

RICHARD HENRY TAWNEY
1880–1962

The agrarian problem in the sixteenth century. 1912, New York 1961.
Poverty as an industrial problem. 1913.
The establishment of minimum rates in the chain-making industry under the Trade Boards Act of 1909. 1914.
The establishment of minimum rates in the tailoring industry under the Trade Boards Act of 1909. 1915.

The acquisitive society. New York 1920, London 1921.
Secondary education for all: a policy for Labour, edited for the Education Advisory Committee of the Labour Party by R. H. Tawney. [1922].
Tudor economic documents. 3 vols 1924, New York 1963. Ed Tawney, with E. Power.
The British Labor Movement. New Haven 1925.
Wilson, T. A discourse upon usury, with an historical introduction by Tawney. 1925, New York 1963.
Religion and the rise of capitalism. 1926, New York [1926].
Studies in economic history: the collected papers of George Unwin. 1927. Ed with memoir by Tawney.
Equality. 1931, [1931] (rev), New York [1931], London 1952 (rev with new ch), New York 1961, London 1964 (introd by R. M. Titmuss), New York 1965.
Land and labour in China. 1932, New York 1964.
The reorganisation of education in China. 1932. With C. H. Becker.
The attack and other papers. 1953, New York 1953.
Business and politics under James I: Lionel Cranfield as merchant and minister. Cambridge 1958.
The radical tradition: twelve essays on politics, education and literature. 1964, New York 1964. Ed R. Hinden; includes a selection of pamphlets, lectures.
Tawney edited Stud in Economic and Social History *from 1934* (*with E. Power*), *and was joint editor with E. Lipson of* Economic History Rev *1926–33*.

ALAN JOHN PERCIVALE TAYLOR
b. 1906

The Italian problem in European diplomacy 1847–9. Manchester 1934.
Germany's first bid for colonies 1884–5: a move in Bismarck's European policy. 1938, New York 1967.
The Habsburg monarchy 1815–1918: a history of the Austrian empire and Austria-Hungary. 1941, 1948 (rewritten), New York 1965.
The course of German history: a survey of the development of Germany since 1815. 1945, New York 1946.
From Napoleon to Stalin: comments on European history. 1950.
Rumours of wars. 1952. Essays.
The struggle for mastery in Europe 1848–1918. Oxford 1954.
Bismarck: the man and the statesman. 1955, New York 1955.
Englishmen and others. 1956. Essays.
The trouble makers: dissent over foreign policy 1792–1939. 1957, Bloomington 1958.
Origins of the second world war. 1961, New York 1962.
The first world war: an illustrated history. 1963, New York 1964.
Politics in wartime and other essays. 1964, New York 1965. Includes single lectures previously pbd separately.
English history 1914–45. Oxford 1965 (Oxford History of England 15), 1970 (Pelican).
From Sarajevo to Potsdam. 1966, New York 1967.
War by time-table: how the first World War began. 1969.
Beaverbrook. 1972, 1974 (Pelican).
The second world war. 1974, 1975 (illustr).
Essays in English history. 1976.
Taylor compiled A select list of books on European history 1815–1914 (*with A. Bullock*). *He edited the* Communist Manifesto, *Lord Beaverbrooks's* Abdication of King Edward VIII, *a* History of the twentieth century (*with J. M. Roberts*), Essays presented to Sir Lewis Namier (*with R. Pares*) *and* (*with others*) Churchill's History of the English speaking peoples *and* History of World War I *and* History of World War II. *See* A century of conflict 1850–1950: essays for Taylor, *ed M. Gilbert 1966*.

ARNOLD JOSEPH TOYNBEE
1889-1975

§1

Greek policy since 1882. 1914. Pamphlet.
Armenian atrocities: the murder of a nation, with a speech delivered by Lord Bryce in the House of Lords. 1915, 1915 (rev and enlarged).
Nationality and the war. 1915.
The new Europe: some essays in reconstruction. 1915.
The Belgian deportations. [1916].
The destruction of Poland: a study in German efficiency. [1916]. Pamphlet.
The German terror in Belgium. 1917, New York 1917.
The German terror in France. 1917, New York 1917. Continuation of the above.
'The murderous tyranny of the Turks'. 1917, New York 1917. Pamphlet. Preface by Viscount Bryce.
Turkey: a past and a future. 1917, New York 1917.
The League in the East. 1920. Pamphlet.
The Western question in Greece and Turkey: a study in the contact of civilizations. 1922, 1923 (rev with new preface).
The world after the Peace Conference: being an epilogue to the History of the Peace Conference of Paris [ed H. W. V. Temperley] and a prologue to the Survey of international affairs, 1920-3. 1925, New York 1965.
Turkey. 1926, New York 1927. With K. P. Kirkwood.
The conduct of British Empire foreign relations since the Peace Settlement. 1928.
World order or downfall?: six broadcast talks. [1930].
A journey to China: or things which are seen. 1931.
Britain and the modern world order: a synopsis of talks broadcast April-June 1932. 1932. With J. L. Hammond.
A study of history. 12 vols 1934-61. Vols 1-3, 1935 (corrected); vols 1-10 (abridged by D. C. Somervell, preface by Toynbee) 1946-57, New York 1947-57; 1 vol 1972 (abridged by author and J. Caplan).
— War and civilization. New York 1950, London 1951. Selected by A. V. Fowler from above.
Civilization on trial. New York 1948, London 1948, New York 1960 (with The world and the West, 1953, below).
The prospects of Western civilization. New York 1949 (400 copies). Bampton lectures, on subjects to be treated in vol 12 of A study of history, 1961.
The world and the West: the BBC Reith lectures 1952. 1953, New York 1953, 1960 (with Civilization on trial, 1948, above).
A study of history: what the book is for, how the book took shape. [1954?]. Pamphlet.
An historian's approach to religion, based on Gifford lectures. 1956, New York 1956.
Christianity among the religions of the world. New York 1957, London 1958. Lectures.
Democracy in the atomic age. Melbourne 1957. Lectures.
East to west: a journey round the world. 1958, New York 1958.
Hellenism: the history of a civilization. 1959, New York 1959.
One world and India. [New Delhi] 1960.
Between Oxus and Jumna. 1961, New York 1961. Travel.
America and the world revolution: public lectures, University of Pennsylvania, 1961. 1962, New York 1962.
The economy of the Western hemisphere. 1962. Lectures.
Importance of the Arab world. [Cairo] 1962. Lectures.
The present-day experiment in Western civilization. 1962.
The Toynbee lectures on the Middle East and problems of underdeveloped countries. [Cairo] 1962.
Comparing notes: a dialogue across a generation. [1963]. With P. Toynbee.
Janus at seventy-five. New York 1964. Autobiography.
Between Niger and Nile. 1965. Travel.

Hannibal's legacy: the Hannibalic wars' effect on Roman life. 2 vols 1965.
Change and habit: the challenge of our time. 1966, New York 1966.
Acquaintances. 1967. Reminiscences.
Between Maule and Amazon. 1967. Travel.
Cities of destiny. Ed Toynbee [1967].
The crucible of Christianity: Judaism, Hellenism and the historical background to the Christian faith. Ed Toynbee 1969.
Toynbee on Toynbee. New York 1974.
Mankind and Mother Earth. New York 1976.

§2

Geyl, P. From Ranke to Toynbee: five lectures on histories and historiographical problems. Northampton Mass 1952.
— Toynbee the prophet. JHI 16 1955; rptd (with other essays on Toynbee) in his Debates with historians, Groningen 1955, and in Montague, 1956, below.
— Toynbee's answer. Amsterdam 1961.
Jerrold, D. The lie about the West: a response to Toynbee's challenge. 1954. On The world and the West, 1953.
Blackmur, R. P. Reflections of Toynbee. Kenyon Rev 17 1955; rptd in his A primer of ignorance, New York 1967.
Montagu, A. (ed). Toynbee and history: critical essays and reviews. Boston 1956.
Trevor-Roper, H. Toynbee's millennium. Encounter 8 1957; rptd in his Historical essays, 1957.

GEORGE MACAULAY TREVELYAN
1876-1962

§1

England in the age of Wycliffe. 1899, 1904 (rev), New York 1963.
The Peasants' Rising and the Lollards: a collection of unpublished documents forming an appendix to England in the age of Wycliffe. 1899. Ed Trevelyan, with E. Powell.
England under the Stuarts. 1904, 1925 (rev and corrected), 1946 (rev), New York 1949, London 1960 (with new bibliography) (Pelican).
The poetry and philosophy of George Meredith. 1906, New York 1966.
Garibaldi's defence of the Roman republic 1848-9. 1907.
Garibaldi and the thousand: Naples and Sicily 1859-60. 1909.
English songs of Italian freedom, selected with an introduction 1911.
Garibaldi and the making of Italy. 1911.
Clio, a muse, and other essays literary and pedestrian. 1913, 1919 (enlarged, as The recreations of an historian), 1930 (enlarged, as Clio, a muse and other essays).
The life of John Bright. 1913, Boston 1913.
Scenes from Italy's war. London 1919, Boston 1919.
Lord Grey of the Reform Bill: being the life of Charles, second Earl Grey. 1920.
British history in the nineteenth century 1782-1901. 1922, 1937 (enlarged as British history in the nineteenth century and after 1782-1919), New York 1962.
Manin and the Venetian revolution of 1848. 1923.
History of England. 1926, 1937 (rev and enlarged), 1952 (corrected), Garden City NY 1953, London 1956 (with illustrations, as Illustrated history of England), 1959 (abridged, as A shortened history of England) (Pelican).
Must England's beauty perish? a plea on behalf of the National Trust. 1929.
Select documents of Queen Anne's reign down to the union with Scotland 1702-7. Ed Trevelyan, Cambridge 1929.

England under Queen Anne. 3 vols 1930–4.
Sir George Otto Trevelyan: a memoir. 1932.
Garibaldi: being Garibaldi's defence of the Roman republic, Garibaldi and the thousand, Garibaldi and the making of Italy. 3 pts 1933.
Grey of Fallodon: being the life of Sir Edward Grey, afterwards Viscount Grey of Fallodon. 1937, Boston 1937.
The English revolution 1688–9. 1938, New York [1939].
English social history: a survey of six centuries, Chaucer to Queen Victoria. 1942, 4 vols 1949–52 (with illustrations, as Illustrated English social history).
Trinity College: an historical sketch. Cambridge 1943.
An autobiography and other essays. 1949.
A layman's love of letters. 1954 (Clark lectures 1953).
Trevelyan pbd an edn of The poetical works of George Meredith, *1912,* Selected poetical works of George Meredith, *1955, and pbd* The Meredith pocket book, *1906. He also pbd an edn of Macaulay's* Lays of ancient Rome and other historical poems, *1928, and compiled* Carlyle: an anthology, *1953.*

§2

Plumb, J. H. G. M. Trevelyan. 1951 (Br Council pamphlet).
Clark, G. N. Trevelyan. Proc Br Acad 49 1963.

HUGH REDWALD TREVOR-ROPER, BARON DACRE
b. 1914

Archbishop Laud 1573–1645. 1940, 1962 (corrected, with new preface), Hamden Conn 1962.
The last days of Hitler. 1947, New York 1947, London 1950 (new introd), 1952 (omitting some footnotes and appendices), 1965 (with new introd and footnotes), 1962 (rev), New York 1962 (with new preface).
The gentry 1540–1640. [1953].
Hitler's table talk 1941–4. 1953. Introd, The mind of Adolf Hitler, by Trevor-Roper.
The Bormann letters. 1954. Ed Trevor-Roper.
Historical essays. 1957, New York 1957 (as Men and events: historical essays), 1966 (as Historical essays).
The testament of Adolf Hitler. 1961. Selections with introd by Trevor-Roper.
Hitler's war directives 1939–45. 1964, New York 1965 (as Blitzkrieg to defeat: Hitler's war directives 1939–45). Ed Trevor-Roper from Hitler's Weisungen für die Kriegführung 1939–45 by W. Hubatsch.
The rise of Christian Europe. [1965], New York 1965.
Religion, the Reformation and social change, and other essays. 1967, New York 1968 (as The crisis of the seventeenth century: religion, the Reformation and social change).
The Philby affair: espionage, treason and secret services. 1968.
The plunder of the arts in the seventeenth century. 1970.
A hidden life: the enigma of Sir Edmund Backhouse. 1976.
Princes and artists. 1976.
Trevor-Roper also edited Essays in British history presented to K. Feiling, *1964;* The poems of Richard Corbett, *Oxford 1965 (with J. A. W. Bennett);* The age of expansion: Europe and the world 1559–1660, *1968; and selections from Gibbon and Macaulay.*

GRAHAM WALLAS
1858–1932

The life of Francis Place 1771–1854. 1898, 1918 (rev), New York 1919.
Human nature in politics. 1908, New York 1921.
The great society: a psychological analysis. 1914, New York 1914.
Our social heritage. 1921, New Haven 1921.
The art of thought. 1926, 1945 (abridged by M. Wallas); New York [1926].
Social judgment. Ed M. Wallas 1934, New York [1935].
Men and ideas: essays. Ed M. Wallas 1940.

BEATRICE WEBB, née POTTER
1858–1943

For location of mss see under Sidney Webb, below.

§1

For works written in collaboration with Sidney Webb see under Sidney Webb, below.

The docks; The tailoring trade; The Jewish community. In Life and labour of the people in London, by C. Booth assisted by various contributors, 2 vols 1889–91, 10 vols 1892–97, 17 vols 1902–3.
The Co-operative Movement in Great Britain. 1891, New York 1899, London 1930 (with additional preface).
The economics of factory legislation. In The case for the Factory Acts [by various authors], ed B. Webb 1901; rptd 1909 in Socialism and national minimum, by B. Webb, B. L. Hutchins and the Fabian Soc.
The case for the national minimum [by various authors]. Ed B. Webb 1913.
The wages of men and women: should they be equal? [1919].
My apprenticeship. 1926, New York 1926. Autobiography.
[Credo]. In Living philosophies, by Albert Einstein [et al], New York 1931; rptd (with postscript, An interposition) in I believe, [by] W. H. Auden [et al], London 1940.
Our partnership. Ed B. Drake and M. I. Cole 1948, New York 1948. Autobiography.

Diaries

Beatrice Webb's diaries 1912–24, 1924–32. Ed M. I. Cole 2 vols 1952–56.
Visit to New Zealand in 1898: B. Webb's diary, with entries by S. Webb. Wellington 1959.
American diary 1898. Ed D. A. Shannon, Madison 1963.
The Webbs' Australian diary 1898. Ed A. G. Austin, Melbourne 1965.

§2

Cole, M. I. In her Women of today, 1938.
— Beatrice Webb. 1945.
Cole, G. D. H. Beatrice Webb as an economist. Economic Jnl 53 1943; rptd in The Webbs and their work, ed M. I. Cole 1949.
Tawney, R. H. Beatrice Webb. Proc Br Acad 29 1943; rptd in his Attack and other papers, 1953.
Leavis, F. R. Mill, Beatrice Webb and the 'English school'. Scrutiny 16 1949; rptd as introd to his edn of Mill on Bentham and Coleridge, 1950.
Letwin, S. B. The pursuit of certainty: Hume, Bentham, Mill, Beatrice Webb. Cambridge 1965.
Muggeridge, K. and R. Adam. Beatrice Webb: a life. 1967.

SIDNEY JAMES WEBB,
1ST BARON PASSFIELD
1859–1947

The British Library of Political and Economic Science has the Webbs' research collections on trade unionism and local government on which their History of trade unionism, Industrial democracy *and* English local government *were based. It also has their private papers: the Passfield Papers.*

§ 1

Works by S. Webb alone, or with authors other than Beatrice Webb:

The basis of socialism: historic. In Fabian essays in socialism, ed G. B. Shaw 1889, ed H. G. Wilshire, New York 1891, ed Shaw 1908 (with new preface), 1920 (with introd by S. Webb), 1931 (with new preface by Shaw), 1948 (with postscript by Shaw entitled Sixty years of Fabianism).
Socialism in England. [Baltimore] 1889, London 1890 (rev), 1908 (with introductory ch).
The eight hours day. [1891]. With H. Cox.
The London programme [of reforms in the administration of the metropolis]. 1891, 1895 (as Vestry and guardian elections, parish councils: the London programme. With new introductory ch).
The reform of London. 1892. An 'Eighty' Club pamphlet.
Labour in the longest reign 1837–97. 1897. Rptd, with alterations, from the Wholesale Co-operative Soc's Annual for 1893.
London education. 1904.
The basis & policy of socialism. 1908. With the L.C.C. and the Fabian Soc. Rptd (rev) from Fabian Tracts.
Secondary education. 1908. Appendix to A century of education, by H. B. Binns.
Social movements. In Cambridge modern history vol 12, Cambridge 1910; London [1916] (pbd separately with appendix as Towards social democracy? a study of social evolution during the past three-quarters of a century).
Grants in aid: a criticism and a proposal. 1911, 1920 (rev and enlarged).
Great Britain after the war. 1916. With A. Freeman.
How to pay for the war: being ideas offered to the Chancellor of the Exchequer by the Fabian Research Department. Ed S. Webb 1916.
The restoration of trade union conditions. 1917, New York 1917.
The works manager today. 1917.
The story of the Durham miners 1662–1921. 1921.
The future of Soviet communism. In What is ahead of us? by G. D. H. Cole [et al], [1937].
The evolution of local government. 1951. Lectures, rptd from Municipal Jnl 1899.

Works written in collaboration with Beatrice Webb:

The history of trade unionism. 1894, 1920 (rev and extended to 1920), New York 1920.
Industrial democracy. 2 vols 1897, 1 vol 1902 (with new introd), 1920 (with new introd).
Problems of modern industry. 1898, 1902 (with new introd). Essays, each previously pbd separately.
The history of liquor licensing in England, principally from 1700 to 1830. 1903, 1963 (as vol 11 of reissue of English local government, below), Hamden Conn 1963.
Bibliography of road making and maintenance in Great Britain. 1906.
English local government from the Revolution to the Municipal Corporations Act. 9 vols 1906–29, 11 vols 1963 (with new introds by various authors).
The break-up of the poor law: being part one of the Minority Report of the Poor Law Commission. Ed S. and B. Webb 1909.

The public organisation of the labour market: being part two of the Minority Report of the Poor Law Commission. Ed S. and B. Webb 1909.
English poor law policy. 1910, 1963 (as vol 10 of reissue of English local government, above), Hamden Conn 1963.
The state and the doctor. 1910.
The prevention of destitution. 1911.
A constitution for the socialist commonwealth of Great Britain. 1920.
The Consumers' Co-operative Movement. 1921.
The decay of capitalist civilisation. 1923, New York [1923].
Methods of social study. 1932, New York 1968.
Soviet communism: a new civilisation? 2 vols 1935, New York 1936, London 1937 (title without question-mark; with postscript), 1941 (new introd by B. Webb).
Is Soviet communism a new civilisation? 1936. Pamphlet. Reprint of epilogue to Soviet communism, above.
Soviet communism: dictatorship or democracy? 1936. Pamphlet.
The truth about Soviet Russia. Consists mainly of B. Webb's introd to the 1941 reissue of their Soviet communism: a new civilisation, above.

Diaries

Visit to New Zealand in 1898: Beatrice Webb's diary, with entries by S. Webb. Wellington 1959.
The Webbs' Australian diary 1898. Ed A. G. Austin, Melbourne 1965.

§ 2

Tawney, R. H. The Webbs and their work. 1945 (pamphlet); rptd in The development of economic thought: great economists in perspective, ed H. W. Spiegel, New York [1952] and in Tawney's Attack and other papers, London 1953.
— The Webbs in perspective. 1953. Pamphlet.
Cole, M. I. Social services and the Webb tradition. 1946. Pamphlet.
— (ed). The Webbs and their work. 1949. Essays by various authors.
— Beatrice and Sidney Webb. 1955. Pamphlet.
— The story of Fabian socialism. 1961.
Laski, H. J. The Webbs and Soviet communism. 1947.
Russell, B. In his Portraits from memory, 1956.

DAME CICELY VERONICA
WEDGWOOD
b. 1910

Strafford 1593–1641. 1935, 1961 (extensively rev as Thomas Wentworth, first Earl of Strafford 1593–1641: a revaluation), New York 1962.
The Thirty Years War. 1938, New Haven 1939, London 1957 (Penguin) (slightly corrected, with new introd).
Oliver Cromwell. 1939, New York 1956, London 1962 (with rev bibliographical note), New York 1966 (as The life of Cromwell), London 1973 (rev).
Battlefields in Britain. 1944 (Britain in pictures).
William the Silent: William of Nassau Prince of Orange 1533–84. 1944, New Haven 1944.
Canetti, E. Auto da fé. Tr C. V. Wedgwood 1946.
Velvet studies. 1946. Historical essays rptd.
Richelieu and the French monarchy. 1949, New York 1950, 1962 (rev).
Reading history. 1950 (Reader's guides).
Seventeenth-century English literature. 1950.
The last of the Radicals: Josiah Wedgwood MP. 1951.
Montrose. 1952, Hamden Conn 1966.
Edward Gibbon. 1955 (Br Council pamphlet).
The great rebellion: 1, The King's peace 1637–41. 1955, New York 1955. 2, The King's war 1641–7. 1958, New York 1959.

Poetry and politics under the Stuarts. Cambridge 1960, Ann Arbor 1964.
Truth and opinion: historical essays. 1960, New York 1960, 1967 (as The sense of the past).
The trial of Charles I. 1964, New York 1964 (as A coffin for King Charles: the trial and execution of Charles I).
The political career of Peter Paul Rubens. 1975.

Woolf edited International Rev *1919 and* Nation *1922. He helped to found* Political Quart *in 1930 and, with W. A. Robson, was joint editor 1931–59. With Virginia Woolf he founded the Hogarth Press in 1917 and, with G. H. W. Rylands, edited* Hogarth Lectures on Literature *from 1927; he contributed regularly to* New Statesman.
See D. Wilson, Woolf: a political biography, *1978.*

LEONARD SIDNEY WOOLF
1880–1969

The village in the jungle. 1913, New York 1926. Novel.
The wise virgins: a story of words, opinions and a few emotions. 1914. Novel.
Economic imperialism. 1920, New York 1920.
Empire and commerce in Africa: a study in economic imperialism. [1920] (Labour Research Department).
Socialism and co-operation. 1921.
Stories of the East. Richmond 1921; rptd in Diaries in Ceylon 1908–11, 1962, below.
Fabian essays on co-operation. Ed Woolf 1923.
Fear and politics: a debate at the Zoo. 1925 (Hogarth Essays).
Essays on literature, history, politics etc. 1927.
Hunting the highbrow. 1927 (Hogarth Essays).
Imperialism and civilization. 1928, New York [1928].
After the deluge: a study of communal psychology. 2 vols 1931–9, New York 1931–9.
The intelligent man's way to prevent war. 1933. By various authors, ed Woolf.
Quack, quack! 1935, New York [1935]. Essays on un-reason and superstition in politics, belief and thought.
The League and Abyssinia. 1936. Pamphlet.
Barbarians at the gate. 1939, New York [1939] (as Barbarians within and without).
The hotel. 1939, New York 1963 (with new introd). Play.
The war for peace. 1940.
The international post-war settlement. [1944] (Fabian pamphlet).
Foreign policy: the Labour Party's dilemma. 1947 (Fabian pamphlet).
The early Fabians and British socialism. In Shaw and society: an anthology and a symposium, with contributions by Woolf [et al]. Ed C. E. M. Joad 1953.
Principia politica: a study of communal psychology. 1953, New York 1953. Intended as vol 3 of After the deluge, 1931–9, above.
Sowing: an autobiography of the years 1880–1904. 1960, New York 1960.
Growing: an autobiography of the years 1904–11. 1961, New York 1962.
Diaries in Ceylon 1908–11: records of a colonial administrator; and Stories from the East: three short stories on Ceylon. Dehiwala 1962, London 1963.
Beginning again: an autobiography of the years 1911–18. 1964, New York 1964.
A calendar of consolation: a comforting thought for every day in the year. 1967, New York 1968.
Downhill all the way: an autobiography of the years 1919–39. 1967, New York 1967.
The journey not the arrival matters: an autobiography of the years 1939–69. 1969, New York 1970.

SIR CHARLES LEONARD WOOLLEY
1880–1960

Dead towns and living men: pages from an antiquary's notebook. 1920, 1954 (rev and enlarged), New York 1956.
The Sumerians. Oxford 1928, New York 1965.
The excavations at Ur and the Hebrew records. 1929.
Ur of the Chaldees: a record of seven years of excavation. 1929, 1950 (rev), New York 1965.
Digging up the past. 1930, New York 1931, London 1954 (rev), New York 1954.
The development of Sumerian art. 1935.
Abraham: recent discoveries and Hebrew origins. 1936, New York 1936.
A forgotten kingdom: a record of the results obtained from the excavation of two mounds in the Turkish Hatay. 1953, Baltimore 1953, London 1959 (rev).
Spadework: adventures in archaeology. 1953, New York 1953 (as Spadework in archaeology).
Excavations at Ur: a record of twelve years' work. 1954, New York [1954], London 1955 (corrected).
Alalakh: an account of the excavations at Tell Atchana in the Hatay 1937–49. 1955. With C. J. Gadd and R. D. Barnett.
History unearthed: a survey of eighteen archaeological sites throughout the world. 1958, New York 1962.
Mesopotamia and the Middle East. 1961, New York 1961 (as The art of the Middle East including Persia, Mesopotamia and Palestine).
The young archaeologist. Edinburgh [1961].
As I seem to remember. 1962.

GEORGE MALCOLM YOUNG
1882–1959

Gibbon. 1932, New York 1933, London 1948 (with new introd).
Early Victorian England 1830–65. 2 vols 1934, New York 1951. Ed Young, who wrote the introd, Portrait of an age, later pbd separately (rev) as Victorian England: portrait of an age, 1936, 1953 (with new introd), New York 1953; ed G. K. Clark, Oxford 1977.
Charles I and Cromwell: an essay. 1935.
Daylight and champaign: essays. 1937.
The government of Britain. 1941 (Britain in Pictures).
Today and yesterday: collected essays and addresses. 1948.
Last essays. 1950.
Stanley Baldwin. 1952. *See D. C. Somervell,* Stanley Baldwin: an examination of some features of Young's biography, *1953.*
Young edited selections from Hardy, Meredith and Macaulay.

III. PHILOSOPHERS, THEOLOGIANS, WRITERS ON NATURAL SCIENCE AND ON PSYCHOLOGY

General Studies

Passmore, J. A hundred years of philosophy. 1957, 1966 (rev and enlarged).

Warnock, G. J. English philosophy since 1900. Oxford 1958, 1969 (rev).

Henn, T. R. Science in writing: a selection of passages from the writings of scientific authors, with notes and a section on the writing of scientific prose. 1960.

Quinton, A. Thought. In Edwardian England 1901–14, ed S. Nowell-Smith, Oxford 1964.

SAMUEL ALEXANDER
1859–1938

Moral order and progress: an analysis of ethical conceptions. 1889.

Locke. 1908.

Space, time and deity: the Gifford lectures, 1916–18. 2 vols 1920, 1927 (with a new preface), 1966 (foreword by D. Emmet), New York 1966.

Beauty and other forms of value. 1933, New York [1968].

Philosophical and literary pieces, edited, with a memoir, by his literary executor (John Laird). 1939.

SIR ALFRED JULES AYER
b. 1910

Language, truth and logic. 1936, 1946 (rev), New York 1952, London 1971 (Pelican).

The foundations of empirical knowledge. 1940.

The British empirical philosophers: Locke, Berkeley, Hume, Reid and J. S. Mill. 1952, New York 1968. Anthology ed Ayer and R. Winch.

Philosophical essays. 1954.

The problem of knowledge. 1956.

The Vienna Circle. In The revolution in philosophy, by A. J. Ayer [et al], 1956.

Logical positivism. 1959, Glencoe Ill 1959. Anthology, ed with introd by Ayer.

The concept of a person and other essays. 1963.

The humanist outlook. 1968. Anthology, ed Ayer.

The origins of pragmatism: studies in the philosophy of Charles Sanders Peirce and William James. 1968, San Francisco 1968.

Metaphysics and common sense. 1969.

The origins of pragmatism. 1968.

The central questions of philosophy. 1973, 1976 (Pelican).

Russell. 1974.

Part of my life. 1977. Autobiography.

JOHN DESMOND BERNAL
1901–71

Bernal's literary papers have been deposited in the library of Birkbeck College.

The world, the flesh and the devil: an enquiry into the future of the three enemies of the rational soul. 1929.

The social function of science. 1939, New York 1939, Cambridge Mass 1967 (rev).

The freedom of necessity. 1949. Essays.

The physical basis of life. 1951.

Marx and science. 1952, New York 1952.

Science and industry in the nineteenth century. 1953.

Science and society. Moscow 1953. In Russian.

Science in history. 1954, 1965 (rev), New York 1965, 4 vols London 1969 (rev).

World without war. 1958, New York 1958, London 1961 (rev).

A prospect of peace. 1960. Based on World without war, above.

Science for a developing world: a symposium. Ed J. D. Bernal 1962.

The origin of life. 1967.

CHARLIE DUNBAR BROAD
1887–1971

Perception, physics and reality: an enquiry into the information that physical science can supply about the real. Cambridge 1914.

Scientific thought. 1923, New York 1923.

The mind and its place in nature. 1925, New York 1925.

Five types of ethical theory (Spinoza, Butler, Hume, Kant, Sidgwick). 1930, New York 1930.

Examination of McTaggart's philosophy. 2 vols Cambridge 1933–8.

Ethics and the history of philosophy: selected essays. 1952.

Religion, philosophy and psychical research: selected essays. 1953.

Autobiography. In The philosophy of Broad, ed P. A. Schilpp, New York 1959 (for 1960).

A reply to my critics. In The philosophy of Broad, ed P. A. Schilpp, New York 1959 (for 1960).

Lectures on psychical research. 1962, New York 1962.

Induction, probability and causation: selected papers. Dordrecht 1968.

Broad edited McTaggart's Nature of existence, 1927, and wrote the introd to McTaggart's Some dogmas of religion, 1930.

ROBIN GEORGE COLLINGWOOD
1889–1943

§1

Croce, B. The philosophy of Giambattista Vico. Tr Collingwood, 1913, New York 1913.

Religion and philosophy. 1916.

Roman Britain. 1923, Oxford 1932 (corrected), 1934 (corrected), 1942 (corrected).

Speculum mentis: or, the map of knowledge. Oxford 1924.

Outlines of a philosophy of art. 1925.

Croce, B. An autobiography. Tr Collingwood, Oxford 1927.

Faith and reason: a study of the relations between religion and science. 1928.

The archaeology of Roman Britain. 1930, 1969 (rev and enlarged by I. Richmond).

Bruce, J. C. The handbook to the Roman Wall. 9th edn ed [and largely rewritten by] R. G. Collingwood, Newcastle-upon-Tyne 1933.

An essay on philosophical method. Oxford 1933.

Roman Britain and the English settlements. Oxford 1936, 1937 (corrected) (Oxford History of England 1). With J. N. L. Myres.

The principles of art. Oxford 1938, New York 1958.

An autobiography. 1939.
The first mate's log of a journey to Greece in the schooner yacht Fleur de Lys in 1939. 1940.
An essay on metaphysics. Oxford 1940.
The new Leviathan: or man, society, civilization and barbarism. Oxford 1942, 1944 (corrected).
The idea of nature. Ed T. M. Knox, Oxford 1945, New York 1960.
The idea of history. Ed T. M. Knox, Oxford 1946, New York 1956.
Essays in the philosophy of art. Ed A. Donagan, Bloomington [1964].
Essays in the philosophy of history. Ed W. Debbins, Austin 1965.
The Roman inscriptions of Britain, vol 1: inscriptions on stone. Oxford 1965. With R. P. Wright.
Faith and reason: essays in the philosophy of religion. Ed L. Rubinoff, Chicago 1968.

§2

McCallum, R. B. R. G. Collingwood 1889–1943; T. M. Knox, Notes on Collingwood's philosophical works; I. A. Richmond, Appreciation of Collingwood as an archaeologist. Proc Br Acad 29 1943.
Tomlin, E. W. F. R. G. Collingwood. 1953, 1961 (rev) (Br Council pamphlet).
Donagan, A. The later philosophy of Collingwood. Oxford 1962. Appendix III contains letters from Collingwood to Croce.

JOHN WILLIAM DUNNE
1875–1949

§1

Sunshine and the dry fly. 1924.
An experiment with time. 1927, New York 1927, London 1938 (rev).
The serial universe. 1934, New York 1938.
The league of North-West Europe: a solution to the present European crisis. [1936].
The jumping lions of Borneo. 1937, New York [1938].
The new immortality. 1938.
An experiment with St George. 1939, New York [1939] (as St George and the witches).
Nothing dies. 1940, 1951 (rev).
Intrusions? 1955.

§2

Broad, C. D. Dunne's theory of time. In his Religion, philosophy and psychical research, 1953.
Borges, J. L. Time and J. W. Dunne. In his Other inquisitions 1937–52, Austin 1964.

SIR ARTHUR STANLEY EDDINGTON
1882–1944

Stellar movements and the structure of the universe. 1914.
Report on the relativity theory of gravitation. 1918.
Space, time and gravitation: an outline of the general relativity theory. Cambridge 1920, New York 1959.
The mathematical theory of relativity. Cambridge 1923, 1924 (enlarged).

The internal constitution of the stars. Cambridge 1926, New York 1959.
Stars and atoms. Oxford 1927, New Haven 1927.
The nature of the physical world. Cambridge 1928, New York 1928.
Science and the unseen world. 1929, New York 1929.
The expanding universe. Cambridge 1933, New York 1933.
New pathways in science. Cambridge 1935, New York 1935.
Relativity theory of protons and electrons. Cambridge 1936, New York 1936.
The philosophy of physical science. Cambridge 1939, New York 1939, Cambridge 1949 (corrected).
Fundamental theory. Ed E. T. Whittaker, Cambridge 1946.

JOHN BURDON SANDERSON HALDANE
1892–1964

Daedalus: or science and the future. 1924 (for 1923), New York [1924].
Callinicus: a defence of chemical warfare. 1925, New York [1925].
Animal biology. Oxford 1927. With J. S. Huxley.
The last judgment: a scientist's vision of the future of man. New York 1927.
Possible worlds, and other essays. 1927, New York 1928.
Enzymes. 1930, Cambridge Mass 1965.
The causes of evolution. 1932, New York 1932.
The inequality of man, and other essays. 1932, New York 1933 (as Science and human life).
Biology in everyday life. 1933. With J. R. Baker.
Fact and faith. 1934.
Science and the supernatural: a correspondence between A. Lunn and Haldane. 1935, New York 1935.
Heredity and politics. 1938, New York [1938].
How to be safe from air raids. 1938.
The Marxist philosophy and the sciences. 1938, New York [1939].
Science and everyday life. 1939, New York 1940.
Science and you. [1939].
Keeping cool, and other essays. 1940, New York [1940] (as Adventures of a biologist).
Science in peace and war. 1940.
New paths in genetics. 1941, New York 1942.
A banned broadcast, and other essays. 1946.
Science advances. 1947, New York 1947.
What is life? New York 1947, London 1949.
Is evolution a myth?: a debate. 1949. With D. Dewar and C. M. Davies.
Everything has a history. 1951. Essays.
The biochemistry of genetics. 1954, New York 1954.
The unity and diversity of life. Delhi 1958.
Science and Indian culture. Calcutta 1965.
Haldane was a regular contributor to Daily Worker *and* Reynold's News.

GODFREY HAROLD HARDY
1877–1947

Orders of infinity: the 'Infinitärcalcül' of Paul Du Bois-Reymond. Cambridge 1910, 1924 (rev).
Collected papers of Srinivasa Ramanujan. Ed G. H. Hardy [et al], Cambridge 1927, New York 1962.
A mathematician's apology. Cambridge 1940, 1967 (foreword by C. P. Snow).
Ramanujan: twelve lectures on subjects suggested by his life and work. Cambridge 1940, New York [1959?].

Bertrand Russell and Trinity: a college controversy of the last war. Cambridge 1942 (priv ptd), 1970 (with introd by C. D. Broad).

Collected papers. 7 vols Oxford 1966–79.

Hardy edited and wrote a number of mathematical treatises, alone and with others, and contributed several hundred papers to mathematical journals.

HERBERT HENSLEY HENSON
1863–1947

Light and heaven: historical and social sermons to general congregations. 1897.

Apostolic Christianity: notes and inferences mainly based on S. Paul's Epistles to the Corinthians. 1898.

Ad rem: thoughts for critical times in the church. [1899].

Cross-bench views of current church questions. 1902.

Godly union and concord. 1902, New York 1902.

Preaching to the time in St Margaret's Westminster during the Coronation year. 1902.

Studies in English religion in the seventeenth century. 1903.

Notes on popular rationalism. 1904.

The value of the Bible and other sermons 1902–4. 1904.

Moral discipline in the Christian church. 1905.

Religion in the schools: addresses on fundamental Christianity. 1906.

Christian marriage. 1907.

Christ and the nation: Westminster and other sermons. 1908.

The national church: essays on its history and constitution and criticisms of its present administration. 1908.

The liberty of prophesying. 1909.

Westminster sermons. 1910.

The road to unity: an address delivered to the National Council of the Evangelical Free Churches. [1911].

The creed in the pulpit. [1912]. Sermons.

Puritanism in England. 1912.

Notes of my ministry. 1913.

War-time sermons. 1915.

Robertson of Brighton 1816–53. 1916.

Christian liberty, and other sermons 1916–17. 1918.

Anglicanism. 1921.

In defence of the English church. [1923].

Notes on spiritual healing. 1925.

Church and parson in England. 1927.

The Book and the vote. 1928. On the revision of the Book of Common Prayer.

Disestablishment. 1929.

The Oxford groups. 1933, New York 1934 (as The Oxford group movement).

Christian morality: natural, developing, final. Oxford 1936.

Ad clerum. 1937.

The Church of England. Cambridge 1939.

Last words in Westminster Abbey. 1941.

Retrospect of an unimportant life. 3 vols 1942–50. Autobiography.

Bishoprick papers. 1946.

Letters. Ed E. F. Braley 2 vols 1950–4.

Theology and life. 1957, New York 1957. Sermons.

LANCELOT THOMAS HOGBEN
1895–1975

Alfred Russel Wallace. 1918.

Exiles of the snow, and other poems. 1918.

The nature of living matter. 1930.

Principles of animal biology. 1930, 1940 (rev), New York 1940.

Genetic principles in medicine and social science. 1931.

A journey to Nineveh, and other verses. 1932. By 'Kenneth Calvin Page' [i.e. Hogben].

Nature and nurture. 1933, New York 1933, London 1939 (rev).

Mathematics for the million: a popular self-educator. 1936, New York [1937], London 1937 (rev), New York 1940 (rev), 1943 (rev), London 1951 (rev), New York 1951, London 1953 (rev), 1967 (rev).

The retreat from reason. 1936, New York [1937].

What is ahead of us? 1937. With G. D. H. Cole.

Political arithmetic: a symposium of population studies. 1938. Ed Hogben.

Science for the citizen: a self-educator based on the social background of scientific discovery. 1938, New York 1938, London 1943 (rev), 1951 (rev), New York 1951, London 1956 (rev), New York [1956?].

Dangerous thoughts. 1939, New York 1940.

Author in transit. New York [1940].

Interglossa: a draft of an auxiliary for a democratic world order, being an attempt to apply semantic principles to language design. 1943 (Pelican).

An introduction to mathematical genetics. 1946.

From cave painting to comic strip: a kaleidoscope of human communication. 1949, New York 1949.

Chance and choice by cardpack and chessboard: an introduction to probability in practice by visual aids. 2 vols 1950–5, vol 1 New York 1950.

Statistical theory—the relationship of probability, credibility and error.

Mathematics in the making. 1960, Garden City NY 1961 (for 1960).

Essential world English. 1963, New York 1963.

Science in authority: essays. 1963, New York 1963.

The mother tongue. 1964, New York 1965 (for 1964).

Whales for the Welsh: a tale of war and peace, with notes for those who teach or preach. 1967.

SIR JULIAN SORELL HUXLEY
1887–1975

The individual in the animal kingdom. Cambridge 1912.

Essays of a biologist. 1923, New York 1923.

Essays in popular science. 1926, New York 1927.

Religion without revelation. 1927, New York 1927, London 1941 (abridged), 1957 (rev), New York 1957.

Ants. 1930, New York 1930, London 1935 (enlarged).

Bird-watching and bird behaviour. 1930. Broadcast talks.

Africa view. 1931, New York 1931.

What dare I think? the challenge of modern science to human action and belief. 1931, New York 1931.

The captive shrew and other poems of a biologist. Oxford 1932, New York 1933.

Problems of relative growth. 1932, New York 1932.

A scientist among the Soviets. 1932, New York 1932.

The elements of experimental embryology. Cambridge 1934, New York 1963. With G. A. de Beer.

If I were dictator. 1934, New York 1934.

Scientific research and social needs. 1934.

We Europeans: a survey of 'racial' problems. 1935, New York 1936. With A. C. Haddon.

The uniqueness of man. 1941, New York 1941 (as Man stands alone).

Evolution: the modern synthesis. 1942, New York 1943, London 1963 (rev).

On living in a revolution. 1944, New York 1944. Essays.

Evolution and ethics 1893–1943. 1947. By T. H. Huxley and J. Huxley; includes J. Huxley, Evolutionary ethics, 1943 (Romanes lecture).

Man in the modern world. 1947, New York 1948. Essays selected from the Uniqueness of man and On living in a revolution.

Soviet genetics and world science: Lysenko and the meaning of heredity. 1949, New York 1949 (as Heredity, East and West: Lysenko and world science).
Evolution in action. 1953, New York 1953.
From an antique land: ancient and modern in the Middle East. 1954, New York 1954.
New bottles for new wine: essays. 1957, New York 1960 (as Knowledge, morality and destiny: essays).
Biological aspects of cancer. 1958, New York 1958.
The story of evolution. 1958, 1969 (as The wonderful world of evolution).
Essays of a humanist. 1964.
Charles Darwin and his world. 1965. With H. B. D. Kettlewell.
Huxley edited T. H. Huxley's Diary of the voyage of HMS Rattlesnake, *1935;* The science of life, *1925 (with H. G. and G. P. Wells); the collections of essays,* The new systematics, *1940 and* The humanist frame, *1961; and wrote or edited numerous popular scientific books in collaboration with E. N. da C. Andrade, J. B. S. Haldane* (Animal biology, *1927), A. C. Hardy et al.*

WILLIAM RALPH INGE
1860–1954

Society in Rome under the Caesars. 1888, New York 1888.
Christian mysticism. 1899, 1933 (new preface), New York 1956.
Faith and knowledge: sermons. Edinburgh 1904.
Studies of English mystics. 1906, Freeport NY 1969.
Truth and falsehood in religion. 1906, New York 1907.
All Saints' sermons, 1905-7. 1907.
Personal idealism and mysticism. 1907, New York 1907.
Faith. 1909, New York 1910 (as Faith and its psychology).
Speculum animae: four devotional addresses. 1911.
The church and the age. 1912.
Types of Christian saintliness. 1915.
The philosophy of Plotinus. 2 vols 1918, New York 1968.
Outspoken essays. 2 sers 1919, 1922, New York 1968, 1969.
Liberalism in religion. 1924. Pamphlet.
Personal religion and the life of devotion. 1924, New York 1924.
England. 1926, New York 1926, London 1933 (rev), 1953 (rev), New York 1953.
Lay thoughts of a dean. New York 1926.
The Platonic tradition in English religious thought. 1926, New York 1926.
The church in the world: collected essays. 1927, Freeport Ny 1969.
Protestantism. 1927, Garden City NY 1928, London 1935 (rev).
Assessments and anticipations. 1929, New York 1929 (as Labels and libels).
Christian ethics and modern problems. 1930, New York 1930.
The social teaching of the church. 1930, New York [1930].
What we mean by hell. In What is the real hell?, by W. R. Inge [et al], 1930.
More lay thoughts of a dean. 1931.
God and the astronomers. 1933.
Things new and old: sermons and addresses. 1933.
Vale. 1934. Autobiography.
The gate of life. 1935. Sermons.
A rustic moralist. 1937.
Dean Inge indicts the Red Government of Spain. [1938].
Our English Bible, by W. R. Inge [et al]. 1938.
Our present discontents. 1938. Essays.
A pacifist in trouble. 1939. Articles.
The fall of the idols. 1940.
Talks in a free country. 1942. Imaginary dialogues.
God, King and Empire: a trilogy, by W. R. Inge [et al]. 1947.

Mysticism in religion. [1947], Chicago 1948.
The end of an age and other essays. 1948, New York 1949.
Diary of a Dean: St Paul's 1911-34. [1949], New York 1950.
Goodness and truth. Ed A. F. Judd 1958, New York 1958 (as The things that remain). Sermons.
The awakening of the soul: an introduction to Christian mysticism. Ed A. F. Judd 1959.
Inge was a regular contributor to a number of newspapers, especially Evening Standard.

SIR JAMES HOPWOOD JEANS
1877–1946

The dynamical theory of gases. Cambridge 1904, 1916 (rev and enlarged), 1921 (rev and enlarged), 1925 (rev), New York 1954.
An elementary treatise on theoretical mechanics. Boston Mass [1907].
The mathematical theory of electricity and magnetism. Cambridge 1908, 1911 (rev), 1920 (rev), 1925 (rev).
Report on radiation and the quantum-theory. 1914.
Problems of cosmogony and stellar dynamics. Cambridge 1919.
Astronomy and cosmogony. Cambridge 1928, 1929 (rev), New York 1961.
Eos: or the wider aspects of cosmogony. 1928, New York [1929], 1931 (as Man and the stars).
The universe around us. Cambridge 1929, New York [1929], Cambridge 1930 (rev), New York 1931, Cambridge 1933 (rev), 1944 (rev), New York 1944.
The mysterious universe. Cambridge 1930, 1930 (corrected), New York 1930, Cambridge 1931 (rev), New York [1932].
The stars in their courses. Cambridge 1931, New York 1931.
The new background of science. Cambridge 1933, New York 1933, Cambridge 1934 (rev), New York 1934.
Through space and time. Cambridge 1934, New York 1934.
Man and the universe. In Scientific progress, by Jeans [et al], 1936. Lectures.
Science and music. Cambridge 1937, New York 1937.
An introduction to the kinetic theory of gases. Cambridge 1940, New York 1940.
Physics and philosophy. Cambridge 1942, New York 1943.
The growth of physical science. Cambridge 1947, New York 1948; ed P. J. Grant, Cambridge 1951.

CYRIL EDWIN MITCHINSON JOAD
1891–1953

Essays in common sense philosophy. 1919, 1933 (rev).
Common-sense ethics. 1921.
Common-sense theology. [1922]. Extracts rptd as Unorthodox dialogues on education and art, 1930.
Introduction to modern philosophy. 1924.
Introduction to modern political theory. Oxford 1924.
Samuel Butler 1835-1902. 1924, Boston 1924.
Mind and matter: the philosophical introduction to modern science. [1925], New York 1925.
Thrasymachus: or the future of morals, 1925, New York 1925, London 1936 (rev, as The future of morals).
After-dinner philosophy. 1926. By Joad and J. Strachey.
The Babbitt Warren. 1926, New York 1927. A satire on the United States.
The bookmark, 1926. Essays.
The mind and its workings. 1927, New York 1928.
Diogenes: or the future of leisure. [1928], New York 1928.

The future of life: a theory of vitalism. 1928, New York 1928.

Great philosophies of the world. 1928, New York 1930, London 1937 (rev).

The meaning of life, as shown in the process of evolution. 1928.

Matter, life and value. 1929.

The present and future of religion. 1930, New York 1930.

The horrors of the countryside. 1931. Pamphlet.

The story of civilization. 1931.

Philosophical aspects of modern science. 1932, New York 1964.

Under the fifth rib: a belligerent autobiography. 1932, New York 1933, London 1935 (as The book of Joad: a belligerent autobiography).

Counter attack from the East: the philosophy of Radhakrishnan. 1933.

Guide to modern thought. 1933, New York 1933, London 1948 (Pan books; rev and enlarged).

Is Christianity true? a correspondence between A. Lunn and Joad. 1933, 1943 (with new introd by Joad).

Liberty to-day. 1934, New York [1935], London 1938 (rev).

Manifesto: being the book of the Federation of Progressive Societies and Individuals. Ed Joad 1934.

Return to philosophy: being a defence of reason, an affirmation of values and a plea for philosophy. 1935, New York 1936.

The dictator resigns. 1936.

Guide to philosophy. 1936, New York 1936.

The story of Indian civilization. 1936.

The testament of Joad. 1937.

Guide to the philosophy of morals and politics. 1938, New York 1946.

Guide to modern wickedness. 1939.

How to write, think and speak correctly. Ed Joad [1939].

Why war? 1939 (Penguin Special).

Journey through the war mind. 1940.

Philosophy for our times. 1940.

What is at stake, and why not say so? 1940.

The Brains Trust book: answers to 'Any questions?'. Ed H. Thomas. [1942]. With A. B. Campbell, J. S. Huxley et al.

God and evil. 1942, New York 1943.

An old countryside for new people. London [1942]. Pamphlet.

Pieces of mind. 1942. Selections from his works, by Joad.

The adventures of the young soldier in search of the better world. 1943, New York 1944.

Philosophy. 1944, Greenwich Conn 1962.

About education. 1945.

How our minds work. 1946, New York 1947.

The untutored townsman's invasion of the country. 1946.

More opinions. 1947.

Decadence: a philosophical inquiry. 1948, New York 1949.

The English counties. 1948, [1957] (rev by B. Webster Smith), New York 1959. Ed Joad.

A year more or less. 1948. Autobiographical essays.

The principles of parliamentary democracy. 1949.

Shaw. 1949.

A critique of logical positivism. 1950, Chicago 1950.

An introduction to contemporary knowledge. Leeds [1950].

The pleasure of being oneself. 1951, New York 1951.

A first encounter with philosophy: an introduction especially designed for young men and women. [1952].

The recovery of belief: a restatement of Christian philosophy. 1952.

Folly farm. 1954. Fiction.

ERNEST JONES
1879–1958

Papers on psychoanalysis. 1913, 1918 (rev and enlarged), New York 1961.

Treatment of the neuroses. 1920, New York 1963.

Essays in applied psycho-analysis. 1923, 2 vols 1951 (enlarged). First ch rptd (rev) as Hamlet and Oedipus, below.

Psycho-analysis. 1928, New York 1929, 1948 (rev and enlarged, as What is psychoanalysis?), London 1949.

The elements of figure skating. 1931, 1952 (rev and enlarged).

On the nightmare. 1931, New York 1931 (as Nightmare, witches and devils).

Hamlet and Oedipus. 1949, New York [1949].

Sigmund Freud: life and work. 3 vols 1953–7, New York 1953–7 (as The life and work of Sigmund Freud); 1 vol edn abridged by L. Trilling and S. Marcus, New York 1961, London 1961.

Sigmund Freud: four centenary addresses. New York 1956.

Free associations: memories of a psycho-analyst. 1959, New York 1959. Autobiography.

Jones also edited Social aspects of psycho-analysis (*1924*) *and a* Glossary for the use of translators of psycho-analytical works (*1928*); *he was founder and editor of the* International Jnl of Psychoanalysis *1920–39, and editor of the* International psycho-analytical library.

RONALD ARBUTHNOTT KNOX
1888–1957

§1

Naboth's vineyard in pawn: three sermons on the Church of England in the past, in the present and in the future. 1913; rptd in The Church in bondage, 1914, below.

Some loose stones: being a consideration of certain tendencies in modern theology. 1913, New York 1913, 1915 (with new preface and additional note).

The Church in bondage. 1914. Sermons 1911–14.

An hour at the front. 1914, 1916 (abridged, as Ten minutes at the front). Prayers.

Reunion all round, or Jael's hammer laid aside: being a plea for the inclusion within the Church of England of all Mahometans, Jews, Buddhists, Brahmins, Papists and Atheists, by the author of Absolute and Abitofhell. 1914; rptd in Essays in satire, 1928, below.

Absolute and Abitofhell: being a satire in the manner of Dryden on a newly-issued work entitl'd Foundations [ed B. H. Streeter], by RAK. 1915 (Fulham Books 4). First pbd Oxford Mag 28 Nov 1912 and 27 Feb 1913; rptd in Essays in satire, 1928 below.

Bread or stone: four conferences on impetrative prayer. 1915.

An apologia. 1917 (priv ptd). For distribution to members of the Society of SS. Peter and Paul after Knox's conversion.

The essentials of spiritual unity. 1918.

A spiritual Aeneid. 1918, New York 1918, London 1950 (corrected, adds 'After 33 years'), 1958 (introd by E. Waugh).

Meditations on the Psalms. 1919.

Patrick Shaw-Stewart. 1920.

Q. Horati Flacci Carminum librum quintum, a R. Kipling and C. Graves anglice redditum, edidit A. Godley. Oxford 1920. Parody.

Memories of the future: being memories of the years 1915–72, written in 1988 by Opal, Lady Porstock. Ed [or rather written by] Knox 1923.

A book of acrostics. 1924.

Sanctions: a frivolity. 1924. Novel.

Virgil. Aeneid Books vii to ix, partly in the original and partly in English verse translation. Ed [and tr] Knox, Oxford 1924.

The viaduct murder. 1925, New York 1926. Detective novel.

An open-air pulpit. 1926. Essays, mainly first pbd in Evening Standard.

Other eyes than ours. 1926. Novel.

The belief of Catholics. 1927, New York 1927, London 1939 (with a new preface and slight corrections) ('What I Believe' ser).

The three taps: a detective story without a moral. 1927, New York 1927.

Anglican cobwebs. [1928]. Substance of course of sermons.

Essays in satire. 1928, New York 1930.

The footsteps at the lock. 1928. Detective novel.

The mystery of the kingdom and other sermons. 1928.

The rich young man: a fantasy. [1928]. On the Crucifixion.

The Church on earth. 1929, New York 1929.

On getting there. 1929. Essays first pbd in Universe and Evening Standard.

Caliban in Grub Street. 1930, New York 1930. On current attitudes towards religion.

Broadcast minds. 1932. A criticism of the works of scientific publicists such as H. G. Wells, J. Huxley, B. Russell, H. L. Mencken.

Difficulties: being a correspondence about the Catholic religion between Knox and Arnold Lunn. 1932, 1952 (adds letter).

The body in the silo. [1933], New York 1934 (as Settled out of court). Detective novel.

Still dead. 1934, New York 1934. Detective novel.

Barchester pilgrimage. 1935, New York 1936. Tales in continuation of Trollope's novels, in his style.

Heaven and Charing Cross: sermons on the Holy Eucharist. 1935, New York 1936. 3 sermons rptd in The window in the wall, 1956, below.

The Holy Bible: an abridgement and rearrangement. 1936, New York 1936.

Double cross purposes. 1937. Detective novel.

Let dons delight: being variations on a theme in an Oxford common-room. 1939, New York 1939. Imaginary dialogues.

Captive flames: a collection of panegyrics. 1940, New York 1941.

In soft garments: a collection of Oxford conferences. 1942.

I believe: the religion of the Apostles' creed. Reading 1944. Abridged revisions of sermons pbd as The Creed in slow motion, 1949, below.

God and the atom. 1945, New York 1945.

A retreat for priests. 1946, New York 1946.

The Mass in slow motion. 1948, New York 1948. Sermons.

The Creed in slow motion. 1949, New York 1949. Sermons.

The trials of a translator. New York 1949, London 1949 (as On Englishing the Bible; adds 1 essay). Mainly first pbd in Clergy Rev.

Enthusiasm: a chapter in the history of religion, with special reference to the xvii and xviii centuries. Oxford 1950, New York 1950.

The Gospel in slow motion. New York 1950, London 1950. Sermons.

Stimuli. 1951, New York 1951. Sermons first pbd in Sunday Times.

The hidden stream: a further collection of Oxford conferences. 1952, New York 1953.

A New Testament commentary for English readers. 3 vols New York 1952–6, London 1953–6.

Off the record. 1953, New York 1954. Selected letters on religious matters.

A retreat for lay people. 1955, New York 1955.

The window in the wall and other sermons on the Holy Eucharist. 1956, New York 1957 (for 1956).

Bridegroom and bride. 1957, New York 1957. Essays on marriage.

On English translation: the Romanes lecture. Oxford 1957; rptd in next.

Literary distractions. 1958, New York 1958.

The priestly life: a retreat. New York 1958, London 1959.

Lightning meditations. New York [1959], London 1959. First pbd in Sunday Times.

Proving God: a new apologetic. [1959]. Preface by E. Waugh. 4 chs from an unfinished work.

Retreat for beginners. New York [1960], London 1961 (as Retreat in slow motion).

The layman and his conscience: a retreat. New York 1961, London 1962 (without subtitle).

Translations of the Bible, the Liturgy and other Devotional Works

The Holy Gospel of Jesus Christ according to Matthew. [1941] (priv ptd).

The New Testament of our Lord and Saviour Jesus Christ, newly translated from the Vulgate. 1944 (priv ptd), 1945 (first authorized edn with slight changes), New York 1946. The 4 Gospels and Acts were each separately issued in 1949.

The Epistles and Gospels for Sundays and holidays. Tr with notes 1946.

The Book of Psalms in Latin and English with the Canticles used in the Divine Office. 1947, 1964 (ed H. Richards, The Golden Lib). English tr and notes by Knox.

The Old Testament, newly translated from the Vulgate: vol 1, Genesis to Esther, New York 1948, London 1949; vol 2, Job-Machabees. 1949, New York 1950; 1 vol 1958 (as The shorter Knox Bible: Old Testament). An abridgement, ed L. Johnson.

Holy Week: the text of the Holy Week Offices with a new translation. 1951, New York 1951.

The Holy Bible: a translation from the Latin Vulgate. 1955, New York 1956. First 1 vol edn.

Autobiography of a saint: Thérèse of Lisieux. [1958].

The imitation of Christ, by Thomas à Kempis. Tr Knox and M. Oakley [1959]. Completed by Oakley after Knox's death.

Knox also contributed trns to the revision of The Westminster hymnal, *1940, and the revision of* The manual of prayers, *1942, (withdrawn 1943).*

§2

Waugh, E. Mgr Ronald Knox. Horizon 17 1948.
—— The life of Knox. 1959.
Speaight, R. A modern Virgilian. [1959].
—— Knox the writer. 1966.
Corbishley, T. Knox the priest. 1964.

JOHN McTAGGART ELLIS McTAGGART
1866–1925

§1

Studies in the Hegelian dialectic. Cambridge 1896, New York 1964.

Studies in Hegelian cosmology. Cambridge 1901.

Some dogmas of religion. 1906, 1930 (with memoir by C. D. Broad), New York 1968 (1906 edn rptd).

A commentary on Hegel's logic. Cambridge 1910, New York 1964.

Dare to be wise: an address delivered before the Heretics Society in Cambridge. 1910. Rptd in Philosophical studies, 1934, below.

Human immortality and pre-existence. 1915, New York 1915. First pbd as chs 2 and 4 of Some dogmas of religion, 1906, above.

The nature of existence. 2 vols (vol 2 ed C. D. Broad), Cambridge 1921, 1927, Grosse Pointe Michigan 1968.

Philosophical studies. Ed S. V. Keeling, Cambridge 1934, New York 1934.

§2

Broad, C. D. McTaggart. Proc Br Acad 13 1927; rptd in Some dogmas of religion, 1930, above, and in Broad's Ethics and the history of philosophy, 1952.
—— Examination of McTaggart's philosophy. 2 vols Cambridge 1933–8.
Dickinson, G. L. J. McT. E. McTaggart. Cambridge 1931.

JAMES MOFFATT
1870–1944

The historical New Testament: being the literature of the New Testament arranged in the order of its literary growth and according to the dates of the documents—a new translation edited with prolegomena, historical tables, critical notes and an appendix. Edinburgh 1901, 1901 (rev).
The New Testament: a new translation. 1913, 1914 (rev), 1922 (parallel edn with the Authorized version), New York [1922].
The Old Testament: a new translation. 2 vols [1924], New York [1924–5].
The Bible: a new translation, containing the Old and New Testaments. 1926, New York [1926] (as The Holy Bible, containing the Old and New Testaments: a new translation), London 1935 (rev, as A new translation of the Bible, containing the Old and New Testaments), New York [1935]. A reissue of the two preceding.

Moffatt also pbd devotional works, surveys of theological literature, anthologies and collections of religious and literary quotations, and selections from his trns of the Bible. He also edited the letters of J. Denney [1922], selections from the writings of J. Owen (1904) and J. Tillotson (1926), The expositor's year book (1926, 1927) and the Moffatt New Testament Commentary (18 vols 1928–50). He was executive secretary, 1930–44, to the American Standard Bible Committee responsible for the Revised Standard Version of the Bible (pbd 1946–52).

GEORGE EDWARD MOORE
1873–1958

§1

Principia ethica. Cambridge 1903.
Ethics. [1912], New York 1912.
Philosophical studies. 1922, New York 1922.
Proof of an external world. Proc Br Acad 25 1939; rptd in Philosophical papers, 1959, below.
An autobiography; A reply to my critics. In The philosophy of Moore, ed P. A. Schilpp, Evanston 1942, New York 1952 (adds Addendum to my reply).
Russell's Theory of descriptions. In The philosophy of Russell, ed P. A. Schilpp, Evanston Ill 1942.
Some main problems of philosophy. 1953, New York 1953. Lectures given 1910–11, with appendix and notes.
Visual sense-data. In British philosophy in the mid-century: a Cambridge symposium, ed C. A. Mace 1957, New York 1957.
Philosophical papers. 1959, New York 1959.
Common-place book 1919–53. Ed C. Lewy 1962 (for 1963).
Lectures on philosophy. Ed C. Lewy [1966]. Lectures given 1925–34.
Moore edited Mind *1921–47.*

§2

Schilpp, P. A. (ed). The philosophy of Moore. Evanston 1942, New York 1952 (rev).

Keynes, J. M. In his Two memoirs, 1949. The effect of Principia ethica on Bloomsbury.
W. B. Yeats and T. Sturge Moore: their correspondence 1901–37. Ed U. Bridge 1953. Moore's philosophy discussed at length by his brother and Yeats.
Johnstone, J. K. Bloomsbury philosophy. In his Bloomsbury group, 1954.
Woolf, L. In his Sowing, 1960.
Braithwaite, R. B. G. E. Moore. Proc Br Acad 47 1961; rptd in Moore, ed A. Ambrose and Lazerowitz, 1970.
Klemke, E. D. The epistemology of Moore. Evanston 1969.
—— (ed). Studies in the philosophy of Moore. Chicago 1969.

NOEL JOSEPH TERENCE MONTGOMERY NEEDHAM
b. 1900

Mechanistic biology and the religious consciousness. In Science, religion and reality, ed Needham 1925, New York 1925, 1955 (with introductory essay by G. Sarton).
Man a machine: in answer to a romantic and unscientific treatise written by E. Rignano & entitled Man not a machine. 1927, New York [1928].
Materialism and religion. 1929. Pamphlet.
The sceptical biologist: ten essays. 1929, New York [1930].
Chemical embryology. 3 vols Cambridge 1931, New York 1963.
The great amphibium: four lectures on the position of religion in a world dominated by science. 1931.
Order and life. New Haven 1936, Cambridge 1936.
The Nazi attack on international science. 1941.
Biochemistry and morphogenesis. Cambridge 1942.
Time, the refreshing river: essays and addresses 1932–42. 1943, New York 1943.
Chinese science. 1945.
History is on our side: a contribution to political religion and scientific faith. 1946, New York 1947.
Science and civilisation in China. Cambridge 1954–.
Chinese astronomy and the Jesuit mission: an encounter of cultures. 1958. Pamphlet.
Heavenly clockwork: the great astronomical clocks of medieval China. Cambridge 1960. With W. Ling and D. J. de Solla Price.
Science and China's influence on the world. In The legacy of China, ed R. S. Dawson, Oxford 1964.
The grand titration: science and society in East and West. 1969.
Within the four seas: the dialogue of East and West. 1969.

MICHAEL POLANYI
1891–1976

Atomic reactions. 1932.
The contempt of freedom: the Russian experiment and after. 1940.
Full employment and free trade. Cambridge 1945.
Science, faith and society. Oxford 1946, Chicago 1964.
The logic of liberty: reflections and rejoinders. 1951, Chicago 1958.
Personal knowledge: towards a post-critical philosophy. 1958, Chicago 1958.
The study of man. 1959, Chicago 1959.
Beyond nihilism. Cambridge 1960.
The tacit dimension. 1967.
Knowing and being. 1969, Chicago 1969. Essays, ed M. Grene.

HENRY HABBERLEY PRICE
b. 1889

Perception. 1932, 1950 (rev), 1961 (new preface).
Hume's theory of the external world. Oxford 1940.
Thinking and experience. 1953, Cambridge Mass 1953.
Belief. 1969, New York 1969.

WILLIAM HALSE RIVERS RIVERS
1864–1922

The Todas. 1906.
The influence of alcohol and other drugs on fatigue. 1908.
The history of Melanesian society. 2 vols Cambridge 1914.
Kinship and social organization. 1914.
Instinct and the unconscious: a contribution to a biological theory of the psycho-neuroses. Cambridge 1920.
Conflict and dream. 1923, New York 1923.
Psychology and politics, and other essays. 1923. With an appreciation by C. S. Myers.
Medicine, magic and religion. Ed G. Elliot Smith 1924, New York 1924.
Social organization. Ed W. J. Perry 1924.
Psychology and ethnology. Ed G. Elliot Smith 1926, New York 1926.
With J. H. Ward Rivers edited Br Jnl of Psychology *from 1904 and was one of the supervisors of the* Cambridge archaeological and ethnological ser *from 1906. He contributed* Report on anthropological research outside America *to* Reports upon the present condition and future needs of the science of anthropology, *Washington DC 1902, and edited* Essays on the depopulation of Melanesia, *Cambridge 1922.*

BERTRAND ARTHUR WILLIAM RUSSELL, 3RD EARL RUSSELL
1872–1970

A detailed catalogue of the archives of Russell: archive administrator and editor B. Feinberg 1967 (300 copies) *contains lists of the Amberley papers, mss of books, articles and speeches, personal and public correspondence; the archives are held by McMaster Univ, Hamilton Ontario.*

§1

German social democracy: six lectures, with an appendix on social democracy and the women question in Germany by A. Russell. 1896, 1965 (with new preface and without appendix), New York [1965].
An essay on the foundations of geometry. Cambridge 1897, New York 1956 (foreword by M. Kline). French trn (Paris 1901) has revisions and annotations.
A critical exposition of the philosophy of Leibniz; with an appendix of leading passages. Cambridge 1900, London 1937 (with new introd). French trn (Paris 1908) has new preface.
The principles of mathematics. Vol 1, Cambridge 1903, London 1937 (with new introd), New York 1938. All pbd.
To the electors of the Wimbledon division of Surrey. 1907. Election manifesto.
Anti-Suffragist anxieties. [1910]. People's Suffrage Federation pamphlet.
Philosophical essays. 1910, 1966 (rev), New York 1967. For '2nd edn' *see* Mysticism and logic, 1918, below.
Principia mathematica. 3 vols Cambridge 1910–13, 1925–7 (rev); abridged edn of vol 1 pbd 1962 (as Principia mathematica to *56). With A. N. Whitehead; Russell was responsible for all new material in 1925–7 edn.

The problems of philosophy. [1912], New York [1912].
Our knowledge of the external world as a field for scientific method in philosophy. Chicago 1914, London 1914, 1926 (rev), New York 1929 (with new preface).
The philosophy of Bergson, with a reply by H. W. Carr and a rejoinder by Mr Russell. Cambridge 1914; rptd in A history of western philosophy, 1945, below.
Scientific method in philosophy: the Herbert Spencer lecture. Oxford 1914; rptd in Mysticism and logic, 1918, below.
War—the offspring of fear. [1914]. Union of Democratic Control pamphlet.
Justice in war-time. Manchester 1915, Chicago 1916 (includes The policy of the Entente, below), London 1916, Chicago 1917 (rev), London 1917.
The philosophy of pacifism. [1915]. Pamphlet. Also ptd in Towards ultimate harmony: report of Conference on Pacifist Philosophy of Life, pbd for the League of Peace and Freedom 1916.
The policy of the Entente 1904–14: a reply to Professor Gilbert Murray [i.e. to his pamphlet, The foreign policy of Sir Edward Grey 1906–15, Oxford 1915]. Manchester [1915]; rptd in Justice in war-time (1916 edn), above.
Bertrand Russell and the War Office. [1916]. Pamphlet; rptd in Justice in war-time, (1917 edn), above.
The case of Ernest F. Everett. [1916]. No-Conscription Fellowship leaflet; discussion of the case of a conscientious objector which led to Russell's prosecution; rptd in the Autobiography of Russell 1914–44, 1967, below.
Principles of social reconstruction. 1916, New York 1917 (as Why men fight: a method of abolishing the international duel).
Rex vs. Russell: report of the proceedings before the Lord Mayor. 1916. No-Conscription Fellowship pamphlet; a speech in his own defence.
Political ideals. [1916]. Pamphlet; rptd in Political ideals, New York 1917, below.
What are we fighting for? [1916]. No-Conscription Fellowship leaflet.
Why not peace negotiations? [1916]. No-Conscription Fellowship leaflet.
Political ideals. New York 1917, London 1963 (with new foreword), New York 1964. Lecture ser.
Mysticism and logic and other essays. 1918, New York 1929 (with new preface). Includes 2nd and 3rd essays of Philosophical essays, above.
Roads to freedom: socialism, anarchism and syndicalism. 1918, 1919 (rev), New York 1919 (as Proposed roads to freedom), 1949 (rev).
Introduction to mathematical philosophy. 1919, New York 1919.
The practice and theory of Bolshevism. 1920, New York 1920 (as Bolshevism: practice and theory), London 1949 (rev), New York 1964.
The analysis of mind. 1921, New York 1921.
Free thought and official propaganda. 1922, New York 1922. Lecture; rptd in Sceptical essays 1928, below.
The problem of China. 1922, New York 1922, London [1926] (with postscript), 1966 (with new foreword).
The ABC of atoms. 1923, New York 1923, London 1924 (rev).
A free man's worship, with a special preface. Portland Maine 1923, Girard Kansas 1927 (as What can a free man worship?). Rptd from Philsophical essays, 1910.
The prospects of industrial civilization. 1923, New York 1923, 1959 (with new preface by Dora Russell). With Dora Russell.
Bolshevism and the West: a debate on the resolution 'that the Soviet form of government is applicable to Western civilization'; S. Nearing, affirmative; B. Russell, negative. 1924, New York 1924 (as Debate: resolved that the Soviet form of government is applicable to Western civilization).
How to be free and happy. New York 1924. Lecture.

Icarus: or, the future of science. 1924, New York 1924; rptd in The future of science, 1959, below.

The ABC of relativity. 1925, New York 1925, London 1958 (rev, ed F. Pirani), Fair Lawn NJ 1958, London 1969 (rev).

What I believe. 1925, New York 1925; rptd in Why I am not a Christian, 1927, below.

On education, especially in early childhood. 1926, New York 1926 (as Education and the good life). Pt 2 rptd as Education of character, New York 1961.

The analysis of matter. 1927, New York 1927, New York 1954 (introd by L. E. Denoun), London 1954.

An outline of philosophy. 1927, New York [1927] (as Philosophy).

Why I am not a Christian. 1927, [New York] 1927.

Sceptical essays. 1928, New York 1928.

A liberal view of divorce. Girard Kansas [1929]. Pamphlet.

Marriage and morals. 1929, New York 1929.

The conquest of happiness. 1930, New York 1930.

Debate! Is modern marriage a failure? Resolved: that the present relaxing of family ties is in the interest of the good life; B. Russell, affirmative; J. C. Powys, negative. New York 1930.

Has religion made useful contributions to civilization?: an examination and a criticism. 1930, Girard Kansas 1930. Pamphlet.

The scientific outlook. 1931, New York 1931, 1949 (rev).

Education and the social order. 1932, New York 1932 (as Education and the modern world).

Freedom and organization, 1814-1914. 1934, New York 1934 (as Freedom versus organization). Rptd 1965, pts 1, 2 as Legitimacy versus industrialism 1814-48; pts 3, 4 as Freedom versus organization 1774-1914.

In praise of idleness, and other essays. 1935, New York 1935.

Religion and science. 1935, New York [1935].

Determinism and physics: being the 18th Earl Grey Memorial Lecture. Newcastle-upon-Tyne 1936.

Which way to peace? 1936.

The Amberley papers: the letters and diaries of Lord and Lady Amberley [Bertrand Russell's parents]. Ed Bertrand and Patricia Russell 2 vols 1937, New York 1937. Selection.

Education for democracy: an address. 1937.

Power: a new social analysis. 1938, New York 1938.

An inquiry into meaning and truth. 1940, New York 1940.

How to become a philosopher: the art of rational conjecture; How to become a logician: the art of drawing inferences; How to become a mathematician: the art of reckoning. Girard Kansas 1942, New York 1968 (as The art of philosophizing).

How to read and understand history: the past as the key to the future. Girard Kansas 1943. Pamphlet; rptd in Understanding history, 1957, below.

An outline of intellectual rubbish: a hilarious catalogue of organized and individual stupidity. Girard Kansas 1943. Pamphlet; rptd in Unpopular essays, 1950, below.

The value of free thought: how to become a truth-seeker and break the chains of mental slavery. Girard Kansas 1944. Pamphlet; rptd in Understanding history, 1957, below.

A history of Western philosophy and its connection with political and social circumstances from the earliest times to the present day. New York 1945, London 1946, 1961 (rev).

Ideas that have helped mankind. Girard Kansas 1946. Pamphlet.

Is materialism bankrupt?: mind and matter in modern science. Girard Kansas 1946. Pamphlet; rptd in Understanding history, 1957, below.

Physics and experience: the Henry Sidgwick lecture. Cambridge 1946.

The faith of a rationalist. [1947], Girard Kansas 1947. Pamphlet.

Philosophy and politics. 1947; rptd in Unpopular essays, 1950, below.

Human knowledge: its scope and limits. 1948, New York 1948.

Towards world government. [1948]. New Commonwealth pamphlet.

Am I an atheist or an agnostic?: a plea for tolerance in the face of new dogmas. Girard Kansas 1949.

Authority and the individual: the Reith lectures 1948-9. 1949, New York [1949], Boston 1960 (adds Terminal essay, Philosophy and politics).

Unpopular essays. 1950, New York [1951?].

The impact of science on society. New York 1951, London 1952 (enlarged), New York 1953.

New hopes for a changing world. 1951, New York [1952?].

How near is war? 1952. Pamphlet.

What is freedom? 1952. Pamphlet; rptd (rev) in Fact and fiction, 1961, below.

The good citizen's alphabet. 1953, New York 1958, London 1970 (adds History of the world in epitome, 1962). Drawings by F. Themerson, captions by Russell.

Satan in the suburbs, and other stories. 1953, New York 1953.

What is democracy? 1953. Pamphlet; rptd in Fact and fiction, 1961, below.

History as an art: the Herman Ould Memorial Lecture. Aldington Kent 1954; rptd in Portraits from memory, 1956, below.

Human society in ethics and politics. 1954, New York 1955.

Nightmares of eminent persons, and other stories. 1954, New York 1955.

Man's duel from the hydrogen bomb. 1955. Pamphlet; rptd in Portraits from memory, 1956, below.

Logic and knowledge: essays 1901-50. Ed R. C. Marsh 1956, New York 1956.

Portraits from memory, and other essays. 1956, New York 1956.

Understanding history, and other essays. New York 1957.

The will to doubt. New York 1958.

Common sense and nuclear warfare. 1959, New York 1959.

The future of science, with a 'self-portrait' of the author. New York 1959.

My philosophical development. 1959, New York 1959. With appendix, Russell's philosophy, by A. Wood.

Wisdom of the West: a historical survey of Western philosophy in its social and political setting. Ed P. Foulkes 1959, New York 1959.

Act or perish. [1960]. By Rev Michael Scott and Russell (but written by Russell). The statement that launched the Committee of 100.

Russell speaks his mind. Cleveland 1960, London [1960]. Text of a ser of television interviews by W. Wyatt in 1959.

Civil disobedience. Birmingham 1961. Speech.

Education of character. New York 1961. Pt 2 of On education, especially in early childhood, 1926, above.

Fact and fiction. 1961, New York 1962. Essays and stories.

Has man a future? 1961, New York 1962.

Win we must. Birmingham 1961. Speech; rptd in the Autobiography of Russell vol 3, 1969, below.

Essays in skepticism. New York 1962.

History of the world in epitome: for use in Martian infant schools. 1962. Drawings by F. Themerson; rptd in The good citizen's alphabet (1970 edn), above.

You are to die. [1962]. Leaflet issued at the time of the Cuban crisis.

Unarmed victory. 1963, New York 1963.

Legitimacy versus industrialism 1814-48. 1965. Pts 1, 2 of Freedom and organization, 1934, above.

Freedom versus organization 1776-1914. 1965. Pts 3, 4 of Freedom and organization, 1934, above.

Danger in South-East Asia. [1965]. Leaflet.

The Labour party's foreign policy. 1965. Speech.

Appeal to the American conscience. [1966]. Russell Peace Foundation pamphlet on Vietnam; rptd in War crimes in Vietnam, 1967, below.

The autobiography of Russell (1872–1914; 1914–44; 1944–67). 3 vols 1967–9; vols 1, 2 Boston [1967–8], vol 3 (subtitled 1944–69) New York [1969?].

War crimes in Vietnam. 1967, New York [1967].

§2

Santayana, G. The philosophy of Russell. In his Winds of doctrine, 1913, New York 1925.

Bradley, F. H. In his Essays on truth and reality, Oxford 1914.

Russell, J. F. S., 2nd Earl Russell. My life and adventures. 1923. Autobiography of Russell's brother.

Dewey, J. and H. M. Kallen (ed). The Russell case. New York 1941. Essays by various authors on the revocation of Russell's appointment to the chair of philosophy in the College of the City of New York.

Hardy, G. H. Russell and Trinity: a college controversy of the last war. Cambridge 1942 (priv ptd), 1970 (with introd by C. D. Broad).

Schilpp, P. A. (ed). The philosophy of Russell. Evanston 1944, 1946 (rev), New York 1951 (rev), 2 vols 1963 (rev).

Lawrence, D. H. Letters to Russell. Ed H. T. Moore, New York 1948. Russell's letters have not survived.

Pears, D. F. Logical atomism: Russell and Wittgenstein. In The revolution in philosophy, by A. J. Ayer [et al], 1956.

—— Russell and the British tradition in philosophy. 1967.

Wood, A. Russell: the passionate sceptic. 1957.

Schoenman, R. (ed). Russell—philosopher of the century: essays in his honour. 1967.

Lewis, J. Russell: philosopher and humanist. 1968.

GILBERT RYLE
1900–76

Philosophical arguments. Oxford 1945. Lecture.

The concept of mind. 1949, New York 1959.

Systematically misleading expressions. In Essays on logic and language, ed A. Flew, Oxford 1951, New York 1951. By Ryle et al.

Dilemmas. Cambridge 1954. Lectures.

Feelings. In Aesthetics and language: essays, ed W. Elton, Oxford 1954. By Ryle et al.

The theory of meaning. In British philosophy in the mid-century: a Cambridge symposium, ed C. A. Mace 1957, New York 1957.

A puzzling element in the notion of thinking. [1958]. Lecture.

A rational animal. 1962. Lecture.

Plato's progress. Cambridge 1966.

Thinking and reflecting. In The human agent: Royal Institute of Philosophy lectures vol 1, 1966–7, 1968.

The thinking of thoughts. Saskatoon 1968. Lecture.

Ryle edited Mind *from 1947.*

LIZZIE SUSAN STEBBING
1885–1943

A modern introduction to logic. 1930, 1933 (rev), New York 1961.

Logic in practice. 1934, 1954 (rev C. W. K. Mundle).

Imagination and thinking. 1936. With C. Day Lewis; 2 addresses.

Philosophy and the physicists. 1937, New York 1958. A discussion of the views of Eddington and Jeans.

Thinking to some purpose. 1939 (Pelican).

Ideals and illusions. 1941.

A modern elementary logic. 1943, 1952 (rev C. W. K. Mundle).

WILLIAM TEMPLE
1881–1944

The faith and modern thought. 1910.

Principles of social progress. Melbourne 1910.

The nature of personality. 1911.

Foundations: a statement of Christian belief in terms of modern thought by seven Oxford men. Ed B. H. Streeter 1912. By Temple et al.

The kingdom of God. 1912.

Repton school sermons: studies in the religion of the Incarnation. 1913.

Studies in the spirit and truth of Christianity. 1914.

Church and nation. 1915.

Plato and Christianity. 1916.

A challenge to the church. 1917. On the National mission 1916.

Competition: a study in human motive. 1917. By Temple et al.

Issues of faith. 1917.

Mens creatrix: an essay. 1917.

Fellowship with God. 1920. Sermons.

Life of Bishop Percival. 1921.

The universality of Christ. 1921, New York [1922], London 1962 (as About Christ; with Christ's revelation of God, 1925).

Christus veritas: an essay. 1924, New York 1924 (as Christ the truth). Sequel to Mens creatrix, above.

Christ in his church: a charge delivered at his primary visitation [of the Manchester diocese] 1924. 1925.

Personal religion and the life of fellowship. 1926.

Essays in Christian politics and kindred subjects. 1927.

Christianity and the state. 1928.

Christian faith and life. 1931, New York 1931, London 1963 (with foreword by F. R. Barry).

Thoughts on some problems of the day: a charge delivered at his primary visitation [of the York diocese]. 1931.

Nature, man and God. 1934, New York 1949.

Basic convictions. New York 1936, London 1937.

Christianity in thought and practice. 1936, New York 1936.

The church and its teaching today. New York 1936.

The preacher's theme today. 1936, New York 1936 (as The centrality of Christ).

Readings in St John's gospel, 2 ser 1939, 1940, 1 vol 1945.

The hope of a new world. 1940. Broadcast talks.

Thoughts in war-time. 1940.

Citizen and churchman. 1941.

Christianity and social order. 1942, New York 1942 (Penguin Special).

Palm Sunday to Easter. 1942, New York 1942.

The Church looks forward. 1944, New York 1944.

Religious experience and other essays and addresses. Ed A. E. Baker 1958.

SIR D'ARCY WENTWORTH THOMPSON
1860–1948

A glossary of Greek birds. Oxford 1895, London 1936 (illustr).

On growth and form. Cambridge 1917, 1942 (rev), 1961 (abridged J. T. Bonner).

Science and the classics. 1940. Collected articles and addresses.

A glossary of Greek fishes. 1947.

Thompson wrote many official papers and reports on fishery statistics and oceanography, and translated Aristotle's Historia animalium *and H. Müller's* Fertilisation of flowers, *1883*. *He contributed to* The legacy of Greece *and* The companion to Greek studies.

EVELYN UNDERHILL
1875–1941

The miracles of Our Lady Saint Mary, brought out of divers tongues. 1905, New York 1906.
Mysticism. 1911, 1912 (rev), 1930 (rev), New York 1930.
The path of the eternal wisdom by 'John Cordelier' [i.e. E. Underhill]. 1911.
A book of contemplation, the which is called The cloud of unknowing, in which a soul is oned with God. Ed E. Underhill 1912.
The spiral way: being meditations upon the fifteen mysteries of the soul's ascent, by 'John Cordelier'. 1912, 1922 (rev).
The mystic way: a psychological study in Christian origins. 1913.
One hundred poems of Kabir. Tr R. Tagore, assisted by E. Underhill 1914. Introd by E. Underhill.
Practical mysticism: a little book for normal people. 1914, New York [1915].
Mysticism and war. 1915. Pamphlet.
Ruysbroeck. 1915.
Ruysbroeck, J. van. The adornment of the spiritual marriage; The sparkling stone; The book of supreme truth. Ed E. Underhill 1916. Tr from the Flemish by C. A. W. Dom.
Jacopone da Todi, poet and mystic 1228–1306: a spiritual biography. 1919.
The essentials of mysticism and other essays. 1920, New York 1960.
The life of the spirit and the life of to-day. 1922, New York [1922].
Hylton, W. The scale of perfection, newly edited from manuscript sources by E. Underhill. 1923.
The mystics of the Church. [1925], New York 1926.
Concerning the inner life. 1926, New York [1926].
Man and the supernatural. 1927, New York [1928].
Life as prayer. Edinburgh [1928]. Pamphlet.
The house of the soul. 1929, New York [1930].
Worship. [1929]. Pamphlet.
The golden sequence: a fourfold study of the spiritual life. 1932, New York [1933].
The inside of life. [1932]. Pamphlet.
Medieval mysticism. In The Cambridge medieval history vol 7, Cambridge 1932.
Mixed pasture: twelve essays and addresses. 1933, New York 1933. On the spiritual life.
The school of charity: meditations on the Christian creed. 1934.
What is mysticism? [1936]. Pamphlet.
Worship. 1936, New York 1937. A different work from the pamphlet pbd in 1929.
The parish priest and the life of prayer. 1937. 2 addresses.
The spiritual life: four broadcast talks. 1937, New York 1937.
The mystery of sacrifice: a meditation on the Liturgy. 1938.
Eucharistic prayers from the ancient liturgies. Ed E. Underhill 1939.
Abba: meditations based on the Lord's Prayer. 1940.
The fruits of the spirit. 1942, 1949 (enlarged).
Light of Christ: addresses given at the house of retreat, Pleshey 1932. 1944, New York 1945. With memoir by L. Menzies.
Meditations and prayers. 1949. Booklet.
Shrines and cities of France and Italy. 1949. Ed L. Menzies from an early diary 1901–7. Written and illustr E. Underhill.

Letters

Letters. Ed C. Williams 1943.

ALFRED NORTH WHITEHEAD
1861–1947

§1

A treatise on universal algebra, with applications. Vol 1, Cambridge 1898, New York 1960. No more vols pbd.
The axioms of projective geometry. Cambridge 1906, New York [1960?].
The axioms of descriptive geometry. Cambridge 1907, New York 1960.
Principia mathematica. 3 vols Cambridge 1910–13, 1925–7 (rev); abridged edn of vol 1 pbd 1962 (as Principia mathematica to *56). With B. Russell, who was responsible for all the new matter in the rev edn.
An introduction to mathematics. 1911, New York 1911, London 1927 (rev), 1942 (rev under the direction of J. H. C. Whitehead), New York 1948.
The organisation of thought: educational and scientific. 1917, Philadelphia 1917. The larger pt rptd (rev) in The aims of education and other essays, below.
An enquiry concerning the principles of natural knowledge. Cambridge 1919, 1925 (rev).
The concept of nature. Cambridge 1920, Ann Arbor 1957. Companion vol to An enquiry concerning the principles of natural knowledge, above.
The principle of relativity, with applications to physical science. Cambridge 1922.
Science and the modern world. New York 1925, Cambridge 1926.
Religion in the making. New York 1926, Cambridge 1926; rptd in Essays in science and philosophy, below.
Symbolism: its meaning and effect. New York 1927, Cambridge 1928.
Process and reality: an essay in cosmology. Cambridge 1929, New York 1929.
The function of reason. Princeton 1929, London 1929.
The aims of education and other essays. New York 1929, London 1959 (foreword by Lord Lindsay).
Adventures of ideas. New York 1933, Cambridge 1933.
Nature and life. Chicago [1934], Cambridge 1934.
Modes of thought. New York 1938, Cambridge 1938.
Essays in science and philosophy. New York 1947, London 1948, New York 1957 (as Science and philosophy).
Dialogues of Whitehead as recorded by L. Price. 1954, Boston 1954.

§2

Emmet, D. M. Whitehead's philosophy of organism. 1932, 1966 (corrected).
—— In her Nature of metaphysical thinking, 1945.
—— A. N. Whitehead. Proc Br Acad 33 1947.
Smith, J. Evaluations III: Whitehead. Scrutiny 3 1935.
Das, R. The philosophy of Whitehead. 1938.
Schilpp, P. A. (ed). The philosophy of Whitehead. Evanston 1941, New York 1951 (rev).
Russell, B. Portraits from memory: I, Whitehead. Listener 10 July 1952.
—— In his Autobiography vol 1 1967.
Leclerc, I. Whitehead's metaphysics: an introductory exposition. 1958.
—— (ed). The relevance of Whitehead: philosophical essays. 1961.
Mays, W. The philosophy of Whitehead. 1959.
Jnl of Philosophy 58 1961. Whitehead centennial issue, ed G. L. Kline; rptd as Whitehead: essays on his philosophy, ed G. L. Kline. Englewood Cliffs NJ 1963.
Sherburne, D. W. A. A Whiteheadian aesthetic. New Haven 1961.
—— (ed). A key to Whitehead's Process and reality. New York 1966.
Pittenger, W. N. Alfred North Whitehead. 1969.

ARTHUR JOHN TERENCE DIBBEN WISDOM
b. 1904

Interpretation and analysis, in relation to Bentham's theory of definition. 1931.
Problems of mind and matter. Cambridge 1934.
Other minds. Oxford 1952, New York 1952.
Philosophy and psycho-analysis. Oxford 1953 (for 1952), New York 1953.
Paradox and discovery. Oxford 1965 (for 1966).

LUDWIG JOSEF JOHANN WITTGENSTEIN
1889–1951

§1

Logisch-philosophische Abhandlung. Annalen der Natur-philosophie 14 1921; London 1922 (as Tractatus logico-philosophicus, German text with Eng trn by C. K. Ogden, introd by B. Russell), New York 1922, London 1933 (corrected), 1955 (with index), 1961 (German text with a new trn by D. F. Pears and B. F. McGuinness, introd by Russell), New York 1961, London 1963 (corrected).
Some remarks on logical form. Aristotelian Soc Suppl Vol 9 1929; rptd in Essays on Wittgenstein's Tractatus, ed I. M. Copi and R. W. Beard 1966.
Philosophical investigations. Ed G. E. M. Anscombe, R. Rhees and G. H. von Wright, Oxford 1953, New York 1953, Oxford 1958 (rev), 1967 (with index); tr Anscombe; German and English texts.
Moore, G. E. Wittgenstein's lectures in 1930–3. Mind 63 1954, 64 1955; rptd in Moore's Philosophical papers, 1959.
Remarks on the foundations of mathematics. Ed G. H. von Wright, R. Rhees and G. E. M. Anscombe, Oxford 1956, New York 1956. Tr Anscombe; German and English texts.
Preliminary studies for the Philosophical investigations, generally known as the Blue and Brown books. Oxford 1958, New York 1958, Oxford 1960 (corrected), 1969 (with index). Dictated to students, Cambridge 1933–5.
Notebooks 1914–16. Ed G. H. von Wright and G. E. M. Anscombe, Oxford 1961, New York 1961. Tr Anscombe. 3 notebooks not destroyed used in the preparation of the Tractatus, 1922.
Philosophische Bemerkungen. Oxford 1964 (aus dem Nachlass herausgegeben von R. Rhees).
A lecture on ethics. Philosophical Rev 74 1965. Transcript of shorthand notes by F. Waismann of a paper given at Cambridge 1929 or 1930.
Lectures and conversations on aesthetics, psychology and religious belief compiled from notes taken by Y.

Smithies, R. Rhees and J. Taylor. Ed C. Barrett, Oxford 1966, Berkeley 1966.
Waismann, F. Wittgenstein und der Wiener Kreis, aus dem Nachlass herausgegeben von B. F. McGuinness. Oxford 1967. Discussion between Wittgenstein, Waismann and M. Schlick transcribed from Waismann's shorthand notes.
Zettel. Ed G. E. M. Anscombe and G. H. von Wright. Oxford 1967. Tr Anscombe. Unpbd fragments, German and English texts.
On certainty. (Über Gewissheit). Ed G. E. M. Anscombe and G. H. von Wright. Oxford 1969. Tr D. Paul and Anscombe; German and English texts.
Prototractatus: an early version of Tractatus logico-philosophicus. Ed B. F. McGuinness, T. Nyberg and G. H. von Wright, with a trn by D. F. Pears and B. F. McGuinness 1971.

Letters

Englemann, P. Letters with a memoir. Oxford 1967. Tr L. Furtmüller and B. F. McGuinness; the letters in parallel German and English texts.
Letters to C. K. Ogden. Ed G. H. von Wright, Oxford 1973.

§2

Ramsey, F. P. Mind 32 1923. Essay-review of Tractatus, 1922; rptd in his The foundations of mathematics, 1931 and in Copi and Beard, 1966, below.
Black, M. Some problems connected with language. Proc Aristotelian Soc 39 1938; rptd as Wittgenstein's Tractatus, in his Language and philosophy, Ithaca 1949, and in Copi and Beard, 1966, below.
—— A companion to Wittgenstein's Tractatus. Cambridge 1964.
Ryle, G. Ludwig Wittgenstein. Analysis 12 1951; rptd in Copi and Beard, 1966 and in Fann, 1967, below.
Moore, G. E. Wittgenstein's lectures in 1930–3. Mind 63 1954, 64 1955; rptd in his Philosophical papers, 1959.
Russell, B. In his Logic and knowledge, ed R. C. Marsh 1956.
—— In his My philosophical development, 1959.
Malcolm, N. Wittgenstein: a memoir, with a biographical sketch by G. H. von Wright. Oxford 1958, 1966 (rev).
Anscombe, G. E. M. An introduction to Wittgenstein's Tractatus. 1959, 1963 (rev), 1967 (rev).
Copi, I. M. and R. W. Beard (ed). Essays on Wittgenstein's Tractatus. 1966. An anthology.
Fann, K. T. (ed). Wittgenstein—the man and his philosophy: an anthology. New York 1967.
—— Wittgenstein's conception of philosophy. Oxford 1969.
Winch, P. (ed). Studies in the philosophy of Wittgenstein. 1969.
Pears, D. Wittgenstein. 1971.
Kenny, A. Wittgenstein. 1973, 1975 (Pelican).

IV. WRITERS ON TRAVEL, THE COUNTRYSIDE AND SPORT

GERTRUDE MARGARET LOWTHIAN BELL
1868–1926

Safar Nameh—Persian pictures: a book of travel. 1895 (anon), 1928 (as Persian pictures, with preface by E. D.

Ross), New York 1928, London 1937 (introd by V. Sackville-West), 1947 (preface by A. J. Arberry).
Poems from the Divan of Hafiz. Tr G. Bell 1897, 1928 (preface by E. D. Ross).
The desert and the sown. 1907, New York 1907 (as Syria: the desert and the sown), London 1928.
The thousand and one churches. 1909. With W. M. Ramsay.

Amurath to Amurath. 1911. Travels in Asia Minor and Persia.

Palace and mosque at Ukhaiḍir: a study in early Mohammadan architecture. Oxford 1914.

The Arab War—confidential information for general headquarters from G. Bell: being despatches reprinted from the secret Arab Bulletin. [1940].

Gertrude Bell also prepared an official report Review of the civil administration of Mesopotamia, *1920. Her private library is now at the University of Newcastle.*

Letters

The letters of Gertrude Bell. Ed Lady Bell 2 vols 1927, New York 1927.

The earlier letters of Gertrude Bell. Ed E. Richmond 1937, New York [1937].

Burgoyne, E. Gertrude Bell from her personal papers 1889–1914. 2 vols 1958.

'GEORGE BOURNE', GEORGE STURT
1890–1927

The ms of Sturt's Journal *is in the BM, with other mss.*

A year's exile. 1898. A tale.

The Bettesworth book: talks with a Surrey peasant. 1901, 1911 (with author's note).

Memoirs of a Surrey labourer: a record of the last years of Frederick Bettesworth. 1907.

The ascending effort. 1910.

Change in the village. 1912, New York 1912.

Lucy Bettesworth. 1913.

William Smith, potter and farmer 1790–1858. 1920.

A farmer's life, with a memoir of the farmer's sister. 1922.

The wheelwright's shop. Cambridge 1923.

A small boy in the sixties. Cambridge 1927.

The journals 1890–1902. Ed G. Grigson 1941.

The journals 1890–1927: a selection. Ed E. D. Mackerness 2 vols Cambridge 1967.

ROBERT BYRON
1905–41

Europe in the looking-glass: reflections of a motor drive from Grimsby to Athens. 1926.

The station: Athos, treasures and men. 1928, New York 1928, London 1949 (introd by C. Sykes), New York 1949.

The Byzantine achievement: an historical perspective. 1929, New York 1929.

The birth of western painting. 1930, New York 1931. With D. T. Rice.

An essay on India. 1931.

The appreciation of architecture. 1932.

First Russia, then Tibet. 1933.

Innocence & design, by Richard Waughburton [Byron and C. Sykes]. 1935. Fiction.

The road to Oxiana. 1937, 1950 (introd by D. T. Rice).

Byron was special correspondent in India for Daily Express *1929. He pbd a travel guide to Wiltshire and contributed to U. Pope,* Survey of Persian art, *1938.*

SIR NEVILLE CARDUS
1889–1975

A cricketer's book. 1922.

Days in the sun: a cricketer's journal. 1924.

The summer game: a cricketer's journal. [1929].

Cricket. 1930 (English Heritage ser).

Good days: a book of cricket. 1934.

Australian summer. [1937]. The test matches 1936–7.

Music for pleasure. Sydney 1942.

English cricket. 1945 (Britain in Pictures).

Ten composers. 1945, 1958 (rev as A composers eleven, with additional ch on Bruckner), New York 1959.

Autobiography. 1947.

The Ashes: with background of the Tests and pen pictures of the 1948 Australian team. [1948].

Second innings. 1950. Autobiographical reminiscences.

Cricket all the year. 1952.

Kathleen Ferrier: a memoir. Ed Cardus 1954, New York 1955.

Close of play. 1956. Essays on cricket.

Talking of music. 1957, New York 1957. Mainly rptd from Manchester Guardian.

Sir Thomas Beecham: a memoir. 1961.

Gustav Mahler: his mind and his music. 1965, New York [1965].

The delights of music: a critic's choice. 1966.

Since 1917 Cardus contributed regularly to Manchester Guardian (Guardian), *mainly on cricket and music. He also contributed to* Sydney Morning Herald *1941–7.*

BERNARD RICHARD MEIRION DARWIN
1876–1961

The golf courses of the British Isles. 1910, 1925 (rev, as The golf courses of Great Britain).

Tee shots, and others. 1911. Essays.

A friendly round. 1922. Essays from the Times.

A round of golf on the LNER. York [1924].

Eton v. Harrow at Lords. 1926.

Green memories. [1928].

The English public school. 1929.

Second shots: casual talks about golf. 1930.

Out of the rough. [1932]. Essays on golf.

Dickens. 1933, New York 1933.

Playing the like. 1934. Essays on golf.

W. G. Grace. 1934.

John Gully and his times. 1935, New York 1935.

Rubs of the green. 1936. Essays on golf.

A round of golf. [1937].

Life is sweet, brother. 1940. Autobiographical reminiscence.

Pack clouds away. 1941. Autobiographical reminiscence.

Golf between two wars. 1944.

Golfing by-paths. 1946. Essays from Country Life.

War on the line: the story of the Southern Railway in wartime. 1946.

Every idle dream. 1948. Essays.

James Braid. 1952.

Golf. 1954.

The world that Fred made: an autobiography. 1955.

Darwin also pbd tales and verses for children, mostly with his wife E. M. Darwin. He contributed to Country Life *from 1908 and was on the staff of the* Times *1919–53, after which he wrote leaders.*

ROBERT PETER FLEMING
1907–71

Brazilian adventure. 1933, New York 1934, [1942] (with foreword by C. Fadiman).

Variety: essays, sketches and stories. 1933.

One's company: a journey to China. 1934, New York 1934, London 1948 (with News from Tartary, below, as Travels in Tartary).

News from Tartary: a journey from Peking to Kashmir. 1936, New York 1936, London 1948 (as Travels in Tartary, with One's company, above).

The flying visit. 1940, New York 1940. Fiction.
A story to tell, and other tales. 1942, New York 1942.
The sixth column: a singular tale of our times. 1951, New York 1951.
A forgotten journey. 1952. Diary of a journey through Russia, Manchuria and Northern China in 1934.
Special operations. Ed P. J. F. Howarth 1955. By Fleming [et al]; accounts by British agents of underground movements during the Second World War.
My aunt's rhinoceros and other reflections. 1956, New York 1958. Essays.
Invasion 1940: an account of the German preparations and the British counter-measures. 1957, New York 1957 (as Operation Sea lion: the projected invasion of England in 1940).
With the Guards to Mexico! and other excursions. 1957.
The Gower Street poltergeist. 1958. Rptd from Spectator.
The siege at Peking. 1959, New York 1959.
Bayonets to Lhasa: the first full account of the British invasion of Tibet in 1904. 1961, New York 1961.
Goodbye to the Bombay bowler. 1961. Rptd from Spectator.
The fate of Admiral Kolchak. 1963, New York 1963.
Fleming contributed to Spectator *from 1931 and to* Times *from 1932.*
See D. Hart-Davis, Fleming: a biography, *1974.*

ROBERT BONTINE CUNNINGHAME GRAHAM
1852–1936

§1

Father Archangel of Scotland and other essays. 1896. With his wife Gabriela.
Mogreb-el-Acksa: a journey in Morocco. 1898, 1921 (rev); ed E. Garnett, New York 1930.
The Ipané. 1899, New York 1925. Stories and sketches.
Thirteen stories. 1900, New York 1942.
A vanished Arcadia: being some account of the Jesuits in Paraguay 1607 to 1767. 1901, New York 1924.
Success. 1902. Stories and sketches.
Hernando de Soto, together with an account of one of his captains, Gonçalo Silvestre. 1903, New York 1924.
Progress and other sketches. 1905.
His people. 1906. Stories and sketches.
Faith. 1909. Stories and sketches.
Hope. 1910. Stories and sketches.
Charity. 1912. Stories and sketches.
A hatchment. 1913. Stories and sketches.
Scottish stories. 1914.
Bernal Diaz del Castillo: being some account of him taken from his True history of the conquest of New Spain. 1915.
Brought forward. 1916. Stories and sketches.
A Brazilian mystic: being the life and miracles of Antonio Conselheiro. 1920, New York 1920.
Cartagena and the banks of the Sinú. 1920, New York 1921.
The conquest of New Granada: being the life of Gonzalo Jimenez de Quesada. 1922.
The conquest of the River Plate. 1924, New York 1924.
Doughty deeds: an account of the life of Robert Graham of Gartmore, poet and politician 1735–97. 1925.
Pedro de Valdivia, conqueror of Chile. 1926.
Redeemed and other sketches. 1927.
José Antonio Páez. 1929.

The horses of the Conquest. 1930; ed R. M. Denhardt, Norman Oklahoma 1949.
Writ in sand. 1932. Stories and sketches.
Portrait of a dictator: Francisco Solano Lopez, Paraguay 1865–70. 1933.
Mirages. 1936. Essays and sketches.

§2

West, H. F. A modern conquistador: Graham, his life and works. 1932.
—— Don Roberto. Hanover NH 1936 (priv ptd).
Hudson, W. H. Letters to Graham. Ed R. Curle 1941.
'Hugh MacDiarmid' (C. M. Grieve). Cunninghame Graham: a centenary study. Glasgow [1952].
Conrad, J. Letters to Cunninghame Graham. Ed C. T. Watts 1969.
Watts, C. and L. Davies. Cunninghame Graham: a critical biography. Cambridge 1979.

DAME FREYA MADELINE STARK
b. 1893

Baghdad sketches. Baghdad 1932, London 1937 (enlarged), New York [1938].
The valleys of the Assassins and other Persian travels. 1934.
The southern gates of Arabia: a journey in the Hadhramaut. 1936, New York [1936].
Seen in the Hadhramaut. 1938, New York 1939. A collection of photographs with a preface.
A winter in Arabia. 1940, New York 1940.
Letters from Syria. 1942.
East is West. 1945, New York 1945 (as The Arab island: the Middle East 1939–43).
Perseus in the wind. 1948, Boston 1956. Essays.
Traveller's prelude. 1950, Baltimore 1962. Autobiography.
Beyond Euphrates: autobiography 1928–33. 1951.
The coast of incense: autobiography 1933–9. 1953.
Ionia: a quest. 1954, New York [1954].
The Lycian shore. 1956, New York 1956.
Alexander's path from Caria to Cilicia. [1958], New York 1958.
Riding to the Tigris. [1959], New York 1960.
Dust in the lion's paw: autobiography 1939–46. [1961], New York 1962.
Rome on the Euphrates: the story of a frontier. [1966], New York 1967.
The zodiac arch. 1968, New York 1969. Essays and stories.
Space, time & movement in landscape. [1969].
Freya Stark contributed articles to Times *etc on Arab problems both during and after World War II. She also wrote poems and short stories, mostly for* Cornhill Mag.

FLORA THOMPSON
1877–1947

Bog-myrtle and peat. 1921. Verse.
Lark Rise. 1939, New York 1939.
Over to Candleford. 1941, New York 1941.
Candleford Green. 1943, New York 1943.
Lark Rise to Candleford: a trilogy. Oxford 1945, New York 1945. Contains the 3 previous novels. Introd by H. J. Massingham.

INDEX

INDEX